standard catalog of

1903-1990

by Robert Lichty

FIRST EDITION

COPYRIGHT MCMXC

Published by Krause Publications, Inc.
700 E. State St.
Iola, WI 54990
Telephone: 715-445-2214

INTERNATIONAL STANDARD BOOK NUMBER: 0-87341-140-4
LIBRARY of CONGRESS NUMBER: 90-60574

Printed in the United States of America

CATALOG STAFF

PUBLISHER: John A. Gunnell
EDITOR: James T. Lenzke
PHOTO RESEARCH: Kenneth Buttolph
DATA PROCESSING: Bruce Denny
COVER DESIGN: Paul Tofte
BOOKS MANAGER: Pat Klug

CONTENTS

FOREWORD

Traditionally, the concept behind Krause Publications' Standard Catalogs is to compile massive amounts of information about motor vehicles and present it in a standard format which the hobbyist, collector or professional dealer can use to answer some commonly asked questions.

Those questions include: What year, make and model is the vehicle? What did it sell for new? How rare is it? What is special about it? Some answers are provided by photos and others by the fact-filled text.

Chester L. Krause of Krause Publications is responsible for the overall concept of creating the Standard Catalog series covering American automobiles. David V. Brownell, editor of *Special-Interest Autos*, undertook preliminary work on the concept while serving as editor of *Old Cars Weekly* in the 1970s. Then editor John A. Gunnell assumed the project in 1978. The first Standard Catalog, covering postwar models (1946-1975) was published in 1982, while Beverly Rae Kimes continued writing and researching *The Standard Catalog of American Cars* (1805-1942), which was published in 1985. In 1987 *The Standard Catalog of Light Duty American Trucks* (1900-1986), was published by John Gunnell, while the second edition of the 1946-1975 volume was printed. In 1988, the 1805-1942 volume by Kimes appeared in second edition form. Also in 1988, James M. Flammang authored *The Standard Catalog of American Cars* (1976-1986), which went into its second edition in 1990. Currently the four-volume set of Standard Catalogs enjoys good sales in the automotive/truck collector hobby, and provides a wealth of detailed information that car and truck collectors, hobbyists, restorers and investors will not find from any other publishing house.

The scope of these catalogs has been to cover the major manufacturers, which have survived into the 1990s: Chrysler, Ford and General Motors as well as companies they have absorbed and companies no longer with us today. Independent companies such as Checker, Hudson, Kaiser-Frazer, Nash, Packard, Studebaker and Willys are included in the earlier catalogs, as well as some 200 producers of low-volume nameplates from Airscoot to Yenko. In each case, the data compiled encompasses a physical description; list of known equipment and original specifications; technical data; historical footnotes and appraisal of the car's current "ballpark value."

In each catalog, all compilations were made by an experienced editiorial team consisting of the Automotive Staff of Krause Publications and numerous contributors who are recognized experts on a certain marque or specific area of automotive history. A major benefit of combining teamwork with expertise has been the gathering of many significant facts about each model.

No claims are made about the catalogs being history textbooks or encyclopedias. Nor are they repair manuals or "bibles" for motor vehicle enthusiasts. They are, rather, intended as a contribution to the pursuit of greater knowledge about the many wonderful automobiles and trucks built in the United States since 1805. They are much larger in size, broader in scope and more deluxe in format than any previously published collectors' guides, buyers' digests or pricing guides.

The long-range goal of Krause Publications is to make all of the these catalogs as nearly perfect as possible. At the same time, we expect such catalogs will always raise new questions and bring forth new facts that were not previously unearthed in the countless hours of research by our team. All contributors are requested to maintain an ongoing file of new research, corrections and additional photos which can be used to refine and expand future editions.

We thank the editors and contributors to the three volume *Standard Catalog of American Cars* for providing much of the material herein. For it is through their research and editing effort that we produce this *Catalog of Ford*, with an assurance that most of the information which we've combined herewith from those three catalogs is accurate and well-researched. Additionally, we have included some of the best Ford, Lincoln, Mercury and Mustang-oriented articles from past issues of *Old Cars Weekly* authored by experts in the field. Should you have access to expanded information that you wish to share, please don't hesitate to contact the editors, in care of Krause Publications, *Standard Catalog of Ford*, 700 East State Street, Iola, WI 54990.

Other catalogs currently available are: *The Standard Catalog of American Cars 1805-1942; The Standard Catalog of American Cars 1946-1975; The Standard Catalog of American Cars 1976-1986;* and *The Standard Catalog of Light Duty American Trucks 1900-1986*. With the publication of this *Standard Catalog of Ford*, simultaneously Krause Publications is releasing *The Standard Catalog of Chevrolet 1912-1990* by Pat Chappell, and *The Standard Catalog of Chrysler 1924-1990* by John Lee. For ordering information and current prices write: Krause Publications/Old Cars Weekly, 700 East State Street, Iola, WI 54990.

ABBREVIATIONS

A/C	Air conditioning
A.L.A.M.	Assoc. of Licensed Automobile Mfgs.
Adj.	Adjustable
Aero.	Fastback
AM, FM, AM/FM	Radio types
Amp.	Amperes
Approx.	Approximate
Auto.	Automatic
Auxil.	Auxiliary
Avail.	Available
Avg.	Average
BxS	Bore x Stroke
Base	Base (usually lowest-priced) model
Bbl.	Barrel (carburetor)
B.H.P.	Brake horsepower
BSW	Black sidewall (tire)
Brk/Brkwd/Brkwood	Brookwood
Brdcl.	Broadcloth
Bus.	Business (i.e. Business Coupe)
C-A	Carryall
C.C.	Close-coupled
Cabr.	Cabriolet
Carb.	Carburetor
Capr.	Caprice
Cass.	Cassette (tape player)
Cav.	Cavalier
CB	Citizens Band (radio)
Celeb.	Celebrity
CEO	Chief Executive Officer
CFI	Cross Fire (fuel) Injection
Chvt.	Chevette
C.I.D.	Cubic inch displacement
Cit.	Citation
Clb	Club (Club Coupe)
Clth.	Cloth-covered roof
Col.	Colonnade (coupe body style)
Col.	Column (shift)
Conv/Conv.	Convertible
Conv. Sed.	Convertible Sedan
Corp Limo	Corporate Limousine
Cpe	Coupe
Cpe P.U.	Coupe Pickup
C.R.	Compression ratio
Crsr.	Cruiser
Cu. In.	Cubic Inch (displacement)
Cust.	Custom
Cyl.	Cylinder
DeL.	DeLuxe
DFRS	Dual facing rear seats
Dia.	Diameter
Disp.	Displacement
Dr.	Door
Ea.	Each
E.D.	Enclosed Drive
E.F.I.	Electronic Fuel Injection
E.W.B.	Extended Wheelbase
Eight	Eight-cylinder engine
8-tr.	Eight-track
Encl.	Enclosed
EPA	Environmental Protection Agency
Equip.	Equipment
Est. Wag.	Estate Wagon
Exc.	Except
Exec.	Executive
F.	Forward (3F - 3 forward speeds)
F.W.D.	Four-wheel drive

Fam.	Family
Fml.	Formal
"Four"	Four-cylinder engine
4WD	Four-wheel drive
4-dr.	Four-door
4-spd.	Four-speed (transmission)
4V	Four-barrel carburetor
FP	Factory Price
Frsm.	Foursome
Frt.	Front
FsBk	Fastback
Ft.	Foot/feet
FWD	Front wheel drive
G.B.	Greenbrier
GBR	Glass-belted radial (tire)
Gal.	Gallon
GM	General Motors (Corporation)
GT	Gran Turismo
G.R.	Gear Ratio
H	Height
H.B.	Hatchback
H.D.	Heavy Duty
HEI	High Energy Ignition
H.O.	High-output
H.P.	Horsepower
HT/HT Hdtp.	Hardtop
Hr.	Hour
Hwg.	Highway
I	Inline
I.D.	Identification
Imp	Impala
In.	Inches
Incl.	Included or Including
Int.	Interior
King/Kingwd.	Kingswood
Lan	Landau (coupe body style)
Lb. or Lbs.	Pound-feet (torque)
LH	Left hand
Lift.	Liftback (body style)
Limo	Limousine
LPO	Limited production option
Ltd.	Limited
Lthr. Trm.	Leather Trim
L.W.B.	Long wheelbase
Mag.	Wheel style
Mast.	Master
Max.	Maximum
MFI	Multi-port Fuel Injection
M.M.	Millimeters
Monte.	Monte Carlo
MPG	Miles per gallon
MPH	Miles per hour
Mstr.	Master
N/A	Not available (or not applicable)
NC	No charge
N.H.P.	Net horsepower
No.	Number
Notch or N.B.	Notchback
OHC	Overhead cam (engine)
OHV	Overhead valve (engine)
O.L.	Overall length
OPEC	Organization of Petroleum Exporting Countries
Opt.	Optional
OSRV	Outside rear view
O.W. or O/W	Opera window
OWL	Outline White Letter (tire)

Oz.	Ounce
P	Passenger
Park/Parkwd	Parkwood
PFI	Port fuel injection
Phae.	Phaeton
Pkg.	Package (e.g.option pkg)
Prod.	Production
Pwr.	Power
R	Reverse
RBL	Raised black letter (tire)
Rbt.	Runabout
Rds.	Roadster
Reg.	Regular
Remote	Remote control
Req.	Requires
RH	Right-hand drive
Roch.	Rochester (carburetor)
R.P.M.	Revolutions per minute
RPO	Regular production option
R.S. or R/S	Rumbleseat
RV	Recreational vehicle
RVL	Raised white letter (tire)
S	Gm lowtrim model designation
S.A.E.	Society of Automotive Engineers
SBR	Steel-belted radials
Sed.	Sedan
SFI	Sequential fuel injection
"Six"	Six-cylinder engine
S.M.	Side Mount
Spd.	Speed
Spec.	Special
Spt.	Sport
Sq. In.	Square inch
SR	Sunroof
SS	Super Sport
Sta. Wag.	Station wagon
Std.	Standard
Sub.	Suburban
S.W.B.	Short Wheelbase
Tach.	Tachometer
Tax.	Taxable (horsepower)
TBI	Throttle body (fuel) injection
Temp.	Temperature
THM	Turbo Hydramatic (transmission)
3S	Three-seat
Trans.	Transmission
Trk.	Trunk
2-Dr.	Two-door
2 V	Two-barrel (carburetor)
2WD	Two-wheel drive
Univ.	Universal
Utl.	Utility
V.	Venturi (carburetor)
V-6, V-8	Vee-type engine
VIN	Vehicle Identification Number
W	With
W/O	Without
Wag.	Wagon
w (2w)	Window (two window)
W.B.	Wheelbase
Woodie	Wood-bodied car
WLT	White-lettered tire
WSW	White sidewall (tire)
W.W.	Whitewalls
W. Whl.	Wire wheel

PHOTO CREDITS

Whenever possible, throughout the Catalog, we have strived to picture all cars with photographs that show them in their most original form. All photos gathered from reliable outside sources have an alphabetical code following the caption which indicates the photo source. An explanation of these codes is given below. Additional photos from Krause Publications file are marked accordingly. With special thanks to the editors of the previous *Standard Catalogs of American Cars* for their original research and obtaining many of these photos of Chevrolet over the years.

(AA)	Applegate & Applegate
(CH)	Chevrolet
(CP)	Crestline Publishing
(GM)	General Motors
(HAC)	Henry Austin Clark, Jr.
(HFM)	Henry Ford Museum
(IMSC)	Indianapolis Motor Speedway Corporation

(JAC)	John A. Conde
(JG)	Jesse Gunnell
(NAHC)	National Automotive History Collection
(OCW)	Old Cars Weekly
(PC)	Pat Chappell
(PH)	Phil Hall
(WLB)	William L. Bailey

INTRODUCTION

By Bob Lichty

This new standard catalog, focusing on Ford Motor Company products, is a compilation of photos, articles, specifications tables and current value listings of all Ford, Edsel, Lincoln and Mercury automobiles including Mustang and Thunderbird. As such, the introduction to this book should recognize the valued contributions of writers and historians whose work is included in its pages.

Realizing that many automotive hobbyists have a preference for a specific brand (or marque) of cars or various marques built by a single corporation, it seemed logical that a catalog formatted along those lines would be appealing. Therefore, the author was asked to handle the editing of such a catalog from material existing at Krause Publications.

The primary source of photos showing the styling and features of Ford Motor Company cars was the *Old Cars* photo archives, a vast collection containing over 14,000 pictures, advertisements and illustrations of automobiles.

This archives includes automakers' publicity stills, photos obtained from specialized vendors such as Applegate & Applegate, pictures taken at hobby shows by the *Old Cars* staff and news photos snapped at thousands of hobby events. In addition, where photographs were unavailable, illustrations from sales and technical literature and advertisements were used to show what the cars looked like when they were new.

The catalog begins with a selection of informative histories and articles which have appeared in *Old Cars* since the launch of that weekly tabloid in 1971. These stories were enhanced with attractive new photos and graphics designed by Phil LaFranka. They were then organized in a manner which provides a look at the background histories and product developments of FoMoCo branches including Ford, Edsel, Lincoln and Mercury.

Inside the catalog, you'll find nearly 60 articles, some of which were first published so many years ago that they are now, themselves, considered "classics." They highlight Ford milestones from the times of the Model T to around 1973.

Of course, the "meat" of the book is the lengthy and detailed specifications tables which present, in standardized format, styling and engineering features of virtually all of the FoMoCo cars. You'll find engine sizes, horsepower ratings, wheelbases, measurements and tire sizes — just to name a few things.

Thanks for the gathering of these facts go to the authors of three other catalogs previously published by Krause Publications. They are *The Standard Catalog of American Cars 1805-1942* by Beverly Rae Kimes and Austin Clark, Jr.; *The Standard Catalog of American Cars 1946-1975* by John A. Gunnell; and *The Standard Catalog of American Cars 1976-1986* by Jim Flammang.

The final element that came into use in this catalog was the presentation of current "ballpark prices" for Fords, Thunderbirds, Mustangs, Edsels, Lincolns and Mercurys. These were sourced from the *Old Cars Price Guide*, which is compiled as a bimonthly magazine edited by Ken Buttolph and James T. Lenzke. The prices are formatted according to Krause Publication's time-tested 1-to-6 condition scale, so that Ford fans who use the catalog can determine their cars' values in a variety of conditions.

ABOUT THE AUTHOR

Bob Lichty has been an active old car enthusiast since he was a young boy. During the summers, he spent weeks with his aunt and uncle, the owners of a Ford garage. Everyone in the Lichty family owned Fords, so it was only natural that Bob would become a Ford lover, too.

As a teenager in the '60s, Bob's Ford interest peaked. This was during the company's exciting "Total Performance" years.

Bob Lichty has owned hundreds of collector cars over the past 20 years. They ranged from dozens of Fords to what he describes as "more esoteric marques, thrown in for good variety." He has owned at least 14 examples of his favorite Fords, the 1955-'56 models.

Lichty considers himself privileged to have spent his entire working career in the automobile industry and the old car hobby. He started as an advertising artist for B.F. Goodrich, the tire-maker headquartered in his native town of Akron, Ohio. Bob then moved into the publishing field, with his artwork appearing in national publications such as *Rod & Custom* and *Hot Rod*. Soon, articles written by Lichty began to show up in the same magazines.

Within the old car hobby, Bob's first full-time job was with *Hemmings Motor News*. He then moved to the position of advertising manager at *Old Cars*, shortly after its inception. In years since then, Lichty operated his own collector car dealership in Southern California. He has been the marketing director for Carlisle Productions, the producer of six annual collector car events in Carlisle, Pa., for the past seven years.

Bob lives in Carlisle with his wife, Donna, and their two sons.

BODY STYLES

Body style designations describe the shape and character of an automobile. In earlier years automakers exhibited great imagination in coining words to name their products. This led to names that were not totally accurate. Many of those **'car words'** were taken from other fields: mythology, carriage building, architecture, railroading, and so on. Therefore, there was no 'correct' automotive meaning other than that brought about through actual use. Inconsistences have persisted into the recent period, though some of the imaginative terms of past eras have faded away. One manufacturer's 'sedan' might resemble another's 'coupe.' Some automakers have persisted in describing a model by a word different from common usage, such as Ford's label for Mustang as a 'sedan.' Following the demise of the true pillarless hardtop (two- and four-door) in the mid-1970s, various manufacturers continued to use the term 'hardtop' to describe their offerings, even though a 'B' pillar was part of the newer car's structure and the front door glass may not always have been frameless. Some took on the description 'pillared hardtop' or 'thin pillar hardtop' to define what observers might otherwise consider, essentially, a sedan. Descriptions in this catalog generally follow the manufacturers' choice of words, except when they conflict strongly with accepted usage.

One specific example of inconsistency is worth noting: the description of many hatchback models as 'three-door' and 'five-door,' even though that extra 'door' is not an entryway for people. While the 1976-1986 domestic era offered no real phaetons or roadsters in the earlier senses of the words, those designations continue to turn up now and then, too.

TWO-DOOR (CLUB) COUPE: The Club Coupe designation seems to come from club car, describing the lounge (or parlor car) in a railroad train. The early postwar club coupe combined a shorter-than-sedan body structure with the convenience of a full back seat, unlike the single-seat business coupe. That name has been used less frequently in the 1976-86 period, as most notchback two-door models (with trunk rather than hatch) have been referred to as just 'coupes.' Moreover, the distinction between two-door coupes and two-door sedans has grown fuzzy.

TWO-DOOR SEDAN: The term sedan originally described a conveyance seen only in movies today: a wheelless vehicle for one person, borne on poles by two men, one ahead and one behind. Automakers pirated the word and applied it to cars with a permanent top, seating four to seven (including driver) in a single compartment. The two-door sedan of recent times has sometimes been called a pillared coupe, or plain coupe, depending on the manufacturer's whim. On the other hand, some cars commonly referred to as coupes carry the sedan designation on factory documents.

TWO-DOOR (THREE-DOOR) HATCHBACK COUPE: Originally a small opening in the deck of a sailing ship, the term 'hatch' was later applied to airplane doors and to passenger cars with rear liftgates. Various models appeared in the early 1950s, but weather-tightness was a problem. The concept emerged again in the early 1970s, when fuel economy factors began to signal the trend toward compact cars. Technology had remedied the sealing difficulties. By the 1980s, most manufacturers produced one or more hatchback models, though the question of whether to call them 'two-door' or 'three-door' never was resolved. Their main common feature was the lack of a separate trunk. 'Liftback' coupes may have had a different rear-end shape, but the two terms often described essentially the same vehicle.

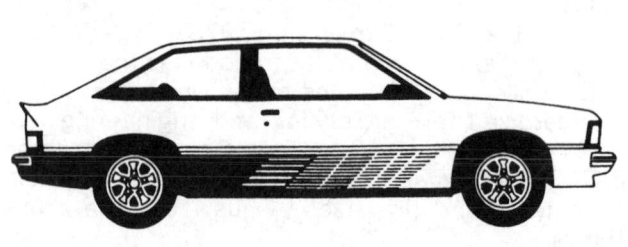

TWO-DOOR FASTBACK: By definition, a fastback is any automobile with a long, moderately curving, downward slope to the rear of the roof. This body style relates to an interest in streamlining and aerodynamics and has gone in and out of fashion at various times. Some (Mustangs for one) have grown quite popular. Others have tended to turn customers off. Certain fastbacks are, technically, two-door sedans or pillared coupes. Four-door fastbacks have also been produced. Many of these (such as Buick's late 1970s four-door Century sedan) lacked sales appeal. Fastbacks may or may not have a rear-opening hatch.

TWO-DOOR HARDTOP: The term hardtop, as used for postwar cars up to the mid-1970s, describes an automobile styled to resemble a convertible, but with a rigid metal (or fiberglass) top. In a production sense, this body style evolved after World War II, first called 'hardtop convertible.' Other generic names have included sports coupe, hardtop coupe or pillarless coupe. In the face of proposed rollover standards, nearly all automakers turned away from the pillarless design to a pillared version by 1976-77.

COLONNADE HARDTOP: In architecture, the term colonnade describes a series of columns, set at regular intervals, usually supporting an entablature, roof or series of arches. To meet Federal rollover standards in 1974 (standards that never emerged), General Motors introduced two- and four-door pillared body types with arch-like quarter windows and sandwich type roof construction. They looked like a cross between true hardtops and miniature limousines. Both styles proved popular (especially the coupe with louvered coach windows and canopy top) and the term colonnade was applied. As their 'true' hardtops disappeared, other manufacturers produced similar bodies with a variety of quarter-window shapes and sizes. These were known by such terms as hardtop coupe, pillared hardtop or opera-window coupe.

FORMAL HARDTOP: The hardtop roofline was a long-lasting fashion hit of the postwar car era. The word 'formal' can be applied to things that are stiffly conservative and follow the established rule. The limousine, being the popular choice of conservative buyers who belonged to the Establishment, was looked upon as a formal motorcar. So when designers combined the lines of these two body styles, the result was the Formal Hardtop. This style has been marketed with two or four doors, canopy and vinyl roofs (full or partial) and conventional or opera-type windows, under various trade names. The distinction between a formal hardtop and plain pillared-hardtop coupe (see above) hasn't always followed a strict rule.

CONVERTIBLE: To Depression-era buyers, a convertible was a car with a fixed-position windshield and folding top that, when raised, displayed the lines of a coupe. Buyers in the postwar period expected a convertible to have roll-up windows, too. Yet the definition of the word includes no such qualifications. It states only that such a car should have a lowerable or removable top. American convertibles became extinct by 1976, except for Cadillac's Eldorado, then in its final season. In 1982, though, Chrysler brought out a LeBaron ragtop; Dodge a 400; and several other companies followed it a year or two later.

ROADSTER: This term derives from equestrian vocabulary where it was applied to a horse used for riding on the roads. Old dictionaries define the roadster as an open-type car designed for use on *ordinary* roads, with a single seat for two persons and, often, a rumbleseat as well. Hobbyists associate folding windshields and side curtains (rather than roll-up windows) with roadsters, although such qualifications stem from usage, not definition of term. Most recent roadsters are either sports cars, small alternative-type vehicles or replicas of early models.

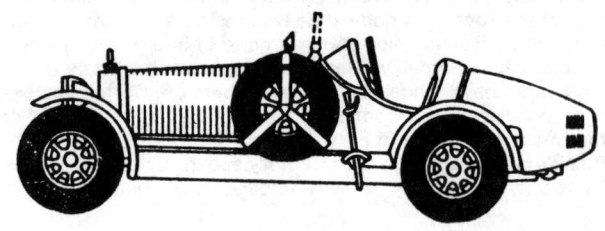

RUNABOUT: By definition, a runabout is the equivalent of a roadster. The term was used by carriage makers and has been applied in the past to light, open cars on which a top is unavailable or totally an add-on option. None of this explains its use by Ford on certain Pinto models. Other than this inaccurate usage, recent runabouts are found mainly in the alternative vehicle field, including certain electric-powered models.

FOUR-DOOR SEDAN: If you took the wheels off a car, mounted it on poles and hired two weightlifters (one in front and one in back) to carry you around in it, you'd have a true sedan. Since this idea isn't very practical, it's better to use the term for an automobile with a permanent top (affixed by solid pillars) that seats four or more persons, including the driver, on two full-width seats.

FOUR-DOOR HARDTOP: This is a four-door car styled to resemble a convertible, but having a rigid top of metal or fiberglass. Buick introduced a totally pillarless design in 1955. A year later most automakers offered equivalent bodies. Four-door hardtops have also been labeled sports sedans and hardtop sedans. By 1976, potential rollover standards and waning popularity had taken their toll. Only a few makes still produced a four-door hardtop and those disappeared soon thereafter.

FOUR-DOOR PILLARED HARDTOP: Once the 'true' four-door hardtop began to fade away, manufacturers needed another name for their luxury four-doors. Many were styled to look almost like the former pillarless models, with thin or unobtrusive pillars between the doors. Some, in fact, were called 'thin-pillar hardtops.' The distinction between certain pillared hardtops and ordinary (presumably humdrum) sedans occasionally grew hazy.

FOUR-DOOR (FIVE-DOOR) HATCHBACK: Essentially unknown among domestic models in the mid-1970s, the four-door hatchback became a popular model as cars grew smaller and front-wheel-drive versions appeared. Styling was similar to the orignal two-door hatchback, except for — obviously — two more doors. Luggage was carried in the back of the car itself, loaded through the hatch opening, not in a separate trunk.

LIMOUSINE: This word's literal meaning is 'a cloak.' In France, Limousine means any passenger vehicle. An early dictionary defined limousine as an auto with a permanently enclosed compartment for 3-5, with a roof projecting over a front driver's seat. However, modern dictionaries drop the separate compartment idea and refer to limousines as large luxury autos, often chauffeur-driven. Some have a movable division window between the driver and passenger compartments, but that isn't a requirement.

TWO-DOOR STATION WAGON: Originally defined as a car with an enclosed wooden body of paneled design (with several rows of folding or removable seats behind the driver), the station wagon became a different and much more popular type of vehicle in the postwar years. A recent dictionary states that such models have a larger interior than sedans of the line and seats that can be readily lifted out, or folded down, to facilitate light trucking. In addition, there's usually a tailgate, but no separate luggage compartment. The two-door wagon often has sliding or flip-out rear side windows.

FOUR-DOOR STATION WAGON: Since functionality and adaptability are advantages of station wagons, four-door versions have traditionally been sales leaders. At least they were until cars began to grow smaller. This style usually has lowerable windows in all four doors and fixed rear side glass. The term 'suburban' was almost synonymous with station wagon at one time, but is now more commonly applied to light trucks with similar styling. Station wagons have had many trade names, such as Country Squire (Ford) and Sport Suburban (Plymouth). Quite a few have retained simulated wood paneling, keeping alive the wagon's origin as a wood-bodied vehicle.

LIFTBACK STATION WAGON: Small cars came in station wagon form too. The idea was the same as bigger versions, but the conventional tailgate was replaced by a single lift-up hatch. For obvious reasons, compact and subcompact wagons had only two seats instead of the three that had been available in many full-size models.

DIMENSIONS

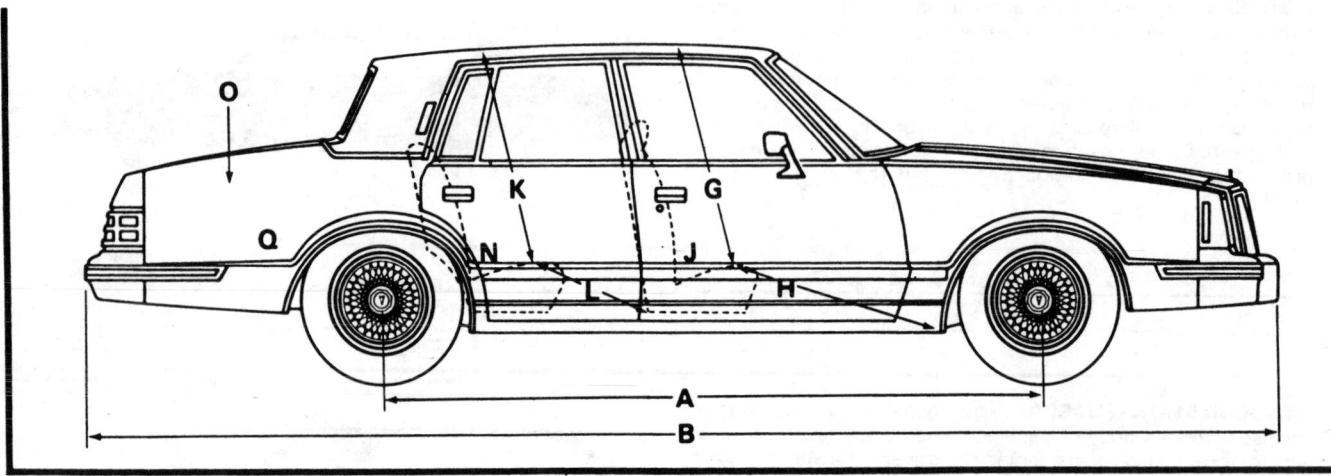

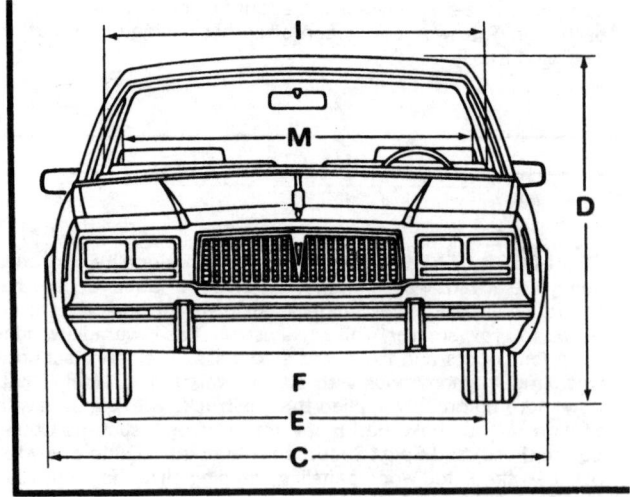

DIMENSIONS
Exterior:
A Wheelbase
B Overall length
C Width
D Overall height
E Tread, front
F Tread, rear
Interior—front:
G Headroom
H Legroom
I Shoulder room
J Hip room
Interior—rear:
K Headroom
L Legroom
M Shoulder room
N Hip room
O Trunk capacity (liters/cu. ft.)
P Cargo index volume (liters/cu. ft.)
Q Fuel tank capacity (liters/gallons)

INDEX TO ARTICLES

MIGHTY MERCURY

GENERAL INFORMATION

INTRODUCTION TO THE BEST OF OLD CARS WEEKLY CONTRIBUTIONS

Over the years, contributors to *Old Cars* have written numerous stories and articles about Ford Motor Company products. Their subjects ranged from histories of Henry Ford, Sr. — and the other men who made FoMoCo a reality — to the "is-it-collectible?" 1973 Cougar.

In the words of many experts and analysts, from Peter Winnewisser to Tim Howley, the history of FoMoCo marques has been looked at, dissected, analyzed, criticized, poked fun at and praised.

By carefully selecting from the works of these writers, we wound up with a wonderful collection of Ford, Mustang, Thunderbird, Edsel, Lincoln and Mercury stories gathered together here for your reading pleasure. They range from appreciations of the "Tin Lizzy," to examinations of how Henry Ford orchestrated the introduction of the Model A.

You'll read of the sporty and fast V-8 powered "Deuce," the safety-conscious mid-'50s "Vickies" and the four-passenger "Squarebirds" that are now gaining collector attention. You'll learn facts about the sensible Falcon and the "cool cat" Cougar.

Nearly 60 stories will take you through more than 85 years of Ford history and product developments. You will hear about woodies, roadsters, ragtops, factory show cars, "California customs," retractables, race cars, pace cars and Shelbys.

The articles included in the front portion of the catalog tell about historic cars and the men who built them. Ford's good times and bad times are both covered, since both played a role in Dearborn, Mich. lore and legend.

You'll get facts about which FoMoCo cars are biggest, priciest and fastest. You'll get opinions about which are the best models to add to your personal collection.

Originally penned for *Old Cars*, the stories we present here have been contributed from a variety of experts — professional journalists, hobby writers, members of the Society of Automotive Historians, specialized technical advisors from specific marque clubs and columnists who regularly cover the automotive beat from Dearborn to Daytona Beach.

STORIES BY YOUR FAVORITE WRITER

Ford Model T

Model T Times

by Glenrose Nash

1909 Ford Model T at the Henry Ford Museum

In 1908, a unique individual appeared on the American scene. She was called Lizzie. She had no last name, and the adjective "Tin" preceded her given name. She was part of a big family — the Fords — Model T branch. True, she was a machine, but what a machine! Henry Ford's biographer, Allen Nevins, says, "People, as they dealt with its temperamental, skittish ways, almost unanimously cherished an intimate affection for the unpredictable creature...with all its superiority, dependability, and simplicity, it combined an arch and mercurical eccentricity. It was more like a human being (of feminine gender) than any other car ever known to man. To buy one was to embark on a great event."

What was the little creature really like? It stood seven feet in height and had a wheelbase of eight feet, four inches — certainly strange proportions in our day! Nevertheless, with its four-cycle, 20 horsepower motor, it did the job of furnishing cheap, dependable transportation. The fuel tank, placed under the seat, a feature which caused quite a problem in filling it, held 10 gallons (in the touring car). It weighed 1,200 pounds. Not two, but four

square lights, one pair mounted on each side of the hood just below the windshield and one pair about where we would expect lights now. The shape was awkward, no flowing lines. The tops of the fenders were flat, the hood squarish. The big steering wheel jutted high and wide toward the driver. Wheels with sturdy spokes echoed the look of sturdiness. Windshields folded to half-height in pleasant weather when the top was down. Seats were high and narrow, although later the back seat was widened to accommodate three people. The running board was wide enough to hold luggage or a tool chest. Color was a dark green at first, but by 1912 all models were black. The vehicle might have looked strange, but compared to the various horseless carriages that preceded it, the result was little short of a miracle.

Of course, mistakes had to be corrected. Bearings in the rear axle had to be replaced often. Transmission bands' linings burned out. The front and rear wheels were different sizes. There were no front doors in the touring car. Starting in cold weather (by cranking) was difficult, to say the least.

In 1914, improvements included: Klaxon horn; acetylene gas headlamp; curved rear fenders; smoother line on front fenders; hood louvres; unbraced windshield; demountable rims (sold extra).

By 1917, the following: larger, better-shaped radiator; rounded hood; nickel and black enamel trim; better muffler.

In 1918: self-starter; improved engine.

By 1925: all-steel bodies; door on driver's side in open runabout; fuel tank under cowl; choice of colors.

The Model T has been called the greatest single model in automobile history. Most importantly, it opened up a new way of life for the working man and his family. Perhaps not immediately, for the initial touring car sold for $850, the roadster for $825. However, as Henry Ford perfected the continuous moving assembly line in 1912-13, prices decreased. The 1914 Model T brought $490 for a touring car, $440 for a runabout, and $690 for a town car. By that time, more than a half-million Americans had a Model T stowed away in a converted barn or makeshift garage behind the house. Cinders from the coal furnace that most people had in their homes furnished a driveway out of the mud.

The little vehicle was a magic carpet to transport townspeople beyond the city limits and rural families to Main Street. A few concrete roads were being built, some only one lane wide. Asphalt and macadam were more common. In town, often brick streets were found. Service stations began to spring up here and there. Ford dealers made sure that a complete line of parts were available. The menfolk often tinkered with their own automobile. These sturdy cars had an average life expectancy of eight years, and their owners gave them all the tender loving care possible. Use was judiciously restricted to "pleasure driving." City women still walked downtown for shopping and sent a child on a bicycle to the neighborhood store. The weekly main order was delivered. Milk, meat, and sometimes bakery goods and fresh produce arrived at the door by horse-drawn vehicle. Working people rode a bicycle or walked to their place of employment. The street car did a lively business within the community, and the interurban between towns.

The recreational use of the little four-cylinder car was the big thing! Now a Sunday could be planned around a small trip of anywhere from 25 to 50 miles without buying a train ticket for each member of the family. Besides, back roads (and there were few others) could be explored. A distant lake or river might be a place to spread a picnic lunch on its banks. Grown sons and daughters, as well as relatives or friends, could stay in touch. A fair or concert out of town was within reach. Horizons expanded

as the fortunes of the Ford Motor Co. and its competitors grew. This versatile automobile did not, of course, exist in a vacuum. In 1913 General Motors and the Dodge Brothers were producing good cars, but most were higher priced and therefore beyond the reach of the lowly working man. By 1922, the Overland was selling for $895, and a six-cylinder Essex had a price below $1,000. In 1926, Chevrolet sold for $875. Other cars in the early 1900s were such products as the Rio, the Hupmobile, Marmon, Renault, Pierce-Arrow, Studebaker, and others not as well-known.

That the Ford held up well was demonstrated by the many contests, both for speed and endurance. As early as

1914 Model T (restored).

1927 Ford Model T at an old car show.

1909, of six cars entered in a transcontinental race from New York to Seattle, two of them Fords, one of the latter came in first. High above the road, or sometimes, west of Missouri, above a path, the sturdy little "critter" managed to cross the mountains and slither through mud to win. However, when it was found that the two drivers had changed engines part way across country, the car was disqualified.

At this point in the Model T story, the writer cannot resist turning to family experience. Since I was only two years old, the year my father bought his first Ford — 1920 — I was blissfully unaware of the intricacies of the little automobile. However, I have pictures of it parked proudly in the driveway by our house in Galesburg, Illinois. It was an open model which sported what was known as a California top, a rigid, all-weather enclosure — much better than the isinglass side curtains, which snapped on and off. It came equipped with a crank to start it, but soon an electric starter was installed. That year this little beauty without the extras mentioned sold for $440. If it had been more, we could never have dreamed of buying a car. A former chicken house was expanded to provide shelter for the latest addition to our family (probably much more exciting to the two older brothers than their sister's birth two years before).

The first car that I really remember clearly was our second — the closed-in four-door sedan, bought in 1924. It featured, besides the more comfortable interior, high-pressure balloon tires with demountable rims. How proud I felt, bouncing about on the rear seat while my Father, with Mother beside him, took us on an evening drive or a Sunday trip! Now we could often visit my grandmother seven miles away or traverse a forty-mile stretch to the Mississippi, maybe even drive fifty miles to the city of Peoria.

We roamed the rural roads of Knox County, Illinois, constantly, and I can find my way on their much-improved modern surfaces now. We saw so much — the Brickyard, the CB&Q (now Burlington Northern) long tunnel under the extensive yard, the "Humps" out in the yards, Spoon River, the fair grounds, coal banks, the Boy Scout Camp, one-room school houses, several lakes, and parks and endless fields and farms. How confined our existence had been before the arrival of this fine conveyance! I grew up to be one of those people who had never been on a train. It wasn't until I was twenty-two and went away to teach school that I had that experience. There was no need. It was then, without a car of my own, that I remembered those Sunday trips, especially.

My brothers had saved money all during their paper-route and odd-job days, and each was able to buy a Model T. My older brother bought a coupe in 1924. Two years later my other brother bought a used 1924 model. My most dramatic memory (and most likely his, too) was when a wheel on my older brother's coupe came off and rolled up in someone's front yard. Later, he bought a Model A roadster with a rumbleseat. What a thrill it was to ride in it!

During those good-old days of the mid '20s, routes were marked by colored stripes on telephone poles. Very steep hills were avoided due to lack of power. Mud was often a hazard. Nevertheless we took advantage of an innovation in labor practices — the one-week vacation with pay. Previously, it had been too expensive for the whole family to buy train tickets, hotel accommodations, and three meals a day. Now things were different. Gasoline cost the same if only one person rode in the car or four or five crowded

in. Not only that, but tourist camps sprang up along the way. Food supplies were packed from home and a tent rolled up and carried in an enclosure on the running board. Room and board was suddenly almost as cheap as staying at home. In fact, my father figured that fifty dollars would see him, my mother, and me through the week. It did. At least, for us Midwesterners. The Dells in Wisconsin, Lincoln's birthplace in Kentucky, the Sand Dunes along Lake Michigan, and the Ozarks were accessible. At about thirty-five miles per hour, it took a week just to get to these destinations and back, but Mom could tell the neighbors; Dad, his co-workers; and the kids, their classmates, about where they had been.

In later years, improvements were made in overnight facilities. Rooms for tourists in private homes and tourist cabins became available. The latter were suited for housekeeping, so Mother could still prepare the meals and put up lunches for the next day's travel. Some were grouped around a gas station or little store. Those beside a "road-house" where liquor was sold were not considered proper for a family. Picnic tables and little fireplaces often went with the tourist "court." Local hotels were still located in small towns, and a night in one of these was often the highlight of a vacation.

Women began to take over the wheel. Now they could do the errands and drive various members of the family about. Some, however, including my mother, never felt confident enough to learn the new skill. Most of my generation were not so hesitant. We did not need to take a driver's test or apply for a license to drive. Complicated signs, rules of the road, parking decks, and divided highways did not exist. Some young women were even bold enough to set out on long trips. In 1932, Darlene and Marge Dorgan, Ruby Moran, Winifred Swearingen, and Ruby McDonald of Bradford, Illinois set out for The Dells, Wisconsin in a 1926 Ford touring car. It was to be the first of many trips which would total 100,000 miles. The girls even met Henry Ford at the factory and had their picture taken with him. On some of the trips, other young women took the place of some of the original five. Recently the group, who came to call themselves the Gypsy Coeds, held a reunion to talk over old times in touring fifty years ago.

By 1927, Henry Ford had brought out the Model A, with seven body types and eight colors. Its lines were lower and smoother, and it had a comfortable ride due to better shock absorbers and springs. It had a unique feature — safety glass — in the windshield. The four-door was $750; the two-door, $495; and the coupe, $494.

In 1932, a V-8 was announced, and this roomier, heavier car sold for $460 to $650. Looking back, Henry Ford could indeed be proud. He was now almost seventy. He had ushered in an age of pure driving pleasure. Seatbelts were not needed as people drove slowly and enjoyed the view. The old brick streets in town were bumpy, but the word "pothole" had not been invented. Monstrous semis didn't menace the roads. All vehicles were compact models in the twenties and thirties.

Unfortunately, perhaps we are traveling more, but enjoying it less. Frantic commuting or speeding down the interstate with no intimate look at farmhouses and villages cannot compare with those early, exploratory trips into the countryside. Without the mass-produced, inexpensive Model T our world might not have opened up so extensively. Although modern travel by automobile can be frustrating, we are grateful for the chance to be a part of it. Thank you, Mr. Ford!

The 1915 Ford T Was Doc's Cultured Carrier

by Gerald Perschbacher

Doc Fredericks was loved by everyone. And everyone loved his Model T Ford touring, also.

Story goes that he bought the car when he was fresh out of medical school, that he paid for it partly with cash, a little with some things he bartered, and a lot with the promise for free calls on any youngster under the age of 10, a promise he had made to the Ford dealer in town. And the promise kept him jumping in a town of 7,000.

The Ford dealer had a large family — six boys and seven girls, if I recall the final count. I'm sure Doc never forgot, since he had delivered 11 of them. The dealer was shrewd.

I guess Doc Fredericks was, too, only he never put it on for anyone to see.

A typical day would see him drive down Main Street, top down in the breeze, heading to some medical emergency which mostly consisted of treatment with some linament, a cotton bandage, and some tall tale that took the sting away. Everyone said he set more arms than Carter had pills, too.

Doc could have afforded a nice, new Chrysler when they came out in the mid-'20s, or some shiny Packard 120 when it hit the market like bricks in 1935. But he stayed with his Model T Ford.

"Never anything like it, son," he told me once, when I stared wide-eyed at all the medical paraphernalia he had tucked on the floor in back and packed onto the rear seat. I remember standing there, smelling the black leather, petting the brass headlight rims. He told me it was the last year for rims like those. He seemed to take immense pride in everything he said about the touring car.

"Just high enough and wide enough for me to carry all my needs," he confided. "And long enough, too, with 100 inches between front and rear wheels."

"Gosh, Doc, what is all that in back?" I asked in awe.

"Your carpenter daddy would say, 'the tools of my trade,' my instruments, linaments, bandages, and culture dishes. Because I carry so much equipment to take good culture specimens, I call my T a cultured carrier," he laughed. And I did, too. It was the way he said it.

The T always shone and seldom saw dirt on it longer than a day. And I never recall having seen it muddy. No. Doc kept it spruced up, like a little limousine.

One Friday night I took out to the wrong part of town, got into a crap game with some bigger boys who were new to town, and got the whipping of my life. Doc Fredericks found me heaped like trash by the gutter, mended my aches and bruises, and escorted me home in the back seat of his T. I remember the hurts, but I recall the ride even more vividly. It was the first car I ever had ridden in, since Daddy was of the old, horse-sense school.

I remember asking him one question as he readied to leave. "Doc, why do you keep the old Model T?"

"Some folks in town think I've had some bad debts, but I keep the T because it's trustworthy. I could have bought a much larger car back in '15, and I could have paid cash for this one too. But I didn't. I keep the T to keep me humble and keep me serving."

The tapered firewall design was new for '15 and added a crude, aerodynamic look to the front. The one-millionth Model T was made that year.

1919 Model T Ford 3-door Touring Car

The year 1919 was a significant one in the history of Ford Motor Co. A financial restructuring of business and financial dealings made Henry and Edsel Ford the sole owners of the firm. On Jan. 1, Edsel was named company president.

Old Henry rocked the automobile industry by instituting a $6 per day minimum wage for his workers. He still had plenty of profits left — enough to construct the world's largest, single industry manufacturing complex adjacent to the Rouge River, in Detroit.

On the production front, the Fordson tractor was introduced to provide American agriculturists with a reliable, but low cost piece of farm machinery.

Publishing was another field that felt the Ford influence, when Henry started printing his *Dearborn Independent* newspaper in 1919.

With so many diverse responsibilities to think about, it was not surprising that few real changes were seen in the 1919 Model T cars. The black-painted steel radiators, rounded hoods with six louvers, and nickel-plated hubcaps adopted in 1917 were carried over, again, for 1919.

Closed-bodied cars received a few new options including an electric starter system and demountable tire rims. But, by and large, there was little reason to modernize the Model T, since sales were strong and buyers seemed very satisfied with the product their money was buying.

The "three-door" Model T touring car was one of the most popular Ford body styles. There was a door stamping on the front driver's side of the car, but only for a balanced appearance. The door was a "dummy" type that was not cut out. This was to discourage foolhardy Ford owners from stepping out into oncoming traffic. Only the rear door on the left-hand side of the car actually opened, as did both front and rear righthand doors. The price for this model was $525.

Like other Model Ts, the touring car was perched on a 100-inch wheelbase. Actual measurements taken from our feature car show a front tread of 57½ inches and a one-inch narrower rear tread. Tires were large but narrow 30x3½ inch types mounted on wooden spoke wheels. They were all-black rubber, of course.

The T's mono-block, four-cylinder powerplant had a 3¾x4 inch bore and stroke. It displaced 2.9 liters or, if you prefer Americanized figures, 176.7 cubic inches. Brake horsepower developed was 20 at 1600 R.P.M.

Power was transmitted to the drivetrain via a planetary, two-speed transmission. Nothing fancy, but quite sufficient to get the Ford owner from Point A to Point B. A 10-gallon gasoline tank was used.

The 1919 Model T Ford three-door touring car was a popular model that sold for $525 when new.

Ford's 1926 Model T

by Gerald Perschbacher

"Those whose consciences are clear, who know that they have done their duty and have not denied their obligations to humanity, who have not thought themselves better or more deserving than their fellow-creatures — these do not have to take refuge in fears. They are free to scan the future and to greet whatever it may have in store."

These words emphasized by Henry Ford addressed the fear of change. Spoken in the early 1920s, the words were prophetic as the venerable Model T Ford lost popularity and sales. A new move, strong and bold, was needed if the Ford Motor Co. was to survive. But Henry wanted a few more miles squeezed out of his Model T.

In 1926 Ford added glamour to his creation, offering a nickeled radiator shell, a lower chassis, lightweight pistons, and a choice of colors. The Fordor sedan was high and boxy, like a top hat, and sold for $545, the cheapest Model T sedan up to that time. That same price would carry over for 1927.

Henry stated production with the first 1926 Model T being number 12,225,528 in November 1925. Near the end of July '26, Model T number 14,000,000 had been produced, a milestone in automobile mass production which was not invented by Henry Ford but certainly perfected by him.

When it came to colors, the coupe and Tudor sedan were finished in "deep channel green," while the Fordor sedan came "in a rich Windsor maroon." Advertisements mentioned that "fenders are larger, longer and more attractive, conforming to stream-like treatment. The hood is also longer; louvres on sides are redesigned and increased in number.

"Seats are set further back, lowered and designed to permit easy relaxation. Lowering the car's center of gravity tends to give greater sense of security and to increase roadability. Improvements in both the transmission and rear wheel brakes, with wider drums and bands, makes braking smoother and more positive. Running boards are wider and near the ground; doors are designed for easier entrance and exit. Balloon tires, $25 extra."

The Fordor was unlike other cars in the Ford lineup for 1926, since it carried the typical square fuel tank under the seat which made it difficult to refuel. Other models could be regassed from the outside without major inconvenience, an advancement for the Model T.

The Fordor carried lightweight cast-iron pistons and used fuel more efficiently with better vaporization than before. The four-cylinder motor developed about 20 horsepower, and the wheelbase stretched on a 100-inch length. Beginning in January 1926, headlights were mounted atop a tie-bar which ran between front fenders.

The Ford company brought in profits of $75,000,000 for 1926, a drop from the $100,000,000 in 1924. Henry knew that the days were numbered for "The Universal Car" — the Model T Ford.

It was in 1926, the year that Ford established the five-day work week, that Henry announced that the famous Model T Ford would have its last hurrah in 1927.

Cheapest of the Ford Model T 4-dr sedans was the 1926 version which sold for $545

Ford Model A

Henry Orchestrated Media, Public Setting the Stage for Model A

by Robert C. Ackerson

A review of the events leading up to and surrounding the development of the Model A Ford reveals much of the operation of the Ford Motor Co. a half century ago.

Perhaps most interesting in view of the tremendous volume of material that has been written about Henry Ford and his company is the inability of any writer to accurately pinpoint the date when Henry Ford officially gave the order to commence work on a successor to the Model T. Allan Nevins and Frank Hill in *Ford: Expansion and Challenge 1915-1933* conclude that "the exact chronology of the work on the new prototype is hazy." In December 1926 Henry Ford emphatically denied that he was planning a new car. Any work taking place at Ford that outsiders could construe as indicating that such was the case, Ford said, was to "keep our engineers busy — prevent them tinkering too much with the Ford car." This attempt to stifle speculation was unsuccessful not because it

sounded silly but rather because the force of the argument to the contrary had become so powerful and pervasive that to suggest any other course of action for the Ford Motor Co. was without foundation.

The primary factor suggesting that Ford had no real choice but to come forth with a new model can be simply stated: the market had changed and the product he was marketing had not. From the production of the first Model T on Oct. 1, 1908 until its end in 1927 the Model T was designed and priced for the "first time" car buyer. This was of course the key to Ford's success and while admittedly he was not the first to recognize the potential of manufacturing such an automobile the sheer magnitude of the industrial empire he erected upon this foundation represents an achievement even his most severe critics begrudgingly admire.

But by 1925 his policy of steadily reducing the price of

The new 1928 Model A. The smart Fordor sedan, with its closed rear quarters, exuded style.

the Model T seemed to have reached the point of diminishing returns. That year was the biggest the automotive industry had experienced but Ford sales, rather than paralleling this growth, had suffered a small decline. The following year came even more serious news, for the first time in Ford history a drop in price did not act as a catalyst upon sales. The country was becoming more prosperous and with more income came a desire for more than just basic transportation. Thus while Ford sales had slipped from 1,870,000 in 1924 to 1,675,000 in 1925 the more expensive Chevrolet had moved from a 280,000 sales mark to an impressive and disturbing (to Ford's lieutenants) 470,000. Furthermore, Ford's policy of price cutting had been adopted by his competitors. From 1922 to 1926 Ford lowered the price on his sedan from $645 to $565. But in the same span of time the Overland Four had been reduced $300 to $595, the Dodge from $1,785 to $895, and the Maxwell from $1,485 to $995. Put another way, whereas at the start of the decade the Model T had virtually no competition even remotely near its price, by 1926 there were nearly a dozen American marques offering models priced under $1,000. Equally important, in the same span of time average per capita earnings had increased 10% thus enabling more new car buyers to seriously consider lifting their sights beyond the Model T.

On Jan. 20, 1926 Ernest C. Kanzler took what numerous Ford historians have recognized as an act of great personal courage. In a six page memorandum to Henry Ford he outlined the company's predicament: "with every additional car our competitors sell they get stronger and we get weaker...We have not gone ahead in the last few years...Our Ford customers...are going to other manufacturers."

Six months later on July 20 Kanzler was gone but apparently the following month Ford gave an oral order to begin work on a new model Ford. Charles Sorenson, his great production master, is quoted by Nevins and Hill as saying, "We've got to design a car for the market, a four-cylinder one" after he started to transform Ford's acceptance of reality into a counterattack by the Ford Motor Co.

Thus even though Henry Ford in February 1927 was still steadfastly denying that a new Ford car was on the way just the opposite was the case.

Finally on May 25, 1927, the rumors took substance; the Ford Motor Company announced it would build a new car to replace the Model T. The following day the 15,000,000th Model T was built at Ford's Highland Park plant. Speculation about what type of automobile would succeed the Model T became one of the major news stories of the day. Even prior to May 25, 1927, rumors were rife about the form a new Ford would take. Some prophets declared that Ford would unveil an eight-cylinder automobile with a price tag under $1,000. Others forecast that a new two-cylinder Ford was on the way. Perhaps Ford would call his new creation the Edison, suggested other sources. In the summer of 1927 even more radical remarks issued forth from the rumor mill. The new Ford would have 12 cylinders or even be diesel powered were typical examples of their form.

On a more realistic plane, industrial analysts centered their attention on the economic and market importance Henry Ford's new car would have. Would it have the same impact as the Model T? With Chevrolet on the move could Ford mount a successful counterattack?

Those who were anticipating a car with the same impact upon America as the Model T were to be disappointed. It's probably true that Ford would have been mightily pleased to introduce a car with radical design features (hence the X-8 engine project upon which Eugene Farkas labored on from 1924 to 1926) but such was not to be the case. In this light some Ford historians have suggested that the Model A was best seen as an "interim car" intended to span the gap between the Model T and a successor with qualities that would enable it to monopolize the market in a similar fashion. Counterbalancing this argument is the hypothesis that Henry Ford fully expected the Model A to have a life span equal to the Model T. Neither case was of course possible of realization in the late 1920s. The Model T was a special case unto itself and it's highly doubtful if any automobile will ever be able to exercise a similar impact on society.

In this regard perhaps it's best to describe the Model A, in 1927, as being highly competitive in overall design to its competitors but hardly possessing attributes that could in any way be conceived as revolutionary. Edsel Ford readily conceded this point, noting, "There is nothing radical about the new car. In fact, it is more conventional than the old Model T." Years later, in 1957, John R. Bond, in an evaluation of the Model A's engine design (*Road and Track*, February 1957), viewed it as "anything but a modern design, even in 1927." Yet as we shall see design was not the Model As claim to greatness.

The dimension and scope of the changes that had to be made at the Ford Motor Co. in preparation for the debut of the Model A in late 1927 were without precedent in industrial history. Indeed it was not without reason that Henry Ford on his birthday in 1927 said, "Sixty-four today and the biggest job of my life ahead." Ford was probably right on this account in more than one respect. No doubt he had delayed far too long in giving the go-ahead for work to commence on a successor to the Model T but after finally accepting the inevitable he had a crystal clear vision of what had to be done. The new car had to offer more speed and comfort than the Tin Lizzie yet maintain Ford's traditional price advantage and reputation for qual-

The Model A went right to work, even if it did have a touch of class. The '29 phaeton hauled two policeman and an early radio set.

By 1929 the Model A was firmly entrenched in society. Even the wealthy might buy a Ford, such as this station wagon, for picking up arrivals at the railroad station. (Photo courtesy of the Henry Ford Museum)

ity. This was an enormous task requiring the designing of an automobile virtually all of whose 5,580 parts were different from those on the Model T. Added to the challenge this task posed was the pressure exerted upon Ford by the public's great expectations. The impact of the Ford Motor Co. on American life and the interest it generated in the public's mind was aptly demonstrated by the attention every word uttered and each mode by any company official attracted in the media during the six months preceding the Model A's introduction.

Furthermore the Model A was born into a world far different from that which welcomed the Model T. Now a Ford automobile faced strong, entrenched competition in what was once its sole domain, the low-priced field. Whereas at one time the Ford had been the innovator he was now forced to adapt himself to playing a new game, the rules of which had been written by others. In 1928 other men such as Alfred Sloan, Bill Knudsen, and Walter Chrysler had already grasped the importance of styling and technical advances in the sale of an automobile. Let Henry Ford's critics say what they will about him but when the challenge faced in 1928 is considered from purely a technical point of view; the excellence of his response is sufficient to judge that phase of Ford's life as his finest hour. Allan Nevin alluded to this point when he wrote in *Ford: Expansion and Challenge, 1915-1933* that "Ford plunged into the new undertaking with an eagerness of spirit and clarity of vision that characterized him at his best."

In comparison to the facilities existing at General Motors and Chrysler, the research and development resources at Ford were of the Stone Age variety. Ray Dahlinger, Ford's official tester, was prone to submit only two reports to the designers: either the item was "damn good" or it was "no damn good." There was no middle ground as far as Dahlinger was concerned. At the Ford Motor Co. the testing and designing processes took place as if they were separated by barriers of space and language. Every component of the Model A was subjected to virtually all tortures capable of being inflicted upon an inanimate object. Then the designers would receive the mangled corpse and be forced to perform a post mortem examination upon the remains to determine the cause of its demise.

Yet this approach had some benefits and when united with Henry Ford's mechanical brilliance and unfailing vision of what was or was not practical the result was truly one of the outstanding cars of all time, a car Gordon Buehrig has characterized as "probably the highest quality small car ever built." If nothing else the Model A was perhaps the most complex item ever developed under rule of trial and error and Allan Nevin's assessment that Ford's "mechanical genius was worth more than laboratory refinements" should not be easily dismissed in this respect. Moreover Ford's dedication to the integrity of any product bearing his name and his almost naive disregard of the costs of production incurred by such a policy ensured that the Model T's successor would be of superior quality. Regarding this point Henry Ford told a *Detroit News* reporter in December 1927 that "We paid no attention to the cost or the time we took. When you are thinking about things like that you can't do a good job. This was a good job. We got things done the way we wanted them."

It is of course true that the Ford camp in 1927 no longer counted among its ranks engineers of the stature of C.H. Wills but those who remained still represented a pool of

A famous poster, "Features of the New Ford." Examples may be found hanging in Ford showrooms to this day. The poster introduced the Model A to America.

talent that when led by Henry Ford were up to the challenge confronting them. Men such as Joseph Galamb, Eugene Farkas, Frank Johnson, and Laurence Sheldrick all acquitted themselves well in this regard. In addition when it came time to gear up the Rouge plant for production of the Model A, Ford could turn to two of the best men in the business, William Sorenson and Pete Martin.

Although an experimental model without body was operational early in 1927 it wasn't until Aug. 10 that Edsel Ford could report to an anxious nation that "the new Ford automobile is an accomplished fact. The engineering problems affecting its design and equipment and affecting also its manufacture have all been solved.

No less a formidable task was the revamping of the Ford production lines to begin spewing forth Model As. *The New York Times* called this changeover "probably the biggest replacement of plant in the history of American industry." Certainly if the Rouge had been the wonder of the industrial world when it was producing Model Ts, it became, during the changeover to the new Ford, an industrial miracle made manifest. Virtually at every point of production new machinery that dwarfed that used for the manufacture of the Model T was moved into position. Tools of a highly specialized nature were used in a scale that had no equal elsewhere in the world. The total cost of the equipment and renovation which comprised what Nevin characterized as "a memorable epic of industrial achievement" was, according to *The New York Times*, $18,000,000.

On Oct. 11, 1927, work had progressed to the point where Edsel Ford could announce that the Model As assembly line would soon be operational. At the same time Edsel Ford also revealed that Ford dealers had already received down payments for the Model A from 125,000 people. Less than two weeks later, on Oct. 20, Henry Ford stamped serial number "A1" into the first Model A engine off its assembly line. Finally on Nov. 25 Ford made public the date when the Model A would go on display. Dec. 2 would be "The Day" for millions of Americans.

The actual cost of designing the Model A and renovating the Rouge plant for its production was estimated by Henry Ford to have totalled some $100,000,000. His method for arriving at this figure was typically straight forward. "All I know," said Ford, "is that when we started actually to work out this change of models we had $350,000,000 in the bank. Now we have worked it out and we have $250,000,000 in the bank. That means we have spent $100,000,000 in the operation."

Surprisingly the six months between the cessation of Model T production and the introduction of the Model A did not provide Chevrolet with as great a sales opportunity as might be expected. Sales in 1927 fell one million units below the 1926 level, apparently reflecting the decision of many potential new car buyers to wait and see what the new Ford had to offer.

Beginning on Nov. 28 Ford placed the first of five full-page advertisements in some two-thousand newspapers from coast to coast. Not until the fourth day was a picture of the Model A included. This was to a certain extent somewhat anti-climatic since earlier in November virtually every newspaper in touch with the automotive scene had carried a photograph of a Model A Tudor sedan taken by an enterprising reporter outside a Brighton, Mich. restaurant.

The public's response to the unveiling of the Model A was of such intensity that it instantly became an event worthy of inclusion into the folklore of the Ford automobile. Within 36 hours of its public debut over 10 million Americans got a first hand glimpse of the Model Ts successor. In New York City alone, 50,000 people placed orders for new Fords and within two weeks the Ford Motor Co. had 400,000 advance orders in its possession.

In contrast to this outpouring of enthusiasm, Model A production remained disappointingly low throughout 1927 and even when the new year began it stood at only 150 units a day. Eventually, however, production began a steady upward climb and by February 1929 the first million Model As had been built. During 1928 as would be expected, Chevrolet outsold Ford with the sale of a million cars. Ford had to settle for second place with its sales mark just under the 800,000 level. The following year, however, Ford rebounded into the top position, building 1,851,092 Model As and controlling 34% of the U.S. market.

The Model As life span was of course not nearly as long as that of the Model T. The twin forces of the Depression and the vastly changed structure of the automobile market saw to that. On Aug. 31, 1931 Model A production came to an end; a total of 4,320,446 Model A Fords had been built. From the outset of its production life the Model A enjoyed a considerably diffrent public image than did the Model T. Whereas the Model T, in spite of all efforts to the contrary, was seen as offering little more than basic transportation, the Model A enjoyed a much higher social standing. Such varied public figures as Mary Pickford, Will Rogers, John D. Rockefeller, and Carl Sandburg owned Model As and were proud of it. If for no other reason the Model A deserves the position it has been allocated in Ford history. Yet of course its claim to fame goes far beyond such an intangible issue. In short, the Model A was an outstandingly good automobile. In workmanship, style, and performance, it was on a par with far more expensive automobiles and indeed it is only the Model As low initial price that causes some enthusiasts to deny it the status of a classic.

In 1954 Frank Rowsome, Jr. wrote a memorable article on the Model A for *Popular Science* which appeared in that magazine's September 1954 issue. Rowsome recalled, obviously with a good deal of nostalgia, his experiences with a Model A. Noting that it "invariably started" he wrote that "one Maine winter, with temperatures around 20 below zero, I caught it on the first turn every morning for weeks." No surprise that Rowsome described the Model A as "one of the most wonderfully satisfying cars ever built...an uncommonly willing car, like a friendly farm dog." Yet perhaps unknowingly Mr. Rowsome paid the Model A the highest tribute when he compared it with the nation's new automobiles. "Twenty-six years from now," he predicted, "...darn few of us will recall the glistening 1954 models with the same warm affection with which we now remember the Model A."

Without much fear of contradiction, it's fair to pronounce his prediction as 100% correct.

Ford Oval-Window Coupe Features Distinct Styling

by Peter Winnewisser

Produced only in 1928 and 1929, the Ford Model A business coupe was an attractive practical car designed to meet the needs of business executives, salesmen, physicians, and others whose activities kept them on the road. Family practitioners loved it, as evidenced by its nickname, the doctor's coupe.

Domestic production of the Model A Ford totaled 4,320,446 units. Less than two percent of these (74,987 cars) were type 54A business coupes. This low production figure is one of the reasons why these models are relatively rare in comparison with sport and standard coupes. It's also probable that many of those which did survive past World War II were turned into sport coupes when they reached the hands of some eager restorer.

Introduced in the spring of 1928, the business coupe had a bit of the sport coupe effect without the landau irons (although these were later available as a dealer installed accessory). It was distinguished by a non-folding "soft" top extending down over the rear quarter to the belt line of the car. This roof covering was made of high-grade black artificial leather heavily coated with nitro-cellulose to withstand weather. The leather was stretched tightly over heavy wooden bows and continued forward to cover the visor.

The bow effect was carried out in the interior rear quarter with trimming in harmony with the cushions. Convenient door pockets for papers or small books, plus a spacious parcel shelf, added to the car's utility.

In 1928 only one interior trim scheme was available: blue check cloth with gray body cloth. Exterior colors were the same as those available on other models.

Two practical features of the business coupe were an enlarged window in the rear (introduced late in 1928) and a spacious (14 cubic feet) luggage area with no interior trim, but with an ample 35⅜-inch deck opening. The trunk lid was provided with a handle lock and supports to hold it in place when lifted. When closed, the door folded into gutters which allowed water to run down into a spillway and then onto the road, making the compartment waterproof. For those who preferred, a rumbleseat was available at extra cost.

In 1929 an oval quarter window (porthole) was added to the business coupe. Most, if not all of these models, had this feature. It was unique because no other Model A had this kind of window. It was discontinued, along with the business coupe, for the 1930 model year. Also available that year were several new interior trim schemes and a choice of new exterior colors.

According to *Old Cars Price Guide* (winter 1985), the value of a 1928 business coupe in no. 1 condition is $11,000. The 1929 oval window coupe is estimated at a surprisingly low $9,200. Current owners might disagree with these figures but, in any event, they are a long way from the original $525 selling price.

Model A enthusiasts who frequent the antique auto show circuit will occasionally spot an oval window coupe in the lineup. One of these is owned by Ron Van Allen of Bridgeport, N.Y. A professional auto refinisher and restorer, Van Allen completed a restoration of his coupe early in 1984. Painted a striking jet black with a black long grain leather top, the car was shown 10 times last year and garnered 13 awards including "best of show" at the New York State Fair Grand Concours d'Elegance.

Side quarter view on Ron Van Allen's 1929 Oval Window Coupe clearly shows the porthole or oval window. Van Allen is from Bridgeport, N.Y. and did a complete ground-up restoration of his unusual coupe.

Henry's Personal Model A

by Tom LaMarre

"The Model T is the most perfect automobile in the world," Henry Ford once said.

Ford gave grudging approval to its replacement, the Model A, but insisted that the new car project not begin until the last Model T left the shop.

The legendary assembly line came to a stop, costing Ford an estimated $100 million. In the meantime, there were endless battles between Edsel Ford and his father regarding the Model A.

Despite his loyalty to the Model T, Henry Ford eventually did acquire a Model A for his personal use — a 1929 coupe. The car's success was proven by then. The millionth Model A was built on Feb. 4, 1929; the two-millionth car followed on July 24, 1929.

Henry's Model A, which was black with red striping (his favorite color), differed in some respects from the regular production model. Experimental brake drums, cowl ventilators, custom upholstery, and a holder for Vichy mineral water (which Ford favored for his health at that time) were some of the personal touches for Henry.

As a Model A owner, he was in good company. Mary Pickford was enrolled as purchaser number one when her husband, Douglas Fairbanks, bought her a 1928 sport coupe as a gift. Another owner of a 1928 coupe was Dolores Del Rio. Joan Crawford owned a 1929 town car, while Franklin D. Roosevelt owned a 1929 cabriolet.

Ford's personal car, a 1929 coupe, was finished in black with red striping.

1930 Model A Roadster Gave Value Above Price

"The new Ford is a value far above the price," read the cover of the handsome sales catalog. Characterized by a number of styling refinements and minor technical changes, the 1930 Model A was the only Ford of its type officially promoted as "new and improved" by the new company that built it.

The untrained eye could have difficulty distinguishing a '30 model from the '29, but the changes are apparent to old car lovers. On most body styles, revisions to the cowl area will be noted. New streamline moldings can also be seen. Ford claimed longer, lower, gracefully flowing lines. The hood was raised somewhat and a higher, narrower radiator was used. The stainless steel radiator shell (Ford called it "rustless" steel) had a new, one-half turn type cap which, like the fuel filler lid, was flat and knurled. Plated, hemisphere-shaped headlights were used.

New, smaller wheels were a specifications change. They were welded-steel spoke types wearing larger 4.75 x 19 inch balloon tires. This helped lower the overall vehicle height. This, said FoMoCo, "gives greater safety and additional riding comfort." What actually happened was that they lowered the center of gravity by bringing the car closer to the ground.

The DeLuxe roadster was an unusually attractive body style incorporating performance and open car pleasure. A specially designed sport top of tan colored material was fitted. The top bows were natural wood.

At a price of $520, this car had a rumbleseat as standard equipment. Like the upholstery used in the driver's compartment, that in the auxiliary seat was of tan colored genuine leather. The windshield and wild wings featured shatterproof Triplex glass. Additional features included welled fenders, truck rack, rearview mirror (attached to driver's windshield post), cowl lamps, windshield wiper, full length bumpers, top boot, and five-spoke wheels finished in a color that harmonized with the body hue.

The 1930 cars retained the remarkable Model A engine, an L-head four-cylinder, cast en bloc type motor. With a 3⅞x4¼-inch bore and stroke, piston displacement was 200.5 cubic inches. SAE/NACC horsepower ratings, at 24.03, were identical. Brake horsepower totaled 40 at 2200 rpm. The engine was said to give unusual acceleration, smoothness, speed, and power without sacrificing reliability and economy. Gasoline economy in the 20-30 mpg range was claimed for Model As.

The Model A would do 55-65 mph when pressed. Torque tube drive was carried over from Model T Ford days. Carburetion was via a one-barrel Zenith unit. The ignition system was of the company's own design and manufacture. The overall gear ratio was 3.77:1.

The Model A had a 103.5 inch wheelbase with Houdaille double-acting shock absorbers front and rear. A three-quarter irreversible type steering gear of worm-and-sector design gave a turning radius of 17 feet. Transverse springs were a Ford trademark. Four-wheel brakes were used. They were of the internal-expanding type with mechanical actuation. The service brakes were fully enclosed for protection against mud, water, and sand.

Many other items were standard on all Model As, including: a speedometer, gasoline gauge on the instrument panel, dash lighting, combination tail and stop lamp, oil indicator rod, and theft-proof ignition lock. The DeLuxe roadster had a shipping weight of 2,230 pounds.

Our feature car is from Walter E. Cuny's Falls Motors Limited auto collection of Genoa, Ill. It is equipped with a number of extra-cost accessories including a radiator grille guard, "Quail" type hood mascot, plated sidemount covers with strap-on pedestal type mirrors, dual rearview mirrors, dual spotlights, and a tan colored rumbleseat roof. It personifies Ford's promotional theme highlighting the "new" 1930 Model A as a "notable example of high quality at a low price."

1930 Model A Ford DeLuxe Roadster   (Photo Courtesy W.E. Cuny)

Model A Fordor Popular in '31

Ford Motor Co. reached an automotive milestone when it sold its 20-millionth automobile in 1931. The most popular and best selling Ford body style that season was the Model A Fordor sedan.

Like other 1931 models, the Fordor sedan had some new characteristic features. They included one-piece runningboard aprons, a corrugated instrument panel, and a panel in the radiator shell of DeLuxe models which was painted the same color as the body.

Technically, the 1931 Model A was a refined version of the previous type. Power was provided by a Ford-built four-cylinder, L-head engine with a bore and stroke of $3\frac{7}{8}$ x $4\frac{1}{4}$ inches. It had a piston displacement of 200.5 cubic inches and used a Zenith carburetor and Ford type ignition system. National Automobile Chamber of commerce (NACC) net horsepower rating was 24.03 and the gross horsepower was listed as being 40 b.h.p. @2200 rpm. Overall gear ratio was 3.77:1.

The Model A was built on a trim, 103.5 inch wheelbase and used 4.75 x 19 inch tires. The Fordor sedan sold for a mere $630 and had a shipping weight of 2,488 pounds.

The Model A Fordor sedan was Ford Motor Company's most popular 1931 body type.

1931 Model A Convertible Sedan

This rare open Ford was produced for slightly more than six months with a total worldwide production of only 5,072. Its distinctive one-of-a-kind body style had a rigid upper-side body style above the windows in an attempt to lower the noise which was considered objectionable in the phaetons. The fabric top slid on rails and stored behind the rear seat in a flat stack which was covered with a boot. The retail price was high at $640, but genuine leather seats were standard equipment. This extremely rare model, along with over 150 other Fords, is on permanent display at the famous Towe Ford Museum in Deer Lodge, Mont. The Towe Museum has every year and every model Ford built between 1903 and 1953. They also claim to have every body style roadster and phaeton from 1928 to 1938!

The Towe Museum is open year round and is located midway between Yellowstone National Park and Glacier National Park on Interstate 90. For more information contact the Museum at 1106 Main Street, Deer Lodge, MT 59722 (406) 846-3111.

'31 Ford Model A convertible sedan

Ford Early V-8

Ford's '32 Roadster was Sporty and Fast

Ford Motor Co. introduced a line of all-new cars in March 1932 as the replacement for its popular but somewhat old-fashioned Model A series. These cars had longer, lower bodies highlighted by a handsome V-type radiator grille which added to their modern appearance. Everything about them looked just right for 1932 and still does today.

New technical advances included use of a fuel pump, floor mounted starter buttons, coincidental ignition lock, Houdaille double-acting shock absorbers and rubber mounted spring shackles. For safety's sake the gas tank was moved to the rear of the cars. The Ford transmission featured silent second gear.

Two engines were available. The lower-priced Model Bs had a 200.5 cubic inch four-cylinder powerplant which developed 50 horsepower. Cars in the Ford V-18 series used a 221 cubic inch V-8 producing 65 horsepower. This was the first American V-8 priced to suit the budget of the "common man." For identification, the Model Bs said "Ford" on the hubcaps, while the higher-priced line had V-8 emblems there and on the bow-shaped headlight tie-bar.

Three roadsters were included in each of the two lines: one featuring two-passenger seating and having a rear luggage compartment; the second a standard job with a rumbleseat; and the third having a rumbleseat and DeLuxe trim. Prices were $410, $435, and $450, respectively, for Model B roadsters and $460, $485, and $500 for V-18s. DeLuxe equipment included a chrome spare tire cover, pin striping, cowl lights, and wheels painted to match the body color.

The roadster body style designated an open car with a folding windshield which did not have roll-up door windows. When driving in cold or inclement weather, protection for driver and passengers was afforded by snap on side curtains. The roadster was the sporty model in the 1932 Ford lineup.

1932 Ford convertible

1932 Ford Roadster.

by Peter Winnewisser

1935 Restyling

After four years of declining sales and loss of sales leadership, the Ford Motor Co. pulled out all the stops with its restyled 1935 models. They were promoted as cars of "greater beauty, greater comfort and greater safety." Henry Ford was thrilled. "The 1935 Ford V-8 is the best car we have ever produced," he boasted.

The buying public agreed. Attracted by more streamlined body styling, smoother ride, elimination of front opening doors (except the rear doors on sedans) and competitive pricing, Americans preferred the V-8 to other low-priced cars in 1935.

A broad selection of body styles, leadership in open cars, and the only low-cost V-8 engine helped Ford forge to the front in the competitve motor world. It was a dramatic victory — the only years in the '30s when Ford sales and production would outstrip Chevrolet. Final production score: Ford, 942,439; Chevrolet, 793,437.

The 1935 Ford Model 48 was a neat package with a distinctive look that set it off from the previous Model 40. Styling changes included a new body with its front end distinguished by a full length v-shaped grille. It had a clip on horizontal break strips, slanted hood louvres (accentuated by stainless steel beading), bullet-shaped headlamps, and parking lights incorporated. The large, rounded fenders flowed gracefully into the running-boards.

Although retaining the 90 hp V-8 engine, Ford introduced some engineering refinements. They included forced-draft crankcase ventilation to exhaust gases and water vapor. Improvements were also made to the clutch, brakes (although still mechanical), frame, rear axle, and steering.

Advances in styling and engineering are only part of the 1935 story. The new Ford was also a better riding car. Few would argue with a contemporary poem about the V-8 which claimed, "Oh, it glides o'er the road with the greatest of ease, and it rides front or back just as smooth as you please."

This comfortable ride was due mainly to what the company termed "center-poise" suspension. This design moved the engine forward 8.5 inches and improved the spring suspension. The net effect of this was that the passengers rode cradled between the wheels. With better weight distribution, the car provided a smoother ride, as well as more stability at high speeds.

Riding quality was enhanced by smaller, but wider wheels with a four-inch rim and larger, softer, 16 x 6:00 tires. These fat tires also added to the overall appearance of the car.

In the open car field, Ford outclassed its competition by a wide margin in 1935. According to the *Standard Catalog of American Cars 1805-1942*, Chevrolet produced less than 1,400 open cars that year, while Ford built in excess of 32,000 in four models (roadster, phaeton, cabriolet, and convertible sedan). The classiest of the group were the roadster and phaeton.

The Model 48-750 deluxe phaeton had everything going for it: looks, performance, ride, and price ($580). When loaded with accessories, as it usually was, the phaeton made an impressive sight.

Produced only in the deluxe style, it came equipped with top boots, side curtains, wind wings, leather upholstery, glove box, ashtray, and dust hood. The top irons,

windshield frame, stanchions, and rear window frames were bright chrome plated.

For inclement weather, side curtains were installed on steel rods inserted in special door grommets. When not in use they were stored in an envelope behind the rear seat cushion.

The phaeton was available in any of seven deluxe color combinations: black, green, two grays, two blues, and maroon. Two of these (Duncan blue and Coach maroon) were used only on special order, at added cost. The body color was accented by a single pin stripe five-eights of an inch below the belt line. Black or colored wheels were provided at the buyer's discretion.

Our feature car is owned by Dick White of Oneida, N.Y. It is a typical example and illustrates why Ford open cars were the classiest in the low-priced field in 1935.

White completely restored his vineyard green phaeton in 1983. One of only 6,073 produced, the car is in no. 1 condition. It is valued by *Old Cars Price Guide* at $27,000. A similar car was recently advertised in *Old Cars Weekly*. for $35,000.

Accessories on the car include a clock mirror, heater,

radio, dual outside mirrors, license plate frames, tonneau windshield, rear mounted spare locking hubcap, greyhound radiator ornament, two-speed Columbia rear end, and banjo steering wheel (actually a 1936 item, according to White).

An avid Ford man who specializes in Model As and V-8s, White prefers the '35 to other Fords of that era. "I like the looks of it," he says. "It's the last year with the 32-spoke wire wheels and exposed horns, and it rides like a heavy car."

In some circle, the 1935 Ford doesn't get much respect. "Why would you want to write about a '35 Ford?" inquired one V-8 enthusiast with whom we discussed this article. In the past, V-8 devotees turned more to the 1934 and 1936 models. It's not improbable that quite a few 1936 Fords on the road today began life as '35s.

On the other hand, there are those who would argue that the '35 Ford is a class act. Enthusiasts, such as Dick White, would certainly agree with the unknown poet quoted above, when he concludes his ode to the 1935 Ford: "It's a peach! It's a beaut! It's a wow!"

Low-Priced Fords of 1939

America had lifted itself from the depths of the Depression by 1939. Her people could see the great promise that the future held, but only through the dark shadow cast by current world events.

In New York, millions attended the World's Fair to see glimpses of what tomorrow could bring. San Francisco's International Exposition took others on a visit to "Treasure Island." On Oct. 25, in Wilmington, Del., the experimental sale of a new kind of women's stockings — made of a plastic material called nylon — showed the world what scientists could do with coal, air, and water. What even more wondrous accomplishments would the 1940s bring?

Great hopes for tomorrow could not, however, wipe out the realities of the day. In September, England declared war on Germany. America was not yet directly involved in the growing conflict, but her industries were already working feverishly to supply free Europe with needed armaments.

With the nation's dual focus on future hopes and current realities, perhaps it was only natural that Ford had two different-looking lines of cars on the market in 1939. Its Deluxe model had all-new, more modern styling that hinted at what the '40s would bring. The lower-priced models, on the other hand, had nearly the same image as the 1938 Ford DeLuxe.

These cars were characterized by a V-type nose and horizontal radiator grille bars, left and right. Headlights were mounted inboard of the fenders, where they blended into the "catwalk" area. A bright metal molding trimmed the upper belt line and continued, forward, along the hood sides. There it "hooked" around a Ford script just behind the grille.

Officially, Ford dropped the "standard" designation and referred to its low-priced cars as "Ford V-8s." They came in two separate series, as determined by the type of V-8 engine used. The 922A series used the company's small 136 cid./60 hp V-8 and was known as the V-8-60 series. It included three body styles, all having the "old-fashioned" sheet metal. The five-window coupe sold for $599, and Tudor sedan was $640, and the Fordor sedan went for $686.

There was also a 91A series, which used Ford's larger 221 cid./85 hp V-8. Sometimes referred to as the V-8-85 series, it included a total of 10 cars; four with the "old-fashioned" (standard) look and six with updated DeLuxe sheet metal. The four lower-priced cars came only in closed body styles: the five-window coupe at $640, the Tudor sedan at $681, the Fordor sedan at $727, and the station wagon at $840.

Low-priced cars in both series had the same 112-inch wheelbase, although the V-8-60 models had smaller 16 x 5.50 tires. Size 16 x 6.00 tires were standard equipment for the V-8-85s. Lockheed hydraulic brakes, a 1939 innovation for Ford, were used on all cars in both series.

The V-8-60 power plant had a diminutive 2.6 x 3.2 inch bore and stroke and three main bearings. The compression ratio was 6.61:1 and a new, dual-downdraft Ford

1939 Ford "standard" V-8 Fordor sedan.

carburetor was fitted. Peak horsepower came at 3500 rpm and the torque rating was 94 lbs.-ft. at 2500 rpm. A 4.44:1 rear axle was teamed with the small engine. Although heavily promoted as an economy option, the "small-block" never really found favor with buyers.

Three main bearings were also used in the V-8-85 engine, which had a 3-1/16 x 3¾ inch bore and stroke and 6.15:1 compression. This engine was improved, from 1938 specifications, through the use of the crankshaft, piston rings, camshaft, and valve train refinements also found in 1939's all-new 95 hp Mercury V-8. Again, a dual-downdraft Ford carburetor was fitted. Horsepower peaked at 3800 rpm in the bigger "mill," while maximum torque of 155 lbs.-ft. was measured at 3800 rpm. A numerically lower 3.78:1 ratio rear axle was used in V-8-85 drive trains.

Except for the design of front end sheet metal, the less expensive V-8-85s (91As) were virtually the same as the Deluxe V-8-85s, although they lacked the banjo steering wheel, glove box lock, stem-wind clock, left door arm rest, wheel trim rings, and dual visors and taillights that came with the DeLuxe equipment package. In addition, convertibles and convertible sedans were offered only in the Deluxe 91A car-line.

Although the 1938-like styling made the lower-priced cars look old-fashioned, it was not an unattractive design at all. In fact, subtle refinements to the grille and the hood side panels created a rather handsome overall appearance that seemed slightly richer-looking than that of many other low-priced 1939 cars. Inside the new Fords, instruments were grouped at the left-hand side, in front of the driver, while a grille for the optional radio was located at the center of the dash. The interior was nicely appointed, in the style of the period, for a car of this price class.

The Ford suspension still featured flexible cantilever springs of transverse design at the front. Double-acting hydraulic shock absorbers were also standard. The cars had an overall length of 179.5 inches and sedans stood 68⅝ inches high. The front tread measured 55.5 inches, while the rear tread was a wider 58.25 inches. The three-speed sliding gear transmission, with floor shifter, was mated to the engine via a single dry-plate clutch with molded asbestos lining.

Ford's two lower-priced 1939 series (922A and 91A) contributed somewhere near 200,000 units to the company's 532,152 assemblies between late 1938 and early 1940. Production records at the Henry Ford Museum show that body style figures for the 91A series "standard" models were 38,197 for the five-window coupe, 124,866 for the Tudor, 28,151 for the Fordor, and 3,277 for the station wagon. In addition, 4,281 sedan delivery trucks, with the "old-fashioned" passenger car sheet metal, were made. There are no records on 922A output, although this may have been considered an engine option. If so, the number of 922As built would be included in these totals. If not, there's some missing numbers not recorded in the archives.

1939 Ford "Standard" Station Wagon

Ford's 1940 Standard Tudor Sedan

by Gerald Perschbacher

In 1940 the Standard Tudor sedans were the second most popular kids on the Ford block. With 105,458 members in the gang, the Standard Tudors appealed to a broad cross-section of American society.

The Standard series carried the older V-8 engine with 136 inches developing 60 horsepower at 3500 rpm, which was noticeably less than the 85 to 90 horsepower which delivered a compression ratio of 6.6 to 1 and a pressure of 158 pounds at 2800 rpm maximum.

Salesmanship was at its best in Ford advertisements in '40. "Boy, you shoulda seen me breeze by Doc Tompkins, comin' up Elm Street hill," began one advertisement. Its point was performance: "The only place you'll find eight-cylinder performance is in an eight-cylinder engine. That's why the Ford V-8 stands alone in the low-price field! You can read about Ford performance — you can hear about it from pleased and proud Ford owners — or you can feel it for yourself."

The new Ford was leading the way in sales among professional aviators in '40. "A recent survey among 206 American Airlines' captains and first officers showed that 96 owned Ford, Mercury or Lincoln-Zephyr cars. This is impressive testimony to the excellence of Ford engineering."

With its slim 112-inch wheelbase and trim overall weight of 2,909 pounds, the Standard Tudor sedan looked just right to ladies and was priced attractively at $701. One ad begins, "Who says a woman doesn't know her own mind? I've known mine ever since I saw the new Ford V-8."

"Joe started it," the ad reads. "He came home last night and made some cracks at our old car. So I said, "Out with it, my man, just which new car have you been looking at?' And he said, 'Oh, not any, really. Might look around a bit. But I did watch a swell new Ford go by downtown today.'

"So this afternoon I took a long look at the new Ford myself. That's easy to do! And the salesman was grand. Never mentioned fan belts or fuel pumps or anything like that. He just let me look around and open things and ask questions. Pretty soon, I began to get as excited as Joe was — then we went for a ride."

Part of the Standard's salesmanship centered on quiet, comfortable, roomy rides and capitalized on the addition of four more inches for leg room in the back seat. Fingertip gearshift mounted to the steering column was amazingly smooth and easy to operate, especially with three people in the front seat. And women were attracted to the speed of the V-8 mentioned in the sales pitches.

The Standard Tudor carried the old grille from 1939 but boasted new sealed-beam headlights which were standard for the industry in 1940 as a safety improvement. The windshield was fixed, window ventilators were standard, and windshield wipers were mounted below the windshield. A good number of owners realized good gas economy, probably because of the smaller V-8.

Although considered a Plain Jane in its day, today the 1940 Standard Tudor by Ford can sell for $6,000 in good original or restored condition.

1940 Ford "Standard" Tudor Sedan

Postwar America had a Ford in its future

by Robert C. Ackerson

One of the major advantages enjoyed by American cars over their British counterparts in the early postwar years was the relative youthfulness of their design. Whereas the U.S. manufacturers had managed to sustain production until early 1942, the British, for the most part, had to call it quits nearly 2½ years earlier. As a result when peacetime production resumed, the Americans were in effect one full styling cycle ahead of the British. This was great if you were totally taken by the mid-'30s look but if you were one of the good old boys who hung around Ford Country, none of those foreign cars could hold a candle to a '46 Ford. During the early months of 1945 when the war's end became increasingly imminent, Ford began its famous "There's a Ford in your future!" series of advertisements. Although they could be faulted for promising more than the first postwar Ford could possibly deliver, these ads surely were appealing to Americans eager to return back to the way things once had been. Of course it didn't quite turn out that way but at least for a little while, in the crystal ball of these Ford ads, Americans caught a glimpse of the good old days. It would be a time when, promised Ford, "You'll take your ease in style...go high, wide and handsome" and discover that "It'll be more fun 'getting there.'" The new Ford car that would make all this possible would be "big, roomy and sturdy," an automobile whose "smart lines will surely rate a 'second look' on street and highway." All that was needed for Ford to "start production plans" was the "go ahead" from Uncle Sam.

As the war came to an end in the summer of 1945, Ford backed up that promise with action. In its June 3, 1945 issue, the *New York Times* carried a photo of the 1946 Ford and reported the first Fords to be built since February 1942 were expected to be in production within 60 to 90 days. Just over a month later, *Business Week* (July 14, 1945) carried a photo of Henry Ford II driving the first postwar Ford (a white two-door sedan) off the assembly line on July 3, 1945. Although Ford's plans to formally introduce the 1946 Ford on Sept. 22 had to be scrapped due to part shortages, the public did get a chance to give it the once-over on Oct. 26 and by the middle of January 1946 daily Ford output had exceeded the 1300 mark. Although these Fords with their solid front axles have at times been regarded as anachronistic automobiles from the days when Henry Ford held sway at Dearborn, a close look at their immediate predecessors suggests this judgment might just be a bit too harsh.

In 1941 Ford introduced automobiles that, for the first time, shared body shells with the more expensive Mercury. This cozy arrangement, which set the pattern for the years ahead, made the new Ford somewhat larger than it had been in 1940. Indeed, it was "the biggest Ford ever built." Its wheelbase grew two inches to 114 and overall weight was up a substantial 300 pounds. With a body width of just over 73 inches the front seat in the four-door sedan was seven inches wider than previously. Not all of its fans greeted Ford's new size and look with enthusiasm. To many, Ford had lost its lithe, light look and gained a bulky, almost obese appearance. But on the other hand Ford, it could be argued with equal fervor, was marketing a car whose larger windshield and side windows had an appearance that was more forward-looking (sorry Chrysler) than Plymouth's and at least as contemporary as Chevrolet's. But lest anyone gained the impression that Ford had just introduced, new styling for 1941 and left its underalls unchanged its ads reported that "The biggest news is in the new glide of this big new car! Softer springs, big improved shock absorbers and new stabilizer all blend into a gentle, easy-going 'boulevard' ride." These claims were far from being mere boasts. Ford did reduce its spring rates, use larger shock absorbers, and its wider frame (which had earlier been used on the 1940 Mercury) was 100% more rigid than that of the 1940 Ford. True enough, the Ford's suspension was still archaic, with its solid axles and transverse leaf springs, but it enabled an eager-beaver driver to cor-

ner his '41 Ford with considerable alacrity.

In 1941 there were nearly seven million Ford cars on American roads and Ford was justifiably proud that nearly two million of them were over 10 years old. But slowly these Fords with either four-cylinder or V-8 engines made room for those 1941 models equipped with the first six-cylinder engine of modern Ford history. Ford regarded this engine as "the most modern six in the industry." This claim tended (and intentionally so) to downplay the six's performance capability. The six at 590 pounds weighed just eight pounds less than the V-8 and with 225.8 cubic inches was competitive in size to the V-8 which displaced 221 cubic inches. Although Ford publicly rated both engines at 90 hp, the six was actually slightly more powerful and developed its peak horsepower at 3300 rpm which was 500 rpm under the top of the V-8's power curve. Also

The 1942 Ford was an all-new car. Styling, with minor changes, would endure through the 1948 model year.

1942 Ford Convertible

giving the six a big edge in low-speed over the V-8 was its 180 lbs-ft of torque developed at 2000 rpm. The V-8 on the other hand was churning out only 155 lbs-ft at 2200 rpm. The price differential between Fords equipped with these engines was just $15 with the price advantage going to the six. Visually the only distinction between six- and eight-cylinder Fords were their hood emblems which, depending upon the engine installed, carried either a 6 or 8 numeral. Both engines had solid valve lifters and were nearly identical in weight.

In 1942 the price differential between the two engines was lowered to just $10. This minor cost adjustment was accompanied by a reshuffling of the engine-model series combinations Ford offered. When the six had first been introduced in May 1941 it was the standard engine for the bottom of the rung Special models and optional in the higher grade DeLuxe and Super DeLuxe lines. The Ford Special was also offered with the V-8 engine. Three models were available in the Special line, a coupe, plus two and four-door sedans. The price spread between the lower priced Ford Special coupe with a six-cylinder engine and the most expensive Super DeLuxe model, the V-8 sta-

tion wagon was $261. For his $729 the owner of a Special coupe was purchasing an automobile identical in terms of mechanical design to the more costly versions. However, its standard equipment list was skimpy, consisting of such bare necessities as a single taillight, horn, and windshield wiper. Most interesting of all, according to a Ford, Mercury, Lincoln price list dated May 20, 1941, the Ford Specials were "furnished in black only." For 1942 the six was available in both the Special and DeLuxe lines but not for the most expensive Super DeLuxe models. This arrangement made sense only from the perspective of those who naturally assumed the V-8 was the superior engine. From a performance perspective it was an illogical move as we've earlier indicated. Ford, in spite of Henry Ford's dislike for six-cylinder engines, assumed a somewhat equivocal stance in its advertising regarding the relative merits

The 1947 Ford Super Deluxe two-door sedan was almost identical to the '46 version.

of its V-8 and six-cylinder engines. "Both," it explained, "are 90 horsepower, both basically rugged, reliable, low on gas and oil use...We believe the Ford V-8 engine, now even more responsive, is the finest ever put in a low-price car. The smooth new Six is the most modern '6' in America."

Before production of 1942 Fords came to an end on Feb. 10, 1942, just 160,211 had been produced. In the early days of 1942 with the United States at war and it becoming very obvious that cessation of automobile assembly was on the horizon, Ford advertising took on a somber tone. For example, Ford told readers of *Country Gentleman* (January 1942) that "you will ask a lot of the car you choose in these unusual times. You will ask a lot in what it must have today. You may ask a lot in the length of service that you put it to."

In terms of styling the 1942 Ford was not, as would be expected, radically different from the 1941 models. It was, though, one of the better examples of American styling found among the 1942 cars. Slightly wider bumpers and a more rectangular shaped grille retaining a vertical bar theme gave the Ford a less rotund appearance.

The 1948 Ford four-door sedan was well-accepted when new although it appeared instantly dated when the all-new '49 models were introduced in June 1948.

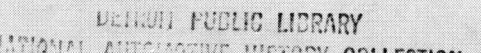
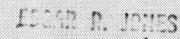

1946 FORD
with many advancements —now in production!

There's a *Ford* in your future!

Here is the most beautiful Ford car ever built— with more improvements than many pre-war yearly models. . . . Under the broad hood there's new and greater power. Plus improved economy in oil and gasoline. . . . Roomy, colorful interiors invite you to relax in luxury. New-type springs assure a full-cushioned level ride. Brakes are newly-designed hydraulics—for quick, smooth, quiet stops. . . . Ask your Ford Dealer about the smartest Ford cars ever built. **FORD MOTOR COMPANY**

9

This ad, remembered fondly today, was published widely in late 1945 as the new '46 Fords entered production.

44

Other changes included rectangular parking lights moved inboard from their former position above the headlights, rear fender gravel shields, and concealed runningboards. There were also those signs of the times common to most 1942 American cars; more plastic interior trim and the use of other metals such as molybdenum alloy instead of nickel for engine valves, gears, and shafts. Ford assured its potential customers that "under what is new, you will find it good. Defense requirements have brought no cuts in its basic excellence. We have never built a better Ford to own or drive."

Although the first postwar Ford, as we've earlier mentioned, wasn't quite as dramatic an automobile as Ford teaser ads suggested, it did, as Ford claimed, contain more mechanical improvements than were often found in new models introduced in the prewar years. Its brakes, although having the same 12-inch drums and 162 square inches of swept area, were praised for their improved performance and a number of design changes in both the V-8 and six engines made them superior to their 1942 counterparts in several key areas. The biggest change of course was the adoption of the 239.4 cid, 59A block V-8 which had previously powered Ford trucks for use in Ford passenger cars. With a 6.75:1 compression ratio, 3-3/16 inch bore, and 3-3/16 stroke it produced 100 horsepower at 3800 rpm. Ford described it as the "most powerful engine ever to power a Ford car" and Tom McCahill's road test found in the February 1946 issue of *Mechanix Illustrated* credited it with a top speed of approximately 84 mph and a zero to 60 mph time of just under 20 seconds. Before the war some owners of both the V-8 and six-cylinder Fords had complained of excessive oil consumption. The 1946 models with four-ring (one more than in 1941) aluminum pistons plus superior valve seat cooling represented a strong Ford effort to solve this problem. Ford trimmed its lineup to just two series, Super DeLuxe and DeLuxe, in 1946, with the convertible, station wagon, and sedan-coupe models available only in Super DeLuxe form. Common to both series were such features as twin horns, dual windshield wipers, two taillights, an ignition keyhole light, lockable glove box, and an interior trunk light. In addition, the Super DeLuxe models were delivered with a long list of additional features, including but not limited to twin sun visors, electric cigarette lighter, twin dashboard mounted ashtrays, clock, horn ring, and crank controls for the front door window vents.

The new Ford's front grille retained the 1942 shape but adopted a horizontal-bar theme that made its visual identification as a new car very easy. In view of what was yet to come from Detroit, it's interesting to note that *The New York Times* (June 3, 1945) described this grille as "massive." The front parking lights remained in their prewar position but were given a different shape that was more ornate and less graceful than the 1942 version.

On April 22, 1946, Ford extended the Super DeLuxe series to include the Sportsman's Convertible Coupe (Ford later referred to this model as the "Sportsman Convertible" and the 1947 version carried "Sportsman" side and rear body script) whose wooded body sections represented, said Ford, "a natural blending of the station wagon and the ever-popular convertible. Outside and inside," continued Ford, " there never was a car like this before! The new Ford Sportsman's convertible is really two cars in one! Ford designers have combined the paneled smartness of the station wagon and the touch-a-button convenience of a convertible!"

This Ford woodie did not really gain a great deal of popularity as a new car. No doubt its $2,041 price tag was partially responsible for its phasing out during the 1947 model run. By contrast the Ford station wagon whose bodies were built by Ford as its Iron Mountain, Michigan facility was the best selling automobile of its type in the United States. It's interesting to observe that Ford also touted the station wagon as "really two cars in one," a vehicle that was a "roomy eight-passenger sedan or with both rear seats removed, a family utility carryall."

Ford was advertising its 1946 models as late as March 1947 and when the 1947 version did appear it was as expected only moderately changed in appearance and mechanically identical to the 1946 Ford. The red tracer paint that highlighted the older model's grille was dropped for 1947. The addition of a hood mounted emblem added unnecessary clutter to the Ford's front end although in fairness to Ford its frontal appearance now with circular parking lights positioned beneath the headlights still was quite attractive. In its very first issue, dated June 1947, *Road and Track* tested a 1947 Ford V-8 and described it as a "high performance car" whose top speed was 81.3 mph. *Road and Track* also reported on the performance of a pair of Fords in a hillclimb held at Mohansic Lake, north of New York City. A 1946 Ford two-door sedan, said *Road and Track*, fitted with a "specially built motor left the starting line with a roar from its twin exhausts." Its time for the climb was 42.1 seconds which compared favorably with the winning run of 41.2 seconds set by a supercharged BMW. Not far behind at 43 seconds was a "fast 1941 Ford convertible."

For the abbreviated 1948 model year Ford limited changes to a new steering column lock, very minor trim revisions, reshaped door handles, and a new hood ornament.

There was more than a mere touch of irony in those ads for the 1948 models that proclaimed "There's a Finer Ford in your future." Just a little more than a year after the death of Henry Ford in April 1947, a dramatic new Ford would appear and with new bodies and suspensions they would symbolize the real beginning of the Ford renaissance.

Stepping Back In Time Previewing the '49 Ford

by Tim Howley

We've just walked through our *Old Cars* time capsule, and stepped into New York's Waldorf Astoria for a press preview of the new 1949 Ford. The date is June 8, 1948, and we're at the biggest new car press party in history. The public will get its first glimpse of the all-new postwar Ford at dealer showrooms June 18.

We've just come out of the elevator, and directly in front of us are five quarter-size models of the stunning new Fords. Words can hardly describe them. We've seen slab sided cars before. But it took Ford to really bring off the postwar look. The lines are square rather than rounded. The new Ford uses a minimum of trim. The entire effect is one of restraint. Even the sedans look as handsome as the convertibles and coupe. Ford has set the styling for the '50s.

To our right is a huge "Forty-Niner" exhibit. A gold prospector, standing beside a new Ford Custom club coupe, is handing out nugget souvenirs. To our left is a bright red '49 Ford convertible. It's attractive young female occupants are waving at us. Oh, oh, it's starting to rain, and up

goes the top on the car that's destined to be America's favorite convertible of the future. Now, let's see if we can work our way through this excited crowd for a good look at the cars in the main ballroom.

Some of the cars are on a giant merry-go-round. There's also a Ferris wheel with two full-size chassis twisting and turning as they revolve so we can see all the details of construction. All around us are cutaway engines and special exhibits of the new Ford features. If you're used to Ford's transverse springing and turtleback styling, all we can say is that the only thing the '49 Ford has in common with last year's model is a 114-inch wheelbase. The most obvious difference is the styling. The car is completely new from the attractive new spinner type grille to the bustle back which practically doubles luggage capacity.

Now we're looking at Ford's new ladder type frame. The cross-member frame is gone, and so is the antiquated torque tube drive. It's been replaced by the new Hotchkiss drive. The transverse rear buggy springs have been

The 1949 model was the first all-new postwar Ford. The slab sided look and the clean lines were stunning. The also new 1949 Chevrolet looked dated in comparison.

replaced by semi-elliptics in the rear so that all driving and braking forces are transmitted through the springs instead of radius rods and the torque tube. The rigid transverse front springs and the front radius rods are gone, too. Ford's new front springs are the coil type combined with a completely new steering linkage system.

But the biggest change is that the engine has been moved five inches forward so that rear seat passengers will no longer be sitting over the axle. The transmission, differential, and brakes are all new, and designed for easier servicing. The engine is still a flathead V-8 rated at 100 horsepower. But when you look at the cutaway models you'll see lots of improvements. Ford engineers have cut oil consumption, improved the manifolding bearings, and redesigned the cooling system to allow the engine to run 12 degrees cooler than earlier models. The new V-8 eliminates all the hot spots that gave so much trouble in the earlier models. We notice that the crab distributor up front has disappeared. There's a new, easy-to-service, conventional type distributor mounted in front, on top of the right cylinder bank. There's also a six-cylinder engine. Both engines come with a standard three-speed synchromesh transmission with or without optional overdrive. Ford says they probably won't have an automatic transmission for another two or three years, and an overhead valve V-8 is still a long way off.

Everybody here in the ballroom is talking about Hydra-Coil front springs, Para-Flex rear springs, and something Ford's advertising department calls "Mid-Ship Ride." We've been talking to several motor magazine editors who have already road-tested the new Ford. The reactions are mixed. Passengers say the car rides like a dream; they can hardly believe it's a Ford. But drivers complain about hard steering at low speeds. Reportedly, the car is especially hard to park. We've heard several complaints about understeer in cornering and tire scrub. On the positive side, they're raving about the excellent gas mileage the new Ford delivers. Early reports indicate that a V-8 with overdrive will deliver about 22 mpg on the road and the 6 with overdrive will deliver nearly 25 mpg tops.

There's only one thing that disappoints us about the new Ford. And that's somewhat shoddy construction. Doors, hood, trunk, and body panels don't appear to fit too well. We suspect there will be a lot of owner complaints about rattles and leaks. Chrome and stainless trim have a slapped-on look. Interiors, as beautiful as they are, don't look like they will wear as well as on earlier models. But you have to understand that the new Ford was designed and put into production in a record time of only 14 months. The car that was to have been the '49 Ford is now the '49 Mercury, designed during the war. Back in 1946, Ford management decided to build their new postwar Ford from scratch, and style would be the thing. Style is what sells in today's fast changing low-priced market. Ford believes that the public will overlook the bugs if their new offering is truly a trend setter. They aren't even waiting for normal October introduction time. They want to put their new models on the streets this summer. They'll be working out the bugs through the model year. Later 1949 models and the 1950 model will no doubt be a lot better automobiles. Ford spent $72 million just in tool-

ing up for the '49, and they intend to go right on improving it.

There are four models in the standard line — a coupe and a club coupe, a two-door and a four-door. The coupe and club coupe share the same body, but the coupe has no back seat. While attractive on the outside, the standard model has a frighteningly spartan interior. In the custom series there is a club coupe, two-door, four-door, convertible, and a wooden-bodied station wagon. The station wagon comes only in a two-door version, and is the most radically styled wagon we have ever seen.

Viewing these new Fords from the year 1948, it's hard to believe that they will ever become collector's items. They certainly mark a Ford milestone. But we wonder if they will ever last long enough to be collected. Ford is certainly going through a revolution these days. Engineering can be improved for years into the future. But we wonder if the revolutionary '49 Ford marks the final stage in American automobile design. Where can Ford go from here? That's what we wonder as we stand in the crowd at the Waldorf Astoria on this historic Ford day of June 8, 1948.

The 1949 flathead V-8 was rated at 100 horsepower.

Riding the Crest of the '50s Fords — Crestliner

by Gerald Perschbacher

"It has the look — it has the room — it has the feel — it's the '50 Ford!"

Ford's flair in advertisements waved the banner for the new, true "Fashion Car" for 1950. Advertisements boasted "more hip and shoulder room than any other car in Ford's class! Plenty of leg room both front and rear. No wonder people say the '50 Ford is one fine car in the low-price field!

"Ever handle a car that you can steer with finger-tip ease — stop with a feather touch on the brake pedal? That's the '50 Ford with 35 percent easier acting King-Size Brakes!

"Fifty ways new — that's Ford for '50! For example, just get the feel of the new 100 hp V-8! So quiet it whispers, so alive it puts you out front in any traffic situation!"

Ford was stretching its new look into a second year by 1950.

Many things weren't as new as the salesmen would have you think. The V-8 engine with 100 hp at 3600 rpm was a leftover from 1949; in its basic form it was a holdover from the very first postwar Ford V-8. But there was one great, new addition for Ford in '50: the Crestliner.

Christened as the Custom Deluxe Crestliner two-door sedan, with V-8 engine, the new baby was a shot of high-octane sporting blood into the sagging sales force. In '50, the car sales market softened, and postwar dollars tightened up. A car salesman had to earn his pay in this crucial year, and the Crestliner was one way to do it.

Only 8,703 Crestliners sold in the '50 model year, but the price was good for a salesman's commission. At $1,711 the Crestliner was the fourth highest priced car in the Ford stable. Only the two station wagons and the convertible had heftier prices.

The Crestliner was the lightest-weight, high-priced Ford, tipping the scales at 3,050 pounds — more than 200 pounds lighter than the convertible and almost 500 pounds lighter than the station wagon. With its production total, it was least of the lineup, also.

The Crestliner was crowned with a vinyl top, ample extra chrome (such as the sweeping, Corvette-like band that sparkled each side), a special steering wheel, and special paint along with full wheel covers. The car truly was princely.

Wheelbase was standard Ford at 114 inches. The company pushed the "Hushed Ride" and such innovations as "Magic Air" heater with an increased airflow of 25 percent, larger re-styled parking lights framed generously with chrome and positioned above the front bumper and below the headlights, wider sunvisors inside, water-sealed and dust-free brakes, larger defroster opening (increased 44 percent), new rotary door locks, and a splashy choice of 11 new colors, "baked on to keep that showroom complexion."

In that tough sales year of 1950, Ford pushed its products hard. Longevity was emphasized, durability was underlined. And even the Ford slogan was updated: "There's a Ford in your future — with a future built in!"

50s Ford

Back in 1954, when the Korean War was over and the performance race was on, Ford had a revolutionary car that now is more ignored than a Mustang at a Model T convention. And that's all right with me, because the speculators haven't yet sent prices soaring on "My Secret Love," the 1954 Ford.

What's so special about '54s? Maybe it's the fact that, like the 1937s, they're not so special with the Ford set. I've yet to see them featured in even the most avid Ford publications. Yet the nearly forgotten '54 may one day turn out to be the most memorable Ford of all.

Ford had two big firsts that year: the first overhead valve V-8 in the low-priced three, plus (along with Mercury) the first balljoint front suspension on anything but a luxury or sports car. Some say the '54 is a baby Lincoln in disguise; actually, the '54 Mercury is the baby Lincoln. The Ford has its own distinct personality and charm. It is a truly unique, one-year-only kind of Ford.

The '54 shares its body skin and basic styling with the 1952-'53 models, making it appear to be linked strongly to late flatheads. In practice, '54 Fords aren't even tolerated at flathead events. Underneath, they have an all-new suspension system, new chassis, and a half-inch longer wheelbase than the '53. Chrome and stainless treatment is quite different than that of the '53, and the bright, kitchen-colored interiors are completely redesigned, the dashboard being the most radical design departure of all.

The biggest news, of course, was under the old Ford bonnet, where Ford engineers had buttoned in a compact, oversquare ohv V-8, the biggest single Ford engine improvement since the 1932 flathead V-8. Ford had been working on overheads for a long time before 1954. In 1952, both the Lincoln and the Ford Six went to overhead design. Both the new "Y Block" jobs, the Ford 239 and the Mercury 256, were scaled down versions of the husky Lincoln ohv V-8. Rated at 130 hp at 4,200 rpm, and with torque at 214 from 1,800 to 2,200 rpm, the 239 gave 20 more horsepower than the '53 flathead without increase displacement.

For the first time in a Ford V-8, bore was larger than stroke, giving less piston travel and more space for larger valves. The 7.2-to-1 compression ratio could be raised to 12-to-1 or even higher. Cast rather than forged, the crankshaft now had five main bearings instead of three. There was a total of eight counterweights for smoother operation and greater resistance to vibration.

Early overheads have been much maligned by both earlier and later Ford enthusiasts. In theory, they were a tremendous improvement over the flathead. Surface area in the combustion chambers were reduced for less heat loss through the cooling jacket; valve size was increased and timing improved. Better engine breathing was permitted through improved porting and manifolding. Solid lifters in both the Ford and Mercury were a lot more trouble-free than Lincoln's hydraulics.

Why, then, do these engines have such poor reputations? For one thing, by standards of the later 292 and 312 and even the 272, they were gutless. But this was far more the fault of the two-speed Fordomatic than the engines, which, when equipped with overdrive, were not bad movers at all. The real problem was one of lubrication, particularly to the cam bearings and rocker arms. It took many years for Ford to get its lubrication down to the science it is today, and all the early overheads suffer from lubrication deficiencies. Cooling systems also tend to build up scale at the backs of the blocks. It's very hard today to find a good rebuildable Ford 239 or Mercury 256, and it's almost as difficult to find 272s, 292s, and 312s.

The biggest 1954 feature — other than the engine — was a miniaturized version of Lincoln's MacPherson ball-

The Not-So-Special Special

by Tim Howley

Forerunner — perhaps — of the LTD series, plush '54 Ford Crestline sedan was nicely detailed. That was the year Ford really went to work on their interiors.

Steering wheel was big and high in '54 Ford. Dash used warning lights for first time, featured Astra-dial speedometer. (Howley photo)

joint front suspension, developed for the Mexican Road Racing cars. Ford's MacPherson didn't exactly invent the system; he copied the Jaguar system, and Jaguar, in turn, had refined it from several European cars dating back to the '30s. MacPherson went to balljoints only to make his struts work. Up until that time, kingpins were the standard of the industry because engineers were convinced that balljoints, while satisfactory for small European cars, would break under the weight of big American models. The Lincoln victories in the Mexican Road Races proved the industry wrong, and within a few years balljoints became the standard.

In the balljoint system, each front wheel is connected by two simple ball-and-socket joints to the spring-supported arms coming out on each side of the frame. One is connected to the top supporting arm, the other to the bottom, permitting four-way movement with a dual purpose: up and down for the road shocks, back and forth for the turning movements. The benefits are many. Lubrication points in the 1954 Ford front suspension were reduced from 16 to four, repair work was greatly simplified, alignment made infinitely easier. The entire units could be replaced in minutes, rather than hours. Both handling and ride were also greatly improved.

Just how does the 1954 peform? Uncle Tom McCahill, who described it as ''Abe Lincoln as a boy'' or the ''Mexican Jumping Bean, junior size,'' claimed he could get up to 60 from 0 in 14.9 to 15.3 seconds, about four seconds faster than a '53. I find this hard to believe of a '54 Fordomatic, when even the '55 with the 272 engine could do no better than 14.5 seconds. I'd be more inclined to go by less enthusiastic reports, which claimed about 18.5 seconds from a standing start. A '53 could beat it up to 30 mph, but the '54 had just a little more punch at higher speeds.

A 1954 Ford could cruise comfortably all day in the 60 to 70 mph range, delivering 13 to 17 mpg with Fordomatic. Top speed was 92 to 94 mph. Naturally, the seldom found overdrive equipped cars deliver better performance and better gas and any '54 Ford will run a lot better on premium fuel than on regular, which is suggested in the owner's manual.

Braking on the '54 Ford is better than average, especially with power brakes, a $41 option. There is some slewing in panic stops over 50 mph, as the car tends to be a little front heavy. This is easily eliminated with two passengers in the back seat. On the other hand, overall performance is greatly reduced with three or four people in the car, proving that, for practical purposes, the engine was just too small.

The car's best feature is its handling, with or without $134 optional power steering. The '54 Ford had the best roadability of any small or medium-size car on the road that year; it felt stable and cornered well at all speeds. There was some tendency to wander at higher speeds, but we must remember that this would actually now be considered a compact car. I suppose that, by modern standards, you might say it leans too heavily into the turns, but you really have to compare it to other cars of the time to realize what a vast difference the MacPherson balljoint front suspension made. My favorite '54 Ford combination is a six with overdrive. I've always had a lot of respect for the Ford six in those years, both for performance and economy. Besides, with a six, power steering was unnecessary.

Any 1954 Ford is quite comfortable riding at all speeds. The new suspension system absorbed more of the road shocks than the old. With the remarkably quiet engine, the only noise you'll hear over 60 is from the wind and tires.

Ford gave its customers a lot of choice in the '54, with three distinct lines — the Mainline, Customline, and

Crestline. All power equipment — including power steering and brakes, power windows, and four-way power seats — was offered for the first time. The luxurious Crestline four-door sedan was an entirely new model that year and could only be compared to the later LTD series. It was the last year that Ford offered a club coupe in its standard line, and the first year that a wide selection of interior colors and fabrics were offered. Interiors might easily have been the most colorful of any from the bright fifties. I can remember slick, tough vinyls in colors like colonial white, yellow, bright red, soft blue, salmon pink, and peppermint green. Some of the convertible and hardtop dashboards were done up in pearl white and were exceptionally striking.

The dashboard was the most noticeable feature on the '54 Ford. Atop the dash, the speedometer sported a transparent plastic dome and was called the "Astra-dial." Designed to reflect sun and headlight glare onto the back of the numerals, it proved to be a major annoyance to drivers and was discontinued after the 1955 model year.

For safety and convenience, all instruments were recessed in a burnished metal panel. On one hand, Ford showed respect for the motorist by giving him a manually operated choke, but on the other Ford insulted him with oil and generator "idiot lights" for the first time.

No review of 1954 Fords would be complete without mention of the Skyliner Victoria with its plexiglass bubble top over the driver's compartment. The blue-green transparent top was the ultimate Ford gimmick, and an expensive option at about $300 extra. It filtered out 60 percent of the sun's heat rays and 72 percent of the sky glare, had five times the impact resistance of glass (but scratched easily), tended to warp in the warm climates and crack in the cold regions. If you didn't like looking green as a Martian when you drove a '54 Ford (or Merc), there was another extra. For a few bucks more you could get a little vinyl curtain that would zip up in an instant. Incidentally, a tinted see-through top was also a convertible option, but never caught on. Ford never bothered explaining the reason for the starlite top; it was just another excuse to sell a car. The idea was abandoned during 1956, but has now been revived in the Lincoln under the name of "Moon Roof."

It's still not too difficult to find a '54 Ford bubbletopper. Ford built 13,344 of the model, and a lot of them have been saved. For that matter, all '54 Ford models are still fairly plentiful and at quite reasonable prices.

Ford gave its buyers a lot for their money in 1954, and a '54 Ford will give a collector a lot of car for his money even now. The only extra you may want are deluxe wheel covers. Ford didn't even offer these standard on the bubbletoppers or Crestline sedans. A car of many paradoxes — that pretty, pert little '54 Ford.

1954 Ford Crestline Skyliner hardtop

1954 Ford Country Squire wagon was found resting in the shade at recent Florida auction. Darling of suburbanites, the '54 Country Squire is rare today.

1955-56 Fords had Thunderbird Style, Power

1955 Crown Victoria 2dr Hardtop

by Robert C. Ackerson

After the photo finish sales race in 1954 with Chevrolet, hopes were high at Ford that 1955 could be the year when Chevrolet would be swallowed up in the wake of a Ford sales bonanza. Just about every *Old Cars Weekly* reader knows that at year's end it was Chevrolet that was the year's big winner in more ways than one. In the production race, Chevrolet was the champion, 1,830,038 to 1,764,524. Out in the jungle of NASCAR short track competition, the king was Chevrolet, and when it came to styling, well, it's hard to fault that masterpiece that was a 1955 Chevrolet Bel Air convertible. On this latter point, Ford designers must have really spent a lot of time scratching their heads. After all, everybody loved the line of the Thunderbird and transferring its looks to the Ford sedans seemed to be a real, sure-fire shortcut to sales success.

Now lest anyone gets the notion that we're kicking Ford just a bit too hard, let's note that Ford output did take a big jump forward from the 1954 level of 1,394,762 but Chevrolet came out of the gate so quick and fast that Ford never really got into the race. But in the long view this disadvantage really represents the foundation for Ford's future greatness as a high performance automobile. Ford never came forth with an engine during the '50s that quite matched the glamour of Chevrolet's class "265" but the gap was narrowed considerably by borrowing larger engines from Big Brother Mercury and by organizing a first class racing team that in 1956 proved more than capable of coping with the Chevrolets in NASCAR competition.

There's also one other key feature of the 1955 Fords that deserves recognition and that's the great success of the Fairlane series. Most Ford historians correctly regard the 1957 version as the first of the really big Fords but the 1955 Fairlanes actually got Ford moving into this very lucrative sector of the market.

Although we've conceded that Chevrolet had a styling edge over Ford, the appearance of their cars was the number one reason why participants in *Popular Mechanics*' survey of 1955 Ford owners purchased their cars. It's also worth noting that the long lambasted two-tone body finishes that were common to most 1955 cars was a popular feature among Ford owners. *Popular Mechanics* (July 1955) reported that 87% of Ford owners liked the bright new colors and their two-tone combinations, while only 10% professed displeasure. There were, however, some murmurs of discontent about excessive body rattles and poor body and assembly that were portents of bad times yet to come, not just for Ford but for just about every American auto manufacturer.

But if these cries were to grow more vocal as time passed, there was more than enough happiness to go

Wherever you go... *wherever she goes*

...Lifeguard Design goes with both of you!

If ever there was a time to join the quarter million families who own two Fords, it's *now!* For now you not only give *your* family two-Ford freedom, you also give them the priceless added safety of Lifeguard Design. There's a new Lifeguard steering wheel, new Lifeguard door latches, a new Lifeguard rear-view mirror. And, at very little extra cost, you can have seat belts and Lifeguard padding for sun visors and control panel for even greater protection.

Then, too, you'll have new confidence in the instant passing might of Ford's new Thunderbird Y-8 . . . the standard eight at no extra cost in Ford Fairlane and Station Wagon models. And wherever you drive, you'll bask in the envious glances which Ford's Thunderbird styling draws everywhere.

Why not own TWO!

FORD ...the fine car at half the fine car price!

Ford promoted its "Lifeguard Safety Features" widely in 1956.

1956 Ford Customline four-door sedan.

around in 1955. Leading the Ford offerings was a scrupulous Fairlane Crown Victoria. Ford had resurrected the old Victoria name in 1951 for its new hardtop but the Crown "Vic" was a venture into auto exotica. Admittedly, it was essentially a two-door Fairlane. But only the crass and cynical would dare affront us with that nasty fact back in those days because that combination of a superdip side fender spear plus its chrome tiara made the Crown Victoria more than one teenager's dream boat. And when the optional plastic front roof section was added, it was almost too painful to dream about owning a Vicky in geometry class! There were, of course, lesser Fords built, but it was really hard to get terribly excited about Customlines or Mainline Fords. They were just too drab for a school boy's fantasy and besides, who would want to be seen in one of them anyway? Even Ford seemed to sense that the future belonged to the Fairlane. While Customlines were available in two or four door sedan versions, and the bottom of the pile Mainline offered these models plus a really somber Business Sedan, the Fairlane came on strong with two Crown Victoria variations, two and four-door sedans, a "normal" hardtop Victoria plus the Sunliner convertible.

We all knew that Ford was the nation's station wagon boss and with five versions it wasn't taking any chances of losing its grip. Chevrolet did outflank Ford's wagon train

with the Nomad, but with the eight-passenger Country Squire and Country Sedan plus the two-door six-passenger Ranch Wagons (in either Custom or Standard form) and a six-passenger Country Sedan, Ford wasn't shy about proclaiming that its station wagons were "Handsome for Calling" and "Handy for Hauling."

Although the 1955 Fords looked considerably larger than the 1954 versions, there was very little change in their physical dimensions. Both models had identical, 115.5 inch wheelbases and the 1955 sedans were at 198.5 inches, a mere 0.2 inches longer. The 1954 station wagons actually outstretched the newer models by half an inch!

Along with Chevrolet and Plymouth, Ford's 1955 models had a new frame for 1955. Ford claims it was lower, by nearly two inches. Just a year earlier Ford had adopted the Lincoln-like ball-joint front suspension which was a key factor in its recognition by *Motor Trend* as the top handling car tested during 1954. Coming off of this winning performance, Ford was content to fine tune its suspension system for 1955. The length of the rear leaf springs was extended slightly and the front wheel spindles were inclined three degrees. With more power on tap, Ford engineers opted for larger, 11- instead of 10-inch diameter brake drums all around. Those on the front wheels were 2¼ inches wide and those at the rear mea-

1955 Ford Fairlane Sunliner convertible

sured 1¾ inches in width. Ford really didn't enjoy any real advantage over the opposition in stopping ability since Plymouth was using 11-inch front and rear brake drums and Chevrolet, as it had in 1954, was fitting its cars with eleven inch drums on all four wheels.

If you were making your first foray to the local Ford dealer to check out the '55s that fabulous autumn, it took a few minutes to eyeball Ford's new look before it was time to give the interior the once-over. As I remember the ritual, one of the first items to be scrutinized was the speedometer's top reading, and for 1955 Ford didn't let us good old boys down. Whereas the 1954 speedometer's numerals lead to a maximum of 110 mph, the '55s reached out to 120 mph! None of this 85 mph nonsense found on today's pedal cars!

The Fairlanes, as expected, had the fanciest trim and upholstery but every Ford had what *Motor Trend* (February 1955) regarded as the "top instrument panel in the popular price field." Few owners were thrilled to discover that water would often seep through the front venti-panes when they were opened for ventilation (wasn't that what they were for?) during rain storms. It also wasn't very exciting during winter snowfalls to watch the windshield wipers leave lots of windshield area untouched. But since Ford wasn't alone in suffering these growing pains during

the early years of the wraparound winshield era, we took this unpleasantness pretty much in stride.

But nobody who had stacks of *Hot Rod*, *Hop Up* and countless other automobile magazines growing in the basement or under the bed was willing to settle for such casual action when it came to performance. Ford's engine lineup, on paper at least, looked pretty good. If you were really concerned about annually saving a few tankfuls of less than a quarter per gallon gas, Ford was happy to sell you a car with the 223 cid which was boosted to 120 hp at 4000 rpm and 195 ft-lb at 2400 rpm for 1955. As we've detailed in earlier installments of this Ford history this was a fine little engine but in the horsepower rating game of the '50s it was not a big attention grabber.

Ford was keeping a close watch on what Chevrolet was up to with its new V-8 and tailored its V-8 lineup as close to Chevrolet's as was feasible. Thus the basic 272 cid V-8 with a single two-barrel carburetor and 7.6:1 compression ratio came out of the box with 162 hp at 4400 rpm and 258 ft-lb at 2200 rpm. The standard engine for the top-billed Fairlanes was a 272 cid V-8 with an 8.5:1 compression ratio, four-barrel carburetor, and dual exhausts which, claimed Ford, was good for 182 hp at 4400 rpm and 268 ft-lb at 2200 rpm. These engines, by virtue of their 3.62 inch bore and 3.60 inch stroke, were consider-

1956 Ford Fairlane Sunliner convertible

ably larger than the 1954 version (239 cubic inches, 3.50 inch bore, 3.60 inch stroke). Other alterations for 1955 included a new cam and the use of 18mm, "Turbocharge," gasketless spark plugs.

It wasn't the gearbox to choose for maximum accleration, but the Fordomatic transmission for 1955 was revamped to allow first gear starts. All that was needed was a sharp depression of the acclerator, and just about everyone could perform that trick without much persuasion!

Although 59% of Ford owners responding to *Popular Mechanics'* owner's suvery ranked "performance and power" as the best feature of their cars, an acceleration contest between equivalent Fords and Chevrolets was usually a vexing experience for the Ford driver. For the most part Ford six owners weren't likely to be overly concerned about acceleration, but for the record, a Ford six with overdrive and a 4.11 axle could acclerate from zero to 60 in approximately 16 seconds. This was a respectable for a six but in contrast, the 14.5 second time needed by a 162 hp Ford V-8 with Fordomatic was downright disappointing since a comparable Chevrolet got there over two seconds quicker! Even a Fordomatic Fairlane with 182 hp engine had a difficult time dealing with the performance of the Powerglide Chevrolet powered by the standard, 265 cid V-8. Floyd Clymer's test of such a Ford in the July 1955 issue of *Popular Mechanics* netted a best

zero to 60 capability of 13.9 seconds. Ford was claiming that its V-8 had "Trigger Torque" power but it usually seemed that in any dragstrip showdown, the Chevrolet got the jump on Ford and emerged the shoot-out victor.

Ford's response to Chevrolet's "The Hot One" blitz was a curious one. It did, as we'll detail shortly, counter with a major performance-racing campaign but its opening shots for the model year stressed safety and depicted the 1956 Ford as "the fine car at half the fine car price." When the new models debuted in the autumn of 1955, *Motor Trend* (November 1955) reported that "the 1956 Ford will kick off a brand new public relations philosophy for Ford Motor Company. Safety will be stressed on at least an equal footing with performance and horsepower."

Ford based most of its safety features upon data compiled by the Automotive Safety Research Program at Cornell University, studies conducted by the Indiana State Police, and its own research program. The Cornell project concluded that the three most common causes of automotive accident related injuries were the result of on occupant being thrown from a car, the passengers striking the windshield, or the driver colliding with the steering wheel. The Indiana State Police also reported that an individual's chances of survival in an automotive accident doubled if they were not thrown from the car. As a result one of the most highly touted features of Ford's "Lifeguard" design was a new door latch constructed of spe-

cial hardened steel whose longer length greatly reduced the chances of the door flying open under impact. Ford had offered seatbelts in 1955 but the 1956 version with a loop strength of 4000 pounds, which was 1000 pounds above the minimum strength specifications established by Cornell, received considerably greater publicity. Nearly as important in terms of their contribution to occupant safety were redesigned front seat tracks that were less susceptible to breaking loose in a collision. Ford also supplied new more securely anchored rear seat cushions. More visible was the optional vinyl plastic foam padding for the dash and visors that Ford claimed was five times more shock absorbent than sponge rubber. Ford also provided a rearview mirror with beveled edges and an adhesively backed glass surface that prevented shattering as well as a deep-dished steering wheel as standard equipment. Unfortunately for Ford these laudable features really didn't have the mid-'50s sales appeal of horsepower and performance. However, Ford wasn't exactly left holding an empty bag since it adopted the 292 cid V-8 used by both Mercury and Thunderbird in 1955. This V-8 had been marketed in late 1955 as Ford's Police Interceptor engine with a rating of 205 horsepower. In its general format it was essentially the 272 cid V-8 with a larger, 3.75 inch bore. In early 1956 the 205 hp version continued to be available on special order. Far more common were 292 cid V-8s with 202 hp (when linked to Fordomatic) and a 200 hp rating for cars equipped with either the manual gearbox or overdrive. But whereas 205 hp Chevrolets had no trouble breaking the 10 second, zero to 60 mph mark, the 202 hp Fords found it insurmountable. A 202 hp Ford with overdrive tested by *Speed Age* (May 1956) came close with a 10.21 second run. Ford fanatics probably framed this issue because it also reported that a 205 hp stick-shift Chevy ran a bog slow, zero to 60 mph time of 11.3 seconds. But other road test results were less encouraging. *Motor Life* (February 1956) and *Motor Trend* (February 1956) both ran a 202 hp Fairlane

equipped with Fordomatic from zero to 60 mph and reported identical 11.6 second times. At the Santa Ana, California drag strip a three-speed, 205 hp Chevrolet was its class record holder with a speed of 86.20 mph. By contrast the hottest Ford was capable of 84.74 mph. And if there were any Ford diehards who were still unwilling to accept the reality of Chevrolet's "The Hot One's Even Hotter" claim, *Motor Life* (March 1956) provided their coup de grace. In that issue a road test of a 205 hp Chevrolet with the two-speed Powerglide transmission reported it was capable of repeated zero to 60 mph times ranging from 8.4 to 9.4 seconds.

The smaller, 272 cid Ford V-8 was continued in 1956 and along with the 292 V-8 it was fitted with a new, higher lift cam, stronger valves and rocker arms, larger intake ports plus a reshaped combustion chamber that allowed for greater fuel turbulence. A new 12-volt ignition system was common to all Fords and perhaps because it looked around and discovered it was the last U.S. automaker to retain a manual choke. Ford used an automatic choke for its V-8s. But traditionalists could still find some solace knowing that the Ford Six still used a manual unit. When ordered with Fordomatic, the 272 cid V-8 was given an 8.4:1 compression ratio and a horsepower rating of 176 at 4400 rpm. These relative figures dropped to 8.0:1 and 173 at 4400 rpm when either a manual transmission or overdrive was ordered. The Ford Six, still displacing 223 cubic inches was boosted to 137 hp at 4000 rpm for 1956.

Early in the year, Ford and Chevrolet had their annual wheel to wheel contest at the Daytona Speed Weeks and by virtue of Ford's strong showing in the NASCAR races it was awarded the Pure Oil Manufacturer's Trophy with 584 points to Chevrolet's 566. However, Chevrolet's 81.39 mph speed in the standing start, one mile run bettered Ford's 80.84 mph and in the flying-mile competition Chevrolet's 121.33 mph speed put it comfortably ahead of Ford's best effort of 118.13 mph.

1955 Ford Country Sedan station wagon as depicted in the '55 sales catalog

The Failed Safe '56 Ford

by Tim Howley

Safety is nothing new under the automobile sun. Back in 1956, year of disasters like Elvis Presley songs, Kim Novak movies, and the *Andrea Doria* sinking, Ford mounted a multi-million dollar advertising campaign based on safety. It resulted in Ford's second biggest post-war mistake, second only to the Edsel. Buyers simply didn't want safer cars, just prettier cars. It literally took an act of Congress to get car buyers into a safety mood. Today, the '56 Ford, a classic in its own right, is a classic

could see that at the time.

During that year, Ford and Chrysler made a $200,000 grant to Cornell University's Medical College for expansion of the school's automobile crash injury research program. Henry Ford II said that Cornell's research to date had been of considerable help in developing features designed to reduce injuries in traffic accidents.

Ford began testing their cars for safety as early as 1953, and results were first evident in the '56 models.

Jerry Lew's blue and white 1956 Ford Fairlane Sunliner convertible after extensive body work.

example of the safety car that failed. It's a fortunate collector who can find one with the original unpopular safety equipment.

Ford had a good thing going in the "Nifty Fifties." The classic Thunderbird styling was reflected throughout the entire line. The 1955 Ford was sold on style and performance. For the first half of the year, Ford led Chevrolet in sales and ended the year a close second, even though Chevrolet could out-produce them by 7,000 units a day. Perhaps the high-performance '55 Chevrolet Bel Air V-8 was a little too radical for conservative Chevrolet buyers. The car with the great V-8 reputation was still the Ford overhead in its second year. Ford's 1955 styling was radical, but the public accepted it, and '56 promised to be Ford's best year in history.

Ford decided not to tamper with a good thing. The '56 model would be a tastefully face-lifted version of the '55. The main difference would not be in the car's manufacture but in the advertising. Ford marketing men honestly believed they could build performance and sell safety. It wouldn't work, but nobody of any importance in Detroit

Standard equipment included Ford's new "deep dish" lifeguard steering wheel with hub three inches below the rim. The seat track was designed to keep from sliding forward in a head-on crash. New lifeguard double-grip door latches were designed to resist popping loose under impact.

All these features were standard equipment. The whole frame and major body members had been beefed up in '55 for extra rigidity. The idea behind Ford's wraparound windshield was better visibility. Unfortunately, the blind spot was only moved back in a few inches. The curved glass distorted traffic approaching from the side and windshield replacements were expensive for insurance men. The whole industry finally decided to drop wraparound windshields in the early '60s. Already collectors are having difficulty replacing them in their '50s cars.

Ford wasn't completely dedicated to safety during those years. Apparently, executives simply thought that people would pay a little extra for it. Aircraft type anchored seat belts, thickly padded dashboard crash panel, and padded sun visors were all optional. Buyers thought the seat belts looked a bit ominous. Salesmen

Standard equipment on 1956 Fords was deep dish steering wheel with spokes that gave with impact.

quickly pointed out that the padded dash and visors were stylish. The belts were only a part of the "style-safety" package. Besides, the shatterproof rearview mirror was standard equipment. Longtime Ford salesmen now recall that the '56 Ford safety package was difficult to sell.

Ford gave up their attractive but hard to read "Astra-dome" instrument panel in '56 in favor of the easier to read dials. All were white figures mounted on a black and silver background. The idiot lights stayed.

I knew a number of '56 Ford owners. They all raved about the car's good looks and snappy performance and cursed the seat belts. Research showed that less than six percent of the buyers were influenced by the safety pitch. In fact, research strongly indicated that the safety story was turning buyers away to Chevrolet. The safety pitch is forgotten now. Collectors, like original owners, go for the '56 Ford's classic Thunderbird styling. The car is simply beautiful, and a delight to drive. A good '56 Ford will still handle and corner as effortlessly as the day it was new. They never tried to drive the driver. Ford had come a long way from the cumbersome '49s.

For '56, Ford offered six station wagons, a stunning Sunliner convertible, the attractive Crown Victoria (one version with a plexiglass greenhouse top), and their first four-door hardtop. You could pick from an array of Easter egg colors including tangerine, pink, yellow, purple, and turquoise. I've always loved those shocking mid-'50s car colors, and was sorry to see Detroit go back to the more conservative colors of the '30s and '40s.

When new, '56 Fords had a so-so reputation. Buyers complained about poor gas mileage, body squeaks, leaks, rattles, and generally poor quality workmanship. The interior vinyl, while bright, was cheap, and quickly took on a flophouse look. The dual exhausts through the bumpers soon rusted the bumpers. The soft stainless steel grille dented easily. By 1959 or '60, most '56 Fords looked worse than cars 10 years their seniors. They soon became the most popular cars in the worst parts of town. I guess most of them just quietly rusted away into oblivion. When the headlights finally fell out, that was the end. Little wonder that '56 Ford Fairlanes are scarce items

now, and command increasingly high prices.

We witnessed a decent (but not perfect) four-door hardtop go for $1,000 in Scottsdale, Ariz. We saw a mint tangerine convertible sell for $3,000 in Anaheim, Calif. Within the last few years, '56 Ford Fairlanes have become very hot. Since few have been saved, they're probably a lot rarer than Thunderbirds now.

Our feature car belongs to Jerry Lew, a San Francisco Bay area title insurance officer and Ford-Mercury enthusiast. Jerry has a collection of flathead Fords and Mercs housed in a 10-car garage under his new home in Moraga, Calif. "I built a garage with an attached house," Jerry says. "Now I'm buying back all the cars I was foolish enough to sell off when I was in my teens. The '56 Ford convertible is one of my favorites. I don't particularly care what the car is worth. I just like its styling." The car was rough when Jerry bought it. He spent more money on the bodywork than most non-collectors would pay for a decent running '56 Ford. He pulled the engine out of a parts convertible. But he likes '56 Fords so much that he still intends to restore the parts car.

Jerry bought and restored his '56 for only two reasons. He loved the colors — blue and white. And the padded dash was perfect.

"You just don't find them with good dash padding," Jerry points out. "Most of the time, when the padding starts to go, the guys just peel the whole thing off. I was really fortunate in finding a convertible with a dash this nice." Jerry is what you might call a dashboard nut. He's been known to restore whole cars around a perfect dashboard. That's precisely what he's doing to the '56 Ford, the safety car that failed. Jerry said, like the people in the television commercials, "Gee, I didn't know that."

Collectors, like buyers 34 years ago, are unimpressed with the safety features of the '56 Ford. The marque lost out to Chevrolet in sales that year. Ford was beaten badly. Finally, in 1957, Ford outsold Chevrolet. Learning from their mistake the previous year, Ford sold style in '57. We suspect that Fords have always been as safe as any cars on the road, but we have a hunch that safety never sold a single Ford. The safety pitch of '56 wasn't exactly one of Ford's "better ideas."

1957-1959
A New Kind of Ford

Ford was all-new for '57. That year it was America's best-selling car. (Pre-production prototype)

Ford used big tail lamps in '57 and again in '59. They would become a Ford trademark.

By Robert C. Ackerson

As we recounted in the last installment of this survey of modern Ford history, Ford in the mid-'50s was preparing the foundation for a major assault upon Chevrolet's seemingly impregnable position as America's number one selling automobile. If success was to be measured by permanent possession of the sales leadership then Ford's effort wasn't successful. But on the other hand, Ford did win the sales race in 1957 and was outproduced by Chevrolet in 1959 by just 44,230 cars. Pushing Chevrolet down a peg was a mighty hard task back in those days.!

One other point needs to be said about the influence of the mid-'50s sales battle upon Ford's corporate psyche. It seemed to bring out the best of its performance tradition along with a real willingness to venture out into new areas of automotive innovation. Keep in mind this was the company that was less than a decade from the Mustang, only a few years from the Falcon, which really deserves recognition as a modern day Model A, and of course destined to provide a whole generation of super-powered super stars for the NASCAR super tracks.

But we're getting ahead of ourselves just a bit. Our main point of interest at the moment is the 1957 Ford and that model, as unlikely as it appears was spurred on by the same forces that brought the Edsel into being. There's no need at this point to recount that less than dashing scenario in Ford history, but it's certainly worth noting that, unlike General Motors, Ford was woefully weak in the then growing and highly profitable medium priced car field. If ever there was a time when Alfred Sloan's dictum concerning the wisdom of producing a car for every pocketbook was providing bundles of profits for GM it was then. Ford wasn't doing all that bad, of course, but whereas GM could send out convoys of Pontiacs, Oldsmobiles and Buicks to satisfy America's yearning for automobiles that seemed to tell everyone that its owner was on the way up, Ford had to make do with a relatively thin line of Mercurys. Although the hoopla surrounding the Edsel's development and introduction plus its sensational sales failure has tended to overshadow the significance of the 1957 Ford, it played a major and far more successful role in the company's sales offensive.

In terms of Ford design history the 1957 model would have been a landmark regardless of its merits since it was the first example of a styling department supervised by George W. Walker who became Ford's director of styling in May 1955. Admittedly much of the groundwork that provided the 1957 Ford's inspiration had already been completed by that time but that simply puts credit where it's deserved. What's really important is that when Ford decided to strengthen its market position, the bits and pieces for a really attractive automobile with a Ford label were in hand.

With substantial justification therefore, George Walker was proud of the 1957 Fords in general and the Fairlane models in particular. Overall he described them as possessing a "fleeter, lighter, faster line." Although not every Ford product that received his approval was applauded for its restrained use of chrome trim, the new Ford reflected Walker's contention that "good simple lines are the best expression of forward motion. With sculptured sheet metal we can try to lead the public away from chrome."

Not surprisingly, most critics of the time agreed with Walker's analysis. Tom McCahill, (*Mechanix Illustrated*, November 1956) told his legions of faithful readers, "The Fairlane 500 is as good looking a car as you'll find in the low-priced field and has enough outright glamour to satisfy the giddiest of hearts without resorting to just plain bad taste to knock your eye out."

The Ford's styling wasn't totally without fault however.

The pods for the headlights gave the Ford a frog-like look that wasn't particularly appealing; *Motor Life*, (December 1956) regarded them as the Ford's weakest point and reported "the most universal reaction here is 'why did they do it?'" Although the Ford's simple front grillework suggested its creators were looking over their shoulders at the 1956 Chevrolet, it represented a pleasing blend of horizontal and vertical bars that was easy on the eyes. Similarly the Ford's canted rear fender fins blended nicely with its "Jet-Tube" taillights to combine a neo-classical Ford look with the latest styling craze to sweep across Detroit. George Walker was surprisingly blase about this development, observing that "Later, maybe we will drop them on their sides, and after that there's nothing left to do but leave them off."

The impact of Ford's "equaflair" styling was expressed in its most dramatic fashion in the Fairlane and Fairlane 500 series. With an 118 inch wheelbase and overall length of 107.7 inches, these cars were nine inches longer and four inches lower than the 1956 Fairlanes. Ford wasted no time in touting the Fairlane's physical bulk. Potential customers were advised that "There's no car in your field that is longer..." The Fairlane 500 was "so low and so wide...so heavy and big and so roomy inside...Even *medium* priced cars find it hard to compete." Surveying the current mood of the automobile market and the new Fairlane, George Walker asked "...how can you call this Ford a 'small car'? People want a Lincoln at Ford prices and we have to give it to them." Writing in *Hot Rod* (January 1957) Racer Brown concurred at least in part with Walker's sentiments. "Gone are the days when the Ford could be referred to as a 'small car'" he noted. "Instead," said Brown "the new Ford borders on the 'barge-like' although it escapes this definition by virtue of several redeeming features."

Ford provided a full complement of Fairlane and Fairlane 500 (in some ads Ford referred to the 500 as the Fairlane "Five Hundred") models including two- and four-door "thin pillar" sedans plus corresponding hardtop models known respectively as the Club Victoria and Town Victoria. The only convertible, at least until the arrival of the retractable hardtop in December 1956, the Sunliner, was available only in Fairlane 500 form.

Ford's interior design for 1957 wasn't quite as dramatically new as its exterior but it rated good grades for both attractiveness and practicality. The standard "deep-dish" steering wheel was reduced in diameter by half inch from the year earlier unit and its lower position relative to the driver made long distance motoring more pleasant. Also contributing to the Ford's appealing interior environment were seats with greater support and an easier to read instrument panel. Not such great ideas were its tiny rearview mirror and awkwardly positioned front door locks which were located just inside the front vent windows. *Motor Trend* (January 1957) predicted: "Thieves will welcome this handy push button." However the rest of us appreciated the quick action of the Ford's window lift mechanism. The driver's window for example, needed just 1⅝ turns of the winder to be raised or lowered.

With 37 different fabric-color combinations and a choice of either the standard nylon or optional vinyl upholstery, most customers had little difficulty finding an interior that satisfied their decorating whims.

Whatever doubts anyone at Ford might have had about the wisdom of increasing the Fairlane's size were blown away by the tremendous sales success of the 188 inch wheelbase models. Actually, it was the Fairlane 500 series that was the show stealer. Production of 500s exceeded that of the plainer Fairlanes by a comfortable six to one margin. While output of the lower priced Custom and Cus-

The three different positions of Ford's famous 1957 retractable hardtop. Called the Skyliner, the "retractable" was a part of the Ford line in 1957, 1958 and 1959. It's a highly desirable collector item today.

The last retractable was the 1959 Skyliner. Early ones (such as this example) featured Fairlane 500 script on the rear fenders while later ones were called Galaxies.

tom 300 models was a respectable 475,805, production of Fairlane 500's was, at 632,816, even more impressive.

We don't want to create the impression however that the Custom and Custom 300 Fords were devoid of any socially redeeming features. The overwhelming amount of their mechanical elements were shared with the Fairlanes but their shorter (116 inch) wheelbase and lack of hardtop models worked against their sales appeal during an era when upward mobility demanded ownership of an automobile with lots of length and no center pillars. Ford's five station wagons, ranging from the top of the line Country Squire to the no-nonsense Ranch Wagon were also based upon the 116 inch wheelbase chassis.

A number of sources have placed the development cost of the 1957 Ford at $200 million. While part of this amount might possibly have lead to the Mercury and Edsel models that were spun off the Ford line there's no doubt that Ford spent a bundle on its cars.

For that kind of expenditure Ford received an automobile with much more than a new shape and size. *Motor Trend* (November 1956) reported it was "a new car that's really new—The '57 Ford should prove to be all that Ford lovers had hoped for."

Much of this newness was found in the Ford's new frame whose design allowed the floor and seats to be positioned between the side rails. This format, which had been pioneered by Hudson nearly two decades earlier, plus a tapered driveshaft and fourteen inch wheels were the primary contributors to the Ford's lowered profile.

Ford had been an innovator with its excellent ball-joint front suspension and for 1957 only some minor refinements were needed to maintain Ford's reputation for good handling. The total number of front end components was reduced by combining all elements of the upper and lower arms into just two units. Simply by redesigning the lower arm to be angled backward 20 degrees Ford was able to provide a smoother ride and less front end dip in braking. At the rear, all Fords except station wagon models (which have five) were fitted with four leaf springs. The main leaf was 25% heavier than its 1956 counterpart and with a length of 55 inches, the rear springs were two inches longer than those used in 1956. Most of this extra length was found forward of the axle, a feature which along with the near total outboard location of the spring encouraged Tom McCahill to report (*Mechanix Illustrated*, November 1956) that the Ford cornered "as flat as a mailman's feet." It's also interesting that although the extra inches of wheelbase added bulk to the Ford's overall size they helped improve its weight distribution to a respectable 55.4% front, 44.6% rear ratio. We don't want to create the impression that the Ford was the world's top handling sedan. It could, if the driver became a bit overzealous on turns, break away with little warning and *Motor Trend* (January 1957) complained that "There is a certain un-Ford-like wallowing when coming out of severe highway dips...."

Ford's early season engine lineup consisted of a trio of V-8s and its familiar 223 cid six. Leading the pack was the 312 cid Thunderbird Special V-8 which was optional in all models and standard in none of them! Its four-barrel "low silhouette" carburetor was substantially redesigned for 1957 to not only provide a lower height and allow for the use of an inexpensive replaceable paper element air cleaner but to reduce fuel starvation on sharp turns. A new, higher lift cam and larger valves helped improve the breathing of all Ford V-8s and with a 9.7:1 compression ratio the Thunderbird Special was rated at 245 hp at 4500 rpm. Contributing to this output was a dual exhaust system which was offered only for the Thunderbird Special.

The standard engine for all Fairlane and station wagon models was the 292 cid Thunderbird V-8. With a 9.0:1 compression ratio and two-barrel carburetor it reported

in with a 212 horsepower output when linked to Ford-O-Matic. When a three-speed gearbox was ordered its horsepower dropped to 206. Ford's smallest V-8, a 272 cid, 8.6:1 compression ratio creation with a two-barrel carburetor and 190 horsepower was reserved for the Custom and Custom 300 models.

With a respectable 144 horsepower on tap at 4200 rpm. Ford's six-cylinder engine was available in all models except the retractable hardtop.

But the "real stuff" from Ford first showed off its potential at Bonneville in September 1956. This was, of course, the super-charged version of the 312 V-8. In its production form it was offered with an 8.5:1 compression ratio, 256° duratin cam and a supercharge boost of approximately five pounds. However it's generally recognized that its 300 horsepower at 4800 rpm was conservative. At Bonneville the blown Ford set many new AAA records with speeds of up to 131 mph.

Ford had contracted with McCulloch for its total production run of VR superchargers and for a time it

All '58 Fairlane 500s featured gold-colored trim down the body sides.

appeared the blown Fords would become a common commodity in performance circles. At Daytona, they were all over the beach and the best of the bunch reached 131 mph. Later in the year one of these fleet Fords lapped the Indianapolis track at 117 mph. On the drag strips they were equally impressive, proving capable of speeds in the 96 to 100 mph zone and elapsed time in the high 14 second area. This engine was available in any 1957 Ford or Thunderbird and while its price of $447.60 did not include any chassis modifications, there were plenty of heavy-duty components available to make the supercharged Ford a very capable road machine. When prepared for NASCAR competition these models had their boost raised to six pounds and carried a 290° cam. A reasonable estimate of their horsepower output was 340.

Although NASCAR's decision to ban superchargers, fuel injection and multi-carburetor setups for Grand National competition shortly after the season began, cut short what promised to be a memorable Chevy versus Ford versus everybody else year of racing, the supercharged Ford

left its mark upon racing history. Jerry Unser won the Pikes Peak climb in 15 minutes, 39.2 seconds. And the same Ford that earlier had set hundreds of speed and endurance records at Bonneville was driven to a new cross-country, New York to Los Angeles record by Danny Eames and Chuck Daigh. Their average speed for 2913 miles was 61.18 mph.

This achievement was, of course, just one of many events and developments that made 1957 such a historic automotive year. Certainly not the least exciting occasion was Ford's introduction of the world's first *mass-produced* retractable hardtop on Dec. 8, 1956 at the National Automobile Show in New York City. While Ford's supercharged engine was its performance reply to Chevrolet's fuel injection system, it's fair to suggest the hand assembled prototype displayed in New York was Ford's technical response to Chevrolet's engineering prowess implied in the FI system.

The Skyliner (this name had first been used in 1954 for Ford's semi-bubble top model) was based upon the 118-

undoubtedly contributed to a good deal of showroom traffic that lead to the sale of a more conventional model.

Any automobile history concerning postwar automobiles has to address the issue of quality and workmanship since it was in those areas that so many manufacturers sowed the seeds of future customer discontent. The 1957 Fords took their first share of criticism for shortfalls in these categories. Regarding the assembly of its test car, *Motor Trend* (January 1957) reported it was "startlingly bad in this respect. Nothing seemed to fit. Great gobs of lead were hanging on the rakish left rear fin... The left rear door wouldn't shut unless the window was open. The trunk, like the hood, was nearly impossible to latch." *Hot Rod* (January 1957) while giving its test car the benefit of the doubt as possibly an early model off the assembly line, reported, "The fit of the hood, doors, and trunk was only fair and as such, certainly sub-standard for Ford." The logic that explains why early buyers of a new model had to put up with below-par assembly standard, has always escaped me but in fairness to Ford it wasn't the only auto

The two-door Ranch Wagon was Ford's bottom-of-the-line hauler for '58.

inch wheelbase chassis but an extended rear deck added an additional three inches of overall length. Many critics of this automobile never tired of reminding their readers of its very limited luggage capacity, which was essentially confined to a 24 inch x 30 inch x 15 inch space under its rear deck lid. But on the other hand Ford was offering a complex top system that had been tested without failure through ten thousand cycles and regardless of this weakness and its limited production life, this particular Ford was an impressive example of its manufacturer's technical strength.

Whether the top was being raised or lowered its operation was a dramatic scene to witness. Within a 40 second time span, seven electric motors (drawing no more current than required to operate a conventional convertible top) manipulated the rear deck and the top in a precise fashion that never failed to impress those who invariably gathered for the occasion.

The Skyliner never was a big seller with only 20,766 sold in 1957, but its ability to attract attention by the truckload

manufacturer to engage in such field research. Nonetheless all too many 1957 Fords exposed their owners to the torments of dust and water leaks plus the great nemesis common to cars of the '50s, the plague of the rust worms.

But let's not take too much away from the 1957 Ford. It was exciting to look at a sensational performer in its supercharged form and its model production run of 1,655,068 units outpaced Chevrolet's 1,515,177 mark.

But as 1957 faded away the battle between Ford and Chevrolet took on a new complexion. Unlike 1957 when Ford had the advantage of a new look and Chevrolet was making do with a revision of a body style in its third year of production, 1958 saw the situation somewhat altered. Chevrolet, this time around was the car with a new appearance while Ford had to defend its sales position with a facelifted model. This was by no means an impossible situation for Ford, but it required an automobile with an appearance both pleasing and fresh. Unfortunately for Ford, its 1958 model failed on both counts. The primary

mistake made by its stylists was the abandonment of basic good taste in favor of a mentality that had been manifested by the 1957 Mercury. In general this resulted in an automobile whose styling was dominated by uncoordinated shapes and forms, uninspired styling cliches and a general lack of logic. The Ford's front end was a hopelessly confused collection of (on the Fairlane 500) fender mounted "gun sights," a false hood scoop, dual headlights complete with chrome tipped visors and huge amounts of brightwork that encased the honeycombed grille work in a prison of poor design. A similar disaster awaited the viewer when he examined the Fairlane 500's flanks. There he discovered a huge side spear with a gold anodized aluminum insert shaped with little regard to the car's basic form. Ford also made a serious error by tampering with the popular form of its circular taillights. For 1958 oblong-shaped lights were used at the rear that at best were unhappy reminders of those used by Edsel. Tom McCahill recalled in *Mechanix Illustrated*, (December 1957) that "when I first saw the new Ford running

1958 Ford Custom 300 four-door sedan

around the Dearborn track last May...I remarked to a company engineer, 'God! Look at those taillights!' I believe he answered, 'Yeah, but you get used to them!'" McCahill also had little use for the Fairlane 500's prior mentioned front fender decorations which he regarded as "about as useful as an elephant tail on a fox."

There were other misfeasances of the stylist's trade such as the awkwardly curved shape pressed into the trunk lid and the series of flutes running from front to rear along the Ford's hood that served little purpose but to add even more confusion to an already cluttered appearance. *Motor Life*, February 1958, was being extremely diplomatic when it noted that "the reputed cost of the changeover is far greater than the improvement obtained. It doesn't seem as if Ford got its money's worth this trip." Tom McCahill, after testing the 1958 Ford (*Mechanix Illustrated*, December 1957) concluded: "I think the '57 Ford looked better than the '58. I also think from a looks standpoint that the Chevy Impala for '58 will give Ford one helluva race."

Ford Motor Company reportedly spent the tidy sum of $185 million on its lineup of Ford, Mercury and Lincoln automobiles and a good deal of this expenditure was to develop a new family of V-8s. The larger 410 and 430 cubic inch versions were initially reserved for use in Mercury, senior Edsel, Lincoln and Continental models. The smaller (by comparison only) 332 and 352 cid V-8s were shared by Ford and the less expensive Edsel series. These engines with their wedge-shaped combustion chambers, very large bearings and valve dimensions seemed to possess a fair degree of performance potential but Ford made little effort to explore this area with any degree of seriousness. The 352 Interceptor Special V-8 which was available only in Fairlane 500 models was rated at 300 horsepower at 4600 rpm and 395 lb-ft torque at 2800 rpm. These specifications plus a 10.2:1 compression ratio and a standard four barrel carburetor seemed fairly impressive, but the cold hard facts from the drag strip weren't particularly exciting. Zero to 60 mph times with an automatic transmission usually were in the vicinity of 10 seconds.

Pretty Ford Galaxie convertible with conventional top design outsold the retractable hardtop. This one was the Sunliner while the retractable was called the Skyliner.

However, in fairness to the Interceptor Special, part of the problem was the 2.69:1 rear axle ratio supplied as standard equipment.

The 300 horsepower V-8 plus the 265 horsepower Interceptor 332 Special which carried a 9.5:1 compression ratio and a four-barrel carburetor were the only engines available with Ford's new Cruise-O-Matic automatic transmission. In theory, if not in practice this was a high-performance unit with two drive ranges. In D1 the transmission provided full throttle acceleration through all three forward gears. In D2 the intial take off was made in second gear, thus accleration was considerably more leisurely. But the motoring press exhibited little enthusiasm for Cruise-O-Matic in either format, chosing instead to register complaints about the mediocre performance provided by the combination of a 300 hp engine, a 2.69:1 rear axle and Cruise-O-Matic. *Motor Life* (February 1958) observed that "The Cruise-O-Matic, oddly, doesn't appear to have any advantages that could have caused it to be developed."

This sentiment was also one which commonly greeted Ford-Aire, Ford's entry in the air-suspension carnival. With a $156 price tag and the ability to maintain a constant car height under all conditions, Ford-Aire did have some appeal. But like virtually every other system from its competitors, Ford sent its rubber bladder wonder to a quick end and offered it only in 1958.

With a production run of just over 950,000 automobiles, Ford stumbled badly in 1958, trailing Chevrolet at year's end by over 216,000 units. In fairness to Ford it should be noted that only Rambler and Thunderbird moved up the production ladder in 1958. It wasn't a year of strong domestic sales and thus part of the Ford decline was attributed to a generally soft market. But that can't really hide the negative sales appeal of the 1958 Ford's appearance. It simply wasn't the equal of the 1957 in this regard and represents one of the few times in modern Ford history when it erred badly on such a crucial point. However to its credit, the newer model did represent progress in the area of quality control. After completing its road test of a 1958 Ford, *Motor Life* (February 1958), reported, "One of the chief impressions gained from all this driving

is that the car was of exceptional quality of assembly, in contrast not only to earlier Fords but rival makes as well...It was one of the quickest bodies yet encountered from Detroit."

In essence Ford, because of this asset was in a stronger position to take advantage of a revived market for automobiles than a number of other American producers. It hadn't lost too many friends because of sloppy assembly during 1958 and thus if it could bounce back in 1959 with a better looking automobile it might just push Chevrolet out of "Number One Country."

From more than one perspective the 1959 version of the Chevrolet vs. Ford was one of the most interesting to take place during that decade. But without doubt the most intriguing was the divergent styling philosophies the two cars represented. GM had been stung badly by the sudden onslaught and subsequent popularity of Chrysler's bold new styling in 1957. In comparison to competing models from Dodge, DeSoto and Chrysler, the Oldsmobiles and Buicks of that year appeared, in spite of being first year editions of new body shells, to be relics left over from an earlier styling cycle. The reaction of GM to this seldom experienced situation was vigorous and dramatic. Under the direction of Harley Earl, the GM designers created a line of automobiles that in terms of sheer size, bulk and of course fins were fully capable of delivering powerful sales broadsides to the Chrysler Corp. automotive fleet. Obviously not wishing to be left in drydock, Ford could have jumped into the fray with its own particular brand of Chrysler "Me Tooism" but it chose not to do so. Instead, Ford regained considerable sales ground and the respect of countless thousands of discriminating car buyers by producing one of the best styled automobiles of its history.

Ford styling chief, George Walker had been for many years an advocate of "crisp" body design. In effect he favored automobiles on which most body lines were straight, corners were well defined and an overall "sculptured" effect was achieved. Thus, roof lines receiving Walker's approval were flat and thin; curves were used to avoid a boxy look and soft, rounded appearance was rejected in favor of a more formal profile.

1959 Ford Country Sedan station wagon

A common explanation of the 1959 Ford look from company executives usually included the idea that Ford was building automobiles not jet planes and that in styling the new models, Ford designers had used a "common sense" rather than "excess" approach.

Whatever the rationale, the final product was sensational. Ford artfully dodged the fin dilemma by sweeping the rear fender line backward from a graceful midpoint dip that contributed to a look of class, distinction and sophistication. At the rear the fender enclosed high mounted back-up lights and two very large circular taillights mounted so low in the rear deck that the rear bumper was dished to provide sufficient space for their use. Ford didn't shy away from the use of chrome in 1959 but like the rest of the '59's styling components it was used with a sense of purpose, namely to accentuate a clearly defined design theme.

It's not really surprising as a result that instead of stirring up controversy, the 1959 Ford's appearance elicited many favorable responses. Al Berger of the *Speed Age* staff believed the Ford's styling changes were "for the better, not just for the sake of change...All the frills have been eliminated—the quadruple taillights, the dummy air scoop on the hood, the deep trench in the rear deck and the dirt-catching grooves on the roof have gone the way of all styling gimmicks."

Shortly after the Ford line was presented a second shock wave was sent through the ranks of its opposition by the introduction of half a dozen Galaxie models that mated the Thunderbird roofline with the excellent form of the Fairlane 500. The results were spectacular. Neither Chevrolet or Plymouth had anything that directly competed with the Galaxie. Although only their roofline distinguished the Galaxies from the Fairlane 500's, they became Ford's most popular series with total production totalling 464,336 units.

Each one of these cars undoubtedly brought Ford a tidy profit but there were other basic changes in the Ford lineup that were equally important as money makers. Ranking high as a common sense cost cutting move was the decision to use the 188 inch chassis for every Ford series and model. This of course added extra inches of length to the Custom 300 and station wagon models but if this displeased anyone, a reduction in body width from 78 inches to 76.6 inches probably cancelled out any potential negative sales impact.

Ford also slimmed down its initial engine lineup for 1959 offering only single versions of the 332 and 352 cubic inch V-8's. The 352 retained its 300 horsepower rating but a drop in compression ratio from 10.2 to 9.6:1 reduced its torque to 380 lb-ft. at 2800 rpm. Whereas the 332 cid V-8 had been offered with either 240 or 265 horsepower in 1958, it was now available only with 225 horsepower, a single two-barrel carburetor and 8.9:1 compression ratio. Although the 223 cid six remained unchanged, the 292 cid V-8 did not escape the V-8 power slippage for 1959. Its peak horsepower was slightly diluted to an even 200 at 4400 rpm.

After introducing Cruise-O-Matic in 1958, Ford sent the old three speed Ford-O-Matic, which had been supplied by Borg-Warner to the showers. Its Ford-built replacement was less expensive, $190 to $180, less complex with 27.4% fewer parts and thanks to the use of alumimum for its casing and bell housing about fifty pounds lighter. However, with only two forward speeds, versatility and acceleration were not among its strongest virtues. For example, the new Ford-O-Matic could be run to just over 60 mph in first gear but with no intermediate gear it had little strength above that point. There actually wasn' all that much excitement in the Ford-O-Matic's acceleration anyway. A *Motor Life* (January 1959) road test of a 225 horsepower version yielded an uninspiring 15 second time for the zero to 60 mph run.

But there were other Fords with the 300 horsepower—325 cid V-8 that could reach 60 mph in 10-seconds and certainly this more than adequate performance, the Ford's good looks and respectable workmanship qualified 1959 as a vintage Ford year. Ford liked to call its 1959 models "the world's most beautifully proportioned cars" and while that might have been a bit exaggerated, even the most anti-Dearborn type had to concede that Ford had more than acquitted itself for the "Crime of '58."

'58 Ford Retractable
HARD TO TOP

Resembling a venus flytrap, the 1958 Ford Fairlane retractable hardtop steals its share of stare even today.

By Gerald Perschbacher

Every baseball game teaches the spectators a lesson in life. When opportunity comes whizzing across the plate, we may take a big swing and miss; but it's only strike one. What was learned from our first mistake or miscalculation can be applied to a second try when opportunity comes again. If then we swing and miss, we learn more. With feet firmly planted in the batter's box of life, we await the wind up and the pitch of yet a third opportunity. On our third swing may rest a career and a future.

It was the Ford Motor Co. which stepped to the plate in 1957 through '59 facing the third pitch for a retractable hardtop.

The idea was not new. The first modern car with the feature of a retractable hardtop was introduced to the American public amid brass bands and corporate flag-waving by the Chrysler Corp. The year was 1940, and the car was the Chrysler Thunderbolt.

Sleek and more aerodynamic in looks than any other contemporary, the Chrysler Thunderbolt was conceived in the fertile minds of designers Alex Tremulis and Ralph Roberts. Tremulis was spreading his wings of exciting design at the Briggs Manufacturing Co.; Roberts was an inside man from Chrysler itself.

Once conceived, the concept was nurtured through birth by the LeBaron Body Co., custom coach builders to the elite. A family of six Thunderbolts were brought into this life, and all carried full aluminum bodies, skirted wheels, concealed headlights, one seat for passengers (to accommodate three), and the feature that mystified crowds wherever the car was shown for publicity purposes — the retractable hardtop.

It was a very small top, but the space to store it created a challenge for the designers. The top was electronically controlled as was the rear deck. Most publicity shots, however, played down the hideaway hardtop. The Chrysler Corp. had stepped to the plate, thought six times about a retractable hardtop, took its swing, but there were no practical results.

Enter batter number two; the Playboy for 1947. A former Packard dealer by the name of Louis Horowitz and a former Pontiac man named Charles D. Thomas originated the concept of a fairly inexpensive car of small stature and forgettable styling and appointments.

The car was austere and lackluster. The fit and finish had little integrity. Priced at slightly under $1,000 by the factory in Buffalo, the car carried an appealing name (for most people) but only a four-cylinder Continental engine that had little, if any extra power to "play." But the car did carry a true fold-down hardtop. Basically a two-passenger vehicle, the 90-inch wheelbase did not allow for a lot of mechanical plumbing to raise and lower the top automatically. The Playboy's hardtop disappeared manually. A total of under 100 Playboys were made before the company closed its doors on the 1951 model.

It took the brawn and bucks of the Ford Motor Co. to suit up the first truly successful retractable hardtop and send it out on the field for 1957. Perhaps it was an outgrowth from the "see-through" sun top which saw the last light of sun at the end of the 1956 model run. It is believed that the company spent five years planning for actual production which resulted in the Skyliner retractable hardtop at a factory price of $2,942.

Its shipping weight of 3,916 pounds reflected the extra hardware required to pop the top. That weight was nearly 500 pounds greater than Ford's heaviest convertible, the Sunliner. The new retractable Skyliner appeared in the Fairlane 500 V-8 Series which boasted a 118-inch wheelbase which stretched to just under 211 inches in overall length, a good three inches longer than the standard Fairlane models. The car had the potential to do a nice job of running the bases with a 272-cubic inch V-8 engine pushing out 190 horsepower at 4500 rpm. The retractable hardtop was first on Ford's batting list of sedans.

The new hideaway top was more than three inches shorter than the standard cut, and the trunk opened its jaws opposite normal procedure in order to gulp down the top within 60 seconds after the driver pushed the button. The whole trick was a $20 million game plan by the company in order to test sales in an area never exploited. Ford's retractable Fairlane stepped to the batter's box for 1957, planted its feet in te dust of competition, and heaved its sales bat high over its shoulder. But what was the call when the ball streaked to the plate?

In production numbers, the result was not staggering. 2,766 retractables played the game for '57, 14,713 joined the league in '58; and 12,915 suited up for '59 with a uniform change that blazed the name Galaxie instead of Fairlane. Style changes for '60 outdated the design without costly styling conversions. Though not remarkable in production, the Ford retractable was the most successful of the three much-publicized retractable hardtops herein mentioned.

Financial gain is but one scoreboard for success. Another is publicity mileage. Having a baseball glove unlike anybody else's in the neighborhood brings inquisitive young players to your doorstep to see what everyone is talking about. No doubt the retractable hardtop served this purpose for Ford in building up traffic coming into Ford showrooms from coast to coast. A lot of those buyers may not have walked away with a retractable Ford, but chances were good that another player in Ford's lineup would sign over to new owners.

The Ford Fairlane retractable hardtop might not have hit a home run, but it did help Ford win the pennant with almost 37,000 more new passenger car registrations over Chevrolet for 1957. And Ford's retractable hardtop may not have been a Hank Aaron or a Babe Ruth, but it certainly was a Lou Brock when it came to stealing attention!

60s Ford

The Full-Size 1960-61 Fords
More Style, More Horsepower

By Robert C. Ackerson

Ford celebrated its 80th anniversary in 1983 and an awful lot of people believed 1983 would be a year when Ford's economic fortunes made a major turnabout. We're not going to delve into the whys and wherefores of Ford's recovery at this point but the catch and effective "Have you driven a ford lately?" theme is a tip-off. Ford is at its best being Ford, not GM or anyone else and it seems to this writer that Ford, after some years of meandering is again on track and ready to get back into the fray as a builder of some pretty interesting automobiles.

Looking back at 1960 there's more than a hint that what ailed Ford during that season was its temporary loss of "Fordism." The model year production figures seem to sum up Ford's dilemma pretty well. Whereas Ford produced 1,481,071 units of its super-sharp 1959 models. It was only able to find enough customers for 911,034 Fords in 1960. That presidential election year wouldn't be

remembered as one of the Armerican economy's best performances and Ford wasn't the only U.S. auto manufacturer to experience a sales decline. Yet, the suspicion remains strong that a major factor was its new look for 1960. But unlike the 1958's there was little in the Ford's appearance to fault. It was contemporary, not overly endowed with chrome and original, but certainly not extreme. It did, however, suffer an identity crisis and it was Tom McCahill who zeroed in on this flaw. In his report on the new Ford he wrote (*Mechanix Illustrated*, February 1960): "Style-wise the 1960 Ford is so different from any other Ford ever made that if the name didn't appear anywhere on the car it would be impossible for the most dyed-in-the-wool automobile man to determine what make he was looking at without raising the hood or looking under the body." But this would be the last year for a long, long time that McCahill could make such a state-

1960 Ford Fairlane 4-dr sedan

ment. Ford, it seems, gave up trying to convince its customers that they really didn't want to drive Fords that looked like Fords. For the rest of the decade Ford produced cars that evolved very slowly from a styling position containing all the key elements of the Ford look. Chevrolet, even with its radical '59s, had never swayed far from its traditional marque identity. Ford finally caught on to what Chevrolet was up to after 1960!

But nonetheless Ford stepped out with a sensational new Starliner hardtop model that year and it's difficult to fault the appearance of that Ford. Since a good deal of money had been spent to give the '60s their new look, Ford wanted to reach every prospective buyer with that message. "Ford is famous for a 'beautifully proportioned' concept of styling" it explained, "and the 1960's are styled within this tradition..... yet with a world of difference." The result included a lower hoodline, a windshield nearly 20% larger than in 1959 and the replacement of the old dogleg cornerposts with "Easy Entrance" windshield pillars. In the case of the Starliner, Ford stylists endowed it with a "sports car flavor and the open-air freedom of a two-door hardtop." The Starliner was attractive and Ford was correct by claiming its appearance "set it apart from all others." But at the same time Ford was not offering a hardtop with the square back roofline which had been extremely popular among purchasers of 1959 Fords. Thus whereas Ford had produced nearly 122,000 two-door hardtop Galaxies in 1959 total output of Starliners was only 68,641. It's also possible that Ford was moving a bit too rapidly in altering the status of its various model designations to suit the buying public. For 1960 the Custom 300 series was replaced by a line of Fairlanes and the Fairlane 500s which as recently as 1958 had enjoyed top billing, were relegated to third position in the lineup. If this didn't lead to some confusion then Ford made sure

some existed by sending out some conflicting signals about the Galaxie, Starliner and Sunliner models. Some sources regard the Starliner and Sunliner as part of the Galaxie series but Ford in its *Buyer's Digest of New Car Facts* for '60 noted in regard to the Starliner that "it offers all the Galaxie advantages found in the Town Victoria (a four-door hardtop) plus a wonderfully different roof and rear window design that proudly establish the Starliner as an exclusive model."

With a 119 inch wheelbase and an overall length of 213.7 inches the 1960 Fords were the largest models in the company's history and with a width of 81.5 inches they had the rather questionable honor of being the widest cars built in the United States. To accommodate this larger body a new chassis and suspension system were used in 1960. In general they followed the design format of 1959 although Ford claimed the frame was 25% stronger.

When the new models were introduced on Oct. 9, 1959 there was little in their specifications to suggest Ford was about to reverse its nearly three-year-old-performance decline. There were some minor developments, such as lighter weight (due to increased use of aluminum castings) Ford-O-Matic and Cruise-O-Matic transmissions, both of which, Ford said, had been recalibrated for improved performance. But a look up and down the engine lineup failed to turn up anything new that held much promise on the dragstrip. The 332cid V-8 was no longer available and the 300hp Thunderbird 352 Special V-8 possessed virtually no credentials as a performance engine. A somewhat less energetic Thunderbird 352 V-8 was offered with a two-barrel carburetor, 235hp and 8.9:1 compression ratio but of course neither it nor the Thunderbird 292 V-8 (185 hp, 8.8:1 compression ratio) were anything more than moderately stressed V-8s ideal for sale to the mass mar-

The full-size 1960 Ford was totally re-engineered and it looked brand new too. The wraparound windshield with its protruding "dogleg" was gone but Chevrolet-like horizontal rear fins were part of the new package.

ket. The standard-in-all-models 223 cid six was sporting a unique side-mounted air cleaner mandated by the lower hoodline for 1960 but this obviously was not destined to be regarded as a momentous development.

Yet, help was on the way to Ford's beseiged performances. It was long overdue but finally in December 1959 Ford announced a very welcome addition to its engine line that promised enough power to achieve performance parity with Chevrolet.

For approximately another $150 above the cost of the 300 hp, 352 cid engine (which listed for $177.40) Ford unveiled, with considerable and justifiable pride, its 352 Special 4V V-8. Dave Evans, the Ford project engineer for this program along with engine engineer Don Sullivan and chassis engineer John Cowley were barely able to restrain their sense of pleasure that "Ford was back!" *Motor Life* (January 1960) quoted Evans as predicting the new engine "will deliver an honest 150 mph!" At Daytona it came mighty close, enabling a Ford to average 145.4 mph for five laps. Less than a week after that impressive run the same car lapped Ford's Romeo, Michigan track at 152.2 mph.

Although the Special 4V was based upon the 352 cid engine, it fully deserved being called a "special" engine. A look at its power ratings left no doubt about that. With 360 hp at 6000 rpm and 380 lb-ft of torque at 3400 rpm it was obviously not your average Ford V-8. Sitting atop an aluminum manifold that weighed forty pounds less than the version used on the Thunderbird 352 Special V-8 was a Holley four-barrel with a 540 cfm capacity. Also unique to this engine were new cast iron headers. Internal alterations were not radical but they were effective. A higher, 10.6:1 compression ratio was obtained by slightly filling in the area around the valve heads and an increased rev capability was achieved by mating Falcon pushrods with

the solid lifters and rockers that had been used back in 1958. Both the intake and exhaust valve diameters at 2.03 and 1.56 inches respectively were unchanged but the exhaust valves were now drop-forged rather than being cast units. Along with a new, higher-lift cam and larger clearances, slightly heavier valve springs were used. To handle the Special's 36 horsepower a clutch with 2400 pounds of spring pressure was standard along with a stronger driveshaft. Ford also offered the "Interceptor" suspension system with its stronger springs and shocks for use with this engine and dealers were also able to supply many other extreme use chassis and driveshaft components including heavy-duty rear axles and spindles, even stiffer springs plus three-inch wide brake drums with hardened linings.

Output of Fords with this engine was very limited. By Jan. 15, 1960, for example, only 24 had been produced. However, those that were available turned in some impressive performances. The "typical" 360 hp Ford with its dual exhausts (in the words of *Motor Trend)* emitting "a subdued, guttural growl" was capable of zero to 60 mph runs approximately seven seconds when equipped with the stock three-speed overdrive transmission and a 4.86:1 rear axle. *Motor Life* (July 1960) tested a version fitted with the three-speed gearbox and 4.11 axle, and reported a standing start, quarter-mile time and speed respectively of 14.81 seconds and 94.71 mph. At the Daytona Speed Week a 360 hp Ford recorded an unofficial two-way speed through the flying mile of 142.5 mph. Since a Chrysler 300F with a four-speed transmission later achieved an average of 144.927 mph, it's apparent that the Ford was one of the fastest sedans in the world. However when official speed runs began, NASCAR took a look at the Ford's 3.22:1 axle and 15 inch wheels and declared them ineligible for competition use since they

1961 Ford Sunliner convertible

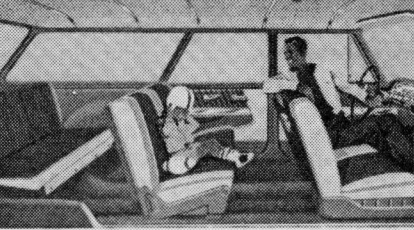

Power-operated rear window now standard on all '61 Ford 9-passenger wagons and the 6-passenger Country Squire! So handy for loading small items!

All seats face forward. In 9-passenger Ford wagons, everybody rides facing front the way people like to ride! Seat backs flatten flush with the floor for cargo carrying.

Built big for big cargo! And you get a wider rear opening...low loading level...flush tailgate...all make loading and unloading easier for '61.

Beautifully proportioned
to the CLASSIC FORD LOOK

New, for 1961—Ford's famous Country Squire is available in both 6- and 9-passenger models.

BEAUTIFULLY BUILT
TO TAKE CARE OF ITSELF

Beautifully built to do more for you, too, with new seven-inch-wider tailgate, new roll-down rear window and a whole wagonful of built-for-people comfort features no other wagon can match.

A station wagon buyer's guide for '61 would have to put the new Ford Wagon at the top of its list. No other wagon delivers so much, in such style, and at such a favorable price.

In the first place, you choose from America's most complete line ...6 new models...from Country Squire, the Thunderbird of station wagons, to the low priced Ranch Wagon. And there's other important news. Just turning the wheel is 25% easier when parking. New rear springing and wide-tread design give you a smoother ride.

What else is new in the world's most popular wagons? Well, here's a wagon that lubricates itself ... cleans its own oil ... adjusts its own brakes ... guards its own body ... takes care of its own finish. In short, a wagon beautifully built to take care of itself!

HERE'S HOW THE '61 FORD TAKES CARE OF ITSELF
...THE FIRST 1961 CAR THAT DEALERS HAVE WARRANTED
FOR 12,000 MILES OR ONE FULL YEAR

Lubricates itself — You'll normally go 30,000 miles without a chassis lubrication.

Cleans its own oil — You'll go 4,000 miles between oil changes with Ford's Full-Flow oil filter.

Adjusts its own brakes — New truck-size brakes adjust themselves automatically.

Guards its own muffler — Ford mufflers are double-wrapped and aluminized — normally will last three times as long as ordinary mufflers.

Protects its own body — All vital underbody parts are specially processed to resist rust and corrosion, even to galvanizing the body panels beneath the doors.

Takes care of its own finish — New Diamond Lustre Finish never needs wax.

Extended Warranty — Ford Dealers were the first to extend their warranty on the '61 cars for 12,000 miles or one full year, whichever comes first. Ask your dealer for details. FORD DIVISION, Ford Motor Company.

An honor to be proud of, this is the medal presented by the international fashion authority, Centro per l'Alta Moda Italiana, to the 1961 Ford for functional expression of classic beauty.

'61 FORD STATION WAGONS

The 1961 Ford Country Squire, with its familiar "wood-trimmed" look, was the top-of-the-line wagon. For some reason, Ford elected to carry over its old-fashioned tailgate/rear window design long after the competition had switched to a roll-down rear window.

were not included on Ford's AMA specifications sheet. Although Ford offered many axles ranging up to 5.83:1 it had listed only 3.56 and 3.89 ratios with the AMA. A similar slip up made the Ford's 15 inch wheels NASCAR outlaws. As a result the fastest official Ford time at Daytona was a disappointing 130.010 mph.

This wasn't the end of the controversy that seemed to settle around Ford's first hot performer since 1957. *Motor Life* (June 1960) really stirred matters up by reporting that a 360 hp Ford had turned in a quarter-mile speed of 105.50 mph! *Motor Life* in its evaluation of drag racing performances by Ford, Chevrolet, Plymouth and Pontiac explained that "to obtain reliable figures, the best speeds for each of the fastest makes and models were compiled from drag strips in Alabama, Arizona, Arkansas, California, Florida, Louisiana, New Mexico, Oklahoma, Rhode Island and Virginia." This didn't satisfy some fans of Pontiac, Chevrolet and Plymouth who reacted with letters in which they challenged, questioned and in general refused to believe the Ford's ability to reach a terminal quarter-mile speed of 105 mph.

Ford had also been taken to task by some owners of the 360 hp models who complained about a lack of power and valve float above 6000 rpm. These weren't the type of field reports that pleased Ford and a number of modifications were made on 360 hp engines produced after February 1960. These included the use of a K-series distributor and new valve springs and retainers.

While, as we will soon detail, Ford increased the intensity of its push into the rank of the high performers in 1961, it was also a year when other significant developments took place both in Ford's styling and engineering. Although the same basic body shell was carried over from 1960, the changes made for 1961 were remarkable. The '61 Fords sported new sheet metal from the belt line down and while this change could have been bad news, Ford once again turned back to basics and utilized an arrangement of circular taillights and canted rear fender fins with great success. After looking the new Ford over, *Motor Trend* (October 1960), concluded, "From the rear, the fin and light arrangement shows some resemblance to the 1957 model." This was good news. And it was in conjunction with a new, full-width, concave grille that also had that "Ford look." There was also a worthwhile down scaling of the Ford's overall dimensions that, while having no impact upon passenger space, removed some unnecessary bulk. Its stem to stern length was reduced by nearly four inches to 209.9 inches and those 81.1 inches of width found on the '60 were shaved down to 79.9 inches. Ford was still a large automobile but with a shorter rear deck and very successful facelift it was, said *Motor Life* (March 1961), "clean, sleek and crisp." Not surprisingly Ford was in complete agreement with this analysis. For example, one Ford advertisement described the new Galaxie as a "styling trend-setter...beautifully proportioned to the Classic Ford Look..." In an analysis of contemporary styling presented by *Motor Trend* in its December 1960 issue, a former Detroit automotive stylist sided with Ford, noting, "Ford appears to have learned the lesson of not forgetting the importance of identity in the annual styling race. The whole rear of the Ford is one happy family of well designed elements that say Ford, Ford, Ford. The front is a powerful but simple presentaion."

However, the 1961 Ford also had its detractors. Another stylist participating in *Motor Trend's* styling critique asserted, "The biggest guessing game in the business is going in at Ford and somebody guessed wrong. After having the best looking car in 1960, Ford has done a quick about-face and reverted to the mediocrity that has characterized Ford in off years." Then there was the GM stylist who told *Car Life* (February 1961): "The new Ford should certainly sell; it has all the best GM in its styling." There was some truth in this assertion. For example, if just four little letters were removed from the Ford's hood it could pass from a frontal viewpoint, for a Buick or Cadillac.

Ford made a major effort, in addition to this surprisingly controversial restyling to enhance the sales appeal of its new models by improving their quality and increasing the time interval between major servicing routines. Before production began on the 1961's, Ford issued more stringent quality specifications to its component suppliers that, in part, called for more uniform chrome plating, higher stainless steel standards and thicker coatings for aluminum parts. Ford also upgraded the quality of materials used in the 1961's interior and stressed higher assembly line standards. These changes for the better, said *Motor Trend* (July 1961), "set the new Ford apart from its predeccessor...Ford does not yet display the best craftsmanship in the low-price field but it is much closer to doing so than in several years."

Ford's new, longer interval lubrication schedule was due to the use of a new grease with a molybdenum-disulphide base that had a tremendous affinity for metal. All lubrication points had polyurethane caps and liners to protect against contamination and when it was time for service, grease fittings were temporarily installed in place of threaded plugs. Ford didn't establish a mileage limit between service stops when the new model first appeared since it regarded driving conditions as more critical than mileage in this regard. However, this really wasn't a matter easily understood by the average motorist and Ford soon recommended 30,000 miles between chassis lubrication.

Ford also expended considerable effort to improve the ride quality of its automobiles for 1961. All body mounts were constructed of butyl rubber in an effort to reduce transmission of road noise to the interior and by using thinner main springs at the rear (except on two-door sedans and hardtops) Ford engineers gained a softer ride. These changes plus recalibrated shock absorbers, and the use of teflon and nylon suspension bushings were developments that eventually would enable Fords to challenge some of the world's most expensive automobiles to some memorable "Quiet Man" competitions.

In what had almost become an annual effort to confuse the customer, Ford did some reshuffling of its model line for 1961 that moved the Starliner hardtop and Sunliner convertible into the Galaxie series, dropped the slow-selling two-door Fairlane business coupe and added an attractive Galaxie two-door hardtop.

When the new models were introduced it also seemed that Ford was sending mixed signals concerning its performance plans for 1961. Good news arrived in the form of a new 390 cubic inch displacement for its largest V-8. However, except for the Police Special version which developed 330 hp at 5000 rpm, the 390 was rated at 300 hp. It's likely, judging from the ability of a 300 hp/390 cid Ford with Cruise-O-Matic to break the 10 second mark from zero to 60 mph that its horsepower rating was more realistic than that of the older 352 version. In an apparent effort to come closer to telling the whole truth about horsepower. Ford also lowered the horsepower rating of the 352 cid V-8 with a two-barrel carburetor to 220 for 235. Its 292 cid V-8 was derated 10 horsepower to 175.

But Ford had no need to issue any retractions about the potency of its new high performance engine for 1961 which became available after mid-November. Compared to the older 352 cid engine the new version, like other 390 V-8s, had a longer, 3.780 inch stroke and larger 4.050 inch bore. But beyond this point there were few items

commonly shared by this 375 horsepower mountain of motor muscle and other more ordinary 390s. The high performance 390 did not use regular production cylinder blocks, instead, a different set of casting patterns were used that provided much stronger and thicker bulkheads between the cylinders. A small but vital feature to ensure adequate engine lubrication was the repositioning of the pressure relief valve at the end of the oil system and the use of larger oil passages. By using grooved main bearing journals, Ford engine engineers made certain they received their fair share of the Ford's oil supply which was funneled through a heavy-duty, full flow oil filter.

From subjecting the 375 hp engine blocks to a special dye test to assure they harbored no weak spots to x-raying their pistons as a final quality check Ford made certain these engines were structurally equal to the rigors of their appointed destiny. Along with these upgraded production standards Ford added a new aluminum intake manifold with larger passages plus a Holley 600 cfm four barrel carburetor to its high performance entourage for 1961. Officially the results were 375hp at 6000 rpm and 427 ft-lb of torque at 3400rpm. However, *Hot Rod* (December 1960) reported that "actual corrected horsepower on a precision built engine with 11.1:1 compression and all other components carefully selected is just a shade over a horse per inch."

At this point in the great performance age of the American automobile the state of the art chassis and suspension development was lagging behind the power potential of most of the super cars. But a review of the special chassis features of the 375/390 Ford indicated its maker was learning fast. Included in the standard package were heavy-duty springs and shocks at all four wheels plus larger, front brake drums that boosted lining area to 234 square inches from 212.5. These linings were of the same fade-resistant material used on the Ford police interceptors. The Ford's 15 inch wheels were fitted with 6.70 x 15 tires as standard equipment but 7.10 x 15s were available as an option. A number of tire brands were supplied by Ford but most 375 Fords were delivered with Firestone "500" four ply nylon tires that were intended for use at sustained speeds of 120 mph.

The only transmission offered for this special Ford was a three-speed manual that could be fitted with overdrive. As power was supplied to the rear wheels it passed through a sturdy 10.5 inch clutch with 2495 pounds of spring pressure, a husky three inch diameter driveshaft (the stock version measured 2.75 inches), across heavier U-joints and into a four pinion differential.

During the summer Ford added a Borg-Warner built fourspeed as a 375/390 option. With ratios of 2.37, 1.78, 1.37 and 1.0, the 375/390-four-speed combination made its competition debut at the Pikes Peak hill climb and while Louis Unser (1961 Chevrolet) was the class winner with a run of 15 minutes, six seconds, Curtis Turner's Ford was just 2.4 seconds behind. The order of finish at the Winternationals held at Pomona, California were, for Ford fans, unfortunately the same. Don Nicholson's 1961 Chevrolet was the S/S stock eliminator with a 13.59 second—105.88 mph quarter-mile run but the Fords were strong contenders with several entries also achieving speeds of 105 mph.

Late in 1960 Ford drivers had lapped the Romeo, Mich. track at 158.8 mph with a hardtop Ford powered by the 375 engine. *Hot Rod* (December 1969) noted that "the engineers insist that if they had really pulled out all the stops, they could have hit 160 mph." However, that year's Daytona 500, where the big boys played, was strictly Indian Country as the Pontiacs finished 1-2-3. Yet, Ford was also getting the knack of putting on its war paint. Finishing in fourth position was Fred Lorenzen's Ford and among the thirteen 1961 Fords entered, Curtis Turner had been the fastest qualifier at 153.4 mph.

Ford obviously was, if not yet on a roll, certainly well along on the road back to performance of championship caliber. Its final salvo for 1961 was a warning shot to its General Motors and Chrysler competition that Ford was far from running out of better performance ideas. The addition of a new aluminum intake manifold sporting three Holley two-barrels boosted Ford's top power output to 401 hp at 6000 rpm and 430 ft-lbs at 3500 rpm.

The dawn of the age of Total Performance was close at hand.

1962–64 Galaxie 500 XL Ford's Performance Daze

By Robert C. Ackerson

It could be argued (and it was) that with the introduction of the Fairlane series in 1962 Ford was taking the first step toward "downsizing" its automobiles years before that expression entered our motoring vocabulary. With the Fairlane getting plenty of attention (plus a name already made famous by a big Ford), the line-up of regular-sized Fords was trimmed of all two-door station wagons plus the Starliner two-door hardtop. The base series of Galaxie 100s consisted only of two- and four-door sedan models while the sportier two and four door hardtops and convertibles were reserved for the top-of-the-line Galaxie 500s.

This restructuring of Ford's offerings lead *Motor Trend* to speculate about the big Ford's possible demise as the company standard bearer. In its review of the new models, *Motor Trend* (November 1961) explained that "if the Galaxie goes well, then the car of this type will survive in volume—if not, well then the Fairlane is the answer and the Ford of the future...If it fails, this may be its last year as the standard Ford, and then it will retire to the status of a special type." To say the least this type of prophesying was off base. Production of full-size Fords did decline in 1962 but the slip was relatively minor, consisting of just 68,753 cars. With a total output of 722,647, the Galaxies remained the corporate leaders. The Fairlane was, to be

1964 Galaxie 500/XL 4-dr hardtop

sure, a major success with sales exceeding 386,000 but neither the big Ford's nor the Falcon's popularity suffered as a result. An expanding economy, plus a strong product lineup gave Ford a production run second only to 1955.

Certainly not the least significant attraction of the 1962 Ford was its appearance. After 1958 it became increasingly difficult to find fault with Ford styling and the 1962s stand out as one of the best examples of Ford design competence. With a 209 inch overall length they were large autombles but their clean lines, now totally free of fender fins and devoid of any overtones of General Motors influence gave them anything but an ungainly appearance.

There were plenty of new options for 1962 such as two-speed wipers, load-leveling shocks and a remote control trunk release to suit the tastes of Ford's most particular customers but vying with styling as the major selling point for just about everyone in the automobile business was performance. As we've seen, Ford, after Chevrolet's

power rampage, didn't get back into the performance ring until 1960. Late in 1961, after the triple carburetor 390 cid V-8 with 401 hp had debuted, Ford had offered the Borg-Warner four-speed gearbox with any of its 390 cid engines. This type of rapid progress lead many Ford enthusiasts to expect something new when the 1962 models debuted on Sept. 29, 1961. But since the initial engine line up was unchanged from 1961's most left their Ford dealers on Sept. 21, 1961 just a bit disappointed. Undoubtedly eager Ford salesmen had done their best explaining the operation of the new clutch interlock for three speed manual gearboxes that greatly reduced the chances of accidentally chipping a gear tooth and the new, longer life mufflers Ford was installing. But those Good Old Ford Boys wanted more ammunition under the hood to go Chevrolet hunting and it just wasn't there. But once in a while you have to be a little patient!

Just in time for some slightly delayed New Year's celebrations Ford piped on board a new 406 cid V-8 packing 405 horsepower at 5800 rpm. This Thunderbird Special 406 carried over the triple carbs (a 385 horsepower version with a single four-barrel carburetor were also available), cam, valve gear, ignition, bearings and exhaust system of the 401 horsepower—390 cid engine. However, there were some major changes that reflected Ford's growing expertise in developing modern, high performance automobiles. The 406 block with its larger 4.23

gear found at the rear in place of the 8.75 inch unit used in 1961. A three-inch diameter driveshaft was also fitted along with a four pinion differential.

With the standard 3.56:1 axle the typical 405 hp Ford was capable of zero to 60 runs in seven seconds and quarter-mile marks of 15.5 seconds and 92 mph. This was quick motion by any standard for a stock sedan but in the crucible of drag racing competition Roger Huntington had to report (*Car Life*, November 1962) that against the Chevys in SS/S competition at the NHRA Winternationals, Ford still came away a loser. Although they were running the quarter-mile in 12.7 seconds and reaching speeds of 110-112 mph. Huntington explained; "Most of the Fords seemed to be down on brute horsepower." A 1962 Ford with the 330 hp/390 cid V-8 did win A/S class against the strong 335 hp/348 cid Chevrolets but upon discovery of several non-stock features such as high strength valve springs it ws disqualified.

However, the Winternationals drag competition provided a look at what Ford was planning for 1963. Attracting plenty of attention in the FX (Factory Experimental) class were light-weight Fords with fiberglass front fenders, hoods and rear decks. These goodies plus alumimum inner fender panels and bumpers lopped several hundred pounds from the Ford's weight to bring it down to approximately 3300 pounds. Eventually Ford would turn to the lighter Fairlane for its drag racing ventures but that

1962 Galaxie 500 2-dr hartop

inch bore used a totally different casting which provided thicker cylinder walls. To cope with the 406's added power, stronger pistons and connecting rods were installed and the oil relief valve was set at 60 instead of 45 psi. Dual valve springs with greater maximum load were also used on the 406.

Included in the $379.70 price tag of the 406 engine (one of which was Ford's 30 millionth V-8) was a comprehensive performance package whose most obvious feature was the excellent Borg-Warner four speed with ratios of 2.36, 1.78, 1.41 and 1.0. Less apparent, until the 406 Ford got into motion were its stiffer by 20 percent than stock springs and shocks. Ford didn't offer sintered brake linings but three-inch brake drums fitted with harder linings did a respectable job of hauling those two tons of Ford down from a maximum velocity not far from 140 mph.

Ford also added substantial strength to its high performance driveline. For example a nine inch diameter ring

wouldn't really get moving until 1964. The FX Galaxies at the NHRA runoffs also sported engine components such as dual Holley four-barrel carbs, new cylinder heads with larger exhaust valves and a 300° duration cam that would be readily available in 1963.

Although the 409 Chevrolets humbled the 406 Ford in drag racing a Ford driven by Curtis Turner won the July 4th running of the Pikes Peak Hill Climb. In NASCAR competition Ford was the victor of the Atlanta 500 (which due to rain was shortened to 328 miles), the Rebel 300 at Darlington and the Charlotte World 600. In the latter race, which was held on May 27, 1962, Nelson Stacy's Ford averaged 125.552 mph for a new 600 mile race record. Although Ford also won the Southern 500 at Darlington, The Daytona 500 had been a major Ford setback. Of four Fords entered, only Fred Lorenzen's managed to last the duration to finish in fifth position behind three Pontiacs and Richard Petty's Plymouth.

Although Ford did emerge victorious over Pontiac in the

earlier mentioned races, *Motor Trend* (March 1963) noted, "It was invariably Pontiac that set the best times —still the surest indication of superior equipment." Also suggesting rather convincingly that Ford still had to burn the midnight oil over it's performance homework were the final results of the 53 race NASCAR season:

Race	Race Victories
Pontiac	22
Chevrolet	14
Plymouth	11
Ford	6

A similar tale was told by a review of the NASCAR driver's standings:

1. Joe Weatherly (Pontiac)
2. Richard Petty (Plymouth)
3. Ned Jarrett (Chevrolet)
4. Jack Smith (Pontiac)
5. Rex White (Ford)

But Ford hadn't come so far in such a short time to be content with this type of "Total Performance" and its 1963 lineup reflected not only an even greater emphasis on performance but also continued development of Ford's luxury car image. As a mid-year sales stimulant, Ford had offered the Galaxie 500 XL form in 1962. The most notable XL features included bucket seats, floor-mounted shifter and an engine-turned instrument panel insert. Although production totalled just over 41,000, the Galaxie 500/XL offering was extended from the two-door hardtop and convertible bodies to include the four-door Victoria hardtop and the 1963½ fastback coupe which as we will soon detail, was destined to play an important role in Ford's racing successes during 1963 and 1964.

Although some publications regarded Ford's styling changes for 1963 as "minor" there was no difficulty in identifying the 1963 model as a new Ford. From any angle such key Ford features as circular taillights, a wide grille and a restrained use of side trim were key features that linked the 1963 Ford to its predecessors. At the same time, however, a move away from the curvaceous form of the '62 gave the new model a fresh and appealing appearance.

But for those who were interested in how the new Ford would "go" a real eye opener was the Riverside 500 which took place in mid-January 1963. This was not by any means the first encounter of NASCAR-type stock cars on a course where sports cars usually played. But it was, said *Car Life* (April 1963) "a six-hour show of just how far Detroit has progressed in the past 10 years." We don't want to create the impression that this was one of the greatest races of all time. The use of the pace car to control the speed of the competitors whenever the yellow caution flag was shown, was annoying to many spectators and since the final four laps were run in that fashion Dan Furney's victory had some of its luster removed. However, it was a stunning and convincing demonstration both of Ford's new 427 cid V-8 engine and the 1963½ fastback body style.

Ford, in the midst of its Total Performance program wasn't the least bashful about touting the considerble virtues of this dynamic combination of looks and power. In one memorable advertisement illustrating a Ford kicking up some dust as it rounded a sharp turn, Ford boasted; "To top this you have to spend 5,750,000 lire...or shed four passengers...In road performance the all-out version of Ford's Sports Hardtop with 425 hp engine, four-speed gearbox and the *standard* heavy-duty suspension and brakes, has no full-size rivals in all the world...in fact, only the top echelon of the two-seaters can generate anymore go!"

The 427 engine was in terms of its origin a bored and stroked version of the older 406 with a 4.23 inch bore and 3.78 stroke. But there was also plenty of design changes

to convince any critic that Ford's interest in Total Performance was genuine. Beginning with crossbolted main bearing caps (numbers 2, 3, and 4) lighter weight, impact extruded aluminum pistons and stronger connecting rods, the 427 engine abounded with features that make it far superior to the discontinued 406. With twin four-barrel carburetors this Thunderbird 427 cid High Performance V-8 produced 425 hp at 6000 rpm and 480 lb-ft of torque at 3700 rpm. Since NASCAR did not allow multi-carb units to run on its super tracks Fords also offered the 427 with a single 4-barrel with rating of 410 hp at 5600 rpm and 476 lb-ft at 3400 rpm.

Although some nitpickers questioned Ford's use of the Fastback label for its new 1963½ model, there was a good solid reason for its existence regardless of what Ford chose to call it. Simply put, there was more to race-winning than horsepower, handling stability and braking capability. Ford still had a great deal to learn about aerodynamics as it was soon to discover in the early stages of the GT-40 program but it fully understood that the squared-off roof of the Galaxie was costing it NASCAR race victories. By adopting the sports roof for NASCAR competition Ford was able to field an automobile that could maintain a 160 mph speed with one hundred less horsepower than required by the older version.

Ford introduced the Fastback model along with the Falcon Sprint at Monte Carlo where Ford Motor Co. Vice President Benson Ford made no apologies for Ford's growing involvement in motor sport. "The public," he claimed, "is demanding and getting cars that are more fun, more sumptuous, perhaps, but also more responsive, more tastefully designed, of improved quality and durability and with more economical and trouble-free operation...Once again, racing is affecting the course of a vast industry—and by doing so it must inevitably affect future history. Most obviously, it is stimulating interest, concern, even passion for autombles with the general public."

Mr. Ford was being too modest. Not only was the "general public" developing a passion for performance automobiles but the Ford Motor Co. was becoming extremely proficient at building automobiles with an abundant of passion satisfying attributes.

One of the best examples of Ford's expertise at tailoring its products to suit a very specific and limited performance market was the lightweight Fastback model whose only purpose in life was to let it all hang out on the drag strip. Taking a tip from its own history Ford offered this two-door hardtop only in a white and red, exterior-interior color combination. In standard production form most Ford models outweighed their Chevrolet and Plymouth counterparts. This might have been perceived as a sales advantage but on the drag strip it became a multi-hundred pound handicap. Although the drag-racing model's steel body was identical to other Ford's, all bolt-on items such as doors, trunk lid, hood and front fenders were constructed of fiberglass. Alumimum was used for the Ford's front and rear bumpers. Its interior, instead of being the scrumptious haven from the outside world that was found on production models offered only the basics; skinny, front bucket seats, cheap floor mats and absolutely no sound deadening! Furthermore the Ford could not be ordered with such basics as a radio, heater, or clock. Other weight shedding measures, which in total lopped nearly 700 pounds from the Galaxie's usual 4150 pound weight, included the use of the frame normally used on the 300 series Fords and an aluminum bell housing for the standard Borg-Warner four-speed gearbox which was a 34 pound weight-saver. Ford installed special heat treated gears with ratios of 2.36, 1.66, .123 in this transmission.

With 425 horsepower these Galaxies which the NHRA declared eligible for both Super Stock and Stock Eliminator competition were capable of quarter-mile marks of 12

seconds and 118 mph. No wonder *Hot Rod* (July 1963) asserted, "the engine produced by Ford today is a tremendous improvement over that of 1962...From the 352 high performance of 1960 to this 427 engine, there has been a constant flow of improvement." But before the competition season came to a close Ford offered a "Mark II" version of the 427 V-8 with new cylinder heads having larger ports and valves, an aluminum high-rise manifold, stronger connecting rods, forged steel crankshaft and a ten quart oil pan.

The tremendous performance of the 427 NASCAR Ford was vividly demonstrated in a road test of a Holman-Moody prepared model conducted by *Car Life* magazine. Although it was officially rated at 410 hp, the true output of the 427 after it had received the Holman-Moody treatment was far closer to 500 horsepower. With a 3.50:1 rear axle the Ford's top speed was approximately 155 mph. Even with this gearing however, the Ford was a strong sprinter with *Car Life* (February 1964) reporting the following acceleration times:

0-30 mph—2.3 seconds
0-60 mph—6.3 seconds
0-100 mph—13.2 seconds
Standing start ¼ mile—14.2 seconds/105 mph

These figures were extremely impressive but even the capability of the 427 Ford paled in comparison to the speeds attained by a Ford with a super-sized, 483 cid V-8 at Bonneville back in October 1962. This particular car was originally a Galaxie convertible but a fastback roof had been installed in order to transform it into a NASCAR racer. With all those cubic inches at their disposal, drivers Fred Lorenzen, Don White and Ralph Moody had little difficulty in setting 46 new national and international records from 25 kilometers to 500 miles. In addition to averaging 163.85 mph for 500 miles (from a standing start), the Ford attained a top speed of 176.978 mph. Its fastest lap around the 10-mile circular track was 169.4 mph.

All the emphasis upon speed and performance at Ford over-shadowed several notable developments such as a new three speed, all synchomesh gearbox that was standard on all full-size Fords except those with the high performance engines. While this new feature was just beginning its production life in 1963, the elimination of the 292 V-8 from Ford's engine lineup closed the book on the family of V-8 engines that had originated with the overhead valve, 239 cid V-8 of 1954.

Ford had also stepped up its effort to further upgrade its ride quality for 1963. Although such expressions as a "new antiharsh" suspension and "tuned spring technique" could have been dismissed merely as examples from 1963's advertising vocabulary they did in reality describe several changes in suspension geometry and design that contributed both to the Galaxie's good cornering and ride. Both the front and rear suspension were designed to allow a slight horizontal movement of the wheels as they passed over small bumps. In effect there was shock absorption in both the horizontal and vertical planes.

Motor Trend (April 1963) not only liked the Ford's road manners but also reported: "That built-in quality Ford's becoming known for is evident on exterior and interior of everything from the least expensive to the most expensive of the Galaxie line. These are solid cars, and from what we've seen of them personally they usually come from the factory with everything put together just right."

This "just right" perspective of the Ford line by *Motor Trend* obviously carried over into 1964 when Ford received *Motor Trend*'s Car of the Year Award for "engineering advancement in the concept of Total Perfor-

mance, based on high performance testing in open competition." Ford defined Total Performance as "the ability of a vehicle to fully accomplish its intended function." In a sense the 16 different Ford models in three separate series (Custom 300, Galaxie 500 and Galaxie 500/XL) were well suited to appeal to buyers regardless of the extent of their financial resources and their interest in high performance. Ford's 138 hp six was the standard engine for all models except for the Galaxie 500/XL which used a 195 hp-289 cid version of the lightweight V-8 that had first appeared in the 1962 Fairlane. The only other significant change in Ford's engine lineup as the model year began was the replacement of the 200 hp, 352 cid V-8 with a version fitted with a four (instead of two) barrel carburetor and a 250 hp rating.

There was no difficulty in identifying the 1964 Ford. Although its famous circular taillights were now virtually a Ford trademark they were as pleasing as ever and the instantly famous fastback roofline was now extended to an attractive four-door hardtop in the Galaxie 500 and 500/XL series. While the Ford's heavily sculptured flanks gave it a light, lithe look its road weight was increased by nearly 300 pounds. Ford justified this avoirdupois advance by claiming "a substantial improvement in ride and handling characteristics is immediately noticeable in the 1964 Ford with increased weight in the body and suspension system. Big car feel and surer, safer control are the result of a 200-300 pound weight advantage over traditional standard car weights. Most of this weight advantage is in important areas such as frame, body, front suspension and rear suspensions."

The 1964 dream machine for Ford fans was undoubtedly one of the three (two- and four-door hardtops plus a convertible) Galaxie 500/XL models equipped with the "Super High-Performance" 427 engine and chassis option. With its standard bucket seats, floor shift and center console plus 425 very able and ambitous horses, such an XL was a suave and sexy machine that still is an attention getter. Chrysler's 426 Hemis had the edge over the Ford 427 in terms of brute power but as an untemperamental super car that was readily available and reasonably priced the Ford was a very appealing product capable of zero to 60 mph runs in the seven second region.

Although the 426 Hemi Plymouths swept the first three places at Daytona in January, the Ford racing record for 1964 included victories in every NASCAR race of over one hundred miles after the Daytona 500 to the Southern 500 run on Labor Day. In addition, Fords finished 1-2-4-5 at the Jan. 19, 1964 running of the Riverside 500 where Fred Lorenzen set a new stock car lap record of 102.5 mph and Dan Gurney's race winning Ford reached a speed of 156 mph.

When John Bond of *Road & Track* visited Dearborn in late 1963 he left totally impressed by Ford's commitment to performance. "Not even in the days of Mercer, Stutz, Duesenberg, etc." he wrote in *Road & Track*, "have we seen such a concerted effort towards all-out racing from one manufacturer in all facets of the sport."

The 1964 models were not, of course, the ultimate examples of Ford's Total Performance philosophy but they did bring an era of sorts to a close. After 1965 the big Fords seemed to mature almost as if they were animated objects. They grew in size, gained more weight and gradually lost some of the qualities that made a Ford a Ford. By no means was Ford alone in moving toward the middle-of-the-road in many crucial areas of design but in retrospect the resulting loss of identity took away some of Ford's great automotive heritage that was so apparent in the appearance and performance of the 1964 models.

for people who won't take "dull" for an answer!

FALCON SQUIRE WAGON. This one's the hit of the compact wagon show. It's got all-star features: woodlike steel side paneling ... luxurious interior trim ... optional bucket seats with a console in between ... and the loadspace is over 7 feet long! Price of admission? The Falcon Squire costs less than many standard compact wagons. Yet it comes with extras like deep-pile carpeting and power tailgate window, to mention a few. For a private audition, see your Ford Dealer.

A PRODUCT OF
Ford
MOTOR COMPANY

live it up
with a lively
One from
FORD

FALCON FAIRLANE GALAXIE THUNDERBIRD

The Successful Falcon Was Sensible Machine

By Robert C. Ackerson

In spite of its rather humble demeanor and relatively short life span (1960-1970), the Falcon deserves more than just a passing glance in any overview of Ford history. From both a psychological and economic point of view its success was a major boost for the Ford Motor Co. Debuting in late 1959, it came on the heels of the Edsel debacle and since it became a major success it restored the credibility of market research in the eyes of many people. To put it another way FoMoCo not only asked the right questions of people (sometimes it failed to do so in regard to the Edsel), but it also paid careful attention to such items as population and income growth plus the competition the automobile faced for the consumer's dollar from other sources. When it evaluated the market prior to the Falcon's introduction Ford's attention to details (plus keeping an eye on what its competitors were up to) paid off handsomely.

Certainly not a small factor in the Falcon's success was its faithfulness to Ford tradition. Both the Model T and Model A were in their basic design down to earth, practical automobiles and the significance of this fact upon automotive history is, of course, profound. Henry Ford II recognized this by remarking that. "The economic impact and the interest value of such a development (the advent of the American compact car) could well be comparable in significance to the appearance of the Model T and Model A on the American scene." In its analysis of the Falcon in its November, 1959 issue *Road and Track* recognized the Falcon's virtues in this regard by writing, "As far as we are concerned the new Falcon 6 is a reasonably close facsimile, at least in terms of what the Model A might have been if it had continued with year-to-year improvements. Automobile design can never stand still, but the basic concept of the new Falcon is pretty much that of the Model A — good, solid honest transportation."

The steps leading to the Falcon are fascinating. As early as 1945 Ford was considering the production of a small car. While none of the projects Dearborn engaged on in this area came to life as American products, they were transferred to Ford's European facilities in such forms as the French Vedette, the German Taunus and the British Consul and Zephyr models.

Actual work on the Falcon project began in late 1956 under the "XK Thunderbird" label. During its existence the project's title became "Lavion," "Astrion" and then finally "Falcon." As work on the 20 full-size clay models that would lead 'to the finished product progressed a shift was made away from styling themes that would relate the Falcon to other Ford products. Instead it was decided to endow it with soft rounded lines rather than the crisp sharp features characteristic of Ford-built cars since 1955. Yet in its final form the Falcon was easily identifiable as a Ford automobile.

The Falcon was designed and styled around six basic objectives that harked back to the days of the Model T and A. In Ford's words it was to be a car with the characteristics of "light weight, low cost, full size (six-passenger capacity), low upkeep, performance equivalent to the standard Ford 6 and high economy." A comparison with a 1959 Ford Fairlane 500 sedan reveals how successful the Falcon met the standard of roominess set for it. Whereas the full-size Ford had a wheelbase of 118 inches and an overall length of 208 inches the Falcon rested on a 109.5 inch wheelbase and measured 181.1 inches from stem to stern. Yet it offered more front seat head and leg room than the Fairlane; exceeded it in rear seat headroom and nearly matched its rear seat legroom.

The Ford engineers assigned to the Falcon program worked under a mandated maximum curb weight limit of 2400 pounds. In its final form, ready to go, it weighed in at 2382 pounds. Much of the credit for this low figure was due to the Falcon engine. Total weight of this cast iron, 144.4 cubic inch six was a mere 345.5 pounds. In comparison the standard Ford 6 weighed 525 pounds. The Falcon engine was noteworthy for more than just its lightweight. For its size it produced good torque (138 lb-ft at 2000 rpm), had an ultra short stroke, 2.5 inch and a reasonable horsepower rating of 90. Its basic, straightforward design, again a mark of its heritage, was in contrast to the unorthodox pancake, aircooled six of its arch rival, the Corvair, which carried overtones of the infamous copper-cooled Chevrolet of the early 1920s.

The Falcon's performance was definitely on the mild side. Falcons with three-speed manual transmissions could move from zero to 60 in 17.7 seconds. This wasn't too bad but when saddled to a scaled down version of the two-speed Fordomatic automatic transmission this time was extended to a leisurely 25.1 seconds. Part of the fault here was the Falcon's 3.10 rear axle ratio, a shortcoming which was partially remedied by the availability of a 3.56:1 ratio early in the 1960 model run.

As might be expected the motoring press found the Corvair with all its technical features a more fascinating item to write about. *Motor Trend* in a three-way 2500 mile test judged the Corvair superior overall to both the Valiant and the Falcon. Surely to Ford's corporate chagrin the Falcon was rated last. Not surprisingly, the Corvair also received *Motor Trend's* nod as the "Car of the Year."

Ford's television advertising, while not identifying the Corvair by name, clearly had the Chevrolet product in mind with comments such as the following: (referring to the Falcon) "The engine's up front and reduce chances of oversteering, or skidding out of control in emergency stops . . ." "The gas tank is safely in the rear, instead of up front 'in the laps' of the driver and front-seat passengers . . ." "Optional hot water heater eliminates fumes and danger of gasoline-fueled heater inside the car . . ."

Within two months the Falcon, Corvair and Valiant, along with the Rambler and Studebaker Lark began to lock horns in racing competition. The first compact car race was held in November 1959 at the Continental Divide Raceway near Denver, Colo. This was a six-hour event which was won by a Rambler American with a Volkswagen in second place. Falcons finished third and fourth with Corvairs behind in sixth and seventh places. The no-show of the Chrysler Valiants was to shortly prove rather ironical.

Prior to the 12 hour race, a two hour race for compact cars was held at Sebring on Dec. 12, 1959. Two Jaguar 3.4 liter sedans with engines brought up to D-type specs along with two Lark V-8s prepared by Holman and Moody and driven by Curtis Turner and Fireball Roberts rode roughshod over their competition. The Jaguars finished first and third with the Larks second and fourth. Only one Falcon was entered. Driven by Denise McCluggage it finished in seventh position.

In retrospect however, these were just bush league events in comparison to what what took place during the 1960 Daytona Speed Weeks. In addition to all the competition activities scheduled, NASCAR also included events for compact cars that utilized both an infield road racing course and the banked oval. To put it bluntly the Valiant ran off with all the marbles this time around. With their "Hyper-Paks" the Valiants, officially rated at 148 hp but in reality possessing nearly 200 hp, were head and shoulders above their Corvair and Falcon competitors. In the ten lap race around the oval the Valiants finished one, two, three with the leading car averaging 122.282 mph. In

1960 Falcon Deluxe 4dr Sedan

the event using both the road course and the banked section Valiants filled the top seven positions. The Falcons driven by Joe Weatherly and Curtis Turner were outclassed but yet possessed some intriguing modifications that included a three carburetor manifold carrying Holley two-barrel carbs, 9.4:1 compression ratio and a milled head. These Falcons with approximately 140 hp could turn 8000 rpm and accelerate from zero to 60 in just 10.8 seconds. However, the Daytona Valiants needed only 7.1 seconds for the same run. Thus the factory performance kit for the Falcon was pulled off the market in quick order.

Partially compensating for this move was the marketing by Paxtom Products of Santa Monica, Calif. of a supercharger applicable to the Falcon as well as the Corvair and Valiant. An intriguing "one-off" Falcon built by Bill Stroppe for William Clay Ford was powered by a 312 cid Mercury V-8 overbored 0.060 inches to provide a displacement of 320 cubic inches. In addition to this modification its engine also had a 10.0:1 compression ratio, Racer Brown Street cam and a four barrel carburetor.

With the Falcon the best selling car in its class Ford saw little reason to change it in 1961. There were a number of minor trim modifications including the placement of a Falcon symbol behind the front fender wells and a new convex grille that set the 1961 model apart from older Falcons. A welcomed move by those unhappy with the Falcon's acceleration was the availability of a 170 cid engine producing 101 hp at 4400 rpm. This engine with redesigned crankshaft, connecting rods and pistons weighed just seven pounds more than the original Falcon engine which was down-graded to a 85 bhp rating for 1961. With a three speed manual transmission Falcons thus equipped accelerated from zero to 60 mph in 14.3 seconds.

The Falcon began to lose some of its innocence in 1962 with the offering of the Futura model. For approximately $250 the customer was offered a trim package that included fancy "polka-dot" wheel cover, three "teardrop" chrome trimpieces on each rear quarter panel, semi-bucket front seats (individually adjustable, and a small storage-console between the front seats. Futuras also were equipped with narrow strip white wall tires.

The high point of Ford Falconry however came in early 1963 when the 1963½ Falcon Sprint was introduced. (A convertible had been offered earlier along with the other 1963 Falcons.) Coinciding with its press presentation in Monte Carlo was the Sprints' entry in the 1963 Monte Carlo rally While they didn't win, one Sprint driven by Swedish ice-racing champion Bo Ljungfelt set the fatest time in all the timed tests and finished second overall.

These Rally Sprints were equipped with the usual items considered "de rigueur" at Monte Carlo. For power they relied upon a 260 hp, 289 cid Cobra engine capable of 7000 rpm. Thus a zero to 60 mph time of 7.5 seconds was not beyond the realm of possibility. Production Sprints were considerably tamer, being equipped with 164 hp, 260 cid V-8s. Yet they possessed sufficient sporting qualities for *Car and Driver* at the end of its Sprint test to conclude that it "can certainly qualify as a fine sports sedan in the manner of a 3.8 Jag."

When the Mustang was introduced in 1964 the marketing of the Falcon as an automobile with sporting pretensions became rather redundant. At the same time the market for compact cars became a no-growth segment of the total sales picture thus pushing the Falcon and the other American compacts out of the public limelight. Finally of course when Ford unveiled the Maverick in 1970 the Falcon's fate was sealed. The rather unceremonious demise of the Falcon belies its role in Ford History. It marked a dramatic turnaround from the Edsel disaster for Ford and played a fairly significant, though short lived, role in Ford's Total Performance campaign.

Selling the Sprint: Falcon's Best for '64

By Gerald Perschbacher

It sat in a forlorn corner of the car lot, having more years on it than most of the other cars that had been traded in.

"Nobody will even look at that Falcon," the used car manager said when it came on the scene in a recent deal on a summer's day. "We'll be stuck with this one for a long time."

I was new to the business then in 1975. I thought anything with four wheels and enough gumption to get out of the way of its own shadow was a good product to hawk. Bold as I was, brash with determination, I told Bill, "I'll bet

Ford's Falcon Sprint for 1964 was fourth in production total for the Futura series that year, with 13,830 Sprint hardtops leaving the factory. In excellent condition, today the car could bring $6,000 in collector circles.

I find a buyer for the Falcon, and by Saturday, too."

"That's a tall order for anyone, especially someone new to car sales," Bill said. "I'd think about that if I were you."

I boiled. "I said I would sell the car, and that's what I'll do — and if I don't, I'll hang up this job Saturday." Bill looked up, fixed is eyes on mine, and bellowed, "You're on."

I knew I would strike a nerve with Bill if I put my new job on the line in a bet. His son was after the job, but old Mr. Garner, who owned the largest dealership in town, saw fit to take me over Bill's son. Now Bill had a chance to get his way.

I smiled as I walked out of the office, but not for long. Saturday was only four days away. I had no prospects; the car needed reconditioning, although minor, and I had work to do for an evening class in auto mechanics.

I had to make the best of it, so I tore into the Falcon, studying it as I cleaned it, polished, buffed, detailed and appraised the situation. And I hit the books, too.

Wheelbase 109.5 inches, overall length 181.6 inches, weight 2,813 pounds, V-8 engine with 260 cubic inches and 164 hp at 4,400 rpm. The figures ingrained themselves.

With only 18,400 miles, the Falcon Sprint was your typical little old lady's car. It had a scratch on the passenger's side, a battle scar from a close scrape in a garage, I guessed. And this little old lady must have been a chain smoker. Nicotine coated the inside.

For the best part of my first day, I cleaned and prepped. Bill watched from the window, taking a jaunt close by whenever a customer nosed around the lot.

My first prospect was a factory worker with a young family. "Great car for the kids, no worry of them falling out the back doors on a two-door." I said. He kicked the tires and grunted as he passed by.

My second prospect stuck his nose under the hood when I told him about the V-8 and how it kicked up the trail dust and put the small car out front fast. "But will it stay out front?" he asked, then walked over to an Oldsmobile 88.

Six more prospects wandered around the car, bending down to catch as many glimpses as possible: all lookers, no cash.

Depression set in. I phone relatives, friends, even a couple of enemies from high school days. Then I dug into the car again, gave it more detailing, sprucing it up to the hilt. Bill kept watching.

Saturday morning he greeted me with a loud shout. "You'll never guess it, so here's the scoop. A guy put down $500 on that Falcon Sprint last night after you went home. You were right on your bet, and I'm glad. For all the work you put into that car, you earned the sale five times over. Guess you proved me wrong," he said.

I found out later that Bill was more bluff than anything. Two days after the sale, I saw his son sporting around town behind the wheel of the Sprint — a gift from his father.

Ford's Ultimate Musclecar

by Bill Siuru

In 1964, you could walk into your friendly Ford dealership and order a car that was ready for the drag strip without any modifications on your part. That is, if you could prove you could handle such a performer. This was the Ford Thunderbolt, a very formidable machine on the race track and drag strip. The T-Bolts were essentially hand assembled from the high performance components in Ford's parts bin and from outside suppliers of speed equipment.

To make the Thunderbolt, Ford started with the relatively lightweight 1964 Fairlane two-door sedan. Under the hood they installed a huge 427 cid V-8 powerplant that was rated at 425 horsepower, although the actual output

The 1964 Thunderbolt was one of the few dragsters made and sold by a car manufacturer. (Photo by Siuru)

was probably closer to 500 after modifications. Modifications to the engine compartment were needed to fit this big engine. The engine was equipped with two four-barrel carburetors, hi-rise aluminum cylinder heads, and had a 14:1 compression ratio. To get the needed air flow to the carburetors, two six-inch diameter "stove pipes" were used. The inlets were where the highbeams normally were fitted in a Fairlane.

The Thunderbolt buyer had a choice of either an automatic or close-ratio four-speed transmission. Also there was a 4:57 or 4:71 rear end to choose from. Stock wheels consisted of seven-inch wide tires in the rear and four-inch ones in front. Slick tires were standard on the rear. The cars came ready for the drag strip, being equipped with traction bars and a drive shaft loop.

The car was assembled at Ford's Dearborn assembly plant, but before it was completed it was sent to Dearborn Steel Tubing Co. for modifications to make it a Thunderbolt. Ford did everything possible to keep the Thunderbolt's total weight down. The hood, with its giant rear facing air scoop, and front fenders were made of fiberglass. A few of the early editions even had fiberglass doors. The cars came with either fiberglass or aluminum bumpers. Plexiglass replaced normal glass in the car's rear, side, and vent windows. The Thunderbolt came with lightweight bucket seats and a minimum of ornamentation.

The Thunderbolt weighed in at 3,200 pounds, 400 pounds more than a standard Fairlane two-door sedan, but remember that the 427 engine and added performance equipment weighed considerably more than the standard equipment six-cylinder. To improve the Thunderbolt's weight distribution, the car's heavy duty battery was placed in the trunk.

The Thunderbolts were not intended for street use. In fact, dealers were warned that these cars should only be sold to the "knowing, capable enthusiast." Incidentally, because it was a racing machine it did not come with the usual Ford warranty. Right out of the dealer's showroom, the Thunderbolt could turn in quarter mile times of just over 11 seconds and speeds of over 120 mph.

There is a debate about the number of Thunderbolts actually made. Some say 60, other owners think 100. The first 11 were "factory" cars, the remainder were available to individual dragsters and racers. The first 11 were painted Vintage Burgundy, the rest came in Wimbledon White. Few of the latter cars were left plain white, but were either repainted other colors or at least received some trim modifications like racing stripes or flames.

The Thunderbolts listed at $3,980, about $1,700 more than a regular two-door Fairlane. It is rumored that Ford lost money on every car. It is estimated that it cost Ford $5,200 to build each car. However, the publicity and advertising were worth the money.

Ford ads stated that the Thunderbolts were ready for racing, all you needed were the keys. And indeed they were ready to go after the competition, namely the lightweight Dodges and Plymouths with their 426 cid hemi V-8s which were eating up the drag strips and raceways around the country. They did very well setting records that would stand for a considerable amount of time.

Thunderbird

Ford Thunderbird 1955-1957

by James F. Petrik

America had produced sports cars, as well as sporty two-passenger cars, from before 1900 until the early '30s, at which time the Depression doomed such machines impractical or frivolous.

After World War II, the small English sports cars reached our shores in increasing numbers, even though absolute sales were still not very large. Such a car, with a noisy four-cylinder engine, 1920-type weather protection, and 1929 styling, had a limited appeal.

Around 1949, the Jaguar XK-120 revolutionized the sports car movement with sleek styling and smooth high-speed performance. This car became a status symbol, even among those who had no interest in racing or sports cars.

At this time, American cars, in increasing numbers, were being equipped with automatic transmissions. Starting in 1951, power steering became available, and power brakes, seat, and windows were also becoming popular. The public was demanding these features, and it was inevitable that a sporting two-seater, complete with luxury equipment, would eventually be produced.

Since there seem to be two contradictory legends as to just exactly when and how the beginning of the Thunderbird actually occurred, we will skip to the General Motors Motorama, in January of 1953, that gave the world the first view of the Corvette. A Ford corporate product letter in February of 1953 initiated the crash program to build a sports car. Ford needed glamour and publicity in a hurry, so the car had to be a V-8, made out of familiar material, and had to be styled so that the public would associate it with the Ford car.

To save precious time, rather than build models of the various styling creations, full-size profile renderings were made, cut out and mounted upright, so that they could be viewed like regular automobiles.

To speed the car's development, a used Ford sedan was purchased, then cut and rewelded to suit. It was given a 102-inch wheelbase (just like Jaguar and Corvette), the various components were correctly placed and angled, and the space problems were worked out. Italian sports cars were a big thing then, so this car was given the name

"Burnetti" after William Burnett, the Ford Division chief engineer, who suggested this approach.

Although it was impossible to get the car into production before the fall of 1954 (as a 1955 model), Ford had to have a styling model ready for display at the auto show in Detroit, opening on Saturday, Feb. 20, 1954. A wooden mock-up that looked real was the display car. This lovely car had to have a name.

Throughout the development period, various names had been suggested. Lewis D. Crusoe (Ford vice-president and general manager) liked the name "Savile." However, he promised a $250 suit of clothes to the employee submitting the name chosen. The name "Thunderbird" was submitted by a stylist, Alden "Gib" Giberson, who had lived in the southwest. In Indian legend, the Thunderbird symbolized power, swiftness, and prosperity. It was considered a helper of man because by flapping its wings it was believed to cause thunder and lightning, and bring rain to the parched fields. The "Thunderbird" name became official on Feb. 15, 1954.

In the spring and summer of '54 one began to see pictures and articles in the various magazines on Ford's new sports car. By the time the car was introduced, most of the car magazines were saying that Ford never called the car a sports car. Let us correct that right now. The first known showroom brochure, showing the car with a 1954 license plate called the T-Bird a sports car. This folder had the wrong engine and tire size listed, incidentally. The Thunderbird advertisement in the Aug. 16, 1954 issue of *Sports Illustrated* also mentioned "sports car." Some Ford shop manuals so late as to cover the 1957 Thunderbird still called the car "Ford Sports Car."

Most of the publicity photographs of the Thunderbird for the press kits and other publicity releases were taken during the summer of 1954, and they do not show the car in its final form. None of these shows the chrome trim at the bottom of the fender skirt, and some of the cars had chrome-trimmed headlight rims, as used on the Ford Fairlane series, but never really used on the Thunderbird. Although the name "Fairlane" had not as yet been chosen for the fanciest 1955 Ford series, the wooden Thunder-

This photo of a 1955 Thunderbird shows good soft top detailing.

Never used, the 1956 "Five-Window Hardtop" gave the maximum visibility.

"The Fairlane Bird" was a prototype.

bird model shown in February of 1954 had that word in script above the grille and on the gas tank door in the trunk lid.

The writer doubts that the following statement has ever before appeared in print, but a careful study of all the evidence proves without a doubt that for a few brief moments (one week??..two weeks??) in automotive history that: "The Fairlane-trimmed Thunderbird (known as the 'Fairlane Bird' due to the chrome strip on each side) actually WAS the 1955 Thunderbird."

The evidence is as follows:

1. There are at least three different magazine advertisements by Ford, some are one-page and some are two-page, showing the Thunderbird with this trim. These advertisements all came out in late October 1954, just at the time the regular Thunderbird went on to display. The best known of these is the one on the back cover of *Motor Trend* magazine, for November 1954.

2. In addition to the Ford advertisements, there was one at that time by one of Ford's suppliers, the Champion Spark Plug Co. The Thunderbird was the hottest thing going then and any concern having anything to do with this car wanted to cash in on the prestige car.

3. All prototypes and mock-ups were photographed either in the styling studio or in the display yard. Only production cars or special show cars would be taken to an affluent neighborhood to pose for glamour photographs. At that time, at least one pretty female model would be hired to be part of these scenes.

4. Then there is the matter of the catalog. According to

rumor, these catalogs (showing the Thunderbird with the chrome strip) were printed and sent to the parts depots for later distribution to the dealers. Before distribution could take place, these catalogs were ordered to be destroyed. A few are still in existence, however, and the writer has one. These are almost identical to the "main" catalog, and bear the same publication number and date (FD-7520-8/54).

If the car had not been intended for production, there would have been no magazine advertising, no glamour photos, and no catalogs.

The chrome strips were the idea of Mr. Crusoe. Some of his associates have said that this was one of his few mistakes. The stylists did not want the strips, so they were removed at the last moment. Since expensive tooling had been made, these could have been a profitable accessory. Ford Motor Co. made the real mistake. As far as can be determined, only two of these cars were made, the light green one, and the black one belonging to Mr. Crusoe. His car also had wire wheel covers and a continental spare tire mounting.

Regarding continental kits, there seemed to be a few slightly different kits available. None were shown in regular Thunderbird catalogs, but some of these kits were dealer-installed. There is at least one instance where the continental kit was factory-installed. This one was late in the year, on a car with serial number P5FH-247117.

The dealer's cost for this item was $110.98.

The Thunderbird made its debut on Oct. 22, 1954, and was reported to have garnered 4000 orders its first day.

An open 1957 model, mounted on the turntable in the display yard.

Ford had hoped to sell 10,000 Thunderbirds per year. They never did catch up on the orders and eventually sold 16,155 of the 1955 model. It was the right product at the right time. Mounted on a 102-inch wheelbase with an overall length of 175.3 inches, and with a tread of 56 inches, front and rear, it was a full-size two-passenger car, not a midget. Originally, the car was available in three colors (Thunderbird blue, raven black, and torch red), each with color-keyed upholstery. In the spring, snowshoe white and goldenrod yellow were added. The base price was $2695, but when full power and automatic were added, plus fender skirts, windshield washers, whitewalls, back-up lights, tinted glass, and the soft top (hardtop was standard), the price could look like $3800 or more. On the 1955 model only, the power seat was standard equipment.

Among the nice touches were a beautiful engine-turned dashboard, a tachometer, and a carpeted floor. Although Westclox and Borg made clocks for Ford, the 1955 Thunderbird had a clock (with sweep-second hand) made by the Telechron Clock Divison of General Electric. The dashboard had a 150 mph speedometer with see-through top illumination called "Astra-dial." The steering wheel had a three-inch in-and-out adjustment. Black rayon was the original soft top material but, late in the year, white vinyl became available. No sun visors were on the 1955 models. A very popular item was the engine dress-up kit. These cars also had an inside hood release.

The first production Thunderbird was built Sept. 9, 1954, and had serial number P5FH-100005. It is now owned by George Watts of Villa Park, Calif. The last 1955 Thunderbird (whereabouts unknown) had serial number P5FH-260557, and was built on Sept. 16, 1955.

The 292 cubic inch Mercury engine was used in the Thunderbird, with 193 hp at 440 rpm in those cars having the three-speed manual transmission, and also in those overdrive. The cars with Fordomatic were rated 198 hp at 4400 rpm.

The 1956 Thunderbird sought to correct what few shortcomings the 1955 model had. After all, the 1955 Thunderbird had outsold the Corvette by a ratio of more than five to one.

The most obvious change was the addition of the spare tire mounting. The Thunderbird for 1956 had a continental kit as standard equipment. This left more usable room in the trunk compartment. This also increased the overall length by 10 inches. Another much-needed addition was actually an option. The portholes in the hardtop did help to eliminate a rather dangerous blind spot. Before the porthole hardtop was decided upon, there was an alternative top, with a window just aft of the door window. This was sometimes referred to as the "five-window hardtop." This top would have given better visibility than the portholes, but it was ruled against. The final decision not to use this was probably because it looked too much like the new Continental Mark II, or perhaps because a 1954 Corvette show car had one like it. It was seriously considered, however, because a background sketch in the 1956 Ford Fairlane shows a Thunderbird with this top.

There were minor changes in the taillights. The insignia

A 1957 softtop model, taken by the Ford factory in Germany.

above the grille was changed from the crossed checkered flags on the 1955 model to the Thunderbird emblem. Side cowl vents were used to keep feet cooler in hot weather. Two-tone paint combinations were now optional, and the rear bumper was changed to make room for the spare tire in the center of the car. On each corner was an exhaust outlet, *not* one of Ford's better ideas. Interior sun visors were standard, as was the 12-volt electrical system. The engines were larger and more powerful. Glass wind wings were added at the front of the doors, to keep the passengers from being buffeted by the wind.

Safety was a big thing at Ford this year. The door latches were of the type that would not let the doors fly open in case of an accident, and the steering wheel was dished and would "give" when struck by the driver's body. Padded dash and visors were an option, as were seat belts. All Ford products had these safety items and the *Motor Trend* "Car of the Year Award" was given to the Ford Motor Co. for this effort.

The wheelbase and tread was the same as on the 1955 model, as was the tire size (6.70-15), but the overall length was now 185.2 inches. A total of 15,631 of this model was built. The first one was built on the 17th of October, 1955, and went to Lewis Crusoe. It had a white hardtop, and the body was in prime coat. The serial number was P6FH-102661. The last 1956 model was P6FH-359516 and was built about August 24, 1956.

All the options were again available. The Thunderbird began the year with seven colors and 13 two-tone combinations. In March 1956, two more colors were added, and

there were 19 two-tone options. The car could be ordered with the top and the body painted the same color.

Cars with three-speed transmissions had a 292 cubic inch engine rated 202 hp at 4600 rpm. Those with over-drive had a 312 cubic engine of 215 hp at 4600 rpm. The Fordomatic cars had 312 cubic inches and 225 hp at 4600 rpm. Late in the model year, a dual four-barrel carburetor setup was available for the manual transmission options, and was rated at 260 hp. The basic list price was now up to $3162.

The 1957 Thunderbird was restyled from the earlier ones, although the same basic body shell and wheelbase was retained. The front end was redesigned, the rear deck and side panels changed, making the car about four inches shorter overall than the 1956 model. The spare tire was back inside the trunk as trunk room had been increased. Accessory manufacturers furnished continental kits, however, for those needing more room.

For greater differential durability, a straddle-mounted pinion was used. A nice feature was automatic radio volume control. The faster the car went, the louder the volume. A gadget that most people had disconnected was the automatic power seat return (Dial-O-Matic). When the ignition was shut off, the seat went to the rearward position; when the ignition was turned on, the seat returned to the selected setting. This was not a great idea.

Accessories and safety features were all again available, as were the two types of hardtops. The dashboard was revised, with a 140 mph speedometer and no transparent top housing, like the earlier Thunderbirds had.

94

When a Thunderbird was sent overseas, the only item changed was the installation of a metric speedometer. On the 1955 and 1956 models, this meant that the 150 mph now read 240 kph. The conversion is almost perfect, as 149.14 mph does equal the 240 kph. In some foreign countries, American headlights are illegal, and some cars were shipped without headlights. There is no record of the factory ever building a right-hand drive model, but at least two owners had them converted to the configuration.

The tread and wheelbase remained the same as the earlier cars, and the overall length was 181.4 inches. The tire size was changed to 7.50-14. The base price was still $3162, and 21,380 of this model were built. The first 1957 model was built on Sept. 14, 1956 and the serial number was D7FH-100010. Production did not cease when the regular 1957 production stopped, so these cars were built with the 1958 Fords until Dec. 13, 1957. The last Thunderbird had serial number E7FH-395813.

Soft tops were available in four colors this year. There were originally ten paint colors, and there were five colors added or substituted for the 1957 colors when the 1957 Thunderbirds were being built along with the 1958 Fords. There were 34 two-tone combinations, all with color-keyed upholstery.

The 292 cubic-inch engine was available only with the three-speed manual transmission. This was rated 212 hp at 4500 rpm. The overdrive transmission and the Fordomatic cars had the 312 cubic inch engine that was rated 245 hp at 4500 rpm. There were two dual four-barrel options, both of 312 cubic inch displacement, and each available with any transmission. One was rated 270 hp at 4800 rpm, and the other, the racing version, was rated at 285 hp. There were also 208 cars made with the 312 cubic inch supercharged engine, rated 300 hp at 4800 rpm.

All of the two-passenger Thunderbirds had a floor-mounted shift lever, regardless of engine or transmission. All production Thunderbirds had chrome trim on the bottom of the fender skirts. In the spring of 1955, a triangular chrome stone shield was added to the front lower portion of the skirts. All 1956 and 1957 models must have these in a concourse.

The porthole hardtop models had no insignia on them. The 1955 hardtop had the Ford crest insignia, the 1956 non-porthole hardtop had no insignia, and the 1957 non-porthole hardtop had a round emblem with a V-shaped Thunderbird device.

The total three-year production figure stands at 53,166, a memorable achievement for a two-passenger luxury car in this country.

1958 Hardtop.

The Squarebirds

1958–1960

by James E. Petrik

With the two-passenger Thunderbird selling so nicely, why would anyone want to change the format? For profit, mostly. While the little Bird was selling better than had been anticipated, it was never going to be a high-volume seller. The history of two-passenger cars in this country, at least up to that time, had never been very great, sales-wise. Cars were a family thing, and that meant four or five people were to be seated. Most of the people buying Thunderbirds bought them for style or prestige, with performance a poor third, according to a market study made during 1956. Not only did most owners ignore any "sports car" image or usage, but one of the main objections to the little Thunderbird was its lack of passenger and luggage room. Thunderbird styling and Thunderbird engines were selling Ford cars, however.

Dropping the two-passenger model was not all that easy. Originally there was some thought that for 1958, there would be both two- and four-passenger Thunderbirds, the two-passenger model finally getting a power-operated soft top. Even in 1961, there was some thought of reusing some of the sheet metal from the little Thunderbirds in developing what became the Mustang.

The 1958 Thunderbird was new throughout. New body (new type of construction, the unitized type) and frame combined, a new size, and a new motor.

Right here, we have two mysteries regarding the 1958

model. The first is that while the new engine was 352 cubic inches, and was rated 300 hp at 4400 rpm (this engine was available with the three-speed manual, three-speed manual with overdrive, and the new Cruise-O-Matic automatic transmission), the main catalog printed in March mentions the availability of a 430 cubic inch engine, rated 375 hp at 4800 rpm. This was the Lincoln engine and was available only with Cruise-O-Matic. Were any actually produced and sold?? There was a prototype model tested by *Motor Trend* magazine, and this big engine could reduce the zero-to-60 mph time by two seconds, and the zero-to-one hundred mph time by 11 seconds. No production figures were ever given for this option.

The second mystery concerns what happened on March 17 (St. Patrick's Day), 1958. The weekly industry newspaper, *Automotive News*, dated March 24, 1958, mentions that Ford's 50-millionth vehicle was built that day, and it was a Thunderbird. A trade magazine, *Automotive Industries*, mentions that a green Thunderbird hardtop was driven off the assembly line that day and it was Ford Motor Co.'s 50-millionth vehicle since the first production gas vehicle was built in 1903. In addition, there is a photo of a 1958 Thunderbird hardtop, seemingly white (or very light green) with a sign by the rear wheel saying "Ford's 50 Millionth." If one were to look in the book by

1959 Convertible

Silverado Publishing Co. entitled "The Ford Road" (the 75th Anniversary Book) on page 157, one would see a picture of a 1959 White Ford Galaxie four-door sedan with a big sign above saying "Ford's 50 Millionth." This also shows Henry Ford II with other notables at this ceremony, as well as a 1903 Model A Ford and their "Levacar." The Galaxie was built April 29, 1959 at the Dearborn Assembly Plant. Which was the right car? Hobbyists have found that Ford sometimes plays tricks with serial numbers and production figures. One never really knows.

This all-new car now had a wheelbase of 113 inches (an increase of 11 inches), an overall length of 205.4 inches (up 24 inches from 1957). The front tread was 60 inches, with the rear tread now 57 inches. The new tire size was 8.00-14.

This was the first model to have front window vent panes, and this car also won the *Motor Trend* "Car of the Year" Award, for a combination of safety, comfort, compactness, and performance.

To keep the overall height down, the passengers sat deep in the compartment, and this necessitated a large transmission hump and driveshaft tunnel. Ordinarily, that would have been bad, but the Thunderbird designers came up with a real winner. Separate the passengers with a large console, making the car strictly four-passenger. This became a Thunderbird item that others copied.

The 1958 model was the only Thunderbird to have coil spring rear suspension until the 1967 model made its appearance. The thought was that an air suspension system would be optional, but this was never offered.

The car had rather angular lines but did come out very good-looking. As with most 1958 cars, four headlights became standard. The grille framing and the front bumper were combined in one huge stamping. The grille insert was a thin sheet stamping with many round holes in it. There were two bumper guards mounted on the lower part of the grille frame opening, in the center portion. There were two taillights on each side of the car and the "grille" around each taillight group was a painted stamped part, with the pattern matching the front grille. If the optional back-up lights were used, the fixtures were mounted in with the outboard taillights on each side. The outside top part of the rear fenders had slight tailfins. These extended forward just slightly past the door handles. An outward crease came from the top of the headlight and went straight back to about the center of the door where it then curved downward. The word "Thunderbird" was in script just back of the headlights on each side. On the lower part of the front door, a spear-pointed convex section went rearward, blending into the side of the rear bumper. The fender skirt, if used, was a part of this side sculpture. On the door part of this spear, there

1960 Hardtop

were five sets of vertical bars, about seven bars per set. The hood had a low wide scoop, and on top of each front fender there was a "gunsight-type" ornament. The base of the hardtop, on the sides, had a chrome band with horizontal ribbing. Just above this and just to the rear of the side windows were round emblems. These were about the same size as on the 1957 non-porthole hardtop.

The dash instruments on the 1958 model were of black background with white numerals, just opposite of that used on the 1959 and 1960 models. Most luxury items were still accessories at this stage of Thunderbird history.

The 1958 Thunderbird hardtop went into production on Jan. 13, 1958, while it was June before the convertible version became available. The first-year version had a semi-automatic top, power-operated. The next year the top became fully automatic.

This year saw 12 single colors, 34 two-tone combinations, and 10 interior choices. There were seven different cloth tops for the convertible, four exterior colors, but one exterior color (white) had four different lining color choices.

The hardtop had a base price of $3631, and the convertible was $3929. Most of these cars were loaded with accessories to a far higher price.

There were 35,758 hardtops and 2,134 convertibles built, for a total of 37,892 cars. This was almost double the 1957 total that even had an extended production period. This was a superb showing, as 1958 was an extremely depressed year regarding automobile sales. Just about every brand was doing about 60 percent of the previous year's sales.

The 1959 model was very close to being like the 1958 model, as the wheelbase, tread, overall length, and tire size were identical. This model had regular semi-elliptic leaf rear springs.

The spear point on the door now had a chrome "point" on it, and the five sets of vertical bars on the spears were now gone. The script "Thunderbird" was now on the spear, just aft of the point. The ornaments on the front fenders no had a Thunderbird insignia on them. A new design wheel cover was used for this year and also 1960.

The grille insert for the 1959 model was a series of horizontal bars. As could be expected, this horizontal bar motif was also used in the area around the taillights.

As with the 1959 model, most accessories were extra cost items, but most of these cars had plenty of these nice luxury "toys."

The standard engine was once again the 352 cubic inch mill, rated 300 hp at 4400 rpm, available with all three transmissions, the three-speed, three-speed with overdrive, and the Cruise-O-Matic option. This year, the 430 cubic inch Lincoln engine was available for $177 extra.

98

The only transmission available for this option was the Cruise-O-Matic. This engine was now rated at 350 hp at 4800 rpm.

Eighteen single colors, 15 of them exclusively Thunderbird, were available, all in the new Diamond-Lustre Finish. This eliminated waxing, until the car wax industry invented a new type of wax for cars that did not need waxing. There were 41 two-tone combinations, as well as fourteen interior choices. Again there were seven top choices.

On the side of the roof, where the round emblem was on the '58 models, there now appeared a small Thunderbird emblem, bird shaped.

Basic list prices were $3696 for the hardtop and $3979 for the convertible. The hardtop found 57,195 buyers and the convertible saw the production total 10,261, for a grand total of 67,456.

The nicest of the three-year series was the 1960 Thunderbird. Although the same size as the previous two years, and using the same body shell, the small changes made this a nicer and more popular car.

The standard engine this year was the 352 cubic inch motor, rated 300 hp at 4600 rpm, and the optional engine ($177) was again the 430 cubic inch Lincoln engine, rated 350 hp at 4600 rpm. As before, the small engine had three transmission choices, and the large engine had only the automatic box.

The main new option this year was the sun roof in the hardtop. This cost an extra $212.40 and was manually operated. About 2536 of these cars were produced, and the sunroof would not be seen again until the 1969 models came out.

The grille insert for 1960 was square mesh design, with three vertical bars and one horizontal bar added. This gave the car a rather "toothy" appearance. The square mesh was also around the taillights, of which there were three on each side this year. The back-up lights were mounted in the inboard lights this time. The chrome points were removed from the door spears, although the script "Thunderbird" remained in place. The rear fenders, just forward of the taillights now had three sets of three vertical bars each thereon. The front fender ornaments were oval-shaped with a Thunderbird insignia in them.

If the car was equipped with a sun roof, a chrome rail was installed on the forward edge of the roof, to deflect the passing air up over the opening. This was also the last year a front chrome trim band was used on the convertible roofs. The insignia on the hardtop this year was a large one, right in the center of the sail panel. The chrome bands at the base of the hardtop were not quite as high as previously. They were smooth the first few months of production, then they became ribbed, as the earlier models had been.

In July 1960, two Thunderbird hardtops were made of stainless steel. This project was in conjunction with the Allegheny Ludlum Steel Corp. The car weighed 3957 pounds, the same as the standard Thunderbird. The bodies were made of the Type 302 stainless steel, with a satin finish. The trim was Type 430 stainless with a mirror finish.

This year saw 19 single colors, none of which were exclusively Thunderbird. There were 15 interior choices, and three colors of convertible roof (black, white, and blue). For two-tone combinations, Ford went crazy this year. There were 28 color combinations, but each and every one of these could be reversed, making 56 possibilities.

Base price of the hardtop was $3755, and the convertible was $4222. There were a total of 78,447 hardtops, including the sun roof models, and 11,860 convertibles. This makes a grand total of 92,843 cars. This model had the greatest sales of the whole Thunderbird family, until Ford tried to compete with small cheap cars for the 1977 model.

The real collector's item for this year, due to rarity (and desirability) would be a sunroof hardtop with the 430 cubic inch engine. Only 3,900 cars (4.2%) had the large engine in 1960. This is one odd trait that seems to cover all Thunderbirds. When more than one engine option was available, the large engine never did sell very well so the Thunderbird never had the performance image it could have had.

Interior view of a 1960 hardtop, showing the sunroof in the open position.

1961-63 Thunderbird Expanding The Line

by James F. Petrik

If one were to ask most real Thunderbird enthusiasts what the Thunderbird's "golden years" or "shining hours" were as applied to the four-passenger models, 1961-'63 would most certainly be the period. Completely restyled, and with a new engine, some of their most exciting models would make their appearance.

This model was far more rounded than the previous "Squarebirds" and some thought that the front end looked rather boat-like. This front combined the grille

1961 Convertible. Photo courtesy Indianapolis Motor

1961 Hardtop. This is the last year that used wide whitewall tires.

framing and the bumper into one expensive piece of metalwork. The grille insert was mainly made up of horizontal bars, with a few vertical bars in the background. A vestigal air scoop was on top of the hood again for this series. The reason for the front end of this group was to make it possible to make the 1963 model a front-wheel drive car. The design work had been completed and test models made. While the car was a success as far as the mechanics went, it was wisely decided to drop the whole idea. The cost would have been greater, maintenance higher, tire wear greater, and on a heavy car, front wheel alignment would be difficult. Another good reason was that with front-wheel drive, the cockpit could have been cleaned up. The Thunderbird image was of the double-cockpit-with-console, however, and so no cleaned-up cockpit was wanted or needed. Thunderbird was not trying for six passengers back then.

In each of the years in the 1961-'63 series, the cars had two large round taillights, one on each side. On top of each rear fender was a very slight fin, something popular in those days. For these three years, the back-up lights were in the rear bumper, just outboard of the center-mounted license plate. The 1961 model is distinguished

by four horizontal chrome strips on the rear portion of each rear fender, and by the word "Thunderbird" in script on the front part of the front fender side, at about the same height as the headlights.

Standard equipment this year included power steering, power brakes, and the automatic transmission (Cruise-O-Matic). The new engine displaced 390 cubic inches, and was rated 300 hp at 4600 rpm.

The 1961 Thunderbird was available as a hardtop and as a convertible, and no sunroof was offered. This had not been a big seller the previous year, about 2.75 percent of the year's total. Unitized body-and-frame construction was again employed. A Thunderbird insignia was on the roof quarter panel of the hardtops in this series. New this year were the Day-Night mirror bonded to the windshield, electric windshield wipers, and self-adjusting brakes. An interesting option was the Swing-Away steering wheel, which moved to the right for ease on entry and exit. This wheel movement could occur only with the transmission lever in the "Park" position.

1962 Thunderbird Landau, a newcomer to the lineup

A gold-colored Thunderbird convertible was chosen as Pace Car for the golden anniversary of the Indianapolis Speedway.

This was the last model to have the wide white-sidewall tires as optional equipment. The 1961 model was available in 19 single colors, seven of them exclusive to the Thunderbird. There were 30 two-tone combinations available. Sixteen interior choices and three convertible top colors (black, white, and blue, all with black lining) gave the prospective buyer something to think about.

The wheelbase was 113 inches, the overall length was 205.0 inches, and the tread was 61 inches, front, and 60 inches rear. Tire size was 8.00-14, still rather small (in the writer's opinion) for a car of this weight and power.

The price of the hardtop was $4170, and the convertible was $4637.

There were 73,051 of 1961 model, 10,516 of these were convertibles, and 62,535 were the hardtops.

On Oct. 12, 1961, all loyal Thunderbird people rushed to their dealer's showrooms to see the latest models. They found that the "Dynamic Duo" had become a quartet. In addition to the convertible and the hardtop, there

1962 Sports Roadster. The genuine wire wheels and the tonneau cover headrests put this model two steps ahead of all other convertibles of that vintage.

was a formal hardtop, called a "Landau." This was a name harking back to the classic era, and the car had a vinyl roof and "S"-irons as well. Some called it a "Thunderbird in a tuxedo." The big news was the special convertible now available, with genuine chrome wire wheels and a lift-off fiberglass tonneau cover, with headrests (for the front seat passengers) that covered the rear compartment. This converted the car to a two-passenger model and the correct name of this offering was "Sports Roadster." With tonneau cover removed, the car was a four-passenger convertible. The convertible top and windows could be actuated with the tonneau cover in place. This model also had a special insignia just under the word "Thunderbird" on the front fender. A grab bar on the dashboard, in front of the passenger, was included on the Roadster.

The size of this model was identical to the 1961 model, as was the tire size. The Sports Roadster with wire wheels had to have inner tubes in the tires to hold the air.

Like the 1961 model, the 390 cubic inch engine was standard, as was power steering, power brakes, and Cruise-O-Matic. A three two-barrel carburetor setup was optional, this giving 340 hp at 5000 rpm, and cost $242.10 extra.

1963 Sports Roadster. The rarest and prettiest of the Roadsters.

1963 Thunderbird Hardtop.

The Swing-Away steering wheel became standard on this model. In late spring, some of these cars appeared with a horizontal chorme accessory stripe on the sides.

This model had three rectangular bars on each rear fender, the bars having horizontal grooves in them. The grille insert for this model was of a few horizontal chrome bars with small chrome rectangles placed between the bars, like a waffle effect.

There were 18 single colors, and 20 two-tone combinations for the hardtop. Twelve of the single colors were exclusively Thunderbird. Later on, one additional color became available. There were 19 interior choices, as well as two vinyl roof colors (black and white) for the Landau. There were only seven colors available for the Sports Roadster. As in 1961, the convertible top had three color options.

The prices for these cars were hardtop, $4321; Landau, $4398; convertible, $4788; Sports Roadster, $5439. The production figures were hardtop and Landau (grouped together) 69,554. The convertible had 7,030, while the Sports Roadster had only 1,427. Of this 1,427, the 340 hp option was on 120 of these cars. This makes 78,011, which was about 5,000 more than the previous year.

The 1963 Thunderbird was considered by many to be the best-looking of this three-year group. Basically, the models were the same as the previous year. The script "Thunderbird" was now on the rear fender. The front fender now had a crease in it that extended very near to the rear door edge, turned downward, and faded into the door. Just below this, in the center of the door, there were three sets of slanting chrome strips, five strips to each set. The grille insert for 1963 was mostly of thin vertical bars. Below the fender crease was the special insignia location on the Sports Roadster (really the same location as on the 1962 model).

The Landau this year had simulated walnut trimming, and also a walnut-colored steering wheel, rather than being color-keyed as on the 1962 model.

The dimensions and tire size were the same as the previous two years. Some of the changes on this model were the use of an alternator instead of a generator, and this was the first model to use hydraulic windshield wipers, run by the power steering pump. Metal-clad brake and accelerator pedals were new this year. Power steering and brakes, as well as Cruise-O-Matic and Swing-Away Steering Wheel, were standard equipment, as well as an AM radio. As an accessory, a tachometer was now available. The brakes were improved to make them more fade-resistant. Oddly enough, with the 300 hp engine, a single exhaust was used. With the 340 hp option, dual exhausts were again used, this still costing $242.10 extra. A nice option was the AM/FM radio.

The Thunderbird this year was available in 24 single colors, with 24 two-tone combinations, and 17 interior choices. Eleven of the colors were exclusive to the Thunderbird. The Sports Roadster was to be had in eight colors. There were four (black, white, brown, and blue) vinyl roof colors for the Landau, and the convertible top was again available in three colors (black, white, and blue) with black lining.

Prices were up about $125 from the 1962 models. The hardtop was now $4445; Landau, $4548; convertible, $4912; and the Sports Roadster was $5563.

Now for some real class. In January of 1963, the Special Limited Edition Landau (only 2000 made) was premiered in the Principality of Monaco. These cars were all painted white, with white leather interior, and a white steering wheel. The interior wood trim was simulated rosewood, not walnut. The top was a maroon vinyl, called rose beige. On the dash was a special "gold" nameplate carrying the car's special serial number (one to 2000). This car cost $4748 and was known as the "Princess Grace" model by salesmen and Thunderbird enthusiasts. The cars also carried special wheel covers with simulated knock-off hub spinners.

There was one special show car made this year, the "ITALIEN." This had to be the sleekest of all Thunderbirds. When viewed from the side it was a fastback, but in reality it was a notchback, like the original 1965 Mustang fastback. This car had wire wheels, special taillight trim, and special trim on the front fenders and doors.

There seems to be some disagreement as to how many cars were made this year, but the following list is from the Ford Division (who is not always correct). Hardtop, 42,806; Landau, 12,139; convertible, 5,913; Limited Edition Landau, 2,000; and Sports Roadster, 455, of which only 37 had the 340 hp option. This totalled 63,313, which is down almost 15,000 from the preceding year. This was probably because GM offered new competition, the Grand Prix and the Riviera. The Avanti was also now present, though not a large factor.

1963 Thunderbird Landau...the formal Thunderbird.

1967-1971 Thunderbird Four-Door Sedans

by James F. Petrik

In the autumn of 1966, a dyed-in-the-wool Thunderbird enthusiast had good reason to feel disappointment. His (or her) favorite automobile, introduced 12 years earlier as a convertible, would no longer be able to have its top folded. As an even greater shock, the Thunderbird would be available as a four-door Landau, in addition to the familiar two-door hardtop and two-door Landau. Did the country really need another four-door sedan?

Ford had this to say about the car, in a salesman's selling instruction booklet: "Heretofore, a buyer of Ford Motor Co. cars had no place to go between the Mercury Park Lane and the Lincoln Continental. Now he has Thunderbird. You have a strong sales wedge with the four-door Landau, an entry capable of breaking the Cadillac, Buick Electra, and Olds 98 domination of a selected buying segment. Thunderbird has been grabbing about 45% of the upper medium-price hardtop market against Riviera and Toronado. Market research indicates that 27% of the Grand Prix, Riviera, and Starfire owners would prefer a four-door. That's a lot of people, a most inviting conquest market."

In spite of what was said above, the factory had made no preliminary market survey. There had been no influx of mail asking about such a car. Just what prompted Ford to even think about it? It all began as a sketch in the styling studio. Stylists are always thinking of far-out things to draw, and while some of their renderings are rather radical, they also come up with some real winners. Legend has it that Lee Iacocca came through the styling studio one day and saw a rendering of a dark maroon four-door Thunderbird with a black vinyl roof. This car had center-opening doors and a sail panel on the rear door where it was hinged to the body. He was so impressed with the concept that he ordered the stylists to get this car design completed as quickly as possible. Iacocca did have quite a knack of knowing what the customers wanted, and when. The Mustang and the Mustang II are very good examples of that.

Was this new model a success? The first year saw 24,967 of these made. Compare that with 21,093 convertibles, the total of the 1964, 1965, and 1966 model years. With both air conditioning and restrictive govern-

The '67 Landau was the first of the four-door Thunderbirds. Notice the center-opening rear doors.

ment regulations becoming more common, it seemed as if the convertible would not be missed. The word "fun" had gone out of our automotive vocabulary.

In the '20s and '30s, many four-door cars had center-opening doors. This is where the front doors had the hinges at the front, and the rear door had the hinges at the rear, the door handles being in the center of the door space. By the '40s, most cars had all doors hinged at the front. In 1967, only the Lincoln Continental had center-opening doors, exclusive of the Thunderbird. On the Thunderbird, this door arrangement required that part of the top, or "sail," below the "S"-iron be fastened to the door and open with it. This gave head room to the person getting in or out of the rear seat.

No longer would the unitized construction be used, as these cars had a separate body-and-frame construction. In fact, two wheelbases were required. The two-door models used a 115-inch wheelbase, while the four-door Landaus used a 117-inch wheelbase. Both front and rear treads on all models were 62 inches.

Some features missing from previous models were the vent-panes in the front door windows, and the fender skirts that would be seen no more. The headlights were hidden behind doors, but the full-width taillight continued.

The Swing-Away steering wheel of yore became the Tilt-Away wheel, which, when swung aside, also tilted for ease of entry and exit. Power front disc/rear drum brakes were again standard, with the federally mandated dual master cylinders. Also again standard were the automatic parking brake release and Sequential Turn Signals. New this year was an all-coil spring suspension, the first time a Thunderbird had coil springs in the rear since the 1958 model. One might say that any luxury feature that was not standard was most certainly available as an option.

The four-door Landau had an overall length of 209.4 inches. The tire size was 8.15-15, and the basic list price was $4858.25.

The standard engine was 390 cubic inches, rated 315 hp at 4600 rpm. The optional engine was 428 cubic inches with 345 hp at 4600 rpm. The new Select-Shift Cruise-O-Matic was the only available transmission. There were 20 single paint colors available, with 15 interiors, and the vinyl roof was available in a choice of four colors.

The 1968 Thunderbirds were very similar to the 1967 models. On the four-door Landau, the wheelbase, tread, overall length, tire size, and standard engine were the same as for the 1967 model. The Tilt-Away steering wheel became an option this year. Federally mandated safety items this year included side-mounted front (amber) and rear (red) reflectors or lights. The energy-absorbing steering column was also used this year. The grille was changed very slightly. A rear lamp monitor (showing which lights were burning) was a nice accessory. Some new features were a rear window defogger and cornering lights. The three-passenger Flight Bench front seat was a new feature, but the bucket seats and console were optional.

An optional engine was the new 429 cubic inch mill, with 360 hp at 4600 rpm. As of Jan. 1, 1968, this became the only Thunderbird engine. This was a welcome change as the Thunderbird was getting rather heavy. The Select-Shift Cruise-O-Matic was again the only transmission available.

Ford seemed rather reticent from this point on about listing colors and upholstery options, but there were 20 paint choices, more than 15 interiors, and four vinyl roof options that were available.

The basic list price was $4847.28 and the bucket seat and console option was $64.77. There were 4,674 of the bucket seat model, and 17,251 with the bench seats, a

The 1971 model was the last of the curiously styled four-door Thunderbirds.

total of 21,925. This figure is down more than 3,000 cars from the previous year.

The 1969 four-door Landau was very much like the 1968 model, with a slightly different front, and the rear no longer had the full-width taillights. The center portion was no longer illuminated. The Sequential Turn Signal feature was retained, however. All the luxury features were either standard or optional. The Tilt-Away steering wheel was again an option this year. Two new items were the electric rear window defroster, a most welcome feature for winter weather, and an electrically operated sun roof. Hard to tell what Ford was thinking about, but when the car had a sun roof, this car was called a "five-door" model. Most people do not go in or out of the roof. The cost was up to $453 for this option, as compared to the $212 for the 1960 manually operated sun roof. Front seat head restraints were required by law this year. Wheelbase, tread, length, etc. were the same as the 1967 and 1968 models, but the tire size was now 8.55-15 or 8.45-15, whichever was available.

There were 20 colors available, and no vinyl roof colors were listed, but it should be safe to assume four colors.

1968 two-door Landau.

1968 four-door Landau.

Various price lists floated around through the year, but $5043 looks like a good base price for the bench seat model, while the bucket seats and console would cost about $65 extra.

The 429 cubic inch engine, 360 hp at 4600 rpm, and Select-Shift Cruise-O-Matic transmission was the only available power train this year. There were 1,983 of these cars with the bucket seat option and 13,712 of the bench-seat models made a total of 15,995. The four-door production kept dwindling every year.

1970 saw the beginning of the sixth series Thunderbird. This would be a two-year series. The four-door Landaus for all five years seemed to have the same body shell, although the two-door models kept everyone confused with an endless display of side window and roof variations. The new models were one inch lower and about six inches longer, due to an entirely new front end design that had the radiator grille stick way out and come to a point. The wheelbase was retained at 117.0 inches, and the tread was 62 inches, front and rear.

The headlights were no longer concealed, but the radio antenna and the windshield wipers were. The full-width taillights were again used, still with Sequential Turn Signals. Radial ply tires became standard, and the size was now 215-R15. Full-width front seat was again standard, with high-back bucket seats and console a $78 option.

Most luxury equipment was still standard, with few remaining items optional. This year the steering wheel was only tilting, Ford's "better idea" (Swing-Away) was dropped. Power-operated sun roof was still an expensive option, and for $194, one could get the Sure-Track Brake Control System, to insure swift straight line stops under all road conditions.

This year there were 31 colors to choose from, with many upholstery options in a total of seven colors. No vinyl roof color options were listed, but there were at least four to choose from.

Motive power was still the 429 cubic inch engine, of 360 hp at 4600 rpm, coupled to the Select-Shift Cruise-O-Matic Transmission. The base price for the bench front seat model was $5182. The bucket seat model got popular this year, as 5,005 of this type were built, with 3,396 of the bench seat type, for a grand total of only 8,401.

The last of the four-door Thunderbirds made their debut for the 1971 model year. This model was exactly the same size as the 1970 model, with the tire size now H78-15 belted bias, or 215-15 steel-belted radial whitewall (Michelin). The Michelin tires had a very narrow white band, and the other tires had two narrow white bands. Only the two-door Thunderbirds had the bucket seat and console option this year. The four-door model had a solid or split bench front seat choice. Some exterior appearance options were color-keyed wheel covers, bodyside moldings with protective color-keyed inserts, and wheel lip moldings. Full-width taillights with Sequential Turn Signals were again employed, as were all the previous luxury items. The tilt steering wheel was again an option, as were items like electric rear window defrost.

Twenty-four paint colors were available, but some applied only to certain models. This year saw five vinyl roof colors, and many interior options.

This was the last year that such high horsepower ratings would be given, 360 hp at 4600 rpm for the 429 cubic inch engine. As usual, the Select-Shift Cruise-O-Matic transmission was the only transmission furnished. The base price of the car was $5516 ($4858 back in 1967), and the extra cost of the split bench seat is not known. Production figures show 4,238 cars with the split bench, and 2,315 with the solid bench seat, a total of 6,553 cars. This is way down from the 1967 total of 24,967 four-door Landaus. Actually, all Thunderbird production was down, going from 77,956 in 1967 to the 36,055 of 1971.

Mustang

1964½ Mustang — Zippy Chariot

by Gerald Perschbacher

Bob drove it regularly around town. The dark green Mustang was a zippy little chariot at his command, his first sporty car.

"It's not at all like my '56 Chevy — the Blue Bomb," Bob would say with speedy enthusiasm. "I really like my Mustang."

A part of the early postwar baby boom, Bob and I couldn't even think about buying our own cars when the '64 Mustang hit the showroom in April of that year. We were green behind the wheel, older than schoolboys but too wet behind the ears for full adulthood. But the green Mustang was a godsend to two growing "men."

We'd hit the pavement in the coupe, which originally was tagged by the Ford dealer at $2,368.

"It's a '64 model," the dealer said back then. "Well, really, it's almost a '65. Let's call it a '64½ just to be accurate."

No lightweight at 2,572 pounds, the pert Mustang "features a very tidy 108-inch wheelbase and comes equipped with a 170 cubic inch six-cylinder engine and three-speed, floor-mounted manual transmission," the salesman told Bob's dad. Just like Bob, his father was prone to let thoughts of sporty looks and performance race through his mind. Soon his wallet was pulled out, some cash laid down, and a contract was readied to be signed.

The '64½ was supposed to seat four people, but I never believed it. The one time I rode in back, we climbed up and down the Ozarks, winding and weaving. I became roadsick. It took about 50 miles of riding up front before I was well again. The back seat was a sales advantage, maybe; or fit for children and other "small people." It certainly didn't fit a six-footer!

Bob and his parents probably realized the car's shortcomings in the rear, too. The car — bought for family use — became a second car, later to be turned over to Bob to bounce back and forth to school. Luxury it wasn't.

Bob didn't care. He rode in front in the black bucket seat. And he liked to ride that shift stick, too.

"This generation wants economy and sportiness, handling and performance, all wrapped up in one set of wheels," echoed the salesman's words. Some sales hype, in print, "There is a market out there, searching for a car. Ford Motor Co. committed itself to design that car. It is to carry four people, weight under 2,500 pounds, and cost less than $2,500." It came close when the car left the assembly line, but still struck out on two of the counts.

Bob's car had a hood that seemed longer than the whole car. Styling was a big percentage of the work put into the '64½ Mustang. Everybody liked the looks of it, and time has treated the style well after more than 20 years.

Bob never apologized for the six-under-the-hood, but you could see his eyes brighten when he said how his dad turned down the high-performance, 289-cubic inch V-8 with its 271 hp. Lee Iacocca knew what he had created back in '64 — a dream put into steel and rubber. Many people wanted a part in the dream, too.

The Ford people said, "The result was overwhelming. The first-year sales estimate of 100,000 units was surpassed in four months. Some 22,000 orders were taken the first day. In just 12 months, more than 417,000 Mustangs were sold, a record for first-year sales.

"Mustang had an enormous appeal among young people, with more than half of the first-year buyers under 34 years old," factory wits would wag. "The surprise was that 16 percent of buyers were in the 45-55 age bracket. The Mustang seemed to bridge just about every gap in the market."

The upper-age bracket included Bob's dad; but I think he had the car in mind for Bob all along.

Holding the auto record as the best selling model in the shortest time is the 1964½ Ford Mustang. (Prototype)

Shelby Mustang
"Stirred The Emotions"

The 1965 Shelby Mustang GT-350 transformed the image of the Mustang into something spectacular.

by Robert C. Ackerson

Just recently a national automotive publication was taken to task by some of its readers for devoting considerable space to a dual road test of the Lamborghini Countach S and Ferrari 512 Boxer. The source of their discontent wasn't the testing of these cars as such but rather because they were portrayed as the ultimate in supercars. Owners of older sports cars were quick to point out their cars could approach the Ferrari/Lamborghini performance sphere at prices, to say the least, considerably less than the $100,000 asked for these automobiles.

Behind this mini-protest lies a larger truth, namely that the last dozen years or so have been tough times for performance cars. There are great cars in production today and to be sure, a lot of contemporary automobiles are going to be sought-after collectibles down the road a couple of decades. But in this context the old car fan of today appears to be infinitely more fortunate than his 21st century counterpart. The cars that light his fire today, more often than not, were designed to squeeze the last BTU out of a gallon of low octane gasoline or conform with governmental decrees mandating a minimum bumper height. Instead, they were made to out-corner, out-accelerate and in every other important criteria of performance outhustle their more mundane brethren.

It's not surprising that Ford was the greatest American practitioner of this form of automotive magic. Its very origins were rooted in performance and racing. In the 1960s its leaders, infused with desire to overhaul Chevrolet in sales, reasoned that one way to achieve that goal was by producing automobiles that could dust off their Chevrolet counterparts, whether they met on the dragstrip, race track, back country road or city boulevard.

Thus it came to pass that one Carroll Shelby met one Lee Iacocca in 1965. Iacocca wanted the Mustang's image (certainly not exactly that of a gutless wonder) to gain a few extra lumens of brightness by becoming a class champion in SCCA production sports car racing. Shelby, already involved in preparing the GT-40s for their eventual string of triumphs at LeMans, was just the man to transform the good Mustang into the great Mustang.

In a nutshell that's how the GT-350 came to pass. Only 562 were constructed during 1965 but these were cars so stunning in performance that their place in automobile history is completely out of proportion to their numbers. Consider the impression they made upon the motoring press early in 1965. "What Shelby has done," said *Car and Driver* (May 1965), "is to convert the Mustang fastback coupe into a road-going version of a NASCAR stocker....Not a lady's car by any stretch of the imagination, probably not even a gentleman's car for that matter, but surely a man's car, in the tradition of the Blower Bentley or the Cad-Allard." John Christy of *Sports Car Graphic* wrote in that magazine's June 1965 issue that "it was quite obvious that this car is easily the equal of anything that Europe has to offer in the GT category, even at three times the price....It is pure and simple, a sports car in every sense of the word." *Road and Track* (May 1965) concluded, "All in all, the GT-350 is pretty much a brute of a car...the GT-350 seems more suited to the dropout than the serious scholar." John Christy, not willing to let this semi-slur go unchallenged, retorted (*Sports Car Graphic*, July 1965), "...it is hardly suited for dropouts." If nothing else, the GT-350 was an automobile that obviously stirred the emotions of anyone who drove it!

Mustangs destined to become GT-350s were delivered to Shelby American sans hoods and rear seats. However, they were far from being derelicts. All were equipped with the Mustang's performance handling kit, the 271 hp "High Performance" 289 cid V-8 and a Warner T-10, close-ratio four-speed gearbox. These features made the Mustang a car to be respected but they were just the basic building blocks for the creation of the GT-350. That began when the standard, 0.84 inch front stabilizer bar was replaced with a one-inch version. While the front spring rates remained unchanged at 105 lbs./in, the use of large Koni adjustable shocks set at their stiffest positions plus the lowering, by one inch, of the upper control arm left no doubt about Shelby's plans for the GT-350.

The modifications to the Mustang's rear suspension were limited to the use of Koni shocks, plus a pair of trailing torque-control arms. But in conjunction with the revised front suspension they resulted in far less body lean in the corners and more importantly approximately 30% less front wheel lean. Thus the GT-350's road manners were like those of the archetype vintage British sports car. The ride was spine-jarring but on smooth surfaces, the corners were taken fast and flat. There was nothing neo-classic about wheels and tires selected by Shelby for the GT-350; 15-inch Kelsey-Hayes "mag-type" wheels with six-inch rims fitted with Goodyear Blue Streak tires rated for 130 mph. Kelsey-Hayes also supplied the GT-350's 11-inch front disc brakes, equipped with racing pads. At the rear were 10-inch x 2.5-inch drum brakes normally used on the large Ford station wagons. When installed on a GT-350 they were fitted with sintered-metal linings. Rounding out the GT-350's altered underpinnings was faster, 19:1 steering and, on approximately half of the 1965 models, a battery relocated in the trunk to improve front-rear weight distribution.

To propel the GT-350 to a speed where Shelby's efforts became worthwhile, the 271 hp V8 was given a dose of snake tonic that boosted output to 306 hp at 6000 rpm. The most prominent changes included use of a Ford-built high-rise intake manifold plus a Holley four-barrel carburetor with special jetting calibrated to be compatible with free-flowing welded-tube headers. A larger than stock (6.5 quart instead of five quart capacity) cast aluminum oil pump with internal baffles to minimize oil frothing was also installed as was a larger 15 quart radiator.

Although there were occasional murmurs of discontent about the GT-350's appearance lacking identity, it had a distinct, straight-to-the-point look that even its critics had to admit was appealing. The only body color available was Wimbledon white set off by dark blue stripes with GT-350 lettering positioned in the lower body panels. A dealer installed option that did little to help the GT-350 blend into the automotive wall paper was wide, dark blue racing stripes running down its centerline.

Although the interior was basically stock Mustang, there were enough changes to remind its occupants that they were in a vehicle intended primarily for rapid transit. Grafted onto the dash was a small instrument pod containing an oil pressure gauge (reading to 80 psi) and a tachometer, redlined at 6500 rpm and measuring to 8000 rpm. A fiberglass platform behind the front seats provided space for both luggage and the spare tire. The loss of two rear seats probably cost Shelby a few sales but once the driver buckled up those big, three-inch wide safety belts and wrapped his hands around the wood-rimmed, aluminum steering wheel with its hub-mounted Cobra emblem, the lack of space for four hardly mattered.

Shelby advertised many of the GT-350's performance features as options that he promised would be "oats for your Mustang." For example, the 715 cfm, four-barrel carburetor and aluminum high-rise manifold was available for $169.95, the solid-lifter cam kit retailed for $76.55 and the big 10 inch by 2.5 inch drum brakes with metallic linings could be yours for $96.64. The GT-350's "No-

Spin'' ratchet-type differential, which was more commonly found in trucks than cars listed for $173.71. Not offered as after market items was the GT-350's fiberglass hood with its center-mounted air scoop and NASCAR-type locking pins. This item plus the removal of virtually all noise and heat insulation gave the GT-350 a ready-for-the-road weight of approximately 3000 pounds, or some 200 pounds less than a high performance Mustang.

Contemporary road test results confirmed what was obvious from a study of GT-350 specifications; it was one of the best performing small-engined American sports cars of all time. It was a rare GT-350 that could not accelerate from zero to 60 mph in less than seven seconds, run from zero to 100 mph in under 19 seconds and exceed 90 mph in a quarter mile run. This wasn't race-winning performance but that matter was taken care of by the racing version of the Shelby Mustang, the GT-350R. Its price of $5,950 was well above the road model's $4,547 but even a partial review of its standard equipment suggest customers got plenty for their money. The use of a racing cam, careful engine reassembly with all components balanced and blueprinted, ported and polished heads, plus a cold air plenum chamber, gave the 350R, in the words of a Shelby spokesman, ''considerably more'' power than the ''stock'' GT-350 engine. Realistic estimates of its output ranged from 325 to 350 horsepower. There was little need to alter the basic GT-350 format so the Shelby men left well enough alone. However, front and rear brake cooling ducts were installed and the front disc brakes were equipped with extra hard pads. To further reduce weight, all body glass except for the windshield was replaced with Plexiglas. The removal of the small rear quarter vents and use of aluminum panels to seal over the resulting hoods saved 50 pounds. At the front a fiberglass apron replaced the stock bumper and gravel pan. A large capacity (34 gallon) fuel tank with a quick release cap was also installed as were true bucket seats, roll bar, shoulder harness and fire extinguisher.

Total production of the GT-350R was very low, numbering only about two dozen. But each one was ''pre-raced'' at the Willow Springs track and for three consecutive years (1965, 1966, 1967), the GT-350R was the SCCA's Class B-Production National Champion.

The GT-350 was revamped in 1966 but its basic character remained undefiled. *Car and Driver* (May 1966) concluded that ''for 1966 the car has been considerably refined, though it's still a tough, for-men-only machine.'' The use of longer exhaust pipes extending to the rear axle, instead of exiting just ahead of the rear wheels, lowered the interior noise level by a decibel or two, and the clangorous ratchet-type limited slip differential was replaced by a more civilized unit. The new models were visually identified externally by their rear quarter windows, rear brake scoops a la the 1965 competition model, and a horizontally barred grille. A couple of knuckle raps on the engine hood of a 1966 model revealed that it was now made of steel. Shelby also abandoned the ''you can have it any color as long as it's Wimbledon white'' policy for 1966, offering the GT-350 in candy apple red, guardsman blue, ivy green, raven black, and Wimbledon white. The interior of the 1966 GT-350 also differed from its predecessor's. Fold down rear seats were now installed (although in theory they were optional) and if it wasn't exactly luxurious, the use of the Mustang GT's dash and steering wheel could be perceived as a sign at least to GT-350 purists that decadence was creeping into the GT-350. A similar conclusion could be reached about the availability of the C-4 automatic transmission as a GT-350 option. But this reworked version of Cruise-O-Matic was no slough, and Joe Granatelli claimed it could out-accelerate a four-speed GT-350.

In April 1966 the Model SN Paxton Supercharger became a $670 option. Shelby Mustangs so equipped were known as GT-350S models although they did not carry any special identification. The use of a supercharger required a number of minor engine changes, the most apparent being the use of a 460 cfm Autolite carburetor. With at least 390 horsepower on tap the GT-350S was a very quick automobile. *Motor Trend* (August 1966) reported a zero to 60 mph time of six seconds and quarter-mile marks of 14 seconds — 102 mph and this with an automatic transmission!

1966 was also the one and only year for the GT-350H model. A total of 936 of these cars were purchased by Hertz and for $17 a day plus 17 a mile anyone with a driver's license could make like Ken Miles.

Total GT-350 production for 1966 was 2,380 cars, a big jump from the small batch of 1965 model year cars turned out. The next year sales reached the 3,225 level. But these Shelbys were evolving rapidly away from the character of the early models. They were far more refined and while certainly very fine performers and fun to drive, were intended to be Grand Tourers rather than out-and-out sports cars. Neither Shelby nor Ford can really be blamed for this transformation. The market for supercars in general was moving away from the brash behavior of the early '60s high performance machines and since both firms were in business to make money and not just cars, it was only logical for them to follow the market. But the refinement of the final Shelby Mustangs makes the early models all the more special. They clearly have the credentials to be regarded as modern classics. They are rare, possess a distinctive appearance, and perhaps most importantly, still perform in the same manner that gave a lucky few the rides of their lives back in the mid-'60s.

Mustang Fever

by Tim Howley

This page is dedicated to every kid who ever dreamed of his first car and to all those fathers who have the power to grant or deny that dream. For there has finally come to pass in this household of old car traditions and late model car intrusions that great American institution known as the teenage car. Late model car without a future, or hobby car of tomorrow? You decide.

Our oldest son, Bill, grew up on a passing parade of collectible automobiles. He was barely four when we bought an Auburn in 1965. Since then he's been exposed to everything from Apperson to Zephyr. I think he was one of the few first-graders who knew that a Duesenberg was not a big German car built by Ettore Bugatti. Like all kids, he developed old car preferences of his own. When you're 16 a 11-year-old pony car can be pretty old.

About a year ago this new word began popping up at the dinner table. The word was "Mustang." Specifically, 1967 Mustang fastback. As I had it explained to me, "Dad, the '67 Mustang fastback is a modern classic. When was the last time we saw one at an auction?" And "Aren't you glad I don't want a brand new piece of junk?" Now how do you argue with one like that? At first you dismiss the whole thing with a grumpy, "Go out in the garage and polish the '56 Lincoln, kid. You're not even old enough to have a driver's license."

Ha, that was only the beginning. There came an endless succession of ads clipped out of newspapers, phone numbers of Mustang sellers scribbled by the telephone, and, finally, on the kitchen calendar, under July 26: "Bill's birthday. Don't forget '67 Mustang fastback. Red."

The birthday came and went. Soon there was the driver's examination. Ha, ha. He failed. There was at last the Mustang reprieve. But not for long. The second time he passed. Now the pursuit of the Mustang fastback gained the full momentum of an army of German tanks under full attack.

I retreated to my last beachhead. Realizing that Mustang fastbacks are not as common as coupes, I knew I could buy a little more time. But not much. The end finally came late in the afternoon of Sunday, Feb. 12, at a place called Graham Auto Sales in National City, just south of San Diego, Calif. After the old man had made up excuses to pass on some 85 Mustangs over a period of 13 months, the end came swift and without pain. This Mustang wasn't red like he wanted. It was sort of a clockwork orange. But it had the black interior and all the rallye equipment. It ran better than most, and probably hadn't been drag raced for a good eight years. What more can you ask of a '67 Mustang fastback? The price was $1,495. I couldn't argue with that. Total defeat came when the salesman took me up on a $1,300 offer. Well, it's a rare car. Ford produced only 71,042 Mustang fastbacks for '67. While this one was not quite a GT, it had most of the GT equipment, including

390 engine, rallye wheels, full sports instrumentation and special suspension.

The pool table was quickly removed from the empty side of the garage. The dirt bikes no doubt will soon disappear, and the '60 T-Bird (what the old man thought he should have) will soon be on the market. We have now entered our Mustang era, like it or not.

What is this Mustang attraction? We oldsters, who dodder around in our vintage tin, might well take a look at the very late collectibles and the people who are into them. The '60s spawned a whole new breed of exciting cars — the GTOs, the Camaros, the Cougars, the Barracudas, and above all, the Mustangs. Not since the Model A has any car stirred up collector interest like the early Mustangs. They are as great a force on the hobby today as they were on the public years ago. Just observe the behavior at any major auction. These Mustang convertibles barely qualify as vintage cars, yet they command prices of $3,000 or more. Interest in them transcends all age and economic barriers. They are...well...Mustangs. The hottest things that have happened to car collecting since two-seater Thunderbirds.

The Mustang was the car that started the whole pony car rage, and did for the '60s what the Model A did for the late '20s and the '55 to '57 Chevrolet Bel Air V-8 did for the '50s. The Mustang set a whole new trend to longer hoods and shorter rear decks. Its influence can be seen to this day in Toyotas, Datsuns and Capris. And no other car in history has gone from fun transportation to collectibility quite as quickly as the Mustang.

I suppose I could explain Bill's Mustang mania quite easily. We had a new '67 Mustang coupe, which we disposed of after six short months. At the tender age of six it made quite an impression. He was denied his childhood illusion. But I strongly suspect it goes a whole lot deeper, and touches the deepest nerve center of a whole new generation of car enthusiasts. Perhaps when Lee Iacocca envisioned the first of the pony cars, he felt not only the pulse of the American car buying public of the early '60s, but that of a coming generation of car savers. The Mustang sprang from his hunch that there had to be a market out there for such a car. A hunch that was dramatically proven by research. It was more than a market. It was a whole feeling of the times, a feeling that has been denied by the dull decade of the Seventies.

Back in 1961, people were writing in, asking Ford to revive the old two-seater Thunderbird. Ford styling already had a number of small bucket type sporty jobs in the bag. These soon evolved into the Allegros, of which 13 were built and demonstrated. One of the little experiments was the Mustang I. It was an aluminum bodied sports type with an amidship V-4 engine. Dan Gurney drove one at Watkins Glen in the fall of 1962, and the

crowd went wild.

From all of these experimentals a whole new series of clays evolved. Once the decision was made to actually build a new small car, a design competition was held between Ford's three corporate studios to come up with the basic shape. Joe Oros' Ford Division studio produced the winning clay model in only two weeks, and the finished cars were rolling off the assembly lines just 18 months later.

The final Mustang was really a body engineering job because the basic chassis, engine, suspension, and driveline components were all carried over from the Falcon and Fairlane. The name Mustang was one of several suggested, but the one that seemed to fit best. It hinted of speed, power and freedom. It promised, once again, Ned Jordan's "Somewhere West of Laramie," a land of spirited young cowgirls riding lean and raggy into distant sunsets, of rough riding cowboys and lone prairies, of movieland adventure in the romantic old west. The spirit of the Jordan Playboy was ready to ride once more.

The Mustang was unveiled April 17, 1964. It carried a base price of $2,368 for the six-cylinder coupe, F.O.B., Detroit. From there, the western sky was the limit. Never before in history, or since, has a car come with so many options. You could go all the way from a very sporty economy car to practically an out-and-out sports job. Ford advertising called the new Mustang "The Unexpected."

1967 Mustang GT fastback

Within days it had garnered more media exposure than any car in 40 years. It took only four months to sell the first 100,000, and by the end of the 1965 model year, nearly 681,000 cars had been sold, an all-time industry record for first year sales. The millionth Mustang came in March 1966. By the time the '67 models hit the showrooms, almost 1.4 million Mustangs had been sold.

Looking back now you can see why the car made a tremendous impression on the kiddies of the '60s, those same people who today are driving cars. A whole generation of Americans saw Detroit's last great advance. And they saw it at a time when car collecting was coming of age. And now as they come of age, and Detroit offers them little more than plastic promises, where do they turn? Back to the pony cars of the '60s. And who are we, as parents, to say they are making the wrong decisions? We have taught them collector car values. And

1967 Mustang Fastback

1967 Mustang fastback

they are coming to appreciate the collectibles that they can remember, drive, and enjoy. Which is precisely what this old car hobby is all about. We oldsters see it over a span of 30 years or more. Our offspring see it in a more compact period. The difference is one of time, but not one of ultimate values.

Carroll Shelby saw it all the day the first Mustang hit the streets. He started a craze that you have to see to believe. In July 1978 there was another Shelby American Convention, this time in Pasadena, Calif. Spend a day with this group and you will understand what car collecting today, and tomorrow, is all about. For here is some of the greatest new excitement in car circles now!

I'm not sure that a '67 Mustang qualifies yet on any scale. The real interest at the moment is in the '65 and '66 models and, of course, in the early Shelbys. But the '67 and '68 models have a charm all their own that the new collectors should be quick to recognize. Usually the second go-around loses a lot of the flavor of the first. Not so with the second series Mustangs. They had stronger new styling without losing the intent of the original. I have always been especially fond of '67-'68 interior treatment. No, Ford did not attempt to spoil a good thing, although sales fell sharply in '67 and again in '68. I'm not sure why. Possibly, the originals had, for the most part, saturated the thirsty market.

Mustang had an unbelievable number of extras in those second two years. You could go all the way up to a 390 V-8 in '67 and a 427 Cobra V-8 in '68. There was Tilt-Away

steering, Select-Shift Cruise-O-Matic which would let you go fully automatic or shift manually. You could opt for power front disc brakes, air conditioning, a convenience control panel, and at least three different interiors.

Bill's Mustang is almost, but not quite, a GT. It seems to lack only fog lamps, quad exhausts, and special trim and stripes to make it official. But it has the 390 with chromed valve covers and air cleaner, the tachometer, the simulated wood-grained steering wheel, the heavy duty suspension and sports type wheel covers. I would venture to say that with the incredible list of options available, almost every one of the 3.4 million Mustangs built is, in its own way, one of a kind.

According to Bill, the last Mustang "worth having" is the '69. Who am I to argue? Ford tried hard to recapture its youth market with the '69, '70 and '71 models with their monster engines. But the sheer size of the later Mustangs fought the whole reason for their initial popularity. America loved its little upstart Mustang, and the bigger it got the more the purists turned back to the original. Production dropped 299,824 units for 1969 down to 125,093 for 1972, and up only to 134,867 for 1973. Ford's Mustang II only proves they never should have tampered with the original.

I suppose one Mustang in our garage will soon mean another, and a parts car, and parts, and whole new kind of meets, swaps, etc. Would anybody like to buy a '54 Ford Victoria, or a '60 T-Bird, or better yet, a '56 Lincoln?

1969 Mach I 428 CJ/SCJ: Fastest Mustang of All?

Zero to 60 in 5.5 seconds! One-quarter mile in 13.9 seconds! Performance like that might be a little short of breaking the sound barrier, but few enthusiasts will argue the fact that the 1969 Ford Mustang Mach I with 428 Cobra Jet engine was suitably named.

Mustang sales were slipping by late 1968, when a new model called the Mach I appeared. This was at a time when Detroit still believed that *performance* sold automobiles.

Even the least powerful Mach I had the get-there-quick, performance image with fastback (Ford called it "Sportsroof") styling, a blacked-out hood and cowl, dual racing mirrors, reflective tape stripes a hairy-looking — but nonfunctional — hood scoop and fat tires on chrome styled steel wheels.

Ford didn't stop in the appearance department, however. Under-the-hood goodies for the lowest-priced Mach I started with a 351 Windsor V-8. It stirred up 250 hp which flowed to the rear axle via a standard three-speed manual gear box.

Mach I was a bit of a handler, too. It had various competition suspension components including heavy springs, stiff shocks and a hefty front sway bar.

For those willing to spend more, FoMoCo provided several extra horsepower engines. They included a hot 302 with 290 horses, the old 390 with 320 hp the 429 CJ-R (375 hp) and *three* versions of the 428 cid Cobra Jet V-8.

The 428 CJ engines had a big Holley four-barrel, 390 GT cam and 427 low-riser heads. Version no. I came with a nonfunctional hood scoop. A Ram-Air package ($133 extra) was part of version no. 2. Then there was the 428 Super Cobra Jet engine. It combined the functional "shaker" scoop with beefy rear axles and "LeMans" type con rods.

Published drag strip results show the 428 CJ Mach I made a strong claim for the title of "Quickest Mustang." In addition to the acceleration times given at the start of this article, it had a top speed of 121 mph (not the fastest for a Mustang).

The standard Mach I sold for $3,122 and tipped the scales at 3175 pounds. The 428 CJ engine options started at $224 and ran about $357 with Ram-Air included. A well optioned car was about $3,700 and 3,700 pounds.

Total production of 1969 Mach Is was a solid 72,458 units. Over 13,000 of them are believed to have been 428 CH/SCJ powered, so some of these brutally fast Mustangs are still around. About 9.4 percent would be a good ballpark figure.

Mach I package came only on Sportsroof; included hood pins, chrome wheels and interior goodies.

116

Edsel

Ford's Famous Failure Has Devoted Following

by Tim Howley

1960 Edsel convertible

Need we say more!

1960 Edsel Corsair Convertible

Ford's 75th anniversary in 1978 marked another anniversary, one they'd just as soon have forgotten. That year the Edsel was 20 years old! For years, Ford wouldn't even talk about the Edsel. Its designer, Roy Brown, was sent off to Great Britain to take charge of the Cortina. He's back now. And, at 75, even the most serious of serious Ford Committees can look back on the Edsel with a smile. Henry Ford II forgave the car officially, pointing out that Edsels have become collector's items. The Edsel's advertising agency, Foote, Cone & Belding, is no longer stigmatized by the industry. Foote, Cone has been handling the Mazda account now for several years.

So the Edsel is alive and well and no longer being restored only in Poland. Like Sputnik, the hoola-hoop and the Purple People Eater, it has come back out of the faddy '50s. It is very "in" to drive a 1958 Edsel now. Edsel prices haven't exactly hit the ceiling, but virtually every single one of the Edsel's innovations has since been copied by some other make and has met with success. Experts now say it wasn't the car, but the times.

Ford spent $250 million to make it the car of the decade, not too far out, but just far enough to shock slightly. There was a touch of Alfa-Romeo plus a little bit of Archie Bunker's LaSalle to the vertical front grille. The whole idea was to have a grille that looked different from everybody else's. The broad, very long hood, leaning forward into the slim nose, smacked of Classic cars of the early '30s. There was even a hood ornament that was reminiscent of the old Boyce Motometers. The overall effect was a distinctive change from all the me-too styling that dominated the industry for years.

The Edsel was the most carefully researched automobile to that date. As early as 1948, Ford had recognized a real need for the car. Chevrolet buyers were moving up to Pontiacs and Buicks. Plymouth buyers to Dodges and DeSotos, but Ford buyers were not moving up to Mercurys in the numbers possible with a broader range of medium priced offerings. Long before the car was even designed, Ford went out and asked the public what it wanted. They even asked the public what they wanted it to be named. Though, finally, Henry Ford II said he didn't care what the research said about appealing names, the name would be Edsel, and that would be it.

As the Edsel moved closer to production in 1955, you have to remember that the public mood was in favor of such a car. People wanted more horsepower, tailfins, three-tone paint jobs, wrap-around windshields, bigness. 1955 was a 7.9 million car year. It was 1955 optimism which led to the excesses of 1958. So what happened? An unexpected recession came in the later part of 1957. The little upstart Volkswagen became a national hero almost overnight. All of the 1958 models had it tough. Edsel, the newcomer, with little more to offer than bigness and

power, was the hardest hit of all. It was a great embarrassment to Ford who had gone out and wooed away a lot of ex-GM and Chrysler dealers to sell their new car.

If dealers were a problem, so was the press, which didn't exactly give it the expected round of applause. Most looked upon it as, well, here's another new car . . . so. *Consumer Reports* was the most critical of all. CU really loathed the car. But there was a lot more to the 1958 Edsel than met the critical eye of the press. The two larger series, the Citation and the Corsair, had a colossal V-8 engine, a Lincoln-Mercury 430 cut down to 410 cid. The dashboard looked like the binnacle of a yacht. There was a huge, drum speedometer perched on top. A flashing light warned you when you reached any speed that you had pre-selected on your speedometer. There was even a tachometer for those who appreciated it.

One of the Edsel's best received features was the push-button automatic transmission, which proved to be a lot more dependable than Packard's Ultramatic. Even today, few Edsel owners will complain about it.

As for engines, the 118 inch wheelbase Ranger and Pacer shared the same overhead V-8, a hefty displacement of 361 inches, a slightly bored out version of the Ford 352. Horsepower was rated at 303. The Corsair and Citation had the big 410 rated at 345 hp. Both engines had 10.5 to 1 compression ratio.

The Edsel's reviewers complained about economy, about suspension, about steering, about cornering, etc., but few complained about power. There was absolutely no feeling of engine effort all the way up to 90. Engine and body noise were extremely low. By 1958 standards, the Edsel was a very well engineered, designed and produced car. A lot of them stayed on the road for a very long time.

In one last ditch effort, Ford restyled the car of 1959. The grille was much more conservative. The dash was very close to that of a 1959 Ford. In fact, the 1959 Edsel was so much like a 1959 Ford there really wasn't much reason for the Ford buyer to move up a notch, and few of them did.

Ford would have dropped the whole thing right then and there, but they were committed to a three-year plan. There would still be a third year Edsel, an all new bodied car, and looking more like a Ford than ever before. Ford politely pulled the Edsel off the stage early in the 1960 model year, after only 2846 of the 1960 units were built. Nothing more was heard of the Edsel until the Edsel Owner's Club was organized in 1968. Edsel Owners now boast some 3,000 members and hold meets from coast to coast, a few right under the eyes of Ford. The Edsel Owner's celebrated the 20th anniversary of E-Day.

Lincoln

Obtaining Rare Lincoln Took "Personal" Touch

Henry M. Leland was president and founder of the Lincoln Motor Car Co., a Detroit-based auto manufacturing firm. Lincoln was sold to Ford Motor Co. in 1922. Ten years later, Ford's prestige branch introduced the all-new 12-cylinder series "KB" on a 145 inch wheelbase chassis. A wide range of 22 body styles with factory or custom coachwork were seen that season.

The car featured in this article is the Model 12-244B Judkins two-passenger coupe and is part of San Sylmar, Calif. Merle Norman Classic Beauty Collection. This car sold for $5,100 when new and was purchased for the collection with $5,000 in cash. The previous owner was a man who lived in San Francisco who didn't write English or have a telephone. Tom Powels and J.B. Nethercutt looked him up personally to make the offer and bring the car into San Sylmar.

The magnificent 12-cylinder engine used in the Series "KB" was of L-head design with a V-type block configuration. Bore and stroke measurements of 3¼ x 4½ inches gave a piston displacement of 448 cid. This motor featured Stromberg carburetion, an Autolite ignition system and developed 150 bhp at 3400 rpm. Net horsepower using National Automobile Chamber of Commerce (N.A.C.C.) formulas was 50.7.

Production of Series KB models began on Jan. 1, 1932 and serial numbers KB1 through KB1666 were stamped on the cars. Styling features characteristic of the line were: V-type radiator, twin horns, front fender parking lights and a sloping windshield and pillar treatment. The five door ventilators in the hood and the radiator shutters were thermostatically controlled.

The feature car is finished in a medium tan color with moldings and window frames in medium brown. The padded leather top is dark brown, as are the steel wire wheel rims. Black enamel is used on the fenders and frame covers and the body moldings are striped in creamy white. Options and accessories include dual covered side-mount spare tires with rearview mirrors, white sidewall tires and a trunk rack. Factory tire size for the 1932 "KB" Series was 7.50 x 18 inches.

The car's 12-cylinder engine is linked to a three-speed Silent Synchromesh transmission. Free-wheeling, controlled by a dash lever, is standard equipment. Vacuum-boosted mechanical brakes are employed and double action hydraulic shock absorbers are used. Overall gear ratio is 4.58:1 and a 28-gallon fuel tank is mounted towards the rear of the chassis. The brake vacuum booster can be adjusted via a steering column lever to vary pressure.

The Lincoln "KB" models were not only pretty and prestigious, but also could perform on a par with such Classics as the Duesenberg J and the Cadillac V-16. Automotive historian Maurice Hendry (*Best of Old Cars Weekly*, Vol. 4; Page 267) determined top speed at 95 mph and found the Lincolns capable of reaching 30 mph in seven seconds; 60 mph in 20 seconds; and 80 mph in 35 seconds from a 10 mph rolling start. The powerful motor also had a couple of unusual features like a 65-degree block angle and an exhaust pipe that ran in front of and below the block.

Total production of just 23 Judkins-bodied coupes of this type was recorded for the 1932 model run. That makes this particular survivor an exceptional rarity in the world of historic automobiles.

Twin horns, wipers and taillamps are seen on this 1932 Lincoln Model "KB" Judkins two-passenger coupe. Large, nickel-plated headlamps are attached to the front fenders by a bright metal tie-bar. (Photo courtesy Merle Norman Classic Beauty Collection)

The Lincoln-Zephyr

A Sleek, Styling Leader

1938 Lincoln-Zephyr convertible sedan

By Robert C. Ackerson

It's really doubtful if the proverbial car designed by committee actually exists. Virtually without exception, automobiles, whether they're hand crafted beauties or down to earth four-door sedans produced by the millions, bear the influence of a key personality who, for better or worse, leaves his mark for others to pass judgment upon.

What really sets the great cars apart from the also-rans and the nondescripts is the genius of their designers. And although the Lincoln-Zephyr for years was overshadowed by the brilliance of the Lincoln Continental's appearance, it is today regarded by contemporary enthusiasts as one of the most important American automobiles of the late thirties; a tribute to the talent of its original designer, John Tjaarda and the good tast of Edsel Ford.

The environment surrounding the Lincoln-Zephyr's developement was dominated, at least initially, by the need of pragmatic businessmen at the Briggs body company and to a degree the Ford Motor Co., to shore up their operations against the onslaught of the Great Depression. John Tjaarda came to Briggs with an impressive resume. While working at Locke and Co. in Rochester, N.Y., he had designed numerous custom bodies for such stately chassis as Duesenberg, Packard and Pierce-Arrow. During his stay at General Motors styling, Tjaarda helped set the stage for GM's styling leadership. At Briggs his assignment to prepare designs primarily for Ford but upon occasion for other clients was overshadowed by one dominant reality: Briggs was suffering a serious business decline. In order to reverse this trend and at the same time mend relations with Ford where it was felt Briggs was "playing favorites" with Chrysler, a proposal for a new Ford product was prepared in considerable secrecy. There's no doubt that Tjaarda deserves center stage position as the talent behind the car which was to become the Lincoln-Zephyr. But at the same time it's well worth the effort to recognize the influence of Lancia's Lambda model of 1921 which had pioneered the adaptation of aircraft-type body construction principles for the automobile. A dozen years later such practice, while still the exception rather than the norm, had gained wide acceptance among designers of Tjaarda's stature. Similarly, it was a time when streamlining was coming into vogue. Both the Chrysler Airflow and the Raymond Loewy-designed Hupmobile of 1934 were production manifestations, but not until Tjaarda had finished his labors was there an American car that combined a pleasing appearance with, at least for the times, an aerodynamic form. Then there was the matter of engine location. Doctor Porsche's rear-engined Auto Union grand prix cars were on their way and with serious consideration being given to rear-engined production cars on both sides of the Atlantic, Tjaard'a "pusher car" prototype came as no surprise. However, the public's luke-warm attitude towards a rear-engined automobile (only 50% favored it in pre-production showing of the Tjaadra design) lead to its abandonment. The scientific integrity of Briggs' measurement of otherwise favorable reaction to Tjaadra's when it was shown in Chicago and New York in 1934 probably was not as sophisticated as modern consumer reaction techniques but there was no reason to doubt the public's approval of its appearance.

1936 Lincoln-Zephyr 2-dr sedan

1936 Lincoln-Zephyr two-door sedan interior

Years later, the New York Museum of Art added its official sanction to the public's verdict by recognizing the 1938 Lincoln-Zephyr as an automobile with "impeccable, studied elegance."

Not to anyone's real surprise, Edsel Ford reacted with enthusiasm to the Tjaarda styling prototype, and with a 1936 model year introduction goal progress on the Lincoln-Zephyr's development was rapid. Its introduction as a medium priced car was logical given the economic environment and while it never matched the sales of the 120 Packard, it contributed significantly to the preservation of Lincoln as a marque. It's also interesting to point out that the Lincoln-Zephyr was (with the exception of the Continental) to be the last new Lincoln until the debut of the 1949 models.

Initial plans for the Zephyr called for its use of Ford V-8 modified to produce 100 hp. However Edsel Ford, aware of the Zephyr's public image as a Lincoln product, assigned Frank Johnson, Lincoln's chief engineer, the task of designing a new V-12 engine. This powerplant proved as is common knowledge, to be the Zephyr's most controversial feature. In *Motor Trend* (July 1954), Tjaarda wrote that "because of basic limitations in the construction — manufacturing economy was essential, and it used some unsuitable Ford componets — the V-12 was never an outstanding engine." Other judgments, or perhaps indictments of the V-12 point to its poor crankcase ventilation, inadequate lubrication and the limited experience of Ford mechanics with the Zephyr engine. However, matched against these criticisms are the improvements Lincoln made to the V-12 in the years subsequent to its introduction and the popularity and great success of the V-12 engine in Europe where it powered many low-production sports and high performance automobiles.

Although the 1936 Zephyr was available in just two models (two and four door sedans, priced respectively at $1275 and $1320), sales were brisk, totalling 14,994. In contrast, sales of the K series Lincoln numbered only 1515. The natural adversaries of the Zephyr, the LaSalle and 120 Packard bracketed its production level with the Packard the runaway leader at 55,024 and the LaSalle considerably closer with an output of 13004. But neither of these cars really represented the solid step forward that did the Zephyr. The LaSalle was a beautifully styled

1940 Lincoln-Zephyr club coupe

away from the status quo need not be bizarre or ungainly.

Although the Zephyr would be equipped with mechanical brakes until 1939 (and a solid front axle with a transverse leaf spring for its entire production life), its road performance was excellent. Its 75°, V-12 engine with four main bearings, aluminum heads, alloy steel pistons and single, twin throat downdraft carburetor displaced 267.3 cubic inches and developed 110 hp at 3900 rpm. Its maximum torque output was 186 ft-lbs. In their test of the 1936 Lincoln-Zephyr both *The Autocar* and *The Motor* were impressed with the American V-12. *The Motor* depicted it as an automobile with "a fine performance" and *The Autocar* which reported a 16 second, zero to 60 mph time and a top speed of nearly 91 mph noted that "on the open road quite a mild opening of the throttle pedal sends the speedometer needle leaping toward the 70 mark with no actual impression of speed."

1939 Lincoln-Zephyr sedan

car and in that sense one of GM's most important automobiles. The Packard, while a tremendous sales success, was strictly conventional both in its appearance and engineering. In contrast to both cars the Zephyr was both innovative and original. Whatever its weaknesses, the availability of a V-12 engine in a medium priced war *was* news. The use of unit-body construction with its combination of strength and lightweight was a break with past tradition and not only was its appearance esthetically outstanding, but it also demonstrated that a dramatic move

Changes made in the 1937 Lincoln-Zephry were minimual. Externally the new model was identified by the five double vertical "bright days" of its grille which as before was painted the same color as the body. The side hood engine vents were now fitted with thin vertical bars matching those of the grille. Also contributing to the Zephyr's well-integrated front-end appearance was a reshaped bumper forming a graceful wide-angle V. Ford was quick to correct one major design flaw of the 1936 model, the poor accessibility to its trunk space. Since the

spare tire blocked the way, entrance to the luggage space of the 1936 vesion was through the rear seat. Not exactly what mid-America expected in a medium-priced automobile. The use of a spare tire bracket with a swivel mount the following year was a simple and efficient solution. Although the interiors of the first Zephyr was restrained and attractive, and thus hard to fault, Lincoln spent a good deal of time and effort revamping its appearance for 1937. The most interesting changes included the provision of two glove compartments, a center console containing the speedometer, clock, plus fuel level, oil pressure, engine temperature and ammeter gauges. Carried over from the 1936 was the chrome tubing surrounding the seatbacks.

Aided by two new models, a three-passenger coupe (which became the Zephyr leader at $1165) and a Town-Limousine fitted with a glass partition, production of the

1941 Lincoln-Zephyr sedan

Lincoln-Zephyr fell just short of 30,000 cars in 1937. LaSalle's output stood at 32,000 and the Packard One-Twenty's at 50,100.

In contrast to the conservative advertising of the K model linking Lincoln with an automotive age that was on the wane, the Zephyr vigorously promoted as a car that was pointing toward the future. It was, said Lincoln, ''a modern ship of the Land.'' And years before Porsche used a similar theme in the early '60s, Lincoln-Zephyr ads proclaimed that ''this car has four wheels, but there the

similarity between the Lincoln-Zephyr and others ends.'' Perhaps the definitive advertisement for the 1937 Zephyr illustrated the Burlington Zephyr streamliner train flashing by in the background as a Lincoln-Zephyr in rather elegant fashion motors by. The captions was simply, ''The newest things on wheels.''

In what might well be the best postwar example of how to make an attractive automobile even more so, the Lincoln-Zephyr was given reshaped rear fenders and new front end sheet metal for 1938. The result was nothing

short of stunning, particularly in the case of the three passenger coupe model. Every element of its appearance had that "just right" look, not a piece of chrome was out of place nor could a single flaw be found in the Lincoln's smooth body contours. Although none of them were of the same magnitude as the Zephyr's new styling, the 1938 models did feature several interesting mechanical changes. The most apparent, was a dash-mounted shift lever pointing to the Zephyr's adoption of a steering column positioned shifter in 1940. In addition, the V-12 was equipped with hydraulic valve lifters, a larger diameter steering wheel was fitted and the battery was positioned under the hood. In spite of these mechanical changes, the Zephyr's outstanding appearance and the addition of two new convertible coupe and sedan models, production slumped to 19,111 units as poor economic conditions reduced total industry sales.

With the Model K Lincoln headed for extinction and the Zephyr scheduled for new bodies in 1940, only small changes were made in its appearance for the 1939 model year, although the enclosure of the Zephyr's running boards was of historical interest. This was also the year that Ford Motor Co. belatedly made the switch over to hydraulic brakes.

Changes were considerably more substantial the following year: new bodies with more interior space, increased window area, a one piece rear window plus a larger trunk. None of these changes affected the Zephyr's basic appearance although the concurrent modernization of the Ford and Mercury models tended to dilute the impact of the Zephyr's new styling. More important than the adoption of a steering column gear shift arrangement was the V-12's larger 2⅞ inch bore which increased displacement to 292 cubic inches and raised horsepower output to 120. There was also some reshuffling of the Zephyr's model lineup. The convertible sedan and coupe-sedan versions were dropped (the latter's production had been just 3629 for 1938 and 1939 and a two-door club coupe was added.

The last two years of Lincoln prewar production did not take the Zephyr's philosophy to its final form, that was to occur in the 1946-48 model years. Yet, the 1941-42 models, while still attractive and, today, desirable automobiles, were no longer styling leaders. In just five years the relative design positions of Lincoln and Packard had been completely reversed. The 1941 Clipper was bringing the future into the here and now, the 1941 Zephyr was a best a dated design brought up to date. This disparity became even more apparent in 1942 as the Zephyr's larger fenders and two-tier front end seemed to belong to a different time span than the rest of the body. But these criticisms not withstanding, the Lincoln-Zephyr aside from its contribution to the economic recovery of the Briggs Company and its role in preserving Lincoln as one of America's great cars, was an automobile whose virtures far exceeded the limits of its short-comings. Total Lincoln-Zephyr production from 1936 through 1942 totalled 130,194, a respectable output by any standards. The Zephyr's role as a styling leader, its status as the progenitor of the Lincoln-Continental plus, (whatever flaws went along for the ride), its V-12 engine paved the way for its present (and growing) popularity among automobile hobbyists.

The author wishes to acknowledge the valuable assistance of Chad Coombs, editor-in-chief of *The Way of the Zephyr*, the official publication of The Lincoln Zephyr Owner's Club, 2107 Steinruck Road, Elizabethtown, PA 17022.

1942 Lincoln-Zephyr four-door sedan

Lincoln Continental History

by Joey Evans

1940 Lincoln Continental MKI Cabriolet

When Ford took over Lincoln in 1922, Edsel Ford became solely responsible for the car's destiny. Ralph Roberts, a founder of LeBaron, once said that he considered Edsel to be one of the most gifted automobile stylists of his time. He said that Edsel knew what he wanted and he could identify the elements of style which gave a coherent blend of solidarity, dignity and grace to any automotive project he touched. Famous industrial stylist Walter Dorwin Teague wrote of Edsel Ford in this manner: "I found in him an extreme sensitiveness united with an unself-conscious modesty that left no need for the kind of

compensations that publicity has to offer. By choice, he moved quietly behind the scenes where public eyes could not follow him. Thus the fact that among his many superb qualities he was also a great designer was known to few except those who had the privilege of collaborating with him in this field."

Edsel Ford died in 1943, at the very moment that his automobile design genius was beginning to be appreciated. And he left as his most memorable work the Lincoln Continental, a name that was only an afterthought, and a styling achievement that ranks among the greatest

works of 20th century industrial design. In the beginning, Edsel Ford was thinking of a continental-styled car for his own personal use, not necessarily of a Lincoln Continental. Ford's founding-father stylist, E.T. "Bob" Gregorie, has recalled that Edsel had a "one-of-a-kind" Ford built about once a year in the early '30s.

THE JENSEN FORDS

In 1934 Edsel had Gregorie design a sleek speedster which was carried out on a Ford chassis. Edsel considered having it put into limited production by the same people who built the Brewster-bodied town cars. But they weren't interested. Finally he shipped his second chassis to Jensen in England, where the 1935 Jensen-Ford was developed. If you study a Jensen carefully you will begin to see predictions of the Lincoln Continental. The low silhouette, long hood, low doors and sweeping fenders all give some hint of Edsel's thinking. But the Jensen-Ford was never very successful. Maybe that is why Edsel Ford looked even further into the future.

He travelled Europe widely, became keenly aware of continental design trends, attended the European auto shows and carefully took the pulse of the sports and luxury car buyer. In September 1938 he returned to Detroit with an idea for another special convertible coupe to be

name was ever considered. They used the name in such a generic sense that the Continental emblem did not appear until the 1941 model year, though the name was used in all the literature from the very beginning.

Evidently, Edsel did a number of preliminary sketches, but the first actual sketch was done by Gregorie using a yellow crayon on a 1/10 scale blueprint of the 1939 Lincoln Zephyr. Gregorie lowered and lengthened the entire car, making the hood extremely long, giving the car a distinct trunk and eliminating the runningboards. Stylists wanted to hide the spare tire in the trunk, but Edsel persisted that the car be "strictly continental," meaning the tire would be completely exposed, without even a metal or fabric tire cover. A 1/10 clay was then done in Gregorie's office. The clay has long since disappeared, but two photographs attest to the fact that it was done and dated October 1938. The clay was largely a rework of the Lincoln Zephyr with inserts in the front fenders and with a rear that was most unique, but the car would use the Zephyr floor pan, wheelhouses and basic body panels. A full-sized clay was never made in order to save time. The first prototype was built from a full-sized draft, which must have been no easy accomplishment.

THE FIRST CONTINENTAL

1940 Lincoln Continental coupe

built for his personal use, and possibly for limited production. Some sources say it was Gregorie who proposed the first Lincoln Continental. In truth, the two were so tuned to the latest European concepts and to each other's design tastes that only one car could have been developed. For a time they considered executing their ideas on a Ford chassis, or possibly as an extension of the new Mercury. However, it was finally decided that a Lincoln-Zephyr chassis would be the most appropriate, both for design and marketing reasons. Edsel was doubtless very much aware of the Darrin on the Packard 120 chassis and also of the Cadillac 60 Special. The name of the new Ford creation came as naturally as the svelte lines. When Ford and Gregorie talked about the continental cars they always referred to the word "Continental." No other

The actual car was made on a production Lincoln-Zephyr convertible 125-inch wheelbase chassis with all Zephyr running gear. There were no special mechanical modifications. Special body parts were hammered out over wooden forms, and there was extensive use of lead throughout. The car may have weighed 5,000 pounds, and must have been a rather poor performer with its 267 cid V-12 engine. Twelve inches was added to the hood and front fenders. A four-inch section was removed from the doors. The rear deck was possibly the car's most unusual feature. It was made as high as possible without interfering with the car's flowing lines, and was so much separated from the fenders that it had almost a boattailed appearance.

The car employed a standard '39 Zephyr instrument

higher than on the first car and standard Lincoln-Zephyr door handles were used. On this car the gearshift was placed in the steering column in order to test the 1940 steering linkage. The first car was scrapped during 1939. The second was purchased by Gregorie in late September 1939. Eventually this second car went to California where it miraculously escaped destruction, though not the ravages of time. It was discovered by collectors about 20 years ago, and is in the hands of a collector to this day. It is doubtful that a third 1939 prototype was ever built. If, indeed, Benson and Henry II were given cars they must have been very early 1940 models.

1940 MODELS

While the second 1939 prototype was being constructed a decision was made to put the Continental into limited production for the 1940 model year. To make the body parts special low cost dies were set up, wood covered with metal. The windshield frame was an aluminum casting. Front fenders and hood were stamped on Zephyr dies, but an insert was designed which could be added to those dies to extend the Continental panels seven inches. In spite of all the shortcuts, the Continental remained as much a custom car as a production car, and the amount of lead used was of necessity quite excessive. Factory officials always opposed the car because it was so cost-inefficient to produce. As long as Edsel lived the project went ahead anyway. But after his death the opposition continued to be voiced until the car was finally taken out of production.

The first production Continental, Series H-86268, was assembled and photographed on Oct. 3, 1939 and shipped to Chester, Pa. on Oct. 6. Its factory price was $2,840. It had the standard 1940 Lincoln Zephyr V-12 which had 292 cubic inch displacement and developed 120 hp at 3,900 rpm. This first car is unaccounted for today, but several more must have been assembled very quickly as a Continental cabriolet was exhibited in New York, Oct. 15-22. Several more made their appearances about this time, and by the end of 1939, 25 Continentals had been built, all designated 1940 models. Official production began in Dec. 13, 1939 and ceased on July 10, 1940. The two oldest known 1940 Continentals are now both in Harrah's Automobile Collection. In all, 350 cabriolets and 54 coupes were built for the model year, and the survival rate is amazing. Approximately 230 are known to survive, though many are basket cases to this day.

The coupe warrants special note. The first Continental coupe was completed April 3, 1940. It was a pilot model that was extensively photographed and shortly salvaged. The differences between the cabriolet and the coupe were relatively minor. The doors on the coupe employ channel window framing, probably more for cost reasons than for styling effect. The coupe is in essence a hardtop, although a center post is employed for rigidity. This was not the first car with channel window frames. This feature was used on the Cadillac 60 Special beginning with the introductory model in 1938 and on the 1939 Mercury club coupe. On both the Mercury and the Lincoln Continental it foretold of hardtop styling which General Motors popularized in 1949.

1940 Continentals are especially interesting as almost no two are exactly alike in detail. During the 1940 model year numerous changes were made. Some of these were the later additions of license light assembly, bottom moldings, tire cover, gravel guards and rear splash shields. Any 1940 Continental today is a valuable find. But every caution should be taken for authentication. These cars were so cobbled down through the years that frequently many authentic and hard to find items have been replaced by unauthentic pieces which would be detected only by an expert.

1941 Lincoln Custom limousine

cluster, but without the floor console. The steering wheel was probably from the '39 Mercury which was at the time perceived as being more modern than the Zephyr steering wheel. Save the ball and spear hood ornament, and door handles, there were virtually no trim parts to the car. It was built strictly from stock "off-the-shelf" Ford and Lincoln Zephyr parts, recalls retired Ford stylist Bob Thomas, who was there at the time.

The serial number was H-74750, and the car was completed in late February 1939 after Edsel had left for his winter vacation in Florida. The car was finished in eagle gray with gray leather trim, and as soon as it was finished it was shipped to Edsel in Hobe Sound, Fla. From this point on the car is surrounded as much in legend as in fact. There can be no doubt that the car stirred up an immediate sensation wherever it was seen, but it was not without its problems.

Edsel even phoned Gregorie saying that he was pleased with the car but it leaked like a sieve. It is claimed that Edsel returned from Florida with 200 orders. If so, copies of these orders have never been found. It is further claimed that Edsel immediately requested the construction of two more 1939 prototypes, one for his son Benson and the other for his son Henry Ford II. This second and third prototype theory has been the subject of much collector debate for years. Factory records, especially photographs, indicate that only a second prototype was built. It was painted in black, was completed in June, and bore the serial number H-82410. This car was somewhat different from the first in that only eight inches were added to the hood and front fenders. This allowed the doors to be moved further forward so that both front and rear seating room could be increased. The trunk was raised even

Refined Luxury in the 1953 Lincoln

by Gerald Perschbacher

When the 1953 new car market opened and American buyers went shopping to see the produce of the domestic automakers, Cadillac was on the top shelf of horsepower, with its V-8 rated at 210, but Lincoln was second with its V-8 cranking out 205 horsepower.

In the areas of maneuverability and handling, Chrysler Corp.'s Chrysler and DeSoto were rated favorably, but the Lincoln was in its own box right alongside. Again, it was near the top.

Among the pick-of-the-bunch luxury cars, the '53 Lincoln weighed in at 4,062 pounds. It was at least 200 to 400 pounds lighter than the Cadillac, about 400 pounds lighter than the Chrysler and Custom Imperial and almost a match for the Buick Roadmaster. Only one direct competitor — the Packard — was about 100 pounds lighter than the freshly picked Lincoln.

Since coupons were hard to come by when the buyer went shopping in that automobile market, price played a part in deciding which tomatoes to squeeze. Lincoln for '53 ranged from $3,522 to $4,031, about $300 higher than Packard, nearly $500 more than the highest-priced Buick Roadmaster, but reasonably similar to Cadillac 62 and the Chrysler New Yorker.

The 1953 Lincoln may not have been the most powerful car in its day and was neither the safest or most luxurious. But it was a head taller than the previous year's Lincoln crop in refinements and luxury.

The factory farmers in the Lincoln field were proud of their new produce, calling it "the touch of casual magnificence, designed for the world you move in." That idea would also apply to those dreamers who wished they moved in better worlds.

Automobile writers liked the flavorful Lincoln, but they seldom raved. Consensus marked this new crop as a ripe and tasty staple for any well-to-do garage. The car came on a 123-inch wheelbase with overall length just a straw over 214 inches. A Cosmopolitan sprang up from the factory some 6,562 strong for the two-door hardtop sport coupe and 7,560 strong for the four-door sedan. The Capri jumped into the marketplace with three models: the two-door hardtop coupe with 12,916 produced; the four-door sedan with 11,352 made; and the two-door convertible with only 2,372 placed in the market.

The Cosmopolitan was a good buy. It was about $300 cheaper, but all the stock characteristics were the same. Special touches in the trim and appointments set the two series apart, but only the experienced shopper could notice the difference.

The Lincoln for '53 sprouted a garden full of gizmos for the lazy man. Power steering often headed the list, with power braking, electric windows, and power front seat adjustment lining up behind. A bundle of goodies like that could be yours for about $420, but most buyers back then seldom dickered or complained. For them, a Lincoln was usually a step up and visual proof of financial security. To worry too much about price was below most Lincoln owners!

Twelve different colors of paint were available to Lincoln buyers. Castle tan, embassy brown metallic, colonial blue, majestic maroon metallic, crown blue metallic, Oxford gray metallic, empire green metallic and palace gray and cinebar red were carried over from 1952. In addition, vassar yellow and Coventry green gray — Mercury colors with different names — were offered.

The 1953 Lincoln may not have been the best Lincoln. But from the 1946 through 1955 sales season, the '53 ranked second in overall production, behind the 1949 crop. With its refinements firmly establishing it in the luxury market, and cooking strong on a big V-8, the '53 Lincoln did its owners proud.

The 1953 Lincoln Cosmopolitan hardtop carried a factory price of $3,322 and upheld the Lincoln tradition of quality and luxury.

Continental Mk II History

by Joey Evans

Ever since the classic Lincoln Continental was discontinued in 1948, dealer requests mounted for reintroduction of the model. At one point, a Continental was considered based on the 1949 Lincoln Cosmopolitan Series. Designer Bob Thomas recalls that it actually got as far as the clay stage. But management felt that the rounded lines of 1949-1951 era Lincolns did not lend themselves to classic Continental styling. Moreover, continuance of a car worthy of the name "Lincoln Continental" was not a top priority at the Ford Motor Co. during its period of postwar rebirth.

For 1952, the Lincoln-Mercury Division decided to position its new obv Lincoln Capri not against Cadillac but against the Oldsmobile 98. This new marketing strategy was implemented during the 1953-'54 era with cars that were second to none in the field of performance. But they were somewhat lacking in true luxury car appeal. Still, the image of a Lincoln Continental never vanished from the minds of the designers, management and, most important, the Ford family. For it meant the ultimate in prestige at the very top of the Ford line. Early in 1952, Henry Ford II, now chairman of the board, appointed the Davis Committee to look into costs and concepts for a new ultra-luxury car plus a second upper-middle class car to put Ford in a better competitive position against GM. The recommendations of the Davis Committee ultimately resulted in

1956 Lincoln Continental Mark II coupe.

1940 Lincoln Continental Mark I convertible.

the introduction of the 1956 Lincoln Continental Mark II and the 1958 Edsel, two projects which were ultimately doomed. And both projects demonstrated some of the best engineering and design thinking of the decade. The cars were right; the market was wrong.

The Davis Committee initially targeted the price of the Continental at approximately $8,000, realizing that the volume might be so limited that the company might not even break even. (By the time the car was introduced, the price tag was nearly $10,000, and the company lost approximately $1,000 a unit.) But the Davis Committee strongly recommended approval if only for the institutional and advertising value of a Lincoln Continental comeback. Keep in mind the competitive situation at the time. Cadillac was preparing its 1953 Eldorado convertible. Packard was planning its Caribbean. Even the more moderately priced makes, Buick and Oldsmobile, were ready to launch the Fiesta and Skylark convertibles in the $5,000 range. And Chrysler had its Imperials in the luxury sedan and limousine field. To cap it all off, Rolls-Royce was becoming an increasing factor in this country. What did Lincoln have to offer? By late 1952, a musclecar that was winning the Mexican Road Race hands down, but nothing built to win a place in the luxury car arena. A Lincoln Continental had to be built, if only for psychological reasons.

WILLIAM CLAY FORD HEADED THE PROJECT.

In July 1952 a Special Projects Office was created with William Clay Ford as manager. He was the youngest of Edsel's three sons and was anxious for the opportunity to separate himself from his older brothers. William Clay Ford was ably assisted in this project by John Reinhart, designer; Harley Copp, chief engineer; and Gordon Buehrig, body engineer.

The original 1940-1948 Continental was little more than a modified Lincoln incorporating an enormous amount of custom body work. The mechanical quality was no better or worse than that of the Lincoln V-12. Fit and finish, while good for a semi-custom car, was lacking in overall quality control. The car won its reputation on looks, not on overall excellence. Any new Continental would have to measure up to the truly great classics of the '30s in every respect and give the appearance of a lineal descendant of the original Continental. Recreation of a classic in contemporary form was no easy assignment. William Clay Ford had a far greater task before him than his father had 14 years earlier.

The Special Products Division (in 1955) gave birth to the Lincoln Continental Division, which was completely separate from the Lincoln-Mercury Division. It was not even allowed to draw stylists from other Divisions. Bob Thomas and Ray Smith came over from American Motors. Others were from the old Ford Trade School. All played important roles in both overall design and details. Working under John Reinhart, they started out by drawing what they thought might have been Lincoln Continentals had

the model been continued from 1949 right up through 1952. By December 1952, the Executive Committee was invited in for an initial preview. Reportedly, Henry Ford II remarked, ''I wouldn't give a dime for that.'' So it was back to the drawing boards.

REINHART'S ''MODERN FORMAL'' DESIGN WINS.

At this point the project took an interesting turn into history. Had Henry Ford II been more favorably impressed with the original efforts, the Mark II might have emerged looking very much like the Mark I in mid-'50s dress. But William Clay Ford and John Reinhart decided to call in four outside designers to get a variety of ideas. They called upon Walter Buell Ford, V. Gardner, the team of R. Miller and A. Grisinger, and, finally, George Walker. The five design teams worked throughout the winter, and in April 1953 a second design presentation was made. Basic design direction was broken into two categories. ''Modern Informal,'' tending more towards a very contemporary mid-'50s look, and ''Modern Formal,'' tending more towards a simple timeless design.

Walter Buell Ford went Modern Informal, to such an extreme that his designs could now be interpreted as cars of the late '60s. Gardner played it safe with true 1941-1948 era Continental coupes all done up in a mid-'50s mode. Miller and Grisinger went mid-'50s modern, ala Loewy and Darrin. George Walker hedged his bets going from mid-'50s modern to '40s Continental done in '50s dressing. Reinhart and the Special Projects group came up with something rather unique, perhaps influenced by Henry Ford II's initial reaction. Their design was neither a direct lift from the original Continental or a mid-Fifties chromed bomber. It was a car of freshly original line and form in a true modern classic mode. And it incorporated a long hood and spare tire hump on the trunk. Two features which spoke softly of the Continental's past distinction.

All designs were done in line drawings showing three views, and none was signed. Members of the executive committee, one at a time, viewed the renderings, and were not given the slightest clue as to who were the creators. The result was that Reinhart's Design #9 won hands down, and thus the Continental Mark II was conceived as a truly unique descendant of the original.

The project now moved into high gear. A three-eighths clay was already in progress. There was no time for a full-size clay until later, so the three-eighths model was shown to the Executive Committee in 3-D, ala the latest Hollywood movies. The project moved forward in absolute secrecy until a meeting of the Lincoln Continental Owners Club on Oct. 16, 1954.

There, William Clay Ford made a public announcement that as part of the 1955 Ford Motor Co. offering there would be a ''high quality, low volume, prestige automobile to be known as the Lincoln Continental.'' Thereafter, the Mark II received a wide amount of publicity building up to the car's formal introduction at the Paris Auto Show, Oct. 6, 1955.

Considering just the publicity alone generated around this car, both before and after introduction, the Ford Motor Company received untold millions in free advertising. This certainly must have greatly aided overall sales during the 1956 and 1957 banner years. While the Continental turned out to be a losing project, it did, indeed, give the Ford Motor Company the prestige they were seeking at that time.

UNIQUE FRAME, STANDARD ENGINE.

Because the overall height could not exceed 58 inches, a new type of frame was developed to cradle the passengers between the frame side rails. This was a then very unique combination ''Y'' and ladder type frame of incredible strength and rigidity. This type of frame was later brought back in the mid-Sixties on Ford and Mercury, and was then the much touted ''perimeter frame.'' One

unusual engineering feature was a rather complicated driveshaft incorporating three universal joints fed into a Hotchkiss rear end. The purpose was to achieve the lowest possible tunnel height. Beyond this, the running gear was pretty much stock 1956 Lincoln. But engine and transmission components were machined to the highest tolerances. All engines received a dynamometer test, then were partially disassembled for inspection. Transmissions were road tested in another vehicle before installation. Nuts and bolts were torqued to aircraft standards. The chassis was dynamometer tested and tuned. Wheel alignment was held to super-fine tolerances. Wheels, tires and drums were all balanced. Chrome plating was three times as durable as SAE standards. The Continental people were not trying to build something ultra unique, like the Tucker, but simply the highest quality American car it was possible to build using the best technology of the period. And appearances did not tell you the entire story. If you simply looked under the hood, the only differences from the stock Lincoln appeared to be chromed valve covers and air cleaner.

The painting process will give you a clue to the overall standards. First, sheet metal body panels and supporting structure were assembled on the chassis and adjusted to fit within very narrow tolerances. Then the panels were removed and tagged to their frame. At this point the frame went along one line to have its running gear installed, while the body panels went through a custom painting process. No dipping, no spray booths, no mass-production methods.

A painter stood in the open and sprayed on two coats of primer, after which the paint was water-sanded by hand and then baked. Then came two coats of surfacer followed by hand-sand and bake. Then two coats of lacquer, followed by hand oil-sanding and baking. Then two more coats of color followed by hand-rubbing and hand polishing.

From here the body went to the trim line where it was fitted with broadcloths as rich as the finest fur felts, or the highest quality brocades and nylons, or Matelasse, or leathers from Bridge of Weir, Scotland. Here, too, the instruments were installed in a dash panel which was an integral part of the body superstructure. The instruments were of the highest precision calibre, including even a tachometer. They were so jewel-like in their look and performane that they were indeed worthy of a Tiffany label. Heat and vent controls had already been installed in a special panel below the radio and above the transmission hump. These were lever-type aircraft-like controls. They added much to the overall look of the cockpit, but were no more practical than any of their era. Interestingly enough, air conditioning was just about the only option available on the Mark II. Otherwise, the car was sold completely equipped without the usual inexhaustible list of options. A credit to the Mark II's product planners.

After painting, installation of interior and trim, the body and chassis were reunited, given several more quality control inspections, and finally the car was extensively road tested. The Continental plant had its own half mile test track. Part of this track was fitted with railroad ties so the car could be thoroughly racked. The test driver was even required to make certain adjustments himself. Then there was one more series of inspections. And lastly, each car was buttoned up in a tailored car cover with a felt fleece inner lining. For further protection during shipment, the car (under its cover) was finally covered by a plastic bag. No further dealer inspection or preparation was required. The dealer simply took the handsome radial wheel covers out of the trunk and mounted them on the wheels. The new Mark was now ready for the road.

DRIVING THE MARK II.

A well restored or carefully maintained original Mark II is

a pleasure to drive, utterly quiet, solid as a bank vault, and surprisingly good handling even on mountain roads. Floyd Clymer conducted a test drive of the Mark II for *Popular Mechanics* in 1956. He drove 817 miles, over mountains, across desert, and under a variety of California road conditions. Clymer noted that the car combined the solid quality of cars of the '20s with a semi-sports car feel very much like the Thunderbird, only better. Clymer and others who tested the Mark II were impressed with the comfort on long trips, the comfortable driver positioning behind the wheel, and the sure, responsive steering. No test driver ever boasted about the performance, although most found it adequate to the task. Clymer got a speedometer reading of 118 mph on a dry lake bed.

The Mark II was a car of many compliments and few complaints. Owners were extensively surveyed by *Popular Mechanics* and most were highly enthusiastic about the car. However, one Arkansas executive did sum up the negative viewpoint with these words: "I hardly think anyone would buy this car except for prestige. It's hard to get into. Uncomfortable in the back seat. No particular speed. Everything very average except price."

The cold fact was that the Continental was very high priced compared to the Premiere which offered many of the same qualities at less than half the price in the hardtop version. And for $5,000 one could purchase a fully equipped Premiere convertible. The Lincolns had virtually the same running gear as the Mark IIs, though not quite so carefully machined and tested. The Lincolns had very much the same riding and handling qualities as the Mark IIs. Even though they were built by a separate Division, their quality appears to have benefitted very much from the Mark II project. There were a number of complaints with early 1956 Lincolns, but later on in the year the quality was superb. The 1957 model was even better. At 285 hp the 1956 engine was admittedly somewhat underpowered for both the Lincoln and the Mark II. For 1957, the horsepower was up to 300 for both cars for a noticeable improvement in performance. There were other minor improvements, including an improved Turbo-Drive transmission.

The question that remains is — why would a buyer choose a Mark II over a Premiere? Production figures show that many did not. The Lincoln-Mercury Division produced 50,322 Premieres and Capris for the 1956 model year, a record to that date. Production was down to 41,123 for the 1957 model year. Compare this to the official figures that the Ford Motor Co. has given for the Continental Mark II. 1,251 units produced during the closing months of 1955, 1,307 for 1956, and only 442 for 1957. Total production was only 3,000! In the beginning the car was not considered to have any model year. Some years later the company declared that all cars built beginning Oct. 1, 1956, would be considered 1957 models.

WHY DID THE MARK II FAIL?

The car was built to endure; the marketing plan was not. The car had timeless styling and restrained use of trim that have made it much admired in later years. Yet these were not qualities which evidently appealed to large numbers of affluent buyers in 1956. The car had many innovative features that buyers perhaps did not see. Consider, for instance, the unique wraparound windshield design. It incorporated an ultra-thin pillar not possible with conventional construction. This pillar was located entirely inboard of the windshield glass, and was sealed and retained by a new method. It was far superior to the traditional wraparound windshield that was the trend at the time, and it allowed the driver to be positioned close to the controls without shortening the classic Continental hood. But how many potential buyers really noticed such subtle features as this and many more?

Yes, quite a number of notable people purchased Mark IIs, Frank Sinatra for one. But an equal number chose instead the Premiere and laughed all the way to the bank. Walt Disney chose a bright lavender hardtop, and openly boasted to associates that it was a lot smarter buy than the Mark II.

At first Mark II sales took off quite briskly, then suddenly nosedived. Some will contend that the dealer setup may have had something to do with it. It was very costly for Lincoln-Mercury dealers to qualify to sell the Mark. Of some 1,300 dealers only about 650 agreed to take on the car, and then many of them sold only one or two. There were also many stories about dealers who sold units at full price or over full price while others discounted the car a thousand dollars or more. Everyone can give you inside reasons why the Mark II failed, but in the final analysis nobody is really sure.

The price certainly was a factor. A $10,000 price tag was just a bit ridiculous in those pre-inflated years. And Lincoln was not alone in offering a car priced right out of sight. Cadillac's Eldorado Brougham, introduced late in 1956 to compete with the Mark II, was even less successful. it seemed that the four-passenger Thunderbird (1958-1960) was a lot closer in price to what the target market really wanted. It also has been said that Detroit could not deliver the quality it promised simply due to the nature of the American labor market. In the end, the Mark II was discontinued in May 1957 and its plant was converted over for production of the 1958 Edsel.

Years later, Gordon Buehrig gave this observation which was printed in *Continental Comments*, the national magazine of the Lincoln Continental Owners Club. He said, "A car which had so much going for it had to have something going against it to fail. It is obvious if the Continental Mark II were to be the best car in the world then it would have to be put together better than any other. It would have to be put together with the same dedication to perfection that was so evident in the design and engineering. In the American labor market it is impossible to find such craftsmen."

THE MARK II TODAY.

Best estimates put Mark II survival rate at around 2,000 cars. A 97-100 point Mark II now is about a $15,000 car, which means it has indeed depreciated since it was built. You can buy a very good one in the $10,000 range. The supply is plentiful; the market is not particularly strong. The Mark II represents one of the best investments in getting a lot of car for considerably under the price of a Classic. However, the resale market at this time is uncertain, so the Mark II is not the best car from a purely speculative standpoint.

There are virtually no specially built models. The car was offered only in a two-door hardtop model. A convertible was seriously considered, but only one was built with factory authorization.

There was, however, such a wide choice of colors and upholstery patterns and combinations that virtually no two Mark IIs are exactly alike. Moreover, the cars were so highly priced when new that they became collectors' items almost overnight, and there are still quite a number of them around with low mileage. There is one final factor which may have a tremendous impact on the Mark II in years to come. Since the last Mark II rolled off the line Lincoln has built one collectible car after another. The increasing interest in all Lincoln Continental Marks assures collectibility of all of them for many years to come. And certainly the elegant Mark II has to be right at the head of the pack. The Ford Motor Co. never built a more costly production car and probably never will.

Lincoln From 1958 To 1960 Remembered

by Gary Schwertley

The late 1950s saw some of Detroit's wildest efforts in the area of styling and also that of salesmanship. Lincoln was no exception to this trend, and the car planned for and introduced in 1958 turned out to be a most interesting and unusual automobile. Since Lincoln-Mercury had spent a huge sum tooling up for the '58s, they became committed to a continuing series. In this way, the '59 and '60 Lincolns followed in the path of the '58s.

Every recent book written about post-World War II Lincolns mentions these cars to some limited extent, but mostly with regard to their styling excesses (which alone make these cars interesting in their own right). The other point the books underscore is that of a poor sales record. Facts not mentioned in the books, however, would relate to some astounding engineering boo-boos and interesting mechanical puzzles. This area of engineering and production shortcomings made these cars a nightmare for service managers and mechanics as well as salesmen. It should be noted, however, that 1958 was a company-wide bad year. There is perhaps some cosmic connection between this fact and the vexation that hounded this series of Lincolns and Continentals.

'58-'60 Lincoln enthusiasts, few though they may be, should not take this article as a latter-day mud sling. This author writes of them only as a result of lingering interest and fascination in these Lincolns.

In the '58-'60 period, Lincoln continued to have a separate line for Lincoln and Continental. While the two models were different in some cosmetic ways, mechanically and basic design-wise they were essentially the same. Gone was the distinct apparent difference as between the Continental Mark II's and the '56-'57 Lincolns. The salient feature on the Continental lacking on the Lincoln is of course the inverted rear glass with the lowering feature. With the Continentals of this series there is the first installment of the twice-used Mark III, IV, and V designations.

For Lincoln, 1958 was a year of innovation. This was their first production stab at "Uniframe Body" construction since the Lincoln-Zephyr. A tag affixed to the cars of this series near the driver's door scuffplate announced the Uni-frame Body's attributes as "comfort, security and durability."

Another innovation was rear coil spring suspension.

1959 Lincoln Continental Town Car

When this "new" idea was applied to '58 Lincolns, the early models in some cases gave their owners something to talk about at the club. The rear trailing arms were weak; the driver would take off from a stop and the trailing arms would come unglued. The rear axle assembly would pivot down, coming off the springs. At the same time, the brake lines would snap, and you would have no brakes. This loss of brakes was of little consequence, however, since in the meantime the driveshaft had gotten yanked out of the transmission. The driveshaft did not fall into the street, however. There was an add-on metal plate right behind the transmission to decrease body and drive-line

1958 Lincoln Premiere 2-dr hardtop

vibrations. It was one of a number of post-production stopgaps that vainly attempted to reduce vibration. It did serve some useful purpose, though, in that it kept the driveshaft more or less in the car when the rear suspension disaster occurred. The '59 models had some of these rear end problems, but to a much lesser extent. In 1960, Lincoln went back to leaf springs in the rear — they had had enough of coils in the back for the time being.

One innovation of the time was the crankshaft-driven power steering pump introduced in 1958. This was a very good design as it turns out, and was used on Lincolns up to 1969. Unfortunately, it was not fully utilized as installed on the '58-'60 Lincoln series. Later, starting in 1961, the same pump was used to drive hydraulic windshield wipers. For '58-'60, the Lincolns were stuck with vacuum wipers — but with a huge vacuum motor! The hydraulic wipers used after 1960 were quite good; you could hardly stop them without breaking a wiper arm. These had their drawback, however, like everything else. Every once in a while one of these hydraulic hoses would break — the variable for the owner was where you happened to be driving when it broke.

1959 Lincoln Continental Mark IV convertible

'58 and '59 Lincolns had an instrument cluster that put practically all the instruments and controls behind one huge plastic "lens." From day one, practically not a single car of this type could be found without a big crack running down the center of it. An NOS lens for '58-'59 Lincolns was recently advertised for sale. At first glance, this would appear to have been an opportunity not to be missed. Such a part in unbroken form is surely a find at this point. On second thought, however, one would almost be a fool to buy this part and install it, only to have it also become cracked like the lens it would replace. It could be displayed on the wall, perhaps, something like a trophy — the last intact example remaining.

Although in 1957 Lincoln used a robot top mechanism on convertible models, 1958 was the first year a nearly fully retractable top design was utilized. On the '58-'60 Continentals, the back panel ahead of the deck lid opened when the top was lowered. In the down position, the top folded neatly into a compartment and the back panel covered it up. I have described the top as "nearly fully retractable" only because a small portion of each side

roof rail was still exposed when the top was completely lowered. Lincoln engineers had thought of this contingency, however, and provided two fiberglass covers to hide even these small areas. These covers came in the luggage compartment from the factory and were neatly stored in their own baggie. Trouble with them was that through use, the locks would get weak and they would blow off while the car was in motion. More common, though, was that the owner would install them wrong and the locks would not be engaged, with the same fiberglass-shattering results. To this day, even when you do see one of these cars, it usually will not have the glass covers present. Indeed, some '58-'60 Continental convertible buffs are not aware of them, never having seen a car in later years with them.

These tops as used on the '58-'60 Continental convertibles were complicated, but not nearly so troublesome as the ones used later on the '61-'67 models. The back glass on these even rolled down the same as it did on the steel-topped Continentals of the same years; in fact, the first part of the top-lowering cycle was of necessity the lower-

ing of this glass. What strikes me as strange about the design of these tops are those two large blisters in the back panel and those portions of the top side rails that the fiberglass covers hide. The covers themselves form part of this blister when the top is down. Of course, the top would not work without these blisters. It is as if the engineers designed the top, then tried to fit the robot back panel and found that the whole works wouldn't fit with the top down. It troubles me that those blisters just aren't congruent with the rest of the body design.

An all-new engine was used in the '58 Lincolns and Continentals — the 430 cubic inch. Although through further development in subsequent years the engine proved to be quite a good one, in its introductory year it proved troublesome. For one thing, it became quite evident early on that L-M had used too "hot" of an engine for a large luxury vehicle driven for the most part by older car buyers. Engine detonation quickly became an owner complaint and Lincoln-Mercury launched a campaign to detune and lower the compression of these engines. The campaign entailed numerous fixes, and not all applied to every vehicle. The build date of a given unit was the deciding factor in what modification was applied, as the engines had undergone design changes as they were originally being produced. Campaign modifications included: regrinding the valve seats in the cylinder heads from 30° to 45°; changing valves; doubling head gaskets to reduce compression; changing valve springs; adding valve spring shims; changing carburetors. It should be noted that these problems were not limited to the 430 engines, but also plagued the other Ford engines in this family such as the Mercury 383 and the Edsel 410.

Further along the lines of innovation, L-M engineers came up with a dual purpose oil pump. One half pumped oil and the other half provided vacuum for the wipers and various accessories. It seems the vacuum side of the pump had a welch plug in it that sometimes would fall out and into the oil pan. The first '58s that were encountered with this problem drove the service people nuts. The vacuum pump without this plug would make a knocking sound in the engine that was initially quiet.

Nowadays, these dual-purpose oil/vacuum pumps are nearly impossible to find. Some years back, a '59 Continental being overhauled at a dealer in Long Beach, CA nearly became a permanent fixture of the service department there. Luckily, "Ernie's Barge," as it was affectionately (part of the time) called, was an employee's car and the owner was not in too big of a hurry. It was finally decided to install a later 430 conventional oil pump and a rather large vacuum reserve tank.

One spectacular design coming out of 1958 for Lincoln was the 430 "Super Marauder" engine, optionally planned for Mercury as well. This idea might have gotten past the drawing board, but not much further than the parts book. Evidently not much more than prototypes were made after the engineering and sales debacle of 1958 hit Ford like a ton of bricks early in the production year. This was a hotter version of the Lincoln 430, with two huge, thirsty four barrels perched on top of the manifold, both covered by an impressive chrome air cleaner. I suppose if someone had one of these today it would be worth something as a curiosity.

By 1960, Lincoln has rectified most of the ills of the '58s. The '60 Lincolns, especially, even looked fairly good. The Lincoln rear roof area had been redesigned and given a less flamboyant look. The body was squared off some and looked solid and less conventional. The '60s still had the basic huge, boxy look, though, and Continental stuck with the inverted, roll-down back window for one more year.

Under the skin, though, the '60s were fine cars. There was a Lincoln-Mercury factory program to monitor a few selected cars for quality control. These cars were identified by a brass tag with a number on it, located near the vehicle ID plate. The factory kept very close track of these "brass tag" cars and records were maintained of every service function performed on them. It has also been said that these brass tag units were used in some cases as test beds for '61 components. Failed component assemblies for these units were tagged, identified with brass tag unit number, and shipped to the factory for analysis. The brass tags were marked, as an example, "WIXOM 2115." Wixom, MI, of couse, being the factory where all the '58-'60 Lincolns were built.

Some other improvements made on the '60 Lincolns besides the change in coachwork and the rear suspension was the redesign of the instrument panel and simplified carburetion (changed to a Carter ABD two barrel, which was also used on the later '61 and '62 models). Unfortunately, the '60s still retained the centrally-mounted Ranco valve for the heaters with long sensor tubes snaking over to each air duct in the cowl. Maintenance-wise, a few problems were retained due to the basic body shell design. A good example is the procedure for changing the starter, which required unbolting the engine mounts and jacking the engine up a few inches before you could even begin with the starter itself.

Even with the good outweighing the bad in 1960, the cars were written off by the factory from a sales standpoint. The '60 Lincolns were merely marking time for Lincoln-Mercury until the '61 models could be marketed. 1960 Lincoln production is quite low, with less than 25,000 being built that model year. It is interesting to note the wide array of body styles, paint and soft trim options available to buyers of 1960 Lincolns and Continentals, particularly in view of the limited numbers built. By contrast, the '61 and later "flat-sided" Lincoln Continentals were offered in rather limited lines of body and trim options.

What with the initial bad sale figures, subsequently lower production, oftentimes shorter than expected life in service and late recognition as collectibles, many styles of these '58-'60 Lincolns are quite rare today. A good example here is the 1960 Continental convertible. Since fewer than 1,500 were built originally, these are a very rare automobile today.

Continentals of the Early Sixties Carry Timeless, Tasteful Appearance

By Don Narus

"Classic beauty in a smart new size." "This is the luxury motorcar that stands apart from all other cars." "The car that cannot be outdated." Such pardonable puffery can apply to only one car of the '60s: Lincoln's elegant series of Continentals produced from 1961 through 1965. During those years this timeless design forged a new direction for American luxury car styling and was awarded the bronze medal of the Industrial Design Institute while reviving Lincoln prestige, and, not incidentally, their sales penetration of the luxury market.

These svelte cars hit the market in November 1960 like a splash of ice-cold water in the public's face. After three years of attempting to sell gaudy, overstated, super-sculptured, overgrown behemoths, the 1961 Continental design provided a renaissance in Lincoln styling, distinguished by restraint, simplicity, and quiet elegance from headlight to taillight. Some confusion exists on exactly who was responsible for the styling coup, and it is variously attributed to Elwood Engel, George Walker and Eugene Bordinat. But credits aside, it was a triumph of design.

In another turnabout, the Continental was offered in

The unique 1961 Lincoln Continental four-door convertible.

just two models, the four-door sedan and the remarkable four-door convertible. Eleven models were offered in 1960.

Compared to its luxury contemporaries, the 1961 Continental was a compact car. Built on a 123 inch wheelbase and powered by a 430 cid engine, it offered buyers agility and luxury in one smart package.

To carry through its return to classic elegance, front and rear doors opened at the center. Interior appointments were lavish but tasteful, and automatic transmission, power windows, heater, transistorized radio, power door locks, and deep, foam cushioned seats were all standard at a price of $6,067 for the sedan and $6,713 for the convertible. The sedan tipped the scales at 4,927 pounds, the convertible weighed in at a whopping 5,215 pounds.

The sedan had the most rigid unit frame construction ever produced. But the convertible lacked the steadying influence of the steel roof, and early production models suffered very noticeable body shake from 51 to 62 m.p.h. A mid-year change eliminated this problem by adding 20 pound cast-iron balancers at all four corners of the car.

With the new body design came a stepped-up quality

1964 Lincoln Continental convertible.

1964 Lincoln Continental 4-dr sedan

142

control program which was the envy of other manufacturers. Every Continental was subjected to a 12-mile road test covering 189 check points involving chassis, engine, suspension, and running gear components. Generators were individually "run-in" before installation. A special device was developed to check wiring after its installation. All engine parts were gauged individually before assembly. Each engine was checked on a test stand before it was installed in a car. A "black light" was used to check for leaks of fluids and lubricants.

With these elaborate safeguards, Lincoln could confidently offer a two-year, 24,000 mile warranty on the Continentals.

Those customers who handed over $6,700 for a Continental convertible in 1961 might have left the showroom with a slightly nagging feeling of trepidation about the operation of the top, but the raising and lowering mechanism, complicated though it was, had its technological foundation in the '57-'59 Ford Skyliners, so was not an untried, unproven system by any means. Lincoln, though, hedged their bets by building in access points in the rear deck and underneath the car as well as by removal of the

1962 Lincoln Continental convertible

1965 Lincoln Continental convertible

rear seat.

Continental owners also discovered a neat bypass of the regular electrics, should these throw a fit while the top was partially up or down. This consisted of placing the transmission lever in reverse or low and turning on the ignition. Through some electronic miracle connected with the lockout for the neutral and park positions on the transmission, current flows and, voila, the top mechanism continues to work. Raises hob with the battery, though.

The early Continentals do have their weak points. Brakes, for instance, are just not up to the job in relation to the car's weight and speed potential. The tansmissions are delicate compared to the robust construction of the rest of the car and overheating can cook them beyond repair without warning. But their virtues far outweigh their faults, and 1961 models launched the modern Continental era auspiciously and very successfully.

"... Its hallmark is surpassing good taste. The classic beauty which is Lincoln Continental's exclusively does not depend upon ostentation. Lincoln Continental for 1962 wears a limited-edition look of elegance that time will not dim." These words appeared in the brochure for the 1962 Lincoln Continental. They set the pace for what would follow for the next four years. Minor improvements, with slight changes to a thoroughly excellent design. One such minor improvement was in the steering wheel, it was moved three-quarters of an inch higher for more comfort. Another was moving of the headlights one inch higher. The dip stick was now self sealing, to prevent dust from entering the crankcase. There was a new grille and rear end treatment. The same 123 inch wheelbase was maintained, as was the same power plant. The sedan weighed two pounds more, now at 4,929 and cost was upped to $6,074. The convertible weighed in at 5,213 pounds, and sold for $6,720. Sales for 1962 totaled 31,535 units.

In July 1963 *Motor Trend* said of the Continental, 'On long open road trips you really know you're in a luxury car. If you listen hard you can hear a slight murmur, but its not something you're naturally aware of. Interior and exterior detailing on the Continental is above reproach. Everything fits as it should and only the highest quality upholstery and carpeting materials are used. "Again, slight changes to grille and rear deck for 1963. The wheelbase remained the same, as did the engine at 430 cid. Horsepower, however, was boosted to 320 at 4600 rpm. Sedan weight was again increased to 4,950 lbs. and sold for $6,270. The convertible weight was boosted to 5,360 pounds and sold for $6,916 up almost $200 from the previous year.

Once again, in what was now true Lincoln tradition, the body design for 1964 remained unchanged, with slight changes to grille and rear deck. The wheelbase was lengthened to 126 inches but engine size remained at 430 cid, developing 320 hp at 4600 rpm. Although the outside remained the same, the interior underwent a complete change. The dash was redesigned. Air conditioning could now be incorporated with subtle dash louvers. Wheel size was increased to 15 inches. A semi-custom limousine, first introduced on a limited basis in 1963, was again offered on a limited basis. Built by Lehmann-Peterson of Chicago, the cars could also be ordered with a division window. That same year the White House fleet took delivery of another Lincoln Presidential limousine. 37,750 units were produced for the year. A sedan sold for $6,270. A convertible for $6,916.

With the exception of the special order Lehmann-Peterson Executive limousine, only two models continued to be offered for 1965. A completely new grille and hood was installed in the same timeless body design. The 1965 front end strongly resembled the Mercury of the same year. Parking lights were incorporated into the front fenders without really destroying the fender line. 1965 proved to be the best selling year for Lincoln since the introduction of their compact luxury car in 1961. A total of 45,470 units were produced. One of the more popular accessories available this year was the "Vinyl Roof." Full leather interior in the roll over pleat style were standard on convertibles, optional on sedans.

In addition to leather, sedan buyers had a choice of largo cloth or wool broadcloth. Wheelbase continued at 126 inches. The special order Executive limousine was three feet longer than the standard sedan and featured such things as padded vinyl roof with a rear opera window, for greater privacy. Inside the rear compartment there were rear facing companion seats permanently positioned. The compartment was carpeted in mouton. Options included: a built-in television set in a hand rubbed walnut cabinet, a telephone compartment, built-in dictating machine or a refrigerator. Price tag for this super luxury car was around $16,500 in comparison to the standard sedan which sold for $6,166, without air (air conditioning ran another $500). The convertible carried a $6,800 price tag.

The body design begun in 1961 ended with the 1965 model. The basic lines of this design, however, have continued on to the present. Enduring. Timeless. Hallmarks of the milestone Continentals.

Mercury

'46 Mercury Sedan Coupe: a Sporty and Spirited Car

Early Mercurys were little more than hopped-up, dressed-up Fords. From the beginning, the new "Merc" had a reputation for sporty looks and spirited performance.

With smooth notchback styling and an extra-horsepower engine, the six-passenger sedan coupe was one of 1946's more attractive buys. This handsome two-door looked great and performed the same way.

Like other Mercs, the sedan coupe was rushed back into production soon after World War II ended. Although the company had done some preliminary work on an all-

Options on this '46 Merc sedan coupe include whitewalls, wheel trim rings, fog lamps, fender skirts, OSRV mirrors and radio. Note the roof-mounted radio antenna.

new postwar model, those sold between 1946 and 1948 were little more than updated '42s. The sedan coupe had been popular before the war and came back strong immediately afterwards.

Because no major retooling was done, Ford had Mercurys back on the market as early as Nov. 1, 1945. At this point, however, the number of available models was limited and national distribution had not yet been re-established. It took until Feb. 8, 1946, for things to get back into full swing.

By the end of the year, there were six models on the market. They ranged from the two-door sedan ($1,448) to a wood-trimmed Sportsman's convertible ($2,209). The sedan coupe was designated a Model 72 — part of the 69M Series — and proved to be the year's second best-selling body style. It had a production run of 24,163 units.

This popular model was basically a two-door club coupe with "five-window" styling. There were large windows with vent panes in each of the doors, individual swing-out rear quarter windows and a rectangular rear window. The windshield was of split-V type.

The interior of the sedan coupe was richly appointed for a car of its price class. It featured a plastic steering wheel, full horn ring, bright metal trim, and an instrument panel finished in metallic lacquer.

The front seat was of split-bench design; the seatbacks folded to allow entrance to the rear. The back seat was a narrow, solid bench type. With a full load of six passengers, things in the rear of the coupe were snug.

A new grille was the most noticeable change in the '46 Mercurys. It had thin vertical bars surrounded by a body color trim piece. The bars were segmented into rectangular groupings, four on either side of the nose. A Mercury nameplate was positioned above this elaborate ensemble and underneath were four vertical ribs with the word "eight" lettered between them. All of this was underscored with twin oval openings filled with chrome, horizontal bars.

A distinction of '46 models was a bright metal rub strip running along the beltline from the front of the hood to the rear of the body. There were also twin horizontal moldings on the sides of all fenders. Standard features of Mercurys included a flathead V-8 engine, mid-section seating, double-acting hydraulic shocks, self-centering hydraulic brakes, torque tube drive, balanced weight distribution, long "Slow Motion" springs, two-way chassis stabilization (stabilizer bar and anti-sway bar), rubber insulated spring shackles and metal spring covers.

The V-8 engine used in all Mercs featured a short, dynamically balanced crankshaft made from a special alloy metal. This crank was said to be extra rugged and could handle the Merc's high power-to-weight ratio.

Mercury motor numbers and serial numbers are identical. Restorers can find them in a number of places on a car including: 1) the left frame member ahead of the cowl; 2) the rear of the engine on top of the clutch housing; and 3) on the left side of the frame near the front engine support. The 1946 numbers ran from 99A-650280 to 99A-1412707.

1955 Montclair Hardtop: Mercury's "Low-Rider"

New style features for the 1955 Mercury models included an all-new body with a redesigned bumper grille, hood type headlights, new side moldings, and distinctive taillights.

Promoted as a new "low silhouette" series, the Montclair was sort of a factory-built "lowrider," although it was strictly a top-of-the-line car. Its characteristic trim features were round front fender medallions with "Montclair" scripts behind them and a chrome drop-belt molding running from the front to rear window pillars.

The Montclairs were built off the same 119-inch wheelbase used for other Mercury sedans, coupes and covertibles. They sat lower on their haunches, however. The sedan, for example, was just 58.6 inches high, a full 2½ inches lower than 1955 Monterey and Custom sedans.

Overall length for all 1955 Mercs was 206.3 inches, but the Montclair's lower silhouette made it look extra long. It also gave the impression of a narrower overall width, although this measurement was an identical 76.4 inches for all Mercs, too.

A "full-scope" wraparound windshield led off the long list of new-for-1955 Mercury features. Other innovations that year included tubeless tires; a full-flow oil filter; Hotchkiss drive; oversize hydraulic brakes; weatherproofed ignition; 18 mm anti-fouling spark plugs; aluminum alloy pistons; and an automatic choke. King pins were replaced with ball joints for easier, steadier steering, better control and freer cornering action.

Two "super-torque" V-8s were offered in Montclairs, depending on transmission choice. Standard in cars with three-speed manual or overdrive transmission was a 188 hp V-8 with 7.6:1 compression. Montclair models with Merc-O-Matic Drive came with a 198 hp V-8 having 8.5:1 high-compression heads.

Popular accessories available for 1955 Mercs included power brakes, power steering, power window controls, radio, heater, and white sidewall tires.

The Montclair lineup included a four-door sedan, two-door hardtop, Sun Valley hardtop and convertible at prices between $2,685 and $2,712. Series production totalled 104,667 cars.

Mercury built a total of 71,588 Montclair steel-top two-door hardtops in 1955. Also available was a Sun Valley hardtop, with plexiglass roof insert.

Mercury Convertible Cruiser

by Robert C. Ackerson

Although Mercury had long enjoyed a reputation as one of America's "hot cars," it had to wait until 1957 to have its second opportunity to pace the Indianapolis 500.

As was the tradition at Indy, a pace car dinner was held in early January at which Mercury's general manager, F.C. Reith, accepted Alex Hulman's invitation to supply the 1957 race's pace car.

Hulman told his audience that "Mercury's outstanding contributions to automotive development in their 1957 cars led us to select it as the pace car for this year's Indianapolis 500-mile race." Hulman also noted that "Mercury's entirely new and advanced styling combined with many unique engineering and mechanical advances influenced our choice."

In response to these kind words, Reith said that "Mercury is distinctly honored by the recognition given us by Mr. Hulman and the Speedway. We feel that the 1957 Mercury Convertible Cruiser pace car — designed specifically to lead the fastest field ever to compete at Indianapolis — will give a good account of itself and help make the 1957 race another memorable occasion in automotive history."

Mercury watchers were probably a bit befuddled by Reith's reference to a "Convertible Cruiser" since the 1957 lineup's leader, the Turnpike Cruiser, had been available only as a hardtop. But on the same date as the pace car dinner, Jan. 7, Reith also unveiled the new Mercury convertible before several hundred journalists.

The pace car was painted Sun Glitter and was fitted with a black top. The rear panel side indentations were finished in a silver bright color.

Other features unique to the Convertible Cruiser included front fender ornaments consisting of a Mercury crest and winged checkered flags which were illuminated and served as directionals. On the rear deck was another lighted ornament in which the Mercury head was placed between two checkered flags. In addition, a "Dream Car" spare tire mount was standard on the Convertible Cruiser. This feature was optional on other models.

Emphasizing the added length this gave the Mercury convertible was a broad, bright metal applique on the rear fender that ran from the wheel well to the rear bumper. Rounding out the special trim of the Convertible Cruiser were Turnpike Cruiser wheel covers and rear bumper pod safety reflectors.

The Convertible Cruiser's interior featured an all-vinyl crush grain upholstery in Sun Glitter and black along with black carpeting. The instrument panel was that of the Turnpike Cruiser and had black padding with chrome and white controls. The instrumentation included a tachometer and a clock that automatically computed elapsed time and miles traveled. An engraved plaque was placed on the extreme right side of the dash on each of the 1265 convertibles built, citing them as true replicas of the pace car.

Also fitted were padded sun visors and a "special safety" steering wheel with a flat top sector that, according to Mercury, permitted the driver "to see over its rim for an unobstructed view of the road." The engine of the Convertible Cruiser was the 368 cid, 290 hp V-8 that was standard on the Turnpike Cruisers. Also fitted was Merc-O-Matic transmission with "keyboard" controls plus power steering and brakes.

With a price tag of $4,103, the Convertible Cruiser was the most expensive Mercury for 1957. It was also the second Mercury to pace the Indy 500. Earlier, in 1950, Benson Ford had driven a Mercury to pace the field in that year's race. Receiving the actual 1957 pace car was race winner Sam Hanks.

1957 Mercury Convertible Cruiser.

Breezeway Merc

by Tom LaMarre

It was billed the "Exclusive Look" for 1963. And what made the full-size Mercury different from any other car was its breezeway roof design with retractable rear window.

The reverse-slant roof blended perfectly with the Merc's all-new styling. At the same time, it gave the car a family resemblance to the Lincolns of a few years earlier. The similarities between the '63 Merc and the '59 Lincoln Mark IV are especially striking. Not only do they share the same roof style, but also the same small fins with chrome trim and very similar rear ends. The taillight clusters mounted on the full-width chrome panels are almost lookalikes on the two cars.

But the Mercury featured smooth overall styling instead of the sculptured look of the big Lincoln. Maybe that's why the resemblance never really occurred to me when my parents bought a Monterey Custom four-door sedan in the spring of 1963. Inside and out, the Mercury was finished in a shade called pink frost, a taupe sort of color that now seems to be very popular on GM cars (Cadillac lists it as "woodland haze").

Memories of the car lead me to say "Bring back the breezeway," for the roof was practical as well as beautiful. Gone was the task of cleaning snow and ice off the back window. A dashboard-mounted control actuated the retractable window, usually lowering it just enough for our basset hound to stick his nose out.

The full-size Mercury line was comprised of the Monterey, Monterey Custom, and Monterey S-55. The powerful Marauder made its debut in mid-season as a 1963½ model. Prices ranged from $2,887 for the Monterey four-door sedan to $3,900 for the S-55 convertible coupe. All Montereys had a 120-inch wheelbase as did the Colony Park station wagon. Overall length was 215 inches.

Things were new under the hood, too. A 300 hp version of the 390 engine was optional, compared to the 250 hp rating of the standard 390. But even this was tame compared to the engines offered in the Marauder fastback hardtops. The 427 cubic inch "Marauder" engine developed 415 hp, while the "Super Marauder" was rated at 425 hp. The sleek Monterey Marauder was available in both the Custom and S-55 series; I still remember the black S-55 Marauder that my father had as a loaner while the sedan was in for service.

With Parnelli Jones at the wheel, a Marauder won the Pike's Peak Hill Climb on July 4th, setting a record time of 14:17.4 minutes. Jones and his Marauder received widespread coverage in all of the auto magazines that year, along with an extensive Mercury advertising campaign based on the Pike's Peak champion.

A good deal of publicity also surrounded the prodution of the 60 millionth Ford-built vehicle, an S-55 finished in gold with a white interior. As for me, I'll take a pink frost breezeway sedan.

This postcard highlights Mercury's breezeway window. Retractable rear window was a Mercury feature for years.

Pit Stop: 1966 Mercury Comet Cyclone GT

by Linda Clark

It was a mod world in 1966. Women's skirts were shorter, and men's hair was longer. Notre Dame went for the tie instead of a win in its dream football game against Michigan State, and it appeared America was going for the same in Vietnam.

In Detroit, the musclecar craze triggered by Pontiac's GTO was in high gear, however, and Mercury stole some of the thunder with its own Cyclone GT in 1966. To remind us of Mercury's serious performance intentions, the Cyclone GT was chosen as the Indianapolis 500 pace car. After bidding itself into providing the mandatory matched set of Cyclone GT convertibles for the revered Memorial Day race, some 100 pace car replicas found their way to Indiana, where they transported parade queens and celebrities in conjunction with Indy 500 festivities. Unlike other automakers, Mercury made no attempt to market the replica pace cars through dealers.

The base Cyclone model had premiered in mid-1964, and the high-performance Cyclone GT in the fall of 1965, along with the rest of the 1966 Comet line. Initially, the regular Cyclone was offered only as a two-door hardtop with bucket seats. The only engine offered in the Cyclone was Ford's familiar 225 hp 289 cid V-8. Promoted by Lincoln-Mercury as its performance leader, the Cyclone was distinguished by its own grille and optional fiberglass hood (derived from the legendary drag racing Comets of 1964-65) with non-functional hood scoops. With a four-speed manual transmission and 3:1 axle, the regular Cyclone was capable of an impressive (for its size) zero to 60 time of 8.7 seconds.

From its inception, the Comet/Cyclone had grown on an almost annual basis, and its 1966 incarnation, based on the Ford Fairlane shell, rode on a 116-inch wheelbase, moving it out of the compact and into the intermediate class. For performance nuts, moreover, it made the Cyclone a viable contender against the smaller car/big engine musclecars of the period. Thus, for 1966 Mercury went full blast and brought out the Cyclone GT.

Powered by Ford's popular 335 hp 390 V-8, the Cyclone GT had an optional handling package, front disc brakes and optional four-speed manual or automatic transmission. (A three-speed manual was standard.) Also standard were dual exhausts, drum brakes, a fiberglass hood with twin nonfunctional scoops and "GT" identification and stripes. The 390 V-8 used a four-barrel carburetor and had a 10.5:1 compression ratio. The Merc-O-Matic transmission only came with a GT Sport Shift enabling manual inter-range control via a floor-mounted lever. So equipped, the Cyclone GT was capable of 0-60 mph in seven seconds and quarter-mile runs in the high 14s. And this was in spite of the fact that the 390 engine added some 430 pounds to the standard six-cylinder Comet.

Then director of Mercury high-performance projects, Fran Hernandez, and assistant Paul Preuss oversaw the 1966 pace car effort. The two cars that emerged were candy apple red Cyclone GT convertibles capable of 115 mph cruising speeds. Modifications and engine blueprinting were done at Bud Moore Engineering in Spartanburg, S.C. The pace car rode on Firestone Wide Oval Super Sport tires (7.75 x 14) with optional styled steel wheels. Benson Ford was behind the wheel for the Cyclone GT's parade lap.

Graham Hill won the 500-miler that day, and the Cyclone GT subsequently proved somewhat disappointing in Lincoln-Mercury showrooms. Only 13,812 hardtops and 2,158 convertibles were built. By comparison, Pontiac GTO sold 86,583 in 1966 and Ford's ponycar Mustang 607,568. Ultimately, the 390 powerplant proved to be the Cyclone GT's nemesis, in light of the more potent 389s, 396s and Hemis of the period. But the striking red '66 Cyclone GT convertible pace cars, nevertheless, remain a memorable entry in Mercury's high-performance scrapbook.

The 1966 Mercury Comet Cyclone GT pace car.

The 1967 Mercury was advertised as a "Junior Thunderbird." *Motor Trend's* "Car of the Year."

Cougar
Mercury's Cool Cat
by Robert C. Ackerson

The development of the Cougar as the T-7 project began in early 1963. At that time the Mustang was being fine tuned for its April 1964 introduction and not even the most optimistic Mustang supporters at Ford were anticipating that in its first full production year, Mustang output would total 564,999. There was of course plenty of optimism about the Mustang's sales appeal and over at Lincoln-Mercury there was a strong desire to grab a share of the sales pie of what would soon be called the "pony car" market.

The earliest styling prototype of what was to become the Cougar was not, however, a direct Lincoln-Mercury undertaking. Instead it was a design exercise from Ford's Special Development Studio. Not unexpectedly, it was very Mustang-like in appearance. However, it was also less attractive than the 1964 production model Mustang. Its front end featured a bumper that moved upward at its outer extremities, thus practically encircling both the single headlights plus a broad and wide grille whose overall form suggested that of a giant-sized garden rake. The overall result wasn't particularly pleasing but when the grille was lowered and divided into two sections it provided the key element of the production Cougar's front end look.

Although the Cougar first appeared only in notchback form, a fastback body style showed up in an early 1965 design proposal. This particular design had merit and such elements as its grille, front fender ornamentation and roof line later showed up on the 1967 Mercurys. But as a potential Cougar the car fell short of the mark. Basically it lacked both the distinction which Lincoln-Mercury correctly regarded as essential to the Cougar's sales success and seemed to swap the light and lively Mustang look for an appearance more appropriate for a larger automobile than a trim, sporty four-seater.

This latter criticism points out one of the dilemmas the Cougar's designers had to cope with and eventually over-

come. The Cougar, since it was intended to be higher priced than the Mustang, needed an image that justified its up-market status. At the same time, however, it could cut into the Thunderbird's lucrative sales by appearing too T-birdish. Within the umbrella of what had become known as the S-77 program, the work of several design teams slowly was integrated into a single model incorporating a distinctive hop-up of the rear panels (which removed any vertical Mustang influence) with a very smooth vertical grille treatment (mirrored by a similar wrap-over motif for the taillights). The result was an automobile that demonstrated Lincoln-Mercury's ability to reshape a basically good design into an extremely successful new car without spending a huge sum of money. At a cost of $40 million Mercury had an automobile that used

The 1968 Cougar was only slightly changed. Most noticeable is the addition of side marker lights.

the Mustang's inner skin, deck lid, and roof, plus of course many of its mechanical components yet was anything but a Mustang copycat.

Mercury's early market research included an analysis of how the public would respond to the Cougar name. Since a majority of those interviewed connotated Cougar with such virtues as swiftness, silence and a lithe appearance, there was little doubt at Mercury that the Cougar's name was appropriate. The only discordant note came from Jaguar which was distressed by the close proximity of a Cougar profile to that of a Jaguar. Eventually this Anglo-American tempest in a teapot was resolved by Mercury's willingness to distinctly spell COUGAR directly beneath the chrome cat residing on the Cougar's front grille.

By Feb. 18, 1965 when the final design for the Cougar was approved by management, the tremendous potential of the pony car market was apparent. As an automobile Mercury described as "for the man on his way

to a Thunderbird," the Cougar had all the elements for a successful debut as a 1967 model. Lincoln-Mercury's break-even point for Cougar production was only 60,000 units and as suggested by the Cougar's impressively strong early sales momentum, its goal of a 100,000 output for the model year was conservative.

In terms of major interior and external dimensions, the Cougar and Mustang were quite similar. Of course the Cougar undoubtedly benefited from the Mustang's tremendous sales success. By September 1966 when the Cougar was introduced, Mustang sales totalled 1.5 million and whereas the Cougar's natural competition, the Firebird, had to initially be satisfied with an uncomfortably close relationship with the Camaro, the Cougar was debuting with a carefully conceived design philosophy. Invariably, of course, the Cougar was compared to the Mustang but this usually was to its advantage. For example, *Car Life* (October 1966) told its readers that "there's

a gracefulness and shapeliness about the Cougar that its progenitor doesn't have: there's a faceted, jewel-like quality that gives it an appearance of richness and luxuriousness. *Motor Trend* (November 1966) had a similar evaluation of the Cougar, reporting that its "sleek, sculptured lines rely very little on chrome trim."

As a styling exercise the Cougar was obviously a major success. With a design whose refinement and individuality made it difficult to pick out major clues to its Mustang lineage plus contemporary features as vacuum-operated retractable covers for the dual headlights, the Cougar effectively combined a spirit of sportiness with strong overtones of up-market prestige.

One of the key elements of the Cougar's design philosophy was a very low interior sound level and to this end a strong effort was made to suppress wind noise. Although it was a relatively primitive program by modern standards, all sheet metal, window hardware and weather stripping was designed with this goal in mind. Even the front vent panes had small peripheral beads that were intended to lessen the sound of air flow into the Cougar's interior.

At first glance the Cougar's suspension system seemed commonplace with coil springs and A-arms up front with a live axle plus leaf springs at the rear. However, its front drag strut had an articulated joint, fitted with rubber bushings that allowed a small amount (0.03 inches) of fore-aft movement. This mechanical elbow along with voided rubber bushings for the front spring eyes contributed to a smooth ride by absorbing road shock. At the rear, rubber Iso (as in Isolation) clamps attached the springs to the axle also helped lessen road vibration and noise. The Cougar's 59 inch length rear leaf springs were six inches longer than the Mustang's and were separated by a friction reducing, graphite-impregnated polyethylene element. These features, plus the use of 123.5 pounds of sound proofing enabled Lincoln-Mercury to claim the Cougar had a 15% better "ride" than the Mustang. Judging by the comments of contemporary road testers this was not mere wishful thinking on Lincoln-Mercury's part. "Mustangs tend to ride like their namesakes," said *Car and Driver* (October 1966), "but the much softer Cougar is almost completely free of harshness except on extremely rough roads." *Car Life* (October 1966) approached the Cougar from a slightly different perspective but none-the-less concluded, "There are certain refinements of riding and handling qualities that should make it acceptable to a wider spectrum of consumers."

Although the Cougar's bucket seat frames were identical to those installed on Mustangs, their soft vinyl upholstery plus a neat and uncluttered instrument panel gave the Cougar an interior equal in attractiveness to its exterior. Undoubtedly contributing to these Cougar strong points was the high priority Lincoln—Mercury placed on quality assembly. Not every Cougar was a paragon of precision but Frank E. Zimmerman, Lincoln-Mercury's general sales manager, did report that of the first 3400 Cougars produced, 87% were rated either good or excellent by quality inspectors.

Unlike every other pony car then in production or yet to be, the Cougar was not available with a six-cylinder engine. Its base engine was Ford's familiar 200 hp, 289 cid V-8 fitted with a two-barrel carburetor. For an additional $53, the slightly hotter 225 hp, four-barrel version was offered. And if this didn't provide enough urge and the customer was willing to part with $158, the 390 cid V-8 with a 10.1:1 compression ratio and Holley C70F four-barrel carb was available. Its ratings were 320 hp at 4800 rpm and 427 16-ft at 3200 rpm. All Cougar engines were available with either three or four speed manual gearboxes as well as "Select-Shift Merc-O-Matic" which could be shifted manually if the driver desired.

Purchase of the big Marauder 390 GT V-8 also required installation of the Cougar GT Performance Group which carried a hefty $323.85 price. However, since the heavy 390 V-8 altered the Cougar's front-rear weight distribution from 56%-44% to 59%-41% this was a wise decision by Lincoln-Mercury. The key elements of this option included a considerably firmer suspension with stiffer springs all around and the replacement of all voided suspension bushings with solid units. The standard one-inch diameter shocks were exchanged for 1.1875 inch versions and a slightly larger front anti-roll bar. These fairly substantial charges were accompanied by some major revisions in the Cougar's tire and brake specifications. The standard 7.35 x 14 General Jet Air II tires and five-inch rims were swapped for Firestone Wide Ovals mounted on six-inch rims and Kelsey Hayes 11.38 inch power disc brakes with vented rotors were installed in the front. At the rear slightly wider (2.5 inches instead of 2.25 inches) drum brakes were used. Completing the GT package was a power booster fan, slightly faster steering, a low restriction dual exhaust system plus special exterior identification trim.

Along with just about every other automobile manufacturer, Mercury was determined to corral every possible sale and thus made a strong effort to tailor a Cougar to every conceivable buyer's whims. For example, in addition to the numerous powertrain, transmission and suspension options already mentioned, the Cougar could be equipped with a sports console that enclosed the transmission control, electric clock, and radio. If this didn't convince the potential owner that he or she would be part of the "with it" automotive crowd than a nifty overhead console surely was the clincher. It included a warning light system for low fuel, seat belts, door ajar, and parking brake. In addition two map lights were included and along with the panel lights and rear pillar lights were operated by dash-mounted toggle switches. Although purchase of the Marauder 390 engine was still required, most of the suspension features of the GT package were available as the Performance Handling option.

However, Mercury put heavy emphasis upon the Cougar's fairly extensive standard equipment list as one of its major advantages over other pony cars. "You simply can't put a Cougar together," claimed Mercury, "by starting with a cheaper sports car and piling on options...no matter how much you spent. Because a lot of Cougar ideas aren't even available on them."

The Cougar was touted by its maker to be "the better idea" and overall its critics tended to agree. *Car and Driver* (October 1966) reported that "for 1967, Mercury

Division is serving our cup of tea." In its view, the Cougar was "one pretty good automobile. It doesn't go to the extremes that make the Mustang an 'almost' sports car and the Thunderbird an 'almost' luxury car, but cuts a wide and sensible path down the middle." In a somewhat unusual analysis, *Hot Rod* (October 1966) explained that the idea behind the Cougar was that it "will step along with the best of them, drive the Rolls-Royce owners nuts trying to match its quiet ride and turn a lot of heads on the drive to work or the country club." *Hot Rod* might have been overstating the Cougar's attributes just a bit but it was right on the money by noting that "it will be at least four months before anyone fields a competitor, and by that time the Cougar will be off, roaming through the heartland of suburbia bringing in new customers like you wouldn't believe."

Although Mercury didn't, as we've just suggested, have any real interest in challenging the Rolls-Royce on its own turf, it wasn't the least bit bashful about portraying the Cougar as a strong alternative to other GT-type European automobiles. In early pre-production previews, most participants overestimated its $2,851 base price by an average of $1,000 and from this strong marketing position, the Cougar went on to challenge unnamed but certainly not fictitious competitors. One particularly impressive ad featured an illustration of a sage gold Cougar on the edge of a deserted beach. Behind it sketched an endless ocean. It was the perfect setting for Mercury to explain that "Time was, European car makers had a corner on the sleek market. But by the time your car got stateside, shipping and import charges could add an extra $800 or so to the price tag. Mercury believes a man would sooner have a lot of Cougar, and no salt water costs."

Mercury kept the pressure both on its overseas opposition and on the Pontiac Firebird which was introduced in February 1967 by adding the XR-7 to the Cougar line as a mid-model year offering. Although the XR-7 could be distinguished externally from standard Cougars by its small identification emblem on the C-pillars plus a series of stripes on the rocker panel, the key elements of the XR-7 were found in its interior. The overhead visual check panel was standard as were deluxe front and rear seat belts. The XR-7's instrument panel was finished in simulated walnut and included a tachometer, oil pressure gauge along with an XR-7 plaque. Combination leather-vinyl seats plus door assist straps and map pockets added to the XR-7's European accent. This type of publicity and equipment made it inevitable that sooner or later the Cougar would be directly compared with some of the top European road cars by the motoring press. The most obvious choice was the Jaguar and in its July 1967 issue *Car and Driver* conducted a fairly extensive dual-road test of a Cougar XR-7 and a Jaguar 420 sedan. Mercury had implored the motoring public to "look no further" than the XR-7 "if you have hoped for the custom-crafted appointments of a classic European road car in an all-American package." And while *Car and Driver* didn't give that type of assertion a 100 percent, unqualified endorsement, it came mighty close. "The Jaguar came first" in terms of chronology, noted *Car and Driver*, "but the Cougar is America's most earnest attempt yet to build a Jag-

uar. In this, Mercury has succeeded so well that they have built a better Jaguar than Jaguar...but not by much."

Even more audacious was Roger Ward's comparison road test of an XR-7 versus an Aston Martin DB-6 published in the March 1967 issue of *Popular Mechanics*. Around the three-mile Stardust International Raceway at Las Vegas, Ward found the Aston Martin could maintain a 79.70 mph average while the Cougar's best effort was 76.85 mph. However, Ward reported that "I think I could have picked up much of the five seconds I lost in the Cougar if the car had been prepared differently. However, in straight line acceleration, the four-speed, 320 hp Cougar was more than a match for the far more expensive, 325 hp Aston Martin. Whereas the DB-6 required 8.1 seconds to reach 60 mph, the XR-7 recorded an impressive zero to 60 mph run of 6.1 seconds. Furthermore the Cougar received praise not only for its performance but for its appointments and driveability from Roger Ward. "I found the Cougar," Ward noted, "to be as comfortable as the Aston and its equal in ease of driving...for performance and luxury, I'd say the Cougar is a car for the man who aspires to own an Aston Martin but hasn't got the pocketbook for it."

Early in 1967, Lincoln-Mercury's Leo C. Beebe, who had played a major role in Ford's 1-2-3 victory at LeMans in 1966, left no doubt in anyone's mind that Cougars would be in the thick of Trans Am competition during the 1967 season. Said Beebe: "If you're not in automobile racing, you're not in the automobile business, and we're in the automobile business right up to our ears." "Team Cougar," led by Dan Gurney, didn't win the 1967 Trans Am championship but it came close with four victories. This strong showing effectively demonstrated the performance aspect of the Cougar's nature. Although the Cougar didn't return to the Trans Am wars in 1968 and except for the mandated side warning lights, was externally unchanged for 1968, its performance image was further enhanced by the addition of a new GT-E model. Priced at $4221.42, the GT-E was considerably more expensive than the base model ($2910.42) or the XR-7 ($3208.91). However, its standard engine was a detuned version of Ford's 427 cid NASCAR "wedge" V-8 which was rated conservatively at 390 hp. This engine, which could also be combined with the Cougar GT performance option provided what *Car and Driver* (December 1967) described as "brute, tire-smoking hell-bent-for-action" performance.

Not all Cougar owners were looking for this type of motoring experience and thus the standard Cougar engine for 1968 was a 210 hp, 302 cid V-8. But beyond this level was a 230 hp version plus two 390 cid V-8s with either 280 hp or 325 hp.

Beginning in 1969 the Cougar began an evolutionary movement that to some was most meandering and vague than precise and structured. However, with the pony car market experiencing a sales decline, Lincoln-Mercury couldn't really be faulted for attempting to find a new market niche for the Cougar. But at the same time the first series Cougars stand out as exceptionally well designed, potent and unique pony cars whose many outstanding qualities haven't yet been fully recognized by old car hobbyists.

Don't Forget the 1973 Cougar

Much attention is focused on the Mustang these days, and rightly so. It is an exceptional car. However, it seems that while the Mustang basks in the limelight, its sister car, the Mercury Cougar, is forgotten in the shadows. This is not right. The Cougar has usually been equal to the Mustang in most respects, and often superior to it. In other words, it could be said that the Cougar is a pony of a better color. Let's look at the 1973 Cougar for an example.

Although this was the third year of a style that seemed to remain constant, that was actually not quite true. The grille was modified with a broad top rim, on which the cougar appeared (the cat, not the car). That replaced the round medallion formerly in the center of the grille. The 1973 taillights were made slightly smaller. Also, they were divided with vertical brightwork, instead of the horizontal sections of before.

Wheelbase remained at 112 inches (or 112.1 to be more precise). However, overall length grew three inches to 199.5. The redesigned front bumper, necessitated by new regulations issued by Washington, stuck out further from the body than before. Weight was up around 110 pounds for most models, although the XR-7 convertible, at 3,530, was only 80 pounds heftier.

As had been the Cougar custom beginning with its second model year, four versions were offered. Two body types — hardtop and convertible — were made in two editions. Besides the standard line, there was the deluxe XR-7 series. Exactly what the designation XR-7 means seems to be a mystery, but notice that the Japanese have shown a liking for it. They call a popular Mazda model the RX-7.

What XR-7 meant in practical terms was $177 and $306 added to the list price of the convertible and hardtop, which totalled $3,679 and $3,903, respectively. The extra

The 1973 Cougar.

cost paid for such standard features as rocker panel chrome molding, special wheel covers, vinyl covered roof, leather-finished seats, deluxe seat belts, cherry wood-grain instrument panel and steering wheel inserts, tachometer, alternator and oil pressure gauges, etc.

Often the manufacturers make available a special model for their spring promotion. Ford introduced four "Bronze Age" models, and one of these was a Cougar. Special bronze or brown colors and exclusive trim items were featured on this car.

The introduction of the Bronze Age inadvertently marked the end of another age for the auto industry in general, and the Cougar in particular. The energy crisis punctuated the gung-ho car makers with a long lasting spell of pessimism. That may or may not have been one reason why there were no more Cougar convertibles produced after the 1973 models, or convertibles in any other Mercury line, for that matter.

Cougar ragtop production totals for the 1973 model year were 1,284 standard and 3,165 XR-7 versions. That was the second year that both the XR-7 convertibles and hardtops outsold their standard edition counterparts. From the introduction of the Cougar convertible for 1969, a total of only 25,177 were produced. The relatively low numbers would make them especially attractive to collectors.

Cougar always provided greater standard power in its cars than Mustang. There was never a six-cylinder Cougar before the 1981 models. Even the Mustang's standard V-8 was a 302 cubic inch engine compared to the Cougar's 351 (from 1969 through 1973). The standard engine in the 1973 Cougars was the two-barrel edition of this engine. It was rated at 168 net horsepower. The four-barrel CJ version of the same engine was optional. Its output was not published by Ford, but was believed to be in the 245 to 260 net horsepower range. (For whatever it may be worth, the Canadian horsepower figures, where pollution regulations were somewhat less stringent, were 250 and 300 gross horsepower for the two-barrel and four-barrel engines, respectively.)

Only 4.7 percent of the '73 Cougars were powered with the more potent CJ engine. Here is a list of how popular other equipment was on these Cougars. A mere 0.7 percent, or 424 cars, were fitted with a four-speed manual transmission. Limited shift differential was installed on 4.2 percent.

Power brakes were standard on all '73 Cougars, while power steering was on 99.1 percent, power windows on 14.7 percent, and power seats on 8.4 percent. Only bucket seats were obtainable.

The most popular sound system was a stereo radio in 42.0 percent, with a standard AM radio a close second in 40.5 percent. But 15.6 percent had stereo tape players. Clocks were in 70.6, and 28.0 percent had adjustable steering columns. A remote control left mirror was installed on 91.8 percent of all the 1973 Cougars. That includes all the XR-7 models on which it was standard.

Only 0.8 percent had a tinted windshield, yet 84.5 percent were air-conditioned. Of the hardtops, 82.8 percent were vinyl covered, and 1.6 percent had sun roofs.

155

HOW TO USE THIS CATALOG

APPEARANCE AND EQUIPMENT: Word descriptions identify cars by styling features, trim and (to a lesser extent) interior appointments. Most standard equipment lists begin with the lowest-priced model, then enumerate items added by upgrade models and option packages. Most lists reflect equipment available at model introductions.

I.D. DATA: Information is given about the Vehicle Identification Number (VIN) found on the dashboard. VIN codes show model or series, body style, engine size, model year and place built. Beginning in 1981, a standardized 17 symbol VIN is used. Earlier VINs are shorter. Locations of other coded information on the body and/or engine block may be supplied. Deciphering those codes is beyond the scope of this catalog.

SPECIFICATIONS CHART: The first column gives series or model numbers. The second gives body style numbers revealing body type and trim. Not all cars use two separate numbers. Some sources combine the two. Column three tells number of doors, body style and passenger capacity ('4-dr Sed-6P' means four-door sedan, six-passenger). Passenger capacity is normally the maximum. Cars with bucket seats hold fewer. Column four gives suggested retail price of the car when new, on or near its introduction date, not including freight or other charges. Column five gives the original shipping weight. The sixth column provides model year production totals or refers to notes below the chart. In cases where the same car came with different engines, a slash is used to separate factory prices and shipping weights for each version. Unless noted, the amount on the left of the slash is for the smallest, least expensive engine. The amount on the right is for the least costly engine with additional cylinders. 'N/A' means data not available.

ENGINE DATA: Engines are normally listed in size order with smallest displacement first. A 'base' engine is the basic one offered in each model at the lowest price. 'Optional' describes all alternate engines, including those that have a price listed in the specifications chart. (Cars that came with either a six or V-8, for instance, list the six as 'base' and V-8 'optional'). Introductory specifications are used, where possible.

CHASSIS DATA: Major dimensions (wheelbase, overall length, height, width and front/rear tread) are given for each model, along with standard tire size. Dimensions sometimes varied and could change during a model year.

TECHNICAL DATA: This section indicates transmissions standard on each model, usually including gear ratios; the standard final drive axle ratio (which may differ by engine or transmission); steering and brake system type; front and rear suspension description; body construction; and fuel tank capacity.

OPTIONAL EQUIPMENT LISTS: Most listings begin with drivetrain options (engines, transmissions, steering/suspension and mechanical components) applying to all models. Convenience/appearance items are listed separately for each model, except where several related models are combined into a single listing. Option packages are listed first, followed by individual items in categories: comfort/convenience, lighting/mirrors, entertainment, exterior, interior, then wheels/tires. Contents of some option packages are listed prior to the price; others are described in the Appearance/Equipment text. Prices are suggested retail, usually effective early in the model year. ('N/A' indicates prices are unavailable.) Most items are Regular Production Options (RPO), rather than limited-production (LPO), special-order or dealer-installed equipment. Many options were available only on certain series or body types or in conjunction with other items. Space does not permit including every detail.

HISTORY: This block lists introduction dates, total sales and production amounts for the model year and calendar year. Production totals supplied by auto-makers do not always coincide with those from other sources. Some reflect shipments from the factories rather than actual production or define the model year a different way.

HISTORICAL FOOTNOTES: In addition to notes on the rise and fall of sales and production, this block includes significant statistics, performance milestones, major personnel changes, important dates and places and facts that add flavor to this segment of America's automotive heritage.

156

1957 FORD

1957 FORDS — OVERVIEW — 1957 Fords were completely restyled and bore only a slight resemblance to earlier models. The new Fairlane series (including Fairlane and Fairlane 500 models) was five inches lower; had a two and one-half inch longer wheelbase and measured more than nine inches longer overall compared to 1946 models. The Custom series (including Custom and Custom 300 models) was three inches longer overall and had a one-half inch longer wheelbase than the 1956 models. As an aid in lowering the cars, all models had 14 inch wheels for the first time. Other design changes included a rear-opening hood, streamlined wheel openings and the use of windshield posts that sloped rearward at the bottom. Also, all 1957 Fords sported the latest styling craze, tailfins. Ford referred to these as "high-canted fenders". The big news for the year was the introduction of the Skyliner; the only true hardtop convertible in the world. At the touch of a button, an automatic folding mechanism retracted the top into the trunk, creating a true convertible.

THUNDERBIRD V-8 SERIES — The 1957 model represented the first significant restyling since the T-Bird was first introduced. A longer rear section provided improved storage space. Riding and handling qualities were greatly enhanced by relocating the spare tire in the trunk. As with the large Fords, 1957 Thunderbirds featured fins on the rear fenders. Inside, the 1957 model used the instrument panel from full-sized 1956 Fords, with an engine-turned insert dressing-up the panel.

THUNDERBIRD V-8 SERIES I.D. NUMBERS: Thunderbird models began with the engine designtion, "C7", "D7", or "E7" (depending on engine choice); assembly plant code "F" (Dearborn); body type code "H" (Thunderbird) and, finally, the production number, beginning at 100001 and going up.

THUNDERBIRD V-8 SERIES

Model Number	Body/Style Number	Body Type & Seating	Factory Price	Shipping Weight	Production Total
C7/D7/E7	40	2-dr Conv-2P	3408	3134	21,380

1957 FORD ENGINES

Six-cylinder: Overhead valves. Cast iron block. Displacement: 223 cubic inches. Bore and stroke: 3.62 x 3.60 inches. Compression ratio: 8.6:1. Brake horsepower: 144 at 4200 R.P.M. Carburetion: Holley one-barrel. Four main bearings. Serial number code "A".

V-8: Overhead valves. Cast iron block. Displacement: 272 cubic inches. Bore and stroke: 3.62 x 3.30 inches. Compression ratio: 8.6:1. Brake horsepower: 190 at 4500 R.P.M. Carburetion: Holley two-barrel. Five main bearings. Serial number code "B".

Thunderbird V-8: Overhead valves. Cast iron block. Displacement: 292 cubic inches. Bore and stroke: 3.75 x 3.30 inches. Compression ratio: 9.1:1. Brake horsepower: 212 at 4500 R.P.M. Carburetion: Holley four-barrel. Five main bearings. Serial number code "C".

Thunderbird Special V-8: Overhead valves. Cast iron block. Displacement: 312 cubic inches. Bore and stroke: 3.80 x 3.44 inches. Compression ratio: 9.7:1. Brake horsepower: 245 at 4500 R.P.M. Carburetion: Holley four-barrel. Five main bearings. Serial number code "D".

Thunderbird Special (8V) V-8: Overhead valves. Cast iron block. Displacement: 312 cubic inches. Bore and stroke: 3.80 x 3.44 inches. Compression ratio: 9.7:1 (10.00:1 with Racing Kit). Brake horsepower: 270 at 4800 R.P.M. (285 at 5000 R.P.M. with Racing Kit). Carburetion: two Holley four-barrels. Five main bearings. Serial number code "E".

Thunderbird Special Supercharged V-8: Overhead valves. Cast iron block. Displacement: 312 cubic inches. Bore and stroke: 3.80 x 3.44 inches. Compression ratio: 8.5:1. Brake horsepower: 300 at 4800 R.P.M. (340 at 5300 R.P.M. — NASCAR version). Carburetion: Holley four-barrel with Paxton centrifugal supercharger. Five main bearings. Serial number code "F".

CHASSIS FEATURES: Wheelbase: (Custom, Custom 300 and Station Wagon Series) 116 inches; (Fairlane, Fairlane 500) 118 inches; (Thunerbird) 102 inches. Overall length: (Custom, Custom 300) 201.6 inches; (Fairlane 500 Skyliner V-8 Retractable) 210.8 inches. (All other Fairlane and Fairlane 500) 207.7 inches; (Station Wagons) 203.5 inches; (Thunderbird) 181.4 inches. Tires: (Custom, Custom 300) 7.50 x 14 four-ply tubeless; (Fairlane, Fairlane 500) 7.50 x 14 four-ply tubeless; (Country Sedans and Squires) 8.00 x 14; (Thunderbird) 7.50 x 14 four-ply tubeless.

POWERTRAIN OPTIONS: Three-speed manual was standard. It featured a semi-centrifugal type clutch; three-speed helical gears and synchronizers for second and third gears. Three-speed with automatic overdrive was optional. Specifications were the same as above with automatic overdrive function cutting in at 27 M.P.H., cutting out at 21 M.P.H. Approximate drive ratio: 0.70:1. Manual control below instrument panel. Ford-O-Matic automatic transmission was also optional. This was a torque convertor transmission with automatic planetary gear train; single-stage, three-element hydraulic torque converter; hydro-mechinal automatic controls with no electric or vacuum connections and power flow through fluid member at all times. Six-cylinder rear axle ratios: (Ford-O-Matic) 3.22:1; (manual transmission) 3.89:1 and (automatic overdrive) 4.11:1. V-8 rear axle ratios: (Ford-O-Matic) 3.10:1; (manual transmission) 3.56:1 and (automatic overdrive) 3.70:1.

CONVENIENCE OPTIONS: (Special Thunderbird options or special optional equipment prices for Thunderbirds are set in bold-face type). Custom engine option, 292 cubic inch V-8, ($439). Ford-O-Matic for Ford ($188); **same for Thunderbird ($215).** Automati overdrive transmission for Ford ($108); **same for Thunderbird ($146).** Power steering ($68). Radio ($100). Heater and defroster ($85). **Windshield washers ($10). Power windows ($70). Engine chrome dress-up kit ($25).** Power brakes ($38). Fairlane/station wagon engine option, 312 cubic inch V-8 ($43). Rear fender shields (skirts). Two-tone paint. Backup lamps. Large wheel covers (standard on Fairlane 500). White sidewall tires. Continental tire extension kit. Outside rear view mirror. Lifeguard safety equipment package. Oversized tires. Radio antenna. Non-glare mirror. Other standard factory and dealer-installed options and accessories.

Historical footnotes: Introduction of 1957 Fords and Thunderbirds took place October 1956. The Fairlane 500 Skyliner Retractable Hardtop (convertible) was introduced as a mid-year addition to the line. Overdrive or Ford-O-Matic could now be ordered for any car with any engine. Model year production was 1,655,068 vehicles. Calendar year sales amounted to 1,522,406 Fords and Thunderbirds. Ford out-produced Chevrolet this season, to become America's Number 1 automaker of 1957 (model year basis). The Town Victoria was a four-door pillarless hardtop. The Del Rio was a DeLuxe two-door Ranch Wagon in Fairlane level trim. The Club Victoria was a two-door pillarless hardtop coupe. The Sunliner was a conventional two-door convertible.

FORD — Two ventures named Ford, with no apparent connection to the Dearborn company, were organized for automobile manufacture and seem to have exited the field before any production was seen.

The Ford Automobile Co. of Paterson, N.J., organized in early 1909 with a capital stock of $50,000 by R.W. Bates and G.M. Dorwart.

The Ford Taxicab Corp., a $10,000 venture organized in Portland, Maine during April of 1913 by Newton R. Dexter, Joseph B. Reed and Emery G. Wilson.

1896 Ford, Quadricycle, runabout, HFM

FORD — Dearborn, Michigan — (1903-1990) — Henry Ford was born on a farm in rural Michigan on July 30, 1863 and, as his father later said, grew up with "wheels in his head." At age 16 he took himself to Detroit and a variety of machine shop and other jobs which brought him close to engines. In 1888 he married a lovely young farmer's daughter named Clara Jane Bryant, and in 1891 became an engineer for the Edison Illuminating Co. On Nov. 6, 1893 the Fords' only child, Edsel, was born. On Christmas Eve that year or 1895 (sources differ but the latter is probably correct), Henry, with Clara helping to dribble gasoline into the intake valve, tested his first gasoline engine in the kitchen sink of the Ford home.

Although for a while the practical matters of his employment and providing for his family took precedence, already Henry Ford envisioned building an automobile. An acquaintance of his beat him to it, however, Henry cycling behind Charles Brady King when King tested his first gasoline automobile on the streets of Detroit in March 1896. Henry completed his first car that summer in the shed behind the Ford home, half of the side of which had to be removed to get it out since its inventor had neglected to consider that the door was too small. Once out, the car — he called it a quadricycle — performed well, its drive by leather belt and chain, its two-cylinder four-stroke horizontal engine producing about four hp, which was good for about 20 mph on excursions into the country to the Ford or Bryant farms, with Henry driving, Clara sitting beside with Edsel on her lap. Henry Ford was on his way to becoming a legend.

Although selling the vehicle was not his original inten-tion, when Charles Ainsley offered $200 for it, Ford accepted, using the money to finance his second car, which was completed in late 1897 or early 1898. In mid-1899, his efforts by now having come to the attention of Detroit businessmen with money to invest — including Detroit's mayor William C. Maybury and William H. Murphy, one of the wealthiest men in town — the Detroit Automobile Co. was organized, with Henry Ford as superintendent of a forthcoming automobile production which never came forth. Initially, Henry Ford couldn't make up his mind about what he wished to build, and when he did, his decision, much to the dismay of his backers, was for a race car — which beat a Winton at Grosse Pointe race track in October 1901.

Though only about a dozen cars of any sort had thus far resulted, some of the Ford backers still retained a modi-cum of faith in their superintendent and a new organiza-tion called the Henry Ford Co. resulted on Nov. 30, 1901.

By March 1902, however, disgruntled by a production that was ever forthcoming but never arriving, even the faithful Ford backers had lost faith. Moreover, they had brought in one Henry Martyn Leland as a consultant, which infuriated Ford. He left the company abruptly, tak-ing as settlement $900 and William Murphy's promise not to use the Ford name henceforth. Murphy was good to his word; the car which Henry Leland would now build for the former Ford backers was called the Cadillac.

Meanwhile, Henry Ford set himself up in a shop else-where in town and, with the help of Tom Cooper, built two race cars: the Arrow and the famous 999, a four-cylinder brute displacing an overwhelming 1155.3 cubic inches and in which, at Grosse Pointe in June 1903, Barney Old-field became the first driver to circle a one-mile track in less than a minute: 59.6 seconds was his speed, 999 was the first car Oldfield had ever driven, and his performance made him a star. In January 1904, Henry Ford himself drove a revised version of 999 on the ice at Lake St. Clair to a world land speed record of 91.37 mph.

Meanwhile, Ford had finally decided to become an auto-mobile manufacturer too, with the help of money supplied by coal baron Alexander Young Malcolmson. On June 16, 1903 the Ford Motor Co. evolved from the previous short-lived incorporations of the Ford & Malcomson Co.,

1901 Ford, runabout, OCW

Ltd. and the Fordmobile Co., Ltd., under neither of which had any cars been produced. But one month later, in July 1903, the first Ford Model A runabouts were loaded onto freight cars, and in the 15 months to follow an impressive total of 1700 cars would be built and sold at $750 ($850 with tonneau) apiece. These and all subsequent cars from Ford were renegades, unrecognized by the Association of Licensed Automobile Manufacturers. Rebuffed in his initial attempt to obtain an A.L.A.M. license, Ford elected to fight instead. Though others joined him, it was Ford who protested the loudest and whose maverick stance in contesting the monopolistic Selden Patent group made him a folk hero by January 1911 when, finally, the patent was declared ineffective by court decision.

By late 1904 the Model A had evolved into the C, which was different from the A mainly in the moving of its two-cylinder engine up front under a hood — Model C had a hood but engine still under seat as in Model A and there was a new Ford called the Model B which was a different car altogether save for the two-speed planetary transmission and gravity lubrication system it shared with predecessor Fords.

The B was a vertical in-line 24 hp four with shaft drive and a $2000 price tag, and Henry Ford didn't like it at all. It was built mainly because Malcolmson wanted a piece of the upper-price-market action. As early as 1903, Henry Ford had said, "The way to make automobiles is to make one automobile like another, to make them all alike, to make them come through the factory just alike" — already he was thinking universal car. But the Model B was not that, neither was the two-cylinder 16 hp $1200 Model F of 1905, nor especially the 40 hp six-cylinder $2500 Model K introduced later in 1905, a car Henry Ford positively detested — though, with Frank Kulick driving, one did establish a world record for 24 hours of 47.2 mph and 1135 miles, which bettered the previous mark by 309 miles.

By this time Ford had taken two steps toward the autonomy he desperately wanted; he made plans to extend his manufacturing to engines and running gear (previously this work had been farmed out, to Dodge Brothers especially), and he bought out Alexander Malcolmson (which meant he'd never be forced into building another expensive Ford). Henry Ford was in control now, and knew precisely where he was going. Introduced with the Model K had been the four-cylinder 15/18 hp Model N at $500, underselling the curved dash Oldsmobile (America's best-selling car of that period) and outselling the K by 10 cars to one. By 1906 Ford production topped the 8000 mark, which was good for first place in the industry; in February the N was joined by the R and was followed by the S in the fall of 1907, good sellers too.

In October 1908 the Model T arrived; Henry Ford was through experimenting for almost two decades. This was exactly the car he had wanted to build since 1903. Helping him realize it were Charles Sorenson, Joseph Galamb, Jimmy Smith and especially Childe Harold Wills whose metallurgical experiments with vanadium steel would result in the lightness with durability that was one of the hallmarks of the Model T. Helping him to set the car up for production was Walter Flanders, who would leave the company, however, before the T's introduction to become the "F" of the E-M-F.

The Ford Model T was a remarkable automobile, with 20 hp side-valve four-cylinder engine, two-speed planetary transmission, and a 100-inch wheelbase chassis of blessed simplicity and dogged reliability. (The countless jokes which grew up around the Model T were largely that, and affectionately told.) Considering its price class, the T was a powerful car with 45 mph possible, and it was an economical one too, needing only a gallon of gasoline every 25 miles or so. But more important than what the

Model T was, was what the Model T did. American became a vastly different place in the wake of the Tin Lizzie, and indeed the Ford concept realized with the Model T revolutionized the world.

The mass production of automobiles had its birth in August 1913 when the Ford final (or chassis) assembly line began to move. Although earlier, Ford and others (notably Ransom Eli Olds) had put together some elements (including sequential positioning of machines, men and material) necessary for mass production, it was only with the moving assembly line that a definitive mass production arrived. At Ford, chassis time was cut from 12 1/2 hours to one hour 33 minutes by January 1914, the month Henry Ford introduced the $5 day — and that year Ford produced more than 300,000 Model Ts at the same time the entire rest of the American industry was producing approximately 100,000 less. It was in that year, too, that the Model T, previously available in black, red, green, pearl or French gray, became available in "any color so long as it's black."

Mass production, of course, allowed the Model T to be profitably sold at ever-decreasing prices; introduced at $850, Ford's "Flivver" thereafter enjoyed yearly decreases to a low of $290 in December 1924. The T's price tag was one of the few things to change during the car's lifetime. The radiator shell was revised from brass to black in 1916, electric lights had been introduced in 1915, and January 1919 brought the option of an electric starter — but that was about all into the mid-'20s. In 1922 the Model T passed the million mark in annual sales, and would continue to enjoy million-plus years thereafter, but no longer would the car enjoy its utter dominance in the marketplace.

Everyone at Ford recognized what the emergence of popular competitors like the Chevrolet meant, except Henry Ford who through clever maneuvering shortly after the World War I — which included his resignation from the company and the placing of his son Edsel in the Ford presidency — had rid himself of all other Ford stockholders and thus now had no one to answer to but himself. Initally, Ford answered his associates' complaints regarding the Model Ts old-fashionedness by introducing balloon tires in 1925, and providing the option of wire wheels and the availability of colors other than black in 1926. Ultimately, by the year following and after the building of 15,000,000 Model Ts, even Henry Ford had to admit that the day of his beloved Tin Lizzie was over. The Ford assembly line was shut down at the end of May 1927; when it was started up again six months later, the Model A was on it. Like the T, it was a side-valve four, but twice as powerful at 40 hp, and set in a 103.5-inch wheelbase chassis with three-speed sliding gear transmission and four-wheel brakes. The Tin Lizzie's planetary gearset and two-wheel brakes had by the mid-'20s become two big marks against it, together with its ungainly appearance, this very nicely rectified in the Model A with sprightly body styling attributable mainly to Henry's son Edsel who had been guiding Lincoln fortunes since the Ford takeover of that company in 1922. No car in America had been so feverishly anticipated as the Model A Ford, and rumor ran rife during the half-year following the Ford shutdown until Dec. 2, 1927 when the car made its official debut. Interestingly, among the rumors had been that the new car would be a hybrid of the Lincoln and Ford called the Linford. Though there was a pretty Lincoln look to the car, the Model A with introductory prices as low as $385 was indisputably a Ford.

In the four years to follow, Ford and Chevrolet (which had become no. 1 with the Ford shutdown in '27) divided the production race, the Model A winning in 1929 and 1930, Chevy the victor in 1928 and 1931. Nearly five million Model As had been built by March 31, 1932 when

its successor arrived, the Ford V-8, offering 65 hp for as little as $460. Never before had so many cylinders and so much power been offered for so little. Because Ford enjoyed coming up with the revolutionary and because experimentation with eight-cylinder engines had been ongoing at the company since the mid-'20s, the V-8 was no doubt the car that Henry Ford would have wished to follow the Model T, though its development status had precluded that in 1927. A refined version of the Model A called Model B was introduced along with the V-8 but once the latter car got rolling, the four was forgotten altogether. In 1933 the V-8's wheelbase was increased to 112 inches from the rather short 106.5 with which it had been introduced. In 1934 when the Chevrolet went to independent front suspension, Ford was in the seemingly uncomfortable position of having to justify its continued use of all-round transverse leaf suspension (which had been introduced on the T), but a by-now increasingly stubborn Henry Ford explained it away by saying, "We use transverse springs for the same reason that we use round wheels — because we have found nothing better for the purpose."

In 1935 Ford outsold Chevrolet, but for all other years in the '30s, Chevy was on top. This is not to suggest that the V-8 Ford was an unpopular automobile. It most certainly was popular, its performance potential particularly providing an appeal to the go-faster crowd, whether its member be interested in an illegal fast getaway (as the bank-robbing Clyde Barrow who wrote Henry Ford a testimonial letter) or a legal one (Ford V-8's virtually ruled stock car racing for several years, and Ford racing specials were a mainstay of the Automobile Racing Club of America in the mid-to-late '30s). But many average drivers preferred technical advances and more creature comforts than the V-8 had. In 1936 Chevrolet introduced hydraulic brakes; in 1937 Ford countered with a smaller 60 hp V-8 for a cheaper line of cars, but both it and the traditional V-8 (now at 85 hp) had mechanical brakes. The smaller V-8 was not a success, and Ford dealers began clamouring for a six to sell. But they were not to get it for a while. Among numerous other problems the company had now, the labor situation at Ford during the later '30s was ominous and life-threatening.

As the Ford Motor Co. moved toward the brink of disaster, an aging Henry Ford, always a mercurial man, grew increasingly recalcitrant. His son Edsel, together with long-time Ford associate Charles Sorenson, became convinced that the Ford Motor Co. could only survive despite Henry Ford and not because of him. The Ford V-8 was finally given four-wheel hydraulic brakes for 1939, and the company had a new car that year, another V-8, called the Mercury. About the time it was introduced, Edsel Ford finally convinced his father to produce the car that he and Ford dealers had wanted for several years already. "A Ford Six, At Last" headlined *Business Week* when the new Special was introduced for 1941. It was the first six from Ford since the Model K that Henry had hated so much in 1905, and he had nothing to do with the engine. It was, however, introduced in any color so long as it was black, and the elder Ford may have had something to do with that. (Other colors were quickly added, however.)

A pacifist since his peace ship days of the World War I, Henry Ford remained one as World War II approached and, with Charles Lindbergh, was a member of the America First Committee. His son Edsel was not. Prior to Pearl Harbor, the elder Ford had refused to aid the international war effort, believing in military production geared only for American defense purposes, but following the attack in Hawaii, he ordered a complete changeover to military production even before the War Production Board ordered it. But personal tragedy would strike Henry Ford soon.

On May 26, 1943, his son Edsel, weary and ill from the difficult years when he had become the conscience of the company and an adversary of his father, died of cancer, undulant fever and — as has been written — a broken heart. He was 49 years old. At the funeral Henry Ford stood tight-lipped in grief, and afterwards he appointed himself president of the Ford Motor Co. He was 80 years old. The Ford Motor Co. lay in chaos now. On Sept. 21, 1945 — with the endorsement of his grandmother and his mother, including a threat by the latter to sell her stock — the eldest son of Edsel Ford became the president of the Ford Motor Co., over Henry Ford's objection. On April 7, 1947 Henry Ford was gone; "The Father of the Automobile Dies," headlined *Life* magazine. It would be Henry Ford II who would guide Ford Motor Co. fortunes in the postwar era.

Ford Data Compilation
by Robert C. Ackerson

Model T Data Compilation
by Bruce McCally

1903 FORD

1903 Ford, model A, runabout, OCW

FORD — MODEL A — TWO: The first production automobile produced by the Ford Motor Company, which was incorporated on June 16, 1903, the Model A, was a 2-seater runabout capable of a maximum speed of 30 mph.

With a weight of just 1250 pounds it was an early manifestation of Henry Ford's grasp of the automotive concept that would be fully exhibited in the Model T. As was common to most early automobiles the Model A had a horse buggy (without the horse of course!) appearance. The motor was positioned under the seat and a detachable tonneau provided seating for two additional passengers who gained access to their seats through a rear door.

I.D. DATA: Serial numbers were dash mounted, adjacent to steering column.

Model No.	Body Type & Seating	Price	Weight	Prod. Total
A	Rbt.-2P	850	1250	Note 1
A	Rbt. w/ton.-2P	950	—	Note 1

Note 1: Total production for Model A Series was 670 or 1708, depending upon the source referred to. Ford officially used the 670 figure.

ENGINE: Opposed. Two. Cast iron block. B & S: 4 in. x 4 in. Disp.: 100.4 cu. in. Brake H.P.: 8. Valve lifters: Mechanical. Carb.: Schebler (early), Holley.

CHASSIS: W.B.: 72 in.

TECHNICAL: Planetary transmission. Speeds: 2F/1R. Floor controls. Chain drive. Differential, band brakes. Wooden, spoke wheels.

HISTORICAL: Introduced July 1903. On June 19, 1903 Barney Oldfield drove the Ford 999 to a new one mile record time of 59.6 seconds. Calendar year production: 1708. Model year production: (1903-1904) 1700. The president of Ford was John S. Gray.

1904 FORD

FORD — MODELS AC, C — TWO: These two Ford models replaced the Model A in late 1904. Both were powered by a larger engine developing 10hp. Ford claimed the top speed of both cars was 38mph. The Model AC was essentially a Model A with the new Model C engine. The Model C had its fuel tank positioned under the hood while that of the AC was located beneath the seat. Both cars had a longer, 78 inch wheelbase than that of the Model A.

FORD — MODEL B — FOUR: The Model B was a drastic shift in direction for Henry Ford. With its 4 passenger body, polished wood and brass trim, it was an elegant and expensive automobile. Powered by a 24hp, 318 cubic inch four it was capable of a top speed of 40mph. In place of the dry cells carried by earlier Fords, the Model B was equipped with storage batteries. A 15 gallon fuel tank was also fitted. Other features separating the $2000 Model B from other Fords was its shaft drive and rear hub drum brakes.

I.D. DATA: Location of Serial No.: dash mounted, adjacent to steering column.

1904 Ford, model C, runabout with tonneau, OCW.

Model No.	Body Type & Seating	Price	Weight	Prod. Total
Model A	Rbt.-2P	850	1250	Note 1
Model A	Rbt. w/ton.-2P	950	1250	Note 1
Model AC	Rbt.-2P	850	1250	Note 1
Model AC	Rbt. w/ton.-2P	950	1250	Note 1
Model C	Rbt.-2P	850	1250	Note 1
Model C	Rbt. w/ton.-2P	950	1250	Note 1
Model B	2-dr. Tr.-4P	2000	1700	Note 1

Note 1: Total production in 1904 was 1,695 cars. Ford reported building a total of 670 model As and 1900 models A and AC altogether. Other sources show figures that vary.

ENGINE: [Model A] Cylinder layout: opposed. Two. Cast iron block. B & S: 4 in. x 4 in. Disp.: 100.4 cu. in. Brake H.P.: 8. Valve lifters: Mechanical. Carb.: Holley. [Model AC, C] Cylinder layout: opposed. Two. Cast iron block. B & S: 4-1/4 in. x 4-1/4 in. Disp.: 120.5 cu. in. Brake H.P.: 10. Valve lifters: Mechanical. Carb.: Holley. [Model B] Inline. Four. Cast iron block. B & S: 4-1/4 in. x 5 in. Disp.: 283.5 cu. in. Brake H.P.: 24. Valve lifters: Mechanical. Carb.: Holley.

CHASSIS: [Model A] W.B.: 72 in. [Model B] W.B.: 92 in. [Model C, Model AC] W.B.: 78 in. Tires: 28.

1904 Ford, model B, touring, JAC.

TECHNICAL: [Models A, AC, C] Planetary transmission. Speeds: 2F/1R. Floor shift controls. Cone clutch. Chain drive. Differential band brakes. Wooden spoke wheels. [Model B] Planetary transmission. Speeds: 2F/1R. Floor shift controls. Cone clutch. Shaft drive. Drum brakes. Two rear wheels. Wooden spoke wheels.

HISTORICAL: Date of Introduction: Sept. 1904 (Model C, AC). Calendar year production: 1695. Model year production: (1904-1905) 1745. Antique. The president of Ford was John S. Gray.

1905 FORD

FORD — MODEL F — TWO: The Ford Models C and B were carried into 1905. The Model C was given light yellow painted running gear in place of the former red finish along with wider 3 x 28 wheels.

In February 1905, these Fords were joined by the Model F powered by a 2 cylinder engine developing approximately 16hp. The Model F had a wheelbase of 84 inches and was fitted with a green body, cream colored wheels and running gear.

I.D. DATA: Serial numbers were dash mounted, adjacent to steering column

Model No.	Body Type & Seating	Price	Weight	Prod. Total
C	Rbt.-2P	800	1250	Note 1
C	Rbt. w/ton.	950	1250	Note 1
B	2-dr. Tr.-4P	2000	1700	Note 1
F	2-dr. Tr. Car-4P	1000	1400	Note 1
F	2-dr. Dr. Cpe.-2P	1250	—	Note 1

Note 1: Total production for 1905 was 1,599 cars.

1905 Ford, model B, touring, OCW

ENGINE: [Model C] Opposed. Two. Cast iron block. B & S: 4-1/4 in. x 4-1/2 in. Disp.: 120.5 cu. in. Brake H.P.: 10. Valve lifters: Mechanical. Carb.: Holley. [Model B] Inline. Four. Cast iron block. B & S: 4-1/4 in. x 4 in. Disp.: 283.5 cu. in. Brake H.P.: 24. Valve lifters: Mechanical. Carb.: Holley. [Model F] Opposed. Two. Cast iron block. B & S: 4-1/2 in. x 4 in. Disp.: 127 cu. in. Brake H.P.: 16+. Valve lifters: Mechanical. Carb.: Holley.

CHASSIS: [Model C] W.B.: 78 in. Tires: 28. [Model F] W.B.: 84 in. Tires: 30. [Model B] W.B.: 92 in. Tires: 32.

1905 Ford, model C, runabout with tonneau, OCW

TECHNICAL: [Model C] Planetary transmission. Speeds: 2F/1R. Floor controls. Cone clutch. Chain drive. Differential band brakes. Wooden spoke wheels. Wheel size: 28. [Model B] Planetary transmission. Speeds: 2F/1R. Floor controls. Cone clutch. Shaft drive. Drum brakes on two rear wheels. Wooden spoke wheels. Wheel size: 32. [Model F] Planetary transmission. Speeds: 2F/1R. Floor controls. Cone clutch. Chain drive. Differential band brakes. Wooden spoke wheels. Wheel size: 30.

OPTIONS: Top. Windshield. Lights.

HISTORICAL: Introduced February 1905 (Model F). Calendar year production: 1599. Model year production: (1905-1906) 1599. The President of Ford was John S. Gray.

1906 FORD

1906 Ford, model K, touring, JAC

FORD — MODEL K — SIX: Late in 1905 the Model K Ford, priced at $2500 in touring form debuted. Since Henry Ford was moving close to the final design of his "car for the multitudes", it's not surprising that he cared little for this expensive automobile. Along with the touring model a roadster version was offered that was guaranteed to attain a 60 mph top speed.

1906 Ford, model N, roadster, OCW

FORD — MODEL N — FOUR: The $500 Model N with its front-mounted 4-cylinder engine developing over 15 hp was capable of 45 mph. Its styling, highlighted by such features as twin nickel-plated front lamps and a boat-tail rear deck, plus an 84 inch wheelbase, and a reputation for reliability represented a solid step forward by Henry Ford in his quest for a low-priced car for the mass market.

FORD — MODEL F — TWO: The Model F was continued into 1906 unchanged. No longer available were Models B and C.

I.D. DATA: Dash mounted, adjacent to steering column.

Model No.	Body Type & Seating	Price	Weight	Prod. Total
Model F	2 dr. Tr. Cr.-4P	1100	1400	Note 1
Model K	2 dr. Tr. Cr.-4P	2500	2400	Note 1
Model K	Rbt.-4P	2500	2400	Note 1
Model N	Rbt.-2P	600	800	Note 1

Note 1: Total production was 2,798 or 8,729 depending upon the source referred to. Ford Motor Co. records show both figures.

ENGINE: [Model F] Opposed. 2. Cast iron block. B x S: 4-1/4 in. x 4-1/2 in. Disp: 128 cu. in. Brake H.P.: 10. Valve lifters: Mechanical. Carb.: Holley. [Model K] Inline. Six. Cast iron block. B x S: 4-1/2 in. x 4-1/4 in. Disp.: 405 cu. in. Brake H.P. 40. Valve lifters: Mechanical. Carb.: Holley. [Model N] Inline Four. Cast iron block. B x S: 3-3/4 in. x 3-3/8 in. Disp.: 149 cu. in. Brake H.P.: 15-18. Valve lifters: Mechanical. Carb.: Holley.

CHASSIS: [Series Model F] W.B.: 84. Tires: 30. [Series Model N] W.B.: 84. Tires: 2-1/2'' width. [Series Model K] W.B.: 114/120.

TECHNICAL: [Model F] Transmission: Planetary. Speeds: 2F/1R. Floor shift controls. Cone clutch. Chain drive. Differential band. Wooden spokes. Wheel size: 30. [Model K] Transmission: Planetary. Speeds 2F/1R. Floor shift controls. Disc clutch. Shaft drive. [Model N] Transmission: Planetary. Speeds: 2F/1R. Floor. Disc clutch. Chain drive.

OPTIONS: Cowl lamps. Bulb horn. 3'' wheels (Model N) (50.00).

HISTORICAL: Henry Ford became president of the Ford Motor Company, following the death of John S. Gray on July 6, 1906. A racing version of the Model K set a new world's 24 hr record of 1135 miles of 47.2 mph at Ormond Beach.

1907 FORD

FORD — MODEL K — SIX: The Model K was unchanged for 1907.

FORD — MODEL N — FOUR: The Model N was continued unchanged for 1907. As before it was a handsome automobile with nickel hardware and quarter-circle fenders. Volume production didn't begin until late 1907 when the price rose to $600.

FORD — MODEL R — FOUR: The Model R was introduced in February 1907 as a more elaborate version of the Model N with foot boards in place of the Model N's carriage step. A mechanical lubrication system also replaced the forced-feed oiler of the Model N.

FORD — MODEL S — FOUR: The Model S had the same mechanical and appearance features as that of the Model R, in addition to a single seat tonneau.

I.D. DATA: Serial numbers were dash mounted, adjacent to steering column.

1907 Ford, model K, touring, OCW

Model No.	Body Type & Seating	Price	Weight	Prod. Total
K	2-dr. Tr. Car-4P	2800	2000	—
K	Rbt.-4P	2800	2000	—
N	Rbt.-2P	600	1050	—
R	Rbt.-2P	750	1400	Note 1
S	Rbt. w/ton.-4P	700	1400	—
S	Rds.-2P	750	—	—

Note 1: Total production of the Model R was approximately 2,500 cars.

ENGINE: [Model K] Inline. Six. Cast iron block. B & S: 4-1/2 in. x 4-1/4 in. Disp.: 405 cu. in. Brake H.P.: 40. Valve lifters: Mechanical. Carb.: Holley. [Model N, R, S] Inline. Four. Cast iron block. B & S: 3-3/4 in. x 3-3/8 in. Disp.: 149 cu. in. Brake H.P.: 15-18. Valve lifters: Mechanical. Carb.: Holley.

CHASSIS: [Model K] W.B.: 120 in. [Model N, R, S] W.B.: 84 in. Tires: 3'' width.

1907 Ford, model S, roadster, OCW

TECHNICAL: [Model K] Planetary transmission. Speeds: 2F/1R. Floor controls. Disc clutch. Shaft drive. [Model N, R, S] Planetary transmission. Speeds: 2F/1R. Floor controls. Disc clutch. Chain drive.

HISTORICAL: Calendar year production was 6,775 according to some sources and 14,887 according to others. The president of Ford was Henry Ford.

1908 FORD

FORD — MODELS K, N, R, S — FOUR: For the 1908 model year Ford continued to produce the K, N, R, and S models until production of the Model T began in October 1908.

I.D. DATA: Serial numbers were dash mounted, adjacent to steering column.

Model No.	Body Type & Seating	Price	Weight	Prod. Total
K	2-dr. Tr. Cr.-4P	2800	2000	—
K	Rbt.-4P	2800	2000	—
N	Rbt.-2P	600	1050	—
N	Land.-4P	—	—	—
R	Rbt.-2P	750	1400	—
S	Rbt. w/ton.-4P	750	1400	—
S	Rds.-2P	700	—	—

ENGINE: [Model K] Inline. Six. Cast iron block. B & S: 4-1/2 in. x 4-1/4 in. Disp.: 405. Brake H.P.: 40. Valve lifters: Mechanical. Carb.: Holley. [Model N, R, S] Inline. Four. Cast iron block. B & S: 3-3/4 in. x 3-3/8 in. Disp.: 149. Brake H.P.: 15-18. Valve lifters: Mechanical. Carb.: Holley.

1908 Ford, model S, roadster, OCW

CHASSIS: [Model K] W.B.: 120 in. [Model N, R, S] W.B.: 84 in. Tires: 3'' width.

TECHNICAL: [Model K] Planetary transmission. Speeds: 2F/1R. Floor shift controls. Disc clutch. Shaft drive. [Model N, R, S] Planetary transmission. Speeds: 2F/1R. Floor shift controls. Disc clutch. Chain drive.

HISTORICAL: Calendar year production was 6,015 according to some sources and 10,202 according to others (including early Model T Fords). The president of Ford was Henry Ford.

1909 FORD

1909 Ford, model T, touring, HFM

FORD — EARLY 1909 — MODEL T: The Model T Ford was introduced in October 1908, and was an entirely new car when compared to Ford's previous models. The engine had four cylinders, cast en-bloc; with a removable cylinder head, quite unusual for the time. The engine pan was a one-piece steel stamping and had no inspection plate.

The chassis featured transverse springs, front and rear; a rear axle housing which was drawn steel rather than a casting. Rear axles were non-tapered; the hubs being held with a key and a pin, with the pin being retained by the hub cap. The front axle was a forged "I" beam with spindles which had integral arms.

The use of Vanadium steel almost throughout made for a stronger yet lighter machine which gave the Ford impressive performance for its time.

Wheels were 30'' with 30x3'' tires on the front, and 30x3-1/2'' on the rear. The wheel hub flanges were 5-1/2'' diameter (compared with 6'' from 1911 until the end of production in 1927).

Windshields and tops were optional equipment on the open cars, as were gas headlights, speedometers, robe rails, Prestolite tanks, foot rests, auto chimes, car covers and other accessories which Ford would install at the factory.

The radiator was brass, as were any lamps furnished (oil cowl and tail lamps were standard equipment). The hood had no louvres and was made of aluminum.

Body styles offered were the Touring, Runabout (roadster), Coupe, Town Car and Landaulet.

Bodies were generally made of wood panels over a wood frame, and were offered in red, gray and green; gray being primarily on the Runabouts, red on the Tourings, and green on the Town Cars and Landaulets.

These early cars (first 2500) were so unique that they are generally considered a separate subject when discussing the Model T. Essentially, the engines had built-in water pumps; and the first 800 cars came with two foot pedals and two control levers (the second lever being for reverse) instead of the usual three pedals and one lever.

Front fenders were square tipped, with no bills.

FORD — LATE 1909 - MODEL T: Beginning about car number 2500, the Model T became more or less standardized. Through most of 1909 the windshields and tops on the open cars remained optional, but more and more were delivered with this equipment, as well as gas headlights, factory installed. By the end of the year, they were standard.

Body types and styling continued unchanged. Colors continued as in the early production except that green and red Tourings were both produced, along with a mixture of colors in the other models as well. Red was not offered after June 1909. Black was not listed as an available color and only one of the shipping invoices showed black, but early cars extant today seem to indicate that black was used. This could be due to oxidation of the top color coat, but black early Fords are an enigma to the Model T stu-

1909 Ford, model T, coupe, HAC

dent. The one aluminum-paneled Touring body, built by Pontiac Body, was discontinued about September 1909.

Fenders were similar in design to the earlier 1909's but now had rounded fronts with small "bills."

The engine no longer had the water pump. It was now cooled by thermo-syphon action and set the pattern for all later Model T engines.

I.D. DATA: [Early 1909 (Oct. '08 to Apr. 09)] Serial number was between center exhaust ports on side of engine. Starting: 1 (October 1908). Ending: 2500 (approx.) (The first of the non-water pump engines was 2448, built on April 22, 1909 but there was some mixture of the old and the new in production for a short time.) Calendar year engine numbers: 1 to 309. (October to December 1908). Car numbers were stamped on a plate on the front seat kick panel and these were the same as the engine numbers. Other numbers stamped on the body sills, etc. were manufacturer's numbers and not an identifying number. [1909] Serial number was behind the timing gear on the lower right side of the engine. Starting: 2501 (approx.) Ending: 11145 (approx.) (There is no "break" between the 1909 and 1910 cars. 11146 was the first number assembled in October 1909, the beginning of Ford's fiscal year 1910.). 1909 calendar year engine numbers: 310 to 14161 (approx.) Car numbers were stamped on a plate on the front seat kick panel and these were the same as the engine numbers. Other numbers stamped on the body sills, etc. were manufacturer's numbers and not an identifying number.

Model No.	Body Type & Seating	Price	Weight	Prod. Total
T	Tr.-5P	850 (A)	1200	7728 (B)
T	Rbt.-2P	825 (A)	NA	2351 (B)
T	Town Car-7P	1000 (A)	NA	236 (B)
T	Landaulet-7P	950 (A)	NA	298 (B)
T	Cpe.-2P	950 (A)	NA	47 (B)

Note: 1200 pounds was the figure given for the Touring car and "others in proportion." The bare chassis weighed about 900 pounds.
All body styles except the roadster had two doors; the front compartment being open and without doors on all but the Coupe.
(A) Prices effective October 1, 1908 (at introduction of the Model T).
(B) Fiscal year: October 1, 1908 to September 30, 1909.

1909 Ford, model T, touring, OCW

ENGINE: [Early 1909 (first 2500)] L-head. Four. Cast iron block. B & S: 3-3/4 in. x 4 in. Disp.: 176.7 cu. in. C.R.: 4.5:1 (approx.) Brake H.P.: 22 @ 1600 R.P.M. N.A.C.C. H.P.: 22.5. Main bearings: Three. Valve lifters: Solid. Carb.: Kingston 5-ball, Buffalo. Torque: 83 lbs.-ft. @ 900 R.P.M.
Note: The first 2500 engines had an integral gear-driven water pump and a gear driven fan. There was no babbitt in the upper half of the main bearings. No inspection plate in the crankcase. Valve stems and lifters are exposed (no cover door).
[1909] L-head. Four. Cast iron block. B & S: 3-3/4 in x 4 in. Disp.: 176.7 cu. in. C.R.: 4.5:1 (approx.) Brake H.P.: 22 @ 1600 R.P.M. N.A.C.C. H.P.: 22.5. Main bearings: Three. Valve lifters: Solid. Carb.: Kingston 5-ball, Holley, Buffalo. Torque: 83 lbs.-ft. @ 900 R.P.M.
Note: No water pump; now cooled by thermo-syphon action. There was no babbitt in the upper half of the main bearings. No inspection plate in the crankcase. Valve stems and lifters are exposed (no cover door).

CHASSIS: W.B.: 100 in. O.L.: 10 ft. 8 in. (Chassis) 11 ft. 2-1/2 in. (car). Frt/Rear Tread: 56 in. (60 in. optional until 1916). Tires: 30 x 3 front, 30 x 3-1/2 rear, standard equipment 1909-1925.
Note: Chassis essentially identical except those after mid-1913 have a longer rear crossmember.

TECHNICAL: [Early 1909 (First 800)] Planetary transmission. Speeds: 2F/1R. 2 pedal controls and two levers on floor. (See "General Comments") Multiple disk clutch (24 disks). Torque tube drive. Straight bevel rear axle. Overall ratio: 3.63:1. Brakes: contracting band in transmission. Hand-operated internal expanding in rear wheels. Foot brake stops driveshaft. Parking brake on two rear wheels. Wheel size: 30 in.

OPTIONS: The basic equipment included three oil lamps only. (Two side and one tail.) Options listed included: Windshield. Headlamps. Tops. Horns. Prestolite tanks (instead of the carbide tank). Robe rails. Tire chains. Top boots. Foot rests. Spare tire carriers. Speedometers. Bumpers. No prices were given.

GENERAL COMMENTS

Clutch & Brakes [thru car 800]: Clutch pedal gives low when pressed to floor, high when released, neutral in-between. Reverse lever puts clutch in neutral and applies reverse brake band. Second lever is the parking brake. [1909-1927] Planetary transmission. Speeds: 2F/1R. 3 pedal controls and 1 lever on floor. * Multiple disk clutch (26 disks 1909-1915). (25 disks 1915-1927). Torque tube drive. Straight bevel rear axle. Overall ratio: 3.63:1. Brakes: Contracting band in transmission. Hand-operated internal expanding in rear wheels. Foot brake stops driveshaft. Parking brake on two rear wheels. Wheel size: 30 in. (21 in. optional in 1925, standard in 1926-1927). Drivetrain options: 4 to 1 optional rear axle ratio beginning in 1919.
Clutch & Brakes [after car 800]: Clutch pedal gives low when pressed to floor, high when released, neutral in-between. Control lever puts clutch in neutral and applies parking brake. Center foot pedal applies reverse. Third (right hand) pedal is the service brake, applying transmission brake band.
Model T Wheels: Standard wheels are wooden spoke with demountable rims, an option beginning in 1919. In 1925, 21" wood-spoke demountable rim wood wheels were an option; these became standard in 1926. Beginning January 1926 optional 21" wire wheels became available, and these became standard on some closed cars in calendar year 1927.
In mid-1925 (1926 models) the transmission brake was made about a half-inch wider, and the rear wheel brakes were enlarged to 11" with lined shoes. (1909-1925 were 7" with cast iron shoes no lining).
Springs are transverse semi-elliptic, front and rear.
Model T Steering: 3 to 1 steering gear ratio by planetary gear at top of steering column until mid-1925 when ratio was changed to 5 to 1.

1910 FORD

1910 Ford, model T, OCW

FORD — MODEL T: The 1910 Fords were unchanged from 1909, except for a number of mechanical modifications in the rear axle, and the use of one standard color on all models, dark green. The Landaulet and Coupe were discontinued in 1910 and a new Tourabout (basically a touring car using two separate seat sections) was added. All 1910 Model Ts had windshields.

I.D. DATA: Serial number was behind the timing gear on the lower right side of the engine. Starting: 11146 (approx.) Ending: 31532 (approx.) (there is no "break" between the 1910 and 1911 cars. 31533 was the first number assembled in October 1910, the beginning of Ford's fiscal year 1911. The first "1911" car built was a Torpedo Runabout in which the chassis was assembled October 5, and the final assembly October 26. The first "blue" cars were built during October and are presumed to be "1911" models.) 1910 Calendar year engine numbers: 14162 (approx.) to 34901. Car numbers were stamped on a plate on the front seat kick panel and these were the same as the engine numbers. Other numbers stamped on the body sills, etc. were manufacturer's numbers and not an identifying number.

Model No.	Body Type & Seating	Price	Weight	Prod. Total
T	Tr.-5P	950 (A)	1200	16,890 (B)
T	Tourabout-4P	950 (A)	NA	** (C)
T	Rbt.-2P	900 (A)	NA	1486 (B)
T	Town Car-7P	1200 (A)	NA	377 (B)
T	Landaulet-7P	1100 (A)	NA	2 (B)
T	Cpe.-2P	1050 (A)	NA	187 (B)
T	Chassis	NA	900	108 (D)

Note: 1200 pounds was the figure given for the Touring car, and "others in proportion." The bare chassis weighed about 900 pounds.
All body styles except the Roadster and the Tourabout had two doors; the front compartment being open and without doors on all but the Coupe. The Tourabout was similar to the Touring but had two roadster-like seat sections and no doors.
(A) Prices effective October 1, 1909
(B) Fiscal year, October 1, 1909 to September 30, 1910
(C) Tourings and Tourabouts grouped. 16,890 is the total of the two.
(D) Chassis not shown in the catalog.

ENGINE: L-head. Four. Cast iron block. B & S: 3-3/4 in. x 4 in. Disp.: 176.7 in. C.R.: 4.5:1 (approx.) Brake H.P.: 22 @ 1600 R.P.M. N.A.C.C. H.P.: 22.5. Main bearings: Three. Valve lifters: Solid. Carb.: Kingston 5-ball, Holley, Buffalo (early 1910 only). Torque: 83 lbs.-ft. @ 900 R.P.M.
Note: No water pump; now cooled by thermo-syphon action. There was no babbitt in the upper half of the main bearings. No inspection plate in the crankcase. Valve stems and lifters are exposed (no cover door).

CHASSIS: [1909-1925] W.B.: 100 in. O.L.: 10 ft. 8 in. (Chassis) 11 ft. 2-1/2 in. (car). Frt/Rear Tread: 56 in. (60 in. optional until 1916). Tires: 30 x 3 front, 30 x 3-1/2 rear, standard equipment 1909-1925.

TECHNICAL: Planetary transmission. Speeds: 2F/1R. 3 pedal controls and 1 lever on floor. Multiple disk clutch. Torque tube drive. Straight bevel rear axle. Overall ratio: 3.63:1. Brakes: Contracting band in transmission. Hand-operated internal expanding in rear wheels. Foot brake stops driveshaft. Parking brake on two rear wheels.
Note: Additional technical details will be found in the 1909 "General Comments" box.

OPTIONS: The many options listed for 1909 were not available in 1910. Standard equipment for the open cars now included the windshield, gas headlamps and carbide generator, speedometer and top with side curtains.
Interestingly, the more expensive closed cars (Landaulet, Town Car and Coupe) were equipped with horn and oil lamps only. Headlamps and speedometer were $80 extra.

1911 FORD

1911 Ford, model T, town car, HAC

FORD — MODEL T: Approximately January 1911 the Model T was completely restyled. New fenders, a new but similar radiator, new wheels, new bodies, and during the year, a new engine, front axle and rear axle made the 1911 Ford almost a new beginning.
Bodies were now made with steel panels over a wood framework. A new standard color of dark blue was used on all models.*
Body types continued those offered in 1910. The Tourabout and Landaulet, while listed in the catalogs, were not produced in 1911. The Coupe was phased out; only forty-five being built.
Two new bodies were offered, the Open Runabout and the Torpedo Runabout, both of which differed considerably from the other models in that they had curved fenders, a longer hood, a lower seating arrangement and a lower and longer steering column. In addition, the gas tank was located on the rear deck, behind the seat. The two cars were similar; the Open Runabout not having doors while the Torpedo had one on each side.
Near the end of the year, and then called a "1912" model, a Delivery Car was offered.
Fender construction was also new, setting a general pattern for the bulk of Model T production (until 1926). The front fenders had larger "Gills" than did the 1910 style.
Lamps were all brass; gas headlights and oil (kerosene) side and tail lamps.
The rear axle housing was redesigned. The earlier pressed steel type had gone through a number of modifications in 1909, 1910 and early 1911 but in mid-year a new type with a cast-iron center section appeared. Axles were now taper-end (perhaps changed before the new housing) and the hub flanges were 6" in diameter.
The front axle now used spindles with separate steering arms, and the axle ends were modified to accept the new spindles. The front axle remained relatively unchanged in later years.
* See comments on black cars in 1909.

I.D. DATA: Serial number was behind the timing gear on the lower right side of the engine. Starting: 31533 (approx.). Ending: 70749 (approx.). (There is no "break" between the 1911 and 1912 cars. 70750 was the first number assembled in October 1911, the beginning of Ford's fiscal year 1912.) 1911 Calendar year engine numbers: 34901 to 88900 (approx.).
Car numbers were stamped on a plate on the fire wall and these might be the same as the engine numbers. Ford now used the engine number to identify all cars. Other numbers stamped on the body sills, etc. were manufacturer's numbers and not an identifying number.

Model No.	Body Type & Seating	Price	Weight	Prod. Total
T	Tr.-5P	780 (B)	1200	26,405 (C)
T	Trbt.-4P	725 (B)	NA	0 (C)
T	Rbt.-2P	680 (B)	NA	7845 (E)
T	Torp. Rbt.-2P	725 (B)	NA	(E)
T	Open Rbt.-2P	680 (B)	NA	(E)
T	Twn. Car-7P	960 (A)	NA	315 (C)
T	Lan.-7P	1100 (A)	NA	0 (C)
T	Cpe.-2P	840 (A)	NA	45 (C)
T	Chassis	NA	940	248 (D)

1911 Ford, model T, touring, OCW

Note: 1200 pounds was the figure given for the Touring car, with "others in proportion." The bare chassis weighed about 940 pounds.
All body styles except the Roadster and the Tourabout had two doors; the front compartment being open and without doors on all but the Coupe. The Tourabout was similar to the Touring but had two roadster-like seat sections and no doors.
The Coupe, Landaulet and Tourabout were discontinued before calendar 1911.
(A) Prices for cars without headlamps!
(B) Prices effective October 1, 1910.
(C) Fiscal year, October 1, 1910 to September 30, 1911.
(D) Chassis not shown in catalogs.
(E) Runabouts not broken down by types in production figures.

ENGINE: L-head. Four. Cast iron block. B & S: 3-3/4 in. x 4 in. Disp.: 176.7 cu. in. C.R.: 4.5:1 (approx.). Brake H.P.: 22 @ 1600 R.P.M. N.A.C.C. H.P.: 22.5. Main bearings: Three. Valve lifters: Solid. Carb.: Kingston 5-ball, Holley 4500, Holley H-1 4550. Torque: 83 lbs.-ft. @ 900 R.P.M.
Note: Thermo-syphon. Upper main bearings now babbitted. Valve chambers (2) now enclosed using steel doors held with one stud/nut each. Inspection plate in the crankcase.

CHASSIS: W.B.: 100 in. O.L.: 10 ft. 8 in. (Chassis) 11 ft. 2-1/2 in. (car). Frt/Rear Tread: 56 in. (60 in. optional until 1916). Tires: 30 x 3 front, 30 x 3-1/2 rear, standard equipment 1909-1925.

TECHNICAL: Planetary transmission. Speeds: 2F/1R. 3 pedal controls and 1 lever on floor. Multiple disk clutch. Torque tube drive. Straight bevel rear axle. Overall ratio: 3.63:1. Brakes: Contracting band in transmission. Hand-operated internal expanding in rear wheels. Foot brake stops driveshaft. Parking brake on two rear wheels.
Note: Additional technical details will be found in the 1909 "General Comments" box.

OPTIONS: All cars equipped with headlamps, horn, etc. with no options. Ford even said the warrantee would be voided if any accessories were added, although it's doubtful this ever happened.

1912 FORD

FORD — MODEL T: Approximately January, 1912 the Model T was again restyled, although the appearance was similar to the 1911 cars. The Touring car was now supplied with "fore doors" which enclosed the front compartment. These were removable and many have been lost over the years. The metal side panels of the Touring were now relatively smooth from top to bottom, eliminating the "step" under the seats which marked the 1911's.
The top support straps now fasten to the windshield hinge, rather than to the front of the chassis as they did in prior years.
The Torpedo Runabout was now based on the standard runabout, and the Open Runabout was discontinued. While retaining the curved rear fenders, the front fenders were now standard. The hood and steering column were also the same as those used on the other 1912 cars. The front compartment was enclosed in a manner similar to the 1911 Torpedo.
The "1912" style year lasted only about nine months; an all new "1913" car appeared about September.
The only color on record for 1912 was dark blue but the existence of black cars of the era seems to indicate that black was available as well.

I.D. DATA: Serial number was behind the timing gear on the lower right side of the engine until about 100,000, then just behind the water inlet on the left side of the engine. Also about this time the location was again changed to the standard position above the water inlet, with some mixture of locations for a time. Starting: 70750 (approx.) (Some records show 69877 built on September 30, 1911.) Ending: 157424 (approx.) (There is no "break" between the 1912 and 1913 cars. 157425 was the first number assembled in October 1912, the beginning of Ford's fiscal year 1913.) 1912 Calendar year engine numbers: 88901 to 183563. According to Ford records engines with numbers B1 and B12247 were built at the Detroit plant beginning October 1912 and October 1913 but no records exist as to the exact dates. Car numbers were stamped on a plate on the fire wall. Other numbers stamped on the body sills, etc. were manufacturer's numbers and not an identifying number. Car numbers no longer agreed with the motor numbers and Ford kept no records of them.

1912 Ford, model T, touring, OCW

Model No.	Body Type & Seating	Price	Weight	Prod. Total
T	Tr.-5P	690	1200	50,598 (A)
T	Torp. Runabout-2P	590	NA	13,376 (B)
T	Comm. Rdstr.-2P	590	NA	(B)
T	Town Car-7P	900	NA	802 (A)
T	Delv. Car-2P	700	NA	1845 (A)
T	Cpe.-2P	NA	NA	19 (C)
T	Chassis	NA	940	2133 (C)

Note: 1200 pounds was the figure given for the Touring car, with "others in proportion." The bare chassis weighed about 940 pounds.
The Touring cars had three doors (none for the driver).
(A) Fiscal year, October 1, 1911 to September 30, 1912.
(B) Roadster production figures were combined. The total was 13,376.
(C) Coupes and the Chassis were not shown in the catalogs.

ENGINE: L-head. Four. Cast iron block. B & S: 3-3/4 in. x 4 in. Disp.: 176.7 cu. in. C.R.: 4.5:1 (approx.) Brake H.P.: 22 @ 1600 R.P.M. N.A.C.C. H.P.: 22.5. Main bearings: Three. Valve lifters: Solid. Carb.: Kingston 6-ball*, Holley H-1 4550. Torque: 83 lbs.-ft. @ 900 R.P.M.
Note: Thermo-syphon. Valve chambers (2) now enclosed using steel doors held with one stud/nut each. Inspection plate in the crankcase.
* Kingston carburetor used in limited quantities and does not appear in any of the Ford parts lists.

CHASSIS: W.B.: 100 in. O.L.: 10 ft. 8 in. (Chassis) 11 ft. 2-1/2 in. (car). Frt/Rear Tread: 56 in. (60 in. optional until 1916). Tires: 30 x 3 front, 30 x 3-1/2 rear, standard equipment 1909-1925.

TECHNICAL: Planetary transmission. Speeds: 2F/1R. 3 pedal controls and 1 lever on floor. Multiple disk clutch. Torque tube drive. Straight bevel rear axle. Overall ratio: 3.63:1. Brakes: Contracting band in transmission. Hand-operated internal expanding in rear wheels. Foot brake stops driveshaft. Parking brake on two rear wheels.
Note: Additional technical details will be found in the 1909 "General Comments" box.

OPTIONS: The basic equipment included three oil lamps. (Two side and one tail.) Windshield. Headlamps. Tops. Horns. Top boots. Speedometers.

1913 FORD

FORD — MODEL T: About September 1912 Ford introduced the second new body in the year, the "1913" models. These were the first to set the "pattern" for the next 12 years. The metal side panels now extended from the firewall to the rear, with one door on the left side (Touring Car) at the rear, and two doors on the right.
The doors were unique with this new body; they extended clear to the splash apron. There was no metal support between the front and rear sections of the body and this proved to be a severe problem. The body could flex so much that the doors opened while underway. The initial solution to the problem was to add a steel reinforcement across the rear door sills; then heavier body sills, and then both the heavy sills and the steel reinforcement.
The bottom section of the windshield on the open cars now sloped rearwards; the top section being vertical and folding forward.
The fenders followed the pattern of the 1911-12 cars except that they no longer had the "Bills" at the front.
Side, tail and headlamps were still oil and gas but were now made of steel (painted black) except for the tops and rims which were still brass.

1913 Ford, model T, touring, HFM

The rear axle housings were again redesigned. The center section was now larger (fatter) and the axle tubes were flared and riveted to it.
"Made in USA" now appeared on the radiator under the "Ford." The same notation appeared on many other parts as well and perhaps this was due to the Canadian production. 1913 was the first year in which Ford of Canada manufactured their own engines, etc.
According to Ford data, the 1913 cars were painted dark blue with striping on the very early models. As in earlier years, black is a possibility but it is not documented in any Ford literature.
Body styles offered were the Touring, Runabout and Town Car. The Torpedo with the rear deck mounted gas tank was discontinued. (Ford called the regular runabout a "torpedo" for several years after this.) The Delivery Car, which had proved to be a sales disaster, was also dropped.

I.D. DATA: Serial number was above the water inlet on the left side of the engine. Starting: 157,425 (approx.) October 1912. "1913" cars may have been built earlier. Ending: 248735. (There is no "break" between the 1913 and 1914 cars. The "1914" style Touring was introduced about August 1913, which could make the ending number around 320000 for "1913" cars.) 1913 Calendar year engine numbers: 183564 to 408347. According to Ford records engines with numbers B1 and B12247 were built at the Detroit plant between October 1912 and October 1913 but no records exist as to the exact dates. Numbers stamped on the body sills, etc. were manufacturer's numbers and not an identifying number.

Model No.	Body Type & Seating	Price	Weight	Prod. Total
T	3-dr. Tr.-5P	600 (A)	1200	126,715 (B)
T	2-dr. Rbt.-2P	525 (A)	NA	33,129 (B)
T	4-dr. Twn. Car-7P	800 (A)	NA	1,415 (B)
T	Delivery Car-2P	625 (A)	NA	513 (B)
T	2-dr. Cpe.-2P	NA	NA	1 (C)
T	Chassis	NA	960	8,438 (C)

Note: 1200 pounds was the figure given for the Touring car, with "others in proportion." The bare chassis weighed about 960 pounds.
(A) October 1, 1912.
(B) Fiscal year, October 1, 1912 to September 30, 1913.
(C) Coupes and the Chassis were not shown in the catalogs.

ENGINE: L-head. Four. Cast iron block. B & S: 3-3/4 in. x 4 in. Disp.: 176.6 cu. in. C.R.: 4.0:1 (approx.). Brake H.P.: 20 @ 1600 R.P.M. N.A.C.C. H.P.: 22.5. Main bearings: Three. Valve lifters: Solid. Carb.: Kingston Y (4400), Holley S (4450). Torque: 83 lbs.-ft. @ 900 R.P.M.
Note: Thermo-syphon. Valve chambers (2) now enclosed using steel doors held with one stud/nut each. Inspection plate in the crankcase.
Camshaft modified for less power (less overlap in timing). Modified cylinder head for slightly lower compression.

CHASSIS: W.B.: 100 in. O.L.: 10 ft. 8 in. (Chassis) 11 ft. 2-1/2 in. (car). Frt/Rear Tread: 56 in. (60 in. optional until 1916). Tires: 30 x 3 front, 30 x 3-1/2 rear, standard equipment 1909-1925. Chassis essentially identical except those after mid-1913 have a longer rear crossmember.

TECHNICAL: Planetary transmission. Speeds: 2F/1R. 3 pedal controls and 1 lever on floor. Multiple disk clutch. Torque tube drive. Straight bevel rear axle. Overall ratio: 3.63:1. Brakes: Contracting band in transmission. Hand-operated internal expanding in rear wheels. Foot brake stops driveshaft. Parking brake on two rear wheels.
Note: Additional technical details will be found in the 1909 "General Comments" box.

OPTIONS: All cars equipped with headlamps, horn, etc. with no options. About 1915 the speedometer was discontinued (and the price reduced).
Ford even said the warranty would be voided if any accessories were added, although it's doubtful this ever happened.

1914 FORD

FORD — MODEL T: The 1914 models looked almost identical to the 1913's but the doors were now inset into the side panels, and the body metal extended across the rear door sills, solving the weakness at that point in the 1913's, and setting the pattern for doors until 1926 models.
The windshield, while similar in appearance to the 1913, now folded to the rear. The windshield support rods were given a bend to clear the folded section.
Fenders were modified and now had embossed reinforcing ribs across the widest part and, later, in the apron area of both front and rear fenders. Front fenders had no "Bill" in most 1914 models but a "Bill" was added late in the year. The front fender iron bracket is secured to the fender with four rivets.

1914 Ford, model T, touring, OCW

Black was now *the* Ford color, although Ford Archives records seem to indicate blue was still offered. Interestingly, black was never listed as an available color prior to 1914; this in spite of the many seemingly original pre-1914 black Fords. It is possible black was a common color even in 1909 but there is nothing in the records to prove it.

Lamps continued in the pattern of the 1913's; black and brass.

The chassis frame was modified; now had a longer rear crossmember, eliminating the forged body brackets used since 1909.

A bare chassis was added to the Ford line in 1914. In the fall of the year a Sedan (commonly called a "centerdoor sedan") and a Coupelet (the first "convertible") were introduced but these were "1915 models."

I.D. DATA: Serial number was above the water inlet on the left side of the engine. Starting: 348736 (approx.) October 1913. "1914" cars were built as early as August, which could make the first "1914" cars about 320000. Ending: 670000 (Mid-January, 1915). The new "1915" Ford was introduced in January at the Highland Park plant, but the "1914" style continued for a time at the branches. There is no clear break point in the style years. 1914 calendar year engine numbers: 408348 to 656063. Numbers stamped on the body sills, etc., were manufacturer's numbers and not an identifying number.

Model No.	Body Type & Seating	Price	Weight	Prod. Total
T	3-dr. Tr.-5P	550 (A)	1200	165,832 (B)
T	2-dr. Rbt.-2P	500 (A)	NA	35,017 (B)
T	4-dr. Twn. Car-7P	750 (A)	NA	1,699 (B)
T	Chassis	NA	960	119 (B)

Note: 1200 pounds was the figure given for the Touring car, with "others in proportion." The bare chassis weighed about 960 pounds.
(A) August 1, 1913.
(B) Fiscal year, October 1, 1913 to July 31, 1914.

ENGINE: L-head. Four. Cast iron block. B & S: 3-3/4 in. x 4 in. Disp.: 176.7 cu. in. C.R.: 4.0:1 approx. Brake H.P.: 20 @ 1600 R.P.M. N.A.C.C. H.P.: 22.5. Main bearings: Three. Valve lifters: Solid. Carb.: Kingston Y (4400), Holley G (6040 brass body). Torque: 83 lbs.-ft. @ 900 R.P.M.
Note: Thermo-syphon. Valve chambers (2) now enclosed using steel doors held with one stud/nut each. Inspection plate in the crankcase.

CHASSIS: W.B.: 100 in. O.L.: 10 ft. 8 in. (Chassis) 11 ft. 2-1/2 in. (car). Frt/Rear Tread: 56 in. (60 in. optional until 1916). Tires: 30 x 3 front, 30 x 3-1/2 rear, standard equipment 1909-1925.

TECHNICAL: Planetary transmission. Speeds: 2F/1R. 3 pedal controls and 1 lever on floor. Multiple disk clutch. Torque tube drive. Straight bevel rear axle. Overall ratio: 3.63:1. Brakes: Contracting band in transmission. Hand-operated internal expanding in rear wheels. Foot brake stops driveshaft. Parking brake on two rear wheels.
Note: Additional technical details will be found in the 1909 "General Comments" box.

OPTIONS: The basic equipment included three oil lamps. (Two side and one tail.) Windshield. Headlamps. Tops. Horns. Top boots. Speedometers.

1915-16 FORD

1915 Ford, model T, touring, AA

166

FORD — 1915-1916 — MODEL T: The 1915-style open cars were introduced at the Highland Park plant in January 1915 but the 1914 style continued in some of the branches until as late as April.

The bodies were essentially the same as the 1914 except for the front cowl section. Instead of exposed wood firewall, the metal cowl curved "gracefully" inward to the hood former. The hood and radiator were the same as earlier (except for the louvres in the hood side panels).

The windshield is now upright, with the top section folding to the rear. Electric headlights were standard, these being of the "typical" size and shape of common Model T Fords until 1927.

Headlight rims were brass. Side lights were now of the rounded style, and interchangeable from side to side. The tail lamp was similar but with a red lens in the door, and a clear lens on the side towards the license plate. Side and tail lamps were still kerosene. Side and tail lamps had brass tops and rims but were otherwise painted black. The headlights were powered by the engine magneto.

Fenders in the front again had "Bills" and were the same as the later 1914's. While retaining the same style, later the fender iron bracket was revised and now held with three rivets. Rear fenders were now curved to follow the wheel outline. Neither front nor rear fenders were crowned.

The standard horn in 1915 was a bulb type, mounted under the hood. The hood now had louvres; perhaps so that the horn could be heard. Early in the year, though, Ford began using a magneto-powered horn on some production, and by October 1915 all had the new horn.

The Sedan was unique. Made of aluminum panels, it required special rear fenders and splash aprons. The gasoline tank was located under the rear seat and proved to be quite unsatisfactory because of the poor fuel flow. The body was redesigned during the year and made of steel panels, and the gasoline tank was relocated under the driver's seat.

The Coupelet had a folding top but differed from the Runabout in that the doors had windows and the windshield was like that in the Sedan. It also had a larger turtle deck.

The rear axle was redesigned again, for the last time except for minor modifications. The center section was cast iron and the axle tubes were straight and inserted into it.

The 1916 Fords were but an extension of the 1915's except for the deletion of the brass trim on the lamps. The hood was now made of steel, and all were equipped with the magneto horn.

"Port holes" were added to the side of the Coupelet in an effort to allow the driver a better side view.

The sedan body was redesigned to now use standard fenders and splash aprons, and for a new gas tank under the driver's seat. The new body was all steel.

Body styles offered in 1915 and 1916 were the Touring, Runabout, Sedan, Coupelet and Town Car, in addition to the bare chassis.

I.D. DATA: [1915] Serial number was above the water inlet on the left side of the engine. Starting: 670,000 approx. (January 1915.) the new "1915" Ford was introduced in January at the Highland Park plant, but the "1914" style continued for a time at the branches. There is no clear break point in the style years. Ending: 856,513 (July 24, 1915, end of fiscal 1915.) 1915 Calendar year engine numbers: 656,064 to 1,028,313. Numbers stamped on the body sills, etc. were manufacturer's numbers and not an identifying number. [1916] Serial number was above the water inlet on the left side of the engine. Starting: 856,514 (August 1, 1915.) Ending: 1,362,989 (July 25, 1916, end of fiscal 1916.) 1916 Calendar year engine numbers: 1,028,314 to 1,614,516. Numbers stamped on the body sills, etc. were manufacturer's numbers and not an identifying number.

1915 Ford, model T, runabout, OCW

Model No.	Body Type & Seating	Price	Weight	Prod. Total
1915				
T	3-dr. Tr.-5P	490 (A)	1500	244,181 (B)
T	2-dr. Rbt.-2P	440 (A)	1380	47,116 (B)
T	4-dr. Twn. Car-7P	690 (A)	NA	(B)
T	2-dr. Sed.-5P	975 (A)	1730	989 (B)
T	2-dr. Cpe.-2P	750 (A)	1540	2417 (B)
T	Chassis	410 (A)	980	13,459 (B)

(A) August 1, 1914.
(B) Fiscal year, August 1, 1914 to July 31, 1915.

Model No.	Body Type & Seating	Price	Weight	Prod. Total
1916				
T	3-dr. Tr.-5P	440 (A)	1510	363,024 (B)
T	2-dr. Rbt.-2P	390 (A)	1395	98,633 (B)
T	4-dr. Twn. Car-7P	640 (A)	NA	1972 (B)
T	2-dr. Sed.-5P	740 (A)	1730	1859 (B)
T	2-dr. Cpe.-2P	590 (A)	1540	3532 (B)
T	Chassis	360 (A)	1060	11,742 (B)
T	Ambulance	NA	NA	20,700 (C)

(A) Price effective August 1, 1915.
(B) Fiscal year 1916, August 1, 1915 to July 30, 1916.
(C) Built for military.

ENGINE: L-head. Four. Cast iron block. B & S: 3-3/4 in. x 4 in. Disp.: 176.7 in. C.R.: 4.0:1 approx. Brake H.P.: 20 @ 1600 R.P.M. N.A.C.C. H.P.: 22.5. Main bearings: Three. Valve lifters: Solid. Carb.: Kingston L (6100), Holley G (6040 brass body). Torque: 83 lbs.-ft. @ 900 R.P.M.
Note: Thermo-syphon. Valve chambers (2) now enclosed using steel doors held with one stud/nut each. Inspection plate in the crankcase.

1916 Ford, model T, center door sedan, OCW

CHASSIS: [1915-1916] W.B.: 100 in. O.L.: 10 ft. 8 in. (Chassis) 11 ft. 2-1/2 in. (car). Frt/Rear Tread: 56 in. Tires: 30 x 3 front, 30 x 3-1/2 rear, standard equipment 1909-1925.

TECHNICAL: Planetary transmission. Speeds: 2F/1R. 3 pedal controls and 1 lever on floor. Multiple disk clutch (26 disks 1909-1915). (25 disks 1915-1927). Torque tube drive. Straight bevel rear axle. Overall ratio: 3.63:1. Brakes: Contracting band in transmission. Hand-operated internal expanding in rear wheels. Foot brake stops driveshaft. Parking brake on two rear wheels.
Note: Additional technical details will be found in the 1909 "General Comments" box.

OPTIONS: The basic equipment included three oil lamps. (Two side and one tail.) Windshield. Headlamps. Tops. Horns. Top boots.

1917-18 FORD

1917 Ford, model T, runabout, HAC

FORD — 1917-1918 — MODEL T: The Model T for 1917 looked like an all-new car but was a rather simple evolution from the 1916. The brass radiator and the small hood were gone, as were all bits of brass trim.
New curved and crowned fenders, a new black radiator shell, and a new hood and hood former were the essential changes. The body itself was unchanged. Lamps were also the same as 1916.
The car continued with minor modifications, such as a different mounting base for the windshield, and new rectangular cross-section top sockets replacing the oval ones used since 1915.
Nickel plating on the steering gear box, hub caps and radiator filler neck replaced the earlier brass trim.
A new engine pan came out in 1917 which had a larger front section for a larger fan pulley. The pulley, however, was not enlarged until about 1920.
The "convertible" Coupelet was replaced with a "hard top" Coupelet. While the top could no longer fold, the side window posts could be removed (and stored under the seat) giving the car the hard-top look.
During 1917 the Ford Model TT truck chassis was introduced.
The Town Car was discontinued during the year.

I.D. DATA: [1917] Serial number was above the water inlet on the left side of the engine. Starting: 1362990 (August 1, 1916.) Ending: 2113501 (July 28, 1917, end of fiscal 1917.) 1917 Calendar year engine numbers: 1614517 to 2449179. Numbers stamped on the body sills, etc. were manufacturer's numbers and not an identifying number. [1918] Serial number was above the water inlet on the left side of the engine. Starting: 2113502 (August 1, 1917.) Ending: 2756251 (July 27, 1918, end of fiscal 1918.) 1918 Calendar year engine numbers: 2449180 to 2831426. Numbers stamped on the body sills, etc. were manufacturer's numbers and not an identifying number.

Model No.	Body Type & Seating	Price	Weight	Prod. Total
1917				
T	3-dr. Tr.-5P	360 (A)	1480	568,128 (B)
T	2-dr. Rbt.-2P	345 (A)	1385	107,240 (B)
T	4-dr. Twn. Car-7P	595 (A)	NA	2328 (B)
T	2-dr. Sed.-5P	645 (A)	1745	7361 (B)
T	2-dr. Cpe.-2P	505 (A)	1580	7343 (B)
T	Chassis	325 (A)	1060	41,165 (B)
T	Ambulance	NA	NA	1452 (C)
TT	Truck Chassis	NA	1450	3 (D)

Model No.	Body Type & Seating	Price	Weight	Prod. Total
(A) Price effective August 1, 1916.				
(B) Fiscal year 1917, August 1, 1916 to July 30, 1917.				
(C) Built for military.				
(D) Apparently a pilot run.				
1918				
T	3-dr. Tr.-5P	360 (A)	450 (C)	432,519 (D)
T	2-dr. Rbt.-2P	345 (A)	435 (C)	73,559 (D)
T	4-dr. Twn. Car-7P	595 (A)	NA	2142 (D)
T	2-dr. Sed.-5P	645 (A)	1715	35,697 (D)
T	2-dr. Cpe.-2P	505 (A)	1580	14,771 (D)
T	Chassis	325 (A)	1060	37,648 (D)
T	Ambulance	NA	NA	2136 (E)
TT	Truck Chassis	600 (B)	1450	41,105 (D)
T	Del.	NA	NA	399 (F)
T	Foreign	NA	NA	24,000 (G)

(A) Price effective August 1, 1917.
(B) Price effective October 6, 1917.
(C) Price effective February 21, 1918.
(D) Fiscal year 1918, August 1, 1917 to July 30, 1918.
(E) Built for military.
(F) Not indicated in catalog, perhaps for military.
(G) Cars built in foreign plants and Canada (no breakdown by types).

1918 Ford, model T, center door, sedan, HAC

ENGINE: L-head. Four. Cast iron block. B & S: 3-3/4 in. x 4 in. Disp.: 176.7 cu. in. C.R.: 3.98:1. Brake H.P.: 20 @ 1600 R.P.M. N.A.C.C. H.P.: 22.5. Main bearings: Three. Valve lifters: Solid. Carb.: Kingston L2 (6100), Holley G (6040 iron body). Torque: 83 lbs.-ft. @ 900 R.P.M.
Note: Thermo-syphon. Valve chambers (2) enclosed using steel doors held with one stud/nut each. Inspection plate in the crankcase.
New cylinder head with slightly lower compression and much larger water jacket.

CHASSIS: [1917-1918] W.B.: 100 in. O.L.: 10 ft. 8 in. (Chassis) 11 ft. 2-1/2 in. (car). Frt/Rear Tread: 56 in. Tires: 30 x 3 front, 30 x 3-1/2 rear, standard equipment 1909-1925.

TECHNICAL: Planetary transmission. Speeds: 2F/1R. 3 pedal controls and 1 lever on floor. Multiple disk clutch. (25 disks 1915-1927). Torque tube drive. Straight bevel rear axle. Overall ratio: 3.63:1. Brakes: Contracting band in transmission. Hand-operated internal expanding in rear wheels. Foot brake stops driveshaft. Parking brake on two rear wheels.
Note: Additional technical details will be found in the 1909 "General Comments" box.

OPTIONS: The basic equipment included three oil lamps. (Two side and one tail.) Windshield. Headlamps. Tops. Horns. Top boots.

1919-20 FORD

1919 Ford, model T, runabout, HAC

167

FORD — 1919-1920 — MODEL T: The body styling continued unchanged from 1918 but the Ford was finally given a battery and an electric starter. Beginning as standard equipment on the closed cars only, by mid-1919 it became an option on the open cars. This modification required a new engine block, transmission cover, flywheel, etc. but the general design of these items was unchanged except for the modifications needed to adapt the starter and generator.

Also available for the first time from Ford were wheels with demountable rims as standard equipment on the closed cars, and optional on the open models. When demountable wheels were used, all tires were the same size; 30 by 3-1/2.

With the electrical equipment came an instrument panel for the first time on a Model T (as factory equipment) on cars so equipped. Instrumentation consisted of an ammeter. Controls on the panel were the choke knob and the ignition/light switch. Speedometers were dealer installed options.

The Coupelet was restyled. While looking the same, the door posts were now integral with the doors; no longer removable.

The rear axle was modified slightly. The oil filler hole was lowered to reduce the amount of oil that could be put in, and thus help the oil leak problem at the rear axles. The center section was milled to accept a gasket between the two halves.

The front radius rod was redesigned and now fastened below the axle, adding strength to the assembly.

I.D. DATA: [1919] Serial number was above the water inlet on the left side of the engine. Starting: 2756252 (August 1, 1918.) Ending: 3277851 (July 30, 1919, end of fiscal 1919.) 1919 Calendar year engine numbers: 2831427 to 3659971. Numbers stamped on the body sills, etc. were manufacturer's numbers and not an identifying number. [1920] Serial number was above the water inlet on the left side of the engine. Starting: 3277852 (August 1, 1919.) Ending: 4233351 (July 31, 1920, end of fiscal 1920.) 1920 Calendar year engine numbers: 3659972 to 4698419. Numbers stamped on the body sills, etc. were manufacturer's numbers and not an identifying number.

1919 Ford, model T, touring, OCW

Model No.	Body Type & Seating	Price	Weight	Prod. Total
T	3-dr. Tr.-5P	525 (B)	1500	286,935 (E)
T	2-dr. Rbt.-2P	500 (B)	1390	48,867 (E)
T	2-dr. Sed.-5P	875 (A)	1875	24,980 (E)
T	2-dr. Cpe.-2P	750 (A)	1685	11,528 (E)
T	4-dr. Twn. Car-7P	NA	—	17 (G)
T	Chassis	475 (B)	1060	47,125 (E)
T	Ambulance	NA	—	2227 (F)
TT	Truck Chassis	550 (C)	1477	70,816 (E)
		590 (D)	—	
T	Del.			5847 (G)

(A) Includes starter and demountable wheels.
(B) Price effective August 16, 1918.
(C) Price with solid rubber tires.
(D) Price with Pneumatic tires.
(E) Fiscal year 1919, August 1, 1918 to July 30, 1919.
(F) Built for military.
(G) Not indicated in catalog, perhaps for military.
Note: Starter was an option on the open cars at $75. Weight 95 lbs. Demountable rims were an additional $25. Weight 55 lbs.

1920

T	3-dr. Tr.-5P	575 (B)	1500	165,929 (E)
		675 (A)	1650	367,785 (E)
T	2-dr. Rbt.-2P	550 (B)	1390	31,889 (E)
		650 (A)	1540	63,514 (E)
T	2-dr. Sed.-5P	975 (A)	1875	81,616 (E)
T	2-dr. Cpe.-2P	850 (A)	1760	60,215 (E)
T	Chassis	525 (B)	1060	18,173 (E)
		620 (B)	1210	16,919 (E)
TT	Truck Chassis	660 (C)	1477	135,002 (E)
		640 (D)		

(A) Includes starter and demountable wheels.
(B) Price effective March 3, 1920.
(C) Price with solid rubber tires.
(D) Price with Pneumatic tires.
(E) Fiscal year 1920, August 1, 1919 to July 30, 1920.
Note: Starter was an option on the open cars at $75. Weight 95 lbs. Demountable rims were an additional $25. Weight 55 lbs.

ENGINE: L-head. Four. Cast iron block. B & S: 3-3/4 in. x 4 in. Disp.: 176.7 cu. in. C.R.: 3.98:1. Brake H.P.: 20 @ 1600 R.P.M. N.A.C.C. H.P.: 22.5. Main bearings: Three. Valve lifters: Solid. Carb.: Kingston L4 (6150). Holley NH (6200). Torque: 83 lbs.-ft. @ 900 R.P.M.
Note: Thermo-syphon. Valve chambers (2) enclosed using steel doors held with one stud/nut each. Inspection plate in the crankcase. New light-weight connecting rods.

CHASSIS: [1919-1920] W.B.: 100 in. O.L.: 10 ft. 8 in. (Chassis) 11 ft. 2-1/2 in. (car). Frt/Rear Tread: 56 in. Tires: 30 x 3 front, 30 x 3-1/2 rear, standard equipment 1909-1925. 30 x 3½ all around with demountable rims 1919-1925.

TECHNICAL: [1919-1920] Planetary transmission. Speeds: 2F/1R. 3 pedal controls and 1 lever on floor. Multiple disk clutch. (25 disks 1915-1927). Torque tube drive. Straight bevel rear axle. Overall ratio: 3.63:1. Brakes: Contracting band in transmission. Hand-operated internal expanding in rear wheels. Foot brake stops driveshaft. Parking brake on two rear wheels.
Note: Additional technical details will be found in the 1909 "General Comments" box.

OPTIONS: All cars equipped with headlamps, horn, etc. Starter (75.00). Demountable rims (25.00).

1920-21-22 FORD

1921 Ford model T, roadster, JAC

FORD — MODEL T: Another new body appeared in the open cars in late 1920. It takes an expert to see the difference but different it was. Most noticeable was a new rear quarter panel, now an integral part of the side panel instead of the two-piece assembly used since 1913.

An oval-shaped gas tank (located under the driver's seat) had replaced the previous round type earlier in 1920, and this allowed the seat to be lowered. Seat backs were given a more comfortable angle and the result was a far more comfortable car.

The chassis frame was modified slightly; the running board support brackets were now pressed steel channels instead of the forged brackets with a tie rod used since 1909. Otherwise the basic car was like the previous models.

A new pinion bearing spool was used on the rear axle. The earlier type was an iron casting with enclosed mounting studs. The new spool was a forging and used exposed mounting bolts.

Body styles offered during this period were the Touring, Runabout, Coupelet and Sedan, in addition to the Chassis and the Truck Chassis.

I.D. DATA: (1921) serial number was above the water inlet on the left side of the engine. Starting: 4233352 (August 2, 1920). Ending: 5223135 (July 30, 1921, end of fiscal 1921). 1921 Calendar year engine numbers: 4698420 to 5568071. Numbers stamped on the body sills, etc, were manufacturer's numbers and not an identifying number. (1922) serial number was above the water inlet on the left side of the engine. Starting: 5223136 (August 1, 1921). Ending: 6543606 (September 14, 1922; introduction of first "1923" model). 1922 Calendar year engine numbers: 5638072 to 6953071. Numbers stamped on the body sills, etc. were manufacturer's numbers and not an identifying number.

Model No. 1921	Body Type & Seating	Price	Weight	Prod. Total
T	3-dr. Tr.-5P	440 (A)	1500	84,970 (D)
		415 (B)		
T	3-dr. Tr.-5P	535 (A)	1650	647,300 (E)
		510 (B)		
T	2-dr. Rbt.-2P	395 (A)	1390	25,918 (D)
		370 (B)		
T	2-dr. Rbt.-2P	490 (A)	1540	171,745 (E)
		465 (B)		
T	2-dr. Sed.-5P	795 (A)	1875	179,734 (E)
		760 (B)		
T	2-dr. Cpe.-2P	745 (A)	1760	129,159 (E)
		695 (B)		
T	Chassis	360 (A)	1060	13,356 (D)
		345 (B)		
T	Chassis	455 (A)	1210	23,436 (E)
		440 (B)		
T	Truck Chassis	545 (C)	1477	118,583 (D)
		495 (B)		
T	Foreign & Canada	NA	NA	42,860 (D)

1921 Ford, model T, touring, IMS

(A) Price effective September 22, 1920.
(B) Price effective June 7, 1921.
(C) Price with Pneumatic tires.
(D) August 1, 1920 to December 31, 1921 (Ford began calendar year figures in 1921).
(E) Includes starter and demountable wheels.
Note: Starter was an option on the open cars at $70. Weight 95 lbs. Demountable rims were an additional $25. Weight 55 lbs.

1921 Ford, model T, touring OCW

Model No. 1922	Body Type & Seating	Price	Weight	Prod. Total
T	3-dr. Tr.-5P	355 (A) 348 (B) 298 (C)	1500	80,070 (D)
T	3-dr. Tr.-5P	450 (A) 443 (B) 393 (C)	1650	514,333 (E)
T	2-dr. Rbt.-2P	325 (A) 319 (B) 269 (C)	1390	31,923 (D)
T	2-dr. Rbt.-2P	420 (A) 414 (B) 364 (C)	1540	133,433 (E)
T	2-dr. Sed.-5P	660 (A) 645 (B) 595 (C)	1875	146,060 (E)
T	4-dr. Sed.-5P	725 (C)	1950	4,286 (E)
T	2-dr. Cpe.-2P	595 (A) 580 (B) 530 (C)	1760	198,382 (E)
T	Chassis	295 (A) 285 (B) 235 (C)	1060	15,228 (D)
T	Chassis	390 (A) 380 (B) 330 (C)	1210	23,313 (E)
T	Truck Chassis	445 (A) 430 (B) 380 (C)	1477	135,629 (D)
T	Truck Chassis	475 (C)	1577	18,410 (E)

(A) Price effective September 2, 1921.
(B) Price effective January 16, 1922.
(C) Price effective October 17, 1922.
(D) January 1, 1922 to December 31, 1922. (Includes foreign production.)
(E) Includes starter and demountable wheels.
Note: Starter was an option on the open cars at $70. Weight 95 lbs. Demountable rims were an additional $25. Weight 25 lbs.

1922 Ford, model T, center door sedan, JAC

ENGINE: [1920] L-head. Four. Cast iron block. B & S: 3-3/4 in. x 4 in. Disp.: 176.7 cu. in. C.R.: 3.98:1. Brake H.P.: 20 @ 1600 R.P.M. N.A.C.C. H.P.: 22.5. Main bearings: Three. Valve lifters: Solid. Carb.: Kingston L4 (6150). Holley NH (6200). Torque: 83 lbs.-ft. @ 900 R.P.M.
Note: Thermo-syphon. Valve chambers (2) enclosed using steel doors held with one stud/nut each. Inspection plate in the crankcase. New light-weight connecting rods.

1922 Ford, model T, coupe, OCW

[1921-1922] L-head. Four. Cast iron block. B & S: 3-3/4 in. x 4 in. Disp.: 176.7 cu. in. C.R.: 3.98:1. Brake H.P.: 20 @ 1600 R.P.M. N.A.C.C. H.P.: 22.5. Main bearings: Three. Valve lifters: Solid. Carb.: Kingston L4 (6150), Holley NH (6200). Torque: 83 lbs.-ft. @ 900 R.P.M.
Note: Thermo-syphon. Single valve chamber covered with one steel door half with two stud/nuts or bolts. Beginning in 1922 (#5,530,000 — April, 1922)

CHASSIS: [1909-1925] W.B.: 100 in. O.L.: 10 ft. 8 in. (Chassis) 11 ft. 2-1/2 in. (car). Frt/Rear Tread: 56 in. (60 in. optional until 1916). Tires: 30 x 3 front, 30 x 3-1/2 rear, standard equipment 1909-1925. 30 x 3½ all around with demountable rims 1919-1925. 4:40 x 21 optional in late 1925.
Note: Chassis essentially identical except those after mid-1913 have a longer rear crossmember.

TECHNICAL: Planetary transmission. Speeds: 2F/1R. 3 pedal controls and 1 lever on floor. Multiple disk clutch (25 disks 1915-1927). Torque tube drive. Straight bevel rear axle. Overall ratio: 3.63:1. Brakes: Contracting band in transmission. Hand-operated internal expanding in rear wheels. Foot brake stops driveshaft. Parking brake on two rear wheels.
Note: Additional technical details will be found in the 1909 "General Comments" box.

OPTIONS: No factory options were available.

1923-24-25 FORD

1923 Ford, model T, Fordor sedan, HAC

FORD — 1923 — MODEL T: The 1923 Model T open cars were again restyled. Using the same bodies as the 1921-1922 cars, a new windshield with a sloping angle, and a new "one man" top, the Touring and Runabout looked all new.
   The 1923 model was introduced in the fall of 1922, and was to continue until about June 1923, when another "new" line of Model T's appeared.
   About November 1922, a new "Fordor" Sedan was added to the line. The Fordor body was made of aluminum panels over a wood frame.
   Instrument panels were now standard on all cars. Non-starter open cars had a blank plate where the ammeter would be.
   The early 1923 cars continued the wooden firewall of all previous Fords until early calendar 1923, when the firewall was changed to sheet metal. (This before the styling change in June, mentioned above.)
   The starter and generator were standard equipment on all closed cars, as were the demountable wheels. This equipment was optional on the Runabout and Touring cars.
   1923 was the last year for the Centerdoor Sedan and the Coupe with the forward-opening doors. The "1924" Tudor Sedan and a new Coupe replaced them.

169

1924 Ford, model T, touring, HAC

1924 Ford, model T, coupe, JAC

FORD — 1923-1925 — MODEL T: In June of 1923 the Ford line was restyled again. While those cars built after June but before calendar 1924 are commonly called "1923's", Ford referred to them as 1924's.

The open cars continued the same body, windshield and top as the earlier 1923's, but a new higher radiator and larger hood altered the appearance noticeably. The front fenders were given a lip on the front of the apron to blend in with a new valance under the radiator; these giving the car a more "finished" look.

Two new models replaced the Centerdoor Sedan and the Coupe. These were a new Coupe, now with an integral rear turtle back, and doors that now opened at the rear. A new Tudor Sedan was also introduced, with the doors at the front of the body instead of at the center.

The Fordor Sedan was the same as the earlier one except for the new hood and front fenders. Lower body panels were now steel instead of aluminum.

During 1924 the closed car doors were changed to all metal construction, eliminating the wood framing of previous Sedan and Coupe doors.

In 1924, for the first time Ford offered a "C" cab and a rear platform body on the truck chassis.

The 1924 line continued until about July of 1925 with no major changes except in upholstery material, and construction details.

About May 1925 the Roadster/Pickup and the Closed Cab Truck appeared.

"Balloon" tires (4:40 x 21") mounted on demountable-rim wooden wheels in either black or natural were added as optional equipment in late 1925.

I.D. DATA: [1923] Serial number was above the water inlet on the left side of the engine. Starting: 6,543,607 (September 22, 1922 introduction of 1923 model.) Ending: 7,927,374 (June 30, 1923; introduction of "1924" models.) 1923 Calendar year engine numbers: 6,953,072 to 9,008,371. Numbers stamped on the body sills, etc. were manufacturer's numbers and not an identifying number. [1924] Serial numbers were above the water inlet on the left side of the engine. Starting: 7,927,375 (July 2, 1923 introduction of 1924 models.) Ending: 10,266,471 (July 31, 1924 end of fiscal 1924.) 1924 Calendar year engine numbers: 9,008,372 to 10,994,033. Numbers stamped on the body sills, etc. were manufacturer's numbers and not an identifying number. [1925] Serial number was above the water inlet on the left side of the engine. Starting: 10,266,472 (August 1, 1924, start of fiscal 1925.) Ending: 12,218,728 (July 27, 1925; Start of "1926" models.) 1925 Calendar year engine numbers: 10,994,034 to 12,990,076. Numbers stamped on the body sills, etc. were manufacturer's numbers and not an identifying number.

Model No. 1923	Body Type & Seating	Price	Weight	Prod. Total
T	3-dr. Tr.-5P	298 (A) 295 (B) 295 (C)	1500	136,441 (D)
	3-dr. Tr.-5P	393 (A) 380 (B) 380 (C)	1650	792,651 (E)
T	2-dr. Rbt.-2P	269 (A) 265 (B) 265 (C)	1390	56,954 (D)
	2-dr. Rbt.-2P	364 (A) 350 (B) 350 (C)	1540	238,638 (E)
T	2-dr. Sed.-5P	595 (A) 590 (B) 590 (C)	1875	96,410 (E)
T	4-dr. Sed.-5P	725 (A) 685 (B) 685 (C)	1950	144,444 (E)
T	2-dr. Cpe.-2P	530 (A) 525 (B) 525 (C)	1760	313,273 (E)
T	Chassis	235 (A) 230 (B) 230 (C)	1060	9443 (D)
	Chassis	330 (A) 295 (B) 295 (C)	1210	42,874 (E)
TT	Truck Chassis	380 (A) 370 (B) 370 (C)	1477	197,057 (D)
TT	Truck Chassis	475 (A) 435 (B) 455 (C)	1577	64,604 (E)
TT	Trk. w/body	490 (C)	NA	(F)

(A) Price effective October 17, 1922.
(B) Price effective October 2, 1923.
(C) Price effective October 30, 1923.
(D) January 1, 1923 to December 31, 1923. (Includes foreign production.)
(E) Includes starter and demountable wheels.
(F) Not listed separately from chassis figures.
Note: Starter was an option on the open cars at $65. Weight 95 lbs. Demountable rims were an additional $20. Weight 55 lbs. "C" type truck cab, $65. Truck rear bed, $55 if ordered separately.

Model No. 1924	Body Type & Seating	Price	Weight	Prod. Total
T	3-dr. Tr.-5P	295 (A) 290 (B) 290 (C)	1500	99,523 (D)
	3-dr. Tr.-5P	380 (A) 375 (B) 375 (C)	1650	673,579 (E)
T	2-dr. Rbt.-2P	265 (A) 260 (B) 260 (C)	1390	43,317 (D)
	2-dr. Rbt.-2P	350 (A) 345 (B) 345 (C)	1540	220,955 (E)
T	2-dr. Sed.-5P	590 (A) 580 (B) 580 (C)	1875	223,203 (E)
T	4-dr. Sed.-5P	685 (A) 660 (B) 660 (C)	1950	84,733 (E)
T	2-dr. Cpe.-2P	525 (A) 520 (B) 520 (C)	1760	327,584 (E)
T	Chassis	230 (A) 225 (B) 225 (C)	1060	3921 (D)
	Chassis	295 (A) 290 (B) 290 (C)	1210	43,980 (E)
TT	Truck Chassis	370 (A) 365 (B) 365 (C)	1477	127,891 (D)
TT	Truck Chassis	435 (A) 430 (B) 430 (C)	1577	32,471 (E)
TT	Trk. w/body	490 (A) 485 (B) 485 (C)	NA	38,840 (D)
	Trk. w/body	555 (A) 550 (B) 550 (C)	NA	5649 (E)
TT	Trk. w/stake body	495 (C)	NA	(F)

(A) Price effective October 30, 1923.
(B) Price effective December 2, 1924.
(C) Price effective October 24, 1924.
(D) January 1, 1924 to December 31, 1924. (Includes foreign production.)
(E) Includes starter and demountable wheels.
(F) Not listed separately from body figures.
Note: Starter was an option on the open cars at $65. Weight 95 lbs. Demountable rims were an additional $20. Weight 55 lbs. "C" type truck cab, $65. Truck rear bed, $55 if ordered separately.

1925	Body Type & Seating	Price	Weight	Prod. Total
T	3-dr. Tr.-5P	290 (A) 290 (B) 290 (C)	1500	64,399 (D)
	3-dr. Tr.-5P	375 (A) 375 (B) 375 (C)	1650	626,813 (E)
T	2-dr. Rbt.-2P	260 (A) 260 (B) 260 (C)	1390	34,206 (D)
	2-dr. Rbt.-2P	345 (A) 345 (B) 345 (C)	1536	264,436 (E)
T	2-dr. Pickup-2P	281 (B) 281 (C)	1471	33,795 (G)
	2-dr. Pickup-2P	366 (B) 366 (C)	1621	(G)
T	2-dr. Sed.-5P	580 (A) 580 (B) 580 (C)	1875	195,001 (E)
T	4-dr. Sed.-5P	660 (A) 660 (B) 660 (C)	1950	81,050 (E)
T	2-dr. Cpe.-2P	520 (A) 520 (B) 520 (C)	1760	343,969 (E)
T	Chassis	225 (A) 225 (B) 225 (C)	1060	6523 (D)
	Chassis	290 (A) 290 (B) 290 (C)	1210	53,450 (E)
TT	Truck Chassis	365 (A) 365 (B) 365 (C)	1477	186,810 (D)

Model No.	Body Type & Seating	Price	Weight	Prod. Total
TT	Truck Chassis	430 (A)	1577	62,496 (E)
		430 (B)		
		430 (C)		
TT	Trk. w/body	485 (A)	NA	192,839 (US
		485 (B)		
		485 (C)		
	Trk. w/body	550 (A)	NA	(E, F)
		550 (B)		
		550 (C)		
TT	Trk. w/stake body	495 (A)	NA	(F)
		495 (B)		
		495 (C)		

(A) Price effective October 24, 1924.
(B) Price effective March 4, 1925.
(C) Price effective December 31, 1925 (unchanged from March).
(D) January 1, 1925 to December 31, 1925. (Includes foreign production.)
(E) Includes starter and demountable wheels.
(F) Not listed separately from body figures. (U.S. production only.)
(G) Pickups not separated into starter/non-starter. Figure is for total of the two.
Note: Starter was an option on the open cars at $65. Weight 95 lbs. Demountable rims were an additional $20. Weight 55 lbs. 21" tires and rims $25 extra. Weight 65 lbs. "C" type truck cab, $65. Truck rear bed, $55 if ordered separately. Pickup body for Runabout, $25.

1925 Ford, model T, roadster, OCW

ENGINE: [1923-1924-1925] L-head. Four. Cast iron block. B & S: 3-3/4 in. x 4 in. Disp.: 176.7 cu. in. C.R.: 3.98:1. Brake H.P.: 20 @ 1600 R.P.M. N.A.C.C. H.P.: 22.5. Main bearings: Three. Valve lifters: Solid. Carb.: Kingston L4 (6150). Holley NH (6200). Torque: 83 lbs.-ft. @ 900 R.P.M.
Note: Thermo-syphon. Inspection plate in the crankcase. New light-weight connecting rods.
[1921-1922] L-head. Four. Cast iron block. B & S: 3-3/4 in. x 4 in. Disp.: 176.7 cu. in. C.R.: 3.98:1. Brake H.P.: 20 @ 1600 R.P.M. N.A.C.C. H.P.: 22.5. Main bearings: Three. Valve lifters: Solid. Carb.: Kingston L4 (6150). Holley NH (6200). Torque: 83 lbs.-ft. @ 900 R.P.M. Single valve chamber covered with one steel door held with two stud/nuts or bolts.

CHASSIS: [1923-1924-1925] W.B.: 100 in. O.L.: 10 ft. 8 in. (Chassis) 11 ft. 2-1/2 in. (car). Frt/Rear Tread: 56 in. Tires: 30 x 3 front, 30 x 3-1/2 rear, standard equipment 1909-1925. 30 x 3-1.2 all around with demountable rims 1919-1925. 4:40 x 21 optional in late 1925.

1925 Ford, model T, touring, JAC

TECHNICAL: Planetary transmission. Speeds: 2F/1R. 3 pedal controls and 1 lever on floor. Multiple disk clutch (26 disks 1909-1915). (25 disks 1915-1927). Torque tube drive. Straight bevel rear axle. Overall ratio: 3.63:1. Brakes: Contracting band in transmission. Hand-operated internal expanding in rear wheels. Foot brake stops driveshaft. Parking brake on two rear wheels.
Note: Additional technical details will be found in the 1909 "General Comments" box.

OPTIONS: The basic equipment included three oil lamps only. (Two side and one tail.) Options listed included: Windshield. Headlamps. Tops. Horns. Prestolite tanks (instead of the carbide tank). Robe rails. Tire chains. Top boots. Foot rests. Spare tire carriers. Speedometers. Bumpers. No prices were given.

1926-27 FORD

1926 Ford, model T, touring, OCW

FORD — 1926-1927 — MODEL T: About July 1925 the "Improved Ford" marked the first major restyling of the Model T since 1917. New fenders, running boards, bodies (except for the Fordor), hoods and even a modified chassis made these Fords unique during the era of the Model T.
The Touring was given a door on the driver's side for the first time since 1911 (in U.S. cars; Canadian-built Fords had a driver's side door). The Tudor Sedan and the Coupe were all new, though similar in style to the 1925's. The Fordor Sedan continued the same basic body introduced in late 1922 except for the new cowl, hood, fenders, etc.
The chassis had a new longer rear cross-member, and with a modification of the springs and front spindles, the car was lowered about an inch.
While basically the same running gear as earlier models, the 1926-27 cars had 11-inch rear wheel brake drums, although they were only operated by the "emergency brake" lever. The foot pedals for the low speed and the brake were larger, and the internal transmission brake was made wider for better life and operation.
Initially offered in black, the Coupe and the Tudor were later painted a dark green, while the Fordor Sedan came in a dark maroon, as standard colors. The open cars continued in black until mid-1926.
In 1926, perhaps as "1927" models (Ford didn't name yearly models consistently), colors were added for the open cars; Gunmetal blue or Phoenix brown. Closed cars were offered in Highland green, Royal maroon, Fawn gray, Moleskin and Drake green. By Calendar 1927, anybody could be ordered in any standard Ford color. Black could be had on special order on the pickup body, although Commercial Green was the standard color. Fenders and running boards were black on all models.
When introduced in 1925, standard wheels on the closed cars were the 30 by 3-1/2" demountables, and 30 by 3-1/2 non-demountables on the open cars. By calendar 1926, the 21" balloons were standard on all models.
Wire wheels were offered as an option beginning January 1926. By early 1927, many Ford branches were supplying wire wheels as standard equipment on closed cars.
The gasoline tank was now located in the cowl on all models except the Fordor Sedan, which continued to have it under the driver's seat.
Model T production ended in May 1927 although Ford continued building engines through the year, then a few at a time until August 4, 1941!

I.D. DATA: [1926] Serial number was above the water inlet on the left side of the engine. Starting: 12218729 (July 27, 1925; Start of "1926" models.) Ending: 14049029 (July 30, 1926; end of fiscal 1926.) 1926 Calendar year engine numbers: 12990077 to 14619254. Numbers stamped on the body sills, etc. were manufacturer's numbers and not an identifying number. [1927] Serial number was above the water inlet on the left side of the engine. Starting: 14,049,030 (August 2, 1926 start of fiscal 1927.) Ending: 15006625 (May 25, 1927) (End of Model T Ford car production.)* 1927 Calendar year engine numbers: 14619255 to 15076231.* Numbers stamped on the body sills, etc. were manufacturer's numbers and not an identifying number.
*Most records show 15007032 or 15007033 as the last car but the factory records indicate these numbers were built on May 31, 1927, five days after the car assembly line was stopped. Ford continued building engines through 1927 and at a considerable rate until January 1931 (as many as 12,000 per month after the end of the Model T!). Production averaged about 100 per month in 1931, then dropped to less than ten and ended, finally, on August 4, 1941 with number 15176888.

1926 Ford, model T, Tudor sedan, HAC

1927 Ford, model T, roadster, OCW

CHASSIS: W.B.: 100 in. O.L.: 10 ft. 8 in. (chassis). 11 ft. 2-1/2 in. (car). Frt/Rear Tread: 56 in. Tires: 30 x 3-1/2 all around in early 1926 models. 4:40 x 21 optional in early 1926 and standard in later production.
Note: Chassis essentially identical to 1913-1925 except for a much longer rear cross-member. Chassis lowered about an inch by the use of a different front spindle and spring, and a deeper crown in the rear crossmember.
In mid-1926 the rear crossmember was made with a flanged edge and the chassis was of heavier steel.

TECHNICAL: Planetary transmission. Speeds: 2F/1R. 3 pedal controls and 1 lever on floor. Multiple disk clutch (25 disks 1915-1927). Torque tube drive. Straight bevel rear axle. Overall ratio: 3.63:1. Brakes: Contracting band in transmission. Hand-operated internal expanding in rear wheels. Foot brake stops driveshaft. Parking brake on two rear wheels.
    In January, 1926 optional 21" wire wheels became available, and these became standard on some closed cars in calendar year 1927.
In mid-1925 (1926 models) the transmission brake was made about a half-inch wider, and the rear wheel brakes were enlarged to 11" with lined shoes.
Note: Additional technical details will be found in the 1909 "General Comments" box.

OPTIONS: All cars equipped with headlamps, horn, starter and 21" demountable rims after January 1926. Windshield wiper (hand operated) (.50).* Windshield wiper (vacuum operated) (3.50) (2.00 in 1927). Windshield wings (open cars) (6.50 pr.) (2.50 in 1927). Gypsy curtains (open cars) (3.00 pr.) (1.10 in 1927). Top boot (open cars) (5.00) (4.00 in 1927). Bumpers (front and rear) (15.00). Wire wheels, set of 5 (50.00) (35.00 later 1926). Rear view mirror (open cars) (.75).* Dash lamp (open cars) (.60).* Stop light and switch (2.50). Shock absorbers (9.00 set).
* Standard on closed cars.

1928 FORD

1928 Ford, model A, roadster, AA

FORD — MODEL A — FOUR: The reverting to a Model A designation for the new Ford symbolized the impact this automobile had upon the Ford Motor Company. A far more complex automobile than the Model T, the Model A contained approximately 6800 different parts as compared to the less than 5000 components that comprised the Model T. There were however, similarities. Both cars had 4 cylinder L-head engines and semi-elliptic front and rear transverse springs. But beyond this point the Model A moved far away from the heritage of the Model T. Its engine with a water pump displaced just over 200 cubic inches and with 40hp was virtually twice as powerful as the Model T's and provided a 65mph top speed. Superseding the old magneto ignition was a contemporary battery and ignition system. The Model T's planetary transmission gave way to a three-speed sliding gear unit. Other technical advancements found in the Model A included the use of 4-wheel mechanical brakes and Houdaille, double-action hydraulic shock absorbers.
    The styling of the Model A maintained a link with that of the Model T but with a 103-1/2 inch wheelbase, 4.50 x 21 tires and a high belt line the influence of the Lincoln automobile upon the appearance of the new Ford was unmistakable. Full crown fenders were used and the bodywork of each of the five models initially offered had their body surrounds outlined in contrasting body colors and pin striping. The Model A's 2-piece front and rear bumpers were similar to those used on the 1927 Model T but its new radiator shell with its gentle center V-dip and moderately curved crossbar for the headlights made it impossible to confuse the two Fords.
    The first Model A engine was completed on October 20, 1927 and the following day it was installed in the first Model A assembled. From that day (May 25, 1927) Ford announced it would produce a successor to the Model T, public interest had steadily increased to a level that was finally satisfied on December 2, 1927 when the nationwide introduction of the Model A took place. While many industry observers recognized the passing of the Model T as the end of an era, there was equal appreciation for the extraordinary value the Model A represented and an awareness that it was in all ways more than a worthy successor to the Tin Lizzie.

I.D. DATA: Serial numbers were located on top side of frame near clutch pedal. Starting: Oct. 20-Dec. 31, 1927 - A1; Jan. 1-Dec. 31, 1928 - A5276. Ending: Oct. 20-Dec. 31, 1927 - A5275; Jan. 1-Dec. 31, 1928 - A810122. Engine numbers were located on boss placed on center of left side of block directly below the cylinder head. A prefix letter A was used and a star is found on either end. Starting: Oct. 20-Dec. 31, 1927 - A1; Jan. 1-Dec. 31, 1928 - A5276. Ending: Oct. 20-Dec. 31, 1927 - A5275; Jan. 1-Dec. 31, 1928 - A810122. Model Numbers: 1928 models have a date when the body was manufactured stamped on the upper left side of the firewall.

Model No. 1926	Body Type & Seating	Price	Weight	Prod. Total
T	4-dr. Tr.-5P	290 (A)	1633 (D)	—
T	4-dr. Tr.-5P	375 (A) 380 (B) 380 (C)	1738	364,409 (F)
T	2-dr. Rbt.-2P	260 (A)	1550 (D)	—
T	2-dr. Rbt.-2P	345 (A) 360 (B) 360 (C)	1655	342,575 (F)
T	2-dr. Pickup-2P	281 (A)	NA (D)	N/L (E)
T	2-dr. Pickup-2P	366 (A) 381 (B) 381 (C)	1736	75,406 (F)
T	2-dr. Sed.-5P	580 (A) 495 (B) 495 (C)	1972	270,331 (F)
T	4-dr. Sed.-5P	660 (A) 545 (B) 545 (C)	2004	102,732 (F)
T	2-dr. Cpe.-2P	520 (A) 485 (B) 485 (C)	1860	288,342 (F)
T	Chassis	225 (A)	1167 (D)	—
T	Chassis	290 (A) 300 (B) 300 (C)	1272	58,223 (F)
TT	Truck Chassis	365 (A) 325 (B) 325 (C)	1477	228,496 (G)
TT	Truck Chassis	430 (A) 375 (B) 375 (C)	1577	(F)

Truck Bodies Only

TT	Open Cab	65 65	NA	142,852 (U.S)
TT	Closed Cab	85 85	NA —	(G)
TT	Express Body	55 55	NA —	(G)
TT	Platform Body	50 50	— —	(G)
TT	Expr. w/roof & screen	110 110	— —	(G)

(A) Price effective January 1, 1926.
(B) Price effective June 6, 1926.
(C) Price effective December 31, 1926 (unchanged from June).
(D) Early models with 30 x 3-1/2 non-demountable wheels and no starter. Available only on special order by calendar 1926.
(E) January 1, 1926 to December 31, 1926. (Includes foreign production.)
(F) Includes starter and 21" demountable wheels.
(G) Chassis production figures are for U.S. and foreign. Body figures are for U.S. only and are included in the chassis count. Starter production is not listed separately.
Note: Starter and demountable wheels are standard on all cars. Starter is optional on the truck. Early 1926 cars with 30 by 3-1/2 demountables are 10 pounds lighter.
Pickup body for Runabout, $25.

Model No. 1927	Body Type & Seating	Price	Weight	Prod. Total
T	4-dr. Tr.-5P	380	1738	81,181 (A)
T	2-dr. Rbt.-2P	360	1655	95,778 (A)
T	2-dr. Pickup-2P	381	1736	28,143 (A)
T	2-dr. Sed.-5P	495	1972	78,105 (A)
T	4-dr. Sed.-5P	545	2004	22,930 (A)
T	2-dr. Cpe.-2P	485	1860	69,939 (A)
T	Chassis	300	1272	19,280 (A)
TT	Truck Chassis	325	1477	83,202 (A)
TT	Truck Chassis	375	1577	(B)

Truck Bodies Only

TT	Open Cab	65	NA	41,318 (U.S.)
TT	Closed Cab	85	NA	(C)
TT	Express body	55	NA	(C)
TT	Platform Body	50	NA	(C)
TT	Expr. w/roof & screen	110	NA	(C)

(A) January 1, 1927 to December 31, 1927. (Includes foreign production.)
(B) Includes starter and demountable wheels.
(C) Chassis production figures are for U.S. and foreign. Body figures are for U.S. only and are included in the chassis count. Starter production is not listed separately.
Note: Starter and demountable wheels are standard on all cars. Starter is optional on the truck.
Pickup body for Runabout, $25.
Automobile production ended May 26, 1927 but trucks continued for some time.

ENGINE: L-head. Four. Cast iron block. B & S: 3-3/4 in. x 4 in. Disp.: 176.7 cu. in. C.R.: 3.98:1. Brake H.P.: 20 @ 1600 R.P.M. N.A.C.C. H.P.: 22.5. Main bearings: Three. Valve lifters: Solid. Carb.: Kingston L4 (6150B), Holley NH (6200C), Holley Vaporizer (6250), Kingston Regenerator. Torque: 83 lbs.-ft. @ 900 R.P.M.
Note: Thermo-syphon. Single valve chamber covered with one steel door half with two stud/nuts or bolts.
Transmission housing now bolts to the rear of the cylinder. Fan mounted on the water outlet. Later production used nickel plated head and water connection bolts.

Model No.	Body Type & Seating	Price	Weight	Prod. Total
A	2-dr. Rds. R/S-2/4P	480	2106	Note 1
A	4-dr. Phae.-4P	460	2140	Note 1
A	2-dr. Bus. Cpe.-2P	550	2225	Note 1
A	2-dr. R/S Cpe.2/4P	550	2265	Note 1
A	2-dr. Std. Bus. Rds.	480	2050	Note 1
A	2-dr. Spt. Bus. Cpe.-2P	525	NA	Note 1
A	2-dr. Tudor-4P	550	2340	Note 1
A	4-dr. Fordor-4P	585	2386	Note 1
A	4-dr. Taxi Cab	600	NA	Note 1

Note 1: Body style production was recorded only by calendar year. See list at end of Model A section.

1928 Ford, model A, Fordor sedan, JAC

ENGINE: Inline. L-head. Four. Cast iron block. B & S: 3-7/8 in. x 4-1/4 in. Disp.: 200.5 cu. in. C.R.: 4.22:1. Brake H.P.: 40 @ 2200 R.P.M. SAE H.P.: 24.03. Main bearings: Three. Valve lifters: Mechanical. Carb.: Zenith or Holley double venturi. Torque: 128 lbs.-ft. @ 100 R.P.M.

CHASSIS: W.B.: 103.5 in. Frt/Rear Tread: 56. Tires: 4.50 x 21.

TECHNICAL: Sliding gear transmission. Speeds: 3F/1R. Floor shift controls. Dry multiple disc clutch. Shaft drive. 3/4 floating rear axle. Overall ratio: 3.7:1. Mechanical internal expanding brakes on four wheels. Welded wire wheels. Wheel size: 21.

1928 Ford, model A, phaeton, JAC

OPTIONS: Single sidemount. External sun shade. Radiator ornament. Wind vanes. Rear view mirror. Rear luggage rack. Radiator stone guard. Spare tire lock.

HISTORICAL: Introduced December 2, 1927. Innovations: Safety glass installed in all windows. Calendar year production: 633,594. The president of Ford was Edsel Ford.

1929 FORD

1929 Ford, model A, sport coupe, AA

FORD — MODEL A — FOUR: The most apparent change made in the Model A's appearance, aside from brighter trim and body paint were the exterior door handles on open models. With production rapidly increasing more body styles became available. A Town Car model was introduced on December 13, 1928 followed during 1929 by a wood-bodied station wagon on April 25. Other new styles included a Convertible Cabriolet, several new four door sedans and a Town Sedan. As in 1928 the Model A's base price included many standard equipment features such as a combination tail and stop light, windshield wiper, front and rear bumpers and a Spartan horn.

1929 Ford, model A, taxicab, JAC

I.D. DATA: Serial numbers were located on top side of frame, near clutch pedal. Starting: A 810,123. Ending: A 2742695. Engine no. location: Boss placed on center of left side of block directly below the cylinder head. Starting: A 810123. Ending: A 2724695.

Model No.	Body Type & Seating	Price	Weight	Prod. Total
A	4-dr. Sta. Wag.-4P	650	2500	Note 1
A	2-dr. RS Conv.2-4P	670	2339	Note 1
A	2-dr. RS Spt. Cpe.-2/4P	550	2250	Note 1
A	Mur. Std. Fordor Sed.-4P	625	2497	Note 1
A	Brgg. Std. Fordor Sed.-4P	625	2497	Note 1
A	Brgg. 2W Std. Fordor Sed.-4P	625	2419	Note 1
A	Brgg. Std. Fordor Sed.-4P	625	2497	Note 1
A	Brgg. L.B. Fordor Sed.-4P	625	2500	Note 1
A	2-dr. Tudor Sed.-4P	525	2348	Note 1
A	4-dr. Mur. Twn. Sed.-4P	695	2517	Note 1
A	4-dr. Brgg. Twn. Sed.-4P	695	2517	Note 1
A	2-dr. Std. RS Rds.-2/4P	450	2106	Note 1
A	2-dr. Std. Rds. R/S-2/4P	450	2161	Note 1
A	2-dr. Std. Bus. Cpe.-2P	525	2216	Note 1
A	4-dr. Std. Phae.-4P	460	2203	Note 1
A	4-dr. Std. Cpe.-2P	550	2248	Note 1
A	4-dr. Twn. Cr.-4P	1400	2525	Note 1
A	4-dr. Taxi-4P	800	NA	Note 1

Note 1: Body style production was recorded only by calendar year. See list at end of Model A section.

1929 Ford, model A, Fordor sedan, JAC

ENGINE: Inline. L-head. Four. Cast iron block. B & S: 3-7/8 in. x 4-1/4 in.. Disp.: 200.5 cu. in. C.R.: 4.22:1. Brake H.P.: 40 @ 2200 R.P.M. N.A.C.C. H.P.: 24.03. Main bearings: Three. Valve lifters: Mechanical. Carb.: Zenith or Holley double-venturi. Torque: 128 lbs.-ft. @ 1000 R.P.M.

1929 Ford, model A, town car, JAC

173

CHASSIS: W.B.: 103.5 in. Frt/Rear Tread: 56 in. Tires: 4.50 x 21.

TECHNICAL: Sliding gear. Speeds: 3F/1R. Floor shift controls. Dry multiple disc. Shaft drive. 3/4 floating rear axle. Overall Ratio: 3.7:1. Mechanical internal expanding brakes on four wheels. Welded wire wheels. Wheel Rim Size: 21''.

OPTIONS: Single Sidemount. External Sun Shade. Radiator ornament (3.00). Wind vanes. Rear view mirror. Rear luggage rack. Radiator stone guard. Spare tire lock.

HISTORICAL: Introduced January, 1929. Calendar year sales: 1,310,147 (registrations). Calendar year production: 1,507,132. The president of Ford was Edsel Ford. Production of the first million Model A Fords was completed on February 4, 1929. The 2-millionth Model A Ford was constructed on July 24, 1929.

1930 FORD

1930 Ford, model A, roadster, AA

FORD — MODEL A — FOUR: The Model A was given a substantial face lift for 1930 and it was very effective. Larger 4.75 tires on smaller 19 inch wheels resulted in an overall height reduction which along with wider fenders, a deeper radiator shell and the elimination of the cowl stanchion all were contributors to the Model A's fresh new look. Replacing the older nickel finish for the Ford's exterior brightwork was both nickel and stainless steel trim. During the year a new Victoria model was introduced along with a deluxe version of the phaeton.

I.D. DATA: Top side of frame near clutch panel. Starting: A 2742696. Ending: A4237500. Boss placed on center of left side of block, directly below the cylinder head. Starting Engine No: 1 2742696. Ending: A 4237500.

1930 Ford, model A, phaeton, JAC

Model No.	Body Type & Seating	Price	Weight	Prod. Total
35-B	4-dr. Std. Phae-2P	440	2212	Note 1
40-B	2-dr. Std. Rds.	435	2155	Note 1
40-B	2-dr. Del. Rds. R/S-2-4P	495	2230	Note 1
45-B	2-dr. Std. Cpe.	500	2257	Note 1
45-B	2-dr. Del. Cpe.	550	2265	Note 1
50-B	2-dr. Spt. Cpe. R/S-2-4P	530	2283	Note 1
55-B	2-dr. Tudor Sed.	490	2372	Note 1
68-B	2-dr. Cab.	645	2273	Note 1
150-B	4-dr. Sta. Wag.-4P	650	2482	Note 1
155-C	4-dr. Mu'ry Twn. Sed.-4P	640	2495	Note 1
155-D	4-dr. Briggs Twn. Sed.-4P	650	2495	Note 1
165-C	Std. Mu'ry Fordor Sed.-4P	580	2462	Note 1
165-D	Std. Briggs Fordor Sed.-4P	590	2462	Note 1
170-B	Std. Briggs Fordor 2W Sed.-4P	590	2488	Note 1
170-B	Briggs Fordor 2W Sed.-4P	650	2488	Note 1
180-A	4-dr. Del. Phae-4P	645	2285	Note 1
190-A	2-dr. Vict.-4P	580	2375	Note 1

Note 1: Body style production was recorded only by calendar year. See list at end of Model A section.

ENGINES: In line, L-head. Four. Cast iron block. B. x S.: 3-7/8 in. x 4-1/4 in. Disp.: 200.5 cu. in. C.R.: 4.22:1. Brake H.P. 40 @ 2200 R.P.M. Taxable horsepower: 24.03. Main bearings: Three. Valve lifters: Mechanical. Carb.: Zenith or Holley double-venturi. Torque: 128 lbs.-ft. at 1000 R.P.M.

1930 Ford, model A, coupe, JAC

CHASSIS: W.B.: 103.5 in. Frt/Rear Tread: 56 in. Tires: 4.75 x 19.

TECHNICAL: Transmission: Sliding gear. Speeds: 3F/1R. Floor shift controls. Dry multiple disc clutch. Shaft drive. 3/4 floating rear axle. Overall ratio: 3.77:1. Mechanical internal expanding brakes on four wheels. Welded wire wheels. Wheel size: 19.

1930 Ford, model A, town sedan, JAC

OPTIONS: Single sidemount (20.00). External sun shade. Radiator ornament. Wind vanes. Rear view mirror. Rear luggage rack. Radiator stone guard. Spare tire lock.

HISTORICAL: January, 1930. Calendar year sales: 1055097 (registrations). Calendar year production: 1,155,162. The president of Ford was Edsel Ford.

1931 FORD

1931 Ford, model A, victoria, AA

FORD — MODEL A — FOUR: The final year of Model A production brought revised styling, several new body types and on April 14th production of the 20-millionth Ford, a Fordor sedan. Heading the list of styling changes was a radiator shell with a relief effect, plus running boards fitted with single piece slash aprons. In addition to the 2 and 4 door sedans introduced with a smoother roofline, a revamped cabriolet model was also introduced during 1931. However the star attraction was the convertible sedan which had fixed side window frames over which the top rode up or down on a set of tracks. Standard equipment on the convertible sedan included a side mount.

1931 Ford, model A, roadster, JAC

1931 Ford, model A, Fordor sedan, JAC

I.D. DATA: Serial numbers were located on top side of frame, near clutch pedal. Starting: A4237501. Ending: A4849340. Engine numbers were located on boss placed on center of left side of block, directly below the cylinder head. Starting: A4327501. Ending: A4849340.

Model No.	Body Type & Seating	Price	Weight	Prod. Total
A	4-dr. Std. Phae.-4P	435	2212	Note 1
A	2-dr. Std. Rds.	430	2155	Note 1
A	2-dr. Del. Rds.	475	2230	Note 1
A	2-dr. Std. Cpe.	490	2257	Note 1
A	2-dr. Del. Cpe.	525	2265	Note 1
A	2-dr. Spt. Cpe.	500	2283	Note 1
A	2-dr. Std. Tudor Sed.-4P	490	2462	Note 1
A	2-dr. Del. Tudor Sed.-4P	525	2488	Note 1
A	2-dr. Cab	595	2273	Note 1
A	4-dr. Sta. Wag.-4P	625	2505	Note 1
A	4-dr. Mu'ry Twn. Sed.-4P	630	2495	Note 1
A	4-dr. Briggs Twn. Sed.-4P	630	2495	Note 1
A	4-dr. Std. Fordor Sed.-4P	590	2462	Note 1
A	4-dr. Twn. Sed.-4P	630	2495	Note 1
A	4-dr. Del. Fordor Sed.-4P	630	2488	Note 1
A	Mu'ry Std. Fordor Sed.-4P	590	2462	Note 1
A	Briggs Std. Fordor Sed.-4P	590	2462	Note 1
A	Briggs De. Fordor 2W Sed.-4P	630	2488	Note 1
A	2-dr. Del. Phae.-4P	580	2265	Note 1
A	2-dr. Vic. Cpe.-4P	580	2375	Note 1
A	2-dr. Conv. Sed.-4P	640	2335	Note 1

Note 1: Body style production was recorded only by calendar year. See list at end of Model A section.

ENGINE: Inline. L-head. Four. Cast iron block. B & S: 3-7/8 in. x 4-1/4 in. Disp.: 200.5 cu. in. C.R.: 4.22:1. Brake H.P.: 40 @ 2200 R.P.M. Taxable H.P.: 24.03. Main bearings: Three. Valve lifters: Mechanical. Carb.: Zenith or Holley double venturi. Torque: 128 lbs.-ft. @ 1000 R.P.M.

CHASSIS: W.B.: 103.5. Frt/Rear Tread: 56 in. Tires: 4.75 x 19.

TECHNICAL: Sliding gear transmission. Speeds: 3F/1R. Floor shift controls. Dry multiple disc clutch. Shaft drive. 3/4 floating rear axle. Overall Ratio: 3.77:1. Mechanical internal expanding brakes on four wheels. Welded wire wheels. Wheel size: 19.

OPTIONS: Single sidemount. External sun shade. Radiator ornament. Wind vanes. Rear view mirror. Rear luggage rack. Radiator stone guard. Spare tire lock.

HISTORICAL: Introduced January, 1931. Calendar year sales 528581 (registrations). Calendar year production: 541615. The president of Ford was Edsel Ford.

FORD
Model A Domestic Production Figures
(Calendar Year)

	1927	1928	1929	1930	1931	Totals
Phaeton						
standard	221	47,255	49,818	16,479	4076	117,849
deluxe	—	—	—	3946	2229	6175
Roadster						
standard	269	81,937*	191,529	112,901	5499	392,135
deluxe	—	—	—	11,318	52,997	64,315
*Of these, 51,807 were produced without rumble seat.						
Sport Coupe	734	79,099	134,292	69,167	19,700	302,992
Coupe						
standard	629	70,784	178,982	226,027	79,816	556,238
deluxe	—	—	—	28,937	23,067	52,004
Bus. Coupe	—	37,343	37,644	—	—	74,987
Conv. Cabr.	—	—	16,421	25,868	11,801	54,090
Tudor						
standard	1948	208,562	523,922	376,271	148,425	1,259,128
deluxe	—	—	—	—	21,984	21,984
Fordor (2-window)						
standard	—	82,349	146,097	5279	—	233,725
deluxe	—	—	—	12,854	3251	16,105
Fordor (3-window)						
standard	—	—	53,941	41,133	18,127	113,201
town sedan	—	—	84,970	104,935	55,469	245,374
Conv. Sedan	—	—	—	—	4864	4864
Victoria	—	—	—	6306	33,906	40,212
Town Car	—	89	913	63	—	1065
Station Wagon	—	5	4954	3510	2848	11,317
Taxicab	—	264	4576	10	—	4850

1932 FORD

1932 Ford V-8, DeLuxe 3-window coupe, AA

FORD — MODEL 18 — EIGHT: Once again Henry Ford made automotive history when, on March 31, 1932 he introduced the Ford V-8. This type of engine wasn't a novelty by that time but when offered at traditional Ford low prices this new engine was a true milestone. Henry Ford had this 221 cubic inch displacement engine developed in traditional Ford style — extreme secrecy — a small work force operating under relative primitive conditions — under Henry Ford's close personal supervision.

Its early production life was far from tranquil. Hastily rushed into assembly, many of the 1932 engines experienced piston and bearing failures plus overheating as well as block cracking. However, these problems were soon overcome and for the next 21 years this V-8 would be powering Ford automobiles.

The new Ford was extremely handsome. Both front and rear fenders were fully crowned. The soon-to-be classic radiator shell was slightly V'eed and carried vertical bars. Positioned in the center of the curved headlight tie-bar was Ford's timeless V-8 logo. Apparently sensitive that most of its competitors had longer wheelbases, Ford measured the distance from the center position of the front spring to the center of the rear and claimed it as the V-8's 112 inch wheelbase. Actually its wheelbase was 106 inches.

The new Ford's dash carried all instruments and controls within an engine-turned oval placed in the center of a mahogany colored (early) or walnut (late) grained panel. An anti-theft device was incorporated into the key and ignition switch which was mounted on a bracket attached to the steering column. During the model year Ford incorporated many changes into the design of its new model. One of the most obvious, intended to improve engine cooling was a switch from a hood with 20 louvers to one with 25.

1932 Ford V-8, sport coupe, JAC

FORD — MODEL B — FOUR: Somewhat overwhelmed by the public's response to Model 18, the four-cylinder Model B shared the same body as the V-8, minus V-8 emblems on the headlamp tie bars and with Ford rather than V-8 lettering on its hub caps.

Both types had single transverse leaf springs front and rear. The locating of the rear spring behind the differential and the use of 18 inch wheels gave the Fords a lower overall height than previous models.

I.D. DATA: Top side of frame, near clutch pedal. Starting: [Model B] AB 5000,001 & up. [Model 18] 18-1. Ending: [Model 18] 18-2031126. Prefix "C" indicates Canadian built. Boss placed on center of left side of block, directly below the cylinder head [Model B]. Starting Engine No.: [Model B] AB 5000,005 & up. [Model 18] 18-1. Ending: [Model 18] 18-2031,126.

Model No. Ford V-8	Body Type & Seating	Price	Weight	Prod. Total
18	2-dr. Rds.	460	2203	520
18	2-dr. Del. Rds.	500	2308	6893
18	4-dr. Phae.	495	2369	483
18	4-dr. Del. Phae.	545	2375	923
18	2-dr. Cpe.	490	2398	28,904
18	2-dr. Spt. Cpe.	535	2405	1982
18	2-dr. Del. Cpe.	575	2493	20,506
18	2-dr. Tudor Sed.-4P	500	2508	57,930
18	2-dr. Del. Tudor Sed.-4P	550	2518	18,836
18	4-dr. Fordor Sed.-4P	590	2538	9310
18	4-dr. Del. Fordor Sed.-4P	645	2568	18,880
18	2-dr. Cab. R/S-2-4P	610	2398	5499
18	2-dr. Vic.-4P	600	2483	7241
18	2-dr. Conv. Sed.-4P	650	2480	842
Ford 4-cyl.				
B	2-dr. Rds.	410	2095	948
B	2-dr. Del. Rds.	450	2102	3719
B	4-dr. Phae.	445	2238	593
B	4-dr. Del. Phae.	495	2268	281
B	2-dr. Cpe.	440	2261	20,342
B	2-dr. Spt. Cpe.	485	2286	739
B	2-dr. Del. Cpe.	425	2364	968
B	2-dr. Tudor Sed.-4P	450	2378	36,553
B	2-dr. Del. Tudor Sed.-4P	500	2398	4077
B	4-dr. Fordor Sed.-4P	540	2413	4116
B	4-dr. Del. Fordor Sed.-4P	595	2432	2620
B	2-dr. Cab.-4P	560	2295	427
B	2-dr. Vic.-4P	550	2344	521
B	2-dr. Conv. Sed.-4P	600	2349	41

ENGINE: [Model B] In line, L-head. Four. Cast iron block. B x S: 3-7/8 in. x 4-1/4 in. Disp.: 200.5 cu. in. C.R.: 4.6:1. Brake H.P.: 50. Taxable H.P.: 30. Main bearings: Three. Valve lifters: Mechanical. Carb.: Zenith or Holley double-venturi. [Model 18] 90° V, L-head. Eight. Cast iron block. B x S: 3-1/16 in. x 3-3/4 in. Disp.: 221 cu. in. C.R.: 5.5:1. Brake H.P. 65 @ 3400 R.P.M. SAE H.P.: 30. Main bearings: Three. Valve lifters: Mechanical. Carb.: Special Ford Detroit lubricator downdraft, single barrel, 1-1/2" throat. Torque: 130 lbs.-ft. @ 1250 R.P.M.

CHASSIS: Model 18 & B. W.B.: 106 in. O.L.: 165-1/2. Height: 68-5/8. Frt/Rear Tread: 55.2/56.7. Tires: 5.25 x 18.

TECHNICAL: Transmission: Sliding gear. Speeds: 3F/1R. Floor shift controls. Single dry plate, molded asbestos lining clutch. Shaft drive. 3/4 floating rear axle. Overall ratio: 4.11:1 (early cars - 4.33:1). Mechanical, rod activated brakes on four wheels. Welded wire, drop center rim wheels. Wheel size: 18.

OPTIONS: Single sidemount. Dual sidemount. Clock. Trunk rack. Leather upholstery. Mirror. Twin tail lamps. Bedford cord upholstery. Cowl lamps (Std. models).

HISTORICAL: Introduced: April 2, 1929. Mass production of a low-priced one-piece 90° V-8 engine block. Calendar year sales: 2581927 (registrations). Calendar year production: 287,285. The president of Ford was Edsel Ford.

1933 FORD

1933 Ford V-8, victoria, OCW

FORD — MODEL 40 — EIGHT: In addition to a longer 112 inch wheelbase, X-member double-drop frame, the Model 40 Ford had valenced front and rear fenders, a new radiator design with vertical bars slanted back to match the rear sweep of the windshield and acorn-shaped headlight shells. Curvaceous one-piece bumpers with a center-dip were used at front and rear. Enhancing the Ford's streamlined appearance were the angled side hood louvers. All models regardless of body color were delivered with black fenders and 17 inch wire spoke wheels.

Accompanying these exterior revisions was a new dash arrangement with a reshaped engine-tuned panel enclosing the gauges placed directly in front of the driver. A similarly shaped glove box was placed on the passenger's side.

With its teething problems part of the past, the Ford V-8 by virtue of an improved ignition system, better cooling, higher compression ratio and aluminum cylinder heads developed 75 horsepower.

FORD — MODEL 40 — FOUR: As before the four-cylinder Fords were identical to the eight-cylinder models except for their lack of V-8 trim identification.

I.D. DATA: Serial numbers were located on top side of frame near clutch pedal also, left front pillar, foward portion of left frame member, transmission housing. Starting: [V-8] 18-2031127 and up; [four-cylinder, with prefix "B"] 5185849 & up. Prefix "C" indicates Canadian built. Engine numbers were located on boss placed on center of left side of block, directly below the cylinder head (four-cylinder); On top of clutch housing (V-8). Starting: [V-8] 18-2031127 & up; [four-cylinder] 5185849 & up.

1933 Ford V-8, DeLuxe coupe, JAC

Model No. Ford V-8	Body Type & Seating	Price	Weight	Prod. Total
40	2-dr. Del. Rds. R/S-2/4P	510	2461	4223
40	2-dr. Std. RS Rds.-2/4P	475	2422	126
40	2-dr. Cab R/S-2/4P	585	2545	7852
40	4-dr. Std. Phae.-4P	495	2520	232
40	4-dr. Del. Phae.-4P	545	2529	1483
40	2-dr. 3W Del. Cpe.-2P	540	2538	15894
40	2-dr. 3W Std. Cpe.-2P	490	2534	6585
40	2-dr. 5W Del. Cpe.-2P	540	2538	11244
40	2-dr. 5W Std. Cpe.-2P	490	2534	31797
40	2-dr. Vic.-4P	595	2595	4193
40	2-dr. Del. Tudor Sed.-4P	550	2625	48233
40	2-dr. Std. Tudor Sed.-4P	500	2621	106387
40	4-dr. Del. Fordor Sed.-4P	610	2684	45443
40	4-dr. Std. Fordor Sed.-4P	560	2675	19602
40	4-dr. Sta. Wag.-4P	640	2635	1654
Ford 4-cyl.				
40	2-dr. Del. Rds. R/S-2/4P	460	2278	101
40	2-dr. Std. RS Rds.-2/4P	425	2268	107
40	2-dr. Cab R/S-2/4P	535	2306	24
40	4-dr. Std. Phae.-4P	445	2281	457
40	4-dr. Del. Phae.-4P	495	2290	241
40	2-dr. 3W Del. Cpe.-2P	490	2220	24
40	2-dr. 3W Std. Cpe.-2P	440	2380	189
40	2-dr. 5W Del. Cpe.-2P	490	2299	28
40	2-dr. 5W Std. Cpe.-2P	440	2220	2148
40	2-dr. Vic.-4P	545	2356	25
40	2-dr. Del. Tudor Sed.-4P	500	2520	85
40	2-dr. Std. Tudor Sed.-4P	450	2503	2911
40	4-dr. Del. Fordor Sed.-4P	560	2590	179
40	4-dr. Std. Fordor Sed.-4P	510	2550	682
40	4-dr. Sta. Wag.-4P	590	2505	359

ENGINE: [Model B] Inline. L-head. Four. Cast iron block. B & S: 3-7/8 in. x 4-1/4 in. Disp.: 200.5 cu. in. C.R.: 4.6:1. Brake H.P.: 50. Taxable H.P.: 30. Main bearings: Three. Valve lifters: Mechanical. Carb.: Zenith or Holley double venturi. [Model 40] 90° V, L-head. Eight. Cast iron block. B & S: 3-1/16 in. x 3-3/4 in. Disp.: 221 cu. in. C.R.: 6.3:1. Brake H.P.: 75 @ 3800 R.P.M. Main bearings: Three. Valve lifters: Mechanical. Carb.: Detroit Lubricator downdraft, single barrel 1.25" throat.

CHASSIS: [Model 40] W.B.: 112 in. O.L.: 182-9/10 in. Height: 68 in. Frt/Rear Tread: 55-1/5 in./56-7/10 in. Tires: 5.50 x 17.

TECHNICAL: Sliding gear transmission. Speeds: 3F/1R. Floor shift controls. Single dry plate, woven asbestos lining clutch. Shaft drive. 3/4 floating rear axle. Overall Ratio: 4.11:1. Mechanical internal expanding brakes on four wheels. Welded spoke wheels, drop center rims. Wheel Size: 17 in.

OPTIONS: Radio. Heater. Clock. Radio antenna. Greyhound radiator ornament. Trunk. Trunk rack. Twin tail lamps. Cowl lamps (Std. models). Windshield wings. Dual horns (Std. models). Whitewalls. Leather seats. Dual wipers. Steel spare tire cover. Rumble seat (Coupes).

HISTORICAL: Introduced February 9, 1933. Calendar year sales: 311,113 (registrations). Calendar year production: 334,969. The president of Ford was Edsel Ford. During 1933 Ford conducted a number of economy runs with the Model 40. Under conditions ranging from the Mojave Desert to the Catskill Mountains the Fords averaged between 18.29 and 22.5mpg.

1934 FORD

1934 Ford, V-8, station wagon, AA

FORD — MODEL 40 — EIGHT: Visual changes for 1934 were minor. Different V-8 hub cap emblems (now painted rather than chrome-finished and without a painted surround) were used and the side hood louvers were straight instead of curved. Although the same grille form was continued for 1934 there were changes. The 1934 version had fewer vertical bars and its chrome frame was deeper and flatter. The V-8 grille ornament was placed within an inverted 60° triangle and carried a vertical divider. Other exterior alterations included smaller head and cowl light shells, two rather than one, hood handles and three instead of two body pin stripes. In addition fenders were painted in body color on all models. However, black fenders were available as an option. Closed body models featured front door glass that prior to lowering vertically into the door, moved slightly to the rear. This was usually referred to as "clear vision" ventilation.

The dash panel no longer had the engine-turned panel insert. For 1934 this surface was painted.

DeLuxe models were easily distinguished from their Standard counterparts by their pin-striping, cowl light, twin horns and two taillights.

The principle change in the design of the Ford V-8 consisted of a Stromberg carburetor in place of the Detroit Lubricator unit and a reshaped air cleaner.

Ford also offered its four-cylinder engine in all models at a price $50.00 below that of a corresponding V-8 design. This was the final year for this engine's use in a Ford automobile. The engine was designated Model B; the car was designated Model 40.

I.D. DATA: Serial numbers were on top side of frame, near clutch panel. Also left front pillar forward portion of left frame member transmission housing. Starting No.: 18-451478 and up. Engine numbers on top of clutch housing. Starting Engine No.: 18-457478 & up.

Model No. Ford V-8	Body Type & Seating	Price	Weight	Prod. Total
40 V-8	2-dr. Del. Rds.-2P	525	2461	—
40 V-8	4-dr. Phae.-4P	510	2520	373
40 V-8	4-dr. Del. Phae.-4P	550	2529	3128
40 V-8	2-dr. Cab.-2/4P	590	2545	14,496
40 V-8	2-dr. Std. 5W Cpe.-2P	515	2534	47,623
40 V-8	2-dr. Del. 3W Cpe.-2/4P	555	2538	26,348
40 V-8	2-dr. Del. 5W Cpe.-2/4P	555	2538	26,879
40 V-8	2-dr. Tudor-4P	535	2621	124,870
40 V-8	2-dr. Del. Tudor-4P	575	2625	121,696
40 V-8	4-dr. Fordor-4P	585	2675	22,394
40 V-8	4-dr. Del. Fordor-4P	625	2684	102,268
40 V-8	2-dr. Vic.-4P	610	2595	20,083
40 V-8	4-dr. Sta. Wag.-4P	660	2635	2905
Ford 4-cyl.				
40	2-dr. Del. Rds.-2P	475	2278	—
40	4-dr. Phae.-4P	460	2281	377
40	4-dr. Del. Phae.-4P	510	2290	412
40	2-dr. Cab.-2P	540	2306	12
40	2-dr. Std. 5W Cpe.-2P	465	2220	20
40	2-dr. Del. 3W Cpe.-2/4P	505	2220	7
40	2-dr. Del. 5W Cpe.-2/4P	505	2299	3
40	2-dr. Tudor-4P	485	2503	185
40	2-dr. Del. Tudor-4P	525	2520	12
40	4-dr. Fordor-4P	535	2590	405
40	4-dr. Del. Fordor-4P	575	2590	384
40	2-dr. Vic.-4P	560	2356	—
40	4-dr. Sta. Wag.-4P	610	2505	95

ENGINE: [Model B] Inline. L-head. Four. Cast iron block. B & S: 3-7/8 in. x 4-1/4 in. Disp.: 200.5 cu. in. C.R.: 4.6:1. Brake H.P.: 50. Taxable H.P.: 30. Main bearings: Three. Valve lifters: Mechanical. Carb.: Zenith or Holley double venturi. [Model 40] 90° V, L-head. Eight. Cast iron block. B & S: 3-1/16 in. x 3-3/4 in. Disp.: 221 cu. in. C.R.: 6.3:1. Brake H.P.: 85 @ 3800 R.P.M. Main bearings: Three. Valve lifters: Mechanical. Carb.: Stromberg EE-1 2bbl. downdraft. Torque: 150 lbs.-ft. @ 2200 R.P.M.

CHASSIS: W.B.: 112. O.L.: 182.9 in. Height: 68 in. Frt/Rear Tread: 55.2/56.7 in. Tires: 5.50 x 17.

TECHNICAL: Sliding gear. Speeds: 3F/1R. Floor shift controls. Single dry plate, woven asbestos lining. Shaft drive. 3/4 floating rear axle. Overall Ratio: 4.11:1. Mechanical internal expanding on four wheels. Welded spoke drop center rims. Wheel Size: 17''.

OPTIONS: Radio (ash tray or glove box door mounted). Heater. Clock. Cigar Lighter. Radio Antenna. Seat Covers. Spotlight. Cowl lamps (std. models). Trunk. Whitewalls. Greyhound radiator ornament. Special steel spoke wheels. Oversize balloon tires. Bumper guards. Extra horn, black finish (std. models). Dual windshield wiper. Steel tire cover (std. models). Black painted fendors. Two taillights (std. models).

1934 Ford V-8, cabriolet, JAC

HISTORICAL: Introduced: January, 1934. Calendar year production: 563,921. The president of Ford was Edsel Ford. In April 1934 Clyde Barrow wrote his famous (infamous?) letter to Henry Ford in which he told Ford "what a dandy car you make." At the Ford press preview, held on December 6, 1933 Ford served alcoholic beverages for the first time.

For the first time since 1930 the Ford Motor Company reported a profit ($3,759,311) for 1934.

1935 FORD

1935 Ford, V8, convertible cabriolet, AA

FORD — MODEL 48 — EIGHT: Few Ford enthusiasts would dispute Ford's claim of "Greater Beauty, Greater Comfort, and Greater Safety" for its 1935 models.

The narrower radiator grille lost its sharply V'eed base and four horizontal bars helped accentuate the 1935 model's new, lower and more streamlined appearance. Fender outlines were now much more rounded and the side hood louvers received three horizontal bright stripes. In profile the Ford windshield was seen to be more sharply sloped then previously. No longer fitted were the old cowl lamps since the parking lamps were integral with the headlamps. The headlight shells were body color painted.

For the first time Ford offered a built-in trunk for its 2 and 4-door models and all Fords had front-hinged doors front and rear.

Both Standard and DeLuxe versions shared a painted dash finish with the latter Fords having a set of horizontal bars running down the center section. External distinctions were very obvious. DeLuxe models had bright windshield and grille trimwork as well as dual exposed horns and twin taillights.

Added to the Ford model line up was a Convertible Sedan. No longer available was the Victoria.

I.D. DATA: Serial numbers were located on left side of frame near firewall. Starting No.: 18-1234357. Ending: 18-2207110. Prefix "C" indicates Canadian built. Engine no. location on top of clutch housing. Starting Engine No.: 18-1234357. Ending: 18-2207110.

Model No.	Body Type & Seating	Price	Weight	Prod. Total
48	4-dr. Del. Phae.-4P	580	2667	6073
48	2-dr. Del. Rds. R/S-2/4P	550	2597	4896
48	2-dr. Del. RS Cab.-2/4P	625	2687	17,000
48	4-dr. Del. Conv. Sed.-4P	750	2827	4234
48	2-dr. Std. Cpe. 3W-2P	—	2647	—
48	2-dr. Del. Cpe. 3W-2P	570	2647	31,513
48	2-dr. Std. Cpe. 5W-2P	520	2620	78,477
48	2-dr. Del. Cpe. 5W-2P	560	2643	33,065
48	2-dr. Std. Tudor-4P	510	2717	4,237,833
48	2-dr. Del. Tudor-4P	595	2737	84,692
48	4-dr. Std. Fordor-4P	575	2760	49,176
48	4-dr. Del. Fordor-4P	635	2767	75,807
48	4-dr. Sta. Wag.	670	2896	4536
48	Del. Tudor Sed.-4P	595	2772	87,336
48	Del. Fordor Sed.-4P	655	2787	105,157

ENGINE: 90° V, L-head. Eight. Cast iron block. B & S: 3-1/16 in. x 3-3/4 in. Disp.: 221 cu. in. C.R.: 6.3:1. Brake H.P.: 85 @ 3800 R.P.M. Main bearings: Three. Valve lifters: Mechanical. Carb.: Stromberg EE-1, 2 bbl downdraft. Torque: 144 lbs.-ft. @ 2200 R.P.M.

1935 Ford V-8, DeLuxe roadster, JAC

CHASSIS: W.B.: 112 in. O.L.: 182-3/4 in. Height: 64-5/8 in. Frt/Rear Tread: 55-1/2 / 58-1/4 in. Tires: 6.00 x 16.

TECHNICAL: Sliding gear trans. Speeds: 3F/1R. Floor shift controls. Single dry plate, woven asbestos lining clutch. Shaft drive. 3/4 floating rear axle. Overall Ratio: 4.33:1. Mechanical, internal expanding brakes on four wheels. Welded spoke, drop center rims on wheels. Wheel Size: 16".

1935 Ford V-8, Fordor sedan, JAC

OPTIONS: Radio. Heater. Clock. Cigar lighter. Radio antenna. Seat covers. Spotlight. Cowl lamps (std. models). Trunk. Luggage rack. Whitewalls. Greyhound radiator ornament. Special steel spoke wheels. Oversize balloon tires. Bumper guards. Extra horns black finish (std. models). Dual windshield wipers. Steel tire cover (std. models). Black painted fenders. Two taillights (std. models). Banjo type steering wheel. Rumble seat (coupes and roadsters).

HISTORICAL: Introduction: December, 1934. Calendar year registrations: 826,519. Calendar year production: 942,439. The president of Ford was Edsel Ford. Ford was America's best selling car for 1935. A Ford Convertible Sedan paced the 1935 Indianapolis 500. Ford produced its two-millionth V-8 engine in June 1935.

1936 FORD

1936 Ford V-8 DeLuxe, club cabriolet, AA

FORD — MODEL 68 — EIGHT: The 1936 Fords retained the same basic body of the 1935 models but carried a restyled front end and new rear fenders. The grille, consisting only of vertical bars extended further around the hood sides and the dual horns of the DeLuxe models were placed behind screens set into the fender catwalks.

The Convertible Sedan with its "flat-back" body was superseded by a version with a built-in luggage compartment or "trunk-back" style during the model year.

In place of wire wheels were new pressed steel, artillery wheels with large 12 inch painted hubcaps and chrome centers carrying a very narrow, stylized V-8 logo. The same design was used on the Ford's hood ornament.

Design changes for 1936 included a larger capacity radiator, better engine cooling via new hood side louvers and front vents, and helical-type gears for first and reverse gears. Previously only the second and third gears were of this design. The Ford V-8 now had domed aluminum pistons (replaced by steel versions during the year) and new insert main bearings.

DeLuxe models featured bright work around the grille, headlamps and windshield as well as dual horns and taillights. Those DeLuxe Fords produced later in the model year also had as standard equipment dual windshield wipers, wheel trim rings, clock and rear view mirror.

I.D. DATA: Serial numbers were located on left side of frame near firewall. Starting: 18-2207111. Ending: 18-3331856. Prefix "C" indicates Canadian built. Engine numbers were located on top of clutch housing. Starting: 18-2207111. Ending: 18-3331856.

1936 Ford Deluxe Tudor sedan

Model No.	Body Type & Seating	Price	Weight	Prod. Total
68	2-dr. Del. Rds.-2P	560	2561	3862
68	4-dr. Del. Phae.-4P	590	2641	5555
68	2-dr. Cab.-4P	625	2649	—
68	2-dr. Clb. Cab.-4P	675	2661	4616
68	4-dr. Conv. Trk. Sed.-4P	780	2916	—
68	4-dr. Conv. Sed.-4P	760	2791	5601
68	2-dr. Del. 3W Cpe.-2P	570	2621	21,446
68	2-dr. Std. 5W Cpe.-2P	510	2599	78,534
68	2-dr. Del. 5W Cpe.-2P	555	2641	29,938
68	2-dr. Std. Tudor Sed.-4P	520	2659	174,770
68	Std. Tudor Tr. Sed.-4P	545	2718	—
68	2-dr. Del. Tudor Sed.-4P	565	2691	20,519
68	Del. Tudor Tr. Sed.-4P	590	2786	125,303
68	4-dr. Std. Fordor Sed.-4P	580	2699	31,505
68	Std. Fordor Tr. Sed.-4P	605	2771	—
68	4-dr. Del. Fordor Sed.-4P	625	2746	42,867
68	Del. Fordor Tr. Sed.-4P	650	2816	159,825
68	4-dr. Sta. Wag.	670	3020	7044

ENGINE: 90° V, inline. Eight. Cast iron block. B & S: 3-1/16 in. x 3-3/4 in. Disp.: 221 cu. in. C.R.: 6.3:1. Brake H.P.: 85 @ 3800 R.P.M. Taxable H.P.: 30. Main bearings: Three. Valve lifters: Mechanical. Carb.: Ford 67-9510A 2 bbl downdraft. Torque: 148 lbs.-ft. @ 2200 R.P.M.

CHASSIS: W.B.: 112 in. O.L.: 182-3/4 in. Height: 68-5/8 in. Frt/Rear Tread: 55-1/2 in./58-1/4 in. Tires: 6.00 x 16.

TECHNICAL: Sliding gear transmission. Speeds: 3F/1R. Floor shift controls. Single dry plate, moulded asbestos lining clutch. Shaft drive. 3/4 floating rear axle. Overall Ratio: 4.33:1. Mechanical, internal expanding brakes on four wheels. Pressed steel wheels, drop center rim. Wheel Size: 16.

OPTIONS: Radio (five versions from 44.50). Heater (14.00). Clock (9.75). Cigar lighter. Radio antenna. Seat covers. Spotlight. Rumble seat (coupes, roadster) (20.00). Luggage rack (7.50). Banjo steering wheel. "Spider" wheel covers (3.75 early). Wind wings (10.00). Combination oil-pressure, gas gauge (3.75). Dual windshield wipers (3.00). Leather upholstery. Electric air horns.

HISTORICAL: Introduced October, 1935. Ford was the overall winner of the 1936 Monte Carlo Rally. Calendar year registrations: 748,554. Calendar year production: 791,812. The president of Ford was Edsel Ford.

1937 FORD

FORD — MODEL 78 — EIGHT: The 1937 models were the first Fords to have their headlights mounted in the front fenders and possess an all steel top. The 1937 Fords styling reflected the strong influence of the Lincoln-Zephyr. The grille with horizontal bars and a center vertical bar cut a sharp V into the side hood area. As had been the case for many years the side hood cooling vents reflected the grille's general form.

Ford offered sedans with either a "slant-back" or "trunk-back" rear deck. All Ford sedans had access to the trunk area through an external lid. In addition, a new coupe with a rear seat was introduced. All models had a rear-hinged alligator-type hood.

1937 Ford V-8, 5-window coupe, AA

The operation of the 221 cid V-8 was further improved by the use of a higher capacity water pump, larger insert bearings and cast alloy steel pistons. Replacing the rod-operated mechanical brake system was a version using a cable linkage.

As in previous years Ford offered both Standard and DeLuxe models with the latter possessing interiors with walnut woodgrain window molding and exterior trim bright work. Standard models had painted radiator grilles and windshield frames. A burl mahogany woodgrain finish was applied to their interior window trim.

Ford introduced a smaller version of its V-8 with a 2-3/5 inch bore and 3-1/5 inch stroke. Its displacement was 136 cubic inches. This 60 hp engine was available only in the Standard Ford models.

I.D. DATA: Left side of frame near firewall. Starting: [Model 74] 54-6602. [Model 78] 18-3331857. Ending: [Model 74] 54-358334. [Model 78] 18-4186446. Prefix "C" indicates Canadian built. Top of clutch housing. Starting Engine No.: [Model 74] 54-6602; [Model 78] 18-3331857. Ending: [Model 74] 54-358334; [Model 78] 18-4186446.

1937 Ford V-8, Tudor sedan, AA

Model No.	Body Type & Seating	Price	Weight	Prod. Total
78	2-dr. Del. Rds.-2P	696	2576	1250
78	4-dr. Del. Phae.-5P	750	2691	3723
78	2-dr. Del. Cab.	720	2616	10,184
78	2-dr. Del. Clb. Cab.	760	2636	8001
78	2-dr. Del. Conv. Sed.	860	2861	4378
78	2-dr. Del. Cpe. 5W-3P	660	2506	26,738
78	Del. Clb. Cpe. 5W-4P	720	2616	16,992
78	2-dr. Del. Tudor Sed.-5P	675	2656	33,683
78	Del. Tudor Tr. Sed.-5P	700	2679	—
78	4-dr. Del. Fordor Sed.-5P	735	2671	22,885
78	Del. Fordor Tr. Sed.-5P	760	2696	98,687
78	4-dr. Sta. Wag.-5P	755	2991	9304
78	2-dr. Std. Tudor Sed.-5P	610	2616	308,446
78	Std. Tudor Tr. Sed.-5P	635	2648	—
78	4-dr. Std. Fordor Sed.-5P	670	2649	49,062
78	Std. Fordor Tr. Sed.-5P	695	2666	45,531
78	2-dr. Std. Cpe. 5W-3P	585	2496	90,347

Note 1: The five standard bodies when ordered with the 60 hp V-8 were designated as Model 74 Fords and weighed over 200 lbs. less.

ENGINE: [Model 78] 90° V, inline. 8. Cast iron block. B & S: 3-1/16 in. x 3-3/4 in. Disp.: 221 cu. in. C.R.: 6.3:1. Brake H.P.: 85 @ 3800 R.P.M. Taxable H.P.: 30.01. Main bearings: Three. Valve lifters: Mechanical. Carb.: Stromberg 67-9510A 2bbl downdraft. Torque: 153 lbs.-ft. @ 2200 R.P.M. [Model 74] 90° V, inline. 8. Cast iron block. B & S: 2-3/5 in. x 3-1/5 in. Disp.: 136 cu. in. C.R.: 6.6:1. Brake H.P. 60 @ 3600 R.P.M. Taxable H.P. 21.6. Main bearings: Three. Valve lifters: Mechanical. Carb.: Stromberg 922A-9510A 2bbl. downdraft. Torque: 94 lbs.-ft. @ 2500 R.P.M.

1937 Ford V-8, station wagon, JAC

TECHNICAL: Transmission: Sliding gear. Speeds: 3F/1R. Floor shift controls. Single dry plate, molded asbestos lining clutch. Shaft drive. 3/4 floating rear axle. Overall Ratio: 4.33:1. Mechanical, internal expanding brakes on 4 wheels. Pressed steel, drop center rim wheels. Wheel size: 16".

OPTIONS: Fender skirts. Radio. Heater. Clock (mirror clock & glove box clock). Cigar lighter. Radio antenna. Side view mirror. Dual wipers. Sport light. Dual taillights (std. on DeLuxe models). Fog lamps. Locking gas cap. Glove box lock. Defroster. Draft deflectors. Vanity mirror. Wheel trim bands. DeLuxe hubcaps. White sidewall tires. Center bumper guard. DeLuxe steering wheel. Sliding glass panels (Sta. Wag.) (20.00).

HISTORICAL: Introduction: November, 1937. First year for 60 hp V-8, first year for rear fender skirts. Calendar year sales: 765,933 (registrations). Calendar year production: 848,608. The president of Ford was Edsel Ford.

1938 FORD

1938 Ford V-8, DeLuxe, station wagon, AA

FORD — DELUXE — MODEL 81A — EIGHT: Ford adopted a new marketing strategy for 1938 in which its Standard models carried the same basic front sheet metal used in 1937 while the DeLuxe models were given a substantially revised appearance. A curved grille outline with horizontal bars and a separate set of side hood louvers distinguished the more costly DeLuxe models. Interior alterations consisted of a new instrument panel with a centrally located radio speaker grille and recessed control knobs. As before, the windshield opening knob was centered high on the dash.

FORD — STANDARD — MODEL 82A — EIGHT: The 60hp Ford V-8 engine was standard only in the three models offered in the Standard line. These Fords were also available with the 221cid V-8. The Standard Ford grille featured horizontal bars that extended into the side hood region for engine cooling.

I.D. DATA: Serial numbers were located on left frame side member near fire wall. Starting: 81A — 18-4186447; 82A — 54-358335 & up. Ending: 81A — 18-4661100. Engine numbers were located on top of clutch housing. Starting: 81A — 18-4186447; 82A — 54-358335 & up. Ending: 81A — 18-4661100.

Model No.	Body Type & Seating	Price	Weight	Prod. Total
81A	2-dr. Std. Cpe.-2P	625	2575	34,059
81A	2-dr. Std. Tudor Sed.-5P	665	2674	106,117
81A	4-dr. Std. Fordor Sed.-5P	710	2697	30,287
81A	4-dr. Sta. Wag.-5P	825	2981	6944
81A	4-dr. Del. Phae.-5P	820	2748	1169
81A	2-dr. Del. Clb. Conv.-5P	800	2719	6080
81A	2-dr. Del. Conv. Cpe.-3P	770	2679	4702
81A	4-dr. Del. Conv.-5P	900	2883	2703
81A	2-dr. Del. Cpe.-3P	685	2606	22,225
81A	2-dr. Del. Clb. Cpe.-5P	745	2688	7171
81A	2-dr. Del. Tudor Sed.-5P	725	2742	101,647
81A	DeL. Fordor Sed.-5P	770	2773	92,020

Note 1: The three Standard bodies when ordered with the 60hp V-8 were designated as Model 81A Fords.

1938 Ford, V-8, Standard coupe, HAC

ENGINE: [Model 81A] 90° V, inline. Eight. Cast iron block. B & S: 3-1/16 in. x 3-3/4 in. Disp.: 221 cu. in. C.R.: 6.12:1. Brake H.P.: 85 @ 3800 R.P.M. Taxable H.P.: 30. Main bearings: Three. Valve lifters: Mechanical. Carb.: Chandler-Groves and Stromberg 21A-9510A, 2bb1 downdraft. Torque: 146 lbs.-ft. @ 2000 R.P.M. [Model 82A] 90° V, inline. Eight. Cast iron block. B & S: 2-3/5 in. x 3-1/5 in. Disp.: 136 cu. in. C.R.: 6.6:1. Brake H.P.: 60 @ 3500 R.P.M. Taxable H.P.: 21.6. Main bearings: Three. Valve lifters: Mechanical. Carb.: Chandler-Groves and Stromberg 9221-95101, 2bb1 downdraft. Torque: 94 lbs.-ft. @ 2500 R.P.M.

CHASSIS: Models 81A & 82A. W.B.: 112 in. O.L.: 179-1/2 in. Height: 68-5/8 in. Frt/Rear Tread: 55-1/2 in./58-1/4 in. Tires: 6.00 x 16 (Model 82A — 5.50 x 16).

TECHNICAL: Sliding gear transmission. Speeds: 3F/1R. Floor shift controls. Single dry plate, molded asbestos lining clutch. Shaft drive. 3/4 floating rear axle. Overall Ratio: 4.33:1. Mechanical, internal expanding brakes on four wheels. Pressed steel wheels, drop-center rims. Wheel Size: 16''.

OPTIONS: Fender skirts. Bumper guards. Radio. Heater. Clock (mirror and glove box). Cigar lighter. Seat covers. Side view mirror. Dual wipers. Sportlight. Dual taillights (Std. models). Fog lights. Locking gas cap. Glove box lock. Defroster. Draft deflectors. Vanity mirror. Wheel trim bands. DeLuxe hub caps. White sidewall tires. DeLuxe steering wheel. License plate frame.

HISTORICAL: Introduced November, 1937. Ford secured its second victory in the Monte Carlo Rally. Calendar year registrations: 363,688. Calendar year production: 410,048. The president of Ford was Edsel Ford.

1939 FORD

1939 Ford V-8, DeLuxe, coupe, AA

FORD — DELUXE — MODEL 91A — EIGHT: The 1939 Fords were again divided into Standard and DeLuxe models. The former carried the general styling of the 1938 DeLuxe Ford. Thus they had a sharply V'eed grille with horizontal bars, headlights mounted inboard of the fenders and small side hood louvers. The DeLuxe models had a much more modern appearance. Their teardrop-shaped headlights blended smoothly into the leading edges of the front fenders and a grille set lower in the hood than as previous models carried vertical bars. Simple chrome trim replaced the hood louvers and a more smoother body profile was featured. The most significant technical development was the adoption by Ford of Lockheed hydraulic brakes.

FORD — STANDARD — MODEL 922A — EIGHT: Only four body styles were offered in the Standard series. Customers could chose either the 60 hp or 85 hp engines.
Standard models were not equipped with the banjo steering wheel, glove box lock and clock found on DeLuxe Fords.

I.D. DATA: Serial numbers were located on the left side member near firewall. Starting No. Model: 91A — 18-4661001. Model 922A — 54-506501 & up. Ending: 91A-18-210700. Engine no. location was top of clutch housing. Starting Engine No.: Model 91A — 18-4661001. Model 922A — 54-506501 & up. Ending: Model 91A — 18-5210700.

Model No.	Body Type & Seating	Price	Weight	Prod. Total
922A	Std. 2-dr. Cpe.-3P	640	2710	38,197
922A	Std. 2-dr. Tudor Sed.-5P	680	2830	124,866
922A	Std. 2-dr. Fordor Sed.-5P	730	2850	—
922A	Std. 4-dr. Sta. Wag.-5P	840	3080	3277
91A	2-dr. DeL. Conv. Cpe.-3P	790	2840	10,422
91A	4-dr. DeL. Conv. Sed.-5P	920	2935	3561
91A	2-dr. DeL. Cpe.-3P	700	2752	33,326
91A	2-dr. DeL. Tudor Sed.-5P	745	2867	144,333
91A	DeL. Fordor Sed.-5P	790	2898	—
91A	4-dr. DeL. Sta. Wag.-5P	920	3095	6155

Note 1: The Standard models were available with the 60 hp or 85 hp engines.

1939 Ford, V-8, DeLuxe, station wagon, OCW

180

1939 Ford V-8, Fordor sedan, JAC

ENGINE: [85hp] 90° V, inline. Eight. Cast iron block. B & S: 3-1/16 in. x 3-3/4 in. Disp.: 221 cu. in. C.R.: 6.15:1. Brake H.P.: 90 @ 3800 R.P.M. Taxable H.P.: 30. Main bearings: Three. Valve lifters: Mechanical. Carb.: Stromberg 21A-951A, 2 bbl downdraft. Torque: 155 lbs-ft. @ 2200 R.P.M. [60 hp] 90° V, inline. Eight. Cast iron block. B & S: 2-3/5 in. x 3-1/5 in. Disp.: 136 cu. in. C.R.: 6.6:1. Brake H.P.: 60 @ 3500 R.P.M. Taxable H.P.: 21.6. Main bearings: Three. Valve lifters: Mechanical. Carb.: Stromberg 922A-9510A, 2 bbl downdraft. Torque: 94 lbs-ft. @ 2500 R.P.M.

CHASSIS: Series 91A-922A. W.B.: 112 in. O.L.: 179-1/2 in. Height: 68-5/8 in. Frt/Rear Tread: 55-1/2 / 58-1/4 in. Tires: 6.00 x 16. (60hp-5.50 x 16).

TECHNICAL: Sliding gear trans. Speeds: 3F/1R. Floor shift controls. Single dry plate, molded asbestos lining clutch. Shaft drive. 3/4 floating rear axle. Overall Ratio: 4.33:1. Lockheed hydraulic brakes on four wheels. Pressed steel, drop-center rim on wheels. Wheel Size: 16''.

OPTIONS: Bumper guards. Radio. Heater. Clock. Seat covers. Sideview mirror. Sport light. Fog lamps. Locking gas cap. Draft deflectors. Vanity mirror. Wheel dress up rings. DeLuxe hub caps. White sidewall tires. License plate frames. Fender skirts.

HISTORICAL: Introduced: November 4, 1938. Lockheed hydraulic brakes. Calendar year registrations: 481,496. Calendar year production: 532,152. The president of Ford was Edsel Ford.

1940 FORD

1940 Ford Deluxe, convertible coupe, AA

FORD V-8, MODEL 01A — EIGHT: The 1940 Fords featured extremely handsome styling by Eugene Gregorie. All models were fitted with sealed beam headlights and a steering column-mounted shift lever. DeLuxe models had chrome headlight trim rings with the parking light cast into its upper surface. The DeLuxe grille combined a center section with horizontal bars and secondary side grids whose horizontal bars were subdivided into three sections by thicker molding. Hubcaps for these top level Fords featured bright red "Ford DeLuxe" lettering and trim rings finished in the body color. The DeLuxe instrument panel was given a maroon and sand two-tone finish which matched that of the steering wheel. Model 01A carried the 85 hp engine and was available in both Standard dnd DeLuxe versions.

FORD — MODEL 022A — EIGHT: Distinguishing the 60 Standard Fords was their grille and hood that were very similar to those of the 1939 DeLuxe models. Their headlight shells were finished in the body color and the integral parking lamp lacked the ribbed surround used on the DeLuxe model. The vertical grille bars were painted to match the body color. DeLuxe hubcaps had a series of concentric rings surrounding a blue V-8.
The Standard dash and steering wheel had a Briarwood Brown finish and the instrument panel had a larger speedometer face. Both Standard and DeLuxe Fords had front vent windows.
For the final year the Ford V-8 60 was available for Standard models.

I.D. DATA: Left frame side member near firewall. Starting: [Model 01A] 18-5210701; [Model 022A] 54-506501 & up. Ending: [Model 01A] 18-5896294. Top of clutch housing. Starting Engine No.: [Model 01A] 18-5210701; [Model 022A] 54-506401 & up. Ending Engine No.: [Model 01A] 18-5896294.

1940 Ford V-8 DeLuxe station wagon, OCW

Model No.	Body Type & Seating	Price	Weight	Prod. Total
022A	2-dr. Std. Cpe.-3P	660	2763	33,693
022A	2-dr. Std. Tudor Sed.-5P	700	2909	150,933
022A	4-dr. Std. Fordor Sed.-5P	750	2936	25,545
022A	4-dr. Std. Sta. Wag.-5P	875	3249	4469
022A	2-dr. Bus. Cpe.-5P	680	2801	16,785
01A	2-dr. Del. Conv. Cpe.-5P	850	2956	23,704
01A	2-dr. Del. Cpe.-3P	721	2791	27,919
01A	2-dr. Del. Tudor Sed.-5P	765	2927	171,368
01A	4-dr. Del. Fordor Sed.-5P	810	2966	91,756
01A	4-dr. Del. Sta. Wag.	950	3262	8730
01A	2-dr. Del. Bus. Cpe.-5P	745	2831	20,183

ENGINE: [85 hp Engine] 90° V, inline. Eight. Cast iron block. B & S: 3-1/16 in. x 3-3/4 in. Disp.: 221 cu. in. C.P.: 6.15:1. Brake H.P. 85 @ 3800 R.P.M. Taxable H.P.: 30. Main bearings: Three. Valve lifters: Mechanical. Carb.: Chandler-Groves 21A-9510A, 2bbl downdraft. Torque: 155 lbs.-ft. @ 2200 R.P.M. [60 hp Engine] 90° V, inline. Eight. Cast iron block. B & S: 2-3/5 in. x 3-1/5 in. Disp.: 135 cu. in. C.R.: 6.6:1. Brake H.P.: 60 @ 3500 R.P.M. Taxable H.P. 21.6. Main bearings: Three. Valve lifters: Mechanical. Carb.: Chandler-Groves 922A-9510A 2bbl downdraft. Torque: 94 lbs.-ft. @ 2500 R.P.M.

CHASSIS: 01A & 022A. W.B.: 112 in. O.L.: 188-1/4 in. Height: 68 in. Frt/Rear Tread: 55-3/4 / 58-1/4. Tires: 6.00 x 16. (60 hp - 5.50 x 16).

TECHNICAL: Transmission: Sliding gear. Speeds: 3F/1R. Floor. Steering column-mounted shift lever. Single dry plate, molded asbestos lining clutch. Shaft drive. 3/4 floating rear axle. Overall Ratio: 4.33:1. Lockheed hydraulic brakes on 4 wheels. Pressed steel, drop-center rims wheels. Wheel size: 16 in.

OPTIONS: Fender skirts. Bumper guards. Radio. Heater. Cigar lighter. Radio antenna. Seat covers. Sideview mirror. Right hand side mirror. Sport light. Fog lamps. Locking gas cap. Defroster. Vanity mirror. DeLuxe wheel rings. DeLuxe hubcaps. White sidewall tires. Gravel deflectors. License plate frame. Two-tone paint.

HISTORICAL: Introduction: October 1940. Calendar year sales: 542,755 (registrations). Calendar year production: 599,175. The president of Ford was Edsel Ford.

1941 FORD

1941 Ford, Super DeLuxe, club coupe, AA

FORD — SUPER DELUXE — SIX or EIGHT: The 1941 Fords were with fresh styling and a revamped chassis easily recognized as new models. All versions were mounted on a longer by two inches wheelbase of 114 inches and by virtue of a wider body featured substantially increased interior dimensions. Emphasizing Ford's rounder, more curved body form was a new three-piece grille that consisted of a neo-traditional vertical center section with two auxillary units set low on either side. Running boards were continued but due to the body's greater width were far less noticeable than on earlier Fords. Further accentuating the lower and wider nature of the 1941 Ford was the position of the headlights, which were further apart in the fenders.

Super DeLuxe Fords were easily identified by the bright trim on their running board edges and chrome grille sections. The Super DeLuxe bumpers had ridges along their bottom edge. A mid-year (March) revision to Super DeLuxe models added bright trimwork to the front and rear fenders, windshield, rear and side windows. Super DeLuxe script was placed in the inboard position of the left front fender. Bright rear taillight surrounds were installed. In addition the standard features of the Super DeLuxe included a trunk light, glove box mounted clock, bright wheel trimmings, twin visors, wipers and plastic Kelobra grain dash trim. The wheels had either Vermillion or Silver Gray stripes. Seven body styles were offered in Super DeLuxe form.

1941 Ford, Super DeLuxe, 4-dr. sedan, OCW

FORD — DELUXE — SIX or EIGHT: DeLuxe series Fords lacked the trunk light, glove box clock, wheel trim rings and unique license plate guard found on the Super DeLuxe models. Their instrument panels were finished in Ebony grain and among standard features were a glove box lock, dual wipers and sun visors. There was no striping on the DeLuxe Ford wheels which were painted black regardless of body color. Those on the Super DeLuxe models were painted to match the color of the body and fenders. Only the center grille portion was chromed on DeLuxe models.

Both Super DeLuxe and DeLuxe Fords were available with either Ford's V-8 engine, now rated at 90hp or for $15 less a new 26cid flathead six also credited with 90hp. Among its design features were four main bearings, a vibration damper, forged connecting rods, molybdenum-chrome alloy steel valve seat inserts and solid valve lifters. The six cylinder engine was a mid-year offering and its availability required new hood trim. Prior to the Sixes' introduction the molding was a plain trim piece with horizontal liner. With the availability of two engines it now carried either a V-8 or 6 identification with a blue background.

FORD — STANDARD — SERIES 11A — SIX: The three Standard models were offered only in a Harbor grey finish and without the V-8 engine option. In addition the windshield divider was a black, rather than stainless steel molding and like the DeLuxe Fords only the center grille section was chromed. In addition the Standard Fords were equipped with a single taillight, horn, windshield wiper and sun visor. Lacking from their interior were such appointments as arm rests, dome light, cigarette lighter and glove box lock.

I.D. DATA: Serial numbers were on left frame member directly behind front engine mount. Starting No.: 6 cyl-1GA-1 V-8 18-5986295. Ending: 6 cyl-1GA-34800 -8 18-6769035. Prefix "C" indicates Canadian built. Engine numbers located on top of clutch housing. Starting Engine No.: 6 cyl-1GA-1 V-8 18-5986295. Ending: 6 cyl-1GA-34800 V-8 18-6769035.

1941 Ford, Super DeLuxe, 2-dr. sedan, OCW

Model No.	Body Type & Seating	Price	Weight	Prod. Total
Sup. DeL.	2-dr. Conv.-6P	950	3187	30,240
Sup. DeL.	2-dr. Cpe.-3P	775	2969	22,878
Sup. DeL.	2-dr. Cpe.-4P	800	3001	10,796
Sup. DeL.	2-dr. Cpe. Sed.-6P	850	3052	45,977
Sup. DeL.	2-dr. Tudor-6P	820	3110	185,788
Sup. DeL.	4-dr. Fordor-6P	860	3146	88,053
Sup. DeL.	4-dr. Sta. Wag.-6P	1015	3419	9485
DeLuxe	2-dr. Cpe.-3P	730	2953	33,598
DeLuxe	2-dr. Cpe.-4P	750	2981	12,844
DeLuxe	2-dr. Tudor-6P	775	3095	177,018
DeLuxe	4-dr. Fordor-6P	815	3121	25,928
DeLuxe	4-dr. Sta. Wag.-6P	965	3412	6116
Special	2-dr. Cpe.-3P	706	2878	9823
Special	2-dr. Tudor-6P	735	2983	27,189
Special	4-dr. Fordor-6P	775	3033	3838

Note: Weights are for V-8 equipped models.

ENGINE: [V-8] 90° V Inline. Eight. Cast iron block. B & S: 3-1/16 in. x 3-3/4 in. Disp.: 221 cu. in. C.R.: 6.15:1. Brake H.P.: 90 @ 3800 R.P.M. Taxable H.P.: 30. Main bearings: Three. Valve lifters: Mechanical. Carb.: Ford 21A-9510A 2bbl. downdraft. Torque: 156 lbs.-ft. @ 2200 R.P.M. [6 Cylinder] Inline. L-head. Six. Cast iron block. B & S: 3-3/10 in. x 4-2/5 in. Disp.: 225.8 cu. in. C.R.: 6.7:1. Brake H.P.: 90 @ 3300 R.P.M. Taxable H.P.: 30. Main bearings: Four. Valve lifters: Mechanical. Carb.: Ford 1GA-9510A 1bbl. Torque: 180 lbs.-ft. @ 2000 R.P.M.

CHASSIS: Special, DeLuxe, Super DeLuxe. W.B.: 114 in. O.L.: 194.3 in. Height: 68.15 in. Frt/Rear Tread: 55.75/58.25 in. Tires: 6.00 x 16.

TECHNICAL: Sliding gear transmission. Speeds: 3F/1R. Column controls. Semi-centrifugal, moulded asbestos linings. Shaft drive. 3/4 floating rear axle. Overall Ratio: 3.78:1. Hydraulic brakes on four wheels. Pressed steel, drop center rim wheels. Wheel Size: 16".

OPTIONS: Fender skirts (12.50). Radio. Heater (hot air 23.00, hot water 20.00). Clock. Seat covers. Side view mirror. Passenger side mirror. Sport light. Locking gas cap. Glove compartment lock. Defroster. Vanity mirror. Radio foot control. Wheel trim rings. DeLuxe hub caps. White sidewall tires. Center bumper guards - front (3.50) rear (2.50). Gravel deflector (1.50).

1941 Ford, DeLuxe, 2-dr. sedan, AA

HISTORICAL: Introduced September, 1941. Calendar year sales: 602013 (registrations). Calendar year production: 600,814. The president of Ford was Edsel Ford. On April 29, 1941 the 29 millionth Ford was constructed.

1942 FORD

1942 Ford, Deluxe, 4-dr. sedan (Army staff car), OCW

FORD — SUPER DELUXE — SIX or V-EIGHT: The 1942 Fords were redesigned with fully concealed running boards plus new front fenders and hood sheet metal. A new grille design featured a very narrow center section in conjunction with side grilles considerably larger and more squared off than previously. The Super Deluxe grille had its bright work accentuated by blue painted grooves. Used only on these top of the line Fords were front and rear bumpers with ridges along their upper surface. The Super DeLuxe script was now positioned just below the left headlight. The taillights on all models were now horizontally positioned but only those on the Super DeLuxe had bright trim plates. Also unique to Super DeLuxe Fords were bright trim surrounds for the windshield, rear window and side windows. Wheel covers were painted to match body color and carried three stripes. Trim rings were standard.

Interior features included an electric clock, left front door arm rests, a steering wheel with a full circle horn ring and crank-operated front vent windows. The instrument panel was finished in Sequoia Grain. Assist cords were installed on sedan and sedan coupe models.

FORD — DELUXE — SERIES 21A: Common to all 1942 Fords was a revised frame design that was lower by one inch than the 1941 version, lower and wider leaf springs, a two inch wider tread and dual lateral stabilizer bars. DeLuxe models were equipped with the bumpers used for the 1941 Super DeLuxe Ford models. Their grille frames were painted body color. Unique to the DeLuxe Ford was its center grille panel with "DeLuxe" spelled out vertically in bright letters before a blue background. Wheel covers were painted to match body color. The DeLuxe instrument panel was finished in Crackle Mohagany grain.

1942 Ford, Super DeLuxe, coupe-sedan HAC

FORD — SPECIAL — SERIES 2GA — SIX: The three Special models shared their grille design and bumpers with the DeLuxe models but lacked the latter's bumper guards. Black wheel covers were standard and like those on all 1942 Fords carried blue Ford script.

The transition to a war time economy brought many material substitutes in the 1942 models. Among the more obvious was the use of plastic interior components and the replacement of nickel by molybdenum in valves, gears and shafts. The final 1942 model Fords were produced on February 10, 1942.

I.D. DATA: Serial numbers located on left frame member directly behind front engine mount. Starting: 6 cyl. — IGA-34801; V-8 — 18-6769036. Ending: 6 cyl. — IGA-227,523; V-8 — 18-6925878. Prefix "C" indicates Canadian built. Engine numbers were located on top of clutch housing. Starting: IGA-34801; V-8 — 18-6769036. Ending: 6 cyl. — IGA-227523; V-8 — 18-6925898.

Model No.	Body Type & Seating	Price	Weight	Prod. Total
2GA	2-dr. Cpe.-3P	780	2910	1606
2GA	2-dr. Tudor-6P	815	3053	3187
2GA	4-dr. Fordor-6P	850	3093	27,189
21A	2-dr. Cpe.-3P	810	2978	5936
21A	2-dr. Cpe. Sed.-5P	875	3065	5419
21A	2-dr. Tudor-6P	840	3141	27,302
21A	4-dr. Fordor-6P	875	3161	5127
21A	4-dr. Sta. Wag.-6P	1100	3460	567
Sup. DeL.	2-dr. Conv.-5P	1080	3238	2920
Sup. DeL.	2-dr. Cpe.-3P	850	3050	5411
Sup. DeL.	2-dr. Cpe. Sed.-5P	910	3120	13,543
Sup. DeL.	2-dr. Tudor-6P	885	3159	37,199
Sup. DeL.	4-dr. Fordor-6P	920	3200	24,846
Sup. DeL.	4-dr. Sta. Wag.-6P	1100	3468	5483

ENGINE: [V-8] 90° V, inline. Eight. Cast iron block. B & S: 3-1/16 in. x 3-3/4 in. Disp.: 221 cu. in. C.R.: 6.2:1. Brake H.P.: 96 @ 3800 R.P.M. Taxable H.P.: 30. Main bearings: Three. Valve lifters: Mechanical. Carb.: Ford 21A-9510A. Torque: 156 lbs.-ft. @ 2200 R.P.M. [6-cyl.] Inline. L-head. Six. Cast iron block. B & S: 3-3/10 in. x 4-2/5 in. Disp.: 225.8 cu. in. C.R.: 6.7:1. Brake H.P.: 90 @ 3300 R.P.M. Taxable H.P.: 30. Main bearings: Four. Valve lifters: Mechanical. Carb.: Ford IGA-9510A 1bb1. Torque: 180 lbs.-ft. @ 2000 R.P.M.

CHASSIS: Special, DeLuxe, Super DeLuxe. W.B.: 114 in. O.L.: 194.4 in. Height: 68.15 in. Frt/Rear Tread: 58 in./60 in. Tires: 6.00 x 16.

TECHNICAL: Sliding gear transmission. Speeds: 3F/1R. Column controls. Semi-centrifugal, molded asbestos lining clutch. Shaft drive. 3/4 floating rear axle. Overall Ratio: 3.78:1. Hydraulic brakes on four wheels. Pressed steel wheels, drop center rims. Wheel Size: 16".

OPTIONS: Fender skirts. Bumper guards (center). Radio (39.00). Heater (air-$23, water $20). Clock. Side view mirror. Passenger side mirror. Sport light. Locking gas cap. Fog lights. Seat covers. Defroster. Visor-vanity mirror. Radio foot control. Wheel trim rings. White sidewall tires (15.00). Bumper end guards (2.75 a pair). Oil filter (6.14). License plate frames.

HISTORICAL: Introduced September 12, 1941. Calendar year production: 43,407. Model year production: 160,211. The president of Ford was Edsel Ford.

STANDARD CATALOG OF
FORD
1946-1975

As was the case with the other major automakers, Ford entered the postwar market with a slightly restyled version of its 1942 models. The car-hungry market responded as if it were a completely new design and public demand dictated that the car remain nearly the same from 1946 through 1948.

by John Smith

When Henry Ford died in 1947, the wheels at Ford Motor Co. began to turn more smoothly and development of the all-new 1949 models began. Gone were the obsolete transverse rear springs and torque tube driveshaft. The new body was much lower, although shorter, than the previous year's models. Once again, the buying public flocked to the Ford showrooms eager to buy the slab-sided offering from Dearborn. Ford wisely decided to continue the same cars with very minor trim changes into the 1950 model year. The basic body style was used again in 1951, only this time the trim changes were more apparent. Model year 1951 also hailed the introduction of one of the most beautifully proportioned cars ever to come off of the Dearborn assembly lines, the 1951 Ford Victoria. Going hand-in-hand with the introduction of the hardtop Victoria was the introduction of the first fully automatic Ford-O-Matic transmission.

Ford continued to be "the car" to have if you were a performance enthusiast. Even though the old flathead V-8 was outperformed by the new overhead valve offerings from general motors, many more speed parts were available for the flathead and that was as much a reson for their popularity as anything.

Continuing with a strong second place position in the low-priced field in the early '50s. Ford sales hovered near the one million mark for the first three years of the decade. A very significant change, in 1954, was introduction of the first overhead valve V-8 in Ford Division's history. Another innovation was the company's first ball joint front in use seemingly forever. Perhaps the most significant event of the year, however, was the late summer introduction of the Thunderbird. The beautiful little two-seater challenged both the European sports cars the G.I.s had fallen in love with during the war and also, the new Chevrolet Corvette.

Model year 1955 brought the introduction of a beautiful line of new Fairlanes, named after Henry Ford's mansion in Dearborn, Mich. Even though these mid-century Fords were warmly greeted by the public — and sold better than any models built since the war — the year's highlight event was taking place across town, with introduction of the ubiquitious small-block Chevrolet V-8.

For 1956, Ford once again decided to leave well enough alone in the styling department and offered a beautiful 1956 lineup to the public. Even though they looked similar to 1955s, the new models were flashier — a very important factor for the '50s. Ford introduced the sporty two-door station wagon the "Parklane" to compete with Chevrolet's Nomad. The great horsepower race of the '50s was in full swing by 1956 and all manufacturers were offering "power pack" options normally consisting of a four-barrel carburetor, slightly stronger cam, and, of course, dual exhausts. Ford offered its version for a new 312 cubic inch V-8.

1964 saw a continued emphasis by Ford toward total performance. The big Galaxies, Fairlanes and Falcons continued to offer almost identical product lines and performance options carried over from the '63½s. Falcons received the biggest styling changes in spite of the mid-year introduction of the revolutionary Mustang. (Mustangs are covered in their own section of this book.)

A high-water mark in the horsepower race, for all manufacturers including Ford, was 1957. Chevrolet introduced the famous fuel-injected 283 cubic inch V-8 engine and, in answer, Ford offered the supercharged "312" V-8. Conservatively rated at 300 horsepower, these supercharge motors were strong enough to handle any competition. The NASCAR versions, which put out in excess of 340 horsepower, absolutely dominated the stock car tracks during that year. If the supercharged version of the 312 was a little too wild for your tastes, you could order the engine in several different configurations, including two with twin four-barrel carburetion. Chevrolet was experiencing moderate success with its sport station wagon, the Nomad. To continue its answer to that challenge, Ford offered the Del Rio Ranch Wagon. In essence, Del Rios were base two-door Ranch Wagons sporting Custom 300 side trim and a fancy interior. Even though they did not enjoy the success or subsequent following of the Nomad, they were one-the-less very pleasant cars to look at. The fancier Parklane was discontinued after one year.

Mechanical innovations highlighted Ford model year 1958, while styling changes were made in the trim department. Even though 1957 and 1958 models look considerably different, they are still basically the same car. New for 1958 was the famous "FE" series of 332 and 352 cubic inch V-8s, which grew into the "390" and the awesome "427." Also new for 1958, and offered for the first time in a Ford Division product, was the three-speed Cruise-O-Matic transmission. A novel spension called Level-Aire-Ride, was offered this year only. Quality problems plagued the 1958 models and, as a consequence, only one million were made, the lowest production figure since 1952.

The following season witnessed introduction of a car that many consider to be the most beautiful Ford ever built, the 1959 Galaxie. For stylists took a Fairlane 500 two-door hardtop and added a Thunderbird inspired roof. The combination was so attractive that it was awarded the Gold Medal for Exceptional Styling at the Brussels World's Fair. With engines of up to 300 horsepower, they were spirited performers, also.

Even though they are not particularly well liked by many, the 1960 Fords were among the smoothest and most aerodynamic cars to come out of Dearborn. With other manufacturers producing engines well into the mid-300 horsepower range, Ford was being left behind and, in response, offered the 360 horsepower 352 cubic inch V-8. While the other automakers were offering four-speed manual transmissions, Ford continued to offer only a three-speed manual with overdrive, which undoubtedly helped mileage, but hurt performance. The biggest news for 1960, however, was introduction of the compact Falcon. The most successful one of the compact offerings

from the big three auto makers, the Falcon was extremely simple and straightforward, both in styling and mechanical features.

Throughout the early '60s, Ford continued on a steady-as-shh-goes course, offering the intermediate size Fairlane in 1962. Model year 1963 will be remembered as a high-water mark in the performance books at Ford. Not only was a new V-8 offered in the compact Falcon, but NASCAR and drag racing competition dictated the development and introduction of the most powerful engine ever to come from Dearborn, the incredible 427. These engines were "race-only" offerings, although some did find their way onto the streets. They produced 410 horsepower with one four-barrel carburetor and 425 horsepower with two. Fords absolutely dominated NASCAR racing with the "427" for the next four years and the record number of wins that they established in those seasons still stands as the most NASCAR victories for any one marque. Another highlight was the introduction of a car which many consider to be the most beautiful car of the '60s, the 1963½ Galaxie 500 fastback. The body style was designed in answer to the demands of the NASCAR people who had nothing more aerodynamic to drive than the standard notch back Galaxie hardtops.

The 1965 season witnessed introduction of another significnt contribution to the low-priced field, the lxuurious LTD. This plush entury was embraced by luxury-hungry consumers on a tight budget. More than 100,000 were sold during the first year of production. The Fairlane was redesigned in 1965 and the Falcon continued to use the same basic body style first introduced in 1964.

The next year saw a slight redesigning in the full-size Ford lineup and, also, the introduction of the limited-production seven-liter Galaxie models. These two-door hardtops and convertibles featured the new 428 cubic inch V-8 engine, Cruise-O-Matic automatic transmission or four-speed manual transmission and power front disc brakes as standard equipment. With only 8,705 of the hardtops and 2,368 of the convertibles being produced, they are highly sought after collector's items today. The big news in 1966 was the complete redesigning of the intermediate Fairlane Series, which was made large enough to accommodate big-block Ford V-8s.

The full-size Galaxies were restyled for 1967 and presented a very attractive package to the buying public. Fairlanes continued to use the same body as in 1966 with only minor restyling. For 1967, NASCAR allowed the use of the intermediate size bodies in Grand National racing. The Fairlanes took the place of the Galaxies on the high-banks, with Ford continuing to dominate the big races.

For 1968, the entire lineup received only minor restyling, with the exception of the intermediate Fairlane. Mid-year introduction time witnessed the introduction of one of the strongest engines ever to come from the Dearborn drawing boards, the incredible Corbra jet 428. Very conservatively rated at 335 horsepower, actual output was more in the area of 400 horsepower.

As in the late '50s, another great horsepower race was in full swing during the late '60s, with each manufacturer trying to out-power the other. Ford was right in the swing of things with the 428 CJ Mustang and Fairlane.

Engine and drivetrain options continued unchanged for 1970 but, in 1971, manufacturers produced the most awesome cars ever introduced to the general public. Ford produced the Boss 351 Mustang, the 429 SCJ Torino Cobras and the 429 SCJ Mustangs. Insurance companies were tightening the noose on "Supercar" owners by that time and 1971 is recognized as the last year for most true high-performance products from Detroit.

Ford made a significant contribution in the economy car field for 1971. In answer to the growing import threat and new sub-compacts from AMC and Chevrolet, Ford introduced its very successful Pinto. While competitors, like the Vega, were plagued with quality control and engineering problems, the simple Pinto continued to be a strong seller until it was finally withdrawn from the market — in 1980 — to make room for the Escort.

The balance of the years from 1971 through 1975 are not attracting a great deal of enthusiast interest as yet, although several specific models have future potential. Those 1972 LTD and 1973 Mustang convertibles will undoubtedly gain popularity with collectors in the next few years.

Ford has long produced a car which appealed to the masses. Even though the marque was outsold by giant Chevrolet for most years since the war (except 1957 and 1959) many Fords continue to generate appeal with collectors. Fords of the '50s were among the best looking cars; the Fords of the '60s were among the fastest and Fords of the '70s may someday be acclaimed as the most dependable and comfortable ever built.

1946 FORD

1946 FORDS — OVERVIEW — All 1946 Fords were, in essence, restyled 1942 models, utilizing the same drivetrain as the pre-war models. The grille was restyled with horizontal bars on the outside of the rectangular opening, instead of the flush-mounted grille of the 1942 model. The remainder of the body was virtually the same as the pre-war model.

DELUXE SERIES — (ALL ENGINES) — The DeLuxe series was the base trim level for 1946 and included rubber moldings around all window openings, a horn button instead of a ring, one sun visor and arm rests only on the driver's door.

DELUXE SIX-CYLINDER I.D. NUMBERS: DeLuxe six-cylinder models began with the designation, ''6GA'', with production numbers beginning at 227524 and going to 326417.

DELUXE SIX-CYLINDER

Model Number	Body/Style Number	Body Type & Seating	Factory Price	Shipping Weight	Production Total
6GA	73A	4-dr Sedan-6P	1198	3187	Note 1
6GA	70A	2-dr Sedan-6P	1136	3157	Note 1
6GA	77A	2-dr Coupe-3P	1074	3007	Note 1

NOTE 1: See DeLuxe V-8 Series listing. Production was counted by series and body style only, with no breakouts by engine type.

DELUXE V-8 SERIES I.D. NUMBERS: DeLuxe V-8 powered models began with the designation, ''69A'', with production numbers beginning at 650280 and going to 1412707.

DELUXE V-8

Model Number	Body/Style Number	Body Type & Seating	Factory Price	Shipping Weight	Production Total
69A	73A	4-dr Sedan-6P	1248	3220	9,246
69A	70A	2-dr Sedan-6P	1185	3190	74,954
69A	70A	2-dr Coupe-3P	1123	3040	10,670

PRODUCTION NOTE: Total series output was 94,870 units. In addition, there were 84 chassis produced with closed drive front end, two chassis produced with open drive front end. Ford does not indicate the number of each model produced with sixes and V-8s. Therefore, all figures given above show total production of each body style with both types of engines.

1946 Ford, Super DeLuxe 4-dr sedan, V-8 (AA)

SUPER DELUXE SERIES — (ALL ENGINES) — The Super DeLuxe Series was the top trim level for 1946 and included chrome moldings around all windows, a horn ring, two sun visors, arm rests on all doors, passenger assist straps on the interior ''B'' pillars for easier rear seat egress, horizontal chrome trim on the body and leather interior on the convertible models.

SUPER DELUXE SIX-CYLINDER I.D. NUMBERS: Super DeLuxe six-cylinder models began with the same ''6GA'' designation and used the same production numbers as the DeLuxe models.

SUPER DELUXE SIX-CYLINDER

Model Number	Body/Style Number	Body Type & Seating	Factory Price	Shipping Weight	Production Total
6GA	73B	4-dr Sedan-6P	1273	3207	Note 1
6GA	70B	2-dr Sedan-6P	1211	3157	Note 1
6GA	72B	2-dr Coupe Sed-6P	1257	3107	Note 1
6GA	77B	2-dr Coupe-3P	1148	3007	Note 1
6GA	79B	4-dr Sta Wag-8P	1504	3457	Note 1

NOTE 1: See Super DeLuxe V-8 series listing. Production was counted by series and body style only, with no breakouts by engine type.

SUPER DELUXE V-8 SERIES I.D. NUMBERS: Super DeLuxe V-8 models began with the same ''69A'' designation and used the same production numbers as the DeLuxe models.

SUPER DELUXE V-8

Model Number	Body/Style Number	Body Type & Seating	Factory Price	Shipping Weight	Production Total
69A	73B	4-dr Sedan-6P	1322	3240	92,056
69A	70B	2-dr Sedan-6P	1260	3190	163,370
69A	72B	2-dr Cpe Sed-6P	1307	3140	70,826
69A	77B	2-dr Coupe-3P	1197	3040	12,249
69A	76	2-dr Clb Conv-6P	1488	3240	16,359
69A	71	SptMan Conv-6P	1982	3340	723
69A	79B	4-dr Sta Wag-8P	1553	3490	16,960

PRODUCTION NOTE: Total series output was 372,543 units. In addition, there were 26 chassis produced with closed drive front end, three chassis produced with open drive front end and eight chassis-only produced. Ford does not indicate the number of each model produced with sixes or V-8s. Therefore, all figures given above show total pro-

duction of each body style. With both types of engines, except in the case of convertibles, which come only with V-8 power.

1946 FORD ENGINES
Six-cylinder: L-head. Cast iron block. Displacement: 226 cubic inches. Bore & stroke: 3.30 x 4.40 inches. Compression ratio: 6.8:1. Brake horsepower: 90 at 3300 R.P.M. Carburetor: Holley single-barrel model 847F. Four main bearings.
V-8: L-head. Cast iron block. Displacement: 239 cubic inches. Bore and stroke: 3.19 x 3.75 inches. Compression ratio: 6.8:1. Brake horsepower: 100 at 3800 R.P.M. Carburetor: Holley two-barrel model 94. Three main bearings.

CHASSIS FEATURES: Wheelbase: 114 inches. Overall length: 198.2 inches. Tires: 6.00 x 16.

1947 FORD

1947 FORDS — OVERVIEW — 1947 Fords were unchanged from the previous year and were, in fact, retitled 1946 models with updated Series and Model numbers.

DELUXE SERIES — (ALL ENGINES) — The DeLuxe series was the base trim level for the 1947 and included rubber moldings around all window openings, a horn button instead of a ring, one sun visor and arm rests only on the driver's door.

DELUXE SIX-CYLINDER SERIES I.D. NUMBERS: DeLuxe six-cylinder models began with the designation, ''7GA''. Production numbers were 71GA-326418 to 71GA-414366; also (beginning 10/3/47) 77HA-0512 to 77HA-9038.

DELUXE SIX

Model Number	Body/Style Number	Body Type & Seating	Factory Price	Shipping Weight	Production Total
7GA		4-dr Sedan-6P	1270	3213	Note 1
7GA		2-dr Sedan-6P	1212	3183	Note 1
7GA		2-dr Coupe-3P	1154	3033	Note 1

NOTE 1: See DeLuxe V-8 Series listing. Production was counted by series and body style only, with no breakouts by engine type.

DELUXE V-8 SERIES I.D. NUMBERS: DeLuxe V-8 models began with the designation, ''79A'', with the production numbers beginning at 799A-1412708 and going to 799A-2071231.

DELUXE V-8

Model Number	Body/Style Number	Body Type & Seating	Factory Price	Shipping Weight	Production Total
79A		4-dr Sedan-6P	1346	3246	44,563
79A		2-dr Sedan-6P	1288	3216	44,523
79A		2-dr Coupe-3P	1230	3066	10,872

PRODUCTION NOTE: Total series output was 99,958 units. In addition, there were 23 chassis produced with closed drive front ends. Ford does not indicate the number of each model produced with sixes of V-8 engines. Therefore, all production figures given above show total production of each body style with both types of engines.

1947 Ford Sportsman convertible

SUPER DELUXE SERIES — (ALL ENGINES) — The Super DeLuxe Series was the top trim level for 1947 and included chrome moldings around all windows, a horn ring, two sun visors, arm rests on all doors, passenger assist straps on the interior ''B'' pillars for easier rear seat egress, horizontal chrome trim on body and leather interior on the convertible models.

SUPER DELUXE SIX-CYLINDER I.D. NUMBERS: Super DeLuxe six-cylinder models began with the designation, ''7GA'' and used the same production numbers as the DeLuxe models.

SUPER DELUXE SIX

Model Number	Body/Style Number	Body Type & Seating	Factory Price	Shipping Weight	Production Total
7GA		4-dr Sedan-6P	1372	3233	Note 1
7GA		2-dr Sedan-6P	1309	3183	Note 1
7GA		2-dr Cpe Sed-6P	1330	3133	Note 1
7GA		2-dr Coupe-3P	1251	3033	Note 1
7GA		4-dr Sta Wag-8P	1893	3487	Note 1

NOTE 1: See Super DeLuxe V-8 listing. Production was counted by series and body style only, with no breakouts by engine type.

SUPER DELUXE V-8 SERIES I.D. NUMBERS: Super DeLuxe V-8 models began with the same ''79A'' designation and used the same production numbers as the DeLuxe models.

SUPER DELUXE V-8

Model Number	Body/Style Number	Body Type & Seating	Factory Price	Shipping Weight	Production Total
79A		4-dr Sedan-6P	1440	3266	116,744
79A		2-dr Sedan-6P	1382	3216	132,126
79A		2-dr Cpe Sed-6P	1409	3166	80,830
79A		2-dr Coupe-3P	1330	3066	10,872
79A		Club Convertible-6P	1740	3266	22,159
79A		SptsMan Conv	2282	3366	2,274
79A		Station Wagon-8P	1972	3520	16,104

PRODUCTION NOTE: Total series output was 385,109 units. In addition, there were 23 chassis produced with closed drive front ends. Ford does not indicate the number of each model produced with sixes or V-8s. Therefore, all figures given above show total production of each body style with both types of engines, except in the case of convertibles, which came only with V-8 power.

1947 FORD ENGINES

Six-cylinder: L-head. Cast iron block. Displacement: 226 cubic inches. Bore & stroke: 3.30 x 4.40 inches. Compression ratio: 6.8:1. Brake horsepower: 90 at 3300 R.P.M. Carburetor: Holley single-barrel model 847F. Four main bearings.
V-8: L-head. Cast iron block. Displacement: 239 cubic inches. Bore and stroke: 3.19 x 3.75 inches. Compression ratio: 6.8:1. Brake horsepower: 100 at 3800 R.P.M. Carburetor: Holley two-barrel model 94. Three main bearings.

CHASSIS FEATURES: Wheelbase: 114 inches. Overall length 198.2 inches. Tires: 6.00 x 16.

1948 FORD

1948 FORDS — OVERVIEW — 1948 Fords continued to share the 1946-1947 bodies with only slight trim changes. The parking lights were moved below the headlights from the former location between them. They were now round, instead of rectangular.

DELUXE SERIES — (ALL ENGINES) — The DeLuxe series was the base trim level for 1948 and included rubber moldings around window openings, a horn button instead of horn ring, one sun visor and one arm rest only on the driver's door.

DELUXE SIX-CYLINDER I.D. NUMBERS: DeLuxe six-cylinder models began with the designation, "87HA", with production numbers beginning at 0536 and going to 73901.

DELUXE SIX

Model Number	Body/Style Number	Body Type & Seating	Factory Price	Shipping Weight	Production Total
87HA	73A	4-dr Sedan-6P	1270	3213	Note 1
87HA	70A	2-dr Sedan-6P	1212	3183	Note 1
87HA	72A	2-dr Coupe-3P	1154	3033	Note 1

NOTE 1: See DeLuxe V-8 Series listing. Production was counted by series and body style, with no breakout by engine type.

DELUXE V-8 I.D. NUMBERS: DeLuxe V-8 powered models began with the designations "89A", with production numbers beginning with 899A-1984859 and going to 899A-2381447.

DELUXE SIX

Model Number	Body/Style Number	Body Type & Seating	Factory Price	Shipping Weight	Production Total
89A	73A	4-dr Sedan-6P	1346	3246	N.A.
89A	70A	2-dr Sedan-6P	1288	3216	23,356
89A	77A	2-dr Coupe-3P	1230	3066	5,048

PRODUCTION NOTE: Total series output was 28,404 units (not including the four-door sedan, for which production figures are not available). Ford does not indicate the number of each model produced with sixes or V-8s. Therefore, all production figures given above show total production of each body style with both types of engines.

SUPER DELUXE SERIES — (ALL ENGINES) — The Super DeLuxe series was the top trim level for 1948 and included chrome moldings around the windows, horn ring, two sun visors, arm rests on all doors, passenger assist straps on the interior "B" pillar for easier rear seat egress, horizontal chrome trim on the body and leather interior on the convertible models.

1948 Ford, Super DeLuxe 4-dr sedan, V-8 (AA)

SUPER DELUXE SIX-CYLINDER I.D. NUMBERS: Super DeLuxe six-cylinder models began with the same "87HA" designation and used the same production numbers as the DeLuxe models.

SUPER DELUXE SIX

Model Number	Body/Style Number	Body Type & Seating	Factory Price	Shipping Weight	Production Total
87HA	73B	4-dr Sedan-6P	1372	3233	Note 1
87HA	70B	2-dr Sedan-6P	1309	3183	Note 1
87HA	72B	2-dr Coupe Sed-6P	1330	3133	Note 1
87HA	77B	2-dr Coupe-3P	1251	3033	Note 1
87HA	79B	4-dr Sta Wagon-8P	1893	3487	Note 1

NOTE 1: See Super DeLuxe V-8 Series listing. Production was counted by series and body style only, with no breakouts by engine type.

SUPER DELUXE I.D. NUMBERS: Super DeLuxe V-8 powered models began with the same "89A" designation and used the same production numbers as the DeLuxe models.

SUPER DELUXE V-8

Model Number	Body/Style Number	Body Type & Seating	Factory Price	Shipping Weight	Production Total
89A	73B	4-dr Sedan-6P	1440	3266	71,358
89A	70B	2-dr Sedan-6P	1382	3216	82,161
89A	72B	2-dr Cpe Sed-6P	1409	3166	44,828
89A	77B	2-dr Coupe-3P	1330	3066	
89A	76B	2-dr Club Conv-6P	1740	3266	12,033
89A	71B	SptMan Conv-6P	2282	3366	28
89A	79B	4-dr Sta Wag-8P	1972	3520	8,912

PRODUCTION NOTE: Total series output was 219,320 units (not including the two-door Coupe, for which production figures are not available). Ford does not indicate the number of each model produced with sixes or V-8 engines. Therefore, all figures given show total production of each body style with both types of engines, except in the case of convertibles, which came only with V-8 power.

1948 FORD ENGINES

Six-cylinder: L-head. Cast iron block. Displacement: 226 cubic inches. Bore & stroke: 3.30 x 4.40 inches. Compression ratio: 6.8:1. Brake horsepower: 95 at 3300 R.P.M. Carburetion: Holley single-barrel model 847F. Four main bearings.
V-8: L-head. Cast iron block. Displacement: 239 cubic inches. Bore & stroke: 3.19 x 3.75 inches. Compression ratio: 6.8:1. Brake horsepower: 100 at 3800 R.P.M. Carburetion: Holley two-barrel model 94. Three main bearings.

CHASSIS FEATURES: Wheelbase: 114 inches. Overall length: 198.2 inches. Tires: 6.00 x 16.

1949 FORD

1949 FORDS — OVERVIEW — 1949 represented the first totally new automobile produced by Ford since the end of World War II. The chassis was the wishbone type, with longitudinal rear springs replacing the transverse springs used on earlier models. Styling featured a heavy chrome molding curving from the top of the grille down to the gravel deflector, with 'FORD' in large block letters mounted above the grille molding. There was a horizontal chrome bar in the center of the grille, extending the full width of the opening, with parking lamps mounted on the ends of the bar. In the center of the bar was a large spinner, with either a '6' or '8' designation, indicating engine choice. The body was slab-sided, eliminating the rear fender bulge altogether. A chrome strip near the bottom of the body extended from the front fender openings back to the gas cap. Models for 1949 included the base Ford series, and the top line Custom series.

FORD SERIES — (ALL ENGINES) — The Ford series was the base trim level for 1949 and included rubber window moldings, a horn button instead of horn ring, one sun visor and an arm rest only on the driver's door.

FORD SIX SERIES I.D. NUMBERS: Ford six-cylinder models began with the designation, "98HA", with production numbers beginning at 101 and going to 173310.

FORD SIX SERIES

Model Number	Body/Style Number	Body Type & Seating	Factory Price	Shipping Weight	Production Total
98HA	73A	4-dr Sedan-6P	1472	2990	Note 1
98HA	70A	2-dr Sedan-6P	1425	2945	Note 1
98HA	72A	2-dr Clb Cpe-6P	1415	2925	Note 1
98HA	72C	2-dr Bus Cpe-3P	1333	2871	Note 1

NOTE 1: See Ford V-8 Series listing. Production was counted by series and body style only, with no breakout per engine type.

FORD V-8 SERIES I.D. NUMBERS: Ford V-8 models began with the designation, "98BA", with production numbers beginning at 101 and going to 948236.

FORD V-8 SERIES

Model Number	Body/Style Number	Body Type & Seating	Factory Price	Shipping Weight	Production Total
98BA	73A	4-dr Sedan-6P	1546	3030	44,563
98BA	70A	2-dr Sedan-6P	1499	2985	126,770
98BA	72A	2-dr Clb Cpe-6P	1523	2965	4,170
98BA	72C	2-dr Bus Cpe-3P	1420	2911	28,946

PRODUCTION NOTE: Total series output was 204,449 units. Ford does not indicate the number of each model produced with sixes or V-8s. Therefore, all production figures given above show total production of each body style.

1949 Ford, Custom 2-dr sedan, V-8 (AA)

CUSTOM SERIES — (ALL ENGINES) — The Custom series was the top trim level for 1949 and included chrome window moldings, a horn ring, two sun visors, passenger assist straps on the interior B pillars for easier rear seat egress and horizontal chrome trim along the lower half of the body.

CUSTOM SIX SERIES I.D. NUMBERS: Custom six-cylinder models began with the same "98HA" designation and used the same production numbers as the Ford series.

CUSTOM SIX SERIES

Model Number	Body/Style Number	Body Type & Seating	Factory Price	Shipping Weight	Production Total
98HA	73B	4-dr Sedan-6P	1559	2993	Note 1
98HA	70B	2-dr Sedan-6P	1511	2948	Note 1
98HA	72B	2-dr Clb Cpe-6P	1511	2928	Note 1
98HA	76	2-dr Conv-6P	1886	3234	Note 1
98HA	79	2-dr Sta Wag-8P	2119	3523	Note 1

NOTE 1: See Custom V-8 Series listing. Production was counted by series and body style only with no breakout per engine type.

CUSTOM V-8 SERIES I.D. NUMBERS: Custom V-8 models began with the same "98HA" designation and used the same production numbers as the Ford series.

CUSTOM V-8 SERIES

Model Number	Body/Style Number	Body Type & Seating	Factory Price	Shipping Weight	Production Total
98BA	73B	4-dr Sedan-6P	1638	3033	248,176
98BA	70B	2-dr Sedan-6P	1590	2988	433,316
98BA	72B	2-dr Clb Cpe-6P	1596	2968	150,254
98BA	76	2-dr Conv-6P	1949	3274	51,133
98BA	79	2-dr Sta Wag-8P	2264	3563	31,412

PRODUCTION NOTE: Total series output was 914,291 units. Ford does not indicate the number of each model produced with sixes or V-8s. Therefore, all production figures given above show total production of each body style.

1949 FORD ENGINES
6-cylinder: L-head. Cast iron block. Displacement: 226 cubic inches. Bore and stroke: 3.30 x 4.40 inches. Compression ratio: 6.8:1. Brake horsepower: 95 at 3300 R.P.M. Carburetor: Holley one-barrel model 847FS. Four main bearings. Serial number code "H".
V-8: L-head. Cast iron block. Displacement: 239 cubic inches. Bore and stroke: 3.19 x 3.75 inches. Compression ratio: 6.8:1. Brake horsepower: 100 at 3600 R.P.M. Carburetor: Holley two-barrel model AA-1. Three main bearings. Serial number code "B".

CHASSIS FEATURES: Three-speed manual transmission with a semi-centrifugal type clutch; three speed helical gears and synchronizers for second and third gears was standard equipment. Three speed with automatic overdrive was optional. The automatic overdrive function cut in at 27 miles per hour and cut out at 21 miles per hour. Approximate drive ratio was 0.70:1. Wheelbase: 114 inches. Overall length: (Passenger cars) 196.8 inches; (Station wagons) 208 inches. Overall width: 72.8 inches. Rear axle gear ratios with standard transmission: (Passenger car) 3.73:1. (Station wagon) 3.92:1. Rear axle gear ratio with automatic overdrive: (Passenger car) 4.10:1; (Station wagon) 4.27:1. Tires: (Passenger car) 6.00 x 16; (Station wagon) 7.10 x 15.

1950 FORD

1950 FORDS — OVERVIEW — The 1950 Fords seemed identical to 1949 models, but were said to include "50 improvements for '50". Some of these improvements were, recessed gas filler neck, redesigned hood ornaments, flat-top horn ring, three-bladed cooling fan and pushbutton handles on exterior doors. An assembly plant designation was used in the serial numbers for the first time. (See production note).

PRODUCTION NOTE: Assembly plant designations were as follows: AT – Atlanta; BF – Buffalo; CS – Chester; CH – Chicago; DL – Dallas; DA – Dearborn; EG – Edgewater; HM – Highland Park; KC – Kansas City; LB – Long Beach; LU – Louisville; MP – Memphis; NR – Norfold; RH – Richmond; SP – Somerville; SR – Twin City (St. Paul).

DELUXE SERIES — (ALL ENGINES) — The DeLuxe series was the base trim level for 1950, and included rubber window moldings, a horn button instead of horn ring, one sun visor, and an arm rest only on the driver's door.

DELUXE SIX SERIES I.D. NUMBERS: DeLuxe six-cylinder models began with the designation, "OHA" followed by an assembly plant code and, finally, the unit's production number according to the final assembly plant. (See production note). Each plant began at 100001 and went up.

DELUXE SIX SERIES

Model Number	Body/Style Number	Body Type & Seating	Factory Price	Shipping Weight	Production Total
OHA	D73	4-dr Sedan-6P	1472	3050	Note 1
OHA	D70	2-dr Sedan-6P	1424	2988	Note 1
OHA	D72C	2-dr Bus Cpe-3P	1333	2933	Note 1

NOTE 1: See DeLuxe V-8 Series listing. Production was counted by series and body style only, with no breakout per engine type.

DELUXE V-8 SERIES I.D. NUMBERS: DeLuxe V-8 models began with the designation, "OBA" followed by an assembly plant code and, finally, the unit's production number according to the final assembly location. (See production note). Each plant began at 100001 and went up.

DELUXE V-8 SERIES

Model Number	Body/Style Number	Body Type & Seating	Factory Price	Shipping Weight	Production Total
OBA	D73	4-dr Sedan-6P	1545	3078	77,888
OBA	D70	2-dr Sedan-6P	1498	3026	275,360
OBA	D72C	2-dr Bus Cpe-3P	1419	2965	35,120

PRODUCTION NOTE: Total series output was 388,368 units. Ford does not indicate the number of each model produced with sixes or V-8s. Therefore, all production figures given above show total production of each body style.

1950 Ford, Custom club coupe, V-8 (AA)

CUSTOM DELUXE SERIES — (ALL ENGINES) — The Custom DeLuxe series was the top trim level and included chrome window moldings, chrome horn ring, two sun visors, arm rests on all doors, passenger assist strap on the interior "B" pillars for easier rear seat egress and chrome strips along the lower half of the body, with the model identification at the front edge of the chrome strip.

CUSTOM DELUXE SERIES SIX I.D. NUMBERS: Custom DeLuxe six-cylinder models began with the same "OHA" designation and used the same production numbers as DeLuxe models.

CUSTOM DELUXE SIX SERIES

Model Number	Body/Style Number	Body Type & Seating	Factory Price	Shipping Weight	Production Total
OHA	C73	4-dr Sedan-6P	1558	3062	Note 1
OHA	C70	2-dr Sedan-6P	1511	2999	Note 1
OHA	C72	2-dr Clb Cpe-6P	1511	2959	Note 1
OHA	C79	Sta Wag-6P	2028	3491	Note 1

NOTE 1: See DeLuxe V-8 Series listing. Production was counted by series and body style only, with no breakout per engine type.

CUSTOM DELUXE V-8 I.D. NUMBERS: Custom DeLuxe V-8 models began with the same "OBA" designation and used the same production numbers as the DeLuxe models.

1950 Ford, Custom DeLuxe Crestliner 2-dr sedan, V-8 (AA)

CUSTOM DELUXE V-8 SERIES

Model Number	Body/Style Number	Body Type & Seating	Factory Price	Shipping Weight	Production Total
OBA	C73	4-dr Sedan-6P	1637	3093	247,181
OBA	C73	2-dr Sedan-6P	1590	3031	398,060
OBA	C70C	2-dr Crestliner-6P	1711	3050	8,703
OBA	C72	2-dr Clb Cpe-6P	1595	3003	85,111
OBA	C76	2-dr Conv-6P	1948	3263	50,299
OBA	C79	2-dr Sta Wag-6P	2107	3531	29,017

PRODUCTION NOTE: Total series output was 818,371 units. Ford does not indicate the number of each model produced with sixes or V-8s. Therefore, all production figures given above show total production of each body style with both types of engines, except in the case of Crestliners and convertibles, which came only with V-8 power.

1950 FORD ENGINES
Six-cylinder: L-head. Cast iron block. Displacement: 226 cubic inches. Bore and stroke: 3.30 x 4.40 inches. Compression ratio: 6.8:1. Brake horsepower: 95 at 3300 R.P.M. Carburetor: Holley one-barrel model 847F5. Four main bearings. Serial number code "H".
V-8: L-head. Cast iron block. Displacement: 239 cubic inches. Bore and stroke: 3.19 x 3.75 inches. Compression ratio: 6.8:1. Brake horsepower: 100 at 3600 R.P.M. Carburetor: Holley two-barrel model AA-1. Three main bearings. Serial number code "B".

CHASSIS FEATURES: The standard Ford transmission was a three-speed manual type with semi-centrifugal type clutch; three-speed helical gearset and synchronizers for second and third gears. A three-speed manual gearbox with automatic overdrive was optional. Specifications were similar to 1949. Wheelbase: (all models) 114 inches. Overall length: (Passenger cars) 196.8 inches; (Station wagons) 208 inches. Overall width: (all models) 72.8 inches. Tires: (standard) 6.00 x 16; (optional) 6.70 x 15; (Station wagon) 7.10 x 15. Rear axle gear ratios with standard transmission: (Passenger car) 3.73:1. (Station wagon) 3.92:1. Rear axle gear ratio with automatic overdrive: (Passenger car) 4.10:1; (Station wagon) 4.17:1.

Historical footnotes: The two-door sedan with short top was the Club Coupe. The two-door station wagon was the Country Squire. The Crestliner was a special two-door sedan with vinyl top covering; extra chrome; special steering wheel; special paint and full wheel covers.

1951 FORD

1951 Ford, DeLuxe 2-dr sedan, V-8 (AA)

1951 FORDS — OVERVIEW — While the 1951 Fords shared body components with the 1949-1950 models, a few trim changes made a substantial difference in looks. The horizontal bar in the grille had the single large spinner replaced by two smaller spinners, which were mounted at the ends of the bar. The taillight lenses were redesigned slightly and the license plate cover was reshaped. Inside, a completely different instrument panel was used and all instruments were grouped in front of the driver.

DELUXE SERIES — (ALL ENGINES) — The DeLuxe series was the base trim level for 1951 and included rubber window moldings, a horn button instead of horn ring, one sun visor and an arm rest only on the driver's door.

DELUXE SIX SERIES I.D. NUMBERS: DeLuxe six-cylinder model numbers began with the designation "1HA" followed by an assembly plant code and, finally, the unit's production numbers according to the final assembly location. (See production note). All plants began with 100001 and went up.

DELUXE SIX SERIES

Model Number	Body/Style Number	Body Type & Seating	Factory Price	Shipping Weight	Production Total
1HA	73	4-dr Sedan-6P	1465	3089	Note 1
1HA	70	2-dr Sedan-6P	1417	3023	Note 1
1HA	72C	2-dr Bus Cpe-3P	1324	2960	Note 1

NOTE: See DeLuxe V-8 series listing. Production was counted by Series and body style only with no breakout per engine type.

DELUXE V-8 SERIES I.D. NUMBERS: DeLuxe V-8 models began with the designation, "1BA", assembly code and, finally, the unit's production numbers, according to the final assembly location. (See production note). All plants began with 100001 and went up.

DELUXE V-8 SERIES

Model Number	Body/Style Number	Body Type & Seating	Factory Price	Shipping Weight	Production Total
1BA	73	4-dr Sean-6P	1540	3114	54,265
1BA	70	2-dr Sedan-6P	1492	3062	146,010
1BA	72C	2-dr Bus Cpe-3P	1411	2997	20,343

PRODUCTION NOTE: Total series output was 220,618 units. Ford does not indicate the number of each model produced with sixes or V-8s. Therefore, all production figures given above show total production of each body style.

1951 Ford, Custom DeLuxe Victoria 2-dr hardtop, V-8 (AA)

CUSTOM DELUXE SERIES — (ALL ENGINES) — The Custom DeLuxe series was the top trim level for 1951 and included chrome window moldings, chrome horn ring, two sun visors, arm rests on all doors, passenger assist straps on interior "B" pillars for easier rear seat egress and horizontal chrome strips on the body exterior.

CUSTOM DELUXE SIX I.D. NUMBERS: Custom DeLuxe, six-cylinder models began with the same "1HA" designation and used the same production numbers as the DeLuxe models.

CUSTOM DELUXE SIX SERIES

Model Number	Body/Style Number	Body Type & Seating	Factory Price	Shipping Weight	Production Total
1HA	73	4-dr Sedan-6P	1553	3089	Note 1
1HA	70	2-dr Sedan-6P	1505	3023	Note 1
1HA	72B	2-dr Clb Cpe-6P	1505	2995	Note 1
1HA	79	2-dr Sta Wag-8P	2029	3510	Note 1

NOTE 1: See Custom DeLuxe V-8 Series. Production was counted by series and body style only with no breakouts per engine type.

CUSTOM DELUXE V-8 I.D. NUMBERS: Custom DeLuxe V-8 models began with the same "1BA" designation and used the same production numbers as the DeLuxe models. (See production note).

CUSTOM DELUXE V-8 SERIES

Model Number	Body/Style Number	Body Type & Seating	Factory Price	Shipping Weight	Production Total
1BA	73B	4-dr Sedan-6P	1633	3114	232,691
1BA	70B	2-dr Sedan-6P	1585	3062	317,869
1BA	70C	2-dr Crestliner-6P	1595	3065	8,703
1BA	72C	2-dr Clb Cpe-6P	1590	3034	53,263
1BA	60	2-dr Victoria-6P	1925	3188	110,286
1BA	76	2-dr Conv-6P	1949	3268	40,934
1BA	79	2-dr Sta Wag-8P	2110	3550	29,017

PRODUCTION NOTE: Total series output was 792,763 units. Ford does not indicate the number of each model produced with sixes or V-8's. Therefore, all production figures given above are total production of each body style with both engines, except in the case of Crestliners, Victorias and Convertibles, which came only with V-8 power.

1951 FORD ENGINES
Six-cylinder: L-head. Cast iron block. Displacement: 226 cubic inches. Bore and stroke: 3.30 x 4.40 inches. Compression ratio: 6.8:1. Brake horsepower: 95 at 3600 R.P.M. Carburetor: Holley one-barrel moddel 847FS. Four main bearings. Serial number code "H".
V-8: L-head. Cast iron block. Displacement: 239 cubic inches. Bore and stroke: 3.19 x 3.75 inches. Compression ratio: 6.8:1. Brake horsepower: 100 at 3600 R.P.M. Carburetor: Ford two-barrel model 8BA. Three main bearings. Serial number code "B".

CHASSIS FEATURES: The Standard Ford transmission was a three-speed manual type with semi-centrifugal clutch, three-speed helical gearset and synchronizers for second and third gears. Three-speed transmission with automatic overdrive (see 1949 specifications) was optional at $92 extra. Two-speed Ford-O-Matic transmission was optional at $159 extra. This was a torque converter type transmission with three-speed (automatic intermediate gear for starting) automatic planetary geartrain and single stage, three element, hydraulic torque converter. Wheelbase: (all models) 114 inches. Overall length: (Passenger cars) 196.4 inches; (Station wagons) 208 inches. Overall width: (all models) 72.9 inches. Rear axle gear ratios with manual transmission: (standard) 3.73:1; (optional) 4.10:1. Rear axle gear ratio with automatic overdrive: 4.10:1. Rear axle ratio with Ford-O-Matic: 3.31:1. Tires: (standard) 6.00 x 16; (optional) 6.70 x 15 and (station wagon) 7.10 x 15.

Historical footnotes: The two-door sedan with short top was the Club Coupe. The two-door station wagon was the Country Squire. The Crestliner was a special two-door sedan with vinyl roof covering; extra chrome; special steering wheel; special paint and full wheel covers. The Victoria was a new pillarless two-door hardtop.

1952 FORD

1952 Ford, Mainline Ranch Wagon (station wagon), V-8 (AA)

1952 FORDS OVERVIEW — 1952 represented the first totally new body for Ford since 1949. The new models featured a one-piece curved windshield, full-width rear window, protruding round parking lights, round three-bladed spinner in the center of the grille bar, simulated scoop on the rear quarter panels, gas filler pipe and neck concealed behind the license plate, redesigned instrument panel and suspended clutch and brake pedals.

MAINLINE SERIES — (ALL ENGINES) — The Mainline series was the base trim level for 1952 and included rubber window moldings, a horn button instead of horn ring, one sun visor and an arm rest only on the driver's door.

MAINLINE SIX SERIES I.D. NUMBERS: Mainline, six-cylinder models began with the designation, "A2", assembly plant code and finally the unit's production numbers according to the final assembly location. (See production note). Each plant began at 100001 and went up.

MAINLINE SIX SERIES

Model Number	Body/Style Number	Body Type & Seating	Factory Price	Shipping Weight	Production Total
A2	73A	4-dr Sedan-6P	1530	3173	Note 1
As	70A	2-dr Sedan-6P	1485	3070	Note 1
A2	72C	2-dr Bus Cpe-3P	1389	2984	Note 1
A2	59A	2-dr Sta Wag-6P	1832	3377	Note 1

NOTE 1: See Mainline V-8 Series listing. Production was counted by series and body style only, with no breakout per engine type.

MAINLINE V-8 SERIES I.D. NUMBERS: Mainline V-8 models began with the designation, "B2", assembly plant code and, finally the unit's production numbers, according to the final assembly location (See production note). Each plant began at 100001 and went up.

MAINLINE V-8 SERIES

Model Number	Body/Style Number	Body Type & Seating	Factory Price	Shipping Weight	Production Total
B2	73A	4-dr Sedan-6P	1600	3207	41,277
B2	70A	2-dr Sedan-6P	1555	3151	79,931
B2	72C	2-dr Bus Cpe-3P	1459	3085	10,137
B2	59A	2-dr Sta Wag-6P	1902	3406	32,566

PRODUCTION NOTE: Total series output was 163,911 units. Ford does not indicate the number of each model produced with sixes or V-8s. Therefore, all production figures given above show total production of each body style.

CUSTOMLINE SERIES — (ALL ENGINES) — The Customline series was the interme-diate trim level for 1952 and included chrome window moldings, chrome horn ring, two sun visors, arm rests on all doors, passenger assist straps on interior "B" pillars for easier rear seat egress, a horizontal chrome strip on the front fenders and a chrome opening on the rear quarter panel scoop.

CUSTOMLINE SIX SERIES I.D. NUMBERS: Customline, six-cylinder models began with the same "A2" designation and used the same production numbers as the Mainline models. (See production note).

CUSTOMLINE SIX SERIES

Model Number	Body/Style Number	Body Type & Seating	Factory Price	Shipping Weight	Production Total
A2	73B	4-dr Sedan-6P	1615	3173	Note 1
A2	70B	2-dr Sedan-6P	1570	3070	Note 1
A2	72B	2-dr Clb cpe-6P	1579	3079	Note 1

NOTE 1: Customline V-8 Series listing. Production was counted by series and body style only with no breakout per engine type.

CUSTOMLINE V-8 SERIES I.D. NUMBERS: Customline V-8 models began with the same "B2" designation and used the same production numbers as the Mainline models. (See production note).

CUSTOMLINE V-8 SERIES

Model Number	Body/Style Number	Body Type & Seating	Factory Price	Shipping Weight	Production Total
B2	73B	4-dr Sedan-6P	1685	3207	188,303
B2	70B	2-dr Sedan-6P	1640	3151	175,762
B2	72B	2-dr Clb Cpe-6P	1649	3153	26,550
B2	79C	4-dr Sta Wag-6P	2060 .	3617	11,927

PRODUCTION NOTE: Total series output was 402,542 units. Ford does not indicate the number of each model produced with sixes and V-8s. Therefore, all production figures are total production of each body style.

1952 Ford, Crestline Victoria 2-dr hardtop, V-8 (AA)

CRESTLINE SERIES: The Crestline series was the top trim level for 1952 and was offered only with V-8 engines. This series included all trim in the Customline series, plus wheel covers and additional chrome trim along the bottom of the side windows.

CRESTLINE SERIES I.D. NUMBERS: (V-8 only) Crestline models began with the same "B2" designation and used the same production numbers as the Mainline and Custom-line V-8 models.

CRESTLINE SERIES

Model Number	Body/Style Number	Body Type & Seating	Factory Price	Shipping Weight	Production Total
B2	60B	2-dr Victoria-6P	1925	3274	77,320
B2	76B	2-dr Sunliner-6P	2027	3339	22,534
B2	79B	4-dr Sta Wag-8P	2186	3640	5,426

1952 FORD ENGINES

Six-cylinder: Overhead valves. Cast iron block. Displacement: 215 cubic inches. Bore and stroke: 3.56 x 3.60 inches. Compression ratio: 7.0:1. Brake horsepower: 101 at 3500 R.P.M. Carburetion: Holley one-barrel model 847FS. Four main bearings. Serial number code "A". V-8: L-head. Cast iron block. Displacement 239 cubic inches. bore and stroke: 3:19 x 3.75 inches. Compression ratio: 7.2:1. Brake horsepower: 110 at 3800 R.P.M. Carburetion: Ford two-barrel model 8BA. Three main bearings. Serial number code "B".

CHASSIS FEATURES: The standard transmission was a three-speed manual type of the usual design. Three-speed manual with automatic overdrive (see 1949 specifications) was a $102 option. Ford-O-Matic transmission was a $170 option. Ford-O-Matic fea-tured a torque converter transmission with automatic planetary geartrain; single stage three-element hydraulic torque converter; hydraulic mechanical automatic controls with no electrical or vacuum connections; forced air cooling; and power flow through the fluid member at all times. Wheelbase: (all models) 115 inches. Overall length: (all models) 197.8 inches. Overall width: (all models) 73.2 inches. Rear axle gear ratios: (manual transmission) 3.90:1; (overdrive) 4.10:1; (optional overdrive) 3.15:1; (Ford-O-Matic) 3.31:1; (optional with Ford-O-Matic) 3.54:1. Tires: (standard) 6.00 x 16; (optional) 6.70 x 15.

CONVENIENCE OPTIONS: A completely new line of custom accessories was brought out by the Ford Motor Company to match 1952 styling. Several interesting additions on the list were a speed governor; turn indicators; illuminated vanity mirror; engine compartment light; five-tube DeLuxe radio; seven-tube Custom radio; spring wound clock; electric clock; color keyed rubber floor mats; wheel discs; wheel trim rings; rear fender skirts; rocker panel trim strips; hand brake signal lamp and Magic Air heater and defroster.

Historical footnotes: The Crestline Victoria was a two-door pillarless hardtop. The Sun-liner in the same series was a two-door convertible. The four-door all-metal station wagon in the Crestline series was called the Country Squire. It came with wood grained side trim appliques. The Mainline two-door Station wagon was called the Ranch Wagon. The Customline four-door station wagon was called the Country Sedan. First year for overhead valve six-cylinder engine. The 1952 Fords were introduced to the public Feb-ruary 1, 1952. Over 32 percent of cars built this year had Ford-O-Matic gear shifting. Over 20 percent of cars built with manual transmissions had the overdrive option. The Ford station wagon led the industry with 30.9 percent of the output for this body style. Of total production for the 1952 calendar year (617,725 units) it was estimated that a full 621,783 Fords were built with V-8 engines!

1953 FORD

1953 Ford, Mainline two-door sedan, 6-cyl

1953 FORDS OVERVIEW — 1953 Fords utilized 1952 bodies with moderate trim updat-ing. The grille incorporated a larger horizontal bar with three vertical stripes on either side of a large spinner. The length of this bar was increased and wrapped around the front edges of the fenders. Parking lights were rectangular instead of round. The Ford crest appeared in the center of the steering wheel hub and contained the words, "50th Anniversary 1903-1953." Beginning in 1953, Ford adopted a new coding system for serial numbers, which can be broken down as follows: The first symbol designates the engine type; (A0 215 cubic inch six-cylinder; (B) 239 cubic inch V-8; (P) 255 cubic inch Law Enforcement V-8. The second symbol designates the model year: '3' for 1953; '4' for 1954 '5' for 1955, etc. The third symbol designates the final assembly plant (See Production Note A). The fourth symbol designates the body type (See Production Note B). The fifth through tenth digits indicate the number of the unit built at each assembly plant, beginning with 100000.

PRODUCTION NOTE A: In 1953, Ford assembly plants were identified by the following designations:
A – Atlanta; B – Buffalo; C – Chester; G – Chicago; F – Dearborn; E – Edgewater; E – Mahwah; H – Highland Park; K – Kansas City; L – Long Beach; M – Memphis; N – Norfolk; R – Richmond; R – San Jose; S – Somerville; P – Twin City (St. Paul).

PRODUCTION NOTE B: Body type symbols were: C – Sunliner; R – Customline Ranch Wagon; W – Mainline Ranch Wagon; X – Country Sedan; V – Victoria; T – Crestline four-door Sedan: S – Sedan Delivery; G – Mainline and Customline two-door Sedan, two-door Coupe and four-door Sedan.

MAINLINE SERIES — (ALL ENGINES) — The Mainline series was the base trim level for 1953 and included rubber window moldings, horn button instead of horn ring, one sun visor and an arm rest only on the driver's door.

MAINLINE SIX SERIES I.D. NUMBERS: Mainline six-cylinder models began with the designation, "A3", followed by assembly plant code, body type and, finally, the unit's production number. (See production note). Each plant began at 100001 and went up.

MAINLINE SIX SERIES

Model Number	Body/Style Number	Body Type & Seating	Factory Price	Shipping Weight	Production Total
A3	73B	4-dr Sedan-6P	1783	3115	Note 1
A3	70B	2-dr Sedn-6P	1734	3067	Note 1
A3	72B	2-dr Clb Cpe-6P	1743	3046	Note 1

NOTE 1: See Mainline V-8 Series listing. Production was counted by series and body style only, with no breakout per engine type.

MAINLINE V-8 SERIES I.D. NUMBERS: Mainline V-8 models began with the desgina-tion, "B3", assembly plant code, body type code, and, finally, the unit's production number according to the final assembly location. (See production note). Each plant began at 100001 and went up.

MAINLINE V-8 SERIES

Model Number	Body/Style Number	Body Type & Seating	Factory Price	Shipping Weight	Production Total
B23	73A	4-dr Sedan-6P	1766	3181	66,463
B3	70A	2-dr Sedan-6P	1717	3136	152,995
B3	72C	2-dr Bus Cpe-3P	1614	3068	16,280
B3	59A	2-dr Sta Wag-6P	2095	3408	66,976

PRODUCTION NOTE: Total series output was 302,714 units. Ford does not indicate the number of each model produced with sixes or V-8s. Therefore, all production figures given above are total production of each body style with both engines.

CUSTOMLINE SERIES — (ALL ENGINES) — The Customline series was the interme-diate trim level for 1953 and included chrome window moldings, chrome horn half-ring, two sun visors, arm rests on all doors, passenger assist straps on interior "B" pillars for easier rear seat egress, a horizontal chrome strip on the front fenders and a chrome opening on the rear quarter panel scoop. There was another horizontal chrome strip from the scoop opening to the back of the body.

CUSTOMLINE SIX SERIES I.D. NUMBERS: Customline six-cylinder models began with the same "A3" designation and used the same production numbers as the Mainline models.

1953 Ford, Customline 4-dr sedan, V-8 (AA)

CUSTOMLINE SIX SERIES

Model Number	Body/Style Number	Body Type & Seating	Factory Price	Shipping Weight	Production Total
A3	73B	4-dr Sedan-6P	1783	3115	Note 1
A3	70B	2-dr Sedan-6P	1734	3067	Note 1
A3	72B	2-dr Clb Cpe-6P	1743	3046	Note 1

NOTE 1: See Customline V-8 Series listing. Production was counted by Series and body style only with no breakout per engine type.

CUSTOMLINE V-8 SERIES I.D. NUMBERS: Customline, V-8 models began with the same "B3" designation and used the same production numbers as the Mainline models.

CUSTOMLINE V-8 SERIES

Model Number	Body/Style Number	Body Type & Seating	Factory Price	Shipping Weight	Production Total
B3	73B	4-dr Sedan-6P	1858	3193	374,487
B3	70B	2-dr Sedan-6P	1809	3133	305,433
B3	72B	2-dr Clb Cpe-6P	1820	3121	43,999
B3	79B	4-dr Sta Wag-6P	2267	3539	37,743

PRODUCTION NOTE: Total series output was 761,662 units. Ford does not indicate the number of each model produced with sixes or V-8s. Therefore, all production figures given above are total production of each body style with both engines, except for station wagons (Country Sedan), which came only with V-8 power.

CRESTLINE SERIES — The Crestline series was the top trim level for 1953 and was offered only with V-8 engines. This series included all trim in the Customline series, plus wheel covers and additional chrome trim along the bottom of the side widows.

CRESTLINE I.D. NUMBERS: Crestline models began with the same "B3" designation and used the same production numbers as the Mainline and Customline V-8 models.

CRESTLINE SERIES

Model Number	Body/Style Number	Body Type & Seating	Factory Price	Shipping Weight	Production Total
B3	60B	2-dr Victoria-6P	2120	3250	128,302
B3	76B	2-dr Sunliner-6P	2230	3334	40,861
B3	79C	4-dr Sta Wag-6P	2403	3609	11,001

1953 FORD ENGINES

Six-cylinder: Overhead valves. Cast iron block. Displacement: 215 cubic inches. Bore and stroke: 3.56 x 3.60 inches. Compression ratio: 7.0:1 Brake horsepower: 101 at 3500 R.P.M. Carburetion: Holley one-barrel model 1904F. Four main bearings. Serial number code "A".

V-8: L-head. Cast iron block. Displacement: 239 cubic inches. Bore and stroke: 3.19 x 3.75 inches. Compression ratio: 7.2:1. Brake horsepower: 110 at 3800 R.P.M. Carburetion : Holley two-barrel model 2100. Three main bearings. Serial number code "B".

CHASSIS FEATURES: Three-speed manual transmission was standard. This unit featured a semi-centrifugal type clutch; three-speed helical gears with synchronizers for second and third gears. Three-speed manual transmission with automatic overdrive was a $108 option. Specifications were the same above with automatic overdrive function cutting in 27 miles per hour, cutting out at 21 miles per hour. Approximate drive ratio was: 0.70:1. Manual control was provided below the instrument panel. Ford-O-Matic automatic transmission was a $184 option. This was a torque converter type transmission with automatic planetary geartrain; single stage, three-element hydraulic torque converter; hydraulic-mechanical automatic controls and no electrical or vacuum connections. Power was transmitted through the fluid member at all times. Wheelbase: 115 inches. Overall length: 197.8 inches. Overall width: 74.3 inches. Tires: 6.70 x 15 (standard) 7.10 x 15 (station wagon). Rear axle gear ratios: (standard transmission) 3.90:1; (optional) 4.10:1; (automatic overdrive) 4.10:1; (Ford-O-Matic) 3.31:1.

POWERTAIN OPTIONS: None available.

CONVENIENCE OPTIONS: Power steering ($125). Power brakes ($35). Ford-O-Matic transmission ($184). Overdrive ($108). Six-tube DeLuxe radio ($88). Eight-tube Custom radio ($100). Recirculation type heater ($44). DeLuxe heater ($71). Electric clock ($15). Directional signals ($15). Windshield washer ($10). Tinted glass ($23). White sidewall tires ($27).

Historical footnotes: The Mainline two-door all-metal station wagon was called the Ranch Wagon. The Customline four-door all-metal station wagon was called the Country Sedan. The Crestline four-door all-metal station wagon with wood grain applique side trim was called the Country Squire. The Victoria was a pillarless two-door hardtop. The Sunliner was a two-door convertible. Introduction of 1953 models took place December 12, 1953. On a model year basis 1,240,000 cars were built, of which total 876,300 were estimated to be V-8 powered units. Ford opened a new Technical Service Laboratory at Livonia, Michigan this year. A specially trimmed Sunliner convertible paced the 1953 Indianapolis 500 Mile Race. Master Guide power steering was introduced June 16, 1953.

190

1954 FORD

1954 Ford, Mainline 2-dr business coupe, 6-Cyl (AA)

1954 FORDS — OVERVIEW — 1954 Fords utilized the 1952-1953 bodies with moderate trim updating. The grille incorporated a large horizontal bar with large slots on either side of a centrally located spinner. Round parking lights were located at either end of the horizontal bar. Many new convenience options were added for 1954. Among them, were power windows, four-way power seats and power brakes. Ball joints replaced king pins in the front suspension. The big news from Ford Division in 1954, however, was a new V-8 engine, with overhead valves. This new engine was rated at 130 horsepower, or nearly 25 percent more than the 1953 flathead. Even the introduction of the new V-8 overshadowed by the biggest news of all; the February 20, 1954 announcement of an all new personal luxury car called the Thunderbird to be introduced in the 1955 model year.

MAINLINE SERIES — (ALL ENGINES) — The Mainline series was the base trim level for 1954 and included rubber window moldings, horn button instead of horn ring, one sun visor and an arm rest only on the driver's door.

MAINLINE SIX SERIES I.D. NUMBERS: Mainline six-cylinder models began with the designation, "A4", followed by assembly plant code, body type code and, finally, the unit's production number according to the final assembly location. (See production note). Each plant began at 100001 and went up.

MAINLINE SIX SERIES

Model Number	Body/Style Number	Body Type & Seating	Factory Price	Shipping Weight	Production Total
A4	73A	4-dr Sedan-6P	1701	3142	Note 1
A4	70A	2-dr Sedan-6P	1651	3086	Note 1
A4	72C	2-dr Bus Cpe-3P	1548	3021	Note 1
A4	59A	2-dr Sta Wag-6P	2029	3338	Note 1

NOTE 1: See Mainline V-8 Series listing. Production was counted by series and body style only, with no breakout per engine type.

MAINLINE V-8 SERIES I.D. NUMBERS: Mainline, V-8 models began with the designation, "U4", assembly plant code, body type and, finally, the unit's production number according to the final assembly location. (See production note). Each plant began at 100001 and went up.

MAINLINE V-8 SERIES

Model Number	Body/Style Number	Body Type & Seating	Factory Price	Shipping Weight	Production Total
U4	73A	4-dr Sedan-6p	1777	3263	55,371
U4	70A	2-dr Sedan-6p	1728	3207	123,329
U4	72C	2-dr Bus Cpe-3P	1625	3142	10,665
U4	59A	2-dr Sta Wag-6P	2106	3459	44,315

PRODUCTION NOTE: Total series output was 233, 680 units. Ford does not indicate the number of each model produced with sixes and V-8s. Therefore, all production figures given above are total production of each body style with both engines.

1954 Ford, Country Sedan 4-dr station wagon, V-8 (AA)

CUSTOMLINE SERIES — (ALL ENGINES) — The Customline series was the intermediate trim level for 1954 and included chrome window moldings, chrome half-horn ring, two sun visors, arm rests on all doors, passenger assist straps on interior "B" pillars for easier rear seat egress, a horizontal chrome strip along the entire length of the body and a chrome stone shield near the bottom of the rear quarter panels.

CUSTOMLINE SIX SERIES I.D. NUMBERS: Customline six-cylinder models began with the same "A4" designation and used the same production numbers as the Mainline series. (See production note).

CUSTOMLINE SIX SERIES

Model Number	Body/Style Number	Body Type & Seating	Factory Price	Shipping Weight	Production Total
A4	73B	4-dr Sedan-6P	1793	3155	Note 1
A4	70B	2-dr Sedan-6P	1744	3099	Note 1
A4	72B	2-dr Clb Cpe-6P	1753	3080	Note 1
A4	59B	2-dr Sta Wag-6P	2122	3344	Note 1
A4	79B	4-dr Sta Wag-6P	2202	3513	Note 1

NOTE 1: Customline V-8 Series listing. Production was counted by series and body style only with no breakout per engine type.

CUSTOMLINE V-8 SERIES I.D. NUMBERS: Customline, V-8 models began with the same "U4" designation, and used the same production numbers as the Mainline series. (See production note).

CUSTOMLINE V-8 SERIES

Model Number	Body/Style Number	Body Type & Seating	Factory Price	Shipping Weight	Production Total
U4	73B	4-dr Sedan-6p	1870	3276	262,499
U4	70B	2-dr Sedan-6P	1820	3220	293,375
U4	72B	2-dr Clb Cpe-6P	1830	3201	33,951
U4	59B	2-dr Sta Wag-6P	2198	3465	36,086
U4	79B	4-dr Sta Wag-6P	2279	3634	48,384

PRODUCTION NOTE: Total series output was 674,295 units. Ford does not indicate the number of each model produced with sixes or V-8s. Therefore, all production figures given above are total production of each body style with both engines.

1954 Ford Crestline Skyliner 2-dr hardtop (glass roof), V-8

CRESTLINE SERIES — (ALL ENGINES) — The Crestline series was the top trim level for 1954, and included a six-cylinder engine for the first time since the series began in 1950. This series included all the Customline trim, plus three chrome hash marks behind the quarter panel stone shields, chrome "A" pillar moldings, additional chrome trim along the bottom of the side windows and wheel covers.

CRESTLINE SIX I.D. SERIES NUMBERS: Crestline, six-cylinder models began with the same "A4" designation and used the same production numbers as the Mainline and Customline models. (See production note).

CRESTLINE SIX SERIES

Model Number	Body/Style Number	Body Type & Seating	Factory Price	Shipping Weight	Production Total
A4	73C	4-dr Sedan-6P	1898	3159	Note 1
A4	60B	2-dr Victoria-6P	2055	3184	Note 1
A4	60F	2-dr Skyliner-6P	2164	2104	Note 1
A4	76B	2-dr Sunliner-6P	2164	3231	Note 1
A4	79C	4-dr Sta Wag-8P	2339	3536	Note 1

NOTE 1: See Mainline V-8 Series listing. Production was counted by series and body style only, with no breakout per engine type.

CRESTLINE V-8 SERIES I.D. NUMBERS: Crestline, V-8 models began with the same "U4" designation and used the same production numbers as the Mainline and Crestline V-8 models. (See production notes).

CRESTLINE V-8 SERIES

Model Number	Body/Style Number	Body Type & Seating	Factory Price	Shipping Weight	Production Total
U4	73C	4-dr Sedan-6P	1975	3280	99,677
U4	60B	2-dr Victoria-6P	2131	3305	95,464
U4	60F	2-dr Skyliner-6P	2241	3325	13,144
U4	76B	2-dr Sunliner-6P	2241	3352	33,685
U4	76C	4-dr Sta Wag-8P	2415	3684	12,797

PRODUCTION NOTE: Total series output was 254,7687 units. Ford does not indicate the number of each model produced with sixes or V-8s. Therefore, all production figures are total production of each body style with both engines.

CHASSIS FEATURES: Wheelbase: 115 inches. Overall length: (passenger cars) 198.3 inches. (station wagons) 198.1 inches. Overall width: 73.5 inches. Tires: (standard) 6.70 x 15; (station wagon) 7.10 x 15.

1954 FORD ENGINES

Six-cylinder: Overhead valves. Cast iron block. Displacement: 223 cubic inches. Bore and stroke: 3.62 x 3.60 inches. Compression ratio: 7.2:1. Brake horsepower: 115 at 3900 R.P.M. Carburetion: Holley one-barrel model 1904F. Four main bearings. Serial number code "A".

V-8: Overhead valves. Cast iron block. Displacement: 239 cubic inches. Bore and stroke: 3.50 x 3.10 inches. Compression ratio: 7.2:1. Brake horsepower: 130 at 4200 R.P.M. Carburetion: Holley two-barrel model AA-1. Five main bearings. Serial number code "U".

Law enforcement V-8: Overhead valves. Displacement: 256 cubic inches. Bore and stroke: 3.62 x 3.10 inches. Compression ratio: 7.5:1. Brake horsepower: 160 at 4400 R.P.M. Carburetion: Holley four barrel. Five main bearings. Serial number code "P".

POWERTRAIN OPTIONS: Three-speed manual transmission was standard equipment. It featured a semi-centrifugal type clutch; three-speed helical gears and synchronizers for second and third gears. Three-speed with automatic overdrive was optional. Specifications were the same as above with automatic overdrive function cutting in at 27 miles per hour, cutting out at 21 miles per hour. Approximate drive ratio: 0.70:1. Manual control was mounted below the instrument panel. Ford-O-Matic automatic transmission was optional. This was a torque converter type transmission with automatic planetary geartrain; single stage, three-element hydraulic torque converter; hydraulic-

mechanical automatic controls with no electrical or vacuum connnections and power flow through the fluid member at all times. Rear axle gear ratios: (Ford) 3.90:1; (Ford with overdrive) 4.10:1; (Ford with Ford-O-Matic) 3.31:1;

CONVENIENCE OPTIONS: Automatic overdrive ($110). Ford-O-Matic transmission ($184). Power steering ($134). Power brakes ($41). Radio ($88-99). Heater and defroster ($44-71). Power windows ($102). Power seat ($64). White sidewall tires ($27 exchange). Note: Power windows available on Customline and Crestline only.

Historical footnotes: Public presentation of the original 1954 Ford line was made January 6, 1954. Three new models, Crestline Skyliner, Crestline Sunliner and Ranch Wagon were introduced. The Ranch Wagon was a two-door station wagon in the Mainline series, but now had Customline appearance features. The Customline two-door sedan with short top was the Club Coupe. The Customline four-door station wagon was the Country Sedan. The Crestline four-door station wagon with wood grained trim was the Country Squire. The Victoria was a Crestline two-door pillarless hardtop. The Skyliner was a Crestline two-door pillarless hardtop with green tinted plastic insert in roof over front seat. The Sunliner was the Crestline convertible. Of the total 1,165,942 Fords built in the 1954 calendar year, industry sources estimate that 863,096 units had V-8 engines installed. The 1,000,000th car of the 1954 production run was turned out August 24, 1954. Slow motion production of cars built to 1955 specifications began October 25, 1954.

1955 FORD

1955 Ford Fairlane Club sedan, 2-dr sedan, V-8

1955 FORDS — OVERVIEW — 1955 Fords were totally redesigned, inside and out, from the 1954 version. The bodies were longer, lower and wider. Even though the 1955 models used the same backlighted speedometer, first introduced in 1954, the rest of the instrument panel was new. A new Fairlane series replaced the Crestliner as the top trim level. At the front, large, round parking lights were mounted in a concave grille underneath the headlights. The Ford crest was mounted above the word Fairlane, in script, on the front of the hood, and again, on the doors above the chrome Fairlane stripe. This stripe began at the tops of the front fenders, moved back along the tops of the fenders, over the side of the doors, into a dip and then to the rear of the car. The Fairlane series also featured chrome eyebrows on the headlight doors. The contemporary interest in horsepower and speed was reflected in two new, larger, overhead valve V-8 engines. Perhaps some of the most exciting news was the introduction on Oct. 22, 1954 of the all-new '55 two-passenger Thunderbird. The announced base price was $2695.

MAINLINE SERIES — (ALL ENGINES) — The Mainline series was the base trim level for 1955 and included rubber window moldings, a horn button instead of chrome horn ring, one sun visor and an arm rest only on the driver's door.

MAINLINE SIX I.D. NUMBERS: Mainline, six-cylinder models began with the designation, "A5" followed by assembly plant code, body type code and, finally, the unit's production number, according to the final assembly location. Each plant began at 100001 and went up. (See production note).

MAINLINE SIX SERIES

Model Number	Body/Style Number	Body Type & Seating	Factory Price	Shipping Weight	Production Total
A5	73A	4-dr Sedan-6P	1753	3106	Note 1
A5	70A	2-dr Sedan-6P	1707	3064	Note 1
A5	70D	2-dr Bus Cpe-3P	1606	3026	Note 1

NOTE 1: See Mainline V-8 Series listing. Production was counted by series and body style only, with no breakout per engine type.

MAINLINE V-8 I.D. NUMBERS: Mainline, V-8 models began with the designation, "U5" (272 cubic inch V-8) or "P5" (292 cubic inch V-8), followed by assembly plant code, body type code and, finally, the unit's production number according to final assembly location. (See production note). Each plant began at 100001 and went up.

MAINLINE SERIES V-8

Model Number	Body/Style Number	Body Type & Seating	Factory Price	Shipping Weight	Production Total
U5/P5	73A	4-dr Sedan-6P	1853	3216	41,794
U5/P5	70A	2-dr Sedan-6P	1807	3174	76,698
U5/P5	70D	2-dr Bus Cpe-3P	1706	3136	8,809

PRODUCTION NOTE: Total series output was 127,301 units. Ford does not indicate the number of each model produced with sixes or V-8s. Therefore, all production figures given above are total production of each body style with both engines.

1955 Ford, Customline 2-dr sedan, V-8 (AA)

CUSTOMLINE SERIES — (ALL ENGINES) — The Customline series was the intermediate trim level for 1955 and included chrome window moldings, chrome horn half-ring, two sun visors, arm rests on all doors, passenger assist straps on two-door interior "B" pillars for easier rear seat egress, a horizontal chrome strip along the entire length of the body and Customline in script on the rear fenders.

CUSTOMLINE SIX I.D. NUMBERS: Customline six-cylinder models began with the same "A5" designation and used the same production numbers as the Mainline series. (See production note).

CUSTOMLINE SIX SERIES

Model Number	Body/Style Number	Body Type & Seating	Factory Price	Shipping Weight	Production Total
A5	73B	4-dr Sedan-6P	1845	3126	Note 1
A5	70B	2-dr Sedan-6P	1801	3084	Note 1

NOTE 1: See Customline V-8 Series listing. Production was counted by series and body style only, with no breakout per engine type.

CUSTOMLINE V-8 I.D. NUMBERS: Customline V-8 models began with the same "U5" or "P5" designation and used the same production numbers as the Mainline series. (See production note).

CUSTOMLINE SIX SERIES

Model Number	Body/Style Number	Body Type & Seating	Factory Price	Shipping Weight	Production Total
U5/P5	73B	4-dr Sedan-6P	1945	3236	235,417
U5/P5	70B	2-dr Sedan-6P	1901	3194	236,575

PRODUCTION NOTE: Total series output was 471,992 units. Ford does not indicate the number of each model produced with sixes and V-8s. Therefore, all production figures are total production of each body style with both engines.

FAIRLANE SERIES — (ALL ENGINES) — The Fairlane series was the top trim level for 1955 and indicated chrome window and "A" pillar moldings (hardtops and Sunliner), chrome eyebrows on the headlight doors and a chrome side sweep molding, plus all Customline trim (except the side chrome).

FAIRLANE SIX I.D. NUMBERS: Fairlane six-cylinder models began with the same "A5" designation and used the same production numbers as the Mainline and Customline Series. (See production note).

1955 Ford, Fairlane Skyliner Crown Victoria 2-dr sedan, V-8

FAIRLANE SIX SERIES

Model Number	Body/Style Number	Body Type & Seating	Factory Price	Shipping Weight	Production Total
A4	73C	4-dr Town Sed-6P	1960	3134	Note 1
A4	70C	2-dr Club Sed-6P	1914	3088	Note 1
A4	60B	2-dr Victoria-6P	2095	3184	Note 1
A4	64A	2-dr Crown Vic-6P	2202	3246	Note 1
A4	64B	2-dr Crown Vic Sky	2272	3264	Note 1
A4	76B	2-dr Sunliner-6P	2224	3248	Note 1

NOTE 1: See Fairlane V-8 Series listing. Production was counted by series and body style only, with no breakout per engine type.

FAIRLANE V-8 I.D. NUMBERS: Fairlane, V-8 models began with the same "U5" or "P5" designation and used the same production numbers as the Mainline and Customline Series. (See production note).

FAIRLANE V-8 SERIES

Model Number	Body/Style Number	Body Type & Seating	Factory Price	Shipping Weight	Production Total
U5/P5	73C	4-dr Town Sed-6P	2060	3268	254,437
U5/P5	70C	2-dr Club Sed-6P	2014	3222	173,311
U5/P5	60B	2-dr Victoria-6P	2195	3318	113,372
U5/P5	64A	2-dr Crown Vic-6P	2302	3380	33,165
U5/P5	64B	2-dr Crown Vic Sky	2372	3388	1,999
U5/P5	76B	2-dr Sunliner-6P	2324	3382	49,966

PRODUCTION NOTE: Total series output was 626,250 units. Ford does not indicate the number of each model produced with sixes or V-8s. Therefore, all production figures given above are total production of each body style with both engines.

STATION WAGON SERIES — (ALL ENGINES) — Station Wagons were, for the first time, included in their own series. The Ranch Wagon was the base trim level two-door wagon. Six and eight-passenger Country Sedans were the intermediate level and the Country Squire was the top trim level wagon. The level of trim equipment paralleled the Mainline, Customline and Fairlane series of passenger cars.

STATION WAGON SIX I.D. NUMBERS: Station Wagon, six-cylinder models began with the same "A5" designation and used the same production numbers as the conventional cars. (See production note).

STATION WAGON SIX SERIES

Model Number	Body/Style Number	Body Type & Seating	Factory Price	Shipping Weight	Production Total
A5	59A	2-dr Ranch Wag-6P	2043	3309	Note 1
A5	59B	2-dr Cus Ranch Wag	2109	3327	Note 1
A5	79B	4-dr Ctry Sed-6P	2156	3393	Note 1
A5	79B	4-dr Ctry Sed-8P	2287	3469	Note 1
A5	79C	4-dr Ctry Squire	2392	3471	Note 1

NOTE 1: See Station Wagon V-8 Series listing. Production was counted by series and body style only, with no breakout per engine type.

STATION WAGON V-8 SERIES I.D. NUMBERS: Station Wagon V-8 models began with the same "U5" or "P5" designation and used the same production numbers as the conventional cars. (See production note).

STATION WAGON V-8 SERIES

Model Number	Body/Style Number	Body Type & Seating	Factory Price	Shipping Weight	Production Total
U5/P5	59A	2-dr Ranch Wag-6P	2143	3443	40,493
U5/P5	59B	2-dr Cus Ranch Wag	2209	3461	43,671
U5/P5	79D	4-dr Ctry Sed-6P	2256	3527	53,075
U5/P5	79B	4-dr Ctry Sed-8P	2387	3603	53,209
U5/P5	79C	4-dr Ctry Squire	2492	3605	19,011

PRODUCTION NOTE: Total series output was 209,459 units. Ford does not indicate the number of each model produced with sixes or V-8s. Therefore, all production figures given above are total production of each body style.

THUNDERBIRD (V-8) — SERIES 40A — A bright, high-spirited car, the Thunderbird was equipped with the new overhead valve V-8 engine, boosted to higher horsepower ratings with the additional of a four-barrel carburetor and dual exhausts. A host of power-assist options including steering, windows, seat and brakes were available. The three-speed manual transmission was standard equipment, but overdrive and Ford-O-Matic automatic transmissions were optional accessories. Road clearance was only 5-1/2 inches, far less than the conventional Ford cars of the same year. The Thunderbird, with it's two-seater personal car appeal, came from the factory with a fibreglass hardtop. A rayon convertible top was an extra-cost option priced $290. Full-scale production began during the week of Sept. 5, 1954. The 292 cubic inch engine came with two compression ratios, 8.1 (193 h.p.) and 8.5 (198 h.p.). The lower ratio was used with the manual transmission only. The Thunderbird production line continued until Sept. 16, 1955. In addition to being started before the '54 model run was completed, it continued after the '56 model year began on Sept. 6, 1955. Only Thunderbirds were being assembled at the start and finish of the '55 model year run. This means that the first 1500 and the last 500 serial numbers from the series 100001 through 260557 were assigned only to Thunderbirds. The intervening numbers were assigned to the mixed production of Thunderbirds and the regular passenger car lines.

THUNDERBIRD SERIES I.D. NUMBERS: (V-8 only) Thunderbirds began with the designation "P4", followed by assembly plant code, body type code and, finally, the unit's production number.

1955 Ford, 2-dr Thunderbird convertible, V-8 (AA)

THUNDERBIRD SERIES

Model Number	Body/Style Number	Body Type & Seating	Factory Price	Shipping Weight	Production Total
P5	40	2-dr Conv-2P	2944	2980	16,155

THUNDERBIRD CHASSIS FEATURES: Wheelbase: 102 inches. Overall length: 175.3 inches. Overall width: 70.3 inches. Tires: 6.70 x 15 tubeless.

1955 FORD ENGINES

Six-Cylinder: Overhead valves. Cast iron block. Displacement: 223 cubic inches. Bore and stroke: 3.62 x 3.60 inches. Compression ratio: 7.5:1. Brake horsepower: 120 at 4000 R.P.M. Carburetion: Holley single-barrel. Four main bearings. Serial number code "A".

V-8: Overhead valves. Cast iron block. Displacement: 272 cubic inches. Bore and stroke: 3.62 x 3.30 inches. Compression ratio: 7.6:1. Brake horsepower: 162 at 4400 R.P.M. (182 at 4400 R.P.M. with the four-barrel "Power Pack"). Carburetion: Holley two-barrel. Five main bearings. Serial number code "U".

Thunderbird V-8: Overhead valves. Cast iron block. Displacement: 292 cubic inches. Bore and stroke: 3.75 x 3.30 inches. Compression ratio: 8.1:1 (8.5:1 with Ford-O-Matic). Brake horsepower: 193 at 4400 R.P.M. (198 at 4400 R.P.M. with Ford-O-Matic). Carburetion: Holley four-barrel. Five main bearings. Serial number code "P".

POWERTRAIN OPTIONS: Three-speed manual was standard equipment. It featured a Semi-centrifugal type clutch; three-speed helical gears and synchronizers for second and third gears. Three-speed with automatic overdrive was optional at $110. Specifications were the same as above with automatic overdrive function cutting in at 27 M.P.H., cutting out at 21 M.P.H. Approximate drive ratio: 0.70:1. Manual control below instrument panel.

CHASSIS FEATURES: Wheelbase: (Passenger car) 115.5 inches; (Station wagon) 115.5 inches; (Thunderbird) 102 inches. Overall length: (Passenger cars) 198.5 inches; (Station wagon) 197.6 inches; (Thunderbird) 175.3 inches. Overall width: (Ford) 75.9 inches. (Thunderbird) 70.3 inches. Tires: (Station wagons) 7.10 x 15 tubeless; (All other cars) 6.70 x 15 tubeless. Front tread: (Ford) 58 inches; (Thunderbird) 56 inches. Rear tread: (Ford) 56 inches; (Thunderbird) 56 inches.

CONVENIENCE OPTIONS: Overdrive transmission ($110). Ford-O-Matic automatic transmission ($178). Radio ($99). Heater ($71). Power brakes ($32). Power seat ($64). Power windows ($102). White sidewall tires ($27 exchange). Soft-top for Thunderbird, in addition to hardtop ($290). Soft-top for Thunderbird, as substitute for hardtop ($75). Power steering ($91). Other standard factory and dealer-installed type options and accessories.

Historical footnotes: The Town Sedan is a DeLuxe Fairlane four-door sedan. The Club Sedan is a DeLuxe Fairlane two-door sedan. The Victoria is a Fairlane two-door pillarless hardtop. The Crown Victoria is a Fairlane two-door pillared hardtop with "basket handle" roof trim. The Crown Victoria Skyliner is a similar model with forward half of top constructed from transparent green plexiglass. The Sunliner is the two-door Fairlane convertible. The Ranch Wagon has Mainline trim level; the Custom Ranch Wagon has Customline trim; the Country Sedan is a four-door station wagon with Customline trim and the Country Squire is a Fairlane trim level station wagon with wood-grained side appliques. Production of 1955 Fords began October 25, 1954 and ended August 30, 1955. The 1955 Ford was introduced to the public November 12, 1954. Production of 1955 Thunderbirds began September 7, 1954 and ended Sept. 16, 1955. The 1955 Thunderbird was introduced to the public October 22, 1954. Of the total 1,435,002 cars built from October 1954 to September 1955, the majority were V-8s. During the 1955 calendar year 1,546,762 Ford V-8s and 217,762 Sixes were manufactured. Also on a calendar year basis, 230,000 Fords had power steering; 31,800 had power brakes; 22,575 (of all FoMoCo products) had air-conditioning; 197,215 cars had overdrive and 1,014,500 cars had automatic transmissions. The 1955 run was the second best in Ford Motor Company history, behind 1923 when Model Ts dominated the industry. A new factory in Mahwah, N.J. opened this year, to replace one in Edgewater, N.J. A new factory in San Jose, California replaced a one-third as big West Coast plant in Richmond, California. A new factory was also opened in Louisville, Kentucky, replacing a smaller facility in the same city. Robert S. McNamara was Vice-President and General Manager of Ford Division; J.O. Wright was Assistant General Sales Manager; C.R. Beacham was General Sales Manager; Holmes Brown was Public Relations Director and G.C. Eldredge was Advertising Manager.

1956 FORD

1956 FORD — OVERVIEW — Ford reused the 1955 body again with the exception of differences in the top configuration two-door hardtops of each year, the addition of the Fairlane level Parklane 2-dr. Sport wagon and a Customline Victoria 2-dr. hardtop. Oval parking lights replaced the round ones used on the 1955 models and the chrome trim was revised moderately from the previous year. The 1956 models used larger taillights with chrome rings around the lenses. Inside was where the 1956 model was completely new. Safety was a very popular theme in 1956 and new Fords featured a completely redesigned instrument panel with optional padding and padded sun visors. Also, the steering wheel featured a 2½ inch recessed hub, supposedly designed to lessen injury to the driver in the event of an accident. Seat belts were also offered for the first time in 1956.

MAINLINE SERIES — (ALL ENGINES) — The Mainline series was the base trim level for 1956 and included rubber window moldings, a horn button instead of horn ring, one sun visor and an arm rest on the driver's door only.

MAINLINE SIX SERIES I.D. NUMBERS: Mainline six-cylinder models began with the designation, "A6", followed by assembly plant code, body type code and finally, the unit's production number, according to the final assembly location. (See production note). Each plant began at 100001 and went up.

MAINLINE SIX SERIES

Model Number	Body/Style Number	Body Type & Seating	Factory Price	Shipping Weight	Production Total
A6	73A	4-dr Sedan-6P	1895	3127	Note 1
A6	70A	2-dr Sedan-6P	1850	3087	Note 1
A6	70D	2-dr Bus Sed-3P	1748	3032	Note 1

NOTE 1: See Mainline V-8 Series listing. Production was counted by series and body style only, with no breakout per engine type.

MAINLINE V-8 SERIES I.D. NUMBERS: Mainline V-8 models began with the designation, "U6" (272 cubic inch V-8), "M6" (292 cubic inch V-8), or "P6" (312 cubic inch V-8), followed by assembly plant code, body type code and finally, the unit's production number, according to the final assembly location. (See production note). Each plant began with 100001 and went up.

MAINLINE V-8 SERIES

Model Number	Body/Style Number	Body Type & Seating	Factory Price	Shipping Weight	Production Total
U/M/P-6	73A	4-dr Sedan-6P	1995	3238	49,448
U/M/P-6	70A	2-dr Sedan-6P	1950	3198	106,974
U/M/P-6	70D	2-dr Bus Sed-3P	1848	3143	8,020

PRODUCTION NOTE: Total series output was 164,442 units. Ford does not indicate the number of each model produced with sixes or V-8s. Therefore, all production figures given above are total production of each body style with both engines.

CUSTOMLINE SERIES — (ALL ENGINES) — The Customline series was the intermediate trim level for 1956 and included chrome window moldings, horn ring, two sun visors, arm rests on all doors, passenger assist straps on two-door interior "B" pillars, for easier rear seat egress; a chrome strip along the entire length of the body with the series identification just above, and forward of the rear wheel opening. Trunk lid identification consists of a Ford crest with horizontal chrome bars on either side of the crest.

CUSTOMLINE SIX SERIES I.D. NUMBERS: Customline, six-cylinder models began with the same "A6" designation and used the same production numbers as the Mainline series. (See production note).

CUSTOMLINE SIX SERIES

Model Number	Body/Style Number	Body Type & Seating	Factory Price	Shipping Weight	Production Total
A6	73B	4-dr Sedan-6P	1985	3147	Note 1
A6	70B	2-dr Sedan-6P	1939	3107	Note 1
A6	64D	2-dr Vic-6P	2093	3202	Note 1

1956 Ford, Customline 4-dr sedan, 6-cyl (AA)

NOTE 1: See Customline V-8 Series listing. Production was counted by series and body style only, with no breakout per series.

CUSTOMLINE V-8 SERIES I.D. NUMBERS: Customline V-8 models began with the same "U6", "M6", or "P6" designation and used the same production numbers as the Mainline series. (See production note).

CUSTOMLINE V-8 SERIES

Model Number	Body/Style Number	Body Type & Seating	Factory Price	Shipping Weight	Production Total
U/M/P-6	73B	4-dr Sedan-6P	2086	3258	170,695
U/M/P-6	70B	2-dr Sedan-6P	2040	3218	164,828
U/M/P-6	64D	2-dr Vic-6P	2193	3345	33,130

PRODUCTION NOTE: Total series output was 368,653 units. Ford does not indicate the number of each model produced with sixes or V-8s. Therefore, all production figures given above are total production of each body style with both engines.

FAIRLANE SERIES — (ALL ENGINES) — The Fairlane series was the top trim level for 1956 and included chrome window moldings, chrome "A" pillar moldings on Sunliners, chrome side sweep moldings with simulated exhaust outlets at the back of the trim, Fairlane script below the Ford crest on the hood and a large, V-shaped insignia on the trunk lid. Also, V-8 equipped Fairlanes had rear bumpers with slots in each end for passage of the dual, exhausts, which were standard with either V-8 engine.

FAIRLANE SIX-CYLINDER I.D. NUMBERS: Fairlane six-cylinder models began with the same "A6" designation and used the same production numbers as the Mainline and Customline series. (See production note).

FAIRLANE SIX-CYLINDER SERIES

Model Number	Body/Style Number	Body Type & Seating	Factory Price	Shipping Weight	Production Total
A6	73C	4-dr Town Sed-6P	2093	3147	Note 1
A6	70C	2-dr Club Sed-6P	2047	3107	Note 1
A6	57A	4-dr Town Vic-6P	2249	3297	Note 1
A6	64C	2-dr Club Vic-6P	2194	3202	Note 1
A6	64A	2-dr Crown Vic-6P	2337	3217	Note 1
A6	64B	Crown Vic Skyliner	2407	3227	Note 1
A6	76B	2-dr Sunliner-6P	2359	3312	Note 1

NOTE 1: See Fairlane V-8 Series listing. Production was counted by series and body style only, with no breakout per engine type.

FAIRLANE V-8 SERIES I.D. NUMBERS: Fairlane, V-8 models began with the same "U6", "M6", or "P6" designations and used the same production numbers as the Mainline and Customline series. (See production note).

FAIRLANE V-8 SERIES

Model Number	Body/Style Number	Body Type & Seating	Factory Price	Shipping Weight	Production Total
U/M/P-6	73C	4-dr Town Sed-6P	2194	3290	244,872
U/M/P-6	70C	2-dr Club Sed-6P	2147	3250	142,629
U/M/P-6	57A	4-dr Town Vic-6P	2349	3440	32,111
U/M/P-6	64C	2-dr Club Vic-6P	2294	3345	177,735
U/M/P-6	64A	2-dr Crown Vic-6P	2438	3360	9,209
U/M/P-6	64B	Crown Vic Skyliner	2507	3370	603
U/M/P-6	76B	2-dr Sunliner-6P	2459	3455	58,147

PRODUCTION NOTE: Total series output was 645,306 units. Ford does not indicate the number of each model produced with sixes and V-8s. Therefore, all production figures given above are total production of each body style with both engines.

1956 Ford, Country Squire 4-dr station wagon, V-8 (AA)

STATION WAGON SERIES — (ALL ENGINES) — Station Wagons continued as their own series for 1956. The Ranch Wagon was the base trim level two-door wagon; Country Sedans were the intermediate trim level and Country Squires were the top trim level with simulated wood-grain exterior paneling. The level of equipment paralleled the Mainline, Customline and Fairlane series of passenger cars.

STATION WAGON SIX-CYLINDER I.D. NUMBERS: Station Wagon, six-cylinder models began with the same "A6" designation, and used the same production numbers as the conventional cars. (See production note).

STATION WAGON SIX-CYLINDER SERIES

Model Number	Body/Style Number	Body Type & Seating	Factory Price	Shipping Weight	Production Total
A6	59A	2-dr Ranch Wag-6P	2185	3330	Note 1
A6	59B	2-dr Cus Ranch Wag	2249	3345	Note 1
A6	59C	2-dr Parklane Wag	2428	3360	Note 1
A6	79D	4-dr Cntry Sed-6P	2297	3420	Note 1
A6	79B	4-dr Cntry Sed-8P	2428	3485	Note 1
A6	79C	4-dr Cntry Squire	2533	3495	Note 1

NOTE 1: See Station Wagon V-8 Series listing. Production was counted by series and body style only, with no breakout per engine type.

STATION WAGON V-8 SERIES I.D. NUMBERS: Station Wagon V-8 models began with the same ''U6'', ''M6'' or ''P6'' designation and used the same production numbers as the passenger cars. (See production note).

STATION WAGON V-8 SERIES

Model Number	Body/Style Number	Body Type & Seating	Factory Price	Shipping Weight	Production Total
U/M/P-6	59A	2-dr Ranch Wag-6P	2285	3473	48,348
U/M/P-6	59B	2-dr Cus Ranch Wag	2350	3488	42,317
U/M/P-6	59C	2-dr Parklane Wag	2528	3503	15,186
U/M/P-6	79D	4-dr Cntry Sed-6P	2397	3536	—
U/M/P-6	79B	4-dr Cntry Sed-8P	2528	3628	85,374
U/M/P-6	79C	4-dr Cntry Squire	2633	3638	23,221

PRODUCTION NOTE: Total series output was 214,446 units (not including six passenger Country Sedans, for which figures were unavailable). Ford does not indicate the number of each model produced with sixes or V-8 engines. Therefore, all production figures given above are total production of each body style with both engines.

THUNDERBIRD SERIES — (V-8) — Although the 1956 Thunderbird shared the same body as the 1955, there were a few significant changes which make the 1956 model very unique. Probably the most visible change is the outside location of the spare tire, which gave much more room in the trunk and, unfortunately, put so much weight behind the rear wheels, that handling and steering were adversely affected. Also, the 1956 Thunderbird included wind wings on the windshield, cowl vents on each fender and a different rear bumper configuration with the simplified exhausts routed out the ends of the bumper.

1956 Ford, Thunderbird 2-dr convertible, V-8 HFM

THUNDERBIRD V-8 I.D. NUMBERS: Thunderbird models began with the designation ''M6'' or ''P6'', assembly plant code ''F'' (Dearborn), body type code ''H'' (Thunderbird) and, finally, the production number beginning at 100001 and going up.

THUNDERBIRD SERIES

Model Number	Body/Style Number	Body Type & Seating	Factory Price	Shipping Weight	Production Total
M6/P6	40A	2-dr Conv-2P	3151	3088	15,631

1956 FORD ENGINES

Six-cylinder: Overhead valves. Cast iron block. Displacement: 223 cubic inches. Bore and stroke: 3.62 x 3.60 inches. Compression ratio: 8.0:1. Brake horsepower: 137 at 4200 R.P.M. Carburetion Holley single-barrel. Four main bearings. Serial number code ''A''.

V-8: Overhead valves. Cast iron block. Displacement: 272 cubic inches. Bore and stroke: 3.62 x 3.30 inches. Compression ratio: 8.0:1. Brake horsepower: 173 at 4400 R.P.M. (176 at 4400 R.P.M. with Ford-O-Matic). Carburetion: Holley two-barrel. Five main bearings. Serial number code ''U''.

Thunderbird V-8: Overhead valves. Cast iron block. Displacement: 292 cubic inches. Bore and stroke: 3.75 x 3.30 inches. Compression ratio: 8.4:1. Brake horsepower: 200 at 4600 R.P.M. (202 at 4600 R.P.M. with Ford-O-Matic). Carburetion: Holley four-barrel. Five main bearings. Serial number code ''M.''

Thunderbird Special V-8: Overhead valves. Cast iron block. Displacement: 312 cubic inches. Bore and stroke: 3.80 x 3.44 inches. Compression ratio: 8.4:1. Brake horsepower 215 at 4600 R.P.M. (225 at 4600 R.P.M. with Ford-O-Matic). Carburetion: Holley four-barrel. Five main bearings. Serial number code ''P''.

POWERTRAIN OPTIONS: Three-speed manual was standard equipment. It featured a semi-centrifugal type clutch; three-speed helical gears and synchronizers for second and third gears. Three-speed with automatic overdrive was optional. Specifications were the same as above with automatic overdrive function cutting in at 27 M.P.H., cutting out at 21 M.P.H. Approximate drive ratio: 0.70:1. Manual control below instrument panel. Ford-O-Matic automatic transmission was optional. This was a torque converter transmission with automatic planetary gear train; single stage, three-element hydraulic torque converter; hydro-mechanical automatic controls with no electric or vacuum connections and power flow through fluid member at all times. Six-cylinder rear axle ratios: (Ford-O-Matic) 3.22:1; (manual transmission) 3.89:1 and (overdrive) 3.89:1. V-8 rear axle ratios: (Ford-O-Matic) 3.22:1; (manual 3.78:1 and (overdrive) 3.89:1.

FORD CHASSIS FEATURES: Wheelbase: 115.5 inches. Overall length: 198.5 inches (197.6 inches on Station Wagons). Overall width: 75.9 inches. Tires: 6.70 x 15 4-ply tubeless, 7.10 x 15 4-ply tubeless on Victorias with Ford-O-Matic and on Ranch wagons, 7.10 x 15 6-ply tubeless on Country Sedans and Country Squire wagons.

THUNDERBIRD CHASSIS FEATURES: Wheelbase: 102 inches. Overall length: 175.3 inches (185 inches including Continental kit). Overall width: 70.3 inches. Tires: 6.70 x 15 4-ply tubeless.

CONVENIENCE OPTIONS: (Thunderbird options and prices are set in bold face type.) Automatic overdrive transmission ($110-**$148**). Ford-O-Matic transmission ($178-**215**). Power Steering for Mainline models ($91). Power steering for other models (**$51-64**). Power seat ($60). Radio ($100). Heater ($85). Power brakes ($32). Thun-

---

derbird V-8 for Fairlane models ($123). **Thunderbird Special V-8 for Thunderbirds ($123). Power brakes ($40). Windshield washers ($10). Wire wheel covers ($35). Power windows ($70). Chrome engine dress-up kit ($25).** Rear fender shields. Full wheel discs. White sidewall tires. Continental tire kit. Tinted windshield. Tinted glass. Life-Guard safety equipment. Two-tone paint finish. Front and rear bumper guards. Grille guard package. Rear guard package. Rear mount radio antenna. Other standard factory and dealer-installed options and accessories.

Historical footnotes: Production of 1956 Fords started Sept. 6, 1955 and the '56 Thunderbird began production on Oct. 17, 1955. The Parklane station wagon was a DeLuxe Fairlane trim level two-door Ranch Wagon. The Crown Victoria Skyliner featured a plexiglas tinted transparent forward roof, the last year for this type construction. The Sunliner was a two-door convertible. The new Y-block Thunderbird V-8 came with double twin-jet carburetion; integrated automatic choke; dual exhausts; turbo-wedge shaped combustion chambers and automatic Power Pilot. A 12-volt electrical system and 18-mm anti-fouling spark plugs were adopted this season. Model year sales peaked at 1,392,847 units. Calendar year production hit 1,373,542 vehicles. (Both figures include Thunderbird sales and production).

1957 FORD

1957 FORDS — OVERVIEW — 1957 Fords were completely restyled and bore only a slight resemblance to earlier models. The new Fairlane series (including Fairlane and Fairlane 500 models) was five inches lower; had a two and one-half inch longer wheelbase and measured more than nine inches longer overall compared to 1946 models. The Custom series (including Custom and Custom 300 models) was three inches longer overall and had a one-half inch longer wheelbase than the 1956 models. As an aid in lowering the cars, all models had 14 inch wheels for the first time. Other design changes included a rear-opening hood, streamlined wheel openings and the use of windshield posts that sloped rearward at the bottom. Also, all 1957 Fords sported the latest styling craze, tailfins. Ford referred to these as ''high-canted fenders''. The big news for the year was the introduction of the Skyliner; the only true hardtop convertible in the world. At the touch of a button, an automatic folding mechanism retracted the top into the trunk, creating a true convertible.

CUSTOM SERIES — (ALL ENGINES) — The Custom series was the base trim level for 1957 and included chrome window moldings, a horn button instead of a horn ring, one sun visor and an arm rest on the driver's door only. An abbreviated version of the 1955 Fairlane sweep type chrome trim began behind the front door and went back along the body sides.

CUSTOM SIX SERIES I.D. NUMBERS: Custom, six-cylinder models began with the designation, ''A7'', followed by assembly plant code, body type code and, finally, the unit's production numbers according to the final assembly location. (See production note). Each plant began at 100001 and went up.

CUSTOM SIX SERIES

Model Number	Body/Style Number	Body Type & Seating	Factory Price	Shipping Weight	Production Total
A7	73A	4-dr Sedan-6P	2042	3197	Note 1
A7	70A	2-dr Sedan-6P	1991	3154	Note 1
A7	70D	2-dr Bus Cpe-3P	1889	3145	Note 1

NOTE 1: See Custom V-8 Series listing. Production was counted by series and body style only, with no breakout per engine type.

CUSTOM V-8 I.D. NUMBERS: Custom V-8 models began with the engine designation code, followed by assembly plant code, body type code and, finally, the unit's production numbers, according to the final assembly location. (See production note). Each plant began at 100001 and went up.

CUSTOM V-8 SERIES

Model Number	Body/Style Number	Body Type & Seating	Factory Price	Shipping Weight	Production Total
NA	73A	4-dr Sedan-6P	2142	3319	68,924
NA	70A	2-dr Sedan-6P	2091	3276	116,963
NA	70D	2-dr Bus Coupe-3P	1979	3267	6,888

PRODUCTION NOTE: Total series output was 192,775 units. Ford does not indicate the number of each model produced with sixes and V-8s. Therefore, all production figures given above are total production of each body style with both engines. ''Model numbers'' were now equivalent to V-8 engine code designations, which varied with specific powerplant attachments.

1957 Ford, Custom 300 4-dr. sedan, V-8

CUSTOM 300 MODELS — (ALL ENGINES) — The Custom 300 was the top trim level in the short wheelbase Custom series and included chrome window moldings; chrome horn ring; two sun visors; arm rests on all doors and a slightly modified version of the new Fairlane sweep, featuring a gold anodized insert between two chrome strips. The word 'FORD' was spelled out in block letters above the grill and a small Ford crest appeared on the trunk lid.

CUSTOM 300 SIX SERIES I.D. NUMBERS: Custom 300 six-cylinder models began with the same "A7" designation and used the same production numbers as the Custom models. (See production note.)

CUSTOM 300 SIX SERIES

Model Number	Body/Style Number	Body Type & Seating	Factory Price	Shipping Weight	Production Total
A7	73B	4-dr Sedan-6P	2157	3212	Note 1
A7	70B	2-dr Sedan-6P	2105	3167	Note 1

NOTE 1: See Custom 300 V-8 Series listing. Production was counted by series and body style only, with no breakouts per engine type.

CUSTOM 300 V-8 SERIES I.D. NUMBERS: Custom 300 V-8 models began with the same engine designations and used the same production numbers as the Custom models. (See production note.)

CUSTOM 300 V-8 SERIES

Model Number	Body/Style Number	Body Type & Seating	Factory Price	Shipping Weight	Production Total
NA	73B	4-dr Sedan-6P	2257	3334	194,877
NA	70B	2-dr Sedan-6P	2205	3289	160,360

PRODUCTION NOTE: Total series output was 355,237 units. Ford does not indicate the number of each model produced with sixes or V-8s. Therefore, all production figures given above are total production of each body style with both engines. "Model.Numbers" were equivalent to V-8 engine code designations, which varied with specific powerplant attachments.

1957 Ford, Fairlane Town Sedan 4-dr. sedan, V-8 AA

FAIRLANE SERIES — (ALL ENGINES) — The Fairlane model was the base trim level for the longer wheelbase Fairlane series and included chrome window moldings with slightly less chrome around the "C" pillar than the Fairlane 500 model and a considerably different side stripe than the higher-priced model. The Fairlane side chrome began just behind the front door. It then followed the fin forward to its source, dropped over the side and swept back, at a 45-degree angle, to a point just above the wheel opening. From there it ran straight back to the rear bumper. The word Fairlane appeared in script, on the side of the front fenders, and above the grille. A large V-shaped Fairlane crest appeared on the trunk lid.

FAIRLANE SIX SERIES I.D. NUMBERS: Fairlane, six-cylinder models began with the same "A7" designation and used the same production numbers as the Custom series. (See production note).

FAIRLANE SIX SERIES

Model Number	Body/Style Number	Body Type & Seating	Factory Price	Shipping Weight	Production Total
A7	58A	4-dr Town Sed-6P	2286	3315	Note 1
A7	64A	2-dr Club Sed-6P	2235	3270	Note 1
A7	57B	4-dr Town Vic-6P	2357	3350	Note 1
A7	63B	2-dr Club Vic-6P	2293	3305	Note 1

NOTE 1: See Fairlane V-8 Series listing. Production was counted by series and body style only, with no breakouts per engine type.

FAIRLANE V-8 SERIES I.D. NUMBERS: Fairlane V-8 models began with the same engine designations and used the same production numbers as the Custom series. (See production note).

FAIRLANE V-8 SERIES

Model Number	Body/Style Number	Body Type & Seating	Factory Price	Shipping Weight	Production Total
NA	58A	4-dr Town Sed-6P	2386	3437	52,060
NA	64A	2-dr Club Sed-6P	2335	3392	39,843
NA	57B	4-dr Town Vic-6P	2457	3471	12,695
NA	63B	2-dr Club Vic-6P	2393	3427	44,127

PRODUCTION NOTE: Total series output was 148,725 units. Ford does not indicate the number of each model produced with sixes and V-8s. Therefore, all production figures given above are total production of each body style with both engines. "Model Numbers" were no equivalent to V-8 engine code designations, which varied with specific power plant attachments.

1957 Ford. Fairlane 500 2-dr Sunliner convertible, V-8

FAIRLANE 500 MODELS — (ALL ENGINES) — The Fairlane 500 was the top trim level in the Fairlane series and included all the trim used on the Fairlane models plus slightly more chrome on the "C" pillars and different side trim. The side trim was a modified version of the Fairlane sweep which included a gold anodized insert between two chrome strips. It began on the sides of the front fenders, dipping near the back of the front doors, merging into a strip and following the crest of the fins to the rear of the body.

FAIRLANE 500 SIX SERIES I.D. NUMBERS: Fairlane 500 six-cylinder models began with the same "A7" designation and used the same production numbers as the Fairlane models and Custom series. (See production note.)

FAIRLANE 500 SIX SERIES

Model Number	Body/Style Number	Body Type & Seating	Factory Price	Shipping Weight	Production Total
A7	58B	4-dr Town Sed-6P	2333	3300	Note 1
A7	64B	2-dr Club Sed-6P	2281	3285	Note 1
A7	57A	4-dr Town Vic-6P	2404	3365	Note 1
A7	63A	2-dr Club Vic-6P	2339	3320	Note 1
A7	76B	Sunliner Conv-6P	2505	3475	Note 1

NOTE 1: See Fairlane 500 V-8 Series listing. Production was counted by series and body style, with no breakouts per engine type.

FAIRLANE 500 V-8 SERIES I.D. NUMBERS: Fairlane 500 V-8 models began with the same engine designations and used the same production numbers as the Fairlane models and the Custom series. (See production note).

FAIRLANE 500 V-8 SERIES

Model Number	Body/Style Number	Body Type & Seating	Factory Price	Shipping Weight	Production Total
NA	58B	4-dr Town Sed-6P	2433	3452	193,162
NA	64B	2-dr Club Sed-6P	2381	3407	93,753
NA	57A	4-dr Town Vic-6P	2504	3487	68,550
NA	63A	2-dr Club Vic-6P	2439	3442	183,202
NA	63A	2-dr Club Vic-6P	2439	3442	183,202
NA	76B	Sunliner Conv-6P	2605	3497	77,728
NA	51A	Skyliner Conv-6P	2942	3916	20,766

PRODUCTION NOTE: Total series output was 637,161 units. Ford does not indicate the number of each model produced with sixes and V-8s. Therefore, all production figures given above are total production of each body style. "Model Numbers" were now equivalent to V-8 engine code designations, which varied with specific powerplant attachments. All convertibles are two-door styles; all Skyliner retractable convertibles are V-8 powered.

STATION WAGON SERIES — (ALL ENGINES) — The Ranch Wagon was the base trim level two-door station wagon for 1957. Country Sedans were the intermediate level with four-door styling. Country Squires were the top trim level, also with four-door styling. The level of equipment paralleled Custom, Custom 300 and Fairlane 500 models of passenger cars.

STATION WAGON SIX SERIES I.D. NUMBERS: Station Wagon six-cylinder models began with the same "A7" designation and used the same production numbers as the passenger cars. (See production note).

STATION WAGON SIX SERIES

Model Number	Body/Style Number	Body Type & Seating	Factory Price	Shipping Weight	Production Total
A7	59A	2-dr Ranch Wag-6P	2301	3398	Note 1
A7	59B	2-dr Del Rio-6P	2397	3405	Note 1
A7	79D	4-dr Ctry Sed-6P	2451	3468	Note 1
A7	79C	4-dr Ctry Sed-9P	2556	3557	Note 1
A7	79E	4-dr Ctry Squire	2684	3571	Note 1

NOTE 1: See Station Wagon V-8 Series listing. Production was counted by series and body style, with no breakouts per engine type.

STATION WAGON V-8 SERIES I.D. NUMBERS: Station Wagon V-8 models began with the same engine designations and used the same production numbers as the passenger cars. (See production note).

STATION WAGON V-8 SERIES

Model Number	Body/Style Number	Body Type & Seating	Factory Price	Shipping Weight	Production Total
NA	59A	2-dr Ranch Wag-6P	2401	3520	60,486
NA	59B	2-dr Dl Rio-6P	2497	3527	46,105
NA	79D	4-dr Ctry Sed-6P	2551	3590	135,251
NA	79C	4-dr Stry Sed-9P	2656	3679	49,638
NA	79E	4-dr Ctry Squire	2784	3693	27,690

PRODUCTION NOTE: Total series output was 319,170 units. Ford does not indicate the number of each model produced with sixes and V-8s. Therefore, all production figures given above are total production of each body style with both engines. "Model Numbers" were now equivalent to V-8 engine code designations, which varied with specific powerplant attachments. The Country Squire had simulated wood-grained exterior paneling.

1957 Ford, Thunderbird 2-dr convertible (with hardtop), V-8 (AA)

THUNDERBIRD V-8 SERIES — The 1957 model represented the first significant restyling since the T-Bird was first introduced. A longer rear section provided improved storage space. Riding and handling qualities were greatly enhanced by relocating the spare tire in the trunk. As with the large Fords, 1957 Thunderbirds featured fins on the rear fenders. Inside, the 1957 model used the instrument panel from full-sized 1956 Fords, with an engine-turned insert dressing-up the panel.

THUNDERBIRD V-8 SERIES I.D. NUMBERS: Thunderbird models began with the engine designation, "C7", "D7", or "E7" (depending on engine choice); assembly plant code "F" (Dearborn); body type code "H" (Thunderbird) and, finally, the production number, beginning at 100001 and going up.

THUNDERBIRD V-8 SERIES

Model Number	Body/Style Number	Body Type & Seating	Factory Price	Shipping Weight	Production Total
C7/D7/E7	40	2-dr Conv-2P	3408	3134	21,380

1957 FORD ENGINES

Six-cylinder: Overhead valves. Cast iron block. Displacement: 223 cubic inches. Bore and stroke: 3.62 x 3.60 inches. Compression ratio: 8.6:1. Brake horsepower: 144 at 4200 R.P.M. Carburetion: Holley one-barrel. Four main bearings. Serial number code "A".

V-8: Overhead valves. Cast iron block. Displacement: 272 cubic inches. Bore and stroke: 3.62 x 3.30 inches. Compression ratio: 8.6:1. Brake horsepower: 190 at 4500 R.P.M. Carburetion: Holley two-barrel. Five main bearings. Serial number code "B".

Thunderbird V-8: Overhead valves. Cast iron block. Displacement: 292 cubic inches. Bore and stroke: 3.75 x 3.30 inches. Compression ratio: 9.1:1. Brake horsepower: 212 at 4500 R.P.M. Carburetion: Holley four-barrel. Five main bearings. Serial number code "C".

Thunderbird Special V-8: Overhead valves. Cast iron block. Displacement: 312 cubic inches. Bore and stroke: 3.80 x 3.44 inches. Compression ratio: 9.7:1. Brake horsepower: 245 at 4500 R.P.M. Carburetion: Holley four-barrel. Five main bearings. Serial number code "D".

Thunderbird Special (8V) V-8: Overhead valves. Cast iron block. Displacement: 312 cubic inches. Bore and stroke: 3.80 x 3.44 inches. Compression ratio: 9.7:1 (10.00:1 with Racing Kit). Brake horsepower: 270 at 4800 R.P.M. (285 at 5000 R.P.M. with Racing Kit). Carburetion: two Holley four-barrels. Five main bearings. Serial number code "E".

Thunderbird Special Supercharged V-8: Overhead valves. Cast iron block. Displacement: 312 cubic inches. Bore and stroke: 3.80 x 3.44 inches. Compression ratio: 8.5:1. Brake horsepower: 300 at 4800 R.P.M. (340 at 5300 R.P.M. — NASCAR version). Carburetion: Holley four-barrel with Paxton centrifugal supercharger. Five main bearings. Serial number code "E".

POWERTRAIN OPTIONS: Three-speed manual was standard. It featured a semi-centrifugal type clutch; three-speed helical gears and synchronizers for second and third gears. Three-speed with automatic overdrive was optional. Specifications were the same as above with automatic overdrive function cutting in at 27 M.P.H., cutting out at 21 M.P.H. Approximate drive ratio: 0.70:1. Manual control below instrument panel. Ford-O-Matic automatic transmission was also optional. This was a torque convertor transmission with automatic planetary gear train; single-stage, three-element hydraulc torque converter; hydro-mechincal automatic controls with no electric or vacuum connections and power flow through fluid member at all times. Six-cylinder rear axle ratios: (Ford-O-Matic) 3.22:1; (manual transmission) 3.89:1 and (automatic overdrive) 4.11:1. V-8 rear axle ratios: (Ford-O-Matic) 3.10:1; (manual transmission) 3.56:1 and (automatic overdrive) 3.70:1.

CHASSIS FEATURES: Wheelbase: (Custom, custom 300 and Station Wagon Series) 116 inches: (Fairlane, Fairlane 500) 118 inches; (Thunderbird) 102 inches. Overall length: (Custom, Custom 300) 201.6 inches: (Fairlane 500 Skyliner V-8 Retractable) 210.8 inches. (All other Fairlane and Fairlane 500) 207.7 inches; (Station Wagons) 203.5 inches; (Thunderbird) 181.4 inches. Tires: (Custom, Custom 300) 7.50 x 14 four-ply tubeless; (Fairlane, Fairlane 500) 7.50 x 14 four-ply tubeless; (Country Sedans and Squires) 8.00 x 14; (Thunderbird) 7.50 x 14 four-ply tubeless.

CONVENIENCE OPTIONS: (Special Thunderbird options or special optional equipment prices for Thunderbirds are set in bold-face type). Custom engine option, 292 cubic inch V-8, ($439). Ford-O-Matic for ($188); **same for Thunderbird ($215).** Automatic overdrive transmission for Ford ($108); **same for Thunderbird ($146).** Power steering ($68). Radio ($100). Heater and defroster ($85). Windshield washers ($10). **Power windows ($70).** Engine chrome dress-up kit ($25). Power brakes ($38). Fairlane/station wagon engine option. 312 cubic inch V-8 ($43). Rear fender shields (skirts). Two-tone paint. Backup lamps. Large wheel covers (standard on Fairlane 500). White sidewall tires. Continental tire extension kit. Outside rear view mirror. Lifeguard safety equipment package. Oversized tires. Radio antenna. Non-glare mirror. Other standard factory and dealer-installed options and accessories.

Historical footnotes: Introduction of 1957 Fords and Thunderbirds took place October 1956. The Fairlane 500 Skyliner Retractable Hardtop (convertible) was introduced as a mid-year addition to the line. Overdrive or Ford-O-Matic could now be ordered for any car with any engine. Model year production was 1,655,068 vehicles. Calendar year sales amounted to 1,522,406 Fords and Thunderbirds. Ford out-produced Chevrolet this season, to become America's Number 1 automaker of 1957 (model year basis). The Town Victoria was a four-door pillarless hardtop. The Del Rio was a DeLuxe two-door Ranch Wagon in Fairlane level trim. The Club Victoria was a two-door pillarless hardtop coupe. The Sunliner was a conventional two-door convertible.

1958 FORD

1958 FORDS — OVERVIEW — Even though 1958 Fords shared the same basic body with 1957 models, there were many new styling ideas. A simulated air scoop hood and honeycomb grille were borrowed from Thunderbird stylists. A sculptured rear deck lid, plus dual headlamps created a much more futuristic looking car than the previous model. Cruise-O-matic three-speed automatic transmission was offered for the first time in 1958, as were 332 and 352 cubic inch V-8 engines. Also new for 1958 (and offered only in 1958) was the Ford-Aire suspension system, for use in Fairlane series cars and Station Wagons.

CUSTOM 300 SERIES — ALL ENGINES — The Custom 300 series was the base trim level for 1958 and included chrome window moldings, a horn button instead of a horn ring, one sun visor, an arm rest on the drivers door only and a single chrome strip on the body side. This molding began on the side of the front fender, continued horizontally to the back of the front door, then turned down and joined a horizontal chrome strip which continued to the back of the body. A Styletone trim option duplicated this side trim, except the lower horizontal strip was a double strip with a gold anodized insert.

CUSTOM 300 SIX SERIES I.D. NUMBERS: Custom 300 Six-cylinder models began with the designation, "A8", followed by assembly plant code, body type code, and, finally, the unit's production numbers, according to the final assembly location (See production note). Each plant began at 100001 and went up.

1958 Ford, Custom 2-dr sedan, 6-cyl

CUSTOM SIX SERIES

Model Number	Body/Style Number	Body Type & Seating	Factory Price	Shipping Weight	Production Total
A8	73A	4-dr Sedan-6P	2119	3227	Note 1
A8	70A	2-dr Sedan-6P	2065	3197	Note 1
A8	70D	2-dr Bus Coupe-3P	1977	3174	Note 1

NOTE 1: See Custom V-8 Series listing. Production was counted by series and body style only, with no breakout per engine type.

CUSTOM 300 I.D. NUMBERS: Custom 300, V-8 models began with the engine designation code, assembly plant code, body type code, and, finally, the unit's production numbers, according to the final assembly location (See production note). Each plant began at 100001 and went up.

CUSTOM V-8 SERIES

Model Number	Body/Style Number	Body Type & Seating	Factory Price	Shipping Weight	Production Total
NA	73A	4-dr Sedan-6P	2256	3319	163,368
NA	70A	2-dr Sedan-6P	2202	3289	173,441
NA	70D	2-dr Bus Coupe-3P	2114	3266	4,062

PRODUCTION NOTE: Total series output was 340,871 units. Ford does not indicate the number of each model produced with sixes or V-8s. Therefore, all production figures given above are total production of each body style with both engines. Individual "model numbers" not available, see 1957 Ford V-8 production note.

FAIRLANE MODELS — ALL ENGINES — The Fairlane model was the base trim level for the longer wheelbase Fairlane series. It included chrome window moldings, with slightly less chrome around the "C" pillar than Fairlane 500 models. Also a considerably different side stripe was used compared to the higher priced model. The base Fairlane side chrome had two strips. The lower molding began at the rear of the front wheel opening, then went straight to the back of the front door. From there it began to gradually curve upward. The upper strip began at the front of the fender and went straight back, to the back of the front door. It then began to curve gradually downward, merging with the lower strip directly over the rear wheel opening. A Fairlane script appeared on the rear fenders and directly above the grille opening. Mid-year Fairlanes came with an addition sweep spear of anodized aluminum trim centered in the panel created by the before mentioned trim. In addition mid-year Fairlanes featured 3 porthole trim pieces on the rear where the Fairlane script would appear.

FAIRLANE SIX SERIES I.D. NUMBERS: Fairlane six-cylinder models began with the same "A8" designation and used the same production numbers as the Custom 300 series (See production note).

FAIRLANE SIX SERIES

Model Number	Body/Style Number	Body Type & Seating	Factory Price	Shipping Weight	Production Total
A8	58A	4-dr Town Sed-6P	2250	3376	Note 1
A8	64A	2-dr Club Sed-6P	2196	3307	Note 1
A8	57B	4-dr Town Vic-6P	2394	3407	Note 1
A8	63B	2-dr Club Vic-6P	2329	3328	Note 1

NOTE 1: See Fairlane V-8 Series listing. Production was counted by series and body style only, with no breakout per engine type.

FAIRLANE SIX SERIES I.D. NUMBERS: Fairlane V-8 models began with the same engine designations and used the same production numbers as the Custom 300 series (See production note).

FAIRLANE V-8 SERIES

Model Number	Body/Style Number	Body Type & Seating	Factory Price	Shipping Weight	Production Total
NA	58A	4-dr Town Sed-6P	2374	3468	57,490
NA	64A	2-dr Club Sed-6P	2320	3399	38,366
NA	57B	4-dr Town Vic-6P	2517	3499	5,868
NA	63B	2-dr Club Vic-6P	2453	3420	16,416

PRODUCTION NOTE: Total series output was 118,140 units. Ford does not indicate the number of each model produced with sixes or V-8s. Therefore, all production figures given above are total production of each body style with both engines.

1958 Ford, Fairlane 500 Skyliner 2-dr retractable hardtop, V-8

FAIRLANE 500 MODELS — ALL ENGINES — The Fairlane 500 models had the top trim level in the Fairlane series. It included all the trim used in the Fairlane models plus slightly more chrome on the "C" pillars and different side trim. The side trim was a double runner chrome strip with a gold anodized insert. The top chrome strip began on the side of the front fender, sloped slightly, and terminated at the top of the rear bumper. The lower molding split from the upper strip where the front door began, dropped in a modified Fairlane sweep and merged with the upper strip at the rear bumper. Fairlane scripts appeared above the grille and on the trunk lid and the Fairlane 500 script appeared on the rear fenders, above the chrome side trim.

FAIRLANE 500 SIX SERIES I.D. NUMBERS: Fairlane 500 six-cylinder models began with the same "A8" designation and used the same production numbers as the Fairlane models and Custom series (See production note).

FAIRLANE 500 SIX SERIES

Model Number	Body/Style Number	Body Type & Seating	Factory Price	Shipping Weight	Production Total
A8	58B	4-dr Town Sed-6P	2403	3380	Note 1
A8	64B	4-dr Club Sed-6P	2349	3313	Note 1
A8	57A	4-dr Town Vic-6P	2474	3419	Note 1
A8	63A	2-dr Club Vic-6P	2410	3316	Note 1
A8	76B	Sunliner Conv-6P	2625	3478	Note 1

NOTE 1: See Fairlane 500 V-8 Series listing. Production was counted by series and body style, with no breakouts per engine type.

FAIRLANE 500 V-8 SERIES I.D. NUMBERS: Fairlane 500 V-8 models began with the same engine designation and used the same production numbers as the Fairlane models and Custom series (See production note).

FAIRLANE 500 V-8 SERIES

Model Number	Body/Style Number	Body Type & Seating	Factory Price	Shipping Weight	Production Total
NA	58B	4-dr Town Sed-6P	2527	3510	105,698
NA	64B	2-dr Club Sed-6P	2473	3443	34,041
NA	57A	4-dr Town Vic-6P	2598	3549	36,059
NA	63A	2-dr Club Vic-6P	2534	3446	80,439
NA	76B	Sunliner Conv-6P	2749	3637	35,029
NA	51A	Skyliner Conv-6P	3138	4094	14,713

PRODUCTION NOTE: Total series output was 306,429 units. Ford does not indicate the number of each model produced with sixes and V-8s. Therefore, all production figures given above are total production of each body style with both engines. All convertibles are two-door styles; all Skyliner retractable convertibles are V-8 powered.

STATION WAGON SERIES — ALL ENGINES — The Ranch Wagon was the base trim level two-door and four-door station wagons for 1958. Country Sedans were intermediate level station wagons and Country Squires were the top trim level. The level of equipment paralleled Custom, Custom 300 and Fairlane 500 models of passenger cars.

STATION WAGON SIX SERIES I.D. NUMBERS: Station Wagon six-cylinder models began with the same "A8" designation, and used the same production numbers as the passenger cars (See production note).

STATION WAGON SIX SERIES

Model Number	Body/Style Number	Body Type & Seating	Factory Price	Shipping Weight	Production Total
A8	59A	2-dr Ranch Wag-6P	2372	3480	Note 1
A8	79A	4-dr Ranch Wag-6P	2426	3543	Note 1
A8	59B	2-dr Del Rio-6P	2478	3504	Note 1
A8	79D	4-dr Ctry Sed-6P	2532	3555	Note 1
A8	79C	4-dr Ctry Sed-9P	2639	3625	Note 1
A8	79E	4-dr Ctry Sq-9P	2769	3672	Note 1

NOTE 1: See Station Wagon V-8 Series listing. Production was counted by series and body style, with no breakouts per engine type.

STATION WAGON V-8 SERIES I.D. NUMBERS: Station Wagon V-8 models began with the same engine designations, and used the same production numbers as the passenger cars (See production note).

STATION WAGON V-8 SERIES

Model Number	Body/Style Number	Body Type & Seating	Factory Price	Shipping Weight	Production Total
NA	59A	2-dr Ranch Wag-6P	2479	3607	34,578
NA	79A	4-dr Ranch Wag-6P	2533	3670	32,854
NA	59B	2-dr Del Rio-6P	2585	3631	12,687
NA	79D	4-dr Ctry Sed-6P	2639	3682	68,772
NA	79C	4-dr Ctry Sed-9P	2746	3752	20,702
NA	79E	4-dr Ctry Sq-9P	2876	3799	15,020

PRODUCTION NOTE: Total series output was 184,613 units. Ford does not indicate the number of each model produced with sixes and V-8s. Therefore, all production figures given above are total production of each body style with both engines. The Country Squire station wagon has simulated wood-grained exterior paneling.

1958 Ford, Thunderbird Tudor hardtop coupe, V-8 (AA)

THUNDERBIRD SERIES — V-8 — 1958 was the first year for the four-passenger "Square Birds." The hardtop was introduced on Jan. 13, 1958 with the convertible not showing up until June of 1958. The new personal Thunderbirds were over 18 inches longer and 1000 pounds heavier than their 1957 counterparts. The new T-Bird featured an extended top with squared-off "C" pillar. It had chrome trim along the base of the top and a small Thunderbird crest directly above the trim. A massive, one-piece bumper surrounded a honeycomb grille. The honeycomb look was duplicated in stamped and painted steel around the four circular taillights. A Thunderbird script appeared on the front fenders and five heavy, cast stripes appeared on the door, at the feature line. Inside, bucket seats and a vinyl covered console were used for the first time in a Thunderbird. Also for the first time, Thunderbirds were offered as either a hardtop or convertible, each being a separate model.

THUNDERBIRD V-8 SERIES I.D. NUMBERS: Thunderbird models began with the engine designation, "H8", assembly plant code "Y" (Wixom), body type code "H" (Thunderbird), and, finally, the unit's production number, beginning at 100001 and going up.

THUNDERBIRD V-8 SERIES

Model Number	Body/Style Number	Body Type & Seating	Factory Price	Shipping Weight	Production Total
H8	63A	Tudor H.T.-4P	3630	3708	35,758
H8	76A	2-dr Conv-4P	3914	3903	2,134

1958 FORD ENGINES:
Six-cylinder: Overhead valves. Cast iron block. Displacement: 223 cubic inches. Bore and stroke: 3.62 x 3.60 inches. Compression ratio: 8.6:1. Brake horsepower: 145 at 4200 R.P.M. Carburetion: Holley one-barrel. Four main bearings. Serial number code "A".

V-8: Overhead valves. Cast iron block. Displacement: 292 cubic inches. Bore & stroke: 3.75 x 3.30 inches. Compression ratio: 9.1:1. Brake horsepower: 205 at 4500 R.P.M. Carburetion: Holley two-barrel. Five main bearings. Serial number code "C".

Interceptor V-8: Overhead valves. Cast iron block. Displacement: 332 cubic inches. Bore and stroke: 4.00 x 3.30 inches. Compression ratio: 9.5:1. Brake horsepower: 240 at 4600 R.P.M. Carburetion: Holley two-barrel. Five main bearings. Serial number code "B".

Interceptor Special V-8: Overhead valves. Cast iron block. Displacement: 332 cubic inches. Bore and stroke: 4.00 x 3.30 inches. Compression ratio: 9.5:1. Brake horsepower: 265 at 4600 R.P.M. Carburetion: Holley four-barrel. Five main bearings. Serial number code "G".

Interceptor 352 Special V-8: Overhead valves. Cast iron block. Displacement: 352 cubic inches. Bore and stroke: 4.00 x 3.50 inches. Compression ratio: 10.2:1. Brake horsepower: 300 at 4600 R.P.M. Carburetion: Holley four-barrel. Serial number code "H".

POWERTRAIN OPTIONS: Three-speed manual transmission was standard equipment. If featured semi-centrifugal type clutch; three-speed helical gears, with synchronizers for second and third gears. Three-speed with automatic overdrive was optional. Specifications were the same as above with automatic overdrive function cutting in at 27 MPH, cutting out at 21 MPH. Approximate drive ratio: 0.70:1. Manual control below instrument panel. Ford-O-Matic automatic transmission was optional. This was a torque converter transmission with automatic planetary gear train; single-stage, three-element hydraulic torque converter; hydro-mechanical automatic controls with no electrical or vacuum connections and power flow through fluid member at all times. Cruise-O-Matic automatic transmission was also optional. This unit was the same as Fordomatic, except for having three-speeds forward. It was a high-performance automatic transmission with two selective drive ranges for smooth 1-2-3 full-power starts, or 2-3 gradual acceleration and axle ratio of 2.69:1 for fuel economy. Six-cylinder rear axle ratios: (Fordomatic) 3.22:1; (manual transmission) 3.89:1 and (automatic overdrive) 4.11:1. V-8 rear axle ratios: (Cruise-O-Matic 2.69:1; (Fordomatic) 3.10:1; (manual transmission) 3.56:1 and (automatic overdrive) 3.70:1.

CHASSIS FEATURES: Wheelbase: (Custom 300 and station wagons) 116.03 inches; (Fairlane, Fairlaine 500) 118.04; (Thunderbird) 113 inches. Overall length: (Custom 300) 202 inches; (station wagons) 202.7 inches; (Skyliner retractable) 211 inches; (other Fairlane, Fairlaine 500) 207 inches; (Thunderbird) 205.4 inches. Overall width; (all Fords) 78 inches; (Thunderbirds) 77 inches. Tires: (nine-passenger wagons) 8.00 x 14; (Skyliner retractable) 8.00 x 14; (all other Fords) 7.50 x 14; (Thunderbirds) 8.00 x 14.

CONVENIENCE OPTIONS: (Equipment and prices in bold face type are for Thunderbird. Ford-O-Matic drive ($180). Cruise-O-Matic ($197). Ford-Aire suspension ($156). Overdrive ($108). Power brakes ($37). Power steering ($69). Front power windows ($50); on Custom 300 'business' two-door ($64). Front and rear power windows ($101). Manual four-way adjustable seat ($17). Four-way power adjustable seat ($64). Six-tube radio and antenna ($77). Nine-tube Signal-Seeking radio and antenna ($99). White sidewall tires, four-ply, size 7.50 x 14 ($33). White sidewall tires, four-ply, size 8.00 x 14 ($50). Wheel covers ($19 and standard on Fairlane 500). Styleton two-tone paint ($22). Tinted glass ($20). Backup lights ($10). Custom 300 DeLuxe interior trim ($24). Electric clock ($15 and standard on Fairlane 500). Windshield washer ($12). Positive action windshield wiper ($11). Lifeguard safety package with padded instrument panel and sun visors ($19). Lifeguard safety package, as above, plus two front seat belts ($33). Polar Air Conditioner includes tinted glass ($271). Select Air Conditioner includes tinted glass ($395). Interceptor 265 horsepower V-8 in Custom 30 ($196); in Fairlane ($183). Interceptor Special 300 horsepower V-8 in Fairlane 500 ($159); in station wagon ($150). Note: Interceptor engine prices are in place of base six-cylinder prices. Automatic overdrive ($108). Heater and defroster ($80). Base Interceptor 332 cubic inch V-8 in Custom 300 models ($59). Interceptor Special V-8 in Fairlanes and station wagons ($54). Heater and defroster in Fairlanes and station wagons ($85). **Thunderbird: Power steering ($69). Heater and defroster ($95). Whitewall tires ($36 exchange). Leather interior ($106). Other dealer-installed options and accessories.**

Historical footnotes: Dealer introductions for 1958 Fords were held November 7, 1957. Dealer introductions for 1958 Thunderbirds were held February 13, 1958. Production at three factories — Memphis, Buffalo and Somerville — was phased out this season. In June, 1958, a new plant, having capacity equal to all three above, was opened at Loraine, Ohio. On a model year basis, 74.4 percent of all Fords built in the 1958 run had V-8 power. Sixty-eight percent of these cars had automatic transmission. Model year production of Fords and Thunderbirds totaled 987,945 cars. Calendar year sales of Fords and Thunderbirds peaked at 1,038,560 units. The Thunderbird was, along with the Rambler, one of only two U.S. marques to see sales increases for 1958, a recession year in the country. The Town Victoria was a four-door pillarless hardtop style. The Club Victoria was a two-door pillarless hardtop style. The Custom 300 two-door sedan was also called the business sedan. The Sunliner was a conventional two-door convertible style. The Skyliner was a retractable hardtop-convertible.

1959 FORD

1959 FORDS — OVERVIEW — 1959 Fords are considered by many to be the most beautifully styled Fords ever built. They were, in fact, awarded the Gold Medal for Exeptional Styling at the Brussels World Fair. With elegance and understated class, the car showed remarkable good taste and restraint. At a time when other car manufacturers were attempting to make their cars look like they were capable of inter-stellar travel or supersonic speeds, Ford excised restraint. Ford designers merely swept the rear fenders feature lines to the back of the car, formed a housing for the backup lights and curved the lower portion around an over-sized taillight for a startling effect. At the front end, the fenders were flattened across the top and housed the dual headlights. They had a sculptured effect at the sides where they rolled over the side trim. The 1959 Fords were long, low and had an exceptionally flat hood. There was relatively little chrome trim. Bright colors were used for incredible effects. A new 350 horsepower 430 cubic inch V-8 engine was optional (in the Thunderbird series) and a wider grille extended from side to side. The parking lights were recessed into the bumper and, late in 1958, a new series called the Galaxie was introduced as the top line model. Galaxie stylists had adapted the roof line of the Thunderbird to the standard Fairlane 500 body and produced truly beautiful results. The Custom line was dropped, making the Custom 300 the base trim level for 1959.

CUSTOM 300 SERIES — (ALL ENGINES) — The Custom 300 series was the base trim level for 1959 and included chrome window moldings, a horn button instead of horn ring, one sun visor, an arm rest only on the drivers door and a single chrome strip on the body side. The chrome strip followed the lines of the Fairlane sweep, but used only a single strip.

CUSTOM 300 SIX SERIES I.D. NUMBERS: Custom 300, six-cylinder models began with the designation, "A9" followed by assembly plant code, body type code, and finally, the unit's production numbers according to the final assembly location. (See production note). Each plant began at 100001 and went up.

CUSTOM 300 SIX SERIES

Model Number	Body/Style Number	Body Type & Seating	Factory Price	Shipping Weight	Production Total
A9	58E	4-dr Sedan-6P	2273	3385	Note 1
A9	64F	2-dr Sedan-6P	2219	3310	Note 1
A9	64G	2-dr Bus Cpe-3P	2132	3283	Note 1

NOTE 1: See Custom 300 V-8 Series listing. Production was counted by series and body style only, with no breakout per engine type.

CUSTOM 300 V-8 SERIES I.D. NUMBERS: Custom 300 V-8 models began with the engine designation code, assembly plant code, body type code, and finally, the unit's production numbers according to the final assembly location. (See production note). Each plant began at 100001 and went up.

CUSTOM 300 V-8 SERIES

Model Number	Body/Style Number	Body Type & Seating	Factory Price	Shipping Weight	Production Total
NA	58E	4-dr Sedan-6P	2391	3486	249,553
NA	64F	2-dr Sedan-6P	2337	3411	228,573

PRODUCTION NOTE: Total series output was 482,210 units. Ford does not indicate the number of each model produced with sixes or V-8s. Therefore, all production figures given above are total production of each body style with both engines.

FAIRLANE MODELS — (ALL ENGINES) — The Fairlane model was the intermediate trim level for 1959 and included chrome window moldings, a horn ring, two sun visors, arm rests on all doors and a more complicated side trim than the Custom series. The trim was a two-piece design, which could feature an optional silver anodized insert between the two pieces forming the 1959 version of the Fairlane sweep.

FAIRLANE SIX SERIES I.D. NUMBERS: Fairlane, six-cylinder models began with the same "A9" designation and used the same production numbers as the Custom 300 series. (See production note).

FAIRLANE SIX SERIES

Model Number	Body/Style Number	Body Type & Seating	Factory Price	Shipping Weight	Production Total
A9	58A	4-dr Town Sedan-6P	2411	3415	Note 1
A9	64A	2-dr Club Sedan-6P	2357	3332	Note 1

NOTE 1: See Fairlane V-8 Series listing. Production was counted by series and body style, with no breakouts per engine type.

FAIRLANE V-8 SERIES I.D. NUMBERS: Fairlane, V-8 models began with the same engine deisgnations, and used the same production numbers as the Custom 300 series. (See production note).

FAIRLANE V-8 SERIES

Model Number	Body/Style Number	Body Type & Seating	Factory Price	Shipping Weight	Production Total
NA	58A	4-dr Town Sedan-6P	2529	3516	64,663
NA	64A	2-dr Club Sedan-6P	2475	3433	35,126

PRODUCTION NOTE: Total series output was 97,789 units. Ford does not indicate the number of each model produced with sixes or V-8s. Therefore, all production figures given above are total production of each body style with both engines.

1959 Ford, Fairlane 500 Galaxie Town Victoria 4-dr. hardtop, V-8

1959 Ford, Fairlane 500 Club Victoria 2-dr. hardtop, V-8 AA

FAIRLANE 500 SERIES — (ALL ENGINES) — Prior to the introduction of the Galaxie, the Fairlane 500 was the top trim level for 1959, and included all the trim used in the Fairlane series, including the optional insert. In addition a large aluminum panel surrounded the rear wheel opening and ran to the rear bumper. Optional stainless steel fender skirts could be ordered to expand the large chrome area.

FAIRLANE 500 SIX SERIES I.D. NUMBERS: Fairlane 500, six-cylinder models began with the same "A9" designation and used the same production numbers as the Fairlane models and Custom models. (See production note).

FAIRLANE 500 SIX SERIES

Model Number	Body/Style Number	Body Type & Seating	Factory Price	Shipping Weight	Production Total
A9	58B	4-dr Town Sed-6P	2530	3417	Note 1
A9	64B	2-dr Club Sed-6P	2476	3338	Note 1
A9	57A	4-dr Town Vic-6P	2602	3451	Note 1
A9	63A	2-dr Club Vic-6P	2537	3365	Note 1

NOTE 1: See Fairlane 500 V-8 listing. Production was counted by series and body style, with no breakout per engine type.

FAIRLANE 500 V-8 SERIES I.D. NUMBERS: Fairlane 500 V-8 models began with the same engine designation, and used the same production numbers as the Fairlane models and Custom models. (See production note).

FAIRLANE 500 V-8 SERIES

Model Number	Body/Style Number	Body Type & Seating	Factory Price	Shipping Weight	Production Total
NA	58B	4-dr Town Sed-6P	2648	3518	35,670
NA	64B	2-dr Club Sed-6P	2594	3439	10,141
NA	57A	4-dr Town Vic-6P	2720	3552	9,308
NA	63A	2-dr Club Vic-6P	2655	3466	23,892

PRODUCTION NOTE: Total series output was 79,011 units. Ford does not indicate the number of each model produced with sixes or V-8s. Therefore, all production figures given above are total production of each body style with both engines.

GALAXIE SERIES — (ALL ENGINES) — The Galaxie was the new top line series for 1959. The only difference in the Galaxie, and the Fairlane 500 series was the styling of the top. Galaxies used the standard top, with a Thunderbird style "C" pillar. The combinations formed one of the best looking cars ever to come out of Dearborn.

GALAXIE SIX SERIES I.D. NUMBERS: Galaxie, six-cylinder models used the same "A9" designation and used the same production numbers as the Custom, Fairlane and Fairlane 500 models. (See production note).

GALAXIE SIX SERIES

Model Number	Body/Style Number	Body Type & Seating	Factory Price	Shipping Weight	Production Total
A9	54A	4-dr Town Sed-6P	2582	3405	Note 1
A9	64H	2-dr Club Sed-6P	2528	3377	Note 1
A9	75A	4-dr Town Vic-6P	2654	3494	Note 1
A9	65A	2-dr Club Vic-6P	2589	3338	Note 1
A9	76B	2-dr Sunliner-6P	2839	3527	Note 1

NOTE 1: See Galaxie V-8 Series listing. Production was counted by series and body style, with no breakouts per engine type.

GALAXIE V-8 SERIES I.D. NUMBERS: Galaxie, V-8 models began with the same engine designation, and used the same production numbers as the Custom, Fairlane, and Fairlane 500 models. (See production note).

GALAXIE V-8 SERIES

Model Number	Body/Style Number	Body Type & Seating	Factory Price	Shipping Weight	Production Total
NA	54A	4-dr Town Sed-6P	2700	3506	183,108
NA	64H	2-dr Club Sed-6P	2646	3478	52,848
NA	75A	4-dr Town Vic-6P	2772	3595	47,728
NA	65A	2-dr Club Vic-6P	2707	3439	121,869
NA	51A	2-dr Skyliner-6P	3346	4064	12,915
NA	76B	2-dr Sunliner-6P	2957	3628	45,868

PRODUCTION NOTE: Total series output was 464,336 units. Ford does not indicate the number of each model produced with sixes or V-8s. Therefore, all production figures given above are total production of each body style for both engines. The Sunliner is a conventional two-door convertible. The Skyliner is a retractable hardtop convertible and came only with V-8 power.

STATION WAGON SERIES — (ALL ENGINES) — The Ranch Wagons were the base trim level two-door and four-door station wagons for 1959. Country Sedans were the intermediate trim level. Country Squires were the top trim level. The level of equipment paralleled Custom, Fairlane and Galaxie models of passenger cars.

STATION WAGON SIX SERIES I.D. NUMBERS: Station Wagon, six-cylinder models began with the same "A9" designation and used the same production numbers as the conventional cars. (See production note).

STATION WAGON SIX SERIES

Model Number	Body/Style Number	Body Type & Seating	Factory Price	Shipping Weight	Production Total
A9	59C	2-dr Ranch Wag-6P	2567	3590	Note 1
A9	71H	4-dr Ranch Wag-6P	2634	3685	Note 1
A9	59D	2-dr Ctry Sed-6P	2678	3613	Note 1
A9	71F	4-dr Ctry Sed-6P	2745	3718	Note 1
A9	71E	4-dr Ctry Sed-9P	2829	3767	Note 1
A9	71G	4-dr Ctry Sq-9P	2958	3758	Note 1

NOTE 1: See Station Wagon V-8 Series listing. Production was counted by series and body style, with no breakout per engine.

STATION WAGON V-8 SERIES I.D. NUMBERS: Station Wagon V-8 models began with the same engine designations and used the same production numbers as the conventional cars. (See production note.)

STATION WAGON V-8 SERIES

Model Number	Body/Style Number	Body Type & Seating	Factory Price	Shipping Weight	Production Total
NA	59C	2-dr Ranch Wag-6P	2685	3691	45,558
NA	71H	4-dr Ranch Wag-6P	2752	3786	67,339
NA	59D	2-dr Ctry Sedan-6P	2796	3714	8,663
NA	71F	4-dr Ctry Sedan-6P	2863	3819	94,601
NA	71E	4-dr Ctry Sedan-9P	2947	3868	28,881
NA	71G	4-dr Ctry Sq-9P	3076	3859	24,336

PRODUCTION NOTE: Total series output was 269,378 units. Ford does not indicate the number of each model produced with sixes or V-8. Therefore, all production figures given above are total production of each body style with both engines.

1959 Ford, Thunderbird Tudor hardtop coupe, V-8 (AA)

THUNDERBIRD — V-8 SERIES - Thunderbird for 1959 saw only a few cosmetic changes to the basis 1958 body style. The honeycomb grille was replaced by a horizontal bar grille and the new look was duplicated in the small grilles behind the taillights. The four side stripes used on the 1958 model were removed and a chrome arrow took their place on the side. The instrument panel dial faces were white for 1959, instead of the black used in previous years.

THUNDERBIRD V-8 SERIES I.D. NUMBERS: Thunderbird models began with the engine designation, "H9", assembly plant code "Y" (Wixom), body type code and, finally, the units production number, beginning at 100001 and going up.

THUNDERBIRD V-8 SERIES

Model Number	Body/Style Number	Body Type & Seating	Factory Price	Shipping Weight	Production Total
H9	63A	Tudor H.T.	3696	3813	57,195
H9	76A	2-dr Conv-4P	3979	3903	10,261

1959 FORD ENGINES

Six-cylinder. Overhead valves. Cast iron block. Displacement: 223 cubic inches. Bore and stroke: 3.62 x 3.60 inches. Compression ratio: 8.6:1. Brake horsepower: 145 at 4000 R.P.M. Carburetion: Holley one-barrel. Four main bearings. Serial number code "A".

V-8: Overhead valves. Cast iron block. Displacement: 292 cubic inches. Bore & stroke: 3.75 x 3.30 inches. Compression ratio: 8.8:1. Brake horsepower: 200 at 4400 R.P.M. Carburetion: Holley two-barrel. Five main bearings. Serial number code "C".

Thunderbird 332 Special V-8: Overhead valves. Cast iron block. Displacement: 332 cubic inches. Bore and stroke: 4.00 x 3.30 inches. Compression ratio: 8.9:1. Brake horsepower: 225 at 4400 R.P.M. Carburetion: Holley two-barrel. Five main bearings. Serial number code "B".

Thunderbird 352 Special V-8: Overhead valves. Cast iron block. Displacement: 352 cubic inches. Bore and stroke: 4.00 x 3.50 inches. Compression ratio: 9.6:1. Brake horsepower: 300 at 4600 R.P.M. Carburetion: Holley four-barrel. Five main bearings. Serial number code "H".

Thunderbird 430 Special V-8: (Available only in Thunderbird and with Cruise-O-Matic transmission only) Overhead valves. Cast iron block. Displacement: 430 cubic inches. Bore and stroke: 4.30 x 4.70 inches. Compression ratio: 10.0:1. Brake horsepower: 350 at 4400 R.P.M. Carburetion: Holly four-barrel.

POWERTRAIN OPTIONS: Three-speed manual transmission was standard. It featured a semi-centrifugal type clutch; three-speed helical gears and synchronizers for second and third gears. Three-speed with automatic overdrive was optional. Specifications were the same as above with automatic overdrive function cutting in at 27 M.P.H., cutting out at 21 M.P.H. Approximate drive ratio: 0.70:1. Manual control below instrument panel. Ford-O-Matic transmission was also optional. This was a torque converter transmission with automatic planetary gear train; single-stage, three-element hydraulic torque converter; hydro-mechanical controls with no electric or vacuum connections and power flor through fluid member at all times. Six-cylinder rear axle gear ratios: (Ford-O-Matic) 3.56:1; (manual transmission) 3.56:1; (optional with automatic overdrive) 3.56:1. V-8 rear axle gear ratios: (Ford-O-Matic with 292 V-8) 3.10:1; (Ford-O-Matic with 332/352 V-8) 2.91:1; (Cruise-O-Matic with 292 V-8) 3.10:1; (Cruise-O-Matic with 332 V-8) 2.91:1; (Cruise-O-Matic with 352 V-8) 2.69:1; (manual transmission) 3.56:1. Equa-Lock rear axle gear ratios: 3.70:1 or 3.10:1.

CHASSIS FEATURES: Wheelbase: (all Fords) 118 inches; (Thunderbird) 113 inches. Overall length: (Skyliner) 208.1 inches; (all other models) 208 inches. Overall width: (Ford) 76.6 inches; (Thunderbird) 77 inches. Tires: (Thunderbirds, Skyliners, nine-passenger station wagons and Sunliners with automatic transmission) 8.00 x 14 four-ply tubeless; (all other models) 7.50 x 14 four-ply tubeless.

FORD CONVENIENCE OPTIONS: Ford-O-Matic Drive ($190). Cruise-O-Matic ($231). Automatic overdrive ($108). Power brakes ($43). Power steering ($75). Front and rear power window lifts ($102). Four-Way power seat ($64). Radio and pushbutton antenna ($59). Signal seeking radio and antenna ($83). Fresh Air heater and defroster ($75). Recirculating heater and defroster ($48). White sidewall tires, four-ply, 7.50 x 14 ($33); 8.00 x 14 ($50). Wheel covers as option ($17). Styleton two-tone paint ($26). Tinted glass ($26). Backup lights ($10). Custom 300 and Ranch Wagon DeLuxe ornamentation package ($32). Electric clock ($15). Windshield washer ($14). Two-speed windshield wipers ($7). Lifeguard safety package including padded instrument panel and sun visor ($19); plus pair front seat safety belts ($8). Polar Aire Conditioner with tinted glass ($271). Select Aire Conditioner with tinted glass ($404). Heavy-duty 70-amp battery ($8). Equa-Lock differential ($39). Four-way manual seat ($17). Fairlane side molding ($11). Fairlane 500 rocker panel molding. Thunderbird special 225 horsepower 332 cubic inch V-8 ($141 over base Six). Thunderbird Special 300 horsepower 352 cubic inch V-8 ($167 over base Six). Standard 292 cubic inch two-barrel V-8, all except Skyliner ($118). Other standard dealer-installed accessories such as floor mats, seat covers, fender skirts, etc.

THUNDERBIRD CONVENIENCE OPTIONS: Dual-Range Cruise-O-Matic transmission ($242). Overdrive ($145). Powerbrakes ($43). Power steering ($75). Four-way power driver's seat ($86). Front and rear power windows ($102). Heavy-duty 70-amp battery ($8). Fresh Air heater/defroster ($83). Pushbutton radio and antenna ($105). Select Air Conditioner ($446). Front seat belts ($23). Backup lights ($110). Tinted glass ($38). Wondershield washer ($14). Outside rear view mirror ($5). Conventional tu-tone paint ($26). Full wheel covers ($17). Rear fender shields ($27). Five 8.00 x 14 four-ply Rayon white sidewall tubeless tires ($36 exchange). Undercoating ($13). Thunderbird Special 350 horsepower V-8 ($177); leather interior ($106) and other standard dealer-installed accessories.

Historical footnotes: Dealer introduction for the 1959 Ford line was held October 17, 1958. Thunderbirds were introduced to the public ten days later. Model year production of Fords and Thunderbird was 1,462,140 units, while calendar year sales peaked at 1,528,592 cars. Special model nomenclature was similar to previous years. In March, 1958, Ford reported it had reduced the cost of making an automobile by $94 per unit between 1954 and 1958. On a model year basis, 78.1 percent of all 1959 Fords had V-8 power and 71.7 percent featured automatic transmission.

1960 FORD

1960 FORDS — OVERVIEW — Fords were totally redesigned from the ground up for 1960. They shared nothing with the previous models except engines and drivelines. While 1960 styling was considered controversial by many, it remains one of the smoothest designs ever to come from the Dearborn drawing boards. The new models were longer, lower and wider than their predecessors and were very restrained, especially when compared to some of their contemporaries. All 1960 Fords featured a single chrome strip from the top of the front bumper, sweeping up to the top of the front fender, then back, horizontally along the belt line, to the back of the car where it turned inward and capped the small horizontal fin. Large semi-circular taillights were housed in an aluminum escutcheon panel below the fins and directly above a large chrome bumper. At the front end, a large, recessed mesh grille housed the dual headlights. The Fairlane series contained the word Ford spaced along the recessed section of the full-width hood and used four cast stripes along the rear quarter panel for trim. The Fairlane script was on the sides of the front fenders. The Galaxie series used a Ford crest, in script, on the deck lid and on the front fenders. A single chrome strip began near the center of the front door and continued back to the taillights on the side, with a ribbed, aluminum stone shield behind the rear wheel opening. This season also saw the introduction of the Falcon. Ford's entrant into the compact car race was a pleasingly styled, uncomplicated little car, being available in two-door and four-door sedans and station wagons. The styling left little doubt that they were Ford products, but was remarkably simple and attractive.

NUMBERING SYSTEM NOTE: Ford changed it's serial number code once again in 1960 and the serial number code can be broken down as follows: First symbol: indicates year 0 - 1960, 1 - 1961, etc; Second symbol: assembly plant (See production note). Third and fourth symbols: body type. Fifth symbol: engine choice (See engine section). The last six digits are the unit's production number, beginning at 100001 and going up, at each of the assembly plants.

PRODUCTION NOTE: The New assembly plant codes can be broken down as follows: A - Atlanta; C - Chester; D - Dallas; E - Mahwah; F - Dearborn; P - Twin Cities; G - Chicago; L - Lorain; J - Los Angeles; K - Kansas City; N - Norfold; Z - St. Louis; R - San Jose; S - Pilot Plant; T - Metuchen; U - Louisville and Y - Lincoln (Wixom).

1960 Ford, Fairlane 500 4-dr sedan, 6-cyl

FAIRLANE SERIES — (ALL ENGINES) — The Fairlane series was the base trim level for 1960 and included chrome moldings around windshield and rear windows, two sun visors, arm rests on all doors and no extra chrome side trim.

FAIRLANE 6-CYL SERIES I.D. NUMBERS: Fairlane six-cylinder models began with the number 0, followed by the assembly plant code, body type code, engine designation and, finally, the unit's production number, according to the final assembly location. (See production note.)

FAIRLANE 6-CYL SERIES

Model Number	Body/Style Number	Body Type & Seating	Factory Price	Shipping Weight	Production Total
V	32	4-dr Sedan-6P	2311	3605	Note 1
V	31	2-dr Sedan-6P	2257	3531	Note 1
V	32	2-dr Bus Cpe-3P	2170	3504	Note 1

NOTE 1: See Fairlane V-8 Series listing. Production was counted by series and body style only, with no breakout per engine type.

FAIRLANE V-8 SERIES I.D. NUMBERS: Fairlane V-8 models began with the number '0', followed by assembly plant code, body type code, engine designation code and, finally, the unit's production number. (See production note.)

FAIRLANE V-8 SERIES

Model Number	Body/Style Number	Body Type & Seating	Factory Price	Shipping Weight	Production Total
NA	32	4-dr Sedan-6P	2424	3706	110,373
NA	31	2-dr Sedan-6P	2370	3632	93,561
NA	33	2-dr Bus Cpe-3P	2283	3605	1,733

PRODUCTION NOTE: Total series output was 205,667 units. This figure included 572 Custom 300 four-door sedans and 302 Custom 300 two-door sedans which were used in fleets (Taxis, Police cruisers, etc). Ford does not indicate the number of each model produced with sixes and V-8s. Therefore, all production figures given above are total production of each body style with both engines.

FAIRLANE 500 SERIES — (ALL ENGINES) — The Fairlane 500 was the intermediate trim level and included all the Fairlane trim, plus four chrome stripes on the rear fenders and the Fairlane crest on the hood.

FAIRLANE 500 6-CYL SERIES I.D. NUMBERS: Fairlane 500 six-cylinder models used the same serial number sequence as the Fairlane models. (See production note.)

FAIRLANE 500 6-CYL SERIES

Model Number	Body/Style Number	Body Type & Seating	Factory Price	Shipping Weight	Production Total
V	42	4-dr Town Sed-6P	2388	3609	Note 1
V	41	2-dr Club Sed-6P	2334	3535	Note 1

NOTE 1: See Fairlane 500 V-8 Series listing. Production was counted by series and body style only, with no breakout per engine type.

FAIRLANE 500 V-8 I.D. NUMBERS: Fairlane 500 V-8 models used the same serial number sequence as the Fairlane models. (See production note.)

FAIRLANE 500 V-8 SERIES

Model Number	Body/Style Number	Body Type & Seating	Factory Price	Shipping Weight	Production Total
	41	4-dr Town Sed-6P	2501	3710	153,234
	41	2-dr Club Sed-6P	2447	3636	91,041

PRODUCTION NOTE: Total series output was 224,275 units. Ford does not indicate the number of each model produced with sixes or V-8s. Therefore, all production figures given above are total production of each body style with both engines.

1960 Ford, Galaxie Starliner 2-dr hardtop coupe, V-8

GALAXIE AND GALAXIE SPECIAL SERIES — (ALL ENGINES) — The Galaxie and Galaxie Special series were the top trim level for 1960 and included chrome A pillar moldings, chrome window moldings, horizontal chrome strip on the side of the body, ribbed aluminum stone shields behind the rear wheels, Galaxie script on the front fenders and trunk lid and the Ford crest on the hood. The Galaxie Special series included the Starliner and Sunliner with all the high-level trim, except that the Galaxie script on the trunk lid was replaced with either the Sunliner or Starliner script.

GALAXIE AND GALAXIE SPECIAL 6-CYL SERIES I.D. NUMBERS: Galaxie and Galaxie special, six cylinder models used the same serial number sequence as the Fairlane series. (See production note).

GALAXIE AND GALAXIE SPECIAL 6-CYL SERIES

Model Number	Body/Style Number	Body Type & Seating	Factory Price	Shipping Weight	Production Total
V	52	4-dr Town Sed-6P	2603	3633	Note 1
V	51	2-dr Club Sed-6P	2549	3552	Note 1
V	54	4-dr Town Vic-6P	2788	3752	Note 1
V	53	2-dr Starliner-6P	2610	3566	Note 1
V	55	2-dr Sunliner-6P	2860	3750	Note 1

NOTE 1: See Galaxie and Galaxie Special V-8 Series listing. Production was counted by series and body style only, with no breakout per engine type.

GALAXIE AND GALAXIE SPECIAL SERIES I.D. NUMBERS: Galaxie and Galaxie special V-8 models used the same serial number sequence as the Fairlane series. (See production note).

GALAXIE AND GALAXIE SPECIAL V-8 SERIES

Model Number	Body/Style Number	Body Type & Seating	Factory Price	Shipping Weight	Production Total
NA	52	4-dr Town Sed-6P	2716	3734	103,784
NA	51	2-dr Club Sed-6P	2662	3653	31,866
NA	54	4-dr Town Sed-6P	2716	3734	104,784
NA	53	2-dr Starliner-6P	2723	3667	68,641
NA	55	2-dr Sunliner-6P	2973	3841	44,762

PRODUCTION NOTE: Total series output was 289,268 units. Ford does not indicate the number of each model produced with sixes or V-8s. Therefore, all production figures given above are total production of each body style with both engines.

STATION WAGON SERIES — (ALL ENGINES) — The Ranch Wagon was the base trim level station wagon, Country Sedans were the intermediate level of equipment and Country Squires were the top trim level. The level of equipment paralleled Fairlane, Fairlane 500 and Galaxie models of conventional cars.

STATION WAGON 6-CYL SERIES I.D. NUMBERS: Station Wagon, six-cylinder models used the same serial number sequence as Fairlane and Galaxie models of conventional cars.

STATION WAGONS 6-CYL SERIES

Model Number	Body/Style Number	Body Type & Seating	Factory Price	Shipping Weight	Production Total
V	61	2-dr Ranch Wag-6P	2586	3830	Note 1
V	62	4-dr Ranch Wag-6P	2656	3947	Note 1
V	64	4-dr Ctry Sed-6P	2752	3961	Note 1
V	66	4-dr Ctry Sed-9P	2837	4007	Note 1
V	68	4-dr Ctry Sq-9P	2967	4021	Note 1

STATION WAGON 6-CYL SERIES I.D. NUMBERS: Station Wagons, V-8 models used the same serial number sequence as Fairlane and Galaxie models of conventional cars. (See production note.)

STATION WAGON V-8 SERIES

Model Number	Body/Style Number	Body Type & Seating	Factory Price	Shipping Weight	Production Total
NA	61	2-dr Ranch Wag-6P	2699	3931	27,136
NA	62	4-dr Ranch Wag-6P	2769	4048	43,872
NA	64	4-dr Ctry Sed-6P	2865	4062	59,302
NA	66	4-dr Ctry Sed-9P	2950	4108	19,277
NA	68	4-dr Ctry Sq-9P	3080	4122	22,237

PRODUCTION NOTE: Total series output was 171,824 units. Ford does not indicate the number of each model produced with sixes or V-8s. Therefore, all production figures given above are total production of each body style with both engines.

FALCON 6-CYL SERIES — The Falcon was Ford's contribution to the compact car field. While being nearly three feet shorter overall than the full-size Fords, the Falcon offered an interior spacious enough for occupants more than six-feet tall. The compact station wagon offered more than enough cargo space for the majority of buyers. Falcon styling was very simple and utlra-conservative. The body was slab-sided, with just a slightly recessed feature line. Two single headlights were mounted inside the grille opening and the grille itself was an aluminum stamping consisting of horizontal and vertical bars. The name Ford appeared on the hood, in front of the power bulge type simulated scoop. At the rear, the word Falcon, in block letters, appeared between the two round taillights. Power was supplied by a 144 cubic inch six-cylinder engine. Transmission choices included the standard three-speed synchromesh manual transmission or optional two-speed Fordomatic automatic transmission.

1960 Ford, Falcon DeLuxe 2-dr station wagon, 6-cyl

FALCON 6-CYL SERIES I.D. NUMBERS: Falcon models used the same serial number sequence as the full-size Fords. (See production note), except the engine code was "S".

FALCON 6-CYL SERIES

Model Number	Body/Style Number	Body Type & Seating	Factory Price	Shipping Weight	Production Total
S	58A	4-dr Sedan-6P	1974	2317	167,896
S	64A	2-dr Sedan-6P	1912	2282	193,470
S	71A	4-dr Sta Wag-6P	2287	2575	46,758
S	59A	2-dr Sta Wag-6P	2225	2540	27,552

PRODUCTION NOTE: Total series output was 435,676 units.

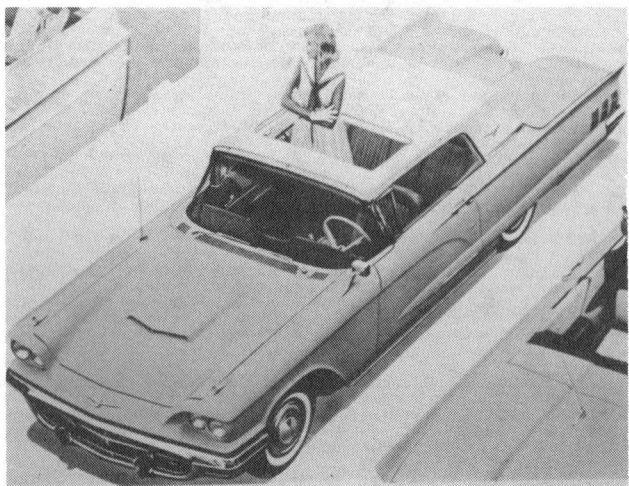

1960 Ford Thunderbird Tudor hardtop coupe with sun roof otpion, V-8

THUNDERBIRD V-8 SERIES: The 1960 Thunderbird used the same body as the previous two years, with only trim updating. This was the last of the 'Square Birds', with the highly sculptured fender and body lines. The grille was the same pattern of small squares used in 1957 and was located behind a large horizontal chrome bar with three vertical dividers. The grille pattern was duplicated behind the taillights. Three taillights were used per side, instead of two, as in previous years. The Thunderbird script appeared on the door. Script was unique to 1960. Script in other years was sometimes shared ('63-'64). The 430 V-8 was again an option available only with automatic transmission. The most significant change for 1960 was the addition of a manually-operated sunroof and 2,536 cars were produced with this option.

THUNDERBIRD V-8 SERIES I.D. NUMBERS: Thunderbird models began with the number '0' assembly plant code 'Y' (Wixom), body type code, engine type code 'Y' or 'J' and, finally, the unit's production number beginning at 100001 and going up.

THUNDERBIRD V-8 SERIES

Model Number	Body/Style Number	Body Type & Seating	Factory Price	Shipping Weight	Production Total
Y/J	71	2-dr H.T. Cpe-4P	3755	3799	80,938
Y/J	73	2-dr Conv-4P	4222	3897	11,860

1960 FORD ENGINES

Six-cylinder: Overhead valves. Cast iron block. Displacement: 144 cubic inches. Bore and stroke: 3.50 x 2.50 inches. Compression ratio: 8.7:1. Brake horsepower: 85 at 4200 R.P.M. Carburetion: Holley single barrel. Four main bearings. Serial number code 'S'.

Ford six-cylinder: Overhead valves. Cast iron block. Displacement: 223 cubic inches. Bore and stroke: 3.62 x 3.60 inches. Compression ratio: 8.4:1. Brake horsepower: 145 at 4000 R.P.M. Carburetion: Holley single barrel. Four main bearings. Serial number code 'V'.

V-8: Overhead valves. Cast iron block. Displacement: 292 cubic inches. Bore and stroke: 3.75 x 3.30 inches. Compression ratio: 8.8:1. Brake horsepower: 185 at 4200 R.P.M. Carburetion: Holley two-barrel. Five main bearings. Serial number code 'W'.

Interceptor V-8: Overhead valves. Cast iron block. Displacement: 352 cubic inches. Bore and stroke: 4.00 x 3.50 inches. Compression ratio: 8.9:1. Brake horsepower: 235 at 4400 R.P.M. Carburetion: Holley two-barrel. Five main bearings. Serial number code 'X'.

Interceptor Special V-8: Overhead valves. Cast iron block. Displacement: 352 cubic inches. Bore and stroke: 4.00 x 3.50 inches. Compression ratio: 9.6:1. Brake horsepower: 300 at 4600 R.P.M. Carburetion: Holley four-barrel. Five main bearings. Serial number code 'Y'.

Interceptor Special V-8: Overhead valves. Cast iron block. Displacement: 352 cubic inches. Bore and stroke: 4.00 x 3.50 inches. Compression ratio: 10.6:1. Brake horsepower: 360 at 6000 R.P.M. Carburetion: Holley four-barrel. Five main bearings. Serial number code 'R'.

Thunderbird Special V-8: Overhead valves. Cast iron block. Displacement: 430 cubic inches. Bore and stroke: 4.30 x 3.50 inches. Compression ratio: 10.2:1. Brake horsepower: 350 at 4400 R.P.M. Carburetion: Holley four-barrel. Five main bearings. Serial number code 'J'.

POWERTRAIN OPTIONS: Engine choices are detailed above. Transmission selections were the same available in 1959. Prices and power teams are indicated in optional equipment listing below. Ford axle ratios were the same provided in 1959.

CHASSIS FEATURES: Wheelbase: (All Fords and Thunderbirds) 119 inches; (Falcons) 109.5 inches. Overall length: (All Fords) 213.7 inches; (Thunderbirds) 205.32 inches; (Falcon passenger cars) 181.2 inches; (Falcon station wagons) 189 inches. Overall width: (Fords) 81.5 inches; (Thunderbirds) 77 inches; (Falcons) 70 inches. Overall height, sedan: (Fords) 55 inches; (Thunderbirds) 52.5 inches; (Falcons) 54.5 inches. Tires: (Ford passenger cars-closed body) 7.50 x 14; (Ford convertibles and station wagons and Thunderbird) 8.00 x 14; (Falcon passenger cars) 6.00 x 13; (Falcon station wagon) 6.50 x 13.

FORD CONVENIENCE OPTIONS: Standard 185 horsepower V-8 engine ($113.00). Two-barrel 235 horsepower V-8 ($147.80). Four-barrel 300 horsepower V-8 ($177.40). Polar air-conditioning including Tinted Glass and V-8 ($271). Select-Air air-conditioning including Tinted Glass and V-8 ($404). Backup lights ($11). Heavy-duty 70-amp battery ($8). Equa-Lock differential ($39). Electric Clock ($15). Fresh Air heater/defroster ($75). Recirculating heater/defroster ($47). Four-way manual seat ($17). Rocker, panel molding($14). Padded dash and visors ($25). Tutone paint ($19). Power brakes ($43). Power seat ($64). Power steering ($77). Front and rear power windows ($102). Pushbutton radio and antenna ($59). Front seat belts ($21). Tinted glass ($43). Cruise-O-Matic ($211). Ford-O-Matic with 6-cylinder ($180). Ford-O-Matic with V-8 ($190). Overdrive ($108). Wheel covers ($17). Windshield washer 9$14). Two-speed windshield wipers ($10). Tires — Ford offered numerous tire options such as white sidewall and oversized models.

FALCON CONVENIENCE OPTIONS: Heavy-duty battery ($8). DeLuxe trim package ($66). Fresh Air heater/defroster ($68). Two tone paint ($17). Manual radio and antenna ($54). Safety equipment: padded dash and visors ($19); front seat safety belts ($21). Whitewall tires ($29). Automatic transmission ($159). Wheel covers ($16). Windshield washer ($13). Electric windshield wiper ($10).

THUNDERBIRD CONVENIENCE OPTIONS: Cruise-O-Matic ($242). Overdrive ($145). Radio and antenna ($113). Fresh Air heater ($83). Air conditioner ($466). Tinted glass ($38). White sidewall tires, rayon, size 8.00 x 14 ($36). White sidewall tires, nylon, size 8.00 x 14 ($64). Engine, V-8, 350 horsepower ($177). Power steering ($75). Power windows ($102). Power brakes ($43). Four-Way power driver's seat ($92). Outside, left or right mirror ($5). Backup lights ($10). Windshield washers ($14). Rear fender shield ($27). Front seat belts ($23). Leather interior ($106). Heavy-duty 70-amp battery, standard on convertible, on other models: ($8). Two-Tone Paint ($26). Underseal ($14). Sliding roof for hardtop ($212).

Historical footnotes: All three lines of 1960 Fords were introduced to the public on October 8, 1959. Falcon station wagons were added to the new compact series in March, 1960. Although Ford did not provide production breakouts by engine type, trade publications recorded that 67.5 percent of all Fords (excluding Thunderbirds and Falcons) had V-8 engines installed. All Falcons were Sixes and all Thunderbirds were V-8 powered. Automatic transmissions were installed in 67.1 percent of all Fords, 44.5 percent of all Falcons and 97.9 percent of all Thunderbirds built during the model run. Ford's share of the overall automobile market dropped to 22.55 percent this year, compared to 27.33 percent in 1959. Model year production peaked at 911,034 Fords, 435,676 Falcons and 92,843 Thunderbirds. Model year series production was as follows: (Custom 300) 900; (Fairlane) 204,700; (Fairlane 500) 244,300; (Galaxie) 289,200; (station wagon) 171,800; (Thunderbird) 92,800. Just 297,400 six-cylinder Fords were produced for the model year.

1961 FORD

1961 FORDS — OVERVIEW — 1961 saw the third major restyling of the full-sized Ford line in as many years. From the beltline down, the 1961 Fords were completely new. The upper body structure was retained from the 1960 lineup. A full-width concave grille with a horizontal dividing bar highlighted front end styling. The Ford name, in block letters, replaced the crest used in previous years on Fairlane models and the series designation appeared on the front fenders, behind the headlights. The horizontal, full-length fin, used in 1960, was replaced with a smaller, canted fin, nearly identical in size and shape to the fin used on 1957-1958 Custom series cars. Large, round taillights were used once again and a horizontal chrome strip, very similar to one used on 1960 models, was used once again. It was complemented by a ribbed, aluminum stone guard on the Galaxie series. 1961 saw the beginning of the great horsepower race of the 1960s and Ford cracked the magic 400 barrier with a new engine; the 401 horsepower, 390 cubic inch V-8. The Falcon continued virtually unchanged from 1960, with only an updated convex grille in place of the concave unit used the previous year. A 170 cubic inch, six-cylinder engine became optional throughout the line. The biggest styling changes for 1961 took place in the Thunderbird series. Replacing the 1958-1960 Square Bird, was a much longer, more rounded Thunderbird. A massive front bumper surrounded the grille, which was stamped aluminum and carried a horizontal grid pattern. A single chrome strip began at the top of the front bumpers, swept up and back and outlined the small, canted fins back to the taillights. Four cast stripes were stacked on the side, immediately in front of the taillights. A smooth deck lid replaced the heavily sculptured lid used during the previous three years. Two large, round taillights replaced the six lights used in 1960. Beginning in 1961, Cruise-O-Matic transmission, Power Steering and Power Brakes became standard equipment on all Thunderbirds.

1961 Ford, Fairlane Town Sedan 4-dr. sedan, 6-cyl

FAIRLANE SERIES — (ALL ENGINES) — The Fairlane series was the base trim level for 1961 and included chrome moldings around the windshield and rear window, two sun visors, a horn button instead of horn ring, arm rest on all doors and no extra side chrome.

FAIRLANE 6-CYL I.D. NUMBERS: Fairlane, six-cylinder models began with the number '1', followed by the assembly plant code, body type code, engine designation 'V' and, finally, the unit's production number according to the final assembly location. (See production note). Each plant began at 100001 and went up.

FAIRLANE 6-CYL SERIES

Model Number	Body/Style Number	Body Type & Seating	Factory Price	Shipping Weight	Production Total
V	32	4-dr Town Sedan-6P	2315	3585	Note 1
V	31	4-dr Club Sedan-6P	2261	3487	Note 1

NOTE 1: See Fairlane V-8 Series listing. Production was counted by series and body style only, with no breakouts per engine type.

FAIRLANE V-8 SERIES I.D. NUMBERS: Fairlane V-8 models began with the number '1', followed by assembly plant code, body type code, engine designation code and, finally, the unit's production number according to final assembly location. (See production note). Each plant began at 100001 and went up.

FAIRLANE V-8 SERIES

Model Number	Body/Style Number	Body Type & Seating	Factory Price	Shipping Weight	Production Total
NA	32	4-dr Town Sedan-6P	2431	3683	66,924
NA	31	2-dr Club Sedan-6P	2377	2685	97,208

PRODUCTION NOTE: Total series output was 164,132 units. This figure includes 303 Custom 300 four-door sedans and 49 Custom 300 two-door sedans which were used in fleet service (Taxis, Police cruisers, etc.). Ford does not indicate the number of each model produced with sixes or V-8s. Therefore, all production figures given above are total production of each body style with both engines.

FAIRLANE 500 SERIES — (ALL ENGINES) — The Fairlane 500 was the intermediate trim level and included all the Fairlane trim plus a chrome horn ring and a single horizontal chrome stip running from the back of the front wheel well to the rear bumper.

FAIRLANE 500 V-8 SERIES I.D. NUMBERS: Fairlane 500 V-8 models used the same serial number sequence as the Fairlane models. (See production note).

FAIRLANE 500 6-CYL SERIES

Model Number	Body/Style Number	Body Type & Seating	Factory Price	Shipping Weight	Production Total
V	42	4-dr Town Sedan-6P	2430	3593	Note 1
V	41	2-dr Club Sedan-6P	2376	3502	Note 1

NOTE 1: See Fairlane 500 V-8 Series listing. Production was counted by series and body style, with no breakouts per engine type.

FAIRLANE 500 6-CYL I.D. NUMBERS: Fairlane 500, six-cylinder models used the same serial number sequence as the Fairlane models. (See production notes).

FAIRLANE 500 V-8 SERIES

Model Number	Body/Style Number	Body Type & Seating	Factory Price	Shipping Weight	Production Total
NA	42	4-dr Town Sedan-6P	2546	3691	98,917
NA	41	4-dr Club Sedan-6P	2492	3600	42,468

PRODUCTION NOTE: Total series output was 141,385 units. Ford does not indicate the number of each model produced with sixes or V-8s. Therefore, all production figures given above are total production of each body style with both engines.

1961 Ford, Galaxie Sunliner 2-dr convertible, 6-cyl

GALAXIE SERIES — (ALL ENGINES) — The Galaxie series was the top trim level for 1961 and included chrome 'A' pillar moldings; chrome window moldings; horizontal chrome strip on the side of the body; ribbed aluminum stone shield behind the rear wheel opening; a stamped aluminum escutcheon panel between the taillights (duplicating the pattern of the grille) and either Galaxie, Starliner, or Sunliner scripts on the trunk lid.

GALAXIE 6-CYL SERIES I.D. NUMBERS: Galaxie, six-cylinder models used the same serial number sequence as the Fairlane series. (See production note).

GALAXIE 6-CYL SERIES

Model Number	Body/Style Number	Body Type & Seating	Factory Price	Shipping Weight	Production Total
V	52	4-dr Town Sed-6P	2590	3570	Note 1
V	51	2-dr Club Sed-6P	2536	3488	Note 1
V	54	4-dr Town Vic-6P	2662	3588	Note 1
V	57	2-dr Club Vic-6P	2597	3545	Note 1
V	53	2-dr Starliner-6P	2597	3517	Note 1
V	55	2-dr Sunliner-6P	2847	3694	Note 1

NOTE: See Galaxie V-8 Series listing. Production was counted by series and body style with no breakouts per engine type.

GALAXIE V-8 SERIES I.D. NUMBERS: Galaxie, V-8 models used the same serial number sequence as the Fairlane series. (See production note).

GALAXIE V-8 SERIES

Model Number	Body/Style Number	Body Type & Seating	Factory Price	Shipping Weight	Production Total
NA	52	4-dr Town Sed-6P	2706	3668	141,823
NA	51	2-dr Club Sed-6P	2652	3586	27,780
NA	54	4-dr Town Vic-6P	2778	3686	30,342
NA	57	2-dr Club Vic-6P	2713	3643	75,437
NA	53	2-dr Starliner-6P	2713	3615	29,669
NA	55	2-dr Sunliner-6P	2963	3792	44,614

PRODUCTION NOTE: Total series output was 349,665 units. Ford does not indicate the number of each model produced with sixes or V-8s. Therefore, all production figures are total production of each body style with each engine.

STATION WAGON SERIES — (ALL ENGINES) — The Ranch Wagon was the base trim level Station Wagon, Country Sedans were the intermediate level and Country Squire were the top time level. The level of equipment paralleled Fairlane, Fairlane 500 and Galaxie models of passenger cars.

STATION WAGON 6-CYL I.D. NUMBERS: Station Wagon six-cylinder models used the same serial number sequence as Galaxie and Fairlane series conventional cars. (See production note).

STATION WAGON 6-CYL SERIES

Model Number	Body/Style Number	Body Type & Seating	Factory Price	Shipping Weight	Production Total
V	61	2-dr Ranch Wag-6P	2586	3816	Note 1
V	62	4-dr Ranch Wag-6P	2656	3911	Note 1
V	64	4-dr Ctry Sed-6P	2752	3934	Note 1
V	66	4-dr Ctry Sed-9P	2856	3962	Note 1
V	67	4-dr Ctry Squire	2941	3930	Note 1
V	68	4-dr Ctry Squire	3011	3966	Note 1

NOTE 1: See Station Wagon V-8 Series listing. Production was counted by series and body style, with no breakouts per engine type.

STATION WAGON V-8 SERIES I.D. NUMBERS: Station Wagon, V-8 models used the same serial number sequence as Fairlane and Galaxie models of passenger cars. (See production note).

STATION WAGON V-8 SERIES

Model Number	Body/Style Number	Body Type & Seating	Factory Price	Shipping Weight	Production Total
NA	61	2-dr Ranch Wag-6P	2702	3914	12,042
NA	62	4-dr Ranch Wag-6P	2772	4009	30,292
NA	64	4-dr Ctry Sed-6P	2868	4032	46,311
NA	66	4-dr Ctry Sed-9P	2972	4060	16,356
NA	67	4-dr Ctry Squire	3057	4036	16,961
NA	68	4-dr Ctry Squire	3127	4064	14,657

PRODUCTION NOTE: Total series output was 136,619 units. Ford does not indicate the number of each model produced with sixes or V-8s. Therefore, all production figures given above are total production of each body style with both engines.

FALCON 6-CYL SERIES — The Falcon contined unchanged from 1961, with the exception of a new convex grille. A new 170 cubic inch six-cylinder was added to the lineup and the Futura two-door sedan was added to give a sporty flair to the compact car line. The Futura was the same body shell, equipped with a bucket seat interior and a center console.

OVER 550,000

1961 Ford, Falcon DeLuxe 4-dr, 6-cyl

FALCON I.D. NUMBERS: Falcon model used the same serial number sequence as the full-size Fords, except the engine code was either 'S' or 'U'.

FALCON 6-CYL SERIES

Model Number	Body/Style Number	Body Type & Seating	Factory Price	Shipping Weight	Production Total
S/U	12	4-dr Sedan-6P	1974	2289	159,761
S/U	11	2-dr Sedan-6P	1912	2254	149,982
S/U	17	2-dr Futura Sed-5P	2160	2322	44,470
S/U	22	4-dr Sta Wag-6P	2268	2558	87,933
S/U	21	2-dr Sta Wag-6P	2225	2525	32,045

PRODUCTION NOTE: Total series output was 474,191 units.

1961 Ford, Thunderbird 2-dr convertible, V-8

THUNDERBIRD V-8 SERIES — The 1961 Thunderbirds were totally new cars. They were longer, lower, wider and heavier than the previous years. Cruise-O-Matic automatic transmission, power steering, power brakes and the new 390 cubic inch V-8 engine were standard equipment on all Thunderbirds for 1961.

THUNDERBIRD V-8 SERIES I.D. NUMBERS: Thunderbird models began with the number '1', assembly plant code 'Y' (Wixom), body type code, engine type code 'Z' and, finally, the unit's production number beginning at 100001 and going up.

THUNDERBIRD V-8 SERIES

Model Number	Body/Style Number	Body Type & Seating	Factory Price	Shipping Weight	Production Total
Z	71	2-dr H.T. Cpe-4P	4170	3958	62,535
Z	73	2-dr Conv-4P	4637	4130	10,516

1961 FORD ENGINES

Falcon six-cylinder: Overhead valves. Cast iron block. Displacement: 144 cubic inches. Bore and stroke: 3.50 x 2.50 inches. Compression ratio: 8.7:1. Brake horsepower: 85 at 4200 R.P.M. Carburetion: Holley one-barrel. Four main bearings. Serial numbers code 'S'.

Falcon 170 six-cylinder: Overhead valves. Cast iron block. Displacement: 170 cubic inches. Bore and stroke: 3.50 x 2.94 inches. Compression ratio: 8.7:1. Brake horsepower: 101 at 4400 R.P.M. Carburetion: Holley one-barrel. Four main bearings. Serial number code 'U'.

Ford six-cylinder: Overhead valves. Cast iron block. Displacement: 223 cubic inches. Bore and stroke: 3.62 x 3.60 inches. Compression ratio: 8.4:1. Brake horsepower: 135 at 4000 R.P.M. Carburetion: Holley one-barrel. Four main bearings. Serial number code 'V'.

V-8: Overhead valves. Cast iron block. Displacement: 292 cubic inches. Bore and stroke: 3.75 x 3.30 inches. Compression ratio: 8.8:1. Brake horsepower: 175 at 4200 R.P.M. Carburetion: Holley two-barrel. Five main bearings. Serial number code 'W'.

Interceptor V-8: Overhead valves. Cast iron block. Displacement: 352 cubic inches. Bore and stroke: 4.00 x 3.50 inches. Compression ratio: 8.9:1. Brake horsepower: 220 at 4400 R.P.M. Carburetion: Holley two-barrel. Five main bearings. Serial number code 'X'.

Thunderbird V-8: Overhead valves. Cast iron block. Displacement: 390 cubic inches. Bore and stroke: 4.05 x 3.78 inches. Compression ratio: 9.6:1. Brake horsepower: 300 at 4600 R.P.M. Carburetion: Holley four-barrel. Five main bearings. Serial number code 'Z'.

Thunderbird Special V-8: Overhead valves. Cast iron block. Displacement: 390 cubic inches. Bore and stroke: 4.05 x 3.78 inches. Compression ratio: 10.6:1. Brake horsepower: 375 at 6000 R.P.M. Carburetion: Holley four-barrel. Five main bearings. Serial number code 'R'.

Thunderbird Special (6V) V-8: Overhead valves. Cast iron block. Displacement: 390 cubic inches. Bore and stroke: 4.05 x 3.78 inches. Compression ratio: 10.6:1. Brake horsepower: 401 at 6000 R.P.M. Carburetion: three Holley two-barrels. Five main bearings. Serial number code 'R'.

CHASSIS FEATURES: Wheelbase: (Thunderbird) 113 inches; (Falcon) 109.5 inches; (all other models) 119 inches. Overall length: (Thunderbird) 205 inches; (Falcon station wagons) 189 inches; (other Falcons) 181.2 inches; (all other models) 209.9 inches. Front tread: (Thunderbird and Ford) 61 inches; (Falcon) 55 inches. Rear tread: (Thunderbird and Ford) 60 inches; (Falcon) 54.5 inches. Tires: (Thunderbird and Ford station wagons) 8.00 x 14; (Fords) 7.50 x 14; (Falcon station wagon) 6.50 x 13; (other Falcons) 6.00 x 13.

FALCON CONVENIENCE OPTIONS: Backup lights ($11). Heavy-duty battery ($8). Crankcase vent system ($6). DeLuxe trim package ($78). Engine, 170 cubic inches; 101 horsepower ($37). Fresh Air heater/defroster ($73). Station Wagon luggage rack ($35). Two tone paint ($19). Manual radio and antenna ($54). Safety Equipment including padded dash and visors ($22); plus front seat belts ($21). Electric tailgate windows for station wagons ($30). Automatic transmission ($163). Wheel covers ($16). Windshield washer ($14). Electric windshield wiper ($10). Plus numerous oversize and white sidewall tire options.

THUNDERBIRD CONVENIENCE OPTIONS: Radio and antenna ($113). Fresh Air heater ($83). Select Aire air-conditioner ($463). Tinted glass ($43). White sidewall tires, rayon, 8.00 x 14 ($42); nylon ($70). Power windows ($106). Four-way driver's power seat ($92). Outside, left or righthand mirror ($5). Windshield washers ($14). Rear fender shields ($27). Front seat belts ($23). Leather interior ($106). Heavy-duty, 70-amp battery ($8). Two-tone paint ($26). Equa-Lock differential ($39). Movable steering control ($25).
NOTE: Crankcase ventilation system standard on California cars only.

FORD CONVENIENCE OPTIONS: Standard 175 horsepower V-8 Engine ($116). Two-barrel, 220 horsepower V-8 ($148). Four-barrel, 300 horsepower V-8 ($197). Polar air-conditioner, including tinted glass ($271). Select air-conditioner, including tinted glass ($436). Backup lights ($11). Heavy-duty, 70-amp battery ($8). Crankcase vent system ($6). Equa-Lock differential ($39). Electric clock ($15). Magic Aire heater/defroster ($75). Recirculating heater/defroster ($47). Four-way manual seat ($17). Rocker panel molding ($16). Padded dash and visors ($24). Tutone paint ($22). Power brakes ($43). Power seat ($64). Power steering ($82). Power tailgate window ($32). Front and rear power windows ($102). Pushbutton radio and antenna ($59). Front seat belts ($21). Tinted glass ($43). Cruise-O-Matic transmission ($212). Ford-O-matic transmission with six-cylinder engine ($180); Ford-O-Matic transmission with eight-cylinder engine ($190); Overdrive transmission ($108). Wheel covers ($19). Windshield washer ($14). two-speed windshield wipers ($12). Plus numerous oversize and white sidewall tire options with price variations by style, engine and use of air conditioning.

Historical footnotes: Lee A. Iacocca was in his second season at the Ford helm this year. Calendar year output totaled 1,362,186 cars. Market penetration was up to 24 percent as model year production peaked at 163,600 Fairlanes; 141,500 Fairlane 500s; 349,700 Galaxies; 136,600 station wagons; 73,000 Thunderbirds; 129,700 standard Falcons; 224,500 DeLuxe Falcons and 135,100 Falcon station wagons. Dealer introduction dates were September 29 for Fords and Falcons, November 12 for Thunderbirds. The full-size line production totals included 201,700 six-cylinder cars, while all Falcons were Sixes and all Thunderbirds V-8s.

1962 FORD

1962 FORDS — OVERVIEW — In 1962, Ford continued it's policy of making major styling changes in least one line. The 1962 Galaxies and full size line were restyled and the end result is recognized as one of the cleaner designs to come from Dearborn. Except for one horizontal feature line at the beltline, the body was slabsided. The model designation was carried in script along the rear fender. Ford continued the tradition of large round taillights throughout the entire line, with the taillights on Galaxies being separated by a stamped aluminum escutcheon panel. The model designation was spelled out in block letters across the trunk lid. At the front end, a full-width grille carried a horizontal grid pattern and was capped on each end by the dual headlight. The Ford crest was centered at the front of the hood throughout the full-size line. The Falcon line continued unchanged from the previous year, except for the addition of an updated grille. The convex grille bars carried a vertical pattern. Also, a wood-grained version of the Falcon four-door station wagon was added to the DeLuxe series and was known as the Falcon Squire. A bucket seat 2-dr. sedan sport model was added to the line as the Futura. Like the Falcon line, the 1962 Thunderbirds received only minor cosmetic changes for the new year. The new 'Birds had a smooth hood no longer using the two ridges characteristic only of 1961 models. The 1962 taillights were also slightly different than the previous year, with a chrome ring around the center of the lens. The big news for 1962 was the introduction of the intermediate size Fairlanes. The new model was nearly 12 inches shorter than the full size Galaxies, yet was nearly eight inches longer than the compact Falcon. At the time of their introduction, the Fairlanes were compared to the 1949-1950 Fords in length and width. They were nearly identical, but were considerably lower. No one would ever guess the Fairlane was anything, but a Ford. They utilized the characteristic round taillights, 'high-canted' fenders and a grille which was nearly identical to the Galaxie line. This year saw a continuation of the great '60s, horsepower race and in to do combat with the GM and Chrysler offerings. Ford introduced the famous '406' V-8, producing 405 HP. The resizing of the Fairlane also saw the introduction of a completely new line of small V-8 engines. At 221 cubic inches, the new motor was the same displacement as the first 'flathead' V-8. It was of thin-wall casting design and was the first in a series of lightweight V-8s.

GALAXIE SERIES — (ALL ENGINES) — The Galaxie series was the base trim level for 1962 and included chrome moldings around the windshield and rear window, two sun visors, a chrome horn ring, arm rests on all doors and a single horizontal chrome strip at the belt line.

GALAXIE 6-CYL I.D. NUMBERS: Galaxie six-cylinder models began with the number '2', followed by the assembly plant code, body type code, engine designation 'V' and, finally, the unit's production number according to the final assembly location. (See production note). Each plant began at 100001 and went up.

GALAXIE 6-CYL SERIES

Model Number	Body/Style Number	Body Type & Seating	Factory Price	Shipping Weight	Production Total
V	52	4-dr Sedan-6P	2507	3583	Note 1
V	51	2-dr Sedan-6P	2453	3478	Note 1

NOTE 1: See Galaxie V-8 Series listing. Production was counted by series and body style only, with no breakouts per engine type.

GALAXIE V-8 I.D. NUMBERS: Galaxie V-8 models began with the number '2', followed by the assembly plant code, body type code, engine designation code and, finally, the unit's production number according to the final assembly location. (See production note). Each plant began at 100001 and went up.

GALAXIE V-8 SERIES

Model Number	Body/Style Number	Body Type & Seating	Factory Price	Shipping Weight	Production Total
NA	52	4-dr Sedan-6P	2616	3684	115,594
NA	51	2-dr Sedan-6P	2562	3589	54,930

PRODUCTION NOTE: Total series output was 170,524 units. Ford does not indicate the number of each model produced with sixes or V-8s. Therefore, all production figures given above are total production of each body style with both engines.

1962 Ford Galaxie 500 2-dr hardtop, V-8

GALAXIE 500 SERIES — (ALL ENGINES) — The Galaxie 500 Series was the top trim level for 1962 and included chrome 'A' pillar moldings, chrome window moldings, a color-keyed horizontal chrome strip at the beltline, chrome rocker panel moldings, quarter panel moldings and a chrome trim strip with a Ford crest at the base of the 'C' pillar, on the top.

GALAXIE 500 6-CYL I.D. NUMBERS: Galaxie 500 six-cylinder models used the same serial number sequence as the Galaxie series. (See production note).

GALAXIE 500 6-CYL SERIES

Model Number	Body/Style Number	Body Type & Seating	Factory Price	Shipping Weight	Production Total
V	62	4-dr Town Sed-6P	2667	3568	Note 1
V	61	2-dr Club Sed-6P	2613	3476	Note 1
V	64	4-dr Town Vic-6P	2739	3577	Note 1
V	63	2-dr Club Vic-6P	2674	3505	Note 1

NOTE 1: See Galaxie 500 V-8 Series listing. Production was counted by series and body style with no breakouts per engine type.

GALAXIE 500 V-8 SERIES I.D. NUMBERS: Galaxie 500 V-8 models used the same serial number sequence as the Galaxie series. (See production note).

GALAXIE 500 V-8 SERIES

Model Number	Body/Style Number	Body Type & Seating	Factory Price	Shipping Weight	Production Total
NA	62	4-dr Town Sed-6P	2776	3679	174,195
NA	61	2-dr Club Sed-6P	2722	3587	27,824
NA	64	4-dr Town Vic-6P	2848	3688	30,778
NA	63	2-dr Club Vic-6P	2783	3616	87,562
NA	65	2-dr Sunliner-6P	3033	3782	42,646

PRODUCTION NOTE: Total series output was 404,600 units. Ford does not indicate the number of each model produced with sixes or V-8s. Therefore, all production figures are total production of each body style with each engine.

GALAXIE 500XL SERIES — (V-8) — The Galaxie 500XL series was new for 1962, and was the sporty series of the Galaxie line. The "XLs" included all the trim of the Galaxie 500 models, but offered bucket seats and a floor mounted shift lever, as well as an engine-turned insert in the instrument panel, and on the side stripe.

GALAXIE 500XL I.D. NUMBERS: Galaxie 500XL models used the same serial number sequence as the Galaxie and Galaxie 500 series. (See production note).

GALAXIE 500XL SERIES V-8

Model Number	Body/Style Number	Body Type & Seating	Factory Price	Shipping Weight	Production Total
	NA	2-dr Club Vic-5P	3108	3625	28,412
	NA	2-dr Sunliner-5P	3358	3804	13,183

PRODUCTION NOTE: Total series output was 41,595 units.

STATION WAGON SERIES — (ALL ENGINES) — The Ranch Wagon was the base trim level Station Wagon, Country Sedans were the intermediate level and Country Squires were the top trim level. The level of equipment paralleled Galaxie, Galaxie 500 and Galaxie 500XL models of passenger cars.

STATION WAGON 6-CYL I.D. NUMBERS: Station Wagon six-cylinder models used the same serial number sequence as Galaxie series of passenger cars. (See production note).

STATION WAGON 6-CYL SERIES

Model Number	Body/Style Number	Body Type & Seating	Factory Price	Shipping Weight	Production Total
V	17	4-dr Ranch Wag-6P	2733	3905	Note 1
V	72	4-dr Ctry Sed-6P	2829	2829	Note 1
V	74	4-dr Ctry Sed-9P	2933	3946	Note 1
V	76	4-dr Ctry Sq-6P	3018	3942	Note 1
V	78	4-dr Ctry Sq-9P	3088	3959	Note 1

NOTE 1: See Station Wagon V-8 Series listing. Production was counted by series and body style, with no breakouts per engine type.

STATION WAGON V-8 SERIES I.D. NUMBERS: Station Wagon V-8 models used the same serial number sequence as Galaxie series of passenger cars. (See production note).

STATION WAGON V-8 SERIES

Model Number	Body/Style Number	Body Type & Seating	Factory Price	Shipping Weight	Production Total
NA	71	4-dr Ranch Wag-6P	2842	4016	33,674
NA	72	4-dr Ctry Sed-6P	2938	4039	47,635
NA	74	4-dr Ctry Sed-9P	3042	4057	16,562
NA	78	4-dr Ctry Sq-9P	3197	4057	15,666

PRODUCTION NOTE: Total series output was 129,651 units. Ford does not indicate the number of each model produced with sixes or V-8s. Therefore, all production figures given above are total production of each body style with both engines.

FAIRLANE SERIES — (ALL ENGINES) — The Fairlane was the new intermediate size line of Fords for 1962. With styling very similar to the 1961 full size Fords there was no doubt of the Fairlane's heritage. The Fairlane line included the base Fairlane models and the top Fairlane 500 models. The new models also introduced the famous 221 series small-block Ford V-8, with the new thin-wall casting technique, producing the lightest complete V-8 engine of the time.

FAIRLANE SERIES — (ALL ENGINES) — The Fairlane was the base trim level of the line and included chrome windshield and rear window moldings, a horn button instead of horn ring, arm rests on all doors, a single horizontal Fairlane sweep type strip (which followed the belt level feature line), the Ford crest on the hood and the word Ford, in block letters, on the trunk lid.

FAIRLANE SIX SERIES I.D. NUMBERS: Fairlane six-cylinder models began with the number '2', followed by the assembly plant code, body type code, engine designation 'U' and, finally, the unit's production number according to the final assembly location. (See production note). Each plant began at 100001 and went up.

FAIRLANE SIX SERIES

Model Number	Body/Style Number	Body Type & Seating	Factory Price	Shipping Weight	Production Total
U	32	4-dr Sedan-6P	2216	2791	Note 1
U	31	2-dr Sedan-6P	2154	2757	Note 1

NOTE 1: See Fairlane V-8 Series listing. Production was counted by series and body style only, with no breakouts per engine type.

FAIRLANE V-8 SERIES I.D. NUMBERS: Fairlane V-8 models began with the number '2', followed by the assembly plant code, body type code, engine designation code 'L' and, finally, the unit's production number according to final assembly location. (See production note). Each plant began at 100001 and went up.

FAIRLANE V-8 SERIES

Model Number	Body/Style Number	Body Type & Seating	Factory Price	Shipping Weight	Production Total
L	32	4-dr Sedan-6P	2319	2949	45,342
L	31	2-dr Sedan-6P	2257	2915	34,264

PRODUCTION NOTE: Total series output was 79,606 units. Ford does not indicate the number of each model produced with sixes or V-8s. Therefore, all production figures given above are total production of each body style.

1962 Ford Fairlane 500 2-dr Sports Coupe, V-8

FAIRLANE 500 SERIES — (ALL ENGINES) — The Fairlane 500 models were the top trim level of the line and included chrome window moldings, a chrome horn ring, arm rests on all doors, simulated chrome inserts on the door upholstery, a two-piece chrome Fairlane sweep with a ribbed aluminum insert and two sun visors. The Sport Coupe 2-dr. sedan included bucket seats and special identification was introduced mid-year.

FAIRLANE 500 SIX I.D. NUMBERS: Fairlane 500 six-cylinder models used the same serial numbers sequence as the Fairlane models. (See production note).

FAIRLANE 500 SIX SERIES

Model Number	Body/Style Number	Body Type & Seating	Factory Price	Shipping Weight	Production Total
U	42	4-dr Sedan-6P	2507	2808	Note 1
U	41	2-dr Sedan-6P	2304	2774	Note 1
U	47	2-dr Spt Cpe-5P	2504	2870	Note 1

NOTE 1: See Fairlane 500 V-8 Series listing. Production was counted by series and body style, with no breakouts per engine type.

FAIRLANE 500 V-8 SERIES I.D. NUMBERS: Fairlane 500 V-8 models used the same serial number sequence as the Fairlane models. (See production note).

FAIRLANE 500 V-8 SERIES

Model Number	Body/Style Number	Body Type & Seating	Factory Price	Shipping Weight	Production Total
L	42	4-dr Sedan-6P	2407	2966	129,258
L	41	2-dr Sedan-6P	2345	2932	68,624
L	47	2-dr Spt Cpe-5P	2607	3002	19,628

PRODUCTION NOTE: Total series output was 217,510 units. Ford does not indicate the number of each model produced with sixes or V-8s. Therefore, all production figures given above are total production of each body style.

1962 Ford, Falcon Squire 4-dr station wagon, 6-cyl

FALCON SERIES — 6-CYL — The Falcon continued unchanged from 1961, with the exception of a new convex grille with vertical bars and a new Galaxie style top configuration. There were two separate Falcon lines for 1962; the Standard and DeLuxe Series, rather than the DeLuxe trim package, which was optional on all 1960 and 1961 Falcons. Also new was the Falcon Squire station wagon.

STANDARD FALCON I.D. NUMBERS: The standard series Falcon used the same serial number sequence as the full-size Fords, except the engine code was either 'S' or 'U'. (See production note).

STANDARD SERIES FALCON

Model Number	Body/Style Number	Body Type & Seating	Factory Price	Shipping Weight	Production Total
S/U	12	4-dr Sedan-6P	2047	2299	Note 1
S/U	11	2-dr Sedan-6P	1985	2262	Note 1
S/U	22	4-dr Sta Wag-6P	2341	2595	Note 1
S/U	21	2-dr Sta Wag-6P	2298	2559	Note 1

NOTE 1: See DeLuxe Falcon listing. Production was counted by body style, with no breakouts per level of trim.

DELUXE FALCON I.D. NUMBERS: DeLuxe Falcon models, used the same serial number sequence as the full-size Fords, except the engine code was either 'S' or 'U'. (See production note).

DELUXE SERIES FALCON

Model Number	Body/Style Number	Body Type & Seating	Factory Price	Shipping Weight	Production Total
S/U	12	4-dr Sedan-6P	2133	2319	126,041
S/U	11	2-dr Sedan-6P	2071	2282	143,650
S/U	17	2-dr Futura Sedan-5P	2232	2347	17,011
S/U	22	4-dr Sta Wag-6P	2427	2621	66,819
S/U	21	2-dr Sta Wag-6P	2384	2584	Note 1
S/U	26	4-dr Squire Wag-6P	2603	2633	22,583

PRODUCTION NOTE: Total series output was 396,129 units. Ford does not indicate the total number of Standard models and DeLuxe models produced. Therefore, all production figures are total production of each body style with both level of trim.

1962 Ford Thunderbird 2-dr Sports Roadster, V-8 (AA)

THUNDERBIRD SERIES — (V-8) — Except for minor exterior trim changes, the 1962 Thunderbirds were identical to their 1961 counterparts. The new Landau hardtop featured a vinyl top as standard equipment. It was the first time such a top was offered on the Thunderbird line. Also new for 1962, was the Sports Roadster. In an attempt to bring back the sporty appearance of the old two-seat T-Birds, Ford offered the Thunderbird convertible with a fiberglass tonneau cover for the back seats. The cover included two streamlined headrests, which contributed to a very sleek looking car when the top was down. The 390 cubic inch "M" series engine was a new option for '62.

THUNDERBIRD I.D. NUMBERS: Thunderbird models began with the number '2', assembly plant code 'Y' (Wixom), body type code, engine type code 'Z' and, finally, the units production number beginning at 100001 and going up.

THUNDERBIRD SERIES

Model Number	Body/Style Number	Body Type & Seating	Factory Price	Shipping Weight	Production Total
Z	83	2-dr HT Cpe-6P	4321	4132	68,127
Z	83	2-dr Lan HT Cpe-4P	4398	4144	Note 1
Z	85	2-dr Conv-4P	4788	4370	9,844
Z	85	2-dr Spts Rds Conv	5439	4471	Note 1

NOTE 1: Total series output was 78,011 units. Ford does not indicate the number of Landau hardtops and Sports Roadsters produced, separate from the standard hardtops and convertibles. Therefore, all production figures are total production of each

NOTE 2: The Body/Style Number for the Sports Roadster was "85" for the first 558 units at which time it was changed to "89" for the balance of that model year production. The change to "89" took place with serial number 2Y 89 Z 127027. The last "85" Sports Roadster serial number was 2Y 85 Z 114640.

1962 FORD ENGINES

Falcon six-cylinder: Overhead valves. Cast iron block. Displacement: 144 cubic inches. Bore and stroke: 3.50 xZ 2.50 inches. Compression ratio: 8.7:1. Brake horsepower: 85 at 4200 R.P.M. Carburetion: Holley one-barrel. Seven main bearings. Serial number code 'S'.

Falcon 170 six-cylinder: Overhead valves. Cast iron block. Displacement: 170 cubic inches. Bore and stroke: 3.50 x 2.94 inches. Compression ratio: 8.7:1. Brake horsepower: 101 at 4400 R.P.M. Carburetor: Holley one-barrel. Seven main bearings. Serial number code 'U'.

Ford six-cylinder: Overhead valves. Cast iron block. Displacement: 223 cubic inches. Bore and stroke: 3.62 x 3.60 inches. Compression ratio: 8.4:1. Brake horsepower: 138 at 4200 R.P.M. Carburetion: Holley one-barrel. Four main bearings. Serial number code 'V'.

Fairlane V-8: Overhead valves. Cast iron block. Displacement: 221 cubic inches. Bore and stroke: 3.50 x 2.87 inches. Compression ratio: 8.7:1. Brake horsepower: 145 at 4400 R.P.M. Carburetion: Holley two-barrel. Five main bearings. Serial number code 'L'.

Ford V-8: Overhead valves. Cast iron block. Displacement: 292 cubic inches. Bore and stroke: 3.75 x 3.30 inches. Compression ratio: 8.8:1. Brake horsepower: 170 at 4200 R.P.M. Carburetion: Holley two-barrel. Five main bearings. Serial number code 'W'.

Interceptor V-8: Overhead valves. Cast iron block. Displacement: 352 cubic inches. Bore and stroke: 4.00 x 3.50 inches. Compression ratio: 8.9:1. Brake horsepower: 220 at 4300 R.P.M. Carburetion: Holley two-barrel. Five main bearings. Serial number code 'X'.

Interceptor 390 V-8: Overhead valves. Cast iron block. Displacement: 390 cubic inches. Bore and stroke: 4.05 x 3.78 inches. Compression ratio: 9.6:1. Brake horsepower: 300 at 4600 R.P.M. Carburetion: Holley four-barrel. Five main bearings. Serial number code 'Z'.

Thunderbird 390 V-8: Overhead valves. Cast iron block. Displacement: 390 cubic inches. Bore and stroke: 4.05 x 3.78 inches. Compression ratio: 10.5:1. Brake horsepower: 340 at 5000 R.P.M. Carburetion: Three Holley two-barrels. Five main bearings. Serial number code 'M'.

Thunderbird 406 V-8: Overhead valves. Cast iron block. Displacement: 406 cubic inches. Bore and stroke: 4.13 x 3.78 inches. Compression ratio: 11.4:1. Brake horsepower: 385 at 5800 R.P.M. Carburetion: Holley four barrel. Five main bearings. Serial number code 'B'.

Thunderbird Special 406 V-8: Overhead valves. Cast iron block. Displacement: 406 cubic inches. Bore and stroke: 4.13 x 3.78 inches. Compression ratio: 11.3:1. Brake horsepower: 405 at 4800 R.P.M. Carburetion: Three Holley two-barrels. Five main bearings. Serial number code 'G'.

CHASSIS FEATURES: Wheelbase: (Falcon) 109.5 inches; (Fairlane) 115.5 inches; (Thunderbird) 113 inches; (all others) 119 inches. Overall length: (Falcon station wagons) 189 inches; (other Falcons) 181.1 inches; (Fairlanes) 197.6 inches; (all Fords) 209.3 inches; (Thunderbird) 205 inches. Tires: (Fairlane Six and Falcon station wagons) 6.50 x 13; (Falcons) 6.00 x 13; (Fairlane V-8) 7.00 x 14; (Fairlane '260' V-8) 7.00 x 13; (Ford station wagons) 8.00 x 14; (other Fords) 7.50 x 14.

FALCON CONVENIENCE OPTIONS: Backup lights ($11). Heavy-duty battery ($8). Squire bucket seats and console ($120). Crankcase ventilation system ($6). DeLuxe trim package ($87). Engine, 170'' 101 horsepower ($38). Tinted glass ($27). Windshield tinted glass ($13). Station wagons luggage rack ($39). Two tone paint ($19). Pushbutton radio and antenna ($59). **Safety Equipment including padded dash and front visors ($22).** Seat safety belts ($21). Electric tailgate windows ($30). Automatic transmission ($163). Vinyl trim for Sedan (DeLuxe trim package required) ($25). **Wheel covers ($16).** Windshield washer ($14). Electric windshield wiper ($10).

FORD CONVENIENCE OPTIONS: Polar Aire air-conditioning with eight-cylinder ($271). Select Aire air-conditioning with eight-cylinder ($361). Backup lights, standard Galaxie 500 ($11). Heavy-duty battery, 70-amp. ($8). Crankcase ventilation system ($6). Equa-Lock differential ($39). Electric clock, standard Galaxie 500 ($15). Recirculating heater and defroster ($28 deduct option). Chrome luggage rack ($39). Four-way manual seat ($17). Rocker panel molding ($16). Padded dash and visors ($24). Tutone paint ($22). Power brakes ($43). Power seat ($64). Power steering ($82). Power tailgate window ($32). Front and rear power windows ($102). Pushbutton radio and antenna ($59). Front seat belts ($21). Tinted glass ($40). Tinted windshield ($22). Cruise-O-Matic transmission ($190). Fordomatic with six-cylinder ($180). Fordomatic with V-8 ($190). Overdrive transmission ($108). Four-speed manual transmission 375 horsepower or 401 horsepower V-8 required ($188). Vinyl trim, Galaxie 500 except convertible ($26). DeLuxe wheel covers ($26). Wheel covers ($19). Windshield washer and wipers, 2-speed ($20).

THUNDERBIRD CONVENIENCE OPTIONS: Radio and antenna ($113). Engine, 340 horsepower Tri-carb V-8 ($242). Select Air air-conditioning ($415). Tinted glass ($43). Rayon white sidewall tires, 8.00 x 14 ($42). Nylon white sidewall tires, 8.00 x 14 ($70). Power windows ($106). Four-way power seat, driver or passenger ($92). Outside, Rear view mirror, ($5). Windshield washers ($14). Rear fender shields ($27). Front seat belts ($23). Seat bolsters and inserts, leather ($106). Heavy-duty battery, 70-amp ($8). Two-tone paint ($26). Chrome wire wheels ($373).

Historical footnotes: The 1962 Falcon was introduced September 29, 1961. The 1962 Galaxie and station wagon lines appeared the same day. The new Thunderbirds were introduced October 12, 1961. The Fairlane series did not debut until November 16, 1961. Ford announced the introduction of the first transistorized ignition system, for production cars, in March, 1962. A total of 30,216 Fairlanes with the 260 cubic inch V-8 installed. A total of 722,647 Galaxies, 386,192 Fairlanes, 381,559 Falcons and 75,536 Thunderbirds were built this year, second only to the record production season 1955. Mid-year models included the Galaxie 500/XL hardtop and convertible, the Fairlane 500 Sports Sedan and the Falcon Sports Futura. Lee A. Iacocca was Vice-President and general manager of the Ford Division again this year.

1963 FORD

1963 FORDS — OVERVIEW — In 1963, for the fifth year in a row, the full-size Ford line was completely restyled. As in 1962, the sides were devoid of any sculpture lines, except for the beltline feature line. The model designation was carried in script on the fender immediately behind the front wheel opening. Once again, the taillights were large round units mounted at the top of the rear fenders, with a stamped aluminum escutcheon panel being used on the Galaxie 500 series. The model designation was spelled out in block letters across the trunk lid. The grille was a full width aluminum stamping, again carrying a horizontal grid, and featuring a large Ford crest in the center, which was acutally the hood release. The word FORD was spelled out in block letters across the front of the hood. For 1963, the famous small-block 260 and 289 engines replaced the old 292 cubic-inch Y-block, which had been in continuous production since 1956, as the standard V-8 option. Also, with the other car makers continuing to escalate the horsepower race, Ford introduced the most powerful engines in its history; the 410 and 425 horsepwer 427s.

FORD 300 SERIES — (ALL ENGINES) — The Ford 300 was the base trim level for 1963 and included chrome moldings around the windshield and rear window, two sun visors, a chrome horn ring, arm rests on all doors, and no chrome side trim.

FORD 300 SIX I.D. NUMBERS: Ford 300, six-cylinder models began with the number '3', followed by the assembly plant code, engine designation 'V' and, finally, the unit's production number, according to the final assembly location. Each plant began at 100001 and went up. (See production note).

FORD 300 SIX SERIES

Model Number	Body/Style Number	Body Type & Seating	Factory Price	Shipping Weight	Production Total
V	54	4-dr Sedan-6P	2378	3645	Note 1
V	53	2-dr Sedan-6P	2324	3565	Note 1

NOTE 1: See Ford 300 V-8 Series listing. Production was counted by series and body only. No engine breakouts.

FORD 300 V-8 SERIES I.D. NUMBERS: Ford 300 V-8 models began with the number '3', followed by the assembly plant code, body type code, engine designation code and, finally, the unit's production number, according to the final assembly location. Each plant began at 100001 and went up. (See production note).

FORD 300 SERIES

Model Number	Body/Style Number	Body Type & Seating	Factory Price	Shipping Weight	Production Total
NA	54	4-dr Sedan-6P	2387	3640	44,142
NA	53	2-dr Sedan-6P	2433	3560	26,010

PRODUCTION NOTE: Total series output was 70,152 units. Ford does not indicate the number of each model produced with Sixes or V-8s. Therefore, all production figures given above are total production of each body style with both engines.

GALAXIE SERIES — (ALL ENGINES) — The Galaxie was the intermediate trim level for 1963 and included all the 300 series trim, plus a single chrome strip running horizontally along the lower body sides and two chrome fender ornaments on the front fenders.

GALAXIE SIX SERIES I.D. NUMBERS: Galaxie, six-cylinder models used the same serial number sequence as the '300' series. (See production note).

GALAXIE SIX SERIES

Model Number	Body/Style Number	Body Type & Seating	Factory Price	Shipping Weight	Production Total
V	52	4-dr Sedan-6P	2507	3665	Note 1
V	51	2-dr Sedan-6P	2453	3575	Note 1

NOTE 1: See Galaxie V-8 Series listing. Production was counted by series and body only. No engine breakouts.

GALAXIE V-8 SERIES I.D. NUMBERS: Galaxie V-8 models used the same serial number sequence as the '300' series. (See production note).

GALAXIE V-8 SERIES

Model Number	Body/Style Number	Body Type & Seating	Factory Price	Shipping Weight	Production Total
NA	52	4-dr Sedan-6P	2616	3660	82,419
NA	51	2-dr Sedan-6P	2562	3850	30,335

PRODUCTION NOTE: Total series output was 112,754 units. Ford does not indicate the number of each model produced with Sixes or V-8s. Therefore, all production figures given above are total production of each body style with both engines.

GALAXIE 500 SERIES — (ALL ENGINES) — The Galaxie 500 Series was the top trim level for 1963, and included chrome 'A' pillar moldings, chrome window moldings, two horizontal chrome strips on the side; one at the feature line and another, shorter one, beginning at the front of the front door and going to the back of the car, where it swept up and merged with the upper strip. Between the two chrome pieces, just in front of the taillights, were six cast 'hash marks'.

GALAXIE 500 SIX SERIES I.D. NUMBERS: Galaxie 500, six-cylinder models used the same serial number sequence as the '300' and Galaxie Series. (See production note).

GALAXIE 500 SIX SERIES

Model Number	Body/Style Number	Body Type & Seating	Factory Price	Shipping Weight	Production Total
V	62	4-dr Town Sedan-6P	2667	3685	Note 1
V	61	2-dr Club Sedan-6P	2613	3605	Note 1
V	64	4-dr Town Vic-6P	2739	3700	Note 1
V	63	2-dr Club Vic-6P	2674	3620	Note 1
V	66	2-dr Fstbk Cpe-6P	2674	3620	Note 1
V	65	2-dr Sunliner-6P	2924	3775	Note 1

NOTE 1: See Galaxie 500 V-8 Series listing. Production was counted by series and body only. No engine breakouts.

GALAXIE 500 V-8 I.D. NUMBERS: Galaxie 500, V-8 models used the same serial number sequence as the '300' and Galaxie series. (See production note).

GALAXIE 500 V-8 SERIES

Model Number	Body/Style Number	Body Type & Seating	Factory Price	Shipping Weight	Production Total
NA	62	4-dr Town Sedan-6P	2776	3680	205,722
NA	61	2-dr Club Sedan-6P	2722	3600	21,137
NA	64	4-dr Town Vic-6P	2848	3695	26,558
NA	63	2-dr Club Vic-6P	2783	3615	49,733
NA	66	2-dr Fstbk Cpe-6P	2783	3615	100,500
NA	65	2-dr Sunliner-6P	3033	3770	36,876

PRODUCTION NOTE: Total series output was 440,526 units. Ford does not indicate the number of each model produced with Sixes or V-8s. Therefore, all production figures given above are total production of each body style with both engines.

1963 Ford, Galaxie XL 2-dr convertible, V-8 (AA)

GALAXIE 500XL SERIES — (V-8) — Galaxie 500XL models used the same serial number sequence as the Galaxie and Galaxie 500 Series. (See production note).

GALAXIE 500XL V-8 SERIES

Model Number	Body/Style Number	Body Type & Seating	Factory Price	Shipping Weight	Production Total
NA	62	4-dr Town Vic-5P	3333	3750	12,596
NA	67	2-dr Club Vic-5P	3628	3670	29,713
NA	68	2-dr Fstbk Cpe-5P	3268	3670	33,870
NA	69	2-dr Sunliner-5P	3518	3820	18,551

PRODUCTION NOTE: Total series output was 94,730 units.

STATION WAGON SERIES — (ALL ENGINES) — The Country Sedans were the base trim level Station Wagons for 1963, with the Country Squires being the top trim level. The trim paralleled the Galaxie and Galaxie 500 models of conventional cars.

STATION WAGON SIX SERIES I.D. NUMBERS: Station Wagon six-cylinder models used the same serial number sequence as Galaxie and Galaxie 500 series of conventional cars. (See production note).

STATION WAGON SIX SERIES

Model Number	Body/Style Number	Body Type & Seating	Factory Price	Shipping Weight	Production Total
V	72	4-dr Ctry Sed-6P	2829	3990	Note 1
V	74	4-dr Ctry Sedan-9P	2933	4005	Note 1
V	76	4-dr Ctry Squire-6P	3018	4005	Note 1
V	78	4-dr Ctry Squire-9P	2933	4015	Note 1

NOTE 1: See Station Wagon V-8 Series listing. Production was counted by series and body only. No engine breakouts.

STATION WAGON V-8 SERIES I.D. NUMBERS: Station Wagon V-8 models used the same serial number sequence as Galaxie and Galaxie 500 models of conventional cars. (See production note).

STATION WAGON V-8 SERIES

Model Number	Body/Style Number	Body Type & Seating	Factory Price	Shipping Weight	Production Total
NA	72	4-dr Ctry Sedan-6P	2938	3985	64,954
NA	74	4-dr Ctry Sedan-9P	3042	4000	22,250
NA	76	4-dr Ctry Squire-9P	3127	4000	19,922
NA	78	4-dr Ctry Squire-9P	3197	4010	19,246

PRODUCTION NOTE: Total series output was 126,372 units. Ford does not indicate the number of each model produced with Sixes or V-8s. Therefore, all production figures given above are total production of each body style with both engines.

1963 FAIRLANES — OVERVIEW — The Fairlane was a carryover from 1962, with some minor trim changes. Two new models were added to the lineup, however. They were the Fairlane 500 Hardtop and the Fairlane 500 Sport Coupe. With their pillarless styling, they added a sporty look to the otherwise conservative Fairlane lineup.

FAIRLANE SERIES — (ALL ENGINES) — The 1963 carried over from the 1962 model year, with very few changes in chrome trim. The addition of two two-door hardtop models added a sporty touch to the conservative Fairlane lineup.

FAIRLANE SIX SERIES I.D. NUMBERS: Fairlane, six-cylinder models began with the number '3', followed by the assembly plant code, body type code, engine designation "U" and finally, the unit's production number, according to the final assembly location. Each plant began at 100001 and went up.

FAIRLANE SIX SERIES

Model Number	Body/Style Number	Body Type & Seating	Factory Price	Shipping Weight	Production Total
U	32	4-dr Sedan-6P	2216	2855	Note 1
U	31	2-dr Sedan-6P	2154	2815	Note 1
U	38	4-dr Ranch Wag-6P	2525	3195	Note 1

NOTE 1: See Fairlane V-8 Series listing. Production was counted by series and body only. No engine breakouts.

FAIRLANE V-8 SERIES I.D. NUMBERS: Fairlane, V-8 models began with the number '3', followed by the assembly plant code, body type code, engine designation code and, finally, the units's production number, according to the final assembly location. Each plant began at 100001 and went up. (See production note).

FAIRLANE V-8 SERIES

Model Number	Body/Style Number	Body Type & Seating	Factory Price	Shipping Weight	Production Total
NA	32	4-dr Sedan-6P	2319	2987	44,454
NA	31	2-dr Sedan-6P	2257	2924	28,984
NA	38	4-dr Ranch Wag-6P	2628	3327	24,006

PRODUCTION NOTE: Total series output was 97,444 units. Ford does not indicate the number of each model produced with Sixes or V-8s. Therefore, all production figures given above are total production of each body style with both engines.

1963 Ford, Fairlane 500 4-dr station wagon, V-8

FAIRLANE 500 SERIES — (ALL ENGINES) — The Fairlane 500 models were the top trim level of the line and included chrome window moldings, a chrome horn ring, arm rests on all doors, a version of the 'Fairlane sweep' which very strongly resembled the chrome used on 1959 full-size Fairlane 500s, three chrome exhaust ports located on the rear fenders, just ahead of the taillights, and a stamped aluminum escutcheon panel between the taillights, with the Ford crest situated in the center, on the gasoline filler cap.

FAIRLANE 500 SIX SERIES I.D. NUMBERS: Fairlane 500, six-cylinder models used the same serial number sequence as the Fairlane models. (See production note).

FAIRLANE 500 SIX I.D. NUMBERS: Fairlane 500, six-cylinder models used the same serial number sequence as the Fairlane models. (See production note).

FAIRLANE 500 SIX SERIES

Model Number	Body/Style Number	Body Type & Seating	Factory Price	Shipping Weight	Production Total
U	42	4-dr Sedan-6P	2304	2870	Note 1
U	41	2-dr Sedan-6P	2242	2830	Note 1
U	43	2-dr H.T. Cpe-6P	2324	2850	Note 1
U	47	2-dr Spt Cpe-5P	2504	2870	Note 1
U	48	4-dr Ranch Wag-6P	2613	3210	Note 1
U	49	4-dr Squire-6P	2781	3220	Note 1

NOTE 1: See Fairlane V-8 Series listing. Production was counted by series and body only. No engine breakouts.

FAIRLANE 500 I.D. NUMBERS: Fairlane 500 V-8 models used the same serial number sequence as the Fairlane models. (See production note).

FAIRLANE 500 SERIES

Model Number	Body/Style Number	Body Type & Seating	Factory Price	Shipping Weight	Production Total
NA	42	4-dr Sedan-6P	2407	3002	103,175
NA	41	2-dr Sedan-6P	2345	2962	34,764
NA	43	2-dr H.T. Cpe-6P	2427	2982	41,641
NA	47	2-dr Spt Cpe-5P	2607	3002	28,268
NA	48	4-dr Ranch Wag-6P	2716	3342	29,612
NA	49	4-dr Squire-6P	2884	3352	7,983

PRODUCTION NOTE: Total series output was 246,443 units, including 277 Fairlane Squires with optional bucket seat interiors. Ford does not indicate the number of each model produced with sixes or V-8s. Therefore, all production figures given above are total production of each body style with both engines.

1965 FALCONS — OVERVIEW — The Falcon line continued to use the body shell introduced in 1960, but was updated with a new convex grille featuring a horizontal grid, and more bold use of chrome. The big news in the Falcon line was the addition of the two-door Hardtop and the sporty convertible. These two body styles were available in the Futura series and the new high-powered Sprint series. A team of specially prepared 1963 Falcon Spring hardtops terrorized the European rally circuit, with some very un-Falcon performances.

FALCON SERIES — (ALL ENGINES) — The Falcon continued to use the same body as in previous years and had a new convex grille with a horizontal grid pattern, chrome side trim, and slightly revised taillight lenses, with additional chrome around the inside of the lens. The DeLuxe models of 1962 were replaced by the Futura models for 1963 and included the addition of a two-door hardtop, a convertible and offered V-8 power for the first time in the series' history.

STANDARD SERIES — (ALL ENGINES) — Falcon Standard series cars were the base trim level for 1963 and included chrome windshield and rear window moldings, two horns, two sun visors, arm rests on the front doors only and a horn button instead of a chrome horn ring.

STANDARD SERIES I.D. NUMBERS: Falcon Standard series cars used the same serial number sequence as the full-size Fords and the Fairlane (See production note).

STANDARD FALCON SERIES

Model Number	Body/Style Number	Body Type & Seating	Factory Price	Shipping Weight	Production Total
NA	02	4-dr Sedan-6P	2047	2345	62,365
NA	01	2-dr Sedan-6P	1985	2305	70,630

1963 Ford, Falcon Futura 2-dr convertible, 6-cyl (AA)

FUTURA SERIES — (ALL ENGINES) — The Futura series was the top trim level for 1963 and included a chrome horn ring; rear arm rests and ash trays; two horns; Futura wheel covers instead of hub caps; the round 'Futura' symbol on the top 'C' pillar; chrome side window moldings; chrome windshield and rear window moldings; a horizontal chrome strip between the tail lights and a horizontal arrow style chrome strip on the body side. The Sport Coupe and Sprint versions also included wire wheel covers and bucket seats.

FUTURA I.D. NUMBERS: Futura models used the same serial number sequence as the full size Fords, Fairlane models and Standard series Falcons (See production note).

FUTURA SERIES

Model Number	Body/Style Number	Body Type & Seating	Factory Price	Shipping Weight	Production Total
NA	16	4-dr Sedan-6P	2165	2355	31,736
NA	19	2-dr Sedan-6P	2116	2315	16,674
NA	17	2-dr Sedan-5P	2237	2350	10,344
NA	18	2-dr HT Cpe-6P	2198	2455	17,524
NA	18	2-dr Spts HT-5P	2319	2490	10,972
NA	18	2-dr Sprint-5P	2603	2875	10,479
NA	15	2-dr Conv-6P	2470	2655	18,942
NA	15	2-dr Spt Conv-5P	2591	2690	12,250
NA	15	2-dr Sprint Conv-4P	2837	2998	4,602

PRODUCTION NOTE: Total series output was 265,518 units. Ford does not indicate the number of each model produced with sixes or V-8s. Therefore, all production figures given above are total production of each body style with both engines.

1963 THUNDERBIRDS — OVERVIEW — While using the same body as the 1961-1962 T-Birds, the 1963 model is, perhaps, the most easily recognizable of the entire series. The major difference in the 1963 model, and the two previous models, is a mid-body feature line which moves back, horizontally, from the front of the car and then dips down near the back of the front door. Three sets of five cast 'hash marks' are used on

the side of the door, just ahead of the feature line dip. In January, 1963, a Limited Edition Thunderbird Landau was introduced and was available only with Maroon exterior color, white top, white steering wheel and white leather interior. This model is often referred to as the Monaco Edition, as it was introduced in Monaco, Morocco.

1963 Ford, Thunderbird 2-dr hardtop coupe, V-8

THUNDERBIRD SERIES — (V-8) — The 1963 Thunderbird continued to use the same body as the past two years. However, the new side feature stripe makes it the most easily recognizable of the three-year body style. A single exhaust system was included as standard equipment for the first and only time and a 340 horsepower 390 cubic inch V-8 was again an option. It featured three two-barrel carburetors.

THUNDERBIRD I.D. NUMBERS: Thunderbird models began with number '3', assembly plant code 'Y' (Wixom), body type code, engine type code 'M' or 'Y', and, finally, the unit's production number, beginning at 100001 and going up.

THUNDERBIRD SERIES

Model Number	Body/Style Number	Body Type & Seating	Factory Price	Shipping Weight	Production Total
Y/M	83	2-dr HT Cpe-4P	4445	4195	42,806
Y/M	87	2-dr Land HT-4P	4548	4320	14,139
Y/M	85	2-dr Conv-4P	4912	4205	5,913
Y/M	89	2-dr Spt Rds-4P	5563	4395	455

PRODUCTION NOTE: Total series output was 63,313 units.

1963 FORD CHASSIS FEATURES: Wheelbase: 119 inches. Overall length 209.0 inches. Tires: 7.50 x 14 four-ply tubeless blackwalls (8.00 x 14 four-ply tubeless blackwalls on station wagons).

1963 FAIRLANE CHASSIS FEATURES: Wheelbase: 115.5 inches. Overall length: 197.6 inches (201.8 inches on station wagons). Tires: 6.50 x 13 four-ply blackwall tubeless (7.00 x 14 four-ply blackwall tubeless on station wagons).

FALCON CHASSIS FEATURES: Wheelbase: 109.5 inches. Overall length: 181.1 inches. Tires: 6.00 x 13 four-ply tubeless blackwall (6.50 x 13 four-ply tubeless on station wagons and convertibles).

THUNDERBIRD CHASSIS FEATURES: Wheelbase: 113 inches. Overall length: 205 inches. Tires: 8.00 x 14 four-ply tubeless whitewalls.

1963 FORD ENGINES

Falcon six-cylinder: Overhead valves. Cast iron block. Displacement: 144 cubic inches. Bore and stroke: 3.50 x 2.50 inches. Compression ratio: 8.7:1. Brake horsepower: 85 at 4200 R.P.M. Carburetion: Holley single barrel. Seven main bearings. Serial number code "S".

Falcon/Fairlane 170 six-cylinder: Overhead valves. Cast iron block. Displacement: 170 cubic inches. Bore and stroke: 3.50 x 2.94 inches. Compression ratio: 8.7:1. Brake horsepower: 101 at 4400 R.P.M. Carburetion: Holley single barrel. Seven main bearings. Serial number code "U".

Ford six-cylinder: Overhead valves. Cast iron block. Displacement: 223 cubic inches. Bore and stroke: 3.62 x 3.60 inches. Compression ratio: 8.4:1. Brake horsepower: 138 at 4200 R.P.M. Carburetion: Holley single barrel. Four main bearings. Serial number code "V".

Fairlane V-8: Overhead valves. Cast iron block. Displacement: 221 cubic inches. Bore and stroke: 3.75 x 330 inches. Compression ratio: 8.8:1. Brake horsepower: 145 at 4400 R.P.M. Carburetion: Holley two-barrel. Five main bearings. Serial number code "L".

Challenger 260 V-8: Overhead valves. Cast iron block. Displacement: 260 cubic inches. Bore and stroke: 3.80 x 2.87 inches. Compression ratio: 8.7:1. Brake horsepower: 164 at 4400 R.P.M. Carburetion: Holley two-barrel. Five main bearings. Serial number code "F".

High Performance Challenger 289 V-8: Overhead valves. Cast iron block. Displacement: 289 cubic inches. Bore and stroke: 3.00 x 2.87 inches. Compression ratio: 10.5:1. Brake horsepower: 271 at 6000 R.P.M. Carburetion: Holley four-barrel. Five main bearings. Serial number code "K".

Interceptor V-8: Overhead valves. Cast iron block. Displacement: 352 cubic inches. Bore and stroke: 4.00 x 3.50 inches. Compression ratio: 8.9:1. Brake horsepower: 220 at 4300 R.P.M. Carburetion: Holley two-barrel. Five main bearings. Serial number code "X".

Thunderbird V-8: Overhead valves. Cast iron block. Displacement: 390 cubic inches. Bore and stroke: 4.05 x 3.78 inches. Compression ratio: 9.6:1. Brake horsepower: 300 at 4600 R.P.M. Carburetion: Holley four-barrel. Five main bearings. Serial number code "Z".

Thunderbird Special V-8: Overhead valves. Cast iron block. Displacement: 390 cubic inches. Bore and stroke: 4.05 x 3.78 inches. Compression ratio: 9.6:1. Brake horsepower: 330 at 5000 R.P.M. Carburetion: Holley four-barrel. Five main bearings. Serial number code "Z". (Available in Thunderbirds only).

Thunderbird Special "six-barrel" V-8: Overhead valves. Cast iron block. Displacement: 390 cubic inches. Bore and stroke: 4.05 x 3.78 inches. Compression ratio: 10.5:1. Brake horsepower: 340 at 5000 R.P.M. Carburetion: three Holley two-barrels. Five main bearings. Serial number code "M".

Thunderbird 406 V-8: Overhead valves. Cast iron block. Displacement: 406 cubic inches. Bore and stroke: 4.13 x 3.78 inches. Compression ratio: 11.4:1. Brake horsepower: 385 at 5800 R.P.M. Carburetion: Holley four-barrel. Five main bearings. Serial number code "B".

Thunderbird Special "six-barrel" V-8: Overhead valves. Cast iron block. Displacement: 406 cubic inches. Bore and stroke: 4.13 x 3.78 inches. Compression ratio: 11.4:1. Brake horsepower: 405 at 5800 R.P.M. Carburetion: three Holley two-barrels. Five main bearings. Serial number code "G".

Thunderbird High-Performance V-8: Overhead valves. Cast iron block. Displacement: 427 cubic inches. Bore and stroke: 4.23 x 3.78 inches. Compression ratio: 11.5:1. Brake horsepower: 410 at 5600 R.P.M. Carburetion: Holley four-barrel. Five main bearings. Serial number code "Q".

Thunderbird High-Performance 8V V-8: Overhead valves. Cast iron block. Displacement: 427 cubic inches. Bore and stroke: 4.23 x 3.78 inches. Compression ratio: 11.5:1. Brake horsepower: 425 at 6000 R.P.M. Carburetion: two Holley four-barrels. Five main bearings. Serial number code "R".

1963 FORD TRANSMISSIONS: Same as 1962.

CONVENIENCE OPTIONS: Popular '300' and Galaxie series option included the 289 cubic inch V-8 engine ($109). Cruise-O-Matic automatic transmission ($212). Power steering ($81). Power brakes ($43). White sidewall tires ($33). Popular Galaxie 500 and Galaxie 500XL options included the 390 cubic inch V-8 engine ($246). Cruise-O-Matic automatic transmission ($212). Four-speed manual transmission ($188). Power steering ($81). Power brakes ($43). Two-tone paint ($22). White sidewall tires ($33). Windshield washers ($20). Backup lights ($10). Electric clock ($14). Radio ($58). AM/FM radio ($129). Popular station wagon options included power tailgate window ($32). Luggage rack ($45). Electric clock ($14). There were 758 Country Squires produced with the optional bucket seat interior at $141 extra. Popular Fairlane and Fairlane 500 options included the 260 cubic inch engines ($103 or $154). Fordomatic automatic transmission ($189). Four-speed manual transmissions with V-8s ($188). AM radio ($58). Power steering ($81). Power tailgate window on station wagons ($32). Luggage rack on station wagons ($45). Two-tone paint ($22). White sidewall tires ($34). Padded dashboard and sun visors ($24). Popular Falcon options included the 170 cubic inch six-cylinder engine ($437). The 260 cubic inch V-8s ($158 or $196). Fordomatic automatic transmission ($163). Four-speed manual transmission ($90 with six-cylinder or $188 with V-8). Power tailgate window on station wagons ($29). Two-tone paint ($19). AM radio ($58). White sidewall tires ($29). Backup lights ($10). Deluxe trim package for sedans ($37). Popular Thunderbird options included power windows ($106). Power seats ($92). Passenger power seats ($92). AM/FM radio ($83). Tinted glass ($43). Windshield washers ($13). Wire wheels ($343).

Historical footnotes: The "Fairlane 500 Sports Coupe" was a two-door pillarless hardtop. The "Falcon Sprint" was a compact, high-performance V-8 powered Falcon. The "Galaxie Fastback" was a full size two-door hardtop with more gently sloping roofline than conventional hardtop, to produce less wind resistance.

1964 FORD

1964 FORDS OVERVIEW — As is the case in the previous six years, the 1964 Fords were totally restyled. This year it wasn't just the regular Ford which came under the stylist's brush, but the entire line from the compact Falcon to the prestigious Thunderbird. Engine choices remained virtually unchanged for 1964.

FORD CUSTOM SERIES — (ALL ENGINES) — Full size Fords were completely revamped for 1964. They were recognizable as Ford products only because of their traditional large, round taillights. The grille carried a horizontal grid highlighted with three vertical ribs. The Ford name, in block letters, was seen on all models, but side trim differed considerably. A sheetmetal feature line began on the front fender at belt line level. It continued horizontally, to the rear of the car, and dipped down. A lower sheetmetal feature line began behind the front wheels and continued, horizontally, toward the rear of the car. There it swept upward and merged with the upper feature line. All models using optional, large displacement V-8s, carried the engine designation symbol on the lower front fender. The Custom series was the base trim level. It included chrome windshield and rear window moldings; two sun visors, a chrome horn ring, arm rests on all doors and three cast 'stripes' on the front fenders, just behind the headlights.

CUSTOM SIX SERIES I.D. NUMBERS: Custom six-cylinder models began with the numbers '4', followed by the assembly plant code, engine designation 'V' and, finally, the unit's production number, according to the final assembly location. Each plant began at 100001 and went up (See production note).

CUSTOM SIX SERIES

Model Number	Body/Style Number	Body Type & Seating	Factory Price	Shipping Weight	Production Total
V	54	4-dr Sedan-6P	2404	3621	Note 1
V	53	2-dr Sedan-6P	2350	3521	Note 1

NOTE 1: See production note below.

CUSTOM V-8 SERIES I.D. NUMBERS: Custom V-8 models began with the number '4', followed by the assembly plant code, body type code, engine designation code and, finally, the unit's production number, according to the final assembly location. Each plant began at 100001 and went up (See production note).

CUSTOM V-8 SERIES

Model Number	Body/Style Number	Body Type & Seating	Factory Price	Shipping Weight	Production Total
NA	54	4-dr Sedan-6P	2513	3617	57,964
NA	53	2-dr Sedan-6P	2459	3527	41,359

PRODUCTION NOTE: Total series output was 99,323 units. Ford does not indicate the number of each model produced with Sixes or V-8s. Therefore, all production figures given above are total production of each body style with both engines.

CUSTOM 500 SERIES — (ALL ENGINES) — The Custom 500 was the upper trim level of the base-line Custom Series and included chrome windshield and rear window moldings; Nylon carpeting (instead of the rubber mats used in the Custom models); arm rests with ash trays on all doors; two sun visors and all trim used in the Custom models, plus a single horizontal chrome strip on the exterior body side.

CUSTOM 500 SIX SERIES I.D. NUMBERS: Custom 500, six-cylinder models used the same Serial Number sequence as the Custom models (See production note).

CUSTOM 500 SERIES

Model Number	Body/Style Number	Body Type & Seating	Factory Price	Shipping Weight	Production Total
V	52	4-dr Sedan-6P	2507	3661	Note 1
V	51	2-dr Sedan-6P	2453	3561	Note 1

NOTE 1: See production note below.

CUSTOM 500 V-8 SERIES I.D. NUMBERS: Custom 500, V-8 models used the same Serial Number sequence as the Custom models (See production note).

CUSTOM 500 V-8 SERIES

Model Number	Body/Style Number	Body Type & Seating	Factory Price	Shipping Weight	Production Total
NA	52	4-dr Sedan-6P	2616	3657	68,828
NA	51	2-dr Sedan-6P	2562	3557	20,619

PRODUCTION NOTE: Total series output was 89,447 units. Ford does not indicate the number of each model produced with Sixes or V-8s. Therefore, all production figures given above are total production of each body style with both engines.

GALAXIE 500 SERIES — (ALL ENGINES) — The Galaxie 500 was the intermediate trim level for 1964 and included all Custom trim, plus chrome fender top ornamentation, chrome window frames, the Ford crest on the roof 'C' piller and a full length chrome strip (which split at the rear of the front doors and included an aluminum insert forward of that point). 'Galaxie 500', in script, was included in the aluminum insert, at the front of the stripe. A stamped aluminum insert also hightlighed the rear treatment and included 'Galaxie 500' in script, on the right side of the insert. Two-tone vinyl trim was used on the side of the doors and on the seats.

GALAXIE 500 SIX SERIES I.D. NUMBERS: Galaxie 500, six-cylinder models used the same Serial Number sequence as the Custom series (See production note).

GALAXIE SIX SERIES

Model Number	Body/Style Number	Body Type & Seating	Factory Price	Shipping Weight	Production Total
V	62	4-dr Town Sed-6P	2667	3676	Note 1
V	61	2-dr Club Sed-6P	2613	3576	Note 1
V	64	4-dr Town Vic-6P	2739	3691	Note 1
V	66	2-dr Club Vic-6P	2674	3586	Note 1
V	65	2-dr Sunliner Conv-6P	2936	3761	Note 1

NOTE 1: See production note below. **ADDITIONAL NOTE:** The two-door convertible is called the Sunliner.

GALAXIE 500 V-8 SERIES I.D. NUMBERS: Galaxie 500, V-8 models used the same Serial Number sequence as the Custom series (See production note).

GALAXIE 500 V-8 SERIES

Model Number	Body/Style Number	Body Type & Seating	Factory Price	Shipping Weight	Production Total
NA	62	4-dr Town Sed-6P	2776	3672	198,805
NA	61	2-dr Club Sed-6P	2722	3572	13,041
NA	64	4-dr Town Vic-6P	2848	3687	49,242
NA	66	2-dr Club Vic-5P	2783	3582	206,998
NA	65	2-dr Sunliner Conv-5P	3045	3757	37,311

PRODUCTION NOTE: Total series output was 505,397 units. Ford does not indicate the number of each model produced with Sixes or V-8s. Therefore, all production figures given above are total production of each body style with both engines.

GALAXIE 500XL SERIES — (V-8) — Galaxie 500XL was the top trim level for 1964 and included all the trim features of the Galaxie models, plus, bucket seats and floor mounted transmission shifter; polished door trim panels; dual-lens courtesy/warning lights in the doors; rear reading lights in hardtops and Galaxie 500XL badges on the body exterior. The 289 cubic inch, 195 horsepower V-8 engine was standard on all 'XLs'.

GALAXIE 500 XL I.D. NUMBERS: Galaxie 500 XLs used the same Serial Number sequence as the Custom and Galaxie series (See production note).

GALAXIE SERIES

Model Number	Body/Style Number	Body Type & Seating	Factory Price	Shipping Weight	Production Total
NA	60	4-dr Town Vic-5P	3287	3722	14,661
NA	68	2-dr Club Vic-5P	3222	3622	58,306
NA	69	2-dr Conv-5P	3484	3787	15,169

PRODUCTION NOTE: Total series output was 88,136 units.

1964 Ford, Country Squire, 4-dr station wagon, V-8

STATION WAGON SERIES — (ALL ENGINES) — The Country Sedans were the base trim level station wagons for 1964, with the Country Squires being the top trim level. The trim paralleled the Galaxie 500 and Galaxie 500XL models of conventional cars.

STATION WAGON SIX SERIES I.D. NUMBERS: Station wagon, six-cylinder models used the small Serial Number sequence as Custom and Galaxie 500 series of conventional cars (See production note).

STATION WAGON SIX SERIES

Model Number	Body/Style Number	Body Type & Seating	Factory Price	Shipping Weight	Production Total
V	72	4-dr Ctry Sed-6P	2829	3975	Note 1
V	74	4-dr Ctry Sed-9P	2933	3985	Note 1
V	76	4-dr Ctry Squire-6P	3018	3990	Note 1
V	78	4-dr Ctry Squire-9P	3088	4000	Note 1

NOTE 1: See production note below.

STATION WAGON V-8 SERIES I.D. NUMBERS: Station Wagon, V-8 models used the same Serial Number sequence as Custom and Galaxie 500 models of conventional cars (See production note).

STATION WAGON V-8 SERIES

Model Number	Body/Style Number	Body Type & Seating	Factory Price	Shipping Weight	Production Total
NA	72	4-dr Ctry Sed-6P	2938	3971	68,578
NA	74	4-dr Ctry Sed-9P	3042	3981	25,661
NA	76	4-dr Ctry Squire-6P	3127	3986	23,570
NA	78	4-dr Ctry Squire-9P	3197	3996	23,120

PRODUCTION NOTE: Total series output was 140,929 units. Ford does not indicate the number of each model produced with Sixes or V-8s. Therefore, all production figures given above are total production of each body style with both engines.

FAIRLANE SERIES — (ALL ENGINES) — The 1964 Fairlane styling featured new sheetmetal for the body sides and rear, which seemed to add to the Fairlane's 'Total Performance' image. The rear fenders featured a smoother top than 1963, with a complete absence of fins. The sides were sculptured into a convex shape, which flowed forward from the sides of the taillights and terminated in a chrome scoop. The grille carried the familiar horizontal gride with thin vertical dividers.

FAIRLANE V-8 SERIES I.D. NUMBERS: Fairlane V-8 models began with number '4', followed by the assembly plant code, body type code, engine designation code and, finally, the unit's production number, according to the final assembly location. Each plant began at 100001 and went up (See production note).

FAIRLANE SIX SERIES

Model Number	Body/Style Number	Body Type & Seating	Factory Price	Shipping Weight	Production Total
U/T	32	4-dr Sedan-6P	2224	2828	Note 1
U/T	31	2-dr Sedan-6P	2183	2788	Note 1
U/T	38	2-dr Sta Wag-6P	2520	3223	Note 1

NOTE 1: See production note below. **ADDITIONAL NOTE:** The station wagon was called the Ranch wagon.

FAIRLANE SIX SERIES I.D. NUMBERS: Fairlane, six-cylinder models began with the number '4', followed by the assembly plant code, body type code, engine designation 'U' or 'T' and, finally, the unit's production number, according to the final assembly location. Each plant began at 100001 and went up.

FAIRLANE V-8 SERIES

Model Number	Body/Style Number	Body Type & Seating	Factory Price	Shipping Weight	Production Total
NA	32	4-dr Sedan-6P	2324	2962	36,693
NA	31	2-dr Sedan-6P	2283	2922	20,421
NA	38	2-dr Sta Wag-6P	2620	3357	20,980

PRODUCTION NOTE: Total series output was 78,094 units. Ford does not indicate the number of each model produced with Sixes or V-8s. Therefore, all production figures given above are total production of each body style with both engines.

1964 Ford Fairlane 500 2-dr hardtop Sports Coupe, V-8

FAIRLANE 500 SERIES — (ALL ENGINES) — The Fairlane 500 models were the top trim level of the line and included chrome window moldings; a chrome horn ring; arm rests on all doors; a twin-spear side molding running the full length of the body, (with an accent color of red, black or white, between the spears). In addition, chrome, fender top ornaments and the Ford crest appeared on the 'C' pillar of the more DeLuxe model of the series. Fairlane 500 models also had carpeting.

FAIRLANE 500 SIX SERIES I.D. NUMBERS: Fairlane 500, six-cylinder models used the same serial number sequence as the Fairlane models (See production note).

FAIRLANE 500 SIX SERIES

Model Number	Body/Style Number	Body Type & Seating	Factory Price	Shipping Weight	Production Total
U/T	42	4-dr Town Sed-6P	2306	2843	Note 1
U/T	41	2-dr Club Sed-6P	2265	2813	Note 1
U/T	43	2-dr HT Cpe-6P	2330	2858	Note 1
U/T	47	2-dr HT Spt Cpe-5P	2491	2878	Note 1
U/T	48	4-dr Cust Sta Wag	2601	3243	Note 1

NOTE 1: See production note below.

FAIRLANE 500 V-8 SERIES I.D. NUMBERS: Fairlane 500, V-8 models used the same serial number sequence as the Fairlane models (See production note).

FAIRLANE 500 V-8 SERIES

Model Number	Body/Style Number	Body Type & Seating	Factory Price	Shipping Weight	Production Total
NA	42	4-dr Town Sed-6P	2406	297	86,919
NA	41	2-dr Club Sed-6P	2365	2913	23,477
NA	43	2-dr HT Cpe-6P	2430	2992	42,733
NA	47	2-dr HT Spt Cpe-5P	2591	3012	12,431
NA	48	4-dr Cust Sta Wag	2701	3377	24,962

PRODUCTION NOTE: Total series output was 199,522 units. Ford does not indicate the number of each model produced with sixes or V-8s. Therefore, all production figures given above are total production of each body style with both engines.

1964 Ford, Falcon Sprint 2-dr hardtop coupe, V-8

FALCON SERIES — (ALL ENGINES) — The 1964 Falcons reflected the 'Total Performance' image in their new styling. A more aggressive, angled grille lead a completely restyled body. As in 1963, the base trim level was the standard series, and the top trim level was the Futura. The hightly styled sculptured body sides gave the 1964 Falcons a racy appearance and added rigidity to the sheetmetal. A convex feature line began on the front fenders, but sloped slightly and increased in width gradually, until it met the taillights. The word Ford, was spelled out across the hood in block letters and Falcon was spelled out in block letters between the taillights. The new grille featured a rectangular design that was angularly recessed and complimented the side profile. As in the past years, the Falcons continued to use single headlamps. Standard Falcon cars were the base trim level for 1964. They included chrome windshield and rear window moldings, twin horns, two sun visors, arm rests on the front doors only and a horn button instead of a chrome horn ring.

STANDARD FALCONS SERIES I.D. NUMBERS — (ALL ENGINES): Standard series Falcons used the same Serial Number sequence as the full-size Fords and the Fairlane line (See production note).

STANDARD FALCON SERIES

Model Number	Body/Style Number	Body Type & Seating	Factory Price	Shipping Weight	Production Total
NA	02	4-dr Sedan-6P	2040	2400	28,411
NA	01	2-dr Sedan-6P	1985	2365	36,441

FALCON FUTURA SERIES — (ALL ENGINES) — The Futura series was the top trim level for 1964 and included a chrome horn ring; rear arm rests with ash trays; twin horns; Futura wheel covers (instead of hub caps); chrome hood ornament; Futura symbol on the front fender; chrome side window moldings; chrome windshield and rear window moldings; two horizontal sloping chrome strips on the body side and four cast hash marks on the rear fender in front of the taillights. The Sprint versions of the Futura hardtop and convertible also featured a V-8 engine, bucket seats and wire wheel covers.

FALCON FUTURA I.D. NUMBERS: Futura models used the same Serial Number sequence as the full size Fords, Fairlanes and standard series Falcons (See production note).

FALCON FUTURA SERIES

Model Number	Body/Style Number	Body Type & Seating	Factory Price	Shipping Weight	Production Total
NA	16	4-dr Sedan-6P	2165	2410	38,032
NA	19	2-dr Sedan-6P	2116	2375	16,261
NA	17	2-dr Sedan-6P	2237	2350	212
NA	17	2-dr HT Cpe-6P	2198	2515	32,608
NA	11	2-dr Spts HT-5P	2314	2545	8,322
NA	15	2-dr Conv-6P	2470	2710	13,220
NA	12	2-dr Spts Conv-5P	2586	2735	2,980
NA	13	2-dr Sprint HT-5P	2425	2813	13,830
NA	14	2-dr Sprint Conv-5P	2660	3008	4,278

PRODUCTION NOTE: Total series output was 130,103 units. This figure includes 285 Sprint hardtops built without consoles, 626 Sprint convertibles built with bench seats. Ford does not indicate the number of each model produced with Sixes or V-8s. Therefore, all production figures given above are total production of each body style with both engines. The Sprint models came only with V-8 engines and five-passenger (bucket) seating.

FALCON STATION WAGON SERIES — (ALL ENGINES) — Falcon station wagons became a separate series for the first time in 1964 and included the base Standard series, the intermediate DeLuxe series and the top-line Squire wagon.

FALCON STATION WAGON I.D. NUMBERS: Falcon station wagons used the same Serial Number sequence as the full-size Fords, Fairlanes and Falcon sedans (See production note).

FALCON STATION WAGON SERIES

Model Number	Body/Style Number	Body Type & Seating	Factory Price	Shipping Weight	Production Total
NA	22	4-dr Sta Wag-6P	2349	2695	17,779
NA	21	2-dr Sta Wag-6P	2315	2660	6,034
NA	24	4-dr DeL Sta Wag	2435	2715	20,697
NA	26	4-dr Squire Wag-6P	2611	2720	6,766

PRODUCTION NOTE: Total series output was 51,276 units. Ford does not indicate the number of each model produced with Sixes or V-8s. Therefore, all production figures given above are total production of each body style with both engines.

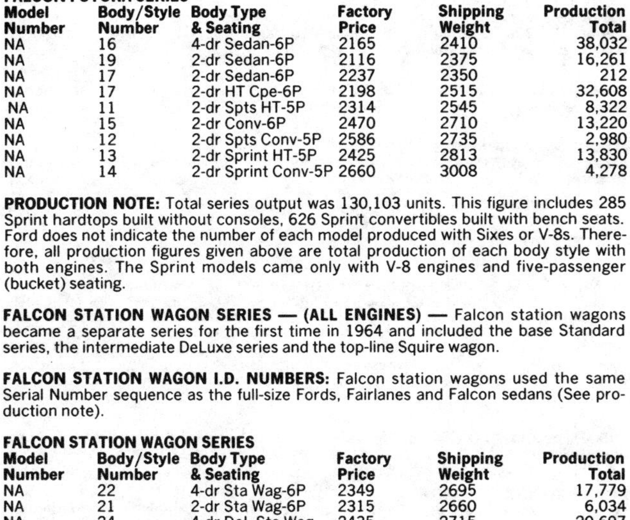

1964 Ford, Thunderbird convertible

THUNDERBIRD SERIES — (V-8) — The 1964 Thunderbirds were also completely restyled and featured longer hoods and shorter roof lines than previous offerings. The side panels were highly sculptured. They had mirror-image feature lines at the belt line and lower body side. The front end was more aggressive and featured a larger power dome (scoop) on the hood. The headlights were spaced farther apart than in previous years. The rear of the 1964 T-Bird featured rectangular taillights set within a massive bumper. The Thunderbird name, in script, was located just behind the front wheels on the front fenders and Thunderbird, in block letters, was spaced along the front of the hood. The factory-built Sports Roadster was dropped, but dealers continued to add this kit, as an option, on a few 1964 Thunderbirds.

THUNDERBIRD I.D. NUMBERS: Thunderbird models began with the number '4', assembly plant code 'Y' (Wixom), body type code, engine type code 'Z' and, finally, the unit's production number, beginning at 100001 and going up.

THUNDERBIRD SERIES

Model Number	Body/Style Number	Body Type & Seating	Factory Price	Shipping Weight	Production Total
Z	83	2-dr HT Cpe-4P	4486	4431	60,552
Z	87	2-dr Landau-4P	4589	4586	22,715
Z	85	2-dr Conv-4P	4853	4441	9,198

PRODUCTION NOTE: Total series output was 92,465 units.

CHASSIS FEATURES: Wheelbase: (Full-size Fords) 119 inches; (Fairlanes) 115.5 inches; (Falcons) 109.5 inches; (Thunderbirds) 113.2 inches. Overall length: (Full-size Fords) 209.9 inches; (Fairlane passenger models) 197.6 inches; (Fairlane station wagons) 201.8 inches; (Falcon Sprints) 181.1 inches; (Falcon passenger cars) 181.6 inches; (Falcon station wagons) 189 inches; (Thunderbirds) 205.4 inches. Tires: (Ford Custom) 7.00 x 14; (Ford station wagons) 8.00 x 14; (all other Fords) 7.50 x 14; (Fairlane passenger cars) 6.50 x 14); (Fairlane station wagons) 7.00 x 14; (Falcon Sprint) 6.50 x 13; (Falcon convertibles) 6.50 x 13; (Falcon station wagons) 6.50 x 13; (Regular Falcons) 6.00 x 13; (Thunderbird) 8.15 x 15.

POWERTRAIN OPTIONS: Falcon six-cylinder: Overhead valves. Cast iron block. Displacement: 144 cubic inches. Bore and stroke: 3.50 x 2.50 inches. Compression ratio: 8.7:1. Brake horsepower: 85 at 4200 R.P.M. Carburetion: Holley one-barrel. Seven main bearings. Serial Number code 'S'.

Falcon/Fairlane/Mustang six-cylinder: Overhead valves. Cast iron block. Displacement: 170 cubic inches. Bore and stroke: 3.50 x 2.94 inches. Compression ratio: 8.7:1. Brake horsepower: 101 at 4400 R.P.M. Carburetion: Holley one-barrel. Seven main bearings. Serial Number code 'U'.

Mustang six-cylinder: Overhead valves. Cast iron block. Displacement: 200 cubic inches. Bore and stroke: 3.68 x 3.13 inches. Compression ratio: 8.7:1. Brake horsepower: 116 at 4400 R.P.M. Carburetion: Holley single-barrel. Seven main bearings. Serial Number code 'T'.

Ford six-cylinder: Overhead valves. Cast iron block. Displacement: 223 cubic inches. Bore and stroke: 3.62 x 3.60 inches. Compression ratio: 8.4:1. Brake horsepower: 138 at 4200 R.P.M. Carburetion: Holley one-barrel. Four main bearings. Serial Number code 'V'.

V-8: Overhead valves. Cast iron block. Displacement: 260 cubic inches. Bore and stroke: 3.80 x 2.87 inches. Compression ratio: 8.8:1. Brake horsepower: 164 at 4400 R.P.M. Carburetion: Holley two-barrel. Five main bearings. Serial Number code 'F'.

Challenger 289 V-8: Overhead valves. Cast iron block. Displacement: 289 cubic inches. Bore and stroke: 4.00 x 2.87 inches. Compression ratio: 9.0:1. Brake horsepower: 195 at 4400 R.P.M. Carburetion: Holley two-barrel. Five main bearings. Serial Number code 'C'.

Challenger 289 four-barrel V-8: Overhead valves. Cast iron block. Displacement: 289 cubic inches. Bore and stroke: 4.00 x 2.87 inches. Compression ratio: 9.8:1. Brake horsepower: 225 at 4800 R.P.M. Carburetion: Holley four-barrel. Five main bearings. Serial Number code 'A'.

High Performance Challenger 289 V-8: Overhead valves. Cast iron block. Displacement: 289 cubic inches. Bore and stroke: 4.00 x 2.87 inches. Compression ratio: 10.5:1. Brake horsepower: 271 at 6000 R.P.M. Carburetion: Holley four-barrel. Five main bearings. Serial Number code 'K'.

Interceptor V-8: Overhead valves. Cast iron block. Displacement: 352 cubic inches. Bore and stroke: 4.00 x 3.50 inches. Compression ratio: 9.3:1. Brake horsepower: 250 at 4400 R.P.M. Carburetion: Holley four-barrel. Five main bearings. Serial Number code 'X'.

Thunderbird V-8: Overhead valves. Cast iron block. Displacement: 390 cubic inches. Bore and stroke: 3.05 x 3.78 inches. Compression ratio: 10.0:1. Brake horsepower: 300 at 4600 R.P.M. Carburetion: Holley four-barrel. Five main bearings. Serial Number code 'Z'.

Thunderbird Special V-8: Overhead valves. Cast iron block. Displacement: 390 cubic inches. Bore and stroke: 4.05 x 3.78 inches. Compression ratio: 10.0:1. Brake horsepower: 330 at 5000 R.P.M. Carburetion: Holley four-barrel. Five main bearings. Serial Number code "P".

Thunderbird High Performance V-8: Overhead valves. Cast iron block. Displacement: 427 cubic inches. Bore and stroke: 4.23 x 3.78 inches. Compression ratio: 11.5:1. Brake horsepower: 410 at 5600 R.P.M. Carburetion: Holley four-barrel. Five main bearings. Serial Number code "Q".

Thunderbird Super High-Performance V-8: Overhead valves. Cast iron block. Displacement: 427 cubic inches. Bore and stroke: 4.23 x 3.78 inches. Compression ratio: 11.5:1. Brake horsepower: 425 at 6000 R.P.M. Carburetion: Two Holley four-barrels. Five main bearings. Serial Number code "R" 1964 Ford transmissions: Same as 1963. 1964 Ford rear axle ratios: Same as 1963.

CONVENIENCE OPTIONS: Popular Custom and Galaxie series options included 288 cubic inch V-8 engine ($109). 390 cubic inch V-8 engine ($246). Cruise-O-Matic automatic transmission ($189 or $212). Four-speed manual transmission ($188). Power steering ($86). Power brakes ($43). Power windows ($102). Tinted windshield ($21). AM radio ($58). Vinyl roof on two-door victorias ($75). Wheel covers ($45). White sidewall tires ($33). Popular station wagon options included the 390 cubic inch V-8 engine ($246). Cruise-O-Matic automatic transmission ($212). Power steering ($86). Power brakes ($43). Power tailgate window ($32). Luggage rack ($45). White sidewall tires ($33). Electric clock ($14). Radio ($58 for AM, $129 for AM/FM). Popular Fairlane and Fairlane 500 options included the 260 cubic inch V-8 engine ($100). The 2889 cubic inch V-8 engine ($145). Fordomatic automatic transmission ($189). Cruise-O-Matic automatic transmission ($189). Four-speed manual transmissions with V-8 engines ($188). AM radio ($58). Power steering ($86). Power tailgate window on station wagons ($32). Luggage rack on station wagons ($45). Two-tone paint ($22). White sidewall tires ($33). Wheel covers ($18). Vinyl roof on two-door hardtops ($75). Popular Falcon options included the 170 cubic inch six-cylinder engine ($17). The 260 cubic inch V-8 engine ($170). Fordomatic automatic transmission ($177). Four-speed manual transmission ($92 with six-cylinder, $188 with V-8). AM radio ($58). Two-tone paint ($19). White sidewall tires ($30). Backup lights ($10). DeLuxe trim package for standard sedans ($43). Popular Falcon station wagon options included all those of the sedans plus power tailgate window ($30). Popular Thunderbird options included air

conditioning ($415). Tinted windows ($43). Leather seats ($106). Power seats ($184). Power windows ($106). AM/FM radio ($83). White sidewall tires ($42). Fiberglass Tonneau cover for convertibles ($269). DeLuxe wheel covers ($16).

Historical footnotes: The full-size Fords, Fairlanes and Falcons were introduced September 27, 1963 and the Mustang appeared in dealer showrooms during April, 1964. Model year production peaked at 1,015,697 units. Calendar year production of 1,787,535 cars was recorded. Lee A. Iacocca was the chief executive officer of the company this year. Note also that Ford introduced the famous Fairlane Thunderbolt drag cars and also the single-overhead cam hemi-engine that Ford tried to use for NASCAR racing. It was disallowed due to insufficient number produced for homogolation.

1965 FORD

1965 Ford, Galaxie 500 4-dr sedan, V-8

1965 FORDS — OVERVIEW — As well as several of the lines being completely restyled once again for 1965, the new 'Total Performance' Ford lineup represented five full car lines, with 44 models, the widest choice of models in Ford Division's history. The 1965 full size Fords were billed as the "Newest since 1949". Luxury and comfort were featured with the big Fords, which used rear coil springs for the first time, new interior styling. 'Silent Flow' ventilation systems were standard on four-door hardtops. In keeping with the new luxury image, the Galaxie 500 LTD interior trim option was offered for the first time, in two and four-door hardtops. Completely restyled once again, the full size Fords possessed incredibly clean styling with very sharp, square lines, and almost no curves. The new grilles featured thin horizontal bars which followed the leading edge contour of the hood and was framed by the new vertical dual headlights. From the side, a single, horizontal feature line divided the less prominent beltline and lower body lines. As in 1964, all full size Fords carried the engine designation symbol on the front fender behind the front wheel, for the larger, optional V-8 engines.

FORD CUSTOM SERIES — (ALL ENGINES) — The Custom series was the base trim level full size Ford for 1965, and included chrome windshield and rear window moldings, two sun visors, a chrome horn ring, arm rests on all doors, and the "Custom" name on the front fender. The taillights were round lenses in a rectangular housing. The Ford name appeared in block letters across the front of the hood and on the vertical section of the trunk lid.

CUSTOM I.D. NUMBERS: (Six-cylinder models) Custom, Six-cylinder models began with the number "5", followed by the assembly plant code, engine designation code "V", and finally, the unit's production number, according to the final assembly location. Each plant began at 100001 and went up. (See production note).

CUSTOM SIX SERIES

Model Number	Body/Style Number	Body Type & Seating	Factory Price	Shipping Weight	Production Total
V	54	4-dr Sedan-6P	2366	3350	Note 1
V	62	2-dr Sedan-6P	2313	3278	Note 1

NOTE 1: See DeLuxe Series V-8 listing.

CUSTOM I.D. NUMBERS: (V-8 models) Custom, V-8 model began with the number "5", followed by the assembly plant code, body type code, engine designation code, and finally, the units production number, according to the final assembly location. Each plant began at 100001 and went up. (See production note).

CUSTOM EIGHT SERIES

Model Number	Body/Style Number	Body Type & Seating	Factory Price	Shipping Weight	Production Total
NA	54	4-dr Sedan-6P	2472	3400	96,393
NA	62	2-dr Sedan-6P	2420	3328	49,034

PRODUCTION NOTE: Total series output was 145,427 units. Ford does not indicate the number of each model produced with Six and V-8 engines. Therefore, all production figures are total production of each body style.

CUSTOM 500 SERIES — (ALL ENGINES) — The Custom 500 was the upper trim level of the base-line Custom series, and included chrome windshield and rear window moldings, nylon carpeting over the rubber mats used in the Custom models, arm rests, with ash trays, on all doors, two sun visors, and all the trim used in the Custom models, plus a short horizontal chrome strip along the front fender and front door.

CUSTOM 500 I.D. NUMBERS: (Six-cylinder models) Custom 500, Six-cylinder model used the same serial number sequence as the Custom models. (See production note).

CUSTOM 500 SIX SERIES

Model Number	Body/Style Number	Body Type & Seating	Factory Price	Shipping Weight	Production Total
V	54B	4-dr Sedan-6P	2467	3380	Note 1
V	62B	2-dr Sedan-6P	2414	3308	Note 1

NOTE 1: See Custom 500 V-8 listing.

CUSTOM 500 I.D. NUMBERS: (V-8 models) Custom 500, V-8 models used the same serial number sequence as the Custom models. (See production note).

CUSTOM 500 V-8 SERIES

Model Number	Body/Style Number	Body Type & Seating	Factory Price	Shipping Weight	Production Total
NA	54B	4-dr Sedan-6P	2573	3430	71,727
NA	62B	2-dr Sedan-6P	2520	3358	19,603

PRODUCTION NOTE: Total series output was 91,330 units. Ford does not indicate the number of each model produced with Six and V-8 engines. Therefore, all production figures are total production of each body style.

GALAXIE 500 SERIES (ALL ENGINES) — The Galaxie 500 was the intermediate trim level for 1965, and included all the Custom trim, plus a chrome hood ornament, Ford crest in the center of the trunk lid, chrome window frames, the Ford crest on the roof "C" pillar, 'Galaxie 500', in block letters at the front of the front fenders, chrome rocker panel trim, hexagonal taillights with chrome 'cross-hairs' trim and backup lights. Two-tone vinyl trim was used on the inside of the doors and on the seats.

GALAXIE 500 I.D. NUMBERS: (Six-cylinder models) Galaxie 500, Six-cylinder models used the same serial number sequence as the Custom series. (See production note).

GALAXIE 500 6-CYL SERIES

Model Number	Body/Style Number	Body Type & Seating	Factory Price	Shipping Weight	Production Total
V	54A	4-dr Sedan-6P	2623	3412	Note 1
V	57B	4-dr HT-6P	2708	3452	Note 1
V	63B	2-dr HT-6P	2630	3352	Note 1
V	76A	2-dr Conv-6P	2889	3556	Note 1

NOTE 1: See Galaxie 500 V-8 Series listing.

GALAXIE 500 I.D. NUMBERS: (V-8 models) Galaxie 500, V-8 models used the same serial number sequence as the Custom series. (See production note).

GALAXIE 500 V-8 SERIES

Model Number	Body/Style Number	Body Type & Seating	Factory Price	Shipping Weight	Production Total
NA	54A	4-dr Sedan-6P	2730	3462	181,183
NA	57B	4-dr HT-6P	2815	3502	49,982
NA	63B	2-dr HT-6P	2737	3402	157,284
NA	76A	2-dr Conv-6P	2996	3616	31,930

PRODUCTION NOTE: Total series output was 420,379 units. Ford does not indicate the number of each model produced with Six and V-8 engines. Therefore, all production figures are total production of each body style.

GALAXIE 500XL SERIES — (V-8) — Galaxie 500XL was the sport trim version of the Galaxie 500 two-door hardtop and two-door convertible, and included all Galaxie 500 trim, plus bucket seats and floor-mounted shift lever, polished door trim panels with carpeting on the lower portion of the doors, dual-lens courtesy/warning lights in the door panels, rear reading lights in hardtops and Galaxie 500XL badges on the body exterior. The 200 horsepower, 289 cubic inch V-8 engine and Cruise-O-Matic automatic transmission were standard in both "XL" body styles.

GALAXIE 500XL I.D. NUMBERS: Galaxie 500XLs used the same serial number sequence as the Custom and Galaxie series. (See production note).

GALAXIE 500XL V-8 SERIES

Model Number	Body/Style Number	Body Type & Seating	Factory Price	Shipping Weight	Production Total
NA	63C	2-dr HT-5P	3167	3507	28,141
NA	76B	2-dr Conv-5P	3426	3675	9,849

PRODUCTION NOTE: Total series output was 37,900 units.

GALAXIE 500 LTD SERIES — (V-8) — The Galaxie 500 LTD was the new top trim level for 1965, and included all the Galaxie 500 trim plus, 200 horsepower, 289 cubic inch V-8 engine and Cruise-O-Matic automatic transmission as standard equipment. Also included thickly padded seats, with 'pinseal' upholstery, simulated walnut appliques on the lower edge of the instrument panel, Gabardine finish headlining and sun visors, front and rear door courtesy/warning lights, courtesy lights in the rear roof pillars on the interior and under the instrument panel, glove box and ash tray lights, and a self-regulating clock.

GALAXIE 500 LTD I.D. NUMBERS: Galaxie 500 LTD used the same serial number sequence as the Custom and Galaxie 500 series. (See production note).

GALAXIE 500 LTD V-8 SERIES

Model Number	Body/Style Number	Body Type & Seating	Factory Price	Shipping Weight	Production Total
NA	57F	4-dr HT-6P	3245	3588	68,038
NA	63F	2-dr HT-6P	3167	3496	37,691

PRODUCTION NOTE: Total series output was 105,729 units.

STATION WAGONS SERIES — (ALL ENGINES) — The Ranch Wagon was once again the base trim level Station Wagon for 1965, with the Country Sedans being the intermediate level and the Country Squires being the top trim level. The trim paralleled the Custom 500, Galaxie 500 and Galaxie 500 LTD models of conventional cars.

STATION WAGON I.D. NUMBERS: (Six-cylinder models) Station Wagon, six-cylinder models used the same serial number sequence as Custom, and Galaxie 500 series of conventional cars. (See production note).

STATION WAGON SERIES SIX

Model Number	Body/Style Number	Body Type & Seating	Factory Price	Shipping Weight	Production Total
V	71D	4-dr Ranch Wag-6P	2707	3841	Note 1
V	71B	4-dr Ctr Sed-6P	2797	3851	Note 1
V	71C	4-dr Ctry Sed-10P	2899	3865	Note 1
V	71E	4-dr Ctry Sq-6P	3041	3895	Note 1
V	71A	4-dr Ctry Sq-10P	3109	3909	Note 1

NOTE 1: See Station Wagon V-8 Series listing.

STATION WAGON I.D. NUMBERS: (V-8 models) Station Wagon, V-8 models used the same serial number sequence as Custom, and Galaxie 500 model of conventional cars. (See production note).

STATION WAGON V-8 SERIES

Model Number	Body/Style Number	Body Type & Seating	Factory Price	Shipping Weight	Production Total
NA	71D	4-dr Ranch Wag-6P	2813	3891	30,817
NA	71B	4-dr Ctry Sed-6P	2904	3901	59,693
NA	71C	4-dr Ctry Sed-10P	3005	3915	32,344
NA	71E	4-dr Ctry Sq-6P	3147	3945	24,308
NA	71A	4-dr Ctry Sq-10P	3216	3959	30,502

PRODUCTION NOTE: Total series output was 177,664 units. Ford does not indicate the number of each model produced with Six and V-8 engines. Therefore, all production figures are total production of each body style.

1965 FORD FAIRLANE — OVERVIEW — The 1965 Fairlane featured new sheet metal below the beltline, for new front, rear and side appearance. Overall length and width were increased, resulting in the first total restyling of the line since it's introduction in 1962. The front end featured a wide horizontal grille and horizontal dual head lights. The hood incorporated a small peak in the center that swept forward over the leading edge and met a similar accent line in the grille. Overall profile was changed with a higher fender line that carried farther back, for a more massive look. For the first time since introduction, Fairlane taillights were not round, but, rather, rectangular and were accented with chrome 'cross-hairs' accents across the lens face. The optional backup lights were mounted in the center of the lens.

FAIRLANE MODELS — (ALL ENGINES) — The Fairlane was the base trim level for the line and included chrome windshield and rear window moldings, chrome horn ring, front and rear arm rests, cigarette lighter, vinyl coated rubber floor mats, and the Fairlane name in block letters at the front of the front fenders.

FAIRLANE I.D. NUMBERS: (Six-cylinder models) Fairlane, Six-cylinder models began with the number "5", followed by the assembly plant code, body type code, engine designation "T", and finally, the unit's production number, according to the final assembly location. Each plant began at 100001 and went up.

FAIRLANE SIX SERIES

Model Number	Body/Style Number	Body Type & Seating	Factory Price	Shipping Weight	Production Total
T	54A	4-dr Sedan-6P	2223	2858	Note 1
T	62A	2-dr Sedan-6P	2183	2806	Note 1
T	71D	4-dr Sta Wag-6P	2512	3183	Note 1

NOTE 1: See Fairlane V-8 Series listing.

FAIRLANE I.D. NUMBERS: (V-8 models) Fairlane, V-8 models began with the number "5", followed by the assembly plant code, body type code, engine designation code, and finally, the unit's production number, according to the final assembly location. Each plant began at 100001 and went up. (See production note.)

FAIRLANE V-8 SERIES

Model Number	Body/Style Number	Body Type & Seating	Factory Price	Shipping Weight	Production Total
NA	54A	4-dr Sedan-6P	2329	3055	25,378
NA	62A	2-dr Sedan-6P	2288	2998	13,685
NA	71D	4-dr Sta Wag-6P	2618	3375	13,911

PRODUCTION NOTE: Total series output was 52,974 units. Ford does not indicate the number of each model produced with Six and V-8 engines. Therefore, all production figures are total production of each body style.

FAIRLANE 500 SERIES — (ALL ENGINES) — The Fairlane 500 models were the top trim level of the line, and included chrome window moldings, a chrome horn ring, front and rear arm rest, a Ford crest on the roof "C" pillar, a chrome hood ornament, a single horizontal chrome strip with an aluminum insert, Ford, in block letters across the rear escutcheon panel, with two chrome strips between the taillights and a Ford crest in the center of the panel. The Fairlane 500 models also used carpet instead of the vinyl floor mats found in Fairlane models.

FAIRLANE 500 I.D. NUMBERS: (Six-cylinder models) Fairlane 500, Six-cylinder models used the same serial number sequence as the Fairlane models. (See production note.)

1965 Ford Fairlane 500 2-dr hardtop Sports Coupe, V-8

FAIRLANE 500 SIX SERIES

Model Number	Body/Style Number	Body Type & Seating	Factory Price	Shipping Weight	Production Total
T	54B	4-dr Sedan-6P	2303	2863	Note 1
T	62B	2-dr Sedan-6P	2263	2806	Note 1
T	65A	2-dr HT-6P	2327	2877	Note 1
T	65B	2-dr Spts Cpe-5P	2484	2888	Note 1
T	71B	4-dr Sta Wag-6P	2592	3220	Note 1

NOTE 1: See Fairlane 500 V-8 Series listing.

FAIRLANE 500 I.D. NUMBERS: (V-8 models) Fairlane 500, V-8 models used the same serial number sequence as the Fairlane models. (See production note.)

FAIRLANE 500 V-8 SERIES

Model Number	Body/Style Number	Body Type & Seating	Factory Price	Shipping Weight	Production Total
NA	54B	4-dr Sedan-6P	2409	3055	77,836
NA	62B	2-dr Sedan-6P	2369	2997	16,092
NA	65B	2-dr HT-6P	2432	3069	41,405
NA	65B	2-dr Spt Cpe-5P	2590	3080	15,141
NA	71B	4-dr Sta Wag-6P	2697	3412	20,506

PRODUCTION NOTE: Total series output was 170,980 units. Ford does not indicate the number of each model produced with Six and V-8 engines. Therefore, all production figures are total production of each body style.

1965 Ford, Falcon Futura 2-dr convertible, V-8

1965 FALCON'S — OVERVIEW — While continuing to use the 1964 body shell, trim changes made the 1965 Falcon look considerably different than the previous year. The grille was a thin horizontal bar design, which was divided into two sections by a wider vertical bar at the center. A vertical, three-colored crest was used on the center divider. The round taillights utilized chrome 'cross-hairs' for accent, and the optional backup lights were mounted in the center of the lens.

FALCON SERIES — (ALL ENGINES) — Falcons were the base trim level for 1965, and included chrome windshield and rear window moldings, two horns, two sun visors, arm rests on the front doors only, and a horn button instead of a chrome horn ring. A new Falcon emblem with black, paint-filled Falcon letters was attached to the front fender behind the wheel opening.

FALCON I.D. NUMBERS: (ALL ENGINES) Falcons used the same serial number sequence as the full-size Fords and the Fairlane line. (See production note.)

FALCON SERIES

Model Number	Body/Style Number	Body Type & Seating	Factory Price	Shipping Weight	Production Total
NA	54A	4-dr Sedan-6P	2038	2410	30,186
NA	62A	2-dr Sedan-6P	1977	2370	35,858

FUTURA SERIES — (ALL ENGINES) — The Futura series was the top trim level for 1965, and included a chrome horn ring, arm rests front and rear, with ash trays, 2 horns, Futura wheel covers instead of hub caps, a chrome hood ornament, Futura symbol on the front fender behind the wheel well, chrome windshield and rear window moldings and side window moldings, a full-length, spear-type chrome-molding, with either red, white or black painted insert.

FUTURA I.D. NUMBERS: (ALL ENGINES) Futura models used the same serial number sequence as the full-size Fords, Fairlanes, and Falcons. (See production note.)

FUTURA SERIES

Model Number	Body/Style Number	Body Type & Seating	Factory Price	Shipping Weight	Production Total
NA	54B	4-dr Sedan-6P	2146	2410	33,985
NA	62B	2-dr Sedan-6P	2099	2375	11,670
NA	63B	2-dr HT-6P	2179	2395	24,451
NA	63B	2-dr HT-5P	2226	2380	1,303
NA	76A	2-dr Conv-6P	2428	2675	6,191
NA	76B	2-dr Conv-5P	2481	2660	124
NA	63D	2-dr Sprint HT-5P	2425	2813	2,806
NA	76D	2-dr Sprint Conv-5P	2660	3008	300

PRODUCTION NOTE: Total series output was 171,442 units, including 13,824 four-door Sedans, and 13,850 two-door Sedans with the DeLuxe trim option in the Falcon model line. Ford does not indicate the number of each model with Six and V-8 engines. Therefore, all production figures are total production of each body style. **ADDITIONAL NOTE:** Models 63B and 76B have bucket seats.

FALCON STATION WAGON SERIES — (ALL ENGINES) — Falcon Station wagons included the Falcon as the base trim level, Futura Wagon as the intermediate level and Squire as the top trim level.

STATION WAGON I.D. NUMBERS: — (ALL ENGINES) Falcon Station Wagons used the same serial number sequence as the full-size Fords, Fairlanes and Falcon sedans. (See production note).

FALCON STATION WAGON SERIES

Model Number	Body/Style Number	Body Type & Seating	Factory Price	Shipping Weight	Production Total
NA	71A	4-dr Falcon Wag-6P	2317	2680	14,911
NA	59A	2-dr Falcon-6P	2284	2640	4,891
NA	71B	4-dr Futura Wag-6P	2453	2670	12,548
NA	71C	4-dr Squire Wag-6P	2608	2695	6,703

PRODUCTION NOTE: Total series output was 39,053 units. Ford does not indicate the number of each model produced with Six and V-8 engines. Therefore, all production figures are total production of each body style.

1965 Ford, Thunderbird 2-dr convertible, V-8

1965 THUNDERBIRD OVERVIEW — Except for minor trim changes, the 1965 Thunderbird was the same as the 1964 model. Disc brakes and sequential turn signals were added to the 1965 list of features, as well as reversible keys and keyless locking system. Also available were vacuum operated, power door locks (introduced as part of an optional safety group in 1964), and a remote trunk release. A simulated, chrome 'scoop' was incorporated in the front fender immediately to the rear of the front wheel openings. A new Thunderbird crest replaced the Thunderbird name across the front of the hood, for 1965. A restyled Thunderbird emblem was used on the roof "C" pillar and new wheel covers were used for 1965. The new horizontal grille featured 6 vertical bars and 8 horizontal bars.

THUNDERBIRD SERIES — With a few trim changes, the 1965 Thunderbird continued to use the same body as introduced in 1964. A new grille was used within the existing shell, and a Thunderbird emblem replaced the block Thunderbird letters on the front of the hood. A die-cast front fender ornament, in the form of a forward-canted exhaust-outlet was located directly behind the front wheelwell. A Thunderbird emblem was used on the roof "C" pillar and new wheel covers were used for 1965.

THUNDERBIRD I.D. NUMBERS: Thunderbird models began with the number "5", assembly plant code "Y" (Wixom), body type code, engine type code "Z", and finally, the unit's production number, beginning at 100001 and going up.

THUNDERBIRD SERIES

Model Number	Body/Style Number	Body Type & Seating	Factory Price	Shipping Weight	Production Total
A	63A	2-dr HT-4P	4394	4470	42,652
Z	63B	2-dr Landau-4P	4495	4478	25,474
Z	76A	2-dr Conv-4P	4851	4588	6,846

PRODUCTION NOTE: Total series output was 74,972 units.

1965 FORD CHASSIS FEATURES: Wheelbase: 119 inches. Overall length: 210 inches. Tires: 7.35 x 15 4-ply tubeless blackwall (8.15 x 15 4-ply tubeless blackwall on Station Wagons).

1965 FAIRLANE CHASSIS FEATURES: Wheelbase: 116 inches. Overall length: 198.4 inches, (203.2 inches on Station Wagons). Tires: 6.94 x 14 4-ply tubeless blackwall (7.35 x 14 4-ply tubeless on Station Wagons).

FALCON CHASSIS FEATURES: Wheelbase: 109.5 inches. Overall length: 181.6 inches (190 on Station Wagons). Tires: 6.50 x 13 (7.00 x 13 on Station Wagons). All tires were 4-ply tubeless blackwall.

THUNDERBIRD CHASSIS FEATURES: Wheelbase: 113.2 inches. Overall length: 205.4 inches. Tires: 8.15 x 15 4-ply tubeless blackwall.

1965 FORD TRANSMISSIONS
Same as 1963, with the following exception: The Borg-Warner T-10 4-speed transmission was replaced for 1965, with the Ford produced T&C "top-loader" 4-speed.

1965 FORD REAR AXLE RATIOS:
Same as 1963.

1965 FORD ENGINES
Falcon/Fairlane/Mustang 6-cylinder: Overhead valves. Cast iron block. Displacement: 170 cubic inches. Bore and stroke: 3.50 x 2.94 inches. Compression ratio: 9.1:1. Brake horsepower: 105 at 4400 R.P.M. Carburetion: Holley single-barrel. Seven main bearings. Serial number code "U".

Falcon/Fairlane/Mustang 6-cylinder: Overhead valves. Cast iron block. Displacement: 200 cubic inches. Bore and stroke: 3.68 x 3.13 inches. Compression ratio: 9.2:1. Brake horsepower: 120 at 4400 R.P.M. Carburetion: Holley single-barrel. Seven main bearings. Serial number code "T".

Ford 6-cylinder: Overhead valves. Cast iron block. Displacement: 240 cubic inches. Bore and stroke: 4.00 x 3.18 inches. Compression ratio: 9.2:1. Brake horsepower: 150 at 4000 R.P.M. Carburetion: Holley single barrel. Seven main bearings. Serial number code "V".

Challengar 289 V-8: Overhead valves. Cast iron block. Displacement: 289 cubic inches. Bore and stroke: 4.00 x 2.87 inches. Compression ratio: 9.3:1. Brake horsepower: 200 at 4400 R.P.M. Carburetion: Holley two barrel. Five main bearings. Serial number code "C".

Challenger 289 4V V-8: Overhead valves. Cast iron block. Displacement: 289 cubic inches. Bore and stroke: 4.00 x 2.87 inches. Compression ratio: 10.0:1. Brake horsepower: 225 at 4800 R.P.M. Carburetion: Holley four-barrel. Five main bearings. Serial number code "A".

High Performance 289 V-8: Overhead valves. Cast iron block. Displacement: 289 cubic inches. Bore and stroke: 4.00 x 2.87 inches. Compression ratio: 10.5:1. Brake horsepower: 271 at 6000 R.P.M. Carburetion: Holley four-barrel. Five main bearings. Serial number code "K".

Interceptor V-8: Overhead valves. Cast iron block. Displacement: 352 cubic inches. Bore and stroke: 4.00 x 3.50 inches. Compression ratio: 9.3:1. Brake horsepower: 250 at 4400 R.P.M. Carburetion: Holley four-barrel. Five main bearings. Serial number code "X".

Thunderbird V-8: Overhead valves. Cast iron block. Displacement: 390 cubic inches. Bore and stroke: 4.05 x 3.78 inches. Compression ratio: 10.0:1. Brake horsepower: 300 at 4600 R.P.M. Carburetion: Holley four-barrel. Five main bearings. Serial number code "Z".

Thunderbird Special V-8: Overhead valves. Cast iron block. Displacement: 390 cubic inches. Bore and stroke: 4.05 x 3.78 inches. Compression ratio: 10.0:1. Brake horsepower: 330 at 5000 R.P.M. Carburetion: Holley four-barrel. Five main bearings. Serial number code "P".

Thunderbird Super High-Performance V-8: Overhead valves. Cast iron block. Displacement: 427 cubic inches. Bore and stroke: 4.23 x 3.78 inches. Compression ratio: 11.5:1. Brake horsepower: 425 at 6000 R.P.M. Carburetion: Two Holley four barrels. Five main bearings. Serial number code "R".

1965 AND 1966 FORD ENGINE SECTION:
"SOHC 427 4V V8: Hemispherical combustion chambers with overhead valves and overhead camshafts for each engine bank. Cast iron block and cylinder heads. Displacement: 427 cubic inches. Bore and stroke: 4.23 x 3.78. Compression ratio: 12.1:1. Brake horsepower: 616 @ 7000 RPM. Carburetion: Holley four barrel. Five main bearings. Engine was only available "over the counter" for $2500, thus, no engine code was provided.

SOHC 427 BV V8: Hemispherical combustion chambers with overhead camshafts for each engine bank. Cast iron block and cylinder heads. Displacement: 427 cubic inches. Bore and stroke: 4.23 x 3.78. Compression ratio: 12.1:1. Brake horsepwoer: 657 @ 7500 RPM. Carburetion: Two Holley four barrels. Five main bearings. Availability as 4V version.

CONVENIENCE OPTIONS: Popular Custom and Custom 500 model options included the 289 cubic inch V-8 engine ($109). Cruise-O-Matic automatic transmission ($189). Power steering ($97). AM radio ($58). Wheel covers ($25). White side wall tires ($34). Popular Galaxie 500 and Galaxie 550 XL options included the 390 cubic inch V-8 engine ($246). Cruise-O-Matic automatic transmission ($190). 4-speed manual transmission ($188 — no charge on XLs). Power steering ($97). Power brakes ($43). Power windows ($102). Tinted windshield ($40). Air conditioning ($36). AM radio ($58). Vinyl roof ($76). Wheel covers ($26). White sidewall tires ($34). Popular LTD options included the 390 cubic inch V-8 engine ($137). Power steering ($97). Power brakes ($43). Power windows ($102). Tinted windshield ($40). Air conditioning ($364). AM radio ($72); AM/FM radio ($142). Vinyl roof ($76). White sidewall tires ($34). Popular Station Wagon options included the 390 cubic inch V-8 engine ($246). Cruise-O-Matic automatic transmission ($190). Power steering ($97). Power brakes ($43). Tinted windows ($40). Power tailgate window ($32). Luggage rack ($45). AM radio ($58). White sidewall tires ($34). Wheel covers ($25). Popular Fairlane and Fairlane 500 options included 289 cubic inch V-8 engine ($108), or High-Performance 289 cubic inch V-8 ($430). Cruise-O-Matic automatic transmission ($190). 4-speed manual transmission ($188). AM radio ($58). Power steering ($86). Power tailgate window on Station Wagons ($32). Luggage rack on Station Wagons ($45). White sidewall tires ($34). Wheel covers ($22). Vinyl roof on two-door hardtops ($76). Popular Falcon options included the 200 cubic inche 6-cylinder engine ($45), or the 289 cubic inch V-8 engine ($153). Cruise-O-Matic automatic transmission ($182 or $172 with 6-cylinder). Front bucket seats ($69). AM radio ($58). Two-tone paint ($19). White sidewall tires ($30). Sprint package ($222, 273 on convertibles). Luggage rack ($45). Popular Falcon Station Wagon options included all those of the sedans, plus the following: Power tailgate window ($30). Luggage rack ($45). Popular Thunderbird options included Air conditioning ($425). Tinted windshield ($43). Leather seats ($106). Power seats ($184). Power windows ($106). AM/FM radio ($84). White sidewall tires ($44). Vacuum trunk release ($13). DeLuxe wheel covers ($16).

Historical footnotes: Model names were dropped for 1965, in favor of designating the car by it's actual body style, i.e., "Club Victoria" became "two-door Hardtop," and "Sunliner" became "two-door Convertible", etc. The 427 cubic inch single-overhead cam engine was installed in the Fairlane Thunderbolt drag cars.

1966 FORD

1966 FORDS — OVERVIEW — For 1966, Ford continued its policy of major restyling in several of the model lines. While 1965 and 1966 full-size Fords bear a resemblance to each other, they are quite different cars. The hood is the only interchangeable exterior body component. The 1966 models featured more rounded lines than the previous year, even though the feature lines were in the same location.

FORD CUSTOM SERIES — (ALL ENGINES) — The Custom series was the base trim level full-size Ford for 1966 and included chrome windshield and rear window moldings; two sun visors; a chrome horn ring; arm rests on all doors and the Custom name, in script, on the rear fender. The taillights had square lenses, with centrally-mounted backup lights surrounded by a chorme bezel. The Ford name appeared, in block letters, across the front of the hood and across the vertical section of the trunk lid.

CUSTOM SIX SERIES IDENTIFICATION NUMBERS: Custom six-cylinder models began with the number '6', followed by the assembly plant code, engine designation code 'V' and, finally, the unit's production number according to the final assembly location. Each plant began at 100001 and went up (See production note).

CUSTOM SIX SERIES

Model Number	Body/Style Number	Body Type & Seating	Factory Price	Shipping Weight	Production Total
V	54B	4-dr Sedan-6P	2415	3433	Note 1
V	62B	2-dr Sedan-6P	2363	3333	Note 1

NOTE 1: See production note below.

CUSTOM V-8 SERIES IDENTIFICATION NUMBERS: Custom V-8 models began with the number '6', followed by the assembly plant code, body type code, engine designation code and, finally, the unit's production number according to the final assembly location. Each plant began at 100001 and went up (See production note).

CUSTOM V-8 SERIES

Model Number	Body/Style Number	Body Type & Seating	Factory Price	Shipping Weight	Production Total
NA	54B	4-dr Sedan-6P	2539	3477	72,245
NA	62B	2-dr Sedan-6P	2487	3377	32,292

PRODUCTION NOTE: Total series output was 138,238 units. Ford does not indicate the number of each model produced with sixes or V-8s. Therefore, all production figures given above are total production of each body style with both engines.

CUSTOM 500 SERIES — (ALL ENGINES) — The Custom 500 was the upper trim level of the base-line Custom series and included chrome windshield and rear window moldings; Nylon carpeting instead of the rubber mats used in the Custom models; arm rests (with ash trays) on all doors; two sun visors and all trim used in the Custom models. There was also a horizontal chrome strip along the side feature line and the designation '500', in a die-cast block with black-painted background, in front of the Custom script. A small Ford crest was located in the chrome side strip, on the front of the front fenders.

CUSTOM 500 SIX SERIES IDENTIFICATION NUMBERS: Custom 500 six-cylinder models used the same Serial Number sequence as the Custom models (See production note).

CUSTOM 500 SIX SERIES

Model Number	Body/Style Number	Body Type & Seating	Factory Price	Shipping Weight	Production Total
V	54B	4-dr Sedan-6P	2514	3444	Note 1
V	62B	2-dr Sedan-6P	2464	3375	Note 1

NOTE 1: See production note below.

CUSTOM 500 V-8 SERIES IDENTIFICATION NUMBERS: Custom 500 V-8 models used the same Serial Number sequence as the Custom models. (See production note).

CUSTOM 500 V-8 SERIES

Model Number	Body/Style Number	Body Type & Seating	Factory Price	Shipping Weight	Production Total
NA	54B	4-dr Sedan-6P	2639	3488	109,449
NA	62B	2-dr Sedan-6P	2588	3419	28,789

PRODUCTION NOTE: Total series output was 138,238 units. Ford does not indicate the number of each model produced with Sixes or V-8s. Therefore, all production given above figures are total production of each body style with both engines.

GALAXIE 500 SERIES — (ALL ENGINES) — The Galaxie 500 was the intermediate trim level for 1966 and included all the Custom trim, plus a chrome hood ornament; Ford crest in the feature line on the front fender; stamped aluminum rocker panel moldings and a stamped aluminum insert, between two chrome strips on the vertical section of the trunk lid, with Ford, in block letters, spaced evenly across. Two-tone vinyl trim was used on the inside of the doors and on the seats. Simulated wood appliques were used on the instrument panel trim pieces.

GALAXIE 500 SIX SERIES IDENTIFICATION NUMBERS: Galaxie 500 six-cylinder models used the same Serial Number sequence as the Custom and Custom 500 models (See production note).

GALAXIE 500 SIX SERIES

Model Number	Body/Style Number	Body Type & Seating	Factory Price	Shipping Weight	Production Total
V	54A	4-dr Sedan-6P	2658	3456	Note 1
V	57B	4-dr FsBk Sed-6P	2743	3526	Note 1
V	63B	2-dr FsBk Cpe-6P	2685	3437	Note 1
V	76A	2-dr Conv-6P	2914	3633	Note 1

NOTE 1: See production note below.

GALAXIE 500 V-8 SERIES IDENTIFICATION NUMBERS: Galaxie 500 V-8 models used the same Serial Number sequence as the Custom and Custom 500 series (See Production note).

GALAXIE 500 V-8 SERIES

Model Number	Body/Style Number	Body Type & Seating	Factory Price	Shipping Weight	Production Total
NA	54A	4-dr Sedan-6P	2784	3500	171,886
NA	57B	4-dr FsBk Sed-6P	2869	3570	54,886
NA	63B	2-dr FsBk Cpe-6P	2791	3481	198,532
NA	76A	2-dr Conv-6P	3041	3677	27,454

PRODUCTION NOTE: Total series output was 452,758 units. Ford does not indicate the number of each model produced with Sixes or V-8s. Therefore, all production given above figures are total production of each body style with both engines.

GALAXIE 500XL SERIES — (V-8) — Galaxie 500XL was the sport trim version of the Galaxie 500 two-door hardtop and two-door convertible and included all Galaxie 500 trim, plus bucket seats and floor-mounted shift lever; polished door trim panels with carpeting on the lower portion of the doors; dual-lens courtesy/warning lights in the door panels; rear reading lights (in hardtops) and Galaxie 500XL badges on the body exterior. The 200 horsepower, 289 cubic inch V-8 engine and Cruise-O-Matic automatic transmission were standard in both 'XL' body styles.

GALAXIE 500XL IDENTIFICATION NUMBERS: Galaxie 500XLs used the same Serial Number sequence as the Custom and Galaxie series (See production note).

GALAXIE 500XL SERIES

Model Number	Body/Style Number	Body Type & Seating	Factory Price	Shipping Weight	Production Total
NA	63C	2-dr FsBk-5P	3208	3616	25,715
NA	76B	2-dr Conv-5P	3456	3761	6,360

PRODUCTION NOTE: Total series output was 32,075 units.

1966 Ford, Galaxie 500 '7-Litre' 2-dr hardtop sports coupe, V-8

GALAXIE 500 7-LITRE SERIES — The '7-Litre' was the high-performance version of the Galaxie 500XL and was equipped with the 345 horsepower, 428 cubic inch V-8 engine as standard equipment, along with the Cruise-O-Matic automatic transmission. The four-speed manual transmission was available as a no-cost option for those who chose to be even more sporting. Along with the 428 engine, standard equipment also included a sport steering wheel (of simulated English walnut); bucket seats; floor shift; low restriction dual exhaust and a non-silenced air cleaner system. Also standard were the power disc brakes.

GALAXIE 500 7-LITRE IDENTIFICATION NUMBERS: Galaxie 500 7-Litres used the same Serial Number sequence as the Custom and Galaxie series (See production note).

GALAXIE 500 7-LITRE SERIES

Model Number	Body/Style Number	Body Type & Seating	Factory Price	Shipping Weight	Production Total
Q	63D	2-dr FsBk-5P	3596	3914	8,705
Q	76D	2-dr Conv-5P	3844	4059	2,368

PRODUCTION NOTE: Total series output was 11,073 units.

GALAXIE 500 LTD SERIES — (V-8) — The Galaxie 500 LTD was the top trim level for 1966 and included all the Galaxie 500 trim, plus the 200 horsepower, 289 cubic inch (V-8) engine; Cruise-O-Matic automatic transmission; thickly padded seats (with 'pinseal' upholstery); simulated walnut appliques on the lower edge of the instrument panel (and in the door inserts); Gabardine finish headliner and sun visors; front and rear door courtesy/warning lights; courtesy lights on the rear interior roof pillars and under the instrument panel; glove box and ash tray lights and a self-regulating clock.

GALAXIE 500 LTD IDENTIFICATION NUMBERS: Galaxie 500 LTDs used the same Serial Number sequence as the Custom and Galaxie 500 series (See production note).

GALAXIE 500 LTD SERIES

Model Number	Body/Style Number	Body Type & Seating	Factory Price	Shipping Weight	Production Total
NA	57F	4-dr HT Sed-6P	3278	3649	69,400
NA	63F	2-dr FsBk Cpe-6P	3201	3601	31,696

PRODUCTION NOTE: Total series output was 101,096 units.

STATION WAGON SERIES — (ALL ENGINES) — The Ranch Wagon was the base trim level Station Wagon for 1966. The Country Sedans were the intermediate level and the Country Squires were the top trim level. The trim paralleled the Custom 500, Galaxie 500 and Galaxie 500 LTD models of conventional cars.

STATION WAGON SIX SERIES IDENTIFICATION NUMBERS: Station Wagon six-cylinder models used the same Serial Number sequence as Custom and Galaxie 500 series of conventional cars (See production note).

STATION WAGON SIX SERIES

Model Number	Body/Style Number	Body Type & Seating	Factory Price	Shipping Weight	Production Total
V	71D	4-dr Ranch Wag-6P	2793	3919	Note 1
V	71B	4-dr Ctry Sed-6P	2882	3934	Note 1
V	71C	4-dr Ctry Sed-9P	2999	3975	Note 1
V	71E	4-dr Ctry Sq-6P	3182	4004	Note 1
V	71A	4-dr Ctry Sq-9P	3265	4018	Note 1

NOTE 1: See production note below.

STATION WAGON V-8 SERIES IDENTIFICATION NUMBERS: Station Wagon V-8 models used the same Serial Number sequence as Custom and Galaxie 500 models of conventional cars (See production note).

STATION WAGON V-8 SERIES

Model Number	Body/Style Number	Body Type & Seating	Factory Price	Shipping Weight	Production Total
NA	71D	4-dr Ranch Wag-6P	2900	3963	33,306
NA	71B	4-dr Ctry Sed-6P	2989	3978	55,616
NA	71C	4-dr Ctry Sed-9P	3105	4019	36,633
NA	71E	4-dr Ctry Sq-6P	3289	4048	27,645
NA	71A	4-dr CtrySq-9P	3372	4062	47,953

PRODUCTION NOTE: Total series output was 195,153 units. Ford does not indicate the number of each model produced with Sixes and V-8s. Therefore, all production figures given above are total production of each body style with both engines.

1966 FAIRLANE — OVERVIEW — Major restyling was given to the Fairlane lineup, which included 13 different models. They were longer, lower and wider, and featured new suspensions both front and rear. The full-width grille featured a horizontal grid with a large divider bar and the Fairlane crest in the center of the grille. The headlights were vertically stacked and angled back, at the bottom, for a more aggressive look. A full-length horizontal feature line was used for emphasis and the model designation, in block letters, was located on the rear fender. The taillights were rectangular and featured a chrome ring around the outside and around the centrally located backup lights. Engine choices ranged from the 200 cubic inch, 120 horsepower six-cylinder engine, up to the mighty, 335 horsepower, 390 cubic inch 'GT' V-8 engine. For the first time, three convertibles were added to the lineup of hardtops and sedans. There was a total of 13 different models.

FAIRLANE MODELS — (ALL ENGINES) — The Fairlane was the base trim level for the 1966 and included chrome windshield and rear window moldings; chrome rain gutter molding; chrome horn ring; front and rear arm rests; cigarette lighter; vinyl coated rubber floor mats and the Fairlane name, in block letters, on the front fenders.

FAIRLANE SIX SERIES IDENTIFICATION NUMBERS: Fairlane six-cylinder models began with the number '6', followed by the assembly plant code, body type code, engine designation 'T' and, finally, the unit's production number according to the final assembly location. Each plant began at 100001 and went up.

FAIRLANE SIX SERIES

Model Number	Body/Style Number	Body Type & Seating	Factory Price	Shipping Weight	Production Total
T	54	4-dr Sedan-6P	2280	2792	Note 1
T	62	2-dr Sedan-6P	2240	2747	Note 1
T	71	4-dr Sta Wag-6P	2589	3182	Note 1

NOTE 1: See production note below.

FAIRLANE V-8 SERIES IDENTIFICATION NUMBERS: Fairlane V-8 models began with the number '6', followed by the assembly plant code, body type code, engine designation code and, finally, the unit's prodution number according to the final assembly location. Each plant began at 100001 and went up (See production note).

FAIRLANE V-8 SERIES

Model Number	Body/Style Number	Body Type & Seating	Factory Price	Shipping Weight	Production Total
NA	54A	4-dr Sedan-6P	2386	2961	26,170
NA	62A	2-dr Sedan-6P	2345	2916	13,498
NA	71D	4-dr Sta Wag-6P	2694	3351	12,379

PRODUCTION NOTE: Total series output was 52,047 units. Ford does not indicate the number of each model produced with Sixes or V-8s. Therefore, all production figures given above are total production of each body style with both engines.

1966 Ford, Fairlane GT 2-dr convertible, V-8

FAIRLANE 500 SERIES — (ALL ENGINES) — The Fairlane 500 was the intermediate trim level for 1966 and included all the Fairlane trim, plus polished aluminum rocker panel moldings; a Fairlane crest in the center of the grille; color-keyed carpets (front and rear) and Fairlane 500 identification, in block letters, on the rear fenders. A Fairlane crest and Fairlane script also appeared on the righthand vertical section of the trunk lid.

FAIRLANE 500 SIX SERIES IDENTIFICATION NUMBERS: Fairlane 500 six-cylinder models used the same Serial Number sequence as the Fairlane models (See production note).

FAIRLANE 500 SIX SERIES

Model Number	Body/Style Number	Body Type & Seating	Factory Price	Shipping Weight	Production Total
T	54B	4-dr Sedan-6P	2357	2798	Note 1
T	62B	2-dr Sedan-6P	2317	2754	Note 1
T	63B	2-dr HT Cpe-6P	2378	2856	Note 1
T	76B	2-dr Conv-6P	2603	3084	Note 1
T	71B	4-dr Sta Wag-6P	2665	3192	Note 1
T	71E	4-dr Squire Wag-6P	2796	3200	Note 1

NOTE 1: See production note below.

FAIRLANE 500 V-8 SERIES IDENTIFICATION NUMBERS: Fairlane 500 V-8 models used the same Serial Number sequence as the Fairlane models (See production note).

FAIRLANE 500 V-8 SERIES

Model Number	Body/Style Number	Body Type & Seating	Factory Price	Shipping Weight	Production Total
NA	54B	4-dr Sedan-6P	2463	2967	68,635
NA	62B	2-dr Sedan-6P	2423	2923	14,118
NA	63B	2-dr HT Cpe-6P	2484	3025	75,947
NA	76B	2-dr Conv-6P	2709	3253	9,299
NA	71B	4-dr Sta Wag-6P	2770	3361	19,826
NA	71E	4-dr Squire Wag-6P	2901	3369	11,558

PRODUCTION NOTE: Total series output was 199,383 units. Ford does not indicate the number of each model produced with Sixes or V-8s. Therefore, all production figures given above are total production of each body style with both engines.

FAIRLANE 500XL SERIES — (ALL ENGINES) — The Fairlane 500XL was the sporty version of the Fairlane 500 series and included all the Fairlane 500 features, plus bucket seats and console; special name plaques and exterior trim; DeLuxe wheel covers; red safety lights and white courtesy lights in the door arm rests.

FAIRLANE 500XL SIX SERIES IDENTIFICATION NUMBER: Fairlane 500XL six-cylinder models used the same Serial Number sequence as the Fairlane and Fairlane 500 models (See production note).

Model Number	Body/Style Number	Body Type & Seating	Factory Price	Shipping Weight	Production Total
T	63C	2-dr HT Cpe-5P	2543	2884	Note 1
T	76C	2-dr Conv-5P	2768	3099	Note 1

NOTE 1: See production note below.

FAIRLANE 500XL V-8 SERIES IDENTIFICATION NUMBERS: Fairlane 500XL V-8 models used the same Serial Number sequence as the Fairlane and Fairlane 500 models (See production note).

FAIRLANE 500XL V-8 SERIES

Model Number	Body/Style Number	Body Type & Seating	Factory Price	Shipping Weight	Production Total
NA	63C	2-dr HT Cpe-5P	2649	3053	23,942
NA	76C	2-dr Conv-5P	2874	3268	4,560
NA	63D	2-dr GT HT-5P	2843	3493	33,015
NA	76D	2-dr GT Conv-5P	3068	3070	4,327

PRODUCTION NOTE: Total series output was 65,844 units. Ford does not indicate the number of each model produced with Sixes or V-8s. Therefore, all production figures given above are total production of each body style with both engines.

ADDITIONAL NOTE: The Fairlane GT models came only with the 390 cubic inch V-8 engine.

1966 Ford, Falcon Futura 2-dr coupe, V-8

1966 FALCONS — OVERVIEW — The Falcon series also received a total restyling for 1966, with a longer hood, shorter trunk and rounder lines than in 1965. The beautiful two-door hardtops were discontinued for 1966, with the Futura sport coupe carrying the sporty image for the year.

FALCON SERIES — (ALL ENGINES) — The Falcons were the base trim level of the compact Falcon line for 1966 and included chrome windshield, rear window and rain gutter moldings; twin horns and sun visors; arm rests on the front doors only and a horn button, instead of a chrome horn ring. The Falcon script was located behind the front wheel well, on the front fender, and Ford was spelled out, in block letters, across the front of the hood. Falcon was spelled out, in block letters, across the vertical section of the trunk lid.

FALCON IDENTIFICATION NUMBERS: (ALL ENGINES) — Falcons used the same Serial Number sequence as the full-size Ford and the Fairlane line (See production note).

FALCON SERIES

Model Number	Body/Style Number	Body Type & Seating	Factory Price	Shipping Weight	Production Total
NA	54A	4-dr Sedan-6P	2114	2559	34,685
NA	62A	2-dr Sedan-6P	2060	2519	41,432
NA	71A	4-dr Sta Wag-6P	2442	3037	16,653

PRODUCTION NOTE: Total series output was 92,770 units. Ford does not indicate the number of each model produced with Sixes or V-8s. Therefore, all production figures given above are total production of each body style with both engines.

FUTURA SERIES — (ALL ENGINES) — The Futura series was the top trim level for 1966 and included all the standard Falcon features, plus a cigarette lighter; rear arm rests and ash trays; chrome horn ring; Nylon carpeting; special Futura moldings, trim, emblems and nameplates and chrome side window frames. In addition, the sports coupe also featured the 120 horsepower, 200 cubic inch six-cylinder engine; bucket seats in front; special nameplates and special wheel covers.

FUTURA IDENTIFICATION NUMBERS: (ALL ENGINES) — Futura models used the same Serial Number sequence as the full-size Fords, Fairlanes and Falcons (See production note).

FALCON FUTURA SERIES

Model Number	Body/Style Number	Body Type & Seating	Factory Price	Shipping Weight	Production Total
NA	54B	4-dr Sedan-6P	2237	2567	34,039
NA	62B	2-dr Clb Cpe-6P	2183	2527	21,997
NA	62C	2-dr Spt Cpe-5P	2328	2597	20,289
NA	71B	4-dr Squire Wag-6P	2553	3045	13,574

PRODUCTION NOTE: Total series output was 89,899 units. Ford does not indicate the number of each model produced with Sixes and V-8s. Therefore, all production figures are total production of each body style with both engines.

1966 Ford, Thunderbird 2-dr Landau sports coupe, V-8

THUNDERBIRD SERIES — (OVERVIEW) — Even though it used the body shell of the previous two years, the 1966 Thunderbird looked completely new. The grille was more sharply angled back and featured an egg-crate backing for a massive Thunderbird emblem which appeared to float in the grille. At the rear, a single, massive taillight stretched from side to side, with a single backup light being part of the Thunderbird emblem in the center of the lens. The name Thunderbird appeared, in script, just ahead of the taillights on the rear fender. Another Thunderbird emblem appeared on the roof 'C' pillar. More horsepower was available in the form of the optional 345 horsepower, 428 cubic inch V-8 engine.

THUNDERBIRD IDENTIFICATION NUMBERS: Thunderbird models began with the number '6', assembly plant code 'Y' (Wixom), body type code, engine type codes 'Z' or 'Q' and, finally, the unit's production number, beginning at 100001 and going up.

Model Number	Body/Style Number	Body Type & Seating	Factory Price	Shipping Weight	Production Total
Z/Q	63A	2-dr HT Cpe-4P	4395	4386	13,389
Z/Q	63B	2-dr HT Twn Sed-4P	4451	4359	15,633
Z/Q	63D	2-dr Landau-4P	4552	4367	35,105
Z/Q	76A	2-dr Conv-4P	4845	4496	5,049

PRODUCTION NOTE: Total series output was 69,176 units.

1966 FORD CHASSIS FEATURES: Wheelbase: 119 inches. Overall length: 210 inches (210.9 inches on station wagons). Tires: 7.35 x 15 four-ply tubeless blackwell (8.45 x 15 four-ply tubeless blackwell on station wagons).

1966 FAIRLANE CHASSIS FEATURES: Wheelbase: 116 inches (113 inches on station wagons). Overall length: 197 inches (199.8 inches on station wagons). Tires: 6.95 x 14 four-ply tubeless blackwall (7.75 x 14 four-ply tubeless blackwall on station wagons).

FALCON CHASSIS FEATURES: Wheelbase: 110.9 inches (113 inches on station wagons). Overall length: 184.3 inches (198.7 inches on station wagons). Tires: 6.50 x 13 four-ply tubeless blackwalls (7.75 x 14 four-ply tubeless blackwall on station wagons).

THUNDERBIRD CHASSIS FEATURES: Wheelbase: 113.2 inches. Overall length: 205.4 inches. Tires: 8.15 x 15 four-ply tubeless blackwall.

1966 FORD ENGINES
Falcon/Fairlane six-cylinder: Overhead valves. Cast iron block. Displacement: 170 cubic inches. Bore and stroke: 3.50 x 2.94 inches. Compression ratio: 9.1:1. Brake horsepower: 105 at 4400 R.P.M. Carburetion: Holley one-barrel. Seven main bearings. Serial Number code 'U'.

FALCON/FAIRLANE/MUSTANG SIX-CYLINDER: Overhead valves. Cast iron block. Displacement: 200 cubic inches. Bore and stroke: 3.68 x 3.13 inches. Compression ratio: 9.2:1. Brake horsepower: 120 at 4400 R.P.M. Carburetion: Holley one-barrel. Seven main bearings. Serial Number code 'T'.

FORD SIX-CYLINDER: Overhead valves. Cast iron block. Displacement: 240 cubic inches. Bore and stroke: 4.00 x 3.18 inches. Compression ratio: 9.2:1. Brake horsepower: 150 at 4000 R.P.M. Carburetion: Holley one-barrel. Seven main bearings. Serial Number code 'V'.

CHALLENGER 289 V-8: Overhead valves. Cast iron block. Displacement: 289 cubic inches. Bore and stroke: 4.00 x 2.87 inches. Compression ratio: 9.3:1. Brake horsepower: 200 at 4400 R.P.M. Carburetion: Holley two-barrel. Five main bearings. Serial Number code 'C'.

CHALLENGER 289 V-8: Overhead valves. Cast iron block. Displacement: 289 cubic inches. Bore and stroke: 4.00 x 2.87 inches. Compression ratio: 10.0:1. Brake horsepower: 225 at 4800 R.P.M. Carburetion: Holley four-barrel. Five main bearings. Serial Number code 'A'.

HIGH-PERFORMANCE 289 V-8: Overhead valves: Cast iron block. Displacement: 289 cubic inches. Bore and stroke: 4.00 x 2.87 inches. Compression ratio: 10.5:1. Brake horsepower: 271 at 6000 R.P.M. Carburetion: Holley four-barrel. Five main bearings. Serial Number code 'K'.

INTERCEPTOR V-8: Overhead valves. Cast iron block. Displacement: 352 cubic inches. Bore and stroke: 4.00 x 3.50 inches. Compression ratio: 9.3:1. Brake horsepower: 250 at 4400 R.P.M. Carburetion: Holley four-barrel. Five main bearings. Serial Number code 'X'.

THUNDERBIRD V-8: Overhead valves. Cast iron block. Displacement: 390 cubic inches. Bore and stroke: 4.05 x 3.78 inches. Compression ratio: 9.5:1. Brake horsepower: 275 at 4400 R.P.M. Carburetion: Holley two-barrel. Five main bearings. Serial Number code 'H'.

THUNDERBIRD FOUR-BARREL V-8: Overhead valves. Cast iron block. Displacement: 390 cubic inches. Bore and stroke: 4.05 x 3.78 inches. Compression ratio: 10.5:1. Brake horsepower: 315 at 4600 R.P.M. Carburetion: Holley four-barrel. Five main bearings. Serial Number code 'Z'.

GT 390 V-8: Overhead valves. Cast iron block. Displacement: 390 cubic inches. Bore and stroke: 4.05 x 3.78 inches. Compression ratio: 11.0:1. Brake horsepower: 335 at 4800 R.P.M. Carburetion: Holley four-barrel. Five main bearings. Serial Number code 'S'.

THUNDERBIRD HIGH-PERFORMANCE V-8: Overhead valves. Cast iron block. Displacement: 427 cubic inches. Bore and stroke: 4.23 x 3.78 inches. Compression ratio: 11.0:1. Brake horsepower: 410 15 5600 R.P.M. Carburetion: Holley four-barrel. Five main bearings. Serial Number code 'W'.

THUNDERBIRD SUPER HIGH-PERFORMANCE V-8: Overhead valves. Cast iron block. Displacement: 427 cubic inches. Bore and stroke: 4.23 x 3.78 inches. Compression ratio: 11.5:1. Brake horsepower: 425 at 6000 R.P.M. Carburetion: Two (2) Holley four-barrels. Five main bearings. Serial Number code 'R'.

THUNDERBIRD SPECIAL V-8: Overhead valves. Cast iron block. Displacement: 428 cubic inches. Bore and stroke: 4.13 x 3.98 inches. Compression ratio: 10.5:1. Brake horsepower: 345 at 4600 R.P.M. Carburetion: Holley four-barrel. Five main bearings. Serial Number code 'Q'.

ENGINES: "SOHC 427 4V V8: Hemispherical combusion chambers with overhead valves and overhead camshafts for each engine bank. Cast iron block and cylinder heads. Displacement: 427 cubic inches. Bore and stroke: 4.23 x 3.78. Compression ratio: 12.1:1. Brake horsepower: 616 @ 7000 RPM. Carburetion: Holley four barrel. Five main bearings. Engine was only available "over the counter" for $2500, thus, no engine code was provided.

SOHC 427 8V V8: Hemispherical combustion chambers with overhead valves and overhead camshafts for each engine bank. Cast iron block and cylinder heads. Displacement: 427 cubic inches. Bore and stroke: 4.23 x 3.78. Compression ratio: 12.1:1. Brake horsepower: 657 @ 7500 RPM. Carburetion: Two Holley four barrels. Five main bearings. Availability as 4V version.

POLICE INTERCEPTOR V-8: Overhead valves. Cast iron block. Displacement: 428 cubic inches. Bore and stroke: 4.13 x 3.98 inches. Compression ratio: 10.5:1. Brake horsepower: 360 at 5400 R.P.M. Carburetion: Holley four-barrel. Five main bearings. Serial Number code 'P'.

1966 FORD TRANSMISSIONS:
Same as 1965.

1966 FORD REAR AXLE RATIOS:
Same as 1965.

CONVENIENCE OPTIONS: Popular Custom and Custom 500 options included the 289 cubic inch V-8 engine ($106). Cruise-O-Matic automatic transmission ($184). Power steering ($94). AM radio ($57). Wheel covers ($22). White sidewall tires ($33). Popular Galaxie 500/Galaxie 500XL/Galaxie 500 7-Litre and Galaxie 500 LTD options included the 390 cubic inch V-8 engine ($101 for two-barrel engine; $153 for four-barrel engine and not available in 7-Litre models). Power steering ($94). Power brakes ($42). Power windows ($99). Tinted windshield ($21). Air conditioning $353). AM radio ($57). AM/FM radio ($133). Vinyl roof on two-door hardtops ($74); on four-door hardtops ($83). White sidewall tires ($33). Popular station wagon options included all those in the Galaxie 500 models plus, power tailgate window ($31). Luggage rack ($44). Third passenger seat ($29). Popular Fairlane and Fairlane 500 series options included the 289 cubic inch V-8 engine ($105 and not available on GT). 390 cubic inch V-8 engine ($206 and standard on GT). Cruise-O-Matic automatic transmission ($184 with 289 V-8; $214 with 390 V-8). Four-speed manual transmission ($183). AM radio ($57). Power steering ($84). Power tailgate window on station wagons ($31). Luggage rack on station wagons ($44). Two-tone paint ($21). White sidewall tires ($33). Wheel covers ($21). Vinyl roof on two-door hardtops ($76). Popular Falcon options included the 200 cubic inch six-cylinder engine ($26). The 289 cubic inch V-8 engine ($131). Cruise-O-Matic automatic transmission ($167 with six-cylinder engine; $176 with 289 V-8). Power Steering ($84). Power tailgate on station wagons ($44). AM radio ($57). Vinyl roof on two-door models ($74). Wheel covers ($21). White sidewall tires ($32). Popular Thunderbird options included air conditioning ($413). The 428 cubic inch V-8 engine ($64). Six-Way power seats ($193). Power windows ($103). Cruise control ($129). AM/FM radio ($82). Two-tone paint ($25). White sidewall tires with red stripe ($43).

Historical footnotes: The full-sized Fords were introduced October 1, 1966 and all the Ford lines appeared in dealer showrooms the same day. Model year production peaked at 2,093,832 units. Calendar year sales of 2,038,415 cars were recorded. Donald N. Frey was the chief executive officer of the company this year. On a calendar year sales basis, Ford was the Number 2 maker in America this year and held a 23.71 percent share of total market. Only 237 Ford Motor Company products, of all types, had 427 cubic inch V-8s installed during the 1966 calendar year.

1967 FORD

1967 FORDS — OVERVIEW — As in the previous 10 years, Ford continued to restyle at least one of the model lines. The 1967 full-size Fords were completely restyled from the previous year, sharing only drivetrains with the 1966 models. The new models were more round, with rounder tops and fenders. At the front end, stacked quad headlights were used once again, but the grille was all new. It was a double stamped aluminum piece, featuring horizontal bars, divided by five vertical bars. The center portion of the grille projected forward and this point was duplicated in the forward edge of the hood and in the bumper configuration. The bodyside feature lines were in the same location as the 1966 models, but were somewhat less pronounced. The taillights were vertically situated rectangular units with chrome moldings and chrome crosshairs surrounding the standard equipment backup lights. All 1967 Fords are easily recognizeable by the Energy-Absorbing steering wheels used in every model. A very large, deeply padded hub predominates the wheel. Also, all 1967 Fords were equipped with a dual master cylinder for the first time.

FORD CUSTOM SERIES — (ALL ENGINES) — The Custom Series was the base trim level Ford for 1967 and included chrome windshield and rear window moldings; a chrome horn ring; nylon carpeting, the Custom name in script on the front fenders and the Ford name, in block letters, spaced across the front of the hood and across the vertical section of the trunk lid.

CUSTOM SIX-CYLINDER I.D. NUMBERS: Custom six-cylinder models began with the number '7', followed by the assembly plant code, engine designation code 'V' and, finally, the unit's production number, according to the final assembly location. Each plant began at 100001 and went up (See production note).

CUSTOM SIX SERIES

Model Number	Body/Style Number	Body Type & Seating	Factory Price	Shipping Weight	Production Total
V	54E	4-dr Sed-6P	2496	3469	Note 1
V	62E	2-dr Sed-6P	2441	3411	Note 1

CUSTOM V-8 SERIES I.D. NUMBERS: Custom V-8 models began with the number '7', followed by the assembly plant code, body type code, engine designation code, and, finally, the unit's production number, according to the final assembly location. Each plant began at 100001 and went up (See production note).

CUSTOM V-8 SERIES

NA	62E	4-dr Sed-6P	2602	3507	41,417
NA	62E	2-dr Sed-6P	2548	3449	18,107

PRODUCTION NOTE: Total series output was 59,524 units. Ford does not indicate the number of each model produced with sixes and V-8s. Therefore, all production figures given above are total production of each body style with both engines.

CUSTOM 500 SERIES — (ALL ENGINES) — The Custom 500 was the upper trim level of the base-line Custom Series and included all the Custom trim, plus special Custom 500 exterior trim and choices of four different upholsteries on the interior.

CUSTOM 500 SIX-CYLINDER SERIES I.D. NUMBERS: Custom 500 six-cylinder models used the same Serial Number sequence as the Custom models (See production note).

CUSTOM 500 SIX SERIES

Model Number	Body/Style Number	Body Type & Seating	Factory Price	Shipping Weight	Production Total
V	54B	4-dr Sed-6P	2551	3471	Note 1
V	62B	2-dr Sed-6P	2595	3513	Note 1

NOTE 1: See Custom 500 V-8 series listing. Production was counted by series and body style only, with no breakout per engine type.

CUSTOM 500 V-8 SERIES I.D. NUMBERS: Custom 500, V-8 models used the same Serial Number sequence as the Custom models (See production note).

CUSTOM 500 V-8 SERIES

Model Number	Body/Style Number	Body Type & Seating	Factory Price	Shipping Weight	Production Total
NA	54B	4-dr Sed-6P	2701	3509	83,260
NA	62B	2-dr Sed-6P	2659	3451	18,146

PRODUCTION NOTE: Total series output was 101,406 units. Ford does not indicate the number of each model produced with Sixes and V-8s. Therefore, all production figures given above are total production of each body style with both engines.

GALAXIE 500 SERIES — (ALL ENGINES) — The Galaxie 500 was the intermediate trim level for 1967 and included all the Custom Series trim, plus stamped aluminum lower bodyside moldings; chrome side window moldings; simulated wood-grain appliques on the instrument panel and inner door panels and a stamped aluminum trim panel on the vertical section of the trunk lid. The name, Galaxie 500, in block letters, was located on the rear fenders and the Ford crest was located on the trunk lid above the aluminum trim panel.

GALAXIE 500 SIX-CYLINDER SERIES I.D. NUMBERS: Galaxie 500 six-cylinder models used the same Serial Number sequence as the Custom Series (See production note).

GALAXIE 500 SIX SERIES

Model Number	Body/Style Number	Body Type & Seating	Factory Price	Shipping Weight	Production Total
V	54A	4-dr Sed-6P	2732	3481	Note 1
V	57B	4-dr FsBk Sed-6P	2808	3552	Note 1
V	63B	2-dr FsBk Cpe-6P	2755	3484	Note 1
V	76A	2-dr Conv-6P	3003	3660	Note 1

NOTE 1: See Galaxie 500 V-8 Series listing. Production was counted by Series and body style only, with no breakout per engine type.

GALAXIE 500 V-8 SERIES I.D. NUMBERS: Galaxie 500, V-8 models used the same Serial Number sequence as the Custom and Custom 500 models (See production note).

GALAXIE 500 V-8 SERIES

Model Number	Body/Style Number	Body Type & Seating	Factory Price	Shipping Weight	Production Total
NA	54A	4-dr Sed-6P	2838	3519	130,063
N	57B	4-dr FsBk Sed-6P	2743	3526	57,087
NA	63B	2-dr FsBK Cpe-6P	2861	3522	197,388
NA	76A	2-dr Conv-6P	3110	3704	19,068

PRODUCTION NOTE: Total series output was 403,606 units. Ford does not indicate the number of each model produced with Sixes and V-8s. Therefore, all production figures given above are total production of each body style with both engines.

GALAXIE 500XL V-8 SERIES — (ALL ENGINES) — The Galaxie 500XL was the sport trim version of the two-door Fastback and two-door Convertible and included the 200 horsepower '289' V-8 engine and Select-Shift Cruise-O-Matic transmission as standard equipment. Also, the model line included bucket seats and front console; all Galaxie 500 trim; special ornamentation; automatic courtesy and warning lights in the door panels and chrome trim on the foot pedals.

GALAXIE 500XL V-8 SERIES I.D. NUMBERS: Galaxie 500XLs used the same Serial Number sequence as the Custom and Galaxie Series (See production note).

GALAXIE 500XL V-8 SERIES

Model Number	Body/Style Number	Body Type & Seating	Factory Price	Shipping Weight	Production Total
NA	63C	2-dr FsBk Cpe-5P	3243	3594	18,174
NA	76B	2-dr Conv-5P	3493	3704	5,161

PRODUCTION NOTE: Total series output was 23,335 units.

1967 Ford, LTD 2-dr hardtop sports coupe, V-8

LTD V-8 SERIES — (ALL ENGINES) — The LTD was the top trim level full-size Ford for 1967 and was considered it's own series for the first time since introduced in 1965. LTDs included all the Galaxie 500 trim, plus the 200 horsepower 289 V-8 engine and Select-Shift Cruise-O-Matic automatic transmission as standard equipment. Other regular features were flow-through ventilation system; distinctive LTD trim and ornamentation; special wheel covers; simulated wood-grain on the instrument panel and door panels; automatic courtesy and warning lights in the doors; deep-foam cushioning in the seating surfaces; pull-down arm rests front and rear; color-keyed steering wheel and vinyl top on two-door hardtops.

LTD V-8 SERIES I.D. NUMBERS: LTDs used the Serial Number sequence as the Custom and Galaxie Series (See production note).

LTD V-8 SERIES

Model Number	Body/Style Number	Body Type & Seating	Factory Price	Shipping Weight	Production Total
NA	54F	4-dr Sed-6P	3298	3795	12,491
NA	57F	4-dr HT Sed-6P	3363	3676	51,978
NA	63F	2-dr HT Cpe-6P	3362	3626	46,036

PRODUCTION NOTE: Total series output was 110,505 units.

STATION WAGON SERIES — (ALL ENGINES) — The Ranch Wagon was the base trim level station wagon for 1967, with the Country Sedans being the intermediate level and the Country Squires being the top trim level. The trim paralleled the Custom 500, Galaxie 500 and LTD models of conventional cars.

STATION WAGON SIX-CYLINDER SERIES I.D. NUMBERS: Station wagon six-cylinder models used the same Serial Number sequence as Custom and Galaxie 500 Series of conventional cars.

STATION WAGON SIX SERIES

Model Number	Body/Style Number	Body Type & Seating	Factory Price	Shipping Weight	Production Total
V	71D	4-dr Ranch Wag-6P	2836	3911	Note 1
V	71B	4-dr Ctry Sed-6P	2935	3924	Note 1
V	71C	4-dr Ctry Sed-9P	3061	4004	Note 1
V	71E	4-dr Ctry Squire-6P	3234	3971	Note 1
V	71A	4-dr Ctry Squire-9P	3359	4011	Note 1

NOTE 1: See station wagon V-8 series listing. Production was counted by series and body style only, with no breakout per engine type.

STATION WAGON V-8 SERIES I.D. NUMBERS: Station wagon V-8 models used the same Serial Number sequence as the Custom and Galaxie 500 Series of conventional cars (See production note).

STATION WAGON V-8 SERIES

Model Number	Body/Style Number	Body Type & Seating	Factory Price	Shipping Weight	Production Total
NA	71D	4-dr Ranch Wag-6P	2943	3949	23,932
NA	71B	4-dr Ctry Sed-6P	2042	3962	50,818
NA	71C	4-dr Ctry Sed-9P	3168	4042	34,377
NA	71E	4-dr Ctry Squire-6P	3340	4009	25,600
NA	71A	4-dr Ctry Squire-9P	3466	4049	44,024

PRODUCTION NOTE: Total series output was 178,751 units. Ford does not indicate the number of each model produced with Sixes and V-8s. Therefore, all production figures given above are total production of each body style with both engines.

1967 FAIRLANES OVERVIEW — The Fairlane continued to use the body introduced in 1966 with minor trim changes. The new grille was a single aluminum stamping instead of the two grilles used in the previous model and the taillights were divided horizontally by the backup light, instead of vertically as in 1966.

FAIRLANE MODELS — (ALL ENGINES) — The Fairlane was the base trim level for 1967 and included chrome windshield and rear window moldings; chrome rain gutter moldings; a chrome horn ring; front and rear arm rests; cigarette lighter; vinyl coated rubber floor mats and a single horizontal chrome trim strip along the bodyside, with the Fairlane name, in block letters, at the forward end.

FAIRLANE SIX-CYLINDER SERIES I.D. NUMBERS: Fairlane six-cylinder models began with the number '7', followed by the assembly plant code, body type code, engine designation 'T' and, finally, the unit's production number, according to the final assembly location. Each plant began at 100001 and went up.

FAIRLANE SIX-CYLINDER SERIES

Model Number	Body/Style Number	Body Type & Seating	Factory Price	Shipping Weight	Production Total
T	54	4-dr Sed-6P	2339	2782	Note 1
T	62	2-dr Sed-6P	2297	2747	Note 1
T	71	4-dr Sta Wag-6P	2643	3198	Note 1

NOTE 1: See Fairlane V-8 Series listing. Production was counted by series and body style only, with no breakout per engine type.

FAIRLANE V-8 SERIES I.D. NUMBERS: Fairlane V-8 models began with the number '7', followed by the assembly plant code, body type code, engine designation code and, finally, the unit's production number, according to the final assembly location. Each plant began at 100001 and went up (See production note).

FAIRLANE V-8 SERIES

Model Number	Body/Style Number	Body Type & Seating	Factory Price	Shipping Weight	Production Total
NA	54A	4-dr Sed-6P	2445	2951	19,740
NA	62A	2-dr Sed-6P	2402	2916	10,628
NA	71D	4-dr Sta Wag-6P	2748	3367	10,881

PRODUCTION NOTE: Total series output was 41,249 units. Ford does not indicate the number of each model produced with Sixes and V-8s. Therefore, all production figures given above are total producton of each body style with both engines.

1967 Ford, Fairlane 500 4-dr sedan, V-8

FAIRLANE 500 SERIES — (ALL ENGINES) — The Fairlane 500 was the intermediate trim level for 1967 and included all the Fairlane trim, plus special Fairlane 500 trim and moldings; Color-Keyed Carpet front and rear and a choice of four Nylon and Vinyl upholsteries. Also included was a stamped aluminum lower bodyside molding which contained the Fairlane name, in block letters, at the forward edge and another aluminum stamping containing the Ford name, in block letters, located on the vertical section of the trunk lid.

FAIRLANE 500 SIX-CYLINDER SERIES I.D. NUMBERS: Fairlane 500, six-cylinder models used the same Serial Number sequence as the Fairlane models (See production note).

FAIRLANE 500 SIX SERIES

Model Number	Body/Style Number	Body Type & Seating	Factory Price	Shipping Weight	Production Total
T	54B	4-dr Sed-6P	2417	2802	Note 1
T	62B	2-dr Sed-6P	2377	2755	Note 1
T	63B	2-dr HT Cpe-6P	2439	2842	Note 1
T	76B	2-dr Conv-6P	2664	3159	Note 1
T	71B	4-dr Sta Wag-6P	2718	3206	Note 1
T	71E	4-dr Squire Wag-6P	2902	3217	Note 1

NOTE 1: See Fairlane 500 V-8 Series listing. Production was counted by series and body style only, with no breakout per engine type.

FAIRLANE 500 V-8 SERIES I.D. NUMBERS: Fairlane 500 V-8 models used the same Serial Number sequence as the Fairlane models (See production note).

FAIRLANE 500 V-8 SERIES

Model Number	Body/Style Number	Body Type & Seating	Factory Price	Shipping Weight	Production Total
NA	54B	4-dr Sed-6P	2522	2971	52,552
NA	62B	2-dr Sed-6P	2482	2924	8,473
NA	NA	2-dr HT Cpe-6P	2545	3011	70,135
NA	76B	2-dr Conv-6P	2770	3328	5,428
NA	71B	4-dr Sta Wag-6P	2824	3375	15,902
NA	71E	4-dr Squire Wag-6P	3007	3386	8,348

PRODUCTION NOTE: Total series output was 159,838 units. Ford does not indicate the number of each model produced with Sixes and V-8s. Therefore, all production figures given above are total production of each body style with both engines.

FAIRLANE 500XL SERIES — (ALL ENGINES) — The Fairlane 500XL was the sporty version of the Fairlane 500 Series and included all the Fairlane 500 features, plus bucket seats and console; special name plaques and exterior trim; DeLuxe wheel covers and red safety lights and white courtesy lights in the lower interior door panels.

FAIRLANE 500XL SIX-CYLINDER SERIES I.D. NUMBERS: Fairlane 500XL six-cylinder models used the same Serial Number sequence as the Fairlane and Fairlane 500 models (See production note).

FAIRLANE 500XL SIX SERIES

Model Number	Body/Style Number	Body Type & Seating	Factory Price	Shipping Weight	Production Total
T	63C	2-dr HT Cpe-5P	2619	2870	Note 1
T	76C	2-dr Conv-5P	2843	3187	Note 1

NOTE 1: See Fairlane 500XL V-8 Series listing. Production was counted by series and body style only, with no breakout per engine type.

FAIRLANE 500XL V-8 SERIES I.D. NUMBERS: Fairlane 500XL V-8 models used the same Serial Number sequence as the Fairlane and Fairlane 500 models (See production note).

FAIRLANE 500XL V-8 SERIES

Model Number	Body/Style Number	Body Type & Seating	Factory Price	Shipping Weight	Production Total
NA	63C	2-dr HT Cpe-5P	2724	3039	14,871
NA	76C	2-dr Conv-5P	2950	3356	1,943
NA	63D	2-dr GT HT Cpe-5P	2839	3301	18,670
NA	76D	2-dr GT Conv-5P	3064	3607	2,117

PRODUCTION NOTE: Total series output was 37,601 units. Ford does not indicate the number of each model produced with Sixes and V-8s. Therefore, all production figures given above are total production of each body style with both engines.

1967 Ford, Falcon Futura 2-dr sedan, V-8

1967 FALCON — OVERVIEW — Like the Fairlane lineup, the 1967 Falcons continued to use the body introduced in 1966, with only minor trim changes. The most noticeable change in the two years, was the scoop-like indentations behind the front wheel openings, on the front fenders. The grille was nearly identical, with a horizontal and vertical dividing bar being the only difference.

FALCON SERIES — (ALL ENGINES) — The Falcons were the base trim level of the compact Falcon line for 1967 and included chrome windshield, rear window and rain gutter moldings; arm rests on the front doors only and a horn button, instead of the chrome horn ring found on Futura models. The Falcon name, in script, was located on the rear fender, just ahead of the taillights and, in block letters, across the vertical section of the trunk lid.

FALCON SERIES I.D. NUMBERS — (ALL ENGINES) — Falcons used the same Serial Number sequence as the full-size Ford and Fairlane lines (See production note).

FALCON SERIES

Model Number	Body/Style Number	Body Type & Seating	Factory Price	Shipping Weight	Production Total
NA	54A	4-dr Sed-6P	2167	2551	13,554
NA	62A	2-dr Sed-6P	2118	2520	16,082
NA	71A	4-dr Sta Wag-6P	2497	3030	5,553

PRODUCTION NOTE: Total series output was 35,198 units. Ford does not indicate the number of each model produced with Sixes and V-8s. Therefore, all production figures given above are total production of each body style with both engines.

FUTURA SERIES — (ALL ENGINES) — The Futura Series was the top trim level for 1967 and included all the standard Falcon features, plus a cigarette lighter; arm rests and ash trays on all doors; a chrome horn ring; Nylon carpting; special Futura moldings; trim, emblems and nameplates and chrome side window frames. In addition, the sports coupe offered front bucket seats; special nameplates; a map light; ash tray; glove box and trunk lights; 7.35 x 14 tires; a side accent stripe; remote-control driver's mirror and DeLuxe seat belts.

FUTURA SERIES I.D. NUMBERS: Futura models used the same Serial Number seqence as the full-size Fords, Fairlanes and Falcons (See production note).

FUTURA SERIES

Model Number	Body/Style Number	Body Type & Seating	Factory Price	Shipping Weight	Production Total
NA	54B	4-dr Sed-6P	2322	2559	11,254
NA	62B	2-dr Sed-6P	2280	2528	6,287
NA	62C	2-dr HT Spts Cpe-5P	2437	3062	7,053
NA	71B	4-dr Squire Wag-6P	2609	2556	4,552

PRODUCTION NOTE: Total series output was 29,146 units. Ford does not indicate the number of each model produced with Sixes and V-8s. Therefore, all production figures given above are total production of each body style with both engines.

THUNDERBIRD SERIES — (ALL ENGINES) — The 1967 Thunderbirds were totally restyled once again. The front end featured a full-width grille with hidden headlights and a large Thunderbird emblem floating in the center of the grille. As in 1966, the rear end featured a large, single taillight lens with a horizontal trim strip in the center. In addition, there were backup lights, in the center of the strip, giving the impression of a large round taillight. For the first time in the Thunderbird's history, a four-door sedan, called the 'Landau Sedan' was offered. This Landau was different than the sedans in that the rear doors opened to the front, giving the nickname 'suicide doors.'

1967 Ford, Thunderbird 4-dr Landau Sedan, V-8 (AA)

THUNDERBIRD SERIES I.D. NUMBERS — (ALL ENGINES) — Thunderbird models began with the number '7', assembly plant code 'Y' (Wixom), body type code, engine type code 'Z' or 'Q' and, finally, the unit's production number, beginning at 100001 and going up.

THUNDERBIRD SERIES

Model Number	Body/Style Number	Body Type & Seating	Factory Price	Shipping Weight	Production Total
Z/Q	65A	2-dr HT-4P	4603	4348	15,567
Z/Q	65B	2-dr Landau-4P	4704	4256	37,422
Z/Q	57B	4-dr Landau-4P	4825	4348	24,967

PRODUCTION NOTE: Total series output was 77,956 units.

FORD CHASSIS FEATURES: Wheelbase: 119 inches. Overall length: (station wagons) 213.9 inches; (other models) 213 inches. Tires: (sedans) 7.75 x 15 four-ply tubeless blackwall; (hardtops) 8.15 x 15 four-ply tubeless blackwall; (station wagons) 8.45 x 15 four-ply tubeless blackwall.

FAIRLANE CHASSIS FEATURES: Wheelbase: (station wagons) 113 inches; (other models) 116 inches. Overall length: (station wagons) 199.8 inches; (other models) 197 inches. Tires: (hardtops and station wagons) 7.15 x 14 four-ply tubeless blackwall; (other models) 6.95 x 14 four-ply tubeless blackwall.

FALCON CHASSIS FEATURES: Wheelbase: (station wagons) 113 inches; (other models) 110.9 inches. Overall length: (station wagons) 198.7 inches; (other models) 184.3 inches. Tires: (sport coupe) 7.35 x 14 four-ply tubeless blackwall; (station wagons) 7.75 x 14 four-ply tubeless blackwall; (other models) 6.50 x 13 four-ply tubeless blackwall.

THUNDERBIRD SERIES CHASSIS FEATURES: Wheelbase: (four-door Landau) 117 inches; (other models) 115 inches. Overall length: (four-door Landau) 209.9 inches; (other models) 206.9 inches. Tires: 8.15 x 15 four-ply tubeless blackwall.

FORD ENGINES
Same as 1966 (however, a tunnel-port 427 was available as an over-the-counter kit, with tunnel-port intake on special cylinder heads and special intake manifold).

FORD TRANSMISSIONS
Same as 1966.

FORD REAR AXLE RATIOS
Same as 1966.

CONVENIENCE OPTIONS FOR FULL-SIZE FORDS: 200 horsepower/289 cubic inch V-8 engine ($107). 275 horsepower/390 cubic inch V-8 engine ($78 in XLs and LTDs; $184 in all others). 315 horsepower/390 cubic inch V-8 engine ($158 in XLs and LTDs; $265 in all others). Cruise-O-Matic automatic transmission ($188 to $220 depending on engine choice). Four-speed manual transmission ($184). Power steering ($95). Power brakes ($42). Tinted windshield ($21). Air conditioning ($356). AM radio ($57). AM/FM radio ($134). Vinyl roof on two-door hardtops ($74); on four-door hardtops ($83). White sidewall tires ($35).

CONVENIENCE OPTIONS FOR STATION WAGONS: Included all those in the Custom and Galaxie 500 models, plus power tailgate window ($32). Luggage rack ($44). DeLuxe adjustable luggage rack ($63).

CONVENIENCE OPTIONS FOR FAIRLANES: Included the 200 horsepower/289 cubic inch V-8 engine ($106). 390 cubic inch V-8 engines ($184 for two-barrel version, $264 for four-barrel version). Cruise-O-Matic automatic transmission ($188 to $220). Four-speed manual transmission ($184). Power steering ($84). Power tailgate window in station wagons ($32). Luggage rack on station wagons ($44). Two-tone paint ($22). White sidewall tires ($34). Wheel covers ($41). Vinyl roofs on two-door hardtops ($74).

CONVENIENCE OPTIONS FOR FALCONS: Included the 200 cubic inch six-cylinder engine ($26). 289 cubic inch V-8 engine ($132). Four-barrel 289 cubic inch V-8 engine ($183). Cruise-O-Matic automatic transmission ($187). Four-speed manual transmission ($184). Power steering ($84). Power tailgate window on station wagons ($32). Tinted windshield ($21). Luggage rack on station wagons ($44). AM radio ($57). Eight-track stereo tape ($128). Two-tone paint ($19). Vinyl roof on two-door sedans ($74). Wheel covers ($21). White sidewall tires ($32).

CONVENIENCE OPTIONS FOR THE THUNDERBIRD SERIES: Included the 345 horse-power, 428 cubic inch V-8 engine ($91). Six-way power seats ($98 — driver's seat only). Power windows ($104). Cruise Control ($130). Air conditioning ($421). AM/8-track stereo radio ($128). AM/FM radio ($90). AM/FM multiplex stereo radio ($164). Two-tone paint ($25). White sidewall tires with red band ($52).

Historical footnotes: The 1967 Fords were introduced September 30, 1966. The grand total of assemblies for the 1967 model year was 1,742,311 units. This included, 877,128 Fords; 238,688 Fairlanes; 76,500 Falcons; 472,121 Mustangs and 77,956 Thunderbirds. Calendar year production for all the above lines peaked at 240,712 units. As far as sales and production, it was a good year for America's Number 2 maker. However, Vice President and General Manager M.S. McLaughlin did have other things to deal with, such as a 57 day United Auto Worker's strike. It was the longest lasting labor dispute in Ford history and culminated in a three-year contract agreement that included unprecedented wage and benefits packages. A posivite note was the performance of the Ford GT-40 in the European Grand Prix racing circuit. A trio of these cars, running at LeMans, finished first, second and third. It was the first time American entries had ever captured the championship honors in the prestigious race.

1968 FORD

1968 FORDS — OVERVIEW — For the first time in ten years, only one of the Ford lines received major restylings. The remainder of the model lineup stayed basically the same as in 1967. The 1968 full-size Fords were basically 1967 body shells with updated front ends. The two years look completely different, to be sure, but there is very little that changed behind the windshield. The new grillework was less protruding than the 1967 version and offered hidden headlights on the upper lines. It was a honeycomb grille with a single, centrally located vertical dividing bar. The Ford name, in block letters, and the Ford crest, in a small emblem on the driver's side headlight door, appeared. The rooflines were a little more formal than the previous year and the tail-lights, although retaining the same shape, were divided horizontally by the backup lights, rather than vertically. The large, padded hub, used on the steering wheels of all 1967 Fords, was replaced by a more conventional pad covering the entire center spoke. More Federally mandated safety regulations appeared in the form of front and rear fender marker lights. Powerwise, the mighty 427 cubic inch V-8 engine was detuned to 390 horsepower, by limiting carburetion to a single four-barrel and replacing the wild, solid-lifter camshaft with a more timid hydraulic lifter cam. At mid-year, the 427 was discontinued and replaced by the equally famous and powerful Cobra Jet 428 and Super Cobra Jet 428 V-8s. These engines dominated the Super Stock classes at the drag races in 1968, when installed in the light Mustang bodies. Also, the new lightweight '385' series engines, displacing 429 cubic inches, became the top power option in the big Thunderbirds.

FORD CUSTOM SERIES — (ALL ENGINES) — The Custom Series was the base trim level Ford for 1968 and included chrome windshield and rear window moldings; a chrome horn ring; Nylon carpeting; the Custom name, in script, on the rear fenders and Ford, in block letters, across the front of the hood.

CUSTOM SIX-CYLINDER SERIES I.D. NUMBERS: Custom six-cylinder models began with the number '8', followed by the assembly plant code, engine designation 'V' and, finally, the unit's production number, according to the final assembly location. Each plant began at 100001 and went up (See production note).

CUSTOM SIX SERIES

Model Number	Body/Style Number	Body Type & Seating	Factory Price	Shipping Weight	Production Total
V	54E	4-dr Sed-6P	2642	3478	Note 1
V	62E	2-dr Sed-6P	2584	3451	Note 1

NOTE 1: See Custom V-8 Series listing. Production was counted by series and body style only, with no breakout per engine type.

CUSTOM V-8 SERIES I.D. NUMBERS: Custom V-8 models began with the number '8', followed by the assembly plant code, body type code, engine designation code and, finally, the unit's production number, according to the final assembly location. Each plant began at 100001 and went up (See production note).

CUSTOM V-8 SERIES

Model Number	Body/Style Number	Body Type & Seating	Factory Price	Shipping Weight	Production Total
NA	54E	4-dr Sed-6P	2749	3518	45,980
NA	62E	2-dr Sed-6P	2691	3491	18,485

PRODUCTION NOTE: Total series output was 64,465 units. Ford does not indicate the number of each model produced with Sixes or V-8s. Therefore, all production figures given above are total production of each body style with both engines.

CUSTOM 500 SERIES — (ALL ENGINES) — The Custom 500 was the upper trim level of the base-line Custom Series and included all the Custom trim, plus special Custom 500 exterior trim, a single horizontal chrome strip along the bodyside feature line and choices of four different upholsteries on the interior.

CUSTOM 500 SIX-CYLINDER SERIES I.D. NUMBERS: Custom 500 six-cylinder models used the same Serial Number sequence as the Custom models (See production note).

CUSTOM 500 SIX SERIES

Model Number	Body/Style Number	Body Type & Seating	Factory Price	Shipping Weight	Production Total
V	54B	4-dr Sed-6P	2741	3491	Note 1
V	62B	2-dr Sed-6P	2699	3440	Note 1

NOTE 1: See Custom 500 V-8 Series listing. Production was counted by series and body style only, with no breakout per engine type.

CUSTOM 500 V-8 SERIES I.D. NUMBERS: Custom 500 V-8 models used the same Serial Number sequence as the Custom models (See production note).

CUSTOM 500 V-8 SERIES

Model Number	Body/Style Number	Body Type & Seating	Factory Price	Shipping Weight	Production Total
NA	54B	4-dr Sed-6P	2848	3531	49,398
NA	62B	2-dr Sed-6P	2806	3480	8,938

PRODUCTION NOTE: Total series output was 58,336 units. Ford does not indicate the number of each model produced with Sixes and V-8s. Therefore, all production figures given above are total production of each body style with both engines.

1968 Ford, Galaxie 500 2-dr convertible, V-8

GALAXIE 500 SERIES — (ALL ENGINES) — The Galaxie 500 was the intermediate trim level for 1968 and included all the Custom Series trim, plus stamped aluminum rocker panel moldings; simulated wood-grain appliques on the instrument panel and inner door panels and a stamped aluminum trim panel on the vertical section of the trunk lid. The name Ford, in block letters, was located on the vertical section of the trunk, on the passenger side of the car. The name Galaxie 500, in script, was located on the rear fenders, just in front of the taillights.

GALAXIE 500 SIX-CYLINDER SERIES I.D. NUMBERS: Galaxie 500 six-cylinder models used the same Serial Number sequence as the Custom Series (See production note).

GALAXIE 500 SIX SERIES

Model Number	Body/Style Number	Body Type & Seating	Factory Price	Shipping Weight	Production Total
V	54A	4-dr Sed-6P	2864	3496	Note 1
V	57B	4-dr HT Sed-6P	2936	3542	Note 1
V	63B	2-dr FsBk Cpe-6P	2881	3514	Note 1
V	65C	2-dr HT Cpe-6P	2916	3520	Note 1
V	76A	2-dr Conv-6P	3108	3659	Note 1

NOTE 1: See Galaxie 500 V-8 Series listing. Production was counted by series and body style only, with no breakout per engine type.

GALAXIE 500 V-8 SERIES I.D. NUMBERS: Galaxie 500 V-8 models used the same Serial Number sequence as the Custom Series (See production note).

GALAXIE 500 V-8 SERIES

Model Number	Body/Style Number	Body Type & Seating	Factory Price	Shipping Weight	Production Total
NA	54A	4-dr Sed-6P	2971	3536	117,877
NA	57B	4-dr HT Sed-6P	3043	3582	55,461
NA	63B	2-dr FsBk Cpe-6P	2988	3554	69,760
NA	65C	2-dr HT Cpe-6P	3023	3560	84,332
NA	76A	2-dr Conv-6P	3215	3699	11,832

PRODUCTION NOTE: Total series output was 339,262 units. Ford does not indicate the number of each model produced with Sixes and V-8s. Therefore, all production figures given above are total production of each body style with both engines.

GALAXIE 500XL V-8 SERIES — (ALL ENGINES) — The Galaxie 500XL was the sport trim version of the Galaxie 500 two-door fastback and two-door convertible and included the 210 horsepower, 302 cubic inch V-8 engine and Select-Shift Cruise-O-Matic automatic transmission as standard equipment. Also, the model line included bucket seats and front console; hidden headlights; special 'XL' crest in the center of the hood; automatic courtesy and warning lights in the door panels and chrome trim on the foot pedals.

GALAXIE 500XL V-8 SERIES I.D. NUMBERS: Galaxie 500XLs used the same Serial Number sequence as the Custom Series and standard Galaxie 500 models (See production note).

GALAXIE 500XL V-8 SERIES

Model Number	Body/Style Number	Body Type & Seating	Factory Price	Shipping Weight	Production Total
NA	63C	2-dr FsBk Cpe-5P	3092	3608	50,048
NA	76B	2-dr Conv-5P	3321	3765	6,066

PRODUCTION NOTE: Total series output was 56,114 units.

LTD V-8 SERIES — (ALL ENGINES) — The LTD was the top trim level full-size Ford for 1968 and included all the Galaxie 500 trim, plus the 210 horsepower, 302 cubic inch V-8 engine and Select-Shift Cruise-O-Matic automatic transmission as standard equipment. Also included in the LTD package was flow-through ventilation; distinctive LTD trim and ornamentation; special wheel covers; simulated wood-grain appliques on the instrument panel and inner door panels; automatic courtesy and warning lights in the doors; deep-foam cushioning in the seating surfaces; pull-down arm rests, front and rear; color-keyed steering wheel and vinyl top on two-door hardtops.

LTD V-8 SERIES I.D. NUMBERS: LTDs used the same Serial Number sequence as the Custom and Galaxie Series (See production note).

LTD V-8 SERIES

Model Number	Body/Style Number	Body Type & Seating	Factory Price	Shipping Weight	Production Total
NA	54C	4-dr Sed-6P	3135	3596	22,834
NA	57F	4-dr HT Sed-6P	3206	3642	61,755
NA	65A	2-dr HT Cpe-6P	3153	3679	54,163

PRODUCTION NOTE: Total series output was 138,752 units.

STATION WAGON SERIES — (ALL ENGINES) — The Ranch Wagon was the base trim level station wagon for 1968, with the Custom Ranch Wagons and the Country Sedans being the intermediate trim level and the Country Squires being the top trim level. The trim paralleled the Custom, Custom 500, Galaxie 500 and LTD models of conventional cars.

STATION WAGON SIX-CYLINDER SERIES I.D. NUMBERS: Station wagon six-cylinder models used the same Serial Number sequence as Custom and Galaxie 500 Series of conventional cars (See production note).

STATION WAGON SIX SERIES

Model Number	Body/Style Number	Body Type & Seating	Factory Price	Shipping Weight	Production Total
V	71D	4-dr Ranch Wag-6P	3000	3905	Note 1
V	71H	4-dr Cus Wag-6P	3063	3915	Note 1
V	71J	4-dr Cus Wag-9P	3176	3961	Note 1
V	71B	4-dr Ctry Sed-6P	3181	3924	Note 1
V	71C	4-dr Ctry Sed-9P	3295	3981	Note 1

NOTE 1: See station wagon V-8 Series listing. Production was counted by series and body style only, with no breakout per engine type.

STATION WAGON V-8 SERIES I.D. NUMBERS: Station wagon V-8 models used the same Serial Number sequence as the Custom and Galaxie 500 Series of conventional cars (See production note).

STATION WAGON V-8 SERIES

Model Number	Body/Style Number	Body Type & Seating	Factory Price	Shipping Weight	Production Total
NA	71D	4-dr Ranch Wag-6P	3107	3945	18,237
NA	71H	4-dr Cus Wag-6P	3170	3955	18,181
NA	71J	4-dr Cus Wag-9P	3283	4001	13,421
NA	71B	4-dr Ctry Sed-6P	3288	3964	39,335
NA	71C	4-dr Sed-9P	3402	4021	29,374
NA	71E	4-dr Ctry Sq-6P	3539	4013	33,994
NA	71A	4-dr Ctry Sq-9P	3619	4059	57,776

PRODUCTION NOTE: Total series output was 210,318 units. Ford does not indicate the number of each model produced with Sixes and V-8s. Therefore, all production figures given above are total production of each body with both engines. It was during 1968 that Ford gained the title: 'Wagon Master', because of the outstanding sales record of that particular body style in all the lines.

1968 FAIRLANE — OVERVIEW — The Fairlane line was the one chosen for major restyling for the new year. It was undoubtedly one of the nicest looking Fairlanes ever to come out of Detroit. It had a full-width grille, containing horizontally mounted quad headlights, and smooth sides with a single horizontal feature line running front to rear. The taillights were vertically situated, rectangular units, with a centrally located backup light. The word Ford was spaced evenly across the trunk lid, in block letters. The top-line Fairlane models for 1968 were called Torino, with the Fairlane 500 being demoted to intermediate trim level.

FAIRLANE MODELS — (ALL ENGINES) — The Fairlane was the base trim level for 1968 and included chrome windshield and rear window moldings; chrome rain gutters and side window frames; a chrome horn ring; front and rear arm rests; cigarette lighter; vinyl-coated rubber floor mats and the Fairlane name, in script, on the side of the rear fender. The Ford name was spelled out, in block letters, across the front of the hood and across the vertical section of the trunk lid.

FAIRLANE SIX-CYLINDER SERIES I.D. NUMBERS: Fairlane six-cylinder models began with the number '8', followed by the assembly plant code, body type code, engine designation 'T' and, finally, the unit's production number, according to the final assembly location. Each plant began at 100001 and went up.

FAIRLANE SIX-CYLINDER SERIES

Model Number	Body/Style Number	Body Type & Seating	Factory Price	Shipping Weight	Production Total
T	54A	4-dr Sed-6P	2464	2889	Note 1
T	65A	2-dr HT Cpe-6P	2456	2931	Note 1
T	71B	4-dr Sta Wag-6P	2770	3244	Note 1

NOTE 1: See Fairlane V-8 Series listing. Production was counted by series and body style only, with no breakouts per engine type.

FAIRLANE V-8 SERIES I.D. NUMBERS: Fairlane V-8 models began with the number '8', followed by the assembly plant code, body type code, engine designation code and, finally, the unit's production number, according to the final assembly location. Each plant began at 100001 and went up (See production note).

FAIRLANE V-8 SERIES

Model Number	Body/Style Number	Body Type & Seating	Factory Price	Shipping Weight	Production Total
NA	54A	4-dr Sed-6P	2551	3083	18,146
NA	65A	2-dr HT Cpe-6P	2544	3125	44,683
NA	71B	4-dr Sta Wag-6P	2858	3422	14,800

PRODUCTION NOTE: Total series output was 77,629 units. Ford does not indicate the number of each model produced with Sixes and V-8s. Therefore, all production figures given above are total production of each body style with both engines.

FAIRLANE 500 SERIES — (ALL ENGINES) — The Fairlane 500 was the intermediate trim level for 1967 and included all the Fairlane trim, plus special Fairlane 500 trim and moldings; color-keyed carpeting, front and rear and a choice of four Nylon and vinyl upholsteries. Also included was an aluminum dividing bar, in the center of the vertical portion of the trunk lid, and a horizontal dividing bar, in the center of the grille. The Fairlane 500 name, in script, appeared on the rear fender, just ahead of the taillights.

FAIRLANE 500 SIX-CYLINDER SERIES I.D. NUMBERS: Fairlane 500, six-cylinder models used the same Serial Number sequence as the Fairlane models (See production note).

FAIRLANE 500 SIX SERIES

Model Number	Body/Style Number	Body Type & Seating	Factory Price	Shipping Weight	Production Total
T	54B	4-dr Sed-6P	2520	2932	Note 1
T	63B	2-dr FsBk Cpe-6P	2543	2994	Note 1
T	65B	2-dr HT Cpe-6P	2568	2982	Note 1
T	76B	2-dr Conv-6P	2822	3136	Note 1
T	71D	4-dr Sta Wag-6P	2857	3274	Note 1

NOTE 1: See Fairlane 500 V-8 Series listing. Production was counted by series and body style only with no breakout per engine type.

FAIRLANE 500 V-8 SERIES I.D. NUMBERS: Fairlane 500 V-8 models used the same Serial Number sequence as the Fairlane models (See production note).

FAIRLANE 500 V-8 SERIES

Model Number	Body/Style Number	Body Type & Seating	Factory Price	Shipping Weight	Production Total
NA	54B	4-dr Sed-6P	2631	3121	42,390
NA	63B	2-dr FsBk Cpe-6P	2653	3177	32,452
NA	65B	2-dr HT Cpe-6P	2679	3136	33,282
NA	76B	2-dr Conv-6P	2910	3323	3,761
NA	71D	4-dr Sta Wag-6P	2968	3466	10,190

PRODUCTION NOTE: Total series output was 122,075 units. Ford does note indicate the number of each model produced with Sixes and V-8s. Therefore, all production figures given above are total production of each body style with both engines.

1968 Ford, Fairlane Torino GT 2-dr hardtop sports coupe, V-8

FAIRLANE GT SERIES — (ALL ENGINES) — The Fairlane GT was the sporty version of the Fairlane 500 Series and included all the Fairlane 500 features, plus the 210 horsepower, 302 cubic inch V-8 engine; bucket seats and console; special name plaques and exterior trim; DeLuxe wheel covers and red safety and white courtesy lights on the interior door panels, as standard equipment.

FAIRLANE GT V-8 SERIES I.D. NUMBERS: Fairlane GT V-8 models used the same Serial Number sequence as the Fairlane and Fairlane 500 models (See production note).

FAIRLANE GT V-8 SERIES

Model Number	Body/Style Number	Body Type & Seating	Factory Price	Shipping Weight	Production Total
Na	63D	2-dr FsBk Cpe-5P	2747	3208	74,135
NA	65D	2-dr HT Cpe-5P	2772	3194	23,939
NA	76D	2-dr Conv-5P	3001	3352	5,310

PRODUCTION NOTE: Total series output was 103,384 units.

FAIRLANE TORINO SERIES — (ALL ENGINES) — The Fairlane Torino was the top trim level for 1968 and included all the Fairlane 500 trim, plus a lower bodyside molding; special emblems and trim inside and out and a Torino crest on the 'C' pillars of the two-door hardtop and four-door sedan.

FAIRLANE TORINO SIX-CYLINDER SERIES I.D. NUMBERS: Fairlane Torino six-cylinder models used the same Serial Number sequence as the Fairlane and Fairlane 500 models (See production note).

FAIRLANE TORINO SIX-CYLINDER SERIES

Model Number	Body/Style Number	Body Type & Seating	Factory Price	Shipping Weight	Production Total
T	54C	4-dr Sed-6P	2688	2965	Note 1
T	65C	2-dr HT Cpe-6P	2710	3001	Note 1
T	71E	4-dr Squire-6P	3032	3336	Note 1

NOTE 1: See Torino V-8 Series listing. Production was counted by series and body style only, with no breakout per engine type.

FAIRLANE TORINO V-8 SERIES I.D. NUMBERS: Fairlane Torino V-8 models used the same Serial Number sequence as the Fairlane and Fairlane 500 models (See production note).

FAIRLANE TORINO V-8 SERIES

Model Number	Body/Style Number	Body Type & Seating	Factory Price	Shipping Weight	Production Total
NA	54C	4-dr Sed-6P	2776	3159	17,962
NA	65C	2-dr HT Cpe-6P	2798	3195	35,964
NA	71E	4-dr Squire-6P	3119	3514	14,773

PRODUCTION NOTE: Total series output was 68,699 units. Ford does not indicate the number of each model produced with Sixes and V-8s. Therefore, all production figures given above are total production of each body style with both engines.

1968 Ford, Falcon Futura 4-dr station wagon, V-8

1968 FALCON — OVERVIEW — The 1968 Falcons again used the same body shell as the previous two years, with only minor trim changes. The most noticeable change in the entire car is that the taillights were square, instead of the round type used on the car since its introduction in 1960. The grille was a stamped aluminum piece, with a rectangular mesh pattern, divided by the Falcon crest, in the center. The simulated exhaust port, used on the front fender of the 1967 Falcons, was not continued into the year 1968.

FALCON SERIES — (ALL ENGINES) — The Falcons were the base trim level of the compact Falcon line for 1968 and included chrome windshield, rear window and rain gutter moldings; arm rests on the front doors only and a horn button, instead of the chrome horn ring found on the Futura models. The Falcon name, in script, appeared on the rear fenders, just ahead of the taillights and in block letters, across the vertical section of the trunk lid.

FALCON SERIES I.D. NUMBERS — (ALL ENGINES) — Falcons used the same Serial Number sequence as the full-size Fords and the Fairlane lines (See production note).

FALCON SERIES

Model Number	Body/Style Number	Body Type & Seating	Factory Price	Shipping Weight	Production Total
NA	54A	4-dr Sed-6P	2301	2714	29,166
NA	62A	2-dr Sed-6P	2252	2659	36,443
NA	71A	4-dr Sta Wag-6P	2617	3132	15,576

PRODUCTION NOTE: Total series output was 81,185 units. Ford does not indicate the number of each model produced with Sixes and V-8s. Therefore, all production figures given above are total production of each body style with both engines.

FUTURA SERIES — (ALL ENGINES) — The Futura Series was the top trim level for 1968 and included all the standard Falcon features, plus a cigarette lighter; arm rests and ash trays on all doors; a chrome horn ring; Nylon carpeting; special Futura moldings; trim, emblems and nameplates and chrome side window frames. In addition, the sports coupe offered front bucket seats; special nameplates; a map light; ash tray; glove box and trunk lights; 7.35 x 14 tires; a side chrome accent stripe; remote-control outside driver's mirror and DeLuxe seat belts.

FUTURA SERIES I.D. NUMBERS: Futura models used the same Serial Number sequence as the full-size Fords, Fairlanes and Falcons (See production note).

FUTURA SERIES

Model Number	Body/Style Number	Body Type & Seating	Factory Price	Shipping Weight	Production Total
NA	54B	4-dr Sed-6P	2456	2719	18,733
NA	62B	2-dr Sed-6P	2415	2685	10,633
NA	62C	2-dr Spts Cpe-5P	2541	2713	10,077
NA	71B	4-dr Squire-6P	2728	3123	10,761

PRODUCTION NOTES: Total series output was 50,204 units. Ford does not indicate the number of each model produced with Sixes and V-8s. Therefore, all production figures given above are total production of each body style with both engines.

THUNDERBIRD SERIES — (ALL ENGINES) — The 1968 Thunderbird was a restyled version of the 1967 model, with very minor trim updating. The grille was very slightly revised from the 1967 offering and the taillights were mildly updated. New wheel covers completed the facelifting of the Thunderbird for 1968.

THUNDERBIRD SERIES I.D. NUMBER — (ALL ENGINES) — Thunderbird models began with the number '8', assembly plant code 'Y' (Wixom), body type code, engine type code 'Z' or 'N' and, finally, the unit's production number, beginning at 100001 and going up (See production note).

THUNDERBIRD SERIES

Model Number	Body/Style Number	Body Type & Seating	Factory Price	Shipping Weight	Production Total
N/Z	65A	2-dr HT Cpe-6P	4716	4366	9,977
N/Z	65A	2-dr Landau-4P	4845	4372	33,029
N/Z	57B	4-dr Landau-4P	4924	4458	21,925

PRODUCTION NOTE: Total series output was 64,931 units. This figure inclues 4,557 two-door hardtops; 13,924 two-door Landaus and 17,251 four-door Landaus equipped with bench seats.

1968 FORD CHASSIS FEATURES: Wheelbase: 119 inches. Overall length: (station wagons) 213.9 inches; (other models) 213.3 inches. Tires: (hardtops) 8.15 x 15 four-ply tubeless blackwall; (station wagons) 8.45 x 15 four-ply tubeless blackwall; (other models) 7.75 x 15 four-ply tubeless blackwall.

1968 FAIRLANE CHASSIS FEATURES: Wheelbase: (station wagons) 113 inches; (other models) 116 inches. overall length: (station wagons) 203.9 inches; (other models) 201 inches. tires: (station wagons) 7.75 x 14 tubeless blackwall; (FTs) F870 x 14; (other models) 7.35 x 14 tubeless blackwall.

FALCON CHASSIS FEATURES: Wheelbase: (station wagons) 113 inches; (other models) 110.9 inches. Overall length: (station wagons) 198.7 inches; (other models) 184.3 inches. Tires: (station wagons) 7.75 x 14 four-ply tubeless blackwall; (other models) 6.95 x 14 four-ply tubeless blackwall.

THUNDERBIRD SERIES CHASSIS FEATURES: Wheelbase: (four-door Landau) 117 inches; (other models) 115 inches. Overall length: (four-door Landau) 209.9 inches; (other models) 206.9 inches. Tires: (four-door Landau) 8.45 x 15 tubeless blackwall; (other models) 8.15 x 15 four-ply tubeless blackwall.

1968 FORD ENGINES

Falcon/Fairlane six-cylinder. Overhead valves. Cast iron block. Displacement: 170 cubic inches. Bore and stroke: 3.50 x 2.94 inches. Compression ratio: 8.7:1. Brake horsepower: 100 at 4000 R.P.M. Carburetion: Holley one-barrel. Seven main bearings. Serial Number code 'U'.

Falcon/Fairlane/Mustang six-cylinder. Overhead valves. Cast iron block. Displacement: 200 cubic inches. Bore and stroke: 3.68 x 3.13 inches. Compression ratio: 8.8:1. Brake horsepower: 115 at 3800 R.P.M. Carburetion: Holley one-barrel. Seven main bearings. Serial Number code 'T'.

Ford six-cylinder. Overhead valves. Cast iron block. Displacment: 240 cubic inches. Bore and stroke: 4.00 x 3.18 inches. Compression ratio: 9.2:1. Brake horsepower: 150 at 4000 R.P.M. Carburetion: Holley one-barrel. Seven main bearings. Serial Number code 'V'.

Challenger 289 V-8. Overhead valves. Cast iron block. Displacement: 289 cubic inches. Bore and stroke: 4.00 x 2.87 inches. Compression ratio: 8.7:1. Brake horsepower: 195 at 4600 R.P.M. Carburetion: Holley two-barrel. Five main bearings. Serial Number code 'C'.

302 V-8. Overhead valves. Cast iron block. Displacement: 302 cubic inches. Bore and stroke: 4.00 x 3.00 inches. Compression ratio: 9.0:1. Brake horsepower: 210 at 4000 R.P.M. Carburetion: Motorcraft two-barrel. Five main bearings. Serial Number code 'F'.

302 four-barrel V-8. Overhead valve. Cast iron block. Displacement: 302 cubic.inches. Bore and stroke: 4.00 x 3.00 inches. Compression ratio: 10.0:1. Brake horsepower: 230 at 4800 R.P.M. Carburetion: Motorcraft four-barrel. Five main bearings. Serial Number code 'J'.

Thunderbird V-8: Overhead valves. Cast iron block. Displacement: 390 cubic inches. Bore and stroke: 4.05 x 3.78 inches. Compression ratio: 9.5:1. Brake horsepower: 265 at 4400 R.P.M. Carburetion: Motorcraft four-barrel. Five main bearings. Serial Number code 'H'.

Thunderbird V-8: Overhead valves. Cast iron block. Displacement: 390 cubic inches. Bore and stroke: 4.05 x 3.78 inches. Compression ratio: 10.5:1. Brake horsepower: 280 at 4400 R.P.M. Carburetion: Motorcraft four-barrel. Five main bearings. Serial Number code 'H'.

Thunderbird four-barrel V-8. Overhead valves. Cast iron block. Displacement: 390 cubic inches. Bore and stroke: 4.05 x 3.78 inches. Compression ratio: 10.5:1. Brake horsepower: 315 at 4600 R.P.M. Carburetion: Motorcraft four-barrel. Five main bearings. Serial Number code 'Z'.

GT 390 V-8. Overhead valves. Cast iron block. Displacement: 390 cubic inches. Bore and stroke: 4.05 x 3.78 inches. Compression ratio: 10.5:1. Brake horsepower: 325 at 4800 R.P.M. Carburetion: Holley four-barrel. Five main bearings. Serial Number code 'S'.

Thunderbird High-Performance V-8. Overhead valves. Cast iron block. Displacement: 427 cubic inches. Bore and stroke: 4.23 x 3.78 inches. Compression ratio: 10.9:1. Brake horsepower: 390 at 4600 R.P.M. Carburetion: Motorcraft four-barrel. Five main bearings. Serial Number code 'W'.

Cobra Jet 428 V-8. Overhead valves. Cast iron block. Displacement: 428 cubic inches. Bore and stroke: 4.13 x 3.98 inches. Compression ratio: 10.7:1. Brake horsepower: 335 at 5600 R.P.M. Carburetion: Holley four-barrel. Five main bearings. Serial Number code 'Q'.

Super Cobra Jet 428 V-8: Overhead valves. Cast iron block. Displacement: 428 cubic inches. Bore and stroke: 4.13 x 3.98 inches. Compression ratio: 10.5:1. Brake horsepower: 360 at 5400 R.P.M. Carburetion: Holley four-barrel. Serial Number code 'R'.

Thunderbird 428 V-8. Overhead valves. Cast iron block. Displacement: 428 cubic inches. Bore and stroke: 4.13 x 3.98 inches. Compression ratio: 10.5:1. Brake horsepower: 340 at 5400 R.P.M. Carburetion: Motorcraft four-barrel. Serial Number code 'Q'.

Thunder-Jet 429 V-8: Overhead valves. Cast iron block. Displacement: 429 cubic inches. Bore and stroke: 4.36 x 3.59 inches. Compression ratio: 10.5:1. Brake horsepower: 360 at 4600 R.P.M. Carburetion: Motorcraft four-barrel. Serial Number code 'K'.

1968 FORD TRANSMISSION: Same as 1967.

1968 FORD REAR AXLE RATIOS: Same as 1967.

CONVENIENCE OPTIONS FOR FULL-SIZE FORDS: 210 horsepower: 302 cubic inch V-8 engine ($110). 265 horsepower, 390 cubic inch V-8 engine ($78 in XLs and LTDs; $184 in others). 315 horsepower 390 cubic inch V-8 engine ($158 in XLs and LTDs; $265 in others). Cruise-O-Matic automatic transmission ($188 to $220, depending on engine choice). Power steering ($95). Power brakes ($42). Tinted windshield ($95). Air conditioning ($356). AM radio ($57). AM/FM stereo radio ($134). Vinyl roof ($74 on two-door hardtops; $83 on four-door models). White sidewall tires ($35).

CONVENIENCE OPTIONS FOR STATION WAGONS: Included all those in the Custom and Galaxie 500 models of conventional cars, plus power tailgate window ($32). Luggage rack ($44). DeLuxe adjustable luggage rack ($63).

CONVENIENCE OPTIONS FOR FAIRLANES AND TORINOS: Included the 210 horsepower, 302 cubic inch V-8 engine ($107, standard on GT models). 390 cubic inch V-8 engines ($184 for two-barrel version; $264 for the four-barrel version). Cruise-O-Matic automatic transmission ($188 to $220, depending on engine choice). Four-speed manual transmission ($184). AM radio ($57). Power steering ($84). Power tailgate window in station wagons ($32). Luggage rack on station wagons ($44). Two-tone paint ($22). White sidewall tires ($34). Wheel covers ($41). Vinyl roofs on two-door hardtops ($74).

CONVENIENCE OPTIONS FOR FALCONS: Included the 200 cubic inch six-cylinder engine ($26). 289 cubic inch V-8 engine ($132). 302 cubic inch V-8 engine ($183). Cruise-O-Matic automatic transmission ($187). Four-speed manual transmission ($184). Power steering ($84). Power tailgate window on station wagons ($32). Tinted windshield ($21). Luggage rack on station wagons ($44). AM radio ($57). Eight-track stereo tape player ($128). Two-tone paint ($19). Vinyl roof on two-door sedans ($74). Wheel covers ($21). White sidewall tires ($32).

CONVENIENCE OPTIONS FOR THE THUNDERBIRD SERIES: Included the 429 cubic inch Tunder-Jet V-8 engine. Six-Way power driver's seat ($98). Power windows ($104). Cruise Control ($130). Air conditioning ($421). AM/8-track stereo radio ($128). AM/FM Multiplex stereo radio ($164). Two-tone paint ($25). White sidewall tires with red band ($52).

Historical footnotes: Ford products captured over 20 checkered flags in NASCAR stock car racing during 1968, with Ford driver David Pearson taking the overall championship. In USAC competition, Ford pilot A.J. Foyt was top driver of the year. Benny Parsons and Cale Yarborough also made Ford racing history this year, driving Fairlanes and Torinos in ARCA contests. A specially-trimmed Torino convertible paced the 52nd Indianapolis 500 mile race. The new Fords were introduced to the public on September 22, 1967. In Europe, Ford GT-40s competed in the international class races, attempting to repeat the success of 1967, when similar machines finished first, second and third in the French Grand Prix, at LeMans. Early in 1968, Semon E. 'Bunkie' Knudsen became the chief executive officer of Ford Motor Company. Knudsen had held a similar position with Pontiac and Chevrolet during some of the most exciting years in automotive history.

1969 FORD

1969 FORDS — OVERVIEW — The year 1969 started out as a scramble for new Ford Motor Company products. It was almost to the point where a scorecard was needed to keep track of all the models. A new series on scene was the Cobra, Ford's performance line in the Fairlane Series. Not to be left out, the Mustang stable added the hot Mach I and the luxurious Grande. The big news for 1969 came at mid-year introduction time, when another horse, the Maverick, was introduced. The Maverick was designed to be direct competition for the Volkswagen and was intended to influence those who liked a small and economical car. With a base price of $1995, it was the only Ford under $2000. For the first time, economy was heavily promoted, with Ford announcing that the Maverick would average 22 miles per gallon. By design, the Maverick was introduced April 17, 1969, exactly five years to the day, after the phenomenally successful Mustang.

FORD CUSTOM SERIES — (ALL ENGINES) — The 1969 full-size Fords were totally restyled and shared nothing with the previous year's offering. The lines of the new models were even more round than in 1968 and they looked more like big, luxury cars than Fords. Luxury, in fact, was very highly promoted. Velour interiors and vinyl tops were the order of the day in the LTD lineup. All full-size Fords shared the same body lines, with the LTD receiving it's own front end treatment, thus further segregating it from the 'ordinary' Galaxie Series. The Custom Series was the base trim level Ford for 1969 and included chrome windshield and rear window moldings; a chrome horn ring; Nylon carpeting; the Custom name, in script on the rear fender (just in front of the rear marker light); the Ford name, in block letters, across the rear escutcheon panel and a single horizontal chrome strip along the center of the body.

CUSTOM SIX-CYLINDER SERIES I.D. NUMBERS: Custom six-cylinder models began with the number '9', followed by the assembly plant code, engine designation 'V' and, finally, the unit's production number, according to the final assembly location. Each plant began at 100001 and went up (See production note).

CUSTOM SIX SERIES
Model Number	Body/Style Number	Body Type & Seating	Factory Price	Shipping Weight	Production Total
V	54E	4-dr Sed-6P	2674	3608	Note 1
V	62E	2-dr Sed-6P	2632	3585	Note 1
V	71D	4-dr Ranch Wag-6P	3074	4069	Note 1

NOTE 1: See Custom V-8 Series listing. Production was counted by series and body style only, with no breakout per engine type.

CUSTOM V-8 SERIES I.D. NUMBERS: Custom V-8 models began with the number '9', followed by the assembly plant code, body type code, engine designation code and, finally, the unit's production number, according to the final assembly location. Each plant began at 100001 and went up (See production note).

CUSTOM V-8 SERIES
Model Number	Body/Style Number	Body Type & Seating	Factory Price	Shipping Weight	Production Total
NA	54E	4-dr Sed-6P	2779	3648	45,653
NA	62E	2-dr Sed-6P	2737	3625	15,439
NA	71D	4-dr Ranch Wag-6P	3179	4109	17,489

PRODUCTION NOTE: Total series output was 78,581 units. Ford does not indicate the number of each model produced with Sixes and V-8s. Therefore, all production figures given above are total production of each body style with both engines.

CUSTOM 500 SERIES — (ALL ENGINES) — The Custom 500 was the upper trim level of the base-line Custom Series and included all the Custom trim, plus special Custom 500 exterior trim and choices of four different upholsteries on the interior.

CUSTOM 500 SIX-CYLINDER SERIES I.D. NUMBERS: Custom 500 six-cylinder models used the same Serial Number sequence as the Custom models (See production note).

CUSTOM 500 SERIES
Model Number	Body/Style Number	Body Type & Seating	Factory Price	Shipping Weight	Production Total
V	54B	4-dr Sed-6P	2773	3620	Note 1
V	62B	2-dr Sed-6P	2731	3570	Note 1
V	71H	4-dr Ranch Wag-6P	3138	4082	Note 1
V	71J	4-dr Ranch Wag-10P	3251	4132	Note 1

NOTE 1: See Custom 500 V-8 Series listings. Production was counted by series and body style only, with no breakout per engine type.

CUSTOM 500 V-8 SERIES I.D. NUMBERS: Custom 500 V-8 models used the same Serial Number sequence as the Custom models (See production note).

CUSTOM 500 V-8 SERIES
Model Number	Body/Style Number	Body Type & Seating	Factory Price	Shipping Weight	Production Total
NA	54B	4-dr Sed-6P	2878	3660	45,761
NA	62B	2-dr Sed-6P	2836	3610	7,585
NA	71H	4-dr Ranch Wag-6P	3243	4122	16,432
NA	71J	4-dr Ranch Wag-10P	3556	4172	11,563

PRODUCTION NOTE: Total series output was 81,341 units. Ford does not indicate the number of each model produced with Sixes and V-8s. Therefore, all production figures given above are total production of each body style with both engines.

GALAXIE 500 SERIES — (ALL ENGINES) — The Galaxie 500 was the intermediate trim level for 1969 and included all the Custom Series trim, plus stamped aluminum lower body side moldings and pleated interior trim.

GALAXIE 500 SIX-CYLINDER SERIES I.D. NUMBERS: Galaxie 500 six-cylinder models used the same Serial Number sequence as the Custom Series.

GALAXIE 500 SIX SERIES
Model Number	Body/Style Number	Body Type & Seating	Factory Price	Shipping Weight	Production Total
V	54A	4-dr Sed-6P	2897	3670	Note 1
V	64B	2-dr FsBk Cpe-6P	2913	3680	Note 1
V	65C	2-dr FT Cpe-6P	2965	3635	Note 1
V	57B	4-dr HT Sed-6P	2966	3705	Note 1
V	76A	2-dr Conv-6P	3142	3840	Note 1
V	71B	4-dr Ctry Sed-6P	3257	4067	Note 1
V	71C	4-dr Ctry Sed-10P	3373	3092	Note 1

NOTE 1: See Galaxie 500 V-8 Series listing. Production was counted by series and body style only, with no breakout per engine type.

GALAXIE 500 V-8 SERIES I.D. NUMBERS: Galaxie 500 V-8 models used the same Serial Number sequence as the Custom Series (See production note).

GALAXIE 500 V-8 SERIES
Model Number	Body/Style Number	Body Type & Seating	Factory Price	Shipping Weight	Production Total
NA	54A	4-dr Sed-6P	3002	3710	104,606
NA	63B	2-dr FsBk Cpe-6P	3018	3720	63,921
NA	65C	2-dr FT Cpe-6P	3070	3675	71,920
NA	57B	4-dr HT Sed-6P	3071	3745	64,031
NA	76A	2-dr Conv-6P	3247	3880	6,910
NA	71B	4-dr Ctry Sed-6P	3362	4107	36,287
NA	17C	4-dr Ctry Sed-10P	3487	4132	11,563

PRODUCTION NOTE: Total series output was 359,238 units. Ford does not indicate the number of each model produced with Sixes and V-8s. Therefore, all production figures given above are total production of each body style with both engines.

GALAXIE 500XL SERIES — (ALL ENGINES) — The Galaxie 500XL was the sport trim version of the Galaxie 500. It came in 'Sportsroof' (two-door fastback coupe) and convertible styles. Standard equipment included bucket seats; wheel covers; die-cast grille; retractable headlights; pleated, all-vinyl interior trim and five vertical hash marks at the forward part of the front fenders, in addition to all the standard Galaxie 500 trim.

GALAXIE 500XL SIX-CYLINDER SERIES I.D. NUMBERS: The Galaxie 500XL six-cylinder models used the same Serial Number sequence as the Custom and Galaxie 500 Series (See production note).

GALAXIE 500XL SIX SERIES
Model Number	Body/Style Number	Body Type & Seating	Factory Price	Shipping Weight	Production Total
V	63C	2-dr FsBk Cpe-5P	3052	3785	Note 1
V	76B	2-dr Conv-5P	3280	3935	Note 1

NOTE 1: See Galaxie 500XL V-8 Series listing. Production was counted by series and body style only, with no breakout per engine data.

1969 Ford, XL 2-dr hardtop coupe, V-8

GALAXIE 500XL V-8 SERIES I.D. NUMBERS: Galaxie 500XLs used the same Serial Number sequence as the Custom and Galaxie 500 Series (See production note).

GALAXIE 500XL V-8 SERIES
Model Number	Body/Style Number	Body Type & Seating	Factory Price	Shipping Weight	Production Total
NA	63C	2-dr FsBk Cpe-5P	3157	3825	54,557
NA	76B	2-dr Conv-5P	3385	3975	7,402

PRODUCTION NOTE: Total series output was 61,959 units. Ford does not indicate the number of each model produced with Sixes and V-8s. Therefore, all production figures given above are total production of each body style with both engines.

LTD V-8 SERIES — (ALL ENGINES) — The LTD was the top trim level full-size Ford for 1969 and included all the Galaxie 500 trim, plus the 220 horsepower, 302 cubic inch V-8 engine; Select-Shift Cruise-O-Matic automatic transmission; electric clock; bright exterior moldings and dual accent paint stripes. The LTD station wagon models (Country Squires) also had simulated wood-grain appliques on the bodysides. All LTDs also came with retractable headlights and die-cast grilles.

LTD V-8 SERIES I.D. NUMBERS: LTDs used the same Serial Number sequence as the Custom and Galaxie 500 Series (See production note).

LTD V-8 SERIES
Model Number	Body/Style Number	Body Type & Seating	Factory Price	Shipping Weight	Production Total
NA	54C	4-dr Sed-6P	3192	3745	63,709
NA	57F	4-dr Sed-6P	3261	3840	113,168
NA	65A	2-dr FT Cpe-6P	3234	3745	111,565
NA	71E	4-dr Ctry Sq-6P	3644	4202	46,445
NA	71A	4-dr Ctry Sq-10P	3721	4227	82,790

PRODUCTION NOTE: Total series output was 417,677 units.

1969 FAIRLANE — (OVERVIEW) — Performance was the key word in the Fairlane lineup for 1969. Virtually all models, except four-door sedans, looked very fast. And most of them were. When equipped with the new Cobra Jet 428, the Fairlanes were awesome, as well as beautiful. They shared the same body as the 1968 models, with only very minor trim updating. The taillights were revised slightly and were more square in shape than the 1968 type. The grille was revised slightly, with a more prominent center dividing bar than in 1968. At mid-year introduction time, the incredible Talladega Torino was released, in extremely limited quantities, to qualify the body style for use in NASCAR racing. The front end was extended several inches and used a flat grille—mounted at the front of the opening, rather than back several inches as on standard models. Also, the rear bumper from a standard Fairlane was used, up front, because it was more aerodynamic than the original front bumper. All Talladegas were equipped with the Cobra Jet 428 engine and gave a choice of either Select-Shift Cruise-O-Matic automatic transmission, or the bulletproof 'top-loader' four-speed manual gear box.

FAIRLANE MODELS — (ALL ENGINES) — The Fairlane was the base trim level for 1969 and included chrome windshield and rear window moldings; chrome rain gutters and side window frames; a chrome horn ring; front and rear arm rests; cigarette lighter; vinyl-coated rubber floor mats and the Fairlane name, in script, on the passenger side of the escutcheon panel. The Ford name was spelled out, in block letters, across the front of the hood and on the vertical section of the trunk lid.

FAIRLANE SIX-CYLINDER SERIES I.D. NUMBERS: Fairlane six-cylinder models began with the number '9', followed by the assembly plant code, body type code, engine designation 'T' and, finally, the unit's production number, according to the final assembly location. Each plant began at 100001 and went up (See production note).

FAIRLANE SIX-CYLINDER SERIES

Model Number	Body/Style Number	Body Type & Seating	Factory Price	Shipping Weight	Production Total
T	54A	4-dr Sed-6P	2471	3010	Note 1
T	65A	2-dr HT Cpe-6P	2482	3025	Note 1
T	71B	4-dr Sta Wag-6P	2824	3387	Note 1

NOTE 1: See Fairlane V-8 Series listing. Production was counted by series and body style only, with no breakout per engine data.

FAIRLANE V-8 SERIES I.D. NUMBERS: Fairlane V-8 models began with the number '9', followed by the assembly plant code, body type code, engine designation code and, finally, the unit's production number, according to the final assembly location. Each plant began at 100001 and went up (See production note).

FAIRLANE V-8 SERIES

Model Number	Body/Style Number	Body Type & Seating	Factory Price	Shipping Weight	Production Total
NA	54A	4-dr Sed-6P	2561	3120	27,296
NA	65A	2-dr HT Cpe-6P	2572	3133	85,630
NA	71D	4-dr Sta Wag-6P	2914	3387	10,882

PRODUCTION NOTE: Total series output was 123,808 units. Ford does not indicate the number of each model produced with Sixes and V-8s. Therefore, all production figures given above are total production of each body style with both engines.

FAIRLANE 500 SERIES — (ALL ENGINES) — The Fairlane 500 was the intermediate trim level for 1969 and included all Fairlane trim, plus special 500 trim and moldings; color-keyed carpeting (front and rear) and a choice of four Nylon and vinyl upholsteries. Also included was an aluminum trim panel in the center of the rear escutcheon panel, between the taillights. The Fairlane 500 name, in script, appeared on the side of the rear fender, just in front of the taillights.

FAIRLANE 500 SIX-CYLINDER SERIES I.D. NUMBERS: Fairlane 500 six-cylinder model used the same Serial Number sequence as the Fairlane models (See production note).

FAIRLANE 500 SIX SERIES

Model Number	Body/Style Number	Body Type & Seating	Factory Price	Shipping Weight	Production Total
T	54B	4-dr Sed-6P	2551	3029	Note 1
T	65B	2-dr FT Cpe-6P	2609	3036	Note 1
T	63B	2-dr FsBk Cpe-6P	2584	3083	Note 1
T	76B	2-dr Conv-6P	2834	3220	Note 1
T	71B	4-dr Sta Wag-6P	2934	3415	Note 1

NOTE 1: See Fairlane 500 V-8 Series listing. Production was counted by series and body style only, with no breakout per engine type.

FAIRLANE 500 V-8 SERIES I.D. NUMBERS: Fairlane 500 V-8 models used the same Serial Number sequence as the Fairlane models (See production note).

FAIRLANE 500 V-8 SERIES

Model Number	Body/Style Number	Body Type & Seating	Factory Price	Shipping Weight	Production Total
NA	54B	4-dr Sed-6P	2641	3135	40,888
NA	65B	2-dr FT Cpe-6P	2699	3143	28,179
NA	63B	2-dr FsBk Cpe-6P	2674	3190	29,849
NA	76B	2-dr Conv-6P	2924	3336	2,264
NA	71B	4-dr Sta Wag-6P	3024	3523	12,869

PRODUCTION NOTE: Total series output was 114,049 units. This figure includes 3,379 Formal Hardtop coupes (FT Cpe) produced with bucket seats; 7,345 Sportroofs (FsBk Cpe) produced with bucket seats and 219 convertibles produced with bucket seats. Ford does not indicate the number of each model produced with Sixes and V-8s. Therefore, all production figures are total production of each body style.

1969 Ford, Torino GT 2-dr convertible, V-8

FAIRLANE TORINO SERIES — (ALL ENGINES) — The Fairlane Torino was the top trim level for 1969 and included all the Fairlane 500 trim, plus a polished aluminum rocker panel molding; special emblems and trim (inside and out) and a Torino crest on the 'C' pillars on the two-door hardtop and four-door sedan versions.

FAIRLANE TORINO SIX-CYLINDER SERIES I.D. NUMBERS: Fairlane Torino six-cylinder models used the same Serial Number sequence as the Fairlane and Fairlane 500 models (See production note).

FAIRLANE TORINO SIX-CYLINDER SERIES

Model Number	Body/Style Number	Body Type & Seating	Factory Price	Shipping Weight	Production Total
T	54C	4-dr Sed-6P	2716	3075	Note 1
T	65C	2-dr FT Cpe-6P	2737	3090	Note 1
T	71E	4-dr Squire-6P	3090	3450	Note 1

NOTE 1: See Fairlane Torino V-8 Series listing. Production was counted by series and body style only, with no breakout per engine type.

FAIRLANE TORINO V-8 SERIES I.D. NUMBERS: Fairlane Torino V-8 models used the same Serial Number sequence as the Fairlane and Fairlane 500 models (See production note).

FAIRLANE TORINO V-8 SERIES

Model Number	Body/Style Number	Body Type & Seating	Factory Price	Shipping Weight	Production Total
NA	54C	4-dr Sed-6P	2806	3180	11,971
NA	65C	2-dr FT Cpe-6P	2827	3195	20,789
NA	71E	4-dr Squire-6P	3180	3556	14,472

PRODUCTION NOTE: Total series output was 47,232 units. Ford does not indicate the number of each model produced with Sixes and V-8s. Therefore, all production figures given above are total production of each body style with both engines.

FAIRLANE TORINO GT SERIES — (ALL ENGINES) — The Fairlane Torino GT was the sporty version of the Fairlane 500 Series and included all the Fairlane 500 features, plus the 220 horsepower, 302 cubic inch V-8 engine; bucket seats and console; special name plaques and exterior trim; styled steel wheels; lower body side striping on two-door hardtop and two-door convertible versions and a body side 'C' stripe on the two-door Sportsroof (FsBk Cpe) version. A high-performance version of this model, known as the Torino Cobra, was also offered. It included the 335 horsepower, 428 cubic inch V-8 engine and four-speed manual transmission as standard equipment, as well as F70 x 14 wide oval tires.

FAIRLANE TORINO GT I.D. NUMBRS — (ALL ENGINES) — Fairlane Torino GTs used the same Serial Number sequence as the Fairlane and Fairlane 500 models (See production note).

FAIRLANE TORINO GT SERIES

Model Number	Body/Style Number	Body Type & Seating	Factory Price	Shipping Weight	Production Total
NA	65D	2-dr FT Cpe-5P	2848	3173	17,951
NA	63D	2-dr FsBk Cpe-5P	2823	3220	61,319
NA	76D	2-dr Conv-5P	3073	3356	2,552

FAIRLANE TORINO GT COBRA SUB-SERIES

Model Number	Body/Style Number	Body Type & Seating	Factory Price	Shipping Weight	Production Total
NA	65A	2-dr HT Cpe-5P	3208	3490	NA
NA	63B	2-dr FsBk Cpe-5P	3183	3537	NA

PRODUCTION NOTE: Total series output was 81,822 units, including the Cobra models (for which separate production figures are unavailable). Ford does not indicate the number of each model produced with Sixes and V-8s. Therefore, all production figures are total production of each body style with both engines.

1969 Ford, Falcon 2-dr sedan, V-8

1969 FALCON — (OVERVIEW) — Falcons continued to use the same body style as in the past three years, with no major changes in either sheetmetal or trim. An optional V-8, new safety steering wheel and redesigned side marker lamps were the most noticeable revisions from the past. A full-width anodized aluminum grille helped impart a 'big car' appearance

FALCON SERIES — (ALL ENGINES) — The Falcons were the base trim level for 1969 and included chrome windshield; rear window and rain gutter moldings; arm rests on the front doors only and a horn button, instead of the chrome ring found on the Futura models. The Falcon name, in script, appeared on the rear fender sides and on the vertical section of the trunk lid (on the passenger side).

FALCON SERIES I.D. NUMBERS — (ALL ENGINES) — Falcons used the same Serial Number sequence as the full-size Fords and the Fairlane lines (See production note).

FALCON SERIES

Model Number	Body/Style Number	Body Type & Seating	Factory Price	Shipping Weight	Production Total
NA	54A	4-dr Sed-6P	2316/2431	2735	22,719
NA	62A	2-dr Sed-6P	2226/2381	2700	29,263
NA	71A	4-dr Sta Wag-6P	2643/2733	3110	11,568

PRODUCTION NOTE: Total series output was 63,550 units. Ford does not indicate the number of each model produced with Sixes and V-8s. Therefore, all production figures are total production of each body style.
ADDITIONAL NOTE: The prices above the slash are for Six/below slash for V-8.

FUTURA SERIES — (ALL ENGINES) — The Futura Series was the top trim level for 1969 and included all the standard Falcon features, plus a cigarette lighter; arm rests and ash trays on all doors; a chrome horn ring; Nylon carpeting; special Futura moldings, trim, emblems and nameplates and chrome side window frames. In addition, the sports coupe offered front bucket seats; special nameplates; a map light; ash tray, glove box and trunk lights; 7.35 x 14 tires; a side chrome accent stripe; polished aluminum rocker panel moldings and wheel well trim; a remote-control outside driver's mirror and DeLuxe seat belts.

FUTURA SERIES I.D. NUMBERS — (ALL ENGINES) — Futura models used the same Serial Number sequence as the full-size Fords, Fairlanes and Falcon models (See production note).

FUTURA SERIES

Model Number	Body/Style Number	Body Type & Seating	Factory Price	Shipping Weight	Production Total
NA	54B	4-dr Sed-6P	2481/2571	2748	11,850
NA	62B	2-dr Sed-6P	2444/2534	2715	6,482
NA	62C	2-dr Spt Cpe-5P	2581/2671	2738	5,931
NA	71B	4-dr Sta Wag-6P	2754/2844	3120	7,203

PRODUCTION NOTE: Total series output was 31,466 units. Ford does not indicate the number of each model produced with Sixes and V-8s. Therefore, all production figures are total production of each body style.
ADDITIONAL NOTE: The prices above slash are for Six/below slash for V-8.

MAVERICK SERIES — (ALL ENGINES) — The Maverick was the mid-year introduction model for 1969. It used a Falcon chassis and 170 cubic inch six-cylinder engine to power the only body style available — a two-door sedan.

MAVERICK SERIES I.D. NUMBERS — (ALL ENGINES) — The Mavericks used the same Serial Number sequence as the full-size Fords, Fairlanes and Falcons. (See production note).

MAVERICK SERIES

Model Number	Body/Style Number	Body Type & Seating	Factory Price	Shipping Weight	Production Total
T	91	2-dr Sed-6P	1995	2411	127,833

PRODUCTION NOTE: Total series output was 127,833 units.

1969 Ford, Thunderbird 2-dr Landau, V-8

THUNDERBIRD SERIES — (ALL ENGINES) — The Thunderbird continued to use the same body as the previous two years with minor trim changes and new frontal and taillight arrangements. The grille featured a horizontal division bar with the Thunderbird emblem in the center and three vertical moldings. The taillights of the 1969 Thunderbirds were large, rectangular units, with a single backup light mounted in the center of the escutcheon panel. A power-operated sun roof was once again offered in the Thunderbird Sun Roof Landau.

THUNDERBIRD SERIES I.D. NUMBERS — (ALL ENGINES) — Thunderbird models began with the number '9', assembly plant code 'Y' (Wixom), body type code, engine type code 'N' or 'Z' and, finally, the unit's production number, beginning at 100001 and going up (See production note).

THUNDERBIRD SERIES

Model Number	Body/Style Number	Body Type & Seating	Factory Price	Shipping Weight	Production Total
N/Z	65C	2-dr HT-4P	4807	4348	5,913
N/Z	65D	2-dr Landau-4P	4947	4360	27,664
N/Z	57C	4-dr Landau-4P	5026	4460	15,650

PRODUCTION NOTE: Total series output was 49,227 units. This figure includes 2,361 hardtops equipped with bucket seats; 12,425 Landau hardtops equipped with bucket seats and 1,983 Landau four-doors equipped with bucket seats.

FORD CHASSIS FEATURES: Wheelbase: 121 inches. Overall length: (station wagons) 216.9 inches; (other models) 213.9 inches. Tires: (station wagons) 9.00 x 15 four-ply tubeless blackwall; (other models) 8.25 x 15 four-ply tubeless blackwall.

FAIRLANE CHASSIS FEATURES: Wheelbase: (station wagons) 113 inches; (other models) 116 inches. Overall length: (station wagons) 203.9 inches; (other models) 201 inches. Tires: (convertibles) 7.75 x 14 four-ply blackwall; (Cobras) F70 x 14; (other models) 7.35 x 14 four-ply tubeless blackwall.

FALCON CHASSIS FEATURES: Wheelbase: (station wagons) 113 inches; (other models) 110.9 inches. Overall length: (station wagon) 198.7 inches; (other models) 184.3 inches. Tires: (station wagons) 7.75 x 14 four-ply tubeless blackwall; (sports coupe) 7.35 x 14 four-ply tubeless blackwall; (other models) 6.95 x 14 four-ply tubeless blackwall.

MAVERICK CHASSIS FEATURES: Wheelbase: 103 inches. Overall length: 179.4 inches. Tires: 6.00 x 13 four-ply tubeless blackwall.

THUNDERBIRD SERIES CHASSIS FEATURES: Wheelbase: (four-door Landau) 117 inches; (other models) 115 inches. Overall length: (four-door Landau) 209.9 inches; (other models) 206.9 inches. Tires: (four-door Landau) 8.45 x 15 four-ply tubeless; (other models) 8.15 x 15 four-ply tubeless whitewall.

1969 FORD ENGINES
Falcon six-cylinder. Overhead valves. Cast iron block. Displacement: 170 cubic inches. Bore and stroke: 3.50 x 2.94 inches. Compression ratio: 8.7:1. Brake horsepower: 100 at 4000 R.P.M. Carburetion: Holley one-barrel. Seven main bearings. Serial Number code 'U'.

Falcon/Fairlane/Mustang six-cylinder. Overhead valves. Cast iron block. Displacement: 200 cubic inches. Bore and stroke: 3.68 x 3.13 inches. Compression ratio: 8.8:1. Brake horsepower: 115 at 3800 R.P.M. Carburetion: Motorcraft one-barrel. Seven main bearings. Serial Number code 'T'.

Ford/Mustang six-cylinder. Overhead valve. Cast iron block. Displacement: 240 cubic inches. Bore and stroke: 4.00 x 3.18 inches. Compression ratio: 9.2:1. Brake horsepower: 150 at 4000 R.P.M. Carburetion: Motorcraft one-barrel. Seven main bearings. Serial Number code 'V'.

Ford six-cylinder. Overhead valves. Cast iron block. Displacment: 250 cubic inches. Bore and stroke: 3.68 x 3.91 inches. Compression ratio: 9.0:1. Brake horsepower: 155 at 4000 R.P.M. Carburetion: Motorcraft one-barrel. Seven main bearings. Serial Number code 'L'.

302 V-8. Overhead valves. Cast iron block. Displacement: 320 cubic inches. Bore and stroke: 4.00 x 3.00 inches. Compression ratio: 9.5:1. Brake horsepower: 220 at 4600 R.P.M. Carburetion: Motorcraft two-barrel. Five main bearings. Serial Number code 'F'.

Boss 302 V-8. Overhead valves. Cast iron block. Displacement: 302 cubic inches. Bore and stroke: 4.00 x 3.00 inches. Compression ratio: 10.5:1. Brake horsepower: 290 at 5600 R.P.M. Carburetion: Holley four-barrel. Five main bearings.

351 V-8. Overhead valve. Cast iron block. Displacement: 351 cubic inches. Bore and stroke: 4.00 x 3.50 inches. Compression ratio: 9.5:1. Brake horsepower: 250 at 4600 R.P.M. Carburetion: Motorcraft two-barrel. Five main bearings. Serial Number code 'H'.

351 Four-Barrel V-8. Overhead valves. Cast iron block. Displacement: 351 cubic inches. Bore and stroke: 4.00 x 3.50 inches. Compression ratio: 10.7:1. Brake horsepower: 290 at 4800 R.P.M. Carburetion: Motorcraft four-barrel. Five main bearings. Serial Number code 'M'.

Interceptor V-8. Overhead valves. Cast iron block. Displacement: 390 cubic inches. Bore and stroke: 4.05 x 3.78 inches. Compression ratio: 9.5:1. Brake horsepower: 265 at 4400 R.P.M. Carburetion: Motorcraft two-barrel. Five main bearings. Serial Number code 'H'.

Thunderbird V-8: Overhead valves. Cast iron block. Displacement: 390 cubic inch. Bore and stroke: 4.05 x 3.78 inches. Compression ratio: 10.5:1. Brake horsepower: 280 at 4400 R.P.M. Carburetion: Motorcraft two-barrel. Five main bearings.

390 GT V-8. Overhead valves. Cast iron block. Displacement: 390 cubic inches. Bore and stroke: 4.05 x 3.78 inches. Compression ratio: 10.5:1. Brake horsepower: 320 at 4600 R.P.M. Carburetion: Holley four-barrel. Five main bearings. Serial Number code 'S'.

Cobra Jet 428 V-8. Overhead valves. Cast iron block. Displacement: 428 cubic inches. Bore and stroke: 4.13 x 3.98 inches. Compression ratio: 10.6:1. Brake horsepower: 335 at 5200 R.P.M. Carburetion: Holley four-barrel. Five main bearings. Serial Number code 'Q'.

Super Cobra Jet 428 V-8. Overhead valves. Cast iron block. Displacement: 428 cubic inches. Bore and stroke: 4.13 x 3.98 inches. Compression ratio: 10.5:1. Brake horsepower: 360 at 5400 R.P.M. Carburetion: Holley four-barrel. Five main bearings.

Thunder Jet 429 V-8. Overhead valves. Cast iron block. Displacement: 429 cubic inches. Bore and stroke: 4.36 x 3.59 inches. Compression ratio: 10.5:1. Brake horsepower: 320 at 4500 R.P.M. Carburetion: Motorcraft two-barrel. Five main bearings. Serial Number code 'K'.

Thunder Jet 429 Four-Barrel V-8. Overhead valves. Cast iron block. Displacement: 429 cubic inches. Bore and stroke: 4.36 x 3.59 inches. Compression ratio: 10.5:1. Brake horsepower: 360 at 4600 R.P.M. Carburetion: Motorcraft four-barrel. Five main bearings. Serial Number code 'N'.

Boss 429 V-8. Overhead valves. Cast iron block. Displacement: 429 cubic inches. Bore and stroke: 4.36 x 3.59 inches. Compression ratio: 11.3:1. Brake horsepower: 375 at 5600 R.P.M. Carburetion: Holley four-barrel. Five main bearings.

1969 FORD TRANSMISSIONS: Same as 1968.

1969 FORD REAR AXLE RATIOS: Same as 1968.

FORD CONVENIENCE OPTIONS: 265 horsepower, 390 cubic inch V-8 engine ($58). 320 horsepower, 429 cubic inch V-8 engine ($163). 360 horsepower, 429 cubic inch V-8 engine ($237). Cruise-O-Matic automatic transmission ($222). Power steering ($100). Power brakes ($65 — Front discs). Tinted windshield ($45). Air conditioning ($389). AM radio ($61). AM/FM stereo radio ($181). Vinyl roof ($100). White sidewall tires ($33).

FAIRLANE/FAIRLANE TORINO CONVENIENCE OPTIONS: 220 horsepower, 302 cubic inch V-8 engine (no charge). 351 cubic inch V-8 engine ($84). Cruise-O-Matic automatic transmission ($222). Four-speed manual transmission ($194 — standard on Cobras). AM radio ($61). Power steering ($100). Power tailgate window on station wagons ($35). Luggage rack on station wagons ($47). Two-tone paint ($27). White sidewall tires ($34). Vinyl roofs on two-door hardtops and four-door sedans ($90).

FALCON CONVENIENCE OPTIONS: 200 cubic inch six-cylinder engine ($26). 302 cubic inch V-8 engine ($79). Cruise-O-Matic automatic transmission ($175). Power steering ($89). Power tailgate window on station wagons ($35). Tinted windshield ($32). AM radio ($61). Wheel covers ($21).

MAVERICK CONVENIENCE OPTIONS: Cruise-O-Matic automatic transmission ($175). AM radio ($61). White sidewall tires ($34).

THUNDERBIRD CONVENIENCE OPTIONS: 429 cubic inch Thunder Jet V-8 engine ($237). Six-Way power seats ($99). Power windows ($109). Cruise-Control ($97). Air conditioning ($427). Climate Control air conditioning ($499). AM/FM stereo radio ($150). AM/8-track stereo ($128). Exterior Protection Group on two-doors ($25); on four-doors ($29).

Historical footnotes: The 1969 Ford lines were publically introduced on September 27, 1968. Calendar year production for America's Number Two automaker hit the 1,743,442 unit level this year. A total of 1,880,384 Fords were registered as new cars during calendar 1969. Semon E. Knudsen was, again, president of the company and continued to actively pursue a strong high-performance image. Stock car driver Richard Petty was enticed to drive for Ford in 1969, after a successful stint with Plymouth. He captured the checkered flag in the Riverside 500 Grand National Race. David Pearson, also driving Fords, won the NASCAR championship with 26 Grand National victories. The car was a special Talladega streamlined Torino that sold for $3680. A total of 754 were built during January and February of 1969. It was the next to last season for the compact Falcon, which could not be modified to meet Federal safety regulations at reasonable cost. The Falcon nameplate was used on a budget-priced Torino added as a late-year model in 1970, then dropped entirely. Ford called its fastback cars "Sportsroof" models and used the name "Squire" on its fanciest station wagons.

1970 FORD

1970 FORDS — OVERVIEW — For model year 1970, Ford continued to expand its lineup with more and more models within each series. The full-size Fords were only slightly restyled for 1970, with a revamped rear end treatment. The taillights of the new model were positioned lower in the body and the grille was updated.

FORD CUSTOM SERIES — (ALL ENGINES) — The Custom Series was the base trim level for 1970 and included chrome windshield and rear window moldings; Nylon carpeting; the Custom name, in script, on the rear fenders and the Ford name, in block letters, across the front of the hood and in the rear escutcheon panel. The Custom 500 models offered the same trim, with the addition of the horizontal chrome strip along the mid-section of the body and a brushed aluminum trim strip at the front of the hood.

CUSTOM SIX-CYLINDER SERIES I.D. NUMBERS: Custom six-cylinder models began with the number '0', followed by the assembly plant code, engine designation 'V' and, finally, the unit's production number, according to the final assembly location. Each plant began at 100001 and went up (See production note).

CUSTOM SIX SERIES

Model Number	Body/Style Number	Body Type & Seating	Factory Price	Shipping Weight	Production Total
V	54E	4-dr Sed-6P	2771	3527	Note 1
V	54B	4-dr Sed-6P	2872	3567	Note 1

NOTE 1: See Custom V-8 Series listing. Production was counted by series and body style only, with no breakout per engine type.

CUSTOM V-8 SERIES I.D. NUMBERS: Custom V-8 models began with the number '0', followed by the assembly plant code, body type code, engine designation code and, finally, the unit's production number according to the final assembly location. Each plant began at 100001 and went up (See production note).

CUSTOM V-8 SERIES

Model Number	Body/Style Number	Body Type & Seating	Factory Price	Shipping Weight	Production Total
NA	54E	4-dr Sed-6P	2850	3563	42,849
NA	71D	4-dr Ranch Wag-6P	3305	4079	15,086
NA	54B	4-dr Sed-6P	2951	3603	41,261
NA	71H	4-dr Ranch Wag-6P	3368	4049	15,304
NA	71J	4-dr Ranch Wag-10P	3481	4137	9,943

PRODUCTION NOTE: Total series output was 124,443 units. Ford does not indicate the number of each model produced with Sixes and V-8s. Therefore, all production figures given above are total production of each body style with both engines.

GALAXIE 500 SERIES — (ALL ENGINES) — The Galaxie 500 was the intermediate trim level for 1969 and included all the Custom trim; plus a pleated vinyl interior; chrome side window and rain gutter moldings and polished aluminum wheel opening moldings.

GALAXIE 500 SIX-CYLINDER SERIES I.D. NUMBERS: Galaxie 500 six-cylinder models used the same Serial Number sequence as the Custom Series (See production note).

GALAXIE 500 SIX SERIES

Model Number	Body/Style Number	Body Type & Seating	Factory Price	Shipping Weight	Production Total
V	54A	4-dr Sed-6P	3026	3540	Note 1
V	57B	4-dr HT Sed-6P	3096	3611	Note 1
V	65C	2-dr FT Cpe-6P	3094	3550	Note 1
V	63B	2-dr FsBk Cpe-6P	3043	3549	Note 1

NOTE 1: See Galaxie 500 V-8 Series listing. Production was counted by series and body style only, with no breakout per engine type.

GALAXIE 500 V-8 SERIES I.D. NUMBERS: Galaxie 500 V-8 models used the same Serial Number sequence as the Custom Series (See production note).

GALAXIE 500 V-8 SERIES

Model Number	Body/Style Number	Body Type & Seating	Factory Price	Shipping Weight	Production Total
NA	54A	4-dr Sed-6P	3137	3661	101,784
NA	57B	4-dr HT Sed-6P	3208	3732	53,817
NA	65C	2-dr FT Cpe-6P	3205	3671	57,059
NA	63B	2-dr FsBk Cpe-6P	3154	3670	50,825
NA	71B	4-dr Ctry Sed-6P	3488	4089	32,209
NA	71C	4-dr Ctry Sed-10P	3600	4112	22,645

PRODUCTION NOTE: Total series output was 318, 339 units. Ford does not indicate the number of each model produced with Sixes and V-8s. Therefore, all production figures given above are total production of each body style with both engines.

FORD XL SERIES — (ALL ENGINES) — The Ford XL was the sport trim version of the full-size two-door convertible and two-door fastback models and included the features of the Galaxie 500s, plus the 302 cubic inch V-8 engine; bucket seats; special wheel covers; LTD style die-cast grille; retractable headlights; pleated, all-vinyl interior trim and the XL designation, in block letters, in the center of the front of the hood.

FORD XL V-8 SERIES I.D. NUMBERS: Ford XLs used the same Serial Number sequence as the Custom and Galaxie 500 Series (See production note).

FORD XL V-8 SERIES

Model Number	Body/Style Number	Body Type & Seating	Factory Price	Shipping Weight	Production Total
NA	63C	2-dr FsBk Cpe-5P	3293	3750	27,251
NA	76B	2-dr Conv-5P	3501	3983	6,348

PRODUCTION NOTE: Total series output was 33,599 units.

1970 Ford, LTD Brougham, 2-dr hardtop sports coupe, V-8

FORD LTD V-8 SERIES — (ALL ENGINES) — The LTD was the top trim level full-size Ford for 1970 and included all the Galaxie 500 trim, plus the 250 horsepower, 351 cubic inch V-8 engine; Cruise-O-Matic automatic transmission; electric clock; bright exterior moldings and dual accent paint stripes. The LTD station wagon models (Country Squires) also included simulated wood-grain appliques on the bodysides. All LTDs also included retractable headlights and a die-cast grille. The absolute top trim level for 1970 was the LTD Brougham two and four-door hardtops and four-door sedan. These were LTDs with more lavish interiors than the regular LTD offered. Exterior trim remained the same as the standard LTD.

FORD LTD V-8 SERIES I.D. NUMBERS: LTDs used the same Serial Number sequence as the Custom and Galaxie 500 Series (See production note).

FORD LTD V-8 SERIES

Model Number	Body/Style Number	Body Type & Seating	Factory Price	Shipping Weight	Production Total
NA	54C	4-dr Sed-6P	3307	3701	78,306
NA	57F	4-dr HT Sed-6P	3385	3771	90,390
NA	65A	2-dr HT Cpe-6P	3356	3727	96,324
NA	71E	4-dr Ctry Sq-6P	3832	4139	39,837
NA	71A	4-dr Ctry Sq-10P	3909	4185	69,077
LTD BROUGHAM SUB-SERIES					
NA	54	4-dr Sed-6P	3502	3829	NA
NA	57	4-dr HT Sed-6P	3579	4029	NA
NA	65	2-dr HT Cpe-6P	3537	3855	NA

PRODUCTION NOTE: Total series output was 373,934 units. Production is not broken down between LTD models and LTD Brougham models. Therefore, production figures represent total LTD model production.

1970 FAIRLANE/TORINO — OVERVIEW — The Fairlane/Torino Series was completely restyled, with a very sleek body shell and rounded fender contours. The top-line Torino Series featured hidden headlights as part of it's luxury package. The powerful Cobra models offered a functional hood scoop and rear window louvers as part of the Cobra package. The mid-year 1969 introduction of the Maverick caused Falcon sales to plummet and, for 1970, the Falcon was nothing more than the lowest-price Fairlane model. It was available only as a two-door sedan.

FAIRLANE SERIES — (ALL ENGINES) — The Fairlane was the base trim level of the intermediate Fairlane/Torino Series and included chrome windshield, rear window and rain gutter moldings; front and rear door arm rests; cigarette lighter; Nylon carpeting; the Fairlane 500 name, in script, on the rear fenders above the side marker lights; two chrome hash marks on the front fenders, behind the front wheel opening, and the Ford name, in block letters, on the driver's side of the hood and across the escutcheon panel.

FAIRLANE 500 SIX-CYLINDER SERIES I.D. NUMBERS: Fairlane 500 six-cylinder models began with the number '0', followed by the assembly plant code, body type code, engine designation 'L' and, finally, the unit's production number, according to the final assembly location. Each plant began at 100001 and went up (See production note).

1970½ Ford Falcon, 2-dr sedan, V-8

FAIRLANE 500 SIX-CYLINDER SERIES

Model Number	Body/Style Number	Body Type & Seating	Factory Price	Shipping Weight	Production Total
FALCON SUB-SERIES					
L	54A	4-dr Sed-6P	2500	3116	Note 1
L	62A	2-dr Sed-6P	2460	3100	Note 1
L	71D	4-dr Sta Wag-6P	2767	3155	Note 1
FAIRLANE 500 SUB-SERIES					
L	54B	4-dr Sed-6P	2627	3116	Note 1
L	65B	2-dr HT Cpe-6P	2660	3128	Note 1
L	71B	4-dr Sta Wag-6P	2957	3508	Note 1

NOTE 1: See Fairlane 500 V-8 Series listing. Production was counted by series and body style only, with no breakout per engine type.

FAIRLANE 500 V-8 SERIES I.D. NUMBERS: Fairlane 500 V-8 models began with the number '0', followed by the assembly plant code, body type code, engine designation code and, finally, the unit's production number, according to the final assembly location. Each plant began at 100001 and went up (See production note).

FAIRLANE 500 V-8 SERIES

Model Number	Body/Style Number	Body Type & Seating	Factory Price	Shipping Weight	Production Total
NA	54A	4-dr Sed-6P	2528	3216	30,443
NA	62A	2-dr Sed-6P	2479	3200	26,071
NA	71D	4-dr Sta Wag-6P	2856	3255	10,539
NA	54B	4-dr Sed-6P	2716	3216	25,780
NA	65B	2-dr HT Cpe-6P	2750	3228	70,636
NA	71B	4-dr Sta Wag-6P	3047	3608	13,613

PRODUCTION NOTE: Total series output was 177,091 units. Ford does not indicate the number of each model produced with Sixes and V-8s. Therefore, all production figures given above are total production of each body style with both engines.

TORINO SERIES — (ALL ENGINES) — The Torino was the intermediate trim level for the intermediate size Fairlane/Torino Series and included all the Fairlane 500 trim, plus a single horizontal chrome strip along the bodyside. The Torino name appeared in script, on the driver's side of the hood and in block letters on the side of the front fenders, behind the front wheel opening.

TORINO SIX-CYLINDER SERIES I.D. NUMBERS: Torino, six-cylinder models used the same Serial Number sequence as the Fairlane 500 models (See production note).

TORINO SIX-CYLINDER SERIES

Model Number	Body/Style Number	Body Type & Seating	Factory Price	Shipping Weight	Production Total
L	54C	4-dr Sed-6P	2689	3158	Note 1
L	57C	4-dr HT Sed-6P	2795	3189	Note 1
L	65C	2-dr HT pe-6P	2722	3173	Note 1
L	63C	2-dr FsBk Cpe-6P	2810	3211	Note 1
L	71C	4-dr Sta Wag-6P	3074	3553	Note 1

NOTE 1: See Torino V-8 Series listing. Production was counted by series and body style only, with no breakout per engine type.

TORINO V-8 SERIES I.D. NUMBERS: Torino V-8 models used the same Serial Number sequence as the Fairlane 500 models (See production note).

TORINO V-8 SERIES

Model Number	Body/Style Number	Body Type & Seating	Factory Price	Shipping Weight	Production Total
NA	54C	4-dr Sed-6P	2778	3258	30,117
NA	57C	4-dr HT Sed-6P	2885	3289	14,312
NA	65C	2-dr HT Cpe-6P	2812	3273	49,826
NA	63C	2-dr FsBk Cpe-6P	2899	3311	12,490
NA	71C	4-dr Sta Wag-6P	3164	3653	10,613

PRODUCTION NOTE: Total series output was 117,358 units. Ford does not indicate the number of each model produced with Sixes and V-8s. Therefore, all production figures given above are total production of each body style with both engines.

TORINO BROUGHAM SERIES — (ALL ENGINES) — The Torino Brougham was the top trim level of the Torino Series for 1970 and included all the Torino trim, plus polished aluminum wheel well and rocker panel moldings; retractable headlights; wheel covers and the 220 horsepower, 302 cubic inch V-8 engine. The station wagon version included all of the above features, plus simulated wood-grain appliques and power front disc brakes.

TORINO BROUGHAM SERIES I.D. NUMBERS — (ALL ENGINES) — Torino Broughams used the same Serial Number sequence as the Fairlane 500 and Torino models (See production note).

TORINO BROUGHAM V-8 SERIES

Model Number	Body/Style Number	Body Type & Seating	Factory Price	Shipping Weight	Production Total
NA	57E	4-dr HT Sed-6P	3078	3309	14,543
NA	57E	2-dr HT Cpe-6P	3006	3293	16,911
NA	71E	4-dr Sq Sta Wag-6P	3379	3673	13,166

PRODUCTION NOTE: Total series output was 44,620 units.

TORINO GT AND COBRA SERIES — (ALL ENGINES) — The Torino GT was the sport version of the Torino Series and included all the Torino trim, plus outside color-keyed dual racing interior mirrors; hood scoop; trim rings with hub caps; courtesy lights; carpeting; padded seats; GT emblems; 250 horsepower 351 cubic inch V-8 engine and E70 x 15 fiberglass-belted white sidewall tires (F70 x 15 tires on convertibles versions). The Torino Cobra was the high-performance version of the Torino Series and included all the Torino trim, plus the 360 horsepower, 429 cubic inch V-8 engine; four-speed manual transmission; competition suspension; seven inch wide wheels with hub caps; black center hood; hood locking pins; bright exterior moldings; courtesy lights; Cobra emblems and F70 x 15 fiberglass-belted black sidewall tires with raised white letters.

TORINO GT AND TORINO COBRA SERIES I.D. NUMBERS — (ALL ENGINES) — Torino GT and Cobra models used the same Serial Number sequence as Fairlane 500 and Torino models (See production note).

TORINO GT AND COBRA V-8 SERIES

Model Number	Body/Style Number	Body Type & Seating	Factory Price	Shipping Weight	Production Total
TORINO GT					
NA	63F	2-dr FsBk Cpe-6P	3105	3366	56,819
NA	76F	2-dr Conv-6P	3212	3490	3,939
TORINO GT COBRA					
NA	63H	2-dr FsBk Cpe-6P	3270	3774	7,675

PRODUCTION NOTE: Total series output was 68,433 units.

1970 Ford, Maverick DeLuxe 2-dr sedan, 6-cyl

MAVERICK SERIES — (ALL ENGINES) — The Maverick continued unchanged for 1970. Customer demand was so great for the 1969 version that Ford officials decided to leave a good thing alone and continued to offer the same car for 1970.

MAVERICK SERIES — (ALL ENGINES) — The 1970 Maverick was unchanged in any way from the 1969 version (See 1969).

PRODUCTION NOTE: Total series output was 451,081 units.

THUNDERBIRD SERIES — (ALL ENGINES) — The 1970 Thunderbird featured a new grille, with a protruding center section, which was found to be very delicate and caused insurance companies to charge very high premiums to Thunderbird owners. The entire car was lower than in previous years and featured an inverted 'U' taillight arrangement. The length and lowness of the new Thunderbird was accented by a single horizontal feature line along the mid-section of the body. Color-keyed wheel covers added to the rich look of the new Thunderbirds.

1970 Ford, Thunderbird 2-dr hardtop sports coupe, V-8

THUNDERBIRD SERIES I.D. NUMBERS — (ALL ENGINES) — Thunderbird models began with the number '0', assembly plant code 'Y' (Wixom), body type code, engine type code 'N' and, finally, the unit's production number, beginning at 100001 and going up (See production note).

THUNDERBIRD SERIES

Model Number	Body/Style Number	Body Type & Seating	Factory Price	Shipping Weight	Production Total
N	65C	2-dr HT-4P	4961	4354	5,116
N	65D	2-dr Landau-4P	5104	4630	36,847
N	57C	4-dr Landau-4P	5182	4464	8,401

PRODUCTION NOTE: Total series output was 50,364 units. This figure includes 1,925 two-door hardtops equipped with bucket seats; 16,953 two-door Landaus equipped with bucket seats and 5,005 four-door Landaus equipped with bucket seats.

FORD CHASSIS FEATURES: Wheelbase: 121 inches. Overall length: (station wagons) 216.9 inches; (other models) 213.9 inches. Tires: (Custom six-cylinder) F78 x 15 four-ply blackwall tubeless; (Custom and Custom 500 V-8) G78 x 15 four-ply tubeless blackwall; (Galaxie 500 and LTD) H78 x 15 four-ply tubeless blackwall.

FAIRLANE 500 AND TORINO CHASSIS FEATURES: Wheelbase: (station wagon) 114 inches; (other models) 117 inches. Overall length: (station wagon) 209 inches; (other models) 206.2 inches. Tires: (convertibles) F70 x 14 four-ply tubeless blackwall; (station wagons) G78 x 14; (GTs) E70 x 14; (other models) E78 x 14.

THUNDERBIRD SERIES CHASSIS FEATURES: Wheelbase: (two-doors) 114.7 inches; (other models) 117.1 inches. Overall length: 215 inches. Tires 215 x 15 radial blackwalls.

1970 FORD ENGINES

Maverick six-cylinder. Overhead valves. Cast iron block. Displacement: 170 cubic inches. Bore and stroke: 3.50 x 2.94 inches. Compression ratio: 9.0:1. Brake horsepower: 105 at 4400 R.P.M. Carburetion: Holley one-barrel. Seven main bearings. Serial Number code 'U'.

Maverick six-cylinder. Overhead valves. Cast iron block. Displacement: 200 cubic inches. Bore and stroke: 3.68 x 3.13 inches. Compression ratio: 8.0:1. Brake horsepower: 120 at 4400 R.P.M. Carburetion: Motorcraft one-barrel. Seven main bearings. Serial Number code 'T'.

Ford/Mustang six-cylinder. Overhead valves. Cast iron block. Displacement: 240 cubic inches. Bore and stroke: 4.00 x 3.18 inches. Compression ratio: 9.2:1. Brake horsepower: 150 at 4000 R.P.M. Carburetion: Motorcraft one-barrel. Seven main bearings. Serial Number code 'V'.

Ford six-cylinder. Overhead valves. Cast iron block. Displacement: 250 cubic inches. Bore and stroke: 3.68 x 3.91 inches. Compression ratio: 9.0:1. Brake horsepower: 155 at 4400 R.P.M. Carburetion: Motorcraft one-barrel. Seven main bearings. Serial Number code 'L'.

302 V-8. Overhead valves. Cast iron block. Displacement: 302 cubic inches. Bore and stroke: 4.00 x 3.00 inches. Compression ratio: 9.5:1. Brake horsepower: 220 at 4600 R.P.M. Carburetion: Motorcraft two-barrel. Five main bearings. Serial Number code 'F'.

Boss 302 V-8. Overhead valves. Cast iron block. Displacement: 302 cubic inches. Compression ratio: 10.6:1. Brake horsepower: 290 at 5800 R.P.M. Carburetion: Holley four-barrel. Five main bearings.

351 V-8. Overhead valves. Cast iron block. Displacement: 351 cubic inches. Bore and stroke: 4.00 x 3.50 inches. Compression ratio: 9.5:1. Brake horsepower: 250 at 4600 R.P.M. Carburetion: Motorcraft two-barrel. Five main bearings. Serial Number code 'H'.

351 Four-Barrel V-8. Overhead valves. Cast iron block. Displacement: 351 cubic inches. Bore and stroke: 4.00 x 3.50 inches. Compression ratio: 11.0:1. Brake horsepower: 300 at 5400 R.P.M. Carburetion: Motorcraft four-barrel. Five main bearings.

390 V-8. Overhead valves. Cast iron block. Displacement: 390 cubic inches. Bore and stroke: 4.05 x 3.78 inches. Compression ratio: 9.5:1. Brake horsepower: 270 4400 R.P.M. Carburetion: Motorcraft two-barrel. Five main bearings. Serial Number code 'H'.

Cobra Jet 428 V-8. Overhead valve. Cast iron block. Displacement: 428 cubic inches. Bore and stroke: 4.13 x 3.98 inches. Compression ratio: 10.6:1. Brake horsepower: 335 at 5200 R.P.M. Carburetion: Holley four-barrel. Five main bearings. Serial Number code 'Q'.

Super Cobra Jet 428 V-8. Overhead valves. Cast iron block. Displacement: 428 cubic inches. Bore and stroke: 4.13 x 3.98 inches. Compression ratio: 10.5:1. Brake horsepower: 360 at 5400 R.P.M. Carburetion: Holley four-barrel. Five main bearings.

Thunder Jet 429 V-8. Overhead valves. Cast iron block. Displacement: 429 cubic inches. Bore and stroke: 4.36 x 3.59 inches. Compression ratio: 10.5:1. Brake horsepower: 320 at 4400 R.P.M. Carburetion: Motorcraft two-barrel. Five main bearings. Serial Number code 'K'.

Thunder Jet 429 Four-Barrel V-8. Overhead valves. Cast iron block. Displacement: 429 cubic inches. Bore and stroke: 4.36 x 3.59 inches. Compression ratio: 10.5:1. Brake horsepower: 360 at 4600 R.P.M. Carburetion: Motorcraft four-barrel. Five main bearings. Serial Number code 'N'.

Police Interceptor 429 V-8. Overhead valves. Cast iron block. Displacement: 429 cubic inches. Bore and stroke: 4.36 x 3.59 inches. Compression ratio: 11.3:1. Brake horsepower: 370 at 5400 R.P.M. Carburetion: Holley four-barrel. Five main bearings. Serial Number code 'P'.

Boss 429 V-8. Overhead valves. Cast iron block. Displacement: 429 cubic inches. Bore and stroke: 4.36 x 3.59 inches. Compression ratio: 11.3:1. Brake horsepower: 375 at 5600 R.P.M. Carburetion: Holley four-barrel Five main bearings.

Ram Air Boss 429 V-8: Same specifications as Boss 429.

1970 FORD TRANSMISSIONS: Same as 1969.

1969 FORD REAR AXLE RATIOS: Same as 1969.

FORD CONVENIENCE OPTIONS: Power disc brakes ($65). Power steering ($105). Air conditioning ($389). Cruise-O-Matic automatic transmission ($201-$222). Tinted windshield ($45). AM radio ($61). AM/FM radio ($240). Vinyl roof ($105). White sidewall tires ($34). Custom Series 265 horsepower, 390 cubic inch V-8 engine ($131). Galaxie 500/XL/LTD 265 horsepower, 390 cubic inch V-8 engine ($86). Custom Series 320 horsepower, 429 cubic inch V-8 engine ($213). Galaxie 500/XL/LTD 320 horsepower, 429 cubic inch V-8 inch ($168). LTD Luxury trim package ($104).

FAIRLANE/TORINO CONVENIENCE OPTIONS: Power steering ($100). Air conditioning ($389). Cruise-O-Matic automatic transmission ($201-$222). Four-speed manual transmission ($194). AM radio ($61). Station wagon power tailgate window ($35). Station wagon roof top luggage rack ($46). White sidewall tires ($34). Vinyl roof on two-door and four-door hardtops and sedan ($95). Fairlane/Torino 351 cubic inch V-8 engine ($45).

THUNDERBIRD CONVENIENCE OPTIONS: Air conditioning ($427). Six-Way power seats ($198). Power side windows ($110). Cruise-Control ($97). Air conditioning with Climate Control ($499). AM/FM stereo radio ($150). AM radio with 8-track tape player ($150). Brougham interior package ($162). Limited-edition Fiera Brougham option package ($304).

1970 Ford, Falcon 2-dr sedan, V-8

Historical footnotes: The full-sized Fords were introduced in September, 1969 and the Falcon/Torino appeared in dealer showrooms at mid-year. Model year production peaked at 1,326,533 units. Calendar year production of 1,647,918 cars was recorded. Due to the new, reverse-curve Torino rear window design (and increased competition from the aerodynamic Dodge Daytona and Plymouth Superbird), Ford elected to race 1969 models this year. Only six stock car flags were taken by FoMoCo drivers. The DeTomaso Pantera, an Italian-built specialty sports car powered by a 310 horsepower 351 cubic inch Ford 'Cleveland' V-8 made its debut in 1970. During the early months of 1970, the Falcon compact was still marketed in three styles, two and four-door sedans and station wagons, but was replaced by the larger Fairlane based '70½ Falcon during the summer.

1971 FORD

1971 FORDS — OVERVIEW — The complete restyling of two model lines and the introduction of the sub-compact Pinto line characterized 1972, a year which also saw the end of two Ford trademarks. The Fairlane was dropped, along with the 'FE' series, big-block V-8 engine. The Fairlane name ceased to exist with the end of the 1970 model year and the big-block engine, in 390 and 428 cubic inch sizes, was gradually phased-out during the production run. It was replaced by a new 400 cubic inch 'Cleveland' V-8 and the 429 cubic inch V-8.

FORD CUSTOM SERIES — (ALL ENGINES) — The full-size Fords received a total restyling. The grille was a full-width horizontal unit, with a larger, vertical center section which protruded forward. The hood peaked the center section of the grille and became wider toward the windshield. The Custom Series was the base trim level full-size Ford for 1971 and included chrome windshield and rear window moldings; Nylon carpeting and the Custom name, in block letters, on the rear fenders and rear escutcheon panel. The Custom 500 models included all the Custom trim, plus polished aluminum wheel well moldings; argent and chrome appliques on the instrument panel; rear deck moldings and Custom 500 ornamentation. The Custom and Custom 500 models were available with either the 140 horsepower 240 cubic inch six-cylinder engine or the 210 horsepower 302 cubic inch V-8 engine as standard equipment.

CUSTOM SERIES I.D. NUMBERS: Custom models began with the number '1', followed by the assembly plant code, engine designation code and, finally, the unit's production number, according to the final assembly location. Each plant began at 100001 and went up (See production note).

CUSTOM SERIES

Model Number	Body/Style Number	Body Type & Seating	Factory Price	Shipping Weight	Production Total
BASE CUSTOM					
NA	54B	4-dr Sed-6P	3288/3363	3683/3724	41,062
NA	71B	4-dr Ranch Wag-6P	3890	4190	16,696

Model Number	Body/Style Number	Body Type & Seating	Factory Price	Shipping Weight	Production Total
CUSTOM 500					
NA	54D	4-dr Sed-6P	3426/3501	3688/3729	33,765
NA	71D	4-dr Ranch Wag-6P	3982	4215	25,957

PRODUCTION NOTE: Total series output was 117,480 units. The price and weight to the left of the slant bar indicate six-cylinder equipped models and the price and weight to the right of the slant bar indicate V-8 powered models.

GALAXIE 500 SERIES — (ALL ENGINES) — The Galaxie 500 was the intermediate trim level full-size Ford for 1971 and included all the Custom trim, plus wood-grain appliques on the interior doors and instrument panel; bodyside moldings, with black- painted inserts; partial polished aluminum wheel well moldings; chrome window frames; deck and rear quarter extension moldings; Galaxie 500 ornamentation; 240 horsepower; 351 cubic inch V-8 engine and F78 x 15 belted black sidewall tires (H78 x 15 tires on Country Sedans).

GALAXIE 500 SERIES I.D. NUMBERS: Galaxie 500 models used the same Serial Number sequence as the Custom Series (See production note).

GALAXIE 500 SERIES

Model Number	Body/Style Number	Body Type & Seating	Factory Price	Shipping Weight	Production Total
NA	54F	4-dr Sed-6P	3246/3367	3668/3826	98,130
NA	57F	4-dr HT Sed-6P	3665/3786	3723/3881	46,595
NA	65F	2-dr HT Cpe-6P	3628/3749	3668/3826	117,139
NA	71F	4-dr Ctry Sed-6P	4074	4241	60,487
NA	71D	4-dr Ctry Sed-10P	4188	4291	NA

PRODUCTION NOTE: Total series output was 322,351 units. This figure does not include the ten- passenger four-door Country Sedan, for which separate production figures breakouts are not available. The price and weight to the left of the slant bar indicate six-cylinder equipped models and the price and weight to the right of the slant bar indicate V-8 powered models.

FORD LTD SERIES — (ALL ENGINES) — A more formal roofline was used in the LTD Series and the interiors were completely restyled, with the emphasis on luxury or a luxury appearance in the lower-priced lines. The taillights were rectangular and were located at either end of the rear escutcheon panel, with the LTDs featuring an additional red, plastic reflector in the center. This gave the illusion of a single, full-width taillight. The LTD was the top trim level full-size Ford for 1971 and included all the Galaxie 500 trim, plus power front disc brakes; electric clock; luxury seat trim (except convertibles); lefthand outside rear view mirror; Nylon carpeting; power top on convertibles and G78 x 15 belted tires (in place of F78 x 15) on convertibles. The LTD Country Squire station wagons also included wheel covers; power tailgate window; simulated wood-grain appliques on the bodyside panels; pleated vinyl trim and H78 x 15 belted black sidewall tires. The LTD Brougham Series included all the LTD trim, plus wheel covers; unique Brougham seat trim; DeLuxe steering wheel; front door courtesy light; cut-pile carpeting; front seat center arm rest and polished seat side shields; rear door courtesy light switches; special LTD 'C' pillar ornamentation and high-back bucket seats on the two-door hardtop.

LTD SERIES I.D. NUMBERS: LTDs used the same Serial Number sequence as the Custom and Galaxie 500 Series (See Production note).

LTD SERIES

Model Number	Body/Style Number	Body Type & Seating	Factory Price	Shipping Weight	Production Total
BASE LTD					
NA	53H	4-dr Sed-6P	3931	3913	92,260
NA	57H	4-dr HT Sed-6P	3969	3908	48,166
NA	65H	2-dr FT Cpe-6P	3923	3853	103,896
NA	76H	2-dr Conv-6P	4094	4091	5,750
NA	71H	4-dr Ctry Sq-6P	4308	4308	130,644
NA	71	4-dr Ctry Sq-10P	4496	4358	NA
LTD BROUGHAM					
NA	53K	4-dr Sed-6P	4094	3949	26,186
NA	57K	4-dr HT Sed-6P	4140	3944	27,820
NA	65K	2-dr HT Cpe-6P	4097	3883	43,303

PRODUCTION NOTE: Total Series output was 478,025 units. This figure includes the four-door, ten-passenger Country Squire, for which separate production figure breakouts are not available.

1971 Ford, Torino Cobra 2-dr hardtop sports coupe, V-8

TORINO SERIES — (ALL ENGINES) — Torinos for 1971 were merely 1970 bodies with updated trim and a very slightly revised grille. Standard equipment on the base Torino Series included chrome windshield, rear window and rain gutter moldings; front and rear arm rest on the doors and the Torino name, in block letters, on the rear fenders. The Torino 500 Series had all the base Torino trim, plus color-keyed carpeting; cloth and vinyl interior trim; deck lid dock cover; Aargent-painted egg crate grille and polished aluminum wheel well and rocker panel moldings.

TORINO AND TORINO 500 SERIES I.D. NUMBERS: Torino and Torino 500s began with the number '1', followed by the assembly plant code, body type code, engine designation code and, finally, the unit's production number, according to the final assembly location. Each plant began at 100001 and went up (See production note).

TORINO AND TORINO 500 SERIES

Model Number	Body/Style Number	Body Type & Seating	Factory Price	Shipping Weight	Production Total
BASE TORINO					
NA	54A	4-dr Sed-6P	2672/2767	3141/3220	29,501
NA	62A	2-dr HT Cpe-6P	2706/2801	3151/3230	37,518
NA	71D	4-dr Sta Wag-6P	3023/2950	3498/3577	21,570
TORINO 500					
NA	54C	4-dr Sed-6P	2855/2950	3146/3225	35,650
NA	57C	4-dr HD Sed-6P	2959/3054	3210/3289	12,724
NA	65C	2-dr HT Cpe-6P	2887/2982	3156/3235	89,966
NA	63C	2-dr FsBk Cpe-6P	2943/3038	3212/3291	11,150
NA	71C	4-dr Sta Wag-6P	3170/3265	3560/3639	23,270

PRODUCTION NOTE: Total series output was 261,349 units. The price and weight to the left of the slant bar indicate six-cylinder equipped models and the price and weight to the right of the slant bar indicate V-8 powered models.

TORINO BROUGHAM/TORINO GT/TORINO COBRA SERIES — (ALL ENGINES) — The Torino Brougham was the top trim level Torino for 1971 and included all the Torino 500 equipment, plus wheel covers; chrome exterior moldings; soundproofing package; Brougham ornamentation; cloth interior trims (in choice of four colors) and 210 horsepower, 302 cubic inch V-8 engine. The Squire wagon also included power front disc brakes; simulated wood-grain paneling on the bodysides and G78 x 14 belted black sidewall tires. The Torino GT was the sporty version of the Brougham Series and included all the basic Brougham trim, plus color-keyed outside racing mirrors (remote control on lefthand mirror); GT identification on the grille and rocker panels; simulated hood scoop; hub caps with trim rings; chrome trim on the foot pedals; full-width taillight and E70 x 14 white sidewall Wide-Oval tires. The convertible also had a power top. The Torino Cobra was the high-performance version of the Brougham Series and included all the Brougham trim, plus 285 horsepower, 351 cubic inch 'Cleveland' V-8 engine; four-speed manual transmission with Hurst shifter; special Cobra identification; heavy-duty suspension; seven inch wide, Argent-painted wheels with chrome hub caps; black grille and lower escutcheon panel; black-finished hood with non-reflective paint; polished aluminum wheel well moldings; F70 x 14 white sidewall Wide Oval tires; 55 ampere heavy-duty battery; dual exhausts and pleated vinyl seat trim.

TORINO BROUGHAM/GT/COBRA SERIES I.D. NUMBERS: — (ALL ENGINES) — Torino Brougham/GT/Cobra models used the same Serial Number sequence as the Torino and Torino 500 Series. (See production note).

TORINO BROUGHAM/GT/COBRA SERIES

Model Number	Body/Style Number	Body Type & Seating	Factory Price	Shipping Weight	Production Total
NA	57E	4-dr Brgm HT Sed	3248	3345	4,408
NA	65E	2-dr Brgm HT Cpe	3175	3390	8,593
NA	71E	4-dr Squire Wag-6P	3560	3663	15,805
NA	63F	2-dr GT Spt Cpe-6P	3150	3346	31,641
NA	76F	2-dr GT Conv-6P	3408	3486	1,613
NA	63H	2-dr Cobra HT Cpe	3295	3594	3,054

PRODUCTION NOTE: Total series output was 65,114 units. Styles 57E, 65E and 63H are six-passenger models.

1971 Ford, Maverick 'Grabber' 2-dr sedan, V-8

MAVERICK SERIES — (ALL ENGINES) — The 1971 Maverick was unchanged from the previous two years, except for the addition of a four-door sedan and a 'Grabber' version of the two-door sedan. Also the 302 cubic inch V-8 engine was available for the first time. The 302 proved to be a brisk performer in the small body and the special edition of the two-door sedan, called the 'Grabber' was introduced to further enhance the performance image.

MAVERICK SERIES I.D. NUMBERS — (ALL ENGINES) — Maverick used the same Serial Number sequence as the full-size Fords and Torinos (See production note).

MAVERICK SERIES

Model Number	Body/Style Number	Body Type & Seating	Factory Price	Shipping Weight	Production Total
NA	54A	4-dr Sed-6P	2235/2404	2610/2803	73,208
NA	62A	2-dr Sed-6P	2175/2344	2478/2671	159,726
NA	62D	2-dr Grabber-6P	2354/2523	2570/2763	38,963

PRODUCTION NOTE: Total series output was 271,897 units. The price and weight to the left of the slant bar indicate six-cylinder equipped models and the price and weight to the right of the slant bar indicate V-8 powered models.

1971 PINTO — (OVERVIEW) — The new Pinto was introduced to serve the ever-growing small car market and to complete with Chevrolet's Vega and American Motor's Gremlin. Pintos were available with either a British-built 1600 cubic centimeter overhead valve four-cylinder engine, or a second, more powerful (and much more popular) German-built 2000 cubic centimeter motor, which was also a Four. Both engines used a four-speed manual transmission, but only the larger engine was available with the three-speed Cruise-O-Matic automatic transmission. While good fuel economy was the main objective of the new Pinto, those equipped with the larger engine and four-speed manual transmission provided quite brisk performance by any standards.

1971 Ford, Pinto 2-dr sedan, 4-cyl

PINTO SERIES — (ALL ENGINES) — The Pinto was the new sub-compact offering, built to compete with imports and domestic sub-compacts. It came only as a two-door sedan at first. Standard equipment included ventless door windows; high-back, slim line bucket seats; all-vinyl upholstery; two-pod instrument cluster; glove box; interior dome light; floor-mounted transmission controls; rack and pinion steering; hot water heater; DirectAire Ventilation system and 6.00 x 13 Rayon blackwall tires. In mid-season a three-door Runabout was added to the Pinto line. Its standard equipment was the same as above, plus fold-down rear seat with load floor color-keyed carpeting and passenger compartment color-keyed carpeting.

PINTO SERIES I.D. NUMBERS — (ALL ENGINES) — Pintos used the same Serial Number sequence as the full-size Fords, Torinos, Mavericks and Mustangs (See production note).

PINTO SERIES

Model Number	Body/Style Number	Body Type & Seating	Factory Price	Shipping Weight	Production Total
NA	62B	2-dr Sed-4P	1919	1949	288,606
NA	64B	2-dr Runabout-4P	2062	1994	63,796

PRODUCTION NOTE: Total series output was 352,402 units.

1971 Ford, Thunderbird 2-dr Landau, V-8

THUNDERBIRD SERIES — (ALL ENGINES) — The Thunderbird was essentially a 1970 model with only slight trim revisions. The grille had slightly wider bright metal blades at every third rung, giving a horizontally segmented look. There were also nine vertical division bars. New front side marker lamps with a one-piece lens were used. In addition, the front bumper wraparound edge was more massive.

THUNDERBIRD SERIES I.D. NUMBERS — (ALL ENGINES) — Thunderbirds began with the number '1', assembly plant code 'Y' (Wixom), body type code, engine code 'N' and finally, the unit's production number, beginning at 100001 and going up (See production note).

THUNDERBIRD SERIES

Model Number	Body/Style Number	Body Type & Seating	Factory Price	Shipping Weight	Production Total
N	65A	2-dr HT Cpe-4P	5295	4399	9,146
N	65B	2-dr Landau-4P	5438	4370	20,356
N	57C	4-dr Landau-4P	5516	4509	6,553

PRODUCTION NOTE: Total series output was 36,055 units. This figure includes 2,992 two-door hardtops equipped with bucket seats; 8,133 two-door Landaus equipped with bucket seat and 4,238 four-door Landaus equipped with the split bench seat.

FORD CHASSIS FEATURES: Wheelbase: 121 inches. Overall length: 216.2 inches (219.2 inches on station wagons). Tires: F78 x 15 belted black sidewall (G78 x 15 on Galaxie 500s and LTDs and H78 x 15 on station wagons).

TORINO SERIES CHASSIS FEATURES: Wheelbase: 117 inches (114 on station wagons). Overall length: 206.2 inches (209 on station wagons). Tires: E78 x 14 belted blackwall (unless noted).

MAVERICK CHASSIS FEATURES: Wheelbase: 103 inches. Overall length: 179.4 inches. Tires: 6.00 x 13 (6.50 x 13 on V-8 models).

PINTO SERIES CHASSIS FEATURES: Wheelbase: 115 inches (115 inches on four-door Landaus). Overall length: 215 inches. Tires: H78 x 15 belted black sidewall.

THUNDERBIRD SERIES CHASSIS FEATURES: Wheelbase: 115 inches (115 inches on four-door Landaus). Overall length: 215 inches. Tires: H78 x 15 belted black sidewall.

1971 FORD ENGINES:
Pinto Four: Overhead valves. Cast iron block. Displacement: 98 cubic inches. Bore and stroke: 3.19 x 3.06 inches. Compression ratio: 8.4:1. Brake horsepower: 75 at 5000 R.P.M. Carburetor: one-barrel. Five main bearings.

Pinto Four: Overhead cam. Cast iron block. Displacement: 122 cubic inches. Bore and stroke: 3.58 x 3.03 inches. Compression ratio: 9.0:1. Brake horsepower: 100 at 5600 R.P.M. Carburetion: Ford/Weber two-barrel. Five main bearings.

227

Maverick six-cylinder: Overhead valves. Cast iron block. Displacement: 170 cubic inches. Bore and stroke: 3.50 x 2.94 inches. Compression ratio: 8.7:1. Brake horsepower: 100 at 4200 R.P.M. Carburetion: Motorcraft one-barrel. Seven main bearings. Serial Number code 'U'.

Maverick six-cylinder: Overhead valves. Cast iron block. Displacement: 200 cubic inches. Bore and stroke: 3.68 x 3.13 inches. Compression ratio: 8.7:1. Brake horsepower: 115 at 4000 R.P.M. Carburetion: Motorcraft one-barrel. Seven main bearings. Serial Number code 'T'.

Ford/Maverick/Mustang six-cylinder: Overhead valves. Cast iron block. Displacement: 250 cubic inches. Bore and stroke: 3.68 x 3.91 inches. Compression ratio: 9.0:1. Brake horsepower: 145 at 4000 R.P.M. Carburetion: Motorcraft one-barrel. Seven main bearings. Serial Number code 'L'.

Ford six-cylinder: Overhead valves. Cast iron block. Displacement: 240 cubic inches. Bore and stroke: 4.00 x 3.18 inches. Compression ratio: 8.9:1. Brake horsepower: 140 at 4000 R.P.M. Carburetion: Motorcraft one-barrel. Seven main bearings. Serial Number code 'V'.

302 V-8: Overhead valves. Cast iron block. Displacement: 302 cubic inches. Bore and stroke: 4.00 x 3.00 inches. Compression ratio: 9.0:1. Brake horsepower: 210 at 4600 R.P.M. Carburetion: Motorcraft two-barrel. Five main bearings. Serial Number code 'F'.

351 V-8: Overhead valves. Cast iron block. Displacement: 351 cubic inches. Bore and stroke: 4.00 x 3.50 inches. Compression ratio: 9.0:1. Brake horsepower: 240 at 4600 R.P.M. Carburetion: Motorcraft two-barrel. Five main bearings. Serial Number code 'H'.

351 'Cleveland' two-barrel V-8: Overhead valves. Cast iron block. Displacement: 351 cubic inches. Bore and stroke: 4.00 x 3.50 inches. Compression ratio: 9.0:1. Brake horsepower: 240 at 4600 R.P.M. Carburetion: Motorcraft two-barrel. Five main bearings. Serial Number code 'H'.

351 'Cleveland' four-barrel V-8: Overhead valves. Cast iron block. Displacement: 351 cubic inches. Bore and stroke: 4.00 x 3.50 inches. Compression ratio: 10.7:1. Brake horsepower: 285 at 5400 R.P.M. Carburetion: Holley four-barrel. Five main bearings. Serial Number code 'M'.

Boss 351 V-8: Overhead valves. Cast iron block. Displacement: 351 cubic inches. Bore and stroke: 4.00 x 3.50 inches. Compression ratio: 11.1:1. Brake horsepower: 330 at 5400 R.P.M. Carburetion: Holley four-barrel. Five main bearings. Serial Number code 'Q'.

390 V-8: Overhead valves. Cast iron block. Displacement: 390 cubic inches. Bore and stroke: 4.05 x 3.78 inches. Compression ratio: 8.6:1. Brake horsepower: 225 at 4400 R.P.M. Carburetion: Motorcraft two-barrel. Five main bearings. Serial Number code 'Y'.

400 'Cleveland' V-8: Overhead valves. Cast iron block. Displacement: 400 cubic inches. Bore and stroke: 4.00 x 4.00 inches. Compression ratio: 9.0:1. Brake horsepower: 260 at 4400 R.P.M. Carburetion: Motorcraft two-barrel. Five main bearings. Serial Number code 'S'.

Thunder Jet 429 four-barrel V-8: Overhead valves. Cast iron block. Displacement: 429 cubic inches. Bore and stroke: 4.36 x 3.59 inches. Compression ratio: 10.5:1. Brake horsepower: 360 at 4600 R.P.M. Carburetion: Motorcraft four-barrel. Five main bearings. Serial Number code 'N'.

Cobra Jet 429 V-8: Overhead valves. Cast iron block. Displacement: 429 cubic inches. Bore and stroke: 4.36 x 3.59 inches. Compression ratio: 11.3:1. Brake horsepower: 370 at 5400 R.P.M. Carburetion: Holley four-barrel. Five main bearings. Serial Number code 'C'.

Super Cobra Jet 429 V-8: Overhead valves. Cast iron block. Displacement: 429 cubic inches. Bore and stroke: 4.36 x 3.59 inches. Compression ratio: 11.3:1. Brake horsepower: 375 at 5600 R.P.M. Carburetion: Holley four-barrel (with Ram-Air induction). Five main bearings. Serial Number code 'J'.

1971 FORD TRANSMISSIONS: Same as 1970.

1971 FORD REAR AXLES: Same as 1970.

FORD CONVENIENCE OPTIONS: 260 horsepower 400 cubic inch V-8 engine. 255 horsepower 390 cubic inch V-8 engine ($98). 320 horsepower 429 cubic inch V-8 engine ($168). 360 horsepower 429 cubic inch V-8 engine ($268). Cruise-O-Matic automatic transmission ($217 to $238 depending on engine choice). Power steering ($115). Power front disc brakes ($52). Tinted windshield ($54). Air conditioning ($420). Cruise control ($84). AM radio ($66). AM/FM radio ($240). Vinyl roof on passenger cars ($113); on station wagons ($142). White sidewall tires ($34).

TORINO CONVENIENCE OPTIONS: 240 horsepower 351 cubic inch V-8 engine ($45).; 285 horsepower 351 cubic inch V-8 engine ($93). 370 horsepower Cobra Jet 429 cubic inch V-8 engine, in Cobra ($279); in all other Torinos ($372). Cruise-O-Matic automatic transmission, base Torino ($217); Cobra ($238). Four-speed manual transmission ($250). AM radio ($66). Power steering ($115). Power tailgate window on station wagons ($35). Luggage rack on station wagon ($52). Vinyl roof ($95). White sidewall tires ($34).

MAVERICK CONVENIENCE OPTIONS: 115 horsepower 200 cubic inch six-cylinder engine ($39). 145 horsepower 250 cubic inch six-cylinder engine ($79). 210 horsepower 302 cubic inch V-8 engine. Cruise-O-Matic automatic transmission ($183). AM radio ($61). Power Steering ($95). White sidewall tires ($34).

PINTO CONVENIENCE OPTIONS: 100 horsepower 122 cubic inch four-cylinder overhead cam engine ($50). Cruise-O-Matic automatic transmission ($175). AM radio ($61). Chrome window moldings ($60). White sidewall tires ($33).

THUNDERBIRD CONVENIENCE OPTIONS: Six-way power seats ($207). Power windows ($133). Cruise-Control ($97). Air conditioning ($448); with Climate control ($519). AM/FM stereo radio ($150); or AM/8-track stereo ($150). Electric rear window defogger ($48).

Historical footnotes: The full-sized Fords were introduced September 18, 1970 and the other lines appeared in dealer showrooms the same day. Model year production peaked at 1,910,924 units. Calendar year production of 2,176,425 cars was recorded. (NOTE: The model year figure includes only Fords, Torinos, Mavericks, Pintos and Thunderbirds, while the calendar year figure covers all passenger and station wagon models). The Pinto Runabout was a two-door hatch back coupe. The more expensive full-sized Ford four-door sedans were advertised as 'pillared hardtops' this year. Fords captured only three NASCAR races in 1971, as the performance era wound to its close. Lee Iacocca became the President of Ford Motor Company this season.

228

1972 FORD

1972 FORDS — OVERVIEW — For 1972, only two of the model lines received major restyling: the Torino and Thunderbird. All others either remained the same or received only very minor trim changes. It was a significant year in the respect that all engines were required to run on regular gasoline requiring a maximum compression ratio of around 9.0:1. Also, engines were no longer rated at brake horsepower. Beginning in 1972, all engines were rated in SAE Net horsepower, or the *theoretical* horsepower after deducting for the drain caused by the accessories and transmission. This fact notwithstanding, the 351 'Cleveland' V-8 still generated nearly 300 SAE Net horsepower, making it one of the most powerful engines being produced that year. Pollution requirements and rising insurance rates, plus the lower compression ratios, meant considerably restricted performance. As a result, 1971 is almost universally considered to be the end of the 'muscle car' era.

FORD CUSTOM AND CUSTOM 500 SERIES — (ALL ENGINES) — For 1972, the full-size Fords received only minor trim updating in the form of a slightly restyled grille set within the same grille opening. There was also a slightly more protective front bumper. The rest of the body styling remained unchanged. The Custom was the base trim level for 1971 and included chrome windshield and rear window moldings; Nylon carpeting; ignition key warning buzzer; 351 cubic inch V-8 engine and Cruise-O-Matic automatic transmission (six-cylinder versions were available for fleet and taxi use, but will not be covered here due to limited collector interest). Power steering and F78 x 15 belted black sidewall tires were also standard. The Custom 500 versions included all the Custom trim, plus lower back panel and wheel lip moldings and cloth and vinyl seating surfaces. Station wagons also included H78 x 15 belted black sidewall tires and power tailgate window.

CUSTOM SERIES I.D. NUMBERS: Custom models began with the number '2', followed by the assembly plant code, engine designation code and, finally, the unit's production number, according to the final assembly location. Each plant began at 100001 and went up (See production note).

CUSTOM SERIES

Model Number	Body/Style Number	Body Type & Seating	Factory Price	Shipping Weight	Production Total
BASE CUSTOM					
NA	54B	4-dr Sed-6P	3288	3759	33,014
NA	71B	4-dr Ranch Wag-6P	3806	4317	13,064
CUSTOM 500					
NA	54D	4-dr Sed-6P	3418	3764	24,870
NA	71D	4-dr Ranch Wag-6P	3895	4327	16,834

PRODUCTION NOTE: Total series output was 87,782 units. Station wagon production was not broken down between six and ten-passenger wagons.

GALAXIE 500 SERIES — (ALL ENGINES) — The Galaxie 500 was the intermediate trim level full-size Ford for 1972 and included all the Custom 500 trim, plus wheel lip and deck lid moldings, rocker panel moldings and wood-grain appliques on the instrument panel.

GALAXIE 500 SERIES I.D. NUMBERS: Galaxie 500 models used the same Serial Number sequence as the Custom Series (See production note).

GALAXIE 500 SERIES

Model Number	Body/Style Number	Body Type & Seating	Factory Price	Shipping Weight	Production Total
NA	54F	4-dr Sed-6P	3685	3826	104,167
NA	57F	4-dr HT Sed-6P	3720	3881	28,939
NA	65F	2-dr HT Cpe-6P	3752	3826	80,855
NA	71F	4-dr Ctry Sed-6P	4028	4308	55,238

PRODUCTION NOTE: Total series output was 269,199 units. Station wagon production was not broken down between six and ten-passenger wagons.

1972 Ford, LTD Country Squire 4-dr station wagon, V-8

FORD LTD SERIES — (ALL ENGINES) — The LTD was the top trim level full-size Ford for 1972 and included all the Galaxie 500 trim, plus power front disc brakes; electric clock; luxury seat trim (except convertibles); rear bumper guards; wood-grain accents on interior door panels; front door courtesy lights; chrome trim on foot pedals; chrome arm rest bases; F78 x 15 belted black sidewall tires on two-door hardtops and G78 x 15 size on all others except wagons. Country Squire wagons also included full wheel covers and reflective rear wood-grain paneling, in addition to the wood-grain paneling on the body sides. LTD Brougham included all the standard LTD features, plus full wheel covers; rocker panel moldings; unique Brogham seat and door trim; high-back, flight-bench seats with center arm rest; cut-pile carpeting; rear door courtesy light switches; front and rear dual arm rests and G78 x 15 belted black sidewall tires.

LTD SERIES I.D. NUMBERS: LTDs used the same Serial Number sequence as the Custom and Galaxie 500 Series (See production note).

LTD

Model Number	Body/Style Number	Body Type & Seating	Factory Price	Shipping Weight	Production Total
BASE LTD					
NA	53H	4-dr Sed-6P	3906	3913	104,167
NA	57H	4-dr HT Sed-6P	3941	3908	33,742
NA	65H	2-dr HT Cpe-6P	3898	3853	101,048
NA	76H	2-dr Conv-6P	4073	4091	4,234
NA	71H	4-dr Ctry Sq-6P	4318	4308	121,419

Model Number	Body/Style Number	Body Type & Seating	Factory Price	Shipping Weight	Production Total
LTD BROUGHAM					
NA	53K	4-dr Sed-6P	4047	3949	36,909
NA	57K	4-dr HT Sed-6P	4090	3944	23,364
NA	65K	2-dr HT Cpe-6P	4050	3883	50,409

PRODUCTION NOTE: Total series output was 475,292 units. Station wagon production was not broken down between six and ten-passenger wagons.

1972 Ford, Gran Torino Sport 2-dr hardtop sport coupe, V-8

1972 TORINO — OVERVIEW — The 1972 Torino was one of two models completely restyled. The 'Coke bottle' shape was even more pronounced for 1972, than in previous years. There were rounded front fender profiles, and a rear fender line which swept up toward the roof 'C' pillar, then tapered toward the rear of the car. Behind the car was a massive rear bumper, which housed rectangular taillights at each end. The grille was slightly reminiscent of the Cobra, being a large oval between the quad headlights. Automotive writer Tom McCahill observed that he thought the 1972 Torinos looked like, "land-locked Tunas sucking air". The top profile of the four-door sedans was more round than in previous years, and the two-door fastback 'Sportsroof' featured an extremely low roofline.

TORINO SERIES — (ALL ENGINES) — Two basic lines of intermediate-sized Ford Torinos were left. Both the base Torino models and the top-line Gran Torinos were restyled from end-to-end. The Torino models featured chrome windshield, rear window and rain gutter moldings; high-back bench seats, all-vinyl seat and door trim; floor mats; hub caps with trim rings; 250 cubic inch six-cylinder engine and three-speed manual transmission. The Torino station wagon also included power front disc brakes and three-way tailgate. The Gran Torino was the top trim level for 1972 and included all the Torino trim, plus manual front disc brakes cloth and vinyl trim on seats and interior door panels; carpeting; lower body side, wheel well and deck lid moldings; dual-note horn; trunk mat; DeLuxe steering wheel and chrome trim on the foot pedals. The Gran Torino Squire wagon also included the 140 horsepower, 302 cubic inch V-8 engine; DeLuxe pleated vinyl interior trim; wheel covers and wood-grain appliques on the body sides, tailgate and instrument panel. The Gran Torino Sport was the sports version of the Gran Torino line and included all the Gran Torino features, plus the 140 horsepower, 302 cubic inch V-8 engine; pleated, all vinyl trim; hood scoops; color-keyed dual racing mirrors and a unique grille.

TORINO AND GRAN TORINO SERIES I.D. NUMBERS: Torino and Gran Torino models began with the number '2', followed by the assembly plant code, body type code, engine designation code and, finally, the unit's production number, according to the final assembly location. Each plant began at 100001 and went up (See production note).

Model Number	Body/Style Number	Body Type & Seating	Factory Price	Shipping Weight	Production Total
BASE TORINO					
NA	53B	4-dr HT Sed-6P	2641/2731	3469/3548	33,486
NA	65B	2-dr HT Cpe-6P	2673/2762	3369/3448	33,530
NA	71B	4-dr Sta Wag-6P	2955/3045	3879/3958	22,204
NA	53D	4-dr Sed-6P	2856/2947	3476/3555	102,300
GRAN TORINO					
NA	65D	2-dr HT-6P	2878/2967	3395/3474	132,284
NA	71D	4-dr Sta Wag-6P	3096/3186	3881/3960	45,212
NA	63R	2-dr FsBk Cpe-6P	3094	3496	60,794
NA	65R	2-dr Spt HT Cpe-6P	3094	3474	31,239
NA	71K	4-dr Squire Wag-6P	3486	4042	35,595

PRODUCTION NOTE: Total series output was 496,645 units. The price and weight to the left of the slant bar are for six-cylinder equipped models and the price and weight to the right of the slant bar are for V-8 powered models.

1972 Ford, Maverick 4-dr sedan, V-8

MAVERICK SERIES — (ALL ENGINES) — The Maverick Series was unchanged from the 1971 models.

MAVERICK SERIES I.D. NUMBERS: Mavericks used the same Serial Number sequence as the full-size Fords and Torino models (See production note).

MAVERICK SERIES

Model Number	Body/Style Number	Body Type & Seating	Factory Price	Shipping Weight	Production Total
NA	54A	4-dr Sed-6P	2245/2406	2833/2826	73,686
NA	62A	2-dr Sed-6P	2190/2350	2538/2731	145,931
NA	62D	2-dr Grabber-6P	2359/2519	2493/2786	35,347

PRODUCTION NOTE: Total series output was 254,964 units. The price and weight to the left of the slant bar are for six-cylinder equipped models and the price and weight to the right of the slant bar are for V-8 powered models.

1972 Ford, Pinto Runabout 3-dr hatch back coupe, 4-cyl

PINTO SERIES — (ALL ENGINES) — The Pintos were unchanged from the 1971 models, with the exception of a larger rear window on Runabout models and the addition of a two-door station wagon.

PINTO SERIES I.D. NUMBERS — (ALL ENGINES) — Pintos used the same Serial Number sequence as the full-size Fords, Torinos, Mavericks and Mustangs (See production note).

PINTO SERIES

Model Number	Body/Style Number	Body Type & Seating	Factory Price	Shipping Weight	Production Total
NA	62B	2-dr Sed-4P	1960	1968	181,002
NA	64B	2-dr Runabout-4P	2078	2012	197,920
NA	73B	2-dr Sta Wag-4P	2265	2293	101,483

PRODUCTION NOTE: Total series output was 480,405 units.

1972 Ford, Thunderbird 2-dr formal sports coupe, V-8

THUNDERBIRD SERIES — (ALL ENGINES) — Thunderbirds were completely restyled for 1972, a year that witnessed the introduction of the largest Thunderbirds ever. They were based on the Lincoln Continental Mark IV chassis and used the Mark IV body, with only minor changes, inside and outside. While the Thunerbird had lost most of its sportiness, it had gained all the luxury features of the Continental. The grille was a centrally located opening featuring horizontal grille bars between the quad headlights. The top had a very low profile, with a large 'C' pillar. At the rear, a single taillight lens was used once again, giving a massive appearance.

THUNDERBIRD SERIES I.D. NUMBES — (ALL ENGINES) — Thunderbirds began with the number '2', assembly plant code 'J' (Los Angeles) or 'Y' (Wixom), body type code, engine code 'A' or 'N' and, finally, the unit's production number, beginning at 100001 and going up.

THUNDERBIRD SERIES

Model Number	Body/Style Number	Body Type & Seating	Factory Price	Shipping Weight	Production Total
A/N	65K	2-dr HT-6P	5293	4420	57,814

FORD CHASSIS FEATURES: Same as 1971.

TORINO AND GRAN TORINO CHASSIS FEATURES: Wheelbase: (four-door models) 118 inches; (other models) 114 inches. Overall length: (two-door models) 203.7 inches; (four-door models) 207.3 inches; (station wagons) 211.6 inches. Tires: (Torino two-door models) E78 x 14; (Gran Torino and Torino four-door models) F78 x 14; (station wagons) H78 x 14; (Gran Torino Sport hardtop) E70 x 14; (Gran Torino Sport fastback) F70 x 14. All tires were belted black sidewall.

MAVERICK CHASSIS FEATURES: Wheelbase: 103 inches. Overall length: 179.4 inches. Tires: (V-8s) C78 x 14 tubeless blackwall; (other models) 6.45 x 14 tubeless blackwall.

PINTO SERIES CHASSIS FEATURES: Wheelbase: 94 inches. Overall length: 163 inches. Tires: 6.00 x 13 Rayon black sidewall (A78 x 13; A70 x 13 and 175R13 tires were optional).

THUNDERBIRD SERIES CHASSIS FEATURES: Wheelbase: 120.4 inches. Overall length: 214 inches. Tires: 215R15 belted Michelin radial blackwalls.

1972 FORD ENGINES
Pinto Four-cylinder. Overhead valves. Cast iron block. Displacement: 98 cubic inches. Bore and stroke: 3.19 x 3.06 inches. Compression ratio: 8.0:1. Net horsepower: 54 at 4600 R.P.M. Carburetion: Motorcraft one-barrel. Five main bearings.

Pinto Four-cylinder. Overhead cam. Cast iron block. Displacement: 122 cubic inches. Bore and stroke: 3.58 x 3.03 inches. Compression ratio: 8.2:1. Net horsepower: 86 at 5400 R.P.M. Carburetion: Ford/Weber two-barrel. Five main bearings. Serial Number code 'X'.

Maverick Six-cylinder. Overhead valves. Cast iron block. Displacement: 170 cubic inches. Bore and stroke: 3.50 x 2.94 inches. Compression ratio: 8.3:1. Net horsepower: 82 at 4400 R.P.M. Carburetion: Motorcraft one-barrel. Seven main bearings. Serial Number code 'U'.

Ford Six-cylinder. Overhead valves. Cast iron block. Displacement: 240 cubic inches. Bore and stroke: 4.00 x 3.18 inches. Compression ratio: 8.5:1. Net horsepower: 103 at 3800 R.P.M. Carburetion: Motorcraft one-barrel. Seven main bearings. Serial Number code 'V'.

Maverick/Mustang/Torino Six-cylinder. Overhead valves. Displacement: 250 cubic inches. Bore and stroke: 3.68 x 3.91 inches. Compression ratio: 8.0:1. Net horsepower: 98 at 3400 R.P.M. Carburetion: Motorcraft one-barrel. Seven main bearings. Serial Number code 'L'.

302 V-8. Overhead valves. Cast iron block. Displacement: 302 cubic inches. Bore and stroke: 4.00 x 3.00 inches. Compession ratio: 8.5:1. Net horsepower: 140 at 4000 R.P.M. Carburetion: Motorcraft two-barrel. Five main bearings. Serial Number code 'F'.

351 'Windsor' V-8. Overhead valves. Cast iron block. Displacement: 351 cubic inches. Bore and stroke: 4.00 x 3.50 inches. Compression ratio: 8.3:1. Net horsepower: 153 at 3800 R.P.M. Carburetion: Motorcraft two-barrel. Five main bearings. Serial Number code 'H'.

351 'Cleveland' V-8. Overhead valves. Cast iron block. Displacement: 351 cubic inches. Bore and stroke: 4.00 x 3.50 inches. Compression ratio: 8.6:1. Net horsepower: 163 at 3800 R.P.M. Carburetion: Motorcraft two-barrel. Five main bearings. Serial Number code 'H'.

351 'Cleveland' Four-barrel V-8. Overhead valves. Cast iron block. Displacement: 351 cubic inches. Bore and stroke: 4.00 x 3.50 inches. Compression ratio: 8.6:1. Net horsepower: 248 at 5400 R.P.M. Carburetion: Holley four-barrel. Five main bearings. Serial Number code 'M'.

351 HO 'Cleveland' V-8. Overhead valves. Cast iron block. Displacement: 351 cubic inches. Bore and stroke: 4.00 x 3.50 inches. Compression ratio: 8.6:1. Net horsepower: 266 at 5400 R.P.M. Carburetion: Holley four-barrel. Five main bearings. Serial Number code 'Q'.

400 'Cleveland' V-8. Overhead valves. Cast iron block. Displacement: 400 cubic inches. Bore and stroke: 4.00 x 4.00 inches. Compression ratio: 8.5:1. Net horsepower: 172 at 4000 R.P.M. Carburetion: Motorcraft two-barrel. Five main bearings. Serial Number code 'S'.

Thunder Jet 429 V-8. Overhead valves. Cast iron block. Displacement: 429 cubic inches. Bore and stroke: 4.36 x 3.59 inches. Compression ratio: 8.5:1. Net horsepower: 205 at 4400 R.P.M. Carburetion: Motorcraft four-barrel. Five main bearings. Serial Number code 'K'.

Thunderbird 429 V-8. Overhead valves. Cast iron block. Displacement: 429 cubic inches. Bore and stroke: 4.36 x 3.59 inches. Compression ratio: 8.5:1. Net horsepower: 212 at 4400 R.P.M. Carburetion: Motorcraft four-barrel. Five main bearings. Serial Number code 'A'.

Thunderbird 460 V-8. Overhead valves. Cast iron block. Displacement: 460 cubic inches. Bore and stroke: 4.36 x 3.85 inches. Compression ratio: 8.5:1. Net horsepower: 224 at 4400 R.P.M. Carburetion: Motorcraft four-barrel. Five main bearings. Serial Number code 'A'.

1972 FORD TRANSMISSIONS: Same as 1971.

1972 FORD REAR AXLE RATIOS: Same as 1971.

FORD CONVENIENCE OPTIONS: 172 horsepower, 400 cubic inch V-8 engine ($95). 205 horsepower, 429 cubic inch V-8 engine ($222). Power front disc brakes, standard on LTDs ($50). Tinted windshield ($53). Air conditioning ($409); with climate control ($486). Cruise-Control ($99). AM radio ($64). AM/FM stereo radio ($234). Vinyl roof ($110); on station wagons ($148). White sidewall tires ($34).

TORINO/GRAN TORINO CONVENIENCE OPTIONS: 163 horsepower, 351 cubic inch 'Cleveland' V-8 engine ($44). 248 horsepower, 351 cubic inch 'Cleveland' V-8 engine, two-door models only ($127). 205 horsepower, 429 cubic inch V-8 engine ($99). Cruise-O-Matic automatic transmission ($21 to $211 depending on engine choice). Four-speed manual transmission ($200). AM radio ($64). AM/FM stereo radio ($208). Power steering ($112). Power tailgate window on station wagons ($34). Luggage rack on station wagons ($77). Vinyl roof ($93). White sidewall tires ($34).

MAVERICK CONVENIENCE OPTIONS: 200 cubic inch six-cylinder ($38). 250 cubic inch six-cylinder engine ($77). 302 cubic inch V-8 engine. Cruise-O-Matic automatic transmission ($177). AM radio ($59). Power steering ($92). White sidewall tires ($34).

PINTO CONVENIENCE OPTIONS: 86 horsepower, 122 cubic inch four-cylinder overhead cam engine ($49). Cruise-O-Matic automatic transmission ($170). AM radio ($59). Chrome window moldings. Luxury Decor Group ($137). Wheel covers ($23). White sidewall tires ($42).

THUNDERBIRD CONVENIENCE OPTIONS: Six-Way power seats ($201). Power windows ($130). Cruise-Control ($103). Tilt steering wheel ($51). Climate Control air conditioning ($505). AM/FM stereo radio ($146). Electric rear window defogger ($36). Power sunroof ($505). Vinyl roof ($137). Turnpike convenience group ($132).

Historical footnotes: The 1972 Ford line was introduced September 24, 1971. New options appearing this season included electric sliding sun roofs; electric deck lid release; tailgate power lock and bodyside moldings with vinyl inserts. Sun roofs were installed on 0.6 percent of all 1972 FoMoCo products, including Lincolns and Mercuries. As far as the Ford lines — Ford/Torino/Maverick/Pinto/Club Wagon/Thunderbird and Mustang — were concerned, model year output peaked at 1,855,201 vehicles this year. The calendar year production total was counted as 1,868,016 units. Henry Ford II was Ford Motor Company Board Chairman and Lee Iacocca was the firm's President. Ford Division (also called Ford Marketing Corporation) was headed by J.B. Naughton, who held the title of Vice-President and Divisonal General Manager. The year 1972 was sales record-breaker and marked the first time in history that Ford dealers sold more than three million cars and trucks. For information about Ford trucks and commercial vehicles see Krause Publication's *The Complete Encyclopedia of Commercial Vehicles.*

1973 FORD

1973 FORDS OVERVIEW — For 1973, the full-size Fords were the only models to receive significant restyling. The rest of the Ford lines received only very minor trim updating. More Federally mandated safety requirements were initiated, in the form of the massive (and incredibly ugly) 'park bench' safety bumpers. These bumpers were supposed to be able to tolerate direct impact at five miles per hour, with no resultant damage. Pollution standards were tightened. The existing engines were further detuned or more emissions control equipment was added, making for some of the poorest performing and least fuel efficient motors ever built. The Arab embargo, of oil products imported from the Middle East, also brought fuel economy to the spotlight and manufacturers began striving for improved mileage at the expense of performance and efficiency.

FULL-SIZE FORD SERIES — (ALL ENGINES) — Full-size Fords were restyled for 1973. The emphasis was placed on a more rounded profile, similar to the Torino Series of the previous year. The 'Mercedes style' grille was the current craze and big Fords had their own version, complete with a spring-loaded hood ornament on the high trim-level models. At the rear, two rectangular taillights were used on all models and were very similar to those used on the lower-priced lines of the 1972 full-size Fords. The Custom 500 was the base trim level Ford for 1973 and included chrome windshield and rear window moldings; Nylon carpeting; ignition key warning buzzer; 351 cubic inch V-8 engine; Cruise-O-Matic automatic transmission; power steering and G78 x 15 belted black sidewall tires. The Galaxie 500 was the intermediate trim level and included all the Custom 500 features, plus lower back panel wheel lip moldings; cloth and vinyl seating surfaces; rocker panel moldings and wood-grain appliques on the instrument panel. The LTD was the top trim level and included all the Galaxie 500 features, plus deep-cushioned low-back bench seats; electric clock; DeLuxe two-spoke steering wheel; chrome trim on the foot pedals; polished aluminum trim around the rear edge of the hood; bodyside moldings with vinyl inserts and HR78 x 15 steel-belted radial tires. The LTD Brougham had all the LTD features, plus high-back Flight-Bench seats with center arm rests; ash tray and front door courtesy lights; full wheel covers; cut-pile carpeting; carpeted lower door panels; polished rocker panel moldings and extensions; automatic seatback release (on two-door models); vinyl roof and color-keyed seat belts. The Ranch Wagon contained all the features of the Galaxie 500 models, plus J78 x 15 tires. The Country Sedan contained all the features found in the Ranch Wagon, plus dual-note horn; wood-grain appliques on the instrument panel and front and rear door panels; special sound package; bodyside moldings and a chrome plated grille. The Country Squires contained all the features found in the LTDs, plus J78 x 15 tires and 400 cubic inch V-8 engine.

FORD SERIES I.D. NUMBERS — (ALL ENGINES) — Fords began with the number '3', followed by the assembly plant code, engine designation code and, finally, the unit's production number, according to the final assembly location. Each plant began at 100001 and went up (See production note).

FORD SERIES

Model Number	Body/Style Number	Body Type & Seating	Factory Price	Shipping Weight	Production Total
CUSTOM 500					
NA	53D	4-dr Sed-6P	3606	4078	42,549
NA	71D	4-dr Ranch Wag-6P	4050	4550	22,432
GALAXIE 500					
NA	53F	4-dr Sed-6P	3771	4110	85,654
NA	57F	4-dr HT Sed-6P	3833	4120	25,802
NA	65F	2-dr HT Cpe-6P	3778	4059	70,808
NA	71F	4-dr Ctry Sed-6P	4164	4581	51,290
LTD					
NA	53H	4-dr Sed-6P	3958	4150	122,851
NA	57H	4-dr HT Sed	4001	4160	28,608
NA	65H	2-dr HT Cpe-6P	3950	4100	120,864
NA	71H	4-dr Ctry Sq-6P	4401	4642	142,933
LTD BROUGHAM					
NA	53K	4-dr Sed-6P	4113	4179	49,553
NA	57K	4-dr HT Sed-6P	4103	4189	22,268
NA	65K	2-dr HT Cpe-6P	4107	4128	68,901

PRODUCTION NOTE: Total series output was 941,054 units.
ADDITIONAL NOTE: The LTD four-door sedan was called a pillared hardtop.

1973 TORINO — (OVERVIEW) — 1973 Torinos were unchanged from the 1972 models, with the exception of a revised grille. The opening was more rectangular than the 1972 version and blended well with the large front bumper. The remainder of the car was identical to the 1972 model. Improvements included larger standard rear brakes, an interior hood release and optional spare tire lock.

TORINO AND GRAN TORINO SERIES — (ALL ENGINES) — The 1973 Torino and Gran Torino models were very slightly modified from 1972 specifications. The Torino models were the base trim level and featured chrome windshield, rear window and rain gutter moldings; high-back bench seats; all-vinyl seat and door trim; floor mats; hub caps; 250 cubic inch six-cylinder engine and three-speed manual transmission. The Torino station wagon also included power front disc brakes and three-way tailgate. The Gran Torino was the top trim level for 1973 and included all the Torino trim, plus manual front disc brakes; cloth and vinyl trim on seats and interior door panels; carpeting; lower bodyside, wheel well and deck lid moldings; dual-note horn; trunk mat; DeLuxe two-spoke steering wheel and chrome trim on the foot pedals. The Gran Torino Squire wagon also included the 138 horsepower 302 cubic inch V-8 engine; DeLuxe pleated vinyl interior trim; wheel covers and wood-grain appliques on the bodysides, tailgate and instrument panel. The Gran Torino Sport was the sports version of the Gran Torino line and included all the Gran Torino features, plus the 138 horsepower 302 cubic inch V-8 engine; pleated, all-vinyl trim; hood scoops; color-keyed dual racing mirrors and a unique grille.

TORINO AND GRAN TORINO SERIES I.D. NUMBERS — (ALL ENGINES) — The Torino and Gran Torino models began with the number '3', followed by the assembly plant code, body type code, engine designation code and, finally, the unit's production number, according to the final assembly location. Each plant began at 100001 and went up (See production note).

TORINO SERIES

Model Number	Body/Style Number	Body Type & Seating	Factory Price	Shipping Weight	Production Total
NA	53B	4-dr Sed-6P	2701/2796	3597/3683	37,524
NA	65B	2-dr HT Cpe-6P	2732/2826	3528/3615	28,005
NA	71B	4-dr Sta Wag-6P	3198	4073	23,982

Model Number	Body/Style Number	Body Type & Seating	Factory Price	Shipping Weight	Production Total
GRAN TORINO SERIES					
NA	53D	4-dr Sed-6P	2890/2984	3632/3719	98,404
NA	65D	2-dr HT Cpe-6P	2921/3015	3570/3656	138,962
NA	71D	4-dr Sta Wag-6P	3344	4096	60,738
NA	71K	4-dr Squire-6P	3559	4124	40,023
NA	63R	2-dr Spt FsBk Cpe	3154	3670	51,853
NA	65R	2-dr Spt HT Cpe	3154	3652	17,090
GRAN TORINO BROUGHAM					
NA	53K	4-dr Sed-6P	3051/3140	3632/3719	NA
NA	65K	2-dr HT Cpe-6P	3071/3160	3590/3656	NA

PRODUCTION NOTE: Total series output was 496,581 units. Separate breakouts were not available for Gran Torino Broughams. Styles 53B, 53D and 53K were called four-door pillared sedans. Styles 63R and 65R were six-passenger (6P) models.
ADDITIONAL NOTE: Prices and weights above slant bar are for Sixes/below slant bar for V-8s.

MAVERICK SERIES — (ALL ENGINES) — The Maverick series was basically unchanged from the 1972 models. There was, however, a slightly new appearance up front because of the flatter, reinforced bumper.

MAVERICK SERIES I.D. NUMBERS: Mavericks used the same Serial Number sequence as full-sized Fords and Torino models (See production note).

1973 Ford, Maverick 'Grabber' 2-dr sedan, V-8

MAVERICK SERIES

Model Number	Body/Style Number	Body Type & Seating	Factory Price	Shipping Weight	Production Total
NA	54A	4-dr Sed-6P	2297/2419	2737/2900	110,382
NA	62A	2-dr Sed-6P	2240/2362	2642/2800	148,943
NA	62	2-dr Grabber-6P	2419/2541	2697/2855	32,350

PRODUCTION NOTE: Total series output was 291,675 units. The prices and weights to the left of the slant bar indicate six-cylinder equipped models and the prices and weights to the right of the slant bar indicate V-8 powered models.

1973 Ford, Pinto Squire 2-dr station wagon, 4-cyl

PINTO SERIES — (ALL ENGINES) — The Pinto exterior remained basically the same as in the 1972 model year with the exception of front and rear bumpers. Front bumper guards were made standard equipment this year (but deleted in later years). Pinto styles included the two-door (sometimes called three-door) Runabout, which had a large rear hatch with gas-operated springs; plus the two-door sedan and station wagon. Because of the bumper design changes, the Pinto was actually about one and a half inches longer this year although the true body length was not changed.

PINTO SERIES I.D. NUMBERS — (ALL ENGINES) — Pintos used the same Serial Number sequence as the full-size Fords, Torinos, Mavericks and Mustangs (See production note).

PINTO SERIES

Model Number	Body/Style Number	Body Type & Seating	Factory Price	Shipping Weight	Production Total
NA	62B	2-dr Sed-4P	1997	2124	116,146
NA	64B	2-dr Runabout-4P	2120	2162	150,603
NA	73B	2-dr Sta Wag-4P	2319	2397	217,763

PRODUCTION NOTE: Total series output was 484,512 units.

1973 Ford, Thunderbird 2-dr formal sports coupe, V-8

THUNDERBIRD SERIES — (ALL ENGINES) — The 1973 Thunderbird continued to use the same body as introduced in 1972, with a few minor changes. An opera window was added to help eliminate the blind spot created by the massive 'C' pillar. Other product improvements included suspension system refinements; increased front and rear headroom and steel-belted radial tires with white sidewalls as standard equipment. An inside hood release and spare tire lock were also new. The 1973 Thunderbird had an egg-crate grille in place of the bar type used the previous year. The two headlamps on either side of the grille were mounted in individual, square-shaped bezels. An unslotted bumper with vertical grille guards and new fender-notched parking lamp treatment were seen. The remainder of the car was unchanged.

THUNDERBIRD SERIES I.D. NUMBERS — (ALL ENGINES) — Thunderbirds began with the number '3', assembly plant code 'J' (Los Angeles) or 'Y' (Wixom), body type code, engine designation code 'A' or 'N' and, finally, the unit's production number, beginning at 100001 and going up.

THUNDERBIRD SERIES

Model Number	Body/Style Number	Body Type & Seating	Factory Price	Shipping Weight	Production Total
A/N	65K	2-dr HT Cpe-6P	5577	4572	87,269

FORD CHASSIS FEATURES: Same as 1971.

TORINO AND GRAN TORINO CHASSIS FEATURES: Same as 1972.

MAVERICK CHASSIS FEATURES: Same as 1972.

PINTO CHASSIS FEATURES: Same as 1972.

THUNDERBIRD CHASSIS FEATURES: Same as 1972.

1973 FORD ENGINES
Pinto Four-cylinder. Overhead cam. Cast iron block. Displacement: 122 cubic inches. Bore and stroke: 3.58 x 3.03 inches. Compression ratio: 8.2:1. Net horsepower: 86 at 5400 R.P.M. Carburetion: Ford/Weber two-barrel. Five main bearings. Serial Number code 'X'.

Maverick Six-cylinder. Overhead valves. Cast iron block. Displacement: 200 cubic inches. Bore and stroke: 3.68 x 3.13 inches. Compression ratio: 8.3:1. Net horsepower: 84 at 3800 R.P.M. Carburetion: Motorcraft single-barrel. Seven main bearings. Serial Number code 'U'.

Maverick/Mustang/Torino Six-cylinder. Overhead valves. Cast iron block. Displacement: 250 cubic inches. Bore and stroke: 3.68 x 3.91 inches. Compression ratio: 8.0:1. Net horsepower: 88 at 3200 R.P.M. Carburetion: Motorcraft single-barrel. Seven main bearings. Serial Number code 'L'.

302 V-8. Overhead valves. Cast iron block. Displacement: 302 cubic inches. Bore and stroke: 4.00 x 3.00 inches. Compression ratio: 8.0:1. Net horsepower: 135 at 4200 R.P.M. Carburetion: Motorcraft two-barrel. Five main bearings. Serial Number code 'F'.

351 'Windsor' V-8. Overhead valves. Cast iron block. Displacement: 351 cubic inches. Bore and stroke: 4.00 x 3.50 inches. Compression ratio: 8.0:1. Net horsepower: 156 at 3800 R.P.M. Carburetion: Motorcraft two-barrel. Five main bearings. Serial Number code 'H'.

351 'Cleveland' V-8. Overhead valves. Cast iron block. Displacement: 351 cubic inches. Bore and stroke: 4.00 x 3.50 inches. Compression ratio: 8.0:1. Net horsepower: 154 at 4000 R.P.M. Carburetion: Motorcraft two-barrel. Five main bearings. Serial Number code 'H'.

351 'Cobra Jet Cleveland V-8. Overhead valves. Cast iron block. Displacement: 351 cubic inches. Bore and stroke: 4.00 x 3.50 inches. Compression ratio: 8.0:1. Net horsepower: 266 at 5400 R.P.M. Carburetion: Holley four-barrel. Five main bearings. Serial Number code 'Q'.

400 'Cleveland' V-8. Overhead valves. Cast iron block. Displacement: 400 cubic inches. Bore and stroke: 4.00 x 4.00 inches. Compression ratio: 8.0:1. Net horsepower: 163 at 3800 R.P.M. Carburetion: Motorcraft two-barrel. Five main bearings. Serial Number code 'S'.

Thunder Jet 429 V-8. Overhead valves. Cast iron block. Displacement: 429 cubic inches. Bore and stroke: 4.36 x 3.59 inches. Compression ratio: 8.0:1. Net horsepower: 197 at 4400 R.P.M. Carburetion: Motorcraft four-barrel. Five main bearings. Serial Number code 'K'.

Thunderbird 429 V-8. Overhead valves. Cast iron block. Displacement: 429 cubic inches. Bore and stroke: 4.36 x 3.59 inches. Compression ratio: 8.0:1. Net horsepower: 201 at 4400 R.P.M. Carburetion: Motorcraft four-barrel. Five main bearings. Serial Number code 'N'.

Thunderbird 460 V-8. Overhead valves. Cast iron block. Displacement: 460 cubic inches. Bore and stroke: 4.36 x 3.85 inches. Compression ratio: 8.0:1. Net horsepower: 219 at 4400 R.P.M. Carburetion: Motorcraft four-barrel. Five main bearings. Serial Number code 'A'.

ENGINE NOTE: Beginning with the 250 cubic inch six-cylinder engine, Ford rated each engine with two or three different horsepower ratings, depending on the model each engine was installed in. Horsepowers shown in the engine section represent the lowest rating for each engine (except the '460', which shows the highest rating). As body size and weight increased between models, horsepower ratings increased correspondingly. (i.e. — the '302' cubic inch V-8 was rated at 135 horsepower when installed in the Maverick and rated at 138 horsepower when installed in a Gran Torino). Most engine ratings varied between one and five horsepower, with the '460' varying 17 horsepower.

1973 FORD TRANSMISSIONS: Same as 1972.

1973 FORD REAR AXLE RATIOS: Same as 1972.

FORD CONVENIENCE OPTIONS: 171 horsepower, 400 cubic inch V-8 engine ($95). 198 horsepower, 429 cubic inch V-8 engine. 202 horsepower, 460 cubic inch V-8 engine ($222). Tinted windshield ($53). Air conditioning ($409); with Climate Control ($486). Cruise Control ($99). AM radio ($64). AM/FM stereo radio ($234). Viny roof ($110); on station wagons ($148). White sidewall tires ($33).

TORINO/GRAN TORINO CONVENIENCE OPTIONS: 159 horsepower, 351 cubic inch 'Cleveland' V-8 engine ($44). 168 horsepower, 400 cubic inch 'Cleveland' V-8 engine. 197 horsepower, 429 cubic inch V-8 engine ($99). Cruise-O-Matic automatic transmission ($211). Four-speed manual transmission ($200). AM radio ($64). AM/FM stereo radio ($208). Power steering ($112). Power tailgate window on station wagons ($34). Luggage racks on station wagons ($77). Vinyl roof ($93). White sidewall tires ($34).

MAVERICK CONVENIENCE OPTIONS: 200 cubic inch six-cylinder engine ($77). 135 horsepower, 302 cubic inch V-8 engine. Cruise-O-Matic automatic transmission ($177). AM radio ($59). Power steering ($92). White sidewall tires ($33).

PINTO CONVENIENCE OPTIONS: 86 horsepower, 122 cubic inch four-cylinder overhead cam engine ($49). Cruise-O-Matic automatic transmission ($170). AM radio ($59). Luxury decor group ($137). Wheel covers ($23). White sidewall tires ($42).

THUNDERBIRD CONVENIENCE OPTIONS: Six-Way power seats ($201). Power windows ($130). Cruise Control ($103). Tilt steering wheel ($51). Climate Control air conditioning ($505). AM/FM stereo radio ($146). Electric rear window defogger ($36). Power sunroof ($505). Vinyl roof ($137). Turnpike convenience group ($132).

Historical footnotes: The 1973 Ford line, except for Club Wagons, was publicly introduced on September 22, 1972. Highlights of the year included the new impact-absorbing bumpers and an increased emphasis on making cars theft and vandal-proof. For example, a new fixed-length type radio antenna was adopted; inside hood release mechanisms became a regular feature in some models and a spare tire lock was a new, extra-cost option. The Ford LTD was honored, by *Motor Trend* magazine, as the "Full-sized Sedan of the Year", while *Road Test* magazine went further, calling it their "Car of the Year". Calendar year sales of 1,716,975 units were recorded. This included Club Wagons and some 1975 Fords (including Granada and Elite) made late in the calendar year. Model year production (1974 models only) hit 1,843,340 units, with 26,917 Falcon Club Wagons included. That gave the company a 22.69 percent share of America's total market. Important FoMoCo executives included Board Chairman, Henry Ford II; Corporate President, Lee Iacocca and Ford Marketing Corporation Vice-President and Divisional General Manager B.E. Bidwell.

1974 FORD

1974 FORDS — (OVERVIEW) — With the exception of a totally restyled Mustang, 1974 Fords were basically 1973 models with refinements and slight trim updating. Emphasis continued to be placed on a luxury look and the addition of safety equipment. More Federally mandated safety requirements were initiated, primarily in the form of massive rear 'safety' bumpers designed to withstand direct impact, at five miles per hour, without damage. When combined with the front safety bumpers adopted in 1973, the weight of a typical car was up nearly 350 pounds! Pollution standards were also further tightened, which, combined with the weight increases, made 1974 models generally more sluggish than any available in the recent past. Pintos and Mavericks saw little technical innovation and all other lines were now limited to just V-8s under the hood. Torinos could be had with '302', '351', '400' and '460' engines. The bigger cars came with a base 351 cubic inch V-8 or one of three options. They were a higher output '351', the '400' or the '460'. The latter engine was the only one offered in Thunderbirds, as the powerful '429' was gone for all time.

1974 Ford, LTD 4-dr pillared hardtop (sedan), V-8

FULL-SIZED FORDS — (ALL ENGINES) — The full-sized Fords were slightly retrimmed versions of 1973 models. The main difference between cars of the two years appeared at the front. Extension caps were no longer used on the front fender corners, so that the vertical parking lamp lens was taller than the previous type and had a ribbed appearance. The overall shape of the grille was the same, but inserts with a finer mesh pattern were used. Also, the central section — below the protruding area of the hood — was surrounded by a rectangular housing that segmented it from the rest of the grille. This gave more of a 'Mercedes-Benz' look to the front of the car, or what some refer to as neo-classical styling. To heighten this image, a stand-up hood ornament was added to models with high-level trims. The profile of the 1974 Ford was much the same as previously seen, except that an upper, full-length horizontal feature line paralleled the upper body edge. It swept from the top of the parking lamps, to the rear of the car. In addition, the lower feature line now continued ahead of the forward wheel opening. Newly designed wheel covers were seen and the rear end treatment was also enriched. The Custom 500 was the base trim level offering and included chrome windshield and rear window moldings; Nylon carpeting; ignition key warning buzzer; power steering; automatic transmission; G78 x 15 belted black sidewall tires and the 351 cubic inch motor. The Galaxie 500 was the intermediate trim level and included all Custom 500 features, plus lower back panel and wheel lip moldings; cloth and vinyl seats; rocker panel moldings and wood-grain appliques on the instrument panel. The LTD was the top trim level and included all the Galaxie 500 features, plus deep-cushioned, low-back bench seats; electric clock; DeLuxe two-spoke steering wheel; chrome trim on the foot pedals; polished aluminum trim for the rear hood edge and HR78 x 15 steel-belted radial tires. The LTD Brougham had all LTD features, plus high-back Flight-Bench seats with center arm rest; ash tray and front door courtesy lights; full wheel covers; cut-pile carpeting; carpeted lower door panels; polished rocker panel moldings (with extensions); automatic seatback release (in two-door styles); vinyl roof and color-keyed seat belts. The Ranch Wagon contained all the features of the Galaxie 500, plus J78 x 15 tires. The Country Sedan added a dual-note horn; wood-grain instrument panel applique; wood-grain front and rear door panel trim; special sound insulation package; bodyside moldings and a special chrome plated grille. The Country Squire contained all features found in LTDs, plus J78 x 15 tires and a base 400 cubic inch V-8.

FORD SERIES I.D. NUMBERS: Fords began with the number '4', followed by the assembly plant code, engine designation code and, finally, the unit's production number, according to final assembly location. Each plant began at 100001 and went up (See production note).

FULL-SIZED FORD SERIES

Model Number	Body/Style Number	Body Type & Seating	Factory Price	Shipping Weight	Production Total
CUSTOM 500/RANCH WAGON					
NA	53D	4-dr Sed-6P	3911	4180	28,941
NA	71D	4-dr Sta Wag-6P	4417	4654	12,104
GALAXIE 500/COUNTRY SEDAN					
NA	53F	4-dr Sed-6P	4093	4196	49,661
NA	57F	4-dr HT Sed-6P	4166	4212	11,526
NA	65F	2-dr HT Cpe-6P	4140	4157	34,214
NA	71F	4-dr Ctry Sed-6P	4513	4690	22,400
LTD/COUNTRY SQUIRE					
NA	53H	4-dr Sed-6P	4299	4262	72,251
NA	57H	4-dr HT Sed-6P	4367	4277	12,375
NA	65H	2-dr HT Cpe-6P	4318	4215	73,296
NA	71H	4-dr Ctry Sq-6P	4827	4742	64,047
LTD BROUGHAM					
NA	53K	4-dr Sed-6P	4576	4292	30,203
NA	57K	4-dr HT Sed-6P	4646	4310	11,371
NA	65K	2-dr HT Cpe-6P	4598	4247	39,084

PRODUCTION NOTES: Total series output was 519,916 units. Styles 53F, 53H and 53K were called four-door pillared hardtops.

1974 TORINO/GRAN TORINO — OVERVIEW — New grilles, front bumpers and some optional revisions in roof pillar treatments characterized the Torino models of 1974. The grille used a finer mesh and was now segmented by seven vertical division bars, with the parking lamps hidden behind the insert instead of being mounted on it. The bumper had a slightly more prominent center protrusion with the rubber-faced guards moved a bit closer together. Opera window treatments could be ordered, at extra cost, to 'fancy-up' the rear pillar of coupes. Side trim was revised to eliminate the wide, horizontally ribbed decorative panels used on high-trim models the previous season. Introduced at mid-year was the Gran Torino Elite Series featuring full-length side trim with vinyl inserts; a chrome center molding across the grille; single headlamps (in square bezels) and parking lamps notched into the corners of front fenders. Stand-up hood ornaments were seen on many 1974 Torino models. The Torino Series was the base trim level and featured windshield, rear window and rain gutter moldings; high-back bench seats; all-vinyl upholstery and trim; floor mats; hub caps; three-speed manual transmission; HR78 x 14 tires (G78 x 14 on hardtops) and a base '302' V-8. The Torino station wagon also included power front disc brakes; H78 x 14 tires and a three-way tailgate. The Gran Torino was the top trim level and included all above items, plus manual front disc brakes; cloth and vinyl seat trims; carpeting; lower bodyside, wheel well and deck lid moldings; dual-note horn; trunk mat; DeLuxe two-spoke steering wheel and chrome foot pedal trim. The Gran Torino Squire wagon also had DeLuxe pleated vinyl interior trim; wheel covers; wood-grain bodyside appliques; wood-grain tailgate trim and wood-grain dashboard inserts. The Gran Torino Sport was the sporty version of the Gran Torino line. Its standard extras included pleated, all-vinyl trim; hood scoops; color-keyed dual outside racing mirrors and a unique grille.

TORINO/GRAN TORINO SERIES I.D. NUMBERS: The Torino and Gran Torino models began with the number '4', followed by the assembly plant code, body type code, engine designation code and, finally, the unit's production number, according to the final assembly location. Each plant began at 100001 and went up (See production note).

TORINO/GRAN TORINO SERIES

Model Number	Body/Style Number	Body Type & Seating	Factory Price	Shipping Weight	Production Total
TORINO					
NA	53B	4-dr Sed-6P	3176	3793	31,161
na	65B	2-dr HT Cpe-6P	3310	3509	22,738
NA	71B	4-dr Sta Wag-6P	3755	4175	15,393
GRAN TORINO					
NA	53D	4-dr Sed-6P	3391	3847	72,728
NA	65D	2-dr HT Cpe-6P	3485	3647	76,290
NA	71D	4-dr Sta Wag-6P	3954	4209	29,866
GRAN TORINO SPORT/SQUIRE					
NA	71K	4-dr Squire-6P	4237	4250	22,837
NA	65R	2-dr HT Spt Cpe	3761	3771	23,142
GRAN TORINO BROUGHAM					
NA	53K	4-dr Sed-6P	3903	3887	11,464
NA	65K	2-dr HT Cpe-6P	3912	3794	26,402
GRAN TORINO ELITE					
NA	65M	2-dr HT Cpe-6P	4374	4092	96,604

PRODUCTION NOTES: Total series output was 428,086 units. Styles 53D and 53K were called four-door pillared hardtops. Style 65R was a six-passenger model. All 1974 Torinos were V-8 powered.

1974 Ford, Maverick 4-dr sedan, 6-cyl

MAVERICK SERIES — (ALL ENGINES) — The Maverick had a very slight frontal restyling for 1974, as energy-absorbing bumpers were adopted this year. A horizontal slot appeared in the center of the face bar, where the license plate had formerly been positioned. DeLuxe models featured side moldings with vinyl inserts; wheel cutout trim moldings and, on cars with vinyl roofs, a Maverick nameplate on the rear roof pillar. On all models, a similar nameplate was carried at the lefthand side of the grille.

MAVERICK SERIES I.D. NUMBES: Mavericks used the same Serial Number system as other Ford products (See production note).

MAVERICK SERIES

Model Number	Body/Style Number	Body Type & Seating	Factory Price	Shipping Weight	Production Total
NA	54A	4-dr Sed-6P	2824/2982	2851/3014	137,728
NA	62A	2-dr Sed-6P	2742/2949	2739/2902	139,818
NA	62D	2-dr Grabber-6P	2923/3081	2787/2950	23,502

PRODUCTION NOTE: Total series output was 301,048 units. The prices and weights to the left of the slant bar are for Six/to the right of the slant bar are for V-8.

1974 Ford, Pinto Runabout 3dr-door hatch back coupe, 4-cyl

PINTO SERIES — (ALL ENGINES) — This was the year that energy-absorbing bumpers were added to the Pinto, too. This brought an obvious change to the front of the car, as the air slot opening in the gravel pan could no longer be seen. Also eliminated was the center-mounted license plate holder. It didn't look right with the massive new bumper, but then, hardly anything else did either. The bumper was plain on the base trim models, but came with rubber-faced, vertical guards and a black vinyl impact strip on models with the DeLuxe Decor package. Pinto wagons could be had with optional trim packages that included simulated wood-grain exterior paneling and rooftop luggage racks.

PINTO SERIES I.D. NUMBERS: Pintos used the same Serial Number system as full-sized Fords, Torinos and Mavericks (See production note).

PINTO SERIES

Model Number	Body/Style Number	Body Type & Seating	Factory Price	Shipping Weight	Production Total
NA	62B	2-dr Sed-4P	2527	2372	132,061
NA	64B	2-dr Hatch-4P	2631	2402	174,754
NA	73B	2-dr Sta Wag-4P	2771	2576	237,394

PRODUCTION NOTES: Total series output was 544,209 units. The two-door hatch back coupe was called the Pinto Runabout.

1974 Ford, Thunderbird 2-dr Formal hardtop coupe, V-8 (PH)

THUNDERBIRD SERIES — (ALL ENGINES) — The Thunderbird was left pretty much alone for 1974, except that the 460 cubic inch V-8 was new under the hood. The side script plate was in its same location — above the side molding at the trailing edge of the front fender — but was slightly larger in size.

THUNDERBIRD SERIES I.D. NUMBERS: Thunderbirds began with the number '4', followed by the assembly plant code 'J' (Los Angeles) or 'Y' (Wixom), body type code, engine designation code 'A' and, finally, the unit's production number, beginning at 100001 and going up.

THUNDERBIRD SERIES

Model Number	Body/Style Number	Body Type & Seating	Factory Price	Shipping Weight	Production Total
A	65K	2-dr HT Cpe-6P	7221	4825	58,443

FORD CHASSIS FEATURES: Wheelbase: 121 inches. Overall length: (passenger cars) 223 inches; (station wagons) 226 inches. Width: 80 inches. Tires: Refer to text.

TORINO CHASSIS FEATURES: Wheelbase: (two-door) 114 inches; (four-door) 118 inches. Overall length: (two-door passenger car) 212 inches; (four-door passenger car) 216 inches; (station wagons) 222 inches. Width: (passenger cars) 80 inches; (station wagon) 79 inches. Tires: Refer to text.

MAVERICK CHASSIS FEATURES: Wheelbase: (two-door) 103 inches; (four-door) 109.9 inches. Overall length: (two-door) 187 inches; (four-door) 194 inches. Width: 71 inches. Tires: (two-door) 6.45 x 14; (four-door) C78 x 14; (Grabber) D70-14.

PINTO CHASSIS FEATURES: Wheelbase: 94.2 inches. Overall length: (passenger car) 169 inches; (station wagon) 179 inches. Width: 70 inches. Tires: (passenger car) 6.00 x 13; (station wagon) A78 x 13.

THUNDERBIRD CHASSIS FEATURES: Wheelbase: 120.4 inches. Overall length: 225 inches. Width: 80 inches. Tires: LR78 x 15.

1974 FORD ENGINES

Pinto Four-cylinder. Overhead cam. Cast iron block. Displacement: 122 cubic inches. Bore and stroke: 3.58 x 3.03 inches. Compression ratio: 8.2:1. Net horsepower: 86 at 5400 R.P.M. Carburetion: Ford/Weber two-barrel. Five main bearings. Serial Number code 'X'.

Pinto/Mustang Four-cylinder. Overhead cam. Cast iron block. Displacement: 139 cubic inches. Bore and stroke: 3.78 x 3.13 inches. Compression ratio: 8.6:1. Net horsepower: 80. Carburetion: Motorcraft two-barrel. Five main bearings. Serial Number code 'Y'.

Maverick Six-cylinder. Overhead valves. Cast iron block. Displacement: 200 cubic inches. Bore and stroke: 3.68 x 3.13 inches. Compression ratio: 8.3:1. Net horsepower: 84 at 3800 R.P.M. Carburetion: Motorcraft one-barrel. Seven main bearings. Serial Number code 'T'.

Maverick Six-cylinder. Overhead valves. Cast iron block. Displacement: 250 cubic inches. Bore and stroke: 3.68 x 3.91 inches. Compression ratio: 8.0:1. Net horsepower: 91 at 3200 R.P.M. Carburetion: Motorcraft one-barrel. Seven main bearings. Serial Number code 'L'.

302 V-8 Overhead valves. Cast iron block. Displacement: 302 cubic inches. Bore and stroke: 4.00 x 3.00 inches. Compression ratio: 8.0:1. Net horsepower: 140 at 3800 R.P.M. Carburetion: Motorcraft two-barrel. Five main bearings. Serial Number code 'F'.

351 'Windsor' V-8. Overhead valve. Cast iron block. Displacement: 351 cubic inches. Bore and stroke: 4.00 x 3.50 inches. Compression ratio: 8.2:1. Net horsepower: 163 at 4200 R.P.M. Carburetion: Motorcraft two-barrel. Five main bearings. Serial Number code 'H'.

351 'Cleveland' V-8. Overhead valves. Cast iron block. Displacement: 351 cubic inches. Bore and stroke: 4.00 x 3.50 inches. Compression ratio: 8.0:1. Net horsepower: 162 at 4000 R.P.M. Carburetion: Motorcraft two-barrel. Five main bearings. Serial Number code 'H'.

351 'Cleveland' Four-barrel V-8. Overhead valves. Cast iron block. Displacement: 351 cubic inches. Bore and stroke: 4.00 x 3.50 inches. Compression ratio: 7.9:1. Net horsepower: 255 at 5600 R.P.M. Carburetion: Motorcraft four-barrel. Five main bearings. Serial Number code 'Q'.

400 V-8. Overhead valves. Cast iron block. Displacement: 400 cubic inches. Bore and stroke: 4.00 x 4.00 inches. Compression ratio: 8.0:1. Net horsepower: 170 at 3400 R.P.M. Carburetion: Motorcraft two-barrel. Five main bearings. Serial Number code 'S'.

Thunderbird 460 V-8. Overhead valves. Cast iron block. Displacement: 460 cubic inches. Bore and stroke: 4.36 x 3.85 inches. Compression ratio: 8.0:1. Net horsepower: 215 at 4000 R.P.M. (220 horsepower in Thunderbirds). Carburetion: Carter four-barrel. Five main bearings. Serial Number code 'A'.

1974 FORD TRANSMISSIONS: Same as 1973.

1974 FORD REAR AXLE RATIOS: Same as 1973.

FORD OPTIONS: 170 horsepower 400 cubic inch V-8, in Country Squires (standard); in other models ($94). 215 horsepower 460 cubic inch V-8 ($304). Tinted glass ($55). Air conditioning, standard type ($426); Climate Control type ($506). Cruise Control ($103). AM radio ($67). AM/FM radio ($243). Vinyl roof, on passenger cars ($115); on station wagons ($148); on LTD Brougham (standard). White sidewall tires ($33). AM/FM stereo with tape player ($378). Power seats ($106). Power windows ($134). Sunroof ($516). Country Squire Brougham option ($202). Country Squire Luxury package option ($545). Brougham Luxury Package option ($380).

TORINO OPTIONS: 162 horsepower 351 cubic inch 'Cleveland' V-8 ($46). 170 horsepower 400 cubic inch V-8 ($140). 215 horsepower 460 cubic inch V-8 ($245). 225 horsepower 351 cubic inch 'Cleveland' four-barrel V-8 ($132). Cruise-O-Matic transmission; with small V-8 ($219); with '460' V-8 ($241). AM radio ($67). AM/FM stereo radio ($217). Power steering ($117). Power disc brakes, on station wagons (standard); on passenger cars ($71). Power tailgate window ($35). Station wagon luggage rack ($80). Vinyl roof ($96). White sidewall tires ($33). Station wagon third passenger seat ($67). Sun roof ($490). AM/FM stereo radio with tape player ($378).

MAVERICK OPTIONS: 250 cubic inch Six ($42). 140 horsepower 302 cubic inch V-8 ($122). Cruise-O-Matic transmission ($212). AM radio ($61). Power steering ($106). White sidewall tires ($33). Vinyl top ($83). Air conditioning ($383). Luxury Decor Group, except Grabber ($332).

PINTO OPTIONS: 90 horsepower 140 cubic inch Four ($52). Cruise-O-Matic transmission ($212). AM radio ($61). AM/FM stereo radio ($222). Luxury Decor Group ($137). Full wheel covers ($23). Forged aluminum wheels ($154). White sidewall tires ($44). Vinyl top ($83). Air conditioning ($383). Station wagon Squire package ($241).

THUNDERBIRD OPTIONS: Six-Way power seats ($105). Cruise Control ($107). Climate Control air conditioning ($74). Electric rear window defogger ($85). Power Moonroof ($798). Sunroof ($525). AM/FM radio with stereo tape ($311). Turnpike Convenience Group, includes Cruise Control, trip odometer and manual reclining passenger seat ($138). Burgundy Luxury Group package ($411).

OPTIONAL EQUIPMENT NOTES: Cruise-O-Matic automatic transmission and power front disc brakes were standard equipment on Torino station wagons. Automatic transmission, power steering and power front disc brakes were standard equipment on LTD, Custom 500, Galaxie and Thunderbird. Air conditioning, power windows and AM radio were also standard equipment in Thunderbirds.

Historical footnotes: Ford's 1974 model year resulted in 1,843,340 assemblies, including Falcon Club Wagons. Calendar year output was 1,716,975 units, again including the Falcon Club Wagon. (The Falcon Club Wagon was a light truck that Ford included, statistically, with passenger car production.) The chief executives of the company were the same as in 1973. Model year declines of some 130,000 units were caused by lagging buyer interest in 'big' Fords and Thunderbirds. Meanwhile, assemblies of the Mustang II tripled. Ford Motor Company's headquarters were listed as Southfield Road (at Rotunda Drive), P.O. Box 1509, Dearborn, MI 48121.

1975 FORD

1975 Ford, Gran Torino Brougham 4-dr pillared hardtop, V-8

1975 FORDS — OVERVIEW — With the exception of the slightly restyled full-size Fords, the 1975 models were, once again, basically the same as the year before. The big Fords were attractively facelifted with the addition of a larger, Mercedes-style grille and new taillights. The most significant change occurred with the two-door hardtop model. The true pillarless hardtop was replaced by a coupe with fixed quarter windows and large 'opera' windows. The 1975 Torinos were unchanged from the previous year. In an effort to segregate the very popular Elite from the rest of the line, the Gran Torino name was dropped and this car was now called the Elite. Once again, the Maverick and Pinto were unchanged, except for some very minor grille updating in each line. The big news for 1975 was the addition of the new Granada Series. The Granada was a new intermediate size car, offered in four-door sedan and two-door sedan. As Ford was very proud to point out, the four-door bore more than a passing resemblance to the Mercedes-Benz. Granadas could be fitted with options that created anything from a taxi to a mini-limousine. They came powered by engines ranging from the very sedate 250 cubic inch six-cylinder, up to the 351 'Windsor' V-8. The latter motor produced not-so-sedate performance and these Granadas were, in fact, among the fastest of the 1975 Fords. The Thunderbird was exactly the same car as produced in 1974, with one small exception. The steering wheel had slightly different spokes (as did the steering wheels on all new Fords, except the Pinto). Pollution standards were stiffened once again and, in 1975, all cars were required to burn unleaded gasoline. The majority of the new models came with catalytic converters on the exhaust systems, to help reduce emissions and contaminates.

1975 Ford, LTD Landau 2-dr hardtop coupe, V-8

FULL-SIZE FORD SERIES — (ALL ENGINES) — The Custom 500 was the base trim level Ford for 1975. It included chrome windshield and rear window moldings; Nylon carpeting; ignition key warning buzzer; 351 cubic inch V-8 engine; Cruise-O-Matic automatic transmission; power steering and G78 x 15 belted black sidewall tires. The LTD was the intermediate trim level. It included all the Custom 500 features, plus wheel lip moldings; cloth and vinyl seating surfaces; rocker panel moldings and wood-grain appliques on the instrument panel. The LTD Brougham was the top trim level and included all the LTD features, plus deep-cushioned low-back bench seats; electric clock; DeLuxe two-spoke steering wheel; chrome trim on the foot pedals; polished aluminum trim around the rear edge of the hood; bodyside moldings with vinyl inserts and HR78 x 15 steel-belted radial tires. The LTD Landau had all the Brougham features, plus high-back Flight Bench seats (with center arm rests); ash tray and front door courtesy lights; full wheel covers; cut-pile carpeting; carpeted lower door panels; polished rocker panel moldings with extensions; automatic seatback release (on two-door models); vinyl roof and color-keyed seat belts. The Ranch Wagon contained all the features of the LTD models, plus JR78 x 15 steel-belted radial tires. The Country Sedan contained all the features found on the Ranch Wagon, plus dual-note horn; wood-grain appliques on the instrument panel and front and rear door panels; special sound package; bodyside moldings and a chrome plated grille. The Country Squires contained all the features found in the LTD Country Sedans, plus JR78 x 15 steel-belted radial tires and the 400 cubic inch V-8 engine.

FORD SERIES I.D. NUMBERS — (ALL ENGINES) — Fords began with the number '5', followed by the assembled plant code, engine designation code and, finally, the unit's production number, according to the final assembly location. Each plant began at 100001 and went up (See production note).

FORD SERIES

Model Number	Body/Style Number	Body Type & Seating	Factory Price	Shipping Weight	Production Total
CUSTOM 500					
NA	53D	4-dr Sed-6P	4380	4377	31,043
NA	71D	4-dr Ranch Wag-6P	4970	4787	6,930
LTD					
NA	53H	4-dr Sed-6P	4615	4408	82,382
NA	60H	2-dr o/w Cpe-6P	4656	4359	47,432
NA	71H	4-dr Ctry Sed-6P	5061	4803	22,935
LTD BROUGHAM					
NA	53K	4-dr Sed-6P	5016	4419	32,327
NA	60K	2-dr o/w Cpe-6P	5050	4391	24,005
NA	71K	4-dr Ctry Sq-6P	5340	4845	41,550
LTD LANDAU					
NA	53L	4-dr Sed-6P	5370	4446	32,506
NA	60L	2-dr o/w Cpe-6P	5401	4419	26,919

PRODUCTION NOTES: Total series output was 390,714 units. Station wagon production was not broken down between six and ten-passenger wagons. The new Body Type designation o/w Cpe indicates the two-door coupe with opera windows.

TORINO/GRAN TORINO/ELITE SERIES — (ALL ENGINES) — The Torino line was the same as the previous year. The Torino models were the base trim level and featured chrome windshield, rear widow and rain gutter moldings; high-back bench seats; all-vinyl seat and door trim; floor mats; hub caps; 302 cubic inch V-8 engine and three-speed manual transmission. The Torino station wagon also included power front disc brakes and three-way tailgate. The Gran Torino was the intermediate trim level for 1975 and included all the Torino features, plus manual front disc brakes; cloth and vinyl trim on seats and interior door panels; carpeting; lower bodyside, wheel well and deck lid moldings; dual-note horn; trunk mat; DeLuxe two-spoke steering wheel and chrome trim on the foot pedals. The Gran Torino Squire wagon also included the

148 horsepower 351 cubic inch V-8 engine; Cruise-O-Matic automatic transmission; DeLuxe pleated vinyl interior trim; wheel covers and wood-grain appliques on the body-sides, tailgate and instrument panel. The Gran Torino Brougham was the highest trim level and included all the Gran Torino features, plus power front disc brakes; power steering; cloth seating surfaces; bodyside moldings and padded vinyl top. The Elite continued to offer the same features as in 1974.

TORINO/GRAN TORINO/ELITE SERIES I.D. NUMBERS — (ALL ENGINES) — The Torino, Gran Torino and Elite models began with the number '5', assembly plant code, body type code, engine designation code and, finally, the unit's production number, according to the final assembly location. Each plant began at 100001 and went up (See production note).

TORINO/GRAN TORINO/ELITE SERIES

Model Number	Body/Style Number	Body Type & Seating	Factory Price	Shipping Weight	Production Total
TORINO					
NA	53B	4-dr Sed-6P	3957	4059	22,928
NA	65B	2-dr o/w Cpe—6P	3954	3987	13,394
NA	71B	4-dr Sta Wag-6P	4336	4412	13,291
GRAN TORINO					
NA	53D	4-dr Sed-6P	4258	4090	53,161
NA	65D	2-dr o/w Cpe-6P	4234	3998	35,324
NA	71D	4-dr Sta Wag-6P	4593	4456	23,951
TORINO BROUGHAM					
NA	53K	4-dr Sed-6P	4791	4163	5,929
NA	65K	2-dr o/w Cpe-6P	4759	4087	4,849
TORINO SPORT					
NA	65R	2-dr Spt HT-6P	4744	4044	5,126
ELITE					
NA	65M	2-dr HT Cpe-6P	4721	4160	123,372

PRODUCTION NOTE: Total series output was 318,482 units.

1975 Ford, Maverick 2-dr sedan, 6-cyl

MAVERICK SERIES — (ALL ENGINES) — Originally scheduled to be replaced by the new Granada, the Maverick's existence was extended after the energy scare of 1974. The sedans and the sporty Grabber coupe featured refinements to interior and exterior trim; thicker, cut-pile carpeting; a DeLuxe steering wheel as standard equipment and a 200 cubic inch base V-6. Ford block lettering was added along the hood lip and the slot in the center of the front bumper was slightly decreased in width. New options included power front disc brakes and a deck lid mounted luggage rack. A catalytic converter was required with the base engine, while the optional 350 cubic inch Six or 302 cubic inch V-8 came without this unpopular piece of equipment. Radial tires were also added to the regular equipment list. Buyers were given a choice of Blue, Black or Tan interior combinations (as in the past) or new, light Green trim.

MAVERICK SERIES I.D. NUMBERS — (ALL ENGINES) — Mavericks used the same Serial Number sequence as the full-size Fords and Torino models (See production note).

MAVERICK SERIES

Model Number	Body/Style Number	Body Type & Seating	Factory Price	Shipping Weight	Production Total
NA	54A	4-dr Sed-6P	3025/3147	2820/2971	90,695
NA	62A	2-dr Sed-6P	3061/3183	2943/3094	63,404
NA	62D	2-dr Grabber-6P	3224/3346	2827/2979	8,473

PRODUCTION NOTE: Total series output was 162,572 units. The price and weight to the left of the slant bar apply to six-cylinder equipped models and the price and weight to the right of the slant bar apply to V-8 powered models.

PINTO SERIES — (ALL ENGINES) — Changes to the Pinto were also of the minor type this year. There was little reason to go any further, since good fuel economy was helping sell the car. The optional 2.8 liter V-6 was available only with Cruise-O-Matic attachments and only in the station wagon, but wasn't very popular. Only 16 percent of all buyers added optional six-cylinder motors. Some other new accessories included power steering; power front disc brakes and a fuel-economy warning light. Standard motivation came from a U.S.-built 2.3 liter L-4 equipped with either four-speed manual or three-speed automatic transmission.

1975 Ford, Pinto Runabout 3-dr hatch back coupe, 4-cyl

PINTO SERIES

Model Number	Body/Style Number	Body Type & Seating	Factory Price	Shipping Weight	Production Total
NA	62B	2-dr Sed-4P	2769	2495	64,081
NA	64B	3-dr Hatch-4P	2967/3220	2528/2710	68,919
NA	73B	2-dr Sta Wag-4P	3094/3347	2692/2874	90,763

PRODUCTION NOTE: Total series output was 223,763 units. The price and weight to the left of the slant bar apply to four-cylinder equipped models and the price and weight to the right of the slant bar apply to V-6 powered models.

1975 Ford, Granada 4-dr sedan, V-8

GRANADA SERIES — (ALL ENGINES) — Ford referred to the Granada as a 'precision-sized' compact car. It was built off the Maverick four-door platform and came as a two-door coupe and four-door sedan. Its styling had a luxury flavor and was heavily influenced by European design themes. Even as a base model, it was quite elegant amongst cars in its class. The super-rich Ghia-optioned Granada went a step further where luxury was concerned. The 200 cubic inch L-6 was base Granada powerplant when attached to the three-speed manual gearbox. Ghias came standard with a 250 cubic inch L-6; digital clock; DeLuxe sound package and wide range of fancy seating surfaces. The base model could be ordered with the bigger Six. Two-barrel V-8s, of 302 or 351 cubic inches, were provided in both levels. Dealer sales of Granadas in the United States peaked at 241,297 cars, cutting substantially into the popularity of Mustang II.

GRANADA SERIES I.D. NUMBERS — (ALL ENGINES) — Granadas used the same Serial Number sequence as full-size Fords, Torinos, Mavericks and Pintos (See production note).

GRANADA SERIES

Model Number	Body/Style Number	Body Type & Seating	Factory Price	Shipping Weight	Production Total
BASE					
NA	54H	4-dr Sed-6P	3756/3784	3293/3355	118,168
NA	66H	2-dr Sed-6P	3698/3826	3230/3306	100,810
GHIA					
NA	54K	4-dr Sed-6P	4240/4326	3361/3423	43,652
NA	66K	2-dr Sed-6P	4182/4268	3311/3373	40,028

PRODUCTION NOTE: Total series output was 302,649 units. The price and weight to the left of the slant bar apply to six-cylinder equipped models and the price and weight to the right of the slant bar apply to V-8 powered models.

1975 Ford, Thunderbird 2-dr formal coupe, V-8

THUNDERBIRD SERIES — (ALL ENGINES) — The Thunderbird had certainly come a long ways since its 'two-seater' days. It was now FoMoCo's top-of-the-line personal/luxury car. A highly promoted new feature was the Sure-Trac rear brake anti-skid device. There were other chassis refinements, like four-wheel power disc brakes and the Hydro-Boost hydraulic brake boosting system. Standard features included automatic transmission; power steering; power brakes; power windows; air conditioning and AM/FM radio. Optional, for collector types, were Silver or Copper Luxury Groups with a special, heavy-grained half-vinyl roof; velour or leather seats; DeLuxe trunk lining and specific wheel covers.

THUNDERBIRD SERIES I.D. NUMBERS — (ALL ENGINES) — Thunderbirds began with the number '5', assembly plant code 'J' (Los Angeles) or 'Y' (Wixom), body type code, engine designation code 'A' and, finally, the unit's production number, beginning at 100001 and going up.

THUNDERBIRD SERIES

Model Number	Body/Style Number	Body Type & Seating	Factory Price	Shipping Weight	Production Total
A	65K	2-dr HT Cpe-6P	7701	4893	42,685

FORD CHASSIS FEATURES: Wheelbase: 121 inches. Overall length: (passenger cars) 224 inches; (station wagon) 226 inches. Width: 80 inches. Tires: HR78 x 15.

TORINO CHASSIS FEATURES: Wheelbase: (two-door) 114 inches; (four-door) 118 inches. Overall length: (two-door) 214 inches; (four-door) 218 inches; (station wagon) 223 inches. Width: 80 inches. Tire: HR78 x 14.

MAVERICK CHASSIS FEATURES: Wheelbase: (two-door) 103 inches; (four-door) 109.9 inches. Overall length: (two-door) 187 inches; (four-door) 194 inches. Width: 71 inches. Tires: (Grabber) DR70 x 14; (other two-doors) BR78 x 14; (four-doors) CR78 x 14.

PINTO CHASSIS FEATURES: Wheelbase: (passenger cars) 94.4 inches; (station wagon) 94.7 inches. Overall length: (passenger cars) 169 inches; (station wagons) 179 inches. Width: 70 inches. Tires: (all models) BR78 x 13B.

GRANADA CHASSIS FEATURES: Wheelbase: 109.9 inches. Overall length: (base models) 198 inches. (Ghia) 200 inches. Width: 74 inches. Tires: (Ghia four-door) ER78-14; (other models) DR78-14.

THUNDERBIRD CHASSIS FEATURES: Wheelbase: 120.4 inches. Overall length: 226 inches. Width: 80 inches. Tires: LR78 x 15.

1975 FORD ENGINES

Pinto Four-cylinder. Overhead cam. Cast iron block. Displacement: 144 cubic inches. Bore and stroke: 3.78 x 3.13 inches. Compression ratio: 8.6:1. Net horsepower: 83. Carburetion: Motorcraft two-barrel. Five main bearings. Serial Number code 'Y'.

Pinto/Mustang V-6. Overhead valves. Cast iron block. Displacement: 159 cubic inches. Bore and stroke: 3.50 x 2.70 inches. Compression ratio: 8.0:1. Net horsepower: 97. Carburetion: Holley two-barrel. Four main bearings. Serial Number code 'Z'.

Maverick Six-cylinder. Overhead valves. Cast iron block. Displacement: 200 cubic inches. Bore and stroke: 3.68 x 3.13 inches. Compression ratio: 8.3:1. Net horsepower: 75 at 3200 R.P.M. Carburetion: Motorcraft one-barrel. Seven main bearings. Serial Number code 'T'.

Maverick/Granada Six-cylinder. Overhead valves. Cast iron block. Displacement: 250 cubic inches. Bore and stroke: 3.68 x 3.91 inches. Compression ratio: 8.0:1. Net horsepower: 72 at 2900 R.P.M. Carburetion: Motorcraft one-barrel. Seven main bearings. Serial Number code 'L'.

302 V-8. Overhead valves. Cast iron block. Displacement: 302 cubic inches. Bore and stroke: 4.00 x 3.00 inches. Compression ratio: 8.0:1. Net horsepower: 129 at 3800 R.P.M. Carburetion: Motorcraft two-barrel. Five main bearings. Serial Number code 'F'.

351 'Windsor' V-8. Overhead valves. Cast iron block. Displacement: 351 cubic inches. Bore and stroke: 4.00 x 3.50 inches. Compression ratio: 8.2:1. Net horsepower: 143 at 3600 R.P.M. Carburetion: Motorcraft two-barrel. Five main bearings. Serial Number code 'H'.

351 'Modified' V-8. Overhead valves. Cast iron block. Displacement: 351 cubic inches. Bore and stroke: 4.00 x 3.50 inches. Compression ratio: 8.0:1. Net horsepower: 148 at 3800 R.P.M. Carburetion: Motorcraft two-barrel. Five main bearings. Serial Number code 'H'.

400 V-8. Overhead valves. Cast iron block. Displacement: 400 cubic inches. Bore and stroke: 4.00 x 4.00 inches. Compression ratio: 8.0:1. Net horsepower: 158 at 3800 R.P.M. Carburetion: Motorcraft two-barrel. Serial Number code 'S'.

Thunderbird 460 V-8. Overhead valves. Cast iron block. Displacement: 460 cubic inches. Bore and stroke: 4.36 x 3.85 inches. Compression ratio: 8.0:1. Net horsepower: 218 at 4000 R.P.M. Carburetion: Motorcraft four-barrrel. Five main bearings. Serial Number code 'A'.

FORD CONVENIENCE OPTIONS: 158 horsepower 400 cubic inch V-8 engine ($94, standard on Country Squires). 218 horsepower 460 cubic inch V-8 engine ($304). Tinted glass ($55). Air conditioning ($426). Climate Control ($506). Cruise Control ($103). AM radio ($67). AM/FM stereo radio ($243). Vinyl roof ($115); on station wagons ($148); on LTD Landau (standard). White sidewall tires ($33).

TORINO/GRAN TORINO/ELITE CONVENIENCE OPTIONS: 158 horsepower 400 cubic inch V-8 engine ($54). 218 horsepower 460 cubic inch V-8 engine ($245). AM radio ($67). AM/FM stereo radio ($217). Power steering ($117). Power front disc brakes ($71); on station wagons (standard). Power tailgate window on station wagons ($35). Luggage rack on station wagons ($80). Vinyl top ($96). Air conditioning ($426). White sidewall tires ($33).

MAVERICK CONVENIENCE OPTIONS: 129 horsepower 302 cubic inch V-8 engine. Cruise-O-Matic automatic transmission ($212). AM radio ($61). Power steering ($106). Luxury Decor Package ($392). White sidewall tires ($33).

PINTO CONVENIENCE OPTIONS: 159 cubic inch V-6 engine ($229). Cruise-O-Matic automatic transmission ($212). AM radio ($61). AM/FM stereo radio ($222). Luxury Decor Group ($137). Forged aluminum wheels ($154). White sidewall tires ($33).

GRANADA CONVENIENCE OPTIONS: 129 horsepower 302 cubic inch V-8 engine. 143 horsepower 351 'Windsor' V-8 engine. Cruise-O-Matic automatic transmission ($222). Power steering ($106). Power brakes ($45). AM radio ($61). AM/FM stereo radio ($222). Vinyl roof ($83). Air conditioning ($426). White sidewall tires ($33).

THUNDERBIRD CONVENIENCE OPTIONS: Six-Way power seats ($105). Cruise-Control ($107); with Turnpike Convenience Group (standard). Climate-Control air conditioning ($74). Electric rear window defroster ($85). Power moonroof ($798). Turnpike Convenience Group includes: Cruise-Control, trip odometer and manual passenger seat recliner ($138).

Historical footnotes: The 1975 Ford line was introduced September 27, 1974. Model year sales, by United States dealers, included 282,130 Pintos; 207,944 Mustang IIs; 142,964 Mavericks; 241,297 Granadas; 158,798 Torinos; 102,402 Elite; 297,655 LTDs and 37,216 Thunderbirds. The production of 1975 models, in U.S. factories hit 1,302,205 cars. Calendar year production of Fords, in this country, peaked at 1,302,844 units. These figures *do not* include Falcon club wagons of which 17,431 were made for both the model and calendar years. Top executives influencing Ford Division policy were Henry Ford II, Lee Iacocca and B.E. Bidwell. It was the final season for the long-lasting Custom 500 nameplate.

No make offered a more complete line than Ford in 1976-1989, from subcompact Pinto through full-size LTD and Thunderbird. Engines reached all the way up to a 460 cid V-8, which would remain available through 1978. After five years in the lineup, Pinto was about to get some

1976 Granada Sports Coupe (F)

trouble in the form of serious accusations about fire hazards. Some hideous blazes had resulted from rear-end collisions. Less-vulnerable gas tanks were installed in Pintos built after 1976, but the adverse publicity hurt sales in subsequent years as well.

1977 Pinto three-door Runabout (F)

Maverick was in its next-to-last season, dangling a Stallion package in an attempt to lure youthful drivers. Pinto had one too, but both were for looks rather than action. Ford had high hopes for Granada, introduced in 1975 with Mercedes-like styling and a four-wheel disc brake option. Torino and Elite made up the mid-size lineup. Thunderbird

1977 Granada Ghia coupe (F)

236

not only carried a 202 horsepower engine, but came in a selection of luxury paint options to dress up its huge body. Ford sales had shrunk in 1975, but rebounded somewhat this year, partly as a result of the new "California strategy" that delivered special option packages only to West Coast customers.

1978 Fairmont sedan (F)

The big T-Bird didn't last much longer, replaced for 1977 by a downsized edition that was actually a modification of the new LTD II. T-Bird cost far less in this form — but also carried less standard equipment and a modest 302 cid V-8. Production soared far above the level of the last big 'bird. Torino and Elite both faded away, and Maverick was about to do so. Granada became the first American car to offer a standard four-speed (overdrive) gearbox. GM had downsized its full-size models, but LTD kept its immense dimensions until 1979.

1980 LTD Crown Victoria Country Squire station wagon (JG)

Few realized it at the time, but the basic structure of the new Fairmont for 1978 soon would serve as the basis for a whole line of FoMoCo rear-drive models. MacPherson struts held up Fairmont's front end — a suspension style that would grow more common as front-wheel drives arrived. Fairmont powerplants ran the gamut: four, six, or V-8. A Euro-styled ES edition became available, but most of the attention went to the Futura Sport Coupe, marked by wide B-pillars in a wrapover roofline reminiscent of Thunderbird's. Granada tried the Euro route too, with a blackout-trimmed ESS variant. Pinto's Cruising Wagon and Sports Rallye packages seemed less memorable, if practical. Thunderbird added a Town Landau model, but collectors are more likely to turn to the Diamond Jubilee Edition, offered this year only.

Two years after GM's downsizing of Caprice/Impala, Ford finally shrunk its LTD. Engines shrunk too, with a 302 V-8 standard and 351 the biggest. A luxurious Heritage model took the place of the single-year Diamond Jubilee T-Bird. Pinto added equipment and an ESS package and found more customers, while the smaller LTD had trouble

in the sales department. LTD II never had caught on, and dropped away after '79. It was Thunderbird's turn for downsizing in 1980, as a modest 255 cid standard V-8 went under the hood. Best bet for collectors: the Silver Anniversary T-Bird. The "Crown Victoria" name reappeared in the LTD roster this year, bringing back memories of the sharpest mid-1950s Ford. LTDs also had a new automatic overdrive transmission. Every Ford model endured a loss of sales, but so did most other domestic makes.

1981 Fairmont Futura sedan (JG)

Heralding a new Ford era, the front-wheel-drive Escort arrived for 1981, carrying a CHV (hemi) engine. Escort became Ford's best seller and, a year later, best-selling domestic model. Granada slimmed down to Fairmont size, with Fairmont's base four-cylinder engine. After two years powered by a 302 cid V-8, LTD dropped to a 255. That wasn't the most startling engine change, however: Thunderbird now carried a standard six-cylinder powerplant.

Sporty performance seemed paramount for the 1982

1981 LTD coupe (JG)

model year, with the arrival not only of a Mustang GT but a two-seater EXP, based on the Escort platform. Ford now offered its own V-6 engine, while LTDs could get a 351 V-8 only if destined for police hands. T-bird not only continued the base inline six, but made a 255 V-8 the biggest possibility. A 20 percent sales decline didn't harm Ford's market share, since other makes weren't finding too many customers either.

The massive Thunderbirds of the 1970s seemed fully forgotten as the 10th generation arrived for 1983. This one was loaded with curves — and before long, a possible turbocharged, fuel-injected four-cylinder engine. With close-ratio five-speed and "quadra-shock" rear suspension. T-bird's Turbo Coupe became quite an attraction, helping sales to more than double. A little shuffling of names produced a "new" LTD (closely tied to the dropped Granada), while the big rear-drives became "LTD Crown Victoria."

1986 Tarus GL wagon (JG)

Turbocharging even hit EXP and Escort GT for 1984. EXP altered its form, adding the "bubbleback" liftgate from the faded Mercury LN7. Another front-drive model joined up: the compact Tempo with High Swirl Combustion engine, a replacement for Fairmont. Both Tempo and Escort could be ordered with a Mazda-built diesel — a curious decision since diesels were on their way out in other makes. Led by Thunderbird, sales hit their highest point since 1979, but Escort lost the best-seller label to Chevrolet's Cavalier.

LTD continued its high-performance, V-8 engine LX touring sedan into 1985, which was generally a carryover year. Tempos now came with standard five-speed gearboxes. Incentive programs helped sales (and Ford's market share) to rise noticeably. A revised Escort emerged before the 1986 model year, including an attractive GT model with high-output engine.

Not many new models received as much publicity as the front-drive Taurus, leader of the 1986 pack. And few cars looked as different from the model they replaced than Taurus versus LTD. Plenty of customers liked Taurus's grille-free aero look, as did *Motor Trend* with its Car of the Year award. Overall sales fell, however, after three years of increases, leaving Ford with less than 12 percent of the total market (imports included).

Potentially collectible Fords include a number of the

1986 Escort LX sedan (JG)

upper-level and special-edition Thunderbirds: Diamond Jubilee, Turbo Coupe, perhaps a recent Fila. Fans of little Fords may like the 1985-'86 Escort GT, though plenty of them seem to be around. EXP never really caught the fancy of the two-seater customer and enthusiasts don't seem overly excited either. Fairmont and Granada had their strong points as new (and used) cars, but whether an ES blackout option or Futura roofline makes them desirable later on is another matter. Unfortunately, only Mustang offered a convertible during the 1976-'86 period.

1976 FORD

Not much was dramatically different at Ford for 1976, after some significant changes a year earlier. Full-size models had been restyled in 1975, gaining a Mercedes-like grille. The Granada mid-size was new that year, with obvious Mercedes styling touches, while the Elite name went on the former Gran Torino. Pillarless two-door hardtop models had faded away by 1975, replaced by a new six-window coupe style with fixed quarter windows and large opera windows. Installation of catalytic converters expanded for 1976, accompanied by ample gas mileage boosts. Fuel economy improvements this year resulted from revised carburetor calibrations and lower rear axle ratios. All models used no-lead gas. The model lineup was the same as 1975, except that Custom 500 (equivalent to LTD) was now available only to fleet buyers. Special Pinto (and Mustang) models were produced for West Coast consumption. Corporate body colors for 1976 were: black, silver metallic, medium slate blue metallic, candyapple red, dark red, bright red, medium blue metallic, bright blue metallic, bright dark blue metallic, light blue, bright medium blue, dark yellow green metallic, dark jade metallic, light or dark green, copper metallic, medium chestnut metallic, dark brown metallic, saddle bronze metallic, tan, yellow orange, bright yellow, cream, dark yellow, chrome yellow, light gold, light jade, medium green gold, medium ginger metallic, dark brown, medium orange metallic, tangerine, and white. Additional colors were available on certain models, including diamond bright and diamond flare finishes, as well as three crystal metallic colors.

1976 Pinto Stallion hatchback coupe (F)

PINTO — FOUR/V-6 — Ford's subcompact, introduced in 1971, had a new front-end look this year. Appearance changes included a new argent-painted egg crate grille of one-piece corrosion-resistant plastic, bright bezels for the single round headlamps, bright front lip hood molding, and 'Ford' block letters centered above the grille. That new grille was peaked and angled forward slightly, with a tighter crosshatch pattern than before, and held square inset parking lamps. Backup lights were integral with the horizontal taillamps. Bodies held front and rear side marker lights. For the first time, standard interiors had a choice of all vinyl or sporty cloth-and-vinyl. Four new interior trim fabrics were offered, along with a new bright red interior color. Three four-passenger bodies were offered: two-door sedan, 'three-door' Runabout hatchback, and two-door wagon. Wagons had flipper rear compartment windows and a liftgate-open warning light, as well as tinted glass. Major fuel economy improvements resulted from catalysts, new carburetor calibrations, and a lower (3.18:1) rear axle ratio with the standard 140 cu. in. (2.3-liter) OHC four and fully synchronized four-speed manual gearbox with floor shift lever. Optional was a 170.8 cu. in. (2.8-liter) two- barrel V-6, which came only with Cruise-O-Matic transmission. Pinto's front suspension used independent short/long arms with ball joints. At the rear were longitudinal semi-elliptic leaf springs with rubber Iso-clamps at the axle. Rear springs had four leaves except wagons, five leaves. Pinto had front disc/rear drum brakes, rack-and-pinion steering, and unibody construction. New this year was a low-budget Pony MPG two-door, wearing minimal chrome trim and plain hubcaps. The fuel economy leader Pinto, dubbed an "import fighter," had 3.00:1 axle ratio, a slip-clutch cooling fan, and new calibrations for the 2.3-liter engine. Pinto standard equipment included a heater/defroster with DirectAire ventilation, bucket seats, mini-console, inside hood release, dome light, glovebox, dual padded sunvisors, and B78x13 tires. Runabouts and wagons had a fold-down back seat and deluxe seatbelts. Six-cylinder models required automatic transmission. Runabouts had a carpeted load area. A new Squire option for Runabouts added simulated woodgrain vinyl paneling on bodyside and lower back panel, similar to the Squire wagon option. Squire also displayed bright surround and Bpillar moldings as well as belt, drip and window frame moldings. Targeting younger drivers was a sporty new Stallion option featuring special silver body paint and taping, black window and door moldings, and blacked-out wiper arms, hood, grille and lower back panel. Black tape treatment went on rocker panel and wheel lip areas; Stallion (horse) decals on front fenders. Stallion also included dual racing mirrors, styled steel wheels with trim rings, A70 x 13 tires with raised white letters, and a "competition" handling suspension. A Luxury Decor Group included woodtone instrument panel applique, custom steering wheel, passenger door courtesy light switch, and rear seat ashtray. Joining the individual option list this year were an AM radio with tape player, the half-vinyl roof, rocker panel moldings, and leather-wrapped steering wheel.

1976 Maverick "Luxury Decor" sedan (F)

1976 Maverick Stallion coupe (F)

MAVERICK — SIX/V-8 — Initially scheduled for disappearance when the new Granada arrived in 1975, Maverick hung on a while longer as concern about the fuel crisis continued. This year's grille was a forward-slanting horizontal-bar design, split into two sections by a center vertical divider bar. Rectangular park/signal lamps were mounted in the bright argent plastic grille; backup lights integral with the taillamps. Single round headlamps continued. The front bumper held twin slots, and the hood showed a sculptured bulge. Inside was a new foot-operated parking brake. Front disc brakes were now standard. Base engine was the 200 cu. in. (3.3-liter) inline six with one-barrel carburetor. Options: 250 cu. in. six with one-barrel, or the 302 V-8 with two-barrel. All three came with either three- speed manual or automatic transmission. Maverick's fuel tank had grown from 16 to 19.2 gallons during the 1975 model year. Gas mileage was improved by lowering rear axle ratio to 2.79:1, recalibrating engines, and adding back-pressure modulation of the EGR system. The compact, unibodied Maverick used a ball-joint front suspension with short and long arms. Hotchkiss rear suspensions had longitudinal semi-elliptic (three-leaf) springs. Standard equipment included fully-synchronized three-speed column shift, C78 x 14 bias-ply tires, hubcaps, ventless windows with curved glass, front/rear side marker lights, European-type armrest with door pull assist handle, and lockable glovebox. A padded instrument panel held two round cluster pods for gauges. Standard bench seats were trimmed in Random stripe cloth and vinyl. Two-doors had a flipper rear quarter window. A Stallion dress-up package, similar to Pinto's, included black grille and moldings; unique paint/tape treatment on hood, grille, decklid, lower body, and lower back panel; plus large Stallion decal on front quarter panel. The package also included dual outside mirrors, raised white-letter steel-belted radials on styled steel wheels, and "competition" suspension. Two-doors had a new optional three-quarter vinyl roof; four-doors, as "halo" vinyl roof. Other options included individually reclining bucket seats; paint stripes that extended along bodyside and over the roof (on vinyl-topped two-doors); and AM and AM/FM radios with stereo tape players.

1976 Granada Ghia sedan (F)

GRANADA — SIX/V-8 — Ford called Granada "the most successful new-car nameplate in the industry in 1975," after its debut. For 1976, fuel economy improved and the "precision-size" compact held a new standard vinyl bench seat and door trim, but not much changed otherwise. Granada's chromed grille showed a 6x5 pattern of wide holes, with a 2 x 2 pattern within each hole. On each side of the single round headlamps were small, bright vertical sections patterned like the grille. Wide- spaced 'Ford' letters stood above the grille. On the fender extensions were wraparound front parking lights and signal/marker lenses. Each wraparound tri-color horizontal-style taillamp was divided into an upper and lower section, with integral side marker lights. Backup lamps sat inboard of the taillamps. Sporting a tall, squared-off roofline and European-influenced design, the five-passenger Granada strongly resembled a Mercedes up front. Ford hardly hit that fact, bragging that "Its looks and lines remind you of the Mercedes 280 and the Cadillac Seville." Bodies featured bright wraparound bumpers, plus bright moldings on windshield, backlight, drip rail, door belt, door frame, and wheel lip. Two-door Granadas had distinctive opera windows. Four-doors had a bright center pillar molding with color-keyed insert. Two- and four-door sedans were offered, in base or Ghia trim. Standard equipment included a three-speed manual transmission, front disc/rear drum brakes, heater/defroster, inside hood release, DR78 x 14 blackwall steel-belted radials, anti-theft decklid lock, burled walnut woodtone instrument panel appliques, locking glovebox, two rear seat ashtrays, lighter, and full wheel covers. Base engine was the 200 cu. in. (3.3-liter) inline six with one-barrel carb. Optional: a 250 cu. in. six, 302 cu. in. V-8, and 351 cu. in. V-8. Granada Ghia added a Ghia ornament on the opera window glass; color-keyed bodyside molding with integral wheel lip molding; left-hand remote-control mirror; dual accent paint stripes on bodyside, hood and decklid; trunk carpeting; and lower back panel applique color-keyed to the vinyl roof. Inside Ghia was a "floating pillow" sew design on independent reclining or flight bench seats, map pockets and assist handle on back of front seats, day/night mirror, and luxury steering wheel with woodtone applique on the rim. Under Ghia's hood was the larger 250 cu. in. six-cylinder engine. For economy, axle ratios were reduced to 2.75:1 and 2.79:1. Granada's front suspension used short/long control arms with ball joints and coil springs. At the rear were semi-elliptic four-leaf springs. Steering was the recirculating ball type. Four-wheel power disc brakes had become optional during the 1975 model year, along with Sure-Trak anti-skid brakes, power seats, Traction-Lok

axle, power moonroof, and space-saver spare tire. Those continued for 1976. New options this year included speed control, tilt steering wheel, AM radio with stereo tape player, power door locks, and heavy-duty suspension. A Luxury Decor option (for four-door Ghia only) included black/tan two-tone paint, four-wheel disc brakes, lacy-spoke cast aluminum wheels, large Ghia badge on C-pillar, and front/rear bumper rub strips. Inside, that option had velour cloth and super-soft vinyl upholstery with larger door armrest, soft glovebox and ashtray doors, rear center armrest, console with warning lights, leather-wrapped steering wheel, and lighted visor vanity mirror. A Sports Sedan package for two-doors included a floor shift lever, special paint, color-keyed wheels, pinstripes, and leather-wrapped steering wheel. Mercury's Monarch was Granada's corporate twin, differing only in grille/taillamp design and trim details. Both evolved from the Maverick platform.

1976 Gran Torino two-door hardtop (F)

TORINO — V-8 — Nine models made up the mid-size Torino lineup this year: base, Gran Torino and Brougham two- and four-doors, and a trio of wagons. Gran Torino Sport was dropped. Two-doors rode a 114 in. wheelbase; four-doors measured 118 in. between hubs. The similar-size Elite was a separate model (below). Fuel economy was improved by recalibrating engine spark and back-pressure EGR, and lowering the rear axle ratio to 2.75:1. Five body colors were new. Torino and Gran Torino got a new saddle interior. Appearance was similar to 1975. Side-by-side quad round headlamps flanked a one-piece plastic grille with tiny crosshatch pattern, divided into six sections by vertical bars. Clear vertical parking/signal lamps hid behind twin matching outer sections, making eight in all. 'Ford' block letters stood above the grille. Two-door Torinos retained the conventional pillarless design, while four-doors were referred to as "pillared hardtops." Bodies held frameless, ventless curved side glass. Standard engine was the 351 cu. in. (5.8-liter) V-8 with two-barrel carburetor and solid-state ignition. SelectShift Cruise-O-Matic, power front disc/rear drum brakes, power steering, and HR78 x 14 steel-belted radial tires were standard. Two V-8s were optional: a 400 cu. in. two-barrel and the big 460 four-barrel. Torino's front suspension used single lower control arms, strut bar and ball joints. Coil springs brought up the rear. Bodies sat on a separate torque box perimeter-type frame. Standard equipment included a cloth/vinyl front bench seat with adjustable head restraints, vinyl door trim panels, recessed door handles, day/night mirror, heater/defroster, and inside hood release. Broughams added a split bench seat. Torino and Gran Torino wore hubcaps; Broughams added wheel covers, as well as opera windows and a vinyl roof. Wagons had a three-way tailgate and locking storage compartment. Squire wagons added a power tailgate window, full wheel covers, and woodgrain paneling with side rails. New options included a bucket seat console (on Gran Torino two-door); opera windows for the base Torino two-door (as well as other models); space-saver spare tire; and engine immersion heater. Also optional: an automatic parking brake release and electric decklid release.

1976 Elite two-door hardtop (F)

ELITE — V-8 — Although the Elite nameplate arrived just a year earlier, its body had been around a while longer, then called Gran Torino. Appearance changes were slight this year on the pillarless two-door hardtop body, which rode a 114 in. wheelbase. Elite sported a "luxury" sectioned grille with vertical bars and horizontal center bar. Its floating egg crate design formed a two-row, eight-column arrangement. Each of the 16 "holes" held a crosshatch pattern. The grille protruded forward in segments, and the bumper extended forward at its center and ends. A stand-up hood ornament held the Elite crest. Single round headlamps in square housings had bright bezels, while vertical parking/signal lamps sat in front fendertip extensions. Wide vinyl-insert bodyside moldings were color-keyed to the vinyl roof. Large wraparound taillamps had bright bezels and integral side marker lights (with red reflector on lower back panel applique). On the rear roof pillar were two tiny side-by-side opera windows, to the rear of regular quarter windows. Bodies also displayed bright tapered wide wheel lip moldings. Six body colors were new, while a standard gold vinyl roof replaced the former brown. Either a full vinyl roof or a new half-vinyl version was available, at no extra charge. To boost gas mileage, the standard axle changed from 3.00:1 to 2.75:1. Standard equipment included the 351 cu. in. (5.8-liter) two-barrel V-8 with SelectShift Cruise-O-Matic, power steering and brakes, four-wheel coil springs, and HR78 x 15 SBR tires. The standard bench seat had Westminster pleated knit cloth and vinyl trim. Woodtone accented the instrument cluster/panel, steering wheel and door panels. Also standard: front bumper guards, heater/defroster, DirectAire ventilation, clock, full wheel covers, and bright window moldings. An Interior Decor group included individually adjustable split bench seats with choice of cashmere-like cloth or all-vinyl

trim, shag carpeting, visor vanity mirror, dual-note horn, and eight-pod instrument panel with tachometer. Bucket seats with console and floor shift became optional this year. Other new options: space-saver spare tire, turbine-spoke cast aluminum wheels, AM/FM stereo search radio, electric decklid release, automatic parking brake release, and engine immersion heater.

1976 LTD Landau four-door pillared hardtop (F)

FULL-SIZE LTD/CUSTOM 500 — V-8 — LTD was the only full-size Ford available to private buyers this year, as the Custom 500 badge went on fleet models only. The ten-model lineup included two- and four-door base, Brougham and Landau LTD models; Custom 500 four-door and wagon; and base and Country Squire LTD wagons. Four-doors were called "pillared hardtops." Landau and Country Squire models had hidden headlamps. Brougham and Landau two-doors carried half-vinyl roofs; four-doors got a "halo" vinyl roof. Front-end appearance changed slightly with a switch to dark argent paint on the secondary surface of the chromed grille. Otherwise, little change was evident other than a new wheel cover design. LTD's crosshatch grille peaked slightly forward. Headlamp doors held a horizontal emblem. Tri-section wraparound front parking/signal lenses stood at fender tips. On the hood was a stand-up ornament. Two-doors had a six-window design, with narrow vertical windows between the front and rear side windows. Vinyl-insert bodyside moldings were standard. All models had a reflective rear applique. Six body colors were new. At mid-year, Country Squire lost the long horizontal chrome strip along its woodgrain bodyside panel. Base engine was the two-barrel 351 cu. in. (5.8-liter) V-8, but wagons carried the 400 cu. in. engine. A 460 V-8 with dual exhausts was optional on all models. Standard equipment included power steering and brakes, SelectShift Cruise-O-Matic, steel-belted radials, power ventilation system, and front bumper guards. Brougham, Landau and wagon also had rear guards. Police models with the 460 V-8 and three-speed automatic had first-gear lockout. Front suspensions used single lower arms with strut bar and ball joints. At the rear were coil springs with three-link rubber cushion and track bar. Rear axle ratios changed to 2.75:1 and engines were recalibrated, in an attempt to boost gas mileage. Wagons had a fuel tank of only 21 gallons, versus 24.3 gallons on hardtops. An 8-gallon auxiliary tank was available. Wagons now had standard hydro-boost rear brakes. A parking brake warning light became standard on all models. Decklid and ignition switch locks offered improved anti-theft protection. Other new options: four-wheel power disc brakes, adjustable-level air shocks, dual-tone paint treatment (Brougham and Landau) in four combinations, and AM/FM search radio. Inside were standard full-width bench seats with cloth/vinyl trim; cut-pile carpeting; full-length padded armrests; and woodtone instrument panel and door appliques. LTD bodies held bright belt, drip and wheel lip moldings. Landau added concealed headlamps, a convenience group, half vinyl roof (on two-door), front cornering lamps, wide color-keyed bodyside moldings, and unique narrow center pillar windows. Also on Landaus: padded door panels with woodtone accents, fold-down center armrests, and a digital clock.

1976 Thunderbird two-door hardtop (F)

THUNDERBIRD — V-8 — Apart from a trio of trim/paint Luxury Group packages, not much was new on the personal-luxury Thunderbird for 1976. T-Bird's bulged-out grille consisted of rectangular holes in a crosshatch pattern, with 'Thunderbird' block letters above. Quad round headlamps in squarish housings didn't fit snugly together but were mounted separately, with a little body-colored space between each pair. Large sectioned wraparound parking and cornering lamps stood at fender tips. T-Bird's opera windows were less tall than most, and narrow roll-down rear windows also were installed. Full-width segmented-design taillamps had four bulbs in each pod. Standard equipment included the big 460 cu. in. (7.5-liter) V-8 with four-barrel carburetor, SelectShift Cruise-O-Matic, 2.75:1 rear axle, SelectAire conditioner, vinyl roof, vinyl-insert bodyside moldings, JR78 x 15 steel-belted radials, power steering and brakes, power windows, and cornering lamps. Rear suspension, as before, was the "stabul" four-link system. Inside was a baby burled walnut woodtone instrument panel applique and new AM radio. Also standard: automatic parking brake release, front and rear bumper guards with white insert rub strips, split bench seats with fold-down armrests, remote-control left mirror, full wheel covers, twin padded pull-down armrests, lined luggage area, and courtesy lights. New options included a power lumbar seat, AM/FM search radio, AM/FM quadrasonic 8 track tape player, engine block heater, and Kasman cloth interior trim. An automatic headlamp dimmer was added to the Light Group. Also available: a power-operated moonroof made with one-way glass. The new Creme/Gold Luxury Group featured two-tone paint (gold

glamour paint on bodyside and creme accent on hood, deck, greenhouse and bodyside molding). Also included was a gold padded half-vinyl roof, deep-dish aluminum wheels, and gold Thunderbird emblem in opera window. There was a choice of two-tone Creme/Gold leather or gold media velour seating surface. The right-hand instrument panel was finished with gold applique. A Bordeaux Luxury Group included Bordeaux glamour paint, fully padded half-vinyl roof in silver or dark red, wide bodyside moldings to match the vinyl roof, dual hood and bodyside paint stripes, and simulated wire wheel covers. Inside was a choice of red leather or red media velour. There was also a Lipstick (red) package with white striping. Thunderbirds came in 21 colors, including the Luxury Group choices.

I.D. DATA: Ford's 11-symbol Vehicle Identification Number (VIN) is stamped on a metal tab fastened to the instrument panel, visible through the windshield. The first digit is a model year code ('6' 1976). The second letter indicates assembly plant: 'A' Atlanta, GA; 'B' Oakville, Ontario (Canada); 'E' Mahwah, NJ; 'G' Chicago; 'H' Lorain, Ohio; 'J' Los Angeles; 'K' Kansas City, MO; 'P' Twin Cities, Minn.; 'R' San Jose, CA; 'T' Metuchen, NJ; 'U' Louisville, KY; 'W' Wayne, MI; 'Y' Wixom, MI. Digits three and four are the body serial code, which corresponds to the Model Numbers shown in the tables below (e.g., '10' Pinto 2-dr. sedan). The fifth symbol is an engine code: 'Y' L4-140 2Bbl.; 'Z' V6170 2Bbl.; 'T' L6200 1Bbl.; 'L' L6250 1Bbl.; 'F' V8302 2Bbl.; 'H' V8351 2Bbl.; 'S' V8400 2Bbl.; 'A' V8460 4Bbl.; 'C' Police V8460 4Bbl. Finally, digits 6-11 make up the consecutive unit number of cars built at each assembly plant. The number begins with 100,001. A Vehicle Certification Label on the left front door lock face panel or door pillar shows the manufacturer, month and year of manufacture, GVW, GAWR, certification statement, VIN, body code, color code, trim code, axle code, transmission code, and domestic (or foreign) special order code.

PINTO (FOUR/V-6)

Model Number	Body/Style Number	Body Type & Seating	Factory Price	Shipping Weight	Production Total
10	62B	2-dr. Sedan-4P	3025/3472	2452/2590	92,264
10	62B	2-dr. Pony Sed-4P	2895/--	2450/--	Note 1
11	64B	2-dr. Hatch-4P	3200/3647	2482/2620	92,540
11	64B	2-dr. Sqr Hatch-4P	3505/3952	2518/2656	Note 2
12	73B	2-dr. Sta Wag-4P	3365/3865	2635/2773	105,328
12	73B	2-dr. Sqr Wag-4P	3671/4171	2672/2810	Note 2

Note 1: Pony production included in base sedan figure. **Note 2:** Squire Runabout hatchback and Squire Wagon production are included in standard Runabout and station wagon totals.

MAVERICK (SIX/V-8)

| 91 | 62A | 2-dr. Sedan-4P | 3117/3265 | 2763/2930 | 60,611 |
| 92 | 54A | 4-dr. Sedan-5P | 3189/3337 | 2873/3040 | 79,076 |

GRANADA (SIX/V-8)

| 82 | 66H | 2-dr. Sedan-5P | 3707/3861 | 3119/3226 | 161,618 |
| 81 | 54H | 4-dr. Sedan-5P | 3798/3952 | 3168/3275 | 187,923 |

GRANADA GHIA (SIX/V-8)

| 84 | 66K | 2-dr. Sedan-5P | 4265/4353 | 3280/3387 | 46,786 |
| 83 | 54K | 4-dr. Sedan-5P | 4355/4443 | 3339/3446 | 52,457 |

TORINO (V-8)

25	65B	2-dr. HT Cpe-6P	4172	3976	34,518
27	53B	4-dr. HT Sed-6P	4206	4061	17,394
40	71B	4-dr. Sta Wag-6P	4521	4409	17,281

1976 Gran Torino Brougham four-door pillared hardtop (F)

GRAN TORINO (V-8)

30	65D	2-dr. HT Cpe-6P	4461	3999	23,939
31	53D	4-dr. HT Sed-6P	4495	4081	40,568
42	71D	4-dr. Sta Wag-6P	4769	4428	30,596
43	71K	4-dr. Sqr Wag-6P	5083	4454	21,144

GRAN TORINO BROUGHAM (V-8)

| 32 | 65K | 2-dr. HT Cpe-6P | 4883 | 4063 | 3,183 |
| 33 | 53K | 4-dr. HT Sed-6P | 4915 | 4144 | 4,473 |

ELITE (V-8)

Model Number	Body/Style Number	Body Type & Seating	Factory Price	Shipping Weight	Production Total
21	65H	2-dr. HT Cpe-6P	4879	4169	146,475

CUSTOM 500 (V-8)

52	60D	2-dr. Pill. HT-6P	N/A	N/A	7,037
53	53D	4-dr. Pill. HT-6P	4493	4298	23,447
72	71D	4-dr. Ranch Wag-6P	4918	4737	4,633

LTD (V-8)

62	60H	2-dr. Pill. HT-6P	4780	4257	62,844
63	53H	4-dr. Pill. HT-6P	4752	4303	108,168
74	71H	4-dr. Sta Wag-6P	5207	4752	30,237
74	71H	4-dr. DFRS Wag-10P	5333	4780	Note 3
76	71K	4-dr. Ctry Sqr-6P	5523	4809	47,379
76	71K	4-dr. DFRS Sqr-10P	5649	4837	Note 3

Note 3: Wagons with dual-facing rear seats (a $126 option) are included in standard station wagon and Country Squire wagon totals.

LTD BROUGHAM (V-8)

| 68 | 60K | 2-dr. Pill. HT-6P | 5299 | 4299 | 20,863 |
| 66 | 53K | 4-dr. Pill. HT-6P | 5245 | 4332 | 32,917 |

LTD LANDAU (V-8)

| 65 | 60L | 2-dr. Pill. HT-6P | 5613 | 4346 | 29,673 |
| 64 | 53L | 4-dr. Pill. HT-6P | 5560 | 4394 | 35,663 |

THUNDERBIRD (V-8)

| 87 | 65K | 2-dr. HT Cpe-6P | 7790 | 4808 | 52,935 |

FACTORY PRICE AND WEIGHT NOTE: For Maverick and Granada, prices and weights to left of slash are for six-cylinder, to right for V-8 engine. For Pinto, prices and weights to left of slash are for four-cylinder, to right for V-6 engine.

ENGINE DATA: BASE FOUR (Pinto): Inline. Overhead cam. Four-cylinder. Cast iron block and head. Displacement: 140 cu. in. (2.3 liters). Bore & stroke: 3.78 x 3.13 in. Compression ratio: 9.0:1. Brake horsepower: 92 at 5000 R.P.M. Torque: 121 lbs.-ft. at 3000 R.P.M. Five.00 main bearings. Hydraulic valve lifters. Carburetor: 2Bbl. Holley-Weber 9510. VIN Code: Y. **OPTIONAL V-6 (Pinto):** 60-degree, overhead-valve V-6. Cast iron block and head. Displacement: 170.8 cu. in. (2.8 liters). Bore & stroke: 3.66 x 2.70 in. Compression ratio: 8.7:1. Brake horsepower: 103 at 4400 R.P.M. Torque: 149 lbs.-ft. at 2800 R.P.M. Four main bearings. Solid valve lifters. Carburetor: 2Bbl. Motorcraft 9510 (D6ZE-BA). VIN Code: Z. **BASE SIX (Maverick, Granada):** Inline. Overhead valve. Six-cylinder. Cast iron block and head. Displacement: 200 cu. in. (3.3 liters). Bore & stroke: 3.68 x 3.13 in. Compression ratio: 8.3:1. Brake horsepower: 81 at 3400 R.P.M. Torque: 151 lbs.-ft. at 1700 R.P.M. Seven main bearings. Hydraulic valve lifters. Carburetor: 1Bbl. Carter YFA 9510. VIN Code: T. **BASE SIX (Granada Ghia); OPTIONAL (Maverick, Granada):** Inline. Overhead valve. Six-cylinder. Cast iron block and head. Displacement: 250 cu. in. (4.1 liters). Bore & stroke: 3.68 x 3.91 in. Compression ratio: 8.0:1. Brake horsepower: 87 at 3600 R.P.M. (Maverick/Ghia, 90 at 3000). Torque: 190 lbs.-ft. at 2000 R.P.M. (Ghia, 187 at 1900). Seven main bearings. Hydraulic valve lifters. Carburetor: 1Bbl. Carter YFA 9510. VIN Code: L. **OPTIONAL V-8 (Maverick, Granada):** 90-degree, overhead valve V-8. Cast iron block and head. Displacement: 302 cu. in. (5.0 liters). Bore & stroke: 4.00 x 3.00 in. Compression ratio: 8.0:1. Brake horsepower: 138 at 3600 R.P.M. (Granada, 134 at 3600). Torque: 245 lbs.-ft. at 2000 R.P.M. (Granada, 242 at 2000). Five main bearings. Hydraulic valve lifters. Carburetor: 2Bbl. Ford 2150A 9510. VIN Code: F. **BASE V-8 (Torino, Elite, LTD); OPTIONAL (Granada):** 90-degree, overhead valve V-8. Cast iron block and head. Displacement: 351 cu. in. (5.8 liters). Bore & stroke: 4.00 x 3.50 in. Compression ratio: 8.0:1. (Torino, 8.1:1). Brake horsepower: 152 at 3800 R.P.M. (Torino, 154 at 3400). Torque: 274 lbs.-ft. at 1600 R.P.M. (Torino, 286 at 1800). Five main bearings. Hydraulic valve lifters. Carburetor: 2Bbl. Ford 2150A. VIN Code: H. **BASE V-8 (500/LTD wagon); OPTIONAL (Torino, Elite, LTD):** 90-degree, overhead valve V-8. Cast iron block and head. Displacement: 400 cu. in. (6.6 liters). Bore & stroke: 4.00 x 4.00 in. Compression ratio: 8.0:1. Brake horsepower: 180 at 3800 R.P.M. Torque: 336 lbs.-ft. at 1800 R.P.M. Five main bearings. Hydraulic valve lifters. Carburetor: 2Bbl. Ford 2150A. VIN Code: S. **BASE V-8 (Thunderbird); OPTIONAL (Torino, Elite, LTD):** 90-degree, overhead valve V-8. Cast iron block and head. Displacement: 460 cu. in. (7.5 liters). Bore & stroke: 4.36 x 3.85 in. Compression ratio: 8.0:1. Brake horsepower: 202 at 3800 R.P.M. Torque: 352 lbs.-ft. at 1600 R.P.M. Five main bearings. Hydraulic valve lifters. Carburetor: 4Bbl. Motorcraft 9510 or Ford 4350A 9510. VIN Code: A.

Note: A Police 460 cu. in. V-8 ws also available for LTD.

CHASSIS DATA: Wheelbase: (Pinto) 94.5 in.; (Pinto wag) 94.8 in.; (Maverick 2dr.) 103.0 in.; (Maverick 4dr.) 109.9 in.; (Granada) 109.9 in.; (Torino) 114.0 in.; (Torino 4dr./wag) 118.0 in.; (Elite) 114.0 in.; (Custom 500/LTD) 121.0 in.; (TBird) 120.4 in. Overall length: (Pinto) 169.0 in.; (Pinto wag) 178.8 in.; (Maverick 2dr.) 187.0 in.; (Maverick 4dr.) 193.9 in.; (Granada) 197.7 in.; (Torino 2dr.) 213.6 in.; (Torino 4dr.) 217.6 in.; (Torino wag) 222.6 in.; (Elite) 216.1 in.; (LTD 2dr.) 223.9 in.; (LTD wag) 225.6 in.; (TBird) 225.7 in. Height: (Pinto) 50.6 in.; (Pinto wag) 52.0 in.; (Maverick) 52.9 in.; (Granada) 53.3-53.4 in.; (Torino 2dr.) 52.6 in.; (Torino 4dr.) 53.3 in.; (Torino wag) 54.9 in.; (Elite) 53.1 in.; (LTD 2dr.) 53.7 in.; (LTD 4dr.) 54.8 in.; (TBird) 52.8 in. Width: (Pinto) 69.4 in.; (Pinto wag) 69.7 in.; (Maverick) 70.5 in.; (Granada) 74.0 in.; (Granada Ghia) 74.5 in.; (Torino) 79.3 in.; (Torino) 79.9 in.; (Elite) 78.5 in.; (LTD) 79.5 in.; (LTD wag) 79.9 in.; (LTD wag) 79.7 in. Front Tread: (Pinto) 55.0 in.; (Maverick) 56.5 in.; (Granada) 59.0 in.; (Torino) 63.4 in.; (Elite) 63.0 in.; (LTD) 64.1 in.; (TBird) 62.9 in. Rear Tread: (Pinto) 55.8 in.; (Maverick) 56.5 in.; (Granada) 57.7 in.; (Torino wag) 63.1 in.; (Elite) 3.1 in.; (LTD) 64.3 in.; (TBird) 62.8 in. Standard Tires: (Pinto) A78 x 13 or B78 x 13; (Maverick) C78 x 14, except DR78 x 14 w/V-8 engine; (Granada) DR78 x 14; (Torino) HR78 x 14; (Elite) HR78 x 15; (LTD) HR78 x 15 exc. wagon, JR78 x 15; (TBird) JR78 x 15.

TECHNICAL: Transmission: Three-speed manual transmission (column shift) standard on Maverick/Granada. Gear ratios: (1st) 2.99:1; (2nd) 1.75:1; (3rd) 1.00:1; (Rev) 3.17:1. Four-speed floor shift standard on Pinto: (1st) 3.65:1; (2nd) 1.97:1; (3rd) 1.37:1; (4th) 1.00:1; (Rev) 3.66:1 or 3.95:1. Pinto station wagon: (1st) 4.07:1; (2nd) 2.57:1; (3rd) 1.66:1; (4th) 1.00:1; (Rev) 3.95:1. Select-Shift three-speed automatic standard on other models, optional on all; column lever but floor shift optional on Maverick, Granada, Torino and Elite (standard on Pinto). Pinto (L4140) automatic gear ratios: (1st) 2.47:1; (2nd) 1.47:1; (3rd) 1.00:1; (Rev) 2.11:1. Pinto (V-6)/Maverick/Granada/Torino (V8351)/Elite (V8351) auto. gear ratios: (1st) 2.46:1; (2nd) 1.46:1; (3rd) 1.00:1; (Rev) 2.20:1. Torino/Elite/LTD/TBird (V8400/460): ratios: (1st) 2.46:1; (2nd) 1.46:1; (3rd) 1.00:1; (Rev) 2.18:1. LTD (V8351): (1st) 2.40:1; (2nd) 1.47:1; (3rd) 1.00:1; (Rev) 2.00:1. Standard final drive ratio: (Pinto four) 3.18:1 w/4spd, 3.18:1 or 3.40:1 w/auto.; (Pinto Pony) 3.00:1; (Pinto V-6) 3.40:1; (Maverick) 2.79:1; (Granada) 2.79:1 or 2.75:1 w/3spd and 2.75:1, 3.00:1 or 3.07:1 w/auto.; (Torino/Elite) 2.75:1; (LTD/T-Bird) 2.75:1 exc. Police 460 V-8, 3.00:1. Steering: (Pinto) rack and pinion: (others) recirculating ball. Front Suspension: (Pinto/Maverick/Granada) rigid axle w/semi-elliptic leaf springs; (Torino/Elite) rigid axle w/lower trailing arms, upper oblique torque arms and coil trailing links and anti-sway bar; (Torino/Elite/LTD/Thunderbird) coil springs with single lower control arm, lower trailing links, strut bar and anti-sway bar. Rear Suspension: (Pinto/Maverick/Granada) rigid axle w/semi- elliptic leaf springs; (Torino/Elite) rigid axle w/lower trailing arms, upper oblique torque arms and coil springs; (LTD) rigid axle w/lower trailing radius arms, upper torque arms and coil springs, three-link w/track bar; (Thunderbird) "stabul" four-link system with coil springs and anti-sway bar. Brakes: Front disc, rear drum; four-wheel discs available on Granada, LTD and Thunderbird. Ignition: Electronic. Body construction: (Pinto/Maverick/Granada) unibody; (Torino/Elite/LTD) separate body and perimeter box frame; (Thunderbird) separate body and perimeter frame with torque box. Fuel tank: (Pinto) 13 gal.; (Pinto wag) 14 gal.; (Maverick/Granada) 19.2 gal.; (Torino/Elite) 26.5 gal.; (Torino wag) 21.3 gal.; (LTD) 24.3 gal. exc. wagon, 21 gal.; (TBird) 26.5 gal.

DRIVETRAIN OPTIONS: Engines: 250 cu. in., 1Bbl. six: Maverick/Granada ($96). 302 cu. in., 2Bbl. V-8: Granada ($154); Granada Ghia ($88). 351 cu. in., 2Bbl. V-8: Granada ($200); Granada Ghia ($134). 400 cu. in., 2Bbl. V-8: Torino/Elite/LTD ($100). 460 cu. in., 4Bbl. V-8: Torino/Elite ($292); LTD ($353); LTD wagon ($251). Dual exhaust: TBird ($72). Transmission/Differential: SelectShift Cruise-O-Matic: Pinto ($186); Maverick/Granada ($245). Floor shift lever: Maverick/Granada ($27). Traction-Lok differential: Granada ($48); Torino/Elite ($53); LTD ($54); TBird ($55). Optional axle ratio: Pinto/Maverick/Granada ($13); Torino/Elite/LTD/TBird ($14). Power Accessories: Power brakes: Pinto ($54); Maverick ($53); Granada ($57). Four-wheel power disc brakes: Granada ($210); LTD ($170); TBird ($184). Sure-Track brakes: Granada ($227); TBird ($378). Power steering: Pinto ($117); Maverick/Granada ($124). Suspension: H.D. susp.: Maverick ($16); Granada ($29); LTD ($18); TBird ($29). H.D. handling susp.: Torino ($18-$32); Elite ($92). Adjustable air shock absorbers: LTD ($43). Other: Engine block heater: Pinto/Maverick/Granada ($17); Torino/Elite/LTD/TBird ($18). H.D. battery: Maverick/Granada ($14); LTD ($17). H.D. electrical system: Torino ($29); Elite ($80). Extended-range fuel tank: LTD ($99). Trailer towing pkg. (light duty): Granada ($42); LTD ($53). Trailer towing pkg. (medium duty): Torino/Elite ($59); LTD ($46-$145). Trailer towing pkg. (heavy duty): Torino ($87-$121); Elite ($121); LTD ($132-$230); TBird ($92). California emission system: Maverick/Granada ($46); Torino/Elite/LTD/TBird ($50). High-altitude option: Torino/Elite/LTD/TBird ($13).

PINTO CONVENIENCE/APPEARANCE OPTIONS: Option Packages: Stallion option ($283). Luxury decor group ($241). Convenience light group ($70-$102). Protection group ($73-$134). Comfort/Convenience: Air conditioner ($420). Rear defroster, electric ($70). Tinted glass ($46). Leather-wrapped steering wheel ($33). Dual color-keyed mirrors ($42). Entertainment: AM radio ($71); w/stereo tape player ($192). AM/FM radio ($129). AM/FM stereo radio ($173). Exterior: Sunroof, manual ($230). Half vinyl roof ($125). Metallic glow paint ($54). Roof luggage rack ($52-$75). Rocker panel moldings ($19). Wheels: Forged aluminum wheels ($82-$172). Styled steel wheels ($92-$119). Wheel covers ($28). Trim rings ($29). Tires: A78 x 13 WSW. A70 x 13 RWL. B78 x 13 BSW/WSW. BR78 x 13 SBR BSW/WSW. BR70 x 13 RWL.

MAVERICK CONVENIENCE/APPEARANCE OPTIONS: Option Packages: Stallion option ($329). Exterior decor group ($99). Interior decor group ($106). Luxury decor group ($508). Luxury interior decor ($217). Deluxe bumper group ($28-$61). Convenience group ($34-$64). Protection group ($24-$39). Light group ($22-$34). Security lock group ($16). Comfort/Convenience: Air cond. ($420). Rear defogger ($40). Tinted glass ($45-$59). Fuel monitor warning light ($18). Dual color-keyed mirrors ($13-$25). Entertainment: AM radio ($71); w/tape player ($192). AM/FM radio ($128). AM/FM stereo radio ($210); w/tape player ($299). Exterior: Vinyl roof ($94). Metallic glow paint ($54). Lower bodyside paint ($55). Bodyside or bodyside-roof accent paint stripe ($27). Decklid luggage rack ($51). Rocker panel moldings ($19). Bumper guards, front or rear ($17). Interior: Reclining bucket seats ($147). Cloth bucket seat trim ($24). Vinyl seat trim ($25). Color-keyed deluxe seatbelts ($17). Wheels: Forged aluminum wheels ($98-$187). Styled steel wheels ($59-$89). Hubcap trim rings ($35) except (NC) with decor group. Tires: C78 x 14 WSW. BR78 x 14 BSW. CR78 x 14 BSW/WSW. DR78 x 14 BSW/WSW. DR70 x 14 RWL. Space-saver spare ($13) except (NC) with radial tires.

GRANADA CONVENIENCE/APPEARANCE OPTIONS: Option Packages: Sports sedan option ($482). Exterior decor group ($128). Interior decor group ($181). Luxury decor group ($642). Convenience group ($31-$75). Deluxe bumper group ($61). Light group ($25-$37). Protection group ($24-$39). Visibility group ($30-$47). Security lock group ($17). Comfort/Convenience: Air cond. ($437). Rear defogger ($43). Rear defroster, electric ($76). Fingertip speed control ($96). Power windows ($95-$133). Power door locks ($63-$88). Power four-way seat ($119). Tinted glass ($47). Leather-wrapped steering wheel ($14-$33). Luxury steering wheel ($18). Tilt steering wheel ($54). Fuel monitor warning light ($18). Digital clock ($40). Horns and Mirrors: Dual-note horn ($6). Color-keyed outside mirrors ($29-$42). Lighted visor vanity mirror ($40). Entertainment: AM radio ($71); w/tape player ($192). AM/FM radio ($142). AM/FM stereo radio ($210); w/tape player ($299). Exterior: Power moonroof ($786). Power sunroof ($517). Vinyl or half vinyl roof ($102). Metallic glow paint ($54). Bodyside/decklid paint stripes ($27). Bodyside/decklid accent moldings ($28). Black vinyl insert bodyside moldings ($35). Rocker panel moldings ($19). Decklid luggage rack ($33). Interior: Console ($65). Reclining seats ($60). Leather seat trim ($181). Deluxe cloth seat trim ($88). Trunk carpeting ($20). Trunk dress-up ($33). Color-keyed seatbelts ($17). Wheels: Styled steel wheels ($41-$60); w/trim rings ($76- $95). Lacy spoke aluminum wheels ($112-$207). Tires: E78 x 14 BSW/WSW. DR78 x 14 WSW. ER78 x 14 BSW/WSW. FR78 x 14 BSW/WSW. Space-saver spare (NC).

TORINO/ELITE CONVENIENCE/APPEARANCE OPTIONS: Option Packages: Squire Brougham option: Torino ($184). Interior decor group: Elite ($384). Accent group: Torino ($45). Deluxe bumper group ($50-$67). Light group ($41-$43). Convenience group: Tornio ($33-$84); Elite ($49). Protection group ($26-$42). Security lock group ($18). Comfort/Convenience: Auto-temp control air cond. ($88). Anti-theft alarm system ($84). Rear defroster, electric ($99). Windshield/rear window defroster, Power windows ($104-$145). Power tailgate window: Torino wag ($43). Power door locks ($68-$109). Electric decklid release ($17). Six-way power seat ($130). Automatic seatback release ($30). Reclining passenger seat ($70). Leather-wrapped steering wheel ($36). Luxury steering wheel ($20). Tilt steering wheel ($59). Fuel sentry vacuum gauge ($13-$32). Fuel monitor warning light ($20). Electric clock: Torino ($18). Horns and Mirrors: Dual-note horn ($7). Remote driver's mirror, chrome ($14). Remote-control color-keyed mirrors ($32-$46). Lighted visor vanity mirror ($43). Entertainment: AM radio ($78). AM/FM stereo radio ($229); w/tape player ($326). AM/FM stereo search radio: Elite ($386). Dual rear speakers ($39). Exterior: Power moonroof: Elite ($859). Power sunroof ($545). Vinyl roof: Torino ($112); Elite (NC). Opera windows: Torino ($50). Fender skirts: Torino ($41). Rocker panel moldings ($26). Vinyl-insert bodyside moldings: Torino ($38). Metallic glow paint ($59). Dual accent paint stripes ($29). Bumper guards, front or rear: Torino ($18). Luggage rack: Torino ($82-$91). Interior: Bucket seats ($146) exc. Elite w/decor group (NC). Rear-facing third seat: Torino wag ($104). Vinyl bench seat trim: Torino ($22). Pleated vinyl bench seat trim ($22-$28). Duraweave vinyl seat trim: Torino ($55). Vinyl split bench seat: Torino (NC). Color-keyed seatbelts ($18). Trunk trim ($36). Wheels: Deluxe wheel covers: Torino ($37). Luxury wheel covers ($58-$95). Wire wheel covers: Elite ($99). Magnum 500 wheels w/trim rings: Torino ($141-$178). Turbine spoke cast aluminum wheels: Elite ($226). Torino Tires: H78 x 14 BSW/WSW. HR78 x 14 WSW. HR78 x 14 six- ply BSW/WSW. JR78 x 14 WSW. HR78 x 15 BSW/WSW. Space-saver spare (NC). Elite Tires: HR78 x 15 SBR WSW ($39). HR70 x 15 SBR WSW ($59). Space-saver spare (NC).

LTD CONVENIENCE/APPEARANCE OPTIONS: Option Packages: Landau luxury group ($472-$708). Brougham option: wagon ($396); Squire ($266). Harmony color group ($99). Convenience group ($97-$104). Light group ($76-$79). Deluxe bumper group ($41-$59). Protection group ($47-$78). Security lock group ($18). Comfort/Convenience: Air cond. ($353); w/auto-temp control ($486). Anti-theft alarm system ($566). Rear defogger ($43). Rear defroster, electric ($83). Fingertip speed control ($87-$107). Power windows ($108-$161). Power mini-vent and side windows ($232). Power door locks ($68-$109). Six-way power driver's seat ($132); driver and passenger ($259). Automatic seatback release ($30). Tinted glass ($64). Luxury steering wheel ($20). Tilt steering wheel ($59). Fuel monitor warning light ($20). Electric clock ($18). Digital clock ($25-$43). Lighting, Horns and Mirrors: Cornering lamps ($43). Dual-note horn ($6). Driver's remote mirror ($14). Entertainment: AM radio ($78). AM/FM stereo radio ($229); w/tape player ($326). AM/FM stereo search radio ($386). Dual rear speakers ($39). Exterior: Sunroof, manual ($632). Full vinyl roof ($126) exc. wagon ($151) and Brougham/Landau two-door (NC). Half vinyl roof ($126). Fender skirts ($42). Metallic glow paint ($59). Dual accent paint stripes ($29). Rocker panel moldings ($26). Vinyl-insert bodyside moldings ($41). Rear bumper guards ($18). Luggage rack ($82-$96). Interior: Dual-facing rear seats: wagon ($126). Split bench seat w/passenger recliner ($141). Leather interior trim ($222). All-vinyl seat ($22). Duraweave vinyl trim ($55). Recreation table ($58). Color-keyed seatbelts ($18). Deluxe cargo area ($83-$126). Lockable side stowage compartment ($43). Luggage area trim ($36). Wheels: Full wheel covers ($30). Deluxe wheel covers ($63- $93). Tires: H78 x 15 BSW/WSW. J78 x 15 BSW/WSW. HR78 x 15 WSW. JR78 x 15 BSW/WSW. LR78 x 15 BSW/WSW.

THUNDERBIRD CONVENIENCE/APPEARANCE OPTIONS: Option Packages: Bordeaux luxury group ($624-$700). Creme/gold luxury group ($717-$793). Lipstick luxury group ($337-$546). Turnpike group ($180). Convenience group ($84). Protection group ($79-$87). Light group ($164). Power lock group ($86). Security lock group ($18). Comfort/Convenience: Auto-temp control air cond. ($88). Anti- theft alarm system ($84). Rear defroster, electric ($99). Windshield/rear window defroster, electric ($355). Fingertip speed control ($120). Tinted glass ($29-$66). Power mini-vent windows ($79). Six-way power driver's seat ($132); driver and passenger ($250). Power lumbar support seats ($86). Reclining passenger seat ($70). Automatic seatback release ($30). Tilt steering wheel ($68). Fuel monitor warning light ($20). Lighting and Mirrors: Cornering lamps ($43). Lighted driver's visor vanity mirror ($43). Entertainment: AM/FM stereo radio ($145); w/tape player ($249). AM/FM stereo search radio ($298). AM/FM quadrasonic radio w/tape player ($382). Power antenna ($39). Exterior: Power moonroof ($879); sunroof ($716). Starfire paint ($204). Wide color-keyed vinyl-insert bodyside molding ($121). Dual bodyside/hood paint stripes ($33). Interior: Leather trim ($239). Kasman cloth trim ($96). Super-soft vinyl seat trim ($55). Trunk dress-up ($59). Wheels: Deluxe wheel covers ($67). Simulated wire wheel covers ($88) exc. with creme/gold group ($163 credit). Deep-dish aluminum wheels ($251) exc. with Bordeaux/lipstick luxury group ($163). Tires: JR78 x 15 SBR WSW ($41). LR78 x 15 SBR wide WSW ($59). Space-saver spare ($86).

HISTORY: Introduced: October 3, 1975. Model year production: 1,861,537 (incl. Mustangs). Total production for the U.S. market of 1,714,258 units (incl. Mustangs) consisted of 342,434 four- cylinder, 390,750 sixes and 981,074 V-8s. Calendar year production (U.S.): 1,459,109 (incl. Mustangs). Calendar year sales by U.S. dealers: 1,682,583 (incl. Mustangs); total sales gave Ford a 19.9 percent share of the market. Model year sales by U.S. dealers: N/A. NOTE: Totals do not include Club Wagons.

Historical Footnotes: Ford sales had declined sharply in the 1975 model year, down over 21 percent. That left Ford with only a 22 percent market share. Full-size models had sold best. Even the success of the Granada (new for 1975) hadn't been as great as anticipated. Continuing their interest in small, economical cars, Ford had introduced Pinto Pony and Mustang II MPG models late in the 1975 model year. Sales swung upward again for the 1976 model year, even though few major changes were evident in the lineup. Part of the reason was Ford's new "California strategy," which offered special option packages for West Coast buyers only, in an attempt to take sales away from the imports. It proved quite successful this year. Prices took a sizable jump as the model year began, then were cut back in January. Production fell for Pinto, Mustang II and Maverick in the 1976 model year, but overall production zoomed up almost 19 percent—especially due to Granada demand. Model year sales followed a similar pattern, up 18.5 percent for the year. Major changes in Ford personnel had taken place late in the 1975 model year. Henry Ford II, Lee Iacocca and B.E. Bidwell were the top Ford executives. Pinto was once described as "a car nobody loved, but everybody bought." This was the last year of the allegedly unsafe Pinto gas tank and filler neck, which had resulted in a number of highly publicized and grotesque accident-caused fires that led to massive product-liability lawsuits. The new Maverick Stallion was meant to look like a '60s muscle car, but offered no more performance than other Mavericks. Granada, on the other hand, had proven to be one of the fastest Fords, at least with a "Windsor" 351 cu. in. V-8 under its hood.

1977 FORD

Biggest news for 1977 was the downsizing of Thunderbird (which had actually grown a bit in the past few years). Torino and Elite were dropped, and Pinto restyled with a sportier look. Maverick hung on for one more season without change, and nothing dramatic happened to Granada or LTD. Later in the model year, though, a new Abodied LTD II replaced the abandoned Torino. On the mechanical side, Dura-Spark ignition was supposed to help meet the more stringent emissions standards.

PINTO — FOUR/V-6 — Revised front and rear styling hit Ford's subcompact, offered again in two-door sedan, "three-door" Runabout and station wagon form. Up front was a new "soft" nose with sloping hood and flexible fender extension and stone deflector assembly. The new horizontal-bar crosshatch grille, made of rigid plastic, tilted backward. Twin vertical rectangular park/signal lamps stood on each side of the bright grille, with recessed round headlamps at the outside. Soft urethane headlamp housings were taller than before, but the grille itself was narrower. As in the previous design, 'Ford' letters stood above the grille. At the rear of the two-door sedan and three-door Runabout were new, larger horizontal dual-lens taillamps. New extruded anodized aluminum bumpers went on the front and rear. New body colors were added, and a new vinyl roof grain was available. Runabouts had a new optional all-glass third

1977 Pinto three-door Runabout (F)

door. Inside was new cloth trim, optional on the base high-back bucket seats. A new lower (2.73:1) rear axle ratio went with the standard OHC 140 cu. in. (2.3-liter) four-cylinder engine, which hooked up to a wide-ratio four-speed manual gearbox. The low-budget Pony came with rack-and-pinion steering, front disc brakes, all-vinyl or cloth/vinyl high-back front bucket seats, mini-console, color-keyed carpeting, and argent hubcaps. The base two-door sedan included a color-keyed instrument panel and steering wheel, bright backlight trim, plus bright drip and belt moldings. Runabouts had a fold-down rear seat, rear liftgate, and rubber mat on the load floor. All models except the Pony could have a 170.8 cu. in. (2.8- liter) V-6 instead of the four. Pinto got a shorter manual-transmission shift lever to speed up gear-changes. A new Sports option included a tachometer, ammeter and temperature gauge, new soft-rim sports steering wheel, front stabilizer bar, higher-rate springs, and higher axle ratio. A new Cruising Wagon, styled along the lines of the Econoline Cruising Van, aimed at youthful buyers. It included a front spoiler, blanked rear quarters with glass portholes, styled wheels, Sports Rallye equipment, and carpeted rear section. Other major new options included a flip-up removable sunroof, manual four-way bucket seat, Runabout cargo area cover, two-tone paint, simulated wire wheel covers, and high-altitude option. An Interior Decor Group included Alpine cloth plaid trim on low-back bucket seats.

1977 Maverick coupe (F)

MAVERICK — SIX/V-8 — For its final season, Maverick changed little except for some new body and interior colors, two new vinyl roof colors, and a new vinyl-insert bodyside molding. New options included wire wheel covers, four-way manual bucket seats, and high-altitude option. The optional 302 V-8 got a new variable-Venturi carburetor. All engines gained Dura-Spark ignition. There was also a new wide-ratio three-speed manual shift. Revised speedometers showed miles and kilometers. The Decor Group added a halo vinyl roof. Standard powerplant was the 200 cu. in. (3.3-liter) six; optional, either a 250 cu. in. six or 302 cu. in. V-8. Standard equipment included front disc brakes (manual), three-speed column-shift manual transmission, foot parking brake with warning light, and 19.2-gallon gas tank. The full- width bench seat had Random stripe cloth and vinyl trim. Also standard: color-keyed carpeting; armrests with door pull assist handle; flip-open rear quarter windows; bright hubcaps; and bright drip rail and wheel lip moldings.

1977 Granada sedan (JG)

GRANADA — SIX/V-8 — Styling of the Mercedes-emulating Granada remained similar to 1976, with nine new body colors available. According to Ford's catalog, that carryover design "Looks like cars costing three times as much." A new fully-synchronized four-speed manual transmission with overdrive fourth gear became standard, replacing the former three-speed. That made Granada the first domestic model to offer an overdrive four-speed as standard equipment (except in California,

1977 Granada Sports Coupe (F)

where it was unavailable). Actually, it was the old three-speed gearbox with an extra gear hooked on. Base engine was the 200 cu. in. (3.3-liter) inline six with Dura-Spark ignition. Also standard were front disc brakes, inside hood release, wiper/washer control on the turn signal lever, DR78 x 14 steel-belted radial tires, hood ornament, vinyl-trim bench seats, cigar lighter, and full wheel covers. The body sported window, drip, belt and wheel lip moldings. Two-doors displayed opera lamps. Granada Ghia added a left-hand remote-control mirror, wide color-keyed vinyl-insert bodyside moldings (integral with wheel lip moldings), flight bench seats, and unique wire-style wheel covers. Alternate engine choices were the 250 cu. in. inline six, 302 V-8, and 351 V-8. A new variable-Venturi carburetor for the 302 V-8 was used only in California. Four basic models were offered: Granada and Ghia two- and four-door sedans. A Sport Coupe package with odense-grain half-vinyl roof became available later. It included white-painted styled steel wheels with bright trim rings, louvered opera window applique, color-keyed lower back panel applique, and rubber bumper guards (front/rear) with wide rub strips. Sport Coupes also had new taillamp lenses with black surround moldings; black wiper arms and window moldings; color-keyed sport mirrors; leather-wrapped sports steering wheel; and reclining bucket seats in simulated perforated vinyl. New Granada options included four-way manual bucket seats, automatic-temperature-control air conditioning, illuminated entry, front cornering lamps, simulated wire wheel covers, white lacy-spoke cast aluminum wheels, wideband whitewall radials, electric trunk lid release, and high-altitude option.

1977 LTD II hardtop coupe (F)

LTD II — V-8 — Serving as a replacement for the abandoned Torino, the new A-bodied LTD II had similar dimensions, and long-hood styling that wasn't radically different. Wheelbase was 114 inches for the two-door, 118 inches for four-door models. Overall length ranged from 215.5 to 223.1 inches. The goal, according to Ford, was to combine "LTD's traditional high level of workmanship with Mustang's sporty spirit." A wide choice of models was offered: 'S', base and Brougham in two- door hardtop, four-door pillared hardtop or four-door wagon body styles (same selection as Torino). Wagons were offered only this year, and LTD II would last only into the 1979 model year. Among the more noticeable styling features were vertically-stacked quad rectangular headlamps, and doors with a straight beltline. Sharply-tapered opera windows on wide roof pillars stood to the rear of (and higher than) the regular quarter windows of two-doors (except for the 'S' model). Four-doors were also a six-window design. Wraparound parking/signal lamps were fendertip-mounted, and the hood ornament was new. The chrome-plated grille had a crosshatch pattern similar to the full-size LTD, but with a sharper peak. Angled, sharp-edged wraparound vertical tail-lamps stood at rear quarter panel tips. Inside, LTD II had new seat trim and new styles, plus new-look door trim and instrument cluster. Standard engine dropped from the 351 of the last Torino to a 302 V-8, now with Dura-Spark ignition and a lower axle ratio. Standard equipment on the budget-priced 'S' included SelectShift automatic transmission; power steering and brakes; coolant recovery system; and Kirsten cloth/vinyl bench seat. The basic LTD II had Ardmore cloth/vinyl flight bench seat, deluxe door trim, rear panel applique, hood ornament, and rocker panel and wheel lip moldings. The top-line Brougham added Doral cloth/vinyl split bench seats, dual horns, electric clock, dual accent paint stripes, and wide color- keyed vinyl-insert bodyside moldings. Standard engine was the 302 cu. in. V-8 with two-barrel carb (351 in California) hooked to SelectShift Cruise-O- Matic. Important new options included the opera windows, illuminated entry, day/date quartz clock, sports steering wheel, cornering lamps, monaural AM/FM radio, stereo radio with quadrasonic tape player, wide whitewall radials, wire wheel covers, and (for two-doors) a half-vinyl roof. Announced for mid-year introduction was a Brougham Creme/Blue package, offered in Creme or dark blue metallic body color with creme or blue vinyl roof. Creme vinyl split-bench seats had blue accent straps and welts.

LTD/CUSTOM 500 — V-8 — Rivals may have shrunk their big cars, but Ford's remained fully full-size once again. According to the factory, that gave LTD a "wider stance, and more road-hugging weight." New colors and fabrics entered LTD interiors this year, but not much else was different. Powertrain changes included improved 351 and 400 cu. in. V-8s with new Dura- Spark ignition, as well as lower rear axle ratios and standard coolant recovery system. New options included illuminated entry, quadrasonic tape player, simulated wire wheel covers, forged aluminum wheels, and wide whitewall radial tires. LTD Brougham was dropped, but the top-rung Landau model took over its position in the pricing lineup. Six basic models were available: LTD and Landau two- and four-door, LTD wagon, and Country Squire wagon. As in 1976, the Custom 500 was for fleet buyers only. LTD's front end looked similar to 1976.

1977 LTD Landau four-door pillared hardtop (F)

crosshatch grille had four horizontal divider bars and 15 vertical bars, with 'Ford' block letters across the upper header. Three-section wraparound parking/signal lamps stood at fender tips. Standard LTD equipment included a 351 cu. in. (5.8- liter) V-8 with Dura-Spark ignition, SelectShift automatic transmission, power brakes and steering, front bumper guards, Redondo cloth/vinyl bench seat, glovebox and ashtray lamps, hood ornament, and bright hubcaps. Vinyl-insert moldings highlighted door belt, drip, hood, rear, rocker panels, and wheel lips. Landau models added concealed headlamps, as well as an Ardmore cloth/vinyl flight bench seat, electric clock, half or full vinyl roof, rear bumper guards, full wheel covers, wide color-keyed bodyside moldings, and dual-note horn. A Landau Creme and Blue package was announced for mid- year, with choice of color combinations. Creme body color came with a creme or blue vinyl roof; dark blue body with creme or blue vinyl roof. Inside was a creme super-soft vinyl luxury group, and split bench seats with blue welts.

1977 Thunderbird Town Landau hardtop coupe (F)

THUNDERBIRD — V-8 — All-new sheetmetal and sharp downsizing to a 114 inch wheelbase helped concealed the fact that the shrunken Thunderbird was essentially an adaptation of the newly- introduced LTD II. Even if buyers noticed, they might not have cared, since T-Bird's price was also sharply cut by about $2700 from its 1976 level. However, this Thunderbird had less standard equipment and more options than before. Overall length was cut by 10 inches in this new "contemporary" package, ranking as mid- rather than full- size, but with the same six-passenger capacity. This year's side view was much different. A chrome wrapover roof molding with little beveled-glass opera windows stood on the wide, solid B-pillars between the door window and large far-rear coach window, with thin C-pillar. Both of those rear side windows sat higher than the door window. Distinctive features also included concealed headlamps behind large flip-up doors, and functional fender louvers. The chrome-plated crosshatch grille with bright surround molding was similar to the prior design, but with dominant horizontal bars. Park/signal lenses stood at front fender tips. At the rear were new tall, full-width taillamps and a sculptured decklid. A 'Thunderbird' nameplate stood on the deck section that extended down between the taillamps. The hinged grille's lower edge was designed to swing rearward under impact, to avoid damage from slow-speed collision. A smaller engine was installed this year: the 302 cu. in. (5.0-liter) V-8 with new Dura-Spark ignition; but California buyers got a 351 V-8. Both the 351 and 400 cu. in. V-8s were optional. To improve handling, Thunderbird had higher-rate rear springs, larger front stabilizer bar, and standard rear stabilizer bar. Standard fittings included HR78x15 steel-belted radial tires, SelectShift automatic transmission, power steering and brakes, coolant recovery system, Wilshire cloth/vinyl bench seats, AM radio, electric clock, wheel covers, and hood ornament. Moldings for roof wrapover, wheel lips, rocker panels, hood rear, and belt also were standard. Inside was a new five-pod instrument cluster with European-type graphics and simulated burled woodgrain. Sew style of the standard bench seat was new, with optional split-bench and bucket seats. Town Landau added an aluminum roof wrapover applique; unique stripes on upper bodysides, hood/grille opening panel, headlamp doors and decklid; accent paint on wheels and fender louvers; die-cast hood ornament with color-coordinated acrylic insert; and 'Town Landau' script silk-screened on opera windows. Also included: turbine-spoke cast aluminum wheels, dual sport mirrors, cornering lamps, Town Landau plaque at the right of the instrument panel, and an owner's nameplate in 22K gold finish. Major new options included an illuminated entry system, day/date quartz clock, leather-wrapped sports steering wheel, console, turbine-style cast aluminum wheels, automatic- temperature air conditioning, and front and rear vinyl roof. An optional Exterior Decor Group could accent T-Bird's wrapover roof treatment. An Interior Decor Group contained Ardmore and Kasman Knit cloth upholstery, fold-down center armrests, reclining passenger seat, passenger visor vanity mirror, and color-keyed seatbelts. A Silver/Lipstick feature package, announced for mid- year, featured Silver metallic or Lipstick Red body color with Silver or Lipstick Red vinyl roof. Inside was a Dove Grey all-vinyl decor group with either split-bench or bucket seats, with Lipstick Red accent straps and welts, Dove Grey door and quarter trim, and Lipstick carpet molding.

I.D. DATA: As before, Ford's 11-symbol Vehicle Identification Number (VIN) is stamped on a metal tab fastened to the instrument panel, visible through the windshield. Coding is similar to 1976. Model year code changed to '7' for 1977. Code 'Y' for Wixom assembly plant was dropped. One engine code was added: 'Q' modified V8351 2Bbl.

PINTO (FOUR/V-6)

Model Number	Body/Style Number	Body Type & Seating	Factory Price	Shipping Weight	Production Total
10	62B	2-dr. Sedan-4P	3237/3519	2315/2438	48,863
10	62B	2-dr. Pony Sed-4P	3099/--	2313/--	Note 1
11	64B	2-dr. Hatch-4P	3353/3635	2351/24/4	74,237
12	73B	2-dr. Sta Wag-4P	3548/3830	2515/2638	79,449
12	73B	2-dr. Sqr Wag-4P	3891/4172	2552/2675	Note 2

Note 1: Pony production included in base sedan figure. **Note 2:** Squire Wagon production is included in standard station wagon total. **Pinto Production Note:** Totals include 22,548 Pintos produced as 1978 models but sold as 1977 models (6,599 two-door sedans, 8,271 hatchback Runabouts, and 7,678 station wagons).

MAVERICK (SIX/V-8)

91	62A	2-dr. Sedan-4P	3322/3483	2782/2947	40,086
92	54A	4-dr. Sedan-5P	3395/3556	2887/3052	58,420

GRANADA (SIX/V-8)

82	66H	2-dr. Sedan-5P	4022/4209	3124/3219	157,612
81	54H	4-dr. Sedan-5P	4118/4305	3174/3269	163,071

GRANADA GHIA (SIX/V-8)

84	66K	2-dr. Sedan-5P	4452/4639	3175/3270	34,166
83	54K	4-dr. Sedan-5P	4548/4735	3229/3324	35,730

LTD II (V-8)

30	65D	2-dr. HT Cpe-6P	4785	3789	57,449
31	53D	4-dr. Pill. HT-6P	4870	3904	56,704
42	71D	4-dr. Sta Wag-6P	5064	4404	23,237
43	71K	4-dr. Squire Wag-6P	5335	4430	17,162

LTD II 'S' (V-8)

25	65B	2-dr. HT Cpe-6P	4528	3789	9,531
27	53B	4-dr. Pill. HT-6P	4579	3894	18,775
40	71B	4-dr. Sta Wag-6P	4806	4393	9,636

LTD II BROUGHAM (V-8)

32	65K	2-dr. HT Cpe-6P	5121	3898	20,979
33	53K	4-dr. Pill. HT-6P	5206	3930	18,851

CUSTOM 500 (V-8)

52	60D	2-dr. Pill. HT-6P	N/A	N/A	4,139
53	53D	4-dr. Pill. HT-6P	N/A	N/A	5,582
72	71D	4-dr. Ranch Wag-6P	N/A	N/A	1,406

LTD (V-8)

62	60H	2-dr. Pill. HT-6P	5128	4190	73,637
63	53H	4-dr. Pill. HT-6P	5152	4240	160,255
74	71H	4-dr. Sta Wag-6P	5415	4635	90,711
76	71K	4-dr. Ctry Sqr-6P	5866	4674	Note 3

Note 3: Country Squire production, and that of wagons with dual-facing rear seats (a $134 option for both standard and Country Squire wagon), is included in basic wagon totals.

LTD LANDAU (V-8)

65	60L	2-dr. Pill. HT-6P	5717	4270	44,396
64	53L	4-dr. Pill. HT-6P	5742	4319	65,030

THUNDERBIRD (V-8)

87	60H	2-dr. HT Cpe-6P	5063	3907	318,140

THUNDERBIRD TOWN LANDAU (V-8)

87	60H	2-dr. HT Cpe-6P	7990	4104	Note 4

Note 4: Town Landau production is included in basic Thunderbird total.

FACTORY PRICE AND WEIGHT NOTE: For Maverick and Granada, prices and weights to left of slash are for six-cylinder, to right for V-8 engine. For Pinto, prices and weights to left of slash are for four-cylinder, to right for V-6 engine.

ENGINE DATA: BASE FOUR (Pinto): Inline. Overhead cam. Four-cylinder. Cast iron block and head. Displacement: 140 cu. in. (2.3 liters). Bore & stroke: 3.78 x 3.13 in. Compression ratio: 9.0:1. Brake horsepower: 89 at 4800 R.P.M. Torque: 120 lbs.-ft. at 3000 R.P.M. Five main bearings. Hydraulic valve lifters. Carburetor: 2Bbl. Motorcraft 5200. VIN Code: Y. OPTIONAL V-6 (Pinto): 60-degree, overhead-valve V-6. Cast iron block and head. Displacement: 170.8 cu. in. (2.8 liters). Bore & stroke: 3.66 x 2.70 in. Compression ratio: 8.7:1. Brake horsepower: 93 at 4200 R.P.M. Torque: 140 lbs.-ft. at 2600 R.P.M. Four main bearings. Solid valve lifters. Carburetor: 2Bbl. Motorcraft 2150. VIN Code: Z. BASE SIX (Maverick, Granada): Inline. Overhead valve. Six-cylinder. Cast iron block and head. Displacement: 200 cu. in. (3.3 liters). Bore & stroke: 3.68 x 3.13 in. Compression ratio: 8.5:1. Brake horsepower: 96 at 4400 R.P.M. Torque: 151 lbs.-ft. at 2000 R.P.M. Seven main bearings. Hydraulic valve lifters. Carburetor: 1Bbl. Carter YFA. VIN Code: T. BASE SIX (Granada Ghia); OPTIONAL (Maverick, Granada): Inline. Overhead valve. Six-cylinder. Cast iron block and head. Displacement: 250 cu. in. (4.1 liters). Bore & stroke: 3.68 x 3.91 in. Compression ratio: 8.1:1. Brake horsepower: 98 at 3400 R.P.M. Torque: 182 lbs.-ft. at 1800 R.P.M. Seven main bearings. Hydraulic valve lifters. Carburetor: 1Bbl. Carter YFA. VIN Code: L. BASE V-8 (LTD II, Thunderbird); OPTIONAL (Maverick, Granada): 90-degree, overhead valve V-8. Cast iron block and head. Displacement: 302 cu. in. (5.0 liters). Bore & stroke: 4.00 x 3.00 in. Compression ratio: 8.4:1. Brake horsepower: 130-137 at 3400-3600 R.P.M. (some Granadas, 122 at 3200). Torque: 243-245 lbs.-ft. at 1600-1800 R.P.M. (some Granadas, 237 at 1600). Five main bearings. Hydraulic valve lifters. Carburetor: 2Bbl. Motorcraft 2150. VIN Code: F. NOTE: Horsepower and torque ratings of the 302 V 8 varied slightly, according to model. OPTIONAL V-8 (LTD II, Thunderbird): 90-degree, overhead valve V-8. Cast iron block and head. Displacement: 351 cu. in. (5.8 liters). Bore & stroke: 4.00 x 3.50 in. Compression ratio: 8.3:1. Brake horsepower: 149 at 3200 R.P.M. Torque: 291 lbs.-ft. at 1600 R.P.M. Five main bearings. Hydraulic valve lifters. Carburetor: 2Bbl. Motorcraft 2150. Windsor engine. VIN Code: H. OPTIONAL V-8 (Granada): Same as 351 cu. in. V-8 above, but Brake H.P.: 135 at 3200 R.P.M. Torque: 275 lbs.-ft. at 1600 R.P.M. BASE V-8 (LTD II wagon, LTD); OPTIONAL (Granada Ghia, LTD II, Thunderbird): Same as 351 cu. in. V-8 above, but Compression: 8.0:1. Brake H.P.: 161 at 3600 R.P.M. Torque: 285 lbs.-ft. at 1800 R.P.M. VIN Code: Q. BASE V-8 (LTD wagon); OPTIONAL (LTD II, Thunderbird, LTD): 90-degree, overhead valve V-8. Cast iron block and head. Displacement: 400 cu. in. (6.6 liters). Bore & stroke: 4.00 x 4.00 in. Compression ratio: 8.0:1. Brake horsepower: 173 at 3800 R.P.M. Torque: 326 lbs.-ft. at 1600 R.P.M. Five main bearings. Hydraulic valve lifters. Carburetor: 2Bbl. Motorcraft 2150. VIN Code: S. OPTIONAL V-8 (LTD): 90-degree, overhead valve V-8. Cast iron block and head. Displacement: 460 cu. in. (7.5 liters). Bore & stroke: 4.36 x 3.85 in. Compression ratio: 8.0:1. Brake horsepower: 197 at 4000 R.P.M. Torque: 353 lbs.-ft. at 2000 R.P.M. Five main bearings. Hydraulic valve lifters. Carburetor: 4Bbl. Motorcraft 4350. VIN Code: A.

Note: A Police 460 cu. in. V-8 was also available for LTD.

CHASSIS DATA: Wheelbase: (Pinto) 94.5 in.; (Pinto wag) 94.8 in.; (Maverick 2dr.) 103.0 in.; (Maverick 4dr.) 109.9 in.; (Granada) 109.9 in.; (LTD II 2dr.) 114.0 in.; (LTD II 4dr./wag) 118.0 in.; (Custom 500/LTD) 121.0 in.; (TBird) 114.0 in. Overall Length: (Pinto) 169.0 in.; (Pinto wag) 178.8 in.; (Maverick 2dr.) 187.0 in.; (Maverick 4dr.) 193.9 in.; (Granada) 197.7 in.; (LTD II 2dr.) 215.5 in.; (LTD II 4dr.) 219.5 in.; (LTD II wag) 223.1 in.; (LTD) 224.1 in.; (LTD wag) 225.6 in.; (TBird) 215.5 in. Height: (Pinto) 50.6 in.; (Pinto wag) 52.0 in.; (Maverick) 53.4-53.5 in.; (Granada) 53.2-53.5 in.; (LTD II 2dr.) 52.6 in.; (LTD II 4dr.) 53.3 in.; (LTD II wag) 54.9 in.; (LTD 2dr.) 53.8 in.; (LTD 4dr.) 54.8 in.; (LTD wag) 56.7 in.; (TBird) 53.0 in. Width: (Pinto) 69.4 in.; (Pinto wag) 69.7 in.; (Maverick) 70.5 in.; (Granada) 74.0 in.; (Granada 4dr.) 74.5 in.; (LTD II) 78.0 in.; (LTD II wag) 79.6 in.; (LTD) 79.5 in.; (LTD wag) 79.9 in.; (TBird) 78.5 in. Front Tread: (Pinto) 55.0 in.; (Maverick) 56.5 in.; (Granada) 59.0 in.; (LTD II) 63.6 in. (LTD) 64.1 in. (TBird) 63.2 in. Rear Tread: (Pinto) 55.8 in.; (Maverick) 56.5 in.; (Granada) 57.7 in.; (LTD II) 63.5 in.; (LTD) 64.3 in. (TBird) 63.1 in. Standard Tires: (Pinto) A78 x 13; (Maverick) C78 x 14, except DR78 x 14 w/V-8 engine; (Granada) DR78 x 14 SBR BSW; (LTD II) HR78 x 14 SBR; (LTD) HR78 x 15 exc. wagon, JR78 x 15; (TBird) HR78 x 15 SBR BSW.

TECHNICAL: Transmission: Three-speed manual transmission (column shift) standard on Maverick. Gear ratios: (1st) 3.56:1; (2nd) 1.90:1; (3rd) 1.00:1; (Rev) 3.78:1. Four-speed overdrive manual standard on Granada: (1st) 3.29:1; (2nd) 1.84:1; (3rd) 1.00:1; (4th) 0.81:1; (Rev) 3.29:1. Four-speed floor shift standard on Pinto: (1st) 3.98:1; (2nd) 2.14:1; (3rd) 1.42:1; (4th) 1.00:1; (Rev) 3.99:1. Pinto station wagon: (1st) 3.65:1; (2nd) 1.97:1; (3rd) 1.37:1; (4th) 1.00:1; (Rev) 3.66:1. Select-Shift three-speed automatic standard on other models, optional on all. Pinto automatic gear ratios: (1st) 2.46-2.47:1; (2nd) 1.46-1.47:1; (3rd) 1.00:1; (Rev) 2.11:1 or 2.19:1. Maverick/Granada/LTD II/LTD/TBird gear ratios: (1st) 2.46:1; (2nd) 1.46:1; (3rd) 1.00:1; (Rev) 2.14:1 to 2.19:1. LTD II/LTD/TBird w/V8351 or V8400: (1st) 2.40:1; (2nd) 1.47:1; (3rd) 1.00:1; (Rev) 2.00:1. Standard final drive ratio: (Pinto four) 2.73:1 w/4spd, 3.18:1 w/auto.; (Pinto V-6) 3.00:1; (Maverick) 2.79:1 or 3.00:1; (Granada) 3.00:1 or 3.4:1; (LTD II) 2.50:1; (LTD) 2.47:1; (TBird) 2.50:1 exc. w/V8400, 3.00:1. Steering: (Pinto) rack and pinion; (others) recirculating ball. Front Suspension: (Pinto) coil springs with short/long control arms, lower leading arms, and anti-sway bar on wagon; (others) coil springs with control arms, lower trailing links and anti-sway bar. Rear Suspension: (Pinto/Maverick/Granada) rigid axle w/semi- elliptic leaf springs; (LTD II/Thunderbird) rigid axle w/lower trailing radius arms, upper oblique torque arms, coil springs and anti-sway bar; (LTD) rigid axle w/lower trailing radius arms, upper torque arms and coil springs, three-link w/track bar. Brakes: Front disc, rear drum; four-wheel discs available on Granada and LTD. Ignition: Electronic. Body construction: (Pinto/Maverick/Granada) unibody; (LTD II/LTD/TBird) separate body and perimeter box frame. Fuel tank: (Pinto) 13 gal.; (Pinto wag) 14 gal.; (Maverick/Granada) 19.2 gal.; (LTD II) 26 gal. exc. wag, 21.3 gal.; (LTD) 24.2 gal. exc. wagon, 21 gal.; (TBird) 26.5 gal.

DRIVETRAIN OPTIONS: Engines: 170 cu. in. V-6: Pinto ($289). 250 cu. in., 1Bbl. six: Maverick/Granada ($102). 302 cu. in., 2Bbl. V-8: Maverick ($161); Granada ($164). 351 cu. in., 2Bbl. V-8: Granada ($212); LTD II/TBird ($66). 400 cu. in., 2Bbl. V-8: LTD II/TBird ($155); LTD II wagon ($100); LTD ($107). 460 cu. in., 4Bbl. V-8: LTD ($297); LTD wagon ($189). Transmission/Differential: SelectShift Cruise-O-Matic: Pinto ($196); Maverick/Granada ($259). Floor shift lever: Granada ($28). Traction-Lok differential: LTD ($57); TBird ($54). Optional axle ratio: Pinto ($14); TBird ($14); LTD ($16). Power Accessories: Power brakes: Pinto ($58); Maverick ($57); Granada ($60). Four-wheel power disc brakes: Granada ($222); LTD ($180). Power steering: Pinto ($124); Maverick/Granada ($131). Suspension: H.D. susp.: Maverick ($17); Granada ($38); LTD ($20). Handling susp.: TBird ($79). H.D. handling susp.: LTD II ($9-$33). Adjustable air shock absorbers: LTD ($46). Other: H.D. battery: Pinto/Maverick ($16); LTD II/TBird ($17); LTD ($18). H.D. alternator: LTD II/TBird ($45). Trailer towing pkg. (heavy duty): LTD II ($93-$151); LTD ($125); TBird ($138). California emission system: Maverick/Granada ($48); LTD ($53); TBird ($70). High- altitude option: Pinto/Maverick/Granada ($39); LTD ($42); TBird ($22).

PINTO CONVENIENCE/APPEARANCE OPTIONS: Option Packages: Cruising wagon option, incl. bodyside tape stripe ($416). Sports rallye pkg. ($89). Exterior decor group ($122-$128). Interior decor group ($160). Convenience light group ($73-$108). Deluxe bumper group ($65). Protection group ($122-$142). Comfort/Convenience: Air conditioner ($446). Rear defroster, electric ($73). Tinted glass ($48). Dual sport mirrors ($45). Entertainment: AM radio ($76); w/stereo tape player ($204). AM/FM radio ($135). AM/FM stereo radio ($184). Exterior: Sunroof, manual ($243). Flip-up open air roof ($147). Half vinyl roof ($133). Glass third door ($13). Metallic glow paint ($58). Two-tone paint/tape treatment ($5- $51). Special paint/tape w/luggage rack: cruising wag ($58). Black narrow vinyl-insert bodyside moldings ($37). Roof luggage rack ($80). Rocker panel moldings ($20). Interior: Four-way driver's seat ($33). Load floor carpet ($23). Cargo area cover ($30). Wheels: Wire wheel covers ($79-$119). Forged aluminum wheels ($57-$183). Styled steel wheels ($98-$127). Wheel covers ($29). Tires: A78 x 13 WSW. A70 x 13 RWL. B78 x 13 BSW/WSW. BR78 x 13 BSW/WSW. BR70 x 13 RWL.

MAVERICK CONVENIENCE/APPEARANCE OPTIONS: Option Packages: Exterior decor group ($105). Interior decor group ($112). Deluxe bumper group ($65). Convenience group ($49-$67). Protection group ($34-$41). Light group ($36). Comfort/Convenience: Air cond. ($446). Rear defogger ($42). Tinted glass ($47-$63). Dual sport mirrors ($14-$27). Entertainment: AM radio ($76); w/tape player ($204). AM/FM radio ($135). AM/FM stereo radio ($222); w/tape player ($317). Exterior: Vinyl roof ($100). Metallic glow paint ($58). Wide vinyl-insert bodyside moldings ($64). Bumper guards, front and rear ($36). Interior: Four-way reclining driver's bucket seat ($33). Reclining vinyl bucket seats ($129). Cloth reclining bucket seats ($25). Vinyl seat trim ($27). Wheels: Wire wheel covers ($86-$119). Lacy spoke aluminum wheels ($218-$251). Styled steel wheels ($100-$131). Tires: C78 x 14 WSW ($33). CR78 x 14 SBR BSW ($89). CR78 x 14 SBR WSW ($121). DR78 x 14 SBR BSW ($89-$112). DR78 x 14 SBR WSW ($121-$144). Space-saver spare ($14) except (NC) with radial tires.

GRANADA CONVENIENCE/APPEARANCE OPTIONS: Option Packages: Sports coupe option ($483-$511). Interior decor group ($192). Luxury decor group ($618). Convenience group ($34-$80). Deluxe bumper group ($65). Light group ($27- $40). Cold weather group ($18-$64). Heavy-duty group ($16- $48). Protection group ($25-$41). Visibility group ($33-$49). Comfort/Convenience: Air cond. ($464); auto-temp ($505). Rear defogger ($46). Rear defroster, electric ($81). Fingertip speed control ($102). Illuminated entry system ($49). Power windows ($101-$141). Power door locks ($66-$93). Power decklid release ($17). Power four-way seat ($127). Tinted glass ($49). Tilt steering wheel ($58). Digital clock ($42). Lighting and Mirrors: Cornering lamps ($42). Dual sport mirrors ($30-$45). Lighted right visor vanity mirror ($42). Entertainment: AM radio ($76); w/tape player ($204). AM/FM radio ($151). AM/FM stereo radio ($222); w/tape player ($317). Exterior: Power moonroof ($833). Full or half vinyl roof ($108). Metallic glow paint ($58). Bodyside/decklid paint stripes ($28). Bodyside/decklid accent moldings ($29). Black vinyl insert bodyside moldings ($37). Rocker panel moldings ($20). Decklid luggage rack ($54). Interior: Console ($69). Four-way driver's seat ($33). Reclining seats ($64). Leather seat trim ($192). Cloth bench seat ($12). Cloth flight bench seat ($19). Deluxe cloth seat/door trim ($93). Color-keyed seatbelts ($18). Wheels: Deluxe wheel covers ($20) exc. Ghia (NC). Wire wheel covers ($65-$86). Styled steel wheels w/trim rings ($81- $101). Lacy spoke cast aluminum wheels ($119-$219). Tires: DR78 x 14 SBR WSW. ER78 x 14 SBR BSW/WSW. FR78 x 14 SBR BSW/WSW/wide WSW. Space-saver spare (NC).

1977 LTD Country Squire wagon (JG)

LTD II CONVENIENCE/APPEARANCE OPTIONS: Option Packages: Squire Brougham option ($203). Sports instrumentation group ($103-$130). Exterior decor group ($225-$276). Accent group ($58). Deluxe bumper group ($72). Light group ($46-$49). Convenience group ($101-$132). Power lock group ($92-$125). Comfort/Convenience: Air cond. ($505); w/auto-temp control ($546). Rear defroster, electric ($87). Fingertip speed control ($93-$114). Illuminated entry system ($51). Tinted glass ($57). Power windows ($114-$158). Power tailgate window: wag ($43). Six-way power seat ($143). Leather-wrapped steering wheel ($39-$61). Tilt steering wheel ($63). Day/date clock ($20-$39). Lighting and Mirrors: Cornering lamps ($43). Remote driver's mirror, chrome ($14). Dual sport mirrors ($51). Entertainment: AM radio ($72). AM/FM radio ($132). AM/FM stereo radio ($192); w/tape player ($266); w/quadrasonic tape player ($399). AM/FM stereo search radio ($349). Dual rear speakers ($43). Exterior: Full vinyl roof ($111-$162). Half vinyl roof ($111). Opera windows ($51). Vinyl-insert bodyside moldings ($39). Metallic glow paint ($62). Two-tone paint ($49-$88). Dual accent paint stripes ($30). Luggage rack ($100). Interior: Bucket seats w/console ($158) exc. Brougham (NC). Rear-facing third seat: wag ($100). Vinyl seat trim ($22). Color-keyed seatbelts ($18). Wheels: Deluxe wheel covers ($36). Luxury wheel covers ($59- $95). Wire wheel covers ($99). Turbine spoke cast aluminum wheels ($234-$270). Tires: H78 x 14 SBR WSW ($45). HR78 x 14 wide-band WSW ($16- $61). JR78 x 14 SBR WSW ($26-$71). HR78 x 15 SBR WSW ($45).

LTD CONVENIENCE/APPEARANCE OPTIONS: Option Packages: Landau luxury group ($403-$563). Convenience group ($88-$136). Light group ($36-$38). Deluxe bumper group ($43-$63). Protection group ($50-$59). Comfort/Convenience: Air cond. ($514); w/auto-temp control ($600). Rear defogger ($46). Rear defroster, electric ($88). Fingertip speed control ($92-$113). Illuminated entry system ($54). Power windows ($114-$170). Power mini-vent and side windows ($246). Power door locks ($72-$116). Six-way power driver's seat ($139); driver and passenger ($275). Tinted glass ($68). Tilt steering wheel ($63). Electric clock ($20). Digital clock ($26-$46). Lighting and Mirrors: Cornering lamps ($46). Driver's remote mirror ($16). Lighted visor vanity mirror ($42-$46). Entertainment: AM radio ($83). AM/FM radio ($147). AM/FM stereo radio ($242); w/tape player ($346); w/quadrasonic tape player ($450). AM/FM stereo search radio ($409). Dual rear speakers ($42). Exterior: Full vinyl roof ($134) exc. Landau two-door (NC). Half vinyl roof ($134). Fender skirts ($45). Metallic glow paint ($63). Dual accent paint stripes ($30). Rocker panel moldings ($28). Vinyl-insert bodyside moldings ($43). Rear bumper guards ($20). Luggage rack ($101). Interior: Dual-facing rear seats: wagon ($134). Split bench seat w/passenger recliner ($149). Leather seat trim ($236). All-vinyl seat trim ($24). Duraweave vinyl trim ($59). Color-keyed seatbelts ($20). Lockable side storage compartment ($46). Wheels: Full wheel covers ($32). Deluxe wheel covers ($67-$99) Wire wheel covers ($105-$137). Deep-dish aluminum wheels ($251-$283). Tires: HR78 x 15 SBR WSW. JR78 x 15 SBR BSW/WSW/wide WSW. LR78 x 15 SBR WSW.

THUNDERBIRD CONVENIENCE/APPEARANCE OPTIONS: Option Packages: Interior luxury group ($724). Exterior decor group ($317-$368). Interior decor group ($299). Deluxe bumper group ($72). Instrumentation group ($103-$111). Convenience group ($88-$96). Protection group ($43-$47). Light group ($46). Power lock group ($92). Comfort/Convenience: Air cond. ($505); auto-temp ($546). Rear defroster, electric ($87). Fingertip speed control ($93- $114). Illuminated entry system ($51). Tinted glass ($61). Power windows ($114). Six-way power seat ($143). Automatic seatback release ($32). Leather-wrapped steering wheel ($39- $61). Tilt steering wheel ($63). Day/date clock ($20). Lighting and Mirrors: Cornering lamps ($43). Driver's remote mirror, chrome ($14). Dual sport mirrors ($51). Lighted passenger visor vanity mirror ($42-$46). Entertainment: AM/FM radio ($59). AM/FM stereo radio ($120); w/tape player ($193); w/quadrasonic tape player ($326). AM/FM stereo search radio ($276). AM radio delete ($72 credit). Dual rear speakers ($43). Exterior: Power moonroof ($888). Vinyl roof, two-piece ($132). Metallic glow paint ($62). Two-tone paint ($49). Bright wide bodyside moldings ($39). Black vinyl-insert bodyside moldings ($39). Wide color-keyed vinyl-insert bodyside moldings ($51). Dual accent paint stripes ($39).

Interior: Bucket seats w/console ($158) exc. (NC) w/decor group. Leather seat trim ($241). Vinyl seat trim ($22). Color-keyed seatbelts ($18). Wheels: Wire wheel covers ($99) exc. w/decor group ($47 credit). Turbine spoke aluminum wheels ($88-$234). Tires: HR78 x 15 SBR WSW ($45). HR78 x 15 SBR wide WSW ($61). HR70 x 15 SBR WSW ($67). Space-saver spare (NC).

HISTORY: Introduced: October 1, 1976. Model year production: 1,840,427 (incl. Mustangs). Total passenger-car production for the U.S. market of 1,703,945 units (incl. Mustangs) included 236,880 four-cylinder, 262,840 sixes and 1,184,225 V-8s. Calendar year production (U.S.): 1,714,783 (incl. Mustangs). Calendar year sales by U.S. dealers: 1,824,035 (incl. Mustangs). Model year sales by U.S. dealers: 1,749,529 (incl. Mustangs).

NOTE: Totals above do not include Club Wagons, of which 32,657 were sold in the model year.

Historical Footnotes: Both the new LTD II and the shrunken Thunderbird were meant to rival Chevrolet's Monte Carlo and Pontiac Grand Prix. Far more T-Birds came off the line for 1977 than had their predecessors the year before: 301,787 of the new downsized versions versus just 48,196 of the '76 biggies. While Thunderbird's price was cut dramatically this year, LTD cost nearly 7 percent more than in 1976. Since gasoline prices weren't rising, Ford's lineup of relatively small cars wasn't doing as well as hoped. Slight price cuts of smaller models, after their 1977 introduction, didn't help. As a result, plants producing smaller Fords shut down nearly two months earlier for the '78 changeover than did those turning out full-size models. During the model year, Maverick production halted, to be replaced by the new Fairmont compact. A UAW strike against Ford during the model year didn't affect production much, as it was nearly identical to 1976 output. Since the California strategy of special models available on the West coast had been successful the year before, Ford continued that approach.

1978 FORD

Ford's diamond jubilee (75th anniversary) was celebrated for an entire year, topped off by the Diamond Jubilee Edition Thunderbird. New this year was the compact Fairmont, replacing the Maverick which had not been selling well. Granada gained a restyle for the first time since its 1975 debut. Thunderbird now offered a sports decor package. A Pulse Air or Thermactor II emissions control device replaced the complicated standard Thermactor air pump system.

1978 Pinto three-door hatchback (F)

PINTO — FOUR/V-6 — New body and interior colors made up most of the changes in Ford's rear-drive subcompact model. Pintos now carried split-cushion "bucket" style rear seats. New options included white-painted forged aluminum wheels and an accent stripe treatment in four color combinations. New interior colors were jade, tangerine and blue. Seven body colors were available, as well as vinyl roofs in jade or chamois. Pinto's model lineup was the same as before: two-door sedan, three-door hatchback Runabout, and station wagon. Base engine remained the 140 cu. in. (2.3-liter) overhead-cam four, with four-speed manual gearbox. The optional 2.8-liter V-6 engine got a new lightweight plastic fan. Optional power rack-and-pinion steering added a new variable-ratio system similar to that used on Fairmont/Zephyr. A Sports Rallye Package included a tachometer, sport steering wheel, front stabilizer bar, heavy-duty suspension, and 3.18:1 axle. The Rallye Appearance package contained dual racing mirrors, black front spoiler, gold accent stripes, and blacked-out exterior moldings. The Cruising Wagon option returned, with front spoiler, graphic multi-colored paint striping, cargo area carpeting, styled steel wheels, dual sport mirrors, and steel side panels with round tinted porthole windows near the rear. At mid-year a panel delivery Pinto was added, with full-length flat cargo floor and metal side panels. Most regular production options were available on the panel Pinto (plus a rear-window security screen).

1978 Fairmont sedan (JG)

FAIRMONT — FOUR/SIX/V-8 — With the demise of Maverick came a new, more modern compact model. Fairmont and Zephyr (its corporate twin from Mercury) shared the new unitized "Fox" body/chassis platform which began development in the early 1970s and would later carry a number of other FoMoCo models. Fairmont was designed with an emphasis on efficiency and fuel economy, achieved by means of reduced weight and improved aerodynamics. At the same time, Ford wanted to make the best use of interior space, combining the economy of a compact with the spaciousness of a mid-size. Fairmont also offered easy serviceability and maintenance, with a roomy engine compartment and good accessibility. Styling was influenced by Ford's Ghia design studios in Turin, Italy, with clean, straightforward lines. Zephyr differed only in grille design and trim details. The standard Fairmont grille had two horizontal bars and one vertical divider over a subdued crosshatch pattern. Single rectangular headlamps flanked vertical rectangular signal lamps. A single bright molding surrounded the headlamps, park/signal lamps, and grille. Taillamps contained integral backup lamps. Doors and front seatbacks were thinner than Maverick's.

1978 Fairmont Futura Sport Coupe (F)

Fairmont also had a higher roofline and lower beltline. Under the chassis was a new suspension system using MacPherson struts and coil springs up front, and four-link coil spring design at the rear. Front coil springs were mounted on lower control arms instead of around the struts, as in other applications. Rack-and-pinion steering could have unique variable-ratio power assist at extra cost. Base engine was the 140 cu. in. (2.3-liter) "Lima" four, as used in Pintos and Mustangs—the first four-cylinder powerplant in a domestic Ford compact. Options included a 250 cu. in. (3.3-liter) inline six and 302 cu. in. (5.0-liter) V-8. A four-speed manual gearbox was standard, but V-8 models required automatic. Four-cylinder models had standard low- back bucket seats, while sixes and eights held a bench seat. Bodies sported bright grille, headlamp and parking lamp bezels; plus bright windshield, backlight and drip moldings. Standard equipment included B78 x 14 blackwall tires, hubcaps, and bright left-hand mirror. Wagons had CR78 x 14 tires. Wheelbase was 105.5 inches. The opening model lineup included two- and four-door sedans and a station wagon. An ES option (Euro styled), added later, displayed a blacked-out grille and cowl grille, rear quarter window louvers, black window frames and lower back panel, and turbine-spoked wheel covers. Also included: a sports steering wheel, color-keyed interior trim, and unique black instrument panel with gray engine turnings. Its specially-tuned suspension included a rear stabilizer bar. Vent louvers were also available as an individual option. A different looking Futura Sport Coupe, with roofline reminiscent of Thunderbird, joined the original sedans and wagon in December, touted as a sporty luxury model. Futura's unique styling features included quad rectangular headlamps above rectangular parking lamps, a large-pattern crosshatch grille, hood ornament, bright window frames, slanted rear end with wraparound taillamps, wide wrapover roof design, and horizontal louvers in center roof pillars. The coupe, which borrowed a subtitle formerly used on the 1960s Falcon, also added accent paint striping, black luggage area, full-length vinyl bodyside moldings with bright inserts, bright belt moldings, wheel lip moldings, and deluxe wheel covers. Inside, the five-passenger Futura had pleated vinyl bucket seats, woodtone appliques on the dash, and color-keyed seatbelts. William P. Benton, Ford's vice-president (and Ford Division General Manager) said Fairmont Futura "has the best fuel economy in its class, leg, shoulder and hip room of a mid-size car, and responsive handling, plus a rich new look and an array of luxury touches." Four-cylinder powered, with four-speed manual shift, it could deliver 26 MPG on the EPA scale. Options included a divided vinyl roof and seven two- tone combinations, plus color-keyed turbine wheel covers.

GRANADA — SIX/V-8 — Granada and its twin, the Mercury Monarch, took on a fresh look this year with new bright grilles, rectangular headlamps, parking lamps, front bumper air spoiler, wide wheel lip moldings, new wraparound taillamps, and lower back panel appliques. Also new on two-doors were "twindow" opera windows split by a bright center bar. This was the first major restyle since the pair's 1974 debut, and the first quad rectangular headlamps in the Ford camp. The spoiler and hood-to-grille-opening panel seal, and revised decklid surface, helped reduce aerodynamic drag. The new crosshatch grille showed a tight pattern, split into sections by two horizontal dividers. A 'Ford' badge went on the lower driver's side of the grille. Rectangular headlamps stood above nearly-as-large rectangular parking lamps, both in a recessed housing. Two-door and four-door sedans were offered again, in base or Ghia trim. Granada Ghia had wide bodyside moldings. A new ESS (European Sports Sedan) option package included a blackout vertical grille texture as well as black rocker panels, door frames and bodyside moldings; black rubber bumper guards and wide rub strips; and a unique interior. ESS had color-keyed wheel covers, a heavy-duty suspension, dual sport mirrors, decklid and hood pinstriping, leather-wrapped steering wheel, FR78 x 14 SBR tires, and individual reclining bucket seats. ESS also had unique half- covered, louvered quarter windows. Low on the cowl was an 'ESS' badge, above 'Granada' script. Other options included an AM/FM stereo with cassette tape player, and a 40-channel CB transceiver. Five new Granada colors were offered this year, and a valino vinyl roof came in three new color choices. The base 200 cu. in. six from 1977 was replaced by a 250 cu. in. (4.1-liter) version, with 302 cu. in. (5.0-liter) V-8 optional. The V-8 could now have a variable-venturi carburetor. The bigger 351 cu. in. V-8 was abandoned.

1978 LTD II Brougham hardtop coupe (F)

LTD II — V-8 — Station wagons left the LTD II lineup this year, since the new Fairmont line included a wagon. Otherwise, models continued as before in 'S', base and Brougham series. Broughams had a full-length bodyside trim strip. Standard engine was again the 302 cu. in. (5.0-liter) V-8 with Cruise-O-Matic transmission, power front disc brakes, and power steering. Options included the 351 and 400 cu. in. V-8 engines, a heavy-duty trailer towing package (for the 400 V-8), and a Sports Appearance package. Two-doors could either have a solid panel at the rear, or the extra (higher) far rear coach-style window. A new bumper front spoiler, hood-to-grille-opening panel seal, revised decklid surface, and new fuel tank air deflector were supposed to cut aerodynamic drag and boost economy. Bumper-to-fender shields were new, too. A revised low-restriction fresh-air intake went on V-8 engines. A new mechanical spark control system was limited to the 351M and 400 cu. in. V-8s. Newly optional this year: a 40-channel CB radio. Mercury Cougar was corporate twin to the LTD II.

1978 LTD Landau pillared sedan (F)

LTD/CUSTOM 500 — V-8 — Full-size Fords were carried over for 1978, with new body colors available but little change beyond a new front bumper spoiler, rear floorpan air deflector, and other aerodynamic additions. The decklid was new. As before, LTD came in two-door or four-door pillared hardtop form, as well as plain-bodyside and Country Squire (simulated wood paneled) station wagons. Custom 500 was the fleet model, sold in Canada. Station wagons could now have optional removable auxiliary cushions for the dual facing rear seats. Among the more than 70 options were new two-tone body colors for the LTD Landau. Air conditioners now allowed the driver to control heating and cooling. A downsized LTD would arrive for 1979, so this was a waiting season.

1978 Thunderbird Town Landau hardtop coupe (JG)

THUNDERBIRD — V-8 — Styling of Ford's personal luxury coupe was similar to that of the downsized 1977 model. Six new body colors, four vinyl roof colors, bold striped cloth bucket seat trim, and new russet interior trim were offered. But the biggest news was the limited-production Diamond Jubilee Edition, commemorating Ford's 75th anniversary. Billed as "the most exclusive Thunderbird you can buy," it included several items never before offered on a TBird. Diamond Jubilee had a unique monochromatic exterior in Diamond Blue metallic or Ember metallic; distinctive matching thickly-padded vinyl roof and color-keyed grille texture; unique quarter-window treatment; accent striping; jewel-like hood ornament; cast aluminum wheels; and bodyside moldings. 'Diamond Jubilee Edition' script went in the opera windows, a hand-painted 'D.J.' monogram on the door (with owner's initials). Also included were color-keyed bumper guard/rub strips and turbine aluminum wheels. Inside was unique "biscuit" style cloth split bench seat trim, leather-covered steering wheel, twin illuminated visor vanity mirrors, seatbelt warning chimes, "super sound" package, and other luxury options. Even the keys were special. Diamond Blue models had a blue luxury cloth interior; Ember bodies, a chamois-color interior. Standard features also included whitewall tires, AM/FM stereo search radio with power antenna, dual sport mirrors, manual passenger recliner, and a hand-stitched leather-covered instrument panel pad above the tachometer and gauge set. Finishing off the interior were ebony woodtone appliques, and 22K gold-finish owner's nameplate. Thunderbird's Town Landau, introduced as a mid-year 1977 model, continued in 1978. Its roofline displayed a brushed aluminum wrapover applique. Also included were pinstriping, script on the opera windows, a color-coordinated jewel-like hood ornament, cast aluminum wheels with accent paint, wide vinyl-insert bodyside moldings, six-way power driver's seat, power windows and door locks, cornering lamps, and interior luxury group. Town Landau came in 14 body colors. Standard fittings also included whitewall tires, accent stripes, lighted visor vanity mirror, and dual sport mirrors. Inside were crushed velour split bench seats with fold-down center armrests. Six velour trim colors were available, along with optional leather seating surfaces. Dashes held burled walnut woodtone appliques. Also on Town Landau: SelectAire conditioner, AM/FM stereo search radio, day/date clock, and trip odometer. Thunderbird's Sports Decor Group included a bold blackout grille, unique imitation decklid straps, paint stripes, twin remote mirrors, spoke-style wheels, and tan vinyl roof with color-keyed rear window moldings. New options included a power radio antenna and 40-channel CB. Standard engine remained the 302 cu. in. (5.0-liter) V-8 with SelectShift automatic, power steering and brakes. Both 351 and 400 cu. in. V-8s were optional. Cougar XR7 was Thunderbird's Mercury counterpart.

I.D. DATA: As before, Ford's 11-symbol Vehicle Identification Number 'VIN' is stamped on a metal tab fastened to the instrument panel, visible through the windshield. Coding is similar to 1976-77. Model year code changed to '8' for 1978.

PINTO (FOUR/V-6)

Model Number	Body/Style Number	Body Type & Seating	Factory Price	Shipping Weight	Production Total
10	62B	2-dr. Sedan-4P	3336/3609	2337/2463	62,317
10	62B	2-dr. Pony Sed-4P	2995/--	2321/--	Note 1
11	64B	3-dr. Hatch-4P	3451/3724	2381/2507	74,313
12	73B	2-dr. Sta Wag-4P	3794/4067	2521/2637	52,269
12	73B	2-dr. Sqr Wag-4P	4109/4382	2555/2672	Note 2

Note 1: Pony production included in base sedan figure. **Note 2:** Squire Wagon production is included in standard station wagon total.

Pinto Production Note: Totals do not include 22,548 Pintos produced as 1978 models but sold as 1977s (see note following 1977 listing).

1978 Fairmont station wagon (JG)

FAIRMONT (FOUR/SIX)

93	36R	2-dr. Spt Cpe-5P	4044/4164	2605/2648	116,966
91	66B	2-dr. Sedan-5P	3589/3709	2568/2611	78,776
92	54B	4-dr. Sedan-5P	3663/3783	2610/2653	136,849
94	74B	4-dr. Sta Wag-5P	4031/4151	2718/2770	128,390

Fairmont Engine Note: Prices shown are for four-cylinder and six-cylinder engines. A V-8 cost $199 more than the six.

GRANADA (SIX/V-8)

81	66H	2-dr. Sedan-5P	4264/4445	3087/3177	110,481
82	54H	4-dr. Sedan-5P	4342/4523	3122/3212	139,305

GRANADA GHIA (SIX/V-8)

81	66K	2-dr. Sedan-5P	4649/4830	3147/3237	Note 3
82	54K	4-dr. Sedan-5P	4728/4909	3230/3320	Note 3

GRANADA ESS (SIX/V-8)

81	N/A	2-dr. Sedan-5P	4836/5017	3145/3235	Note 3
82	N/A	4-dr. Sedan-5P	4914/5095	3180/3270	Note 3

Note 3: Granada Ghia and ESS production is included in base Granada totals above.

LTD II (V-8)

30	65D	2-dr. HT Cpe-6P	5069	3773	76,285
31	53D	4-dr. Pill. HT-6P	5169	3872	64,133

LTD II 'S' (V-8)

25	65B	2-dr. HT Cpe-6P	4814	3746	9,004
27	53B	4-dr. Pill. HT-6P	4889	3836	21,122

LTD II BROUGHAM (V-8)

30	65K	2-dr. HT Cpe-6P	5405	3791	Note 4
31	53K	4-dr. Pill. HT-6P	5505	3901	Note 4

Note 4: Brougham production is included in LTD II totals above.

LTD LANDAU (V-8)

64	60L	2-dr. Pill. HT-6P	5898	4029	27,305
65	53L	4-dr. Pill. HT-6P	5973	4081	39,836

CUSTOM 500 (V-8)

Model Number	Body/Style Number	Body Type & Seating	Factory Price	Shipping Weight	Production Total
52	60D	2-dr. Pill. HT-6P	N/A	N/A	1,359
53	53D	4-dr. Pill. HT-6P	N/A	N/A	3,044
72	71D	4-dr. Ranch Wag-6P	N/A	N/A	1,196

Production Note: Custom 500 was produced for sale in Canada. Totals include an LTD 'S' two-door and Ranch wagon for sale in U.S.

LTD (V-8)

62	60H	2-dr. Pill. HT-6P	5335	3972	57,466
63	53H	4-dr. Pill. HT-6P	5410	4032	112,392
74	71H	4-dr. Sta Wag-6P	5797	4532	71,285
74	71K	4-dr. Ctry Sqr-6P	6207	4576	Note 5

Note 5: Country Squire production, and that of wagons with dual-facing rear seats (a $143 option for both standard and Country Squire wagon), is included in basic wagon totals.

THUNDERBIRD (V-8)

87	60H	2-dr. HT Cpe-6P	5411	3907	333,757

THUNDERBIRD TOWN LANDAU (V-8)

87/607	60H	2-dr. HT Cpe-6P	8420	4104	Note 6

Note 6: Town Landau production is included in basic Thunderbird total.

1978½ Thunderbird Diamond Jubilee hardtop coupe (F)

THUNDERBIRD DIAMOND JUBILEE EDITION (V-8)

87/603	60H	2-dr. HT Cpe-6P	10106	4200	18,994

FACTORY PRICE AND WEIGHT NOTE: Pinto/Fairmont prices and weights to left of slash are for four-cylinder, to right for six-cylinder engine. For Granada, prices and weights to left of slash are for six-cylinder, to right for V-8 engine.

ENGINE DATA: BASE FOUR (Pinto, Fairmont): Inline. Overhead cam. Four-cylinder. Cast iron block and head. Displacement: 140 cu. in. (2.3 liters). Bore & stroke: 3.78 x 3.13 in. Compression ratio: 9.0:1. Brake horsepower: 88 at 4800 R.P.M. Torque: 118 lbs.-ft. at 2800 R.P.M. Five main bearings. Hydraulic valve lifters. Carburetor: 2Bbl. Motorcraft 5200. VIN Code: Y. OPTIONAL V-6 (Pinto): 60-degree, overhead-valve V-6. Cast iron block and head. Displacement: 170.8 cu. in. (2.8 liters). Bore & stroke: 3.66 x 2.70 in. Compression ratio: 8.7:1. Brake horsepower: 90 at 4200 R.P.M. Torque: 143 lbs.-ft. at 2200 R.P.M. Four main bearings. Solid valve lifters. Carburetor: 2Bbl. Motorcraft 2150. VIN Code: Z. OPTIONAL SIX (Fairmont): Inline. Overhead valve. Six-cylinder. Cast iron block and head. Displacement: 200 cu. in. (3.3 liters). Bore & stroke: 3.68 x 3.13 in. Compression ratio: 8.5:1. Brake horsepower: 85 at 3600 R.P.M. Torque: 154 lbs.-ft. at 1600 R.P.M. Seven main bearings. Hydraulic valve lifters. Carburetor: 1Bbl. Carter YFA. VIN Code: T. BASE SIX (Granada): Inline. Overhead valve. Six-cylinder. Cast iron block and head. Displacement: 250 cu. in. (4.1 liters). Bore & stroke: 3.68 x 3.91 in. Compression ratio: 8.5:1. Brake horsepower: 97 at 3200 R.P.M. Torque: 210 lbs.-ft. at 1400 R.P.M. Seven main bearings. Hydraulic valve lifters. Carburetor: 1Bbl. Carter YFA. VIN Code: L. BASE V-8 (LTD II, Thunderbird, LTD); OPTIONAL (Fairmont, Granada): 90-degree, overhead valve V-8. Cast iron block and head. Displacement: 302 cu. in. (5.0 liters). Bore & stroke: 4.00 x 3.00 in. Compression ratio: 8.4:1. Brake horsepower: 134 at 3400 R.P.M. (Fairmont, 139 at 3600). Torque: 248 lbs.-ft. at 1600 R.P.M. (Fairmont, 250 at 1600). Five main bearings. Hydraulic valve lifters. Carburetor: 2Bbl. Motorcraft 2150. VIN Code: F. BASE V-8 (LTD wagon); OPTIONAL (LTD II, LTD): 90-degree, overhead valve V-8. Cast iron block and head. Displacement: 351 cu. in. (5.8 liters). Bore & stroke: 4.00 x 3.50 in. Compression ratio: 8.3:1. (LTD, 8.0:1). Brake horsepower: 144 at 3200 R.P.M. (LTD, 145 at 3400). Torque: 277 lbs.-ft. at 1600 R.P.M. (LTD, 273 at 1800). Five main bearings. Hydraulic valve lifters. Carburetor: 2Bbl. Motorcraft 2150. Windsor engine. VIN Code: H. OPTIONAL V-8 (LTD II, Thunderbird): Modified version of 351 cu. in. V-8 above Compression: 8.0:1. Brake H.P.: 152 at 3600 R.P.M. Torque: 278 lbs.-ft. at 1800 R.P.M. VIN Code: Q. OPTIONAL V-8 (LTD II, Thunderbird, LTD): 90-degree, overhead valve V-8. Cast iron block and head. Displacement: 400 cu. in. (6.6 liters). Bore & stroke: 4.00 x 4.00 in. Compression ratio: 8.0:1. Brake horsepower: 166 at 3800 R.P.M. (LTD, 160 at 3800). Torque: 319 lbs.-ft. at 1800 R.P.M. (LTD, 314 at 1800). Five main bearings. Hydraulic valve lifters. Carburetor: 2Bbl. Motorcraft 2150. VIN Code: S. OPTIONAL V-8 (LTD): 90-degree, overhead valve V-8. Cast iron block and head. Displacement: 460 cu. in. (7.5 liters). Bore & stroke: 4.36 x 3.85 in. Compression ratio: 8.0:1. Brake horsepower: 202 at 4000 R.P.M. Torque: 348 lbs.-ft. at 2000 R.P.M. Five main bearings. Hydraulic valve lifters. Carburetor: 4Bbl. Motorcraft 4350. VIN Code: A.

Note: A Police 460 cu. in. V-8 was also available for LTD.

CHASSIS DATA: Wheelbase: (Pinto) 94.5 in.; (Pinto wag) 94.8 in.; (Fairmont) 105.5 in.; (Granada) 109.9 in.; (LTD II 2dr.) 114.0 in.; (LTD II 4dr.) 118.0 in.; (Custom 500/LTD) 121.0 in.; (TBird) 114.0 in. Overall Length: (Pinto) 169.3 in.; (Pinto wag) 179.1 in.; (Fairmont) 193.8 in. exc. Futura coupe, 195.8 in.; (Granada) 197.7 in.; (LTD II 2dr.) 215.5 in.; (LTD II 4dr.) 219.5 in.; (LTD) 224.1 in.; (LTD wag) 225.7 in.; (LTD Landau) 226.8 in.; (TBird) 215.5 in. Height: (Pinto) 50.6 in.; (Pinto wag) 52.1 in.; (Fairmont) 53.5 in.; (Fairmont Futura cpe) 52.2 in.; (Fairmont wag) 54.7 in.; (Granada) 53.2-53.3 in.; (LTD II 2dr.) 52.6 in.; (LTD II 4dr.) 53.3 in.; (LTD 2dr.) 53.8 in.; (LTD 4dr.) 54.8 in.; (LTD wag) 56.7 in.; (TBird) 53.0 in. Width: (Pinto) 69.4 in.; (Pinto wag) 69.7 in.; (Fairmont) 71.0 in.; (Granada) 74.0 in.; (LTD II) 78.6 in.; (LTD) 79.5 in.; (LTD wag) 79.7 in.; (TBird) 78.5 in. Front Tread: (Pinto) 55.0 in.; (Fairmont) 56.6 in.; (Granada) 59.0 in.; (LTD II) 63.6 in. (LTD) 64.1 in. (TBird) 63.2 in. Rear Tread: (Pinto) 55.8 in.; (Fairmont) 57.0 in.; (Granada) 57.7 in.; (LTD II) 63.5 in.; (LTD) 64.3 in. (TBird) 63.1 in. Standard Tires: (Pinto) A78 x 13; (Fairmont) B78 x 14, except CR78 x 14 on wagon; (Granada) DR78 x 14 SBR BSW; (Granada Ghia) ER78 x 14; (LTD II) HR78 x 14 SBR BSW; (LTD) HR78 x 15 exc. wagon, JR78 x 15 and 2dr. w/V8302 engine, GR78 x 15; (TBird) HR78 x 15 SBR BSW.

TECHNICAL: Transmission: Three-speed manual transmission standard on Fairmont six. Gear ratios: (1st) 3.56:1; (2nd) 1.90:1; (3rd) 1.00:1; (Rev) 3.78:1. Four-speed overdrive manual standard on Granada: (1st) 3.29:1; (2nd) 1.84:1; (3rd) 1.00:1; (4th) 0.81:1; (Rev) 3.29:1. Four-speed floor shift standard on Pinto/Fairmont four: (1st) 3.98:1; (2nd) 2.14:1; (3rd) 1.42:1; (4th) 1.00:1; (Rev) 3.99:1. SelectShift three-speed automatic standard on other models, optional on all. Pinto/Fairmont four-cylinder automatic gear ratios: (1st) 2.47:1; (2nd) 1.47:1; (3rd) 1.00:1; (Rev) 2.11:1. LTD II/TBird w/V8351 or V8400: (1st) 2.40:1; (2nd) 1.47:1; (3rd) 1.00:1; (Rev) 2.00:1. Other models: (1st) 2.46:1; (2nd) 1.46:1; (3rd) 1.00:1; (Rev) 2.18:1 to 2.20:1. Standard final drive ratio: (Pinto) 2.73:1 w/4spd; (Fairmont) 3.08:1 or 2.73:1 w/manual, 2.47:1 w/auto.; (Granada) 3.00:1 w/4spd, 2.47:1 w/auto.; (LTD II) 2.75:1 or 2.50:1; (LTD) 2.75:1 or 2.47:1; (TBird) 2.75:1 w/V8302, 2.50:1 w/other V-8 engines. Steering: (Pinto/Fairmont) rack and pinion; (others) recirculating ball. Front Suspension: (Pinto) coil springs with short/long control arms, lower leading arms, and anti-sway bar on wagon; (Fairmont) MacPherson struts with coil springs mounted on lower control arms; (others) coil springs w/lower trailing links and anti-sway bar. Rear Suspension: (Pinto/Granada) rigid axle w/semi-elliptic leaf springs; (Fairmont) four-link coil springs; (LTD II/TBird) rigid axle w/lower trailing radius arms, upper oblique torque arms, coil springs and anti-sway bar; (LTD) rigid axle w/lower trailing radius arms, upper torque arms and coil springs, three-link w/track bar. Brakes: Front disc, rear drum; four-wheel discs available on Granada and LTD. Ignition: Electronic. Body construction: (Pinto/Fairmont/Granada) unibody; (LTD II/LTD/TBird) separate body and perimeter box frame. Fuel tank: (Pinto) 13 gal.; (Pinto wag) 14 gal.; (Fairmont) 16 gal.; (Granada) 18 gal.; (LTD II) 21 gal.; (LTD) 24.2 gal. exc. wagon, 21 gal.; (TBird) 21 gal.

DRIVETRAIN OPTIONS: Engines: 170 cu. in. V-6: Pinto ($273). 200 cu. in., 1Bbl. six: Fairmont ($120). 302 cu. in., 2Bbl. V-8: Fairmont ($319); Granada ($181). 351 cu. in., 2Bbl. V-8: LTD II/LTD/TBird ($157). 400 cu. in., 2Bbl. V-8: LTD II/LTD/TBird ($283); LTD wagon ($126). 460 cu. in., 4Bbl. V-8: LTD ($428); LTD wagon ($271). Transmission/Differential: SelectShift Cruise-O-Matic: Pinto ($281); Fairmont ($368); Fairmont wagon ($281); Granada ($193). Floor shift lever: Fairmont/Granada ($30). First-gear lockout delete: LTD/LTD II ($7). Traction-Lok differential: LTD II/TBird ($59); LTD ($62). Optional axle ratio: Pinto ($13); LTD ($14). Brakes & Steering: Power brakes: Pinto ($64); Fairmont/Granada ($63). Four-wheel power disc brakes: Granada ($300); LTD ($187-$197). Power steering: Pinto ($131); Fairmont ($140); Granada ($148). Semi-metallic front disc pads: LTD/LTD II ($8). Suspension: H.D. susp.: Granada ($27); LTD ($65); TBird ($20). Handling susp.: Fairmont ($30). H.D. handling susp.: LTD II ($36). Adjustable air shock absorbers: LTD ($50). Other: H.D. battery: Fairmont ($17); LTD II/LTD/TBird ($18). H.D. alternator: LTD II/LTD/TBird ($50). Trailer towing pkg. (heavy duty): LTD II/TBird ($184); LTD ($139). California emission system: Pinto/Fairmont/Granada ($69); LTD II/TBird ($75); LTD ($138-$295). High-altitude option (NC).

PINTO CONVENIENCE/APPEARANCE OPTIONS: Option Packages: Cruising wagon option ($365-$401). Cruising wagon paint/tape treatment ($59). Sports rallye pkg. ($76- $96). Rallye appearance pkg. ($176-$201). Exterior decor group ($30-$40). Interior decor group ($149-$181). Interior accent group ($28-$40). Convenience/light group ($81-$143). Deluxe bumper group ($70). Protection group ($83-$135). Comfort/Convenience: Air conditioner ($459). Rear defroster, electric ($77). Tinted glass ($53); windshield only ($25). Cigar lighter ($5). Trunk light ($5). Driver's sport mirror ($16). Dual sport mirrors ($49). Day/night mirror ($7). Entertainment: AM radio ($65); w/digital clock ($47-$119); w/stereo tape player ($119-$192). AM/FM radio ($48-$120). AM/FM stereo radio ($89-$161). Exterior: Flip-up open air roof ($167). Half vinyl roof ($125). Glass third door ($25). Metallic glow paint ($40). Two-tone paint/tape treatment ($40-$49). Accent tape stripe ($49-$59). Black narrow vinyl-insert bodyside moldings ($39). Bumper guards ($37). Roof luggage rack ($59). Rocker panel moldings ($22). Lower bodyside protection ($30). Interior: Four-way driver's seat ($33). Load floor carpet ($23). Cargo area cover ($25). Wheels: Wire wheel covers ($90). Forged aluminum wheels ($173-$252); white ($187-$265). Styled steel wheels ($78). Tires: A78 x 13 WSW. A70 x 13 RWL. B78 x 13 BSW/WSW. BR78 x 13 BSW/WSW. BR70 x 13 RWL.

1978 Fairmont ES Sport Coupe (JG)

FAIRMONT CONVENIENCE/APPEARANCE OPTIONS: Option Packages: ES option: sedan ($300). Squire option ($365). Exterior decor group ($214). Exterior accent group ($96). Interior decor group ($176-$301). Interior accent group ($89-$94). Deluxe bumper group ($70). Convenience group ($29-$60). Appearance protection group ($36-$47). Light group ($35-$40). Comfort/Convenience: Air cond. ($465). Rear defogger ($47). Rear defroster, electric ($84). Tinted glass ($52); windshield only ($25). Sport steering wheel ($36). Electric clock ($18). Cigar lighter ($6). Interval wipers ($29). Liftgate wiper/washer: wag ($78). Trunk light ($4). Left remote mirror ($19). Dual bright mirrors ($13-$36). Day/night mirror ($8). Entertainment: AM radio ($72); w/8track tape player ($192). AM/FM radio ($120). AM/FM stereo radio ($176); w/8track or cassette player ($243). Exterior: Vinyl roof ($89-$124). Metallic

glow paint ($46). Two-tone paint ($42). Accent paint stripe ($30) exc. Futura (NC). Pivoting front vent windows ($37-$60). Rear quarter vent louvers ($33). Bodyside moldings ($39). Rocker panel moldings ($22). Bumper guards, front and rear ($37). Luggage rack ($72). Lower bodyside protection ($30-$42). Interior: Bucket seat, non-reclining ($72). Bench seat ($72 credit). Cloth seat trim ($19-$37). Vinyl seat trim ($22). Lockable side storage box ($19). Wheels: Hubcaps w/trim rings ($34) exc. Futura (NC). Deluxe wheel covers ($33). Turbine wheel covers ($33-$66). Wire wheel covers ($48-$114). Cast aluminum wheels ($210-$276). Tires: B78 x 14 WSW. BR78 x 14 BSW/WSW. C78 x 14 BSW/WSW. CR78 x 14 BSW/WSW. DR78 x 14 SBR BSW/WSW/RWL.

GRANADA CONVENIENCE/APPEARANCE OPTIONS: Option Packages: Luxury interior group ($476). Interior decor group ($211). Convenience group ($30-$89). Deluxe bumper group ($70). Light group ($30-$43). Cold weather group ($37- $54). Heavy-duty group ($37-$54). Protection group ($25-$43). Visibility group ($4-$58). Comfort/Convenience: Air cond. ($494); auto-temp ($535). Rear defogger ($47). Rear defroster, electric ($84). Fingertip speed control ($55-$102). Illuminated entry system ($49). Power windows ($116-$160). Power door locks ($76-$104). Power decklid release ($19). Auto. parking brake release ($8). Power four-way seat ($90). Tinted glass ($54); windshield only ($25). Tilt steering wheel ($58). Digital clock ($42). Lighting and Mirrors: Cornering lamps ($42). Trunk light ($4). Left remote mirror ($14). Dual remote mirrors ($31- $46). Dual sport mirrors ($42-$53). Day/night mirror ($8). Lighted right visor vanity mirror ($34). Entertainment: AM radio ($72); w/tape player ($192). AM/FM radio ($135). AM/FM stereo radio ($176); w/8track or cassette player ($243); w/quadrasonic tape ($365). AM/FM stereo search radio ($319). CB radio ($270). Exterior: Power moonroof ($820). Full or half vinyl roof ($102). Metallic glow paint ($46). Bodyside/decklid paint stripes ($29). Bodyside accent moldings ($33). Vinyl insert bodyside moldings ($39). Rocker panel moldings ($23). Interior: Console ($75). Four-way driver's seat ($33). Reclining seats (NC). Leather seat trim ($271). Flight bench seat (NC). Cloth flight bench seat ($54). Deluxe cloth seat/door trim: Ghia/ESS ($99). Color-keyed seatbelts ($19). Wheels: Deluxe wheel covers ($37) exc. Ghia/ESS (NC). Wire wheel covers ($59-$96). Styled steel wheels w/trim rings ($59-$96). Lacy spoke aluminum wheels ($205-$242); white ($218-$255). Tires: DR78 x 14 SBR WSW. ER78 x 14 SBR BSW/WSW. FR78 x 14 SBR BSW/WSW/wide WSW. Inflatable spare (NC).

LTD II CONVENIENCE/APPEARANCE OPTIONS: Option Packages: Sports appearance pkg. ($216-$363). Sports instrumentation group ($111-$138). Sports touring pkg. ($287- $434). Deluxe bumper group ($76). Light group ($49-$54). Convenience group ($107-$139). Power lock group ($100-$132). Front protection group ($46-$58). Comfort/Convenience: Air cond. ($543); w/auto-temp control ($588). Rear defroster, electric ($93). Fingertip speed control ($104-$117). Illuminated entry system ($54). Tinted glass ($62); windshield only ($28). Power windows ($126- $175). Power door locks ($71-$101). Six-way power seat ($149). Auto. parking brake release ($9). Leather-wrapped steering wheel ($51-$64). Tilt steering wheel ($70). Electric clock ($20). Day/date clock ($22-$42). Lighting, Horns and Mirrors: Cornering lamps ($46). Trunk light ($4). Dual-note horn ($7). Remote driver's mirror ($16). Dual chrome mirrors ($7). Dual sport mirrors ($29- $58). Lighted visor vanity mirror ($33-$37). Entertainment: AM radio ($79). AM/FM radio ($132). AM/FM stereo radio ($192); w/tape player ($266); w/quadrasonic tape player ($399). AM/FM stereo search radio ($349). CB radio ($295). Dual rear speakers ($46). Exterior: Full or half vinyl roof ($112). Opera windows ($51). Vinyl-insert bodyside moldings ($42). Wide bright bodyside moldings ($42). Rocker panel moldings ($29). Metallic glow paint ($62) exc. (NC) w/sports pkg. Two-tone paint ($53). Dual accent paint stripes ($33). Lower bodyside protection ($33). Interior: Bucket seats w/console ($211) exc. Brougham ($37). Vinyl seat trim ($24). Cloth/vinyl seat trim ($24). Front floor mats ($20). H.D. floor mats ($9). Color-keyed seatbelts ($21). Wheels: Deluxe wheel covers ($38). Luxury wheel covers ($62- $100). Wire wheel covers ($105-$143) exc. (NC) w/sports pkg. Cast aluminum wheels ($196-$301). Tires: HR78 x 14 SBR WSW ($46). HR78 x 14 wide-band WSW ($66). HR78 x 14 SBR RWL ($62). HR78 x 15 SBR WSW ($68). Inflatable spare (NC).

LTD CONVENIENCE/APPEARANCE OPTIONS: Option Packages: Landau luxury group ($457-$580). Convenience group ($96-$146). Light group ($26-$38). Deluxe bumper group ($50-$72). Protection group ($45-$53). Comfort/Convenience: Air cond. ($562); w/auto-temp control ($607). Rear defogger ($50). Rear defroster, electric ($93). Fingertip speed control ($104-$117). Illuminated entry system ($54). Power windows ($129-$188). Power door locks ($82- $153). Six-way power driver's seat ($149); driver and passenger ($297). Tinted glass ($75); windshield only ($28). Tilt steering wheel ($70). Auto. parking brake release ($8). Electric clock ($21). Digital clock ($28-$49). Lighting, Horns and Mirrors: Cornering lamps ($46). Trunk light ($4). Dual-note horn ($7). Driver's remote mirror ($16). Dual remote mirrors ($32-$47). Lighted visor vanity mirror ($33-$37). Entertainment: AM radio ($79). AM/FM radio ($132). AM/FM stereo radio ($192); w/tape player ($266); w/quadrasonic tape player ($399). AM/FM stereo search radio ($349). Dual rear speakers ($46). Exterior: Power moonroof ($896). Full vinyl roof ($141) exc. Landau two-door (NC). Half vinyl roof ($141). Metallic glow paint ($62). Dual accent paint stripes ($33). Rocker panel moldings ($29). Vinyl-insert bodyside moldings ($42). Rear bumper guards ($22). Luggage rack ($80). Interior: Dual-facing rear seats: wagon ($143). Split bench seat w/passenger recliner ($141-$233). Leather seat trim ($296). All-vinyl seat trim ($24). Duraweave vinyl trim ($50). H.D. floor mats ($9). Color-keyed seatbelts ($21). Lockable side stowage compartment ($33). Wheels: Full wheel covers ($38). Deluxe or color-keyed wheel covers ($61-$99). Wire wheel covers ($99-$137). Deep-dish aluminum wheels ($263-$301). Tires: GR78 x 15 SBR WSW. HR78 x 15 SBR BSW/WSW. JR78 x 15 SBR BSW/WSW/wide WSW. LR78 x 15 SBR WSW.

THUNDERBIRD CONVENIENCE/APPEARANCE OPTIONS: Option Packages: Sports decor group ($396-$446). Interior luxury group ($783). Exterior decor group ($332-$382). Interior decor group ($316). Deluxe bumper group ($76). Sports instrumentation group ($111-$118). Convenience group ($93-$103). Protection group ($46-$50). Light group ($49). Power lock group ($100). Sound insulation pkg. ($29). Comfort/Convenience: Air cond. ($543); auto-temp ($588) exc. special editions ($45). Rear defroster, electric ($93). Fingertip speed control ($104-$117). Illuminated entry system ($54). Tinted glass ($66); windshield only ($28). Power windows ($126). Six-way power seat ($149). Automatic seatback release ($33). Auto. parking brake release ($9). Leather- wrapped steering wheel ($51-$64). Tilt steering wheel ($70). Day/date clock ($22). Lighting and Mirrors: Cornering lamps ($46). Trunk light ($4). Driver's remote mirror, chrome ($16). Dual sport mirrors ($8-$58). Lighted visor vanity mirror ($33-$37). Entertainment: AM/FM radio ($53). AM/FM stereo radio ($113); w/tape player ($187); w/quadrasonic tape player ($320) exc. special editions ($50). AM/FM stereo search radio ($270). CB radio ($295). AM radio delete ($79 credit). Power antenna ($45). Dual rear speakers ($46). Exterior: Power moonroof ($691). Vinyl roof, two-piece ($138). Metallic glow paint ($62). Two-tone paint ($53). Dual accent paint stripes ($46). Bright wide bodyside moldings ($42). Vinyl bodyside moldings ($42). Wide color-keyed bodyside moldings ($54). Rocker panel moldings ($29). Bumper guards ($42). Interior: Bucket seats w/console ($211) exc. ($37) w/decor group. Leather/vinyl seat trim ($296). Vinyl seat trim ($24). Front floor mats ($20). Trunk trim ($39). Color-keyed seatbelts ($21). Wheels: Wire wheel covers ($105). Styled wheels ($146). Tires: GR78 x 15 WSW ($46). HR78 x 15 BSW ($22). HR78 x 15 SBR WSW ($20-$68). HR78 x 15 SBR wide WSW ($88). HR70 x 15 SBR WSW ($22-$90). Inflatable spare (NC).

HISTORY: Introduced: October 7, 1977 except Fairmont Futura Coupe, December 2, 1977. Model year production: 1,929,254 (incl. Mustangs). Total passenger-car production for the U.S. market of 1,777,291 units (incl. Mustangs) included 285,878 four- cylinder, 511,500 sixes and 979,913 V-8s. Calendar year production (U.S.): 1,698,136 (incl. Mustangs). Calendar year sales by U.S. dealers: 1,768,753 (incl. Mustangs). Model year sales by U.S. dealers: 1,830,417 (incl. Mustangs).

NOTE: Totals above do not include Club Wagons, of which 43,917 were sold in the model year; or imported Fiestas, which recorded sales of 81,273).

Historical Footnotes: Model year sales increased modestly for 1978, though production slipped a bit. Major recalls of more than 4 million vehicles, however (and investigations of many more), did Ford's reputation no good. Most serious were the Pintos recalled for gas tanks that might burst into flame, followed by automatic transmissions that were alleged to jerk suddenly from "park" to "reverse" (a situation that never was fully resolved). At this time, too, Ford president Lee Iacocca was replaced by Philip Caldwell; and Iacocca reemerged within a few months as the new head of Chrysler. The new compact Fairmont sold far better than its predecessor Maverick: 417,932 Fairmonts versus just 105,156 Mavericks sold in 1977. Fairmont sold even better as a first- year car than had Mustang when it was introduced. 1977 had been Thunderbird's best sales year, and it sold well in 1978 too. Granada and LTD II sales plummeted for the model year. Fairmont was "the most successful new-car nameplate ever introduced by a domestic manufacturer and Ford's top selling car line in 1978," said Walter S. Walla, Ford Division General Manager. It was also highly rated by the auto magazines. Readers of *Car and Driver* called it "most significant new American car for 1978." Computer-assisted design techniques had been used to develop the Fairmont/Zephyr duo, along with over 320 hours of wind-tunnel testing. Corporate Average Fuel Economy (CAFE) standards began this year. Automakers' fleets would be required to meet a specified average miles-per-gallon rating each year for the next decade, with 27.5 MPG the ultimate goal. Fairmont, in fact, was designed with the CAFE ratings in mind, which required that Fords average 18 MPG. This year's model introduction meetings had been held in the Detroit and Dearborn area for the first time since 1959. More than 15,000 dealers, general managers and spouses attended. The international emphasis was highlighted by a "flags of the world of Ford" display at the world headquarters, in a special ceremony. On the import front, Ford began to import the tiny front-wheel drive Fiesta from its German plant.

1979 FORD

Full-size Fords finally received their expected downsizing, two years later than equivalent General Motors models. Mustang (listed separately) also offered some big news for 1979 with a total restyle. Pinto got a more modest alteration, while Thunderbird switched grilles. CAFE standards rose from 18 to 19 MPG this year, prompting powertrain refinements. The 2.3-liter four on Pinto/Fairmont got an aluminum or plastic fan, oil filler cap and rear cover plate. The 2.8-liter V-6 got a new camshaft design. An aluminum intake manifold went on the 302 cu. in. V-8 in LTD and some Granadas. The 351 cu. in. V-8 ('W' version), optional in LTD, LTD II and Thunderbird, lost up to 40 pounds by switching to an aluminum intake manifold, water pump and rear cover.

1979 Pinto three-door Runabout (F)

PINTO — FOUR/V-6 — Restyling brought the subcompact Pinto a new front-end look with single rectangular headlamps in bright housings, as well as a new sloping hood and fenders, and horizontal-style argent grille. Single vertical parking lamps stood inboard of the headlamps, which were recessed farther back than the parking lamps. The slat-style grille contained three horizontal divider bars. 'Ford' block letters stood at the hood front. New sculptured-look front/rear aluminum bumpers had black rub strips and end sections. Small backup lenses were at inner ends of the new sedan/Runabout horizontal-design taillamps, extending through the upper, center and lower sections. Full wheel covers took on a new design. Inside, a new instrument panel and pad held rectangular instrument pods. The redesigned cluster now included a speedometer graduated in miles and kilometers, fuel gauge, and warning lights with symbols. New body and interior colors were available. As before, two-door sedan, "three-door" hatchback Runabout and station wagon models were offered. A Cruising Package became optional on both Runabouts and wagons, featuring multi-color bodyside paint/tape treatment and black louvers on the wagon's liftgate window. There was also a new ESS option for sedans and Runabouts, with black grille and exterior accents, black-hinged glass third door, wide black bodyside moldings, and sports-type equipment. Other new options included lacy-spoke cast aluminum wheels, AM/FM stereo radio with cassette, separate light and convenience groups (formerly combined), heavy-duty battery, and a revised Exterior Decor group. Pinto's standard equipment list grew longer this year, adding an AM radio, power brakes, electric rear defroster, and tinted glass. The low-budget Pony lacked some of these extras. Standard engine remained the 140 cu. in. (2.3-liter) overhead-cam four, with four-speed gearbox; automatic and V-6 optional. Oil-change intervals were raised to 30,000 miles. The V-6 added a higher-performance camshaft, while V-6 automatic transmissions were meant to offer higher R.P.M. shift points to improve acceleration.

FAIRMONT — FOUR/SIX/V-8 — Appearance of the year-old compact didn't change this year. Model lineup included two-door and four-door sedans, a station wagon, and the uniquely-styled Futura coupe. Seven new body colors and four new vinyl roof colors were available. Availability of the distinctive tu-tone paint treatment was expanded to sedans, as well as the Futura. A four-speed overdrive manual

1979 Fairmont Squire wagon (F)

transmission with new single-rail shifter design replaced the former three-speed, with either the 200 cu. in. (3.3-liter) inline six or 302 cu. in. (5.0- liter) V-8. (V-8s formerly came only with automatic.) Base engine remained the 140 cu. in. (2.3-liter) four, with non- overdrive four-speed manual gearbox. The six was now offered on California wagons. Ignition and door locks were modifed to improve theft- resistance. A lower axle ratio (2.26:1) came with the V-8 and automatic. Inside was a new dark walnut woodtone instrument cluster applique. New options included tilt steering, new- design speed control, performance instruments (including tachometer and trip odometer), ultra-fidelity premium sound system, remote decklid release, styled steel wheels with trim rings, and flip-up open-air roof. Wide vinyl-insert bodyside moldings were available on Futura. The Futura Sports Group included unique tape striping, charcoal argent grille and color-keyed turbine wheel covers, but dispensed with the usual hood ornament. Futura again sported a unique front end with quad rectangular headlamps, wrapover roof pillar, wide tapered Bpillars, and wraparound taillamps. Fairmont's ES package was offered again. It included a blackout grille, black cowl grille, bright belt moldings, black window frames and quarter window vent louvers, black/bright bodyside moldings, dual black sail-mount sport mirrors (left remote), turbine wheel covers, handling suspension with rear stabilizer bar, and 5.5 inch wheels.

1979 Granada Ghia coupe (F)

GRANADA — SIX/V-8 — Billed as "An American Classic" (playing on its Mercedes lookalike origins), Granada changed little for 1979. Few customers had chosen four-wheel disc brakes, so that option was dropped. Both the standard 250 cu. in. (3.3-liter) inline six and 302 cu. in. (5.0-liter) V-8 came with a four-speed overdrive manual gearbox that used a new enclosed single-rail shift mechanism. As before, two- and four-door sedans were produced, in base, Ghia or ESS trim. Four new body colors and two new vinyl roof colors were offered, along with a paint and tape treatment option. Base models got all-bright versions of the '78 Ghia wheel cover. A thin, contemporary wheel lip molding replaced Ghia's former wider moldings. Ghia seats had a new sew style, as well as all-vinyl door trim with carpeted lower panels. Leather/vinyl trim was now available with bucket seats in the Interior Decor group. New soft Rossano cloth became optional on the base flight bench seat. New Willshire cloth luxury trim was available. Bright moldings replaced the color-keyed moldings on the vinyl roof. A new lightweight aluminum intake manifold went on V-8s in four-doors. Electronic voltage regulators were new. Ignition locks offered improved theft-resistance. New options included tone-on-tone paint in five color combinations. Dropped were white lacy-spoke aluminum wheels, Traction-Lok axle, and the Luxury Interior Group. This year's ESS option was identified by 'Granada' script above the 'ESS' badge, rather than below, on the lower cowl. Granada ESS had blacked-out grille and exterior trim, color-keyed wheel covers and dual mirrors, decklid and hood pinstriping, individually reclining bucket seats with Euro headrests, and leather-wrapped steering wheel. Optional speed control for the ESS included a black leather-wrapped steering wheel.

1979 LTD II hardtop coupe (F)

LTD II — V-8 — Not enough buyers had found LTD II appealing, so this would be its third and final season. Not much was new this year, except for a redesigned front bumper spoiler, corrosion-resistant plastic battery tray, and electronic voltage regulator. Seven body colors were new, as were front and full vinyl roofs. Broughams had new interior fabric selections. All models had standard flight bench seating with fold-down center armrest. The 400 cu. in. V-8 option was abandoned. Base engine remained the 302 cu. in. (5.0-liter) V-8, with 351 V-8 optional. Automatic transmission was standard. A newly optional 27.5 gallon gas tank suggested that LTD II's economy problems hadn't quite been corrected by the use of a lighter weight front bumper this year, or by carburetor refinements. Rear bumper guards became standard, and the ignition lock was modified. The Sports Touring Package included two- tone paint with tape breaks on the bodyside/hood/lower back panel, as well as a grille badge and Magnum 500 wheels with HR78 x 14 RWL tires. A Sports Appearance Group for two-doors had bold tri-color tape stripes. As before, two-door hardtop and four-door pillared hardtop bodies were offered, in base, Brougham or 'S' trim. The low-cost 'S' model had an upgraded bench seat and woodtone instrument panel applique this year.

1979 LTD Country Squire station wagon (F)

LTD — V-8 — Substantial downsizing made this year's LTD the ninth all-new full-size model in the company's history. Still built with body-on-frame construction, it was intended to be space- efficient as well as fuel-efficient, a result of over 270 hours of wind-tunnel testing. Riding a 114.4 inch wheelbase (7 inches shorter than before), the reduced LTD managed to increase its former interior space while shrinking on the outside. A conventionaL sedan design replaced the former pillared hardtop style. Door openings grew larger, and doors thinner. Both the cowl and hood were lower. So was the car's beltline. Glass area expanded. Overall, the new design was slightly taller and more boxy. Inside, LTD's seating position was higher. LTD's tighter crosshatch grille was split into two side- by-side sections by a narrow vertical divider, and topped by a wide upper bar. The grille looked flatter than before. 'Ford' letters went on the driver's side of the upper grille header. Base models displayed single rectangular headlamps with outboard fendertip signal lamps, while quad rectangular headlamps above rectangular park/signal lamps went on Landau and Squire models. Front marker lenses wrapped around fender sides, matching the headlamps and parking lamps. A tall, narrow ornament adorned the hood. Two-doors were four-window design with a slim coach-style quarter window. Landaus had new rear-pillar coach lamps. Country Squire wagons showed a new woodtone applique treatment. Large vertical rectangular taillamps were rather wide, each with a small backup lens below. The recessed license plate housing was in the decklid's center, with 'Ford' letters on left of decklid. Inside were thin-back seats with foam padding over flex-o-lator cushion support, and a four- spoke soft-rim steering wheel. A steering-column stalk held the dimmer, horn and wiper/washer controls. Door-lock plungers moved to the armrests to improve theft-resistance. Lockable side stowage compartments became standard on wagons. Base engine, except on wagons with California emissions, was the 302 cu. in. (5.0-liter) V-8. That engine had a new single accessory-drive belt operating the fan/water pump, alternator, and power steering pump. A variable-venturi carburetor became standard on both the 302 and the optional 351 V-8 engines. Up front was a new short/long Aarm coil spring front suspension with link-type stabilizer bar; at the rear, a new four-bar link coil spring setup. Front disc brakes used a new pin-slider design. LTD's option list still included speed control, tilt steering, automatic-temperature-control air conditioning, heavy-duty trailer towing package, and the 351 V-8, along with other popular extras. New options this year were: special handling suspension system, premium stereo sound, digital clock with time/date/elapsed time, flight bench seating with dual reclining seatbacks, power antenna, and 40-channel CB radio. Also available: window-frame-mounted mirrors, bumper rub strips, electronic AM/FM stereo search radio with Quadrasonic8 tape player, AM/FM stereo radio with cassette, tu-tone paint/tape treatment, and Exterior Accent Group. The Convenience Group added a trip odometer and low fuel/low washer fluid warning lights. A "resume" feature was added to the fingertip speed control; a left-hand recliner added to split bench seats. Options dropped included the 400 and 460 V-8 engines, Traction-Lok, four-wheel disc brakes, leather seat trim, color-keyed wheel covers, deep-dish aluminum wheels, and fender skirts.

1979 Thunderbird Heritage Edition hardtop coupe (F)

THUNDERBIRD — V-8 — A much bolder, heavier-looking box-texture grille greeted TBird customers this year. A large 4x4 grid pattern (just three horizontal and three vertical bars) stood in front of thin vertical bars. A new spoiler went below the front bumper. Clear fendertip parking lamps with adjoining amber marker lenses each held three horizontal divider strips. Separate large rectangular taillamps, replacing the

former full-width units, were essentially a rectangle within a rectangle, with TBird emblem in the center. A single backup lamp stood between them, centered over new standard rear bumper guards. Thunderbird also had a new electronic voltage regulator, and carburetor refinements on the standard 302 cu. in. (5.0-liter) V-8. Door and ignition locks were modified for theft protection. Eight body colors, five vinyl roof colors, and four interior trim colors were new. Standard seating was now the flight bench design with Rossano cloth seating surfaces and large fold-down front armrest. Front fenders held a vertical set of "louvers." Bodysides showed narrow opera windows, with large rear swept-back side windows. Headlamp covers held a wide insignia, plus 'Thunderbird' script on the left one. A posh new Heritage model replaced the Diamond Jubilee edition. 'Heritage' script went on the huge blank Cpillar, as that model had no rear side window. Heritage had two monochromatic body color themes in maroon or light medium blue, with formal padded vinyl roof. Equipment included 36- ounce cut-pile carpeting, split bench seats in soft velour cloth (or optional leather seating surfaces), leather- wrapped steering wheel, sports instrument panel with tachometer and gauges, driver's lighted visor vanity mirror, and AM/FM stereo radio. Town Landau had a brushed aluminum wrapover applique, color-keyed hood ornament, cast aluminum wheels with accent paint, and wide vinyl-insert bodyside moldings. New options included an extended-range 27.5-gallon gas tank (standard on Town Landau and Heritage), AM/FM stereo radio with cassette, mud/stone deflectors, and ultra-soft leather/vinyl upholstery (for Heritage). Bucket seats and a console could be ordered separately, or as a no-cost extra with the Interior Decor Group.

I.D. DATA: Ford's 11-symbol Vehicle Identification Number (VIN) is stamped on a metal tab fastened to the instrument panel, visible through the windshield. The first digit is a model year code ('9' 1979). The second letter indicates assembly plant: 'A' Atlanta, GA; 'B' Oakville, Ontario (Canada); 'E' Mahwah, NJ; 'G' Chicago; 'H' Lorain, Ohio; 'J' Los Angeles; 'K' Kansas City, MO; 'S' St. Thomas, Ontario; 'T' Metuchen, NJ; 'U' Louisville, KY; 'W' Wayne, MI. Digits three and four are the body serial code, which corresponds to the Model Numbers shown in the tables below (e.g., '10' Pinto 2-dr. sedan). The fifth symbol is an engine code: 'Y' L4-140 2Bbl.; 'Z' V6170 2Bbl.; 'T' L6200 1Bbl.; 'L' L6250 1Bbl.; 'F' V8302 2Bbl.; 'H' V8351 2Bbl. Finally, digits 6-11 make up the consecutive unit number of cars built at each assembly plant. The number begins with 100,001. A Vehicle Certification Label on the left front door lock face panel or door pillar shows the manufacturer, month and year of manufacture, GVW, GAWR, certification statement, VIN, body code, color code, trim code, axle code, transmission code, and special order code.

PINTO (FOUR/V-6)

Model Number	Body/Style Number	Body Type & Seating	Factory Price	Shipping Weight	Production Total
10	62B	2-dr. Sedan-4P	3629/3902	2346/2446	75,789
10	41E	2-dr. Pony Sed-4P	3199/ --	2329/ --	Note 1
11	64B	3-dr. Hatch-4P	3744/4017	2392/2492	69,383
12	73B	2-dr. Sta Wag-4P	4028/4301	2532/2610	53,846
12	41E	2-dr. Pony Wag-4P	3633/ --	N/A	Note 1
12	73B	2-dr. Sqr Wag-4P	4343/4616	2568/2646	Note 2

Note 1: Pony production included in base sedan and wagon figures. **Note 2:** Squire Wagon production is included in standard station wagon total.

1979 Fairmont Futura sedan (F)

FAIRMONT (FOUR/SIX)

93	36R	2-dr. Spt Cpe-5P	4071/4312	2546/2613	106,065
91	66B	2-dr. Sedan-5P	3710/3951	2491/2558	54,798
92	54B	4-dr. Sedan-5P	3810/4051	2544/2611	133,813
94	74B	4-dr. Sta Wag-5P	4157/4398	2674/2741	100,691

Fairmont Engine Note: Prices shown are for four-cylinder and six- cylinder engines. A V-8 cost $283 more than the six.

GRANADA (SIX/V-8)

81	66H	2-dr. Sedan-5P	4342/4625	3051/3124	76,850
82	54H	4-dr. Sedan-5P	4445/4728	3098/3169	105,526

GRANADA GHIA (SIX/V-8)

81/602	66K	2-dr. Sedan-5P	4728/5011	3089/3160	Note 3
82/602	54K	4-dr. Sedan-5P	4830/5113	3132/3203	Note 3

GRANADA ESS (SIX/V-8)

81/433	N/A	2-dr. Sedan-5P	4888/5161	3105/3176	Note 3
82/433	N/A	4-dr. Sedan-5P	4990/5273	3155/3226	Note 3

Note 3: Granada Ghia and ESS production is included in base Granada totals above.

250

1979 LTD Landau sedan (F)

LTD II (V-8)

Model Number	Body/Style Number	Body Type & Seating	Factory Price	Shipping Weight	Production Total
30	65D	2-dr. HT Cpe-6P	5445	3797	18,300
31	53D	4-dr. Pill. HT-6P	5569	3860	19,781

LTD II 'S' (V-8)

25	65B	2-dr. HT Cpe-6P	5198	3781	834
27	53B	4-dr. Pill. HT-6P	5298	3844	9,649

Production Note: LTD 'S' was for fleet sale only.

LTD II BROUGHAM (V-8)

30	65K	2-dr. HT Cpe-6P	5780	3815	Note 4
31	53K	4-dr. Pill. HT-6P	5905	3889	Note 4

Note 4: Brougham production is included in LTD II totals above.

LTD (V-8)

62	66H	2-dr. Sedan-6P	5813	3421	54,005
63	54H	4-dr. Sedan-6P	5913	3463	117,730
74	74H	4-dr. Sta Wag-6P	6122	3678	37,955
74	74K	4-dr. Ctry Sqr-6P	6615	3719	29,932

LTD Production Notes: Production of wagons with dual-facing rear seats (a $145-$149 option for both standard and Country Squire wagon) is included in basic wagon totals. Totals also include production of Custom 500 models for Canadian market (2,036 two-doors, 4,567 four-doors and 1,568 wagons).

LTD LANDAU (V-8)

64	66K	2-dr. Sedan-6P	6349	3472	42,314
65	54K	4-dr. Sedan-6P	6474	3527	74,599

THUNDERBIRD (V-8)

87	60H	2-dr. HT Cpe-6P	5877	3893	284,141

THUNDERBIRD TOWN LANDAU (V-8)

87/607	60H	2-dr. HT Cpe-6P	8866	4284	Note 5

THUNDERBIRD HERITAGE EDITION (V-8)

87/603	60H	2-dr. HT Cpe-6P	10687	4178	Note 5

Note 5: Town Landau and Heritage production is included in basic Thunderbird total.

FACTORY PRICE AND WEIGHT NOTE: Pinto/Fairmont prices and weights to left of slash are for four-cylinder, to right for six-cylinder engine. For Granada, prices and weights to left of slash are for six-cylinder, to right for V-8 engine.

ENGINE DATA: BASE FOUR (Pinto, Fairmont): Inline. Overhead cam. Four-cylinder. Cast iron block and head. Displacement: 140 cu. in. (2.3 liters). Bore & stroke: 3.78 x 3.13 in. Compression ratio: 9.0:1. Brake horsepower: 88 at 4800 R.P.M. Torque: 118 lbs.-ft. at 2800 R.P.M. Five main bearings. Hydraulic valve lifters. Carburetor: 2Bbl. Motorcraft 5200. VIN Code: Y. **OPTIONAL V-6** (Pinto): 60-degree, overhead-valve V-6. Cast iron block and head. Displacement: 170.8 cu. in. (2.8 liters). Bore & stroke: 3.66 x 2.70 in. Compression ratio: 8.7:1. Brake horsepower: 102 at 4400 R.P.M. Torque: 138 lbs.-ft. at 3200 R.P.M. Four main bearings. Solid valve lifters. Carburetor: 2Bbl. Motorcraft 2150 or 2700VV. VIN Code: Z. **OPTIONAL SIX** (Fairmont): Inline. Overhead valve. Six-cylinder. Cast iron block and head. Displacement: 200 cu. in. (3.3 liters). Bore & stroke: 3.68 x 3.13 in. Compression ratio: 8.5:1. Brake horsepower: 85 at 3600 R.P.M. Torque: 154 lbs.-ft. at 1600 R.P.M. Seven main bearings. Hydraulic valve lifters. Carburetor: 1Bbl. Carter YFA or Holley 1946. VIN Code: T. **BASE SIX** (Granada): Inline. Overhead valve. Six-cylinder. Cast iron block and head. Displacement: 250 cu. in. (4.1 liters). Bore & stroke: 3.68 x 3.91 in. Compression ratio: 8.6:1. Brake horsepower: 97 at 3200 R.P.M. Torque: 210 lbs.-ft. at 1400 R.P.M. Seven main bearings. Hydraulic valve lifters. Carburetor: 1Bbl. Carter YFA. VIN Code: L. **BASE V-8** (LTD II, Thunderbird,

LTD); OPTIONAL (Fairmont, Granada): 90-degree, overhead valve V-8. Cast iron block and head. Displacement: 302 cu. in. (5.0 liters). Bore & stroke: 4.00 x 3.00 in. Compression ratio: 8.4:1. Brake horsepower: (LTD) 129 at 3600 R.P.M.; (LTD II/TBird) 133 at 3400; (Fairmont) 140 at 3600; (Granada) 137 at 3600. Torque: (LTD) 223 lbs.- ft. at 2600 R.P.M.; (LTD II/TBird) 245 at 1600; (Fairmont) 250 at 1800; (Granada) 243 at 2000. Five main bearings. Hydraulic valve lifters. Carburetor: 2Bbl. Motorcraft 2150 or 2700VV. VIN Code: F. OPTIONAL V-8 (LTD, Thunderbird): 90-degree, overhead valve V-8. Cast iron block and head. Displacement: 351 cu. in. (5.8 liters). Bore & stroke: 4.00 x 3.50 in. Compression ratio: 8.3:1. Brake horsepower: 135 or 142 at 3200 R.P.M. Torque: 286 lbs.-ft. at 1400 R.P.M. Five main bearings. Hydraulic valve lifters. Carburetor: 2Bbl. Motorcraft 7200VV. Windsor engine. VIN Code: H. OPTIONAL V-8 (LTD II, LTD, Thunderbird): Modified version of 351 cu. in. V-8 above Compression: 8.0:1. Brake H.P.: 151 at 3600 R.P.M. Torque: 270 lbs.-ft. at 2200 R.P.M. Carb: Motorcraft 2150.

CHASSIS DATA: Wheelbase: (Pinto) 94.5 in.; (Pinto wag) 94.8 in.; (Fairmont) 105.5 in.; (Granada) 109.9 in.; (LTD II 2dr.) 114.0 in.; (LTD II 4dr.) 118.0 in.; (LTD) 114.4 in.; (TBird) 114.0 in. Overall Length: (Pinto) 168.8 in.; (Pinto wag) 178.6 in.; (Fairmont) 193.8 in. exc. Futura coupe, 195.8 in.; (Granada) 197.8 in.; (LTD II 2dr.) 217.2 in.; (LTD II 4dr.) 221.2 in.; (LTD) 209.0 in.; (LTD wag) 212.9 in.; (TBird) 217.2 in. Height: (Pinto) 50.6 in.; (Pinto wag) 52.1 in.; (Fairmont) 53.5 in.; (Fairmont Futura cpe) 52.3 in.; (Fairmont wag) 54.4 in.; (Granada) 53.2 in.; (LTD II 2dr.) 52.6 in.; (LTD II 4dr.) 53.3 in.; (LTD) 54.5 in.; (LTD wag) 56.7 in.; (TBird) 52.8 in. Width: (Pinto) 69.4 in.; (Pinto wag) 69.7 in.; (Fairmont) 71.0 in.; (Granada) 74.0 in.; (LTD II) 78.6 in.; (LTD) 77.5 in.; (LTD wag) 79.3 in.; (TBird) 78.5 in. Front Tread: (Pinto) 55.0 in.; (Fairmont) 56.6 in.; (Granada) 59.0 in.; (LTD II) 63.6 in. (LTD) 62.2 in. (TBird) 63.2 in. Rear Tread: (Pinto) 55.8 in.; (Fairmont) 57.0 in.; (Granada) 57.7 in.; (LTD II) 63.5 in.; (LTD) 62.0 in. (TBird) 63.1 in. Standard Tires: (Pinto) A78 x 13; (Fairmont) B78 x 14, except CR78 x 14 on wagon; (Granada) DR78 x 14 SBR BSW; (Granada Ghia) ER78 x 14; (LTD II) HR78 x 14 SBR BSW; (LTD) FR78 x 14 SBR BSW exc. wagon, GR78 x 14; (TBird) GR78 x 15 SBR BSW.

TECHNICAL: Transmission: Four-speed manual standard on Pinto/Fairmont four: (1st) 3.98:1; (2nd) 2.14:1; (3rd) 1.42:1; (4th) 1.00:1; (Rev) 3.99:1. Four-speed overdrive manual standard on Fairmont/Granada six/V-8. Six-cylinder: (1st) 3.29:1; (2nd) 1.84:1; (3rd) 1.00:1; (4th) 0.81:1; (Rev) 3.29:1. V-8 ratios: (1st) 3.07:1; (2nd) 1.72:1; (3rd) 1.00:1; (4th) 0.70:1; (Rev) 3.07:1. Three-speed automatic standard on other models, optional on all. Pinto/Fairmont four-cylinder (and Fairmont six) gear ratios: (1st) 2.47:1; (2nd) 1.47:1; (3rd) 1.00:1; (Rev) 2.11:1. LTD II/TBird w/V8351: (1st) 2.40:1; (2nd) 1.47:1; (3rd) 1.00:1; (Rev) 2.00:1. Other models: (1st) 2.46:1; (2nd) 1.46:1; (3rd) 1.00:1; (Rev) 2.18:1 to 2.20:1. Standard final drive ratio: (Pinto) 2.73:1 or 3.08:1; (Fairmont) 3.08:1 exc. 2.73:1 w/six and auto., 2.26:1 w/V-8 and auto.; (Granada) 3.00:1 w/4spd; (LTD II) 2.75:1 or 2.47:1; (LTD) 2.26:1 exc. wag, 2.73:1 or 2.26:1; (TBird) 2.75:1 exc. w/V8351, 2.47:1. Steering: (Pinto/Fairmont) rack and pinion; (others) recirculating ball. Front Suspension: (Pinto) coil springs with short/long control arms, and anti-sway bar with V-6; (Fairmont) MacPherson struts with coil springs on lower control arms and link-type anti-sway bar; (Granada/LTD II/TBird) coil springs with short/long control arms and anti-sway bar; (LTD) long/short control arms w/coil springs and link-type stabilizer. Rear Suspension: (Pinto/Granada) rigid axle w/semi-elliptic leaf springs; (Fairmont) four-bar link coil springs; (LTD II/TBird) rigid axle w/lower trailing radius arms, upper oblique torque arms, coil springs and anti-sway bar; (LTD) rigid axle w/four-bar link and helical coil springs. Brakes: Front disc, rear drum. Ignition: Electronic. Body construction: (Pinto/Fairmont/Granada) unibody; (LTD II/LTD/TBird) separate body and perimeter box frame. Fuel tank: (Pinto) 11.7 gal.; (Pinto wag) 14 gal.; (Fairmont) 16 gal.; (Granada) 18 gal.; (LTD II) 21 gal.; (LTD) 19 gal. exc. wagon, 20 gal.; (TBird) 21 gal. exc. 27.5 gal. on Town Landau and Heritage.

DRIVETRAIN OPTIONS: Engines: 170 cu. in. V-6: Pinto ($273). 200 cu. in., 1Bbl. six: Fairmont ($241). 302 cu. in., 2Bbl. V-8: Fairmont ($524); Granada ($283). 351 cu. in., 2Bbl. V-8: LTD II/LTD/TBird ($263). Transmission/Differential: Cruise-O-matic trans.: Pinto ($307); Fairmont ($401); Fairmont wagon ($307); Granada ($307). Floor shift lever: Fairmont/Granada ($31). Traction- Lok differential: LTD II/TBird ($64). Optional axle ratio: Pinto ($13); LTD ($18). Brakes & Steering: Power brakes: Pinto/Fairmont/Granada ($70). Power steering: Pinto ($141); Fairmont ($149); Granada ($155). Suspension: H.D. susp.: Fairmont ($19-$25); Granada ($20); LTD II ($41); LTD/TBird ($22). Handling susp.: Fairmont ($41); LTD ($42). Adjustable air shock absorbers: LTD ($54). Other: H.D. battery ($18-$21). H.D. alternator: LTD II/LTD ($50). Engine block heater ($13-$14). Trailer towing pkg. (heavy duty): LTD ($161-$192). California emission system: Pinto ($69); Fairmont/Granada ($76); others ($83). High- altitude option ($33-$36).

PINTO CONVENIENCE/APPEARANCE OPTIONS: Option Packages: ESS pkg. ($236-$261). Cruising pkg. ($330- $566); tape delete ($55 credit). Sport pkg. ($96-$110). Exterior decor group ($20-$40). Interior decor group ($137- $207). Interior accent group ($5-$40). Convenience group ($24-$61). Deluxe bumper group ($52). Protection group ($33- $36). Light group ($25-$37). Comfort/Convenience: Air conditioner ($484). Rear defroster ($84). Tinted glass ($59). Cigar lighter ($5). Trunk light ($5). Driver's sport mirror ($18). Dual sport mirrors ($52). Day/night mirror ($10). Entertainment: AM radio: Pony ($65). AM radio w/digital clock ($47-$119); w/stereo tape player ($119-$192). AM/FM radio ($48-$120). AM/FM stereo radio ($89-$161); w/cassette player ($157-$222). Radio flexibility option ($90). Exterior: Flip-up open air roof ($199). Glass third door ($25). Metallic glow paint ($41). Two-tone paint/tape treatment ($76). Accent tape stripe ($76). Black narrow vinyl-insert bodyside moldings ($39). Premium bodyside moldings ($10-$48). Rear bumper guards ($19). Roof luggage rack ($63). Mud/stone deflectors ($23). Lower bodyside protection ($30). Interior: Four-way driver's seat ($35). Load floor carpet ($24). Cargo area cover ($28). Front floor mats ($18). Wheels: Wire wheel covers ($99). Forged aluminum wheels ($217-$289); white ($235-$307). Lacy spoke alum. wheels ($217-$289). Styled steel wheels ($54). Tires: A78 x 13 WSW ($43). BR78 x 13 BSW ($148); WSW ($191). BR70 x 13 RWL ($228).

1979 Fairmont Futura Sport Coupe (F)

FAIRMONT CONVENIENCE/APPEARANCE OPTIONS: Option Packages: ES option ($329). Futura sports group ($102). Ghia pkg. ($207-$498). Squire option ($399). Exterior decor group ($223). Exterior accent group ($82). Interior decor group ($170-$311). Interior accent group ($80-$84). Instrumentation group ($77). Deluxe bumper group ($57). Convenience group ($33-$65). Appearance protection group ($36-$47). Light group ($27-$43). Comfort/Convenience: Air cond. ($484). Rear defogger ($51). Rear defroster, electric ($90). Fingertip speed control ($104-$116). Power windows ($116-$163). Power door locks ($73-$101). Power decklid release ($22). Power seat ($94). Tinted glass ($59); windshield only ($25). Sport steering wheel ($39). Tilt steering ($69-$81). Electric clock ($20). Cigar lighter ($7). Interval wipers ($35). Rear wiper/washer ($63). Map light ($7). Trunk light ($7). Left remote mirror ($17). Dual bright mirrors ($37-$43). Day/night mirror ($10). Entertainment: AM radio ($72); w/8track tape player ($192). AM/FM radio ($120). AM/FM stereo radio ($176); w/8track or cassette player ($243). Premium sound system ($67). Radio flexibility ($93). Exterior: Flip-up open air roof ($199). Full vinyl roof ($90). Metallic glow paint ($48). Two-tone paint ($51); special ($51-$207). Accent stripe ($28). Pivoting front vent windows ($48). Rear quarter vent louvers ($35). Vinyl bodyside moldings ($39); wide black vinyl ($41). Rocker panel moldings ($25). Bright window frames ($18). Bumper guards, rear ($20). Luggage rack ($76). Lower bodyside protection ($30-$42). Interior: Vinyl bucket seats, non-reclining ($72). Bench seat ($72 credit). Cloth/vinyl seat trim ($20-$42). Vinyl seat trim ($24). Front floor mats ($18). Lockable side storage box ($20). Wheels: Hubcaps w/trim rings ($37). Deluxe wheel covers ($37). Turbine wheel covers ($39-$76). Wire wheel covers ($50-$127). Styled steel wheels ($40-$116). Cast aluminum wheels ($251-$327). Tires: B78 x 14 WSW. BR78 x 14 BSW/WSW. C78 x 14 BSW/WSW. CR78 x 14 BSW/WSW. DR78 x 14 SBR BSW/WSW/RWL.

1979 Granada Ghia coupe

GRANADA CONVENIENCE/APPEARANCE OPTIONS: Option Packages: Interior decor group ($211). Convenience group ($35-$94). Deluxe bumper group ($78). Light group ($41- $46). Cold weather group ($30-$60). Heavy-duty group ($18- $60). Protection group ($24-$47). Visibility group ($5-$70). Comfort/Convenience: Air cond. ($514); auto-temp ($555). Rear defogger ($51). Rear defroster, electric ($90). Fingertip speed control ($104-$116). Illuminated entry system ($52). Power windows ($120-$171). Power door locks ($78-$110). Power decklid release ($22). Auto. parking brake release ($8). Power four-way seat ($94). Tinted glass ($64); windshield only ($25). Tilt steering wheel ($69). Digital clock ($47). Lighting and Mirrors: Cornering lamps ($43). Trunk light ($5). Left remote mirror ($17). Dual remote mirrors ($37- $54). Dual sport mirrors ($46-$63). Day/night mirror ($11). Lighted right visor vanity mirror ($36). Entertainment: AM radio ($72); w/tape player ($192). AM/FM radio ($135). AM/FM stereo radio ($176); w/8track or cassette player ($243); w/quadrasonic tape ($365). AM/FM stereo search radio ($319). CB radio ($270). Radio flexibility ($93). Exterior: Power moonroof ($899). Full or half vinyl roof ($106). Metallic glow paint ($48). Bodyside/decklid paint stripes ($36). Two-tone paint/tape ($163). Bodyside accent moldings ($43). Black vinyl insert bodyside moldings ($39). Rocker panel moldings ($25). Lower bodyside protection ($31). Interior: Console ($99). Four-way driver's seat ($34). Reclining seats (NC). Leather seat trim ($271). Flight bench seat (NC). Cloth/vinyl flight bench seat ($54). Deluxe cloth/vinyl trim (NC). Front floor mats ($18). Color-keyed seatbelts ($19). Wheels: Deluxe wheel covers ($41) exc. Ghia/ESS (NC). Wire wheel covers ($108) exc. Ghia/ESS ($67). Styled steel wheels w/trim rings ($83-$124). Cast aluminum wheels ($248-$289). Tires: DR78 x 14 SBR WSW. ER78 x 14 SBR BSW/WSW. FR78 x 14 SBR BSW/WSW/wide WSW. Inflatable spare (NC).

LTD II CONVENIENCE/APPEARANCE OPTIONS: Option Packages: Sports appearance pkg.: 2dr. ($301-$449). Sports instrumentation group ($121-$151). Sports touring pkg.: 2dr. ($379-$526). Deluxe bumper group ($63). Light group ($51-$57). Convenience group ($120-$155). Power lock group ($111-$143). Protection group ($49-$61). Comfort/Convenience: Air cond. ($562); w/auto-temp control ($607). Rear defroster, electric ($99). Fingertip speed control ($113-$126). Illuminated entry system ($57). Tinted glass ($70); windshield only ($28). Power windows ($132- $187). Six-way power seat ($163). Tilt steering wheel ($75). Electric clock ($22). Day/date clock ($22-$45). Lighting, Horns and Mirrors: Cornering lamps ($49). Dual-note horn ($9). Remote driver's mirror ($18). Dual sport mirrors ($9-$68). Lighted visor vanity mirror ($34-$39). Entertainment: AM radio ($79). AM/FM radio ($132). AM/FM stereo radio ($192); w/tape player ($266); w/quadrasonic tape player ($399). AM/FM stereo search radio ($349). CB radio ($295). Dual rear speakers ($46). Radio flexibility ($105). Exterior: Full or half vinyl roof ($116). Opera windows ($54). Vinyl-insert bodyside moldings ($42). Wide bright bodyside moldings ($42-$71). Rocker panel moldings ($29). Metallic glow paint ($64) exc. (NC) w/sports pkg. Two-tone paint ($82). Dual accent paint stripes ($33). Front bumper guards ($26). Mud/stone deflectors ($25). Lower bodyside protection ($33-$46). Interior: Bucket seats w/console ($211) exc. Brougham ($37). Vinyl seat trim ($26). Cloth/vinyl seat trim ($26). Front floor mats ($20). H.D. floor mats ($9). Color-keyed seatbelts ($22). Wheels/Tires: Deluxe wheel covers ($45). Luxury wheel covers ($66-$111). Wire wheel covers ($116-$161) exc. (NC) w/sports pkg. Cast aluminum wheels ($200-$361). HR78 x 14 SBR WSW ($47). GR78 x 15 SBR WSW ($48).

1979 LTD Landau sedan (JG)

1979 LTD II two-door hardtop

LTD CONVENIENCE/APPEARANCE OPTIONS: Option Packages: Interior luxury group: Landau ($705); Country Squire ($758). Exterior accent group ($29-$66). Convenience group ($68-$99). Light group ($32-$41). Protection group ($46-$55). Comfort/Convenience: Air cond. ($597); w/auto-temp control ($642). Rear defogger ($57). Rear defroster, electric ($100). Fingertip speed control ($113-$126). Illuminated entry system ($57). Power windows ($137-$203). Power door locks ($87- $161). Power driver's seat ($164); driver and passenger ($329). Tinted glass ($83); windshield only ($28). Tilt steering wheel ($76). Auto. parking brake release ($8). Electric clock ($24). Digital clock ($32-$55). Lighting, Horns and Mirrors: Cornering lamps ($49). Trunk light ($4). Dual-note horn ($9). Driver's remote mirror, door or sail mount ($18). Dual remote mirrors ($37-$55). Lighted visor vanity mirror ($36-$41). Entertainment: AM radio ($79). AM/FM radio ($132). AM/FM stereo radio ($192); w/tape player ($266). AM/FM stereo search radio w/quadrasonic tape player ($432). CB radio ($295). Power antenna ($47). Dual rear speakers ($46). Deluxe sound pkg. ($55); luxury pkg. ($42). Premium sound system ($74-$158). Radio flexibility ($105). Exterior: Full or half vinyl roof ($143). Metallic glow paint ($64). Two-tone paint/tape ($86-$118). Hood striping ($14). Rocker panel moldings ($29). Vinyl-insert bodyside moldings ($43). Bumper guards, front or rear ($26). Bumper rub strips ($54). Luggage rack ($113). Lower bodyside protection ($33- $46).

Interior: Dual-facing rear seats: wagon ($145-$149). Flight bench seat ($99). Dual flight bench seat recliner ($58). Split bench seat w/passenger recliner ($187-$233). All-vinyl seat trim ($26). Duraweave vinyl trim ($52). Front floor mats ($20). H.D. floor mats ($9). Trunk trim ($41-$46). Color- keyed seatbelts ($24). Wheels: Full wheel covers ($39). Luxury wheel covers ($64). Wire wheel covers ($145). Tires: FR78 x 14 WSW ($47). GR78 x 14 BSW ($30). GR78 x 14 WSW ($47-$77). HR78 x 14 (wagon): BSW ($30); WSW ($77). Conventional spare ($13).

THUNDERBIRD CONVENIENCE/APPEARANCE OPTIONS: Option Packages: Sports decor group ($459-$518). Interior luxury group ($816). Exterior decor group ($346-$405). Interior decor group ($322). Sports instrumentation group ($87-$129). Convenience group ($108-$117). Protection group ($49-$53). Light group ($51). Power lock group ($111). Luxury sound insulation ($30). Comfort/Convenience: Air cond. ($562); auto-temp ($607) exc. Twn Lan/Heritage ($45). Rear defroster ($99). Fingertip speed control ($113-$126). Illuminated entry system ($57). Tinted glass ($70); windshield only ($28). Power windows ($132). Six-way power seat ($163). Automatic seatback release ($36). Seatbelt warning chime ($22). Tilt steering wheel ($75). Day/date clock ($24). Lighting and Mirrors: Cornering lamps ($49). Driver's remote mirror, chrome ($18). Dual sport mirrors ($9-$68). Lighted visor vanity mirror ($34-$39). Entertainment: AM/FM radio ($53). AM/FM stereo radio ($113); w/tape player ($187); w/quadrasonic tape player ($320) exc. Twn Lan/Heritage ($50). AM/FM stereo search radio ($270). CB radio ($295). AM radio delete ($79 credit). Power antenna ($47). Dual rear speakers ($46). Radio flexibility ($105). Exterior: TRoof ($747). Power moonroof ($691). Vinyl roof, two-piece ($132). Metallic glow paint ($64). Two-tone paint ($82). Dual accent paint stripes ($46). Bright wide bodyside moldings ($42). Vinyl bodyside moldings ($42). Wide color- keyed vinyl bodyside moldings ($53). Rocker panel moldings ($29). Bumper rub strips ($37). Mud/stone deflectors ($25). Lower bodyside protection ($33-$46). Interior: Bucket seats w/console ($211) exc. ($37) w/decor group. Leather seat trim ($243-$309). Vinyl seat trim ($26). Front floor mats ($20). Trunk trim ($43). Color-keyed seatbelts ($22). Wheels/Tires: Wire wheel covers ($118). Styled wheels ($166). Cast aluminum wheels ($150-$316). GR78 x 15 WSW ($47). HR78 x 15 BSW ($25). HR78 x 15 WSW ($72). HR70 x 15 WSW ($29-$100). Inflatable spare (NC).

HISTORY: Introduced: October 6, 1978. Model year production: 1,835,937 (incl. Mustangs). Total passenger-car production for the U.S. market of 1,670,106 units (incl. Mustangs) included 448,627 four-cylinder, 485,842 sixes and 735,637 V-8s. Calendar year production (U.S.): 1,345,427 (incl. Mustangs). Calendar year sales by U.S. dealers: 1,499,098 (incl. Mustangs). Model year sales by U.S. dealers: 1,541,600 (incl. Mustangs).

NOTE: Totals above do not include Club Wagons, of which 42,449 were sold in the model year; or imported Fiestas, which recorded sales of 77,733.

Historical Footnotes: To attempt to meet the CAFE requirement of 19 MPG gas mileage this year, Ford pushed sales of the new downsized LTD. Buyers seemed to want the big V-8 rather than economical fours and sixes, prompting Ford to increase the price of the V-8 model. LTD sales fell rather sharply, putting the reduced-size model far behind Caprice/Impala. LTD II production ceased in January 1979, amid flagging sales. Sales declined considerably for model year 1979, down 15 percent. A gasoline crisis in mid-year didn't help; but mainly, Ford had lagged behind other companies in downsizing its big-car lineup. Pinto sales were good, even though the outmoded design couldn't truly rival the new subcompacts. And sales of the new Mustang were most impressive—nearly 70 percent above the final figure for its second-generation predecessor. A replacement for the Pinto was scheduled for 1981, dubbed "Erika." That would, of course, be changed to Escort by the time the new front-drive subcompact was introduced. Not until then would Ford have a true rival to Chevrolet's Chevette. Lee Iacocca had been fired by Henry Ford II soon after the model year began. Philip Caldwell then became president.

1980 FORD

Ford's emphasis this year lay in economy, highlighted by its new lockup overdrive automatic transmission. The 1980 CAFE goal for automakers' fleets was 20 MPG (up from 19 MPG in 1979). Thunderbird was the star of the lineup in its new downsized form. LTD II was gone, and Pinto was in its final season. On the powerplant front, a turbocharged four was announced as a Fairmont option, but didn't quite materialize, presumably due to mechanical difficulties. A smaller (255 cu. in.) V-8 replaced the former 302 as a Fairmont option, and became standard on the new mid-size TBird. LTD's new automatic overdrive transmission boasted an economy improvement of 19 percent over a comparable 1979 model.

1980 Pinto three-door hatchback (JG)

PINTO — FOUR — All Pintos had four-cylinder engines for 1980, as the optional V-6 disappeared. The standard 140 cu. in. (2.3- liter) four received improvements to boost its highway gas mileage. Styling was virtually identical to 1979, with seven new body colors and three new interior trim colors available. The low-budget Pony now wore steel-belted radial tires. Batteries were maintenance-free, and cars carried a restyled scissors jack. Radios played a Travelers' Advisory band, and the station wagon's Cruising Package option was revised. This was Pinto's final season, as the new front-drive Escort was ready for production. The Rallye Pack option, introduced late in 1979 on hatchback and wagon, was expanded this year. Model lineup continued as before: two-door sedan, "three-door" hatchback Runabout, two-door station wagon, and Pony sedan or wagon. Pony lacked the base model's tinted glass, rear defroster, AM radio, bumper rub strips, and vinyl-insert bodyside moldings, as well as bright window frame, belt and 'B' pillar moldings. Pinto's ESS package included a charcoal grille and headlamp doors, black windshield and backlight moldings, dual black racing mirrors, glass third door with black hinges, blackout paint treatment, black wheel lip moldings, 'ESS' fender insignia, and black window frames. The price was $281 to $313.

1980 Fairmont sedan (JG)

FAIRMONT — FOUR/SIX/V-8 — Powerplants were the major news in the Fairmont arena this year. Most notable was the announcement of a turbocharged four, but evidently that one never quite made production. A new 255 cu. in. (4.2-liter) V-8 did, though, replacing the former 302 option. It was available only with automatic. Both the 255 and the 200 cu. in. (3.3-liter) inline six had a new lightweight starter. Base engine remained the 140 cu. in. (2.3-liter) four, with four-speed manual gearbox. Manual-shift transmissions had a new self-adjusting clutch. New high-pressure P-metric steel-belted radial tires became standard on all models. A mini spare tire and maintenance-free battery were standard, while all radios added a Travelers' Advisory band. Fairmont came in nine new body colors and two new two-tone color schemes (with accent color in the bodyside center). A four-door sedan joined the Futura coupe at mid-year, wearing the unique Futura crosshatch grille. Futuras had standard halogen headlamps (except where prohibited by state laws). Otherwise, styling was similar to 1978-79. The Futura coupe had a woodgrain dash applique, quad halogen headlamps, trunk light, bright window frame moldings, vinyl bodyside moldings, and wheel lip and door belt moldings. The Futura sports group, priced at $114, included color-keyed turbine wheel covers, charcoal/argent grille, and youth-oriented tape stripes; the customary hood ornament, louvers and accent stripe were deleted. The optional sport steering wheel switched from brushed aluminum to black finish. Fairmont's $378 ES sedan option package included a blackout grille, front/rear rub strips, black cowl grille, black window frames and quarter window vent louvers, and vinyl-insert bodyside moldings. Also included: dual black remote sport mirrors, turbine wheel covers, black sport steering wheel, rear bumper guards, handling suspension, and black lower back panel.

1980 Granada Ghia sedan (F)

GRANADA — SIX/V-8 — Apart from seven new body colors and three new vinyl roof colors, little changed on the compact Granada sedans. A new lightweight starter went under the hood, a better scissors jack in the trunk, and Ardmore cloth upholstery on the seats. Maintenance-free batteries were standard. Joining the option list were a heavy-duty 54-amp battery, mud/stone guards, and revised electronic search stereo radios and tape players. "Tu-tone" paint cost $180. Standard engine was the 250 cu.

in. (4.1-liter) inline six, with 302 cu. in. (5.0- liter) V-8 optional. California Granadas required the new 255 cu. in. V-8. Granada came in two- or four-door sedan form again: base, Ghia or ESS trim. Granada Ghia carried dual body/hood/decklid accent stripes, black/argent lower back panel applique, left remote mirror, wide vinyl-insert bodyside moldings, and burled walnut woodtone door trim. The sporty Granada ESS held a blacked-out grille. dual remote mirrors, black bodyside moldings with bright inserts, black rocker panel paint, hood/decklid paint stripes, bucket seats with chainmail vinyl inserts, leather-wrapped steering wheel, louvered opera window applique, and wide wheel lip moldings.

1980 LTD Crown Victoria sedan (F)

LTD — V-8 — Reshuffling of the model lineup hit the full-size line for 1980. This year's selection included budget-priced LTD 'S', base LTD, and LTD Crown Victoria sedans. An 'S' edition also joined the LTD (plain-body) and Country Squire (woodgrain) station wagon choices. Crown Victoria (same name as the mid-1950s high-line Ford) replaced the former Landau as top-of-the-line sedan. A new four-speed automatic transmission with overdrive top gear became optional on all models with the 351 cu. in. (5.8-liter) V-8, and on sedans with the base 302 (5.0-liter) V-8. Also new this year: standard P-metric radial tires with higher pressure, standard maintenance-free battery, and halogen headlamps (except LTD 'S'). Crown Victoria and Country Squire carried a new wide hood ornament design, while standard LTDs had no ornament at all. Country Squire wagons had simulated woodgrain panels with planking lines. New black rocker panel moldings and lower bright moldings with rear extensions went on the Crown Victoria. So did a new rear half-vinyl roof with "frenched" seams and brushed

1980 LTD Crown Victoria Country Squire station wagon (JG)

aluminum roof wrapover moldings. Both LTD and Crown Vic sedans displayed new decklid tape stripes. Front bumper guards were standard. New options included the Traction-Lok axle; cast aluminum wheels; auto-headlamp on/off/delay system; leather-wrapped luxury steering wheel; and electronic stereo search radio with cassette player and Dolby sound. Appearance was similar to 1979. Each checkerboard grille section had a 15 x 7 hole pattern (30 across), topped by a heavy upper header bar. 'S' had a different front end and grille, with round headlamps and parking lamps inset into the grille. Other models showed quad headlamps. Bodyside beltline striping was higher this year. Two-door opera windows had a more vertical look. LTD had three police packages available: 302 cu. in. V-8, regular 351 V-8, and high-output 351 (with dual exhausts and modified camshaft). Police packages included heavy-duty alternators, a 2.26:1 axle for the 5.0 liter (3.08:1 for the 5.8 liter), 71 ampere-hour battery, heavy-duty power brakes, 140 MPH speedometer, heavy-duty suspension, GR70 x 15 blackwall police radials, and conventional spare tire. Police automatic transmissions had a first-gear lockout and oil cooler.

1980 Thunderbird Silver Anniversary hardtop coupe (F)

THUNDERBIRD — V-8 — For its 25th year in the lineup, Thunderbird got a new size and a new standard engine. This year's version rode a 108.4 inch wheelbase (formerly 114) and carried a standard 255 cu. in. (4.2-liter) V-8. That engine had the same stroke as the 302 V-8 (now optional), but a smaller bore. For the first time in a decade and a half, this TBird also wore a unitized body, essentially the same as the Fairmont

platform. Instead of the former six-passenger capacity, the ninth-generation edition was intended for just four. It weighed over 700 pounds less than before. Modified MacPherson struts made up the front suspension, with four-bar-link coil springs at the rear. Thunderbird had power-assisted, variable-ratio rack-and-pinion steering. Axle ratios were lowered, to boost mileage. A new four-speed overdrive automatic transmission was optional with the 302 V-8. Styling features included traditional concealed headlamps, full-width wraparound taillamps, a lower beltline, unique (but traditional) wraparound parking lamps, and a strong mid-bodyside sculpture theme. Single opera windows to the rear of a wrapover roof band on the solid wide C pillars held a Thunderbird emblem. At front and rear were soft color- keyed urethane bumper systems. The eggcrate grille showed an 8 x 6 "hole" pattern, with the pattern repeated in a bumper slot below. Trim panels on the headlamp covers extended outward and around the fender sides to contain side marker lenses. Taillamp panels had a notch at the center, and wide Thunderbird emblem on each lens. Base and Town Landau models were offered at first. Town Landau added air conditioning, autolamp delay system, tinted glass, jewel-like hood ornament, electronic instrument cluster, cornering lamps, dual remote mirrors, and owner's nameplate with 22K gold finish. Also included: upper bodyside/hood/decklid paint/tape striping, AM/FM stereo search radio, padded half-vinyl roof with wrapover band and coach lamps, power driver's seat, power windows, and turbine-spoke cast aluminum wheels. A Silver Anniversary model, added at mid-year, came in a selection of color combinations: Silver Anniversary Glow (with black wrapover band and silver vinyl roof, or silver band and black roof); Black (with silver wrapover and black vinyl roof, or black wrapover and silver roof); Light Grey (silver wrapover band and black viyl roof); Red Glow (silver wrapover and red vinyl roof); Midnight Blue metallic (silver wrapover band and midnight blue vinyl roof); or Black Silver Glow two-tone (silver wrapover and black vinyl roof). All Silver Anniversary models had Dove Grey interiors, plus standard automatic overdrive transmission. Three distinct roof treatments were available: base, Exterior Luxury Group (on Town Landau), and Silver Anniversary. TBirds also had new high-pressure P-metric radial tires, maintenance-free battery, mini spare tire, new wheels and covers, new two-tier instrument panel, and a four- spoke soft-rim steering wheel. Dual seatback recliners went on all split bench seats. Sculptured window-frame-mounted mirrors were optional. Other new options were: electronic instrument cluster including digital speedometer; TR type low-profile wide aspect ratio tires on cast aluminum wheels with special suspension tuning; keyless entry system; electronic garage door opener; diagnostic warning light system; six-speaker premium sound system; and flip-up removable moon roof. Many of these extras were standard on Town Landau and/or Silver Anniversary. Thunderbird's mate over at Mercury was the Cougar XR7.

I.D. DATA: As before, Ford's 11-symbol Vehicle Identification Number (VIN) is stamped on a metal tab fastened to the instrument panel, visible through the windshield. Coding is the same as 1979, except engine codes (symbol five) changed as follows: 'A' L4-140 2Bbl.; 'A' turbo L4140 2Bbl.; 'B' L6200 1Bbl.; 'C' L6250 1Bbl.; 'D' V8255 2Bbl.; 'F' V8302 2Bbl.; 'G' V8351 2Bbl. Model year code changed to '0' for 1980.

PINTO (FOUR)

Model Number	Body/Style Number	Body Type & Seating	Factory Price	Shipping Weight	Production Total
10	62B	2-dr. Sedan-4P	4223	2385	84,053
10	41E	2-dr. Pony Sed-4P	3781	2377	Note 1
11	64B	3-dr. Hatch-4P	4335	2426	61,842
12	73B	2-dr. Sta Wag-4P	4622	2553	39,159
12	41E	2-dr. Pony Wag-4P	4284	2545	Note 1
12/604	73B	2-dr. Sqr Wag-4P	4937	2590	Note 2

Note 1: Pony production included in base sedan and wagon figures. Panel deliver Pintos also were produced. **Note 2:** Squire Wagon production is included in standard station wagon total.

1980 Fairmont Squire wagon (F)

FAIRMONT (FOUR/SIX)

91	66B	2-dr. Sedan-5P	4435/4604	2571/ --	45,074
92	54B	4-dr. Sedan-5P	4552/4721	2599/ --	143,118
94	74B	4-dr. Sta Wag-5P	4721/4890	2722/ --	77,035

FAIRMONT FUTURA (FOUR/SIX)

93	36R	2-dr. Spt Cpe-5P	4837/5006	2612/ --	51,878
92	N/A	4-dr. Sedan-5P	5070/5239	N/A	5,306

Fairmont Engine Note: Prices shown are for four-cylinder and six- cylinder engines. A 255 cu. in. V-8 cost $119 more than the six.

1980 Granada sedan (JG)

GRANADA (SIX/V-8)

Model Number	Body/Style Number	Body Type & Seating	Factory Price	Shipping Weight	Production Total
81	66H	2-dr. Sedan-5P	4987/5025	3063/3187	60,872
82	54H	4-dr. Sedan-5P	5108/5146	3106/3230	29,557

GRANADA GHIA (SIX/V-8)

81/602	66K	2-dr. Sedan-5P	5388/5426	3106/3230	Note 3
82/602	54K	4-dr. Sedan-5P	5509/5547	3147/3271	Note 3

GRANADA ESS (SIX/V-8)

81/933	N/A	2-dr. Sedan-5P	5477/5515	3137/3261	Note 3
82/933	N/A	4-dr. Sedan-5P	5598/5636	3178/3302	Note 3

Note 3: Granada Ghia and ESS production is included in base Granada totals above. Granada Engine Note: Prices shown are for six-cylinder and V8255 engines. A 302 cu. in. V-8 cost $150 more than the 255 V-8.

1980 LTD sedan (JG)

LTD (V-8)

62	66H	2-dr. Sedan-6P	6549	3447	15,333
63	54H	4-dr. Sedan-6P	6658	3475	51,630
74	74H	4-dr. Sta Wag-6P	7007	3717	11,718

LTD 'S' (V-8)

N/A	66D	2-dr. Sedan-6P	N/A	N/A	553
61	54D	4-dr. Sedan-6P	6320	2464	19,283
72	74D	4-dr. Sta Wag-6P	6741	3707	3,490

LTD CROWN VICTORIA (V-8)

64	66K	2-dr. Sedan-6P	7070	3482	7,725
65	54K	4-dr. Sedan-6P	7201	3524	21,962
76	74K	4-dr. Ctry Sqr-6P	7426	3743	9,868

LTD Production Note: Production of wagons with dual-facing rear seats (a $146-$151 option for both standard and Country Squire wagon) is included in basic wagon totals.

THUNDERBIRD (V-8)

87	66D	2-dr. HT Cpe-4P	6432	3118	156,803

1980 Thunderbird Town Landau hardtop coupe (JG)

THUNDERBIRD TOWN LANDAU (V-8)

87/607	66D	2-dr. HT Cpe-4P	10036	3357	Note 4

THUNDERBIRD SILVER ANNIVERSARY (V-8)

87/603	66D	2-dr. HT Cpe-4P	11679	3225	Note 4

Note 4: Town Landau and Silver Anniversary production is included in basic Thunderbird total.

FACTORY PRICE AND WEIGHT NOTE: Fairmont prices and weights to left of slash are for four-cylinder, to right for six-cylinder engine. Granada prices and weights to left of slash are for six-cylinder, to right for 255 cu. in. V-8 engine.

ENGINE DATA: BASE FOUR (Pinto, Fairmont): Inline. Overhead cam. Four-cylinder. Cast iron block and head. Displacement: 140 cu. in. (2.3 liters). Bore & stroke: 3.78 x 3.13 in. Compression ratio: 9.0:1. Brake horsepower: 88 at 4600 R.P.M. Torque: 119 lbs.-ft. at 2600 R.P.M. Five main bearings. Hydraulic valve lifters. Carburetor: 2Bbl. Motorcraft 5200. VIN Code: A. OPTIONAL SIX (Fairmont): Inline. Overhead valve. Six-cylinder. Cast iron block and head. Displacement: 200 cu. in. (3.3 liters). Bore & stroke: 3.68 x 3.13 in. Compression ratio: 8.6:1. Brake horsepower: 91 at 3800 R.P.M. Torque: 160 lbs.-ft. at 1600 R.P.M. Seven main bearings. Hydraulic valve lifters. Carburetor: 1Bbl. Holley 1946. VIN Code: B. BASE SIX (Granada): Inline. Overhead valve. Six-cylinder. Cast iron block and head. Displacement: 250 cu. in. (4.1 liters). Bore & stroke: 3.68 x 3.91 in. Compression ratio: 8.6:1. Brake horsepower: 90 at 3200 R.P.M. Torque: 194 lbs.-ft. at 1660 R.P.M. Seven main bearings. Hydraulic valve lifters. Carburetor: 1Bbl. Carter YFA. VIN Code: C. BASE V-8 (Thunderbird); OPTIONAL (Fairmont, Granada): 90-degree, overhead valve V-8. Cast iron block and head. Displacement: 255 cu. in. (4.2 liters). Bore & stroke: 3.68 x 3.00 in. Compression ratio: 8.8:1. Brake horsepower: (Fairmont) 119 at 3800 R.P.M.; (TBird) 115 at 3800. Torque: (Fairmont) 194 lbs.-ft. at 2200 R.P.M.; (TBird) 194 at 2200. Five main bearings. Hydraulic valve lifters. Carburetor: 2Bbl. Motorcraft 2150. VIN Code: D. BASE V-8 (LTD, Thunderbird Silver Anniversary); OPTIONAL (Granada, Thunderbird): 90-degree, overhead valve V-8. Cast iron block and head. Displacement: 302 cu. in. (5.0 liters). Bore & stroke: 4.00 x 3.00 in. Compression ratio: 8.4:1. Brake horsepower: (LTD) 130 at 3600 R.P.M.; (TBird) 131 at 3600; (Granada) 134 at 3600. Torque: (LTD) 230 lbs.-ft. at 1600 R.P.M.; (TBird) 231 at 1600; (Granada) 232 at 1600. Five main bearings. Hydraulic valve lifters. Carburetor: 2Bbl. Motorcraft 2150 or 2700VV. VIN Code: F. OPTIONAL V-8 (LTD): 90-degree, overhead valve V-8. Cast iron block and head. Displacement: 351 cu. in. (5.8 liters). Bore & stroke: 4.00 x 3.50 in. Compression ratio: 8.3:1. Brake horsepower: 140 at 3400 R.P.M. Torque: 265 lbs.-ft. at 2000 R.P.M. Five main bearings. Hydraulic valve lifters. Carburetor: 2Bbl. Motorcraft 7200VV. Windsor engine. VIN Code: G.

NOTE: A high-output version of the 351 cu. in. V-8 was available for police use.

CHASSIS DATA: Wheelbase: (Pinto) 94.5 in.; (Pinto wag) 94.8 in.; (Fairmont) 105.5 in.; (Granada) 109.9 in.; (LTD) 114.3 in.; (TBird) 108.4 in. Overall Length: (Pinto) 170.8 in.; (Pinto wag) 180.6 in.; (Fairmont) 195.5 in. exc. Futura coupe, 197.4 in.; (Granada) 199.7 in.; (LTD) 209.3 in.; (LTD wag) 215.0 in.; (TBird) 200.4 in. Height: (Pinto) 50.5 in.; (Pinto wag) 52.0 in.; (Fairmont) 52.9 in.; (Fairmont Futura cpe) 51.7 in.; (Fairmont wag) 54.2 in.; (Granada) 53.2-53.3 in.; (LTD) 54.7 in.; (LTD wag) 57.4 in.; (TBird) 53.0 in. Width: (Pinto) 69.4 in.; (Pinto wag) 69.7 in.; (Fairmont) 71.0 in.; (Granada) 74.5 in.; (LTD) 77.5 in.; (LTD wag) 79.3 in.; (TBird) 74.1 in. Front Tread: (Pinto) 55.0 in.; (Fairmont) 56.6 in.; (Granada) 59.0 in.; (LTD) 62.2 in.; (TBird) 58.1 in. Rear Tread: (Pinto) 55.8 in.; (Fairmont) 57.0 in.; (Granada) 57.7 in.; (LTD) 62.0 in. (TBird) 57.0 in. Standard Tires: (Pinto) BR78 x 13 SBR exc. Pony, A78 x 13; (Fairmont) P175/75R14; (Granada) DR78 x 14 SBR BSW exc. Ghia, ER78 x 14 and ESS, FR78 x 14; (LTD) P205/75R14 BSW exc. wagon, P215/75R14; (TBird) P185/75R14 SBR BSW.

TECHNICAL: Transmission: Four-speed manual standard on Pinto/Fairmont four: (1st) 3.98:1; (2nd) 2.14:1; (3rd) 1.42:1; (4th) 1.00:1; (Rev) 3.99:1. Four-speed overdrive manual standard on Fairmont/Granada six: (1st) 3.29:1; (2nd) 1.84:1; (3rd) 1.00:1; (4th) 0.81:1; (Rev) 3.29:1. Three-speed automatic standard on other models, optional on all. Pinto/Fairmont four-cylinder gear ratios: (1st) 2.47:1; (2nd) 1.47:1; (3rd) 1.00:1; (Rev) 2.11:1. Other models: (1st) 2.46:1; (2nd) 1.46:1; (3rd) 1.00:1; (Rev) 2.18:1 to 2.20:1. Four-speed overdrive automatic available on Thunderbird w/V8302 and LTD: (1st) 2.47:1; (2nd) 1.47:1; (3rd) 1.00:1; (4th) 0.67:1; (Rev) 2.00:1. Standard final drive ratio: (Pinto) 3.08:1 w/4spd; (Fairmont) 3.08:1 exc. 2.73:1 w/six and auto., 2.26:1 w/V-8 and auto.; (Granada) 3.00:1 w/4spd, 2.79:1 w/V-8 and auto.; (LTD) 2.26:1 exc. wag 2.73:1, and 3.08:1 w/4spd overdrive auto.; (TBird) 2.26:1 exc. w/4spd auto., 3.08:1. Steering: (Pinto/Fairmont/TBird) rack and pinion; (others) recirculating ball. Front Suspension: (Pinto) coil springs with short/long control arms, and anti-sway bar with V-6; (Fairmont) MacPherson struts with coil springs on lower control arms and link-type anti-sway bar; (Granada) coil springs with short/long control arms and anti-sway bar; (LTD) long/short control arms w/coil springs and link-type stabilizer; (Thunderbird) modified MacPherson struts. Rear Suspension: (Pinto/Granada) rigid axle w/semi-elliptic leaf springs; (Fairmont/TBird) four-bar link coil springs; (LTD) rigid axle w/four-bar link and helical coil springs. Brakes: Front disc, rear drum. Ignition: Electronic. Body construction: (Pinto/Fairmont/Granada/TBird) unibody; (LTD) separate body and perimeter box frame. Fuel tank: (Pinto) 13 gal. exc. wag, 14; (Fairmont) 16 gal.; (Granada) 18 gal.; (LTD) 19 gal.; (TBird) 17.5 gal.

DRIVETRAIN OPTIONS: Engines: Turbo 140 cu. in. four: Fairmont ($481). 200 cu. in. six: Fairmont ($169). 255 cu. in. V-8: Fairmont ($288); Granada ($38). 302 cu. in. V-8: Granada ($188); TBird ($150). 351 cu. in. V-8: LTD ($150). Transmission/Differential: Select-shift auto. trans.: Pinto/Fairmont/Granada ($340). Four-speed overdrive automatic trans.: LTD/TBird ($138). Floor shift lever: Fairmont/Granada ($38). Traction-Lok differential: LTD ($69). Optional axle ratio: Pinto/Fairmont ($15); LTD ($19). Brakes/Steering/Suspension: Power brakes: Pinto/Fairmont/Granada ($78). Power steering: Pinto ($160); Fairmont/Granada ($165). H.D. susp.: Granada/LTD/TBird ($23). Handling susp.: Fairmont ($44); LTD ($43). Adjustable air shock absorbers: LTD ($55). Other: H.D. battery ($20-$21). Engine block heater ($15). Trailer towing pkg., heavy duty: LTD ($164-$169). California emission system: Pinto/Fairmont ($253); Granada ($275); LTD ($235); TBird ($238). High-altitude option ($36).

PINTO CONVENIENCE/APPEARANCE OPTIONS: Option Packages: ESS pkg. ($281-$313). Cruising pkg. ($355-$606); tape delete ($70 credit). Rally pack: hatch ($369); wagon ($625). Sport pkg. ($103-$118). Exterior decor group ($24-$44). Interior decor group ($165-$238). Interior accent group ($5-$50). Convenience group ($26-$118). Protection group ($36-$40). Light group ($41). Comfort/Convenience: Air conditioner ($538). Rear defroster, electric ($96). Tinted glass ($65). Cigar lighter ($8). Trunk light ($5). Driver's remote mirror ($18). Dual sport mirrors ($58). Day/night mirror ($11). Entertainment: AM radio: Pony ($80). AM/FM radio ($65-$145). AM/FM stereo radio ($103-$183); w/cassette player ($191-$271). Radio flexibility option ($31). Exterior: Flip-up open air roof ($206-$219). Glass third door ($31). Metallic glow paint ($45). Two-tone paint/tape ($80). Accent tape stripe ($80). Black narrow vinyl-insert bodyside moldings ($43). Premium bodyside moldings ($11-$54). Bumper rub strips ($34). Roof luggage rack ($71). Mud/stone deflectors ($25). Lower bodyside protection ($34). Interior: Four-way driver's seat ($38). Load floor carpet ($28). Cargo area cover ($30). Front floor mats ($19). Wheels/Tires: Wire wheel covers ($104). Forged aluminum wheels ($225-$300); white ($256-$331). Lacy spoke alum. wheels ($225-$300). Styled steel wheels ($56). BR78 x 13 WSW ($50). BR70 x 13 RWL ($87).

FAIRMONT CONVENIENCE/APPEARANCE OPTIONS: Option Packages: ES option ($378). Futura sports group ($114). Ghia pkg.: Futura cpe ($193); std. sedan ($566). Squire option ($458). Exterior decor group ($260). Exterior accent group ($95). Interior decor group ($184-$346). Interior accent group ($110-$115). Instrument cluster ($85). Convenience group ($29-$51). Appearance protection group ($46-$53). Light group ($30-$48). Comfort/Convenience: Air cond. ($571). Rear defroster, electric ($101). Fingertip speed control ($116-$129). Power windows ($135-$191). Power door locks ($88-$125). Power decklid release ($24). Power seat ($166). Tinted glass ($71). Sport steering wheel ($43). Leather-wrapped steering wheel ($44). Tilt steering ($78-$90). Electric clock ($23). Cigar lighter ($8). Interval wipers ($39). Rear wiper/washer ($79). Left remote mirror ($19). Dual bright remote mirrors ($54-$60). Entertainment: AM radio ($93). AM/FM radio ($145). AM/FM stereo radio ($183).

w/8track player ($259); w/cassette player ($271). Premium sound system ($94). Radio flexibility ($63). Exterior: Flip-up open air roof ($219). Full or half vinyl roof ($118). Metallic glow paint ($54). Two-tone paint ($56); metallic ($154-$169). Accent stripe ($33). Pivoting front vent windows ($50). Rear quarter vent louvers ($41). Vinyl-insert bodyside moldings ($44); wide black vinyl ($45). Rocker panel moldings ($30). Bright window frames ($24). Bumper guards, rear ($23). Bumper rub strips ($40). Luggage rack ($88). Mud/stone deflectors ($25). Lower bodyside protection ($34-$48). Interior: Non-reclining bucket seats ($31-$50). Bench seat ($50 credit). Cloth/vinyl seat trim ($28-$44). Vinyl seat trim ($25). Front floor mats ($19). Lockable side storage box ($23). Wheels/Tires: Hubcaps w/trim rings ($41). Deluxe wheel covers ($41). Turbine wheel covers ($43); argent ($43-$84). Wire wheel covers ($74-$158). Styled steel wheels ($49-$133). Cast aluminum wheels ($268-$351). P175/75R14 WSW ($50). P185/75R14 BSW ($31); WSW ($81); RWL ($96). Conventional spare ($37).

GRANADA CONVENIENCE/APPEARANCE OPTIONS: Option Packages: Interior decor group ($243). Convenience group ($39-$108). Light group ($46-$51). Cold weather group ($31-$65). Heavy-duty group ($20-$65). Protection group ($29- $53). Visibility group ($6-$66). Comfort/Convenience: Air cond. ($571); auto-temp ($634). Rear defroster, electric ($101). Fingertip speed control ($116- $129). Illuminated entry system ($58). Power windows ($136- $193). Power door locks ($89-$125). Power decklid release ($25). Power four-way seat ($111). Tinted glass ($71). Tilt steering wheel ($78). Digital clock ($54). Lighting and Mirrors: Cornering lamps ($50). Dual remote mirrors ($41-$60). Dual sport mirrors ($50-$69). Lighted right visor vanity mirror ($41). Entertainment: AM radio ($93). AM/FM radio ($145). AM/FM stereo radio ($183); w/8track player ($259); w/cassette ($271). AM/FM stereo search radio ($333); w/8track ($409); w/cassette and Dolby ($421). Radio flexibility ($63). Exterior: Power moonroof ($998). Full or half vinyl roof ($118). Metallic glow paint ($54). Bodyside/decklid paint stripes ($49). Two-tone paint/tape ($180). Bodyside accent moldings ($50). Black vinyl insert bodyside moldings ($44). Rocker panel moldings ($30). Bumper rub strips ($41). Mud/stone deflectors ($25). Lower bodyside protection ($34). Interior: Console ($110). Four-way driver's seat ($38). Reclining bucket seats (NC). Deluxe cloth/vinyl seat (NC). Flight bench seat (NC). Cloth/vinyl flight bench seat ($60). Leather seat trim ($277). Front floor mats ($19). Color-keyed seatbelts ($23). Wheels: Luxury wheel covers ($46) exc. Ghia (NC). Wire wheel covers ($119) exc. Ghia/ESS ($73). Styled steel wheels w/trim rings ($91-$138). Cast aluminum wheels ($275-$321). Tires: DR78 x 14 SBR WSW. ER78 x 14 SBR BSW/WSW. FR78 x 14 SBR BSW/WSW/wide WSW. Inflatable spare ($37).

LTD CONVENIENCE/APPEARANCE OPTIONS: Option Packages: Interior luxury group ($693-$741). Convenience group ($68-$98). Power lock group ($114-$166). Light group ($33-$43). Protection group ($48-$58). Comfort/Convenience: Air cond. ($606); w/auto-temp control ($669). Rear defroster, electric ($103). Fingertip speed control ($116). Illuminated entry system ($58). Power windows ($140-$208). Power door locks ($89-$120). Power driver's seat ($168); driver and passenger ($335). Tinted glass ($85). Autolamp on/off delay ($63). Leather-wrapped steering wheel ($44). Tilt steering wheel ($78). Auto. parking brake release ($10). Electric clock ($24). Digital clock ($38-$61). Seatbelt chime ($23). Interval wipers ($40). Lighting, Horns and Mirrors: Cornering lamps ($48). Trunk light ($5). Dual-note horn ($10). Driver's remote mirror ($19). Dual remote mirrors ($38-$56). Lighted right visor vanity mirror ($35-$41); pair ($42-$83). Entertainment: AM radio ($93). AM/FM radio ($145). AM/FM stereo radio ($183); w/8track tape player ($259); w/cassette ($271). AM/FM stereo search radio ($333); w/8track ($409); w/cassette ($421). CB radio ($316). Power antenna ($49). Dual rear speakers ($40). Premium sound system ($94). Radio flexibility ($66). Exterior: Full or half vinyl roof ($145). Metallic glow paint ($65). Two-tone paint/tape ($75). Dual accent paint stripes ($33). Hood striping ($14). Pivoting front vent windows ($50). Rocker panel moldings ($29). Vinyl-insert bodyside moldings ($45). Bumper guards, rear ($26). Bumper rub strips ($56). Luggage rack ($115). Lower bodyside protection ($34- $46). Interior: Dual-facing rear seats: wagon ($146-$151). Flight bench seat ($56). Leather split bench seat ($349). Dual flight bench seat recliners ($55). Split bench seat w/ recliners ($173-$229). All-vinyl seat trim ($28). Duraweave vinyl trim ($50). Front floor mats ($19); front/rear ($30). Trunk trim ($46-$51). Trunk mat ($14). Color-keyed seatbelts ($24). Wheels/Tires: Luxury wheel covers ($70). Wire wheel covers ($138). Cast aluminum wheels ($310). P205/75R14 WSW ($50). P215/75R14 BSW ($29); WSW ($50-$79). P225/75R14 WSW ($79- $107). P205/75R15 WSW ($55-$87). Conventional spare ($37).

THUNDERBIRD CONVENIENCE/APPEARANCE OPTIONS: Option Packages: Exterior luxury group ($489). Interior luxury group ($975). Exterior decor group ($359). Interior decor group ($348). Protection group ($39-$43). Light group ($35). Power lock group ($113). Comfort/Convenience: Air cond. ($571); auto-temp ($634) exc. Twn Lan/Anniv. ($63). Rear defroster ($101). Fingertip speed control ($116-$129). Illuminated entry system ($58). Keyless entry ($106-$119). Garage door opener w/lighted vanity mirrors ($130-$171). Autolamp on/off delay ($63). Tinted glass ($71); windshield only ($29). Power windows ($136). Four-way power seat ($111). Six-way power driver's seat ($166). Auto. parking brake release ($10). Leather-wrapped steering wheel ($44). Tilt steering wheel ($78). Electronic instrument cluster ($275-$313). Diagnostic warning lights ($50). Digital clock ($38). Interval wipers ($39). Lighting, Horns and Mirrors: Cornering lamps ($50). Trunk light ($5). Dual-note horn ($9). Driver's remote mirror, chrome ($18). Dual remote mirrors ($69). Lighted right visor vanity mirror ($35-$41). Entertainment: AM/FM radio ($53). AM/FM stereo radio ($90); w/8track player ($166); w/cassette ($179). AM/FM stereo search radio ($240); w/8track ($316) exc. Twn Lan/Anniv. ($76); w/cassette ($329) exc. Twn Lan/Anniv. ($89). CB radio ($316). AM radio delete ($81 credit). Power antenna ($49). Dual rear speakers ($38). Premium sound system ($119-$150). Radio flexibility ($66). Exterior: Flip-up open-air roof ($219). Vinyl half roof ($133). Metallic glow paint ($60). Two-tone paint/tape ($106- $163). Dual accent bodyside paint stripes ($40). Hood/bodyside paint stripes ($16-$56). Wide vinyl bodyside moldings ($54). Wide door belt moldings ($31-$44). Rocker panel moldings ($30). Mud/stone deflectors ($25). Lower odyside protection ($34-$46). Interior: Bucket seats w/console ($176) exc. (NC) w/decor group. Recaro buckets w/console ($166-$254) exc. Twn Lan (NC). Leather seat trim ($318-$349). Vinyl seat trim ($26). Front floor mats ($19). Trunk trim ($44). Color-keyed seatbelts ($23). Wheels/Tires: Wire wheel covers ($50-$138). Luxury wheel covers ($88). P195/75R14 BSW ($26); WSW ($50). TR WSW tires on alum. wheels: base ($441-$528). Conventional spare ($37).

HISTORY: Introduced: October 12, 1979. Model year production: 1,167,581 (incl. Mustangs). Total passenger-car production for the U.S. market of 1,048,044 units (incl. Mustangs) included 426,107 four-cylinder, 334,298 sixes and 287,639 V-8s. Of the fours, 1,158 were Fairmont turbos (and 12,052 Mustang turbos). Calendar year production (U.S.): 929,639 (incl. Mustangs). Calendar year sales by U.S. dealers: 1,074,675 (incl. Mustangs). Model year sales by U.S. dealers: 1,124,192 (incl. Mustangs, but not incl. 68,841 imported Fiestas).

NOTE: Starting this year, Club Wagons (vans) were no longer classed as passenger cars.

Historical Footnotes: Early in 1980, the "Erika" subcompact to come for 1981 was renamed Escort (and Mercury Lynx). Sales for the model year fell over 28 percent, touching every car in the lineup but headed by LTD's 43 percent drop. LTD was advertised during this period as rivaling Rolls-Royce for smooth, quiet ride qualities. The restyled and downsized Thunderbird didn't find many buyers either. Two assembly plants closed during 1980, at Mahwah, New Jersey and Los Angeles. Still, Ford expected to spend $2 billion for expansion and retooling at other domestic acilities. Foremost hope for the future was the new Escort being readied for 1981 introduction. Philip E. Benton became head of the Ford Division, following the retirement of Walter S. Walla.

1981 FORD

The new front-wheel drive Escort "world car" arrived for 1981, to assist Ford in reaching a healthy share of subcompact buyers. Granada had all-new sheetmetal with shorter wheelbase and length, but claimed six-passenger capacity. Fairmont Futura added a wagon, while there was a new top-of-the-line Thunderbird. Several Ford models could be ordered with either a four, six or eight-cylinder engine. New base powertrain for the full-size LTD was the small (255 cu. in.) V-8. Corporate body colors for 1981 were: Black, Bright Bittersweet, Candyapple Red, Medium or Bright Red, Light Medium Blue, Medium Dark Brown, Bright Yellow, Cream, Chrome Yellow, Tan, Antique Cream, Pastel Chamois, Fawn, and White. Also available was a selection of metallics including: Silver, Medium Grey, Light Pewter, Medium Pewter, Maroon, Dark Blue, Bright Blue, Medium Dark Spruce, Dark Brown, Dark Pine, and Dark Cordovan. Some Ford products also could choose from up to nine "Glamour" colors and 16 clearcoat polish paint selections.

1981 Escort GLX three-door hatchback (F)

ESCORT — FOUR — Because it evolved from Ford's international experience, the new front-wheel-drive Escort was called a "world car." It was also dubbed "international" size, as Ford's attempt to rival the imports. A $3 billion development program had been initiated in the early 1970s to produce Escorts for sale both in the U.S. and Europe. The engine alone cost $1 billion to develop. The U.S. version of the all-new overhead-cam, Compound Valve Hemispherical (CVH) engine had to meet federal emissions standards, too. The transverse-mounted engine was called hemi-head because of its hemispherical-shaped combustion chambers, calling to mind some far more muscular hemis of past decades. Displacing just 97.6 cu. in., it was the smallest engine in American Ford history. Cylinder head and intake manifold were aluminum. The CVH design put the spark plug close to the center of the combustion chamber. Escort had many maintenance-free features, including self-adjusting brakes, lubed-for-life wheel bearings and front suspension, preset carb mixtures, hydraulic valve lifters, fixed caster and camber settings at the front end, and self-adjusting clutches. Ford General Manager Phillip E. Benton Jr. said "all of the Escort's major components and systems such as the engine, transaxle...suspension and body were especially designed for the car, with no carryover parts or components." "Three-door" hatchback and four-door liftgate bodies were offered. Both were 65.9 inches wide, on a 94.2 inch wheelbase. Five trim levels included base, L, GL, GLX, and sporty SS. Escort's four-speed manual transaxle was fully synchronized, with wide-ratio gearing. Optional three-speed automatic used a new split-torque design in intermediate and high, which divided torque between the converter and a direct mechanical hookup to the dual driveshafts. Escort had four- wheel independent suspension, rack-and-pinion steering, standard halogen headlamps, maintenance-free battery, fluidic windshield washer, and inertia seatback release. Front suspension used MacPherson struts with strut-mounted coil springs and a stabilizer bar. At the rear were independent trailing arms with modified MacPherson struts and coil springs, mounted on stamped lower control arms. P-metric (P155/80R) radial tires rode 13 in. steel wheels, with cast aluminum wheels optional. The hatchback Escort was 7 inches shorter than the old Pinto Runabout, while the wagon was 15 inches shorter than the Pinto version. Seats were higher than Pinto's, and glass area greatly enlarged. Escort's eggcrate grille had a 7 x 4 hole pattern. Recessed single rectangular headlamps sat in bright housings. Outboard were wraparound park/signal lamps. Wraparound taillamps were angled at the front edge. Backup lamps stood inboard, toward the license plate housing. 'Ford' and 'Escort' lettering went on the hatch lid, below large sloping, curved hatch glass. Wagons had vertical wraparound taillamps and a less-sloped rear window. Standard equipment for the base Escort included an AM radio, two-speed wipers, lighter, three-speed heater/defroster, inside hood release, high-back vinyl front bucket seats, bench-type folding rear seat, argent grille, bright bumpers, door-mounted driver's mirror, day/night mirror, courtesy lights, and semi-styled steel wheels with black hub covers and lug covers. Bright moldings went on the windshield surround, drip rail, and rear window surround. Escort L added bright headlamp housings, a bright grille, bright driver's mirror, matte black rocker panel paint, bodyside paint stripe, and bright belt molding. Escort GL included deluxe bumper rub

1981 Escort GLX four-door Liftgate (JG)

strips and end caps, bright window frame moldings, vinyl-insert bodyside moldings with argent stripe, bright wheel hub covers and trim rings, bright lower back surround molding, high-back reclining bucket seats, four-spoke "soft feel" steering wheel, consolette, visor vanity mirror, and rear ashtrays. Escort GLX added dual color-keyed remote-control sport mirrors, bumper guards, low-back reclining bucket seats, woodtone instrument cluster applique, console with graphic warning display, digital clock, roof grab handles, locking glovebox, styled steel wheels with bright trim rings, interval wipers, and P165/80R13 blackwall SBR tires. Escort SS included black bumpers, argent stripe bumper end caps, black grille and headlamp housings, blackout moldings and rocker panel paint, dual black remote sport mirrors, bodyside/rear tape striping with decal, styled steel wheels with bright trim rings and argent hub covers, high-back reclining vinyl bucket seats, handling suspension, and instrumentation group. Options included a console with graphic display module, intermittent wipers, and pivoting front vent windows. Gas mileage estimates reached 30 MPG city and 44 MPG highway. Early criticisms from the press and elsewhere prompted Ford to deliver a number of running changes right from the start, in an attempt to increase the car's refinement. First-year versions suffered several recalls. Mercury Lynx was Escort's corporate twin.

1981 Fairmont sedan (F)

FAIRMONT — FOUR/SIX/V-8 — In addition to the usual sedans and Futura coupe, Fairmont delivered a station wagon this year under the Futura badge. The four-door, steel-sided wagon had Futura's quad rectangular headlamps and distinctive grille, as well as body brightwork and an upgraded interior. Squire (woodgrain) trim was available at extra cost. Fairmonts also added new standard equipment, including power front disc brakes, bucket seats, deluxe sound package to reduce road noise, dual-note horn, bright window frames, visor vanity mirror, glovebox lock, and rear seat ashtray. The option list expanded to include a console with diagnostic warning lights and digital clock (as on Mustang), illuminated entry system, Traction-Lok rear axle (V-8 only), lighted visor vanity mirror, and Michelin TR type tires. Both the 200 cu. in. (3.3-liter) six and 255 cu. in. (4.2-liter) V-8 now had a viscous-clutch fan drive. Base engine remained the 140 cu. in. (2.3-liter) four, with four-speed manual gearbox. The elusive turbo four was no longer listed as a possibility. Neither was the six with four-speed manual gearbox. That four-speed now had a self-adjusting clutch. Fairmont's base four-cylinder produced EPA estimates of 34 MPG highway and 23 MPG city. Fairmont's new grille had a tight crosshatch pattern, with two horizontal dividers to split it into three rows, each two "holes" high. As before, large vertical parking lamps stood inboard of the rectangular headlamps. Wide (non- wraparound) taillamps had vertical ribbing, with backup lenses at inner ends. Four-doors had a six-window design with narrow quarter windows that tapered to a point at the top. Wagons carried vertical wraparound taillamps, with backup lenses alongside the license plate.

1981 Granada GLX sedan (F)

GRANADA — FOUR/SIX/V-8 — For its final two years in the lineup, Granada received an aerodynamic restyle that was supposed to deliver a 21 percent improvement in fuel economy. Ford called it "the industry's most changed American-built sedan for 1981." This Granada was 3 inches shorter than its predecessor, but with more leg, hip and shoulder room inside, and more luggage space. Wheelbase was Fairmont-sized. In fact, Granada's chassis was based on the familiar "Fox" platform, with coil springs all around. The fully unitized body weighed 400 pounds less than the 1980 version. Drag coefficient rated a low 0.44. Under this year's hood was a standard 140 cu. in. (2.3-liter) OHC four, as in Fairmont and Mustang, with four-speed manual shift. Also available: the 200 cu. in. (3.3-liter) inline six and 255 cu. in. (4.2-liter) V-8. Automatic was standard with the bigger engines. New for 1981 was a MacPherson strut front suspension, a pin-slider front disc brake system, front bucket seats on all models, revised instrument panel with two-pod instrument cluster, and stalk-mounted controls for turn signals, horn, dimmer, and wiper. P-metric steel-belted radial tires rode 14 in. stamped steel wheels. Granada also sported halogen headlamps. Three Granada series were offered: L, GL, and GLX (replacing base, Ghia and ESS). As before, body styles included only the two- and four-door sedans. The new upright bright grille had a tight crosshatch pattern with wide slots in 10 x 10 hole arrangement, with 'Ford' lettering on the upper header bar (driver's side). Quad rectangular headlamps were

1981 Granada GL coupe (JG)

used, with wraparound marker lenses and small horizontal amber parking lamps set in the front bumper. Wide taillamps (full-width except for the recessed license plate area) had backup lamps halfway toward the center. Each taillamp was divided into an upper and lower segment. Pinstripes flowed along the hood creases, and there was a stand-up see-through hood ornament. A small square badge was mounted ahead of the front door. Mercury Cougar was Granada's corporate companion.

1981 LTD coupe (JG)

LTD — V-8 — Full-size Fords no longer carried a standard full-size engine. LTD's new standard powertrain consisted of the 255 cu. in. (4.2-liter) V-8 and automatic overdrive transmission, which had been introduced in 1980 as an option on LTD and Thunderbird. That transmission also featured a lockup clutch torque converter. Three-speed automatic was abandoned. Two other V-8s were optional: 302 cu. in. (5.0-liter) or 351 cu. in. (5.8-liter), both with two-barrel carburetors. The latter produced 145 horsepower. A high-output 351 delivering 20 more horsepower was available only for police cars. LTD's lineup included four-door sedans in base, 'S' and Crown Victoria trim; two-door sedans in base and Crown Vic; and four-door wagons in all three series. Switching to a smaller base powerplant didn't seem to help mileage enormously, as the EPA estimate was a modest 16 MPG. New standard equipment included halogen headlamps on 'S' models, and separate ignition and door keys. Remote mirrors were now door-mounted rather than sail-mounted. Joining the option list were puncture-resistant tires and a convex remote-control passenger mirror. Country Squire switched from a seatbelt buzzer to chime. Appearance was the same as 1980. Taillamps had vertical ribbing, with small backup lenses below. The license plate was recessed in the decklid. Rear marker lenses followed the angle of quarter panel tips.

1981 Thunderbird Heritage hardtop coupe (F)

THUNDERBIRD — Six/V8 — Some TBird enthusiasts were doubtless shocked by the news: this year's edition carried a standard six-cylinder engine. The old familiar inline six at that, displacing just 200 cu. in. (3.3-liter). It came with standard SelectShift automatic. (Actually, the inline six had become a credit option during the 1980 model year.) The formerly standard 255 cu. in. (4.2-liter) V-8 became optional, as was a 302 cu. in. (5.0-liter) engine and automatic overdrive transmission for either V-8. Base models were better trimmed this year. In fact, all models offered items that had formerly been part of the Exterior Luxury Group. New standard equipment included halogen headlamps, viscous fan clutch, vinyl-insert bodyside moldings, wide door belt moldings, remote control left mirror, and deluxe color-keyed seatbelts. Automatic-temperature-control air conditioners added a defog mode. Three Thunderbird series were offered: base, Town Landau, and Heritage (replacing the former Silver Anniversary model). Town Landau also added equipment, including luxury wheel covers and a color-keyed wrapover band with small opera windows for the rear half-vinyl roof (similar to the treatment used on the 1980 Silver Anniversary TBird). Heritage carried a standard 255 cu. in. V-8. Appearance was similar to 1980, except that the front bumper no longer held a lower grille pattern. Huge full-width taillamps held Thunderbird emblems on each side. The decklid protruded halfway between each taillamp half. The license plate sat in a recessed opening low on the bumper. With wrapover roof band, opera windows were tiny. New options included a convertible-like Carriage Roof, Traction-Lok axle, pivoting front vent windows, convex remote mirror (passenger side), and self-sealing puncture-resistant tires.

I.D. DATA: Ford had a new 17-symbol Vehicle Identification Number (VIN), again stamped on a metal tab fastened to the instrument panel, visible through the windshield. Symbols one to three indicates manufacturer, make and vehicle type: '1FA' Ford passenger car. The fourth symbol ('B') denotes restraint system. Next comes a letter 'P', followed by two digits that indicate body type: Model Number, as shown in left column of tables below. (Example: '91' Fairmont two-door sedan.) Symbol eight indicates engine type: '2' L498 2Bbl.; 'A' L4-140 2Bbl.; 'B' L6200 1Bbl.; 'D' V8255 2Bbl.; 'F' V8302 2Bbl.; 'G' V8351 2Bbl. Next is a check digit. Symbol ten indicates model year ('B' 1981). Symbol eleven is assembly plant: 'A' Atlanta, GA; 'B' Oakville, Ontario (Canada); 'G' Chicago; 'H' Lorain, Ohio; 'K' Kansas City, MO; 'X' St. Thomas, Ontario; 'T' Metuchen, NJ; 'U' Louisville, KY; 'W' Wayne, MI. The final six digits make up the sequence number, starting with 100001. A Vehicle Certification Label on the left front door lock face panel or door pillar shows the manufacturer, month and year of manufacture, GVW, GAWR, certification statement, VIN, and codes for such items as body type, color, trim, axle, transmission, and special order information.

1981 Escort three-door hatchback (JG)

ESCORT (FOUR)

Model Number	Body/Style Number	Body Type & Seating	Factory Price	Shipping Weight	Production Total
05	61D	3-dr. Hatch Sed-4P	5158	1962	Note 1
08	74D	4-dr. Liftgate-4P	5731	2074	Note 1
05/60Q	61D	3-dr. L Hatch-4P	5494	1964	Note 1
08/60Q	74D	4-dr. L Liftgate-4P	5814	2075	Note 1
05/60Z	61D	3-dr. GL Hatch-4P	5838	1987	Note 1
08/60Z	74D	4-dr. GL Lift-4P	6178	2094	Note 1
05/602	61D	3-dr. GLX Hatch-4P	6476	2029	Note 1
08/602	74D	4-dr. GLX Lift-4P	6799	2137	Note 1
05/936	61D	3-dr. SS Hatch-4P	6139	2004	Note 1
08/936	74D	4-dr. SS Lift-4P	6464	2114	Note 1

Note 1: Total Escort production came to 192,554 three-door hatchbacks and 128,173 four-door liftbacks. Breakdown by trim level not available.

Escort Body Type Note: Hatchback Escorts are variously described as two- or three-door; Liftgate models are sometimes referred to as station wagons.

FAIRMONT (FOUR/SIX)

Model Number	Body/Style Number	Body Type & Seating	Factory Price	Shipping Weight	Production Total
20	66	2-dr. 'S' Sed-5P	5701/5914	N/A	N/A
20	66B	2-dr. Sedan-5P	6032/6245	2564/2617	23,066
21	54B	4-dr. Sedan-5P	6151/6364	2614/2667	104,883
23	74B	4-dr. Sta Wag-5P	6384/6597	2721/2788	59,154

1981 Fairmont Futura Squire station wagon (JG)

FAIRMONT FUTURA (FOUR/SIX)

Model Number	Body/Style Number	Body Type & Seating	Factory Price	Shipping Weight	Production Total
22	36R	2-dr. Coupe-5P	6347/6560	2619/2672	24,197
21/605	54B	4-dr. Sedan-5P	6361/6574	2648/2701	Note 2
23/605	74B	4-dr. Sta Wag-5P	6616/6829	2755/2822	Note 2

Note 2: Production totals listed under base Fairmont sedan and wagon also include Futura models.

GRANADA (FOUR/SIX)

Model Number	Body/Style Number	Body Type & Seating	Factory Price	Shipping Weight	Production Total
26	66D	2-dr. L Sedan-5P	6474/6687	2707/2797	35,057
27	54D	4-dr. L Sedan-5P	6633/6848	2750/2840	86,284
26/602	66D	2-dr. GL Sed-5P	6875/7088	2728/2818	Note 3
27/602	54D	4-dr. GL Sed-5P	7035/7248	2777/2867	Note 3
26/933	66D	2-dr. GLX Sed-5P	6988/7201	2732/2822	Note 3
27/933	54D	4-dr. GLX Sed-5P	7148/7361	2784/2874	Note 3

Note 3: Granada GL and GLX production is included in base Granada totals above.

Fairmont/Granada Engine Note: Prices shown are for four- and six-cylinder engines. A 255 cu. in. V-8 cost $50 more than the six.

1981 LTD Country Squire station wagon (JG)

LTD (V-8)

Model Number	Body/Style Number	Body Type & Seating	Factory Price	Shipping Weight	Production Total
32	66H	2-dr. Sedan-6P	7607	3496	6,279
33	54H	4-dr. Sedan-6P	7718	3538	35,932
38	74H	4-dr. Sta Wag-6P	8180	3719	10,554
39	74K	4-dr. Ctry Sqr-6P	8640	3737	9,443

LTD 'S' (V-8)

Model Number	Body/Style Number	Body Type & Seating	Factory Price	Shipping Weight	Production Total
31	54D	4-dr. Sedan-6P	7522	3490	17,490
37	74D	4-dr. Sta Wag-6P	7942	3717	2,465

LTD CROWN VICTORIA (V-8)

Model Number	Body/Style Number	Body Type & Seating	Factory Price	Shipping Weight	Production Total
34	66K	2-dr. Sedan-6P	8251	3496	11,061
35	54K	4-dr. Sedan-6P	8384	3538	39,139

LTD Production Note: Production of wagons with dual-facing rear seats (a $143 option) is included in basic wagon totals.

THUNDERBIRD (SIX/V-8)

Model Number	Body/Style Number	Body Type & Seating	Factory Price	Shipping Weight	Production Total
42	66D	2-dr. HT Cpe-4P	7551/7601	3004/3124	86,693

1981 Thunderbird Town Landau hardtop coupe (JG)

THUNDERBIRD TOWN LANDAU (SIX/V-8)

Model Number	Body/Style Number	Body Type & Seating	Factory Price	Shipping Weight	Production Total
42/60T	66D	2-dr. HT Cpe-4P	8689/8739	3067/3187	Note 4

THUNDERBIRD HERITAGE (V-8)

Model Number	Body/Style Number	Body Type & Seating	Factory Price	Shipping Weight	Production Total
42/607	66D	2-dr. HT Cpe-4P	11355	3303	Note 4

Note 4: Town Landau and Heritage production is included in basic Thunderbird total.

MODEL NUMBER NOTE: Some sources include a prefix 'P' ahead of the two-digit model number. **FACTORY PRICE AND WEIGHT NOTE:** Fairmont/Granada prices and weights to left of slash are for four-cylinder, to right for six-cylinder engine. Thunderbird prices and weights to left of slash are for six-cylinder, to right for V-8 engine.

ENGINE DATA: BASE FOUR (Escort): Inline. Overhead cam. Four-cylinder. Cast iron block; aluminum head. Displacement: 97.6 cu. in. (1.6 liters). Bore & stroke: 3.15 x 3.13 in. Compression ratio: 8.8:1. Brake horsepower: 65 at 5200 R.P.M. Torque: 85 lbs.-ft. at 3000 R.P.M. Five main bearings. Hydraulic valve lifters. Carburetor: 2Bbl. Holley-Weber 5740. VIN Code: 2. BASE FOUR (Fairmont, Granada): Inline. Overhead cam. Four-cylinder. Cast iron block and head. Displacement: 140 cu. in. (2.3 liters). Bore & stroke: 3.78 x 3.13 in. Compression ratio: 9.0:1. Brake horsepower: 88 at 4600 R.P.M. Torque: 118 lbs.-ft. at 2600 R.P.M. Five main bearings. Hydraulic valve lifters. Carburetor: 2Bbl. Holley 6500. VIN Code: A. BASE SIX (Thunderbird); OPTIONAL (Fairmont, Granada): Inline. Overhead valve. Six-cylinder. Cast iron block and head. Displacement: 200 cu. in. (3.3 liters). Bore & stroke: 3.68 x 3.13 in. Compression ratio: 8.6:1. Brake horsepower: 88 at 3800 R.P.M. Torque: 154 lbs.-ft. at 1400 R.P.M. Seven main bearings. Hydraulic valve lifters. Carburetor: 1Bbl. Holley 1946. VIN Code: B. BASE V-8 (LTD); OPTIONAL (Fairmont, Granada, Thunderbird): 90-degree, overhead valve V-8. Cast iron block and head. Displacement: 255 cu. in. (4.2 liters). Bore & stroke: 3.68 x 3.00 in. Compression ratio: 8.2:1. Brake horsepower: 115 at 3400

R.P.M.; (LTD, 120 at 3400). Torque: 195 lbs.-ft. at 2200 R.P.M.; (LTD, 205 at 2600). Five main bearings. Hydraulic valve lifters. Carburetor: 2Bbl. Motorcraft 2150 or 7200VV. VIN Code: D. OPTIONAL V-8 (LTD, Thunderbird): 90-degree, overhead valve V-8. Cast iron block and head. Displacement: 302 cu. in. (5.0 liters). Bore & stroke: 4.00 x 3.00 in. Compression ratio: 8.4:1. Brake horsepower: 130 at 3400 R.P.M. Torque: 235 lbs.-ft. at 1600 R.P.M.; (LTD, 235 at 1800). Five main bearings. Hydraulic valve lifters. Carburetor: 2Bbl. Motorcraft 2150 or 7200VV. VIN Code: F. OPTIONAL V-8 (LTD): 90-degree, overhead valve V-8. Cast iron block and head. Displacement: 351 cu. in. (5.8 liters). Bore & stroke: 4.00 x 3.50 in. Compression ratio: 8.3:1. Brake horsepower: 145 at 3200 R.P.M. Torque: 270 lbs.-ft. at 1800 R.P.M. Five main bearings. Hydraulic valve lifters. Carburetor: 2Bbl. Motorcraft 7200VV. Windsor engine. VIN Code: G.

NOTE: A high-output version of the 351 cu. in. V-8 was available. Brake H.P.: 165 at 3600 R.P.M. Torque: 285 lbs.- ft. at 2200 R.P.M.

CHASSIS DATA: Wheelbase: (Escort) 94.2 in.; (Fairmont/Granada) 105.5 in.; (LTD) 114.3 in.; (TBird) 108.4 in. Overall Length: (Escort hatch) 163.9 in.; (Escort Lift) 165.0 in.; (Fairmont) 195.5 in. exc. Futura coupe, 197.4 in.; (Granada) 196.5 in.; (LTD) 209.3 in.; (LTD wag) 215.0 in.; (TBird) 200.4 in. Height: (Escort) 53.3 in.; (Fairmont) 52.9 in.; (Fairmont Futura 2dr.) 51.7 in.; (Fairmont wag) 54.2 in.; (Granada) 53.0 in.; (LTD) 54.7 in.; (LTD wag) 57.4 in.; (TBird) 53.0 in. Width: (Escort) 65.9 in.; (Fairmont/Granada) 71.0 in.; (LTD) 77.5 in.; (LTD wag) 79.3 in.; (TBird) 74.1 in. Front Tread: (Escort) 54.7 in.; (Fairmont/Granada) 56.6 in.; (LTD) 62.2 in. (TBird) 58.1 in. Rear Tread: (Escort) 56.0 in.; (Fairmont/Granada) 57.0 in.; (LTD) 62.0 in. (TBird) 57.0 in. Standard Tires: (Escort) P155/80R13 SBR BSW; (Fairmont/Granada) P175/75R14 SBR BSW; (LTD) P205/75R14 SBR WSW exc. wagon, P215/75R14; (TBird) P195/75R14 SBR WSW.

TECHNICAL: Transmission: Four-speed manual standard on Fairmont/Granada four: (1st) 3.98:1; (2nd) 2.14:1; (3rd) 1.42:1; (4th) 1.00:1; (Rev) 3.99:1. Four-speed manual transaxle standard on Escort: (1st) 3.58:1; (2nd) 2.05:1; (3rd) 1.21:1; (4th) 0.81:1; (Rev) 3.46:1. Three-speed automatic standard on other models, optional on all. Gear ratios on Fairmont/Granada four, Fairmont six and some TBirds: (1st) 2.47:1; (2nd) 1.47:1; (3rd) 1.00:1; (Rev) 2.11:1. Other models: (1st) 2.46:1; (2nd) 1.46:1; (3rd) 1.00:1; (Rev) 2.19:1. Four-speed overdrive automatic standard on LTD, available on Thunderbird V-8: (1st) 2.40:1; (2nd) 1.47:1; (3rd) 1.00:1; (4th) 0.67:1; (Rev) 2.00:1. Standard final drive ratio: (Escort) 3.59:1 w/4spd, 3.31:1 w/auto.; (Fairmont/Granada) 3.08:1 exc. 2.73:1 w/six, 2.26:1 w/V-8; (LTD) 3.08:1. (TBird) 2.73:1 w/six and auto., 2.26:1 w/255 V-8 and 3spd auto., 3.08:1 w/4-spd automatic. Drive Axle: (Escort) front; (others) rear. Steering: (LTD) recirculating ball; others (rack and pinion). Front Suspension: (Escort/Granada) MacPherson strut-mounted coil springs with lower control arms and stabilizer bar; (Fairmont/Thunderbird) modified MacPherson struts with lower control arms, coil springs and link-type anti-sway bar; (LTD) long/short control arms w/coil springs and link-type stabilizer bar. Rear Suspension: (Escort) independent trailing arms w/modified MacPherson struts and coil springs on lower control arms; (Fairmont/Granada/LTD) four-link live axle with coil springs; (Thunderbird) four-link live axle system with coil springs and anti-sway bar. Brakes: Front disc, rear drum. Ignition: Electronic. Body construction: (LTD) separate body and frame; (others) unibody. Fuel tank: (Escort) 10 gal.; (Fairmont/Granada) 14 or 16 gal.; (LTD) 20 gal.; (TBird) 18 gal.

DRIVETRAIN OPTIONS: Engines: 200 cu. in. six: Fairmont/Granada ($213). 255 cu. in. V-8: Fairmont/Granada ($263); TBird ($50). 302 cu. in. V-8: TBird ($91) exc. Heritage ($41); LTD sedan ($41). 351 cu. in. V-8: LTD sedan ($83); LTD wagon ($41). H.O. 351 cu. in. V-8: LTD ($139-$180). Transmission/Differential: Automatic transaxle: Escort ($344). Select-shift auto. trans.: Fairmont/Granada ($349). Four-speed overdrive automatic trans.: TBird ($162). Floor shift lever: Fairmont/Granada ($43). Traction-Lok differential: Fairmont/Granada/TBird ($67); LTD ($71). Optional axle ratio: Escort ($15); Granada ($16). Brakes/Steering/Suspension: Power brakes: Escort ($79). Power steering: Escort ($163); Fairmont/Granada ($168). H.D. susp.: Fairmont/Granada ($22); LTD/TBird ($23). Handling susp.: Escort ($37); Fairmont/LTD ($45). Adjustable air shock absorbers: LTD ($57). Other: H.D. battery ($20). H.D. alternator: LTD ($46). Extended-range gas tank: Escort ($32). Engine block heater ($16). Trailer towing pkg., heavy duty: LTD ($176). California emission system ($46). High-altitude option ($38).

1981 Escort GLX Squire wagon (JG)

ESCORT CONVENIENCE/APPEARANCE OPTIONS: Option Packages: Squire wagon pkg. ($256). Instrument group ($77). Protection group ($49). Light group ($39). Comfort/Convenience: Air conditioner ($530). Rear defroster, electric ($102). Fingertip speed control ($132). Tinted glass ($70); windshield only ($28). Digital clock ($52). Intermittent wipers ($41). Rear wiper/washer ($100). Dual remote sport mirrors ($56). Entertainment: AM/FM radio ($63). AM/FM stereo radio ($100); w/cassette player ($187). Dual rear speakers ($37). Premium sound ($91). AM radio delete ($61 credit). Exterior: Flip-up open air roof ($154-$228). Metallic glow paint ($45). Two-tone paint/tape ($104). Front vent windows, pivoting ($55). Remote quarter windows ($95). Vinyl-insert bodyside moldings ($41). Bumper guards, front or rear ($23). Bumper rub strips ($34). Roof luggage rack ($74). Roof air deflector ($26). Lower bodyside protection ($60). Interior: Console ($98). Low-back reclining bucket seats ($30). Reclining front seatbacks ($55). Cloth/vinyl seat trim ($28); vinyl (NC). Deluxe seatbelts ($23). Wheels/Tires: Wheel trim rings ($44). Aluminum wheels ($193- $330). P155/80R13 WSW ($55). P165/80R13 BSW ($19); WSW ($55- $74).

FAIRMONT CONVENIENCE/APPEARANCE OPTIONS: Option Packages: Squire option ($200). Interior luxury group ($232-$256). Instrument cluster ($88). Appearance protection group ($50). Light group ($43). Comfort/Convenience: Air cond. ($585). Rear defroster, electric ($107). Fingertip speed control ($132). Illuminated entry ($60). Power windows ($140-$195). Power door locks ($93-$132). Remote decklid release ($27). Power seat ($122). Tinted glass ($76); windshield only ($29). Leather-wrapped steering wheel ($49). Tilt steering ($80-$93). Electric clock ($23). Interval wipers ($41). Rear wiper/washer ($85). Lighting and Mirrors: Map light ($9); dual-beam ($13). Trunk light ($6). Left remote mirror ($15). Dual bright remote mirrors ($55). Lighted visor vanity mirror ($43). Entertainment: AM/FM radio ($51). AM/FM stereo radio ($88); w/8track player ($162); w/cassette player ($174). Twin rear speakers ($37). Premium sound system ($91). Radio flexibility ($61). AM radio delete ($61 credit). Exterior: Flip-up open air roof ($228). Full or half vinyl roof ($115). Metallic glow paint ($55). Two-tone paint ($128- $162). Accent paint stripe ($34). Pivoting front vent windows ($55). Liftgate assist handle: wag ($16). Rocker panel moldings ($30). Bumper guards, rear ($23). Bumper rub strips ($43). Luggage rack: wagon ($90). Lower bodyside protection ($37-$49). Interior: Console ($168). Bench seat ($24 credit). Cloth seat trim ($28-$54). Flight bench seat (NC); w/vinyl trim ($26). Front floor mats ($18-$20). Locking storage box ($24). Deluxe seatbelts ($23). Wheels/Tires: Wire wheel covers ($76-$117). Styled steel wheels ($52-$94). P175/75R14 WSW ($55). P185/75R14 WSW ($86). P190/65R390 BSW on TRX alum. wheels ($470-$512). Conventional spare ($39).

GRANADA CONVENIENCE/APPEARANCE OPTIONS: Option Packages: Interior sport group ($282-$295). Light group ($45). Cold weather group ($67). Protection group ($51). Comfort/Convenience: Air cond. ($585). Rear defroster ($107). Fingertip speed control ($89-$132). Illuminated entry system ($60). Power windows ($140-$195). Power door locks ($93- $132). Power decklid release ($27). Power flight bench seat ($122); split bench ($173). Tinted glass ($76); windshield only ($29). Steering wheel: sport ($26-$39); leather-wrapped ($49); tilt ($80-$94). Electric clock ($23). Interval wipers ($41). Lighting and Mirrors: Cornering lamps ($51). Map light ($13). Trunk light ($6). Remote right mirror ($52). Lighted right visor vanity mirror ($43). Entertainment: AM/FM radio ($51). AM/FM stereo radio ($88); w/8track player ($162); w/cassette ($174). Premium sound ($91). Radio flexibility ($61). AM radio delete ($61 credit). Exterior: Flip-up open-air roof ($228). Full or half vinyl roof ($115). Metallic glow paint ($55). Bodyside/decklid paint stripes ($50). Two-tone paint ($146-$162). Pivoting front vent windows ($55). Vinyl insert bodyside moldings ($45). Bumper guards, rear ($23). Bumper rub strips ($43). Mud/stone deflectors ($26). Lower bodyside protection ($37). Interior: Console ($168). Split bench seat: GL/GLX ($178). Cloth seat trim ($45-$62). Flight bench seat (NC). Front floor mats ($18-$20). Color-keyed seatbelts ($23). Wheels/Tires: Luxury wheel covers: L ($43); GL/GLX (NC). Wire wheel covers ($124); GL/GLX ($80). Cast aluminum wheels ($308-$350). P175/75R14 WSW ($55). P185/75R14 BSW ($32); WSW ($86); RWL ($102). 190/65R390 BSW on TRX aluminum wheels ($468-$512). Conventional spare ($39).

1981 LTD Crown Victoria sedan (JG)

LTD CONVENIENCE/APPEARANCE OPTIONS: Option Packages: Interior luxury group ($693-$765). Convenience group ($70-$101). Power lock group ($93-$176). Light group ($37). Protection group ($57). Comfort/Convenience: Air cond. ($624); w/auto-temp control ($687). Rear defroster, electric ($107). Fingertip speed control ($135). Illuminated entry system ($59). Power windows ($143-$211). Power driver's seat ($173); driver and passenger ($346). Tinted glass ($87); windshield only ($29). Autolamp on/off delay ($65). Leather-wrapped steering wheel ($45). Tilt steering wheel ($80). Auto. parking brake release ($10). Electric clock ($23). Digital clock ($40-$63). Seatbelt chime ($23). Interval wipers: fleet only ($41). Lighting and Mirrors: Cornering lamps ($48). Remote right mirror ($39). Lighted right visor vanity mirror ($38); pair ($43-$80). Entertainment: AM/FM radio ($51). AM/FM stereo radio ($88); w/8track tape player ($162) exc. Crown Vic ($74); w/cassette ($174) exc. Crown Vic ($87). AM/FM stereo search radio ($234) exc. Crown Vic ($146); w/8track ($221-$309); w/cassette ($233-$321). Power antenna ($48). Dual rear speakers ($39). Premium sound system ($116-$146). Radio flexibility ($65). AM radio delete ($61 credit). Exterior: Full or half vinyl roof ($141). Metallic glow paint ($67). Two-tone paint/tape ($44-$78). Dual accent paint stripes ($34). Hood striping ($15). Pivoting front vent windows ($55). Rocker panel moldings: Ctry Squire ($29). Vinyl-insert bodyside moldings ($44). Bumper guards, rear ($27). Bumper rub strips ($46). Luggage rack ($84). Lower bodyside protection ($34-$46). Interior: Dual-facing rear seats: wagon ($146). Cloth/vinyl flight bench seat ($59). Leather seating ($361). Dual flight bench seat recliners ($56). Cloth/vinyl split bench seating ($178-$237). All-vinyl seat trim: Crown Vic/Ctry Squire ($28); Duraweave vinyl ($54). Front floor mats ($20). Trunk trim ($45). Wheels/Tires: Luxury wheel covers ($72). Wire wheel covers ($135). Cast aluminum wheels ($338). P215/75R14 WSW ($30). P225/75R14 WSW ($30-$61). P205/75R15 WSW ($10-$40); puncture- resistant ($95-$125). Conventional spare ($39).

THUNDERBIRD CONVENIENCE/APPEARANCE OPTIONS: Option Packages: Interior luxury group ($1039) exc. Town Landau ($584). Exterior decor group ($341). Interior decor group ($349). Protection group ($45). Light group ($30). Power lock group ($120). Comfort/Convenience: Air cond. ($585); auto-temp ($652) exc. Twn Lan/Heritage ($67). Rear defroster ($107). Fingertip speed control ($132). Illuminated entry system ($60). Keyless entry ($122). Garage door opener w/lighted vanity mirrors ($134-$177). Autolamp on/off delay ($65). Tinted glass ($76); windshield only ($29). Power windows ($140). Four-way power seat ($122). Six-way power driver's seat ($173). Auto. parking brake release ($10). Leather-wrapped steering wheel ($45). Tilt steering wheel ($80). Electronic instrument cluster ($282-$322). Diagnostic warning lights: base ($51). Digital clock ($40). Interval wipers ($41). Lighting and Mirrors: Cornering lamps ($51). Remote right mirror ($52). Lighted right visor vanity mirror ($41). Entertainment: AM/FM radio ($51). AM/FM stereo radio ($88); w/8track player ($74-$162); w/cassette ($87-$174). AM/FM stereo search radio ($146-$234); w/8track ($221-$309) exc. Heritage ($74); w/cassette ($233-$321) exc. Heritage ($87). Power antenna ($48). Dual rear speakers ($37). Premium sound system ($116-$146). Radio flexibility ($65). AM radio delete ($61 credit). Exterior: Carriage roof ($902). Flip-up open-air roof ($228). Vinyl half roof ($130). Metallic glow paint ($70). Two-tone paint ($111-$180). Dual accent bodyside paint stripes: base ($41). Hood/bodyside paint stripes ($16-$57). Pivoting front vent windows ($55). Wide door belt moldings ($45). Rocker panel moldings ($30). Mud/stone deflectors ($26). Lower bodyside protection ($34-$48). Interior: Bucket seats w/console ($182) exc. (NC) w/decor group. Recaro bucket seats w/console ($376-$461) exc. Heritage ($213). Leather seat trim ($359). Vinyl seat trim ($28-$29). Front floor mats ($13); carpeted ($20). Trunk trim ($44). Wheels/Tires: Wire wheel covers ($38-$135). Luxury wheel covers ($98). Self-sealing tires ($85). TR WSW tires on alum. wheels ($428-$563). Conventional spare ($39).

HISTORY: Introduced: October 3, 1980. Model year production: 1,054,976 (incl. Mustangs). Total passenger-car production for the U.S. market of 1,030,915 units (incl. Mustangs) included 531,507 four-cylinder, 287,673 sixes and 211,735 V-8s. (Total includes 71,644 early '82 EXPs, all four-cylinder.) Calendar year production (U.S.): 892,043 (incl. Mustangs). Calendar year sales by U.S. dealers: 977,220 (incl. Mustangs). Model year sales by U.S. dealers: 1,058,044 (incl. Mustangs, 27,795 leftover Pintos and 41,601 early '82 EXPs, but not incl. 47,707 imported Fiestas).

Historical Footnotes: Escort quickly managed to become the best-selling Ford model, selling 284,633 examples. Obviously, Escort was primed to compete with Chevrolet's five-year-old Chevette. Otherwise, sales slumped somewhat. The restyled and downsized Granada sold better than in 1980, however, finding 105,743 buyers. Total model year sales were down over 7 percent, but that wasn't so bad considering the 28 percent decline from 1979 to 1980 (which also saw Ford/Lincoln/Mercury's market share shrink to a record low 16.5 percent). Mustang didn't sell nearly as well as hoped, even with a series of rebates offered during the year, dropping 29.5 percent for the model year. Model year production was closer to the 1980 figure, down just over 3 percent as opposed to a whopping 39 percent decline in the previous season. Calendar year production and sales both fell too, but not to a shocking level. This was a bad year all around for the industry. Car prices and interest rates had been rising steadily during this inflationary period, while the country also remained in a recession economy. Escort evolved from the "Erika" project, which first began in 1972. The goal: to produce a car that could be revised to suit both European and American tastes, using parts that could either be provided locally or imported. Both a 1.3-liter and 1.6-liter engine were planned, but only the bigger one found its way under domestic Escort hoods. Ford spent some $640 million to renovate its Dearborn, Michigan plant to manufacture Escort's 1.6-liter CVH engine. The engines were also built at a Ford facility in Wales. Additional future production was planned for Lima, Ohio, and for a new plant to be built in Mexico. The 1981 CAFE goal was 22 MPG.

1982 FORD

In addition to the new high-performance Mustang GT, 1982 brought a new two-seater EXP to the Ford fold, the first two-passenger model since the '55 Thunderbird. Escort added a four-door hatchback sedan, while Granada added a station wagon. Otherwise, 1982 was largely a carryover year. Ford's first domestic V-6 engine became available this year in Granada and Thunderbird. Weighing only a few pounds more than a four, it had an aluminum head, intake manifold and front cover. Ford's famous script returned this year after a long absence, in the form of a blue oval emblem at the front and rear of each model. Fairmont/Granada/Thunderbird sixes now had lockup torque converters in their SelectShift automatics, which worked in all three forward speeds. The government's fuel economy (CAFE) standard this year was 24 MPG.

1982 Escort GLX five-door hatchback (JG)

ESCORT — FOUR — A new four-door hatchback sedan joined Escort's initial "three-door" (actually two-door) hatchback and four-door liftback wagon. Base and SS wagons were dropped. L, GL and GLX Escorts now had bright headlamp housings. Power front disc brakes had become standard on wagons late in the 1981 model year, and continued this year. New stainless steel wheel trim rings (formerly stamped aluminum) arrived on GL, GLX and GT models. Escort had a new low-restriction exhaust and larger (P165/80R13) tires in all sizes. Ford's oval script emblem replaced 'Ford' block letters on the liftgate, which also held 'Escort' lettering. An electric hatch release was now standard on GLX hatchbacks (optional elsewhere). There was a running change in the four-speed manual transaxle, with different third and fourth gear ratios. Third gear changed from 1.23:1 to 1.36:1, and fourth from 0.81:1 to 0.95:1. Air-conditioned models included a switch that disconnected the unit for an instant when the gas pedal was floored. Like other Ford models, this year's Escort also displayed the blue script oval up front. Otherwise, appearance was similar to 1981. Base Escorts had an argent painted grille, wraparound amber parking lamps, single rectangular halogen headlamps, short black bumper end caps, semi-styled steel wheels with black and argent hub covers, and black wheel nut covers. Sedans had wraparound tri-color taillamps; red taillamps went on wagons. Inside were vinyl high-back front bucket seats, a black two-spoke steering wheel, black instrument panel with ashtray, bronzetone cluster, and color-keyed soft-feel pad. Escort L added bright headlamp doors, bright grille with integral Ford oval, brushed center-pillar applique, matte black rocker panels, bodyside paint stripes, black taillamp extensions, an 'L' badge on the liftgate, and blackout front end. Escort GL added deluxe bumper end caps and rub strips, 'GL' badge in back, front air dam, vinyl-insert bodyside moldings with argent insert, and bright window frame and lower back surround moldings. Inside, the GL had high-back reclining bucket seats and a four-spoke soft-feel color-keyed steering wheel. GLX stepped upward with interval wipers, dual color-keyed remote sport mirrors, 'GLX' badge, front and rear bumper guards, low-back reclining bucket seats in GLX vinyl or cloth/vinyl, woodtone instrument cluster applique, P165/80R13 tires, and console with graphic warning display. Escort GT (formerly SS) added a handling suspension, black bumpers with deluxe rub strips and deluxe end caps, front air dam, roof grab handles, black grille and headlamp doors, and Ford oval on the black grille's header bar. Blackout treatment went on windshield molding, drip moldings, quarter window and door frames, quarter window moldings, dual remote sport mirrors, door handles and lock covers, center pillar applique, rocker panels, belt and back window moldings, lower back surround molding, and taillamp extensions. Bodyside and rear end tape stripes showed an identifying decal. New options included shearling and leather (or leather alone) seat inserts, and an AM/FM stereo with 8track player. The optional Squire exterior now had lighter-color walnut woodtone trim. Escorts had a larger (11.3 gallon) gas tank this year. EPA ratings reached 31 MPG city (47 MPG highway) on the base Escort with four-speed.

EXP — FOUR — First shown at the Chicago Auto Show, then introduced in April as an early '82 model, EXP was the first two-seater Ford offered in 25 years. Comparing EXP to the original Thunderbird, Ford Division General Manager Louis E. Lataif said: "We're introducing another two-seater with the same flair, but the EXP will be a very affordable, very fuel efficient car matched to the lifestyles of the eighties." For comparison, the sporty new coupe weighed a thousand pounds less than the original Thunderbird. EXP was also 2 inches lower and 5 inches shorter. EXP's rakish non-boxy body rode an Escort/Lynx 94.2 inch wheelbase, with that car's front-drive running gear, four-wheel independent suspension, and dashboard. EXP was longer, lower and narrower than Escort. Performance wasn't (yet) its strong suit, however, since EXP weighed about 200 pounds more than Escort but carried the same small engine.

1982 EXP three-door hatchback (F)

Standard features included steel-belted radial tires, power front disc/rear drum brakes, halogen headlamps, rack- and-pinion steering, reclining high-back bucket seats, four- spoke sport steering wheel, and easy-to-read instrument panel and console with full instrumentation. Underhood was the 97.6 cu. in. (1.6-liter) CVH engine with standard four-speed overdrive manual transaxle. Several standard equipment additions were incorporated as a running change. They included tinted glass, an electronic day/date digital clock, power liftgate release, maintenance-free 48 ampere-hour battery, engine compartment light, ashtray light, and headlamps-on warning buzzer. Both EXP and Mercury's LN7, its corporate cousin, had a sharply-sloped windshield, wheel arches with prominent lips, and wide bodyside moldings not far below the top of the wheel opening line. Biggest difference was in the back end. Ford's coupe was a notchback with lift-up hatch, while Mercury's LN7 fielded a big "bubbleback" back window. EXP's minimalist grille consisted merely of twin side-by-side slots in the sloped front panel (LN7 had ten). Single quad hedlamps sat in "eyebrow" housings. Large wraparound taillamps came to a point on the quarter panel. Parking lamps stood in the bumper, well below the headlamps. Priced considerably higher than Escort, EXP carried an ample list of standard equipment. It included power brakes, tachometer, engine gauges, full carpeting, electric back-window defroster, power hatchback release, digital clock, and cargo area security shade. Manual-transaxle models had a sport-tuned exhaust. Automatic models had a wide-open- throttle cutout switch for the optional air conditioning compressor clutch. A rather modest option list included a flip-up open-air roof, premium stereo system, and leather (or shearling and leather) seating surfaces. An optional TR handling package included special wheels and Michelin TRX tires in P165/70R365 size, and a larger-diameter front stabilizer bar. Shock valving, spring rates and caster/camber settings were modified for firmer ride and tighter handling. As the full model year began, Ford offered an optional (no-extra-cost) 4.05:1 final drive ratio for better performance. Later came a close-ratio gearbox with 3.59:1 final drive ratio, intended for the same purpose. Finally, in March 1982, an 80-horsepower edition of the CVH four became available. It had higher (9.0:1) compression, a bigger air cleaner intake, lower-restriction exhaust and dual-outlet exhaust manifold, larger carburetor venturis, and higher-lift camshaft.

1982 Fairmont Futura sedan (JG)

FAIRMONT FUTURA — FOUR/SIX/V8 — All Fairmount models acquired the Futura name this year as the lineup shrunk to a single series: just a two- and four-door sedan, and sport coupe. the station wagon was dropped, and the 255 cu. in. (4.2-liter) V-8 was available only in police and taxi packages. Base engine was the 140 cu. in. (2.3-liter) four, with 3.3-liter inline six optional. Optional SelectShift automatic with the six included a new lockup torque converter. Fairmont's new front end look featured a bold grille with strong divider forming a 6x2 grid, with each "hole" containing a tight internal crosshatch pattern. Quad rectangular headlamps now stood above quad park/signal lamps, like LTD but without its wraparound side marker lenses. Instead, Fairmont had small marker lenses set low on front fenders. The rear held the same vertically-ribbed taillamps as before. Front fenders held a Futura badge. Deluxe wide lower bodyside moldings met partial wheel lip moldings. Interiors held new high-gloss woodtone door trim and instrument panel appliques (formerly walnut). In back was a new deep-well trunk. AM radios added dual front speakers, and a new flash-to-pass feature was added to the headlamp lever. There was also a new gas cap tether. The former optional sweep-hand electric clock switched to quartz-type, and the available extended-range fuel tank held 20 gallons (formerly 16). Discontinued options were the leather-wrapped steering wheel, vinyl front floor mats, and right lighted visor vanity mirror.

1982 Granada GL Squire station wagon (JG)

GRANADA — FOUR/SIX/V-6 — Following its major restyle and downsizing for 1981, Granada looked the same this year but added a pair of station wagons (L and GL series). New station wagon options included a luggage rack, two-way liftgate (with flip-up window), rear wiper/washer, and Squire package. Fuel filler caps were now tethered. Flash-to-pass control on the steering column was new this year. Sedans could get an optional extended-range fuel tank. No more V-8s went under Granada hoods. A new optional "Essex" 232 cu. in. (3.8-liter) V-6 producing 112 horsepower was said to offer V-8 power; and it weighed just 4 pounds more than the base 140 cu. in. (2.3-liter) four. An inline six also remained available (standard on wagons). The V-6 got an EPA rating of 19 MPG city and 26 MPG highway. A new torque converter clutch providing a direct connection became standard on SelectShift automatic for the six and V-6 engines. This would be Granada's final season, but its basic design carried on in the form of a restyled LTD.

1982 LTD Crown Victoria sedan (JG)

LTD — V-8 — After a long history, the 351 cu. in. (5.8-liter) V-8 no longer was available for private full-size Fords, but continued as an option for police models. Little changed on this year's LTD lineup, apart from seven new body colors. Ford ovals were added to front grilles and rear decklids (or tailgates). All monaural radios had dual front speakers and wiring for rear speakers. The sweep-hand clock added quartz operation. A new medium-duty trailer towing option replaced the former heavy-duty one. New optional wire wheel covers incorporated a locking feature. Base engine was a 255 cu. in. (4.2-liter) V-8; optional, the 302 cu. in. (5.0-liter) V-8. Also optional for 1982 was a Tripminder computer that combined a trip odometer with quartz clock to show vehicle speed, real or elapsed time, and fuel flow. Touching buttons could display instant or average MPG, amount of fuel used, trip mileage, average trip speed, and total trip time. Thunderbird could also get one. With 114.3 inch wheelbase, LTD was the biggest Ford. Wide amber parking lamps stood below quad headlamps. Amber marker lenses had a large section above a smaller one, to follow the line of the headlamp/parking lamp. The fine checkerboard grille pattern was divided by a vertical center bar, with Ford oval at driver's side. An 'Automatic Overdrive' badge went ahead of the door. Vertically ribbed taillamps held 'LTD' lettering, with small backup lamps below the taillamps. 'LTD' letters also decorated the 'C' pillar.

1982 Thunderbird Heritage hardtop coupe (JG)

THUNDERBIRD — SIX/V-6/V-8 — Engine choices grew smaller yet on the '82 Thunderbird, as the familiar 302 cu. in. (5.0-liter) V-8 was abandoned. The 200 cu. in. (3.3-liter) inline six became standard on base 'birds, new 232 cu. in. (3.8-liter) V-6 optional, with 255 cu. in. (4.2-liter) V-8 the biggest that could be bought. SelectShift transmission with the inline six had a new lockup torque converter. Three models were offered again: base, Town Landau, and Heritage. TBird's gas tank grew from 18 to 21 gallons. Exterior trim had more black-accented areas. A new optional Tripminder computer not only showed time and speed, but figured and displayed elapsed time, distance traveled, average or present MPG, fuel used, and average speed. There was a new wire wheel cover option with locking feature, and a new luxury vinyl roof option (standard on Town Landau). Appearance was similar to 1981, with the same huge taillamps. Concealed headlamps again had a clear lens-like trim panel on each cover, which extended outward far around the fender to form large wraparound signal/marker lenses. Those lenses were all clear except for an amber section toward the wheel. The crosshatch grille had an 8 x 6 pattern of wide holes. 'Thunderbird' lettering was set in the grille header. A wide see-through hood ornament held a Thunderbird insignia. That emblem also highlighted lenses and back pillars.

I.D. DATA: Ford's 17-symbol Vehicle Identification Number (VIN) again was stamped on a metal tab fastened to the instrument panel, visible through the windshield. The first three symbols ('1FA') indicate manufacturer, make and vehicle type. The fourth symbol ('B') denotes restraint system. Next comes a letter 'P', followed by two digits that indicate body type: Model Number, as shown in left column of tables below. (Example: '05' Escort two-door hatchback.) Symbol eight indicates engine type: '2' L498 2Bbl.; 'A' L4-140 2Bbl.; 'B' or 'T' L6200 1Bbl.; '3' V6232 2Bbl.; 'D' V8255 2Bbl.; 'F' V8302 2Bbl.; 'G' V8351 2Bbl. Next is a check digit. Symbol ten indicates model year ('C' 1982). Symbol eleven is assembly plant: 'A' Atlanta, GA; 'B' Oakville, Ontario (Canada); 'G' Chicago; 'H' Lorain, Ohio; 'K' Kansas City, MO; 'X' St. Thomas, Ontario; 'Z' St. Louis, MO; 'R' San Jose, CA; 'T' Edison, NJ; 'W' Wayne, MI. The final six digits make up the sequence number, starting with 100001. A Vehicle Certification Label on the left front door lock face panel or door pillar shows the manufacturer, month and year of manufacture, GVW, GAWR, certification statement, VIN, and codes for such items as body type, color, trim, axle, transmission, and special order information.

ESCORT (FOUR)

Model Number	Body/Style Number	Body Type & Seating	Factory Price	Shipping Weight	Production Total
05	61D	2-dr. Hatch-4P	5462	1920	Note 1
06	58D	4-dr. Hatch-4P	5668	N/A	Note 1
05	61D	2-dr. L Hatch-4P	6046	1926	Note 1
06	58D	4-dr. L Hatch-4P	6263	2003	Note 1
08	74D	4-dr. L Sta Wag-4P	6461	2023	Note 1
05	61D	2-dr. GL Hatch-4P	6406	1948	Note 1
06	58D	4-dr. GL Hatch-4P	6622	2025	Note 1
08	74D	4-dr. GL Sta Wag-4P	6841	2043	Note 1
05	61D	2-dr. GLX Hatch-4P	7086	1978	Note 1
06	58D	4-dr. GLX Hatch-4P	7302	2064	Note 1
08	74D	4-dr. GLX Sta Wag-4P	7475	2079	Note 1
05	61D	2-dr. GT Hatch-4P	6706	1963	Note 1

Note 1: Total Escort production came to 165,660 two-door hatchbacks, 130,473 four-door hatchbacks, and 88,999 station wagons. Breakdown by trim level not available. Bodies are sometimes referred to as three-door and five-door.

EXP (FOUR)

01	67D	3-dr. Hatch Cpe-2P	7387	2047	98,256

FAIRMONT FUTURA (FOUR/SIX)

22	36R	2-dr. Spt Cpe-5P	6517/7141	2597/2682	17,851
20	66B	2-dr. Sedan-5P	5985/6619	2574/2659	8,222
21	54B	4-dr. Sedan-5P	6419/7043	2622/2707	101,666

GRANADA (FOUR/SIX/V-6)

26	66D	2-dr. L Sedan-5P	7126/7750	2673/2791	12,802
27	54D	4-dr. L Sedan-5P	7301/7925	2705/2823	62,339
28	74D	4-dr. L Sta Wag-5P	-- /7983	-- /2965	45,182
26	66D	2-dr. GL Sed-5P	7543/8167	2699/2817	Note 2
27	54D	4-dr. GL Sed-5P	7718/8342	2735/2853	Note 2
28	74D	4-dr. GL Wag-5P	-- /8399	-- /2995	Note 2
26	66D	2-dr. GLX Sed-5P	7666/8290	2717/2835	Note 2
27	54D	4-dr. GLX Sed-5P	7840/8464	2753/2871	Note 2

Note 2: Granada GL and GLX production is included in basic Granada L totals above.

Fairmont/Granada Engine Note: Prices shown are for four- and six- cylinder engines. Six-cylinder price includes $411 for the required automatic transmission. A 232 cu. in. V-6 cost $70 more than the inline six in a Granada.

LTD (V-8)

32	66H	2-dr. Sedan-6P	8455	3496	3,510
33	54H	4-dr. Sedan-6P	8574	3526	29,776
38	74H	4-dr. Sta Wag-6P	9073	3741	9,294

LTD 'S' (V-8)

31	54D	4-dr. Sedan-6P	8312	3522	22,182
37	74D	4-dr. Sta Wag-6P	8783	3725	2,973

LTD CROWN VICTORIA (V-8)

34	66K	2-dr. Sedan-6P	9149	3523	9,287
35	54K	4-dr. Sedan-6P	9294	3567	41,405
39	74K	4-dr. Ctry Sqr-6P	9580	3741	9,626

THUNDERBIRD (SIX/V-8)

42	66D	2-dr. HT Cpe-4P	8492/8733	3000/3137	45,142

THUNDERBIRD TOWN LANDAU (SIX/V-8)

42/60T	66D	2-dr. HT Cpe-4P	9703/9944	3063/3200	Note 3

THUNDERBIRD HERITAGE (V-6/V-8)

42/607	66D	2-dr. HT Cpe-4P	12742/12742	3235/3361	Note 3

Note 3: Town Landau and Heritage production is included in basic Thunderbird total.

MODEL NUMBER NOTE: Some sources include a prefix 'P' ahead of the two- digit model number. **FACTORY PRICE AND WEIGHT NOTE:** Fairmont/Granada prices and weights to left of slash are for four-cylinder, to right for six-cylinder engine. Thunderbird prices and weights to left of slash are for inline six- cylinder, to right for V-8 engine. Thunderbird could also have a V-6 engine (standard on the Heritage) for the same price as the V-8.

ENGINE DATA: BASE FOUR (Escort, EXP): Inline. Overhead cam. Four-cylinder. Cast iron block and aluminum head. Displacement: 97.6 cu. in. (1.6 liters). Bore & stroke: 3.15 x 3.13 in. Compression ratio: 8.8:1. Brake horsepower: 70 at 4600 R.P.M. Torque: 89 lbs.-ft. at 3000 R.P.M. Five main bearings. Hydraulic valve lifters. Carburetor: 2Bbl. Motorcraft 740. VIN Code: 2. NOTE: An 80-horsepower high-output version of the 1.6-liter four arrived later in the model year. **BASE FOUR (Fairmont,**

Granada): Inline. Overhead cam. Four-cylinder. Cast iron block and head. Displacement: 140 cu. in. (2.3 liters). Bore & stroke: 3.78 x 3.13 in. Compression ratio: 9.0:1. Brake horsepower: 86 at 4600 R.P.M. Torque: 117 lbs.-ft. at 2600 R.P.M. Five main bearings. Hydraulic valve lifters. Carburetor: 2Bbl. Holley 6500 or Motorcraft 5200. VIN Code: A. BASE SIX (Granada wagon, Thunderbird); OPTIONAL (Fairmont, Granada): Inline. Overhead valve. Six-cylinder. Cast iron block and head. Displacement: 200 cu. in. (3.3 liters). Bore & stroke: 3.68 x 3.13 in. Compression ratio: 8.6:1. Brake horsepower: 87 at 3800 R.P.M. Torque: 151-154 lbs.-ft. at 1400 R.P.M. Seven main bearings. Hydraulic valve lifters. Carburetor: 1Bbl. Holley 1946. VIN Code: B or T. OPTIONAL V-6 (Granada, Thunderbird): 90-degree, overhead valve V-6. Cast iron block and aluminum head. Displacement: 232 cu. in. (3.8 liters). Bore & stroke: 3.80 x 3.40 in. Compression ratio: 8.65:1. Brake horsepower: 112 at 4000 R.P.M. Torque: 175 lbs.-ft. at 2000 R.P.M. Four main bearings. Hydraulic valve lifters. Carburetor: 2Bbl. Motorcraft 2150. VIN Code: 3. BASE V-8 (LTD); OPTIONAL (Thunderbird): 90-degree, overhead valve V-8. Cast iron block and head. Displacement: 255 cu. in. (4.2 liters). Bore & stroke: 3.68 x 3.00 in. Compression ratio: 8.2:1. Brake horsepower: 122 at 3400 R.P.M.; (TBird, 120 at 3400). Torque: 209 lbs.-ft. at 2400 R.P.M.; (TBird, 205 at 1600). Five main bearings. Hydraulic valve lifters. Carburetor: 2Bbl. Motorcraft 2150 or 7200VV. VIN Code: D. Note: The 255 cu. in. V-8 was also offered in Fairmont police cars. BASE V-8 (LTD wagon); OPTIONAL (LTD sedan): 90-degree, overhead valve V-8. Cast iron block and head. Displacement: 302 cu. in. (5.0 liters). Bore & stroke: 4.00 x 3.00 in. Compression ratio: 8.4:1. Brake horsepower: 132 at 3400 R.P.M. Torque: 236 lbs.-ft. at 1800 R.P.M. Five main bearings. Hydraulic valve lifters. Carburetor: 2Bbl. Motorcraft 2150A or 7200VV. VIN Code: F. HIGH-OUTPUT POLICE V-8 (LTD): 90-degree, overhead valve V-8. Cast iron block and head. Displacement: 351 cu. in. (5.8 liters). Bore & stroke: 4.00 x 3.50 in. Compression ratio: 8.3:1. Brake horsepower: 165 at 3600 R.P.M. Torque: 285 lbs.-ft. at 2200 R.P.M. Five main bearings. Hydraulic valve lifters. Carburetor: 2Bbl. VV. VIN Code: G.

CHASSIS DATA: Wheelbase: (Escort/EXP) 94.2 in.; (Fairmont/Granada) 105.5 in.; (LTD) 114.3 in.; (TBird) 108.4 in. Overall Length: (Escort hatch) 163.9 in.; (Escort wagon) 165.0 in.; (EXP) 170.3 in.; (Fairmont) 195.5 in. exc. Futura oupe, 197.4 in.; (Granada) 196.5 in.; (LTD) 209.3 in.; (LTD wag) 215.0 in.; (LTD Crown Vic) 211.0 in.; (TBird) 200.4 in. Height: (Escort hatch) 53.1 in.; (Escort wag) 53.3 in.; (EXP) 50.5 in.; (Fairmont) 52.9 in.; (Futura cpe) 51.7 in.; (Granada) 53.0 in.; (Granada wag) 54.2 in.; (LTD) 54.7 in.; (LTD wag) 57.4 in.; (TBird) 53.3 in. Width: (Escort) 65.9 in.; (EXP) 63.0 in.; (Fairmont/Granada) 71.0 in.; (LTD) 77.5 in.; (LTD wag) 79.3 in.; (TBird) 74.1 in. Front Tread: (Escort/EXP) 54.7 in.; (Fairmont/Granada) 56.6 in.; (LTD) 62.2 in. (TBird) 58.1 in. Rear Tread: (Escort/EXP) 56.0 in.; (Fairmont/Granada) 57.0 in.; (LTD) 62.0 in. (TBird) 57.0 in. Standard Tires: (Escort/EXP) P165/80R13 SBR BSW; (Fairmont/Granada) P175/75R14 SBR BSW; (LTD) P205/75R14 SBR WSW exc. wagon, P215/75R14; (TBird) P195/75R14 SBR WSW.

TECHNICAL: Transmission: Four-speed manual standard on Fairmont/Granada four: (1st) 3.98:1; (2nd) 2.14:1; (3rd) 1.42:1; (4th) 1.00:1; (Rev) 3.99:1. Four-speed manual transaxle standard on Escort/EXP: (1st) 3.58:1; (2nd) 2.05:1; (3rd) 1.21:1 or 1.36:1; (4th) 0.81:1 or 0.95:1; (Rev) 3.46:1. Three-speed automatic standard on Fairmont/Granada and TBird six: (1st) 2.46:1 or 2.47:1; (2nd) 1.46:1 or 1.47:1; (3rd) 1.00:1; (Rev) 2.11:1 or 2.19:1. Escort/EXP three-speed automatic: (1st) 2.79:1; (2nd) 1.61:1; (3rd) 1.00:1; (Rev) 1.97:1. Four-speed overdrive automatic standard on LTD and Thunderbird V-6/V-8: (1st) 2.40:1; (2nd) 1.47:1; (3rd) 1.00:1; (4th) 0.67:1; (Rev) 2.00:1. Standard final drive ratio: (Escort/EXP) 3.59:1 w/4spd, 3.31:1 w/auto.; (Fairmont/Granada four) 3.08:1; (Fairmont/Granada six) 2.73:1; (Granada V-6) 2.47:1; (LTD) 3.08:1 exc. w/V8351, 2.73:1; (TBird six) 2.73:1; (TBird V-6/V-8) 3.08:1. Drive Axle: (Escort/EXP) front; (others) rear. Steering: (LTD) recirculating ball; (others) rack and pinion. Front Suspension: (Escort/EXP) MacPherson strut-mounted coil springs and stabilizer bar; (Fairmont/Granada/TBird) modified MacPherson struts with lower control arms, coil springs and anti-sway bar; (LTD) long/short control arms w/coil springs and stabilizer bar. Rear Suspension: (Escort/EXP) independent trailing arms w/modified MacPherson struts and coil springs on lower control arms; (others) four-link rigid axle with coil springs. Brakes: Front disc, rear drum; power assisted (except Escort). Ignition: Electronic. Body construction: (Escort/EXP/Fairmont/Granada/TBird) unibody; (LTD) separate body and frame. Fuel tank: (Escort/EXP) 11.3 gal.; (Fairmont/Granada) 16 gal.; (LTD) 20 gal.; (TBird) 21 gal.

DRIVETRAIN OPTIONS: Engines: H.O. 1.6-liter four: Escort ($57). Fuel-saver 1.6- liter four: Escort (NC). Fuel-saver 140 cu. in. four: Fairmont (NC). 200 cu. in. six: Fairmont/Granada ($213). 232 cu. in. V-6: Granada ($283) exc. wagon ($70); Thunderbird ($241). 255 cu. in. V-8: TBird ($241) exc. Heritage (NC). 302 cu. in. V-8: LTD sedan ($59). Transmission/Differential: Automatic transaxle: Escort/EXP ($411). Auto. transmission.: Fairmont/Granada ($411). Floor shift lever: Fairmont/Granada ($49). Traction-Lok differential: Fairmont/Granada/TBird ($76); LTD ($80). Optional axle ratio: Escort/EXP/Fairmont/Granada (NC). Brakes & Steering: Power brakes: Escort ($93). Power steering: Escort/EXP ($190); Fairmont/Granada ($195). Suspension: H.D. susp.: Granada ($24); LTD/TBird ($26). Handling susp.: Escort ($139-$187) exc. GLX ($41); Fairmont ($52); LTD ($49). TR performance susp. pkg.: EXP ($405) w/TR sport aluminum wheels; ($204) w/steel wheels. Other: H.D. battery ($22-$26). H.D. alternator: EXP ($27); LTD ($52). Extended-range gas tank: Fairmont/Granada ($46). Engine block heater ($17-$18). Trailer towing pkg., medium duty: LTD ($200-$251). California emission system ($64-$65). High-altitude emissions (NC).

ESCORT CONVENIENCE/APPEARANCE OPTIONS: Option Packages: Squire wagon pkg. ($293). Instrument group ($87). Appearance protection group ($55). Light group ($30). Comfort/Convenience: Air conditioner ($611). Rear defroster, electric ($120). Remote liftgate release ($30). Tinted glass ($82); windshield only ($32). Digital clock ($57). Interval wipers ($48). Rear wiper/washer ($117). Dual remote sport mirrors ($66). Entertainment: AM radio ($61). AM/FM radio ($76) exc. base ($137). AM/FM stereo radio ($106) exc. base ($167); w/cassette or 8track player ($184) exc. base ($245). Dual rear speakers ($39). Exterior: Metallic glow paint ($61). Two-tone paint/tape ($122-$161). Front vent windows, pivoting ($60). Remote quarter windows ($109). Vinyl-insert bodyside moldings ($45). Bumper guards, front or rear ($26). Bumper rub strips ($41). Luggage rack ($93). Roof air deflector ($29). Lower bodyside protection ($68). Interior: Console ($111). Low-back reclining bucket seats ($33-$98). High-back reclining bucket seats ($65). Cloth/vinyl seat trim ($29); vinyl (NC). Shearling/leather seat trim ($109-$138). Deluxe seatbelts ($24). Wheels/Tires: Wheel trim rings ($48). Aluminum wheels ($232- $377). P165/80R13 WSW ($58).

EXP CONVENIENCE/APPEARANCE OPTIONS: Comfort/Convenience: Appearance protection group ($48). Air conditioner ($611). Fingertip speed control ($151). Tinted glass ($82). Right remote mirror ($41). Entertainment: AM/FM radio ($76). AM/FM stereo radio ($106); w/cassette or 8track player ($184). Premium sound ($105). AM radio delete ($37 credit). Exterior: Flip-up open air roof ($276). Metallic glow paint ($51). Two-tone paint/tape ($122). Luggage rack ($93). Lower bodyside protection ($68). Interior: Low-back bucket seats ($33). Cloth/vinyl seat trim ($29); vinyl (NC). Leather seat trim ($138). Shearling/leather seat trim ($138). Wheels/Tires: Cast aluminum wheels ($232). P165/80R13 RWL ($72).

FAIRMONT/GRANADA CONVENIENCE/APPEARANCE OPTIONS: Option Packages: Granada Squire option ($282). Interior luxury group: Fairmont ($282). Instrument cluster: Fairmont ($100). Cold weather group: Granada ($77). Appearance protection group ($57-$59). Light group ($49-$51). Comfort/Convenience: Air cond. ($676). Rear defroster, electric ($124). Fingertip speed control ($155). Illuminated entry ($68). Power windows ($165-$235). Power door locks ($106-$184). Remote decklid release: Fairmont ($32). Power seat: Fairmont ($139). Power split bench seat: Granada ($196). Tinted glass: Granada ($88). Tinted windshield ($32). Leather-wrapped steering wheel: Granada ($55). Tilt steering ($95). Quartz clock ($32). Interval wipers ($48). Liftgate wiper/washer: wagon ($99). Lighting and

1982 Fairmont Futura sedan (JG)

Mirrors: Cornering lamps: Granada ($59). Map light: Fairmont ($10); Granada dual-beam ($15). Trunk light ($7). Left remote mirror: Fairmont ($22). Dual bright remote mirrors: Fairmont ($65); right only, Granada ($60). Lighted right visor vanity mirror ($46); pair ($91). Entertainment: AM/FM radio ($39-$54). AM/FM stereo radio ($85); w/8track or cassette player ($172). Twin rear speakers: Fairmont ($39). Premium sound system ($105). AM radio delete ($61 credit). Exterior: Flip-up open air roof ($276). Full or half vinyl roof ($137-$140). Metallic glow paint ($63). Two-tone paint ($105-$144). Accent paint stripes ($39-$57). Pivoting front vent windows ($63). Two-way liftgate: wag ($105). Rocker panel moldings: Fairmont ($33). Protective bodyside moldings: Granada ($49). Bumper guards, rear ($28). Bumper rub strips ($50). Luggage rack: Granada ($115). Lower bodyside protection ($41). Interior: Console ($191). Vinyl flight bench seat: Fairmont ($29) w/interior luxury. Cloth/vinyl seat trim: Fairmont ($29). Vinyl seat trim: Granada ($29). Flight bench seat (NC). Split bench seat: Granada ($230). Front floor mats ($13-$22). Wheels/Tires: Luxury wheel covers: Granada ($49) exc. GL/GLX (NC). Wire wheel covers ($80-$152). Turbine wheel covers: Fairmont ($54). Styled steel wheels: Fairmont ($54-$107). Cast aluminum wheels: Granada ($348-$396). P175/75R14 WSW ($66). P185/75R14 BSW: Granada ($38). P185/75R14 WSW ($104) exc. wagon ($66). P185/75R14 RWL: Granada ($121) exc. wagon ($83). P190/65R390 BSW on TRX alum. wheels ($529-$583). Conventional spare ($51).

LTD CONVENIENCE/APPEARANCE OPTIONS: Option Packages: Interior luxury group ($727-$807). Convenience group ($90-$116). Power lock group ($106-$201). Light group ($43). Protection group ($67). Comfort/Convenience: Air cond. ($695); w/auto-temp control ($761). Rear defroster, electric ($124). Fingertip speed control ($155). Illuminated entry system ($68). Power windows ($165-$240). Power driver's seat ($198); driver and passenger ($395). Tinted glass ($102); windshield only ($32). Autolamp on/off delay ($73). Leather-wrapped steering wheel ($51). Tilt steering wheel ($95). Auto. parking brake release ($12). Tripminder computer ($215-$293). Quartz clock ($32). Digital clock ($46-$78). Seatbelt chime ($27). Interval wipers ($48). Lighting and Mirrors: Cornering lamps ($55). Remote right mirror ($43). Lighted right visor vanity mirrors ($46-$91). Entertainment: AM/FM radio ($41-$54). AM/FM stereo radio ($85); w/8track or cassette tape player ($172) exc. Crown Vic ($87). AM/FM stereo search radio ($232) exc. Crown Vic ($146); w/8track or cassette ($233-$318). Power antenna ($55). Dual rear speakers ($41). Premium sound system ($133- $167). AM radio delete ($61 credit). AM/FM delete: Crown Vic ($152 credit). Exterior: Full or half vinyl roof ($165). Metallic glow paint ($66). Two-tone paint/tape ($66-$105). Dual accent bodyside paint stripes ($39). Hood striping ($17). Pivoting front vent windows ($63). Rocker panel moldings ($32). Vinyl-insert bodyside moldings ($51). Bumper guards, rear ($30). Bumper rub strips ($52). Luggage rack ($104). Lower bodyside protection ($39-$52). Interior: Dual-facing rear seats: wagon ($167). Leather seating ($412). Dual flight bench seat recliners ($65). Split bench seating ($139-$204). All-vinyl seat trim ($28); Duraweave vinyl ($62). Front floor mats ($15-$21). Trunk trim ($49). Wheels/Tires: Luxury wheel covers ($82). 15 in. wheel covers ($49). Wire wheel covers ($152). Cast aluminum wheels ($384). P215/75R14 WSW ($36). P225/75R14 WSW ($36-$73). P205/75R15 WSW ($11-$47); puncture-resistant ($112-$148). Conventional spare ($51).

THUNDERBIRD CONVENIENCE/APPEARANCE OPTIONS: Option Packages: Interior luxury group ($1204) exc. Town Landau ($683). Exterior decor group ($385). Interior decor group ($372). Protection group ($51). Light group ($35). Power lock group ($138). Comfort/Convenience: Air cond. ($676); auto-temp ($754) exc. Heritage ($78). Rear defroster ($126). Fingertip speed control ($155). Illuminated entry system ($68). Keyless entry ($139). Tripminder computer ($215-$261). Autolamp on/off delay ($73). Tinted glass ($88); windshield only ($32). Power windows ($165). Six-way power driver's seat ($198). Auto. parking brake release ($12). Leather-wrapped steering wheel ($51). Tilt steering wheel ($95). Electronic instrument cluster ($321-$367). Diagnostic warning lights ($59). Digital clock ($46). Interval wipers ($48). Lighting and Mirrors: Cornering lamps ($59). Remote right mirror ($60). Lighted right visor vanity mirrors ($46-$91). Entertainment: AM/FM radio ($39-$54). AM/FM stereo radio ($85); w/8track or cassette player ($87-$172). AM/FM stereo search radio ($146-$232); w/8track or cassette ($318) exc. Twn Lan ($233) and Heritage ($87). Power antenna ($55). Dual rear speakers ($39). Premium sound system ($133-$167). AM radio delete ($61 credit). Exterior: Carriage roof ($766-$973). Flip-up open-air roof ($276). Vinyl rear half roof ($156-$320). Metallic glow paint ($80). Two-tone paint ($128-$206). Dual accent bodyside paint stripes ($49). Hood/bodyside paint stripes ($16-$65). Pivoting front vent windows ($63). Wide door belt moldings ($51). Rocker panel moldings ($33). Lower bodyside protection ($39-$54). Interior: Bucket seats w/console ($211) exc. (NC) w/decor group. Split bench seat ($208). Luxury split bench ($124). Recaro bucket seats w/console ($405-$523) exc. Heritage ($222). Leather seat trim ($409). Vinyl seat trim ($28-$30). Front floor mats, carpeted ($22). Trunk trim ($48). Wheels/Tires: Wire wheel covers ($45-$152). Luxury wheel covers ($107). Self-sealing tires ($106). TR WSW tires on alum. wheels ($490-$643). Conventional spare ($51).

HISTORY: Introduced: September 24, 1981 except EXP, April 9, 1981. Model year production: 1,035,063 (incl. Mustangs). Total production for the U.S. market of 888,669 units (incl. Mustangs) included 461,524 four-cylinder, 251,145 sixes and 176,000 V-8s. Calendar year production (U.S.): 690,655 (incl. Mustangs). Calendar year sales by U.S. dealers: 925,490 (incl. Mustangs). Model year sales by U.S. dealers: 888,633 (incl. Mustangs).

Historical Footnotes: Escort became the best selling domestic car this model year, finding 321,952 buyers (up over 13 percent from 1981). Still, total Ford Division sales for the model year declined by close to 20 percent: only 888,633 versus 1,105,751 in 1981. And 1981 had posted a loss as well. FoMoCo's market share held at the depressing 16.5 percent level of the prior year. *Car and Driver* readers had voted Escort "Most Significant New Domestic Car" for 1981, and it beat Chevrolet's Chevette this year. Granada gained sales in its recently downsized form, but other models did not. Mustang dropped by almost one-third, Fairmont and Thunderbird by more than 40 percent. EXP did not sell as well as hoped for after its spring 1981 debut, so within a couple of months incentives were being offered. Sales rose a bit later, partly due to a more peppy high- output EXP 1.6-liter engine that debuted in mid-year. Two new plants (San Jose, California and St. Thomas, Ontario) were assigned to assemble the Escort/EXP subcompacts. Escort was also assembled at Wayne, Michigan and Edison, New Jersey. Production of Thunderbird for the model year fell dramatically, by more than half. As the 1983 model year began, Ford offered what was then low-interest financing (10.75 percent rate) to customers who would buy one of the leftover '82 models. In January 1982, the UAW agreed to an alternating-shift arrangement at certain plants. Workers would work 10 days, then take 10 days off. That way, a skilled work force remained available for the day when increased production again became necessary. Ford's advertising theme at this time was: "Have you driven a Ford lately?"

1983 FORD

A dramatically modern 10th-generation Thunderbird showed the aero styling that was becoming the standard for sporty— and even luxury—models. Escort added a revised GT model, based on the European XR3. The high-output 1.6-liter four, added at mid-year 1982, could power both Escort and EXP. The new short-wheelbase LTD sedan was basically a rebodied Granada. The LTD nameplate also continued on the bigger LTD Crown Victoria.

Ford LTD

1983 Escort GT three-door hatchback (F)

ESCORT — FOUR — America's best selling car in 1982 lost its base model this year, dropping to four series. That made Escort L the new base model, with stepups to GL, GLX, and a sporty GT. The new GT was said to be more akin to the high-performance XR3, which had been the image car of the European Escort line. Its 1.6-liter four had multi-port fuel injection. GT also carried five-speed manual shift with 3.73:1 final drive, a TR performance suspension with Michelin TRX tires, functional front and rear spoilers, molded wheel lip extensions (flares), and flared tailpipe extension. GT standards also included foglamps (below the bumper), flat black exterior trim, unique taillamp treatment, a new reclining sport seat, specially-tuned exhaust, special steering wheel, and console and full instrumentation featuring arc yellow graphics. GT was claimed to run 0-60 MPH in about 11 seconds. The high-output carbureted 97.6 cu. in. (1.6-liter) four, introduced as a 1982.5 option, continued available on any Escort except the GT. The base 1.6-liter had new fast-burn technology to improve fuel economy. Escort might have any of three suspension levels: base, handling, and TRX performance. All manual-shift models had a standard upshift indicator that showed when to shift into the next higher gear for best mileage. All Escorts now had all-season SBR tires and a larger (13-gallon) gas tank. Five-speed was available with either the high-output or EFI engine. Escort's Fuel-Saver package came with economy 3.04:1 final drive and wide-ratio four-speed gearbox. Apart from minor details, appearance was the same as 1982. GL and GLX had a new wide bodyside molding with argent stripe (introduced at mid-year 1982). GLX no longer had front and rear bumper guards. GL now had standard low-back reclining bucket seats. All except L had a new locking gas filler door with inside release. Optional knit vinyl seat trim replaced regular vinyl on GL and GLX. New Escort options were: remote-controlled convex right-hand mirror, remote-release fuel filler door (standard on upper Escorts), and P175/80R13 tires. Other options included a luggage rack for hatchbacks, roof air deflector, shearling and leather seat trim, and dual rear speakers.

Ford EXP

1983 EXP HO Sport Coupe (JG)

EXP — FOUR — This year's EXP looked the same, but had a wider choice of engines and transaxles. Standard powertrain was a refined 97.6 cu. in. (1.6-liter) four with two-barrel carburetor and fast-burn capability, hooked to four-speed manual transaxle with overdrive fourth gear. The high-output 1.6-liter introduced as a 1982.5 option was available with either automatic or a new optional five-speed gearbox. That engine produced 80 horsepower, versus 70 for the base four. Newly optional this year was a multi-port fuel-injected version of the four. Acceleration to 60 MPH was supposed to be cut by 3 seconds with the new powerplant. Five-speed gearboxes came with 3.73:1 final drive ratio. Shift control for the optional automatic transaxle was revised to a straight-line pattern. EXP had a larger (13-gallon) gas tank. Interiors were more color-keyed this year, including the console and instrument panel (which had arc yellow gauge graphics); the former panel was black. Seats had a new sew style and more porous knit vinyl that would be cooler in summer. A remote-control locking fuel filler door was now standard. New options included a right-hand remote-control convex mirror, remote fuel door release, sport performance bucket seats, and P175/80R13 tires. Michelin TRX tires and TR wheels were now available with base suspension. The luggage rack, 4.05:1 drive ratio and conventional remote right mirror were deleted from the option list. As before, a Ford script oval stood above the twin grille slots. 'EXP' letters and Ford oval decorated the decklid. Small backup lenses were near inner ends of full-width wraparound taillamps.

1983 LTD four-door sedan (JG)

LTD — FOUR/SIX/V-6 — The familiar LTD nameplate took on two forms for 1983: a new, smaller five-passenger model, and the old (larger) LTD Crown Victoria (listed below). This new LTD was built on the 'L' body shell. Among its features were gas-pressurized shocks and struts, as introduced in 1982 on the new Continental. LTD came in a single well-equipped series: just a four-door sedan and wagon. Sedans carried the 140 cu. in. (2.3-liter) four with four-speed as base powertrain; wagons, the 250 cu. in. (3.3-liter) inline six with three-speed automatic. A 3.8-liter "Essex" V-6 became optional, with four-speed overdrive automatic. So was a propane-powered four, intended to attract fleet buyers. The base 2.3-liter engine had a new single-barrel carburetor and fast-burn technology. LTD had flash-to-pass on the headlamp lever, as well as rack-and-pinion steering. Wheelbase was 105.5 inches, just like the Granada it replaced. In fact this was the familiar Fairmont platform, in yet another variant. Aerodynamic design features included a 60-degree rear-window angle, addition of a front valance and spoiler, and aero-styled decklid. Drag coefficient was claimed to be 0.38 (low for a sedan). LTD's sloping front end displayed a slanted grille that consisted of thin vertical strips dominated by three heavier horizontal divider bars. A Ford oval adorned the center of the heavy upper header bar. Quad rectangular headlamps were deeply recessed. Park lamps sat below the bumper strip; wraparound side markers at front fender tips. The sloping rear end held horizontal tri-color wraparound taillamps with upper and lower segments, and backup lenses halfway toward the center (similar to 1982 Granada). Standard wide vinyl-insert bodyside moldings met with bright partial wheel lip moldings. The instrument panel stemmed from the 1982 Thunderbird. Tire tread design was the wraparound European style, with all-season capability. Mercury Marquis was LTD's corporate twin. Both measured between compact and mid-size.

1983 LTD Country Squire station wagon (JG)

FAIRMONT FUTURA — FOUR/SIX — For its final season, Fairmont continued with little change. The lineup had been simplified into a single series for the 1982 model year. This time, the 4.2-liter V-8 was dropped completely, leaving only a base four and optional inline six. The 140 cu. in. (2.3-liter) switched from 1Bbl. to 2Bbl. carburetion and added fast-burn technology and long-reach spark plugs, plus a redesigned exhaust manifold. Two- and four-door sedans were offered again, along with a two-door coupe. A low-budget 'S' series also was introduced. The Traction-Lok axle was now available with TR-type tires. New options included a 100-amp alternator (LPO option). Flight bench seating and a headlamp-on warning buzzer were added to the interior luxury group. Dual rear speakers were discontinued as an option. Radios got a new look and graphics. In short, not much change. For 1984, the rear-drive Fairmont, which had sold quite well during its six-year life and remained popular with fleet and taxi buyers, would be replaced by the new front-drive Tempo.

LTD CROWN VICTORIA — V-8 — Full-size Fords carried on with little change and a longer name. The model lineup first consisted of two- and four-door sedans and Country Squire (woodgrain) station wagon, in just one luxury level. Later came a low-budget 'S' pair of sedans and plain-bodied wagon. Base engine was the fuel-injected 302 cu. in. (5.0-liter) V-8 with four-speed overdrive automatic. Base tires grew one size, to P215/75R14. Country Squire now had a standard AM/FM radio. All models had a new fuel cap tether. The right-hand remote mirror option was now a convex type. A new, bolder double-crosshatch design grille had a 12x4 hole pattern with internal crosshatching in each hole, and a heavy upper header. The Ford script oval sat at the left portion of the grille. Quad rectangular headlamps stood above rectangular parking lamps, and the assembly continued around the fender tips to enclose signal/marker lenses. Sedans also had a new taillamp design. Country Squire had revised woodtone appearance without the former planking lines. New options included a remote-control locking fuel door, locking wire wheel covers, and new-generation electronic radios. Two trailer-towing packages were offered. Options deleted were dual rear speakers, monaural AM/FM radio, full and half vinyl roofs, seatbelt reminder chime, rear bumper guards, and dual flight bench recliner seats.

THUNDERBIRD — V-6/V-8 — In its tenth and smaller form, Thunderbird took on a striking aero look. "Conceived for today with an eye on tomorrow" was the way the factory catalog described it. The new version was built on the 'S' shell, with 104 inch wheelbase (down from 108). Extensive aerodynamic testing resulted in an air drag coefficient of 0.35 (lower than any tested domestic competitor in its class). Aero design features included concealed drip moldings, a sloping hood, tapered fenders and quarter panels, sharply raked windshield and backlight, contoured parking lamps, and integrated decklid spoiler. Inside, Thunderbird had a standard deep-well luggage compartment, assist straps, storage bins integral with door trim panels, and a console with padded armrest/lid. Engineering features of the new design included gas-

1983 Thunderbird hardtop coupe (F)

pressurized, modified MacPherson struts at the front suspension and gas shocks at the four-bar-link rear. Base engine was the 232 cu. in. (3.8-liter) V-6 with SelectShift three-speed automatic and locking torque converter. Optional: a fuel-injected 302 cu. in. (5.0-liter) V-8 with four-speed overdrive automatic. The Town Landau series was deleted. So was the 4.2-liter V-8 and the inline six. Flash-to-pass became standard. So was variable-ratio, power rack-and-pinion steering. Much more curvaceous and smooth than former 'Birds, the new one had exposed quad rectangular halogen headlamps in deeply recessed housings, with cornering/marker lenses at the edge of each headlamp housing. Parking lamps were well below the front bumper strip. The sloping grille showed an eggcrate (8x6) pattern and heavy upper header. Full-width wraparound taillamps met the recessed license plate housing in a sloping back panel. Backup lenses stood near the center of each taillamp. Trim was minimal, with little of the former TBird's sculptured look. Wide bodyside moldings continued all around the car to meet the bumper rub strips. Options included electric remote outside mirrors, an automatic- dimming rear-view mirror, pivoting front vent windows, keyless entry, clearcoat metallic paint, remote locking fuel door, voice alert, and a canvas-wrapped emergency kit containing tools and first aid items (which stored in a quarter-panel well). Mercury Cougar was similar in design, but with a different side-window look. The new Thunderbird was expected to appeal to younger buyers than previous editions. All the more so a little later when the Turbo Coupe appeared. Louis E. Lataif spoke for Ford in calling it "the ultimate road machine—a complete high- performance package." The turbocharged 2.3-liter four was Ford's first use of a "blow-through" design. That put the turbocharger *ahead* of the throttle, giving faster response by maintaining slight pressure in the intake system. This helped overcome the low-speed lag of conventional turbos. The engine also had Bosch multi-port fuel injection, forged-aluminum pistons, an oil cooler, aluminum rocker covers, and the fourth generation (EECIV) of electronic engine control systems. Compression was cut to 8.0:1 from the usual 9.5:1. Standard was a five-speed manual transmission with performance-type close-ratio gearing. Fifth gear was a 0.86:1 overdrive. The shift linkage had a short throw between gears. Turbos had a 3.45:1 final drive ratio. A new Ford rear suspension called "quadra-shock" was offered for the first time on the Turbo

1983 Thunderbird Turbo coupe (JG)

Coupe. It was a special four-bar-link coil spring system with two hydraulic axle dampers mounted horizontally toward the rear, between brackets on axle and body rail. Like other models, Turbo Coupe had gas-pressurized struts and shocks. The unique front fascia included two recessed Marchal foglamps. A wide charcoal-color bodyside molding and bumper rub strip system encircled the whole car. Headlamp housings were black. There was also a special fluted B pillar molding, and other charcoal or black accents. Goodyear Eagle P205/70HR14 blackwall performance tires rode unique aluminum wheels. Turbo Coupe's instrument panel was special black and brushed finish, including a tachometer with boost and overboost lights; plus a row of diagnostic warning lights and a digital clock. Controls for the dual electric mirrors were on the console. Standard fittings included a leather-wrapped steering wheel and shift knob, Traction-Lok axle, bodyside and decklid paint stripes, black door handles and lock bezels, and charcoal headlamp doors. Lear-Siegler articulated bucket seats had inflatable lumbar support along with open- mesh head restraints. Turbo Coupe's special handling suspension with performance tires was available on other models. Illuminated entry was new standard on the Heritage model, as were dual bright electric remote-control mirrors, electronic instruments, tinted glass, lighted vanity mirrors, and a premium sound system. Also included: tilt steering, digital clock, power locks, autolamp on/off/delay system, bodyside moldings, bumper rub strip extensions, wire wheel covers, a special grille ornament, and striping on hood, bodyside and decklid. Heritage seats were velour cloth trim and a Thunderbird seatback emblem. Front seats held a Velcro- closed driver's map pocket. The instrument panel displayed Prima Vera woodtone appliques. Heritage had unique quarter windows and electro-luminescent coach lamps, Customers later received an anodized aluminum plaque with their signature.

I.D. DATA: Ford's 17-symbol Vehicle Identification Number (VIN) again was stamped on a metal tab fastened to the instrument panel, visible through the windshield. The first three symbols ('1FA') indicate manufacturer, make and vehicle type. The fourth symbol ('B') denotes restraint system. Next comes a letter 'P', followed by two digits that indicate body type: Model Number, as shown in left column of tables below. (Example: '04' Escort L two-door hatchback; the numbering system changed this year.) Symbol eight indicates engine type: '2' L498 2Bbl.; '4' H.O. L498 2Bbl.; '5' L498 EFI; 'A' L4-140 1Bbl.; 'D' Turbo L4140 EFI; 'X' L6200 1Bbl.; '3' V6232 2Bbl.; 'F' V8302 2Bbl.; 'G' V8351 2Bbl. Next is a check digit. Symbol ten indicates model year ('D' 1983). Symbol eleven is assembly plant: 'A' Atlanta, GA; 'B' Oakville, Ontario (Canada); 'G' Chicago; 'H' Lorain, Ohio; 'K' Kansas City, MO; 'S' St. Thomas, Ontario; 'Z' St. Louis, MO; 'R' San Jose, CA; 'T' Edison, NJ; 'W' Wayne, MI. The final six digits make up the sequence number, starting with 100001. A Vehicle Certification Label on the left front door lock face panel or door pillar shows the manufacturer, month and year of manufacture, GVW, GAWR, certification statement, VIN, and codes for such items as body type, color, trim, axle, transmission, and special order information.

ESCORT (FOUR)

Model Number	Body/Style Number	Body Type & Seating	Factory Price	Shipping Weight	Production Total
04	61D	2-dr. L Hatch-4P	5639	1932	Note 1
13	58D	4-dr. L Hatch-4P	5846	1998	Note 1
09	74D	4-dr. L Sta Wag-4P	6052	2026	Note 1
05	61D	2-dr. GL Hatch-4P	6384	1959	Note 1
14	58D	4-dr. GL Hatch-4P	6601	2025	Note 1
10	74D	4-dr. GL Sta Wag-4P	6779	2052	Note 1
06	61D	2-dr. GLX Hatch-4P	6771	1993	Note 1
15	58D	4-dr. GLX Hatch-4P	6988	2059	Note 1
11	74D	4-dr. GLX Sta Wag-4P	7150	2083	Note 1
07	61D	2-dr. GT Hatch-4P	7339	2020	Note 1

Note 1: Total Escort production came to 151,386 two-door hatchbacks, 84,649 four-door hatchback sedans, and 79,335 station wagons. Breakdown by trim level not available. Bodies are sometimes referred to as three- and five-door.

EXP (FOUR)

01	67D	3-dr. Hatch Cpe-2P	6426	2068	19,697
01/301B	67D	3-dr. HO Cpe-2P	7004	N/A	Note 2
01/302B	67D	3-dr. HO Spt Cpe-2P	7794	N/A	Note 2
01/303B	67D	3-dr. Luxury Cpe-2P	8225	N/A	Note 2
01/304B	67D	3-dr. GT Cpe-2P	8739	N/A	Note 2

Note 2: Production of step-up models is included in basic EXP total above.

FAIRMONT FUTURA (FOUR/SIX)

37	36R	2-dr. Coupe-4P	6666/7344	2601/2720	7,882
35	66B	2-dr. Sedan-5P	6444/7122	2582/2701	3,664
36	54B	4-dr. Sedan-5P	6590/7268	2626/2745	69,287

FAIRMONT 'S' (FOUR)

35/41K	66B	2-dr. Sedan-5P	5985/6663	2569/2688	Note 3
36/41K	54B	4-dr. Sedan-5P	6125/6803	2613/2732	Note 3

Note 3: Fairmont 'S' production is included in Futura sedan totals above.

1983 LTD Brougham sedan (JG)

LTD (FOUR/SIX)

39	54D	4-dr. Sedan-5P	7777/8455	2788/2874	111,813
39/60H	54D	4-dr. Brghm-5P	8165/8843	2802/2888	Note 4
40	74D	4-dr. Sta Wag-5P	-- /8577	-- /2975	43,945

Note 4: Brougham production is included in basic sedan total.

Fairmont/LTD Engine Note: Prices shown are for four- and six-cylinder engines. Six-cylinder price includes $439 for the required automatic transmission. A 232 cu. in. V-6 cost $70 more than the inline six in an LTD.

LTD CROWN VICTORIA (V-8)

42	66K	2-dr. Sedan-6P	10094	3590	11,414
43	54K	4-dr. Sedan-6P	10094	3620	81,859
44	74K	4-dr. Ctry Sqr-6P	10253	3773	20,343
43/41K	54K	4-dr. 'S' Sed-6P	9130	N/A	Note 5
44/41K	74K	4-dr. 'S' Wag-6P	9444	N/A	Note 5
44/41E	74K	4-dr. Sta Wag-6P	10003	N/A	Note 5

Note 5: Production of 'S' models and basic station wagon is included in basic sedan and Country Squire totals above.

THUNDERBIRD (V-6/V-8)

46	66D	2-dr. HT Cpe-4P	9197/9485	2905/2936	121,999

THUNDERBIRD HERITAGE (V-6/V-8)

46/607	66D	2-dr. HT Cpe-4P	12228/12516	3027/ --	Note 6

THUNDERBIRD TURBO COUPE (FOUR)

46/934	66D	2-dr. HT Cpe-4P	11790	N/A	Note 6

Note 6: Turbo Coupe and Heritage production is included in basic Thunderbird total.

MODEL NUMBER NOTE: Some sources include a prefix 'P' ahead of the two- digit model number. **FACTORY PRICE AND WEIGHT NOTE:** Fairmont/LTD prices and weights to left of slash are for four-cylinder, to right for six-cylinder engine. Thunderbird prices and weights to left of slash are for V-6, to right for V-8 engine.

ENGINE DATA: BASE FOUR (Escort, EXP): Inline. Overhead cam. Four-cylinder. Cast iron block and aluminum head. Displacement: 98 cu. in. (1.6 liters). Bore & stroke: 3.15 x 3.13 in. Compression ratio: 8.8:1. Brake horsepower: 70 at 4600 R.P.M. Torque: 88 lbs.-ft. at 2600 R.P.M. Five main bearings. Hydraulic valve lifters. Carburetor: 2Bbl. Motorcraft 740. VIN Code: 2. OPTIONAL FOUR (Escort, EXP): High-output version of 1.6-liter four above Horsepower: 80 at 5400 R.P.M. Torque: 88 lbs.-ft. at 3000 R.P.M. VIN Code: 4. BASE FOUR (Escort GT); OPTIONAL (Escort, EXP): Fuel-injected version of 1.6-liter four above Compression ratio: 9.5:1. Horsepower: 88 at 5400 R.P.M. Torque: 94 lbs.- ft. at 4200 R.P.M. VIN Code: 5. BASE FOUR (Fairmont, LTD): Inline. Overhead cam. Four-cylinder. Cast iron block and head. Displacement: 140 cu. in. (2.3 liters). Bore & stroke: 3.78 x 3.13 in. Compression ratio: 9.0:1. Brake horsepower: 90 at 4600 R.P.M. Torque: 122 lbs.-ft. at 2600 R.P.M. Five main bearings. Hydraulic valve lifters. Carburetor: 1Bbl. Carter YFA. VIN Code: A. NOTE: A 140 cu. in. (2.3-liter) propane four was also available for LTD. TURBOCHARGED FOUR (Thunderbird Turbo Coupe): Same as 140 cu. in. four above, with fuel injection and turbocharger Compression ratio: 8.0:1. Horsepower: 142 at 5000 R.P.M. Torque: 172 lbs.-ft. at 3800 R.P.M. VIN Code: D. OPTIONAL SIX (Fairmont, LTD): Inline. Overhead valve. Six-cylinder. Cast iron block and head. Displacement: 200 cu. in. (3.3 liters). Bore & stroke: 3.68 x 3.13 in. Compression ratio: 8.6:1. Brake horsepower: 92 at 3800 R.P.M. Torque: 156 lbs.-ft. at 1400 R.P.M. Seven main bearings. Hydraulic valve lifters. Carburetor: 1Bbl. Holley 1946. VIN Code: X. BASE V-6 (Thunderbird); OPTIONAL (LTD): 90-degree, overhead valve V-6. Cast iron block and aluminum head. Displacement: 232 cu. in. (3.8 liters). Bore & stroke: 3.80 x 3.40 in. Compression ratio: 8.65:1. Brake horsepower: 110 at 3800 R.P.M. Torque: 175 lbs.-ft. at 2200 R.P.M. Four main bearings. Hydraulic valve lifters. Carburetor: 2Bbl. Motorcraft 2150 or 7200VV. VIN Code: 3. BASE V-8 (Crown Victoria); OPTIONAL (LTD, Thunderbird): 90-degree, overhead valve V-8. Cast iron block and head. Displacement: 302 cu. in. (5.0 liters). Bore & stroke: 4.00 x 3.00 in. Compression ratio: 8.4:1. Brake horsepower: 130 at 3200 R.P.M. Torque: 240 lbs.-ft. at 2000 R.P.M. Five main bearings. Hydraulic valve lifters. Electronic fuel injection. VIN Code: F. NOTE: Crown Victoria also announced a high-output version rated 145 horsepower at 3600 R.P.M., 245 lbs.-ft. at 2200 R.P.M. HIGH-OUTPUT POLICE V-8 (Crown Victoria): 90-degree, overhead valve V-8. Cast iron block and head. Displacement: 351 cu. in. (5.8 liters). Bore & stroke: 4.00 x 3.50 in. Compression ratio: 8.3:1. Brake horsepower: 165 at 3600 R.P.M. Torque: 290 lbs.-ft. at 2200 R.P.M. Five main bearings. Hydraulic valve lifters. Carburetor: 2Bbl. VV. VIN Code: G.

CHASSIS DATA: Wheelbase: (Escort/EXP) 94.2 in.; (Fairmont/LTD) 105.5 in.; (Crown Vic) 114.3 in.; (TBird) 104.0 in. Overall Length: (Escort) 163.9 in.; (Escort wagon) 165.0 in.; (EXP) 170.3 in.; (Fairmont) 195.5 in. exc. Futura coupe, 197.4 in.; (LTD) 196.5 in.; (Crown Vic) 211.1 in.; (Crown Vic wag) 215.0 in.; (TBird) 197.6 in. Height: (Escort) 53.3 in.; (EXP) 50.5 in.; (Fairmont) 52.9 in.; (Futura cpe) 51.7 in.; (LTD) 53.6 in.; (LTD wag) 54.3 in.; (Crown Vic) 55.3 in.; (Crown Vic wag) 56.8 in.; (TBird) 53.2 in. Width: (Escort/EXP) 65.9 in.; (Fairmont/LTD) 71.0 in.; (Crown Vic) 77.5 in.; (Crown Vic wag) 79.3 in.; (TBird) 71.1 in. Front Tread: (Escort/EXP) 54.7 in.; (Fairmont/LTD) 56.6 in.; (Crown Vic) 62.2 in. (TBird) 58.1 in. Rear Tread: (Escort/EXP) 56.0 in.; (Fairmont/LTD) 57.0 in.; (Crown Vic) 62.0 in. (TBird) 58.5 in. Standard Tires: (Escort/EXP) P165/80R13 SBR BSW; (Escort GT/EXP luxury cpe) P165/70R365 Michelin TRX; (Fairmont) P175/75R14 SBR BSW; (LTD) P185/75R14 SBR BSW; (Crown Vic) P215/75R14 SBR WSW; (TBird) P195/75R14 SBR WSW; (TBird Turbo Cpe) P205/70HR14. Tranmission: Four-speed manual standard on LTD: (1st) 3.98:1; (2nd) 2.14: 1; (3rd) 1.49:1; (4th) 1.00:1; (Rev) 3.99:1. Escort four-speed manual transaxle (1st) 3.23:1; (2nd) 1.90:1; (3rd) 1.23:1; (4th) 0.81:1; (Rev) 3.46:1. Four- speed manual on Escort/EXP: (1st) 3.58:1; (2nd) 2.05:1; (3rd) 1.23:1 or 1.36:1; (4th) 0.81:1 or 0.95:1; (Rev) 3.46:1. Five- speed manual on Escort/EXP: (1st) 3.60:1; (2nd) 2.12:1; (3rd) 1.39:1; (4th) 1.02:1; (5th) 1.02:1; (Rev) 3.62:1. (Note: separate final drive for 5th gear.) TBird Turbo Coupe five- speed: (1st) 4.03:1; (2nd) 2.37:1; (3rd) 1.50:1; (4th) 1.00:1; (5th) 0.86:1; (Rev) 3.76:1. TBird Turbo Coupe five- speed with 3.73:1 axle ratio: (1st) 3.76:1; (2nd) 2.18:1; (3rd) 1.36:1; (4th) 1.00:1; (5th) 0.86:1; (Rev) 3.76:1. Three-speed automatic standard on LTD and TBird six: (1st) 2.46:1 or 2.47:1; (2nd) 1.46:1 or 1.47:1; (3rd) 1.00:1; (Rev) 2.11:1 or 2.19:1. Escort/EXP three-speed automatic: (1st) 2.79:1; (2nd) 1.61:1; (3rd) 1.00:1; (Rev) 1.97:1. Four-speed overdrive automatic standard on LTD V-6, Crown Victoria and Thunderbird V-8: (1st) 2.40:1; (2nd) 1.47:1; (3rd) 1.00:1; (4th) 0.67:1; (Rev) 2.00:1. Standard final drive ratio: (Escort/EXP) 3.59:1 w/4spd, 3.04:1 w/fuel saver, 3.73:1 w/5spd, 3.31:1 w/auto.; (Fairmont) 3.08:1 exc. w/six, 2.73:1; (LTD four) 3.45:1; (LTD six) 2.73:1; (LTD V-6) 3.08:1; (Crown Vic) 3.08:1; (TBird) 3.45:1 w/5spd, 2.47:1 w/3spd automatic, 3.08:1 w/4spd auto. Drive Axle: (Escort/EXP) front; (others) rear. Steering: (Crown Vic) recirculating ball; (others) rack and pinion. Front Suspension: (Escort/EXP) MacPherson struts with lower control arms, coil springs and stabilizer bar; (Fairmont/LTD/TBird) modified MacPherson struts with lower control arms, coil springs and anti-sway bar; (Crown Vic) long/short control arms w/coil springs and stabilizer bar. LTD and TBird had gas-filled shock absorbers. Rear Suspension: (Escort/EXP) independent trailing arms w/modified MacPherson struts and coil springs on lower control arms; (Fairmont/LTD/Crown Vic) rigid axle w/four-link coil springs; (Thunderbird) four-link rigid axle with coil springs and electronic level control; (TBird Turbo Coupe) "quadra-shock" four-bar-link assembly with two hydraulic, horizontal axle dampers. Gas-filled shocks on LTD and TBird. Brakes: Front disc, rear drum; power assisted (except Escort). Ignition: Electronic. Body construction: (Crown Vic) separate body and frame; (others) unibody. Fuel tank: (Escort/EXP) 13.0 gal.; (Fairmont/LTD) 16.0 gal.; (Crown Vic) 18.0 gal.; (Crown Vic wagon) 18.5 gal.; (TBird) 21 gal.

DRIVETRAIN OPTIONS: Engines: H.O. 1.6-liter four: Escort ($70-$73); EXP GT ($70). Fuel-saver 1.6-liter four: Escort (NC). Turbo 140 cu. in. four: LTD ($896). 200 cu. in. six: Fairmont/LTD ($239). 232 cu. in. V-6: LTD ($309) exc. wagon ($70). 302 cu. in. V-8: Thunderbird ($288). Transmission/Differential: Close-ratio four-speed trans.: Escort (NC). Five-speed manual trans.: Escort ($76). Automatic transaxle: Escort/base EXP ($439) exc. GT and other EXP ($363). Select-shift auto. transmission.: Fairmont/LTD ($439). Overdrive auto. trans.: LTD ($615) exc. wagon ($176); Thunderbird ($176). Floor shift lever: Fairmont/LTD ($49). Traction-Lok differential: Fairmont/LTD/Crown Vic/TBird ($95). Optional axle ratio: Fairmont (NC). Brakes & Steering: Power brakes: Escort ($95). Power steering: Escort/EXP ($210); Fairmont/LTD ($218). Suspension: H.D. susp.: Fairmont ($24); Crown Vic/TBird ($26). Handling susp.: Escort ($199) exc. GLX ($41); Fairmont ($52); Crown Vic ($49). TR performance susp. pkg.: Escort ($41) w/Michelin TRX tires; EXP luxury or GT ($41). Other: H.D. battery ($26). H.D. alternator: EXP ($27). Extended-range gas tank: Fairmont/LTD ($46). Engine block heater ($17-$18). Trailer towing pkg., medium duty: Crown Vic ($200-$251); heavy duty ($251-$302). Trailer towing pkg.: TBird ($251). California emission system ($46-$76). High- altitude emissions (NC).

ESCORT CONVENIENCE/APPEARANCE OPTIONS: Option Packages: Squire wagon pkg. ($350). Instrument group ($87). Appearance protection group ($39). Light group ($43). Comfort/Convenience: Air conditioner ($624). Rear defroster, electric ($124). Fingertip speed control ($170). Tinted glass ($90); windshield only, LPO ($38). Digital clock ($57). Interval wipers ($49). Rear wiper/washer ($117). Dual remote sport mirrors ($67). Entertainment: AM radio: L ($61). AM/FM radio ($82) exc. L ($143). AM/FM stereo radio ($109) exc. base ($170); w/cassette or 8track player ($199) exc. L ($260). Premium sound ($117). Exterior: Flip-up open-air roof ($217-$310). Clearcoat metallic paint ($305). Metallic glow paint ($51). Two-tone paint/tape ($134-$173). Dual bodyside paint stripes ($39). Front vent windows, pivoting ($60). Remote quarter windows ($109). Vinyl-insert bodyside moldings ($45). Bumper guards, front or rear ($28). Bumper rub strips ($41). Luggage rack ($93). Lower bodyside protection ($68). Interior: Console ($111). Fold-down center armrest ($55). Low-back reclining bucket seats: L ($98). High-back reclining bucket seats: L ($65). Vinyl low-back reclining bucket seats: GL/GLX ($24). Vinyl high-back bucket seats: L ($24). Color- keyed front mats ($22). Wheels/Tires: Wheel trim rings ($54). Cast aluminum wheels ($226-$383). TR sport aluminum wheels ($568) exc. GLX ($411) and GT ($201). TR styled steel wheels ($210-$367). P165/80R13 SBR WSW ($59). P175/80R13 SBR BSW ($20); WSW ($78).

EXP CONVENIENCE/APPEARANCE OPTIONS: Comfort/Convenience: Air conditioner ($624). Rear defroster: base ($124). Tinted glass: HO ($90). Entertainment: AM/FM radio ($82). AM/FM stereo radio ($109); w/cassette or 8track player ($199) exc. luxury cpe ($90). Premium sound ($117). AM radio delete ($37 credit). AM/FM stereo delete: luxury cpe ($145 credit). AM/FM stereo/cassette delete: GT ($235 credit). Exterior: Flip-up open air roof ($310). Metallic glow paint ($51). Two-tone paint/tape ($146). Sport tape stripe ($41). Lower bodyside protection ($68). Interior: Low-back sport cloth or knit vinyl bucket seats (NC). Low-back sport performance seats ($173). Leather/vinyl seat trim ($144). Shearling low-back bucket seats ($227). Wheels: TR sport aluminum wheels: GT (NC).

FAIRMONT CONVENIENCE/APPEARANCE OPTIONS: Option Packages: Interior luxury group ($294). Instrument cluster ($100). Appearance protection group ($32-$60). Light group ($55). Comfort/Convenience: Air cond. ($724). Rear defroster, electric ($135). Fingertip speed control ($170). Illuminated entry ($82). Power windows ($180-$255). Power door locks ($120-$170). Remote decklid release ($40). Four-way power seat ($139). Tinted glass ($105). Tinted windshield ($38). Tilt steering ($105). Quartz clock ($35). Interval wipers ($49). Lighting and Mirrors: Trunk light ($7). Left remote mirror: S ($22). Dual bright remote mirrors: S ($68). Lighted visor vanity mirrors, pair ($100). Entertainment: AM radio: S ($61). AM/FM radio ($59-$120). AM/FM stereo radio ($109-$170); w/8track or cassette player ($199-$260). Premium sound system ($117). AM radio delete ($61 credit). Exterior: Flip-up open air roof ($310). Full or half vinyl roof ($152). Metallic glow paint ($63). Two-tone paint ($117- $156). Accent paint stripes: S ($39). Pivoting front vent windows ($63). Rocker panel moldings ($33). Bumper guards, rear ($28). Bumper rub strips ($50). Lower bodyside protection ($41). Interior: Console ($191). Cloth/vinyl seat trim ($35). Bench seat (NC). Front floor mats ($15-$24). Wheels/Tires: Wire wheel covers ($87-$152). Turbine wheel covers: S ($66). Styled steel wheels ($60-$126). Steel wheels, 5.5 in.: fleet LPO ($18-$74). P175/75R14 SBR WSW ($72). P185/75R14 BSW: fleet ($44). P185/75R14 WSW ($116). P190/65R390 Michelin BSW TRX ($535-$601).

LTD CONVENIENCE/APPEARANCE OPTIONS: Option Packages: Squire option ($282). Brougham decor option: wagon ($363). Power lock group ($170-$210). Cold weather group ($77). Appearance protection group ($60). Light group ($38). Comfort/Convenience: Air cond. ($724); auto-temp ($802). Rear defroster, electric ($135). Fingertip speed control ($170). Illuminated entry ($76). Autolamp on-off delay ($73). Power windows ($255). Six-way power driver's seat ($207); dual ($415). Tinted glass ($105). Tinted windshield: fleet ($38). Leather-wrapped steering wheel ($59). Tilt steering ($105). Electronic instrument cluster ($289-$367). Tripminder computer ($215-$293). Digital clock ($78). Diagnostic warning lights ($59). Auto. parking brake release ($12). Interval wipers ($49). Liftgate wiper/washer: wagon ($99). Lighting and Mirrors: Cornering lamps ($60). Map light: fleet ($15). Right remote convex mirror ($60). Lighted visor vanity mirrors ($51-$100). Entertainment: AM/FM radio ($59). AM/FM stereo radio ($109); w/8track or cassette player ($199). Electronic-tuning AM/FM stereo radio ($252); w/cassette ($396). Premium sound system ($117-$151). AM radio delete ($61 credit). Exterior: Flip-up open air roof ($310). Full vinyl roof ($152). Metallic glow paint ($63). Two-tone paint ($117). Pivoting front vent windows ($63). Two-way liftgate: wag ($105). Protective bodyside moldings, LPO ($49). Bumper guards, rear ($28). Bumper rub strips ($56). Luggage rack: wagon ($126). License frames ($9). Lower bodyside protection ($41). Interior: Console ($100). Vinyl seat trim ($35). Split bench seat (NC). Individual seats w/console ($61). Leather seat trim ($415). Front floor mats ($23). Wheels/Tires: Luxury wheel covers ($55). Wire wheel covers ($159-$198). Styled wheels ($178). Cast aluminum wheels ($402). P185/75R14 BSW ($38); WSW ($72). P195/75R14 WSW ($72- $116). Puncture-sealant P195/75R14 WSW ($228). Conventional spare ($63).

CROWN VICTORIA CONVENIENCE/APPEARANCE OPTIONS: Option Packages: Interior luxury group ($830-$911). Convenience group ($95-$116). Power lock group ($123-$220). Light group ($48). Protection group ($68). Comfort/Convenience: Air cond. ($724); w/auto-temp control ($802). Rear defroster, electric ($135). Fingertip speed control ($170). Illuminated entry system ($76). Power windows ($180-$255). Power driver's seat ($210); driver and passenger ($420). Remote fuel door lock ($24). Tinted glass ($105); windshield only, fleet ($38). Autolamp on/off delay ($73). Leather-wrapped steering wheel ($59). Tilt steering wheel ($105). Auto. parking brake release ($12). Tripminder computer ($215-$261). Quartz clock: S ($35). Digital clock ($61-$96). Interval wipers ($49). Lighting and Mirrors: Cornering lamps ($60). Remote right mirror ($43). Lighted visor vanity mirrors ($100). Entertainment: AM/FM stereo radio: S ($106); w/8track or cassette tape player ($112-$218). AM/FM stereo search radio ($166-$272); w/8track or cassette ($310-$416). Power antenna ($60). Premium sound system ($145-$179). AM radio delete: S ($61 credit). AM/FM delete ($152 credit). Exterior: Metallic glow paint ($77). Two-tone paint/tape ($78). Dual accent bodyside paint stripes: S ($39). Pivoting front vent windows ($63). Rocker panel moldings: Ctry Squire ($32). Vinyl-insert bodyside moldings ($55). Bumper rub strips ($52). Luggage rack: Ctry Sq ($110). License frames ($9). Lower bodyside protection ($39-$52). Interior: Dual-facing rear seats: Ctry Sq ($167). Leather seat trim ($418). Split bench seating ($139). All-vinyl seat trim ($34); Duraweave vinyl, wagon ($96). Carpeted floor mats ($33). Trunk trim ($49). Wheels/Tires: Luxury wheel covers ($88). 15 in. wheel covers: S ($49). Wire wheel covers ($159-$198). Cast aluminum wheels ($390). P225/75R14 WSW ($42-$43). P205/75R15 WSW ($17); puncture-resistant ($130). Conventional spare ($63).

THUNDERBIRD CONVENIENCE/APPEARANCE OPTIONS: Option Packages: Interior luxury group: base ($1170). Exterior accent group ($343). Luxury carpet group ($48-$72). Traveler's assistance kit ($65). Light group ($35). Power lock group ($172). Comfort/Convenience: Air cond. ($732); auto-temp ($802). Rear defroster ($135). Fingertip speed control ($170). Illuminated entry system ($82). Keyless entry ($163) exc. Heritage ($88). Anti-theft system ($159). Remote fuel door lock ($26). Tripminder computer ($215-$276). Autolamp on/off delay ($73). Tinted glass ($105); windshield only, LPO ($38). Power windows ($193). Six-way power driver's seat ($222); dual ($444). Auto. parking brake release ($12). Leather-wrapped steering wheel ($59). Tilt steering wheel ($105). Electronic instrument cluster ($321-$382). Electronic voice alert ($67). Diagnostic warning lights ($59). Digital clock ($61). Interval wipers ($49). Lighting and Mirrors: Cornering lamps ($68). Dual electric remote mirrors ($94). Electronic-dimming day/night mirror ($77). Lighted visor vanity mirrors, pair ($106). Entertainment: AM/FM stereo radio: base ($109); w/8track or cassette player ($199) exc. Turbo Cpe ($90). Electronic- tuning AM/FM stereo search radio ($144-$252); w/cassette ($396) exc. Turbo Cpe ($288) and Heritage ($144). Power antenna ($66). Premium sound system ($179). AM radio delete ($61 credit). Exterior: Flip-up open-air roof ($310). Clearcoat paint ($152). Two-tone paint/tape ($148-$218). Charcoal lower accent treatment: Turbo Cpe ($78). Hood paint stripe ($16). Dual accent bodyside/decklid paint stripes ($55). Hood/decklid/bodyside paint stripes ($71). Pivoting front vent windows ($76). Wide bodyside moldings: base ($57). Bright rocker panel moldings ($39). Bumper rub strip extensions ($52). License frames ($9). Lower bodyside protection ($39-$54). Interior: Articulated seats ($183-$427). Leather seat trim ($415-$659). Vinyl seat trim ($37). Front floor mats, carpeted ($22). Wheels/Tires: Wire wheel covers ($45-$159); locking ($84-$198) exc. Heritage ($20). Luxury wheel covers ($113). Styled wheels ($65-$178). Puncture-sealing tires ($124). P205/70R14 performance WSW ($62). P205/70HR14 performance BSW ($152). TRX performance BSW ($471-$649) exc. Turbo Cpe ($154). Conventional spare ($63).

HISTORY: Introduced: October 14, 1982 except Thunderbird, February 17, 1983 and Thunderbird Turbo Coupe, April 1, 1983. Model year production: 928,146 (incl. Mustangs). Total production for the U.S. market of 914,666 units (incl. Mustangs and 55,314 early '84 Tempos) included 423,532 four-cylinder, 313,353 sixes and 177,781 V-8s. That total included 12,276 turbo fours. Calendar year production (U.S.): 1,008,799 (incl. Mustangs). Calendar year sales by U.S. dealers: 1,060,314 (incl. Mustangs). Model year sales by U.S. dealers: 996,694 (incl. Mustangs and 70,986 early '84 Tempos).

Historical Footnotes: Once again, Escort was the best-selling car in the country. That helped Ford's model year sales to rise 12 percent over 1982, but the total stood well below the 1981 total of 1.1 million. Next in line for sales honors were the new smaller LTD and full-size LTD Crown Victoria. The new aero-styled T-Bird sold far more copies than its predecessor--more than twice the 1982 total. Ford still ranked No. 2 in the domestic auto industry, but Oldsmobile had become a potent contender for that spot. Ford was judged second in the industry in quality, behind the Lincoln-Mercury division but ahead of rival GM and Chrysler. Low-rate (10.75 percent) financing was extended in December 1982 to include '83 models as well as the leftover 1982s. Continuing demand kept the big rear-drive Ford alive, as did improved fuel supplies. The new Tempo was introduced in May 1983, but as an early '84 model.

1984 FORD

Ford was trying hard to conquer the youth market— especially the affluent young motorist—with offerings like the SVO Mustang, Thunderbird Turbo Coupe, and new turbo EXP. Fairmont was gone after a six-year run, but the brand-new Tempo took its place in the compact market. Horn buttons returned to the steering wheel hub once again on most models. The inline six finally disappeared. The turbocharged 1.6- liter four, available for Escort and EXP, featured a high-lift camshaft and EEC-IV electronic controls. It delivered boost up to 8 PSI, raising horsepower by some 35 percent.

1984 Escort GL five-door hatchback (JG)

ESCORT — FOUR — Diesel power was the first big news under Ford subcompact hoods, as the company's first passenger-car diesel engine became available on both Escort and Tempo. Produced by Mazda, the 2.0-liter diesel four came with five-speed manual (overdrive) transaxle. A little later came a different kind of four: a turbocharged, fuel-injected version of Escort's 97.6 cu. in. (1.6-liter) engine, ready for the GT model. Turbos hooked up to a five-speed manual gearbox, in a package that included firmer suspension and special wheels/tires. Three other 1.6-liter engines were available: base carbureted, high-output, and fuel-injected. Model availability was revised. In addition to the carryover L and GL, and the sporty GT, there was a new LX (replacing GLX). LX had the fuel-injected four, TR suspension, blackout body trim, overhead console with digital clock, full instruments (including tach), and five-speed transaxle. Appearance changes were limited to details. Escort GT now sported black polycarbonate bumpers. Inside was a new soft-feel instrument panel with integral side-window demisters, and new steering wheel. Escort's horn button moved to the center of the steering wheel. A new-design rear seat, standard on GL, GT and LX, folded down to form a flatter load floor. Each side could fold independently. LX bodies showed dark moldings with "discreet" bright accents. Power ventilation replaced the "ram air" system. New Escort options were: overhead console with digital clock; floor console with graphic warning display module and covered storage area; new electronic radios; graphic equalizer; tilt steering; and power door locks. A lighted visor vanity mirror was added to the light group.

1984 EXP Turbo coupe (JG)

EXP — FOUR — Turbocharged power brought EXP a strong performance boost this year. The new turbo model had a unique front air dam and rear decklid spoiler, with easy-to-spot taped 'Turbo' nomenclature on doors and rear bumper. It also had two-tone paint with black lower section, unique Cpillar applique, black wheel flares, and black rocker panel moldings. The turbo package also included a tighter suspension with Koni shock absorbers, Michelin P185/65R365 TRX tires on new cast aluminum wheels, and five-speed manual transaxle. Base powertrain was upgraded to the high-output 1.6-liter engine, also mated to five-speed manual. EXP had a completely revised exterior. The silhouette was altered dramatically by adding a "bubbleback" liftgate. EXP also had new blackout taillamps, color-keyed bumper rub strips and mirrors, and a revised front air dam. Both the liftgate and taillamps came from Mercury's LN7, companion to EXP that was discontinued this year. Inside was a standard overhead console with digital clock, new instrument panel with performance cluster and tachometer, and new steering wheel with center horn control. Cloth low-back bucket seats were standard. Styled steel wheels were a new design. New options included a tilt steering wheel, electronic radios with graphic equalizer, clearcoat paint, and illuminated visor vanity mirror. Options deleted were: shearling and leather seat trims, AM/FM stereo with 8track, and AM/FM monaural radio. Both EXP and Escort had a new clutch/starter interlock system. New competitors for EXP included Honda's CRX and Pontiac Fiero.

1984 Tempo GLX coupe (JG)

TEMPO — FOUR — Ford's second front-drive model, replacement for the departed rear-drive Fairmont, arrived as an early '84 model, wearing what Ford called "rakish contemporary styling." General Manager Louis E. Lataif said "it continues the modern aerodynamic design theme established with the '83 Thunderbird, but with its own particular flair." Less enthusiastic observers sometimes referred to Tempo's aero shape as a "jellybean" design. Aircraft-type door configurations were indeed shared with the '83 Thunderbird. Door tops extended up into the roof to create a wraparound effect. That also eliminated the need for an exterior drip molding, and allowed easier entry/exit. Tempo's body-color plastic grille consisted of three horizontal slots, one above the other, with a Ford oval at the center of the middle one. Alongside the grille were single quad recessed halogen headlamps. Tapered amber wraparound signal/marker lenses started at the outer end of each headlamp housing. Horizontal taillamps at ends of rear panels tapered down in a curve on the quarter panels. A bodyside "character line" ran just below the beltline, sweeping upward a bit at the back. The nose was sloped; the rear end stubby. Two- and four-door sedans were offered, on a 99.9 inch wheelbase, the latter with six-window design and rounded window corners. Tempo came in L, GL, and GLX trim. This was essentially a stretched version of Escort's chassis, but with a different suspension. A new 140 cu. in. (2.3-liter) HSC (high swirl combustion) four-cylinder engine was developed specially for Tempo. Displacement was identical to the familiar 2.3-liter four used in Fairmont/LTD, but bore/stroke dimensions differed in this OHV design, which actually evolved from the old inline six. This was the first production fast-burn engine, controlled by an EEC-IV onboard computer as used in the Thunderbird Turbo Coupe. The engine had 9.0:1 compression and was announced as producing 90 horsepower (though later sources give a lower rating). For this year only, a carburetor was used. Tempo could have either a close-ratio five-speed manual or automatic transaxle, or a Fuel Saver four-speed (which was standard). In addition to rack-and- pinion steering, Tempo had fully independent quadra-link rear suspension using MacPherson struts; also a MacPherson strut front suspension and stabilizer bar. Power front disc brakes were standard. Inside, Tempo had low-back bucket seats with cloth trim; color-keyed molded door trim panels with integral storage bins; a storage bin above the radio (on the instrument panel); color-keyed vinyl sunvisors with elastic band on driver's side; a carpeted package tray; and a consolette. An optional TR handling package included Michelin P185/65R365 TRX tires on new-design cast aluminum wheels, and a special handling suspension. Other notable options included a factory-installed anti-theft system, remote-release fuel filler door, illuminated entry, light-duty trailer towing package, and electronic AM/FM stereo search sound systems. Several changes were made for the full 1984 model year. Most noteworthy was the addition of a 2.0-liter diesel option with five-speed manual overdrive. The horn button was relocated to the steering wheel; fuel tank enlarged; and two options were added (tachometer and sport performance seat). Mercury's Topaz was nearly identical except for trim and the list of options available.

1984 LTD/LX four-door sedan (JG)

LTD — FOUR/V-6/V-8 — Though basically unchanged after its 1983 debut, LTD received a few fresh touches that included argent accents on bodyside moldings and (optional) bumper rub strips, and a revised instrument panel woodtone applique. A new Aframe steering wheel with center horn button replaced the former four-spoke design. Headlamp doors now had dark argent paint, instead of light argent. Parking and turn lamp lenses switched from clear white to amber, and bulbs from amber to clear. Most noteworthy new body feature was the unique formal roof treatment added to the Brougham four-door sedan. It had a distinctive solid rear pillar and "frenched" back window treatment, and included a full Cambria cloth roof. The inline six-cylinder engine finally disappeared. Manual transmission with the base 140 cu. in. (2.3-liter) four was dropped. A 302 cu. in. (5.0-liter) EFI high-output V-8 was available only on police sedans. That made a 232 cu. in. (3.8-liter) V-6, now fuel-injected, the only regular option (standard on wagons). All engines added EECIV controls. Propane power was available again, but found few takers. Base and Brougham sedans were offered again, along with a station wagon. Base models could get some of Brougham's expanded standard trim as part of the Interior Luxury Group. Power steering and three-speed automatic were made standard, with four-speed automatic available in V-6 models. New LTD options included a flight bench seat (said to be the single most requested feature).

265

1984 LTD Crown Victoria sedan (JG)

LTD CROWN VICTORIA — V-8 — Crown Vic's new grille featured a light argent second surface, and a new optional Brougham roof for the four-door had a formal look. It included a padded full vinyl top, a more upright rear window with "frenched" treatment, and electro-luminiscent coach lamps on the center pillar. Interiors had a new vinyl grain pattern. Otherwise, the full- size Ford was a carryover, available again as a two- or four- door sedan, and pair of wagons. The Crown Victoria station wagon was just a Country Squire without simulated wood trim. The wide grille had a 12 x 4 hole crosshatch pattern (plus a 2 x 2 pattern within each segment). Wide amber parking lamps went below the quad headlamps. Amber signal/marker lenses consisted of a large lens above a small one. 'LTD Crown Victoria' lettering went ahead of the front door, just above the crease line. Sole standard engine was the 302 cu. in. (5.0-liter) fuel-injected V-8. The high- performance 351 cu. in. (5.8-liter) V-8 with variable-venturi carburetor was available only with police package.

1984 Thunderbird Elan hardtop coupe (JG)

THUNDERBIRD — FOUR/V-6/V-8 — Visible changes were few on Ford's personal luxury coupe, but the model lineup was revised. The Heritage series was renamed elan (Ford didn't capitalize the name). And a new Fila model was developed in conjunction with Fila Sports, Inc., an Italian manufacturer of apparel for active leisure sports (mainly tennis and skiing). Fila had exclusive light oxford gray over charcoal paint, with unique red and blue tape stripes emulating the graphics of the company's logo. Bright trim was minimal, with body-color grille and wheels, and charcoal windshield and backlight moldings. Inside, Fila had charcoal components. Articulated seats were trimmed in oxford white leather, with perforated leather inserts; or oxford gray luxury cloth with perforated cloth inserts. Turbo Coupe added charcoal greenhouse moldings and a new viscous clutch fan, as well as a starter/clutch interlock system

1984 Thunderbird Turbo coupe (JG)

and oil-temperature warning switch. All TBirds now had standard bumper rub strip extensions, and a modified appearance of the birds on taillamps. Electronic fuel injection went on the base 232 cu. in. (3.8-liter) V-6. Counterbalanced springs replaced the hood's prior prop rod. Steering wheels (except Turbo Coupe's) were now A frame design, with horn button in the center. Sole engine option was the 302 cu. in. (5.0-liter) fuel-injected V-8. Turbo Coupe retained the 140 cu. in. (2.3-liter) turbocharged four, but now came with automatic transmission as well as the five-speed manual gearbox. Each model had a slightly curved 8 x 6 hole crosshatch grille pattern with wide Thunderbird insignia in the tall header bar. Staggered, recessed quad headlamps flanked the grille. Amber (formerly clear) parking lamps were set into the bumper. Small amber wraparound marker lenses were used. 'Thunderbird' insignias went on back pillars. Mercury Cougar was mechanically identical, but a bit different in styling.

I.D. DATA: Ford's 17-symbol Vehicle Identification Number (VIN) again was stamped on a metal tab fastened to the instrument panel, visible through the windshield. The first three symbols ('1FA') indicate manufacturer, make and vehicle type. The fourth symbol ('B') denotes restraint system. Next comes a letter 'P', followed by two digits that indicate body type: Model Number, as shown in left column of tables below. (Example: '04' Escort L two-door hatchback). Symbol eight indicates engine type: '2' L498 2Bbl.; '4' H.O. L498 2Bbl.; '5' L498 EFI; '8' Turbo L498 FI; 'H' Diesel L4121 'A'

L4-140 1Bbl.; 'R' or 'J' HSC L4140 1Bbl.; '6' Propane L4140; 'W' Turbo L4140 EFI; '3' V6232 2Bbl.; 'F' V8302 2Bbl.; 'G' V8351 2Bbl. Next is a check digit. Symbol ten indicates model year ('E' 1984). Symbol eleven is assembly plant: 'A' Atlanta, GA; 'B' Oakville, Ontario (Canada); 'G' Chicago; 'H' Lorain, Ohio; 'K' Kansas City, MO; 'X' St. Thomas, Ontario; 'Z' St. Louis, MO; 'T' Edison, NJ; 'W' Wayne, MI. The final six digits make up the sequence number, starting with 100001. A Vehicle Certification Label on the left front door lock face panel or door pillar shows the manufacturer, month and year of manufacture, GVW, GAWR, certification statement, VIN, and code for such items as body type and color, trim, axle ratio, transmission, and special order data.

ESCORT (FOUR)

Model Number	Body/Style Number	Body Type & Seating	Factory Price	Shipping Weight	Production Total
04	61D	2-dr. Hatch-4P	5629	1981	Note 1
13	58D	4-dr. Hatch-4P	5835	2024	Note 1
04	61D	2-dr. L Hatch-4P	5885	1981	Note 1
13	58D	4-dr. L Hatch-4P	6099	2034	Note 1
09	74D	4-dr. L Sta Wag-4P	6313	2066	Note 1
05	61D	2-dr. GL Hatch-4P	6382	2033	Note 1
14	58D	4-dr. GL Hatch-4P	6596	2086	Note 1
10	74D	4-dr. GL Sta Wag-4P	6773	2115	Note 1
15	58D	4-dr. LX Hatch-4P	7848	2137	Note 1
11	74D	4-dr. LX Sta Wag-4P	7939	2073	Note 1

ESCORT GT (FOUR)

07	61D	2-dr. Hatch-4P	7593	2103	Note 1
07	61D	2-dr. Turbo Hatch-4P	N/A	2239	Note 1

Note 1: Total Escort production came to 184,323 two-door hatchbacks, 99,444 four-door hatchback sedans, and 88,756 station wagons. Breakdown by trim level not available. Bodies are sometimes referred to as three- door and five-door.

Diesel Engine Note: Diesel-powered Escorts came in L and GL trim, priced $558 higher than equivalent gasoline models.

EXP (FOUR)

01 /A80	67D	3-dr. Hatch Cpe-2P	6653	2117	23,016
01 /A81	67D	3-dr. Luxury Cpe-2P	7539	2117	Note 2
01 /A82	67D	3-dr. Turbo Cpe-2P	9942	2158	Note 2

Note 2: Production of luxury and turbo coupe models is included in basic EXP total above.

1984 Tempo GLX sedan (JG)

TEMPO (FOUR)

18	66D	2-dr. L Sedan-5P	6936	2249	Note 3
21	54D	4-dr. L Sedan-5P	6936	2308	Note 3
19	66D	2-dr. GL Sed-5P	7159	2276	Note 3
22	54D	4-dr. GL Sed-5P	7159	2339	Note 3
20	66D	2-dr. GLX Sed-5P	7621	2302	Note 3
23	54D	4-dr. GLX Sed-5P	7621	2362	Note 3

Note 3: Total Tempo production came to 107,065 two-doors and 295,149 four-doors.

Diesel Engine Note: Diesel-powered Tempos cost $558 more than equivalent gasoline models.

1984 LTD Country Squire station wagon (JG)

LTD (FOUR/V-6)

39	54D	4-dr. Sedan-5P	8605/9014	2804/2881	154,173
39/60H	54D	4-dr. Brghm-5P	9980/10389	2812/2889	Note 4
40	74D	4-dr. Sta Wag-5P	-- /9102	-- /2990	59,569

Note 4: Brougham production is included in basic sedan total.

LTD CROWN VICTORIA (V-8)

Model Number	Body/Style Number	Body Type & Seating	Factory Price	Shipping Weight	Production Total
42	66K	2-dr. Sedan-6P	10954	3546	12,522
43	54K	4-dr. Sedan-6P	10954	3587	130,164
44	74K	4-dr. Ctry Sqr-6P	11111	3793	30,803
43/41K	54K	4-dr. 'S' Sed-6P	9826	N/A	Note 5
44/41K	74K	4-dr. 'S' Wag-6P	10136	N/A	Note 5
44/41E	74K	4-dr. Sta Wag-6P	10861	N/A	Note 5

Note 5: Production of 'S' models and basic station wagon is included in basic sedan and Country Squire totals above.

THUNDERBIRD (V-6/V-8)

Model Number	Body/Style Number	Body Type & Seating	Factory Price	Shipping Weight	Production Total
46	66D	2-dr. HT Cpe-4P	9633/10253	2890/3097	170,533
46/607	66D	2-dr. Elan Cpe-4P	12661/13281	2956/3163	Note 6
46/606	66D	2-dr. Fila Cpe-4P	14471/14854	3061/3268	Note 6

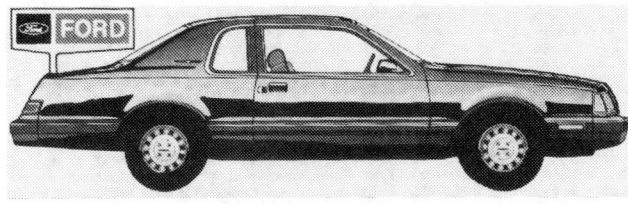

1984 Thunderbird hardtop coupe (JG)

THUNDERBIRD TURBO COUPE (FOUR)

Model Number	Body/Style Number	Body Type & Seating	Factory Price	Shipping Weight	Production Total
46/934	66D	2-dr. HT Cpe-4P	12330	2938	Note 6

Note 6: Turbo Coupe and Elan/Fila production is included in basic Thunderbird total.

MODEL NUMBER NOTE: Some sources include a prefix 'P' ahead of the two-digit model number **FACTORY PRICE AND WEIGHT NOTE:** LTD prices and weights to left of slash are for four-cylinder, to right for V-6 engine. Thunderbird prices and weights to left of slash are for V-6, to right for V-8 engine.

ENGINE DATA: BASE FOUR (Escort): Inline. Overhead cam. Four-cylinder. Cast iron block and aluminum head. Displacement: 97.6 cu. in. (1.6 liters). Bore & stroke: 3.15 x 3.13 in. Compression ratio: 9.0:1. Brake horsepower: 70 at 4600 R.P.M. Torque: 88 lbs.-ft. at 2600 R.P.M. Five main bearings. Hydraulic valve lifters. Carburetor: 2Bbl. Motorcraft 740. VIN Code: 2. BASE FOUR (EXP); OPTIONAL (Escort): High-output version of 1.6-liter four above Horsepower: 80 at 5400 R.P.M. Torque: 88 lbs.-ft. at 3000 R.P.M. VIN Code: 4. BASE FOUR (Escort LX, GT); OPTIONAL (Escort, EXP): Fuel-injected version of 1.6-liter four above Horsepower: 84 at 5200 R.P.M. Torque: 90 lbs.-ft. at 2800 R.P.M. VIN Code: 5. TURBO FOUR (Escort, EXP): Same as 1.6-liter four above, with fuel injection and turbocharged Compression ratio: 8.0:1. Horsepower: 120 at 200 R.P.M. Torque: 120 lbs.-ft. at 3400 R.P.M. VIN Code: 8. DIESEL FOUR (Escort, Tempo): Inline. Overhead cam. Four-cylinder. Cast iron block and aluminum head. Displacement: 121 cu. in. (2.0 liters). Bore & stroke: 3.39 x 3.39 in. Compression ratio: 22.5:1. Brake horsepower: 52 at 4000 R.P.M. Torque: 82 lbs.-ft. at 2400 R.P.M. Solid valve lifters. Fuel injection. VIN Code: H. BASE FOUR (Tempo): Inline. Overhead valve. Four-cylinder. Cast iron block and head. Displacement: 140 cu. in. (2.3 liters). Bore & stroke: 3.70 x 3.30 in. Compression ratio: 9.0:1. Brake horsepower: 84 at 4400 R.P.M. Torque: 118 lbs.-ft. at 2600 R.P.M. Five main bearings. Hydraulic valve lifters. Carburetor: 1Bbl. Holley 6149. High Swirl Combustion (HSC) design. VIN Code: R (U.S.) or J (Mexico). BASE FOUR (LTD): Inline. Overhead cam. Four-cylinder. Cast iron block and head. Displacement: 140 cu. in. (2.3 liters). Bore & stroke: 3.78 x 3.13 in. Compression ratio: 9.0:1. Brake horsepower: 88 at 4000 R.P.M. Torque: 122 lbs.-ft. at 2400 R.P.M. Five main bearings. Hydraulic valve lifters. Carburetor: 1Bbl. Carter YFA. VIN Code: A. PROPANE FOUR (LTD): Same as 140 cu. in. four above, but for propane fuel Compression ratio: 10.0:1. Brake horsepower: 88 at 4000 R.P.M. Torque: 122 lbs.-ft. at 2400 R.P.M. VIN Code: 6. TURBOCHARGED FOUR (Thunderbird Turbo Coupe): Same as 140 cu. in. four above, with fuel injection and turbocharger Compression ratio: 8.0:1. Horsepower: 145 at 4600 R.P.M. Torque: 180 lbs.-ft. at 3600 R.P.M. VIN Code: W. BASE V-6 (Thunderbird): OPTIONAL (LTD): 90-degree, overhead valve V-6. Cast iron block and aluminum head. Displacement: 232 cu. in. (3.8 liters). Bore & stroke: 3.80 x 3.40 in. Compression ratio: 8.7:1. Brake horsepower: 120 at 3600 R.P.M. Torque: 205 lbs.-ft. at 1600 R.P.M. Four main bearings. Hydraulic valve lifters. Throttle-body fuel injection. VIN Code: 3. BASE V-8 (Crown Victoria): OPTIONAL (Thunderbird): 90-degree, overhead valve V-8. Cast iron block and head. Displacement: 302 cu. in. (5.0 liters). Bore & stroke: 4.00 x 3.00 in. Compression ratio: 8.4:1. Brake horsepower: 140 at 3600 R.P.M. Torque: 250 lbs.-ft. at 1600 R.P.M. Five main earings. Hydraulic valve lifters. Electronic fuel injection (TBI). VIN Code: F. NOTE: Crown Victoria wagons had a high-output 302 cu. in. V-8 rated 155 horsepower at 3600 R.P.M., 265 lbs.-ft. at 2000 R.P.M. HIGH-OUTPUT POLICE V-8 (Crown Victoria): 90-degree, overhead valve V-8. Cast iron block and head. Displacement: 351 cu. in. (5.8 liters). Bore & stroke: 4.00 x 3.50 in. Compression ratio: 8.3:1. Brake horsepower: 180 at 3600 R.P.M. Torque: 285 lbs.-ft. at 4000 R.P.M. Five main bearings. Hydraulic valve lifters. Carburetor: 2Bbl. VV. VIN Code: G.

CHASSIS DATA: Wheelbase: (Escort/EXP) 94.2 in.; (Tempo) 99.9 in.; (LTD) 105.6 in.; (Crown Vic) 114.3 in.; (TBird) 104.0 in. Overall Length: (Escort) 163.9 in.; (Escort wagon) 165.0 in.; (EXP) 170.3 in.; (Tempo) 176.2 in.; (LTD) 196.5 in.; (Crown Vic) 211.1 in.; (Crown Vic wag) 215.0 in.; (TBird) 197.6 in. Height: (Escort) 53.3-53.4 in.; (EXP) 50.5 in.; (Tempo 2dr.) 2.5 in. (Tempo 4dr.) 52.7 in.; (LTD) 53.6 in. (LTD wag) 54.3 in.; (Crown Vic) 55.3 in.; (Crown Vic wag) 56.8 in.; (TBird) 53.2 in. Width: (Escort/EXP) 65.9 in.; (Tempo) 66.2 in.; (LTD) 71.0 in.; (Crown Vic) 77.5 in. (Crown Vic wag) 79.3 in.; (TBird) 71.1 in. Front Tread: (Escort/EXP) 54.7 in.; (Tempo) 54.7 in.; (LTD) 56.6 in.; (Crown Vic) 62.2 in. (TBird) 58.1 in. Rear Tread: (Escort/EXP) 56.0 in.; (Tempo) 57.6 in.; (LTD) 57.0 in.; (Crown Vic) 62.0 in. (TBird) 58.5 in. Standard Tires: (Escort) P165/80R13 SBR BSW; (Escort GT) P165/70R365 Michelin TRX; (Escort Turbo GT) P185/65R365 Michelin TRX; (Tempo) P175/80R13 SBR BSW; (LTD) P185/75R14; (Crown Vic) P215/75R14 SBR WSW; (TBird) P195/75R14 SBR WSW; (TBird Turbo Cpe) P205/70HR14 BSW.

TECHNICAL: Transmission: Four-speed manual standard on Tempo: (1st) 3.23:1; (2nd) 1.92:1; (3rd) 1.23:1; (4th) 0.81:1; (Rev) 3.46:1. Escort four-speed manual transaxle (1st) 3.23:1; (2nd) 1.90:1; (3rd) 1.23:1; (4th) 0.81:1; (Rev) 3.46:1. Alternate Escort four-speed manual: (1st) 3.58:1; (2nd) 2.05:1; (3rd) 1.23:1 or 1.36:1;

(4th) 0.81:1 or 0.95:1; (Rev) 3.46:1. Five-speed manual on Escort/EXP/Tempo: (1st) 3.60:1; (2nd) 2.12:1; (3rd) 1.39:1; (4th) 1.02:1; (5th) 1.02:1; (Rev) 3.62:1. (Note: separate final drive for 5th gear.) Tempo diesel five-speed manual: (1st) 3.93:1; (2nd) 2.12:1; (3rd) 1.39:1; (4th) 1.02:1; (5th) 0.98:1; (Rev) 3.62:1. TBird Turbo Coupe five-speed: (1st) 4.03:1; (2nd) 2.37:1; (3rd) 1.50:1; (4th) 1.00:1; (5th) 0.86:1; (Rev) 3.76:1. Three-speed automatic standard on LTD: (1st) 2.46:1 or 2.47:1; (2nd) 1.46:1 or 1.47:1; (3rd) 1.00:1; (Rev) 2.11:1 or 2.19:1. Escort/EXP/Tempo three-speed automatic: (1st) 2.79:1; (2nd) 1.61:1; (3rd) 1.00:1; (Rev) 1.97:1. Four-speed overdrive automatic standard on LTD propane four, Crown Victoria and Thunderbird: (1st) 2.40:1; (2nd) 1.47:1; (3rd) 1.00:1; (4th) 0.67:1; (Rev) 2.00:1. Standard final drive ratio: (Escort/EXP) 3.59:1 w/4spd, 3.73:1 w/5spd, 3.31:1 w/auto., 3.52:1 w/diesel; (Tempo) 3.04:1 w/4spd, 3.33:1 w/5spd, 3.23:1 w/auto., 3.73:1 w/diesel; (LTD four) 3.27:1; (LTD V-6) 2.73:1 or 3.27:1; (LTD propane four) 3.08:1; (Crown Vic) 3.08:1; (TBird) 3.45:1 w/5spd, 2.73:1 w/3spd automatic and V-6, 3.27:1 w/4spd auto. and V-6, 3.08:1 w/4spd auto. and V-8, 3.73:1 w/turbo and auto. Drive Axle: (Escort/EXP/Tempo) front; (others) rear. Steering: (Crown Vic) recirculating ball; (others) rack and pinion. Front Suspension: (Escort/EXP) MacPherson struts with lower control arms, coil springs and stabilizer bar; (Tempo) MacPherson struts with stabilizer bar; (LTD/TBird) modified MacPherson struts with lower control arms, coil springs and anti-sway bar; (Crown Vic) long/short control arms w/coil springs and stabilizer bar. LTD and TBird had gas-filled struts. Rear Suspension: (Escort/EXP) independent trailing arms w/modified MacPherson struts and coil springs on lower control arms; (Tempo) fully independent quadra-link with MacPherson struts; (LTD/Crown Vic) rigid axle w/four-link coil springs; (Thunderbird) four-link rigid axle with coil springs and electronic level control; (TBird Turbo Coupe) "quadra-shock" four-bar-link assembly with two hydraulic, horizontal axle dampers. Gas-filled shocks on LTD and TBird. Brakes: Front disc, rear drum; power assisted (except Escort). Ignition: Electronic. Body construction: (Crown Vic) separate body and frame; (others) unibody. Fuel tank: (Escort/EXP) 13.0 gal.; (Tempo) 14.0 gal.; (LTD) 16.0 gal.; (Crown Vic) 20.0 gal.; (TBird) 21 gal.

DRIVETRAIN OPTIONS: Engines: Fuel-saver 1.6-liter four: Escort (NC). Propane 140 cu. in. four: LTD ($896). 232 cu. in. V-6: LTD ($409). 302 cu. in. V-8: Thunderbird ($383). Transmission/Differential: Five-speed manual trans.: Escort/Tempo ($76). Automatic transaxle: Escort ($439) exc. LX/GT and EXP ($363); Tempo ($439). Auto. transmission.: TBird Turbo Cpe ($315). Overdrive auto. trans.: LTD ($237). Traction-Lok differential: LTD/Crown Vic/TBird ($95). Brakes & Steering: Power brakes: Escort ($95). Power steering: Escort/EXP ($215); Tempo ($223). Suspension: H.D. susp.: Tempo (NC); Crown Vic/TBird ($26). Handling susp.: Escort L ($199); Escort GL ($95). Soft ride susp. pkg.: Tempo (NC). Other: H.D. battery ($27). H.D. alternator: EXP ($27); LTD ($52). Extended-range gas tank: LTD ($46). Engine block heater ($18). Trailer towing pkg.: LTD ($398); Crown Vic ($200-$251); TBird ($251). California emission system: Escort/EXP ($46); others ($99). High-altitude emissions (NC).

ESCORT CONVENIENCE/APPEARANCE OPTIONS: Option Packages: Squire wagon pkg. ($373). Instrument group ($87). Power door lock group ($124-$176). Light group ($67). Comfort/Convenience: Air conditioner ($643). Rear defroster, electric ($130). Fingertip speed control ($176). Tinted glass ($95); windshield only ($48). Tilt steering ($104). Overhead console w/digital clock ($82). Interval wipers ($50). Rear wiper/washer ($120) exc. LX ($46). Entertainment: AM radio: L ($39). AM/FM radio ($82) exc. L ($121). AM/FM stereo radio ($109) exc. L ($148); w/cassette player ($204) exc. L ($243). Electronic-tuning AM/FM stereo ($252-$291); w/cassette ($396-$435). Graphic equalizer ($176). Premium sound ($117). Exterior: Flip-up open-air roof ($315). Clearcoat metallic paint (NC). Glamour paint ($51). Two-tone paint/tape ($134- $173). Dual bodyside paint stripes ($39). Front vent windows, pivoting ($63). Vinyl-insert bodyside moldings ($45). Bumper guards, front or rear ($28). Bumper rub strips ($48). Luggage rack ($100). Lower bodyside protection ($68). Interior: Console ($111). Vinyl seat trim ($24). Color-keyed front mats ($22). Wheels/Tires: Wheel trim rings ($54). Cast aluminum wheels ($279). TR aluminum wheels ($201). Styled steel wheels ($104 credit). P165/80R13 SBR WSW ($59). P175/80R13 SBR BSW (NC).

EXP CONVENIENCE/APPEARANCE OPTIONS: Comfort/Convenience: Air conditioner ($643). Fingertip speed control ($176). Tinted glass ($95). Tilt steering ($104). Lighted visor vanity mirror ($50). Entertainment: AM/FM stereo radio ($109); w/cassette player ($204) exc. luxury cpe ($95). Electronic-tuning AM/FM stereo ($252) exc. luxury cpe ($144) and Turbo ($49); w/cassette ($396) exc. luxury cpe ($288) and Turbo ($193). Graphic equalizer ($176). Premium sound ($117). AM radio delete ($39 credit). AM/FM stereo delete: luxury cpe ($148 credit). AM/FM stereo/cassette delete: Turbo ($243 credit). Exterior: Flip-up open air roof ($315). Clearcoat paint ($161). Lower two-tone paint/tape ($146). Sport tape stripe ($41). Stripe delete (NC). Medium bodyside moldings ($45). Lower bodyside protection ($68). Interior: Low-back knit vinyl bucket seats (NC). Sport performance seats ($173). Front floor mats ($22). Wheels: TR aluminum wheels ($369). TR styled steel wheels ($168). Cast aluminum wheels ($238). P165/80R13 RWL ($90). P165/70R365 TRX (NC).

TEMPO CONVENIENCE/APPEARANCE OPTIONS: Option Packages: TR performance pkg. w/aluminum wheels ($366- $424). Sport appearance group: GL 2dr. ($299). Power lock group ($202-$254). Appearance protection group ($71). Light/convenience group ($50-$85). Comfort/Convenience: Air cond. ($743). Rear defroster, electric ($140). Fingertip speed control ($176). Illuminated entry ($82). Anti-theft system ($159). Power windows ($272). Power decklid release ($41). Six-way power seat ($224). Tinted glass ($110); windshield ($48). Tilt steering ($110). Sport instrument cluster ($71-$87). Digital clock ($61). Interval wipers ($50). Lighting and Mirrors: Left remote mirror ($23); right ($70). Dual remote mirrors ($93). Lighted visor vanity mirrors, pair ($100-$112). Entertainment: AM radio ($59). AM/FM stereo radio ($109); w/cassette player ($204). Electronic-tuning AM/FM stereo ($252); w/cassette ($396). Premium sound system ($117). AM radio delete ($39 credit). Exterior: Flip-up open air roof ($315). Metallic glamour glow paint ($63). Black lower body accent paint ($78-$194). Narrow bodyside moldings ($61). Bumper guards, front/rear ($56). Bumper rub strips ($48). Interior: Console ($111). Fold-down front armrest ($55). Vinyl seat trim ($35). Carpeted front floor mats ($13). Trunk trim ($30). Wheels/Tires: Luxury wheel covers ($59). Styled steel wheels ($59) exc. GL/GLX (NC). P175/80R13 WSW ($72).

LTD CONVENIENCE/APPEARANCE OPTIONS: Option Packages: Squire option ($282). Brougham decor option: wagon ($363). Interior luxury group ($388). Power lock group ($213-$254). Cold weather group ($77). Light group ($38). Police pkg. ($859-$1387). Taxi pkg. ($860). H.D. fleet pkg. ($210). Comfort/Convenience: Air cond. ($743); auto-temp ($809). Rear defroster, electric ($140). Fingertip speed control ($176). Illuminated entry ($82). Autolamp on-off delay ($73). Power windows ($272). Six-way power driver's seat ($224); dual ($449). Tinted glass ($110). Tinted windshield ($48). Leather-wrapped steering wheel ($59). Tilt steering ($110). Electronic instrument cluster ($289-$367). Tripminder computer ($215-$293). Digital clock ($78). Diagnostic warning lights ($83). Interval wipers ($50). Liftgate wiper/washer: wagon ($99). Lighting and Mirrors: Cornering lamps ($68). Right remote convex mirror ($61). Lighted visor vanity mirrors ($57-$106). Entertainment: AM/FM stereo radio ($109); w/cassette player ($204). Electronic-tuning AM/FM stereo radio w/cassette ($396). Premium sound system ($151). AM radio delete ($39 credit). Exterior: Full vinyl roof ($152). Metallic glow paint ($63). Two-tone ($128). Pivoting front vent windows ($79). Two-way liftgate: wag ($105). Protective bodyside moldings ($55). Bumper guards, rear ($28). Bumper rub strips ($56). Luggage rack: wagon ($126). Lower bodyside protection ($41). Interior: Vinyl seat trim ($35). Split or flight bench seat (NC). Individual seats w/console ($61). Leather seat trim ($415). Front floor mats, carpeted ($23). Wheels/Tires: Luxury wheel covers ($55). Wire wheel covers ($165); locking ($204). Styled wheels ($178). Styled steel wheels w/trim rings ($54). P185/75R14 WSW ($72). P195/75R14 BSW ($38); WSW ($116). Puncture-sealant P195/75R14 WSW ($240). Conventional spare ($63).

LTD CROWN VICTORIA CONVENIENCE/APPEARANCE OPTIONS: Option Packages: Interior luxury group ($954-$1034). Convenience group ($109-$134). Power lock group ($140-$238). Light group ($48). Protection group ($68). Police pkg. ($279-$398). Comfort/Convenience: Air cond. ($743); w/auto-temp control ($809). Rear defroster, electric ($140). Fingertip speed control ($176). Illuminated entry system ($82). Power windows ($198-$272). Power driver's seat ($227); driver and passenger ($454). Remote fuel door lock ($35). Tinted glass ($110); windshield only ($48). Autolamp on/off delay ($73). Leather- wrapped steering wheel ($59). Tilt steering wheel ($110). Auto. parking brake release ($12). Tripminder computer ($215- $261). Digital clock ($61). Interval wipers ($50). Lighting and Mirrors: Cornering lamps ($68). Remote right mirror ($46). Lighted visor vanity mirrors ($106). Entertainment: AM/FM stereo radio: S ($106); w/cassette tape player ($112-$204). Electronic-tuning AM/FM stereo radio w/cassette ($166) exc. S ($416). Power antenna ($66). Premium sound system ($151-$179). Radio delete ($148 credit). Exterior: Metallic glow paint ($77). Two-tone paint ($117). Dual accent bodyside paint stripes ($39). Pivoting front vent windows ($79). Rocker panel moldings ($18-$38). Vinyl-insert bodyside moldings ($61). Bumper rub strips ($59). Luggage rack ($110). Lower bodyside protection ($39-$52). Interior: Dual-facing rear seats: Ctry Sq ($167). Leather seat trim ($418). Split bench seating ($139). All-vinyl seat trim ($34); Duraweave vinyl ($96). Carpeted front floor mats ($21). Trunk trim ($49). Wheels/Tires: Wire wheel covers ($165); locking ($204). Cast aluminum wheels ($390). P225/75R14 WSW ($42-$43). P205/75R15 WSW ($17); puncture-sealant ($178). P215/75R14 BSW ($66 credit). Conventional spare ($63).

1984 Thunderbird FILA hardtop coupe (JG)

THUNDERBIRD CONVENIENCE/APPEARANCE OPTIONS: Option Packages: Interior luxury group ($1223). Exterior accent group ($299). Luxury carpet group ($72). Traveler's assistance kit ($65). Light group ($35). Power lock group ($177). Comfort/Convenience: Air cond. ($743); auto-temp ($809). Rear defroster ($140). Fingertip speed control ($176). Illuminated entry system ($82). Keyless entry ($116-$198). Anti-theft system ($159). Remote fuel door lock ($37). Tripminder computer ($215-$276). Autolamp on/off delay ($73). Tinted glass ($110); windshield only ($48). Power windows ($198). Six-way power driver's seat ($227); dual ($454) exc. Fila ($227). Auto. parking brake release ($12). Leather-wrapped steering wheel ($59). Tilt steering wheel ($110). Electronic instrument cluster ($321-$382). Electronic voice alert ($67). Diagnostic warning lights ($89). Low oil warning light ($24). Digital clock: base ($61). Interval wipers ($50). Lighting and Mirrors: Cornering lamps ($68). Electro- luminescent coach lamps ($84). Dual electric remote mirrors ($86). Electronic-dimming day/night mirror ($77). Lighted visor vanity mirrors, pair ($106). Entertainment: AM/FM stereo radio: base ($109); w/cassette player ($204) exc. Turbo Cpe ($95). Electronic-tuning AM/FM stereo search radio ($144-$252); w/cassette ($396) exc. Turbo Cpe ($288) and Elan ($144). Power antenna ($66). Premium sound system ($179). AM radio delete ($39 credit). Exterior: Flip-up open-air roof ($315). Metallic clearcoat paint ($183). Two-tone paint/tape ($148-$218). Charcoal lower accent treatment ($78). Hood paint stripe ($16). Dual accent bodyside/decklid paint stripes ($55). Hood/decklid/bodyside paint stripes ($71). Pivoting front vent windows ($79). Wide bodyside moldings ($57). Rocker panel moldings ($39). License frames ($9). Lower bodyside protection ($39-$54). Interior: Articulated seats ($183-$427). Leather seat trim ($415). Vinyl seat trim ($37). Front floor mats, carpeted ($22). Wheels/Tires: Wire wheel covers, locking ($26-$204). Luxury wheel covers ($113). Styled wheels ($65-$178). Puncture- sealing tires ($124). P205/70R14 BSW (NC). P205/70R14 WSW ($62). P205/70HR14 performance BSW ($152). Cast aluminum TRX wheels w/BSW performance tires ($471-$649) exc. Turbo Cpe ($154). Conventional spare ($63).

HISTORY: Introduced: September 22, 1983 except Tempo, May 1983. Model year production: 1,496,997 (incl. Mustangs). Total production for the U.S. market of 1,294,491 units (incl. Mustangs) included 711,698 four-cylinder, 323,985 sixes and 258,808 V-8s. That total included 25,581 turbo fours and 24,879 diesel engines. Calendar year production (U.S.): 1,145,028 (incl. Mustangs). Calendar year sales by U.S. dealers: 1,300,644 (incl. Mustangs). Model year sales by U.S. dealers: 1,262,498 (incl. Mustangs).

Historical Footnotes: Sales hit their highest mark since 1979 for the model year. That was a 27 percent jump over 1983. Thunderbird showed the strongest rise. Escort lost its title as top- selling car in the nation to Chevrolet's Cavalier. EXP sales had never been promising, and declined again this year, even after the turbo edition had been offered. Escort/Tempo's 2.0- liter diesel, from Mazda Motor Corp., showed sluggish sales as well. As an indication of the importance placed upon advertising to the youth market, Edsel B. Ford II was named advertising manager in late 1983. Tempo design had begun in 1979 under a "Topaz" project (the name ultimately given to the Mercury version).

1985 FORD

Thunderbird enjoyed a modest restyle, but nothing too dramatic occurred for the 1985 model year. LTD had added a high-performance, V-8 powered LX touring sedan late in the '84 season, which continued this year. Base models were upgraded, now including as standard various popular items that were formerly optional. Such simplification of the model lineup cut production costs and (presumably) made selection easier for buyers. Manual gearboxes for Escort and Thunderbird were improved. Tempo now had a standard fuel- injected 2.3-liter four and five-speed transaxle, as well as a high-performance engine option.

1985 Escort GL five-door hatchback (JG)

ESCORT — FOUR — Reverse gear on both the four- and five-speed manual transaxle moved to a new position this year, intended to make shifting easier. On five-speeds, it moved from the upper left to the lower right. (The change began on Thunderbird Turbo Coupe and Mustang SVO for '84.) Mechanical radios had a new flat-face design. Starting in mid-year 1984, clearcoat paints were made available on the Escort L and GL. Otherwise, little was new on Ford's subcompact two- and four-door hatchbacks as the model year began. Later on, though, a restyled 1985.5 Escort appeared, powered by a new 1.9-liter four-cylinder engine. Standard engine for the first series was again the CVH 97.6 cu. in. (1.6-liter) carbureted four, with four-speed gearbox. A high-output version was available, as well as one with electronic fuel injection and another with a turbocharger. The 2.0-liter diesel was offered again, too. Five-speed manual and three-speed automatic transmissions were available. Escort's three-row grille design had thin vertical bars across each row to form a crosshatch pattern, with Ford oval in the center. Base and L Escorts had a bright grille and blackout front-end treatment, halogen headlamps, heater/defroster, four-speed gearbox, rack-and-pinion steering, short black bumper end caps, bright bumpers, side window demisters, day/night mirror, and cloth/vinyl high-back reclining front bucket seats. Bright moldings went on the windshield surround, backlight, belt, headlamps and drip rail; color- keyed moldings on the A pillar. Escort L. had a brushed aluminum B pillar applique. Wagons and diesels had standard power brakes. Escort GL added a front air dam, long black bumper end caps with argent stripe, remote locking fuel door, dual bodyside paint stripes, AM radio, low-back seats, and additional bright moldings. Escort LX included front/rear bumper guards, power brakes, blackout body treatment, digital clock, foglamps, locking glovebox, TR performance suspension and styled steel wheels, black tri-oval steering wheel, and five-speed manual tranxale. GT models carried wide black bodyside moldings with argent striping, dual black remote racing mirrors, power brakes, TR performance suspension, tape stripes and decals, five-speed transaxle, black wheel spats, remote liftgate release, foglamps, and sport-tuned exhaust. Turbo GT had aluminum TR wheels; non-turbos, steel wheels with bright trim rings. Turbos also had standard power steering.

EXP — FOUR — Like the Escort sedans, the two-seater EXP got a revised location for reverse gear (below 5th gear). Radios and cassette players showed a new flat-face design. Base engine was the fuel-injected 97.6 cu. in. (1.6-liter) four. The Turbo Coupe was available again, wearing aluminum wheels with low-profile performance tires and Koni shock absorbers. This was EXP's final season in its original form. Standard equipment included an AM rdio, tinted rear- window glass, halogen headlamps, digital clock, power brakes, tachometer, handling suspension, remote locking fuel door, black bumper rub strips, black left-hand remote sport mirror, and black moldings. Inside were low-back cloth/vinyl reclining bucket seats. EXP's Luxury Coupe added an AM/FM stereo radio, interval wipers, luxury cloth seats with four- way (manual) driver's side adjuster, remote liftgate release, dual remote mirrors, rear defroster, and tinted glass. Turbo Coupe included a front air dam, black rocker panel moldings, AM/FM stereo with cassette, lower tu-tone paint/tape treatment, power steering, TR suspension and aluminum wheels, wheel spats, and rear spoiler.

1985 Tempo Sport GL coupe (JG)

TEMPO — FOUR — Throttle-body fuel injection was added to Tempo's 2300 HSC (High Swirl Combustion) engine after a year of carburetion. A new high-output version had a new cylinder head and intake manifold, and drove a special 3.73:1 final drive ratio. Five-speed manual overdrive transaxles were now standard in all Tempo series, with revised reverse gear position (now below 5th gear). GLX Tempos now had a sport instrument cluster, front center armrest, power lock group, illuminated entry, light convenience group, tinted glass, AM/FM stereo radio, power steering, and tilt steering wheel. Just before the '85 model year, the fuel tank grew from 14 to 15.2 gallons. There were new see-through reservoirs for brake, power steering and washer fluid levels. This year's instrument panel included side window demisters, plus contemporary flat-face radio design and a storage shelf. New options included graphic equalizer, clearcoat metallic paints, and styled road wheels (standard on GL and GLX).

1985 Tempo GLX sedan (JG)

Tempo again came in three series: L, GL and GLX. Base Tempos came with AM radio, cloth/vinyl reclining low-back bucket seats, bodyside accent stripes, dual decklid stripes (two-doors), power brakes, bright bumpers with black end caps, and black left-hand mirror. GL added a blackout back panel treatment, bumper end cap extensions, bumper rub strips, digital clock, map pocket, black bodyside moldings, styled wheels, interval wipers, and dual striping on four- door decklids. A high-performance Sport GL performance option included the high-output (HSO) engine, seven-spoke aluminum wheels with locking lug nuts, P185/70R14 blackwall tires, improved suspension components, graduated bodyside taping, dual remote mirrors, sport performance cloth seats, and grey bumpers with blue inserts.

LTD — FOUR/V-6/V-8 — Modest restyling gave LTD a new horizontal grille for its third season, plus new sedan taillamps. Otherwise, only minor trim changes were evident. The new grille had three horizontal bars, with the Ford script oval incorporated into the body. As before, the whole front end was angled, and displayed a large upper grille header bar. The new taillamps had a larger lighted area. LTD also had new black vinyl-clad bodyside moldings with argent accent stripe, and a new, smoother-looking brushed stainless B-pillar molding. Base models wore new deluxe wheel covers. The base 140 cu. in. (2.3-liter) engine added low-friction piston rings, with a boost in compression. Wagons had a standard 232 cu. in. (3.8-liter) V-6. Standard tires grew one size, to 195/75R14 all-season tread. New options included dual electric remote mirrors and black vinyl rocker panel moldings. Optional styled road wheels changed color to light argent. Joining the base and Brougham sedan and LTD wagon later in the model year was a new high-performance LX touring sedan. It carried a high-output version of the fuel-injected 302 cu. in. (5.0-liter) V-8, coupled to four-speed overdrive automatic transmission and a 3.27:1 Traction-Lok rear axle. The performance sedan also had a special handling suspension with rear stabilzer bar, fast 15:1 steering gear, and Goodyear Eagle GT performance tires. LX had its own distinctive look, highlighted by body-color grille, charcoal and red-orange accents, twin chromed exhaust extensions, and styled road wheels. Inside LX was a center console with floor shifter, tachometer, and unique front bucket seats with inflatable lumbar support. Both base and Brougham sedans had an AM radio, SelectShift automatic transmission, locking glovebox, power brakes and steering, reclining split-bench seating with cloth upholstery, left-hand remote mirror, dual bodyside and hood accent stripes, and bright moldings. Brougham added a digital clock, light group, seatback map pockets, lighted visor vanity mirror (passenger), luxury cloth upholstery, automatic parking brake release, and luxury door trim panels with cloth inserts.

LTD CROWN VICTORIA — V-8 — Except for an aluminum front bumper on station wagons and some new body and vinyl colors, full-size Fords showed no significant body change. To improve the ride, Crown Vic got new gas-filled shock absorbers, pressurized with nitrogen. An ignition diagnostics monitor was added to the EEC-IV electronic engine controls. The horn control moved from the stalk to the center of the steering wheel. Flash-to- pass was added this year. A single key was now used for door and ignition locks. Lower bodyside panels now had urethane coating for extra corrosion protection. Model lineup for the biggest rear-drives remained the same: two- and four-door sedan (standard or 'S'), along with plain-bodied and Country Squire (woodgrain) wagons. The sole 302 cu. in. (5.0-liter) V-8 engine, with fuel injection, came with four-speed automatic overdrive transmission. A new optional automatic load leveling suspension (available later in the model year) used an electronic sensor and air- adjustable rear shocks. With a heavy-duty trailer towing package, Crown Vic and Country Squire could again tow trailers up to 5,000 pounds. Standard equipment included chrome bumpers with guards, left-hand remote-control mirror, dual-note horn, cloth/vinyl reclining flight bench seating, power steering and brakes, and deluxe wheel covers. The budget-priced 'S' models lacked such items as the padded half (rear) vinyl roof, dual accent tape striping, quartz clock, brushed lower decklid applique, and various moldings. 'S' models had an AM radio; others an AM/FM stereo.

1985 Thunderbird Elan hardtop coupe (JG)

THUNDERBIRD — FOUR/V-6/V-8 — A new color-keyed grille and full-width wraparound taillamps with inboard backup lamps made up the evident changes on Ford's personal luxury coupe. There was also a new Thunderbird emblem, which appeared on taillamp lenses, C pillars and upper grille header. Inside was a new instru- instrument panel with digital speedometer and anglog gauges, door trim panels, and a third rear seatbelt. Standard interiors had a shorter center console, so three people could sit in back. Turbo Coupe's 140 cu. in. (2.3-liter) four- cylinder engine got electronic boost control and higher flow- rate fuel injectors for more power, water-cooled bearings, and a new five-speed gearbox with revised gear ratios. Standard tire size was now 205/70R14 except for Turbo Coupe, which wore performance 225/60VR15 tires on 7 inch wheels. Joining the option list were power front seat recliners for comfort and a graphic equalizer to improve audio entertainment. Fully electronic instruments were optional on all TBirds except the Turbo Coupe. Base 'birds had the standard 232 cu. in. (3.8-liter) V-6 with three-speed automatic transmission, power steering and brakes, mini spare tire, knit cloth 60/40 split bench reclining seats, AM/FM stereo radio, quartz clock, and bumper rub strips. Bright moldings went on the drip rail, windshield surround, backlight, and windows. Charcoal bodyside moldings had vinyl inserts. Thunderbird Elan added wide bodyside moldings, power windows, interval wipers, dual electric remote mirrors, diagnostic warning lights, digital clock, tinted glass, AM/FM stereo with cassette, decklid and bodyside accent stripes, and a light group. Fila included the autolamp delay system, speed control, leather-wrapped tilt steering wheel, four-speed overdrive automatic transmission, cast aluminum wheels, electronic-tuning radio with cassette, cornering lamps, power locks, illuminated entry, and articulated sport seats. The driver's seat had six-way power adjustment and power lumbar support. Fila also had a color- keyed grille instead of the usual brightwork, as well as charcoal paint with dark charcoal lower accents and charcoal windshield/backlight moldings.

I.D. DATA: Ford's 17-symbol Vehicle Identification Number (VIN) again was stamped on a metal tab fastened to the instrument panel, visible through the windshield. Coding was similar to 1984. Model year code changed to 'F' for 1985. Engine code 'W' for HSC L4140 FI was added; code '6' for propane four dropped. A Vehicle Certification Label on the left front door lock face panel or door pillar shows the manufacturer, month and year of manufacture, GVW, GAWR, certification statement, VIN, and codes for such items as body type, color, trim, axle, transmission, and special order information.

ESCORT (FOUR)

Model Number	Body/Style Number	Body Type & Seating	Factory Price	Shipping Weight	Production Total
04/41P	61D	2-dr. Hatch-4P	5620	1981	Note 1
13/41P	58D	4-dr. Hatch-4P	5827	2034	Note 1
04	61D	2-dr. L Hatch-4P	5876	1981	Note 1
13	58D	4-dr. L Hatch-4P	6091	2034	Note 1
09	74D	4-dr. L Sta Wag-4P	6305	2066	Note 1
05	61D	2-dr. GL Hatch-4P	6374	2033	Note 1
14	58D	4-dr. GL Hatch-4P	6588	2086	Note 1
10	74D	4-dr. GL Sta Wag-4P	6765	2115	Note 1
15	58D	4-dr. LX Hatch-4P	7840	2137	Note 1
11	74D	4-dr. LX Sta Wag-4P	7931	2073	Note 1

ESCORT GT (FOUR)

07	61D	2-dr. Hatch-4P	7585	2103	Note 1
07/935	61D	2-dr. Turbo Hatch-4P	8680	2239	Note 1

1985.5 ESCORT — Second Series (FOUR)

31	N/A	2-dr. Hatch-4P	5856	2089	Note 1
31	N/A	2-dr. L Hatch-4P	6127	2096	Note 1
36	N/A	4-dr. L Hatch-4P	6341	2154	Note 1
34	N/A	4-dr. L Sta Wag-4P	6622	2173	Note 1
32	N/A	2-dr. GL Hatch-4P	6642	2160	Note 1
37	N/A	4-dr. GL Hatch-4P	6855	2214	Note 1
35	N/A	4-dr. GL Sta Wag-4P	7137	2228	Note 1

Note 1: Ford reported production of the second (1985.5) Escort series at 100,554 two-door hatchbacks, 48,676 four-door hatchback sedans, and 36,998 station wagons, but did not include the initial series. Other sources give total Escort production for the model year of 212,960 two- doors, 111,385 four-doors, and 82,738 wagons. Breakdown by trim level not available. Bodies are sometimes referred to as three-door and five- door.

Diesel Engine Note: Diesel-powered Escorts came in L and GL trim, priced $558 higher than equivalent gasoline models.

EXP (FOUR)

01/A80	67D	3-dr. Hatch Cpe-2P	6697	2117	26,462
01/A81	67D	3-dr. Luxury Cpe-2P	7585	2117	Note 2
01/A82	67D	3-dr. Turbo Cpe-2P	9997	N/A	Note 2

Note 2: Production of luxury and turbo coupe models is included in basic EXP total above.

TEMPO (FOUR)

18	66D	2-dr. L Sedan-5P	7052	2249	Note 3
21	54D	4-dr. L Sedan-5P	7052	2308	Note 3
19	66D	2-dr. GL Sed-5P	7160	2276	Note 3
22	54D	4-dr. GL Sed-5P	7160	2339	Note 3
20	66D	2-dr. GLX Sed-5P	8253	2302	Note 3
23	54D	4-dr. GLX Sed-5P	8302	2362	Note 3

Note 3: Total Tempo production came to 72,311 two-doors and 266,776 four-doors. A turbocharged Tempo GTX, priced at $9870, was announced but apparently not produced.

Diesel Engine Note: Diesel-powered Tempos cost $479 more than equivalent gasoline models.

LTD (FOUR/V-6)

39	54D	4-dr. Sedan-5P	8874/9292	2804/2881	162,884
39/60H	54D	4-dr. Brghm-5P	9262/9680	2812/2889	Note 4
40	74D	4-dr. Sta Wag-5P	-- /9384	-- /2990	42,642

LTD LX BROUGHAM (V-8)

39/938	54D	4-dr. Sedan-5P	11421	N/A	Note 4

Note 4: Brougham production is included in basic sedan total.

LTD CROWN VICTORIA (V-8)

42	66K	2-dr. Sedan-6P	11627	3546	13,673
43	54K	4-dr. Sedan-6P	11627	3587	154,612
44	74K	4-dr. Ctry Sqr-6P	11809	3793	30,825
43/41K	54K	4-dr. 'S' Sed-6P	10609	N/A	Note 5
44/41K	74K	4-dr. 'S' Wag-6P	10956	N/A	Note 5
44/41E	74K	4-dr. Sta Wag-6P	11559	N/A	Note 5

Note 5: Production of 'S' models and basic station wagon is included in basic sedan and Country Squire totals above.

Police Model Note: Crown Victoria 'S' police models sold for $10,929 with the 302 cu. in. V-8 and $11,049 with 351 cu. in. V-8. engine.

1985 Thunderbird Turbo coupe (JG)

THUNDERBIRD (V-6/V-8)

Model Number	Body/Style Number	Body Type & Seating	Factory Price	Shipping Weight	Production Total
46	66D	2-dr. HT Cpe-5P	10249/10884	2890/3097	151,851
46/607	66D	2-dr. Elan Cpe-5P	11916/12551	2956/3163	Note 6
46/606	66D	2-dr. Fila Cpe-5P	14974/15609	3061/3268	Note 6

THUNDERBIRD TURBO COUPE (FOUR)

46/934	66D	2-dr. HT Cpe-5P	13365	2938	Note 6

Note 6: Turbo Coupe and Elan/Fila production is included in basic Thunderbird total.

MODEL NUMBER NOTE: Some sources include a prefix 'P' ahead of the two- digit model number. **FACTORY PRICE AND WEIGHT NOTE:** TD prices and weights to left of slash are for four-cylinder, to right for V-6 engine. Thunderbird prices and weights to left of slash are for V-6, to right for V-8 engine.

ENGINE DATA: BASE FOUR (Escort): Inline. Overhead cam. Four-cylinder. Cast iron block and aluminum head. Displacement: 97.6 cu. in. (1.6 liters). Bore & stroke: 3.15 x 3.13 in. Compression ratio: 9.0:1. Brake horsepower: 70 at 4600 R.P.M. Torque: 88 lbs.-ft. at 2600 R.P.M. Five main bearings. Hydraulic valve lifters. Carburetor: 2Bbl. Holley 740. VIN Code: 2. Note: Second Series Escorts, introduced at mid-year, carried a new 1.9-liter engine; see 1986 listing for specifications. BASE FOUR (EXP); OPTIONAL (Escort): High-output version of 1.6-liter four above Horsepower: 80 at 5400 R.P.M. Torque: 88 lbs.-ft. at 3000 R.P.M. VIN Code: 4. BASE FOUR (Escort LX/GT); OPTIONAL (Escort): Fuel-injected version of 1.6-liter four above Horsepower: 84 at 5200 R.P.M. Torque: 90 lbs.-ft. at 2800 R.P.M. VIN Code: 5. TURBO FOUR (Escort, EXP): Same as 1.6-liter four above, with fuel injection and turbocharger Compression ratio: 8.0:1. Horsepower: 120 at 5200 R.P.M. Torque: 120 lbs.-ft. at 3400 R.P.M. VIN Code: 8. DIESEL FOUR (Escort, Tempo): Inline. Overhead cam. Four-cylinder. Cast iron block and aluminum head. Displacement: 121 cu. in. (2.0 liters). Bore & stroke: 3.39 x 3.39 in. Compression ratio: 22.5:1. Brake horsepower: 52 at 4000 R.P.M. Torque: 82 lbs.-ft. at 2400 R.P.M. Five main bearings. Solid valve lifters. Fuel injection. VIN Code: H. BASE FOUR (Tempo): Inline. Overhead valve. Four-cylinder. Cast iron block and head. Displacement: 140 cu. in. (2.3 liters). Bore & stroke: 3.70 x 3.30 in. Compression ratio: 9.0:1. Brake horsepower: 86 at 4000 R.P.M. Torque: 124 lbs.-ft. at 2800 R.P.M. Five main bearings. Hydraulic valve lifters. Throttle-body fuel injection. High Swirl Combustion (HSC) design. VIN Code: X. OPTIONAL FOUR (Tempo): High-output version of HSC four above Horsepower: 100 at 4600 R.P.M. Torque: 125 lbs.-ft. at 3200 R.P.M. VIN Code: S. BASE FOUR (LTD): Inline. Overhead cam. Four-cylinder. Cast iron block and head. Displacement: 140 cu. in. (2.3 liters). Bore & stroke: 3.78 x 3.13 in. Compression ratio: 9.5:1. Brake horsepower: 88 at 4000 R.P.M. Torque: 122 lbs.-ft. at 2400 R.P.M. Five main bearings. Hydraulic valve lifters. Carburetor: 1Bbl. Carter YFA. VIN Code: A. PROPANE FOUR (LTD): Same as 140 cu. in. four above, but for propane fuel Compression ratio: 10.0:1. Brake horsepower: 88 at 4000 R.P.M. Torque: 122 lbs.-ft. at 2400 R.P.M. VIN Code: 6. TURBOCHARGED FOUR (Thunderbird Turbo Coupe): Same as 140 cu. in. four above, with fuel injection and turbocharger Compression ratio: 8.0:1. Horsepower: 155 at 4600 R.P.M. Torque: 190 lbs.-ft. at 2800 R.P.M. VIN Code: W. BASE V-6 (LTD wagon, Thunderbird); OPTIONAL (LTD): 90-degree; overhead valve V-6. Cast iron block and aluminum head. Displacement: 232 cu. in. (3.8 liters). Bore & stroke: 3.80 x 3.40 in. Compression ratio: 8.7:1. Brake horsepower: 120 at 3600 R.P.M. Torque: 205 lbs.-ft. at 1600 R.P.M. Four main bearings. Hydraulic valve lifters. Throttle-body fuel injection. VIN Code: 3. BASE V-8 (Crown Victoria); OPTIONAL (Thunderbird): 90-degree, overhead valve V-8. Cast iron block and head. Displacement: 302 cu. in. (5.0 liters). Bore & stroke: 4.00 x 3.00 in. Compression ratio: 8.4:1. Brake horsepower: 140 at 3200 R.P.M. Torque: 250 lbs.-ft. at 1600 R.P.M. Five main bearings. Hydraulic valve lifters. Electronic fuel injection (TBI). VIN Code: F. OPTIONAL HIGH-OUTPUT V-8 (Crown Victoria): Same as 302 cu. in. V-8 above, except Horsepower: 155 at 3600 R.P.M. Torque: 265 lbs.-ft. at 2000 R.P.M. BASE V-8 (LTD LX): Same as 302 cu. in. V-8, above, except Compression ratio: 8.3:1. Horsepower: 165 at 3800 R.P.M. Torque: 245 lbs.-ft. at 2000 R.P.M. HIGH-OUTPUT POLICE V-8 (Crown Victoria): 90-degree, overhead valve V-8. Cast iron block and head. Displacement: 351 cu. in. (5.8 liters). Bore & stroke: 4.00 x 3.50 in. Compression ratio: 8.3:1. Brake horsepower: 180 at 3600 R.P.M. Torque: 285 lbs.-ft. at 2400 R.P.M. Five main bearings. Hydraulic valve lifters. Carburetor: 2Bbl. 7200VV. VIN Code: G.

CHASSIS DATA: Wheelbase: (Escort/EXP) 94.2 in.; (Tempo) 99.9 in.; (LTD) 105.6 in.; (Crown Vic) 114.3 in.; (TBird) 104.0 in. Overall Length: (Escort) 163.9 in.; (Escort wagon) 165.0 in.; (EXP) 170.3 in.; (Tempo) 176.2 in.; (LTD) 196.5 in.; (Crown Vic) 211.0 in.; (Crown Vic wag) 215.0 in.; (TBird) 197.6 in. Height: (Escort) 53.3-53.4 in.; (EXP) 50.5 in.; (Tempo) 52.7 in.; (LTD) 53.8 in.; (LTD wag) 54.4 in.; (Crown Vic) 55.3 in.; (Crown Vic wag) 56.8 in.; (TBird) 53.2 in. Width: (Escort/EXP) 65.9 in.; (Tempo) 68.3 in.; (LTD) 71.0 in.; (Crown Vic) 77.5 in.; (Crown Vic wag) 79.3 in.; (TBird) 71.1 in. Front Tread: (Escort/EXP/Tempo) 54.7 in.; (LTD) 56.6 in.; (Crown Vic) 62.2 in. (TBird) 58.1 in. Rear Tread: (Escort/EXP) 56.0 in.; (Tempo) 57.6 in.; (LTD) 57.0 in.; (Crown Vic) 62.0 in. (TBird) 58.5 in. Standard Tires: (Escort/EXP) P165/80R13 SBR BSW; (Escort L) P175/80R13; (Escort LX/GT) P165/70R365 Michelin TRX; (Escort/EXP Turbo) P185/65R365 Michelin TRX; (Tempo) P175/80R13 SBR BSW; (LTD) P195/75R14 SBR BSW exc. LX and police, P205/70HR14 Goodyear Eagle BSW; (Crown Vic) P215/75R14 SBR WSW; (TBird) P205/70R14 SBR BSW; (TBird Turbo Cpe) P225/60VR15 performance BSW.

TECHNICAL: Transmission: Escort four-speed manual transaxle: (1st) 3.23:1; (2nd) 1.92:1; (3rd) 1.23:1; (4th) 0.81:1; (Rev) 3.46:1. Alternate Escort four-speed manual: (1st) 3.58:1; (2nd) 2.05:1; (3rd) 1.23:1; (4th) 0.81:1; (Rev) 3.46:1. Five- speed manual on Escort/EXP/Tempo: (1st) 3.60:1; (2nd) 2.12:1; (3rd) 1.39:1; (4th) 1.02:1; (5th) 1.02:1; (Rev) 3.62:1. (Note: separate final drive for 5th gear.) Escort/Tempo diesel five-speed manual: (1st) 3.93:1; (2nd) 2.12:1; (3rd) 1.39:1; (4th) 0.98:1; (5th) 0.98:1; (Rev) 3.62:1. TBird Turbo Coupe five-speed: (1st) 4.03:1; (2nd) 2.37:1; (3rd) 1.49:1; (4th) 1.00:1; (5th) 0.81:1; (Rev) 3.76:1. Three-speed automatic standard on LTD, Thunderbird turbo/V-6: (1st) 2.46:1 or 2.47:1; (2nd) 1.46:1 or 1.47:1; (3rd) 1.00:1; (Rev) 2.11:1 or 2.19:1. Escort/EXP/Tempo three-speed automatic: (1st) 2.79:1; (2nd) 1.61:1; (3rd) 1.00:1; (Rev) 1.97:1. Four- speed overdrive automatic standard on LTD V-6, Crown Victoria and Thunderbird: (1st) 2.40:1; (2nd) 1.47:1; (3rd) 1.00:1; (4th) 0.67:1; (Rev) 2.00:1. Standard final drive ratio: (Escort/EXP) 3.59:1 w/4spd, 3.73:1 w/5spd, 3.31:1 w/auto., 3.52:1 w/diesel; (Tempo) 3.33:1 w/5spd, 3.23:1 w/auto., 3.73:1 w/diesel or H.O. engine; (LTD four) 3.27:1; (LTD V-6) 2.73:1 w/3spd auto.; (Crown Vic) 3.08:1; (TBird) 3.45:1 w/turbo, 2.73:1 w/3spd automatic and V-6, 3.27:1 w/4spd auto. and V-6, 3.08:1 w/V-8. Drive Axle: (Escort/EXP/Tempo) front; (others) rear. Steering: (Crown Vic) recirculating ball; (others) rack and pinion. Front Suspension: (Escort/EXP/Tempo) MacPherson struts with lower control arms, coil springs and stabilizer bar; (LTD/TBird) modified MacPherson struts with lower control arms, coil springs and anti-sway bar; (Crown Vic) long/short control arms w/coil springs and stabilizer bar. LTD, Crown Vic and TBird had gas-filled struts/shocks. Rear Suspension: (Escort/EXP) independent trailing arms w/modified MacPherson struts and coil springs on lower control arms; (Tempo) fully independent quadra-link with MacPherson struts; (LTD/Crown Vic/TBird) rigid axle w/four- link coil springs; (TBird Turbo Coupe) "quadra-shock" four- bar-link assembly with two hydraulic, horizontal axle dampers. Gas-filled shocks on LTD, Crown Vic and TBird. Brakes: Front disc, rear drum; power assisted (except Escort). Ignition: Electronic. Body construction: (Crown Vic) separate body and frame; (others) unibody. Fuel tank: (Escort/EXP) 13.0 gal.; (Tempo) 15.2 gal.; (LTD) 16.0 gal.; (Crown Vic) 18.0 gal.; (Crown Vic wag) 18.5 gal.; (TBird) 20.6 gal.

DRIVETRAIN OPTIONS: Engines: H.O. 1.6-liter four: Escort ($73). 232 cu. in. V-6: LTD ($418). 302 cu. in. V-8: Thunderbird ($398). Transmission/Differential: Five-speed manual trans.: Escort ($76). Automatic transaxle: Escort ($439) exc. LX/GT and EXP ($363); Tempo ($266-$363). Auto. transmission.: TBird Turbo Cpe ($315). First gear lockout delete: LTD, Crown Vic 'S' ($7). Overdrive auto. trans.: TBird ($237). Traction-Lok differential: LTD/Crown Vic/TBird ($95). Brakes/Steering/Suspension: Power brakes: Escort ($95). Power steering: Escort/EXP ($215); Tempo ($223). H.D. susp.: Crown Vic/TBird ($26); LTD LPO ($43). Handling susp.: Escort L ($199); Escort GL ($95); Crown Vic ($49). Auto. load leveling: Crown Vic ($200). Other: H.D. battery ($27). H.D. alternator: Escort/EXP ($27). Extended-range gas tank: LTD ($46). Engine block heater ($18). Trailer towing pkg.: Crown Vic ($251-$302); TBird ($251). California emission system: Escort/EXP ($46); others ($99). High-altitude emissions (NC).

ESCORT CONVENIENCE/APPEARANCE OPTIONS: Option Packages: Squire wagon pkg. ($373). Instrument group ($87). Convenience group ($206-$341). Light group ($67). Comfort/Convenience: Air conditioner ($643). Rear defroster, electric ($139). High-capacity heater ($76). Fingertip speed control ($176). Power door locks ($124-$176). Tinted glass ($95); windshield only LPO ($48). Tilt steering ($104). Overhead console w/digital clock ($82). Interval wipers ($50). Rear wiper/washer ($120) exc. LX ($46). Dual remote sport mirrors ($68). Entertainment: AM radio: base/L ($39). AM/FM radio ($82) exc. base/L ($121). AM/FM stereo radio ($109) exc. base/L ($148); w/cassette player ($148) exc. base/L ($295). Electronic- tuning AM/FM stereo w/cassette ($409-$448). Premium sound ($138). Exterior: Flip-up open-air roof ($315). Clearcoat metallic paint ($91) exc. LX/GT (NC). Two-tone paint/tape ($134-$173). Dual bodyside paint stripes ($39). Front vent windows, pivoting ($63). Vinyl-insert bodyside moldings ($45). Bumper guards, front or rear ($28). Bumper rub strips ($48). Luggage rack: wag ($100). Interior: Console ($111). Vinyl seat trim ($24). Cloth/vinyl low-back bucket seats: L ($33). Color-keyed front mats ($22). Wheels/Tires: Wheel trim rings ($54). Cast aluminum wheels ($279). TR aluminum wheels: LX/GT ($201). Styled steel wheels fleet only ($104 credit). P165/80R13 SBR WSW ($59).

EXP CONVENIENCE/APPEARANCE OPTIONS: Comfort/Convenience: Air conditioner ($643). Fingertip speed control ($176). Tinted glass ($95). Tilt steering ($104). Lighted visor vanity mirror ($50). Entertainment: AM/FM stereo radio: base ($109); w/cassette player ($256) exc. luxury cpe ($148). Electronic-tuning AM/FM stereo w/cassette ($409) exc. luxury cpe ($300) and Turbo ($152). Premium sound ($138). AM radio delete ($39 credit). AM/FM stereo delete: luxury cpe ($148 credit). AM/FM stereo/cassette delete: Turbo ($295 credit). Exterior: Flip-up open air roof ($315). Clearcoat paint ($91). Lower two-tone paint/tape ($146). Paint/tape delete LPO (NC). Medium bodyside moldings: Turbo ($45). Lower bodyside protection ($68). Interior: Four-way driver's seat: base ($55). Low-back vinyl bucket seats: base (NC). Cloth sport performance seats: luxury cpe ($173). Front floor mats ($22). Wheels/Tires: TR aluminum wheels: luxury cpe ($370). TR styled steel wheels: luxury cpe ($168). Cast aluminum wheels: luxury cpe ($238). P165/80R13 RWL ($90). P165/70R365 Michelin TRX (NC).

TEMPO CONVENIENCE/APPEARANCE OPTIONS: Option Packages: Sport performance pkg.: GL ($900-$911). Power lock group ($202-$254). Luxury option group: GL/LX ($755-$855). Select option group: GL ($401). Comfort/Convenience: Air bag, driver's side: GL 4dr. fleet only ($815). Air cond. ($743). Rear defroster, electric ($140). Fingertip speed control: GL/GLX ($176). Power windows ($272). Power decklid release ($40). Remote fuel door release LPO ($26). Six-way power driver's seat ($224). Tinted glass ($110); windshield fleet ($48). Tilt steering: GL ($110). Sport instrument cluster ($87). Dual sport remote mirrors ($93). Entertainment: AM/FM stereo radio: L/GL ($109); w/cassette player ($148-$256). Electronic-tuning AM/FM stereo w/cassette ($152-$409). Graphic equalizer ($107-$218). AM radio delete ($39 credit). Exterior: Clearcoat paint ($91). Lower body accent paint ($78-$118). Interior: Vinyl seat trim LPO ($35). Leather seat trim: GLX ($300). Carpeted front floor mats fleet ($13). Wheels/Tires: Styled wheels: L ($73). P175/80R13 WSW ($72).

LTD CONVENIENCE/APPEARANCE OPTIONS: Option Packages: Squire option ($282). Interior luxury group: wagon ($388). Power lock group ($213-$254). Light group ($38). Police pkg. ($901-$1429). Taxi pkg. ($860). Comfort/Convenience: Air cond. ($743); auto-temp ($809). Fingertip speed control ($176). Illuminated entry ($82). Autolamp on-off delay ($73). Power windows ($272). Six-way power driver's seat ($224); dual ($449). Tinted glass ($110). Tinted windshield fleet ($48). Leather-wrapped steering wheel ($59). Tilt steering ($110). Tripminder computer ($215- $293). Digital clock ($78). Diagnostic warning lights ($89). Auto. parking brake release LPO ($12). Interval wipers ($50). Liftgate wiper/washer: wagon ($99). Lighting and Mirrors: Cornering lamps ($68). Right remote convex mirror ($61). Dual electric remote mirrors ($96). Lighted visor vanity mirrors ($57-$106). Entertainment: AM/FM stereo radio ($109); w/cassette player ($256). Electronic-tuning AM/FM stereo radio w/cassette ($409). Premium sound system ($138). AM radio delete ($39 credit). Exterior: Formal roof, cloth or vinyl ($848). Full vinyl roof ($152). Two-tone paint ($117). Pivoting front vent windows ($79). Two-way liftgate: wag ($105). Bright protective bodyside moldings w/vinyl insert ($55). Rocker panel moldings ($40). Bumper guards, rear ($28). Bumper rub strips ($56). Luggage rack: wagon ($126). Lower bodyside protection ($41). Interior: Vinyl seat trim ($35). Flight bench seat (NC). Front floor mats, carpeted ($23). Wheels/Tires: Luxury wheel covers ($55). Wire wheel covers, locking ($204). Cast aluminum wheels: LX ($224). Styled wheels ($178). Styled steel wheels w/trim rings fleet ($54). P195/75R14 WSW ($72). P205/70R14 WSW ($134). Puncture- sealant P195/75R14 WSW ($202). Conventional spare LPO ($63).

NOTE: Many LTD options listed above were not available for the LX Brougham.

LTD CROWN VICTORIA CONVENIENCE/APPEARANCE OPTIONS: Option Packages: Interior luxury group ($949-$1022). Convenience group ($109-$134). Power lock group ($140-$238). Light group ($48). Comfort/Convenience: Air cond. ($743); w/auto-temp control ($809). Rear defroster, electric ($140). Fingertip speed control ($176). Illuminated entry system ($82). Power windows ($198-$272). Power driver's seat ($227); driver and passenger ($454). Remote fuel door lock ($35). Tinted glass ($110); windshield only LPO ($48). Autolamp on/off delay ($73). Leather-wrapped steering wheel ($59). Tilt steering wheel ($110). Auto. parking brake release ($12). Tripminder computer ($215-$261). Quartz clock: S ($35). Digital clock ($61-$96).

Interval wipers ($50). Lighting and Mirrors: Cornering lamps ($68). Remote right mirror ($46). Lighted visor vanity mirrors ($106). Entertainment: AM/FM stereo radio: S ($109); w/cassette tape player ($148-$256). Electronic-tuning AM/FM stereo radio w/cassette ($300) exc. S LPO ($409). Power antenna ($66). Premium sound system ($168). Radio delete: AM ($39 credit); AM/FM ($148 credit). Exterior: Fully padded Brougham vinyl roof ($793). Two-tone paint/tape ($117). Dual accent bodyside paint stripes: S LPO ($39). Pivoting front vent windows ($79). Rocker panel moldings ($18-$38). Vinyl-insert bodyside moldings ($61). Bumper rub strips ($59). Luggage rack: wagon ($110). License frames ($9). Interior: Dual-facing rear seats: wagon ($167). Leather split bench seat ($418). Cloth/vinyl split bench seating ($139). All-vinyl seat trim ($34); Duraweave vinyl, wagon ($96). Carpeted front/rear floor mats ($33). Trunk trim ($37). Wheels/Tires: Wire wheel covers, locking ($204). Cast aluminum wheels ($390). P205/75R15 WSW ($17); puncture- sealant ($178). P215/70R15 WSW ($79). Conventional spare ($63).

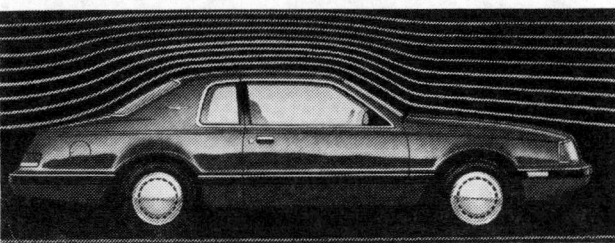

1985 Thunderbird Elan hardtop coupe (JG)

THUNDERBIRD CONVENIENCE/APPEARANCE OPTIONS: Option Packages: Light group ($35). Power lock group ($213). Comfort/Convenience: Air cond. ($743); auto-temp ($905). Rear defroster ($140). Fingertip speed control ($176). Illuminated entry system ($82). Keyless entry ($116-$198). Anti-theft system ($159). Tripminder computer ($215-$276). Autolamp on/off delay ($73). Tinted glass ($110); windshield only LPO ($48). Power windows ($198). Six-way power driver's seat ($227); dual ($454) exc. Fila ($227). Dual power seat recliners ($189). Auto. parking brake release: base ($12). Leather-wrapped steering wheel ($59). Tilt steering wheel ($110). Electronic instrument cluster ($270-$330). Diagnostic warning lights ($89). Low oil warning light: base ($24). Digital clock: base ($61). Interval wipers ($50). Lighting and Mirrors: Cornering lamps ($68). Dual electric remote mirrors ($96). Electronic-dimming day/night mirror ($77). Lighted visor vanity mirrors, pair ($106). Entertainment: AM/FM stereo radio w/cassette player ($148). Electronic-tuning AM/FM stereo search radio w/cassette ($300) exc. Elan ($152). Power antenna ($66). Graphic equalizer ($252). Premium sound system ($168). AM/FM radio delete ($148 credit). Exterior: Flip-up open-air roof ($315). Metallic clearcoat paint ($183). Two-tone paint/tape ($163-$218). Hood paint stripe ($16). Dual accent bodyside/decklid paint stripes: base ($55). Hood/decklid/bodyside paint stripes: base ($71). Pivoting front vent windows ($79). Wide bodyside moldings ($57). Bright rocker panel moldings ($39). License frames ($9). Interior: Articulated sport seats ($183-$427). Heated seats ($157). Leather seat trim ($415). Vinyl seat trim: base ($37). Front floor mats, carpeted ($22). Wheels/Tires: Wire wheel covers, locking ($204). Cast aluminum wheels ($343). Styled wheels ($178). P205/70R14 WSW ($62). P215/70R14 WSW ($99). P215/70HR14 performance BSW ($215). Conventional spare ($63).

HISTORY: Introduced: October 4, 1984. Model year production: 1,265,221 (incl. Mustangs, but with incomplete Escort total from Ford). Total production for the U.S. market of 1,389,103 units (incl. Mustangs) included 828,320 four-cylinder, 270,461 sixes and 290,322 V-8s. That total included 24,708 turbo fours and 10,246 diesel engines. Calendar year production (U.S.): 1,098,532 (incl. Mustangs). Calendar year sales by U.S. dealers: 1,386,195 (incl. Mustangs). Model year sales by U.S. dealers: 1,443,993 (incl. Mustangs).

Historical Footnotes: Sales rose 14 percent for the 1985 model year, partly as a result of incentive programs late in the season. Ford's market share rose to a healthy 17.2 percent, up from 16 percent the year before. All seven series showed an increase, led by Escort which revealed a 21 percent rise. Tempo did well, too. Ford raised prices only 1.3 percent (average) this year, though Crown Victoria went up over 6 percent and Mustangs were actually cheaper.

1986 FORD

The new front-drive, mid-size Taurus was the big news for 1986. Its aerodynamic styling went considerably beyond the Tempo design, taking its cue from European Fords. Taurus hardly resembled the rear-drive LTD that it was meant to replace. Mercury's Sable was similar, but with its own set of body panels and features. A reworked Escort had appeared as a mid-year 1985 model, but the restyled EXP two-seater wouldn't arrive until later in this model year.

1986 Escort LX wagon (JG)

ESCORT — FOUR — This year's Escort actually arrived as a 1985.5 model, carrying a bigger (1.9-liter) four-cylinder engine under its hood. The model lineup was revised. An LX series replaced the former GL, and the temporarily-abandoned GT was reintroduced. Pony was the name for the base hatchback (same name as the low-budget Pinto of the late 1970s). "Official" diesel models were dropped, but the 2.0-liter diesel engine remained available as an option. A new two-slot body-color grille held the Ford script oval in the center of the single horizontal bar. Aero-style headlamps met the amber wraparound parking lenses. Wraparound taillamps had two horizontal ribs. Inside was a new black four-spoke steering wheel. Options included tilt steering, speed control, and air conditioning. Escort's base engine was carbureted, hooked to a four- speed manual transaxle. Automatic shift was optional. As before, Escort had four-wheel independent suspension. Pony had standard power brakes, day/night mirror, dome light, cloth/vinyl low-back reclining bucket seats, and P175/80R13 tires. Escort L added an AM radio and load floor carpet. LX included remote fuel door lock, remote liftgate release, wide vinyl bodyside moldings, bumper rub strips, and styled steel wheels. In addition to a high-output 1.9-liter engine with port fuel injection and five-speed manual transaxle, Escort GT had a performance suspension with new front and rear stabilizer bars, as well as P195/60HR15 tires on eight-spoke aluminum wheels. Also included: front and rear body-color partial fascias; foglamps; console with graphic display; leather- wrapped steering wheel; body-color wheel spats with integral rocker panel moldings; rear spoiler; and body-color narrow bodyside moldings. One easy-to-spot styling feature was GT's offset grille, with slots occupying just two-thirds of the panel instead of full-width. A 'GT' decal sat on the solid passenger side of the "grille" panel.

1986 Escort EXP Sport Coupe (F)

EXP — FOUR — After a brief absence from the lineup, the two-seater EXP returned in restyled form with a sleek new front-end design, including air dam and aero headlamps. Also new was a bubble-back styled rear hatch with integral spoiler. Otherwise, the new four-window coupe design looked similar to 1985 at the rear, but markedly different up front. Ford's blue script oval stood above a single-slot grille. Aero headlamps met wraparound marker lenses. Parking lamps were mounted below, in the bumper region, alongside a wide center slot. Large 'EXP' recessed lettering was easy to spot on the wide C pillar. Wraparound full-width taillamps (split by the license plate's recessed housing) were divided into upper/lower segments, and tapered downward to a point on each quarter panel. Luxury Coupe and Sport Coupe versions were offered, with 1.9-liter fast-burn four, five-speed manual transaxle, and four-wheel independent suspension. Luxury Coupe had the carbureted engine, along with a tachometer and trip odometer, reclining low-back bucket seats trimmed in cloth/vinyl (or all vinyl), AM/FM stereo radio, overhead console, and left remote mirror. A fuel-injected high-output version of the four went into the Sport Coupe, which also had special handling components, performance bucket seats, center console with graphic systems monitor, foglamps, dual electric mirrors, and low-profile 15 in. handling tires on cast aluminum wheels. Special Option Groups contained such items as speed control, flip-up open air roof, and premium sound system.

1986 Tempo LX coupe (JG)

TEMPO — FOUR — After only two seasons in the lineup, Tempo got new front and rear styling. The new grille consisted simply of twin wide slots below a blue Ford oval in the sloping, body- colored center panel. Aerodynamic halogen headlamps continued outward to meet clear parking lamps, wrapping around to amber side marker lenses that tapered downward to a rounded "point." (The former Tempo had conventional recessed headlamps.) Tempo also had a color-keyed lower front valence panel. Wide, dark gray bodyside moldings held bright inserts. This year's taillamps were wraparound full-width style. Dark gray partial front and rear bumper covers had side extensions with bright insert. Completing the look were aero-style mirrors. Inside was a new-design four-spoke deep-dish steering wheel. A push-pull headlamp switch replaced the toggle unit. New door sill scuff plates were added. A new LX series replaced the GLX. Both GL and LX tires were upgraded to 14 inch size. Sport GL went to 15 inches, and had red interior accent colors to replace the former blue. New options included P185/70R14 whitewalls, decklid luggage rack, 2.0-liter diesel (except in California), and premium sound system. Diesel power was an option rather than a distinct model. Also available: a supplemental air bag restraint system, sport instrument cluster, and lower accent paint treatment. In addition to the basic GL and LX models, Select GL and Sport GL packages were offered. GL included full cloth reclining front bucket seats, power front disc/rear drum brakes, and such conveniences as interval wipers and a digital clock. Tempo LX included styled wheels, tilt steering, power door locks, a full array of courtesy lights, bright argent lower back panel applique, and AM/FM stereo radio (which could be deleted). A Select GL package added power steering, tinted glass, dual sail-mounted remote electric mirrors, and AM/FM stereo radio (also open to deletion for credit). Sport GL had a special handling suspension, as well as a high specific output (HSO) version of the standard 2300 HSC (high swirl combustion) four. All had a standard five-speed manual transaxle. Automatic was optional on GL and Select GL, as was the 2.0-liter diesel four with five-speed.

1986 Taurus LX sedan (JG)

TAURUS — FOUR/V-6 — Most striking of the aerodynamic new mid-size, front-drive Taurus's styling features was the lack of a grille. The solid body-colored panel between aero halogen headlamps held nothing other than a Ford oval, set in a larger oval opening. The only other opening up front was a wide center air-intake slot, far down between horizontally-ribbed bumper segments. Those wide single-section headlamps (with integrated turn signal lamps) continued around the fender side to meet small amber lenses. Clear side marker lenses were farther down, below the bodyside/bumper molding. The 'Taurus' nameplate (and model identification) went low on the door, in or just below the bodyside molding. At the rear were wraparound taillamps. Taurus wagons had narrow vertical taillamps, and center high-mount stoplamp above the liftgate. That distinctive liftgate design had a back window that tapered inward at the top. Taurus had flush-mounted glass all around, and shingled one-piece doors. Aero styling gave an impressive drag coefficient: as low as 0.33 for the sedan. Four series were offered: L, GL, LX, and (later) a sporty MT5, in six-window sedan or wagon form. Base engine was a new 153 cu. in. (2.5-liter) fuel-injected HSC four, though early models came only with the 183 cu. in. (3.0-liter) V-6. Later optional (standard on GL/LX and wagons), that V-6 had multi-port fuel injection. The 2.5-liter four could have a three-speed automatic transaxle with centrifugally locking clutch; the V-6 turned to a four-speed overdrive automatic transaxle. A five-speed manual transaxle was available only with the four. The four-cylinder engine was derived from

1986 Taurus GL wagon (JG)

Tempo's High Swirl Combustion design. Sedans had fully independent MacPherson strut suspension, front and rear. Wagons had independent short and long arm type rear suspension, which was more compact to add cargo space. Polycarbonate bumpers were corrosion-proof and resilient. The driver-oriented instrument panel featured a swept-away design with three analog backlit instrument clusters. An electronic cluster was optional. Tactile-type switches had raised or depressed sections so drivers could determine the function by touch. Windshield wipers had 20 in. blades and an articulated driver's side arm for a full wipe all the way to the pillar. Standard equipment included power brakes and steering, gas-filled shocks and struts, all-season steel-belted radials, driver's side footrest, locking glovebox, dual-note horn, black left-hand remote mirror, AM radio, and reclining cloth flight bench seats. Wagons had a 60/40 split fold-down rear seat, cargo tie-downs, rear bumper step pad, and dual cargo area lights. MT5 came with five-speed manual transaxle and floor shift lever, and included interval wipers, electronic-tuning AM/FM stereo with digital clock, tinted glass, tachometer, dual electric remote mirrors, color-keyed rocker panel moldings, and bucket seats. MT5 sedans had blackout treatment on 'B' and 'C' pillars. Taurus GL was similar to MT5 but with four-speed automatic and without a tachometer. The top-ranked LX had air conditioning, remote fuel door release, cornering lamps, power locks, black/bright bodyside moldings, power cloth split bench seats with adjustable front lumbar support, tilt steering, power windows, and lighted visor vanity mirrors. Options included an Insta-Clear heated windshield, power moonroof, keyless entry, and electronic climate control. Wagons could get a rear-facing third seat, liftgate wiper/washer, and folding load floor extension that could also serve as a picnic table. Preferred Equipment Packages included such options as speed control, rear window defroster, air conditioning, and electronic entertainment systems. At first glance, Taurus looked very much like the related Mercury Sable, developed under the same program; but the sedans shared no sheetmetal at all. Wagons differed up front, but were the same from the windshield on back. The pair did share drivetrains and running gear, plus most equipment.

LTD — FOUR/V-6 — Ford's rear-drive mid-size was scheduled for abandonment at mid-year, now that the front-drive Taurus had arrived. For its final partial season, the 232 cu. in. (3.8-liter) V-6 became standard (though the four was listed as a credit option). The high-performance LX sedan didn't make the lineup this year, and not much was new apart from the newly required center high-mount stop lamp. Quite a few low-rate options were dropped, and the four-speed automatic overdrive transmission became optional. LTD was virtually identical to Mercury Marquis, both riding the old Granada platform. Models included base and Brougham sedans, and the base wagon.

1986 LTD Crown Victoria sedan (JG)

LTD CROWN VICTORIA — V-8 — Big rear-drives had more than a spark of life remaining in Ford's plans. Crown Victoria added a new sedan and wagon series this year: the top-level LX and Country Squire LX. Each model incorporated a standard (previously optional) interior luxury group. LX had reclining split bench seats upholstered in velour cloth or vinyl (leather seating surfaces optional). Equipment included power windows and a digital clock, as well as a variety of luxury trim extras. Sequential multi-port fuel injection replaced the former central injection on the standard 302 cu. in. (5.0-liter) V-8 engine, which came with four-speed overdrive automatic. No options were available, except the 351 cu. in. V-8 for police models. The 302 got a number of internal changes, including fast-burning combustion chambers, higher compression, roller tappets, low-tension piston rings, and viscous clutch cooling fan. Wagons now had a mini spare tire rather than the conventional one. All series had automatic parking brake release, a tethered gas cap, and right-hand visor mirror. A rear bumper step pad became standard on wagons. The new high-mount brake lamp was mounted on the package tray on sedans, on tailgate of wagons. Standard equipment included an AM/FM stereo radio with four speakers, quartz clock, front/rear courtesy lights, cloth flight bench seat with dual recliners, and remote driver's mirror. Split bench seats were optional. P205/75R15 tires became standard this year. Seven exterior colors were new, along with five vinyl roof colors. Country Squire's simulated woodgrain panels switched from cherry to dark cherry. Optional this year were dual electric remote mirrors for LX and a conventional spare tire for wagons. Traction-Lok axle was now included with the heavy-duty trailer towing packages. Preferred Equipment Packages grouped such options as six-way power driver's seat, power lock group, and speed control. Styling was similar to 1985. Full-size Fords had an upright crosshatch grille with relatively large holes in a 12x4 pattern. Quad rectangular headlamps stood above amber park/signal lenses, and the whole assembly continued outward to meet twin amber lenses around the fender tips. The entire front end showed a straight-up, symmetrical design. Small marker lenses sat quite low on the front fenders, just ahead of wheel openings. Red rear side marker lenses were vertical, near quarter panel tips. In back, each squarish vertical taillamp consisted of four raised segments.

1986 Thunderbird hardtop coupe (JG)

THUNDERBIRD — FOUR/V-6/V-8 — Thunderbird dropped down to three models this year as the Fila series left the lineup. Both the base 232 cu. in. (3.8-liter) V-6 and optional 302 cu. in. (5.0-liter) V-8 engines now had viscous engine mounts (which had been standard on the 2.3-liter turbo in 1985). The V-8 switched to multi-port fuel injection and added roller tappets, low-tension piston rings, and fast-burn combustion chambers. P215/70R14 blackwalls were now standard (except on Turbo Coupe). V-6 models came with three-speed SelectShift automatic; V-8s with four-speed overdrive automatic. All models now had an electronic-tuning AM/FM stereo radio. Six body colors and three interior trim colors were new. Elan's interior cloth trim was revised for a plusher appearance. A woodtone instrument panel applique was added. Standard equipment included variable-ratio power rack-and-pinion steering, power front disc/rear drum brakes, and gas-pressurized shocks and struts. Inside were reclining cloth split bench seats. Thunderbird elan (accent over the e) had upgraded trim and such conveniences as power windows, dual electric remote mirrors, interval wipers, system sentry, a digital clock, and lighted visor mirrors. Turbo Coupe again carried the 2.3-liter turbocharged four, with five-speed close-ratio manual shift and special Goodyear performance tires. Articulated front sport seats adjusted several ways. New options were: power moonroof (delayed availability) and a collapsible spare tire (including a 12-volt air compressor that plugged into the lighter). Preferred Equipment Packages included such extras as illuminated entry, electronic instrument cluster, and a power lock group. Styling was similar to 1985. Recessed, staggered quad rectangular headlamps were flanked by amber wraparound signal/marker lenses at matching height. TBird's grille had four thin, bright horizontal bars over a blackout pattern. Small amber parking lamps were down in the bumper rub strip. Wraparound taillamps again held a Thunderbird emblem in each lens. Emblems also went on the Cpillar and grille header. Thunderbird was similar to Mercury's Cougar.

I.D. DATA: Ford's 17-symbol Vehicle Identification Number (VIN) again was stamped on a metal tab fastened to the instrument panel, visible through the windshield. The first three symbols ('1FA') indicate manufacturer, make and vehicle type. The fourth symbol ('B') denotes restraint system. Next comes a letter 'P', followed by two digits that indicate body type: Model Number, as shown in left column of tables below. (Example: '31' Escort L two-door hatchback). Symbol eight indicates engine type: '9' L4113 2Bbl.; 'J' H.O. L4113 Fl; 'H' Diesel L4121; 'X' HSC L4140 Fl; 'S' H.O. HSC L4140 Fl; 'W' Turbo L4140 EFI; 'D' L4153 Fl; 'U' V6183 Fl; '3' V6232 2Bbl.; 'F' V8302 2Bbl.; 'G' V8351 2Bbl. Next is a check digit. Symbol ten indicates model year ('G' 1986). Symbol eleven is assembly plant: 'A' Atlanta, GA; 'B' Oakville, Ontario (Canada); 'G' Chicago; 'H' Lorain, Ohio; 'K' Kansas City, MO; 'X' St. Thomas, Ontario; 'T' Edison, NJ; 'W' Wayne, MI. The final six digits make up the sequence number, starting with 100001. A Vehicle Certification Label on the left front door lock face panel or door pillar shows the manufacturer, month and year of manufacture, GVW, GAWR, certification statement, VIN, and codes for such items as body type, color, trim, axle, transmission, and special order information.

ESCORT (FOUR)

Model Number	Body/Style Number	Body Type & Seating	Factory Price	Shipping Weight	Production Total
31/41P	N/A	2-dr. Pony Hatch-4P	6052	2089	Note 1
31	N/A	2-dr. L Hatch-4P	6327	2096	Note 1
36	N/A	4-dr. L Hatch-4P	6541	2154	Note 1
34	N/A	4-dr. L Sta Wag-4P	6822	2173	Note 1
32	N/A	2-dr. LX Hatch-4P	7284	2160	Note 1
37	N/A	4-dr. LX Hatch-4P	7448	2214	Note 1
35	N/A	4-dr. LX Sta Wag-4P	7729	2228	Note 1
33	N/A	2-dr. GT Hatch-4P	8112	2282	Note 1

Note 1: For the model year, a total of 228,013 two-door hatchbacks, 117,300 four-door hatchback sedans, and 84,740 station wagons were produced. Breakdown by trim level not available. Bodies are sometimes referred to as three-door and five-door.

EXP (FOUR)

01	N/A	2-dr. Spt Cpe-2P	7186	N/A	Note 2
01/931	N/A	2-dr. Luxury Cpe-2P	8235	N/A	Note 2

Note 2: Total EXP production was 30,978.

TEMPO (FOUR)

19	66D	2-dr. GL Sed-5P	7358	2363	Note 3
22	54D	4-dr. GL Sed-5P	7508	2422	Note 3
20	66D	2-dr. GLX Sed-5P	8578	2465	Note 3
23	54D	4-dr. GLX Sed-5P	8777	2526	Note 3

Note 3: Total Tempo production came to 69,101 two-doors and 208,570 four-doors.

TAURUS (FOUR/V-6)

29	54D	4-dr. L Sedan-6P	9645/10256	2749/2749	Note 4
30	74D	4-dr. L Sta Wag-6P	-- /10763	-- /3067	Note 4
29/934	54D	4-dr. MT5 Sed-6P	10276/ --	2759/ --	Note 4
30/934	74D	4-dr. MT5 Wag-6P	10741/ --	2957/ --	Note 4
29/60D	54D	4-dr. GL Sedan-6P	-- /11322	-- /2909	Note 4
30/60D	74D	4-dr. GL Wag-6P	-- /11790	-- /3108	Note 4
29/60H	54D	4-dr. LX Sedan-6P	-- /13351	-- /3001	Note 4
30/60H	74D	4-dr. LX Wag-6P	-- /13860	-- /3198	Note 4

Note 4: Total Taurus production came to 178,737 sedans and 57,625 station wagons.

LTD (FOUR/V-6)

39	54D	4-dr. Sedan-5P	9538/10032	2801/2878	58,270
39	54D	4-dr. Brghm-5P	9926/10420	2806/2883	Note 5
40	74D	4-dr. Sta Wag-5P	-- /10132	-- /2977	14,213

Note 5: Brougham production is included in basic sedan total.

LTD CROWN VICTORIA (V-8)

42	66K	2-dr. Sedan-6P	13022	3571	6,559
43	54K	4-dr. Sedan-6P	12562	3611	97,314
44	74K	4-dr. Ctry Sqr-6P	12655	3834	20,164
44/41E	74K	4-dr. Sta Wag-6P	12405	3795	Note 6
43/41K	54K	4-dr. 'S' Sed-6P	12188	3591	Note 6
44/41K	74K	4-dr. 'S' Wag-6P	12468	3769	Note 6

1986 LTD Crown Victoria Country Squire station wagon (JG)

LTD CROWN VICTORIA LX (V-8)

42/60H	66K	2-dr. Sedan-6P	13752	3608	Note 6
43/60H	54K	4-dr. Sedan-6P	13784	3660	Note 6
44/41E/60H	74K	4-dr. Sta Wag-6P	13567	3834	Note 6
44/60H	74K	4-dr. Ctry Sqr-6P	13817	3873	Note 6

Note 6: Production of 'S' and LX models and basic station wagon is included in basic sedan and Country Squire totals above.

Police Crown Victoria Note: A Police model (P43/41K/55A) 'S' sedan cost $11,813 with 302 cu. in. V-8, or $11,933 with 351 cu. in. V-8 engine.

THUNDERBIRD (V-6/V-8)

46	66D	2-dr. HT Cpe-5P	11020/11805	2923/3101	163,965
46	66D	2-dr. Elan Cpe-5P	12554/13339	2977/3155	Note 7

THUNDERBIRD TURBO COUPE (FOUR)

46	66D	2-dr. HT Cpe-5P	14143	3016	Note 7

Note 7: Turbo Coupe and Elan production is included in basic Thunderbird total.

MODEL NUMBER NOTE: Some sources include a prefix 'P' ahead of the two- digit model number. **FACTORY PRICE AND WEIGHT NOTE:** LTD and Taurus prices and weights to left of slash are for four-cylinder, to right for V-6 engine. Thunderbird prices and weights to left of slash are for V-6, to right for V-8 engine.

ENGINE DATA: BASE FOUR (Escort): Inline. Overhead cam. Four-cylinder. Cast iron block and aluminum head. Displacement: 113 cu. in. (1.9 liters). Bore & stroke: 3.23 x 3.46 in. Compression ratio: 9.0:1. Brake horsepower: 86 at 4800 R.P.M. Torque: 100 lbs.-ft. at 3000 R.P.M. Five main bearings. Hydraulic valve lifters. Carburetor: 2Bbl. Holley 740. VIN Code: 9. BASE FOUR (Escort GT); OPTIONAL (Escort): High-output, multi-port fuel-injected version of 1.9-liter four above Horsepower: 108 at 5200 R.P.M. Torque: 114 lbs.- ft. at 4000 R.P.M. VIN Code: J. DIESEL FOUR (Escort, Tempo): Inline. Overhead cam. Four-cylinder. Cast iron block and aluminum head. Displacement: 121 cu. in. (2.0 liters). Bore & stroke: 3.39 x 3.39 in. Compression ratio: 22.7:1. Brake horsepower: 52 at 4000 R.P.M. Torque: 82 lbs.-ft. at 2400 R.P.M. Five main bearings. Solid valve lifters. Fuel injection. VIN Code: H. BASE FOUR (Tempo): Inline. Overhead valve. Four-cylinder. Cast iron block and head. Displacement: 140 cu. in. (2.3 liters). Bore & stroke: 3.70 x 3.30 in. Compression ratio: 9.0:1. Brake horsepower: 86 at 4000 R.P.M. Torque: 124 lbs.-ft. at 2800 R.P.M. Five main bearings. Hydraulic valve lifters. Throttle-body fuel injection. High Swirl Combustion (HSC) design. VIN Code: X. OPTIONAL FOUR (Tempo): High-output version of HSC four above Horsepower: 100 at 4600 R.P.M. Torque: 125 lbs.-ft. at 3200 R.P.M. VIN Code: S. BASE FOUR (Thunderbird Turbo Coupe): Inline. Overhead cam. Four-cylinder. Cast iron block and head. Displacement: 140 cu. in. (2.3 liters). Bore & stroke: 3.78 x 3.13 in. Compression ratio: 8.0:1. Brake horsepower: 155 at 4600 R.P.M. (145 at 4400 with automatic). Torque: 190 lbs.-ft. at 2800 R.P.M. (180 at 3000 with automatic). Five main bearings. Hydraulic valve lifters. Port fuel injection. VIN Code: W. BASE FOUR (late Taurus): Inline. Overhead valve. Four-cylinder. Cast iron block and head. Displacement: 153 cu. in. (2.5 liters). Bore & stroke: 3.70 x 3.60 in. Compression ratio: 9.0:1. Brake horsepower: 88 at 4600 R.P.M. Torque: 130 lbs.-ft. at 2800 R.P.M. Five main bearings. Hydraulic valve lifters. Electronic fuel injection. VIN Code: D. BASE V-6 (Taurus LX/wagon); OPTIONAL (Taurus): 60-degree, overhead valve V-6. Cast iron block and head. Displacement: 183 cu. in. (3.0 liters). Bore & stroke: 3.50 x 3.10 in. Compression ratio: 9.25:1. Brake horsepower: 140 at 4800 R.P.M. Torque: 160 lbs.-ft. at 3000 R.P.M. Four main bearings. Hydraulic valve lifters. Multi-port fuel injection. VIN Code: U. BASE V-6 (LTD, Thunderbird): 90-degree, overhead valve V-6. Cast iron block and aluminum head. Displacement: 232 cu. in. (3.8 liters). Bore & stroke: 3.80 x 3.40 in. Compression ratio: 8.7:1. Brake horsepower: 120 at 3600 R.P.M. Torque: 205 lbs.-ft. at 1600 R.P.M. Four main bearings. Hydraulic valve lifters. Throttle-body fuel injection. VIN Code: 3. BASE V-8 (Crown Victoria); OPTIONAL (Thunderbird): 90-degree, overhead valve V-8. Cast iron block and head. Displacement: 302 cu. in. (5.0 liters). Bore & stroke: 4.00 x 3.00 in. Compression ratio: 8.9:1. Brake horsepower: 150 at 3200 R.P.M. Torque: 270 lbs.-ft. at 2000 R.P.M. Five main bearings. Hydraulic valve lifters. Sequential (port) fuel injection. VIN Code: F. HIGH-OUTPUT POLICE V-8 (Crown Victoria): 90-degree, overhead valve V-8. Cast iron block and head. Displacement: 351 cu. in. (5.8 liters). Bore & stroke: 4.00 x 3.50 in. Compression ratio: 8.3:1. Brake horsepower: 180 at 3600 R.P.M. Torque: 285 lbs.-ft. at 2400 R.P.M. Five main bearings. Hydraulic valve lifters. Carburetor: 2Bbl. VIN Code: G.

CHASSIS DATA: Wheelbase: (Escort/EXP) 94.2 in.; (Tempo) 99.9 in.; (Taurus) 106.0 in.; (LTD) 105.6 in.; (Crown Vic) 114.3 in.; (TBird) 104.0 in. Overall Length: (Escort) 166.9 in.; (Escort wagon) 168.0 in.; (EXP) 168.4 in.; (Tempo) 176.2 in.; (Taurus) 188.4 in.; (Taurus wag) 191.9 in.; (LTD) 196.5 in.; (Crown Vic) 211.0 in.; (Crown Vic wag) 215.0 in.; (TBird) 197.6 in. Height: (Escort) 53.3-53.5 in.; (EXP) 50.9 in.; (Tempo) 52.7 in.; (Taurus) 54.4 in.; (Taurus wag) 55.2 in.; (LTD) 53.8 in.; (LTD wag) 54.4 in.; (Crown Vic) 55.3 in.; (Crown Vic wag) 56.8 in.; (TBird) 53.2 in. Width: (Escort/EXP) 65.9 in.; (Tempo) 68.3 in.; (Taurus) 70.7 in.; (LTD) 71.0 in.; (Crown Vic) 77.5 in.; (Crown Vic wag) 79.3 in.; (TBird) 71.1 in. Front Tread: (Escort/EXP/Tempo) 54.7 in.; (Taurus) 61.5 in.; (LTD) 56.6 in.; (Crown Vic) 62.2 in. (TBird) 58.1 in. Rear Tread: (Escort/EXP) 56.0 in.; (Tempo) 57.6 in.; (Taurus) 60.5 in.; (Taurus wag) 59.9 in.; (LTD) 57.0 in.; (Crown Vic) 62.0 in. (TBird) 58.5 in. Standard Tires: (Escort Pony/L) P165/80R13 SBR BSW; (Escort L wag/LX) P175/80R13; (Escort GT) P195/60HR15 BSW; (EXP) P185/70R14 SBR; (Tempo) P185/80R14 SBR BSW; (Taurus) P195/70R14 BSW; (Taurus GL/LX) P205/70R14; (LTD) P195/75R14 BSW; (Crown Vic) P205/75R15 SBR WSW; (TBird) P215/70R14 SBR BSW; (TBird Turbo Cpe) P225/60VR15 Goodyear unidirectional "Gatorback" BSW.

TECHNICAL: Transmission: Four-speed manual transaxle standard on Escort Pony/L; five-speed standard on Escort LX/GT, EXP, Tempo, and Thunderbird Turbo Coupe. Gear ratios N/A. Three-speed automatic standard on LTD, Thunderbird turbo/V-6: (1st) 2.46:1 or 2.47:1; (2nd) 1.46:1 or 1.47:1; (3rd) 1.00:1; (Rev) 2.11:1 or 2.19:1. Taurus four/Escort/Tempo three-speed automatic: (1st) 2.79:1; (2nd) 1.61:1-1.62:1; (3rd) 1.00:1; (Rev) 1.97:1. Four-speed overdrive automatic standard on LTD V-6, Crown Victoria and Thunderbird: (1st) 2.40:1; (2nd) 1.47:1; (3rd) 1.00:1; (4th) 0.67:1; (Rev) 2.00:1. Taurus V-6 four-speed overdrive automatic: (1st) 2.77:1; (2nd) 1.54:1; (3rd) 1.00:1; (4th) 0.69:1; (Rev) 2.26:1. Standard final drive ratio: (Escort) 3.52:1 w/4spd, 2.85:1 w/fuel saver, 3.73:1 w/5spd, 3.23:1 w/auto., 3.52:1 w/diesel; (EXP) N/A; (Tempo) 3.23:1 exc. 3.73:1 w/diesel or H.O. engine; (Taurus four) 3.23:1; (Taurus V-6) 3.37:1; (LTD) 2.73:1 w/3spd auto., 3.27:1 w/4-spd auto.; (Crown Vic) 2.73:1; (TBird) 3.45:1 w/turbo, 2.73:1 w/3spd automatic and V-6, 3.27:1 w/4spd auto. and V-6, 3.08:1 w/V-8. Drive Axle: (Escort/EXP/Tempo/Taurus) front; (others) rear. Steering: (Crown Vic) recirculating ball; (others) rack and pinion. Front Suspension: (Escort/EXP/Tempo) MacPherson struts with lower control arms, coil springs and stabilizer bar; (EXP) N/A; (Taurus) MacPherson struts with control arms, coil springs and stabilizer bar; (LTD/TBird) modified MacPherson struts with lower control arms, coil springs and anti-sway bar; (Crown Vic) long/short control arms w/coil springs and stabilizer bar. LTD, Crown Vic and TBird had gas-filled struts/shocks. Rear Suspension: (Escort/EXP) independent trailing arms w/modified MacPherson struts and coil springs on lower control arms; (EXP) N/A; (Tempo) fully independent trailing quadra-link with MacPherson struts; (Taurus) MacPherson struts w/parallel suspension arms and coil springs; (Taurus wag) upper/lower control arms, coil springs and stabilizer bar; (LTD/Crown Vic/TBird) rigid axle w/four links and coil springs; (TBird Turbo Coupe) "quadra-shock" four-bar-link assembly with two hydraulic, horizontal axle dampers. Gas- filled shocks on LTD, Crown Vic and TBird. Brakes: Front disc, rear drum (power assisted). Ignition: Electronic. Body construction: (Crown Vic) separate body and frame; (others) unibody. Fuel tank: (Escort) 10.0 gal.; (Escort wag) 13.0 gal.; (EXP) N/A; (Tempo) 15.2 gal.; (Taurus/LTD) 16.0 gal.; (Crown Vic) 18.0 gal.; (Crown Vic wag) 18.5 gal.; (TBird) 20.6 gal.

DRIVETRAIN OPTIONS: Engines: Diesel 2.0-liter four: Escort ($591); Tempo ($509). 140 cu. in. four: LTD ($494 credit). 182 cu. in. V-6: Taurus L sed ($611). 302 cu. in. V-8: Thunderbird ($548). Transmission/Differential: Five-speed manual trans.: Escort ($76). Automatic transaxle: Escort ($466) exc. LX/GT and EXP ($390); Tempo ($448). Auto. transmission.: TBird Turbo Cpe ($315). Floor shift lever: Taurus GL/LX (NC). First gear lockout delete: Crown Vic ($7). Overdrive auto. trans.: TBird ($237); LTD ($245). Traction-Lok differential: LTD/Crown Vic/TBird ($100). Steering/Suspension: Power steering: Escort/EXP ($226); Tempo ($223). H.D. susp.: Escort/Taurus/-Crown Vic ($26); LTD ($43). Handling susp.: Crown Vic ($49). Auto. load leveling: Crown Vic ($200). Other: H.D. battery ($27). H.D. alternator: Escort/EXP ($27); Crown Vic ($54). Extended-range gas tank: Taurus/LTD ($46). Engine block heater ($18). Trailer towing pkg.: Crown Vic ($377-$389). California emission system: Escort/EXP ($46); others ($99). High-altitude emissions (NC).

ESCORT CONVENIENCE/APPEARANCE OPTIONS: Option Packages: Instrument group ($87). Climate control/convenience group ($742-$868). Premium convenience group ($306-$390). Protection convenience gorup ($131-$467). Select L pkg. ($397). Light group ($67). Comfort/Convenience: Air conditioner ($657). Rear defroster, electric ($135). Fingertip speed control ($176). Tinted glass ($99). Tilt steering ($115). Overhead console w/digital clock ($82). Interval wipers ($50). Rear wiper/washer ($126). Dual remote sport mirrors ($68). Entertainment: AM radio ($39). AM/FM stereo radio ($109) exc. base ($148); w/cassette player ($256) exc. base/L ($295) and GT ($148). Radio delete: L/LX ($39 credit); GT ($148 credit). Premium sound ($138). Exterior: Clearcoat paint ($91). Two-tone paint ($61-$156). Front vent windows, pivoting ($63). Wide vinyl bodyside moldings ($45). Bumper guards, front/rear ($56). Bumper rub strips ($48). Luggage rack: wag ($100). Interior: Console ($111). Vinyl seat trim ($24). Wheels/Tires: Bright wheel trim rings ($54). Styled wheels ($128-$195). P165/80R13 SBR WSW ($59). Full-size spare ($63).

EXP CONVENIENCE/APPEARANCE OPTIONS: Option Packages: Climate control/convenience group ($841-$868). Sun/Sound group ($612). Convenience group ($300-$455). Comfort/Convenience: Air conditioner ($657). Rear defroster ($135). Fingertip speed control ($176). Console w/graphic systems monitor ($111). Tinted glass ($99). Tilt steering ($115). Interval wipers ($50). Dual electric remote mirrors ($88). Lighted visor vanity mirror ($50). Entertainment: AM/FM stereo radio w/cassette player ($148). Premium sound ($138). Radio delete ($148 credit). Exterior: Flip-up open air roof ($315). Clearcoat paint ($91). Interior: Cargo area cover ($59). Vinyl seat trim ($24).

TEMPO CONVENIENCE/APPEARANCE OPTIONS: Option Packages: Sport GL pkg. ($934). Select GL pkg. ($340-$423). Power lock group ($207-$259). Power equipment group ($291-$575). Convenience group ($224-$640). Comfort/Convenience: Air bag restraint system ($815). Air cond. ($743). Rear defroster, electric ($145). Fingertip speed control ($176). Power windows ($207-$282). Six-way power driver's seat ($234). Tinted glass ($113); windshield ($48). Tilt steering ($115). Sport instrument cluster ($87). Dual electric remote mirrors ($111). Entertainment: AM/FM stereo radio ($109); w/cassette player ($148-$256). Electronic-tuning AM/FM stereo w/cassette ($279) exc. w/Sport GL pkg. ($23). Premium sound ($138). Radio delete ($39-$295 credit). Exterior: Clearcoat metallic paint ($91). Lower body accent paint ($78). Decklid luggage rack ($100). Interior: Console ($116). Front center armrest ($55). Vinyl seat trim ($35). Leather seat trim ($300). Wheels/Tires: Styled wheels ($178). P185/70R14 WSW ($72).

TAURUS CONVENIENCE/APPEARANCE OPTIONS: Option Packages: Exterior accent group ($49-$99). Power lock group ($180-$221). Light group ($48-$51). Comfort/Convenience: Air cond. ($762). Electronic climate control air cond.: GL ($945); LX ($183). Rear defroster ($145). Insta-clear windshield ($250); N/A on MT5. Fingertip speed control ($176). Illuminated entry ($82). Keyless entry ($202). Power windows ($282). Six-way power driver's seat ($237); dual ($473). Remote fuel door release: MT5/GL ($37). Tinted glass: L ($115); windshield only LPO ($48). Leather-wrapped steering wheel ($59). Tilt steering ($115). Electronic instrument cluster ($305); N/A on MT5. Autolamp on/off delay ($73). Diagnostic warning lights ($89). Auto. parking brake release: L/GL ($12). Digital clock: L ($78). Interval wipers: L ($50). Rear wiper/washer: wag ($124). Lighting and Mirrors: Cornering lamps ($68). Dual electric remote mirrors: L ($59-$96). Dual lighted visor vanity mirrors ($104-$116). Entertainment: AM/FM stereo radio: L/MT5 ($157). Electronic-tuning AM/FM stereo w/cassette/Dolby ($127-$284). Power antenna ($71). Premium sound system ($168). Radio delete: L ($39 credit); others ($196 credit). Exterior: Power moonroof ($701). Clearcoat paint ($183). Bodyside/decklid paint stripe ($57). Rocker panel moldings: L ($55). Luggage rack delete: L wag LPO ($105 credit). Interior: Bucket seats (NC). Split bench seating: L ($276). Vinyl seat trim ($39). Leather seat trim: LX sed ($415). Rear-facing third seat: wag ($155). Reclining passenger seat ($45). Load floor extension: wag ($66). Cargo area cover: wag ($66). Carpeted floor mats ($43). Wheels/Tires: Luxury wheel covers ($65). Styled wheels, 14 in. ($113-$178). Cast aluminum wheels, 15 in. ($326-$390). P195/70R14 WSW ($72). P205/70R14 BSW ($38); WSW ($72-$110). P205/65R15 BSW ($46-$84); WSW ($124-$162). Conventional spare ($63).

LTD CONVENIENCE/APPEARANCE OPTIONS: Option Packages: Squire option ($282). Interior luxury group ($388). Power lock group ($218-$259). Light group ($38). Comfort/Convenience: Air cond. ($762). Rear defroster ($145). Fingertip speed control ($176). Autolamp on-off delay ($73). Power windows ($282). Six-way power driver's seat ($234). Tinted glass ($115). Tinted windshield ($48). Leather-wrapped steering wheel ($59). Tilt steering ($115). Digital clock ($78). Auto. parking brake release ($12). Interval wipers ($50). Lighting and Mirrors: Cornering lamps ($68). Right remote convex mirror ($61). Dual electric remote mirrors ($96). Lighted visor vanity mirrors ($57-$106). Entertainment: AM/FM stereo radio ($109); w/cassette player ($256). Premium sound system ($138). AM radio delete ($39 credit). Exterior: Full vinyl roof ($152). Clearcoat metallic paint ($183). Two-tone paint w/tape stripe ($117). Pivoting front vent windows ($79). Two-way liftgate: wag ($105). Rocker panel

moldings ($40). Bumper guards, rear ($28). Bumper rub strips ($56). Luggage rack: wagon ($126). Lower bodyside protection ($41). Interior: Vinyl seat trim ($35). Flight or split bench seat (NC). Front floor mats, carpeted ($23). Wheels/Tires: Luxury wheel covers ($55). Wire wheel covers, locking ($212). Styled wheels ($178). Styled steel wheels w/trim rings ($54). P195/75R14 WSW ($72). P205/70R14 WSW ($134). Conventional spare ($63).

LTD CROWN VICTORIA CONVENIENCE/APPEARANCE OPTIONS: Option Packages: Convenience group ($109-$134). Power lock group ($143-$243). Light group ($48). Police pkg. ($291-$411). Comfort/Convenience: Air cond. ($762); w/auto-temp control ($828). Rear defroster, electric ($145). Fingertip speed control ($176). Illuminated entry system ($82). Power windows ($282). Power six-way driver's seat ($237); driver and passenger ($473). Tinted glass ($115); windshield only ($48). Autolamp on/off delay ($73). Leather-wrapped steering wheel ($59). Tilt steering wheel ($115). Tripminder computer ($215-$261). Quartz clock: S ($35). Digital clock ($61-$96). Interval wipers ($50). Lighting and Mirrors: Cornering lamps ($68). Remote right convex mirror ($46). Dual electric remote mirrors ($100). Entertainment: AM/FM stereo radio: S ($109); w/cassette tape player ($148-$256). Electronic-tuning AM/FM stereo radio w/cassette ($300) exc. S ($409). Power antenna ($73). Premium sound system ($168). Radio delete: AM ($39 credit). Exterior: Brougham vinyl roof ($793). Two-tone paint/tape ($117). Dual accent bodyside stripes ($39). Pivoting front vent windows ($79). Rocker panel moldings ($18-$38). Vinyl-insert bodyside moldings ($61). Bumper rub strips ($59). Luggage rack: wagon ($110). Interior: Dual-facing rear seats: wagon ($167). Leather seat trim ($433). Reclining split bench seats ($144). All-vinyl seat trim ($100). Duraweave vinyl ($100). Carpeted front floor mats ($21); front/rear ($33). H.D. floor covering ($27). Wheels/Tires: Wire wheel covers, locking ($205). Cast aluminum wheels ($390). P205/75R15 puncture-sealant ($161). P215/70R15 WSW ($62). Conventional spare ($63).

THUNDERBIRD CONVENIENCE/APPEARANCE OPTIONS: Option Packages: Light group ($35). Power lock group ($220). Comfort/Convenience: Air cond. ($762); auto-temp ($924). Rear defroster ($145). Fingertip speed control ($176). Illuminated entry system ($82). Keyless entry ($198). Anti-theft system ($215). Tripminder computer ($215-$276). Autolamp on/off delay ($73). Tinted glass ($115); windshield only ($49). Power windows ($207). Six-way power driver's seat ($238); dual ($476). Dual power seat recliners ($189). Leather-wrapped steering wheel ($59). Tilt steering wheel ($115). Electronic instrument cluster ($270-$330). Diagnostic warning lights ($89). Digital clock ($61). Interval wipers ($50). Lighting and Mirrors: Cornering lamps ($68). Dual electric remote mirrors ($96). Lighted visor vanity mirrors, pair ($106). Entertainment: Power antenna ($71). Graphic equalizer ($218). Premium sound system ($168). AM/FM radio delete ($196 credit). Exterior: Power moonroof ($701). Metallic clearcoat paint ($183). Two-tone paint/tape ($183-$218). Dual accent paint stripes ($55). Pivoting front vent windows ($79). Wide bodyside moldings ($57). Interior: Articulated sport seats ($183). Leather seat trim ($415). Soft vinyl seat trim ($37). Front floor mats, carpeted ($22). Wheels/Tires: Wire wheel covers, locking ($212). Cast aluminum wheels ($343). Styled wheels ($178). P215/70R14 WSW ($62). Conventional spare ($63). Inflatable spare ($122).

HISTORY: Introduced: October 3, 1985 except Taurus, December 26, 1985 and EXP, mid-year. Model year production: 1,559,959 (incl. Mustangs). Total production for the U.S. market of 1,424,374 units (incl. Mustangs) included 845,607 four-cylinder, 380,402 sixes and 198,365 V-8s. That total included 23,658 turbo fours and 7,144 diesel engines. Calendar year production (U.S.): 1,221,956 (incl. Mustangs). Calendar year sales by U.S. dealers: 1,397,141 (incl. Mustangs). Model year sales by U.S. dealers: 1,332,097 (incl. Mustangs).

Historical Footnotes: Sales fell this model year, after three straight years of rises. Moreover, Ford's market share shrunk markedly (from 13.1 percent overall in 1985 to just 11.9 percent in '86). Ford's share when considering only domestic-built autos declined less sharply, from 17.2 percent down to 16.5 percent. Only Mustang showed a sales increase. Escort continued as America's best seller. The Escort/EXP duo found 416,147 buyers this year. Tempo was the second best-selling Ford, for the third year in a row. Crown Vic hung on because of continuing popularity of full-size rear-drives, partly due to moderated gas prices. Throughout the year, low-interest financing was offered, at record-breaking rates. Ford offered a new three-year unlimited mileage powertrain warranty (with deductibles). Because of production delays, the new Taurus (and related Mercury Sable) weren't introduced until December 1985. The new aero mid-size sold well, however. V-6 engines for Taurus were in short supply, keeping production from reaching an even higher level. Taurus was the result of a $3 billion development program, and was named *Motor Trend* Car of the Year. Even before production, it got a lot of publicity. Auto show attendees were even asked their opinions on whether Taurus should or should not have a conventional grille. (Those who preferred a solid panel eventually "won.") Ford claimed that a 1985 owner survey showed that "Ford makes the best-built American cars," based on reports of problems people had with 198184 models. Ford's main slogan at this time: "Quality is Job 1."

FORD

1987-1990

Ford broke records in 1987; $4.6 billion in net income (better than General Motors) and $71.6 billion in worldwide sales. Earnings from U.S. operations alone hit $3.4 billion.

Donald E. Peterson was chairman and CEO for the company, with William C. Ford, Harold A. Poling and Stanley A. Seneker on his top management team. Thomas J. Wagner took over as Ford Division general manager. Domestic new car sales climbed six percent, despite general flatness of the industry.

Leading the sales race was the Escort/EXP series, although the one-year-old Taurus proved the real key to success, with its sales more than doubling from '86. The only change in products was the disappearance of the LTD which, though dropped after 1985, had some 51,000 sales in model year 1986. The popularity of the Taurus made up the difference completely. In fact, all six other Ford carlines declined somewhat in deliveries.

New for '87 was a four-wheel-drive Tempo and a five-liter Thunderbird Sport model. The Festiva, a Korean-built captive import, bowed in the spring as an '88 model, but it was American-made Fords which ruled the market. Model year sales of domestic-built models saw Ford, with 1,422,489 units sold, come in ahead of Chevrolet's 1,390,281. Chevy, however, inched ahead with the Japanese-made Sprint and Spectrum counted. In September, a costly labor agreement helped Ford avert a strike.

Unchanged management guided Ford through 1988, with corporate sales and earnings breaking records for the third year in a row. World sales were $92.4 billion, with $53 billion in net income again topping General Motors. Model year dealer sales of new cars, including the Festiva, rose to 1,535,145 units. This put Ford in first place, ahead of Chevrolet's grand total by 66,000 cars.

The new, Mazda-built Probe and the Festiva accounted for most of Ford's sales increase. Mustangs, restyled Tempos and Thunderbirds also gained more buyers, while the Escort/EXP, Taurus and Crown Victoria lost some ground. Escort, however, was still America's number one seller, with Taurus second.

Product news focused on the Probe, an Americanized version of Mazda's front-drive 626 with GT trim and a 145 hp turbo four available. Other Fords received refinements to drivetrains and option packages.

There seemed to be no stopping Ford and 1989 proved it with a 40,000 car sales increase and 4/10ths percent market share increase. Two possible future collector models bowed: the SHO (Super High-Output) Taurus sedan with a standard 24-valve three-liter/220 hp V-6 and the T-bird Super Coupe with a 3.8-liter/215 hp supercharged V-6. They had production runs of 1,558 and 1,243 units respectively.

The Escort approached its three millionth sale since 1981. The Tempo and Taurus dropped slightly in sales, while the Festiva climbed upwards to 60,000 units.

Management changes saw Donald Peterson step down from the chairman's position effective March 1, 1990. He was replaced by Harold Poling. Philip E. Benton Jr. became president and chief operating officer. Big corporate news included Ford's 1989 purchase of Jaguar, the English luxury automaker for $2.5 billion.

Thunderbird marked its 35th anniversary with the start of the 1990 model year and was changed little. Most other models were also largely unaltered, except for a complete updating of the Escort. The new version, designed by Mazda, bowed in the spring of 1990 as a '91 model. The "old" Escort continued to be built in Edison, N.J., for several months.

Other 1990 product changes included a front and rear restyling of the Probe, a Taurus police car package and a new grille and tail lamps for the Festiva import. Sales of 1.5 million cars were predicted, by Ford, at the start of the 1990 model years.

1987 FORD

1987 FORD — Once again, Ford's subcompact Escort ranked number one in sales for the model year. Also for the 1987 model year, Taurus became the second best-selling passenger car in the country. As soon as the mid-size Taurus began its rise to become a hot seller, Ford's LTD left the lineup for good. Sales of the full-size, rear-drive LTD Crown Victoria slid this year, but its place in the lineup was assured regardless. Tempo added a four-wheel-drive option this year, while Thunderbird took on some new sheet metal and glass (but kept its same overall profile).

1987 LTD Crown Victoria LX four-door sedan

LTD CROWN VICTORIA — V-8 — Only a few equipment changes arrived with the '87 full-size Fords. Air conditioning, tinted glass and a digital clock were now standard equipment. Two- and four-door sedans and a four-door station wagon, in base and LX trim levels, were all powered by a 5.0-liter V-8 with four-speed overdrive automatic transmission.

1987 Escort GL four-door hatchback

ESCORT — FOUR — Fuel injection replaced the carburetor on Escort's base 1.9-liter four-cylinder engine. As before, Escort GT was powered by a high-output version of the four, with multi-point injection. Some shuffling of model designations and the deletion of the LX series meant this year's offering consisted of Pony, GL and GT models. Automatic motorized front seat belts were introduced during the model year. Joining the option list: a fold-down center armrest and split fold-down rear seat.

EXP — FOUR — Ford's tiny two-seater came in two forms: Luxury Coupe with the base 1.9-liter four-cylinder engine, or Sport Coupe with the high-output powerplant. EXP enjoyed a restyling for reintroduction as a 1986.5 model, after a brief departure from the lineup. Rather than a distinct model, EXP was now considered part of the Escort series.

1987 Thunderbird Turbo Coupe

THUNDERBIRD — FOUR/V-6/V-8 — Even though the personal-luxury coupe's profile didn't undergo a dramatic alteration, the sheetmetal was all new this year. So were aero-style headlamps and flush-fitting side glass, as well as full-width taillamps. A new sport model with 5.0-liter V-8 joined the lineup, and the former Elan was now called LX. A 232 cu. in. (3.8-liter) V-6 hooked to four-speed overdrive automatic was the standard powertrain for base and LX models, with V-8 optional. The former three-speed automatic was gone. T-Bird's Turbo Coupe got a boost under the hood from the intercooled 2.3-liter four, which was formerly seen in the Mustang SVO. The Turbo also had Automatic Ride Control, functional hood scoops, 16-inch unidirectional tires, a standard five-speed manual gearbox, and four-wheel disc brakes with anti-locking.

I.D. DATA: Ford's 17-symbol Vehicle Identification Number (VIN) was stamped on a metal tab fastened to the instrument panel, visible through the windshield. The first three symbols ('1FA') indicate manufacturer, make and vehicle type. The fourth symbol ('B') denotes restraint system. Next comes a letter 'P', followed by two digits that indicate Model Number, as shown in left column of tables below. (Example: '20' - Escort Pony two-door hatchback). Symbol eight indicates engine type. Next is a check digit. Symbol ten indicates model year ('H' - 1987). Symbol eleven is assembly plant. The final six digits make up the sequence number, starting with 100001.

1987 Tempo All-Wheel-Drive four-door sedan

TEMP — FOUR — Front-drive only through its first three seasons, the compact Tempo added a part-time four-wheel-drive option this year. "Shift-on-the-fly" capability allowed engagement of 4WD while in motion, simply by touching a dashboard switch. Models with that option, which was intended for use only on slippery roads, got an "All Wheel Drive" nameplate. 4WD models also included the high-output version of the 2.3-liter four-cylinder engine. Power steering was now standard on all Tempos, while the driver's airbag became a regular production option (RPO) instead of a limited-production item. A revised three-speed automatic transmission contained a new fluid-linked converter, eliminating the need for a lockup torque converter.

ESCORT (FOUR)

Model Number	Body/Style Number	Body Type & Seating	Factory Price	Shipping Weight	Production Total
20	61D	2-dr. Pony Hatch-4P	6436	2180	Note 1
21	61D	2-dr. GL Hatch-4P	6801	2187	Note 1
25	58D	4-dr. GL Hatch-4P	7022	2222	Note 1
28	74D	4-dr. GL Sta Wag-4P	7312	2274	Note 1
23	61D	2-dr. GT Hatch-4P	8724	2516	Note 1

Note 1: For the model year, a total of 206,729 two-door hatchbacks, 102,187 four-door hatchback sedans, and 65,849 station wagons were built.

EXP (FOUR)

18		2-dr. Spt Cpe-2P	8831	2388	Note 2
17		2-dr. Luxury Cpe-2P	7622	2291	Note 2

Note 2: Total EXP production was 25,888.

TEMP (FOUR)

31	66D	2-dr. GL Sed-5P	8043	2462	Note 3
36	54D	4-dr. GL Sed-5P	8198	2515	Note 3
32	66D	2-dr. LX Sed-5P	9238	2562	Note 3
37	54D	4-dr. LX Sed-5P	9444	2617	Note 3
33	66D	2-dr. Spt GL Sed-5P	8888	2667	Note 3
38	54D	4-dr. Spt GL Sed-5P	9043	2720	Note 3
34	66D	2-dr. AWD Sed-5P	9984	2667	Note 3
39	54D	4-dr. AWD Sed-5P	10138	2720	Note 3

Note 3: Total Temp production came to 70,164 two-doors and 212,468 four doors.

TAURUS (FOUR/V-6)

50	54D	4-dr. L Sedan-6P	10491/11163	—/2982	Note 4
55	74D	4-dr. L Sta Wag-6P	—/11722	—/3186	Note 4
51	54D	4-dr. MT5 Sed-6P	11966/—	2886/—	Note 4
56	74D	4-dr. MT5 Wag-6P	12534/—	3083/—	Note 4
52	54D	4-dr. GL Sedan-6P	11498/12170	—/3045	Note 4
57	74D	4-dr. GL Wag-6P	—/12688	—/3242	Note 4
53	54D	4-dr. LX Sedan-6P	—/14613	—/3113	Note 4
58	74D	4-dr. LX Wag-6P	—/15213	—/3309	Note 4

Note 4: Total Taurus production came to 278,562 sedans and 96,201 station wagons.

LTD CROWN VICTORIA (V-8)

70	66K	2-dr. Sed-6P	14727	3724	5,527
73	54K	4-dr. Sed-6P	14355	3741	105,789
78	74K	4-dr. Ctrv Sqr-6P	14507	3920	17,562
76	74K	4-dr. Sta Wag-6P	14235	3920	Note 5
72	54K	4-dr. 'S' Sed-6P	13860	3708	Note 5
75	74K	4-dr. 'S' Wag-6P	14228	3894	Note 5

1987 Taurus LX sedan

TAURUS — FOUR/V-6 — Sales of the aero-styled front-drive Taurus began to take off soon after its mid-1986 debut, so little change was needed for the 1987 model year. Base powerplant for the L and MT5 series, and the GL sedan, was a 2.5-liter four, with a 3.0-liter V-6 optional in all except the MT5. Other models had the V-6 as standard, with four-speed overdrive automatic transmission. The MT5 came with a standard five-speed gearbox: L/GL with a three-speed automatic. Mercury's Sables, with similar styling, were all V-6 powered this year.

LTD CROWN VICTORIA LX (V-8)

Model Number	Body/Style Number	Body Type & Seating	Factory Price	Shipping Weight	Production Total
71	66K	2-dr. Sed-6P	15421	3735	Note 5
74	54K	4-dr. Sed-6P	15454	3788	Note 5
77	74K	4-dr. Sta Wag-6P	15450	4000	Note 5
79	74K	4-dr. Ctry Sqr-6P	15723	4000	Note 5

Note 5: Production of 'S' and LX models and basic station wagon is included in basic sedan and Country Squire totals above.

THUNDERBIRD (V-6/V-8)

60	66D	2-dr. HT Cpe-5P	12972/13611	3133/3176	Note 6
61	66D	2-dr. Spt Cpe-5P	—/15079	—/3346	Note 6
62	66D	2-dr. LX Cpe-5P	15383/16022	3176/3315	Note 6

THUNDERBIRD TURBO COUPE (FOUR)

64	66D	2-dr. HT Cpe-5P	16805	3380	Note 6

Note 6: Total production, 128,135 Thunderbirds.
FACTORY PRICE AND WEIGHT NOTE: Taurus prices and weights to left of slash are for four-cylinder, to right for V-6 engine. Thunderbird prices and weights to left of slash are for V-6, to right for V-8 engine.

1987 LTD Country Squire station wagon

ENGINE DATA: BASE FOUR (Escort): Inline. Overhead cam. Four-cylinder. Cast iron block and aluminum head. Displacement: 113 cu. in. (1.9 liters). Bore & stroke: 3.23 x 3.46 in. Compression ratio: 9.0:1. Brake horsepower: 90 at 4600 RPM. Torque: 106 lbs.-ft. at 3400 RPM. Five main bearings. Hydraulic valve lifters. Throttle-body fuel injection. BASE FOUR (Escort GT, EXP Spt coupe): High-output, MFI version of 1.9-liter four above — Horsepower: 115 at 5200 RPM. Torque: 120 lbs.-ft. at 4400 RPM. DIESEL FOUR (Escort): Inline. Overhead cam. four-cylinder. Cast iron block and aluminum head. Displacement: 121 cu. in. (2.0 liters). Bore & stroke: 3.39 x 3.39 in. Compression ratio: 22.7:1. Brake horsepower: 58 at 3600 RPM. Torque: 84 lbs.-ft. at 3000 RPM. Five main bearings. Solid value lifters. Fuel injection. BASE FOUR (Tempo): Inline. Overhead valve. Four-cylinder. Cast iron block and head. Displacement: 140 cu. in. (2.3 liters). Bore & stroke: 3.70 x 3.30 in. Compression ratio: 9.0:1. Brake horsepower: 86 at 3800 RPM. Torque: 120 lbs.-ft. at 3200 RPM. Five main bearings. Hydraulic valve lifters. Throttle-body fuel injection. High Swirl Combustion (HSC) design. BASE FOUR (Tempo 4WD or Sport): High-output version of HSC four above — Horsepower: 94 at 4000 RPM. Torque: 126 lbs.-ft. at 3200 RPM. BASE FOUR (Thunderbird Turbo Coupe): Inline. Overhead cam. Four-cylnder. Cast iron block and head. Displacement: 140 cu. in. (2.3 liters). Bore & stroke: 3.78 x 3.13 in. Compression ratio: 8.0:1. Brake horsepower: 190 at 4600 RPM. (150 at 4400 with automatic). Torque: 240 lbs.-ft. at 3400 RPM. (200 at 3000 with automatic). Five main bearings. Hydraulic valve lifters. Port fuel injection. BASE FOUR (Taurus): Inline. Overhead valve. Four-cylinder. Cast iron block and head. Displacement: 153 cu. in. (2.5 liters). Bore & stroke: 3.70 x 3.60 in. Compression ratio: 9.0:1 Brake horsepower: 90 at 4400 RPM. Torque: 140 lbs.-ft. at 2800 RPM. Five main bearings. Hydraulic valve lifters. Throttle-body fuel injection. BASE V-6 (Taurus LX): OPTIONAL (Taurus): 60-degree, overhead valve V-6. Cast iron block and head. Displacement: 182 cu. in. (3.0 liters). Bore & stroke: 3.50 x 3.10 in. Compression ratio: 9.3:1. Brake horsepower: 140 at 4800 RPM. Torque: 160 lbs.-ft. at 3000 RPM. Four main bearings. Hydraulic valve lifters. Multi-port fuel injection. BASE V-6 (Thunderbird): 90-degree, overhead valve V-6. Cast iron block and aluminum head. Displacement: 232 cu. in. (3.8 liters). bore & stroke: 3.80 x 3.40 in. Compression ratio: 8.7:1. Brake horsepower: 120 at 3600 RPM. Torque: 205 lbs.-ft. at 1600 RPM. Four main bearings. Hydraulic valve lifters. Throttle-body fuel injection. BASE V-8 (LTD Crown Victoria): OPTIONAL (Thunderbird): 90-degree, overhead valve V-8. Cast iron block and head. Displacement: 302 cu. in. (5.0 liters). Bore & stroke: 4.00 x 3.00 in. Compression ratio: 8.9:1. Brake horsepower: 150 at 3200 RPM. Torque: 270 lbs.-ft. at 2000 RPM. Five main bearings. Hydraulic valve lifters. Sequential (port) fuel injection.

CHASSIS DATA: Wheelbase: (Escort/EXP) 94.2 in.; (Tempo) 99.9 in.; (Taurus) 106.0 in.; (Crown Vic) 114.3 in.; (T-Bird) 104.2 in. **Overall Length:** (Escort 166.9 in.; (Escort wagon) 168.0 in.; (EXP) 168.4 in.; (Tempo) 176.5 in.; (Taurus) 188.4 in.; (Taurus wag) 191.9 in.; (Crown Vic) 211.0 in.; (Crown Vic wag) 215.0 in.; (T-Bird) 202.1 in. **Height:** (Escort) 53.3-53.5 in.; (EXP) 50.9 in.; (Tempo) 52.7 in.; (Taurus) 54.3 in.; (Taurus wag) 55.1 in.; (Crown Vic) 55.3 in.; (Crown Vic wag) 57.1 in.; (T-Bird) 53.4 in. **Width:** (Escort/EXP) 65.9 in.; (Tempo) 68.3 in.; (Taurus) 70.6 in.; (Crown Vic) 77.5 in.; (Crown Vic wag) 79.3 in.; (T-Bird) 71.1 in. **Front Tread:** (Escort/EXP) 54.7 in.; (Tempo) 54.9 in.; (Taurus) 61.5 in.; (Crown Vic) 62.2 in. (T-Bird) 58.1 in. **Rear Tread:** (Escort/EXP) 56.0 in.; (Tempo) 57.6 in.; (Taurus) 60.5 in.; (Taurus wag) 59.9 in.; (Crown Vic) 62.0 in.; (T-Bird) 58.5 in. **Standard Tires:** (Escort Pony) P165/80R13; (Escort GL 4-dr/wag) P165/80R13; (Escort GT) P195/60HR15: (EXP) P185/70R14; (Tempo) P185/70R14; (Taurus) P195/70R14; (Taurus GL/LX) P205/70R14; (Crown Vic) P205/75R15; (T-Bird) P215/70R14; (T-Bird Spt) P215/70HR14; (T-Bird Turbo Cpe) P225/60VR16 Goodyear Eagle GT "Gatorback."

TECHNICAL: Transmission: Four-speed manual transaxle standard on Escort. Five-speed standard on Escort GT, EXP, Tempo, Taurus MT5 and Thunderbird Turbo. Three-speed automatic standard on Taurus L/GL. Four-speed overdrive automatic standard on Taurus LX/Crown Vic/T-Bird. **Drive Axle:** (Escort/EXP/Tempo/Taurus) front; (others) rear. **Steering:** (Crown Vic) recirculating ball; (others) rack/pinion. **Front Suspension:** (Escort/EXP/Tempo) MacPherson struts with lower control arms, coil springs and stabilizer bar; (Taurus) MacPherson struts with control arms, coil springs and stablilizer bar; (T-Bird) modified MacPherson struts with lower control arms, coil springs and anti-sway bar; (Crown Vic) upper/lower control arms w/coil springs and stabilizer bar. **Rear Suspension:** (Escort/EXP) trailing arms w/modified MacPherson struts and coil springs on lower control arms; (Tempo) independent trailing four-link with MacPherson struts; (Taurus sedan) MacPherson struts w/parallel suspension arms and coil springs; (Taurus wag) upper/lower control arms, coil springs and stabilizer bar; (Crown Vic/T-Bird) rigid axle w/four links and coil springs. **Brakes:** Front disc, rear drum (power assisted) except (Thunderbird Turbo Coupe) four-wheel discs with anti-lock. **Body construction:** (Crown Vic) separate body and frame; (others) unibody. **Fuel tank:** (Escort/EXP) 13.0 gal.; (Tempo) 15.4 gal.; (Tempo 4WD) 13.7 gal.; (Taurus) 16.0 gal.; (Crown Vic) 18.0 gal.; (T-Bird) 22.1 gal.

DRIVETRAIN OPTIONS: Engines: Diesel 2.0-liter four: Escort (NC). 3.0-liter V-6: Taurus L/GL ($672). 5.0-liter V-8: Thunderbird ($639). **Transmission/Differential:** Five-speed manual trans.: Escort ($76). Automatic transaxle: Escort GL ($490); EXP ($415); Tempo ($482). Auto. transmission: T-Bird Turbo Cpe ($515). Traction-Lok differential: Crown Vic ($100). **Steering/Suspension:** Power steering: Escort/EXP ($235). H.D./handling susp.: Taurus/Crown Vic ($26). Auto. load leveling: Crown Vic ($200). Trailer towing pkg.: Crown Vic ($387-$399).

1987 Escort GL station wagon

ESCORT/EXP CONVENIENCE/APPEARANCE OPTIONS:
Premium Equipment Group. Bumper guards and rub strips, overhead console with digital clock, tachometer, trip odometer and coolant temperature gauge, dual power mirrors, power steering, GL w/gas engine ($496). GL w/diesel engine ($409). Front & rear bumper guards ($56). Bumper rub strips ($48). Overhead console w/clock ($82). Tachometer, trip odometer & coolant temp gauge ($87). Dual power mirrors ($88). Power steering ($235). Climate Control Group; Air conditioning, heavy-duty battery, rear defogger, tinted glass, intermittent wipers; GL w/gas engine, EXP Luxury Coupe ($920). GL w/diesel, GT or EXP Sport Coupe ($893). Air conditioning ($688). Heavy-duty battery ($27). Rear defogger ($145). Tinted glass ($105). Intermittent wipers ($55). Luxury Group; Light/Security Group, front center armrest, cruise control, split folding rear seatback, tilt steering column; GL ($395). Light/Security Group, GL ($91). GT ($67). Front center armrest, Escort ($55). Cruise control ($176). Split folding rear seatback, Escort ($49). Tilt steering column ($124). Convenience Group. Cargo area cover, dual power mirrors, dual visor mirrors, (lighted right), cruise control, power steering, tilt steering column EXP Luxury Coupe ($473). EXP Sport Coupe ($309). Cargo area cover, EXP ($59). Dual power mirrors, EXP ($88). Visor mirrors (lighted right), EXP ($50). Sun and Sound Group. Overhead console w/graphic systems monitor, removable sunroof, AM/FM ST w/cassette, premium Sound System EXP Luxury Coupe ($597). EXP Sport Coupe ($566). Console w/graphic systems monitor, EXP ($56). Removable sunroof, EXP ($355). AM/FM ST w/cassette, EXP ($148). Premium Sound System ($138). Luggage rack ($110). Clearcoat paint, GL & EXP ($91). AM radio ($39). AM/FM Stereo, Pony ($159). GL ($120). AM/FM Stereo w/cassette, AM/FM stereo, Pony ($306). GL ($267). GT, EXP ($148). Cast aluminum wheels ($293). Styled road wheels ($195). Rear wiper/washer ($126).

TEMP CONVENIENCE/APPEARANCE OPTIONS:
Select GL Pkg., Tinted glass, dual power mirrors w/AM/FM Stereo ED ($191). w/o radio ($124). Tinted glass ($120). Dual power mirrors ($111). AM/FM Stereo ET radio ($93). Power Equipment Group. Power Lock Group (includes remote fuel filler and trunk releases), power driver's seat, power windows. 2-door GL. Sport or All Wheel Drive ($560). 4-door GL, Sport or All wheel Drive ($635). LX 2-door ($323). LX 4-door ($347). Power Lock Group, 2-doors ($237). 4-doors ($288). Power driver's seat ($251). Power windows, 2-doors ($222). 4-doors ($296). Convenience Group. Front center armrest. Preimum Sound System, AM/FM ST ET cassette, speed control, tilt steering column; GL ($643). Select GL ($565). Sport GL ($418). LX ($371). All Wheel Drive ($510). Front center armrest ($55). Premium Sound System ($138). AM/FM Stereo ET cassette, GL ($250). LX or Select GL ($157). Speed control ($176). Tilt steering column ($124). Lower accent paint treatment ($78). Air bag, GL ($815). LX ($751). Air conditioning ($773). Console ($116). Rear defogger ($145). Sport instrument cluster ($87). Decklid luggage rack ($115). AM/FM Stereo ($93). AM/FM Stereo ET cassette, GL ($250). LX, Select GL or All Wheel Drive ($157). AM delete, GL ($65 credit). AM/FM ST delete LX or All-Wheel Drive ($157 credit). Sport GL or w/Convenience Group ($315 credit). Styled road wheels ($178). California emissions pkg ($99). Clearcoat metallic paint ($91). All vinyl seat trim ($35).

1987 Taurus LX station wagon

TAURUS CONVENIENCE/APPEARANCE OPTIONS:
Exterior accent group, MT-5 sedan ($91). MT-5 wagon ($49). Automatic air conditioning, LX ($183). GL ($945). Manual air conditioning ($788). Autolamp system ($73). Heavy-duty battery ($27). Cargo area cover, wagons ($66). Digital clock ($78). Cornering lamps ($68). Rear defogger ($145). Engine block heater ($18). Remote fuel door & decklid release ($91), w/remote liftgate release, wagons ($41). Extended range fuel tank ($46). Tinted glass ($120). Illuminated entry system ($82). Electronic instrument cluster ($351). Keyless entry system ($202). Light group, L, GL & MT-5 sedans ($48). L, GL & MT-5 wagons ($52). Diagnostic alert lights ($89). Load floor extension, wagons ($66). Power door locks ($195). Dual power mirrors, L sedan ($96). L wagon ($59). Dual illuminated visor mirrors, L ($116). GL & MT-5 ($104). Rocker panel moldings ($55). Power moonroof ($741). Clearcoat paint ($183). Automatic parking brake release ($12). AM/FM Stereo ET radio ($141). AM/FM Stereo w/cassette, L ($268). GL, MT-5 & LX ($137). Premium sound system ($168). Power antenna ($76). AM radio delete, L ($65 credit). AM/FM stereo delete GL, MT-5 & LX ($206 credit). Rear-facing third seat, wagons ($155). Reclining passenger seat ($45). Power driver's seat ($251). Dual power seats, LX ($502). Others ($251). Speed control ($176). Tilt steering column ($124). Leather-wrapped steering wheel ($59). Paint

stripe ($57). Sliding vent windows ($79). Rear wiper/washer, wagons ($126). Finned wheel covers, L, GL & MT-5 ($65). Locking spoked wheel covers L, GL & MT-5 ($205). LX ($140). Aluminum wheels, L, GL & MT-5 ($390). LX ($326). Styled road wheels, L, GL & MT-5 ($178). LX ($113). Power windows ($296). Insta-Clear windshield ($250). Intermittent wipers ($55). California emissions pkg ($99). Split bench seats ($276). Leather seat trim ($415). Vinyl seat trim ($39).

LTD CROWN VICTORIA CONVENIENCE/APPEARANCE OPTIONS:
Conventional spare tire ($73). Automatic A/C & rear defogger ($211). Autolamp system ($73). Heavy-duty battery ($27). Bumper rub strips ($59). Convenience group; Remote decklid or tailgate release, intermittent wipers, trip odometer, low fuel & oil warning lights; exc. LX ($135), w/Power Lock Group ($85). Cornering lamps ($68). Rear defogger ($145). Engine block heater ($18). Illuminated entry system ($82). Light group ($48). Power lock group, Power door locks, remote fuel door release, 2-doors ($207). 4-doors & wagons ($257). Deluxe luggage rack ($115). Right remote mirror ($46). Vinyl insert bodyside moldings ($66). Two-tone paint/tape treatment ($117). AM/FM Stereo w/cassette ($137). Power antenna ($76). AM/FM radio delete ($206 credit). Premium Sound System ($168). Power driver's seat ($251). Dual power seats ($502). Dual facing rear seats, wagon ($173). Cruise control ($176). Leather-wrapped steering wheel ($59). Tilt steering column ($124). Tripminder computer ($215). Pivoting front vent windows ($79). Locking wire wheel covers ($212). Cast aluminum wheels ($390). Power windows & mirrors ($393). Intermittent wipers ($55). Brougham half vinyl roof ($665). Split bench seat ($139). All-vinyl seat trim ($34). Duraweave vinyl seat trim ($96). Leather seat trim ($418). P215/70R15 tires ($72).

THUNDERBIRD CONVENIENCE/APPEARANCE OPTIONS:
Heavy-duty battery ($27). Electronic Equipment Group; Keyless entry system, automatic climate control, base ($634). Sport, Turbo Coupe ($365). LX ($577). Luxury Light/Convenience Group; Autolamp system, cornering lamps, lighted visor mirrors, illuminated entry system, Light group, base ($461). Base w/Electronic Equipment ($379). Sport & Turbo ($426). Sport & Turbo w/Electronic Equipment ($344). LX ($244). Dual power seats, base, LX & Sport ($302). LX w/articulated seats, Turbo ($251). Power antenna ($76). Digital clock, base ($61). Rear defogger ($145). Engine block heater ($18). Power Lock Group; Power door locks remote fuel filler & truck releases ($249). Dual power mirrors ($96). Power moonroof, base, Sport or Turbo ($841). LX or w/Luxury/Light Group ($741). AM/FM Stereo delete ($206 credit). AM/FM Stereo ET cassette ($137). Graphic Equalizer ($218). Premium Sound System ($168). Power driver's seat ($251). Speed control ($176). Leather-wrapped steering wheel ($59). Tilt steering column ($124). Locking wire wheel covers, LX ($90). Cast aluminum wheels, base ($343). Styled road wheels ($122). Power windows ($222). Intermittent wipers ($55). California emissions pkg ($99). Two-tone paint, base ($218). LX ($163). Clearcoat paint ($183). Articulated sport seats (std. Turbo) ($183). Vinyl trim ($37). Leather trim ($415).

HISTORY: Introduced: October 2, 1986. Model year production: 1,474,116 (total), including Mustangs. Calendar year production (U.S.): 1,317,787 (incl. Mustangs). Calendar year sales by U.S. dealers: 1,389,886 (incl. Mustangs). Model year sales by U.S. dealers: 1,422,489 (incl. Mustangs).

1988 FORD

Escort and EXP started off the year in their former form, but were replaced by a modestly modified Second Series in the spring. For the first time in nearly a decade, the full-size LTD Crown Victoria got a notable restyling. Tempo earned a more modest restyle, while Taurus added some performance with a new engine choice.

During 1987, Taurus had become Ford's top seller, displacing the Escort. In addition to the domestic models, Ford now offered a Korean-built Festiva subcompact, designed by Mazda.

1988½ Escort GT hatchback coupe

ESCORT — FOUR — For the first half of the model year, Escort continued with little change except that an automatic transmission became optional for the base Pony. The diesel engine option was dropped during the 1987 model year. Also during the model year, motorized automatic front shoulder belts were made standard. A facelifted Second Series Escort arrived at mid-year. Changes at that time included new fenders, taillamps, bodyside moldings, quarter panels and plastic bumpers, plus a switch to 14-inch tires. The upgraded GT got a new grille and rear spoiler.

EXP — FOUR Only one model remained for the first half of the model year, the Luxury Coupe, as the Sport Coupe dropped out. A Second Series EXP arrived at mid-year, but this would be the final season for the subcompact two-seater.

TEMPO — FOUR — Restyling of Ford's compact sedans included a new two-slot grille aero-styled headlamps (integrated with parking lamps and side marker lenses), wrap-around taillamps, and new bumpers. The four-door also got mostly new body panels and new window designs, while the two-door changed a bit less. A new analog instrument panel contained a standard temperature gauge. Motorized front shoulder belts automatically pivoted around the seats. Under the hood, multi-point fuel injection was now used on both the standard and high-output 2.3-liter four-cylinder engines. The standard four got a boost of 12 horsepower. All Wheel Drive was now available only in the four-door model. The high-output engine was standard in the GLS series and the AWD this year.

TAURUS — FOUR/V-6 — Performance fans had a new engine to choose from under Taurus hoods this year: a 3.8-liter V-6. Horsepower was the same as that of the 3.0-liter V-6, but the bigger engine developed 55 more pounds-feet of torque. All models except the base L and MT5 sedans could get the 3.8-liter powerplant, which came only with four-speed overdrive automatic transmission. The MT5 wagon was dropped this year, so only the MT5 sedan came with the four-cylinder engine and five-speed manual transmission. L/GL sedans also had the four as standard, but with three-speed automatic. All station wagons (and the LX sedans) had a standard 3.0-liter V-6 with four-speed automatic. Taurus L models had some equipment additions, including a dual reclining split front bench seat, dual power mirrors, trip odometer, electronically-tuned stereo radio, and tinted glass.

LTD CROWN VICTORIA — V-8 — No two-doors remained in the full-size Ford lineup for 1988. The four-door sedans and wagons got a front and rear restyle (including new grille and hood, bumpers with rub strips, and trunk lid). Sedans also gained wrap-around taillamps. Whitewall P215/70R15 tires became standard, along with intermittent wipers, a trip odometer, low fuel and oil-level warning lights, an automatic headlamp on/off system, and front-door map pockets. Base models added a remote-control mirror on the passenger side. Joining the options was the Insta-Clear heated windshield. Both base and LX models were powered by a 150-horsepower, 5.0-liter V-8 engine with four-speed overdrive automatic.

1988 Thunderbird coupe

THUNDERBIRD — FOUR/V-6/V-8 — Multi-point fuel injection replaced the former single-point system in Thunderbird's base V-6 engine this year, boosting horsepower by 20. Inside that engine was a new balance shaft to produce smoother running. Dual exhausts were now standard with the 5.0-liter V-8, which was standard on the Sport model and optional on the base/LX editions. As before, the Turbo Coupe carried a turbocharged 2.3-liter four. Also standard on the Turbo: a five-speed gearbox, anti-lock braking, electronic ride control and 16-inch tires. Sport models switched from a standard electronic instrument cluster to analog gauges, and came with articulated sport seats.

I.D. DATA: Ford's 17-symbol Vehicle Identification Number (VIN) was stamped on a metal tab fastened to the instrument panel, visible through the windshield. The first three symbols ('1FA') indicate manufacturer, make and vehicle type. The fourth symbol denotes restraint system. Next comes a letter 'P', followed by two digits that indicate Model Number, as shown in left column of tables below. (Example: '20' • Escort Pony two-door hatchback). Symbol eight indicates engine type. Next is a check digit. Symbol ten indicates model year ('J' • 1988'). Symbol eleven is assembly plant. The final six digits make up the sequence number, starting with 100001.

ESCORT (FOUR)

Model Number	Body/Style Number	Body Type & Seating	Factory Price	Shipping Weight	Production Total
20	61D	2-dr. Pony Hatch-4P	6632	2180	Note 1
21	61D	2-dr. GL hatch-4P	6949	2187	Note 1
25	58D	4-dr. GL Hatch-4P	7355	2222	Note 1
28	74D	4-dr. GL Sta Wag-4P	7938	2274	Note 1
23	61D	2-dr. GT Hatch-4P	9055	2516	Note 1
90	61D	2-dr. Pony Hatch-4P	6747	N/A	Note 1
91	61D	2-dr. LX Hatch-4P	7127	2258	Note 1
95	58D	4-dr. LX Hatch-4P	7457	2295	Note 1
98	74D	4-dr. LX Sta Wag-4P	8058	2307	Note 1
93	61D	2-dr. GT Hatch-4P	9093	N/A	Note 1

EXP (FOUR)

17		2-dr. Luxury Cpe-2P	8073	2291	Note 1

EXP SECOND SERIES (FOUR)

88		2-dr. Luxury Cpe-2P	8201	2359	Note 1

Note 1: Total production of both series, including EXP, was 422,035 (251,911 two-door, 113,470 four-door and 56,654 station wagons).

TEMPO (FOUR)

31	66D	2-dr. GL Sed-5P	8658	2536	Note 2
36	54D	4-dr. GL Sed-5P	8808	2585	Note 2
37	54D	4-dr. LX Sed-5P	9737	2626	Note 2
39	54D	4-dr. AWD Sed-5P	10413	2799	Note 2
33	66D	2-dr. GLS Sed-5P	9249	2552	Note 2
38	54D	4-dr. GLS Sed-5P	9400	2601	Note 2

Note 2: Total Tempo production came to 313,262 (49,930 two-door and 263,332 four-door.)

TAURUS (FOUR/V-6)

50	54D	4-dr. L Sedan-6P	11699/12731	—/3005	Note 3
55	74D	4-dr. L Sta Wag-6P	—/12884	—/3182	Note 3
51	54D	4-dr. MT5 Sed-6P	12835/—	2882/—	Note 3
52	54D	4-dr. GL Sedan-6P	12200/12872	—3049	Note 3
57	74D	4-dr. GL Wag-6P	—/13380	—/3215	Note 3
53	54D	4-dr. LX Sedan-6P	—/15295	—/3119	Note 3
58	74D	4-dr. LX Wag-6P	—/15905	—/3288	Note 3

Note 3: Total Production was 387,577 (294,576 sedans and 93,001 wagons.)

LTD CROWN VICTORIA (V-8)

73	54K	4-dr. Sedan-6P	15218	3779	Note 4
72	54K	4-dr. 'S' Sed-6P	14653	3742	Note 4
76	74K	4-dr. Sta Wag-6P	15180	3991	Note 4
74	74K	4-dr. Ctry Sqr-6P	15613	3998	Note 4

LTD CROWN VICTORIA LX (V-8)

74	54K	4-dr. Sedan-6P	16134	3820	Note 4
77	74K	4-dr. Sta Wag-8P	16210	3972	Note 4
79	74K	4-dr. Ctry Sqr-8P	16643	4070	Note 4

Note 4: Total production came to 110,249 sedans and 14,940 wagons.

THUNDERBIRD (V-6/V-8)

Model Number	Body/Style Number	Body Type & Seating	Factory Price	Shipping Weight	Production Total
60	66D	2-dr. HT Cpe-5P	13599/14320	3215/3345	Note 5
61	66D	2-dr. Spt Cpe-5P	—/16030	—/3450	Note 5
62	66D	2-dr. LX Cpe-5P	15885/16606	3259/3389	Note 5
THUNDERBIRD TURBO COUPE (FOUR)					
64	66D	2-dr. HT Cpe-5P	17250	3415	Note 5

Note 5: Total production, 147,243 Thunderbirds.

FACTORY PRICE AND WEIGHT NOTE: Taurus prices and weights to left of slash are for four-cylinder, to right for V-6 engine. Thunderbird prices and weights to left of slash are for V-6, to right for V-8 engine.

ENGINE DATA:BASE FOUR (Escort): Inline. Overhead cam. Four-cylinder. Cast iron block and aluminum head. Displacement: 113 cu. in. (1.9 liters). Bore & stroke: 3.23 x 3.46 in. Compression ratio: 9.0:1. Brake horsepwoer: 90 at 4600 RPM; Torque: 106 lbs.-ft. at 3400 RPM. Five main bearings. Hydraulic valve lifters. Throttle-body duel injection. **BASE FOUR** (Escort GT): High-output. MFI version of 1.9-liter four above—Horsepower: 115 at 5200 RPM. Torque: 120 lbs.-ft at 4400 RPM. **BASE FOUR** (Tempo): Inline. Overhead valve. Four-cylinder. Cast iron block and head. Displacement: 140 cu. in. (2.3 liter). Bore & stroke: 3.70 x 3.30 in. Compression ratio: 9.0:1. Brake horsepower: 98 at 4400 RPM. Torque: 124 lbs.-ft. at 2200 RPM. Five main bearings. Hydraulic valve lifters. Multi-point fuel injection. High Swirl Combustion (HSC) design. **BASE FOUR** (Tempo 4WD or Sport): High-output version of HSC four above—Horsepower: 100 at 4400 RPM. Torque: 130 lbs.-ft. at 2600 RPM. **BASE FOUR** (Thunderbird Turbo Coupe): Inline. Overhead cam. Four-cylinder. Cast iron block and head. Displacement: 140 cu. in. (2.3 liters). Bore & stroke: 3.78 x 3.13 in. Compression ratio: 8.0:1. Brake horsepower: 190 at 4600 RPM. (150 at 4400 with automatic). Torque: 240 lbs.-ft. at 3400 RPM. (200 at 3000 with automatic). Five main bearings. Hydraulic valve lifters. Port fuel injection. **BASE FOUR:** (Taurus). Inline. Overhead valve. Four-cylinder. Cast iron block and head. Displacement: 153 cu. in. (2.5 liters). Bore & stroke: 3.70 x 3.60 in. Compression ratio: 9.0:1. Brake horsepower: 90 at 400 RPM. Torque: 130 lbs.-ft. at 2600 RPM. Five main bearings. Hydraulic valve lifters. Throttle-body fuel injection. **BASE V-6** (Taurus LX/Wagons): OPTIONAL (Taurus L sedan): 60-degree, overhead valve V-6. Cast iron block and head. Displacement: 182 cu. in. (3.0 liters). Bore & stroke: 3.50 x 3.10 in. Compression ratio: 9.3:1. Brake horsepower: 140 at 4800 RPM. Torque: 160 lbs.-ft at 3000 RPM. Four main bearings. Hydraulic valve lifters. Multi-port fuel injection. **BASE V-6** (Thunderbird); OPTIONAL (Taurus): 90-degree, overhead valve V-6. Cast iron block and aluminum head. Displacement: 232 cu. in. (3.8 liters). Bore & stroke: 3.80 x 3.40 in. Compression ratio: 9.0:1. Brake horsepower: 140 at 3800 RPM. Torque: (Taurus) 215 lbs.-ft. t 2200 RPM; (T-bird) 215 lbs.-ft at 2400. Four main bearings. Hydraulic valve lifters. Multi-point fuel injection. **BASE V-8** (LTD Crown Victoria); OPTIONAL (Thunderbird): 90-degree, overhead valve V-8. Cast iron block and head. Displacement: 302 cu. in. (5.0 liters). Bore & stroke: 4.00 x 3.00 in. Compression ratio: 8.9:1. Brake horsepower: (Crown Vic) 150 at 3200 RPM; (T-bird) 155 at 3400. Torque: (Crown Vic) 270 lbs.-ft at 2000 RPM; (T-bird) 265 at 2200. Five main bearings. Hydraulic valve lifters. Sequential (port) fuel injection.

CHASSIS DATA: Wheelbase: (Escort/EXP) 94.2 in.; (Tempo) 99.9 in.; (Taurus) 106.0 in.; (Crown Vic) 114.3 in.; (T-bird) 104.2 in. **Overall Length:** (Escort) 166.9 in.; (Escort wagon) 168.0 in.; (EXP) 168.4 in.; (Tempo) 176.5 in.; (Taurus) 188.4 in.; (Taurus wag) 191.9 in.; (Crown Vic) 211.0 in.; (Crown Vic wag) 216.0 in.; (T-bird) 202.1 in. **Height:** (Escort) 53.3-53.5 in.; (EXP) 50.9 in.; (Tempo) 52.7 in.; (Taurus) 54.3 in.; (Taurus wag) 55.1 in.; (Crown Vic) 55.5 in.; (Crown Vic wag) 57.0 in.; (T-bird) 53.4 in.**Width:** (Escort/EXP) 65.9 in.; (Tempo) 68.3 in.; (Taurus) 70.6 in.; (Crown Vic) 77.5 in.; (Crown Vic wag) 79.3 in.; (T-bird) 71.1 in. **Front Tread:** (Escort/EXP) 54.7 in.; (Tempo) 54.9 in.; (Taurus) 61.5 in.; (Crown Vic) 62.2 in.; (T-bird) 58.1 Rear Tread: (Escort/EXP) 56.0 in.; (Tempo) 57.6.; (Taurus) 60.5 in.; (Taurus wag) 59.9.; (Crown Vic) 62.0 in.; (T-bird) 58.5 in. **Standard Tires:** (Escort Pony) P175/80R13; (Escort GL 4-dr/wag) P165/80R13; (Second Series Escort) P175/70R14; (Escort GT) P195/60HR15; (EXP) P185/70R14; (Tempo) P185/70R14; (Taurus) P195/70R14; (Taurus LX) P205/70R14; (Crown Vic) P205/70R15; (T-Bird) P215/70R14; (T-bird Spt) P215/70HR14; (T-bird Turbo Cpe) P225/60VR16 Goodyear Eagle GT.

TECHNICAL: Transmission: Four-speed manual transaxle standard on Escort. Five-speed standard on Escort GT, EXP Tempo, Taurus MT5 and Thunderbird Turbo. Three-speed automatic standard on Taurus L/GL. Four-speed overdrive automatic standard on Taurus LX/wagons, Crown Vic and T-bird. **Drive Axle:** (Escort / EXP / Tempo / Taurus) front; (others) rear. **Steering:** (Crown Vic) recirculating ball; (others) rack/pinion. **Front Suspension:** (Escort/EXP/Tempo) MacPherson struts with lower control arms, coil springs and stabilizer bar; (Taurus) MacPherson struts with control arms, coil springs and stabilizer bar; (T-bird) modified MacPherson struts with lower control arms, coil springs and anti-sway bar; (Crown Vic) upper/lower control arms w/coil springs and stabilizer bar. **Rear Suspension:** (Escort/EXP) trailing arms w/modified MacPherson struts and coil springs on lower control arms; (Tempo) independent trailing four-link with MacPherson struts; (Taurus sedan) MacPherson struts w/parallel suspension arms and coil springs; (Taurus wag) upper/lower control arms, coil springs, and stabilizer bar; (Crown Vic/T-Bird) rigid axle w/four links and coil springs. **Brakes:** Front disc, rear drum (power assisted). **Body construction:** (Crown Vic) separate body and frame; (others) unibody. **Fuel tank:** (Escort/EXP) 13.0 gal.; (Tempo) 15.4 gal.; (Tempo 4WD) 13.7 gal.; (Taurus) 16.0 gal.; (Crown Vic) 18.0 gal.; (T-Bird) 22.1 gal.

DRIVETRAIN OPTIONS: Engines: 3.0-liter V-6: Taurus L ($672). 3.8-liter V-6: Taurus LX, L/GL wagons ($396); other Taurus ($1068). 5.0-liter V-8: Thunderbird ($721). **Transmission/Differential:** Five-speed manual trans.: Escort ($76). Automatic transaxle: Escort GL ($490); EXP ($415); Tempo ($482). Auto. transmission: T-Bird Turbo Cpe ($515). Traction-Lok differential: Crown Vic ($100). **Steering/Suspension:** Power steering: Escort/EXP ($235). H.D./handling susp.: Escort/Taurus/Crown Vic ($26). Auto. load leveling: Crown Vic ($195). Trailer towing pkg.: Crown Vic ($387-$399).

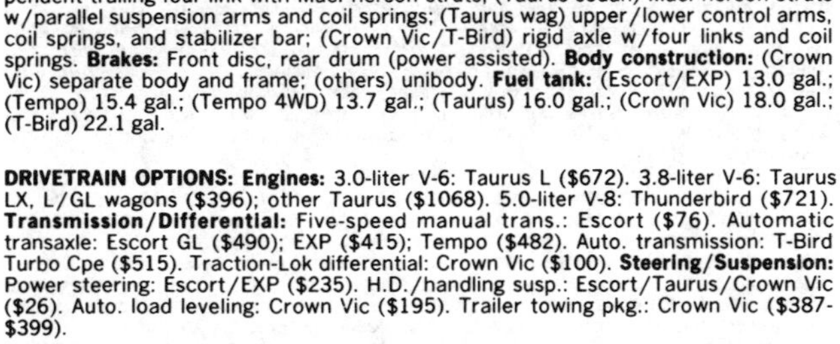

1988 Escort hatchback sedan

ESCORT/EXP CONVENIENCE/APPEARANCE OPTIONS:
EXP Special Value Pkg. ($961). Escort GT Special Value Pkg. ($815). 4 Spd. Man. Transaxle Pkg., Transaxle, 4 Spd Man., Wide Vinyl Bodyside moldings, Elect. AM/FM Stereo, Elect. Digital Clock/Overhead Console, Power Steering, Tinted Glass, Interval Wipers, Bumper Guards, Bumper Rub Strips, Rear Defroster, Instrumentation Grp., Light/Security Grp, Dual Elect. Remote Cntrl Mirrors, Trim Rings/Center Hubs ($582). Auto. Transaxle Pkg., Wide Vinly Bodyside Mldgs., Elect. AM/FM Stereo Radio, Digital Clock/Overhead Console, Tinted Glass, Interval Wipers, Bumper Guards, Bumper Rub Strips, Instrumentation Grip, Dual Elect. Remote-Control Mirrors, Trim Rings/Center Hubs ($823). Sun & Sound Group (EXP) Console w/Graphic Systems Monitor ($56). Flip-Up Open Air Roof ($355). Elect. AM/FM Stereo Radio ($137). Premium Sound System ($138). EXP Lux Coupe ($586). Manual Air Cond. ($688). Frt. Center Armrest ($55). H.D. Battery ($27). F&R Bumper Guards ($56). Bumper Rub Strips ($48). Cargo Area Cover ($70). Two Tone Paint ($159). Elect. Digital Clock/Overhead Console ($82). Rr. Window Defroster ($145). Tinted Glass ($105). Instrumentation Grp. ($87). Light/Security Grp., GL ($91); GT ($67). Dlx Luggage Rack ($115). Color-Keyed Remote-Cntrl. Mirrors ($88). Wide Vinyl Bodyside Moldings ($50). Clearcoat Paint, GL/EXP ($91); GT (Two-Tone) ($152). AM Radio ($39). Electronic AM/FM Stereo, Pony ($206); GL ($167). Electronic AM/FM Cass. Tape, Pony ($343); GL ($304); GT & EXP ($137). Premium Sound System ($138). Speed Control ($182). Split Fold Down Rr. Seat ($49). Tilt Wheel ($124). Trim Rings/Center Hubs ($67). Vinyl Trim ($37). Styled Road Wheels ($195). Interval Windshield Wipers ($55). Rr. Window Wiper/Washer ($126). H.D. Alternator ($27). Frt. Lic. Plate Bracket (NC). Calif. Emissions System (NC). Engine Block Heater ($18). Full Size Spare Tire ($73). TIRES: P165/80Rx13WSW ($73).

TEMPO CONVENIENCE/APPEARANCE OPTIONS:
Preferred Equip. Pkgs.: 2-Door GL ($245); 4-Door GL ($295); 4-Door GL ($1013); 4-Door LX ($748); 4-Door LX ($984). Manual Air Conditioner ($773). Frt. Center Armrest ($55). Rr. Window Defroster ($145). Sport Instrument Cluster ($87). Decklid Luggage Rack ($115). Pwr. Lock Group, 2-Door Models ($237); 4-Door Models ($287). Dual Electric Remote Control Mirrors ($111). AM/FM Stereo Radio w/Cass ($141). Power Driver's Seat ($251). Premium Sound System ($138). Speed Control ($182). Tilt Steering Wheel ($124). Supplemental Air Bag Restraint System, GL ($815); LX ($751). Polycast Wheels ($178). Power Side Windows, 4 Dr ($296). Calif. Emissions ($99). Clearcoat Metallic Paint ($91). Lower Accent Paint Treatment ($159). All Vinyl Seat & Trim ($37). H.D. Battery ($27). Frt. Lic. Plate Bracket (NC). Eng. Block Immersion Heater ($94). Styled Steel Wheels/Trim Rings (NC). P185/70Rx14 WSW ($82).

TAURUS CONVENIENCE/APPEARANCE OPTIONS:
Preferred Equip. Pkgs., L (201A) ($1203); 4 Dr. Gl Sedan (203A) ($1366), (204A) ($1808); 4 Dr. GL Wagon (203A) ($1316), (204A) ($1758); LX (207A) ($559), (208A) ($1495); 4 Dr. MT-5 Sedan (212A) ($972). Elect. Climate Control Air Conditioning, L or GL ($971); LX or Pkgs. 201A, 203A or 204A ($183). Manual Air Cond. ($788). Autolamp System ($73). H.D. Battery ($27). Cargo Area Cover ($66). Electronic Digital Clock ($78). Cornering Lamps ($68). Rr. Window Defroster ($145). Eng. Block Immersion Heater ($18). F&R Floormats ($43). Remote Fuel Door/Decklid Release, Sdns ($91). Remote Fuel Door Release, Wgns ($41). Extended Range Fuel Tank ($46). Illum. Entry System ($82). Diagnostic ($89). Electronic, LX ($239); All Other, exc. MT-5 ($351). Keyless Entry System, w/Pkg. 207A ($121); All Other ($202). Light Group ($59). Load Flr Extension, "Picnic Table" ($66). Power Door Locks ($195). Dual Illum Visor Mirrors L ($116). GL or MT-5 ($104). Rocker Panel Moldings ($55). Power Moonroof ($741). Clearcoat Paint ($183). Auto Parking Brake Release ($12). High Level audio System w Pkg 207A ($167). w/Pkg 212A ($335). All Other ($472). Elect. AM/FM Stereo Search Radio w/Cass ($137). Premium Sound System ($168). Power Radio Antenna ($76). Rr. Facing Third Seat ($155). 6-Way Pwr. Driver Seat ($251). 6-Way Dual Pwr. Seats, LX or Pkg. 204A or 212A ($251); All Other ($502). Speed Control ($182). Tilt Steering Column ($124). Leather Wrapped Strg. Wheel ($59). Paint Stripe ($57). Rr. Window Washer/Wiper ($126). Calif. Emissions ($99). Bucket Seats (NC). Leather Seat Trim, LX ($415); GL & MT-5 ($518); Vinyl Seat Trim, L ($51); All Other ($37). Frt. Lic. Plate Bracket (NC). Frt. Floor Mats ($26). Bolt-on Lux., wheel covers, w/Pkg. 203A or 204A ($21); All Other ($85). Finned Wheelcovers ($65). Custom 15" (Locking) wheelcovers, L or GL ($212); LX, or Pkg. 203A or 204A ($148); Pkgs. 207A or 208A ($34); MT-5 ($127). Cast Alum. Wheels, L or GL ($227); MT-5 ($141); LX, or Pkg. 203A or 204A ($162); Pkgs. 207A or 208A ($49). Styled Road Wheels, L or GL ($178); MT-5 ($93); LX or Pkg. 203A or 204A ($113). Pwr. Side Windows ($296). Insta-Clear Windshield ($250). Interval Windshield Wipers ($55). P205/70Rx14WSW Tires ($82). P205/65Rx15BSW Tires ($65). P205/65Rx15WSW Tires ($146). Conventional Spare Tire ($73).

LTD CROWN VICTORIA CONVENIENCE/APPEARANCE OPTIONS:
Preferred Equip. Pkgs., 4 Dr. LTD Crown Victoria (110A) ($472); 4 Dr. LTD Crown Victoria LX (111A) ($699). 4 Dr. LTD Crown Victoria LX (112A) ($988); 4 Dr. LTD Crown Victoria LX (113A) ($1564); 4 Dr. LTD Crown Victoria & Country Squire Wgn (130A) ($587), (131A) ($1385); 4 Dr. LTD Country Squire Wagon (130A) ($472), (131A) ($1270); 4 Dr. LTD Crown Victoria LX & Country Squire LX Wgn (132A) ($756); (133A) ($1191); 4 Dr. LTD Crown Victoria S (120A) ($352), (121A) ($1085). Auto. Temp. Control Air Cond. w/Pkgs. 110A, 111A, 112A, 130A, 131A or 132A ($66); All Other ($211). High Level Audio System, w Pkg. 112A or 132A ($335); w/Pkg. 113A or 133A ($167); Other Models ($472). H.D. Battery ($27). Frt. License Plate Bracket (NC). Cornering Lamps ($68). Rr. Window Defroster ($145). F&R Color-Keyed Carpet Floor Mats ($43). Eng. Block Immersion Heater ($18). Illum. Entry System ($82). Light Group ($59). Power Lock Group ($245). Dlx Luggage Rack ($115). Vinyl Insert Bodyside Moldings ($66). Two-Tone Paint/Tape Treatment ($159). Elect. AM/FM Stereo Search Radio w/Cass. Tape Player & Dolby Noise Reduction System ($137). Pwr. Radio Antenna ($76). Premium Sound System ($168). Pwr. 6-Way Driver Seat ($251). Dual Control Power Seats w/Pkgs. 111A, 112AS, 113A, 131A, 132A or 133A ($251); Other Models ($502). Dual Facing Rr. Seats ($173). Speed Control ($182). Leather Wrapped Steering Wheel ($59). Tilt Steering Wheel ($124). Tripminder Computer ($215). Pivoting Frt. Vent Windows ($79). Lckg. Wire Style Wheelcovers ($212). Cast Alum. Wheels ($390). Pwr. Side Windows, Incl. Dual Elect. Remote Mirrors ($379). Insta-Clear Windshield ($250). Brghm Hall Vinyl Roof ($665). Calif. Emissions ($99). All Vinyl Seat Trim ($37). Duraweave Vinyl Seat Trim ($96). Leather Seat Trim ($415). 100 Ampere Alternator ($52). F&R Bumper Guards ($62). Remote Decklid Release ($50). First Gear Lock-Out Delete ($7). Frt. Floor Mats (Color-Keyed) ($26). H.D. Blk. Floor Covering F&R ($27). Dual Accent Bodyside Paint Stripes ($61). Dlx. 15" Wheelcovers ($49).

THUNDERBIRD CONVENIENCE/APPEARANCE OPTIONS:
Preferred Equip. Pkgs., Standard Model (151A) ($1273), Premium Sound System Added & Rear Defroster Deleted ($1296), Graphic Equalizer Added & Rr. Defroster Deleted ($1346); Sport (154A) ($852), Premium Sound System Added & Rr. Defroster Deleted ($885), Graphic Equalizer Added & Rr. Defroster Deleted ($925); LX (162A) ($804), Premium Sound System Added & Rr. Defroster Deleted ($827), Graphic Equalizer Added & Rr. Defroster Deleted ($877); Turbo Coupe (157A) (NC), Premium Sound System Added & Rr. Defroster Deleted ($23), Graphic Equalizer Added & Rr. Defroster Deleted ($72). H.D. Battery, 58 Amp ($27). Electronic Equip. Group, Base ($634); Sport & Turbo Coupe ($365); LX ($577). Frt. Floor Mats ($33). Luxury Light/Convenience Group, Base ($472); Base w/Electronic Equip. Grp. ($390); Sport & Turbo Coupe ($426); Sport & Turbo Cpe w/Electronic Equip. Grp. ($344); LX ($244). Dual Pwr. Seats, LX or 151A ($302); 154A or 157A ($251). Pwr. Antenna ($76). Premium Luxury Pkg. w/151A ($832); Turbo Coupe w/157A & Sport w/154A ($669). Frt. License Plate Bracket (NC). Rr. Window Defroster ($145). Eng. Block Immersion Heater ($18). Illum. Entry System ($82). Power Lock Group ($237). Dual Electronic Remote Cntrl. Mirrors ($96). Power Moonroof, Base Turbo Cpe & Spt ($841); LX, or w/Lux./Light Group ($741). Electronic AM/FM Stereo w/Cass. Tape Player ($137). Graphic Equalizer ($218). Premium Sound System ($168). Power, 6-Way Driver Seat ($251). Dual Power Seats, Base ($554); Turbo Cpe or Sport ($502). Speed Control ($182). Leather-Wrapped Strg. Wheel ($59). Tilt Strg Wheel ($124). Bodyside & Decklid Stripes ($55). Lckg. Wire Style Wheelcovers, LX or w/151A (Over Styled Road

Wheels) ($90); Base (Over Luxury Wheelcovers) ($212). Cast Aluminum Wheels, LX, Spt or w/151A ($89); Base ($211). Styled Road Wheels ($122). Pwr. Side Windows ($222). Interval Windshield Wipers ($55). Calif. Emissions System ($99). Two-Tone Paint Treatment, Base ($213); LX, or w/151A (Over Bodyside & Decklid Stripes, or LX) ($159). Clearcoat Paint ($183). Leather Trim ($415). P215/70Rx14WSW Tires ($73). Conventional Spare Tire ($73).

HISTORY: Introduced: October 1, 1987 except (Tempo) November 1987 and (Escort/EXP Second Series) May 12, 1988. Model year production: 1,606,531 total (incl. Mustangs). Calendar year production (U.S.); 1,305,883 (incl. Mustangs). Calendar year sales by U.S. dealers: 1,527,504 (incl. Mustangs). Model year sales by U.S. dealers: 1,471,343 (incl. Mustangs).

1989 FORD

While the subcompact EXP dropped out of Ford's lineup, a new sporty coupe arrived: the Probe, a product of a joint venture between Ford and Mazda but built in Michigan. Also new this year was a totally restyled Thunderbird, including a Super Coupe with supercharged V-6 engine. That SC was named *Motor Trend* Car Of The Year. Taurus also jumped on the performance bandwagon with a ''Super High Output'' engine in its SHO edition, cutting 0-60 time down to the 8-second neighborhood.

1989 Escort GT hatchback coupe

ESCORT — FOUR — Following its mild facelift during the 1988 model year, the front-drive Ford subcompact entered 1989 with little change. With the EXP two-seater gone, the remaining Escort lineup included only the Pony and GT (both in two-door hatchback form only), and the LX (in three body styles). This year's models has gas-charged struts. The base 1.9-liter four produced 90 horsepower, while the GT's high-output version delivered 115 horsepower, with multi-point fuel injection.

1989 Tempo AWD four-door sedan

TEMPO — FOUR — Little change was evident on this year's compact Tempo sedan, which received a notable aero facelift a year earlier. GL models added nitrogen-pressurized shock absorbers. GLS had a new standard front center armrest. All models got an emissions-system warning light. A stretchable cargo tie-down net went into GLX, LX and All-Wheel Drive models.

PROBE — FOUR — Instead of serving as a replacement for the long-lived rear-drive Mustang, the new Probe became a separate model with its own following. Body and interior of the front-drive, two-door hatchback coupe were designed by Ford. Chassis and powertrain were shared with the Mazda MX-6 coupe, which is no surprise since both were produced at the same plant in Flat Rock, Michigan. Three models were available: base and GL, powered by a 110-horsepower Mazda 2.2-liter (12-valve) four; and the GT, with a turbocharged/intercooled variant of the four, rated 145 horsepower. A five-speed manual gearbox was standard; four-speed automatic optional on GL/LX. Standard equipment also included cloth reclining front bucket seats (driver's seat height-adjustable), power brakes and steering, tachometer, gauges, AM/FM stereo radio, tinted backlight and quarter windows, cargo cover, full console, and a digital clock. The LX added full tinted glass, intermittent wipers, tilt steering column (and instrument cluster), power windows, overhead console (with map light), lumbar/bolster adjustments on the driver's seat, rear defogger, and remote fuel door/liftgate releases.

The sporty GT, available only with five-speed, also added front/rear disc brakes, alloy wheels, automatically-adjustable performance suspension, foglamps, its own front/rear fascia, and P195/60VR15 tires on alloy wheels. Both front seats had lumbar adjustment. Only the GT could get optional anti-lock braking.

1989 Taurus SHO sedan

TAURUS — FOUR/V-6 — Most of the attention this year went to the new Taurus SHO, a high-performance model with special dual-overhead-cam 3.0-liter V-6 (four valves per cylinder) that churned out 220 horsepower. The engine was built by Yamaha, and the sole transmission was a Mazda-built five-speed manual (designed by Ford). SHO also included disc brakes on all four wheels, a special handling suspension, dual exhausts, and P215/65R15 performance tires on aluminum alloy wheels. For a distinctive look, the SHO added a set of rather subtle ground-effects body panels, including wheel spats, headed by a front air dam with foglamps. Interior touches included a leather-wrapped steering wheel, analog gauges, special power front sport seats with lumbar adjustment, 140-mph speedometer, 8000-rpm tachometer, a rear defogger, cruise control, console with cup holders and armrest, and power windows. With the demise of the MT5 model, SHO was the only Taurus available with manual shift. Other models had slight revisions to grille, headlamps and taillamps.

1989 LTD Crown Victoria four-door sedan

LTD CROWN VICTORIA — V-8 — Since it enjoyed a significant facelift a year earlier, the full-size rear-drive Ford returned with little change for 1989. Base and LX trim levels were offered, a four-door sedan and station wagon body styles, all powered by a 150-horsepower 5.0-liter V-8 with four-speed overdrive automatic. Standard equipment included air conditioning, tinted glass and automatic headlamp on/off. On the dashboard, an engine-systems warning light replaced the former low-oil indicator.

THUNDERBIRD — V-6 — Still rear-drive and arriving a little later than the other Ford models, the sharply restyled Thunderbird rode a much longer (113-inch) wheelbase but was nearly an inch lower and 3.4 inches shorter than its predecessor. Width grew by 1.6 inches, and the interior gained considerable room. All four wheels now had independent suspension. The Turbo Coupe was gone, so both base and LX 'Birds had the 232 cu. in. (3.8-liter) V-6 engine with four-speed overdrive automatic. Both rode 15-inch tires this year, instead of the former 14-inchers. The LX featured digital instruments (including a tachometer) and speed-sensitive power steering. The base 'Bird had analog guages. All models came with air conditioning and power windows. Cloth reclining front bucket seats, tinted glass, intermittent wipers, dual remote mirrors, a full-length console, visor mirrors, power brakes/steering and AM/FM stereo radio were standard. The LX added a power driver's seat, illuminated entry system, power locks, cruise control, power mirrors, folding rear armrest, lighted visor mirrors, radio with cassette player, leather-wrapped steering wheel (with tilt column) and remote gas door and decklid releases.

The V-8 engine option was gone, but performance fans had a much different choice: the new Super Coupe, with a supercharged (intercooled) version of the V-6 under its hood and a standard five-speed manual gearbox. Aero body flaring and dual exhausts made the SC distinctive, while standard four-wheel disc brakes came with anti-locking (optional on the base and LX models). An Automatic Adjustable Suspension allowed selection of shock-absorber damping for a soft or firm ride. Performance tires were 16-inch size. Inside were analog instruments, including a tachometer and boost gauge, plus power articulated front seats with inflatable lumbar bolsters and adjustable backrest wings. Also on the SC: foglamps, soft-feel steering wheel, power mirrors and a folding rear armrest.

I.D. DATA: Ford's 17-symbol Vehicle Identification Number (VIN) was stamped on a metal tab fastened to the instrument panel, visible through the windshield. The first three symbols indicate manufacturer, make and vehicle type. The fourth symbol denotes restraint system. Next comes a letter (usually 'P'), followed by two digits that indicate Model Number, as shown in left column of tables below. (Example: '90' - Escort Pony two-door hatchback). Symbol eight indicates engine type. Next is a check digit. Symbol ten indicates model year ('K' - 1989). Symbol eleven denotes assembly plant. The final six digits make up the sequence number, starting with 000001 (except Probe, 500001).

ESCORT (FOUR)					
Model Number	Body/Style Number	Body Type & Seating	Factory Price	Shipping Weight	Production Total
90		2-dr. Pony Hatch-4P	6964	2235	
91		2-dr. LX Hatch-4P	7349	2242	
95		4-dr. LX Hatch-4P	7679	2313	
98		4-dr. LX Sta Wag-4P	8280	2312	
93		2-dr. GT Hatch-4P	9315	2442	

TEMPO (FOUR)

Model Number	Body/Style Number	Body Type & Seating	Factory Price	Shipping Weight	Production Total
31	66D	2-dr. GL Sed-5P	9057	2529	
36	54D	4-dr. GL Sed-5P	9207	2587	
37	54D	4-dr. LX Sed-5P	10156	2628	
39	54D	4-dr. AWD Sed-5P	10860	2787	
33	66D	2-dr. GLS Sed-5P	9697	2545	
38	54D	4-dr. GLS Sed-5P	9848	2603	
PROBE (FOUR)					
20		2-dr. GL Cpe-4P	10459	2715	
21		2-dr. LX Cpe-4P	11443	2715	
21		2-dr. GT Cpe-4P	13593	2870	
TAURUS (FOUR/V-6)					
50	54D	4-dr. L Sedan-6P	11778/12450	2901/3020	
55	74D	4-dr. L Sta Wag-6P	—/13143	—/3172	
52	54D	4-dr. GL Sedan-6P	12202/12874	2927/3046	
57	74D	4-dr. GL Wag-6P	—/13544	—/3189	
53	54D	4-dr. LX Sedan-6P	—/15282	—/3076	
58	74D	4-dr. LX Wag.-6P	—/16524	—/3220	
54	54D	4-dr. SHO Sed-6P	—/19739	—/3078	

Note: Taurus prices and weights to left of slash are for four-cylinder, to right for V-6 engine.

LTD CROWN VICTORIA (V-8)					
73	54K	4-dr. Sedan-6P	15851	3730	
72	54K	4-dr. 'S' Sed-6P	15434	3696	
76	74K	4-dr. Sta Wag-6P	16209	3941	
78	74K	4-dr. Ctry Sqr-6P	16527	3935	
LTD CROWN VICTORIA LX (V-8)					
74	54K	4-dr. Sedan-6P	16767	3770	
77	74K	4-dr. Sta Wag-8P	17238	3915	
79	74K	4-dr. Ctry Sqr-8P	17556	4013	
THUNDERBIRD (V-6/V-8)					
60		2-dr. HT Cpe-5P	14612	3542	
62		2-dr. LX Cpe-5P	16817	3554	
64		2-dr. Super Cpe-5P	19823	3701	

1989 Taurus LX station wagon

ENGINE DATA: BASE FOUR (Escort): Inline. Overhead cam. Four-cylinder. Cast iron block and aluminum head. Displacement: 113 cu. in. (1.9 liters). Bore & stroke: 3.23 x 3.46 in. Compression ratio: 9.0:1. Brake horsepower: 90 at 4600 RPM. Torque: 106 lbs.-ft. at 3400 RPM. Five main bearings. Hydraulic valve lifters. Throttle-body fuel injection. BASE FOUR (Escort GT): High-output, MFI version of 1.9-liter four above — Horsepower: 115 at 5200 RPM. Torque: 120 lbs.-ft. at 4400 RPM. BASE FOUR (Probe): Inline. Overhead cam. Four-cylinder. Cast iron block. Displacement: 133 cu. in. (2.2 liters). Bore & stroke: 3.39 x 3.70 in. Compression ratio: 8.6:1. Brake horsepower: 110 at 4700 RPM. Torque: 130 lbs.-ft. at 3000 RPM. Hydraulic valve lifters. Port fuel injection. **TURBOCHARGED FOUR (Probe GT):** Same as 2.2-liter four above, with turbocharger and intercooler — Compression ratio: 7.8:1. Horsepower: 145 at 4300 RPM. Torque: 190 lbs.-ft. at 3500 RPM. **BASE FOUR (Tempo):** Inline. Overhead valve. Four-cylinder. Cast iron block and head. Displacement: 140 cu. in. (2.3 liters). Bore & stroke: 3.70 x 3.30 in. Compression ratio: 9.0:1. Brake horsepower: 98 at 4400 RPM. Torque: 124 lbs.-ft. at 2200 RPM. Five main bearings. Hydraulic valve lifters. Multi-point fuel injection. High Swirl Combustion (HSC) design. **BASE FOUR (Tempo 4WD or Sport):** High-output version of HSC four above — Horsepower: 100 at 4400 RPM. Torque: 130 lbs.-ft. at 2600 RPM. **BASE FOUR (Taurus):** Inline. Overhead valve. Four-cylinder. Cast iron block and head. Displacement: 153 cu. in. (2.5 liters). Bore & stroke: 3.70 x 3.60 in. Compression ratio: 9.0:1. Brake horsepower: 90 at 4400 RPM. Torque: 130 lbs.-ft. at 2600 RPM. Five main bearings. Hydraulic valve lifters. Throttle-body fuel injection. **BASE V-6 (Taurus LX/wagons): OPTIONAL (Taurus):** 60-degree, overhead valve V-6. Cast iron block and head. Displacement: 182 cu. in. (3.0 liters). Bore & stroke: 3.50 x 3.10 in. Compression ratio: 9.3:1. Brake horsepower: 140 at 4800 RPM. Torque: 160 lbs.-ft. at 3000 RPM. Four main bearings. Hydraulic valve lifters. Multi-port fuel injection. **BASE V-6 (Taurus SHO):** Duel-overhead-cam V-6 (24 valve). Cast iron block and head. Displacement: 182 cu. in. (3.0 liters). Bore & stroke: 3.50 x 3.10 in. Compression ratio: 9.8:1. Brake horsepower: 220 at 6000 RPM. Torque: 200 lbs.-ft. at 4800 RPM. Four main bearings. Hydraulic valve lifters. Sequential fuel injection. **BASE V-6 (Thunderbird): OPTIONAL: (Taurus):** 90-degree, overhead valve V-6. Cast iron block and aluminum head. Displacement: 232 cu. in. (3.8 liters). Bore & stroke: 3.80 x 3.40 in. Compression ratio: 9.0:1. Brake horsepower: 140 at 3800 RPM. Torque: (Taurus) 215 lbs.-ft. at 2200 RPM; (T-Bird) 215 lbs.-ft. at 2400. Four main bearings. Hydraulic valve lifters. Port fuel injection. **SUPERCHARGED V-6 (Thunderbird Super Coupe):** Same as 232 cu. in. (3.8-liter) V-6 above, except — Compression ratio: 8.2:1. Horsepower: 210 at 4000 RPM. Torque: 315 lbs.-ft. at 2600 RPM. **BASE V-8 (LTD Crown Victoria):** 90-degree, overhead valve V-8. Cast iron block and head. Displacement: 302 cu. in. (5.0 liters). Bore & stroke: 4.00 x 3.00 in. Compression ratio: 8.9:1. Brake horsepower: 150 at 3200 RPM. Torque: 270 lbs.-ft. at 2000 RPM. Five main bearings. Hydraulic valve lifters. Sequential (port) fuel injection.

CHASSIS DATA: Wheelbase: (Escort) 94.2 in.; (Tempo) 99.9 in.; (Probe) 99.0 in.; (Taurus) 106.0 in.; (Crown Vic) 114.3 in.; (T-Bird) 113.0 in. **Overall Length:** (Escort) 166.9 in.; (Escort wagon) 168.0 in.; (Tempo) 176.5 in.; (Probe) 177.0 in.; (Taurus) 188.4 in.; (Taurus wag) 191.9 in.; (Crown Vic) 211.0 in.; (Crown Vic Wag) 216.0 in.; (T-Bird) 198.7 in. **Height:** (Escort) 53.3-53.5 in.; (Tempo) 52.7 in.; (Probe) 51.8 in.; (Taurus) 54.3 in.; (Taurus wag) 55.1 in.; (Crown Vic) 55.5 in.; (Crown Vic wag) 57.0 in.; (T-Bird) 52.7 in. **Width:** (Escort) 65.9 in.; (Tempo) 68.3 in.; (Probe) 67.9 in.; (Taurus) 70.6 in.; (Crown Vic) 77.5 in.; (Crown Vic wag) 79.3 in.; (T-Bird) 72.7 in. **Front Tread:** (Escort) 54.7 in.; (Tempo) 54.9 in.; (Probe) 57.3 in.; (Taurus) 61.5 in.; (Crown Vic) 62.2 in.; (T-Bird) 61.4 in. **Rear Tread:** (Escort) 56.0 in.; (Tempo) 57.6 in.; (Probe) 57.7 in.; (Taurus) 60.5 in.; (Taurus wag) 59.9 in.; (Crown Vic) 62.0 in.; (T-Bird) 60.2 in. **Standard Tires:** (Escort Pony) P175/70R14; (Escort GT) P195/60HR15; (Tempo) P185/70R14; (Probe) P185/70SR14; (Probe GT) P195/60VR15; (Taurus) P195/70R14; (Taurus LX) P205/70R14; (Taurus SHO) P215/65R15; (Crown Vic) P215/70R15; (T-Bird) P205/70R15; (T-Bird Super Cpe) P225/60VR16.

TECHNICAL: Transmission: Four-speed manual transaxle standard on Escort Pony. Five-speed standard on Escort LX wagon and GT, Tempo, Probe, Taurus SHO and Thunderbird Super Coupe. Three-speed automatic standard on Taurus four. Four-speed overdrive automatic standard on Taurus V-6, Crown Vic and T-Bird. **Drive Axle:** (Crown Vic/T-Bird) rear; (others) front. **Steering:** (Crown Vic) recirculating ball; (others) rack/pinion. **Front Suspension:** (Escort/Tempo) MacPherson struts with lower control arms, coil springs and stabilizer bar; (Probe) MacPherson struts with asymmetrical control arms, strut-mounted coil springs and stabilizer bar; (Taurus) MacPherson struts with control arms, coil springs and stabilizer bar; (Crown Vic) upper/lower control arms w/coil springs and stabilizer bar; (T-Bird) independent long spindle with short/long arms, coil springs and stabilizer bar. **Rear Suspension:** (Escort) trailing arms w/modified MacPherson struts and coil springs on lower control arms; (Tempo) independent trailing four-link with MacPherson struts; (Probe) independent struts, four-bar with single trailing arms, coil springs and stabilizer bar. (Taurus sedan) MacPherson struts w/parallel suspension arms and coil springs; (Taurus wag) upper/lower control arms, coil springs and stabilizer bar; (Crown Vic) rigid axle w/four links and coil springs; (Thunderbird) independent with upper/lower arms, coil springs and stabilizer bar. **Brakes:** Front disc, rear drum (power assisted) except (Probe GT, Taurus SHO and T-Bird Super Coupe) front/rear disc. **Body construction:** (Crown Vic) separate body and frame; (others) unibody. **Fuel tank:** (Escort) 13.0 gal.; (Tempo) 15.4 gal.; (Tempo 4WD) 13.7 gal.; (Probe) 15.1 gal.; (Taurus) 16.0 gal.; (Crown Vic) 18.0 gal.; (T-Bird) 19.0 gal.

DRIVETRAIN OPTIONS: Engines: 3.0-liter V-6: Taurus L/GL sed ($672). 3.8-liter V-6: Taurus GL wagon ($400); other Taurus ($1072). **Transmission/Differential:** Five-speed manual trans.: Escort LX sed ($76). Automatic transaxle: Escort ($490) except LX wagon ($415); Temp ($515); Probe ($617). Automatic transmission: T-Bird Super Coupe ($539). Traction-Lok differential: Crown Vic/T-Bird ($100); T-Bird SC ($21). **Steering/Suspension:** Power steering: Escort ($235). H.D./handling susp.: Taurus/Crown Vic ($26). Auto. load leveling: Crown Vic ($195). Trailer towing pkg: Crown Vic ($387-$399).

1989 Escort LX station wagon

CONVENIENCE/APPEARANCE OPTIONS: (330A) Escort GT Special Value Pkg. ($815). LX Series (320A) 5 Spd Manual Transaxle Pkg incl: Power Steering, Electronic Digital Clock, Overhead Console, Rr Window Defroster, Tinted Glass, Instrumentation Grp, Light Security Grp, Dual Electric Remote Cntrl, Mirrors, Wide Vinyl Bodyside Moldings, Electronic AF/FM Stereo Radio, Luxury Wheel Covers, Interval Windshield Wipers, 2 & 4 DR LX HB ($560). 4 DR LX Wagon ($484). (321A) Automatic Transaxle Pkg. incl: all 320A except Auto. Transaxle instead of 5 Spd Manual 2 & 4 DR LX HB ($938). 4 DR LX Wgn ($863). Manual Air Conditioner ($720). H.D. Battery ($27). Digital Clock, Overhead Console ($82). Rr Window Defroster ($150). Tinted Glass ($105). Instrumentation Grp. ($87). Light/Security Grp. LX ($91). GT ($67). Dlx Luggage Rack ($115). Color-Keyed Electric Remote Control Mirrors ($98). Wide Vinyl Bodyside Moldings ($50). Clearcoat Paint LX ($91). GT (incl Two-Tone) ($183). Two-Tone Paint ($91). AM Radio ($54). Electronic AM/FM Stereo Pony ($206). LX ($152). Electronic AM/FM Cass Tape Pony ($343). LX ($289). GT & Exp ($137). Premium Sound System ($138). Speed Control ($191). Split Fold Down Rr Seat ($50). Pwr Steering ($235). Tilt Steering ($124). Luxury Wheel Covers ($71). Vinyl Trim ($37). Polycast Wheels ($193). Interval Windshield Wipers ($55). Rr Window Wiper/Washer ($126). H.D. Alternator ($27). Frt License Plate Bracket (NC). Calif Emissions System (NC). Eng Block Heater ($20). Full Size Spare Tire ($73). P175/70R14 WSW Tires, LX ($73). Preferred Equip Pkgs: (226A) 2 Door GL ($449). 4 Door GL ($499). (227A) 4 Door GL ($1250). (229A) 2 Dr GLS ($1220). (229A) 4 Dr GLS ($1270). (233A) 4 Dr LX ($863). (234A) 4 Dr LX ($1099). (232A) 4 Dr AWD ($352). Manual Air Conditioner ($807). Rr Window Defroster ($150). Sport Instrument Cluster ($87). Decklid Luggage Rack ($115). Pwr Lock Group 2 Dr ($246). 4 Dr ($298). Dual Electric Remote Control Mirrors ($121). AM/FM Stereo Radio w/Cass ($137). Power Driver's Seat ($261). Premium Sound System ($138). Speed Control ($191). Sports Appearance Group ($1178). Tilt Steering Wheel ($124). Supplemental Air Bag Restraint System GL ($815). LX ($751). Polycast Wheels ($193). 4 Dr Power Side Windows ($306). Calif Emissions ($100). Clearcoat Metallic Paint ($91). Lower Accent Paint Treatment ($159). All Vinyl Seat & Trim ($37). Frt Lic Plate Bracket (NC). Eng Block Immersion Heater ($20). Styled Steel Wheels/Trim Rings (NC). Tires: P185/70Rx14 WSW ($82). Preferred Equip Pkgs: (251A) Tinted Glass, Interval Wipers, Light Grp, Dual Electric Remote Grp, Tilt Strg Column & Cluster, Rr Window Defroster ($334). (253A) Electronic Instrument Cluster. Electronic Control Air Cond, Illum Entry, Leather Wrapped Strg Wheel & Transaxle Shift Knob, Pwr Driver's seat, Trip Computer, Rr Washer/Wiper, Walk-in Passenger Seat, Pwr Windows, Spd Control, Pwr Dr Locks, AM/FM Electronic Cass w/Prem Sound/ Pwr Antenna ($2214). (261A) Anti-Lock Braking System, Electronic Air Cond, Illum Entry, Leather Wrapped Strg Wheel & Transaxle Shift Knob, Pwr Driver's Seat, Trip Computer, Vehicle Maintenance Monitor (Overhead Console), Rr Washer/Wiper, Walk-in Passenger Seat, Pwr Windows, Spd Control, Pwr Dr Locks, AM/FM Electronic Cass w/Prem Sound/Pwr Antenna ($2621). Air Conditioner Manual, w/Pkg 250A, incl tinted glass ($927). Other models ($807). Rr Window Defroster ($150). Pwr Dr Locks ($155). Speed Control ($191). Flip-up Open Air Roof ($355). Alum Wheels w/GL ($290). w/LX ($237). AM/FM Electric Stereo Radio w/Prem Sound ($168). AM/FM Electronic Cass. w/Premium Sound/Pwr Antenna ($344). AM/FM Prem Electronic Cass w/Prem Sound/CD player, Pwr Antenna w/Pkgs 251A, 252A, or 260A ($1052). W/Pkgs 253A or 261A ($708). Frt Lic Plate Bracket (NC). Calif Emission System (NC). Eng Block Heater ($20). GL (204A) ($1749). LX (207A) ($777). (208A) Sedan ($1913). (208A) Wagon ($1513). SHO (211A) ($533). Elect Climate Control Air Conditioning Pkg 202A ($971). SHO, LX or Pkg 204A ($183). Air Cond, Manual ($807). Autolamp System ($73). H.D. Battery ($27). Cargo Area Cover ($66). Cornering Lamps ($68). Rr Window Defroster ($150). Eng Block Immersion Heater ($20). F&R Floor Mats ($43). Remote Fuel Door/Decklid or Liftgate Release ($91). Extended Range Fuel Tank ($46). Illum Entry System ($82). Diagnostic Instrument Cluster ($89). Electronic Instruments LX ($239). GL ($351). Keyless Entry System w/Pkg 207A or 211A ($137). Other Models ($218). Light Group ($59). Load Flr Extension, "Picnic Table" ($66). Power Door Locks ($205). Dual Illum Visor Mirrors ($100). Rocker Panel Moldings ($55). Power Moonroof ($741). Clearcoat Paint ($183). Auto Parking Brake Release ($12). High Level Audio System w/Pkg 204A ($335). W/Pkg 207A ($167). Other Models ($472). Elect AM/FM Stereo Search Radio w/Cass ($137). Premium Sound System ($168). Power Radio Antenna ($76). Ford JBL Audio System ($488). Rr Facing Third Seat ($155). 6-Way Pwr Driver Seat ($261). Dual 6-Way Pwr Seats LX, or Pkg 204A or 211A ($261). Other Models ($502). Speed Control ($191). Tilt Steering Column ($124). Leather Wrapped Strg Wheel ($63). Paint Stripe ($61). Rr Window Washer/Wiper ($126). Finned Wheel Covers ($65). Custom 15" (Locking) Wheel Covers w/Pkg 202A ($212). W/Pkg 204A

($148). Cast Alum Wheels L or GL ($279). LX or Pkg 204A ($215). Pkgs 207A or 208A ($49). Styled Road Wheels GL ($193). LX or 204A ($128). Pwr Side Windows ($306). Insta-Clear Windshield ($250). Interval Windshield Wipers ($55). Calif Emissions ($100). Bucket Seats (NC). Leather Seat Trim LX & SHO ($489). GL ($593). Vinyl Seat Trim, L ($51). GL ($37). Frt Lic Plate Bracket (NC). Frt Floor Mats ($26). Bolt-on Luxury Wheel Covers w/Pkg 204A ($21). Other Models ($85). Tires: P205/70Rx14 WSW ($82). P205/65Rx15 BSW ($65). P205/65Rx15 WSW ($146). Conventional Spare Tire ($73). 4 Dr LTD Crown Victoria LX (111A) ($383). 4 Dr LTD Crown Victoria LX (112A) ($938). 4 Dr LTD Crown Victoria LX (113A) ($1514). 4 Dr LTD Crown Victoria Wgn & Country Squire Wgn (131A) ($1280). 4 Dr LTD Crown Victoria LX Wgn & Country Squire LX Wgn (132A) ($688). (133A) ($1191). 4 Dr LTD Crown Victoria S (120B) ($66). (121A) ($802). Auto Temp Control Air Cond w/Pkgs 111A, 112A, 131A or 132A ($66). Other Models ($216). High Level Audio System w/Pkg 112A or 132A ($335). W/Pkg 113A or 133A ($167). Other Models ($472). H.D. Battery ($27). Frt License Plate Bracket (NC). F&R Bumper Guards ($62). Cornering Lamps ($68). Rr Window Defroster ($150). Color-Keyed Floor Mats, F&R Carpet ($43). Eng Block Immension Heater ($20). Illum Entry System ($82). Light Group ($59). Power Lock Group ($255). Vinyl Insert Bodyside Moldings ($66). Clearcoat Paint ($226). Two-Tone Paint/Tape Treatment ($159). Elect AM/FM Stereo Search Radio w/Cass Tape Player & Dolby Noise Reduction System ($137). Pwr Radio Antenna ($76). Premium Sound System ($168). Pwr, 6-Way Driver Seat ($261). Dual Control, Power Seats w/Pkgs 112A, 131A, or 132A ($251). Other Models ($522). Dual Facing Rr Wag Seats ($173). Speed Control ($191). Leather Wrapped Steering Wheel ($63). Tilt Steering Wheel ($124). Tripminder Computer ($215). Pivoting Frt Vent Windows ($79). Vinyl Roof Delete ($200 credit). Style Lckg Wire Wheel Covers ($228). Cast Alum Wheels ($440). Pwr Side Windows incl: Dual Electr Remote Mirrors ($389). Insta-Clear Windshield ($250). Brghm Half Vinyl Roof ($665). Calif Emissions ($100). All Vinyl Seat Trim ($37). Duraweave Vinyl Seat Trim ($96). Leather Seat Trim ($489). 100 Ampere Alternator ($52). Electronic Digital Clock ($96). Remote Decklid Release ($50). First Gear Lock-Out Delete ($7). Frt Floor Mats (Color-Keyed) ($26). H.D. Blk, F&R Floor Covering ($27). Dual Accent Bodyside Paint Stripes ($61). Dlx, 15'' Wheel Covers ($49). (151B) Standard, Dual Electric Remote Mirrors, Bright Window Mldgs, Elect AM/FM Stereo Radio w/Cass Player/Clock, Spd Cntrl & Tilt Strg Wheel, Pwr Lock Group, 6-Way Pwr Driver's seat, 6-Way Pwr Pass Seat, Styled Wheel Covers, Rr Window Defroster, Lux Light/Convenience Grp ($1235). (162A) LX, Rr Window Defrost, 6-Way Pwr Pass Seat, Cast Alum Wheels w/BSW P215/70R15 Tires Premium Luxury Grp, (Lux Light/Convenience Grp, Floor Mats, Keyless Entry System, Electronic Prem Cass Radio w/Prem Sound, Pwr Antenna) ($735). (157B) Super Coupe Elect AM/FM Stereo Radio w/Cass Player/Clock, Spd Control & Til Strg Wheel, Pwr Lock Grp, 6-Way Pwr Driver's Seat, 6-Way Pwr Pass Seat, Rr Window Defroster (NC). (61E) Premium Luxury Group, Floor Mats, Keyless Entry System, Lux Light/Convenience Grp, Electronic Prem Cass Radio w/Prem Sound, Pwr Antenna ($420). Super Coupe w/Pkg 157B ($761). Anti-Lock Brake System ($1085). Anti-Theft System ($183). Pwr Moonroof Base w/41X & Super Cpe w/o Lux Light/Conv Grp ($841). LX, or Super Cpe w/Lux Light/Convenience Grp or w/Pkg 151B ($741). Clearcoat Paint ($183). Ford JBL Audio System ($488). Compact Disc Player ($491). Locking Wire Style Wheel Covers LX w/41X, or w/Pkg 151B ($127). Base Model w/41X ($212). LX (NC). Calif Emissions System ($100). Leather Trim, LX ($489). Super Coupe ($622). Frt License Plate Bracket (NC), Cold Weather Group, (eng block heater, 72 ampere H.D. battery, 75 ampere H.D. alternator, Rear Window Defroster, Base & LX) ($45). Super Coupe ($18). Cast Alum Wheels w/Upsize P215/70Rx15 BSW Tires w/Pkg 151B ($213). Base Model w/41X ($299). Tires: P205/70Rx15 WSW ($73). Eagle GT+4 P225/60VRx16 BSW all-season performance, Super Coupe ($73). Conventional Spare Tire, Base or LX ($73).

HISTORY: Introduced: October 6, 1988 except (Thunderbird) December 26, 1988 and (Probe) May 12, 1988. Model year production: 1,234,954 (U.S.) and 1,505,908 (total), including Mustangs. Calendar year sales by U.S. dealers: 1,433,550 (incl. Mustangs). Model year sales by U.S. dealers: 1,512,007 (incl. Mustangs).

1990 FORD

Escort and Taurus had been edged out by an import (Honda Accord) as America's best selling car for calendar year 1989, but a new Escort was being readied for the 1991 model year. The sporty Probe hatchback coupe, introduced for 1989, gained a V-6 engine this year for one of its models. Anti-lock braking was available on both Probe and Taurus models. Performance continued to play a strong role in the Ford lineup, with the availability of the Taurus SHO, Probe GT, and Thunderbird Super Coupe.

1990 Escort LX station wagon

ESCORT — FOUR — Not much was new in the Ford subcompact for 1990, since an all-new version was expected for '91. Rear shoulder belts became standard this year, to complement the motorized front belts. The model lineup was unchanged: Pony two-door hatchback, LX in three body styles, and sporty GT two-door hatchback. The GT version of the 1.9-liter four-cylinder engine produced 110 horsepower, versus 90 horsepower for the base powerplant.

TEMPO — FOUR — Little was new this year for the popular compact Ford sedans, except for the addition of standard floormats and footwell and trunk lights. Polycast wheels got a fresh look. As before, two versions of the 2.3-liter four-cylinder engine were available, and Tempo came in three trim levels (plus the All Wheel Drive four-door). A five-speed manual gearbox was standard, except in the 4WD, which had standard three-speed automatic.

PROBE — FOUR — Most significant of the changes for the sporty Ford front-drive coupe, based on a Mazda MX-6 chassis, was the appearance of a V-6 engine choice. Only the GL came with a standard Mazda-built four-cylinder this year. Probe's GT again carried a turbocharged/intercooled four, and LX got the 140-horsepower, 3.8-liter V-6. This year, too, the GT could have the four-speed overdrive automatic transmission instead of the standard five-speed manual gearbox. Four-wheel disc brakes went on the LX, with anti-lock braking optional. Front seatbelts were now motorized, and back seats also held shoulder belts. As for appearance, all Probes got new taillamps and front/rear fascias. New bodyside moldings and cladding adorned the GT, which also earned a restyle for its alloy wheels. Inside the GT was a new soft-feel steering wheel, while other models got leather on the wheel and gearshift knob. Leather upholstery became optional this year, and both LX and GT tires were bigger than before.

TAURUS — FOUR/V-6 — Anti-lock braking joined the Taurus sedan option list this year, and all models got a standard airbag (with tilt steering) on the driver's side. Inside, the instrument panel was revised and now held coin and cup holders. Otherwise, the popular mid-size front-drive sedans and wagons continued as before, in three trim levels plus the performance-oriented SHO. All but the L sedan could have an optional 3.8-liter V-6 engine instead of the 2.5-liter four or 3.0-liter V-6. Both V-6 engines came with four-speed overdrive automatic. SHO continued its special double-overhead-cam, 24-valve version of the 3.0 V-6, available only with five-speed manual gearbox. New to the option list: a compact-disc player.

1990 LTD Country Squire station wagon

LTD CROWN VICTORIA — V-8 — No major changes were evident in the full-size Ford, but quite a few minor revisions appeared. An airbag was now standard on the driver's side, and a coolant temperature gauge went on the revised instrument panel. Map pockets departed from the doors, but the glove compartment grew in size. A split bench seat replaced the formerly standard full bench arrangement, and all back seats held shoulder belts. New standard equipment also included power windows and mirrors, plus tilt steering. Departing from the option list: the Tripminder computer and pivoting front vent windows. Crown Vics came in a dozen colors this year, including five new ones. Sole powertrain continued to be the 5.0-liter V-8 with four-speed overdrive automatic.

THUNDERBIRD — V-6 — Following its striking 1989 redesign, the rear-drive personal coupe changed little for '90 except for the availability of two new option packages (Power Equipment and Luxury Groups). Base and LX models again carried a standard 3.8-liter V-6 with four-speed overdrive automatic. The Super Coupe held a supercharged (intercooled) version of the V-6, rated 210 horsepower, with standard five-speed manual gearbox.

I.D. DATA: Ford's 17-symbol Vehicle Identification Number (VIN) was stamped on a metal tab fastened to the instrument panel, visible through the windshield. The first three symbols indicate manufacturer, make, and vehicle type. The fourth symbol denotes restraint system. Next comes a letter (usually 'P'), followed by two digits that indicate Model Number, as shown in left column of tables below. (Example: '90' = Escort Pony two-door hatchback). Symbol eight indicates engine type. Next is a check digit. Symbol ten indicates model year ('L' = 1990). Symbol eleven denotes assembly plant. The final six digits make up the sequence number, starting with 000001 (except Probe, 500001).

ESCORT (FOUR)

Model Number	Body/Style Number	Body Type & Seating	Factory Price	Shipping Weight	Production Total
90		2-dr. Pony Hatch-4P	7423	2083	
91		2-dr. LX Hatch-4P	7827	2090	
95		4-dr. LX Hatch-4P	8157	2144	
98		4-dr. LX Sta Wag-4P	8758	2177	
93		2-dr. GT Hatch-4P	9842	2519	
TEMPO (FOUR)					
31	66D	2-dr. GL Sed-5P	9505	2418	
36	54D	4-dr. GL Sed-5P	9655	2467	
37	54D	4-dr. LX Sed-5P	10607	2508	
39	54D	4-dr. AWD Sed-5P	11330	2689	
33	66D	2-dr. GLS Sed-5P	10180	2434	
38	54D	4-dr. GLS Sed-5P	10328	2483	
PROBE (FOUR/V-6)					
20		2-dr. GL Cpe-4P	11574	2715	
21		2-dr. LX Cpe-4P	13113	2715	
21		2-dr. GT Cpe-4P	14838	2715	
Note: Probe LX had a V-6 engine.					
TAURUS (FOUR/V-6)					
50	54D	4-dr. L Sedan-6P	12594/13290	2765/2885	
55	74D	4-dr. L Sta Wag-6P	— /13983	— /3062	
52	54D	4-dr. GL Sedan-6P	13067/13763	3049/3169	
57	74D	4-dr. GL Wag-6P	— /14433	— /3095	
53	54D	4-dr. LX Sedan-6P	— /16095	— /2999	
58	74D	4-dr. LX Wag-6P	— /17338	— /3233	
54	54D	4-dr. SHO Sed-6P	— /21505	— /2985	
Note: Taurus prices and weights to left of slash are for four-cylinder, to right for V-6 engine.					
LTD CROWN VICTORIA (V-8)					
73	54K	4-dr. Sedan-6P	17106	3611	
72	54K	4-dr. 'S' Sed-6P	16479	3591	
76	74K	4-dr. Sta Wag-6P	17512	3795	
78	74K	4-dr. Ctry Sqr-6P	17830	3834	
LTD CROWN VICTORIA LX (V-8)					
74	54K	4-dr. Sedan-6P	17743	3660	
77	74K	4-dr. Sta Wag-8P	18262	3834	
79	74K	4-dr. Ctry Sqr-8P	18580	3873	
THUNDERBIRD (V-6/V-8)					
60		2-dr. HT Cpe-5P	15076	3267	
62		2-dr. LX Cpe-5P	17310	3311	
THUNDERBIRD SUPER COUPE (V-6)					
64		2-dr. HT Cpe-5P	20394	3467	

1990 Escort LX four-door hatchback and two-door hatchback

1990 Tempo LX four-door sedan

ENGINE DATA: BASE FOUR (Escort): Inline. Overhead cam. Four-cylinder. Cast iron block and aluminum head. Displacement: 113 cu. in. (1.9 liters). Bore & stroke: 3.23 x 3.46 in. Compression ratio: 9.0:1. Brake horsepower: 90 at 4600 RPM. Torque: 106 lbs.-ft. at 3400 RPM. Five main bearings. Hydraulic valve lifters. Throttle-body fuel injection. BASE FOUR (Escort GT): High-output, MFI version of 1.9-liter four above — Horsepower: 110 at 5400 RPM. Torque: 115 lbs.-ft. at 4200 RPM. BASE FOUR (Probe): Inline. Overhead cam. Four-cylinder. Cast iron block. Displacement: 133 cu. in. (2.2 liters). Bore & stroke: 3.39 x 3.70 in. Compression ratio: 8.6:1. Brake horsepower: 110 at 4700 RPM. Torque: 130 lbs.-ft. at 3000 RPM. Hydraulic valve lifters. Port fuel injection. TURBOCHARGED FOUR (Probe GT): Same as 2.2-liter four above, with turbocharger and intercooler — Compression ratio: 7.8:1. Horsepower: 145 at 4300 RPM. Torque: 190 lbs.-ft. at 3500 RPM. BASE FOUR (Tempo): Inline. Overhead valve. Four-cylinder. Cast iron block and head. Displacement: 140 cu. in. (2.3 liters). Bore & stroke: 3.70 x 3.30 in. Compression ratio: 9.0:1. Brake horsepower: 98 at 4400 RPM. Torque: 124 lbs.-ft. at 2200 RPM. Five main bearings. Hydraulic valve lifters. Port fuel injection. BASE FOUR (Tempo 4WD or Sport): High-output version of HSC four above — Horsepower: 100 at 4400 RPM. Torque: 130 lbs.-ft. at 2600 RPM. BASE FOUR (Taurus): Inline. Overhead valve. Four-cylinder. Cast iron block and head. Displacement: 153 cu. in. (2.5 liters). Bore & stroke: 3.70 x 3.60 in. Compression ratio: 9.0:1. Brake horsepower: 90 at 4400 RPM. Torque: 130 lbs.-ft. at 2600 RPM. Five main bearings. Hydraulic valve lifters. Throttle-body fuel injection. BASE V-6 (Probe LX, Taurus LX/wagons); OPTIONAL (Taurus): 60-degree, overhead valve V-6. Cast iron block and head. Displacement: 182 cu. in. (3.0 liters). Bore & stroke: 3.50 x 3.10 in. Compression ratio: 9.3:1. Brake horsepower: 140 at 4800 RPM. Torque: 160 lbs.-ft. at 3000 RPM. Four main bearings. Hydraulic valve lifters. Multi-port fuel injection. BASE V-6 (Taurus SHO): Dual-overhead-cam V-6 (24 valve). Cast iron block and head. Displacement: 182 cu. in. (3.0 liters). Bore & stroke: 3.50 x 3.10 in. Compression ratio: 9.8:1. Brake horsepower: 220 at 6200 RPM. Torque: 200 lbs.-ft. at 4800 RPM. Four main bearings. Hydraulic valve lifters. Sequential fuel injection. BASE V-6 (Thunderbird); OPTIONAL (Taurus): 90-degree, overhead valve V-6. Cast iron block and aluminum head. Displacement: 232 cu. in. (3.8 liters). Bore & stroke: 3.80 x 3.40 in. Compression ratio: 9.0:1. Brake horsepower: 140 at 3800 RPM. Torque: (Taurus) 215 lbs.-ft. at 2200 RPM; (T-Bird) 215 lbs.-ft. at 2400 RPM. Four main bearings. Hydraulic valve lifters. Port fuel injection. SUPERCHARGED V-6 (Thunderbird Super Coupe): Same as 232 cu. in. (3.8-liter) V-6 above, except — Compression ratio: 8.2:1. Horsepower: 210 at 4000 RPM. Torque: 315 lbs.-ft. at 2600 RPM. BASE V-8 (LTD Crown Victoria): 90-degree, overhead valve V-8. Cast iron block and head. Displacement: 302 cu. in. (5.0 liters). Bore & stroke: 4.00 x 3.00 in. Compression ratio: 8.9:1. Brake horsepower: 150 at 3200 RPM. Torque: 270 lbs.-ft. at 2000 RPM. Five main bearings. Hydraulic valve lifters. Sequential (port) fuel injection.

CHASSIS DATA: Wheelbase: (Escort) 94.2 in.; (Tempo) 99.9 in.; (Probe) 99.0 in.; (Taurus) 106.0 in.; (Crown Vic) 114.3 in.; (T-Bird) 113.0 in. **Overall Length:** (Escort) 169.4 in.; (Tempo 2-dr) 176.7 in.; (Tempo 4-dr) 177.0 in.; (Probe) 177.0 in.; (Taurus) 188.4 in.; (Taurus wag) 191.9 in.; (Crown Vic) 211.0 in.; (Crown Vic wag) 215.7 in.; (T-Bird) 198.7 in. **Height:** (Escort) 53.7 in.; (Escort wag.) 53.4 in.; (Tempo) 52.8 in.; (Probe) 51.8 in.; (Taurus) 54.6 in.; (Taurus wag) 55.4 in.; (Crown Vic) 55.6 in.; (Crown Vic wag) 56.5 in.; (T-Bird) 52.7 in. **Width:** (Escort) 65.9 in.; (Tempo) 68.3 in.; (Probe) 67.9 in.; (Probe GT) 68.3 in.; (Taurus) 70.8 in.; (Crown Vic) 77.5 in.; (Crown Vic wag) 79.3 in.; (T-Bird) 72.7 in. **Front Tread:** (Escort) 54.7 in.; (Tempo) 54.9 in.; (Probe) 57.3 in.; (Taurus) 61.5 in.; (Crown Vic) 62.2 in.; (T-Bird) 61.6 in. **Rear Tread:** (Escort) 56.0 in.; (Tempo) 57.6 in.; (Probe) 57.7 in.; (Taurus) 60.5 in; (Taurus wag) 59.9 in.; (Crown Vic) 63.3 in.; (T-Bird) 60.2 in. **Standard Tires:** (Escort) P175/70R14; (Escort GT) P195/60HR15; (Tempo) P185/70R14; (Probe) P185/70R14; (Probe LX) P195/70R14; (Probe GT) P205/60VR15; (Taurus) P195/70R14; (Taurus LX) P205/70R14; (Taurus SHO) P215/65R15; (Crown Vic) P215/70R15; (T-Bird) P205/70R15; (T-Bird Super Cpe) P225/60VR16.

TECHNICAL: Transmission: Four-speed manual transaxle standard on Escort Pony. Five-speed standard on Escort LX wagon and GT, Tempo, Probe, Taurus SHO, and Thunderbird Super Coupe. Three-speed automatic standard on Taurus four. Four-speed overdrive automatic standard on Taurus V-6, Crown Vic, and T-Bird. **Drive Axle:** (Crown Vic/T-Bird) rear; (others) front. **Steering:** (Crown Vic) recirculating ball; (others) rack/pinion. **Front Suspension:** (Escort/Tempo) MacPherson struts with lower control arms, coil springs, and stabilizer bar; (Probe) MacPherson struts with asymmetrical control arms, strut-mounted coil springs, and stabilizer bar; (Taurus) MacPherson struts with control arms, coil springs, and stabilizer bar; (Crown Vic) upper/lower control arms w/coil springs and stabilizer bar; (T-Bird) independent long spindle with short/long arms, coil springs, and stabilizer bar. **Rear Suspension:** (Escort) trailing arms w/modified MacPherson struts and coil springs on lower control arms; (Tempo) independent trailing four-link with MacPherson struts; (Probe) independent struts, four-bar with single trailing arms, coil springs, and stabilizer bar. (Taurus sedan) MacPherson struts w/parallel suspension arms and coil springs; (Taurus wag) upper/lower control arms, coil springs, and stabilizer bar; (Crown Vic) rigid axle w/four links and coil springs; (Thunderbird) independent with upper/lower arms, coil springs, and stabilizer bar. **Brakes:** Front disc, rear drum (power assisted) except (Probe LX/GT, Taurus SHO, and T-Bird Super Coupe) front/rear disc. **Body construction:** (Crown Vic) separate body and frame; (others) unibody. **Fuel tank:** (Escort) 13.0 gal.; (Tempo) 15.9 gal.; (Tempo 4WD) 14.2 gal.; (Probe) 15.1 gal.; (Taurus) 16.0 gal.; (Crown Vic) 18.0 gal.; (T-Bird) 19.0 gal.

DRIVETRAIN OPTIONS: Engines: 3.0-liter V-6: Taurus L/GL sed ($696). 3.8-liter V-6: Taurus GL wagon/LX sed ($400); Taurus GL sed ($1096). **Transmission/Differential:** Five-speed manual trans.: Escort LX sed ($76). Automatic transaxle: Escort ($515) except LX wagon ($439); Tempo ($539); Probe ($617). Automatic transmission: T-Bird Super Coupe ($539). Traction-Lok differential: Crown Vic/T-Bird ($100). **Steering/Suspension/Brakes:** Power steering: Escort Pony/LX ($235). Variable-assist power steering: Taurus ($104). H.D./handling susp.: Taurus/Crown Vic ($26). Auto. load leveling: Crown Vic ($195). Trailer towing pkg.: Crown Vic ($378-$405). Anti-lock brakes: Probe LX/GT ($924); Taurus ($985); Thunderbird ($1085).

TEMPO CONVENIENCE/APPEARANCE OPTIONS:
Preferred Equip Pkgs: 2 Dr GL (226A) Incl 5 Spd Manual, Air Cond, Rr Window Defroster, Light Group, Power Lock Grp, pwr decklid release, remote fuel filler door, Dual Electric Remote Control Mirrors, Tilt Wheel ($486); 4 Dr GL ($538). (229A) Special Value GLS 5 Spd Manual, Air Conditioner, Pwr Lock Grp, pwr decklid release, remote fuel filler dr, Tilt Strg Wheel, Pwr Driver's Seat, Prem Sound System, Spd Control 2 Dr GLS ($1267); 4 Dr GLS ($1319). (233A) Special Value LX, Auto Transaxle, Air Conditioner, Rr Defroster, Decklid Luggage Rack, 4 Dr LX ($911). Special Value AWD, Auto Transaxle, Rr Window Defroster, Power Lock Grp, pwr decklid release, remote fuel filler door, Tilt Strg Wheel, Pwr Side Windows, 4 Dr AWD ($378). Air Conditioner ($807). Frt Center Armrest ($55). Rr Window Defroster ($150). Spt Instrument Cluster ($87). Light Grp, ashtray, glove box, eng compartment, dome light door switches (incl. rr doors) & map light ($38). Decklid Luggage Rack ($115). Pwr Lock Grp, pwr dr locks, pwr decklid release, remote fuel filler door (NC); 2 Dr ($246); 4 Dr ($298). Dual Electric Remote Control Mirrors ($121). Electronic AM/FM Stereo Radio w/Cass. ($137). Pwr Driver's Seat ($261). Premium Sound System (4 spkrs & amplifier) ($138). Speed Control ($191). Sports Appearance Grp ($1178). Tilt Steering Wheel ($124). Supplemental Air Bag Restraint System GL ($815); LX or GL w/226A ($690). Polycast Wheels ($193). Pwr Side Windows (4 Dr) ($306). Calif Emissions System ($100). Clearcoat Metallic Paint ($91). Lower Accent Paint Treatment ($159). All Vinyl Seat Trim ($37). Frt License Plate Bracket (NC). Engine Block Immersion Heater ($20). Styled Steel Wheels/Trim Rings (NC). P185/70Rx14 WSW Tires ($82).

ESCORT CONVENIENCE/APPEARANCE OPTIONS:
LX Series (302A) 5 Spd Manual Transaxle Pkg, Electronic Digital Clock/Overhead Console, Rr Window Defroster, Tinted Glass, Instrumentation Grp incl. odometer, temp gauge, white graphics, Light/Security Grp incl illum pass side visor mirror, glove box light, cargo compartment lights (incl liftgate light switch), eng compartment light, ashtray light, rr dr courtesy light switch (4 dr only), headlamps-on chimes, remote liftgate release (hb only), Dual Electric Remote-Cntrl Mirrors, Wide Vinyl Bodyside Moldings, Electronic AM/FM Stereo Radio, Pwr Strg, Luxury Wheel Covers, Interval Wipers, 2 & 4 Dr LX HB ($562); 4 Dr LX Wgn ($486). (321A) Auto Transaxle Pkg, all equipment in 320A but Auto Transaxle 2 & 4 Dr LX HB ($965); 4 Dr LX Wgn ($889). Preferred Equipment Pkg GT (330A) Incl HO 4 Cyl Eng, 5 Spd Transaxle, Air Cond, Rr Defroster, Tinted Glass, Light Security Grp, Electronic AM/FM Stereo Radio Cass, Spd Control, Tilt Strg Wheel, Interval Wipers ($829). Air Conditioner ($720). HD Battery ($27). Electronic Digital Clock/Overhead Console ($82). Rr Window Defroster ($150). Tinted Glass ($105). Instrumentation Group (tachometer, trip odometer, temp gauge, white graphics) ($87). Light/Security Grp, illum pass side visor mirror, glove box light, cargo compartment light (incl. liftgate light switch), eng compart. light, ashtray light, rr dr courtesy light switch (4 dr), headlamps-on chimes, remote liftgate release (hb only) LX ($78); GT ($67). Dlx Luggage Rack ($115). Color-Keyed Electric Remote-Control Mirrors ($98). Wide Vinyl Bodyside Moldings ($50). Clearcoat Paint, LX ($91); GT (incl two-tone paint) ($183). Two-Tone Paint ($91). AM Radio ($54). Electronic AM/FM Stereo, Pony ($206); LX ($152). Electronic AM/FM Cass Tape Player, Pony ($343); LX ($289); GT ($137). Premium Sound System ($138). Speed Control ($191). Split Fold Down Rr Seat ($50). Tilt Steering Wheel ($124). Luxury Wheel Covers ($71). Vinyl Trim ($37). Polycast Wheels ($193). Interval Windshield Wipers ($55). Rear Window Wiper/Washer ($126). H.D. Alternator ($27). Frt License Plate Bracket (NC). Calif Emissions System (NC). Eng Block Heater ($20). Full Size Spare Tire ($73). P175/70R14 WSW Tires, LX ($73).

PROBE CONVENIENCE/APPEARANCE OPTIONS:
Preferred Equip Pkgs (251A) Tinted Glass, Tilt Strg Column & Cluster, Rr Defroster, Convenience Grp Incl Interval Wipers, Light Grp Incl glove box light, underhood lights, fade-to-off dome lamp, headlamps-on warning light, Dual Electric Remote Mirrors ($158); (253A) Electronic Instrument Cluster, Electronic Air Cond Illum. Entry, Pwr Driver's Seat, Trip Computer, Rr Washer/Wiper, Walk-in Pass Seat, Pwr Windows, Spd Control, Pwr Dr Locks, AM/FM Electronic Cass w/Prem Sound/Pwr Antenna, Cargo Tie Down Net ($2088); (261A) Anti-Lock Braking System, Electronic Air Cond, Illum Entry, Pwr Driver's Seat, Trip Computer, Vehicle Maintenance Monitor (Overhead Console) Rr Washer/Wiper, Walk-In Pass Seat, Pwr Windows, Spd Control, Pwr Dr Locks, AM/FM Electronic Cass w/Prem Sound/Pwr Antenna, Dual Illum Visor Vanity Mirrors, Cargo Tie Down Net ($2795). Air Conditioner w/Pkg 250A incl tinted glass ($927); Other Models ($807). Rr Window Defroster ($150). Leather Seating Surface Trim ($489). Pwr Dr Locks ($155). Speed Control ($191). Flip-Up Open Air Roof ($355). Aluminum Wheels w/GL (Pkgs 250A or 251A) ($313); w/LX (Pkg 252A or 253A) ($252). Pwr Windows ($241). AM/FM Electronic Stereo Radio w/Premium Sound ($168). AM/FM Electronic Cass w/Premium Sound/Pwr Antenna ($344). AM/FM Premium Electronic Cass w/Premium Sound/CD Player/Pwr Antenna w/Pkgs 251A, 252A, or 260A ($1052); w/Pkgs 253A or 261A ($709). Calif Emissions System (NC). Frt License Plate Bracket (NC). Eng Block Heater ($20).

TAURUS CONVENIENCE/APPEARANCE OPTIONS:
Preferred Equip Pkg GL (202A) 4-cyl. Engine, Auto Transaxle, Air Cond, Spd Control, Remote Decklid/Liftgate & Fuel Dr Releases, dual beam map light, eng compartment light, dual courtesy lights, headlamps-on reminder chime, Rr Defroster, Rocker Panel Mldgs, Paint Stripe, Pwr Dr Locks, 6-Way Pwr Driver's Seat, Finned Wheel Covers, Power Windows ($1688). LX (207A) 3.0L V6, Air Cond, Rr Window Defroster, Stripe, Pwr Dr. Locks, Electronic AM/FM Stereo Radio Cass, 6-Way Pwr Driver's Seat, Pwr Windows, Cast Alum Wheels (styled wheels may be subsituted), Auto Lamp System, F&R Flr Mats, Illum Entry System, Premium Sound System, Leather-Wrapped Strg Wheel ($748). LX Sedan (208A) 3.8L V6, Spd Control, Remote Decklid/Liftgate & Fuel Dr Releases, dual beam map light, eng compartment light, dual courtesy lights, headlamps-on reminder chime, Rocker Panel Moldings, Paint Stripe, Pwr Dr Locks, Cast Alum Wheels, Autolamp System, Flr Mats, Leather-Wrapped Strg Wheel, Elect Climate Cntrl air cond, Anti-Lock Braking System, High Level Audio System, Electronic Instrument Cluster, Keyless Entry System, Pwr Radio Antenna, 6-Way Pwr Dual Control Seats ($3099); LX Wagon ($1714). SHO (211A) DOHC 3.0L V6/5 Spd Manual, Air Cond, Spd Control, Remote Decklid/Liftgate & Fuel Dr. Releases, dual beam map light, eng compartment light, dual courtesy lights, headlamps-on reminder chime, Rr Window Defroster, Pwr Dr. Locks, 6-Way Pwr Driver's Seat, Pwr Side Windows, Cast Alum Wheels, Autolamp System, F&R Flr Mats, Illum Entry Sys., Leather-Wrapped Strg Wheel, Anti-Lock Braking System, High Level Audio System ($533). (212A) DOHC 3.0L V8/5 Spd Man, Spd Control, Remote Decklid/Liftgate & Fuel Dr Releases, Light Grp, Rear Defroster, Pwr Door Locks, Power Windows, Cast Alum Wheels, Autolamp Sys-

tem, F&R Flr Mats, Leather-Wrapped Strg Wheel, Elect Climate Control Air Cond, Anti-Lock Braking System, High Level Audio System, Keyless Entry System, Power Radio Antenna, Ford JBL Audio System, 6-Way Pwr Dual Control Seats, Leather Seat Trim, Power Moonroof ($2724). Conventional Spare Tire ($73). Electronic Air Conditioning, Pkg 202A ($990); SHO, LX, or Pkg 204A ($183). Manual Air Conditioning ($807). Autolamp System ($73). HD Battery ($27). Cargo Area Cover ($66). Cornering Lamps ($68). Rr Window Defroster ($150). Engine Block Immersion Heater ($20). F&R Floor Mats ($43). Remote Decklid & Fuel Door, Sedans ($91); Wgns (Fuel dr only) ($41). Extended Range Fuel Tank ($46). Illuminated Entry System ($82). Diagnostic Instrument Cluster ($89). Electronic Instrument Cluster, LX ($239); GL ($351). Keyless Entry System w/Pkg 207A or 211A ($137); Other Models ($218). Light Grp dual beam map light, eng compartment light, dual courtesy lights, headlamps-on reminder chime ($59). "Picnic Table" Load Floor Extension ($66). Pwr Door Locks ($205). Dual Illum Visor Mirrors ($100). Rocker Panel Moldings ($55). Pwr Moonroof ($741). Clearcoat Paint ($188). Automatic Parking Brake Release ($12). CD Player ($491). High Level Audio System w/Pkg 204A ($335); w/Pkg 207A ($167); Other Models ($472). Electronic AM/FM Stereo Search Radio w/Cass Player ($137). Premium Sound System ($168). Pwr Radio Antenna ($76). Ford JBL Audio System ($488). Rear Facing Third Seat ($155). 6-Way Pwr Driver's Seat ($261). Dual 6-Way Power Seats, LX or Pkg. 204A or 211A ($261); Other Models ($522). Speed Control ($191). Leather-Wrapped Steering Wheel ($63). Paint Stripe ($61). Rr. Window Washer/Wiper ($126). Finned Wheel Covers ($65). Cast Aluminum Wheels, GL ($279); LX, or Pkg 204A ($215). Styled Road Wheels, GL ($193); LX or Pkg 204A ($128). Pwr Side Windows ($306). Insta-Clear Windshield ($250). Calif Emissions ($100). Bucket Seats (NC). Leather Seat Trim LX & SHO ($489). Vinyl Seat Trim L ($51); GL ($37). Frt License Plate Bracket (NC). Frt Floor Mats ($26). Tilt Steering Column-Delete ($76 credit). P205/70Rx14 WSW ($82). P205/65Rx15 BSW ($65). P205/65Rx15 WSW ($146).

LTD CROWN VICTORIA CONVENIENCE/APPEARANCE OPTIONS:
4 Dr LD Crown Victoria LX (112A) Auto OD Trans, F&R Bumper Guards, Rr Window Defroster, Spd Control, Pwr Lock Grp, Electronic AM/FM Stereo Radio Cass, Light Grp ($420). (113A) all equipment in 112A, 6-Way Pwr Driver's Seat, Cast Alum Wheels, Light Grp, Cornering Lamps, Illum Entry System, Leather-Wrapped Strg Wheel ($859). (114A) Auto OD Trans, F&R Bumper Guards, Spd Control, Power Lock Grp, Cast Alum Wheels, Light Grp, Cornering Lamps, F&R Flr Mats (Color-keyed Carpet), Illum Entry System, Leather-Wrapped Steering Wheel, Auto Climate Control Air Cond, High Level Audio System, Power Antenna, Dual 6-Way Power Seats ($1490). 4 Dr LTD Crown Victoria Wgn & Country Squire Wgn (131A) Auto OD Trans, Bumper Guards (NC). Rear Defroster, Spd Control, Power Lock Grp, Electronic AM/FM Stereo Radio Cass, 6-Way Pwr Driver's Seat, Dual Facing Rr Seats ($938). 4 Dr LTD Crown Victoria LX Wgn & Country Squire LX Wgn (133A) all equipment in (131A), Cast Alum Wheels, HD battery, Cornering Lamps, F&R Color-Keyed Carpet Mats, Illum Entry System, Leather-Wrapped Strg Wheel ($779). (134A) all equipment in (133A) except Rr Defroster, Elect AM/FM Stereo Cass, 6-Way Pwr Driver's Seat, PLUS Auto Climate Control Air Cond, High Level Audio, Pwr Radio Antenna, Dual 6-Way Power Seats ($1117). Auto Temp Air Conditioner w/Pkgs 112A, 113A, 131A or 133A ($66); Other Models ($216). HD Battery ($27). Frt. License Plate Bracket (NC). F&R Bumper Guards ($62). Cornering Lamps ($68). Rr Window Defroster ($150). F&R Color-Keyed Carpet Floor Mats ($43). Eng Block Immersion Heater ($20). Illuminated Entry System ($82). Light Group, dual beam map light, dual courtesy lights, eng compartment light ($59). Pwr Lock Group, pwr dr locks, pwr mirrors on base, remote control decklid release on sdn, pwr doorgate lock on wgn ($255). Vinyl Insert Bodyside Moldings ($66). Clearcoat Paint ($230). Two-Tone Paint/Tape Treatment ($159). High Level Audio System w/Pkg 112A, 113A, 131A or 133A ($335); Other Models ($472). Electronic AM/FM Stereo Search Radio w/Cass Player ($137). Pwr Radio Antenna ($76). Premium Sound System ($168). 6-Way Pwr Driver's Seat ($261). Dual 6-Way Power Seats w/Pkgs 113A, 131A or 133A ($261); Other Models ($522). Dual Facing Rear Seats ($173). Speed

Control ($191). Leather-Wrapped Steering Wheel ($63). Vinyl Roof Delete ($200 credit). Locking Wire Style Wheel Covers ($228). Cast Aluminum Wheels ($440). Insta-Clear Windshield ($250). Brghm Half Vinyl Roof ($665). Calif Emissions ($100). All-Vinyl Seat Trim ($37). Duraweave Vinyl Seat Trim ($96). Leather Seat Trim ($489).

1990 Thunderbird SC Coupe

THUNDERBIRD CONVENIENCE/APPEARANCE OPTIONS:
Preferred Equipment Pkg (151A) Standard Electronic AM/FM Stereo Radio w/Cass Player/Clock, Rr Window Defroster, 6-Way Pwr Pass Seat, Pwr Lock Grp, 6-Way Pwr Driver's Seat, Frt Flr Mats, Keyless Entry, Luxury Group incl Bright Window Mldgs, Spd Control & Tilt Strg Wheel, Dual Electric Remote Mirrors, Styled Road Wheel Covers, Luxury Light Convenience Grp, Cast Alum Wheels w/P215/70R15 BSW Tires ($1288). LX (155A) Rear Defroster, 6-Way Pwr Pass Seat, Keyless Entry System, Electronic Premium Radio Cass w/Prem Sound, Pwr Antenna, Frt Flr Mats, Luxury Grp incl Bright Window Mldgs, Spd control & Tilt Strg Wheel, Dual Electric Remote Mirrors, Styled Road Wheel Covers, Luxury Light/Convenience Grp, Cast Alum Wheels w/P215/70R15 BSW Tires ($819). Anti-Theft System ($183). Keyless Entry Base Model w/o Luxury Grp, or Super Cpe w/o Lux/Light Convenience Grp ($219); LX, Base w/Luxury Grp, or Super Cpe w/Luxury Light/Convenience Grp ($137). Frt. Carpeted Floor Mats ($33). Luxury Light/Convenience Grp (Cornering Lamps, Dual Illum Visor Vanity Mirrors, Illum Entry System, Autolamp System, Auto Day/Night Mirror, Vehicle Maintenance Monitor) ($426). Pwr Moonroof, Super Coupe w/o Luxury Light/Convenience Grp ($841); Base, LX or Super Coupe w/Luxury Light/Convenience Grp ($741). Clearcoat Paint ($188). Electronic Premium Radio Cass w/Premium Sound, Base Model w/o Pkg 151A, Super Cpe w/o Pkg 157A ($442); w/Pkg 151A or 157A ($305). Ford JBL Audio System ($488). Compact Disc Player ($491). Power Antenna ($76). Calif Emissions System ($100). Leather Seating Surfaces Trim, LX ($489); Super Coupe ($622). Frt License Plate Bracket (NC). Cold Weather Grp, eng block heater, H.D. battery, h.d. alternator, rr window defroster, base model w/o 151A, LX w/o 155A or Super Cpe w/Manual Trans & w/o 157A ($195); Super Cpe w/Auto Trans & w/o 157A ($168); Pkgs 151A, 155A, or Super Cpe w/Pkg 157A & Manual Trans ($45); Super Cpe w/Pkg 157A & Auto Trans ($18). Locking Wire Wheel Covers, Base Model w/Pkg 151A ($143); Base w/o 151A ($228). LX w/Pkg 155A & P205/70Rx15 WSW Tires (NC). Cast Alum Wheels w/P215/70Rx15 BSW Tires, Base Model w/Pkg 151A ($213); w/o Pkg 151A ($298). P205/70Rx15 WSW LX & Base ($73). Eagle GT+4 P225/60Rx16 95V All-Season Perf, Super Coupe ($73). Conventional Spare Tires, Base or LX Models ($73).

MUSTANG
1964½-1975

What a coup! to produce an extremely popular car, with virtually no competition. That is exactly what Ford did when they began marketing the Mustang in April 1964. After the record-breaking success of the compact Falcon, Ford saw the need for a small sporty car in the lower price range — a working man's Thunderbird, perhaps.

---

by R. Perry Zavitz
Data compiled by John R. Smith

So, with relatively little effort, a new car was concocted using the Falcon's chassis and many of its components. This Mustang was introduced in mid-1964. The best time to introduce a new car is in the spring. Interest in new cars peaks then. Unlike the fall, there is not the confusion of a profusion of new models.

The 1964½ Mustang, officially considered an early 1965 model, came in a spunky-looking little hardtop coupe and convertible. Its wheelbase was 108 inches, overall length 181.6 inches and weight was just under 2,500 pounds. Base price was $2368 for the hardtop.

The closest competition already on the market was the Corvair Monza Spyder at $2599. The Mustang's standard powerplant was a 170 cubic inch 101 horsepower Six. Admittedly, that was anemic compared to the Spyder's 150 horsepower. But for just a few bucks extra, a 195 horsepower 289 cubic inch V-8 was optional in the Mustang. That was where Ford had the drop on Chevrolet. Virtually any Ford-built engine could be slipped under the Mustang hood. The Corvair was stuck with no such choice because of its flat-Six motor and rear mounting.

The Mustang was an instant hit. So great was its popularity, that the Dearborn factory (shared by Falcon) was not sufficient to meet the demand for new Mustangs. In July, additional production was begun at Ford's San Jose plant. Soon after that, the Falcon assembly line at the Metuchen, N.J., plant was resituated to accommodate Mustang production as well. History books are filled with instances where cars were extremely popular on introduction, but lack of finances and/or production capacity cooled public interest. When the problems were eventually overcome, the buyers were gone. The Mustang is the most outstanding exception to that sad fate.

By the end of 1964, Mustang had scored 263,434 sales. Despite its late start, the Mustang was outsold in the calendar year only by Impala, Galaxie 500, Bel Air and Chevelle. It even surpassed the Falcon, from which it was derived.

When the other Ford lines were altered for 1965, practically no changes were made to the Mustang. The standard six became the larger 200 cubic inch 120 horsepower motor. Only about 2.7 percent of 1964 Mustangs had the six, which grew to over 35 percent popularity in the 1965 models. ther rest, of course, were V-8s. The standard V-8 was the 200 horsepower edition of the "289" engine. Options included 225 horsepower and 271 horsepower versions of the same engine.

A fastback body called the 2+2 was added to the hardtop and convertible choice. The 2+2 was not a hardtop in the sense of having pillarless styling, because it had no rear side windows. In the area where such windows are normally expected there was a set of louvers, used as the outlet for the flow-through ventilation.

Mustangs could be loaded with all the popular power accessories. Automatic or four-speed stick shift transmissions were on the option list, as well as power brakes, power steering and air-conditioning.

On April 17, 1965, the Mustang celebrated its first birthday. It took the cake by setting a new world record of over 418,000 sales in its first year on the market for a new model. It exceeded the previous record set by the Falcon, by about 1,000. It is good to remember that both these achievements came from the same company which, just a few years earlier, made a spectacular blunder with the Edsel.

During calendar 1965, Mustang racked up a total of 518,252 registrations. It was second only to the Chevrolet Impala and almost equalled all models of Dodge combined.

For 1966, again, little change was made. A revised instrument panel, less like the Falcon's, was used. The grille, still the same shape, used horizontal bars. The bright accents were gone, except the horizontal strip on those Mustangs with the $152 GT option. That accessory package (it was not a model) included clear lens fog lights mounted in the outer ends of the grille. The GT also featured racing stripes along the body sills. Only the 225 horsepower or 271 horsepower engines were available with the GT. Faster steering, stiffer suspension and front disc brakes were mechanical features standard on the GTs. Despite the emphasis on, and general trend toward V-8s, only 58 percent of the 1966 Mustangs were so powered — the lowest percentage in marque history.

Production of the 1966 Mustang reached an all-time peak of 607,568. By model year's end, there had been a total of 1,288,5567 Mustangs made.

For 1967, competition in the so-called pony car market was noticeably stiffer. The Mustang had caught other companies unprepared. Only the Plymouth Barracuda (introduced almost simultaneously with the Mustang) and the Dodge Charger could be considered, more or less, in the same class as Mustang. Mercury introduced its version, Cougar, for 1967. Chevrolet made no attempt to respond to the Mustang with the Corvair Monza Spyder, choosing instead to develop an entirely new car for 1967, the Camaro. The Firebird was Pontiac's version of the Camaro, brought out in mid-1967.

An all-new Mustang body was used on the 1967 models. It was said that the original dies were worn-out after making nearly 1.3 million copies, but competition, no doubt, was a major factor in the redesign. Styling, however, stayed almost the same. That was a wise move, because a big change in appearance could have hurt the Mustang's obvious appeal when there were other ponies to pick. The same three body types remained. Also the same engine availibities were offered, plus a big 320 horsepower version of the 390 'cube' Thunderbird V-8. The GT option was obtainable with any V-8 Mustang, which meant some 70 percent of all 1967 editions. Nearly 16 percent of the Mustangs that year had factory air-conditioning.

Production of the 1967 models dropped over 22 percent, to 472,121 units, due to a smaller total Ford produc-

1965 Mustang.

tion that year and increased competition. However, Mustang accounted for 6.2 percent of all 1967 cars built in the United States. Mustang production amounted to slightly more than twice American Motors' total production that year. In the pony car market, Mustang corralled 42.5 percent.

1968 Mustang Sportsroof coupe.

Only subtle appearance changes were made to the 1968 Mustang. The GT option included a choice of stripes. Either the rocker panel type or a reflecting "C" stripe was offered. The latter widened along the front fender ridge, crossed the door to the rear quarter panel, then swept around the depression ahead of the rear wheel and tapered along the bottom of the door.

Some new engine options were offered in 1968. The six and standard V-8 remained, but were down to 115 and 195 horsepower respectively. Optional V-8s included a "302" rated at 230 horsepower; a "390" developing 280 or 325 horsepower and a "427" with 390 horsepower V-8 as well as a 428 cubic inch 335 horsepower job. Seven choices!

Production fell, again in the 1968 season, to 317,404. Mustang accounted for only 3.8 percent of the industry total. It had slipped from second place, in production for 1965, to seventh rank for 1967, but it still remained leader of the pony pack.

A new body for the 1969 kept the Mustang image, but the small appearance changes all seemed to miss the familiar Mustang mark, regretfully. Dual headlights were used, with the outer pair in the fenders. The high-beam inner set were located in the grille ends.

Two new models were added. The Grande was a dressed-up edition of the hardtop. Vinyl roof and a plush interior were two of its standard features. It was priced $231 above the normal hardtop, comparably equipped. The Mach I was a variation of the fastback, now called Sportsroof. Beginning with the 1969 models, the Mustang fastbacks were true hardtops. The rear quarter louvers were gone and more glass area, by way of a small window, abutted the door window.

The Mach I was identifiable by special paint stripes along the sides and across the integral rear spoiler. Only the five optional V-8s were obtainable in the Mach I. They were the 250 and 290 horsepower versions of the 351 cubic inch job; the 320 horsepower 390 "cuber" and the 335 horsepower "428" V-8 with standard carburetion or ram-jet. The latter, the Cobra-Jet Ram Air engine, was quite evident, even in a parked Mustang. The air intake protruded through a large hole in the hood. It was latter called the "shaker" hood.

At the tame end of the engine options, it should be noted that Ford's 250 cubic inch 155 horsepower six-cylinder motor was available for the first time in the Mustang. The standard Six, optional Six and standard 302 cubic inch 220 horsepower V-8 could not be had in the Mach I.

V-8 power was installed in 81.5 percent of the 1969 Mustangs. Automatic transmission installations were running just over 71 percent, but the four-speed stick shift options (a choice of a wide or close-ratio) were found in nearly 11 percent — a record high for Mustang. Power disc brakes were featured on 40.5 percent and power steering on nearly 66 percent of the 1969 Mustangs — both options showing increased acceptance. Nevertheless, total production was down. The most potent powerplant for the Mustang was the 429 V-8, rated at 375 horsepower. Imagine 375 horses to pull a 3,000 pound car! Mustang was extending itself from the fancy little runabout to an all-out performance bomb. Oh yes, the sedate Sixes were still available, but the Mustang also stressed "GO!" The Boss 302 listed for $3720, which was $999 more than the base two-door hotchback hardtop.

A restyled body with a different-looking front end appeared on the 1971 Mustang. The car was slightly lower because of a flatter roof shape. The same six models were available, except the Boss 302 which was renamed Boss

351 — a change necessitated by the 351 cubic inch 330 horsepower motor it used.

Further emphasis on performance was evident by the omission of the "200" six. The standard engine became the 250 cubic inch 145 horsepower six. Standard V-8 was the "302" at 210 horsepower. Options were 240 horsepower, 285 horsepower and 330 horsepower versions of the "351" V-8 and the regular or ram-jet 429 V-8s, both rated at 370 horsepower.

For 1973 the big news in Mustangland was a ragtop, which is noteworthy because it was the final convertible to bear the Ford name. There were 16,302 Mustang ragtops built that model year. Total 1973 Mustang production was up nearly eight percent, to 134,867.

During the 10 Mustang model years (not lumping 1964 with 1965) nearly three million cars were built in an interesting variety, from adequate coupes to road scorching racers. For collectors interested in Ford or specialty type cars, Mustangs are still around awaiting a good home. They can be had with virtually any degree of motor potency, in hardtops, convertibles or fastbacks, with just about any contemporary power accessory. (At the last, over 56 percent of them had factory air-conditioning, nearly 78 percent had power disc brakes and almost 93 percent had power steering.)

Luxury at an affordable price helped make the Mustang so phenomenally popular with the new car buyer. That will probably also hold true for the collector, now, and for some time to come.

1964½ MUSTANG

1964-1/2 Ford Mustang, 2-dr convertible, V-8

1964½ MUSTANG—(ALL ENGINES)—The biggest news for 1964 was not the restyled Galaxie, Fairlane, Falcon or Thunderbird, but, rather, the later introduction of a small, sporty car which caught the rest of the automotive industry totally off guard and caught the hearts of the American car buying public; the Ford Mustang. The Mustang was the mid-year model that set records which have yet to be broken. It combined sporty looks, economy and brisk performance in a package which had a base price of $2368. Mustangs could be equipped to be anything from absolute economy cars, to luxury sports cars. The Mustang, with its lengthened and extended hood, shortened rear deck, sculptured body panels and sporty bucket seats provided a family-size sedan for grocery-getting mothers; an appearance for those people who yearned for another two-seat Thunderbird and plenty of power and handling options for the performance Ford enthusiast. So successful was the Mustang, that a whole assortment of similar cars, by competitive manufacturers, came to be known as 'Pony Cars' or, in other words, cars in the original Mustang image. Mustangs came powered by everything from the very tame 101 horsepower, 170 cubic inch six-cylinder engine, to a wild, solid-lifter high-performance 289 cubic inch V-8, sporting 271 horsepower (and available only with the four-speed manual transmission). The basic standard equipment package found on all 1964-1/2 Mustangs included three-speed manual transmission with floor lever controls; front bucket seats; padded instrument panel; full wheel covers; cloth and vinyl (hardtop) or all-vinyl upholstery; color-keyed carpeting; Sports steering wheel; cigarette lighter; door courtesy lights; glovebox light; and heater and defroster. The original base powerplants were the 170 cubic inch Six or the 260 cubic inch V-8. In the fall of 1964, the 200 cubic inch Six or the 289 cubic inch V-8 became the standard powerplants in the six and eight-cylinder Mustang lines, respectively.

VEHICLE I.D. NUMBERS: Vehicle Identification Numbers and other important encoded information will be found on the Ford Motor Company data plate, located on the rear edge of the left front door. The data plate contains an upper row of codes that reveal body and trim information, plus (at center level) a Vehicle Warranty Number, that reveals other important data. In the upper row, the first three symbols are a body code with '65A' designating hardtop coupe and '76A' designating convertible. The fourth symbol is the paint code, as follows: 'A' – Raven Black; 'B' – Pagoda Green; 'D' – Dynasty Green; 'F' – Guardsman Blue; 'J' – Rangoon Red; 'K' – Silversmoke Gray; 'M' – Wimbledon White; 'P' – Prarie Bronze; 'S' – Cascade Green; 'V' – Sunlight Yellow; 'X' – Vintage Burgandy; 'Y' – Skylight Blue; 'Z' – Chantilly Beige and 'V' – Poppy Red. The next pair of symbols are the trim code. Many different interior trims, too numerous to catalog here, were available. The next group of symbols consisted of two numbers and a letter, which represent the assembly date code. The numbers give the day (i.e. '01' – first day) and the letter designates month of year, following normal progression (i.e. 'A' – January; 'B' – February, etc.), except that the letter 'I' is skipped. The next group of symbols is the DSO (district sales office) code, which is relatively unimportant to collectors. This is followed by a number or letter designating the axle ratio code. A number indicates conventional axle and a letter indicates Equa-Lock. The codes are as follows: '1' or 'A' – 3.00:1; '3' or 'C' – 3.20:1; '4' or 'D' – 3.25:1; '5' or 'E' – 3.50:1; '6' or 'F' – 2.80:1; '7' or 'G' – 3.80:1; '8' or 'H' – 3.89:1 and '9' or 'I' – 4.11:1. The final code on the top row of symbols is a transmission code, as follows: '1' – three-speed manual; '5' – four-speed manual and '6' – C-4 Dual-Range automatic. The first symbol in the Vehicle Warranty Number is a '5' designating 1965 model year (all 1964-1/2 Mustangs were considered 1965 models). The second symbol is a letter designating the assembly point, as follows: Atlanta (A); Dallas (D); Mahwah (E); Dearborn (F); Chicago (G); Lorain (H); Los Angeles (J); Kansas City (K); Michigan Truck (L); Norfolk (N); Twin Cities (P); San Jose (R); Pilot Plant (S); Metuchen (T); Louisville (U); Wayne (W); Wixom (Y) and St. Louis (Z). The next two symbols are the Body Serial Number and agree with the numbers listed in the second column of the specifications charts below (i.e. '07' – two-door hardtop). The fifth symbol is an engine code, which is listed with the engine specifications below. The next group of symbols is the consecutive unit number, beginning with 100001 and up at each factory.

MUSTANG SERIES

Model Number	Body/Style Number	Body Type & Seating	Factory Price	Shipping Weight	Production Total
NA	07	2-dr HT Spt Cpe-4P	2368	2449	97,705
NA	08	2-dr Conv-4P	2614	2615	28,833

PRODUCTION NOTE: Total series output was 121,538 units. In rounded-off figures, 32,700 were Sixes and 88,900 were V-8s.

MUSTANG CHASSIS FEATURES: Wheelbase: 108 inches. Overall length: 181.6 inches. Tires: (with V-8) 7.00 x 13 four-ply tubeless; (with high-performance '289' V-8) 7.00 x 14 four-ply tubeless blackwall; (other models) 6.50 x 13 four-ply tubeless blackwall.

MUSTANG ENGINES

Inline Six. Overhead valves. Cast iron block. Displacement: 170 cubic inches. Bore and stroke: 3.50 x 2.94 inches. Compression ratio: 8.7:1. Brake horsepower: 101 at 4400 R.P.M. Seven main bearings. Hydraulic valve lifters. Carburetion: Ford (Autolite) one-barrel Model C30F-9510-G. Serial Number code 'U'.

Inline Six. Overhead valves. Cast iron block. Displacement: 200 cubic inches. Bore and stroke: 3.68 x 313 inches. Compression ratio: 8.7:1. Brake horsepower: 116 at 4400 R.P.M. Hydraulic valve lifters. Seven main bearings. Carburetor: Ford (Autolite) one-barrel Model C30F-9510-AJ. Serial Number code 'T'.

V-8. Overhead valves. Cast iron block. Displacement: 260 cubic inches. Bore and stroke: 3.80 x 2.87 inches. Compression ratio: 8.8:1. Brake horsepower: 164 at 4400 R.P.M. Five main bearings. Hydraulic valve lifters. Carburetor: Ford (Autolite) two-barrel Model C40F-9510E. Serial Number code 'F'.

Challenger V-8. Overhead valves. Cast iron block. Displacement: 289 cubic inches. Bore and stroke: 4.00 x 2.87 inches. Compression ratio: 9.0:1. Brake horsepower: 210 at 4400 R.P.M. Five main bearings. Hydraulic valve lifters. Carburetor: Ford (Autolite) Model C4AF-9510B. Serial Number code 'C'.

Challenger four-barrel V-8. Overhead valves. Cast iron block. Displacement: 289 cubic inches. Bore and stroke: 4.00 x 2.87 inches. Compression ratio: 9.8:1. Brake horsepower: 220 at 4800 R.P.M. Five main bearings. Hydraulic valve lifters. Carburetor: Ford (Autolite) four-barrel Model C5ZF-9510-C. Serial Number code 'D'.

Challenger high-performance V-8: Overhead valves. Cast iron block. Displacement: 289 cubic inches. Bore and stroke: 4.00 x 2.87 inches. Compression ratio: 10.5:1. Brake horsepower: 271 at 6000 R.P.M. Five main bearings. Solid valve lifters. Carburetor: Ford (Autolite) four-barrel Model C40F-9510-AL. Serial Number code 'K'.

MUSTANG OPTIONS: Accent Group ($27.70). Ford air conditioner ($283.20). Heavy-duty battery ($7.60). Front disc brakes ($58). Full-length center console ($51.50). Console with air conditioning ($32.20). Equa-Lock limited slip differential ($42.50). California type closed emissions system ($5.30). Callenger V-8 ($108). Challenger four-barrel V-8 engine ($162). Challenger high-performance four-barrel V-8 ($442.60). Early year only, 260 cubic inch V-8 ($75). Emergency flashers ($19.60). Tinted glass with banded windshield ($30.90). Banded, tinted windshield only ($21.55). Backup lights ($10.70). Rocker panel moldings ($16.10). Power brakes ($43.20). Power steering ($86.30). Power convertible top ($54.10). Pushbutton radio with antenna ($58.50). Rally-Pac instrumentation with clock and tachometer ($70.80). Deluxe retractable front seat safety belts ($7.55). Special Handling Package ($31.30). Padded sun visors ($5.70). Cruise-O-Matic transmission, with Six ($179.80); with 200 and 225 horsepower V-8s ($189.60). Four-speed manual transmission, with Six ($115.90); with V-8 ($75.80). Hardtop vinyl roof ($75.80). Visibility Group including remote-control mirror; day/nite mirror; two-speed electric wipers and windshield washers ($36). Wheel covers with simulated knock-off hubs ($18.20). Wire wheel covers, size 14 inch, ($45.80). Style steel wheels, size 14 inch ($122.30). **NOTE: The MagicAire heater ($32.20 credit) and front seat belts ($11 credit) were 'delete options'.** Size 6.50 x 13 whitewalls with Six ($33.90). Size 6.95 x 14 tires, blackwall with Six ($7.40); whitewall with Six ($41.30); whitewall with V-8s, except high-performance type ($33.90); black Nylon, except with high-performance V-8 ($15.80); Red Band Nylon with V-8s, except high-performance V-8 ($49.60); Black Nylon or white sidewall Nylon with high-performance V-8 (No Charge).

Historical footnotes: Mustang was introduced April 17, 1964. Model year production peaked at 121,538 units. Lee Iacocca headed an eight-man committee that conceived the idea for the new car. Stylists Joe Oros, Gail Halderman and David Ash de signed the car. So cleanly styled was the new Mustang that it was awarded the Tiffany Award for Excellence in American Design, the first and only automobile ever to be so honored by Tiffany & Company. Not only did the design purists like the new Mustang, so did the public. More than 100,000 were sold in the first four months of production, followed by 500,000 more in the next twelve months. More than 1,000,000 found buyers in less than 24 months. This set an automotive industry sales record which has yet to be equalled or eclipsed. A 1964-1/2 Mustang convertible was also selected as the Indy 500 pace car. Out of all the Mustangs built in the 1964 model run, some 49.2 percent featured an automatic transmission; 19.3 percent four-speed manual transmission; 73.1 percent V-8 engines; 26.9 percent six-cylinder engines; 77.8 percent radio; 99.1 percent heater; 30.9 percent power steering; 7.7 percent power brakes; 88.2 percent whitewalls; 48.3 percent windshield washers; 22.4 percent tinted windshields only; 8.0 percent all tinted glass; 44.6 percent backup lights and 6.4 percent air conditioning

1965 MUSTANG

1965 Ford Mustang, 2-dr hardtop sports coupe, V-8

1965 MUSTANG — (ALL ENGINES) — One brand-new model and a number of very minor revisions were seen in the 1965 Mustang lineup. A 2 + 2 fastback body joined the hardtop and convertible, creating an expanded 'stable' of three 'Pony Cars.' Perhaps the most significant change for 1965 was the use of an alternator in the place of the previously used generator. Engine choices remained the same as in late 1964, with one exception. The old workhorse I-block, 170 cubic inch engine, was replaced by the 200 cubic inch job as base six-cylinder powerplant. A number of small changes and some new options were seen on the 1965 models. While interior door handles on the earliest Mustangs were secured by 'C' type clips, Allen screw attachments were a running production change adopted for later cars. Also, the spacing between the letters in the

lower bodyside nameplates was modified, giving them a five inch measurement or about 1/4 inch longer than before. The push-down door lock buttons were chrome plated, in contrast to the 1964-1/2 type, which was colored to match the interior. Front disc brakes were one new option. So was the GT Package, which included racing stripes as a standard, but deletable, feature. The standard equipment list for 1965 was much the same as before, including heater and defroster; dual sun visors; Sports-type front bumpers; full wheel covers; vinyl upholstery; seat belts; padded instrument panel; automatic courtesy lights; cigarette lighter; front and rear carpets; foam-padded front bucket seats; self-adjusting brakes; Sports steering wheel; five 6.50 x 13 four-ply tubeless black sidewall tires and the 120 horsepower 200 cubic inch Six. The '289' V-8 and 6.95 x 14 size tires were standard in the Mustang V-8 Series.

VEHICLE I.D. NUMBERS: The numbering system and code locations were the same as on previous models. Several additions and deletions in exterior colors were seen. New codes and colors included: Code 'C' = Honey Gold; Code 'I' = Champagne Beige; Code 'O' = Tropical Turquoise and Code 'R' = Ivy Green. Colors deleted were Guardsman Blue (Code 'H'); Cascade Green (Code 'S') and Chantilly Beige (Code 'Z'). The 1965 date codes were changed in regards to the letter used to designate a specific month. Code 'N' designated January, Code 'O' was not used and the remaining months ran in normal alphabetical progression from Code 'P' (for February) through Code 'Z' (for December). The Body Serial Number code for the new two-door fastback was '09'. The 1965 engine Serial Number codes are indicated in the engine data charts below. All other codes were the same used on 1964-1/2 models, except for interior trim codes which are not included in this catalog).

MUSTANG SERIES

Model Number	Body/Style Number	Body Type & Seating	Factory Price	Shipping Weight	Production Total
NA	65A (07)	2-dr HT Cpe-4P	2372	2465	409,260
NA	63A (09)	2-dr FsBk Cpe-4P	2589	2515	77,079
NA	76A (08)	2-dr Conv-4P	2614	2650	73,112

PRODUCTION NOTE: Total model year output was 559,451 units. This figure includes 5,776 Luxury fastbacks; 22,232 Luxury hardtops: 14,905 bench seat equipped hardtops; 5,338 Luxury convertibles and 2,111 convertibles equipped with bench seats. In figures rounded-off to the nearest 100 units, the total included 198,900 Sixes and 360,600 V-8s.

MUSTANG CHASSIS FEATURES: Wheelbase: 108 inches. Overall length: 181.6 inches. Tires: (V-8s) 7.00 x 13 four-ply tubeless blackwalls; (high-performance 289 V-8) 7.00 x 14 four-ply tubeless blackwall; (other models) 6.50 x 13 four-ply tubeless blackwall.

1965 MUSTANG ENGINES

Inline Six. Overhead valves. Cast iron block. Displacement: 200 cubic inches. Bore and stroke: 3.68 x 3.13 inches. Compression ratio: 9.2:1. Brake horsepower: 120 at 4400 R.P.M. Seven main bearings. Hydraulic valve lifters. Carburetor: Ford (Autolite) two-barrel Model C50F-9510-E. Serial Number code 'T'.

Challenger V-8. Overhead valves. Cast iron block. Displacement: 289 cubic inches. Bore and stroke: 4.00 x 2.87 inches. Compression ratio: 9.3:1. Brake horsepower: 200 at 4400 R.P.M. Five main bearings. Hydraulic valve lifters. Carburetor: Ford (Autolite) two-barrel Model C5ZF-9510-A. Serial Number code 'C'.

Challenger four-barrel V-8. Overhead valves. Cast iron block. Displacement: 289 cubic inches. Bore and stroke: 4.00 x 2.87 inches. Compression ratio: 10.0:1. Brake horsepower: 225 at 4800 R.P.M. Five main bearings. Hydraulic valve lifters. Carburetion: Ford (Autolite) four-barrel Model C5ZF-9510-C. Serial Number code 'A'.

Challenger high-performance V-8. Overhead valves. Cast iron block. Displacement: 289 cubic inches. Bore and stroke: 4.00 x 2.87 inches. Compression ratio: 10.5:1. Brake horsepower: 271 at 6000 R.P.M. Five main bearings. Solid valve lifters. Carburetor: Ford (Autolite) four-barrel Model C40F-9510-AL. Serial Number code 'K'.

MUSTANG OPTIONS: Accent Group, on hardtop and convertible ($27.70); on fastback coupe ($14.20). Ford air conditioner ($283.20). Heavy-duty battery ($7.60). Front disc brakes with V-8 and manual brakes only ($58). Full-length center console ($51.50). Console for use with air conditioner ($32.20). Equa-Lock limited-slip differential ($42.50). California type closed emissions system ($5.30). Challenger 200 horsepower V-8 ($108). Challenger four-barrel 225 horsepower V-8 ($162). Challenger 271 horsepower high-performance V-8 including Special Handling Package and 6.95 x 14 Nylon tires ($442.60). Emergency flashers ($19.60). Tinted glass with banded windshield ($30.90). Tinted-banded windshield glass ($21.55). Backup lights ($10.70). Rocker panel moldings, except fastback coupe ($16.10). Power brakes ($43.20). Power steering ($86.30). Power convertible top ($54.10). Pushbutton radio with antenna ($58.50). Rally-Pac instrumentation with clock and tachometer ($70.80). DeLuxe retractable front seat safety belts ($7.55). Special Handling package, with 200 or 225 horsepower V-8s ($31.30). Padded sun visors ($5.70). Cruise-O-Matic transmission, with Six ($179.80); with 200 and 225 horsepower V-8s ($189.60). Four-speed manual transmission, with Six ($115.90); with V-8 ($188). Vinyl roof, on two-door hardtop only ($75.80). Visibility Group, includes remote-control outside rearview mirror; day/nite inside rearview mirror; two-speed electric wipers and windshield washers ($36). Wheel covers with knock-off hubs ($18.20). Fourteen inch wire wheel covers ($45.80). Fourteen inch styled steel wheels ($122.30). **NOTE:** Delete options and tire options same as 1964-1/2 models.

Historical footnotes: The 1965 Mustang was officially introduced on October 1, 1964. Model year production peaked at 559,451 cars. Of these, 53.6 percent were equipped with automatic transmission; 14.5 percent with four-speed manual transmissions; 64.4 percent with V-8 engines; 35.6 percent with Sixes; 78.9 percent with radio; 98.9 percent with heaters; 24.9 percent with power steering; 4.3 percent with power brakes; 97 percent with bucket seats; 98.8 percent with front seat safety belts; 83.6 percent with white sidewall tires; 47.3 percent with windshield washers; 24.8 percent with tinted windshields; 9 percent with all-tinted glass; 38.6 percent with backup lights; 9.1 percent with air conditioning; 3.9 percent with dual exhausts and 2 percent with limited-slip differential. A total of 1.3 percent of all 1965 Mustangs, or 6,996 cars, were sold with the 271 horsepower V-8 (Code 'K') and all of these units had four-speed manual transmission. An interesting historical point is that Mustangs made in Germany were called Ford T-5 models, since the right to the Mustang name in that country belonged to another manufacturer.

1966 MUSTANG

1966 MUSTANG — (ALL ENGINES) — The 1966 Mustang continued to sell like 'hot cakes', in spite of only very minor restyling in the trim department. The grille featured a floating Mustang emblem in the center, with no horizontal or vertical dividing bars. Brand new trim, on the rear fender, featured three chrome strips leading into the simulated scoop. This was the first year of Federally mandated safety standards and all

1966 Ford Mustang, 2-dr convertible, V-8

1966 Fords included seat belts; padded instrument panel; emergency flashers; electric wipers and windshield washers as standard equipment. In addition, the list of regular Mustang features was comprised of the following: front bucket seats; pleated vinyl upholstery and interior trim; Sports type steering wheel; five dial instrument cluster; full carpeting; heater and defroster; lefthand door outside rearview mirror; backup lamps; door courtesy lights; rocker panel moldings; full wheel covers; three-speed manual transmission with floor lever control and 200 cubic inch 120 horsepower six-cylinder engine. The fastback coupe also came with special Silent-Flo ventilation and the base V-8 engine was the 200 horsepower version of the '289'.

MUSTANG I.D. NUMBERS — (ALL ENGINES) — The numbering system and code location was the same as on previous models, although the size and color of the data plate itself was changed. The plate was narrower and the warranty number (formerly on the lower row) was now at the top lefthand corner of the plate. The data on the upper row of codes (body code, color code, trim code, etc.) was moved to a narrow, unfinished band that crossed the data plate, horizontally, nearly at its center. Another change was that previously data plates finished in black had indicated cars painted in conventional enamel, while gray finish had indicated cars done in acrylic enamel. This color-coding system was reversed for 1966. Reading along the top row of codes, the first symbol became a '6' to indicate 1966 model year. The next symbol was a letter designating the assembly plant (with the same codes as previously used). The next two symbols were the Body Serial Code ('07' = hardtop coupe; '09' = fastback coupe; '08' = convertible). The fifth symbol was a letter designating the type of engine, as indicated in the engine data listings below. The next six symbols in the upper row of codes were the consecutive unit number. The first three symbols in the lower row of codes represented the Body Style Number, as indicated in the second column of the charts below. The fourth symbol was a letter indicating the exterior color, as follows: Code 'A' = Raven Black; Code 'F' = Light Blue; Code 'H' = Light Beige; Code Code 'K' = Dark Blue Metallic; Code 'M' = Wimbledon White; Code 'P' = Medium Palomino Metallic; Code 'R' = Dark Green Metallic; Code 'T' = Candyapple Red; Code 'U' = Medium Turquoise Metallic; Code 'V' = Emberglo Metallic; Code 'X' = Maroon Metallic; Code 'Y' = Light Blue Metallic; Code 'Z' = Medium Sage Metallic; Code '4' = Medium Silver Metallic; Code '5' = Signal Flare Red and Code '8' = Springtime Yellow. The fifth and sixth symbols were the interior trim code (not cataloged here). The next three symbols were the assembly date code, following the system used in 1964 (i.e. 21A = twenty-first day of January). The tenth and eleventh symbols were numbers designating the District Sales Office code. The next symbol was a number designating the type of axle and the last (thirteenth) symbol on the lower row was the transmission code. Axle codes and transmission codes are the same as those listed in the 1964 Mustang I.D. Number section.

MUSTANG SERIES

Model Number	Body/Style Number	Body Type & Seating	Factory Price	Shipping Weight	Production Total
NA	65A (07)	2-dr HT Cpe-4P	2416	2488	499,751
NA	63A (09)	2-dr FsBk Cpe-4P	2607	2519	35,698
NA	76A (08)	2-dr Conv-4P	2653	2650	72,119

PRODUCTION NOTE: Total series output was 607,568 units. This figure included 7,889 Luxury fastbacks; 55,938 Luxury hardtops; 21,397 hardtops equipped with bench seats; 12,520 Luxury convertibles, and 3,190 convertibles equipped with bench seats. In figures rounded-off to the nearest 100 units, the total included 253,200 Sixes and 354,400 V-8s.

1966 MUSTANG ENGINES

Inline Six. Overhead valves. Cast iron block. Displacement: 200 cubic inches. Bore and stroke: 3.68 x 3.125 inches. Compression ratio: 9.2:1. Brake horsepower: 120 at 4400 R.P.M. Seven main bearings. Hydraulic valve lifters. Carburetor: Ford (Autolite) one-barrel Model C60F-9510-AD. Serial Number code 'T'.

V-8. Overhead valves. Cast iron block. Displacement: 289 cubic inches. Bore and stroke: 4.00 x 2.875 inches. Compression: 9.3:1. Brake horsepower: 200 at 4400 R.P.M. Five main bearings. Hydraulic valve lifters. Carburetor: Ford (Autolite) two-barrel Model C6DF-9510-A. Serial Number code 'C'.

V-8. Overhead valves. Cast iron block. Displacement: 289 cubic inches. Bore and stroke: 4.00 x 2.875 inches. Compression: 10.1:1. Brake horsepower: 225 at 4800 R.P.M. Five main bearings. Hydraulic valve lifters. Carburetor: Ford (Autolite) four-barrel Model C6ZF-9510-A. Serial Number code 'A'.

V-8. Overhead valves. Cast iron block. Displacement: 289 cubic inches. Bore and stroke: 4.00 x 2.875 inches. Compression ratio: 10.5:1. Brake horsepower: 271 at 6000 R.P.M. Five main bearings. Solid valve lifters. Carburetor: Ford (Autolite) four-barrel Model C60F-9510-C. Serial Number code 'K'.

MUSTANG CHASSIS FEATURES: Wheelbase: 108 inches. Overall length: 181.6 inches. Tires: (Six) 6.50 x 13 four-ply tubeless blackwall; (V-8 7.00 x 13 four-ply tubeless blackwall; (high-performance V-8) 7.00 x 14 four-ply tubeless blackwall.

MUSTANG OPTIONS: Challenger 289 cubic inch V-8 ($105.63). Challenger four-barrel 289 cubic inch 225 horsepower 289 cubic inch V-8 ($158.48). High-performance 289 cubic inch 271 horsepower 289 cubic inch V-8, in standard Mustang ($433.55); in Mustang GT ($381.97). **NOTE:** The total cost of the high-performance engine was $327.92 on regular Mustangs and $276.34 on Mustang GTs, plus the cost of the base V-8 attachment over the Six (which was $105.63). Cruise-O-Matic automatic transmission, with Six ($175.80); with standard V-8s ($185.39); with high-performance V-8 ($216.27). Four-speed manual floor-shift transmission, with Six ($113.45); with all V-8s ($184.02). Power brakes ($42.29). Power steering ($84.47). Power convertible top ($52.95). Heavy-duty 55 ampere battery ($7.44). Manual disc brakes, with V-8 only ($56.77). GT Equipment group, with high-performance V-8 only, includes: dual exhausts; fog lamps; special ornamentation; disc brakes; GT racing stripes (rocker panel moldings deleted) and Handling Package components ($152.20). Limited-slip differential ($41.60). Rally-Pack instrumentation, includes clock and tachometer

($69.30). Special Handling Package, with 200 and 225 horsepower V-8 engines, includes increased rate front and rear springs; larger front and rear shocks; 22:1 overall steering ratio and large diameter stabilizer bar ($30.64). Fourteen inch styled steel wheels, on V-8 models only ($93.84). Two-speed electric windshield wipers ($12.95). Tinted-banded windshield only ($21.09). All glass tinted with banded windshield ($30.25). DeLuxe, retractable front seat safety belts and warning lamp ($14.53). Visibility Group, includes remote-control outside rearview mirror; day/nite inside mirror and two-speed electric wipers ($29.81). Ford air conditioner ($310.90). Stereo tape player, AM radio mandatory($128.49). Full-width front seat with arm rest, for Styles 65A and 76A only, ($24.42). Rear deck luggage rack, except fastback ($32.44). Radio and antenna ($57.51). Accent striping, less rear quarter ornamentation ($13.90). Full-length center console ($50.41). Console for use with air conditioning ($31.52). DeLuxe steering wheel with simulated wood-grained rim ($31.52). Interior Decor Group, includes special interior trim; DeLuxe wood-grain steering wheel; rear window door courtesy lights and pistol grip door handles ($94.13). Vinyl top, on hardtop ($74.36). Simulated wire wheel covers ($58.24). Wheel covers with simulated knock-off hubs ($19.48). Closed crankcase emissions system, except with high-performance V-8 ($5.19). Exhaust emissions control system, except with high-performance V-8 ($45.45). Tire options, exchange prices listed indicate cost above base equipment: 6.95 x 14 four-ply rated whitewall ($33.31); Nylon blackwall ($15.67); Nylon whitewall ($48.89); Nylon with dual Red Band design, on cars with high-performance V-8 (no charge); all other ($48.97). **Notes:** No charge for substitution of Nylon blackwalls or whitewalls on cars with high-performance V-8. MagicAire heater could be deleted for $45.45 credit. Air conditioning, three-speed manual transmission, power steering and U.S. Royal tires not available in combination with high-performance V-8. Power brakes and accent striping not available with GT Equipment Group. Full-width front seat not available in cars with Interior Decor Group, or Model 63A or cars with console options.

Historical footnotes: The 1966 Mustangs were introduced October 1, 1965, the same day as all other Fords. Model year production hit 607,568 Mustangs with the little 'Pony' pulling down a significant 7.1 percent share of all American car sales. Of all Mustangs built during the 1966 model run, only 7.1 percent had four-speed transmissions; 62.8 percent automatic transmission; 58.3 percent V-8 engines; 79.3 percent radio; 98.8 percent heater; 28.9 percent power steering; 3.3 percent power brakes; 9.5 percent vinyl tops; 29.1 percent tinted windshields; 7.3 percent all tinted glass; 6.7 percent disc brakes; 5 percent dual exhausts; 2.6 percent limited-slip differential; 17.9 percent a non-glare inside rearview mirror. 85.3 percent whitewalls and 9.5 percent air conditioning. Henry Ford II was Ford Motor Company Board Chairman and Arjay Miller was the President. The Ford Division, which was actually responsible for Mustang sales, was headed by M.S. McLaughlin who had the titles of Vice-President and General Manager. For 1966, Mustang was the third best-selling individual nameplate in the American industry, an outstanding achievement for a car only three model years old.

1967 MUSTANG

1967 Ford Mustang GTA, 2-dr fastback 2+2 sports coupe, V-8

MUSTANG SERIES — (ALL ENGINES) — For the first time since its mid-1964 introduction the Mustang was significantly changed. The styling was similar to the original, in its theme, but everything was larger. The grille featured a larger opening. The feature lines on the side led to a larger simulated scoop. The taillights took the form of three vertical lenses on each side of a concave indentation panel, with a centrally located gas cap. Standard equipment included all Ford Motor Company safety features, plus front bucket seats; full carpeting; floor-mounted shift; vinyl interior trim; heater; wheel covers and cigarette lighter. The fastback came with wheel covers; special emblems and rocker panel moldings. There were five engine choices ranging from a 120 horsepower 200 cubic inch Six to a 320 horsepower 390 cubic inch V-8. New options available included Select Shift Cruise-O-Matic.

MUSTANG SERIES

Model Number	Body/Style Number	Body Type & Seating	Factory Price	Shipping Weight	Production Total
NA	07	2-dr HT Spt Cpe-4P	2461	2578	356,271
NA	09	2-dr FsBk Cpe-4P	2592	2605	71,042
NA	08	2-dr Conv-4P	2698	2738	44,808

MUSTANG SERIES I.D. NUMBERS — (ALL ENGINES) — Mustangs used the same Serial Number sequence as full-sized Fords, Fairlanes and Falcons (See production note).

PRODUCTION NOTE: Total series output was 472,121 units, including both Sixes and V-8s. This figure includes 22,228 Luxury hardtops; 8,190 hardtops with bench seats; 17,391 Luxury fastbacks; 4,848 Luxury convertibles and 1,209 convertibles equipped with bench seats. In figures rounded-off to the nearest 100, the model year output of 1967 Mustangs included 141,500 Sixes and 330,600 V-8s.

MUSTANG CHASSIS FEATURES: Wheelbase: 108 inches. Overall length: 183.6 inches. Tires: 6.95 x 14 four-ply tubeless blackwall.

MUSTANG ENGINES

Mustang six-cylinder. Overhead valves. Cast iron block. Displacement: 200 cubic inches. Bore and stroke: 3.68 x 3.13 inches. Compression ratio: 9.2:1. Brake horsepower: 120 at 4400 R.P.M. Carburetion: Holley one-barrel. Seven main bearings. Serial Number code 'T'.

Challenger 289 V-8. Overhead valves. Cast iron block. Displacement: 289 cubic inches. Bore and stroke: 4.00 x 2.87 inches. Compression ratio: 9.3:1. Brake horsepower: 200 at 4400 R.P.M. Carburetion: Holley two-barrel. Five main bearings. Serial Number code 'C'.

Challenger 289 V-8. Overhead valves. Cast iron block. Displacement: 289 cubic inches. Bore and stroke: 4.00 x 3.87 inches. Compression ratio: 10.0:1. Brake horsepower: 225 at 4800 R.P.M. Carburetion: Holley four-barrel. Five main bearings. Serial Number code 'A'.

High-Performance 289 V-8. Overhead valves. Cast iron block. Displacement: 289 cubic inches. Bore and stroke: 4.00 x 2.87 inches. Compression ratio: 10.5:1 Brake horsepower: 271 at 6000 R.P.M. Carburetion: Holley four-barrel. Five main bearings. Serial Number code 'K'.

Four-Barrel V-8: Overhead valves. Cast iron block. Displacement: 390 cubic inches. Bore and stroke: 4.05 x 3.78 inches. Compression ratio: 10.5:1. Brake horsepower: 315 at 4600 R.P.M. Carburetion: Holley four-barrel. Five main bearings. Serial Number code 'Z'.

CONVENIENCE OPTIONS: 200 horsepower V-8 ($106). 225 horsepower V-8 ($158). 271 horsepower V-8, included with GT Equipment Group, ($434). 320 horsepower V-8 ($264). Cruise-O-Matic three-speed automatic transmission; six-cylinder ($188); 200 and 225 horsepower V-8s ($198); 271 and 320 horsepower V-8s ($232). Four-speed manual; six-cylinder or 225 horsepower V-8 ($184); other V-8s ($233). Heavy-duty three-speed manual, required with 390 V-8 ($79). Power front disc brakes ($65). Power steering ($84). Power top, convertible ($53). GT Equipment Group, V-8s only ($205). Limited-slip differential ($42). Competition Handling Package, with GT Group only ($62). Styled-steel wheels, 2+2 ($94); others ($115). Tinted windows and windshield ($30). Convenience control panel ($40). Fingertip speed control, V-8 and Cruise-O-Matic required, ($71). Remote-control left door mirror, standard 2+2 ($10). Saftey-glass rear window, convertible ($32). Select-Aire conditioning ($356). Pushbutton AM radio ($58). Pushbutton AM/FM radio ($134). Stereo-Sonic tape system, AM radio required, ($128). Folding rear seat and access door, 2+2, sport deck option, ($65). Full-width front seat, not available with 2+2, ($24). Tilt-Away steering wheel ($60). Deck lid luggage rack, not available on 2+2, ($32). Comfort-weave vinyl trim, not available on convertible, ($25). Center console, radio required, ($50). DeLuxe steering wheel ($32). Exterior Decor Group ($39). Lower back panel grille ($19). Interior Decor Group, convertibele ($95); others ($108). Two-tone paint, lower back grille ($13). Accent stripe ($14). Vinyl roof, hardtop ($74). Wheel covers, standard 2+2, ($21). Wire wheel covers, 2+2 ($58); others ($80). Typical whitewall tire option ($33). Rocker panel moldings, standard on 2+2, ($16). Magic-Aire heater, delete option ($32).

Historical footnotes: The 1967 Mustang was introduced September 30, 1966. Model year output peaked at 472,121 units. Dealer sales totaled 377,827 units, a 31.2 percent decline due to increased competition in the sports/personal car market, plus a strike in the final business quarter. Henry Ford II was Chairman of Ford Motor Company. Mustang's creator, Lee Iacocca, was an Executive Vice-President in charge of North American Operations and was definitely on his way up to the corporate ladder, thanks to the success his 'Pony Car' had seen. Meanwhile, at Ford Corporation, one J.B. Naughton moved up to the slot of Vice-President and General Sales Manager. About seven percent of all 1967 Mustangs had four-speed manual tranmissions; 98 percent had bucket seats; nearly 15 percent vinyl tops and some 16 percent air conditioning. A rare feature was dual exhausts, found only on about 25,000 cars.

1968 MUSTANG

1968 Ford Mustang, 2-dr convertible, V-8

MUSTANG SERIES — (ALL ENGINES) — The 1968 Mustang continued to use the same body shell introduced the previous year, with minor trim changes. The Mustang emblem appear to float in the center of the grille, with no horizontal or vertical bars attached to the emblem. Also, the side scoop had much cleaner chrome trim than the previous year, with no horizontal stripes connected to it.

MUSTANG SERIES I.D. NUMBERS — (ALL ENGINES) — Mustangs used the same Serial Number sequence as full-size Fords, Fairlanes and Falcons. (See 1968 Ford section).

MUSTANG SERIES

Model Number	Body/Style Number	Body Type & Seating	Factory Price	Shipping Weight	Production Total
NA	65A	2-dr HT Cpe-4P	2602	2635	249,447
NA	63A	2-dr FsBk Cpe-4P	2712	2659	42,325
NA	76A	2-dr Conv-4P	2814	2745	25,376

PRODUCTION NOTE: Total series output was 317,148 units. This figure included 9,009 DeLuxe hardtops; 6,113 hardtops equipped with bench seats; 7,661 DeLuxe fastbacks; 256 fastbacks equipped with bench seats; 853 DeLuxe hardtops equipped with bench seats and 3,339 DeLuxe convertibles.

MUSTANG CHASSIS FEATURES: Wheelbase: 108 inches. Overall length: 183.6 inches. Tires: 6.95 x 14 four-ply tubeless blackwall (E70 x 14 four-ply tubeless blackwall, with Wide-Oval sport tire option).

MUSTANG ENGINES
Mustang six-cylinder. Overhead valves. Cast iron block. Displacement: 200 cubic inches. Bore and stroke: 3.68 x 3.13 inches. Compression ratio: 8.8:1. Brake horsepower: 115 at 3800 R.P.M. Carburetion: Holley one-barrel. Seven main bearings. Serial Number code 'T'.

Ford six-cylinder. Overhead valves. Cast iron block. Displacment: 250 cubic inches. Bore and stroke: 3.68 x 3.91 inches. Compression ratio: 9.0:1. Brake horsepower: 155 at 4000 R.P.M. Carburetion: Motorcraft one-barrel. Seven main bearings. Serial Number code 'L'.

Challenger 289 V-8. Overhead valves. Cast iron block. Displacement: 289 cubic inches. Bore and stroke: 4.00 x 2.87 inches. Compression ratio: 8.7:1. Brake horsepower: 195 at 4600 R.P.M. Carburetion: Holley two-barrel. Five main bearings. Serial Number code 'C'.

302 V-8. Overhead valves. Cast iron block. Displacement: 302 cubic inches. Bore and stroke: 4.00 x 3.00 inches. Compression ratio: 9.0:1. Brake horsepower: 220 at 4000 R.P.M. Carburetion: Motorcraft two-barrel. Five main bearings. Serial Number code 'F'.

302 four-barrel V-8. Overhead valve. Cast iron block. Displacement: 302 cubic inches. Bore and stroke: 4.00 x 3.00 inches. Compression ratio: 10.0:1. Brake horsepower: 230 at 4800 R.P.M. Carburetion: Motorcraft four-barrel. Five main bearings. Serial Number code 'J'.

GT 390 V-8. Overhead valves. Cast iron block. Displacement: 390 cubic inches. Bore and stroke: 4.05 x 3.78 inches. Compression ratio: 10.5:1. Brake horsepower: 325 at 4800 R.P.M. Carburetion: Holley four-barrel. Five main bearings. Serial Number code 'S'.

High-Performance V-8. Overhead valves. Cast iron block. Displacement: 427 cubic inches. Bore and stroke: 4.23 x 3.78 inches. Compression ratio: 10.9:1. Brake horsepower: 390 at 4600 R.P.M. Carburetion: Motorcraft four-barrel. Five main bearings. Serial Number code 'W'.

Cobra Jet 428 V-8. Overhead valves. Cast iron block. Displacement: 428 cubic inches. Bore and stroke: 4.13 x 3.98 inches. Compression ratio: 10.7:1. Brake horsepower: 335 at 5600 R.P.M. Carburetion: Holley four-barrel. Five main bearings. Serial Number code 'Q'.

MUSTANG OPTIONS: 250-cid one-barrel 155 horsepower inline Six (not available). 289-cid two-barrel 195 horsepower V-8 ($106). 302-cid two-barrel 220 horsepower V-8 (not available). 302-cid four-barrel 230 horsepower ($172). 390-cid four-barrel 325 horsepower V-8 ($264). 427-cid four-barrel 390 horsepower V-8 (not available). 428-cid four-barrel 335 horsepower V-8 (not available). Select-Shift Cruise-O-Matic three speed automatic; six-cylinder ($19); 289 V-8s ($201); 390 V-8 ($233). Four-speed manual, not available with six-cylinder; 289 V-8s ($184); 390 V-8 ($233). Power front disc brakes, V-8s only, required with 390 V-8 or GT Equipment Group ($54). Power steering ($84). Power top, convertible ($53). GT Equipment Group, 230 or 325 horsepower V-8s with power brakes, not available with Sports Trim Group of optional wheel covers, ($147). Tachometer, V-8s only ($54). Limited-slip differential, V-8s only ($79). Glass backlight, convertible ($39). Tinted glass ($30). Convenience Group, console required with Select-Aire ($32) Fingertip speed control, V-8 and Select-Shift required ($74). Remote-control left door mirror ($10). Select-Aire conditioner ($360). Pushbutton AM radio ($360). AM/FM stereo radio ($61). Stereo-Sonic Tape System, AM radio required, ($181). Sport deck rear seat, 2+2 only ($65). Full-width front seat, hardtop, 2+2 only, not available with console, ($32). Tilt-Away steering wheel ($66). Center console, radio required ($54). Interior Decor Group; convertibles and models with full-width front seat ($110); others without full-width front seat ($124). Two-tone hood paint ($19). Accent paint stripe ($14). Vinyl roof, hardtop ($74). Wheel covers, not available with GT or V-8 Sports Trim Group ($34). Whitewall tires ($33).

Historical footnotes: The 1968 Mustangs were introduced in September, 1967. Model year production peaked at 317,148 units. The 427 powered Mustang was capable of moving from 0-60 miles per hour in around six seconds. The price for this motor was $775 above that of the base Mustang V-8. Only a handful of 1968 models were made with 427 or 428 cubic engines. Side marker lights and other new Federally mandated safety features were required on all Mustangs built this year.

1969 MUSTANG

1969 Ford Mustang, Grande 2-dr hardtop sports coupe, V-8

MUSTANG SERIES — (ALL ENGINES) — The Mustang was somewhat different for 1969. It was enlarged considerably and slightly restyled for the new year. For the first time, Mustangs had quad headlights, the outboard units being mounted in deeply recessed openings at the outer edges of the fenders. The inboard units were mounted inside the grille opening. The side scoop was now located high on the rear fenders of fastback models. It was in the same location as before on the hardtops and convertibles, but faced rearward. High-performance was the theme, at Ford in 1969, and the hot new Mustangs were in the spotlight. The sizzling Mach I came with a 351 cubic inch V-8 as standard equipment. the 390 and Cobra Jet 428 engines were optional. Trans-AM road racing was very popular at this time. To compete with the Chevrolet Camaro and Dodge Challenger R/T Ford introduced the famous and powerful Boss 302 Mustang. Apparently the company engineers did their homework when they designed the Boss 302, because it won the championship in Trans-Am competiton that year. The top engine option for 1969 Mustangs became the incredibly awesome and huge Boss 429. Even though these monsters came with a factory horsepower rating of 375, actual output was in the neighborhood of 515 horsepower with a four-barrel carburetor. They were definitely not machines for the weak-spirited individual. Only now, after being out of production for more than 12 years, is the true potential of these engineering masterpieces being fully realized.

MUSTANG SERIES I.D. NUMBERS — (ALL ENGINES) — Mustangs used the same Serial Number sequence as full-size Fords, Fairlanes, Falcons and Mavericks. (See 1969 Ford section).

MUSTANG SERIES

Model Number	Body/Style Number	Body Type & Seating	Factory Price	Shipping Weight	Production Total
NA	65A	2-dr HT Cpe-4P	2618/2723	2690	127,954
NA	63A	2-dr FsBk Cpe-4P	2618/2723	2713	61,980
NA	76A	2-dr Conv-4P	2832/2937	2800	14,746
NA	65E	2-dr Grande HT-4P	2849/2954	2981	22,182
NA	63C	2-dr Mach I FsBk-4P	/3122	3175	72,458

PRODUCTION NOTE: Total series output was 299,824 units. This figure included 5,210 DeLuxe hardtops; 4,131 hardtops equipped with bench seats; 5,958 DeLuxe fastbacks; 504 DeLuxe hardtops equipped with bench seats and 3,439 DeLuxe convertibles.

MUSTANG ENGINES
Mustang six-cylinder. Overhead valves. Cast iron block. Displacement: 200 cubic inches. Bore and stroke: 3.68 x 3.13 inches. Compression ratio: 8.8:1. Brake horsepower: 115 at 3800 R.P.M. Carburetion: Motorcraft one-barrel. Seven main bearings. Serial Number code 'T'.

Ford six-cylinder. Overhead valves. Cast iron block. Displacment: 250 cubic inches. Bore and stroke: 3.68 x 3.91 inches. Compression ratio: 9.0:1. Brake horsepower: 155 at 4000 R.P.M. Carburetion: Motorcraft one-barrel. Seven main bearings. Serial Number code 'L'.

302 V-8. Overhead valves. Cast iron block. Displacement: 320 cubic inches. Bore and stroke: 4.00 x 3.00 inches. Compression ratio: 9.5:1. Brake horsepower: 220 at 4600 R.P.M. Carburetion: Motorcraft two-barrel. Five main bearings. Serial Number code 'F'.

351 V-8. Overhead valve. Cast iron block. Displacement: 351 cubic inches. Bore and stroke: 4.00 x 3.50 inches. Compression ratio: 9.5:1. Brake horsepower: 250 at 4600 R.P.M. Carburetion: Motorcraft two-barrel. Five main bearings. Serial Number code 'H'.

351 Four-Barrel V-8. Overhead valves. Cast iron block. Displacement: 351 cubic inches. Bore and stroke: 4.00 x 3.50 inches. Compression ratio: 10.7:1. Brake horsepower: 290 at 4800 R.P.M. Carburetion: Motorcraft four-barrel. Five main bearings. Serial Number code 'M'.

390 GT V-8. Overhead valves. Cast iron block. Displacement: 390 cubic inches. Bore and stroke: 4.05 x 3.78 inches. Compression ratio: 10.5:1. Brake horsepower: 320 at 4600 R.P.M. Carburetion: Holley four-barrel. Five main bearings. Serial Number code 'S'.

Cobra Jet 428 V-8. Overhead valves. Cast iron block. Displacement: 428 cubic inches. Bore and stroke: 4.13 x 3.98 inches. Compression ratio: 10.6:1. Brake horsepower: 335 at 5200 R.P.M. Carburetion: Holley four-barrel. Five main bearings. Serial Number code 'Q'.

Super Cobra Jet 428 V-8. Overhead valves. Cast iron block. Displacement: 428 cubic inches. Bore and stroke: 4.13 x 3.98 inches. Compression ratio: 10.5:1. Brake horsepower: 360 at 5400 R.P.M. Carburetion: Holley four-barrel. Five main bearings.

MUSTANG CHASSIS FEATURES: Wheelbase: 108 inches. Overall length: 187.4 inches. Tires: C78 x 14 four-ply tubeless blackwall (E78 x 14 four-ply on small V-8 equipped models and F70 x 14 four-ply on large V-8 equipped models).

MUSTANG OPTIONS: 250-cid one-barrel 155 horsepower inline Six, not available in Mach I, ($26). 302-cid two-barrel 220 horsepower V-8, not available in Mach I, ($105). 351-cid two-barrel 250 horsepower V-8, standard in Mach I, ($163). 351-cid four-barrel 290 horsepower V-8, Mach I ($26); others ($189). 390-cid four-barrel 320 horsepower V-8, Mach I ($100); others ($158). 428-cid four-barrel 335 horsepower V-8, Mach I ($224); others ($288). 428-cid four-barrel Cobra Jet V-8, Mach I, including Ram Air, ($357); others ($421). Select-Shift Cruise-O-Matic transmission; six-cylinder engines ($191); 302 and 351 V-8s ($201); 390 and 428 V-8s ($222). Four-speed manual; 302 and 351 V-8s ($205); 390 and 428 V-8s ($254). Power disc brakes, not available with 200-cid inline Six, ($65). Power steering ($95). Power top, convertible ($53). GT Equipment Group, not available on Grande or with six-cylinder or 302-cid V-8, ($147). Tachometer, V-8s only ($54). Handling suspension, not available on Grande or with six-cylinder and 428 V-8 engines, ($31). Competition suspension, standard Mach I and GT; 428 V-8 required, ($31). Glass backlight, convertible ($39). Limited-slip differential, 250 inline Six and 302 V-8 ($42). Traction-Lok differential, not available Sixes and 302 V-8s ($64). Intermittent windshield wipers ($17). High-back front bucket seats, not available in Grande, ($85). Color-keyed dual racing mirrors, standard in Mach I and Grande, ($19). Power ventilation, not available with Select-Aire, ($40). Electric clock, standard Mach I and Grande, ($16). Tinted windows and windshield ($32). Speed control, V-8 and automatic transmission required ($74). Remote-control left door mirror ($13). Select-Aire conditioner, not available 200 inline Six or 428 V-8 with four-speed ($380). Pushbutton AM radio ($61). AM/FM stereo radio ($181). Stereo-Sonic tape system, AM radio required, ($134). Rear seat speaker, hardtop and Grande ($13). Rear seat deck, Sports Roof and Mach I ($97). Full-width front seat, hardtop, not available with console, ($32). Tilt-Away steering wheel ($66). Rim-Blow DeLuxe steering wheel ($36). Console ($54). Interior Decor Group, not available on Mach I, and Grande, ($101); with dual racing mirrors ($88). DeLuxe Interior Decor Group, SportsRoof and convertible ($133); with dual racing mirrors ($120). DeLuxe seatbelts with reminder light ($16). Vinyl roof, hardtop ($84). Wheel covers, not available Mach I, GT, Grande; included with exterior Decor Group, ($21). Wire wheel covers, not available Mach I, GT; standard on Grande, with Exterior Decor Group ($58); without Exterior Decor Group ($80). Exterior Decor Group, not available on Mach I and Grande, ($32). Chrome styled steel wheels, standard on Mach I; not available on Grande or with 200 inline Six, ($117); with GT Equipment Group ($78); with Exterior Decor Group ($95). Adjustable head restraints, not available on Mach I, ($17).

Historical footnotes: The 1969 Mustangs were introduced in September, 1968. Model year production peaked at 299,824 units. Bunkie Knudsen was the chief executive officer of the company this year. The new fastback styling was called the "Sportsroof" treatment. The fantastic Boss 302 Mustang was styled and detailed by Larry Shinoda. Its standard equipment included the special competition engine; staggered shock absorbers; heavy-duty springs; stout CJ four-speed gear box; power front disc brakes; heavy-duty rear drums; special ignition system (with high R.P.M. cut-out feature) and F60 x 15 Goodyear Polyglas tires. A total of 1,934 Boss 302 Mustangs were built, almost twice as many as needed to qualify the model for SCCA Trans-Am racing.

1970 MUSTANG

1970 Ford Mustang, 'Boss 302' 2-dr Sportsroof coupe, V-8

MUSTANG SERIES — (ALL ENGINES) — For 1970, Mustangs were slightly revised versions of the 1969 models. The biggest change was the return to single headlights. They were located inside the new, larger grille opening. Simulated air intakes were seen where the outboard lights were on the 1969 models. The rear was also slightly restyled. There were flat taillight moldings and a flat escutcheon panel, taking the place of the concave panel and lights used in 1969. The year 1970 saw the introduction of the famous 351 'Cleveland' V-8 engine, in two-barrel and four-barrel configurations. Standard equipment in Mustangs included vinyl high-back bucket seats; carpeting; floor mounted shift lever; instrument gauges; E78 x 15 tires and either the '200' Six or the '302' V-8. The Grande came with all above, plus DeLuxe two-spoke steering wheel; color-keyed racing mirrors; wheel covers; electric clock; bright exterior moldings; dual outside paint stripes and luxury trim bucket seats. Convertibles had power-operated tops. The Mach I featured vinyl buckets; hood scoop; competition suspension; color-keyed racing mirrors; console mounted shift controls; DeLuxe steering wheel with rim-blow feature; rocker panel moldings; rear deck lid tape stripe; deep-dish sport wheel covers; carpeting; E70-15 fiberglass-belted whitewall tires and the 250 horsepower 351 cubic inch two-barrel V-8. The Mustang Boss 302 had, in addition to the above and the features mentioned in historical footnote, quick ratio steering; functional front spoiler and Space Saver spare tire.

MUSTANG SERIES I.D. NUMBERS — (ALL ENGINES) — Mustangs used the same Serial Number sequence as full-size Fords, Fairlane 500s, Torinos and Mavericks (See 1970 Ford section).

MUSTANG SERIES

Model Number	Body/Style Number	Body Type & Seating	Factory Price	Shipping Weight	Production Total
NA	65B	2-dr HT Cpe-4P	2721/2822	2721/2923	82,569
NA	63B	2-dr FsBk Cpe-4P	2771/2872	2745/2947	45,934
NA	76B	2-dr Conv-4P	3025/3126	2831/3033	7,673
NA	65E	2-dr Grande HT-4P	2926/3028	2806/3008	13,581
NA	63C	2-dr Mach I FsBk-4P	3271	3240	40,970
NA	63	2-dr Boss 302 FsBk	3720	3227	6,318

PRODUCTION NOTE: Total series output was 190,727. Mustang prices and weights to the left of the slant bar are for six-cylinder equipped models/prices and weights to the right are for V-8 equipped models.

MUSTANG CHASSIS FEATURES: Wheelbase: 108 inches. Overall length: 187.4 inches. Tires: C78 x 14 four-ply tubeless blackwall (E78 x 14 four-ply on cars equipped with small V-8s and F70 x 14 four-ply on those with large V-8s). Boss 302 and Boss 429s used F70 x 15 tires.

MUSTANG ENGINES
See 1970 Ford engine data.

Maverick six-cylinder. Overhead valves. Cast iron block. Displacement: 200 cubic inches. Bore and stroke: 3.68 x 3.13 inches. Compression ratio: 8.0:1. Brake horsepower: 120 at 4400 R.P.M. Carburetion: Motorcraft one-barrel. Seven main bearings. Serial Number code 'T'.

Ford/Mustang six-cylinder. Overhead valves. Cast iron block. Displacement: 240 cubic inches. Bore and stroke: 4.00 x 3.18 inches. Compression ratio: 9.2:1. Brake horsepower: 150 at 4000 R.P.M. Carburetion: Motorcraft one-barrel. Seven main bearings. Serial Number code 'V'.

Ford six-cylinder. Overhead valves. Cast iron block. Displacement: 250 cubic inches. Bore and stroke: 3.68 x 3.91 inches. Compression ratio: 9.0:1. Brake horsepower: 155 at 4400 R.P.M. Carburetion: Motorcraft one-barrel. Seven main bearings. Serial Number code 'L'.

302 V-8. Overhead valves. Cast iron block. Displacement: 302 cubic inches. Bore and stroke: 4.00 x 3.00 inches. Compression ratio: 9.5:1. Brake horsepower: 220 at 4600 R.P.M. Carburetion: Motorcraft two-barrel. Five main bearings. Serial Number code 'F'.

Boss 302 V-8. Overhead valves. Cast iron block. Displacement: 302 cubic inches. Compression ratio: 10.6:1. Brake horsepower: 290 at 5800 R.P.M. Carburetion: Holley four-barrel. Five main bearings.

351 V-8. Overhead valves. Cast iron block. Displacement: 351 cubic inches. Bore and stroke: 4.00 x 3.50 inches. Compression ratio: 9.5:1. Brake horsepower: 250 at 4600 R.P.M. Carburetion: Motorcraft two-barrel. Five main bearings. Serial Number code 'H'.

351 Four-Barrel V-8. Overhead valves. Cast iron block. Displacement: 351 cubic inches. Bore and stroke: 4.00 x 3.50 inches. Compression ratio: 11.0:1. Brake horsepower: 300 at 5400 R.P.M. Carburetion: Motorcraft four-barrel. Five main bearings.

Cobra Jet 428 V-8. Overhead valve. Cast iron block. Displacement: 428 cubic inches. Bore and stroke: 4.13 x 3.98 inches. Compression ratio: 10.6:1. Brake horsepower: 335 at 5200 R.P.M. Carburetion: Holley four-barrel. Five main bearings. Serial Number code 'Q'.

Super Cobra Jet 428 V-8. Overhead valves. Cast iron block. Displacement: 428 cubic inches. Bore and stroke: 4.13 x 3.98 inches. Compression ratio: 10.5:1. Brake horsepower: 360 at 5400 R.P.M. Carburetion: Holley four-barrel. Five main bearings.

Boss 429 V-8. Overhead valves. Cast iron block. Displacement: 429 cubic inches. Bore and stroke: 4.36 x 3.59 inches. Compression ratio: 11.3:1. Brake horsepower: 375 at 5600 R.P.M. Carburetion: Holley four-barrel Five main bearings.

MUSTANG OPTIONS: 250 horsepower 351 cubic inch V-8, in Mach I (standard); in other Mustangs ($45). 300 horsepower 351 cubic inch V-8 in Mach I ($48); in other Mustangs ($93). 335 horsepower 428 cubic inch Cobra-Jet V-8 engine with Ram-Air induction, in Mach I ($376); in other Mustangs ($421). Cruise-O-Matic automatic transmission ($222). Four-speed manual transmission ($205). Power steering ($95). Power front disc brakes ($65). Limited-Slip differential ($43). Styled steel wheels ($58). Magnum 500 chrome wheels ($129). AM radio ($61). AM/FM stereo radio ($214). AM/8-track stereo ($134). Center console ($54). Tilt steering wheel ($45). Exterior Decor group ($78). Vinyl roof ($84); on Grande ($26). Wheel covers ($26). Rocker panel moldings ($16).

Historical footnotes: The 1970 Mustangs were introduced in September, 1969. Model year production peaked at 190,727 units. Bunkie Knudsen was the chief executive officer of the company this year, but was in his last year at the helm. Ford Motor company chairman, Henry Ford II, fired Knudsen in 1971. Knudsen, of course, was famous for creating Pontiac's 'performance image' in the early 1960s. Part of the problem was that auto sales were becoming less relative to high-performance marketing techniques in the early 1970s. For example, Ford ceased its official racing activities late in the calendar year. Others, however, suggested that Knudsen was the victim of Ford's traditional family controlled management system. He had tried to overstep the limits of his power and, for this, was dismissed on short notice.

1971 MUSTANG

1971 Ford Mustang, 'Boss 351' 2-dr Sportsroof coupe, V-8

MUSTANG SERIES — (ALL ENGINES) — The 1971 Mustangs were completely restyled. They were over two inches longer and had a new hood and concealed windshield wipers. The styling left little doubt that the cars were Mustangs, but they were lower, wider and heavier than any previous models. A full-width grille, incorporating the headlights within its opening, was again seen in the center. The Mustang corral was again seen in the center. The roof had a thinner appearance. New door handles fit flush to the body. New on the options list were the Special Instrumentation Group package; electric rear window defogger and a Body Protection Group package that included side moldings and front bumper guards. The fastback-styled 'Sportsroof' was now available dressed in a vinyl top. Sadly, two of the most exotic engines were gone. The Boss 302 and Boss 429 powerplants had bitten the dust. Although rumours persist that five cars *were* assembled with the 'Boss 429', they are, as yet, unconfirmed. There was a new Boss 351 Mustang that provided a more refined package, with a better weight distribution layout than the front-heavy Boss 429. Standard equipment on base Mustangs included color-keyed Nylon carpeting; floor-shift; high-back bucket seats; steel guardrail door construction; DirectAire ventiliation system; concealed windshield wipers with cowl air inlets; mini console with ash tray; arm rests; courtesy lights; cigar lighter; heater and defroster; all-vinyl interior; glove box; E78-14 belted black sidewall tires; power convertible top and either the '250' Six or '302' V-8. The Mustang Grande Coupe had the same basic features, plus bright pedal pads; DeLuxe high-back bucket seats in cloth trim; DeLuxe instrument panel; DeLuxe two-spoke steering wheel; electric clock; molded trim panels with integral pull handles and arm rests; right rear quarter panel trim with ash tray; dual paint accent stripes; dual color-keyed racing mirrors (left remote-control); rocker panel moldings; vinyl roof; wheel covers and wheel lip moldings. The Mustang Mach I had all of the basic equipment, plus color-keyed spoiler, hood moldings, fender moldings and racing mirrors; a unique grille with Sportlamps; competition suspension; trim rings and hub caps; high-back bucket seats; honeycomb texture back panel applique; pop-open gas cap; deck lid paint stipe; black or Argent Silver finish on lower bodyside (with bright molding at upper edge); E70 x 14 whitewalls and the two-barrel '302' V-8. A NASA styled hood scoop treatment was a no-cost option. The Mustang Boss 351 had even more extras. In addition to the basic equipment, this model featured a fuctional NASA hood scoop; black or Argent Silver painted hood; hood lock pins; Ram-Air engine callouts; color-keyed racing mirrors (left remote-con-

trolled); unique grille with Sportslamps; hub caps with rim rings; bodyside tape stripes in black or Argent Silver; color-keyed hood and front fender moldings; Boss 351 callout nomenclature; dual exhausts; power disc brakes; Space Saver spare tire; competition suspension with staggered rear shocks; 3.91:1 rear axle gear ratio with Traction-Lok differential; electronic R.P.M. limiter; Boss 351 cubic inch V-8 (finished in black and shipped 'knocked-down'); 80 ampere battery; Instrumentation Group; F60-15 white-letter tires; 330 horsepower High-Output 351 cubic inch V-8 with four-barrel carburetion; special cooling package and wide-ratio four-speed manual gear box with Hurst shifter.

MUSTANG SERIES I.D. NUMBERS — (ALL ENGINES) — Mustangs used the same Serial Number sequence as the full-size Fords, Torinos and Mavericks (See 1971 Ford section).

MUSTANG SERIES

Model Number	Body/Style Number	Body Type & Seating	Factory Price	Shipping Weight	Production Total
NA	65D	2-dr HT Cpe-4P	2911/3006	2937/3026	65,696
NA	63D	2-dr FsBk Cpe-4P	2973/3068	2907/2993	23,956
NA	76D	2-dr Conv-4P	3227/3322	3059/3145	6,121
NA	65F	2-dr Grande-4P	3117/3212	2963/3049	17,406
NA	63	2-dr Boss 351-4P	4124	3281	NA
NA	63R	2-dr Mach I	3268	3220	36,449

PRODUCTION NOTE: Total series output was 149,678 units. The price and weight to the left of the slant bar apply to six-cylinder equipped models and the price and weight to the right of the slant bar apply to V-8 powered models.

MUSTANG CHASSIS FEATURES: Wheelbase: 109 inches. Overall length: 187.5 inches. Tires: E78 X 14 belted blackwall.

MUSTANG ENGINES
See 1971 Ford engine data.

Ford/Maverick/Mustang six-cylinder: Overhead valves. Cast iron block. Displacement: 250 cubic inches. Bore and stroke: 3.68 x 3.91 inches. Compression ratio: 9.0:1. Brake horsepower: 145 at 4000 R.P.M. Carburetion: Motorcraft one-barrel. Seven main bearings. Serial Number code 'L'.

302 V-8: Overhead valves. Cast iron block. Displacement: 302 cubic inches. Bore and stroke: 4.00 x 3.00 inches. Compression ratio: 9.0:1. Brake horsepower: 210 at 4600 R.P.M. Carburetion: Motorcraft two-barrel. Five main bearings. Serial Number code 'F'.

351 V-8: Overhead valves. Cast iron block. Displacement: 351 cubic inches. Bore and stroke: 4.00 x 3.50 inches. Compression ratio: 9.0:1. Brake horsepower: 240 at 4600 R.P.M. Carburetion: Motorcraft two-barrel. Five main bearings. Serial Number code 'H'.

351 'Cleveland' four-barrel V-8: Overhead valves. Cast iron block. Displacement: 351 cubic inches. Bore and stroke: 4.00 x 3.50 inches. Compression ratio: 10.7:1. Brake horsepower: 285 at 5400 R.P.M. Carburetion: Holley four-barrel. Five main bearings. Serial Number code 'M'.

Boss 351 V-8: Overhead valves. Cast iron block. Displacement: 351 cubic inches. Bore and stroke: 4.00 x 3.50 inches. Compression ratio: 11.1:1. Brake horsepower: 330 at 5400 R.P.M. Carburetion: Holley four-barrel. Five main bearings. Serial Number code 'Q'.

Cobra Jet 429 V-8: Overhead valves. Cast iron block. Displacement: 429 cubic inches. Bore and stroke: 4.36 x 3.59 inches. Compression ratio: 11.3:1. Brake horsepower: 370 at 5400 R.P.M. Carburetion: Holley four-barrel. Five main bearings. Serial Number code 'C'.

Super Cobra Jet 429 V-8: Overhead valves. Cast iron block. Displacement: 429 cubic inches. Bore and stroke: 4.36 x 3.59 inches. Compression ratio: 11.3:1. Brake horsepower: 375 at 5600 R.P.M. Carburetion: Holley four-barrel (with Ram-Air induction). Five main bearings. Serial Number code 'J'.

CONVENIENCE OPTIONS FOR MUSTANG SERIES: 240 horsepower 351 cubic inch V-8 engine ($45). 285 horsepower 351 cubic inch 'Cleveland' V-8 engine ($93). 370 horsepower Cobra Jet 429 cubic inch V-8 engine ($372). Cruise-O-Matic automatic transmission ($217-$238). Four-speed manual transmission ($216). Power steering ($115). Power front disc brakes ($70). Limited-Slip differential ($48). Magnum 500 chrome wheels ($129). AM radio ($66). AM/FM stereo radio ($214). AM/8-track stereo ($129). Center console ($60). Electric rear window defogger ($48). NASA style hood scoops (no charge). Drag-Pac rear axle 3.91:1 ratio ($155); 4.11:1 ratio ($207). Vinyl roof ($26). White sidewall tires ($34).

Historical footnotes: The 1971 Mustang were introduced September 19, 1970. Model year production peaked at 149,678 units. Calendar year sales of 127,062 cars were recorded. J.B. Naughton was the chief executive officer of the Ford Division this year. This branch of the corporation was also known as Ford Marketing Corporation. Of all Mustangs built in the model year 1971, some 5.3 percent had four-speed manual transmissions; 5.6 percent had stereo eight-track tape players; 1.9 percent had power windows and 29 percent had vinyl roofs.

1972 MUSTANG

MUSTANG SERIES — (ALL ENGINES) — The Mustang was a very versatile package. The original, in 1964-1/2, was promoted as a Sports/Personal car. Later, the Mustang became, first a luxury auto and, then, a high-performance 'machine'. Actually, the basic car itself was changed very little in overall concept. Yet, for 1972, it was suddenly being called Ford's ''Sports Compact.'' It came in five two-door styles, two hardtops; two Sportsroofs (fastbacks) and a convertible. Styling was generally unaltered, the only appearance refinements being a color-keyed front bumper and redesigned deck latch panel nameplate. Instead of spelling Mustang, in block letters on the rear, a chrome signature script was being used. The powerful 429 cubic inch V-8 was no longer offered. The 'Cleveland' 351 cubic inch four-barrel job was the hairiest powerplant around. Standard equipment, in all body styles, included concealed wipers; rocker panel and wheel lip moldings; lower back panel applique with bright moldings; color-keyed dual racing mirrors; recessed exterior door handles; wheel covers: Direct-Aire ventilation; heater and defroster; high-back bucket seats and bonded door trim panels with pull-type handles and arm rests. At this point, the specific equipment in different styles started varying. For instance, the hardtop and Sportsroof featured carpeting; mini-consoles; courtesy lights; DeLuxe two-spoke steering wheel with wood-toned inserts; three-speed floor shift; E78 x 14 black belted tires and a base 250 cubic

inch Six. In addition to all of this, the Sportsroof also featured fixed rear quarter windows (except with power lifts) and a tinted backlight. The Mustang convertible also had a five-ply power-operated top; color-keyed top boot; tinted windshield and glass backlight; bright, upper back panel moldings; knitted vinyl seat trim; molded door handles and black instrument panel appliques. The Mustang Grande featured — in addition to the above — a vinyl top with Grande script nameplates; unique bodyside tape stripes; unique wheel covers; floor mat in trunk; Lambeth cloth and vinyl interior trim; bright pedal moldings; DeLuxe camera grain instrument panel with wood-toned appliques; panel mounted electric clock and rear ash trays. The Mach I Sportsroof featured the following standard extras: competition suspension; NASA type hood scoops as no-cost option (with base V-8 only); front spoiler-type bumper; color-keyed hood and rear fender moldings; black grille with integral Sportslamps; black or Argent Silver painted lower body; front and rear valance panels; rear tape stripes with Mach I decals; wheel trim rings and hub caps; E70 x 14 bias-belted whitewall tires and '302' two-barrel V-8.

1972 Ford, Mustang 2-dr hardtop sports coupe, V-8

MUSTANG SERIES I.D. NUMBERS: Mustangs used the same Serial Number sequence as the full-sized Fords, Torinos and Mavericks. (See 1972 Ford section).

MUSTANG SERIES

Model Number	Body/Style Number	Body Type & Seating	Factory Price	Shipping Weight	Production Total
NA	65D	2-dr HT Cpe-4P	2729/2816	2941/3025	57,350
NA	63D	2-dr FsBk Cpe-4P	2786/2873	2909/2995	15,622
NA	76D	2-dr Conv-4P	3015/3101	3061/3147	6,401
NA	65F	2-dr Grande-4P	2915/3002	2965/3051	18,045
NA	63R	2-dr Mach I-4P	3053	3046	27,675

PRODUCTION NOTE: Total series output was 125,405 units. The prices and weights to the left of the slant bar apply to six-cylinder equipped models and the prices and weights to the right of the slant bar apply to V-8 powered models. The Mach I Sportsroof came only with V-8 power.

MUSTANG CHASSIS FEATURES: Wheelbase: 109 inches. Overall length: 190 inches. Width: 75 inches. Tires: E78 x 14. (Note: Additional tire sizes are denoted in text, when used as standard equipment on specific models).

MUSTANG ENGINES
See 1972 Ford Series engine data.

Maverick/Mustang/Torino Six-cylinder. Overhead valves. Displacement: 250 cubic inches. Bore and stroke: 3.68 x 3.91 inches. Compression ratio: 8.0:1. Net horsepower: 98 at 3400 R.P.M. Carburetion: Motorcraft one-barrel. Seven main bearings. Serial Number code 'L'.

302 V-8. Overhead valves. Cast iron block. Displacement: 302 cubic inches. Bore and stroke: 4.00 x 3.00 inches. Compression ratio: 8.5:1. Net horsepower: 140 at 4000 R.P.M. Carburetion: Motorcraft two-barrel. Five main bearings. Serial Number code 'F'.

351 'Cleveland' V-8. Overhead valves. Cast iron block. Displacement: 351 cubic inches. Bore and stroke: 4.00 x 3.50 inches. Compression ratio: 8.6:1. Net horsepower: 163 at 3800 R.P.M. Carburetion: Motorcraft two-barrel. Five main bearings. Serial Number code 'H'.

351 'Cleveland' Four-barrel V-8. Overhead valves. Cast iron block. Displacement: 351 cubic inches. Bore and stroke: 4.00 x 3.50 inches. Compression ratio: 8.6:1. Net horsepower: 248 at 5400 R.P.M. Carburetion: Holley four-barrel. Five main bearings. Serial Number code 'M'.

351 HO 'Cleveland' V-8. Overhead valves. Cast iron block. Displacement: 351 cubic inches. Bore and stroke: 4.00 x 3.50 inches. Compression ratio: 8.6:1. Net horsepower: 266 at 5400 R.P.M. Carburetion: Holley four-barrel. Five main bearings. Serial Number code 'Q'.

MUSTANG OPTIONS: 177 horsepower 351 cubic inch 'Cleveland' V-8 ($41). 266 horsepower 351 cubic inch 'Cleveland' B-8 engine ($115). 275 horsepower 351 cubic inch High-Output V-8 with four-barrel carburetion ($841-$870). Cruise-O-Matic transmission ($204). Four-speed manual transmission ($193). Power steering 9$103). Power front disc brakes ($62). Limited-slip differential ($43). Magnum 500 chrome wheels ($108-$139). Center console ($53-$97). Vinyl roof ($79). White sidewall tires ($34).

Historical footnotes: The 1972 Mustangs were introduced September 24, 1971. Calendar year sales, by United States dealers, stopped at 120,589 units, a decline from the previous season. Model year production stopped at 111,015 cars. Of these, 2.7 percent had four-speed manual transmission; 3.9 percent had Tilt-Telescope steering; 6.2 percent wore optional styled wheels and 32.3 percent had vinyl tops. There were no changes in top Ford management, although B.E. Bidwell would soon be elected Vice-President and General Manager of Ford Marketing Corportion.

1973 MUSTANG

1973 Ford, Mustang 2-dr convertible, V-8

MUSTANG SERIES — (ALL ENGINES) — The 1973 Mustangs were virtually the same as the 1972 models. The Mustang convertible was the only car of that body style still offered by Ford, as well as one of the few remaining rag-tops in the entire industry. All Mustangs featured a high-impact molded urethane front bumper that was color-keyed to the body. One design change for the new season was a revised cross-hatch design in the grille. New Mustang exterior colors and interior trims were provided. New options included forged aluminum wheels and steel-belted radial-ply tires. Headlights, still of single-unit design, were housed inside square panels that flanked the grille on each side. New features of the grille itself included a 'floating' Pony badge at the center and an egg crate style insert with vertical parking lights in the outboard segments. A new front valance panel was of unslotted design. Standard equipment included the '250' Six or '302' V-8; three-speed manual transmission; floor-mounted shift control; E78 x 14 black sidewall tires; rocker panel and wheel lip moldings; lower back panel applique with bright molding; chrome, rectangular lefthand door mirror; all-vinyl upholstery and door trim; mini front console; color-keyed loop-pile carpets; DeLuxe two-spoke steering wheel (with woodtone insert); cigarette lighter; seat belt reminder system and door courtesy lamps. The fastback 'Sportsroof' style also included a tinted back window and fixed rear quarter windows. The convertible added under-dash courtesy lights; power-operated vinyl top; glass backlight; knit-vinyl seat trim and power front disc brakes. Standard extras on the Mustang Grande, in addition to base equipment, was comprised of dual, color-keyed racing mirrors; vinyl roof; bodyside tape striping; special wheel covers; trunk mat; Lambeth cloth and vinyl seat trim; molded door panels with integral arm rests; bright pedal pads; DeLuxe instrument panel and electric clock. Also available was the Mustang Mach I, which came with all of the following: competition suspension package; choice of two hood designs (one with NASA-type scoops); size E70-14 whitewall tires, of bias-belted, wide-oval construction; color-keyed dual racing mirrors; black grille and back panel appliques; back panel tape stripe; wheel trim rings and hub caps; tinted back window; all-vinyl upholstery and trim (with high-back bucket seats) and the 136 SAE Net horsepower version of the two-barrel 302 cubic inch V-8.

MUSTANG SERIES I.D. NUMBERS — (ALL ENGINES) — Mustangs used the same Serial Number sequence as the full-size Fords, Torinos and Mavericks (See 1973 Ford section).

MUSTANG SERIES

Model Number	Body/Style Number	Body Type & Seating	Factory Price	Shipping Weight	Production Total
NA	65D	2-dr HT Cpe-4P	2760/2847	2984/3076	51,430
NA	63D	2-dr FsBk Cpe-4P	2820/2907	2991/3083	10,820
NA	76D	2-dr Conv-4P	3102/3189	3106/3198	11,853
NA	65F	2-dr Grande-4P	2946/3033	2982/3074	25,274
NA	63R	2-dr Mach I-4P	3088	3090	35,440

PRODUCTION NOTE: Total series output was 134,867 units. The price and weights to the left of the slant bar indicate six-cylinder equipped models and the price and weight to the right of the slant bar indicate V-8 powered models. The Mach I was available only with V-8 power.

MUSTANG SERIES CHASSIS FEATURES: Same as 1972, except that length increased by four inches to a total of 194 inches overall.

MUSTANG SERIES ENGINES
Mustang six-cylinder. Overhead valves. Cast iron block. Displacement: 250 cubic inches. Bore and stroke: 3.68 x 3.91 inches. Compression ratio: 8.0;1. Net horsepower: 88 at 3200 R.P.M. Carburetion: Motorcraft single-barrel. Seven main bearings. Serial Number code 'L'.

302 V-8. Overhead valves. Cast iron block. Displacement: 302 cubic inches. Bore and stroke: 4.00 x 3.00 inches. Compression ratio: 8.0:1. Net horsepower: 135 at 4200 R.P.M. Carburetion: Motorcraft two-barrel. Five main bearings. Serial Number code 'F'.

351 'Windsor' V-8. Overhead valves. Cast iron block. Displacement: 351 cubic inches. Bore and stroke: 4.00 x 3.50 inches. Compression ratio: 8.0:1. Net horsepower: 156 at 3800 R.P.M. Carburetion:. Motorcraft two-barrel. Five main bearings. Serial Number code 'H'.

351 'Cleveland' V-8. Overhead valves. Cast iron block. Displacement: 351 cubic inches. Bore and stroke: 4.00 x 3.50 inches. Compression ratio: 8.0:1. Net horsepower 154 at 4000 R.P.M. Carburetion: Motorcraft two-barrel. Five main bearings. Serial Number code 'H'.

MUSTANG OPTIONS: 302 cubic inch two-barrel V-8, standard in Mach I; in other models ($87). 351 cubic inch two-barrel V-8 ($128). 351 cubic inch four-barrel V-8, including 55 amp alternator; heavy-duty 55 amp battery; special intake manifold; special valve springs and dampers; large-capacity 4300-D carburetor; 2.5 inch diameter dual exhaust outlets; modified camshaft and four-bolt main bearing caps. Requires Cruise-O-Matic 3.25 axle ratio or four-speed manual 3.50 axle ratio transmission, power front disc brakes, competition suspension ($194). California emission testing ($14). Select-Shift Cruise-O-Matic transmission ($204). Four-speed manual with Hurst shifter, not available with six-cylinder ($193). Power front disc brakes, standard convertible; required with 351 V-8s, ($62). Power windows ($113). Power steering, required with Tilt-Away steering wheel, ($103). Select-Aire conditioning, including extra cooling package; not available on six-cylinder with three-speed manual transmission ($368). Console, in Grande ($53); in other models ($68). Convenience Group, including trunk light; glove compartment light; map light; underhood light; 'lights on' warning buzzer; automatic seatback releases; under-dash courtesy lights (standard on convertible); parking brake warning light and glove compartment lock ($46). Electric rear window defroster, not available with convertible or six-cylinder ($57). Tinted glass, convertible ($14); others ($36). Instrumentation Group, including tachometer, trip odometer and oil pressure, ammeter and temperature gauges; included with Mach I Sports Interior, not available on six-cylinders; Grande without console ($55); others ($71). Color-keyed dual racing mirrors, standard Grande, Mach I, ($23). AM radio ($59). AM/FM stereo radio ($191). Sport deck rear seat Sportsroof, Mach I only ($86). DeLuxe three-spoke Rim-Blow steering wheel ($35). Tilt-Away steering wheel, power steering required, ($41). DeLuxe leather-wrapped two-spoke steering wheel ($23). Stereo-Sonic Tape System, AM radio required ($120). Intermittent windshield wipers ($23). Optional axle ratios ($12). Traction-Lok differential ($43). Heavy-duty 70 amp per hour battery, standard hardtop and convertible with 351 two-barrel in combination with Instrument Group or Select-Aire, ($14). Extra-cooling package, standard with Select-Aire, not available on six-cylinders, ($13). Dual Ram Induction, 351 two-barrel V-8, including functional NACA-type hood with black or argent two-tone paint, hood lock pins, 'Ram-Air' engine decals, ($58). Rear deck spoiler, Sportsroof, Mach I only ($29). Competition suspension, including extra heavy-duty front and rear springs, extra heavy-duty front and rear shock absorbers; standard Mach I; not available on six-cylinders ($28). DeLuxe seat and shoulder belts, standard convertible except shoulder belts ($15). DeLuxe Bumper Group including rear rubber bumper inserts and full-width horizontal strip ($25). Rear bumper guards ($14). Decor Group, including black or argent lower bodyside paint with bright upper edge moldings, unique grille with sport lamps, trim rings with hubcaps; deletes rocker panel and wheel lip moldings with Decor Group, ($51). Door edge guards, included with Protection Group, ($6). Color-keyed front floor mats ($13). Metallic Glow paint ($35). Two-tone hood paint, Mach I ($18); others ($34). Protection Group, including vinyl-insert bodyside moldings, spae tire lock, door edge guards; deletes bodyside tape stripe on grande, not available on Mach I or with Decor Group ($23); others ($36). Vinyl roof, hardtops, including C-pillar tri-color ornament; standard Grande, ($80). three-quarter vinyl roof, Sportsroof only ($52). Mach I Sports Interior, V-8 Sportsroof, Mach I only, including knitted vinyl trim, high-back bucket sets with accent stripes, Instrumentation Group, door trim panels with integral pull handles and arm rests, color-accented deep embossed carpet runners, DeLuxe black instrument panel applique with woodtone center section, bright pedal pads, rear seat ashtry, ($115). Black or argent bodyside stripes, with Decor Group only ($23). Trim rings with hubcaps, standard on Mach I and with Decor Group, Grande ($8); others ($31). Sports wheel covers, Grande ($56); Mach I, Decor Group ($48); others ($79). Forged aluminum wheels, Grande ($119); Mach 1, Decor Group ($111); others ($142).

Historical footnotes: Most 1973 Mustangs, 90.4 percent were equipped with the automatic, 6.7 percent had the three-speed manual, 2.9 percent had the four-speed manual, 92.9 percent had power steering, 77.9 percent had power brakes; 5.6 percent had a tilting steering wheel, 62.8 percent had tinted glass, 3.2 percent had power windows and 56.2 percent were sold with an air conditioner.

1974 MUSTANG

1974 Ford, Mustang II 2-dr hatch back coupe, 4-cyl

MUSTANG II SERIES — (ALL ENGINES) — Ford Motor Company introduced its all-new Mustang II in 1974. It was billed as the 'right car at the right time'. The new Pony measured seven inches shorter than the original 1965 Mustang and was a full 13 inches shorter than the 1973. Sales of the new entry were sluggish at first, since the company loaded most cars in the early mix with a lot of optional equipment. It didn't take long, however, for the marketing men to see that the car had greatest appeal as an economy job. The Mustang II was a combination of design motifs derived from both sides of the Atlantic. The Italian coachbuilding firm of Ghia, recently acquired by Ford Motor Company, did some of the primary design work, while other ingredients came straight from the Ford/Mercury/Lincoln styling studios. Four models were available, the notch back coupe, three-door fastback, Ghia notch back coupe and fastback Mach I. Standard equipment included a 2.3 liter Four; four-speed manual transmission with floor shift; solid state ignition; front disc brakes; tachometer; steel-belted whitewalls; low-back front bucket seats; vinyl upholstery and door trim; color-keyed carpeting; woodtone instrument panel applique; European type arm rests and full wheel covers. The 2+2 model added a fold-down rear seat and styled steel wheels. The Ghia notch back coupe also had ,in addition to the base equipment, color-keyed DeLuxe seat belts; dual color-keyed remote-control door mirrors; Super Sound Package;shag carpeting; woodtone door panel accents; digital clock; super-soft vinyl or Westminster cloth interior trim; color-keyed vinyl roof and spoke-style wheel covers. The Mach I had all 2+2 equipment, plus 2.8-liter V-6 engine; dual color-keyed remote-control door mirrors; Wide-Oval steel-belted BSW radial tires; black lower bodyside paint; decklid striping and styled steel wheels with trim rings.

MUSTANG II SERIES I.D. NUMBERS — (ALL ENGINES) — Mustang II models used the same Serial Number sequence as full-size Ford, Torinos.

MUSTANG II SERIES

NA	60F	2-dr HT Cpe-4P	3081	2620	177,671
NA	69F	3-dr FsBk-4P	3275	2699	74,799
NA	60H	2-dr Ghia Cpe-4P	3427	2866	89,477
NA	69R	2-dr Mach I-4P	3621	2778	44,046

PRODUCTION NOTE: Total series output was 385,993 units.

MUSTANG II SERIES CHASSIS FEATURES: Wheelbase: 96.2 inches. Overall length: 175 inches. Tires: B78 x 13 belted blackwall (BR78 x 13 on Ghia model).

FORD MUSTANG ENGINES
Mustang four-cylinder. Overhead cam. Cast iron block. Displacement: 140 cubic inches. Bore and stroke: 3.78 x 3.13 inches. Compression ratio: 8.6:1. SAE Net horsepower: 85. Carburetion: Motorcraft two-barrel. Five main bearings. Serial Number code 'Y'.

Mustang V-6. Overhead valves. Cast iron block. Displacement: 169 cubic inches. Bore and stroke: 3.66 x 2.70 inches. Compression ratio: 8.0:1. SAE Net horsepower 105. Carburetion: two-barrel. Serial Number code 'Z'.

MUSTANG OPTIONS: 2.8-liter (171 cubic inch) 105 horsepower V-6, standard in Mach I; in other Mustang IIs ($229). Select-Shift Cruise-O-Matic ($212). Convenience Group includes: dual color-keyed remote-control door mirrors; right visor vanity mirror; inside day/night mirror; parking brake boot and rear ash tray, on Mustangs with Luxury Interior Group ($41); on Mach I or Mustangs with Rallye Package ($21); on other Mustangs ($57). Light Group includes: underhood, glovebox, map, ash tray and instrument panel courtesy lights, plus trunk or cargo area courtesy light and warning lamps for parking brake, 'door ajar' and 'headlamps-on' ($44). Luxury Interior Group includes: super-soft vinyl upholstery; DeLuxe door panels with large arm rests and woodtone accents; DeLuxe rear quarter trim; 25 ounce cut-pile carpeting; sound package; parking brake boot; door courtesy lamps; rear ashtray; standard in Ghia, in other Mustangs ($100). Maintenance Group includes: shop manual; spare bulbs; fire extinguisher; flares; warning flag; fuses; tire gauge; bungee cord; lube kit; trouble light; pliers; screwdriver and crescent wrench ($44). Rallye Package, 2.8 V-8 required—not available on Ghia, includes Traction-Lok differential; steel-belted RWL tires; extra-cooling package; competition suspension; dual color-keyed remote-control door mirrors; styled steel wheels; sport exhaust system; digital clock and leather-wrapped steering wheel; on Mach I ($150), on 2+2 ($284), on others ($328). Select-Aire conditioning ($383). Anti-theft alarm system ($75). Traction-Lok differential ($45). Heavy-duty battery ($14). Color-keyed DeLuxe seat belts, standard in Ghia, in others ($17). Front and rear bumper guards ($37). Digital clock, standard in Ghia, in others ($36). Console ($43). Electric rear window defroster ($59). California emission equipment ($19). Full tinted glass ($37). Dual color-keyed door mirrors, standard in Ghia and Mach I; in others ($36). Rocker panel moldings ($14). Vinyl-insert bodyside moldings ($50). Glamour paint ($36). Pinstripes ($14). Power brakes ($45). Power steering ($106). Radios, AM ($61); AM/FM monaural ($124); AM/FM stereo ($222); AM/FM stereo with tape player ($346). Competition suspension, including heavy-duty springs; adjustable shocks; rear anti-roll bar and 195/70 B/WL tires ($37). Flip-out quarter windows, for 2+2 and Mach I fastbacks only ($29). Vinyl roof, hardtop only— standard on Ghia; on other models ($83). Fold-down rear seat ($61). Super Sound Package, standard in Ghia; in others ($22). Leather-wrapped steering wheel ($30). Sun roof ($149). Luggage compartment trim ($28). Picardy velour cloth trim, Ghia ($62). Wheel trim rings, standard on Ghia; on others ($32).

Historical footnotes: The new Mustang II was initially released as a luxury sub-compact in mid-1973 and, by the end of model year 1974, had recorded an impressive record of 338,136 assemblies, which compared to only 193,129 sales of the 'big' Mustangs sold the previous model year.

1975 MUSTANG

1975 Ford, Mustang II Ghia 2-dr coupe, 4-cyl

MUSTANG II — (FOUR/SIX) — SERIES O — Throughout its five years of availability, the Mustang II would see very little change. A 'moonroof' option and extra-cost V-8 engine were the major revisions for 1975. The design of the steering wheel was modified. A two-spoke type was used again, but the spokes bent downwards at each end instead of running nearly straight across, as in the 1974 models. Ghia models had a new roofline, with thicker, 'blind' rear quarters. This made the opera windows somewhat smaller. Another Ghia addition was a stand-up hood ornament. New hub caps were featured with most decor-levels and, on cars with catalytic converters, unleaded fuel decals were affixed to the gas filler cap. In mid-year, several changes took effect. The first was a slightly plainer Ghia coupe with restyled hub caps and no hood ornament. The second was the Mustang II MPG, an economy leader that gave 26-28 highway miles per gallon. Standard equipment on the basic notchback hardtop included solid state ignition; front disc brakes; tachometer; steel-belted BR78 x 13 black sidewall tires; low-back front bucket seats; vinyl upholstery and trim; wood-grained dash appliques; arm rests; full wheel covers; four-speed manual transmission with floor shift and the 2.3 liter Four. The standard 2+2 fastback added a fold-down rear seat and styled steel wheels. the Ghia coupe had all base equipment plus DeLuxe color-keyed seat belts; dual color-keyed, remote controlled OSRV door mirrors; radial whitewalls; Super Sound package; shag carpeting; wood-grained door accent panels; digital clock; choice of Westminster cloth or super-soft vinyl trim; color-keyed vinyl roof and spoke-style wheel covers. The Mach I fastback model had all equipment used on the 2+2, plus color-keyed, remote-control OSRV door mirrors; steel-belted BR70 x 13 wide oval tires; black lower bodyside paint; specific rear deck lid striping; styled steel wheels and with trim rings and the 2.8 liter V-6 engine.

VEHICLE I.D. NUMBERS: Vehicle Identification Numbers were located on the top left hand surface of the instrument panel and had eleven symbols. The first symbol '5' designated 1975 model year. The second symbol designated the assembly plant. The third symbol '0' designated Mustang. The fourth symbol designated the Body Style Number, as follows: '2' = two-door notch back coupe; '3' = three-door fastback coupe; '4' = two-door Ghia notch back coupe and '5' + two-door fastback Mach I coupe. The fifth symbol designated the engine. The last six symbols were the sequential unit number beginning at 100001 and up. The third and fourth symbols in the VIN (first and second columns of the chart below) were the same as the Ford Model Number.

MUSTANG II SERIES

Model Number	Body/Style Number	Body Type & Seating	Factory Price	Shipping Weight	Production Total
MUSTANG II LINE					
0	2	2-dr Cpe-4P	3529/3801	2660/2775	85,155
0	3	3-dr FsBk Cpe-4P	3818/4090	2697/2812	30,038
0	4	2-dr Ghia Cpe-4P	3938/4210	2704/2819	52,320
MUSTANG II MACH I LINE					
0	5	3-dr FsBk Cpe-4P	4188	2879	21,062

NOTE: In the specifications chart above, prices and weights above slash apply to Fours/below slash to V-6s.

MUSTANG II SERIES ENGINES

BASE 2.3 LITRE FOUR
Inline Four. Overhead valves and camshaft. Cast iron block. Displacement: 140 cubic inches. Bore and stroke: 3.78 x 3.12 inches. SAE Net horsepower: 83. Hydraulic valve lifters. Carburetor: Motorcraft two-barrel Model 5200.

BASE 2.8 LITRE V—6
V-6. Overhead valves and camshaft. Cast iron block. Displacement: 170.8 inches. Bore and stroke: 3.66 x 2.70 inches. SAE Net horsepower: 97. Carburetor: Motorcraft two-barrel Model 5200.

OPTIONAL 5.0 LITRE V-8
V-8. Overhead valves. Cast iron block. Displacement: 302 cubic inches. Bore and stroke: 4.002 x 3.00 inches. SAE Net horsepower: 122. Carburetor: Motorcraft two-barrel Model 2150.

CHASSIS FEATURES: Wheelbase: (all models) 96.2 inches. Overall length: (all models) 175 inches. Front tread: (all models) 55.6 inches. Rear tread: (all models) 55.8 inches. Tires: Refer to text.

POWERTRAIN OPTIONS: Four-speed manual transmission with floor shift (standard). Select-Shift Cruise-O-Matic ($227). Mach I 2.8 litre, 171 cubic inch V-6 engine, in Mach I (no charge); in other models ($253). 5.0 litre, 302 cubic inch V-8 engine, in Mach I ($172); in other models ($199). Traction-Lok differential ($46). Heavy-duty battery ($14). Extended range fuel tank ($18).

CONVENIENCE OPTIONS: Exterior Accent Group ($151). Select-Aire conditioning ($401). Anti-Theft alarm system ($71). DeLuxe color-keyed seat belts, in Ghia (standard); in other models ($51). Front and rear bumper guards ($31). Digital quartz electic clock ($37). Console ($63). Electric rear window defroster ($59). California emissions equipment ($41). Fuel monitor warning light ($14). Deck lid Luggage rack ($43). Dual, color-keyed OSRV door mirrors, standard Ghia/Mach I; on others ($36). Rocker panel moldings ($14). Color-keyed vinyl insert type bodyside moldings ($51). Power steering ($111). Glass moonroof ($422). Radio, AM ($63); AM/FM ($124); AM/FM stereo ($213); with 8-track ($333). Glamour paint ($43). Vinyl roof for hardtop coupe, standard with Ghia; on others ($83). Fold-down rear seat, standard in fastbacks; on others ($61). Leather-wrapped steering wheel ($30). Pin striping ($18). Sun roof ($195). Competition suspension, includes heavy-duty springs; adjustable shock absorbers; rear anti-roll bar and 195/70 blackwall or White Line tires, on Ghia or others with Exterior Accent Group ($43); on Mach I ($25); on others ($55). Velour cloth interior trim ($63). Flip-out rear quarter windows, on fastbacks ($31).

CONVENIENCE OPTION PACKAGES: Convenience-Group, includes dual, color-keyed, remote-controlled OSRV door mirros; righthand visor/vanity mirror; inside day/nite mirror; parking brake boot and rear ashtray, with Luxury Interior Group ($48); with Mach I or models with Rallye Package or Exterior Accent Group ($29); on other models ($65). **Light Group,** includes underhood; glove box; ashtray; dashboard courtesy lights plus map light, 'door ajar' and head lamps-on warning lights ($33). **Security Lock Group,** includes locking gas cap; inside hood release lock and spare tire lock ($14). **Luxury Interior Group,** includes Super-Soft vinyl seats; door trim with large arm rests; DeLuxe rear quarter trim; door courtesy lights; color-keyed seat belts; shag carpets; parking brake boot; rear ashtray and Super-Sound package ($100). **Ghia Silver Luxury Group,** (for Ghia coupe only), includes Silver metallic paint; silver Normande-grain half-vinyl roof; standup hood ornament; Cranberry striping; Silver bodyside moldings; all-Cranberry interior in Media volour cloth; color-keyed sun visors and headliner; plus center console ($151). **Maintenance Group,** includes shop manual; bulbs; fire extinguisher; flares; warning flag; fuses; tire gauge; bungee cloth; lube kit; trouble light; pliers; screw driver and crescent wrench ($45). **Rallye Package,** includes Traction-Lok differential; 195/70 RWL tires; extra-cooling package; bright exhaust tips; competition suspension package; dual, color-keyed, remote-control OSRV door mirrors; leather-wrapped steering wheel and styled steel wheels with trim rings, on Mach I ($168); on 2+2 ($218); on other models ($262). **Protection Group,** includes door edge guards; front floor mats and license plate frames; on Mach I ($19); on others ($27).

Historical footnotes: The 1975 Mustang II lineup was introduced in September, 1974, with the plainer Ghia coupe and Mustang II M.P.G. bowing at mid-year. Modwl year production of 188,575 cars was recorded. Lee Iacocca was chief executive officer of the company this year. The new Mustang II V-8 was capable of a top speed above 105 miles per hour and could cover the standing start 1/4 mile in 17.9 seconds with a terminal speed of 77 miles per hour.

MUSTANG
1976-1986

1974 Mustang II

Disappointment was doubtless a common reaction among ponycar fans, when Mustang II replaced the former edition for 1974. Ford's claim that it was the "right car at the right time" may well have been accurate, especially in view of the gas crisis. Yet it was far removed from the original concept of a decade past—and farther yet from the scorching performance versions that greeted the early 1970s. Still, the new and smaller Mustang sold a lot better than its ample predecessor. Sales fell after the opening year, but remained well above the level of 1971-73.

1976 Mustang Cobra II 2+2 coupe (F)

As 1976 rolled around, Mustang came with a four, German-made V-6, or small-block (302 cu. in.) V-8 engine. The two-door hardtop had a restrained look, while the 2--2 hatchback showed more sporty lines. Ghia was the luxury edition, while Mach 1 sounded a lot more exciting than reality dictated. A silver Stallion appearance group added few thrills, and even the new blackout-trimmed Cobra II package was stronger on bold looks than performance.

Cobra II became more colorful by 1977, and a T-Roof became available, but not much changed otherwise. For its next (and final) season, Mustang II added a V-8 powered King Cobra selection with giant snake on the hood. Though ranking with collectible Mustangs, the King added little to Mustang's performance capability.

Customers eagerly awaited the next Mustang, which took on a far different form—a design that was destined for long life. Notchback (two-door) and hatchback (three-door) bodies were offered again, but the new aero wedge shape could hardly be compared with Mustang II.

1980 Mustang "Carriage Roof" coupe (F)

By year's end, five different engines had been installed under Mustang hoods: base four, carryover V-6, replacement inline six, 302 V-8, and a new turbocharged four. Both the turbo and V-8 produced 140 horsepower. The Cobra option package could have either engine. Sport and TRX packages helped Mustang's handling. To tempt contemporary customers and later collectors, about 6,000 Indy Pace Car replicas were produced. Sales zoomed upward for the model year, but slipped back close to pre-1979 levels later.

1982 Mustang 5.OL coupe (F)

Cobra for 1980 adopted some styling touches from the Pace Car, including a slat-style grille, foglamps and hood scoop. While turbo power went up, the 302 cu. in. V-8 disappeared temporarily, replaced by a 255. A new carriage roof was designed to resemble a convertible, but the real thing would arrive a couple of years later. Not much changed for 1981, except for the availability of a new five-speed gearbox. But a year later the "Boss" 302 V-8 was back, stronger than before (while the turbo took a breather for one season). Mustang's revised model lineup now included a GT instead of the old Cobra option, yet sales declined for the third year in a row.

The awaited convertible Mustang arrived for 1983, along with a restyled front and rear end. Replacing the V-8's carburetor with a four-barrel boosted horsepower up to 175. At the other end, the base four's carb switched from two barrels to one. When the turbo emerged again, it had new multi-port fuel injection. Borg-Warner's close-ratio five-speed could help GT Mustangs hit 60 MPH in the seven-second neighborhood.

1984 Mustang SVO coupe (F)

1984½ Mustang GT-350 20th Anniversary convertible (JG)

Several years earlier, Ford had formed a Special Vehicle Operations Department to oversee racing and limited-edition production. The first regular-production fruit of their labor appeared for 1984: the Mustang SVO, with an air-to-air intercooler on its turbocharged four-cylinder engine. SVO's five-speed had a Hurst linkage, wheels held big 16-inch tires, and it stopped with discs on all wheels. A non- intercooled turbo went into GT models. Sales edged upward again in 1984, and further yet in the next two years.

All Mustangs for 1985 sported a single-slot grille similar to SVO's. Roller tappets and a performance camshaft gave GT's carbureted 302 V-8 a 210-horsepower rating, 30 more than the fuel-injected V-8. Sequential fuel injection went into V-8s for 1986, adding 20 horsepower; but the four-barrel version faded away. SVO turbos now managed to produce 200 horsepower, ready for the Hurst-shifted five-speed.

Expensive when new, SVO is surely one of the Mustangs worth hanging onto. Far more exotic would be the McLaren Mustang, but only 250 were produced in 1981. A mid-1980s GT wouldn't be a bad choice either, with so many more available. Quite a few of the '79 Pace Car replicas went on sale, too, and might be worth a look. King Cobras of 1978 have attracted some interest, as have some of the "ordinary" Cobra versions. Of course, some people consider just about every Mustang to be worth owning, if not exactly collectible.

1984 through the present Mustang emphasized the hi-performance GT models and in both convertible and hatchback. Ford even threatened to discontinue the traditional Mustang in favor of the Mazda based Probe. A flood of letters from V-8 hi-performance firms urged Ford to produce both cars.

1976 MUSTANG

1976 Mustang II Stallion 2+2 coupe (F)

MUSTANG II — FOUR/V-6/V-8 — Restyled in a new smaller size in 1974, Mustang came in two basic body styles: a two-door hardtop and three-door 2+2 hatchback. The two-door was commonly referred to by Ford as a sedan rather than a coupe, which distinguished it from the old (larger) coupe design. The "three-door" model had only two doors for people, and was designated either a hatchback or fastback, both terms accurately describing the sloping lift-up rear design. Two-doors came in base or Ghia trim; fastbacks in base or Mach 1 form. Fastbacks had fold- down rear seats, while the hardtops displayed a formal-look roofline. An MPG series, carrying fewer standard items and a smaller price tag, had joined the Mustang lineup in mid-year 1975 and continued in 1976. This year's highlights included significant fuel economy gains, some new options, and a new sport exterior dress-up package for the 2+2 and Mach 1. The former horizontal stainless steel bumper inserts were replaced by black bumper rub strips with white stripes. The wiper/washer control had moved to the turn signal lever in mid-year 1975, and continued there this year. To improve economy, Mustang II got a lower optional 2.79:1 axle ratio. An optional wide-ratio transmission was available with that rear-end ratio. New options included sporty plaid trim on seating surfaces; expanded availability of Ghia luxury coupe colors; whitewall tires; and an AM radio with stereo tape player. Styling was similar to 1975, except for a new air scoop below the front bumper. Rectangular parking/signal lamps were inset right into the forward-slanting grille, which had a 14 x 6 hole crosshatch pattern. The grille was narrower at the top than at the base, with a traditional Mustang (horse) emblem in its center. Separate 'Ford' block letters stood above the grille, facing upward. Single round headlamps were recessed into squarish housings. The front bumper protruded forward in the center, matching the width of the grille. Rub strips wrapped only slightly onto the bumper sides. Door sheetmetal had a sculptured, depressed area that began near the back and extended for a short distance on the quarter panel, following the contour of the wheel opening. The curvaceous bodyside crease ran below the door handle. Two-doors had a 'B' pillar and conventional quarter window. Fastbacks had sharply tapered quarter windows that came to a point at the rear. Each European-style taillamp consisted of three side-by-side sections, with a small backup lens at the bottom of each center section and large amber turn signal lenses. Large 'Ford' block letters stood on the panel between the taillamps, above the license plate housing. Bodies had a a one-piece fiberglass-reinforced front end nd color-keyed urethane-coated bumpers. Standard features included wheel lip moldings, side marker lights with die-cast bezels, recessed door handles, and slim high-lustre exterior trim moldings. Inside were low-back all-vinyl front bucket seats with full-width head restraints, tachometer, speedometer, ammeter, fuel and temperature gauges, European- type armrests with integral pull handles, a two-spoke steering wheel, and lockable glovebox. Simulated burled walnut woodtone accents went on the instrument panel and shift knob. Mustang had a unitized body and chassis with front isolated mini-frame, Hotchkiss-type rear suspension, and rack-and-pinion steering. The rear suspension consisted of longitudinal semi-elliptic leaf springs (four leaves), while the independent front suspension used ball joints, a stabilizer bar, and compression-type struts. Standard engine was a 140 cu. in. (2.3-liter) four with four-speed floor shift. Optional: a 302 cu. in. (5.0-liter) V-8 with Cruise-O- Matic, or 171 cu. in. (2.8-liter) V-6 with four-speed manual. Mach 1 had the V-6 as standard. A four-speed manual gearbox became available with the V-8 later in the season. Front disc brakes were standard; power brakes (and steering) optional. Ghias included a quartz digital clock, bodyside molding, BR78 x 13 steel-belted radial whitewalls, padded half or full vinyl roof, hood ornament, dual remote mirrors, crushed velour seat surfaces, full console, and bodyside paint stripes. Mach 1 added the 2.8-liter V-6, dual remote racing mirrors, BR70 x 13 raised-white-letter tires on styled steel wheels, and rear tape and fender decals. Black paint went on lower bumpers, lower bodyside, and between rear taillamps. Ghias had wire-type wheel covers; Mach 1 included wheel trim rings. Three Luxury Groups were available: Silver, Tan Glow, and Silver Blue Glow (the latter two colors new this year). Two special option packages were offered: a new Stallion group intended to appeal to youthful buyers, and the more notorious Cobra II. The sporty silver Stallion package featured a two-tone paint and tape treatment (on fastback models); a large Stallion decal on front fenders (at the cowl); dual racing mirrors; styled steel wheels with raised- white-letter tires; and a competition suspension. Black paint highlighted the greenhouse, lower body, hood, grille, decklid, and lower back panel. On the ultimate option, large 'Cobra II' decal lettering at the door bottoms was easy to spot from a distance. Cobra II sported a black grille with cobra emblem, front air dam, simulated hood scoop, rear spoiler, and rocker-panel racing stripes. Dual wide stripes ran from the grille, over the hood and roof, onto the deck area. Front fenders displayed large cobra (snake) decals. Louvers covered the triangular flip-out quarter windows. Inside was a sport steering wheel and brushed-aluminum trim on dash and door panels, plus dual remote-control mirrors. Cobra II carried a standard V-6 ngine and four-speed, with raised-white-letter tires on styled steel wheels. Only one body color scheme was offered at first: white with blue striping.

I.D. DATA: Mustang's 11-symbol Vehicle Identification Number (VIN) is stamped on a metal tab fastened to the instrument panel, visible through the windshield. The first digit is a model year code ('6' 1976). The second letter indicates assembly plant: 'F' Dearborn, MI; 'R' San Jose, CA. Digits three and four are the body serial code, which corresponds to the Model Numbers shown in the tables below: '02' 2-dr. HT; '03' 3-dr. 22 hatchback; '04' Ghia 2-dr. HT; '05' Mach 1 3-dr. 22 hatchback. The fifth digit is an engine code: 'Y' L4-140 2Bbl.; 'Z' V6170 2Bbl.; 'F' V8302 2Bbl. Finally, digits 6-11 make up the consecutive unit number, starting with 100,001. A Vehicle Certification Label on the left front door lock face panel or door pillar shows the manufacturer, month and year of manufacture, GVW, GAWR, certification statement, VIN, body code, color code, trim code, axle code, transmission code, and domestic (or foreign) special order code.

MUSTANG II (FOUR/V-6)

Model Number	Body/Style Number	Body Type & Seating	Factory Price	Shipping Weight	Production Total
02	60F	2-dr. Notch Cpe-4P	3525/3791	2678/2756	78,508
03	69F	3-dr. 2+2 hatch-4P	3781/4047	2706/2784	62,312

1976 Mustang II Ghia coupe (F)

MUSTANG GHIA (FOUR/V-6)

04	60H	2-dr. Notch Cpe-4P	3859/4125	2729/2807	37,515

MUSTANG MACH 1 (V-6/V-8)

05	69R	3-dr. 22 Hatch-4P	4209/4154	2822/ --	9,232

FACTORY PRICE/WEIGHT NOTE: Figures to left of slash are for four- cylinder engine, to right of slash for V-6 engine (Mach 1, V-6 and V-8). A V-8 engine on base or Ghia initially was priced $212 higher than the V-6, but later cost $54 less than a V-6.

ENGINE DATA: BASE FOUR: Inline, overhead cam, four-cylinder. Cast iron block and head. Displacement: 140 cu. in. (2.3 liters). Bore & stroke: 3.78 x 3.13 in. Compression ratio: 9.0:1. Brake horsepower: 92 at 5000 R.P.M. Torque: 121 lbs.-ft. at 3000 R.P.M. Five main bearings. Hydraulic valve lifters. Carburetor: 2Bbl. Holley-Weber 9510. VIN Code: Y. OPTIONAL V-6: 60-degree, overhead valve V-6. Cast iron block and head. Displacement: 170.8 cu. in. (2.8 liters). Bore & stroke: 3.66 x 2.70 in. Compression ratio: 8.7:1. Brake horsepower: 103 at 4400 R.P.M. Torque: 149 lbs.-ft. at 2800 R.P.M. Four main bearings. Solid valve lifters. Carburetor: 2Bbl. Holley-Weber 9510. German-built. VIN Code: Z. OPTIONAL V-8: 90-degree, overhead valve V-8. Cast iron block and head. Displacement: 302 cu. in. (5.0 liters). Bore & stroke: 4.00 x 3.00 in. Compression ratio: 8.0:1. Brake horsepower: 134 at 3600 R.P.M. Torque: 247 lbs.-ft. at 1800 R.P.M. Five main bearings. Hydraulic valve lifters. Carburetor: 2Bbl. Motorcraft 9510. VIN Code: F.

CHASSIS DATA: Wheelbase: 96.2 in. Overall length: 175.0 in. Height: (Notch cpe) 50.0 in.; (Hatch) 49.7 in. Width: 70.2 in. Front Tread: 55.6 in. Rear Tread: 55.8 in. Wheel Size: 13 x 5 in. Standard Tires: B78 x 13 exc. (Ghia) BR78 x 13; (Mach 1) BR70 x 13 RWL SBR. Sizes CR70 x 13 and 195/70R13 were available.

TECHNICAL: Transmission: Four-speed manual transmission (floor shift) standard. Gear ratios: (1st) 4.07:1; (2nd) 2.57:1; (3rd) 1.66:1; (4th) 1.00:1; (Rev) 3.95:1. Four-cylinder four-speed: (1st) 3.50:1; (2nd) 2.21:1; (3rd) 1.43:1; (4th) 1.00:1; (Rev) 3.38:1. Select-Shift three-speed automatic optional (initially standard on V-8). Four-cylinder: (1st) 2.47:1; (2nd) 1.47:1; (3rd) 1.00:1; (Rev) 2.11:1. V-6/V-8 automatic: (1st) 2.46:1; (2nd) 1.46:1; (3rd) 1.00:1; (Rev) 2.20:1. Standard final drive ratio: 2.79:1 w/4spd, 3.18:1 w/auto.; (V-6) 3.00:1; (V-8) 2.79:1. Steering: Rack and pinion. Front Suspension: Compression strut with lower trailing links, stabilizer bar and coil springs. Rear Suspension: Hotchkiss rigid axle w/semi-elliptic leaf springs (four leaves) and anti-sway bar. Brakes: Front disc, rear drum. Disc dia.: 9.3 in. outer, 6.2 in. inner. Drum dia.: 9.0 in. Ignition: Electronic. Body construction: Unibody w/front isolated mini-frame. Fuel tank: 13 gal.

DRIVETRAIN OPTIONS: Engines: 140 cu. in. four ($272 credit from base V-6 price). Transmission/Differential: Cruise-O-Matic trans. ($239). Optional axle ratio ($13). Traction-Lok differential ($48). Brakes/Steering/Suspension: Power brakes ($54). Power steering ($117). Competition suspension ($29-$191). Other: H.D. 53-amp battery ($14). Extended-range fuel tank ($24). Engine block heater ($17). California emission system ($49).

CONVENIENCE/APPEARANCE OPTIONS: Option Packages: Cobra II pkg. ($325). Cobra II modification pkg. ($287). Rallye package: Mach 1 ($163); 22/hardtop ($267-$399). Ghia luxury group ($177). Stallion option ($72). Exterior accent group ($169). Luxury interior group ($117). Convenience group ($35). Light group ($28-$41). Protection group ($36-$43). Comfort/Convenience: Air cond. ($420). Rear defroster, electric ($70). Tinted glass ($46). Leather-wrapped steering wheel ($33). Electric clock ($17). Digital clock ($40). Fuel monitor warning light ($18). Anti-theft alarm ($83). Security lock group ($16). Horns and Mirrors: Dual-note horn ($6). Color-keyed mirrors ($42). Entertainment: AM radio ($71); w/tape player ($192). AM/FM radio ($128). AM/FM stereo radio ($173); w/tape player ($299). Exterior: Glass moonroof ($470). Manual sunroof ($230). Vinyl roof ($86). Half-vinyl roof: Ghia (NC). Glamour paint ($54). Two-tone paint/tape ($84). Pinstriping ($27). Bumper guards, front/rear ($34). Color-keyed vinyl-insert bodyside molding ($60). Rocker panel moldings ($19). Pivoting rear quarter windows ($33). Decklid luggage rack ($51). Interior: Console ($71). Fold-down rear seat ($72). Velour cloth trim ($99). Color-keyed deluxe seatbelts ($17). Wheels and Tires: Cast aluminum spoke wheels ($96-$182). Forged aluminum wheels ($96-$182). Styled steel wheels: 22/HT ($51); Ghia (NC). Trim rings ($35). B78 x 13 BSW ($84). B78 x 13 WSW ($33-$52). BR78 x 13 BSW ($97). BR78 x 13 WSW ($33-$130 BR70 x 13 RWL ($30-$160). CR70 x 13 WSW ($10- $169). 195/70R13 WSW ($22-$191). 195/70R13 RWL ($12-$203). 195/70R13 wide WSW ($5-$208).

HISTORY: Introduced: October 3, 1975. Model year production (U.S.): 187,567. Total production for the U.S. market of 172,365 included 91,880 four-cylinder, 50,124 V-6, and 30,361 V-8 Mustangs. Calendar year production (U.S.): 183,369. Calendar year sales: 167,201. Model year sales by U.S. dealers: N/A.

Historical Footnotes: Mustang, America's best selling small specialty car, had been outselling Monza, Starfire and Skyhawk combined. The optional V-6, also used on the imported Mercury Capri, was made in Germany. A V-8 powered Cobra II could do 0-60 MPH in around 9 seconds.

1977 MUSTANG

1977 Mustang II Ghia coupe (F)

MUSTANG II — FOUR/V-6/V-8 — No significant styling changes were evident on Mustang for 1977, though new colors were offered and both four and V-6 engines lost power. As before, hardtop (notchback) and three-door fastback models were available. Simulated pecan replaced the burled walnut woodgrain interior appliques. California models used a variable-venturi carburetor. Joining the option list were simulated wire wheel covers, painted cast aluminum spoke wheels, a flip-up removable sunroof, four-way manual bucket seats, and high-altitude option. The bronze-tinted glass sunroof panels could either be propped partly open, or remove completely for storage in the trunk. That TBar roof package included a wide black band across the top (except with the Cobra II). Mustang's engine/transmission selection continued as before. Neither a V-6, nor a V-8 with four-speed manual gearbox, was offered in California. The basic two-door hardtop carried a standard 140 cu. in. (2.3-liter) four-cylinder engine with Dura-Spark ignition, four-speed manual gearbox, front disc brakes, color-keyed urethane bumpers, low-back bucket seats with vinyl trim, B78 x 13 tires, and full wheel covers. Bright moldings highlighted the windshield, drip rail, belt, back window and center pillar. Mustang 2+2 hatchbacks included a front spoiler at no extra cost (which could be deleted), along with a sport steering wheel, styled steel wheels, B78 x 13 bias-belted raised-white-letter or 195R/70 whitewall tires, blackout grille, and brushed aluminum instrument panel appliques. Ghia added a half-vinyl roof, pinstripes, unique wheel covers, and bodyside moldings with color-keyed vinyl inserts. Ghia interiors could have Media Velour cloth with large armrests. Stepping up another notch, Mach 1 carried a standard 2.8-liter V-6 and sported a black paint treatment on lower bodyside and back panel. Also included: dual sport mirrors, Mach 1 emblem, and raised-white-letter BR70 x 13 (or 195R/70) steel-belted radial tires on styled steel wheels with trim rings. Cobra II changed its look after the model year began. Big new tri-color tape stripes went on the full bodyside and front spoiler, front bumper, hood, hood scoop, roof, decklid and rear

1977 Mustang Cobra II 2+2 coupe (F)

spoiler. 'Cobra II' block lettering was low on the doors at first, later halfway up as part of the huge center bodyside tape stripe. The decklid spoiler displayed a Cobra snake decal, and another snake highlighted the black grille. Early Cobras also had snake cowl decals. Flat black greenhouse moldings, vertical-style quarter-window louvers (without the snake) and rear-window louvers also became standard. So was a narrow band of flat black along the upper doors. Cobra II equipment also included dual black sport mirrors, rear-opening hood scoop, BR70 or 195/R70 x 13 RWL tires, and brushed

aluminum door trim inserts. The required power brakes cost extra. Cobra II was now offered in four color choices, not just the original white with blue striping. Selections were white body with red, blue or green stripes; or black with gold stripes. A new Rallye package included dual racing mirrors, heavy-duty springs and cooling, adjustable shocks, and rear stabilizer bar. Mustang's Sports Performance package included a 302 cu. in. V-8 with two-barrel carb, heavy-duty four-speed manual gearbox, power steering and brakes, and P195R/70 radial tires. Ghia's Sports Group was available with black or tan body, including a vinyl roof and many color-coordinated components in black or chamois color. Also included was a three-spoke sports steering wheel, cast aluminum wheels with chamois-color spokes, and trunk luggage rack with straps and buckles. The later-arriving 2+2 Rallye Appearance Package replaced the Stallion option. It included dual gold accent stripes on hood and bodysides; flat black wiper arms, door handles, lock cylinders, and antenna; dual black sport mirrors; and argent styled steel wheels with trim rings. A gold-color surround molding highlighted the black grille (which lost its horse emblem). Also included: gold taillamp accent moldings and dual gold accent stripes in bumper rub strips. A black front spoiler was a no-cost option. Black and Polar White body colors were offered with the package. Inside were black or white vinyl seats with gold ribbed velour Touraine cloth inserts and gold welting, and gold accent moldings on door panels.

I.D. DATA: As before, Mustang's 11-symbol Vehicle Identification Number (VIN) is stamped on a metal tab fastened to the instrument panel, visible through the windshield. Coding is similar to 1976. Model year code changed to '7' for 1977.

MUSTANG II (FOUR/V-6)

Model Number	Body/Style Number	Body Type & Seating	Factory Price	Shipping Weight	Production Total
02	60F	2-dr. Notch Cpe-4P	3702/3984	2627/2750	67,783
03	69F	3-dr. 2+2 Hatch-4P	3901/4183	2672/2795	49,161

MUSTANG GHIA (FOUR/V-6)

04	60H	2-dr. Notch Cpe-4P	4119/4401	2667/2790	29,510

MUSTANG MACH 1 (V-6/V-8)

05	69R	3-dr. 2+2 Hatch 4P	4332/4284	2785/--	6,719

FACTORY PRICE/WEIGHT NOTE: Figures to left of slash are for four-cylinder engine, to right of slash for V-6 engine (Mach 1, V-6 and V-8). A V-8 engine on base or Ghia initially was priced $234 higher than the V-6.

PRODUCTION NOTE: Totals shown include 20,937 Mustangs produced as 1978 models, but sold as 1977 models (9,826 model 02, 7,019 model 03, 3,209 Ghia, and 883 Mach 1).

ENGINE DATA: BASE FOUR: Inline, overhead cam, four-cylinder. Cast iron block and head. Displacement: 140 cu. in. (2.3 liters). Bore & stroke: 3.78 x 3.13 in. Compression ratio: 9.0:1. Brake horsepower: 89 at 4800 R.P.M. Torque: 120 lbs.-ft. at 3000 R.P.M. Five main bearings. Hydraulic valve lifters. Carburetor: 2Bbl. Motorcraft 5200. VIN Code: Y. OPTIONAL V-6: 60-degree, overhead valve V-6. Cast iron block and head. Displacement: 170.8 cu. in. (2.8 liters). Bore & stroke: 3.66 x 2.70 in. Compression ratio: 8.7:1. Brake horsepower: 93 at 4200 R.P.M. Torque: 140 lbs.-ft. at 2600 R.P.M. Four main bearings. Solid valve lifters. Carburetor: 2Bbl. Motorcraft 2150. German-built. VIN Code: Z. OPTIONAL V-8: 90-degree, overhead valve V-8. Cast iron block and head. Displacement: 302 cu. in. (5.0 liters). Bore & stroke: 4.00 x 3.00 in. Compression ratio: 8.4:1. Brake horsepower: 139 at 3600 R.P.M. Torque: 247 lbs.-ft. at 1800 R.P.M. Five main bearings. Hydraulic valve lifters. Carburetor: 2Bbl. Motorcraft 2150. VIN Code: F.

CHASSIS DATA: Wheelbase: 96.2 in. Overall length: 175.0 in. Height: (Notch cpe) 50.3 in.; (Hatch) 50.0 in. Width: 70.2 in. Front Tread: 55.6 in. Rear Tread: 55.8 in. Standard Tires: B78 x 13 exc. (Ghia) BR78 x 13; (Mach 1) BR70 x 13.

TECHNICAL: Transmission: Four-speed manual transmission (floor shift) standard. V-8 gear ratios: (1st) 2.64:1; (2nd) 1.89:1; (3rd) 1.34:1; (4th) 1.00:1; (Rev) 2.56:1. Four/V-6 four-speed: (1st) 3.50:1; (2nd) 2.21:1; (3rd) 1.43:1; (4th) 1.00:1; (Rev) 3.38:1. Select-Shift three-speed automatic optional. Four-cylinder (1st) 2.47:1; (2nd) 1.47:1; (3rd) 1.00:1; (Rev) 2.11:1. V-8 automatic: (1st) 2.46:1; (2nd) 1.46:1; (3rd) 1.00:1; (Rev) 2.19:1. Standard final drive ratio: (four) 3.18:1; (V-6/V-8) 3.00:1. Steering/suspension/brakes/body: same as 1976. Fuel tank: 13 gal. exc. w/V-8, 16.5 gal.

DRIVETRAIN OPTIONS: Engines: 140 cu. in. four ($289 credit from base V-6 price). 170 cu. in. V-6 ($289). 302 cu. in. V-8 ($230). Other: Cruise-O-Matic trans. ($253). Power brakes ($58). Power steering ($124). H.D. battery ($16). California emission system ($52). High-altitude emissions ($39).

CONVENIENCE/APPEARANCE OPTIONS: Option Packages: Cobra II pkg. ($535). Sports performance pkg. ($451-$607) exc. Mach 1 ($163). Rallye package ($43-$88). Ghia sports group ($422). Exterior accent group ($216). Appearance decor group ($96-$152). Luxury interior group ($124). Convenience group ($37-$71). Light group ($29-$43). Protection group ($39-$46). Comfort/Convenience: Air cond. ($446). Rear defroster, electric ($73). Tinted glass ($48). Leather-wrapped steering wheel ($35-$49). Digital clock ($42). Dual sport mirrors ($45). Entertainment: AM radio ($76); w/tape player ($204). AM/FM radio ($135). AM/FM stereo radio ($184); w/tape player ($317). Exterior: Flip-up open air roof ($147). Manual sunroof ($243). Full vinyl roof ($90). Front spoiler (NC). Metallic glow paint ($58). Pinstriping ($28). Color-keyed vinyl-insert bodyside moldings ($64). Rocker panel moldings ($20). Decklid luggage rack ($54). Interior: Console ($76). Four-way driver's seat ($33). Fold-down rear seat ($77). Media Velour cloth trim ($105). Color-keyed deluxe seatbelts ($18). Wheels and Tires: Wire wheel covers ($33-$86). Forged aluminum wheels ($102-$193); white ($153-$243). Lacy spoke aluminum wheels ($102-$193). Styled steel wheels ($37- $90). Trim rings ($37). B78 x 13 BSW/WSW. BR78 x 13 BSW/WSW. BR70 x 13 RWL. 195/70R13 WSW/wide WSW/RWL.

HISTORY: Introduced: October 1, 1976. Model year production (U.S.): 153,173. Total production for the U.S. market of 141,212 included 71,736 four-cylinder, 33,326 V-6, and 36,150 V-8 Mustangs. Calendar year production (U.S.): 170,315. Calendar year sales: 170,659. Model year sales by U.S. dealers: 161,513.

Historical Footnotes: After a very strong showing following the 1974 restyle, Mustang sales had begun to sag somewhat in 1975 and '76. The Cobra packages looked dramatic, and performed well enough with a V-8, but Mustang couldn't find enough customers in this form. Production declined significantly this year. A four-cylinder Mustang with manual four-speed managed a 26 MPG city/highway rating in EPA estimates.

1978 MUSTANG

1978 Mustang coupe (JG)

MUSTANG II — FOUR/V-6/V-8 — New colors and interior trims made up most of the changes for 1978. The 2.8-liter V-6 got a plastic cooling fan. A new electronic voltage regulator gave longer-life reliability than the old electro-mechanical version. New this year was optional variable-ratio power steering, first introduced on the Fairmont. New inside touches included separate back-seat cushions, revised door and seat trim, new carpeting, and new tangerine color. Six new body colors added late in the 1977 model year were carried over this time. As before, clear rectangular horizontal parking lamps set into the crosshatch black grille. Angled outward at its base, that grille had a 14 x 6 hole pattern, with Mustang (horse) badge in the center. Separate 'Ford' letters stood above the grille. Single round headlamps continued this year. Engine choices were the same as in 1977. So were the two body styles: two-door hardtop (notchback) or "three-door" 22 fastback (hatchback). Base and Ghia notchback models were offered; base and Mach 1 hatchbacks. Standard equipment included the 140 cu. in. (2.3-liter) four-cylinder engine with electronic ignition, four-speed transmission, front disc brakes, rack-and-pinion steering, tachometer, and ammeter. Mustang's Cobra II package (for hatchback only) ontinued in the form introduced at mid-year in 1977. Tri-color tape stripes decorated bodysides and front spoiler, front bumper, hood, hood scoop, roof, decklid and rear spoiler. Huge 'Cobra' block letters went on the center bodyside tape stripe and decklid spoiler; a Cobra decal on the back spoiler; and Cobra II snake emblem on the black grille. The package also included flat black greenhouse moldings, black quarter-window and backlight louvers, black rocker panels and dual racing mirrors, a narrow black band along upper doors, rear-opening hood scoop, Rallye package, and flipper quarter windows (except with T-Roof option). Styled steel wheels with trim rings held BR70 RWL tires (195/70R with V-8, or with V-6 engine and air conditioner). King Cobra, new this year, might be viewed as a regular Cobra and more of the same, with plenty of striping and lettering. The King did without the customary bodyside striping, but sported a unique tape treatment including a giant snake decal on the hood and pinstriping on the greenhouse, decklid, wheel lips, rocker panels, belt, over-the-roof area, and around the side windows. Up front was a tough-looking spoiler. The 302 cu. in. (5.0-liter) V-8 was standard on the King, with four-speed transmission and power brakes/steering. A 'King Cobra' nameplate went on each door and the back spoiler; '5.0L' badge on the front hood scoop. King Cobra also had rear quarter flares, a black grille and moldings, and color-keyed dual sport mirrors. Raised-white-letter tires rode lacy spoke aluminum wheels with twin rings and Cobra symbol on the hubs. A Fashion Accessory Group, aimed at women, consisted of a four-way adjustable driver's seat, striped cloth seat inserts, illuminated entry, lighted driver's vanity visor mirror, coin tray, and door pockets. It came in nine body colors. The simulated convertible T-Roof, with dual removable tinted glass panels, was now entering its first full model year as an option on the 22 and Mach 1 hatchbacks. Mustang's Ghia sports group came with black, blue or chamois body paint and a chamois or black vinyl half-roof, along with vinyl-insert bodyside moldings and pinstripes. Aluminum wheels had chamois-color lacy spokes. Inside was all-vinyl chamois or black seat trim, black "engine-turned" dash appliques, and a leather-wrapped steering wheel.

I.D. DATA: As before, Mustang's 11-symbol Vehicle Identification Number (VIN) is stamped on a metal tab fastened to the instrument panel, visible through the windshield. Coding is similar to 1976-77. Model year code changed to '8' for 1978.

MUSTANG II (FOUR/V-6)

Model Number	Body/Style Number	Body Type & Seating	Factory Price	Shipping Weight	Production Total
02	60F	2-dr. Notch Cpe-4P	3555/3768	2608/2705	81,304
03	69F	3-dr. 22 Hatch-4P	3798/4011	2654/2751	68,408

MUSTANG GHIA (FOUR/V-6)

04	60H	2-dr. Notch Cpe-4P	3972/4185	2646/2743	34,730

MUSTANG MACH 1 (V-6/V-8)

05	69R	3-dr. 22 Hatch-4P	4253/4401	2733/ --	7,968

FACTORY PRICE/WEIGHT NOTE: Figures to left of slash are for four-cylinder engine, to right of slash for V-6 engine (Mach 1, V-6 and V-8). A V-8 engine on base or Ghia initially was priced $148 higher than the V-6.

PRODUCTION NOTE: Totals shown do not include 20,937 Mustangs produced as 1978 models, but sold as 1977 models (see note with 1977 listing).

ENGINE DATA: BASE FOUR: Inline, overhead cam, four-cylinder. Cast iron block and head. Displacement: 140 cu. in. (2.3 liters). Bore & stroke: 3.78 x 3.13 in. Compression ratio: 9.0:1. Brake horsepower: 88 at 4800 R.P.M. Torque: 118 lbs.-ft. at 2800 R.P.M. Five main bearings. Hydraulic valve lifters. Carburetor: 2Bbl. Motorcraft 5200. VIN Code: Y. OPTIONAL V-6: 60-degree, overhead valve V-6. Cast iron block and head. Displacement: 170.8 cu. in. (2.8 liters). Bore & stroke: 3.66 x 2.70 in. Compression ratio: 8.7:1. Brake horsepower: 90 at 4200 R.P.M. Torque: 143 lbs.-ft. at 2200 R.P.M. Four main bearings. Solid valve lifters. Carburetor: 2Bbl. Motorcraft 2150. German-built. VIN Code: Z. OPTIONAL V-8: 90-degree, overhead valve V-8. Cast iron block and head. Displacement: 302 cu. in. (5.0 liters). Bore & stroke: 4.00 x 3.00 in. Compression ratio: 8.4:1. Brake horsepower: 139 at 3600 R.P.M. Torque: 250 lbs.-ft. at 1600 R.P.M. Five main bearings. Hydraulic valve lifters. Carburetor: 2Bbl. Motorcraft 2150. VIN Code: F.

CHASSIS DATA: Wheelbase: 96.2 in. Overall length: 175.0 in. Height: (Notch cpe) 50.3 in.; (Hatch) 50.0 in. Width: 70.2 in. Front Tread: 55.6 in. Rear Tread: 55.8 in. Standard Tires: B78 x 13 SBR; (Ghia) BR78 x 13 SBR; (Mach 1) BR70 x 13 SBR RWL.

TECHNICAL: Transmission: Four-speed manual transmission (floor shift) standard. V-8 gear ratios: (1st) 2.64:1; (2nd) 1.89:1; (3rd) 1.34:1; (4th) 1.00:1; (Rev) 2.56:1. Four-cylinder four-speed: (1st) 3.50:1; (2nd) 2.21:1; (3rd) 1.43:1; (4th) 1.00:1; (Rev) 3.38:1. V-6 four-speed: (1st) 4.07:1; (2nd) 2.57:1; (3rd) 1.66:1; (4th) 1.00:1; (Rev) 3.95:1. Select-Shift three-speed automatic optional. Four-cylinder: (1st) 2.47:1; (2nd) 1.47:1; (3rd) 1.00:1; (Rev) 2.11:1. V-6/V-8 automatic: (1st) 2.46:1; (2nd) 1.46:1; (3rd) 1.00:1; (Rev) 2.19:1. Standard final drive ratio: (four) 3.18:1; (V-6) 3.00:1 w/4spd, 3.40:1 w/auto.; (V-8) 2.79:1. Steering/suspension/brakes/body: same as 1976-77. Fuel tank: 13 gal. exc. w/V-8 engine, 16.5 gal.

DRIVETRAIN OPTIONS: Engine/Transmission: 140 cu. in. four ($213 credit from base V-6 price). 170 cu. in. V-6 ($213). 302 cu. in. V-8 ($361) exc. Mach 1 ($148). Cruise-O-Matic trans. ($281). Brakes/Steering: Power brakes ($64). Power steering ($131). Other: Engine block heater ($12). California emission system ($69). High-altitude emissions (NC).

CONVENIENCE/APPEARANCE OPTIONS: Option Packages: Cobra II pkg.: hatch ($677-$700). King Cobra pkg.: hatch ($1253). Fashion accessory pkg.: 2dr. ($207). Rally package ($43-$93). Rally appearance pkg. ($163). Ghia sports group ($361). Exterior accent group: pinstripes, wide bodyside moldings, dual remote sport mirrors, and whitewalls on styled wheels ($163-$245). Appearance decor group: lower body two-tone, pinstripes, styled wheels, brushed aluminum dash applique ($128-$167). Luxury interior group ($149-$155). Convenience group: interval wipers, vanity and day/night mirrors, and pivoting rear quarter windows on hatchback ($34- $81). Light group ($40-$52). Appearance protection group ($24-$36). Comfort/Convenience: Air cond. ($459). Rear defroster, electric ($77). Tinted glass ($53). Leather-wrapped steering wheel ($34-$49). Entertainment: AM radio ($72); w/tape player ($192). AM/FM radio ($120). AM/FM stereo radio ($161); w/8track or cassette tape player ($229). Exterior: TRoof "convertible" option ($587-$629). Flip-up open air roof ($167). Full vinyl roof ($99). Front spoiler ($8). Metallic glow paint ($40). Pinstriping ($30). Color- keyed bodyside moldings ($66). Rocker panel moldings ($22). Bumper guards, front and rear ($37). Lower bodyside protection ($30). Interior: Console ($75). Four-way driver's seat ($33). Fold-down rear seat ($90). Willshire cloth trim ($100). Ashton cloth/vinyl trim ($12). Color-keyed deluxe seatbelts ($18). Wheels and Tires: Wire wheel covers ($12-$90). Forged aluminum wheels ($173-$252); white ($187-$265). Lacy spoke aluminum wheels ($173-$252); white ($187-$265). Styled steel wheels ($59-$78). Trim rings ($39). B78 x 13 WSW. BR78 x 13 BSW/WSW. BR70 x 13 RWL. 195/70R13 WSW/wide WSW/RWL.

HISTORY: Introduced: October 7, 1977. Model year production: 192,410. Total production for the U.S. market of 173,423 units included 85,312 four-cylinder, 57,060 V-6, and 31,051 V-8 Mustangs. Calendar year production: 240,162. Calendar year sales by U.S. dealers: 199,760. Model year sales by U.S. dealers: 179,039.

Historical Footnotes: This would be the final year for Mustang II, as an all-new Mustang was planned for 1979. Although plenty of Mustangs were built during the 1974-78 period, Cobra II production was modest. King Cobra, offered only for 1978, is the rarest of the lot.

1979 MUSTANG

1979 Mustang Sport Option coupe (JG)

MUSTANG — FOUR/V-6/SIX/V-8 — All-new sheetmetal created what appeared to be an all-new Mustang for 1979. Its chassis came from Fairmont, though, shortened and modified to hold the new body metal. The familiar curved crease in the bodyside was gone. At a time when most cars were shrinking, the new Mustang managed to gain 4 inches in length—and 20 percent more passenger space. Weight was down by some 200 pounds, however. The aerodynamic wedge design featured a sloping front and hood, and sculptured roofline. A lowered window line gave Mustang large glass area for improved visibility. As in the prior version, two-door notchback and three-door hatchback bodies were offered, in base and Ghia levels. There was also a Sport package, and a high-performance TRX package. As before, Ford generally referred to the two-door as a sedan, while the third door of the "three-door" was a hatch rather than an entry for people. The new hatchback did not have the sharply-angled fastback shape of the former Mustang. The notchback two-door did look more like a sedan than its predecessor, though enthusiasts still tend to view it as a coupe (especially since a convertible would appear on that body a few years later). Mercury Capri was similar, but offered only in hatchback form. Both bodies had sail-shaped quarter windows that were wider at the base, but the hatchback's were much narrower at the top, almost triangle-shaped.

1979 Mustang 5.0L Sport Option coupe (F)

Both models had a set of tall louver-like ribs formed in a tapered panel on the 'C' pillar, angled to match the quarter window's rear edge, but the hatchback had one more of them. Staggered, recessed quad rectangular headlamps replaced the former single round units. The outer units sat a little farther back than the inner pair. The new black crosshatch grille (with 10 x 5 hole pattern) angled forward at the base and no longer held a Mustang badge. It did have 'Ford' lettering at the driver's side. Rectangular amber parking/signal lamps were mounted in the bumper, just below the outboard headlamps. Narrow amber front side marker lenses followed the angle of front fender tips. Well below the front bumper was an air scoop with five holes. On the hood, above the grille, was a round tri-color Mustang emblem. A '2.8' or '5.0' badge on front fenders, at the cowl ahead of the door, denoted a V-6 or V-8 engine under the hood. Taillamps were wider than before, now wrapping around each quarter panel. In addition to the German-built 170 cu. in. (2.8-liter) V-6 and 302 cu. in. (5.0-liter) V-8, both carried over from 1978, there was a new engine option: a turbocharged 140 cu. in. (2.3-liter) four. Base engine remained a non-turbo four. Later in the year, Ford's inline six replaced the V-6 as irst option above the base model. The turbo was also optional in other Mustangs. A V-8 model could have a new four-speed manual overdrive transmission, with "peppy" 3.07:1 first gear and 0.70:1 overdrive. A single (serpentine) belt now drove engine accessories. Mustang's new front suspension used a hydraulic shock strut to replace the conventional upper arm. Rear suspension was a new four-bar link-and-coil system, replacing the old leaf-spring Hotchkiss design. Two handling/suspension options were offered. The basic handling suspension with 14-inch radial tires included different spring rates and shock valving, stiffer bushings in front suspension and upper arm in the rear, and a special rear stabilizer bar. The second level package came with a Michelin TRX tire option, an ultra-low aspect ratio tire (390 MM) introduced on the European Granada. Its 15.35 inch size demanded special metric wheels. That package also included unique shock valving, increased spring rates, and wider front/rear stabilizer bars. All Mustangs had full instruments including tachometer, trip odometer, and gauges for fuel, oil pressure, alternator and temperature. Mustangs also had bucket seats, simulated woodgrain instrument panel applique, and stalk-mounted controls for horn, headlamp dimmer, and wiper/washer. At the chassis, standard equipment included rack-and-pinion steering, manual front disc brakes, and a front stabilizer ar. Also standard: vinyl door trim with carpeted lower panel, squeeze-open lockable glovebox, day/night mirror, lighter, black remote driver's mirror, and full wheel covers. Fastbacks had black rocker panel moldings, full wraparound bodyside moldings with dual accent stripe insert, and semi- styled wheels with black sport hub covers and trim rings. Quite a few options joined the list, including a sport-tuned exhaust, cruise control, tilt steering, leather seat trim, and interval windshield wipers. Ghia Mustangs used many color-keyed components including dual remote-control mirrors, quarter louvers, and bodyside molding inserts. Ghia also had turbine-style wheel covers, BR78 x 14 radial tires, pinstripes, body-color window frames, a 'Ghia' badge on decklid or hatch, low-back bucket seats with European-type headrests, and convenience pockets in color-keyed door panels. Interiors came in six leather colors and five of soft cloth. The costly ($1173) Cobra package included a 2.3-liter turbocharged four, turbo hood scoop with 'Turbo' nameplate, 190/65R x 390 TRX tires on metric forged aluminum wheels, and special suspension. A 302 cu. in. V-8 was available instead of the turbo. Cobras had blacked-out greenhouse trim, black lower bodyside tape treatment, and wraparound bodyside moldings with dual color-keyed inserts. Also included: color- keyed grille and quarter louvers, dual sport mirrors, black bumper rub strips with dual color-keyed inserts, an 8000 R.P.M. tachometer, engine-turned instrument cluster panel, sport-tuned exhaust, and bright tailpipe extension. Rocker panel moldings were deleted. Optional hood graphics cost $78 extra.

I.D. DATA: Mustang's 11-symbol Vehicle Identification Number (VIN) is stamped on a metal tab fastened to the instrument panel, visible through the windshield. The first digit is a model year code ('9' 1979). The second letter indicates assembly plant: 'F' Dearborn, MI; 'R' San Jose, CA. Digits three and four are the body serial code, which corresponds to the Model Numbers shown in the tables below: '02' 2-dr. notchback; '03' 3-dr. hatchback; '04' Ghia 2-dr. notchback; '05' Ghia 3-dr. hatchback. The fifth digit is an engine code: 'Y' L4-140 2Bbl.; 'W' turbo L4140 2Bbl.; 'Z' V6170 2Bbl.; 'T' L6200 (late); 'F' V8302 2Bbl. Finally, digits 6-11 make up the consecutive unit number, starting with 100,001. A Vehicle Certification Label on the left front door lock face panel or door pillar shows the manufacturer, month and year of manufacture, GVW, GAWR, certification statement, VIN, and codes for body type, color, trim, axle, transmission, and special order data.

MUSTANG (FOUR/V-6)

Model Number	Body/Style Number	Body Type & Seating	Factory Price	Shipping Weight	Production Total
02	66B	2-dr. Notch-4P	4071/4344	2431/2511	156,666
03	61R	3-dr. Hatch-4P	4436/4709	2451/2531	120,535

MUSTANG GHIA (FOUR/V-6)

04	66H	2-dr. Notch-4P	4642/4915	2539/2619	56,351
05	61H	3-dr. Hatch-4P	4824/5097	2548/2628	36,384

PRODUCTION NOTE: Approximately 6,000 Indy Pace Car Replicas were built, offered for sale at mid-year.

FACTORY PRICE/WEIGHT NOTE: Figures to left of slash are for four- cylinder engine, to right of slash for V-6 engine. A V-8 engine was priced $241 higher than the V-6.

ENGINE DATA: BASE FOUR: Inline, overhead cam, four-cylinder. Cast iron block and head. Displacement: 140 cu. in. (2.3 liters). Bore & stroke: 3.78 x 3.13 in. Compression ratio: 9.0:1. Brake horsepower: 88 at 4800 R.P.M. Torque: 118 lbs.-ft. at 2800 R.P.M. Five main bearings. Hydraulic valve lifters. Carburetor: 2Bbl. Motorcraft 5200. VIN Code: Y. TURBO FOUR: Same as 140 cu. in. four above, but with turbocharger Brake H.P.: 140 at 4800 R.P.M. Torque: N/A. Carburetor: 2Bbl. Holley 6500. VIN Code: W. OPTIONAL V-6: 60-degree, overhead valve V-6. Cast iron block and head. Displacement: 170.8 cu. in. (2.8 liters). Bore & stroke: 3.66 x 2.70 in. Compression ratio: 8.7:1. Brake horsepower: 109 at 4800 R.P.M. Torque: 142 lbs.-ft. at 2800 R.P.M. Four main bearings. Solid valve lifters. Carburetor: 2Bbl. Ford 2150 or Motorcraft 2700VV. German-built. VIN Code: Z. NOTE: A 200 cu. in. inline six became optional late in the model year; see 1980 listing for specifications. OPTIONAL V 8: 90-degree, overhead valve V-8. Cast iron block and head. Displacement: 302 cu. in. (5.0 liters). Bore & stroke: 4.00 x 3.00 in. Compression ratio: 8.4:1. Brake horsepower: 140 at 3600 R.P.M. Torque: 250 lbs.-ft. at 1800 R.P.M. Five main bearings. Hydraulic valve lifters. Carburetor: 2Bbl. Motorcraft 2150. VIN Code: F.

CHASSIS DATA: Wheelbase: 100.4 in. Overall length: 179.1 in. Height: 51.8 in. Width: 69.1 in. Front Tread: 56.6 in. Rear Tread: 57.0 in. Standard Tires: B78 x 13 BSW exc. (Ghia) BR78 x 14 SBR BSW.

TECHNICAL: Transmission: Four-speed manual (floor shift) standard on four-cylinder. Gear ratios: (1st) 3.98:1; (2nd) 2.14:1; (3rd) 1.42:1; (4th) 1.00:1; (Rev) 3.99:1. Turbo four-speed: (1st) 4.07:1; (2nd) 2.57:1; (3rd) 1.66:1; (4th) 1.00:1; (Rev) 3.95:1. Four-speed overdrive manual transmission standard on V-8. Gear ratios: (1st) 3.07:1; (2nd) 1.72:1; (3rd) 1.00:1; (4th) 0.70:1; (Rev) 3.07:1. Select-Shift three-speed automatic optional. Four-cylinder: (1st) 2.47:1; (2nd) 1.47:1; (3rd) 1.00:1; (Rev) 2.11:1. V-6/V-8 automatic: (1st) 2.46:1; (2nd) 1.46:1; (3rd) 1.00:1; (Rev) 2.18:1 or 2.19:1. Standard final drive ratio: 3.08:1 except 3.45:1 w/turbo, 2.47:1 w/V-8 and auto. (early models differed). Steering: Rack and pinion. Front Suspension: Modified MacPherson hydraulic shock struts with coil springs and stabilizer bar. Rear Suspension: Four-bar link and coil spring system; anti- sway bar with V-8. Brakes: Front disc, rear drum. Disc dia.: 9.3 in. (10.4 in. w/V-8). Rear drum dia.: 9 in. Ignition: Electronic. Body construction: unibody w/front isolated mini-frame. Fuel tank: 11.5 gal. exc. with V-6/V-8 engine, 12.5 gal.

DRIVETRAIN OPTIONS: Engine/Transmission: Turbo 140 cu. in. four ($542). 170 cu. in. V-6 ($273). 302 cu. in. V-8 ($514). Sport-tuned exhaust ($34). Automatic trans. ($307). Brakes & Steering: Power brakes ($70). Variable-ratio power steering ($141). Other: Handling suspension ($33). Engine block heater ($13). H.D. battery ($18). California emission system ($76). High- altitude emissions ($33).

CONVENIENCE/APPEARANCE OPTIONS: Option Packages: Cobra pkg. ($1173). Cobra hood graphics ($78). Sport option ($175). Exterior accent group ($72). Interior accent group ($108-$120). Light group ($25-$37). Protection group ($33-$36). Power lock group ($99). Comfort/Convenience: Air cond. ($484). Rear defroster, electric ($84). Fingertip speed control ($104-$116). Tinted glass ($59); windshield only ($25). Leather-wrapped steering wheel ($41-$53). Tilt steering wheel ($69-$81). Interval wipers ($35). Rear wiper/washer ($63). Lighting and Mirrors: Trunk light ($5). Driver's remote mirror ($18). Dual remote mirrors ($52). Entertainment: AM radio ($72); w/digital clock ($119); w/tape player ($192). AM/FM radio ($120). AM/FM stereo radio ($176); w/8track or cassette tape player ($243). Premium sound system ($67). Dual rear speakers ($42). Radio flexibility option ($90). Exterior: Flip-up open air roof ($199). Full vinyl roof ($102). Metallic glow paint ($41). Lower two-tone paint ($78). Bodyside/decklid pinstripes ($30). Wide bodyside moldings ($66). Narrow vinyl-insert bodyside moldings ($39). Rocker panel moldings ($24). Mud/stone deflectors ($23). Lower bodyside protection ($30). Interior: Console ($140). Four-way driver's seat ($35). Cloth seat trim ($20). Ghia cloth seat trim ($42). Accent cloth seat trim ($29). Leather seat trim ($282). Front floor mats ($18). Color-keyed deluxe seatbelts ($20). Wheels and Tires: Wire wheel covers ($60-$99). Turbine wheel covers ($10-$39). Forged metric aluminum wheels ($259-$298). Cast aluminum wheels ($251-$289). Styled steel wheels w/trim rings ($55-$94). B78 x 13 WSW ($43). C78 x 13 BSW ($25); WSW ($69). B78 x 14 WSW ($66). C78 x 14 BSW ($48). BR78 x 14 BSW ($124); WSW ($43-$167). CR78 x 14 WSW ($69-$192); RWL ($86- $209). TRX 190/65R 390 Michelin BSW ($117-$241). Tire Note: Lower prices are for Mustang Ghia.

HISTORY: Introduced: October 6, 1978. Model year production: 369,936. Total production for the U.S. market of 332,024 units included 181,066 four-cylinder (29,242 with turbocharger), 103,390 sixes, and 47,568 V-8 Mustangs. Calendar year production: 365,357. Calendar year sales by U.S. dealers: 304,053. Model year sales by U.S. dealers: 302,309.

Historical Footnotes: If the second-generation Mustang had lacked some of the pizazz of the original pony car, the "new breed" third- generation edition offered a chance to boost the car's image. The optional turbocharged 2.3-liter four was said to offer "V-8 performance without sacrificing fuel economy." In Ford tests, the Mustang turbo went 0-55 MPH in just over 8 seconds (a little quicker than a V-8). Gas mileage reached well into the 20s. A V-8 version was named pace car for the Indy 500, prompting the production of a Pace Car Replica later in the year. Ready for the 1980s, Mustang now offered a pleasing blend of American and European design. Of many styling proposals, the final one came from a team led by Jack Telnack of the Light Truck and Car Design Group. Plastic and aluminum components helped cut down the car's weight, and it was considerably roomier inside than the former Mustang II. Drag oefficient of 0.44 (for the fastback) was the best Ford had ever achieved. Customers must have liked the new version, as Mustang leaped from No. 22 to No. 7 in the sales race.

1980 MUSTANG

1980 Mustang Sport Option coupe (JG)

MUSTANG — FOUR/SIX/V-8 — Appearance of the modern, resized Mustang changed little in its second season, except for a new front/rear look on the sporty Cobra model. Two-door notchbacks also had an aerodynamic revision to their decklids. Mustang's taillamps consisted of five sections on each side, plus a backup lens section inboard (toward the license plate). A larger section at the outside wrapped around onto each quarter panel. Decklids held 'Ford' and 'Mustang' lettering. Bodyside moldings stretched all the way around the car, meeting bumper strips. Body striping came down ahead of the front marker lenses. Four-cylinder models had no fender identifier; others were marked with a liter figure. Base and Ghia models were offered again, in notchback or hatchback form. Base notchbacks had black bumper rub strips; hatchback bumpers had dual argent stripe inserts. Hatchbacks also had full wraparound, wide black bodyside moldings with dual argent inserts. Both models carried high-back vinyl bucket seats. Notchback rear pillar louvers were color-keyed, while the hatchback's were black. Ghia added low-back bucket seats with Euro-style headrests, a roof assist handle, color- keyed window frames, dual remote mirrors, pinstriping, 14 inch tires, turbine wheel covers, and Ghia insignia on decklid or hatch. Available again was the Cobra option, raised in price to $1482. Cobra's slat-style three-hole grille, hood scoop (with simulated rear opening), front air dam (with built-in foglamps) and rear spoiler were restyled with the '79 Indy Pace Car replica in mind. Cobra's tape treatment was also revised, and it carried the TRX suspension. Features included black lower Tu-Tone treatment, special bodyside and quarter window taping, dual black sport mirrors, sport-tuned exhaust with bright tailpipe extension, black bumper rub strips, 190/65R x 390 TRX tires on forged metric aluminum wheels, engine-turned instrument cluster panel with Cobra medallion, bodyside molding with dual color-keyed accent stripes, 8000 R.P.M. tach. and the turbo engine. 'Cobra' lettering went on quarter windows. A 255 cu. in. (4.-liter) V-8 replaced the former 302, but engines were otherwise the same as before. The 200 cu. in. (3.3-liter) inline six had replaced the former V-6 as a powerplant option during 1979. Both the non-turbocharged 2.3-liter four and inline six could have a four-speed manual gearbox (overdrive fourth with the six), while all engines could have automatic. All models now had high-pressure Pmetric radial tires and halogen headlamps. Maintenance-free batteries were standard, and radios added a Travelers' Advisory Band. Semi-metallic front disc brake pads were included with optional engines. Two suspension options were available: The standard package and a modified "Special Suspension System" that included Michelin TRX tires on special forged aluminum wheels. A new Carriage Roof option for the notchback model was supposed to resemble a convertible, even though the car had a solid 'B' pillar. It used diamond-grain vinyl. Other new options included a root luggage rack, cargo area cover (hatchback), liftback window louvers, and Recaro adjustable seatback bucket seats with improved thigh support. Inside door handles were relocated to the upper door.

I.D. DATA: As before, Mustang's 11-symbol Vehicle Identification Number (VIN) is stamped on a metal tab fastened to the instrument panel, visible through the windshield. Engine codes changed this year. The first digit is a model year code ('0' 1980). The second letter indicates assembly plant: 'F' Dearborn, MI; 'R' San Jose, CA. Digits three and four are the body serial code, which corresponds to the Model Numbers shown in the tables below: '02' 2-dr. notchback; '03' 3- dr. hatchback; '04' Ghia 2-dr. notchback; '05' Ghia 3-dr. hatchback. The fifth digit is an engine code: 'A' L4-140 2Bbl.; 'A' turbo L4140 2Bbl.; 'T' L6200 1Bbl.; 'D' V8255 2Bbl. Finally, digits 6-11 make up the consecutive unit number, starting with 100,001. A Vehicle Certification Label on the left front door lock face panel or door pillar shows the manufacturer, month and year of manufacture, GVW, GAWR, certification statement, VIN, and codes for body type and color, trim, axle, transmission, and special order information.

MUSTANG (FOUR/SIX)

Model Number	Body/Style Number	Body Type & Seating	Factory Price	Shipping Weight	Production Total
02	66B	2-dr. Notch-4P	4884/5103	2497/2532	128,893
03	61R	3-dr. Spt Hatch-4P	5194/5413	2531/2566	98,497

MUSTANG GHIA (FOUR/SIX)

04	66H	2-dr. Notch-4P	5369/5588	2565/2600	23,647
05	61H	3-dr. Hatch-4P	5512/5731	2588/2623	20,285

FACTORY PRICE/WEIGHT NOTE: Figures to left of slash are for four- cylinder engine, to right of slash for six-cylinder. A V-8 engine cost $119 more than the six.

ENGINE DATA: BASE FOUR: Inline, overhead cam, four-cylinder. Cast iron block and head. Displacement: 140 cu. in. (2.3 liters). Bore & stroke: 3.78 x 3.13 in. Compression ratio: 9.0:1. Brake horsepower: 88 at 4600 R.P.M. Torque: 119 lbs.-ft. at 2600 R.P.M. Five main bearings. Hydraulic valve lifters. Carburetor: 2Bbl. Motorcraft 5200. VIN Code: A. TURBO FOUR: Same as 140 cu. in. four above, but with turbocharger Brake H.P.: 150 at 4800 R.P.M. Torque: N/A. Carburetor: 2Bbl. Holley 6500. OPTIONAL SIX: Inline, overhead valve six-cylinder. Cast iron block and head. Displacement: 200 cu. in. (3.3 liters). Bore & stroke: 3.68 x 3.13 in. Compression ratio: 8.6:1. Brake horsepower: N/A. Torque: N/A. Seven main bearings. Hydraulic valve lifters. Carburetor: 2Bbl. Holley 1946. VIN Code: T. OPTIONAL V-8: 90-degree, overhead valve V-8. Cast iron block and head. Displacement: 255 cu. in. (4.2 liters). Bore & stroke: 3.68 x 3.00 in. Compression ratio: 8.8:1. Brake horsepower: 119 at 3800 R.P.M. Torque: 194 lbs.-ft. at 2200 R.P.M. Five main bearings. Hydraulic valve lifters. Carburetor: 2Bbl. Motorcraft 2150. VIN Code: D.

CHASSIS DATA: Wheelbase: 100.4 in. Overall length: 179.1 in. Height: 51.4 in. Width: 69.1 in. Front Tread: 56.6 in. Rear Tread: 57.0 in. Standard Tires: P185/80R13 BSW exc. (Ghia) P175/75R14.

TECHNICAL: Transmission: Four-speed manual (floor shift) standard on four-cylinder. Gear ratios: (1st) 3.98:1; (2nd) 2.14:1; (3rd) 1.42:1; (4th) 1.00:1; (Rev) 3.99:1. Turbo four-speed: (1st) 4.07:1; (2nd) 2.57:1; (3rd) 1.66:1; (4th) 1.00:1; (Rev) 3.95:1. Four-speed overdrive manual transmission standard on six. Gear ratios: (1st) 3.29:1; (2nd) 1.84:1; (3rd) 1.00:1; (4th) 0.81:1; (Rev) 3.29:1. Select-Shift three-speed automatic optional. Four-cylinder: (1st) 2.47:1; (2nd) 1.47:1; (3rd) 1.00:1; (Rev) 2.11:1. Turbo/six/V-8 automatic: (1st) 2.46:1; (2nd) 1.46:1; (3rd) 1.00:1; (Rev) 2.19:1. Standard final drive ratio: 3.08:1 w/four, 2.26:1 w/V-8 and auto., 3.45:1 w/turbo. Steering: Rack and pinion. Front Suspension: Modified MacPherson hydraulic shock struts with coil springs and stabilizer bar. Rear Suspension: Four-bar link and coil spring system. Brakes: Front disc, rear drum. Ignition: Electronic. Body construction: Unibody w/front isolated mini-frame. Fuel tank: 11.5 gal. exc. w/V-8 engine, 12.5 gal.

DRIVETRAIN OPTIONS: Engine/Transmission: Turbo 140 cu. in. four ($481). 200 cu. in. six ($219). 255 cu. in. V-8 ($338) exc. w/Cobra pkg. ($144 credit). Sport-tuned exhaust: V-8 ($38). Select-shift automatic trans. ($340). Optional axle ratio ($18). Brakes & Steering: Power brakes ($78). Power steering ($160). Other: Handling suspension ($35). Engine block heater ($15). H.D. battery ($20). California emission system ($253). High- altitude emissions ($36).

CONVENIENCE/APPEARANCE OPTIONS: Option Packages: Cobra pkg. ($1482). Cobra hood graphics ($88). Sport option: black rocker/belt moldings and door/window frames, full wraparound bodyside molding with dual argent stripe insert, sport wheel trim rings and steering wheel ($168-$186). Exterior accent group ($63). Interior accent group ($120-$134). Light group ($41). Appearance protection group ($38-$41). Power lock group ($113). Comfort/Convenience: Air cond. ($583). Rear defroster, electric ($96). Fingertip speed control ($116-$129). Tinted glass ($65); windshield only ($29). Leather-wrapped steering wheel ($44-$56). Tilt steering wheel ($78-$90). Interval wipers ($39). Rear wiper/washer ($79). Lighting and Mirrors: Trunk light ($5). Driver's remote mirror ($19). Dual remote mirrors ($58). Entertainment: AM radio ($93). AM/FM radio ($145). AM/FM stereo radio ($183); w/8track tape player ($259); w/cassette player ($271). Premium sound system ($94). Dual rear speakers ($38). Radio flexibility option ($63). Exterior: Flip-up open air roof ($204-$219). Carriage roof ($625). Full vinyl roof ($118). Metallic glow paint ($46). Lower two-tone paint ($88). Bodyside/decklid pinstripes ($34). Accent tape stripes ($19-$53). Hood scoop ($31). Liftgate louvers ($141). Narrow vinyl-insert bodyside moldings ($43); wide ($74). Rocker panel moldings ($30). Roof luggage rack ($86). Mud/stone deflectors ($25). Lower bodyside protection ($34). Interior: Console ($166). Four-way driver's seat ($38). Recaro high-back bucket seats ($531). Cloth/vinyl bucket seats ($21-$46). Vinyl low-back bucket seats (NC). Accent cloth/vinyl seat trim ($30). Leather low-back bucket seats ($345). Cargo area cover ($44). Front floor mats ($19). Color-keyed seatbelts ($23). Wheels and Tires: Wire wheel covers ($79-$121). Turbine wheel covers ($10-$43). Forged metric aluminum wheels ($313-$355). Cast aluminum wheels ($279-$321). Styled steel wheels w/trim rings ($61-$104). P185/80R13 WSW ($50). P175/75R14 BSW ($25); WSW ($50-$75). P185/75R14 BSW ($25-$49); WSW ($75-$100); RWL ($92-$117). TRX 190/65 x 390 BSW ($125-$250).

HISTORY: Introduced: October 12, 1979. Model year production: 271,322. Total production for the U.S. market of 241,064 units included 162,959 four-cylinder (12,052 with turbocharger), 71,597 sixes, and 6,508 V-8 Mustangs. Calendar year production: 232,517. Calendar year sales by U.S. dealers: 225,290. Model year sales by U.S. dealers: 246,008.

Historical Footnotes: Mustang's base 2.3-liter four-cylinder engine was said to deliver an ample boost in gas mileage this year. Short supplies of the German-made V-6 had prompted Ford to switch to the familiar inline six during the 1979 model year. After a whopping sales increase for 1979, Mustang slackened this year. Still, most observers felt the new model showed a vast improvement over the Mustang II and would give Ford another strong hold on the ponycar market.

1981 MUSTANG

1981 Mustang T-top coupe (F)

MUSTANG — FOUR/SIX/V-8 — For Mustang's third season in this form, little change was evident. A variety of manual transmission ratios was offered, both four-speed and new five-speed. First offered only on four-cylinder models (standard or turbocharged), the five-speed cost an extra $152. Its fifth gear was an overdrive ratio, but the lower four did not offer close-ratio gearing. Some critics found fault with the five-speed's shift pattern, which put fifth gear right next to fourth. The standard 140 cu. in. (2.3-liter) four-cylinder overhead-camshaft engine was rated at 23 MPG city (34 highway) with four-speed manual gearbox. Two other engines (inline six and 255 cu. in. V-8) were optional, along with a total of seven transmissions. Turbocharged models no longer came with automatic shift. For identification, both 'Ford' and 'Mustang' block lettering stood on the hatch or decklid. As usual, Ford tended to describe the notchback two-door model as a "sedan," though most observers call it a coupe. Joining the option list was a TRoof with twin removable tinted glass panels, offered on either the two-door notchback or three-door hatchback. Other new options included reclining bucket seats (either high- or low-back), power windows, and remote right convex mirror. An optional console included a graphic display module that contained a digital clock with elapsed time, and warned of low fuel or washer level as well as inoperative lights. Mustangs could also get a Traction-Lok rear axle. Ghia was a separate model again, while Cobra was a $1588 option package. Cobra equipment was similar to 1979-80, including 190/65R x 390 TRX tires on forged metric aluminum wheel, an 8000 R.P.M. tachometer, lower two-tone paint, 'Cobra' tape treatment, hood scoop, sport-tuned exhaust, dual black sport mirrors, black bumper rub strips, bodyside moldings with dual accent stripes, and black greenhouse moldings. Cobra had a built-in front spoiler, black quarter- window louvers, Cobra medallion on dash and door trim, and a handling suspension. A V-8 engine could replace the standard turbo four, for a $346 credit. Taping could be deleted from the Cobra package, if desired, knocking $65 off the price; but the bold hood decal cost $85 extra. Offered

late in 1980 was the limited-production, much- modified McLaren Mustang, similar in appearance to the IMSA show car. McLaren had no grille, a low (and large) front spoiler, working hood scoops, prominent fender flares, and Firestone HPR radial tires on BBS alloy wheels. The variable- boost turbo engine produced 175 horsepower. A total of 250 McLarens were built, priced at $25,000.

I.D. DATA: Like other Ford products, Mustang had a new 17-symbol Vehicle Identification Number (VIN), again stamped on a metal tab fastened to the instrument panel, visible through the windshield. The first three symbols specify manufacturer, make and vehicle type: '1FA' Ford passenger car. Symbol four ('B') denotes restraint system. Next comes a letter 'P', followed by two digits that indicate body type: '10' 2-dr. notchback; '15' 3-dr. hatchback; '12' Ghia 2-dr. notchback; '13' Ghia 3-dr. hatchback. Symbol eight indicates engine type: 'A' L4-140 2Bbl.; 'A' turbo L4140 2Bbl.; 'T' L6200 1Bbl.; 'D' V8255 2Bbl. Next is a check digit. Symbol ten indicates model year ('B' 1981). Symbol eleven is assembly plant: 'F' Dearborn, MI; 'R' San Jose, CA. The final six digits make up the sequence number, starting with 100001. A Vehicle Certification Label on the left front door lock face panel or door pillar shows the month and year of manufacture, GVW, GAWR, VIN, and codes for body type and color, trim, axle, transmission, accessories, and special order information.

MUSTANG (FOUR/SIX)

Model Number	Body/Style Number	Body Type & Seating	Factory Price	Shipping Weight	Production Total
10	66B	2-dr. Notch-4P	6171/6384	2524/2551	77,458
15	61R	3-dr. Spt Hatch-4P	6408/6621	2544/2571	77,399

MUSTANG GHIA (FOUR/SIX)

12	66H	2-dr. Notch-4P	6645/6858	2558/2585	13,422
13	61H	3-dr. Hatch-4P	6729/6942	2593/2620	14,273

FACTORY PRICE/WEIGHT NOTE: Figures to left of slash are for four- cylinder engine, to right of slash for six-cylinder engine. A V-8 engine was priced $50 higher than the six.

ENGINE DATA: BASE FOUR: Inline, overhead cam, four-cylinder. Cast iron block and head. Displacement: 140 cu. in. (2.3 liters). Bore & stroke: 3.78 x 3.13 in. Compression ratio: 9.0:1. Brake horsepower: 88 at 4600 R.P.M. Torque: 118 lbs.-ft. at 2600 R.P.M. Five main bearings. Hydraulic valve lifters. Carburetor: 2Bbl. Motorcraft 5200 or Holley 6500. VIN Code: A. TURBO FOUR: Same as 140 cu. in. four above, but with turbocharger Brake H.P.: N/A. Torque: N/A. OPTIONAL SIX: Inline, overhead valve six-cylinder. Cast iron block and head. Displacement: 200 cu. in. (3.3 liters). Bore & stroke: 3.68 x 3.13 in. Compression ratio: 8.6:1. Brake horsepower: 94 at 4000 R.P.M. Torque: 158 lbs.-ft. at 1400 R.P.M. Seven main bearings. Hydraulic valve lifters. Carburetor: 2Bbl. Holley 1946. VIN Code: T. OPTIONAL V-8: 90-degree, overhead valve V-8. Cast iron block and head. Displacement: 255 cu. in. (4.2 liters). Bore & stroke: 3.68 x 3.00 in. Compression ratio: 8.2:1. Brake horsepower: 115 at 3400 R.P.M. Torque: 195 lbs.-ft. at 2200 R.P.M. Five main bearings. Hydraulic valve lifters. Carburetor: 2Bbl. Motorcraft 7200VV or 2150. VIN Code: D.

CHASSIS DATA: same as 1980.

TECHNICAL: Transmission: Four-speed manual (floor shift) standard on four-cylinder. Gear ratios: (1st) 3.98:1; (2nd) 2.14:1; (3rd) 1.42:1; (4th) 1.00:1; (Rev) 3.99:1. Turbo four-speed: (1st) 4.07:1; (2nd) 2.57:1; (3rd) 1.66:1; (4th) 1.00:1; (Rev) 3.95:1. Four-speed overdrive manual transmission standard on six. Gear ratios: (1st) 3.29:1; (2nd) 1.84:1; (3rd) 1.00:1; (4th) 0.81:1; (Rev) 3.29:1. Other models: (1st) 3.98:1; (2nd) 2.14:1; (3rd) 1.42:1; (4th) 1.00:1; (Rev) 3.99:1. Five-speed manual overdrive optional: (1st) 4.05:1; (2nd) 2.43:1; (3rd) 1.48:1; (4th) 1.00:1; (5th) 0.82:1; (Rev) 3.90:1. Turbo five- speed: (1st) 3.72:1; (2nd) 2.23:1; (3rd) 1.48:1; (4th) 1.00:1; (5th) 0.76:1; (Rev) 3.59:1. Select-Shift three-speed automatic optional: (1st) 2.46:1 or 2.47:1; (2nd) 1.46:1 or 1.47:1; (3rd) 1.00:1; (Rev) 2.11:1 or 2.19:1. Standard final drive ratio: (four) 3.08:1 exc. 3.45:1 w/5spd; (six) 3.45:1 w/4spd, 2.73:1 w/auto.; (V-8) 2.26:1. Steering: Rack and pinion. Front Suspension: Modified MacPherson struts with lower control arms, coil springs and stabilizer bar. Rear Suspension: Four-bar link and coil spring system with lower trailing arms and transverse linkage bar. Brakes: Front disc, rear drum. Ignition: Electronic. Body construction: Unibody. Fuel tank: 12.5 gal.

DRIVETRAIN OPTIONS: Engine/Transmission: Turbo 140 cu. in. four ($610). 200 cu. in. six ($213). 255 cu. in. V-8 ($263) exc. w/Cobra pkg. ($346 credit). Sport-tuned exhaust: V-8 ($39); w/turbo and auto. (NC). Five-speed manual trans. ($152). Select-shift automatic trans. ($349). Traction-Lok differential ($63). Optional axle ratio ($20). Brakes & Steering: Power brakes ($76). Power steering ($163). Other: Handling suspension ($43). Engine block heater ($16). H.D. battery ($20). California emission system ($46). High- altitude emissions ($38).

CONVENIENCE/APPEARANCE OPTIONS: Option Packages: Cobra pkg. ($1588); tape delete ($65 credit). Cobra hood graphics ($90). Sport option ($52-$72). Interior accent group ($126-$139). Light group ($43). Appearance protection group ($41). Power lock group ($93- $120). Comfort/Convenience: Air cond. ($560). Rear defroster, electric ($107). Fingertip speed control ($132). Power windows ($140). Tinted glass ($76); windshield only ($29). Leather-wrapped steering wheel ($49-$61). Tilt steering wheel ($80-$93). Interval wipers ($41). Rear wiper/washer ($85). Lighting and Mirrors: Trunk light ($6). Driver's remote mirror ($20). Dual remote mirrors ($56). Entertainment: AM/FM radio ($51). AM/FM stereo radio ($88); w/8track tape player ($162); w/cassette player ($174). Premium sound system ($91). Dual rear speakers ($37). Radio flexibility option ($61). AM radio delete ($61 credit). Exterior: TRoof ($874). Flip-up open air roof ($213-$228). Carriage roof ($644). Full vinyl roof ($115). Metallic glow paint ($48). Two-tone paint ($121-$155). Lower two-tone paint ($90). Pinstriping ($34). Accent tape stripes ($54). Hood scoop ($32). Liftgate louvers ($145). Rocker panel moldings ($30). Roof luggage rack ($90). Mud/stone deflectors ($26). Lower bodyside protection ($37). Interior: Console ($168). Recaro high-back bucket seats ($732). Cloth/vinyl bucket seats ($22-$48). Accent cloth/vinyl seat trim ($30). Leather low-back bucket seats ($359). Cargo area cover: hatch ($45). Front floor mats ($18- $20). Color-keyed seatbelts ($23). Wheels and Tires: Wire wheel covers ($77-$118). Turbine wheel covers ($10-$41). Forged metric aluminum wheels ($340). Cast aluminum wheels ($305). Styled steel wheels w/trim rings ($60-$101). P185/80R13 WSW ($49). P175/75R14 BSW ($24); WSW ($49-$73). P185/75R14 BSW ($24-$49); WSW ($73-$97); RWL ($90- $114). TRX 190/65R x 390 BSW ($122-$146).

HISTORY: Introduced: October 3, 1980. Model year production: 182,552. Total production for the U.S. market of 162,593 Mustangs included 101,860 four-cylinder, 55,406 sixes, and only 5,327 V-8 engines. Calendar year production: 153,719. Calendar year sales by U.S. dealers: 154,985. Model year sales by U.S. dealers: 173,329.

Historical Footnotes: Mustang prices rose sharply this year, as did those of other Ford products. The new TRoof met all federal body structure regulations, as a result of body modifications that included the use of H-shaped reinforcements. Both production and sales slipped considerably, but this was a weak period for the industry as a whole. Ford's Special Vehicle Operations department started up in September 1980, headed by Michael Kranefuss. Its goal: limited production performance cars and motorsport activities. Several racing Mustangs got factory assistance, including a turbo model driven in IMSA GT events and a TransAm model. A turbo-powered IMSA "concept car" with big Pirelli tires and huge fender flares toured the auto show circuit.

1982 MUSTANG

1982 Mustang 5.0L Sport Option coupe (JG)

MUSTANG — FOUR/SIX/V-8 — "The Boss is Back!" declared Ford ads. Biggest news of the year was indeed the return of the 302 cu. in. (5.0-liter) V-8, coupled with the temporary disappearance of the turbo four. Performance-oriented Mustangs could have a high-output 302 with four-speed manual overdrive transmission, a combination that had last been offered in 1979. This year's 302 V-8 had a bigger (356 CFM) two-barrel carburetor, larger- diameter (freer-flowing) exhaust system, and low-restriction air cleaner with dual inlets. That setup delivered considerably faster acceleration than the '79 version, able to hit 60 MPH in less than 8 seconds. Base engine was the 140 cu. in. (2.3-liter) four; also optional, a 255 cu. in. (4.2- liter) V-8, and 200 cu. in. inline six. A lockup torque converter (all three gears) was included on automatics with the inline six or small V-8 engine. A high-altitude emissions system was available with all engines. Appearance changed little for 1981, but model designations were revised. The new lineup included an L, GL, and GLX, as well as a GT that replaced the former Cobra option. Mustang L was the new base model, with full wheel covers, full wraparound bodyside moldings, and an AM radio. New standard equipment included seatbelts with tension relievers, a remote-control left-hand mirror, new flash-to- pass headlamp feature, and new screw-on gas cap tethered to the filler neck. There was also a switch to 14inch wheels with Pmetric (P175/75R14) steel-belted radial tires. Four- cylinder Mustangs with air conditioning had an electro-drive cooling fan. Radios had dual front speakers plus wiring for two more. Mustang's GT (first designated an SS) added P185/75R14 blackwall steel-belted radials on cast aluminum wheels, a handling suspension, dual black remote mirrors, and built-in foglamps. Styling features included body-colored front fascia with integral spoiler and air dam, three-slot grille, color- keyed rear spoiler, and body-color cowl grille. 'GT' identification went on the liftgate. Body-color headlamp frames replaced the black doors on other models. Black bodyside moldings had a black plastic insert and aluminum end caps. Equipment included a Traction-Lok differential, power brakes and steering, and a console with digital clock and diagnostic warning module. Blackout treatment continued on interior components. An optional TR performance package could enhance the handling qualities of all Mustang models. It included Michelin TRX tires on forged metric aluminum wheels, and a handling suspension with rear stabilizer bar.

I.D. DATA: Mustang's 17-symbol Vehicle Identification Number (VIN), stamped on a metal tab fastened to the instrument panel, is visible through the windshield. The first three symbols specify manufacturer, make and vehicle type: '1FA' Ford passenger car. Symbol four ('B') denotes restraint system. Next comes a letter 'P', followed by two digits that indicate body type: '10' 2-dr. notchback sedan; '16' 3-dr. hatchback; '12' GLX 2-dr. notchback; '13' GLX 3-dr. hatchback. Symbol eight indicates engine type: 'A' L4-140 2Bbl.; 'B' L6200 1Bbl.; 'D' V8255 2Bbl.; 'F' V8302 2Bbl. Next is a check digit. Symbol ten indicates model year ('C' 1982). Symbol eleven is assembly plant: 'F' Dearborn, MI. The final six digits make up the sequence number, starting with 100001. A Vehicle Certification Label on the left front door lock face panel or door pillar shows the month and year of manufacture, VIN, and codes for body type and color, trim, axle ratio, transmission, and special order information.

MUSTANG (FOUR/SIX)

Model Number	Body/Style Number	Body Type & Seating	Factory Price	Shipping Weight	Production Total
10	N/A	2-dr. L Notch-4P	6345/7062	2511/2635	Note 1
10	66B	2-dr. GL Notch-4P	6844/7468	2528/2652	45,316
16	61B	3-dr. GL Hatch-4P	6979/7390	2565/2689	69,348
12	66H	2-dr. GLX Notch-4P	6980/7604	2543/2667	5,828
13	61H	3-dr. GLX Hatch-4P	7101/7725	2579/2703	9,926

MUSTANG GT (V-8)

16	N/A	3-dr. Hatch-4P	-- /8308	-- /2629	Note 2

Note 1: Production of L model is included in GL total. Note 2: Ford figures include GT production in GL hatchback total above. Other industry sources report a total of 23,447 GT models produced.

FACTORY PRICE/WEIGHT NOTE: Figures to left of slash are for four- cylinder engine, to right of slash for six-cylinder. (The higher amount includes the cost of an automatic transmission.) A 255 cu. in. V-8 engine was priced $70 higher than the six; a 302 V-8 was $189 higher.

ENGINE DATA: BASE FOUR: Inline, overhead cam, four-cylinder. Cast iron block and head. Displacement: 140 cu. in. (2.3 liters). Bore & stroke: 3.78 x 3.13 in. Compression ratio: 9.0:1. Brake horsepower: 86 at 4600 R.P.M. Torque: 117 lbs.-ft. at 2600 R.P.M. Five main bearings. Hydraulic valve lifters. Carburetor: 2Bbl. Motorcraft 5200 or Holley 6500. VIN Code: A. OPTIONAL SIX: Inline, overhead valve six-cylinder. Cast iron block and head. Displacement: 200 cu. in. (3.3 liters). Bore & stroke: 3.68 x 3.13 in. Compression ratio: 8.6:1. Brake horsepower: 87 at 3800 R.P.M. Torque: 154 lbs.-ft. at 1400 R.P.M. Seven main bearings. Hydraulic valve lifters. Carburetor: 2Bbl. Holley 1946. VIN Code: B. OPTIONAL V-8: 90-degree, overhead valve V-8. Cast iron block and head. Displacement: 255 cu. in. (4.2 liters). Bore & stroke: 3.68 x 3.00 in. Compression ratio: 8.2:1. Brake horsepower: 120 at 3400 R.P.M. Torque: 205 lbs.-ft. at 1600 R.P.M. Five main bearings. Hydraulic valve lifters. Carburetor: 2Bbl. Motorcraft 2150 or 7200VV. VIN Code: D. OPTIONAL HIGH-OUTPUT V-8: 90-degree, overhead valve V-8. Cast iron block and head. Displacement: 302 cu. in. (5.0 liters). Bore & stroke: 4.00 x 3.00 in. Compression ratio: 8.3:1. Brake horsepower: 157 at 4200 R.P.M. Torque: 240 lbs.-ft. at 2400 R.P.M. Five main bearings. Hydraulic valve lifters. Carburetor: 2Bbl. Motorcraft 2150A. VIN Code: F.

CHASSIS DATA: Wheelbase: 100.4 in. Overall length: 179.1 in. Height: 51.4 in. Width: 69.1 in. Front Tread: 56.6 in. Rear Tread: 57.0 in. Standard Tires: P175/75R14 BSW exc. GT, P185/75R14.

TECHNICAL: Transmission: Four-speed manual (floor shift) standard on four-cylinder. Gear ratios: (1st) 3.98:1; (2nd) 2.14:1; (3rd) 1.49:1; (4th) 1.00:1; (Rev) 3.99:1. Four-speed overdrive manual transmission standard on V-8. Gear ratios: (1st) 3.07:1; (2nd) 1.72:1; (3rd) 1.00:1; (4th) 0.70:1; (Rev) 3.07:1. Five-speed manual overdrive optional: (1st) 3.72:1; (2nd) 2.23:1; (3rd) 1.48:1; (4th) 1.00:1; (5th) 0.76:1; (Rev) 3.59:1. Select-Shift three-speed automatic optional on four- cylinder, standard on six: (1st) 2.47:1; (2nd) 1.47:1; (3rd) 1.00:1; (Rev) 2.11:1. Converter clutch automatic available with six/V-8: (1st) 2.46:1; (2nd) 1.46:1; (3rd) 1.00:1; (Rev) 2.19:1. Standard final drive ratio: 2.73:1 except four w/5spd, 3.45:1; four w/auto. or 302 V-8 w/4spd, 3.08:1. Steering/Suspension/Brakes: same as 1981. Body construction: unibody. Fuel tank: 15.4 gal.

DRIVETRAIN OPTIONS: Engine/Transmission: 200 cu. in. six ($213). 255 cu. in. V-8 ($263) exc. w/GT ($57 credit). 302 cu. in. V-8 ($452) exc. w/TR performance pkg. ($402). Five-speed manual trans. ($196). Select-shift automatic trans. ($411). Traction-Lok differential ($76). Optional axle ratio (NC). Brakes/Steering/Suspension: Power brakes ($93). Power steering ($190). TR performance suspension pkg. ($533-$583) exc. GT ($105). Handling suspension ($50). Other: Engine block heater ($17). H.D. battery ($24). California emission system ($46). High-altitude emissions (NC).

CONVENIENCE/APPEARANCE OPTIONS: Option Packages: Light group ($49). Appearance protection group ($48). Power lock group ($139). Comfort/Convenience: Air cond. ($676). Rear defroster, electric ($124). Fingertip speed control ($155). Power windows ($165). Tinted glass ($88); windshield only ($32). Leather-wrapped steering wheel ($55). Tilt steering wheel ($95). Interval wipers ($48). Rear wiper/washer ($101). Lighting and Mirrors: Trunk light ($7). Remote right mirror ($41). Entertainment: AM/FM radio ($76). AM/FM stereo radio ($106); w/8track or cassette player ($184). Premium sound system ($105). Dual rear speakers ($39). AM radio delete ($61 credit). Exterior: TRoof ($1021). Flip-up open air roof ($276). Carriage roof ($734). Full vinyl roof ($137). Metallic glow paint ($54). Two-tone paint ($138-$177). Lower two-tone paint ($104). Accent tape stripes ($62). Hood scoop ($38). Liftgate louvers ($165). Black rocker panel moldings ($33). Lower bodyside protection ($41). Interior: Console ($191). Recaro high-back bucket seats ($834). Cloth/vinyl seats ($23-$51). Leather low-back bucket seats ($409). Cargo area cover ($51). Front floor mats, carpeted ($22). Wheels and Tires: Wire wheel covers ($91-$141). Cast aluminum wheels ($348-$398). Styled steel wheels w/trim rings ($72- $122). P175/75R14 WSW ($66). P185/75R14 BSW ($30); WSW ($66- $96); RWL ($85-$116).

HISTORY: Introduced: September 24, 1981. Model year production: 130,418. Total production for the U.S. market of 119,314 Mustangs included 54,444 four-cylinder, 37,734 sixes, and 27,136 V-8 engines. Calendar year production: 127,370. Calendar year sales by U.S. dealers: 119,526. Model year sales by U.S. dealers: 116,804.

Historical Footnotes: Option prices rose sharply this year, by around 20 percent on the average. Production of V-8 engines also rose sharply, with five times as many coming off the line as in 1981. Mustang sales declined by almost one-third this year. A convertible model was announced, but didn't appear until the 1983 model year.

1983 MUSTANG

1983 Mustang GT 5.0L convertible (F)

MUSTANG — FOUR/V-6/V-8 — A restyled nose and rear end improved Mustang's aerodynamics, but the model was otherwise essentially a carryover for 1983. All Mustangs had a new angled-forward front end and new front fascia, with deeply recessed headlamp housings. A narrower grille design tapered inward slightly at the base, with a Ford oval in its center. Rectangular parking lamps stood at bumper level, as before, below the outboard headlamps. Taillamps continued the wraparound design, but in restyled form. The use of galvanized and zincrometal coatings was expanded. The high-output 302 cu. in. V-8 edition displayed a new hood scoop design. Most noteworthy, though, was the return of the ragtop. A new convertible (part of the GLX series) came with any powertrain except the 2.3-liter four with automatic. Unlike the Chrysler LeBaron, Mustang convertibles had a glass backlight and roll-down quarter windows, along with a power top. Engine choices changed considerably for (and during) 1983. A 232 cu. in. (3.8-liter) "Essex" V-6, offered in Mustang for the first time, delivered a 2-second improvement in 0-60 time over the previous 3.3-liter inline six. The high-output 302 cu. in. (5.0-liter) V-8 with four-speed manual continued this year, but a four-barrel carburetor replaced the former two-barrel. Horsepower jumped to 175 (formerly 157). The V-8 also got an aluminum intake manifold and freer exhaust flow. It was standard on the GT. The base 140 cu. in. (2.3-liter) four switched from two-barrel to single-barrel carburetion. Later in the season, a new 140 cu. in. OHC turbo arrived, with multi-port fuel injection. The last previous turbo four, in 1981, had been carbureted. Turbo models could not have air conditioning. Both the inline six and 255 cu. in. (4.2-liter) V-8 were dropped. A new manual five-speed gearbox, optional with the four, had Ford's U-shaped shift motion between fourth and fifth gear. A Borg-Warner T5 close-ratio five-speed arrived later for the GT's high-output 5.0-liter V-8, hooked to a 3.27:1 final drive. An upshift indicator light option (with manual transmission) was available, to show the most fuel-efficient shift points. All Mustang tires increased by at least one size, while the optional handling suspension got tougher anti-sway bars and retuned springs/shocks. It was now available without the formerly-required Michelin TRX tires. Joining the option list were: cloth sport performance low-back bucket seats; turbine wheel covers; restyled wire wheel covers; convex right-hand mirror; new special two-tone paint and tape treatment; and TRX tires and wheels without the TR performance suspension. Several options were deleted, including the rear wiper/washer, dual rear speakers, carriage roof, liftgate louvers, accent tape stripe, and Recaro seats. Standard equipment on the L (base) Mustang included black bumper rub strips, halogen headlamps, three-speed heater/defroster, woodtone instrument panel aplique, quarter- window louvers, black remote left mirror, AM radio, and four- spoke steering wheel with woodgrain insert. Also standard: four-speed manual gearbox, full wheel covers, argent accent striping, cigarette lighter, and high-back reclining bucket seats with vinyl upholstery. Mustang GL added black rocker panel, door and window frame moldings; dual accent bodyside pinstripes; a black sport steering wheel; lower-carpeted door trim panels; right visor vanity mirror; and low-back bucket seats. Mustang GLX came with dual bright remote-control mirrors, woodgrain-insert four-spoke steering wheel, bright rocker panel moldings, map pockets in the driver's door trim panel, and a light group. The GLX convertible included power brakes, tinted glass, dual black remote-control mirrors, black rocker moldings, and automatic transmission. Mustang GT carried a standard Traction-Lok rear axle, power brakes and steering, black grille, rear spoiler, black hood scoop, handling suspension, and five-speed manual gearbox. GT models could have Michelin TRX tires on cast aluminum wheels and a console with digital clock and diagnostic module, but no dual accent bodyside pinstriping. Black windshield, window and door frames completed the GT's appearance.

I.D. DATA: As before, Mustang's 17-symbol Vehicle Identification Number (VIN) was stamped on a metal tab fastened to the instrument panel, visible through the windshield. Symbols one to three specify manufacturer, make and vehicle type: '1FA' Ford passenger car. Symbol four ('B') denotes restraint system. Next comes a letter 'P', followed by two digits that indicate body type: '26' 2-dr. notchback sedan; '28' 3-dr. hatchback; '27' 2-dr. convertible. Symbol eight indicates engine type: 'A' L4-140 1Bbl.; 'D' turbo L4140 FI; '3' V6232 2Bbl.; 'F' V8302 4Bbl. Next is a check digit. Symbol ten indicates model year ('D' 1983). Symbol eleven is assembly plant: 'F' Dearborn, MI. The final six digits make up the sequence number, starting with 100001. A Vehicle Certification Label on the left front door lock face panel or door pillar shows the manufacturer, month and year of manufacture, GVW, GAWR, certification statement, VIN, and codes for body type, color, trim, axle, transmission, and special order information.

MUSTANG (FOUR/V-6)

Model Number	Body/Style Number	Body Type & Seating	Factory Price	Shipping Weight	Production Total
26	66B	2-dr. L Notch-4P	6727/7036	2532/2621	Note 1
26/60C	66B	2-dr. GL Notch-4P	7264/7573	2549/2638	Note 1
28/60C	61B	3-dr. GL Hatch-4P	7439/7748	2584/2673	Note 1
26/602	66B	2-dr. GLX Notch-4P	7398/7707	2552/2641	Note 1
28/602	61B	3-dr. GLX Hatch-4P	7557/7866	2587/2676	Note 1
27/602	N/A	2-dr. GLX Conv.-4P	-- /9449	-- /2759	Note 1

MUSTANG GT (V-8)

28/932	61B	3-dr. Hatch-4P	-- /9328	-- /2891	Note 1
27/932	N/A	2-dr. Conv.-4P	-- /13479	N/A	Note 1

MUSTANG TURBO GT (FOUR)

28/932	61B	3-dr. Hatch-4P	9714/ --	N/A	Note 1

Note 1: Ford reports total production of 33,201 two-doors, 64,234 hatchbacks, and 23,438 convertibles.

FACTORY PRICE/WEIGHT NOTE: Figures to left of slash are for four- cylinder engine, to right of slash for V-6. A 4Bbl. 302 cu. in. V-8 engine cost $1044 more than the V-6 ($595 more on the GLX convertible). The price of the GLX convertible jumped sharply after the model year began, to $12,467.

ENGINE DATA: BASE FOUR: Inline, overhead cam, four-cylinder. Cast iron block and head. Displacement: 140 cu. in. (2.3 liters). Bore & stroke: 3.78 x 3.13 in. Compression ratio: 9.0:1. Brake horsepower: 90 at 4600 R.P.M. Torque: 122 lbs.-ft. at 2600 R.P.M. Five main bearings. Hydraulic valve lifters. Carburetor: 1Bbl. Carter YFA. VIN Code: A. OPTIONAL TURBO FOUR: Same as 140 cu. in. four above, but with turbocharger and electronic fuel injection Compression ratio: 8.0:1. Brake H.P.: 142 at 5000 R.P.M. Torque: 172 lbs.-ft. at 3800 R.P.M. VIN Code: D. OPTIONAL V-6: 90-degree, overhead valve V-6. Cast iron block and aluminum head. Displacement: 232 cu. in. (3.8 liters). Bore & stroke: 3.80 x 3.40 in. Compression ratio: 8.7:1. Brake horsepower: 112 at 4000 R.P.M. Torque: 175 lbs.-ft. at 2600 R.P.M. Four main bearings. Hydraulic valve lifters. Carburetor: 2Bbl. Motorcraft 2150. VIN Code: 3. OPTIONAL V-8: 90-degree, overhead valve V-8. Cast iron block and head. Displacement: 302 cu. in. (5.0 liters). Bore & stroke: 4.00 x 3.00 in. Compression ratio: 8.3:1. Brake horsepower: 175 at 4000 R.P.M. Torque: 245 lbs.-ft. at 2400 R.P.M. Five main bearings. Hydraulic valve lifters. Carburetor: 4Bbl. Holley 4180. VIN Code: F.

CHASSIS DATA: Wheelbase: 100.4 in. Overall length: 179.1 in. Height: 51.9 in. Width: 69.1 in. Front Tread: 56.6 in. Rear Tread: 57.0 in. Standard Tires: P185/75R14 SBR BSW exc. GT, P205/70HR14 or Michelin P220/55R390 TRX.

TECHNICAL: Transmission: Four-speed manual (floor shift) standard on four-cylinder. Gear ratios: (1st) 3.98:1; (2nd) 2.14:1; (3rd) 1.49:1; (4th) 1.00:1; (Rev) 3.99:1. Four-speed overdrive manual transmission standard on V-8. Gear ratios: (1st) 3.07:1; (2nd) 1.72:1; (3rd) 1.00:1; (4th) 0.70:1; (Rev) 3.07:1. Five-speed manual overdrive optional: (1st) 3.72:1; (2nd) 2.23:1; (3rd) 1.48:1; (4th) 1.00:1; (5th) 0.76:1; (Rev) 3.59:1. Turbo five-speed: (1st) 4.03:1; (2nd) 2.37:1; (3rd) 1.50:1; (4th) 1.00:1; (5th) 0.86:1; (Rev) 3.76:1. Alternate turbo five-speed: (1st) 3.76:1; (2nd) 2.18:1; (3rd) 1.36:1; (4th) 1.00:1; (5th) 0.86:1; (Rev) 3.76:1. V-8 five-speed: (1st) 2.95:1; (2nd) 1.94:1; (3rd) 1.34:1; (4th) 1.00:1; (5th) 0.73:1; (Rev) 2.76:1. Select-Shift three-speed automatic optional on four-cylinder, standard on six: (1st) 2.47:1; (2nd) 1.47:1; (3rd) 1.00:1; (Rev) 2.11:1. V-6 ratios: (1st) 2.46:1; (2nd) 1.46:1; (3rd) 1.00:1; (Rev) 2.19:1. Standard final drive ratio: 3.08:1 w/4spd, 3.45:1 w/5spd, 3.08:1 or 2.73:1 w/auto. Steering: Rack and pinion. Front Suspension: Modified MacPherson struts with lower control arms and stabilizer bar. Rear Suspension: Rigid axle w/four-bar link and coil springs. Brakes: Front disc, rear drum. Ignition: Electronic. Body construction: Unibody. Fuel tank: 15.4 gal.

DRIVETRAIN OPTIONS: Engine/Transmission: 232 cu. in. V-6 ($309). 302 cu. in. V-8 ($1343) exc. conv. ($595). Five-speed manual trans. ($595). Select-shift automatic trans. ($439). Traction-Lok differential ($95). Optional axle ratio (NC). Brakes/Steering/Suspension: Power brakes ($93). Power steering ($202). Handling suspension ($252). Other: Engine block heater ($17). H.D. battery ($26). California emission system ($76). High-altitude emissions (NC).

CONVENIENCE/APPEARANCE OPTIONS: Option Packages: Sport performance pkg. ($196). Light group ($55). Appearance protection group ($60). Power lock group ($160). Comfort/Convenience: Air cond. ($724). Rear defroster, electric ($135). Fingertip speed control ($170). Power windows ($180). Tinted glass ($105); windshield only ($38). Leather-wrapped steering wheel ($59). Tilt steering wheel ($105). Interval wipers ($49). Remote right mirror ($44). Entertainment: AM/FM radio ($82). AM/FM stereo radio ($109); w/8track or cassette player ($199). Premium sound system ($117). AM radio delete ($61 credit). Exterior: TRoof ($1055). Flip-up open air roof ($310). Metallic glow paint ($54). Two-tone paint ($150-$189). Liftgate louvers: hatch ($171). Rocker panel moldings ($33). Lower bodyside protection ($41). Interior: Console ($191). Cloth/vinyl seats ($29-$57). Leather low-back bucket seats ($415). Front floor mats, carpeted ($22). Wheels and Tires: Wire wheel covers ($98-$148). Turbine wheel covers (NC). Cast aluminum wheels ($354-$404). Styled steel wheels w/trim rings ($78-$128). P185/75R14 WSW ($72). P195/75R14 WSW ($108). P205/75R14 BSW ($224). TRX P220/55R390 BSW ($327-$551).

HISTORY: Introduced: October 14, 1982 except convertible, November 5, 1982. Model year production: 108,438. Total production for the U.S. market of 108,438 Mustangs included 27,825 four-cylinder, 47,766 sixes, and 32,847 V-8 engines. Calendar year production: 124,225. Calendar year sales by U.S. dealers: 116,976. Model year sales by U.S. dealers: 116,120.

Historical Footnotes: Mustang's convertible actually began life as a steel-topped notchback, modified by an outside contractor. The car itself was assembled at Dearborn, then sent to Cars & Concepts in Brighton, Michigan for installation of the top and interior trim. Mustang GT was said to deliver a seven-second 0-60 time (quickest of any standard domestic model), as well as cornering that matched exotic cars. All that plus fuel economy in the mid-20s.

1984 MUSTANG

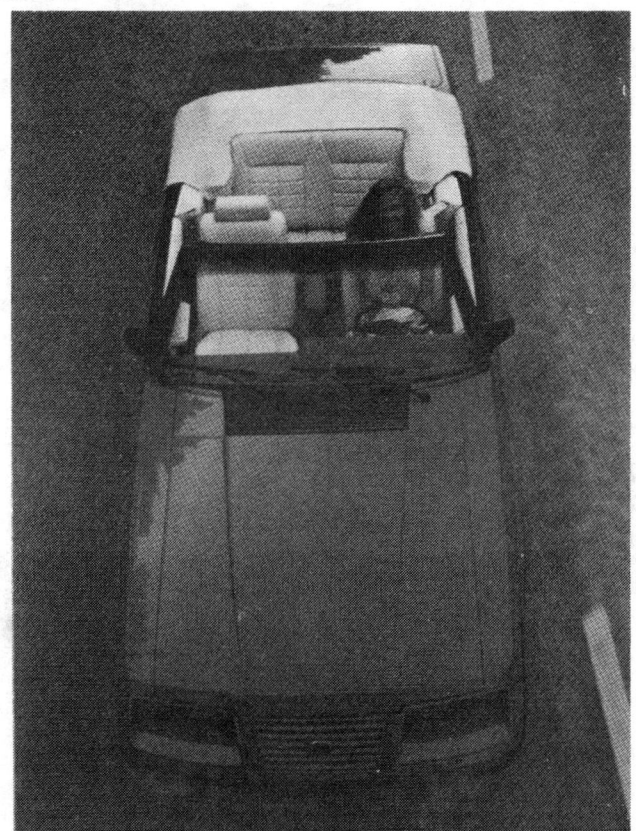

1984 Mustang 3.8L convertible (JG)

(front and rear). Four-wheel disc brakes were standard. SVO had a much different front-end look than the standard Mustang, with a "grille-less" front fascia and integrated foglamps. Just a single slot stood below the hood panel, which contained a Ford oval. Large single rectangular headlamps were deeply recessed, flanked by large wraparound lenses. A polycarbonate dual-wing rear spoiler was meant to increase rear-wheel traction, while rear-wheel "spats" directed airflow around the wheel wells. SVO's price tag was more than double that of a base Mustang. Offered in "three-door" hatchback form, SVO came only in black, silver metallic, dark charcoal metallic, or red metallic. Interiors were all charcoal. Only six major options were available for SVO, because it had so much standard equipment. Those were: air conditioning, power windows, power door locks, cassette player, flip-up sunroof, and leather seat trim.

1984 Mustang SVO coupe (JG)

Standard SVO equipment included an 8000 R.P.M. tachometer; quick-ratio power steering; Traction-Lok rear axle; leather-wrapped steering wheel, shift knob and brake handle; unique instrument panel appliques; narrow bodyside moldings; and unique C-pillar and taillamp treatments. A premium/regular fuel switch recalibrated the ignition instantly. Revised pedal positioning allowed "heel and toe" downshifting, and had a footrest for the left foot during hard cornering. Standard models looked the same as in 1983. Throughout the line were new steering wheels with center horn, new instrument panel appliques, and split folding rear seats. All manual transmissions now had a clutch/starter interlock, so the engine couldn't start unless the clutch was depressed. Mustang instrument panels had red lighting this year. Buyers could also select a more modest turbo model, without the intercooler. Mustang's GT Turbo had been introduced in spring 1983, and continued for '84. GT customers also had a choice of V-8 engines, and an available overdrive automatic transmission. The series lineup was simplified this year. The L series, previously two-door notchback only, was now also available in "three-door" hatchback form. GL and GLX models of 1983 were

1984 Mustang GT 5.0L HO Sport Coupe (JG)

MUSTANG — FOUR/V-6/V-8 — Performance-minded Mustangers enjoyed fresh temptation this year in the new SVO. Developed by Ford's Special Vehicle Operations department, SVO carried an air-to-air intercooler on its 140 cu. in. (2.3-liter) turbocharged, fuel-injected four-cylinder engine. That helped boost horsepower up to 175, and improve low-end performance. The SVO package included a Borg-Warner T5 five-speed manual gearbox with Hurst linkage, four-wheel disc brakes, performance suspension with adjustable Koni gas-filled shocks, P225/50VR16 Goodyear NCT tires on cast aluminum 16 x 7 in. wheels, and functional hood scoop. SVO could, according to Ford, hit 134 MPH and get to 60 MPH in just 7.5 seconds. Inside were multi-adjustable articulated leather bucket seats. SVO's shock absorbers and struts had three settings: cross-country (for front and rear), GT (front only), and competition

gone, replaced by a single LX series. A convertible was offered again this year, in both LX and GT form. The GT series displayed a new front air dam, with road lamps available. GT also added gas-filled shock absorbers and a handling suspension. Elsewhere on the powerplant front, the optional 232 cu. in. (3.8-liter) V-6 switched to throttle-body fuel injection and gained some horsepower. A fuel-injected high-output 5.0-liter V-8 came with automatic overdrive transmission. A higher-output version of the four-barrel V-8, producing 205 horsepower, was announced for December arrival but delayed.

I.D. DATA: Mustang's 17-symbol Vehicle Identification Number (VIN) again was stamped on a metal tab fastened to the instrument panel, visible through the windshield. The first three symbols specify manufacturer, make and vehicle type: '1FA' Ford passenger car. Symbol four ('B') denotes restraint system. Next comes a letter 'P', followed by two digits that indicate body type: '26' 2-dr. notchback sedan; '28' 3-dr. hatchback; '27' 2-dr. convertible. Symbol eight indicates engine type: 'A' L4-140 1Bbl.; 'W' turbo L4140 FI; '3' V6232 FI; 'F' V8302 FI; 'M' V8302 4Bbl. Next is a check digit. Symbol ten indicates model year ('E' 1984). Symbol eleven is assembly plant: 'F' Dearborn, MI. The final six digits make up the sequence number, starting with 100001. A Vehicle Certification Label on the left front door lock face panel or door pillar shows the manufacturer, month and year of manufacture, GVW, GAWR, certification statement, VIN, and codes for body type and color, trim, axle, transmission, and special order information.

MUSTANG (FOUR/V-6)

Model Number	Body/Style Number	Body Type & Seating	Factory Price	Shipping Weight	Production Total
26	66B	2-dr. L Notch-4P	7098/7507	2538/2646	Note 1
28	61B	3-dr. L Hatch-4P	7269/7678	2584/2692	Note 1
26/602	66B	2-dr. LX Notch-4P	7290/7699	2559/2667	Note 1
28/602	61B	3-dr. LX Hatch-4P	7496/7905	2605/2713	Note 1
27/602	66B	2-dr. LX Conv.-4P	--/11849	--/2873	Note 1

L/LX Price/Weight Note: Figures to left of slash are for four-cylinder engine, to right of slash for V-6. A 4Bbl. 302 cu. in. V-8 engine cost $1165 more than the V-6 ($318 more on the LX convertible).

1984½ Mustang GT-350 20th Anniversary convertible (F)

MUSTANG GT (TURBO FOUR/V-8)

| 28/932 | 61B | 3-dr. Hatch-4P | 9762/9578 | 2753/2899 | Note 1 |
| 27/932 | 66B | 2-dr. Conv.-4P | 13245/13051 | 2921/3043 | Note 1 |

GT Price and Weight Note: Figures to left of slash are for turbo four, to right for V-8.

1984 Mustang SVO coupe (JG)

MUSTANG SVO (TURBO FOUR)

| 28/939 | 61B | 3-dr. Hatch-4P | 15596 | 2881 | Note 1 |

Note 1: Ford reports total production of 37,680 two-doors, 86,200 hatchbacks and 17,600 convertibles.

ENGINE DATA: BASE FOUR: Inline, overhead cam, four-cylinder. Cast iron block and head. Displacement: 140 cu. in. (2.3 liters). Bore & stroke: 3.78 x 3.13 in. Compression ratio: 9.0:1. Brake horsepower: 88 at 4000 R.P.M. Torque: 122 lbs.-ft. at 2400 R.P.M. Five main bearings. Hydraulic valve lifters. Carburetor: 1Bbl. Carter YFA. VIN Code: A. OPTIONAL TURBO FOUR: Same as 140 cu. in. four above, but with turbocharger and electronic fuel injection Compression ratio: 8.0:1. Brake H.P.: 145 at 4600 R.P.M. Torque: 180 lbs.-ft. at 3600 R.P.M. VIN Code: W. SVO TURBO FOUR: Same as standard turbo four above, but Brake H.P.: 175 at 4400 R.P.M. Torque: 210 lbs.-ft. at 3000 R.P.M. OPTIONAL V-6: 90-degree, overhead valve V-6. Cast iron block and aluminum head. Displacement: 232 cu. in. (3.8 liters). Bore & stroke: 3.80 x 3.40 in. Compression ratio: 8.7:1. Brake horsepower: 120 at 3600 R.P.M. Torque: 205 lbs.-ft. at 1600 R.P.M. Four main bearings. Hydraulic valve lifters. Electronic fuel injection (TBI). VIN Code: 3. OPTIONAL V-8: 90-degree, overhead valve V-8. Cast iron block and head. Displacement: 302 cu. in. (5.0 liters). Bore & stroke: 4.00 x 3.00 in. Compression ratio: 8.3:1. Brake horsepower: 175 at 4000 R.P.M. Torque: 245 lbs.-ft. at 2200 R.P.M. Five main bearings. Hydraulic valve lifters. Carburetor: 4Bbl. Holley 4180C. VIN Code: M. OPTIONAL V-8: Fuel injected version of 302 cu. in. V-8 above Brake H.P.: 165 at 3800 R.P.M. Torque: 245 lbs.-ft. at 2000 R.P.M. VIN Code: F.

NOTE: A high-output version of the carbureted V-8, rated 205 horsepower at 4400 R.P.M., was announced but delayed.

CHASSIS DATA: Wheelbase: 100.5 in. Overall length: 179.1 in. except SVO, 181.0 in. Height: 51.9 in. Width: 69.1 in. Front Tread: 56.6 in. except SVO, 57.8 in. Rear Tread: 57.0 in. except SVO, 58.3 in. Standard Tires: P185/75R14 SBR BSW exc. GT, P205/70HR14.

TECHNICAL: Transmission: Four-speed manual (floor shift) standard on four-cylinder. Gear ratios: (1st) 3.98:1; (2nd) 2.14:1; (3rd) 1.49:1; (4th) 1.00:1; (Rev) 3.99:1. Standard turbo five-speed: (1st) 4.03:1; (2nd) 2.37:1; (3rd) 1.50:1; (4th) 1.00:1; (5th) 0.86:1; (Rev) 3.76:1. Standard V-8 five-speed: (1st) 2.95:1; (2nd) 1.94:1; (3rd) 1.34:1; (4th) 1.00:1; (5th) 0.63:1; (Rev) 2.76:1. Select-Shift three-speed automatic optional on four-cylinder: (1st) 2.47:1; (2nd) 1.47:1; (3rd) 1.00:1; (Rev) 2.11:1. Four-speed overdrive automatic standard on V-6: (1st) 2.40:1; (2nd) 1.47:1; (3rd) 1.00:1; (4th) 0.67:1; (Rev) 2.00:1. Standard final drive ratio: (four) 3.08:1 w/4spd, 3.27:1 w/auto.; (V-6) 3.08:1; (V-8) 3.08:1 w/5spd, 2.73:1 w/3spd auto., 3.27:1 w/4spd auto.; (turbo) 3.45:1. Steering: Rack and pinion. Front Suspension: Modified MacPherson struts with lower control arms and stabilizer bar; SVO added adjustable gas-pressurized shocks. Rear Suspension: Rigid axle w/four-bar link and coil springs; SVO and GT Turbo added an anti-sway bar. Brakes: Front disc, rear drum except SVO, four-wheel disc brakes. Ignition: Electronic. Body construction: Unibody. Fuel tank: 15.4 gal.

DRIVETRAIN OPTIONS: Engine/Transmission: 232 cu. in. V-6 ($409). 302 cu. in. V-8 pkg. ($1574) exc. LX conv. ($727). Five-speed manual trans. (NC). Three-speed automatic trans. ($439). Four-speed overdrive auto. trans. ($551). Traction-Lok differential ($95). Optional axle ratio (NC). Brakes/Steering/Suspension: Power brakes ($93). Power steering ($202). Handling suspension ($252) exc. w/VIP pkg. ($50). Other: Engine block heater ($18). H.D. battery ($27). California emission system ($99). High-altitude option (NC).

CONVENIENCE/APPEARANCE OPTIONS: Option Packages: SVO competition preparation pkg.: delete air cond., power locks, AM/FM/cassette and power windows ($1253 credit). VIP pkg. for L/LX with AM/FM stereo or tilt wheel ($93); both ($196). VIP pkg. for GT ($110). 20th anniversary VIP pkg.: GT ($25-$144). Light/convenience group ($55-$88). Power lock group ($177). Comfort/Convenience: Air cond. ($743). Rear defroster, electric ($140). Fingertip speed control ($176). Power windows ($198). Tinted glass ($110). Tilt steering wheel ($110). Interval wipers ($50). Remote right mirror ($46). Entertainment: AM/FM stereo radio ($109); w/cassette player ($222) exc. SVO or w/VIP pkg. ($113). Premium sound system ($151). AM radio delete ($39 credit). Exterior: TRoof ($1074) exc. w/VIP pkg. ($760). Flip-up open air roof ($315). Metallic glow paint ($54). Two-tone paint: L/LX ($150-$189). Lower two-tone paint ($116). Liftgate louvers: hatch ($171). Rocker panel moldings ($39). Lower bodyside protection ($41). Interior: Console ($191). Articulated sport seats ($196). High-back vinyl bucket seats: L ($29); low-back, LX/GT ($29). Leather bucket seats ($189). Front floor mats, carpeted ($22). Wheels and Tires: Wire wheel covers ($98). Cast aluminum wheels ($354). Styled steel wheels w/trim rings ($78). P185/75R14 WSW ($72). P195/75R14 WSW ($108). P205/75R14 BSW ($224). TRX P220/55R390 BSW ($327-$551) exc. GT ($27 credit).

HISTORY: Introduced: September 22, 1983. Model year production: 141,480. Total production for the U.S. market of 129,621 Mustangs included 46,414 four-cylinder, 47,169 sixes, and 36,038 V-8 engines. Calendar year production: 140,338. Calendar year sales by U.S. dealers: 138,296. Model year sales by U.S. dealers: 131,762.

Historical Footnotes: Ford's Special Vehicle Operations Department had been formed in 1981 to supervise the company's renewed involvement in motorsports (among other duties), and to develop special limited-edition high-performance vehicles. SVO was the first of those offered as a production model. *Motor Trend* called SVO "the best driving street Mustang the factory has ever produced." *Road & Track* claimed that SVO "outruns the Datsun 280ZX, outhandles the Ferrari 308 and Porsche 944...and it's affordable." Its hefty price tag meant SVO was targeted toward more affluent, car-conscious consumers.

1985 MUSTANG

MUSTANG — FOUR/V-6/V-8 — Changes for 1985 focused mainly on Mustang's front end and mechanical matters. All models wore a new front-end look with a four-hole integral air dam below the bumper, flanked by low rectangular parking lamps. GT also had integral foglamps. A "grille" similar to SVO—essentially one wide slot with angled sides in a sloping front panel—appeared on all Mustangs. That panel displayed a Ford oval. Taillamps were full-width (except for the license plate opening), with backup lenses at the upper portion of each inner section. A Ford script oval stood above the right taillamp. Most Mustang exterior trim and accents switched from black to a softer charcoal shade. All models had new charcoal front and rear bumper rub strips and bodyside moldings. Also new: charcoal hood paint/tape treatment, a revised decklid decal, and GT nomenclature (where applicable) molded into the bodyside molding. The base L series was dropped, making LX the bottom-level Mustang. Standard LX equipment now included power brakes and steering, remote-control right-side mirror, dual-note horn, interval windshield wipers, and an AM/FM stereo radio. Also available were the GT and SVO, as well as LX and GT convertibles. As before, both notchback and hatchback codies were offered. New standard interior features included a console, low-back bucket seats (on LX), articulated sport seats (on GT), luxury door trim panels, and covered visor mirrors. The convertible's quarter trim panels were revised to accommodate a refined seatbelt system. Mechanical radio faces switched to a contemporary flat design. All Mustangs had larger tires this year, and added urethane lower bodyside protection. New GT tires were P225/60VR15 Goodyear Eagle

Total driving performance has helped make Ford Mustang the choice of police forces in 15 states.

1985 Mustang Special Pursuit 5.0L coupe (JG)

unidirectional "Gatorbacks" on 15 x 7 in. cast aluminum wheels. Added to the option list: a new electronic AM/FM stereo radio with cassette player. The 140 cu. in. (2.3-liter) four remained standard, but buyers had quite a choice of other powerplants, as usual. Mustang GT's high-output carbureted 302 cu. in. (5.0-liter) V-8 gained a high-performance camshaft, plus roller tappets and a two-speed accessory drive system. That engine now produced 210 horsepower, while its mating five-speed manual gearbox had a tighter shift pattern and new gear ratios. The high-output, fuel-injected V-8 also gained strength, reaching 180 horsepower. The turbocharged SVO returned a little late, now wearing Eagle 50-series tires on 16-inch wheels. Both the 3.8-liter V-6 and 5.0-liter V-8 had a new oil warning light.

I.D. DATA: Mustang's 17-symbol Vehicle Identification Number (VIN) again was stamped on a metal tab fastened to the instrument panel, visible through the windshield. Coding was similar to 1984. Model year code changed to 'F' for 1985. Coding for the SVO turbocharged four changed to 'T'.

MUSTANG LX (FOUR/V-6)

Model Number	Body/Style Number	Body Type & Seating	Factory Price	Shipping Weight	Production Total
26/602	66B	2-dr. Notch-4P	6885/8017	2559/2667	Note 1
28/602	61B	3-dr. Hatch-4P	7345/8477	2605/2713	Note 1
27/602	66B	2-dr. Conv.-4P	--/11985	--/2873	Note 1

LX Price/Weight Note: Figures to left of slash are for four-cylinder engine, to right of slash for V-6 (including the price of the required automatic transmission). A 4Bbl. 302 cu. in. V-8 engine cost $561 more than the V-6 ($152 more on the LX convertible).

MUSTANG GT (V-8)

28/932	61B	3-dr. Hatch-4P	9885	2899	Note 1
27/932	66B	2-dr. Conv.-4P	13585	3043	Note 1

1985 Mustang SVO coupe (JG)

MUSTANG SVO (TURBO FOUR)

28/939	61B	3-dr. Hatch-4P	14521	2881	Note 1

Note 1: Ford reports total production of 56,781 two-doors, 84,623 hatchbacks and 15,110 convertibles.

ENGINE DATA: BASE FOUR: Inline, overhead cam, four-cylinder. Cast iron block and head. Displacement: 140 cu. in. (2.3 liters). Bore & stroke: 3.78 x 3.13 in. Compression ratio: 9.0:1. Brake horsepower: 88 at 4000 R.P.M. Torque: 122 lbs.-ft. at 2600 R.P.M. Five main bearings. Hydraulic valve lifters. Carburetor: 1Bbl. Carter YFA. VIN Code: A. SVO TURBO FOUR: Same as 140 cu. in. four above, but with turbocharger and electronic fuel injection Compression ratio: 8.0:1. Brake H.P.: 175 at 4400 R.P.M. Torque: 210 lbs.-ft. at 3000 R.P.M. VIN Code: T. OPTIONAL V-6: 90-degree, overhead valve V-6. Cast iron block and aluminum head. Displacement: 232 cu. in. (3.8 liters). Bore & stroke: 3.80 x 3.40 in. Compression ratio: 8.7:1. Brake

horsepower: 120 at 3600 R.P.M. Torque: 205 lbs.-ft. at 1600 R.P.M. Four main bearings. Hydraulic valve lifters. Electronic fuel injection (TBI). VIN Code: 3. OPTIONAL V-8: O-degree, overhead valve V-8. Cast iron block and head. Displacement: 302 cu. in. (5.0 liters). Bore & stroke: 4.00 x 3.00 in. Compression ratio: 8.3:1. Brake horsepower: 180 at 4200 R.P.M. Torque: 260 lbs.-ft. at 2600 R.P.M. Five main bearings. Hydraulic valve lifters. Electronic fuel injection. VIN Code: F. OPTIONAL HIGH-OUTPUT V-8: Same as 302 cu. in. V-8 above, but with Holley 4Bbl. carburetor Brake H.P.: 210 at 4400 R.P.M. Torque: 270 lbs.- ft. at 3200 R.P.M. VIN Code: M.

CHASSIS DATA: Wheelbase: 100.5 in. Overall length: 179.3 in. except SVO, 180.8 in. Height: 52.1 in. Width: 69.1 in. Front Tread: 56.6 in. except SVO, 57.8 in. Rear Tread: 57.0 in. except SVO, 58.3 in. Standard Tires: P195/75R14 SBR WSW exc. GT, P225/60VR15 SBR BSW; and SVO, P225/50VR16 Eagle BSW.

TECHNICAL: Transmission: Four-speed manual (floor shift) standard on four-cylinder. Gear ratios: (1st) 3.98:1; (2nd) 2.14:1; (3rd) 1.42:1; (4th) 1.00:1; (Rev) 3.99:1. SVO turbo five-speed: (1st) 3.50:1; (2nd) 2.14:1; (3rd) 1.36:1; (4th) 1.00:1; (5th) 0.78:1; (Rev) 3.39:1. Standard V-8 five-speed: (1st) 3.35:1; (2nd) 1.93:1; (3rd) 1.29:1; (4th) 1.00:1; (5th) 0.68:1; (Rev) 3.15:1. Select-Shift three-speed automatic optional on four- cylinder: (1st) 2.47:1; (2nd) 1.47:1; (3rd) 1.00:1; (Rev) 2.11:1. V-6 three speed automatic: (1st) 2.46:1; (2nd) 1.46:1; (3rd) 1.00:1; (Rev) 2.19:1. Four-speed overdrive automatic standard on V-8: (1st) 2.40:1; (2nd) 1.47:1; (3rd) 1.00:1; (4th) 0.67:1; (Rev) 2.00:1. Standard final drive ratio: (four) 3.08:1 w/4spd; (V-6) 2.73:1; (V-8) 3.08:1 w/5spd, 3.27:1 w/4spd auto.; (turbo) 3.45:1. Steering: Rack and pinion, power-assisted. Front Suspension: Modified MacPherson struts with lower control arms and stabilizer bar; SVO added adjustable gas- pressurized shocks. Rear Suspension: Rigid axle w/four-bar link and coil springs; GT/SVO added an anti-sway bar. Brakes: Front disc, rear drum (power-assisted) except SVO, four-wheel discs. Ignition: Electronic. Body construction: Unibody. Fuel tank: 15.4 gal.

DRIVETRAIN OPTIONS: Engine/Transmission/Suspension: 232 cu. in. V-6: LX ($439). 302 cu. in. V-8 pkg. ($1000) exc. LX conv. ($152). Five-speed manual trans.: LX ($124). Three-speed automatic trans.: LX ($439). Four-speed overdrive auto. trans.: LX ($676); GT ($551). Traction-Lok differential ($95). Optional axle ratio (NC). Handling suspension: LX ($258). Other: Engine block heater ($18). H.D. battery ($27). California emission system ($99). High-altitude option (NC).

CONVENIENCE/APPEARANCE OPTIONS: Option Packages: SVO competition preparation pkg.: delete air cond., power locks, AM/FM stereo/cassette and power windows ($1417 credit). Light/convenience group ($55). Power lock group ($177-$210). Comfort/Convenience: Air cond. ($743). Rear defroster, electric ($140). Fingertip speed control ($176). Power windows ($198) exc. conv. ($272). Tinted glass ($110). Tilt steering wheel: LX ($110). Entertainment: AM/FM stereo radio w/cassette player: LX/GT ($148). Electronic AM/FM stereo w/cassette: LX/GT ($300). Premium sound system: LX/GT ($138). Radio delete ($148 credit). Exterior: TRoof: hatch ($1074). Flip-up open air roof: hatch ($315). Lower two-tone paint ($116). Single wing spoiler: SVO (NC). Interior: Console ($191). Low-back vinyl bucket seats: LX ($29). Leather sport performance bucket seats: LX conv. ($780); GT conv. ($415); SVO ($189). LX Wheels and Tires: Wire wheel covers ($98). Styled steel wheels ($178). P205/75R14 WSW ($109). P205/70VR14 BSW ($238). P225/60VR15 SBR BSW ($665).

HISTORY: Introduced: October 4, 1984. Model year production: 156,514. Total production for the U.S. market of 143,682 Mustangs included 79,885 four-cylinder, 18,334 sixes, and 45,463 V-8 engines. Calendar year production: 187,773. Calendar year sales by U.S. dealers: 157,821. Model year sales by U.S. dealers: 159,741.

Historical Footnotes: This year's GT proved that the V-8 had a future under Mustang hoods, even with the turbocharged SVO available. For one thing, the GT was a lot cheaper. It also performed more sedately than a turbo under ordinary conditions, yet was able to deliver impressive performance whenever needed. *Motor Trend* applauded the arrival of the potent 210-horsepower V-8 for delivering "lovely axle-creaking torque reminiscent of another time."

1986 MUSTANG

1986 Mustang GT convertible (JG)

MUSTANG — FOUR/V-6/V-8 — Model lineup was the same as in 1985: LX two-door sedan or hatchback (and convertible), GT hatchback and convertible, and SVO. LX had full bodyside striping, power brakes and steering, and such extras as interval wipers, luxury sound package, and an AM/FM stereo radio (which could be deleted for credit). Base engine remained the 140 cu. in. (2.3-liter) OHC four, with four-speed manual gearbox. V-8 engines now had sequential port fuel injection. The 232 cu. in. (3.8-liter) V-6 with throttle-body injection also was optional again, and standard on the LX convertible. Appearance was essentially the same as in 1985. The sloping center front-end panel held a Ford oval at the top, and a single wide opening below. Quad rectangular headlamps were deeply recessed. Parking lamps stood far down on the front end. Side marker lenses were angled to match the front fender tips. Taillamps were distinctly divided into upper and lower sections by a full-width divider bar. 'Mustang' lettering stood above the left taillamp, a Ford oval above the right. Three new body colors were offered. Turbine wheel covers switched from bright/argent to bright/black. Mustang's rear axle was upgraded to 8.7 inches with the standard 2.73:1 axle ratio (8.8 inch with others), for use with the 5.0-liter V-8. Viscous engine mounts were added on the 3.8-liter V-6 and the V-8, as used on the turbo four starting in mid-year 1985. One key now operated door locks and ignition. The two-door LX notchback had its high-mount brake lamp added to the package tray; GT and SVO were modified to take it on the spoilers. Hatchback LX models added a spoiler to house that brake lamp, while LX and GT convertibles installed a luggage rack with integrated brake lamp. Preferred Equipment Packages included such items as air conditioning, styled wheels, and Premium Sound System. Mustang GT carried a new high-output 302 cu. in. (5.0- liter) V-8 with multi-port fuel injection. Rated 200 horsepower, with EECIV electronic engine controls, it was hooked to a five-speed manual (overdrive) transmission, or automatic overdrive. GT included a special suspension, Goodyear Eagle VR performance tires, quick-ratio power steering, and articulated front sport seats. The four-barrel V-8 was abandoned. All Mustang V-8s with five-speed manual also added an upshift indicator light. SVO, the "ultimate Mustang," carried a computer- controlled 200-horsepower 2.3-liter four with intercooled turbocharger and multi-port fuel injection. A five-speed manual, with Hurst shifter that offered short, quick throws, was standard. So were disc brakes all around.

I.D. DATA: Mustang's 17-symbol Vehicle Identification Number (VIN) again was stamped on a metal tab fastened to the instrument panel, visible through the windshield. Coding was similar to 198485. Model year code changed to 'G' for 1986.

MUSTANG LX (FOUR/V-6)

Model Number	Body/Style Number	Body Type & Seating	Factory Price	Shipping Weight	Production Total
26	66B	2-dr. Notch-4P	7189/8153	2601/2722	Note 1
28	61B	3-dr. Hatch-4P	7744/8708	2661/2782	Note 1
27	66B	2-dr. Conv.-4P	--/12821	--/2908	Note 1

LX Price/Weight Note: Figures to left of slash are for four-cylinder engine, to right of slash for V-6 (including the price of the required automatic transmission). A 302 cu. in. V-8 engine cost $1120 more than the four ($106 more on the LX convertible).

MUSTANG GT (V-8)

28	61B	3-dr. Hatch-4P	10691	2976	Note 1
27	66B	2-dr. Conv.-4P	14523	3103	Note 1

MUSTANG SVO (TURBO FOUR)

28/937	61B	3-dr. Hatch-4P	15272	3028	Note 1

Note 1: Ford reports total production of 106,720 two-doors (including convertibles) and 117,690 hatchbacks.

ENGINE DATA: BASE FOUR: Inline, overhead cam, four-cylinder. Cast iron block and head. Displacement: 140 cu. in. (2.3 liters). Bore & stroke: 3.78 x 3.13 in. Compression ratio: 9.5:1. Brake horsepower: 88 at 4200 R.P.M. Torque: 122 lbs.-ft. at 2600 R.P.M. Five main bearings. Hydraulic valve lifters. Carburetor: 1Bbl. Carter YFA. VIN Code: A. SVO TURBO FOUR: Same as 140 cu. in. four above, but with turbocharger and electronic fuel injection Compression ratio: 8.0:1. Brake H.P.: 200 at 5000 R.P.M. Torque: 240 lbs.-ft. at 3200 R.P.M. VIN Code: T. OPTIONAL V-6: 90-degree, overhead valve V-6. Cast iron block and aluminum head. Displacement: 232 cu. in. (3.8 liters). Bore & stroke: 3.80 x 3.40 in. Compression ratio: 8.7:1. Brake horsepower: 120 at 3600 R.P.M. Torque: 205 lbs.-ft. at 1600 R.P.M. Four main bearings. Hydraulic valve lifters. Electronic fuel injection (TBI). VIN Code: 3. OPTIONAL V-8: 90-degree, overhead valve V-8. Cast iron block and head. Displacement: 302 cu. in. (5.0 liters). Bore & stroke: 4.00 x 3.00 in. Compression ratio: 9.2:1. Brake horsepower: 200 at 4000 R.P.M. Torque: 285 lbs.-ft. at 3000 R.P.M. Five main bearings. Hydraulic valve lifters. Sequential fuel injection. VIN Code: M.

CHASSIS DATA: Wheelbase: 100.5 in. Overall length: 179.3 in. except SVO, 180.8 in. Height: 52.1 in. exc. conv., 51.9 in. Width: 69.1 in. Front Tread: 56.6 in. except SVO, 57.8 in. Rear Tread: 57.0 in. except SVO, 58.3 in. Standard Tires: P195/75R14 SBR WSW exc. GT, P225/60VR15 SBR BSW; and SVO, P225/50VR16 "Gatorback" BSW.

TECHNICAL: Transmission: Four-speed manual (floor shift) standard on four-cylinder. Five-speed manual standard on turbo and V-8. Gear ratios N/A. Select-Shift three-speed automatic optional on four-cylinder, standard on V-6. Gear ratios: (1st) 2.47:1; (2nd) 1.47:1; (3rd) 1.00:1; (Rev) 2.11:1. V-6 three-speed automatic: (1st) 2.46:1; (2nd) 1.46:1; (3rd) 1.00:1; (Rev) 2.19:1. Four-speed overdrive automatic available with V-8: (1st) 2.40:1; (2nd) 1.47:1; (3rd) 1.00:1; (4th) 0.67:1; (Rev) 2.00:1. Standard final drive ratio: (four) 3.08:1 w/4spd, 3.27:1 w/auto.; (V-6) 2.73:1; (V-8) 2.73:1 w/5spd, 3.27:1 w/4spd auto.; (turbo) 3.73:1. Steering: Rack and pinion, power-assisted. Front Suspension: Modified MacPherson struts with lower control arms and stabilizer bar; SVO added adjustable gas- pressurized shocks. Rear Suspension: Rigid axle w/four-bar link and coil springs; GT/SVO added an anti-sway bar and dual shocks on each side. Brakes: Front disc, rear drum (power-assisted) except SVO, four-wheel disc brakes. Ignition: Electronic. Body construction: Unibody. Fuel tank: 15.4 gal.

DRIVETRAIN OPTIONS: Engine/Transmission/Suspension: 232 cu. in. V-6: LX ($454). 302 cu. in. V-8 pkg. ($1120) exc. LX conv. ($106). Five-speed manual trans.: LX ($124). Three-speed automatic trans.: LX ($510); std. on conv. Four-speed overdrive auto. trans.: LX ($746); GT ($622). Other: Engine block heater ($18). H.D. battery ($27). California emission system ($102). High-altitude option (NC).

CONVENIENCE/APPEARANCE OPTIONS: Option Packages: SVO competition preparation pkg.: equipment deleted ($1451 credit). Light/convenience group ($55). Power lock group ($182-$215). Comfort/Convenience: Air cond. ($762). Rear defroster, electric ($145). Fingertip speed control ($176). Power windows ($207) exc. conv. ($282). Tinted glass ($115). Tilt steering wheel ($115). Entertainment: AM/FM stereo radio w/cassette player: LX/GT ($148). Electronic seek/scan AM/FM stereo w/cassette: LX/GT ($300). Premium sound system ($138). Radio delete ($148 credit). Exterior: TRoof: hatch ($1100). Flip-up open air roof: hatch ($315). Lower charcoal accent paint ($116). Single wing spoiler: SVO (NC). Interior: Console w/clock and systems monitor ($191). Vinyl bucket seats: LX ($29). Articulated leather sport bucket seats: LX conv. ($807); GT conv. ($429). Leather seat upholstery: SVO ($189). LX Wheels and Tires: Wire wheel covers ($98). Styled steel wheels ($178). P205/75R14 WSW ($109). P225/60VR15 on cast aluminum wheels ($665).

HISTORY: Introduced: October 3, 1985. Model year production: 224,410. Total production for the U.S. market of 198,358 Mustangs included 107,340 four-cylinder, 38,422 sixes, and 52,596 V-8 engines. Calendar year production: 177,737. Calendar year sales by U.S. dealers: 167,699. Model year sales by U.S. dealers: 175,598.

Historical Footnotes: Mustang was the only Ford model to show a sales increase for 1986. Mercury's similar Capri would not return for another year, but Mustang was prepared to carry on in ordinary and high-performance trim. Turbocharging forced a hefty amount of horsepower out of SVO's small four-cylinder engine, delivering acceleration that rivaled big old V-8s.

MUSTANG
1987-1990

The Mustang entered 1987 as a rear-drive hatchback model produced by Ford Division of Ford Motor Co., with headquarters in Detroit, Mich. All '87 Mustangs were made at the Dearborn assembly plant between Sept. 30, 1986 and Oct. 13, 1987. The factory operated two shifts and built an average of 45.9 Mustangs per hour — 163,392 for the model year.

Gone this season was the SVO (Special Vehicle Operations) version of the Mustang. Horsepower of the GT's five-liter engine rose to 225. It also featured an aero ground-effects package, fog lamps and unique tail lamp treatment for both convertibles and hatchbacks. LX Mustangs came in sedan, convertible and hatchback styles stressing luxury. New for the year were a redesigned instrument panel, pod-mounted headlamp switches and a console. The standard transmission was now a five-speed manual, and a four-speed automatic was also introduced.

Industry analysts had expected the Mustang's popularity to wane when the Mazda-made Probe bowed in mid-1988, but they guessed wrong. Instead, sales leaped to 170,601, more than 40,000 cars above the goal set in the fall. Workers on two shifts at Dearborn built 46 Mustangs per hour between July 31, 1987 and Aug. 3, 1988.

There was little change in the cars, except a higher sticker price. The least expensive Mustang listed for $9,209 versus $8,645 the previous year. Ford executives must have been happy with a 4.4 percent sales increase in spite of $600 higher prices. So much so, in fact, that plans were made to modernize the factory and keep the Mustang alive through the 1990s.

The 25th anniversary of the Mustang was highlighted in 1989, when a new LX 5-liter series was introduced. Model year sales increased to 172,218 units and the "pony car's" market share held steady at 2.3 percent.

Production of Mustangs built to 1989 specifications began Aug. 31, 1988 and ended Sept. 5, 1989. An average of 46 units per hour was maintained at the factory in Dearborn. This pushed the nameplate's all-time sales total over six million cars since April 1, 1964, when it bowed at the New York World's Fair. Mustang collectors whispered of a "Silver Anniversary" edition GT with a 351 V-8, twin turbos and 400 hp being sourced from race car builder Jack Rousch, but with sales galloping, Ford insisted that the first 1964½ model was originally planned as a 1965 Mustang, meaning the anniversary would come in 1990. It's likely that Ford management saw some sense in waiting a year, as a limited-edition car could be a good sales motivator in a slacker market.

1990 Ford Mustang GT convertible

When the 1990 models appeared, there was little change obvious in the Mustang lineup. Sedans, hatchbacks and ragtops again came in the LX and LX 5L series, with hatchbacks and convertibles available as GTs. A 2.3-liter four remained the LX engine with the 220 hp 5-liter HO V-8 reserved for LX 5L and GT versions.

A limited-edition metallic emerald green convertible with white interior was announced for release in the spring. The rumored 351-powered 25-year edition was deemed too costly to produce, according to knowledgeable sources.

1987 MUSTANG

Mercury's Capri was out of the lineup after 1986, leaving Mustang as Ford's sole pony-car. The turbocharged SVO Mustang also departed, leaving only an LX and GT model. Also gone: the V-6 engine.

1987 Mustang GT hatchback coupe

MUSTANG — FOUR/V-8 — Ford's ponycar got a fresh look for 1987 with a significant restyling — the first one since its debut for 1979. Changes included new front and rear fascias, a switch to aero headlamps, and the addition of substantial lower bodyside moldings. The GT had a lower air dam with integrated foglamps and air scoops, as well as 'Mustang GT' lettering formed into its flared rocker panel moldings and rear fascia. The GT hatchback also had a large spoiler that held the required high-mount stop lamp. Wide taillamps on the GT were covered by a louver-like slotted applique. Inside all Mustangs was a new instrument panel that showed a more European look, accompanied by a two-spoke steering wheel. Multi-point fuel injection replaced the former carburetor on the base four-cylinder engine, while the V-8 got a boost from 200 up to 225 horsepower. A five-speed manual gearbox was now standard, with four-speed overdrive automatic optional.

I.D. DATA: Mustang's 17-symbol Vehicle Identification Number (VIN) again was stamped on a metal tab fastened to the instrument panel, visible through the windshield. Coding was similar to 1984-86. Model year code (symbol ten) changed to 'H' for 1987.

MUSTANG LX (FOUR/V-8)

Model Number	Body/Style Number	Body Type & Seating	Factory Price	Shipping Weight	Production Total
40	66B	2-dr. Notch-4P	8043/9928	2724/3000	Note 1
41	61B	3-dr. Hatch-4P	8474/10359	2782/3058	Note 1
44	66B	2-dr. Conv.-4P	12840/14725	2921/3197	Note 1

LX Price/Weight Note: Figures to left of slash are for four-cylinder engine, to right of slash for V-8.

MUSTANG GT (V-8)

42	61B	3-dr. Hatch-4P	11835	3080	Note 1
45	66B	2-dr. Conv.-4P	15724	3214	Note 1

Note 1: Ford reports total production of 64,704 two-doors (including convertibles) and 94,441 hatchbacks. Other sources claim totals of 58,100 two-doors, 80,717 hatchbacks, and 20,328 convertibles.

ENGINE DATA: BASE FOUR (LX): Inline, overhead cam, four-cylinder. Cast iron block and head. Displacement: 140 cu. in. (2.3 liters). Bore & stroke: 3.78 x 3.13 in. Compression ratio: 9.5:1. Brake horsepower: 90 at 3800 RPM. Torque: 130 lbs.-ft. at 2800 RPM. Five main bearings. Hydraulic valve lifters. Port fuel injection. BASE V-8 (GT); OPTIONAL (LX): 90-degree, overhead valve V-8. Cast iron block and head. Displacement: 302 cu. in. (5.0 liters). Bore & stroke: 4.00 x 3.00 in. Compression ratio: 9.2:1. Brake horsepower: 225 at 4000 RPM. Torque: 300 lbs.-ft. at 3200 RPM. Five main bearings. Hydraulic valve lifters. Sequential fuel injection.

CHASSIS DATA: Wheelbase: 100.5 in. Overall length: 179.6 in. Height: 52.1 in. exc. conv., 51.9 in. Width: 69.1 in. Front Tread: 56.6 in. Rear Tread: 57.0 in. Standard Tires: P195/75R14 except GT, P225/60VR16 Goodyear Eagle GT Gatorback.

TECHNICAL: Transmission: Five-speed manual (floor shift) standard. Four-speed overdrive automatic available. **Steering:** Rack and pinion, power-assisted. **Front Suspension:** Modified MacPherson struts with lower control arms and stabilizer bar (gas shocks on GT). **Rear Suspension:** Rigid axle w/four links and coil springs (stabilizer bar on GT). **Brakes:** Front disc, rear drum (power-assisted). **Body construction:** Unibody. **Fuel tank:** 15.4 gal.

DRIVETRAIN OPTIONS: Engine/Transmission/Suspension: 5.0-liter V-8 pkg.: LX ($1885). Four-speed overdrive auto. trans. ($515).

CONVENIENCE/APPEARANCE OPTIONS:
Climate Control Group (Air conditioning, heavy-duty battery, rear defogger, tinted glass), LX coupe w/four ($1005); LX coupe w/V8 ($978); LX conv. w/four ($740); LX coupe w/V8 ($713); GT coupe ($858); GT conv. ($713). Air conditioning ($788). Heavy-duty battery ($27). Rear defogger ($145). Tinted glass ($120). Climate Control Group w/Premium Sound instead of rear defogger, LX coupes w/four ($1028); LX coupes w/V8 ($1001); LX conv. w/four ($908); LX conv. w/V8, GT ($881). Climate Control Group w/Custom Equipment Group and Premium Sound instead of rear defogger, LX coupes w/four ($860); LX coupes w/V8 ($833); LX conv. w/four ($740); LX conv. w/V8, GT ($713). Custom Equipment Group (Graphic EQ, dual power mirrors, lighted visor mirrors, tilt steering column, power windows) LX coupes w/four ($624); LX conv. ($538); GT coupe ($500); GT conv. ($414). Graphic Equalizer ($218). Dual power mirrors ($60). Lighted visor mirrors ($100). Tilt steering column, LX ($124). Power windows, coupes ($222); convertibles ($296). Special Value Group (Power Lock Group [includes remote fuel filler & decklid/hatch releases], AM/FM w/cassette, speed control, styled road wheels), LX w/V8 ($735); GT ($519). Power Lock Group, LX ($244); GT ($206). AM/FM Stereo w/cassette ($137). Speed control ($176). Styled road wheels, LX ($178). Bodyside molding insert stripe ($49). AM/FM Stereo delete ($206 credit). Flip-up/open-air sunroof ($355). T roof, LX ($1737); LX w/Climate Control Group ($1667); LX w/Special Value Group ($1543); LX w/Custom Equipment Group ($1505); GT ($1608); GT w/Special Value Group ($1401); GT w/Custom Equipment Group ($1341). Premium Sound System ($168). Wire wheel covers, LX ($98). Leather articulated sport seats, LX conv. ($780); GT conv. ($415).

1988 MUSTANG

In the wake of the 1987 restyling, Mustang entered this model year with minimal change.

1988 Mustang GT hatchback coupe

MUSTANG — FOUR/V-8 — As in 1987, two powerplants were available for the Ford ponycar: a 2.3-liter four-cylinder engine rated 90 horsepower, or a 225-horsepower V-8 (standard on the GT). A five-speed manual floor shift was standard, with four-speed overdrive automatic optional.

I.D. DATA: Mustang's 17-symbol Vehicle Identification Number (VIN) again was stamped on a metal tab fastened to the instrument panel, visible through the windshield. Coding was similar to 1984-87. Model year code (symbol ten) changed to 'J' for 1988.

MUSTANG LX (FOUR/V-8)

Model Number	Body/Style Number	Body Type & Seating	Factory Price	Shipping Weight	Production Total
40	66B	2-dr. Notch-4P	8726/10611	2751/3037	Note 1
41	61B	3-dr. Hatch-4P	9221/11106	2818/3105	Note 1
44	66B	2-dr. Conv.-4P	13702/15587	2953/3209	Note 1

LX Price/Weight Note: Figures to left of slash are for four-cylinder engine, to right of slash for V-8.

MUSTANG GT (V-8)

42	61B	3-dr. Hatch-4P	12745	3193	Note 1
45	66B	2-dr. Conv.-4P	16610	3341	Note 1

Note 1: A total of 179,565 Mustangs were produced for the U.S. market (71,890 two-doors, 74,331 hatchbacks, and 33,344 convertibles).

ENGINE DATA: BASE FOUR (LX): Inline, overhead cam, four-cylinder. Cast iron block and head. Displacement: 140 cu. in. (2.3 liters). Bore & stroke: 3.78 x 3.13 in. Compression ratio: 9.5:1. Brake horsepower: 90 at 3800 RPM. Torque: 130 lbs.-ft. at 2800 RPM. Five main bearings. Hydraulic valve lifters. Port fuel injection. BASE V-8 (GT); OPTIONAL (LX): 90-degree, overhead valve V-8. Cast iron block and head. Displacement: 302 cu. in. (5.0 liters). Bore & stroke: 4.00 x 3.00 in. Compression ratio: 9.5:1. Brake horsepower: 225 at 4200 RPM. Torque: 300 lbs.-ft. at 3200 RPM. Five main bearings. Hydraulic valve lifters. Sequential fuel injection.

CHASSIS DATA: Wheelbase: 100.5 in. Overall length: 179.6 in. Height: 52.1 in. exc. conv., 51.9 in. Width: 69.1 in. Front Tread: 56.6 in. Rear Tread: 57.0 in. Standard Tires: P195/75R14 except (GT) P225/60VR16 Goodyear Eagle GT Gatorback.

TECHNICAL: Transmission: Five-speed manual (floor shift) standard. Four-speed overdrive automatic available. **Steering:** Rack and pinion, power-assisted. **Front Suspension:** Modified MacPherson struts with lower control arms and stabilizer bar (gas shocks on GT). **Rear Suspension:** Rigid axle w/four links and coil springs (stabilizer bar on GT). **Brakes:** Front disc, rear drum (power-assisted). **Body construction:** Unibody. **Fuel tank:** 15.4 gal.

DRIVETRAIN OPTIONS: 5.0-liter V-8 pkg.: LX ($1885). Four-speed overdrive auto. trans. ($515).

CONVENIENCE/APPEARANCE OPTIONS:
Preferred Equip. Pkgs., LX Sdn or HB w/four (NC); LX Sdn or HB w/V8 ($615); LX convertible w/four (NC); LX Convertible w/V8 ($555); GT Hatchback ($615); GT Convertible ($555). Manual Control Air Cond ($788). Pwr. Side Windows ($222). Tilt Strg Wheel ($124). Dual Illum. Visor Mirrors ($100). Custom Equipment Group, LX ($1034); LX Convertible ($934); GT ($910); GT Convertible ($810). Bodyside Mldg. Insert Stripe ($49). Rr. Window Defroster ($145). Graphic Equalizer ($218). Pwr. Lock Grp. ($237). Dual Electric Remote Mirrors ($60). Electronic AM/FM Radio Cassette ($137). Flip-Up Open Air Roof ($355). T Roof, LX ($1800); w/Preferred Equip. Pkg. ($1505); w/Custom Equip. Grp. ($1459); w/Custom Equip. Grp & Preferred Equip. Pkg. ($1163); GT ($1659); w/Preferred Equip. Pkg. ($1363); w/Custom Equip. Grp. ($1437); w/Custom Equip. Grp. & Preferred Equip. Pkg. ($1141). Premium Sound System ($168). Speed Control ($182). Wire Style Wheel Covers ($178). Styled Road Wheels ($178). Frt. Lic. Plate Bracket (NC). Eng. Block Immersion Heater ($18). Calif. Emissions System ($99). High Alt. Emissions System (NC). Lower Titanium Accent Treatment Ext. Paint, GT (NC). Leather Articulated Spt Seats, LX Convertible ($780); GT Convertible ($415); Vinyl Seat Trim ($37). P195/75Rx14 WSW Tires ($82).

HISTORY:
Introduced: October 1, 1987. Model year production: 211,225 (total). Calendar year production: 200,089. Calendar year sales by U.S. dealers: 170,080. Model year sales by U.S. dealers: 170,601.

1989 MUSTANG

1990 Mustang LX 5.0L two-door hatchback

Ford's ponycar entered the 1989 marketplace with little change, except that the LX, when equipped with an available V-8 engine, was now called "LX 5.0L Sport."

1989 Mustang LX 5.0L Sport hatchback coupe

MUSTANG — FOUR/V-8 — Once again, two powerplants were available for Ford's ponycar: a 90-horsepower four or 225-horsepower V-8. Standard on the GT, the V-8 was optional in LX Mustangs. When installed in an LX, the V-8 package included articulated sport seats (as in the GT). Both convertible models now had standard power windows and door locks.

I.D. DATA: Mustang's 17-symbol Vehicle Identification Number (VIN) again was stamped on a metal tab fastened to the instrument panel, visible through the windshield. Coding was similar to 1984-88. Model year code (symbol ten) changed to 'K' for 1989.

MUSTANG LX (FOUR/V-8)

Model Number	Body/Style Number	Body Type & Seating	Factory Price	Shipping Weight	Production Total
40	66B	2-dr. Notch-4P	9050/11410	2754/3045	
41	61B	3-dr. Hatch-4P	9556/12265	2819/3110	
44	66B	2-dr. Conv.-4P	14140/17001	2966/3257	

LX Price/Weight Note: Figures to left of slash are for four-cylinder engine, to right of slash for V-8.

MUSTANG GT (V-8)

Model Number	Body/Style Number	Body Type & Seating	Factory Price	Shipping Weight	Production Total
42	61B	3-dr. Hatch-4P	13272	3194	
45	66B	2-dr. Conv.-4P	17512	3333	

ENGINE DATA: BASE FOUR (LX): Inline, overhead cam, four-cylinder. Cast iron block and head. Displacement: 140 cu. in. (2.3 liters). Bore & stroke: 3.78 x 3.13 in. Compression ratio: 9.5:1. Brake horsepower: 90 at 3800 RPM. Torque: 130 lbs.-ft. at 2800 RPM. Five main bearings. Hydraulic valve lifters. Port fuel injection. **BASE V-8 (GT); OPTIONAL (LX):** 90-degree, overhead valve V-8. Cast iron block and head. Displacement: 302 cu. in. (5.0 liters). Bore & stroke: 4.00 x 3.00 in. Compression ratio: 9.2:1. Brake horsepower 225 at 4200 RPM. Torque: 300 lbs.-ft. at 3200 RPM. Five main bearings. Hydraulic valve lifters. Sequential fuel injection.

CHASSIS DATA: Wheelbase: 100.5 in. **Overall length:** 179.6 in. **Height:** 52.1 in. exc. conv., 51.9 in. **Width:** 69.1 in. **Front Tread:** 56.6 in. **Rear Tread:** 57.0 in. **Standard Tires:** P195/70R14 except (LX 5.0L Sport and GT) P225/60VR15.

TECHNICAL: Transmission: Five-speed manual (floor shift) standard. Four-speed overdrive automatic available. **Steering:** Rack and pinion, power-assisted. **Front Suspension:** Modified MacPherson struts with lower control arms and stabilizer bar (gas shocks on GT). **Rear Suspension:** Rigid axle w/four links and coil springs (stabilizer bar on GT). **Brakes:** Front disc, rear drum (power-assisted). **Body construction:** Unibody. **Fuel tank:** 15.4 gal.

DRIVETRAIN OPTIONS: Four-speed overdrive auto. trans. ($515).

CONVENIENCE/APPEARANCE OPTIONS: Preferred Equip. Pkgs LX w/four, Special Value Grp, Pwr Lock Grp, Dual Electric Remote Mirrors, Electronic AM/FM Radio w/Cass Player & Clock, Speed Control, Styled Road Wheels, Pwr Side Windows, LX Sdn or HB (NC); LX Convertible (NC). LX V8 Sport GT, Special Value Grp, Pwr Lock Grp, Dual Electric Remote Mirrors, Electronic AM/FM Radio w/Cass Player & Clock, Spd Control, Power Windows, Custom Equipment Grp Air Cond, Manual Control, Dual Illum Visor Mirrors, Tilt Wheel, Prem Sound System, Sedans or Hatchbacks ($1006); Convertibles ($487). Group Opts. Custom Equipment Group (four LX Series only) Manual Control, Dual Illum Visor Mirrors, Tilt Wheel, Premium Sound System, LX Sdn & HB ($1180); LX Convertible ($1080). Bodyside Molding Insert Stripe ($61). Rear Window Defroster ($150). Flip-Up Open Air Roof ($355). Wire Style Wheel Covers ($193). Calif. Emissions System ($100). High Alt. Emissions System (NC). Lower Titanium Accent Treatment Ext. Paint, GT (NC). Leather Articulated Sport Seats, LX Convertible ($855); LX V8 Sport Convertible or GT Convertible ($489). Vinyl Seat Trim ($37). Frt. License Plate Bracket (NC). P195/75Rx14 WSW Tires ($82).

HISTORY: Introduced: October 6, 1988. Model year production: 209,769. Calendar year sales by U.S. dealers: 161,148. Model year sales by U.S. dealers: 172,218.

1990 MUSTANG

Safety led Mustang into 1990, as a driver's airbag and rear shoulder belts became standard. Otherwise, the familiar rear-drive ponycar continued as before, for its twelfth season in this form.

MUSTANG — FOUR/V-8 — Body styles and powertrains were the same as prior years: coupe, hatchback, and convertible, with 2.3-liter four or 5.0-liter V-8. No longer did Mustang's interior hold a tilt steering column or console armrest, but door panels now held map pockets. The LX 5.0L, with V-8 engine, came with the heftier suspension and bigger tires from the GT, but without the GT's spoilers and air dams. Clearcoat paint was now optional, as was leather interior trim for the V-8 hatchbacks.

I.D. DATA: Mustang's 17-symbol Vehicle Identification Number (VIN) again was stamped on a metal tab fastened to the instrument panel, visible through the windshield. Coding was similar to 1984-89. Model year code (symbol ten) changed to 'L' for 1990.

MUSTANG LX (FOUR/V-8)

Model Number	Body/Style Number	Body Type & Seating	Factory Price	Shipping Weight	Production Total
40	66B	2-dr. Notch-4P	9638/12107	2634/2715	
41	61B	3-dr. Hatch-4P	10144/12950	2634/2715	
44	66B	2-dr. Conv.-4P	14495/17681	2871/2952	

LX Price/Weight Note: Figures to left of slash are for four-cylinder engine, to right of slash for LX 5.0L Sport V-8.

MUSTANG GT (V-8)

Model Number	Body/Style Number	Body Type & Seating	Factory Price	Shipping Weight	Production Total
42	61B	3-dr. Hatch-4P	13929	3065	
45	66B	2-dr. Conv.-4P	18303	3213	

ENGINE DATA: BASE FOUR (LX): Inline, overhead cam, four-cylinder. Cast iron block and head. Displacement: 140 cu. in. (2.3 liters). Bore & stroke: 3.78 x 3.13 in. Compression ratio: 9.5:1. Brake horsepower: 88 at 4000 RPM. Torque: 132 lbs.-ft. at 2600 RPM. Five main bearings. Hydraulic valve lifters. Port fuel injection. **BASE V-8 (GT); OPTIONAL (LX):** 90-degree, overhead valve V-8. Cast iron block and head. Displacement: 302 cu. in. (5.0 liters). Bore & stroke: 4.00 x 3.00 in. Compression ratio: 9.0:1. Brake horsepower: 225 at 4200 RPM. Torque: 300 lbs.-ft. at 3200 RPM. Five main bearings. Hydraulic valve lifters. Sequential fuel injection.

1990 Mustang LX 5.0L convertible

CHASSIS DATA: Wheelbase: 100.5 in. **Overall length:** 179.6 in. **Height:** 52.1 in. **Width:** 68.3 in. **Front Tread:** 56.6 in. **Rear Tread:** 57.0 in. **Standard Tires:** P195/75R14 except (LX 5.0L Sport and GT) P225/60VR15.

TECHNICAL: Transmission: Five-speed manual (floor shift) standard. Four-speed overdrive automatic available. **Steering:** Rack and pinion, power-assisted. **Front Suspension:** Modified MacPherson struts with lower control arms and stabilizer bar (gas shocks on GT). **Rear Suspension:** Rigid axle w/four links and coil springs (stabilizer bar on GT). **Brakes:** Front disc, rear drum (power-assisted). **Body construction:** Unibody. **Fuel tank:** 15.4 gal.

DRIVETRAIN OPTIONS: Four-speed overdrive auto. trans. ($539).

CONVENIENCE/APPEARANCE OPTIONS: Preferred Equip Pkgs. LX w/four Special Value Grp, Pwr Equipment Grp, Pwr Lock Grp, Dual Electric Remote Mirrors, Pwr Side Windows, Spd Cntrl, Electronic AM/FM Radio w/Cass Player & Clock, LX Sdn or HB (NC); LX Convertible (NC). LX V8 Sport GT Special Value Grp, Pwr Equipment Grp, Pwr Lock Grp, Dual Electric Remote Mirrors, Power Windows, Electronic AM/FM Radio w/Cass Player & Clock, Spd Control, Custom Equip. Grp, Air Condtioner, Dual Illum Visor Mirrors, Premium Sound System, Sedans or Hatchbacks ($1003); Convertibles ($496). Custom Equipment Grp, four LX Series only, Air Conditioner, Mirrors, Dual Illum Visor LX Sdn & HB ($907); LX Convertible ($807). Rr Window Defroster ($150). Flip-Up Open Air Roof ($355). Wire Style Wheel Covers ($193). Premium Sound System, Incl 6 prem spkrs & 4 channel amplifier 80 watts ($168). Calif Emissions ($100). High Alt Emissions (NC). Clearcoat Exterior Paint ($91). Lower Titanium Accent Treatment, GT ($159). Leather Seating Surfaces on Articulated Spt Seats ($489). Vinyl Seat Trim ($37). Frt License Plate Bracket (NC). Eng Block Immersion Heater ($20). P195/75Rx14 WSW Tires ($82).

EDSEL
1958-1960

1958 Edsel Pacer convertible

The history of the Edsel began years before the first cars bearing the name appeared. In early 1952 Henry Ford II appointed the "Davis Committee" to investigate the possibilities of creating an additional car line. Ford announced in August 1956 that it was in the process of establishing five regional sales offices that would operate, under the direction of the Ford Motor Co.'s Special Products Division, to form the core of a new, coast-to-coast network of Edsel dealers.

Data compiled by Dale Rapp
Introduction by Linda Clark

This marketing program was put into effect the following month and, on Oct. 15, 1956, the selection of 24 district sales managers was made. J.C. Doyle was named general sales and marketing manager and had, as his assistants, N.K. VanDerzee and R.F.G. Copeland. Named to head the new organization, as Edsel general manager (as well as Ford vice-president), was R.E. Krafve.

As the winter and spring months of 1957 rolled by, countless miles of newsprint and film were employed in introducing the "new Edsel line," to a supposedly anxious public. The fanfare surrounding the coming of the cars was filled with startling numbers. "More than $250,000,000 will be spent in designing the new line of cars," claimed W.H. Huber's Sales Promotions Department. Then, on Jan. 21, 1957, R.E. Krafve predicted, "The new Edsel line of cars will surpass the originally announced first-year sales goal of 200,000 units."

Such glowing publicity spewed forth from Edsel Division headquarters, in Ecorse Township, Mich., with amazing regularity. And no doubt the company had faith in its own messages, since production facilities for 1958 models were established all over the country, in places

such as Mahwah, N.J.; Sommerville, Mass.; Wayne, Mich.; Louisville, Ky., Milpitas and Los Angeles, Calif.

The 1958 Edsel was introduced in the United States on

1958 Edsel Pacer 2 dr. hardtop

Sept. 4, 1957 — but not to the expected rave reviews or standing ovations. Nor were there long lines of potential buyers standing outside Edsel showrooms. The Edsel was introduced in Canada one week later, on Sept. 11, 1957. In a generally bad season for automobile sales, thousands of Americans — shocked by high new car prices — decided to curtail purchases or try the imported economy models. Edsel built 3,729 cars in July 1957; 19,876 the following month and 18,815 the next. By that time dealers were fully stocked. When the market downturn revealed itself, production was cut to 7,566 October "builds" and just 2,483 cars the remaining months of the year. Model year business hit the brakes at 63,110.

By mid-January 1958, operations of the Edsel Division were combined with those of Mercury, Lincoln and English Fords, in the renamed M-E-L Division, headquartered at

Ford's Dearborn facilities. Ben D. Mills, another Ford Group vice president, was put in charge of M-E-L and C.E. Bowie handled the responsibilities of general sales manager. Marketing was divided up by each of the lines, with separate managers for Mercury, Lincoln, imported cars and Edsels. In the latter area, L.C. Beebe was in charge. Each car line was merchandised and advertised individually, with separate dealer franchises for each as well. Edsel advertising was handled by Kenyon and Eckhardt, the Mercury agency, while Lincoln/English Ford ads were done elsewhere.

The initial Edsel lineup featured 18 models in four series

1958 Edsel Pacer convertible

which were named: Ranger, Pacer, Corsair and Citation (on the marketing ladder). Available body styles included two- and four-door sedans, hardtops and station wagons, plus convertibles in Pacer and Citation trim.

The Ranger and Pacer models rode on a 118.04 inch wheelbase while the Corsair and Citation shared a 124.05 inch wheelbase. Edsel offered no less than five station wagons which rode on a 116 inch wheelbase and came as two or three-seat Bermudas and Villagers, as well as the economy, two-seat job, known as the Roundup.

Compared with its Chrysler and General Motors con-

1958 Edsel Citation 4 dr hardtop

temporaries in model year 1958, the Edsel's profile was clean and attractive and its interior almost as lush as the Kaiser that had expired in 1955. In addition to its most distinctive feature, the "horse-collar" grille, Edsel offered

1959 Edsel Villager station wagon

"Teletouch" automatic transmission — controlled by pushbuttons in the center of the steering wheel hub — on 1958 models. A wide choice of power-assisted options was also available. Two V-8s, a 361 cubic inch engine in the Ranger, Pacer and station wagon models and a 410 cubic inch engine in the higher series Corsair and Citation, were also offered.

"EDSEL . . . already an expression of good taste," read the advertisements for 1959 editions of the car, which it was claimed, offered luxury features at Plymouth-Chevrolet-Ford style prices. This was certainly a change from the original concept, in which Edsels were aimed at the very upper level of the medium-price class inhabited by makes like Buick, Oldsmobile and DeSoto.

The 1959 lineup consisted of 16 models. There were

1960 Edsel Ranger convertible

three each of sedans and hardtops (the latter style offering trios in both two- and four-door form); a pair of pillarless four-doors; four wagons and a lone convertible. Although the number of models was down, the number of dealers increased (by a significant 80 percent), which gave hope that the new model year might take a turn for the better. The distribution system was also streamlined a bit, so that dealers would no longer be overstocked with cars. This freed-up dollars that might be better spent in local advertising and promotional efforts. Things were not, however, going smoothly in Edselland. Model year sales dropped to 44,891 units.

1958 EDSEL

1958 Edsel, Ranger 2-dr sedan, V-8 (AA)

RANGER — (V-8) — Series A — The all-new 1958 Edsel, said to be the product of nine years of planning, was publicly launched on September 4, 1957, as a product of the Edsel Division of Ford Motor Company. Although obviously based on contemporary Fords and Mercurys, in its day the Edsel was described as being, "Entirely new to the industry." It was aimed at the medium-priced car field and came in four different lines with prices from $2,484 to a high of $3,796. The two lower-priced series, Ranger and Pacer, were built off the 118 inch wheelbase platform that 1958 Fords utilized. The two higher-priced lines, Corsair and Citation, were on a 124 inch wheelbase and had what was, essentially, a stretched version of the Mercury's chassis and sheetmetal components. However, when compared to Ford and Mercury counterparts, on a model-for-model basis, the Edsels offered more power, more luxury, more standard equipment and more radical styling. They were intended to enter the sales battle against cars like Buick, Oldsmobile and Chrysler New Yorker which Ford, heretofore, had only Mercury to compete with. In trying to make the Edsel into a car that buyers would view as something really different Ford Motor Company — at first — went to the trouble of establishing a separate Edsel Division, with headquarters in Ecorse Township, Michigan. It was the first time in automotive history that any major manufacturer had set up a large dealer organization (1,200 to 1,400 outlets) prior to the introduction and marketing of a completely new line of automobiles. Also, the Edsels radical styling was part of the effort to give the new models their own personality. The frontal treatment was conceived as a modern interpretation of the Classic Packard's tall, vertical center grille, with smaller grilles at each side, Unfortunately, the public thought that the center grille looked like horse collar and thats what it was soon being called. This horse collar grille split the center of the car and was flanked by twin rectangular openings having horizontal grille bars and parking lamps at the outboard ends. Both the grille and the lamps wrapped around the front body corners. The front bumper was also split and had a concave indention that took on a projectile-like contour. The center of the hood had a broad peak or bulge, which protruded to meet the horse collar. The name Edsel, in gold block letters, ran vertically down the center of the grille, inside a horse collar shaped inner molding. The top of the hood was decorated with a standup hood ornament. Two headlamps were placed in each fender, being horizontally positioned and set into oval shaped openings. Pacer body side styling was characterized, at the front, by a sort of reverse angled, fin-shaped feature line running along the front fender and door. At the rear, was a sporty-looking indention, usually referred to as a 'scallop'. It was outlined with a thin chrome molding and had large chrome letters inside, which spelled out the new car's name. Body panels and rooflines on the smaller models had a Ford look, while those on the big Edsels came straight from the Mercury studio. The rear end reverted to a more radical theme with a depressed center bumper, boomerang-shaped horizontal taillamps and the deck lid depressed below the level of the flat, but rounded, fender tops. Station wagons of all types had certain styling distinctions, which are described in the outline of the Station Wagon Series given below. The Ranger was the base trim-level Edsel. Rangers could be identified by suitable model signature scripts placed above and ahead of the front wheel openings; lack of front fender and lack of roof edge reveal moldings and a slightly plainer appearance in general. Ranger sedans were equipped with front and rear arm rests; three ash trays; two coat hoods; Black rubber floor mats and White vinyl headliners. Trims available for these cars were Code 'A' (Green cloth); Code 'B' (Blue cloth) and Code 'C' (Grey and Black cloth). Ranger hardtops were equipped the same as sedans, except for the type of upholstery. Trims available for both two and four-door pillarless styles were Code 'K' (White vinyl and Green cloth); Code 'M' (White vinyl and Blue cloth) and Code 'N' (White vinyl and Black cloth). Three-speed manual transmission with column controls, a 361 cubic inch 303 horsepower V-8 with four-barrel carburetion and 8.00 x 14 four-ply tires were featured as well.

VEHICLE I.D. NUMBERS: Encoded information designating engine, model year, assembly plant, body style and consecutive unit production number was found on the upper line of the data plate, affixed to the lefthand front door post of all 1958 Edsels. The first symbol was a letter designating the type of engine, as follows: 'W' — 361 cubic inch V-8 or 'X' — 410 cubic inch V-8. The second symbol was an '8', designating 1958 model year. The third symbol was another letter, designating assembly plant, as follows: 'U' = Louisville, Kentucky; 'R' = San Jose, California: 'S' = Somerville, Massachusetts; 'E' = Mahwah, New Jersey; 'W' = Wayne, Michigan and 'J' = Los Angeles, California. The fourth symbol was another letter, which designated the style of the body, as follows: 'C' = Ranger two-door sedan; 'F' = Ranger/Pacer four-door sedan; 'G' = Ranger/Pacer two-door hardtop; 'H' = Ranger/Pacer four-door hardtop; 'R' = pacer convertible; 'S' = Roundup 2 dr. wagon; 'T' Villager/Bermuda 4 dr. 6 pass. wagon; 'V' = Villager Bermuda 4 dr. 9 pass. wagon; 'W' = Corsair/Citation two-door hardtop; :X' = Corsiar/Citation four-door hardtop; 'Y' = Citation convertible. The following symbols (six numbers) were the consecutive unit production number. Consecutive numbers at each plant began at 700001 and up. Additional encoded information designating Body Type, exterior color, interior trim, date of assembly, transmission type and rear axle was listed on the lower part of the data plate. The Body Type codes consisted of two numbes followed by a single letter as shown in the second column of the specifications charts below. The exterior color code consisted of three letters, the first indicating main body color; the second indicating top color and the third indicating the color that the scallop was painted. The codes and colors were as follows: Code 'A' = Jet Black; 'B' = Silver Grey Metallic; Code 'C' = Ember Red; Code 'D' = Turquoise; Code 'E' = Snow White (*); Code 'F' = Powder Blue (**); Code 'G' = Horizon Blue; Code 'H' = Royal Blue Metallic; Code 'J' = Ice Green; Code 'K' = Spring Green; Code 'L' = Spruce Green Metallic; Code 'M' = Charcoal Brown Metallic; Code 'N' = Driftwood (*); Code 'Q' = Jonquil Yellow; Coce 'R' = Sunset Coral (*); Coce 'T' = Chalf Pink (**); Code 'U' = Copper Metallic and Code 'X' = Gold Metallic. **Note:** (*) indicates colors for Ranger / Pacer / Wagons only and (**) indicates colors for Corsair / Citation only. The interior trim code was a single letter, as described in text covering each model. The date code consisted of one or two numbers and a letter. The numbers designated the day of the month that the car was built. The letter indicated the month of production with 'A' = January; 'B' = February, etc. The letter "I" was not used and the month of July 1957 (Code G), Aug. 57 (Code H), July 1958 (Code U), and Aug. 58 (Code V). Transmission codes were numerical, as follows: '1' = standard manual; '2' = overdrive; '3' = column-lever automatic and '4' = Tel-Touch pushbutton automatic. A letter was used to designate different rear axles, as follws: 'A' = 2.91:1; 'B' = 3.32:1; 'C' = 3.70:1 and 'D' = 3.89:1.

RANGER SERIES

Model Number	Body/Style Number	Body Type & Seating	Factory Price	Shipping Weight	Production Total
A	64A	2-dr Sed-6P	2484	3729	4,615
A	58A	4-dr Sed-6P	2557	3805	31
A	63A	2-dr HT-6P	2558	3724	32
A	57A	4-dr HT-6P	2643	3796	33

RANGER SERIES ENGINE
V-8 Overhead valves. Cast iron block. Displacement: 361 cubic inches. Bore and stroke: 4.05 x 3.50. Compression ratio: 10.5:1. Brake horsepower: 303 at 4600 RPM. Five main bearings. Hydraulic valve lifters. Carburetor: four-barrel Ford or Holley.

NOTE: This engine was the 352 Ford V-8 with a slight overbore. The block and heads were painted yellow. The air cleaner and valve covers were painted white. There were red 'E 400' markings on the valve covers to designate torque (not horsepower).

1958 Edsel, Pacer 2-dr hardtop sport coupe, V-8

PACER — (V-8) — SERIES B — The Pacer represented the second step up in the Edsel product lineup. It used the same body as Rangers, with slightly more trim, extra equipment and fancier upholstery fittings. Pacers could be externally identified by the Pacer front fender scripts and the use of a slightly curved, fin-shaped molding on the sides of front fenders and doors. Available body styles were similar to those in the Ranger Series, except that the two-door sedan wasn't available, but a two-door convertible was. Pacer sedans were equipped with four built-in arm rests; two ash trays; cigarette lighter; two coat hooks; chromed inside rearview mirror; one-third/two-thirds design front seat; color-keyed rubber floor mats and a White vinyl headliner. Trims available in the sedan were Code 'E' (Brown cloth); Code 'E' (Green cloth) and Code 'F' (Blue cloth). Pacer hardtops carried the same equipment as sedans, but different trims were used. They were, as follows: Code 'R' (White vinyl and Brown cloth); Code 'S' (White vinyl and Coral cloth); Code 'AX' (White vinyl and Red cloth); Code 'AY' (White vinyl and Turquoise cloth); Code 'T' (Green cloth and vinyl) and Code 'V' (Blue cloth and vinyl). Pacer convertibles were built with four built-in arm rests; three ash trays; cigarette lighter; courtesy lights under instrument panel; rear arm rest lights and chrome inside rearview mirror. They also had one-third/two-third seat designs color-keyed rubber floor mats and vinyl-coated convertible tops in a choice of Black, White, Turquoise or Coral. Convertible interior trims were, as follows: Code 'AJ' (White and Coral vinyl); Code 'AN' (White and Black vinyl); Code 'AV' (White and Turquoise vinyl) or Code 'AZ' (White and Red vinyl).

PACER SERIES B

Model Number	Body/Style Number	Body Type & Seating	Factory Price	Shipping Weight	Production Total
B	58B	4-dr Sed-6P	2700	3826	5262
B	63B	4-dr HT-6P	2770	3773	5710
B	57B	4-dr HT-6P	2828	3857	4765
B	76B	2-dr Conv-6P	3766	4311	1876

NOTE: The designation (*) in production total column indicates that the figure is an estimate. Exact figures are not available, due to a change in record keeping during the production run.

PACER SERIES ENGINE
See 1958 Edsel ranger Series engine data.

CORSAIR — (V-8) — SERIES A — The third step up in the 1958 Edsel lineup was the Corsair Series, which was comprised of two and four-door hardtops on the 124 inch wheelbase. Cars in this line had the look of contemporary Mercurys with greater overall length and a roof styled with an overhanging rear edge and wraparound backlight. For identification, there were Corsiar front fender scripts; fin-shaped side moldings across the upper mid-section of front fenders and doors; chrome outline moldings on the rear fender scallop; bright Edsel block letteing within the rear fender scallop; Edsel block lettering positioned vertically within the horse collar center grille; rocker panel moldings and heavy chrome trim along the edge of the roof and rear body pillars. Vertical guards were optional on each of the front bumpers, being positioned quite close to the horse collar grille. the Corsair and Citation shared many chassis and inner body components with the 1957/58 Mercury. Therefore, only a few components from the Ranger / Pacer Series would interchange with the Corsair / Citation Series. Examples of parts that were common between the two types included the hood ornaments; center and side grilles; front bumpers, Tele-Touch motors except harness, headlight doors, and starter. Standard equipment on Corsair hardtops included built-in front and rear arm rests; ash trays; cigarette lighter; two coat hooks; courtesy lights on the instrument panel; chromed inside rearview mirror; one-third / two-third design front seat; White vinyl headliner and color-keyed floor carpeting. Trim codes available for Corsairs were Code 'B' (Blue cloth and vinyl); Code 'C' (White vinyl and Turquoise cloth; Code 'D' (Green cloth and vinyl); Code 'E' (White vinyl and Gold cloth; Coce 'X' (Gray vinyl and Red cloth) and code 'Y' (White vinyl and Copper cloth).

CORSAIR SERIES A

Model Number	Body/Style Number	Body Type & Seating	Factory Price	Shipping Weight	Production Total
A	63A	2dr HT-6P	3311	4134	3327
A	57A	4-dr HT-6P	3390	4235	5989

CORSAIR SERIES ENGINE
V-8. Overhead valves. Cast iron block. Displacement: 410 cubic inches. Bore and stroke: 4.20 x 3.70 inches. Compression ratio: 10.5:1. Brake horsepower: 345 at 4600 RPM. Five main bearings. Hydraulic valve lifters. Carburetor: four-barrel Holley.

1958 Edsel, Citation 4-dr hardtop sedan, V-8 (HFM)

CITATION — (V-8) — SERIES B — The Citation was the top-of-the-line Edsel offering. It shared the same body which the Corsair fetured, but came with more DeLuxe interiors and trim. There were Citation front fender scripts; model medallions on the rear roof pillar and a special decorative arrangement within the scallop on the rear fender sides. Inside the scallop, an additional, projectile-shaped beauty panel was formed by chrome outline moldings. Also, a large medallion was placed directly below the upper, inner molding, towards the rear. On most two-tone cars the scallop and roof was painted one color and the body another. Tri-tone color combinations were available only on Pacer, Corsair, and Citation hardtops, but only a limited set of Tri-color options was available. A wide variety of two or three-tone combinations could be achieved with the 19 colors available. Standard equipment on Citation hardtops included all items found on Corsairs, plus padded dashborad; electric clock and glove compartment light. Interior trims available in Citation hardtops were: Code 'AA' (Black vinyl and Gray cloth); Code 'H' (Blue cloth and vinyl); Code 'J' (White vinyl and Turquoise cloth); Code 'K' (Green cloth and vinyl); Code 'L' (White vinyl and Gold cloth; Code 'Z' (Pink vinyl and Brown cloth) and Code 'AB' (White vinyl and Copper cloth). The Citation convertible came with the same equipment as hardtops, plus dual exhausts and vinyl-coated convertible tops available in Black, White, Turquoise and Copper. Convertible color schemes were, as follows: Code 'AC' (Brown and Pink vinyl); Code 'AD' (Red and White vinyl); Code 'AE' (Copper and White vinyl); Code 'S' (Turquoise and White vinyl) and Code 'T' (Gold and White vinyl).

CITATION SERIES A

Model Number	Body/Style Number	Body Type & Seating	Factory Price	Shipping Weight	Production Total
B	63B	2-dr HT-6P	3500	4136	2520
B	57B	4-dr HT-6P	3580	4230	5003
B	76B	2-dr Conv-6P	3766	4311	930

CITATION SERIES ENGINE
See 1958 Edsel Corsair Series engine data.

STATION WAGONS — (V-8) — MIXED SERIES CODING — The 1958 Edsel station wagons were all built off the 116 inch wheelbase Ford station wagon platform and utilized the basic sheetmetal of two or four-door 1957 Ford station wagons. Front end sheetmetal was shared with the Edsel Ranger/Pacer Series. The wagon has boomerang shaped taillights housed in a chrome bezel. Three models were available. The Roundup was a two-door station wagon with seating for six. A Roundup script was placed at the front fender tip and a projectile-shaped contrast panel was formed by a chrome outline molding. The 'projectile' went from the rear of the car to the middle of the front door. All wagons were equipped with four arm rests; ash trays; cigarette lighter; two coat hooks; dome and courtesy lights and White vinyl headliner. The Roundup came with black rubber floor mats and a conventional split front seat. The Villager station wagon was a four-door model, which came with six or nine-passenger seating. It had all items that were standard on the roundup, plus a solid front bench seat. Trim codes available for both wagons discussed above were: Code 'BA' (White and Green vinyl); Code 'BB' (White and Blue vinyl); Code 'BC' (Black vinyl and Gold Saran) and Code 'BD' (Red vinyl with Gold Saran). The Bermuda was the top-line station wagon. It had four-doors and either six or nine-passenger seating. Bermudas had simulated wood-grain exterior paneling; color-keyed rubber floor mats; one-third/two third design front seat and chromed inside rearview mirror. Trim included 'AT' (two-tone Blue vinyl); Code 'AJ' (White and Coral vinyl: Code 'AS' two-tone Green vinyl; Coce 'AU' (Driftwood vinyl and Brown Saran) and Code 'AV' (White and Turquoise vinyl).

STATION WAGON SERIES

Model Number	Body/Style Number	Body Type & Seating	Factory Price	Shipping Weight	Production Total
ROUNDUP					
NA	59A	2-dr Sta Wag-6P	2841	3761	757
VILLAGER					
NA	79C	4-dr Sta Wag-6P	2898	3827	2535
NA	79A	4-dr Sta Wag-9P	2955	3900	768
BERMUDA					
NA	79D	4-dr Sta Wag-6P	3155	3853	1421

STATION WAGON SERIES ENGINES
See 1958 Edsel Ranger Series engine data.

CHASSIS FEATURES: Wheelbase: (Ranger/Pacer) 118 inches; (all station wagons) 116 inches; (Corsair/Citation) 124 inches. Overall length: (Ranger/Pacer) 213.1 inches; (all station wagons) 205.4 inches; (Citation/Corsiar) 218.8 inches. Front tread: (Ranger/Pacer) 59.44 inches; (station wagons) 58.97 inches; (Corsair/Citation) 59.38 inches. Rear tread: (Ranger/Pacer) 59 inches; (station wagons) 56.40 inches; (Corsair/Citation) 59 inches. Tires: (Citation/Corsair) 8.50 x 14; (all others) 8.00 x 14.

POWERTRAIN OPTIONS: Three-speed manual transmission with column lever control was standard in Rangers, Pacers and all station wagons. Three-speed automatic transmission with pushbutton Teletouch Drive was standard and mandatory in Corsair/Citation. Overdrive transmission, in Ford-based models ($127.45). Three-speed automatic with column lever control ($217.70). Three-speed automatic transmission with Teletouch control, in Ford-based models ($231.40). Dual exhausts, on Citation convertible (standard equipment); on other models ($23.45).

CONVENIENCE OPTIONS: Power steering ($84.95). Power brakes ($38.25). Power windows ($100.95). Four-Way power seats ($76.45). Dial-A-Temp heater and defroster ($92.45). Dial-A-Temp air conditioning with heater, on Ranger/Pacer ($417.70); on Corsair/Citation ($460.15). Push-button radio with manual antenna ($95.25). Station-seeking radio with electric antenna ($143.90). Rear seat speaker ($16). Tachometer ($14.95). Electric clock, standard in Citation ($15.94). Compass. Push-button chassis lubricator, on Corsair/Citation only ($42.50). Padded instrument panel ($22.65). Front seat belts. Windshield washer ($11.50). Tinted glass ($34). Backup lights ($8.50). Full wheel covers ($12.75). Full wheel covers with appliques and spinner. Front bumper guards. Rear bumper guards. Engine compartment light. Glove compartment light. Luggage compartment light. Inside non-glare rearview mirror. Rocker panel moldings. Hooded outside mirror. Foam front seat cushion, standard in Corsair/Citation ($21.25). Foam rear seat cushion. Carpeting, standard in Corsair/Citation ($12.30). License plate frames. Courtesy lights. Oil filter, standard with Corsair/Citation ($9.15).Paper air cleaner. Two-tone paint on top or scallop ($17). Tri-tone paint. Size 8.00 x 14 whitewall tires. Pacer ($40.35); Corsair/Citation ($44.25). Size 8.50 x 14 whitewall tires. Undercoating. Vacuum-booster windshield wipers ($11.70).Electric windshield wipers. Rear-mounted antennas, single or dual. Excess speed warning light. parking brake warning light. Fuel level warning light. Oil level warning light. Open door warning light. Padded sun visors (included in padded dash safety package). Exhaust deflectors single or dual. Seat covers. Contour floor mats, front and rear. Locking fuel tank cap. Curb signals. Traffic light reflector. Standard-stye outside mirror left and right. Spot light, left and right. Electric luggage compartment opener. Inside-outside temperature gauge. Rear door safety locks four-door only. Fuel and vacuum booster pump. Extra cooling radiator and fan. Electric door locks. Air suspension ride.

Historical footnotes: The Edsel received one of the biggest and longest lasting new car build-ups in automotive history. As early as August 7, 1956, Ford announced that its Special Products Division was in the process of establishing five regional sales offices through which to market an all-new car called the Edsel. The following October 15, the company appointed 24 district sales managers to oversee Edsel sales in major cities. On January 11, 1957, Ford informed the world that the Edsel would be far more radical than any of its other products and that equally radical sales techniques would be adopted to marketing of the car. Then days later, corporate officals predicted 200,000 sales in the first year and set their sights accordingly. After having named the car, publicly on November 19, 1956, Ford released the names and characteristics of each Edsel Series on February 5, 1957. To build even more interest, a Mach 10, 1957 press release identified five factories where Edsels were to be assembled, adding that a sixth factory, on the West Coast, would be added soon. Edsel production began in July, 1957, under the direction of R.E. Krafve, a Ford Motor Company Vice-President who was named General Manager of the Edsel Divivsion. The new division built 3,729 units in July; 19,876 units in August; 18,815 units in September; 7,566 units in October; 2,483 units in November and 2,138 units in December for a total of 54,607 cars in calendar 1957. Model year output was recorded as 63,110 cars for only 1.5 percent of the total U.S. market. Of this figure, 4,900 cars were built at Wayne, Michigan; 6,400 at Mahwah, New Jersey; 33,300 at Louisville, Kentucky; 7,100 at San Jose, California and 11,400 at Somerville, New Jersey. In mid-January, 1958, Ford combined the operations of Edsel, Mercury, Lincoln and English Ford to create a new Mercury-Edsel-Lincoln Division. Of all Edsels built in 1958, 91.9 percent had automatic transmission; 48.7 percent had power steering; 43.3 percent had power brakes; 7.6 percent had power seats; 5.6 percent had power windows; 80.3 percent had radios; 89.4 percent had a heater; 73.2 percent had white sidewall tires; 32.9 percent had tinted glass; 61.4 percent had windshield washers; 43.3 percent had backup lights; 28.4 percent had dual exhausts; 1.6 percent had air conditioning; 2 percent had overdrive and all had V-8 engines. Although universally recognized as a failure in the area of sales, it is interesting to note that, in its first year, the Edsel set an all-time record for deliveries of a brand-new medium-priced automobile.

1959 EDSEL

1959 Edsel, Ranger 4-dr sedan, V-8

RANGER — (V-8) — The Edsel Marketing Division had expected to sell 200,000 cars during 1958, but soon admitted that there was a problem. The company went on record as saying that the Edsel had an identity crisis. Since the first models covered such a wide market spectrum, buyers were unable to determine exactly where the Edsel fit in. Consequently, the Pacer and Citation Series were discontinued for 1959. More emphasis was placed on slotting the remaining models into the bottom end of the low-priced field. As previously indicated, the Edsel line joined Lincolns, Mercurys and English Fords in the new M-E-L marketing division. Upon instituting this regrouping, Henry Ford II — President of the corporation — stated that, "Unified direction of the organizations responsible for the five M-E-L Division product lines (which included English Anglia, Prefect, Consul, Zephyr and Zodiac cars and Thames Van trucks) will strengthen the profit potential of our dealer and assist in increasing the company's efficiency". J.J. Nance was named General manager of M-E-L at its formation, but on September 4, 1959, Ben D. Mills was appointed to the same post. Edsel launched its new 1959 program with the theme of "a new kind of car". Economy was stressed more than before. The Ranger was built off a new, 120 inch wheelbase platform, with a 292 cubic inch V-8 engine as base powerplant. It shared some common sheetmetal with the 1959 Ford. Overall styling changes were quite obvious, although the original theme was not totally disregarded either. The horse collar grille was retained in a modified form. It was now filled with horizontal blades and an Edsel badge at the top. The standup hood ornament disappeared and the parking lamps were moved into the split front bumpers. The side grilles each had three 'stacks' of short prominent, moldings. There were also less noticeable moldings inbetween, which ran from the grille to the dual, horizontal headlamps. The hood still had a broad peak above the top of the

grille. The front of the body was flatter and more shelf-like and the scallop at the rear was nearly gone. A different type of sweepspear treatment was used, which had a distinct scallop shape for each line. On Rangers, it consisted of a full-length upper molding, combined with a lower molding that ran to the door, then dipped in a curved 'V' and continued in a taper to the rear, where it rejoined the top molding. The area between the moldings was often painted in a color other than that on the main body (and often matched the roof). Widely-spaced block letters spelled out Edsel, in chrome, with a few letters on each side of the front door break line. A Ranger script was placed near the rear body corner, under the sweep spear. The rear end still had a wing-like image, but no longer with the taillights in the 'wings'. They were now placed into the rear deck latch panel, slightly above the horizontal centerline. The taillights consisted of three circular lenses, placed horizontally against chrome grille panels housed in wedge-shaped chrome surrounds. A massive one-piece bumper (with a dip below the license plate) ran fully across the rear of the cars. The deck lid still had a wide, center depression with a simulated chrome air vent at the rear. Roof treatments looked like those on the big 1958 Edsels, with a rear overhang and a large, wraparound back light with angular-looking edges. A grooved aluminum trim plate was used on the rear roof pillar. Standard equipment on all models included an air cleaner; positive action windshield wipers; front foam seat cushions; electric clock; cigarette lighter and carpeting (except wagons). Rangers were also equipped with four arm rests; front and rear ash trays; two coat hooks; color-keyed vinyl headliner and a conventional split front seatback. Trim codes on this series were: Code '23' (two-tone Green vinyl and Signet cloth); Code '24' (two-tone Blue vinyl and Signet cloth); Code '25' (White and Buff vinyl and Gold puff cloth and Code '501' (Silver and Black vinyl with Black star cloth).

VEHICLE I.D. NUMBERS: The numbering system and code locations were basically the same as on 1958 Edsels. The first symbol in the top row of codes on the data plate designated engine type, as follows: 'A' = Six; 'C' = 292 cubic inch V-8: 'B' = 332 cubic inch V-8 and 'W' = 361 cubic inch V-8. The second symbol was changed to a '9' to designate 1959 model year. Third symbols were the same for each Ford factory, but Edsels were now built only at Louisville, Kentucky (Code 'U'). Body style and consecutive numbering systems were unchanged, although less codes were used in 1959. On the lower row of codes, Body Type designations were as listed in the specification charts below. Exterior color codes were unchanged, as follows: Code 'A' = Jet Black: Code 'B' = Moonrise Gray; Code 'C' = Gold Metallic; Code 'D' = Redwood Metallic; Code 'E' = Snow White; Code 'F' = President Red; Code 'G' = Talisman Red; Code 'H' = Desert Tan; Code 'J' = Velvet Maroon; Code 'K' = Platinum Gray Metallic; Code 'L' = Star Blue Metallic; Code 'M' = Jet Stream Blue; Code 'N' = Light Aqua; Code 'P' = Blue Aqua; Code 'Q' = Petal Yellow; Code 'R' = Mist Green and Code 'S' = Jadeglint Green Metallic. Interior trim codes are explained in the text. Date codes were as before, except that only the letters of normal progression are used. Transmission codes were the same as before, although few types were available. Axle codes were changed as follows: '1' = 3.10:1; '2' = 3.56:1; '3' = 3.70:1; '4' = 3.89:1; '5' = 2.91:1 and '6' = 2.69:1.

RANGER SERIES V-8

Model Number	Body/Style Number	Body Type & Seating	Factory Price	Shipping Weight	Production Total
NA	64C	2-dr Sed-6P	2629	3545	7,778
NA	58D	4-dr Sed-6P	2684	3775	12,814
NA	63F	2-dr HT-6P	2691	3690	5,474
NA	57F	4-dr HT-6P	2756	3680	2,352

NOTE: The prices and weights given above are for Ranger V-8s. A six-cylinder engine was a 'delete option' for 1959. Subtract $84 from the above prices for Sixes and deduct 99 pounds.

RANGER SERIES ENGINES

BASE V-8
V-8. Overhead valves. Cast iron block. Displacement: 292 cubic inches. Bore and stroke: 3.75 x 3.30 inches. Compression ratio: 8.8:1. Brake horsepower: 200 at 4400 RPM. Five main bearings. Hydraulic valve lifters. Carburetor: two-barrel Ford.

NOTE: This engine was available, as standard equipment. It came with the cylinder block and heads painted black; the air cleaner and valve covers painted gold.

OPTIONAL V-8s
332 V-8. Overhead valves, cast iron block. Displacement 332 cubic inches. Bore and stroke 4.00 x 3.30 inches. Compression ratio 8.9:1. Brake horsepower 225 at 4400 RPM. 5 main bearings. Hydraulic valve lifters. Carburetor 2 barrel Ford. **361 V-8.** Overhead valves, cast iron block. Displacement 361 cubic inches. Bore and stroke 4.05 x 3.50 inches. Compression ratio 10.5:1. Brake horsepower 300 at 4400 RPM. Five main bearings. Hydraulic valve lifters. Carburetor 4 barrel Ford.

OPTIONAL SIX
Inline overhead valve Six. Cast iron block. Displacement: 223 cubic inches. Bore and stroke: 3.62 x 3.60 inches. Compression ratio: 8.4:1. Brake horsepower: 145 at 4000 RPM. Four main bearings. Hydraulic valve lifters. Carburetor; one barrel Holley.

NOTE: This engine was available, as a delete option, only in the Ranger Series. It came with the cylinder block and heads painted black; air cleaner and valve covers paint red.

1959 Edsel, Corsair 4-dr hardtop sedan, V-8

CORSAIR — (V-8) — The Corsair was now nothing more than a Ranger with fancier trim and longer list of standard features. Both series were built off the same platform. The biggest external difference between the two lines was the side trim and variations in the body styles offered. The upper sweep spear molding on Corsairs actually started as a front hood lip accent, moved around the edge of the front fender, then began a long, subtle curve to the taillights. Upon hitting the taillight, it moved back across the quarter panel, then curved upwards and tapered to a point of the front fender tip. The area between the two moldings, at the rear, was filled with a scallop-shaped contrast panel, also outlined in chrome. A medallion was positioned at the forward tip of the 'scallop'. There was also a series identification script on the lower rear quarter panel, under the trim. Standard equipment on closed body styles included all Ranger items, except a one-third/two-thirds type seat design was used. Trim combinations included all of the following: Code '38' (Aqua vinyl and Reception cloth); Code '39' (Redwood vinyl and Reception cloth); Code '40' (Gold vinyl and Black Reception cloth); Code '51' (Black vinyl and Black mesh cloth); Code '53' (Green vinyl and Green Reception cloth) and Code '54' (Blue vinyl and Reception cloth). Code '39' (Redwood vinyl and Reception cloth, was an alternate choice. Standard equipment on the Corsair convertible was the same as for closed cars, plus dual exhausts and a vinyl coated top with vinyl boot. The ragtops featured all-vinyl interior trims in the following combinations: Code '41' (Gold and White); code '42' (Black, White and Silver); Code '43' (Turquoise and White) and Code '44' (Black and Red).

CORSAIR SERIES V-8

Model Number	Body/Style Number	Body Type & Seating	Factory Price	Shipping Weight	Production Total
NA	58B	4-dr Sed-6P	2812	3695	3,301
NA	63B	2-dr HT-6P	2819	3780	2,315
NA	57B	4-dr HT-6P	2885	3710	1,694
NA	76E	2-dr Conv-6P	3072	3790	1,343

CORSAIR SERIES ENGINE
V-8. Overhead valves. Cast iron block. Displacement: 332 cubic inches. Bore and stroke: 4.00 x 3.30 inches. Compression ratio: 8.9:1. Brake horsepower: 225 at 4400 R.P.M. Five main bearings. Hydraulic valve lifters. Carburetor: two-barrel Model PB9E-9510-B.

STATION WAGONS — (V-8) — VILLAGER SERIES — Only the Villager station wagon survived into 1959. It shared frontal treatments and side trim with the Ranger line of passenger models. Distinct styling was seen at the rear. The taillights consisted of two circular lenses set against a chrome grillework that was housed in a short, horizontal oval, which was banded in chrome. At the lower portion of the rear body, a full-width, oval-shaped panel stretched across the Villager. It contained Edsel block lettering at its center and backup lights at each outboard end. A chrome outline molding encircled the panel and incorporated a rectangular nameplate at the topcenter. It carried the Villager name in letters. Directly above this ornament, a combination lock button and handle was positioned. Villager rear fender tops formed a small, crisp tailfin and the bumper was a distinctive type, which was reshaped at the center to hold the license plate. Only the four-door wagon was available and it came with either six or nine-passenger seating. Standard equipment included four arm rests; two ash trays; cigarette lighter; color-keyed rubber floor mats; printed cardboard headliner with plastic bows and a solid-back bench seat. Available interior trims were: Code '30' (two-tone green vinyl and Gold puff cloth); Code '31' (White and Red vinyl and Gold puff cloth); Code '32' (Buff and White vinyl and Straw vinyl) and code '52' (two-tone Blue vinyl with Gold puff cloth).

VILLAGER SERIES

Model Number	Body/Style Number	Body Type & Seating	Factory Price	Shipping Weight	Production Total
NA	71E	4-dr Sta Wag-6P	2971	3840	5,687
NA	71F	4-dr Sta Wag-9P	3055	3930	2,133

NOTE: The prices and weights given above are for Villager V-8s. The six-cylinder engine was a 'delete option.' For 1959 Villager Sixes subtract $84 from prices above and deduct 99 pounds.

VILLAGER SERIES ENGINES
See 1959 Edsel Corsair Series for base 332 cubic inch V-8 specifications. See 1959 Ranger Series for optional 223, and 361 engine spec.

CHASSIS FEATURES: Wheelbase: (Villager) 118 inches; (all others) 120 inches. Overall length: (Villager) 210.1 inches; (all others) 210.9 inches. Front tread: (all models) 59 inches. Rear tread: (all models) 56.4 inches. Tires: (Ranger with standard shift) 7.50 x 14 four-ply; (all others) 8.00 x 14 four-ply.

POWERTRAIN OPTIONS: A three-speed manual transmission with column control was standard equipment with the 233, 292 and 332 cubic inch engines. Two-speed Mile-O-Matic transmission was optional on all models with any engine, but was rarely used in attachment with the 361 cubic inch Super Express V-8 ($189.60). Three-speed Dual-Drive automatic transmission was optional only with the Super Express V-8 ($230.80). Overdrive transmission was not officially listed as a factory option for 1959 Edsels. However, at least four 1959 models are known to have been specially ordered and factory-built with such attachments. In such cases, the space on the space on the data plate for the transmission code is left blank. **NOTE:** One of these cars is a Ranger six driven on a daily basis by contributor Dale Rapp. This car delivers 20-22 miles per gallon fuel economy today). Dual exhausts, on convertible (standard equipment); on other V-8 models ($31.90). Heavy-duty clutch ($17).

CONVENIENCE OPTIONS: Power brakes ($42.25). Four-Way power seat ($70.20). Power steering ($81.80). Power windows ($102.05). Lever-Temp heater ($74.45). Polar-Aire air conditioning with Dial-Temp heater/defroster ($431.20). Dial-Temp heater/defroster ($90.10). Back-up lights ($9.42). Eight-tube pushbutton radio ($64.95). Signal-Seeking radio ($89.20). Rear seat radio speaker ($10.70). Safety Package, including padded windshield header and dashboard ($20.60). Wheel covers ($16.60). Wheel covers with applique ($28). Windshield washer ($13.95). Tinted glass ($37.90). Two-tone top paint ($21.55). Electric windshield wipers ($8.40). Size 8.00 x 14 four-ply white sidewall tire ($35.68). Rocker panel molding ($17). Heavy-duty rear springs ($4.86). Heavy-duty front springs ($6.50). Heavy-duty shock absorbers ($14.60). Seat belts. Single or dual rear-mounted radio antenna. Continental tire carrier. Engine compartment light. Luggage compartment light. Courtesy lights. Contour floor mats. Fuel tank lock. Curb signals. Inside non-glare rearview mirror. License plate frames. Traffic light reflectors. Standard type outside rearview mirror. Hooded type outside rearview mirror. Single or dual spotlights. Seat covers. Rear door safety locks. Parking brake warning light. Station wagon rooftop carrier. Compass. Tissue dispenser. Litter container. Remote-control outside rearview mirror. Also available was the Visibility Group option package including backup lights; windshield washer; hooded outside rearview mirror; courtesy and glove box lights and non-glare inside rearview mirror ($35.40).

Historical footnotes: The 1959 Edsel lineup was pubicly introduced on October 31, 1958. Model year output peaked at 44,891 units, for 0.8 percent market penetration. Calendar year production hit 29,677 units. Ben D. Mills was the General Manger of the Mercury-Edsel-Lincoln Division. All Edsels made to 1959 specifications were assembled at the Louisville, Kentucky assembly plant. On a model year basis, 80.5 percent of all Edsels had automatic transmissions; 30.5 pecent power steering; 18.9 percent power brakes: 2.3 percent power seats; 1.5 percent power windows; 75.5 percent radios; 95 percent heater/defrosters; 72.1 percent white sidewall tires; 8.2 percent tinted glass; 19.8 percent windshield washers; 12.2 percent electric windshield wipers; 31.7 percent backup lights; 2.9 percent dual exhausts; 2.2 percent air conditioning; 77.6 percent V-8 engines and 22.4 percent six-cylinder engines. Production during calendar year 1959 included 5,880 cars in January; 3,819 in February; 4.035 in March; 4,031 in April; 2,959 in May; 2,575 in June; 1.971 in July; 1,561 in August; 889 in September; 1,767 in October; 190 in November and none in December. The cars made in November were built to 1960 model specifications, of course, and were the last batch of Edsels ever made. The close of production was officially announced on November 19, 1959.

1960 EDSEL

1960 Edsel, Ranger 2-dr convertible, V-8

EDSEL RANGER — (V-8) — In February, 1959, Henry Ford II attempted to dispel the rumors, circulating in the automotive industry, about the Edsel's forthcoming desire. The Ford Motor Company President assured the world that the Edsel was to be a permanent member of the Ford family of cars. He said that he was certain the Edsel would prove successful and profitable in the long run and also revealed that the introduction date for 1960 models had already been set. These cars made their debut in October and featured a completely new body with numerous engineering improvements. Features included a lower silhouette, longer overall length and greater body width. Offered only in Ranger and Villager configurations, the 1960 Edsel provided engines ranging from the 145 horsepower Six to a 300 horsepower V-8. The horse collar grille was abandoned and, in its place, was an attractive design with dual headlamps 'floating' against a chrome grid. The grille was split, at the center, by a pinch-waist panel. A one-piece front bumper appeared on Edsels for the first time and incorporated a license plate housing at the center. The front parking lamps were integrated into the fenders in projectile-shaped housings. The new Edsel profile was straight from the Ford studios, with the exception of trim and decorations. A thin chrome molding swept from behind the upper front wheel cutout to the extreme lower corner of the rear body. Edsel block letters were placed above the molding at the trailing edge of the rear quarter, while Ranger of Villager scripts appeared on the cowl side. At the rear, there was a wide, horizontal deck latch panel with a concave indentation and Edsel block lettering spaced across the center portion. Twin, vertical taillamps were positioned at each end of the car. They were somewhat oval-shaped, with the top portion rising higher than the upper edge of the deck. The rear quarter top surfaces were formed into two narrow bulges on each side, which mated with the taillamps. The rear bumper was a one-piece unit, with a center license plate indentation and vertical 'ribs' on each side, directly below the vertical taillamp lenses. Standard equipment on all models included an electric clock; air cleaner; front foam cushion oil filter; positive action windshield wipers; cigarette lighter; turn signals and carpets (except on station wagons). In addition, the Ranger convertible featured a DeLuxe trim package and standard dual exhausts. Also found inside all Rangers were four arm rests; front and rear ash trays; two coat hooks and vinyl, color-keyed headlings. Standard trims available in Ranger sedans and hardtops were: Code '20' (Silver vinyl and Black pebble cloth); Code '22' (Blue vinyl and Black pebble cloth); Code '23' (Green vinyl and Brown pebble cloth); code '24' (Gold vinyl and Brown pebble cloth) and Code '25' (Red vinyl and Black pebble cloth). Also available in these styles were DeLuxe combinations including: Code '11' (Silver vinyl and Gray Champagne cloth); Code '15' (Red vinyl and Gray Champagne cloth) and Code '17' (Turquoise vinyl and Champage cloth). The DeLuxe combination used in Ranger convertibles were: Code '54' (two-tone Gold vinyl); code '55' (Red and Silver vinyl); Code '56' (Black vinyl); Code '57' (two-tone Turquoise vinyl).

VEHICLE I.D. NUMBERS: The numbering system and code locations were basically the same as on previous models. The first symbol in the top row of codes on the date plate designated engine type, as follows: 'V' = 223 cubic inch Six; 'W' = 292 cubic inch V-8 and 'Y' = 352 cubic inch V-8. The second symbol was changed to '0' to designate 1960 model year. The third symbol 'U' on all 1960 Edsels designated assembly at Louisville, Kentucky factory. The fourth Body Style code was changed to a two-digit number, as follows: '11' = two-door sedan; '12' = four-door sedan; '13' = two-door hardtop; '14' = six-passenger station wagon and '18' = nine-passenger station wagon. The consecutive numbering system was unchanged. On the lower row of codes, Body Type designations were as listed in the second colunn of the specifications charts below. Exterior color codes were changed, as follows: Code 'A' = Black velvet; Code 'C' = Turquoise; Code 'E' = Cadet Blue Metallic; Code 'F' = Hawaiian Blue; Code 'H' = Alaskan Gold Metallic; Code 'J' = Regal Red; Code 'K' = Turquoise Metallic; Code 'M' = Polar White; Code 'N' = Sahara Beige; Code 'Q' = Lilac Metallic; Code 'R' = Buttercup Yellow; Code 'T' = Sherwood Green Metallic; Code 'U' = Bronze Rose Metallic; Code; 'W' = Sea Foam Green and Code 'Z' = Cloud Silver Metallic. Interior trim codes are explained in the text. Date codes were as in 1959 (Actually, all production took place during 1959). Transmission codes were unchanged. Axle codes were as follows: '1' = 3.56:1; '2' = 3.89:1; '3' = 3.10:1; '6' = 2.91:1; 'A' = 3.56:1; with Equa-Lock; 'B' = 3.89:1 with Equa-Lock and 'C' = 3.10:1 with Equa-Lock.

RANGER SERIES V-8

Model Number	Body/Style Number	Body Type & Seating	Factory Price	Shipping Weight	Production Total
NA	64A	2-dr Sed-6P	2643	3601	777
NA	58A	4-dr Std Sed-6P	2697	3700	1,126
NA	58B	4-dr DeL Sed-6P	2736	3700	162
NA	63A	2-dr Std HT	2705	3641	243
NA	63B	2-dr DeL HT	2743	3641	52
NA	57A	4-dr Std HT	2770	3718	104
NA	57B	4-dr DeL HT	2809	3718	31
NA	76B	Conv-6P	3000	3836	76

NOTES: An 'A' Suffix after the Body Type Number indicates standard interior trim; a 'B' suffix indicates DeLuxe interior trim. Production figures are broken out accordingly. Prices for DeLuxe trim models were determined by adding the retail price of the Edsel DeLuxe trim package to the price of the same model in standard trim. Weights are assumed to be about the same. All styles have six-passenger seating.

ADDITIONAL NOTE: Prices and weights are for Rangers with the standard V-8 engine. The six-cylinder engine was available as a 'delete option' again. To determine the original cost of a six-cylinder Edsel, subtract $84 from the V-8 price. To determine the original weight of a six-cylinder Edsel, subtract 99 pounds from the V-8 weight.

RANGER SERIES ENGINES

BASE V-8
V-8. Overhead valves. Cast iron block. Displacement: 292 cubic inches. Bore and stroke: 3.75 x 3.30 inches. Compression ratio: 8.8:1. Five main bearings. Hydraulic valve lifters. Carburetor: two-barrel Model B9A-9510-A. **NOTE:** The cylinder block and heads were painted black. The valve covers and air cleaner were painted Red.

OPTIONAL V-8
V-8 Overhead valves. Cast iron block. Displacement 352 cubic inches. Bore and stroke 4.00 x 3.50 inches compression ratio 9.6:1. Five main bearings. Hydraulic valve lifters. Carburetor 4 barrel Ford. **NOTE:** The cylinder block and heads were painted black. The valve covers and air cleaner were painted turquoise green.

OPTIONAL SIX
See 1959 Edsel Ranger Series six-cylinder engine data. (N.A. in convertible).

STATION WAGON — (V-8) — VILLAGER SERIES — The Edsel station wagon for 1960 had the same general styling seen on the passenger cars. As usual, however, there were slight changes at the rear to accomodate the wagon body structure. This amounted to the upper rear fender feature line running straight across, above the taillamps, and then sweeping back to intersect the top of the concave lower panel. There was Edsel block lettering within the center of the lower panel, a Villager script directly above (on the tailgate) and, at the top of the gate, a chrome ornament that served as a handle containing the lock and latch mechanisms. As in the past, the wagon continued to offer an access arrangement wih the upper liftgate and lower drop-down tailgate. The 1960 Villager came only in four-door styles, with a choice of six or nine-passenger seating configurations. Villagers had the same standard equipment as other lines, except that color-keyed rubber floor mats and printed cardboard headliners were utilized. Interior trims included Code '32' (Blue vinyl and Ivy-stripe rib cloth); Code '33' (Green vinyl and Ivy-stripe rib cloth); Code '35' (Red vinyl and Ivy-stripe cloth) and Code '50' (Silver and Black vinyl).

VILLAGER SERIES

Model Number	Body/Style Number	Body Type & Seating	Factory Price	Shipping Weight	Production Total
NA	71F	4-dr Sta Wag-6P	2989	4029	216
NA	71E	4-dr Sta Wag-9P	3072	4046	59

NOTE: Prices and weights are for Villagers with the standard V-8 engine. The six-cylinder engine was available as a 'delete option'. To determine the original cost of a six-cylinder Villager, subtract $84 from the V-8 price. To determine the original weight of a six-cylinder Villager, subtract 99 pounds from the V-8 weight.

CHASSIS FEATURES: Wheelbase: (all models) 120 inches. Overall length: (Ranger) 216 inches; (Villager) 214.8 inches. Front tread: 61 inches. Rear tread: 60 inches. Tires: (Villager) 8.00 x 14; (Ranger) 7.50 x 14.

POWERTRAIN OPTIONS: A three-speed manual transmission was standard on all base models, but cars with the optional 352 cubic inch 'Super Express' V-8 included automatic transmission as a mandatory option. Two-speed Mile-O-Matic automatic transmission, available in any model ($189.60). Three-speed Dual-Power Drive automatic transmission, available with the Super Express V-8 only ($230.80). The 352 cubic inch 300 horsepower Super Express V-8, available as optional equipment over the base V-8 ($58). **NOTE:** Dual exhausts were standard equipment with the Super Express V-8.

CONVENIENCE OPTIONS: Power steering ($81.80). Power brakes ($43.25). Power windows ($102.05). Four-Way power seat ($70.20). Lever-Temp heater and defroster ($74.45). Lever-Temp air conditioning with tinted glass and heater ($403.80). Polar-Air air conditioner. Backup lights ($9.50). Pushbutton radio ($64.95). Rear seat speaker, except convertibles ($10.70). Single or dual rear-mounted antenna. Rocker panel moldings, except Villager ($17). Tinted glass ($37.90). Two-tone paint ($17). Full wheel cover ($16.60). Wheel covers with applique and spinner ($30.10). Windshield washer ($13.85). Electric windshield wipers ($8.40). Whitewall tires ($35.70). Inside non-glare rear view mirror. Standard outside mirror. Hooded outside mirror. Single spot light with mirror. Remote-control outside mirror. Padded instrument panel. Padded sun visors. Courtesy lights. Glove box light. Luggage compartment light. Parking brake warning light. Equa-lock differential. Seat belts. Heavy-duty cooling system. Fender skirts. Tissue dispenser. Litter bag. Locking fuel cap. Remote-control deck lid opener. Luggage rack, Villager. License plate frames. Rubber floor mats, front and rear. Rear door safety locks, four-door.

CONVENIENCE OPTIONS: DeLuxe trim package ($38.60). Visibility Group, includes backup lights; windshield washer; inside non-glare mirror; outside hooded mirror ($30.90). Convenicene Group A, includes heater and defroster; radio; Mile-O-Matic Drive; two-tone paint and full wheel covers ($362.60). Convenience Group B, inclues heater and defroster; radio; Dual-Power drive; two-tone paint; wheel covers with applique and white sidewall tires ($453).

Historical footnotes: The 1960 Edsels were introduced on October 15, 1959. The Edsel was discontinued on November 19, 1959. Model year output amounted to 2,846 cars all of which were built in calendar 1959. Of these, 889 were made in September; 1,767 were made in October and 190 were built in November. All assemblies were made at the Louisville, Kentucky factory. Since the first Edsel was built, in 1957, a total of 110,847 were made. After November 19, 1959, Ben D. Mills became General Manager of Ford Motor Company's 'new' Lincoln-Mercury Division. The much heralded — and now famous — Edsel was no more.

LINCOLN
1921-1942

LINCOLN — Detroit, Michigan — (1920-1942 et. seq.)
— He named the company for the President for whom he had first voted in 1864; initially, it was not intended for automobile manufacture at all, and its organization was the product of circumstance. In early 1917 Henry Martyn Leland had walked out of Cadillac following unpleasant words both he and his son Wilfred had with William C. Durant of General Motors.

A lot of people left GM that way, the confrontation in this case being, according to the Lelands, the reluctance of Durant to convert Cadillac to Liberty aviation engine production for the war effort. Already Henry Leland was 74 years old, but his stature in the industry and his passionate patriotism resulted in his new Lincoln Motor Co. being given a government contract to build some 6000 Liberty engines and a $10,000,000 advance to do it. But the Armistice came quickly, too quickly for the Lelands to have established a solid footing with their new company.

Faced with a huge factory, a work force of about 6000 men and mounting debts, they made a quite logical decision. The man who had given America the Cadillac motorcar would now provide the country with the Lincoln. Capital stock for the venture — $6.5 million of it — was subscribed within three hours of being placed on sale.

This was a terrific beginning; unfortunately, it would prove to be one of only two high points the Lelands would enjoy during their short tenure with the car. The other was the trade press response to the engineering of the Lincoln itself. Like any Leland product, the Lincoln was precision built. Its 60° V-8 engine with its characteristic fork-and-blade connecting rods, was rugged and compact, developed 81 bhp and ensured a 70 mph performance. Full-pressure lubrication and a massive torque tube drive highlighted the chassis. But two factors convened to make the Lincoln less appealing. First, its coachwork had been assigned to Leland's son-in-law whose previous speciality seems to have been ladies' millinery.

The Lincoln look was strictly old-hat, dowdy even, with styling reminiscent of the prewar era past, not a breath of the flapper flamboyance that would mark the '20s. Second, because of late supplier deliveries and Leland's penchant for engineering perfection, the car was delayed, arriving in the marketplace in September 1920 — not the planned January — which missed an entire selling season and hit the postwar recession. The Lelands were convinced they could set matters right, and contacted Brunn in Buffalo about coachwork. But still, the Lincoln board directors could only see the figures — 3407 cars produced by Feb. 4, 1922 vis-a-vis the projected 6000 for the first year alone — and on that day, over the vigorous objection of the Lelands, they put the company into receivership and up for sale. It was bought for $8 million by Henry Ford.

Though the car hadn't appealed to many customers, Ford took a fancy to the Lincoln for several intertwined reasons. His Model T was America's best-selling cheap car by leagues; offering a luxury automobile at over 10 times the price (the Lincoln was introduced as a $5000 range car) probably tweaked his interest, and certainly that of his son Edsel whose refined sense of the aesthetic was certainly not satisfied with his father's "Tin Lizzie."

Moreover, in 1902, Henry Leland had made his Cadillac out of the frazzled remains of a company Henry Ford himself had started and which he left in disgust after, among other vexations, listening to Leland's uncomplimentary comments about his car.

Buying out Leland now must have been a splendid satisfaction. It may have been further vengeance, or the genuine admiration Ford had for Henry Leland, but initially the plan was for the Lelands to remain with the company. This was a marriage made in hell, however, and the Lelands left after four months, seeing Henry Ford thereafter only in court during the lawsuit they instituted regarding reimbursement to original creditors and stockholders.

Meanwhile, Edsel Ford became the president of the Lincoln Motor Co. By December 1922, just 10 months after the Ford purchase of the company, 5512 Lincolns had been sold, over 2,000 more cars than the Lelands had delivered in 17 months. The Leland fears to the contrary, the product had not been compromised; indeed it had been improved, with aluminum pistons and better cylinder head cooling immediately, and an increase in wheelbase to 136 inches (from 130) for 1923.

Sales that year rose to 7875. Under Ford aegis, the Lincoln remained a robust car, favored by the Detroit Police Flying Squad amongst other progressive law enforcement agencies, the cars for the police sometimes being provided four-wheel brakes which production versions wouldn't have until 1927.

Perhaps more importantly, under Edsel Ford's direction, the Lincoln became a beautiful car, with series production of designs from the masters of America's coachbuilding craft. By 1929 the Model L Lincoln was up to 90 hp and 90 mph, and leading it down the road was a graceful greyhound mascot, selected by Edsel and produced by Gorham. In 1931 the Model K (that designation having been used on Henry Ford's first foray into the luxury car field in 1908, incidentally) replaced the L, a refined V-8 offering 120 hp, 145-inch wheelbase and duo-servo brakes. Clearly, it was an interim model. In 1932 the Ford became a V-8, and though the Lincoln Model K V-8 was continued that year, the Lincoln grabbing the headlines was the new V-12 Model KB with 447.9 cubic inches, 150 hp and 95+ mph performance.

Interestingly, the more expensive and custom-built KB (with price tags ranging from $4300 to $7200) fared rather well against the V-8 Model K (at $2900 to $3350) that year, with 1641 of the former built, 1765 of the latter. In 1933 the V-8 was replaced by a smaller 382-cubic-inch 125 hp V-12 designated KA and set in a 136-inch wheelbase chassis as opposed to the KB's 145. But that depth-of-depression year brought sales of only 587 KB's and 1420 KA's. Building two different engines for a plummeting luxury car market didn't make a great deal of sense, and in 1934 both were dropped and replaced with a 414-cubic-inch 150 hp unit with aluminum cylinder heads.

All Lincolns into the early postwar years would be V-12 powered, though precious few of them would be the K series as sales of these big Lincolns continued to dwindle while the '30s wore on. Just 120 of the big K's would be built in 1939-1940, the most famous of which was President Roosevelt's "Sunshine Special," FDR carrying forth a Presidential preference for Lincolns which had begun

with Calvin Coolidge and which would endure to the present day.

But prestige was not what made Lincoln financially respectable in the later '30s. The Zephyr did, and when it arrived for 1936, Lincoln sales soared from the under 4000 cars in '35 to over 22,000. Originally intended to use a modified version of the Ford V-8, the Zephyr instead, at Edsel Ford's direction, became a 75° 267-cubic-inch 110 hp V-12 with aluminum alloy heads, cast steel pistons and a reputation for sluggishness and unreliability it has had ever to live with, not always fairly. (The engine was used in England in the Allard, Atalanta and Brough Superior.)

The chassis with its transverse springs and mechanical four-wheel brakes represented a specification only to be whispered about, but the synchromesh gearbox was fine and the unitized construction was worthy of a shout, as was the very fresh (and later imitated) styling courtesy of John Tjaarda and Briggs, and refined for production by E.T. "Bob" Gregorie of Lincoln.

With some models listing under $1500, the Zephyr was the lowest-priced V-12 offered on the American market since Errett Lobban Cord's Auburn of the early '30s. It didn't change appreciably in the years to follow, though 1938 saw the gearshift lever spring from the dashboard, 1939 at last brought hydraulic brakes, and in 1940 the by-now-popular column-mounted gearshift arrived on the Zephyr. With the demise of the big K in 1940 — the last cars carrying prophetic black cloisonne emblems replacing the former red or blue — there was room for a new car in the Lincoln lineup, though the one which arrived did so rather by accident.

It was in September 1938 that, returning from a trip to Europe, Edsel Ford asked Bob Gregorie to design a special custom job for him that would be "strictly continental." Whether a Lincoln or Ford would be used, or the chassis of the company's new car called Mercury, was a matter decided in favor of the first named. And thus it was that the Continental was born of the Zephyr. Ford's personal car engendered such comment wherever he took it that production seemed a good and viable idea. On Oct. 2, 1939, the new Contiental Cabriolet was introduced at the Ford Rotunda in Dearborn as a model of the Lincoln Zephyr. A coupe followed in May 1940, and in September that year the word "Zephyr" was dropped and the car became simply the Lincoln Continental.

A total of 1990 Continentals were built before the war put an end to all automobile production. The Continental would return after the war, but without Edsel Ford. Henry's son, whose unerring good taste had made a ravishing beauty of the Lincoln, died on May 26, 1943.

1921-42 Lincoln Data Compilation
by Robert C. Ackerson

1921 LINCOLN

1921 Lincoln, model L, coupe, AA

LINCOLN — MODEL L — EIGHT: The styling of the first Lincoln was conservative to the point of being uninspired. However in terms of its design the Lincoln was an automobile of grandeur. Rightly identified in automotive history as the "Master of Precision" its creator, Henry M. Leland, was 75 years old when the company he and his son founded produced its first automobile. Leland had already made his mark in the automotive industry as a supplier of engines to Ransom E. Olds, the creator of the first Cadillac in 1903 and the prime force behind their quality. Under Leland's presidency Cadillac won the 1908 Dewar Trophy in England, introduced its self-starter and all-electric system in 1912 and two years later the first American 90° V-8 automobile engine.

After breaking with William Durant in 1917 Leland proceeded to form the Lincoln Motor Company to produce Liberty aircraft engines for the U.S. government. However this effort came to a close after 6500 engines had been delivered. The next step in Leland's career was the development and production of the Lincoln automobile, of which its engine and chassis design attracted considerable attention. Key engine features included a 60° instead of 90° Vee and fork and blade connecting rods. The chassis was noted for its strong torque-tube drive and Alemite lubrication fittings.

I.D. DATA: Serial numbers were on right side of cowl, top of clutch housing and transmission case. Starting: 1 (1920), 835 (1921). Ending: 834 (1920), 3151 (1921). Engine numbers were on left side of crankcase between cylinders 1 and 2. Starting: 1 (1920), 835 (1921). Ending: 834 (1920), 3151 (1921).

Model No.	Body Type & Seating	Price	Weight	Prod. Total
101	4-dr. Tr. (perm top)-7P	4600	—	1015
102	2-dr. Rds.-3P	—	—	78
103	4-dr. Phae.-5P	—	—	278
104	2-dr. Cpe.-4P	—	—	451
105	4-dr. Sed.-5P	—	—	352
106	4-dr. Limo. gls. part.-7P	6600	—	101
107	4-dr. Twn. Brgm.-7P	6600	—	10
108	4-dr. Sed.-7P	—	—	26
109	4-dr. Twn. Car-7P	6600	—	19
110	4-dr. Berl. gls. part-7P	—	—	6
111	2-dr. Brun. Rds.-3P	—	—	68
112	2-dr. Brun. Phae. Del.-7P	—	—	196
113	4-dr. Sed.-4P	—	—	50
114	4-dr. Jud. Sed. gls. part- 7P	—	—	29
115	4-dr. Jud. Berl. gls. part- 5P	—	—	25
122	Chassis only	4000	—	253

ENGINE: 60° V, L-head. Eight. Cast iron block. B & S: 3-3/8 in. x 5 in. Disp.: 357.8 cu. in. C.R.: 4.8:1. Brake H.P.: 81 @ 2600 R.P.M. Main bearings: Three. Valve lifters: Mechanical. Carb.: Stromberg updraft.

CHASSIS: [Types 101-105 and 107] W.B.: 130 in. Frt/Rear Tread: 60 in. Tires: 33 x 5. [Types 106, 108-115, 122] W.B.: 136 in. Frt/Rear Tread: 60 in. Tires: 33 x 5.

TECHNICAL: Sliding gear transmission. Speeds: 3F/1R. Floor shift controls. Multiple disc, dry plate clutch. Shaft drive. Full floating rear axle. Overall Ratio: 4.58:1. Mechanical brakes on two rear wheels. Twelve spoke wooden artillery wheels, demountable rims. Wheel Size: 23 in.

OPTIONS: Front bumper. Rear bumper. Dual sidemount. Sidemount cover(s).

HISTORICAL: Introduced: September, 1920. A Lincoln won a Los Angeles to Phoenix race in April 1921. Innovations: circuit breaker electrical system, Alemite pressure gun lubrication, automatic tire pump, thermostatic radiator shutters, sealed cooling system with condenser tank. Calendar year production: 2957 (1920 and 1921). Model year sales: 674. Model year production: 2957*. The president of Lincoln was Henry Martyn Leland. Considerable discrepancies exist in early production and sales records for the Lincolns. Thus these and subsequent figures should be considered only approximate levels.

320

1922 LINCOLN

1922 Lincoln, model L, touring, OCW

LINCOLN — MODEL L — EIGHT: The postwar depression that overwhelmed William Durant's best efforts to retain control of General Motors and put Henry Ford to a severe test forced the Lincoln Motor Company into receivership in November 1921. Subsequently the firm was purchased by Henry Ford for $8 million on February 4, 1922.

Changes in the Lincoln's design were minor. The acquisition of Lincoln by Ford was made evident by a new radiator badge that had the Lincoln name sandwiched by "Ford Detroit" and placed within an oval shell. The older more ornate, version had carried the words "Leland Built". Design changes included an improved cylinder head for better engine cooling (on cars after serial number 7820) and the use of aluminum in place of the older cast iron versions. Also phased in after car number 8500 was a new timing chain and sprockets.

In June 1922 both Henry Leland and his son acrimoniously left Lincoln and Edsel Ford became the company's president. Under total Ford control the above noted engineering changes were made as well as a price reduction of $1000 on all models with non-custom bodies. Aided by the economy's recovery these moves caused a major reversal in Lincoln sales which after totalling only 150 cars in January and February reached 5512 for the remaining ten months of 1922.

I.D. DATA: Serial numbers were located on right side of cowl, top of clutch housing and transmission case. Starting: 3152. Ending: 8709. Engine numbers were located on left side of crankcase between cylinder 1 and 2. Starting: 3152. Ending: 8709.

Model No.	Body Type & Seating	Price	Weight	Prod. Total
101	4-dr. Tr. (perm top)-7P	3800	—	483
102	2-dr. Rds.-3P	—	—	6
103	4-dr. Phae.-5P	—	—	37
104	2-dr. Cpe.-4P	3900	—	441
105	4-dr. Sed.-5P	4200	—	344
107	4-dr. Twn. Brgm.-7P	—	—	2
109	4-dr. Twn. Car-7P	—	—	12
111	2-dr. Brun. Rds.-3P	3800	—	178
112	4-dr. Brun. Phae. Delx.-4P	3800	—	771
113	4-dr. Sed.-4P	3800	—	353
114	4-dr. Jud. Sed. gls. part.-7P	—	—	22
115	4-dr. Jud. Berl. gls. part.-5P	—	—	29
116	4-dr. FW Sed.-7P	—	—	6
117	4-dr. Brun. Sed.-7P	4900	—	718
118	4-dr. Brun. Limo. gls. part.-7P	—	—	554
119	4-dr. FW Limo. gls. part.-7P	5800	—	20
120	4-dr. Brun. Twn. Car-7P	7200	—	6
121	4-dr. Brun. Limo. gls. part.-7P	5100	—	2
122	Chassis	3400	—	287
124A	4-dr. Tr.-7P	3300	—	1136
125	4-dr. Sed.-4P	5200	—	59
126	2-dr. Brun. Cpe.-2P	4400	—	1
127	4-dr. Jud. Sed.-4P	—	—	104
128	4-dr. Jud. Berline-4P	5200	—	74
129	4-dr. Brun. Sed.-7P	4700	—	1
702	2-dr. Jud. Cpe.-2P	—	—	1

1922 Lincoln, Model L. 4 pass. sedan, HAC

ENGINE: 60° V, L-head. Eight. Cast iron block. B & S: 3-3/8 in. x 5 in. Disp.: 357.8 cu. in. C.R.: 4.8:1. Brake H.P.: 90 @ 2800 R.P.M. Main bearings: Three. Valve lifters: Mechanical. Carb.: Stromberg updraft.

CHASSIS: [Series 101-105] W.B.: 130 in. Frt/Rear Tread 60 in. Tires: 33 x 5. [All others] W.B.: 136 in. Frt/Rear Tread: 60 in. Tires: 33 x 5.

TECHNICAL: Sliding gear transmission. Speeds: 3F/1R. Floor shift controls. Multiple disc, dry plate clutch. Shaft drive. Full floating rear axle. Overall Ratio: 4.58:1. Mechanical brakes on two rear wheels. Twelve spoke wooden artillery wheels, demountable rims. Wheel Size: 23 in.

OPTIONS: Front bumper. Rear bumper. Dual sidemount. Sidemount cover(s).

HISTORICAL: Introduced: January, 1922. Calendar year production: 5512. The president of Lincoln was Edsel Ford - after June 1922.

1923 LINCOLN

1923 Lincoln, model L, touring, OCW

LINCOLN — MODEL L — EIGHT: After the Ford takeover, the Lincoln Motor Company became an independent operation whose stock was 100 percent owned by the Ford Motor Company. However, with the Lelands completely out of the picture, it was absorbed into Ford.

Principle changes for 1923 were headlined by the elimination of the 130 inch wheelbase chassis. During the model year a number of changes occurred, including the use of Houdaille hydraulic shock absorbers.

I.D. DATA: Serial numbers were located on the right side of cowl, top of clutch housing and transmission case. Starting: 8710. Ending: 16,434. Engine numbers were located on left side of crankcase between cylinders 1 and 2. Starting Engine No.: 8710. Ending: 16,434.

Model No.	Body Type & Seating	Price	Weight	Prod. Total
111	2-dr. Brun. Rds.-2P	3800	NA	54
112	4-dr. Brun. Del. Phae.-4P	3800	—	15
117	4-dr. Brun. Sed.-7P	4900	—	971
118	4-dr. Brun. Limo.-7P	—	—	563
120	4-dr. Brun. Fwn. Car-6P	—	—	50
121	4-dr. Brun. Limo. gls. part-7P	—	—	18
122	Chassis	—	—	177
123A	4-dr. Brun. Phae.-4P	—	—	1061
124A	4-dr. Tr.-4P	—	—	1182
125	4-dr. Jud. Sed.-4P	—	—	365
126	2-dr. Brun. Cpe.-4P	—	—	816
127	4-dr. Jud. Sed. 3W-4P	—	—	532
128	4-dr. Jud. Ber. gls. part-4P	—	—	238
129	4-dr. Brun. Sed.-5P	—	—	1195
130	2-dr. Brun. Rds.-3P	—	—	48
131	4-dr. Brun. Cab.-6P	—	—	14
132	4-dr. Jud. Sed. 2W-4P	—	—	93
133	4-dr. Jud. Sed. 3W-4P	—	—	269
	4-dr. FW Cab. Coll. Tp.-7P	6200	—	—

1923 Lincoln, model L. 5 pass. coupe. HAC

ENGINE: 60° V, L-head. Eight. Cast iron block. B & S: 3-3/8 in. x 5 in. Disp.: 357.8 cu. in. C.R.: 4.8:1. Brake H.P.: 90 @ 2800 R.P.M. Taxable H.P.: 39.2. Main bearings: Three. Valve lifters: Mechanical. Carb.: Stromberg 03 updraft.

CHASSIS: W.B.: 136 in. Frt/Rear Tread 60 in. Tires: 33 x 5.

TECHNICAL: Sliding gear transmission. Speeds: 3F/1R. Floor shift controls. Multiple disc, dry plate clutch. Shaft drive. Full floating rear axle. Overall Ratio: 4.58:1; opt. 4.90:1. Mechanical brakes on two rear wheels (Lincolns for police use had 4 wheel brakes). 12 spoke wooden artillery wheels with demountable rims. Wheel Size: 23 in.

OPTIONS: Front bumper. Rear bumper. Dual sidemount. Sidemount cover(s). Drum headlights.

HISTORICAL: Introduced: January, 1923. Calendar year registration: 7875. Calendar year production: 7875. The company president was Edsel Ford.

1924 LINCOLN

1924 Lincoln, model L, touring, OCW

LINCOLN — MODEL L — EIGHT: Although there was no single styling change in the Lincoln's appearance that could even remotely be regarded as revolutionary the sum total of the revisions made for 1924 resulted in a more modern and decidedly more attractive appearance. All models had as standard equipment the nickel-plated drum-style headlights that had been optional in 1923. A higher radiator with a nickel-plated shell enabled a smoother hoodline to be used. The radiator shutters were now vertical instead of horizontal. The Lincoln's oval grille emblem no longer carried the "Ford Detroit" lettering. On all models except type 702 (a Judkin-bodied coupe) new fenders with a smoother and wider design were installed.

Although no changes were made in the Lincoln's engine's basic specifications a new cam reshaped for smoother valve operation was installed.

I.D. DATA: Serial numbers were located on right side of cowl, top of clutch housing and transmission case. Starting: 16435. Ending: 23614. Engine numbers were located on left side of crankcase between cylinders 1 and 2. Starting: 16435. Ending: 23614.

Model No.	Body Type & Seating	Price	Weight	Prod. Total
117	4-dr. Brun. Sed.-7P	—	—	271
118	4-dr. Brun. Limo.-7P	5100	—	128
120	4-dr. Brun. Twn. Car-6P	—	—	12
121	4-dr. Brun. Limo.-7P	—	—	8
122	Chassis	3600	—	79
123A	4-dr. Brun. Phae.-4P	4000	—	829
124A	4-dr. Tr.-7P	4000	—	601
126	2-dr. Brun. Cpe.-4P	4600	—	424
127	4-dr. Jud. Sed. 3W-4P	4800	—	2
128	4-dr. Jud. Ber.-4P	5400	—	111
129	4-dr. Brun. Sed.-5P	4900	—	351
130	2-dr. Brun. Rds.-3P	4000	—	188
131	2-dr. Brun. Cab-6P	—	—	13
132	4-dr. Jud. Sed. 2W-4P	—	—	358
133	4-dr. Jud. Sed. 3W-4P	—	—	889
134	4-dr. Jud. Sed.-7P	—	—	846
135	4-dr. Brun. Limo.-7P	6400	—	482
136	4-dr. Brun. Sed.-7P	—	—	928
137	4-dr. Brun. Cab-5P	—	—	6
138	4-dr. Brun. Twn. Car-5P	6400	—	8
139	4-dr. FW Limo.-7P	6000	—	29
140	4-dr. Jud. Ber.-4P	5400	—	20
140	4-dr. Brun. Open Drive Limo.-5P	6400	—	—

ENGINE: 60° V, L-head. Eight. Cast iron block. B & S: 3-3/8 in. x 5 in. Disp.: 357.8 cu. in. C.R.: 4.8:1. Brake H.P.: 90 @ 2800 R.P.M. Taxable H.P.: 39.2. Main bearings: Three. Valve lifters: Mechanical. Carb.: Stromberg 03 updraft.

CHASSIS: W.B.: 136 in. Frt/Rear Tread 60 in. Tires: 33 x 5.

TECHNICAL: Sliding gear transmission. Speeds: 3F/1R. Floor shift controls. Multiple disc, dry plate clutch. Shaft drive. Full floating rear axle. Overall Ratio: 4.58:1. Opt. 4.90:1. Mechanical brakes on two rear wheels (Lincolns for police use had 4 wheel brakes). 12 spoke wooden artillery wheels, demountable rims. Wheel Size: 23 in.

OPTIONS: Front bumper. Rear bumper. Dual sidemount. Sidemount cover(s). Natural wood finish wheels. Disc wheels. Rudge-Whitworth wire wheels. Painted radiator shell.

HISTORICAL: Introduced: January, 1924. Calendar year registrations: 5672. Calendar year production: 7,053. The president of Ford was Edsel Ford. The 1924 models were the first Lincolns to have a spark setting mark on the clutch ring and fly wheel.

1925 LINCOLN

1925 Lincoln, model L, touring, OCW

LINCOLN — MODEL L — EIGHT: The absence of cowl lights made it easy to identify the 1925 Lincoln. Also giving them a distinctive appearance was the Gorham-produced greyhound radiator ornament. Initially this was an option but during the year it was included in the Lincoln's standard equipment. Other changes included a longer and smoother operating emergency brake lever plus factory installed front and rear bumpers for all models. Early in the model year run a steering ratio of 15:1 replaced the older 12-2/3:1 ratio.

I.D. DATA: Serial numbers were located on right side of cowl, top of clutch housing and transmission case. Starting: 23615. Ending: 32029. Engine numbers were located on left side of crankcase between cylinder 1 and 2. Starting Engine No.: 23615. Ending: 32029.

Model No.	Body Type & Seating	Price	Weight	Prod. Total
122	Chassis	3800	—	121
123A	4-dr. Brun. Phae.-4P	4000	—	689
123B	4-dr. Brun. Spt. Phae.-4P	—	—	25
123C	4-dr. Brun. Spt. Phae. TC-4P	—	—	1
124A	4-dr. Tr.-7P	4000	—	418
124B	4-dr. Brun. Spt. Tr. TC-7P	4200	—	324
124C	4-dr. Brun. Spt. Tr.-7P	—	—	3
126	2-dr. Brun. Cpe.-4P	4600	—	204
128	4-dr. Jud. Berl.-4P	5600	—	31
130	2-dr. Brun. Rds.-2P	4000	—	126
132	4-dr. Jud. Sed. 2W-4P	—	—	146
133	4-dr. Jud. Sed. 3W-4P	—	—	548
134	4-dr. Brun. Sed.-7P	—	—	829
135	4-dr. Brun. Limo. gls. part.-7P	—	—	443
136	4-dr. Brun. Sed.-5P	—	—	541
137	4-dr. Brun. Cab.-5P	6600	—	58
138	4-dr. Brun. Twn. C.-7P	—	—	18
139	4-dr. FW Limo.-7P	—	—	297
140	4-dr. Jud. Berl. gls. part. 2W-4P	—	—	248
141	2-dr. LeB. Cpe. Rds.-2P	—	—	95
142	4-dr. Holbrk. Coll. Cab-7P	7200	—	11
143	2-dr. Brun. Cpe.-4P	—	—	470
144A	4-dr. LeB. Trk. Sed. 2W-4P	—	—	159
144B	4-dr. LeB. Trk. Sed. 3W-4P	—	—	433
145A	4-dr. Brun. Brgm. gls. part.-7P	—	—	15
146	4-dr. Diet. Sed.-5P	—	—	1095
147A	4-dr. Diet. Sed.-7P	—	—	398
147B	4-dr. Diet. Berl.-7P	—	—	214
148A	4-dr. Diet. Brgm.-6P	6800	—	3
149A	4-dr. Diet. Coll. Cab	—	—	12
150A	Burial C'ch.	—	—	1
702	2-dr. Jud. Cpe.-2P	5100	—	345
2557	Special	—	—	2
2686	Special Rds.	—	—	11
123D	4-dr. Spt. Phae.-4P	—	—	106
	4-dr. Brun. Twn. C.-5P	6400	—	—
	4-dr. Brun. Open-D Limo.	6400	—	—
	4-dr. FW Limo.-7P	6000	—	—
	4-dr. Jud. Berl. 3W-4P	5400	—	—

1925 Lincoln, model L. limousine, JAC

ENGINE: 60° V, L-head. Eight. Cast iron block. B & S: 3-3/8 in. x 5 in. Disp.: 357.8 cu. in. C.R.: 4.8:1. Brake H.P.: 90 @ 2800 R.P.M. Taxable H.P.: 39.2. Main bearings: Three. Valve lifters: Mechanical. Carb.: Stromberg 03 updraft.

CHASSIS: W.B.: 136 in. Frt/Rear Tread: 60 in. Tires: 33 x 5.

TECHNICAL: Sliding gear transmission. Speeds: 3F/1R. Floor shift controls. Multiple disc, dry plate clutch. Shaft drive. Full floating rear axle. Overall Ratio: 4.58:1; opt. 4.90:1. Mechanical brakes on two rear wheels (Lincolns for police use had 4 wheel brakes). 12 spoke wooden artillery wheels with demountable rims. Wheel Size: 23 in.

I.D. DATA: Serial numbers were located on right side of cowl, top of clutch housing and transmission case. Starting: 16435. Ending: 23614. Engine numbers were located on left side of crankcase between cylinders 1 and 2. Starting: 16435. Ending: 23614.

OPTIONS: Dual sidemount. Sidemount cover(s). Natural wood finish wheels. Disc wheels. Rudge-Whitworth wire wheels. Painted radiator shell. 7.00 x 21 balloon tires.

HISTORICAL: Introduced: January, 1925. Calendar year registrations: 6808. Calendar year production: 8451. The company president was Edsel Ford.

1926 LINCOLN

1926 Lincoln, model L, Dietrich, coupe roadster, OCW

LINCOLN — MODEL L — EIGHT: Exterior changes were virtually non-existent in the Lincoln's appearance but a number of interior revisions and engine modifications contributed to the best sales year yet for Lincoln. During the model year a non-movable 19 inch wheel with a smaller cross section and molded to form finger grips on its lower surface replaced the older tilt-type 18 inch unit. The headlight tilting lever was now located below the horn button on the hub and both the wheel and spokes were of black walnut construction.

Beneath the Lincoln hood, a new centrifugal-type carburetor air cleaner was readily noticeable. A new distributor cam that Lincoln said provided more efficient high-speed operation was standard.

I.D. DATA: Serial numbers were located on right side of cowl, top of clutch housing and transmission case. Starting: 32030. Ending: 39899. Engine numbers were located on left side of crankcase between cylinders 1 and 2. Starting: 32030. Ending: 39899.

Model No.	Body Type & Seating	Price	Weight	Prod. Total
122	Chassis	—	—	154
123A	4-dr. Phae.-4P	4000	—	147
123B	4-dr. Spt. Phae.-4P	4500	—	283
123C	4-dr. Brun. Spt. Phae. TC-4P	—	—	41
124A	4-dr. Tr.-7P	—	—	93
124B	4-dr. Brun. Spt. Tr. TC-7P	4500	—	324
124C	4-dr. Brun. Spt. Tr.-7P	—	—	12
130	2-dr. Brun. Rds.-3P	—	—	99
136	4-dr. Brun. Sed.-5P	6400	—	3
137	4-dr. Brun. Cab.-5P	6600	—	52
139	4-dr. FW Limo.-7P	6000	—	60
140	4-dr. Jud. Berl 2W gls. part.-4P	5400	—	273
141	2-dr. Leb. Cpe. Rds. Aux. St.-2P	—	—	150
142	4-dr. Holbrk. Coll. Cab-7P	7200	—	13
143	2-dr. Brun. Cpe.-4P	—	—	308
144A	4-dr. Leb. Trk. Sed. 2W-4P	4800	—	513
144B	4-dr. Leb. Trk. Sed. 3W-4P	4800	—	1350
145A	4-dr. Brun. Brgm. gls. part.-7P	6400	—	42
145B	4-dr. Brun. Open Limo.	—	—	3
146	4-dr. Diet. Sed.-5P	6800	—	558
147A	4-dr. Diet. Sed.-7P	—	—	1590
147B	4-dr. Diet. Berl.-7P	6800	—	1180
148A	4-dr. Diet. Brgm.-6P	6800	—	2
149A	4-dr. Diet. Coll. Cab-5P	7200	—	2
150A	Burial C'ch.	—	—	8
150B	150" wb Chassis	—	—	37
151	2-dr. Lke. Rds.-2P	—	—	101
152	4-dr. Diet. Sed.-5P	—	—	653
153A	4-dr. Holbrk. Coll. Cab-5P	7200	—	10
154	2-dr. Diet. Cpe. R/S-2P	—	—	263
155	4-dr. Leb. Coll. Spt. Cab-5P	—	—	7
157	4-dr. Wilby Land.-6P	6700	—	10
702	2-dr. Jud. Cpe.-2P	5300	—	371

ENGINE: 60° V, L-head. Eight. Cast iron block. B & S: 3-3/8 in. x 5 in. Disp.: 357.8 cu. in. C.R.: 4.8:1. Brake H.P.: 90 @ 2800 R.P.M. Taxable H.P.: 39.2. Main bearings: Three. Valve lifters: Mechanical. Carb.: Stromberg 03 updraft.

1926 Lincoln, model L, 7-pass. sedan, JAC

CHASSIS: W.B.: 136 in. Frt/Rear Tread: 60 in. Tires: 33 x 5.

TECHNICAL: Sliding gear transmission. Speeds: 3F/1R. Floor shift controls. Multiple disc, dry plate clutch. Shaft drive. Full floating rear axle. Overall Ratio: 4.58:1, Opt. 4.90:1. Mechanical brakes on two rear wheels (Lincolns for police use had 4 wheel brakes). 12 spoke wooden artillery wheels, demountable rims. Wheel Size: 23 in.

1926 Lincoln, model L, Locke sport roadster, JAC

OPTIONS: Dual sidemount. Sidemount cover(s). Natural wood finish wheels. Disc wheels. Buffalo wire wheels. 7.00 x 21 balloon tires. Monogram (5.00). Tonneau cowl & rear windshield (400.00).

HISTORICAL: Introduced: January, 1926. Calendar year registrations: 7711. Calendar year production: 8787. The president of Lincoln was Edsel Ford

1927 LINCOLN

1927 Lincoln, model L, 3-window sedan, OCW

LINCOLN — MODEL L — EIGHT: Identifying the 1927 Lincolns were bullet-shaped headlight shells enclosing new lamps with dual filaments providing high and low beams in place of the older tilting beam arrangement. Also updated were the Lincoln's rear lights which now consisted of a red lens-taillight, amber lens-brake light and a white lens-backup light. Another revision taking place during 1927 was the use of running boards with black-ribbed rubber rather than a linoleum covering. Although not easily detected, the 1927 Lincolns were one inch lower than previously, due to new 32 x 6.75 tires and a 1/2 inch reduction in spring camber. A new instrument panel placed all instruments within an oval surface.

After offering front wheel brakes for police use since 1923, Lincoln installed mechanical 4-wheel brakes on all its 1927 models. This was described as a "six brake system" in reference to the hand brake control over the rear brakes and the operation of the front and rear brakes by the foot pedal.

The technical changes for 1927 included a new lighter weight clutch system with fewer parts plus a standard equipment "coincidental lock" for the ignition and steering wheel.

I.D. DATA: Serial numbers were located on right side of cowl, top of clutch housing and transmission case. Starting: 39900. Ending: 47499. Engine numbers were located on left side of crankcase between cylinders 1 & 2. Starting: 39900. Ending: 47499.

Model No.	Body Type & Seating	Price	Weight	Prod. Total
122	Chassis	3500	—	83
123B	4-dr. Brun. Spt. Phae.-4P	4700	—	8
123C	4-dr. Brun. Spt. Phae. TC-4P	—	—	1
124A	4-dr. Tr.-7P	—	—	2
124B	4-dr. Brun. Spt. Tr. TC-7P	—	—	6
143	2-dr. Brun. Cpe.-4P	—	—	46
144A	4-dr. Leb. Trk. Sed. 2W-4P	4600	—	400
144B	4-dr. Leb. Trk. Sed. 3W-4P	4800	—	926
145A	4-dr. Brun. Brgm.-7P	6800	—	63
146	4-dr. Diet. Sed.-5P	5100	—	3
147A	4-dr. Diet. Sed.-7P	5300	—	1193
147B	4-dr. Diet. Ber.-7P	—	—	1005
150B	150'' wb Chassis	3700	—	22
151	2-dr. Lke. Rds.-2P	4600	—	178
152	4-dr. Diet. Sed.-5P	—	—	917
153A	4-dr. Holbrk. Coll. Cab-5P	7200	—	7
154	2-dr. Diet. Cpe. R/S-2P	—	—	580
155	4-dr. Leb. Coll. Spt. Cab-5P	7300	—	7
156	2-dr. Leb. Cpe.-4P	—	—	293
157	4-dr. Wilby Ber.-6P	—	—	12
158	4-dr. Jud. Ber.-5P	—	—	100
159	4-dr. Brun. Cab-5P	—	—	54
160	4-dr. Wilby Limo.-7P	6000	—	164
161	4-dr. Jud. Ber.-5P	—	—	352
162A	4-dr. Leb. Cab 2W-5P	—	—	—
162B	4-dr. Leb. Lan. 3W-5P	—	—	Note 1
162C	4-dr. Leb. Brgm. 3W-5P	—	—	Note 1
	4-dr. Brun. Cab-7P	—	—	—
	4-dr. Brun. Brgm.-7P	—	—	—
	4-dr. Jud. Ber.-7P	—	—	—
	4-dr. Jud. Ber. 2W-4P	5500	—	—
	4-dr. Holbrk. Cab-7P	7400	—	—
	4-dr. Lab. Cab-7P	7600	—	—
	4-dr. Wilby Ber. Land.-6P	6500	—	—
163A	4-dr. Lke. Spt. Phae.-4P	—	—	167
163B	4-dr. Lke. Dbl. Cwl. Spt. Phae.-4P	—	—	90
164A	4-dr. Lke. Spt. Tr.-7P	—	—	173
702	2-dr. Jud. Cpe.-2P	5300	—	205
Cus. Jobs		—	—	72

Note 1: Total combined production for the Leb. Lan. and Leb. Brgm. was 20.

1927 Lincoln, model L, Locke dual cowl phaeton, HAC

ENGINE: 60° V, L-head. Eight. Cast iron block. B & S: 3-3/8 in. x 5 in. Disp.: 357.8 cu. in. C.R.: 4.8:1. Brake H.P.: 90 @ 2800 R.P.M. Taxable H.P.: 39.2. Main bearings: Three. Valve lifters: Mechanical. Carb.: Stromberg 03 updraft.

CHASSIS: W.B.: 136 in. Frt/Rear Tread: 60 in. Tires: 32 x 6.75.

TECHNICAL: Sliding gear transmission. Speeds: 3F/1R. Floor shift controls. Multiple disc, dry plate clutch. Shaft drive. Full floating rear axle. Overall Ratio: 4.58:1, Opt. 4.90:1. Mechanical internal expanding brakes on four wheels. 12 spoke wooden artillery wheels, demountable rims. Wheel Size: 20 in.

OPTIONS: Dual sidemount. Sidemount cover(s). Natural wood finish wheels. Steel disc wheels. Buffalo wire wheels. Monogram. Tonneau cowl and rear windshield.

HISTORICAL: Introduced: January, 1927. Innovations: four wheel mechanical brakes, dual filament headlights. Calendar year registrations: 6460. Calendar year production: 7149. The president of Lincoln was Edsel Ford.

1928 LINCOLN

LINCOLN — MODEL L — EIGHT: Lincoln did not endorse the concept of model years, explaining, "There are no yearly or periodic Lincoln models; the Lincoln has reached such a state of development that drastic changes are neither necessary or desirable. Whenever it is possible to achieve an improvement in the Lincoln, it is made interchangeable with previous design." This philosophy was illustrated by the use of new mufflers during 1928 that dealers were able to retrofit to earlier Lincolns.

1928 Lincoln, model L, Locke sport roadster, OCW

Of greater importance was the use of a larger engine that began very late in 1927 and was carried over into 1928. By virtue of a 1/8'' bore increase the Lincoln V-8 now displaced 384.8 cubic inches. Other changes occurring at this time included a slight boost in compression ratio to 4.81:1, larger 1-7/8 inch rather than 1-3/4 inch intake valves, a reshaped combustion chamber and the use of counterweights on the crankshaft. Also debuting in 1928 was an engine oil filter and conical valve springs. Other technical changes included new steering tube bearings and lighter-weight rear axle.

Appearance revisions consisted of cowl lights shaped in the form of Lincoln's front and rear lamps, chrome-plated bumpers and five-stud, steel spoke wheels.

I.D. DATA: Serial numbers were located on right side of cowl, top of clutch housing and transmission case. Starting: 47500. Ending: 54500. Engine numbers were located on left side of crankcase between cylinders 1 and 2. Starting: 47500. Ending: 54500.

Model No.	Body Type & Seating	Price	Weight	Prod. Total
122	Chassis	—	—	105
144A	4-dr. LeB. Trk. Sed. 2W-4P	4800	—	263
144B	4-dr. LeB. Trk. Sed. 3W-4P	4800	—	529
145A	4-dr. Brun. Brgm.-7P	6400	—	3
147A	4-dr. Diet. Sed.-7P	5000	—	1023
147B	4-dr. Diet. Ber.-7P	5200	—	709
150B	150'' wb Chassis	—	—	24
151	2-dr. Lke. Rds.-2P	4600	—	65
152	4-dr. Diet. Sed.-5P	4800	—	835
153A	4-dr. Holbrk. Coll. Cab.-5P	7200	—	8
154	2-dr. Diet. Cpe. R/S-2P	4600	—	54
155	4-dr. LeB. Coll. Spt. Cab.-5P	7300	—	9
156	2-dr. LeB. Cpe.-4P	4600	—	230
157	4-dr. Wilby Ber.-6P	6500	—	6
159	4-dr. Brun. Cab.-5P	6600	—	12
160	4-dr. Wilby Limo.-7P	6000	—	483
161	4-dr. Jud. Ber.-5P	5500	—	348
162A	4-dr. LeB. Cab. 2W-5P	7350	—	Note 1
162B	4-dr. LeB. Lan. 3W-5P	7350	—	Note 1
162C	4-dr. LeB. Brgm. 3W-5P	—	—	Note 1
163A	4-dr. Lke. Spt. Phae.-4P	4600	—	226
163B	4-dr. Lke. Dbl. Cwl. Spt. Phae.-4P	—	—	150
164A	4-dr. Lke. Spt. Tr.-7P	4600	—	323
165	2-dr. Clb. Rds. R/S-2P	—	—	347
166	4-dr. Brun. Brgm.-7P	—	—	86
167	4-dr. Diet. Conv. Sed.-5P	—	—	38
168A	4-dr. Sed.-7P	—	—	1
168B	4-dr. Limo.-7P	—	—	1
169A	4-dr. Twn. 2W Sed.-5P	—	—	88
169B	4-dr. Twn. 3W Sed.-5P	—	—	140
170	2-dr. Jud. Cpe.-2P	—	—	14
171	4-dr. Diet. Conv. Cpe.-4P	6500	—	6
172	4-dr. Jud. Ber.-5P	—	—	1
702	2-dr. Jud. Cpe.-2P	5000	—	110
Custom				59

Note 1: Total combined production of the Leb. Cab., Leb. Lan. and Leb. Brgm. was 66.

1928 Lincoln, model L, club roadster, HAC

ENGINE: 60° L-head. Eight. Cast iron block. B & S: 3-1/2 in. x 5 in. Disp.: 384.8. C.R.: 4.81:1. Brake H.P.: 90 @ 2800 R.P.M. Taxable H.P.: 39.2. Main bearings: Three. Valve lifters: Mechanical. Carb.: Stromberg 03 updraft.

CHASSIS: W.B.: 136 in. Frt/Rear Tread: 60 in. Tires: 32 x 6.75. Opt. 20 x 7.00.

TECHNICAL: Sliding gear transmission. Speeds: 3F/1R. Floor shift controls. Multiple disc, dry plate clutch. Shaft drive. Full floating rear axle. Overall Ratio: 4.58:1 opt. 4.90:1. Mechanical internal expanding brakes on four wheels. Steel spoke wheels. Wheel Size: 20 in.

324

OPTIONS: Dual Sidemount. Sidemount cover(s). Wooden artillery wheels. Steel disc wheels (all-welded ''safety wheels''). Buffalo wire wheels. Monogram. Tonneau cowl and windshield.

HISTORICAL: Introduced: January, 1928. Innovations: standard oil filter, counter balanced crankshaft. Calendar year registrations: 6039. Calendar year production: 6362. The president of Lincoln was Edsel Ford.

1929 LINCOLN

1929 Lincoln, roadster, AA

LINCOLN — MODEL L — EIGHT: The 1929 Lincoln's appearance was highlighted by a higher, narrower and somewhat squarer radiator shell topped by a larger filler cap. In addition, the old leather windshield visor was replaced by a dark glass version. Many models had laminated safety glass and all 1928 Lincolns had twin windshield wipers.

Interior changes consisted of a new engine temperature gauge, (which corresponded with the repositioning of the cigar lighter to the dashboard from its previous instrument panel location) and an electric rather than spring-wound clock.

Technical changes were not extensive consisting of the use of rubber engine mounts, increased (from 30 to 50 pounds), oil pressure and a stronger starter-generator.

I.D. DATA: Serial numbers were located on right side of cowl, top of clutch housing and transmission case. Starting: 54501. Ending: 61699. Engine numbers were located on left side of crankcase between cylinders 1 and 2. Starting: 54501. Ending: 61699.

1929 Lincoln, model L. town sedan, JAC

Model No.	Body Type & Seating	Price	Weight	Prod. Total
122	Chassis	3300	—	75
150B	150'' wb Chassis	3500	—	43
151	2-dr. Lke. Rds.-2P	4650	—	7
153A	4-dr. Holbrk. Coll. Cab.-5P	6800	—	2
155	4-dr. LeB. Coll. Spt. Cab.-5P	7400	—	3
156	2-dr. LeB. Cpe.-4P	5300	—	138
157	4-dr. Wilby Ber.-6P	—	—	5
160	4-dr. Wilby Limo.-7P	6200	—	155
162A	4-dr. LeB. Cab. 2W-5P	7400	—	Note 1
162B	4-dr. LeB. Lan. 3W-5P	—	—	Note 1
162C	4-dr. LeB. Brgm. 3W-5P	—	—	Note 1
163A	4-dr. Lke. Spt. Phae.-4P	4650	—	88
163B	4-dr. Lke. Dbl. Cwl. Spt. Phae.-4P	—	—	58
164A	4-dr. Lke. Spt. Tr.-7P	—	—	88
164B		—	—	18
165	2-dr. Clb. Rds. R/S-2P	4900	—	225
166	4-dr. Brun. Brgm.-7P	7400	—	78
167	4-dr. Diet. Conv. Sed.-7P	6900	—	60
168A	4-dr. Sed.-7P	5100	—	1380
168B	4-dr. Limo.-7P	5300	—	837
169A	4-dr. Twn. 2W Sed.-5P	4900	—	658
169B	4-dr. Twn. 3W Sed.-5P	—	—	1513
170	2-dr. Clb. Cpe.-2P	5200	—	270
171	4-dr. Diet. Conv. Cpe.-4P	6000	—	69
172	4-dr. Jud. Ber.-5P	5800	—	360
173A	4-dr. Sed. 2W-5P	4900	—	22

Model No.	Body Type & Seating	Price	Weight	Prod. Total
173B	4-dr. Sed. 3W-5P	4900	—	436
174	4-dr. Wilby Limo.-7P	6200	—	228
175	4-dr. Brun. Brgm.-5P	7200	—	50
176A	4-dr. Spt. Phae.-4P	4650	—	92
176B	4-dr. Spt. Phae. Dbl. Cwl.-4P	5050	—	42
177	4-dr. Spt. Tr.-7P	4650	—	174
178	4-dr. LeB. Spt. Sed.-5P	—	—	42
179	2-dr. Cpe.-4P	4800	—	209
180	4-dr. Brun. Brgm. 2W-7P	7200	—	24
181	2-dr. Diet. Conv. Cpe.-4P	6500	—	8
182	4-dr. Diet. Conv. Sed.-5P	6900	—	10
183	4-dr. Sed.-5P	5000	—	27
184	4-dr. LeB. Brgm.-5P	—	—	2

Note 1: Total combined production of the Leb. Cab., Leb. Land. and Leb. Brgm. was 74.

ENGINE: 60° V, L-head. Eight. Cast iron block. B & S: 3-1/2 in. x 5 in. Disp.: 384.8 cu. in. C.R.: 4.81:1. Brake H.P.: 90 @ 2800 R.P.M. Taxable H.P.: 39.2. Main bearings: Three. Valve lifters: Mechanical. Carb.: Stromberg 03 updraft.

CHASSIS: [Model L] W.B.: 136 in. Frt/Rear Tread: 60 in. Tires: 32 x 6.75. Opt. 20 x 7.00.

1929 Lincoln, model L, phaeton, JAC

TECHNICAL: Sliding gear transmission. Speeds: 3F/1R. Floor shift controls. Multiple disc, dry plate clutch. Shaft drive. Full floating rear axle. Overall Ratio: 4.58:1 opt. 4.90:1. Mechanical external expanding brakes on four wheels. Steel spoke wheels. Wheel Size: 20 in.

OPTIONS: Dual Sidemount. Sidemount cover(s). Wooden artillery wheels. Steel disc wheels. Buffalo wire wheels. Monogram. Tonneau cowl and windshield.

HISTORICAL: Introduced: January 1, 1929. Calendar year sales: 6399 (6151 registrations). Calendar year production: 7672. Model year production: 7641. The president of Lincoln was Edsel Ford.

1930 LINCOLN

1930 Lincoln, model L, roadster, DW

LINCOLN — MODEL L — EIGHT: With the L series Lincoln scheduled for replacement in 1931 only minor changes were to be found in the Lincoln's format for 1930. The Brunn seven-passenger brougham, Willoughby six-passenger landaulet and the seven-passenger cabriolets by Brunn and Holbrook were no longer available. An open, convertible model took the place of the club roadster. Lincoln made a concession to modern tastes by offering fenders painted to match body colors for the first time. More precise control was now provided by the adoption of worm and roller type steering.

I.D. DATA: Serial numbers were located on right side of cowl, top of clutch housing and transmission case. Starting: 61700. Ending: 66000. Engine numbers were located on left side of crankcase between cylinders 1 and 2. Starting: 61700. Ending: 66000.

1930 Lincoln, model L, Judkins two-window berline, JAC

Model No.	Body Type & Seating	Price	Weight	Prod. Total
122	Chassis	—	—	30
165	2-dr. Clb. Rds. R/S-2P	—	—	12
172	4-dr. Jud. Ber.-5P	5600	—	72
174	4-dr. Wilby Limo.-7P	—	—	244
175	4-dr. Brun. Brgm.-5P	—	—	44
176A	4-dr. Spt. Phae.-4P	—	—	53
176B	4-dr. Spt. Phae. Dbl. Cwl.-4P	—	—	90
177	4-dr. Spt. Tr.-7P	—	—	79
178	4-dr. Leb. Spt. Sed.-5P	5300	—	8
179	2-dr. Cpe.-4P	—	—	275
180	4-dr. Brun. Brgm. 2W-7P	—	—	68
181	2-dr. Diet. Conv. Cpe.-4P	—	—	42
182	4-dr. Diet. Conv. Sed.-5P	—	—	40
183	4-dr. Sed.-5P	—	—	541
184	4-dr. Leb. Brgm.-5P	—	—	49
185	2-dr. Leb. Conv. Rds.-2P	6900	—	100
186	4-dr. Jud. Ber.-5P	5600	—	100
187	4-dr. Wilby Panel Brgm.-4P	7000	—	5
188	2-dr. Der. Conv. Rds.-2P	—	—	1
189	4-dr. Der. Conv. Phae.-5P	6000	—	21
190	2-dr. Jud. Cpe.-2P	5000	—	25
191	2-dr. Lke. Spt. Rds.-2P	4500	—	15

1930 Lincoln, model L, 7-pass. sedan, JAC

ENGINE: 60° V, L-head. Eight. Cast iron block. B & S: 3-1/2 in. x 5 in. Disp.: 384.8 cu. in. C.R.: 4.81:1. Brake H.P.: 90 @ 2800 R.P.M. Taxable H.P.: 39.2. Main bearings: Three. Valve lifters: Mechanical. Carb.: Stromberg 03 updraft.

CHASSIS: W.B.: 136 in. Frt/Rear Tread: 60 in. Tires: 32 x 6.75. Opt. 20 x 7.00.

TECHNICAL: Sliding gear transmission. Speeds: 3F/1R. Floor shift controls. Multiple disc clutch. Shaft drive. Full floating rear axle. Overall Ratio: 4.58:1. Opt. 4.90:1. Mechanical external expanding brakes on four wheels. Steel spoke wheels. Wheel Size: 20 in.

1930 Lincoln, model L, LeBaron convertible roadster, JAC

OPTIONS: Dual sidemount. Sidemount cover(s). Wooden artillery wheels. Steel disc wheels. Buffalo wire wheels. Monogram. Tonneau cowl and windshield.

HISTORICAL: Introduced: January, 1930. Calendar year registrations: 4356. Calendar year production: 3515. Model year production: 3212. The president of Lincoln was Edsel Ford.

1931 LINCOLN

1931 Lincoln, model K, Murphy dual cowl phaeton, OCW

LINCOLN — SERIES 201 — MODEL K — EIGHT: The Model K represented a dramatic shift away from the confines of the Model L design, although that car's great engine in updated form was continued.

The use of a new 145 inch wheelbase frame with six cross members and cruciform braces plus 7.00 x 19 tires gave the new Lincoln a low, sleek profile. Accentuating this look were numerous other styling changes. A new peaked radiator shape, a longer hood plus higher windows were key contributors. Only slightly less dramatic were the new bowl-shaped headlight shells and imposing dual trumpet horns with town and country settings. The graceful flow of the Lincoln fenders plus the rounded form of the front and rear bumpers were further examples of a well-coordinated design.

Both free wheeling and synchromesh on 2nd and 3rd gears were introduced on the 1931 models. In addition, a new double dry disc clutch was installed. Lincoln retained both a floating rear axle and torque tube drive with slight revisions. The old steel rod and Perrot braking system was replaced by a cable operated Bendix Duo-Servo system. Also introduced in 1931 were double acting Houdaille hydraulic shock absorbers at all four wheels.

In addition to a new Stromberg carburetor and more efficient manifolding, the Lincoln V-8 was now fitted with 5 main bearings plus separate generator and starter units. A mechanical fuel pump replaced the obsolete vacuum system.

I.D. DATA: Serial numbers were located on the right side of cowl, top of clutch housing and transmission case. Starting: 66001. Ending: 70000. Engine numbers were located on left side of crankcase between cylinders 1 and 2. Starting: 66001. Ending: 70000.

Model No.	Body Type & Seating	Price	Weight	Prod. Total
201	Chassis			61
202A	4-dr. Dbl. Cwl. Spt. Phae.-5P	4600	5245	77
202B	4-dr. Spt. Phae.-5P	4400	5175	60
203	4-dr. Spt. Tr.-7P	4400	5250	45
204-A	4-dr. Twn. Sed. 2W-5P	4600	5205	211
204-B	4-dr. Twn. Sed. 3W-5P	4600	5205	447
205	4-dr. Sed.-5P	4700	5440	552
206	2-dr. Cpe.-5P	4600	5235	225
207-A	4-dr. Sed.-7P	4900	5420	521
207-B	4-dr. Limo.-7P	5100	5370	387
207-C	4-dr. Limo.-7P	5100	5370	14
208-A	4-dr. All. W. Non-Clp. Brun. Cab-5P	7400	5340	30
208-B	4-dr. All W. Semi-Clp. Brun. Cab-5P	7400	5440	—
209	4-dr. All. W. Brgm. Brun.-5P	7200	5370	34
210	4-dr. Diet. Conv. Cpe.-4P	6400	5220	25
211	4-dr. Diet. Sed.-5P	6800	5250	65
212	4-dr. Der. Phae.-4P	6200	5040	11
213-A	4-dr. Jud. Ber. 2W-4P	5800	5420	—
213-B	4-dr. Jud. Ber. 3W-4P	5800	5460	171
214	2-dr. LeB. Conv. Cpe.-2/4P	4700	5070	275
215	4-dr. Wilby Limo.-6P	6100	5370	151
216	4-dr. Wilby Panel Brgm.-7P	7400	5400	15
217-A	4-dr. All W. Non-Up Leb. Cab-7P	7100	5320	Note 1
217-B	4-dr. All W. Semi-Clp. Leb. Cab-7P	7300	5420	Note 1
218	2-dr. Jud. Cpe.-2P	5200	5180	86
219	2-dr. Diet. Cpe.-2P	—	—	35
220	150" wb Chassis	—	—	3
221	155" wb Chassis	—	—	3
	Special	—	—	26
	RHD	—	—	21

1931 Lincoln, model K, town sedan, JAC

326

Note 1: Total combined production of the All W. Non-Up Leb. Cab. and All W. Semi-Clp. Leb. Cab. was 21.

ENGINE: 60° V, L-head. Eight. Cast iron block. B & S: 3-1/2 in. x 5 in. Disp.: 384.8 cu. in. C.R.: 4.95:1. Brake H.P.: 120 @ 2900 R.P.M. N.A.C.C. H.P.: 43. Main bearings: Five. Valve lifters: Mechanical. Carb.: Stromberg DD3 downdraft 2bbl.

CHASSIS: W.B.: 145 in. Frt/Rear Tread: 60 in. Tires: 19 x 7.00.

1931 Lincoln, model K, Judkins 2 pass. coupe. JAC

TECHNICAL: Sliding gear transmission. Speeds: 3F/1R. Floor shift controls. Double dry disc clutch. Full floating rear axle. Shaft drive. Overall Ratio: 4.58:1, 4.90:1, 4.23:1 (standard). Bendix Duo-Servo mechanical brakes on four wheels. Steel spoke wheels. Wheel Size: 19 in.

OPTIONS: Dual sidemount.

HISTORICAL: Introduced: January, 1931. Innovations: First American use of a two-barrel down-draft carburetor. Free wheeling was introduced on the 1931 Lincolns. Calendar year registrations: 3466. Calendar year production: 3592. Model year production: 3540. The president of Lincoln was Edsel Ford.

1932 LINCOLN

1932 Lincoln, model K, coupe, AA

LINCOLN — SERIES 501 — MODEL KA — EIGHT: Lincoln significantly altered its marketing stance in 1932. The KA series models were priced lower than previous K models and was offered in seven standard body styles. On a 136 inch wheelbase chassis the KA Lincoln featured a sharply pointed front grille, one-piece front and rear bumpers and thermostatically-operated hood shutters.

LINCOLN — SERIES 231 — MODEL KB — TWELVE: The KB shared the modern appearance of the medium-priced KA but since it represented a new peak of Lincoln excellence the KB had many distinctive features. Its cloisonne' emblem was blue (that of the KA was red), its radiator shell was noticeably thinner and of course its wheelbase was 145 inches. As was the case with the 1931 Model K, the KA was available in nine standard and fourteen factory custom bodies. Of even greater interest was the KA's new V-12 engine. The terms "massive" and "rugged" have often been applied to this engine with good reason. Displacement was 447.9 cubic inches, installed weight exceeded a ½ ton and the valves measured 2 inches in diameter. The forged-steel crankshaft was carried in 7 main bearings.

I.D. DATA: Serial numbers were located on the right side of cowl, top of clutch housing and transmission case. Starting: KA-70001; [KB] KB1. Ending: KA-72041; [KB] KB1666. Engine numbers were located on left side of crankcase between cylinders 1 and 2. Starting: KA-70001; [KB] KB1. Ending: KA-72041; [KB] KB1666.

Model No. Series 501 KA	Body Type & Seating	Price	Weight	Prod. Total
501	Chassis	—		7
502	2-dr. Cpe.-2P	3200	5220	—
502	2-dr. Cpe.-2/4P	3245	5090	86
503		—		40
504	4-dr. Twn. Sed.-4P	3100	5450	147
505	4-dr. Sed.-5P	3200	5430	921
506	2-dr. Vict.-5P	3200	5345	265
507-A	4-dr. Sed.-7P	3300	5435	508
507-B	4-dr. Limo.-7P	3350	5520	122
508	4-dr. Phae.-4P	3000	5145	29
510	2-dr. Rds.-2P	2900	4925	—
	RHD			5

Model No. Series 231 KB	Body Type & Seating	Price	Weight	Prod. Total
231	Chassis	—	—	18
232-A	4-dr. Mphy. Dbl. Cwl. Spt. Phae.-4P	4500	5625	30
232-B	4-dr. Mphy. Spt. Phae.-4P	4300	5600	13
233	4-dr. Spt. Tr.-7P	4300	5720	24
234-A	4-dr. Twn. Sed. 2W-5P	4500	5740	123
234-B	4-dr. Twn. Sed. 3W-5P	4500	5740	200
235	4-dr. Sed.-5P	4600	5750	216
236	2-dr. Cpe.5-P	4400	5750	83
237-A	4-dr. Sed.-7P	4700	5855	266
237-B	4-dr. Limo.-7P	4900	5885	41
237-C	4-dr. Limo.-7P	4900	5885	135
238	4-dr. Brun. all w. Cab.-5P	7200	5585	14
239	4-dr. Brun. all w. Brgm.-7P	7000	5920	13
240	4-dr. Diet. Spt. Ber.-5P	6500	5605	8
241	4-dr. Diet. Conv. Sed.-5P	6400	5720	20
242-A	2-dr. Diet. Cpe.-2/4P	5150	5710	—
242-B	2-dr. Diet. Cpe.-2P	5000	5710	17
243-A	4-dr. Jud. Ber. 2W-5P	5700	5860	—
243-B	4-dr. Jud. Ber. 3W-5P	5700	5860	74
244-A	2-dr. Jud. Cpe.-2/4P	5350	5610	—
245	4-dr. Wilby Limo.-7P	5900	5950	64
246	4-dr. Wilby Pan. Brgm.-4P	7100	5855	4
247	4-dr. Waths Conv. Vict.-5P	5900	5470	10
248	2-dr. Conv. Rds.-2/4P	4600	5535	112
249	2-dr. Muphy Spt. Rds.	6800	5605	3
250	150'' wb Chassis	—	—	1
	Specials	—	—	3
	RHD	—	—	10

1932 Lincoln, model KB, 7-pass. sedan, JAC

ENGINE: [Series KA] 60° V, L-head. Eight. Cast iron block. B & S: 3-1/2 in. x 5 in. Disp.: 384.8 cu. in. C.R.: 5.23:1. Brake H.P.: 125 @ 2900 R.P.M. Main bearings: Five. Valve lifters: Mechanical. Carb.: Stromberg DD3 downdraft 2bhl. [Series KB] 60° V, L-head. Twelve. Cast iron block. B & S: 3-1/4 in. x 4-1/2 in. Disp.: 447.9 cu. in. C.R.: 5.25:1. Brake H.P.: 150 @ 3400 R.P.M. Taxable H.P.: 50.7. Main bearings: Seven. Valve lifters: Mechanical. Carb.: Stromberg DD downdraft 2bbl. Torque: 292 lbs.-ft. @ 1200 R.P.M.

CHASSIS: [Series KA] W.B.: 136 in. Frt/Rear Tread: 60 in. Tires: 18 x 7.00. [Series KB] W.B.: 145 in. O.L.: 214 in. Frt/Rear Tread: 60 in. Tires: 18 x 7.50.

TECHNICAL: Sliding gear transmission. Speeds: 3F/1R. Floor shift controls. Double dry disc clutch. Shaft drive. Full floating rear axle. Overall Ratio: 4.58:1; 4.90:1; 4.23:1 (standard). Bendix Duo-Servo mechanical brakes on four wheels. Steel spoke wheels. Wheel Size: 18 in.

OPTIONS: Dual sidemount.

HISTORICAL: Calendar year registrations: 3179. Calendar year production: 3388. Model year production: Series 501 (KA)-2132, Series 231 (KB)-1515. The company president of Lincoln was Edsel Ford.

1933 LINCOLN

1933 Lincoln, model K, Brunn convertible victoria, AA

LINCOLN — SERIES 511 — MODEL KA — TWELVE: Lincoln concluded the era of the classic V-8 engine with its fork and blade connecting rods by introducing a new 67° V-12 for the KA series. Its displacement was 381.7 cubic inches. Aluminum pistons were installed and the crankshaft was carried in four bearings. The detachable cylinder heads were constructed of cast iron. This engine while based upon the KB V-12 was simpler and less expensive to produce.

A total of 12 models were available in KA form and their styling was once again substantially revised. Lincoln adopted hood louvers rather than shutters for both KA and KB models and an elegant chrome mesh grille sloped backward for a more streamlined profile. Early models continued to use the older clamshell type fenders but mid-way through the model year valanced-type versions were adopted and Lincoln agreed to retro-fit them to the early 1933 models at no cost to owners.

LINCOLN — SERIES 251 — MODEL KB — TWELVE: The KB had the same basic styling of the KA but its considerably larger size and available custom bodywork left no chance of being mistaken for a KA. A new double-drop frame was introduced for 1933.

I.D. DATA: Serial numbers were located on right side of cowl, top of clutch housing and transmission case. Starting: [KA] KB2001; [KB] KB2001. Ending: [KA] KA1140; [KB] KB2604. Engine numbers were located on left side of crankcase between cylinders 1 and 2. Starting: [KA] KA1; [KB] KB2001. Ending: [KA] KA1140; [KB] KB2604.

1933 Lincoln, model KB, coupe, HAC

Model No. Series 511 KA	Body Type & Seating	Price	Weight	Prod. Total
511	Chassis	—	—	Note 1
512-A	2-dr. Cpe.-2/4P	3145	5210	Note 1
512-B	2-dr. Cpe.-2P	3100	5190	Note 1
513-A	2-dr. Conv. Rds.-2/4P	3200	5050	85
514	4-dr. Twn. Sed.-5P	3100	5235	201
515	4-dr. Sed.-5P	3200	5270	320
516	2-dr. Vict.-5P	3200	5200	109
517-A	4-dr. Sed.-7P	3300	5440	190
517-B	4-dr. Limo.-7P	3350	5465	111
518-A	4-dr. Dbl. Cwl. Phae.-5P	3200	5040	12
518-B	4-dr. Phae.-5P	3000	5030	12
519	4-dr. Phae.-7P	3200	5040	10
520-A	2-dr. Rds.-2/4P	2745	5030	Note 2
520-B	2-dr. Rds.-2P	2700	5020	Note 2
	Specials	—	—	1
	RHD	—	—	4
Series 251 KB				
251	Chassis	—	—	4
252-A	4-dr. Dbl. Cwl. Spt. Phae.-4P	4400	5500	9
252-B	4-dr. Spt. Phae.-4P	4200	5410	6
253	4-dr. Spt. Tr.-7P	4300	5500	6
254-A	4-dr. Twn. Sed. 2W-5P	4400	5590	39
254-B	4-dr. Twn. Sed. 3W-5P	4400	5590	41
255	4-dr. Sed.-5P	4500	5790	52
256	4-dr. Vict. Cpe.-5P	4300	5710	18
257-A	4-dr. Sed.-7P	4600	5820	110
257-B	4-dr. Limo.-7P	4800	5840	105
258-C	4-dr. Brun. Non. Clp. Cab.-7P	6900	5685	—
258-D	4-dr. Brun. Smi. Clp. Cab.-5P	6900	5685	8
14	4-dr. Brun. Brgm.-7P	6900	5730	13
260	2-dr. Brun. Conv. Cpe.-5P	5700	5470	—
260	2-dr. Diet. Spt. Ber.-5P	—	—	15
261	4-dr. Diet. Conv. Sed.-5P	6100	5600	15
263-A	4-dr. Jud. Ber. 2W-4P	5500	5710	Note 3
263-B	4-dr. Jud. Ber. 3W-4P	5500	5710	Note 3
264-D	2-dr. Jud. Cpe.-2P	5000	5720	12
265-B	4-dr. Wilby Limo.-7P	5700	5840	40
266-B	4-dr. Wilby Pnl. Brgm.	7000	5840	2
267-B	2-dr. LeB. Conv. Rds.-2/4P	4500	5490	37
2197	2-dr. Diet. Cpe.-2P	4900	—	8
1308	4-dr. Jud. Sed. Limo.-7P	5800	—	1
	155'' wb Chassis	—	—	1
	Specials	—	—	16
	RHD	—	—	3

Note 1: Total combined production of the Series 511 KA 2-dr. coupes was 44.
Note 2: Total combined production of the Series 511 KA 2-dr. rdsts. was 12.
Note 3: Total combined production of the Series 251 KB 4-dr. Jud. Ber. (2W and 3W) was 36.

ENGINE: [KA] 67° V, L-head. Twelve. Cast iron block. B & S: 3 in. x 4-1/2 in. Disp.: 381.7. Brake H.P.: 125 @ 3400 R.P.M. N.A.C.C. H.P.: 43.2. Main bearings: Four. Valve lifters: Mechanical. Carb.: Stromberg EE22 downdraft, 2bhl. [KB] 65° V, L-head. Twelve. Cast iron block. B & S: 3-1/4 in. x 4-1/2 in. Disp.: 447.9. C.R.: 5.25:1. Brake H.P.: 150 @ 3400 R.P.M. N.A.C.C. H.P.: 50.7. Main bearings: Seven. Valve lifters: Mechanical. Carb.: Stromberg DD downdraft 2bbl. Torque: 292 lbs.-ft. @ 1200 R.P.M.

CHASSIS: [Series KA] W.B.: 136 in. Frt/Rear Tread: 60 in. Tires: 18 x 7.00. [Series KB] W.B.: 145 in. O.L.: 214 in. Frt/Rear Tread: 60 in. Tires: 18 x 7.50.

TECHNICAL: Sliding gear transmission. Speeds: 3F/1R. Floor shift controls. Double dry disc clutch. Shaft drive. Full floating rear axle. Overall Ratio: 4.58:1, 4.90:1, 4.23:1 (std.). Bendix Duo-Servo mechanical brakes on four wheels. Steel spoke wheels. Wheel Size: 18 in. Drivetrain Options: Free-wheeling std. on KB, opt. on KA.

OPTIONS: Dual sidemount.

HISTORICAL: Calendar year production: 2007. Model year production: 1647 (1114-KA, 533-KB). The president of Lincoln was Edsel Ford.

1934 LINCOLN

1934 Lincoln, model KB, Willoughby sport sedan, AA

LINCOLN — SERIES 521 — MODEL KA — TWELVE: In effect there was only a single Lincoln series for 1934. However the use of KA and KB prefixes for serial numbers as well as the use of different series numbers for the 136 inch and 145 inch wheelbase chassis warrants their separation into KA and KB series.

Lincoln styling was little changed for 1934. Radiator shells in both series were now painted body color instead of being chrome plated and all models had hood shutters rather than louvers. Smaller headlights further enhanced the Lincoln's refined front end appearance.

1934 Lincoln, model KB, touring JAC

LINCOLN — SERIES 271 — MODEL KB — TWELVE: The Senior Lincoln shared a draftless ventilation system with the KA models. In addition, all 1934 Lincolns were fitted with asymmetric headlights which had an additional passing feature in which only the left headlight would be lowered. Powering these 145 inch wheelbase Lincolns was a larger version of the KA V-12. Among its features were aluminum cylinder heads providing a 6.28:1 compression ratio and an engine oil cooler.

I.D. DATA: Serial numbers were located on right side of cowl, top of clutch housing and transmission case. Starting: 136'' wheelbase KA1501, 145'' wheelbase KB3001. Ending: 136'' wheelbase KA3176, 145'' wheelbase KB3744. Engine numbers were located on left side of crankcase between cylinders 1 and 2. Starting: 136'' wheelbase KA1501, 145'' wheelbase KB3001. Ending: 136'' wheelbase KA3176, 145'' wheelbase KB3744.

Model No.	Body Type & Seating	Price	Weight	Prod. Total
Series 521 (136'' wheelbase)				
521	Chassis	—	—	21
522-A	2-dr. Cpe.-2/4P	3250	4959	Note 1
522-B	2-dr. Cpe.-2P	3200	4929	Note 1
523	2-dr. Conv. Rds.-2/4P	3400	3934	75
524	4-dr. Twn. Sed.-5P	3450	5044	450
525	4-dr. Sed.-5P	3400	5044	425
526	2-dr. Vict.-5P	3400	5029	115
527-A	4-dr. Sed.-7P	3500	5203	275
527-B	4-dr. Limo.-7P	3550	5228	175
531	4-dr. Conv. Sed. Phae.	3900	5029	75
	RHD	—	—	8
Series 271 (145'' wheelbase)				
271	Chassis	—	—	12
272-A		—	—	2
272-B		—	—	—
273	4-dr. Tr.-7P	4200	5125	20
277-A	4-dr. Sed.-7P	4500	5510	210
277-B	4-dr. Limo.-7P	4700	5570	215
278-A	4-dr. Brun. Semi-Clp. Cab-5P	6800	5335	—
278-B	4-dr. Brun. Non-Clp. Cab-5P	6800	5315	13
279	4-dr. Brun. Brgm.-7P	6800	5480	15
280	2-dr. Brun. Conv. Cpe.-5P	5600	5045	Note 2
280-?	2-dr. Diet. Conv. Rd.	—	—	Note 2
281	4-dr. Diet. Conv. Sed.-5P	5600	5330	25
282	4-dr. Jud. Sed. Limo.-7P	5700	5605	Note 3
282-?	2-dr. Diet. Cpe.-2P	—	—	Note 3
283-A	4-dr. Jud. Ber. 2W-4P	5400	5495	37
283-B	4-dr. Jud. Ber. 3W-4P	5400	5520	17
285	4-dr. Wilby Limo.-7P	5600	5605	77
287	2-dr. Leb. Conv. Rds.-2/4P	4400	5085	45
	Special			7
	RHD			5

Note 1: The total combined production of the Series 521 2-dr. coupes was 60.
Note 2: The total combined production of the Series 271 Brunn conv. cpe. and Dietrich conv. rds. was 25.
Note 3: The total combined production of the Series 271 Judkins sed. limo. and Dietrich coupe was 27.

1934 Lincoln, model KB, LeBaron roadster, JAC

ENGINE: 67° V, L-head. Twelve. Cast iron block. B & S: 3-1/8 in. x 4-1/2 in. Disp.: 414 cu. in. C.R.: 6.38:1. Brake H.P.: 150 @ 3800 R.P.M. Taxable H.P.: 46.8. Main bearings: Four. Valve lifters: Mechanical. Carb.: Stromberg EE22 downdraft 2bb1.

CHASSIS: [Series 521] W.B.: 136 in. Frt/Rear Tread: 60 in. Tires: 18 x 7.00. [Series 271] W.B.: 145 in. O.L.: 214 in. Height: 72 in. Frt/Rear Tread: 60 in. Tires: 18 x 7.50.

1934 Lincoln, model KB, Judkins two-window berline, JAC

TECHNICAL: Sliding gear transmission. Speeds: 3F/1R. Floor shift controls. Double dry disc clutch. Shaft drive. Full floating rear axle. Overall Ratio: 4.58:1, 4.90:1, 4.23:1 (Standard). Bendix Duo-Servo mechanical brakes on four wheels. Steel spoke wheels. Wheel Size: 18 in.

OPTIONS: Dual sidemount.

HISTORICAL: Calendar year registrations: 3024. Model year production: 2411 (1671 - 136'' wheelbase, 740 - 145'' wheelbase). The president of Lincoln was Edsel Ford.

1935 LINCOLN

1935 Lincoln, model K, LeBaron convertible coupe, AA

LINCOLN — SERIES 301 — MODEL K — TWELVE: The long wheelbase Lincolns were available in three factory body styles for 1935. Other configurations were offered as in earlier years by Brunn, LeBaron, Judkins and Willoughby. Whereas the new bodies were moved forward 4½ inches on the 136 inch wheelbase models, those for the 145 inch wheelbase version were moved a full 9 inches to the front. In either case Lincoln claimed the result was an improved ride and a lower center of gravity.

Technical changes while less dramatic than the Lincoln's new appearance were still noteworthy. A new cam provided a smoother level of operation and along with a new exhaust system contributed to improved performance and a lower overall noise level.

Transmission changes included the use of helical cut gears for 2nd and 3rd plus the use of needle roller bearings in the clutch. A fully automatic spark control was also a first-time feature for the Lincoln.

1935 Lincoln, model K, 4-dr sedan, JAC

LINCOLN — SERIES 541 — MODEL K — TWELVE: Lincoln limited the use of the 136 inch wheelbase chassis in 1935 to its two-door factory custom and five-passenger standard bodies. The exceptions to this policy was the availability of the LeBaron coupe, sedan, phaeton and convertible roadster plus a Brunn convertible Victoria with this wheelbase.

Regardless of their wheelbase all Lincolns had new styling dominated by a more rounded, softer appearance. A sloping rear deck, similar to that of the 1934 Willoughby Sport Sedan was adopted as was a honeycomb mesh radiator grille. With the radiator cap now placed under the hood, the Lincoln's greyhound hood ornament was permanently mounted. Other changes enabling the 1935 Lincolns to be quickly perceived as new models were their one-piece bumpers with twin vertical bars, horizontal hood ventilators extending nearly to the windshield and smaller headlights that were further elongated to add another element of fleetness. Their shells were now body-color painted.

Interior changes were highlighted by a new dash with two large dials containing the instruments and a placement was provided for a radio. The glove box was also enlarged.

I.D. DATA: Serial numbers were located on right side of cowl, top of clutch housing and transmission case. Starting: K 3501. Ending: K 4919. Engine numbers were located on left side of crankcase between cylinders 1 and 2. Starting: K 3501. Ending: K 4919.

1935 Lincoln, model K, LeBaron convertible sedan, JAC

Model No.	Body Type & Seating	Price	Weight	Prod. Total
Series 541 (136" wb)				
541	Chassis	—	—	1
542	2-dr. Leb. Conv. Rds.-2/4P	4600	5335	30
543	4-dr. Sed. 2W-5P	4300	5690	170
544	4-dr. Sed. 3W-5P	4300	5680	278
545	2-dr. Cpe.-5P	4200	5535	44
546	2-dr. Leb. Conv. Sed. Phae.-5P	5000	5665	20
547	2-dr. Brun. Conv. Vict.-5P	5500	5440	15
548	2-dr. Leb. Cpe.-2P	4600	5335	23
	RHD	—	—	5
Series 301 (145" wb)				
301	Chassis	—	—	8
302	4-dr. Tr.-7P	4200	5155	15
303-A	4-dr. Sed.-7P	4600	5840	351
303-B	4-dr. Limo.-7P	4700	5935	282
304-A	4-dr. Brun. Semi-Clp. Cab-5P	—	—	13
304-B	4-dr. Brun. Non-Clp. Cab-5P	—	—	13
305	4-dr. Brun. Brgm.-7P	—	—	10
307	4-dr. Leb. Conv. Sed.-5P	5500	5965	20
308	4-dr. Jud. Limo.-7P	—	—	18
309-A	4-dr. Jud. Ber. 2W-5P	—	—	34
309-B	4-dr. Jud. Ber. 3W-5P	—	—	13
310	4-dr. Wilby Limo.-7P	—	—	40
311	4-dr. Wilby Spt. Sed.-5P	—	—	5
8	Specials	—	—	8
	RHD	—	—	18

ENGINE: 67° V, L-head. Twelve. Cast iron block. B & S: 3-1/8 in. x 4-1/2 in. Disp.: 414 cu. in. C.R.: 6.38:1. Brake H.P.: 150 @ 3800 R.P.M. Taxible H.P.: 46.8. Main bearings: Four. Valve lifters: Mechanical. Carb.: Stromberg EE22 downdraft 2bbl.

CHASSIS: [Series 541] W.B.: 136 in. Frt/Rear Tread: 60 in. Tires: 17 x 7.50. [Series 301] W.B.: 145 in. O.L.: 214. Frt/Rear Tread: 60 in. Tires: 17 x 7.50.

TECHNICAL: Sliding gear transmission. Speeds: 3F/1R. Floor shift controls. Double dry disc clutch. Shaft drive. Full floating rear axle. Overall Ratio: 4.58:1, 4.90:1, 4.23:1 (Std.). Bendix Duo-Servo mechanical brakes on four wheels. Steel spoke wheels. Wheel Size: 17 in.

OPTIONS: Dual sidemount. Radio. Heater. Clock.

HISTORICAL: Model year production: 1411 (Series 541-581, Series 301-830). The president of Lincoln was Edsel Ford.

1936 LINCOLN

1936 Lincoln-Zephyr, 4-dr. sedan, OCW

LINCOLN-ZEPHYR — TWELVE: The Lincoln-Zephyr was both one of the most handsome American cars of the thirties and one of the most revolutionary. The word teardrop was applicable to its overall form, taillights, fender skirts and grille emblem. The sloping rear deck, curved side window corners, simple grille form with horizontal bars in combination with headlights fully molded into the front fenders were successfully coordinated in an appearance that gave life to the expression "streamlined".

The dramatic exterior appearance of the Zephyr was mirrored by its interior motif. Twin circular dials containing the oil temperature, fuel, battery gauges and the speedometer was reminiscent of earlier Lincolns. In the dash center was a circular ash tray and directly beneath two large dials were the controls for the instrument panel light, throttle, choke and cigarette lighter. The dual windshield wipers were operated by a button just above the ash tray. The starter button was to the driver's left while the steering wheel hub contained the switch controlling the exterior lights. A steering wheel/ignition lock was installed on the steering column.

The Zephyr's pleated upholstery was available in taupe broadcloth or tan bedford cord. Leather was offered as an option.

The engineering design format of the Zephyr was headed by its integral body-frame construction and all-steel roof, the first offered by Ford Motor Company. Suspension was by transverse springs with solid front and rear axles.

To power the Lincoln-Zephyr a V-12 was developed from the Ford V-8 design. In essence the Zephyr engine was a 75 degree version of the Ford V-8 with four additional cylinders. Twin water pumps were used as was a single down-draft carburetor. Other key features included alloy steel pistons, aluminum cylinder heads and a one piece block casting.

I.D. DATA: Serial numbers were located on right side of cowl, top of clutch housing and transmission case. Starting: H1. Ending: H15528. Engine on left side of crankcase between cylinder 1 and 2. Starting: H1. Ending: H15528.

Model No.	Body Type & Seating	Price	Weight	Prod. Total
902	4-dr. Sed.-6P	1320	3349	12,272
902	4-dr. Sed. RHD-6P			908
903	2-dr. Sed.-6P	1275	3289	1814

ENGINE: 75° V, L-head. Twelve. Cast iron block. B & S: 2-3/4 in. x 3-3/4 in. Disp.: 267.3 cu. in. C.R.: 6.7:1. Brake H.P.: 110 @ 3900 R.P.M. Taxable H.P.: 36.3. Main bearings: Four. Valve lifters: Mechanical. Carb.: Stromberg downdraft 2bbl. Torque: 186 lbs.-ft. @ 2000 R.P.M.

CHASSIS: W.B.: 122 in. O.L.: 202.5 in. Height: 69 in. Frt/Rear Tread: 55.5/58.25 in. Tires: 16 x 7.00.

TECHNICAL: Sliding gear transmission. Speeds: 3F/1R. Floor shift controls. Single dry plate, centrifugal clutch. Shaft drive. 3/4 floating rear axle. Overall Ratio: 4.44:1. Mechanical brakes on four wheels. Pressed steel, drop-center rims wheels. Wheel Size: 23 in. Drivetrain Options: Columbia two-speed rear axle.

OPTIONS: Clock. Leather upholstery. Fitted luggage.

HISTORICAL: Introduced: November, 1935. Innovations: Aerodynamic design, low priced V-12 motoring, float indicator for oil level. Model year production; 14,994. The president of Lincoln was Edsel Ford.

1936 Lincoln, model K, LeBaron, coupe AA

LINCOLN — SERIES 300 — MODEL K — TWELVE: All Lincolns, regardless of wheelbase carried the K label and a 300 series model number. Changes in the year-old body shell consisted of a more sharply (27 degrees instead of 20 degrees) rearward sloping windshield, a grille with more prominent horizontal bars and fenders with smoother and more rounded edges. Substantially changing the Lincoln's front end appearance was the lowering of the headlights. Standard pressed steel wheels with larger hubcaps replaced the older wire version. A new interior feature was the under-dash placement of the handbrake.

Technical changes included the use of dual windshield wiper motors, a five rather than four engine mount system and an all-helical gear transmission.

I.D. DATA: Serial numbers were located on right side of cowl, top of clutch housing and transmission case. Starting: K 5501. Ending: K 7014. Engine numbers were located on left side of crankcase between cylinders 1 and 2. Starting: K 5501. Ending: K 7014.

Model No.	Body Type & Seating	Price	Weight	Prod. Total
321	145" wheelbase Chassis			9
322	136" wheelbase Chassis			6
323	4-dr. Tr.-7P	4200	5276	8
324-A	4-dr. Sed. 2W-5P	4300	5426	103
324-B	4-dr. Sed. 3W-5P	4300	5476	297
326	2-dr. Cpe.-5P	4200	5266	36
327-A	4-dr. Sed.-7P	4600	5591	368
327-B	4-dr. Limo.-7P	4700	5641	370
328	2-dr. Brun. Conv. Vict.-5P	5500	5176	10
329-A	4-dr. Brun. Non Clp. Cab.-5P	—	—	10
329-B	4-dr. Brun. SC Cab.-5P	—	—	10
330	2-dr. LeB. Conv. Rds.-2/4P	4700	5136	20
331	4-dr. Brun. Brgm.-7P	—	—	20
332	2-dr. LeB. Cpe.-2/4P	4700	5126	25
333	4-dr. LeB. Conv. Sed. Phae.-5P	5000	5296	30
334	4-dr. LeB. Conv. Sed.-5P	5500	5381	15
335	4-dr. Jud. Sed. Limo.-7P	—	—	26
337-A	4-dr. Jud. Ber. 2W-5P	—	—	51
337-B	4-dr. Jud. Ber. 3W-5P	—	—	13
339	4-dr. Wilby Limo.-7P	—	—	62
341	4-dr. Wilby Spt. Sed.-5P	—	—	11
	RHD (136" wb)	—	—	4
	RHD (145" wb)	—	—	15
	Specials	—	—	15

ENGINE: 67° V, L-head. Twelve. Cast iron block. B & S: 3-1/8 in. x 4-1/2 in. Disp.: 414 cu. in. C.R.: 6.38:1. Brake H.P.: 150 @ 3800 R.P.M. Taxable H.P.: 46.8. Main bearings: Four. Valve lifters: Mechanical. Carb.: Stromberg EE22 downdraft 2bbl.

CHASSIS: W.B.: 136/145 in. Frt/Rear Tread: 60 in. Tires: 17 x 7.50.

TECHNICAL: Sliding gear transmission. Speeds: 3F/1R. Floor shift control. Double dry disc clutch. Shaft drive. Full floating rear axle. Overall Ratio: 4.58:1, 4.90:1, 4.23:1 (std.). Bendix Duo-Servo mechanical brakes on four wheels. Pressed steel disc wheels. Wheel Size: 17 in.

OPTIONS: Dual sidemount. Radio. Heater. Clock.

HISTORICAL: Model year production: 1515. The president of Lincoln was Edsel Ford.

1937 LINCOLN

1937 Lincoln-Zephyr, 4-dr. sedan, OCW

LINCOLN-ZEPHYR — TWELVE: The positive public reaction to the original Lincoln-Zephyr was underscored by a doubling of its popularity in 1937. As expected of a new car beginning its second year the Zephyr wasn't radically changed for 1937. However a new instrument panel with twin glove compartments bracketing a center console carrying the controls and instruments was featured. The speedometer was placed within a large circular dial with a smaller unit positioned directly below contained the clock. On either side were vertical dials with the fuel and oil level gauges placed in the unit to the left. The right side unit enclosed the temperature and battery gauges.

Easier access to the trunk was provided by a revised spare tire bracket which now folded outward when the trunk lid was opened.

Styling changes while limited in scope made it easy to identify a 1937 Lincoln-Zephyr. The grille now carried 5 pairs of vertical bars and a new side molding swept upward from the grille bar prior to extending along the upper belt line in its way to the rear deck. In addition, the front bumper was slightly less V'eed than previously and a more ornate set of hood vents were used which matched the grille texture.

I.D. DATA: Serial numbers were located on right side of cowl, top of clutch housing and transmission case. Starting: H 15529. Ending: H 45529. Engine numbers were located on left side of crankcase between cylinders 1 and 2. Starting: H 15529. Ending: H 45529.

1937 Lincoln, model K, Brunn convertible sedan, JAC

Model No.	Body Type & Seating	Price	Weight	Prod. Total
700	2-dr. Cpe. Sed.-6P	1245	3329	1500
720	2-dr. Cpe.-6P	1165	3214	5199
730	4-dr. Sed.-6P	1265	3369	23159
737	4-dr. Twn. Limo.-6P	1425	3398	139

ENGINE: 75° V, L-head. Twelve. Cast iron block. B & S: 2-3/4 in. x 3-3/4 in. Disp.: 267.3 cu. in. C.R.: 6.7:1. Brake H.P.: 110 @ 3900 R.P.M. N.A.C.C. H.P.: 36.3. Main bearings: Four. Valve lifters: Mechanical. Carb.: Stromberg downdraft 2bbl. Torque 186 lbs.-ft. @ 2000 R.P.M.

CHASSIS: Chassis: 122 in. O.L.: 202.5 in. Height: 69 in. Frt/Rear Tread: 55.5/58.25. Tires: 16 x 7.00.

TECHNICAL: Sliding gear transmission. Speeds: 3F/1R. Floor shift controls. Single dry plate, centrifugal clutch. Shaft drive. 3/4 floating rear axle. Overall Ratio: 4.44:1. Mechanical brakes on 4 wheels. Pressed steel wheels, drop center rims. Wheel Size: 16 in. Drivetrain Options: Columbia two-speed rear axle.

OPTIONS: Radio. Heater. Leather upholstery. Fitted luggage.

HISTORICAL: Calendar year production: 29293. Model year production: 29997. The company president was Edsel Ford.

1937 Lincoln, model K, LeBaron convertible sedan, AA

LINCOLN — MODEL K — TWELVE: Lincoln continued to place a priority on custom body styles with a total of 17 versions available, along with 4 standard body types in 1937. For the first time the Lincoln V-12 was fitted with hydraulic valve lifters. Other technical changes for 1937 included a positioning of the V-12 further forward on the chassis as well as the use of altered engine mounts.

New styling that blended the headlights into the front fender form and gave the Lincolns even more of a rounded, smooth appearance represented the last major changes that would be made in the design of the K Lincoln.

I.D. DATA: Serial numbers were located on right side of cowl, top of clutch housing and transmission case. Starting: K 7501. Ending: K 8490. Engine numbers were located on left side of crankcase between cylinders 1 and 2. Starting: K 7501. Ending: K 8490.

Model No.	Body Type & Seating	Price	Weight	Prod. Total
353	4-dr. Wilby Tr.-7P	5550	—	7
354-A	4-dr. Sed. 2W-5P	4450	5492	48
354-B	4-dr. Sed. 3W-5P	4450	5522	136
356	2-dr. Wilby Cpe.-5P	5550	—	6
357-A	4-dr. Sed.-7P	4750	5697	212
357-B	4-dr. Limo.-7P	4850	5647	248
358	2-dr. Brun. Conv. Vict.-5P	5550	5346	13
359-A	4-dr. Brun. Non-Clp. Cab-5P	6650	—	10
359-B	4-dr. Brun. Semi-Clp. Cab	6750	5646	7
360	2-dr. Leb. Conv. Rds.-2/4P	4950	—	15
361	4-dr. Brun. Brgm.-7P	6750	5681	29
362	2-dr. Leb. Cpe.-2P	4950	5172	24
363-A	4-dr. Leb. Conv. Sed. part.-5P	5650	—	12
363-B	4-dr. Leb. Conv. Sed.-5P	5450	5547	37
365	4-dr. Jud. Sed. Limo.-7P	5950	5732	27
367-A	4-dr. Jud. Ber. 2W-5P	5650	5622	47
367-B	4-dr. Jud. Ber. 3W-5P	5750	5682	19
369	4-dr. Wilby Limo.-7P	5850	5801	60
371	4-dr. Wilby Spt. Sed.-5P	6850	—	6
373	4-dr. Wilby Pnl. Brgm.-7P	7050	—	4
375	4-dr. Brun. Tr. Cab-5P	6950	—	10

ENGINE: 67° V, L-head. Twelve. Cast iron block. B & S: 3-1/8 in. x 4-1/2 in. Disp.: 414 cu. in. C.R.: 6.38:1. Brake H.P.: 150 @ 3800 R.P.M. Taxable H.P.: 46.8. Main bearings: Four. Valve lifters: Hydraulic. Carb.: Stromberg EE22 downdraft 2bb1.

CHASSIS: W.B.: 136 in./145 in. Frt/Rear Tread: 60 in. Tires: 17 x 7.50.

TECHNICAL: Sliding gear transmission. Speeds: 3F/1R. Floor shift controls. Double dry disc clutch. Shaft drive. Full floating rear axle. Overall Ratio: 4.58:1, 4.90:1, 4.23:1 (Std.). Bendix Duo-Servo mechanical brakes on four wheels. Pressed steel disc wheels. Wheel Size: 17 in.

OPTIONS: Dual sidemount. Radio. Heater. Clock. Cigar lighter.

HISTORICAL: Model year production: 977. The president of Lincoln was Edsel Ford.

1938 LINCOLN

1938 Lincoln-Zephyr, convertible sedan, AA

LINCOLN-ZEPHYR — TWELVE: The Lincoln-Zephyr received a major styling revision utilizing new front sheet metal and rear fenders as well as a longer, 125 inch wheelbase. The grille now was divided and consisted of very thin, horizontal chrome bars. This design set the theme for the rest of the Lincoln-Zephyr's exterior body trim. The narrow belt line molding enhanced the low profile of the Zephyr which was further accentuated by the four side hood bars. Furthering the integration of the Zephyr's various body trim components into an extremely coherent styling format was the unobtrusive hood ornament which flowed downward to accentuate the 2-piece grille design. At the rear the fenders were like those up front, larger and more elongated than previously. The teardrop shaped headlights were incorporated into the smooth form of the fenders.

Following up on the construction of 3 prototype convertible sedans were two production open models, a convertible coupe and convertible sedan.

Interior revisions were numerous. The metal surrounds for the seats used in 1936 and 1937 were removed, a larger banjo-type, 18 inch steering wheel was installed and a new biscuit upholstery pattern was introduced. Closed model seats were available in striped tan broadcloth or tan bedford cloth as well as tan leather. The convertible models were upholstered in tan leather and whipcord. Lincoln once again rearranged the Zephyr's dash gauges for gas, oil, temperature and battery functions. Pointing the way to the column-mounted shift lever which Lincoln would introduce in 1940, was a convoluted shift handle that protruded from the center console.

I.D. DATA: Serial numbers were located on right side of cowl, top of clutch housing and transmission case. Starting: H 45530. Ending: H 64640. Engine numbers were located on left side of crankcase between cylinders 1 and 2. Starting: H 45530. Ending: H 64640.

Model No.	Body Type & Seating	Price	Weight	Prod. Total
700	2-dr. Cpe. Sed.-6P	1355	3409	800
720	2-dr. Cpe.-6P	1295	3294	2600
730	4-dr. Sed.-6P	1375	3444	14,520
737	4-dr. Twn. Limo.-6P	1550	3474	130
740	4-dr. Conv. Sed.-6P	1790	3724	461
760-B	2-dr. Conv. Cpe.-6P	1650	3489	600

ENGINE: 75° V, L-head. Twelve. Cast iron block. B & S: 2-3/4 in. x 3-3/4 in. Disp.: 267.3 cu. in. Overall Ratio: 6.7:1. Brake H.P.: 110 @ 3900 R.P.M. Taxable H.P.: 36.3. Main bearings: Four. Valve lifters: Hydraulic. Carb.: Chandler Gloves AA1 downdraft 2bbl. Torque: 186 lbs.-ft @ 2000 R.P.M.

CHASSIS: W.B.: 125 in. O.L.: 210 in. Height: 63-1/4 in. Frt/Rear Tread 55-1/2 / 58-1/4. Tires: 16 x 7.00.

TECHNICAL: Sliding gear transmission. Speeds: 3F/1R. Floor located controls. Single dry plate clutch. Shaft drive. 3/4 floating rear axle. Overall Ratio: 4.44:1. Mechanical brakes on 4 wheels. Pressed steel wheels, drop center rim. Wheel size: 16 in. Drivetrain options: Columbia 2-speed rear axle.

OPTIONS: Bumper guards. Radio. Heater. Leather upholstery. Wind wings. Whitewall tires. Fitted luggage.

HISTORICAL: Calendar year production: 19751. Model year production: 19111. The president of Lincoln was Edsel Ford. A Zephyr sedan was second among 26 entrants in the 1938 Gilmore Economy run with a 23.47 MPG.

LINCOLN — MODEL K — TWELVE: The 1938 K Lincoln's grille was given a new look via the use of 18 rather than 30 horizontal bars as used previously. Due to the elimination of thermostatically controlled hood shutters the side engine louvers were also revised. Built-in trunks were found on all standard sedan models and both the side belt line molding and exterior door handles were of stainless steel construction.

Minor changes to the Lincoln's upholstery plus rheostat dash-panel lighting highlighted the Lincoln's interior.

Technical changes consisted of improved synchomesh and brakes with a greater resistance to fading.

I.D. DATA: Serial numbers were located on right side of cowl, top of clutch housing and transmission case. Starting: K 9001. Ending: K9450. Engine numbers were located on left side of crankcase between cylinders 1 and 2. Starting: K 9001. Ending: K 9450.

1938 Lincoln, model K, 4 dr. sedan, JAC

Model No.	Body Type & Seating	Price	Weight	Prod. Total
403	4-dr. Wilby Tr.-7P	5900	—	5
404-A	4-dr. Sed. 2W-5P	4900	5527	9
404-B	4-dr. Sed. 3W-5P	4900	5532	49
406	2-dr. Wilby Cpe.-5P	5900	5407	4
407-A	4-dr. Sed.-7P	5100	5672	78
407-B	4-dr. Limo.-7P	5200	5762	91
408	4-dr. Brun. Conv. Vict.-5P	5900	5322	8
409-A	4-dr. Brun. Sm. Clp. Cab.-5P	7000	5716	6
409-B	4-dr. Brun. Non Clp. Cab.-5P	6900	5696	5
410	2-dr. Leb. Conv. Rds.-2-4P	5300	—	8
411	4-dr. Brun. Brgm.-5P	7000	5806	13
412	2-dr. Leb. Cpe.-2P	5300	5227	12
413-A	4-dr. Leb. Conv. Sed.-5P	5800	5462	15

ENGINE: 67°V, L-head. Twelve. Cast iron block. B & S: 2-1/8 in. x 4-1/2 in. Disp.: 414 cu. in. C.R.: 6.38:1. Brake H.P.: 150 @ 3800 R.P.M. Taxable H.P. 46.8. Main bearings: Four. Valve lifters: Hydraulic. Carb.: Stromberg EE1 downdraft 2bbl.

CHASSIS: W.B.: 136/145 in. O.L.: 213 in. Frt/Rear Tread: 60 in. Tires: 17 x 7.50.

TECHNICAL: Sliding gear transmission. Speeds: 3F, 1R. Floor shift controls. Double dry disc clutch. Shaft drive. Full floating rear axle. Overall Ratio: 4.58:1. Bendix Duo-Servo mechanical brakes on 4 wheels. Pressed steel disc wheels. Wheel Size: 17 in.

OPTIONS: Dual sidemount. Sidemount cover(s). Radio. Heater. Clock. Cigar lighter.

HISTORICAL: Model year production: 416. The president of Lincoln was Edsel Ford.

1939 LINCOLN

1939 Lincoln-Zephyr, convertible coupe, AA

LINCOLN-ZEPHYR — TWELVE: The use of hydraulic brakes highlighted the Lincoln-Zephyr's technical changes for 1939. The other change of any consequence was the use of a voltage-regulator rather than a generator cut-out. This feature was also found on Zephyrs produced towards the end of the 1938 model run.

Among styling changes found on the 1939 Lincoln-Zephyr was a larger grille shape with vertical bars, two rather than four side hood bars and a more vertical front prow. The lower body panels now enclosed the running boards. Both the front and rear bumpers were reshaped. The front unit had a two-part center section while at the rear the bumper was less pointed than previously.

The Zephyr's dash continued to feature symmetrically positioned dual glove boxes and ash trays plus the centrally located speedometer. For 1939 this circular panel also contained the gauges for battery oil, fuel and engine temperature. A battery-condition gauge replaced the ammeter.

Once again a new upholstery scheme was used with vertical pleats and the optional leather was offered in tan, red, gray and brown. In addition a new custom interior option (standard on the Town Limousine) was offered.

I.D. DATA: Serial numbers were located on right side of cowl, top of clutch housing and transmission case. Starting: H 64641. Ending: H 85640. Engine numbers were located on left side of crankcase between cylinders 1 and 2. Starting: H 64641. Ending: H 85640.

Model No.	Body Type & Seating	Price	Weight	Prod. Total
H-70	2-dr. Cpe. Sed.-6P	1330	3600	800
H-72	2-dr. Cpe.-6P	1320	3520	2500
H-73	4-dr. Sed.-6P	1360	3620	16,663
	4-dr. Tun.-Limo.-6P	1700	3670	95
H-74	4-dr. Conv. Sed.-6P	1790	3900	302
H-76	2-dr. Conv. Cpe.-6P	1700	3790	640

ENGINE: 75° V, L-head. Twelve. Cast iron block. B & S: 2-3/4 in. x 3-3/4 in. Disp.: 267.3 cu. in. C.R.: 6.7:1. Brake H.P.: 110 @ 3900 R.P.M. Taxable H.P.: 36.3. Main bearings: Four. Valve lifters: Hydraulic. Carb.: Stromberg downdraft 2bbl. Torque: 186 lbs.-ft. @ 2000 R.P.M.

CHASSIS: W.B.: 125 in. O.L.: 210 in. Height: 69-1/2 in. Frt/Rear Tread: 55-1/2/58-1/4 in. Tires: 16 x 7.00.

TECHNICAL: Sliding gear transmission. Speeds: 3F/1R. Floor shift controls. Single dry disc plate clutch. Shaft drive. 3/4 floating rear axle. Overall Ratio: 4.44:1. Bendix hydraulic internal expanding brakes on four wheels. Pressed steel, dropped center wheels. Wheel Size: 16 in. Drivetrain Options: Columbia 2-speed rear axle.

OPTIONS: Bumper guards. Radio. Heater. Leather upholstery. Wind wings. Whitewall tires. Fitted luggage. Custom interior.

HISTORICAL: Calendar year production: 22578. Model year production: 21000. The president of Lincoln was Edsel Ford.

1939 Lincoln, model K, Willoughby limousine, OCW

LINCOLN — MODEL K — TWELVE: Changes in the Lincoln K were limited to the use of a different model Stromberg carburetor and wider steel wheel rims with steel spokes added to the back side for greater strength.

Specific production figures for the last of the K Lincoln are unavailable. If any were built in 1940 they were unchanged from the 1939 version.

I.D. DATA: Serial numbers were located on right side of cowl, top of clutch housing and transmission case. Starting: K 9451. Ending: K 9674. Engine numbers were located on left side of crankcase between cylinder 1 and 2. Starting: K 9451. Ending: K 9674.

Model No.	Body Type & Seating	Price	Weight	Prod. Total
403	4-dr. Tr.-7P	—	—	1
404-A	4-dr. Sed. 2W-5P	4800	5735	2
404-B	4-dr. Sed. 3W-5P	4800	5740	12
406	2-dr. Wilby Cpe.-5P	5800	5615	1
407-A	4-dr. Sed.-7P	5000	5880	25
407-B	4-dr. Limo.-7P	5100	5970	58
408	2-dr. Brun. Conv. Vict.-5P	5800	5530	2
409-A	4-dr. Brun. Non. Clp. Cab.-5P	6800	6010	1
409-B	4-dr. Brun. Smi. Cpl. Cab.-5P	6900	6030	1
410	2-dr. LeB. Conv. Rds.-2/4P	5200	5505	2
411	4-dr. Brun. Brgm.-7P	6900	6120	2
412	2-dr. LeB. Cpe.-2P	5200	5425	4
413-A	4-dr. LeB. Conv. Sed.-5P	5700	5670	3
413-B	4-dr. LeB. Conv. Sed. Part.-5P	5900	5780	6
415	4-dr. Jud. Limo.-7P	6200	5950	2
417-A	4-dr. Jud. Ber. 2W-5P	5900	5770	2
417-B	4-dr. Jud. Ber. 3W-5P	6000	5840	1
419	4-dr. Wilby Limo.-7P	6100	6140	4
421	4-dr. Wilby Spt. Sed.-5P	6900	6030	1
423	4-dr. Wilby Pnl. Brgm.-5P	—	—	1
425	4-dr. Brun. Tr. Cab.-5P	7100	5870	2

ENGINE: 67° V, L-head. Twelve. Cast iron block. B & S: 3-1/8 in. x 4-1/2 in. Disp.: 414 cu. in. C.R.: 6.38:1. Brake H.P.: 150 @ 3800 R.P.M. Taxable H.P.: 46.8. Main bearings: Four. Valve lifters: Hydraulic. Carb.: Stromberg downdraft 2bbl.

CHASSIS: W.B.: 136/145 in. Frt/Rear Tread: 60 in. Tires: 17 x 7.50.

TECHNICAL: Sliding gear transmission. Speeds: 3F/1R. Floor shift controls. Double dry disc clutch. Shaft drive. Full floating rear axle. Overall Ratio: 4.58:1; 4.90:1; 4.23:1 (std.) Bendix Duo-Servo mechanical brakes on four rear wheels. Wheel size: 17 in.

OPTIONS: Dual sidemount. Sidemount cover(s). Radio. Heater. Clock. Cigar lighter.

HISTORICAL: Model year production: 133. The president of Lincoln was Edsel Ford.

1940 LINCOLN

LINCOLN-ZEPHYR — TWELVE: The use of a redesigned body shell for the Zephyr which was to remain in use until 1949 cushioned the demise of the K Lincolns and buoyed the Lincoln-Zephyr into the mainstream of Lincoln's marketing strategy. The major styling-features for 1940 consisted of larger, by 22% glass area, front window vent windows and the inboard positioning of the taillight. In addition, the one-piece rear window, lack of running boards and the use of sealed-beam headlights made it easy to identify the 1940 Lincoln-Zephyr.

Once again a rearranged instrument panel was introduced for the Lincoln-Zephyr. The circular case for the speedometer and instruments was now located directly behind the steering column (which for the first time carried the "Finger-Tip Gearshift") and a single, large glove box was placed in front of the passenger seat. The optional radio was installed on the upper dash panel just above the centrally located radio grille. To the left of the speaker was the clock.

All interior appointments had a mahogany metal finish and a two-spoke steering wheel was installed.

By virtue of a large 2-7/8 inch bore the Zephyr's engine now displaced 292 cubic inches and was rated at 120hp.

In addition to the production model Lincoln-Zephyrs, a small number of custom-built versions were constructed during 1940. Three of these carried Brunn Town car bodies. In addition three Custom series limousines were completed.

1940 Lincoln-Zephyr, 4-dr. sedan, JAC

CONTINENTAL — TWELVE: The outstanding nature of the Lincoln-Zephyr's styling was further demonstrated by its transformation into one of America's most beautiful classics, the Continental. Compared to the Zephyr, the Continental was 3 inches lower and had a longer, by 7 inches, hood. During the 1940 model run many styling developments took place. These included the installation of a spare tire cover, rear bumper splash shields and rubber rear fender gravel shields. Also changed was the location of the license bracket which was moved from the body to the bumper. Continentals were fitted with the instrument panel of the Lincoln-Zephyr Town Limousine and featured a gold colored finish for the interior trim and hardware.

With the exception of a side-mounted engine air cleaner the Continental's mechanical composition was essentially that of other Lincoln-Zephyrs. However Continental engines had polished aluminum heads and manifolds and chromed acorn cylinder head nuts.

I.D. DATA: Serial numbers were located on right side of cowl, top of clutch housing and transmission case. Starting: H 85641. Ending: H 107687. Engine numbers were located on left side of crankcase between cylinders 1 and 2. Starting: H 85641. Ending: H 107687.

1940 Lincoln-Zephyr, coupe, AA

Model No.	Body Type & Seating	Price	Weight	Prod. Total
72A	2-dr. Cpe.-2P	1360	3375	1256
72AS	2-dr. Cpe.-4P	1400	3465	316
73	4-dr. Sed.-6P	1400	3535	15764
	4-dr. Twn. Sed.-7P	1740	3575	98
76	2-dr. Conv. Cpe.-6P	1770	3635	700
77	2-dr. Clb. Cpe.-6P	1400	3465	3500
H-32	4-dr. Limo.-7P	—	—	4
H-36	4-dr. Brun. Twn. Car-5P	—	—	4
56	2-dr. Cont. Cab.-5P	2840	3615	350
57	2-dr. Cont. Cpe.-5P	—	—	54

ENGINE: 75° V, L-head. Twelve. Cast iron block. B & S: 2-7/8 in. x 3-3/4 in. Disp.: 292 cu. in. C.R.: 7.2:1. Brake H.P.: 120 @ 3500 R.P.M. Taxable H.P.: 39.3. Main bearings: Four. Valve lifters: Hydraulic. Carb.: Holley downdraft 2bbl. Torque: 220 lbs.-ft. @ 2000 R.P.M.

CHASSIS: W.B.: 125 in. O.L.: 209-1/2 in. Height: 69-1/2 (Continental 63). Frt/Rear Tread: 55-1/2 / 58-1/4 in. Tires: 16 x 7.00.

TECHNICAL: Sliding gear transmission. Speeds: 3F/1R. Column shift controls. Single dry plate clutch. Shaft drive. 3/4 floating rear axle. Overall Ratio: 4.44:1. Bendix hydraulic internal expanding brakes on four wheels. Pressed steel, dropped center wheels. Wheel Size: 4-1/2 K - 16. Drivetrain Options: Columbia 2 speed rear axle.

1940 Lincoln-Zephyr sedan coupe, OCW

1940 Lincoln-Continental cabriolet, JAC

1940 Lincoln-Continental coupe, AA

OPTIONS: Bumper guards. Radio. Heater. Leather upholstery. Wind wings. Whitewall tires. Fitted luggage. Custom interior.

HISTORICAL: Introduced October 2, 1939. Calendar year production: 24021. Model year production: 22046. The president of Lincoln was Edsel Ford.

1941 LINCOLN

1941 Lincoln-Zephyr, 4-dr. sedan, AA

LINCOLN — ZEPHYR — TWELVE: Lincolns for 1941 were available as either Zephyr, Custom or Continental models with the Zephyr providing the basic styling — engineering platform for all three versions.

The new Zephyrs had a wide grille outline molding, front fender mounted parking lights, more heavily chromed and reshaped taillights and a combined trunk lid and rear deck light. The front and rear bumpers were also slightly altered and a new hubcap design was introduced.

Interior alterations were similarly of a minor nature. The clock and ash tray were now circular in shape as were the door handles. Additional upholstery fabrics were also available.

For the first time Borg-Warner overdrive was optional and a power top was standard on the convertible model.

LINCOLN — CONTINENTAL — TWELVE: Since the Continental had used the Zephyr's new styling for its 1940 debut, only superficial appearance changes distinguished the 1941 version, although separate tooling was now used for the Continental. Both interior and exterior door handles were of the push-button type and the same styling changes found on the 1941 Zephyr models were also carried over to the Continental. Lincoln Continental script was found both on the hood and spare tire hubcap of the 1941 model. Road hubcaps carried Lincoln V-12 inscriptions. During the 1941 model run minor refinements took place in the appearance of the Continental's hood ornament, V-12 emblem and taillight form. Both turn signals and vacuum window lifts were standard. Interior selection consisted of blue cord/leather, green cord/leather and tan cord matched with either tan or red leather. All-leather upholstery was available in colors of green, black, blue, red or tan. The instrument panel had a mahogany finish.

1941 Lincoln-Continental coupe, OCW

LINCOLN — CUSTOM — TWELVE: With a wheelbase 13 inches longer than the other 1941 Lincolns and a more luxurious interior the Custom series represented a reasonable reincarnation of the K Lincoln spirit. The Custom carried a Continental hood ornament and Zephyr club coupe front doors. The Custom's side hood molding had previously been used on the 1940 Lincoln Zephyr.

Custom interiors were of a very high quality. A pinstripe broadcloth upholstery was available in blue, green and tan-brown. A cord pattern was offered in tan-brown. Optional custom interiors were also available.

I.D. DATA: Serial numbers were located on right side of cowl, top of clutch housing and transmission case. Starting: H 107688. Ending: H 129690. Engine numbers were located on left side of crankcase between cylinders 1 and 2. Starting: H 107688. Ending: H 129690.

Model No.	Body Type & Seating	Price	Weight	Prod. Total
Lincoln-Zephyr				
72A	2-dr. Cpe.-3P	1432	3560	972
72B	2-dr. Cpe.-5P	1464	3580	178
73	4-dr. Sed.-6P	1493	3710	14,469
76	2-dr. Conv. Cpe.-6P	1801	3840	725
77	2-dr. Clb. Cpe.-6P	1493	3640	3750
36	4-dr. Brun. Twn. Cr.-5P	—	—	5
Lincoln-Continental				
56	2-dr. Cab.-5P	2778	3860	400
57	2-dr. Cpe.-5P	2727	3890	850
Lincoln-Custom				
31	4-dr. Sed.-7P	2622	4250	355
32	4-dr. Limo.-7P	2751	4270	295

1941 Lincoln-Continental cabriolet, HFM

ENGINE: 75° V, L-head. Twelve. Cast iron block. B & S: 2-7/8 in. x 3-3/4 in. Disp.: 292 cu. in. C.R.: 7.2:1. Brake H.P.: 120 @ 3500 R.P.M. Taxable H.P.: 39.3. Main bearings: Four. Valve lifters: Hydraulic. Carb.: Holley downdraft 2bbl. Torque: 220 lbs.-ft. @ 2000 R.P.M.

CHASSIS: [Zephyr] W.B.: 125 in. O.L.: 210 in. Height: 69-1/2 in. Frt/Rear Tread: 55-1/2 in./60-3/4 in. Tires: 16 x 7.00. [Custom] W.B.: 138 in. O.L.: 225.3 in. Height: 70.5. Frt/Rear Tread: 55-1/2 in./60-3/4 in. Tires: 16 x 7.00. [Continental] W.B.: 125 in. O.L.: 209-8/10 in. Height: 63 in. Frt/Rear Tread: 55-1/2 in./60-3/4 in. Tires: 16 x 7.00.

TECHNICAL: Sliding gear transmission. Speeds: 3F/1R. Column shift controls. Single dry plate clutch. Shaft drive. 3/4 floating rear axle. Overall Ratio: 4.44:1. Bendix Hydraulic, internal expanding brakes on four wheels. Pressed steel, dropped center wheels. Wheel Size: 5K-16. Drivetrain Options: Columbia 2-speed rear axle. Borg-Warner overdrive.

OPTIONS: Bumper guards. Radio. Heater. Custom interior (100.00). Leather upholstery. Wind wings. Whitewall tires. Fitted luggage.

HISTORICAL: Calendar year production: 17756 (Lincoln-Zephyr: 20094, Lincoln-Continental: 1250, Lincoln-Custom: 650). Model year production: 21994. The president of Lincoln was Edsel Ford. In the 1941 Gilmore Economy Run the first place winner was a Lincoln Custom with a ten-miles-per-gallon average of 57.827 or 21.03 mpg. The second place car was a Lincoln Zephyr at 57.749 t.m.p.g. or 22.96 mpg. Both cars had Columbia 2-speed rear axles and Borg-Warner overdrive.

1942 LINCOLN

1942 Lincoln, Continental, coupe, OCW

1942 Lincoln-Zephyr, 4-dr. sedan, AA

LINCOLN-ZEPHYR — TWELVE: The 1942 Lincoln-Zephyr was longer, wider and lower. A two-part grille with horizontal bars accentuated the Lincoln's more massive form. Adding to the popular horizontal-line styling theme common to so many 1942 automobiles were the new headlight trim plates containing the parking and directional lights. Common to all 1942 Lincolns were exterior push-button door latches.

Although chassis revisions included longer front springs and a wider front tread, the big technical news was the availability of the Liquimatic 2-speed automatic transmission. This complex and ultimately unsuccessful venture combined overdrive, a fluid coupling and a semi-automatic transmission.

1942 Lincoln, Continental, cabriolet, AA

CONTINENTAL — TWELVE: Common to all 1942 Lincolns was a larger, 306 cubic inch V-12 rated at 130 hp. A lower 7.0:1 compression ratio was specified and cast iron heads replaced the aluminum versions. The Continental also shared the Zephyr's new styling format.

CUSTOM — TWELVE: The Custom shred a rearranged dashboard with the Zephyr. The circular speedometer was placed just to the right of the steering column with a panel containing fuel, temperature, oil and battery gauges to its immediate left. A very large radio speaker grille occupied the center section. A clock, whose size and shape matched that of the speedometer plus a Lincoln plaque provided design symmetry on the right side of the dash.

I.D. DATA: Serial numbers were located on right side of cowl, top of clutch housing and transmission case. Starting: H 129691. Ending: H 136254. Engine numbers were located on left side of crankcase between cylinders 1 and 2. Starting: H 129691. Ending: H 136254.

Model No.	Body Type & Seating	Price	Weight	Prod. Total
Lincoln-Zephyr				
72-A	2-dr. Cpe.-3P	1748	3790	Note 1
72-B	2-dr. Cpe.-5P	—	3790	Note 1
73	4-dr. Sed.-6P	1801	3980	4418
76	2-dr. Conv. Cpe.-6P	2274	4190	191
77-A	2-dr. Clb. Cpe.-6P	1801	3810	253
Lincoln Continental				
56	2-dr. Cab.-5P	3174	4020	136
57	2-dr. Cpe.-5P	3174	4060	200
Lincoln Custom				
31	4-dr. Sed.-7P	3117	4380	47
32	4-dr. Limo.-7P	3248	4400	66

Note 1: The total combined production of these models was 1236.

ENGINE: 75° V, L-head. Twelve. Cast iron block. B & S: 2-15/16 in. x 3-3/4 in. Disp.: 292 cu. in. C.R.: 7.0:1. Brake H.P.: 130 @ 4000 R.P.M. Taxable H.P.: 39.9. Main bearings: Four. Valve lifters: Hydraulic. Carb.: Holley downdraft 2bbl. Torque 220 lbs.-ft. @ 2000 R.P.M.

CHASSIS: [Zephyr] W.B.: 125 in. O.L.: 218.7 in. Height: 68-1/2. Frt/Rear Tread: 59/60-3/4. Tires: 15 x 7.00. [Custom] W.B.: 138 in. Frt/Rear Tread 59/60-3/4. Tires: 15 x 7.00. [Continental] W.B.: 125 in. O.L.: 217 in. Height: 63-1/10 (Cabriolet). Frt/Rear Tread: 59/60-3/4. Tires: 15 x 7.00.

TECHNICAL: Sliding gear transmission. Speeds: 3F/1R. Column shift controls. Single dry plate clutch. Shaft drive. 3/4 floating rear axle. Overall Ratio: 4.22:1. Bendix hydraulic, internal expanding brakes on 4 wheels. Pressed steel, dropped center wheels. Drivetrain Options: Columbia 2-speed rear axle. Borg-Warner overdrive. Liquimatic (189.00).

OPTIONS: Bumper guards. Radio. Heater. Clock. Custom interior (95.00). Leather upholstery. Wind wings. Whitewall tires. Fitted luggage.

HISTORICAL: Introduced: September 30, 1942. Innovations: Liquimatic transmission. Calendar year production: 1276. Model year production: 6547 (Zephyr: 6098, Continental: 336, Custom: 113). The president of Lincoln was Edsel Ford. 1942 model year production ended January 31, 1942.

LINCOLN
1946-1975

Like most American cars, the 1946-1948 Lincolns were warmed-over prewar models. When you had a gorgeous automobile like the Continental, that wasn't bad. It was one of those rare cars that became an instant Classic. Although highly regarded for its styling, sales were not good. But it did help Lincoln's image.

1946-74 Lincoln Date Compilation by Charles Webb

When the first postwar Lincolns debuted in early 1948 (1949 models), the company had nothing to compare with the Continental. The top-of-the-line Cosmopolitan looked too much like the standard Lincoln series, which in turn resembled Mercury, with whom it shared bodies.

In 1952, Lincoln dramatically changed its appearance. It bore no resemblance to the previous year's model, but shared the corporate look all Ford Motor Co. cars had that year. Although Lincolns had participated in previous Pan American Road races, this was the first year the make dominated the event, winning the first four spots (using 1953 models).

The "hot car" image nurtured by the racing victories was fully exploited by the company. As an ad for 1955 models said, "The first function of a fine car is outstanding performance." Fortunately for Lincoln, the Pan American Road Race was discontinued in 1954. Its days as a Road Race winner were about to end. Chrysler came out with its potent 300 in 1955.

The Continental returned in 1956. The beautiful Mark II captured the spirit of the original Continental, yet was thoroughly modern in design. Despite early waiting lists, it suffered the same fate as its predecessor: low demand.

The 1956 Lincoln was also very attractive. If anyone had doubts about Lincoln's status as a prestige car, they were vanquished this year. Regrettably, styling was jazzed up a bit for 1957. And the following year, Lincoln was completely changed.

The 1958 to 1960 models were the biggest American cars of the postwar era. In certain parts of the country, owners were obligated by law to place red reflectors on the rear of their new Lincolns and amber clearance lights on the front. These huge Lincolns came on the automotive scene at a time when Detroit was being widely critized for building cars that were too big. Lincoln sales declinded in 1958 and continued to drop until the resyled 1961s were introduced.

As in 1956, the 1961 Continental showed the world just how beautiful a production American automobile could be. It made most of its contemporaries look like they had been designed by Soupy Sales. Stylistically, it was the most influential car of the decade. Lincoln kept the same basic styling until 1969.

One benefit of doing so was it established a "Lincoln look." Cadillac had long been aware of the value of continuity in styling, something early postwar Lincolns didn't have. With an easily identifiable look all its own, Ford Motor Co. was able to make its less expensive cars classier by giving them Lincoln styling traits.

In the spring of 1968, the 1969 Continental Mark III was introduced. It looked like a Mark II that had gone "Hollywood." The Mark III proved to be very popular and a sales success. Its design would influence Lincoln styling throughout the 1970s.

1946 LINCOLN

1946 Lincoln, 4-dr sedan, V-12 (AA)

LINCOLN SERIES — SERIES 66H — The new 1946 Lincolns were warmed over 1942s. They had a more massive bumper, different nameplate on the sides of the hood and a heavier grille with horizontal and vertical bars. The pushbutton Continental style door openers introduced on the 1942 models were kept.

LINCOLN I.D. NUMBERS: Serial numbers were the same as engine numbers. They ranged from H1366,255 to 138,051; H138,052 to 152,839. The first letter (H) indicates the series (66H).

LINCOLN Model Number	Body/Style Number	Body Type & Seating	Factory Price	Shipping Weight	Production Total
66H	73	4-dr Sedan-6P	2337	3980	Note 1
66H	76	2-dr Conv-6P	2883	4210	Note 1
66H	77	2-dr Clb Cpe-6P	2318	3380	Note 1

NOTE 1: Total production of all body types was 16,645 units.

LINCOLN ENGINE
V-12: L-head. Cast iron block. Displacement: 305 cubic inches. Bore and stroke: 2.93 x 375 inches. Compression ratio: 7.20:1. Brake horsepower: 130 at 3600 R.P.M. Four main bearings. Carburetor: Chandler-Grove two-barrel.

1946 Lincoln-Continental, 2-dr cabriolet, V-12

CONTINENTAL SERIES — SERIES 66H — The Continental was a luxurious, beautiful, handcrafted automobile built for boulevard cruising. The 1946 model received a larger, cirss-cross pattern grille and a heavier bumper. Lincoln Continental was written in chrome on the side of the hood.

CONTINENTAL I.D. NUMBERS: See Lincoln I.D. numbers.

CONTINENTAL Model Number	Body/Style Number	Body Type & Seating	Factory Price	Shipping Weight	Production Total
66H	52	2-dr Conv-5P	4474	4090	201
66H	57	2-dr Club Cpe-5P	4392	4100	265

CONTINENTAL ENGINE
See 1946 Lincoln Series 66H engine data.

CHASSIS FEATURES: Wheelbase: 125 inches. Overall length: 216 inches. Front tread: 59 inches. Rear tread: 60.6 inches. Tires: 7.00 x 15.

POWERTRAIN OPTIONS: A three-speed manual transmission was standard. Overdrive was optional.

CONVENIENCE OPTIONS: Custom interior ($149 in Lincoln sedan and coupe). Radio. Whitewall tires. Heater.

Historical footnotes: The 1946 Continental was pace car at the 1946 Indianapolis 500.

1947 LINCOLN

1947 Lincoln, 2-dr convertible, V-12

LINCOLN SERIES — SERIES 76H — Styling changes for 1947 were minor. The push-button door handles were replaced by conventional ones. And the word 'Lincoln' was written in chrome on both sides of the hood. The raised hexagon center wheel covers of the previous year were replaced by plainer ones.

LINCOLN I.D. NUMBERS: Serial numbers were the same as engine numbers. They ranged from 7H152,840 to 174,289.

LINCOLN Model Number	Body/Style Number	Body Type & Seating	Factory Price	Shipping Weight	Production Total
76H	73	4-dr Sedan-6P	2554	4015	Note 1
76H	76	2-dr Conv-6P	3142	4245	Note 1
76H	77	2-dr Clb Cpe-6P	2533	3915	Note 1

NOTE 1: Total production of all body types was 19,891 units.

LINCOLN ENGINE
V-12: L-head. Cast iron block. Displacement: 305 cubic inches. Bore and stroke: 2.93 x 3.75 inches. Compression ratio: 7.20:1. Brake horsepower: 130 at 3600 R.P.M. Four main bearings. Carburetor: Chandler-Grove two-barrel.

1947 Lincoln-Continental, 2-dr coupe, V-12 (TVB)

CONTINENTAL SERIES — SERIES 76H — The best way to tell a 1947 Continental from a 1946 (or 1948) is to ask the owner. The only exterior changes were in the wheel covers and, in mid-model year, the hood ornament. Mechanical improvements were made to the generator and starter drive.

CONTINENTAL I.D. NUMBERS: See Lincoln I.D. Numbers.

CONTINENTAL Model Number	Body/Style Number	Body Type & Seating	Factory Price	Shipping Weight	Production Total
76H	52	2-dr Conv-5P	4746	4135	738
76H	57	2-dr Clb Cpe-6P	4662	4125	831

CONTINENTAL ENGINE
See 1947 Lincoln Series 76H engine data.

CHASSIS FEATURES: Wheelbase: 125 inches. Overall length: 216 inches. Front tread: 59 inches. Rear tread: 60.6 inches. Tires: 7.00 x 15.

POWERTRAIN OPTIONS: A three-speed manual transmission was standard. Overdrive was optional.

CONVENIENCE OPTIONS: Custom interior, in Lincoln sedan and coupe ($168). Whitewall tires. Radio. Heater.

1948 LINCOLN

1948 Lincoln, 4-dr sedan, V-12

LINCOLN SERIES — SERIES 876H — Lincoln Division was working frantically to bring out the new postwar model. So the 1948s were basically just leftover 1947s.

LINCOLN I.D. NUMBERS: Serial numbers were the same as engine numbers. They ranged from 8H174,290 to 182,129.

LINCOLN Model Number	Body/Style Number	Body Type & Seating	Factory Price	Shipping Weight	Production Total
876H	73	4-dr Sedan-6P	2554	4015	Note 1
876H	76	2-dr Conv-6P	3142	4245	Note 1
876H	77	2-dr Clb Cpe-6P	2533	3915	Note 1

NOTE 1: Total production of all body types was 6,470.

LINCOLN ENGINE
V-12: L-head. Cast iron block. Displacement: 305 cubic inches. Bore and stroke: 2.93 x 3.75 inches. Compression ratio: 7.20:1. Brake horsepower: 130 at 3600 R.P.M. Four main bearings. Carburetor: Chandler-Grove two-barrel.

1948 Lincoln-Continental, 2-dr cabriolet, V-12

CONTINENTAL SERIES — SERIES 876H — The Continental was virtually unchanged for 1948.

CONTINENTAL I.D. NUMBERS: See Lincoln I.D. numbers.

CONTINENTAL Model Number	Body/Style Number	Body Type & Seating	Factory Price	Shipping Weight	Production Total
876H	56	Conv-6P	4746	4135	452
876H	57	2-dr Clb Cpe-6P	4662	4125	847

CONTINENTAL ENGINE
See 1948 Lincoln Series 876H engine data.

CHASSIS FEATURES: Wheelbase: 125 inches. Overall length: 216 inches. Front tread: 59 inches. Rear tread: 60.6 inches. Tires: 7.00 x 15.

POWERTRAIN OPTIONS: A three-speed manual transmission was standard. Overdrive was optional.

CONVENIENCE OPTIONS: Custom interior ($168 in Lincoln sedan and coupe). Whitewall tires. Radio. Heater.

Historical footnotes: In 1951, the Museum of Modern Art selected the Continental as one of eight automotive 'works of art.' Eight years later, *Time* magazine ranked it in their top 10 choice of the 100 best-designed commercial products.

1949 LINCOLN

1949 Lincoln, 4-dr sedan, V-8 (AA)

LINCOLN SERIES — SERIES 9EL — The first all-new postwar Lincolns were introduced on April 22, 1948. They had a more streamlined appearance than the 1948s. However, the new, two-piece windshield seemed a bit out of sync with the 'modern' styling. At a distance, it was hard to tell a Lincoln from a Mercury. Recessed headlights and a shinier front end set it apart.

LINCOLN I.D. NUMBERS: Serial numbers were the same as engine numbers. They started at 9EL1 and went up to 9EL73,559.

LINCOLN Model Number	Body/Style Number	Body Type & Seating	Factory Price	Shipping Weight	Production Total
9EL	72	2-dr Club Cpe-6P	2527	3959	Note 1
9EL	74	4-dr Sport Sed-6P	2575	4009	Note 1
9EL	76	2-dr Conv-6P	3116	4224	Note 1

NOTE 1: Total 9EL Series production was 38,384 units.

LINCOLN ENGINE
V-8: L-head. Cast iron block. Displacement: 336.7 cubic inches. Bore and stroke: 3.5 x 4.37 inches. Compression ratio: 7.00:1. Brake horsepower: 152 at 3600 R.P.M. Carburetor: Holley two-barrel.

1949 Lincoln, Cosmopolitan 4-dr Sport Sedan, V-8 (AA)

COSMOPOLITAN SERIES — SERIES 9EH — The Continental was gone. The new top-of-the-line Lincoln was the Cosmopolitan. While it resembled the standard series, most of the sheetmetal was different. A one-piece windshield and what appeared to be a huge horizontal gob of chrome on each front fender, were a couple of its main distinguishing features. Power windows and power seats were standard.

COSMOPOLITAN I.D. NUMBERS: Serial numbers ranged from 9EH1 to 73,563.

COSMOPOLITAN Model Number	Body/Style Number	Body Type & Seating	Factory Price	Shipping Weight	Production Total
9EH	72	2-dr Club Cpe-6P	3186	4194	7,685
9EH	73	4-dr Town Sed-6P	3238	3274	7,302
9EH	74	4-dr Sport Sed-6P	3238	4259	18,906
9EH	76	2-dr Conv-6P	3948	4419	1,230

PRODUCTION NOTE: The Town Sedan was the only 1949 Lincoln with fastback styling.

COSMOPOLITAN ENGINE
See 1949 Lincoln Series 9EL engine data.

CHASSIS FEATURES: Wheelbase: (Series 9EL) 121 inches; (Cosmopolitan) 125 inches. Overall length: (Series 9EL) 213 inches; (Cosmopolitan) 220.5 inches. Front tread: 58.5 inches. Rear tread: 60 inches. Tires: 8.20 x 15.

POWERTRAIN OPTIONS: A three-speed manual transmission was standard. 'Touch-O-Matic' overdrive was optional. Late in the model year, Hydra-Matic automatic transmission became optional.

CONVENIENCE OPTIONS: Hand brake signal. Radio. Vacuum antenna. Power windows. Heater.

Historical footnotes: Lincolns won two of the nine National Association for Stock Car Auto Racing (NASCAR) Grand National races held in 1949. The 1949 Lincoln's recessed headlights were originally planned to be hidden.

1950 LINCOLN

1950 Lincoln, 2-dr coupe, V-8 (AA)

LINCOLN SERIES — SERIES OEL — A new horizontal bar grille with vertical elements enhanced the appearance of the standard Lincoln. Its name was in the same location, on the front fender, as last year, but was larger. In mid-model year, the Lido Coupe was added to the line. It featured a vinyl top and custom interior.

LINCOLN I.D. NUMBERS: OEL Series serial numbers ranged from 50LP5,001L to 20,082L and 50LA5,001L to 72,521. Assembly plant codes: LA - Los Angeles; LP - Lincoln Plant; SL - St. Louis.

LINCOLN

Model Number	Body/Style Number	Body Type & Seating	Factory Price	Shipping Weight	Production Total
OEL	L-72	2-dr Club Cpe-6P	2529	4090	Note 1
OEL	L-72C	2-dr Lido Cpe-6P	2721	4145	Note 1
OEL	L-74	4-dr Spt Sed-6P	2576	4115	11,741

NOTE 1: Total production of body styles L-72 and L-72C was 5,748.

LINCOLN ENGINE
V-8: L-head. Cast iron block. Displacement: 336.7 cubic inches. Bore and stroke: 3.5 x 4.37 inches. Compression ratio: 7.00:1. Brake horsepower: 152 at 3600 R.P.M. Carburetor: Holley 885-FFC two-barrel.

COSMOPOLITAN SERIES — SERIES OEH — The Cosmopolitan received a new grille and dash for 1950. Its name was now written in chrome on the lower front fenders. The Cosmopolitan Capri had a padded leather roof and custom interior. It also had an additional horizontal gobs of chrome on the rear quarter panels parallel to the ones on the front fenders. The Capri was introduced to make up for Lincoln's lack of a two-door hardtop.

COSMOPOLITAN I.D. NUMBERS: Cosmopolitan serial numbers ranged from 50LP5,001L to 15,701H. See Lincoln I.D. numbers for assembly plant code.

1950 Lincoln, Cosmopolitan 4-dr sedan, V-8

COSMOPOLITAN

Model Number	Body/Style Number	Body Type & Seating	Factory Price	Shipping Weight	Production Total
OEH	H-72	2-dr Club Cpe-6P	3187	4375	1,315
OEH	H-72C	2-dr Capri Cpe-6P	3406	4385	509
OEH	H-74	4-dr Sport Sed-6P	3240	4410	8,332
OEH	H-76	2-dr Conv-6P	3950	4640	536

COSMOPOLITAN ENGINE
See 1950 Lincoln Series OEL engine data.

CHASSIS FEATURES: Wheelbase: (Series OEL) 121 inches; (Cosmopolitan) 125 inches. Overall length: (Series OEL) 213.8 inches; (Cosmopolitan) 212.2 inches. Front tread: 58.5 inches. Rear tread: 60 inches. Tires: (Series OEL) 8.00 x 15; (Cosmopolitan) 8.20 x 15.

POWERTRAIN OPTIONS: A three-speed manual transmission was standard. Overdrive and Hydra-Matic automatic transmission were extra-cost options.

CONVENIENCE OPTIONS: Heater. Power windows (standard in Cosmopolitan). Power antenna. Whitewall tires. Radio.

Historical footnotes: Lincolns won two of the 19 NASCAR Grand National races held in 1950.

1951 LINCOLN

1951 Lincoln, 4-dr sedan, V-8 (TVB)

LINCOLN SERIES — SERIES 1EL — The front of the 1951 Lincoln looked like a 1950 model that had gotten into a fight and lost. The grille bar only extended from the center section between the bumper guards. A forward slanting, vertical piece was added to the front fender side chrome. The word Lincoln was written behind it. The glamorous Lido coupe came with a canvas or vinyl roof, fender skirts, rocker panel molding and custom interior.

LINCOLN I.D. NUMBERS: Series 1EL serial numbers began with either 41LP5,001L or 51LA5,001L.

LINCOLN

Model Number	Body/Style Number	Body Type & Seating	Factory Price	Shipping Weight	Production Total
1EL	L-72B	2-dr Clb Cpe-6P	2505	4065	Note 1
1EL	L72C	2-dr Lido Cpe-6P	2702	4100	Note 1
1EL	L-74	4-dr Sport Sed-6P	2553	4130	12,279

NOTE 1: Total production for body styles L-72B and L-72C was 4,482 units.

LINCOLN ENGINE
V-8: L-head. Cast iron block. Displacement: 336.7 cubic inches. Bore and stroke: 3.5 x 4.38 inches. Compression ratio: 7.00:1. Brake horsepower: 154 at 3600 R.P.M. Carburetor: Holley 885-FFC two-barrel.

1951 Lincoln, Cosmopolitan 4-dr sedan, V-8

COSMOPOLITAN SERIES — SERIES 1EH — Except for the chrome rocker panels, the new Cosmopolitan looked pretty much like the standard Lincoln. The distinctive gobs of chrome on the front fenders of the previous two years were mercifully removed. Also, the Cosmopolitan name was placed on the upper front fenders. Next to the convertible, the snazziest model was the Capri coupe. It featured a canvas or vinyl roof, DeLuxe upholstery and (like all Cosmopolitans) fender skirts.

COSMOPOLITAN I.D. NUMBERS: Cosmopolitan serial numbers ranged from 51LP5,001H to 20,813H.

COSMOPOLITAN

Model Number	Body/Style Number	Body Type & Seating	Factory Price	Shipping Weight	Production Total
1EH	H-72B	2-dr Club Cpe-6P	3129	4340	1,476
1EH	H-72C	2-dr Capri Cpe-6P	3350	4360	1,251
1EH	H-74	4-dr Sport Sed-6P	3182	4415	12,229
1EH	H-76	2-dr Conv-6P	3891	4615	857

COSMOPOLITAN ENGINE
See 1951 Lincoln Series 1EL.

CHASSIS FEATURES: Wheelbase: (Series 1EL) 121 inches; (Cosmopolitan) 125 inches. Overall length: (Series 1EL) 214.8 inches; (Cosmopolitan) 222.5 inches. Front tread: 58.5 inches. Rear tread: 60 inches. Tires (Series 1EL) 8.00 x 15; (Cosmopolitan) 8.20 x 15.

POWERTRAIN OPTIONS: A three-speed manual transmission was standard. Overdrive and Hydra-Matic automatic transmission were optional.

CONVENIENCE OPTIONS: Heater. Power windows. Whitewall tires. Radio.

Historical footnotes: This season set an all-time output record for Lincoln at 390,439 cars . . . more than the company had ever sold since being acquired by Ford Motor Company in 1922. In November, 1951, the 124 inch wheelbase series was discontinued. This season's dealer introductions were staged for November 15, 1950. Production of models built to 1951 specifications was quartered at Detroit and Los Angeles assembly plants, although a new factory in Wayne, Michigan, was nearly completed this season and went into operations for production of 1952 Lincolns. Benson Ford was the general manager of the Lincoln-Mercury Division this year.

1952 LINCOLN

1952 Lincoln, Cosmopolitan 4-dr sedan, V-8 (AA)

COSMOPOLITAN SERIES — SERIES 2H — Lincoln was completely restyled for 1952. It had a lean, racy look. The bumper and grille were integrated. Instead of being recessed, the headlights seemed to stick out slightly from the fenders. Side trim consisted of a nearly full-length spear which divided a wide, slanted rear fender molding. The large vertical taillights were vaguely similar to last year's. A wraparound windshield and rear window added a 'modern' touch to the car's styling. New ball-joint suspension improved its handling and ride.

COSMOPOLITAN I.D. NUMBERS: Cosmopolitan serial numbers ranged from 52LP5,001 to 52WA29,217H. Assembly plant code: LA - Los Angeles; LP - Lincoln plant; SL - St. Louis; WA - Wayne, Michigan.

COSMOPOLITAN

Model Number	Body/Style Number	Body Type & Seating	Factory Price	Shipping Weight	Production Total
2H	60C	2-dr HT Spt Cpe-6P	3293	4155	4,545
2H	73A	4-dr Sedan-6P	3198	4125	Note 1

NOTE 1: Total production for Cosmopolitan and Capri four-door sedans was 15,854.

COSMOPOLITAN ENGINE
V-8: Overhead valves. Cast iron block. Displacement: 317.4 cubic inches. Bore and stroke: 3.8 x 3.5 inches. Compression ratio: 7.50:1. Brake horsepower: 160 at 3900 R.P.M. Carburetor: Holley two-barrel.

1952 Lincoln, Capri 2-dr hardtop sport coupe, V-8 (AA)

CAPRI SERIES — SERIES 2H — The Capri was now Lincoln's top-of-the-line model. The sedan featured fabric and leather upholstery. Like the Cosmopolitan that it resembled, its gas tank filler was hidden behind the rear license plate.

CAPRI I.D. NUMBERS: Capri serial numbers ranged from 52LA5,001H to 52LA7,761H; 52SL5,001H to 52SL5,072H; plus those found in the Cosmopolitan I.D. numbers section.

CAPRI

Model Number	Body/Style Number	Body Type & Seating	Factory Price	Shipping Weight	Production Total
2H	60A	2-dr HT Cpe-6P	3518	4235	5,681
2H	73B	4-dr Sedan-6P	3331	4140	Note 1
2H	76A	2-dr Conv-6P	3665	4350	1,191

NOTE 1: See Cosmopolitan note.

CAPRI ENGINE
See 1952 Lincoln Cosmopolitan Series engine data.

CHASSIS FEATURES: Wheelbase: 123 inches. Overall length: 214 inches. Front tread: 58.5 inches. Rear tread: 58.5 inches. Tires: 8.00 x 15.

POWERTRAIN OPTIONS: Hydra-Matic automatic transmission was standard. A 'maximum duty kit' was available for owners who wanted to race their Lincolns.

CONVENIENCE OPTIONS: Heater. Power front seat and power windows (both standard in convertible). Whitewall tires. Radio. Spotlight. Grille guard.

Historical footnotes: Lincolns came in first, second, third and fourth at the 1952 Pan American Road Race in Mexico. However, 1953 models were used.

1953 LINCOLN

COSMOPOLITAN SERIES — SERIES 8H — With the exception of an emblem inside a chrome 'V' on the upper section of the grille and the word Lincoln printed across the face of the hood, styling was basically the same as last year.

COSMOPOLITAN I.D. NUMBERS: Serial numbers in 1953 ranged from 53WA5,001H to 39,566H; 53LA5,001H to 10,995H and 53SL5,001H. See 1952 Cosmopolitan I.D. numbers for assembly plant codes.

COSMOPOLITAN

Model Number	Body/Style Number	Body Type & Seating	Factory Price	Shipping Weight	Production Total
8H	60C	2-dr HT Spt Cpe-6P	3322	4155	6,562
8H	73A	4-dr Sedan-6P	3226	4135	7,560

COSMOPOLITAN ENGINE
V-8: Overhead valves. Cast iron block. Displacement: 317.5 cubic inches. Bore and stroke: 3.8 x 3.5 inches. Compression ratio: 8.00:1. Brake horsepower: 205 at 4200 R.P.M. Five main bearings. Carburetor: Holley 2140 four-barrel.

1953 Lincoln, Capri 2-dr convertible, V-8

CAPRI SERIES — SERIES 8H — The most expensive series continued to be the Capri. Except for the chrome rocker panels, it was difficult to tell them from Cosmopolitans.

CAPRI I.D. NUMBERS: See Cosmopolitan I.D. numbers.

CAPRI

Model Number	Body/Style Number	Body Type & Seating	Factory Price	Shipping Weight	Production Total
8H	60A	2-dr HT Cpe-6P	3549	4165	12,916
8H	73B	4-dr Sedan-6P	3453	4150	11,352
8H	76A	2-dr Conv-6P	3699	4310	2,372

CAPRI ENGINE
See 1953 Cosmopolitan Series engine data.

CHASSIS FEATURES: Wheelbase: 123 inches. Overall length: 214.1 inches. Front tread: 58.5 inches. Rear tread: 58.5 inches. Tires: 8.00 x 15; (Convertible) 8.20 x 15.

POWERTRAIN OPTIONS: Hydra-Matic automatic transmission was standard.

CONVENIENCE OPTIONS: Power brakes. Four-way power seat. Power steering. Electric windows. Tinted windows. Whitewall tires. Radio.

Historical footnotes: For the second year in a row, Lincolns captured the top four spots in the Pan American Road Race. A fire at General Motors' Livonia, Michigan transmission plant stopped production of the Hydra-Matic equipped Lincolns for 55 days. This reportedly caused Lincoln to lose 7,000 sales. Eighty-seven percent of 1953 Lincolns had power brakes and sixty-nine percent had power steering.

1954 LINCOLN

COSMOPOLITAN SERIES — Lincolns grew an inch in length and width this year. The Lincoln name was now written on the front fenders. The wide, slanted rear fender chrome piece was replaced by a rear fender stone shield. The straight, side molding was higher and longer than that used on the 1953s. The company emblem and 'V' were on the face of the hood and the top bumper/grille bar was straight.

COSMOPOLITAN I.D. NUMBERS: Serial numbers ranged from 54WA5,001H to 36,840H and 54LA5,001H to 9,891H. See 1952 Cosmopolitan I.D. numbers for assembly plant codes.

COSMOPOLITAN

Model Number	Body/Style Number	Body Type & Seating	Factory Price	Shipping Weight	Production Total
NA	60C	2-dr HT Spt Cpe-6P	3625	4155	2,994
NA	73A	4-dr Sedan-6P	3522	4135	4,447

COSMOPOLITAN ENGINE
V-8: Overhead valves. Cast iron block. Displacement: 317.5 cubic inches. Bore and stroke: 3.8 x 3.5 inches. Compression ratio: 8.0:1. Brake horsepower: 205 at 4200 R.P.M. Five main bearings. Carburetor: Holley 2140 four-barrel.

1954 Lincoln, Capri 2-dr convertible, V-8 (AA)

CAPRI SERIES — Except for the chrome rocker panels and roof trim, it was hard to tell a Capri from a Cosmopolitan without looking at the nameplate.

CAPRI I.D. NUMBERS: See Cosmopolitan I.D. numbers.

CAPRI Model Number	Body/Style Number	Body Type & Seating	Factory Price	Shipping Weight	Production Total
NA	60A	2-dr HT Cpe-6P	3869	4250	14,003
NA	73B	4-dr Sedan-6P	3711	4245	13,598
NA	76A	2-dr Conv-6P	4031	4310	1,951

CAPRI ENGINE
See 1954 Cosmopolitan Series engine data.

CHASSIS FEATURES: Wheelbase: 123 inches. Overall length: 215 inches. Tires: 8.00 x 15; (Convertible) 8.20 x 15.

POWERTRAIN OPTIONS: Hydra-Matic automatic transmission was standard.

CONVENIENCE OPTIONS: Power brakes. Power steering. Four-Way power seat. Tinted glass. Whitewall tires. Radio. Heater.

Historical footnotes: Lincolns took first and second place at the 1954 Pan American Road Race.

1955 LINCOLN

CUSTOM SERIES — The 1955 Lincoln was a refined version of the 1954 model. Removal of the lower vertical bars on the grille gave it a cleaner look. The headlight treatment seemed very Ford-like. The Lincoln name was (as in 1953) printed on the front of the hood. Although the full length side chrome spear remained, the rear fender stone shield was changed. The taillight design and hood ornament were also new. Custom two-door hardtops came with chrome rocker panels.

CUSTOM I.D. NUMBERS: Serial numbers ranged from 55WA5,001H to 28,595H and 55LA5,001H to 8,519H.

CUSTOM Model Number	Body/Style Number	Body Type & Seating	Factory Price	Shipping Weight	Production Total
NA	60C	2-dr HT Spt Cpe-6P	3666	4185	1,362
NA	73A	4-dr Sedan-6P	3563	4235	2,187

CUSTOM ENGINE
V-8: Overhead valves. Cast iron block. Displacement: 341 cubic inches. Bore and stroke: 3.93 x 3.5 inches. Compression ratio: 8.50:1. Brake horsepower: 225 at 4400 R.P.M. Carburetor: Holley four-barrel.

CAPRI SERIES — Its nameplate, chrome rocker panels and a different rear roof pillar trim, distinguished the exterior of the Capri from the lower-priced Custom. The convertible had leather upholstery.

CAPRI I.D. NUMBERS: See Custom I.D. numbers.

CAPRI Model Number	Body/Style Number	Body Type & Seating	Factory Price	Shipping Weight	Production Total
NA	60A	2-dr HT Cpe-6P	3910	4305	11,462
NA	73B	4-dr Sedan-6P	3752	4245	10,724
NA	76A	2-dr Conv-6P	4072	4415	1,487

CAPRI ENGINE
See 1955 Custom Series engine data.

CHASSIS FEATURES: Wheelbase: 123 inches. Overall length: 215.6 inches. Tires: 8.00 x 15; (Convertible and cars with air conditioning) 8.20 x 15.

1955 Lincoln, Capri 2-dr hardtop sport coupe, V-8

POWERTRAIN OPTIONS: Turbo-Drive automatic transmission was standard.

CONVENIENCE OPTIONS: Air conditioning. Power steering. Power brakes. Power windows. Tinted glass. Heater. Radio. Power seats. Whitewall tires.

Historical footnotes: Ninety-three percent of 1955 Lincolns had power steering; ninety-four percent power brakes; ninety-one percent power seats; eighty-two percent power windows; ninety-eight percent power radios; ninety-nine percent heater and eighty-nine percent tinted glass. This was the first year Lincoln used its own automatic transmission. It had been equipping cars with GM's Hydra-Matic. Also, on April 18, 1955, Lincoln became a separate division of the Ford Motor Company. Since October 1945 it had been part of the Lincoln-Mercury Division.

1956 LINCOLN

CAPRI SERIES — Lincoln was attractively restyled for 1956. It was based on the XL-500 and XM-800 dream cars. It had hooded headlights and a bumper-integrated, center horizontal bar grille with thinner horizontal bars above and below it. Taillight treatment was similar to last year. Bumper ports beneath the taillights served as exhaust exits. Full length, tire-level side molding was incorporated onto the standard fender skirts. All 1956 Lincolns came equipped with power steering, automatic transmission and dual exhaust.

CAPRI I.D. NUMBERS: Serial numbers ranged from 56WA-5,001L to 480,056 and 56LA5,001L to 122,88L. See 1952 Cosmopolitan I.D. numbers.

CAPRI Model Number	Body/Style Number	Body Type & Seating	Factory Price	Shipping Weight	Production Total
NA	60E	2-dr HT Spt Cpe-6P	4119	4305	4,355
NA	73A	4-dr Sedan-6P	4212	4315	4,436

CAPRI ENGINE
V-8: Overhead valves. Cast iron block. Displacment: 368 cubic inches. Bore and stroke: 4 x 3.65 inches. Compression ratio: 9.0:1. Brake horsepower: 285 at 4600 R.P.M. Carburetor: Lincoln four-barrel.

1956 Lincoln, Premiere 2-dr hardtop coupe, V-8

PREMIERE SERIES — It is easy to see why the Premiere hardtop was able to win an award from the Industrial Designers Institute for excellence in automotive design. Outside of rear fender medallions and fancier wheel covers, it was difficult to tell the Premiere from the less costly Capri. Like all Ford Motor Company products in 1956, the Premiere had a lot of safety features. Improved door latches, deep-dish steering wheel, heavily padded seat backs and door panels were standard. Power windows and four-way power front seat were standard.

PREMIERE I.D. NUMBERS: See Capri I.D. numbers.

PREMIERE Model Number	Body/Style Number	Body Type & Seating	Factory Price	Shipping Weight	Production Total
NA	60B	2-dr HT Cpe-6P	4601	4357	19,619
NA	73B	4-dr Sedan-6P	4601	4347	19,465
NA	76B	2-dr Conv-6P	4747	4452	2,447

PREMIERE ENGINE
See 1956 Capri Series engine data.

CHASSIS FEATURES: Wheelbase: 126 inches. Overall length: 223 inches. Overall width: 79.9 inches. Tires: 8.00 x 15; (Convertible and cars with air conditioning) 8.20 x 15.

POWERTRAIN OPTIONS: Turbo-Drive automatic transmission was standard.

CONVENIENCE OPTIONS: Air conditioning. Power brakes. Pushbutton lubrication. Power windows. Power Four-Way front seat. Automatic headlight dimmer. Heater. Radio. Whitewall tires.

Historical footnotes: Ninety-eight percent of 1956 Lincolns were equipped with power brakes; 85 percent power seats; 86 percent power windows; 94 percent radios; 99 percent heaters and 98 percent whitewall tires. In 1956, Lincoln switched from 6-volt to a 12-volt electrical system.

1956 Lincoln-Continental, Mark II 2-dr hardtop coupe, V-8

MARK II SERIES — The Continental returned this year with the introduction of the Mark II. It made its debut on October 6, 1955 at the Paris Auto Show. Long hood, short deck, restrained use of chrome and near perfect proportions; the Mark II showed the world just how beautiful a production American automobile can be. Like its Continental predecessors, it was an instant classic. Yet it was not an imitation of the original. The Mark II was unmistakenly modern in design. Being priced in the then lofty $10,000 range seemed to only accentuate how special this car was.

MARK II I.D. NUMBERS: Not available.

MARK II

Model Number	Body/Style Number	Body Type & Seating	Factory Price	Shipping Weight	Production Total
NA	60A	2-dr Spt Cpe-6P	9966	4825	2,550

MARK II ENGINE
V-8: Overhead valves. Cast iron block. Displacement: 368 cubic inches. Bore and stroke: 4 x 3.65 inches. Compression ratio: 10.00:1. Brake horsepower: 300 at 4800 R.P.M. Carburetor: Carter four-barrel.

CHASSIS FEATURES: Wheelbase: 126 inches. Overall length: 218.5 inches. Overall width: 77.5 inches. Tires: 8.00 x 15; (Cars with air conditioning) 8.20 x 15.

POWERTRAIN OPTIONS: Turbo-Drive automatic transmission was standard.

CONVENIENCE OPTIONS: The only option was air-conditioning. Power steering; power brakes; power seat; radio; whitewall tires and a heater were all standard equipment.

1957 LINCOLN

1957 Lincoln, Capri 2-dr hardtop sport coupe, V-8

CAPRI SERIES — Lincolns received a facelift this year that was stylistically equivalent to putting a beehive hairdo on the Mona Lisa. The main change included the addition of two more headlights (actually they functioned as auxiliary lights), wider parking and signal lights, full-length center body side chrome and exaggerated tailfin enclosed taillights.

CAPRI I.D. NUMBERS: Serial numbers ranged from 57WA5,001L to 46,232L. See 1952 Cosmopolitan I.D. numbers for assembly plant codes.

CAPRI

Model Number	Body/Style Number	Body Type & Seating	Factory Price	Shipping Weight	Production Total
NA	57A	4-dr Landau HT Sed	5294	4538	1,451
NA	58A	4-dr Sedan-6P	2794	4349	1,476
NA	60A	2-dr HT Cpe-6P	4649	4373	2,973

CAPRI ENGINE
V-8: Overhead valves. Cast iron block. Displacement: 368 cubic inches. Bore and stroke: 4 x 3.65 inches. Compression ratio: 10.00:1. Brake horsepower: 300 at 4800 R.P.M. Carburetor: Carter four-barrel.

1957 Lincoln, Premiere 4-dr Landau hardtop sedan, V-8 (AA)

PREMIERE SERIES — Except for the nameplate and star medallion on the front fenders, exterior differences between the Premiere and Capri were nil. Advertising promoted the 300 horsepower V-8 as a 'safety feature'. Power seats, power steering, electric windows and power brakes were standard.

PREMIERE I.D. NUMBERS: See Capri I.D. numbers.

PREMIERE

Model Number	Body/Style Number	Body Type & Seating	Factory Price	Shipping Weight	Production Total
NA	57B	4-dr Landau HT Sed	5294	4538	11,223
NA	58B	4-dr Sedan-6P	5294	4527	5,139
NA	60B	2-dr HT Cpe-6P	5149	4451	15,185
NA	76B	2-dr Conv-6P	5381	4676	3,676

PREMIERE ENGINE
See 1957 Capri Series engine data.

CHASSIS FEATURES: Wheelbase: 126 inches. Overall length: 224.6 inches. Front tread: 58.5 inches. Rear tread: 60 inches. Tires: 8.00 x 15; (Convertible and cars with air conditioning) 8.20 x 15.

POWERTRAIN OPTIONS: Turbo-Drive automatic transmission was standard. Directed-power differential was optional.

CONVENIENCE OPTIONS: Air conditioning. Tinted glass. Whitewall tires. Front license plate frame. Padded instrument panel. Seat belts. Spotlight. Power vent windows. Three-tone leather trim. Six-Way power seat. Auxiliary driving lights. Electric door locks. Automatic headlight dimmer. Town and Country radio. Power radio antenna. Pushbutton lubrication. Dual control heater. Padded sun visors.

Historical footnotes: Only 22 percent of 1957 Lincolns came equipped with air conditioning.

1957 Lincoln-Continental, Mark II 2-dr hardtop, V-8 (AA)

MARK II SERIES — This was the second and last year for the beautiful Mark II. Outside of a slightly lighter frame, it was identical to last year's model. A convertible was offered. Only two were built. Power steering; power brakes; carpeting; radio; heater; power seats; power windows and whitewall tires were standard.

MARK II I.D. NUMBERS: Not available.

MARK II

Model Number	Body/Style Number	Body Type & Seating	Factory Price	Shipping Weight	Production Total
NA	60A	2-dr HT Spt Cpe-6P	9695	4797	444
NA	76A	2-dr Conv-4P	10,000	NA	2

MARK II ENGINE
V-8: Overhead valves. Cast iron block. Displacement: 368 cubic inches. Bore and stroke: 4 x 3.65 inches. Compression ratio: 10.00:1. Brake horsepower: 300 at 4800 R.P.M. Carburetor: Carter four-barrel.

CHASSIS FEATURES: Wheelbase: 126 inches. Overall length: 218.5 inches. Overall width: 77.5 inches. Tires: 8.00 x 15; (Cars with air conditioning) 8.20 x 15.

POWERTRAIN OPTIONS: Turbo-Drive automatic transmission was standard.

CONVENIENCE OPTIONS: The only option was air conditioning.

1958 LINCOLN

CAPRI SERIES — The Capri was totally restyled for 1958. It had a unique roof design, slanting headlight pods, stylized front and rear bumpers and wraparound front and rear windows. The grille was mainly horizontal, with several vertical accent bars that seemed to make the car look wider than it already was. The side chrome spears were lower and not as long as those used on last year's model. Automatic transmission; power steering; power brakes; windshield washers; padded instrument panel and a V-8 engine were standard on all 1958 Lincolns.

CAPRI I.D. NUMBERS: Serial numbers ranged from H8Y-400,001 to 429,624. The first letter (H) stood for the 430 cubic inch V-8 with four-barrel carburetor. The first letter (J) stood for the same engine with three (3) two-barrel carburetors. The second digit (8) referred to the year (1958). The 'Y' referred to the Wixom, Michigan assembly plant. The fourth digit indicated the series and body styles as follows: 'A' - 1958-1958 Capri two-door hardtop; 1959 four-door sedan; 1959 four-door hardtop sedan. 'B' - 1958 Capri four-door hardtop; 1959 Premier four-door sedan; 1959 Premier four-door hardtop; 1959 Premiere two-door hardtop; 1959 Continentals. 'D' - 1959 Premier four-door hardtop. 'E' or 'F' - 1958 Continental two-door hardtop. 'K' - Capri four-door sedan. 'L' - 1958 Premier four-door sedan. 'M' - 1958 Continental four-door sedan. The fifth digit ('4') refers to the Lincoln Division. The last five digits are the production numbers.

CAPRI

Model Number	Body/Style Number	Body Type & Seating	Factory Price	Shipping Weight	Production Total
NA	53A	4-dr Sedan-6P	4951	4799	1,184
NA	57A	4-dr Landau HT Sed	4951	4810	3,084
NA	63A	2-dr HT Cpe-6P	4803	4735	2,591

CAPRI ENGINE
V-8: Overhead valves. Cast iron block. Displacement: 430 cubic inches. Bore and stroke: 4.29 x 3.7 inches. Compression ratio: 10.50:1. Brake horsepower: 375 at 4800 R.P.M. Carburetor: Holley 4150 four-barrel.

1958 Lincoln, Premier 4-dr Landau hardtop sedan, V-8

PREMIERE SERIES — A chrome rocker panel, a star at the forward tip of the side chrome spear and its distinct nameplate were the easiest ways to tell the Premier series from the lower priced Capri. Buyers could get either leather and fabric or all-fabric upholstery.

PREMIERE I.D. NUMBERS: See Capri I.D. numbers.

PREMIERE

Model Number	Body/Style Number	Body Type & Seating	Factory Price	Shipping Weight	Production Total
NA	53B	4-dr Sedan-6P	5505	4802	1,660
NA	57B	4-dr HT Sed-6P	5505	4798	5,572
NA	63B	2-dr HT Cpe-6P	5259	4734	3,043

PREMIERE ENGINE
See 1958 Capri engine data.

1958 Lincoln-Continental, Mark III 2-dr convertible, V-8

CONTINENTAL MARK III — The Mark II of 1956-1957 had as much in common with the new Mark III as a thoroughbred Kentucky Derby winner has with TV's 'Mr. Ed', the talking horse. A criss-cross pattern aluminum grille, full-length lower-body molding and a grid pattern rear panel were exclusive to the Mark III. The Coupe and four-door had an unusual rear window that could be lowered. The coupe's roof style was shared with the convertible. The Mark III had the same standard equipment as the Premieres and Capris.

CONTINENTAL I.D. NUMBERS: See Capri I.D. numbers.

CONTINENTAL

Model Number	Body/Style Number	Body Type & Seating	Factory Price	Shipping Weight	Production Total
NA	54A	4-dr Sedan-6P	6012	4888	1,283
NA	65A	2-dr HT Cpe-6P	5765	4802	2,328
NA	68A	2-dr Conv-6P	6223	4927	3,048
NA	75A	4-dr HT Sed-6P	6012	4884	4,891

CONTINENTAL ENGINE
See 1958 Capri engine data.

CHASSIS FEATURES: Wheelbase: 131 inches. Overall length: 229 inches. Tires: 9.00 x 14; (Optional on Mark III) 9.50 x 14.

POWERTRAIN OPTIONS: Turbo-Drive automatic transmission was standard. Directed power differential was optional. A 430 cubic inch V-8 with three (3) two-barrel carburetors and 400 horsepower at 4600 R.P.M. was available at extra cost.

CONVENIENCE OPTIONS: Special paint ($39.10). Air-conditioner and heater ($610.70). Power windows ($120.40). Power vent windows ($66). Power Six-Way seat over manual ($106.50). Six-Way power seat over Four-Way ($45.20). Whitewall tires, five, Rayon ($55.50); five Nylon whitewall tires ($85.40). Tinted glass ($48.40). Automatic headlight dimmer ($49.50). Translucent sun visors ($26.90). Power lubricator ($43). Leather interior, except standard in convertible, ($100). Seat belts ($23.70). Air suspension.

Historical footnotes: One of the least popular options in 1958 was air suspension. Only two percent of Lincolns came with it. Lincoln switched to unitized body construction this year. The chassis was eliminated. The suspension, driveline and engine units were fastened to the body structure.

1959 LINCOLN

CAPRI SERIES — The 1959 Capri was a couple inches shorter than last year's model, but at 227 inches, nobody confused it with a Rambler American. The canted headlights were integrated into the restyled grille. Side chrome was a bit gaudier. Brushed-aluminum trim covered the lower quarter panel and was connected to a chrome spear above the rear tires that continued almost to the front fender. The rear panel pattern was redesigned.

CAPRI I.D. NUMBERS: See 1958 Capri I.D. numbers.

CAPRI

Model Number	Body/Style Number	Body Type & Seating	Factory Price	Shipping Weight	Production Total
NA	53A	4-dr Sedan-6P	5090	5030	1,312
NA	57A	4-dr HT Sed-6P	5090	5000	4,417
NA	63A	2-dr HT Cpe-6P	4902	4925	2,200

CAPRI ENGINE
V-8. Overhead valves. Cast iron block. Displacement: 430 cubic inches. Bore and stroke: 4.29 x 3.7 inches. Compression ratio: 10.00:1. Brake horsepower: 350 at 4400 R.P.M. Carburetor: Carter AFB-2853S four-barrel.

1959 Lincoln, Premiere 2-dr hardtop coupe, V-8

PREMIERE SERIES — Once again, the best way to identify a Premiere was to look for its nameplate. On the outside, it looked the same as the lowest-priced Lincoln series. All 1959 Lincolns were equipped with automatic transmission; power brakes; power steering; dual exhausts; electric clock; windshield washer and remote-control outside mirror. In addition, Premieres came with power windows, rear license plate frame and Four-Way power front seat.

PREMIERE I.D. NUMBERS: See 1958 Capri I.D. numbers.

PREMIERE

Model Number	Body/Style Number	Body Type & Seating	Factory Price	Shipping Weight	Production Total
NA	53B	4-dr Sedan-6P	5594	5030	1,282
NA	57B	4-dr HT Sed-6P	5594	5015	4,606
NA	63B	2-dr HT Cpe-6P	5347	4920	1,963

PREMIERE ENGINE: See 1959 Capri Series engine data.

CONTINENTAL MARK IV — The Mark IV featured a criss-cross pattern grille, full-length lower body molding (but *no* side spear), four taillights and reverse slant rear window that could be lowered. Even the back window of the convertible was made of glass and was retractable. Mark IVs were equipped with Six-Way power seats; tinted glass; 'Travel-Tuner' radio with dual speakers; power vent windows and were available in three metallic paints exclusive to the series.

1959 Lincoln-Continental, Mark IV 4-dr Landau hardtop sed, V-8

CONTINENTAL MARK IV I.D. NUMBERS: See 1958 Capri I.D. numbers.

CONTINENTAL MARK IV

Model Number	Body/Style Number	Body Type & Seating	Factory Price	Shipping Weight	Production Total
NA	23A	Executive Limo-6P	10,230	5450	49
NA	23B	Formal Sed-6P	9208	5450	78
NA	54A	4-dr Sedan-6P	6845	5155	955
NA	65A	2-dr HT Cpe-6P	6598	5050	1,703
NA	68A	2-dr Conv-6P	7056	5175	2,195
NA	75A	4-dr HT Sed-6P	6845	5155	6,146

CONTINENTAL MARK IV ENGINE: See 1959 Capri Series engine data.

CHASSIS FEATURES: Wheelbase: 131 inches. Overall length: 227.1 inches. Tires: 9.50 x 14.

POWERTRAIN OPTIONS: Turbo-Drive automatic transmission was standard. A power differential was optional for $52.

CONVENIENCE OPTIONS: Travel Tuner radio ($144.20). FM tuner radio ($114). Leather upholstery ($85). Remote control trunk release ($40). Power lubricator ($40). Electronic headlight dimmer ($51). Power vents ($65). Six-Way power seats ($98). Tinted glass ($48). Power windows ($94.70). Air-conditioner with heater ($385).

Historical footnote: Almost all 1959 Lincolns (99.6 percent) had a radio and 40.8 percent came with an air-conditioner.

1960 LINCOLN

LINCOLN SERIES — The biggest changes for 1960 were, a full-length mid-body chrome spear; larger tailfins wrapped in chrome; new instrument panel; altered horizontal theme grille; more conventional style front bumper and Ford-like square roofline. The backup and taillights were rectangular. All 1960 Lincolns came with power brakes; power steering; heater and defroster; undercoating; whitewall tires; clock; radio; windshield washer; padded dash; center rear arm rest and dual exhaust.

LINCOLN I.D. NUMBERS: Lincoln serial numbers contained eleven digits. The first indicated model year, as follows: '0' – 1960; '1' – 1961 etc. The second indicated the assembly plant as follows: 'Y' – Wixom, Michigan; 'S' – Allen Park, Michigan. The third and fourth digits referred to the series and body style model numbers. The fifth indicated the type of engine as follows: 'A' – 460 cubic inch V-8 with four-barrel carb; 'G' – 462 cubic inch V-8 with four-barrel carb; 'S' – 400 cubic inch V-8 with two-barrel carb. The last six digits were the sequential vehicle production numbers.

LINCOLN

Model Number	Body/Style Number	Body Type & Seating	Factory Price	Shipping Weight	Production Total
NA	53A	4-dr Sedan-6P	5441	5016	1,093
NA	57A	4-dr HT Sed-6P	5441	5012	4,397
NA	63A	2-dr HT Cpe-6P	5253	4929	1,670

LINCOLN ENGINE
V-8: Overhead valves. Cast iron block. Displacement: 430 cubic inches. Bore and stroke: 4.29 x 3.7 inches. Compression ratio: 10.00:1. Brake horsepower: 315 at 4100 R.P.M. Carburetor: Carter ABD-2965S two-barrel.

PREMIERE SERIES — The Premiere looked virtually the same as the standard Lincoln, except for a small front fender medallion. All Premieres came with power windows, rear compartment reading lights and four-way power seats.

PREMIERE I.D. NUMBERS: See Lincoln I.D. numbers.

PREMIERE

Model Number	Body/Style Number	Body Type & Seating	Factory Price	Shipping Weight	Production Total
NA	53B	4-dr Sedan-6P	5945	5072	1,010
NA	57B	4-dr HT Sed-6P	5945	5068	4,200
NA	63B	2-dr HT Cpe-6P	5696	4987	1,364

PREMIERE ENGINE
See 1960 Lincoln Series engine data.

CONTINENTAL MARK V — A criss-cross "dot-in-a-square" pattern grille; circular tail and backup lights; lower front fender chrome bars and a reverse slanted, retractable rear window, set the top-of-the-line Mark V apart from the other series. Standard features included a Six-Way power seat, tinted glass and power vent windows.

CONTINENTAL MARK V.I.D. NUMBERS: See Lincoln I.D. numbers.

CONTINENTAL MARK V

Model Number	Body/Style Number	Body Type & Seating	Factory Price	Shipping Weight	Production Total
NA	23A	4-dr Executive-6P	10,230	5495	34
NA	23B	4-dr Town Car-6P	9207	5286	136
NA	54A	4-dr Sedan-6P	6854	5157	807
NA	65A	2-dr HT Cpe-6P	6598	5070	1,461
NA	68A	2-dr Conv-6P	7056	5176	2,044
NA	75A	4-dr HT Sed-6P	6845	5153	6,604

1960 Lincoln-Continental, Mark V 2-dr convertible, V-8

CONTINENTAL MARK V ENGINE
See 1960 Lincoln Series engine data.

CHASSIS FEATURES: Wheelbase: 131 inches. Overall length: 227.2 inches. Overall width: 80.3 inches. Tires: 9.50 x 14.

POWERTRAIN OPTIONS: Turbo-Drive automatic transmission was standard. A directed power differential was a $57.50 option.

1960 Lincoln-Continental, Mark V Executive 4-dr limousine, V-8

CONVENIENCE OPTIONS: Air-conditioner with heater ($475.20). Electronic headlight dimmer ($56). Electric door locks, on two-doors ($39.45); on four-doors ($63.65). Power lubricator ($46.90). FM radio attachment ($129). Four-Way power seat ($87). Six-Way power seat, over a manual seat ($118.95). Six-Way power seat over a Four-Way power seat ($49.50). Power vent windows ($75.60). Remote control trunk lid ($45.60). Chrome curb guard ($26.90).

Historical footnotes: Almost half of all 1960 Lincolns (49 percent) came equipped with an air-conditioner. Lincolns had a new Hotchkiss rear suspension.

1961 LINCOLN

1961 Lincoln-Continental, 4-dr sedan, V-8

CONTINENTAL SERIES — Once again, Lincoln proved it could produce a strikingly beautiful car. The 1961 Continental became one of the most influential automobile designs of the 1960s. The four headlights were imbedded in a criss-cross pattern grille (with emphasis on the horizontal bars). The front and rear wraparound bumpers blended well into the overall design. Side trim was limited to full-length upper body molding and a chrome rocker panel. The rear doors opened to the center. All 1961 Continentals had automatic transmission; a radio with rear speaker; heater; power brakes; power steering; power windows; walnut applique or padded instrument panel; carpeting and power door locks.

CONTINENTAL I.D. NUMBERS: See 1960 Lincoln I.D. numbers.

CONTINENTAL

Model Number	Body/Style Number	Body Type & Seating	Factory Price	Shipping Weight	Production Total
NA	53A	4-dr Sedan-6P	6067	4927	22,303
NA	74A	4-dr Conv-6P	6713	5215	2,857

PRODUCTION NOTE: Four Lincoln-Continental four-door hardtops may have been built.

CONTINENTAL ENGINE
V-8. Overhead valves. Cast iron block. Displacement: 430 cubic inches. Bore and stroke: 4.29 x 3.7 inches. Compression ratio: 10.00:1. Brake horsepower: 300 at 4100 R.P.M. Carburetor: Carter ABD two-barrel.

CHASSIS FEATURES: Wheelbase: 123 inches. Overall length: 212.4 inches. Tires: (Sedan) 9.00 x 14; (Convertible) 9.50 x 14.

POWERTRAIN OPTIONS: Turbo-Drive automatic transmission was standard. A directed power differential was optional for $57.50.

CONVENIENCE OPTIONS: Air-conditioner with heater ($504.60). Six-Way power seat ($118.95). Speed control ($96.80). Special interior trim ($100). Tinted glass ($53.65).

Historical footnotes: Sixty-five percent of 1961 Continentals were equipped with an air-conditioner. Every new Continental underwent a 12-mile road test before it left the factory. The Industrial Design Institute awarded the designers of the 1961 Lincoln-Continental a bronze medal. Few other automobiles have ever been so honored.

1962 LINCOLN

1962 Lincoln-Continental, 4-dr convertible phaeton, V-8

CONTINENTAL SERIES — Removal of the front bumper guards, the use of a new type of individual headlight trim, a narrower center grille bar and a semi-honeycomb style grille treatment (repeated on the rear panel) were the main changes for 1962. The new Continentals were also slightly lower, longer and narrower than the 1961 models. Broadcloth upholstery was standard in the sedan, all-vinyl in the convertible. Like last year's model, the convertible top retracted into the trunk. All Continentals had power brakes; automatic transmission; power steering; power windows; a radio with a rear speaker; carpeting; electric clock; power door locks; walnut applique or padded instrument panel; dual exhaust and folding center arm rests.

CONTINENTAL I.D. NUMBERS: See 1960 Lincoln I.D. numbers.

CONTINENTAL

Model Number	Body/Style Number	Body Type & Seating	Factory Price	Shipping Weight	Production Total
NA	53A	4-dr Sedan-6P	6074	4929	27,849
NA	74A	4-dr Conv-6P	6720	5213	3,212

CONTINENTAL ENGINE
V-8. Overhead valves. Cast iron block. Displacement: 430 cubic inches. Bore and stroke: 4.29 x 3.7 inches. Compression ratio: 10.00:1. Brake horsepower: 300 at 4100 R.P.M. Carburetor: Carter ABD two-barrel.

CHASSIS FEATURES: Wheelbase: 123 inches. Overall length: 213 inches. Tires: (Sedan) 9.00 x 14; (Convertible) 9.50 x 14.

POWERTRAIN OPTIONS: Turbo-Drive automatic transmission was standard. A directed power differential cost an extra $57.50.

CONVENIENCE OPTIONS: Air-conditioner and heater ($505.60). Automatic headlight dimmer ($45.60). Special interior trim ($100). Power vent windows ($75.60). Electric radio antenna ($32.60). Automatic trunk release ($53.40). Six-Way power seat ($118.95). Speed control ($96.80). Tinted glass ($53.65).

Historical footnotes: Almost three out of four 1962 Continentals were sold with air-conditioning, 96 percent came with power seats.

1963 LINCOLN

1963 Lincoln-Continental, 4-dr sedan, V-8

CONTINENTAL SERIES — A different rear panel design and new grille treatment were the main changes for 1963. The Continental was also about a third of an inch longer. The dash was changed slightly to give more knee room. All new Continentals came equipped with: automatic transmission; power brakes; power windows; heater; Six-Way power seat; power radio antenna; radio with rear speaker; dual exhausts; carpeting; electric clock; power steering; walnut applique or padded instrument panel; power vent windows; chrome curb guards; visor vanity mirror; remote control outside rear view mirror and power door locks.

CONTINENTAL I.D. NUMBERS: See 1960 Lincoln I.D. numbers.

CONTINENTAL

Model Number	Body/Style Number	Body Type & Seating	Factory Price	Shipping Weight	Production Total
NA	82	4-dr Sedan-6P	6270	4950	28,095
NA	86	4-dr Conv-6P	6916	5360	3,138

CONTINENTAL ENGINE
V-8. Overhead valves. Cast iron block. Displacement: 430 cubic inches. Bore and stroke: 4.29 x 3.7 inches. Compression ratio: 10.00:1. Brake horsepower: 320 at 4600 R.P.M. Carburetor: Carter AFB four-barrel.

CHASSIS FEATURES: Wheelbase: 123 inches. Overall length: 213.3 inches. Tires: (Sedan) 9.00 x 14; (Convertible) 9.50 x 14.

POWERTRAIN OPTIONS: Turbo-Drive automatic transmission was standard. A directed power differential could be ordered for $57.50.

CONVENIENCE OPTIONS: Air-conditioner and heater ($504.60). Tinted glass ($53.65). Power trunk lock ($53.40). Speed control ($96.80). Front seat belts ($16.80). Automatic headlight dimmer ($45.60). AM/FM pushbutton radio ($84.70). Special leather trim, except standard in convertible ($100).

Historical footnote: Seventy-three percent of all 1963 Continentals had air conditioners, 94.4 percent tinted glass and 20.6 percent a locking differential.

1964 LINCOLN

1964 Lincoln-Continental, 4-dr convertible phaeton, V-8

CONTINENTAL SERIES — The Continental grew a bit in 1964. Still, styling changes continued to be mild. Among them were, a new dash; full-length lower body molding; flat side glass; horizontal theme rear end trim and the replacement of the thick center grille bar, formerly connecting the headlights, by five vertical bars. All Continentals were equipped with automatic transmission; radio; power seats; power windows; power brakes and power steering.

CONTINENTAL I.D. NUMBERS: See 1960 Lincoln I.D. numbers.

CONTINENTAL

Model Number	Body/Style Number	Body Type & Seating	Factory Price	Shipping Weight	Production Total
NA	82	4-dr Sedan-6P	6292	5055	32,969
NA	86	4-dr Conv-6P	6938	5393	3,328

CONTINENTAL ENGINE
V-8: Overhead valves. Cast iron block. Displacement: 430 cubic inches. Bore and stroke: 4.29 x 3.7 inches. Compression ratio: 10.00:1. Brake horsepower: 320 at 4600 R.P.M. Carburetor: Carter C3VE-9510B four-barrel.

CHASSIS FEATURES: Wheelbase: 126 inches. Overall length: 216.3 inches. Width: 78.6 inches. Tires: 9.15 x 15.

POWERTRAIN OPTIONS: Turbo-Drive automatic transmission was standard. A directed power differential was optional.

CONVENIENCE OPTIONS: Air-conditioner and heater ($504.60). Speed control ($96.80). Tinted glass ($53.65). AM/FM pushbutton radio ($84.70). Power trunk lock ($53.40). Automatic headlight dimmer ($45.60). Moveable steering wheel.

Historical footnotes: One of the least popular Lincoln options in 1964 was the moveable steering wheel. Only seven percent of the cars came with this feature.

1965 LINCOLN

1965 Lincoln-Continental, 4-dr sedan, V-8

CONTINENTAL SERIES — The Continental received a relatively major facelift in 1965. Although basic styling remained the same, it had a flat horizontal grille theme and wraparound signal lights. The hood was also new. Among the many standard features were, automatic transmission; power steering; dual exhausts; visor vanity mirror; trip odometer; transistorized radio with rear speaker; undercoating; walnut applique or padded instrument panel; heater and defroster; Six-Way power seat; power radio antenna; remote control outside rear view mirror; power brakes; carpeting; windshield washer and power door locks.

CONTINENTAL I.D. NUMBERS: See 1960 Lincoln I.D. numbers.

CONTINENTAL

Model Number	Body/Style Number	Body Type & Seating	Factory Price	Shipping Weight	Production Total
NA	82	4-dr Sedan-6P	6292	5075	36,824
NA	86	4-dr Conv-6P	6798	5475	3,356

CONTINENTAL ENGINE
V-8: Overhead valves. Cast iron block. Displacement: 430 cubic inches. Bore and stroke: 4.29 x 3.7 inches. Compression ratio: 10.00:1. Brake horsepower: 320 at 4600 R.P.M. Carburetor: Carter C3VE-9510B four-barrel.

CHASSIS FEATURES: Wheelbase: 126 inches. Overall length: 216.3 inches. Width: 78.6 inches. Tires: 9.15 x 15.

POWERTRAIN OPTIONS: Turbo-Drive automatic transmission was standard. A directed power differential was a $57.50 option.

CONVENIENCE OPTIONS: Air-conditioner and heater ($504.50). Vinyl roof ($104.30). Individually adjustable front seats ($281.40). Power trunk lock ($53.40). Automatic headlight dimmer ($45.60). Emergency flasher ($12.80). AM/FM pushbutton radio ($84.70). Speed control ($96.80). Moveable steering wheel ($60.00). Special leather trim, except standard in convertible ($100). Tinted glass ($53.65). Door edge guards ($6.90). Closed crankcase emission reduction system ($5.30).

Historical footnotes: Only about one in four 1965 Continentals had a moveable steering wheel, but 90.6 percent were sold with air-conditioning.

1966 LINCOLN

CONTINENTAL SERIES — The Continental grew another four inches in 1966. The turn signals returned to the bumper, which now extended to the front tire openings. An emblem was on the front fender above the bumper. For the first time in five years, the taillights did not wraparound the rear fenders. Other changes included a return to curved side glass and a new instrument panel. Among the many standard features were; automatic transmission; power seats; power steering; front disc brakes; power windows; carpeting and windshield washer.

1966 Lincoln-Continental, 4-dr convertible phaeton, V-8

CONTINENTAL I.D. NUMBERS: See 1960 Lincoln I.D. numbers.

CONTINENTAL

Model Number	Body/Style Number	Body Type & Seating	Factory Price	Shipping Weight	Production Total
NA	82	4-dr Sedan-6P	5750	5085	35,809
NA	86	4-dr Conv-6P	6383	5480	3,180
NA	89	2-dr HT Cpe-6P	5485	4985	15,766

CONTINENTAL ENGINE
V-8. Overhead valves. Cast iron block. Displacement: 462 cubic inches. Bore and stroke: 4.38 x 3.830 inches. Compression ratio: 10.25:1. Brake horsepower: 340 at 4600 R.P.M. Carburetor: Carter C6VF-9510B four-barrel.

CHASSIS FEATURES: Wheelbase: 126 inches. Overall length: 220.9 inches. Width: 79.7 inches. Tires: 9.15 x 15.

POWERTRAIN OPTONS: Turbo-Drive automatic transmission was standard. Directed power differential and a 3.00:1 rear axle were optional.

CONVENIENCE OPTIONS: Air-conditioner and heater ($504.60). Vinyl roof ($104.30). Individually adjustable front seats ($281.40). Power trunk lock ($53.40). Automatic headlight dimmer ($45.60). AF/FM pushbutton radio ($84.70). Speed control ($96.80). Moveable steering wheel ($60). Tinted glass ($53.65).

Historical footnotes: Slightly more than one in three Continentals had a moveable steering wheel, 93.5 percent came with air-conditioning, 14.3 percent with a locking differential and 97.7 percent with tinted glass.

1967 LINCOLN

1967 Lincoln-Continental, 4-dr sedan, V-8

CONTINENTAL SERIES — Styling changes for 1967 were minor. Once again the center section of the grille was slightly protruding. The grille pattern featured horizontal bars accentuated by vertical ones. All new Continentals were equipped with; automatic transmissions; power steering; power brakes; power windows; visor vanity mirror; trip odometer; front and rear seat belts; Two-Way power seat; dual exhaust; carpeting; electric clock; remote control outside mirror; windshield washer and heater and defroster. The convertible also had leather trim, remote control trunk release and rear glass window.

CONTINENTAL I.D. NUMBERS: See 1960 Lincoln I.D. numbers.

CONTINENTAL

Model Number	Body/Style Number	Body Type & Seating	Factory Price	Shipping Weight	Production Total
NA	82	4-dr Sedan-6P	5795	5049	32,331
NA	86	4-dr Conv-6P	6449	5505	2,276
NA	89	2-dr HT Cpe-6P	5553	4940	11,060

CONTINENTAL ENGINE
V-8. Overhead valves. Cast iron block. Displacement: 462 cubic inches. Bore and stroke: 4.38 x 3.830 inches. Compression ratio: 10.25:1. Brake horsepower: 340 at 4600 R.P.M. Carburetor: Carter 4362 four-barrel.

CHASSIS FEATURES: Wheelbase: 126 inches. Overall length: 220.9 inches. Width: 79.7 inches. Tires: 9.15 x 15.

POWERTRAIN OPTIONS: Select Shift Turbo-Drive automatic transmission was standard. Directed power differential and a high torque axle were optional at extra cost.

1967 Lincoln-Continental, 4-dr Lehman-Peterson limousine, V-8

CONVENIENCE OPTIONS: Manual air-conditioner ($471.05). Air-conditioner with automatic temperature control ($523.55). Leather with vinyl trim, standard in convertible, ($124.30). Automatic headlight dimmer ($50.05). Emission control exhaust ($50). Speed actuated power door locks, in convertible and sedan ($68.50); in coupe, ($44.85). Six-Way power seat ($83.23). Six-Way power seat with passenger side recliner and power adjustable headrest ($181.68). Two-Way contour power seat, individually adjustable, with passenger side recliner ($290.58). Individually adjustable power contour seat, Six-Way for driver, Two-Way reclining for passenger ($373.86). Power vent windows ($71.64). AM radio with power antenna ($161.27). AM/FM signal seeking radio with power antenna ($244.54). AM radio and stereosonic tape system with power antenna ($244.54). Shoulder belts ($32). Embassy roof for coupe, ($131.60); for sedan ($136.85). Tilting steering wheel ($58.74). Remote control trunk release with warning light ($33.19). Tinted glass ($52.53). Speed control ($94.77).

Historical footnote: Most 1967 Continentals, 96.5 percent, were sold with an air-conditioning.

1968 LINCOLN

1968 Lincoln-Continental, 2-dr hardtop sport coupe, V-8

CONTINENTAL SERIES — A new hood accentuated the protruding center section of the 1968 Lincoln-Continental grille. Wraparound signal lights, similar to those on the 1965 models, and wraparound taillights returned. Otherwise, styling was little changed from the previous year. All 1968 Continentals were equipped with automatic transmission; power steering; seat belts; remote-control outside rear view mirror; windshield washer; power windows; dual exhaust; electric clock; padded instrument panel; four-way emergency flashers; power disc brakes and Two-Way power seat.

CONTINENTAL I.D. NUMBERS: See 1960 Lincoln I.D. numbers.

CONTINENTAL

Model Number	Body/Style Number	Body Type & Seating	Factory Price	Shipping Weight	Production Total
NA	81	2-dr HT Cpe-6P	5736	4883	9,415
NA	82	4-dr Sedan-6P	5970	4978	29,719

CONTINENTAL ENGINE
V-8. Overhead valves. Cast iron block. Displacement: 462 cubic inches. Bore and stroke: 4.38 x 3.830 inches. Compression ratio: 10.25:1. Brake horsepower: 340 at 4600 R.P.M. Carburetor: Carter C8VF-9510E four-barrel.

CHASSIS FEATURES: Wheelbase: 126 inches. Overall length: 221 inches. Tires: 9.15 x 15.

POWERTRAIN OPTIONS: Turbo-Drive automatic transmission was standard. A directed power differential and a high torque (3.00:1) axle were optional.

CONVENIENCE OPTIONS: Manual control air-conditioner ($503.90). Air-conditioner with automatic temperature control ($523.55). Remote control righthand outside mirror ($13.15). Automatic headlight dimmer ($50.05). Front seat shoulder belts ($32). Rear seat shoulder belts ($32). Tinted glass ($52.53). Rear window defogger ($42.50). Spare tire cover ($10.95). Manually adjustable head rests ($52.50). Power door locks in coupe ($47.45); in sedan ($68.50). Combination AM radio with stereo-sonic tape system, including two front and rear speakers and power antenna ($244.54). AM/FM signal-seeking radio with power antenna ($244.54). Vinyl covered roof ($136.85). Automatic ride leveler suspension ($97.15). Individually adjustable contour seats with Six-Way power for driver, Two-Way power reclining passenger side ($334.46). Six-Way power bench seat ($83.28). Six-Way power seat with reclining passenger side ($142.28). Tilting steering wheel ($66.95). Speed control $94.77). Power vent windows ($71.64). Stereo-sonic tape system ($130.10). Leather with vinyl trim ($137.26). Five, four-ply dual chamber whitewall tires ($196.80).

1969 LINCOLN

CONTINENTAL SERIES — The most noticeable changes made to the 1969 Lincoln were a revised grille pattern and the appearance of the Continental name printed above the grille. This was the last year the basic 1961 Continental body shell (and unit body construction) was used. Among the standard features were, automatic transmission; power steering; power brakes; self-adjusting front disc brakes; dual exhaust; vanity mirror; power windows and Two-Way power seat.

CONTINENTAL I.D. NUMBERS: See 1960 Lincoln I.D. numbers.

CONTINENTAL

Model Number	Body/Style Number	Body Type & Seating	Factory Price	Shipping Weight	Production Total
NA	81	2-dr HT Cpe-6P	5813	4916	9,032
NA	82	4-dr Sedan-6P	9046	5011	29,351

CONTINENTAL ENGINE
V-8: Overhead valves. Cast iron block. Displacement: 460 cubic inches. Bore and stroke: 4.36 x 3.85 inches. Compression ratio: 10.50:1. Brake horsepower: 365 at 4600 R.P.M. Carburetor: Autolite C8VF-9510J four-barrel.

1969 Lincoln-Continental, Mark III 2-dr coupe, V-8

CONTINENTAL MARK III SERIES — The big news at Lincoln was the introduction of the Mark III. It arrived in April of 1968, but was sold as a 1969 model. It bore absolutely no resemblance to the Mark III of 1958. Rather, it was a personal luxury car in the long-hood, short-deck tradition of the Mark II. The rear deck spare tire hump was also reminiscent of the first 'Mark'. However, basic styling was in tune with the standard Lincolns. Among the many standard features offered on the Mark III were the same items available on the Continental plus individually adjustable front seats; front and rear center folding arm rests; Flow-Thru ventilation system and rear lamp monitoring system.

CONTINENTAL MARK III I.D. NUMBERS: See 1960 Lincoln I.D. numbers.

CONTINENTAL MARK III

Model Number	Body/Style Number	Body Type & Seating	Factory Price	Shipping Weight	Production Total
NA	89	2-dr HT Cpe-5P	6741	4475	30,858

CONTINENTAL MARK III ENGINE
See 1969 Continental Series engine data.

CHASSIS FEATURES: Wheelbase: (Continental) 126 inches; (Mark III) 117.2 inches. Overall length: (Continental) 224 inches; (Mark III) 216 inches. Tires: (Continental) 9.15 x 15; (Mark III) 8.55 x 15.

POWERTRAIN OPTIONS: Select-Shift automatic transmission was standard. A directed power differential and high torque axle were optional.

CONVENIENCE OPTIONS: Manual air-conditioner ($503.70). Automatic temperature control air-conditioner ($523.30). Automatic headlight dimmer ($51.20). Rear window defogger with environment control in Continental ($42). Rear window defogger in Mark III ($26.30). Rear window defroster in Mark III ($85.30). Remote-control deck lid release ($40.70). Leather with vinyl interior ($137.80). Power door locks in two-doors ($47.30); in four-doors ($68.20). Six-Way power seat in Continental ($89.20). Six-Way power seat in Mark III ($179.70). Six-Way power seat with reclining passenger side seat, in Continental ($149.60); in Mark III ($238.70). Power vent windows in Continental (72.20). AM radio with power antenna ($161.40). AM/FM signal-seeking radio with power antenna in Continental ($244). AM radio/sterosonic tape system with power antenna, in Continental ($245.30); in Mark III ($258.40). AM/FM radio with power antenna, in Continental ($288.60); in Mark III ($326.60). Vinyl roof ($152.20). Individually adjustable seats, in Continental ($334.50). Speed control ($94.50). Sure-Track brake system in Mark III ($195.80). Tilting steering wheel ($72.20). Tinted glass ($56.40). Town Car interior in Continental ($249.20). Four-ply fiberglass belted 9.15 x 15 whitewall tires ($196.80).

Historical footnote: All but 0.3 percent of Mark IIIs had an air- conditioner. Just over one in three came with a moveable steering wheel. The vast majority of 1969 Continentals, 83.8 percent were sold with a vinyl roof.

1970 LINCOLN

1970 Lincoln-Continental, 4-dr sedan, V-8

CONTINENTAL SERIES — The Continental was restyled for 1970. A resemblance to past models was clearly evident. Hidden headlights, a protruding grille (with horizontal grille pieces) and wraparound front fenders gave it a sort of refined 'Batmobile' look. The Continental also had a new bumper-integrated taillight rear end treatment. The doors were wider, on both the hardtop and sedan. The sedan's rear door now opened in the conventional way. Standard equipment included, automatic transmission; fender skirts; custom pin stripe; padded windshield pillar; map and reading lights; cut-pile carpeting; electric clock; vanity mirror; simulated wood-grain dash panel applique; power windows; power steering; power front disc brakes; front and rear ash trays and cigarette lighters; Two-Way power bench seat and flashing side marker lights.

CONTINENTAL I.D. NUMBERS: See 1960 Lincoln I.D. numbers.

CONTINENTAL

Model Number	Body/Style Number	Body Type & Seating	Factory Price	Shipping Weight	Production Total
NA	81	2-dr HT Cpe-6P	5976	4669	3,073
NA	82	4-dr Sedan-6P	6211	4719	28,622

CONTINENTAL ENGINE
V-8: Overhead valves. Cast iron block. Displacement: 460 cubic inches. Bore and stroke: 4.36 x 3.85 inches. Compression ratio: 10.00:1. Brake horsepower: 365 at 4600 R.P.M. Carburetor: four-barrel.

1970 Lincoln-Continental, Mark III 2-dr coupe, V-8

CONTINENTAL MARK III SERIES — The biggest changes in the 1970 Mark III were hidden windshield wipers and new wheel covers. The signal and taillights were also altered. The parking lights now remained on when the headlights were being used. In addition to the items standard on the Continental, the Mark III also came equipped with: Sure-Track brake system; Cartier electric chronometer; walnut dash panel and steering wheel applique; head console with warning lights; spare tire cover; rear lamp monitor system and vinyl roof.

CONTINENTAL MARK III I.D. NUMBERS: Serial numbers start at 0( )89( )800,001. See 1960 Lincoln I.D. numbers for serial numbers code.

CONTINENTAL MARK III

Model Number	Body/Style Number	Body Type & Seating	Factory Price	Shipping Weight	Production Total
NA	89	2-dr HT Cpe-6P	7281	4675	21,432

CONTINENTAL MARK III ENGINE
See 1970 Continental engine data.

CHASSIS FEATURES: Wheelbase: (Continental) 127 inches; (Mark III) 117.2 inches. Overall length: (Continental) 224 inches; (Mark III) 216 inches. Tires: (Continental) 9.15 x 15; (Mark III) 225 x 15.

POWERTRAIN OPTIONS: Select-Shift automatic transmission was standard. Traction-Lok differential and higher ratio rear axle were optional.

CONVENIENCE OPTIONS: Manual air-conditioner ($503.70). Automatic temperature control air-conditioner ($523.20). Automatic headlight dimmer ($51.20). Cross-Country ride package in Continental ($17.10). Automatic ride control ($97.10). Sun roof in Mark III ($459.10). Leather with vinyl interior, in Mark III ($164); in Continental ($157.40). 'Moondust' paint ($131.20). Remote-control deck lid release in Mark III ($40.70). Power door locks in Mark III ($47.30). Six-Way power seat, in Continental ($89.20); in Mark III ($179.70). Six-Way power seat with reclining passenger side seat, in Continental ($149.60); in Mark III ($242.70). Twin Comfort Six-way/Two-way power

seats in Continental ($220.40). Twin Comfort Six-way/Two-way power seats with reclining passenger seat ($280.70). AM radio with power antenna ($161.40). AM/FM radio with power antenna ($301.70). AM radio with Stereosonic tape system and power antenna ($296.50).

Historical footnotes: All but four percent of 1970 Continentals came with an air-conditioner and tinted glass. Most Marks IIIs, 83.9 percent, had a tilting steering wheel. Many chassis parts on Lincoln's new body mounted on a frame construction, were interchangeable with full-size Mercurys and Fords. The 1970 Mark III was the first American car to come with steel-belted radial tires as standard equipment.

1971 LINCOLN

1971 Lincoln-Continental, 4-dr sedan, V-8

CONTINENTAL SERIES — Styling was little changed from 1970. Unlike last year, the grille's horizontal bars were not extended to the headlight covers. This toned down the front end a bit. Standard equipment included; automatic temperature control air-conditioning; automatic transmission; power front disc brakes; power steering; Two-Way power seat; fender skirts; cut-pile carpeting; carpeted luggage compartment; folding center arm rests in front and rear; remote-control outside mirror; vanity mirror; tinted glass; electric clock; trip odometer and power ventilation system.

CONTINENTAL I.D. NUMBERS: Serial numbers started with 1 ( ) ( ) ( ) ( )800,001. See 1960 Lincoln I.D. numbers for serial numbers code.

CONTINENTAL

Model Number	Body/Style Number	Body Type & Seating	Factory Price	Shipping Weight	Production Total
NA	81	2-dr HT Cpe-6P	7172	5032	8,205
NA	82	4-dr Sedan-6P	7419	5072	27,346

CONTINENTAL ENGINE
V-8. Overhead valves. Cast iron block. Displacement: 460 cubic inches. Bore and stroke: 4.36 x 3.85 inches. Compression ratio: 10.00:1. Brake horsepower: 365 at 4600 R.P.M. Carburetor: four-barrel.

1971 Lincoln-Continental, Mark III 2-dr coupe, V-8

CONTINENTAL MARK III SERIES — The Mark III was virtually unchanged for 1971. It had the same standard features as the Continental plus, high-back front seats with individual arm rests; Cartier chronometer; monitor system for brakes; spare tire cover and vinyl roof (five vinyl top covers were available).

CONTINENTAL MARK III I.D. NUMBERS: Serial numbers start at 1 ( )89( )800,001. See 1960 Lincoln I.D. numbers for serial numbers code.

CONTINENTAL MARK III

Model Number	Body/Style Number	Body Type & Seating	Factory Price	Shipping Weight	Production Total
NA	89	2-dr HT Cpe-5P	8421	5003	27,091

CONTINENTAL MARK III ENGINE: Same as Continental.

CHASSIS FEATURES: Wheelbase: (Continental) 127 inches; (Mark III) 117.2 inches. Overall length: (Continental) 225 inches; (Mark III) 216.1 inches. Tread width: (Continental) 64.3 inches; (Mark III) 62.3 inches. Tires: 225-15 steel belted Michelin.

POWER TRAIN OPTIONS: Select-Shift automatic transmission was standard. Traction-Lok differential and higher ratio rear axle were optional.

CONVENIENCE OPTIONS: Sure Track brake system, standard in Mark III; in Continental ($196.80). Front bumper guards, in Continental ($19.70). Rear window defogger ($31.50). Automatic headlight dimmer ($51.20). Automatic load adjuster, in Continental ($97.10). Power deck lid release, in Mark III ($46). Power door locks, in Mark III ($49.90). Lock release group, in Continental ($106.30). Moondust metallic paint ($131.20). Six-Way power seat, in Continental ($91.90); in Mark III, ($183.70). Six-Way power bench seat with recliner, in Continental ($152.50). Six-Way power seat with reclining passenger seat, in Mark III ($242.70) . Six-Way/Two-Way twin comfort power seat, in Continental ($223). Rear window defroster ($85.30). Six-Way/Two-Way twin comfort power seat, in Mark III ($246.60). Six-Way/Two-Way power twin comfort seat with passenger recliner, in Continental ($283.30). Cross-Country ride package ($17.10). Speed control ($94.50). AM signal-seeking radio $161.40). AM/FM stereo radio ($306.90). AM radio with stereo tape system ($301.70). Vinyl roof, in Continental ($156.10). Leather seat trim, in Continental ($173.20); in Mark III ($183.70). Tilting steering wheel ($72.20). Luxury wheel covers, in Continental ($59.10). Intermittent windshield wipers, in Continental ($26.30).

Historical footnotes: Only 12.3 percent of 1971 Continentals had a locking differential. Most Mark IIIs, 88 percent, came with a tilting steering wheel. Nineteen seventy-one was the golden anniversary of Lincoln.

1972 LINCOLN

CONTINENTAL SERIES — Full-length upper body moldings and a new criss-cross pattern grille, were the most noticeable styling changes for 1972. A hood ornament with the Lincoln emblem was also added. Standard equipment included, fender skirts; automatic temperature control air-conditioning; power front disc brakes; cut-pile carpeting; electric clock; carpeted luggage compartment; lefthand remote-control outside rear view mirror; front and rear arm rests; tinted glass; visor vanity mirror; AM radio with power antenna; Two-Way power seat; power ventilation; power windows and seat belts.

CONTINENTAL I.D. NUMBERS: Serial numbers started with 2( )( )( )A80,001. See 1960 Lincoln I.D. numbers for serial numbers code.

1972 Lincoln-Continental, 4-dr sedan, V-8

CONTINENTAL

Model Number	Body/Style Number	Body Type & Seating	Factory Price	Shipping Weight	Production Total
NA	81	2-dr HT Cpe-6P	7068	4906	10,408
NA	82	4-dr Sedan—6P	7302	4958	35,561

CONTINENTAL ENGINE
V-8: Overhead valves. Cast iron block. Displacement: 460 cubic inches. Bore and stroke: 4.36 x 3.85 inches. Compression ratio: 8.50:1. SAE net horsepower: 212 at 4400 R.P.M. Carburetor: four-barrel.

1972 Lincoln-Continental, Mark IV 2-dr coupe, V-8

CONTINENTAL MARK IV SERIES — The new Mark IV was four inches longer, about half an inch lower and a fraction of an inch wider than last year's Mark III. The radiator style grille was longer and used fewer vertical bars. It also bore a Mark IV emblem and a hood ornament on top. A new roof design featured an oblong opera window. Four rectangular bumper integrated taillights replaced the vertical wraparound ones. The distinctive spare-tire hump on the trunk remained. The Mark IV had more leg and shoulder room for rear seat passengers. In addition to the standard features offered on the Continental, the Mark IV was equipped with, Sure Track power brake system; spare tire cover; luxury wheel covers; Cartier electric clock; Six-Way power Twin Comfort lounge seat; vinyl roof and automatic seat back release.

CONTINENTAL MARK IV I.D. NUMBERS: Serial numbers start at 2( )89A800,001. See 1960 Lincoln I.D. numbers for serial numbers code.

CONTINENTAL MARK IV

Model Number	Body/Style Number	Body Type & Seating	Factory Price	Shipping Weight	Production Total
NA	89	2-dr HT Cpe-6P	8640	4792	48,591

CONTINENTAL MARK IV ENGINE
V-8: Overhead valves. Cast iron block. Displacement: 460 cubic inches. Bore and stroke: 4.36 x 3.85 inches. Compression ratio: 8.50:1. SAE net horsepower: 224 at 4400 R.P.M. Carburetor: four-barrel.

CHASSIS FEATURES: Wheelbase: (Continental) 127 inches; (Mark IV) 120.4 inches. Overall length: (Continental) 225 inches; (Mark IV) 220.1 inches. Tires: 225-15 Michelin radial.

POWER TRAIN OPTIONS: Select-Shift automatic transmission was standard. Traction-Lok differential and a higher ratio rear axle were optional.

CONVENIENCE OPTIONS: Sure Track brake system, on Continental ($191.83). Opera window, in Mark IV ($81.84). Front bumper guards ($19.19). Rear window defroster ($83.13). Automatic headlight dimmer ($49.88). Cornering lamps, in Mark IV ($35.81). Moondust metallic paint ($127.88). Power lock/release group, in Continental ($103.59). Lock convenience group, in Mark IV ($93.36). AM/FM stereo radio ($141.96). AM radio with stereo tape player ($136.84). Seats with leather trim, in Continental ($168.80); in Mark IV ($179.04). Leather trimmed seats with passenger recliner ($61.39 extra in Mark IV). Six-Way power bench seat with passenger recliner ($148.35 Continental). Six-Way power bench seat, in Continental ($89.52). Six-Way/Two-Way power Twin Comfort seats, in Continental ($217.40). Six-Way/Two-way power Twin Comfort seats with passenger recliner, in Continental ($276.23). Tilting steering wheel ($70.35). Town Car package for Continental four-door sedan ($446.67). Town Car package with leather trim for Continental four-door sedan ($635.47). Speed control ($92.08). Vinyl roof, on Continental ($152.19). Luxury wheel covers, on Continental ($57.56).

Historical footnotes: Most 1972 Continentals, 77.3 percent came with a tilting steering wheel.

1973 LINCOLN

1973 Lincoln-Continental, 4-dr sedan, V-8

CONTINENTAL SERIES — The Continental name was printed above the grille of the 1973 model. It hadn't been seen in this location for three years. An improved bumper with bumper guards was another change. Otherwise, the new Continental looked virtually the same as last year's. Among the standard features were: automatic transmission; power steering; white sidewall tires; DeLuxe wheel covers; dual custom strips; power windows; Two-Way power seat; AM radio with power antenna; cut-pile carpeting; seat belt warning buzzer; electric clock; folding center arm rests in front and rear; carpeted luggage compartment; tinted glass; remote control lefthand outside mirror; visor mounted vanity mirror; spare tire lock and cornering lights.

CONTINENTAL I.D. NUMBERS: Serial numbers started with 3 ( ) ( ) ( )A800,001. See 1960 Lincoln I.D. numbers for serial numbers code.

CONTINENTAL

Model Number	Body/Style Number	Body Type & Seating	Factory Price	Shipping Weight	Production Total
NA	81	2-dr HT Spt Cpe-6P	7230	5016	13,348
NA	82	4-dr Sedan-6P	7474	5049	45,288

CONTINENTAL ENGINE
V-8. Overhead valves. Cast iron block. Displacement: 460 cubic inches. Bore and stroke: 4.36 x 3.85 inches. Compression ratio: 8.00:1. SAE net horsepower: 219 at 4400 R.P.M. Carburetor: four-barrel.

CONTINENTAL MARK IV SERIES — The main changes to the new Mark IV were restyled, wraparound signal lights and an improved front bumper that covered up the lower part of the grille (this area had been exposed in 1972). The Mark IV featured the same standard items as the Continental, plus vinyl roof; opera windows; Twin Lounge seats with Six-Way power; cloth and vinyl upholstery; deep cut-pile carpeting; reading lights; carpeted spare tire cover; Cartier electric clock; inside hood latch release; Sure-Track brake system and customer monograms.

CONTINENTAL MARK IV I.D. NUMBERS: Serial numbers start at 3( )89A800,001. See 1960 Lincoln I.D. numbers for serial number code.

CONTINENTAL MARK IV

Model Number	Body/Style Number	Body Type & Seating	Factory Price	Shipping Weight	Production Total
NA	89	2-dr HT Spt Cpe-5P	8984	4908	69,437

1973 Lincoln-Continental, Mark IV 2-dr coupe, V-8

CONTINENTAL MARK IV ENGINE
V-8. Overhead valves. Cast iron block. Displacement: 460 cubic inches. Bore and stroke: 4.36 x 3.85 inches. Compression ratio: 8.00:1. SAE net horsepower: 208 at 4400 R.P.M. Carburetor: four-barrel.

CHASSIS FEATURES: Wheelbase: (Continental) 127 inches; (Mark IV) 120.4 inches. Overall length: (Continental) 229.5 inches; (Mark IV) 224 inches. Tires: 230R15 steel-belted radial.

POWERTRAIN OPTIONS: Select-Shift automatic transmission was standard Traction-Lok differential and a high ratio rear axle were optional.

CONVENIENCE OPTIONS: Town Car package including power vent windows, rear door quarter arm rest inserts, 'C' pillar lights and vinyl covered 'B' pillar, on four-door models; also, on both two and four-door models, including vinyl roof; seat back robe cords; seat back carpet inserts; personalized owner's initials; distinctive Town Car insignia; flocked headlining and sun visors and glove box vanity mirror: for two-door Continentals ($567); for four-door Continentals ($635). Sun roof ($611.28). Rear window defroster ($83.13). Remote control righthand mirror $26.67. Tilting steering wheel ($70.35). Automatic headlight dimmer ($49.88). Mark IV Silver Luxury group, including silver grained vinyl roof, red interior and silver 'Moondust' metallic paint, ($400). AM/FM stereo radio ($141.96). AM radio with stereo tape system ($136.84). Continental seats with leather trim ($168.80). Seats with leather trim and passenger recliner ($240.43). Six-Way/Two-Way Twin Comfort power seats, in Continental ($217.40). Six-Way/Two-Way Twin Comfort power seats with recliner, in Continental ($276.23). Six-Way power bench seat in Continental ($89.52). Six-Way power bench seat with recliner, in Continental ($148.35). Bodyside vinyl insert molding ($33.25). Interval windshield wipers ($25.57).

Historical footnotes: Ninety-three percent of 1973 Mark IVs came with a tilting steering wheel.

1974 LINCOLN

1974 Lincoln-Continental, 4-dr Town Car sedan, V-8

CONTINENTAL SERIES — The Continental received a minor, but attractive facelift this year. New wraparound signal lights, clean headlight doors and a vertical bar style grille seemed to have been influenced by the Mark IV. Standard features included power windows; power ventilation system; Six-Way power seat; automatic temperature control; AM radio with power antenna; Cartier electric clock; visor-mounted vanity mirror; tinted glass; automatic parking brake release; DeLuxe wheel covers; spare tire lock; remote control outside rear view mirror; power steering; fender skirts; power front disc brakes; cornering lights and carpeted luggage compartment.

CONTINENTAL I.D. NUMBERS: Serial numbers started with 4( )( )( )A800,001. See 1960 Lincoln I.D. numbers for serial numbers code.

CONTINENTAL

Model Number	Body/Style Number	Body Type & Seating	Factory Price	Shipping Weight	Production Total
NA	81	2-dr HT Spt Cpe-6P	8053	5366	7,318
NA	82	4-dr Sedan-6P	8238	5361	29,351

CONTINENTAL ENGINE
V-8: Overhead valves. Cast iron block. Displacement: 460 cubic inches. Bore and stroke: 4.36 x 3.85 inches. Compression ratio: 8.00:1. SAE net horsepower: 215 at 4000 R.P.M. Carburetor: four-barrel.

1974 Lincoln-Continental, Mark IV 2-dr coupe, V-8

CONTINENTAL MARK IV SERIES — The Mark IV's styling was virtually unchanged for 1974. However, new sound insulation and thicker carpeting helped give it a quieter ride. In addition to most of the standard features offered on Continentals, the Mark IV came equipped with Sure Track power brake system; carpeted spare tire cover; digital clock; rear bumper guard: luxury steering wheel; front and rear rub strips; vinyl roof; Six-Way Twin Comfort power seat and engine compartment light.

CONTINENTAL MARK IV I.D. NUMBERS: Serial numbers start at 4( )89A800,001. See 1960 Lincoln I.D. numbers for serial number code.

CONTINENTAL MARK IV

Model Number	Body/Style Number	Body Type & Seating	Factory Price	Shipping Weight	Production Total
NA	89	2-dr HT Spt Cpe-6P	10,194	5362	57,316

CONTINENTAL MARK IV ENGINE
V-8: Overhead valves. Cast iron block. Displacement: 460 cubic inches. Bore and stroke: 4.36 x 3.85 inches. Compression ratio: 8.00:1. SAE net horsepower 220 at 4000 R.P.M. Carburetor: four-barrel.

CHASSIS FEATURES: Wheelbase: (Continental) 127.2 inches; (Mark IV) 120.4 inches. Overall length: (Continental) 232.6 inches; (Mark IV) 228.4 inches. Tires: (Continental) 234R15 steel belted radial; (Mark IV) 230 x 15 steel belted radial.

POWERTRAIN OPTIONS: Select-Shift automatic transmission was standard. Traction-Lok differential and high ratio rear axle were optional.

CONVENIENCE OPTIONS: Anti-theft alarm system ($77). Sure-Track brake system, on Continental ($191.82). Quick Defrost defroster, in Mark IV ($306.70). Rear window defroster ($83.13). Dual exhaust, on Mark IV ($52). Righthand remote control outside rear view mirror ($26.67). Illuminated visor vanity mirror ($86.70). Body side moldings with vinyl insert ($33.25). Moondust metallic paint ($127.88). Diamond Fire metallic paint ($167). AM/FM multiplex radio ($141.96). AM/FM Multiplex radio with stereo tape system, in Continental ($26.33); in Mark IV ($127.37). Speed control ($92.08). Bench seat with passenger recliner, in Continental ($58.83). Six-Way Twin Comfort power seat, in Continental ($217.15). Six-Way Twin Comfort power seat with passenger recliner, in Continental ($278.48). Tilting steering wheel ($70.35). Sun roof ($611.28). Power sun roof with steel panel, in Mark IV ($611.28). Space Saver spare tire, for Mark IV ($77.40). Leather interior trim, in Mark IV ($179.04); in Continental ($168.80). Mark IV velour interior trim ($179.70). Vinyl roof, on Continental ($152.19). Luxury wheel covers, on Continental ($76). Power vent windows, in Continental four-door ($68). Interval windshield wipers ($25.57). Mark IV Silver Luxury package including silver grained vinyl roof, silver metallic paint, red leather or velour interior, or silver leather interior ($400). As above, with power glass sun roof ($777.40). Mark IV Gold Luxury package including gold grained vinyl roof, gold diamond fire metallic paint, tan leather interior with brown suede accents and tan components ($438 Mark IV). As above, with power glass sun roof ($770.40). Town Car package including vinyl roof; Six-Way power bench seat in vinyl with leather seating surfaces; full-width head restraints; front seat back robe cords; carpeted front seat backs; glove box vanity mirror; flocked headlining and sun visors; distinctive insignia; and personalized initials, in two-door Continentals ($567.47); in four-door Continentals ($635.47).

1975 LINCOLN

1975 Lincoln-Continental 2-dr Town coupe, V-8

CONTINENTAL SERIES — Several changes were made to the Continental for 1975. Among these were, a new roof design; new taillights; rotary valve steering gear; new brakes; Continental name written in chrome on the rear fenders; full-length lower body molding; a vertical bar grille containing several heavier accent bars and the extension of the grille below the upper front bumper. Some of the many standard Continental features included, power steering; power front discs brakes; solid-state ignition; automatic temperature control air-conditioning; tinted glass; power windows; AM/FM Multiplex stereo radio with power antenna; Cartier digital clock; vinyl roof; power door locks; power trunk lid release; tilting steering wheel; trip odometer; door edge guards; DeLuxe wheel covers; Six-Way cloth and vinyl power seat; cut-pile carpeting; door-closing assist straps; folding center arm rests; visor mounted vanity mirror; lefthand remote-control outside rear view mirror; spare tire cover and lock; personalized initials and license plate frames.

CONTINENTAL I.D. NUMBERS: Serial numbers started with 5( )( )( )A800,001. See 1960 Lincoln I.D. numbers for serial number code.

CONTINENTAL

Model Number	Body/Style Number	Body Type & Seating	Factory Price	Shipping Weight	Production Total
NA	81	2-dr HT Spt Cpe-6P	9214	5219	21,185
NA	82	4-dr Sedan-6P	9656	5229	33,513

CONTINENTAL ENGINE
V-8: Overhead valves. Cast iron block. Displacement: 460 cubic inches. Bore and stroke: 4.36 x 3.85 inches. Compression ratio: 8.00:1. SAE net horsepower: 215 at 4000 R.P.M. Carburetor: four-barrel.

1975 Lincoln-Continental, Mark IV 2-dr coupe, V-8

CONTINENTAL MARK IV SERIES — The 1975 Mark IV was a virtual clone of last year's model. However, there was a new Landau vinyl roof option. It featured a 'frenched' rear window and bright chrome band vaguely reminiscent of the 1955-1956 Ford Crown Victories. Standard features included most of those offered on the Continental plus, four-wheel disc brakes; wiper-mounted windshield washers; speed control; Six-Way power Twin Comfort lounge seats with cloth upholstery and engine compartment light.

CONTINENTAL MARK IV I.D. NUMBERS: Serial numbers start at 5Y89A800,001. See 1960 Lincoln I.D. numbers for serial number code.

CONTINENTAL MARK IV

Model Number	Body/Style Number	Body Type & Seating	Factory Price	Shipping Weight	Production Total
NA	89	2-dr HT Spt Cpe-6P	11,082	5145	47,145

CONTINENTAL MARK IV ENGINE
V-8: Overhead valves. Cast iron block. Displacement: 460 cubic inches. Bore and stroke: 4.36 x 3.85 inches. Compression ratio: 8.00:1. SAE net horsepower: 220 at 4000 R.P.M. Carburetor: four-barrel.

CHASSIS FEATURES: Wheelbase: (Continental) 127.2 inches; (Mark IV) 120.4 inches. Overall length: (Continental) 232.9 inches; (Mark IV) 228.1 inches. Tires: (Continental) 234R15 steel belted radial; (Mark IV) 230 x 15 steel belted radial.

POWERTRAIN OPTIONS: Select-Shift automatic transmission was standard. Traction-Lok differential and high ratio rear axle were optional.

CONVENIENCE OPTIONS: Town Car/Town Coupe package included power vent windows; coach lamps; exterior nameplate; Six-Way power seat with leather seating surfaces; special seat trim and door panels; deep cut-pile carpeting; glove box vanity mirror; luggage compartment carpeting and interior nameplate with gold accent, in Continental two-door ($567.47); in Continental four-door ($635.47). Mark IV Silver Luxury group ($400). Lipstick and White Mark IV luxury group ($400). Mark IV forged aluminum wheels ($287). AM/FM stereo radio with tape player ($139). Leather interior trim, in Continental ($168.80); in Mark IV ($179.04). Rear window defroster (83.13). Speed-control, on Continental ($92.08). Six-Way Twin Comfort seat with passenger recliner, in Mark IV ($61.39). Add $97.40 for above with power lumber back support. Moondust metallic paint ($141.96). Diamond fire metallic paint ($167). Right-hand remote control outside rear view mirror ($26.67). Power sun roof ($611.28). Mark IV power sun roof with glass panel ($777.40). Space Saver spare tire ($77.40). Anti-theft alarm system ($77).

LINCOLN
1976-1986

Descriptions of Lincoln in 1976 and beyond sound more like they belong in a fashion magazine than an automobile catalog. Bill Blass? Givenchy? Pucci and Cartier? Each of those internationally known apparel designers put his name and ideas on a Designer Series "Mark" Lincoln. Each displayed the designer's signature on opera windows, as well as a golden plate on the dash. Affluent customers must have liked the idea, just as ordinary folks wore jeans with designer names on the back pocket. Lincoln sales leaped upward this year.

1976 Continental sedan (L)

As the era began, just two basic models made up the Lincoln lineup; Continental and Mark IV, both powered by FoMoCo's 460 cid V-8. Mark was known not only for fashionable signatures, but for its Rolls-Royce style vertical-bar grille. Town Car and Town Coupe options added even greater luxury to Continentals.

1978 Versailles sedan (L)

Downsizing hit bodies and engines alike in 1977 as the 400 V-8 became standard, its big brother an option. Styling carried on traditional Lincoln cues, including hidden headlamps and simulated spare tire hump on the reduced Mark V coupe. Continentals adopted the Town Car name and added a Williamsburg special edition. Another breed of Lincoln arrived later in the year: the compact Versailles, ready to battle Cadillac's Seville on a Granada-size platform. Early Versailles models carried a standard 351 cid V-8, but dropped to a 302 for 1978. In honor of Ford's 75th anniversary, Mark V put out a Diamond Jubilee Edition.

Collector's Series versions of both Continental and Mark V joined up for 1979, as Versailles got a bit of restyling. The 400 cid V-8 was now the largest Lincoln powerplant, as the big 460 cid disappeared. Further downsizing came in 1980, as Continental and the new Mark VI managed to look more alike than before. Mark's headlamps remained hidden, while Continental's were now exposed. Base engine for both was now the 302 V-8, with 351 an option — and even that choice would be gone a year later. Marks came in both the customary Designer Series

and a similarly luxurious Signature Series. Versailles, never able to attract enough buyers (perhaps because of its modest origins and high price), dropped out of the lineup after 1980.

1979 Collectors Series sedan/ Continental Mark V coupe (JG)

An all-new Continental for 1982 weighed less than the old Versailles, and could even have a V-6 engine instead of the traditional Lincoln V-8. The former Continental design continued under the Town Car badge, as a four-door only. Mark VI still offered three Designer models and a Signature Series. Continental added a pair of Designer models of its own for 1983 and dropped that V-6 engine choice. Lincoln sales climbed appreciably for the model year.

Mark VII took a dramatically different form for 1984: an aero-styled wedge shape, far removed from its Mark forerunners. It was also shorter. A Mark VII LSC model added capable handling to traditional Lincoln luxuries. Both Continental and Mark could get a turbodiesel engine — though not too many customers seemed to want one, and it didn't last long.

A performance Lincoln? That was the Mark VII LSC, adding more such extras for 1985, including big Eagle GT blackwall tires. Anti-lock braking became optional on both Mark and Continental, and standard the next year. All three models offered Designer and Signature Series. Town Car continued as the "big" conventional Lincoln, reaching record sales levels in 1985 and again in 1986. Plenty of Lincoln buyers, it seemed, preferred the old familiar comforts.

Collectors have a huge selection of Designer Lincolns and other special editions to choose from — several for each model year. Mark coupes tend to attract more attention than the stodgier Continental/Town Car. Among recent models, the Mark VII LSC may not look like a Lincoln (or perform like one), but could be a good bet for the future. Versailles? An interesting idea that never caught on, which could become collectible on that basis alone. Like other Lincolns, it holds a lot of luxury and was especially well constructed. Lincolns of the late '80s continued to offer traditional styling and comfort. The front-drive Lincoln Continental ushered in the aero-look that give Ford a leg up with the Taurus and Sable.

1976 LINCOLN

Lincoln entered the mid-1970s with a pair of big luxury cars. Continental had received a significant facelift for 1975 and continued in that form this year. Mark IV also showed little change for 1976, but added a set of Designer models, signed by well-known names in the fashion world, to lure affluent buyers. Quite a few previously standard items were made optional for 1976, to keep base prices down.

1976 Continental Town Coupe (L)

CONTINENTAL — V-8 — Not much changed in the Continental luxury lineup, which had been substantially redesigned a year earlier, except for several new options and some revisions in standard equipment. A number of former standard items became optional. As before, two body styles were produced: a traditional four-door sedan and distinctive coupe. Posher Town Car and Town Coupe packages also were offered. Wheelbase was 127.2 inches. Continental had a wide six-section vertical-bar grille, with pattern repeated in twin side-by-side bumper slots below. A nameplate decorated the door of the left concealed headlamp. Horizontally-ribbed wraparound park/signal lights stood at fender tips, with separate cornering lamps. The bright Continental star stand-up hood ornament had a fold- down feature. A gold Continental star was laminated into the glass of the two-door's large fixed quarter windows. Front doors held a plaque for owner's initials. Rear fender skirts had bright moldings. The vertical two-pod taillamp assembly had a bright frame and integral side marker light and reflector, with full-width red lower back panel applique. Continental also had bright 'Lincoln Continental' script and 'Lincoln' block letters. Four body colors were added, and the distinctive Jade Green interior was now available in all models. Inside was a standard Cartier-signed digital clock, and the instrument panel had a simulated burled walnut applique. Town Car had special identification on the front fender; Town Coupe, on rear pillar. Both had a vinyl roof and coach lamps on the center pillar, with a new roof band. Interiors had leather seating surfaces and vinyl upholstery. Above the glovebox door was a gold-color Lincoln Town Coupe or Town Car nameplate. For 1976, both Town Coupe and Town Car could be ordered with a coach roof in 14 color choices. It was a thickly-padded vinyl half-roof, rolled and tucked at the rear and quarter windows. A wide molding extended over the roof at the center pillar. Town Car and Town Coupe interiors had loose-pillow seating. Leather and vinyl bench seats were standard in both, with Twin Comfort Lounge seats optional in velour or leather and vinyl. Continental had a separate body on perimeter frame and helical coil spring rear suspension with three-link, rubber- insulated cushioned pivots. Sole engine was the big 460 cu. in. (7.5-liter) V-8. New options included two radio packages: AM/FM stereo search, and the same thing with quadrasonic tape player (an industry first). Forged aluminum wheels were also optional. So was a four-note horn. Four-doors had a new optional opera window set.

1976 Continental MarK IV coupe (L)

MARK IV — V-8 — Lincoln's personal luxury coupe rode a 120.4 inch wheelbase and its "classic" styling changed little this year. New trims and options were available, and the standard equipment list was altered. Most noteworthy, though, was the addition of four Designer Series models, each named for a famous fashion designer: Bill Blass, Cartier, Hubert de Givenchy, and Emilio Pucci. Appearance was similar to 1975, including the expected concealed headlamps. Mark's traditional radiator-style, classic-look grille was rather narrow, made up of thin vertical bars, with a heavy upper header bar that extended down along the grille sides. Its resemblance to Rolls-Royce was no accident. Above the grille was a bright Continental star stand-up hood ornament. Combination wraparound parking and turn signal lamps were inset in leading edges of front fenders. The padded halo vinyl roof had color-keyed surround moldings, with vinyl-clad color-keyed rear window molding. Tiny oval opera windows to the rear of the quarter windows, in the wide rear pillar, held Continental star ornaments. Identification consisted of 'Continental' block letters and script, as well as 'Mark IV' block letters and plaque. Doors displayed the buyer's initials. Bright rocker panel moldings and extensions were included. The simulated spare tire had 'Continental' lettering around the upper perimeter. Horizontal wraparound taillamps stood just above the bumper. Inside were standard Twin Comfort Lounge seats in cloth and vinyl. Mark had the same 460 cu. in. (7.5-liter) V-8 as Continental, with standard 2.75:1 rear axle ratio. A Traction-Lok differential was available, as was a new engine block heater. A number of formerly standard items were made optional, including an AM/FM stereo radio, power door locks, power decklid release, tilt steering column, speed control, paint stripes, and appearance protection group. There were four new optional luxury group interiors: gold/cream, red/rose, light jade/dark jade, and jade/white. Other new colors included dark jade (with a Versailles option), gold, and dove grey. Standard body colors were: black, dove grey, dark red, dark blue metallic, light blue, dark jade metallic, dark brown metallic, cream, tan, and white. Thirteen additional colors were optional. Turning to the Designer Series, the Cartier had dove grey body paint and a Valino grain landau vinyl roof; red and white paint/tape stripes; dove grey bodyside molding; and Twin Comfort Lounge seats in either dove grey Versailles cloth or grey leather seating surfaces. Opera windows carried the golden Cartier signature. Bill Blass had a blue metallic body, cream Normande grain landau vinyl roof, cream and gold paint/tape stripes, and either cream or dark blue bodyside moldings. Twin Comfort seats were either blue majestic cloth or blue leather, with cream accent straps and buttons. The Givenchy Mark displayed aqua blue (turquoise) Diamond Fire body paint, with white Normande grain landau vinyl roof, black and white paint/tape stripes, and white or aqua blue bodyside moldings. Twin Comfort seats wore aqua blue velour cloth or aqua blue leather. Dark red Moondust (burgundy) body paint went on the Pucci, which also had a silver Normande grain landau vinyl roof, silver and lipstick red custom paint/tape stripes, and red or silver bodyside moldings. Twin Comfort seats carried dark red majestic cloth. All four Designer editions had forged aluminum wheels. All had the designer's signature on the opera window, and on a 22K gold plate on the instrument panel (which also carried the owner's name).

I.D. DATA: Lincoln's 11-symbol Vehicle Identification Number (VIN) is stamped on a metal tab fastened to the instrument panel, visible through the windshield. The first digit is a model year code ('6' 1976). The second letter indicates assembly plant: 'Y' Wixom, MI. Digits three and four are the body serial code, which corresponds to the Model Numbers shown in the tables below: '81' Continental 2-dr. HT coupe; '82' Continental 4-dr. HT sedan; '89' Mark IV 2-dr. HT coupe. The fifth symbol is an engine code: 'A' V8460 4Bbl. Finally, digits 6-11 make up the consecutive unit number, starting with 800,001. A Vehicle Certification Label on the left front door lock face panel or door pillar shows the manufacturer, month and year of manufacture, GVW, GAWR, certification statement, VIN, body code, color code, trim code, axle code, transmission code, and domestic (or foreign) special order code.

CONTINENTAL (V-8)

Model Number	Body/Style Number	Body Type & Seating	Factory Price	Shipping Weight	Production Total
81	60B	2-dr. HT Cpe-6P	9142	5035	24,663
82	53B	4-dr. Sedan-6P	9293	5083	43,983

MARK IV (V-8)

89	65D	2-dr. HT Cpe-6P	11060	5051	56,110

ENGINE DATA: BASE V-8: 90-degree, overhead valve V-8. Cast iron block and head. Displacement: 460 cu. in. (7.5 liters). Bore & stroke: 4.36 x 3.85 in. Compression ratio: 8.0:1. Brake horsepower: 202 at 3800 R.P.M. Torque: 352 lbs.-ft. at 1600 R.P.M. Five main bearings. Hydraulic valve lifters. Carburetor: 4Bbl. Motorcraft 4350 (9510).

CHASSIS DATA: Wheelbase: (Continental) 127.2 in.; (Mark IV) 120.4 in. Overall Length: (Cont.) 232.9 in.; (Mark IV) 228.1 in. Height: (Cont. 2-dr.) 55.3 in.; (Cont. 4-dr.) 55.5 in.; (Mark IV) 53.5 in. Width: (Cont.) 80.3 in.; (Mark IV) 79.8 in. Front Tread: (Cont.) 64.3 in.; (Mark IV) 63.1 in. Rear Tread: (Cont.) 64.3 in.; (Mark IV) 62.6 in. Standard Tires: KR78 x 15 SBR WSW.

TECHNICAL: Transmission: Select-Shift three-speed manual transmission (column shift) standard. Gear ratios: (1st) 2.46:1; (2nd) 1.46:1; (3rd) 1.00:1; (Rev) 2.18:1. Standard final drive ratio: 2.75:1. Steering: Recirculating ball, power-assisted. Suspension: Independent front coil springs w/lower trailing links and anti-sway bar; rigid rear axle w/lower trailing radius arms, upper oblique torque arms, coil springs, and transverse linkage (anti-sway) bar. Brakes: Front disc, rear drum. Ignition: Electronic. Body construction: Separate body on perimeter-type (ladder) frame. Fuel tank: (Continental) 24.2 gal.; (Mark IV) 26.5 gal.

DRIVETRAIN OPTIONS: Differential: Higher axle ratio: Cont. ($33). Higher axle ratio w/dual exhausts: Mark ($87). Traction-Lok differential ($61). Brakes & Steering: Sure track brakes ($263). Four-wheel disc brakes: Cont. ($172). Other: Engine block heater ($19). Extended-range fuel tank: Cont. ($100). Trailer towing pkg. III: Mark ($127).

CONVENIENCE/APPEARANCE OPTIONS: Option Packages: Town Car option: Cont. ($731). Town Coupe option: Cont. ($731). Versailles option: Mark ($1033). Mark IV Designer series (Cartier, Blass or Pucci): leather ($1500); Versailles cloth ($2000). Mark IV Givenchy Designer series: leather or velour ($1500). Mark IV luxury group: gold-cream, red rose, dark/light jade, jade-white, saddle- white, lipstick-white, or blue diamond paint ($477-$552). Power lock convenience group ($87-$113). Appearance protection group ($53-$61). Headlamp convenience group ($101). Comfort/Convenience: Rear defroster, electric ($81). Quick- defroster: Mark ($360). Speed control ($117). Power vent windows ($80). Tilt steering wheel ($69). Fuel economy light ($27). Intermittent wipers ($28). Anti-theft alarm ($115). Security lock group ($11-$17). Lighting, Horn and Mirrors: Coach lamps: Cont. ($60). Four- note horn ($17). Right remote mirror ($31). Lighted visor vanity mirrors ($100). Entertainment: AM/FM stereo radio ($148); w/quadrasonic 8- track tape player ($387). AM/FM stereo radio w/tape player: Cont. ($288). Search-tune AM/FM stereo radio ($300). Exterior: Sunroof ($701). Moonroof ($885). Vinyl roof: Cont. ($168). Landau vinyl roof ($113-$512). Coach vinyl roof: Cont. Twn Car/Cpe ($333). Opera windows: Cont. ($84). Moondust paint ($147). Diamond fire paint ($193). Custom paint stripes ($29). Narrow vinyl-insert moldings ($41). Premium bodyside moldings ($113-$143). Interior: Leather interior: Cont. ($220); Mark ($235 credit). Velour seats: Cont. Twn Car/Cpe ($187 credit). Bench seat w/passenger recliner: Cont. ($76). Twin comfort seats: Cont. ($259); w/passenger recliner ($335). Power lumbar seat: Mark ($93). Passenger recliner seat: Mark ($76). Trunk trim option: Cont. ($61). Wheels and Tires: Luxury wheel covers: Cont. ($83). Forged aluminum wheels ($300). LR78 x 15 SBR WSW ($44). Space saver spare: Mark ($96).

HISTORY: Introduced: October 3, 1975. Model year production: 124,756. Calendar year production: 124,880. Calendar year sales by U.S. dealers: 122,003. Model year sales by U.S. dealers: 122,317.

Historical Footnotes: Sales rose by 43 percent for both Lincoln models in the 1976 model year. That made Continental the industry's most successful car (according to Lincoln-Mercury). Production of the new Versailles was scheduled to begin in April 1977, targeted to compete with Cadillac's Seville.

1977 LINCOLN

In the first wave of powerplant downsizing, the restyled Mark lost its big 460 cu. in. standard V-8 and switched to a modest 400 cu. in. version. Continental soon did likewise, keeping the big V-8 was an option. A whole new model arrived later in the season: the Versailles, based on the Ford Granada/Mercury Monarch platform but far most costly, ready to compete with Cadillac's Seville. Standard Continental/Mark colors were: black, dove grey, midnight blue, dark jade metallic, cream, cordovan metallic, light cordovan, and white. Optional: dark red, ice blue, ember, or cinnamon gold Moondust; and silver, black, yellow gold, light jade, or (Mark V only) rose Diamond Fire. Versailles introduced clearcoat paint to domestic cars.

1977 Versailles sedan (JG)

VERSAILLES — V-8 — Lincoln hardly wanted to be left behind when Cadillac's new Seville was attracting plenty of customers. Versailles was its response, introduced very late in the model year (not until spring) as a 1977.5 model. The idea was to combine traditional Lincoln styling with a smaller, more efficient chassis. That was accomplished by turning to the compact Granada/Monarch platform, adding a number of luxury Lincoln touches and vastly improved quality control. Versailles had a radiator-style vertical-bar grille not unlike Continental's (with small emblem in the center of the upper header bar); quad rectangular (exposed) headlamps above clear quad parking/signal lamps; a decklid lid similar in shape to Mark V (with simulated spare tire bulge); and fully padded vinyl roof with "frenched" rear window. Clear wraparound and amber side marker lenses on front fenders matched the height of the headlamp/parking lamp housing and were enclosed by the same bright molding. A stand-up hood ornament featured the Continental star. Full-length high- lustre bodyside moldings had color-keyed vinyl inserts. On the center pillars were Continental-style coach lamps; up top, a padded vinyl roof with Valino pattern (six color choices). At the rear were simple wraparound horizontal taillamps. Forged aluminum wheels were uniquely styled. Versailles came in three metallic colors (cordovan, cinnamon gold and light silver), plus five non-metallic (white, midnight blue, wedgewood blue, light chamois, and midnight cordovan). A lower body two-tone option came in four colors: medium silver metallic, midnight blue, midnight cordovan, or cinnamon gold. Inside were standard flight bench seats, leather-covered armrests, a hand-wrapped leather instrument panel crash pad, and woodgrain cluster and trim panel appliques. Standard equipment included a collapsible spare tire, dual lighted vanity mirrors, digital clock from Cartier, AM/FM stereo search radio, and four-way power seat. A relatively small option list included an illuminated outside thermometer, tilt steering wheel, power decklid release, remote right-hand mirror, whitewalls, power door locks, speed control, forged aluminum wheels, leather/vinyl trim, visor-mounted garage door opener, glass moonroof, CB radio, and illuminated entry. Under the hood (at first) was a 351 cu. in. (5.8-liter) two-barrel V-8 with DuraSpark ignition and SelectShift automatic, hooked to standard 2.50:1 rear axle ratio. California versions carried a 302 cu. in. V-8, which would soon become standard everywhere. Versailles featured unibody construction and a lightweight aluminum hood. Front suspension consisted of helical coil springs (spring over upper arm) with ball joints and drag strut. The Hotchkiss rear had semi-elliptic leaf springs. Four-wheel power disc brakes were standard. Engineering features aimed at refinement and smooth, quiet ride. They included matched, balanced driveline parts, low-friction lower ball joints, double-isolated shocks, reinforced chassis areas, and plenty of insulation. Balanced forged aluminum wheels wore Michelin-X radials. Quality control at the plant was strengthened to the point of dynamometer testing of the engine/transmission, a rigorous water spray test to pinpoint body leaks, and a simulated road test. Bodies received the first clearcoat paint on a regular production car.

CONTINENTAL — V-8 — Model lineup of the big Continental was the same as 1976, including the posh Town Coupe and Town Car options. The restyled front end retained the "classic" vertical chrome- plated grille, but in a narrower form similar to Mark V, along with concealed headlamps and integral parking/turn signal lamps in front fender extensions. Otherwise, appearance was similar to 1976. The strong vertical theme was enhanced by crisp lines of the hood, front fenders, and parking lamps. Continentals had black bumper guard pads and rub strips, a bright stand-up hood ornament, cornering lamps, bright rocker moldings with rear quarter extension, bright full-length fender peak moldings, and rear fender skirts. Premium bodyside moldings had a new vinyl insert grain. Rear quarter windows on two-doors had a Continental star laminated into the glass, Rear ends displayed a full-width red reflective lower back panel applique, vertical two-pod taillamp assembly, and hinged Continental star on the decklid. Five body colors were new. Inside were new head restraints and two new interior colors, as well as a new high-gloss simulated walnut grain on instrument panel, steering wheel, and other components. New options included illuminated entry, fixed-glass moon roof, and CB radio. Base engine announced at first was the big old 460 cu. in. (7.5-liter) V-8, but a 400 cu. in. (6.6-liter) two-barrel V-8 engine with SelectShift automatic later became standard, the 460 four-barrel optional. New DuraSpark ignition gave higher spark plug voltage at startup and low idle speeds, which allowed the wider spark gap needed for burning modern (lean) mixtures. Town Car and Town Coupe added a new Valino grain full vinyl roof and center pillar; coach lamps; and 'Town Coupe' script on rear pillar (or 'Town Car' on front fender). Both had

1977 Continental Town Car (L)

leather seating surfaces, with "loose pillow" design. They also had power vent windows and a six-way power seat. A new special edition also was announced: the Town Car Williamsburg series, in silver or cordovan. It combined two different shades of the same color to give a longer and lower appearance. The silver model had new medium grey metallic paint on bodysides, combined with silver diamond fire on hood, roof and rear deck. The cordovan model had new midnight cordovan bodyside paint, with cordovan metallic hood, roof and rear deck. The silver Williamsburg model also had a silver Valino grain full vinyl roof, dual silver paint stripes, and dove gray natural-grain leather-and-vinyl or media velour upholstery. Cordovan versions carried a cordovan Valino grain vinyl roof, cordovan paint stripes, and cordovan leather-and-vinyl or media velour upholstery. Both Williamsburgs had six-way power Twin Comfort Lounge seats, reclining passenger seat, power vent windows, personalized instrument panel nameplate, lighted visor vanity mirror, carpeted luggage compartment, and dual-beam dome/map lamp.

1977 Continental Mark V coupe (L)

MARK V — V-8 — A new Mark version arrived for 1977, similar to its predecessor but weighing more than 300 pounds less. Downsized, that is, but hardly drastically. Styling was described as "evolutionary," carrying on such familiar details as concealed headlamps, simulated-tire decklid hump, and little horizontal oval porthole windows on the sail panels (with Continental star laminated in the glass). But this version had all-new sheetmetal, grille, bumpers, functional triple fender louvers at the cowl, and vertical taillamps. The overall look was more angular than before, described as "sculptured styling." As before, Mark V had a "classic" (radiator-style) chrome-plated vertical-bar grille, with heavier upper header bar. Front bumper guards were farther apart. Vertical taillamps had thin horizontal trim strips. Mark also had a bright star stand-up hood ornament, blade-like vertical parking lamps, black bumper guard pads and rub strips, premium bodyside moldings with Corinthian grain vinyl insert (choice of color), cornering lamps, bright wheel lip moldings, and personalized owner's initials. The standard roof was painted metal. Interiors held Twin Comfort Lounge seats in pleated design with soft ultravelour fabric. The new instrument panel had a high-gloss walnut woodgrain applique, new lenses with cut crystal appearance, jewelry-like instrument faces, and new Cartier day/date clock. Other standard features included an AM/FM monaural radio with four speakers, power antenna, two- spoke steering wheel, automatic-temperature- control air conditioning, power windows and six-way driver's seat, tinted glass, and four lighted ashtrays with lighters. Standard Mark V colors were black, white, dove grey, midnight blue, dark jade metallic, cream, cordovan metallic, and light cordovan. Optional Moondust colors were dark red, ice blue, cinnamon gold, or ember. Optional Diamond Fire colors: black, rose, silver, light jade, or yellow gold. Base powerplant was reduced to a 400 cu. in. (6.6- liter) two-barrel V-8 with Dura-Spark ignition. Standard equipment included SelectShift three-speed automatic, four- wheel power disc brakes, Michelin steel-belted radial whitewalls, space-saver spare tire, and power steeering. The big 460 V-8 remained available as an option. Other new options included illuminated entry, heated left-hand remote mirror (packaged with electric rear defroster), turbine-style cast aluminum wheels, CB radio, and high-altitude option. Like its predecessor, Mark V was available in Designer models. Bill Blass had midnight blue paint; chamois-color landau vinyl roof with pigskin grain (full vinyl roof optional); pigskin-grain leather-and-vinyl interior in new chamois color; chamois or midnight blue bodyside molding; dual chamois paint stripes on bodyside and decklid, with Bill Blass insignia on front fender; Bill Blass name in opera window; and optional (no extra charge) 22K gold finished instrument panel nameplate with customer's name engraved. Turbine style cast aluminum wheels and six-way power passenger's seat also were included. Cartier's version was similar but with dove grey paint and landau vinyl roof, and dove grey leather-and-vinyl (or majestic velour) interior. Also dove grey bodyside moldings, and a single thin dark red bodyside paint stripe. Decklids held a Cartier interlockingC logo; opera windows, a Cartier signature. The Emilio Pucci model came in black Diamond Fire paint with white landau roof in Cayman grain patent-leather look. A white leather and vinyl interior had black components. Pucci also had black bodyside moldings, a three-quarter length bodyside tape stripe, and Pucci signature in the opera window. Mark's Givenchy edition was painted dark jade metallic, with a unique forward half-vinyl roof in chamois-color pigskin. Interiors were dark jade majestic cloth or leather and vinyl. Chamois-color bodyside moldings and dual paint stripes went on bodyside, hood and decklid. Hood and decklid stripes terminated in a double-G Givenchy insignia. There was also a series of luxury groups: cordovan, midnight blue/cream, gold/cream, light jade/dark jade, red/rose, and majestic velour.

I.D. DATA: Lincoln's 11-symbol Vehicle Identification Number (VIN) is stamped on a metal tab fastened to the instrument panel, visible through the windshield. The first digit is a model year code ('7' 1977). The second letter indicates assembly plant: 'Y' Wixom, MI; 'W' Wayne, MI. Digits three and four are the body serial code, which

corresponds to the Model Numbers shown in the tables below: '81' Continental 2-dr. HT coupe; '82' Continental 4-dr. sedan; '84' Versailles 4dr. sedan; '89' Mark V 2-dr. HT coupe. The fifth symbol is an engine code: 'H' V8351 2Bbl.; 'S' V8400 2Bbl.; 'A' V8460 4Bbl. Finally, digits 6-11 make up the consecutive unit number, starting with 800,001. A Vehicle Certification Label on the left front door lock face panel or door pillar shows the manufacturer, month and year built, GVW, GAWR, VIN, body code, color code, trim code, axle code, transmission code, and special order coding.

VERSAILLES (V-8)

Model Number	Body/Style Number	Body Type & Seating	Factory Price	Shipping Weight	Production Total
84	54M	4-dr. Sedan-5P	11500	3800	15,434

CONTINENTAL (V-8)

81	60B	2-dr. HT Cpe-6P	9474	4836	27,440
82	53B	4-dr. Sedan-6P	9636	4880	68,160

MARK V (V-8)

89	65D	2-dr. HT Cpe-6P	11396	4652	80,321

ENGINE DATA: BASE V-8 (Versailles): 90-degree, overhead valve V-8. Cast iron block and head. Displacement: 351 cu. in. (5.8 liters). Bore & stroke: 4.00 x 3.50 in. Compression ratio: 8.1:1. Brake horsepower: 135 at 3200 R.P.M. Torque: 275 lbs.-ft. at 1600 R.P.M. Five main bearings. Hydraulic valve lifters. Carburetor: 2Bbl. Motorcraft 2150. VIN Code: H. BASE V-8 (Mark V, later Continental): 90-degree, overhead valve V-8. Cast iron block and head. Displacement: 400 cu. in. (6.6 liters). Bore & stroke: 4.00 x 4.00 in. Compression ratio: 8.0:1. Brake horsepower: 179 at 4000 R.P.M. Torque: 329 lbs.-ft. at 1600 R.P.M. Five main bearings. Hydraulic valve lifters. Carburetor: 2Bbl. Motorcraft 2150. VIN Code: S. BASE V-8 (early Continental); OPTIONAL (Mark V): 90-degree, overhead valve V-8. Cast iron block and head. Displacement: 460 cu. in. (7.5 liters). Bore & stroke: 4.36 x 3.85 in. Compression ratio: 8.0:1. Brake horsepower: 208 at 4000 R.P.M. Torque: 356 lbs.-ft. at 2000 R.P.M. Five main bearings. Hydraulic valve lifters. Carburetor: 4Bbl. Motorcraft 4350. VIN Code: A.

CHASSIS DATA: Wheelbase: (Versailles) 109.9 in.; (Continental) 127.2 in.; (Mark V) 120.4 in. Overall Length: (Versailles) 200.9 in.; (Cont.) 233.0 in.; (Mark V) 230.3 in. Height: (Versailles) 54.1 in.; (Cont. 2-dr.) 55.0 in.; (Cont. 4-dr.) 55.2 in.; (Mark V) 53.0 in. Width: (Versailles) 74.5 in.; (Cont. 2-dr.) 79.7 in.; (Cont. 4-dr.) 80.0 in.; (Mark V) 79.7 in. Front Tread: (Versailles) 59.0 in.; (Cont.) 64.3 in.; (Mark V) 63.1 in. Rear Tread: (Versailles) 57.7 in.; (Cont.) 64.3 in.; (Mark V) 62.6 in. Standard Tires: (Versailles) N/A; (Continental) KR78 x 15 SBR WSW; (Mark V) JR78 x 15 SBR WSW;

TECHNICAL: Transmission: SelectShift three-speed manual transmission (column shift) standard. Gear ratios: (1st) 2.46:1; (2nd) 1.46:1; (3rd) 1.00:1; (Rev) 2.18:1. Standard final drive ratio: (Versailles) 2.50:1; (Continental) 2.75:1 except with V8460, 2.50:1; (Mark V) 3.00:1. Steering: Recirculating ball, power-assisted. Suspension: (Versailles) front spring over upper arm w/ball joints and drag struts and coil springs, Hotchkiss rear w/semi-elliptic leaf springs; (others) independent front coil springs w/lower trailing links and anti-sway bar; rigid rear axle w/lower trailing radius arms, upper oblique torque arms, coil springs, and transverse linkage (anti-sway) bar. Brakes: Four-wheel disc except Continental, front disc and rear drum. Ignition: Electronic. Body construction: (Versailles) unibody; (others) separate body on perimeter-type ladder frame. Fuel Tank: (Versailles) N/A; (Continental) 24.2 gal.; (Mark V) 26 gal.

DRIVETRAIN OPTIONS: 460 cu. in. V-8 engine: Mark ($133). Dual exhausts: Mark ($71). Higher axle ratio: Mark ($21). Traction-Lok differential ($65). Four-wheel disc (Sure Track) brakes: Cont. ($461). Sure Track brakes: Mark ($280). Engine block heater ($20). Trailer towing pkg.: Mark ($68-$89). California emission system ($54).

CONTINENTAL/MARK V CONVENIENCE/APPEARANCE OPTIONS: Option Packages: Town Car option: Cont. ($913). Town Coupe option: Cont. ($913). Williamsburg Limited Edition: Cont. (N/A). Mark V Cartier Designer series: leather ($1600); cloth ($2100). Mark V Bill Blass or Emilio Pucci Designer series ($1600). Mark V Givenchy Designer series: leather vinyl ($1600); velour ($2100). Power lock convenience group ($92- $120). Headlamp convenience group ($107). Appearance protection group ($57-$65). Defroster group ($107). Interior light group ($106-$120). Comfort/Convenience: Rear defroster: Cont. ($86). Speed control ($124). Illuminated entry system ($55). Six-way power seat: Cont. ($139); w/recliner ($219) exc. ($81) with Town Car/Cpe. Reclining passenger seat: Mark ($80). Six-way power passenger seat: Mark ($143). Power lumbar seat: Mark ($187). Twin comfort power seats: Cont. ($354-$493). Power vent windows ($85). Tilt steering wheel ($73). Intermittent wipers: Cont. ($30). Lighting and Mirrors: Coach lamps: Cont. ($64). Right remote mirror ($33). Entertainment: AM/FM stereo radio ($143); w/quadrasonic 8- track tape player ($396). AM/FM stereo search radio ($304). CB radio ($285). Exterior: Fixed-glass moonroof: Cont. ($954). Power glass moonroof ($938). Steel roof: Mark ($271 credit). Coach roof: Cont. ($522) exc. ($285) with Town Car/Cpe. Full vinyl roof: Cont. ($178); Mark ($187) exc. ($271 credit) w/Designer series. Opera windows: Cont. ($89). Moondust paint ($155). Diamond fire paint ($205). Custom paint stripes ($31). Rocker panel moldings: Mark ($28). Narrow vinyl-insert moldings: Cont. ($44). Premium bodyside moldings: Cont. ($120). Interior: Leather interior trim: Mark ($252). Velour seats: Town Car/Cpe ($198 credit). Wheels: Luxury wheel covers: Cont. ($88). Forged aluminum wheels: Cont. ($230-$318). Turbine spoke wheels: Cont. ($237- $325).

NOTE: Versailles option list not available; similar to 1978.

HISTORY: Introduced: October 1, 1976 except Versailles, March 28, 1977. Model year production: 191,355. Calendar year production: 211,439. Calendar year sales by U.S. dealers: 181,282. Model year sales by U.S. dealers: 164,208.

Historical Footnotes: Continental was the biggest car on the domestic market, as well as the worst guzzler. It weighed a whopping 5,000 pounds at the curb. The restyled Mark V sold strongly, up by one-third over the score of the last Mark IV. Versailles cost nearly three times as much as the related Mercury Monarch, and not everyone agreed that it was worth the extra price, even with the luxury features and tight construction. The new compact was 32 inches shorter and half a ton lighter than a Continental sedanbut cost nearly $2000 more. Only 8,169 Versailles found buyers in its short opening season. Stretch limousines were produced by various manufacturers, including AHA Manufacturing group in Mississauga, Ontario. That firm did a 12-inch stretch to 139 inch wheelbase, an 18-inch stretch to 145 inches, and even a massive 157 inch version.

1978 LINCOLN

Versailles turned to a smaller V-8 engine in its first complete season, while both Continental and Mark carried on with 400 and 460 cu. in. V-8s. Mark V offered a new Diamond Jubilee Edition to help commemorate FoMoCo's 75th anniversary.

1978 Versailles sedan (L)

VERSAILLES — V-8 — After beginning life in spring 1977 with a 351 cu. in. V-8, Versailles switched to a 302 cu. in. (5.0-liter) V-8 with variable-venturi carburetor for the 1978 model year. That engine had been formerly been installed in California Versailles. Appearance of the four-door sedan was nearly identical this year, and mechanical changes modest: just an improved power steering pump and new electronic engine control system. Versailles had a Continental-style grille, horizontal parking lamps, sculptured aluminum hood with bright Continental star ornament, center-pillar coach lamps, special forged aluminum wheels, and simulated spare tire on the decklid. The fully padded vinyl roof had a "frenched" rear window. Bumper guards had vertical rub strips and a wide horizontal rub strip. Bodies featured a clearcoat paint finish, as well as high-lustre wide upper bodyside moldings with vinyl insert. At the rear were horizontal wraparound taillamps and low-profile bumper guards. Inside touches included leather covering on the instrument panel, steering wheel and armrests. This year's colors were white, midnight blue, wedgewood blue, light chamois, cordovan metallic, light silver metallic, cinnamon gold metallic, dark red metallic, or medium silver metallic in two-tones only. There was a new wire wheel cover option, as well as a remote-mount 40-channel CB radio and lighted outside thermometer. SelectShift automatic transmission was standard, with a 2.50:1 axle ratio.

1978 Continental Town Car (L)

CONTINENTAL — V-8 — Not too much was new on the big Continental, except for different wheel covers. The sculptured bodyside got a new, more contemporary rear fender skirt and wheel lip molding (to match the rocker molding). Interiors had a new wide center folding armrest and revised door armrests. The instrument panel had a new high-gloss woodtone applique, as well as restyled knobs and controls and a padded glovebox door. The "classic" vertical-bar grille and concealed headlamps continued, as did the Town Coupe and Town Car option packages. This year's body colors were: black, white, midnight blue, wedgewood blue, midnight jade, cream, cordovan metallic, dark champagne, midnight cordovan, and dove grey. Optional glamour metallic colors were: dark red, silver, ice blue, light jade, light gold, crystal apricot, champagne, and cinnamon gold. The 400 cu. in. (6.6-liter) V-8 offered improved fuel economy with a low-restriction fresh-air intake, and a new mechanical spark control system. The 460 cu. in. (7.5-liter) V-8 was optional again, except in California. Under the hood was a new electronic voltage regulator and maintenance-free battery; on the dash, a new windshield washer fluid warning light. New options included an integral garage door opener, lighted outside thermometer, and wire wheel covers. The optional CB radio introduced in 1977 now had 40 channels.

355

1978 Continental Mark V coupe (L)

1978 Continental sedan (L)

MARK V — V-8 — Lincoln's personal luxury coupe was limited mainly to mechanical refinements and new standard wheel covers this year, but a special version was offered: the Diamond Jubilee Edition, to commemorate Ford's 75th anniversary. That one came in a choice of special Diamond Blue or Jubilee Gold clearcoat metallic paint. It had a Valino grain landau vinyl roof with matching Valino grain accent molding. Vertical grille bars were color-keyed to the body color, as was the unique hood ornament. There was also a special paint stripe on the hood. Front and rear bumper guard pads had horizontal rub strips color-keyed to the body color. Bright-edged fender louvers and coach lamps were included, and the special opera windows (very small oval, as usual) had 'Diamond Jubilee Edition' script and a simulated diamond chip laminated in the beveled glass. Turbine style cast aluminum wheels were color-keyed to the body. Unique bodyside paint striping was interrupted on the door by personalized customer's initials. On the decklid contour was distinctive Valino grain padded vinyl, with 'Continental' letters spelled out on the simulated spare tire cover. A Valino grain vinyl insert also went in the trunk lock cover. Inside were Diamond Jubilee leather/cloth bucket seats in unique sew style with power lumbar support, along with real and simulated ebony woodgrain inserts. Extras even went so far as unique keys with woodtone applique insert, plus a leather-bound owner's manual and a leather-bound tool kit. A leather-covered console held an umbrella. Diamond Jubilee had dual wide-band whitewall steel-belted radials, illuminated entry, interval wipers, tilt steering, and other extras. Two engines were offered again on Mark V: the 400 cu. in. (6.6-liter) V-8 with SelectShift and 2.75:1 rear axle, or the 460 V-8 with 2.50:1 axle. Body colors were: black, white, midnight blue, wedgewood blue, midnight jade, cream, cordovan metallic, dark champagne, light champagne, midnight cordovan, and dove grey. Moondust metallic colors were optional: dark red, light silver, ice blue, light jade, light gold, crystal apricot, and cinnamon gold. Joining the option list were a digital miles-to-empty indicator, integral garage door opener, lighted outside thermometer, wire wheel covers, and power retractable CB antenna. The four Designer Series were available again. Bill Blass sported midnight cordovan body color with light champagne landau vinyl roof in Valino grain. The Cartier edition came in light champagne body color with light champagne landau vinyl roof. (A standard metal-finished roof was offered at no extra cost; full vinyl roof at extra cost.) Both had light champagne bodyside moldings. Mark's Pucci edition came in light silver metallic body color, with black landau vinyl roof in Cayman grain for a patent-leather look. It had black bodyside moldings and unique paint/tri-tone tape stripes, plus Pucci logo. Givenchy came in midnight jade body color with unique forward half- vinyl roof in light chamois color pigskin. Jade leather and vinyl interior trim had a unique broad lace insert in the seatback, embroidered in the double-G Givenchy logo. Bodyside moldings and dual paint stripes were chamois-colored on the Givenchy.

I.D. DATA: As before, Lincoln's 11-symbol Vehicle Identification Number (VIN) is stamped on a metal tab fastened to the instrument panel, visible through the windshield. Coding is similar to 1977. Model year code changed to '8' for 1978. Engine code 'H' (V8351) was replaced by 'F' (V8302 2Bbl.).

VERSAILLES (V-8)

Model Number	Body/Style Number	Body Type & Seating	Factory Price	Shipping Weight	Production Total
84	54M	4-dr. Sedan-5P	12529	3759	8,931

CONTINENTAL (V-8)

81	60B	2-dr. HT Cpe-6P	9974	4659	20,977
82	53B	4-dr. Sedan-6P	10166	4660	67,110

MARK V (V-8)

89	65D	2-dr. HT Cpe-6P	12099	4567	72,602

Mark V Production Note: Of the total shown, 5,159 were the Diamond Jubilee edition. A total of 16,537 Marks had one of the four Designer packages (8,520 Cartier, 3,125 Pucci, 917 Givenchy, and 3,975 Bill Blass).

ENGINE DATA: BASE V-8 (Versailles): 90-degree, overhead valve V-8. Cast iron block and head. Displacement: 302 cu. in. (5.2 liters). Bore & stroke: 4.00 x 3.00 in. Compression ratio: 8.4:1. Brake horsepower: 133 at 3600 R.P.M. Torque: 243 lbs.-ft. at 1600 R.P.M. Five main bearings. Hydraulic valve lifters. Carburetor: 2Bbl. variable-venturi Motorcraft 2150. VIN Code: F. **BASE V-8** (Continental, Mark V): 90-degree, overhead valve V-8. Cast iron block and head. Displacement: 400 cu. in. (6.6 liters). Bore & stroke: 4.00 x 4.00 in. Compression ratio: 8.0:1. Brake horsepower: 166 at 3800 R.P.M. Torque: 319 lbs.-ft. at 1800 R.P.M. Five main bearings. Hydraulic valve lifters. Carburetor: 2Bbl. Motorcraft 2150. VIN Code: S. **OPTIONAL V-8** (Continental, Mark V): 90-degree, overhead valve V-8. Cast iron block and head. Displacement: 460 cu. in. (7.5 liters). Bore & stroke: 4.36 x 3.85 in. Compression ratio: 8.0:1. Brake horsepower: 210 at 4200 R.P.M. Torque: 357 lbs.-ft. at 2200 R.P.M. Five main bearings. Hydraulic valve lifters. Carburetor: 4Bbl. Motorcraft 4350. VIN Code: A.

CHASSIS DATA: Wheelbase: (Versailles) 109.9 in.; (Continental) 127.2 in.; (Mark V) 120.4 in. Overall Length: (Versailles) 200.9 in.; (Cont.) 233.0 in.; (Mark V) 230.3 in. Height: (Versailles) 54.1 in.; (Cont. 2-dr.) 55.0 in.; (Cont. 4-dr.) 55.2 in.; (Mark V) 52.9 in. Width: (Versailles) 74.5 in.; (Cont. 2-dr.) 79.7 in.; (Cont. 4-dr.) 80.0 in.; (Mark V) 79.7 in. Front Tread: (Versailles) 59.0 in.; (Cont.) 64.3 in.; (Mark V) 63.2 in. Rear Tread: (Versailles) 57.7 in.; (Cont.) 64.3 in.; (Mark V) 62.6 in. Standard Tires: (Versailles) FR78 x 14 SBR WSW; (Continental) 225 x 15 SBR WSW; (Mark V) Michelin 225/230 x 15 SBR WSW.

TECHNICAL: Transmission: SelectShift three-speed manual transmission (column shift) standard. Gear ratios: (1st) 2.46:1; (2nd) 1.46:1; (3rd) 1.00:1; (Rev) 2.18:1. Standard final drive ratio: (Versailles) 2.50:1; (Continental/Mark) 2.75:1 except with V8460, 2.50:1. Steering: Recirculating ball, power-assisted. Suspension/Brakes/Body: same as 1977. Fuel Tank: (Versailles) 19.2 gal.; (Continental) 24.2 gal.; (Mark V) 25 gal.

DRIVETRAIN OPTIONS: 460 cu. in. V-8 engine: Cont./Mark ($187). Dual exhausts: Cont./Mark ($75). Floor shift selector: Versailles ($33). Higher axle ratio: Cont. ($21). Traction-Lok differential: Cont./Mark ($67). Four-wheel disc (Sure Track) brakes: Cont. ($496). Sure Track brakes: Mark ($296). Engine block heater ($20). Trailer towing pkg.: Cont. ($33-$67). Class III trailer towing pkg.: Mark ($72-$95). California emission system ($76). High-altitude option (NC).

VERSAILLES CONVENIENCE/APPEARANCE OPTIONS: Appearance protection group ($76). Reclining bucket seat group ($467). Power lock group ($147). Defroster group ($115). Rear defroster, electric ($88). Garage door opener ($87). Illuminated outside thermometer ($27). Tilt steering wheel ($77). AM/FM stereo radio w/8track tape player ($84 credit); w/quadrasonic 8track ($87). 40channel CB radio ($321). Power glass panel moonroof ($1027). Dual-shade paint ($59). Protective bodyside moldings ($48). Lower bodyside protection ($33). Leather interior trim ($295). Wire wheel covers (NC).

1978 Continental Mark V Diamond Jubilee coupe (L)

CONTINENTAL/MARK V CONVENIENCE/APPEARANCE OPTIONS: Option Packages: Mark V Diamond Jubilee edition ($8000). Williamsburg Limited Edition: Cont. ($1525-$1725). Town Car option: Cont. ($1440). Town Coupe option: Cont. ($1440). Mark V Cartier Designer series: leather/vinyl or velour cloth ($1800). Mark V Emilio Pucci or Givenchy Designer series: leather/vinyl ($1800). Mark V Bill Blass Designer series: leather/vinyl ($1800); ultra-velour cloth ($1533). Mark V luxury groups ($680), but ($775) w/moondust paint. Power lock convenience group ($115-$147). Appearance protection group ($69-$76). Headlamp convenience group ($133). Defroster group ($115). Interior light group ($108-$127). Comfort/Convenience: Speed control ($127). Illuminated entry system ($63). Six-way power seat: Cont. ($151); w/recliner ($236). Reclining passenger seat: Mark ($85). Six-way power passenger seat ($151); Mark ($151). Six-way power lumbar seat: Mark ($107). Twin comfort power seats: Cont. ($547). Power vent windows ($89). Illuminated outside thermometer ($27). Miles-to-empty fuel indicator ($125). Garage door opener ($87). Tilt steering wheel ($77). Intermittent wipers ($35). Lighting and Mirrors: Coach lamps: Cont. ($63). Map/dome light ($19). Right remote mirror ($37). Entertainment: AM/FM stereo radio ($144); w/8track tape player ($203); w/quadrasonic 8-track player ($373). AM/FM stereo search radio ($287). 40channel CB radio ($321). Exterior: Fixed-glass moonroof: Cont. ($1027). Power glass panel moonroof ($1027). Landau vinyl roof: Mark ($484). Steel roof: Mark ($261 credit). Coach roof: Cont. ($547) exc. ($269) with Town Car/Cpe or ($332) w/Williamsburg. Full vinyl roof: Cont. ($215); Mark ($223) exc. ($261 credit) w/Designer series. Opera windows: Cont. ($93). Moondust paint ($189). Custom paint stripes ($53). Rocker panel moldings: Mark ($29). Narrow vinyl-insert moldings: Cont. ($48). Premium bodyside moldings: Cont. ($128). Lower bodyside protection ($33). Interior: Leather interior trim ($267-$295). Velour seats (leather delete): Cont. Twn Car/Cpe ($200 credit). Wheels and Tires: Wire wheel covers ($233). Forged aluminum wheels ($333) exc. (NC) w/Designer Mark. Turbine spoke wheels ($333). Dual wide-band whitewall tires ($52).

HISTORY: Introduced: October 7, 1977. Model year production: 169,620. Calendar year production: 189,523. Calendar year sales by U.S. dealers: 188,487. Model year sales by U.S. dealers: 184,299.

Historical Footnotes: Although Versailles production for the model year dropped sharply, sales this year weren't too far short of twice the total in its first (brief) season: 15,061 versus 8,169. Continental sales rose somewhat for the model year (94,242 versus 83,125), while Mark V gained only modestly. To meet Lincoln-Mercury sales-weighted CAFE requirements, sales of the full-size models had to be held in check, but the company counted on Versailles in its second year.

1979 LINCOLN

Both Continental and Mark V added a new Collector's Series, but otherwise changed little for 1979. Versailles enjoyed a modest, though much-needed restyle, and was the first domestic model to get halogen headlamps. The big 460 cu. in. V-8 disappeared, making a 400 V-8 the biggest Lincoln powerplant.

1979 Versailles "Moon Roof" option sedan (JG)

1979 Versailles "Convertible" option sedan (JG)

VERSAILLES — V-8 — Subtle restyling added 8 inches to the Versailles roofline, giving it a more square, formal "town car" look. Topped with Valino grain vinyl, the roof was fully padded, with a "frenched" back window. Cavalry twill vinyl also was available, with convertible-style back window. New roof accents included a brushed stainless steel wrapover molding, and matching brushed-finish center-pillar appliques with restyled integral coach lamps. Quarter windows were enlarged and door frames revised, allowing wider back doors to open farther. Versailles also added padded vinyl over the simulated spare tire shape on the decklid contour, which carried 'Lincoln' block letters. Wide wraparound taillamps met that "spare." Versailles was the first domestic car with standard halogen headlamps, which cast a "whiter" light. The standard 302 cu. in. (5.0-liter) V-8 had been the first engine to be equipped with electronic engine control (EECI) and variable-venturi carburetor, and continued in that form. Standard equipment included such tempting touches as air conditioning, power windows, four-wheel disc brakes, and speed control. A new electronic AM/FM stereo radio had seek/scan and a Quadrasonic8 tape player. Wire wheel covers were a no-cost option, with aluminum wheels standard.

1979 Continental "Collectors Series" sedan (L)

CONTINENTAL — V-8 — Lincoln's big rear-drive was largely a carryover for 1979, though a Collector's Series was added. Lincoln-Mercury called it the "pinnacle of Lincoln Continental prestige." Some styling features came from the 1978 Mark V Diamond Jubilee Edition, including special paint and a gold-colored grille. Both Town Car and Town Coupe option packages were still available. Wheelbase continued at the lengthy 127 inches. Collector's Series Continentals offered a choice of white or midnight blue clearcoat metallic body paint, with coach roof color-keyed to the body (replacing the full vinyl roof that would otherwise be standard). Up front were gold-painted vertical grille bars. Turbine-style cast aluminum wheels were painted midnight blue between the spokes and the bodyside held unique paint stripes, along with premium lower bodyside moldings keyed to the body color. (Bodyside moldings on other Continentals had a Corinthian grain vinyl insert in customer's choice of color.) 'Collector's Series' script went on the lower corner of the rear pillar of that model. The customary 'Town Car' script on front fender was deleted, and the Collector's Series did not include opera windows. Collector's interior choices were luxury cloth or leather-and-vinyl seat trim in midnight blue. There was a woodtone applique insert in

the steering wheel rim and hub, and a unique hub ornament. Also included: plush midnight blue Tiffany cut-pile carpeting; leather-bound tool kit (containing tools); leather-bound owner's manual; umbrella; power mini-vent windows; illuminated entry; speed control; 63 ampere-hour maintenance-free battery; interval windshield wipers; and a remote-control garage door opener. A Williamsburg option for the Town Car was offered again, in a choice of seven dual-shade color combinations. Williamsburgs included a full vinyl roof, either leather-and-vinyl or velour interior, Twin Comfort Lounge seats, power vent windows, premium bodyside moldings, and so forth. Continental came with the 400 cu. in. (6.6-liter) two-barrel V-8, SelectShift automatic, and 2.47:1 rear axle. Interiors showed expanded use of woodtone appliques on the instrument panel, which added a fuel warning light to replace the former washer fluid light. A new electronic AM/FM stereo radio had digital frequency display.

1979 Continental Mark V "Bill Blass" coupe (L)

MARK V — V-8 — Like Continental, Mark V added a Collector's Series with golden grille this year, to replace the previous Diamond Jubilee Edition. It came with a choice of white or midnight blue clearcoat metallic paint. Standard Collector's equipment included a landau vinyl roof with matching accent moldings, gold-painted vertical grille bars, unique hood ornament and paint stripe, color-keyed front/rear bumper guard pads and horizontal rub strips, bright-edged fender louvers, and coach lamps. 'Collector's Series' script decorated the rear pillar. Turbine aluminum wheels were painted midnight blue between the spokes. A unique bodyside paint stripe was interrupted by the owner's initials on the door. Opera windows were deleted on the Collector's Series, but the decklid lock cover had a vinyl insert. Inside, Mark Collector's had midnight blue power bucket seats in unique sew style (or optional Twin Comfort Lounge seats in white or dark blue leather-and-vinyl). It also had a leather-covered instrument panel, ebony woodtone applique insert in steering wheel rim and hub, blue plush carpeting, leather-covered padded console, leather-bound tool kit and owner's manual, unique keys with woodtone applique insert, power vent windows, illuminated entry, interval wipers, and a number of other luxury touches.

1979 Continental Mark V "Luxury Group" coupe (L)

Otherwise, Mark V appearance chaned little. Padded vinyl now decorated the simulated spare tire on the decklid, which had 'Continental' lettering spaced around its rim. Mark V had only the 400 cu. in. (6.6-liter) two-barrel V-8, with 2.47:1 rear axle ratio. Not much else was different beyond new door/ignition locks and an improved heater. Four Designer Series were offered again, with modest revisions. Bill Blass had a distinctive two-tone paint treatment with hood, decklid and upper bodysides in white; lower bodysides and decklid contour in midnight blue metallic. A white carriage roof had a bright die-cast rear pillar ornament. (If ordered with optional full vinyl roof, the Bill Blass name was in the opera windows.) Blass also had dark blue bodyside moldings and dual gold paint stripes on bodysides and decklid, along with color-keyed turbine-style cast aluminum wheels. Cartier again came in the popular light champagne paint with matching landau vinyl roof, though a standard metal-finished roof was available at no extra cost. It had light champagne bodyside moldings, and a single thin, dark red paint stripe on bodysides. A Cartier interlocking-C logo went on the decklid, and Cartier signature in opera windows. Emilio Pucci's edition had turquoise metallic body paint, a full vinyl roof in midnight blue, white leather-and-vinyl interior trim with midnight blue accents, midnight blue bodyside moldings, Pucci signature in opera windows, and Pucci logo as part of the tri-tone paint stripes. Pucci also had wire wheel covers, whereas the other three had turbine-style cast aluminum wheels. The Givenchy model came in a new crystal blue metallic body paint with crystal blue front half-vinyl roof. Also included: dark crystal blue bodyside moldings and dual tape stripes on bodysides, hood and decklid. Those hood and decklid stripes terminated in a double-G logo. There was also the signature in opera windows. Designer models also had a new electronic-search AM/FM stereo radio with Quadrasonic8 tape player. Mark's Luxury Group series expanded to nine colors this year, from seven in 1978. One of the new ones was white leather-and-vinyl seats with color-keyed components.

I.D. DATA: As before, Lincoln's 11-symbol Vehicle Identification Number (VIN) is stamped on a metal tab fastened to the instrument panel, visible through the windshield. Coding is similar to 1977-78. Model year code changed to '9' for 1979. Engine code 'A' (V8460) was dropped. Consecutive unit (sequence) numbers began with 600,001.

1979 Versailles "Valino Brougham" option sedan (JG)

VERSAILLES (V-8)

Model Number	Body/Style Number	Body Type & Seating	Factory Price	Shipping Weight	Production Total
84	54M	4-dr. Sedan-5P	12939	3684	21,007

CONTINENTAL (V-8)

81	60B	2-dr. HT Cpe-6P	10985	4639	16,142
82	53B	4-dr. Sedan-6P	11200	4649	76,458

MARK V (V-8)

89	65D	2-dr. HT Cpe-6P	13067	4589	75,939

PRICE NOTE: Collector's Series Continental and Mark V were listed as option packages, but also given initial prices as separate models: Continental $16,148 with leather interior, $15,936 with cloth; Mark V $21,326 with bucket seats, $20,926 with Twin Comfort seats.

ENGINE DATA: BASE V-8 (Versailles): 90-degree, overhead valve V-8. Cast iron block and head. Displacement: 302 cu. in. (5.2 liters). Bore & stroke: 4.00 x 3.00 in. Compression ratio: 8.4:1. Brake horsepower: 130 at 3600 R.P.M. Torque: 237 lbs.-ft. at 1600 R.P.M. Five main bearings. Hydraulic valve lifters. Carburetor: 2Bbl. variable-venturi Motorcraft 2150. VIN Code: F. BASE V-8 (Continental, Mark V): 90-degree, overhead valve V-8. Cast iron block and head. Displacement: 400 cu. in. (6.6 liters). Bore & stroke: 4.00 x 4.00 in. Compression ratio: 8.0:1. Brake horsepower: 159 at 3400 R.P.M. Torque: 315 lbs.-ft. at 1800 R.P.M. Five main bearings. Hydraulic valve lifters. Carburetor: 2Bbl. Motorcraft 2150. VIN Code: S.

CHASSIS DATA: Wheelbase: (Versailles) 109.9 in.; (Continental) 127.2 in.; (Mark V) 120.3 in. Overall Length: (Versailles) 201.0 in.; (Cont.) 233.0 in.; (Mark V) 230.3 in. Height: (Versailles) 54.1 in.; (Cont. 2-dr.) 55.2 in.; (Cont. 4-dr.) 55.4 in.; (Mark V) 53.1 in. Width: (Versailles) 74.5 in.; (Cont. 2-dr.) 79.6 in.; (Cont. 4-dr.) 79.9 in.; (Mark V) 79.7 in. Front Tread: (Versailles) 59.0 in.; (Cont.) 64.3 in.; (Mark V) 63.2 in. Rear Tread: (Versailles) 57.7 in.; (Cont.) 64.3 in.; (Mark V) 62.6 in. Standard Tires: (Versailles) FR78 x 14 SBR WSW; (Continental, Mark V) 225 x 15 SBR WSW.

TECHNICAL: Transmission: Select-Shift three-speed manual transmission (column shift) standard. Gear ratios: (1st) 2.46:1; (2nd) 1.46:1; (3rd) 1.00:1; (Rev) 2.18:1. Standard final drive ratio: 2.47:1. Steering/Suspension/Brakes/Body: same as 1977-78. Fuel Tank: (Versailles) 19.2 gal.; (Continental) 24.2 gal.; (Mark V) 25 gal.

DRIVETRAIN OPTIONS: Floor shift selector: Versailles ($36). Higher axle ratio: Cont./Mark ($23). Traction-Lok differential: Cont./Mark ($71). Sure Track disc brakes: Cont. ($525). Sure Track brakes: Mark ($313). H.D. battery ($21). Engine block heater ($21). Trailer towing pkg.: Cont. ($71). Class III trailer towing pkg.: Mark ($84-$107). California emission system ($84). High-altitude option: Cont./Mark (NC).

1979 Versailles "French Window" option sedan (L)

VERSAILLES CONVENIENCE/APPEARANCE OPTIONS: Appearance protection group ($87). Reclining bucket seat group ($491). Power lock group ($155). Defroster group ($121). Rear defroster, electric ($101). Garage door opener ($92). Illuminated outside thermometer ($28). Tilt steering wheel ($81). AM/FM stereo radio w/standard 8track or cassette tape player ($168 credit). 40channel CB radio ($321). Power glass panel moonroof ($1088). Full vinyl or coach roof: Valino grain or Cavalry twill (NC). Dual-shade paint ($63). Protective bodyside moldings ($51). Premium bodyside moldings ($77). Lower bodyside protection ($35). Leather/vinyl interior trim ($312). Wire wheel covers (NC).

CONTINENTAL/MARK V CONVENIENCE/APPEARANCE OPTIONS: Option Packages: Collector's Series: Continental ($4736- $5163); Mark ($7859-$8259). Williamsburg Limited Edition: Cont. ($1617-$1829). Town Car option: Cont. ($1527). Town Coupe option: Cont. ($1527). Mark V Cartier Designer series: leather/vinyl or velour cloth ($1945). Mark V Emilio Pucci Designer series: leather/vinyl interior ($1525). Mark V Bill Blass Designer series: leather/vinyl interior w/carriage roof ($2775); w/full vinyl roof ($1809). Mark V Givenchy Designer series w/broadlace interior ($2145). Mark V luxury groups ($743), but ($843) w/moondust paint. Power lock convenience group ($121-$156). Appearance protection group ($80-$91). Headlamp convenience group ($140). Defroster group ($121). Interior light group ($115-$135). Comfort/Convenience: Rear defroster ($101). Speed control ($140). Illuminated entry system ($65). Six-way power seat: Cont. ($160); w/recliner ($251). Reclining passenger seat: Mark ($91). Six-way power passenger seat: Mark ($159). Power lumbar seat: Mark ($113). Twin comfort power seats: Cont. ($580). Power vent windows ($95). Illuminated outside thermometer ($28). Miles-to-empty fuel indicator: Mark ($133). Garage door opener ($92). Tilt steering wheel ($81). Intermittent wipers ($40). Lighting and Mirrors: Coach lamps: Cont. ($67). Map/dome light ($20). Right remote mirror ($39). Entertainment: AM/FM stereo radio ($144); w/8track tape player ($203); w/cassette player ($203) exc. ($204 credit) w/Collector's. AM/FM stereo search radio w/quadrasonic 8track player ($407). 40channel CB radio ($321). Exterior: Fixed-glass moonroof: Cont. ($1088). Power glass panel moonroof ($555) w/Cont. Collector's. Carriage roof: Mark ($1201). Landau vinyl roof: Mark ($513). Coach roof: Cont. ($580) exc. ($285) with Town Car/Cpe or ($352) w/Williamsburg. Full vinyl roof: Cont. ($228); Mark ($236). Opera windows: Cont. ($99). Moondust paint ($201). Custom paint stripes ($56). Rocker panel moldings: Mark ($31). Narrow vinyl-insert moldings: Cont. ($51). Premium bodyside moldings: Cont. ($136). Lower bodyside protection ($35). Interior: Leather interior trim ($312-$333). Velour seats (leather delete): Cont. Twn Car/Cpe ($212 credit). Wheels and Tires: Wire wheel covers ($247). Forged aluminum wheels ($373). Turbine spoke wheels ($373). Dual wide-band whitewall tires ($54). Inflatable spare tire (NC).

HISTORY: Introduced: October 6, 1978. Model year production: 189,546. Calendar year production: 151,960. Calendar year sales by U.S. dealers: 131,271. Model year sales by U.S. dealers: 149,717.

Historical Footnotes: The big Continental was about to be replaced by a new smaller, lighter version. Sales fell for the model year, quite sharply for the two big Lincolns. Mark V sales had been more than double Cadillac Eldorado's, but the freshly-downsized Eldo threatened Lincoln's supremacy in that league.

1980 LINCOLN

Weights of both big Lincolns dropped considerably as Continental took on an all-new form and Mark VI was similarly redesigned. Each was nearly 800 pounds lighter than its predecessor. New suspensions kept the luxury ride, and both got a new deep-well trunk. Electronic engine control systems were standard on all Lincolns. So was a new four-speed automatic overdrive transmission, which had a mechanical lockup in (overdrive) fourth gear. Continental and Mark were more similar than before, essentially two versions of one modernized traditional design, with Mark the upscale edition. Both rode a "Panther" platform based on the 1979 LTD/Marquis. Base engines also shrunk, down to 302 cu. in. (5.0- liter) size, with 351 cu. in. (5.8-liter) V-8 optional. Other new technical features on both models included halogen headlamps, P-metric radial tires, and a fluidic windshield washer system. A new electronic instrument panel with message center was standard on Mark VI, optional on Continental. It included a digital speedometer, graphic fuel gauge, vehicle warning system and trip computer. Optional on both was keyless entry, operated by a panel of calculator-type pushbuttons in a preprogrammed sequence. All these changes applied to the upper Lincolns, as the smaller Versailles was in its final season.

1980 Versailles "French Window" sedan (JG)

1980 Versailles "Convertible" option sedan (L)

VERSAILLES — V-8 — Only a handful of changes hit the compact Lincoln sedan in its final year. Under the hood was a new starter; in the trunk, an improved jack. Five body colors were new, as well as three vinyl roof colors. So were standard Twin Comfort Lounge seats with recliners. Two Versailles options were dropped: the floor-mounted shift lever and the full vinyl roof. Standard engine was again the 302 cu. in. (5.0-liter V-8) with variable-venturi carburetor. The enlarged and ample standard equipment list included halogen headlamps, leather- wrapped steering wheel, six-way power driver's seat, auto- temp air conditioning, tinted glass, four-wheel disc brakes, new electronic AM/FM stereo search radio and day/date/elapsed time digital clock, and Michelin tires. Appearance was the same as 1979.

1980 Continental "Collectors Series" sedan (L)

CONTINENTAL — V-8 — For the first time in a decade, an all-new Lincoln arrived, featuring a formal roofline, wider swing-away grille, and full-width taillamps. Again built with separate body and frame construction, Continental lost close to 800 pounds. The aero-styled body was more than a foot shorter, now riding a 117.4 inch wheelbase. A traditional Lincoln "classic" vertical-bar chrome- plated grille was now flanked by exposed quad rectangular halogen headlamps, rather than the former concealed lights. The grille was wider than the former version, though not as tall. As before, its pattern repeated in a single bumper slot. Integral parking/turn signal lamps were in front fender extensions, with cornering lamps standard. Bright bumper guards had black pads, and black bumper rub strips held white accent stripes. On the hood was a bright Continental star ornament, bright rear edge molding, and paint stripes. At the rear was a full-width red reflective lower back panel applique (with bright surround molding), vertical taillamps with bright surround moldings, and bumper-mounted backup lamps. Power vent windows and a full vinyl roof with padded rear roof pillar were standard. Inside was a restyled three- pod instrument cluster with new engine temperature gauge. As before, two- and four-door models were offered. Town Car and Town Coupe had their script in the rear quarter window. Both had coach lamps, seatback robe cords, and map pockets. The Williamsburg Town Car series was replaced by individual dual-shade paint options. New dual-shade paint treatments came in five combinations: black with light pewter metallic, maroon with silver metallic, dark cordovan metallic with bittersweet metallic, dark blue metallic with light pewter metallic, or dark champagne metallic with medium fawn metallic. That dual-finish treatment included upper body paint stripes and premium bodyside moldings. The new standard 302 cu. in. (5.0-liter) V-8 had electronic fuel injection and third-generation electronic engine controls (EECIII). Standard four-speed automatic transmission (basically a three-speed with 0.67:1 overdrive gear tacked on) would slip into overdrive at about 35 MPH. A single poly "V" belt on the optional 351 cu. in. (5.8-liter) V-8 drove the water pump, fan, alternator, and power steering pump. Axle ratio was 3.08:1 with the 302 engine, 2.73:1 with the 351 (same as Mark VI). The big 400 cu. in. V-8 was gone. The new coil-spring front suspension used long and short arms, with a stabilizer bar. At the rear was a new four-link coil spring suspension. Michelin Pmetric steel-belted radials were standard. Gas cylinders eased opening of both hood and decklid. An electronic AM/FM stereo search radio was standard. New options included an electronic instrument cluster (with "message center" and 11-function monitor), keyless entry (with five door-mounted pushbuttons), Premium Sound System, and lacy-spoke aluminum wheels. Optional speed control added a "resume" feature.

MARK VI — V-8 — This year, a four-door sedan joined the customary Mark luxury coupe in its freshly downsized form. While the shrunken Mark rode a 114.4 inch wheelbase, though, the sedan's was 3 inches longer (same as Continental). The coupe lost 6 inches of wheelbase and 14 inches in overall length, as well as close to 700 pounds. Styling was undeniably Lincoln, evolved from Mark V, including Rolls-Royce style grille, oval opera windows on wide Cpillars (with Continental star), and easy-to-spot decklid bulge. While the similarly downsized Continental switched to exposed quad headlamps, Mark kept its halogen headlamps hidden behind closed (larger) doors. Body features included a fully padded vinyl roof with "frenched" rear window, wide bright stainless steel/aluminum rocker panel moldings, and standard power vent windows. Four-doors had center-pillar coach lamps. Front fender louvers had bright edges and a simulated adjuster. Premium bodyside moldings came with vinyl insert in choice of colors. Mark also had bright bumper guards with black pads, black bumper rub strips with white accent stripe, bright Continental star hood ornament, and a bright hood rear-edge molding. Slightly taller vertical wraparound parking/signal lights stood again at fender tips. This year's vertical-bar grille pattern was repeated in a wide bumper slot below. Inside was a four-spoke color-keyed steering wheel. Base engine was now the 302 cu. in. (5.0-liter) V-8, with 351 cu. in. variable-venturi V-8 optional. Four-speed overdrive automatic was standard. Unequal-length A-arms replaced former the single arm with drag strut at the front suspension. The four-link rear suspension had shocks angled ahead of the axle. Standard electronic instruments could be deleted. In the trunk was a new mini spare tire. Once again, Mark VI two-doors came in four Designer Series. Bill Blass, painted dark blue metallic on the lower areas, with white upper accents, had a white carriage roof. Leather seating surfaces were midnight blue with white accents (or vice versa). Blass also had dark blue bodyside moldings, dual gold paint stripes on bodyside and decklid contour, Blass logo on rear roof pillar and decklid contour, and color-keyed lacy-spoke cast aluminum wheels. The light/medium pewter metallic Cartier, with medium pewter landau roof, had light pewter bodyside moldings and a single thin, dark red paint stripe on bodyside and decklid. A Cartier logo went on the decklid above the Mark VI script, and Cartier signature in the opera windows. Leather or luxury cloth seating came in light and medium pewter colors. Mark's light/medium fawn metallic Pucci had medium fawn bodyside moldings, tri-band bodyside and decklid contour tape stripes, Pucci signature in opera window, and Pucci logo on rearward fender louver. Givenchy offered bittersweet bodyside moldings, dual bittersweet hood tape stripes, and light fawn bodyside and decklid paint stripes with integral hood/decklid Givenchy logo. Givenchy lettering decorated the opera windows. Body paint was two-tone light fawn and bittersweet metallic, with full vinyl roof in light fawn. Twin Comfort Lounge seats with leather seating surfaces were bittersweet color, accented with Givenchy buttons on seatbacks. Givenchy had wire wheel covers. A new top-of-the-line Signature Series Mark VI (replacing the Collector's Edition) came in dark red or silver metallic paint on both two- and four-door bodies. It had a color-keyed Cavalry twill landau vinyl roof, color- keyed bumper rub strips, body-color accent on parking lamp lenses, vinyl roof wrapover molding with bright accents and coach lamps, and two-tone bodyside and hood accent stripes. 'Signature Series' script went on the rear roof pillar, an owner's monogram on front door. The decklid contour had a padded vinyl treatment. Inside, Signature had dark red leather or cloth seating surfaces, an owner's Signature nameplate on the dash, and plush Allure carpeting on the floor, cowl side, lower doors, center pillar, and in the trunk. Many Mark VI options were standard on the Signature Series, including speed control, six-way power seats, driver and passenger recliners, keyless entry, and Premium Sound System.

I.D. DATA: Lincoln's 11-symbol Vehicle Identification Number (VIN) is stamped on a metal tab fastened to the instrument panel, visible through the windshield. The first digit is a model year code ('0' 1980). The second letter indicates assembly plant: 'Y' Wixom, MI; 'W' Wayne, MI. Digits three and four are the body serial code, which corresponds to the Model Numbers shown in the tables below: '81' Continental 2-dr. coupe; '82' Continental 4-dr. sedan; '84' Versailles 4dr. sedan; '89' Mark VI 2-dr. coupe; '90' Mark VI 4dr. sedan; '96' Mark VI Signature Series. The fifth symbol is an engine code: 'F' V8302 2Bbl. or EFI; 'G' V8351 2Bbl. Finally, digits 6-11 make up the consecutive unit number, starting with 600,001. A Vehicle Certification Label on the left front door lock face panel or door pillar shows the manufacturer, month and year built, GVW, GAWR, VIN, body code, color code, trim code, axle code, transmission code, and special order coding.

VERSAILLES (V-8)

Model Number	Body/Style Number	Body Type & Seating	Factory Price	Shipping Weight	Production Total
84	54M	4-dr. Sedan-6P	14674	3661	4,784

CONTINENTAL (V-8)

81	66D	2-dr. Coupe-6P	12555	3843	7,177
82	54D	4-dr. Sedan-6P	12884	3919	24,056

MARK VI (V-8)

89	66D	2-dr. Coupe-6P	15424	3892	20,647
90	54D	4-dr. Sedan-6P	15824	3988	18,244

MARK VI SIGNATURE SERIES (V-8)

96	66D	2-dr. Coupe-6P	20940	3896	N/A
96	54D	4-dr. Sedan-6P	21309	3993	N/A

ENGINE DATA: BASE V-8 (Versailles): 90-degree, overhead valve V-8. Cast iron block and head. Displacement: 302 cu. in. (5.2 liters). Bore & stroke: 4.00 x 3.00 in. Compression ratio: 8.4:1. Brake horsepower: 132 at 3600 R.P.M. Torque: 232 lbs.-ft. at 1400 R.P.M. Five main bearings. Hydraulic valve lifters. Carburetor: 2Bbl. Motorcraft 2150. VIN Code: F. BASE V-8 (Continental, Mark VI): Same as 302 cu. in. V-8 above, but with electronic fuel injection Brake H.P.: 129 at 3600 R.P.M. Torque: 231 lbs.- ft. at 2000 R.P.M. OPTIONAL V-8 (Continental, Mark VI): 90-degree, overhead valve V-8. Cast iron block and head. Displacement: 351 cu. in. (5.8 liters). Bore & stroke: 4.00 x 3.50 in. Compression ratio: 8.3:1. Brake horsepower: 140 at 3400 R.P.M. Torque: 265 lbs.-ft. at 2000 R.P.M. Five main bearings. Hydraulic valve lifters. Carburetor: 2Bbl. Motorcraft 7200VV. VIN Code: G.

CHASSIS DATA: Wheelbase: (Versailles) 109.9 in.; (Continental) 117.4 in.; (Mark VI 2dr.) 114.4 in.; (Mark VI 4dr.) 117.4 in. Overall Length: (Versailles) 200.7 in.; (Cont.) 219.2 in.; (Mark 2dr.) 216.0 in.; (Mark 4dr.) 219.2 in. Height: (Versailles) 54.1 in.; (Cont./Mark 2dr.) 55.1 in.; (Cont./Mark 4dr.) 55.8 in. Width: (Versailles) 74.5 in.; (Cont./Mark) 78.1 in. Front Tread: (Versailles) 59.0 in.; (Cont./Mark) 62.2 in. Rear Tread: (Versailles) 57.7 in.; (Cont./Mark) 62.0 in. Standard Tires: (Versailles) FR78 x 14 SBR WSW; (Continental, Mark) Michelin P205/75R15 SBR WSW.

TECHNICAL: Transmission: SelectShift three-speed manual transmission (column shift) standard on Versailles. Gear ratios: (1st) 2.46:1; (2nd) 1.46:1; (3rd) 1.00:1; (Rev) 2.19:1. Four-speed automatic overdrive standard on Continental and Mark VI: (1st) 2.40:1; (2nd) 1.47:1; (3rd) 1.00:1; (4th) 0.67:1; (Rev) 2.00:1. Standard final drive ratio: (Versailles) 2.47:1; (Cont./Mark) 3.08:1 except 2.73:1 w/V8351. Steering: Recirculating ball, power-assisted. Suspension: (Versailles) front spring over upper arm w/ball joints and drag struts and coil springs, Hotchkiss rear w/semi-elliptic leaf springs; (Continental/Mark VI) long/short Aarm front w/coil springs and anti-sway bar, four-link coil spring rear. Brakes: (Versailles) four-wheel disc; (others) front disc and rear drum; all power-assisted. Ignition: Electronic. Body construction: (Versailles) unibody; (others) separate body and frame. Fuel Tank: (Versailles) 19.2 gal.; (others) 20.0 gal.

DRIVETRAIN OPTIONS: 351 cu. in. V-8 engine: Cont./Mark ($160). Optional axle ratio ($24). Traction-Lok differential: Cont./Mark ($110). H.D. battery: Cont./Mark ($23). Engine block heater ($23). Trailer towing pkg.: Cont. ($97-$137); Mark ($140-$180). California emission system ($253). High-altitude option: Versailles (NC).

VERSAILLES CONVENIENCE/APPEARANCE OPTIONS: Appearance protection group ($84-$88). Reclining bucket seat group ($416). Power lock group ($169). Defroster group ($132). Rear defroster, electric ($109). Garage door opener ($99). Illuminated outside thermometer ($31). Tilt steering wheel ($81). AM/FM stereo search radio w/8track tape player ($81); w/cassette player ($95). 40channel CB radio ($356). Power glass panel moonroof ($1128). Coach roof, Valino grain (NC). Dual-shade paint ($80). Protective bodyside moldings ($53). Premium bodyside moldings ($83). Lower bodyside protection ($35). Padded decklid applique delete (NC). Leather/vinyl interior trim ($416). Wire wheel covers (NC).

CONTINENTAL/MARK VI CONVENIENCE/APPEARANCE OPTIONS: Option Packages: Mark VI Signature Series ($5485-$5516). Fashion Accent series: Cont. ($600). Town Car option: Cont. ($1089). Town Coupe option: Cont. ($1089). Mark VI Cartier Designer series: leather/vinyl or luxury cloth interior ($2191). Mark VI Emilio Pucci Designer series ($2191). Mark VI Bill Blass Designer series w/carriage roof ($2809); w/full vinyl roof ($1825). Mark VI Givenchy Designer series ($1739). Mark VI luxury groups ($1044). Headlamp convenience group ($141). Defroster group ($132). Comfort/Convenience: Rear defroster ($109). Speed control ($149). Illuminated entry system ($67). Keyless entry ($253- $293). Power door locks ($103-$143). Remote decklid release ($27). Six-way power flight bench seat: Cont. ($171); w/recliners ($312). Reclining passenger seat: Mark ($91); both ($139). Twin comfort six-way power seats: Mark ($171). Twin comfort lounge power seats: Cont. ($1044-$1089) exc. ($45) with Town Car/Cpe. Electronic instrument panel: Cont. ($707); Mark ($707 credit). Garage door opener ($99). Leather-wrapped steering wheel ($47). Tilt steering wheel ($83). Intermittent wipers ($43). Lighting and Mirrors: Coach lamps: Cont. ($71). Touring lamps: Mark ($67). Right remote mirror ($44).

Lighted visor vanity mirror ($123). Entertainment: AM/FM stereo search radio w/cassette ($95) or 8track player ($81). 40channel CB radio ($356). Premium sound system ($160). Exterior: Power glass panel moonroof ($1128) exc. ($817-$888) w/Mark Signature. Carriage roof: Mark ($984). Landau vinyl roof: Mark ($240-$311). Coach vinyl roof: Cont. ($367) exc. ($296) with Town Car/Cpe. Moondust paint ($232). Dual-shade paint: Cont. ($360). Custom paint stripes: Mark ($53). Door edge guards ($16-$24). Premium bodyside moldings: Cont. ($144). Rocker panel molding delete: Mark ($76 credit). Padded decklid applique delete: Mark Signature (NC). License plate frames: rear ($8); front/rear ($16). Lower bodyside protection ($35). Interior: Leather interior trim: Cont. ($368-$435). Floor mats: front ($35); rear ($19). Trunk mat ($15). Wheels and Tires: Wire wheel covers ($255). Lacy spoke or turbine spoke aluminum wheels ($396) exc. (Givenchy) ($141). Wide-band whitewall tires ($36). Conventional spare tire ($40).

NOTE: Mark VI Signature Series was listed first as an option package (with prices shown above), then as a separate model.

HISTORY: Introduced: October 12, 1979. Model year production: 74,908. Calendar year production: 52,793. Calendar year sales by U.S. dealers: 69,704. Model year sales by U.S. dealers: 87,468.

Historical Footnotes: This was the final year for Versailles, which was expensive and guzzled. Its price rose once again, and sales fell to a mere 4,784 for the year. In fact, sales of all three models fell sharply. The total for Lincoln dropped 42 percent. Evidently, downsizing of the "big" Lincolns wasn't enough to attract customers in this difficult period for the industry.

1981 LINCOLN

Without changing appreciably in appearance, the Continental of 1980 became this year's "Town Car," adding more power/comfort choices. A new top-rung Signature Series was added. New options included wire-spoke aluminum wheels and self-sealing tires. Versailles was dropped after 1980 due to shrunken sales. So was the 351 cu. in. V-8, leaving only the fuel-injected 302 powerplant.

1981 Continental Town Car (L)

TOWN CAR — V-8 — Now called the Lincoln Town Car, the former Continental (downsized for 1980) aimed harder at connoisseurs of luxury motoring. Town Car had new standard Twin Comfort Lounge seats with six-way power driver's seat. Coach lamps and premium bodyside moldings were added as standard. Town Car came in 18 body colors: 11 standard, seven optional. Standard auto-temp air conditioning added a "mix" mode, while the optional electronic instrument panel included a message center with fuel economy data. New options were: self-sealing whitewalls, dual-shade paint colors with vinyl roof matching the upper bodyside, Class II trailer towing package, dual power remote mirrors, and wire-spoke aluminum wheels. Coach and carriage roofs were available. Base (indeed only) engine was the fuel-injected 302 cu. in. (5.0-liter) V-8, with four-speed automatic overdrive transmission and 3.08:1 rear axle. The 351 cu. in. V-8 disappeared. Appearance was similar to 1980, except that the grille pattern no longer repeated in a bumper slot. Both the two-door and four-door rode a 117.3 inch wheelbase. The new top-level Signature Series was posher yet. It included a coach roof, 'Signature Series' script on rear roof pillar (and instrument panel), six-way power Twin Comfort Lounge front seats in special "pillowed" sew style, seatback robe cords and map pockets, and padded center-pillar upper trim panel with lower carpeting.

1981 Continental Mark VI sedan (L)

MARK VI — V-8 — Six important options became standard this year: power door locks, power decklid release, intermittent wipers, tilt steering wheel, speed control, and right remote-control mirror. Mark's electronic instrument panel with message center had a new instantaneous fuel economy function. A mix mode was added to the standard automatic-temperature-control air conditioning. Four-doors had new dual-shade paint options. New options this year were: puncture-resistant self-sealing wide whitewalls; power remote mirrors; Class II trailer towing package; and wire-spoke aluminum wheels. The wire wheels and power mirrors became standard on Signature Series, which was otherwise a carryover. Two-doors could have a carriage roof in diamond-grain or Cambria fabric. Of the 21 body colors offered on Mark VI, seven were new: five new standard colors and two optional Moondust colors. Eleven colors in all were standard, eight optional (moondust), and two offered only on the Signature Series. New interior colors were: nutmeg, light fawn, medium fawn, and gold. Powertrain was the same as Town Car's: 302 cu. in. (5.0- liter) fuel-injected V-8 with four-speed overdrive automatic and 3.08:1 axle ratio. No other choices were available. Appearance was unchanged following the 1980 restyle. The Designer Series quartet was revised this year. Cartier came in medium pewter metallic body color. Its interior was luxury group sew style in choice of leather with vinyl or luxury cloth, pewter colored with Cartier logo buttons. The landau vinyl roof was medium pewter. Cartier had dark red accent stripes on bodyside and decklid, and medium pewter bodyside moldings. Standard wheels were color-keyed lacy-spoke aluminum. Mark's Givenchy model had its upper bodyside in black, lower bodyside in dark pewter. Leather with vinyl or luxury cloth interior was pewter colored, with Givenchy logo buttons. Also included: a black landau vinyl roof; red and gold dual accent stripes on hood, bodyside and decklid; black bodyside moldings; and new wire-spoke aluminum wheels. Pucci's edition came in medium fawn metallic, with light fawn interior and Pucci buttons on the seatbacks. It had a fawn full vinyl roof, tri-tone accent stripes on bodyside and decklid, light fawn bodyside moldings, and wire-spoke aluminum wheels. Finally, Bill Blass had its upper bodyside in dark blue metallic, lower bodyside in light fawn metallic. Interior was dark blue with light fawn bolsters and Blass seat buttons; carriage vinyl roof in midnight blue cloth. The Bill Blass had dual dark blue accent stripes on the bodyside, light fawn accent stripes on decklid contour, and light fawn bodyside moldings; plus color-keyed lacy-spoke aluminum wheels.

I.D. DATA: Lincoln had a new 17-symbol Vehicle Identification Number (VIN) this year, again fastened to the instrument panel, visible through the windshield. The first three symbols indicate manufacturer, make and vehicle type: '1LN' Lincoln; '1MR' Continental (Mark). The fourth symbol ('B') denotes restraint system. Next comes a letter 'P', followed by two digits that indicate body type: '93' 2dr. Town Car; '94' 4dr. Town Car; '95' 2dr. Mark VI; '96' 4dr. Mark VI. Symbol eight indicates engine type ('F' V8302). Next is a check digit. Symbol ten indicates model year ('B' 1981). Symbol eleven is assembly plant ('Y' Wixom, MI). The final six digits make up the sequence number, starting with 600001. A Vehicle Certification Label on the left front door lock face panel or door pillar shows the manufacturer, month and year built, GVW, GAWR, VIN, and codes for body type, color, trim, axle, transmission, and special order information.

1981 Continental Town Car (JG)

TOWN CAR (V-8)

Model Number	Body/Style Number	Body Type & Seating	Factory Price	Shipping Weight	Production Total
93	66D	2-dr. Coupe-5P	13707	3884	4,935
94	54D	4-dr. Sedan-6P	14068	3958	27,904

MARK VI (V-8)

95	66D	2-dr. Coupe-5P	16858	3899	18,740
96	54D	4-dr. Sedan-6P	17303	3944	17,958

MARK VI SIGNATURE SERIES (V-8)

95	66D	2-dr. Coupe-5P	22463	3990	N/A
96	54D	4-dr. Sedan-6P	22838	4035	N/A

ENGINE DATA: BASE V-8 (Town Car, Mark VI): 90-degree, overhead valve V-8. Cast iron block and head. Displacement: 302 cu. in. (5.2 liters). Bore & stroke: 4.00 x 3.00 in. Compression ratio: 8.4:1. Brake horsepower: 130 at 3400 R.P.M. Torque: 230 lbs.-ft. at 2200 R.P.M. Five main bearings. Hydraulic valve lifters. Electronic fuel injection. VIN Code: F.

CHASSIS DATA: Wheelbase: (2dr.) 114.3 in.; (4dr.) 117.3 in. Overall Length: (Town Car) 219.0 in. (Mark 2dr.) 216.0 in. (Mark 4dr.) 219.1 in. Height: (2dr.) 55.4 in.; (4dr.) 56.1 in. Width: 78.1 in. Front Tread: 62.2 in. Rear Tread: 62.0 in. Standard Tires: Michelin P205/75R15 SBR WSW.

TECHNICAL: Transmission: Four-speed automatic overdrive standard. Gear ratios: (1st) 2.40:1; (2nd) 1.47:1; (3rd) 1.00:1; (4th) 0.67:1; (Rev) 2.00:1. Standard final drive ratio: 3.08:1. Steering: Recirculating ball, power-assisted. Suspension: Upper/lower front control arms w/coil springs and anti-sway bar, four-link coil spring rear. Brakes: Front disc and rear drum, power-assisted. Ignition: Electronic. Body construction: Separate body and frame. Fuel Tank: 18 gal.

DRIVETRAIN OPTIONS: Traction-Lok differential ($108). H.D. battery ($22). Engine block heater ($22). Trailer towing pkg. ($141-$180). California emission system ($47).

CONVENIENCE/APPEARANCE OPTIONS: Option Packages: Town Car Signature Series ($1144). Mark VI Designer series: Cartier ($2031); Emilio Pucci ($2160); Bill Blass ($3015); Givenchy ($2372). Mark VI luxury groups ($1044). Headlamp convenience group ($149). Defroster group ($135). Comfort/Convenience: Speed control w/resume: Town Car ($153). Illuminated entry system ($67). Keyless entry: Town Car ($257-$294); Mark ($123). Power door locks: Town ($106-$143). Remote decklid release: Town Car ($27). Driver/passenger recliners: Mark ($138); passenger only ($90). Twin comfort six-way power seats: Mark ($170). Twin comfort lounge power seats: Town Car ($260). Twin comfort lounge power seats w/dual recliners: Town ($309) exc. ($48) w/Signature Series. Electronic instrument panel: Town ($706); Mark, delete ($706 credit). Garage door opener ($99). Leather-wrapped steering wheel ($47). Tilt steering wheel: Town ($83). Intermittent wipers: Town ($44). Lighting and Mirrors: Touring lamps: Mark ($67). Right remote mirror: Town ($46). Dual power remote mirrors: Town ($148); Mark ($99). Lighted visor vanity mirrors, pair ($126). Entertainment: AM/FM stereo search radio w/8track player ($81); w/cassette and Dolby ($95). 40channel CB radio ($356). Premium sound system ($160). Exterior: Power glass panel moonroof ($1122). Carriage roof, diamond-grain or cambria fabric: 2dr. ($984). Vinyl coach roof ($240-$315). Moondust paint ($236). Dual-shade paint: Town Car or Mark 4dr. ($246). Custom paint stripes: Mark ($53). Door edge guards ($16-$23). Rocker panel molding delete: Mark ($141 credit). License plate frames: rear ($9); front/rear ($16). Lower bodyside protection ($35). Interior: Leather interior trim: Town ($378-$440); Mark ($470). Floor mats: front ($35); rear ($20). Trunk mat ($16). Wheels and Tires: Wire spoke aluminum wheels ($756) exc. Blass/Cartier ($342). Lacy spoke aluminum wheels ($414) exc. Givenchy/Pucci ($342 credit). Turbine spoke aluminum wheels ($414) exc. Givenchy/Pucci ($342 credit) and Blass/Cartier (NC). Self-sealing whitewall tires ($105). Conventional spare tire ($39).

HISTORY: Introduced: October 3, 1980. Model year production: 69,537. Calendar year production: 64,185. Calendar year sales by U.S. dealers: 63,830. Model year sales by U.S. dealers: 65,248 (plus 334 leftover Versailles models).

Historical Footnotes: Sales were disappointing for the 1981 model year, down by some 25 percent. The Town Car at least came fairly close to its 1980 sales total, but Mark VI found more than 10,000 fewer buyers (down to 34,210).

1982 LINCOLN

A new, smaller Continental debuted this year, weighing less than the old Versailles. Three models now made up the Lincoln lineup: four-door Continental, four-door (Lincoln) Town Car, and Mark VI coupe.

1982 Continental Signature Series sedan (JG)

CONTINENTAL — V-6/V-8 — An all-new "contemporary size" Continental took on the name used by Lincoln for four decades. This modern version rode a 108.7 inch wheelbase and weighed less than 3,600 pounds at the curb. It was 18 inches shorter and 500 pounds lighter than the former version. Base price of $21,302 was considerably higher than either the Town Car or Mark. Four-doored bodied only, Continental came in base model, Signature Series, and Givenchy Designer Series. Under the hood, the 302 cu. in. (5.0-liter) V-8 was standard, but a 232 cu. in. (3.8-liter) V-6 was now available as a no-cost option. Four-speed overdrive automatic was the standard transmission. Continental had variable-ratio power rack-and-pinion steering, four-wheel disc brakes, and a modified MacPherson strut front suspension with stabilizer bar. Nitrogen-pressurized shock absorbers went at all four corners (first time on a domestic car). Standard features included an electronic instrument panel with message center, all-electronic AM/FM stereo search radio, self-sealing steel- belted radials, speed control, illuminated entry, tilt steering, rear defroster, power door locks, power windows, power antenna, interval wipers, and dual power heated outside mirrors (with thermometer in the left one). Six-way power Twin Comfort Lounge front seats had manual recliners. The modest option list included keyless entry and a power glass moonroof. Styling was unmistakably Lincoln, starting with the traditional "classic" vertical-style grille and 'Continental' decklid treatment. Continental had front bumper guards, front and rear bumper rub strips with accent stripe, a Lincoln star hood ornament, and flush-mounted bright windshield molding. Each pair of exposed quad rectangular headlamps met wraparound signal lenses at the fender tips, with cornering and side marker lamps in a single housing. Bumper-mounted backup lamps stood on each side of the license plate bracket. 'Lincoln' script went on the decklid, 'Continental' script on front fenders. There was also a Lincoln Continental rear roof pillar ornament and rear side marker lamps. Front cornering and side marker lamps fit in a single housing. Forged aluminum wheels were standard. Continental's Signature Series had 'Signature Series' script on rear roof pillar, coach lamps in center roof pillar, and wire-spoke aluminum wheels. A bright/brushed full-length narrow upper bodyside molding replaced the standard accent stripe. The owner's identification kit included a signature plate for the instrument panel, and two sets of initials for the outside of front doors. Those items were sent directly to the buyer. The dual-shade

1982 Continental Givenchy Designer Series sedan (JG)

paint treatment on Signature Series came in three special color combinations. A Givenchy Designer Series had dual-shade paint in unique black/medium dark mulberry metallic. Givenchy's rear roof pillar ornament replaced the usual Lincoln Continental ornament and Signature Series script. There was also 'Givenchy' script in the rear quarter window glass. Interior was mulberry cloth luxury cloth or leather. Signature and Designer Series had a new trouble light mounted in the trunk.

MARK VI — V-8 — Appearance of Lincoln's personal luxury coupe and sedan was similar to 1981, with the exception of two new optional specialty roofs: a coach roof (rear half) for two-doors, and a full roof for four-doors. Specialty roofs included a large Cpillar, accented by small vertical quarter windows and slim coach lamps. Roof rear half and moldings could be covered in either Bayville grain vinyl, diamond grain vinyl, Valino vinyl, or Cambria cloth. As before, Mark had concealed headlamps, a simulated spare tire bulge on the decklid, and (on two-doors) tiny horizontal oval opera windows. Standard equipment was similar to 1981, including air conditioning, four-speed overdrive automatic, power brakes and steering, and the fuel-injected 302 cu. in. (5.0-liter) V-8. Eleven paint colors were added, along with three new dual-shade combinations. Both the Givenchy and Cartier Designer Series were scheduled to disappear, but Givenchy reappeared a bit later. The optional leather-wrapped steering wheel was no longer available. A dual exhaust system had become optional in late 1981 and continued this year. Mark's Signature Series came in 13 monotone paint colors, with color-keyed Valino grain coach roof. It also had color-keyed bumper rub strips with white accent stripes. Body-color accents went on parking lamp lenses, and 'Signature Series' script on the Cpillar. This year's Designer Series consisted only of a Bill Blass two-door and Pucci four-door (and later, a Givenchy two-door). The Bill Blass had a choice of three paint and roof treatments: two-tone white with red bodyside accent color, and white diamond-grain vinyl carriage roof; all-white paint with white diamond-grain vinyl carriage roof; or all- black with black Cambria cloth carriage roof. Blass also had black bodyside moldings and dual accent stripes, and double red accent stripes on the decklid contour. The Bill Blass logo went on C pillar and decklid. Mark VI Puccis came in two-tone pastel French vanilla on the top, pastel vanilla metallic on the bottom. The Bayville textured vinyl specialty full roof was pastel French vanilla colored. Bodyside accent stripes were dark brown with gold; decklid pinstripes dark brown with the Pucci logo. That Pucci logo in dark brown was also on the front fender, and on the instrument panel. The Givenchy Designer Series had a dual- shade paint treatment with black upper and medium dark pewter metallic lower, black Valino grain coach roof, and choice of pewter cloth or leather seat trim with Givenchy seat buttons. Givenchy also had black bodyside moldings; red and gold dual accent stripes on hood, bodyside and decklid; Givenchy logo on hood and decklid; 'Givenchy' lettering in opera window; an identification plaque on instrument panel; and wire-spoke aluminum wheels.

(LINCOLN) TOWN CAR — V-8 — Only a four-door Town Car was offered for 1982 (sometimes referred to as, simply, "Lincoln"). The two-door model was dropped. New this year was a Cartier Designer Series, joining the former Signature Series. Appearance was the same as 1981. Sole engine was the fuel-injected 302 cu. in. (5.0-liter) V-8, with electronic controls and four-speed overdrive automatic transmission. Town Car had a 3.08:1 rear axle ratio and an 18-gallon fuel tank. Power door locks were now standard, as was a remote- control decklid release (both formerly optional). Thirteen new paint colors were available. A dual exhaust system had joined the option list in mid-year 1981. The Signature Series added a coach roof, and 'Signature Series' script on the rear roof pillar. The new Cartier model featured two-tone paint: light pewter on top and opal on the bottom. It had a light pewter full vinyl roof in Bayville textured vinyl; opal bodyside moldings; opal and pewter in single red bodyside paint stripe; single red decklid paint stripe with Cartier logo in red tape; Cartier Designer logo in rear quarter windows; and turbine-spoke aluminum wheels. The instrument panel also carried the Cartier logo and identification. Cartier's interior was opal leather with light pewter luxury cloth (or leather in the insert area).

I.D. DATA: Lincoln again had a 17-symbol Vehicle Identification Number (VIN), fastened to the instrument panel, visible through the windshield. The first digit three symbols indicate manufacturer, make and vehicle type: '1LN' Lincoln; '1MR' Continental. The fourth symbol ('B') denotes restraint system. Next comes a letter 'P', followed by two digits that indicate body type: '94' 4dr. Town Car; '95' 2dr. Mark VI; '96' 4dr. Mark VI; '98' 4dr. Continental. Symbol eight indicates engine type: 'F' V8302; '3' V6232 2Bbl. Next is a check digit. Symbol ten indicates model year ('C' 1982). Symbol eleven is assembly plant ('Y' Wixom, MI). The final six digits make up the sequence number, starting with 6000C1. A Vehicle Certification Label on the left front door lock face panel or door pillar shows the manufacturer, month and year built, GVW, GAWR, VIN, and codes for body type, color, trim, axle, transmission, and special order information.

CONTINENTAL (V-6/V-8)

Model Number	Body/Style Number	Body Type & Seating	Factory Price	Shipping Weight	Production Total
98	54D	4-dr. Sedan-5P	21302	3512	23,908
CONTINENTAL SIGNATURE SERIES (V-6/V-8)					
98/603	54D	4-dr. Sedan-5P	24456	3610	Note 1
CONTINENTAL GIVENCHY DESIGNER SERIES (V-6/V-8)					
98/60M	54D	4-dr. Sedan-5P	24803	3610	Note 1
TOWN CAR (V-8)					
94	54D	4-dr. Sedan-6P	16100	3936	35,069

1982 Continental sedan (JG)

TOWN CAR SIGNATURE SERIES (V-8)

Model Number	Body/Style Number	Body Type & Seating	Factory Price	Shipping Weight	Production Total
94/60U	54D	4-dr. Sedan-6P	17394	3952	Note 1

TOWN CAR CARTIER DESIGNER SERIES (V-8)

Model Number	Body/Style Number	Body Type & Seating	Factory Price	Shipping Weight	Production Total
94/605	54D	4-dr. Sedan-6P	18415	3944	Note 1

MARK VI (V-8)

Model Number	Body/Style Number	Body Type & Seating	Factory Price	Shipping Weight	Production Total
95	66D	2-dr. Coupe-6P	19452	3879	11,532
96	54D	4-dr. Sedan-6P	19924	3976	14,804

MARK VI SIGNATURE SERIES (V-8)

Model Number	Body/Style Number	Body Type & Seating	Factory Price	Shipping Weight	Production Total
95/603	66D	2-dr. Coupe-6P	22252	3888	Note 1
96/603	54D	4-dr. Sedan-6P	22720	3985	Note 1

MARK VI DESIGNER SERIES (V-8)

Model Number	Body/Style Number	Body Type & Seating	Factory Price	Shipping Weight	Production Total
95/60M	66D	2-dr. Givenchy-6P	22722	3910	Note 1
95/60N	66D	2-dr. Blass-6P	23594	3910	Note 1
96/60P	54D	4-dr. Pucci-6P	23465	3970	Note 1

Note 1: Production of Signature and Designer Series is included in basic model totals.

Model Number Note: Some sources include a prefix 'P' ahead of the two- digit number; e.g., 'P98' for Continental.

ENGINE DATA: BASE V-8 (Mark VI, Town Car): 90-degree, overhead valve V-8. Cast iron block and head. Displacement: 302 cu. in. (5.2 liters). Bore & stroke: 4.00 x 3.00 in. Compression ratio: 8.4:1. Brake horsepower: 134 at 3400 R.P.M. Torque: 232 lbs.-ft. at 2200 R.P.M. Five main bearings. Hydraulic valve lifters. Electronic fuel injection. VIN Code: F. BASE V-8 (Continental): Same as 302 cu. in. V-8 above, but with 2Bbl. variable- venturi carburetor Brake H.P.: 131 at 3400 R.P.M. Torque: 229 lbs.-ft. at 1200 R.P.M. OPTIONAL V-6 (Continental): 90-degree, overhead valve V-6. Cast iron block and head. Displacement: 232 cu. in. (3.8 liters). Bore & stroke: 3.80 x 3.40 in. Compression ratio: 8.7:1. Brake horsepower: 112 at 4000 R.P.M. Torque: 175 lbs.-ft. at 2600 R.P.M. Four main bearings. Hydraulic valve lifters. Carburetor: 2Bbl. Motorcraft 2150. VIN Code: 3.

NOTE: Some sources list the V-6 as standard Continental engine, with the V-8 a no-cost option.

CHASSIS DATA: Wheelbase: (Continental) 108.7 in.; (Mark 2dr.) 114.3 in.; (Mark/Town 4dr.) 117.3 in. Overall Length: (Cont.) 201.2 in.; (Mark 2dr.) 216.0 in.; (Mark/Town 4dr.) 219.0 in. Height: (Cont.) 55.0 in.; (Mark 2dr.) 55.1 in.; (Mark 4dr.) 56.0 in.; (Town Car) 55.8 in. Width: (Cont.) 73.6 in.; (Mark/Town) 78.1 in. Front Tread: (Cont.) 58.4 in.; (Mark/Town) 62.2 in. Rear Tread: (Cont.) 59.0 in.; (Mark/Town) 62.0 in. Standard Tires: P205/75R15 SBR WSW.

TECHNICAL: Transmission: Four-speed automatic overdrive standard. Gear ratios: (1st) 2.40:1; (2nd) 1.47:1; (3rd) 1.00:1; (4th) 0.67:1; (Rev) 2.00:1. Standard final drive ratio: 3.08:1. Steering: (Continental) rack and pinion; (Mark/Town) recirculating ball; all power-assisted. Suspension: (Continental) modified MacPherson front struts with anti-sway bar, rigid rear axle with upper/lower trailing arms, and gas-pressurized shocks; (others) front control arms w/anti-sway bar, rigid four-link rear axle with lower trailing radius arms and oblique torque arms. Brakes: Front disc and rear drum, power-assisted; except Continental, four-wheel disc brakes. Ignition: Electronic. Body construction: (Continental) unibody; (others) separate body and box-type ladder frame. Fuel Tank: 18 gal. exc. Continental, 22.6 gal.

DRIVETRAIN OPTIONS: Dual exhaust system: Mark/Town ($83) but (NC) w/high-altitude emissions. Traction-Lok differential: Mark/Town ($128). H.D. battery ($28). Engine block heater ($26). Trailer towing pkg. ($223-$306). California emission system ($47). High-altitude emissions (NC).

CONTINENTAL CONVENIENCE/APPEARANCE OPTIONS: Appearance protection group ($47). Keyless entry ($141). Leather-wrapped steering wheel ($59). Dual lighted visor vanity mirrors ($146). Electronic AM/FM radio w/cassette or 8track ($107). Power glass moonroof ($1259). Color-keyed vinyl bodyside molding ($64). Two-tone paint ($298). Moondust paint ($257). Monotone paint: Signature ($298 credit). Leather interior trim ($535). Wire spoke aluminum wheels ($395).

MARK VI/TOWN CAR CONVENIENCE/APPEARANCE OPTIONS: Option Packages: Headlamp convenience group ($175). Defroster group ($151). Comfort/Convenience: Fingertip speed control: Town ($178). Illuminated entry system ($77). Keyless entry ($141). Twin comfort six-way power seats w/recliners: Mark ($354); w/passenger recliner only ($302). Twin comfort power seats w/passenger recliner: Town Car ($288); dual recliners ($340) exc. ($52) w/Signature Series. Electronic instrument panel: Town ($804); Mark, delete ($804 credit). Garage door opener ($110). Tilt steering wheel: Town ($96). Intermittent wipers: Town ($53). Lighting and Mirrors: Touring lamps: Mark ($78). Right remote mirror: Town ($59). Dual remote mirrors w/lighted left thermometer: Town ($173); Mark ($114). Lighted visor vanity mirrors, pair ($146). Entertainment: Electronic AM/FM stereo radio w/8track player ($107); w/cassette and Dolby ($107). 40channel CB radio ($356). Premium sound system ($181). Exterior: Power glass panel moonroof ($1259). Carriage roof: Mark 2dr. ($1057). Full specialty roof: Mark 4dr. ($640) exc. Signature ($368). Specialty coach roof: Mark 2dr. ($1028) exc. Signature ($757). Vinyl coach roof ($272-$357). Moondust paint ($257). Dual-shade paint ($298). Custom accent stripes ($62). Door edge guards ($19-$27). Rocker panel molding delete: Mark ($149 credit). License plate frames: rear ($11); front/rear ($20). Lower bodyside protection ($40). Interior: Leather interior trim: Town ($436-$498). Mark ($535). Floor mats w/carpet inserts: front ($41); rear ($23). Wheels and Tires: Wire wheel covers ($274) exc. Mark Pucci or Town Cartier ($191 credit), or Mark Blass/Givenchy ($586 credit). Wire spoke aluminum wheels ($860) exc. Mark Signature or Town Cartier ($395), or Mark Pucci ($465). Lacy spoke aluminum wheels ($465) exc. Mark Signature ($191), Town Cartier (NC), or Mark Givenchy/Blass ($395 credit). Turbine spoke aluminum wheels ($465) exc. Mark Signature ($191) and Mark Givenchy/Pucci ($395 credit). Self-sealing whitewall tires ($129). Conventional spare tire ($52).

HISTORY: Introduced: September 24, 1981 except Continental, Oct. 1, 1981. Model year production: 85,313. Calendar year production: 97,622. Calendar year sales by U.S. dealers: 93,068. Model year sales by U.S. dealers: 81,653.

Historical Footnotes: Lincoln sales climbed more than 25 percent for 1982— just about the same percentage that they'd declined in the previous model year. Of course, there were three models this year, as opposed to only two in 1981. Obviously, some buyers who might otherwise have chosen another model turned to the new Continental instead. In fact, Mark VI sales dropped considerably, from 34,210 down to just 25,386. All Lincolns were built at Wixom, Michigan, a factory that put in considerable overtime to keep up with production. That production total rose sharply in 1982, up to 47,611 from just 26,651 for the prior calendar year. Lincolns had a 36-month, 36,000-mile warranty.

1983 LINCOLN

All three Lincoln models were mainly carryovers this year. Each came in a choice of Designer or Signature Series, as well as base models. Continental losts its short-lived V-6 option, but offered a long list of standard equipment.

1983 Continental sedan (OCW)

CONTINENTAL — V-8 — Bodies of Lincoln's mid-size "bustleback" four-door sedan showed virtually no change this year, except for an 'Electronic Fuel Injection' plaque on the front fender. That space previously held 'Continental' script. Continental now got the fuel-injected (TBI) version of the familiar 302 cu. in. (5.0-liter) V-8, formerly installed only in the big Lincolns. The 3.8-liter V-6 was discontinued. Four-speed automatic overdrive was again the standard transmission, with a lockup torque converter. A heavy-duty 68 ampere-hour battery was now standard. So was a locking fuel filler door with remote release. Digital electronic instruments were standard. Continental's chassis was actually the old rear- drive "Fox" platform, which originated with Fairmont/Zephyr and also appeared (with shorter wheelbase) in this year's new LTD and Marquis. Standard equipment included four-wheel power disc brakes, self-sealing P205/75R15 whitewall tires, tilt steering, power windows and door locks, speed control, tinted glass, intermittent wipers, cornering lamps, dual power heated mirrors (thermometer on driver's side), stereo search radio, and illuminated entry. Six-way power Twin Comfort Lounge seats were upholstered in Radcliffe cloth. An owner's identification kit included two plaques with owner's initials on front doors, and one for his or her signature on the dash. This year's base model was actually a revision of the Signature Series of 1982, leaving no Signature in the lineup. The Givenchy Designer Series returned again in revised form, joined by an all-new Valentino Designer model. Givenchy was painted Midnight Black and Platinum Mist, with tri-color (grey-blue, magenta, and charcoal) accent striping and unique wraparound roof. Twin Comfort Lounge seats had charcoal Radcliffe cloth or leather seating surfaces. Givenchy identification went on the rear pillar, dash, and quarter windows. Valentino came in a dual-shade combination of its own: Walnut Moondust over Golden Mist, with black and gold accent striping and Valentino logo on the bodyside. Gold decklid accent striping included the Valentino logo. Comfort Lounge seats had Desert Tan Radcliffe cloth or leather seating surfaces, both trimmed with walnut straps and buttons. Valentino also had a leather-wrapped steering wheel. Both Designer Series included coach lamps and cast aluminum wire wheels. A dozen new paint colors were offered this year on "ordinary" Continentals, and seven new dual-shade combinations. Standard colors were: Midnight Black, Cameo White, Platinum Mist, Scarlet Red, Aegean Green Mist, Pastel French Vanilla, Desert Tan, Light Desert Tan, Midnight Blue Mist, and Scarlet Mist. Five moondust colors were optional. Front and rear floor mats were now standard. New options included a three-channel garage door opener, coach lamps, automatic-dimming day/night mirror, and anti-theft alarm system. A bright brushed-aluminum upper bodyside molding option had been added in mid-year 1982.

MARK VI — V-8 — Some shuffling of the Designer Series occurred this year, but otherwise Mark was essentially a carryover with minimal change. Mark had a standard full vinyl roof with opera windows and limousine-style back window, front fender louvers (at the cowl), concealed halogen headlamps, and power vent windows. Standard engine was again the fuel-injected 302 cu. in. (5.0-liter) V-8, with four-speed overdrive automatic. A new all-electronic stereo search radio became standard, while a larger (71 ampere-hour) battery had been standard since mid-year 1982. The Givenchy Designer Series was dropped, as was the four-door specialty roof. But a four-door carriage roof was a new option. Other new options included an automatic dimming day/night mirror, anti-theft alarm, three- channel garage door opener, and locking wire wheel covers. Pucci's Designer Series was now available on both two- and four-door Marks. Body paint was Blue Flannel Mist, with carriage roof in dark blue Cambria cloth. Opera windows were deleted. Inside was a choice of Academy Blue cloth or leather seat trim. Pucci had a wide bright bodyside molding with Midnight Blue vinyl insert, silver sparkle bodyside accent stripes, silver sparkle decklid pinstripe and Pucci logo. 'Emilio Pucci' script went in the rear door quarter window. Pucci's logo also appeared in tape on fender and decklid. Also included: a Mark "star" on rear roof pillar, leather- wrapped steering wheel, and turbine-spoke aluminum wheels. The Bill Blass Designer Series came in two dual-shade combinations: Midnight Black upper and lower, and Light French Vanilla middle, with black Cambria cloth carriage roof; or Light French Vanilla upper/lower and Midnight Black in the middle, with Light French Vanilla Bayville textured vinyl carriage roof. Inside was a choice of French Vanilla cloth or leather seat inserts, with French Vanilla leather bolsters in Signature Series sew style. Midnight Black bodyside moldings, vanilla and black bodyside accent stripes, and vanilla or black decklid accent stripe with the Bill Blass logo were included. (That logo also was on the rear roof pillar and instrument panel.) Bill Blass also had a leather-wrapped steering wheel and wire-spoke aluminum wheels. Rocker panel moldings were deleted. Eleven new paint colors were available on base Marks, and seven new dual-shade combinations. Standard colors were the same as Continental's, except Antique Mahogany Mist replaced Scarlet.

LINCOLN (TOWN CAR) — V-8 — While many sources continued to refer to the traditional big Lincoln sedan as a Town Car, the factory catalog listed it as, simply, "Lincoln." Not much was new, apart from an all-electronic stereo search radio and heavy-duty battery. Eleven new body colors and seven dual-shade combinations were added, along with eight vinyl roof colors. Sole powertrain was again the fuel-injected 302 cu. in. (5.0-liter) V-8 with four-speed overdrive automatic, the same as Mark VI. Standard equipment included auto-temp air conditioning, power antenna, coach and cornering lamps, power side/vent windows, analog clock, remote decklid release, tinted glass, left remote mirror, and full vinyl roof. The Cartier Designer Series had a new Medium Charcoal Moondust over Platinum Mist dual-shade paint treatment. Up top was a Medium Charcoal Moondust padded full vinyl roof in Valino grain. Also included: silver metallic bodyside moldings, a single red bodyside accent stripe, single red decklid accent stripe with Cartier logo in red tape, Cartier designer logo in rear quarter windows, and turbine-spoke aluminum wheels. Cartier's interior was charcoal luxury cloth or leather. Cartier also had a fingertip speed control, and leather-wrapped steering wheel. 'Signature Series' script on the rear quarter pillar and instrument panel identified that model. Twin Comfort Lounge seats came in distinctively sewn Shubert cloth. The coach roof had a "frenched" backlight. Padded center pillars had lower carpeting.

I.D. DATA: Lincoln again had a 17-symbol Vehicle Identification Number (VIN), fastened to the instrument panel, visible through the windshield. The first three symbols indicate manufacturer, make and vehicle type: '1LN' Lincoln; '1MR' Continental. Symbol four ('B') denotes restraint system. Next comes a letter 'P', followed by two digits that indicate body type: '96' 4dr. Town Car; '97' 4dr. Continental; '98' 2dr. Mark VI; '99' 4dr. Mark VI. Symbol eight indicates engine type: 'F' V8302 EFI. Next is a check digit. Symbol ten indicates model year ('D' 1983). Symbol eleven is assembly plant ('Y' Wixom, MI). The final six digits make up the sequence number, starting with 600001. A Vehicle Certification Label on the left front door lock face panel or door pillar shows the manufacturer, month and year built, GVW, GAWR, VIN, and codes for body type, color, trim, axle, transmission, and special order data.

1983 Continental coupe (OCW)

CONTINENTAL (V-8)

Model Number	Body/Style Number	Body Type & Seating	Factory Price	Shipping Weight	Production Total
97	54D	4-dr. Sedan-5P	21201	3719	16,831

CONTINENTAL VALENTINO DESIGNER SERIES (V-8)

97/60R	54D	4-dr. Sedan-5P	22792	3757	Note 1

CONTINENTAL GIVENCHY DESIGNER SERIES (V-8)

97/60M	54D	4-dr. Sedan-5P	22792	3757	Note 1

TOWN CAR (V-8)

96	54D	4-dr. Sedan-6P	17139	4062	53,381

TOWN CAR SIGNATURE SERIES (V-8)

96/60U	54D	4-dr. Sedan-6P	18481	4078	Note 1

TOWN CAR CARTIER DESIGNER SERIES (V-8)

Model Number	Body/Style Number	Body Type & Seating	Factory Price	Shipping Weight	Production Total
96/605	54D	4-dr. Sedan-6P	19817	4070	Note 1

MARK VI (V-8)

98	66D	2-dr. Coupe-6P	20445	4004	12,743
99	54D	4-dr. Sedan-6P	20933	4105	18,113

MARK VI SIGNATURE SERIES (V-8)

98/603	66D	2-dr. Coupe-6P	23340	4013	Note 1
99/603	54D	4-dr. Sedan-6P	23828	4114	Note 1

MARK VI DESIGNER SERIES (V-8)

98/60N	66D	2-dr. Blass-6P	24749	4035	Note 1
98/60P	66D	2-dr. Pucci-6P	24345	N/A	Note 1
99/60P	54D	4-dr. Pucci-6P	24623	4099	Note 1

Note 1: Production of Signature and Designer Series is included in basic model totals.

Model Number Note: Model numbers changed slightly this year. Some sources include a prefix 'P' ahead of the two-digit number; e.g., 'P97' for Continental.

ENGINE DATA: BASE V-8 (all models): 90-degree, overhead valve V-8. Cast iron block and head. Displacement: 302 cu. in. (5.2 liters). Bore & stroke: 4.00 x 3.00 in. Compression ratio: 8.4:1. Brake horsepower: 130 at 3200 R.P.M. Torque: 240 lbs.-ft. at 2000 R.P.M. Five main bearings. Hydraulic valve lifters. Throttle-body (electronic) fuel injection. VIN Code: F. OPTIONAL V-8 (Mark VI): Same as 302 cu. in. V-8 above, but Brake H.P.: 145 at 3600 R.P.M. Torque: 245 lbs.-ft. at 2200 R.P.M.

CHASSIS DATA: Wheelbase: (Continental) 108.6 in.; (Mark 2dr.) 114.3 in.; (Mark/Town 4dr.) 117.3 in. Overall Length: (Cont.) 201.2 in.; (Mark 2dr.) 216.0 in.; (Mark/Town 4dr.) 219.0 in. Height: (Cont.) 54.8 in.; (Mark 2dr.) 55.2 in.; (Mark 4dr.) 56.1 in.; (Town Car) 55.9 in. Width: (Cont.) 73.6 in.; (Mark/Town) 78.1 in. Front Tread: (Cont.) 58.4 in.; (Mark/Town) 62.2 in. Rear Tread: (Cont.) 59.0 in.; (Mark/Town) 62.0 in. Standard Tires: P205/75R15 SBR WSW (self-sealing on Continental).

TECHNICAL: Transmission: Four-speed automatic overdrive standard. Gear ratios: (1st) 2.40:1; (2nd) 1.47:1; (3rd) 1.00:1; (4th) 0.67:1; (Rev) 2.00:1. Standard final drive ratio: 3.08:1. Steering: (Continental) rack and pinion; (Mark/Town) recirculating ball; all power-assisted. Suspension: (Continental) modified MacPherson strut front with anti-sway bar and gas-pressurized shocks, rigid rear axle w/four links, coil springs and gas-pressurized shocks; (Mark/Town Car) short/long front control arms w/coil springs and anti-sway bar, rigid rear axle with four links and coil springs. Brakes: Front disc and rear drum, power-assisted; except Continental, four-wheel disc brakes. Ignition: Electronic. Body construction: (Continental) unibody; (Mark/Town) separate body and frame. Fuel Tank: 18 gal. exc. Continental, 22.3 gal.

DRIVETRAIN OPTIONS: Dual exhaust system ($83) but (NC) w/high-altitude emissions. Traction-Lok differential ($96-$160). Engine block heater ($26). Trailer towing pkg.: Mark/Town ($210-$306). California emission system ($75). High-altitude emissions (NC).

CONTINENTAL CONVENIENCE/APPEARANCE OPTIONS: Platinum luxury group: scarlet red interior, coach lamps, wire spoke aluminum wheels, brushed-aluminum bodyside moldings and leather-wrapped steering wheel ($656). Keyless entry ($89). Garage door opener ($140). Anti-theft alarm ($185). Leather-wrapped steering wheel ($99). Coach lamps ($88). Dual lighted visor vanity mirrors ($149). Automatic-dimming day/night mirror ($89). Electronic AM/FM radio w/cassette or 8track ($170). Power glass moonroof ($1289). Vinyl-insert bodyside molding ($64). Brushed-aluminum upper bodyside molding ($74). Two-tone paint ($320). Moondust paint ($263). License plate frames: rear ($11); front/rear ($20). Leather interior trim ($551). Wire spoke aluminum wheels ($395). Conventional spare tire ($97).

MARK VI/TOWN CAR CONVENIENCE/APPEARANCE OPTIONS: Option Packages: Appearance protection group ($30-$48). Headlamp convenience group ($178). Defroster group ($160). Comfort/Convenience: Fingertip speed control: Town ($188). Illuminated entry system ($77). Keyless entry ($165). Anti- theft alarm ($185). Twin comfort six-way power seats w/recliners: Mark ($357); w/passenger recliner only ($302). Twin comfort power seats w/passenger recliner: Town Car ($302); dual recliners ($357) exc. ($54) with Signature/Cartier. Electronic instrument panel: Town ($804); Mark, delete ($804 credit). Garage door opener ($140). Leather-wrapped steering wheel ($99). Tilt steering wheel: Town ($96). Interval wipers: Town ($60). Lighting and Mirrors: Touring lamps: Mark ($78). Right remote mirror: Town ($59). Dual power remote mirrors w/lighted left thermometer: Town ($174); Mark ($115). Lighted visor vanity mirrors, pair ($149). Automatic-dimming day/night mirror ($89). Entertainment: Electronic AM/FM stereo radio w/8track or cassette player ($170). 40channel CB radio ($356). Premium sound system ($194). Exterior: Power glass panel moonroof ($1289). Carriage roof ($1069-$1102) exc. Signature ($721-$726). Specialty coach roof: Mark 2dr. ($1073) exc. Signature ($779). Vinyl coach roof: Town ($343). Luxury Valino vinyl coach roof: Mark ($294-$381). Moondust paint ($263). Dual-shade paint ($320). Custom accent stripes: Mark ($62). Rocker panel molding delete: Mark ($149 credit). License plate frames: rear ($11); front/rear ($20). Lower bodyside protection ($40). Interior: Leather interior trim ($459-$551) exc. Town Cartier (NC). Floor mats w/carpet inserts: front ($41); rear ($25). Wheels and Tires: Wire wheel covers: Town ($293) exc. Cartier ($145 credit). Locking wire wheel covers ($330) exc. Mark Pucci or Town Cartier ($142 credit), or Mark Blass ($537 credit). Wire spoke aluminum wheels ($867) exc. Mark Pucci or Town Cartier ($395), or Mark Signature ($593). Lacy spoke aluminum wheels ($472) exc. Mark Signature ($191), Town Cartier or Mark Pucci (NC), or Mark Blass ($395 credit). Turbine spoke aluminum wheels ($472) exc. Mark Signature ($191) and Mark Blass ($395 credit). Self-sealing whitewall tires ($139). Conventional spare tire ($64).

HISTORY: Introduced: October 14, 1982. Model year production: 101,068. Calendar year production: 106,528. Calendar year sales by U.S. dealers: 101,574. Model year sales by U.S. dealers: 105,326.

Historical Footnotes: Sales rose sharply for the 1983 model year, reaching a total of 105,326 for the luxury trio (versus 81,653 the year before). Calendar year sales of the bigger Lincolns jumped even more, causing a second shift to be added at the Wixom, Michigan assembly plant. Continental now offered a 36/36,000 warranty on maintenance (free for the first year, with $50 deductible later). The full-line factory catalog referred to independent coachbuilders offering special limousine conversions.

1984 LINCOLN

1984 Continental Town Car (JG)

The aero-styled Mark VII was all new for 1984, almost 6 inches shorter in wheelbase and nearly 400 pounds lighter than before. Aerodynamic features of the Mark VII included a sharply-raked windshield and hidden wipers. Continental alterations were far more modest, focused mainly on the front end. Lincoln added a turbocharged diesel option to both Mark VII and Continental this year, with the engine obtained from BMW. Mark also added an LSC model that combined improved handling with Lincoln's traditional luxury and riding qualities.

CONTINENTAL — SIX/V-8 — A new "aerodynamic" front end gave Continental a more modern look, though not radically different from the 198283 version. Rectangular quad headlamps again flanked a grille made up of thin vertical bars. But the front end had a slightly more sloped appearance, and the grille bars were separated into side-by-side sections. Rectangular parking/signal lamps stood immediately below the headlamps, and the wraparound marker lenses (now split into sections) extended farther back on the fender with an angled rear edge. Separate marker lenses below bumper level were no longer used. Two engine choices were offered this year: the standard gas 302 cu. in. (5.0-liter) V-8 with fuel injection, or the new 2.4-liter turbodiesel. The V-8 had a 3.08:1 axle ratio; the diesel a 3.73:1. Both were coupled to four-speed overdrive automatic transmissions. Electronic air suspension offered automatic level control. The fully electronic automatic-climate-control system featured a digital display, while the dash held an electronic odometer and digital fuel gauge with multi-color graphics. There was also a low oil level warning light and an overhead console, as well as new styles for the cloth and leather seat trim. Cast aluminum wheels were new. Revised instrument and door trim panels had real wood veneer appliques. Fold-away outside mirrors were used. Continental's Givenchy Designer Series had light blue and Midnight Blue glamour clearcoat metallic paint, with tri-color bodyside accent stripe applied at the break line between the two colors. There was a two-color decklid accent stripe with doubleG logo at the center. A rear roof pillar ornament was included. 'Givenchy' script went in the rear quarter window. Twin Comfort Lounge seats came in Admiral Blue luxury cloth (or optional leather at no extra cost). This year's Valentino Designer Series turned to Cabernet wine/medium charcoal glamour clearcoat metallic paint. It had a unique bodyside accent stripe and two-color decklid accent stripe, plus Valentino 'V' logo on the decklid. 'Valentino' script adorned the rear quarter window, and the rear roof pillar held a Valentino ornament. Twin Comfort Lounge seats were charcoal leather and mini-pleated cloth.

1984 Continental Mark VII coupe (JG)

MARK VII — SIX/V-8 — Styling on the all-new "contemporary size premium" Lincoln retained traditional Mark cues, but on a dramatically different form. Aerodynamic appearance included aero headlamps, a wedge profile, and sloping back window. Lincoln described the new Mark as "the most airflow-efficient luxury car built in America, with a drag coefficient of 0.38." This edition was over a foot shorter than the Mark VI, mounted on the same chassis as the Continental sedan (downsized two years earlier). Some observers compared Mark VII's new design to Ford Thunderbird (logically enough) and even to Mercedes 380SEC. Mark had electronic air suspension with automatic three- way level control, nitra-cushion gas-pressurized front struts and rear shocks, and four-wheel power disc brakes. An all-new cockpit-style instrument panel had full electronics. The full-length floor console with gearshift lever included a lockable stowage bin in the armrest, while an overhead console held warning lights and dual-intensity courtesy/reading lamps, Base engine was the 302 cu. in. (5.0- liter) V-8 with EFI and EECIV, hooked to four-speed automatic overdrive transmission. Mark VII could also be ordered with a new inline turbodiesel with dual exhausts, suplied by BMW-Steyr. Power rack-and-pinion steering replaced the old recirculating-ball system. The modern Mark had integrated, flush-mounted aero headlamps that extended well back onto fenders to form marker lenses; a sharply-sloped windshield; wide color-keyed lower bodyside moldings; bright wheel lip and belt moldings; and large nearly-triangular quarter windows. Full-length upper bodyside dual-band paint stripes were standard. The traditional decklid bulge, shaped as a simulated spare tire housing, was back again. So was an upright grille made up of thin vertical bars. Diesel models had a 'Turbo Diesel' badge on the decklid. Eleven new paint colors and six new interior trim colors were available. Standard equipment included front and rear stabilizer bars, tilt steering, speed control, power windows and door locks, locking gas door with remote release, electric rear defroster, and dual remote-control mirrors. Also standard: tinted glass, auto-temp air conditioning, six- way power driver's seat, electronic AM/FM stereo search radio, and P215/70R15 whitewall tires on cast aluminum wheels with center hub ornament. New options included heated driver and passenger seats, a compass/thermometer group for the header, handling package, and portable CB radio. Aimed at the European luxury coupe market, the new LSC Series had a standard handling package and 3.27:1 axle ratio. LSC had quicker-ratio power steering, high-performance P215/65R15 tires on 6 inch aluminum wheels, dark charcoal lower bodyside paint, foglamps, and leather upholstery. There was also a new Versace Designer Series, as well as the popular Bill Blass Designer Series. This year's Blass came in dual-shade clearcoat metallic paint: Goldenrod Glamour with Harvest Wheat. Exterior trim included two-tone cream/dark green bodyside and decklid accent stripes, along with the designer's signature in the quarter window and Bill Blass logo on the decklid. Upholstery was standard two-tone flax and gold ultra-soft leather (or cloth trim at no extra charge). The dash held a Bill Blass logo. Emanating from Gianni Versace of Milan, Italy (a designer of avant-garde clothing), the Mark Versace had a walnut glamour clearcoat metallic body with two-tone tan/bright blue accent stripes on bodyside and decklid, and tan stripes on the hood. Also included: a signature in the quarter window, and Versace logo on the instrument panel. Desert Tan ultra-soft leather went inside, in designer's sew style. Cloth inserts with leather bolster seat trim were available at no extra cost.

TOWN CAR — V-8 — The traditional long-wheelbase Lincoln sedan kept its same form this year, with little change beyond new nitra- cushion gas-pressurized shocks. Tire size rose a notch, to P215/70R15. The dash held a low oil level warning light and revised electronic radio graphics. Full wheel covers were new. Twelve new paint colors and six new dual-shade combinations were offered. A 100-amp alternator had become optional in mid-year 1983. New this year: an optional power decklid pull-down. The optional power six-way driver's seat had a two-position programmable memory. Town Car came only with the 302 cu. in. (5.0-liter) fuel-injected V-8, four- speed overdrive automatic, and 3.08:1 axle. There was a Town Car Signature Series, and a Cartier Designer Series. The Cartier came in a new dual-shade paint treatment: Arctic White with platinum clearcoat metallic, with a new standard Arctic White coach Valino roof that included a "frenched" backlight. Cartier had premium bodyside moldings with platinum vinyl inserts, platinum and red bodyside tape striping, and a single red paint stripe on the decklid with Cartier logo in red tape. The Cartier logo was also laminated in the rear quarter window. Interiors had a choice of Dove Grey luxury cloth or leather upholstery. Town Car Signature had a coach roof, pleat-pillow upholstery, seatback straps and map pockets, and woodtone accents on doors and quarter trim panels.

I.D. DATA: Lincoln again had a 17-symbol Vehicle Identification Number (VIN), fastened to the instrument panel, visible through the windshield. The first three symbols indicate the manufacturer, make and vehicle type: '1LN' Lincoln; '1MR' Continental. Symbol four ('B') denotes restraint system. Next comes a letter 'P', followed by two digits that indicate body type: '96' 4dr. Town Car; '97' 4dr. Continental; '98' 2dr. Mark VII. Symbol eight indicates engine type: 'F' V8302 EFI; 'L' turbodiesel L6146. Next is a check digit. Symbol ten indicates model year ('E' 1984). Symbol eleven is assembly plant ('Y' Wixom, MI). The final six digits make up the sequence number, starting with 600001. A Vehicle Certification Label on the left front door lock face panel or door pillar shows the manufacturer, month and year built, GVW, GAWR, VIN, and codes for such items as body type, color, trim, axle, transmission, and special order data.

CONTINENTAL (V-8)

Model Number	Body/Style Number	Body Type & Seating	Factory Price	Shipping Weight	Production Total
97	54D	4-dr. Sedan-5P	21769	3719	30,468

CONTINENTAL VALENTINO DESIGNER SERIES (V-8)

97/60R	54D	4-dr. Sedan-5P	24217	3757	Note 1

CONTINENTAL GIVENCHY DESIGNER SERIES (V-8)

97/60M	54D	4-dr. Sedan-5P	24242	3757	Note 1

TOWN CAR (V-8)

96	54D	4-dr. Sedan-6P	18071	4062	93,622

TOWN CAR SIGNATURE SERIES (V-8)

96/60U	54D	4-dr. Sedan-6P	20040	4078	Note 1

TOWN CAR CARTIER DESIGNER SERIES (V-8)

96/605	54D	4-dr. Sedan-6P	21706	4070	Note 1

MARK VII (V-8)

98	63D	2-dr. Coupe-5P	21707	N/A	33,344

MARK VII LSC (V-8)

98/938	63D	2-dr. Coupe-5P	23706	N/A	Note 1

MARK VII VERSACE DESIGNER SERIES (V-8)

98/60P	63D	2-dr. Coupe-5P	24406	N/A	Note 1

MARK VII BILL BLASS DESIGNER SERIES (V-8)

98/60N	63D	2-dr. Coupe-5P	24807	N/A	Note 1

Note 1: Production of Signature and Designer Series is included in basic model totals.

Diesel Engine Note: A turbodiesel engine (RPO Code 99L) for Continental or Mark VII cost $1235 extra.

Model Number Note: Some sources include a prefix 'P' ahead of the two- digit number; e.g., 'P97' for Continental.

ENGINE DATA: BASE V-8 (all models): 90-degree, overhead valve V-8. Cast iron block and head. Displacement: 302 cu. in. (5.2 liters). Bore & stroke: 4.00 x 3.00 in. Compression ratio: 8.4:1. Brake horsepower: 140 at 3200 R.P.M. Torque: 250 lbs.-ft. at 1600 R.P.M. Five main bearings. Hydraulic valve lifters. Throttle-body (electronic) fuel injection. VIN Code: F. OPTIONAL V-8 (Town Car): Same as 302 cu. in. V-8 above, with dual exhausts Brake H.P.: 155 at 3600 R.P.M. Torque: 265 lbs.-ft. at 2000 R.P.M. OPTIONAL TURBODIESEL SIX (Continental, Mark VI): Inline, overhead-cam six-cylinder. Cast iron block and aluminum head. Displacement: 149 cu. in. (2.4 liters). Bore & stroke: 3.15 x 3.19 in. Compression ratio: 23.0:1. Brake horsepower: 115 at 4800 R.P.M. Torque: 155 lbs.-ft. at 2400 R.P.M. Four main bearings. Hydraulic valve lifters. Fuel injection. VIN Code: L.

CHASSIS DATA: Wheelbase: (Continental/Mark) 108.5 in.; (Town Car) 117.3 in. Overall Length: (Cont.) 200.7 in.; (Mark) 202.8 in.; (Town) 219.0 in. Height: (Cont.) 55.5 in.; (Mark) 54.0 in.; (Town) 55.9 in. Width: (Cont.) 73.6 in.; (Mark) 70.9 in.; (Town) 78.1 in. Front Tread: (Cont./Mark) 58.4 in.; (Town) 62.2 in. Rear Tread: (Cont./Mark) 59.0 in.; (Town) 62.0 in. Standard Tires: P215/70R15 SBR WSW exc. Mark LSC, P215/65R15 BSW.

TECHNICAL: Transmission: Four-speed automatic overdrive standard. Gear ratios: (1st) 2.40:1; (2nd) 1.47:1; (3rd) 1.00:1; (4th) 0.67:1; (Rev) 2.00:1. Turbodiesel ratios: (1st) 2.73:1; (2nd) 1.56:1; (3rd) 1.00:1; (4th) 0.73:1; (Rev) 2.09:1. Standard final drive ratio: 3.08:1 exc. turbodiesel, 3.73:1 and Mark VII LSC, 3.27:1. Steering: (Continental/Mark) rack and pinion; (Town Car) recirculating ball; all power-assisted. Suspension: (Continental/Mark) modified MacPherson strut front with anti-sway bar, rigid rear axle w/four links and anti-sway bar, electronically-controlled auto-leveling air springs and gas-pressurized shocks at front and rear; (Town Car) short/long front control arms w/coil springs and anti- sway bar, rigid rear axle with four links and coil springs, gas-pressurized front/rear shocks. Brakes: Four-wheel disc except (Town Car) front disc and rear drum; all power-assisted. Ignition: Electronic. Body construction: Unibody except (Town Car) separate body and frame. Fuel Tank: 22.3 gal. exc. Town Car, 18 gal.

DRIVETRAIN OPTIONS: Dual exhaust system: Town Car LPO ($82) but standard w/high-altitude emissions. Handling pkg.: Mark VII ($243). Traction-Lok differential ($96-$160). 100-amp alternator: Town ($62). Engine block heater ($26). Trailer towing pkg. ($209-$306). California emission system ($99). High-altitude emissions (NC).

CONTINENTAL CONVENIENCE/APPEARANCE OPTIONS: Compass/thermometer group ($191). Keyless entry ($122). Garage door opener ($140). Anti-theft alarm ($190). Power decklid pulldown ($79). Dual heated seats ($159). Dual power recliners ($191). Leather-wrapped steering wheel ($99). Coach lamps ($88). Foglamps ($158). Dual lighted visor vanity mirrors ($156). Automatic-dimming day/night mirror ($89). Electronic AM/FM radio w/cassette or 8track ($170). Premium sound system ($206). Portable CB radio ($154). Power glass moonroof ($1289). Vinyl-insert bodyside molding ($70). Brushed-aluminum upper bodyside molding ($74). Dual-shade paint ($320). Moondust paint ($263). License plate frames: rear ($11); front/rear ($22). Leather interior trim: Signature ($551); Givenchy (NC). Wire spoke aluminum wheels: Signature ($686). Forged aluminum wheels ($291) exc. Designer ($395 credit). Puncture-sealant tires ($180). Conventional spare tire ($121).

MARK VII/TOWN CAR CONVENIENCE/APPEARANCE OPTIONS: Option Packages: Headlamp/convenience group ($190). Compass/thermometer group: Mark ($191). Defroster group: Town ($165). Comfort/Convenience: Fingertip speed control: Town ($188). Illuminated entry system ($83). Keyless entry ($205). Anti- theft alarm ($190). Power decklid pulldown ($79). Six-way power seats w/dual recliners: Mark ($225); w/power recliners ($416) exc. Designer ($191). Twin comfort power seats w/passenger recliner: Town Car ($320); dual recliners ($374) exc. ($54) with Signature/Cartier. Dual heated seats: Mark ($159). Electronic instrument panel: Town ($804). Garage door opener ($140). Leather-wrapped steering wheel ($99). Tilt steering wheel: Town ($101). Vent windows: Mark ($73). Interval wipers: Town ($60). Lighting and Mirrors: Foglamps: Mark ($158). Right remote mirror: Town ($59). Dual power remote mirrors: Town ($177). Dual heated outside mirrors: Mark ($49). Lighted visor vanity mirrors, pair ($156). Automatic-dimming day/night mirror ($89). Entertainment: Electronic AM/FM stereo radio w/8track or cassette player ($170). CB radio: Town ($356). Portable CB: Mark ($154). Premium sound system ($206). Exterior: Power glass moonroof ($1289). Carriage roof: Town ($1069) exc. Town Signature ($726). Luxury Valino vinyl coach roof: Town ($343). Moondust paint ($263). Dual-shade paint: Town ($320). License plate frames: rear ($11); front/rear ($22). Interior: Leather interior trim ($459-$551) exc. Town Cartier (NC). Floor mats w/carpet inserts: front ($41); rear ($25). Wheels and Tires: Wire wheel covers: Town ($335) exc. Cartier ($137 credit). Wire spoke aluminum wheels: Town ($867) exc. Cartier ($395), or Signature ($532); Mark ($607-$686). Lacy spoke or turbine spoke aluminum wheels: Town ($472) exc. Signature ($137) or Cartier (NC). Forged aluminum wheels: Mark ($291) exc. Designer ($395 credit). Puncture-sealant whitewall tires ($180). Conventional spare tire: Town ($64); Mark ($121).

HISTORY: Introduced: November 10, 1983 except Town Car, Sept. 22, 1983. Model year production: 157,434. Calendar year production: 168,704. Calendar year sales by U.S. dealers: 151,475. Model year sales by U.S. dealers: 136,753.

Historical Footnotes: Lincoln sales rose 31 percent for the 1984 model year, while the all-new aero Mark VII gained a more modest number of customers. Continental, on the other hand, showed a whopping 71 percent sales gain. The new Mark VII design got extensive wind-tunnel testing at the Lockheed facility in Marietta, Georgia. Results were transmitted instantly to Ford engineers at Dearborn, who could then deduce the likely effect of modifications before the next trial. Mark VII's 0.38 drag coefficient was some 25 percent better than its predecessor, suggesting considerable gain in highway fuel economy. The federal government had first opposed the adoption of European-style aero headlamps, but Ford pressed the issue for two years (later joined by Chrysler) until permission was granted. That change in itself accounted for a 5 percent improvement in aero efficiency, as well as imparting a smooth look to the car's front end. *Ward's Yearbook* described the restyled Mark as "an aerodynamic showpiece."

1985 LINCOLN

Anti-lock brakes arrived as an option on Continental and Mark VII. The ABS system, supplied by the Teves company of Germany, was the first of its kind to be offered on a domestic auto. Electronic suspension became available on the Lincoln Town Car, which got a modest facelift. A mobile telephone became optional, anticipating the craze for cellular car phones that would soon arrive.

CONTINENTAL — SIX/V-8 — Biggest news for the four-door Continental was four-wheel anti-lock braking, standard on the two Designer Series with 5.0-liter V-8, and on all West Coast V-8 models. The system used a mini-computer to monitor all four wheels, and control braking pressure to prevent lockup during a hard stop. Otherwise, apart from a new hood ornament, no change was evident. Continental still had quad rectangular headlamps above rectangular parking lights, leading to sectioned wraparound lenses. Vertical taillamps and the familiar decklid bulge, with 'Continental' lettering around its perimeter and a center emblem, continued as before. Standard engine was the fuel-injected 302 cu. in. (5.0- liter) V-8, with BMW 2.4-liter turbo diesel optional once more (for the last time). A single serpentine accessory drive belt was added to the V-8. Four-speed overdrive automatic was the standard transmission. Standard equipment included auto- temp air conditioning, power four-wheel disc brakes and rack- and-pinion steering, power windows and door locks, electronic AM/FM stereo radio, cast aluminum wheels, overhead console, illuminated entry, tinted glass, and automatic level control. The electronic instrument panel had a message center and systems monitor. Givenchy and Valentino Designer Series were offered again, carrying the same new comfort/convenience package as Mark VII, with seven popular options. Givenchy came in dark rosewood clearcoat metallic paint with special bodyside accent stripe. It had exclusive decklid accent striping with a doubleG logo at the center, a rear roof pillar ornament, and 'Givenchy' script in the rear quarter window. Twin Comfort Lounge seats were upholstered in Mulberry Brown leather (or no-cost optional luxury cloth). Valentino was Midnight Black and Burnished Pewter clearcoat metallic. The unique bodyside and decklid accent stripe included a Valentino 'V' logo on the decklid. The designer's badge went on the rear pillar. Valentino's interior held Sand Beige leather and "vee" cloth seat trim.

1985 Continental Mark VII coupe (JG)

MARK VII — SIX/V-8 — Like Continental, the Mark VII offered anti-lock braking this year. ABS was standard on the LSC, Bill Blass and Versace Series with 302 cu. in. (5.0-liter) V-8, as well as all V-8s in the five Pacific states. In fact, the two models had become quite similar after Mark's downsizing in 1984 to the Continental-size wheelbase. Mark added a new hood ornament, but not much else in appearance changes. Three engines were offered for Mark VII: the regular fuel-injected 5.0-liter V-8 with 2.73:1 axle; a high- performance V-8 (on LSC only) with 3.27:1 rear axle; and the 2.4-liter turbo diesel with 3.73:1 axle. All engines were coupled to four-speed overdrive automatic. V-8s had the new single serpentine accessory drive belt. The high-performance V-8 had a performance camshaft, tubular exhaust manifolds with dual exhausts, aluminum intake manifold, higher-flow- rate throttle body, and low-restriction air cleanerall giving significant acceleration improvement. LSC also had electronic air suspension with special handling components, including stiffer front and rear stabilizer bars, special struts and shocks, and special air springs. New multi-adjustment, articulated sport seats for passenger and driver, with six-way power adjustments, helped to enhance LSC's driver-oriented image. Leather was used extensively inside. LSC's tires were Goodyear Eagle GT P215/65R15 blackwalls with an "aggressive" tread pattern. Much of the regular Mark VII's brightwork was replaced with black or dark charcoal accents for the LSC. A "fluted" dark charcoal full-length lower bodyside molding, with the bodyside painted dark charcoal below the molding, was a distinguishing feature. Also unique to LSC: foglamps and special cast aluminum wheels with exposed lug nuts. Mark's Bill Blass edition came in Silver Sand clearcoat metallic with Burnished Pewter below the lower bodyside moldings. It had two-tone bodyside and decklid accent stripes, designer's name in quarter window, Bill Blass logo on the decklid, and standard Carob Brown leather trim upholstery (or UltraSuede fabric seating surfaces). Either one could have leather designer seat straps to no extra cost. Navy clearcoat metallic was now the color of the Versace Designer Series, with two-tone accent stripes on bodyside and decklid, designer's name in the quarter window, and Admiral Blue ultra-soft leather seats (or at no extra cost, cloth inserts with leather bolster seat trim). A Versace logo went on the dash and floor mats. Standard equipment on the base Mark included power four- wheel disc brakes, power rack-and-pinion steering, front and rear stabilizer bars, tinted glass, digital clock, automatic level control, power windows, cast aluminum wheels, speed control, and electronic AM/FM stereo radio. A new optional comfort/convenience package included eight popular options: power decklid pull-down, keyless entry, illuminated entry, illuminated visor vanity mirrors, six-way power seats (standard on LSC), stereo search radio with cassette, heated remote mirrors, and headlamp convenience system. That package was standard on the Bill Blass and Versace Designer Series.

TOWN CAR — V-8 — "Senior" Lincolns got a facelift for 1985, keeping the same basic (long wheelbase) body and separate chassis. Restyled wraparound parking/signal lamps were still in the front fender tips, outboard of (and separated from) quad rectangular headlamps. But the new grille texture had a tight crosshatch pattern, dominated by vertical bars. Taillamps were now angled slightly, each one divided into two side-by- side sections. Flush bumpers also added a more modern look. Body corners were more rounded, at front and rear. Base engine remained the 302 cu. in. (5.0-liter) EFI V-8 with four-speed automatic overdrive transmission. A higher-output version of the V-8 also was announced. Standard equipment now included speed control, tilt steering, manual reclining seats, right remote-control mirror, and intermittent wipers. A single key now operated door locks and ignition. Seat upholstery fabrics and styles were new this year. The horn button returned to the steering wheel from its former turn- signal stalk location. Signature Series and Cartier Designer Series now had standard keyless entry with illuminated entry, stereo search radio with cassette, and Premium Sound System. The Cartier edition was now painted in Arctic White/Platinum clearcoat metallic, with Arctic White coach Valino vinyl roof and "frenched" backlight. Premium bodyside moldings had light charcoal vinyl inserts. Also included: platinum and red bodyside tape striping, and Cartier logo in red tape on the decklid. Cartier's logo also was laminated in the rear quarter window. Inside was a choice of gray luxury cloth or leather inserts with Oxford White leather bolsters. New options included an automatic-leveling rear suspension (with electronic sensors and air-adjustable shocks), and hands-free mobile phone. Town Car also offered the comfort/convenience package available on Mark VII, with seven popular options.

I.D. DATA: Lincoln again had a 17-symbol Vehicle Identification Number (VIN) fastened to the instrument panel, visible through the windshield. Coding is similar to 1984. Model year code changed to 'F' for 1985. One engine code was added: 'M' H.O. V8302 EFI.

CONTINENTAL (V-8)

Model Number	Body/Style Number	Body Type & Seating	Factory Price	Shipping Weight	Production Total
97/850A	54D	4-dr. Sedan-5P	22573	3719	28,253

CONTINENTAL VALENTINO DESIGNER SERIES (V-8)

97/865A	54D	4-dr. Sedan-5P	26078	3757	Note 1

CONTINENTAL GIVENCHY DESIGNER SERIES (V-8)

97/860A	54D	4-dr. Sedan-5P	25783	3757	Note 1

TOWN CAR (V-8)

96/700A	54D	4-dr. Sedan-6P	19047	4062	119,878

TOWN CAR SIGNATURE SERIES (V-8)

96/705A	54D	4-dr. Sedan-6P	22130	4078	Note 1

TOWN CAR CARTIER DESIGNER SERIES (V-8)

96/710A	54D	4-dr. Sedan-6P	23637	4070	Note 1

MARK VII (V-8)

98/800A	63D	2-dr. Coupe-5P	22399	N/A	18,355

MARK VII LSC (V-8)

98/805A	63D	2-dr. Coupe-5P	24332	N/A	Note 1

MARK VII VERSACE DESIGNER SERIES (V-8)

98/815A	63D	2-dr. Coupe-5P	26578	N/A	Note 1

MARK VII BILL BLASS DESIGNER SERIES (V-8)

98/810A	63D	2-dr. Coupe-5P	26659	N/A	Note 1

Note 1: Production of LSC, Signature and Designer Series is included in basic model totals.

Diesel Engine Note: A turbodiesel engine (RPO Code 99L) for Continental or Mark VII cost $1234 extra on base models, $772 extra for Designer Series or Mark VII LSC.

Model Number Note: Suffixes changed this year. Some sources include a prefix 'P' ahead of the basic two-digit number; e.g., 'P97' for Continental.

ENGINE DATA: BASE V-8 (all models): 90-degree, overhead valve V-8. Cast iron block and head. Displacement: 302 cu. in. (5.2 liters). Bore & stroke: 4.00 x 3.00 in. Compression ratio: 8.4:1. Brake horsepower: 140 at 3200 R.P.M. Torque: 250 lbs.-ft. at 1600 R.P.M. Five main bearings. Hydraulic valve lifters. Throttle-body (electronic) fuel injection. VIN Code: F. OPTIONAL V-8 (Town Car): Same as 302 cu. in. V-8 above, with dual exhausts Brake H.P.: 155 at 3600 R.P.M. Torque: 265 lbs.-ft. at 2000 R.P.M. BASE V-8 (Mark VII LSC): High-output version of 302 cu. in. V-8 above Compression ratio: 8.3:1. Brake H.P.: 180 at 4200 R.P.M. Torque: 260 lbs.-ft. at 2600 R.P.M. VIN Code: M. OPTIONAL TURBODIESEL SIX (Continental, Mark VII): Inline, overhead-cam six-cylinder. Cast iron block and aluminum head. Displacement: 149 cu. in. (2.4 liters). Bore & stroke: 3.15 x 3.19 in. Compression ratio: 23.0:1. Brake horsepower: 115 at 4800 R.P.M. Torque: 155 lbs.-ft. at 2400 R.P.M. Four main bearings. Hydraulic valve lifters. Fuel injection. VIN Code: L.

CHASSIS DATA: Wheelbase: (Continental/Mark) 108.5 in.; (Town Car) 117.3 in. Overall Length: (Cont.) 200.7 in.; (Mark) 202.8 in.; (Town) 219.0 in. Height: (Cont.) 55.6 in.; (Mark) 54.2 in.; (Town) 55.9 in. Width: (Cont.) 73.6 in.; (Mark) 70.9 in.; (Town) 78.1 in. Front Tread: (Cont./Mark) 58.4 in.; (Town) 62.2 in. Rear Tread: (Cont./Mark) 59.0 in.; (Town) 62.0 in. Standard Tires: P215/70R15 SBR WSW exc. Mark VII LSC, P215/65R15 BSW.

TECHNICAL: Transmission: Four-speed automatic overdrive standard. Gear ratios: (1st) 2.40:1; (2nd) 1.47:1; (3rd) 1.00:1; (4th) 0.67:1; (Rev) 2.00:1. Turbodiesel ratios: (1st) 2.73:1; (2nd) 1.56:1; (3rd) 1.00:1; (4th) 0.73:1; (Rev) 2.09:1. Standard final drive ratio: 3.08:1 exc. Mark VII, 2.73:1; Mark VII LSC, 3.27:1; and turbodiesel, 3.73:1. Steering/Suspension/Brakes/Body: same as 1984. Fuel Tank: 22.3 gal. exc. Town Car, 18 gal.

DRIVETRAIN OPTIONS: Dual exhaust system: Town Car ($83) but (NC) w/high-altitude emissions. Traction-Lok differential ($96-$160). 100-amp alternator: Town ($62). Engine block heater ($26). Trailer towing pkg.: Town ($223-$306). California emission system ($99). High-altitude emissions (NC).

CONTINENTAL/MARK VII CONVENIENCE/APPEARANCE OPTIONS: Comfort/convenience pkg.: Cont. ($932); Mark ($1293); Mark LSC ($1068). Compass/thermometer group ($191). Anti-theft alarm ($190). Mobile telephone ($2995-$3135). Dual power recliners ($191). Leather-wrapped steering wheel: Mark ($99). Automatic-dimming day/night mirror ($89). Electronic AM/FM radio w/cassette player and premium sound ($389). Power glass moonroof ($1289). Manual vent windows: Mark ($73). Vinyl-insert bodyside molding: Cont. ($70). Brushed-aluminum upper bodyside molding: Cont. ($74). Dual-shade paint: Cont. ($320). Glamour paint ($263). Leather interior trim ($551) exc. Cont. Givenchy (NC). Wire spoke aluminum wheels ($686). Forged or cast aluminum wheels ($291) exc. Designer ($395 credit). Puncture-sealant tires ($180).

TOWN CAR CONVENIENCE/APPEARANCE OPTIONS: Option Packages:Comfort/convenience pkg. ($607-$821). Headlamp convenience group ($190). Defroster group ($165). Comfort/Convenience: Keyless entry ($205). Anti-theft alarm ($190). Mobile telephone ($2995-$3135). Power decklid pulldown ($79). Twin comfort power seats ($225). Electronic instrument panel ($822). Leather-wrapped steering wheel ($99). Lighting and Mirrors: Dual power remote mirrors ($177). Lighted visor vanity mirrors, pair ($156). Automatic-dimming day/night mirror ($89). Entertainment: Electronic AM/FM stereo radio w/cassette player and premium sound ($389). Exterior: Power glass moonroof ($1289). Carriage roof ($1069) exc. Signature ($726). Luxury Valino vinyl coach roof ($343). Glamour paint ($268). Dual-shade paint ($320). Protective bodyside molding ($70). Interior: Leather interior trim ($459-$521) exc. Cartier (NC). Floor mats w/carpet inserts: front ($41); rear ($25). Wheels and Tires: Wire wheel covers ($335) exc. Cartier ($137 credit). Wire spoke aluminum wheels ($867) exc. Cartier ($395) or Signature ($532). Lacy spoke or turbine spoke aluminum wheels ($472) exc. Signature ($137) or Cartier (NC). Puncture-sealant whitewall tires ($180). Conventional spare tire ($64).

HISTORY: Introduced: October 4, 1984. Model year production: 166,486. Calendar year production: 163,077. Calendar year sales by U.S. dealers: 165,138. Model year sales by U.S. dealers: 165,012.

Historical Footnotes: Customers obviously had a craving for luxury motoring in the traditional style, as sales of Lincoln's Town Car reached a record level. A total of 116,015 found buyers, up a whopping 50 percent from the 1984 figure. The previous record of 94,242 had been set way back in 1978. Continental sales rose only slightly, while the Mark dropped sharply (down to just 20,198, versus 31,502 in the previous model year). The BMW-built turbodiesel found so few buyers that it was discontinued after 1985.

1986 LINCOLN

While option prices remained similar to their 1985 levels, the lists (especially for Continental and Mark VII) shrunk considerably. Both models had ample lists of standard equipment. Among other deletions, the slow-selling turbodiesel engine was dropped. Anti-lock braking became standard on all Continentals and Marks. The V-8 engine added sequential fuel injection, fast-burn combustion chambers, low-tension piston rings, and roller tappets, which delivered a boost in compression and horsepower.

1986 Continental sedan (JG)

CONTINENTAL — V-8 — Lincoln's short-wheelbase, five-passenger luxury four-door sedan showed no appearance change this year. Continental's grille was similar to Mark VII, made up of thin vertical bars with a slightly heavier center bar, and a wide upper header with inset center emblem. Recessed quad rectangular headlamps stood directly above amber-lensed park/signal lamps. The headlamp/park lamp moldings continued around fender tips to surround the large clear/amber marker and cornering lenses, with a molding that angled at the rear. After a couple of years of being branded, simply, "Continental," the mid-size sedan reverted to a "Lincoln" badge. The standard 302 cu. in. (5.0-liter) V-8 switched from throttle-body to sequential (multi-port) fuel injection, again hooked to four-speed overdrive automatic. The anti-lock, four-wheel disc braking system introduced in 1985 continued this year as standard. Electronic air suspension with level control was also standard. The turbodiesel option was abandoned for the '85 model year. Dropped for 1986 were the mobile phone option and Valentino edition. This year's lineup consisted only of the base Continental and Givenchy Designer Series. Standard equipment included keyless entry (and illuminated entry), power decklid pull-down (and remote release), compass/thermometer group, power remote heated mirrors, rear defroster, tinted glass, power windows and door locks, speed control, gas-pressurized shock absorbers, front and rear stabilizer bars, power steering, and P215/70R15 WSw tires on cast aluminum wheels. Also standard: power mini-vent windows, interval wipers, coach lamps, bumper rub strips with argent stripes, dual bodyside and decklid stripes, and electronic instrument panel.

1986 Continental Mark VII coupe (JG)

MARK VII — V-8 — "The car you never expected from Lincoln." That's how the full-line catalog described Mark VII, now entering its third year in aero-styled shape. No significant changes were evident, other than the required high-mount center stop lamp. Mark's grille consisted of many thin vertical bars, dominated by seven slightly heavier vertical bars, with a heavy bright upper header and side surround molding. Inset into the center of the header was a tiny square emblem. Stretched from the grille edge to fender tips were large aero headlamps with integral parking/signal lamps, which met wraparound marker/cornering lenses. Above the left headlamp was 'Lincoln' lettering. Far below the bumper rub strips were LSC's standard foglamps. Three Marks were offered: base, Bill Blass Designer Series, and handling/performance LSC. The latter was powered by an improved high-output 302 cu. in. (5.0-liter) V-8 with sequential (multi-port) fuel injection, tubular exhaust headers and tuned intake manifold, now delivering 200 horsepower. Other models had a more modest 5.0-liter V-8, also driving a four-speed (overdrive) automatic transmission. All Mark VII models now had a standard anti-lock brake system (ABS), introduced on LSC a year earlier. Electronic air suspension with level control continued as standard. The Versace Designer Series was dropped. Formerly optional equipment that became standard this year included keyless entry, power decklid pull-down, Premium Sound System, and power front seat recliners. LSC added a new analog instrument cluster to replace the former electronic display. Standard equipment on base Marks included auto-temp air conditioning, power steering, tilt wheel, P215/70R15 WSW tires on cast aluminum wheels, compass/thermometer, rear defroster, side window defoggers, power windows and door locks, speed control, tinted glass, interval wipers, and AM/FM stereo with cassette player. LSC added dual exhausts with its high-output engine, a handling suspension, P215/65R15 blackwalls, wide bodyside moldings, lower bodyside accent paint, tachometer, and leather seat trim with perforated leather or cloth inserts. Bill Blass had unique lower bodyside clearcoat paint, two-color bodyside/decklid paint stripes, wire-spoke aluminum wheels, and leather or Ultra Suede seat trim.

1986 "Signature Series" Town Car (JG)

TOWN CAR — V-8 — Like its mates, the big four-door Lincoln added sequential fuel injection to its 302 cu. in. (5.0-liter) V-8. That engine also got higher compression, roller tappets, new piston rings, and revised combustion chambers. Town Car's standard equipment list grew, now including the formerly optional dual power remote mirrors, and a defroster group. Three models were fielded again: base Town Car, Signature Series, and Cartier Designer Series. Appearance was the same as 1985. Town Car's classic-look upright grille had a subdued crosshatch pattern dominated by seven vertical bright divider bars, with a bold and bright upper header bar that continued down the sides. The grille stood forward from the headlamp panel, with the space filled in by its wide, bright surrounding side moldings. Each pair of rectangular headlamps was surrounded by a strong, bright molding. Wraparound amber signal lenses were mounted in the fender extensions, with side marker lenses down below the bodyside moldings. Small 'Lincoln' block letters stood above the left headlamp; tiny 'Town Car' script at the cowl, just ahead of the front door. At the rear were vertical taillamps, with a horizontal rectangular backup lamp at the center. Standard equipment included power brakes and steering, rear defroster, auto-temp air conditioning, power windows and door locks, power vent windows, tinted glass, gas-pressurized shocks, speed control, tilt steering, P215/70R15 WSW tires, mini spare tire, full vinyl roof, heated power remote mirrors, and a four-speaker AM/FM stereo radio. Town Car Signature and Cartier both added keyless illuminated entry, a conventional spare tire, wide bright lower bodyside moldings, and six-speaker radio with cassette player and premium sound. Signature had two-color hood/bodyside accent paint stripes and wire wheel covers. Cartier featured dual red hood and single red bodyside/decklid paint stripes, and turbine-spoke aluminum wheels. Both had a half coach roof with wrapover molding and "frenched" back window.

I.D. DATA: Lincoln again had a 17-symbol Vehicle Identification Number (VIN), fastened to the instrument panel, visible through the windshield. The first three symbols indicate manufacturer, make and vehicle type: '1LN' Lincoln. Symbol four denotes restraint system. Next comes a letter 'P', followed by two digits that indicate body type: '96' 4dr. Town Car; '97' 4dr. Continental; '98' 2dr. Mark VII. Symbol eight indicates engine type: 'F' V8302 EFI; 'M' H.O. V8302 EFI. Next is a check digit. Symbol ten indicates model year ('G' 1986). Symbol eleven is assembly plant ('Y' Wixom, MI). The final six digits make up the sequence number, starting with 600001. A Vehicle Certification Label on the left front door lock face panel or door pillar shows the manufacturer, month and year built, GVW, GAWR, VIN, and codes for body, color, trim, axle, transmission, and special order data.

1986 Continental sedan (JG)

CONTINENTAL (V-8)

Model Number	Body/Style Number	Body Type & Seating	Factory Price	Shipping Weight	Production Total
97/850A	54D	4-dr. Sedan-5P	24556	3778	19,012

CONTINENTAL GIVENCHY DESIGNER SERIES (V-8)

97/860A	54D	4-dr. Sedan-5P	26837	3808	Note 1

TOWN CAR (V-8)

96/700B	54D	4-dr. Sedan-6P	20764	4038	117,771

TOWN CAR SIGNATURE SERIES (V-8)

96/705B	54D	4-dr. Sedan-6P	23972	4121	Note 1

TOWN CAR CARTIER DESIGNER SERIES (V-8)

96/710B	54D	4-dr. Sedan-6P	25235	4093	Note 1

MARK VII (V-8)

98/800A	63D	2-dr. Coupe-5P	22399	3667	20,056

MARK VII LSC (V-8)

98/805B	63D	2-dr. Coupe-5P	23857	3718	Note 1

MARK VII BILL BLASS DESIGNER SERIES (V-8)

98/810B	63D	2-dr. Coupe-5P	23857	3732	Note 1

Note 1: Production of LSC, Signature and Designer Series is included in basic model totals.

Model Number Note: Some sources include a prefix 'P' ahead of the basic two-digit number; e.g., 'P97' for Continental. Not all sources include the suffix after the slash.

ENGINE DATA: BASE V-8 (all models): 90-degree, overhead valve V-8. Cast iron block and head. Displacement: 302 cu. in. (5.2 liters). Bore & stroke: 4.00 x 3.00 in. Compression ratio: 8.9:1. Brake horsepower: 150 at 3200 R.P.M. Torque: 270 lbs.-ft. at 2000 R.P.M. Five main bearings. Hydraulic valve lifters. Sequential port (electronic) fuel injection. VIN Code: F. OPTIONAL V-8 (Town Car): Same as 302 cu. in. V-8 above, with dual exhausts Brake H.P.: 160 at 3400 R.P.M. Torque: 280 lbs.-ft. at 2200 R.P.M. BASE V-8 (Mark VII LSC): High-output version of 302 cu. in. V-8 above Compression ratio: 9.2:1. Brake H.P.: 200 at 4000 R.P.M. Torque: 285 lbs.-ft. at 3000 R.P.M. VIN Code: M.

CHASSIS DATA: Wheelbase: (Continental/Mark) 108.5 in.; (Town Car) 117.3 in. Overall Length: (Cont.) 200.7 in.; (Mark) 202.8 in.; (Town) 219.0 in. Height: (Cont.) 55.6 in.; (Mark) 54.2 in.; (Town) 55.9 in. Width: (Cont.) 73.6 in.; (Mark) 70.9 in.; (Town) 78.1 in. Front Tread: (Cont./Mark) 58.4 in.; (Town) 62.2 in. Rear Tread: (Cont./Mark) 59.0 in.; (Town) 62.0 in. Standard Tires: P215/70R15 SBR WSW exc. Mark LSC, P215/65R15 BSW.

TECHNICAL: Transmission: Four-speed automatic overdrive standard. Gear ratios: (1st) 2.40:1; (2nd) 1.47:1; (3rd) 1.00:1; (4th) 0.67:1; (Rev) 2.00:1. Standard final drive ratio: 2.73:1 exc. Mark VII LSC, 3.27:1; Town Car Signature/Cartier, 3.08:1. Steering/Suspension/Body: same as 1984-85. Brakes: Four-wheel disc except (Town Car) front disc and rear drum; all power-assisted; ABS (anti-lock) standard on Continental/Mark. Fuel Tank: 22.1 gal. exc. Town Car, 18 gal.

367

1986 Continental Mark VII LSC coupe (JG)

DRIVETRAIN OPTIONS: Dual exhaust system: Town Car LPO ($83) but standard w/high-altitude emissions. Traction-Lok differential ($101- $165). 100-amp alternator: Town ($67). Engine block heater ($26). Automatic load leveling: Town ($202). Trailer towing pkg.: Town ($159-$306). California emission system ($99).

CONTINENTAL/MARK VII CONVENIENCE/APPEARANCE OPTIONS: Anti-theft alarm ($200). Automatic-dimming day/night mirror ($89). Power glass moonroof ($1319). Vinyl-insert bodyside molding: Cont. ($70). Brushed-aluminum upper bodyside molding: Cont. ($74). Dual-shade paint: Cont. ($320). Glamour paint ($268). Leather interior trim ($551) exc. Cont. Givenchy (NC). Wire spoke aluminum wheels ($693) exc. Designer (NC). Geometric cast aluminum wheels ($298) exc. Designer ($395 credit). Puncture-sealant tires ($190).

TOWN CAR CONVENIENCE/APPEARANCE OPTIONS: Option Packages: Comfort/ convenience pkg. ($698). Headlamp convenience group ($198). Comfort/Convenience: Keyless illuminated entry ($209). Anti- theft alarm ($200). Power decklid pulldown ($79). Six-way power passenger seat ($235). Electronic instrument panel ($822). Leather-wrapped steering wheel ($105). Lighting/Mirrors: Lighted visor vanity mirrors, pair ($156). Automatic-dimming day/night mirror ($89). Entertainment: Electronic AM/FM stereo radio w/cassette player and premium sound ($389). Exterior: Power glass moonroof ($1319). Carriage roof ($1069) exc. Signature ($726). Luxury Valino vinyl coach roof ($343). Glamour paint ($268). Dual-shade paint ($320). Protective bodyside molding ($70). Interior: Leather interior trim ($459-$521) exc. Cartier (NC). Floor mats w/carpet inserts: front ($43); rear ($25). Wheels and Tires: Wire wheel covers ($341) exc. Cartier ($137 credit) and Signature (NC). Wire spoke aluminum wheels ($873) exc. Cartier ($395) or Signature ($532). Lacy spoke or turbine spoke aluminum wheels ($478) exc. Signature ($137) or Cartier (NC). Puncture-sealant whitewall tires ($190). Conventional spare tire ($64).

HISTORY: Introduced: October 3, 1985. Model year production: 156,839. Calendar year production: 183,035. Calendar year sales by U.S. dealers: 177,584. Model year sales by U.S. dealers: 159,320.

Historical Footnotes: Town Car broke its model year sales record for the second year in a row, while Continental sales fell 31 percent. Mark VII sold just a trifle better than in 1985. The main reason for buying a Town Car, according to Lincoln, was "the aura of success it reflects upon its owners." Lincoln called Town Car "the roomiest passenger car in America" (not including wagons and vans), and touted its "regal bearing and formal elegance."

LINCOLN
1987-1990

Ford Motor Co.'s Lincoln-Mercury Division built three cars under the Lincoln nameplate in 1987. Lincoln Town Cars, Mark VII coupes and Continentals were all assembled at a plant in Wixom, Mich., which operated two shifts and built an average 40 cars per hour between Aug. 1, 1986 and Aug. 4, 1987.

A total of 159,320 Lincolns were sold during the 1987 model year. The popularity of the Town Car and Mark VII increased slightly, while the Continental lost about 9,000 customers from 1986. Part of this decrease could be attributed to the fact that a totally new Continental was in the works.

Thomas J. Wagner was general manager of the division headquartered in Detroit's Renaissance Center. Edsel B. Ford II was active in the company as general marketing manager. Product news included a revised Givenchy Designer Series for the rear-drive Continental sedan. The Mark VII rear-drive coupe came in base and LSC versions, with a high-output version of the five-liter Lincoln V-8 in the latter car. A Bill Blass Designer Series Mark VII was available again. The rear-drive Town Car received a new compact disc player option and continued to come in signature and Cartier Designer editions.

In 1988, Ross H. Roberts took over as general manager of Lincoln-Mercury. The Continental became a front-drive sedan that was dramatically different from its predecessors. It was all-new and aerodynamic with a standard 3.8-liter V-6, four-speed automatic transaxle, four-wheel independent suspension and all-disc anti-lock brakes. Priced upwards from $26,602, the new model came in standard or Signature trim levels. Even with production starting three months into the model year, the updated Lincoln still sold 33,507 units, over twice as much in 1987.

Lincoln Town Cars received a new grille and hood ornament, revised interior trim and an electronic AM/FM radio. The wheel covers and rear styling were updated, too. Base-priced at $24,897, the car earned 126,642 sales, down nearly 9,500 from 1987.

Declining in sales by about half as much was the Mark VII, which came in sporty LSC and fancy Bill Blass models priced from $26,904. LSCs got sporty new road wheels and leather seats as a no-cost option. The grille and hood ornament were reworked and a JBL sound system was a new-for-1988 option.

During 1989, the Lincoln Town Car tapered off to 117,806 sales, while the Mark VII coupe climbed to 27,030. In its first full season, the Continental realized 59,054 customers, making Lincoln dealers very happy. From sales of 180,712 cars in 1987, the annual total was now up to 203,890.

New for 1989 was a driver/passenger air bag system for the Continental, an optional anti-theft system for Mark VIIs and new models of the Town Car. Cartier editions had a half-vinyl top and two-tone finish, while Signature versions boasted a half-vinyl coach roof. Mark VIIs came in LSC (with analog gages) and Bill Blass (with electronic instrumentation) models.

For 1990, the Town Car was totally updated. This all-new aerodynamic luxo-mobile had flush aircraft-inspired doors, air bags, speed-sensitive steering, load leveling and an automatic radio antenna. Starting at $28,541, all three editions — base, Signature and Cartier — had a five-liter V-8 linked to a four-speed overdrive transaxle. A new grille, hood ornament, tail lamps and power antenna were seen on the just-under-$30,000 Continental. The Mark VII, also about $30,000, got an air bag system, safer new seat belts, new seats and a message center.

1987 LINCOLN

Because major reworking was expected soon for both Continental and Mark VII, little changed for the 1987 model year.

1987 Continental Givenchy Designer Series four-door sedan

CONTINENTAL — V-8 — Essentially a carryover for 1987, the Continental four-door sedan was powered by a 302 cu. in. (5.0 liter) V-8 with overdrive automatic transmission.

1987 Mark VII coupe

MARK VII — V-8 — Only minor equipment changes arrived with the 1987 Mark VII coupe, since a totally reworked version was expected at mid-year. The standard 302 cu. in. (5.0-liter) V-8 produced 150 horsepower, but the Mark VII LSC version delivered 200.

1987 Town Car Cartier Designer Series four-door sedan

TOWN CAR — V-8 — Continuing as the most popular Lincoln (by far), the full-size Town Car changed little for 1987 except for more extensive use of galvanized metal in the body. A compact-disc player was ready to join the option list, and the Cartier Designer Series got some new body colors and seating fabrics. Powerplant was the same as the Continental and Mark VII: a 5.0-liter V-8 rated 150 horsepower.

I.D. DATA: Lincoln had a 17-symbol Vehicle Identification Number (VIN) fastened to the instrument panel, visible through the windshield. The first three symbols indicate manufacturer, make, and vehicle type: '1LN' - Lincoln. Symbol four denotes restraint system. Next comes a letter 'M',followed by two digits that indicate model number. Symbol eight indicates engine type. Next is a check digit. Symbol ten indicates model year ('H' = 1987). Symbol eleven is assembly plant. The final six digits make up the sequence number, starting with 600001.

Model Number	Body/Style Number	Body Type & Seating	Factory Price	Shipping Weight	Production Total
CONTINENTAL (V-8)					
97	54D	4-dr. Sedan-5P	24602	3799	17,597
CONTINENTAL GIVENCHY DESIGNER SERIES (V-8)					
98	54D	4-dr. Sedan-5P	28902	3826	Note 1
TOWN CAR (V-8)					
81	54D	4-dr. Sedan-6P	22549	4051	76,483
TOWN CAR SIGNATURE SERIES (V-8)					
82	54D	4-dr. Sedan-6P	25541	4106	Note 1
TOWN CAR CARTIER DESIGNER SERIES (V-8)					
83	54D	4-dr. Sedan-6P	26868	4086	Note 1
MARK VII (V-8)					
91	63D	2-dr. Coupe-5P	24216	3722	15,286
MARK VII LSC (V-8)					
93	63D	2-dr. Coupe-5P	25863	3772	Note 1
MARK VII BILL BLASS DESIGNER SERIES (V-8)					
92	63D	2-dr. Coupe-5P	25863	3747	Note 1

Note 1: Production of LSC, Signature, and Designer Series is included in basic model totals.

ENGINE DATA: BASE V-8 (all models): 90-degree, overhead valve V-8. Cast iron block and head. Displacement: 302 cu. in. (5.2 liters). Bore & stroke: 4.00 x 3.00 in. Compression ratio: 8.9:1. Brake horsepower: 150 at 3200 RPM. Torque: 270 lbs.-ft. at 2000 RPM. Five main bearings. Hydraulic valve lifters. Sequential port fuel injection. **BASE V-8 (Mark VII LSC):** High-output version of 302 cu. in. V-8 above — Compression ratio: 9.2:1. Horsepower: 200 at 4000 RPM. Torque: 285 lbs.-ft. at 3000 RPM.

CHASSIS DATA: Wheelbase: (Continental/Mark) 108.5 in.; (Town Car) 117.3 in. **Overall Length:** (Cont.) 200.7 in.; (Mark) 202.8 in.; (Town Car) 219.0 in. **Height:** (Cont.) 55.6 in.; (Mark) 54.2 in.; (Town) 55.9 in. **Width:** (Cont.) 73.6 in.; (Mark) 70.9 in.; (Town) 78.1 in. **Front Tread:** (Cont./Mark) 58.4 in.; (Town) 62.2 in. **Rear Tread:** (Cont./Mark) 59.0 in.; (Town) 62.0 in. **Standard Tires:** P215/70R15 SBR WSW exc. Mark LSC, P215/65R15; BSW.

TECHNICAL: Transmission: Four-speed automatic overdrive standard. **Steering:** (Cont/Mark) rack and pinion; (Town Car) recirculating ball. **Front Suspension:** (Cont./Mark) modified MacPherson struts with lower control arms, electronically-controlled air springs, automatic leveling and stabilizer bar; (Town Car) upper/lower control arms with coil springs and stabilizer bar. **Rear Suspension:** (Cont./Mark) rigid four-link axle with air springs, automatic leveling and stabilizer bar; (Town Car) four-link axle with coil springs. **Brakes:** Four-wheel disc except (Town Car) front disc and rear drum; all power-assisted; ABS (anti-lock) standard on Cont/Mark. **Body construction:** (Cont/Mark) unibody; (Town) separate body and frame. **Fuel Tank:** (Mark VII) 22.1 gal.; (Cont.) 20.3 gal.; (Town Car) 18 gal.

DRIVETRAIN OPTIONS: Traction-Lok differential ($101) except ($175) on base Town Car. Automatic load leveling: Town ($202). Trailer towing pkg: Town ($463-$546).

CONTINENTAL CONVENIENCE/APPEARANCE OPTIONS: Puncture sealant tires ($200). Anti-theft alarm system ($200). Automatic day/night mirror ($89). Brushed aluminum upper bodyside molding ($74). Bodyside protection molding ($70). Power glass moonroof ($1319). Glamour paint ($268). Dual-shade paint ($320). Leather seat trim, base ($560). Ford JBL Audio System ($506). Wire spoke aluminum wheels, base ($693). California emissions system ($99). Engine block heater ($26).

MARK VII CONVENIENCE/APPEARANCE OPTIONS: Puncture sealant tires ($200). Wire spoke aluminum wheels, base ($693). Anti-theft alarm system ($200). Power glass moonroof ($1319). Automatic day/night mirror ($89). Glamour paint ($268). Leather seat trim ($560). Engine block heater ($26). California emissions pkg ($99).

TOWN CAR CONVENIENCE/APPEARANCE OPTIONS: Puncture sealant tires ($200). Locking wire wheel covers Cartier ($137 credit). Base ($341). Lacy spoke aluminum wheels, Signature ($137). Others ($478). Turbine spoke aluminum wheels, Cartier ($395). Signature ($532). Base ($873). Electronic instrument panel ($822). Keyless illuminated entry system ($209). Anti-theft alarm system ($200). Power glass moonroof ($1319). Comfort/Convenience Pkg Power decklid pulldown, illuminated visor mirrors, automatic headlight dimmer, autolamp dealy system, dual power seats, rear floormats ($694). Leather-wrapped steering wheel ($115). Automatic day/night mirror ($89). Bodyside protection molding ($70). Carriage roof, Signature ($726). Others ($1069). Valino luxury coach roof ($343). Ford JBL Audio System ($506). Dual shade paint ($320). Glamour paint ($268). Leather seat trim, Signature ($469). Base ($531). Engine block heater ($26). California emissions pkg ($99). Dual exhaust system ($83). 100-amp. alternator ($67).

HISTORY: Introduced: October 2, 1986. Model year production: 109,366. Calendar year production: 135,951. Calendar year sales by U.S. dealers: 129,091. Model year sales by U.S. dealers: 180,712.

1988 LINCOLN

A dramatically reworked Continental was the big news at Lincoln for 1988, with front-wheel drive and a six-cylinder engine — quite a change from the V-12s of the 1940s and the big V-8s ever since.

CONTINENTAL — V-6 — An all-new front-wheel-drive sedan replaced the former rear-drive Continental. Not only was this the first FWD model from Lincoln, it carried the first engine with fewer than eight cylinders: a 232 cu. inc. (3.8-liter) V-6, as used in Thunderbird and Cougar. The 140-horsepower V-6 had a counter-rotating balance shaft inside its block for smoother running, as well as multi-point fuel injection. It drove a four-speed overdrive automatic transmission.
Slightly longer in wheelbase (109 inches) than its predecessor, the restyled Continental measured more than 4 inches longer overall. Though an inch narrower on the outside, the interior offered more room than before, with seating for six. Leather upholstery was standard, with cloth a no-cost option. The short option list included a compact-disc player, Insta-Clear heated windshield, and power moonroof. Continental's computer-controlled, fully independent suspension included electronic leveling. The four-wheel disc brakes came with a standard anti-lock system.
Standard equipment included automatic climate control, tinted glass, power windows/locks, heated power mirrors, power driver's seat, cruise control, stereo radio/cassette and tilt steering. A Signature Series added a power passenger seat, autolamp system, illuminated/keyless entry and alloy wheels.

MARK VII — V-8 — Introduced early in the spring of 1987, the Mark VII coupe carried on with its rear-drive layout and V-8 engine, but added 25 horsepower. The base model was dropped, leaving only the sporty LSC touring coupe and the classy Bill Blass Designer Series. Standard anti-lock braking included a self-diagnostic provision.

TOWN CAR — V-8 — The traditional Lincoln sedan earned a new grille, taillamps and rear panel this year, for its spring 1987 debut. Interiors wore new fabrics, too. A 150-horsepower, 302 cu. in. (5.0-liter) V-8 with multi-point fuel injection continued to provide the power.

I.D. DATA: Lincoln's 17-symbol Vehicle Identification Number (VIN) was atop the instrument panel, visible through the windshield. The first three symbols indicate manufacturer, make and vehicle type: '1LN' - Lincoln. Symbol four denotes restraint system. Next comes a letter 'M', followed by two digits that indicate model number. Symbol eight indicates engine type. Next is a check digit. Symbol ten is for model year ('J' = 1988). Symbol eleven is assembly plant. The final six digits make up the sequence number, starting with 600001.

1988 Town Car four-door sedan

Model Number	Body/Style Number	Body Type & Seating	Factory Price	Shipping Weight	Production Total
97		4-dr. Sedan-6P	26078	3628	41,287
CONTINENTAL SIGNATURE SERIES (V-6)					
98		4-dr. Sedan-6P	27944	3618	Note 1
TOWN CAR (V-8)					
81	54D	4-dr. Sedan-6P	23126	4093	201,113
TOWN CAR SIGNATURE SERIES (V-8)					
82	54D	4-dr. Sedan-6P	25990	4119	Note 1
TOWN CAR CARTIER DESIGNER SERIES (V-8)					
83	54D	4-dr. Sedan-6P	27273	4107	Note 1
MARK VII LSC (V-8)					
93	63D	2-dr. Coupe-5P	25016	3772	38,259
MARK VII BILL BLASS DESIGNER SERIES (V-8)					
92	63D	2-dr. Coupe-5P	25016	3747	Note 1

Note 1: Production of Signature and Designer Series is included in basic model totals.

ENGINE DATA: BASE V-6 (Continental): 90-degree, overhead valve V-6. Cast iron block and aluminum head. Displacement: 232 cu. in. (3.8 liters). Bore & stroke: 3.80 x 3.40 in. Compression ratio: 9.0:1. Brake horsepower: 140 at 3800 RPM. Torque: 215 lbs.-ft. at 2200 RPM. Four main bearings. Hydraulic valve lifters. Multi-point fuel injection. BASE V-8 (Town Car): 90-degree, overhead valve V-8. Cast iron block and head. Displacement: 302 cu. in. (5.2 liters). Bore & stroke: 4.00 x 3.00 in. Compression ratio: 8.9:1. Brake horsepower: 150 at 3200 RPM. Torque: 270 lbs.-ft. at 2000 RPM. Five main bearings. Hydraulic valve lifters. Sequential port fuel injection. BASE V-8 (Mark VII): High-output version of 302 cu. in. V-8 above — Compression ratio: 9.2:1. Horsepower: 225 at 4000 RPM. Torque: 300 lbs.-ft. at 3200 RPM.

CHASSIS DATA: Wheelbase: (Continental) 109 in.; (Mark) 108.5 in.; (Town Car) 117.3 in. **Overall Length:** (Cont.) 205.1 in.; (Mark) 202.8 in.; (Town Car) 219.0 in. **Height:** (Cont.) 55.6 in.; (Mark) 54.2 in.; (Town) 55.9 in. **Width:** (Cont.) 72.7 in.; (Mark) 70.9 in.; (Town) 78.1 in. **Front Tread:** (Cont.) 62.3 in.; (Mark) 58.4 in.; (Town) 62.2 in. **Rear Tread:** (Cont.) 61.1 in.; (Mark) 59.0 in.; (Town) 62.0 in. **Standard Tires:** (Cont.) P205/70R15; (Mark LSC) P215/65R15; (Mark Bill Blass/Town Car) P215/70R15.

TECHNICAL: Transmission: Four-speed automatic overdrive standard. **Steering:** (Cont/Mark) rack and pinion; (Town Car) recirculating ball. **Front Suspension:** (Cont.) MacPherson struts with integral air springs and two-stage damping; (Mark) modified MacPherson struts with lower control arms, electronically-controlled air springs, automatic leveling and stabilizer bar; (Town Car) upper/lower control arms with coil springs and stabilizer bar. **Rear Suspension:** (Cont.) MacPherson struts with integral air springs and two-stage damping; (Mark) rigid four-link axle with air springs, automatic leveling and stabilizer bar; (Town Car) four-link axle with coil springs. **Brakes:** Four-wheel disc except (Town Car) front disc and rear drum; all power-assisted; ABS (anti-lock) standard on Cont/Mark. **Body construction:** (Cont/Mark) unibody; (Town) separate body and frame. **Fuel Tank:** (Cont.) 18.6 gal.; (Mark VII) 22.1 gal.; (Town Car) 18 gal.

DRIVETRAIN OPTIONS: Traction-Lok differential: Mark/Town ($101). Automatic load leveling: Town ($202). Trailer towing pkg: Town ($463-$546).

CONVENIENCE/APPEARANCE OPTIONS: Keyless Illum Entry System ($209). Front License Plate Bracket (NC). Anti-Theft Alarm System ($200). Power Glass Moonroof ($1319). Memory Seat w/Power Lumbar ($301). Leather-Wrapped Strg Wheel ($115). Ford JBL Audio System ($525). Compact Disc Player ($617). Instaclear Heated Windshield ($253). Comfort/Convenience Pkg ($819). Overhead Console Grp ($226). Cloth Seat Trim (NC). Locking Spoke Wheel Covers, Signature ($137). Locking Spoke Wheel Covers ($341). Styled Aluminum Wheels ($478). Frt License Plate Bracket (NC). Anti-Theft Alarm System ($200). Pwr Glass Moonroof ($1319). Auto Dim Day/Night Mirror ($89). Ford JBL Audio System ($525). Eng Block Heater ($26). Calif Emissions System ($99). TIRES WSW Puncture Sealant, Blass ($200). Lock. Wire-Styled Wheel Covers, Cartier ($137 credit). Signature ($137 credit). Base ($341). Lacy Spoke Alum Wheels, Cartier (NC). Signature (NC). Base ($478). Turbine Spoke Alum Wheels, Cartier (NC). Signature (NC). Base ($478). Wire Spoke Alum, Cartier ($395). Signature ($395). Base ($873). Electronic Instrument Panel ($822). Keyless Illum Entry System ($209). Frt License Plate Bracket (NC). Anti-Theft Alarm System ($200). Pwr Glass Moonroof ($1319). Comfort/Convenience Pkg ($694). Leather-Wrapped Strg Wheel ($115). Auto Dim Day/Night Mirror ($89). Bodyside Protection Mldg ($70). Carriage Roof, Signature ($710). Others ($1069). Valino Lux Coach Roof ($359). Ford JBL Audio System ($525). Compact Disc Player ($617). Dual Shade Paint ($320). Cartier Designer Series (NC). Signature Series ($469). Base ($531). Eng Block Heater ($26). Delete Trim Opt, High Alt ($323). Other ($406). Calif Emissions System ($99). Dual Exhaust, w/High Alt (NC). Other ($83). 100 Ampere Alternator ($67). Tires, WSW Puncture Sealant ($200).

HISTORY: Introduced: March, 1987 except (Continental) December 26, 1987. Model year production: 280,659. Calendar year production: 207,230. Calendar year sales by U.S. dealers: 191,624. Model year sales by U.S. dealers: 183,333.

1989 LINCOLN

This was largely a carryover year for the Lincoln luxury trio: two traditional rear-drive models with V-8 engines and one front-drive with a V-6.

CONTINENTAL — V-6 — A year before, Continental became the first Lincoln with front-wheel drive and a V-6 engine. This year, it was the first domestic automobile with standard airbags for both driver and passenger. The left bag fit into the customary spot in the steering wheel hub: its mate was mounted above the glove compartment. Two trim levels were available again, both powered by a 3.8-liter V-6 with four-speed overdrive automatic transmission. An altered final drive ratio improved response. As before, computer-controlled damping adjusted the suspension to changes in the road surface.

MARK VII — V-8 — Little change was evident in the sport/luxury coupes, which cost the same in either LSC or Bill Blass edition. A computer-malfunction warning light, formerly included only on California cars, now came with all models. The sporty LSC had bigger blackwall tires on alloy wheels, plus leather upholstery and quick-ratio power steering. The luxury-oriented Bill Blass Mark VII came with regular power steering, leather or cloth upholstery, and more chrome body trim. Both had automatic climate control, a self-leveling suspension, and six-way power front seats.

1989 Town Car four-door sedan

TOWN CAR — V-8 — Little changed in the traditional Lincoln sedan. Powerplant remained the 5.0-liter V-8 with 150 horsepower. Standard equipment included power windows and mirrors, automatic climate control, comfort lounge seats, and cruise control. The base model featured a new "Frenched" back window for its standard full vinyl roof. The Signature Series sported a coach roof, while the Cartier came with platinum bodyside moldings and new twin-shade paint.

I.D. DATA: Lincoln's 17-symbol Vehicle Identification Number (VIN) was atop the instrument panel, visible through the windshield. the first three symbols indicate manufacturer, make and vehicle type: '1LN' = Lincoln. Symbol four denotes restraint system. Next comes a letter 'M', followed by two digits that indicate model number. Symbol eight indicates engine type. Next is a check digit. Symbol ten indicates model year ('K' = 1989). Symbol eleven is assembly plant. The final six digits make up the sequence number, starting with 600001.

CONTINENTAL (V-6)

Model Number	Body/Style Number	Body Type & Seating	Factory Price	Shipping Weight	Production Total
97		4-dr. Sedan-6P	27468	3635	
98		4-dr. Sedan-6P	29334	3633	
TOWN CAR (V-8)					
81	54D	4-dr. Sedan-6P	25205	4044	
TOWN CAR SIGNATURE SERIES (V-8)					
82	43D	4-dr. Sedan-6p	28206	4070	
TOWN CAR CARTIER DESIGNER SERIES (V-8)					
83	54D	4-dr. Sedan-6P	29352	4059	
MARK VII LSC (V-8)					
93	63D	2-dr. Coupe-5P	27218	3743	
MARK VII BILL BLASS DESIGNER SERIES (V-8)					
92	63D	2-dr. Coupe-5P	27218	3783	

ENGINE DATA: BASE V-6 (Continental): 90-degree, overhead valve V-6. Cast iron block and aluminum head. Displacement: 232 cu. in. (3.8 liters). Bore & stroke: 3.80 x 3.40 in. Compression ratio: 9.0:1. Brake horsepower: 140 at 3800 RPM. Torque: 215 lbs.-ft. at 2200 RPM. Four main bearings. Hydraulic valve lifters. Multi-point fuel injection. BASE V-8 (Town Car): 90-degree, overhead valve V-8. Cast iron block and head. Displacement: 302 cu. in. (5.2 liters). Bore & stroke: 4.00 x 3.00 in. Compression ratio: 8.9:1. Brake horsepower: 150 at 3200 RPM. Torque: 270 lbs.-ft. at 2000 RPM. Five main bearings. Hydraulic valve lifters. Sequential port fuel injection. BASE V-8 (MARK VII): High-output version of 302 cu. in. V-8 above — Compression ratio: 9.2:1. Horsepower: 225 at 4000 RPM. Torque: 300 lbs.-ft. at 3200 RPM.

CHASSIS DATA: Wheelbase: (Continental) 109 in.; (Mark) 108.5 in.; (Town Car) 117.3 in. **Overall Length:** (Cont.) 205.1 in.; (Mark) 202.8 in.; (Town) 219.0 in. **Height:** (Cont.) 55.6.; (Mark) 54.2 in.; (Town) 55.9 in. **Width:** (Cont.) 72.7 in.; (Mark) 70.9 in.; (Town) 78.1 in. **Front Tread:** (Cont.) 62.3 in.; (Mark) 58.4 in.; (Town) 62.2 in. **Rear Tread:** (Cont.) 61.1 in.; (Mark) 59.0 in.; (Town) 62.0 in. **Standard Tires:** (Cont.) P205/70R15; (Mark LSC) P225/60R16 BSW; (Mark Bill Blass/Town Car) P215/70R15.

TECHNICAL: Transmission: Four-speed overdrive automatic standard. **Steering:** (Cont/Mark) rack and pinion; (Town Car) recirculating ball. **Front Suspension:** (Cont.) MacPherson struts with integral air springs and two-stage damping; (Mark) modified MacPherson struts with lower control arms, electronically-controlled air springs, automatic leveling and stablizer bar: (Town Car) upper/lower control arms with coil springs and stabilizer bar. **Rear Suspension:** (Cont.) MacPherson struts with integral air springs and two-stage damping; (Mark) rigid four-link axle with air springs, automatic leveling and stabilizer bar; (Town Car) four-link axle with coil springs. **Brakes:** Four-wheel disc except (Town Car) front disc and rear drum; all power-assisted; ABS (antiilock) standard on Cont/Mark. **Body construction:** (Cont/Mark) unibody; (Town) separate body and frame. **Fuel Tank:** (Cont.) 18.6 gal.; (Mark VII) 22.1 gal.; (Town Car) 18 gal.

DRIVETRAIN OPTIONS: Traction-Lok differential: Mark/Town ($101). Automatic load leveling: Town ($202). Trailer towing pkg.: Town ($546).

CONTINENTAL CONVENIENCE/APPEARANCE OPTIONS:
Styled Alum Wheels ($478). Keyless Illum. Entry System ($209). Frt. Lic. Plate Bracket (NC). Anti-Theft Alarm System ($200). Pwr Glass Moonroof ($1319). Memory Seat w/Pwr Lumbar ($301). Leather-Wrapped Strg Wheel ($115). Ford JBL Audio System ($525). Compact Disc Player ($627). Instaclear Heated Windshield ($253). Comfort/Convenience Grp ($819). Overhead Console Grp ($226). Cloth Seat Trim (NC). Eng Block Immersion Heater ($26). Calif. Emissions System ($99). TIRES: P205/70 R15 WSW (NC)

MARK VII CONVENIENCE/APPEARANCE OPTIONS:
Frt Lic Plate bracket (NC). Anti-Theft Alarm System ($200). Pwr Glass Moonroof ($1319). Auto Dim Day/Night Mirror ($89). Ford JBL Audio System ($525). Individual Luxury Seats (NC). Eng Block Immersion Heater ($26). Calif. Emissions System ($100).

TOWN CAR CONVENIENCE/APPEARANCE OPTIONS:
Electronic Instrument Panel ($822). Keyless Illum. Entry System ($225). Frt License Plate Bracket (NC). Anti-Theft Alarm System ($225). Pwr Glass Moonroof ($1420). Comfort/Convenience Grp ($694). Leather-Wrapped Strg Wheel ($120). Auto Dim Day/Night Mirror ($89). Bodyside Protection Mldg ($70). Carriage Roof, Signature ($710). Other ($1069). Valino Lux Coach Roof ($359). Ford JBL Audio System ($525). Compact Disc Player ($617). Leather Seat Trim Cartier (NC). Signature Series ($509). Base ($570). Eng block Immersion Heater ($26). Delete Trim Opt, High Alt ($323). other ($406). Calif. Emissions System ($100). Dual Exhaust, w/High Alt (NC). Other ($83). 100 Amp. Alternator ($67). Lock, Wire-Styled Wheel covers Cartier ($137 credit). Signature ($137 credit). Base ($341). Lacy Spoke Alum Wheels Cartier (NC). Signature (NC). Base ($525). Turbine Spoke Alum Wheels Cartier (NC). Signature (NC). Base ($525). Wire Spoke Alum Wheels Cartier ($395). Signature ($395). Base ($873).

HISTORY: Introduced: October 6, 1988 except (Continental) December, 1988. Model year production: 215,966. Calendar year sales by U.S. dealers: 200,315. Model year sales by U.S. dealers: 203,890.

1990 LINCOLN

Dramatically different was the best way to describe the new-for-1990 Town Car, which earned the *Motor Trend* Car of the Year award — first luxury car to achieve that honor in nearly four decades. Far smoother and more rounded than its forerunners (though similar in size), the new Town Car not only looked modern, it functioned with modern efficiency, slicing through the air with a vastly improved coefficient of drag. Lincoln's other two models carried on with minimal change.

CONTINENTAL — V-6 — Only a few changes in trim and equipment could be seen in the front-drive Lincoln. Bolder vertical bars made up a revised grille. A new ornament stood atop the hood, and taillamps gained a slight revision. The power radio antenna now operated automatically, and wire wheel covers left the option list.

MARK VII — V-8 — A restyled grille was the only evident change in Lincoln's two-door coupe duo, but the interior held a new driver's side airbag and rear shoulder belts. The dashboard was new, too. The LSC rode standard BBS alloy wheels, while the luxury-oriented Bill Blass Designer Series showed more chrome trim.

1990 Town Car four-door sedan

TOWN CAR — V-8 — For the first time since its debut a decade earlier, the traditional (and best selling) Lincoln earned a major restyling. Gone was the square look, replaced by gracefully rounded corners (not unlike those in the Continental). Dimensions were similar to its predecessor's, but the car's drag coefficient improved sharply. Still a big luxury automobile, with rear-wheel drive and 5.0-liter V-8 engine, the Town Car continued to sport such extras as opera windows. For safety's sake, twin airbags were installed and anti-lock braking was optional. Aircraft-style doors reached up into the roof. A self-leveling suspension relied upon rear air springs, and power steering was now speed-sensitive. Inside were new seats and a new instrument panel. Dual exhausts were included with the Cartier edition.

I.D. DATA: Lincoln's 17-symbol Vehicle Identification Number (VIN) was atop the instrument panel, visible through the windshield. Symbol ten (model year) changed to 'L' for 1990.

CONTINENTAL (V-6)						
Model Number	**Body/Style Number**	**Body Type & Seating**	**Factory Price**	**Shipping Weight**	**Production Total**	
974		4-dr. Sedan-6P	29258	3618		
CONTINENTAL SIGNATURES SERIES (V-6)						
984		4-dr. Sedan-6P	31181	3628		
TOWN CAR (V-8)						
81F		4-dr. Sedan-6P	27315	3936		
TOWN CAR SIGNATURE SERIES (V-8)						
82F		4-dr. Sedan-6P	30043	3963		
TOWN CAR CARTIER DESIGNER SERIES (V-8)						
83F		4-dr. Sedan-6P	32137	3956		
MARK VII LSC (V-8)						
93		2-dr. Coupe-5P	29437	3715		
MARK VII BILL BLASS DESIGNER SERIES (V-8)						
92		2-dr. Coupe-5P	29215	3690		

ENGINE DATA: BASE V-6 (Continental): 90-degree, overhead valve V-6. Cast iron block and aluminum head. Displacement: 232 cu. in. (3.8 liters). Bore & stroke: 3.80 x 3.40 in. Compression ratio: 9.0:1. Brake horsepower: 140 at 3800 RPM. Torque: 215 lbs.-ft. at 2200 RPM. Four main bearings. Hydraulic valve lifters. Multi-point fuel injection. **BASE V-8** (Town Car): 90-degree, overhead valve V-8. Cast iron block and head. Displacement: 302 cu. in. (5.2 liters). Bore & stroke: 4.00 x 3.00 in. Compression ratio: 8.9:1. Brake horsepower: 150 at 3200 RPM. Torque: 270 lbs.-ft. at 2000 RPM. Five main bearings. Hydraulic valve lifters. Sequential port fuel injection. **BASE V-8 (MARK VII):** High-output version of 302 cu. in. V-8 above — Compression ratio: 9.0:1. Horsepower: 225 at 4200 RPM. Torque: 300 lbs.-ft. at 3200 RPM.

CHASSIS DATA: Wheelbase: (Continental) 109 in.; (Mark) 108.5 in.; (Town Car) 117.4 in. **Overall Length:** (Cont.) 205.1 in.; (Mark) 202.8 in.; (Town) 220.2 in. **Height:** (Cont.) 55.6.; (Mark) 54.2 in.; (Town) 56.7 in. **Width:** (Cont.) 72.7 in.; (Mark) 70.9 in.; (Town) 78.1 in. **Front Tread:** (Cont.) 62.3 in.; (Mark) 58.4 in.; (Town) 62.8 in. **Rear Tread:** (Cont.) 61.1 in.; (Mark) 59.0 in.; (Town) 63.3 in. **Standard Tires:** (Mark LSC) P225/60R16; (others) P215/70R15.

TECHNICAL: Transmission: Four-speed overdrive automatic standard. **Steering:** (Cont/Mark) rack and pinion; (Town Car) recirculating ball. **Front Suspension:** (Cont.) MacPherson struts with integral air springs and two-stage damping; (Mark) modified MacPherson struts with lower control arms, electronically-controlled air springs, automatic leveling and stabilizer bar; (Town Car) upper/lower control arms with coil springs and stabilizer bar. **Rear Suspension:** (Cont.) MacPherson struts with integral air springs and two-stage damping; (Mark) rigid four-link axle with air springs, automatic leveling and stabilizer bar; (Town Car) four-link axle with coil springs, automatic leveling and stabilizer bar; (Town Car) four-link axle with coil springs. **Brakes:** Four-wheel disc except (Town Car) front disc and rear drum; all power-assisted; ABS (anti-lock) standard on Cont/Mark. **Body construction:** (Cont/Mark) unibody; (Town) separate body and frame. **Fuel Tank:** (Cont.) 18.6 gal.; (Mark VII) 22.1 gal.; (Town Car) 18 gal.

DRIVETRAIN OPTIONS: Anti-lock braking: Town ($936). Traction-Lok differential: Mark/Town ($101). Trailer towing pkg.: Town ($335-$417).

CONTINENTAL CONVENIENCE/APPEARANCE OPTIONS:
Keyless Illum. Entry System ($225). Frt. Lic. Plate Bracket (NC). Anti-Theft Alarm System ($225). Pwr Moonroof ($1420). Memory Seat w/Pwr Lumbar ($301). Cellular Phone ($926). Leather-Wrapped Strg Wheel ($120). Ford JBL Audio System ($525). Digital Audio Disc Player ($617). Insta-Clear Heated Windshield ($253). Comfort/Convenience Grp ($819). Overhead Console Grp ($236). Cloth Seat Trim (NC). Eng Block Immersion Heater ($26). Calif. Emissions System ($100). Styled Alum Wheels Signature Series (NC). Standard Series ($556). Geometric Spoke Aluminum Wheels, Signature Series (NC). Standard Series ($556).

MARK VII CONVENIENCE/APPEARANCE OPTIONS:
Frt Lic Plate bracket (NC). Anti-Theft Alarm System ($225). Power Moonroof ($1420). Cellular Phone ($926). AM/FM Stereo w/Compact Disc ($299). Auto Day/Night Rearview Mirror ($89). Ford JBL Audio System ($525). Individual Luxury Seats (NC). Eng Block Immersion Heater ($26). Calif. Emissions System ($100).

TOWN CAR CONVENIENCE/APPEARANCE OPTIONS:
Keyless Illum. Entry System ($225). Anti-Theft Alarm System ($225). Pwr Glass Moonroof ($1420). Programmable Memory Seat ($502). Cellular Phone ($926). Leather-Wrapped Strg Wheel ($120). 4-Wheel Anti-Lock Brake System ($936). AM/FM Stereo w/Digital Disc Player ($299). Passenger Side Airbag ($494). Electrochromic Auto Dimming Rr View Mirror ($99). Ford JBL Audio System ($525). Insta-Clear Windshield ($253). Leather Seat Trim Cartier Designer Series (NC). Signature Series ($570). Base ($570). Comfort/Convenience Grp ($694). Eng block Immersion Heater ($26). Calif. Emissions System ($100). Dual Exhaust, w/High Alt (NC). Other ($83). Geometric Spoke Aluminum Wheels Cartier (NC). Signature (NC). Base ($556). Turbine Spoke Aluminum Wheels Cartier (NC). Signature (NC). Base ($556).

MERCURY
1939-1942

1939 Mercury, convertible coupe, AA

MERCURY — Dearborn, Michigan — (1939-1942) —
"The car that dares to ask 'Why?'," some ads said, and though the question referred to dealt with why a big car couldn't be an economical car too, another question might have been why the Ford Motor Company hadn't

1939 Mercury, town sedan, JAC

introduced the Mercury sooner. The answer to that one undoubtedly was that it had taken that long for Edsel Ford to convince his father to build it. The Mercury was priced in the thousand-dollar range, several hundred dollars

1940 Mercury, coupe, AA

1941 Mercury, town sedan, AA

more than the Ford V-8, several hundred less than the Lincoln Zephyr — and about the same as the upper-range Olds and Dodges and the lower-range Buicks and Chryslers, sales from all of which, it was hoped, the new Mercury would usurp. Its engine was a 95 hp version of the flathead Ford V-8, its styling was inspired by the Zephyr, and it had hydraulic brakes from the beginning. With a wheelbase of 116 inches (increased to 118 in '40) and an overall length of 196 inches, the Mercury was a good-sized car, which fact the Ford company advertised extensively, together with its up-to-20 mpg performance — "few cars of *any* size can equal such economy." By 1941 Ford could also headline that "It's made 150,000 owners change cars!" — and that year another 80,000

1942 Mercury, station wagon, OCW

Mercurys were produced, plus a total of 4430 more in 1942 before the production shutdown for the duration of World War II. Although its prewar history was short, the Mercury had already earned for itself the image of being a fine performer in mph as well as mpg, this "hot car" image quite in keeping with its name, chosen by Edsel Ford, that of the fleet-footed messenger of the gods of Roman mythology. The Mercury was strongly identified as an upmarket Ford during this period; in 1945 the Lincoln-Mercury Division would be established to change that.

1939 MERCURY

1939 Mercury, convertible

MERCURY - (V-8) — SERIES 99A — The Mercury story began in the early 1930s when Ford executives identified the need for a medium-priced car to compete with the Dodge Deluxe, Studebaker Commander and Pontiac Deluxe 8. Around 1937, the company planned to introduce a smaller Ford V-8 model and a larger car. The small car was not built for the domestic market, but the proposed larger car became the Mercury. Edsel Ford personally supervised styling of this car, which was patterned after the lines of the Lincoln-Zephyr V-12. The car looked unique from the rest of the line, though differences were not drastic. The Ford-like grille had horizontal bars, instead of the Ford's vertical grille. Taillamps were barrel-shaped, unlike the Ford "teardrop" units. Mercury fenders were less bulbous, with semi-enclosed wheel openings. Headlamps were teardrop-shaped and flush-mounted. Body trim and ornamentation was distinctive. Standard equipment included dual, cowl-mounted windshield wipers, narrow exposed runningboards, an electric clock, locking glove box, the industry's first two-spoke steering wheel, hydraulic brakes and 6.00 x 16 tires. Closed body types were upholstered in Bedford cord or striped broadcloth. The convertible featured leather seats. Finish colors included black, Jefferson blue, Gull gray, Dartmouth green, Tropical green, Mercury blue metallic, Folkstone gray and Coach maroon bright. Cloud Mist gray and Claret maroon were added as spring colors. Early cars had Ford-Mercury hubcaps, while later cars had Mercury 8 hubcaps.

MERCURY I.D. NUMBERS: Serial number was located on the left frame member, just ahead of cowl. Engine number was located on rear of engine atop clutch housing. Motor serial numbers were identical with serial numbers. Plant codes were: DA (Dearborn, Mich.); LA (Los Angeles, Calif.); ME (Metuchen, N.J.) and SL (St. Louis, Mo.). Starting number: 99A-1. Ending number: 99A-101,700 (approximate).

Model Number	Body/Style Number	Body Type & Seating	Factory Price	Shipping Weight	Production Total
99A	76	2-dr Conv Club Cpe-5P	1018	2995	7,818
99A	70	2-dr. Sed-5P	916	2997	13,216
99A	72	2-dr Cpe Sed-5P	957	3000	8,254
99A	73	4-dr Town Sed-5P	957	3013	39,847

1939 Mercury, two-door sedan

MERCURY ENGINE
V-8. L-head. Cast iron block. Displacement: 239.4 cubic inches. Bore and stroke: 3-3/16 x 3-3/4 inches. Compression ratio: 6.15:1. Brake horsepower: 95 @ 3600 RPM. Maximum torque: 170 lbs.-ft. @ 2100 RPM. Three main bearings. Carburetor: Bendix-Stromberg dual downdraft.

CHASSIS FEATURES: Double-drop X-type frame. Solid I-beam front axle with radius rods. Transverse front leaf springs. Transverse rear leaf springs. Three-speed manual transmission with floor shift. Nine inch, single-plate, semi-centrifugal clutch. Three-quarter floating rear axle with 3.54:1 gear ratio. Wheelbase: 116 inches. Overall length: 195.9 inches. Overall width: 72 inches. Front tread: 55-3/4 inches. Rear tread: 58-1/4 inches. Tires: 16 x 6.00. Fuel tank capacity: 14 gallons.

POWERTRAIN OPTIONS: Overdrive. Rear axle with 3.78:1 gear ratio.

CONVENIENCE OPTIONS: White sidewall tires. Single Roto-Matic radio. Windshield header mounted radio antenna. Hot air heater. Hot water heater. Visor vanity mirror. Draft deflectors. Spotlight. Center front bumper guard. Hub and spoke wheel covers. Road light. Locking gas cap. Two types of oil bath air cleaners. Oil filter. License plate frames. Seat covers. Luggage. Governor.

HISTORICAL FOOTNOTES: Introduced Oct. 8, 1938. Calendar year production: 76,198. U.S. registrations: (1938) 6,835; (1939) 65,884. Mercury was the 11th best-selling car in America in its first year. The Mercury was originally planned as a "Super-Ford" and early models were identified as the "95 horsepower Ford" in factory literature. Two pre-production prototypes were built with non-stock features including roof-mounted windshield wipers and Ford-Mercury hubcaps. The Mercury V-8 could give up to 20 miles per gallon of gas, according to contemporary reports.

1940 MERCURY

1940 Mercury, four-door sedan

MERCURY - (V-8) — SERIES 09A — The 1940 Mercury used a carryover body with numerous improvements. Front door vent windows provided controlled all-weather ventilation. A new grille featured horizontal chrome grille bars on either side of the lower one-half, meeting at a center rail. The nose of the 1940 Mercury was more well-rounded with a new hood latch and ornamentation. A new instrument panel was finished in blue and silver tones. Sealed beam headlamps were adopted. The Mercury Eight name appeared on hubcaps and just below the forward end of the slightly wider belt moldings. Clock spring supports and a new winged handle were added to the rear deck lid. Exterior colors were black, Cloud Mist gray, Folkstone gray, Lyon blue, Sahara sand, Yosemite green, Mandarin maroon and Como blue. Acadia green became available later and Cotswold gray metallic and Garnet were added in the spring. Some two-tone color combinations were also offered on a limited basis. Convertible tops were available in black with vermillion edging or tan-gray with tan edging. Red or Saddle brown leather interiors were offered for open cars. Cloth tops were raised or lowered via a vacuum-powered lift mechanism.

MERCURY I.D. NUMBERS: Serial number was located on the left frame member, just ahead of cowl. Engine number was located on rear of engine atop clutch housing and on left side of frame near left engine support and top of clutch housing. Motor serial numbers were identical with serial numbers. Plant codes were: DA (Dearborn, Mich.); LA (Los Angeles, Calif.); ME (Metuchen, N.J.) and SL (St. Louis, Mo.). Starting number: 99A-101,701. Ending number: 99A-257,100 (approximate).

Model Number	Body/Style Number	Body Type & Seating	Factory Price	Shipping Weight	Production Total
9A	76	2-dr Conv Clb Cpe-5P	1079	3107	9,741
9A	70	2-dr Sed-6P	946	3068	16,243
9A	72	2-dr Cpe Sed-6P	987	3030	16,189
9A	73	4-dr Twn Sed-6P	987	3103	42,806
9A	74	4dr Conv Sed-6P	1212	3249	979

1940 Mercury, convertible coupe

MERCURY ENGINE
V-8. L-head. Cast iron block. Displacement: 239.4 cubic inches. Bore and stroke: 3-3/16 x 3-3/4 inches. Compression ratio: 6.15:1. Brake horsepower: 95 @ 3600 RPM. Maximum torque: 170 lbs.-ft. @ 2100 RPM. Three main bearings. Carburetor: Holley model AA1 dual downdraft.

CHASSIS FEATURES: Double-drop X-type frame. Solid I-beam front axle with radius rods. Transverse front leaf springs. Transverse rear leaf springs. Three-speed manual transmission with column shift. Nine inch, single-plate, semi-centrifugal Long clutch. Three-quarter floating rear axle with 3.54:1 gear ratio. Wheelbase: 116 inches. Overall length: 194-1/8 inches. Front tread: 55-3/4 inches. Rear tread: 58-1/4 inches. Tires: 16 x 6.00. Fuel tank capacity: 17 gallons.

POWERTRAIN OPTIONS: Rear axle with 3.78:1 gear ratio.

CONVENIENCE OPTIONS: White sidewall tires. Single Roto-Matic radio. Windshield header mounted radio antenna. Hot air heater. Hot water heater. Visor vanity mirror. Draft deflectors. Spotlight. Center front bumper guard. Hub and spoke wheel covers. Road light. Locking gas cap. Two types of oil bath air cleaners. Oil filter. License plate frames. Seat covers. Luggage. Governor. Two-tone finish.

HISTORICAL FOOTNOTES: Introduced October 1939. Calendar year production: 82,770. U.S. registrations: 80,418. Mercury was the 11th best-selling car in America in its second year. Worldwide Mercury output was 86,685 cars. The Mercury convertible sedan was an exclusive, one year only model. In addition to its domestic production shown above, this body style had a run of 104 units for export markets.

1941 MERCURY

1941 Mercury, convertible

MERCURY - (V-8) — SERIES 19A — Runningboards were eliminated from 1941 Mercurys and the wheelbase grew two inches longer. A roomier new body, shared with Ford, had a higher silhouette and more squared-off appearance. The windshield and windows were wider and deeper. Two upsweeping horizontal chrome bar grilles appeared on either side of a painted vertical center panel. Recessed circular headlamps were used and separate parking lamps sat atop the front fenders. Other new features included longer door handles, a concealed fuel filler and horizontal wraparound taillamps. Sedan and coupe interiors were done in tan colors with new brown hardware. Numerous new trim moldings decorated the body, hood and fenders. Two new coupes and a station wagon were added, while the convertible sedan disappeared. Colors available included black, Cotswold gray metallic, Capri blue metallic, Cayuga blue, Mayfair maroon, Lochaven green, Harbor gray and Palisade gray. Spring additions were Conestoga tan metallic, Sheffield gray metallic, Florentine blue and Seminole brown.

MERCURY I.D. NUMBERS: Serial number was located on the left frame member, just ahead of cowl. Engine number was located on rear of engine atop clutch housing and on left side of frame near left engine support and top of clutch housing. Motor serial numbers were identical with serial numbers. Plant codes were: DA (Dearborn, Mich.); LA (Los Angeles, Calif.); ME (Metuchen, N.J.) and SL (St. Louis, Mo.). Starting number: 99A-257,101. Ending number: 99A-466,700. (Note: additional numbers also used, as listed in the *Serial Number Book for U.S. Cars 1900-1945*.)

Model Number	Body/Style Number	Body Type & Seating	Factory Price	Shipping Weight	Production Total
19A	77	2-dr 5W Cpe-2P	910	3008	3,313
19A	67	2-dr A/S Cpe-2/4P	936	3049	1,954
19A	72	2-dr Sed Cpe-6P	977	3118	18,263
19A	76	2-dr Conv Clb Cpe-2/4P	1100	3222	8,556
19A	70	2-dr Tudor Sed-6P	946	3184	20,932
19A	73	4-dr Twn Sed-6P	987	3221	42,984
19A	79	4-dr Sta Wag-8P	1141	3468	2,291

MERCURY ENGINE
V-8. L-head. Cast iron block. Displacement: 239.4 cubic inches. Bore and stroke: 3-3/16 x 3-3/4 inches. Compression ratio: 6.30:1. Brake horsepower: 95 @ 3600 RPM. Maximum torque: 176 lbs.-ft. @ 2100 RPM. Three main bearings. Carburetor: Holley model AA1-91 dual downdraft.

CHASSIS FEATURES: New box-sectional frame. Solid I-beam front axle with radius rods. Transverse front leaf springs. Transverse rear leaf springs. Three-speed manual transmission with column shift. Ten inch, single-plate, semi-centrifugal Long clutch (woven molded type lining). Three-quarter floating rear axle with 3.54:1 gear ratio. Wheelbase: 118 inches. Overall length: 200-39/64 inches. Front tread: 55-3/4 inches. Rear tread: 58-1/4 inches. Tires: 16 x 6.50. Fuel tank capacity: 17 gallons.

POWERTRAIN OPTIONS: Rear axle with 3.78:1 gear ratio.

CONVENIENCE OPTIONS: White sidewall tires. Single Roto-Matic radio. Windshield header mounted radio antenna. Hot air heater. Hot water heater. Visor vanity mirror. Draft deflectors. Spotlight. Center front bumper guard. Hub and spoke wheel covers. Road light. Locking gas cap. Two types of oil bath air cleaners. Oil filter. License plate frames. Seat covers. Luggage. Governor. Two-tone finish. Bumper end guards. Outside rearview mirrors. Fender skirts (shields). Hot water rear compartment heater. Extra cooling radiator. Six blade 17-inch fan.

HISTORICAL FOOTNOTES: Introduced October 1940. Calendar year production: 80,085. U.S. registrations: 81,874. Mercury was the 12th best-selling car in America in its third year. Worldwide output was 98,412 cars. Production models were now identified simply as Mercurys, although early 1941 publicity photos show pre-production cars with Mercury Eight emblems. Some photos indicate that slightly smaller, Ford parking lamps with painted bottom halves were used as a running production change. The new Type 67 coupe featured two fold-down auxiliary seats (A/S) in its rear compartment.

1942 MERCURY

1942 Mercury, convertible

MERCURY - (V-8) — SERIES 29A — New, lower streamlined Mercury bodies featured a more massive front end with two groups of wide, horizontal chrome grille bars. Rectangular parking lamps were mounted on either side of the front fender tops, alongside the nose and above the upper grille section. The lower grille section was lower, but wider. Front and rear fenders had double side moldings and fin-like top moldings. The headlamps featured larger, circular bezels. Larger hubcaps and rubber rear fender gravel shields also appeared. The new instrument panel had a central radio grille flanked by a speedometer (on left) and clock (on right). Cars built after Dec. 19, 1941 had bright metal exterior trim "blacked out." A new steering wheel was seen. It had a full-circle horn ring and the Mercury head on the center hub insert.

MERCURY I.D. NUMBERS: Serial number was located on the left frame member, just ahead of cowl. Engine number was located on rear of engine atop clutch housing. Motor serial numbers were identical with serial numbers. Plant codes were: DA (Dearborn, Mich.); LA (Los Angeles, Calif.); ME (Metuchen, N.J.) and SL (St. Louis, Mo.). Starting number: 99A466,701. Ending number: 99A-539,426 (with exceptions).

Model Number	Body/Style Number	Body Type & Seating	Factory Price	Shipping Weight	Production Total
29A	77	2-dr Cpe-3P	995	3073	800
29A	72	2-dr Sed Cpe-6P	1055	3148	5,345
29A	76	2-dr Conv Clb Cpe-5P	1215	3288	969
29A	70	2-dr Sed-6P	1030	3228	4,941
29A	73	4-dr Twn Sed-6P	1065	3263	11,784
29A	79	4-dr Sta Wag-8P	1260	3528	857

*Worldwide production shown above

1942 Mercury, station wagon

MERCURY ENGINE

V-8. L-head. Cast iron block. Displacement: 239.4 cubic inches. Bore and stroke: 3-3/16 x 3-3/4 inches. Compression ratio: 6.40:1. Brake horsepower: 100 @ 3800 RPM. Maximum torque: 176 lbs.-ft. @ 2100 RPM. Three main bearings. Carburetor: Holley AA1 dual downdraft.

CHASSIS FEATURES: Box section frame. Solid I-beam front axle with radius rods. Transverse front leaf springs. Transverse rear leaf springs. Three-speed manual transmission with column shift. Ten inch, single-plate, semi-centrifugal Long clutch. Three-quarter floating rear axle with 3.54:1 gear ratio. Wheelbase: 118 inches. Overall length: 200-39/64 inches. Front tread: 58 inches. Rear tread: 60 inches. Tires: 15 x 6.50. Fuel tank capacity: 17 gallons.

POWERTRAIN OPTIONS: Fluid coupling Liqui-Matic drive optional at extra cost.

CONVENIENCE OPTIONS: White sidewall tires. Single Roto-Matic radio. Windshield header mounted radio antenna. Hot air heater. Hot water heater. Visor vanity mirror. Draft deflectors. Spotlight. Center front bumper guard. Hub and spoke wheel covers. Road light. Locking gas cap. Two types of oil bath air cleaners. Oil filter. License plate frames. Seat covers. Luggage. Governor. Directional signals. Fender skirts. Simulated whitewall wheel trim bands. Bumper end guards. Hot water rear compartment heater. Extra-cooling radiator. Six-blade 17-inch fan. Two-tone finish. Outside rearview mirror.

HISTORICAL FOOTNOTES: Introduced October 1941. Calendar year production: 4,430. U.S. Production: 22,816. Worldwide Production: 24,704 (includes U.S. production from Oct. 3, 1941 to Feb. 10, 1942, plus foreign (mostly Brazilian) output in 1942, 1943, 1944 and 1945. The 1942 Mercury featured "slower motion" springs and thicker body mountings, which resulted in an improved "Sky Ride." A sales slogan for the year was, "The Aviation Idea in an Automobile, More Power Per Pound."

MERCURY
1946-1975

The Lincoln-Mercury division was formed in 1945, but it wasn't until 1949 models appeared, in early 1948, that Mercury was able to shed (temporarily) its image as a glorified Ford.

The 1949 to 1951 Mercurys became very popular with customizers and hot rodders. James Dean, driving one in the classic 1950s youth movie *Rebel Without A Cause*, helped assure these cars cult status.

By Charles Webb

The fancy Ford look returned in 1952. Mercury was supposed to have received a new OHV V-8 that year, but it wasn't ready in time. So the flathead V-8 was kept two more years. The flathead had a reputation as a hot engine. However, this was only because it was so easy to soup-up. Straight from the factory it wasn't all that spectacular.

1949 Mercury coupe

In addition to an OHV V-8, the 1954 Mercury offered one of the most unique cars available that year. Its Sun Valley, like Ford's Skyliner, had a plexiglass section over the front half of the roof. Although not exactly the most practical idea, it did show how innovative Ford Motor Co. was.

Considering they were based on Fords, the 1955 and 1956 Mercurys featured distinctive styling. In 1957, the make received its own body which it shared with no one. That may have been just as well. The man largely responsible for the 1957 Mercury's design years later said the following about it (and its contempories), "You could see how we could get the reputation as real hacks and chrome merchants, because looking at those cars, it would be hard to deny."

Ford once again shared a body with Mercury in 1960 when they introduced the most successful compact Comet.

1961 saw full size Fords and mercurys share bodies and in 1962 and 1963 when the intermediate Fairlane and

1960 Mercury Comet 4-dr. sedan

Meteors also shared bodies.

The "Breezeway" roof, with its retractable rear window (first used on the 1957 Turnpike Cruiser), was reintroduced in 1963. Mercury was the only make to have this unique and useful style roof. Fastback Marauder hardtops were offered because their roofline was more areodynamic and improved the make's chance of winning stock car races.

1969 Mercury Montege MX 2-dr hardtop coupe

"Its now in the Lincoln Continental tradition," proclaimed ads for the 1965 Mercury. That same year, Ford group vice president Lee A. Iacocca was put in charge of a program to improve Lincoln-Mercury sales. He pushed to further identify the make with Lincoln. The results of his efforst are very evident in the 1969 models and up.

While full-size Mercurys became more plush, the compact Comet series expanded and certain models (Caliente and Cyclone) began to earn well-deserved reputations as hot street machines. Mid-size Mercurys of the late 1960s and early 1970s were especially potent when equipped with one of several high-powered engines available.

Mercury entered the 'pony car' market in 1967. Its Cougar was offered with some powerful performance packages the first several years, but, by 1971 became primarily a sporty personal car.

Small Mercurys reappeared in the early 1970s. Comet returned and was joined by Bobcat. The mid-size Monarch came on the scene in 1975.

1946 MERCURY

1946 Mercury, 2-dr sedan, V-8

MERCURY SERIES — SERIES 69M — A new grille was the most noticeable difference between the 1942 and 1946 Mercurys. It had thin, vertical bars surrounded by a trim piece painted the same color as the car. The Liquamatic drive automatic transmission option was also eliminated. The most distinctive new Mercury was the Sportsman convertible. It featured wood body panels.

MERCURY I.D. NUMBERS: Serial numbers were the same as engine numbers. They ranged from 99A50280 to 1,412,707.

MERCURY Model Number	Body/Style Number	Body Type & Seating	Factory Price	Shipping Weight	Production Total
69M	71	2-dr Sptsman Conv	2209	3407	205
69M	70	2-dr Sedan-6P	1448	3240	13,108
69M	72	2-dr Sed Cpe-6P	1495	3190	24,163
69M	73	4-dr Town Sed-6P	1509	3270	40,280
69M	76	2-dr Conv-6P	1711	3340	6,044
69M	79	4-dr Sta Wag-8P	1729	3540	2,797

MERCURY ENGINE
V-8: L-head. Cast iron block. Displacement: 239.4 cubic inches. Bore and stroke: 3.19 x 3.75 inches. Compression ratio: 6.75:1. Brake horsepower: 100 at 3800 R.P.M. Three main bearings. Carburetor: Holley 94 two-barrel.

CHASSIS FEATURES: Wheelbase: 118 inches. Overall length: 201.8 inches. Front tread: 58 inches. Rear tread: 60 inches. Tires: 6.50 x 15.

POWERTRAIN OPTIONS: A three-speed manual transmission was standard.

CONVENIENCE OPTIONS: Radio with foot control. Heater. Fog lamps.

1947 MERCURY

1947 Mercury, 4-dr sedan, V-8 (AA)

MERCURY SERIES — SERIES 79M — Styling changes were slight this year. The Mercury name was placed on the side of the hood. Different hub caps were used. The border around the grille was chrome plated. There was also new trunk trim. More chrome was used on the interior and the dash dial faces were redesigned. The convertible and station wagon came with leather upholstery. The other body styles used fabric.

MERCURY I.D. NUMBERS: Serial numbers were the same as engine numbers. They ranged from 799A1,412,708 to 2,002,282.

MERCURY Model Number	Body/Style Number	Body Type & Seating	Factory Price	Shipping Weight	Production Total
79M	70	2-dr. Sedan-5P	1592	3268	34
79M	72	2-dr. Sed Coupe-6P	1645	3218	29,284
79M	73	Town Sedan-6P	1660	3298	42,281
79M	76	2-dr. Conv-6P	2002	3368	10,221
79M	79	4-dr. Sta Wag-8P	2207	3571	3,558

MERCURY ENGINE
V-8: L-head. Cast iron block. Displacement: 239.4 cubic inches. Bore and stroke: 3.19 x 3.75 inches. Compression ratio: 6.75:1. Brake horsepower: 100 at 3800 R.P.M. Three main bearings. Carburetor: Holley 94 two-barrel.

CHASSIS FEATURES: Wheelbase: 118 inches. Overall length: 201.8 inches. Front tread: 58 inches. Rear tread: 60 inches. Tires: 6.50 x 15.

POWERTRAIN OPTIONS: A three-speed manual transmission was standard.

CONVENIENCE OPTIONS: Radio with foot control. Fog lamps. Heater. Whitewall tires.

1948 MERCURY

1948 Mercury 4-dr station wagon, V-8

MERCURY SERIES — SERIES 89M — If you liked the 1947 Mercurys, you'd like the 1948s. For all practical purposes, they were identical. The major changes this season consisted of different dial faces and no steering column lock.

MERCURY I.D. NUMBERS: Serial numbers were the same as engine numbers. They ranged from 899A1,990,957 to 2,374,315.

MERCURY Model Number	Body/Style Number	Body Type & Seating	Factory Price	Shipping Weight	Production Total
89M	72	2-dr Sed Cpe-6P	1645	3218	16,476
89M	73	4-dr Town Sed-6P	1660	3298	24,283
89M	76	2-dr Conv-6P	2002	3368	7,586
89M	79	4-dr Sta Wag-8P	2207	3571	1,889

MERCURY ENGINE
V-8: L-head. Cast iron block. Displacement: 239.4 cubic inches. Bore and stroke: 3.19 x 3.75 inches. Compression ratio: 6.75:1. Brake horsepower: 100 at 3800 R.P.M. Three main bearings. Carburetor: Mercury two-barrel.

CHASSIS FEATURES: Wheelbase: 118 inches. Overall length: 201.8 inches. Front tread: 58 inches. Rear tread: 60 inches. Tires: 6.50 x 15.

POWERTRAIN OPTIONS: A three-speed manual transmission was standard.

CONVENIENCE OPTIONS: Radio with foot control. Fog lamps. Heater. Whitewall tires.

1949 MERCURY

MERCURY SERIES — SERIES 9CM — The first all-new postwar Mercurys were introduced on April 29, 1948. In a break with tradition they did not look like fancy Fords, but rather, shared Lincoln styling (and basic body shells). The grille resembled a shiny coil divided in the center by a large vertical piece of chrome. A nearly full-length, mid-body chrome spear stretched across the sides. The 1949 Merc also had wraparound front and rear bumpers. The wood bodied station wagon was replaced by one that used only wood trim. As before, the sedan rear doors opened to the center.

MERCURY I.D. NUMBERS: Serial numbers were the same as engine numbers. They ranged from 9CM101 to 302,439.

MERCURY Model Number	Body/Style Number	Body Type & Seating	Factory Price	Shipping Weight	Production Total
9CM	72	2-dr Cpe-6P	1979	3321	120,616
9Cm	74	4-dr Spt Cpe-6P	2031	3386	155,882
9CM	76	2-dr Conv-6P	2410	3591	16,765
9CM	79	2-dr Sta Wag-8P	2716	3626	8,044

1949 Mercury, 4-dr sedan, V-8 (AA)

MERCURY ENGINE
V-8: L-head. Cast iron block. Displacement: 255.4 cubic inches. Bore and stroke: 3.19 x 4 inches. Compression ratio: 6.80:1. Brake horsepower: 110 at 3600 R.P.M. Three main bearings. Carburetor: Holley 885FFC two-barrel.

CHASSIS FEATURES: Wheelbase: 118 inches. Overall length: 206.8 inches. Front tread: 58.5 inches. Rear tread: 60 inches. Tires: 7.10 x 5.

POWERTRAIN OPTIONS: A three-speed manual transmission was standard. Touch-O-Matic overdrive was optional.

CONVENIENCE OPTIONS: Radio. Heater. Rear fender shields. Foam rubber seat cushions. Whitewall tires.

1950 MERCURY

MERCURY SERIES — SERIES OCM — For 1950, the letters of the word Mercury were imbedded in chrome on the front of the hood. The signal lights were chrome encased, in a fashion similar to that used on the 1948 Cadillac. The design of the trunk chrome was altered, as was the tip on the side spear. The biggest change was made to the dash. It was completely restyled. Improvements were made to the carburetor, parking brake and steering. To compete with GM and Chrysler two-door hardtops, Mercury introduced the Monterey coupe. It featured a padded canvas or vinyl top and custom leather interior.

1950 Mercury, Monterey 2-dr coupe, V-8 (AA)

MERCURY I.D. NUMBERS: Serial numbers were the same as engine numbers. For 1950 they were: 50DA1,001M to 79,027M; 50LA1,001M to 44,958M; 50ME1,001M to 97,749M and 50SL1,001M to 110,459M. The plant codes were DA – Dearborn; LA – Los Angeles; ME – Metuchen; SL – St. Louis and W – Wayne.

1950 Mercury, 2-dr station wagon, V-8 (TVB)

MERCURY Model Number	Body/Style Number	Body Type & Seating	Factory Price	Shipping Weight	Production Total
OCM	M-72A	2-dr Cpe-3P	1875	3345	Note 1
OCM	M-72B	2-dr Clb Cpe-6P	1980	3430	Note 1
OCM	M-72C	2-dr Monterey Cpe	2146	3626	Note 1
OCM	M-74	4-dr Spt Sed-6P	2032	3470	132,082
OCM	M-74	2-dr Conv-6P	3412	3710	8,341
OCM	M-79	2-dr Sta Wag-8P	2561	3755	1,746

NOTE 1: A total of 151,489 Mercury coupes were made in 1950.

MERCURY ENGINE:
V-8: L-head. Cast iron block. Displacement: 255.4 cubic inches. Bore and stroke: 3.19 x 4 inches. Compression ratio: 6.80:1. Brake horsepower: 110 at 3600 R.P.M. Three main bearings. Carburetor: Holley 885FFC two-barrel.

CHASSIS FEATURES: Wheelbase: 118 inches. Overall length: (Passenger cars) 206.8 inches; (Station wagon) 213.5 inches. Front tread: 58.5 inches. Rear tread: 60 inches. Tires: 7.10 x 15.

POWERTRAIN OPTIONS: A three-speed manual transmission was standard. Touch-O-Matic overdrive was optional.

CONVENIENCE OPTIONS: Radio. Power windows (standard in convertible). Power seat. Oil bath air cleaner. Heater. Two-tone paint. Whitewall tires.

Historical Notes: The one-millionth Mercury built was a 1950 four-door sedan. Mercurys won two NASCAR Grand National races this year. Mercury was the official pace car at the 1950 Indianapolis 500.

1951 MERCURY

1951 Mercury, 4-dr sedan, V-8 (TVB)

MERCURY SERIES — SERIES 1CM — A new grille that was integrated with the signal lights appeared in 1951. Vertical taillights replaced the horizontal type found on the 1949 and 1950 Mercurys. New, lower, rear quarter panel trim made the wraparound bumper appear to extend even further than before. Chrome gravel shields and rocker panels, a vinyl or canvas roof and custom interior were standard on the Monterey coupe.

MERCURY I.D. NUMBERS: Serial numbers for 1951 were: 51DA51DA10,001M to 67,910M; 51LA10,001M to 46,772M; 51ME10,001M to 103,515M and 51SL10,001M to 127,830M. See 1950 Mercury I.D. numbers for plant codes.

MERCURY Model Number	Body/Style Number	Body Type & Seating	Factory Price	Shipping Weight	Production Total
1CM	M-72B	2-dr Spt Cpe-6P	1947	3485	Note 1
1CM	M-72C	2-dr Monterey Cpe	2116	3485	Note 1
1CM	M-72C	2-dr Monterey Cpe	2127	3485	Note 1
1CM	M-74	4-dr Spt Sed-6P	2000	3550	157,648
1CM	M-76	2-dr Conv-6P	2380	3760	6,759
1CM	M-79	2-dr Sta Wag-8P	2530	3800	3,812

NOTE 1: A total of 142,168 Mercury coupes were made in 1951. **ADDITIONAL NOTE:** The higher priced Monterey included a vinyl top covering.

MERCURY ENGINE
V-8: L-head. Cast iron block. Displacement: 255.4 cubic inches. Bore and stroke: 3.19 x 4 inches. Compression ratio: 6.80:1. Brake horsepower: 112 at 3600 R.P.M. Three main bearings. Carburetor: Holley 885FFC two-barrel.

CHASSIS FEATURES: Wheelbase: 118 inches. Overall length: 206.8 inches; (Station Wagons) 213.5 inches. Front tread: 58.5 inches. Rear tread: 60 inches. Tires: 7.10 x 15.

POWERTRAIN OPTIONS: A three-speed manual transmission was standard. Overdrive and Merc-O-Matic automatic transmission were optional.

CONVENIENCE OPTIONS: Radio. Fender skirts. Heater. Whitewall tires.

Historical footnotes: Approximately one in every three 1951 Mercurys were sold with an automatic transmission. In 1951, Mercurys came in first at two NASCAR Grand National races.

1952 MERCURY

1952 Mercury, 2-dr Custom hardtop coupe, V-8 (AA)

CUSTOM SERIES — SERIES 2M — Like all Ford Motor Company cars, Mercury was completely restyled for 1952. It had frenched headlights; a one-piece curved windshield; wraparound rear window; fake hood scoop; massive integrated bumper/grille and vertical tail/backup lights encased in chrome in manner that made them look like extensions of the rear bumper. The fender level hood line helped give the Custom an aggressive look.

CUSTOM I.D. NUMBERS: Serial numbers for 1952 were: 52SL10,001M to 86,300M; 52LP10,001M to 52WA19,422M; 52LA10,001M to 38,763M and 52ME10,001 to 65,500M. See 1950 Mercury I.D. numbers for plant codes.

CUSTOM Model Number	Body/Style Number	Body Type & Seating	Factory Price	Shipping Weight	Production Total
2M	60E	2-dr Spt Cpe-6P	2100	3435	30,599
2M	70B	2-dr Sedan-6P	1987	3335	25,812
2M	73B	4-dr Sedan-6P	2040	3390	Note 1
2M	79B	4-dr Sta Wag-6P	2525	3795	Note 1
2M	79D	4-dr Sta Wag-8P	2570	3795	Note 1

NOTE 1: The total production of all 1952 Custom and Monterey four-door sedans was 83,475. The total production of all station wagons was 2,487.

CUSTOM ENGINE
V-8: L-head. Cast iron block. Displacement: 255.4 cubic inches. Bore and stroke: 3.19 x 4 inches. Compression ratio: 7.20:1. Brake horsepower: 125 at 3700 R.P.M. Three main bearings. Carburetor: Holley 885FFC two-barrel.

1952 Mercury, Monterey 2-dr convertible, V-8 (AA)

MONTEREY SERIES — SERIES 2M — Except for the chrome rocker panels and fancier wheel covers, exterior styling resembled the lower-priced Custom series. Standard Monterey features included a two-tone paint job and leather and vinyl interior. Suspended pedals were new to both series. The rear doors of Mercury sedans now opened in the conventional manner.

MONTEREY I.D. NUMBERS: See Custom I.D. numbers.

MONTEREY Model Number	Body/Style Number	Body Type & Seating	Factory Price	Shipping Weight	Production Total
2M	60B	2-dr HT Cpe-6P	2225	3520	24,453
2M	73C	4-dr Sedan-6P	2115	3375	Note 1
2M	76B	2-dr Conv-6P	2370	3635	5,261

NOTE 1: See Custom note.

MONTEREY ENGINE
See 1952 Custom Series engine data.

CHASSIS FEATURES: Wheelbase: 118 inches. Overall length: 202.2 inches. Front tread: 58 inches. Rear tread: 56 inches. Tires: 7.10 x 15; (Convertible and station wagons) 7.60 x 15.

POWERTRAIN OPTIONS: A three-speed manual transmission was standard. Overdrive and Merc-O-Matic automatic tranmission were optional.

CONVENIENCE OPTIONS: Radio. 'Merc-O-Matic' heater. Bumper grille guard. Fender skirts (standard on Monterey). Whitewall tires.

Historical footnotes: Almost half of all 1952 Mercurys came with automatic transmission and about 33 percent of the manual shift cars were equipped with a three-speed manual with overdrive. This was the first year for a Mercury two-door hardtop.

1953 MERCURY

CUSTOM SERIES — SERIES 3M — A major styling change for 1953 was made to the grille. It was still integrated with the bumper, but the bumper guards were now bullet-shaped. The trunk featured a new medallion. Side chrome trim consisted of a full-length, mid-body spear and rear fender molding. The doors could stay in position either half-way or fully opened.

CUSTOM I.D. NUMBERS: Serial numbers for 1953 were: 53LA10,001M to 50,946M; 53WA10,001M to 45,383; 53ME10,001M and up and 53SL10,001M to 14,285M. For plant codes see 1950 Mercury I.D. numbers.

CUSTOM Model Number	Body/Style Number	Body Type & Seating	Factory Price	Shipping Weight	Production Total
3M	60E	2-dr Spt Cpe-6P	2117	3465	39,547
3M	70B	2-dr Sedan-6P	2004	3405	50,183
3M	73B	4-dr Sedan-6P	2057	3450	59,794

CUSTOM ENGINE
V-8: L-head. Cast iron block. Displacement: 255.4 cubic inches. Bore and stroke: 3.19 x 4 inches. Compression ratio: 7.20:1. Brake horsepower: 125 at 3800 R.P.M. Three main bearings. Carburetor: Holley 1901FFC two-barrel.

1953 Mercury, Monterey 2-dr convertible, V-8 (AA)

MONTEREY SERIES — SERIES 3M — Two-tone paint, fender skirts and chrome rocker panels were standard on Mercurys top-of-the-line series. The Monterey name was placed on the upper front fenders (except on those built early in the model year). The rear side windows of the station wagon featured sliding glass.

MONTEREY I.D. NUMBERS: See Custom I.D. numbers.

MONTEREY Model Number	Body/Style Number	Body Type & Seating	Factory Price	Shipping Weight	Production Total
3M	60B	2-dr HT Cpe-6P	2244	3465	76,119
3M	73C	4-dr Sedan-6P	2133	3425	64,038
3M	76B	2-dr Conv-6P	2390	3585	8,463
3M	79B	4-dr Sta Wag-6P	2591	3765	7,719

MONTEREY ENGINE
See 1953 Custom Series engine data.

CHASSIS FEATURES: Wheelbase: 118 inches. Overall length: 202.2 inches. Front tread: 58 inches. Rear tread: 56 inches. Tires: 7.10 x 15; (Convertible and station wagon) 7.60 x 15.

POWERTRAIN OPTIONS: A three-speed manual transmission was standard. Overdrive and Merc-O-Matic automatic transmission were optional.

CONVENIENCE OPTIONS: Wheel covers. Power steering. Power seat. Electric windows. Whitewall tires. Bumper grille guard. Radio. Power brakes.

Historical footnotes: An enlarged tailpipe and new, straight-through muffler greatly reduced back pressure. Power brakes were first offered in April of 1953. Fifteen percent of Mercurys were equipped with them. A month later, power steering was introduced. Only eight percent of 1953 Mercurys were sold with this option. The 40 millionth vehicle built by Ford Motor Company was a 1953 Mercury convertible.

1954 MERCURY

CUSTOM SERIES — Wraparound vertical taillights were the most noticeable change made for 1954. The grille was modestly restyled, but was still integrated with the front bumper. 'Mercury' was written in chrome on the rear fenders, above the mid-body spear. New ball joint front suspension improved handling and ride qualities.

CUSTOM I.D. NUMBERS: Serial numbers ranged from 54WA10,001M to 75,348M. See 1960 Mercury I.D. numbers for plant codes.

CUSTOM

Model Number	Body/Style Number	Body Type & Seating	Factory Price	Shipping Weight	Production Total
NA	60E	2-dr HT Cpe-6P	2315	3485	15,234
NA	70B	2-dr Sedan-6P	2194	3435	37,146
NA	73B	4-dr Sedan-6P	2251	3480	32,687

CUSTOM ENGINE
V-8: Overhead valves. Cast iron block. Displacement: 256 cubic inches. Bore and stroke: 3.62 x 3.10 inches. Compression ratio: 7.50:1. Brake horsepower: 162 at 4400 R.P.M. Carburetor: Holley 2140 four-barrel.

1954 Mercury, Monterey Sun Valley 2-dr hardtop, V-8 (AA)

MONTEREY SERIES — The Monterey featured its name written in chrome above the side trim on the rear fender. It had a medallion near the tip of the side chrome spear on the front fenders. Chrome rocker panels and fender skirt were standard. The most unique Monterey was the Sun Valley. The front half of its roof contained a green tinted, plexiglass section. As in previous years, the station wagon had simulated wood trim.

MONTEREY I.D. NUMBERS: See Custom I.D. numbers.

MONTEREY

Model Number	Body/Style Number	Body Type & Seating	Factory Price	Shipping Weight	Production Total
NA	60B	2-dr HT Cpe-6P	2452	3520	79,533
NA	60F	2-dr Sun Valley-6P	2,582	3,535	9,761
NA	73C	4-dr Sedan-6P	2333	3515	65,995
NA	76B	2-dr Conv-6P	2610	3620	7,293
NA	79B	4-dr Sta Wag-8P	2776	3735	11,656

MONTEREY ENGINE
Same as Custom.

CHASSIS FEATURES: Wheelbase: 118 inches. Overall length: 206.2 inches. Tires: 7.10 x 15; (Convertible and station wagon) 7.60 x 15.

POWERTRAIN OPTIONS: A three-speed manual was standard. Overdrive and Merc-O-Matic Drive automatic transmission were optional.

CONVENIENCE OPTIONS: Power steering. Power brakes. Four-Way power seat. Radio. Heater. Fender skirts (Custom). Chrome rocker panels (Custom). Whitewall tires. Solex glass.

1955 MERCURY

1955 Mercury, Custom 2-dr sedan, V-8

CUSTOM SERIES — Mercurys were restyled this year. They were longer, lower and wider. Yet they bore a definite resemblance to the 1954 models. The bumper integrated grille had three heavy vertical bars between the upper and lower bumper. The tall vertical taillights had a 'chubby cheeks' look. The Custom had slightly different side chrome than the other series. Its rear fender molding was plainer. The Custom station wagon did *not* have fake wood trim. All 1955 Mercurys featured a wraparound windshield and hooded headlights.

CUSTOM I.D. NUMBERS: Custom serial numbers were: 55WA10,001M to 94,613M and 55LA10,001M to 48,892. See 1950 Mercury I.D. numbers or plant code.

CUSTOM

Model Number	Body/Style Number	Body Type & Seating	Factory Price	Shipping Weight	Production Total
NA	60E	2-dr HT Cpe-6P	2341	3480	7,040
NA	70B	2-dr Sedan-6P	2218	3395	31,295
NA	73B	4-dr Sedan-6P	2277	3450	21,219
NA	79B	4-dr Sta Wag-6P	2686	3780	13,134

CUSTOM ENGINE
V-8: Overhead valves. Cast iron block. Displacement: 292 cubic inches. Bore and stroke: 3.75 x 3.30 inches. Compression ratio: 7.60:1. Brake horsepower: 188 at 4400 R.P.M. Carburetor: four-barrel.

1955 Mercury, Monterey 4-dr sedan, V-8

MONTEREY SERIES — The rear fender trim was lower on the Monterey than on the Custom. It also had chrome rocker panels and a bright band of molding under the windows. 'Monterey' was written in chrome on the front fenders of the sedan and hardtop. The name was placed on the rear doors of the station wagon. A round medallion was placed next to the nameplate.

MONTEREY I.D. NUMBERS: See Custom I.D. numbers.

MONTEREY

Model Number	Body/Style Number	Body Type & Seating	Factory Price	Shipping Weight	Production Total
NA	60B	2-dr HT Cpe-6P	2465	3510	69,093
NA	73C	4-dr Sedan-6P	2400	3500	70,392
NA	79C	4-dr Sta Wag-8P	2844	3770	11,968

MONTEREY ENGINE
See 1955 Custom Series engine data.

1955 Mercury, Montclair 4-dr sedan, V-8

MONTCLAIR SERIES — In addition to a round medallion and the model name on the front fenders, Montclairs also had a narrow band of chrome under the side windows, which outlined a small panel. They were slightly lower than other Mercurys. The Sun Valley had a tinted plexiglass section over the front half of its roof.

MONTCLAIR I.D. NUMBERS: Serial numbers were: 55ME10,001M to 87,345M and 55SL10,001M to 13,753M.

MONTCLAIR

Model Number	Body/Style Number	Body Type & Seating	Factory Price	Shipping Weight	Production Total
NA	58A	4-dr Sedan-6P	2685	3600	20,624
NA	64A	2-dr HT Cpe-6P	2631	3490	71,588
NA	64B	2-dr Sun Valley	2712	3560	1,787
NA	76B	2-dr Conv-6P	2712	3685	10,668

MONTCLAIR ENGINE
V-8: Overhead valves. Cast iron block. Displacment: 292 cubic inches. Bore and stroke: 3.75 x 3.30 inches. Compression ratio: 8.50:1. Brake horsepower: 198 at 4400 R.P.M. Carburetor: four-barrel.

CHASSIS FEATURES: Wheelbase: (Passenger cars) 119 inches; (Station wagons) 118 inches. Overall length: (Passenger cars) 206.3 inches; (Station wagons) 201.7 inches. Overall height: (Montclairs) 58.6 inches; (Station wagons) 62.45 inches (others) 61.2 inches. Tires: (Convertible) 7.10 x 15; (Station wagons) 7.60 x 15.

POWERTRAIN OPTIONS: A three-speed manual transmission was standard. Overdrive and Merc-O-Matic automatic were optional. A 198 horsepower V-8 was available at extra cost on cars with the automatic.

CONVENIENCE OPTIONS: Power brakes. Power steering. Whitewall tires. Four-Way power seat. Heater. Power windows. Radio. Custom two-tone paint. Custom fender skirts.

1956 MERCURY

1956 Mercury, Medalist 2-dr sedan, V-8

MEDALIST SERIES — The new Medalist was Mercury's lowest priced car. It was introduced in mid-model year. The Medalist featured a more frugal use of side chrome and lacked the front bumper guards found on the more expensive series. Like all 1956 Mercs, it had a big 'M' medallion on the front of the hood and the word 'Mercury' was spelled out in block letters on the center horizontal grille bar.

MEDALIST I.D. NUMBERS: Medalist serial numbers were: 56WA10,001M to 89,958M and 56LA10,001M to 51,292M. See 1950 Mercury I.D. numbers for plant code.

MEDALIST

Model Number	Body/Style Number	Body Type & Seating	Factory Price	Shipping Weight	Production Total
NA	57D	4-dr HT Sed-6P	2458	3530	6,685
NA	64E	2-dr HT Cpe-6P	2389	3545	11,892
NA	70C	2-dr Sedan-6P	2254	3430	20,582
NA	73D	4-dr Sedan-6P	2313	3500	6,653

MEDALIST ENGINE
V-8: Overhead valves. Cast iron block. Displacement: 312 cubic inches. Bore and stroke: 3.8 x 3.44 inches. Compression ratio: 8.00:1. Brake horsepower: 210 at 4600 R.P.M. Carburetor: four-barrel.

CUSTOM SERIES — Chrome window trim was the main styling difference between the Custom and the Medalist. (The Medalist two-door sedan also used slightly less side trim.)

CUSTOM I.D. NUMBERS: See Medalist I.D. numbers.

CUSTOM

Model Number	Body/Style Number	Body Type & Seating	Factory Price	Shipping Weight	Production Total
NA	57C	4-dr HT Sed-6P	2555	3550	12,187
NA	64C	2-dr HT Cpe-6P	2485	3560	20,857
NA	70B	2-dr Sedan-6P	2351	3505	16,343
NA	73B	4-dr Sedan-6P	2410	3520	15,860
NA	76A	2-dr Conv-6P	2712	3665	2,311
NA	79B	4-dr Sta Wag-6P	2819	3860	9,292
NA	79D	4-dr Sta Wag-6P	2722	3790	8,478

CUSTOM ENGINE
See 1956 Medalist Series engine data.

1956 Mercury, Monterey 4-dr sedan, V-68

MONTEREY SERIES — The 1956 Monterey looked a lot like last year's model. The hooded headlights, vertical 'chubby cheek' taillights, and bumper integrated grille were little changed. Montereys featured heavy chrome trim around the side windows and chrome rocker panels. The side body molding made a sort of lightning bolt pattern. 'Monterey' was written in chrome on the front fenders.

MONTEREY I.D. NUMBERS: Monterey serial numbers were: 56ME10,001M to 100,055M; 56SL10,001M to 125,006M. See 1950 Mercury I.D. numbers for plant code.

MONTEREY

Model Number	Body/Style Number	Body Type & Seating	Factory Price	Shipping Weight	Production Total
NA	57B	4-dr HT Sed-6P	2700	3800	10,726
NA	58B	4-dr Spt Sed-6P	2652	3550	11,765
NA	64C	2-dr HT Cpe-6P	2630	3590	42,863
NA	73C	4-dr Sedan-6P	2555	3570	26,735
NA	79C	4-dr Sta Wag-8P	2977	3885	13,280

MONTEREY ENGINE
See 1956 Medalist Series engine data.

1956 Mercury, Montclair 2-dr hardtop, V-8

MONTCLAIR SERIES — Top-of-the-line Montclairs had a narrow color panel surrounded by chrome trim below the side windows and chrome rocker panels. A round medallion was placed near the tip of the front fender side trim. 'Montclair' was written, in chrome, on the front fenders. The four-door Sport sedan was replaced, early in the model year, by a four-door hardtop 'Phaeton.'

MONTCLAIR I.D. NUMBERS: See Monterey serial numbers.

MONTCLAIR

Model Number	Body/Style Number	Body Type & Seating	Factory Price	Shipping Weight	Production Total
NA	57A	4-dr HT Sed-6P	2835	3640	23,493
NA	58A	4-dr Spt Sed-6P	2786	3610	9,617
NA	64A	2-dr HT Cpe-6P	2765	3620	50,562
NA	76B	2-dr Conv-6P	2900	3725	7,762

MONTCLAIR ENGINE
See 1956 Medalist Series engine data.

CHASSIS FEATURES: Wheelbase: (Passenger cars) 119 inches; (Station wagons) 118 inches. Overall length: 206.4 inches. Overall width: 76.4 inches. Tires: 7.10 x 15; (Convertible and Station wagons) 7.60 x 15 inches.

POWERTRAIN OPTIONS: A three-speed manual transmission was standard. Overdrive- and Merc-O-Matic Drive automatic transmission were optional. Cars equipped with an automatic came with a 225 horsepower 312 cubic inch V-8 with four-barrel carburetor. In mid-model year, a new camshaft raised the output in the standard and 225 horsepower V-8s by 10. Also, the M-260 package (two four-barrel carburetors, 260 horsepower) was offered in all series later in the year.

CONVENIENCE OPTIONS: Power lubrication. Power brakes. Power steering. Four-Way power seat. Air conditioning. Seat belts. Whitewall tires. Radio. Power windows. Padded dash.

Historical footnotes: Dual exhausts were standard on all Montclairs and Montereys. Almost 90 percent of all 1956 Mercurys were sold with automatic transmission, 78.4 percent had whitewall tires, 88 percent backup lights and 96 percent heaters. Only 1.1 percent were equipped with an air conditioner. Mercurys won five NASCAR Grand National races in 1956.

1957 MERCURY

MONTEREY SERIES — Mercurys were completely restyled for 1957. For the first time, the make had bodies that were the exclusive to it and not based on Fords or Lincolns. A concave vertical bar grille; front hinged hood; 'V' shaped taillights; upper rear fender and rear deck sculpturing and cowl vent intakes were several of the new features. A chrome 'M' was placed between the grille and bumper. Early models had two headlights; later ones had four.

MONTEREY I.D. NUMBERS: Monterey serial numbers were: 57WA10,001M to 90,490M and 57LA10,001M to 40,854M. See 1950 Mercury I.D. numbers for plant code.

MONTEREY

Model Number	Body/Style Number	Body Type & Seating	Factory Price	Shipping Weight	Production Total
NA	57A	4-dr HT Sed-6P	2763	3915	22,475
NA	58A	4-dr Sedan-6P	2645	3890	53,839
NA	63A	2-dr HT Cpe-6P	2693	3870	42,199
NA	64A	2-dr Sedan-6P	2576	3875	33,982
NA	76A	2-dr Conv-6P	3005	4035	5,003

MONTEREY ENGINE
V-8: Overhead valves. Cast iron block. Displacement: 312 cubic inches. Bore and stroke: 3.8 x 3.44 inches. Compression ratio: 9.70:1. Brake horsepower: 255 at 4600 R.P.M. Carburetor: Holley four-barrel.

1957 Mercury, Montclair 2-dr convertible, V-8

MONTCLAIR SERIES — Chrome headlight rims, nameplates on the upper front fenders and an emblem ornament on the rear shelf of sedans and hardtops were the main differences between Montclairs and Montereys. Convertibles in both series had a plexiglass wraparound rear window.

MONTCLAIR I.D. NUMBERS: See Monterey I.D. numbers.

MONTCLAIR

Model Number	Body/Style Number	Body Type & Seating	Factory Price	Shipping Weight	Production Total
NA	57B	4-dr HT Sed-6P	3317	3925	21,156
NA	58B	4-dr Sedan-6P	3188	3905	19,836
NA	63B	2-dr HT Cpe-6P	3236	3900	30,111
NA	76B	2-dr Conv-6P	3430	4010	4,248

MONTCLAIR ENGINE
See 1957 Monterey Series engine data.

1957 Mercury, Turnpike Cruiser 2-dr hardtop, V-8

TURNPIKE CRUISER SERIES — The Turnpike Cruiser was one of the most gadget laden cars ever built. It was said to have been based on the XM-Turnpike Cruiser, although the opposite is true. All power items were standard. Other special features included: an overhanging roof with retractable rear window; air ducts mounted on top of the windshield (with fake aerial sticking out of them); power seat with a memory dial; rubber instrument bezels; special starter button; clock/odometer; sliding door locks and gold anodized insert in the upper rear fender concave section, which lead to the taillights.

TURNPIKE CRUISER I.D. NUMBERS: Serial numbers were: 57ME10,001M to 85,895M and 57SL10,001M to 98,451M. See 1950 Mercury I.D. numbers for plant code.

TURNPIKE CRUISER

Model Number	Body/Style Number	Body Type & Seating	Factory Price	Shipping Weight	Production Total
NA	65A	2-dr HT Cpe-6P	3758	4005	7,291
NA	75A	4-dr HT Sed-6P	3849	4015	8,305
NA	76S	2-dr Conv-6P	4103	4100	1,265

TURNPIKE CRUISER ENGINE
V-8: Overhead valves. Cast iron block. Displacement: 368 cubic inches. Bore and stroke: 4 x 3.65 inches. Compression ratio: 9.70:1. Brake horsepower: 290 at 4600 R.P.M. Five main bearings. Carburetor: Holley four-barrel.

1957 Mercury, Voyager 4-dr hardtop station wagon, V-8

STATION WAGON SERIES — Station wagons were a separate series this year. The top-of-the-line model was the Colony Park. It featured four-door hardtop styling and fake wood trim. The mid-priced wagon was the Voyager. It had a rear vent window like the Colony Park, but did not have wood trim. The lowest priced wagon, the Commuter, looked about the same as the Voyager, but lacked a rear vent window.

STATION WAGON I.D. NUMBERS: See Turnpike Cruiser I.D. numbers.

STATION WAGON

Model Number	Body/Style Number	Body Type & Seating	Factory Price	Shipping Weight	Production Total
NA	56A	2-dr Commuter-6P	2903	4115	4,885
NA	56B	2-dr Voyager-6P	3403	4240	2,283
NA	77A	4-dr Commuter-6P	2973	4195	11,990
NA	77B	4-dr Colony Park	3677	4240	7,386
NA	77C	4-dr Commuter-8P	3070	4195	5,752
NA	77D	4-dr Voyager-8P	3403	4240	3,716

STATION WAGON ENGINE
Commuter and Voyager same as Monterey. Colony Park same as Turnpike Cruiser.

CHASSIS FEATURES: Wheelbase: 122 inches. Overall length: 211.1 inches. Overall width: 79.1 inches. Tires: 8.00 x 14; (Convertibles and station wagons) 8.50 x14.

POWERTRAIN OPTIONS: A three-speed manual transmission was standard in the station wagons and Monterey. Overdrive and Merc-O-Matic automatic transmission were optional. An automatic was standard in the Turnpike Cruiser and Montclair. A 290 horsepower 368 cubic inch V-8 was optional for the Commuter, Voyager, Montclair and Monterey. The M-335 power package (two four-barrel carbs, 335 horsepower 368 cubic inch V-8) was optional on Montereys.

CONVENIENCE OPTIONS: Continental kit. Seat-O-Matic. Power steering. Power brakes. Radio. Heater. Whitewall tires. Air conditioning.

Historical footnotes: About one-third (32.6 percent) of 1957 Mercurys came with four headlights. All but 3.9 percent had automatic transmission. Three of the least popular options were air conditioning (1.5 percent), power windows (7.3 percent) and overdrive (1.4 percent). In 1959, *Motor Trend* magazine claimed the 1957 Monterey hardtop was one of the most popular used mid-priced cars. Mercury was the official pace car at the 1957 Indianapolis 500 race.

1958 MERCURY

1958 Mercury, Medalist 2-dr sedan, V-8

MEDALIST SERIES — The 1958 Mercury grille was divided into two sections enclosed in the massive bumpers. A chrome 'M' was in the center of the grille. The sculptured rear fenders remained, but the 'V' shaped taillights were altered a bit. There was now a 'projectile' light attached to them. The hood and fenders were new for 1958. Side window trim on the Medalist was painted.

MEDALIST I.D. NUMBERS: Serial numbers were: W500,001 to 547,046. See 1950 Mercury I.D. numbers for plant codes.

MEDALIST

Model Number	Body/Style Number	Body Type & Seating	Factory Price	Shipping Weight	Production Total
NA	58C	4-dr Sedan-6P	2617	3875	10,982
NA	64B	2-dr Sedan-6P	2547	3790	7,750

MEDALIST ENGINE
V-8: Overhead valves. Cast iron block. Displacement: 312 cubic inches. Bore and stroke: 3.80 x 3.44 inches. Compression ratio: 9.70:1. Brake horsepower: 235 at 4600 R.P.M. Five main bearings. Carburetor: Holley four-barrel.

MONTEREY SERIES — A single full-length chrome strip, which started at the headlights, was used on Monterey wagons and two-door hardtop. An extra trim piece, running parallel to the first, extended from the front fender to slightly past the front doors on four-door styles. The rear bumper pods contained concave dividers. The Monterey name was on the front fenders.

MONTEREY I.D. NUMBERS: Serial numbers were: W500,001 to 547,046 and J500,001 and up. Plant code: W = Wayne; J = Los Angeles; T = Metuchen; Z = St. Louis.

MONTEREY

Model Number	Body/Style Number	Body Type & Seating	Factory Price	Shipping Weight	Production Total
NA	57A	4-dr HT Sed-6P	2840	4150	6,909
NA	58A	4-dr Sedan-6P	2721	4160	28,892
NA	63A	2-dr HT Cpe-6P	2769	4075	13,693
NA	64A	2-dr Sedan-6P	2652	4080	10,526
NA	76A	2-dr Conv-6P	3,081	4,225	2,292

MONTEREY ENGINE
V-8: Overhead valves. Cast iron block. Displacement: 383 cubic inches. Bore and stroke: 3.25 x 3.29 inches. Compression ratio: 10.50:1. Brake horsepower: 312 at 4600 R.P.M. Five main bearings. Carburetor: Holley four-barrel.

MONTCLAIR SERIES — Distinguishing features of the Montclair were two full-length side chrome strips, with silver trim between them, and chrome headlight rims. The Turnpike Cruiser was now part of the Montclair series. It featured an overhanging rear roof, retractable rear window and twin air intakes on the roof above both sides of the windshield.

MONTCLAIR I.D. NUMBERS: Serial numbers were the same as for Montereys, plus T500,001 and up and, also, Z500,001 and up.

MONTCLAIR

Model Number	Body/Style Number	Body Type & Seating	Factory Price	Shipping Weight	Production Total
NA	57B	4-dr HT Sed-6P	3365	4165	3,609
NA	58B	4-dr Sedan-6P	3236	4155	4,801
NA	63B	2-dr HT Cpe-6P	3284	4085	5,012
NA	65A	2-dr Trnpike Crus	3498	4150	2,864
NA	85A	4-dr Trnpike Crus	3597	4230	3,543
NA	76B	2-dr Conv-6P	3536	4295	844

MONTCLAIR ENGINE

V-8: Overhead valves. Cast iron block. Displacement: 383 cubic inches. Bore and stroke: 4.29 x 3.29 inches. Compression ratio: 10.50:1. Brake horsepower: 330 at 4600 R.P.M. Five main bearings. Carburetor: Holley four-barrel (standard in Montclair).

V-8: Overhead valves. Cast iron block. Displacement: 430 cubic inches. Bore and stroke: 4.29 x 3.7 inches. Compression ratio: 10.50:1. Brake horsepower: 360 at 4600 R.P.M. Carburetor: Holley four-barrel (standard in Turnpike Cruiser).

1958 Mercury, Park Lane 4-dr hardtop sedan, V-8

PARK LANE SERIES — The new Park Lane was introduced to compete with Buick's Roadmaster. Front fender ornaments, rear roof panel nameplates, chrome headlight rims and rectangular patten trim in the rear bumper pods were styling features of the Park Lane. Like the Montclair, the Park Lane convertible had a wraparound rear window.

PARK LANE I.D. NUMBERS: Serial numbers were: T500,001 and up and, also, Z500,001 and up.

PARK LANE

Model Number	Body/Style Number	Body Type & Seating	Factory Price	Shipping Weight	Production Total
NA	57C	4-dr HT Sed-6P	3944	4390	5,241
NA	63C	2-dr HT Cpe-6P	3867	4280	3,158
NA	76C	2-dr Conv-6P	4118	4405	853

PARK LANE ENGINE

See 1958 Turnpike Cruiser Series engine data.

1958 Mercury, Colony Park 4-dr hardtop station wagon, V-8

STATION WAGON SERIES — The 1958 Mercury wagons were based on the Montclair. The Colony Park had simulated wood trim. Like the Voyager and Commuter, it featured a pillarless hardtop look.

STATION WAGON I.D. NUMBERS: See Park Lane I.D. numbers.

STATION WAGON

Model Number	Body/Style Number	Body Type & Seating	Factory Price	Shipping Weight	Production Total
NA	56A	2-dr Commuter-6P	3035	4400	1,912
NA	56B	2-dr Voyager-6P	3535	4435	568
NA	77A	4-dr Commuter-6P	3105	4485	8,601
NA	77B	4-dr Colony Park-6P	3775	4605	4,474
NA	77C	4-dr Commuter-9P	3201	4525	4,227
NA	77D	4-dr Voyager-6P	3635	4540	2,520

STATION WAGON ENGINE

Commuter, same as Monterey. Voyager and Colony Park, same as Montclair.

POWERTRAIN OPTIONS: A three-speed manual was standard on station wagons, Medalists and Monterey. Overdrive and Merc-O-Matic automatic transmissions were optional. Merc-O-Matic was standard on the Montclair. Multi-Drive automatic was standard on the Park Lane. A 360 horsepower 430 cubic inch V-8 was optional on the Montclair. A 400 horsepower 430 cubic inch V-8 with three two-barrel carburetors was optional on all series. Dual exhausts were a $32.30 option.

CHASSIS FEATURES: Wheelbase: (Park Lane) 125 inches; (others) 122 inches. Overall length: (Station wagons) 214.2 inches; (Park Lane) 220.2 inches; (others) 213.2 inches. Tires: (Convertibles, Park Lane and station wagons) 8.50 x 14; (others) 8.00 x 14.

CONVENIENCE OPTIONS: Tinted glass ($34.40). Two-tone paint ($17.20). Power lubricator ($43). Power steering ($107.50). Power windows ($107.50). Power brakes ($37.70). Four-Way power seat ($69.90). Seat-O-Matic ($96.80). Radio with electric antenna ($149.50). Pushbutton radio ($100). Rear speaker ($16.20). Manual heater and defroster ($91.40). Heater and defroster with Climate Control ($109.49). Electric clock ($15.10). Air conditioner and heater ($458.75). Padded instrument panel

($21.50). Power retracting station wagon window ($32.30). Windshield washer ($14). Speed limit safety monitor ($12.90). Wheel covers ($12.90). Nylon four-ply 8.00 x 14 whitewall tires ($67.40); Rayon four-ply 8.00 x 14 whitewall tires ($41). Foam rubber cushions ($21.50).

Historical footnotes: Only one percent of all 1958 Mercurys came with a manual transmission and overdrive.

1959 MERCURY

1959 Mercury, Monterey 2-dr hardtop, V-8 (AA)

MONTEREY SERIES — Mercurys once again shared a strong family resemblance with Fords, at least from the front. The bumper-integrated grille of last year was replaced by a separate honeycomb grille and plain, wraparound bumper which contained the signal lights. The concave side body sculpturing now extended almost to the front fenders. The wraparound windshield was larger and curved upward. Glass area size of the back window was also increased. The backlights on four-door and two-door hardtop models curved upwards. Four-door and two-door sedans had a unique roof line and a large wraparound rear window. In addition to distinct front fender nameplates, Montereys had a horizontal ribbed rear panel and three chrome bands on the upper rear fenders, in front of the taillights.

MONTEREY I.D. NUMBERS: Monterey serial numbers started at ( )9( )A500,001. Serial number code consisted of 10 symbols. The first represented the engine: P – 312 cubic inch two-barrel; N – 383 cubic inch two-barrel; M – 383 cubic inch four-barrel; L – 430 cubic inch four-barrel; K – 430 cubic inch six-barrel. The second symbol stands for the year (9 – 1959). The third symbol represents the assembly plant: J – California; W – Michigan; Z – Missouri and T – New Jersey. The fourth symbol indicates the series: A – Monterey; B – Montclair; C – Park Lane and D – station wagons. The fifth symbol (5) stands for the Mercury Division. The following group of digits is the sequential vehicle production number.

MONTEREY

Model Number	Body/Style Number	Body Type & Seating	Factory Price	Shipping Weight	Production Total
NA	57A	4-dr HT Sed-6P	2918	4065	11,355
NA	58A	4-dr Sedan-6P	2832	4140	43,570
NA	63A	2-dr HT Sed-6P	2854	4215	17,232
NA	64A	2-dr Sedan-6P	2768	3975	12,694
NA	76A	2-dr Conv-6P	3150	4295	4,426

MONTEREY ENGINES

V-8: Overhead valves. Cast iron block. Displacement: 312 cubic inches. Bore and stroke: 3.79 x 3.43 inches. Compression ratio: 8.75:1. Brake horsepower: 210 at 4400 R.P.M. Five main bearings. Carburetor: Holley 2300 two-barrel.

1959 Mercury, Montclair 2-dr hardtop, V-8 (AA)

MONTCLAIR SERIES — The Montclair had four chrome bands on the upper rear fender, full-length lower body moldings, bright metal 'cubed' grid pattern appliques on the rear panel and special nameplates under the chrome spears on the front fenders. A fabric and vinyl interior, padded dash, windshield washer, electric clock, parking brake warning light and foam rubber cushions were standard.

MONTCLAIR I.D. NUMBERS: Montclair serial numbers started with: ( )9( )B500,001. See Monterey I.D. numbers for code designations.

MONTCLAIR

Model Number	Body/Style Number	Body Type & Seating	Factory Price	Shipping Weight	Production Total
NA	57B	4-dr HT Sed-6P	3437	4275	6,713
NA	58B	4-dr Sedan-6P	3308	4240	9,514
NA	63B	2-dr HT Cpe-6P	3357	4150	7,375

MONTCLAIR ENGINE

V-8: Overhead valves. Cast iron block. Displacement: 383 cubic inches. Bore and stroke: 4.30 x 3.30 inches. Compression ratio: 10.00:1. Brake horsepower: 322 at 4600 R.P.M. Five main bearings. Carburetor: Mercury four-barrel.

1959 Mercury, Park Lane 4-dr hardtop (AA)

PARK LANE SERIES — Styling distinctions of the Park Lane included, chrome-plated projectiles on the rear fender coves, full-length lower body moldings, large aluminum gravel guards on the lower rear quarter panels, bright roof moldings and front fender (instead of hood) ornaments.Rear panel trim was the same as on the Montclair. Once again, the Park Lane convertible (like the Monterey) had a wraparound rear window. Park Lanes came equipped with the same items as Montclairs, plus power steering, power self-adjusting brakes, dual exhaust, backup lights, rear center arm rest and rear cigarette lighter.

PARK LANE I.D. NUMBERS: Serial numbers started at ( )9( )C500,001. See Monterey I.D. numbers for code designations.

PARK LANE

Model Number	Body/Style Number	Body Type & Seating	Factory Price	Shipping Weight	Production Total
NA	57C	4-dr HT Sed-6P	4031	4445	7,206
NA	63C	2-dr HT Cpe-6P	3955	4365	4,060
NA	76C	Conv-6P	4206	4575	1,257

PARK LANE ENGINE

V-8: Overhead valves. Cast iron block. Displacement: 430 cubic inches. Bore and stroke: 4.3 x 3.7 inches. Compression ratio: 10.00:1. Brake horsepower: 345 at 4400 R.P.M. Five main bearings. Carburetor: AFB-2853S four-barrel.

COUNTRY CRUISER STATION WAGON SERIES — The Commuter wagons shared trim styling with Montereys. Voyager and Colony Park station wagon trim was like that used on Montclairs, except the Colony Park had simulated wood panels.

COUNTRY CRUISER STATION WAGONS I.D. NUMBERS: Serial numbers started at ( )9( )D500,001. See Monterey I.D. numbers for code designations.

COUNTRY CRUISER STATION WAGONS

Model Number	Body/Style Number	Body Type & Seating	Factory Price	Shipping Weight	Production Total
NA	56A	2-dr Commuter-6P	3035	4400	1,051
NA	77A	4-dr Commuter-6P	3105	4485	15,122
NA	77B	4-dr Colony Park-6P	3932	4650	5,959
NA	77D	4-dr Voyager-6P	3793	4565	2,496

PRODUCTION NOTE: A two-door Voyager station wagon may have been built and sold in limited quantities.

COUNTRY CRUISER STATION WAGON ENGINES

Voyagers and Colony Parks have the same engine as Montclair. The Commuter powerplant has the following specifications: V-8. Overhead valves. Cast iron block. Displacement: 383 cubic inches. Bore and stroke: 4.29 x 3.29 inches. Compression ratio: 10.00:1. Brake horsepower: 280 at 4400 R.P.M. Carburetor: four-barrel.

POWERTRAIN OPTIONS: A three-speed manual was standard on Montereys and Commuter station wagons. Merc-O-Matic automatic was standard in Montclair, Colony Park and Voyager. It was a $173.30 option in Montereys and Commuters. Multi-Drive Merc-O-Matic was standard in Park Lane and an extra cost option on other series. A 280 horsepower 383 cubic inch V-8 was optional on the Monterey. A 322 horsepower 383 cubic inch V-8 with four-barrel carburetor was optional in Montereys. A 345 horsepower 430 cubic inch V-8 with four-barrel carburetor was optional in Montereys and Montclairs.

CHASSIS FEATURES: Wheelbase: (Park Lane) 128 inches; (others) 126 inches. Overall length: (Station wagons) 218.2 inches; (Park Lane) 222.8 inches; (others) 217.8 inches. Tires: (Monterey) 8.00 x 14; (others) 8.50 x 14.

CONVENIENCE OPTIONS: Pushbutton radio ($68.75). Signal-seeking radio ($90.25). Rear seat radio speaker ($9.30). Electric clock in Monterey and Commuter ($14.20). Windshield washer ($11.75). Tinted glass ($34.90). Tinted windshield ($19.79). Air conditioner with heater ($385). Heater and defroster ($71.15). Heater and defroster with Climate Control ($84.95). Power steering ($83.50). Power brakes ($34.55). Four-Way power seat ($60.40). Seat-O-Matic power seat ($82.20). Power windows ($84.50). Dual exhausts ($25.80). Commuter power tailgate window ($26.80). Safety speed monitor ($12). Padded dash in Monterey and Commuter ($17.10). Backup lights ($8.90). Courtesy light group ($9.30 Monterey). Whitewall tires ($32.95). Two-tone paint ($14.25). Lower back panel reflector ($10.90). Third seat for station wagons ($90.70). Optional Monterey trim ($30.60). Clear plastic seat covers ($29.95). Undercoating ($15). Outside rear view mirror ($6.95). Seat belts ($12.25 each).

Historical footnotes: The majority of 1959 Mercurys, 69.7 percent, came with power steering, 47.2 percent had tinted glass and 52.5 percent had power brakes.

1960 MERCURY

COMET SERIES — Mercury introduced its compact Comet in March of 1960. It was the first car of the make to be powered by a six-cylinder engine. The grille was similar to the one used on full-size Mercurys, but the rear fins and slanting taillights on sedans were distinctive to the Comet. The wagon used a different rear end style and larger,

rounded horizontal taillights. It looked like a dressed-up Falcon. Full-length chrome trim was placed on the body sides.

COMET I.D. NUMBERS: Serial numbers started at OHO( )S800,001. Serial number code: The first symbol designates the year. The second symbol designates the assembly plant as follows: R - California; K - Missouri; H - Ohio. The third and fourth symbols designate the body type as follows: four-door sedan - 12 or 02; two-door sedan - 11 or 01; four-door station wagon - 22 or 07; two-door station wagon - 21 or 06. The fifth symbol designates the engine as follows: S - 144 cubic inch Six; U - 170 cubic inch Six. See Monterey I.D. numbers for V-8s. The last six digits are the sequential vehicle production numbers.

COMET

Model Number	Body/Style Number	Body Type & Seating	Factory Price	Shipping Weight	Production Total
NA	54A	4-dr Sedan-6P	2053	2433	47,416
NA	59A	2-dr Sta Wag-6P	2310	2548	5115
NA	62A	2-dr Sedan-6P	1998	2399	45,374
NA	71A	4-dr Sta Wag-6P	2365	2581	18,426

COMET ENGINE

Six: Overhead valves. Cast iron block. Displacement: 144.3 cubic inches. Bore and stroke: 3.5 x 2.5 inches. Compression ratio: 8.70:1. Brake horsepower: 90 at 4200 R.P.M. Four main bearings. Carburetor: Holley one-barrel.

CHASSIS FEATURES: Wheelbase: (Passenger cars) 114 inches; (Station Wagons) 109.5 inches. Overall length: (Passenger cars) 194.8 inches; (Station Wagons) 191.8 inches. Tires: (Passenger cars) 6.00 x 13; (Station Wagons) 6.50 x 13.

POWERTRAIN OPTIONS: A three-speed manual transmission was standard. Ford-O-Matic automatic was a $172 option.

CONVENIENCE OPTIONS: DeLuxe trim package ($58). Heater and defroster ($74.30). Backup lights ($10.70). Padded instrument panel and visors ($22.40). Two-tone paint ($19.40). Pushbutton radio ($58.80). Electric station wagon tailgate window ($29.90). Whitewall tires, on sedans, ($43.40); on station wagons, ($33). Tinted windshield ($10.30). Wheel covers ($16). Windshield washers ($13.70). Two-speed electric windshield wipers ($9.65).

Historical footnotes: The Comet had originally been planned as the successor to the Edsel. Twenty-four percent of Comets came with tinted glass, four percent had power windows and 62 percent had automatic transmission.

1960 Mercury, Monterey 2-dr hardtop, V-8

MONTEREY SERIES — The basic body shell was unchanged from 1959, but except for the windshield and roof treatment, it was hard to see any resemblance. Unlike the previous two models, the new Mercury looked as if the people who designed the front and rear were from the same planet. The four-door sedan featured a wraparound back window. Flared fins and massive vertical taillights, integrated into the bumper, highlighted the rear end treatment. Outside of full-length upper side body level moldings, the Monterey was relatively free of stylistic 'doo-dads'. Its rear deck panel had enamel finish.

MONTEREY I.D. NUMBERS: Serial numbers started at O( ) ( ) ( ) ( )500,001. Serial number code: The first symbol designates the year. The second the assembly plant as follows: A - Atlanta; B - Oakville, Ontario; E - Mahwah; F - Dearborn; G - Chicago; H - Lorain; J - Los Angeles; K - Kansas City; N - Norfolk; P - Twin Cities; R - San Jose; S - Allen Park; T - Metuchen; U - Louisville; W - Wayne; X - St. Thomas, Ontario; Y - Wixom; Z - St. Louis. The third and fourth numbers designate the body style number. The fifth symbol designates the engine as follows: Four-cylinder - Y; Six-cylinder: S - 144 cubic inch; T - 200 cubic inch (one-barrel); U - (thru 1972) 170 cubic inch (one-barrel); V - (60 to 65) 223 cubic inch (one-barrel); (1966) 240 cubic inch (one-barrel); Z - (1975) 170 cubic inch (two-barrel). Eight-cylinder: A - (1960s) 289 cubic inch (four-barrel), (1973-1975) 460 cubic inch (four-barrel); B - (1960s) 406 cubic inch (four-barrel); C - (1966 to 1967) 289 cubic inch (four-barrel); (1970-1971) 429 cubic inch (four-barrel); F - (1960s) 406 cubic inch (three (3) two-barrels); (1970) 'Boss' 302 cubic inch (four-barrel); H - (1970-1975) 351 cubic inch (two-barrel); J - (1971-1972) Ram Air 429 cubic inch (four-barrel); K - (1960s) 289 cubic inch (four-barrel); (1970-1971) 429 cubic inch (four-barrel); L - (1960s) 221 cubic inch (four-barrel); (1970-1975) 250 cubic inch (one-barrel); M - (1966) 410 cubic inch (four-barrel); (1960s) 430 cubic inch; (1970-1971) 351 cubic inch (four-barrel); N - (1960s) 383 cubic inch (two-barrel); (1970-1973) 429 cubic inch (four-barrel); P - (1960s) 312 cubic inch (two-barrel); (1970-1971) 429 cubic inch (four-barrel); Q - (to 1966) 428 cubic inch (four-barrel); (1970) 429 cubic inch (four-barrel); (1972-1974) 351 cubic inch (four-barrel); R - (1960s) 427 cubic inch (dual four-barrel); (1970) Ram Air 429) cubic inch (four-barrel); S - (1970-1975) 400 cubic inch (four-barrel); W - (1960s) 292 cubic inch (two-barrel); (1966) 427 cubic inch (four-barrel); (1970) 351 cubic inch (four-barrel); X - (1960s) 352 cubic inch (two-barrel), (1966) 352 cubic inch (four-barrel); Y - (1960-1970) 390 cubic inch (two-barrel); Z - (1960s) 390 cubic inch (four-barrel); (1970) Boss 429 cubic inch (four-barrel). The last six digits are the sequential vehicle production numbers.

MONTEREY

Model Number	Body/Style Number	Body Type & Seating	Factory Price	Shipping Weight	Production Total
NA	57A	4-dr HT Sed-6P	2845	4061	9,536
NA	58A	4-dr Sedan-6P	2730	4029	49,594
NA	63A	2-dr HT Cpe-6P	2781	3984	15,790
NA	64A	2-dr Sedan-6P	2631	3952	21,557
NA	76A	2-dr Conv-6P	3077	4161	6,062

MONTEREY ENGINE
V-8. Overhead valves. Cast iron block. Displacement: 312 cubic inches. Bore and stroke: 3.8 x 3.44 inches. Compression ratio: 8.90:1. Brake horsepower: 205 at 4000 R.P.M. Five main bearings. Carburetor: Holley 2300 two-barrel.

MONTCLAIR SERIES — Montclairs could be identified by their distinctive bright metal horizontal bar pattern rear deck panel and three vertical chrome bars on the back doors of four-door models and on the panel in front of the rear tires on two-doors. They also had full-length lower body moldings. A model nameplate appeared on the rear fenders. Standard features included: electric clock, wheel covers, padded dash, courtesy light group and backup lights.

MONTCLAIR I.D. NUMBERS: See Monterey I.D. numbers.

MONTCLAIR

Model Number	Body/Style Number	Body Type & Seating	Factory Price	Shipping Weight	Production Total
NA	57B	4-dr HT Sed-6P	3394	4330	5,548
NA	58B	4-dr Sedan-6P	3280	4298	8,510
NA	63B	2-dr HT Cpe-6P	3331	4253	5,756

MONTCLAIR ENGINE
V-8. Overhead valves. Cast iron block. Displacement: 430 cubic inches. Bore and stroke: 4.3 x 3.7 inches. Compression ratio: 10.00:1. Brake horsepower: 310 at 4100 R.P.M. Five main bearings. Carburetor: Carter ABD-2965S two-barrel.

PARK LANE SERIES — The Park Lane had special 'cubed' pattern, bright metal trim between the trunk lid and rear bumper. Chrome also decorated the rocker and rear quarter panels. In addition, five vertical bars of chrome were placed in a row on the panel in front of the rear tires. Standard features included those found on the Montclair plus power brakes, power steering, windshield washer and inside non-glare mirror.

PARK LAND I.D. NUMBERS: See Monterey I.D. numbers.

PARK LANE

Model Number	Body/Style Number	Body Type & Seating	Factory Price	Shipping Weight	Production Total
NA	57F	4-dr HT Sed-6P	3858	4421	5,788
NA	63F	2-dr HT Cpe-6P	3794	4344	2,974
NA	76D	2-dr Conv-6P	4018	4525	1,525

PARK LANE ENGINE
See 1960 Montclair Series engine data.

1960 Mercury Commuter 4-dr hardtop station wagon, V-8

COUNTRY CRUISER STATION WAGONS SERIES — The Commuter wagon was based on the Monterey series. The simulated wood-trimmed Colony Park came with the same standard equipment as Montclair, plus a power rear window. Both wagons had four-door hardtop styling.

COUNTRY CRUISER STATION WAGONS I.D. NUMBERS: See Monterey I.D. numbers.

COUNTRY CRUISER STATION WAGONS

Model Number	Body/Style Number	Body Type & Seating	Factory Price	Shipping Weight	Production Total
NA	77A	4-dr Commuter-6P	3127	4303	14,949
NA	77B	4-dr Colony Park-6P	3837	4568	7,411

COUNTRY CRUISER STATION WAGON ENGINES
Commuter engine: see 1960 Monterey Series engine data. Colony Park: See 1960 Montclair Series engine data.

CHASSIS FEATURES: Wheelbase: 126 inches. Overall length: 219.2 inches. Tires: (Montclair, Colony Park) 8.50 x 14; (Park Lane) 9.00 x 14; (Other models) 8.00 x 14.

POWERTRAIN OPTONS: A three-speed manual transmission was standard on Montereys and Commuter station wagons. Merc-O-Matic automatic was standard on Montclairs and Colony Park station wagons. Multi-Drive automatic transmission was standard on Park Lane. Merc-O-Matic transmission was optional on Monterey and Commuter. Multi-Drive was also available, but not with the standard engine. Multi-Drive was a $25.50 option on Montclair and Colony Park. A 280 horsepower 383 cubic inch V-8 (four-barrel) and a 310 horsepower 430 cubic inch V-8 were optional on Monterey and Commuter.

CONVENIENCE OPTIONS: Tinted glass ($43.10). Air conditioner with heater ($472.10). Electric clock ($17). Heater and defroster ($78.70). Padded instrument panel in Monterey, Commuter ($21.30). Two-tone paint ($17). Power brakes ($43.20). Power rear tailgate window in Commuter ($32). Four-Way power seats ($76.50). Power steering ($106.20). Power windows ($106.20). Rear fender shields ($11.60). Pushbutton radio ($86). Rear seat radio speaker ($10.70). Tinted windshield ($29. Third seat for station wagons ($113.30). Trim option in Monterey, Commuter ($27.20). Wheel covers Monterey, Commuter ($19.20). Five Rayon whitewall tires ($43.10). Visual aid group ($57).

Historical footnote: Power windows and power seats were relatively unpopular options. Less than eight percent of full-size Mercurys were so equipped in 1960.

1961 MERCURY

COMET SERIES — A new grille and the addition of three vertical chrome pieces to the front fenders were the main difference between the 1961 Comet and last year's model. Mercury considered Comet a 'family-sized' compact. Advertising bragged the make was roomier and longer than most of its competition.

COMET I.D. NUMBERS: See 1960 Comet I.D. numbers.

COMET

Model Number	Body/Style Number	Body Type & Seating	Factory Price	Shipping Weight	Production Total
NA	54A	4-dr Sedan-6P	2053	2411	85,332
NA	59A	2-dr Sta Wag-6P	2310	2548	4199
NA	62A	2-dr Sedan-6P	1998	2376	71,563
NA	71A	4-dr Sta Wag-6P	2353	2581	22,165

COMET ENGINE
Six: Overhead valves. Cast iron block. Displacement: 144.3 cubic inches. Bore and stroke: 3.5 x 2.5 inches. Compression ratio: 8.70:1. Brake horsepower: 85 at 4200 R.P.M. Four main bearings. Carburetor: Holley 1908 one-barrel.

S-22 SERIES — The new S-22 coupe was basically a dressed-up Comet two-door sedan. It was introduced in mid-model year to cash in on the popularity of sporty compacts. Buyers could choose from ten exterior colors. Standard features included front bucket seats with a vinyl-clad steel console between them, deep-loop yarn carpeting, front and rear arm rests, DeLuxe steering wheel and horn ring, rear fender medallion, extra insulation and factory-applied undercoating.

S-22 I.D. NUMBERS: See 1960 Comet I.D. numbers.

S-22

Model Number	Body/Style Number	Body Type & Seating	Factory Price	Shipping Weight	Production Total
NA	62C	2-dr Sedan-5P	2282	2432	14,004

S-22 ENGINE
See 1961 Comet Series engine data.

CHASSIS FEATURES: Wheelbase: (Station wagon) 109.5 inches; (others) 114 inches. Overall length: (wagons) 191.8; (others) 194.8. Tires: (wagons) 6.50 x 13; (others) 6.00 x 13.

POWER TRAIN OPTIONS: A three-speed manual was standard. Ford-O-Matic automatic was optional. A 101 horsepower 170 cubic inch six with one-barrel carburetor was available at extra cost.

CONVENIENCE OPTIONS: Fashion group interior and exterior trim ($86.90). Heater and defroster ($7.430). Backup lights ($10.70). Padded instrument panel and visors ($22.40). Two-tone paint ($19.40). Push-button radio ($58.80). Electric tailgate window ($29.90). Whitewall tires, on passenger cars ($43.40); on station wagons ($33). Tinted windshield ($10.30). Wheel covers ($16). Windshield washers ($13.70). Two-speed electric windshield wipers ($9.65).

PRODUCTION NOTE: Most 1961 Comets, 64.7 percent, were equipped with automatic transmission.

1961 Mercury, Meteor '600' 2-dr sedan, V-8

METEOR 600 SERIES — Mercurys once again began to look like glamourous Fords. The concave, vertical bar grille housed four chrome rimmed headlights. The unusual roof lines of last year were replaced with square, crisp styling. Meteors had a mid-body chrome spear that ran from almost the tip of the rear fender to the front tires. The taillights were small and circular. They extended slightly. An ornament was on top of each front fender.

METEOR 600 I.D. NUMBERS: See 1960 Monterey I.D. numbers.

METEOR 600

Model Number	Body/Style Number	Body Type & Seating	Factory Price	Shipping Weight	Production Total
NA	58A	4-dr Sedan-6P	2587	3714	Note
NA	64A	2-dr Sedan-6P	2533	3647	18,117

NOTE: Four door sedan production total not available.

METEOR 600 ENGINE
Six: Overhead valves. Cast iron block. Displacement: 223 cubic inches. Bore and stroke: 3.62 x 3.6 inches. Compression ratio: 8.40:1. Brake horsepower: 135 at 4000 R.P.M. Four main bearings. Carburetor: one-barrel.

METEOR 800 SERIES — Three horizontal chrome bars on the front fenders, rocker panel molding, chromed tailfin tips and more roof panel trim, helped distinguish the 800 Series from the lower priced 600. Backup lights and an electric clock were a couple of standard extras.

METEOR 800 I.D. NUMBERS: See 1960 Monterey I.D. numbers.

1961 Mercury, Meteor '800' 2-dr hardtop sport coupe, V-8

METEOR 800

Model Number	Body/Style Number	Body Type & Seating	Factory Price	Shipping Weight	Production Total
NA	54A	4-dr Sedan-6P	2765	3762	Note
NA	62A	2-dr Sedan-6P	2711	3680	35,005
NA	65A	2-dr HT-6P	2772	3694	Note
NA	75A	4-dr HT-6P	2837	3780	Note

NOTE: Production totals not available.

METEOR 800 ENGINE
See 1961 Meteor 600 Series engine data.

1961 Mercury, Monterey 2-dr hardtop sport coupe, V-8

MONTEREY SERIES — Chrome rear fender stone guards and full-length body side moldings were the main exterior styling features of the Monterey. The interior was plusher than the other series and a padded dash was standard.

MONTEREY I.D. NUMBERS: See 1960 Monterey I.D. numbers.

MONTEREY

Model Number	Body/Style Number	Body Type & Seating	Factory Price	Shipping Weight	Production Total
NA	54B	4-dr Sedan-6P	2869	3777	22,881
NA	65B	2-dr HT-6P	2876	3709	10,942
NA	75B	4-dr HT-6P	2941	3795	9,252
NA	76A	2-dr Conv-6P	3126	3872	7,053

MONTEREY ENGINE
V-8: Overhead valves. Cast iron block. Displacement: 292 cubic inches. Bore and stroke: 3.75 x 3.3 inches. Compression ratio: 8.80:1. Brake horsepower: 175 at 4200 R.P.M. Five main bearings. Carburetor: Mercury two-barrel.

STATION WAGONS SERIES — The Commuter wagon looked like a Meteor. However, it only had two taillights, instead of six, and they were semi-rectangular rather than round. The Colony Park had imitation wood trim and a power tailgate window. It shared the same standard features as the Monterey.

STATION WAGONS I.D. NUMBERS: See 1960 Monterey I.D. numbers.

STATION WAGONS

Model Number	Body/Style Number	Body Type & Seating	Factory Price	Shipping Weight	Production Total
NA	71A	4-dr Commuter-6P	2922	4115	8,951
NA	71B	4-dr Colony Park-6P	3118	4131	7,887

STATION WAGON ENGINE
Commuter: See 1961 Meteor 600 Series engine data. Colony Park: See 1961 Monterey Series engine data.

CHASSIS FEATURES: Wheelbase: 120 inches. Overall length: (station wagons) 214.4 inches; (others) 214.6 inches. Tires: (Convertible and station wagons) 8.00 x 14; (others) 7.50 x 14.

POWERTRAIN OPTIONS: A three-speed manual transmission was standard. Overdrive was optional on the Meteor and wagons. Merc-O-Matic and Multi-Drive automatics were optional. A 175 horsepower 292 cubic inch V-8 (with two-barrel carburetor) was optional on the Meteor Series and Commuter. A 220 horsepower Marauder 352 cubic inch V-8 (two-barrel); 300 horsepower Marauder 390 cubic inch V-8 (four-barrel) and a 330 horsepower Marauder 390 cubic inch V-8 (four-barrel) were optional. A power rear axle was available.

CONVENIENCE OPTIONS: Air conditioner with heater ($436). Electric clock ($14.60). Courtesy light group ($13.30). Backup lights ($10.70). Heater and defroster ($75.10). Padded instrument panel ($21.30). Power brakes ($43.20). Power tailgate window ($32.30 Commuter). Four-Way power seat ($63.80). Two-tone paint ($22). Power steering ($81.70). Power windows ($102.10). Pushbutton radio ($65). Tinted glass ($43). Station wagon third seat ($70.20). Whitewall tires, on station wagons ($37); on other models ($48). Trim options, on Meteor 800 and Commuter ($27.20). Wheel covers ($19.20). Windshield washer ($13.70). Two-speed windshield wipers ($11.60).

Historical footnotes: The vast majority of 1961 Mercurys had automatic transmission and power steering. About one in 10 came with air conditioning. Mercury once again shared its body shell with Ford.

1962 MERCURY

1962 Mercury, Comet Custom 4-dr sedan, 6-cyl

COMET SERIES — A new, fine-patterned, vertical bar grille, round taillights and the repositioning of the Comet nameplates, from rear to front fenders, were the main styling changes for 1962. The model name was now, officially, Mercury Comet. Increased sound insulation, a roomier trunk and easier to read instrument panel guages were among the less obvious improvements.

COMET I.D. NUMBERS: See 1960 Comet I.D. numbers.

COMET

Model Number	Body/Style Number	Body Type & Seating	Factory Price	Shipping Weight	Production Total
NA	54A	4-dr Sedan-6P	2139	2457	70,227*
NA	69A	2-dr Sta Wag-6P	2483	2642	2,121*
NA	62A	2-dr Sedan-6P	2084	2420	73,800*
NA	71A	4-dr Sta Wag-6P	2526	2679	16,758*

(*) Production figures include Custom and S-22 series.

COMET ENGINE
Six: Overhead valves. Cast iron block. Displacement: 144.3 cubic inches. Bore and stroke: 3.5 x 2.5 inches. Compression ratio: 8.70:1. Brake horsepower: 85 at 4200 R.P.M. Four main bearings. Carburetor: Holley 1909 one-barrel.

COMET CUSTOM SERIES — Outside of the fender nameplates and side window chrome trim, the exterior of the Custom resembled the standard Comet series. However, its interior featured DeLuxe upholstery, white steering wheel, bright horn ring, rear seat arm rest, carpeting, front door dome light switch and cigarette lighter.

COMET CUSTOM I.D. NUMBERS: See 1960 Comet I.D. numbers.

COMET CUSTOM

Model Number	Body/Style Number	Body Type & Seating	Factory Price	Shipping Weight	Production Total
NA	54A	4-dr Sedan-6P	2226	2468	Note *
NA	59B	2-dr Sta Wag-6P	2483	2642	Note *
NA	62B	2-dr Sedan-6P	2171	2431	Note *
NA	71B	4-dr Sta Wag-6P	2526	2679	Note *

NOTE: (*) See Comet production total.

COMET CUSTOM ENGINE
See 1962 Comet Series engine data.

COMET SPECIAL SERIES — The sporty S-22 two-door sedan had six taillights (rather than the four on other Comets), a medallion above the trim on the roof panel and red wheel rims. The all-vinyl interior featured front bucket seats with a storage console between them. Backup lights, whitewall tires and loop-yarn carpeting were among the standard items found on the S-22. The Villager station wagon had simulated wood trim.

COMET SPECIAL I.D. NUMBERS: See 1960 Comet I.D. numbers.

COMET SPECIAL

Model Number	Body/Style Number	Body Type & Seating	Factory Price	Shipping Weight	Production Total
NA	62C	2-dr S-22 Sed-5P	2368	2358	Note *
NA	71C	4-dr Villager Wag	2710	2612	2,318

(*) See Comet production total.

COMET SPECIAL ENGINE
See 1962 Comet Series engine data.

CHASSIS FEATURES: Wheelbase: (Station wagons) 109.5 inches; (others) 114 inches. Overall length: (Station wagons) 191.8 inches; (others) 194.8 inches. Tires: (Station wagons) 6.50 x 13; (others) 6.10 x 13.

POWERTRAIN OPTIONS: A three-speed manual transmission was standard. Merc-O-Matic automatic transmission was a $171.70 option. A 101 horsepower 170 cubic inch six was optional at $45.10.

CONVENIENCE OPTIONS: Backup lights ($10.70). Station wagon luggage rack ($39). Air conditioning ($270.90). Convenience group ($25.80). Padded instrument panel ($16.40). Padded visors ($4.50). Pushbutton radio ($58.80). Two-tone paint ($19.40). Electric tailgate window ($29.75). Tinted glass ($30.90). Tinted windshield ($12.95). Whitewall tires, on passenger cars ($29.90); on station wagons ($33 . Wheel covers ($16). Windshield washers ($13.70). Two-speed electric windshield wipers ($9.65).

Historical footnote: Most 1962 Comets, 64.7 percent were equipped with automatic transmission, 47.4 percent had a radio, 31.9 percent had tinted glass and .9 percent had air conditioning.

1962 Mercury, Meteor Custom 4-dr sedan, V-8

METEOR SERIES — The Meteor was now a mid-size car. It shared the same basic body as Ford's Fairlane, but featured styling similar to the big Mercurys. Meteors had a wavy, fine-pattern vertical bar grille; bumper integrated signal lights; full-length side body moldings (that started above the headlights); a lower chrome spear, which began at the rear bumper and ran about half way across the car (with three thin chrome horizontal bars under it) and cylindrical taillights that stuck out from the tips of the tailfins. Buyers had their choice of 14 solid and 36 two-tone color combinations. The interiors were trimmed in crushed vinyl and cloth.

METEOR I.D. NUMBERS: See 1960 Monterey I.D. numbers.

METEOR

Model Number	Body/Style Number	Body Type & Seating	Factory Price	Shipping Weight	Production Total
NA	54A	4-dr Sedan-6P	2340	2877	9,183
NA	62A	2-dr Sedan-6P	2278	2843	3,935

METEOR ENGINE
Six: Overhead valves. Cast iron block. Displacement: 170 cubic inches. Bore and stroke: 3.5 x 2.94 inches. Compression ratio: 8.70:1. Brake horsepower: 101 at 4400 R.P.M. Four main bearings. Carburetor: Holley 1909 one-barrel.

METEOR CUSTOM SERIES — Chrome side window trim, rocker panel moldings, lower rear-quarter panel gravel shields and more roof side panel brightwork visually distinguished Meteor Customs from standard Meteors. Interiors were available in cloth and vinyl or all-vinyl. Twisted loop carpeting was standard.

METEOR CUSTOM I.D. NUMBERS: See 1960 Monterey I.D. numbers.

METEOR CUSTOM

Model Number	Body/Style Number	Body Type & Seating	Factory Price	Shipping Weight	Production Total
NA	54B	4-dr Sedan-6P	2428	2885	23,484
NA	62A	2-dr Sedan-6P	2366	2851	9,410

METEOR CUSTOM ENGINE
See 1962 Meteor Series engine data.

METEOR S-33 SERIES — The S-33 looked like a Meteor Custom two-door sedan. However, it had special wheel covers, a vinyl interior and front bucket seats with a storage console between them.

METEOR S-33 I.D. NUMBERS: See 1960 Monterey I.D. numbers.

METEOR S-33

Model Number	Body/Style Number	Body Type & Seating	Factory Price	Shipping Weight	Production Total
NA	62C	2-dr Sedan-6P	2509	2851	5,900

METEOR S-33 ENGINE
See 1962 Meteor Series engine data.

CHASSIS FEATURES: Wheelbase: 116.5 inches. Overall length: 203.8 inches. Tires: 6.50 x 14; (7.00 x 14 optional).

POWER TRAIN OPTIONS: A three-speed manual transmission was standard. Overdirve and Merc-O-Matic automatic transmission were optional at extra cost. A 145 horsepower 221 cubic inch V-8 (two-barrel) and a 164 horsepower 260.8 cubic inch V-8 were offered.

CONVENIENCE OPTIONS: Air conditioning ($231.70). Padded instrument panel ($19.95). Outside remote-control rearview mirror ($12). Padded visors ($5.20). Power steering ($81.70). Tinted glass ($40.30). White wall tires ($37). Wheel covers ($18.60). Windshield washer ($13.70). Pushbutton radio ($58.50). Front seat belts ($16.80). Two-tone paint ($22).

Historical footnotes: The vast majority of 1962 Meteors came with a V-8 engine and automatic transmission.

1962 Mercury, Monterey 4-dr hardtop sedan, V-8

MONTEREY SERIES — The most noticeable styling change was seen in the taillights. They protruded from the tailfins. The new grille had a horizontal bar pattern, with an emblem, at its center, connecting the headlights. Side chrome was at two levels, joined in the middle by a slight chrome arch. The Monterey was one inch lower than last year's model.

MONTEREY I.D. NUMBERS: See 1960 Monterey I.D. numbers.

MONTEREY

Model Number	Body/Style Number	Body Type & Seating	Factory Price	Shipping Weight	Production Total
NA	54A	4-dr Sedan-6P	2726	3721	18,975
NA	62A	2-dr Sedan-6P	2672	3644	5,117
NA	65A	2-dr HT-6P	2733	3661	5,328
NA	71A	4-dr Commuter Wag	2920	4069	8,389
NA	75A	4-dr HT-6P	2798	3737	2,691

MONTEREY ENGINE
Six: Overhead valves. Cast iron block. Displacement: 223 cubic inches. Bore and stroke: 3.62 x 3.6 inches. Compression ratio: 8.40:1. Brake horsepower: 138 at 4200 R.P.M. Four main bearings. Carburetor: Holley one-barrel.

MONTEREY CUSTOM SERIES — Full-length lower body moldings and a large, rectangular chrome trim piece on the forward sides of the front fenders, were found on the Custom. The Colony Park station wagon had imitation wood trim, a power tailgate window, carpeting and either cloth and vinyl or all-vinyl interior.

MONTEREY CUSTOM I.D. NUMBERS: See 1960 Monterey I.D. numbers.

MONTEREY CUSTOM

Model Number	Body/Style Number	Body Type & Seating	Factory Price	Shipping Weight	Production Total
NA	54B	4-dr Sedan-6P	2965	3836	27,591
NA	65B	2-dr HT-6P	2972	3772	10,814
NA	71B	4-dr Col Park Wag	3219	4186	9,596
NA	75B	4-dr HT-6P	3037	3851	8,932
NA	76A	Conv-6P	3222	3938	5,489

MONTEREY CUSTOM ENGINE
V-8: Overhead valves. Cast iron block. Displacement: 292 cubic inches. Bore and stroke: 3.75 x 3.3 inches. Compression ratio: 8.80:1. Brake horsepower: 170 at 4200 R.P.M. Five main bearings. Carburetor: Ford two-barrel.

MONTEREY CUSTOM S-55 SERIES — The S-55 was basically a trim and performance option. Front fender ornaments and special wheel covers were the main exterior differences from a standard Custom. The S-55 had front bucket seats, console, red safety-light in the doors, carpeting and a more powerful standard V-8.

MONTEREY CUSTOM S-55 SERIES I.D. NUMBERS: See 1960 Monterey I.D. numbers.

MONTEREY CUSTOM S-55

Model Number	Body/Style Number	Body Type & Seating	Factory Price	Shipping Weight	Production Total
NA	65C	2-dr HT-5P	3488	3772	2,772
NA	76B	2-dr Conv-5P	3738	3938	1,315

MONTEREY CUSTOM S-55 ENGINE
V-8: Overhead valves. Cast iron block. Displacement: 390 cubic inches. Bore and stroke: 4.05 x 3.78 inches. Compression ratio: 9.60:1. Brake horsepower: 300 at 4600 R.P.M. Carburetor: four-barrel.

CHASSIS FEATURES: Wheelbase: 120 inches. Overall length: (Station wagons) 121.1 inches; (others) 215.5 inches. Tires: (Station wagons and convertible) 8.00 x 14; (others) 7.50 x 14.

POWER TRAIN OPTIONS: A three-speed manual transmission was standard. Four-speed manual and Multi-Drive automatic transmissions were optional. A 170 horsepower 292 cubic inch V-8 (two-barrel) was optional in Montereys. A 220 horsepower 352 cubic inch V-8 (two-barrel); 300 horsepower 390 cubic inch V-8 (four-barrel); 330 horsepower 390 cubic inch V-8 (four-barrel); 385 horsepower 406 cubic inch V-8 (four-barrel); 405 horsepower 406 cubic inch V-8 (three (3) two-barrels) and power transfer rear axle were available at extra cost.

CONVENIENCE OPTIONS: Air conditioner with heater ($360.90). Electric clock ($14.60). Backup lights ($10.70). Station wagon luggage rack ($39). Padded dash ($21.30). Padded visors ($5.80). Two-tone paint ($22). Power brakes ($43.20). Power tailgate window, in Commuter ($32.30). Power windows ($102.10). Four-Way power seat ($63.80). Power steering ($81.70). Pushbutton radio ($58.50). Smog reduction system ($5.70). Tinted glass ($43). Tinted windshield ($21.55). Station wagon third seat ($70.20). Wheel covers ($19.20). Windshield washer ($13.70). Two-speed windshield wipers ($7.75). Whitewall tires, on passenger cars ($52.60); on station wagons ($37).

Historical footnotes: Less than five percent of all 1962 Montereys were equipped with a manual transmission. A mere 17 percent were sold with a six-cylinder engine. Mercurys and Checkers were the only medium-priced cars available with a six-cylinder engine in 1962.

1963 MERCURY

1963 Mercury, Comet S-22 2-dr convertible, V-8

COMET SERIES — The new Comet looked a lot like last year's model. Chrome now outlined the side body sculpturing. The four circular taillights protruded from the rear deck panel. The grille featured a horizontal bar theme and the four headlights had chrome rims.

COMET I.D. NUMBERS: See 1960 Comet I.D. numbers.

COMET

Model Number	Body/Style Number	Body Type & Seating	Factory Price	Shipping Weight	Production Total
NA	02	4-dr Sedan-6P	2139	2499	24,230
NA	21	2-dr Sta Wag-6P	2440	2644	623
NA	01	2-dr Sedan-6P	2084	2462	24,351
NA	22	4-dr Sta Wag-6P	2483	2681	4,419

COMET ENGINE
Six: Overhead valves. Cast iron block. Displacement: 144.3 cubic inches. Bore and stroke: 3.5 x 2.5 inches. Compression ratio: 8.70:1. Brake horsepower: 85 at 4200 R.P.M. Four main bearings. Carburetor: Ford C3GF-9510 one-barrel.

COMET CUSTOM SERIES — Chrome window trim and three horizontal bars on the rear quarter panel or on front fenders of wagons, except the Villager, were distinguishing features of the Custom series. The interior came with such items as bright horn ring; rear seat arm rests and ash trays; front door dome light switch; cigarette lighter and carpeting. The Villager wagon had simulated wood trim and a power tailgate window. Front bucket seats were optional.

COMET CUSTOM I.D. NUMBERS: See 1960 Comet I.D. numbers.

COMET CUSTOM

Model Number	Body/Style Number	Body Type & Seating	Factory Price	Shipping Weight	Production Total
NA	12	4-dr Sedan-6P	2226	2508	27,498
NA	23	2-dr Sta Wag-6P	2527	2659	272
NA	11	2-dr Sedan-6P	2171	2471	11,897
NA	13	2-dr HT Cpe-6P	2300	2572	9,432
NA	24	4-dr Sta Wag-6P	2570	2696	5,151
NA	26	4-dr Villager Wag	2754	2736	1,529
NA	15	2-dr Conv-6P	2557	2784	7,354

COMET CUSTOM ENGINE
See 1963 Comet Series engine data.

COMET SPECIAL S-22 SERIES — Six taillights made it easy to identify the Special S-22 Series from the rear. Outside of the front fender ornaments, they looked about the same as Customs. The Custom interiors featured individually adjustable bucket seats with center console and deep, loop-pile carpeting.

COMET SPECIAL S-22 I.D. NUMBERS: See 1960 Comet I.D. numbers.

COMET SPECIAL S—22

Model Number	Body/Style Number	Body Type & Seating	Factory Price	Shipping Weight	Production Total
NA	19	2-dr Sedan-5P	2368	2512	6,303
NA	17	2-dr HT Cpe-6P	2400	2572	5,807
NA	18	2-dr Conv-5P	2710	2825	5,757

COMET SPECIAL S-22 ENGINE
See 1963 Comet Series engine data.

CHASSIS FEATURES: Wheelbase: (Station wagon) 109.5 inches; (other models) 114 inches. Overall length: (Station wagons) 191.8 inches; (other models) 194.8 inches. Tires: (Station wagon and convertible) 6.50 x 13; (other models) 6.00 x 13.

POWERTRAIN OPTINS: A three-speed manual transmission was standard. Four-speed manual and Merc-O-Matic automatic transmissions were optional. A 101 horsepower 170 cubic inch (one-barrel) and a 164 horsepower 260 cubic inch V-8 (two-barrel) were optional.

CONVENIENCE OPTIONS: Backup lights ($10.70). Luggage rack for station wagons ($39). Air conditioning ($270.90). Comet convenience group ($25.80). Padded instrument panel ($16.40). Padded visors ($4.50). Pushbutton radio ($58.80). Two-tone paint ($19.40). Electric tailgate window for station wagons ($29.75). Tinted glass ($30.90). Tinted windshield ($12.95). Whitewall tires on passenger cars ($29.90); on station wagons ($33). Wheel covers ($16). Windshield washers ($13.70). Two-speed electric windshield wipers ($9.65).

Historical footnotes: Just over 64 percent of 1963 Comets were equipped with an automatic transmission.

1963 Mercury, Meteor Custom 2-dr hardtop, V-8

METEOR SERIES — The protruding cone-shaped taillights of 1962 remained on this season's Meteor station wagons, but were replaced on other body types. They now looked like part of the tailfin, rather than an add-on. A slightly sloping full-length chrome spear graced the body side. The grille resembled the one used on the 1962 Comet. Once again, bright metal trim was used on the roof quarter panels.

METEOR I.D. NUMBERS: See 1960 Monterey I.D. numbers.

METEOR

Model Number	Body/Style Number	Body Type & Seating	Factory Price	Shipping Weight	Production Total
NA	32	4-dr Sedan-6P	2340	2959	9,183
NA	31	2-dr Sedan-6P	2278	2920	3,935
NA	38	4-dr Sta Wag-6P	2631	3237	2,359

METEOR ENGINE
Six: Overhead valves. Cast iron block. Displacement: 170 cubic inches. Bore and stroke: 3.5 x 2.94 inches. Compression ratio: 8.70:1. Brake horsepower: 101 at 4400 R.P.M. Four main bearings. Carburetor: Ford C30F-9510-A one-barrel.

METEOR CUSTOM SERIES — Chrome side window trim, full-length lower body moldings and more chrome on the roof quarter panels were features that set the Custom series apart from the standard Meteors. They also had special interiors and carpeting. The Country Cruiser wagon had simulated wood paneling.

METEOR CUSTOM I.D. NUMBERS: See 1960 Monterey I.D. numbers.

METEOR CUSTOM

Model Number	Body/Style Number	Body Type & Seating	Factory Price	Shipping Weight	Production Total
NA	42	4-dr Sedan-6P	2428	2965	14,498
NA	41	2-dr Sedan-6P	2366	2926	2,704
NA	43	2-dr HT Cpe-6P	2448	2944	7,565
NA	49	4-dr Ctry Cruiser	2886	3253	1,485
NA	48	4-dr Sta Wag-6P	2719	3245	3,636

METEOR CUSTOM ENGINE
See 1963 Meteor Series engine data.

METEOR S-33 SERIES — Triple horizontal chrome bars on the front fenders, rear fender insignia and special medallions on the roof quarter panels were exclusive to the S-33. The interior featured front bucket seats with a center console between them.

METEOR S-33 I.D. NUMBERS: See 1960 Monterey I.D. numbers.

METEOR S-33

Model Number	Body/Style Number	Body Type & Seating	Factory Price	Shipping Weight	Production Total
NA	47	2-dr HT Cpe-6P	2628	2964	4,865

METEOR S-33 ENGINE
See 1963 Meteor Series engine data.

CHASSIS FEATURES: Wheelbase: (Passenger cars) 116.5 inches; (Station wagons) 115.5 inches. Overall length: (Passenger cars) 203.8 inches; (Station wagons) 202.3 inches. Tires: 6.50 x 14.

POWERTRAIN OPTIONS: A three-speed manual transmission was standard. Overdrive, four-speed manual and Merc-O-Matic automatic transmissions were optional. A 145 horsepower 221 cubic inch V-8 (two-barrel) and a 164 horsepower 260.8 cubic inch V-8 were available.

CONVENIENCE OPTIONS: Two-speed windshield wipers ($7.75). Air conditioning ($231.70). Padded instrument panel ($19.95). Outside remote-control rearview mirror ($12). Padded visors ($5.20). Power steering ($81.70). Tinted glass ($40.30). Whitewall tires ($37). Wheel covers ($18.60). Windshield washer ($13.70). Pushbutton radio ($58.50). Front seat belts ($16.80). Two-tone paint ($22). Third station wagon seat ($43.50). Station wagon power rear window ($32.30).

Historical footnote: Most Meteors, 79.6 percent, came with an automatic transmission, 91.4 percent had a V-8 engine, 47 percent had power steering, 68.6 percent had a radio, 46 percent had tinted glass and five percent had air conditioning.

1963 Mercury, Monterey 4-dr hardtop sedan, V-8

MONTEREY SERIES — Basic Monterey styling seemed more in tune with the 1961 models than the 1962s. Six taillights were (as in 1961) located in the rear deck panel. Side body moldings ran from the tailfins to the headlights. Chrome trim was on the roof quarter panels. A concave, vertical bar grille housed four chrome-rimmed headlights. Mercury's fondness for unusual designs surfaced again this year. The Breezeway roof featured a roll-down back window. In mid-model year, the Marauder two-door hardtop, with fastback styling, was introduced.

MONTEREY I.D. NUMBERS: See 1960 Monterey I.D. numbers.

MONTEREY

Model Number	Body/Style Number	Body Type & Seating	Factory Price	Shipping Weight	Production Total
NA	52	4-dr Sedan-6P	2887	3994	18,177
NA	51	2-dr Sedan-6P	2834	3854	4,640
NA	57	2-dr Fstbk Spt Cpe	3083	3875	Note 1
NA	53	2-dr HT Cpe-6P	2930	3869	2,879
NA	54	4-dr HT Sed-6P	2995	3959	1,692

NOTE 1: The Marauder Fastback Sport Coupe was introduced as a running addition to the 1963 Mercury line. Specific production totals for this style, model number 57, are not available.

MONTEREY ENGINE
V-8: Overhead valves. Cast iron block. Displacement: 390 cubic inches. Bore and stroke: 4.05 x 3.78 inches. Compression ratio: 8.90:1. Brake horsepower: 250 at 4400 R.P.M. Five main bearings. Carburetor: Ford C3MF-9510 two-barrel.

MONTEREY CUSTOM SERIES — Tire level full-length moldings, three rectangular chrome pieces on the rear fender and front fender nameplates distinguished the Custom from the standard Monterey. All Customs came equipped with backup lights, courtesy light group, electric clock and two-speed windshield wipers.

MONTEREY CUSTOM I.D. NUMBERS: See 1960 Monterey I.D. numbers.

MONTEREY CUSTOM

Model Number	Body/Style Number	Body Type & Seating	Factory Price	Shipping Weight	Production Total
NA	62	4-dr Sedan-6P	3075	3959	39,542
NA	66	2-dr Fstbk Cpe-6P	3083	3887	7,298
NA	63	2-dr HT Cpe-6P	3083	3881	10,693
NA	76	4-dr Sta Wag-6P	3295	4306	6,447

Model Number	Body/Style Number	Body Type & Seating	Factory Price	Shipping Weight	Production Total
NA	76	4-dr Sta Wag-9P	3365	4318	7,529
NA	64	4-dr HT Sed-6P	3148	3971	8,604
NA	65	2-dr Conv-6P	3333	4043	3,783

NOTE: Model number 66, the fastback coupe, was called the Marauder. Models numbered 76 were called Colony Park station wagons.

MONTEREY CUSTOM ENGINE
See 1963 Monterey Series engine data.

MONTEREY S-55 SERIES — The S-55 insignia in front of the rear fender chrome bars and special wheel covers were the most noticeable exterior differences between the S-55 and the Custom. Inside, the S-55 featured vinyl upholstery, front bucket seats with the center console, front and rear arm rests and padded dash. Buyers could have an automatic or a four-speed manual transmission at no extra cost.

MONTEREY S-55 I.D. NUMBERS: See 1960 Monterey I.D. numbers.

MONTEREY S-55
Model Number	Body/Style Number	Body Type & Seating	Factory Price	Shipping Weight	Production Total
NA	68	2-dr Fstbk Cpe-6P	3650	3900	2,317
NA	67	2-dr HT Cpe-6P	3650	3894	3,863
NA	60	4-dr HT Sed-5P	3715	3984	1,203
NA	69	2-dr Conv-5P	3900	4049	1,379

NOTE: Model number 68, the fastback coupe, was called the Marauder.

MONTEREY S-55 ENGINE
See 1963 Monterey Series engine data.

CHASSIS FEATURES: Wheelbase: 120 inches. Overall length: (Passenger cars) 215 inches; (Station wagons) 212.1 inches. Tires: (Passenger cars) 7.50 x 14; (Station wagons) 8.00 x 14.

POWERTRAIN OPTIONS: A three-speed manual transmission was standard on Monterey and Custom series. Multi-Drive automatic or four-speed manual tranmissions were standard in the S-55. Automatic transmission was optional on all series. The four-speed manual transmission was available on all, but the Colony Park. A 300 horsepower cubic inch V-8 (four-barrel); 330 horsepower 390 cubic inch V-8 (four-barrel); 385 horsepower 406 cubic inch (four-barrel) and a 405 horsepower 406 cubic inch V-8 were optional. The last two choices were offered only on cars equipped with a four-speed manual transmission.

CONVENIENCE OPTIONS: Air-conditioner with heater ($360.90). Electric clock ($14.60). Backup lights ($10.70). Station wagon luggage rack ($45.40). Outside remote control rearview mirror ($12). Padded dash ($21.30). Padded visors ($5.80). Two-tone paint ($22). Power brakes ($43.20). Power driver's bucket seat in S-55 ($92.10). Power steering ($106.20). Power windows ($102.10). Pushbutton radio ($58.50). AM/FM radio ($129.30). Front seat belts ($16.80). Swing-away steering wheel ($50). Tinted glass ($43). Tinted windshield ($28). Whitewall tires ($52.60). Monterey sedan trim option ($34.80). Wheel covers ($19.20). Windshield washer ($13.70). Courtesy light group ($14.80). Two-speed windshield wipers ($7.75).

Historical footnotes: The majority of 1963 full-size Mercurys came with automatic transmission, power steering, power brakes, radio and tinted glass. About one in 10 had power windows. Twenty percent were sold with an air-conditioner. Mercury won one NASCAR Grand Nationals race in 1963.

1964 MERCURY

COMET 202 SERIES — The 1964 Comet had a Lincoln Continental style grille. The same theme was repeated on the rear deck panel. A wraparound trim piece was seen on the tips of the front fenders. Three thin, vertical trim slashes were on the sides of the front fenders. The signal lights remained embedded in the front bumper.

COMET 202 I.D. NUMBERS: See 1960 Comet I.D. numbers

COMET 202
Model Number	Body/Style Number	Body Type & Seating	Factory Price	Shipping Weight	Production Total
NA	02	4-dr Sedan-6P	2182	2580	29,147
NA	01	2-dr Sedan-6P	2126	2539	33,824
NA	32	4-dr Sta Wag-6P	2463	2727	5,504

COMET 202 ENGINE
Six: Overhead valves. Cast iron block. Displacement: 170 cubic inches. Bore and stroke: 3.5 x 2.93 inches. Compression ratio: 8.70:1. Four main bearings. Carburetor: Ford C3YF-9510E one-barrel.

COMET 404 SERIES — Full-length body side moldings were the most obvious exterior difference between the Comet 404 and lower priced Comet 202 series. Interior trims were available in cloth and vinyl or all-vinyl. The Villager station wagon featured imitation wood trim.

COMET 404 I.D. NUMBERS: See 1960 Comet I.D. numbers.

COMET 404
Model Number	Body/Style Number	Body Type & Seating	Factory Price	Shipping Weight	Production Total
NA	12	4-dr Sedan-6P	2269	2588	25,136
NA	11	2-dr Sedan-6P	2213	2551	12,512
NA	34	4-dr Sta Wag-6P	2550	2741	6,918
NA	36	4-dr Sta Wag-6P	2734	2745	1,980

NOTE: Model number 36 was called the Villager station wagon.

COMET 404 ENGINE
See 1964 Comet 202 Series engine data.

1964 Mercury, Comet Caliente 2-dr hardtop sport coupe, V-8

CALIENTE SERIES — "Every bit as hot as it looks!", was how sales literature described the Caliente. It had a wide, full-length molding, on its sides and a nameplate on the lower front fenders. A padded instrument panel with walnut grain trim and deep-loop carpeting were a couple of standard luxury features. Caliente hardtops and convertibles were available only in solid colors.

CALIENTE
Model Number	Body/Style Number	Body Type & Seating	Factory Price	Shipping Weight	Production Total
NA	22	4-dr Sedan-6P	2350	2668	27,218
NA	23	2-dr HT Cpe-6P	2375	2688	31,204
NA	25	2-dr Conv-6P	2636	2861	9,039

CALIENTE ENGINE
See 1964 Comet 202 Series engine data.

CYCLONE SERIES — This two-door hardtop was the first macho Comet. Literature told of "under the hood, a whiplash of surging power" and of the "masculine feel of black vinyl in the instrument panel." As a safety feature the "bucket seats are contoured to hold you more securely in turns." (Apparently, Mercury felt a lot of people were falling out of their bucket seats when driving around corners.) Fender nameplates, full-length lower body moldings, vinyl roof coverings and 'chrome wheel look' wheel covers distinguished the Cyclone. A three-spoke steering wheel, front bucket seats with center console and a tachometer were standard. The engine came with special chromed parts, including air cleaner, dip stick, oil filter, radiator cap and rocker arm covers.

CYCLONE I.D. NUMBERS: See 1960 Comet I.D. numbers.

CYCLONE
Model Number	Body/Style Number	Body Type & Seating	Factory Price	Shipping Weight	Production Total
NA	27	2-dr HT Cpe-5P	2655	2688	7,454

CYCLONE ENGINE
V-8: Overhead valves. Cast iron block. Displacement: 289 cubic inches. Bore and stroke: 4 x 2.37 inches. Compression ratio: 9.00:1. Brake horsepower: 210 at 4400 R.P.M. Carburetor: Ford C5MF-9510A two-barrel.

CHASSIS FEATURES: (Passenger cars) 114 inches; (station wagons) 109.5 inches. Overall length: (passenger cars) 195.1 inches; (station wagons) 191.8 inches. Tires (passenger cars) 6.50 x 14; (station wagons) 7.00 x 14.

POWERTRAIN OPTIONS: A three-speed manual transmission was standard. Four-speed manual, Merc-O-Matic and Multi-Drive automatic transmissions were optional. A 116 horsepower 200 cubic inch six (one-barrel); 164 horsepower 260 cubic inch V-8 (two-barrel); 210 horsepower 289 cubic inch V-8 (two-barrel) and a 271 horsepower 289 cubic inch V-8 (four-barrel) were available.

CONVENIENCE OPTIONS: Power steering ($86). Air conditioning ($232). Heavy-duty battery ($7.60). Tinted glass ($27.10). Tinted windshield ($18.10). Station wagon luggage rack ($64.35). Outside remote control rearview mirror ($12). Padded instrument panel ($18.40). Padded visors ($4.50). Two-tone paint ($19.40). Power brakes ($43.20). Pushbutton AM radio ($58.50). Tachometer ($43.10). Wheel covers ($19.20). Windshield washer and wipers ($21.80).

Historical Footnotes: Most 1964 Comets, 68 percent, had automatic transmission, 24 percent had power steering and only four percent had power brakes. A team of Comet Calientes, powered by 271 horsepower 289 cubic inch V-8s, traveled over 100,000 miles at average speeds in excess of 100 miles per hour.

MONTEREY SERIES — Although obviously based on the 1963 models, the new full-size Mercurys now seemed closer in styling to Continentals than Fords. The rear end appeared to be influenced by the 1959 Continental Mark IV. Six rectangular tail/backup lights were set in the rear deck panel. The slightly recessed grille featured bent vertical bars and four chrome rimmed headlights. The signal lights were in the bumper. The unsual Breezeway roof, with its retractable rear window, was offered once again. Full-length upper body moldings and tire level chrome spears decorated the sides.

MONTEREY I.D. NUMBERS: See 1960 Monterey I.D. numbers.

MONTEREY
Model Number	Body/Style Number	Body Type & Seating	Factory Price	Shipping Weight	Production Total
NA	42	4-dr Sedan-6P	2892	3985	20,234
NA	48	4-dr HT Fstbk-6P	2957	4017	4,143
NA	41	2-dr Sedan-6P	2819	3895	3,932
NA	47	2-dr HT Fstbk-6P	2884	3916	8,760
NA	43	2-dr HT Cpe-6P	2884	3910	2,926
NA	45	2-dr Conv-6P	3226	4027	2,592

NOTE: Models number 48 and 47, the pillarless fastback styles, were called Mauraders.

MONTEREY ENGINE
V-8: Overhead valves. Cast iron block. Displacement: 390 cubic inches. Bore and stroke: 4.05 x 3.78 inches. Compression ratio: 9.40:1. Brake horsepower: 250 at 4400 R.P.M. Five main bearings. Carburetor: Ford C4MF-9510D two-barrel.

MONTCLAIR SERIES — Montclairs had three horizontal chrome pieces on the front fenders, nameplates on the rear fenders and a wide band of chrome on the rear quarter panel. Buyers had their choice of cloth and vinyl or all-vinyl interiors.

MONTCLAIR I.D. NUMBERS: See 1960 Monterey I.D. numbers.

MONTCLAIR

Model Number	Body/Style Number	Body Type & Seating	Factory Price	Shipping Weight	Production Total
NA	52	4-dr Sedan-6P	3116	3996	15,520
NA	58	4-dr HT Fstbk-6P	3181	4017	8,655
NA	57	2-dr HT Fstbk-6P	3127	3927	6,459
NA	53	2-dr HT Cpe-6P	3127	3921	2,329

NOTE: Models number 57 and 58, the pillarless fastback styles, were called Mauraders.

MONTCLAIR ENGINE
See 1964 Monterey Series engine data.

PARK LANE SERIES — The Park Lane returned as Mercury's top-of-the-line series. A wide band of tire level chrome trim, running across the body sides, set it apart from other Mercurys. Its interior featured Nylon face, biscuit-design upholstery and large, walnut-tone door panel inserts. The Park Lane convertible, like the Monterey version, came with a glass rear window.

PARK LANE I.D. NUMBERS: See 1960 Monterey I.D. numbers.

PARK LANE

Model Number	Body/Style Number	Body Type & Seating	Factory Price	Shipping Weight	Production Total
NA	62	4-dr Sedan-6P	3348	4035	6,230
NA	68	4-dr HT Fstbk-5P	3413	4056	3,658
NA	67	2-dr HT Fstbk-5P	3359	3966	2,721
NA	63	2-dr HT Cpe-6P	3359	3960	1,786
NA	64	4-dr HT Sed-6P	3413	4050	2,402
NA	65	2-dr Conv-6P	3549	4066	1,967

NOTE: Models number 67 and 68, the pillarless fastback styles, were called Maurauders.

PARK LANE ENGINE
See 1964 Monterey Series engine data.

1964 Mercury, Colony Park 4-dr station wagon, V-8

STATION WAGONS SERIES — The Commuter station wagon was based on the Monterey. The Colony Park had mahogany-toned side paneling.

STATION WAGONS I.D. NUMBERS: See 1960 Monterey I.D. numbers.

STATION WAGONS

Model Number	Body/Style Number	Body Type & Seating	Factory Price	Shipping Weight	Production Total
NA	72	4-dr Commuter-6P	3236	4259	3,484
NA	76	4-dr Colony Park-6P	3434	4275	4,234
NA	72	4-dr Commuter-9P	3306	4271	1,839
NA	76	4-dr Colony Park-9P	3504	4287	5,624

STATION WAGONS ENGINE
See 1964 Monterey Series engine data.

CHASSIS FEATURES: Wheelbase: 120 inches. Overall length: (passenger cars) 215.5; (station wagons) 210.3 inches. Tires: 8.00 x 14.

POWERTRAIN OPTIONS: A three-speed manual transmission was standard. Four-speed manual and Multi-Drive automatic transmissions were optional. The four-speed was not available in station wagons. A power transfer rear axle was offered at extra cost. Optional engines included: 266 horsepower 390 cubic inch V-8 (station wagons only); 300 horsepower 390 cubic inch V-8 (four-barrel); 330 horsepower 390 cubic inch V-8 (four-barrel); 410 horsepower 427 cubic inch V-8 (four-barrel) and 425 horsepower 427 cubic inch V-8 (dual four-barrels). The last two engines were not available in station wagons.

CONVENIENCE OPTIONS: Air conditioner ($430). Heavy-duty battery ($42.50). Bucket seats ($160.90). Console and tachometer ($88.80). Courtesy light group ($23.20). Electric clock in Monterey ($16.10). Power steering ($106). Tinted glass ($43). Tinted windshield ($28). Station wagon luggage rack ($64.40). Padded dash ($21.30). Two-tone paint ($22). Power brakes ($43.20). Six-Way power seats ($96.50). Power windows ($106.20). Pushbutton AM radio ($61.10). AM/FM radio ($148.60). Speed control ($92.70). Tilting steering wheel ($43.10). Windshield washer ($13.70). Vinyl roof ($88.80). Wire wheel covers ($45.20).

Historical Footnotes: Three of the least popular options on full-size Mercurys this year (and their installation rates) were four-speed manual transmission (.9 percent), locking differential (four percent) and tilting steering wheel (two percent). Maurader was the name given full-size Mercury fastback two-door and four-door hardtops. Mercurys won five NASCAR Grand National races in 1964. The Comet Boss Dragster, Mercury's counterpart to Ford's Fairlane Thunderbolt, was introduced.

COMET 202 SERIES — The restyled Comet had vertical headlights which made it look more like a Ford than a Merc. The grille used a horizontal bar theme. Side chrome was limited to the roof quarter panel and three thin horizontal pieces on the front fenders. Wraparound rectangular taillights were used on all body types, except the station wagon, which used suare ones. Front seat belts, a heater and defroster and front and rear arm rests were standard equipment.

COMET 202 I.D. NUMBERS: See 1960 Comet I.D. numbers.

COMET 202

Model Number	Body/Style Number	Body Type & Seating	Factory Price	Shipping Weight	Production Total
NA	01	4-dr Sedan-6P	2163	2335	23,501
NA	02	2-dr Sedan-6P	2108	2295	32,425
NA	32	4-dr Sta Wag-6P	2438	2495	4,814

COMET 202 ENGINE
Six: Overhead valves. Cast iron block. Displacement: 200 cubic inches. Bore and stroke: 3.68 x 3.12 inches. Compression ratio: 9.20:1. Seven main bearings. Carburetor: Ford C50F-9510E one-barrel.

COMET 404 SERIES — Full-length body side chrome and side window moldings set the 404 apart from the 202 series. The Villager Station Wagon had imitation wood paneling and came with a power tailgate window.

COMET 404 I.D. NUMBERS: See 1960 Comet I.D. numbers.

COMET 404

Model Number	Body/Style Number	Body Type & Seating	Factory Price	Shipping Weight	Production Total
NA	11	4-dr Sedan-6P	2248	2340	18,628
NA	12	2-dr Sedan-6P	2193	2305	10,900
NA	34	4-dr Sta Wag-6P	2523	2500	5,226
NA	36	4-dr Sta Wag-6P	2703	2500	1,592

NOTE: Model number 36, a wood-grain panelled station wagon, was called the Villager.

COMET 404 ENGINE
See 1965 Comet 202 Series engine data.

CALIENTE SERIES — The most luxurious Comet remained the Caliente. It had a special horizontal chrome bar taillight treatment that blended into the rear deck panel. In addition, it featured mid tire level molding. Carpeting, a padded dash and door courtesy lights were among the standard items offered on the Caliente. The convertible had a power top.

CALIENTE I.D. NUMBERS: See 1960 Comet I.D. numbers.

CALIENTE

Model Number	Body/Style Number	Body Type & Seating	Factory Price	Shipping Weight	Production Total
NA	22	4-dr Sedan-6P	2327	2370	20,337
NA	23	2-dr HT Cpe 6P	2352	2395	29,247
NA	25	2-dr Conv-6P	2607	2588	6,035

CALIENTE ENGINE
See 1965 Comet 202 Series engine data.

1965 Mercury, Comet Cyclone 2-dr hardtop sport coupe, V-8

CYCLONE SERIES — A vinyl roof, chrome wheels, curb moldings, distinctive grille, designs, two hood scoops, bucket seats with console and a tachometer were standard on the Cyclone two-door hardtop.

CYCLONE I.D. NUMBERS: See 1960 Comet I.D. numbers.

CYCLONE

Model Number	Body/Style Number	Body Type & Seating	Factory Price	Shipping Weight	Production Total
NA	27	2-dr HT Cpe-5P	2625	2994	12,347

CYCLONE ENGINE
V-8: Overhead valves. Cast iron block. Displacement: 289 cubic inches. Bore and stroke: 4 x 2.87 inches. Compression ratio: 9.30:1. Brake horsepower: 200 at 4400 R.P.M. Five main bearings. Carburetor: Ford C5MF-9510A two-barrel.

CHASSIS FEATURES: Wheelbase: (Passenger cars) 114 inches: (109.5) (Station Wagons). Overall length: (passenger cars) 195.3 inches; (station wagons) 191.8 inches. Tires: 6.95 x 14.

POWER TRAIN OPTIONS: A three-speed manual transmission was standard. Four-speed manual and Multi-Drive automatic transmissions were optional. A 200 horsepower Cyclone 289 cubic inch V-8 (two-barrel) and a 225 horsepower Super Cyclone 289 cubic inch V-8 (four-barrel) were optional. A performance handling package could be had for $20.80. A power transfer axle cost $38. A power booster fan was $16.10.

CONVENIENCE OPTIONS: Air conditioner ($257.50). Heavy-duty battery ($7.60). Elapsed-time clock ($20). Courtesy light group ($14.80). Remote-control trunk lid release ($11). Emergency flasher ($12.80). Tinted glass ($27.80). Tinted windshield ($18.10). Backup lights ($10.70). Station wagon luggage rack ($64.35). Remote-control outside rearview mirror ($12). Curb molding ($16.10). Padded dash ($18.40). Padded visors ($4.50). Two-tone paint ($19.40). Power brakes ($43.20). Power steering ($86.30). Station wagon power tailgate window ($29.75). Pushbutton AM radio ($58.50). AM/FM radio ($129.30). Rally Pac ($83); same in Cyclone ($40). Retractable front seat belts ($7.10). Front bucket seats with console in Caliente hardtop and convertible ($131.30). Front bucket seats in two-door sedan only ($70.80). Size 6.95 x 14 whitewall tires. Tachometer ($43.10). Vacuum gauge ($20). Wheel covers ($19.20). Wire wheel covers ($64.40); same on Cyclone ($43.20). Windshield washer and wipers ($21.80). Vinyl roof on hardtop ($75.80).

Historical footnotes: Most 1965 Comets, 65.5 percent, had automatic transmission, 51.3 percent had a six-cylinder engine and only 1.9 percent came with power windows.

MONTEREY SERIES — The 1965 Monterey had a horizontal bar grille with the mid-section protruding slightly. Thin vertical signal lights were located at the tips of the front fenders. Outside of the large front fender trim pieces and rocker panel moldings, the Monterey's sides were relatively clean of 'doodads'. The taillights were vertical and fully integrated into the bumper and rear fenders. Carpeting, front seat belts and a heater and defroster were among the standard features. The Breezeway sedan, with its retractable rear window, was offered once again.

MONTEREY I.D. NUMBERS: See 1960 Monterey I.D. numbers.

MONTEREY

Model Number	Body/Style Number	Body Type & Seating	Factory Price	Shipping Weight	Production Total
NA	44	4-dr Sedan-6P	2782	3853	23,363
NA	43	2-dr Sedan-6P	2711	3788	5,775
NA	47	2-dr HT Fstbk-6P	2843	3823	16,857
NA	42	4-dr Breezeway-6P	2845	3898	19,569
NA	48	4-dr HT Fstbk-6P	2918	3893	10,047
NA	45	2-dr Conv-6P	3165	3928	4762

NOTE: Models number 47 and 48, the pillarless hardtop styles, were called Mauraders. Model number 42, the Breezeway, was a sedan with slanting and retractable rear window styling.

MONTEREY ENGINE
V-8: Overhead valves. Cast iron block. Displacement: 390 cubic inches. Bore and stroke: 4.05 x 3.78 inches. Compression ratio: 9.40:1. Brake horsepower: 250 at 4400 R.P.M. Five main bearings. Carburetor: Ford C5MF-9519-A two-barrel.

MONTCLAIR SERIES — The Montclair had a full-length, chrome middle body spear. Its nameplate was on the rear fenders. As in the Monterey Series, the Breezeway model had chrome trim on the roof quarter panels. In addition to the standard items found in Montereys, Montclair buyers received wheel covers, electric clocks and interval selector windshield wipers.

MONTCLAIR I.D. NUMBERS: See 1960 Monterey I.D. numbers.

MONTCLAIR

Model Number	Body/Style Number	Body Type & Seating	Factory Price	Shipping Weight	Production Total
NA	52	4-dr Breezeway-6P	3074	3933	18,924
NA	58	4-dr HT Fstbk-6P	3145	3928	16,977
NA	57	2-dr HT Fstbk-6P	3072	3848	9,645

NOTE: Models number 57 and 58, the pillarless hardtop styles, were Mauraders. Model number 52, the Breezeway, was a sedan with slanting and retractable rear window styling.

MONTCLAIR ENGINE
See 1965 Monterey Series engine data.

1965 Mercury, Parklane 4-dr hardtop sedan, V-8

PARK LANE SERIES — Rectangular rear fender nameplates, chrome gravel shields and a band of molding above the rocker panels, were three styling features of Park Lanes. They had more luxurious interiors than cars in the other series. Standard equipment included, padded dash, padded visors, courtesy lights, visor-mounted vanity mirrors and a trip odometer.

PARK LANE I.D. NUMBERS: See 1960 Monterey I.D. numbers.

PARK LANE

Model Number	Body/Style Number	Body Type & Seating	Factory Price	Shipping Weight	Production Total
NA	62	4-dr Breezeway-6P	3301	3988	8,335
NA	68	4-dr HT Fstbk-6P	3372	3983	14,211
NA	67	2-dr HT Fstbk-6P	3299	3908	6,853
NA	65	2-dr Conv-6P	3526	4013	3,008

NOTE: Models number 67 and 68, the pillarless hardtop styles, were called Mauraders. Model number 62, the Breezeway, was a sedan with slanting and retractable rear window styling.

PARK LANE ENGINE
V-8: Overhead valves. Cast iron block. Displacement: 390 cubic inches. Bore and stroke: 4.05 x 3.78 inches. Compression ratio: 10.10:1. Brake horsepower: 300 at 4600 R.P.M. Five main bearings. Carburetor: Ford C5AF-9510E four-barrel.

STATION WAGONS SERIES — The third seat, in Mercury wagons equipped with such an option, faced the rear. The rear quarter panels contained wind vanes. The Colony Park had simulated wood paneling.

STATION WAGONS I.D. NUMBERS: See 1960 Monterey I.D. numbers.

STATION WAGONS

Model Number	Body/Style Number	Body Type & Seating	Factory Price	Shipping Weight	Production Total
NA	72	4-dr Commuter-6P	3169	4178	8,081
NA	76	4-dr Colony Park-6P	3364	4213	15,294

STATION WAGONS ENGINE
See 1965 Monterey Series engine data.

CHASSIS FEATURES: (passenger cars) 123 inches; (station wagons) 119 inches. Overall length: (passenger cars) 218.4 inches; (station wagons) 214.5 inches. Tires: 8.15 x 15.

POWER TRAIN OPTIONS: A three-speed manul transmission was standard. Overdrive, four-speed manual and Multi-Drive Merc-O-Matic automatic transmissions were optional. A 255 horsepower 390 cubic inch V-8 (two-barrel) was standard on Montclairs and station wagons equipped with automatic. A 300 horsepower 390 cubic inch V-8 (four-barrel); a 330 horsepower 390 cubic inch V-8 (four-barrel) and a 425 horsepower 427 cubic inch V-8 (dual four-barrel) were optional. The latter engine was offered only with cars that had a four-speed manual gearbox. It was not available in station wagons. A power transfer axle could be had for $42.50.

CONVENIENCE OPTIONS: Air conditioner ($430). Bucket seats in Monterey hardtop and convertible ($160.90). Recling passenger side bucket seat in Park Lane ($45.10). Console and tachometer in Monterey ($88.80). Courtesy light group ($23.20). Remote-control trunk lid release in Monterey sedans ($34.80); in Monterey hardtops and Commuter ($21.90); in Monterey convertible ($14.20). Power door locks in two-doors ($37.30); in four doors ($52.80). Speed-actuated rear door locks ($25.80). Electric clock ($16.10). Tinted windshield ($3.00). Tinted glass ($43). Luggage rack ($64.40). Padded dash ($21.30). Padded visors ($5.80). Two-tone paint ($22). Power antenna ($29.60). Power brakes ($43.20). Four-way power bucket seat, driver's side ($92.10). Six-Way power seats ($96.50). Power windows ($106.20). Power vent windows ($52.80). Pushbutton AM radio ($61.10). AM/FM pushbutton radio with rear speaker ($148.60). Rear seat speaker ($19.30). Studiosonic rear speaker ($53.50). Third seat in station wagons ($76.80). Retractable front seat belts ($7.10). Speed control ($92.70). Sports package in Park Lane two-door hardtop and convertible ($423). Tilting steering wheel ($43.10). Whitewall tires ($40.56). All-vinyl DeLuxe trim in Monterey hardtops and four-door sedans ($70.80). Leather trim in Park Lanes with bench seats ($98.80). Visibility group in Monterey ($30.80). Trip odometer ($8.90). Wheel covers with spinners on Monterey ($38.40); on Montclair and Park Lane ($19.20). DeLuxe wheel covers on Monterey ($19.20). Custom wheel covers on Monterey ($54.10); on Montclair and Park Lane ($34.90). Wire wheel covers on Monterey ($64.40); on Montclair and Park Lane ($45.20). Vinyl roof ($88.80). Windshield washer ($13.70).

Historical footnotes: Just .3 percent of full-size Mercs came with a four-speed manual gear box. Other unpopular options included a tilting steering wheel (6.4 percent) and locking differential (4.5 percent). Mercurys won one NASCAR Grand National race in 1965. The 427 cubic inch single-overhead cam engine was added to the Comet Boss Dragster car for '65.

1966 MERCURY

1966 Mercury, Comet '202' 2-dr sedan, 6-cyl

COMET 202 SERIES — The Comet grew this year, from a compact to an intermediate. A stacked headlight arrangement was continued. The two-level grille consisted of criss-cross pieces. Three bent vertical bars were on the front fenders. A heater and defroster were standard equipment.

COMET 202 I.D. NUMBERS: See 1960 Comet I.D. numbers.

COMET 202

Model Number	Body/Style Number	Body Type & Seating	Factory Price	Shipping Weight	Production Total
NA	01	2-dr Sedan-6P	2206	2779	35,964
NA	02	4-dr Sedan-6P	2263	2823	20,440

COMET 202 ENGINE
Six: Overhead valves. Cast iron block. Displacement: 200 cubic inches. Bore and stroke: 3.68 x 3.13 inches. Compression ratio: 9.20:1. Brake horsepower: 120 at 4400 R.P.M. Carburetor: Ford C3PF-9510-A one-barrel.

CAPRI SERIES — Rocker panel mouldings, front fender medallions and chrome side window trim were styling features of the Capri intermediate. Carpeting was standard.

CAPRI I.D. NUMBERS: See 1960 Comet I.D. numbers.

CAPRI

Model Number	Body/Style Number	Body Type & Seating	Factory Price	Shipping Weight	Production Total
NA	12	4-dr Sedan-6P	2378	2844	15,635
NA	13	2-dr HT Cpe-6P	2400	2876	15,031

CAPRI ENGINE
See 1966 Comet 202 Series engine data.

CALIENTE SERIES — Calientes had chrome trimmed wheel well openings and moldings above the rocker panels. Their interiors were a bit plusher than those on other Comets.

CALIENTE I.D. NUMBERS: See 1960 Comet I.D. numbers.

CALIENTE

Model Number	Body/Style Number	Body Type & Seating	Factory Price	Shipping Weight	Production Total
NA	22	4-dr Sedan-6P	2453	2846	17,933
NA	23	2-dr HT Cpe-6P	2475	2882	25,862
NA	25	2-dr Conv-6P	2735	3143	3,922

CALIENTE ENGINE
See 1966 Comet 202 Series engine data.

1966 Mercury, Comet Cyclone 'GT' 2-dr hardtop spt cpe, V-8

CYCLONE SERIES — A special front fender nameplate, body strips above the rocker panels and a different, horizontal bar grille, made it easy to tell a Cyclone from other Comets. Bucket seats and chromed wheels were standard.

CYCLONE I.D. NUMBERS: See 1960 Comet I.D. numbers.

CYCLONE

Model Number	Body/Style Number	Body Type & Seating	Factory Price	Shipping Weight	Production Total
NA	27	2-dr HT Cpe-5P	2700	3074	6,889
NA	29	2-dr Conv-5P	2961	3321	1,305
NA	26	2-dr GT Conv-5P	3152	3595	2,158
NA	28	2-dr GT Cpe-5P	2891	3315	13,812

CYCLONE ENGINE
V-8: Overhead valves. Cast iron block. Displacement: 289 cubic inches. Bore and stroke: 4 x 2.87 inches. Compression ratio: 9.30:1. Brank horsepower: 200 at 4400 R.P.M. Five main bearings. Carburetor: Ford C40F-9510-AM two-barrel.

STATION WAGONS SERIES — The Voyager was based on the Capri series. The Villager was a bit more luxurious and featured simulated wood grain body panels.

STATION WAGONS I.D. NUMBERS: See 1960 Comet I.D. numbers.

STATION WAGONS

Model Number	Body/Style Number	Body Type & Seating	Factory Price	Shipping Weight	Production Total
NA	06	Voyager-6P	2553	3201	7,595
NA	16	Villager-6P	2,780	3,244	3,880

STATION WAGONS ENGINE
See 1966 Comet 202 Series engine data.

CHASSIS FEATURES: Wheelbase: (Passenger cars) 116 inches; (Station wagons) 113 inches. Overall length: (Passenger cars) 203 inches; (Station wagons) 199.9 inches. Tires: (Passenger cars) 6.95 x 14; (Station wagons) 7.75 x 14.

POWERTRAIN OPTIONS: A three-speed manual transmission standard. Four-speed manual and Merc-O-Matic transmissions were optional. A 200 horsepower 289 cubic inche V-8 (two-barrel); 265 horsepower 390 cubic inch V-8 (two-barrel); 275 horsepower 390 cubic inch V-8 (four-barrel) and a 335 horsepower 390 cubic inch V-8 were offered. The last engine was standard with the GT option. It also included twin hood scoops; body strips; distinctive grille; special emblems; heavy-duty suspension; power booster fan, and dual exhaust. The Cyclone option was called GTA if ordered with an automatic transmission. A power transfer axle was also available.

CONVENIENCE OPTIONS: Air conditioner ($257.50). Heavy-duty battery ($7.60). Elapsed-time clock ($20). Courtesy light group ($14.80). Remote-control trunk lid release ($11). Emergency flasher ($12.80). Tinted glass ($27.10). Tinted windshield ($18.10). Backup lights ($10.70). Station wagon luggage rack ($64.35). Remote-control outside rearview mirror ($12). Curb molding ($16.10). Padded dash ($18.40). Padded visors ($4.50). Two-tone paint ($19.40). Power brakes ($43.20). Power steering ($86.30). Power tailgate window ($29.75). Pushbutton AM radio ($58.50). AM/FM radio ($129.30). Rally Pac, in Cyclone ($40); in other models ($83). Retractable front seat belts ($7.10). Caliente hardtop convertible front bucket seats with console ($131.30). Front bucket seats only in two-door sedan ($79.80). Size 6.95 x 14 white-wall tires. Tachometer ($43.10). Vacuum gauge ($20). Wheel covers ($19.20). Wire wheel covers in Cyclone ($43.20); in other ($64.40). Windshield washer and wipers ($21.80). Vinyl roof on hardtops ($75.80).

HISTORICAL FOOTNOTE: Most 1966 Comets, 72 percent had automatic transmissions. A V-8 engine was ordered in 63.7 percent of these cars. The millionth Comet built was a Caliente four-door sedan. The Cyclone GT was chosen as the official pace car at the 1966 Indianapolis 500 race.

MONEREY SERIES — The new 1966 Mercury grille consisted of horizontal bars and a thin vertical piece in the center. Small signal lights wrapped around the front fenders. Large, chrome ringed taillights, at the ends of the rear fenders, appeared to be bumper-integrated. The Mercury name was written on the hood and trunk lid. A Monterey nameplate appeared on the rear fenders. A large, crisscross pattern trim piece was on the front fenders. Carpeting with fabric and vinly upholstery were standard, except in the convertible, which had an all-vinyl interior.

MONTEREY I.D. NUMBERS: See 1960 Monterey I.D. numbers.

MONTEREY

Model Number	Body/Style Number	Body Type & Seating	Factory Price	Shipping Weight	Production Total
NA	42	4-dr Breezeway-6P	2917	3966	14,174
NA	43	2-dr Sedan-6P	2783	3835	2,487
NA	44	4-dr Sedan-6P	2854	3903	18,998
NA	45	2-dr Conv-6P	3237	4039	3,279
NA	47	2-dr HT Cpe-6P	2915	3885	19,103
NA	48	4-dr HT Sed-6P	2990	3928	7,647

NOTE: Model number 42, the four-door Breezeway, was a sedan with slanting and retractable rear window styling.

MONTEREY ENGINE
V-8: Overhead valves. Cast iron block. Displacement: 390 cubic inches. Bore and stroke: 4.05 x 3.78 inches. Compression ratio: 9.50:1. Brake horsepower: 265 at 4400 R.P.M. Five main bearings. Carburetor: Ford C6AF-9510-AM two-barrel.

1966 Mercury, Montclair 2-dr hardtop, V-8

MONTCLAIR SERIES — Fender-to-fender upper body moldings and chrome rocker panels were two styling features of the Montclair. An electric clock, interval selector windshield wipers, DeLuxe steering wheel and wheel covers were standard.

MONTCLAIR I.D. NUMBERS: See 1960 Monterey I.D. numbers.

MONTCLAIR

Model Number	Body/Style Number	Body Type & Seating	Factory Price	Shipping Weight	Production Total
NA	54	4-dr Sedan-6P	3087	3921	11,856
NA	57	2-dr HT Cpe-6P	3144	3887	11,290
NA	58	4-dr HT Sed-6P	3217	3971	15,767

MONTCLAIR ENGINE
See 1966 Monterey Series engine data.

1966 Mercury, Parklane 4-dr 'Breezeway' sedan, V-8

PARK LANE SERIES — A wide, full-length molding (at tire level) on the body sides and rear deck panel trim, were distinguishing features of the Park Lane.

PARK LANE I.D. NUMBERS: See 1960 Monterey I.D. numbers.

PARK LANE

Model Number	Body/Style Number	Body Type & Seating	Factory Price	Shipping Weight	Production Total
NA	62	4-dr Breezeway-6P	3389	4051	8,696
NA	65	2-dr Conv-6P	3608	4148	2,546
NA	67	2-dr HT Cpe-6P	3387	3971	8,354
NA	68	4-dr HT Sed-6P	3460	4070	19,204

NOTE: Model number 62, the four-door Breezeway, was a sedan with slanting and retractable rear window styling.

PARK LANE ENGINE
V-8: Overhead valves. Cast iron block. Displacement: 410 cubic inches. Bore and stroke: 4.05 x 3.98 inches. Compression ratio: 10.50:1. Brake horsepower: 330 at 4600 R.P.M. Carburetor: Ford C6MF-9510-E four-barrel.

S-55 SERIES — The sporty S-55 had full-length mid-body chrome trim, chrome rocker panels and a rear fender medallion. Bucket seats, a center consol and dual exhausts, were a few of its standard features.

S-55 SERIES I.D. NUMBERS: See 1960 Monterey I.D. numbers.

S-55

Model Number	Body/Style Number	Body Type & Seating	Factory Price	Shipping Weight	Production Total
NA	46	2-dr Conv-5P	3614	4148	669
NA	49	2-dr HT Cpe-5P	3292	4031	2916

S-55 ENGINE
V-8: Overhead valves. Cast iron block. Displacement: 428 cubic inches. Bore and stroke: 4.13 x 3.98 inces. Compression ratio: 10.50:1. Carburetor: Ford C6AF-9510-AD four-barrel.

STATION WAGONS SEREIS — Commuters were trimmed like Montclairs and shared the same standard features. The Colony Park had simulated wood panels and DeLuxe wheel covers. A power tailgate window was standard in the top-of-the-line station wagon.

STATION WAGON I.D. NUMBERS: See 1960 Monterey I.D. numbers.

STATION WAGONS

Model Number	Body/Style Number	Body Type & Seating	Factory Price	Shipping Weight	Production Total
NA	72	4-dr Commuter-6P	3240	4280	6,847
NA	76	4-dr Colony Park-6P	3502	4332	18,894

STATION WAGONS ENGINE
See 1966 Monterey Series engine data.

CHASSIS FEATURES: Wheelbase: (Passenger cars) 123 inches; (Station wagons) 119 inches. Overall: (Passenger cars) 220.4; (Station wagons) 216.5. Tires: (Passenger cars) 8.15 x 15; (Station wagons) 8.45 x 15.

POWERTRAIN OPTIONS: A three-speed manual transmission standard in all but the S-55, which came with either a four-speed manual or Multi-Drive automatic transmission. These transmissions were both optional in the other series, except the four-speed was not available in station wagons. A 275 horsepower 390 cubic inch V-8 (two-barrel); a 330 horsepower 410 cubic inch V-8 (four-barrel) and a 345 horsepower 428 cubic inch V-8 (four-barrel) were offered. A power transfer and a high performance axle were optional.

CONVENIENCE OPTIONS: Air conditioner ($430). Bucket seats in Monterey hardtop and convertible. ($160.90) Reclining passenger side bucket seat in Park Lane ($45.10). Console and tachometer in Monterey ($88.80). Courtesy light group ($23.20). Remote-control trunk lid release ($11). Decor group in Monterey sedans ($34.80); in Monterey hardtop and Commuters ($21.90); in Monterey convertible ($14.20). Power door locks in two-doors ($37.30); in four-doors ($52.80). Speed-actuated rear door locks ($25.80). Electric clock ($16.10). Tinted windshield ($3). Tinted glass ($43). Luggage rack ($64.40). Padded dash ($21.30). Padded visors ($5.80). Two-tone paint ($22). Power antenna ($29.60). Power brakes ($43.20). Four-Way power bucket seat driver's side ($92.10). Six-Way power seats ($96.50). Power windows ($106.20). Power vent windows ($52.80). Pushbutton AM radio ($61.10). AM/FM pushbutton radio with rear speaker ($148.60). Rear seat speaker ($19.30). Studio-sonic rear speaker ($53.50). Third seat in station wagons ($75.80). Retractable front seat belts ($7.10). Sports package in Park Lane two-door hardtop and convertible ($423). Tilting steering wheel ($43.10). Whitewall tires ($40.56). All-vinyl DeLuxe trim in Monterey hardtops and four-door sedans ($70.80). Leather trim in Park Lane bench seats ($98.80). Visibility group in Monterey ($30.80). Trip odometer ($8.90). Wheel covers with spinners in Monterey ($38.40); in Montclair and Park Lane ($19.20). DeLuxe wheel covers on Monterey ($54.10); on Montclair and Park Lane ($34.90). Wire wheel covers on Monterey ($64.40); on Montclair and Park Lane ($45.20). Vinyl roof ($88.80). Windshield washer ($13.70). Cornering lights.

Historical footnotes: The most popular options in full-size 1966 Mercurys included: automatic transmission (98.2 percent) power steering (97 percent) tinted glass (69.7 percent) and power brakes (65.6 percent). Mercurys won two NASCAR Grand National races in 1966.

1967 MERCURY

COMET 202 SERIES — Comet styling was close to that of the Ford Fairlane it was based on. The horizontal grille, with a vertical piece in the center, was framed by stacks of two headlights on each fender. The sides were clean, except for a '202' nameplate on the front fenders. The vertical taillights were on the ends of the rear fenders. About the only *extras* not optional on the '202' were a dome light and a cigarette lighter.

COMET 202 I.D. NUMBERS: See 1960 Comet I.D. numbers.

COMET 202

Model Number	Body/Style Number	Body Type & Seating	Factory Price	Shipping Weight	Production Total
NA	01	2-dr Sedan-6P	2284	2787	14,251
NA	02	4-dr Sedan-6P	2336	2825	10,281

COMET 202 ENGINE
Six: Overhead valves. Cast iron block. Displacement: 200 cubic inches. Bore and stroke: 3.68 x 3.13 inches. Compression ratio: 9.20:1. Brake horsepower: 120 at 4400 R.P.M. Carburetor: Autolite C7DF-9510-A one-barrel.

CAPRI SERIES — The Capri had nearly full-length, mid body side moldings and nameplates on the rear quarter panel. Vinyl and fabric or all-vinyl upholstery, deep loop carpeting and rear arm rests were among standard features.

CAPRI I.D. NUMBERS: See 1960 Comet I.D. numbers.

CAPRI

Model Number	Body/Style Number	Body Type & Seating	Factory Price	Shipping Weight	Production Total
NA	06	4-dr Sedan-6P	2436	2860	9,292
NA	07	2-dr HT Cpe-6P	2459	2889	11,671

CAPRI ENGINE
See 1967 Comet 202 Series engine data.

CALIENTE SERIES — Bright fender ornaments, rocker panel and wheel openings moldings and full-length upper-body pin stripes set the Caliente apart from other Comets. Its interior featured wood-grained dash and door panels, luxury arm rests and paddle-type door handles.

CALIENTE I.D. NUMBERS: See 1960 Comet I.D. numbers.

CALIENTE

Model Number	Body/Style Number	Body Type & Seating	Factory Price	Shipping Weight	Production Total
NA	10	4-dr Sedan-6P	2535	2871	9,153
NA	11	2-dr HT Cpe-6P	2558	2901	9,966
NA	12	3-dr Conv-6P	2818	3170	1,539

CALIENTE ENGINE
See 1967 Comet 202 Series engine data.

1967 Mercury, Comet Cyclone 'GT' 2-dr hardtop coupe, V-8

CYCLONE SERIES — The Cyclone looked about the same as the Caliente, less the fender ornaments. Its grille had fewer horizontal pieces. The rear deck panel was blacked-out and the word Cyclone was spelled out on it. Bucket seats and all-vinyl upholstery were standard.

CYCLONE I.D. NUMBERS: See 1960 Comet I.D. numbers.

CYCLONE

Model Number	Body/Style Number	Body Type & Seating	Factory Price	Shipping Weight	Production Total
NA	15	2-dr HT Cpe-5P	2737	3075	6,101
NA	16	2-dr Conv-5P	2997	2229	809

CYCLONE ENGINE
V-8: Overhead valves. Cast iron block. Displacement: 289 cubic inches. Bore and stroke: 4 x 2.87 inches. Compression ratio: 9.30:1. Brake horsepower: 200 at 4400 R.P.M. Five main bearings. Carburetor: Autolite C7DF-9510-Z two-barrel.

STATION WAGONS SERIES — Two Voyager wagon had a distinctive elongated U-shaped chrome piece on its front fenders. The Villager featured wood-grained side and tailgate panels. It came with crinkle vinyl upholstery and a dual-action tailgate.

STATION WAGONS I.D. NUMBERS: See 1960 Comet I.D. numbers.

Model Number	Body/Style Number	Body Type & Seating	Factory Price	Shipping Weight	Production Total
NA	03	4-dr Voyager-6P	2604	3230	4930
NA	08	4-dr Villager-6P	2841	3252	3140

STATION WAGONS ENGINE
Same as Comet 202.

CHASSIS FEATURES: Wheelbase: (passenger cars) 116 inches; (station wagons) 113 inches. Overall Length: (four-doors and convertibles) 203.5; (two doors) 196 inches; (station wagons) 199.9 inches. Tires: (passenger cars) 7.35 x 14; (station wagons and Cyclone GT) 7.75 x 14.

POWERTRAIN OPTION: A three-speed manual transmission was standard. Four-speed manual and Merc-O-Matic automatic transmissions were optional. A 200 horsepower 289 cubic inch V-8 (two-barrel); 270 horsepower 390 cubic inch V-8 (two-barrel) and a 320 horsepower 390 cubic inch V-8 (four-barrel) were available. The last engine was standard in the Cyclone GT performance package, which also included dual exhausts; racing stripes; wide oval Nylon whitewall tires; heavy-duty suspension; 3.25:1 axle ratio; power booster fan; twin hood scoops and power disc brakes. A performance handling package was offered on cars equipped with the 270 horsepower 390 cubic inch V-8. It featured higher rate front and rear springs, large diameter stabilizer bar and heavy-duty shocks. Buyers could also order a high-performance or power transfer axle.

CONVENIENCE OPTIONS: Air conditioning ($355.95). Heavy-duty battery ($7.44). Bright window frames ($17.70). Electric clock ($15.76). Remote-control deck lid release ($12.65). Tinted windshield ($19.50). Luggage rack on station wagons ($66.99). Right hand side view mirror ($6.95). Outside rearview mirror with remote-control ($9.60). Curb moulding ($15.76). Oxford roof ($84.25). Two-tone paint ($27.06). Power brakes ($42.29). Power disc brakes ($84.25). Four-Way power bench seat ($62.45). Power steering ($95). Power windows ($100.10). AM radio with antenna ($60.05). AM/FM radio with antenna ($133.65). Rear seat speaker ($15.60). DeLuxe seat belts, front and rear with warning light ($10.40). Station wagon third seat with two belts ($51.31). Shoulder belts ($27.06). Stero-sonic tape system ($128.50). Dual-action station wagon tailgate ($45.40). Tachometer ($47.30). Vinyl interior for Comet 202 models ($27.47). Wire wheel covers ($69.52). Styled steel wheels ($115.15). Interval selector windshield wipers ($11.59). Courtesy light group ($19.69). Wide oval, whitewall Nylon tires ($82.94).

Historical footnotes: Three of the most popular Comet options (and their attachment rates) were automatic transmission (82.4 percent), V-8 engine (67.4 percent) and power steering (49.6 percent). A total of 3,419 Cyclone hardtops and 378 convertibles were sold with the GT performance package.

1967 Mercury Cougar 2-dr hardtop sport coupe, V-8

COUGAR SERIES — The new Cougar was basically a dressed-up Mustang. It featured disappearing headlights, wraparound front and rear fenders and triple taillights (with sequential turn signals). The front and rear end styling were similar. Cougars came equipped with all-vinyl bucket seats, three-spoke 'sports-style' steering wheel, deep loop carpeting, DeLuxe seat belts and floor-mounted three-speed manual transmission.

COUGAR I.D. NUMBERS: See 1960 Monterey I.D. numbers.

COUGAR

Model Number	Body/Style Number	Body Type & Seating	Factory Price	Shipping Weight	Production Total
NA	91	2-dr HT Cpe-5P	2851	3005	123,672

COUGAR ENGINE
See 1967 Comet Cyclone Series engine data.

COUGAR XR-7 SERIES — The XR-7 was introduced in mid-model year. Except for a medallion on the roof's quarter panel, it looked like the standard Cougar, but it came with a wood-grained dashboard insert and fancier interior.

COUGAR XR-7 I.D. NUMBERS: See 1960 Monterey I.D. numbers.

COUGAR XR-7

Model Number	Body/Style Number	Body Type & Seating	Factory Price	Shipping Weight	Production Total
NA	93	2-dr HT Cpe-5P	3081	3015	27,221

COUGAR XR-7 ENGINE
See 1967 Comet Cyclone Series engine data.

CHASSIS FEATURES: Wheelbase: 111 inches. Overall length: 190 inches. Tires: 7.35 x 14.

POWERTRAIN OPTIONS: A three-speed manual transmission was standard, except in the XR-7, which came with a four-speed manual gear box. The four-speed was optional in the standard Cougar. Merc-O-Matic Select Shift automatic transmission was optional in both series. A 225 horsepower 289 cubic inch V-8 (four-barrel) and a 320 horsepower 390 cubic inch V-8 (four-barrel) were available. The GT performance package included: 390 cubic inch V-8; performance handling package; wide oval whitewall tires; low back pressure exhausts; power disc brakes and medallions. A power transfer axle was available.

CONVENIENCE OPTIONS: Air conditioner ($355.95). Heavy-duty battery ($7.44). Rear bumper guards ($12.95). Electric clock ($15.76). Courtesy light group ($16.85). Door edge guards ($4.40). Tinted glass ($30.25). Tinted windshield ($21.09). Deck lid luggage carrier ($32.45). Oxford roof ($84.25). Two-tone paint ($27.06). Power brakes ($42.29). Power disc brakes ($84.25). Power steering ($95). AM radio ($60.05). AM/FM radio ($133.65). AM radio with Stereo-Sonic tape system ($188.50). Front bench seat with center arm rest ($24.42). Shoulder belts ($27.06). Speed conrol ($71.30). Sports console ($57). Tilting steering wheel ($60.05). Comfort-weave vinyl interior ($33.05). DeLuxe wheel covers ($18.79). Wire wheel covers (69.51). Visual check panel ($39.50). Styled steel wheels ($115.15).

Historical footnotes: Only 7,412 Cougars came with the optional front bench seat. Just 5.3 percent were equipped with a four-speed manual transmission.

MONTEREY SERIES — The center section of the horizontal bar grille protruded slightly and the signal lights were now located in the front bumpers. Wheel well openings had chrome moldings. The only additional side trim on the Monterey was a front fender criss-cross pattern trim piece and the Monterey name on the side. A fabric and vinyl interior was standard, except in the convertible, which had all-vinyl upholstery. An S-55 sports package was optional on the Monterey convertible and two-door hardtop.

MONTEREY I.D. NUMBERS: See 1960 Monterey I.D. numbers.

MONTEREY

Model Number	Body/Style Number	Body Type & Seating	Factory Price	Shipping Weight	Production Total
NA	44	4-dr Sedan-6P	2904	3798	15,177
NA	44	4-dr Breezeway 6P	2904	3847	5910
NA	45	2-dr Conv-6P	3311	3943	2673
NA	47	2-dr HT Cpe-6P	2985	3820	16,910
NA	48	4-dr HT Sed-6P	3059	3858	8013

NOTE: Model number 44, the four-door Breezeway, was a sedan with slanting and retractable rear window styling.

MONTEREY ENGINE
V-8: Overhead valves. Cast iron block. Displacement: 390 cubic inches. Bore and stroke: 4.05 x 3.78 inches. Compression ratio: 10.50:1. Brake horsepower: 270 at 4400 R.P.M. Five main bearings.
Carburetor: Holley C70F-9510-A four-barrel.

MONTCLAIR SERIES — The Montclair had full-length upper body mouldings. A nameplate was located on the rear fenders. Standard features included DeLuxe wheel covers, electric clock, DeLuxe steering wheel and DeLuxe front and rear seat belts with reminder light. Regular equipment was listed as: carpeting; padded dash and visors; two-speed windshield wipers; windshield washers; emergency flasher; courtesy light group and remote-conrol outside rearview mirror. These same features were also found in Monterey models for 1967.

MONTCLAIR I.D. NUMBERS: See 1960 Mercury I.D. numbers.

MONTCLAIR

Model Number	Body/Style Number	Body Type & Seating	Factory Price	Shipping Weight	Production Total
NA	54	4-dr Sedan-6P	3187	3863	5783
NA	54	4-dr Breezeway-6P	3187	3881	4151
NA	57	2-dr HT Cpe-6P	3244	3848	4118
NA	58	4-dr HT Sed-6P	3316	3943	5870

NOTE: Model number 54, the four-door Breezeway, was a sedan with slanting and retractable rear window styling.

MONTCLAIR ENGINE
See 1967 Monterey Series engine data.

PARK LANE SERIES — Full-length, tire level moldings, wheel well chrome trim and front fender emblems were styling features of the Park Lane. Standard equipment included an automatic parking brake release, rear seat arm rests, vanity mirror, spare tire cover and power front disc brakes.

PARK LANE I.D. NUMBERS: See 1960 Monterey I.D. numbers.

PARK LANE

Model Number	Body/Style Number	Body Type & Seating	Factory Price	Shipping Weight	Production Total
NA	64	4-dr Breezeway-6P	3736	4011	4163
NA	65	2-dr Conv-6P	3984	4114	1191
NA	67	2-dr HT Cpe-6P	3752	3947	2196
NA	68	4-dr HT Sed-6P	3826	3992	5412

NOTE: Model number 64, the four-door Breezeway, was a sedan with slanting and retractable rear window styling.

PARK LANE ENGINE
V-8: Overhead valves. Cast iron block. Displacement: 410 cubic inches. Bore and stroke: 4.05 x 3.98 inches. Compression ratio: 10.50:1. Brakes horsepower: 330 at 4600 R.P.H. Carburetor: C7AF-9510-AE four-barrel.

BROUGHAM SERIES — Broughams were basically similar to the Park Lane models, hich they resembled, but were slight fancier. Extra body insulation, unique interior and exterior ornamentation and wood-grain steering wheel and trim were standard features.

BROUGHAM I.D. NUMBERS: See 1960 Monterey I.D. numbers.

BROUGHAM

Model Number	Body/Style Number	Body Type & Seating	Factory Price	Shipping Weight	Production Total
NA	61	4-dr Breezeway-6P	3896	3980	3325
NA	62	4-dr HT Sed-6P	3986	4000	4189

NOTE: Model number 61, the four-door Breezeway, was a sedan with slanting and retractable rear window styling.

BROUGHAM ENGINE
See 1967 Park Lane Series engine data.

1967 Mercury, Marquis 2-dr hardtop sports coupe, V-8

MARQUIS SERIES — Two noticeable features of the new Marquis two-door hardtop were a vinyl roof and five, full-length, lower body pin stripes. Power front disc brakes; wood-grain interior trim; DeLuxe body insulation; electric clock; courtesy light group; spare tire cover, and plush, fabric and vinyl upholstery were among the many standard items in the Marquis. The front seats had individual fold down arm rests.

MARQUIS I.D. NUMBERS: See 1960 Monterey I.D. numbers.

MARQUIS

Model Number	Body/Style Number	Body Type & Seating	Factory Price	Shipping Weight	Production Total
NA	69	2-dr HT Cpe-6P	3989	3995	6510

MARQUIS ENGINE
See 1967 Park Lane Series engine data.

STATION WAGONS SERIES — The Commuter station wagon had full-length upper body moldings. The Colony Park had wood-grain panels outlined by chrome trim. Both wagons had a heater and defroster and dual-action tailgate. In addition, the Colony Park came with an electric clock; DeLuxe wheel covers; DeLuxe steering wheel; power rear tailgate window; power front disc brakes and all-vinyl or parchment Mosaic fabric interiors.

STATION WAGONS I.D. NUMBERS: See 1960 Monterey I.D. numbers.

STATION WAGONS

Model Number	Body/Style Number	Body Type & Seating	Factory Price	Shipping Weight	Production Total
NA	72	4-dr Commuter-6P	3289	4178	7898
NA	76	4-dr Colony Park-6P	3657	4258	18,680

STATION WAGONS ENGINE
See 1967 Monterey Series engine data.

CHASSIS FEATURES: Wheelbase: (passenger cars) 123 inches; (station wagons) 119 inches. Overall length: (passenger cars) 218.5 inches; (station wagons) 213.5 inches. Tires: (passenger cars) 8.15 x 15; (station wagons) 8.45 x 15.

POWERTRAIN OPTION: A three-speed manual transmission was standard in all, but the Park Lane and Brougham. These came with four-speed manual or Merc-O-Matic Select Shift transmission. Both of these gear boxes were optional in the other series. The four-speed was not available in station wagons. A 330 horsepower 410 cubic inch V-8 (four-barrel); 345 horsepower 427 cubic inch V-8 (four-barrel) and a 360 horsepower 428 cubic inch V-8 (four-barrel) were optional. The 345 horsepower engine was standard in the S-55 performance package, which also included dual exhausts; engine dress-up kit; heavy-duty battery; power disc brakes; DeLuxe wheel covers with spinners; deck lid applique; side paint stripe; door trim panels; bucket seats; sports console; DeLuxe steering wheel; DeLuxe sound package, and S-55 ornamentation. High performance and power transfer axles were available.

CONVENIENCE OPTIONS: Air conditioner ($421.28). Heavy-duty battery ($7.44). Deck lid release with remote control for all passenger cars ($12.65). Door edge guards, in two-doors ($4.40); in four-doors ($6.66). Dual exhausts ($31.52). Electric clock ($15.76). Tinted glass ($42.09). Tinted windshield ($27.41). Automatic headlight dimmer ($41.60). Cornering lights ($33.28). Luggage rack ($62.99). Righthand sideview mirror ($6.95). Remote-control mirror ($9.60). Curb molding ($15.81). Oxford roof, on two-door hardtops ($88.99); on four-door hardtops and sedans ($99.47); on station wagons ($131.65). Two-tone paint ($27.06). Power antenna ($28.97). Power brakes ($42.29). Power door locks, in two-doors ($44.23); in four-doors ($67.62). Power rear windows ($31.62). Six-Way power seats: bucket type ($84.25); bench type ($94.45).

Power seat for S-55: bucket type ($168.40); lounge type ($84.25); driver and passenger ($168.40). Power steering ($103.95). Power vent windows ($51.68). Power windows ($103.95). AM pushbutton radio ($62.15). AM/FM pushbutton radio ($150.84). AM radio with stereo tape system ($190.65). DeLuxe front and rear seat belts ($10.40). Monterey and Commuter shoulder belts ($27.06). Spare tire cover ($3.90). Speed control ($90.74). Tilting steering wheel ($42.19). Station wagon third seat ($95.36). DeLuxe interior trim, in Commuter ($69.30); in Colony Park($77.80). Leather with vinyl trim, in Park Lane and Marquis hardtops ($109.45). Mondero all-vinyl trim in Monterey ($69.30). Visual safety-check panel ($31.42). DeLuxe wheel covers on Monterey and Commuter ($18.79). Wheel covers with spinners, in Monterey ($18.79); in Commuter ($37.59). Wire wheel covers, on Monterey ($69.50); on others ($50.75).

Historical footnotes: A total of 4,451 Commuter and 12,915 Colony Park station wagons came with optional dual center or rear-facing third seats.

1968 MERCURY

COMET SERIES — The new Comet was restyled for 1968. It looked like a full-size Mercury that had gone on a diet. The Comet had a horizontal grille, rocker panel molding, side marker lights —, and chrome-encased, vertical taillights. Among the standard features were an energy-absorbing steering column and steering wheel; front and rear seat belts; shoulder belts; padded dash; padded sun visors; dual brakes with warning light and two-speed windshield wipers and washers.

COMET I.D. NUMBERS: See 1960 Comet I.D. numbers.

COMET

Model Number	Body/Style Number	Body Type & Seating	Factory Price	Shipping Weight	Production Total
NA	01	2-dr HT Cpe-6P	2477	3078	16,693

COMET ENGINE
Six; Overhead valves. Cast iron block. Displacement: 200 cubic inches. Bore and stroke: 3.68 x 3.13 inches. Compression ratio: 8.80:1. Brake horsepower: 115 at 3800 R.P.M. Carburetor: Autolite C80F-9510-E one barrel.

1968 Mercury, Montego MX 2-dr hardtop sports coupe, V-8

MONTEGO SERIES — The Montego looked about the same as the Comet. It had the same standard features as well, plus curb moldings, cigar lighter and glove box lock.

MONTEGO I.D. NUMBERS: See 1960 Comet I.D. numbers.

MONTEGO

Model Number	Body/Style Number	Body Type & Seating	Factory Price	Shipping Weight	Production Total
NA	06	4-dr Sedan-6P	2504	2982	18,492
NA	07	2-dr HT Cpe-6P	2552	3057	15,002

MONTEGO ENGINE
See 1968 Comet Series engine data.

MONTEGO MX SERIES — Full-length upper and lower body trim, chrome wheel well trim and a vinyl top were styling features of the Montego MX. It also had bright metal upper door frames, simulated wood inserts in the lower body molding, wood-grain door trim panels inserts and carpeting.

MONTEGO MX I.D. NUMBERS: See 1960 Comet I.D. numbers.

MONTEGO MX

Model Number	Body/Style Number	Body Type & Seating	Factory Price	Shipping Weight	Production Total
NA	08	4-dr Sta Wag-6P	2876	3379	9,328
NA	10	4-dr Sedan-6P	2657	3007	15,264
NA	11	2-dr HT Cpe-6P	2675	3081	25,827
NA	12	2-dr Conv-6P	2935	3293	3,248

MONTEGO MX ENGINE
See 1968 Comet Series engine data.

CYCLONE SERIES — Cyclones had a mid tire level body tape stripe. Those with the GT option had an upper body level racing stripe; bucket seats; wide tread whitewalls; special wheel covers; all-vinyl interior and special handling package.

CYCLONE I.D. NUMBERS: See 1960 Comet I.D. numbers.

CYCLONE

Model Number	Body/Style Number	Body Type & Seating	Factory Price	Shipping Weight	Production Total
NA	15	2-dr Fstbk Cpe-6P	2768	3254	12,260
NA	17	2-dr HT Cpe-6P	2768	3208	1,368

1968 Mercury, Cyclone GT 2-dr hardtop sports coupe, V-8

CYCLONE ENGINE
V-8: Overhead valves. Cast iron block. Displacement: 302 cubic inches. Bore and stroke: 4 x 3 inches. Compression ratio: 9.0:1. Brake horsepower: 210 at 4600 R.P.M. Carburetor: Autolite C8AF-9510-AF two-barrel.

CHASSIS FEATURES: Wheelbase: (Passenger cars) 116 inches; (Station wagons) 113 inches. Overall length: (Cyclone fastback) 206.1 inches; (others) 206 inches. Tires: 7.74 x 14.

POWERTRAIN OPTIONS: A three-speed manual transmission was standard. Heavy-duty three-speed, four-speed manual and Merc-O-Matic Select Shift automatic transmissions were optional. The heavy-duty three-speed transmission was only available with the 335 horsepower 390 cubic inch V-8. The four-speed manual transmission was not available with the six or 427 cubic inch V-8. A 210 horsepower 302 cubic inch V-8 (two-barrel); 230 horsepower 302 cubic inch V-8 (four-barrel); 265 horsepower 390 cubic inch V-8 (two-barrel); 335 horsepower 390 cubic inch V-8 (four-barrel); 335 horsepower 428 cubic inch V-8 (four-barrel) and a 390 horsepower 427 cubic inch V-8 (four-barrel) were optional. The latter two engines were offered only in hardtops. The 335 horsepower 390 cubic inch V-8 was not available in station wagons. High performance and power transfer axles were optional. A special handling package was offered on V-8 powered two-door hardtops and convertibles. It included: higher rate front and rear springs, a large diameter stabilizing bar and heavy-duty shocks.

CONVENIENCE OPTIONS: Appearance equipment, Brougham interior option includes exterior 'C' piller ornament, unique seat and door trim, Brougham script on instrument panel and DeLuxe steering wheel for Montego MX four-door sedan and two-door hardtop ($77.80). Appearance protection group, includes: vinyl twin front and rear floor mats, door edge guards and license plate frames, for two-doors, ($25.28); for four doors ($29.17). Appearance special equipment group, includes DeLuxe wheel covers; WSW tires; courtesy light group; comfort stream ventilation ($64.85). Decor group includes: wheel lip mouldings; right upper door frames for four-door only; unique lower back panel applique; DeLuxe wheel covers for hardtop only, for hardtop with special appearance equipment group ($42.11); for hardtop without ($60.95); for sedan ($54.45). Light group, includes: two instrument panel lights; glove box light; ash tray light; luggage compartment light; cargo light on wagons; rear door jam switches for four-door models ($19.50). Heavy-duty battery ($7.44). DeLuxe seat belts and seat belt reminder light includes: DeLuxe front seat shoulder belts DeLuxe buckle and color-keyed webbing with black webbing on convertible ($29.61). Front seat shoulder belts includes regular buckle and black webbing; rear seat shoulder belts regular buckle and black webbing; power disc front brakes, electric clock sports console ($50). Rear window defogger ($21.25). Tinted glass ($35.05). Tinted windshield ($21.09). Pair of adjustable headrests ($42.75). Luggage carrier for station wagons only ($62.99). Remote control left hand mirror ($9.60). Two-tone paint ($30.96). AM radio with antenna ($61.40). AM/FM radio stereo with antenna ($184.95). Reflective tape stripe ($16.85). Oxford roof on two-door hardtop ($94.55); on four-door sedan ($94.55). Bucket seats ($110.15). Third seat facing rear in station wagons only ($51.31). Four-Way power bench seat ($62.45). Four-Way power bucket seats ($62.45). Dual rear seat speakers ($26). Power steering ($95). DeLuxe steering wheels ($13.90). Tachometer ($48). Dual-action tailgate for station wagons only ($45.40). Comfort weave vinyl bench seat ($24.47). Ventilation system ($15.60). Visual check group, includes: low fuel, parking brake and door ajar warning lights ($32.45). DeLuxe wheel covers ($21.29). DeLuxe wheel covers with spinners ($20.10). Wheel covers ($41.40). Wire wheel covers with GT group or HT group ($50.75); without ($72.05). Styled steel sheels with GT or HT group ($96.36); without ($117.65). Power rear windows for station wagons ($31.62). Power side windows ($100.10). Two-speed interval selector windshield wipers ($14.19).

Historical footnotes: A tota; of 6,105 fastbacks and 334 two-door hardtops came with the Cyclone GT option. Mercurys won seven NASCAR Grand National races in 1968.

1968 Mercury, Cougar XR-7 2-dr hardtop coupe (GT-E), V-8

COUGAR SERIES — If you liked the 1967 Cougar, you probably liked the 1968. The biggest change was the addition of side marker lights. Standard equipment included; dual hydraulic brake system with warning light; front and rear seat belts; outside rear-view mirror; padded dash; padded sun visors; two-speed windshield wipers and washers; four-way emergency flasher and backup lights.

COUGAR I.D. NUMBERS: See 1960 Monterey I.D. numbers.

COUGAR

Model Number	Body/Style Number	Body Type & Seating	Factory Price	Shipping Weight	Production Total
NA	91	2-dr HT Cpe-5P	2933	3094	81,014

COUGAR ENGINE
See 1968 Cyclone Series engine data.

XR-7 SERIES — Rocker panel moldings, special wheel covers, deck lid medallions and XR-7 plaques on the rear roof pillars set the top-of-the-line Cougar apart from the basic series. Standard equipment included; an overhead console (with map and warning lights); deep loop carpeting; tachometer; trip odometer; gauges; leather trimmed vinyl seats and walnut tone instrument panel.

XR-7 I.D. NUMBERS: See 1960 Monterey I.D. numbers.

XR-7

Model Number	Body/Style Number	Body Type & Seating	Factory Price	Shipping Weight	Production Total
NA	93	2-dr HT Cpe-5P	3232	3134	32,712

XR-7 ENGINE
See 1968 Cyclone Series engine data.

CHASSIS FEATURES: Wheelbase: 111 inches. Overall length: 190.3 inches. Tires: E70 x 14.

POWERTRAIN OPTIONS: A three-speed manual transmission was standard. Heavy-duty three-speed, four-speed manual, and Select Shift Merc-O-Matic automatic transmissions were optional. The heavy-duty three-speed gear box was only available with the 325 horsepower engine. The four-speed manual was not available with the 280 or 390 horsepower V-8s. A 230 horsepower 302 cubic inch V-8 (four-barrel); 280 horsepower 390 cubic inch V-8 (two-barrel); 325 horsepower 390 cubic inch V-8 (four-barrel) and a 335 horsepower 428 cubic inch V-8 (four-barrel) were optional. The 325 horsepower engine was standard with the GT option. This package also included; stiffer front and rear springs, heavy-duty shocks, low back pressure dual exhausts, power booster fan and a large diameter stabilizer bar. The 428 cubic inch V-8 was standard in the 7.0 Litre GT-E package. It featured: twin hood scoops; styled steel wheels; quadruple trumpet exhausts; modified grille and taillight design; silver grey trim on the lower body; extra stiff front and rear springs; heavy-duty shocks and wide-thread radial-ply tires.

CONVENIENCE OPTIONS: Air conditioner ($360.90). Heavy-duty battery ($7.44). DeLuxe seat belt with reminder light ($13.05). DeLuxe front seat shoulder belts ($29.61). DeLuxe rear seat shoulder belts ($29.61). Front seat shoulder belts ($27.06). Power disc brakes ($64.85). Electric clock ($15.76). Sports console ($57). Sports console for XR-7 only ($72.55). Rear window defogger ($21.25). Tinted glass ($30.25). Tinted windshield ($21.09). Door edge guards ($4.40). Rear bumper guards ($12.95). Adjustable front seat headrests ($42.75). Remote control lefthand mirror ($9.60). Visual check panel ($39.50). Two-tone paint ($31.10). AM radio with antenna ($60.90). AM/FM stereo ($21.25). Oxford roof ($41.60). Speed control ($71.30). Power steering ($95). Tilt-away steering wheel ($66.05). Stereo-sonic tape system ($195.15). Three-speed manual transmission ($79). Four-speed manual transmission ($184.02). Four-speed manual transmission with GT group ($105.02). Merc-o-matic transmission with "302" engine ($206.65). Merc-o-matic transmission with "390" engine ($226.10). Merc-o-matic transmission with GT group ($147.10). DeLuxe wheel covers ($21.29). DeLuxe wheel covers with spinners on XR-7 ($18.79). DeLuxe wheel covers, except on XR-7 ($72.05). Styled steel wheels on XR-7 ($96.36). Styled steel wheels ($117.65). BSW tubeless tires ($36.35). WSW tubeless tires ($36.35-$73.40). Red band tubeless tires ($38.95). Space-Saver spare tires ($6.55-$19.50).

Historical footnotes: Only 2.7 percent of all 1968 Cougars were equipped with a four-speed manual gearbox, 86.8 percent had an automatic transmission 87.3 percent power steering and 38.6 percent power brakes. An XR-7 'G' was available on special order. It had hood pins, hood scoop, running lights and a vinyl top with sun roof.

MONTEREY SERIES — The Monterey had a new, equal-size horizontal bar grille which protruded at the center. The vertical signal lights wrapped around the front fenders. Rear end treatment resembled last year's. As before, the back window on cars with the Breezeway option could be lowered. Standard features included; dual brakes with warning light; energy-absorbing steering column and steering wheel; seat belts; padded dash; padded sun visors; outside rearview mirror; side marker lights; heater/defroster; ash tray light; trunk light; four-way emergency flasher; glove box light and shoulder belts.

MONTEREY I.D. NUMBERS: See 1960 Monterey I.D. numbers:

MONTEREY

Model Number	Body/Style Number	Body Type & Seating	Factory Price	Shipping Weight	Production Total
NA	44	4-dr Sedan-6P	3052	3798	30,727
NA	45	2-dr Conv-6P	3436	4114	1,515
NA	47	2-dr HT Cpe-6P	3133	3820	15,145
NA	48	4-dr HT Sed-6P	3207	3858	8,927

MONTEREY ENGINE
V-8: Overhead valves. Cast iron block. Displacement: 390 cubic inches. Bore and stroke: 4.05 x 3.78 inches. Compression ratio: 9.50:1. Brake horsepower: 265 at 4400 R.P.M. Carburetor: Autolite C8AF-9510-M two-barrel.

MONTCLAIR SERIES — DeLuxe wheel covers and full-length, tire level moldings were two exterior differences between the Montclair and the lower-priced Monterey. An electric clock was among the many standard features.

MONTCLAIR I.D. NUMBERS: See 1960 Monterey I.D. numbers.

MONTCLAIR

Model Number	Body/Style Number	Body Type & Seating	Factory Price	Shipping Weight	Production Total
NA	54	4-dr Sedan-6P	3331	3863	7,255
NA	57	2-dr HT Cpe-6P	3387	3848	3,497
NA	58	4-dr HT Sed-6P	3459	3943	4,008

MONTCLAIR ENGINE
See 1968 Monterey Series engine data.

PARK LANE SERIES — The Park Lane had full-length, tire level moldings that looked like two thin parallel strips with a narrow band of chrome between them. The wheel well lips were also chromed and there were three slanted trim pieces on the roof quarter panels. Like all full-size Mercs for 1968, the Park Lane had a redesigned, clustered dash (i.e. dash instruments were placed in close proximity to the driver). The electrical system was improved as well. A seldom-ordered Park Lane option was 'yacht paneling,' a fancy name for exterior wood-grained appliques on passenger cars.

PARK LANE I.D. NUMBERS: See 1960 Monterey I.D. numbers.

PARK LANE

Model Number	Body/Style Number	Body Type & Seating	Factory Price	Shipping Weight	Production Total
NA	64	4-dr Sedan-6P	3552	4011	7,008
NA	65	2-dr Conv-6P	3822	4114	1,112
NA	67	2-dr HT Cpe-6P	3575	3947	2,584
NA	68	4-dr HT Sed-6P	3647	3992	10,390

PARK LANE ENGINE
V-8: Overhead valves. Cast iron block. Displacement: 390 cubic inches. Bore and stroke: 4.05 x 3.78 inches. Compression ratio: 10.50:1. Brake horsepower: 315 at 4600 R.P.M. Carbuetors: Autolite C8AF-9510-B four-barrel.

MARQUIS SERIES — The Marquis was trimmed similar to the Montclair, except it came with a vinyl-covered roof. Its interior was also plusher.

MARQUIS I.D. NUMBERS: See 1960 Monterey I.D. numbers.

MARQUIS

Model Number	Body/Style Number	Body Type & Seating	Factory Price	Shipping Weight	Production Total
NA	69	2-dr HT Cpe-6P	3685	3995	3,965

MARQUIS ENGINE
See 1968 Park Lane Series engine data.

1968 Mercury, Colony Park 4-dr station wagon, V-8

STATION WAGONS SERIES — Both station wagons had full-length, tire level moldings and chrome trimmed wheel openings. The Colony Park had plank style wood-grain applique on its sides. A dual-action tailgate was standard on both.

STATION WAGONS I.D. NUMBERS: See 1960 Monterey I.D. numbers.

STATION WAGONS

Model Number	Body/Style Number	Body Type & Seating	Factory Price	Shipping Weight	Production Total
NA	72	4-drCommuter-6P	3441	4178	8,688
NA	76	4-dr Colony Park-6P	3760	4258	21,179

PRODUCTION NOTE: A total of 5,191 Commuter and 15,505 Colony Park wagons came with either a rear facing or dual-center facing rear seats.

STATION WAGONS ENGINE
See 1968 Monterey Series engine data.

CHASSIS FEATURES: Wheelbase: (Passenger cars) 123 inches; (Station wagons) 119 inches. Overall length: (Passenger cars) 220.1 inches; (Station wagons) 215.4 inches. Tires: 8.15 x 15.

POWERTRAIN OPTIONS: A three-speed manual transmission was standard, except in the Park Lane and Marquis. They came with Select Shift Merc-O-Matic transmission. This automatic was optional in the other series. A 280 horsepower 390 cubic inch V-8 (two-barrel); 315 horsepower 390 cubic inch V-8 (four-barrel); 335 horsepower 390 cubic inch V-8 (four-barrel); 340 horsepower 428 cubic inch V-8 (four-barrel), and 360 horsepower 428 cubic inch V-8 (four-barrel) were optional. High performance and power transfer axles were available.

CONVENIENCE OPTIONS: Appearance and protection group, includes: door edge guards, license plate frames, vinyl twin front and rear floor mats, in two-doors ($25.30); in four-doors ($29.15). Brougham option, includes: exterior Brougham script on 'C' pillar; Brougham script on glove box; unique door trim panels; dual upper body paint stripes; twin comfort lounge seats; luxury level seat trim; in Park Lane four-door models including Oxford roof ($272.05); without Oxford roof ($172.58). Decor group, for Monterey and Commuter sedans, includes: color-keyed interior rear window mouldings on vehicles without Breezeway; DeLuxe steering wheel, rear door courtesy switch ($21.49). Decor group for four-door hardtop and Commuter, includes: bright drip mouldings, DeLuxe steering wheel, rear-door courtesy switch ($21.49). Decor group for two-door hardtop and convertibles includes: DeLuxe steering wheel ($13.90). Whisper-aire air conditioner ($421.28). Power antenna ($28.97). Heavy-duty battery ($7.44). DeLuxe seat belts and seat belt reminder light, includes DeLuxe buckle on all six belts and color-keyed webbing ($13.05). Shoulder belts, includes regular buckle and black webbing, front seat ($27.06); back seat ($27.06). DeLuxe shoulder belts, includes DeLuxe buckle and color-keyed webbing, front seat ($29.61); back seat ($29.61). Power disc brakes ($71.30). Electric clock ($15.76). Spare tire cover ($5.25). Tinted glass ($42.75). Tinted windshield ($27.41). Adjustable front seat head rests ($42.75). Power door locks for two-doors ($45.40); for four-doors ($68.65). Luggage carrier for wagons only ($62.99). Manual righthand side view mirror ($6.95). Remote control lefthand mirror ($9.60). Protective bodyside mouldings ($45.40). Two-tone paint ($30.96). Visual-check panel includes door-ajar warning light, seat belt reminder light, low-fuel reminder light and parking brake warning light ($32.45). AM radio with antenna ($63.40). AM/FM radio stereo with antenna (189.34). Remote control deck lid release ($14). Oxford roof for two-doors ($99.47); for four-door ($99.47); for station wagons ($131.65). Rear-facing third seat in wagons ($128.11). Dual-center-facing seat in wagons ($95.36). Six-Way power seat, bench ($94.80); driver's seat ($84.25); driver's and passenger's side ($168.40). Twin comfort lounge seats ($77.80). Dual rear seat speakers ($25.90). Speed control ($90.74). Power steering ($115.65). Tilt steering wheel ($42.75). Stereo-sonic tape system/AM radio combination ($197.25). Trim includes door panels, seat trim and front seat courtesy lights in Colony Park with DeLuxe interior ($84.25); in Monterey with DeLuxe cloth and vinyl ($84.25). Breezeway ventilation for sedans ($58.35). Comfort stream and heating system ventilation ($40.10). DeLuxe wheel covers ($21.29). DeLuxe wheel covers with medallion for Monterey and Commuter ($40.14); others ($18.79). Wire wheel covers for Monterey and Commuter ($72.05); others ($50.75). Power rear window for Commuter and Colony Park ($31.62). Power side windows ($103.95). Power vent windows ($52.98). Two-speed interval selector windshield wipers ($14.19).

Historical footnotes: The vast majority of 1968 full-size Mercurys, 99.6 percent were equipped with automatic transmission, 99.2 percent had power steering, 42.5 percent had a tilting steering wheel, 59.5 percent had air conditioning and 32.8 percent had power windows.

1969 MERCURY

COMET SERIES — The new Comet had a framed horizontal bar grille. It protruded slightly in the center section, where a Comet emblem was housed. The side marker lights were now at bumper level. Teakwood-toned appliques were used on the instrument panel. The upholstery was cloth and vinyl.

COMET I.D. NUMBERS: See 1960 Comet I.D. numbers.

COMET

Model Number	Body/Style Number	Body Type & Seating	Factory Price	Shipping Weight	Production Total
NA	01	2-dr HT Cpe-6P	2515	3087	14,104

COMET ENGINE
Six. Overhead valves. Cast iron block. Displacement: 450 cubic inches. Bore and stroke: 3.68 x 3.91 inches. Compression ratio: 8.60:1. Brake horsepower: 155 at 4000 R.P.M. Carburetor: Autolite C90F-9510-BD one-barrel.

MONTEGO SERIES — Montegos had moldings above the rocker panels and trunk lid. There were fender-to-fender upper body twin pin stripes. Carpeting and cloth and vinyl, or all-vinyl upholstery were standard.

MONTEGO I.D. NUMBERS: See 1960 Comet I.D. numbers.

MONTEGO

Model Number	Body/Style Number	Body Type & Seating	Factory Price	Shipping Weight	Production Total
NA	06	4-dr Sedan-6P	2538	3060	21,950
NA	07	2-dr HT Cpe-6P	2588	3074	17,785

MONTEGO ENGINE
See 1969 Comet Series engine data.

MONTEGO MX SERIES — Full-length lower body moldings, chromed wheel lip openings, fender-to-fender upper-body chrome trim, trunk lid appliques and wood-tone appliques on the lower dash panel were features of the Montego MX. The convertible had all-vinyl interior and a power top with glass rear window.

MONTEGO MX I.D. NUMBERS: See 1960 Comet I.D. numbers.

MONTEGO

Model Number	Body/Style Number	Body Type & Seating	Factory Price	Shipping Weight	Production Total
NA	08	4-dr Sta Wag-6P	2962	3458	10,590
NA	10	4-dr Sedan-6P	2701	3094	17,738
NA	11	2-dr HT Cpe-6P	2719	3106	22,909
NA	12	2-dr Conv-6P	2979	3356	1,725

PRODUCTION NOTES: A total of 3,621 Montego MX station wagons came with woodgrain side trim. The Brougham option was ordered on 1,590 four-door sedans and 1,226 two-door hardtops. Only 363 of the convertibles were sold with bucket seats.

MONTEGO MX ENGINE
See 1969 Comet Series engine data.

CYCLONE SERIES — The sporty Cyclone fastback had rocker panel and wheel lip opening moldings. It also featured twin racing stripes, which ran from the front bumper and across the sides to the end of the rear fenders. Standard items included: carpeting, all-vinyl upholstery, ventless windows, tinted rear window and wood-tone appliques on the instrument cluster and lower dash.

CYCLONE I.D. NUMBERS: See 1960 Comet I.D. numbers.

CYCLONE

Model Number	Body/Style Number	Body Type & Seating	Factory Price	Shipping Weight	Production Total
NA	15	2-dr Fstbk Cpe-6P	2754	3273	5,882

CYCLONE ENGINE
V-8. Overhead valves. Cast iron block. Displacement: 402 cubic inches. Bore and stroke: 4 x 3 inches. Compression ratio: 9.50:1. Brake horsepower: 220 at 4400 R.P.M. Carburetor: Autolite C8AF-9510-B four-barrel.

CYCLONE CJ SERIES — A blacked-out grille was framed in chrome and had a single chrome piece in the middle running from each end of the grille. There was also a Cyclone emblem in the center, highlighting the front of the Cyclone CJ. Additional features included wheel wheel opening moldings; dual exhausts; a 3.50:1 rear axle; engine dress-up kit; hood tape stripe and competition handling package.

CYCLONE CJ I.D. NUMBERS: See 1960 Comet I.D. numbers.

CYCLONE CJ

Model Number	Body/Style Number	Body Type & Seating	Factory Price	Shipping Weight	Production Total
NA	16	2-dr Fstbk Cpe-6P	3207	3615	3,261

CYCLONE CJ ENGINE
V-8. Overhead valves. Cast iron block. Displacement: 428 cubic inches. Bore and stroke: 4.13 x 3.98 inches. Compression ratio: 10.60:1. Brake horsepower: 335 at 5200 R.P.M. Carburetor: Autolite C8AF-9510-B four-barrel.

CHASSIS FEATURES: Wheelbase (passenger cars) 116 inches; (station wagons) 113 inches. Overall length: (passenger cars) 206.2 inches; (Cyclone and Cyclone CJ) 203.2 inches; (station wagons) 193.8 inches. Tires: (Cyclone) 7.75 x 14; (others) 7.35 x 14.

POWERTRAIN OPTIONS: A three-speed manual transmission was standard except in the Cyclone CJ, which came with a four-speed manual gearbox. Four-speed and Select shift automatic transmissions were optional in the other series. A 220 horsepower 302 cubic inch V-8 (two-barrel); 250 horsepower 351 cubic inch V-8 (two-barrel); 290 horsepower 351 cubic inch V-8 (four-barrel); 320 horsepower 390 cubic inch V-8 (four-barrel); 335 horsepower 428 cubic inch V-8 (four-barrel); 360 horsepower 429 cubic inch V-8 (four-barrel) and a 390 horsepower 427 cubic inch V-8 (four-barrel) were optional. High performance and power transfer axles were available. A special handling package and traction-lok differential were optional.

CONVENIENCE OPTIONS: Heavy-duty battery ($7.80). Electric clock ($15.60). Courtesy light group includes: twin dash panel lights; glove box, and ash tray and luggage compartment lights; cargo light on station wagon and rear door light switch on sedans ($19.50). Cross-country ride package ($13). Competition handling package ($31.10). Curb moldings ($15.60). Decor group, includes: bright wheel lip moldings; trunk lid applique and bright upper door frames in sedans; DeLuxe wheel covers on hardtops and Montego MX with special appearance group ($54.50); on Montegos with special appearance group ($42.80); on Montego without special appearance group ($60.90). Tinted glass ($35). Front head restraints ($17). Hood lock pins for Cyclone and Cyclone CJ ($7.80). Luggage carrier on MX wagons ($46.70). Lefthand remote-control racing mirror on Cyclone and Cyclone CJ ($13). Lefthand remote-control mirror ($10.40). Righthand manual racing ($6.50). MX Brougham, includes: comfort stream ventilation; remote-control mirror; rear roof pillar Brougham identification; luxury-level cloth/vinyl interior; vinyl covered door pull handles; Brougham dash panel nameplate and rim blow steering wheel for Montego MX hardtop or sedan ($90.70). Two-tone paint ($31.10). Dual paint tape-stripes for Cyclone and Cyclone CJ ($31.10). Power disc brakes ($64.80). Power steering ($94.60). Tailgate and power window for MX station wagon ($35). Power windows, except on Comet and Montego, ($104.90). AM radio ($60.90). AM/FM stereo with twin speakers ($185.30). Dual rear-seat speakers, except in convertible and station wagon ($25.90). DeLuxe seat belts for convertibles, includes a seat belt reminder light ($13). DeLuxe front shoulder seat belts, except for convertibles, includes a seat belt reminder light ($15.60). Bucket seats without console for Montego MX, Cyclone hardtops and MX convertible ($110.10). Third seat MX wagon ($51.20). Sports console for Montego MX, Cyclone and Cyclone CJ ($155.70). Special appearance group includes: DeLuxe wheel covers; WSW tires; courtesy light group and comfort stream ventilation, except Cyclone CJ ($64.80). Sports appearance group includes: bucket seats; remote-control lefthand racing mirror; turbine wheel covers and rim blow steering wheel for Cyclone CJ ($149). Rim blow steering wheel ($35). Tachometer ($48). Comfortweave vinyl interior for Montego MX except station wagons and Cyclone ($24.70). Vinyl roof ($99.80). DeLuxe wheel covers with spinners, over hubs ($41.50); other ($20.80). Styled steel wheels, over hubs ($116.60); other ($95.90). Interval windshield wipers ($16.90). Yacht deck paneling for MX wagon ($149).

Historical footnotes: Over five percent of all 1969 Montegos had bucket seats, 26.9 percent had vinyl covered roofs, 1.8 percent had four-speed manual transmission and about one percent came with power seats. Mercurys won four NASCAR Grand National races in 1969.

1969 Mercury, Cougar (Eliminator) 2-dr hardtop coupe, V-8

COUGAR SERIES — The Cougar's grille now had horizontal pieces that protruded slightly at the center. Retractable headlights were used again. Rocker panel strips, wheel well opening moldings and two parallel full-length upper body stripes decorated the Cougar's sides. The backup lights wrapped around the rear fenders and the taillights were trimmed with concave vertical chrome pieces. A vinyl interior with foam-padded bucket seats and carpeting was standard.

COUGAR I.D. NUMBERS: See 1960 Monterey I.D. numbers.

COUGAR

Model Number	Body/Style Number	Body Type & Seating	Factory Price	Shipping Weight	Production Total
NA	65	2-dr HT Cpe-5P	2999	3380	66,331
NA	76	2-dr Conv-5P	3365	3499	5,796

PRODUCTION NOTE: A total of 1,615 Cougar hardtops were ordered with optional front bench seats.

COUGAR ENGINE
V-8. Overhead valves. Cast iron block. Displacement: 351 cubic inches. Bore and stroke: 4 x 3.5 inches. Compression ratio: 9.00:1. Brake horsepower: 250 at 4600 R.P.M. Carburetor: Autolite C9ZF-9510-A two-barrel.

COUGAR XR-7 SERIES — The XR-7 looked about the same as the basic Cougar from the outside. Its standard extras included: rim blow steering wheel; courtesy light group; visual check panel; lefthand, remote-control racing mirror; electric clock; DeLuxe arm rests; walnut-toned instrument panel with tachometer and trip odometer; leather with vinyl upholstery; vinyl door trim panels and special wheel covers.

COUGAR XR-7 I.D. NUMBERS: See 1960 Monterey I.D. numbers.

COUGAR XR-7

Model Number	Body/Style Number	Body Type & Seating	Factory Price	Shipping Weight	Production Total
NA	65	2-dr HT Cpe-5P	3298	3420	23,918
NA	76	2-dr Conv-5P	3578	3539	4,024

COUGAR XR-7 ENGINE
See 1969 Cougar Series engine.

CHASSIS FEATURES: Wheelbase: 111 inches. Overall length: 193.8 inches. Tires: E78 x 14.

POWERTRAIN OPTIONS: A three-speed manual transmission was standard. Heavy-duty three-speed, four-speed manual and Select Shift automatic transmissions were optional. A 290 horsepower 351 cubic inch V-8 (four-barrel); 290 horsepower 302 cubic inch V-8 (four-barrel); 320 horsepower 390 cubic inch V-8 (four-barrel); 335 horsepower 'CJ' 428 cubic inch V-8 (four-barrel) and a 360 horsepower 429 cubic inch V-8 (four-barrel) were available. The 302 cubic inch V-8 was standard in the 'Eliminator' performance package. It featured a two-speed street rear axle; blacked-out grille; ram-air hood scoop; special side body stripe and front and rear spoilers. The 290 horsepower 351 cubic inch V-8 was standard in the '351' performance package. This option included: competition handling package, dual stripes and a power dome hood. The ram-air induction option came with a 428 V-8, hood scoop and F70 x 14 tires. High performance rear axles and heavy-duty traction-lok differential were optional. Also note that two Cougars were produced with the Boss 429 cubic inch engine.

CONVENIENCE OPTIONS: Heavy-duty battery ($7.80). Front bumper guards ($13). Rear window defogger for hardtop ($22.10). Decor group includes: DeLuxe wheel covers; curb molding; rim blow steering wheel; custom grade seat; door and quarter trim; door mounted courtesy lights; rear seat arm rests and windshield pillar and roof rail pads ($90.70). Door edge guards ($5.20). Dual exhausts ($31.10). Tinted glass ($29.80). GT appearance group for Cougar Cyclone, includes: comfortweave vinyl bucket seats; rim blow steering wheel; remote-control lefthand racing mirror; turbine design wheel covers; GT decal; GT dash nameplate and F70 x 14 fiberglass belted tires ($168.40). Front head restraints ($17). Hood lock pins ($7.80). Front and rear rubber floor mats ($13). Lefthand remote-control racing mirror ($13). Lefthand remote-control mirror ($10.40). Two-tone paint ($31.10). Power steering ($99.80). Sun roof with vinyl roof ($459.80). Power windows ($104.90). AM radio ($60.90). AM/FM stereo with twin speakers ($185.30). AM radio and stereosonic tape system ($195.60). Rear seat speaker ($15.60). DeLuxe seat belts in convertibles ($13). DeLuxe front shoulder seat belts, all except convertibles ($15.60). Full-width front seat with center arm rest in hardtop ($24.70). Speed control ($71.30). Sports console ($57.10). Tilt away steering wheel ($68.70). Vinyl roof ($89.40). Visual check panel includes: door-ajar, low-fuel warning lights ($25.90). DeLuxe wheel covers ($20.80). DeLuxe wheel covers, with spinners over hubs ($41.50); other ($20.80). Wire wheel covers, over hubs ($72.60); other ($51.90). Styled steel wheels, over hubs ($95.90); other in hardtops ($16.90). Interval windshield wipers ($16.90).

Historical footnote: The vast majority of 1969 Cougars, 92.4 percent had power steering, 89.4 percent had automatic transmission, 57 percent had tinted glass and 58.9 percent had power brakes.

MONTEREY SERIES — The Monterey had a new, horizontal bar grille with a vertical piece in the center. Signal lights wrapped around the front fenders. The concave, rectangular taillights were clustered in the rear deck panel, which was heavily trimmed with vertical chrome pieces. The wheel well openings, trunk lid and roof quarter panels had moldings. Standard features included: ventless side windows; Nylon carpeting; wood-toned dash and door panels; heater and defroster and dome light. The convertible had an all-vinyl interior, while other body types had cloth and vinyl trims.

MONTEREY I.D. NUMBERS: See 1960 Monterey I.D. numbers.

MONTEREY

Model Number	Body/Style Number	Body Type & Seating	Factory Price	Shipping Weight	Production Total
NA	44	4-dr Sedan-6P	3141	3963	23,009
NA	45	2-dr Conv-6P	3523	4108	1,297
NA	47	2-dr HT Cpe-6P	3220	3927	9,865
NA	48	4-dr HT Sed-6P	3296	3998	6,066
NA	72	4-dr Sta Wag-6P	3519	4272	5,844

PRODUCTION NOTE: A total of 3,839 Monterey wagons came with an optional third seat.

MONTEREY ENGINE
V-8. Overhead valves. Cast iron block. Displacement: 390 cubic inches. Bore and stroke: 4.05 x 3.78 inches. Compression ratio: 9.50:1. Brake horsepower: 265 at 4400 R.P.M. Carburetor: Autolite C9AF-9510-B two-barrel.

MONTEREY CUSTOM SERIES — Rocker panel moldings and DeLuxe wheel covers were two exterior differences between the Custom and the basic Monterey. The Custom also had a DeLuxe steering wheel; leather door pulls; wood-grained vinyl appliques; front seat center arm rest; bright seat side shields; rear door courtesy light switches and Nylon carpeting.

MONTEREY CUSTOM I.D. NUMBERS: See 1960 Monterey I.D. numbers.

MONTEREY CUSTOM

Model Number	Body/Style Number	Body Type & Seating	Factory Price	Shipping Weight	Production Total
NA	54	4-dr Sedan-6P	3360	3968	7,103
NA	56	2-dr HT Cpe-6P	2442	3959	2,898
NA	58	4-dr HT Sed-6P	3516	4000	2,827
NA	74	4-dr Sta Wag-6P	3740	4384	1,920

PRODUCTION NOTE: A total of 967 Monterey Custom station wagons came with a third seat.

MONTEREY CUSTOM ENGINE
See 1969 Monterey Series engine data.

1969 Mercury, Marquis Brougham 4-dr hardtop sedan, V-8

MARQUIS SERIES — The attractive front-end styling of the Marquis was influenced by the Continental Mark III. The integrated bumper grille had a horizontal bar theme and a prominent center section. Hidden headlight covers blended into the grille. Dual lower body pin stripes ran above the full-length bright curb moldings. Except for two backup lights, the rear deck panel was a solid row of concave, rectangular, chrome-accented taillights. The interior featured deep-pile Nylon carpeting, burled-walnut vinyl paneling on the dash and doors, front door courtesy lights, electric clock and a steering wheel with wood-toned spokes and rim.

MARQUIS I.D. NUMBERS: See 1960 Monterey I.D. numbers.

MARQUIS

Model Number	Body/Style Number	Body Type & Seating	Factory Price	Shipping Weight	Production Total
NA	63	4-dr Sedan-6P	3840	4144	31,388
NA	66	2-dr HT Cpe-6P	3902	3927	18,302
NA	68	4-dr HT Sed-6P	3973	4184	29,389
NA	65	2-dr Conv-6P	4107	4380	2,319
NA	76	4-dr Sta Wag-6P	3878	4457	25,604

PRODUCTION NOTE: The Marquis station wagon was called the Colony Park. A total of 18,003 Colony Park station wagons came with the optional third seat.

MARQUIS ENGINE
V-8. Overhead valves. Cast iron block. Displacement: 429 cubic inches. Bore and stroke: 4.36 x 3.59 inches. Compression ratio: 10.50:1. Brake horsepower: 320 at 4400 R.P.M. Carburetor: Autolite C9AF-9510-J two-barrel.

MARAUDER SERIES — The Marauder had a Marquis front end, special tunneled rear window treatment and twin upper body pin stripe. There was a unique sculptured section, with five short, horizontal chrome pieces, just behind the doors. The six tail and two backup lights were embedded in the rear deck panel. Set between them was a blacked-out section with the Marauder name written in chrome. A cloth and vinyl interior was standard.

MARAUDER I.D. NUMBERS: See 1960 Monterey I.D. numbers.

MARAUDER

Model Number	Body/Style Number	Body Type & Seating	Factory Price	Shipping Weight	Production Total
NA	60	2-dr HT Cpe-6P	3351	4009	9,031

MARAUDER ENGINE
See 1969 Monterey Series engine data.

MARAUDER X-100 SERIES — The Marauder X-100 features a two-tone paint job; fender skirts; leather with vinyl interior; rim blow steering wheel; electric clock; glass-belted wide-tread tires and styled aluminum wheels.

MARAUDER X-100 I.D. NUMBERS: See 1960 Monterey I.D. numbers.

MARAUDER X-100

Model Number	Body/Style Number	Body Type & Seating	Factory Price	Shipping Weight	Production Total
NA	61	2-dr HT Cpe-6P	4074	4009	5,635

MARAUDER X-100 ENGINE
V-8. Overhead valves. Cast iron block. Displacement: 429 cubic inches. Bore and stroke: 4.36 x 3.59 inches. Compression ratio: 10.50:1. Brake horsepower: 360 at 4600 R.P.M. Carburetor: four-barrel.

CHASSIS FEATURES: (Station wagons and Marauder) 121 inches; (other models) 124 inches. Overall length: (Marquis) 224.3 inches; (Monterey and Custom) 221.8 inches; (Marauder and X-100) 219.1 inches; (Colony Park) 220.5 inches; (Monterey and Custom station wagons) 218 inches. Tires: (Marquis and station wagons) 8.55 x 15; (X-100) H70 x 15; (other models) 8.25 x 15.

POWERTRAIN OPTIONS: A three-speed manual transmission was standard, except in the Marquis and X-100, both of which came with Select Shift automatic. The automatic transmission was optional in the other models. A 280 horsepower 390 cubic inch V-8 (two-barrel); 320 horsepower 390 cubic inch V-8 (four-barrel); 335 horsepower 428 cubic inch V-8 (four-barrel) and a 360 horsepower 429 cubic inch V-8 (four-barrel) were offered. A competition handling package, which included heavy-duty shocks and larger stabilizer bar, was a $31.10 option on the Marauder and X-100. High performance and power transfer axles were also offered.

CONVENIENCE OPTIONS: Air conditioner ($421). Heavy-duty battery ($6.50). Carpeted load floor on wagons ($15.60). Rear window defogger ($22.10). Electric clock ($15.60). Fender skirts for Marauder ($36.30). Tinted glass ($42.80). Tinted windshield, Fleet only ($27.30). Front head restraints ($17). Luggage-rack carrier for wagons, with Air Deflector ($94.60); without Air Deflector ($73.90). Front and rear rubber floor mats ($13). Outside rearview mirror with remote-control ($10.40). Two-tone paint ($36.30). Two-tone paint Marauder ($45.40). Power antenna ($31.10). Front disc brakes ($71.30). Power locks, in two-doors ($45.40); in four-doors ($68.70). Rear power window on station wagons ($35). Six-Way bench seat ($99.80). Six-Way twin comfort lounge driver's side ($84.20); driver's and passenger's side ($168.40). Power steering ($115.30). Remote-control trunk release ($14.30). Power windows ($110.10). AM radio with antenna ($63.50). AM/FM radio, stereo with antenna ($190.40). AM radio stereosonic tape system ($198.20). Dual rear speakers ($25.90); automatic ride control ($79.10). DeLuxe seat belts with reminder light on all convertibles ($13). DeLuxe front and shoulder seat belts ($15.60). Bucket seat with console, Marauder ($162). Twin comfort lounge, Marquis ($77.80). Center seat facing rear, station wagons ($91.90). Reclining passenger seat, Marauder and Marquis ($41.50). Twin comfort lounge, Marquis CP ($162). Single-key locking system ($3.90). Speed control ($63.50). Rim blow steering wheel, Monterey and Marauder ($35); others ($19.50). Tilt steering wheel ($45.40). All-vinyl DeLuxe trim, Monterey ($28.50). Leather with vinyl trim, Marquis ($110.10). Visual safety-check panel, includes: low fuel, door ajar, headlamps-on warning lights, headlamps-on warning buzzer and seat belt reminder light ($32.40). Vinyl roof on passenger cars ($115.30); on station wagons ($142.50). Styled aluminum wheels, Monterey and Marauder ($116.60). Styled aluminum wheels Monterey, Marquis ($95.90). DeLuxe wheel covers ($20.80). DeLuxe wheel covers with medallion for Monterey and Marauder ($45.40); for Monterey and Marquis ($24.70). Wire wheels, Marauder ($72.60); others ($51.90). Marauder fender skirts ($20.80). Interval selector windshield wipers ($16.90). Appearance protection group, includes: door edge guards; license plate frames; twin vinyl front and rear floor mats for two-doors, except Marauder ($25.90); for four-doors, except Marquis CP ($29.80). Brougham option for Marquis includes exterior 'C' pillar trim; twin comfort lounge seats; upper body peak molding; luxury-level seat trim; unique door trim panels; rear seat center arm rest and vinyl roof ($272). Decor group, includes: wood-grain rim steering wheel, curb molding and DeLuxe wheel covers on Monterey and Monterey station wagons ($57.10). Cooling package ($36).

Historical footnotes: Most full-size 1969 Mercurys, 99.5 percent Montereys; 99.7 percent Customs and 99.5 percent Marauders, were equipped with automatic transmission. Mercury also built the Cyclone Spoiler II, Mercury's equivalent to Ford's NASCAR racer, the Torino Talladega

1970 MERCURY

MONTEGO SERIES — The protruding hood Mercury had been using for the the past few years was carried to extremes on the new Montego. Its grille looked like the front end of a coffin. It had horizontal bars on it and an emblem in the center. The signal lights were placed in the front fenders. Wheel well and roof drip moldings were used. There were four hooded taillights, each evenly divided into four sections by chrome trim pieces. Standard equipment included: concealed wipers, front and rear side markers, cloth and vinyl or all-vinyl interior, wood-tone applique on dash and front and rear arm rests.

MONTEGO I.D. NUMBERS: See 1960 Monterey I.D. numbers.

MONTEGO

Model Number	Body/Style Number	Body Type & Seating	Factory Price	Shipping Weight	Production Total
NA	01	2-dr HT-6P	2473	3161	21,298
NA	02	4-dr Sedan-6P	2560	3246	13,988

MONTEGO ENGINE
Six: Overhead valves. Cast iron block. Displacement: 250 cubic inches. Bore and stroke: 3.68 x 3.91 inches. Compression ratio: 9.00:1. Brake horsepower: 155 at 4000 R.P.M. Carburetor: one-barrel.

MONTEGO MX SERIES — The Montego MX had mid body side molding and chrome trim around the trunk lid on all models; the window frames of four-doors. The interior featured loop carpeting, pleated cloth and vinyl or all-vinyl upholstery and a teakwood applique on the steering wheel.

MONTEGO MX I.D. NUMBERS: See 1960 Monterey I.D. numbers.

MONTEGO MX

Model Number	Body/Style Number	Body Type & Seating	Factory Price	Shipping Weight	Production Total
NA	08	4-dr Sta Wag-6P	2996	3709	5,094
NA	06	4-dr Sedan-6P	2662	3253	16,708
NA	07	2-dr HT Cpe-6P	2563	3186	31,670

MONTEGO MX ENGINE
See 1970 Montego Series engine data.

MONTEGO MX BROUGHAM SERIES — Concealed headlights, chrome rocker panels, wheel well moldings, dual upper body pin stripes, six-pod taillights and silver or black appliques on the rear deck panel set the Brougham apart from the other Montegos. Standard equipment included a cloth and vinyl interior, Nylon loop carpeting and a wood-grain vinyl insert in the steering wheel.

MONTEGO MX BROUGHAM I.D. NUMBERS: See 1960 Monterey I.D. numbers.

MONTEGO MX BROUGHAM

Model Number	Body/Style Number	Body Type & Seating	Factory Price	Shipping Weight	Production Total
NA	10	4-dr Sedan-6P	2712	3153	3,315
NA	11	2-dr HT Cpe-6P	2730	3186	8,074
NA	12	4-dr HT Sed-6P	2844	3206	3,685
NA	18	4-dr Sta Wag-6P	3090	3624	2,682

NOTE: Model number 18, the four-door station wagon, was called the Villager.

MONTEGO MX BROUGHAM ENGINE
See Montego engine data.

1970 Mercury, Cyclone GT 2-dr hardtop sports coupe, V-8

CYCLONE SERIES — The produrbing center section of the Cyclone grille was outlined by a chrome square. It was equally divided into four pieces, with a white circle in the center. Rectangular running lights were embedded in the grille. The lower back panel was either silver or black. Loop carpeting, all-vinyl interior and a competition handling package were standard.

CYCLONE I.D. NUMBERS: See 1960 Monterey I.D. numbers.

CYCLONE

Model Number	Body/Style Number	Body Type & Seating	Factory Price	Shipping Weight	Production Total
NA	15	2-dr HT Cpe-6P	3037	3449	1,695

CYCLONE ENGINE
V-8: Overhead valves. Cast iron block. Displacement: 429 cubic inches. Bore and stroke: 4.36 x 3.59 inches. Compression ratio: 10.50:1. Brake horsepower: 360 at 4600 R.P.M. Carburetor: four-barrel.

CYCLONE GT SERIES — Concealed headlights, non-functional performance scooped hood, full-length lower body side molding, lefthand remote-control and righthand manual racing mirrors, high-back comfortweave vinyl bucket seats, special door panel trim and a three-spoke sports style steering wheel were standard GT features.

CYCLONE GT I.D. NUMBERS: See 1960 Monterey I.D. numbers.

CYCLONE GT

Model Number	Body/Style Number	Body Type & Seating	Factory Price	Shipping Weight	Production Total
NA	16	2-dr HT Cpe-5P	3025	3434	10,170

CYCLONE GT ENGINE
V-8: Overhead valves. Cast iron block. Displacement: 351 cubic inches. Bore and stroke: 4 x 3.5 inches. Compression ratio: 9.50:1. Brake horsepower: 250 at 4600 R.P.M. Carburetor: two-barrel.

CYCLONE SPOILER SERIES — The 'Spoiler' was aptly named. It had front and rear spoilers; exposed headlights; mid body side stripes; traction belted tires; scooped hood; dual racing mirrors; competition handling package and full instrumentation.

CYCLONE SPOILER I.D. NUMBERS: See 1950 Monterey I.D. numbers.

CYCLONE SPOILER

Model Number	Body/Style Number	Body Type & Seating	Factory Price	Shipping Weight	Production Total
NA	17	2-dr HT Cpe-5P	3530	3464	1,631

CYCLONE SPOILER ENGINE
V-8: Overhead valves. Cast iron block. Displacement: 429 cubic inches. Bore and stroke: 4.36 x 3.59 inches. Compression ratio: 11.30:1. Brake horsepower: 370 at 5400 R.P.M. Carburetor: four-barrel.

CHASSIS FEATURES: Wheelbase: (Passenger cars) 117 inches; (Station wagons) 114 inches. Overall length: (Passenger cars) 209.9 inches; (Station wagons) 209 inches. Tires: (Cyclone series) G70-14; (other models) E78-14.

POWERTRAIN OPTIONS: A three-speed manual transmission was standard, except in the Cyclone and Spoiler. Both came with a four-speed manual and Hurst shifter. Four-speed manual and Select-Shift automatic transmissions were optional. A 220 horsepower 351 cubic inch V-8 (two-barrel); 250 horsepower 351 cubic inch V-8 (two-barrel); a 300 horsepower 351 cubic inch V-8 (four-barrel); 360 horsepower Thunder Jet 429 cubic inch V-8 (four-barrel); 370 horsepower Cobra Jet 429 cubic inch V-8 (four-barrel) and a 375 horsepower Super Cobra Jet 429 cubic inch V-8 (four-barrel) were offered. A limited production Boss 429 cubic inch V-8 (four-barrel) was available on special order. Drag pack, drag-pack super and ram-air induction options were offered in the Cyclonne, GT and Spoiler series. A higher ratio rear axle and Track-Lok differential were available at extra cost.

CONVENIENCE OPTIONS: Air-conditioner ($388.60). Heavy-duty 55 amp alternator ($20.80). Heavy-duty battery ($7.80). Extra cooling ($7.80). Cross-country ride ($9.10). Tinted glass ($36.30). Tinted glass windshield, fleet only ($25.90). Heater and defroster ($22.10). Low gear lockout ($6.50). Luggage carrier with adjustable roof rails for MX wagon without air deflector ($54.50); with air deflector ($73.90). Lefthand remote-control racing mirror ($13). Front disc barkes ($64.80). Four-Way bench seat ($73.90). Power steering ($104.90). Power windows ($104.90). Protective vinyl bodyside molding ($25.90). AM radio ($60.90). AM/FM stereo radio ($212.50). Dual rear seat speaker ($27.30). DeLuxe seat and front shoulder belts ($15.60). DeLuxe seat belts with automatic seat back release on two-doors ($38.90). Highback bucket seats with comfort vinyl trim ($119.20). Rear facing third seat MX station wagon ($63.70). Rim-blow steering wheel ($35). Sun roof Montego two-door hardtops ($375.70). Upbeat spectrum stripe MX two-door with bench seats ($32.40). Comfort weave vinyl MX with bench seats ($32.40). Upbeat watch plaid MX with bench seats ($32.40). High level ventilation ($15.50). Vinyl roof ($99.80). DeLuxe wheel covers ($25.90). Luxury wheel covers ($41.50). Styled steel wheels ($38.90). Interval windshield wipers ($25.90). Mud and snow tires ($7.80). F78-14 whitewall tires, with 250 or 302 engines ($31.10); with 351 engines ($49.30). G78-14 whitewall tires, with 351 engine ($49.30); with 429 engines ($64.80); with 351 engines ($46.70). F70-14 traction tires, with 250, 302 engines ($77.80); with 351 engines ($59.60). G70-14 whitewall tires, with 250, 302 engines ($83); with 351 engines ($64.80). G70-14 traction tires, with 250, 302 engines ($95.90); with 351 engine ($77.80); with 429 engine ($59.60). Instrumentation group includes tachometer, oil temperature and ammeter gauges ($77.80). Trailer-towing package includes: 351 two-barrel engine; power disc brakes; competitive handling package; extra-cooling package; heavy-duty alternator; heavy-duty battery, with air conditioner ($151.60); without air conditioner ($159.40).

Historical footnotes: Most 1970 Montegros, 92.6 percent, were equipped with automatic transmission, 87 percent had a V-8 engine, 49.5 percent had air conditioning, 88.1 percent had power steering, 42.1 percent disc brakes and one percent had power seats. Mercurys won four NASCAR Grand National races in 1970.

COUGAR SERIES — The clean Cougar grille of 1969 was replaced by a center hood extension and 'electric shaver' style insert reminiscent of the 1967 and 1968 models. Basic trim was upper body pin stripes, wheel opening and roof moldings and windshield rear window chrome. The interior featured high-back bucket seats, courtesy lights, carpeted door trim panels, vinyl heading and rosewood toned dash panel. The convertible had comfortweave vinyl interior, door mounted courtesy lights, three-spoke steering wheel and power top with folding rear glass window.

COUGAR I.D. NUMBERS: See 1960 Monterey I.D. numbers.

COUGAR

Model Number	Body/Style Number	Body Type & Seating	Factory Price	Shipping Weight	Production Total
NA	91	2-dr HT Cpe-6P	2917	3307	49,479
NA	92	2-dr Conv-5P	3264	3404	2,322

COUGAR ENGINE
See 1970 Cyclone GT engine data.

1970 Mercury, Cougar XR-7 2-dr convertible, V-8

COUGAR XR-7 SERIES — The XR-7 had distinctive wheel covers, rocker panel moldings, remote-control racing mirror and an emblem on the rear roof pillar. Interior features included vinyl high-back bucket seats with leather accents; map pockets on the seat backs; tachometer; trip odometer; rocker switch display; burled walnut vinyl applique on the instrument panel; rear seat arm rests; map and courtesy light; visual check panel; loop yarn Nylon carpeting and an electric clock with elapsed-time indicator.

COUGAR XR-7 I.D. NUMBERS: See 1960 Monterey I.D. numbers.

COURGAR XR-7

Model Number	Body/Style Number	Body Type & Seating	Factory Price	Shipping Weight	Production Total
NA	93	2-dr HT Cpe-6P	3201	3333	18,565
NA	94	2-dr Conv-5P	3465	3430	1,977

COUGAR XR-7 ENGINE
See Cyclone GT Series engine data.

CHASSIS FEATURES: Wheelbase: 111.1 inches. Overall length: 196.1 inches. tires: E78-14.

POWERTRAIN OPTIONS: A three-speed manual transmission was standard. Four-speed manual and Select-Shift automatic transmissions were optional. A 300 horsepower 351 cubic inch V-8 (four-barrel); a 290 horsepower Boss 302 cubic inch V-8 (four-barrel); 335 horsepower Cobra Jet 428 cubic inch V-8 (four-barrel) and a 375 horsepower Boss 429 cubic inch V-8 (four-barrel) were available. The 300 horsepower engine was standard in the Eliminator performance package. The Boss 302 was only offered in the Eliminator. Drag-pack and ram-air induction options could also be ordered. A high performance rear axle and Traction-Lok differential were available at extra cost.

CONVENIENCE OPTIONS: Air-conditioner ($375.70). Electric clock ($15.60). Sports console ($57.10). Tinted glass ($32.40). Tinted windshield, fleet only ($22.10). Heater and defroster ($22.10). Lefthand remote-control racing mirror ($13). Two-tone paint ($31.10). Front disc brakes ($64.80). Power steering ($105.90). AM radio ($60.90). AM/FM stereo radio ($212.50). AM radio/stereo sonic tape ($195.60). Rear seat speaker ($15.60). DeLuxe front seat and shoulder belts ($15.60). Rim-blow steering wheel ($35). Vinyl sun roof ($459.80). Tilt steering wheel ($45.40). Houndstooth cloth and vinyl trim $32.40). Vinyl roof includes roof and bright roof moldings ($89.40). DeLuxe wheel covers ($25.90). Ralley wheel covers over hubs ($41.50); others ($15.60). Wire wheel covers, over hubs ($74.90); others ($48). Styled steel wheels, over hubs ($116.60); others ($90.70). Interval windshield wipers ($25.90). Mud and snow tires ($7.80). Tires: E78-14 whitewall wide tread ($29.80); F70-14 whitewall belted ($63.50); F70-14 traction belted ($76.50); F70-14 traction belted ($13). Appearance protection group includes: front bumper guards, door edge guards, rear floor mats ($31.10). Courtesy light group includes: rear roof pillar, trunk, underhood and map lights, headlamps on warning buzzer with light ($19.50). Decor group includes: DeLuxe wheel covers; curb molding; three-spoke rim-blow steering wheel; custom grade door and quarter trim; door courtesy lights; rear quarter arm rests; comfortweave vinyl high-back bucket seats ($90.70); on Eliminator ($70). Drag-pack option ($207.30). Eliminator option ($129.60). Ram-air induction option includes: ram-air induction system and functional hood scoop in body color; hood stripes (black or argent); color-keyed stripe with CJ 428 logo ($64.80). Visual-check panel includes door-ajar, low-fuel warning lights ($25.90).

Historical footnotes: The majority of 1970 Cougars, 67.6 percent were equipped with power brakes, 95.6 percent had power steering, 63.9 percent tinted glass and 92.2 percent had automatic transmission.

MONTEREY SERIES — The Monterey grille had thin, bi-level horizontal bars outlined in heavier chrome; a slender vertical emblem in the middle; four recessed chrome rimmed headlights and large, wraparound signal lights. There were bright moldings on the wheel well openings, rear roof pillar base and windows. The two large narrow, rectangular deck panel taillights were centrally divided by backup lamps. The interior featured Nylon carpeting; dark teakwood vinyl instrument panel appliques; color-keyed steering wheel; adjustable head restraints; steering column lock; pleated design cloth and vinyl upholstery (all-vinyl in the convertible) and heavy sound insulation.

MONTEREY SERIES — See 1960 Monterey I.D. numbers.

MONTEREY

Model Number	Body/Style Number	Body Type & Seating	Factory Price	Shipping Weight	Production Total
NA	44	4-dr Sedan-6P	3029	3940	29,432
NA	47	2-dr HT Cpe-6P	3107	3904	9,359
NA	48	4-dr HT Sed-6P	3179	3975	5,032
NA	45	2-dr Conv-6P	3429	4085	581
NA	72	4-dr Sta Wag-6P	3440	4249	5,164

Historical footnotes: A total of 3,507 Monterey station wagons were equipped with the optional third rear seat.

MONTEREY ENGINE
V-8: Overhead valve. Cast iron block. Displacement: 390 cubic inches. Bore and stroke: 4.05 x 3.78 inches. Compression ratio: 9.50:1. Brake horsepower: 265 at 4400 R.P.M. Carburetor: two-barrel.

MONTEREY CUSTOM SERIES — The Custom had full-length, mid body chrome spears with vinyl inserts. DeLuxe wheel covers and curb moldings. On the inside was the cloth and vinyl or all-vinyl upholstery, front seat arm rest, teakwood toned inserts in the steering wheel, vinyl covered door pull handles and rear courtesy light switches.

MONTEREY CUSTOM I.D. NUMBERS: See 1960 Monterey I.D. numbers.

MONTEREY CUSTOM

Model Number	Body/Style Number	Body Type & Seating	Factory Price	Shipping Weight	Production Total
NA	54	4-dr Sedan-6P	3288	3945	4,823
NA	56	2-dr HT Cpe-6P	3365	3936	1,194
NA	58	4-dr HT Sed-6P	3436	3987	1,357

MONTEREY CUSTOM ENGINE
See 1970 Monterey engine data.

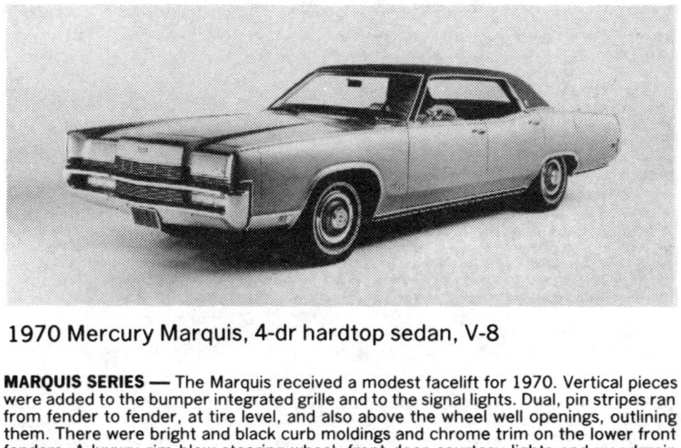

1970 Mercury Marquis, 4-dr hardtop sedan, V-8

MARQUIS SERIES — The Marquis received a modest facelift for 1970. Vertical pieces were added to the bumper integrated grille and to the signal lights. Dual, pin stripes ran from fender to fender, at tire level, and also above the wheel well openings, outlining them. There were bright and black curb moldings and chrome trim on the lower front fenders. A luxury rim blow steering wheel, front door courtesy lights and woodgrain toned door panel inserts graced the Marquis interior.

MARQUIS I.D. NUMBERS: See 1960 Monterey I.D. numbers.

MARQUIS

Model Number	Body/Style Number	Body Type & Seating	Factory Price	Shipping Weight	Production Total
NA	40	4-dr Sedan-6P	3793	4121	14,384
NA	41	2-dr HT Cpe-6P	3952	4072	6,229
NA	42	4-dr HT Sed-6P	3910	4141	8,411
NA	65	2-dr Conv-6P	4047	4337	1,233
N	74	4-dr Sta Wag-6P	3930	4434	2,388
NA	76	4-dr Sta Wag-6P	4,123	4,480	19,204

NOTE: Model number 76, the four-door station wagon, was called the Colony Park.

PRODUCTION NOTE: A total of 1,429 standard Marquis wagons and 14,549 Colony Parks were sold with the optional third seat.

MARQUIS ENGINE
V-8: Overhead valves. Cast iron block. Displacement: 429 cubic inches. Bore and stroke: 4.36 x 3.59 inches. Compression ratio: 10.50:1. Brake horsepower: 320 at 4400 R.P.M. Carburetor: two-barrel.

MARQUIS BROUGHAM SERIES — Instead of pin stripes, the Brougham used upper body moldings which ran from the face of the front fenders to the back of the rear. Also seen on these luxury models were chromed wheel openings and a vinyl roof. The interior featured individually adjustable, twin comfort lounge seats, with two folding arm rests. The door trim panels were wood toned and the door pull handles were covered with vinyl.

MARQUIS BROUGHAM I.D. NUMBERS: See 1960 Monterey I.D. numbers.

MARQUIS BROUGHAM

Model Number	Body/Style Number	Body Type & Seating	Factory Price	Shipping Weight	Production Total
NA	63	4-dr Sedan-6P	4092	4166	14,920
NA	66	2-dr HT Cpe-6P	4151	4119	7,113
NA	68	4-dr HT Sed-6P	4219	4182	11,623

MARQUIS BROUGHAM
See 1970 Marquis Series engine data.

MARAUDER SERIES — Except for its name spelled out in chrome on the face of the hood, the Marauder looked the same as the Marquis from the front. Side trim consisted of twin upper body pin stripes, window moldings and a sculptured section with five short horizontal chrome pieces behind the doors. A tunneled rear window remained a Marauder styling highpoint. The same distinctive taillight treatment used last year was on the 1970 model.

MARAUDER I.D. NUMBERS: See 1960 Monterey I.D. numbers.

MARAUDER

Model Number	Body/Style Number	Body Type & Seating	Factory Price	Shipping Weight	Production Total
NA	60	2-dr HT Cpe-6P	3271	3986	3,397

MARAUDER ENGINE
See Marquis engine data.

MARAUDER X-100 SERIES — Fender skirts, wheel opening moldings and special wheel covers distinguished the X-100 from the standard Marauder. Interior differences included high-back, all-vinyl bucket seats with center console (or twin comfort lounge seats), luxury steering wheel and bright seat side shields.

MARAUDER X-100 I.D. NUMBERS: See 1960 Monterey I.D. numbers.

MARAUDER X-100

Model Number	Body/Style Number	Body Type & Seating	Factory Price	Shipping Weight	Production Total
NA	61	2-dr HT Cpe-6P	3873	4128	2,646

MARAUDER X-100 ENGINE
See 1970 Cyclone Series engine data.

CHASSIS FEATURES: Wheelbase: (Wagons, Marauder and X-100) 121 inches; (others) 124 inches. Overall length: (Marquis and Brougham) 224.3 inches; (Marquis wagons) 220.5 inches; (Monterey and Custom) 221.8 inches; (Monterey wagons) 218 inches; (Marauder and X-100) 219.1 inches. Tires: (Monterey and Custom) G78-15; (Marquis, Brougham, Marauder) H78-15; (Monterey wagons) H70-15 X-100.

POWERTRAIN OPTIONS: A three-speed manual transmission was standard in Marauder, Monterey, and Custom. Select-Shift automatic was standard in Marquis, Brougham and X-100. The automatic was optional in the other series. A 320 horsepower 429 cubic inch V-8 (two-barrel) and a 360 horsepower 429 cubic inch V-8 (four-barrel) were optional. A higher ratio rear axle was available.

CONVENIENCE OPTIONS: Air-conditioner ($421). Heavy-duty 55 amp alternator ($20.80). Heavy-duty 65 amp alternator ($86.80). Heavy-duty battery ($7.80). Carpted load floor wagons ($19.50). Heavy-duty cooling ($36.30). Cross-country ride ($23.40). Electric rear window defroster ($53.20). Door edge guards in two-doors ($6.50); in four-doors ($10.40). Tinted glass ($36.30). Tinted windshield, fleet only ($27.30). Luggage carrier with adjustable roof rails in wagons ($73.90); with air deflector ($94.60). Front and rear floor mats ($13). Two-tone paint ($36.30). Two-tone paint Marauder ($45.40). Power antenna ($31.10). Front disc brakes ($71.30). Power door locks, two-doors ($45.40); four-doors ($68.70); wagons including power lock for tailgate ($77.80). Automatic seat back release ($25.90 two-doors). Six-Way bench seat ($99.80). Power steering ($115.30). Remote control trunk release ($14.30). Power windows ($110.10). Protective vinyl body side moldings in Monterey ($25.90). AM radio ($63.50). AM/FM stereo radio ($239.60). AM radio stereo-sonic tape ($198.20). Automatic ride control ($28.10). DeLuxe front seat and shoulder belts ($15.60). Heavy-duty front-seating, fleet only ($33.70). Center-facing rear seats Mercury wagons includes tailgate step pad ($91.90). Single key locking system ($3.90). Speed control ($63.50). Rim-blow steering wheel ($19.50). Tilt steering wheel ($45.40). DeLuxe vinyl interior Monterey Marauder ($28.50). Vinyl roof ($115.30); wagons ($142.50). DeLuxe wheel covers Monterey and Marauder ($25.90). Luxury wheel covers ($46.70). Styled aluminum wheels, over hubs ($116.60); over DeLuxe ($90.70); Monterey, Marauder X-100 over luxury ($44.10); Marauder over Marauder appearance group ($90.70). Interval windshield wipers ($25.90). Mud and snow tires ($7.80). G78-15 whitewall or blackwall belted Monterey, Custom, Marauder ($31.10). H78-15 whitewall belted on Mercurys ($33.70); on Marauder, Monterey, Custom H70-15 blackwall wide tread ($51.90); on Mercurys ($49.30); on Monterey, Monterey Custom, Marauder ($67.40). Appearance protection group includes: door edge guards; license plate frames; front and rear rubber floor mats, two-door ($25.90); four-door ($29.80). Competition handling group, Marauder ($31.10). Decor group, Monterey, includes: DeLuxe steering wheel (with woodgrain spoke accents); curb molding: DeLuxe wheel covers ($57.10). Marauder appearance group includes: Marauder wheel covers, fender skirts and wheel opening molding ($57.10).

Historical footnotes: Most 1970 Marquis Broughams, 99.6 percent were equipped with air conditioning. Over 99 percent of all full-size Mercurys that had a three-speed manual listed as standard equipment, were sold with an automatic.

1971 MERCURY

1971 Mercury, Comet 2-dr sedan, V-8

COMET SERIES — Comet returned as a compact this year. It looked basically like a Maverick with makeup. The horizontal bar grille protruded slightly (harmonizing with the 'power dome' hood). The center horizontal bar was chromed. Rectangular signal lights were placed alongside the grille. The two headlights were recessed into a chromed background. Side trim consisted of wheel opening moldings and twin pin stripes which ran from the tip of the headlights to the door handles. Taillights were of the pod variety used on Montegos. Standard features included: front and rear arm rests, carpeting, vinyl headliner, cigar lighter, two-spoke steering wheel and light grey-gold check cloth and vinyl upholstery. A do-it-yourself repair manual was offered to Comet buyers.

COMET I.D. NUMBERS: See 1960 Monterey I.D. numbers.

COMET

Model Number	Body/Style Number	Body Type & Seating	Factory Price	Shipping Weight	Production Total
NA	30	2-dr Sedan-4P	2217	2335	54,884
NA	31	4-dr Sedan-4P	2276	2366	28,116

COMET ENGINE
Six: Cast iron block. Displacement: 170 cubic inches. Bore and stroke: 3.68 x 3.91 inches. Compression ratio: 9.00:1. Brake horsepower: 100 at 4200 R.P.M. Carburetor: one-barrel.

CHASSIS FEATURES: Wheelbase: 103 inches. Overall length: 181.7 inches. Tires: 6.45 x 14.

POWERTRAIN OPTIONS: A three-speed manual transmission was standard. Select-Shift automatic was optional for $183. A 115 horsepower 200 cubic inch six (one-barrel); 155 horsepower 200 cubic inch six (one-barrel) and a 210 horsepower 302 cubic inch V-8 (two-barrel) were available at extra cost. A handling and suspension package cost $12 extra.

CONVENIENCE OPITONS: GT package includes: blackout grille; dual body tape stripes; high-back bucket seats; wheel trim rings; hood scoop; dual racing mirrors; bright window frames; DeLuxe door trim panels and black instrument panel ($178.80). Heavy-duty battery ($12). Consolette with clock ($41.80). Rear window defogger ($28.60). Tinted glass ($37). Front and rear bumper guards ($23.90). Two-tone paint ($28.60). Power steering ($115.30). AM radio ($60.80). Vinyl roof ($77.50) Floor-mounted shifters, with automatic or three-speed manual transmissions ($13.10). DeLuxe trim option ($39.40). Vinyl trim ($17.90). DeLuxe wheel covers ($23.90). Convenience group ($26.30). Exterior decor group ($52.50). Air conditioner ($370.60).

Historical footnote Most 1971 Comets, 81 percent, came with automatic transmission, 61.9 percent had a six, 48.3 percent had power steering, 33.2 percent had tinted glass and 24.6 percent had air conditioning.

MONTEGO SERIES — The Montego's protruding grille was toned down a bit for 1971. It now had a criss-cross pattern. Side trim consisted of wheel opening and window moldings. Last year's pod style taillights remained. The instrument panel had wood-grain trim.

MONTEGO I.D. NUMBERS: See 1960 Monterey I.D. numbers.

MONTEGO

Model Number	Body/Style Number	Body Type & Seating	Factory Price	Shipping Weight	Production Total
NA	01	2-dr HT Cpe-6P	2777	3124	9,623
NA	02	4-dr Sedan-6P	2772	3125	5,718

MONTEGO ENGINE
Six: Cast iron block. Displacement: 250 cubic inches. Bore and stroke: 3.68 x 3.91 inches. Compression ratio: 9.00:1. Brake horsepower: 145 at 4000 R.P.M. Carburetor: one-barrel.

MONTEGO MX SERIES — The MX had chrome rocker panels and its name written on the rear fenders. Fancier wheel covers and a slightly plusher interior were the main differences between the MX and the basic Montego.

MONTEGO MX I.D. NUMBERS: See 1960 Monterey I.D. numbers.

MONTEGO MX

Model Number	Body/Style Number	Body Type & Seating	Factory Price	Shipping Weight	Production Total
NA	06	4-dr Sedan-6P	2891	3131	13,559
NA	07	2-dr HT Cpe-6P	2891	3130	13,719
NA	08	4-dr Sta Wag-6P	3215	3547	3,698

MONTEGO MX ENGINE
See 1971 Montego Series engine data.

1971 Mercury, Montego MX Brougham 4-dr hardtop sedan, V-8

MONTEGO MX BROUGHAM SERIES — Upper body twin pin stripes and wheel opening and rocker panel moldings were styling features of the MX Brougham. It also had DeLuxe wheel covers. The upholstery was cloth and vinyl or all-vinyl. The door panels had wood-grain vinyl appliques. The Villager station wagon had wood-toned panels framed with chrome trim. A dual action tailgate was standard.

MONTEGO MX BROUGHAM I.D. NUMBERS: See 1960 Monterey I.D. numbers.

MONTEGO MX BROUGHAM

Model Number	Body/Style Number	Body Type & Seating	Factory Price	Shipping Weight	Production Total
NA	10	4-dr Sedan-6P	3073	3154	1,565
NA	11	2-dr HT Cpe-6P	3085	3171	2,851
NA	12	4-dr HT Sed-6P	3157	3198	1,156
NA	18	4-dr Sta Wag-6P	3456	3483	2,121

NOTE: Model number 18, the four-door station wagon, was called the Villager.

MONTEGO MX BROUGHAM ENGINE
See 1971 Montego Series engine data.

MONTEGO CYCLONE — SERIES — The new Cyclone looked virtually the same as last year's model. It came with a performance hood (having an integral scoop); running lights; cross country ride package; deep loop carpeting; dual racing mirrors; concealed wipers and flow-thru ventilation.

MONTEGO CYCLONE I.D. NUMBERS: See 1960 Monterey I.D. numbers.

MONTEGO CYCLONE

Model Number	Body/Style Number	Body Type & Seating	Factory Price	Shipping Weight	Production Total
NA	15	2-dr HT Cpe-6P	3369	3587	444

MONTEGO CYCLONE ENGINE
V-8: Overhead valves. Cast iron block. Displacement: 351 cubic inches. Bore and stroke: 4. x 3.5 inches. Compression ratio: 10.70:1. Brake horsepower: 285 at 5400 R.P.M. Carburetor: four-barrel.

MONTEGO CYCLONE GT SERIES — The GT had the same standard equipment as the basic Cyclone, plus high-back bucket seats; DeLuxe wheel covers; full instrumentation (tachometer, oil gauge, temperature gauge and ammeter); three-spoke steering wheel and concealed headlights.

MONTEGO CYCLONE GT I.D. NUMBERS: See 1960 Monterey I.D. numbers.

MONTEGO CYCLONE GT

Model Number	Body/Style Number	Body Type & Seating	Factory Price	Shipping Weight	Production Total
NA	16	2-dr HT Cpe-5P	3681	3493	2,287

MONTEGO CYCLONE GT ENGINE
V-8: Overhead valves. Cast iron block. Displacement: 351 cubic inches. Bore and stroke: 4 x 3.5 inches. Compression ratio: 9.00:1. Brake horsepower: 240 at 4600 R.P.M. Carburetor: two-barrel.

MONTEGO CYCLONE SPOILER SERIES — Higher positioned side body stripes and a less potent standard engine were the most noticeable changes made to the Spoiler in 1971. It came with front and rear spoilers, hub caps with bright trim rings and Traction-Lok differential with 3.25:1 gear ratio rear axle.

MONTEGO CYCLONE SPOILER I.D. NUMBERS: See 1960 Monterey I.D. numbers.

MONTEGO CYCLONE SPOILER

Model Number	Body/Style Number	Body Type & Seating	Factory Price	Shipping Weight	Production Total
NA	17	2-dr HT Cpe-5P	3801	3580	353

MONTEGO CYCLONE SPOILER ENGINE
See 1971 Cyclone Series engine data.

CHASSIS FEATURES: Wheelbase: (passenger cars) 117 inches; (station wagons) 114 inches. Overall length: (passenger cars) 209.9 inches; (station wagons) 211.8 inches. Tires: (Montego MX) F78-14; (station wagons and Cyclone GT) G78-14; (Cyclone and Spoiler) G70x14; (other models) E78x14.

POWERTRAIN OPTIONS: A three-speed manual transmission was standard in the Montego, MX and MX Brougham. A four-speed manual gear box with Hurst shifter was standard in the Cyclone and Spoiler. The Cyclone GT came with Select Shift automatic. Four-speed and automatic transmissions were optional in the other series. The four-speed was not offered in station wagons. The cross-country ride package, which included heavy-duty springs, front stabilizer bar and shocks cost $16.90. Ram-air induction was available on Cyclones with the 429 cubic inch Cobra Jet V-8 for $64.80. A higher ratio and Traction-Loc axle were optional. The following V-8 engines were available: 210 horsepower 302 cubic inch (two-barrel); 240 horsepower 351 cubic inch (two-barrel); 285 horsepower 351 cubic inch (four-barrel); 370 horsepower Cobra Jet 429 cubic inch (four-barrel) and 370 horsepower Super Cobra Jet 429 cubic inch (four-barrel).

CONVENIENCE OPTIONS: Heavy-duty battery ($13). Electric clock ($18.20). Extra-duty cooling package ($7.80). Console ($60.90). Rear window defroster ($48). Tinted glass ($42.80). Luggage carrier on MX station wagon ($59.60); on MX station wagon with air deflector ($79.10). Remote-control lefthand mirror ($13). Body side molding ($33.70). Front disc brakes ($70). Four-Way power seat ($77.80). Power steering ($115.30). Power windows ($115.30). Power tailgate window ($35). AM radio ($66.10). AM/FM stereo radio ($218.90). Vinyl covered roof ($99.80). DeLuxe seat

and shoulder belts ($38.90). High-back bucket seats ($132.20). Houndstooth Cyclone interior ($32.40). Third seat for station wagons ($80). Two-tone comfort weave seats in Montego MX ($32.40). Rim-blow steering wheel ($35). Tilting steering wheel ($45.40). Hub caps with trim rings in Cyclones ($31.10). DeLuxe wheel covers ($25.90). Luxury wheel covers ($18.20). Courtesy light group ($20.80). Instrumentation group ($84.20). Trailer towing package ($120.50). Air conditioner ($408).

Historical Footnote: Most 1971 Montegos, 97.1 percent, were equipped with automatic transmission, 91.5 percent had a V-8 engine, 94.5 percent had power steering, 49.5 percent had power brakes, 8.5 percent had power windows and 58.3 percent had an air conditioner. Mercurys won 11 NASCAR Grand National races in 1971.

COUGAR SERIES — The Cougar's front end was restyled. The four headlights were exposed and recessed. The signal lights wrapped around the front fenders. The protruding center grille had vertical bars and was framed in chrome. An ornament was set in its center. Triple, mid tire level, pin stripes ran from fender to fender. There were moldings on the wheel well openings. The rear bumper was integrated into the rear deck panel, which housed the large rectangular taillights. Standard features included: high-back bucket seats; cigar ligher; concealed wipers; consolette with illuminated ash tray; glove box and panel courtesly lights and flow-thru ventilation system.

COUGAR I.D. NUMBERS: See 1960 Monterey I.D. numbers.

COUGAR

Model Number	Body/Style Number	Body Type & Seating	Factory Price	Shipping Weight	Production Total
NA	91	2-dr HT Cpe-5P	3289	3285	34,008
NA	92	2-dr Conv-5P	3681	3415	1,723

COUGAR ENGINE
See 1971 Montego Cyclone GT Series engine data.

1971 Mercury, Cougar XR-7 2-dr hardtop, V-8

COUGAR XR-7 SERIES — The XR-7 had chrome rocker panels, distinctive wheel covers and ornamentation and a unique vinyl covered half-roof. It also provided high-back bucket seats with leather seating surfaces, a fully instrumented dash panel (i.e. tach, trip odometer, toggle switches) and a remote-control lefthand racing mirror. The instrument board and steering wheel had wood-grain appliques. The convertible had a tinted windshield.

COUGAR XR-7 I.D. NUMBERS: See 1960 Monterey I.D. numbers.

COUGAR XF-7

Model Number	Body/Style Number	Body Type & Seating	Factory Price	Shipping Weight	Production Total
NA	93	2-dr HT Cpe-5P	3629	3314	25,416
NA	94	2-dr Conv-5P	3877	3454	1,717

COUGAR XR-7 ENGINE
See 1971 Montego Cyclone GT Series engine data.

CHASSIS FEATURES: Wheelbase: 112.1 inches. Overall length: 196.9 inches. Tires: E78 x 14.

POWERTRAIN OPTIONS: A console-mounted three-speed manual transmission was standard. A four-speed manual gear box with Hurst shifter and Select Shift automatic transmission were optional. The following V-8s were available: 285 horsepower 351 cubic inch (four-barrel) and 370 horsepower Super Cobra Jet 429 cubic inch (four-barrel). A GT package was offered for $129.60. It featured a high-ratio axle; competition suspension; dual racing mirrors; hood scoop (non-functional except with the 429 Cobra Jet V-8 and Ram-Air); performance cooling package; tachometer; rim-blow steering wheel; F78 x 14 whitewall tires; hub caps with bright trim rings; GT fender identification badges and black-finished instrument panel. A higher ratio axle cost $13 extra and a competition handling package was a $32.40 option.

CONVENIENCE OPTIONS: Air conditioner ($408). Heavy-duty battery ($13). Sports console with clock ($76.50). Rear window defroster ($48). Tinted glass ($37.60); on convertibles ($15.60). Lefthand remote-control racing mirror ($15.60). Power front disc brakes ($70). Four-Way power driver's seat ($77.80). Power steering ($115.30). Power windows ($115.30). Vinyl roof with power sun roof ($483.10). AM radio ($66.10). AM/FM stereo radio ($218.90). AM radio with stereo tape system ($200.80). Vinyl roof ($89.40). DeLuxe wheel covers ($25.90). Wire wheel covers ($84.20). Styled steel wheels ($58.30). Appearance protection group ($32.40). Convenience group on closed cars($32.40); on convertibles ($32.40). Decor group ($90.70).

Historical Footnote: Most 1971 Cougars, 96.9 percent, were equipped with automatictransmission, 75 percent had an air conditioner, 98.5 percent had power steering, 77.9 percent had tinted glass, 79.7 percent had disc brakes, 4.6 percent had power seats and 8.9 percent had power windows.

MONTEREY SERIES — The Monterey's wraparound grille was a wave of horizontal bars that came to a point at the center. The four chrome-rimmed headlights were recessed into the grille. Signal lights were located in the front bumper. There was no side trim other than the Monterey name, written in chrome, on the lower quarter panel. The large, rectangular bumper-integrated taillights wrapped around the rear fenders. Standard features included: cloth and vinyl upholstery; carpeting; courtesy and trunk compartment lights; power vent system; recessed outside door handles; dual ash trays and temperature and braking system warning lights.

MONTEREY I.D. NUMBERS: See 1960 Monterey I.D. numbers.

1971 Mercury, Monterey 2-dr hardtop coupe, V-8

MONTEREY

Model Number	Body/Style Number	Body Type & Seating	Factory Price	Shipping Weight	Production Total
NA	44	4-dr Sedan-6P	3423	4028	22,744
NA	47	2-dr HT Cpe-6P	3465	3958	9,099
NA	48	4-dr HT Sed-6P	3533	4024	2,483
NA	72	4-dr Sta Wag-6P	4283	4384	4,160

MONTEREY ENGINE
See 1971 Montego Cyclone GT Series engine data.

MONTEREY CUSTOM SERIES — Rocker panel and lower side window moldings, plus a full-length, mid body side chrome spear, set the Custom apart from the plain Monterey. It also had DeLuxe wheel covers and a plusher interior.

MONTEREY CUSTOM I.D. NUMBERS: See 1960 Monterey I.D. numbers.

MONTEREY CUSTOM

Model Number	Body/Style Number	Body Type & Seating	Factory Price	Shipping Weight	Production Total
NA	54	4-dr Sedan-6P	3958	4105	12,411
NA	56	2-dr HT Cpe-6P	4141	4028	4,508
NA	58	4-dr HT Sed-6P	4113	4104	1,397

MONTEREY CUSTOM ENGINE
V-8: Overhead valves. Cast iron block. Displacement: 400 cubic inches. Bore and stroke: 4 x 4 inches. Compression ratio: 9.00:1. Brake horsepower: 260 at 4400 R.P.M. Carburetor: two-barrel.

MARQUIS SERIES — Changes in the Marquis for 1971 were evolutionary, yet noticable. The word Mercury replaced 'Marquis' on the left headlight door. The protruding type horizontal bar grille was outlined, at the top, by a larger piece of chrome and was no longer centrally divided by the bumper. A full-length chrome stripe ran at slightly above mid tire level. There was chrome trim on the front wheel openings and on the standard fender skirts. The taillight treatment was the same as that used on the Monterey, except for the trunk lid molding and distinct center rear deck panel trim.

MARQUIS I.D. NUMBERS: See 1960 Monterey I.D. numbers.

MARQUIS

Model Number	Body/Style Number	Body Type & Seating	Factory Price	Shipping Weight	Production Total
NA	40	4-dr Sedan-6P	4474	4311	16,030
NA	41	2-dr HT Cpe-6P	4557	4240	7,726
NA	42	4-dr HT Sed-6P	4624	4306	5,491
NA	74	4-dr Sta Wag-6P	4547	4411	2,158
NA	76	4-dr Sta Wag-6P	4806	4471	20,004

NOTE: Model Number 76, a four-door station wagon, was called the Colony Park.

MARQUIS ENGINE
V-8: Overhead valves. Cast iron block. Displacement: 429 cubic inches. Bore and stroke: 4.36 x 3.59. Compression ratio: 10.50:1. Brake horsepower: 320 at 4400 R.P.M. Carburetor: two-barrel.

MARQUIS BROUGHAM SERIES — The Brougham had full-length, upper body moldings, a vinyl covered roof and color-keyed wheel covers (i.e. the center hub of the covers was the same color as the car). Like the basic Marquis, it came with most power equipment standard.

MARQUIS BROUGHAM I.D. NUMBERS: See 1960 Monterey I.D. numbers.

MARQUIS BROUGHAM

Model Number	Body/Style Number	Body Type & Seating	Factory Price	Shipping Weight	Production Total
NA	63	4-dr Sedan-6P	4880	4354	25,790
NA	66	2-dr HT Cpe-6P	4963	4271	14,570
NA	68	4-dr HT Sed-6P	5033	4341	13,781

MARQUIS BROUGHAM ENGINE
See 1971 Marquis Series engine data.

CHASSIS FEATURES: Wheelbase (passenger cars) 124 inches; (station wagons) 121 inches. Overall length: (passenger cars) 224.7 inches; (station wagons) 220.5 inches. Tires: (Monterey) G78 x 15; (Marquis and wagons) H78 x 15.

POWERTRAIN OPTIONS: Select-shift automatic transmission was standard in all, but the basic Monterey sedan and hardtop. They came with a three-speed manual transmission, but could be ordered with the automatic at extra cost. The following V-8 engines were available: 260 horsepower 400 cubic inch (two-barrel); 320 horsepower 429 cubic inch (two-barrel); 360 horsepower 429 cubic inch (four-barrel) and a 370 horsepower 429 cubic inch (four-barrel). Higher ratio and Traction-Lok axles were optional.

CONVENIENCE OPTIONS: Air conditioning ($441.70). Air conditioning with automatic temperature controls ($520.70). Heavy-duty battery ($36.30). Rear window defogger ($31.10). Rear window defroster ($63.50). Tinted glass ($51.90). Cornering lamps ($36.30). Automatic load adjuster ($79.10). Luggage carrier with air deflector ($94.60). Luggage carrier with air deflector on Colony Park ($20.80). Metallic paint ($38.90). Power antenna ($32.40). Power front disc brakes ($71.30). Power door locks in two-doors ($45.40); in four-doors ($68.70). Six-Way power seat ($104.90); driver's side power seat ($89.40); both seats power operated ($178.80). Remote-control trunk release ($14.30). Power steering on Monterey sedan and hardtop ($125.70). Power windows ($132.20). AM radio ($66.10). AM/FM stereo radio ($239.60). AM radio with stereo tape system ($200.80). Dual, rear-seat speakers

($33.70). Vinyl roof on Monterey ($119.20); on station wagons ($142.50). Vinyl 'Halo' roof on Marquis ($128.30). DeLuxe seat and shoulder belts ($15.60). Center-facing third seat on station wagons ($128.60). Reclining passenger seat ($44.10). Twin comfort lounge seats ($77.80). Vinyl interior trim in Monterey ($28.50). Fender skirts in Monterey and Custom ($36.30). Speed control ($68.70). Tilting steering wheel ($45.40). Luxury wheel covers on Monterey ($59.60). Rear window washer on station wagons ($38.90). Convenience group on two-doors ($46.70); on four-doors ($23.40). Appearance protection group ($38.90); same on station wagons ($25.90). Decor group on Monterey ($80.40). Suspension ride package ($23.40). Trailer towing package ($90.70).

Historical Footnote: Most full-size 1971 Mercurys, 90 percent, were equipped with an air conditioner, 28.5 percent had a tilting steering wheel, 27.6 percent had power windows and 90.4 percent had tinted glass.

1972 MERCURY

1972 Mercury, Comet 2-dr sedan, V-8

COMET SERIES — Comet's biggest styling change for 1972 was its dual, full-length upper body pin stripes. Aside from that, it looked the same as last year's model. Standard features included: locking steering column, two-speed windshield wipers/washers, lefthand outside rearview mirror, door-operated courtesy lights, carpeting and heater.

COMET I.D. NUMBERS: See 1960 Monterey I.D. numbers.

COMET

Model Number	Body/Style Number	Body Type & Seating	Factory Price	Shipping Weight	Production Total
NA	30	4-dr Sedan-4P	2398	2674	29,092
NA	31	2-dr Sedan-4P	2342	2579	53,267

COMET ENGINE
Six: Cast iron block. Displacement: 170 cubic inches. Bore and stroke: 3.68 x 3.91 inches. Compression ratio: 9.00:1. SAE net horsepower: 82 at 4400 R.P.M. Carburetor: one-barrel.

CHASSIS FEATURES: Wheelbase: 110 inches. Overall length: (four-door) 187 inches; (two-door) 182 inches. Tires: 6.45 x 14.

POWERTRAIN OPTION: A three-speed manual transmission was standard. Select Shift automatic was optional. A 91 horsepower 200 cubic inch six (one-barrel), 98 horsepower 250 cubic inch six (one-barrel) and a 138 horsepower 302 cubic inch V-8 (two-barrel) were available at extra cost.

CONVENIENCE OPTIONS: GT package included: high-back bucket seats; DeLuxe door trim panels; hood scoop; dual racing mirrors; hub caps with bright trim rings; bright window frames; dual body tape stripes; blackout grille, headlamp doors and lower back panel paint treatment and black dash panel with bright moldings ($173.34). Air conditioner ($359.59). Front and rear bumper guards ($23.11). Consolette with clock ($40.45). Rear-window defogger ($27.73). Door edge guards on two-doors ($5.78); four-doors ($8.10). Tinted windows ($52.01). Body side moldings ($30.05). Two-tone paint ($27.73). Glamour paint ($34.66). Power steering ($92.45). AM radio ($58.94). AM/FM radio ($123.65). Vinyl-covered roof ($72.12). Bucket seats ($72.12). Vinyl trim on two-doors ($17.34). DeLuxe trim ($38.14). Trim rings with hub caps ($27.73). DeLuxe wheel covers ($23.11). Convenience group ($25.54). Exterior decor group ($50.84).

Historical footnotes: Most 1972 Comets, 88 percent, were sold with an automatic transmission, 38.3 percent had a V-8 engine, 38.5 percent had tinted glass, 64.8 percent had power steering, 89 percent had radios, 13.6 percent had bucket seats and 36.3 percent had a vinyl roof.

MONTEGO SERIES — The protruding, chrome outlined grille of the new Montego featured a criss-cross pattern that was carred over to the headlight panels. Wheel well opening moldings were about the only side trim used. The four large rectangular taillights were bumper integrated. Interiors were trimmed in either cloth and vinyl or all-vinyl.

MONTEGO I.D. NUMBERS: See 1960 Monterey I.D. numbers.

MONTEGO

Model Number	Body/Style Number	Body Type & Seating	Factory Price	Shipping Weight	Production Total
NA	02	4-dr Sedan-6P	2843	3454	8,658
NA	03	2-dr HT Cpe-6P	2848	3390	9,963

MONTEGO ENGINE
Six: Cast iron block. Displacement: 250 cubic inches. Bore and stroke: 3.68 x 3.91. Compression ratio: 9.00:1. SAE net horsepower: 95 at 3500 R.P.M. Carburetor: one-barrel.

MONTEGO MX SERIES: Dual upper body pin stripes, running from the front fenders to the rear side windows, and bright rocker panel moldings, were two features of the Montego MX. DeLuxe sound insulation, carpeting and, on the wagon a three-way tailgate, were standard features of the MX line.

MONTEGO MX I.D. NUMBERS: See 1960 Monterey I.D. numbers.

MONTEGO MX

Model Number	Body/Style Number	Body Type & Seating	Factory Price	Shipping Weight	Production Total
NA	04	4-dr Sedan-6P	2951	3485	23,387
NA	07	2-dr HT Cpe-6P	2971	3407	25,802
NA	08	4-dr Sta Wag-6P	3264	3884	6,268

MONTEGO MX ENGINE
See 1972 Montego Series engine data.

1972 Mercury, Montego MX Brougham 2-dr hardtop coupe, V-8

MONTEGO MX BROUGHAM SERIES — Rocker sill, lower rear quarter panel and upper body moldings were styling features of the Montego MX Brougham, which also came with DeLuxe wheel covers, 'flight-bench' folding arm rest seats and a wood-grain applique on the steering wheel. The Villager wagon had wood-grained side body and tailgate paneling.

MONTEGO MX BROUGHAM I.D. NUMBERS: See 1960 Monterey I.D. numbers.

MONTEGO MX BROUGHAM

Model Number	Body/Style Number	Body Type & Seating	Factory Price	Shipping Weight	Production Total
NA	10	4-dr Sedan-6P	3127	3512	17,540
NA	11	2-dr HT Cpe-6P	3137	3433	28,417
NA	18	4-dr Sta Wag-6P	3438	3907	9,237

NOTE: Model number 18, a four-door station wagon, was called the Villager.

MONTEGO MX BROUGHAM ENGINE
See 1972 Montego Series engine data.

MONTEGO GT SERIES — The GT had full-length, tire level side moldings; a performance hood; dual racing mirrors; louvres behind the doors; a tachometer; gauges and a special black-finished instrument panel.

MONTEGO GT I.D. NUMBERS: See 1960 Monterey I.D. numbers.

MONTEGO GT

Model Number	Body/Style Number	Body Type & Seating	Factory Price	Shipping Weight	Production Total
NA	16	2-dr HT Fsk BK-5P	3346	3517	5,820

MONTEGO GT ENGINE
V-8: Overhead valves. Cast iron block. Displacement: 302 cubic inches. Bore and stroke: 4 x 3 inches. Compression ratio: 8.50:1. SAE net horsepower: 140 at 4000 R.P.M. Carburetor: two-barrel.

CHASSIS FEATURES: Wheelbase: (four-doors) 118 inches; (two-doors) 114 inches. Overall length: (four-doors) 213 inches; (two-doors) 209 inches; (station wagons) 216 inches. Front tread: 62.8 inches. Rear tread: 62.9 inches. Tires: (MX and GT) F78 x 14); (station wagons) F78 x 14; (other models) E78 x 14.

POWERTRAIN OPTIONS: A three-speed manual transmission was standard. A four-speed manual gear box (with Hurst shifter) and Select Shift automatic transmission were optional. Buyers of the Cyclone option package (which included: functional dual hood scoop; Traction-Lok differential; wide oval tires; special striping; dual racing mirror and three-spoke steering wheel) could choose either four-speed or automatic transmissions. A 140 horsepower 302 cubic inch V-8 (two-barrel); a 161 horsepower 351 cubic inch V-8 (two-barrel); a 248 horsepower CJ 351 cubic inch V-8; a 168 horsepower 400 cubic inch V-8 (two-barrel) and a 201 horsepower 429 cubic inch V-8 (four-barrel) were optional. A higher ratio axle cost $12.62. Traction-Lok differential sold for $46.76. A competition handling package was $27.76 extra.

CONVENIENCE OPTIONS: Air conditioner ($397.91). Front bumper guards ($15.14). Electric clock ($17.67). Console ($59.32). Tinted windows ($41.66). Carpeted load floor in station wagons ($25.24). Dual racing mirrors ($12.62). Lefthand remote-control mirror ($12.62). Glamour paint ($37.86). Power front disc brakes ($68.14). Power door locks in two-doors ($44.17); in four-doors ($66.89); in station wagons ($75.72). Six-Way power bench seat ($102.22). Power steering ($112.33). Power windows ($112.33). Power tailgate window in station wagons ($34.08) AM radio ($58.94). AM/FM stereo radio ($213.29). Vinyl-covered roof ($97.18). High back bucket seats ($128.72). Rear-facing third seat in station wagons ($75.81). Hub caps with trim rings ($30.29). DeLuxe wheel covers ($25.24). Luxury wheel covers ($17.67). Interval windshield wipers ($25.24). Appearance group on pasenger cars ($31.55); on station wagons ($25.54). Convenience group on two-doors ($47.96); on four-doors ($25.24). Instrumentation group ($99.71). Cross-country ride package ($16.41). Visibility group ($25.24).

Historical footnote: Only 3.3 percent of 1972 Montegos came with bucket seats, 60.8 percent had a vinyl roof, 97.1 percent had a radio, 99.2 percent had automatic transmission, 97.2 percent had a V-8 engine, 97.8 percent had power steering and 14.8 percent had power windows.

MONTEREY SERIES — A waffle pattern grille was the biggest Monterey styling change for 1972. Standard features included: power steering; simulated Cherrywood instrument cluster; color-keyed two-spoke steering wheel; power front disc brakes; Nylon loop carpeting and cloth and vinyl upholstery.

MONTEREY I.D. NUMBERS: See 1960 Monterey I.D. numbers.

MONTEREY

Model Number	Body/Style Number	Body Type & Seating	Factory Price	Shipping Weight	Production Total
NA	44	2-dr Sedan-6P	3793	4136	19,012
NA	46	2-dr HT Cpe-6P	3832	4086	6,731
NA	48	4-dr HT Sed-6P	3896	4141	1,416
NA	74	4-dr Sta Wag-6P	4445	4539	4,644

MONTEREY ENGINE
V-8: Overhead valves. Cast iron block. Displacement: 351 cubic inches. Bore and stroke: 4 x 3.5 inches. Compression ratio: 8.60:1. SAE net horsepower: 163 at 3800 R.P.M. Carburetor: two-barrel.
Station wagon V-8: Overhead valves. Cast iron block. Displacement: 400 cubic inches. Bore and stroke: 4 x 4 inches. Compression ratio: 8.40:1. SAE net horsepower: 172 at 4000 R.P.M. Carburetor: two-barrel.

MONTEREY CUSTOM SERIES — Full-length mid body side moldings, DeLuxe wheel covers and chrome rocker panels helped distinguish Customs from basic Montereys. The Custom's cloth and vinyl interior was also more luxurious.

MONTEREY CUSTOM I.D. NUMBERS: See 1960 Monterey I.D. numbers.

MONTEREY CUSTOM

Model Number	Body/Style Number	Body Type & Seating	Factory Price	Shipping Weight	Production Total
NA	54	4-dr Sedan-6P	3956	4225	16,879
NA	56	2-dr HT Cpe-6P	4035	4175	5,910
NA	58	4-dr HT Sed-6P	4103	4230	1,583

MONTEREY CUSTOM ENGINE
See 1972 Monterey Station Wagon Series engine data.

1972 Mercury, Marquis Brougham 4-dr hardtop sedan, V-8

MARQUIS SERIES — A new ice-cube-tray-pattern grille and similar treatment in the center section of the rear deck panel were the main styling changes for 1972. Standard equipment included: power front disc brakes; power steering; DeLuxe sound insulation; power ventilation; 100 percent Nylon loop carpeting; DeLuxe wheel covers; wood-grain instrument panel; electric clock; map light; luggage compartment light; twin ash tray and courtesy lights.

MARQUIS I.D. NUMBERS: See 1960 Monterey I.D. numbers.

MARQUIS

Model Number	Body/Style Number	Body Type & Seating	Factory Price	Shipping Weight	Production Total
NA	63	4-dr Sedan-6P	4493	4386	14,122
NA	66	2-dr HT Cpe-6P	4572	4336	5,507
NA	68	4-dr HT Sed-6P	4637	4391	1,583
NA	74	4-dr Sta Wag-6P	4445	4539	2,085

MARQUIS ENGINE
V-8: Overhead valves. Cast iron block. Displacement: 429 cubic inches. Bore and stroke: 4.36 x 3.59 inches. Compression ratio: 8.50:1. SAE net horsepower: 208 at 4400 R.P.M. Carburetor: four-barrel. (Station wagons same as Monterey station wagons.)

MARQUIS BROUGHAM SERIES — The Brougham had fender-to-fender, upper body moldings. In addition to standard Marquis features, it came with a vinyl robe cord; cut-pile Nylon carpeting; front door courtesy lights; vanity mirror on the righthand sun-visor; power windows; vinyl roof; color-keyed wheel covers; interior pillar lights and ash trays and lighters in the rear seat arm rests.

MARQUIS BROUGHAM I.D. NUMBERS: See 1960 Monterey I.D. numbers.

MARQUIS BROUGHAM

Model Number	Body/Style Number	Body Type & Seating	Factory Price	Shipping Weight	Production Total
NA	62	4-dr Sedan-6P	4890	4436	38,242
NA	64	2-dr HT Cpe-6P	4969	4386	20,064
NA	67	4-dr HT Sed-6P	5034	4441	12,841
NA	76	4-dr Sta Wag-6P	4550	4579	20,192

MARQUIS BROUGHAM ENGINE
See 1972 Marquis Series engine data. (Station wagons same as Monterey station wagons.)

CHASSIS FEATURES: Wheelbase: (passenger cars) 124 inches; (station wagons) 121 inches. Overall length: (passenger cars) 225 inches; (station wagons) 221 inches. Front tread: 63.3 inches. Rear tread: 64.3 inches. Tires: H78 x 15.

POWERTRAIN OPTIONS: Select-shift automatic transmission was standard. A 172 horsepower 400 cubic inch V-8 (two-barrel); 208 horsepower 429 cubic inch V-8 (four-barrel) and a 224 horsepower 460 cubic inch V-8 were optional.

CONVENIENCE OPTIOS: Air conditioner ($430.58); with automatic temperature controls($507.55) DeLuxe seat and shoulder belts ($50.49). Heavy-duty battery ($12.62). Front bumper guards ($8.84). Electric rear window defroster ($61.84). Tinted glass ($50.49). Cornering lamps ($35.34). Automatic load adjuster ($76.99). Luggage carrier with air deflector on station wagons ($92.13). Glamour paint ($37.86). Sure track brake system ($189.30). Power door locks in two-doors ($44.17); in four-doors ($66.89). Six-Way power bench seat ($102.22). Six-Way left and righthand power seat ($174.16). Power sun roof ($495.97). Power windows ($128.72). Remote-control trunk release ($13.89). AM radio ($64.37). AM/FM stereo radio ($233.47). AM radio

with stereo tape system ($195.62). Vinyl roof Monterey and Custom ($97.18); station wagons ($138.82); Marquis ($124.95). Center-facing third seat ($122.27). Twin comfort lounge seat ($75.72). Speed control ($66.89). Tilting steering wheel ($44.17). Vanity mirror ($3.79). DeLuxe wheel covers Monterey and wagons ($25.24). Luxury wheel covers ($32.82). Interval windshield wipers ($25.24). Rear windshield washer on station wagons ($37.89). Appearance protection group ($37.36). Convenience group on two-doors ($58.05); on four-doors ($35.34). Cross-country ride package ($22.71). Trailer-towing package ($88.34).

Historical footnotes: Most full-size 1972 Mercurys, 73.5 percent, came with a vinyl roof.

1972 Mercury, Cougar XR-7 2-dr hardtop sports coupe, V-8

COUGAR SERIES — The fine, criss-cross pattern on the wraparound front signal lights was replaced by a design of horizontal lines. Otherwise, the 1972 Cougar looked virtually the same as last year's model. Among the standard features were: high-back bucket seats; sequential turn signals; locking steering column; backup lights; consolette with illuminated ash tray; concealed two-speed windshield wipers; dual racing mirrors; two-spoke steering wheel; DeLuxe wheel covers; instrument panel courtesy lights; glove box light and flow-thru ventilation.

COUGAR I.D. NUMBERS: See 1960 Monterey I.D. numbers.

COUGAR

Model Number	Body/Style Number	Body Type & Seating	Factory Price	Shipping Weight	Production Total
NA	91	2-dr HT Cpe-5P	3016	3282	23,731
NA	92	2-dr Conv-5P	3370	3412	1,240

COUGAR ENGINE
V-8: Overhead valves. Cast iron block. Displacement: 351 cubic inches. Bore and stroke: 4 x 3.5 inches. Compression ratio: 8.60:1. SAE net horsepower: 163 at 3800 R.P.M. Carburetor: two-barrel.

COUGAR XR-7 SERIES — The XR-7 came with an emblem in the center of the grille; a half-vinyl roof; bucket seats with leather seating; tachometer; sissy bar; alternator gauge; oil pressure gauge and Nylon carpeting.

COUGAR XR-7 I.D. NUMBERS: See 1960 Monterey I.D. numbers.

COUGAR XR-7

Model Number	Body/Style Number	Body Type & Seating	Factory Price	Shipping Weight	Production Total
NA	93	2-dr HT Cpe-5P	3323	3298	26,802
NA	94	2-dr Conv-5P	3547	3451	1,929

COUGAR XR-7 ENGINE
See 1972 Cougar Series engine data.

CHASSIS FEATURES: Wheelbase: 112.1 inches. Overall length: 196.1 inches. Front tread: 61.5 inches. Rear tread: 61 inches. Tires: E78 x 14.

POWER TRAIN OPTIONS: A three-speed manual transmission was standard. Four-speed manual transmission (with a Hurst shifter) and a Select Shift automatic gear box were offered. A 262 horsepower 351 cubic inch V-8 (four-barrel) and a 266 horsepower CJ 351 cubic inch V-8 were optional. The latter engine came with dual exhaust and competition suspension. The $115.96 GT options package included higher axle ratio; hood scoop; tachometer; performance cooling package; DeLuxe steering wheel; trim rings; black instrument panel and dual racing mirrors. A competition handling package was available for $28.89. Higher ratio axles and Traction-Lok differentials were also available.

CONVENIENCE OPTIONS: Air conditioning ($364.01). Front bumper guards ($13.87). Sports console with clock ($68.18). Rear window defroster ($42.76). Tinted windows in closed cars($33.52); in convertibles ($13.87). Dual racing mirrors with lefthand remote-control ($23.11). Protective body side molding ($30.05). Glamour paint ($34.66). Power front disc brakes ($62.40). Four-Way power seat ($69.34). Power steering ($102.86). Power sun roof ($431.04). Power windows ($102.86). AM radio ($58.94). AM/FM stereo radio ($195.30). AM radio with stereo tape system ($179.12). Vinyl roof ($79.73). Tilting steering wheel ($40.45). Upbeat stripe cloth trim (no charge with decor group). DeLuxe wheel covers ($23.11). Wire wheel covers ($75.12). Interval windshield wipers ($23.11). Appearance protection group ($28.89). Convenience group ($42.76). Exterior decor group ($80.89).

Historical footnotes: The vast majority of 1972 Cougars, 98.5 percent were equipped with an automatic, 87.9 percent had power brakes, 98.1 percent had a radio, 78.9 percent had vinyl roofs, 21.9 percent had tilting steering wheels, 5.7 percent had power seats, and 99.1 percent had power steering.

1973 MERCURY

COMET SERIES — Comet received a new, criss-cross pattern grille and energy-absorbing bumpers. However, basic styling remained the same as it had since 1971. Standard features included: dual hydraulic brakes with warning light system; blend-air heater; wheel lip moldings; rocker panel moldings; carpeting; front and rear ash trays and cloth and vinyl upholstery.

COMET

Model Number	Body/Style Number	Body Type & Seating	Factory Price	Shipping Weight	Production Total
NA	30	4-dr Sedan-4P	2389	2904	28,984
NA	31	2-dr Sedan-4P	2432	2813	55,707

COMET ENGINE
Six: Cast iron block. Displacement: 200 cubic inches. Bore and stroke: 3.68 x 3.13 inches. Compression ratio: 8.30:1. SAE net horsepower: 94 at 3800 R.P.M. Carburetor: one-barrel.

1973 Mercury, Comet 2-dr sedan, 6-cyl

CHASSIS FEATURES: Wheelbase: (two-doors) 103 inches; (four-doors) 109.9 inches. Overall length: (two-doors) 185.4 inches; (four-doors) 192.3 inches. Tires: 6.45 x 14.

POWERTRAIN OPTIONS: A three-speed manual transmission was standard. Select-Shift automatic transmission was optional. An 88 horsepower 250 cubic inch six (one-barrel) and a 138 horsepower 302 cubic inch V-8 (two-barrel) were available at extra cost.

CONVENIENCE OPTIONS: GT package including high-back bucket seats: DeLuxe door trim panels; hood scoop; dual racing mirrors; hub caps with bright trim rings; bright window frames; dual body tape stripe; blacked-out grille; headlamp door, lower back panel and hood paint treatment and black dash panel with bright moldings ($173.34). Air conditioner ($359.59). Front and rear bumper guards ($23.11). Consolette with clock ($40.45). Rear window defogger ($27.73). Door edge guards on two-doors ($5.78); on four-doors ($8.10). Tinted windows ($52.01). Body side moldings ($30.05). Two-tone paint ($27.73). Glamour paint ($34.66). Power steering ($92.45). AM radio ($58.94). AM/FM radio ($123.65). Vinyl covered roof ($72.12). Bucket seats ($72.12). Vinyl trim on two-doors ($17.34). DeLuxe trim ($38.14). Trim rings with hub caps ($27.73). DeLuxe wheel covers ($23.11). Convenience group ($25.54). Exterior decor group ($50.84). Custom option including DeLuxe sound package; grained vinyl roof; radial tires; driver's side remote-control mirror; reclining expanded vinyl bucket seats; mid-side body moldings and distinctive dash ($346).

Historical footnotes: Most 1973 Comets, 91.82 percent, had radios, 35.2 percent had bucket seats, 37.4 percent had vinyl roof, 90 percent had automatic transmissions, 45.9 percent had V-8s and 50.4 percent had tinted glass.

MONTEGO SERIES — Larger, energy-absorbing bumpers were the most noticeable change made to Montegos for 1973. The standard interior was vinyl and cloth.

MONTEGO I.D. NUMBERS: See 1960 Monterey I.D. numbers.

MONTEGO

Model Number	Body/Style Number	Body Type & Seating	Factory Price	Shipping Weight	Production Total
NA	02	4-dr Sedan-6P	2916	3719	7,459
NA	03	2-dr HT Cpe-6P	2926	3653	7,082

MONTEGO ENGINE
Six: Overhead valves. Cast iron block. Displacement: 250 cubic inches. Bore and stroke: 3.68 x 3.91 inches. Compression ratio: 8.00:1. SAE net horsepower: 92 at 3200 R.P.M. Carburetor: one-barrel.

MONTEGO MX SERIES — Like last year, rocker panel moldings and dual, upper body pin stripes helped set the MX apart from the basic Montego. It also had DeLuxe sound insulation and color-keyed deep loop capeting.

MONTEGO MX I.D. NUMBERS: See 1960 Monterey I.D. numbers.

MONTEGO MX

Model Number	Body/Style Number	Body Type & Seating	Factory Price	Shipping Weight	Production Total
NA	10	4-dr Sedan-6P	3009	3772	25,300
NA	11	2-dr HT Cpe-6P	3041	3683	27,812
NA	08	4-dr Sta Wag-6P	3417	4124	7,012

MONTEGO MX ENGINE: For sedans and hardtops see 1973 Montego Series engine data; for station wagons V-8 power was standard, with specifications as follows: V-8: Overhead valves. Cast iron block. Displacement: 302 cubic inches. Bore and stroke: 4 x 3 inches. Compression ratio: 8.00:1. SAE net horsepower: 137 at 4200 R.P.M. Carburetor: two-barrel.

MONTEGO MX BROUGHAM SERIES — Bright upper body moldings and DeLuxe wheel covers were two distinguishing exterior features of the Brougham, which came with 'flight bench' seats. These were bench seats with backs that resembled buckets and a folding arm rest between them. The steering wheel had a wood-grain insert.

MONTEGO MX BROUGHAM I.D. NUMBERS: See 1960 Monterey I.D. numbers.

MONTEGO MX BROUGHAM

Model Number	Body/Style Number	Body Type & Seating	Factory Price	Shipping Weight	Production Total
NA	10	4-dr Sedan-6P	3189	3813	24,329
NA	11	2-dr HT Cpe-6P	3209	3706	40,951
NA	18	4-dr Sta Wag-6P	3606	4167	12,396

NOTE: Model number 18, a four-door station wagon, was called the Villager.

1973 Mercury, Montego MX Brougham 2-dr hardtop coupe, V-8

MONTEGO MX BROUGHAM ENGINE
Sedan and hardtop same as Montego Series engine data. Station wagon same as MX Station wagon engine data.

MONTEGO GT SERIES — New engery-absorbing bumpers and the placing of the letter 'G' over 'T' on the front fender nameplate, were the styling changes made for 1973. Standard features included: DeLuxe sound insulation; DeLuxe wheel covers; sports-type three-spoke steering wheel; deep loop carpeting; dual racing mirrors and performance hood with non-functional dual scoops.

MONTEGO GT I.D. NUMBERS: See 1960 Monterey I.D. numbers.

MONTEGO GT

Model Number	Body/Style Number	Body Type & Seating	Factory Price	Shipping Weight	Production Total
NA	16	2-dr HT Fstbk-6P	3413	3662	4,464

MONTEGO GT ENGINE
See 1973 Montego MX Station wagon engine data.

CHASSIS FEATURES: Wheelbase: (two-door) 114 inches; (four-doors and station wagons) 118 inches. Overall length: (two-doors) 211.3 inches; (four-door) 215.3 inches; (station wagons) 218.5 inches. Tires: (station wagons) F78 x 14 GT or G78 x 14; (other models) E78 x 14.

POWERTRAIN OPTIONS: A three-speed manual transmission was standard. A four-speed manual gear box (with Hurst shifter) and Select-Shift automatic transmission were optional. A 137 horsepower 302 cubic inch V-8 (two-barrel); 161 horsepower 351 cubic inch V-8 (two-barrel); 248 horsepower CJ 351 cubic inch V-8; 168 horsepower 400 cubic inch V-8 (two-barrel) and a 201 horsepower 429 cubic inch V-8 (four-barrel) were optional. A higher ratio axle, Traction-Lok differential and a competitiion handling package were available.

CONVENIENCE OPTIONS: Air conditioner ($397.91). Front bumper guards ($15.14). Electric clock ($17.67). Console ($59.32). Tinted windows ($41.66). Carpeted load floor in station wagon ($25.24). Dual racing mirrors ($25.24). Lefthand remote-control mirror ($12.62). Glamour paint ($37.86). Power front disc brakes ($68.14). Power door locks in two-doors ($44.17); in four-doors ($66.89); in station wagons ($75.72). Six-Way power bench seat ($102.22). Power steering ($112.33). Power window ($121.33). Power tailgate window in station wagons ($34.08). AM radio ($58.94). AM/FM stereo radio ($213.29). Vinyl covered roof ($97.18). High-back bucket seats ($128.72). Rear facing third seat in station wagons ($75.81). Hub caps with trim rings ($30.92). DeLuxe wheel covers ($25.24). Luxury wheel covers ($17.64). Interval windshield wipers ($25.24). Appearance group on station wagons ($25.54); on other models ($31.55). Convenience group on two-doors ($47.96); on four-doors ($25.24). Instrumentation group ($99.71). Cross country ride package ($16.41). Visibility group ($25.24).

Historical footnotes: Just 3.2 percent of 1973 Montegos came with bucket seats, 63.4 percent had vinyl roofs, 97 percent had a radio and 99.2 percent were powered by a V-8 engine.

COUGAR SERIES — Styling changes for 1973 consisted mainly of vertical chrome pieces in the headlight panels, a more refined radiator-look grille and vertical trim pieces on the taillights. Standard equipment included: sequential turn signals; high-back bucket seats; wheel lip moldings; two-spoke color-keyed steering wheel; consolette with ashtray and power front disc brakes.

COUGAR I.D. NUMBERS: See 1960 Monterey I.D. numbers.

COUGAR

Model Number	Body/Style Number	Body Type & Seating	Factory Price	Shipping Weight	Production Total
NA	91	2-dr HT-6P	3372	3396	21,069
NA	92	2-dr Conv-5P	3726	3524	1,284

COUGAR ENGINE
V-8: Overhead valves. Cast iron block. Displacement: 351 cubic inches. Bore and stroke: 4 x 3.5 inches. Compression ratio: 8.00:1. SAE net horsepower: 168 at 4000 R.P.M. Carburetor: two-barrel.

1973 Mercury, Cougar XR-7 2-dr hardtop sports coupe, V-8

COUGAR XR-7 SERIES — Chrome rocker panels and the XR-7 emblem on top of the grille were two ways to tell the top-of-the-line Cougar from the standard one. In addition to the features offered on the basic Cougar line, XR-7 buyers received special wheel covers; toggle switches; remote-control mirror; vinyl roof; tachometer; trip odometer; alternator gauge; oil pressure gauge and a map light. The high-back bucket seats had leather seating surfaces.

COUGAR XR-7 I.D. NUMBERS: See 1960 Monterey I.D. numbers.

COUGAR XR-7

Model Number	Body/Style Number	Body Type & Seating	Factory Price	Shipping Weight	Production Total
NA	93	2-dr HT Cpe-5P	3679	3416	35,110
NA	94	2-dr Conv-5P	3903	3530	3,165

COUGAR XR-7 ENGINE
See 1973 Cougar Series engine data.

CHASSIS FEATURES: Wheelbase: 112.1 inches. Overall length: 199.5 inches. Tires: E78 x 14.

POWERTRAIN OPTIONS: Select-shift automatic transmission was standard. A four-speed manual gear box was optional. A 264 horsepower CJ 351 cubic inch V-8 was available at extra cost. A higher ratio axle and Traction-Lok differential were also available.

CONVENIENCE OPTIONS: Air conditioning ($364.01). Front bumper guards ($13.87). Sports console with clock ($68.18). Rear window defroster ($42.76). Tinted windows ($33.52). Tinted windows in convertibles ($13.87). Dual racing mirrors with lefthand remote-contrl ($23.11). Protective body side molding ($30.05). Glamour paint ($34.66). Power front disc brakes ($62.40). Four-Way power seat ($69.34). Power steering ($102.86). Power sun roof ($431.04). Power windows ($102.86). AM radio ($58.94). AM/FM stereo radio ($195.30). AM radio with stereo tape system ($179.12). Vinyl roof ($79.73). Tilting steering wheel ($40.45). Upbeat stripe cloth trim (no charge with decor group). DeLuxe wheel covers ($23.11). Wire wheel covers ($75.12). Interval windshield wipers ($23.11). Appearance protection group ($28.89). Convenience group ($42.76). Exterior decor group ($80.89).

Historical footnotes: Most 1973 Cougars, 98 percent, had a radio, 94.7 percent had a vinyl roof, 28 percent had a tilting steering wheel, 99.3 percent automatic transmission and 84.5 percent had air conditioning.

MONTEREY SERIES — The new Monterey was about two inches shorter than last year's model, but nobody mistook it for a Comet. Its ice-cube-tray grille was outlined in chrome. The horizontal bars on the recessed headlight panels carried over to the large wraparound signal lights. A full-length, mid body molding spear, chrome wheel well openings and chrome rocker panels graced the Monterey's sides. Six square, chrome trimmed taillights and two backup lights were located on the rear deck panel. Betwen them was trim which matched the grille's pattern. All 1973 Montereys came equipped with power steering, Nylon carpeting, front bumper guards, automatic parking brake release, energy-absorbing bumper and power front disc brakes. A cloth and vinyl interior was standard.

MONTEREY I.D. NUMBERS: See 1960 Monterey I.D. numbers.

MONTEREY

Model Number	Body/Style Number	Body Type & Seating	Factory Price	Shipping Weight	Production Total
NA	44	4-dr Sedan-6P	3961	4225	16,622
NA	46	2-dr HT Cpe-6P	4004	4167	6,452
NA	72	4-dr Sta Wag-6P	4379	4673	4,275

Historical footnotes: One (1) Monterey four-door hardtop was made.

MONTEREY ENGINE
V-8: Overhead valves. Cast iron block. Displacement: 351 cubic inches. Bore and stroke: 4 x 3.5 inches. Compression ratio: 8.00:1. SAE net horsepower: 159 at 4000 R.P.M. Carburetor: two-barrel.
Station wagon V-8: Overhead valves. Cast iron block. Displacement: 400 cubic inches. Bore and stroke: 4 x 4 inches. Compression ratio: 8.00:1. SAE net horsepower: 171 at 3600 R.P.M. Carburetor: two-barrel.

MONTEREY CUSTOM SERIES — The Custom was basically a standard Monterey with a plusher interior and a more powerful engine.

MONTEREY CUSTOM I.D. NUMBERS: See 1960 Monterey I.D. numbers.

MONTEREY CUSTOM

Model Number	Body/Style Number	Body Type & Seating	Factory Price	Shipping Weight	Production Total
NA	54	4-dr Sedan-6P	4124	4295	20,873
NA	56	2-dr HT Cpe-6P	4207	4239	6,962

Historical footnote: Two (2) Monterey Custom four-door hardtops were made.

MONTEREY CUSTOM ENGINE
See 1973 Monterey Station Wagon Series engine data.

MARQUIS SERIES — Changes in the Marquis for 1973 included energy-absorbing bumpers; finger grille squares; wraparound signal lights; a free standing hood ornament and full-length lower body and wheel well opening moldings. Automatic parking brake release; fender skirts; electric clock; inside hood latch release; power front disc brakes and power steering were among the many standard features.

MARQUIS I.D. NUMBERS: See 1960 Monterey I.D. numbers.

MARQUIS

Model Number	Body/Style Number	Body Type & Seating	Factory Price	Shipping Weight	Production Total
NA	62	4-dr Sedan-6P	5072	4547	15,250
NA	66	2-dr HT Cpe-6P	4727	4411	5,973
NA	68	4-dr HT Sed-6P	5206	4565	2,185
NA	74	4-dr Sta Wag-6P	4608	4695	2,464

MARQUIS ENGINE
V-8: Overhead valves. Cast iron block. Displacement: 429 cubic inches. Bore and stroke: 4.36 x 3.59 inches. Compression ratio: 8.00:1. SAE net horsepower: 198 at 4400 R.P.M. Carburetor: four-barrel. The Marquis station wagon used the same engine as the Monterey station wagon.

MARQUIS BROUGHAM SERIES — The Brougham had fender-to-fender upper-body side moldings; power windows; halo vinyl roof; shag cut-pile carpeting; vanity mirror on righthand sun visor; rear pillar and luggage compartment lights and DeLuxe wheel covers with inserts. The Colony Park station wagon came with a three-way tailgate, power rear window and Cherry woodgrain yacht deck exterior paneling.

MARQUIS BROUGHAM I.D. NUMBERS: See 1960 Monterey I.D. numbers.

1973 Mercury, Marquis Brougham 4-dr sedan, V-8

MARQUIS BROUGHAM

Model Number	Body/Style Number	Body Type & Seating	Factory Price	Shipping Weight	Production Total
NA	62	4-dr Sedan-6P	5072	4547	46,624
NA	64	2-dr HT Cpe-6P	5151	4475	22,770
NA	67	4-dr HT Sed-6P	5206	4565	10,613
NA	76	4-dr Sta Wag-6P	4713	4730	23,283

NOTE: Model number 76, a four-door Station wagon, was called the Colony Park.

MARQUIS BROUGHAM ENGINE
See 1973 Marquis Series engine data.

CHASSIS FEATURES: Wheelbase: (Passenger cars) 124 inches; (Station wagons) 121 inches. Overall length: (Passenger cars) 222.5 inches; (station wagons) 223.4 inches. Tires: (Passenger cars) HR78 x 15 steel belted radials; (station wagons) JR78 x 15 steel-belted radials.

POWERTRAIN OPTIONS: Select-Shift automatic transmission was standard. A 171 horsepower 400 cubic inch V-8; 198 horsepower 429 cubic inch V-8 (four-barrel) and a 267 horsepower 460 cubic inch V-8 (four-barrel) were optional.

CONVENIENCE OPTIONS: Air conditioner ($430.58). Air conditioner with automatic temperature controls ($507.55). DeLuxe seat and shoulder belts ($50.49). Heavy-duty battery ($12.62). Front bumper guards ($8.84). Electric rear window defroster ($61.84). Tinted glass ($50.49). Cornering lamps ($35.34). Automatic load adjuster ($75.99). Luggage carrier with air deflector ($92.13). Glamour paint ($37.86). Sure-track brake system ($189.30). Power door locks on two-doors ($44.17); on four-doors ($68.99). Six-Way power bench seat ($102.22). Six-Way in left and righthand power seat ($174.16). Power sun roof ($495.97). Power windows ($128.72). Remote-control trunk release ($13.89). AM radio ($64.37). AM/FM stereo radio ($233.47). AM radio with stereo tape system (195.62). Vinyl roof ($124.95). Center-facing third seat ($122.27). Twin comfort lounge seat ($75.72). Speed control ($66.89). Tilting steering wheel ($44.17). Vanity mirror ($3.79). Luxury wheel covers ($32.82). Interval windshield wipers ($25.24). Rear windshield washer on station wagon ($37.89). Appearance protection group ($37.36). Convenience group on two-doors ($58.05); on four-doors ($35.34). Cross-country ride package ($22.71). Trailer-towing package ($88.34).

Historical footnote: Most full-size Mercurys, 75.7 percent, came with a vinyl roof.

1974 MERCURY

1974 Mercury, Comet 2-dr sedan, 6-cyl

COMET SERIES — New front and rear bumpers and slightly different upper and lower body moldings were the biggest Comet styling changes for 1974. Standard features included dual hydraulic brakes with warning light system; Blend-Air heater; windshield washers; locking steering column; cigar lighter; energy-absorbing steering wheel and two-speed windshield wipers.

COMET I.D. NUMBERS: See 1960 Monterey I.D. numbers.

COMET

Model Number	Body/Style Number	Body Type & Seating	Factory Price	Shipping Weight	Production Total
NA	30	4-dr Sedan-4P	2489	2904	60,944
NA	31	2-dr Sedan-4P	2432	2813	64,751

COMET ENGINE
Six: Overhead valves. Cast iron block. Displacement: 200 cubic inches. Bore and stroke: 3.68 x 3.13 inches. Compression ratio: 8.30:1. SAE net horsepower: 84 at 3800 R.P.M. Carburetor: one-barrel.

CHASSIS FEATURES: Wheelbase: (two-door) 103 inches; (four-door) 109 inches. Overall length: (two-door) 187.7 inches; (four-door) 196.3 inches. Tires: 6.45 x 14.

POWERTRAIN OPTIONS: A three-speed manual transmission was standard. Select-Shift automatic transmission was optional. A 91 horsepower 250 cubic inch Six (one-barrel) and a 140 horsepower 302 cubic inch V-8 were available at extra cost.

CONVENIENCE OPTIONS: Air conditioner ($382.70). Heavy-duty battery ($13.60). Manual front disc brakes ($33.90). Rear window defogger ($30). Tinted glass ($37.50). Solid state ignition ($37.80). Lefthand remote-control dual racing mirrors ($25.10). Bodyside moldings ($32.50). Two-tone paint ($30). Glamour paint ($36.50). Power steering ($106.20). Pushbutton AM radio ($61.40). AM radio with special speakers ($115.50). AM/FM multiplex with dual front door and rear seat speakers ($221.60). AM/FM monoral ($129.10). Embassy roof ($83.20). Bucket seats ($126.40). Floor shifter ($13.80). All-vinyl trim ($13.80). DeLuxe interior ($91.30). DeLuxe wheel covers ($25.10). Forged aluminum wheels with regular equipment ($153.80); with GT option ($123.80). Appearance protection group including floor mats with carpet inserts; door edge guards; license plate frames and spare tire lock on two-door ($36.50); on four-door ($39.10) Bumper protection group including front and rear rubber strips and rear bumper guards on cars without Custom group ($31.32); with Custom group ($23.50). Convenience group including glove box, trunk, instrument panel courtesy and dual dome lights; day/night mirror; color-keyed seat/shoulder belts; DeLuxe and lefthand remote-control racing mirrors, on cars with DeLuxe trim or bucket seats ($31.30); with dual racing mirrors ($39.10); with dual racing mirrors and bucket seats or GT option ($23.50). Custom option including DR78 x 14 steel-belted whitewall radial tires; DeLuxe wheel covers with color-keyed inserts; lefthand remote-control mirror; dual body paint stripe; wheel lip and rocker panel moldings; tan interior; 25 oz. carpeting; higher level NVH package and Odense- grain vinyl roof, on sedans ($408.30); on Villagers ($123.70). GT option including high-back bucket seats; DeLuxe sound insulation; leather-wrapped steering wheel; cut-pile carpeting; color-keyed hood scoop; dual racing mirrors; black hub caps with bright trim rings; blackout hood and black-finished front and lower back panels, on two-doors ($243.70).

Historical footnotes: Most 1974 Comets, 82.2 percent, came with a radio, 36.2 percent had a vinyl roof and 24.1 percent had bucket seats.

MONTEGO SERIES — The slightly protruding, chrome-outlined Montego grille had a criss-cross pattern. The four headlights were nestled in chrome panels. Wheel well openings and center mid body moldings were used on the sides. Taillights were located on the rear deck panel and wrapped around the fenders. Standard features included front disc brakes; impact-resistant bumpers; locking steering column; concealed windshield wipers; inside hood release and color-keyed deep loop carpeting.

MONTEGO I.D. NUMBERS: See 1960 Monterey I.D. numbers.

MONTEGO

Model Number	Body/Style Number	Body Type & Seating	Factory Price	Shipping Weight	Production Total
NA	02	4-dr Sedan-6P	3360	4062	5,674
NA	03	2-dr HT-6P	3327	3977	7,645

MONTEGO ENGINE
V-8: Overhead valves. Cast iron block. Displacement: 302 cubic inches. Bore and stroke: 4 x 3 inches. Compression ratio: 8.00:1. SAE net horsepower: 140 at 3800 R.P.M. Carburetor: two-barrel.

MONTEGO MX SERIES — Rocker panel moldings and nameplates on the lower front fenders, were two identifying traits of the MX. In addition to a slightly plusher interior than the base Montego, the MX had DeLuxe sound insulation.

MONTEGO MX I.D. NUMBERS: See 1960 Monterey I.D. numbers.

MONTEGO MX

Model Number	Body/Style Number	Body Type & Seating	Factory Price	Shipping Weight	Production Total
NA	04	4-dr Sedan-6P	3478	4092	19,446
NA	07	2-dr HT Cpe-6P	3443	3990	20,957
NA	08	4-dr Sta Wag-6P	4083	4426	4,085

MONTEGO MX ENGINE
See 1974 Montego Series engine data.

1974 Mercury, Montego MX Brougham 4-dr sedan, V-8

MONTEGO MX BROUGHAM SERIES — Upper body and lower rear quarter panel moldings, plus a super sound-insulation package and wood-grain applique on the instrument panel were Brougham features. The Villager station wagon had simulated wood-grain body side and tailgate paneling, outlined with bright moldings; power tailgate window; flight-bench seat with center arm rest and imitation Cherry wood instrument and dash panel appliques.

MONTEGO MX BROUGHAM I.D. NUMBERS: See 1960 Monterey I.D. numbers

MONTEGO MX BROUGHAM

Model Number	Body/Style Number	Body Type & Seating	Factory Price	Shipping Weight	Production Total
NA	10	4-dr Sedan-6P	3680	4143	13,467
NA	11	2-dr HT Cpe-6P	3646	4010	20,511
NA	18	4-dr Sta Wag-6P	4307	4463	6,234

NOTE: Model number 18, the four-door station wagon, was called the Villager.

MONTEGO MX BROUGHAM ENGINE
See 1974 Montego Series engine data.

CHASSIS FEATURES: Wheelbase: (two-doors) 114 inches; (four-doors and station wagons) 118 inches. Overall length: (two-doors) 215.5 inches; (four-doors) 219.5 inches; (station wagons) 223.1 inches. Tires: (station wagons) H78 x 14; (Villager Station wagon) HR78 x 14; (other models) G78 x 14.

POWERTRAIN OPTIONS: A three-speed manual transmisson was standard. Select-Shift automatic transmission was optional. A 162 horsepower 351 cubic inch V-8 (two-barrel); 246 horsepower CJ 351 cubic inch V-8; 168 horsepower 400 cubic inch V-8 (two-barrel) and a 244 horsepower 460 cubic inch V-8 (four-barrel) were available. The last engine was not offered in station wagons. The 246 horsepower engine was not available in the MX Brougham series. A high performance axle and Traction-Lok differential were optional.

CONVENIENCE OPTIONS: Air conditioner ($397.91). Automatic temperature control air conditioner ($507.55). Anti-theft alarm system ($79). Traction-Lok differential axle ($46.70). DeLuxe seat belts ($15.14). Load floor carpeting ($25.24). Electric clock ($17.67). Electric rear window defroster in Passenger cars ($46.70); in Station wagons ($61.84). Heavy-duty electrical system ($27.76). Tinted glass ($41.66). Solid-state ignition ($38.20). Luggage carrier with air deflector for station wagons ($76.99). Dual racing mirrors, lefthand mirror remote-control ($38.20). Illuminated visor vanity mirror ($35.60). Body side moldings ($32.82). Front disc brakes for station wagons ($68.14). Power door locks in two-doors ($44.17); in four-doors ($66.89). Six-Way bench seat ($102.22). Power steering ($112.33). Power windows in two-doors ($85.60); in four-noors ($112.33). AM/FM multiplex with stereo tape ($363.20). AM/FM multiplex with dual front door and rear seat speakers ($213.29). Dual rear speakers with AM radio ($30.29). Vinyl roof ($97.18). Embassy roof ($115.80). Rear facing center seat ($75.81). Automatic speed control ($98.70). Tilt steering wheel ($44.80). Standard wheel covers ($25.24). DeLuxe wheel covers on Brougham, Villager ($7.90). Luxury wheel covers ($42.91); same on Brougham, Villager ($17.67). DeLuxe wheel covers ($32.90). Styled steel wheels ($117.10); on Brougham, Villager ($92.10). Opera windows on two-doors with vinyl roof ($80.30). Interval-selector windshield wipers ($25.24). Appearance protection group including floor mats with carpet inserts; door edge guards; license plate frames and spare tire lock ($38.20). Brougham Custom trim option including Arden velour seating surfaces; door panel inserts; comfort lounge seats; luxury steering wheel; Cherry wood cluster cover; instrument panel applique with teakwood inlays; super-soft vinyl seat facings and door panels; trunk side lining boards; DeLuxe color-keyed wheel covers. Door-pull assist straps; 25 oz. carpet; visor vanity mirror and Lavant-grain or Odense-grain Embassy vinyl roof ($315.80). Bumper protection group including front and rear rubber strips and rear bumper guards, on passenger cars ($35.60); on Station wagons ($23.70). Convenience group including remote-control left and visor vanity mirrors; automatic seat back release with two-doors and spare tire extractor on Station wagon, two-doors ($51.40); four-doors ($29); station wagons ($31.60). Cross-country ride package ($16.41). Sports appearance group including fuel; ammeter; oil pressure and temperature gauges; trip odometer; clock; tachometer; sporty hood; dual racing mirrors; black hub caps with bright trim rings; lower body tape stripe; G70 x 14 blackwall tires with raised white letters; lower panel blackout paint; leather-wrapped steering wheel; bright trim pedal pads and H70 x 14 blackwall tires with RL and 460 engine in two-doors ($310.29). Trailer-towing package class II ($32.82); class III ($117.18); station wagons ($80.01). Visibility light group ($29).

Historical footnotes: The vast majority of 1974 Montegos, 90.1 percent, had a radio and 65.7 percent came with a vinyl roof.

1974 Mercury, Cougar XR-7 2-dr hardtop sports coupe, V-8

COUGAR XR-7 SERIES — Front end styling was similar to last year's model, except the grille was wider and had the previous emblem replaced by a hood ornament. Side trim consisted of upper body chrome (running from the tip of the fenders to the rear roof pillars where it connected with a chrome band that went across the roof), full-length upper tire level moldings and a rear roof quarter panel opera window. The rear deck panel taillights wrapped around the fenders. Standard features included: soft, vinyl bucket seats or twin comfort lounge seats; steel-belted radial tires; power steering; performance instrumentation; luxury steering wheel; cut-pile carpeting and inside hood release.

COUGAR XR-7 I.D. NUMBERS: See 1960 Monterey I.D. numbers.

COUGAR XR-7

Model Number	Body/Style Number	Body Type & Seating	Factory Price	Shipping Weight	Production Total
NA	93	2-dr HT Cpe-5P	4706	4255	91,670

COUGAR XF-7 ENGINE
V-8: Overhead valves. Cast iron block. Displacement: 351 cubic inches. Bore and stroke: 4 x 3.5 inches. Compression ratio: 8.00:1. SAE net horsepower: 168 at 4000 R.P.M. Carburetor: two-barrel.

CHASSIS FEATURES: Wheelbase: 114 inches. Overall length: 214.2 inches. Tires: HR78 x 14.

POWERTRAIN OPTIONS: Select-Shift automatic was standard. A 264 horsepower CJ 351 cubic inch V-8; 170 horsepower 400 cubic inch V-8 (two-barrel) and a 220 horsepower 460 cubic inch V-8 were optional. A high performance axle and Traction-Lok differential were available at extra cost.

CONVENIENCE OPTIONS: Air conditioner ($397.54). Automatic temperature control with air conditioner ($475). Anti-theft alarm system ($79). Traction-Lok differential axle ($46.70). DeLuxe seat belts ($15.14). Electric rear window defroster ($61.81). Heavy-duty electrical system ($27.70). Tinted glass ($36.61). Solid-state ignition ($38.20). Lefthand remote-control dual racing mirrors ($38.20). Illuminated visor vanity mirrors ($35.60). Body side moldings ($32.82). Power door locks ($44.80). Six-Way lefthand power seat ($90.80). Electric sun roof ($471.10). Power windows on two-doors ($85.60); on four-doors ($112.33). AM radio with special speakers ($97.40).

AM/FM multiplex with stereo tape ($363.20). AM/FM multiplex with dual front door and rear seat speakers ($213.29). Dual rear speakers with AM radio ($30.30). Vinyl roof ($33.20). Tilt steering wheel ($44.17). Leather-wrapped steering wheel ($6.07). Leather upholstery trim with bucket or twin comfort seats ($167.10). Velour upholstery with twin comfort seats ($77.70). Sporty wheel covers ($61.90). Styled steel wheels ($79). Appearance protection group including floor mats with carpet inserts; door edge guards; license plate frames and spare tire lock ($32.90). Bumper protection group including front and rear rubber strips and rear bumper guards ($35.60). Convenience group including visor vanity mirror; lefthand remote-control mirror and automatic seat back release, on two-doors, includes DeLuxe CC seat belts ($50). Trailer towing package, Class II ($32.90); Class III ($177.10). Visibility light group ($29).

Historical footnotes: Most Cougars, 90.9 percent were equipped with radio, 38.7 percent had bucket seats, 32.6 percent had a tilting steering wheel and 20.6 percent came with speed control.

MONTEREY SERIES — The Monterey had a squares-within-squares, chrome framed grille. This pattern was carried over to the headlight panels. Signal lights wrapped around the front fenders. Rear quarter pillar nameplate and trim, full-length mid-body spear and wheel opening and rocker panel molding were used on the sides. Among the standard features were: Nylon carpeting; glove box light; power steering; automatic parking brake release; solid state ignition and cloth and vinyl interior.

MONTEREY I.D. NUMBERS: See 1960 Monterey I.D. numbers.

MONTEREY

Model Number	Body/Style Number	Body Type & Seating	Factory Price	Shipping Weight	Production Total
NA	44	4-dr Sedan-6P	4367	4559	6,185
NA	46	2-dr HT Cpe-6P	4410	4506	2,003
NA	72	4-dr Sta Wag-6P	4731	4916	1,669

MONTEREY ENGINE
V-8: Overhead valves. Cast iron block. Displacement: 400 cubic inches. Bore and stroke: 4 x 4 inches. Compression ratio: 8.00:1. SAE net horsepower: 170 at 3600 R.P.M. Carburetor: two-barrel.

MONTEREY CUSTOM SERIES — The Custom series script on the rear roof quarter panel, DeLuxe wheel covers, a DeLuxe steering wheel and all-vinyl interior were standard features of the Custom.

MONTEREY CUSTOM I.D. NUMBERS: See 1960 Monterey I.D. numbers.

MONTEREY CUSTOM

Model Number	Body/Style Number	Body Type & Seating	Factory Price	Shipping Weight	Production Total
NA	54	4-dr Sedan-6P	4480	4561	13,113
NA	56	2-dr HT Cpe-6P	4523	4504	4,510

MONTEREY CUSTOM ENGINE
See 1974 Monterey Series engine data.

MARQUIS SERIES — The Marquis grille had rectangular vertical pieces with finder bars within them. The hidden headlight doors had horizontal bars which extened around the wraparound signal lights. Mercury was spelled out in chrome above the grille. Side trim consisted of full-length, lower body moldings. The six square taillights and two backup lights were located in the rear deck panel. Standard features on Marquis included power front disc brakes; power steering; DeLuxe sound insulation; loop-pile carpeting; courtesy lights; fender skirts and power ventilation. The interior was cloth and vinyl.

MARQUIS I.D. NUMBERS: See 1960 Monterey I.D. numbers.

MARQUIS

Model Number	Body/Style Number	Body Type & Seating	Factory Price	Shipping Weight	Production Total
NA	63	4-dr Sedan-6P	5080	4757	6,910
NA	66	2-dr HT Cpe-6P	5080	4698	2,633
NA	68	4-dr HT Sed-6P	4080	4753	784
NA	72	4-dr Sta Wag-6P	4960	4973	1,111

MARQUIS ENGINE
V-8: Overhead valves. Cast iron block. Displacement: 460 cubic inches. Bore and stroke: 4.36 x 3.85 inches. Compression ratio: 8.00:1. SAE net horsepower: 195 at 4400 R.P.M. Carburetor: four-barrel.

1974 Mercury, Marquis Brougham 4-dr sedan, V-8

MARQUIS BROUGHAM SERIES — Full-length upper body molding, halo vinyl roof, power windows; door pull straps; lefthand remote-control mirror; DeLuxe wheel covers with inserts; pillar lights and lights under the instrument panel, were Brougham features.

MARQUIS BROUGHAM I.D. NUMBERS: See 1960 Monterey I.D. numbers.

MARQUIS BROUGHAM

Model Number	Body/Style Number	Body Type & Seating	Factory Price	Shipping Weight	Production Total
NA	62	4-dr Sedan-6P	5519	4833	24,477
NA	64	2-dr HT Cpe-6P	5519	4762	10,207
NA	67	4-dr HT Sed-6P	5519	4853	4,189
NA	76	4-dr Sta Wag-6P	5066	5066	10,802

NOTE: Model number 76, a four-door station wagon, was called the Colony Park.

MARQUIS BROUGHAM ENGINE
See 1974 Marquis engine data.

CHASSIS FEATURES: Wheelbase: (Passenger cars) 124 inches; (Station wagons) 121 inches. Overall length: (Passenger cars) 226.7 inches; (Station wagons) 225.6 inches. Tires: (Passenger cars) HR78 x 15; (Station wagons) JR78 x 15.

POWERTRAIN OPTIONS: Select-Shift automatic transmission was standard. A 195 horsepower 460 cubic inch V-8 was optional. A high performance axle and Traction-Lok differential were available at extra cost.

CONVENIENCE OPTIONS: Air conditioner ($430.58). Anti-theft alarm system, for station wagons without appearance protection group ($79); with appearance protection group ($73.70); Executive wagons without appearance protection group ($84.30); with appearance protection group ($78.95). Heavy-duty battery in Monterey and wagons ($12.62). DeLuxe seat and shoulder belts ($15.14). Electric clock in Monterey ($17.67). Digital clock in Monterey ($39.50). Electric rear window defroster ($61.84). Rear fender skirts except Monterey wagons and Marquis passenger cars ($35.34). Floor mats in Monterey Custom ($23.70). Tinted glass ($50.49). Cornering lights ($35.24). Automatic load adjuster on wagons ($76.99). Luggage carrier with air deflector on wagons ($92.13). Visor vanity illuminated mirror on Monterey and Marquis ($35.60). Body side molding ($32.82); on Monterey, ($14.47). Rocker panel on Monterey Custom ($25). Sure-track power brakes ($189.30 with 460 engines). Six-Way bench seat ($102.22); same on Marquis ($87.08). Six-Way left and right power seat on Marquis ($174.15). Electric power sun roof on Executive wagons ($495.97). Electric windows ($140.79). Power tailgate window on MX wagons ($34.08). Power vent windows (four-doors $64.47). Remote-control trunk release on Executive wagons ($13.89). AM radio with special speakers ($97.40). AM/FM multiplex with stereo tape ($363.20). AM/FM multiplex with dual front-door and rear-seat speakers ($233.47). Dual rear speakers ($32.82). Vinyl roof on Executive wagons ($116.11); on other station wagons ($138.82). Halo roof on Marquis Executive wagons ($124.95). Dual-facing third seat on station wagons ($122.27). Twin comfort lounge seats ($75.72). Vinyl bench seat on Monterey ($27.76). Passenger-side reclining seat ($42.91). Automatic speed control ($66.89). Tilt steering wheel ($44.17). Storage compartment with locks on wagons ($32.90). Recreation table on wagons ($42.11). Trailer brake control ($38.20. Trailer hitch equilizer platform ($88.20). DeLuxe cargo area trim, including lockable storage compartment and padded quarter trim on wagons ($65). Luggage compartment trim on Executive wagons including carpeting, spare tire cover and side lining board ($40.80). Luxury wheel covers ($32.82). Interval selector wipers ($25.24). Rear tailgate window washer on wagons ($37.86). Appearance protection group including floor mats with carpet inserts; door edge guards; license plate frames; spare tire lock; rear mats with carpet inserts and hood lock, on station wagons ($46.10), on Exective wagons Bumper protection group including front and rear rubber strips and rear bumper guards, on station wagons ($23.68) on Executive wagons, ($35.53). Cross-country ride package ($22.71). Decor group including DeLuxe steering wheel and wheel covers, wheel lip and rocker panel moldings on Monterey ($63.16). Grand Marquis luxury trim including digital clock; carpeted trunk with side lining boards and flap; hood and deck lid stripes; perforated vinyl headlining with Corinthian grain vinyl covered visors; assist handles; unique head rest and seat trim; dash panel and cluster applique; door and quarter trim panels; dome map/reading lamp; luxury steering wheel; 25 oz. carpting on Marquis without light group ($325); Marquis with light group ($311.90); wagons without light group ($390.80); wagons with light group ($377.70). Lock convenience group including power door locks; trunk lid release; lefthand remote-control mirror; automatic seat back release on two-doors and power tailgate on station wagons wagons, on two-doors with power windows ($82.89); four-doors with power windows ($80.26); wagons without power windows ($88.16); wagons with power windows ($75.54); two-doors without power windows ($96.05); four-doors without power windows ($93.42). Marquis-Colony Park luxury trim including instrument panel lights; door-pull straps; Brougham level seat; Brougham split bench seat and door trim panels; 25 oz. carpeting; visor vanity mirror; Brougham level sound package; front door courtesy lights; rear door arm rest cigar lighters and Brougham trim ($184.21). Trailer towing package class I ($35.84); class II ($32.82); class III ($88.34). Visibility light group on Monterey ($56.60); on Mercury ($47.40); on Marquis ($39.50).

Historical footnotes: Seventy-eight percent of all full-size 1974 Mercurys came with a vinyl roof.

1975 MERCURY

1975 Mercury, Comet 4-dr sedan, 6-cyl

COMET SERIES — The styling department must have been in hibernation. The new Comet looked virtually the same as last year's model. Standard features included; locking steering column, DeLuxe sound insulation package, deluxe steering wheel, color-keyed instrument panel with lighted dash, dual hydraulic-brake system with warning light and cut-pile carpeting. Buyers had their choice of four colors of cloth and vinyl interior.

COMET I.D. NUMBERS: See 1960 Monterey I.D. numbers.

COMET

Model Number	Body/Style Number	Body Type & Seating	Factory Price	Shipping Weight	Production Total
NA	30	4-dr Sedan-4P	3270	3193	31,080
NA	31	2-dr Sedan-4P	3236	3070	22,768

COMET ENGINE
Six: Overhead valves. Cast iron block. Displacement: 200 cubic inches. Bore and stroke: 3.68 x 3.13 inches. Compression ratio: 8.30:1. SAE net horsepower: 75 at 3800 R.P.M. Carburetor: one-barrel.

CHASSIS FEATURES: Wheelbase: (four-door) 109 inches; (two-door) 103 inches. Overall length: (four-door) 196.9 inches; (two-door) 190 inches. Tires: (four-door) CR78 x 14; (two-door) BR78 x 14.

POWERTRAIN OPTIONS: A three-speed manual transmission was standard. Select-Shift automatic transmission was optional. A 91 horsepower 250 cubic inch six and a 140 horsepower 302 cubic inch V-8 (two-barrel) were available at extra cost.

CONVENINECE OPTIONS: Air conditioner ($382.70). Heavy-duty battery ($13.60). Manual front disc brakes ($33.90). Rear window defogger ($30). Tinted glass ($37.50). Solid-state ignition ($37.80). Lefthand remote-control dual racing mirrors ($25.10). Bodyside moldings ($32.50). Two-tone paint ($30). Glamour paint ($36.50). Power steering ($106.20). Pushbutton AM radio ($61.40). AM radio with special speakers ($115.50). AM/FM multiplex with dual front door and rear seat speakers ($221.60). AM/FM monaural ($129.10). Floor shifter ($13.80). All-vinyl trim ($13.80). DeLuxe interior ($91.30). DeLuxe wheel covers ($25.10). Forged aluminum wheels ($153.80); same with GT option ($123.80). Appearance protection group including floor mats with carpet inserts; door edge guards; license plate frames and spare tire lock in two-doors ($36.50); in four-doors ($39.10). Bumper protection group including front and rear rubber strips and rear bumper guards, on models without Custom group ($31.32); on models with Custom group ($23.50). Convenience group including glove box, trunk, instrument panel courtesy and dual dome lights; day/night mirror; color-keyed seat/shoulder belts; DeLuxe and lefthand remote-control racing mirror, on cars with DeLuxe trim or bucket seats ($31.30); cars with dual racing mirrors ($39.10); cars with dual racing mirrors and bucket seat or GT option ($23.50). Custom option including DR78x14 steel-belted whitewall radial tires; DeLuxe wheel covers with color-keyed inserts; lefthand remote-control mirror; dual body paint stripe; wheel lip and rocker panel moldings; tan interior; 25 oz. carpeting; higher level NVH package and Odense-grain vinyl roof, on sedan ($408.30); on Villager ($123.70). GT option includes high-back bucket seats; DeLuxe sound insulation; leather-wrapped steering wheel; cut-pile carpeting; color-keyed hood scoop; dual racing mirrors; black hub caps with bright trim rings; blackout hood, front and lower back panel, on two-doors ($243.70).

PRODUCTION NOTE: Most 1975 Comets, 82.5 percent, were equipped with a radio, 13.2 percent had bucket seats and 39.2 percent came with a vinyl-covered roof.

BOBCAT SERIES — The new Bobcat was based on Ford's Pinto. It had an attractive, chrome-framed grille with vertical bars and the word Mercury spelled out above it. Both headlights were recessed into bright moldings. The long, rectangular vertical taillights were placed on the rear deck panel.

BOBCAT I.D. NUMBERS: See 1960 Monterey I.D. numbers.

BOBCAT

Model Number	Body/Style Number	Body Type & Seating	Factory Price	Shipping Weight	Production Total
NA	20	3-dr Hatch-4P	3189	NA	20,651
NA	21	2-dr Sta Wag-4P	3481	NA	13,583

NOTE: Model number 20, the three-door hatchback coupe, was called a Runabout. Model number 21, the two-door station wagon, was called the Villager.

BOBCAT ENGINE
Four: Overhead camshaft. Cast iron block. Displacement: 140 cubic inches. Bore and stroke: 3.78 x 3.13 inches. Compression ratio: 8.40:1. SAE net horsepower: 83 at 4800 R.P.M. Carburetor: one-barrel

CHASSIS FEATURES: Wheelbase: (Runabout) 94.5 inches; (Villager) 94.8 inches. Overall length: (Runabout) 169 inches; (Villager) 179 inches. Tires: B78 x 13.

POWERTRAIN OPTIONS: A three-speed manual transmission was standard. Select-Shift automatic transmission was optional. A 97 horsepower 170 cubic inch six was available.

CONVENIENCE OPTIONS: Air conditioning ($416). Vinyl top on Runabout ($83). DeLuxe wheel covers ($25.10). Luggage rack on Villager ($71). Sunroof ($210). AM radio ($61.40). AM/FM radio ($218). Aluminum wheels ($136). Power steering ($106). Sports accent group ($269).

Historical Footnote: Most 1975 Bobcats, 75 percent, came with radios and 10.5 percent had vinyl roofs.

MONARCH SERIES — Mercury called the new Monarch a "precision-size luxury car." It had a chrome-framed grille with vertical bars and Mercury spelled out above it. The two headlights were enclosed in square molding 'boxes' and the signal lights wrapped around the front fenders. Full-length trim (that continued around the rear of the car), wheel lip and window moldings and chrome rocker panels were used on the sides. The wraparound rectangular taillights were located on the rear deck panel. The word Mercury was printed in a chrome-framed section between the taillights. Standard equipment included, individually reclining bucket seats, front disc brakes, foot-operated parking brake, solid-state ignition, locking glove box and inside hood release.

MONARCH I.D. NUMBERS: See 1960 Monterey I.D. numbers.

MONARCH

Model Number	Body/Style Number	Body Type & Seating	Factory Price	Shipping Weight	Production Total
NA	34	4-dr Sedan-5P	3822	3284	34,307
NA	35	2-dr Sedan-5P	3764	3234	29,151

MONARCH ENGINE
See 1975 Comet Series engine data.

1975 Mercury, Monarch 4-dr Ghia sedan, V-8

MONARCH GHIA SERIES — Wide, full-length upper tire level moldings and upper body pin stripes made it easy to distinguished the Ghia from the basic Monarch. It came with a DeLuxe sound insulation package; lefthand remote-control outside mirror; Odense-grain vinyl roof; unique wire spoke wheel covers; carpeted luggage compartment; digital clock and luxury steering wheel.

MONARCH GHIA I.D. NUMBERS: See 1960 Monterey I.D. numbers.

MONARCH GHIA

Model Number	Body/Style Number	Body Type & Seating	Factory Price	Shipping Weight	Production Total
NA	37	4-dr Sedan-5P	4349	3352	22,723
NA	38	2-dr Sedan-5P	4291	3302	17,755

MONARCH GHIA ENGINE
Six: Overhead valve. Cast iron block. Displacement: 250 cubic inches. Bore and stroke: 3.68 x 3.91 inches. Compression ratio: 8.00:1. SAE net horsepower: 72 at 2900 R.P.M. Carburetor: one-barrel.

POWERTRAIN OPTIONS: A three-speed manual transmission was standard. Select-Shift automatic was optional. A 72 horsepower 250 cubic inch six (one-barrel); 129 horsepower 302 cubic inch V-8 (two-barrel) and a 154 horsepower 351 cubic inch V-8 (two-barrel) were available.

CONVENIENCE OPTIONS: Air conditioning ($416). Vinyl roof ($92). AM radio ($61.40). AM/FM stereo radio ($225). AM/FM stereo radio with tape system ($347). Power seats ($104). Power sun roof ($517). Power windows ($85.60). Power steering ($112.33). Power brakes ($68). Rear window defroster ($46.70). Upholstery with leather seating surfaces. Grand Ghia package. Illuminated visor vanity mirror. Decor package including vinyl seat trim with map pocket and assist rails.

Historical Footnotes: Only 6.3 percent of 1975 Monarchs came with a stereo tap system, 50.6 percent had a vinyl roof and 88.4 percent had a radio.

MONTEGO SERIES — Twin slots in the center of the lower front bumper were the main changes to Montego styling for 1975. Standard features included power brakes, power steering, solid state ignition, locking steering column, cut-pile carpeting, concealed windshield wipers and front bumper guards. Buyers could choose from a cloth and vinyl or all-vinyl interior in black, tan, or blue.

MONTEGO I.D. NUMBERS: See 1960 Monterey I.D. numbers.

MONTEGO

Model Number	Body/Style Number	Body Type & Seating	Factory Price	Shipping Weight	Production Total
NA	02	4-dr Sedan-6P	4128	4066	4,142
NA	03	2-dr HT Cpe-6P	4092	4003	4,051

MONTEGO ENGINE
V-8: Overhead valves. Cast iron block. Displacement: 351 cubic inches. Bore and stroke: 4 x 3.5 inches. Compression ratio: 8.00:1. SAE net horsepower: 148 at 3800 R.P.M. Carburetor: two-barrel.

1975 Mercury, Montego MX 2-dr coupe, V-8

MONTEGO MX SERIES — Upper body pin stripes and rocker panel moldings were used on the MX. It also had extra sound insulation and a slightly fancier interior.

MONTEGO MX I.D. NUMBERS: See 1960 Monterey I.D. numbers.

MONTEGO MX

Model Number	Body/Style Number	Body Type & Seating	Factory Price	Shipping Weight	Production Total
NA	04	4-dr Sedan-6P	4328	4111	16,033
NA	07	2-dr HT Cpe-6P	4304	4030	13,666
NA	08	4-dr Sta Wag-6P	4674	4464	4,508

MONTEGO MX ENGINE
See 1975 Montego Series engine data.

MONTEGO MX BROUGHAM SERIES — The Brougham had upper body moldings; door-pull straps; super sound-insulation package; vinyl roof; wood-grain applique on the steering wheel and wiper mounted windshield washer jets. The Villager wagon had wood-grain vinyl paneling on its sides and tailgate; power tailgate window; DeLuxe steering wheel and flight bench seat with folding center arm rest.

MONTEGO MX BROUGHAM I.D. NUMBERS: See 1960 Monterey I.D. numbers.

MONTEGO MX BROUGHAM

Model Number	Body/Style Number	Body Type & Seating	Factory Price	Shipping Weight	Production Total
NA	10	4-dr Sedan-6P	4498	4130	8,235
NA	11	2-dr HT Cpe-6P	4453	4054	8,791
NA	18	4-dr Sta Wag-6P	4909	4522	5,754

NOTE: Model number 18, the four-door station wagon, was called the Villager.

MONTEGO MX BRUGHAM ENGINE
See 1975 Montego Series engine data.

CHASSIS FEATURES: Wheelbase (two-door) 114 inches, (four-door and station wagons) 118 inches. Overall length (two-door) 215.5 inches; (four-door) 219.5 inches; (station wagons) 224.4 inches. Tires: HR78 x 14.

POWERTRAIN OPTIONS: Select-Shift automatic was standard. A 158 horsepower 400 cubic inch V-8 (two-barrel) and a 216 horsepower 460 cubic inch V-8 were optional. A high performance axle and Traction-Lok differential were available at extra cost.

CONVENIENCE OPTIONS: Air conditioner ($397.91). Automatic temperature control air conditioner ($507.55). Anti-theft alarm system ($79). Traction-Lok differential axle ($46.70). DeLuxe seat belts ($15.14). Load floor carpet ($25.24). Electric clock ($17.67). Electric rear window defroster in passenger cars ($46.70); in station wagons ($61.84). Heavy duty electrical system ($27.76). Tinted glass ($41.66). Solid state ignition ($38.20). Luggage carrier with air deflector ($76.99). Dual racing mirrors with remote control lefthand unit ($38.20). Illuminated visor vanity mirror ($35.60). Bodyside moldings ($32.82). Front disc brakes on wagons ($68.14). Power door locks in two-doors ($44.17); four-doors ($66.89). Six-Way bench seat ($124). Power steering ($112.33). Power windows in two-doors ($85.60); four-doors ($112.33). AM/FM multiplex with stereo tape ($383.20). AM/FM multiplex with dual front door and rear seat speakers ($238.29). Dual rear speakers with AM radio ($30.29). Vinyl roof ($97.18). Embassy roof ($115.80). Rear facing center seat ($86). Automatic speed control ($98.70). Tilt steering wheel ($44.80). Standard wheel covers ($25.24). DeLuxe wheel covers for Brougham, Villager ($7.90). Luxury wheel covers ($42.91); same on Brougham, Villager ($17.67). DeLuxe wheel covers ($32.90). Styled steel wheels ($117.10); same on Brougham, Villager ($92.10). Opera windows in two-doors with vinyl roof ($80.30). Interval-selector windshield wipers ($25.24). Appearance protection group including floor mats with carpet inserts; door edge guards; license frames and spare tire lock ($38.20). Brougham Custom trim option including Ardenvelour seating surfaces; door panel inserts; comfort lounge seats; luxury steering wheel; Cherrywood cluster cover; instrument panel applique with teakwood inlays; super-soft vinyl seat facings and door panels; trunk side lining boards; DeLuxe color-keyed wheel covers; door-pull assist straps; 25 oz. carpet; visor vanity mirror and Lavant-grain or Odense-grain Embassy vinyl roof ($384.80). Bumper protection group including front and rear rubber strips and rear bumper guards, on passenger cars ($35.60); on station wagons ($23.70). Convenience group including remote-control lefthand and visor vanity mirrors; automatic seat back release with two-doors and spare tire extractor with station wagons, on two-doors ($51.40); on four-doors ($29); on station wagons ($31.60). Cross-country ride package ($16.41). Sports appearance group including fuel; ammeter; oil pressure and temperature gauges; trip odometer; clock; tachometer; sports hood; dual racing mirrors; black hub caps with bright trim rings; lower body tape stripe; G70x14 blackwall tires with raised white letters (or H70 x 14 blackwall tires with RL and 460 engine) ; lower panel blackout paint; leather-wrapped steering wheel; bright trim pedal pads, for two-doors ($260). Trailer-towing package class II ($32.82); class III ($117.18); station wagons ($80.01). Visibility light group ($29).

Historical Footnotes: Most 1975 Montegos, 89.1 percent, were equipped with a radio, 59.3 percent had vinyl roofs, 3.7 percent had a stereo tape system and 12.4 percent had a tilting steering wheel.

1975 Mercury, Cougar XR-7 2-dr hardtop sports coupe, V-8

COUGAR XR-7 SERIES — Two rectangular openings between the front bumper guards, on the lower bumper, was the extent of styling changes made to Cougars in 1975. They came with power steering; bucket seats with console (or Twin Comfort lounge seats); luxury steering wheel; deep cut-pile carpeting; passenger assist handle; inside hood release; locking steering column and power front disc brakes.

COUGAR XR-7 I.D. NUMBERS: See 1960 Monterey I.D. numbers.

Model Number	Body/Style Number	Body Type & Seating	Factory Price	Shipping Weight	Production Total
NA	93	2-dr HT Cpe-5P	5218	4108	62,987

COUGAR XR-7 ENGINE
See 1975 Montego Series engine data.

CHASSIS FEATURES: Wheelbase: 114 inches. Overall length: 215.5 inches. Tires: HR78 x 14.

POWERTRAIN OPTIONS: Select-Shift automatic was standard. A 158 horsepower 400 cubic inch V-8 (two-barrel) and a 216 horsepower 460 cubic inch V-8 (four-barrel) were optional. A high performance axle and Traction-Lok differential could be ordered.

CONVENIENCE OPTIONS: Air conditioner ($397.54). Automatic temperature control air conditioner ($475). Anti-theft alarm system ($79). Traction-Lok differential axle ($46.70). DeLuxe seat belts ($15.14). Electric rear window defroster ($61.81). Heavy-duty electrical system ($27.70). Tinted glass ($36.61). Solid-state ignition ($38.20). Lefthand remote-control dual racing mirrors ($38.20). Illuminated visor vanity mirror ($35.60). Bodyside moldings ($32.82). Power door locks ($44.80). Six-Way lefthand power seat ($124). Electric sun roof ($525). Power windows, on two-door ($85.60); four-door ($112.33). AM radio with special speakers ($97.40). AM/FM multiplex with stereo tape ($393.20). AM/FM multiplex with dual front door and rear seat speakers ($213.29). Dual rear speakers with AM radio ($30.30). Vinyl roof ($33.20). Tilt steering wheel ($44.17). Leather-wrapped steering wheel ($6.07). Leather upholstery trim with bucket or twin comfort seats ($167.10). Velour upholstery with twin comfort seats ($77.70). Sporty wheel covers ($61.90). Styled steel wheels ($79). Appearance protection group including floor mats with carpet inserts; door edge guards; license plate frames and spare tire lock ($32.90). Bumper protection group including front and rear rubber strips and rear bumper guards ($35.60). Convenience group including visor vanity mirror; lefthand remote-control mirror; automatic seat back release, on two-doors and DeLuxe CC seat belts ($50). Trailer towing package class II ($32.90); class III $117.10. Visibility light group ($29).

MARQUIS SERIES — The 1975 Marquis' chrome framed-grille consisted of six rectangular chrome pieces, each containing five vertical bars. A single vertical bar evenly divided the grille in two. The concealed headlight doors looked like music boxes. Both had an emblem in the center. The wraparound signal lights were circled by four thin chrome bands. Side trim consisted of full-length lower-body molding and upper body pin stripes. Mercury was spelled out on the center rear deck panel between the wraparound, rectangular taillights. Standard features included power steering; power front disc brakes; wood-grain applique on instrument panel; lefthand remote-control mirror; power ventilation system; DeLuxe wheel covers and cut-pile carpeting.

MARQUIS I.D. NUMBERS: See 1960 Monterey I.D. numbers.

MARQUIS

Model Number	Body/Style Number	Body Type & Seating	Factory Price	Shipping Weight	Production Total
NA	63	4-dr Sedan-6P	5115	4513	20,058
NA	66	2-dr HT Cpe-6P	5049	4470	6,807
NA	74	4-dr Sta Wag-6P	5411	4880	1,904

MARQUIS ENGINE
V-8: Overhead valves. Cast iron block. Displacement: 460 cubic inches. Bore and stroke: 4 x 4 inches. Compression ratio: 8.00:1. SAE net horsepower: 158 at 3800 R.P.M. Carburetor: two-barrel.

1975 Mercury, Marquis Brougham 2-dr hardtop coupe, V-8

MARQUIS BROUGHAM SERIES — The Brougham had full-length upper body moldings; vinyl roof; deep cut-pile carpeting; electric clock; power windows; fender skirts; Brougham wheel covers and a visor mounted vanity mirror. The Colony Park station wagon featured simulated Rosewood paneling on the sides and tailgate; flight bench seat with center arm rest; door-pull and seat back assist straps; Brougham wheel covers; DeLuxe seat and shoulder belts; visor mounted vanity mirror and three- way tailgate.

MARQUIS BROUGHAM I.D. NUMBERS: See 1960 Monterey I.D. numbers.

MARQUIS BROUGHAM

Model Number	Body/Style Number	Body Type & Seating	Factory Price	Shipping Weight	Production Total
NA	62	4-dr Sedan-6P	6037	4799	19,667
NA	64	2-dr HT Cpe-6P	5972	4747	7,125
NA	76	4-dr Colony Park-6P	5598	4953	11,652

MARQUIS BROUGHAM ENGINE
Station wagon engine data same as Marquis Series engine data. Sedan and hardtop engine specifications as follows:
V-8: Overhead valves. Cast iron block. Displacement: 460 cubic inches. Bore and stroke: 4.36 x 3.85. Compression ratio: 8.00:1. SAE net horsepower: 218 at 4000 R.P.M. Carburetor: four-barrel.

1975 Mercury, Grand Marquis 4-dr sedan, V-8

GRAND MARQUIS SERIES — A wide, upper tire level band of molding across its sides set the Grand Marquis apart from the other series. It came with deep, shag cut-pile carpeting; dual map-reading lamps; lefthand remote-control mirror; vinyl roof; carpeted luggage compartment; hood and deck lid paint stripes and passenger assist straps.

GRAND MARQUIS I.D. NUMBERS: See 1960 Monterey I.D. numbers.

GRAND MARQUIS

Model Number	Body/Style Number	Body Type & Seating	Factory Price	Shipping Weight	Production Total
NA	60	4-dr Sedan-6P	6469	4815	12,307
NA	61	2-dr HT Cpe-6P	6403	4762	4,945

GRAND MARQUIS ENGINE
See 1975 Marquis Brougham Series engine data.

CHASSIS FEATURES: Wheelbase: (passenger car) 124 inches; (station wagon) 121 inches. Overall length: (passenger car) 229 inches; (station wagon) 227 inches. Tires: (passenger cars) JR78 x 15; (Marquis) HR78 x 15.

POWERTRAIN OPTIONS: Select-Shift automatic transmission was standard. A 218 horsepower 460 cubic inch V-8 (four-barrel) was optional.

CONVENIENCE OPTIONS: Air conditioner ($430.58). Anti-theft alarm system, for station wagons without appearance protection group ($84.30); with appearance protection group ($78.95). Heavy-duty battery, station wagons ($12.62). DeLuxe seat and shoulder belts ($15.14). Digital clock ($39.50). Electric rear window defroster ($61.84). Tinted glass ($50.49). Cornering lights ($35.24). Automatic load adjuster,

station wagons $76.99). Luggage carrier with air deflector ($96.00). Visor vanity illuminated mirror ($35.60). Bodyside moulding ($32.82). Sure track power brakes with 460 cubic inch V-8 ($189.30). Six-Way bench seat ($124). Six-Way left and righthand power seat ($174.16). Electric power sun roof ($495.97). Electric windows ($140.79). Remote control trunk release ($13.89). AM radio with special speakers ($97.40). AM/FM multiplex with stereo tape ($363.20). AM/FM multiplex with dual front door and rear seat speakers ($233.47). Dual rear speakers ($32.82). Vinyl roof ($637). Dual facing third seat, wagons ($122.27). Twin comfort lounge seats ($75.72). Passenger side reclining seat ($42.91). Automatic speed control ($66.89). Tilt steering wheel ($44.17). Storage compartment with locks, station wagons ($32.90). Recreation table, station wagons ($42.11). Trailer brake control ($38.20). Trailer hitch equalizer platform ($88.20). DeLuxe cargo area trim, including lockable storage and padded quarter trim, station wagons ($65). Luggage compartment trim, for station wagons, including: carpeting; spare tire cover and side lining board ($40.80). Luxury wheel covers ($32.82). Interval selector wipers ($25.24). Rear tailgate window washer, station wagons ($37.86). Appearance protection group, including floor mats with carpet inserts; door edge guards; license plate frames; spare tire lock; rear mats with carpet inserts and hood lock, on station wagons ($47.40). Bumper protection group including front and rear rubber bumper strips and rear bumper guards, on station wagons ($23.68); on executive wagons ($35.53). Cross country ride package ($22.71). Grand Marquis luxury trim including digital clock; carpeted trunk with side lining boards and flap; hood and deck lid stripes; perforated vinyl headlining with Corinthian-grain vinyl covered visors; assist handles; unique headrests and seat trim; dash panel and cluster applique; door and quarter trim panels; dome map/reading lamp; luxury steering wheel and 25 oz. carpeting, on Marquis without light group ($325); Marquis with light group ($311.90); station wagons without light group ($390.80); station wagons with light group ($377.70). Marquis/Colony Park luxury trim, including instrument panel lights; door-pull straps; Brougham wheel covers; Brougham split bench seat and door trim panels; 25 oz. carpeting; visor vanity mirror; Brougham level sound package; front door courtesy lights; rear door arm rest cigar lighters and Brougham trim ($184.21). Tailer-towing package class I ($36.84); class II ($32.82) and class III ($88.34). Visability light group ($39.50).

Historical footnotes: Approximately one in three 1974 full-size Mercurys came with speed control.

MERCURY
1976-1986

From the beginning, Mercury suffered an identity problem. Back in 1949, Mercury and Ford were two quite different automobiles. That difference faded somewhat later in the 1950s, but a revival began in the next decade. High-powered Cougars of the late '60s, in particular, renewed Mercury's reputation for performance; and, to a lesser extent, for styling that expressed a separate identity.

That difference didn't last. Through most of the 1976-'86 period, Mercury was just, to put it blunty, a

1976 Comet "Custom Option" sedan (AA)

That difference didn't last. Through most of the 1976-86 period, Mercury was just, to put it bluntly, a plusher and pricier Ford. Sure, their grilles weren't identical, and trim details (even some overall lengths) varied. But down at chassis or engine level, and in the basic body structure, Mercury seemed to offer little that was new or original. What didn't come from Ford — notably styling in the bigger models — came from Lincoln. Style-wise, in fact, Mercury often looked more like a lesser Lincoln than an upscale Ford.

1978 Zephyr Z-7 coupe (M)

Much of the change was solidified earlier in the 1970s when Cougar switched from its role as a slightly bigger Mustang, and became a mid-size instead, closer to Thunderbird. By 1977, the XR-7 badge lost much of its significance. Rather than a singular sporty offering, that model became little more than just another coupe out of a baroquely-trimmed lot, styled after Lincoln Continental's Mark series. By 1980, Cougar grew even closer to T-Bird, hardly more than a clone, just as every other Mercury model had its Ford mate. Bobcat was basically a restyled Pinto, Monarch a fancier Granada, Zephyr nearly identical to Ford's Fairmont. And at the top of the size heap, Marquis and LTD had far more in common than

1979 Grand Marquis sedan (JG)

they had differences. This twin-model concept was known as "badge engineering," and Mercury was one of its most adept practitioners.

Actually, the biggest difference between the two makes may have occurred from 1975-'78 when Mercury fielded a German-built Capri rather than turn to a variant of the reduced-size (domestically built) Mustang II. Even when Mercury finally introduced its version of the all-new Mustang for 1979, it never quite captured the attention of enthusiasts in the same way as Ford's version. That was true even though the chassis was the same, engines the same, just about everything of consequence similar, if not precisely identical. When Ford V-8s were downsized from 302 to 255 cubic inches, so were Mercury's. When Ford models add four-speed overdrive automatics or switch from eight- to six-cylinder power, so do their Mercury counterparts, nearly always at the same time. For instance, when the LTD was downsized in 1979, there was Mercury with a similarly shrunken Marquis.

1983½ Topaz CS sedan (JG)

Still, Mercury managed to survive these years and continues strong today. How did that happen? Well, Mercury was best at turning out mid-size and full-size models which, if not exactly thrilling, at least attracted a regular crop of traditional-minded buyers. Smaller Mercury models never seemed to catch on as well as

1986 Lynx GS wagon (JG)

1986 Grand Marquis Colony Park wagon (JG)

Ford's, but the biggies (and near-biggies) didn't fare badly. Perhaps the best example was the two-seater LN7, introduced in 1982. Ford's EXP, its corporate twin, didn't exactly set the marketplace ablaze; but Mercury's sales record was a disaster.

New-car buyers may have been willing to pay a few hundred dollars extra for a Mercury badge rather than a Ford name on their coupes or sedans, but collectors and enthusiasts might be more reluctant. When you're faced with a basically dull and repetitious lot, how can you select one worthy of hanging onto? Even the models that differed from Ford (or Lincoln) equivalents in some notable way, such as the bubble-back Capri introduced for 1983, aren't likely to send shivers down many spines. If you like a particular Mercury design better than its Ford mate, fine. Buy it, or keep it, or admire it. Otherwise, unless the Merc carries a markedly smaller price tab, there are few compelling reasons to pick it over a comparable Ford. Maybe it's silly, in view of their similarities, but Mustang and T-bird are likely to draw more admiring glances than Capris and Cougars in like condition. Even an Escort GT seems to have a trifle more panache than Mercury's XR3, though if you squint your eyes you can hardly tell them apart.

1976 MERCURY

While the previous model year had brought the longest list of running changes in Lincoln-Mercury history, 1975 was largely a carryover year. The subcompact Bobcat and luxurious Grand Monarch Ghia had been introduced in mid-1975, along with the revised (imported) Capri II. Mercury would not offer a domestic-built cousin to Ford's Mustang until 1979. Otherwise, Mercury offered a model equivalent to each Ford product, typically differing more in body details than basic structure. A number of previously standard items were made optional for 1976 on full-size and luxury models, to keep base prices down. As in the industry generally, fuel economy was a major factor in planning the 1976 lineup. Mercury still offered some "real" pillarless two-door hardtops, but not for long.

1976 Bobcat MPG Runabout (AA)

BOBCAT (MPG) — FOUR/V-6 — Bobcat carried on in its first full season with two body styles: the "three-door" (actually two-door with hatch) Runabout, and a Villager station wagon. Bobcat rode a 94.5 inch wheelbase and had a base 140 cu. in. (2.3-liter) four- cylinder engine with four-speed manual gearbox. A 2.8-liter V-6 was optional. As with most Mercury models, Bobcat was essentially a Ford Pinto with a different hood and grille, and a fancier interior. Bobcat's distinctive grille, made up of thin vertical bars (slightly wider center bar) with bright surround molding, along with a domed hood, identified it as a member of the Lincoln-Mercury family. Large 'Mercury' block letters stood above the grille. Small square running/park/signal lamps with crossbar-patterned bright overlay sat between the single round headlamps and the grille, rather low, just above the bumper. Bodies held front and rear side marker lights, ventless door windows, and fixed quarter windows. Wide, bright wheel lip moldings and bright rocker panel moldings were standard. Also standard: bright windshield, drip rail, side window frame, lower back panel surround, door belt and rear window moldings. At the rear, each wide horizontal three-pod taillamp assembly held a red run/brake/signal light, white backup light and red reflector lens, with bright surround

1976 Bobcat Villager wagon (AA)

molding. Bright wheel covers were standard (styled steel wheels in California). Inside were all-vinyl high-back front bucket seats with integral head restraints. Villager had simulated rosewood-grain appliques with bright surround molding on bodyside and liftgate, a front- hinged center side window, and vertical taillamp assembly with integral backup lights and bright surround molding. Bright 'Bobcat' script and 'Villager' block letters went on the liftgate. The full-upswinging liftgate held fixed glass. New standard equipment included high-back bucket seats, revised door trim panels, and regular seatbelts. Deluxe low- back bucket seats became optional. Runabouts had a new optional simulated woodgrain applique for side and lower back panels. Woodgrain side panels were standard on the Villager wagon. Alpine plaid cloth interior trim in four colors replaced polyknit cloth as an interior option. Other new options included an AM radio with stereo tape player, interval-select wipers, sports vinyl roof with optional sports tape stripes, and engine block heater. Bobcat had rack-and-pinion steering, solid-state ignition, electro-coat primer, and unitized body construction. V-6 models came with power brakes.

COMET — SIX/V-8 — Introduced in 1971, the compact Comet had only minor changes at the front end and grille this year. New blackout paint went on the grille's vertical bars, and around headlamp doors and parking lamps. The wide, bright protruding horizontal-rib center grille was accompanied by bright framed argent side grille panels with integral run/park/signal lamps. Exposed single headlamps now showed blackout housings. Two-doors had front-hinged rear quarter windows; four-doors, roll-down back windows. Both had ventless door windows, bright rocker panels and upper bodyside molding, and a bright gas cap with L-M crest and 'Comet' block letters. Identification was also provided by bright 'Comet' and 'Mercury' script. Two-pod color-keyed taillamp assemblies held integral backup lights. Inside was a two-pod instrument cluster with recessed instruments and a standard front bench seat. Comet's former GT edition was replaced by a Sports Accent Group that included

1976 Comet "Sports Accent" coupe (M)

wide lower bodyside moldings, lower body two-tone paint, dual racing mirrors, belt moldings, styled steel wheels with trim rings, and whitewalls. Two-doors could have an optional half-vinyl roof. A Custom option included new bucket seats, door trim and tinted glass. Five new body colors were offered, as well as a revised Custom interior. Alpine plaid was a new cloth seat trim. There was a new double-action foot-operated parking brake, and a new standard two-spoke steering wheel. Base engine was a 200 cu. in. inline six with one-barrel carb (250 cu. in. in California), with three-speed manual shift. A 302 cu. in. V-8 was optional. Comets had unitized body construction and standard bias-ply blackwall tires. Two- doors rode a 103 inch wheelbase; four-doors, 109.9 inches. Comet was a variant of Ford's Maverick.

1976 Monarch Ghia coupe (M)

MONARCH — SIX/V-8 — Close kin to Ford's Granada, Monarch was described as "precision-size," with 109.9 inch wheelbase. Three models were offered: base, Ghia, and top-rung Grand Monarch Ghia. Little changed this year, except for some engineering improvements that were supposed to improve ride and quiet sound levels inside. Monarch's bright upright grille was made up of thin vertical bars, with a slightly wider center divider bar. Above the grille were 'Mercury' block letters, and a stand-up hood ornament with Monarch 'M' crest and fold-down feature. Single round headlamps sat in color-keyed square frames. Large wraparound park/signal lamps with horizontal ribs were mounted in front fender tips. Bright full-length upper bodyside and decklid moldings were standard. Bright moldings also went on the windshield, full wheel lip, roof drip, and door frame. Full wheel covers displayed a center ornament, composed of three concentric circles on a circular field of red. Two-doors had opera windows. Four-doors included a bright center pillar molding. Three-pod taillamp assemblies included a tri-color lens with white backup lens, and amber-overlayed red brake and turn signal light. The textured back panel applique with bright 'Monarch' block lettering had an integral fuel filler door and hidden gas cap, color coordinated with body paint or vinyl roof. 'Mercury' script stood on the decklid. All-vinyl upholstery was standard. Flight bench seats were now standard in Monarch Ghia. Monarch had a standard 200 cu. in. one-barrel six with three-speed manual (fully synchronized) column shift. A 250 cu. in. inline six was optional, along with 302 and 351 cu. in. V-8s. Monarch used unibody construction. Four-leaf semi- elliptic rear springs were nearly 5 feet long and had stagger-mounted shock absorbers. A new base model had revised standard equipment, including a bench seat, different steering wheel, and revised door trim. Monarch Ghia added a bright driver's side remote mirror, wide odense grain bodyside molding and partial wheel lip molding, and distinctive Ghia wheel covers with simulated spoke motif and round red center ornament, highlighted by three bright concentric circles. A Ghia ornament adorned the opera window of two-doors, or rear pillar of four-doors. Also on Ghia: hood and decklid contour paint stripes, and a full- length upper bodyside paint stripe. A four-door luxury version (Grand Monarch Ghia) joined the lineup in late spring. That one added power windows, power steering, four-wheel power disc brakes, unique seat and door trim, and a fully padded Normande grain vinyl roof with frenched backlight. Bright 'Grand Monarch' script went on the lower fender. Also included on Grand Monarch: cast aluminum spoked wheels, a Normande grain vinyl center pillar pad, Ghia emblem on rear pillar, digital clock, whitewall tires, and unique taillamps. The 250 cu. in. six was standard. Buyers had a choice of saddle and white two-tone leather seating, dark red monotone leather, or dark red monotone cloth. (Leather seating had vinyl door trim.) New options were: console with warning lights (standard on Grand Monarch Ghia), power door locks, speed control, tilt steering, and automatic seatback release as part of the convenience group. Monarch's windshield wiper/washer control had moved to the steering column in mid-1975. Other mid-1975 changes included optional Sure-Track brakes, four-wheel disc brakes, and power seats.

1976 Montego MX Brougham sedan (AA)

1976 Montego MX coupe (AA)

MONTEGO — V-8 — This would be the final outing for Mercury's mid-size, offered in three series: Montego, Montego MX, and Montego MX Brougham. In addition to hardtop coupe and sedan models, two station wagons were available, including the simulated woodgrain-sided MX Villager. Five new body colors raised the total to 16. A landau vinyl roof option was available in six colors for two-doors. Another new option: Twin Comfort Lounge seats (with or without reclining feature) available on MX Brougham and Villager. A 351 cu. in. V-8 engine with SelectShift automatic transmission was standard on all Montegos; 400 and 460 cu. in. V-8 available. Quad round headlamps in bright rectangular frames were flanked by large combination run/park/turn signal lamps that followed the inner surface of the fendertip extensions. A rather narrow, forward-protruding grille carried both horizontal and vertical bars, with horizontal theme dominant. A bright 'Mercury' script went on the upper grille panel and decklid; L-M crest on grille panel and fuel filler door; bright 'Montego' script on lower front fender; and 'Montego' block letters on fuel door. Three-pod taillamp assemblies were used. Bright hubcaps were standard. Inside was a standard low-back front bench seat with adjustable head restraint, upholstered in cloth and vinyl. Standard equipment included power steering and brakes. Front bumper guards held rub strips. Montego MX added bright rocker panel moldings, dual upper body paint stripes, 'Montego MX' script on lower front fender, a lower back panel center surround molding, and bright/black 'Montego MX' name on instrument panel. MX Brougham had deluxe wheel covers with L-M crest in the center, over a brushed metal background with simulated spokes on outer circumference. Also on Broughams: bright upper body peak molding, bright plaque with 'Brougham' script on rear pillar, bright lower rear fender molding, and lower back panel box-textured applique with blackout paint and bright surround molding. Montego MX station wagons came with bright 'Montego' script and 'Mercury' block letters on the three-way tailgate, a vertical three-pod taillamp assembly, bright roof rear and quarter-window moldings, and bright tailgate belt molding. The top-line Villager wagon added full-length simulated woodgrain bodyside and tailgate paneling, surrounded by bright molding (partially black paint-filled). Also on Villager: bright front and rear partial wheel lip moldings, 'Montego MX' script on lower front fender, with Villager plaque. A power tailgate window was included. Montego also had a police package with choice of V-8 engines: 351 cu. in., 400 cu. in. 2Bbl., 460 cu. in. 4Bbl., or Police Interceptor 460 4Bbl. V-8 (with mechanical fuel pump, low-restriction air cleaner and exhaust, and engine oil cooler). Montego's front suspension used single lower arm drag struts and a link-type stabilizer bar. At the rear were helical coil springs in a four-link rubber-cushioned system.

1976 Cougar XR-7 Sports Coupe (M)

COUGAR XR-7 — V-8 — By the mid-1970s, Mercury's Cougar was a far different animal than the version that first appeared in 1967. Mid-size in dimensions, it had a big-car look and styling that emulated the Lincoln Continental Mark IV. Angled horizontal opera windows had been added for 1974, joining the vestigial small quarter windows. The two-door hardtop personal-luxury coupe came with plenty of standard equipment, including a landau vinyl roof and full instrumentation (including tachometer, clock, trip odometer, fuel gauge, ammeter, oil and temp gauges). Standard powerteam was a 351 cu. in. two-barrel V-8 with SelectShift Cruise-O-Matic. 400 cu. in. two-barrel and 460 four-barrel V-8s were optional. Previously standard features, such as a luxury steering wheel, tinted glass, styled steel wheels with trim rings, and bucket seats with console, were made optional this year. New interior options included reclining Twin Comfort Lounge seats, with or without optional velour cloth trim; as well as a cream and gold two-tone interior for the Twin Comfort seats. Other new options: cast aluminum wheels, rocker panel moldings, engine block heater, and AM/FM stereo radio with search feature. A power-operated moon roof had been introduced as an option for 1975, with a sliding panel of tinted one-way glass that could be covered manually by an opaque shade that matched the headliner color and material. Cougar's narrow grille consisted of very thin vertical ribs with a dominant surround molding. Twin side-by-side slots were in the bumper, just below the grille, between the bumper guards. Matching side grilles held quad round headlamps, with parking/turn signal lamps in the front fender extensions. The bright Cougar stand-up hood ornament had a fold-down feature. 'Mercury' script went on both hood and deck. Side marker lights and reflectors were on the front fenders. Horizontal taillamps had integral backup lights, with bright vertical bars, bright partially black paint-filled surround molding, and red reflex rear center applique. Rear side marker lights and reflectors were integral with taillamps. Lower bodyside moldings held color-keyed vinyl inserts. Side windows were ventless and frameless; quarter windows fixed. Bright Cougar ornaments were embedded in the opera window glass. Luxury wheel covers had an L-M crest and Cougar XR-7 ornament on the center hub.

1976 Grand Marquis Ghia sedan (AA)

MARQUIS — V-8 — Eight models in three series made up the full-size line: Marquis, Marquis Brougham, and Grand Marquis. Two wagons were offered, including a simulated woodgrain-sided Colony Park. A 400 cu. in. two-barrel V-8 with three-speed SelectShift was standard on all models. Power front disc/rear drum brakes and power steering were standard. Eight new body colors were added. Otherwise, this was basically a carryover year. Half a dozen separate side-by-side "boxes" made up the Marquis grille, each one holding a set of vertical ribs. Fender tips held large wraparound parking/turn signal/side marker lamps with horizontal lens ribbing. Quad headlamps were hidden behind doors with center emblems. The bright wreath stand-up hood ornament had a fold-down feature. 'Mercury' script stood on the upper grille panel; 'Marquis' script on front fender; a Marquis plaque on rear pillar; and 'Mercury' block letters on rear back panel. Two-doors had fixed quarter windows. Bright rocker panel and lower front/rear fender moldings were standard, along with bright wheel lip moldings. Deluxe wheel covers showed the L-M crest. Wraparound taillamps had horizontal ribs. A textured applique between taillamp assemblies was color-keyed to either the optional vinyl roof or the body color. Inside were low-back front bench seats, rear bench seats trimmed in new cloth and vinyl, and a two-spoke color-keyed steering wheel. Four-doors had a fold-down front seat center armrest (dual on two-doors). Simulated baby burl woodgrain adorned the instrument cluster, with a color-keyed applique over the glovebox door. Front bumper guards had black vertical protection strips. Marquis Brougham added such extras as a vinyl roof, rear fender skirts with bright lip molding, electric clock, power windows, bright full-length fender peak molding, Brougham plaque on lower front fender, and remote-control driver's mirror. Distinctive Brougham wheel covers had a partially plaque-filled Marquis plaque and slots in the outer circumference. The hinged decklid cover showed an L-M crest. Flight bench seats had adjustable low-profile head restraints and a single center folding armrest. Four-doors had rear door courtesy light switches, and a cigar lighter in the back-door armrest ashtrays. Grand Marquis included tinted glass, dual hood

1976 Marquis Brougham hardtop coupe (M)

and decklid paint stripes, full-length bodyside moldings with wide color-keyed vinyl insert, and gold Marquis crest on rear pillar and headlamp covers. Lower front fenders held 'Grand Marquis' script. Interiors held Twin Comfort lounge seats with dual center armrests and leather (or leather and velour) seating surfaces. A digital clock and dome lamp with dual-beam map lights were standard. Marquis station wagons had three-pod vertical taillamps, a bright tailgate belt molding, 'Mercury' block letters across the three-way tailgate, bright L-M crest on the tailgate, and a power back window. Seat upholstery was all vinyl. Rear bumper guards had black vertical rub strips. Colony Park wagons added simulated rosewood-grain paneling on bodyside and tailgate. They were also identified by 'Colony Park' script on lower rear fender, bright full-length fender peak moldings, and Brougham-style wheel covers. Flight bench seats had adjustable low-profile head restraints. New Marquis options included an AM/FM stereo search radio, landau vinyl roof, rocker panel moldings, engine block heater, and forged aluminum wheels. Base Marquis two-doors could get an automatic seatback release. A Tu-Tone group was available on Marquis Brougham and Grand Marquis two-doors. It gave a choice of two distinctive color combinations: tan and dark brown, or cream and gold. Two-tone interior trims in those packages also were available, with colors compatible to the body. The new optional vinyl half-roof for the two-door was offered in a wide range of colors, including two new ones: gold and medium red. There was a full-size Mercury police package, with 460 cu. in. four-barrel V-8 and dual exhausts, automatic transmission with auxiliary oil cooler, 3.00:1 axle ratio, four-wheel power disc brakes, and a list of heavy-duty equipment. It also included a 140 MPH speedometer. Low-gear lockout for the automatic was a limited-production option on the police packages. The packages also were available with other V-8s: 400 2Bbl. (single exhaust); and 460 4Bbl. PI with mechanical fuel pump and dual exhausts.

I.D. DATA: The 11-symbol Vehicle Identification Number (VIN) is stamped on a metal tab fastened to the instrument panel, visible through the windshield. The first digit is a model year code ('6' 1976). The second letter indicates assembly plant: 'A' Atlanta, GA; 'B' Oakville (Canada); 'E' Mahwah, NJ; 'H' Lorain, Ohio; 'K' Kansas City, MO; 'R' San Jose, CA; 'T' Metuchen, NJ; 'W' Wayne, MI; 'Z' St. Louis. Digits three and four are the body serial code, which corresponds to the Model Numbers shown in the tables below (e.g., '20' Bobcat 3-dr. Runabout). The fifth digit is an engine code: 'Y' L4-140 2Bbl.; 'Z' V6170 2Bbl.; 'T' L6200 1Bbl.; 'L' L6250 1Bbl.; 'F' V8302 2Bbl.; 'H' or 'Q' V8351 2Bbl.; 'S' V8400 2Bbl.; 'A' V8460 4Bbl. Finally, digits 6-11 make up the consecutive unit number of cars built at each assembly plant. The number begins with 500,001. A Vehicle Certification Label on the left front door lock face panel or door pillar shows the manufacturer, month and year of manufacture, GVW, GAWR, certification statement, VIN, body code, color code, trim code, axle code, transmission code, and domestic (or foreign) special order code.

1976 Bobcat MPG hatchback coupe (M)

BOBCAT MPG RUNABOUT (FOUR/V-6)

Model Number	Body/Style Number	Body Type & Seating	Factory Price	Shipping Weight	Production Total
20	64H	3-dr. Hatch-4P	3338/3838	2535/ --	28,905

BOBCAT MPG VILLAGER (FOUR/V-6)

22	73H	2-dr. Sta Wag-4P	3643/4143	2668/ --	18,731

COMET (SIX/V-8)

31	62B	2-dr. Fast Sed-4P	3250/3398	-- /2952	15,068
30	54B	4-dr. Sed-5P	3317/3465	-- /3058	21,006

MONARCH (SIX/V-8)

35	66H	2-dr. Sedan-4P	3773/3927	3111/3294	47,466
34	54H	4-dr. Sedan-5P	3864/4018	3164/3347	56,351

MONARCH GHIA (SIX/V-8)

38	66K	2-dr. Sedan-4P	4331/4419	3200/3383	14,950
37	54K	4-dr. Sedan-5P	4422/4510	3250/3433	27,056

MONARCH GRAND GHIA (SIX/V-8)

37	N/A	4-dr. Sedan-5P	5740/5828	3401/3584	Note 1

Note 1: Production included in basic Monarch Ghia total above.

MONTEGO (V-8)

03	65B	2-dr. HT-6P	4299	4057	2,287
02	53B	4-dr. HT Sed-6P	4343	4133	3,403

MONTEGO MX (V-8)

07	65D	2-dr. HT-6P	4465	4085	12,367
04	53D	4-dr. HT Sed-6P	4498	4133	12,666
08	71D	4-dr. Sta Wag-6P	4778	4451	5,012

MONTEGO MX BROUGHAM (V-8)

11	65K	2-dr. HT-6P	4621	4097	3,905
10	53K	4-dr. HT Sed-6P	4670	4150	5,043

MONTEGO MX VILLAGER (V-8)

18	71K	4-dr. Sta Wag-6P	5065	4478	6,412

COUGAR XR-7 (V-8)

93	65F	2-dr. HT Cpe-5P	5125	4168	83,765

MARQUIS (V-8)

66	65H	2-dr. HT-6P	5063	4436	10,450
63	53H	4-dr. Pill. HT-6P	5063	4460	28,212
74	71H	4-dr. 2S Sta Wag-6P	5275	4796	2,493
74	71H	4-dr. 3S Sta Wag-8P	5401	4824	Note 2

1976 Marquis Brougham Pillared Hardtop (AA)

MARQUIS BROUGHAM (V-8)

Model Number	Body/Style Number	Body Type & Seating	Factory Price	Shipping Weight	Production Total
64	65K	2-dr. HT-6P	5955	4652	10,431
62	53K	4-dr. Pill. HT-6P	6035	4693	22,411

GRAND MARQUIS (V-8)

61	65L	2-dr. HT-6P	6439	4679	9,207
60	53L	4-dr. Pill. HT-6P	6528	4723	17,650

MARQUIS COLONY PARK (V-8)

76	71K	4-dr. 2S Sta Wag-6P	5590	4878	15,114
76	71K	4-dr. 3S Sta Wag-8P	5716	4906	Note 2

Note 2: Production totals for three-seat station wagons are included in two-seat figures.

FACTORY PRICE AND WEIGHT NOTE: For Comet and Monarch, prices and weights to left of slash are for six-cylinder, to right for V-8 engine. For Bobcat, prices/weights to left of slash are for four-cylinder, to right for V-6.

ENGINE DATA: BASE FOUR (Bobcat): Inline. Overhead cam. Four-cylinder. Cast iron block and head. Displacement: 140 cu. in. (2.3 liters). Compression ratio: 9.0:1. Brake horsepower: 92 at 5000 R.P.M. Torque: 121 lbs.-ft. at 3000 R.P.M. Five main bearings. Hydraulic valve lifters. Carburetor: 2Bbl. Holley-Weber 9510 (D6EE-AA). VIN Code: Y. OPTIONAL V-6 (Bobcat): 60-degree, overhead-valve V-6. Cast iron block and head. Displacement: 170.8 cu. in. (2.8 liters). Bore & stroke: 3.66 x 2.70 in. Compression ratio: 8.7:1. Brake horsepower: 100 at 4600 R.P.M. Torque: 143 lbs.-ft. at 2600 R.P.M. Four main bearings. Hydraulic valve lifters. Carburetor: 2Bbl. Motorcraft 9510 (D6ZE-BA). VIN Code: Z. BASE SIX (Comet, Monarch): Inline. OHV. Six-cylinder. Cast iron block and head. Displacement: 200 cu. in. (3.3 liters). Bore & stroke: 3.68 x 3.13 in. Compression ratio: 8.3:1. Brake horsepower: 81 at 3400 R.P.M. Torque: 151 lbs.-ft. at 1700 R.P.M. Seven main bearings. Hydraulic valve lifters. Carburetor: 1Bbl. Carter YFA 9510 (D6EE-AA). VIN Code: T. BASE SIX (Monarch Ghia); OPTIONAL (Comet, Monarch): Inline. OHV. Six-cylinder. Cast iron block and head. Displacement: 250 cu. in. (4.1 liters). Bore & stroke: 3.68 x 3.91 in. Compression ratio: 8.0:1. Brake horsepower: 90 at 3000 R.P.M. (Monarch, 87 at 3000). Torque: 190 lbs.-ft. at 2000 R.P.M. (Monarch, 187 at 1900). Seven main bearings. Hydraulic valve lifters. Carburetor: 1Bbl. Carter YFA 9510. VIN Code: L. OPTIONAL V-8 (Comet, Monarch): 90-degree, overhead valve V-8. Cast iron block and head. Displacement: 302 cu. in. (5.0 liters). Bore & stroke: 4.00 x 3.00 in. Compression ratio: 8.0:1. Brake horsepower: 138 at 3600 R.P.M. (Monarch, 134 at 3600). Torque: 245 lbs.-ft. at 2000 R.P.M. (Monarch, 242 at 2000). Five main bearings. Hydraulic valve lifters. Carburetor: 2Bbl. Ford 2150A 9510 (D5DE-AFA). VIN Code: F. BASE V-8 (Montego, Cougar); OPTIONAL (Monarch): 90-degree, overhead valve V-8. Cast iron block and head. Displacement: 351 cu. in. (5.8 liters). Bore & stroke: 4.00 x 3.50 in. Compression ratio: 8.0:1. (Montego, 8.1:1). Brake horsepower: 152 at 3800 R.P.M. (or 154 at 3400). Torque: 274 lbs.-ft. at 1600 R.P.M. (or 286 at 1800). Five main bearings. Hydraulic valve lifters. Carburetor: 2Bbl. Ford 2150A 9510. VIN Code: H. BASE V-8 (Marquis); OPTIONAL (Cougar, Montego): 90-degree, overhead valve V-8. Cast iron block and head. Displacement: 400 cu. in. (6.6 liters). Bore & stroke: 4.00 x 4.00 in. Compression ratio: 8.0:1. Brake horsepower: 180 at 3800 R.P.M. Torque: 336 lbs.-ft. at 1800 R.P.M. Hydraulic valve lifters. Carburetor: 2Bbl. Ford 2150A 9510. VIN Code: S. OPTIONAL V-8 (Cougar, Montego, Marquis): 90-degree, overhead valve V-8. Cast iron block and head. Displacement: 460 cu. in. (7.5 liters). Bore & stroke: 4.36 x 3.85 in. Compression ratio: 8.0:1. Brake horsepower: 202 at 3800 R.P.M. Torque: 352 lbs.-ft. at 1600 R.P.M. Five main bearings. Hydraulic valve lifters. Carburetor: 4Bbl. Motorcraft 9510 or Ford 4350A 9510. VIN Code: A.

CHASSIS DATA: Wheelbase: (Bobcat sed) 94.5 in.; (Bobcat wag) 94.8 in.; (Comet 2-dr.) 103.0 in.; (Comet 4-dr.) 109.9 in.; (Monarch) 109.9 in.; (Cougar) 114.0 in.; (Montego) 114.0 in.; (Montego wag) 118.0 in.; (Marquis) 124.0 in.; (Marquis wag) 121.0 in. Overall Length: (Bobcat sed) 169.0 in.; (Bobcat wag) 178.8 in.; (Comet 2-dr.) 189.5 in.; (Comet 4-dr.) 196.4 in.; (Monarch) 197.7 in.; (Cougar) 215.7 in.; (Montego 2-dr.) 215.7 in.; (Montego 4-dr.) 219.7 in.; (Montego wag) 224.4 in.; (Marquis) 229.0 in.; (Marquis wag) 228.3 in. Height: (Bobcat sed) 50.6 in.; (Bobcat wag) 52.0 in.; (Comet) 52.9 in.; (Monarch) 53.2-53.4 in.; (Cougar) 52.6 in.; (Montego 2.00dr.) 52.6 in.; (Montego 4dr.) 53.3 in.; (Montego wag) 54.9 in.; (Marquis 2-dr.) 53.7 in.; (Marquis 4-dr.) 54.7 in.; (Marquis wag) 56.9 in. Width: (Bobcat sed) 69.4 in.; (Bobcat wag) 69.7 in.; (Comet) 70.5 in.; (Monarch 2-dr.) 74.0 in. exc. Ghia, 74.5 in.; (Monarch 4-dr.) 74.1 in. exc. Ghia, 75.5 in.; (Cougar) 78.5 in.; (Montego 2-dr.) 78.6 in.; (Montego 4-dr./wag) 79.6 in.; (Marquis) 79.6 in.; (Marquis wag) 79.8 in. Front Tread: (Bobcat) 55.0 in.; (Comet) 56.5 in.; (Monarch) 58.5 in.; (Cougar) 63.4 in.; (Montego) 63.4 in.; (Marquis) 64.1 in. Rear Tread: (Bobcat) 55.8 in.; (Comet) 56.5 in.; (Monarch) 57.7 in.; (Cougar) 63.5 in.; (Montego) 63.5 in.; (Marquis) 64.3 in. Standard Tires: (Bobcat) A78 x 13 exc. V-6/wagon, B78 x 13; (Comet) C78 x 14 exc. V-8, CR78 x 14 or DR78 x 14; (Monarch) DR78 x 14 exc. V8351, ER78 x 14; (Cougar) HR78 x 14; (Montego) HR78 x 14; (Marquis) HR78 x 15 exc. wagon, JR78 x 15; (Colony Park) LR78 x 15.

TECHNICAL: Transmission: Three-speed manual transmission (column shift) standard on Comet/Monarch six and V8302. Gear ratios: (1st) 2.99:1 (2nd) 1.75:1; (3rd) 1.00:1; (Rev) 3.17:1. Four-speed floor shift standard on Bobcat. Gear ratios: (1st) 3.65:1; (2nd) 1.97:1; (3rd) 1.37:1; (4th) 1.00:1; (Rev) 3.66:1. Bobcat wagon: (1st) 4.07:1; (2nd) 2.57:1; (3rd) 1.66:1; (4th) 1.00:1; (Rev) 3.95:1. Select-Shift three-speed automatic (column lever) standard on Monarch V-8, Cougar, Montego and Marquis; optional on others. Floor lever optional-on all except full-size. Bobcat L4140 automatic gear ratios: (1st) 2.47:1; (2nd) 1.47:1; (3rd) 1.00:1; (Rev) 2.11:1. Bobcat V-6/Comet/Monarch/Cougar V8351: (1st) 2.46:1; (2nd) 1.46:1; (3rd) 1.00:1; (Rev)

2.20:1. Cougar V8400/460, Montego, full- size: (1st) 2.46:1; (2nd) 1.46:1; (3rd) 1.00:1; (Rev) 2.18:1. Standard final drive ratio: (Bobcat) 3.18:1 w/four, 3.00:1 w/V-6; (Comet) 2.79:1 w/3spd, 2.79:1 or 3.00:1 w/auto.; (Monarch) 2.79:1 w/3spd and 2.75:1, 3.00:1 or 3.07:1 w/auto.; (Cougar) 2.75:1; (Montego) 2.75:1; (Marquis) 2.75:1. Steering: (Bobcat) rack and pinion; (others) recirculating ball. Front Suspension: (Bobcat) coil springs with lower trailing arms, and anti-sway bar on wagon; (Montego) single lower arm drag strut w/coil springs and link-type anti-sway bar; (others) coil springs with short/long arms, lower trailing links and anti-sway bar. Rear Suspension: (Bobcat/Comet/Monarch) rigid axle w/semi- elliptic leaf springs; (Cougar) rigid axle w/lower trailing radius arms, upper oblique torque arms and coil springs; (Montego) four-link rubber-cushioned system w/coil springs; (Marquis) rigid axle w/lower trailing radius arms, upper torque arms and coil springs. Brakes: Front disc, rear drum. Ignition: Electronic. Body construction: (Bobcat/Comet/Monarch) unibody; (others) separate body on perimeter frame; Fuel tank: (Bobcat) 13 gal. exc. wagon, 14 gal.; (Comet) 19.2 gal.; (Monarch) 19.2 gal.; (Cougar) 26.5 gal.; (Montego) 21.3 gal.; (Marquis) 21 gal.

DRIVETRAIN OPTIONS: Engines: 250 cu. in., 1Bbl. six: Comet/Monarch ($96). 302 cu. in., 2Bbl. V-8: Monarch ($154); Monarch Ghia ($88). 351 cu. in., 2Bbl. V-8: Monarch ($200); Monarch Ghia ($134). 400 cu. in., 2Bbl. V-8: Montego/Cougar ($93). 460 cu. in., 4Bbl. V-8: Montego/Cougar ($292); Marquis ($212). Transmission/Differential: SelectShift Cruise-O-Matic: Bobcat ($186); Comet/Monarch ($245). Floor shift lever: Comet/Monarch ($27). Traction-Lok differential: Monarch ($48); Montego/Cougar ($53); Marquis ($54). Optional axle ratio: Bobcat/Comet/Monarch ($13); Montego/Cougar/Marquis ($14). Brakes/Steering: Power brakes: Bobcat ($54); Comet ($53); Monarch ($57). Four-wheel power disc brakes: Monarch ($210); Marquis ($170). Sure-Track brakes: Marquis ($217). Power steering: Bobcat ($117); Comet/Monarch ($124). Suspension: H.D. susp.: Comet ($17); Monarch ($29). Cross-country susp.: Montego/Cougar ($26). Adjustable air shock absorbers: Marquis ($46). Other: Engine block heater: Bobcat/Comet/Monarch ($17); Montego/Marquis/Cougar ($18). H.D. battery: Comet/Monarch ($14-$16); Marquis ($20). H.D. electrical system: Montego/Cougar ($37). Extended-range fuel tank: Marquis ($99). Trailer towing pkg. (light duty): Monarch ($42); Marquis ($53). Trailer towing pkg. (medium duty): Montego/Cougar ($59); Marquis ($46). Trailer towing pkg. (heavy duty): Montego ($82-$121); Cougar/Marquis ($132). Equalizer hitch: Marquis ($99). High-altitude option: Cougar ($13).

BOBCAT CONVENIENCE/APPEARANCE OPTIONS: Option Packages: Sports accent group ($116-$269). Convenience light group ($92). Appearance protection group ($35). Bumper protection ($64). Comfort/Convenience: Air conditioner ($420). Rear defroster, electric ($67). Tinted glass ($46). Interval wipers ($25). Entertainment: AM radio ($71); w/stereo tape player ($192). AM/FM radio ($128). AM/FM stereo radio ($173). Exterior: Sunroof, manual ($230). Sports vinyl roof ($86). Glamour paint ($54). Sports tape striping ($40). Hinged quarter windows ($34). Wide bodyside moldings ($60); narrow ($35). Rocker panel moldings ($19). Runabout woodgrain ($214). Roof luggage rack ($52-$75). Bumper guards ($34). Interior: Deluxe interior ($139). Alpine plaid seat trim ($30). Deluxe seatbelts ($17). Wheels and Tires: Forged aluminum wheels ($53-$136). Styled steel wheels ($48-$83). A78 x 13 WSW. A70 x 13 RWL. B78 x 13 BSW/WSW. BR78 x 13 SBR BSW/WSW. BR70 x 13 RWL.

COMET CONVENIENCE/APPEARANCE OPTIONS: Option Packages: Sports accent group ($235). Custom decor group ($496). Custom interior decor ($222). Bumper group ($30-$64). Convenience/visibility group ($43-$51). Appearance protection group ($8-$39). Security lock group ($16). Comfort/Convenience: Air cond. ($420). Rear defogger ($43). Tinted glass ($42). Fuel monitor warning light ($18). Interval wipers ($25). Entertainment: AM radio ($71); w/tape player ($192). AM/FM radio ($128). AM/FM stereo radio ($216); w/tape player ($299). Exterior: Vinyl roof ($89). Glamour paint ($54). Lower bodyside paint ($55). Tu-tone paint ($33). Bodyside molding ($35). Rocker panel moldings ($19). Decklid luggage rack ($51). Bumper guards, front ($17). Interior: Reclining bucket seats ($119). Alpine plaid seat trim ($30). Vinyl seat trim ($25). Color-keyed deluxe seatbelts ($17). Wheels and Tires: Forged aluminum wheels ($67-$192). Styled steel wheels ($60-$89). Deluxe wheel covers ($29). C78 x 14 WSW. BR78 x 14 BSW. CR78 x 14 BSW/WSW. DR78 x 14 BSW/WSW. DR70 x 14 RWL. Space-saver spare ($13) except (NC) with radial tires.

MONARCH CONVENIENCE/APPEARANCE OPTIONS: Option Packages: 'S' group ($482). Decor group ($181). Convenience group ($31-$75). Bumper group ($64). Light group ($25-$37). Protection group ($24-$39). Visibility group ($34- $47). Security lock group ($17). Comfort/Convenience: Air cond. ($437). Rear defogger ($43). Rear defroster, electric ($73). Fingertip speed control ($96). Power windows ($95-$133). Power door locks ($63-$88). Power four-way seat ($119). Tinted glass ($47). Leather- wrapped steering wheel ($14-$33). Luxury steering wheel ($18). Tilt steering wheel ($54). Fuel monitor warning light ($18). Digital clock ($40). Interval wipers ($25). Horns and Mirrors: Dual-note horn ($6). Dual racing mirrors ($29-$42). Lighted visor vanity mirror ($40). Entertainment: AM radio ($71); w/tape player ($192). AM/FM radio ($142). AM/FM stereo radio ($210); w/tape player ($299). Exterior: Power moonroof ($786). Power sunroof ($517). Full or landau vinyl roof ($102). Glamour paint ($54). Bodyside moldings ($35). Rocker panel moldings ($19). Decklid luggage rack ($51). Interior: Console ($65). Reclining bucket seats ($60). Leather seat trim ($181). Luxury cloth seat trim ($88) exc. (NC) w/Grand Ghia. Trunk carpeting ($20). Trunk dress-up ($33). Color-keyed seatbelts ($17). Wheels/Tires: Styled steel wheels ($35-$54); w/trim rings ($70-$89). Spoke aluminum wheels ($112-$201). E78 x 14 BSW/WSW. DR78 x 14 WSW. ER78 x 14 BSW/WSW. FR78 x 14 BSW/WSW. Space-saver spare (NC).

MONTEGO CONVENIENCE/APPEARANCE OPTIONS: Option Packages: Bumper group ($33-$53). Visibility light group ($82). Convenience group ($20-$66). Protection group ($18-$42). Security lock group ($18). Comfort/Convenience: Air cond. ($483); w/auto-temp control ($520). Defroster, electric ($80). Fingertip speed control ($101). Tinted glass ($53). Power windows ($104-$145). Power tailgate window: wag ($43). Power door locks ($68-$109). Electric decklid release ($17). Six-way power seat ($130). Leather-wrapped steering wheel ($36). Luxury steering wheel ($20). Tilt steering wheel ($59). Fuel sentry vacuum gauge ($34). Fuel monitor warning light ($20). Electric clock ($20). Interval wipers ($28). Horns and Mirrors: Dual-note horn ($7). Remote driver's mirror ($14). Dual racing mirrors ($36-$50). Entertainment: AM radio ($78). AM/FM stereo radio ($236); w/tape player ($339). Dual rear speakers ($39). Exterior: Full or landau vinyl roof ($112). Opera windows ($50). Rocker panel moldings ($26). Bodyside moldings ($38). Glamour paint ($59). Luggage rack ($82-$97). Interior: Twin comfort lounge seats ($164-$234). Polyknit trim ($50). Vinyl trim ($28). Rear-facing third seat: wag ($108). Trunk trim ($36). Wheels/Tires: Deluxe wheel covers ($32). Luxury wheel covers ($37-$68). Styled wheel ($66-$97). H78 x 14 BSW/WSW. HR78 x 14 BSW/WSW. HR78 x 14C BSW/WSW. JR78 x 14 WSW. Space-saver spare (NC).

COUGAR CONVENIENCE/APPEARANCE OPTIONS: Option Packages: Convenience group ($49-$57). Protection group ($34). Light group ($82). Bumper group ($53). Security lock group ($18). Comfort/Convenience: Air cond. ($483); auto-temp ($520). Rear defroster, electric ($80). Fingertip speed control ($101). Tinted glass ($53). Power seat ($130). Power windows ($104). Power door locks ($68). Electric trunk release ($17). Reclining passenger seat ($70). Leather-wrapped steering wheel ($36). Tilt steering wheel ($59). Fuel monitor warning light ($20). Interval wipers ($28). Driver's remote mirror ($14). Dual racing mirrors ($36-$50). Entertainment: AM radio ($78). AM/FM stereo radio ($236); w/tape player ($339). AM/FM stereo search radio ($386). Dual rear speakers ($39). Exterior: Power moonroof ($859); sunroof ($545). Full vinyl roof ($41). Glamour paint ($59). Bodyside molding ($38). Rocker panel moldikngs ($26). Interior: Twin comfort lounge seats ($86). Bucket seats w/console ($143). Leather trim ($222). Velour trim ($96). Trunk dress-up ($36). Wheels/Tires: Styled steel wheels ($93). Cast aluminum wheels ($199). HR78 x 14 SBR WSW ($39). HR78 x 15 SBR WSW ($62). HR70 x 15 WSW ($82). Space-saver spare (NC).

1976 Colony Park station wagon (AA)

MARQUIS CONVENIENCE/APPEARANCE OPTIONS: Option Packages: Grand Marquis option: Colony Park ($305). Tu-tone group ($59-$145). Lock convenience group ($86-$112). Light group ($83-$118). Bumper group ($33-$53). Protection group ($47-$55). Security lock group ($8-$18). Comfort/Convenience: Air cond. ($512); w/auto-temp control ($549). Anti-theft alarm system ($100-$105). Rear defroster, electric ($80). Fingertip speed control ($101). Power windows ($109-$162). Power vent windows ($79). Six-way power driver's seat ($132); driver and passenger ($257). Automatic seatback release ($30). Tinted glass ($66). Deluxe steering wheel ($20). Tilt steering wheel ($59). Fuel monitor warning light ($20). Electric clock ($20). Digital clock ($29-$49). Interval wipers ($28). Lighting and Mirrors: Cornering lamps ($41). Driver's remote mirror ($14). Entertainment: AM radio ($78). AM/FM stereo radio ($236); w/tape player ($339). AM/FM stereo search radio ($386). Dual rear speakers ($39). Power antenna ($39). Exterior: Power sunroof ($632). Full vinyl roof ($126) exc. wagon ($151). Landau vinyl roof ($126). Fender skirts ($41). Glamour metallic paint ($59). Paint stripes ($29). Rocker panel moldings ($26). Vinyl-insert bodyside moldings ($41). Luggage rack: wag ($82-$100). Interior: Twin comfort lounge seats ($86). Reclining passenger seat ($58). Dual-facing rear seats: wagon ($126). Vinyl bench seat ($26). Recreation table: wag ($58). Color- keyed seatbelts ($18). Front/rear mats ($33). Deluxe cargo area ($83-$126). Lockable side stowage compartment: wag ($43). Luggage area trim ($46). Wheels: Brougham wheel covers ($26). Luxury wheel covers ($50-$76). Forged aluminum wheels ($211-$237). Tires: HR78 x 15 WSW. JR78 x 15 BSW/WSW. LR78 x 15B BSW/WSW. LR78 x 15C WSW.

HISTORY: Introduced: October 3, 1975. Model year production: 482,714. Calendar year production (U.S.): 434,877. Calendar year sales by U.S. dealers: 418,749. Model year sales by U.S. dealers: 428,023.

Historical Footnotes: Lincoln-Mercury sales rose almost 24 percent for the 1976 model year, a far better showing than in 1975, which had posted a significant decline. Showing the strongest increase were Monarch and Marquis, rising by some 60 percent. At the smaller end of the Mercury spectrum, Comet fell by nearly 37 percent, while Montego (in its final season) showed a more moderate deline. Led by Monarch, model year production showed a gain of nearly 17 percent. Although General Motors was ready to downsize its full-size models, Ford/Mercury planned to keep its biggies for two more years, including the massive 400 and 460 cu. in. V-8s.

1977 MERCURY

Although the mid-size Montego disappeared, a broad new line of Cougars joined the XR-7. While XR7 competed with Grand Prix, Monte Carlo and Cordoba, the new standard Cougars became rivals to Olds Cutlass and Supreme, Pontiac LeMans, and Buick Century, retaining some of the distinctive sculptured XR7 styling. Engines had "second generation" DuraSpark electronic ignition that produced higher spark-plug voltage. Monarch added a four-speed gearbox (overdrive fourth gear) as standard equipment. Marquis carried on in full-size form, unlike the downsized GM big cars.

1977 Bobcat Runabout (M)

BOBCAT — FOUR/V-6 — Appearance and equipment of Mercury's subcompact changed little this year, except for new colors and trims. Runabouts could have a new optional all-glass third door (hatch). Bumpers were now bright-surfaced, extruded anodized aluminum, which helped cut weight by over 100 pounds. To improve ride/handling, shock absorbers were revalved, and rear-spring front eye bushings stiffened. New DuraSpark ignition offered higher voltage. Inside, the manual gearshift lever was shortened, while a new wide-ratio four-speed was offered. Rear axle ratios were lowered (numerically) too, to help gas mileage. Joining the option list were: a flip-up removable sunroof, manual four-way bucket seats, Sports Group (handling and instrumentation package), simulated wire wheel covers, and high-altitude option. That Sports Group included a tachometer, ammeter and temperature gauges, new soft-rim sports steering wheel, front stabilizer bar, and higher-rate springs. Bobcats had a domed hood, bright metal vertical-textured grille with surround molding, and clear

square park/signal lamps with crosshair bars, positioned between the grille and single round headlamps. Wide-spaced 'Bobcat' block letters stood above the grille. California versions had styled steel wheels, while 49-staters carried deluxe wheel covers. Standard equipment included a lighter, front/rear ashtrays, woodgrain instrument panel applique, wide wheel lip and rocker panel moldings, and manual front disc brakes. Bodies also carried bright side window frame and door belt moldings, and center pillar moldings. At the rear were horizontal tri- pod taillamps with a small backup light in the center of each unit. 'Bobcat' script went in the lower corner of the glass third door. Base engine again was the 140 cu. in. (2.3-liter) four with four-speed floor shift, with 2.8-liter V-6 available. Bias-ply A78 x 13 blackwalls were standard, except in California which required steel-belted radials. Contoured high-back bucket seats came in all-vinyl or Kirsten cloth and vinyl. An 'S' option group included gold-stripe treatment from hood to back panel, blackout trim, styled steel wheels with gold accents, dual racing mirrors, sports suspension with stabilizer bar, and the new glass third door. A Sports Accent Group included styled steel wheels with trim rings, special paint/tape, leather-wrapped steering wheel, deluxe bucket seats, and sound package.

1977 Comet coupe (M)

COMET — SIX/V-8 — Not much changed in the compact Comet, which would not return for 1978. New body and interior colors were offered, along with two new vinyl roof colors. New options included simulated wire wheel covers, two-tone paint, four-way manual bucket seats, high-altitude emissions, and new Decor Groups. The new optional driver's bucket seat adjusted (manually) up and down as well as forward and back. All three engines were modified, including a new variable-venturi carburetor for the California 302 cu. in. V-8. All had improved-response throttle linkage and new DuraSpark ignition. Drivetrains held a new wide-ratio three-speed manual shift, while the 302 V-8 models had a more efficient torque converter. Comet's grille was peaked forward slightly, made up of thin horizontal bars with a dominant horizontal bar in the center and full-width lower grille molding. Aligned with the grille were surround moldings for the clear rectangular park/signal lenses, framed in argent side panels. Those moldings followed the curve of the single round headlamps at their outer edges. Blackout headlamp frames had argent beads. The entire front end had a full-width look. Amber side marker lenses were just ahead of the front wheels, below the bodyside molding. Front bumpers contained two side-by-side slots in the center. Each taillamp consisted of two separate pods. Two-doors had front-hinged rear quarter windows; four- doors, roll-down back door windows. Bright front/rear wheel lip moldings and rocker panel moldings were used, as well as bright upper bodyside and drip rail moldings. Hubcaps were standard, with C78 x 14 blackwall tires. Bright window frames and belt moldings became part of the optional exterior decor group. Several items, including lighter and rear ashtray, were put into a new interior decor group, which also included a deluxe steering wheel, cloth/vinyl or all-vinyl seat trim, and upgraded sound package. Five colors of vinyl were available in the standard interior. Standard equipment included the 200 cu. in. six, three-speed manual shift (but 250 six with automatic in California), lighted front ashtray, European-type armrests and door handles, glovebox, and dome light. The Custom option included a vinyl roof, whitewalls, bodyside paint stripes, full-length molding with color-keyed vinyl inserts, reclining front bucket seats, tinted glass, and leather-wrapped sports steering wheel. That option was billed as having "a little Cougar in it."

1977 Monarch Ghia coupe (M)

MONARCH — SIX/V-8 — "The precision size car with a touch of class." That's how Lincoln-Mercury described Monarch this year. Like other models, it carried a plaque on the dash proclaiming that it was "Ride-Engineered by Lincoln-Mercury." Appearance changed little, however, apart from some new body colors and option choices. New options included four-way manual bucket seats, automatic-temperature-control air conditioning, illuminated entry, front cornering lamps, simulated wire wheel covers, white lacy-spoke cast aluminum wheels, wide-band whitewall radial tires, high-altitude emissions, and electric trunk lid release. Several appearance options had debuted in mid-year 1976 and continued this year, including a landau half-vinyl roof, dual racing mirrors, and styled steel wheels. A new standard four-speed manual floor shift had fourth- gear overdrive. California 302 cu. in. V-8s had a new variable-venturi carburetor. Other mechanical changes included an improved-response throttle linkage; new Dura- Spark ignition; lower rear axle ratios; and new standard coolant recovery system. Monarch's grille was made up of thin vertical bars with bright surround molding and 'Mercury' block lettering above. Horizontally-ribbed park/signal lamps in front fender extensions turned into amber side marker lenses after wrapping around the fender. Twin side-by-side slots were in the front bumper's center. Single round headlamps were recessed in square bright housings. The unique stand-up hood ornament had seven tiny "knobs" atop a pillar within a circle. 'Monarch' script was on the lower cowl, just above the lower bodyside molding. Backup lenses stood at the inner ends of each square-styled tri-pod wraparound taillamp, with tri-color lenses. Two-doors had opera windows; four-doors, rear quarter windows. The textured back panel applique was color-keyed to either the body or vinyl roof. Front and rear full wheel lip moldings, full-length upper bodyside moldings, and bright window frame moldings were standard. Dashboards displayed a simulated burled walnut woodgrain applique. Base engine was again the 200 cu. in. inline six. Standard equipment also included front disc brakes, foot parking brake, blackwall SBR tires, full wheel covers, locking glovebox, and lighter. Monarch Ghia moved up to the 250 cu. in. six and added paint striping on hood contours and decklid, a tapered bodyside paint stripe (replacing the usual darts), and Ghia ornament on opera window of two-doors (rear pillar of four- doors). Full-length lower bodyside moldings had wide color- keyed vinyl inserts. Front and rear partial wheel lip moldings replaced the base Monarch's full wheel lip moldings. Ghia also included map pockets, color-keyed wheel covers (or wire wheel covers), carpeted trunk, day/night mirror, remote driver's mirror, inside hood release, and Flight Bench seat. An 'S' option group included a landau vinyl roof (two-door); goldtone paint/tape stripes on bodysides, hood and decklid; rocker panel moldings; dual remote racing mirrors; styled steel wheels with gold-color accents and trim rings; bucket seats; leather-wrapped steering wheel; heavy-duty suspension; and floor lever with optional automatic. Both models could have the optional 302 cu. in. V-8.

1977 Cougar XR-7 Sports Coupe (M)

COUGAR/XR-7 — V-8 — All-new styling hit Cougar's A-body shell for 1976, as the nameplate expanded to included a set of sedans and wagons as well as the usual XR7 hardtop coupe. Grille, grille opening panel, quad rectangular headlamps, and combination parking/turn signal lamps were all new. Cougar's rear end had new vertical taillamps, backup lights, decklid, quarter panel, and deck opening lower panel. Larger side glass and backlight improved visibility. XR-7 had distinctive new wraparound taillamps, plus a new decklid similar to the Mark V Lincoln. Viewed from the side, the two- and four-door models showed new doors and a straight beltline, as well as a new rear roof (plus optional opera windows). XR-7's profile showed a distinctive large opera window with louvers and a padded landau roof. Base and Villager wagons were offered. Base engine size was reduced from 351 to 302 cu. in., with new Dura-Spark ignition and lower rear axle ratio. Instrument clusters were revised on both Cougars. Air conditioner performance improved with a 40 percent airflow increase. XR7 had a larger-diameter front stabilizer bar, and an added rear stabilizer bar to improve handling. Appearance of the new models was similar to XR-7, but without the louvered opera windows. Taillamps were different, though: two-section vertical units at quarter panel tips, with small backup lenses at outer ends of a wide red center panel below the decklid. Cougar had a distinctive Continental-type swing-away grille made up of vertical bars, divided into two side-by- side sections (each containing three sections). A heavy surround molding positioned the grille well forward of the headlamps, and it extended slightly below the bumper. No bumper slots were used. Moldings above and below the quad rectangular headlamps continued outward to enclose the large fender-tip wraparound park/signal/marker lenses (which were amber at the rear). Above was a bright new stand-up Cougar hood ornament. The red reflective rear center applique in the lower back panel had a bright surround molding. Bright rocker panel moldings, full wheel lip moldings, roof drip rail and window frame moldings, and door belt moldings all were standard. Two-doors had rear quarter window moldings. Inside was a standard cloth and vinyl bench seat. Cougar Brougham added a full vinyl roof (on four-door), upper bodyside paint stripe, bright wide door belt molding, deluxe wheel covers, and Flight bench seat with folding armrest (cloth and vinyl or all vinyl). Opera windows had 'Brougham' script embedded in the glass. Full-length bright bodyside moldings with integral wheel lip moldings replaced the usual full wheel lip and rocker panel moldings. Mercury promoted the XR7 for its sweeping profile, accentuated by its sculptured rear decklid and accent stripes, calling it "bold" and "aggressive." Cougar XR-7 features included the sport-style roofline, fully padded landau vinyl roof. grille extension below the bumper, hood rear edge molding, full wheel lip and rocker panel moldings, and full wheel covers with unique Cougar center insert. Wide opera windows had a trio of vertical louvers at the forward end. Those were accompanied by a small frameless window just to the rear of the door window, in hardtop style. A Cougar ornament adorned the center pillar, while the rear end held a sculptured simulated-spare-tire decklid with lower molding and paint stripe, and 'Cougar' block lettering. Horizontal wraparound taillamps were divided into six sections by vertical strips, wrapping around quarter panel tips, with backup lenses in the second section from the inside. 'Mercury' script went just above the right taillamp. Flight Bench seating with decorative accent stripes came in Ashton cloth or Mateao vinyl. Cougar standard equipment included the 302 V-8 and SelectShift, power brakes and steering, HR78 x 14 tires, two- spoke color-keyed steering wheel, day/night mirror, and inside hood release. XR-7 equipment included HR78 x 15 SBR tires, landau vinyl roof, clock, walnut instrument panel appliques, day/night mirror, dual-note horn, and locking glovebox. Four new XR7 colors were available. Station wagons had a 351 cu. in. V-8, optional on other models. A 400 cu. in. V-8 also was available. Major new options included opera windows, illuminated entry, day/date clock, sports steering wheel, cornering lamps, monaural AM/FM radio, AM/FM stereo search radio, radio with quadrasonic tape player, wide whitewall radials, wire wheel covers, and (two-doors only) front and rear half-vinyl roof.

MARQUIS — V-8 — New body colors and interior fabrics accounted for most of the changes in Mercury's full-size line. Bright vinyl roof surround moldings replaced color-keyed vinyl moldings on Brougham and Grand Marquis. Grand Marquis had newly styled Twin Comfort lounge seats. New options included a power moonroof, illuminated entry, AM/FM stereo radio with quadrasonic8 tape player, simulated wire wheel covers, high- altitude emissions, and wide whitewall radials. The improved standard 400 cu. in. V-8 engine had Dura-Spark ignition and a new standard coolant recovery system, while the rear axle ratio was lowered (numerically). The Colony Park wagon was now a Brougham-level option package. As before, the upright grille consisted of six side-by- side sections, each with five vertical bars, surrounded by a bright molding. Concealed headlamps stood behind rectangular doors with rectangular trim molding and center crest emblem. 'Mercury' script went above the left headlamp. Horizontally- ribbed park/signal lamps stood at fender tips, wrapping around to amber side marker lenses. Front vertical bumper guards had black inserts. Bright rocker panel moldings included front extensions. Inside was a new "Ride-Engineered by Lincoln-Mercury" dash plaque. Front bench seats came in

Ardmore cloth and vinyl, with fold-down center armrest. Standard equipment included three-speed SelectShift, power steering and brakes, and HR78 x 15 blackwall steel-belted radials. Marquis Brougham added a full vinyl roof (on four-doors) or landau vinyl roof (two-doors) with bright surround moldings, fender skirts with bright molding, power windows, clock, and full-length upper body peak molding. Decklid lock covers showed the L-M crest. Flight bench seats came in Willshire cloth and vinyl with folding center armrest. Two- doors had automatic seatback release. Grand Marquis included the 460 4Bbl. V-8, SelectShift, power windows, tinted glass, vinyl roof, digital clock, automatic parking brake release, fender skirts, Twin Comfort Lounge seats, and hood/decklid paint stripes. The big 460 V-8 was not available in California.

I.D. DATA: As before, Mercury's 11-symbol Vehicle Identification Number (VIN) is stamped on a metal tab fastened to the instrument panel, visible through the windshield. Coding is similar to 1976. Model year code changed to '7' for 1977.

BOBCAT RUNABOUT/WAGON (FOUR/V-6)

Model Number	Body/Style Number	Body Type & Seating	Factory Price	Shipping Weight	Production Total
20	64H	3-dr. Hatch-4P	3438/3739	2369/ --	18,405
22	73H	2-dr. Sta Wag-4P	3629/3930	2505/ --	Note 1

BOBCAT VILLAGER (FOUR/V-6)

22	73H	2-dr. Sta Wag-4P	3771/4072	N/A	Note 1

Note 1: Total station wagon production was 13,047 units. Bobcat Runabout and wagon totals include 3,616 vehicles produced in 1978 but sold as 1977 models.

COMET (SIX/V-8)

31	62B	2-dr. Fast Sed-4P	3392/3544	-- /2960	9,109
30	54B	4-dr. Sed-5P	3465/3617	-- /3065	12,436

MONARCH (SIX/V-8)

35	66H	2-dr. Sedan-4P	4092/4279	3123/3277	44,509
34	54H	4-dr. Sedan-5P	4188/4375	3173/3327	55,592

MONARCH GHIA (SIX/V-8)

38	66K	2-dr. Sedan-4P	4659/4749	3244/3398	11,051
37	54K	4-dr. Sedan-5P	4755/4850	3305/3459	16,545

COUGAR (V-8)

91	65D	2-dr. HT Cpe-6P	4700	3811	15,910
90	53D	4-dr. Pill. HT-6P	4832	3893	15,256
92	71D	4-dr. Sta Wag-6P	5104	4434	4,951

1977 Cougar Brougham sedan (M)

COUGAR BROUGHAM (V-8)

95	65K	2-dr. HT Cpe-6P	4990	3852	8,392
94	53K	4-dr. Pill. HT-6P	5230	3946	16,946

COUGAR VILLAGER (V-8)

96	71K	4-dr. Sta Wag-6P	5363	4482	8,569

COUGAR XR-7 (V-8)

93	65L	2-dr. HT Cpe-6P	5274	3909	124,799

MARQUIS (V-8)

66	65H	2-dr. HT-6P	5496	4293	13,242
63	53H	4-dr. Pill. HT-6P	5496	4326	36,103
74	71H	4-dr. 2S Sta Wag-6P	5631	4628	20,363
74	71H	4-dr. 3S Sta Wag-8P	5794	N/A	Note 2

Note 2: Production total for three-seat station wagon is included in two-seat figure.

MARQUIS BROUGHAM (V-8)

Model Number	Body/Style Number	Body Type & Seating	Factory Price	Shipping Weight	Production Total
64	65K	2-dr. HT-6P	6229	4350	12,237
62	53K	4-dr. Pill. HT-6P	6324	4408	29,411

GRAND MARQUIS (V-8)

61	65L	2-dr. HT-6P	6880	4516	13,445
60	53L	4-dr. Pill. HT-6P	6975	4572	31,231

FACTORY PRICE AND WEIGHT NOTE: For Comet and Monarch, prices and weights to left of slash are for six-cylinder, to right for V-8 engine. For Bobcat, prices/weights to left of slash are for four-cylinder, to right for V-6.

ENGINE DATA: BASE FOUR (Bobcat): Inline. Overhead cam. Four-cylinder. Cast iron block and head. Displacement: 140 cu. in. (2.3 liters). Bore & stroke: 3.78 x 3.13 in. Compression ratio: 9.0:1. Brake horsepower: 89 at 4800 R.P.M. Torque: 120 lbs.-ft. at 3000 R.P.M. Five main bearings. Hydraulic valve lifters. Carburetor: 2Bbl. Motorcraft 5200. VIN Code: Y. OPTIONAL V-6 (Bobcat): 60-degree, overhead-valve V-6. Cast iron block and head. Displacement: 170.8 cu. in. (2.8 liters). Bore & stroke: 3.66 x 2.70 in. Compression ratio: 8.7:1. Brake horsepower: 90-93 at 4200 R.P.M. Torque: 139-140 lbs.-ft. at 2600 R.P.M. Four main bearings. Hydraulic valve lifters. Carburetor: 2Bbl. Motorcraft 2150. VIN Code: Z. BASE SIX (Comet, Monarch): Inline. OHV. Six-cylinder. Cast iron block and head. Displacement: 200 cu. in. (3.3 liters). Bore & stroke: 3.68 x 3.13 in. Compression ratio: 8.5:1. Brake horsepower: 96 at 4400 R.P.M. Torque: 151 lbs.-ft. at 2000 R.P.M. Seven main bearings. Hydraulic valve lifters. Carburetor: 1Bbl. Carter YFA. VIN Code: T. BASE SIX (Monarch Ghia); OPTIONAL (Comet, Monarch): Inline. OHV. Six-cylinder. Cast iron block and head. Displacement: 250 cu. in. (4.1 liters). Bore & stroke: 3.68 x 3.91 in. Compression ratio: 8.0:1. Brake horsepower: 98 at 3400 R.P.M. Torque: 182 lbs.-ft. at 1800 R.P.M. Seven main bearings. Hydraulic valve lifters. Carburetor: 1Bbl. Carter YFA. VIN Code: L. BASE V-8 (Cougar); OPTIONAL (Comet, Monarch): 90-degree, overhead valve V-8. Cast iron block and head. Displacement: 302 cu. in. (5.0 liters). Bore & stroke: 4.00 x 3.00 in. Compression ratio: 8.4:1. Brake horsepower: 130-137 at 3400-3600 R.P.M. (some Monarchs, 122 at 3200). Torque: 242-245 lbs.-ft. at 1600-1800 R.P.M. (some Monarchs, 237 at 1600). Five main bearings. Hydraulic valve lifters. Carburetor: 2Bbl. Motorcraft 2150. VIN Code: F. OPTIONAL V-8 (Cougar, Monarch): 90-degree, overhead valve V-8. Cast iron block and head. Displacement: 351 cu. in. (5.8 liters). Bore & stroke: 4.00 x 3.50 in. Compression ratio: 8.3:1. Brake horsepower: 149 at 3200 R.P.M. Torque: 291 lbs.-ft. at 1600 R.P.M. Five main bearings. Hydraulic valve lifters. Carburetor: 2Bbl. Motorcraft 2150. Windsor engine. VIN Code: H. OPTIONAL V-8 (Monarch Ghia): Same as 351 cu. in. V-8 above, but Horsepower: 135 at 3200 R.P.M. Torque: 275 lbs.-ft. at 1600 R.P.M. BASE V-8 (Cougar wagon); OPTIONAL (Cougar): Same as 351 cu. in. V-8 above, but— Compression ratio: 8.0:1. Horsepower: 161 at 3600 R.P.M. Torque: 285 lbs.-ft. at 1800 R.P.M. VIN Code: Q. BASE V-8 (Marquis); OPTIONAL (Cougar): 90-degree, overhead valve V-8. Cast iron block and head. Displacement: 400 cu. in. (6.6 liters). Bore & stroke: 4.00 x 4.00 in. Compression ratio: 8.0:1. Brake horsepower: 173 at 3800 R.P.M. Torque: 328 lbs.-ft. at 1600 R.P.M. Five main bearings. Hydraulic valve lifters. Carburetor: 2Bbl. Motorcraft 2150. VIN Code: S. BASE V-8 (Grand Marquis); OPTIONAL (Marquis): 90-degree, overhead valve V-8. Cast iron block and head. Displacement: 460 cu. in. (7.5 liters). Bore & stroke: 4.36 x 3.85 in. Compression ratio: 8.0:1. Brake horsepower: 197 at 000 R.P.M. Torque: 353 lbs.-ft. at 2000 R.P.M. Five main bearings. Hydraulic valve lifters. Carburetor: 4Bbl. Motorcraft 4350. VIN Code: A.

CHASSIS DATA: Wheelbase: (Bobcat sed) 94.5 in.; (Bobcat wag) 94.8 in.; (Comet 2-dr.) 103.0 in.; (Comet 4-dr.) 109.9 in.; (Monarch) 109.9 in.; (Cougar 2dr.) 114.0 in.; (Cougar 4dr.) 118.0 in.; (Marquis) 124.0 in.; (Marquis wag) 121.0 in. Overall Length: (Bobcat sed) 169.0 in.; (Bobcat wag) 179.1 in.; (Comet 2-dr.) 189.4 in.; (Comet 4-dr.) 196.3 in.; (Monarch) 197.7 in.; (Cougar 2dr.) 215.5 in.; (Cougar 4dr.) 219.5 in.; (Cougar wag) 223.1 in.; (Marquis) 229.0 in.; (Marquis wag) 228.3 in. Height: (Bobcat sed) 50.6 in.; (Bobcat wag) 52.1 in.; (Comet) 52.9 in.; (Monarch) 53.2-53.3 in.; (Cougar) 52.6 in.; (Cougar 4dr.) 53.3 in.; (XR7) 53.0 in.; (Marquis 2-dr.) 53.7-53.8 in.; (Marquis 4-dr.) 54.7-54.8 in.; (Marquis wag) 56.9 in. Width: (Bobcat sed) 69.4 in.; (Bobcat wag) 69.7 in.; (Comet) 70.5 in.; (Monarch 2-dr.) 74.0 in. exc. Ghia, 74.5 in.; (Monarch 4-dr.) 74.1 in. exc. Ghia, 75.5 in.; (Cougar) 78.0 in.; (Marquis) 79.6 in.; (Marquis wag) 79.8 in. Front Tread: (Bobcat) 55.0 in.; (Comet) 56.5 in.; (Monarch) 59.0 in.; (Cougar) 63.6 in.; (Marquis) 64.1 in. Rear Tread: (Bobcat) 55.8 in.; (Comet) 56.5 in.; (Monarch) 57.7 in.; (Cougar) 63.5 in.; (Marquis) 64.3 in. Standard Tires: (Bobcat) A78 x 13 BSW exc. B78 x 14 w/V-6; (Comet) C78 x 14 BSW; (Monarch) DR78 x 14 BSW; (Cougar) HR78 x 14 BSW; (XR7) HR78 x 15 BSW; (Marquis) HR78 x 15; (Marquis wag) JR78 x 15.

TECHNICAL: Transmission: Three-speed manual transmission (column shift) standard on Comet six. Gear ratios: (1st) 3.56:1; (2nd) 1.90:1; (3rd) 1.00:1; (Rev) 3.78:1. Four-speed overdrive floor shift standard on Monarch: (1st) 3.29:1; (2nd) 1.84:1; (3rd) 1.00:1; (4th) 0.81:1; (Rev) 3.29:1. Four-speed floor shift standard on Bobcat sedan: (1st) 3.98:1; (2nd) 2.14:1; (3rd) 1.42:1; (4th) 1.00:1; (Rev) 3.99:1. Bobcat wagon: (1st) 3.65:1; (2nd) 1.97:1; (3rd) 1.37:1; (4th) 1.00:1; (Rev) 3.66:1. Select-Shift three-speed automatic (column lever) standard on Cougar and Marquis, optional on others. Bobcat L4140 automatic gear ratios: (1st) 2.47:1; (2nd) 1.47:1; (3rd) 1.00:1; (Rev) 2.11:1. Bobcat V-6/Comet/Monarch/Cougar/Marquis: (1st) 2.46:1; (2nd) 1.46:1; (3rd) 1.00:1; (Rev) 2.14:1 to 2.19:1. Some Cougar/Marquis: (1st) 2.40:1; (2nd) 1.47:1; (3rd) 1.00:1; (Rev) 2.00:1. Standard final drive ratio: (Bobcat) 2.73:1 w/4spd, 3.18:1 w/auto.; (Bobcat V-6) 3.00:1; (Comet) 3.00:1 w/3spd, 2.79:1 w/250 six and 3spd or any auto.; (Monarch) 3.40:1 w/200 six, 3.00:1 w/250 six or V-8, 2.47:1 w/auto.; (Cougar) 2.50:1 or 2.75:1; (Marquis) 2.47:1 w/V8400, 2.50:1 w/V8460. Steering: (Bobcat) rack and pinion; (others) recirculating ball. Front Suspension: (Bobcat) coil springs with short/long control arms, lower leading arms, and anti-sway bar on wagon; (Comet/Monarch/Cougar) coil springs with short/long arms, lower trailing links and anti-sway bar; (XR7/Marquis) coil springs w/single lower control arms, lower trailing links, strut bar and anti-sway bar. Rear Suspension: (Bobcat/Comet/Monarch) rigid axle w/semi- elliptic leaf springs; (Cougar) rigid axle w/lower trailing radius arms, upper oblique torque arms and coil springs; (Marquis) rigid axle with upper/lower control arms and coil springs. Brakes: Front disc, rear drum. Ignition: Electronic. Body construction: (Bobcat/Comet/Monarch) unibody; (others) separate body on perimeter frame; Fuel tank: (Bobcat) 13 gal. exc. wagon, 14 gal.; (Comet) 19.2 gal.; (Monarch) 19.2 gal.; (Cougar) 26.0 gal.; (Marquis) 24.2 gal.

DRIVETRAIN OPTIONS: Engines: 170 cu. in. V-6: Bobcat ($301). 250 cu. in., 1Bbl. six: Comet/Monarch ($102). 302 cu. in., 2Bbl. V-8: Comet (N/A); Monarch ($93-$163). 351 cu. in., 2Bbl. V-8: Monarch ($142); Cougar ($66). 400 cu. in., 2Bbl. V-8: Cougar ($132); Cougar wag ($66); Marquis (NC). 460 cu. in., 4Bbl. V-8: Marquis ($225). Transmission/Differential: SelectShift Cruise-O-Matic: Bobcat ($197); Comet/Monarch ($259). Floor shift lever: Monarch ($28). Traction-Lok differential: Marquis ($57); Cougar ($54). Optional axle ratio: Cougar ($16); Marquis ($15). Brakes/Steering: Power brakes: Bobcat ($57); Comet ($56); Monarch ($60). Four-wheel power disc brakes: Monarch ($273); Marquis ($180). Power steering: Bobcat ($124); Comet/Monarch ($132). Suspension: H.D. susp.: Monarch ($31). Cross country pkg.: Cougar XR7/wag, Marquis ($27). Other: H.D. battery: Bobcat ($15); Comet ($17); Cougar ($18); Marquis ($21). H.D. alternator: Cougar/Marquis ($45). Engine block heater: Bobcat/Monarch ($18); Marquis ($20). Trailer towing pkg. (heavy duty): Cougar ($117-$157); Marquis ($188). California emission system: Bobcat ($52); Comet/Monarch ($49); Marquis ($53). High-altitude option: Bobcat/Monarch ($38); Marquis ($42).

BOBCAT CONVENIENCE/APPEARANCE OPTIONS: Option Packages: 'S' group ($115). Sports accent group ($285- $308). Sports instrument/handling group ($77-$89). Convenience light group ($68-$125). Bumper group ($68). Protection group ($37). Comfort/Convenience: Air conditioner ($446). Rear defroster, electric ($72). Tinted glass ($49). Driver's remote mirror ($14). Entertainment: AM radio ($75); w/stereo tape player ($203). AM/FM radio ($135). AM/FM stereo radio ($184). Exterior: Sunroof, manual ($244). Flip-up/removable moonroof ($147). Sports vinyl roof ($133). Glass third door ($13). Hinged quarter windows ($36). Glamour paint ($57). Narrow bodyside moldings ($37). Wide color-keyed bodyside moldings ($64). Roof luggage rack ($79). Rocker panel moldings ($20). Interior: Four-way bucket seat ($32). Plaid seat trim ($32). Deluxe interior trim ($147). Load floor carpet ($23). Cargo area cover ($34). Deluxe seatbelts ($18). Wheels/Tires: Wire wheel covers ($86). Forged aluminum wheels ($56-$144). Styled steel wheels ($88). Trim rings ($32). A78 x 13 WSW. B78 x 13 BSW/WSW. BR78 x 13 BSW/WSW. BR70 x 13 RWL.

COMET CONVENIENCE/APPEARANCE OPTIONS: Option Packages: Custom group ($609). Sports accent group ($249). Exterior decor group ($64). Interior decor group ($112). Custom interior ($296). Bumper group ($32-$68). Convenience/visibility group ($65-$80). Protection group ($9-$41). Comfort/Convenience: Air cond. ($46). Electric rear defogger ($46). Tinted window glass ($47). Dual racing mirrors ($14-$28). Entertainment: AM radio ($75); w/tape player ($203). AM/FM radio ($135). AM/FM stereo radio ($229); w/tape player ($317). Exterior: Vinyl roof ($95). Glamour paint ($57). Tu-tone paint ($59). Bodyside moldings ($37). Rocker panel moldings ($20). Interior: Four-way seat ($32). Reclining vinyl bucket seats ($156). Vinyl seat trim ($32). Plaid seat trim ($32). Deluxe seatbelts ($18). Wheels/Tires: Deluxe wheel covers ($31). Wire wheel covers ($22-$116). Cast aluminum wheels ($138-$233). Styled steel wheels ($64-$95). C78 x 14 WSW ($32). CR78 x 14 SBR BSW ($57- $89). CR78 x 14 SBR WSW ($89-$121). DR78 x 14 SBR BSW ($57- $112). DR78 x 14 SBR WSW ($89-$144). Space-saver spare ($14) except (NC) with radial tires.

MONARCH CONVENIENCE/APPEARANCE OPTIONS: Option Packages: 'S' group ($483-$511). Interior decor group ($192). Convenience group ($27-$79). Bumper group ($68). Light group ($40). Cold weather group ($18-$51). Heavy-duty group ($26-$51). Protection group ($26-$41). Visibility group ($4-$50). Comfort/Convenience: Air cond. ($464); auto-temp ($499). Rear defogger ($46). Rear defroster, electric ($78). Fingertip speed control ($98). Illuminated entry system ($50). Power windows ($101-$140). Power door locks ($66-$93). Power decklid release ($17). Power four-way seat ($126). Tinted glass ($50). Tilt steering wheel ($57). Digital clock ($42). Lighting and Mirrors: Cornering lamps ($40). Dual racing mirrors ($31-$45). Lighted right visor vanity mirror ($42). Entertainment: AM radio ($75); w/tape player ($203). AM/FM radio ($151). AM/FM stereo radio ($222); w/tape player ($317). Exterior: Power moonroof ($833). Full or landau vinyl roof ($109). Glamour paint ($57). Bodyside moldings ($37). Rocker panel moldings ($20). Decklid luggage rack ($54). Interior: Console ($69). Four-way seat ($32). Reclining bucket seats ($64). Leather seat trim ($192). Barletta cloth seat ($12). Luxury cloth trim ($93). Color-keyed seatbelts ($18). Wheels/Tires: Deluxe wheel covers ($31) exc. Ghia (NC). Wire wheel covers ($77-$86). Styled steel wheels w/trim rings ($74-$95). Cast aluminum wheels ($118-$213). White aluminum wheels ($138-$232). DR78 x 14 SBR WSW. ER78 x 14 SBR BSW/WSW. FR78 x 14 SBR BSW/WSW/wide WSW.

COUGAR CONVENIENCE/APPEARANCE OPTIONS: Option Packages: Sports instrumentation group ($130-$151). Appearance protection group ($42-$50). Bumper group ($68). Convenience group ($53-$130). Power lock group ($92-$121). Comfort/Convenience: Air cond. ($505); w/auto-temp control ($551). Rear defroster, electric ($82). Fingertip speed control ($78-$97). Illuminated entry system ($51). Tinted glass ($57). Power windows ($114-$158). Power tailgate window: wag ($47). Six-way power seat ($143). Leather-wrapped steering wheel ($61). Tilt steering wheel ($63). Day/date clock ($21-$42). Lighting and Mirrors: Cornering lamps ($50). Remote driver's mirror ($14). Dual racing mirrors ($51). Lighted visor vanity mirror ($42). Entertainment: AM radio ($132). AM/FM radio ($192); w/tape player ($266); w/quadrasonic tape player ($399). AM/FM stereo search radio ($349). Dual rear speakers ($42). Exterior: Power moonroof: XR7 ($934). Full vinyl roof ($111- $161). Landau vinyl roof ($111). Opera windows ($50). Bodyside moldings ($42). Rocker panel moldings ($26). Glamour paint ($63). Two-tone paint ($45-$66). Paint stripes ($33). Luggage rack: wag ($100). Exterior: Twin comfort seats: XR7 ($141). Flight bench seat: wag ($66). Leather seat trim: XR7 ($241). Bucket seats w/console ($41-$207). Rear-facing third seat: wag ($113). Vinyl seat trim ($28). Color-keyed seatbelts ($18). Wheels/Tires: Deluxe wheel covers ($29). Luxury wheel covers ($32-$61). Wire wheel covers ($100-$129). Cast aluminum wheels ($211-$239). Styled wheels: XR7 ($146). Styled wheels w/trim rings ($72-$101). HR78 x 14 SBR WSW ($41-$68). HR78 x 14 wide-band WSW ($55). JR78 x 14 SBR WSW ($68). R7 Tires: HR78 x 15 WSW ($46-$61). HR70 x 15 WSW ($67).

1977 Marquis pillared hardtop (M)

MARQUIS CONVENIENCE/APPEARANCE OPTIONS: Option Packages: Grand Marquis decor ($543). Colony Park option ($315). Tu-tone group ($63-$215). Lock/convenience group ($91-$134). Visibility light group ($46-$86). Protection group ($56). Comfort/Convenience: Air cond. ($543); w/auto-temp control ($582). Rear defroster, electric ($85). Fingertip speed control ($86-$107). Illuminated entry system ($54). Power windows ($116-$172). Power vent windows ($84). Six-way power driver's seat ($139); driver and passenger ($272). Tinted glass ($70). Tilt steering wheel ($63). Digital clock ($31- $52). Interval wipers ($29). Lighting and Mirrors: Cornering lamps ($43). Driver's remote mirror ($15). Lighted visor vanity mirror ($46). Entertainment: AM radio ($82). AM/FM radio (N/A). AM/FM stereo radio ($250); w/tape player ($360); w/quadrasonic tape player ($499). AM/FM stereo search radio ($409). Dual rear speakers ($42). Power antenna ($42). Exterior: Power moonroof ($926). Full vinyl roof ($134). Landau vinyl roof ($134). Fender skirts ($46). Glamour paint ($63). Paint stripes ($31). Rocker panel moldings ($28). Bodyside moldings ($40). Door edge guards ($8-$17). Rear bumper guards ($20). Luggage rack ($106). Interior: Dual-facing rear seats: wagon ($134). Twin comfort seats ($152). Vinyl seat trim ($28). Floor mats ($10). Deluxe seatbelts ($20). Lockable side stowage compartment ($46). Wheels/Tires: Luxury wheel covers ($81). Wire wheel covers ($105). Forged aluminum wheels ($251). HR78 x 15 SBR WSW. JR78 x 15 SBR BSW/WSW/wide WSW. LR78 x 15 SBR WSW.

HISTORY: Introduced: October 1, 1976. Model year production: 531,549 (including 3,616 Bobcats produced as 1978 models but sold as 1977s, but not incl. Canadian Bobcats). Calendar year production (U.S.): 583,055. Calendar year sales by U.S. dealers: 508,132. Model year sales by U.S. dealers: 475,211.

Historical Footnotes: Full-size and luxury models demonstrated a strong sales rise for the 1977 model year, while subcompacts (Bobcat and the imported Capri) declined by nearly 15 percent. That's how it was throughout the industry, though, as customers still craved big cars. The compact Comet and Monarch both declined substantially, while the full-size Marquis found 21 percent more buyers this year, leading the Lincoln-Mercury division in sales. Sales of the specialty Cougar XR7 jumped by 53 percent, from 78,497 in 1976 to an impressive 120,044 this season. The new Cougar models did better than the Montegos they replaced, showing an 18 percent sales rise. Fleet sales were becoming more significant for the Lincoln-Mercury division in the mid-1970s, as dealers pushed harder in their leasing/rental departments.

1978 MERCURY

Comet was gone, replaced by the new Zephyr—close relative of Ford's Fairmont. Based on the "Fox" platform, its chassis would serve as the basis for a variety of FoMoCo products in the coming years. Among its mechanical features were MacPherson struts in the front suspension. Mercury's German-import Capri was in its final season, soon to be replaced by a domestic version based on Mustang. Monarch enjoyed a modest restyle, while the big Marquis continued in its large-scale form for one more year.

1978 Bobcat Villager station wagon (M)

BOBCAT — FOUR/V-6 — Subcompact appearance and equipment changed little this year, except for new body and interior colors. New options included white-painted aluminum wheels and a stripe treatment in four color combinations. The optional 2.8-liter V-6 had a new lightweight plastic fan. Optional power rack-and-pinion steering had a new variable-ratio system similar to Fairmont/Zephyr. Bobcat again had a domed hood, vertical-textured grille with surround moldings, bright-framed round headlamps, and aluminum bumpers. Combination park/signal lamps sat between the grille and headlamps. High-back front bucket seats came in all-vinyl or cloth and vinyl. The rear bench seat had new split bucket-style cushions. Runabout, station wagon and Villager models were offered. Standard equipment included the 140 cu. in. (2.3-liter) OHC four, four-speed manual gearbox, A78 x 13 BSW tires, full fender splash shields, front bucket seats, lighter, front/rear ashtrays, wide wheel lip and rocker panel moldings, wheel covers, and simulated woodgrain instrument panel applique. Power brakes and tinted glass became standard later. Wagons had a liftgate-open warning, high-back bucket seats, three-pod vertical taillamps, hinged rear-quarter windows, cargo area light, wheel lip and rocker panel moldings, and door-operated courtesy lights. Villager wagons added simulated rosewood appliques on bodyside and liftgate, and load floor carpeting.

1978 Zephyr sedan (M)

ZEPHYR — FOUR/SIX/V-8 — Weighing some 300 pounds less than the Comet it replaced, the new Zephyr (and similar Ford Fairmont) came in two-door and four-door sedan form, along with a station wagon. Base engine was a 140 cu. in. (2.3-liter) four with four-speed manual gearbox. Options included both an inline six and small-block V-8. Sixes had three-speed shift. Zephyr had MacPherson strut front suspension with lower control arms, and four-link rear suspension with coil springs. Rack-and-pinion steering was used, and the body was unitized. A total of 13 body colors were available, as well as European- style trim. Quad rectangular headlamps stood directly above

quad clear-lensed park/signal lamps, in a clean front-end style that would become typical. Bright frames surrounded the headlamps and parking lamps. Zephyr's vertical-theme grille consisted of many very thin vertical bars, with 'Mercury' lettering on the driver's side. Bumpers were bright anodized aluminum. Body features also included a bright windshield molding, stand-up hood ornament, and upper bodyside dual accent paint stripes. Twin vertical front fender louvers decorated the cowl. Bright wheel lip, rocker panel, door belt and roof drip moldings were used. Wide horizontally-ribbed taillamps (five ribbed segments) had vertical backup lenses inside, adjoining the license plate recess. Two- and four- door sedans had a wide louver-like design at the rear of the quarter windows or rear door. Doors displayed a thin-line appearance. Low-back bucket seats were upholstered in Colton all-vinyl trim. Steering-column mounted controls operated the wiper/washer, horn, signals and dimmer. Standard equipment included the 2.3-liter OHC four, four-speed manual transmission, high/low ram air ventilation, front disc brakes, foot parking brake, low-back bucket seats (with four-cylinder), bench seats (other engines), woodtone cluster appliques, header-mounted dome lamp, and deluxe wheel covers. Four-doors and wagons had movable quarter windows. B78 x 14 blackwalls were standard except with V-8 engine, which required CR78 x 14. Zephyr's ES option displayed a different front-end look with blackout grille, black rear hood grille, and no hood ornament. ES also had black window frames and rear window ventilation louver, bright full-length lower bodyside moldings, black lower back panel, and styled wheel covers. Inside was a black three-spoke sports steering wheel, black instrument panel and pad, and full-width gunmetal gray instrument panel applique. Dual black outside mirrors were standard. The ES handling suspension included a rear stabilizer bar as well as modified spring rates and shock valving. Rocker panel moldings and upper bodyside paint stripes were deleted. Yet another form was evident on the Zephyr Z-7 sport coupe (kin to Fairmont's Futura Coupe). Most notable was the contemporary wrapover roof design, with very wide B-pillar that held a Z-7 ornament. Z7 also included hood tape stripes, upper bodyside tape stripes, full-length lower bodyside molding, bright window frames, and wraparound taillamps. Rocker panel moldings were deleted. Interiors contained pleated Corinthian vinyl seat trim and a woodtone dash applique. The Villager wagon had woodtone bodyside/tailgate appliques in medium cherry, with bright surround moldings and woodtone inserts. A Luxury Exterior Decor Group included dual accent hood paint stripes, deluxe bodyside protective molding, bright door frame and quarter window moldings, and dual mirrors (driver's remote).

1978 Monarch pillared hardtop (M)

MONARCH — SIX/V-8 — Both Monarch and the closely related Ford Granada entered 1978 with a new look, including new grille, rectangular headlamps, parking lamps, front bumper air spoiler, wide wheel lip moldings, and lower back panel appliques. Two-doors also sported new "twindow" opera windows (two narrow side-by-side windows in the space one would ordinarily occupy). A new ESS option included black vertical grille texture, rocker panels, door frames and bodyside molding; black rubber bumper guards and wide rub strips; and a unique interior. Also optional: AM/FM stereo with cassette tape player and 40-channel CB. Monarch's spoiler and hood-to- grille-opening panel seal, and revised decklid surface, helped reduce aerodynamic drag. The 302 cu. in. V-8 with variable-venturi carburetor was now available. Single rectangular headlamps stood directly above large clear rectangular park/signal lamps, surrounded by a single bright molding. The vertical-bar grille was similar to 1977, but with a heavier upper header bar that reached to the hood top, with no block lettering above. 'Mercury' script went on the side of the grille, with 'Monarch' script again at the cowl area of front fenders. Narrow amber reflector lenses were set back from the front fender tips. Monarch's hood ornament consisted of a castle-like shape within a circle, with seven tiny "knobs" atop the inner segment. Bright front/rear full wheel lip moldings were used, along with a full-length upper bodyside molding. New full- width wraparound taillamps were three-pod design. The red reflective back panel applique held 'Monarch' lettering. Inside was an all-vinyl Flight bench seat. Under the hood, a standard 250 cu. in. (4.1-liter) inline six and four-speed manual overdrive gearbox with floor shift lever. Full wheel covers were standard, along with SBR blackwall tires, an inflatable spare tire, foot parking brake, column-mounted wiper/washer control, and burled woodtone instrument cluster. Monarch Ghia added wire wheel covers, paint stripes on hood and decklid contours, tapered bodyside paint stripes, remote-control driver's mirror, and Ghia ornament on two- door's front quarter panel (or four-door's rear pillar). Ghia's full-length lower bodyside molding had a wide odense grain color-keyed vinyl insert. Burled walnut woodtone accents went on the deluxe steering wheel and door trim panel. Extra conveniences included seatback map pockets, and rear door courtesy lamp switches on the four-door. Ghia also included a dual-note horn, padded door trim with lower carpeting, and driver's remote mirror. The new ESS (Euro-style) option package included a blackout grille; black wipers, black hood paint stripes, and front/rear bumper guards with horizontal rub strip. Also on ESS: bright wide wheel lip moldings, dual racing mirrors, color-keyed wheel covers, black/argent lower back appliques, black bodyside molding with bright mylar insert, black rocker panel paint treatment, and black side window surround moldings. Two-doors had a louvered opera window applique. ESS equipment included a leather-wrapped three-spoke sport steering wheel, day/night mirror, dual-note horn, Flight bench seat, FR78 x 14 BSW tires, and heavy-duty suspension.

COUGAR/XR-7 — V-8 — After just one year of availability, station wagons left the Cougar lineup, since the new Zephyr came in wagon form. Little appearance change was evident either on the basic or XR7 models. Brougham became an option package this year. A 40-channel CB transceiver became optional. A new front bumper air spoiler, hood-to-grille-opening panel seal and other alterations were supposed to reduce XR7 aerodynamic drag, thus improve gas mileage. A revised low-restriction fresh-air intake went on the 302 and larger V-8s. A new mechanical spark control system hit the 351 and 400 cu. in. V-8 engines. Basic Cougars were related to Ford's LTD II, while Cougar shared structural details with Thunderbird. As in 1977, Cougar's Continental-style grille extended slightly below the front bumper. Atop the hood was a bright new stand-up Cougar-head ornament. Signal/marker lamps in front fender extensions were said to "emphasize the wide stance and clean look." The twin-pod vertical taillamp assembly held integral side marker lights. A bright molding surrounded the red reflective rear center applique in the lower back panel. Standard

1978 Cougar XR-7 "Midnight/Chamois Decor" coupe (AA)

Cougar equipment included the 302 cu. in. V-8 and SelectShift three-speed automatic transmission, blackwall SBR tires, power brakes/steering, two-speed wipers, cloth/vinyl bench seat, simulated rosewood dash applique, full wheel lip moldings, bright backlight and windshield moldings, bright taillamp bezels with ornament, and 'Cougar' decklid script. Cougar Brougham added a full vinyl roof (on four-doors), full-length bright bodyside molding with integral wheel lip moldings, and opera windows with 'Brougham' script embedded in the glass. Also on Brougham: upper bodyside paint stripes, bright wide door belt moldings, electric clock, deluxe wheel covers, and Flight bench seat with folding center armrest. Cougar XR7 had a grille extension below the bumper, a hood rear edge molding, sport-style roofline with opera window and louvers, and fully padded landau vinyl roof. Its Flight bench seat came in a new sew style, with accent stripes in Rossano cloth or Mateao vinyl. XR7 had a rear stabilizer bar and 15 in. wheels. 'Cougar' block lettering went on the "sculptured" simulated-spare portion of the decklid. Horizontal wraparound taillamps were divided into five segments, three of them on the back panel with an integral backup lamp in one. Standard XR-7 equipment included the 302 cu. in. V-8, SelectShift, power brakes/steering, baby burl walnut woodtone instrument panel appliques, and day/night mirror. An XR-7 Decor Option included styled wheels, full-length bodyside molding with color-keyed vinyl inserts, color-keyed remote mirrors, Twin Comfort Lounge seats with recliner (or bucket seats with console), and hood stripes. A Midnight/Chamois Decor Option (available later) for XR-7 offered a half vinyl roof with vinyl crossover strap, padded 'Continental' type rear deck, and straight-through paint stripes; plus Midnight Blue and Chamois interior, with Tiffany carpeting.

1978 Marquis pillared hardtop (M)

MARQUIS — V-8 — Full-size models were carryovers, with new body colors but little other change. Station wagons could now have optional removable auxiliary dual seat cushions. As before, they came in pillarless-look two-door hardtop style, and a narrow-pillar four-door. Standard equipment included the 351 cu. in. (5.8-liter) 2Bbl. V-8 (400 cu. in. engine in California and high-altitude areas), SelectShift three-speed automatic, power brakes/steering, HR78 x 15 SBR tires, bench seat in Althea cloth/vinyl, and fold-down center armrest. Marquis again featured a bright vertical box-textured grille, flanked by concealed headlamps with body-color textured pad and Marquis crest. The front end also displayed integral parking/signal/side marker lights, concealed wipers, and a bright stand-up hood ornament. Vertical front bumper guards had black inserts. Rear pillars held a Marquis plaque. Full wheel lip moldings and bright rocker panel moldings with front extensions were standard. Wraparound horizontal-ribbed taillamps had integral rear side marker lights, while the textured color-keyed rear center applique below the decklid had 'Mercury' block letters and little backup lamps at its ends. Marquis Brougham added a landau vinyl roof (two-door) or full vinyl roof (four-door), both with bright surround molding. The full vinyl roof was also available as a no-cost option on two-doors. Brougham also had power windows, fender skirts with bright molding, full-length upper body peak molding, and a decklid lock cover with L-M crest. Brougham wheel covers displayed slots around the circumference and a center crest emblem. Flight bench seats had a folding center armrest and automatic seatback release (on two-door). Moving all the way up, Grand Marquis had a vinyl roof, fender skirts, hood and decklid paint stripes, and a gold Marquis crest on the headlamp cover and the rear pillar. Full-length wide bodyside moldings had color-keyed vinyl inserts; rocker panel extensions and wheel lip moldings were deleted. 'Grand Marquis' script highlighted the decklid. Standard features included tinted glass, a digital clock, dual-beam dome/map light, and Twin Comfort lounge seats in Media velour with dual center folding armrests and headrests with vinyl welts.

I.D. DATA: As before, Mercury's 11-symbol Vehicle Identification Number (VIN) is stamped on a metal tab fastened to the instrument panel, visible through the windshield. Coding is similar to 1976-77. Model year code changed to '8' for 1978. One Canadian assembly plant was added: 'X' St. Thomas, Ontario.

BOBCAT RUNABOUT/WAGON (FOUR/V-6)

Model Number	Body/Style Number	Body Type & Seating	Factory Price	Shipping Weight	Production Total
20	64H	3-dr. Hatch-4P	3537/3810	2389/ --	23,428
22	73H	2-dr. Sta Wag-4P	3878/4151	2532/ --	Note 1

BOBCAT VILLAGER (FOUR/V-6)

Model Number	Body/Style Number	Body Type & Seating	Factory Price	Shipping Weight	Production Total
22	73H	2-dr. Sta Wag-4P	4010/4283	N/A	Note 1

Note 1: Total station wagon production was 8,840 units.

ZEPHYR (FOUR/SIX)

31	66D	2-dr. Sed-5P	3742/3862	2572/2615	27,673
32	54D	4-dr. Sed-5P	3816/3936	2614/2657	47,334
36	74D	4-dr. Sta Wag-5P	4184/4304	2722/2765	32,596

ZEPHYR Z-7 (FOUR/SIX)

35	36R	2-dr. Spt Cpe-5P	4095/4215	2609/2652	44,569

Zephyr Engine Note: A V-8 engine cost $199 more than the six.

MONARCH (SIX/V-8)

35	66H	2-dr. Sedan-5P	4330/4511	3058/3130	38,939
34	54H	4-dr. Sedan-5P	4409/4590	3102/3174	52,775

COUGAR (V-8)

91	65D	2-dr. HT Cpe-6P	5009	3761	21,398
92	53D	4-dr. Pill. HT-6P	5126	3848	25,364

COUGAR XR-7 (V-8)

93	65L	2-dr. HT Cpe-6P	5603	3865	166,508

MARQUIS (V-8)

61	65H	2-dr. HT-6P	5764	4296	11,176
62	53H	4-dr. Pill. HT-6P	5806	4328	27,793
74	71K	4-dr. 2S Sta Wag-6P	5958	4578	16,883
74	71K	4-dr. 3S Sta Wag-8P	N/A	4606	Note 2

Note 2: Production total for three-seat station wagon is included in two-seat figure.

MARQUIS BROUGHAM (V-8)

63	65K	2-dr. HT-6P	6380	4317	10,368
64	53K	4-dr. Pill. HT-6P	6480	4346	26,030

GRAND MARQUIS (V-8)

65	65L	2-dr. HT-6P	7132	4342	15,624
66	53L	4-dr. Pill. HT-6P	7232	4414	37,753

FACTORY PRICE AND WEIGHT NOTE: Monarch prices and weights to left of slash are for six-cylinder, to right for V-8 engine. For Bobcat and Zephyr, prices/weights to left of slash are for four-cylinder, to right for V-6.

ENGINE DATA: BASE FOUR (Bobcat, Zephyr): Inline. Overhead cam. Four-cylinder. Cast iron block and head. Displacement: 140 cu. in. (2.3 liters). Bore & stroke: 3.78 x 3.13 in. Compression ratio: 9.0:1. Brake horsepower: 88 at 4800 R.P.M. Torque: 118 lbs.-ft. at 2800 R.P.M. Five main bearings. Hydraulic valve lifters. Carburetor: 2Bbl. Motorcraft 5200. VIN Code: Y. OPTIONAL V-6 (Bobcat): 60-degree, overhead-valve V-6. Cast iron block and head. Displacement: 170.8 cu. in. (2.8 liters). Bore & stroke: 3.66 x 2.70 in. Compression ratio: 8.7:1. Brake horsepower: 90 at 4200 R.P.M. Torque: 143 lbs.-ft. at 2200 R.P.M. Four main bearings. Hydraulic valve lifters. Carburetor: 2Bbl. Motorcraft 2150. VIN Code: Z. OPTIONAL SIX (Zephyr): Inline. OHV. Six-cylinder. Cast iron block and head. Displacement: 200 cu. in. (3.3 liters). Bore & stroke: 3.68 x 3.13 in. Compression ratio: 8.5:1. Brake horsepower: 85 at 3600 R.P.M. Torque: 154 lbs.-ft. at 1600 R.P.M. Seven main bearings. Hydraulic valve lifters. Carburetor: 1Bbl. Carter YFA. VIN Code: T. BASE SIX (Monarch): Inline. OHV. Six-cylinder. Cast iron block and head. Displacement: 250 cu. in. (4.1 liters). Bore & stroke: 3.68 x 3.91 in. Compression ratio: 8.5:1. Brake horsepower: 97 at 3200 R.P.M. Torque: 210 lbs.-ft. at 1400 R.P.M. Seven main bearings. Hydraulic valve lifters. Carburetor: 1Bbl. Carter YFA or Holley 1946. VIN Code: L. BASE V-8 (Cougar); OPTIONAL (Zephyr, Monarch): 90-degree, overhead valve V-8. Cast iron block and head. Displacement: 302 cu. in. (5.0 liters). Bore & stroke: 4.00 x 3.00 in. Compression ratio: 8.4:1. Brake horsepower: 134-139 at 3400-3600 R.P.M. Torque: 248-250 lbs.-ft. at 1600 R.P.M. Five main bearings. Hydraulic valve lifters. Carburetor: 2Bbl. Motorcraft 2150. VIN Code: F. BASE V-8 (Marquis); OPTIONAL (Cougar): 90-degree, overhead valve V-8. Cast iron block and head. Displacement: 351 cu. in. (5.8 liters). Bore & stroke: 4.00 x 3.50 in. Compression ratio: 8.3:1. Brake horsepower: 145-152 at 3400-3600 R.P.M. Torque: 273-278 lbs.-ft. at 1800 R.P.M. Five main bearings. Hydraulic valve lifters. Carburetor: 2Bbl. Motorcraft 2150. Windsor engine. VIN Code: H. OPTIONAL V-8 (Cougar, Marquis): 90-degree, overhead valve V-8. Cast iron block and head. Displacement: 400 cu. in. (6.6 liters). Bore & stroke: 4.00 x 4.00 in. Compression ratio: 8.0:1. Brake horsepower: 160-166 at 3800 R.P.M. Torque: 314-319 lbs.-ft. at 1800 R.P.M. Five main bearings. Hydraulic valve lifters. Carburetor: 2Bbl. Motorcraft 2150. VIN Code: S. BASE V-8 (Grand Marquis); OPTIONAL (Marquis): 90-degree, overhead valve V-8. Cast iron block and head. Displacement: 460 cu. in. (7.5 liters). Bore & stroke: 4.36 x 3.85 in. Compression ratio: 8.0:1. Brake horsepower: 202 at 4000 R.P.M. Torque: 348 lbs.-ft. at 2000 R.P.M. Five main bearings. Hydraulic valve lifters. Carburetor: 4Bbl. Motorcraft 4350. VIN Code: A.

CHASSIS DATA: Wheelbase: (Bobcat sed) 94.5 in.; (Bobcat wag) 94.8 in.; (Zephyr) 105.5 in.; (Monarch) 109.9 in.; (Cougar 2dr.) 114.0 in.; (Cougar 4dr.) 118.0 in.; (Marquis) 124.0 in.; (Marquis wag) 121.0 in. Overall Length: (Bobcat sed) 169.3 in.; (Bobcat wag) 179.8 in.; (Zephyr) 193.8 in.; (Z7) 195.8 in.; (Monarch) 197.7 in.; (Cougar 2dr.) 215.5 in.; (Cougar 4dr.) 219.5 in.; (Marquis) 229.0 in.; (Marquis wag) 227.1 in. Height: (Bobcat sed) 50.6 in.; (Bobcat wag) 52.1 in.; (Zephyr) 53.5 in.; (Zephyr wag) 54.7 in.; (Z7) 52.2 in.; (Monarch) 53.2-53.3 in.; (Cougar 2dr.) 52.6 in.; (Cougar 4dr.) 53.3 in.; (XR7) 52.9 in.; (Marquis 2-dr.) 53.7-53.8 in.; (Marquis 4-dr.) 54.7-54.8 in.; (Marquis wag) 56.9 in. Width: (Bobcat sed) 69.4 in.; (Bobcat wag) 69.7 in.; (Zephyr) 70.2 in.; (Monarch) 74.0 in.; (Cougar) 78.6 in.; (Marquis) 79.6-79.7 in. Front Tread: (Bobcat) 55.0 in.; (Zephyr) 56.6 in.; (Monarch) 59.0 in.; (Cougar) 63.6 in.; (XR7) 63.2 in.; (Marquis) 64.1 in. Rear Tread: (Bobcat) 55.8 in.; (Zephyr) 57.0 in.; (Monarch) 57.7 in.; (Cougar) 63.5 in.; (XR7) 63.1 in.; (Marquis) 64.3 in. Standard Tires: (Bobcat) A78 x 13 BSW; (Zephyr) B78 x 14 BSW; (Zephyr V-8) CR78 x 14; (Monarch) DR78 x 14 BSW; (Cougar) HR78 x 14 BSW; (XR7) HR78 x 15 BSW; (Marquis) HR78 x 15; (Marquis wag) JR78 x 15.

TECHNICAL: Transmission: Three-speed manual transmission (column shift) standard on Zephyr six. Gear ratios: (1st) 3.56:1; (2nd) 1.90:1; (3rd) 1.00:1; (Rev) 3.78:1. Four-speed overdrive floor shift standard on Monarch: (1st) 3.29:1; (2nd) 1.84:1; (3rd) 1.00:1; (4th) 0.81:1; (Rev) 3.29:1. Four-speed floor shift standard on Bobcat/Zephyr four: (1st) 3.98:1; (2nd) 2.14:1; (3rd) 1.42:1; (4th) 1.00:1; (Rev) 3.99:1. Select- Shift three-speed automatic (column lever) standard on Cougar and Marquis, optional on others. Bobcat L4140 automatic gear ratios: (1st) 2.47:1; (2nd) 1.47:1; (3rd) 1.00:1; (Rev) 2.11:1. Cougar/Marquis with V8351: (1st) 2.40:1; (2nd) 1.47:1; (3rd) 1.00:1; (Rev) 2.00:1. Other automatics: (1st) 2.46:1; (2nd) 1.46:1; (3rd) 1.00:1; (Rev) 2.18:1 to 2.20:1. Standard final drive ratio: (Bobcat) 2.73:1 w/four, 3.40:1 w/V-6; (Zephyr) 3.08:1 w/four, 2.73:1 w/six and 2.47:1 w/V-8; (Monarch) 3.00:1 w/six and 4spd, 2.47:1 w/auto.; (Cougar) 2.75:1 w/V8302, 2.50:1 w/V8351/400. (Marquis) 2.47:1 w/V8400, 2.50:1 w/V8460. Steering: (Bobcat/Zephyr) rack and pinion; (others) recirculating ball. Front Suspension: (Bobcat) coil springs with short/long control arms, lower leading arms, and anti-sway bar on wagon; (Zephyr) MacPherson struts w/coil springs mounted on lower control arm; (others) coil springs w/lower trailing links and anti-sway bar. Rear Suspension: (Bobcat/Monarch) rigid axle w/semi-elliptic leaf springs; (Zephyr) four-link w/coil springs; (Cougar/Marquis) rigid axle with upper/lower control arms and coil springs. Brakes: Front disc, rear drum. Ignition: Electronic. Body construction: (Bobcat/Zephyr/Monarch) unibody; (others) separate body on perimeter frame; Fuel tank: (Bobcat) 11.7 or 13 gal. exc. wagon, 14 gal.; (Zephyr) 16.0 gal.; (Monarch) 18.0 gal.; (Cougar) 21.0 gal.; (Marquis) 24.2 gal. exc. wagon, 21 gal.

DRIVETRAIN OPTIONS: Engines: 170 cu. in. V-6: Bobcat ($273). 200 cu. in., 1Bbl. six: Zephyr ($120). 302 cu. in., 2Bbl. V-8: Zephyr ($319); Monarch ($181). 351 cu. in., 2Bbl. V-8: Cougar ($157). 400 cu. in., 2Bbl. V-8: Cougar ($283); Marquis ($126). 460 cu. in., 4Bbl. V-8: Marquis ($271). Transmission/Differential: SelectShift Cruise-O-Matic: Bobcat/Zephyr ($281); Monarch ($193). Floor shift lever: Zephyr/Monarch ($30). First-gear lockout: Zephyr (NC). Traction-Lok differential: Cougar ($59); Marquis ($63). Optional axle ratio: Bobcat ($13); Marquis ($14). Brakes & Steering: Power brakes: Bobcat (N/A); Zephyr/Monarch ($63). Four-wheel power disc brakes: Monarch ($300); Marquis ($197). Power steering: Bobcat ($131); Zephyr ($140); Monarch ($148). Suspension: H.D. susp.: Monarch ($27). Handling susp.: Zephyr ($30). Cross-country susp.: Cougar ($20); Marquis ($26). Other: H.D. battery: Zephyr ($18); Cougar/Marquis ($20). H.D. alternator: Cougar/Marquis ($49). Engine block heater: Bobcat/Zephyr/Monarch ($12); Cougar ($13); Marquis ($21). Trailer towing pkg. (heavy duty): Cougar ($184); Marquis ($138). California emission system: Bobcat/Zephyr/Monarch ($69); Cougar/Marquis ($75). High-altitude option (NC).

BOBCAT CONVENIENCE/APPEARANCE OPTIONS: Option Packages: Sports accent group ($212-$235). Sports instrument/handling group ($90). Sports pkg. ($108). Convenience/light group ($72-$137). Bumper group ($70). Protection group ($40). Comfort/Convenience: Air conditioner ($459). Rear defroster, electric ($77). Tinted glass (NC). Driver's remote mirror ($14). Day/night mirror ($7). Entertainment: AM radio ($72); w/digital clock ($119); w/stereo tape player ($192). AM/FM radio ($120). AM/FM stereo radio ($161). Exterior: Flip-up/removable moonroof ($167). Sunroof ($259). Sports vinyl roof ($145). Glass third door ($25). Hinged quarter windows ($41). Glamour paint ($40). Narrow bodyside moldings ($39); wide ($67). Roof luggage rack ($59). Rocker panel moldings ($22). Lower bodyside protection ($30). Interior: Four-way bucket seat ($33). Load floor carpet ($23). Cargo area cover ($25). Deluxe interior ($158-$181). Deluxe seatbelts ($18). Wheels/Tires: Wire wheel covers ($20). Forged aluminum wheels ($128); white ($141). Styled steel wheels (NC). Trim rings ($34). BR78 x 13 WSW ($42). BR70 x 13 RWL ($77).

ZEPHYR CONVENIENCE/APPEARANCE OPTIONS: Option Packages: ES option ($180). Villager option ($169). Exterior decor group ($96). Interior decor group ($72). Luxury interior ($199-$289). Bumper protection group ($70). Convenience group ($36). Appearance protection group ($36- $43). Light group ($36-$40). Comfort/Convenience: Air cond. ($465). Rear defogger ($47). Rear defroster, electric ($84). Tinted glass ($52). Sport steering wheel ($36). Electric clock ($20). Cigar lighter ($6). Interval wipers ($29). Liftgate wiper/washer: wag ($78). Map light ($16). Trunk light ($6). Left remote mirror ($14). Dual mirrors ($14-$30). Day/night mirror ($7). Entertainment: AM radio ($72); w/8track tape player ($192). AM/FM radio ($120). AM/FM stereo radio ($176); w/8track or cassette player ($243). Exterior: Vinyl roof ($89). Glamour paint ($46). Two-tone paint ($42). Pivoting front vent windows ($54). Rear vent louvers ($33). Bodyside moldings ($39). Rocker panel moldings ($22). Bright window frames ($24-$29). Bumper guards, front and rear ($37). Luggage rack ($72). Lower bodyside protection ($30-$42). Interior: Bucket seats ($72). Cloth seat trim ($19-$37). Lockable side storage box ($19). H.D. mats ($8). Wheels/Tires: Styled wheel covers ($33). Wire wheel covers ($81). Aluminum wheels ($242). B78 x 14 WSW. BR78 x 14 BSW/WSW. C78 x 14 BSW/WSW. CR78 x 14 BSW/WSW. DR78 x 14 SBR BSW/WSW/RWL.

MONARCH CONVENIENCE/APPEARANCE OPTIONS: Option Packages: ESS option ($524). Ghia option ($426). Interior decor group ($211). Convenience group ($33-$89). Bumper protection group ($70). Light group ($43). Cold weather group ($36-$54). Heavy-duty group ($36-$54). Protection group ($29-$43). Visibility group ($7-$58). Comfort/Convenience: Air cond. ($494); auto-temp ($535). Rear defogger ($47). Rear defroster, electric ($84). Fingertip speed control ($102). Illuminated entry system ($49). Power windows ($116-$160). Power door locks ($76-$104). Power decklid release ($19). Auto. parking brake release ($8). Power four-way seat ($90). Tinted glass ($54). Tilt steering wheel ($58). Digital clock ($42). Lighting and Mirrors: Cornering lamps ($42). Trunk light ($6). Left remote mirror ($14). Right remote mirror ($31). Dual racing mirrors ($39-$53). Day/night mirror ($7). Lighted right visor vanity mirror ($34). Entertainment: AM radio ($72); w/tape player ($192). AM/FM radio ($135). AM/FM stereo radio ($176); w/8track or cassette player ($243); w/quadrasonic tape ($365). AM/FM stereo search radio ($319). CB radio ($270). Exterior: Power moonroof ($820). Full or landau vinyl roof ($102). Glamour paint ($46). Bodyside moldings ($39). Rocker panel moldings ($23). Lower bodyside protection ($30). Interior: Console ($75). Four-way seat ($33). Reclining bucket seats ($84). Leather seat trim ($271). Barletta cloth seat ($54). Luxury cloth seat/door trim ($99). Deluxe seatbelts ($19). Wheels: Deluxe wheel covers ($37) exc. Ghia/ESS (NC). Wire wheel covers ($59-$96). Styled steel wheels w/trim rings ($59-$96). Cast aluminum wheels ($146-$242); white ($159- $255). Tires: DR78 x 14 SBR WSW. ER78 x 14 SBR BSW/WSW. FR78 x 14 SBR BSW/WSW/wide WSW.

COUGAR CONVENIENCE/APPEARANCE OPTIONS: Option Packages: Brougham option ($271-$383). Midnight/chamois decor group: XR7 ($592). Sports instrumentation group ($100-$138). Decor group ($211-$461). Bumper protection group ($76). Light group ($51). Convenience group ($58-$139). Power lock group ($100-$132). Appearance protection group ($45-$53). Comfort/Convenience: Air cond. ($543); w/auto-temp control ($588). Rear defroster, electric ($93). Fingertip speed control ($99-$117). Illuminated entry system ($54). Tinted glass ($66). Power windows ($126-$175). Power seat ($149). Auto. parking brake release ($9). Leather-wrapped steering wheel ($64). Tilt steering wheel ($70). Day/date clock ($22- $42). Lighting, Horns and Mirrors: Cornering lamps ($46). Trunk light ($7). Dual-note horn ($7). Remote driver's mirror ($16). Dual racing mirrors ($58). Lighted visor vanity mirror ($37). Entertainment: AM radio ($79). AM/FM radio ($132). AM/FM stereo radio ($192); w/tape player ($266); w/quadrasonic tape player ($399). AM/FM stereo search radio ($349). CB radio ($295). Upgraded sound ($29). Dual rear speakers ($46). Power antenna: XR7 ($42). Exterior: Power moonroof ($789). Front/landau vinyl roof ($112). Full vinyl roof ($112-$163). Opera windows ($51). Bodyside moldings ($42). Wide bodyside moldings: XR7 ($55). Rocker panel moldings: Brghm ($29). Glamour paint ($62). Two- tone paint ($41-$95). Paint striping ($33). Bumper guards ($42). Lower bodyside protection ($33). Interior: Twin comfort seats w/passenger recliner: XR7 ($175). Bucket seats w/console ($175-$247). Vinyl bench seat ($28). Leather seat: XR7 ($296). Trunk trim ($39). Color- keyed seatbelts ($21). Wheels/Tires: Deluxe wheel covers ($38). Luxury wheel covers ($30-$68). 15 in. wheel covers ($38). Wire wheel covers ($105-$143). Cast aluminum wheels ($118-$303). Styled wheels ($146). Styled wheels w/trim rings ($105-$143) exc. XR7. HR78 x 14 SBR WSW ($46). HR78 x 14 wide-band WSW ($66). HR78 x 15 SBR WSW ($68).

MARQUIS CONVENIENCE/APPEARANCE OPTIONS: Option Packages: Colony Park option ($547). Grand Marquis decor: wag ($559). Tu-tone group ($72-$151). Lock convenience group ($108-$161). Bumper protection group ($59). Appearance protection group ($50-$58). Visibility light group ($47-$96). Comfort/Convenience: Air cond. ($583); w/auto-temp control ($628). Rear defroster, electric ($93). Fingertip speed control ($101-$120). Illuminated entry system ($54). Power windows ($129-$188). Six-way power driver's seat ($149); driver and passenger ($297). Tinted glass ($75); windshield only ($36). Tilt steering wheel ($72). Digital clock ($26-$49). Interval wipers ($32). Lighting and Mirrors: Cornering lamps ($46). Driver's remote mirror ($16). Lighted visor vanity mirror ($33-$37). Entertainment: AM radio ($79). AM/FM stereo radio ($192); w/tape player ($266); w/quadrasonic tape player ($399). AM/FM stereo search radio ($349). Power antenna ($46). Dual rear speakers ($46). Exterior: Power moonroof ($896). Full or landau vinyl roof ($141). Fender skirts ($50). Glamour metallic paint ($62). Paint stripes ($34). Rocker panel moldings ($29). Narrow bodyside moldings ($42). Rear bumper guards: wag ($22). Luggage rack: wag ($80). Lower bodyside protection ($33). Interior: Dual-facing rear seats: wagon ($186). Twin comfort seats ($97); w/passenger recliner ($149). Reclining passenger seat ($63). Vinyl bench seat trim ($29). Deluxe floor mats ($36). Deluxe seatbelts ($21). Lockable side stowage compartment: wag ($22). Wheels/Tires: Luxury wheel covers ($55-$84). Wire wheel covers ($30-$109). Forged aluminum wheels ($236-$264). HR78 x 15 SBR WSW. JR78 x 15 SBR BSW/WSW/wide WSW. LR78 x 15 SBR WSW.

HISTORY: Introduced: October 7, 1977. Model year production: 635,051. Calendar year production (U.S.): 624,229. Calendar year sales by U.S. dealers: 579,498 (incl. 18,035 Capris). Model year sales by U.S. dealers: 571,118.

Historical Footnotes: Model year sales for Lincoln-Mercury division climbed 15 percent, led by Cougar's XR7, setting a new record for the second year in a row. This put LM surprisingly close to Buick in the sales race. A total of 152,591 Cougar XR7 models found buyers. Second best seller was the full-size Marquis, again demonstrating the continued appeal of big cars. Some of the sales, though, may well have been due to the fact that downsizing was expected for 1979, so this would be the last chance for big-car fans. The new compact Zephyr sold far better than had Comet in its final (1977) year. This was the final year for the imported Capri, as a domestic Mercury of that name (closely related to the Ford Mustang) was being readied for the '79 model year.

1979 MERCURY

Two all-new vehicles entered the Mercury stable for 1979: Capri and Marquis. The Capri nameplate moved from a German-made model to a clone of Ford's Mustang. The full-size Marquis was sharply downsized, losing some 800 pounds and 17 inches of overall length. A second generation of electronic controls (EEC-II) was now standard on Marquis with the optional 351W V-8. Bobcat got a significant styling change, with new front/rear appearance. Option availability expanded considerably, especially in Capri and Zephyr, which offered many more options than their predecessors, including speed control (available for first time with manual shift) and tilt steering. AM/FM stereo radios with cassette tape players, formerly offered only on Zephyr and Monarch, were now available in all models. Various engines had a new electronic voltage regulator.

1979 Bobcat "Sports Option" hatchback coupe (M)

BOBCAT — FOUR/V-6 — Rectangular headlamps and a new rakishly sloped, fine-patterned grille dominated by vertical bars gave Mercury's subcompact a fresh front-end look. The hood and front fenders also sloped more than before. Vertical-styled park/signal lamps were inboard of the single headlamps, in the same recessed housings. New front side marker lamps had no surround moldings. A new rear-end appearance on the Runabout included unique horizontal taillamps and exposed black third-door hinges; but the wagon retained its three-pod vertical configuration with integrated backup lights. Bright extruded aluminum bumpers had black rubber end caps. Villager wagons added new rosewood-grain bodyside appliques with simulated wood surround moldings. Inside was a new rectangular instrument cluster, with miles/kilometer speedometer. This was the first Bobcat restyle since its 1975 debut. Five new paint colors were offered. The optional V-6 had a higher-performance camshaft this year, and engines had a new electronic voltage regulator. Standard tires grew to BR78 x 13 steel-belted radials.

1979 Capri RS hatchback coupe (M)

CAPRI — FOUR/V-6/V-8 — No longer did Mercury have to do without a domestically-built equivalent to Ford's Mustang. Capri differed mainly in grille pattern and body details from the Ford ponycar. Unlike Mustang, though, the Mercury version came only in three-door hatchback body style. The company described the shape as a "linear, flowing look highlighted by a sloping roof, soft front and rear bumper coverings, and standard wide bodyside moldings... to create a wraparound effect." Two models were offered: base and Ghia, plus an R/S and Turbo R/S option. The latter included a turbocharged turbo four and TRX tires and suspension. TRX was one of three specially-tuned variants of the Zephyr-type suspension system. It came with new low-profile wide-aspect Michelin 190/65R390 TRX tires. Base engine was a 140 cu. in. (2.3- liter) four. Capri could also have a 2.8-liter V-6 or 302 cu. in. (5.0-liter) V-8. Only on Capri did the optional V-8 have a single belt accessory drive system. That engine also hooked to a four-speed manual overdrive transmission with new single-rail shift design, standard on all Capris. Capri featured a horizontal-bar black and bright grille, flanked by quad rectangular headlamps in bright frames. A sloping hood held color-keyed simulated (non-working) louvers. Wide black bodyside moldings with dual color-keyed center stripe accompanied partial wheel lip moldings. Body trim included upper bodyside paint stripes; black window frame moldings with black frames; black belt and cowl moldings; bright windshield, rear window and drip moldings; black wiper arms; and a black window-frame-mounted remote-control driver's mirror. Soft bumpers were color-keyed. Steel wheels came with hub covers and lug nuts. Large horizontal wraparound taillamps carried integral backup lights. On the mechanical front, Capri had a strut-type coil- spring front suspension with stabilizer, four-bar link coil- spring rear suspension, unitized body, and rack-and-pinion steering. Front high-back bucket seats carried pleated trim. Dashboards held a tachometer and gauges in woodtone cluster applique, with European ISO style identificaton symbols on controls. A three-spoke sport steering wheel was standard. Capri rode a 100.4 inch wheelbase and measured 179.1 inches in length. Standard tires were B78 x 13. Among Capri's new options were tilt steering and speed control (offered for the first time on a FoMoCo car with floor-shift automatic or manual). Capri Ghia came with BR78 x 14 radial tires, dual black remote-control outside mirrors, argent sport wheel covers, a light group, soft-rim sport steering wheel, low-back bucket seats with European headrest, door map pockets, and passenger assist handle on roof rail. Capri R/S option equipment included BR78 x 14 RWL tires and handling suspension; black grille, headlamp housings and quarter louvers; argent sport wheel covers; black greenhouse moldings; hood scoop; dual black window-frame-mounted remote mirrors; and bright tailpipe extension. Tape treatment on bodysides (over the wheels) substituted for the usual pinstripes. Inside were engine-turned instrument panel appliques and Ghia soft door trim panels. With the turbocharged engine and TRX suspension, the Turbo R/S option included a sport-tuned exhaust and tailpipe extension, three- spoke TRX aluminum wheels, and low-back bucket seats with European headrests. Turbo models came only with four-speed manual.

1979 Zephyr sedan (M)

ZEPHYR — FOUR/SIX/V-8 — For its second year in Mercury's lineup, Zephyr looked the same but enjoyed a few mechanical improvements and extra options. Four-speed overdrive manual shift became standard this year for both the 200 cu. in. (3.3-liter) V-6 and 302 cu. in. (5.0-liter) V-8 engines. A new single-rail shift mechanism with enclosed linkage was supposed to eliminate the need for adjustments. California staton wagons could now get the 3.3-liter six. The 302 V-8 with SelectShift had reduced rear axle ratio, now 2.26:1. Options added to Zephyr during the 1978 model

year included power seats, windows and door locks; plus a flip-up removable moonroof. New options this year included speed control, tilt steering, performance instruments, and electric trunk lid release. Eight body colors were new. A revised tone-on-tone paint treatment was available on sedans, and on Z-7 (except ES type, which had its own unique paint treatment). Zephyr police and taxi packages had been introduced during the 1978 model year. Zephyr had a vertical-design grille, quad rectangular headlamps in bright frames, bright rocker panel and wheel lip moldings, deluxe wheel covers, and upper bodyside dual paint stripes. Front bucket seats came with four-cylinder models, but bench seating with six/V-8. In addition to its unique wraprover roof design with wide center pillar, the Z-7 sport coupe added tinted rear window glass, large wraparound taillamps, special hood and bodyside tape stripes, full-length vinyl-insert bodyside molding, bright window frames, and pleated vinyl seat trim. Z-7 deleted the base model's rocker panel moldings. Zephyr wagons had tinted liftgate glass and a cargo area light. Villager wagons added woodtone bodyside and tailgate appliques in medium cherry color, with woodtone-insert bright surround moldings. On the option list, Zephyr ES added a handling suspension and bumper protection group; blackout grille treatment; dual black mirrors (driver's remote); and black cowl grille that was almost full hood width. ES also sported black window frames and rear window ventilation louvers, full-length bright lower bodyside molding, black lower back panel, styled wheel covers with unique all-bright treatment, and gray engine-turned instrument panel and cluster appliques. ES deleted the usual hood ornament, paint stripes, rocker panel and wheel lip moldings.

1979 Monarch Ghia sedan (M)

MONARCH — SIX/V-8 — Blackout paint treatment on the vertical-theme grille was Monarch's major body change this year. Bright vinyl roof moldings replaced the former color-keyed moldings. Engines had new electronic voltage regulators. A new single-rail shift four-speed manual overdrive transmission came in an aluminum case, and a new lightweight aluminum intake manifold went on the 302 cu. in. V-8 (installed in four-doors). Options dropped included four-wheel power disc brakes, and Traction-Lok. Monarchs had single rectangular headlamps, a stand-up hood ornament, bright upper bodyside and wheel lip moldings, full wheel covers, and red reflectorized back panel applique with integral fuel filler door. Base engine was the 250 cu. in. inline six; standard tires, DR78 x 14 blackwall steel- belted radials. All-vinyl Flight Bench seating was standard, as was a burled woodtone instrument cluster. In addition to the base model, Ghia and ES option groups were available. The Ghia option group included a dual-note horn; day/night mirror; paint stripes on hood, upper bodyside and decklid; wire wheel covers; and wide odense grain vinyl bodyside moldings and partial wheel lip moldings. Lettering on the cowl read 'ESS Monarch' (formerly 'Monarch ESS') when that package was installed. The ESS group included FR78 x 14 blackwalls; black wipers and rocker panel treatment; black bodyside moldings with bright inserts; black window frames and center roof pillar; black hood and decklid paint stripes; and louvered opera window appliques (on two-door). Wide wheel lip moldings and color-keyed wheel covers also were included. Four-doors had a black division bar on the back door window. ESS did not have the standard upper bodyside moldings, and offered a choice of all-vinyl Flight bench seat or carryover bucket seats. A leather-wrapped sport steering wheel was standard.

1979 Cougar XR-7 Sports Coupe (M)

COUGAR/XR7 — V-8 — As before, two types of Cougars were available: basic two- and four-door pillared-hardtop models (in base or Brougham trim), and the personal-luxury XR7. Under Cougar's hood was a new electronic voltage regulator, plastic battery tray, and modified carburetor. Base engine was the 302 cu. in. (5.0-liter) V-8. Aerodynamic improvements including a modified under-the-front-bumper spoiler. XR7 had a new black/bright accented grille with body-color tape stripes and new horizontal-style wraparound taillamps (each with two horizontal chrome trim strips). Once again, the XR-7 grille included a lower extension below the front bumper. Other models kept their 1978 styling. New color fabric was available for the XR7 Chamois Decor Group. An extended-range fuel tank became optional. Standard Cougars had a vertical swing-away grille, quad rectangular headlamps, wraparound amber parking lamps with integral side markers, stand-up hood ornament, full wheel lip moldings, and rocker panel moldings. Vertical taillamps had bright bezels and integral side markers. Equipment included SelectShift three-speed automatic, HR78 x 14 tires, power steering and brakes, and rear bumper guards. Cougar Brougham added opera windows; a full vinyl roof (on four-door); upper

bodyside paint stripes; deluxe wheel covers; full-length bright bodyside molding with integral wheel lip moldings; wide bright door belt moldings; and Flight bench seat with folding center armrest. Cougar XR-7 rode 15 in. wheels with GR78 x 15 BSW tires and carried a rear stabilizer bar. Also included; a dual-note horn; special wheel covers with Cougar insert; hood rear edge molding; unique C-pillar treatment and ornament; padded landau vinyl roof with louvered opera window; and the typical sculptured spare-tire decklid design with lower molding. Full wheel lip and rocker panel moldings replaced the usual full- length bright bodyside molding. Dashboards held a simulated walnut instrument cluster faceplate.

1979 Grand Marquis coupe (M)

MARQUIS — V-8 — Two years later than equivalent GM models, the full-size Mercury got its awaited downsizing, losing some 17 inches and over 800 pounds. The new aerodynamically-influenced body came in two- and four-door sedan form, along with station wagons. Underneath was a new long/short A-arm coil-spring front suspension and four-link coil-spring rear suspension. Standard powerplant was now a 302 cu. in. V-8 with variable- venturi carburetor (except wagons with California emissions, a 351 V-8). The big 400 and 460 V-8 engines were gone. Four- wheel disc brakes and Traction-Lok axle also left the option list, along with the power moonroof. Newly optional was an electronic AM/FM stereo search radio with quadrasonic8 tape player and premium sound system. Also joining the option list: an analog clock, digital clock with day/date and elapsed time, AM/FM stereo with cassette, 40-channel CB, and Grand Marquis package. Speed control option included a 'resume' feature. This smaller Marquis had a lower hood, cowl and beltline. The new vertical-theme grille consisted of six separate side-by-side box sections. Concealed headlamps were replaced by exposed quad rectangular headlamps, which led into wraparound park/signal/marker lenses. A new chrome trim strip appeared along the mid-bodyside. So did front fender louvers. At the rear were large horizontal wraparound taillamps with integral side marker lights. Vertical backup lamps were adjacent to the recessed rear license plate bracket. Four-doors had a bright rear door window divider bar. Bright rocker panel, belt, wheel lip, roof drip, windshield, rear window and hood rear edge moldings were standard. Doors were thinner and armrests smaller, adding interior space. A mini spare tire was now used. Under the hood, a new EECII electronic engine control system monitored six functions. Inside was a new four-spoke steering wheel. Flight bench seats were trimmed in Fontainne cloth or optional Ruffino vinyl. Marquis still had a separate body on perimeter frame. Standard equipment included three-speed automatic transmission, power steering and brakes, dual-note horn, bright full wheel covers, stand-up hood ornament, rear roof pillar louvers, and FR78 x 14 SBR blackwall tires. Marquis Brougham added power windows, a full vinyl roof (on four- door) or landau vinyl roof (two-door), bright door frames, hood and decklid paint stripes, deluxe wheel covers, analog clock, and remote driver's mirror. Wide bright lower bodyside moldings included the quarter panels. Two-door Broughams could have the full vinyl roof at no extra cost. The Grand Marquis option added tinted glass, coach lamps, bodyside paint stripes, and wide bright/black lower bodyside moldings. Twin Comfort lounge seats with dual center armrests and reclining passenger seat were upholstered in Kinvara cloth or optional leather and vinyl. Also included: a right visor vanity mirror, dome/dual-beam map light, and pull straps. Marquis wagons had a three-way tailgate and power tailgate window. The Colony Park wagon added full-length bodyside and tailgate rosewood woodtone appliques with bright and woodtone rails, remote driver's mirror, coach lamps, bright door frames, and deluxe wheel covers. Rocker panel and wheel lip moldings were deleted.

I.D. DATA: Mercury's 11-symbol Vehicle Identification Number (VIN) is stamped on a metal tab fastened to the instrument panel, visible through the windshield. The first digit is a model year code ('9' 1979). The second letter indicates assembly plant: 'E' Mahwah, NJ; 'F' Dearborn, MI; 'H' Lorain, Ohio; 'R' San Jose, CA; 'K' Kansas City, MO; 'S' St. Thomas, Ontario; 'T' Metuchen, NJ; 'Z' St. Louis, MO; 'W' Wayne, MI. Digits three and four are the body serial code, which corresponds to the Model Numbers shown in the tables below (e.g., '20' Bobcat hatchback Runabout). The fifth symbol is an engine code: 'Y' L4-140 2Bbl.; 'W' Turbo L4140 2Bbl.; 'Z' V6170 2Bbl.; 'T' L6200 1Bbl.; 'L' L6250 1Bbl.; 'F' V8302 2Bbl.; 'H' V8351 2Bbl. Finally, digits 6-11 make up the consecutive unit number of cars built at each assembly plant. The number begins with 600,001. A Vehicle Certification Label on the left front door lock face panel or door pillar shows the manufacturer, month and year of manufacture, GVW, GAWR, certification statement, VIN, body code, color code, trim code, axle code, transmission code, and special order code.

BOBCAT RUNABOUT/WAGON (FOUR/V-6)

Model Number	Body/Style Number	Body Type & Seating	Factory Price	Shipping Weight	Production Total
20	64H	3-dr. Hatch-4P	3797/4070	2474/--	35,667
22	73H	2-dr. Sta Wag-4P	4099/4372	2565/--	Note 1

BOBCAT VILLAGER (FOUR/V-6)

22	73H	2-dr. Sta Wag-4P	4212/4485	N/A	Note 1

Note 1: Total station wagon production was 9,119 units. Engine Note: An automatic transmission was required with Bobcat V-6 engine, at a cost of $307 more.

CAPRI (FOUR/V-6)

14	61D	3-dr. Fastbk-4P	4481/4754	2548/--	92,432

CAPRI GHIA (FOUR/V-6)

Model Number	Body/Style Number	Body Type & Seating	Factory Price	Shipping Weight	Production Total
16	61H	3-dr. Fastbk-4P	4845/5118	2645/ --	17,712

Capri Engine Note: A V-8 engine cost $241 more than the V-6.

ZEPHYR (FOUR/SIX)

31	66H	2-dr. Sed-5P	3870/4111	2516/2519	15,920
32	54D	4-dr. Sed-5P	3970/4211	2580/2583	41,316
36	74D	4-dr. Sta Wag-5P	4317/4558	2681/2684	25,218

ZEPHYR Z-7 (FOUR/SIX)

35	36R	2-dr. Spt Cpe-5P	4122/4363	2551/2554	42,923

Zephyr Engine Note: A V-8 engine cost $283 more than the six.

MONARCH (SIX/V-8)

33	66H	2-dr. Sedan-5P	4412/4695	3070/3150	28,285
34	54H	4-dr. Sedan-5P	4515/4798	3111/3191	47,594

COUGAR (V-8)

91	65D	2-dr. HT Cpe-6P	5379	3792	2,831
92	53D	4-dr. Pill. HT-6P	5524	3843	5,605

COUGAR XR-7 (V-8)

93	65L	2-dr. HT Cpe-6P	5994	3883	163,716

MARQUIS (V-8)

61	66H	2-dr. Sedan-6P	5984	3507	10,035
62	54H	4-dr. Sedan-6P	6079	3557	32,289
74	74H	4-dr. 2S Sta Wag-6P	6315	3775	5,994

MARQUIS COLONY PARK (V-8)

74	74H	4-dr. 2S Sta Wag-6P	7100	3800	13,758

Wagon Note: Dual facing rear seats for the base Marquis or Colony Park wagon were available for $193.

MARQUIS BROUGHAM (V-8)

63	66K	2-dr. Sedan-6P	6643	3540	10,627
64	54K	4-dr. Sedan-6P	6831	3605	24,682

GRAND MARQUIS (V-8)

65	66L	2-dr. Sedan-6P	7321	3592	11,066
66	54L	4-dr. Sedan-6P	7510	3659	32,349

FACTORY PRICE AND WEIGHT NOTE: Monarch prices and weights to left of slash are for six-cylinder, to right for V-8 engine. For Bobcat and Zephyr, prices/weights to left of slash are for four-cylinder, to right for V-6.

ENGINE DATA: BASE FOUR (Bobcat, Capri, Zephyr): Inline. Overhead cam. Four-cylinder. Cast iron block and head. Displacement: 140 cu. in. (2.3 liters). Bore & stroke: 3.78 x 3.13 in. Compression ratio: 9.0:1. Brake horsepower: 88 at 4800 R.P.M. Torque: 118 lbs.-ft. at 2800 R.P.M. Five main bearings. Hydraulic valve lifters. Carburetor: 2Bbl. Motorcraft 5200. VIN Code: Y. OPTIONAL TURBOCHARGED FOUR (Capri): Same as 140 cu. in. four above, but with turbocharger Horsepower: 140 at 4800 R.P.M. Torque: N/A. Carburetor: 2Bbl. Holley 6500. VIN Code: W. OPTIONAL V-6 (Bobcat, Capri): 60-degree, overhead-valve V-6. Cast iron block and head. Displacement: 170.8 cu. in. (2.8 liters). Bore & stroke: 3.66 x 2.70 in. Compression ratio: 8.7:1. Brake horsepower: 102 at 4400 R.P.M. (Capri, 109 at 4800). Torque: 138 lbs.-ft. at 3200 R.P.M. (Capri, 142 at 2800). Four main bearings. Hydraulic valve lifters. Carburetor: 2Bbl. Motorcraft 2150 or 2700VV. VIN Code: Z. OPTIONAL SIX (Zephyr): Inline. OHV. Six-cylinder. Cast iron block and head. Displacement: 200 cu. in. (3.3 liters). Bore & stroke: 3.68 x 3.13 in. Compression ratio: 8.5:1. Brake horsepower: 85 at 3600 R.P.M. Torque: 154 lbs.-ft. at 1600 R.P.M. Seven main bearings. Hydraulic valve lifters. Carburetor: 1Bbl. Carter YFA or Holley 1946. VIN Code: T. BASE SIX (Monarch): Inline. OHV. Six-cylinder. Cast iron block and head. Displacement: 250 cu. in. (4.1 liters). Bore & stroke: 3.68 x 3.91 in. Compression ratio: 8.6:1. Brake horsepower: 97 at 3200 R.P.M. Torque: 210 lbs.-ft. at 1400 R.P.M. Seven main bearings. Hydraulic valve lifters. Carburetor: 1Bbl. Carter YFA. VIN Code: L. BASE V-8 (Cougar, Marquis); OPTIONAL (Capri, Zephyr, Monarch): 90-degree, overhead valve V-8. Cast iron block and head. Displacement: 302 cu. in. (5.0 liters). Bore & stroke: 4.00 x 3.00 in. Compression ratio: 8.4:1. Brake horsepower: 129-140 at 3400-3600 R.P.M. Torque: 223-250 lbs.-ft. at 1600-2600 R.P.M. Five main bearings. Hydraulic valve lifters. Carburetor: 2Bbl. Motorcraft 2150 or 2700VV. VIN Code: F. OPTIONAL V-8 (Cougar, Marquis): 90-degree, overhead valve V-8. Cast iron block and head. Displacement: 351 cu. in. (5.8 liters). Bore & stroke: 4.00 x 3.50 in. Compression ratio: 8.3:1. Brake horsepower: 135-138 at 3200 R.P.M. Torque: 260-288 lbs.-ft. at 1400-2200 R.P.M. Five main bearings. Hydraulic valve lifters. Carburetor: 2Bbl. Motorcraft 7200VV. Windsor engine. VIN Code: H. OPTIONAL V-8 (Cougar): Modified version of 351 cu. in. V-8 above Compression ratio: 8.0:1. Horsepower: 151 at 3600 R.P.M. Torque: 270 lbs.-ft. at 2200 R.P.M. Carburetor: 2Bbl. Motorcraft 2150.

CHASSIS DATA: Wheelbase: (Bobcat) 94.5 in.; (Bobcat wag) 94.8 in.; (Capri) 100.4 in.; (Zephyr) 105.5 in.; (Monarch) 109.9 in.; (Cougar 2dr.) 114.0 in.; (Cougar 4dr.) 118.0 in.; (Marquis) 114.4 in. Overall Length: (Bobcat) 169.3 in.; (Bobcat wag) 179.8 in.; (Capri) 179.1 in.; (Zephyr) 193.8 in.; (Z7) 195.8 in.; (Monarch) 197.7 in.; (Cougar 2dr.) 215.5 in.; (Cougar 4dr.) 219.5 in. (Marquis) 212.0 in.; (Marquis wag) 217.7 in. Height: (Bobcat) 50.6 in.; (Bobcat wag) 52.1 in.; (Capri) 51.5 in.; (Zephyr) 53.5 in.; (Zephyr wag) 54.7 in.; (Z7) 52.2 in.; (Monarch) 53.2-53.3 in.; (Cougar 2dr.) 52.6 in.; (Cougar 4dr.) 53.3 in.; (XR7) 53.0 in.; (Marquis) 54.5 in.; (Marquis wag) 56.8 in. Width: (Bobcat) 69.4 in.; (Bobcat wag) 69.7 in.; (Capri) 69.1 in.; (Zephyr) 71.0 in.; (Monarch) 74.5 in.; (Cougar) 78.6 in.; (Marquis) 77.5 in.; (Marquis wag) 79.3 in. Front Tread: (Bobcat) 55.0 in.; (Capri) 56.6 in.; (Zephyr) 56.6 in.; (Monarch) 59.0 in.; (Cougar) 63.6 in.; (XR7) 63.2 in.; (Marquis) 62.2 in. Rear Tread: (Bobcat) 55.8 in.; (Capri) 57.0 in.; (Zephyr) 57.0 in.; (Monarch) 57.7 in.; (Cougar) 63.5 in.; (XR7) 63.1 in.; (Marquis) 62.0 in. Standard Tires: (Bobcat) BR78 x 13 SBR; (Capri) B78 x 13; (Capri Ghia) BR78 x 14; (Zephyr) B78 x 14 BSW; (Monarch) DR78 x 14; (Cougar) HR78 x 14; (XR7) GR78 x 15; (Marquis) FR78 x 14; (Marquis wag) GR78 x 14.

TECHNICAL: Transmission: Four-speed manual transmission standard on Capri; automatic optional (gear ratios N/A). Four-speed overdrive floor shift standard on Zephyr/Monarch six: (1st) 3.29:1; (2nd) 1.84:1; (3rd) 1.00:1; (4th) 0.81:1; (Rev) 3.29:1. Zephyr/Monarch V-8: (1st) 3.07:1; (2nd) 1.72:1; (3rd) 1.00:1; (4th) 0.70:1; (Rev) 3.07:1. Four-speed floor shift standard on Bobcat/Zephyr four: (1st) 3.98:1; (2nd) 2.14:1; (3rd) 1.42:1; (4th) 1.00:1; (Rev) 3.99:1. SelectShift three- speed automatic (column lever) standard on Cougar and Marquis, optional on others. Bobcat/Zephyr automatic gear ratios: (1st) 2.47:1; (2nd) 1.47:1; (3rd) 1.00:1; (Rev) 2.11:1. Other automatics: (1st) 2.46:1; (2nd) 1.46:1; (3rd) 1.00:1; (Rev) 2.18:1 to 2.20:1. Standard final drive ratio: (Bobcat) 2.73:1 w/4spd, 3.40:1 w/others; (Capri) 3.08:1 w/four or V-6, 3.45:1 w/turbo, 2.47:1 w/V-8 and auto.; (Zephyr) 3.08:1 exc. 2.73:1 w/six and auto., 2.26:1 w/V-8 and auto.; (Monarch) 3.00:1 w/4spd, 2.79:1 w/auto.; (Cougar) 2.75:1 w/V8302, 2.47:1 w/V8351. (Marquis) 2.26:1 exc. wagon, 2.73:1. Steering: (Bobcat/Capri/Zephyr) rack and pinion; (others) recirculating ball. Front Suspension: (Bobcat) coil springs with short/long control arms, lower leading arms, and anti-sway bar w/V-6; (Capri) modified MacPherson struts w/coil springs and anti- sway bar; (Zephyr) MacPherson struts w/coil springs mounted on lower control arm; (others) coil springs with long/short Aarms and anti-sway bar. Rear Suspension: (Bobcat/Monarch) rigid axle w/semi-elliptic leaf springs; (Capri/Zephyr/Cougar) four-link w/coil springs; (Marquis) rigid axle with upper/lower control arms and coil springs. Brakes: Front disc, rear drum. Ignition: Electronic. Body construction: (Bobcat/Capri/Zephyr/Monarch) unibody; (others) separate body on perimeter frame; Fuel tank: (Bobcat) 11.7 gal. exc. 13 gal. w/V-6 and wagon 14 gal.; (Capri) 11.5 gal. w/four, others 12.5 gal.; (Zephyr) 16.0 gal.; (Monarch) 18.0 gal.; (Cougar) 21.0 gal.; (Marquis) 19 gal. exc. wagon, 20 gal.

DRIVETRAIN OPTIONS: Engines: Turbo 140 cu. in. four: Capri ($542). 170 cu. in. V-6: Bobcat/Capri ($273). 200 cu. in., 1Bbl. six: Zephyr ($241). 302 cu. in., 2Bbl. V-8: Capri ($514); Zephyr ($524); Monarch ($283). 351 cu. in., 2Bbl. V-8: Cougar/Marquis ($263). Sport-tuned exhaust: Capri ($34). Transmission/Differential: SelectShift Cruise-O-Matic: Bobcat/Capri/Monarch ($307); Zephyr ($307-$398). Floor shift lever: Zephyr/Monarch ($31). Traction-Lok differential: Cougar ($64). Optional axle ratio: Bobcat/Capri ($13); Marquis ($16). Brakes & Steering: Power brakes: Bobcat/Capri/Zephyr/Monarch ($70). Power steering: Bobcat/Capri ($141); Zephyr/Monarch ($149). Suspension: H.D. susp.: Monarch ($27); Marquis ($22). Sport handling susp.: Zephyr ($34). Handling pkg.: Marquis ($51). Cross-country susp.: Cougar ($22-$36). Radial sport susp.: Capri ($33). Load levelers: Marquis ($53-$67). Other: H.D. battery ($18-$21). Engine block heater ($13-$14) exc. Marquis ($21). Extended-range fuel tank: Cougar ($33). Trailer towing pkg. (heavy duty): Marquis ($146). California emission system ($76-$83). High-altitude option ($31-$36).

BOBCAT CONVENIENCE/APPEARANCE OPTIONS: Option Packages: Sports accent group ($223-$247). Sports instrument group ($94). Sport pkg. ($72). Deluxe interior ($158-$182). Interior accent group ($42). Convenience group ($55-$96). Appearance protection group ($41-$49). Light group ($33). Comfort/Convenience: Air conditioner ($484). Dual racing mirrors ($36-$52). Day/night mirror ($8. Entertainment: AM radio w/digital clock ($47). AM/FM radio ($48). AM/FM stereo radio ($89); w/tape player ($119); w/cassette player ($157). Radio flexibility option ($90). AM radio delete ($72 credit). Exterior: Flip-up/removable moonroof ($199). Glass third door ($25). Glamour paint ($41). Narrow bodyside moldings ($41). Deluxe bodyside moldings ($51). Rocker panel moldings ($24). Roof luggage rack: wag ($63). Mud/stone deflectors ($22). Lower bodyside protection ($30). Interior: Four-way bucket seat ($35). Load floor carpet ($24). Cargo area cover ($28). Wheels/Tires: Wire wheel covers ($33). Forged or cast aluminum wheels ($164); white forged ($177). BR78 x 13 ($43). BR70 x 13 RWL ($79).

CAPRI CONVENIENCE/APPEARANCE OPTIONS: Option Packages: RS option ($249). Turbo RS option ($1186). Interior accent group ($42-$108). Light group ($16-$28). Appearance protection group ($41-$45). Power lock group ($99). Comfort/Convenience: Air cond. ($484). Rear defroster, electric ($84). Fingertip speed control ($104). Tinted glass ($59); windshield only ($27). Leather-wrapped steering wheel ($36). Tilt steering wheel ($69). Interval wipers ($35). Rear wiper/washer ($63). Right remote mirror ($30). Entertainment: AM radio ($72); w/digital clock ($119). AM/FM radio ($120). AM/FM stereo radio ($176); w/8track or cassette tape player ($243). Premium sound system ($67). Dual rear speakers ($43). Radio flexibility option ($93). Exterior: Flip-up/removable moonroof ($199). Glamour paint ($41). Two-tone paint, black ($48). Rocker panel moldings ($24). Mud/stone deflectors ($22). Lower bodyside protection ($30). Interior: Console ($127). Four-way driver's seat ($35). Danbury or Bradford cloth w/vinyl seat trim ($20). Leather seat trim ($283). Color-keyed deluxe seatbelts ($20). Wheels and Tires: Wire wheel covers ($64). TRX or cast aluminum wheels ($240). Styled steel wheels w/trim rings ($65). B78 x 13 WSW ($43). C78 x 13 BSW ($22); WSW ($65). B78 x 14 WSW ($65). BR78 x 14 BSW ($125); WSW ($43-$168). CR78 x 14 WSW ($65-$190); RWL ($14-$204). TRX 190/65Rx390 Michelin BSW ($51-$241).

ZEPHYR CONVENIENCE/APPEARANCE OPTIONS: Option Packages: ES option ($237). Ghia option ($211-$428). Villager option ($195). Sports instrument group ($78). Exterior decor group ($102). Interior decor group ($72-$108). Luxury interior ($208-$323). Bumper protection group ($58). Convenience group ($31-$51). Appearance protection group ($48-$54). Light group ($35-$41). Comfort/Convenience: Air cond. ($484). Rear defogger ($51). Rear defroster, electric ($90). Speed control ($83-$104). Tinted glass ($59). Power windows ($116-$163). Power door locks ($78-$107). Power seat, four-way ($94). Electric trunk release ($22). Sport steering wheel ($39). Tilt steering ($48-$69). Electric clock ($20). Cigar lighter ($6). Interval wipers ($35). Liftgate wiper/washer: wag ($80). Lighting and Mirrors: Trunk light ($7). Left remote mirror ($17). Dual mirrors ($35). Day/night mirror ($8). Entertainment: AM radio ($72); w/8track tape player ($192). AM/FM radio ($120). AM/FM stereo radio ($176); w/8track or cassette player ($243). Premium sound ($67). Radio flexibility ($93). Exterior: Flip-up/removable moonroof ($199). Vinyl roof ($90). Glamour paint ($48). Two-tone paint ($81-$96). Pivoting front vent windows ($41). Rear vent louvers ($35). Bodyside moldings ($41). Deluxe wide bodyside moldings ($53). Rocker panel moldings ($24). Bright window frames ($25-$30). Bumper guards, rear ($20). Mud/stone deflectors ($22). Roof luggage rack ($76). Lower bodyside protection ($30-$42). Interior: Bucket seats ($72). Ardmore or Brodie cloth seat trim ($39). Kirsten cloth trim ($20). Lockable side storage box ($20). Wheels/Tires: Styled wheel covers ($41). Wire wheel covers ($52-$93). Aluminum wheels ($237-$278). Styled wheels ($54- $95). B78 x 14 WSW. BR78 x 14 BSW/WSW. C78 x 14 BSW/WSW. CR78 x 14 BSW/WSW. DR78 x 14 SBR BSW/WSW/RWL.

MONARCH CONVENIENCE/APPEARANCE OPTIONS: Option Packages: ESS option ($524). Ghia option ($425). Interior decor group ($211). Convenience group ($36-$94). Bumper protection group ($78). Light group ($46). Cold weather group ($57). Heavy-duty group ($57). Appearance protection group ($33-$51). Visibility group ($8-$64). Comfort/Convenience: Air cond. ($514); auto-temp ($555). Rear defogger ($51). Rear defroster, electric ($90). Fingertip speed control ($104). Illuminated entry system ($52). Power windows ($116-$163). Power door locks ($78-$107). Power decklid release ($22). Auto. parking brake release ($8). Power four-way seat ($94). Tinted glass ($64). Tilt steering wheel ($69). Digital clock ($45). Lighting and Mirrors: Cornering lamps ($45). Trunk light ($7). Dual racing mirrors ($42-$59). Lighted right visor vanity mirror ($37). Entertainment: AM radio ($72); w/tape player ($192). AM/FM radio ($135). AM/FM stereo radio ($176); w/8track or cassette player ($243); w/quadrasonic tape ($365). AM/FM stereo search radio ($319). CB radio ($270). Radio flexibility ($93). Exterior: Power moonroof ($849). Full or landau vinyl roof ($106). Glamour paint ($48). Tone-on-tone ($123). Bodyside moldings ($41). Rocker panel moldings ($24). Mud/stone deflectors ($20). Lower bodyside protection ($30). Interior: Console ($84). Four-way seat ($34). Leather seat trim ($283). Rossano cloth seat ($54). Willshire cloth trim ($104). Deluxe seatbelts ($20). Wheels/Tires: Deluxe wheel covers ($40) exc. Ghia/ESS (NC). Wire wheel covers ($69-$108). Styled steel wheels w/trim rings ($75-$114). Cast aluminum wheels ($170-$278). DR78 x 14 SBR WSW. ER78 x 14 SBR BSW/WSW. FR78 x 14 SBR BSW/WSW/wide WSW.

COUGAR CONVENIENCE/APPEARANCE OPTIONS: Option Packages: Brougham option ($266-$382). Brougham decor ($221). XR7 decor group: XR7 ($625). XR7 decor ($487). Sports instrumentation group ($105-$149). Bumper protection group ($63). Light group ($54). Convenience group ($62-$147). Power lock group ($111-$143). Appearance protection group ($66-$76). Comfort/Convenience: Air cond. ($562); w/auto-temp control ($607). Rear defroster, electric ($99). Fingertip speed control ($105-$125). Illuminated entry system ($57). Tinted glass ($79). Power windows ($132-$187). Six-way power seat ($153). Tilt steering wheel ($75). Day/date clock ($22-$46). Seatbelt chime: XR7 ($22). Lighting and Mirrors: Cornering lamps ($49). Remote driver's mirror ($18). Dual racing mirrors ($64). Lighted visor vanity mirror ($39). Entertainment: AM radio ($79). AM/FM radio ($132). AM/FM stereo radio ($192); w/tape or cassetteplayer ($266); w/quadrasonic tape player ($399). AM/FM stereo search radio ($349). CB radio ($295). Upgraded sound: XR7 ($30). Dual rear speakers ($47). Power antenna: XR7 ($47). Radio flexibility ($105). Exterior: Power moonroof ($789). Landau vinyl roof ($116). Full vinyl roof ($170). Opera windows: base ($54). Glamour paint ($54). Two-tone paint ($74-$128). Paint striping ($36). Narrow bodyside moldings ($45). Wide bodyside moldings ($58). Rocker panel moldings: Brghm ($29). Mud/stone deflectors ($24). Lower bodyside protection ($33). Interior: Twin comfort seats w/passenger recliner: XR7/Brghm ($184). Bucket seats w/console ($184-$259). Vinyl bench seat ($30). Flight bench seat ($75). Velour trim: XR7 ($208). Leather seat: XR7 ($309). Trunk trim ($42). Color-keyed seatbelts ($22). Wheels/Tires: Deluxe wheel covers ($43). Luxury wheel covers ($34-$78). Wire wheel covers ($118-$162). Cast aluminum wheels ($136-$345). Styled wheels: XR7 ($166). Styled wheels w/trim rings ($120-$163) exc. XR7. HR78 x 14 SBR WSW ($47). GR78 x 15 WSW ($47). HR78 x 15 SBR WSW ($71).

MARQUIS CONVENIENCE/APPEARANCE OPTIONS: Option Packages: Grand Marquis decor: Colony Park ($586). Convenience group ($78-$93). Lock convenience group ($91- $154). Visibility light group ($18-$47). Appearance protection group ($61-$71). Comfort/Convenience: Air cond. ($597); w/auto-temp control ($642). Rear defroster, electric ($100). Fingertip speed control ($111-$130). Illuminated entry system ($57). Power windows ($137-$203). Six-way power seat ($164); driver and passenger ($329). Tinted glass ($83). Tilt steering wheel ($76). Electric clock ($24). Digital clock ($36-$59). Seatbelt chimes ($22). Lighting and Mirrors: Cornering lamps ($49). Driver's remote mirror ($18). Right remote mirror ($38). Lighted visor vanity mirror ($41). Entertainment: AM radio ($79). AM/FM radio ($132). AM/FM stereo radio ($192); w/tape or cassette player ($266). CB radio ($295). Power antenna ($45). Dual rear speakers ($47). Premium sound system ($74-$158). Radio flexibility ($105). Exterior: Full or landau vinyl roof ($143). Glamous metallic paint ($64). Two-tone paint ($99-$129). Paint striping ($36). Hood striping: Colony Park ($20). Rocker panel moldings: Colony Park ($29). Narrow bodyside moldings ($45). Window frame moldings ($34-$39). Bumper guards, front or rear ($22). Bumper rub strips ($41). Luggage rack: wag ($86). Lower bodyside protection ($33). Interior: Dual-facing rear seats: wagon ($193). Twin comfort seats: Brghm/Colony ($101). Dual seat recliners ($89). Cloth seat trim: Colony ($42). Vinyl seat trim ($34). Polyknit flight bench seat trim: wag ($53). Leather twin comfort seat trim: Grand Marquis/Colony ($261). Trunk trim ($45). Spare tire cover ($13). Deluxe seatbelts ($24). Wheels/Tires: Luxury wheel covers ($64-$93). Wire wheel covers ($89-$118). FR78 x 14 WSW ($47). GR78 x 14 BSW ($23). GR78 x 14 WSW ($47-$71). HR78 x 14 (wagon): BSW ($23); WSW ($71). Conventional spare ($42).

HISTORY: Introduced: October 6, 1978. Model year production: 669,138. Calendar year production (U.S.): 509,450. Calendar year sales by U.S. dealers: 509,999. Model year sales by U.S. dealers: 540,526.

Historical Footnotes: Sales for the '79 model year fell by close to 10 percent for the Lincoln-Mercury division, as motorists worried more about gas mileage. The shrunken Marquis sold far fewer copies than its full-size predecessor of 1978. Model year production rose, however, partly as a result of the new domestically- built Capri; but calendar year production was down considerably. The turbocharger option in the new Capri was supposed to give Mercury a "sporty" image to add to its luxury role.

1980 MERCURY

A new four-speed overdrive automatic transmission, and some weight reductions in the engines, helped give Lincoln- Mercury models considerably better gas mileage. A turbo option was announced for Zephyr as a mid-year addition, but failed to materialize. Capri got a new five-speed gearbox option. Also arriving this year was a new (smaller) Cougar XR7 model. A new powerplant appeared: the 255 cu. in. V-8, replacing the 302 in some models.

BOBCAT — FOUR — Since the front-drive subcompact Lynx would appear for 1981, this would be Bobcat's final year. Little changed in appearance or equipment, apart from a new optional two-tone paint treatment and new sport option. Standard front/rear bumper guards moved inward by 4 inches. Five new paint colors were available. Bobcat again displayed a rakishly-angled, vertical- textured grille with single rectanguar headlamps and vertical park/signal lamps in the same recessed housings. Styled steel wheels came with trim rings. Bodies held bright wide wheel lip moldings; bright rocker panel, side window frame and door belt moldings; and ventless front side windows. Horizontal taillamps had integral backup lights. Aluminum bumpers had black rubber end caps. High-back front bucket seats were standard. Equipment also included the 140 cu. in. (2.3-liter) four with four-speed manual shift; an AM radio (which could be deleted); tinted glass; rear window defroster; front and rear bumper guards with rub strips; and choice of all-vinyl or cloth and vinyl interior. Manual-shift models had a woodgrain shift knob. Two wagons were available

1980 Bobcat "Sport Option" hatchback coupe (M)

again: base and Villager (with full-length rosewood woodtone bodyside applique). New options included mud/stone deflectors (introduced in late 1979). The new Sport option included a front air dam, rear spoiler, and special paint/tape treatment. It included large Bobcat decal lettering on the door as part of the wide stripe treatment. No V-6 engine was offered in this final season.

1980 Capri hatchback coupe (M)

CAPRI — FOUR/SIX/V-8 — Introduced for 1979, Mercury's equivalent to the Ford Mustang looked the same this year, but enjoyed a few mechanical changes. After the new model year began, the turbo engine was to be available with optional automatic as well as the standard four-speed manual shift. A new 255 cu. in. (4.2- liter) V-8 replaced the optional 302. An inline 200 cu. in. six became available late in the model year, replacing the former V-6 as first choice above the base 140 cu. in. (2.3- liter) four. Five-speed shifting became optional with the four at mid-year. New standard equipment included halogen headlamps and metric-size (P185/80R13) steel-belted radials. An AM radio was also made standard later. Wide-aspect, low- profile Michelin TRX tires were again optional. New options included a roof luggage carrier, concealed cargo compartment cover, tri-tone accent tape stripe, and Recaro bucket seats. Capris carried a black/bright horizontal-bar grille and quad rectangular headlamps in bright frames. Color-keyed louvers decorated the hood; black louvers went on the cowl. Semi-styled 13 in. steel wheels had trim rings. Extra-wide wraparound black bodyside moldings held dual color-keyed center stripes. The swing-up hatch had a bright window molding. High-back bucket seats were pleated all-vinyl trim. Standard equipment included the 2.3-liter four with four- speed manual, inside hood release, front stabilizer bar, color-keyed bumpers, full fender splash shields, woodgrain instrument panel applique, full instrumentation (including tachometer), lighter, trip odometer, sport steering wheel, locking glovebox, day/night mirror, and a remote driver's mirror. Ghia added P175/75R14 SBR tires on 14 in. wheels, sport wheel covers, dual black remote mirrors, a Ghia badge, low- back bucket seats with European-style headrests, four-spoke steering wheel with woodtone insert, and a light group. Capri RS included a rear spoiler; non-functional hood scoop; black grille; black right-hand remote mirror; sport wheel covers; and upper bodyside dual accent paint striping. 'RS' tape identification went on the front fender, at the cowl. Blackout headlamp frames, windshield molding, window frame moldings, and third door window molding were RS standards. So was a simulated engine-turned instrument panel. P175/75R14 tires rode 14 in. wheels, with a radial sport suspension. Topping the line, the Turbo RS model had 'Turbo RS' tape identification on the front fender (at cowl); a bright 'Turbo' plaque on the hood scoop; sport-tuned exhaust; three- spoke 15.3 inch forged aluminum wheels; Michelin TRX 190/65R390 low-profile tires; 8000 R.P.M. tachometer; turbo function indicator lights on dash; and rally suspension. Low- back bucket seats had European-style headrests. Turbo engines had a dual bright tailpipe extension (optional with V-8).

1980 Zephyr Z-7 Sports Coupe (AA)

ZEPHYR — FOUR/SIX/V-8 — Biggest news for Zephyr was to be the availability of a turbocharged four-cylinder engine, but that prospect faded away. However, a new 255 cu. in. (4.2-liter) V-8 replaced the former 302. Zephyrs now had high-pressure P-metric SBR tires (P175/75R14) and new quad rectangular halogen headlamps. Manual-shift models had a new self-adjusting clutch. Standard front bumper guards were moved inward a little over 3 inches, but Zephyr was otherwise little changed. Styling features included bright frames around quad headlamp and quad park/signal lamps; a thin-vertical-bar grille; aluminum bumper (with front guards); upper bodyside dual accent stripes; dual front fender louvers; and deluxe wheel covers. Horizontal taillamps had integral backup lenses and bright bezels. Zephyrs had bright wheel lip and rocker panel moldings, bright door belt and roof drip moldings, and all-vinyl low-back bucket seats. Standard equipment included the 140 cu. in. (2.3-liter) four with four-speed manual shift, inside hood release, front stabilizer bar, woodgrain instrument cluster applique, Euro-style front door armrest, and a stand-up hood ornament. Zephyr's Z-7 sport coupe was noted for its contemporary wrapover roof design with upper bodyside accent stripe treatment that continued over the roof. Also standard on Z7: lower bodyside molding with black vinyl insert; bright wheel lip moldings and window frames; Z-7 ornament on wide center pillar; wraparound taillamps; pleated vinyl seat trim; and tinted rear window glass. The Villager wagon had woodtone bodyside paneling appliques. There was also a standard wagon. Ghia packages were available on all models, but the ES option was abandoned.

1980 Monarch Ghia sedan (AA)

MONARCH — SIX/V-8 — Styling remained the same as 1979, but eight new paint colors and three new tone-on-tone combinations were offered. New electronic chimes replaced the buzzer warning system. A new full-width aluminum lower back panel applique with black center replaced the former red reflective applique. Three new vinyl roof colors were available. Again, there was a base model, Ghia option group, and sporty ESS option group. Standard Monarchs had Flight bench seating with fold-down center armrest. Ghia and ESS had a choice of special sculptured Flight bench or bucket seats. Standard equipment included a 250 cu. in. (4.1-liter) inline six with four-speed manual overdrive and floor lever (automatics had column shift), DR78 x 14 BSW SBR tires, inside hood release, vinyl seat trim, lighter, burled woodgrain instrument cluster, locking glovebox, stand-up hood ornament, and full wheel covers. Moldings were included for windshield, wheel lip, backlight, drip, belt, door frame and decklid. Two-doors had opera windows. The optional 302 cu. in. (5.0-liter) V-8 was required in California. Monarch's Ghia option group included accent stripes on hood contours, tapered bodyside accent stripes, wire wheel covers, full-length lower bodyside molding with wide color-keyed vinyl insert, bright driver's remote mirror, accent stripes on decklid and decklid contours, and Ghia decklid ornament. Ghias rode ER78 x 14 tires and carried a dual-note horn, rear door courtesy light switches, vinyl seats, seatback map pockets, and day/night mirror. The ESS option group included black wipers, black hood accent stripes, front/rear bumper guards and horizontal rub strip, bright wide wheel lip moldings, dual racing mirrors, and color-keyed wheel covers. Also on ESS: black bodyside molding with bright mylar insert; black rocker panel paint; black side window surround moldings; louvered opera window applique (two-doors); black rear window division bar (four-doors); black decklid accent stripes; and FR78 x 14 tires. 'ESS' block lettering on front fenders (at cowl) replaced the former 'ESS Monarch' label.

1980 Cougar XR-7 Sports Coupe (AA)

COUGAR XR-7 — V-8 — Aerodynamic styling on an all-new and smaller unitized body changed Cougar substantially. So did a new standard 255 cu. in. (4.1-liter) V-8 instead of the former 302 (which was now optional). Also optional this year was new four-speed automatic overdrive transmission. The new Cougar weighed 700 pounds less than the old, and rode a shorter 108.4 inch wheelbase. More important, the base models were dropped, leaving only the XR7. Cougar now had a strut-type front suspension, four-bar link coil-spring rear suspension, standard variable-ratio power rack-and-pinion steering, sealed-beam halogen headlamps, and P-metric SBR tires (P185/75R14 BSW). Keyless entry was a new option, using door-mounted pushbuttons to activate the door locks and trunk lid. Bodies featured distinctive deep bodyside sculpturing, color-keyed soft front/rear bumper coverings, new vertical-theme taillamps, a padded half-vinyl roof, quarter window louvers, all-new wheels and wheel covers. Passenger capacity dropped to four. Standard equipment included three-speed automatic transmission, power steering and brakes, dual-note horn, front and rear stabilizer bars, brake failure warning light, Flight bench seat, woodgrain instrument panel applique, trip odometer, front/rear center seat dividers, ashtray and glovebox lights, four-spoke steering wheel, analog clock, soft color-keyed bumpers, and quarter-window louvers. Cougar's upright vertical-bar grille with bright surround molding had its pattern repeated in a lower bumper grille opening. Quad rectangular halogen headlamps in bright housings led into wraparound marker lenses. Turn signals were bumper-mounted. Styling touches included a stand-up hood ornament, wide rocker moldings, wheel lip moldings, "frenched" rear window, and dual bodyside

accent stripes. Black door and quarter window frames had bright moldings. An optional Decor Group included such items as full-length wide bodyside moldings (with vinyl inserts to match the roof), hood and decklid accent stripes, bright sail-mount dual remote mirrors, and Twin Comfort lounge seats. A Sports Group (available later) had a striking two-tone treatment and low-profile TR type tires on cast aluminum wheels, with special suspension tuning. The Sports model also had Recaro bucket seats with cloth trim and lumbar/depth/shoulder support adjustment, and power windows. The Luxury Group added such extras as Michelin TRX whitewall tires on cast aluminum wheels, a 5.0-liter V-8, luxury half-vinyl roof, automatic overdrive transmission, split bench seat, electronic instruments, diagnostic warning light module, power windows, lighted visor mirror, quarter courtesy lamp, and hood/decklid paint stripes.

1980 Grand Marquis "Coach Roof" sedan (AA)

MARQUIS — V-8 — Downsized in 1979 to almost full-size, Marquis changed only slightly in appearance this year with new taillamp and lower back panel moldings. New paint combinations put the darker color on top. Halogen headlamps and P-metric (P205/75R14) radial tires were new. So were front bumper guards. Both the base 302 cu. in. (5.0-liter) V-8 and optional 351 cu. in. (5.8-liter) could have four-speed automatic overdrive transmission instead of the standard three-speed automatic. An improved EEC-III system was standard on 351 V-8s, and California 302s. The Traction-Lok option reappeared. Two new versions of the electronic AM/FM stereo search radio, introduced on the '79 Marquis, were offered: plain or with cassette and Dolby. A mid-year 1979 option had been pivoting front vent windows. Joining the option list: turbine-spoke cast aluminum wheels. Again, two and four-door sedans in base, Brougham and Grand Marquis trim were offered, along with base and Colony Park wagons. A bright Marquis crest or 'Grand Marquis' script replaced the former louvers on rear roof pillar. Accent stripes were added to the fender louvers on Grand Marquis. Bodies had bright decklid edge and taillamp surround moldings, bright window frame and lower quarter extension moldings, and Wraparound parking lamps with integral side marker lights. Fender louvers and a wide center pillar were standard. Four-doors had a rear door window divider bar; two-doors, a fixed quarter window. At the back was a black lower back panel, bright rear window molding, horizontal wraparound taillamps with integral side marker lights, and bright decklid lower edge and taillamp surround molding. Flight bench seats had a fold-down center armrest and cloth and vinyl upholstery. Electronic chimes replaced the buzzer as seatbelt warning on Brougham, Grand Marquis and Colony Park. All steering wheels had a woodgrain insert. Two new luxury half-vinyl roofs were available: the standard coach roof on all Grand Marquis models (optional on Brougham), and a formal coach roof optional only on four-door Grand Marquis. Vinyl roofs later switched to smooth french seams and color-keyed back window moldings. Base Marquis standard equipment included power brakes and steering, dual-note horn, four-spoke steering wheel, woodgrain instrument panel applique, day/night mirror, front bumper guards and rub strips, and hood ornament. Brougham added hood accent stripes; full vinyl roof (four-door) or landau vinyl roof (two-door); driver's remote mirror; deluxe wheel covers; wide bright lower bodyside molding with quarter panel extensions; decklid accent stripes; power windows; dash and trunk courtesy lights; and 'Brougham' nameplate on decklid. Grand Marquis added coach lamps, wide bright/black lower bodyside moldings, upper bodyside accent stripes, black painted rocker panel flange, 'Grand Marquis' script on rear roof pillar, and 'Grand Marquis' decklid nameplate. Grand Marquis had standard tinted glass and Twin Comfort lounge seats with dual center folding armrests. Colony Park wagons had full-length bodyside rosewood woodtone appliques, with bright and woodtone rails; plus 'Colony Park' script on quarter panel. Both wagons carried P215/75R14 tires.

I.D. DATA: Mercury's 11-symbol Vehicle Identification Number (VIN) is stamped on a metal tab fastened to the instrument panel, visible through the windshield. Coding is the same as 1979, except engine codes (symbol five) changed as follows: 'A' L4-140 2Bbl.; 'A' Turbo L4140 2Bbl.; 'B' or 'T' L6200 1Bbl.; 'C' L6250 1Bbl.; 'D' V8255 2Bbl.; 'F' V8302 2Bbl.; 'G' V8351 2Bbl. Model year code changed to '0' for 1980.

BOBCAT RUNABOUT/WAGON (FOUR)

Model Number	Body/Style Number	Body Type & Seating	Factory Price	Shipping Weight	Production Total
20	64H	3-dr. Hatch-4P	4384	2445	28,103
22	73H	2-dr. Sta Wag-4P	4690	2573	Note 1

BOBCAT VILLAGER (FOUR)

22	73H	2-dr. Sta Wag-4P	4803	N/A	Note 1

Note 1: Total station wagon production was 5,547 units.

CAPRI (FOUR/SIX)

14	61D	3-dr. Fastbk-4P	5250/5469	2547/2585	72,009

CAPRI GHIA (FOUR/SIX)

16	61H	3-dr. Fastbk-4P	5545/5764	2632/2670	7,975

Capri Engine Note: A V-8 engine cost $119 more than the six.

ZEPHYR (FOUR/SIX)

Model Number	Body/Style Number	Body Type & Seating	Factory Price	Shipping Weight	Production Total
31	66D	2-dr. Sed-5P	4582/4751	2605/2608	10,977
32	54D	4-dr. Sed-5P	4700/4869	2647/2650	40,399
36	74D	4-dr. Sta Wag-5P	4870/5039	2769/2772	20,341

ZEPHYR Z-7 (FOUR/SIX)

35	36R	2-dr. Spt Cpe-5P	4876/5045	2644/2647	19,486

Zephyr Engine Note: A V-8 engine cost $119 more than the six.

MONARCH (SIX/V-8)

33	66H	2-dr. Sedan-5P	5074/5262	3093/3160	8,772
34	54H	4-dr. Sedan-5P	5194/5382	3134/3227	21,746

Monarch Engine Note: Prices are for 302 cu. in. V-8; a 255 V-8 cost only $38 more than the six.

COUGAR XR-7 (V-8)

93	66D	2-dr. HT Cpe-4P	6569	3191	58,028

Cougar Engine Note: Price shown is for 255 cu. in. V-8; a 302 V-8 cost $150 more.

MARQUIS (V-8)

61	66H	2-dr. Sedan-6P	6134	3450	2,521
62	54H	4-dr. Sedan-6P	6722	3488	13,018
74	74H	4-dr. 2S Sta Wag-6P	7071	3697	2,407

MARQUIS BROUGHAM (V-8)

63	66K	2-dr. Sedan-6P	7298	3476	2,353
64	54K	4-dr. Sedan-6P	7490	3528	8,819

MARQUIS COLONY PARK (V-8)

76	74K	4-dr. 2S Sta Wag-6P	7858	3743	5,781

GRAND MARQUIS (V-8)

65	66L	2-dr. Sedan-6P	8075	3504	3,434
66	54L	4-dr. Sedan-6P	8265	3519	15,995

FACTORY PRICE AND WEIGHT NOTE: Monarch prices and weights to left of slash are for six-cylinder, to right for V-8 engine. For Capri and Zephyr, prices/weights to left of slash are for four-cylinder, to right for V-6.

ENGINE DATA: BASE FOUR (Bobcat, Capri, Zephyr): Inline. Overhead cam. Four-cylinder. Cast iron block and head. Displacement: 140 cu. in. (2.3 liters). Bore & stroke: 3.78 x 3.13 in. Compression ratio: 9.0:1. Brake horsepower: 88 at 4600 R.P.M. Torque: 119 lbs.-ft. at 2600 R.P.M. Five main bearings. Hydraulic valve lifters. Carburetor: 2Bbl. Motorcraft 5200. VIN Code: A. OPTIONAL TURBOCHARGED FOUR (Capri): Same as 140 cu. in. four above, but with turbocharger Horsepower: 150 at 4800 R.P.M. Torque: N/A. Carburetor: 2Bbl. Holley 6500. VIN Code: A. OPTIONAL SIX (Capri, Zephyr): Inline. OHV. Six-cylinder. Cast iron block and head. Displacement: 200 cu. in. (3.3 liters). Bore & stroke: 3.68 x 3.13 in. Compression ratio: 8.6:1. Brake horsepower: 91 at 3800 R.P.M. Torque: 160 lbs.-ft. at 1600 R.P.M. Seven main bearings. Hydraulic valve lifters. Carburetor: 1Bbl. Holley 1946. VIN Code: B. BASE SIX (Monarch): Inline. OHV. Six-cylinder. Cast iron block and head. Displacement: 250 cu. in. (4.1 liters). Bore & stroke: 3.68 x 3.91 in. Compression ratio: 8.6:1. Brake horsepower: 90 at 3200 R.P.M. Torque: 194 lbs.-ft. at 1660 R.P.M. Seven main bearings. Hydraulic valve lifters. Carburetor: 1Bbl. Carter YFA. VIN Code: C. BASE V-8 (Cougar); OPTIONAL (Capri, Zephyr): 90-degree, overhead valve V-8. Cast iron block and head. Displacement: 255 cu. in. (4.2 liters). Bore & stroke: 3.68 x 3.00 in. Compression ratio: 8.8:1. Brake horsepower: 115-119 at 3800 R.P.M. Torque: 191-194 lbs.-ft. at 2200 R.P.M. Five main bearings. Hydraulic valve lifters. Carburetor: 2Bbl. Motorcraft 2150. VIN Code: D. BASE V-8 (Marquis); OPTIONAL (Cougar, Monarch): 90-degree, overhead valve V-8. Cast iron block and head. Displacement: 302 cu. in. (5.0 liters). Bore & stroke: 4.00 x 3.00 in. Compression ratio: 8.4:1. Brake horsepower: 130-134 at 3600 R.P.M. Torque: 230-232 lbs.-ft. at 1600 R.P.M. Five main bearings. Hydraulic valve lifters. Carburetor: 2Bbl. Motorcraft 2150 or 2700VV. VIN Code: F. OPTIONAL V-8 (Marquis): 90-degree, overhead valve V-8. Cast iron block and head. Displacement: 351 cu. in. (5.8 liters). Bore & stroke: 4.00 x 3.50 in. Compression ratio: 8.3:1. Brake horsepower: 140 at 3400 R.P.M. Torque: 265 lbs.-ft. at 2000 R.P.M. Five main bearings. Hydraulic valve lifters. Carburetor: 2Bbl. Motorcraft 7200VV. VIN Code: G.

CHASSIS DATA: Wheelbase: (Bobcat) 94.5 in.; (Bobcat wag) 94.8 in.; (Capri) 100.4 in.; (Zephyr) 105.5 in.; (Monarch) 109.9 in.; (Cougar) 108.4 in.; (Marquis) 114.3 in. Overall Length: (Bobcat) 170.8 in.; (Bobcat wag) 180.6 in.; (Capri) 179.1 in.; (Zephyr) 195.5 in.; (Z7) 197.4 in.; (Monarch) 199.7 in.; (Cougar) 200.4 in.; (Marquis) 212.3 in.; (Marquis wag) 218.0 in. Height: (Bobcat) 50.5 in.; (Bobcat wag) 52.0 in.; (Capri) 51.4 in.; (Zephyr) 52.9 in.; (Zephyr wag) 54.2 in.; (Z7) 51.7 in.; (Monarch) 53.2-53.3 in.; (Cougar) 53.0 in.; (Marquis) 54.7 in.; (Marquis wag) 57.4 in. Width: (Bobcat) 69.4 in.; (Bobcat wag) 69.7 in.; (Capri) 69.1 in.; (Zephyr) 71.0 in.; (Monarch) 74.5 in.; (Cougar) 74.1 in.; (Marquis) 77.5 in.; (Marquis wag) 79.3 in. Front Tread: (Bobcat) 55.0 in.; (Capri) 56.6 in.; (Zephyr) 56.6 in.; (Monarch) 59.0 in.; (Cougar) 58.1 in.; (Marquis) 62.2 in. Rear Tread: (Bobcat) 55.8 in.; (Capri) 57.0 in.; (Zephyr) 57.0 in.; (Monarch) 57.7 in.; (Cougar) 57.0 in.; (Marquis) 62.0 in. Standard Tires: (Bobcat) BR78 x 13 SBR BSW; (Capri) P185/80R13 SBR; (Capri Ghia) P175/75R14; (Capri turbo) TRX 190/65R390. (Zephyr) P175/75R14 SBR; (Monarch) DR78 x 14 exc. Ghia, ER78 x 14; (Cougar) P184/75R14 SBR BSW; (Marquis) P205/75R14 SBR; (Marquis wag) P215/75R14.

TECHNICAL: Transmission: Four-speed overdrive floor shift standard on Capri/Zephyr/Monarch six: (1st) 3.29:1; (2nd) 1.84:1; (3rd) 1.00:1; (4th) 0.81:1; (Rev) 3.29:1. Four-speed floor shift standard on Bobcat/Capri/Zephyr four: (1st) 3.98:1; (2nd) 2.14:1; (3rd) 1.42:1; (4th) 1.00:1; (Rev) 3.99:1. Capri turbo: (1st) 4.07:1; (2nd) 2.57:1; (3rd) 1.66:1; (4th) 1.00:1; (Rev) 3.95:1. Select-Shift three-speed automatic standard on Cougar and Marquis, optional on others. Bobcat/Capri/Zephyr automatic gear ratios: (1st) 2.47:1; (2nd) 1.47:1; (3rd) 1.00:1; (Rev) 2.11:1. Other automatics: (1st) 2.46:1; (2nd) 1.46:1; (3rd) 1.00:1; (Rev) 2.18:1 to 2.20:1. Four-speed overdrive automatic standard on Cougar w/V8302: (1st) 2.47:1; (2nd) 1.47:1; (3rd) 1.00:1; (4th) 0.67:1; (Rev) 2.00:1. Standard final drive ratio: (Bobcat) 2.73:1 or 2.79:1 w/4spd, exc. 3.08:1 or 3.00:1 for wagon or either model with auto.; (Capri) 2.73:1 w/four and 4spd, 3.08:1 w/four and auto., 3.08:1 w/six and 4spd, 2.73:1 w/six and auto., 2.26:1 w/V-8 and auto., 3.45:1 w/turbo; (Zephyr) 3.08:1 exc. 2.73:1 w/six and auto., 2.26:1 w/V-8 and auto.; (Monarch) 3.00:1 w/4spd, 2.79:1 w/auto.; (Cougar) 2.26:1 exc. 3.08:1 w/V8302 and overdrive auto.; (Marquis) 2.26:1 exc. 3.08:1 w/V8302 and overdrive auto., 2.73:1 w/V8351; (Marquis wagon) 2.73:1 w/V8302. Steering: (Marquis) recirculating ball; (others) rack and pinion. Front Suspension: (Bobcat) coil springs with short/long control arms and lower leading arms; (Capri) modified MacPherson struts w/coil springs and anti-sway bar; (Zephyr) MacPherson struts w/coil springs mounted on lower control arm; (Cougar) MacPherson struts with anti-sway bar; (Marquis) coil springs with long/short Aarms and anti-sway bar. Rear Suspension: (Bobcat/Monarch) rigid axle w/semi-elliptic leaf springs; (Capri/Zephyr/Marquis) four-link w/coil springs; (Cougar) four-link with coil springs and anti-sway bar. Brakes: Front disc, rear drum. Ignition: Electronic. Body construction: (Marquis) separate body and frame; (others) unibody. Fuel tank: (Bobcat) 13 gal. exc. wagon, 14 gal.; (Capri) 11.5 gal. w/four, 11.9 w/turbo, others 12.5 gal.; (Zephyr) 14 or 16 gal.; (Monarch) 18.0 gal.; (Cougar) 17.5 gal.; (Marquis) 19 gal. exc. wagon, 20 gal.

DRIVETRAIN OPTIONS: Engines: Turbo 140 cu. in. four: Capri ($481). 200 cu. in. six: Capri ($219); Zephyr ($169). 255 cu. in. V-8: Capri ($338); Zephyr ($288); Monarch ($38). 302 cu. in. V-8: Monarch ($188); Cougar ($150). 351 cu. in. V-8: Marquis ($150). Sport-tuned exhaust: Capri ($38). Transmission/Differential: Five-speed manual trans.: Capri ($156). Select-shift auto. trans.: Bobcat/Capri/Zephyr/Monarch ($340). Four-speed overdrive automatic trans.: Marquis/Cougar ($138). Floor shift lever: Zephyr/Monarch ($38). Traction-Lok differential: Marquis ($106). Optional axle ratio: Bobcat/Capri/Zephyr/Marquis ($15). Brakes & Steering: Power brakes: Bobcat/Capri/Zephyr/Monarch ($78). Power steering: Bobcat/Capri ($160); Zephyr/Monarch ($165). Suspension: H.D. susp.: Monarch ($29); Cougar/Marquis ($23). Handling susp.: Capri/Zephyr ($35); Marquis ($51). Adjustable air shock absorbers: Marquis ($55). Other: H.D. battery ($19-$21). Engine block heater ($15). Trailer towing pkg., heavy duty: Marquis ($131-$168). California emission system ($238). High-altitude option ($36).

BOBCAT CONVENIENCE/APPEARANCE OPTIONS: Option Packages: Sport pkg. ($206). Sports accent group ($235-$263). Sports instrument group ($80-$111). Deluxe interior ($173-$200). Interior decor group ($50). Convenience group ($69-$111). Appearance protection group ($38-$41). Light group ($24-$36). Comfort/Convenience: Air conditioner ($538). Dual racing mirrors ($43-$60). Day/night mirror ($10). Entertainment: AM/FM radio ($65). AM/FM stereo radio ($103); w/cassette player ($191). AM radio delete ($76 credit). Exterior: Flip-up/removable moon roof ($219). Glass third door ($31). Glamour paint ($45). Tu-tone paint ($113). Narrow vinyl-insert bodyside moldings ($44). Wide black bodyside moldings ($54). Rocker panel moldings ($28). Roof luggage rack: wag ($71). Mud/stone deflectors ($25). Lower bodyside protection ($31). Interior: Four-way driver's seat ($38). Load floor carpet ($28). Cargo area cover ($30). Front floor mats ($19). Wheels/Tires: Wire wheel covers ($40). Forged or cast aluminum wheels ($185); white forged ($200). BR78 x 13 WSW ($50). BR70 x 13 RWL ($89).

CAPRI CONVENIENCE/APPEARANCE OPTIONS: Option Packages: RS option ($204). Turbo RS option ($1185). Interior accent group ($50-$120). Light group ($20-$33). Appearance protection group ($38-$41). Comfort/Convenience: Air cond. ($538). Rear defroster, electric ($96). Fingertip speed control ($129). Tinted glass ($65). Power door locks ($113). Leather-wrapped steering wheel ($44). Tilt steering wheel ($78). Interval wipers ($39). Rear wiper/washer ($76). Right remote mirror ($36). Entertainment: AM radio ($93). AM/FM radio ($145). AM/FM stereo radio ($183); w/8track tape player ($259); w/cassette player ($271). Premium sound system ($94). Dual rear speakers ($38). Exterior: Flip-up/removable moonroof ($219). Glamour glow paint ($46). Black lower Tu-tone paint ($56). Accent tape stripes: base ($53). Backlight louvers ($141). Rocker panel moldings ($28). Roof luggage rack ($86). Mud/stone deflectors ($25). Lower bodyside protection ($31). Interior: Console ($156). Four-way driver's seat ($38). Recaro bucket seats ($531). Cloth/vinyl bucket seats ($21). Accent cloth/vinyl seat trim ($21). Leather/vinyl bucket seats ($313). Cargo area cover ($34). Color-keyed seatbelts ($24). Wheels and Tires: Wire wheel covers ($89). Forged aluminum wheels ($279). Cast aluminum wheels ($279). Styled steel wheels w/trim rings ($68). P185/80R13 WSW ($50). P175/75R14 BSW (NC); WSW ($50). P185/75R14 BSW ($24); WSW ($74); RWL ($89). TRX 190/65 x 390 BSW ($150).

ZEPHYR CONVENIENCE/APPEARANCE OPTIONS: Option Packages: Ghia pkg.: Z7 ($254); sedan ($499); Villager ($373). Villager option ($226). Luxury exterior decor group ($126). Luxury interior group ($370). Interior accent group ($100). Sports instrument group ($85). Convenience group ($31-$55). Appearance protection group ($43-$53). Light group ($40-$48). Comfort/Convenience: Air cond. ($571). Rear defroster, electric ($101). Fingertip speed control ($108-$129). Power windows ($135-$191). Power door locks ($88-$125). Power decklid release ($25). Power seat ($111). Tinted glass ($71). Sport steering wheel ($43). Leather-wrapped steering wheel ($44). Tilt steering ($78-$99). Electric clock ($24). Cigar lighter ($6). Interval wipers ($39). Rear wiper/washer: wag ($91). Trunk light ($8). Dual bright sculptured remote mirrors ($60). Entertainment: AM radio ($93). AM/FM radio ($145). AM/FM stereo radio ($183); w/8track player ($259); w/cassette player ($271). Premium sound system ($94). Exterior: Flip-up/removable moonroof ($219). Vinyl roof ($118). Glamour paint ($54). Tu-tone paint ($88-$106). Pivoting front vent windows ($50). Rear window vent louvers ($41). Narrow vinyl-insert bodyside moldings ($44); wide black vinyl ($56). Rocker panel moldings ($28). Bright window frames ($24). Bumper guards, rear ($24). Bumper rub strips ($41). Luggage rack: wag ($86). Liftgate assist handle: wag ($13). Mud/stone deflectors ($25). Lower bodyside protection ($31-$44). Interior: Non-reclining bucket seats ($31-$50). Bench seat ($50 credit). Accent cloth seat trim ($40). Base cloth seat trim ($28). Lockable side storage box ($23). Wheels/Tires: Deluxe wheel covers ($41). Styled wheel covers ($46). Wire wheel covers ($120). Styled steel wheels ($99). Cast aluminum wheels ($310). P175/75R14 WSW ($50). P185/75R14 BSW ($24); WSW ($50-$74); RWL ($65-$89). Conventional spare ($37).

MONARCH CONVENIENCE/APPEARANCE OPTIONS: Option Packages: ESS group ($516). Ghia group ($476). Interior decor group ($234). Convenience group ($40). Light group ($51). Cold weather group ($65). Heavy-duty group ($65). Appearance protection group ($30-$53). Visibility group ($71). Comfort/Convenience: Air cond. ($571); auto-temp ($59). Rear defroster, electric ($101). Fingertip speed control ($129). Illuminated entry system ($58). Power windows ($136-$193). Power door locks ($89-$125). Power decklid release ($25). Power four-way seat ($111). Tinted glass ($71). Tilt steering wheel ($78). Auto. parking brake release ($10). Digital clock ($51). Lighting and Mirrors: Cornering lamps ($50). Dual racing mirrors ($49-$68). Lighted right visor vanity mirror ($41). Entertainment: AM radio ($93). AM/FM radio ($145). AM/FM stereo radio ($183); w/8track player ($259); w/cassette ($271). AM/FM stereo search radio ($333); w/8track ($409); w/cassette and Dolby ($421). CB radio ($313). Exterior: Power moonroof ($923). Full or landau vinyl roof ($118). Glamour paint ($54). Tone-on-tone paint ($138). Bodyside moldings ($44). Rocker panel moldings ($28). Bumper rub strips ($41). Mud/stone deflectors ($25). Lower bodyside protection ($31). Interior: Console ($93). Four-way driver's seat ($38).

Reclining bucket seats (NC). Luxury cloth seat ($108). Base cloth flight bench seat trim ($60). Leather seat trim ($313). Color-keyed seatbelts ($24). Wheels/Tires: Luxury wheel covers ($46) exc. Ghia/ESS (NC). Wire wheel covers ($74-$120). Styled steel wheels w/trim rings ($79-$125). Cast aluminum wheels ($190-$310). DR78 x 14 SBR WSW. ER78 x 14 SBR BSW/WSW. FR78 x 14 SBR BSW/WSW/wide WSW.

COUGAR XR-7 CONVENIENCE/APPEARANCE OPTIONS: Option Packages: Luxury group ($1987). Sports group ($1687). Decor group ($516). Appearance protection group ($43-$46). Light group ($35). Power lock group ($113). Comfort/Convenience: Air cond. ($571); auto-temp ($634). Rear defroster ($101). Fingertip speed control ($108-$129). Illuminated entry system ($58). Keyless entry ($231). Garage door opener w/lighted vanity mirrors ($171). Autolamp on/off delay ($63). Tinted glass ($71). Power windows ($136). Four- way power seat ($111). Six-way power driver's seat ($166). Auto. parking brake release ($10). Leather-wrapped steering wheel ($44). Tilt steering wheel ($78). Electronic instrument cluster ($313). Diagnostic warning lights ($50). Digital clock ($38). Seatbelt chimes ($23). Interval wipers ($39). Lighting and Mirrors: Cornering lamps ($50). Driver's remote mirror ($19). Dual remote mirrors ($60). Lighted right visor vanity mirror ($41). Entertainment: AM radio ($93). AM/FM radio ($145). AM/FM stereo radio ($183); w/8track player ($259); w/cassette ($271). AM/FM stereo search radio ($333); w/8track ($409); w/cassette ($421). CB radio ($313). Power antenna ($49). Dual rear speakers ($38). Premium sound system ($119-$150). Exterior: Flip-up/removable moonroof ($219). Luxury half vinyl roof ($125). Vinyl roof delete ($156 credit). Glamour paint ($65). Tu-tone paint ($96-$119). Hood/decklid stripes ($24). Manual vent windows ($50). Wide vinyl-insert bodyside moldings ($56). Rocker panel moldings ($28). Mud/stone deflectors ($25). Lower bodyside protection ($31-$44). Interior: Twin comfort lounge seats ($209). Bucket seats w/console ($176) exc. (NC) w/decor group. Leather seat trim ($303). Trunk trim ($43). Color-keyed seatbelts ($24). Wheels/Tires: Wire wheel covers ($50-$138). Luxury wheel covers ($88). P195/75R14 BSW ($24); WSW ($50). TR 220/55Rx390 WSW tires on alum. wheels: base ($442-$530). Conventional spare ($37).

MARQUIS CONVENIENCE/APPEARANCE OPTIONS: Option Packages: Grand Marquis decor: Colony Park ($581). Convenience group ($80-$98). Power lock group ($90-$164). Visibility light group ($19-$48). Appearance protection group ($51-$61). Comfort/Convenience: Air cond. ($606); w/auto-temp control ($669). Rear defroster, electric ($103). Fingertip speed control ($111-$133). Illuminated entry system ($58). Power windows ($140-$208). Six-way power driver's or bench seat ($168); driver and passenger ($335). Tinted glass ($85). Autolamp on/off delay ($63). Leather-wrapped steering wheel ($44). Tilt steering wheel ($78). Auto. parking brake release ($10). Electric clock ($25). Digital clock ($38-$63). Seatbelt chime ($23). Lighting and Mirrors: Cornering lamps ($50). Driver's remote mirror ($19); passenger's ($41). Lighted right visor vanity mirror ($35-$43). Entertainment: AM radio ($93). AM/FM stereo radio ($183); w/8track tape player ($259); w/cassette ($271). AM/FM stereo search radio ($333); w/8track ($409); w/cassette ($421). CB radio ($313). Power antenna ($49). Dual rear speakers ($38). Premium sound system ($94). Exterior: Full or landau vinyl roof ($145). Coach vinyl roof ($130). Glamour paint ($65). Tu-tone paint ($103-$131). Upper bodyside paint stripes ($36). Hood striping ($14). Hood/decklid paint stripes: base ($23). Pivoting front vent windows ($50). Rocker panel moldings: Colony Park ($29). Narrow bodyside moldings ($44). Bumper guards, rear ($24). Bumper rub strips ($41). Luggage rack: wag ($86-$118). Lower bodyside protection ($31-$44). Interior: Dual-facing rear seats: wagon ($199). Twin comfort seats ($104-$130). Leather seating ($303). Dual seat recliners ($56). All-vinyl seat trim ($34). Cloth trim: wag ($40). Duraweave vinyl trim: wag ($50). Trunk trim ($46). Trunk mat ($14). Color-keyed seatbelts ($25). Wheels/Tires: Luxury wheel covers ($66-$94). Wire wheel covers ($110-$138). Turbine-spoke cast aluminum wheels ($283- $310). P205/75R14 WSW. P215/75R14 BSW/WSW. P225/75R14 WSW. P205/75R15 WSW.

HISTORY: Introduced: October 12, 1979. Model year production: 347,711. Calendar year production (U.S.): 324,518. Calendar year sales by U.S. dealers: 330,852. Model year sales by U.S. dealers: 345,111.

Historical Footnotes: Lincoln-Mercury sales plunged 37 percent for the 1980 model year, drastically below predictions. This would be the final season for Bobcat and Monarch, which would be replaced by the new Lynx and revised Cougar. Bobcat was the slowest- selling Mercury model this year, with Monarch a close second. Sales of both dropped substantially. Plenty of leftover Monarchs remained when the new model year began. Best seller this year was the Zephyr, which found 85,946 buyers. Both sales and production fell sharply for the calendar year, down around 40 percent. Only four Mercury models were expected to reach or exceed the EPA's gas mileage standard, now 20 MPG. Mercury was still perceived as a big, heavy car, at a time when small, lightweight cars were taking over the market.

1981 MERCURY

The new Lynx and Cougar replaced Bobcat and Monarch, both of which had been selling poorly. Like Ford's Escort, Lynx was billed as a "world car." Two models got smaller base engines this year. Cougar XR7 dropped from the 255 cu. in. (4.2-liter) V-8 to a 200 cu. in. (3.3-liter) inline six, while Marquis went from a 5.0-liter V-8 down to 4.2 liters.

1981 Lynx GS hatchback coupe (M)

LYNX — FOUR — Heralding the coming trend toward front-wheel-drive was Mercury's new subcompact "world car," a close twin to Ford Escort. Lynx came in two models and five series: three-door hatchback and four-door liftgate wagon in standard, GL, GS or sporty RS; and with the Villager woodgrain option. The hatchback also came in a fifth, top-of-the-line LS series (a Lincoln-Mercury exclusive). Lynx had four-wheel fully independent suspension, a 97.6 cu. in. (1.6-liter) CVH (Compound Valve Hemispherical) engine, fully synchronized four-speed manual transaxle, and rack-and-pinion steering. Optional: a split-torque three- speed automatic transaxle. A smaller 1.3-liter engine was planned but abandoned. Front suspension consisted of MacPherson struts with strut-mounted coil springs, forged lower control arms, cast steering knuckle, and stabilizer bar. At the rear was an independent trailing-arm suspension with modified MacPherson struts and coil springs on stamped lower control arms. Both Escort and Lynx were designed for easy (and minimal) servicing. Many parts were secured with simple fasteners, including the radiator, fan shroud, oil pan, front fenders, bumpers, grilles, and doors. It was supposed to be easy to replace the battery, headlamps, and exhaust system. Fuses and most bulbs could be replaced without tools. The tight crosshatch-patterned grille was divided into six side-by-side sections by bright vertical bars. Clear wraparound park/signal lamps were outboard of the single rectangular halogen headlamps, which sat within argent housings. Styling included long black front/rear bumper end caps, standard semi-styled steel wheels with white trim rings, bodyside accent striping, and matte black rocker panel paint. Three-doors had high-gloss black center roof pillar appliques and wraparound horizontal taillamps. Four-doors had brushed aluminum center roof pillar appliques. Standard Lynx models had bright wheel lip, window frame, beltline and drip moldings; forward-folding rear bench seat; lighter; day/night mirror; AM radio; and P155/80R13 SBR blackwall tires with European-type wraparound tread patterns. Standard high-back front bucket seats had vinyl upholstery. Options included reclining high- or low-back bucket seats, console with graphic warning display, speed control, premium sound, digital clock, manual pivoting front vent windows, rear wiper/washer, and cast aluminum spoked wheels. Lynx GL added a black air dam, black bumper rub strips with argent accent stripe (front and rear), wide bodyside molding with argent accent stripe, GL badge on hatch or liftgate, and reclining high-back front bucket seats. GL three-door hatchbacks had a black lower back panel surround molding, and both models deleted the matte black rocker panel paint. Lynx GS had front and rear black rubber bumper guards and rub strips, reclining low-back bucket seats, cloth/vinyl seat trim, console with graphic warning display, full instrumentation, GS badge on hatch or liftgate, P165/80R13 SBR BSW tires, intermittent wipers, headlamps-on warning buzzer, and glovebox lock. Two-color upper bodyside accent striping replaced the standard single color. GS also had fully styled steel wheels with bright trim rings, argent hub covers and bright wheel nuts, and dual color-keyed remote mirrors. Lynx RS had a blackout grille with bright 'Mercury' plaque, black bumpers with black rub strip and argent accent stripe, black headlamp housings and windshield molding, and black air dam. Special RS accent stripe/decal treatment replaced the standard upper bodyside accent stripe. RS also had black dual remote mirrors, and blackout treatment on the 'B' pillar applique, 'C' pillar applique, drip and belt moldings, wheel lip moldings, door window frame and quarter window moldings. An RS badge went on the hatch or liftgate. RS also included a handling suspension with larger front stabilizer bar, heavy-duty shocks and stiffer springs, plus P165/80R13 blackwalls. Inside were high-back reclining front bucket seats and a console with graphic warning display. Top-line LS hatchbacks offered all the GS features, plus two-tone paint (four combinations available), hatch accent stripe, pleated velour seat trim, electric rear defroster, AM/FM stereo radio, and burled walnut woodtone appliques on the dash, radio panel and console.

1981 Capri TRX T-Top coupe (JG)

CAPRI — FOUR/SIX/V-8 — Five possibilities greeted Capri customers this year: the base or GS model, RS option, Turbo RS, and Black Magic option. GS replaced the former Ghia. Five-speed manual overdrive became available with either the standard or turbo four-cylinder engine. For 1981, the 200 cu. in. inline six was available with standard four-speed manual overdrive transmission, as well as the optional automatic. Power brakes were now standard, along with 14 in. tires and wheels, and turbine wheel covers. Sport wheel covers were a no-cost option. An AM radio also was standard. New options included a Traction-Lok rear axle and power windows. An optional TRoof came with two removable tinted glass panels. Capri again displayed a black and bright horizontal grille theme with bright headlamp frames, color-keyed hood louvers, black cowl louvers, and black wiper arms. Standard equipment included the 140 cu. in. (2.3-liter) four and four- speed manual shift, and P175/75R14 SBR BSW tires. Powertrain choices included an inline 200 cu. in. (3.3-liter) six, and 255 cu. in. (4.2-liter) V-8, along with the turbo four. Turbos came only with manual shift, V-8s only with automatic. Both the V-8 and turbo had a dual bright tailpipe extension. Capri GS added black dual remote control mirrors, a light group, door map pocket, and four-spoke steering wheel with woodtone insert and GS badge. RS had a large (non-functional) hood scoop; black grille; black headlamp frames and windshield molding; dual black remote mirrors; upper bodyside dual accent stripe (which meant deleting the customary pinstripes); black window frame moldings; and black rear spoiler. RS also included a handling suspension, leather-wrapped steering wheel, and simulated engine-turned instrument panel. Turbo RS models were identified by 'Turbo RS' tape on the front fender, and a bright Turbo plaque on the hood scoop. They also featured a sport-tuned exhaust, three-spoke 15.3 inch forged aluminum wheels, 8000 R.P.M. tachometer, and Rally suspension. Black Magic sported black or white paint with gold accents. The option package included a smallish body-color hood scoop, gold paint on the grille's leading edge, body- color rear spoiler, and Rally suspension. Gold bodyside accent stripes replaced the standard upper bodyside pinstripes. Also included: black bodyside moldings with gold accent stripes; blackout window frame moldings; spoiler; and gold license plate frames. White cars with this option had white taillamp accents and quarter louvers. Black Magic also had Michelin TRX low-profile tires and three-spoke 15.3 inch forged metric aluminum wheels with gold-color finish. Inside were black engine-turned cluster, radio and right-hand appliques. Black vinyl seat trim had gold-color cloth inserts. Black Magic and Turbo models carried TRX 190/65R390 tires.

1981 Zephyr Z-7 Sports Coupe (M)

ZEPHYR — FOUR/SIX/V-8 — Not much changed in Zephyr's appearance, but new standard equipment included power (front disc/rear drum) brakes, narrow protective bodyside moldings, and deluxe sound insulation. A new GS option replaced the former Ghia, available on all except the base wagon. Traction-Lok was now available with the V-8. Inline sixes now required automatic. Also made standard: a glovebox lock and dual-note horn. Zephyr's gas tank grew to 16 gallons except for the four-cylinder, which stayed at 14. Low-back front bucket seats with pleated vinyl trim were standard on all models. Also standard: AM radio, day/night inside mirror, cigar lighter, rear ashtray, and right-hand visor vanity mirror. New options included a console, illuminated entry, and Michelin TRX tires on forged aluminum wheels. Base Zephyr sedans had dual front fender louvers, bright lower bodyside moldings with black vinyl insert, upper bodyside dual accent stripes, and front bumper guards. The vertical-theme grille was made up of thin vertical bars in a uniform pattern (no wider divider bar at any point). Quad rectangular headlamps stood over amber quad rectangular parking lamps. Low-back bucket seats had pleated vinyl trim. Zephyr's Z7 Sport Coupe retained its contemporary wrapover roof design, wraparound taillamps, and upper bodyside accent striping that continued over the roof. A Z-7 ornament was on the center pillar. It had no rocker panel moldings. Standard equipment included tinted rear window glass. Zephyr's GS option added dual accent stripes on the hood, rear quarter window moldings, protective bodyside moldings with integral partial wheel lip moldings, dual bright remote mirrors, and GS decklid badge. Both police and taxi packages were available.

1981 Cougar GS sedan (M)

COUGAR — FOUR/SIX/V-8 — Whereas the 1980 lineup had included only a Cougar XR7, basic Cougars returned this year in the form of a new mid- size five-passenger model, to replace the former Monarch. Two- and four-door sedans were offered, over 3.5 inches narrower than Monarch, but with more hip room in front and rear. Three trim levels were available: base, GS and LS (the latter actually option packages, not separate models). Base engine was now a 140 cu. in (2.3-liter) four with four-speed manual gearbox. Standard tires: P175/75R14 SBR. The hybrid MacPherson strut front suspension placed the coil spring on the lower arm. At the rear: a four-bar link coil spring system. Rack-and-pinion steering with variable-ratio power assist was standard. Manual gearboxes had a self- adjusting clutch. Four-cylinder powered, the new Cougar managed an EPA estimate of 23 MPG (city), as opposed to just 19 for the six-cylinder Monarch it replaced. It also displayed a bit more aerodynamic styling. Cougar sedans had a bright grille with surround molding, made up of very thin vertical bars and a wider center bar, plus three subdued horizontal strips. Quad rectangular halogen headlamps stood in bright housings. Park/turn signal lamps were bumper-mounted. Body features included a Cougar hood ornament, bright bumper with flexible black end caps (front guards standard), bright windshield molding, wide lower bodyside molding with black tape insert and integral partial wheel lip moldings, and full-width wraparound taillamps with integral backups. A Cougar medallion went on the roof pillar, and there was a brushed center pillar applique as well as a color-keyed rear pillar louver applique. Low-back bucket seats wore all-vinyl upholstery. A four-spoke color-keyed steering wheel and AM radio were standard. Basic equipment also included interval wipers, power brakes, dual-note horn, locking glovebox, visor vanity mirror, lighter, trunk mat, hood ornament, full wheel covers, and driver's remote mirror. A 200 cu. in. (3.3-liter) inline six and 255 cu. in. (4.2-liter) V-8 were optional, as was automatic transmission. Cougar GS added such items as hood/bodyside accent stripes, bumper rub strips with white accent stripes, lower bodyside molding with color-keyed vinyl insert, GS badge on front fender, rear bumper guards, upgraded vinyl bucket seat trim, and four-spoke steering wheel with woodtone insert. Cougar LS was available only as a four-door, including ribbed vinyl-insert color-keyed bodyside moldings, a rear half-vinyl roof with color-keyed back window molding, and special bright wheel lip moldings. Also on LS: special bodyside accent stripe, luxury wheel covers, bright passenger remote mirror, LS fender badge, Twin Comfort lounge front seats, cornering lamps, and a light group.

COUGAR XR-7 — SIX/V-8 — After years of V-8 power alone, XR7 dropped down to an inline six as standard engine. Both 255 cu. in. and 302 cu. in. V-8s remained optional, however. Automatic overdrive transmission (introduced in 1980) was now available with both V-8s. The gas tank grew to 18 gallons. New options included puncture-resistant self-sealing tires, Traction-Lok, and pivoting vent windows. Options also

1981 Cougar XR-7 Sports Coupe (M)

included a flip-up removable glass moonroof and keyless entry. Appearance changes included a standard wide bodyside molding with color-keyed vinyl insert, and a wide bright/black belt molding that framed the lower edge of the door and quarter glass. The accent stripe was raised to belt level. Quarter window louvers were removed. The grille and bumper were revised, but still a vertical-bar grille style with bright surround molding. The color-keyed soft bumper covering had a bright insert. Bright rear moldings replaced the "frenched" window design. At the rear was a new standard decklid stripe, plus revised large vertical-theme taillamps (with integral backup lenses) and ornamentation. Later in the season, the vinyl roof wrapover molding was moved forward. New standard equipment included power brakes and variable-ratio power steering. Also standard: the 200 cu. in. (3.3-liter) inline six with automatic transmission, P195/75R14 SBR BSW tires, AM radio, dual-note horn, mini spare tire, halogen headlamps, stand-up hood ornament, upper bodyside paint stripe, analog clock, and half-vinyl roof with black belt molding. XR-7's GS option included hood accent stripes, bright right-hand remote mirror, Twin Comfort lounge seats, woodgrain steering wheel, and luxury wheel covers. LS added power windows and luxury interior trim, as well as door pull straps and electronic seatbelt warning chimes.

1981 Grand Marquis sedan (AA)

MARQUIS — V-8 — A new 255 cu. in. (4.2-liter) V-8, derived from the 302, was standard on base and Brougham Marquis this year. The 302 remained standard on Grand Marquis and on both wagons. The 255 came with automatic overdrive transmission, introduced for 1980 and made standard on all Marquis models for '81. Nine new paint colors were offered, with five new two-tones and three new vinyl roof colors. Among the new options were puncture-resistant self-sealing tires. The optional premium sound system added two more door-mount speakers, making six in all. A high-output 351 cu. in. (5.8-liter) V-8 was available with optional trailer towing or police packages. Tinted glass had become standard on the wagon's tailgate window in mid-year 1980. So had an AM radio on the base sedan and wagon; AM/FM on Brougham, Grand Marquis and Colony Park. For 1981, P205/75R14 SBR whitewalls were standard on all Marquis, and a coach roof on Brougham and Grand Marquis. Rear bumper guards were now standard on Grand Marquis. Appearance was similar to 1980, with a bright vertical- bar grille and quad rectangular halogen headlamps within bright headlamp/parking lamp surround moldings. Front bumper guards and a stand-up hood ornament were standard. Wraparound parking lamps had integral side markers, as did the horizontal wraparound taillamps. Twin fender louvers decorated each side of the car. Marquis Brougham added hood accent stripes, a coach vinyl roof, coach lamps, Brougham decklid nameplate, wide bright lower bodyside molding with quarter panel extensions, deluxe wheel covers, and power windows. The AM/FM stereo had two rear speakers. Twin Comfort lounge seats came in Brougham cloth and vinyl trim. Grand Marquis included tinted glass, wide bright/black lower bodyside molding, upper bodyside accent stripes, black rocker panel flanges, accent stripes on fender louvers, and rear bumper guards. Twin Comfort lounge seats were luxury cloth with dual center folding armrests. The Grand Marquis nameplate went on the rear roof pillar and decklid.

I.D. DATA: Mercury had a new 17-symbol Vehicle Identification Number (VIN), again stamped on a metal tab fastened to the instrument panel, visible through the windshield. Symbols one to three indicate manufacturer, make and vehicle type: '1ME' Mercury passenger car. The fourth symbol ('B') denotes restraint system. Next comes a letter 'P', followed by two digits that indicate body type: Model Number, as shown in left column of tables below. (Example: '31' Zephyr two-door sedan.) Symbol eight indicates engine type: '2' L498 2Bbl.; 'A' L4-140 2Bbl.; 'A' Turbo L4140 2Bbl.; 'B' or 'T' L6200 1Bbl.; 'D' V8255 2Bbl.; 'F' V8302 2Bbl.; 'G' V8351 2Bbl. Next is a check digit. Symbol ten indicates model year ('B' 1981). Symbol eleven is assembly plant: 'A' Atlanta, GA; 'F' Dearborn, MI; 'R' San Jose, CA; 'G' Chicago; 'H' Lorain, Ohio; 'K' Kansas City, MO; 'X' St. Thomas, Ontario; 'T' Metuchen, NJ; 'Z' St. Louis, MO; 'W' Wayne, MI. The final six digits make up the sequence number, starting with 600,001. A Vehicle Certification Label on the left front door lock face panel or door pillar shows the manufacturer, month and year of manufacture, GVW, GAWR, certification statement, VIN, and codes for such items as body type, color, trim, axle, transmission, and special order information.

431

LYNX (FOUR)

Model Number	Body/Style Number	Body Type & Seating	Factory Price	Shipping Weight	Production Total
63	61D	3-dr. Hatch-4P	5603	N/A	Note 1
65	74D	4-dr. Lift-4P	5931	N/A	Note 1
63	61D	3-dr. L Hatch-4P	5665	1935	Note 1
65	74D	4-dr. L Lift-4P	6070	2059	Note 1
63/60Z	61D	3-dr. GL Hatch-4P	5903	1957	Note 1
65/60Z	74D	4-dr. GL Lift-4P	6235	2074	Note 1
63/602	61D	3-dr. GS Hatch-4P	6642	1996	Note 1
65/602	74D	4-dr. GS Lift-4P	6914	2114	Note 1
63/603	61D	3-dr. LS Hatch-4P	7127	2004	Note 1
63/936	61D	3-dr. RS Hatch-4P	6223	1980	Note 1
65/936	74D	4-dr. RS Lift-4P	6563	2098	Note 1

Note 1: Total Lynx production, 72,786 three-door hatchbacks and 39,192 four-door liftgate models.

CAPRI (FOUR/SIX)

67	61D	3-dr. Fastbk-4P	6685/6898	2576/2603	51,786

CAPRI GS (FOUR/SIX)

68	61H	3-dr. Fastbk-4P	6867/7080	2623/2650	7,160

Capri Engine Note: A V-8 engine cost $50 more than the six.

1981 Zephyr Villager station wagon (JG)

ZEPHYR (FOUR/SIX)

70	66D	2-dr. Sed-5P	6103/6316	2532/2585	5,814
N/A	66D	2-dr. S Sed-5P	5769/5982	N/A	N/A
71	54D	4-dr. Sed-5P	6222/6435	2597/2650	34,334
73	74D	4-dr. Sta Wag-5P	6458/6671	2672/2725	16,283

ZEPHYR Z-7 (FOUR/SIX)

72	36R	2-dr. Spt Cpe-5P	6252/6465	2584/2637	10,078

COUGAR (FOUR/SIX)

76	66D	2-dr. Sedan-5P	6535/6748	2682/2772	10,793
77	54D	4-dr. Sedan-5P	6694/6907	2726/2816	42,860

Zephyr/Cougar Engine Note: A 255 cu. in. V-8 engine cost $50 more than the six.

COUGAR XR-7 (SIX/V-8)

90	66D	2-dr. HT Cpe-4P	7799/7849	3000/3137	37,275

R-7 Engine Note: Price shown is for 255 cu. in. V-8; a 302 V-8 cost $41 more.

MARQUIS (V-8)

81	54H	4-dr. Sedan-6P	7811	3493	10,392
87	74H	4-dr. 2S Sta Wag-6P	8309	3745	2,219

MARQUIS BROUGHAM (V-8)

82	66K	2-dr. Sedan-6P	8601	3513	2,942
83	54K	4-dr. Sedan-6P	8800	3564	11,744

MARQUIS COLONY PARK (V-8)

Model Number	Body/Style Number	Body Type & Seating	Factory Price	Shipping Weight	Production Total
88	74K	4-dr. 2S Sta Wag-6P	9304	3800	6,293

GRAND MARQUIS (V-8)

84	66L	2-dr. Sedan-6P	9228	3533	4,268
85	54L	4-dr. Sedan-6P	9459	3564	23,780

FACTORY PRICE AND WEIGHT NOTE: Cougar XR7 prices and weights to left of slash are for six-cylinder, to right for V-8 engine. For Capri, Zephyr and Cougar, prices/weights to left of slash are for four-cylinder, to right for V-6.

ENGINE DATA: BASE FOUR (Lynx): Inline. Overhead cam. Four-cylinder. Cast iron block and aluminum head. Displacement: 97.6 cu. in. (1.6 liters). Bore & stroke: 3.15 x 3.13 in. Compression ratio: 8.8:1. Brake horsepower: 65 at 5200 R.P.M. Torque: 85 lbs.-ft. at 3000 R.P.M. Five main bearings. Hydraulic valve lifters. Carburetor: 2Bbl. Holley-Weber 5740. VIN Code: 2. BASE FOUR (Capri, Zephyr, Cougar): Inline. Overhead cam. Four-cylinder. Cast iron block and head. Displacement: 140 cu. in. (2.3 liters). Bore & stroke: 3.78 x 3.13 in. Compression ratio: 9.0:1. Brake horsepower: 88 at 4600 R.P.M. Torque: 118 lbs.-ft. at 2600 R.P.M. Five main bearings. Hydraulic valve lifters. Carburetor: 2Bbl. Holley 6500. VIN Code: A. OPTIONAL TURBOCHARGED FOUR (Capri): Same as 140 cu. in. four above, but with turbocharger Horsepower: N/A. Torque: N/A. Carburetor: 2Bbl. VIN Code: A. BASE SIX (XR7); OPTIONAL (Capri, Zephyr, Cougar): Inline. OHV. Six-cylinder. Cast iron block and head. Displacement: 200 cu. in. (3.3 liters). Bore & stroke: 3.68 x 3.13 in. Compression ratio: 8.6:1. Brake horsepower: 88-94 at 3800-4000 R.P.M. Torque: 154-158 lbs.-ft. at 1400 R.P.M. Seven main bearings. Hydraulic valve lifters. Carburetor: 1Bbl. Holley 1946. VIN Code: B or T. BASE V-8 (Marquis); OPTIONAL (Capri, Zephyr, Cougar): 90-degree, overhead valve V-8. Cast iron block and head. Displacement: 255 cu. in. (4.2 liters). Bore & stroke: 3.68 x 3.00 in. Compression ratio: 8.8:1. Brake horsepower: 115-120 at 3100-3400 R.P.M. Torque: 195-205 lbs.-ft. at 2000-2600 R.P.M. Five main bearings. Hydraulic valve lifters. Carburetor: 2Bbl. Motorcraft 2150 or 7200VV. VIN Code: D. OPTIONAL V-8 (XR7, Marquis): 90-degree, overhead valve V-8. Cast iron block and head. Displacement: 302 cu. in. (5.0 liters). Bore & stroke: 4.00 x 3.00 in. Compression ratio: 8.4:1. Brake horsepower: 130 at 3400 R.P.M. Torque: 235 lbs.-ft. at 1600 R.P.M. Five main bearings. Hydraulic valve lifters. Carburetor: 2Bbl. Motorcraft 2150 or 2700VV. VIN Code: F. OPTIONAL V-8 (Marquis): 90-degree, overhead valve V-8. Cast iron block and head. Displacement: 351 cu. in. (5.8 liters). Bore & stroke: 4.00 x 3.50 in. Compression ratio: 8.3:1. Brake horsepower: 145 at 3200 R.P.M. Torque: 270 lbs.-ft. at 1800 R.P.M. Five main bearings. Hydraulic valve lifters. Carburetor: 2Bbl. Motorcraft 7200VV. VIN Code: G.

NOTE: A police version of the 351 V-8 was available, rated 165 horsepower at 3600 R.P.M. and 285 lbs.-ft. at 2200 R.P.M.

CHASSIS DATA: Wheelbase: (Lynx) 94.2 in.; (Capri) 100.4 in.; (Zephyr) 105.5 in.; (Cougar) 105.5 in.; (XR7) 108.4 in.; (Marquis) 114.3 in. Overall Length: (Lynx) 163.9 in.; (Lynx lift) 165.0 in.; (Capri) 179.1 in.; (Zephyr) 195.5 in.; (Z7) 197.4 in.; (Cougar) 196.5 in.; (XR7) 200.4 in.; (Marquis) 212.3 in.; (Marquis wag) 218.0 in. Height: (Lynx) 53.3 in.; (Capri) 51.4 in.; (Zephyr) 52.9 in.; (Zephyr wag) 54.2 in.; (Z7) 51.7 in.; (Cougar) 53.0 in.; (XR7) 53.2 in.; (Marquis) 54.7 in.; (Marquis wag) 57.4 in. Width: (Lynx) 65.9 in.; (Capri) 69.1 in.; (Zephyr) 71.0 in.; (Cougar) 68.7 in.; (XR7) 74.1 in.; (Marquis) 77.5 in.; (Marquis wag) 79.3 in. Front Tread: (Lynx) 54.7 in.; (Capri) 56.6 in.; (Zephyr/Cougar) 56.6 in.; (XR7) 58.1 in.; (Marquis) 62.2 in. Rear Tread: (Lynx) 56.0 in.; (Capri) 57.0 in.; (Zephyr/Cougar) 57.0 in.; (XR7) 57.0 in.; (Marquis) 62.0 in. Standard Tires: (Lynx) P155/80R13; (Capri) P175/75R14; (Capri turbo) TRX 190/65R390. (Zephyr/Cougar) P175/75R14 SBR; (XR7) P195/75R14 SBR BSW; (Marquis) P205/75R14 SBR; (Marquis wag) P215/75R14.

TECHNICAL: Transmission: Four-speed manual standard on Lynx. Gear ratios: (1st) 3.58:1; (2nd) 2.05:1; (3rd) 1.21:1; (4th) 0.81:1; (Rev) 3.46:1. Four-speed floor shift standard on Capri/Zephyr/Cougar four: (1st) 3.98:1; (2nd) 2.14:1; (3rd) 1.42:1; (4th) 1.00:1; (Rev) 3.99:1. Four-speed overdrive floor shift standard on Capri six: (1st) 3.29:1; (2nd) 1.84:1; (3rd) 1.00:1; (4th) 0.81:1; (Rev) 3.29:1. Capri turbo four-speed: (1st) 4.07:1; (2nd) 2.57:1; (3rd) 1.66:1; (4th) 1.00:1; (Rev) 3.95:1. Capri five-speed: (1st) 4.05:1; (2nd) 2.43:1; (3rd) 1.48:1; (4th) 1.00:1; (5th) 0.82:1; (Rev) 3.90:1. Capri turbo five-speed: (1st) 3.72:1; (2nd) 2.23:1; (3rd) 1.48:1; (4th) 1.00:1; (5th) 0.76:1; (Rev) 3.59:1. Select-Shift three-speed automatic standard on XR7, optional on others. Gear ratios: (1st) 2.46:1 or 2.47:1; (2nd) 1.46:1 or 1.47:1; (3rd) 1.00:1; (Rev) 2.11:1 to 2.19:1. Lynx three-speed automatic: (1st) 2.80:1; (2nd) 1.60:1; (3rd) 1.00:1; (Rev) 1.97:1. Four-speed overdrive automatic on XR7/Marquis: (1st) 2.40:1; (2nd) 1.47:1; (3rd) 1.00:1; (4th) 0.67:1; (Rev) 2.00:1. Standard final drive ratio: (Lynx) 3.59:1 w/4spd, 3.31:1 w/auto.; (Capri four/turbo) 3.08:1 w/4spd, 3.45:1 w/5spd; (Capri six) 3.08:1 w/4spd, 2.73:1 w/5spd; (Capri V-8) 2.26:1; (Zephyr) 3.08:1 exc. 2.73:1 w/six, 2.26:1 w/V-8; (Cougar) 2.73:1 w/six, 2.26:1 w/V8255 and auto., 3.08:1 w/V-8 and 4-spd auto.; (Marquis) 3.08:1 exc. 2.73:1 w/high-output 351 V-8 and 4spd auto. Steering: (Marquis) recirculating ball; (others) rack and pinion. Front Suspension: (Lynx) MacPherson strut-mounted coil springs w/lower control arms and stabilizer bar; (Capri) modified MacPherson struts w/coil springs and anti-sway bar; (Zephyr/Cougar) MacPherson struts w/coil springs mounted on lower control arm and anti-sway bar; (Marquis) coil springs with long/short Aarms and anti-sway bar. Rear Suspension: (Lynx) independent trailing arms w/modified MacPherson struts and coil springs on lower control arms; (Capri/Zephyr/Cougar/Marquis) four-link w/coil springs; (XR7) four-link with coil springs and anti-sway bar. Brakes: Front disc, rear drum. Ignition: Electronic. Body construction: (Marquis) separate body and frame; (others) unibody. Fuel tank: (Lynx) 10 gal.; (Capri) 12.5 gal.; (Zephyr) 16 gal. exc. 14 gal. w/four; (Cougar) 16 gal.; (XR7) 18 gal.; (Marquis) 19 gal. exc. wagon, 20 gal.

DRIVETRAIN OPTIONS: Engines: Turbo 140 cu. in. four: Capri ($610). 200 cu. in. six: Capri/Zephyr/Cougar ($213). 255 cu. in. V-8: Capri/Zephyr/Cougar ($263); XR7 ($50). 302 cu. in. V-8: Cougar XR7 ($91); Marquis ($41). 351 cu. in. V-8: Marquis ($83); Grand Marquis 4dr., wagon ($41). H.O. 351 cu. in. V-8: Marquis ($139-$180). Sport-tuned exhaust: Capri ($39). Transmission/Differential: Five-speed manual trans.: Capri ($152). Automatic transaxle: Lynx ($344). Select-shift auto. trans.: Capri/Zephyr/Cougar ($349). Four-speed overdrive automatic trans.: Cougar XR7 ($162). Floor shift lever: Zephyr/Cougar ($43). Traction-Lok differential: Capri/Zephyr/Cougar/XR7 ($67); Marquis ($71). Brakes & Steering: Power brakes: Lynx ($79). Power steering: Lynx/Capri ($163); Zephyr ($168); Cougar ($161). Suspension: H.D. susp.: Marquis ($22); Cougar XR7 ($23). Handling susp.: Lynx ($37); Zephyr ($45); Capri/Marquis ($43). Load levelers: Marquis ($57). Other: H.D. battery ($20). Extended-range gas tank: Lynx ($32). Engine block heater ($16). Trailer towing pkg., heavy duty: Marquis ($176-$206). California emission system ($46). High-altitude option ($35-$36).

LYNX CONVENIENCE/APPEARANCE OPTIONS: Option Packages: Villager woodtone option: GL/GS ($224). Appearance protection group ($49). Light group ($39). Comfort/Convenience: Air conditioner ($530). Rear defroster, electric ($102). Fingertip speed control ($132); windshield only ($28). Digital clock ($52). Intermittent wipers ($41). Rear wiper/washer ($100). Dual remote sport mirrors ($56). Entertainment: AM/FM radio ($63). AM/FM stereo radio ($100); w/cassette player ($87-$187). Dual rear speakers ($37). Premium sound ($91). AM radio delete ($61 credit). Exterior: Flip-up/open air roof ($154-$228). Glamour paint ($45). Tu-tone paint ($91). Front vent windows, pivoting ($55). Vinyl-insert bodyside

moldings ($41). Bumper guards, front or rear ($23). Bumper rub strips ($34). Roof luggage rack ($74). Roof air deflector ($26). Lower bodyside protection ($60). Interior: Console ($98). Low-back reclining bucket seats ($30). Reclining front seatbacks ($55). Cloth/vinyl seat trim ($28); vinyl (NC). Deluxe seatbelts ($23). Wheels/Tires: Cast aluminum spoke wheels ($193-$279). P155/80R13 WSW ($55). P165/80R13 BSW ($19); WSW ($55-$74).

CAPRI CONVENIENCE/APPEARANCE OPTIONS: Option Packages: Black magic option ($644). RS option ($234). Turbo RS option ($1191). Light group ($43). Appearance protection group ($41). Comfort/Convenience: Air cond. ($560). Rear defroster, electric ($107). Fingertip speed control ($132). Power windows ($140). Power door locks ($93). Tinted glass ($76). Leather-wrapped steering wheel ($49). Tilt steering wheel ($80-$93). Interval wipers ($41). Rear wiper/washer ($85). Right remote mirror ($37). Entertainment: AM/FM radio ($51). AM/FM stereo radio ($88); w/8track tape player ($162); w/cassette player ($174). Premium sound system ($91). Dual rear speakers ($37). Radio flexibility option ($61). AM radio delete ($61 credit). Exterior: TRoof ($874). Flip-up/open air roof ($213-$228). Glamour paint ($48). Tu-tone paint ($57-$110). Gold accent stripes ($54). Liftgate louvers ($145). Rocker panel moldings ($30). Roof luggage rack ($90). Mud/stone deflectors ($26). Lower bodyside protection ($37). Interior: Console ($168). Recaro bucket seats ($610). Accent cloth/vinyl seat trim ($22). Leather/vinyl seat trim ($359). Front floor mats ($18). Wheels and Tires: Wire wheel covers ($80). Sport wheel covers (NC). Forged metric aluminum wheels ($340). Cast aluminum wheels ($305). Styled steel wheels w/trim rings ($63). P175/75R14 WSW ($55). P185/75R14 BSW (N/A); WSW ($82); RWL ($102). TR 190/65Rx390 BSW ($128).

ZEPHYR CONVENIENCE/APPEARANCE OPTIONS: Option Packages: Villager option ($229). GS option ($327- $383). Instrument cluster ($88). Appearance protection group ($50). Light group ($43). Comfort/Convenience: Air cond. ($585). Rear defroster, electric ($107). Fingertip speed control (N/A). Illuminated entry ($60). Power windows ($140-$195). Power door locks ($93-$132). Remote decklid release ($27). Power seat ($122). Tinted glass ($76). Leather-wrapped steering wheel ($49). Tilt steering ($80-$93). Electric clock ($23). Interval wipers ($41). Rear wiper/washer: wag ($110). Lighting and Mirrors: Dual-beam map light ($13). Trunk light ($6). Left remote mirror ($15). Dual remote mirrors ($55). Lighted visor vanity mirror ($43). Entertainment: AM/FM radio ($51). AM/FM stereo radio ($88); w/8track player ($162); w/cassette player ($174). Twin rear speakers ($37). Premium sound system ($91). Radio flexibility ($61). AM radio delete ($61 credit). Exterior: Flip-up/open air roof (N/A). Full vinyl roof ($115). Glamour paint ($55). Tu-tone paint ($90-$110). Pivoting front vent windows ($55). Tailgate assist handle: wag ($16). Wide vinyl bodyside moldings: Z7 ($55). Rocker panel moldings ($30). Bumper guards, rear ($23). Bumper rub strips ($43). Luggage rack: wagon ($90). Lower bodyside protection ($37-$49). Interior: Console ($168). Bench seat ($24 credit). Cloth/vinyl seat trim ($28). Vinyl trim: Z7 ($26). Front floor mats ($18). Locking storage box ($24). Deluxe seatbelts ($23). Wheels/Tires: Wire wheel covers ($117). Styled steel wheels ($48); w/trim rings ($94). P175/75R14 WSW ($55). P185/75R14 WSW ($86). TR 190/65R390 BSW on TRX alum. wheels ($512). Conventional spare ($39).

COUGAR CONVENIENCE/APPEARANCE OPTIONS: Option Packages: GS option ($371). LS option ($972). Light group ($45). Cold weather group ($67). Appearance protection group ($45). Comfort/Convenience: Air cond. ($585). Rear defroster ($107). Fingertip speed control ($126). Illuminated entry system ($60). Six-way power twin comfort seats ($162). Four-way power flight bench seat ($122). Power windows ($140-$195). Power door locks ($93-$132). Remote decklid release ($27). Tinted glass ($76). Tilt steering wheel ($96). Electric clock ($23). Interval wipers ($41). Lighting and Mirrors: Cornering lamps ($51). Lighted right visor vanity mirror ($43). Entertainment: AM/FM radio ($51). AM/FM stereo radio ($88); w/8track player ($162); w/cassette ($174). Premium sound ($91). Dual rear speakers ($37). Radio flexibility ($61). AM radio delete ($61 credit). Exterior: Flip-up open-air roof ($228). Full or landau vinyl roof ($115). Glamour paint ($55). Tu-tone paint ($66-$162). Bodyside moldings ($45). Bumper rub strips ($41). Mud/stone deflectors ($26). Lower bodyside protection ($37). Interior: Console ($168). Twin comfort seats ($168). Cloth seat trim ($45-$62). Leather seat trim ($340). Deluxe seatbelts ($22). Wheels/Tires: Luxury wheel covers: base ($43). Wire wheel covers ($80-$124). Aluminum wheels ($306-$350). P175/75R14 WSW. P185/75R14 BSW/WSW/RWL. TR on aluminum wheels. Conventional spare.

COUGAR XR7 CONVENIENCE/APPEARANCE OPTIONS: Option Packages: LS option ($715). GS option ($320) exc. ($96) w/LS option. Appearance protection group ($45). Light group ($30). Power lock group ($120). Comfort/Convenience: Air cond. ($585); auto-temp ($652). Rear defroster ($107). Fingertip speed control ($105-$132). Illuminated entry system ($60). Keyless entry ($227). Garage door opener w/lighted vanity mirrors ($177). Autolamp on/off delay ($65). Tinted glass ($76). Power windows ($140). Four- way power seat ($122). Six-way power driver's seat ($173). Auto. parking brake release ($10). Leather-wrapped steering wheel ($45). Tilt steering wheel ($80). Electronic instrument cluster ($322). Diagnostic warning lights ($51). Seatbelt chimes ($23). Digital clock ($40). Interval wipers ($41). Lighting and Mirrors: Cornering lamps ($51). Remote right mirror ($52). Lighted right visor vanity mirror ($41). Entertainment: AM/FM radio ($51). AM/FM stereo radio ($88); w/8track player ($162); w/cassette ($174). AM/FM stereo search radio ($234); w/8track ($309); w/cassette ($321). Power antenna ($48). Dual rear speakers ($37). Premium sound system ($116-$146). Radio flexibility ($65). AM radio delete ($61 credit). Exterior: Carriage roof ($772). Flip-up/open-air roof ($228). Luxury rear vinyl half roof ($165). Vinyl roof delete ($130 credit). Glamour paint ($70). Tu-tone paint ($99). Hood paint stripes ($16). Pivoting front vent windows ($55). Rocker panel moldings ($30). Mud/stone deflectors ($26). Lower bodyside protection ($48). Interior: Bucket seats w/console ($182) exc. (NC) with GS/LS. Recaro bucket seats ($528). Twin comfort lounge seats w/recliners ($215). Leather seat trim ($359). Vinyl seat trim ($28). Front floor mats ($13). Trunk trim ($44). Wheels: Wire wheel covers ($93). Luxury wheel covers ($43).

MARQUIS CONVENIENCE/APPEARANCE OPTIONS: Option Packages: Grand Marquis decor: Colony Park ($491). Convenience group ($70-$101). Power lock group ($93-$176). Light group ($22-$37). Appearance protection group ($57). Comfort/Convenience: Air cond. ($624); w/auto-temp control ($687). Rear defroster, electric ($107). Fingertip speed control ($135). Illuminated entry system ($59). Power windows: base 4dr. ($211). Power seat ($173). Six-way power seats w/recliners ($229). Power twin comfort seats: base ($402). Tinted glass ($87). Autolamp on/off delay ($65). Leather-wrapped steering wheel ($45). Tilt steering wheel ($80). Electric clock ($23). Digital clock ($40-$63). Seatbelt chime ($23). Lighting and Mirrors: Cornering lamps ($49). Remote right mirror ($39). Lighted right visor vanity mirror ($38). Entertainment: AM/FM stereo radio ($88); w/8track tape player ($74) exc. base ($162); w/cassette ($87) exc. base ($174). AM/FM stereo search radio ($146) exc. base ($234); w/tape player ($233-$321). CB radio ($305). Power antenna ($48). Dual rear speakers ($37). Premium sound system ($116). Radio flexibility ($65). AM radio delete ($61 credit). Exterior: Coach vinyl roof: Brghm ($567). Full vinyl roof: base sed ($141). Glamour paint ($67). Tu-tone paint ($100-$134). Paint stripes ($34). Hood striping ($15). Pivoting front vent windows ($55). Rocker panel moldings: Colony Park ($27). Bodyside moldings ($44). Bumper rub strips ($46). Luggage rack: wag ($84). Lower bodyside protection ($46). Interior: Dual-facing rear seats: wagon ($146). Cloth twin comfort seats: wag ($39). Leather twin comfort seating ($361). Duraweave flight bench seats: wag ($54). Vinyl seat trim ($28). Deluxe seatbelts ($24). Trunk trim ($45). Wheels/Tires: Luxury wheel covers ($45-$72). Wire wheel covers ($112-$139). P215/75R14 WSW. P225/75R14 WSW. P205/75R15 WSW/puncture-resistant. Conventional spare.

HISTORY: Introduced: October 3, 1980. Model year production: 389,999. Calendar year production (U.S.): 363,970. Calendar year sales by U.S. dealers: 339,550. Model year sales by U.S. dealers: 354,335 (including 5,730 leftover Bobcats and 13,954 early '82 LN7 models).

Historical Footnotes: After a terrible 1980, the Lynx arrived to give Mercury new hope. First-year sales were heartening, totaling the highest figure since the Comet appeared back in 1960. Model year sales fell only slightly, as a result of the Lynx success. Calendar year sales and production both rose, as did model year production. Cougar XR7 scored far weaker and well below expectations, but the new smaller standard Cougar did better, finding many more buyers than it had a year earlier wearing a Monarch badge. Sales of the full-size Marquis fell, but not drastically. The new LN7, kin to Ford's EXP, debuted in April 1981 but as an early '82 model.

1982 MERCURY

A new four-door Lynx was introduced this year. So was a close-ratio manual transaxle option for both Lynx and the new LN7 two-seater, which arrived in April 1981. Cougar added a station wagon model, and an optional lightweight 232 cu. in. (3.8-liter) V-6 with aluminum heads and plastic rocker arms. Several models had a new lockup torque converter in the SelectShift automatic transmission. A high-output 302 cu. in. (5.0-liter) V-8 became standard on the Capri RS, optional on other Capris.

1982 Lynx GL Villager station wagon (JG)

LYNX — FOUR — A new five-door (actually four "people" doors) hatchback model joined the original two-door hatchback and four-door wagon, but appearance was the same as the original 1981 version. Lynx had quickly become Mercury's best seller. As for mileage, the EPA rating with the base 97.6 cu. in. (1.6- liter) four was 31 city and 47 highway. That CVH engine got a new reduced-restriction exhaust system. The gas tank grew to 11.3 gallons this year, and P165/80R13 tires replaced the former P155 size, but not much else changed. Not until mid- year, at any rate, when a number of mechanical improvements were announced. A high-output 1.6-liter engine was added to the option list in mid-year. So was a new sport close-ratio manual transaxle with higher numerical gear ratios in third and fourth gear, and smaller steps between second and third, and third and fourth. The H.O. powerplant had a higher-lift cam, less-restrictive muffler, stainless steel tubular exhaust header, less-restrictive air intake system, and larger carburetor venturi. Both engines came with a 3.59:1 drive axle ratio (3.31:1 with three-speed automatic).

1982 Lynx LS hatchback sedan (M)

LN7 — FOUR — Even though Lynx was essentially a carryover this year, the two-seater derived from its basic chassis was brand new. Wearing a "bubbleback" third-door treatment, the LN7 coupe displayed an aerodynamic design with 0.34 drag coefficient. The front-wheel drive chassis had four-wheel, fully independent suspension. Powertrain was the same as Lynx: 1.6- liter Compound Valve Hemispherical (CVH) OHC engine with four-speed manual transaxle (overdrive fourth). Mechanically, LN7 was identical to Ford's new EXP. Mercury's version was considered the more radical of the pair, though, as a result of its large wraparound "bubbleback" back window. Both EXP and LN7 had sizable wheel lips, wide bodyside moldings, and steep windshield angle. Large sloped taillamps wrapped around to a point on each quarter panel. Single rectangular halogen headlamps sat in black "eyebrow" housings. Park/signal lamps were mounted below the bumper strip. The LN7 grille consisted of 10 small slots (in two rows) in a sloping body-color panel, versus just two on EXP. Wide black bodyside moldings had argent accent striping. So did the soft black front and rear bumpers. LN7 had dual black door-mounted remote sport mirrors, and a single-color dual bodyside paint stripe. The slotted front fascia held a cat-head ornament, while rear pillars were vertically-louvered. Black paint treatment went on the front pillar, quarter window frame, door frame, and rocker panels. An ample standard equipment list included power brakes, electric rear defroster, AM radio, full performance instrumentation, power liftgate release, self-adjusting clutch linkage, throaty tuned exhaust (with manual shift), interval wipers, and full tinted glass. LN7 also had bright exposed dual exhausts, reclining low-back bucket seats with vinyl trim, tachometer, trip odometer, and temperature gauge. A console held the ammeter, oil pressure gauge and other indicators. Tires were P165/80R13 blackwall steel-belted radials with European-type wraparound tread pattern, on styled steel wheels with trim rings.

1982 Capri L hatchback coupe (CP)

CAPRI — FOUR/SIX/V-8 — Changes in Mercury's variant of Mustang were mainly mechanical this year. Both the optional 200 cu. in. (3.3- liter) inline six with SelectShift automatic, and 255 cu. in. (4.2-liter) V-8, had a new lockup torque converter for the automatic transmission. A new powerteam also was available: the 302 cu. in. (5.0-liter) V-8 with four-speed manual overdrive. That high-output 5.0-liter V-8 had new camshaft timing, low-restriction air cleaner with dual air inlets, large-venturi carburetor, and low-restriction sporty-tuned exhaust. Five-speed manual overdrive with the base 140 cu. in. (2.3-liter) four-cylinder engine later became optional in 45 states. A new base series was added, so the prior base model with console was now Capri L. Selection consisted of base, L, GS, RS, and Black Magic models. This year's gas tank held 15.4 gallons. Flash-to-pass was added to the stalk, and the new screw-on gas cap had a tether. Rear pillar louvers were now body-colored, except for the RS, which had black ones. A console with graphic warning display was now standard on all except the base model. Base Capris had a black and bright horizontal-style grille, front and rear bumpers with color-keyed soft urethane cover, extra-wide wraparound black bodyside molding with dual color-keyed center stripes, turbine wheel covers, upper bodyside pinstripes, black driver's side remote mirror, black and bright window frames, black cowl louver, and color-keyed hood louvers. High-back bucket seats had reclining seatbacks and pleated vinyl trim. Tires were P175/75R14 SBR blackwalls. Capri L had low-back bucket seats, a passenger-side visor vanity mirror, upgraded door trim, console with graphic warning display, and 'L' badge. GS included dual black remote mirrors, 'GS' badge, light group, four-spoke steering wheel with woodtone insert, and driver's door map pocket. Capri RS had a large non-functional hood scoop, black grille, black headlamp frames and windshield molding, dual black remote mirrors, upper bodyside dual accent tape striping, 'RS' tape identification on front fender, black window frame moldings, rear spoiler, and black "third door" window molding. Several revisions hit the RS later on, including a '5.0' badge on the side, dual bright tailpipe outlets, and Rallye suspension with TR performance package replacing the original handling suspension. It also came with Traction-Lok axle, P185/75R14 blackwalls, and power steering. Capri's Black Magic was offered again, with either black or white body color and gold accents. It had a small body- color hood scoop, gold paint on leading edge of grille, and other gold and black trim. Black Magic included a gold cat's head on the fender, and gold license plate frame at the back. Also included: a body-color rear spoiler, Michelin TRX tires on forged metric aluminum wheels with gold-color finish, and rallye suspension. A fuel economy calibration option (with four-cylinder) was added, to attract the economy-minded buyer. It had a feedback fuel system, four-speed manual shift, and 2.73:1 axle (to replace the standard 3.08:1).

1982 Zephyr sedan (CP)

ZEPHYR — FOUR/SIX/V-8 — Not much was new on the Zephyr compact, but the two-door sedan and station wagon were dropped. That left only a two- door (Z7) sport coupe and four-door sedan. Both came in base or GS trim. A new locking torque converter was added to the automatic transmission with optional inline six and 255 cu. in. (4.2-liter) V-8. That V-8 was available only with police and taxi packages. There was a new tethered gas cap and new deep-well trunk design. Tires were P175/75R14 blackwalls. Sedan interiors were upgraded to Z7 level by adding luxury door trim panels, high-gloss woodtone instrument panel appliques, and color-keyed seatbelts. A fuel economy calibration version of the base 140 cu. in. (2.3-liter) four replaced the standard 3.08:1 axle with a 2.73:1, as a no-extra-cost option with restricted options list. It was supposed to deliver 40 MPG on the highway, 25 overall in EPA estimates. Z7 again had the wrapover roof design with broad center pillar and thin rear pillar, no rocker panel moldings, Z7 ornament on the center pillar, and wraparound taillamps. Also standard: tinted rear window glass. GS models had dual accent stripes on the hood, protective bodyside moldings with integral partial wheel lip moldings, a 'GS' badge on the decklid, and dual bright remote mirrors. Rocker panel moldings were deleted from the four-door sedan with GS option.

1982 Cougar LS sedan (CP)

COUGAR — SIX/V-6 — For its second season in this Monarch-based body style, Cougar added a new station wagon model and lost the prospect of V-8 power. Wagons came in either GS or Villager form; sedans were either GS or LS. GS was now the basic level. Passenger capacity increased from five to six, because of the new standard Flight bench seat. Base engine was now the 200 cu. in. (3.3-liter) inline six. SelectShift automatic with locking torque converter was now standard. Manual shift was dropped. An AM radio with dual speakers was now standard. A tether was added to the gas cap, and the tank grew to 16 gallons. Flash-to-pass was added later to the steering column stalk control, while 'GS' badges went on fenders. A rear bumper sight shield was added. Hood and bodyside accent stripes were now standard, along with color-keyed vinyl- insert bodyside moldings. Cougar had a unitized body, strut- type front suspension with spring on lower arm, variable- ratio power-assist rack-and-pinion steering, and four-bar link rear suspension. Cougar LS added unique hood accent stripes that extended across the grille opening panel; bumper rub strips with white accent stripes; ribbed vinyl color-keyed bodyside molding; special bright wheel lip moldings; rear bumper guards; and luxury wheel covers with cat's head center insert. 'LS' badges went on front fenders. LS also added Twin Comfort lounge seats, whereas the GS had a Flight bench seat. The GS station wagon had a bodyside paint stripe in a straight- through design with no kickup, which did not extend onto the liftgate. The Villager wagon deleted the hood accent stripes and had medium rosewood woodtone bodyside paneling appliques. 'Villager' script went on the liftgate and the 'GS' badge was deleted from front fenders. Options included an all-new 232 cu. in. (3.8-liter) V-6, power lock group, and extended-range fuel tank. Options dropped: the floor shifter, console, mud/stone deflectors, and radio flexibility.

1982 Cougar XR-7 Sports Coupe (CP)

COUGAR XR-7 — SIX/V-6/V-8 — No longer available on this year's personal-luxury XR7 was the 302 cu. in. V-8 engine. Three choices were offered, though: base 200 cu. in. (3.3-liter) inline six, new optional aluminum-head 232 cu. in. (3.8-liter) V-6, and 255 cu. in. (4.2-liter) V-8. The two-door hardtop body came in GS and upscale LS form, as the former base model dropped out. Gas tanks grew from 18 to 21 gallons. Four-speed automatic overdrive transmission was standard with the V-6 or V-8, while the base inline six had SelectShift three-speed automatic with a lockup torque converter clutch. Looking at appearance changes, black vinyl-insert bodyside moldings replaced the former color-keyed moldings. Black bumper stripes with white accent stripes replaced bright rub strips. A new half-vinyl roof design with wide black accent and wrapover molding arrived this year. That molding blended into the door belt moldings to give a unified look. The analog clock was now quartz-type. New options included a Tripminder computer. XR7 GS had a vertical-bar grille with bright surround molding, color-keyed soft bumper covering with black rub strips (including white accent stripes), quad rectangular halogen headlamps, amber wraparound park/signal lamps, hood/decklid accent stripes, and upper bodyside paint stripe. Large vertical-theme taillamps had integral backup lenses. Twin Comfort lounge seats had fold-down center armrests and dual recliners. Power brakes and variable-ratio rack-and- pinion steering were standard. Also standard: AM radio, halogen headlamps, and P195/75R14 SBR whitewalls. LS added dual bright remote window-frame-mounted mirrors and luxury wheel covers, plus power windows and tinted glass.

1982 Marquis Brougham sedan (CP)

MARQUIS — V-8 — Full-size Mercury models didn't look much different, but dropped their fender louvers. The former bumper-slot grille extensions were deleted too, replaced by slotless bumpers. Decklid lock covers were replaced with a bezel and ornament. A 302 cu. in. (5.0-liter) V-8 became standard on the Brougham and Grand Marquis four-door sedans this year. Base engine on other models was the 255 cu. in. (4.2-liter) V-8. The 351 cu. in. high-output V-8 was now available only with the police package. All models had four-speed automatic overdrive transmission. AM radios now included two instrument-panel speakers. Electric clocks became quartz. The CB radio option was deleted, as were the radio flexibility option and manual load levelers. One noteworthy new option was a Tripminder computer, which had a multi-function digital clock. It could also compute and display such trip-related information as distance traveled, average speed, instantaneous and trip- average fuel economy, and gallons of fuel consumed. Also joining the option list: a Class II Trailer Towing package, rated up to 3,500 pounds. As before, Marquis had a bright vertical-bar theme grille, front bumper guards, quad rectangular halogen headlamps with bright headlamp/parking lamp surround moldings, and stand-up hood ornament. Wraparound front parking lamps had integral side markers. Bodies also showed a wide center pillar, rear door window divider bar, black lower back panel with vertical backup lamps adjacent to the recessed license plate bracket, and horizontal wraparound taillamps with integral side marker lights. Marquis rode P205/75R14 steel-belted radial whitewalls and carried a mini spare tire. Marquis Brougham added a rear half vinyl roof, coach lamps, hood accent stripes, 'Brougham' decklid nameplate, deluxe wheel covers, and wide bright lower bodyside molding with quarter panel extensions. Inside were Twin Comfort lounge seats in cloth/vinyl. Four-door Broughams had a standard 302 V-8 with variable venturi carburetor. Also standard: an AM/FM stereo radio and power windows. Grand Marquis had upper bodyside accent stripes, wide bright/black lower

bodyside molding, black painted rocker panel flange, nameplate on rear roof pillar and decklid, rear bumper guards, tinted glass, dual-beam dome light, and Twin Comfort seats in luxury cloth. Grand Marquis four-doors carried the 302 V-8. There was still a base Marquis station wagon, and a Colony Park wagon with full-length bodyside rosewood woodtone applique. Wagons had the 302 V-8 and P215/75R14 SBR whitewalls.

I.D. DATA: Mercury's 17-symbol Vehicle Identification Number (VIN) was stamped on a metal tab fastened to the instrument panel, visible through the windshield. Symbols one to three indicates manufacturer, make and vehicle type: '1ME' Mercury passenger car. The fourth symbol ('B') denotes restraint system. Next comes a letter 'P', followed by two digits that indicate body type: Model Number, as shown in left column of tables below. (Example: '71' Zephyr four- door sedan.) Symbol eight indicates engine type: '2' L498 2Bbl.; 'A' L4-140 2Bbl.; 'B' or 'T' L6200 1Bbl.; '3' V6232 2Bbl.; 'D' V8255 2Bbl.; 'F' V8302 2Bbl.; 'G' V8351 2Bbl. Next is a check digit. Symbol ten indicates model year ('C' 1982). Symbol eleven is assembly plant: 'A' Atlanta, GA; 'F' Dearborn, MI; 'R' San Jose, CA; 'G' Chicago; 'H' Lorain, Ohio; 'K' Kansas City, MO; 'X' St. Thomas, Ontario; 'Z' St. Louis, MO; 'W' Wayne, MI; or Edison, NJ. The final six digits make up the sequence number, starting with 600001. A Vehicle Certification Label on the left front door lock face panel or door pillar shows the manufacturer, month and year of manufacture, GVW, GAWR, certification statement, VIN, and codes for such items as body type, color, trim, axle, transmission, and special order information.

LYNX (FOUR)

Model Number	Body/Style Number	Body Type & Seating	Factory Price	Shipping Weight	Production Total
63	61D	3-dr. Hatch-4P	5502	1924	Note 1
64	58D	5-dr. Hatch-4P	5709	1986	Note 1
63	61D	3-dr. L Hatch-4P	6159	1932	Note 1
64	58D	5-dr. L Hatch-4P	6376	1994	Note 1
65	74D	4-dr. L Sta Wag-4P	6581	2040	Note 1
63/60Z	61D	3-dr. GL Hatch-4P	6471	1927	Note 1
64/60Z	58D	5-dr. GL Hatch-4P	6688	1989	Note 1
65/60Z	74D	4-dr. GL Sta Wag-4P	6899	2040	Note 1
63/602	61D	3-dr. GS Hatch-4P	7257	1963	Note 1
64/602	58D	5-dr. GS Hatch-4P	7474	2025	Note 1
65/602	74D	4-dr. GS Sta Wag-4P	7594	2062	Note 1
63/603	61D	3-dr. LS Hatch-4P	7762	1952	Note 1
64/603	58D	5-dr. LS Hatch-4P	7978	2014	Note 1
65/603	74D	4-dr. LS Sta Wag-4P	8099	2052	Note 1
63/936	61D	3-dr. RS Hatch-4P	6790	1961	Note 1

Note 1: Total Lynx production, 54,611 three-door hatchbacks, 40,713 five-door hatchbacks, and 23,835 four-door liftgate station wagons.

LN7 (FOUR)

61	67D	3-dr. Hatch Cpe-2P	7787	2059	35,147

CAPRI (FOUR/SIX)

67	61D	3-dr. Fastbk-4P	6711/7245	N/A	Note 2
67	61D	3-dr. L Fastbk-4P	7245/7869	2591/ --	Note 2

CAPRI BLACK MAGIC (FOUR/SIX)

67	61D	3-dr. Fastbk-4P	7946/8570	2562/2676	Note 2

CAPRI RS (V-8)

67	61D	3-dr. Fastbk-4P	8107	2830	Note 2

CAPRI GS (FOUR/SIX)

68	61H	3-dr. Fastbk-4P	7432/8056	2590/2704	Note 2

Note 2: Total Capri production was 31,525, plus 4,609 GS-level models.

Capri Engine Note: Six-cylinder prices include cost of the required automatic transmission. A 255 cu. in. V-8 engine cost $70 more than the six; a 302 V-8, $189-$239 more.

ZEPHYR (FOUR/SIX)

71	54D	4-dr. Sed-5P	6411/7035	2630/2750	31,698
71/602	54D	4-dr. GS Sed-5P	6734/7358	2643/2763	Note 3

ZEPHYR Z-7 (FOUR/SIX)

72	36R	2-dr. Spt Cpe-5P	6319/6943	2627/2747	7,394
72/602	36R	2-dr. GS Cpe-5P	6670/7294	2637/2757	Note 3

Note 3: Production of GS models is included in basic totals.

Zephyr Engine Note: Six-cylinder prices include cost of the required automatic transmission. A V-8 cost $70 more than the six.

COUGAR (SIX/V-6)

76	66D	2-dr. GS Sed-6P	7983/8053	2937/2941	6,984
77	54D	4-dr. GS Sed-6P	8158/8228	2980/2983	30,672
78	74D	4-dr. GS Wag-6P	8216/8286	3113/3116	19,294
76	66D	2-dr. LS Sed-6P	8415/8485	2973/2976	Note 4
77	54D	4-dr. LS Sed-6P	8587/8657	3022/3025	Note 4

Cougar Engine Note: V-6 engine required power steering (not incl. in above prices).

COUGAR XR-7 (SIX/V-8)

Model Number	Body/Style Number	Body Type & Seating	Factory Price	Shipping Weight	Production Total
90	66D	2-dr. GS Cpe-4P	9094/9235	3152/3289	16,867
90/60H	66D	2-dr. LS Cpe-4P	9606/9847	3161/3298	Note 4

Note 4: Production of LS models is included in GS totals.

Engine Note: A V-6 cost the same as a V-8 under XR7 hoods.

MARQUIS (V-8)

81	54H	4-dr. Sedan-6P	8674	3734	9,454
87	74H	4-dr. 2S Sta Wag-6P	9198	3880	2,487

MARQUIS BROUGHAM (V-8)

82	66K	2-dr. Sedan-6P	9490	3693	2,833
83	54K	4-dr. Sedan-6P	9767	3776	15,312

MARQUIS COLONY PARK (V-8)

88	74K	4-dr. 2S Sta Wag-6P	10252	3890	8,004

GRAND MARQUIS (V-8)

84	66L	2-dr. Sedan-6P	10188	3724	6,149
85	54L	4-dr. Sedan-6P	10456	3809	32,918

FACTORY PRICE AND WEIGHT NOTE: Cougar prices and weights to left of slash are for inline six-cylinder, to right for V-6 engine. For Capri/Zephyr, prices/weights to left of slash are for four-cylinder, to right for V-6.

ENGINE DATA: BASE FOUR (Lynx, LN7): Inline. Overhead cam. Four-cylinder. Cast iron block and aluminum head. Displacement: 97.6 cu. in. (1.6 liters). Bore & stroke: 3.15 x 3.13 in. Compression ratio: 8.8:1. Brake horsepower: 70 at 4600 R.P.M. Torque: 89 lbs.-ft. at 3000 R.P.M. Five main bearings. Hydraulic valve lifters. Carburetor: 2Bbl. Motorcraft 740. VIN Code: 2. BASE FOUR (Capri, Zephyr): Inline. Overhead cam. Four-cylinder. Cast iron block and head. Displacement: 140 cu. in. (2.3 liters). Bore & stroke: 3.78 x 3.13 in. Compression ratio: 9.0:1. Brake horsepower: 86 at 4600 R.P.M. Torque: 117 lbs.-ft. at 2600 R.P.M. Five main bearings. Hydraulic valve lifters. Carburetor: 2Bbl. Holley 6500 or Motorcraft 5200. VIN Code: A. BASE SIX (Cougar, XR7); OPTIONAL (Capri, Zephyr): Inline. OHV. Six-cylinder. Cast iron block and head. Displacement: 200 cu. in. (3.3 liters). Bore & stroke: 3.68 x 3.13 in. Compression ratio: 8.6:1. Brake horsepower: 87 at 3800 R.P.M. Torque: 151-154 lbs.-ft. at 1400 R.P.M. Seven main bearings. Hydraulic valve lifters. Carburetor: 1Bbl. Holley 1946. VIN Code: B or T. OPTIONAL V-6 (Cougar, XR7): 90-degree, overhead valve V-6. Cast iron block and aluminum head. Displacement: 232 cu. in. (3.8 liters). Bore & stroke: 3.80 x 3.40 in. Compression ratio: 8.65:1. Brake horsepower: 112 at 4000 R.P.M. Torque: 175 lbs.-ft. at 2000 R.P.M. Four main bearings. Hydraulic valve lifters. Carburetor: 2Bbl. Motorcraft 2150. VIN Code: 3. BASE V-8 (Marquis); OPTIONAL (Capri, Zephyr, XR7): 90-degree, overhead valve V-8. Cast iron block and head. Displacement: 255 cu. in. (4.2 liters). Bore & stroke: 3.68 x 3.00 in. Compression ratio: 8.2:1. Brake horsepower: 120-122 at 3400 R.P.M. Torque: 205-209 lbs.-ft. at 1600-2400 R.P.M. Five main bearings. Hydraulic valve lifters. Carburetor: 2Bbl. Motorcraft 2150 or 7200VV. VIN Code: D. BASE V-8 (Marquis Brougham, Grand Marquis 4dr.); OPTIONAL (Marquis): 90-degree, overhead valve V-8. Cast iron block and head. Displacement: 302 cu. in. (5.0 liters). Bore & stroke: 4.00 x 3.00 in. Compression ratio: 8.4:1. Brake horsepower: 132 at 3400 R.P.M. Torque: 236 lbs.-ft. at 1800 R.P.M. Five main bearings. Hydraulic valve lifters. Carburetor: 2Bbl. Motorcraft 2150A or 7200VV. VIN Code: F. OPTIONAL V-8 (Capri): High-output version of 302 cu. in. V-8 above Compression ratio: 8.3:1. Horsepower: 157 at 4200 R.P.M. Torque: 240 lbs.-ft. at 2400 R.P.M. POLICE V-8 (Marquis): 90-degree, overhead valve V-8. Cast iron block and head. Displacement: 351 cu. in. (5.8 liters). Bore & stroke: 4.00 x 3.50 in. Compression ratio: 8.3:1. Brake horsepower: 165 at 3600 R.P.M. Torque: 285 lbs.-ft. at 2200 R.P.M. Five main bearings. Hydraulic valve lifters. Carburetor: VV. VIN Code: G.

CHASSIS DATA: Wheelbase: (Lynx/LN7) 94.2 in.; (Capri) 100.4 in.; (Zephyr) 105.5 in.; (Cougar) 105.5 in.; (XR7) 108.4 in.; (Marquis) 114.3 in. Overall Length: (Lynx) 163.9 in.; (Lynx lift) 165.0 in.; (LN7) 170.3 in.; (Capri) 179.1 in.; (Zephyr) 195.5 in.; (Z7) 197.4 in.; (Cougar) 196.5 in.; (XR7) 200.4 in.; (Marquis) 212.3 in.; (Marquis wag) 218.0 in. Height: (Lynx) 53.3 in.; (LN7) 50.5 in.; (Capri) 51.4 in.; (Zephyr) 52.9 in.; (Z7) 51.7 in.; (Cougar) 53.0 in.; (Cougar wag) 54.3 in.; (XR7) 53.2 in.; (Marquis) 55.1 in.; (Marquis wag) 57.2 in. Width: (Lynx/LN7) 65.9 in.; (Capri) 69.1 in.; (Zephyr) 71.0 in.; (Cougar) 71.0 in.; (XR7) 74.1 in.; (Marquis) 77.5 in.; (Marquis wag) 79.3 in. Front Tread: (Lynx/LN7) 54.7 in.; (Capri) 56.6 in.; (Zephyr/Cougar) 56.6 in.; (XR7) 58.1 in.; (Marquis) 62.2 in. Rear Tread: (Lynx/LN7) 56.0 in.; (Capri) 57.0 in.; (Zephyr/Cougar) 57.0 in.; (XR7) 57.0 in.; (Marquis) 62.0 in. Standard Tires: (Lynx/LN7) P165/80R13; (Capri) P175/75R14; (Zephyr/Cougar) P175/75R14 SBR; (XR7) P195/75R14 SBR WSW; (Marquis) P205/75R14 SBR; (Marquis wag) P215/75R14.

TECHNICAL: Transmission: Four-speed manual standard on Lynx. Gear ratios: (1st) 3.58:1; (2nd) 2.05:1; (3rd) 1.21:1 or 1.36:1; (4th) 0.81:1 or 0.95:1; (Rev) 3.46:1. Four-speed floor shift standard on Capri/Zephyr four: (1st) 3.98:1; (2nd) 2.14:1; (3rd) 1.42:1; (4th) 1.00:1; (Rev) 3.99:1. Four-speed overdrive floor shift standard on Capri V-8: (1st) 3.07:1; (2nd) 1.72:1; (3rd) 1.00:1; (4th) 0.70:1; (Rev) 3.07:1. Capri four-cylinder five-speed: (1st) 3.72:1; (2nd) 2.23:1; (3rd) 1.48:1; (4th) 1.00:1; (5th) 0.76:1; (Rev) 3.59:1. SelectShift three-speed automatic standard on Cougar and XR7 six, optional on others. Gear ratios: (1st) 2.46:1 or 2.47:1; (2nd) 1.46:1 or 1.47:1; (3rd) 1.00:1; (Rev) 2.11:1 to 2.19:1. Lynx three-speed automatic: (1st) 2.79:1; (2nd) 1.61:1; (3rd) 1.00:1; (Rev) 1.97:1. Four-speed overdrive automatic on XR7/Marquis: (1st) 2.40:1; (2nd) 1.47:1; (3rd) 1.00:1; (4th) 0.67:1; (Rev) 2.00:1. Standard final drive ratio: (Lynx/LN7) 3.59:1 w/4spd, 3.31:1 w/auto.; (Capri four) 3.08:1 w/4spd or auto., 3.45:1 w/5spd; (Capri six/V-8) 2.73:1; (Capri V-8 w/4spd auto.) 3.08:1; (Zephyr) 3.08:1 exc. 2.73:1 w/six or V-8; (Cougar) 2.73:1 w/six, 2.47:1 with V-6; (XR7) 2.73:1 w/six, 3.08:1 with V-6/V-8. (Marquis) 3.08:1 exc. 2.73:1 w/police 351 V-8. Steering: (Marquis) recirculating ball; (others) rack and pinion. Front Suspension: (Lynx/LN7) MacPherson strut-mounted coil springs w/lower control arms and stabilizer bar; (Capri) modified MacPherson struts w/coil springs and anti-sway bar; (Zephyr/Cougar) MacPherson struts w/coil springs mounted on lower control arm and anti-sway bar; (Marquis) coil springs with long/short Aarms and anti-sway bar. Rear Suspension: (Lynx/LN7) independent trailing arms w/modified MacPherson struts and coil springs on lower control arms; (Capri/Zephyr/Cougar/Marquis) four-link w/coil springs; (XR7) four-link with coil springs and anti-sway bar. Brakes: Front disc, rear drum. Ignition: Electronic. Body construction: (Marquis) separate body and frame; (others) unibody. Fuel tank: (Lynx/LN7) 11.3 gal.; (Capri) 15.4 gal.; (Zephyr) 16 gal.; (Cougar) 16 gal.; (XR7) 21 gal.; (Marquis) 20 gal.

DRIVETRAIN OPTIONS: Engines: 200 cu. in. six: Capri/Zephyr ($213). 232 cu. in. V-6: Cougar ($70); Cougar XR7 ($241). 255 cu. in. V-8: Capri/Zephyr ($283); Capri RS ($57 credit); Cougar XR7 ($241). 302 cu. in. V-8: Capri ($402-$452); Marquis sedan ($59). Transmission/Differential: Five-speed manual trans.: Capri ($196). Automatic transaxle: Lynx/LN7 ($411). Auto. transmission.: Capri/Zephyr ($411). Floor shift lever: Zephyr ($49). Traction-Lok differential: Capri/Zephyr/Cougar/XR7 ($76); Marquis ($80). Optional axle ratio: Lynx/LN7/Capri/Zephyr (NC). Brakes & Steering: Power brakes: Lynx ($93). Power steering: Lynx/LN7/Capri ($190); Zephyr/Cougar ($195). Suspension: H.D. susp.: Zephyr/Cougar ($24); Marquis/Cougar XR7 ($26). Handling susp.: Lynx ($41); Capri ($50); Zephyr ($52); Marquis ($49). Other: H.D. battery ($24-$26). H.D. alternator: LN7 ($27). Extended-range gas tank: Zephyr/Cougar ($46). Engine block heater ($17-$18). Trailer towing pkg., medium duty: Marquis ($200-$251). California emission system ($46-$65). High- altitude emissions (NC).

LYNX CONVENIENCE/APPEARANCE OPTIONS: Option Packages: Villager woodtone pkg.: GL/GS/RS wag ($259). Instrument group ($87). Appearance protection group ($55). Light group ($43). Comfort/Convenience: Air conditioner ($611). Speed control ($151). Remote liftgate release ($30). Tinted glass ($82); windshield only ($32). Digital clock ($57). Interval wipers ($48). Rear wiper/washer ($117). Dual remote sport mirrors ($66). Entertainment: AM radio delete ($61 credit). AM/FM radio ($76). AM/FM stereo radio ($106); w/cassette or 8track player ($184) exc. LS ($78). Premium sound ($105). Dual rear speakers ($39). Exterior: Flip-up/open air roof ($183-$276). Glamour paint ($61) exc. RS. Tu-tone paint ($122) exc. RS. Front vent windows ($60). Narrow bodyside moldings ($45). Bumper guards, front or rear ($26). Bumper rub strips: base/L ($41). Luggage rack ($93). Roof air deflector ($29). Lower bodyside protection ($68). Interior: Console ($111). Low-back reclining bucket seats ($33-$98). High-back reclining bucket seats ($65). Cloth/vinyl seat trim ($29). Vinyl trim: GS (NC). Shearling/leather seat trim ($59-$138). Deluxe seatbelts ($24). Wheels/Tires: Aluminum wheels ($232-$329). P165/80R13 WSW ($58).

LN7 CONVENIENCE/APPEARANCE OPTIONS: Comfort/Convenience: Appearance protection group ($48). Air conditioner ($611). Fingertip speed control ($151). Entertainment: AM/FM radio ($76). AM/FM stereo radio ($106); w/cassette or 8track player ($184). Premium sound ($105). AM radio delete ($37 credit). Exterior: Flip-up open air roof ($276). Glamour paint ($51). Tu-tone paint ($122). Luggage rack ($93). Lower bodyside protection ($68). Interior: Vinyl high-back reclining seats (NC). Cloth/vinyl seat trim ($29). Leather seat trim ($138). Shearling/leather seat trim ($138). Wheels/Tires: Cast aluminum spoke wheels ($232). P165/80R13 RWL ($72).

CAPRI CONVENIENCE/APPEARANCE OPTIONS: Option Packages: TR performance pkg. ($483-$533). Light group ($49). Appearance protection group ($48). Power lock group ($139). Comfort/Convenience: Air cond. ($676). Rear defroster, electric ($124). Fingertip speed control ($155). Power windows ($165). Tinted glass ($88). Leather-wrapped steering wheel ($55). Tilt steering wheel ($95). Interval wipers ($48). Rear wiper/washer ($101). Remote right mirror ($41). Entertainment: AM/FM radio ($76). AM/FM stereo radio ($106); w/8track or cassette player ($184). Premium sound system ($105). Dual rear speakers ($39). AM radio delete ($61 credit). Exterior: TRoof ($1021). Flip-up/open air roof ($276). Carriage roof ($734). Full vinyl roof ($137). Glamour paint ($54). Tu-tone paint ($66-$124). Gold accent stripes ($62). Hood scoop ($72). Liftgate louvers ($165). Rocker panel moldings ($33). Lower bodyside protection ($41). Interior: Recaro bucket seats ($834). Cloth/vinyl seats: base ($23). Cloth/vinyl accent trim: L/RS ($34). Leather/vinyl seats ($409). Wheels and Tires: Wire wheel covers ($91). Cast aluminum wheels ($348). Styled steel wheels w/trim rings ($72). P175/75R14 WSW ($66). P185/75R14 BSW ($30); WSW ($66-$96); RWL ($85-$116).

ZEPHYR/COUGAR CONVENIENCE/APPEARANCE OPTIONS: Option Packages: Cougar Villager option: wag ($282). Power lock group: Cougar ($138-$184). Instrument cluster: Zephyr ($100). Cold weather group: Cougar ($77). Appearance protection group ($57-$59). Light group ($49-$51). Comfort/Convenience: Air cond. ($676). Rear defroster, electric ($124). Fingertip speed control ($155). Illuminated ntry ($68). Power windows ($165-$235). Power door locks: Zephyr ($106-$152). Four-way power seat ($139). Six-way power seats: Cougar ($196). Remote decklid release: Zephyr ($32). Tinted glass ($88). Leather-wrapped steering wheel: Cougar ($55). Tilt steering ($95). Quartz clock ($32). Interval wipers ($48). Liftgate wiper/washer: wagon ($99). Lighting and Mirrors: Cornering lamps: Cougar ($59). Map light: Cougar ($15). Trunk light: Zephyr ($7). Left remote mirror: Zephyr ($22). Dual bright remote mirrors: Zephyr ($65). Right remote mirror: Cougar ($60). Lighted right visor vanity mirror ($46); pair ($91). Entertainment: AM/FM radio ($54). AM/FM stereo radio ($85); w/8track or cassette player ($172). Twin rear speakers: Zephyr ($39). Premium sound system ($105). AM radio delete ($61 credit). Exterior: Flip-up open air roof ($276). Full or half vinyl roof ($137-$140). Glamour paint ($63). Tu-tone paint ($82- $105). Pivoting front vent windows ($63). Two-way liftgate: wag ($105). Rocker panel moldings: Zephyr Z7/GS ($33). Protective bodyside moldings: Cougar ($49). Wide bodyside moldings: Zephyr Z7 ($59). Bumper guards, rear ($28). Bumper rub strips ($50). Luggage rack: wagon ($115). Lower bodyside protection ($41). Interior: Console: Zephyr ($191). Twin comfort seats: Cougar ($204). Cloth/vinyl seat trim: Zephyr ($29). Vinyl seat trim ($29). Leather trim: Cougar LS ($409). Flight bench seat: Zephyr (NC). Floor mats: Zephyr ($13). Wheels/Tires: Luxury wheel covers: Cougar ($49). Wire wheel covers ($104-$152). Styled steel wheels: Zephyr ($54); w/trim rings ($107). Cast aluminum wheels: Cougar ($348-$396). P175/75R14 WSW ($66). P185/75R14 BSW: Cougar ($38). P185/75R14 WSW ($104) exc. wagon ($66). P185/75R14 RWL: Cougar ($121) exc. wagon ($83). TR BSW on alum. wheels ($534-$583). Conventional spare ($51).

COUGAR XR7 CONVENIENCE/APPEARANCE OPTIONS: Option Packages: Appearance protection group ($51). Light group ($35). Power lock group ($138). Comfort/Convenience: Air cond. ($676); auto-temp ($754). Rear defroster ($126). Fingertip speed control ($155). Illuminated entry system ($68). Keyless entry ($277). Tripminder computer ($215-$261). Autolamp on/off delay ($73). Tinted glass ($88). Power windows ($165). Six-way power driver's seat ($198). Auto. parking brake release ($12). Leather-wrapped steering wheel ($51). Tilt steering wheel ($95). Electronic instrument cluster ($367). Diagnostic warning lights ($59). Seatbelt chimes ($27). Digital clock ($46). Interval wipers ($48). Lighting and Mirrors: Cornering lamps ($59). Remote right mirror ($60). Lighted right visor vanity mirrors ($91). Entertainment: AM/FM radio ($54). AM/FM stereo radio ($85); w/8track or cassette player ($172). AM/FM stereo search radio ($232); w/8track or cassette ($318). Power antenna ($55). Dual rear speakers ($39). Premium sound system ($133- $167). AM radio delete ($61 credit). Exterior: Carriage roof ($885). Flip-up open-air roof ($276). Vinyl rear half roof ($187). Vinyl roof delete ($156 credit). Glamour paint ($80). Tu-tone paint ($112). Pivoting front vent windows ($63). Rocker panel moldings ($33). Lower bodyside protection ($54). Interior: Bucket seats w/console (NC). Recaro bucket seats w/console ($523). Leather seat trim ($409). Vinyl seat trim ($28). Trunk trim ($48). Wheels/Tires: Wire wheel covers ($99-$152). Luxury wheel covers: GS ($54). Self-sealing tires ($106). TR tires on alum. wheels ($589-$643). Conventional spare ($51).

MARQUIS CONVENIENCE/APPEARANCE OPTIONS: Option Packages: Grand Marquis decor: Colony Park ($555). Convenience group ($90-$116). Power lock group ($106-$201). Light group ($27-$43). Appearance protection group ($67). Comfort/Convenience: Air cond. ($695); w/auto-temp control ($761). Rear defroster, electric ($124). Fingertip speed control ($155). Illuminated entry system ($68). Power windows ($240). Six-way power flight bench seat: base ($198); reclining ($262). Six-way power twin comfort driver's seat w/recliners ($262); driver and passenger ($460). Tinted glass ($102). Autolamp on/off delay ($73). Leather-wrapped steering wheel ($51). Tilt steering wheel ($95). Tripminder computer ($215-$293). Quartz clock ($32). Digital clock ($46-$78). Seatbelt chime ($27). Lighting and Mirrors: Cornering lamps ($55). Remote right mirror ($43). Lighted right visor vanity mirrors ($91). Entertainment: AM/FM stereo radio ($85-$172); w/8track or cassette tape player ($87-$172). AM/FM stereo search radio ($146-$232); w/8track or cassette ($233-$318). Power antenna ($55). Dual rear speakers ($41). Premium sound system ($133- $167). AM radio delete ($61 credit). AM/FM delete ($152 credit). Exterior: Formal vinyl coach roof: Brghm/Grand 4dr. ($638). Full vinyl roof: base sed ($165). Vinyl roof delete ($71 credit). Glamour paint ($77). Tu-tone paint ($117-$156). Dual accent bodyside stripes ($39). Hood striping ($17). Pivoting front vent windows ($63). Rocker panel moldings ($32). Vinyl- insert bodyside moldings ($51). Bumper guards, rear ($30). Bumper rub strips ($52). Luggage rack ($104). Lower bodyside protection ($39-$52). Interior: Dual-facing rear seats: wagon ($167). Twin comfort lounge seats: base ($139). All-vinyl seat trim: base ($28). Cloth seat trim: wag ($41). Duraweave trim: wag ($62). Leather seating: Grand Marquis ($412). Dual seatback recliners ($65). Trunk trim ($49). Wheels/Tires: Luxury wheel covers ($52-$82). Wire wheel overs ($123-$152). Cast aluminum wheels ($355-$384). P215/75R14 WSW ($36). P225/75R14 WSW ($36-$73). P205/75R15 WSW ($11-$47); puncture-resistant ($112-$148). Conventional spare ($51).

HISTORY: Intro: September 24, 1981 except LN7, April 9, 1981. Production: 380,506. Calendar year production (U.S.): 315,798. Calendar year sales by U.S. dealers: 327,140. Model year sales by U.S. dealers: 319,697 (not including 13,954 early '82 LN7 models sold during 1981 model year).

Historical Footnotes: Sales slumped again this model year, but not so dramatically as in 1981. Mercury's 6.6 percent decline was well under the 16 percent plunge experienced by the domestic auto industry as a whole. The full-size Marquis found more buyers this year, up by almost one-third. Lynx sales proved disappointing, falling well behind the slow-moving EXP, even when the new high-output engine became available. Some observers felt the two-seater's performance didn't match its sporty looks, accounting for lack of buyer interest. In a *Road & Track* test, LN7 took 15 seconds to hit 60 MPH, which wasn't quite sparkling performance for a sporty lightweight. Zephyr and XR-7 sales fell sharply, while the standard Cougar gained a little. Lynx production dropped quite a bit, causing Ford to plan a shutdown of its San Jose, California plant in 1983.

1983 MERCURY

A total restyle hit XR-7, which changed its name to, simply, Cougar. Its aerodynamic design managed a 0.40 drag coefficient. A bubble-back hatchback was added to Capri, along with more engine choices. Two vehicles now carried the Marquis badge: a derivation of the former four-door Cougar on 105.5 inch wheelbase, and Grand Marquis with a 114.3 in. wheelbase. The smaller one had nitrogen-pressurized gas shocks and new sheetmetal. The new front-drive Topaz, replacing the Zephyr, arrived in spring 1983 as an early '84 model.

1983 Lynx R8 hatchback coupe (OCW)

LYNX — FOUR — Mercury's best seller took on a new grille and striping this year, offering a broader selection of engines. The powertrain list included the base 1.6-liter carbureted four with four-speed manual or three-speed automatic; a fuel- injected 1.6; or high-output 1.6. A simplified model lineup included L, GS and LS. Base models and GL were dropped. The new grille had thin vertical bars, as before, but only two wider vertical divider bars (formerly five). The grille emblem moved from the side to the center. Otherwise, appearance was similar to 1982. Interiors were revised, with standard full-width cloth seat trim. Hatchbacks had a removable rear package shelf. Manual-shift models added an upshift indicator light. A high-mileage model (with economy gearing) was available everywhere except California. All except L now had a standard remote-locking fuel filler door. The fuel tank grew to 13 gallons. Standard equipment on Lynx L included four-speed manual shift, P165/80R13 SBR BSW tires on semi-styled steel wheels, four-spoke color-keyed steering wheel, compact spare tire, cloth/vinyl high-back bucket front seats (folding rear bench seat), four-speed heater/defroster, consolette, cargo area cover, and dome lamp. Bright bumpers showed black end caps. Wagons had power brakes. Lynx GS added a black front air dam, AM radio, passenger assist handles, carpeted lower door trim panels, locking gas filler door, power hatch release, dual visor vanity mirrors, two-color upper bodyside accent paint stripes, reclining cloth/vinyl low-back bucket seats with head restraints, and wide bodyside moldings with argent accent stripe. Rocker panel moldings were deleted. Black bumper end caps and rub strips had argent accent stripes. Lynx LS included styled steel wheels, an AM/FM stereo radio, dual remote sport mirrors, velour cloth low-back bucket seats, burled walnut appliques, digital clock, console with graphic warning display, electric back window defroster, and instrument group. The three-door RS now carried a fuel- injected four and five-speed gearbox, plus TR sport suspension and wheels, and Michelin P165/70R365 blackwall TRX tires. Also included with RS: an AM radio, black wheel spats, tape decals, front/rear spoilers, dual black remote sport mirrors, cloth reclining sport bucket seats, black bumper guards and end caps, black console, foglamps, locking fuel filler door, instrument group, and black steering wheel. Wide black bodyside moldings had argent accent stripes. Black moldings were used on the rocker panels, drip, belt, wheel lip, windshield, windows, and lower back panel surround. Blackout treatment extended to the grille, louvered center pillar applique, front roof pillar, wheel housings, dash and license plate area.

LN7 — FOUR — In an attempt to defeat claims of substandard performance, the two-passenger LN7 could now have a high- output version of the CVH 1.6-liter four, hooked to a five- speed manual gearbox. A multi-port fuel-injected four also was available, to improve idling and low-end torque. New options included a four-way adjustable driver's seat and shift indicator light. The gas tank was now 13-gallon. Standard LN7 equipment included the basic 98 cu. in. four with five-speed manual shift, P165/80R13 SBR BSW tires, power brakes, AM radio, C-pillar louvers, black sport steering wheel, interval wipers, digital clock, and electric rear defroster. Also standard: a console, cargo area cover, remote-lock fuel filler door, tachometer, tinted glass, power liftgate release, dual remote black mirrors, and color-keyed scuff plates. Black windshield surround, backlight and wide bodyside moldings were used. Black bumpers had argent stripe and soft fascia. Black paint treatment was evident on the A-pillar, quarter windows, door frames, rocker panels, and back license plate area. Sport models had an AM/FM stereo radio; Grand Sport and RS, an AM/FM stereo with cassette player. Models with the TR package had P165/70Rx365 Michelin BSW tires.

CAPRI — FOUR/V-6/V-8 — Mercury's version of the ponycar distanced itself from Mustang with a new "bubbleback" hatchback design. This year's grille used only one bright horizontal divider bar to separate the pattern into an upper and lower section, unlike the previous multi-bar form. Wraparound taillamps now reached the license plate recess. New standard equipment included a cargo cover. Instruments got more legible graphics. Under Capri hoods, the high-output 302 cu. in. (5.0- liter) V-8 switched from a two- to a four-barrel carburetor and added horsepower. A Borg-Warner five-speed was to be offered with the H.O. engine later in the model year. First step-up engine above the base 140 cu. in. (2.3-liter) four was now the "Essex" 232 cu. in. (3.8-liter) V-6. The base engine changed from a two-barrel to one-barrel carb. A turbo four was announced for spring 1983 arrival (similar to the turbo offered in 1979-81, but fuel-injected). Manual-shift models now had an upshift indicator light. Standard tires grew one size and took on all-season tread. RS tires grew two sizes. Standard Capri equipment included the 140 cu. in. (2.3- liter) four with four-speed manual shift, P185/75R14 SBR BSW tires, power brakes, AM radio, tachometer, trip odometer, aero wheel covers, black bumper rub strips, cargo area cover, black remote driver's mirror, day/night mirror, and halogen headlamps. Extra-wide wraparound black bodyside moldings had dual color-keyed stripes. Bright moldings went on the windshield and roof drip; black molding on the back window; black/bright on window frames. Interiors held high-back vinyl bucket seats with reclining seatbacks (fold-down rear seat), black sport steering wheel, and woodtone dash applique. Capri L added a digital clock, console with graphic warning display, center armrest, low-back bucket seats, and right visor vanity mirror. GS included a woodtone-insert four- spoke steering wheel, black right-hand remote mirror, luxury cloth seats, map pocket, and light group. Capri RS added a Traction-Lok axle, P205/70R14 SBR BSW tires, power steering, leather-wrapped steering wheel, handling suspension, upper bodyside dual accent stripes, tape striping, black windshield and window frame moldings, black right-hand remote mirror, non-working hood scoop, black grille, and black brushed instrument panel. Black Magic came with P220/55R390 Michelin TRX tires on gold 15.3 inch forged metric aluminum wheels, a handling suspension, black leather-wrapped steering wheel, power steering, black hood scoop, black bodyside and window frame moldings, and black right-hand remote mirror. Reclining black vinyl low-back bucket seats had gold cloth inserts. Styling features included gold-accent bodyside taping, and gold accents on fender, grille edge, hood and license frames. Crimson Cat added TR cast aluminum wheels, 'Crimson Cat' tape treatment, sport steering wheel, and dual remote mirrors.

ZEPHYR — FOUR/SIX — Facing its last year in the lineup, Zephyr changed little. The base 140 cu. in (2.3-liter) four now had a one- barrel carburetor instead of two barrels. Manual-shift models had an optional upshift indicator light. The 4.2-liter V-8 was dropped, but Zephyrs could still have a 200 cu. in. (3.3- liter) inline six with locking torque converter in the automatic transmission. The optional Traction-Lok differential could now be ordered with TR-type tires. As in 1982, two trim levels were offered: base and GS, in four-door sedan or sporty coupe form. The Fairmont/Zephyr chassis/body design would continue as the downsized Ford LTD/Mercury Marquis (introduced this year). Zephyr standard equipment included the 2.3-liter four with four-speed manual gearbox, power brakes, deluxe wheel covers, P175/75R14 SBR BSW tires, AM radio, day/night mirror, vinyl low-back bucket seats, two-spoke color-keyed steering wheel, dual upper bodyside accent stripes, front bumper guards, dome lamp, and trunk mat. Bright moldings went on the windshield, back window, roof drip, wheel lip, door belt, rocker panels, and side window frames. Narrow lower bodyside moldings had black inserts. Zephyr's Z7 Sport Coupe added tinted rear window glass, and deleted rocker panel moldings. GS models (Z-7 or sedan) included dual hood accent stripes, four-spoke steering wheel, luxury cloth Flight bench seating, dual bright remote mirrors, and protective bodyside and integral partial wheel lip moldings (no rocker panel moldings).

1983 Marquis Brougham sedan (JG)

MARQUIS — FOUR/SIX/V-6 — Mercury borrowed the rear-drive "Fox" platform to create a new mid-size model bearing the Marquis badge. To avoid confusion, the big one was now called Grand Marquis. This smaller Marquis was basically the former Cougar sedan (and wagon), but with new sheetmetal and redone interior, and a more aero look. It was a six-window design, offered in Two trim levels: base and Brougham. Marquis was closely related to Ford's new LTD, but with a different grille and taillamps. The sloped grille was made up of thin vertical bars with a wider center bar, heavy bright surround molding, and nameplate on the lower driver's side. Quad rectangular headlamps were used, with park/signal lamps mounted in the bumper. Wide taillamps had horizontal ribbing, and the profile showed a 60-degree backlight angle. Marquis used the same drivetrains as LTD, including an optional propane four. Nitrogen gas-pressurized front struts and rear shocks were used. Front suspension had modified MacPherson struts; rear, a four-bar link arrangement. Standard tires were one size bigger than the '82 Cougar. A tethered gas cap was new. A contoured split-front bench seat with individual recliners was standard on automatic-tranmission models. New options included an electronic instrument cluster, six-way power seats, and locking wire wheel covers. A sunroof and extended- range gas tank also were offered. Standard Marquis equipment included a 140 cu. in. (2.3- liter) four with four-speed manual gearbox, AM radio, power brakes, deluxe full wheel covers, P185/75R14 BSW tires, black front bumper guards, lighter, locking glovebox, three-speed heater/defroster, dual-note horn, and trunk mat. A bright remote driver's mirror, day/night mirror, and right visor vanity mirror were standard. Cloth-upholstered Twin Comfort Lounge seats came with seatback recliners. Also included: a mini spare tire and luxury steering wheel with woodtone insert. Dual accent stripes went on hood and upper bodysides. Moldings appeared on window frames, wheel lip, belt, back window, license plate bracket, roof drip and windshield. Bodyside moldings were color-keyed vinyl. Wagons came with the inline 200 cu. in. (3.3-liter) six and automatic shift, tinted liftgate glass, cargo area light, and fold-down rear seat. Marquis Brougham added an illuminated passenger visor vanity mirror, digital clock, electronic warning chimes, full-length armrest, trunk carpeting, and extra interior lights.

1983 Cougar XR-7 Sports Coupe (JG)

COUGAR — V-6/V-8 — Like the closely related Thunderbird, Cougar enjoyed a major restyle. Foremost difference between the two was Cougar's notchback formal appearance with upright backlight and upswept quarter-window shape. TBird had a rounded backlight. Cougar also had a different grille design made up of thin vertical bars. Otherwise, Cougar (no longer called XR-7) looked much like its mate, with rounded contours, sloping front end and raked windshield, and an aero drag coefficient not too much worse than Thunderbird's. Extended- height doors curved inward at the top. Wipers and drip moldings were concealed. Body dimensions dropped a bit, as did Cougar's weight. Cougar's rear-drive "Fox" chassis had coil springs all around. New this year were gas-pressurized shock absorbers. Only two engine choices were offered: base 232 cu. in. (3.8- liter) V-6 or (later) the 302 cu. in. V-8 with throttle-body fuel injection. Four-speed overdrive automatic transmission was optional. Standard Cougar equipment included three-speed automatic transmission, power brakes and steering, AM radio, bumper rub strips, center pillar applique, console with storage bin, analog clock, locking glovebox, hood ornament, brushed instrument panel, and driver's remote mirror. Sport cloth bucket seats included reclining seatbacks. Also standard: a mini spare tire, decklid and bodyside accent stripes, deluxe wheel covers, and P195/75R14 WSW SBR tires. Bright moldings went on the grille surround, concealed drip, door frames, windshield, backlight, and belt. Charcoal lower bodyside moldings had bright accents. Cougar LS added a woodtone instrument panel applique, 'LS' fender badge, tinted glass, coach lamps, dual power remote mirrors, bright rocker panel moldings, luxury cloth seat trim, power windows, luxury wheel covers, hood accent stripes, steering wheel with woodtone insert, and luxury door trim. New options included an anti-theft alarm, emergency kit, and locking fuel filler door. Articulated sport seats and a voice-alert system also joined the option selection.

1983 Grand Marquis LS sedan (JG)

GRAND MARQUIS — V-8 — Still selling well, the biggest Mercury carried on with a revised nameplate and modified grille style. This version, shaped similar to its predecessor, consisted of rather heavy bright vertical bars and a wider center bar, with bright surround molding. Sedans also carried new full-width wraparound taillamps with horizontal ribbing. Backup lenses adjoined the license plate opening, at the inner ends of each taillamp. Grand Marquis came in base and LS trim, in the same three bodies as before: two- and four-door sedan, and four- door Colony Park wagon. Sole engine was the 302 cu. in. (5.0- liter) V-8, now with throttle-body fuel injection. Four-speed overdrive automatic transmission was standard. Sedan tires grew one size. New options included a remote locking fuel filler door and locking wire wheel covers. Marquis was similar to Ford's similarly renamed LTD Crown Victoria, sharing drivetrains and suspension. Standard Grand Marquis equipment included a coach vinyl roof, coach lamps, power windows, power brakes and steering, AM/FM stereo radio, cloth/vinyl Twin Comfort lounge seats, mini spare tire with cover, color-keyed steering wheel, bright wheel covers, bumper guards, analog clock, and dual- note horn. The instrument panel was argent with woodtone applique. Bright moldings went on rocker panels, belt, window frames, wheel lips, taillamps, hood rear edge, windshield, roof drip, grille and parking lamp surround. Wide lower bodyside moldings were used, with color-keyed quarter and rear window moldings. Accent stripes went on the hood and upper bodyside. Grand Marquis LS added tinted glass, luxury cloth Twin Comfort seats, full-length armrests, door pull straps, woodtone applique on door trim panels, front seatback map pocket, dual-beam dome lamp, and a right visor vanity mirror. Colony Park wagons had a three-way tailgate with power tinted window, vinyl-trimmed Twin Comfort seats, conventional spare tire, lockable stowage compartment, woodtone aplique on bodyside and tailgate, bumper step pad, bright/black tailgate window moldings, and bright/woodtone bodyside applique surround moldings. Wagons had no rocker panel, lower bodyside or wheel lip moldings.

I.D. DATA: Mercury's 17-symbol Vehicle Identification Number (VIN) was stamped on a metal tab fastened to the instrument panel, visible through the windshield. Symbols one to three indicates manufacturer, make and vehicle type: '1ME' Mercury passenger car. The fourth symbol ('B') denotes restraint system. Next comes a letter 'P', followed by two digits that indicate body type: Model Number, as shown in left column of tables below. (Example: '86' Zephyr four- door sedan.) Symbol eight indicates engine type: '2' L498 2Bbl.; '4' H.O. L498 2Bbl.; '5' L498 FI; 'A' L4-140 2Bbl.; 'D' Turbo L4140 2Bbl.; 'X' L6200 1Bbl.; '3' V6232 2Bbl.; 'F' V8302 2Bbl.; 'G' V8351 2Bbl. Next is a check digit. Symbol ten indicates model year ('D' 1983). Symbol eleven is assembly plant: 'A' Atlanta, GA; 'F' Dearborn, MI; 'G' Chicago; 'H' Lorain, Ohio; 'K' Kansas City, MO; 'R' San Jose, CA; 'W' Wayne, MI; 'X' St. Thomas, Ontario; 'Z' St. Louis, MO; and Edison, NJ. The final six digits make up the sequence number, starting with 600001. A Vehicle Certification Label on the left front door lock face panel or door pillar shows the manufacturer, month and year of manufacture, GVW, GAWR, certification statement, VIN, and codes for such items as body type, color, trim, axle, transmission, and special order information.

LYNX (FOUR)

Model Number	Body/Style Number	Body Type & Seating	Factory Price	Shipping Weight	Production Total
54	61D	3-dr. L Hatch-4P	5751	1922	Note 1
55	58D	5-dr. L Hatch-4P	5958	1984	Note 1
60	74D	4-dr. L Sta Wag-4P	6166	2026	Note 1
55	61D	3-dr. GS Hatch-4P	6476	1948	Note 1
66	58D	5-dr. GS Hatch-4P	6693	2010	Note 1
61	74D	4-dr. GS Sta Wag-4P	6872	2050	Note 1
58	61D	3-dr. LS Hatch-4P	7529	1950	Note 1
68	58D	5-dr. LS Hatch-4P	7746	2012	Note 1
63	74D	4-dr. LS Sta Wag-4P	7909	2050	Note 1
57	61D	3-dr. RS Hatch-4P	7370	1997	Note 1
65/934	58D	5-dr. LTS Hatch-4P	7334	1920	Note 1

Note 1: Total Lynx production, 40,142 three-door hatchbacks, 28,461 five-door hatchbacks, and 19,192 four-door liftgate station wagons.

LN7 (FOUR)

Model Number	Body/Style Number	Body Type & Seating	Factory Price	Shipping Weight	Production Total
51/A80	67D	3-dr. Hatch Cpe-2P	7398	2076	4,528
51/A8C	67D	3-dr. RS Hatch-2P	8765	N/A	Note 2

LN7 SPORT (FOUR)

Model Number	Body/Style Number	Body Type & Seating	Factory Price	Shipping Weight	Production Total
51/A8A	67D	3-dr. Hatch Cpe-2P	8084	N/A	Note 2

LN7 GRAND SPORT (FOUR)

Model Number	Body/Style Number	Body Type & Seating	Factory Price	Shipping Weight	Production Total
51/A8B	67D	3-dr. Hatch Cpe-2P	8465	N/A	Note 2

Note 2: Total LN7 production is included in figure above.

CAPRI (FOUR/V-6)

Model Number	Body/Style Number	Body Type & Seating	Factory Price	Shipping Weight	Production Total
79/41P	61D	3-dr. Fastbk-4P	7156/7465	2589/2697	Note 3
79	61D	3-dr. L Fastbk-4P	7711/8020	2615/2723	Note 3

CAPRI CRIMSON CAT (FOUR/V-6)

Model Number	Body/Style Number	Body Type & Seating	Factory Price	Shipping Weight	Production Total
79	61D	3-dr. Fastbk-4P	8525/8834	N/A	Note 3

CAPRI BLACK MAGIC (FOUR/SIX)

Model Number	Body/Style Number	Body Type & Seating	Factory Price	Shipping Weight	Production Total
79/932	61D	3-dr. Fastbk-4P	8629/8938	2597/2705	Note 3

CAPRI GS (FOUR/SIX)

Model Number	Body/Style Number	Body Type & Seating	Factory Price	Shipping Weight	Production Total
79/602	61H	3-dr. Fastbk-4P	7914/8223	N/A	Note 3

CAPRI RS (V-8)

Model Number	Body/Style Number	Body Type & Seating	Factory Price	Shipping Weight	Production Total
79	61D	3-dr. Fastbk-4P	9241	2894	Note 3

Note 3: Total Capri production was 25,376.

Capri Engine Note: Six-cylinder prices do not include cost of the required automatic transmission ($439). A high-output 302 cu. in. V-8 engine cost $1034 more than the V-6 on L or GS; $866 more on Black Magic.

ZEPHYR (FOUR/SIX)

Model Number	Body/Style Number	Body Type & Seating	Factory Price	Shipping Weight	Production Total
86	54D	4-dr. Sed-5P	6545/6774	2630/2750	21,732
86/602	54D	4-dr. GS Sed-5P	7311/7550	2696/2881	Note 4

ZEPHYR Z-7 (FOUR/SIX)

Model Number	Body/Style Number	Body Type & Seating	Factory Price	Shipping Weight	Production Total
87	36R	2-dr. Spt Cpe-5P	6442/6681	2627/2747	3,471
87/602	36R	2-dr. GS Cpe-5P	7247/7486	2690/2810	Note 4

Zephyr Price Note: Six-cylinder prices do not include cost of the required automatic transmission ($439).

MARQUIS (FOUR/SIX)

Model Number	Body/Style Number	Body Type & Seating	Factory Price	Shipping Weight	Production Total
89	54D	4-dr. Sedan-5P	7893/8132	N/A	50,169
90	74D	4-dr. Sta Wag-5P	-- /8693	N/A	17,189

MARQUIS BROUGHAM (FOUR/SIX)

Model Number	Body/Style Number	Body Type & Seating	Factory Price	Shipping Weight	Production Total
89	54D	4-dr. Sedan-5P	8202/8441	N/A	Note 4
90	74D	4-dr. Sta Wag-5P	-- /8974	N/A	Note 4

Note 4: Brougham production is included in basic totals above.

Marquis Engine Note: A V-6 engine cost $70 more than the inline six on sedan.

1983 Cougar XR-7 Sports Coupe (OCW)

COUGAR (V-6/V-8)

Model Number	Body/Style Number	Body Type & Seating	Factory Price	Shipping Weight	Production Total
92	66D	2-dr. Cpe-4P	9521/9809	2911/--	75,743
92/603	66D	2-dr. LS Cpe-4P	10850/11138	2911/--	Note 5

Note 5: Production of LS models is included in base or GS totals.

GRAND MARQUIS (V-8)

Model Number	Body/Style Number	Body Type & Seating	Factory Price	Shipping Weight	Production Total
93	66K	2-dr. Sedan-6P	10654	3607	11,117
95	54K	4-dr. Sedan-6P	10718	3761	72,207
93/60H	66K	2-dr. LS Sed-6P	11209	3607	Note 6
95/60H	54K	4-dr. LS Sed-6P	11273	3761	Note 6

GRAND MARQUIS COLONY PARK (V-8)

Model Number	Body/Style Number	Body Type & Seating	Factory Price	Shipping Weight	Production Total
94	74K	4-dr. 2S Sta Wag-6P	10896	3788	12,394

Note 6: LS production is included in basic Grand Marquis totals.

FACTORY PRICE AND WEIGHT NOTE: Cougar prices and weights to left of slash are for V-6, to right for V-8 engine. For Capri/Zephyr/Marquis, prices/weights to left of slash are for four-cylinder, to right for inline six (or V-6).

ENGINE DATA: BASE FOUR (Lynx, LN7): Inline. Overhead cam. Four-cylinder. Cast iron block and aluminum head. Displacement: 97.6 cu. in. (1.6 liters). Bore & stroke: 3.15 x 3.13 in. Compression ratio: 8.8:1. Brake horsepower: 70 at 4600 R.P.M. Torque: 88 lbs.-ft. at 2600 R.P.M. Five main bearings. Hydraulic valve lifters. Carburetor: 2Bbl. Motorcraft 740. VIN Code: 2. **OPTIONAL FOUR** (Lynx, LN7): High-output version of 1.6-liter engine above Horsepower: 80 at 5400 R.P.M. Torque: 88 lbs.-ft. at 3000 R.P.M. VIN Code: 4. **OPTIONAL FOUR** (Lynx, LN7): Fuel-injected version of 1.6-liter engine above Compression ratio: 9.5:1. Horsepower: 88 at 5400 R.P.M. Torque: 94 lbs.- ft. at 4200 R.P.M. VIN Code: 5. **BASE FOUR** (Capri, Zephyr, Marquis): Inline. Overhead cam. Four-cylinder. Cast iron block and head. Displacement: 140 cu. in. (2.3 liters). Bore & stroke: 3.78 x 3.13 in. Compression ratio: 9.0:1. Brake horsepower: 90 at 4600 R.P.M. Torque: 122 lbs.-ft. at 2600 R.P.M. Five main bearings. Hydraulic valve lifters. Carburetor: 1Bbl. Carter YFA. VIN Code: A. **OPTIONAL TURBOCHARGED FOUR** (Capri): Same as 140 cu. in. four above, but with turbocharger Compression ratio: 8.0:1. Horsepower: 142 at 5000 R.P.M. Torque: 172 lbs.-ft. at 3800 R.P.M. VIN Code: D. NOTE: Propane four was available for Marquis. **OPTIONAL SIX** (Zephyr, Marquis): Inline. OHV. Six-cylinder. Cast iron block and head. Displacement: 200 cu. in. (3.3 liters). Bore & stroke: 3.68 x 3.13 in. Compression ratio: 8.6:1. Brake horsepower: 92 at 3800 R.P.M. Torque: 156 lbs.-ft. at 1400 R.P.M. Seven main bearings. Hydraulic valve lifters. Carburetor: 1Bbl. Holley 1946. VIN Code: X. **BASE V-6** (Cougar); **OPTIONAL** (Marquis): 90-degree, overhead valve V-6. Cast iron block and aluminum head. Displacement: 232 cu. in. (3.8 liters). Bore & stroke: 3.80 x 3.40 in. Compression ratio: 8.65:1. Brake horsepower: 110-112 at 3800-4000 R.P.M. Torque: 175 lbs.-ft. at 2200-2600 R.P.M. Four main bearings. Hydraulic valve lifters. Carburetor: 2Bbl. Motorcraft 2150 or 7200VV. VIN Code: 3. **BASE V-8** (Grand Marquis); **OPTIONAL** (Cougar): 90-degree, overhead valve V-8. Cast iron block and head. Displacement: 302 cu. in. (5.0 liters). Bore & stroke: 4.00 x 3.00 in. Compression ratio: 8.4:1. Brake horsepower: 130 at 3200 R.P.M. Torque: 240 lbs.-ft. at 2000 R.P.M. Five main bearings. Hydraulic valve lifters. Fuel injection. VIN Code: F. **OPTIONAL V-8** (Grand Marquis): Carbureted version of 302 cu. in. V-8 above Compression ratio: 8.4:1. Horsepower: 145 at 3800 R.P.M. Torque: 245 lbs.-ft. at 2200 R.P.M. **OPTIONAL V-8** (Capri): High-output version of 302 cu. in. V-8 above Compression ratio: 8.3:1. Horsepower: 175 at 4000 R.P.M. Torque: 245 lbs.-ft. at 2400 R.P.M. Carburetor: 4Bbl. Holley 4180. **POLICE V-8** (Grand Marquis): 90-degree, overhead valve V-8. Cast iron block and head. Displacement: 351 cu. in. (5.8 liters). Bore & stroke: 4.00 x 3.50 in. Compression ratio: 8.3:1. Brake horsepower: 165 at 3600 R.P.M. Torque: 290 lbs.-ft. at 2200 R.P.M. Five main bearings. Hydraulic valve lifters. Carburetor: 2Bbl. VV. VIN Code: G.

CHASSIS DATA: Wheelbase: (Lynx/LN7) 94.2 in.; (Capri) 100.4 in.; (Zephyr/Marquis) 105.5 in.; (Cougar) 104.0 in.; (Grand Marquis) 114.3 in. Overall Length: (Lynx) 163.9 in.; (Lynx lift) 165.0 in.; (LN7) 170.3 in.; (Capri) 179.1 in.; (Zephyr) 195.5 in.; (Z7) 197.4 in.; (Marquis) 196.5 in.; (Grand Marquis) 214.0 in.; (Grand Marquis wag) 218.0 in. Height: (Lynx) 53.3 in.; (LN7) 50.5 in.; (Capri) 51.9 in.; (Zephyr) 52.9 in.; (Z7) 51.7 in.; (Marquis) 53.6 in.; (Marquis wag) 54.3 in.; (Cougar) 53.4 in.; (Grand Marquis) 55.2 in.; (Grand Marquis wag) 56.8 in. Width: (Lynx/LN7) 65.9 in.; (Capri) 69.1 in.; (Zephyr/Marquis) 71.0 in.; (Cougar) 71.1 in.; (Grand Marquis) 77.5 in.; (Grand Marquis wag) 79.3 in. Front Tread: (Lynx/LN7) 54.7 in.; (Capri) 56.6 in.; (Zephyr/Marquis) 56.6 in.; (Capri) 57.0 in.; (Zephyr/Marquis) 57.0 in.; (Cougar) 58.5 in.; (Grand Marquis) 62.0 in. Rear Tread: (Lynx/LN7) 56.0 in.; (Capri) 57.0 in.; (Zephyr/Marquis) 57.0 in.; (Cougar) 58.1 in.; (Grand Marquis) 62.0 in. Standard Tires: (Lynx/LN7) P165/80R13; (Capri) P185/75R14; (Capri RS) P205/70R14; (Zephyr) P175/75R14 SBR; (Marquis) P185/75R14; (Cougar) N/A; (Grand Marquis) P215/75R14 SBR.

TECHNICAL: Transmission: Four-speed manual standard on Lynx. Gear ratios: (1st) 3.58:1; (2nd) 2.05:1; (3rd) 1.23:1 or 1.36:1; (4th) 0.81:1 or 0.95:1; (Rev) 3.46:1. Alternate Lynx four- speed: (1st) 3.23:1; (2nd) 1.90:1; (3rd) 1.23:1; (4th) 0.81:1; (Rev) 3.46:1. Four-speed floor shift standard on Capri/Marquis four: (1st) 3.98:1; (2nd) 2.14:1; (3rd) 1.42:1 or 1.49:1; (4th) 1.00:1; (Rev) 3.99:1. Four-speed standard on Capri V-8: (1st) 3.07:1; (2nd) 1.72:1; (3rd) 1.00:1; (4th) 0.70:1; (Rev) 3.07:1. Lynx/LN7 five-speed manual: (1st) 3.60:1; (2nd) 2.12:1; (3rd) 1.39:1; (4th) 1.02:1; (5th) 1.02:1; (Rev) 3.62:1. Capri four-cylinder five-speed: (1st) 3.72:1; (2nd) 2.23:1; (3rd) 1.48:1; (4th) 1.00:1; (5th) 0.76:1; (Rev) 3.59:1. Capri V-8 five-speed manual:

(1st) 2.95:1; (2nd) 1.94:1; (3rd) 1.34:1; (4th) 1.00:1; (5th) 0.73:1; (Rev) 2.76:1. Capri turbo five-speed manual: (1st) 4.03:1; (2nd) 2.37:1; (3rd) 1.50:1; (4th) 1.00:1; (5th) 0.86:1; (Rev) 3.76:1. Alternate Capri turbo five-speed manual: (1st) 3.76:1; (2nd) 2.18:1; (3rd) 1.36:1; (4th) 1.00:1; (5th) 0.86:1; (Rev) 3.76:1. SelectShift three-speed automatic standard on Capri/Cougar/Marquis six, optional on others. Gear ratios: (1st) 2.46:1 or 2.47:1; (2nd) 1.46:1 or 1.47:1; (3rd) 1.00:1; (Rev) 2.11:1 to 2.19:1. Lynx three- speed automatic: (1st) 2.79:1; (2nd) 1.61:1; (3rd) 1.00:1; (Rev) 1.97:1. Four-speed overdrive automatic on Cougar/Marquis/Grand Marquis: (1st) 2.40:1; (2nd) 1.47:1; (3rd) 1.00:1; (4th) 0.67:1; (Rev) 2.00:1. Standard final drive ratio: (Lynx/LN7) 3.59:1 w/4spd, 3.73:1 w/5spd, 3.31:1 w/auto.; (Capri four) 3.08:1 w/4spd or auto., 3.45:1 w/5spd; (Capri V-6) 2.73:1; (Capri V-8) 3.08:1 w/4spd; (Capri turbo) 3.45:1; (Zephyr four) 3.08:1; (Zephyr six) 2.73:1; (Marquis) 3.45:1 w/four, 2.73:1 w/six, 3.08:1 w/V-8; (Cougar) 2.47:1 w/3spd auto., 3.08:1 with 4spd auto.; (Grand Marquis) 3.08:1. Steering: (Grand Marquis) recirculating ball; (others) rack and pinion. Front Suspension: (Lynx/LN7) MacPherson strut-mounted coil springs w/lower control arms and stabilizer bar; (Capri/Zephyr/Cougar/Marquis) modified MacPherson struts w/coil springs and anti-sway bar; (Grand Marquis) coil springs with long/short Aarms and anti-sway bar. Rear Suspension: (Lynx/LN7) independent trailing arms w/modified MacPherson struts and coil springs on lower control arms; (Capri/Zephyr/Cougar/Marquis/Grand Marquis) four-link w/coil springs. Brakes: Front disc, rear drum. Ignition: Electronic. Body construction: (Grand Marquis) separate body and frame; (others) unibody. Fuel tank: (Lynx/LN7) 13 gal.; (Capri) 15.4 gal.; (Zephyr) 16 gal.; (Marquis) 16 gal.; (Cougar) 21 gal.; (Grand Marquis) 18 gal.; (Grand Marquis wag) 18.5 gal.

DRIVETRAIN OPTIONS: Engines: H.O. 1.6-liter four: Lynx ($70-$73); LN7 RS ($70). Fuel-injected 1.6-liter four: Lynx LS ($367); Lynx LTS ($294). Propane 140 cu. in. four: Marquis ($896). 200 cu. in. six: Zephyr/Marquis ($239). 232 cu. in. V-6: Capri/Marquis ($309) exc. wagon ($70). 302 cu. in. V-8: Capri L/GS ($1343); Capri Black Magic ($866); Capri Redline ($1118); Cougar ($288). Transmission/Differential: Close-ratio four-speed trans.: Lynx (NC). Five-speed manual trans.: Lynx ($76). Automatic transaxle: Lynx ($439) exc. LTS/RS ($363); LN7 ($363). Select-shift auto. transmission.: Capri/Zephyr/Marquis ($439). Overdrive auto. trans.: Marquis ($615) exc. wagon ($176); Cougar ($176). Floor shift lever: Zephyr/Marquis ($49). First-gear lockout delete: Zephyr ($9). Traction-Lok differential: Capri/Zephyr/Marquis/Grand Marquis/Cougar ($95). Optional axle ratio: Capri/Zephyr (NC). Brakes & Steering: Power brakes: Lynx ($95). Power steering: Lynx/LN7 ($210); Capri ($202); Zephyr/Marquis ($218). Suspension: H.D. susp.: Zephyr/Marquis ($24); Grand Marquis/Cougar ($26). Handling susp.: Lynx L/GS ($145); Lynx LS ($41); Zephyr ($52); Grand Marquis ($49). Handling susp. pkg.: Capri ($252). TR performance susp.: Lynx ($41). TR sport susp.: LN7 ($41). Other: H.D. battery ($26). H.D. alternator: LN7 ($27). Extended-range gas tank: Zephyr/Marquis ($46). Engine block heater ($17-$18). Trailer towing pkg., medium duty: Grand Marquis ($200-$251); heavy duty ($251-$302). Trailer towing pkg.: Cougar ($251). California emission system ($46-$76). High-altitude emissions (NC).

LYNX CONVENIENCE/APPEARANCE OPTIONS: Option Packages: TR performance pkg. ($185-$515). Villager woodtone pkg. ($316). Instrument group ($87). Light group ($43). Comfort/Convenience: Air conditioner ($624). Rear defroster, electric ($124). Fingertip speed control ($170). Tinted glass ($90); windshield only ($38). Digital clock ($57). Interval wipers ($49). Rear wiper/washer ($117). Dual remote sport mirrors ($67). Entertainment: AM radio ($61). AM/FM radio ($82) exc. L ($143). AM/FM stereo radio ($109) exc. L ($170); w/cassette or 8track player ($199) exc. L ($260), LS ($90). Premium sound ($117). Exterior: Flip-up open-air roof ($217-$310). Clearcoat metallic paint: RS ($305). Glamour paint ($51). Tu-tone paint ($134-$173). Dual bodyside paint stripes ($39). Front vent windows, pivoting ($60). Remote quarter windows ($109). Vinyl-insert bodyside moldings ($45). Bumper guards, front or rear ($28). Bumper rub strips ($48). Luggage rack ($93). Lower bodyside protection ($68). Interior: Console ($111). Fold-down center armrest ($55). Low-back reclining bucket seats ($98). High-back reclining bucket seats ($65). Vinyl seats ($24). Wheels/Tires: Cast aluminum wheels ($226-$329). P165/80R13 SBR WSW ($59).

LN7 CONVENIENCE/APPEARANCE OPTIONS: Comfort/Convenience: Air conditioner ($624). Entertainment: AM/FM radio ($82). AM/FM stereo radio ($109); w/cassette or 8track player ($199) exc. Sport ($90). Premium sound ($117). AM radio delete ($37 credit). AM/FM stereo delete ($145 credit). AM/FM stereo/cassette delete ($352 credit). Exterior: Flip-up open air roof ($310). Glamour paint ($51). Two-tone paint/tape ($146). Sport tape stripe ($41). Lower bodyside protection ($68). Interior: Cloth, sport cloth or knit vinyl bucket seats (NC). Sport seats ($173). Leather low-back seat trim ($144). Shearling low-back bucket seats ($227).

CAPRI CONVENIENCE/APPEARANCE OPTIONS: Option Packages: Light group ($55). Appearance protection group ($60). Power lock group ($160). Comfort/Convenience: Air cond. ($724). Rear defroster, electric ($135). Fingertip speed control ($170). Power windows ($180). Tinted glass ($105); windshield only ($38). Leather-wrapped steering wheel ($59). Tilt steering wheel ($105). Interval wipers ($49). Remote right mirror ($44). Entertainment: AM/FM radio ($82). AM/FM stereo radio ($109); w/8track or cassette player ($199). Premium sound system ($117). AM radio delete ($61 credit). Exterior: TRoof ($1055). Flip-up open air roof ($310). Glamour paint ($54). Two-tone paint ($78-$137). Rocker panel moldings ($33). Lower bodyside protection ($41). Interior: Console ($191). Cloth/vinyl seats ($29-$40). Leather/vinyl seats ($415). Sport seats ($196). Front floor mats, carpeted ($22). Wheels and Tires: Wire wheel covers ($98). Turbine wheel covers (NC). Cast aluminum wheels ($345). Styled steel wheels w/trim rings ($78). P185/75R14 WSW ($72). P195/75R14 WSW ($108). P205/75R14 BSW ($224). TRX P220/55R390 BSW ($327- $551).

ZEPHYR CONVENIENCE/APPEARANCE OPTIONS: Option Packages: Instrument cluster ($100). Appearance protection group ($32-$60). Light group ($55). Comfort/Convenience: Air cond. ($724). Rear defroster, electric ($135). Fingertip speed control ($170). Illuminated entry ($82). Power windows ($180-$255). Power door locks ($120-$170). Remote decklid release ($40). Four-way power seat ($139). Tinted glass ($105). Tinted windshield ($38). Tilt steering ($105). Quartz clock ($35). Interval wipers ($49). Lighting and Mirrors: Map light ($10). Trunk light ($7). Left remote mirror ($22). Dual bright remote mirrors ($68). Lighted visor vanity mirrors, pair ($106). Entertainment: AM/FM radio ($59). AM/FM stereo radio ($109); w/8track or cassette player ($199). Premium sound system ($117). AM radio delete ($61 credit). Exterior: Flip-up open air roof ($310). Full or half vinyl roof ($152). Glamour paint ($63). Two-tone paint ($117). Pivoting front vent windows ($63). Wide bodyside moldings ($59). Rocker panel moldings ($39). Bumper guards, rear ($28). Bumper rub strips ($50). Lower bodyside protection ($41). Interior: Console ($191). Bucket seats ($21). Cloth/vinyl seat trim ($35). Bench seat (NC). Front floor mats, carpeted ($24). Front/rear rubber mats ($15). Wheels/Tires: Wire wheel covers ($152). Styled steel wheels ($66). Styled steel wheels w/trim rings ($126). Steel wheels, 5.5 in. ($18); H.D. ($74). P175/75R14 SBR WSW ($72). P185/75R14 WSW ($116). TR BSW on aluminum wheels ($601). Conventional spare ($63).

MARQUIS CONVENIENCE/APPEARANCE OPTIONS: Option Packages: Woodtone option ($282). Heavy-duty pkg. ($210). Power lock group ($170-$210). Cold weather group ($77). Appearance protection group ($60). Light group ($38). Comfort/Convenience: Air cond. ($724); auto-temp ($802). Rear defroster, electric ($135). Fingertip speed control ($170). Illuminated entry ($76). Autolamp on-off delay ($73). Power windows ($255). Six-way power driver's seat ($207); dual ($415). Tinted glass ($105). Tinted windshield ($38). Leather-wrapped steering wheel ($59). Tilt steering ($105). Electronic instrument cluster ($289-$367). Tripminder computer ($215-$293). Digital clock ($78). Diagnostic warning lights ($59). Auto. parking brake release ($12). Interval wipers ($49). Liftgate wiper/washer: wagon ($99). Lighting and Mirrors: Cornering lamps ($60). Map light ($15). Right remote convex mirror ($60). Lighted visor vanity mirrors ($51-$100). Entertainment: AM/FM radio ($59). AM/FM stereo radio ($109); w/8track or cassette player ($199). Electronic-tuning AM/FM stereo radio ($252); w/cassette ($396). Premium sound system ($117-$151). AM radio delete ($61 credit). Exterior: Flip-up open air roof ($310). Full vinyl roof ($152). Glamour paint ($63). Two-tone paint ($117). Pivoting front vent windows (N/A). Two-way liftgate: wag ($105). Protective bodyside moldings (N/A). Bumper guards, rear ($28). Bumper rub strips ($56). Luggage rack: wagon ($126). Lower bodyside protection ($41). Interior: Console ($100). Vinyl seat trim ($35). Individual seats w/console ($61). Leather seat trim ($415). Front floor mats ($23). Wheels/Tires: Luxury wheel covers ($55). Wire wheel covers ($159); locking ($198). Styled wheels w/trim rings ($54). Cast aluminum wheels ($402). P185/75R14 BSW ($38); WSW ($72). P195/75R14 WSW ($72-$116). Puncture-sealant P195/75R14 WSW ($240). Conventional spare ($63).

COUGAR CONVENIENCE/APPEARANCE OPTIONS: Option Packages: Luxury carpet group ($72). Traveler's assistance kit ($65). Light group ($35). Power lock group ($172). Comfort/Convenience: Air cond. ($737); auto-temp ($802). Rear defroster ($135). Fingertip speed control ($170). Illuminated entry system ($82). Keyless entry ($163). Anti-theft system ($159). Remote fuel door lock ($26). Tripminder computer ($215-$276). Autolamp on/off delay ($73). Tinted glass ($105); windshield only ($38). Power windows ($193). Six-way power driver's seat ($222); dual ($444). Auto. parking brake release ($12). Leather-wrapped steering wheel ($59). Tilt steering wheel ($105). Electronic instrument cluster ($382). Electronic voice alert ($67). Diagnostic warning lights ($59). Digital clock ($61). Interval wipers ($49). Lighting and Mirrors: Cornering lamps ($68). Electro- luminescent coach lamps ($84). Dual electric remote mirrors ($94). Electronic-dimming day/night mirror ($77). Lighted visor vanity mirrors, pair ($106). Entertainment: AM/FM stereo radio ($109); w/8track or cassette player ($199). Electronic-tuning AM/FM stereo search radio ($252); w/cassette ($396). Power antenna ($66). Premium sound system ($179). AM radio delete ($61 credit). Exterior: Flip-up open-air roof ($310). Luxury vinyl rear half roof ($240). Clearcoat metallic paint ($152). Two-tone paint: LS ($148-$163). Hood striping ($16). Pivoting front vent windows ($76). Rocker panel moldings ($39). License frames ($9). Lower bodyside protection ($39-$54). Interior: Articulated sport seats ($427) exc. LS ($183). Leather seat trim ($415-$659). Vinyl seat trim ($34). Front floor mats, carpeted ($22). Wheels/Tires: Wire wheel covers, locking ($84-$198). Luxury wheel covers ($113). Puncture-sealing tires ($124). P205/70R14 WSW ($62). P205/70HR14 performance BSW ($152). 220/55R390 TRX performance tires on aluminum wheels ($499- $649). Conventional spare ($63).

GRAND MARQUIS CONVENIENCE/APPEARANCE OPTIONS: Option Packages: Grand Marquis LS decor ($616). Convenience group ($95-$116). Power lock group ($123-$220). Light group ($30-$48). Comfort/Convenience: Air cond. ($724); w/auto-temp control ($802). Rear defroster, electric ($135). Fingertip speed control ($170). Illuminated entry system ($76). Power driver's seat ($210); driver and passenger ($420). Remote fuel door lock ($24). Tinted glass ($105); windshield only ($38). Autolamp on/off delay ($73). Leather-wrapped steering wheel ($59). Tilt steering wheel ($105). Tripminder computer ($261). Digital clock ($61). Lighting and Mirrors: Cornering lamps ($60). Remote right mirror ($43). Lighted visor vanity mirrors ($100). Entertainment: AM/FM stereo radio w/8track or cassette tape player ($112). AM/FM stereo search radio ($166); w/8track or cassette ($310). Power antenna ($60). Premium sound system ($145-$179). AM/FM delete ($152 credit). Exterior: Formal coach vinyl roof ($650). Glamour paint ($77). Two-tone paint ($129). Pivoting front vent windows (N/A). Rocker panel moldings ($32). Vinyl-insert bodyside moldings ($55). Bumper rub strips ($52). Luggage rack ($110). Lower bodyside protection ($39-$52). Interior: Dual-facing rear seats: wag ($167). Cloth trim ($48). Leather seat trim ($418). Duraweave vinyl seat trim ($96). Carpeted front floor mats ($21). Wheels/Tires: Luxury wheel covers ($59). Wire wheel covers ($129); locking ($168). Cast aluminum wheels ($361). P225/75R14 WSW ($42-$43). P205/75R15 WSW ($17); puncture- resistant ($130). Conventional spare ($63).

HISTORY: Introduced: September 23, 1982 or October 14, 1982 except Cougar, February 17, 1983. Model year production: 381,721. Calendar year production (U.S.): 432,353. Calendar year sales by U.S. dealers: 409,433. Model year sales by U.S. dealers: 357,617 (not incl. 21,745 early '84 Topaz models).

Historical Footnotes: Grand Marquis was Mercury's best seller for the '83 model year, taking over that spot from the subcompact Lynx. Model year sales jumped nearly 40 percent for the big full- size model. The two-seater LN7 never had found an adequate number of customers, and dropped out after 1983. Ford's similar EXP hung on longer. Capri sales declined a bit, but remained strong enough to carry on. Only about 30 percent of Capris had V-8 power. Topaz, introduced spring as an early '84, found 21,745 buyers in just the few months before the full model year began. Sales were helped by Hertz, which bought 15,200 Tempo/Topaz models for its rental fleet. Cougar sold quite well with its new "reverse-curve" back window styling, though analysts thought the design inferior to Thunderbird's aero- look. Mercury discovered that 40 percent of them were bought by women. Production of Marquis and Grand Marquis rose sharply, adding jobs at the Chicago and St. Louis plants. For the first time, both large and small cars (front-drive Escort/Lynx and rear-drive Grand Marquis) were produced on the same assembly (at St. Thomas, Ontario). Mercury's market share rose from 5.5 percent to 6.1 percent in two years, with credit taken by Lincoln-Mercury General Manager Gordon B. MacKenzie, who took over in 1981. However, MacKenzie soon left Mercury to return to his former spot at Ford of Europe. The new General Manager was Robert L. Rewey Jr.

1984 MERCURY

Mercury's factory sales catalog promised "a new direction in automotive technology." That meant cars that were exciting to drive, pleasing to the eye, "combining innovative design, aerodynamic styling and meticulous engineering." Highlight of the year was the arrival of the front-wheel-drive Tempo compact, which actually emerged as an early '84 model. A diesel four-cylinder engine was available on Lynx and Topaz. Turbos were optional on Lynx and Capri, and standard on the revived Cougar XR-7. Due to sluggish sales, the two-seater LN7 was abandoned.

LYNX — FOUR — "The quality-built small car." So went Mercury's claim for the subcompact Lynx, now in its fourth season. Three- door, five-door and wagon bodies were offered again, with little appearance change. Wraparound taillamps with two horizontal ribs came to a point at their forward limit on the rear quarter panel. Trim levels ran from base and L to GS, sporty RS, RS Turbo, and top-rung LTS (five-door only). Base engine remained the 1.6-liter CVH four, with four-speed manual transaxle. New this year: an optional 2.0-liter diesel engine with five-speed transaxle. Lynx had a "lubed-for-life" chassis, self-adjusting brakes and clutch, rack-and-pinion steering, fully independent suspension, and maintenance-free battery. A new full-width flat-folding rear seat went into L models; new split-folding rear seat on others. Instrument panels and interiors were revised, including new side-window defoggers. The RS Turbo had a fuel-injected turbocharged engine, five-speed manual overdrive transaxle, special suspension with Koni shocks and TR sport cast aluminum wheels with Michelin 185/60R365 TRX traction compound tires, plus power steering and brakes. New options included a tilt steering wheel, power door locks, overhead console with digital clock and map lights, electronic stereo search radio, and graphic equalizer. Also available: air conditioning, electric rear window defroster, flip-up/open-air roof, tinted glass, and Premium Sound System.

1984 Lynx GS hatchback coupe (JG)

1984 Capri GS hatchback coupe (JG)

CAPRI — FOUR/V-6/V-8 — A simplified Capri model lineup included the base GS, high-performance RS, and RS Turbo. Base, L, Black Magic, and Crimson Cat models were dropped. Promoting the Capri turbo, Mercury's factory catalog insisted that "automotive technology didn't became less exhilirating with the passing of the old muscle cars—it merely became more intelligent." The turbocharged four, introduced in 1983 on Mustang GT and TBird Turbo Coupe, produced 145 horsepower at 4600 R.P.M. (60 percent more than standard four). It was hooked to a five-speed manual overdrive transmission and Traction-Lok axle. Capri RS or GS could have a High Output 302 cu. in. (5.0-liter) V-8 with either fuel injection or four-barrel. The four-barrel version (on RS) had a 2.5 inch diameter exhaust and dual outlets, cast aluminum rocker arm covers, and high-lift camshaft. The fuel-injected V-8 now came with automatic overdrive transmission. Fuel injection was added to the 232 cu. in. (3.8-liter) V-6, optional on GS. All Capris had a split rear searback, with each side folding separately. Instrument panels were revised, now with red backlighting. New steering wheels put the horn button on the hub rather than the column stalk. Gas-pressurized shocks were used at front and rear. Bodies had extra-wide wraparound black bodyside moldings with dual color-keyed stripes, bright roof drip and windshield moldings, black rear window molding, and black/bright window frame moldings. Wraparound horizontally- ribbed taillamps were used, and the rear license plate fit in a recessed opening. Standard front seats were cloth/vinyl reclining low-back buckets. Capri had color-keyed hood and rear pillar louvers, and black cowl louvers. The instrument panel was grey suede painted, with applique. Bumpers had integral black rub strips. GS standard equipment included four-speed manual shift, power brakes, turbine wheel covers, trip odometer, tachometer, three-oval black sport steering wheel, integral rear spoiler, AM radio, black left remote mirror, day/night mirror, and dual visor vanity mirrors. Also standard: a dual-note horn, halogen headlamps, locking glovebox, temp/amp/oil gauges, lighter, digital clock, cargo area cover, and console with graphic warning display and stowage bin. Capri RS added a front air dam, power steering, wrapped steering wheel, five-speed manual gearbox, handling suspension, Traction-Lok axle, foglamps, and locking fuel filler door. Styling features included a black right remote mirror, black grille, black rear pillar louver, and tu-tone black/grey instrument panel. RS had black windshield, roof rip and window frame moldings. Turbo RS added identifying decals on fenders and decklid, sport-tuned exhaust with bright tailpipe extension, a hood scoop, cast aluminum valve covers, and heavy-duty battery.

TOPAZ — FOUR — Taking up the rising tide toward front-wheel-drive, Mercury introduced its second model, the compact Topaz, closely tied to Ford's Tempo. Two- and four-door sedans, replacements for the departed Zephyr, carried five passengers. Riding a wheelbase under 100 inches (actually a stretched Lynx platform), Topaz tipped the scales at about 2,200 lbs. The aerodynamically-styled body had a horizontal- bar grille with center emblem. Single rectangular headlamps met amber wraparound front side marker lenses. Euro-style wraparound taillamps tapered downward on each quarter panel. Two-doors had decklid stripes and dual bodyside accent stripes, and a black B pillar molding. Both bodies had a lower back panel applique with argent accents. Two trim levels were offered: GS and LS. Both had standard lower bodyside protection. Color-keyed bodyside moldings were wide in Pacific states, narrow elsewhere. Standard GS features included bright upper/lower grille bars, and window frame, belt, rear window surround and windshield moldings. Bumpers had color-keyed end caps and rub strips. Base engine was a 140 cu. in. (2.3-liter) 2300 HSC (High Swirl Combustion) four with EEC-IV. Displacement was the same as the four that had been around for some years, but bore and stroke were not. This was a different design, derived from the inline six. The standard four-speed manual overdrive transaxle (five-speee in Pacific states) had a self-adjusting clutch. A 2.0-liter diesel also was offered, with five-speed transaxle. Topaz had rack-and-pinion steering and a parallel four-bar-link independent rear suspension. A firm-handling suspension was standard. Interiors held contoured front seats, a locking glovebox, and a color-keyed consolette. Door trim panels were carpeted on the lower section, with built-in storage bins. Cloth/vinyl low-back reclining bucket seats were standard. Standard GS equipment included polycast wheels, two- speed wiper/washer, AM radio (AM/FM in Pacific states), power brakes, lighter, temp gauge, ammeter, locking glovebox, dual- note horn, four-speed heater/defroster, halogen headlamps, color-keyed instrument panel applique, dual color-keyed rmeote mirrors, day/night mirror, and dual visor vanity mirrors. The radio could be deleted for credit. Topaz LS added passenger assist handles, a swivel map light, interval wipers, dual color bodyside accent stripes, color-keyed wide bodyside moldings, decklid moldings (four-door), comfort/convenience group, digital clock, and color-keyed umper end cap extensions. Pacific-state models also had power steering, power door locks, power windows, dual lighted visor vanity mirrors, console with graphic warning display, and illuminated entry. The special Western State Package, adding standard equipment, was offered only in California, Oregon, Washington, Alaska and Hawaii.

MARQUIS — FOUR/V-6 — Descended from the old Cougar, the rear-drive Marquis changed little for its second season. Three-speed SelectShift automatic was now the standard transmission, and the inline six option was dropped. A fuel-injected 232 cu. in. (3.8- liter) V-6 was standard in wagons, optional in sedans. Power steering became standard, and the horn button returned to the center hub of the steering wheel. Gas-pressurized shocks were standard. Thin vertical bars made up the Marquis grille. Angled clear/amber side marker lenses continued back from the housing that contained the quad rectangular headlamps. Amber parking lamps were built into the bumper. Separate clear horizontal rectangular marker lenses were below the bodyside molding, just ahead of the front wheel. At the rear were wraparound taillamps. Front seatbacks had individual recliners. An extra-cost front bench seat expanded capacity to six passengers. Marquis Brougham had Twin Comfort lounge seats with dual recliners and individual fold-down center armrests. Cloth upholstery was standard; vinyl or leather seating surfaces optional. Options included an Electronic Instrument Cluster with Tripminder computer, auto-temp air conditioner, power lock group, and Premium Sound System. Marquis wagons had a standard liftgate-open warning light and cargo area lamp.

1984 Cougar XR-7 Sports Coupe (JG)

COUGAR/XR-7 — FOUR/V-6/V-8 — Following a year out of the lineup, the XR7 name returned this year on a turbocharged Cougar—Mercury's version of the Thunderbird Turbo Coupe. XR7 had a standard five-speed manual or optional (extra cost) three-speed automatic transmissin, along with a handling suspension, high-performance tires, and a tachometer. Turbo models featured Quadra-Shock rear suspension, with two horizontal dampers. Fuel injection went on the basic Cougar's 232 cu. in. (3.8-liter) base V-6 engine. Standard automatic transmissions had a lock-up torque converter. The 302 cu. in. (5.0-liter) V-8 was optional. All engines now had EEC-IV electronic controls. The horn button moved to the center hub of the new steering wheel. Nitrogen gas-pressurized front struts and rear shocks were standard. So was variable-ratio power rack- and-pinion steering. Appearance was similar to 1983, with upswept quarter- window design and wide rear pillars with round emblem. Cougars had deeply recessed quad rectangular headlamps. Wraparound amber side marker lenses extended from the same housing. An optional Electronic Instrument Cluster contained a digital speedometer, graphic fuel gauge, and digital clock. Base Cougars came with automatic transmission, AM radio, bright wheel covers, power brakes and steering, driver's remote mirror, reminder chimes, analog clock, lighter, full console with padded lid, and mini spare tire. Bright moldings went on the grille surround, belt, concealed drip, quarter and back windows, door frames, windshield, and bodyside (with charcoal vinyl insert). Bodies displayed a center pillar applique, charcoal bumper rub strips with extensions, and decklid and upper bodyside accent stripes. Cougar LS added a woodtone applique instrument panel, tinted glass, coach lamps, dual black power remote mirrors, bright rocker panel moldings, power windows, and hood accent stripes. LS also had standard luxury cloth 40/40 seats and a passenger visor vanity mirror. In addition to the turbo engine, Cougar XR-7 had a Traction-Lok axle, tachometer, heavy-duty (54-amp) battery, charcoal floor console with Oxford Grey armrest pad, Oxford Grey headliner, charcoal instrument panel, power windows, and silver metallic polycast wheels. Also on XR7: Oxford Grey tri-band lower tape striping, black leather-wrapped four- spoke steering wheel, clearcoat metallic paint with lower accent, and color-keyed rear window moldings. Seats were Oxford Grey cloth sport buckets.

1984 Marquis Colony Park station wagon (OCW)

GRAND MARQUIS — V-8 — Immodestly described as an "American classic," the full-size (by modern standards, at any rate) Grand Marquis continued with little change, carrying six passengers. Sole engine was the 302 cu. in. (5.0-liter) V-8 with EFI and EEC- IV, coupled to four-speed automatic overdrive. Base and LS trim levels were availble in the two- and four-door sedans. LS had Twin Comfort lounge seats in luxury cloth or optional leather. As before, the upright grille was made up of six vertical bars on each side of a slightly wider center divider bar. Surround moldings of the recessed quad headlamps continued to meet clear park/signal lights at the fender tips, which wrapped around the fenders to a narrow amber lens at the rear. Wraparound horizontally-ribbed taillamps were used. Colony Park and Colony Park LS wagons both had a three- way tailgate with power window, locking stowage compartment, and load floor carpeting. Twin Comfort lounge seats had standard vinyl upholstery, with cloth and knitted vinyl optional; cloth standard on Colony Park LS. Dual-facing optional rear seats held two passengers (for a total of eight). A heavy-duty suspension package included bigger front stabilizer bar, heavy-duty springs and revalved shocks. The heavy-duty (Class III) Trailer Towing Package that could haul 5,000 pounds included a heavy-duty radiator, auxiliary power steering and transmission oil coolers.

I.D. DATA: Mercury's 17-symbol Vehicle Identification Number (VIN) was stamped on a metal tab fastened to the instrument panel, visible through the windshield. Symbols one to three indicates manufacturer, make and vehicle type: '1ME' Mercury passenger car. The fourth symbol ('B') denotes restraint system. Next comes a letter 'P', followed by two digits that indicate body type: Model Number, as shown in left column of tables below. (Example: '54' base Lynx three-door hatchback.) Symbol eight indicates engine type: '2' L498 2Bbl.; '4' H.O. L498 2Bbl.; '5' L498 EFI; '8' Turbo L498 FI; 'H' Diesel L4121; 'A' L4-140 1Bbl.; 'R' or 'J' HSC L4140 1Bbl.; '6' Propane L4140; 'W' Turbo L4140 EFI; '3' V6232 2Bbl. or FI; 'F' V8302 2Bbl. or FI; 'M' V8302 4Bbl.; 'G' V8351 2Bbl. Next is a check digit. Symbol ten indicates model year ('E' 1984). Symbol eleven is assembly plant: 'A' Atlanta, GA; 'B' Oakville, Ontario

(Canada); 'F' Dearborn, MI; 'G' Chicago; 'H' Lorain, Ohio; 'K' Kansas City, MO; 'W' Wayne, MI; 'X' St. Thomas, Ontario; 'Z' St. Louis, MO; and Edison, NJ. The final six digits make up the sequence number, starting with 600001. A Vehicle Certification Label on the left front door lock face panel or door pillar shows the month and year of manufacture, GVW, GAWR, VIN, and codes for such items as body type, color, trim, axle, transmission, and special order information.

LYNX (FOUR)

Model Number	Body/Style Number	Body Type & Seating	Factory Price	Shipping Weight	Production Total
54	61D	3-dr. Hatch-4P	5758	1928	Note 1
65	58D	5-dr. Hatch-4P	5965	1984	Note 1
54	61D	3-dr. L Hatch-4P	6019	1922	Note 1
65	58D	5-dr. L Hatch-4P	6233	N/A	Note 1
60	74D	4-dr. L Sta Wag-4P	6448	N/A	Note 1
55	61D	3-dr. GS Hatch-4P	6495	1948	Note 1
66	58D	5-dr. GS Hatch-4P	6709	N/A	Note 1
61	74D	4-dr. GS Sta Wag-4P	6887	N/A	Note 1
57	61D	3-dr. RS Hatch-4P	7641	N/A	Note 1
68/934	58D	5-dr. LTS Hatch-4P	7879	1920	Note 1

LYNX TURBO (FOUR)

57	61D	3-dr. RS Hatch-4P	8728	1997	Note 1

Note 1: Total Lynx production, 38,208 three-door hatchbacks, 21,090 five-door hatchbacks, and 16,142 four-door liftgate station wagons.

CAPRI GS (FOUR/V-6)

79	61D	3-dr. Fastbk-4P	7758/8167	2615/2723	Note 2

Capri Engine Note: Six-cylinder price does not include cost of the required automatic transmission ($439). The high-output 302 cu. in. V-8 engine cost $1165 more than the V-6.

CAPRI RS TURBO (FOUR)

79	61D	3-dr. Fastbk-4P	9822	2894	Note 2

CAPRI RS (V-8)

79	61D	3-dr. Fastbk-4P	9638	2894	Note 2

Note 2: Total Capri production was 20,642.

TOPAZ (FOUR)

72	66D	2-dr. GS Sedan-5P	7469	2329	32,749
75	54D	4-dr. GS Sedan-5P	7469	2413	96,505
73	66D	2-dr. LS Sedan-5P	7872	2353	Note 3
76	54D	4-dr. LS Sedan-5P	7872	2434	Note 3

Note 3: Production of LS models is included in GS totals.

Diesel Engine Note: A diesel model Topaz cost $8027 (GS) or $8429 (LS).

MARQUIS (FOUR/V-6)

89	54D	4-dr. Sedan-5P	8727/9136	2796/--	91,808
90	74D	4-dr. Sta Wag-5P	--/9224	--/2996	16,004

1984 Marquis Brougham sedan (JG)

MARQUIS BROUGHAM (FOUR/V-6)

89	54D	4-dr. Sedan-5P	9030/9439	2796/--	Note 4
90	74D	4-dr. Sta Wag-5P	--/9498	N/A	Note 4

Note 4: Brougham production is included in basic totals above.

COUGAR (V-6/V-8)

Model Number	Body/Style Number	Body Type & Seating	Factory Price	Shipping Weight	Production Total
92	66D	2-dr. Cpe-4P	9978/10361	2912/--	131,190
92/603	66D	2-dr. LS Cpe-4P	11265/11648	2941/--	Note 5

Cougar Engine Note: The V-8 engine required a four-speed automatic transmission at $237 extra.

COUGAR XR-7 (TURBO FOUR)

92/934	66D	2-dr. Cpe-4P	13065	2900	Note 5

Note 5: Production of LS and XR-7 is included in basic total above.

1984 Grand Marquis LS sedan (JG)

GRAND MARQUIS (V-8)

93	66K	2-dr. Sedan-6P	11576	3607	13,657
95	54K	4-dr. Sedan-6P	11640	3761	117,739
93/60H	66K	2-dr. LS Sed-6P	12131	3607	Note 6
95/60H	54K	4-dr. LS Sed-6P	12195	3761	Note 6

GRAND MARQUIS COLONY PARK (V-8)

94	74K	4-dr. Sta Wag-6P	11816	3788	17,421

Note 6: LS production is included in basic Grand Marquis totals.

FACTORY PRICE AND WEIGHT NOTE: Cougar prices and weights to left of slash are for V-6, to right for V-8 engine. For Capri/Marquis, prices/weights to left of slash are for four-cylinder, to right for V-6.

ENGINE DATA: BASE FOUR (Lynx): Inline. Overhead cam. Four-cylinder. Cast iron block and aluminum head. Displacement: 97.6 cu. in. (1.6 liters). Bore & stroke: 3.15 x 3.13 in. Compression ratio: 9.0:1. Brake horsepower: 70 at 4600 R.P.M. Torque: 88 lbs.-ft. at 2600 R.P.M. Five main bearings. Hydraulic valve lifters. Carburetor: 2Bbl. Motorcraft 740. VIN Code: 2. OPTIONAL FOUR (Lynx): High-output version of 1.6-liter engine above Horsepower: 80 at 5400 R.P.M. Torque: 88 lbs.-ft. at 3000 R.P.M. VIN Code: 4. OPTIONAL FOUR (Lynx): Fuel-injected version of 1.6-liter engine above Compression ratio: 9.5:1. Horsepower: 84 at 5200 R.P.M. Torque: 90 lbs.- at 2800 R.P.M. VIN Code: 5. TURBO FOUR (Lynx): Same as 1.6-liter four above, with fuel injection and turbocharger Compression ratio: 8.0:1. Horsepower: 120 at 5200 R.P.M. Torque: 120 lbs.-ft. at 3400 R.P.M. VIN Code: 8. DIESEL FOUR (Lynx, Topaz): Inline. Overhead cam. Four-cylinder. Cast iron block and aluminum head. Displacement: 121 cu. in. (2.0 liters). Bore & stroke: 3.39 x 3.39 in. Compression ratio: 22.5:1. Brake horsepower: 52 at 4000 R.P.M. Torque: 82 lbs.-ft. at 2400 R.P.M. Five main bearings. Solid valve lifters. Fuel injection. VIN Code: H. BASE FOUR (Topaz): Inline. Overhead valve. Four-cylinder. Cast iron block and head. Displacement: 140 cu. in. (2.3 liters). Bore & stroke: 3.70 x 3.30 in. Compression ratio: 9.0:1. Brake horsepower: 84 at 4400 R.P.M. Torque: 118 lbs.-ft. at 2600 R.P.M. Five main bearings. Hydraulic valve lifters. Carburetor: 1Bbl. Holley 6149. High Swirl Combustion (HSC) design. VIN Code: R (U.S.) or J (Mexico). BASE FOUR (Capri, Marquis): Inline. Overhead cam. Four-cylinder. Cast iron block and head. Displacement: 140 cu. in. (2.3 liters). Bore & stroke: 3.78 x 3.13 in. Compression ratio: 9.0:1. Brake horsepower: 88 at 4000 R.P.M. Torque: 122 lbs.-ft. at 2400 R.P.M. Five main bearings. Hydraulic valve lifters. Carburetor: 1Bbl. Carter YFA. VIN Code: A. BASE TURBO FOUR (Cougar XR-7; OPTIONAL (Capri): Same as 140 cu. in. four above, but with turbocharger Compression ratio: 8.0:1. Horsepower: 145 at 4600 R.P.M. (Capri, 175 at 4400 R.P.M.). Torque: 180 lbs.-ft. at 3800 R.P.M. (Capri, N/A). VIN Code: W. NOTE: Propane four was available for Marquis. BASE V-6 (Cougar); OPTIONAL (Capri, Marquis): 90-degree, overhead valve V-6. Cast iron block and aluminum head. Displacement: 232 cu. in. (3.8 liters). Bore & stroke: 3.80 x 3.40 in. Compression ratio: 8.65:1. Brake horsepower: 120 at 3600 R.P.M. Torque: 205 lbs.-ft. at 1600 R.P.M. Four main bearings. Hydraulic valve lifters. Carburetor: 2Bbl. (or fuel-injected). VIN Code: 3. BASE V-8 (Grand Marquis); OPTIONAL (Cougar): 90-degree, overhead valve V-8. Cast iron block and head. Displacement: 302 cu. in. (5.0 liters). Bore & stroke: 4.00 x 3.00 in. Compression ratio: 8.4:1. Brake horsepower: 140 at 3200 R.P.M. Torque: 250 lbs.-ft. at 1600 R.P.M. Five main bearings. Hydraulic valve lifters. Fuel injection. VIN Code: F. OPTIONAL V 8 (Grand Marquis): Carbureted version of 302 cu. in. V-8 above Compression ratio: 8.4:1. Horsepower: 155 at 3600 R.P.M. Torque: 265 lbs.-ft. at 2000 R.P.M. OPTIONAL V-8 (Capri): Fuel-injected version of 302 cu. in. V-8 above Compression ratio: 8.3:1. Horsepower: 165 at 4000 R.P.M. Torque: 245 lbs.-ft. at 2200 R.P.M. OPTIONAL V-8 (Capri): High-output version of 302 cu. in. V-8 above Compression ratio: 8.3:1. Horsepower: 175 at 4000 R.P.M. Torque: 245 lbs.-ft. at 2200 R.P.M. Carburetor: 4Bbl. Holley 4180C. VIN Code: M. NOTE: High-output version rated 205 H.P. was announced but delayed. POLICE V-8 (Grand Marquis): 90-degree, overhead valve V-8. Cast iron block and head. Displacement: 351 cu. in. (5.8 liters). Bore & stroke: 4.00 x 3.50 in. Compression ratio: 8.3:1. Brake horsepower: 180 at 3600 R.P.M. Torque: 285 lbs.-ft. at 2400 R.P.M. Five main bearings. Hydraulic valve lifters. Carburetor: 2Bbl. VV. VIN Code: G.

CHASSIS DATA: Wheelbase: (Lynx) 94.2 in.; (Capri) 100.5 in.; (Topaz) 99.9 in.; (Marquis) 105.6 in.; (Cougar) 104.0 in.; (Grand Marquis) 114.3 in. Overall Length: (Lynx) 163.9 in.; (Capri) 179.1 in.; (Topaz) 176.5 in.; (Marquis) 196.5 in.; (Cougar) 197.6 in.; (Grand Marquis) 214.0 in.; (Grand Marquis wag) 218.0 in. Height: (Lynx)

53.3 in.; (Capri) 51.9 in.; (Topaz 2dr.) 52.5 in.; (Topaz 4dr.) 52.7 in.; (Marquis) 53.6 in.; (Marquis wag) 54.3 in.; (Cougar) 53.4 in.; (Grand Marquis) 55.2 in.; (Grand Marquis wag) 56.8 in. Width: (Lynx) 65.9 in.; (Capri) 69.1 in.; (Topaz) 66.2 in.; (Marquis) 71.0 in.; (Cougar) 71.1 in.; (Grand Marquis) 77.5 in.; (Grand Marquis wag) 79.3 in. Front Tread: (Lynx) 54.7 in.; (Capri) 56.6 in.; (Topaz) 54.7 in.; (Marquis) 56.6 in.; (Cougar) 58.1 in.; (Grand Marquis) 62.2 in. Rear Tread: (Lynx) 56.0 in.; (Capri/Marquis) 57.0 in.; (Topaz) 57.6 in.; (Cougar) 58.5 in.; (Grand Marquis) 62.0 in. Standard Tires: (Lynx) P165/80R13; (Lynx RS/LTS) 165/70R365 Michelin TRX; (Capri) P185/75R14; (Capri RS) P205/70R14; (Topaz) P175/80R13; (Marquis) P185/75R14; (Cougar) P185/75R14; (XR7) P205/70HR14; (Grand Marquis) P215/75R14 SBR WSW.

TECHNICAL: Transmission: Four-speed manual standard on Lynx/Topaz; five- speed manual or three-speed automatic optional. Four-speed manual standard on Capri; five-speed manual, three-speed or four-speed automatic optional. SelectShift three-speed automatic standard on Cougar/Marquis; four-speed overdrive optional. Five-speed manual standard on Cougar XR7. Four- speed overdrive automatic standard on Grand Marquis. Gear ratios same as equivalent Ford models; see Ford/Mustang listings. Standard final drive ratio: (Lynx) 3.59:1 w/4spd, 3.73:1 w/5spd, 3.31:1 w/auto., 3.52:1 w/diesel; (Capri four) 3.08:1 w/4spd, 3.27:1 w/auto.; (Capri V-6) 3.08:1; (Capri V-8) 3.08:1 w/5spd, 2.73:1 w/auto., 3.27:1 w/4spd auto.; (Capri turbo) 3.45:1; (Topaz) 3.04:1 w/4spd, 3.23:1 w/5spd or auto., 3.73:1 w/diesel; (Marquis) 3.08:1, 3.27:1 or 2.73:1; (Cougar V-6) 2.73:1 w/3spd auto., 3.27:1 with 4spd auto.; (Cougar V-8) 3.08:1; (Cougar XR7 turbo) 3.45:1 w/5spd, 3.73:1 w/auto.; (Grand Marquis) 3.08:1. Steering: (Grand Marquis) recirculating ball; (others) rack and pinion. Front Suspension: (Lynx) MacPherson strut-mounted coil springs w/lower control arms and stabilizer bar; (Topaz) MacPherson struts w/stabilizer bar; (Capri/Cougar/Marquis) modified MacPherson struts w/coil springs and anti-sway bar; (Grand Marquis) coil springs with long/short Aarms and anti- sway bar. Rear Suspension: (Lynx) independent trailing arms w/modified MacPherson struts and coil springs on lower control arms; (Topaz) fully independent quadra-link w/MacPherson struts; (Capri/Cougar/Marquis/Grand Marquis) four-link w/coil springs. Brakes: Front disc, rear drum. Ignition: Electronic. Body construction: (Grand Marquis) separate body and frame; (others) unibody. Fuel tank: (Lynx) 13 gal.; (Capri) 15.4 gal.; (Topaz) 15.2 gal.; (Marquis) 16 gal.; (Cougar) 20.6 gal.; (Grand Marquis) 18 gal.; (Grand Marquis wag) 18.5 gal.

DRIVETRAIN OPTIONS: Engines: Fuel-saver 1.6-liter four: Lynx (NC). H.O. 1.6-liter four: Lynx ($73). Propane 140 cu. in. four: Marquis ($896). 232 cu. in. V-6: Capri/Marquis ($409). 302 cu. in. V-8: Capri ($1372-$1574); Cougar ($383). Transmission/Differential: Five-speed manual trans.: Lynx/Topaz ($76). Automatic transaxle: Lynx ($439) exc. LTS/RS ($363); Topaz ($439). Auto. transmission.: Capri ($439). Overdrive auto. trans.: Capri ($551); Marquis/Cougar ($237). Traction-Lok differential: Capri/Marquis/Grand Marquis/Cougar ($95). Brakes & Steering: Power brakes: Lynx ($95). Power steering: Lynx ($215); Capri ($202); Topaz ($223). Suspension: H.D. susp.: Topaz (NC); Marquis ($43); Grand Marquis/Cougar ($26). Handling susp.: Lynx L ($145); Lynx GS ($41); Grand Marquis ($49). Handling susp. pkg.: Capri ($252) exc. w/VIP pkg. ($50). Soft ride susp. pkg.: Topaz (NC). Other: H.D. battery ($27). Engine block heater ($18). Trailer towing pkg.: Grand Marquis ($200-$302); Cougar ($251). California emission system: Lynx ($46); others ($99). High- altitude emissions (NC).

LYNX CONVENIENCE/APPEARANCE OPTIONS: Option Packages: Villager woodtone pkg. ($339). Instrument group ($87). Power door lock group ($124-$176). Light group ($67). Comfort/Convenience: Air conditioner ($643). Rear defroster, electric ($130). Fingertip speed control ($176). Tinted glass ($95); windshield only ($48). Tilt steering ($104). Overhead console w/digital clock ($82). Interval wipers ($50). Rear wiper/washer ($120). Dual remote sport mirrors ($68). Entertainment: AM radio ($39). AM/FM stereo radio ($109) exc. L ($148); w/cassette player ($204) exc. L ($243). Electronic- tuning AM/FM stereo w/cassette ($396-$435). Premium sound ($117). Radio delete ($39 credit). Exterior: Flip-up open-air roof ($315) exc. Villager ($215). Clearcoat metallic paint (NC). Glamour paint ($51). Dual bodyside paint stripes ($39). Front vent windows, pivoting ($63). Vinyl-insert bodyside moldings ($45). Bumper guards, front or rear ($28). Bumper rub strips ($48). Luggage rack ($100). Lower bodyside protection ($68). Interior: Console ($111). Vinyl seat trim ($24). Wheels/Tires: Wheel trim rings ($54). TR aluminum wheels: LTS/RS ($201). Styled steel wheels ($104 credit). P165/80R13 SBR WSW ($59). P175/80R13 SBR BSW (NC).

CAPRI CONVENIENCE/APPEARANCE OPTIONS: Option Packages: Light group ($55-$88). Power lock group ($177). Comfort/Convenience: Air cond. ($743). Rear defroster, electric ($140). Fingertip speed control ($176). Power windows ($198). Tinted glass ($110). Tilt steering wheel ($110). Interval wipers ($50). Remote right mirror ($46). Entertainment: AM/FM stereo radio ($109); w/cassette player ($222) exc. w/VIP pkg. ($113). Premium sound system ($151). AM radio delete ($39 credit); AM/FM ($148 credit). Exterior: TRoof ($874-$1074). Flip-up open air roof ($315). Glamour paint ($54). Lower bodyside protection ($41). Interior: Sport seats ($196). Vinyl low-back seats ($29). Wheels and Tires: Wire wheel covers ($98). P195/75R14 WSW ($108). P205/70HR14 BSW ($224). TRX 220/55R390 BSW in performance pkg. ($327-$551).

TOPAZ CONVENIENCE/APPEARANCE OPTIONS: Option Packages: TR performance pkg. w/aluminum wheels ($293). Power lock group ($202-$254). Appearance protection group ($71). Light/convenience group ($50-$70). Comfort/Convenience: Air cond. ($743). Rear defroster, electric ($140). Fingertip speed control ($176). Illuminated entry ($82). Anti-theft system ($159). Power windows ($272). Power decklid release ($40). Six-way power seat ($224). Tinted glass ($110); windshield ($48). Tilt steering ($110). Digital clock ($61). Interval wipers ($50). Lighted visor vanity mirrors, pair ($100). Entertainment: AM/FM stereo radio ($109); w/cassette player ($204). Electronic-tuning AM/FM stereo ($252); w/cassette ($396). Premium sound system ($117). AM radio delete ($39 credit). Exterior: Flip-up open air roof ($315). Metallic glamour glow paint ($63). Black lower body accent paint ($78-$133). Bumper guards, front/rear ($56). Interior: Console ($111). Fold-down front armrest ($55). Vinyl seat trim ($35). Carpeted front floor mats ($13). Trunk trim ($30). Tires: P175/80R13 WSW ($72).

MARQUIS CONVENIENCE/APPEARANCE OPTIONS: Option Packages: Woodtone option ($282). Power lock group ($213-$254). Cold weather group ($77). Light group ($38). Police pkg. ($859-$1387). H.D. pkg. ($210). Comfort/Convenience: Air cond. ($743); auto-temp ($809). Rear defroster, electric ($140). Fingertip speed control ($176). Illuminated entry ($82). Autolamp on-off delay ($73). Power windows ($272). Six-way power driver's seat ($224); dual ($449). Tinted glass ($110). Tinted windshield ($48). Leather-wrapped steering wheel ($59). Tilt steering ($110). Electronic instrument cluster ($289-$367). Tripminder computer ($215-$293). Digital clock ($78). Diagnostic warning lights ($89). Auto. parking brake release ($12). Interval wipers ($50). Liftgate wiper/washer: wagon ($99). Lighting and Mirrors: Cornering lamps ($68). Right remote convex mirror ($61). Lighted visor vanity mirrors ($57-$106). Entertainment: AM/FM stereo radio ($109); w/cassette player ($204). Electronic-tuning AM/FM stereo radio w/cassette ($396). Premium sound system ($117-$151). AM radio delete ($39 credit). Exterior: Carriage roof ($848). Full vinyl roof ($152). Glamour paint ($63). Two-tone paint ($117). Pivoting front vent windows ($79). Two-way liftgate: wag ($105). Protective bodyside moldings ($55). Bumper guards, rear ($28). Bumper rub strips ($56). Luggage rack: wagon ($126). Lower bodyside protection ($41). Interior: Vinyl seat trim ($35). Individual seats w/console ($61). Leather seat trim ($415). Front floor mats, carpeted ($23). Wheels/Tires: Luxury wheel covers ($55). Wire wheel covers, locking ($204). Polycast wheels ($178). Styled steel wheels w/trim rings ($54). P185/75R14 WSW ($72). P195/75R14 BSW ($38); WSW ($116). Puncture-sealant P195/75R14 WSW ($240). Conventional spare ($63).

COUGAR CONVENIENCE/APPEARANCE OPTIONS: Option Packages: Luxury carpet group ($72). Traveler's assistance kit ($65). Light group ($35). Power lock group ($177). Comfort/Convenience: Air cond. ($743); auto-temp ($809). Rear defroster ($140). Fingertip speed control ($176). Illuminated entry system ($82). Keyless entry ($198). Anti-theft system ($159). Remote fuel door lock ($37). Tripminder computer ($215-$276). Autolamp on/off delay ($73). Tinted glass ($110); windshield only ($48). Power windows ($198). Six-way power driver's seat ($227); dual ($454). Auto. parking brake release ($12). Leather-wrapped steering wheel ($59). Tilt steering wheel ($110). Electronic instrument cluster ($382). Diagnostic warning lights ($89). Digital clock ($61). Interval wipers ($49). Lighting and Mirrors: Cornering lamps ($68). Electro-luminiscent coach lamps ($84). Dual electric remote mirrors ($96). Electronic-dimming day/night mirror ($77). Lighted visor vanity mirrors, pair ($106). Entertainment: AM/FM stereo radio ($109); w/cassette player ($204). Electronic-tuning AM/FM stereo search radio ($252); w/cassette ($396). Power antenna ($66). Premium sound system ($179). AM radio delete ($39 credit). Exterior: Luxury vinyl half rear roof ($245). Flip-up open-air roof ($315). Metallic clearcoat paint ($183). Hood accent striping ($16). Pivoting front vent windows ($79). Rocker panel moldings ($39). License frames ($9). Lower bodyside protection ($39-$54). Interior: Articulated seats ($183-$427). Leather seat trim ($415). Vinyl seat trim ($37). Front floor mats, carpeted ($22). Wheels/Tires: Wire wheel covers, locking ($90-$204). Luxury wheel covers ($113). Polycast wheels ($65-$178). P195/75R14 puncture-sealing tires ($124). P205/70R14 BSW (NC). P205/70R14 WSW ($62). P205/70HR14 performance BSW ($152). Cast aluminum TRX wheels w/BSW performance tires ($535-$649) exc. XR7 ($318).

GRAND MARQUIS CONVENIENCE/APPEARANCE OPTIONS: Option Packages: LS decor: Colony Park ($621). Convenience group ($109-$134). Power lock group ($140-$238). Light group ($30-$48). Comfort/Convenience: Air cond. ($743); w/auto-temp control ($809). Rear defroster, electric ($140). Fingertip speed control ($176). Illuminated entry system ($82). Power driver's seat ($227); driver and passenger ($454). Remote fuel door lock ($35). Tinted glass ($110); windshield only ($48). Autolamp on/off delay ($73). Leather-wrapped steering wheel ($59). Tilt steering wheel ($110). Tripminder computer ($261). Digital clock ($61). Interval wipers ($50). Lighting and Mirrors: Cornering lamps ($68). Remote right mirror ($44). Lighted visor vanity mirrors ($106). Entertainment: Electronic-tuning AM/FM stereo radio w/cassette ($166). Power antenna ($66). Premium sound system ($151- $179). Radio delete ($148 credit). Exterior: Formal vinyl coach roof: 4dr. ($650). Glamour paint ($77). Two-tone paint ($129). Pivoting front vent windows ($79). Rocker panel moldings ($18-$38). Vinyl-insert bodyside moldings ($61). Bumper rub strips ($59). Luggage rack ($104). Lower bodyside protection ($39-$52). Interior: Dual-facing rear seats: wagon ($167). Cloth twin comfort seats ($48). Leather seat trim ($418). All-vinyl seat trim ($34); Duraweave vinyl ($96). Carpeted front floor mats ($21). Wheels/Tires: Wire wheel covers, locking ($174). Cast aluminum wheels ($361). P225/75R14 WSW ($42-$43). P205/75R15 WSW ($17); puncture-sealant ($178). P215/75R14 BSW ($66 credit). Conventional spare ($63).

NOTE: Many value option packages were offered for each Mercury model.

HISTORY: Introduced: September 22, 1983 except Topaz, April 1983. Model year production: 613,155. Calendar year production (U.S.): 461,504. Calendar year sales by U.S. dealers: 527,198. Model year sales by U.S. dealers: 529,300 (including early '84 Topaz models).

Historical Footnotes: A giant sales leap highlighted the 1984 model year, up about one-third from 484,688 (including 21,745 early Topaz models) to 644,308. Marquis sales rose dramatically, and Cougar wasn't so far from doubling (up 82 percent). Big and luxury models seemed to be doing well, as was the case in the industry as a whole. Lynx and Capri sales slipped notably, though not drastically. LN7 was dropped in 1984, as it had never found a significant number of buyers. Only a few leftovers were sold during the 1984 model year. Lincoln-Mercury now had its own import: the sporty Merkur XR4Ti, from Ford Werke AG in West Germany, rivaling BMW, Audi and Volvo. It was actually sold under a separate franchise.

1985 MERCURY

Cougar got a modest facelift this year, including grille, taillamps and dash. Grand Marquis offered an electronic suspension system. A fuel-injected four-cylinder engine and five-speed manual transaxle were made standard on Topaz. Lynx was a carryover at introduction time, but a Second Series arrived at mid-year, with a larger (1.9-liter) engine under the hood.

1985 Lynx hatchback sedan (CP)

LYNX — FOUR — Since a Second Series Lynx with larger (1.9-liter) CVH four-cylinder engine would arrive as a 1985.5 model, the early carryover version continued with fewer models and engine possibilities. Only the three-door base model survived, along with GS and LS editions. The RS (three-door) and LTS (five-door) were dropped. Also dropped was the port fuel-injected 1.6 engine, leaving only the carbureted version. A new shift pattern for the five-speed transaxle put reverse below fifth gear, instead of by itself at the upper left. All except the base three-door now had power brakes. An AM/FM stereo radio was now standard on GS. The 2.0-liter diesel engine was available again, but turbos faded away. Base Lynx standard equipment included the two-barrel four-cylinder engine, four-speed manual transaxle, P165/80R13 SBR BSW tires on semi-styled steel wheels with bright trim rings, color-keyed door scuff plates, compact spare tire, cargo area cover, consolette, side window demisters, dome light, and day/night mirror. Bright bumpers had black end caps. Cloth reclining high-back

bucket seats were standard. So was a 10-gallon fuel tank. Lynx L added power brakes, an AM radio, black carpeting, 13-gallon fuel tank, black rocker panel paint, and cloth reclining low-back bucket seats. Pacific state models had a five-speed manual transaxle, AM/FM stereo and an instrument group. GS models included a black front air dam, AM/FM stereo radio, styled steel wheels, high-output engine, five-speed transaxle, dual-color upper bodyside accent paint stripes, assist handles, bumper rub strips with argent accent stripe, and color-keyed lower back panel carpeting. Also on GS: a locking glovebox, remote fuel filler door lock/release, and power hatch release. Wide bodyside moldings had argent accent striping, and rocker panels had no black paint. See 1986 listing for description of the Second Series Lynx.

1985 Capri GS hatchback coupe (CP)

CAPRI — FOUR/V-6/V-8 — Appearance of Mercury's Mustang clone was similar to 1984. As usual, Capri had a different grille than Mustang, and horizontal louvers at the rear of the quarter window rather than vertical. Biggest styling difference, though, was the "bubbleback" glass hatch. Roller tappets were added to the 302 cu. in. (5.0-liter) V-8, standard in the RS (later changed to 5.0L name), along with a higher-performance camshaft and two-speed accessory drive. The five-speed manual gearbox got tighter gear ratios and shorter lever travel. Capri GS continued with a standard 140 cu. in. (2.3-liter) four. Other choices included the 232 cu. in. (3.8-liter) V-6, and fuel-injected or four-barrel V-8. The turbo engine was scheduled to reappear, but didn't make it. Both the V-6 and V-8 had a low oil level warning light. Bodies now had charcoal highlights. Standard equipment was added, including an electric rear-window defroster, tinted glass, power steering, interval wipers, and tilt steering. Capri GS standard equipment included the 140 cu. in. four with four-speed manual gearbox, P195/75R14 SBR BSW tires, turbine wheel covers, power windows, tachometer, integral rear spoiler, power brakes, charcoal bumper rub strips, digital clock, console with graphic warning display, and charcoal dual remote mirrors. Capri's charcoal grille had bright edges. Extra-wide wraparound charcoal bodyside moldings were used. Bodies also had dual fender and quarter panel pinstripes, lower bodyside protection, and color-keyed bumpers. Color-keyed louvers went on the hood, rear pillar and quarter panel; charcoal louvers on the cowl. Capri 5.0L included the V-8 engine, P205/70R14 tires, five-speed gearbox, cast aluminum wheels, handling suspension, three-oval black sport steering wheel, foglamps, locking remote gas filler door, front air dam, Traction-Lok, and dual exhausts. Bodies featured a charcoal lower bodyside paint treatment, charcoal moldings and grille, and charcoal rear pillar and quarter panel louvers. Tu-tone articulated sport seats offered adjustable thigh support.

1985 Topaz LS sedan (CP)

TOPAZ — FOUR — Changes to the front-drive compact in its second year were mainly mechanical. Throttle-body fuel injection was added to the standard 140 cu. in. (2.3-liter) four. A new expanded option, the GS Sports Group, included a high-output four with new cylinder head and intake manifold, offered only with manual shift. All manual transaxles were five-speed, with a new shift pattern (reverse moved from upper left to lower right position). Standard equipment now included power steering, tinted glass, and AM/FM stereo, leaving fewer items on the option list. A restyled instrument panel included a package tray and side window defoggers. Child-proof rear door locks were new. Joining the option list: leather seat trim, and a graphic equalizer for audio fans. Topaz had more standard equipment than Tempo—and more yet in Western states. Another difference between the two was Topaz's vertical-style wraparound taillamps, which connected with a full-width ribbed horizontal panel. Topaz GS standard equipment included the five-speed manual transaxle, P175/80R13 SBR BSW tires on polycast aluminum wheels, handling suspension, and tachometer. Styling features included dual bodyside accent stripes, decklid stripes (two-door), dual sport remote mirrors, color-keyed bumper end caps and rub strips, and a black grille. Wide bodyside moldings were color-keyed. Cloth/vinyl low-back reclining bucket seats were standard, along with vinyl lower bodyside protection, consolette, side window demisters, and power brakes. Topaz LS equipment included AM/FM stereo with cassette player, power windows, interval wipers, dual lighted visor vanity mirrors, and tilt steering. LS also had three assist handles, a digital clock, console, remote decklid release, electric rear window defroster, power door locks, illuminated entry, and remote gas filler door lock/release. New optional leather seat trim came only in charcoal.

1985 Marquis sedan (CP)

MARQUIS — FOUR/V-6 — Apart from a revised grille, little change was evident on Mercury's rear-drive mid-size (nearly identical to Ford LTD), redesigned in 1983 on the former Cougar platform. This year's grille had fewer (and wider) vertical bars, and a center bar that was wider yet. New wide wraparound taillamps had horizontal ribbing in a two-tiered, all-red design. The base 140 cu. in. (2.3-liter) four added low-friction rings and gained compression. Standard tires increased to P195/75R14 size, with P205/70R14 newly optional. A high-output V-8 package also was announced, equivalent to LTD's LX model, but failed to appear. A four-door sedan and wagon came in base or Brougham trim. Wagons had a standard 232 cu. in. (3.8-liter) V-6. Standard Marquis equipment included automatic transmission, AM radio, cloth reclining Twin Comfort lounge seats, black front bumper guards, remote driver's mirror, power brakes and steering, and a mini spare tire. Dual hood and upper bodyside accent stripes were used. Wide color-keyed vinyl bodyside moldings had argent striping. Marquis Brougham added a digital clock, lighted passenger visor vanity mirror, luxury cloth reclining Twin Comfort seats, light group, and luxury interior touches. New options included rocker panel moldings, dual power remote mirrors, and Brougham Flight bench seating.

1985 Cougar XR-7 coupe (CP)

COUGAR — FOUR/V-6/V-8 — Two years after its massive restyling, Cougar got a modest facelift. The new grille, styled a la Mercedes, had two horizontal bars and one vertical bar. Its basic shape, though, wasn't much different than before. Taillamps also were revised. A restyled instrument cluster contained a digital speedometer, plus analog fuel and temperature gauges. A full electronic display was optional. XR7 carried an all- analog cluster, and switched to 15 inch wheels. The 60/40 split front seat came with a consolette (not full console). Flatter back seat cushions now held three people. A soft-feel dashboard held side-window defoggers. The turbocharged four-cylinder engine in XR7 was modified for smoother, quiet running, and added horsepower. Five-speed gearboxes got a tighter shift pattern. New standard tires were P205/70R14 on basic models, P225/60VR15 for the XR7. Base models had a standard 232 cu. in. (3.8- liter) V-6 with SelectShift three-speed automatic (four-speed available); or optional 302 V-8 with four-speed overdrive automatic. Standard equipment also included power brakes and steering, four-speaker AM/FM stereo radio, cloth/vinyl reclining Twin Comfort lounge seats, bumper rub strips with extensions, analog clock, side defoggers, and dual-note horn. Upper bodyside accent stripes were standard. Bright moldings went on belt, drip, door frame, quarter and back windows, and windshield. Lower bodyside moldings had charcoal vinyl inserts. Cougar LS added power windows, hood accent stripes, cloth seat trim, bright rocker panel moldings, dual power remote mirrors, tinted glass, coach lamps, and trunk carpeting. XR7 included the turbocharged four with five- speed gearbox, P225/60VR15 performance Goodyear Gatorback BSW tires on cast aluminum wheels, handling suspension, Traction- Lok axle, front air dam, foglamps, and color-keyed dual power remote mirrors. Inside were Oxford Grey cloth sport bucket seats, a black sport steering wheel, digital clock, and charcoal console. Oxford Grey tri-band lower tape stripes, tinted glass, and charcoal moldings were standard on XR7.

1985 Grand Marquis sedan (CP)

GRAND MARQUIS — V-8 — Full-size rear-drives didn't have to change much each year to attract buyers. This year was no exception. Gas- pressurized front struts and rear shocks became standard. The horn button moved from the steering-column stalk to the hub, and a flash-to-pass feature was added. One key now worked both ignition and door locks. An ignition diagnostic monitor was added to EEC-IV engine control. Lower bodysides added chip-resistant urethane coating. Late in the model year, electronic rear leveling was to be made optional. As before, the full-size selection included a two- and four-door sedan, and four-door wagon. Standard equipment included the 302 cu. in. (5.0-liter) V-8 with automatic overdrive transmission, P215/75R14 SBR WSW tires, power brakes/steering, power windows, analog quartz clock, driver's remote mirror, and AM/FM stereo radio. Body features included upper bodyside accent stripes, a coach vinyl roof, bumper guards, and coach lamps. Color-keyed moldings went on quarter windows and roof wraparound of two- doors, and on the rear window; other moldings were bright, including wide lower bodyside moldings. Cloth reclining Twin Comfort lounge seats were standard. Grand Marquis LS added luxury cloth Twin Comfort seats, tinted glass, a folding center rear armrest, dual-beam dome light, and woodtone-applique door trim panels. Colony Park wagons had P215/75R14 WSW tires, conventional spare tire, three-way tailgate with power window, full-length bodyside/rail/tailgate woodtone applique, and vinyl Twin Comfort seats. Mercury's 17-symbol Vehicle Identification Number (VIN) was stamped on a metal tab fastened to the instrument panel, visible through the windshield. Symbols one to three indicates manufacturer, make and vehicle type: '1ME' Mercury passenger car. The fourth symbol ('B') denotes restraint system. Next comes a letter 'P', followed by two digits that indicate body type: Model Number, as shown in left column of tables below. (Example: '72' Topaz GS two- door sedan.) Symbol eight indicates engine type: '2' L498 2Bbl.; '4' H.O. L498 2Bbl.; 'H' Diesel L4121; 'A' L4-140 1Bbl.; 'X' HSC L4140 1Bbl.; 'S' H.O. L4140 FI; 'W' Turbo L4140 EFI; '3' V6232

443

DRIVETRAIN OPTIONS: Engines: H.O. 1.6-liter four: Lynx ($73). 232 cu. in. V-6: Capri ($439); Marquis sedan ($418). 302 cu. in. V-8: Capri ($1238); Cougar ($398). Transmission/Differential: Five-speed manual trans.: Lynx L ($76); Capri GS w/V-8 (NC). Automatic transaxle: Lynx L ($439); Lynx GS ($363); Topaz ($363). SelectShift auto. trans.: Capri ($439); Cougar XR7 ($315). Overdrive auto. trans.: Capri ($551-$676); Cougar ($237). Traction-Lok differential: Marquis/Grand Marquis/Cougar ($95). Brakes & Steering: Power brakes: Lynx ($95). Power steering: Lynx ($215). Suspension: H.D. susp.: Cougar base/LS, Grand Marquis ($26); Marquis LPO ($43). Auto. load leveling: Grand Marquis ($200). Other: H.D. battery ($27). Extended-range gas tank: Marquis sedan ($46). Engine block heater ($18). Trailer towing pkg.: Grand Marquis ($251-$302); Cougar ($251) exc. XR7. California emission system: Lynx ($46); others ($99). High- altitude emissions (NC).

LYNX CONVENIENCE/APPEARANCE OPTIONS: Option Packages: Comfort/convenience group ($259-$384). Comfort/Convenience: Air conditioner ($643). Rear defroster, electric ($130). Fingertip speed control ($176). Power door locks ($124-$176). Tinted glass ($95). Tilt steering ($104). Console w/graphic warning display ($111). Rear wiper/washer ($120). Entertainment: AM/FM stereo radio ($109) exc. base ($148); w/cassette player ($148-$295). Graphic equalizer ($218). Exterior: Clearcoat metallic paint ($91). Two-tone paint ($134-$173). Dual bodyside stripes: L ($39). Black vinyl- insert bodyside moldings ($45). Bumper guards, front or rear ($28). Bumper rub strips ($48) exc. base. Luggage rack: wag ($100). Interior: Vinyl seat trim ($24). Tires: P165/80R13 SBR WSW ($59).

NOTE: Many options were not available on base Lynx.

CAPRI CONVENIENCE/APPEARANCE OPTIONS: Option Packages: TR performance pkg. P220/55VR390 TRX tires on aluminum wheels w/handling suspension: GS ($565) exc. w/V-8 ($377). Power lock group ($177). Comfort/Convenience: Air cond. ($743). Fingertip speed control ($176). Entertainment: Electronic AM/FM stereo w/cassette ($300). Premium sound system ($138). Radio delete ($148 credit). Exterior: TRoof ($1074). Flip-up open air roof ($315). Interior: Low-back vinyl bucket seats: GS ($29). GS Wheels and Tires: Wire wheel covers ($98). Polycast steel wheels ($178). P205/75R14 WSW ($109).

TOPAZ CONVENIENCE/APPEARANCE OPTIONS: Option Packages: Sports group: GS ($439). Comfort/convenience pkg.: GS ($320-$706). TR performance pkg.: P185/65R365 Michelin TRX tires on cast aluminum wheels w/handling suspension ($293). Power lock group ($188-$254). Comfort/Convenience: Air cond. ($743). Rear defroster, electric ($140). Fingertip speed control ($176). Power windows: GS LPO ($272). Six-way power driver's seat LPO ($224). Tilt steering: GS ($110). Entertainment: AM/FM stereo radio w/cassette player: GS ($148). Electronic-tuning AM/FM stereo w/cassette ($78-$300). Graphic equalizer ($218). Exterior: Clearcoat paint ($91). Lower body accent paint ($78). Interior: Vinyl reclining bucket seat trim LPO ($35). Leather seat trim ($300). Wheels/Tires: Styled wheels: GS LPO ($59). P175/80R13 WSW ($72). Conventional spare ($63).

MARQUIS CONVENIENCE/APPEARANCE OPTIONS: Option Packages: Woodtone option: wagon ($282). Power lock group ($213-$254). Light group: base ($38). Comfort/Convenience: Air cond. ($743). Rear defroster ($140). Fingertip speed control ($176). Illuminated entry ($82). Autolamp on-off delay ($73). Power windows ($272). Six-way power driver's seat ($224). Tinted glass ($110). Leather- wrapped steering wheel ($59). Tilt steering ($110). Digital clock: base ($78). Auto. parking brake release LPO ($12). Interval wipers ($50). Lighting and Mirrors: Cornering lamps ($68). Right remote convex mirror ($61). Dual electric remote mirrors ($96). Lighted visor vanity mirrors ($57-$106). Entertainment: AM/FM stereo radio ($109); w/cassette player ($256). Electronic-tuning AM/FM stereo radio w/cassette ($409). AM radio delete ($39 credit). Exterior: Full vinyl roof ($152). Two-tone paint ($117). Pivoting front vent windows ($79). Two-way liftgate: wag ($105). Rocker panel moldings ($40). Bumper guards, rear ($28). Black bumper rub strips w/argent stripe ($56). Luggage rack: wagon ($126). Interior: Vinyl seat trim ($35). Flight bench seat: base (NC). Front floor mats, carpeted ($23). Wheels/Tires: Luxury wheel covers ($55). Wire wheel covers, locking ($204). Polycast wheels ($178). Styled steel wheels w/trim rings fleet ($54). P195/75R14 WSW ($72). P205/70R14 WSW ($134). Conventional spare LPO fleet ($63).

COUGAR CONVENIENCE/APPEARANCE OPTIONS: Option Packages: Headlamp convenience group ($176). Light group ($35). Power lock group ($213). Comfort/Convenience: Air cond. ($743); auto-temp ($905). Rear defroster ($140). Fingertip speed control ($176). Illuminated entry system ($82). Keyless entry ($198). Tinted glass: base ($110). Power windows: base ($198). Six-way power driver's seat ($227); dual ($454). Dual power seat recliners: base/LS ($189). Auto. parking brake release: base/LS ($12). Leather- wrapped steering wheel ($59). Tilt steering wheel ($110). Electronic instrument cluster ($330); N/A XR7. Diagnostic warning lights ($89). Low oil warning light LPO ($24). Digital clock ($61). Interval wipers ($50). Lighting and Mirrors: Cornering lamps ($68). Dual electric remote mirrors: base ($96). Lighted visor vanity mirrors, pair ($106). Entertainment: AM/FM stereo radio w/cassette player ($148). Electronic-tuning AM/FM stereo search radio w/cassette ($300). Power antenna ($66). Graphic equalizer ($252). Premium sound system ($168). AM/FM radio delete ($148 credit). Exterior: Padded half vinyl roof: base/LS ($245). Metallic clearcoat paint ($183). Two-tone paint/tape: base ($163). Hood accent stripe: base ($16). Pivoting front vent windows ($79). Interior: Heated seats ($157). Leather/vinyl seat trim ($415). Vinyl seat trim: base ($37). Front floor mats, carpeted ($22). Wheels/Tires (except XR7): Wire wheel covers, locking ($204). Polycast wheels ($178). P205/70R14 BSW ($62 credit). P215/70R14 WSW ($37). P215/70HR14 performance BSW ($152). Conventional spare ($63).

GRAND MARQUIS CONVENIENCE/APPEARANCE OPTIONS: Option Packages: LS decor: Colony Park ($621). Convenience group ($109-$134). Power lock group ($176-$273). Light group ($30-$48). Comfort/Convenience: Air cond. ($743); w/auto-temp control ($809). Rear defroster, electric ($140). Fingertip speed control ($176). Illuminated entry system ($82). Power driver's seat ($227); driver and passenger ($454). Tinted glass ($110). Autolamp on/off delay ($73). Leather-wrapped steering wheel ($59). Tilt steering wheel ($110). Tripminder computer ($261). Digital clock ($61). Lighting and Mirrors: Cornering lamps ($68). Remote right convex mirror ($46). Lighted visor vanity mirrors ($106). Entertainment: AM/FM stereo radio w/cassette tape player ($148). Electronic-tuning AM/FM stereo radio w/cassette ($300). Power antenna ($66). Premium sound system ($168). AM/FM radio delete ($148 credit). Exterior: Formal coach vinyl roof ($650). Two-tone paint/tape ($129). Hood accent stripes ($18). Pivoting front vent windows ($79). Rocker panel moldings ($18-$38). Narrow vinyl- insert bodyside moldings ($61). Bumper rub strips ($59). Luggage rack: wagon ($110). License frames ($9). Interior: Dual-facing rear seats: wagon ($167). Leather seat trim: LS ($418). All-vinyl seat trim ($34). Cloth trim: wagon ($48). Carpeted front/rear floor mats LPO fleet ($33). Wheels/Tires: Wire wheel covers, locking ($174). Turbine spoke cast aluminum wheels ($361). P205/75R15 WSW ($17); puncture-sealant ($178). P215/70R15 WSW ($79). Conventional spare ($63).

HISTORY: Introduced: October 4, 1984. Model year production: 541,276 (including only mid-year Lynx models). Calendar year production (U.S.): 374,535. Calendar year sales by U.S. dealers: 519,059. Model year sales by U.S. dealers: 555,021.

Historical Footnotes: Grand Marquis sold the best since record-setting 1978, reaching 145,242 buyers (up from 131,515 in 1984). Cougar sales rose about 13 percent; Topaz a bit; Marquis down just a hair. Capri was not doing at all well, finding only 16,829 customers. The imported Merkur wasn't strong either, in its first (short) season. Front-drive may have been the wave of the future by the mid-1980s, but Lincoln-Mercury's rear- drives were doing quite well, not yet ready for retirement.

1986 MERCURY

A new aero-styled Sable, close kin to Ford Taurus, suffered a delayed introduction but replaced the old Marquis (which hung on for this model year). Lynx added a sporty equivalent to Escort's GT. All Lynx models now carried the 1.9-liter engine.

1986 Lynx XR3 hatchback coupe (JG)

LYNX — FOUR — A sporty new XR3 hatchback, similar to Ford's Escort GT, joined the Lynx line, which had arrived in revised form at mid-year 1985. The former 1.6-liter CVH engine had been reworked to reach 1.9-liter displacement. XR3 carried a standard high-output version with multi-port fuel injection, plus 15 inch performance radial tires on aluminum wheels, an asymmetrical grille (again like Escort), foglamps, wheel spats, rocker panel moldings, rear spoiler, and front air dam. Standard five-speed manual or optional three-speed automatic were the two transmission choices. Base, L and GS models were offered, in three- or five-door (actually two and four) hatchback or wagon body styles. The diesel engine option returned (with five-speed gearbox). Lynx carried a new four-spoke steering wheel and new wraparound bumper end treatment, as well as a larger-diameter front stabilizer bar. The 1985.5 Lynx restyle had incorporated new front-end styling and headlamps, along with a revised rear end. Aero headlamps extended outward from the squat angled grille, made up of thin vertical bars with a round center emblem. Above the grille on the driver's side was 'Mercury' block lettering. The headlamps met wraparound park/signal/marker lenses that were amber colored. Horizontally-ribbed, wraparound full-width taillamps extended outward from the recessed rear license plate opening. Small integral, squarish backup lenses were part of each assembly. 'Lynx' lettering (and model identification) went above the left taillamps; 'Mercury' lettering above the right one. Standard Lynx equipment included the 1.9-liter OHC four- cylinder engine, four-speed manual transaxle, power brakes, P175/80R13 BSW SBR tires, semi-styled steel wheels with bright trim rings and argent hub covers with black lug nuts, high-mount rear stoplamp, and black driver's mirror. Bumper end caps extended to wheel openings. Interiors contained low- back reclining front seats with cloth upholstery, a flat- folding rear seat, soft-feel instrument panel, and grained- finish glovebox with coin slots. Lynx L added an AM radio (which could be deleted for credit), bright hood molding, bright hub covers and lug nuts, matte black rocker panel paint, and dual bodyside paint stripes. GS added a five-speed manual transaxle, AM/FM stereo radio, locking fuel filler door with remote release, body- color rocker panels, styled steel wheels, bumper rub strips, wide bodyside molding, roof grab handles, dual visor vanity mirrors, and fold-down front center armrest. XR3's minimalist grille consisted of two slots, one above the other, occuping just two-thirds of the body-color front panel, with 'XR3' identification on the other side. XR3 also had an aerodynamic front air dam with built-in foglamps. Equipment included the high-output engine, P195/60HR15 BSW SBR Goodyear Eagle unidirectional tires on cast aluminum wheels, power steering, overhead console with digital clock, foglamps, full console with graphic warning display, and an instrument group (including tachometer). Also part of XR3: a leather-wrapped steering wheel, cloth sport seats, dual remote mirrors, blackout greenhouse treatment, Midnight Smoke lower bodyside treatment, body-color spoiler, and narrow bodyside moldings.

1986 Capri hatchback coupe (JG)

CAPRI — FOUR/V-6/V-8 — Changes to Mercury's ponycar went mostly under the hood for 1986. The 302 cu. in. (5.0-liter) V-8 added sequential fuel injection, along with roller tappets, new rings, a knock sensor, and tuned intake/exhaust manifolds. Carbureted V-8s were gone. So was the turbo four, which hadn't even arrived for 1985, though it had been announced. Capri's simple model lineup was the same this year: just GS and 5.0L, the latter signifying V-8 power. Capri's ample standard equipment list meant few options were available. Standard equipment included the 140 cu. in. (2.3-liter) four with four-speed manual gearbox, power brakes/steering, tinted glass, interval wipers, electric back window defroster, AM/FM stereo radio, tilt steering, and power windows. GS also had aero wheel covers, upper bodyside paint stripes, a black remote driver's mirror, tachometer and trip odometer, console with graphic warning display, digital clock, and passenger visor vanity mirror. Low-back front bucket seats had cloth upholstery. Options included the 232 cu. in. (3.8-liter) V-6 and three-speed automatic. Capri 5.0 added the 302 cu. in. V-8 and five-speed overdrive manual gearbox, P225/60VR15 tires, hood scoop (non-working), Traction-Lok differential, handling suspension, black brushed-finish dash applique, black remote passenger mirror, upper bodyside dual accent tape stripes, blackout body tgrim, and twin bright tailpipe outlets.

FI; 'F' V8302 2Bbl. or FI; 'M' V8302 4Bbl.; 'G' V8351 2Bbl. Next is a check digit. Symbol ten indicates model year ('F' 1985). Symbol eleven is assembly plant: 'A' Atlanta, GA; 'B' Oakville, Ontario (Canada); 'F' Dearborn, MI; 'G' Chicago; 'H' Lorain, Ohio; 'K' Kansas City, MO; 'W' Wayne, MI; 'X' St. Thomas, Ontario; 'Z' St. Louis, MO; and Edison, NJ. The final six digits make up the sequence number, starting with 600001. A Vehicle Certification Label on the left front door lock face panel or door pillar shows the manufacturer, month and year of manufacture, GVW, GAWR, certification statement, VIN, and codes for such items as body type, color, trim, axle, transmission, and special order information.

LYNX (FOUR)

Model Number	Body/Style Number	Body Type & Seating	Factory Price	Shipping Weight	Production Total
54/41P	61D	3-dr. Hatch-4P	5750	1922	Note 1
54	61D	3-dr. L Hatch-4P	6170	1985	Note 1
65	58D	5-dr. L Hatch-4P	6384	2050	Note 1
60	74D	4-dr. L Sta Wag-4P	6508	2076	Note 1
55	61D	3-dr. GS Hatch-4P	6707	2054	Note 1
66	58D	5-dr. GS Hatch-4P	6921	2121	Note 1
61	74D	4-dr. GS Sta Wag-4P	6973	2137	Note 1

Diesel Engine Note: Lynx diesel models cost $558 more (L) or $415 more (GS).

1985.5 LYNX (FOUR)

51	61D	3-dr. Hatch-4P	5986	2060	Note 1
51	61D	3-dr. L Hatch-4P	6272	2060	Note 1
63	58D	5-dr. L Hatch-4P	6486	2106	Note 1
58	74D	4-dr. L Sta Wag-4P	6767	2141	Note 1
52	61D	3-dr. GS Hatch-4P	6902	2149	Note 1
64	58D	5-dr. GS Hatch-4P	7176	2192	Note 1
59	74D	4-dr. GS Sta Wag-4P	7457	2215	Note 1

Note 1: Total Lynx production for the 1985.5 model year, 20,515 three- door hatchbacks, 11,297 five-door hatchbacks, and 6,721 four-door liftgate station wagons. Further information not available.

CAPRI GS (FOUR/V-6)

79	61D	3-dr. Fastbk-4P	7944/8383	2615/2723	Note 2

Capri Engine Note: Six-cylinder price does not include cost of the required automatic transmission ($439). The high-output 302 cu. in. V-8 engine cost $799 more than the V-6.

CAPRI RS/5.0L (V-8)

79	61D	3-dr. Fastbk-4P	10223	N/A	Note 2

Note 2: Total Capri production was 18,657.

TOPAZ (FOUR)

72	66D	2-dr. GS Sedan-5P	7767	2313	18,990
75	54D	4-dr. GS Sedan-5P	7767	2368	82,366
73	66D	2-dr. LS Sedan-5P	8931	2335	Note 3
76	54D	4-dr. LS Sedan-5P	8980	2390	Note 3

Note 3: Production of LS models is included in GS totals.

Diesel Engine Note: A diesel model Topaz cost $8246 (GS) or $9410- $9459 (LS).

MARQUIS (FOUR/V-6)

89	54D	4-dr. Sedan-5P	8996/9414	2755/ --	91,465
90	74D	4-dr. Sta Wag-5P	-- /9506	-- /2978	12,733

MARQUIS BROUGHAM (FOUR/V-6)

89/60H	54D	4-dr. Sedan-5P	9323/9741	2849/ --	Note 4
90/60H	74D	4-dr. Sta Wag-5P	-- /9805	N/A	Note 4

Note 4: Brougham production is included in basic totals above.

COUGAR (V-6/V-8)

92	66D	2-dr. Cpe-5P	10650/11048	2931/ --	117,274
92/603	66D	2-dr. LS Cpe-5P	11850/12248	2961/ --	Note 5

Cougar Engine Note: The V-8 engine required a four-speed automatic transmission at $237 extra.

COUGAR XR-7 (TURBO FOUR)

Model Number	Body/Style Number	Body Type & Seating	Factory Price	Shipping Weight	Production Total
92/934	66D	2-dr. Cpe-5P	13599	2947	Note 5

Note 5: Production of LS and XR-7 is included in basic total above.

GRAND MARQUIS (V-8)

93	66K	2-dr. Sedan-6P	12240	3607	10,900
95	54K	4-dr. Sedan-6P	12305	3761	136,239
93/60H	66K	2-dr. LS Sed-6P	12789	3607	Note 6
95/60H	54K	4-dr. LS Sed-6P	12854	3761	Note 6

GRAND MARQUIS COLONY PARK (V-8)

94	74K	4-dr. Sta Wag-6P	12511	3788	14,119

Note 6: LS production is included in basic Grand Marquis totals.

FACTORY PRICE AND WEIGHT NOTE: Cougar prices and weights to left of slash are for V-6, to right for V-8 engine. For Capri/Marquis, prices/weights to left of slash are for four-cylinder, to right for V-6.

ENGINE DATA: BASE FOUR (Lynx): Inline. Overhead cam. Four-cylinder. Cast iron block and aluminum head. Displacement: 97.6 cu. in. (1.6 liters). Bore & stroke: 3.15 x 3.13 in. Compression ratio: 9.0:1. Brake horsepower: 70 at 4600 R.P.M. Torque: 88 lbs.-ft. at 2600 R.P.M. Five main bearings. Hydraulic valve lifters. Carburetor: 2Bbl. Holley 740. VIN Code: 2. NOTE: Second Series Lynx, introduced at mid-year, used a new 1.9-liter four; see 1986 listing for specifications. OPTIONAL FOUR (Lynx): High-output version of 1.6-liter engine above Horsepower: 80 at 5400 R.P.M. Torque: 88 lbs.-ft. at 2600 R.P.M. VIN Code: 4. DIESEL FOUR (Lynx, Topaz): Inline. Overhead cam. Four-cylinder. Cast iron block and aluminum head. Displacement: 121 cu. in. (2.0 liters). Bore & stroke: 3.39 x 3.39 in. Compression ratio: 22.5:1. Brake horsepower: 52 at 4000 R.P.M. Torque: 82 lbs.-ft. at 2400 R.P.M. Five main bearings. Solid valve lifters. Fuel injection. VIN Code: 7. BASE FOUR (Topaz): Inline. Overhead valve. Four-cylinder. Cast iron block and head. Displacement: 140 cu. in. (2.3 liters). Bore & stroke: 3.70 x 3.30 in. Compression ratio: 9.0:1. Brake horsepower: 86 at 4000 R.P.M. Torque: 122 lbs.-ft. at 2800 R.P.M. Five main bearings. Hydraulic valve lifters. Fuel injection (TBI). High Swirl Combustion (HSC) design. VIN Code: X. OPTIONAL FOUR (Topaz): High-output version of 140 cu. in. HSC four above Horsepower: 100 at 4600 R.P.M. Torque: 125 lbs.-ft. at 3200 R.P.M. VIN Code: S. BASE FOUR (Capri, Marquis): Inline. Overhead cam. Four-cylinder. Cast iron block and head. Displacement: 140 cu. in. (2.3 liters). Bore & stroke: 3.78 x 3.13 in. Compression ratio: 9.0:1. Brake horsepower: 88 at 4200 R.P.M. Torque: 122 lbs.-ft. at 2600 R.P.M. Five main bearings. Hydraulic valve lifters. Carburetor: 1Bbl. Carter YFA. VIN Code: A. BASE TURBO FOUR (Cougar XR7): Same as 140 cu. in. four above, but with turbocharger Compression ratio: 8.0:1. Horsepower: 155 at 4600 R.P.M. Torque: 190 lbs.-ft. at 2800 R.P.M. VIN Code: W. BASE V-6 (Cougar); OPTIONAL (Capri, Marquis): 90-degree, overhead valve V-6. Cast iron block and aluminum head. Displacement: 232 cu. in. (3.8 liters). Bore & stroke: 3.80 x 3.40 in. Compression ratio: 8.65:1. Brake horsepower: 120 at 3600 R.P.M. Torque: 205 lbs.-ft. at 1600 R.P.M. Four main bearings. Hydraulic valve lifters. Fuel-injected. VIN Code: 3. BASE V-8 (Grand Marquis); OPTIONAL (Cougar): 90-degree, overhead valve V-8. Cast iron block and head. Displacement: 302 cu. in. (5.0 liters). Bore & stroke: 4.00 x 3.00 in. Compression ratio: 8.4:1. Brake horsepower: 140 at 3200 R.P.M. Torque: 250 lbs.-ft. at 1600 R.P.M. Five main bearings. Hydraulic valve lifters. Fuel injection. VIN Code: F. OPTIONAL V-8 (Grand Marquis): High-output version of 302 cu. in. V-8 above Compression ratio: 8.4:1. Horsepower: 155 at 3600 R.P.M. Torque: 265 lbs.-ft. at 2600 R.P.M. OPTIONAL V-8 (Capri): High-output version of 302 cu. in. V-8 above Compression ratio: 8.3:1. Horsepower: 180 at 4200 R.P.M. Torque: 260 lbs.-ft. at 2600 R.P.M. OPTIONAL V-8 (Capri): High-output version of 302 cu. in. V-8 above Compression ratio: 8.3:1. Horsepower: 210 at 4400 R.P.M. Torque: 270 lbs.-ft. at 3200 R.P.M. Carburetor: 4Bbl. Holley. VIN Code: M.

NOTE: Police 351 cu. in. V-8 remained available for Grand Marquis.

CHASSIS DATA: Wheelbase: (Lynx) 94.2 in.; (Capri) 100.5 in.; (Topaz) 99.9 in.; (Marquis) 105.6 in.; (Cougar) 104.0 in.; (Grand Marquis) 114.3 in. Overall Length: (Lynx) 163.9 in.; (Lynx wag) 165.0 in.; (Capri) 179.3 in.; (Topaz) 176.5 in.; (Marquis) 196.5 in.; (Cougar) 197.6 in.; (Grand Marquis) 211.0 in.; (Grand Marquis wag) 215.0 in. Height: (Lynx) 53.3-53.4 in.; (Capri) 52.1 in.; (Topaz) 52.7 in.; (Marquis) 53.8 in.; (Marquis wag) 54.4 in.; (Cougar) 53.4 in.; (Grand Marquis) 55.2 in.; (Grand Marquis wag) 56.8 in. Width: (Lynx) 65.9 in.; (Capri) 69.1 in.; (Topaz) 68.3 in.; (Marquis) 71.0 in.; (Cougar) 71.1 in.; (Grand Marquis) 77.5 in.; (Grand Marquis wag) 79.3 in. Front Tread: (Lynx) 54.7 in.; (Capri) 56.6 in.; (Topaz) 54.7 in.; (Marquis) 56.6 in.; (Cougar) 58.1 in.; (Grand Marquis) 62.2 in. Rear Tread: (Lynx) 56.0 in.; (Capri/Marquis) 57.0 in.; (Topaz) 57.6 in.; (Cougar) 58.5 in.; (Grand Marquis) 62.0 in. Standard Tires: (Lynx) P165/80R13; (Capri) P195/75R14; (Capri 5.0L) P225/60VR15; (Topaz) P175/80R13; (Marquis) P195/75R14; (Cougar) P205/75R14; (XR7) P225/60VR15; (Grand Marquis) P215/75R14 SBR WSW.

TECHNICAL: Transmission: Four-speed manual standard on Lynx; five- speed manual or three-speed automatic optional. Four-speed manual standard on Capri; five-speed manual standard on Capri 5.0L; three-speed or four-speed automatic optional. Five-speed manual standard on Topaz; three-speed automatic optional. SelectShift three-speed automatic standard on Cougar/Marquis; four-speed overdrive optional. Five-speed manual standard on Cougar XR7. Four-speed overdrive automatic standard on Grand Marquis. Gear ratios same as equivalent Ford models; see Ford/Mustang listings. Standard final drive ratio: (Lynx) 3.59:1 w/4spd, 3.73:1 w/5spd, 3.31:1 w/auto., 3.52:1 w/diesel; (Capri four) 3.08:1 w/4spd, 3.27:1 w/auto.; (Capri V-6) 2.73:1; (Capri V-8) 2.73:1 w/5spd or auto., 3.27:1 w/4spd auto.; (Capri turbo) 3.45:1; (Topaz) 3.33:1 w/5spd, 3.23:1 w/auto., 3.73:1 w/diesel or FI four; (Marquis) 3.27:1 or 2.73:1; (Cougar V-6) 2.73:1 w/3spd auto., 3.27:1 with 4spd auto.; (Cougar V-8) 3.08:1; (Cougar XR7 turbo) 3.45:1; (Grand Marquis) 3.08:1. Steering: (Grand Marquis) recirculating ball; (others) rack and pinion. Front Suspension: (Lynx/Topaz) MacPherson strut-mounted coil springs w/lower control arms and stabilizer bar; (Capri/Cougar/Marquis) modified MacPherson struts w/lower control arms, coil springs and anti-sway bar; (Grand Marquis) coil springs with long/short Aarms and anti-sway bar. Rear Suspension: (Lynx) independent trailing arms w/modified MacPherson struts and coil springs on lower control arms; (Topaz) fully independent quadra-link w/MacPherson struts; (Capri/Cougar/Marquis/Grand Marquis) four-link w/coil springs. Brakes: Front disc, rear drum. Ignition: Electronic. Body construction: (Grand Marquis) separate body and frame; (others) unibody. Fuel tank: (Lynx) 10 gal. exc. wag, 13 gal.; (Capri) 15.4 gal.; (Topaz) 15.2 gal.; (Marquis) 16 gal.; (Cougar) 20.6 gal.; (Grand Marquis) 18 gal.; (Grand Marquis wag) 18.5 gal.

1986 Topaz sedan (JG)

TOPAZ — FOUR — Two years after its debut, the front-drive Topaz deserved a change or two. They came in the form of revised front-end styling with aero headlamps, a new grille, and body-color bumpers. Standard tires grew to P185/70R14 size with all-season tread, on 14 inch wheels. Four-way adjustable head restraints were new. The base GS model also got a new standard touring suspension with gas-filled struts. A push/pull headlamp switch replaced the rocker switch, and the wiper/washer control moved from the stalk to the instrument panel. The Sport Group option included new 6 in. aluminum wheels with 15 inch tires, and its high-output engine came only with five-speed manual. Diesel power remained available. The new aerodynamic body featured softly rounded edges and aircraft-inspired doors, with windshield and back window slanted nearly 60 degrees. The sloping front panel contained a single air intake slot, below a bright, horizontally-ribbed upper panel with center round emblem and 'Mercury' lettering on the driver's side. A series of six air intake slots went below the bumper strip. Aero headlamps extended outward to meet wraparound park/signal lenses and amber side markers. At the rear were tall wraparound taillamps. A drag coefficient of 0.36 was recorded for the four-door. Inside was a new four-spoke steering wheel; outside, sail-mounted dual power remote mirrors. Front suspension again used MacPherson struts, with a parallel four-bar arrangement at the back. Standard GS equipment included the HSC 2.3-liter four, five-speed manual transaxle, power brakes and steering, blackwall tires with full wheel covers, low-back cloth reclining front seats, tachometer, AM/FM stereo radio (which could be deleted), side-window demisters, and color-keyed consolette. Dark Smoke bumper rub strips had bright inserts. Other body features: an acrylic grille applique with bright/argent accents, Dark Smoke cowl grille, bright windshield moldings, and black wiper arms. The optional GS Sport Group added Michelin TRX BSW tires on TR cast aluminum wheels with locking lug nuts, and special handling components, along with a high specific output (HSO) version of the 2.3-liter four. A revised intake manifold, higher-lift camshaft, larger cylinder head and other modifications boosted horsepower by 16 percent over the standard engine. It also got a new cast aluminum rocker cover. GS Sport Group also included a graphic display alert module, red inserts in bodyside moldings and bumper rub strips, Dark Smoke greenhouse moldings, and black leather-wrapped steering wheel. Topaz LS included a Touring suspension with gas-filled struts, full console, power windows and door locks, dual lighted visor vanity mirrors, dual-color accent stripes, argent lower taillamp molding, woodgrain instrument cluster accents, and illuminated entry.

1986 Sable LS sedan (JG)

SABLE — FOUR/V-6 — Like Ford's new mid-size Taurus, the closely-related Sable lacked a conventional grille. Unlike Taurus with its mostly solid "grille" panel, Sable sported an illuminated plastic light bar between flush headlamps. Those headlamps extended outward to meet park/signal lamps, and wrap around the fenders into side marker lenses. Below the front bumper rub strip was a set of many vertical slots, arranged in four sections. Bodyside moldings followed a straight line from front to back, above horizontal ribbing in the center segment. At the rear were wide wraparound taillamps (wider than Taurus). Surprisingly, sedans shared no sheetmetal at all. Wagons shared body parts only to the rear of the windshield. The first Sables came only with 181 cu. in. (3.0- liter) fuel-injected V-6 and four-speed overdrive automatic, but a 151 cu. in. (2.5-liter) four and new three-speed automatic would become standard later. Sable's standard cluster included a tachometer and temp gauge. Gas shock absorbers were used in the fully independent suspension. Sable offered seating for six. Two trim levels were offered, GS and LS, in four-door sedan and station wagon form. Standard GS equipment included the 2.5-liter four and three-speed automatic, power brakes/steering, cornering lamps, bumper rub strips, driver's remote mirror, side-window defoggers, passenger assist handles, tachometer, trip odometer, P205/70R14 tires, and a day/night mirror. Wagons had the 3.0-liter V-6 engine and four-speed automatic. Interiors contained a cloth Flight bench seat with driver's side recliner, and fold-down center front armrest. Sable LS added the V-6 engine and four-speed automatic, power windows, remote decklid release, remote gas door release, digital clock, intermittent wipers, dual power remote mirrors, diagnostic

1986 Sable LS wagon (JG)

warning lights, and AM/FM stereo radio. Twin Comfort lounge seats had dual recliners and power lumbar support adjusters. Urethane lower door and rocker panel coating was included. Taurus/Sable came from a $3 billion development program that began in 1980. In early tests, Sable demonstrated an even lower coefficient of drag than Taurus: 0.29 versus 0.32, partly because Sable had two inches more rear overhang.

1986 Marquis sedan (JG)

MARQUIS — FOUR/V-6 — With the new Sable getting all the attention, the car it replaced was almost overlooked. In fact, quite a few examples were sold in this, its final season. The holdover rear-drive mid-size came with a base 140 cu. in. (2.3-liter) four or optional 232 cu. in. (3.8-liter) V-6. Appearance was the same as 1985.

1986 Cougar XR-7 coupe (JG)

COUGAR — FOUR/V-6/V-8 — Mercury's two-door personal-luxury coupe again came in three levels: GS, LS, and the turbocharged XR7. Appearance was similar to 1985. Cougar still displayed an upswept quarter-window design, which was its most notable difference from the closely-related Thunderbird. Base powerplant was the 232 cu. in. (3.8-liter) V-6, with three-speed automatic. The optional 302 cu. in. (5.0-liter) V-8 had new sequential (multi-point) fuel injection and other improvements. Standard tires grew wider, to P215/70R14 size. For the third year in a row, counterbalanced hood springs were promised to replace the prop rod. A standard electronic-tuning stereo radio replaced the manual-tuning version. New options included a power moonroof (arriving later), seven-band graphic equalizer, and inflatable spare tire (complete with air compressor). Standard equipment included power steering/brakes, halogen headlamps, AM/FM stereo, driver's remote mirror, bodyside/decklid accent stripes, vinyl-insert bodyside moldings, analog quartz clock, console, four-spoke steering wheel, and brushed instrument panel applique. Individual cloth/vinyl front seats came with recliners. Cougar LS added tinted glass, power windows, remote passenger mirror, rocker panel moldings, hood accent striping, digital clock, velour upholstery, lighted right visor vanity mirror, and woodtone dash applique. Cougar XR7 included the turbo four with five- speed manual, handling suspension, P205/70HR14 BSW tires on polycast wheels, leather-wrapped steering wheel, tinted glass, and Traction-Lok differential.

1986 Grand Marquis LS sedan (JG)

GRAND MARQUIS — V-8 — Mercury's most popular model, the big rear-drive sedan (and wagon) enjoyed mostly mechanical changes for 1986. The standard 302 cu. in. (5.0-liter) V-8 gained sequential port fuel injection and other internal changes, including roller lifters and tuned intake manifold, with low-tension rings and higher compression ratio. Standard tires grew from 14 to 15 inch diameter. Wagons now had a compact spare tire (conventional optional). Gas caps were tethered. Standard equipment included four-speed overdrive automatic, P215/75R15 whitewalls, AM/FM stereo, wide lower bodyside moldings, power windows, vinyl roof, power brakes/steering, rocker panel and wheel lip moldings, Flight bench seat, gas-filled shocks, hood/decklid paint stripes, and an analog clock. Grand Marquis LS added a visor vanity mirror and luxury interior touches. Colony Park wagons had the woodgrain bodyside and tailgate applique, three-way tailgate with power window, fold-down rear seat, and conventional spare tire. Mercury's 17-symbol Vehicle Identification Number (VIN) was stamped on a metal tab fastened to the instrument panel, visible through the windshield. Symbols one to three indicates manufacturer, make and vehicle type: '1ME' Mercury passenger car. The fourth symbol ('B') denotes restraint system. Next comes a letter 'P', followed by two digits that indicate body type: Model Number, as shown in left column of tables below. (Example: '72' Topaz GS two- door sedan.) Symbol eight indicates engine type: '9' L4113 2Bbl.; 'J' H.O. L4113 MFI; 'H' Diesel L4121; 'A' L4- 140 1Bbl.; 'X' HSC L4140 FI; 'S' H.O. L4140 FI; 'W' Turbo L4140 EFI; 'D' L4153 FI; '3' V6232 FI; 'U' V6183 FI; 'F' V8302 FI; 'M' H.O. V8302 FI; 'G' Police V8351 2Bbl. Next is a check digit. Symbol ten indicates model year ('G' 1986).

Symbol eleven is assembly plant: 'A' Atlanta, GA; 'B' Oakville, Ontario (Canada); 'F' Dearborn, MI; 'G' Chicago; 'H' Lorain, Ohio; 'K' Kansas City, MO; 'W' Wayne, MI; 'X' St. Thomas, Ontario; and Edison, NJ. The final six digits make up the sequence number, starting with 600001. A Vehicle Certification Label on the left front door lock face panel or door pillar shows the manufacturer, month and year of manufacture, GVW, GAWR, certification statement, VIN, and codes for such items as body type, color, trim, axle, transmission, and special order information.

LYNX (FOUR)

Model Number	Body/Style Number	Body Type & Seating	Factory Price	Shipping Weight	Production Total
51	61D	3-dr. Hatch-4P	6182	2060	Note 1
51	61D	3-dr. L Hatch-4P	6472	2060	Note 1
63	58D	5-dr. L Hatch-4P	6886	2106	Note 1
58	74D	4-dr. L Sta Wag-4P	6987	2141	Note 1
52	61D	3-dr. GS Hatch-4P	7162	2149	Note 1
64	58D	5-dr. GS Hatch-4P	7376	2192	Note 1
59	74D	4-dr. GS Sta Wag-4P	7657	2215	Note 1
53	61D	3-dr. XR3 Hatch-4P	8193	2277	Note 1

Note 1: Total Lynx production, 45,880 three-door hatchbacks, 26,512 five-door hatchbacks, and 13,580 four-door liftgate station wagons.

Diesel Engine Note: Lynx diesel models cost $591-$667 more than a gas engine.

CAPRI GS (FOUR/V-6)

79	61D	3-dr. Fastbk-4P	8331/8785	2692/2808	Note 2

Capri Engine Note: Six-cylinder price does not include cost of the required automatic transmission ($510). The high-output 302 cu. in. V-8 engine cost $1330 more than the V-6.

CAPRI 5.0L (V-8)

79	61D	3-dr. Fastbk-4P	10950	3055	Note 2

Note 2: Total Capri production was 20,869.

1986 Topaz coupe (JG)

TOPAZ (FOUR)

72	66D	2-dr. GS Sedan-5P	8085	2313	15,757
75	54D	4-dr. GS Sedan-5P	8235	2368	62,640
73	66D	2-dr. LS Sedan-5P	9224	2335	Note 3
76	54D	4-dr. LS Sedan-5P	9494	2390	Note 3

Diesel Engine Note: A diesel engine cost $509 more than the gasoline-powered Topaz.

SABLE GS (FOUR/V-6)

87	54D	4-dr. Sedan-6P	10700/11311	2812/2812	71.707
88	74D	4-dr. Sta Wag-6P	--/12574	3092	23,931

SABLE LS (V-6)

87	54D	4-dr. Sedan-6P	11776	2812	Note 3
88	74D	4-dr. Sta Wag-6P	13068	3092	Note 3

Note 3: Production of Topaz and Sable LS models is included in GS totals.

MARQUIS (FOUR/V-6)

89	54D	4-dr. Sedan-6P	9660/10154	2883/2935	24,121
90	74D	4-dr. Sta Wag-6P	--/10254	--/2987	4,461

MARQUIS BROUGHAM (FOUR/V-6)

89/60H	54D	4-dr. Sedan-6P	10048/10542	2895/2947	Note 4
90/60H	74D	4-dr. Sta Wag-6P	--/10613	--/2999	Note 4

Note 4: Brougham production is included in basic totals above.

1986 Cougar LS coupe (JG)

COUGAR (V-6/V-8)

Model Number	Body/Style Number	Body Type & Seating	Factory Price	Shipping Weight	Production Total
92	66D	2-dr. Cpe-4P	11421/11969	2918/3096	135,909
92	66D	2-dr. LS Cpe-4P	12757/13305	2918/3096	Note 5

Cougar Engine Note: The V-8 engine required a four-speed automatic transmission at $237 extra.

COUGAR XR-7 (TURBO FOUR)

92	66D	2-dr. Cpe-4P	14377	3015	Note 5

Note 5: Production of LS and XR-7 is included in basic total above.

GRAND MARQUIS (V-8)

93	66K	2-dr. Sedan-6P	13480	3730	5,610
95	54K	4-dr. Sedan-6P	13504	3672	93,919
93/60H	66K	2-dr. LS Sed-6P	13929	3730	Note 6
95/60H	54K	4-dr. LS Sed-6P	13952	3672	Note 6

GRAND MARQUIS COLONY PARK (V-8)

94	74K	4-dr. Sta Wag-6P	13724	3851	9,891

Note 6: LS production is included in basic Grand Marquis totals.

FACTORY PRICE AND WEIGHT NOTE: Cougar prices and weights to left of slash are for V-6, to right for V-8 engine. For Capri/Marquis/Sable, prices/weights to left of slash are for four-cylinder, to right for V-6.

ENGINE DATA: BASE FOUR (Lynx): Inline. Overhead cam. Four-cylinder. Cast iron block and aluminum head. Displacement: 113 cu. in. (1.9 liters). Bore & stroke: 3.23 x 3.46 in. Compression ratio: 9.0:1. Brake horsepower: 86 at 4800 R.P.M. Torque: 100 lbs.-ft. at 3000 R.P.M. Five main bearings. Hydraulic valve lifters. Carburetor: 2Bbl. Holley 740. VIN Code: 9. OPTIONAL FOUR (Lynx): High-output, multi-port fuel injected version of 1.9-liter engine above Horsepower: 108 at 5200 R.P.M. Torque: 114 lbs.-ft. at 4000 R.P.M. VIN Code: J. DIESEL FOUR (Lynx, Topaz): Inline. Overhead cam. Four-cylinder. Cast iron block and aluminum head. Displacement: 121 cu. in. (2.0 liters). Bore & stroke: 3.39 x 3.39 in. Compression ratio: 22.7:1. Brake horsepower: 52 at 4000 R.P.M. Torque: 82 lbs.-ft. at 2400 R.P.M. Five main bearings. Solid valve lifters. Fuel injection. VIN Code: H. BASE FOUR (Topaz): Inline. Overhead valve. Four-cylinder. Cast iron block and head. Displacement: 140 cu. in. (2.3 liters). Bore & stroke: 3.70 x 3.30 in. Compression ratio: 9.0:1. Brake horsepower: 86 at 4000 R.P.M. Torque: 124 lbs.-ft. at 2800 R.P.M. Five main bearings. Hydraulic valve lifters. Fuel injection (TBI). High Swirl Combustion (HSC) design. VIN Code: X. OPTIONAL FOUR (Topaz): High-output version of 140 cu. in. HSC four above Horsepower: 100 at 4600 R.P.M. Torque: 125 lbs.-ft. at 3200 R.P.M. VIN Code: S. BASE FOUR (Capri, Marquis): Inline. Overhead cam. Four-cylinder. Cast iron block and head. Displacement: 140 cu. in. (2.3 liters). Bore & stroke: 3.78 x 3.13 in. Compression ratio: 9.5:1. Brake horsepower: 88 at 4200 R.P.M. Torque: 122 lbs.-ft. at 2600 R.P.M. Five main bearings. Hydraulic valve lifters. Carburetor: 1Bbl. Carter YFA. VIN Code: A. BASE TURBO FOUR (Cougar XR7): Same as 140 cu. in. four above, but with turbocharger Compression ratio: 8.0:1. Horsepower: 155 at 4600 R.P.M. (145 at 4400 with automatic). Torque: 190 lbs.-ft. at 2800 R.P.M. (180 at 3000 w/automatic). VIN Code: W. BASE FOUR (Sable): Inline. Overhead valve. Four-cylinder. Cast iron block and head. Displacement: 153 cu. in. (2.5 liters). Bore & stroke: 3.70 x 3.60 in. Compression ratio: 9.0:1. Brake horsepower: 88 at 4600 R.P.M. Torque: 130 lbs.-ft. at 2800 R.P.M. Five main bearings. Hydraulic valve lifters. Fuel injection (TBI). VIN Code: D. BASE V-6 (Sable LS, wagon); OPTIONAL (Sable): 60-degree, overhead valve V-6. Cast iron block and head. Displacement: 183 cu. in. (3.0 liters). Bore & stroke: 3.50 x 3.10 in. Compression ratio: 9.25:1. Brake horsepower: 140 at 4800 R.P.M. Torque: 160 lbs.-ft. at 3000 R.P.M. Four main bearings. Hydraulic valve lifters. Multi-port fuel injection. VIN Code: U. BASE V-6 (Cougar); OPTIONAL (Capri, Marquis): 90-degree, overhead valve V-6. Cast iron block and aluminum head. Displacement: 232 cu. in. (3.8 liters). Bore & stroke: 3.80 x 3.40 in. Compression ratio: 8.7:1. Brake horsepower: 120 at 3600 R.P.M. Torque: 205 lbs.-ft. at 1600 R.P.M. Four main bearings. Hydraulic valve lifters. Fuel-injected. VIN Code: 3. BASE V-8 (Grand Marquis); OPTIONAL (Cougar): 90-degree, overhead valve V-8. Cast iron block and head. Displacement: 302 cu. in. (5.0 liters). Bore & stroke: 4.00 x 3.00 in. Compression ratio: 8.9:1. Brake horsepower: 150 at 3200 R.P.M. Torque: 270 lbs.-ft. at 2000 R.P.M. Five main bearings. Hydraulic valve lifters. Sequential fuel injection. VIN Code: F. OPTIONAL V-8 (Capri): High-output version of 302 cu. in. V-8 above Compression ratio: 9.2:1. Horsepower: 200 at 4000 R.P.M. Torque: 285 lbs.-ft. at 3000 R.P.M. VIN Code: M.

NOTE: Police 351 cu. in. V-8 remained available for Grand Marquis, rated 180 horsepower at 3600 R.P.M., 285 lbs.-ft. at 2400 R.P.M.

CHASSIS DATA: Wheelbase: (Lynx) 94.2 in.; (Capri) 100.5 in.; (Topaz) 99.9 in.; (Sable) 106.0 in.; (Marquis) 105.6 in.; (Cougar) 104.0 in.; (Grand Marquis) 114.3 in. Overall Length: (Lynx) 166.9 in.; (Lynx wag) 168.0 in.; (Capri) 179.3 in.; (Topaz) 176.2 in.; (Sable) 190.9 in.; (Sable wag) 191.9 in.; (Marquis) 196.5 in.; (Cougar) 197.6 in.; (Grand Marquis) 214.0 in.; (Grand Marquis wag) 218.0 in. Height: (Lynx) 53.3-53.5 in.; (Capri) 52.1 in.; (Topaz) 52.7 in.; (Sable) 55.1 in.; (Marquis) 53.8 in.; (Marquis wag) 54.4 in.; (Cougar) 53.4 in.; (Grand Marquis) 55.2 in.; (Grand Marquis wag) 56.8 in. Width: (Lynx) 65.9 in.; (Capri) 69.1 in.; (Topaz) 68.3 in.; (Sable) 70.7 in.; (Marquis) 71.0 in.; (Cougar) 71.1 in.; (Grand Marquis) 77.5 in.; (Grand Marquis wag)

79.3 in. Front Tread: (Lynx) 54.7 in.; (Capri) 56.6 in.; (Topaz) 54.7 in.; (Sable) 61.6 in.; (Marquis) 56.6 in.; (Cougar) 58.1 in.; (Grand Marquis) 62.2 in. Rear Tread: (Lynx) 56.0 in.; (Capri/Marquis) 57.0 in.; (Topaz) 57.6 in.; (Sable) 60.5 in.; (Sable wag) 59.9 in.; (Cougar) 58.5 in.; (Grand Marquis) 62.0 in. Standard Tires: (Lynx) P165/80R13; (XR3) P195/60HR15; (Capri) P195/75R14; (Capri 5.0L) P225/60VR15; (Topaz) P185/70R14; (Sable) P205/70R14; (Marquis) P195/75R14; (Cougar) P215/70R14; (XR7) P225/60VR15 Goodyear "Gatorback;" (Grand Marquis) P205/75R15 SBR WSW.

TECHNICAL: Transmission: Four-speed manual standard on Lynx; five-speed manual or three-speed automatic optional. Four-speed manual standard on Capri; five-speed manual standard on Capri 5.0L; three-speed or four-speed automatic optional. Five-speed manual standard on Topaz; three-speed automatic optional. SelectShift three-speed automatic standard on Cougar/Marquis; four-speed overdrive optional (standard on Cougar V-8). Three-speed automatic standard on Sable four; four-speed on Sable V-6. Five-speed manual standard on Cougar XR7. Four- speed overdrive automatic standard on Grand Marquis. Gear ratios same as equivalent Ford models; see Ford/Mustang listings. Standard final drive ratio: (Lynx) 3.52:1 w/4spd, 3.73:1 w/5spd, 3.23:1 w/auto., 3.52:1 w/diesel; (Capri four) 3.08:1 w/4spd, 3.27:1 w/auto.; (Capri V-6) 2.73:1; (Capri V-8) 2.73:1 w/5spd or auto., 3.27:1 w/4spd auto.; (Topaz) 3.33:1 w/5spd, 3.23:1 w/auto., 3.73:1 w/diesel or FI four; (Sable) 3.23:1 w/four, 3.37:1 w/V-6; (Marquis) 3.27:1 or 2.73:1; (Cougar V-6) 2.73:1 w/3spd auto., 3.27:1 with 4spd auto.; (Cougar V-8) 3.08:1; (Cougar XR7 turbo) 3.45:1; (Grand Marquis) 2.73:1. Steering: (Grand Marquis) recirculating ball; (others) rack and pinion. Front Suspension: (Lynx/Topaz) MacPherson strut-mounted coil springs w/lower control arms and stabilizer bar; (Capri/Cougar/Marquis) modified MacPherson struts w/lower control arms, coil springs and anti-sway bar; (Sable) MacPherson struts w/control arm, coil springs and anti-sway bar; (Grand Marquis) coil springs with long/short Aarms and anti-sway bar. Rear Suspension: (Lynx) independent trailing arms w/modified MacPherson struts and coil springs on lower control arms; (Topaz) fully independent quadra-link w/MacPherson struts; (Sable) MacPherson struts w/coil springs, parallel suspension arms and anti-sway bar; (Capri/Cougar/Marquis/Grand Marquis) four-link w/coil springs. Brakes: Front disc, rear drum. Ignition: Electronic. Body construction: (Grand Marquis) separate body and frame; (others) unibody. Fuel tank: (Lynx) 10 gal. exc. wag, 13 gal.; (Capri) 15.4 gal.; (Topaz) 15.2 gal.; (Sable) 16 gal.; (Marquis) 16 gal.; (Cougar) 20.6 gal.; (Grand Marquis) 18 gal.; (Grand Marquis wag) 18.5 gal.

DRIVETRAIN OPTIONS: Engines: Diesel 2.0-liter four: Lynx ($591); Topaz ($509). 182 cu. in. V-6: Sable (N/A). 232 cu. in. V-6: Capri ($454); Marquis ($494). 302 cu. in. V-8: Capri ($1784); Cougar ($548). Transmission/Differential: Five-speed manual trans.: Lynx ($76). Automatic transaxle: Lynx L ($466); Lynx GS ($390); Topaz ($448) exc. w/GS sport group ($350). Three-speed auto. transmission.: Capri ($510); Cougar XR7 ($315). Floor shift lever: Sable sedan (NC). Overdrive auto. trans.: Capri GS ($746); Capri 5.0L ($622); Sable GS ($611); Cougar/Marquis ($237). Traction-Lok differential: Marquis/Grand Marquis/Cougar ($100). Steering/Suspension: Power steering: Lynx ($226). H.D. susp.: Lynx/Sable/Grand Marquis ($26); Sable LPO ($26); Marquis ($43). Auto. load leveling: Grand Marquis ($200). Other: H.D. battery ($27). H.D. alternator: Lynx ($27). Extended-range gas tank: Sable/Marquis ($46). Engine block heater ($18). Trailer towing pkg.: Grand Marquis ($377-$389). California emission system: Lynx/EXP ($46); others ($99). High-altitude emissions (NC).

LYNX CONVENIENCE/APPEARANCE OPTIONS: Option Packages: Comfort/convenience pkg. ($298) exc. XR3 ($117) and diesel ($211). Climate control group ($791-$818). Comfort/Convenience: Air conditioner ($657). Rear defroster, electric ($135). Fingertip speed control ($176). Tinted glass ($99). Tilt steering ($115). Console w/graphic systems monitor ($111). Rear wiper/washer ($126). Dual remote mirrors ($68). Entertainment: AM/FM stereo radio: L ($109); base ($148). AM/FM stereo w/cassette player: L ($256); base ($295); GS/XR3 ($148). Radio delete: AM ($39 credit); AM/FM ($148 credit). Premium sound ($138). Exterior: Clearcoat paint ($91). Two-tone paint ($156). Wide vinyl bodyside moldings ($45). Bumper guards, front/rear ($56). Bumper rub strips ($48). Luggage rack: wag ($100). Interior: Vinyl seat trim ($24). Wheels/Tires: Styled wheels ($128). P165/80R13 SBR WSW ($59). Full-size spare ($63).

1986 Capri 5.0L hatchback coupe (JG)

CAPRI CONVENIENCE/APPEARANCE OPTIONS: Option Packages: Power lock group ($182). Comfort/Convenience: Air cond. ($762). Fingertip speed control ($176). Entertainment: Electronic seek/scan AM/FM stereo w/cassette ($300). Premium sound system ($138). Radio delete ($148 credit). Exterior: TRoof ($1100). Flip-up open air roof ($315). Interior: Vinyl bucket seats ($29). Wheels and Tires: Wire wheel covers ($98). Polycast wheels ($178). P205/70R14 WSW ($112).

TOPAZ CONVENIENCE/APPEARANCE OPTIONS: Option Packages: GS sport group ($610). Comfort/convenience pkg. ($330). Convenience group ($246). Power lock group ($141-$259). Comfort/Convenience: Air bag restraint system ($815). Air cond. ($743). Rear defroster, electric ($145). Fingertip speed control ($176). Power windows ($207-$282). Six-way power driver's seat ($234). Tilt steering ($115). Entertainment: AM/FM stereo radio w/cassette player ($148). Electronic-tuning AM/FM stereo w/cassette ($161-$309). Premium sound ($138). Radio delete ($148-$295 credit). Exterior: Clearcoat metallic paint ($91). Lower body accent paint ($78-$118). Interior: Vinyl seat trim ($35). Leather seat trim ($300). Wheels/Tires: Polycast wheels ($178). P185/70R14 WSW ($72).

SABLE CONVENIENCE/APPEARANCE OPTIONS: Option Packages: Power lock group ($186-$257). Light group ($48-$51). Comfort/Convenience: Air cond. ($762). Electronic climate control air cond. ($945). Rear defroster ($145). Heated windshield ($250). Fingertip speed control ($176). Keyless entry ($202). Power windows ($282). Six-way power driver's seat ($237); dual ($473). Tinted glass ($115); windshield only LPO ($48). Leather-wrapped steering wheel ($59). Tilt steering ($115). Electronic instrument cluster ($305). Autolamp on/off delay ($73). Auto. parking brake release: GS ($12). Digital clock: GS ($78). Interval wipers: GS ($50). Rear wiper/washer: wag ($124). Dual lighted visor vanity mirrors: GS ($99). Entertainment: AM/FM stereo w/cassette ($127). Power antenna ($71). Premium sound system ($168). Radio delete LPO ($196 credit). Exterior: Power moonroof ($701). Vent windows ($79). Clearcoat paint ($183). Bodyside accent paint ($57). Luggage rack delete: wag LPO ($105 credit). Interior: Cloth twin comfort reclining seats: GS ($195). Vinyl seat trim: GS ($39). Leather seat trim: LS ($415). Rear- facing third seat: wag ($155). Reclining passenger seat: GS ($45). Picnic tray: wagon ($66). Carpeted floor mats ($43). Wheels/Tires: Polycast wheels ($66). Aluminum wheels ($335). P205/70R14 WSW ($72). P205/65R15 BSW ($46); WSW ($124). Conventional spare ($63).

1986 Marquis Brougham Villager wagon (JG)

MARQUIS CONVENIENCE/APPEARANCE OPTIONS: Option Packages: Woodtone option ($282). Interior luxury group ($388). Power lock group ($218-$259). Light group ($38). Comfort/Convenience: Air cond. ($762). Rear defroster ($145). Fingertip speed control ($176). Autolamp on-off delay ($73). Power windows ($282). Six-way power driver's seat ($234). Tinted glass ($115). Leather-wrapped steering wheel ($59). Tilt steering ($115). Digital clock ($78). Auto. parking brake release ($12). Lighting and Mirrors: Cornering lamps ($68). Right remote convex mirror ($61). Dual electric remote mirrors ($96). Lighted visor vanity mirrors ($57-$106). Entertainment: AM/FM stereo radio ($109); w/cassette player ($256). AM radio delete ($39 credit). Exterior: Full vinyl roof ($152). Clearcoat metallic paint ($183). Two-tone paint w/tape stripe ($117). Pivoting front vent windows ($79). Two-way liftgate: wag ($105). Rocker panel moldings ($40). Bumper guards, rear ($28). Bumper rub strips ($56). Luggage rack: wagon ($126). Interior: Vinyl seat trim ($35). Flight bench seat (NC). Front floor mats, carpeted ($23). Wheels/Tires: Luxury wheel covers ($55). Wire wheel covers, locking ($212). Polycast wheels ($178). Styled steel wheels w/trim rings ($54). P195/75R14 WSW ($72). P205/70R14 WSW ($134). Conventional spare ($63).

COUGAR CONVENIENCE/APPEARANCE OPTIONS: Option Packages: Headlamp convenience group ($176). Light group ($35). Power lock group ($220). Comfort/Convenience: Air cond. ($762); auto-temp ($924). Rear defroster ($145). Fingertip speed control ($176). Illuminated entry system ($82). Keyless entry ($198). Tinted glass ($115). Power windows ($207). Six-way power driver's seat ($238); dual ($476). Dual power seat recliners ($189). Leather-wrapped steering wheel ($59). Tilt steering wheel ($115). Electronic instrument cluster ($330). Diagnostic warning lights ($89). Low-oil alert ($24). Digital clock ($61). Auto. parking brake release ($12). Interval wipers ($50). Lighting and Mirrors: Cornering lamps ($68). Dual electric remote mirrors ($96). Lighted visor vanity mirrors, pair ($106). Entertainment: Electronic-tuning AM/FM stereo w/cassette ($127). Power antenna ($71). Graphic equalizer ($218). Premium sound system ($168). AM/FM radio delete ($196 credit). Exterior: Power moonroof ($701). Luxury vinyl rear half roof ($245). Metallic clearcoat paint ($183). Two-tone paint ($163). Hood accent stripes ($16). Pivoting front vent windows ($79). Interior: Leather seat trim ($415). Vinyl seat trim ($37). Front floor mats, carpeted ($22). Wheels/Tires: Wire wheel covers, locking: base ($212); LS ($90). TRX cast aluminum wheels: base ($612); LS ($490). Polycast wheels: base ($178); LS ($56). P215/70R14 BSW ($62 credit). P215/70HR14 performance BSW ($116). Conventional spare ($63). Inflatable spare ($122).

GRAND MARQUIS CONVENIENCE/APPEARANCE OPTIONS: Option Packages: LS decor ($521). Convenience group ($109- $134). Power lock group ($178-$278). Light group ($30-$48). Comfort/Convenience: Air cond. ($762); w/auto-temp control ($828). Rear defroster, electric ($145). Fingertip speed control ($176). Illuminated entry system ($82). Power six-way driver's seat ($237); driver and passenger ($473). Tinted glass ($118). Autolamp on/off delay ($73). Leather-wrapped steering wheel ($59). Tilt steering wheel ($115). Tripminder computer ($261). Digital clock ($61). Lighting and Mirrors: Cornering lamps ($68). Dual electric remote mirrors ($100). Lighted visor vanity mirrors ($109). Entertainment: AM/FM stereo radio w/cassette tape player ($148). Electronic-tuning AM/FM stereo radio w/cassette ($300). Power antenna ($71). Premium sound system ($168). AM/FM radio delete ($148 credit). Exterior: Formal coach vinyl roof ($650). Two-tone paint/tape ($129). Hood accent stripes ($18). Pivoting front vent windows ($79). Rocker panel moldings ($18-$38). Narrow vinyl- insert bodyside moldings ($61). Bumper rub strips ($59). License frames ($9). Luggage rack: wagon ($110). Interior: Dual-facing rear seats: wagon ($167). Cloth seat trim ($54). All-vinyl seat trim ($34). Leather seat trim ($418). Carpeted front floor mats ($21); front/rear ($33). Wheels/Tires: Wire wheel covers, locking ($176). Turbine spoke cast aluminum wheels ($361). P205/75R15 puncture- sealant ($161). P215/70R15 WSW ($62). Conventional spare ($63).

HISTORY: Introduced: October 3, 1985. Model year production: 791,149. Calendar year production (U.S.): 359,002. Calendar year sales by U.S. dealers: 491,782. Model year sales by U.S. dealers: 474,612.

Historical Footnotes: Every model in the Mercury lineup slipped in the sales race this year. Availability of the new Sable was limited at first, and production flaws (later recalls) were a problem. Rear-drive luxury was still promoted, despite the new front-drive models. Cougar was Lincoln-Mercury's Number One seller, and Capri finally dropped out.

MERCURY
1987-1990

Ford Motor Co. promoted its Escort as a "World Car," but the wide range of products handled by its Lincoln-Mercury dealers seemed to fit the description better. The non-Lincoln models included cars made in the United States, Canada, West Germany and Mexico.

Qualifying as "genuine" domestic cars were the Cougar built in Lorraine, Ohio; the Topaz built in Kansas City, Mo.; the Sable built in Atlanta, Ga. and Chicago, Ill.; the Capri built in Dearborn, Mich.; and the Lynx built in Edison, N.J.

The Topaz and Grand Marquis were both made in Canadian factories, while Ford's Hermosillo, Mexico plant manufactured the Mazda-designed Tracer. And the Merkur Scorpio and XR4Ti — part of a planned new line of imported luxury models — were brought in from West Germany.

Mercury and Merkur new car sales for model year 1987 came to 484,845 units, lead by the Sable. Of possible interest to future collectors was an all-wheel-drive system for the Topaz, which also got a GS Sport package with a high-output engine. Cougars received a four-speed automatic transmission and standard air conditioning. Fuel injection was made standard for the Lynx and Sables added a three-liter V-6 base engine.

Standard Marquis were dropped, along with the Capri, although the latter car had almost 2,000 sales in the model year. Likewise, the Lynx and Tracer sales figures were combined while dealers phased out their inventories of Lynx models.

For 1988, sales of Tracer, Topaz, Sable, Cougar, Grand Marquis and Merkur models totaled 499,881 units. Of interest to enthusiasts was the Cougar's new multi-port fuel injected engine and monochromatic exterior treatments with 16-spoke aluminum wheels (for the XR7). The Topaz had new sheet metal, the Sable got a new engine and the Grand Marquis was made sleeker and given more standard equipment.

Mercury's 50th birthday was celebrated in 1989 with a mid-year Grand Marquis Special Anniversary edition. The Cougar had a nine-inch-longer wheelbase, with a supercharged 215 hp intercooled engine for the XR7. Sables were face-lifted inside and out and all-wheel-drive could now be had on any Topaz. A high-output engine was offered in XR5, LTS and all-wheel-drive Topazes at extra cost.

Mercury and Merkur sales for the '89 model year came to 497,150 units, a modest decrease. This was caused, in part, by an extra-long factory changeover needed to prepare for building the larger Cougar. However, the Cougar's sales did increase eight percent by year's end. Another problem was a labor dispute at the Mexican factory, which held down Tracer production. However, it should be pointed out that dealers sold more Lincolns in this period, giving the division a better overall year in both sales and profits.

For 1990, the Merkur Scorpio was dropped due to lackluster sales, and production of Tracers, in Mexico, was temporarily halted. Other products were little changed, except for the addition of new options, along with standard equipment upgrades. A new Two-plus-Two Capri convertible was built in yet another country — Australia. It was announced as a new spring model.

Mercury sales predictions at the start of the season were optimistic. They called for the retailing of 113,000 Grand Marquis, 118,000 Sables, 100,000 Topaz units, 110,000 Cougars and 40,000 Tracers — almost 500,000 cars total.

1987 MERCURY

Capri, the Mustang clone with a Mercury badge, dropped out of the lineup for 1987. So did the Marquis, like its Ford LTD twin, both replaced by the popular aero-styled Taurus/Sable duo.

1987 Lynx GS wagon

LYNX — FOUR — Biggest news for Mercury's subcompact was the addition of standard fuel injection to replace carburetors on the 1.9-liter four-cylinder engine. This would be Lynx's final year, though the comparable Ford Escort would continue as a top seller. The diesel engine was still available, at no extra charge, except on the sporty XR3.

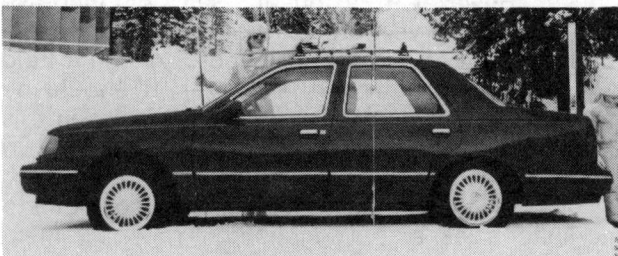

1987 Topaz LS four-door sedan

TOPAZ — FOUR — Nitrogen-filled shock absorbers went into the Topaz suspension for 1987, to help ride/handling a bit. Two notable options joined the list: a new three-speed automatic with fluid-linked torque converter, and a part-time four-wheel-drive system. 4WD was available only with automatic and the high-output engine. A driver's side air bag, available only in limited quantities in 1986, became a regular production option this year.

*Sable GS wagon in Oxford White.
Some features shown may be optional.
See your Lincoln-Mercury dealer for details.*

1987 Sable GS wagon

SABLE — V-6 — Little change was evident on the Mercury version of the hot-selling aero-styled Ford Taurus, as both models entered their second season. Air conditioning became standard on the top-rung LS models. Ford's four-cylinder engine was not offered on Sable, though it continued as a Taurus staple. Instead, Sables had a 3.0-liter V-6 with four-speed overdrive automatic transmission.

1987 Cougar XR-7 coupe

COUGAR — V-6/V-8 — Mercury's mid-size Thunderbird cousin got a restyle for 1987, including a new greenhouse profile, aero headlamps, flush-fit glass, and full-width taillamps. The sporty XR-7 switched from the former turbocharged four to a 5.0-liter V-8. All models now came with standard four-speed overdrive automatic transmission, as manual shifts dropped out of the lineup. The base GS model also disappeared. Both Cougar models came with standard air conditioning and tinted glass. Late in the year, *Motor Trend* tested a special 20th Anniversary edition.

1987 Grand Marquis Colony Park wagon

GRAND MARQUIS — V-8 — Except for the addition of air conditioning as standard equipment, the full-size Mercury (close kin to Ford's LTD Crown Victoria) changed little for 1987. New standard equipment also included an electronic-tuning radio, replacing the former manual version.

I.D. DATA: Mercury's 17-symbol Vehicle Identification Number (VIN) was stamped on a metal tab fastened to the instrument panel, visible through the windshield. Symbols one to three indicate manufacturer, make and vehicle type. The fourth symbol ('B') denotes restraint system. Next comes a letter 'M' (for series), followed by two digits that indicate body type: Model Number, as shown in left column of tables below. (Example: '31' - Topaz GS two-door sedan.) Symbol eight indicates engine type. Next is a check digit. Symbol ten indicates model year ('H' - 1987). Symbol eleven denotes assembly plant. The final six digits make up the production sequence number, starting with 600001.

LYNX (FOUR)

Model Number	Body/Style Number	Body Type & Seating	Factory Price	Shipping Weight	Production Total
20	61D	3-dr. L Hatch-4P	6569	2183	Note 1
21	61D	3-dr. GS Hatch-4P	6951	2202	Note 1
25	58D	5-dr. GS Hatch-4P	7172	2258	12,124
28	74D	4-dr. GS Sta Wag-4P	7462	2277	5,985
23	61D	3-dr. XR3 Hatch-4P	8808	2395	Note 1

Note 1: Total Lynx production, 20,930 three-door hatchbacks.

TOPAZ (FOUR)

Model Number	Body/Style Number	Body Type & Seating	Factory Price	Shipping Weight	Production Total
31	66D	2-dr. GS Sedan-5P	8562	2503	Note 2
33	66D	2-dr. GS Spt Sed-5P	9308	2565	Note 2
36	54D	4-dr. GS Sedan-5P	8716	2557	Note 3
38	54D	4-dr. GS Spt Sed-5P	9463	2621	Note 3
76	54D	4-dr. LS Sedan-5P	10213	2631	Note 3

Note 2: A total of 19,738 two-door sedans were produced.
Note 3: A total of 78,692 four-door sedans were produced.

SABLE GS (V-6)

Model Number	Body/Style Number	Body Type & Seating	Factory Price	Shipping Weight	Production Total
50	54D	4-dr. Sedan-6P	12240	3054	Note 4
55	74D	4-dr. Sta Wag-6P	12793	3228	Note 5

SABLE LS (V-6)

Model Number	Body/Style Number	Body Type & Seating	Factory Price	Shipping Weight	Production Total
53	54D	4-dr. Sedan-6P	14522	3138	Note 4
58	74D	4-dr. Sta Wag-6P	15054	3311	Note 5

Note 4: A total of 91,001 Sable sedans were built.
Note 5: A total of 30,312 Sable wagons were built.

COUGAR (V-6/V-8)

Model Number	Body/Style Number	Body Type & Seating	Factory Price	Shipping Weight	Production Total
60	66D	2-dr. LS Cpe-5P	13595/14234	3133/3272	104,526

COUGAR XR-7 (V-8)

Model Number	Body/Style Number	Body Type & Seating	Factory Price	Shipping Weight	Production Total
62	66D	2-dr. Cpe-5P	15832	3355	Note 6

Note 6: Production of XR-7 is included in basic Cougar total above.

GRAND MARQUIS (V-8)

Model Number	Body/Style Number	Body Type & Seating	Factory Price	Shipping Weight	Production Total
72	66K	2-dr. LS Sed-6P	15323	3764	4,904
74	54K	4-dr. GS Sed-6P	15198	3794	115,599
75	54K	4-dr. LS Sed-6P	15672	3803	Note 7

GRAND MARQUIS COLONY PARK WAGON (V-8)

Model Number	Body/Style Number	Body Type & Seating	Factory Price	Shipping Weight	Production Total
78	74K	4-dr. GS Wag-6P	15462	3975	10,691
79	74K	4-dr. LS wag-6P	16010	4015	Note 7

Note 7: LS production is included in basic Grand Marquis totals.
FACTORY PRICE AND WEIGHT NOTE: Cougar prices and weights to left of slash are for V-6, to right for V-8 engine.

ENGINE DATA: BASE FOUR (Lynx): Inline. Overhead cam. Four-cylinder. Cast iron block and aluminum head. Displacement: 113 cu. in. (1.9 liters). Bore & stroke: 3.23 x 3.46 in. Compression ratio: 9.0:1. Brake horsepower: 90 at 4600 RPM. Torque: 106 lbs.-ft. at 3400 RPM. Five main bearings. Hydraulic valve lifters. Fuel injection. OPTIONAL FOUR (Lynx): High-output, multi-port fuel injected version of 1.9-liter engine above — Horsepower: 115 at 5200 RPM. Torque: 120 lbs.-ft. at 4400 RPM. DIESEL FOUR (Lynx): Inline. Overhead cam. Four-cylinder. Cast iron block and aluminum head. Displacement: 121 cu. in. (2.0 liters). Bore & stroke: 3.39 x 3.39 in. Compression ratio: 22.7:1. Brake horsepower: 58 at 3600 RPM. Torque: 84 lbs.-ft. at 3000 RPM. Five main bearings. Solid valve lifters. Fuel injection. BASE FOUR (Topaz): Inline. Overhead valve. Four-cylinder. Cast iron block and head. Displacement: 140 cu. in. (2.3 liters). Bore & stroke: 3.70 x 3.30 in. Compression ratio: 9.0:1. Brake horsepower: 86 at 3800 RPM. Torque: 120 lbs.-ft. at 3200 RPM. Five main bearings. Hydraulic valve lifters. Fuel injection (TBI). High Swirl Combustion (HSC) design. OPTIONAL FOUR (Topaz): High-output version of 140 cu. in. HSC four above — Horsepower: 94 at 4000 RPM. Torque: 126 lbs.-ft. at 3200 RPM. See note 4. BASE V-6 (Sable): 60-degree, overhead valve V-6. Cast iron block and head. Displacement: 182 cu. in. (3.0 liters). Bore & stroke: 3.50 x 3.10 in. Compression ratio: 9.3:1. Brake horsepower: 140 at 4800 RPM. Torque: 160 lbs.-ft. at 3000 RPM. Four main bearings. Hydraulic valve lifters. Multi-port fuel injection. BASE V-6 (Cougar): 90-degree, overhead valve V-6. Cast iron block and aluminum head. Displacement: 232 cu. in. (3.8 liters). Bore & stroke: 3.80 x 3.40 in. Compression ratio: 8.7:1. Brake horsepower: 120 at 3600 RPM. Torque: 205 lbs.-ft. at 1600 RPM. Four main bearings. Hydraulic valve lifters. fuel-injected. BASE V-8 (Grand Marquis); OPTIONAL (Cougar): 90-degree, overhead valve V-8. Cast iron block and head. Displacement: 302 cu. in. (5.0 liters). Bore & stroke: 4.00 x 3.00 in. Compression ratio: 8.9:1. Brake horsepower: 150 at 3200 RPM. Torque: 270 lbs.-ft. at 2000 RPM. Five main bearings. Hydraulic valve lifters. Sequential fuel injection.

CHASSIS DATA: Wheelbase: (Lynx) 94.2 in.; (Topaz) 99.9 in.; (Sable) 106.0 in.; (Cougar) 104.2 in.; (Grand Marquis) 114.3 in. **Overall Length:** (Lynx) 166.9 in.; (Lynx wag) 168.0 in,; (Topaz) 177.0 in.; (Sable) 190.0 in.; (Sble wag) 191.9 in.; (Cougar) 200.8 in.; (Grand Marquis) 214.0 in.; (Grand Marquis wag) in.; 218.0 in.; **Height:** (Lynx) 53.-53.3 in.; (Topaz) 52.7 in.; (Sable) 54.3 in.; (Sable wag) 55.1 in.; (Cougar) 53.8 in.; (Grand Marquis) 55.5 in.; (Grand Marquis wag) 57.1 in. **Width:** (Lynx) 65.9 in.; (Topaz) 68.3 in.; (Sable) 70.8 in.; (Cougar) 71.1 in.; (Grand Marquis) 77.5 in.; (Grand Marquis wag) 79.3 in. **Front Tread:** (Lynx) 54.7 in.; (Topaz) 54.9 in.; (Sable) 61.6 in.; (Cougar) 58.1 in.; (Grand Marquis) 62.2 in. **Rear Tread:** (Lynx) 56.0 in.; (Topaz) 57.6 in.; (Sable) 60.5 in.; (Sable wag) 59.9 in.; (Cougar) 58.5 in.; (Grand Marquis) 62.0 in. **Standard Tires:** (Lynx) P165/80R13; (XR3) P195/60HR15; (Topaz) P185/70R14; (Topaz GS Sport) P185/65R365; (Sable) P205/70R14; (Cougar) P215/70R14; (XR-7) P205/70HR14; (Grand Marquis) P215/75R15 SBR WSW.

TECHNICAL: Transmission: Four-speed manual standard on Lynx; five-speed manual or three-speed automatic optional. Five-speed manual standard on Topaz; three-speed automatic optional. Four-speed overdrive automatic standard on Sable, Cougar and Grand Marquis. **Steering:** (Grand Marquis) recirculating ball; (others) rack and pinion. **Front Suspension:** (Lynx/Topaz) MacPherson strut-mounted coil springs w/lower control arms and stabilizer bar; (Cougar) modified MacPherson struts w/lower control arms, coil springs and anti-sway bar; (Sable) MacPherson struts w/control arm, coil springs and anti-sway bar; (Grand Marquis) coil springs with long/short A-arms and anti-sway bar. **Rear Suspension:** (Lynx) independent trailing arms w/modified MacPherson struts and coil springs on lower control arms; (Topaz) independent quadra-link w/MacPherson struts; (Sable) MacPherson struts w/coil springs, parallel suspension arms and anti-sway bar; (Cougar/Grand Marquis) four-link w/coil springs. **Brakes:** Front disc, rear drum. **Body construction:** (Grand Marquis) separate body and frame; (others) unibody. **Fuel tank:** (Lynx) 13 gal.; (Topaz) 15.4 gal.; (Topaz 4WD) 13.7 gal.; (Sable) 16 gal.; (Cougar) 22.1 gal.; (Grand Marquis) 18 gal.

DRIVETRAIN OPTIONS: Engines: Diesel four: Lynx (NC). 302 cu. in. V-8: Cougar ($639)/ **Transmission/Differential:** Five-speed manual trans.: Lynx L/GS ($76). Automatic transaxle: Lynx GS ($490); Topaz ($482). Traction-Lok: Grand Marquis ($100). **Steering/Suspension:** Power steering: Lynx ($235). H.D. suspension: Grand Marquis ($26). Trailer towing pkg.: Grand Marquis ($387-399).

LYNX CONVENIENCE/APPEARANCE OPTIONS:
Climate Control Group, GS ($865). XR3 ($838). Comfort/Convenience Group; Overhead console w/digital clock, intermittent wipers, trip odometer, tachometer, temperature gauge, GS ($327). Air conditioning ($688). Bumper guards ($56). Bumper rub strips ($48). Rear defogger ($145). Tinted glass ($105). Dual power mirrors ($88). Wide vinyl bodyside molding ($50). Clearcoat metallic paint ($91). Two-tone paint ($156). AM/FM Stereo, L ($159). GS ($120). AM/FM Stereo with cassette, GS ($267). XR3 ($148). Premium Sound System ($138). Speed control ($176). Tilt steering ($179). w/Comfort/Conv ($124). Split fold-down rear seatback ($49). Front center armrest ($55). Polycast wheels ($128). Vinyl seat trim ($24). Heavy-duty battery ($27). Rear wiper/washer ($126). Engine block heater ($18). Deluxe luggage rack ($110). AM radio delete, GS ($39 credit). AM/FM stereo delete, XR ($159 credit). Vinyl seat trim, L ($24).

TOPAZ CONVENIENCE/APPEARANCE OPTIONS:
Comfort/Convenience Pkg; Fold-down center armrest, intermittent wipers, digital clock, Light Group, remote fuel filler & decklid releases, GS ($409). GS Sport ($368). All Wheel Drive Pkg; Four-wheel drive, high-output engine, GS & LS GS Sport ($800). Air conditioning ($773). Rear defogger ($145). Clearcoat metallic paint ($91). Power Lock Group (std. LS), 2-doors ($237). 4-door ($288). 2-doors w/Comfort/Conv Pkg ($156). 4-doors w/Comfort/Conv Pkg ($207). Lower bodyside accent paint, GS ($78). GS Sport & LS ($118). Premium Sound System ($138). Speed control ($176). Tilt steering column ($124). Styled wheels ($178). Decklid luggage rack ($115). Power windows, 2-doors ($222). 4-doors ($296). Air bag, GS ($815). GS w/Comfort/Conv., LS ($751). AM/FM Stereo delete, GS & GS Sport ($157 credit). AM/FM cassette delete, LS ($315 credit). AM/FM stereo electronic tuning cassette, GS ($157). Heavy-duty battery ($27). Engine block heater ($18). Power driver's seat ($251). California emissions pkg ($99). Vinyl seat trim ($35).

SABLE CONVENIENCE/APPEARANCE OPTIONS:
Conventional spare tire ($73). Automatic air conditioning ($945). Manual air conditioning ($788). Autolamp System ($73). Automatic parking brake release ($12). Digital clock ($78). Dual illuminated visor mirrors ($99). Electronic instrument cluster ($351). Insta-Clear heated windshield ($250). Intermittent wipers ($55). Keyless entry system ($202). Power moonroof ($741). Rear defogger ($145). Sliding vent windows ($79). Cruise control ($176). Tilt steering column ($124). Tinted glass ($120). Light Group, GS sedan ($48). GS wagon ($52). Heavy-duty battery ($27). Heavy-duty suspension ($26). Extended range fuel tank ($46). Power antenna ($76). Power door locks, GS sedans ($285). GS wagons ($237). LS ($195). 6-way power driver's seat ($251). Dual power seats ($502). Power windows ($296). AM/FM stereo electronic tuning cassette ($137). Premium Sound System ($168). AM/FM stereo, delete ($206 credit). Clearcoat paint ($183). Cast aluminum wheels ($335). Locking wire wheel covers ($150). Polycast wheels ($123). Leather-wrapped steering wheel ($59). Leather trim ($415). Vinyl trim ($39). Twin comfort seats, GS ($195). Bucket seats, GS ($195); LS (NC). Picnic tray, wagons ($66). Rear facing third seat, wagons ($155). Rear window wiper/washer, wagons ($126). Luggage rack delete, wagons ($115 credit). Engine block heater ($18).

COUGAR CONVENIENCE/APPEARANCE OPTIONS:
Conventional spare tire ($73). Locking wire wheel covers ($212). Polycast wheels, LS ($178). Power Lock Group ($249). Power windows ($222). Power moonroof ($841). Power driver's seat ($251). Dual power seats, LS ($554). XR-7 ($502). AM-FM Stereo electronic tuning cassette ($137). AM/FM Stereo electronic tuning delete ($206 credit). Premium Sound System ($168). Power antenna ($71). Graphic Equalizer ($218). Clearcoat metallic paint ($183). Two-tone paint ($163). Rear half luxury vinyl roof ($260). Leather seat trim ($415). Automatic air conditioning ($162). Heavy-duty battery ($27). Engine block heater ($18). Rear defogger ($145). Intermittent wipers ($55). Headlamp Convenience Group; Automatic dimmer, Autolamp Delay System ($176). Keyless entry system ($202). Cornering lamps ($68). Light Group ($35). Dual illuminated visor mirrors ($100). Speed control ($176). Leather-wrapped steering wheel, LS ($59). Electronic digital clock ($61). Illuminated entry system ($82). Electronic instrument cluster ($330). Tilt steering column ($124).

GRAND MARQUIS CONVENIENCE/APPEARANCE OPTIONS:
Automatic climate control ($211). Power Antenna ($76). Autolamp Delay System ($73). Digital clock ($61). Convenience Group, Intermittent wipers, power decklid/tailgate release, trip odometer, low fuel, oil & washer fluid warning lights ($135). w/Power Lock Group ($85). Cornering lamps ($68). Rear defogger ($145). Illuminated entry system ($82). Light Group ($48). Power Lock Group, includes remote fuel filler & trunk releases, 2-door ($207). 4-doors, wagons ($257). Deluxe luggage rack ($115). Dual illuminated visor mirrors ($109). Bodyside protection moldings ($66). Two-tone paint w/tape stripes ($179). AM/FM Stereo cassette ($137). AM/FM Stereo electronic tuning delete ($206 credit). Premium Sound System ($168). Formal coach vinyl roof ($665). Power driver's seat ($251). Dual power seats ($502). Dual facing rear seats, wagon ($173). Speed control ($176). Leather-wrapped steering wheel ($59). Tilt steering column ($124). Leather seat trim ($418). Tripminder computer ($261). Pivoting front vent windows ($79). Locking wire wheel covers ($183). Cast aluminum wheels ($361). P215/70R15 tires ($72). Conventional spare tire ($73).

HISTORY: Introduced: October 2, 1986. Model year production: 494,502 (total). Calendar year production (U.S.): 328,509. Calendar year sales by U.S. dealers: 463,860. Model year sales by U.S. dealers: 470,644.

1988 MERCURY

The Lynx subcompact bit the dust this year, while the full-size Grand Marquis and compact Topaz enjoyed a restyling. The aero-look Sable added a larger, more potent powerplant option.

TOPAZ — FOUR — Both four-cylinder engines added power this year, as Mercury's compact took on new sheetmetal. Two sporty models (an XR5 two-door and LS Sport four-door) replaced the former GS Sport edition. The Topaz grille had a vertical-bar pattern, quite different from the related Ford Tempo with its twin-slot grille. Bumpers were now integrated into the body. Wraparound signal/marker lamps flanked aero headlamps. At the rear were full-width wraparound taillamps. Under Topaz hoods, multi-point fuel injection replaced the former single-point system. A new analog instrument cluster contained a tachometer. Motorized automatic front shoulder belts became standard. Front-drive models came with standard five-speed manual shift (automatic optional), but the four-wheel-drive version could only have automatic.

1988 Sable four-door sedan

SABLE — V-6 — Performance fans could order this year's Sable with a new 3.8-liter V-6 option, instead of the standard 3.0-liter. That engine had a counter-rotating balance shaft for smoother running, as well as multi-point fuel injection. Both engines produced 140 horsepower, but the 3.8 delivered considerably more torque. Both air conditioning and tinted glass became standard in all Sables (but could be deleted on the GS). The GS added other formerly-optional items as standard this year: intermittent wipers, separate front seats, digital clock, and a cargo net. Whitewall tires were optional only with the standard steel wheels, not the optional cast aluminum or polycast wheels.

COUGAR — V-6/V-8 — Engine modifications gave Cougar's base V-6 engine an extra 20 horsepower for 1987, and a new balance shaft gave it smoother running. Multi-point fuel injection replaced the former throttle-body (single-point) system. Dual exhausts became standard with the optional V-8, while blackwall tires went on the base LS model.

The sporty XR-7 (V-8 engine only) added body-colored bumpers on both ends, plus a body-color grille, bodyside moldings and mirrors, for a monochromatic look. New 16-spoke cast aluminum wheels came in either argent or body color. Analog instruments replaced the former electronic cluster in the XR-7 dashboard (but the electronic version remained optional). The XR-7 final drive ratio switched from 2.73:1 to 3.08:1 to boost acceleration. Aluminum wheels held 225/60VR15 tires.

GRAND MARQUIS — V-8 — Revised front/rear styling gave the full-size, rear-drive Mercury a new look, as the lineup dropped to four-door sedans and wagons only. The two-door model was gone. This year's bumpers had an integrated appearance, while wraparound taillamps highlighted the rear. Wide lower bodyside moldings were standard on both the GS and LS models. Sedans added a half-vinyl roof (rear only). Whitewall P215/75R15 tires became standard on all models. An automatic headlamp on/off warning system also was standard. Joining the option list: an Insta-Clear heated windshield.

I.D. DATA: Mercury's 17-symbol Vehicle Identification Number (VIN) was stamped on a metal tab fastened to the instrument panel, visible through the windshield. Symbols one to three indicate manufacturer, make and vehicle type. The fourth symbol denotes restraint system. Next comes a letter 'M' (for series), followed by two digits that indicate body type: Model Number, as shown in left column of tables below. (Example: '31' = Topaz GS two-door sedan.) Symbol eight indicates engine type. Next is a check digit. Symbol ten indicates model year ('J' = 1988). Symbol eleven denotes assembly plant. The final six digits make up the production sequence number, starting with 600001.

TOPAZ (FOUR)

Model Number	Body/Style Number	Body Type & Seating	Factory Price	Shipping Weight	Production Total
31	66D	2-dr. GS Sedan-5P	9166	2565	Note 1
33	66D	2-dr. XR5 Sed-5P	10058	2560	Note 1
36	54D	4-dr. GS Sedan-5P	9323	2608	Note 1
37	54D	4-dr. LS Sedan-5P	10591	2651	Note 1
38	54D	4-dr. LTS Sed-5P	11541	2660	Note 1

Note 1: A total of 111,886 Topaz models were produced (16,001 two-door and 95,885 four-door).

SABLE (V-6)

50	54D	4-dr. GS Sed-6P	14145	3097	94,694
53	54D	4-dr. LS Sed-6P	15138	3165	Note 2
55	74D	4-dr. GS Wag-6P	14665	3208	26,591
58	74D	4-dr. LS Wag-6P	15683	3268	Note 2

Note 2: LS production is included in GS totals.

COUGAR (V-6/V-8)

60	66D	2-dr. LS Cpe-5P	14134/14855	3237/3392	119,162

COUGAR XR-7 (V-8)

62	66D	2-dr. Cpe-5P	16266	3485	Note 3

Note 3: Production of XR-7 is included in basic Cougar total above.

GRAND MARQUIS (V-8)

74	54K	4-dr. GS Sed-6P	16100	3828	111,611
75	54K	4-dr. LS Sed-6P	16612	3839	Note 4

GRAND MARQUIS COLONY PARK WAGON (V-8)

78	74K	4-dr. GS Wag-6P	16341	4019	9,456
79	74K	4-dr. LS Wag-6P	16926	4025	Note 4

Note 4: LS production is included in GS totals.

FACTORY PRICE AND WEIGHT NOTE: Cougar price and weight to left of slash is for V-6, to right for V-8 engine.

ENGINE DATA: BASE FOUR (Topaz): Inline. Overhead valve. Four-cylinder. Cast iron block and head. Displacement: 140 cu. in. (2.3 liters). Bore & stroke: 3.70 x 3.30 in. Compression ratio: 9.0:1. Brake horsepower: 98 at 4400 RPM. Torque: 124 lbs.-ft. at 2200 RPM. Five main bearings. Hydraulic valve lifters. Multi-point fuel injection. BASE FOUR (Topaz XR5, LS Sport and AWD): High-output version of 140 cu. in. four above — Horsepower: 100 at 4400 RPM. Torque: 130 lbs.-ft. at 2600 RPM. BASE V-6 (Sable): 60-degree, overhead valve V-6. Cast iron block and head. Displacement: 182 cu. in. (3.0 liters). Bore & stroke: 3.50 x 3.10 in. Compression ratio: 9.3:1. Brake horsepower: 140 at 4800 RPM. Torque: 160 lbs.-ft. at 3000 RPM. Four main bearings. Hydraulic valve lifters. Multi-port fuel injection. BASE V-6 (Cougar); OPTIONAL (Sable): 90-degree, overhead valve V-6. Cast iron block and aluminum head. Displacement: 232 cu. in. (3.8 liters). Bore & stroke: 3.80 x 3.40 in. Compression ratio: 9.0:1. Brake horsepower: (Cougar) 140 at 3800 RPM; (Sable) 140 at 4800. Torque: (Cougar) 215 lbs.-ft. at 2400 RPM; (Sable) 215 at 2200. Four main bearings. Hydraulic valve lifters. Multi-point fuel injection. BASE V-8 (Grand Marquis); OPTIONAL (Cougar): 90-degree, overhead valve V-8. Cast iron block and head. Displacement: 302 cu. in. (5.0 liters). Bore & stroke: 4.00 x 3.00 in. Compression ratio: 8.9:1. Brake horsepower: (Cougar) 155 at 3400 RPM; (Grand Marquis) 150 at 3200. Torque: (Cougar) 265 lbs.-ft. at 2200 RPM; (Grand Marquis) 270 at 2000. Five main bearings. Hydraulic valve lifters. Sequential fuel injection.

CHASSIS DATA: Wheelbase: (Topaz) 99.9 in.; (Sable) 106.0 in.; (Cougar) 104.2 in.; (Grand Marquis) 114.3 in. **Overall Length:** (Topaz 2-dr) 176.7 in.; (Topaz 4-dr) 177.0 in.; (Sable) 190.9 in.; (Sable wag) 191.9 in.; (Cougar) 200.8 in.; (Grand Marquis) 213.5 in.; (Grand Marquis wag) 218.3 in. **Height:** (Topaz) 52.8 in.; (Sable) 54.3 in.; (Sable wag) 55.1 in.; (Cougar) 53.8 in.; (Grand Marquis) 55.4 in.; (Grand Marquis wag) 57.0 in. **Width:** (Topaz 2-dr) 68.3 in. (Topaz 4-dr) 66.8 in.; (Sable) 70.8 in.; (Cougar) 71.1 in.; (Grand Marquis) 77.5 in.; (Grand Marquis wag) 79.3 in. **Front Tread:** (Topaz) 54.9 in.; (Sable) 61.6 in.; (Cougar) 58.1 in.; (Grand Marquis) 62.2 in. **Rear Tread:** (Topaz) 57.6 in.; (Sable) 60.5 in.; (Sable wag) 59.9 in.; (Cougar) 58.5 in.; (Grand Marquis) 62.0 in. **Standard Tires:** (Topaz) P185/70R14; (Sable) P205/70R14; (Cougar) P215/70R14; (XR-7) P225/60VR15; (Grand Marquis) P215/70R15 SBR WSW.

TECHNICAL: Transmission: Five-speed manual standard on Topaz; three-speed automatic optional. Four-speed overdrive automatic standard on Sable, Cougar and Grand Marquis. **Steering:** (Grand Marquis) recirculating ball; (others) rack and pinion. **Front Suspension:** (Topaz) MacPherson strut-mounted coil springs w/lower control arms and stabilizer bar; (Cougar) modified MacPherson struts w/lower control arms, coil springs and anti-sway bar; (Sable) MacPherson struts w/control arm, coil springs and anti-sway bar; (Grand Marquis) coil springs with long/short A-arms and anti-sway bar. **Rear Suspension:** (Topaz) independent quadra-link w/MacPherson struts; (Sable) MacPherson struts w/coil springs, parallel suspension arms and anti-sway bar; (Cougar/Grand Marquis) four-link w/coil springs. **Brakes:** Front disc, rear drums. **Body construction:** (Grand Marquis) separate body and frame; (others) unibody. **Fuel tank:** (Topaz) 15.4 gal.; (Topaz 4WD) 13.7 gal.; (Sable) 16 gal.; (Cougar) 22.1 gal.; (Grand Marquis) 18 gal.

DRIVETRAIN OPTIONS: Engines: 3.8-liter V-6: Sable ($396); 5.0-liter V-8: Cougar ($721). **Transmission/Differential:** Automatic transaxle: Topaz ($482). All Wheel Drive: Topaz ($1257-$1409). Traction-Lok: Cougar/Grand Marquis ($100). **Suspension:** Automatic leveling: Grand Marquis ($195). H.D. suspension: Grand Marquis ($26). Trailer towing pkg: Grand Marquis ($389-$399).

TOPAZ CONVENIENCE/APPEARANCE OPTIONS:
GS Supplemental Restraint System Pkg ($1180). LS Supplemental Restraint System Pkg ($880). Manual Control Air Cond ($773). Comfort/Convenience Grp, GS ($179). Rr Window Defroster ($145). Power Lock Group 2 Dr GS ($237). 2 Dr XR5 ($156). 4 Dr GS ($288). 2 Dr GS w/Comf/Conv Grp ($156). 4 Dr GS w/Comf/Conv Grp ($207). Clearcoat Metallic Paint ($91). Premium Sound System ($138). Speed Control ($182). Tilt Steering Wheel ($124). Polycast Wheels ($178). Decklid Luggage Rack ($115). Power Windows, 4 Dr ($296). All Wheel Drive GS ($1409). XR5, LTS ($1257). LS ($1274). Elect AM/FM Stereo Cass w/Clock GS ($141). GS Driver's Side Airbag ($815). LS Driver's Side Airbag ($622). 6-Way Pwr. Driver's Seat ($251). Locking Spoke Wheel Covers ($212). Calif Emissions System ($99). Frt License Plate Bracket (NC). Eng Block Immersion Heater ($18). Vinyl Seat Trim ($37). TIRES: P185/70R14 WSW ($82). P185/70R14 permance BSW (NC). P185/70R14 Performance WSW ($82).

SABLE CONVENIENCE/APPEARANCE OPTIONS:
PREFERRED EQUIP PKGS: (450B) Sedan ($401). (460A) Sedan ($807). (461A) Sedan ($2213). (455A) Wagon ($638). (456A) Wagon ($1034). (465A) Wagon ($373). (466A) Wagon ($962). (467A) Wagon ($2368). (467A) Wagon ($2353). TIRES: P205/70R14 WSW ($82). P205/65R15 BSW ($65). P205/65R15 WSW ($146). P205/65R15 WSW ($82). Conventional Spare Tire ($73). Cast Alum Wheels ($172). Radial Design Wheel Covers ($157). Polycast Wheels ($123). Air Cond Man Temp Control, Delete (credit). Auto Air Cond ($183). Auto Lamp System ($73). Auto Parking Brake Release ($12). Dual Illum Visor Mirrors ($99). Electronic Instrument Cluster ($351). Insta-Clear Heated Windshield ($250). Keyless Entry System ($202). Power Moonroof ($741). Rr Window Defroster ($145). Fingertip Speed Control ($182). Tilt Strg Wheel ($124). Light Group, GS ($59). H.D. Battery ($27). H.D. Suspension ($26). Extended Range Fuel Tank ($46). Calif Emissions System ($99). Power Lock Group, GS Sedans ($287). GS Wagons ($237). LS ($195). 6-Way Pwr Driver's Seat ($251). 6-Way Pwr Driver & Pass Seat ($502). Power Side Windows ($296). AM/FM Radio w/Cass Player ($137). Premium Sound System ($168). Prem Electronic AM/FM Stereo ($472). Pwr Antenna ($76). Clearcoat Paint ($183). Frt License Plate Bracket (NC). Paint Stripe ($57). F&R Floor Mats ($43). Leather-Wrapped Strg Wheel ($59). Leather Seat Trim ($415). All Vinyl Trim ($37). Individual Bucket Seats, GS (NC). Wagon, Picnic Tray ($66). Rr Facing Third Seat ($155). Liftgate Window Washer/Wiper ($126). Cargo Area Cover ($66). Eng Block Immersion Heater ($18). AM/FM Radio Delete (credit).

COUGAR CONVENIENCE/APPEARANCE OPTIONS:
PREFERRED EQUIP PKGS: (261A) ($895). (261A) w/o WSW Tires ($822). (262B) ($1260). (262B) w/o WSW Tires ($1187). (263A) ($2752). (263A) w/o WSW Tires ($2679). (265A) ($836). (266A) ($1312). Power Lock Group ($237). Power Windows ($222). Power Moonroof, w/262A, 263B, 266A, Lux Light Grp ($741). Pwr Moonroof ($841). 6-Way Pwr Driver's Seat ($251). Dual 6-Way Pwr Seats w/pkg 262 ($302). LS ($554). XR-7 ($502). w/266A ($251). Electronic AM/FM Stereo/Cass ($137). Premium Sound System ($168). Power Antenna ($76). Graphic Equalizer ($218). w/262A, 263B, 266A ($50). Hood Accent Paint Stripes ($16). Clearcoat Metallic Paint ($183). Two-Tone Paint ($159). Leather Seat Trim ($415). Auto Climate Air Cond ($162). H.D. Battery ($27). Eng Block Heater ($18). Electric Rr Window Defroster ($145). Interval Wipers ($55). Auto Park Brake Release ($12). Lux Lamp Group, XR-7 ($176). LS ($244). Keyless Entry System ($202). w/Lux Light Grp, Illum Ent ($121). Speed Control ($182). Leather-Wrapped Strg Wheel ($59). Lux Light Group ($228). Frt Carpet Floor Mats ($33). Illum Entry System ($82). Electronic Instrument Cluster ($270). Tilt Strg Wheel ($124). Frt License Plate Bracket (NC). Calif Emissions System ($99). TIRES: P215/70R14 WSW ($73). Conventional Spare Tire ($73). Locking Wire Style Wheel Covers, w/262A, 263B (NC). Lckg Wire Style Wheel Covers ($212). Polycast Wheels ($178).

GRAND MARQUIS CONVENIENCE/APPEARANCE OPTIONS:
PREFERRED EQUIP PKGS: GS Sedans (156A) ($733). (157A) ($876). LS 4 Door Sedan (171A) ($1071). (172A) ($1330). (173A) ($1743). LS 4 Dr Sdn w/Lckg Wire-Style Wheel Covers ILO Turbine Spoke Alum Wheels (171A) ($903). (172A) ($1152). (173A) ($1565). Colony Park GS (192A) ($1272). (193A) ($1356). Colony Park LS (192A) ($1226). (193A) ($1310). Conventional Spare Tire ($73). (573) Automatic Climate Control ($211). When ordered w/Pkgs (that includes rear defroster) ($66). Electric Rr Window Defroster ($145). Insta-Clear Heated Windshield ($250). Pwr Lock Grp ($245). Pwr Decklid Release ($50). 6-Way Pwr Driver's Seat ($251). Dual 6-Way Pwr Seats ($502). w/Pkgs Containing 6-Way Pwr Driver's Seat ($251). Elec AM/FM Stereo Cassette ($137). High Level Audio System ($472). w/Pkgs 172A or 193A ($304). w/Pkg 173A ($167). Premium Sound System ($168). Pwr Antenna ($76). Frt License Plate Bracket (NC). License Plate Frames ($9). Dlx Luggage Rack ($115). Cornering Lamp ($68). Bodyside Protection Moldings ($66). Two-Tone Paint w/Tape Stripes ($159). Formal Coach Vinyl Roof ($665). Hood Accent Paint Stripes ($18). Leather Wrapped Strg Wheel ($59). F&R Floor Mats ($43). Fingertip Spd Control ($182). Tilt Strg Wheel ($124). Illum Entry System ($82). Light Group ($46). Dual Illum Visor Mirrors ($109). Tripminder ($215). Pivoting Frt Vent Windows ($79). Dual Facing Rr Seats Wag ($173). Cloth Seat Trim, Wagons ($54). Vinyl Seat Trim, Sedans ($37). Leather Seat Trim ($415). Lckg Wire-Styled Wheel Covers ($183). Turbine Spoke Alum Wheels ($361). In pkgs containing Locking Wire-Style Wheel Covers ($178). Calif Emission System ($99). Frt Carpet Floor Mats ($26). Eng Block Immersion Heater ($18).

HISTORY: Introduced: October 1, 1987 except (Topaz) November, 1987. Model year production: 473,400 (total). Calendar year production (U.S.): 293,689. Calendar year sales by U.S. dealers: 486,208 (incl. Tracer). Model year sales by U.S. dealers: 485,613.

1989 MERCURY

Cougar got nearly all the attention for 1989, appearing in a completely new form; and with a supercharged V-6 engine under the hood of the sporty XR7.

1989 Topaz four-door sedan

TOPAZ — FOUR — Little changed in Mercury's compact sedans, which got a moderate restyle for 1988. A driver's side airbag was now available in all except the sporty XR5 two-door.

SABLE — V-6 — Modest revision of Sable's front end included new headlamps and park/signal lamps, as well as full-width illumination of the panel between the headlamps. Sedans changed their taillamp design. The optional 3.8-liter V-6 turned to sequential fuel injection this year.

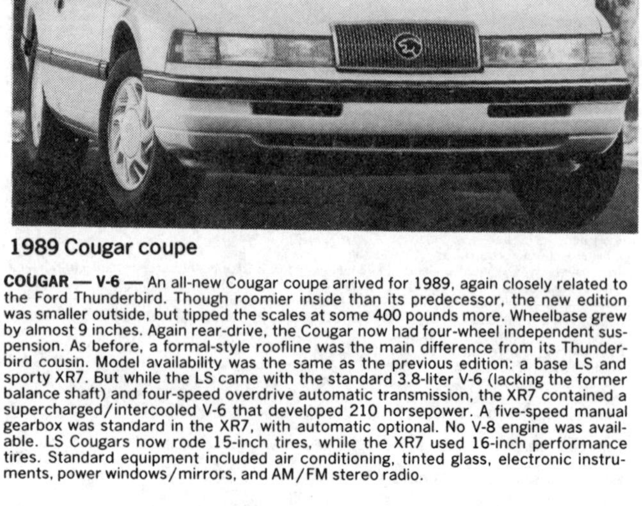

1989 Cougar coupe

COUGAR — V-6 — An all-new Cougar coupe arrived for 1989, again closely related to the Ford Thunderbird. Though roomier inside than its predecessor, the new edition was smaller outside, but tipped the scales at some 400 pounds more. Wheelbase grew by almost 9 inches. Again rear-drive, the Cougar now had four-wheel independent suspension. As before, a formal-style roofline was the main difference from its Thunderbird cousin. Model availability was the same as the previous edition: a base LS and sporty XR7. But while the LS came with the standard 3.8-liter V-6 (lacking the former balance shaft) and four-speed overdrive automatic transmission, the XR7 contained a supercharged/intercooled V-6 that developed 210 horsepower. A five-speed manual gearbox was standard in the XR7, with automatic optional. No V-8 engine was available. LS Cougars now rode 15-inch tires, while the XR7 used 16-inch performance tires. Standard equipment included air conditioning, tinted glass, electronic instruments, power windows/mirrors, and AM/FM stereo radio.

Styling features of the XR7 included monochromatic body treatment and alloy wheels. Anti-lock braking was standard on XR7, which used four-wheel disc brakes rather than the disc/drum arrangement on the LS. Adjustable shock-absorber dampening allowed the selection of a soft or firm ride. Extras on the XR7 included a handling suspension, Traction-Lok axle, sport seats with power bolsters, and analog gauges.

GRAND MARQUIS — V-8 — Little changed in the full-size Mercury, except that clearcoat metallic paint joined the option list this year.

I.D. DATA: Mercury's 17-symbol Vehicle Identification Number (VIN) was stamped on a metal tab fastened to the instrument panel, visible through the windshield. Symbols one to three indicate manufacturer, make and vehicle type. The fourth symbol denotes restraint system. Next comes a letter 'M' (for series), followed by two digits that indicate body type: Model Number, as shown in left column of tables below. (Example: '31' = Topaz GS two-door sedan.) Symbol eight indicates engine type. Next is a check digit. Symbol ten indicates model year ('K' = 1989). Symbol eleven denotes assembly plant. The final six digits make up the production sequence number, starting with 600001.

Model Number	Body/Style Number	Body Type & Seating	Factory Price	Shipping Weight	Production Total
TOPAZ (FOUR)					
31	66D	2-dr. GS Sedan-5P	9577	2567	
33	66D	2-dr. XR5 Sed-5P	10498	2544	
36	54D	4-dr. GS Sedan-5P	9734	2608	
37	54D	4-dr. LS Sedan-5P	11030	2647	
38	54D	4-dr. LTS Sed-5P	11980	2706	
SABLE (V-6)					
50	54D	4-dr. GS Sed-6P	14101	3054	
53	54D	4-dr. LS Sed-6P	15094	3168	
55	74D	4-dr. GS Wag-6P	14804	3228	
58	74D	4-dr. LS Wag-6P	15872	3252	
COUGAR (V-6)					
60	66D	2-dr. LS Cpe-5P	15448	3553	
62	66D	2-dr. XR7 Cpe-5P	19650	3710	
GRAND MARQUIS (V-8)					
74	54K	4-dr. GS Sed-6P	16701	3763	
75	54KK	4-dr. LS Sed-6P	17213	3774	
GRAND MARQUIS COLONY PARK WAGON (V-8)					
78	74K	4-dr. GS Wag-6P	17338	3995	
79	74K	4-dr. LS Wag-6P	17922	3913	

ENGINE DATA: BASE FOUR (Topaz): Inline. Overhead valve. Four-cylinder. Cast iron block and head. Displacement: 140 cu. in. (2.3 liters). Bore & stroke: 3.70 x 3.30 in. Compression ratio: 9.0:1. Brake horsepower: 98 at 4400 RPM. Torque: 124 lbs.-ft. at 2200 RPM. Five main bearings. Hydraulic valve lifters. Multi-point fuel injection. BASE FOUR (Topaz XR5, LST and 4WD): High-output version of 140 cu. in. four above — Horsepower: 100 at 4400 RPM. Torque: 130 lbs.-ft. at 2600 RPM. BASE V-6 (Sable): 60-degree, overhead valve V-6. Cast iron block and head. Displacement: 182 cu. in. (3.0 liters). Bore & stroke: 3.50 x 3.10 in. Compression ratio: 9.3:1. Brake horsepower: 140 at 4800 RPM. Torque: 160 lbs.-ft. at 3000 RPM. Four main bearings. Hydraulic valve lifters. Multi-port fuel injection. BASE V-6 (Cougar); OPTIONAL (Sable): 90-degree, overhead valve V-6. Cast iron block and aluminum head. Displacement: 232 cu. in. (3.8 liters). Bore & stroke: 3.80 x 3.40 in. Compression ratio: 9.0:1. Brake horsepower: 140 at 3800 RPM. Torque: (Cougar) 215 lbs.-ft. at 2400 RPM; (Sable) 215 at 2200. Four main bearings. Hydraulic valve lifters. Multi-point fuel injection. SUPERCHARGED V-6 (Cougar XR7): 90-degree, overhead valve V-6. Cast iron block and aluminum head. Displacement: 232 cu. in. (3.8 liters). Bore & stroke: 3.80 x 3.40 in. Compression ratio: 8.2:1. Brake horsepower: 210 at 4000 RPM. Torque: 315 lbs.-ft. at 2600 RPM. Four main bearings. Hydraulic valve lifters. Multi-point fuel injection. BASE V-8 (Grand Marquis): 90-degree, overhead valve V-8. Cast iron block and head. Displacement: 302 cu. in. (5.0 liters). Bore & stroke: 4.00 x 3.00 in. Compression ratio: 8.9:1. Brake horsepower: 150 at 3200 RPM. Torque: 270 lbs.-ft. at 2000 RPM. Five main bearings. Hydraulic valve lifters. Sequential fuel injection.

CHASSIS DATA: Wheelbase: (Topaz) 99.9 in.; (Sable) 106.0 in.; (Cougar) 113.0 in.; (Grand Marquis) 114.3 in. **Overall Length:** (Topaz 2-dr) 176.7 in.; (Topaz 4-dr) 177.0 in.; (Sable) 190.9 in.; (Sable wag) 191.9 in.; (Cougar) 198.7 in.; (Grand Marquis) 213.5 in.; (Grand Marquis wag) 218.3 in. **Height:** (Topaz) 52.8 in.; (Sable) 54.3 in.; (Sable wag) 55.1 in.; (Cougar) 52.7 in.; (Grand Marquis) 55.4 in.; (Grand Marquis wag) 57.0 in. **Width:** (Topaz 2-dr) 68.3 in. (Topaz 4-dr) 66.8 in.; (Sable) 70.8 in.; (Cougar) 72.7 in.; (Grand Marquis) 77.5 in.; (Grand Marquis wag) 79.3 in. **Front Tread:** (Topaz) 54.9 in.; (Sable) 61.6 in.; (Cougar) 61.4 in.; (Grand Marquis) 62.2 in. **Rear Tread:** (Topaz) 57.6 in.; (Sable) 60.5 in.; (Sable wag) 59.9 in.; (Cougar) 61.2 in.; (Grand Marquis) 62.0 in. **Standard Tires:** (Topaz) P185/70R14; (Sable) P205/70R14; (Cougar) P205/70R15; (XR-7) P225/60VR15; (Grand Marquis) P215/70R15 SBR WSW.

TECHNICAL: Transmission: Five-speed manual standard on Topaz; three-speed automatic optional. Five-speed manual standard on Cougar XR7; four-speed automatic optional. Four-speed overdrive automatic standard on Sable, Cougar LS and Grand Marquis. **Steering:** (Grand Marquis) recirculating ball; (others) rack and pinion. **Front Suspension:** (Topaz) MacPherson strut-mounted coil springs w/lower control arms and stabilizer bar; (Cougar) log spindle SLA with coil springs, gas shocks, upper A-arm, lower arm, tension strut and stabilizer bar; (Sable) MacPherson struts w/control arm, coil springs and anti-sway bar; (Grand Marquis) coil springs with long/short A-arms and anti-sway bar.**Rear Suspension:** (Topaz) independent quadra-link w/MacPherson struts: (Cougar) independent with coil springs, gas shocks, lower 'h' arm, upper arm and stablilizer bar; (Sable) MacPherson struts w/coil springs, parallel suspension arms and anti-sway bar: (Grand Marquis) four-link w/coil springs. **Brakes:** Front dis, rear drum except (Cougar XR7) front/rear discs with anti-lock. **Body construction:** (Grand Marquis) separate body and frame; (others) unibody. **Fuel tank:** (Topaz) 15.4 gal.; (Topaz 4WD) 14.7 gal.; (Sable) 16 gal.; (Cougar) 19.0 gal.; (Grand Marquis) 18 gal.

DRIVETRAIN OPTIONS: Engines: 3.8-liter V-6: Sable ($400). **Transmission/Differential:** Automatic transaxle: Topaz ($515). All Wheel Drive: Topaz ($915-$1441). Automatic transmission: XR7 ($539). Traction-Lok: Cougar/Grand Marquis ($100). **Suspension/Brakes:** Anti-lock brakes: Cougar ($985). Automatic leveling: Grand Marquis ($195). H.D. suspension: Sable/Grand Marquis ($26). Trailer towing pkg.: Grand Marquis ($405).

TOPAZ CONVENIENCE/APPEARANCE OPTIONS:
GS Models Special Value Pkg 361A ($460). Special Value Pkg 363A ($799). GS Supplemental Restraint System Pkg 362A, 4 Dr ($1172). XR5 Model Special Value Pkg 371A ($456). LS Model Special Value Pkg 365A (NC). LS Supplemental Restraint System Pkg 366A ($939). LTS Model LTS Supplrment Restraint System Pkg 376A ($646). Air Conditioner, Manual Control ($788). Comfort/Convenience Grp, GS ($179). Rear Window Defroster ($145). Power Lock Group, 2 Door GS ($237). 2 Door XR5 ($156). 4 Door GS ($288). 2 Dr GS w/Comf/Conv Grp ($156). 4 Dr GS w/Comf/Conv Grp ($207). Clearcoat Metallic Paint ($91). Premium Sound System ($138). Speed Control ($182). Tilt Steering Wheel ($124). Polycast Wheels ($178). Decklid Luggage Rack ($115). Power Windows, 4 Door ($296). All Wheel Drive GS ($1441). GS w/363A ($927). LTS ($1332). LS ($1429). LS w/365A ($915). Electr. AM/FM Stereo Cass w/Clock, GS ($137). Electr. AM/FM Stereo Delete, GS ($245 credit). Electr. AM/FM Cass Delete, XR5, LS, LTS ($382 credit). GS Driver's Side Airbag ($815). LS & LTS Driver's Side Airbag ($622). 6-Way Power Driver's Seat ($251). Locking Spoke Wheel Covers ($212). Calif. Emissions System ($100). Frt. License Plate Bracket (NC). Eng Block Immersion Heater ($20). Vinyl Seat Trim ($37). TIRES: P185/70R14 WSW ($82).

SABLE CONVENIENCE/APPEARANCE OPTIONS:
Preferred Equipment Pkg. 450A ($580). Preferred Equipment Pkg 451A ($1113). Preferred Equip Pkg 452C ($1138). Preferred Equipment Pkg 460A ($496). Preferred Equip Pkg 461A ($1468). Preferred Equipment Pkg 462A ($2161). Air Cond, Man. Temp Control Delete, GS only ($807 credit). Auto Air Conditioning ($183). Auto Lamp System ($73). Auto Parking Brake Release ($12). Dual Illum. Visor Mirrors ($100). Electronic Instrument Cluster ($351). Insta-Clear Heated Windshield ($250). Keyless Entry System ($218). Power Moonroof ($741). Rear Window Defroster ($150). Fingertip Speed Control ($191). Tilt Steering Wheel ($124). Light Group, GS ($59). H.D. Battery ($27). Extd Range Fuel Tank ($46). Calif. Emissions System ($100). Pwr Lock Group, GS ($287). LS ($195). 6-Way Pwr Driver's Seat ($251). 6-Way Pwr Driver & Pass. Seat ($502). w/Pkg 451, 460, 461 or 464 ($251). Power Windows ($296). AM/FM w/Cass Player ($137). Premium Sound System ($168). High Level Audio System ($472). w/Pkg 450, 451 ($335). w/Pkg 461 ($167). Pwr Antenna ($76). Clearcoat Paint ($183). Frt. License Plate Bracket (NC). Paint Stripe ($61). F&R Floor Mats ($43). Leather-Wrapped Strg. Wheel ($59). Leather Seat Trim ($415). All Vinyl Trim ($37). Picnic Tray Wag ($66). Rear Facing Third Seat Wag ($155). Liftgate Window Washer/Wiper Wag ($126). Cargo Area Cover Wag ($66). Eng Block Immersion Heater ($20). AM/FM Radio Delete ($206 credit). TIRES: P205/70R14 WSW ($82). P205/65R15 BSW ($65). P205/65R15 WSW ($146). P205/65R15 WSW ($82). Conventional Spare Tire ($73). Cast Alum Wheels ($224). Polycast Wheels ($138).

COUGAR CONVENIENCE/APPEARANCE OPTIONS:
Cold Weather Group, electric rear window defroster, eng block immersion heater; h.d. battery h.d. alternator ($195). XR7 ($168). w/261, 262, 263 ($45). w/265, 266 ($18). Pwr Lock Group; pwr dr locks; pwr decklid release; remote-release fuel filler door LS ($216). Luxury Lamp Grp; auto headlamp dimmer, autolamp on/off delay system, frt cornering lamps, LS ($244). Luxury Light Grp; underhood light; dual beam dome/map light, instrument panel courtesy lights, dual illum visor vanity mirrors, illuminated entry system ($228). Preferred Equipment Pkg; Tilt str. column, cruise control, electric rear window defroster, Pwr Lock Grp: LS ($636). Preferred Equipment Pkg; P215/70R15 blackwall tires, frt carpeted floor mats, tilt strg column, leather-wrapped strg cruise control, 6-way pwr driver's seat, electric rr window defroster, AM/FM ET stereo radio w/cass; Lux. Light Grp, cast alum wheels pwr Lock Grp ($1081). Preferred Equip Pkg P215/70R15 blackwall tires, frt carpeted flr mats, keyless entry system, diagnostic maintenance monitor, tilt strg column, leather-wrapped strg wheel, cruise control, dual 6-way/6-way pwr seats, electri rr window defroster, high-level AM/FM ET stereo radio w/cass, Lux Light Grp, Luxury Lamp Grp, cast alum wheels, pwr antenna, pwr lock grp ($1814). Preferred Equipment Pkg; tilt strg column, cruise control, 6-way pwr driver's seat, electric rear window defroster, AM/FM ET stereo radio w/cass, Pwr Lock Grp, XR-7; (NC). Preferred Equipment Pkg, color-keyed frt carpeted floor mats, keyless entry system, tilt strg column, cruise control, 6-way pwr driver's seat; electric rr window defroster, high-level AM/FM ET stereo radio w/cass, Luxury Light Grp, Luxury Lamp Grp, pwr antenna, Pwr Lock Grp XR-7 ($862). Pwr Antenna ($76). Anti-Theft System ($183). Diagnostic Maintenance Monitor ($89). Electric Rear Window Defroster ($150). Calif Emission System ($100). Keyless Entry System ($218). w/60A, 262, 263, 265, 266 ($137). Speed Control ($191). Floor Mats, Frt Carpeted Color Keyed ($33). AM/FM ET Stereo Radio w/Cass & Clock ($137). High-Level AM/FM Ed Stereo w/Cass ($441). w/262. 265 ($305). Ford JBL Sound System ($488). Digital Audio Disc Player ($491). Pwr Moonroof; Inclds dual reading lights, pop-up air deflector, sliding sun shade, rear tilt-up ($741). Pwr 6-way driver's seats ($261). Dual 6-way pwr Seats ($522). Leather-Wrapped Steering Wheel ($63). Split Fold-Down Rear Seat ($133). Tilt Wheel ($124). Leather Seat Trim, LS ($489). Leather Seat Trim, XR7 ($489). Warning Lights, Diagnostic Maintenance Monitor, (warning lights for low fuel, low oil, low coolant & low washer fluid, adaptive oil change indicator) LS ($89). Frt License Plate Bracket (NC). Locking Radial Spoke Wheel Covers, w/261 ($228). Styled Sport Wheel Covers ($85). Cast Aluminum 15" wheels ($299). TIRES: P205/70R15 WSW ($73). P225/60VR16 BSW All-Season Performance Tires ($73). Conventional Spare Tire ($73).

GRAND MARQUIS CONVENIENCE/APPEARANCE OPTIONS:
Preferred Equip. Pkgs GS Sedan (156A) ($1055). (157A) ($1313). LS 4-dr sedan (171A) ($1243). (172B) ($1333). GS 4 dr Sedan (157A) w/locking Wire Style Wheel Covers ILO Turbine Spoke Alum. Wheels ($1101). Colony Park GS (192A) Auto OD Trans; Conv. Axle, P215/70R15 All Season WSW Tires; Illum Entry System; Frt Cornering Lamps; Tilt Strg Wheel; Fingertip Spd Control; 6-Way Pwr Driver Seat; Dual Inboard Facing Rear Seats; Electric Rr Window Defroster; Turbine Spoke Alum Wheels; Bodyside protection Mldg; Light Grp; Pwr Lock Group ($1256). (193A) all 92A plus Leather-Wrapped Strg Wheel; Dual Illum Visor Mirrors; Pwr Antenna; Prem Sound System; Electronic AM/FM Stereo Cass Radio ($1509). Colony Park LS (192A) same as GS ($1210). (193A) same as GSA ($1463). (508) Conventional Spare Tire ($85). Auto Climate Cntrl Air Cond ($216). Pkgs 192A, 193A, 171A, 172A, 156A or 157A which include rear Defroster ($66). Elect. Rear Window Defroster ($150). Insta-Clear Heated Windshield ($250). H.D. Battery ($27). Power Lock Group ($255). Pwr Decklid Release ($50). 6-Way Pwr Driver's Seat ($261). Dual 6-Way Pwr Seats ($522). w/Pkgs containing 6-Way Pwr Driver's Seat ($261). Elect AM/FM Stereo Cass ($137). High Level Audio System ($472). w/Pkg 157A ($335). w/Pkgs 172A or 193A ($167). Premium Sound System ($168). Power Antenna ($76). Frt Lic Plate Bracket (NC). Lic Plate Frames ($9). Cornering Lamps ($68). Bodyside Protection Mldgs ($66). Tu Tone Paint w/Tape Stripes ($159). Formal Coach Vinyl Roof ($665). Clearcoat Paint ($226). Hood Accent Paint Stripes ($18). Leather Wrapped Strg Wheel ($63). Floor Mats, F&R ($43). Fingertip Spd Control ($191). Tilt Wheel ($124). Illum Entry System ($82). Light Grp ($46). Dual Illum Visor Mirrors ($109). Tripminder ($215). Pivoting Frt Vent Windows ($79). Dual Facing Rr Seats ($173). Cloth Seat Trim, Wagons ($54). Vinyl Seat Trim, Sedans ($37). Leather Seat Trim ($489). Lckg Wire-Styled Wheel Covers ($228). Turbine Spoke Alum Wheels ($440). Pkgs containing Lckg Wire-Style Wheels ($212). Calif Emissions System ($100). Frt Carpet Flr Mats ($26). Eng Block Immersion Heater ($20).

HISTORY: Introduced: October 6, 1988 except (Cougar) December 26, 1988. Model year production: 294,899 (U.S.); 495,017 (total). Calendar year sales by U.S. dealers: 465,908 (incl. Tracer). Model year sales by U.S. dealers: 485,357.

1990 MERCURY

This was essentially a carryover year for Mercury, all of whose models remained closely related to a model in the Ford lineup. In addition to the four domestically-built models, Mercury dealers had been selling a Mexican-built Tracer, but production halted for 1990, awaiting a revised version for 1991.

TOPAZ — FOUR — Shoulder belts added to rear seats were the only notable change for the Mercury compact. Trunk and footwell lights became standard; so did floormats. Wire wheel covers left the option list. As before, both the standard and high-output 2.3 liter four-cylinder engines were available, the latter standard in the XR5, LTS and four-wheel-drive models.

1990 Sable GS four-door sedan

SABLE — V-6 — Except for the addition of a standard driver's side airbag and optional anti-lock braking (on sedans only), the mid-size Sable sedan and wagons was a carryover for 1990. Inside was a new instrument cluster, with slide-out coin and cupholder trays. Tilt steering became standard; a compact-disc player a new option. Variable-assist power steering now came with the optional 3.8-liter V-6 engine.

1990 Cougar LS coupe

COUGAR — V-6 — Not much changed for 1990 on the Mercury mid-size coupe, which enjoyed a full restyling for 1989, beyond the addition of contoured head restraints and a few option adjustments.

1990 Grand Marquis Colony Park wagon

GRAND MARQUIS — V-8 — Nearly all the changes for the Mercury full-size sedans and wagons went inside: a driver's airbag, new instrument panel, rear shoulder belts, and standard tilt steering. As before, the station wagons could get optional third rear seats for eight-passenger seating. Sedans no longer had standard bumper guards, but they remained on the option list. Rear track width grew by 1.3 inches, because of a different rear axle. A single key now operated doors and ignition.

I.D. DATA: Mercury's 17-symbol Vehicle Identification Number (VIN) was stamped on a metal tab fastened to the instrument panel, visible through the windshield. Symbols one to three indicate manufacturer, make and vehicle type. The fourth symbol denotes restraint system. Next comes a letter 'M' (for series), followed by two digits that indicate body type: Model Number, as shown in left column of tables below. (Example: '31' = Topaz GS two-door sedan.) Symbol eight indicates engine type. Next is a check digit. Symbol ten indicates model year ('L' = 1990). Symbol eleven denotes assembly plant. The final six digits make up the production sequence number, starting with 600001.

TOPAZ (FOUR)

Model Number	Body/Style Number	Body Type & Seating	Factory Price	Shipping Weight	Production Total
31	66D	2-dr. GS Sedan-5P	10027	2447	
33	66D	2-dr. XR5 Sed-5P	10988	2442	
36	54D	4-dr. GS Sedan-5P	10184	2490	
37	54D	4-dr. LS Sedan-5P	11507	2533	
38	54D	4-dr. LTS Sed-5P	12514	2542	
SABLE (V-6)					
50	54D	4-dr. GS Sed-6P	15009	2977	
53	54D	4-dr. LS Sed-6P	16011	3045	
55	74D	4-dr. GS Wag-6P	15711	3088	
58	74D	4-dr. LS Wag-6P	16789	3148	
COUGAR (V-6)					
60	66D	2-dr. LS Cpe-5P	15911	3314	
62	66D	2-dr. XR7 Cpe-5P	20217	3562	
GRAND MARQUIS (V-8)					
74	54K	4-dr. GS Sed-6P	17633	3685	
75	54K	4-dr. LS Sed-6P	18133	3696	
GRAND MARQUIS COLONY PARK WAGON (V-8)					
78	74K	4-dr. GS Wag-6P	18348	3876	
79	74K	4-dr. LS Wag-6P	18920	3882	

ENGINE DATA: BASE FOUR (Topaz): Inline. Overhead valve. Four-cylinder. Cast iron block and head. Displacement: 140 cu. in. (2.3 liters). Bore & stroke: 3.70 x 3.30 in. Compression ratio: 9.0:1. Brake horsepower: 98 at 4400 RPM. Torque: 124 lbs.-ft. at 2200 RPM. Five main bearings. Hydraulic valve lifters. Multi-point fuel injection. BASE FOUR (Topaz XR5, LTS and 4WD): High-output version of 140 cu. in. four above — Horsepower: 100 at 4400 RPM. Torque: 130 lbs.-ft. at 2600 RPM. BASE V-6 (Sable): 60-degree, overhead valve V-6. Cast iron block and head. Displacement: 182 cu. in. (3.0 liters). Bore & stroke: 3.50 x 3.10 in. Compression ratio: 9.3:1. Brake horsepower: 140 at 4800 RPM. Torque: 160 lbs.-ft. at 3000 RPM. Four main bearings. Hydraulic valve lifters. Multi-port fuel injection. BASE V-6 (Cougar); OPTIONAL (Sable): 90-degree, overhead valve V-6. Cast iron block and aluminum head. Displacement: 232 cu. in. (3.8 liters). Bore & stroke: 3.80 x 3.40 in. Compression ratio: 9.0:1. Brake horsepower: 140 at 3800 RPM. Torque: (Cougar) 215 lbs.-ft. at 2400 RPM; (Sable) 215 at 2200. Four main bearings. Hydraulic valve lifters. Multi-point fuel injection. SUPERCHARGED V-6 (Cougar XR7): 90-degree, overhead valve V-6. Cast iron block and aluminum head. Displacement: 232 cu. in. (3.8 liters). Bore & stroke: 3.80 x 3.40 in. Compression ratio: 8.2:1. Brake horsepower: 210 at 4000 RPM. Torque: 315 lbs.-ft. at 2600 RPM. Four main bearings. Hydraulic valve lifters. Multi-point fuel injection. BASE V-8 (Grand Marquis): 90-degree, overhead valve V-8. Cast iron block and head. Displacement: 302 cu. in. (5.0 liters). Bore & stroke: 4.00 x 3.00 in. Compression ratio: 8.9:1. Brake horsepower: 150 at 3200 RPM. Torque: 270 lbs.-ft. at 2000 RPM. Five main bearings. Hydraulic valve lifters. Sequential fuel injection.

CHASSIS DATA: Wheelbase: (Topaz) 99.9 in.; (Sable) 106.0 in.; (Cougar) 113.0 in.; (Grand Marquis) 114.3 in. **Overall Length:** (Topaz 2-dr) 176.7 in.; (Topaz 4-dr) 177.0 in.; (Sable) 192.2 in.; (Sable wag) 193.2 in.; (Cougar) 198.7 in.; (Grand Marquis) 213.6 in.; (Grand Marquis wag) 218.0 in. **Height:** (Topaz) 52.8 in.; (Sable) 54.3 in.; (Sable wag) 55.1 in.; (Cougar) 52.7 in.; (Grand Marquis) 55.6 in.; (Grand Marquis wag) 56.5 in. **Width:** (Topaz) 68.3 in.; (Sable) 70.8 in.; (Cougar) 72.7 in.; (Grand Marquis) 77.5 in.; (Grand Marquis wag) 79.3 in. **Front Tread:** (Topaz) 54.9 in.; (Sable) 61.6 in.; (Cougar) 61.6 in.; (Grand Marquis) 62.2 in. **Rear Tread:** (Topaz) 57.6 in.; (Sable) 60.5 in.; (Sable wag) 59.9 in.; (Cougar) 60.2 in.; (Grand Marquis) 63.3 in. **Standard Tires:** (Topaz) 185/70R14; (Sable) 205/70R14; (Cougar) 205/70R15; (XR7) 225/60VR16; (Grand Marquis) P215/70R15 SBR WSW.

TECHNICAL: Transmission: Five-speed manual standard on Topaz; three-speed automatic optional. Five-speed manual standard on Cougar XR7; four-speed automatic optional. Four-speed overdrive automatic standard on Sable, Cougar LS and Grand Marquis. **Steering:** (Grand Marquis) recirculating ball; (others) rack and pinion. **Front Suspension:** (Topaz) MacPherson strut-mounted coil springs w/lower control arms and stabilizer bar; (Cougar) long spindle SLA with coil springs, gas shocks, upper A-arms, lower arm, tension strut and stabilizer bar; (Sable) MacPherson struts w/control arm, coil springs and anti-sway bar; (Grand Marquis) coil springs with long/short A-arms and anti-sway bar. **Rear Suspension:** (Topaz) independent quadra-link w/MacPherson struts; (Cougar) independent with coil springs, gas shocks, lower 'H' arm, upper arm and stabilizer bar; (Sable) MacPherson struts w/coil springs, parallel suspension arms and anti-sway bar; (Grand Marquis) four-link w/coil springs. **Brakes:** Front disc, rear drum except (Cougar XR7) front/rear discs with anti-lock; anti-locking available on Sable sedan. **Body construction:** (Grand Marquis) separate body and frame; (others) unibody. **Fuel tank:** (Topaz) 15.9 gal.; (Topaz 4WD) 14.7 gal.; (Sable) 16 gal.; (Cougar) 19.0 gal.; (Grand Marquis) 18 gal.

DRIVETRAIN OPTIONS: Engines: 3.8-liter V-6: Sable ($400). **Transmission/Differential:** Automatic transaxle: Topaz ($539). All Wheel Drive: Topaz ($915-1466). Automatic transmission: XR7 ($539). Traction-Lok: Cougar/Grand Marquis ($100). **Steering/Suspension/Brakes:** Variable-assist power steering: Sable ($104). Automatic leveling: Grand Marquis ($195). H.D. suspension: Sable/Grand Marquis ($26). Trailer towing pkg.: Grand Marquis ($405). Anti-lock braking: Sable sedan/Cougar ($985).

1990 Topaz four-door sedan

TOPAZ CONVENIENCE/APPEARANCE OPTIONS:
GS Models Special Value Pkg 361A ($454). Special Value Pkg 363A ($793). XR5 Model Special Value Pkg 371A ($456). LS Model Special Value Pkg 365A (NC). Polycast Wheels ($193). Decklid Luggage Rack ($115). Pwr Windows, 4 Dr ($306). 6-Way Pwr Driver's Seat ($261). Driver-Side Air Bag GS ($815). GS w/361 or 363 ($690). LS or LTS ($622). All Wheel Drive GS ($1466). GS w/363 ($927). LTS ($1356). LS ($1454). LS w/365 ($915). Electronic AM/FM Stereo Cass w/Clock, GS ($137). Calif. Emissions System ($100). Frt. License Plate Bracket (NC). Eng Block Immersion Heater ($20). Lower Accent Paint Treatment ($159). Vinyl Seat Trim ($37). Manual Control Air Cond ($807). Comfort/Convenience Grp, GS ($173). Rear Window Defroster ($150). Power Lock Grp 2-Dr GS ($246). 2 Dr XR5 ($166). 4 Dr GS ($298). 2 Dr GS w/Comf/Conv Grp ($166). 4 Dr GS w/Comf/Conv Grp ($217). Clearcoat Metallic Paint ($91). Premium Sound System ($138). Speed Control ($191). Tilt Strg Wheel ($124). TIRES: P185/70R14 WSW ($82).

SABLE CONVENIENCE/APPEARANCE OPTIONS:
Preferred Equipment Pkg. 450A ($743). Preferred Equipment Pkg 451A ($1032). Preferred Equip Pkg 461A ($1244). Preferred Equipment Pkg 462A ($2036). Auto Air Conditioning ($183). Auto Lamp System ($73). Dual Illum. Visor Mirrors ($100). Electronic Instrument Cluster ($351). Insta-Clear Windshield ($250). Keyless Entry System ($218). Power Moonroof ($741). Rear Window Defroster ($150). Fingertip Speed Control ($191). Luxury Touring Pkg, Sdns ABS, Moonroof Leather Bucket Seats ($2015). Light Group, GS ($59). H.D. Battery ($27). Extd Range Fuel Tank ($46). Calif. Emissions System ($100). Pwr Lock Group, GS Sedans ($296). GS Wagons ($244). LS Sedans ($205). 6-Way Pwr Driver's Seat ($261). 6-Way Pwr Driver & Pass. Seat ($522). w/Pkg 451, 461 or 462 ($261). Power Windows ($306). AM/FM Stereo Cass ($137). Premium Sound System ($168). High Level AM/FM Stereo Cass Audio System ($472). w/Pkg 451 ($335). w/Pkg 461 ($167). JBL Sound System ($488). Digital Compact Disc Player ($491). Pwr Radio Antenna ($76). Clearcoat Paint ($188). Frt. License Plate Bracket (NC). Bodyside Accent Stripes ($61). F&R Floor Mats ($43). Leather-Wrapped Strg. Wheel ($63). Leather Seat Trim ($489). All Vinyl Trim ($37). Picnic Tray Wag ($66). Rear Facing Third Seat Wag ($155). Rear Window Wiper/Washer Wag ($126). Cargo Area Cover Wag ($66). Eng Block Immersion Heater ($20). TIRES: P205/70R14 WSW ($82). P205/65R15 BSW ($65). P205/65R15 WSW ($82-$146). Conventional Spare Tire ($73). Cast Alum Wheels ($224). Polycast Wheels ($138).

COUGAR CONVENIENCE/APPEARANCE OPTIONS:
Preferred Equipment Pkg 261B ($262). Preferred Equipment Pkg 262B ($1164). Preferred Equipment Pkg 263A ($1965). Preferred Equipment Pkg 265B (NC). Preferred Equipment Pkg 266B ($1013). Pwr Lock Group ($246). Diagnostic Maintenance Monitor ($89). Pwr Moonroof ($741). 6-Way Pwer Driver's Seat ($261). Dual 6-Way Pwr Seats in Pkgs w/53A ($261). Dual 6-Way Pwr Seats ($522). Electronic AM/FM Stereo/Cass w/Clock ($137). High Level audio AM/FM Cass w/Clock ($441). w/Pkgs 262, 265 ($304). JBL Sound System ($488). Compact Disc Player ($491). Pwr Antenna ($76). Clearcoat Metallic Paint, LS, Red XR7 ($188). Leather Seat Trim LS ($489). XR7 ($489). Split Fold-Down Rear Seat ($133). Cold Weather Group, LS, XR7 w/MTX ($195). XR7, w/ATX ($168). w/261, 262, 263 ($45). XR7, w/MTX & 265, 266 ($45). XR7 w ATX & 265, 266 ($18). Electric Rear Window Defroster ($150). Light Group ($46). Dual Illum Visor Vanity Mirrors ($100). Illuminated Entry ($82). Luxury Lamp Grp ($244). Headlamp Convenience Grp ($176). Frt Cornering Lamps ($68). Keyless Entry System ($219). w/262, 263, 266 ($137). Speed Control ($191). Tilt Steering Wheel ($124). Leather-Wrapped Strg Wheel ($63). Frt Carpet Floor Mats ($33). Anti-Theft Alarm System ($183). Frt License Plate Bracket (NC). Calif Emission System ($100). TIRES: P205/70R15 WSW ($73). P225/60VR16 BSW All-Season Performance ($73). Conventional Spare Tire ($73). Locking Radial Spoke Wheel Covers ($228). w/Pkg 261 ($143). 15'' Cast Aluminum Wheels ($298). w/Pkg 261 ($213). Styled Sport Wheel Covers ($85).

GRAND MARQUIS CONVENIENCE/APPEARANCE OPTIONS:
GS Sedans; Preferred Equip. Pkg 156A ($975). Preferred Equipment Pkg 157A ($1233). GS 4 dr Sedan w/locking Wire Style Wheel Covers ILO Turbine Spoke Alum. Wheels Preferred Equipment Pkg 157A ($1021). LS 4 Dr Sedan Preferred Equipment Pkg 172A ($1253). Colony Park GS Preferred Equipment Pkg 192A ($1132). Preferred Equipment Pkg 193A ($1385). Colony Park LS Preferred Equipment Pkg 192A ($1086). Preferred Equipment Pkg 193A ($1339). Auto Climate Control ($216). w/Pkgs 192A, 193A, 172A, 156A or 157A which Incl Rear Defroster ($66). Electric Rr Window Defroster ($150). Insta-Clear Heated Windshield ($250). H.D. Battery ($27). Power Lock Group ($255). Power Decklid Release ($50). 6-Way Pwr Driver's Seat ($261). Dual 6-Way Pwr Seats ($522). w/Pkgs containing 6-Way Pwr Driver's Seat ($261). Electronic AM/FM Stereo Cass ($137). High level audio System ($472). w/Pkgs 157A or 172A ($335). w/Pkg 193A ($167). Premium Sound System ($168). Power Antenna ($76). Frt License Plate Bracket (NC). License Plate Frames ($9). Frt Cornering Lamps ($68). Bodyside Protection Moldings, Wag ($66). Tu Tone Paint w/Tape Stripes ($159). Formal Coach Vinyl Roof ($665). Clearcoat paint ($230). Frt Bumper Guards ($38). Rr Bumper Guards ($24). Leather Wrapped Strg Wheel ($63). F&R Floor Mats ($43). Fingertip Speed Control ($191). Illum Entry System ($82). Light Group ($46). Dual Illum Visor Mirrors ($109). Dual Inboard Facing Rr Seats Wag ($173). Cloth Seat Trim, GS Wgn ($54). Vinyl Seat Trim, GS Sdn ($37). Leather Seat Trim, LS Sdn & Wgn ($489). Calif. Emission system ($100). Frt Carpet Flr Mats ($26). Eng Block Immersion Heater ($20). Lckg Wire, Styled Wheel Covers ($228). Turbine Spoke Alum Wheels ($440). In Pkgs containing Locking Wire-Style Wheels ($212). Conventional Spare Tire ($85).

A WORD ABOUT OLD FORDS...

The market for cars more than 10 years is strong. Some buyers of pre-1980 cars are collectors who invest in vehicles likely to increase in value the older they get. Other buyers prefer the looks, size, performance and reliability of yesterday's better-built automobiles.

With a typical 1990 model selling for $12,000 or more, some Americans find themselves priced out of the new-car market. Late-model used cars are pricey too, although short on distinctive looks and roominess. The old cars may use a little more gas, but they cost a lot less.

New cars and late-model used cars depreciate rapidly in value. They can't tow large trailers or mobile homes. Their high-tech engineering is expensive to maintain or repair. In contrast, well-kept old cars are mechanically simpler, but very powerful. They appreciate in value as they grow more scarce and collectible. Insuring them is cheaper too.

Selecting a car and paying the right price for it are two considerations old car buyers face. What models did Ford offer in 1958? Which '63 Thunderbird is worth the most today? What should one pay for a 1970 Mercury convertible?

The Standard Catalog of Ford 1903-1990 answers such questions. The Price Guide section shows most models made between 1903 and 1983. It helps to gauge what they sell for in six different, graded conditions. Models built since 1983 are generally considered ''used cars'' of which few, as yet, have achieved collectible status.

The price estimates contained in this book are current as of the reprint date, June 1991. After that date, more current prices may be obtained by referring to *Old Cars Price Guide* which is available from Krause Publications, 700 E. State St., Iola, WI 54990, telephone (715) 445-2214.

HOW TO USE THE FORD PRICE GUIDE

On the following pages is a **COLLECTOR CAR VALUE GUIDE**. The value of an old car is a ''ballpark'' estimate at best. The estimates contained here are based upon national and regional data compiled by the editors of *Old Cars* and **Old Cars Price Guide**. These data include actual auction bids and prices at collector car auctions and sales, classified and display advertising of such vehicles, verified reports of private sales and input from experts.

Value estimates are listed for cars in six different states of condition. These conditions (1-6) are illustrated and explained in the **VEHICLE CONDITION SCALE** on the following page(s). Values are for complete vehicles, not parts cars, except as noted. Modified car values are not included, but can be estimated by figuring the cost of restoring to original condition and adjusting the figures shown here.

Appearing below is a sample price table listing that illustrates the following elements:

A. MAKE: The make (or marque) appears in large, bold-faced type at the beginning of each value section.

B. DESCRIPTION: The extreme left-hand column indicates vehicle year, model name, body type, engine configuration and, in some cases, wheelbase.

C. CONDITION CODE: The six columns to the right are headed by the numbers 1-to-6 which correspond to the conditions described in the **VEHICLE CONDITION SCALE** in this book.

D. VALUE: The value estimates, in dollars, appear below their respective condition codes and across from the vehicle descriptions.

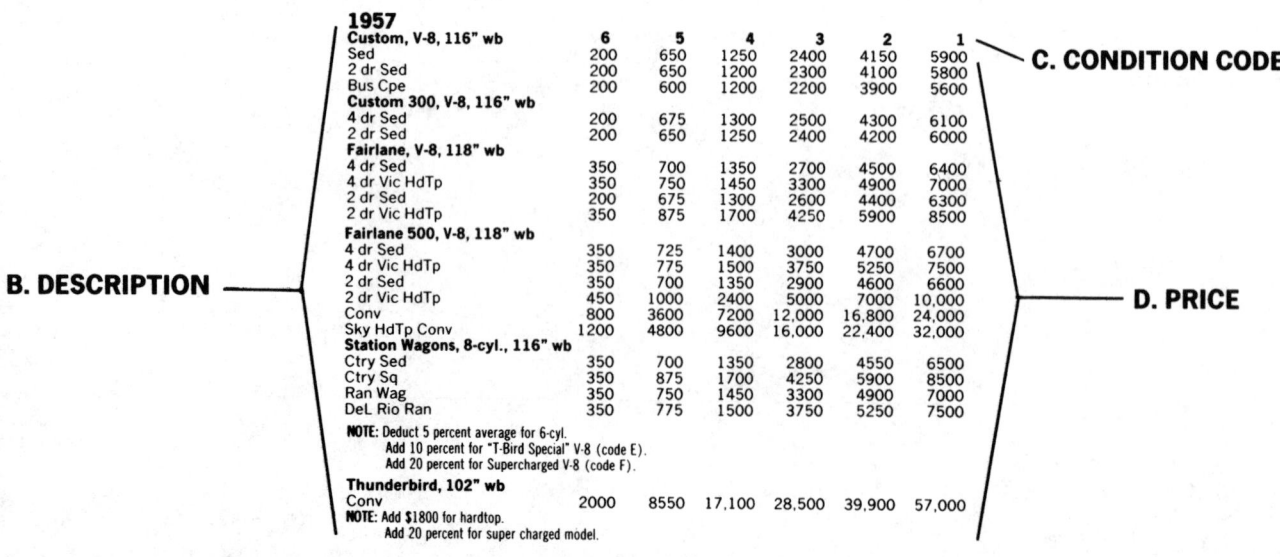

A. MAKE ——— **FORD**

1957	6	5	4	3	2	1
Custom, V-8, 116" wb						
Sed	200	650	1250	2400	4150	5900
2 dr Sed	200	650	1200	2300	4100	5800
Bus Cpe	200	600	1200	2200	3900	5600
Custom 300, V-8, 116" wb						
4 dr Sed	200	675	1300	2500	4300	6100
2 dr Sed	200	650	1250	2400	4200	6000
Fairlane, V-8, 118" wb						
4 dr Sed	350	700	1350	2700	4500	6400
4 dr Vic HdTp	350	750	1450	3300	4900	7000
2 dr Sed	200	675	1300	2600	4400	6300
2 dr Vic HdTp	350	875	1700	4250	5900	8500
Fairlane 500, V-8, 118" wb						
4 dr Sed	350	725	1400	3000	4700	6700
4 dr Vic HdTp	350	775	1500	3750	5250	7500
2 dr Sed	350	700	1350	2900	4600	6600
2 dr Vic HdTp	450	1000	2400	5000	7000	10,000
Conv	800	3600	7200	12,000	16,800	24,000
Sky HdTp Conv	1200	4800	9600	16,000	22,400	32,000
Station Wagons, 8-cyl., 116" wb						
Ctry Sed	350	700	1350	2800	4550	6500
Ctry Sq	350	875	1700	4250	5900	8500
Ran Wag	350	750	1450	3300	4900	7000
DeL Rio Ran	350	775	1500	3750	5250	7500

NOTE: Deduct 5 percent average for 6-cyl.
Add 10 percent for "T-Bird Special" V-8 (code E).
Add 20 percent for Supercharged V-8 (code F).

Thunderbird, 102" wb						
Conv	2000	8550	17,100	28,500	39,900	57,000

NOTE: Add $1800 for hardtop.
Add 20 percent for super charged model.

C. CONDITION CODE

B. DESCRIPTION

D. PRICE

VEHICLE CONDITION SCALE

Excellent

1) EXCELLENT: Restored to current maxiumum professional standards of quality in every area, or perfect original with components operating and appearing as new. A 95-plus point show vehicle that is not driven.

Fine

2) FINE: Well-restored, or a combination of superior restoration and excellent original. Also, an *extremely* well-maintained original showing very minimal wear.

Very Good

3) VERY GOOD: Completely operable original or "older restoration" showing wear. Also, a good amateur restoration, all presentable and serviceable inside and out. Plus, combinations of well-done restoration and good operable components or a partially restored vehicle with all parts necessary to complete and/or valuable NOS parts.

Good

4) GOOD: A driveable vehicle needing no or only minor work to be functional. Also, a deteriorated restoration or a very poor amateur restoration. All components may need restoration to be "excellent," but the vehicle is mostly useable "as is."

Restorable

5) RESTORABLE: Needs *complete* restoration of body, chassis and interior. May or may not be running, but isn't weathered, wrecked or stripped to the point of being useful only for parts.

Parts Car

6) PARTS VEHICLE: May or may not be running, but is weathered, wrecked and/or stripped to the point of being useful primarily for parts.

FORD PRICE GUIDE

FORD

Model A
1903, 2-cyl., Ser. No. 1-670, 8 hp
1904, 2-cyl., Ser. No. 671-1708, 10 hp

	6	5	4	3	2	1
Rbt	1000	3250	5400	10,800	18,900	27,000
Rbt W/ton	1100	3500	5800	11,600	20,300	29,000

Model B
10 hp, 4-cyl.

Tr	Value inestimable

Model C
10 hp, 2-cyl., Ser. No. 1709-2700

Rbt	1000	3250	5400	10,800	18,900	27,000
Rbt W/ton	1100	3500	5800	11,600	20,300	29,000
Dr's Mdl	1000	3250	5400	10,800	18,900	27,000

Model F
16 hp, 2-cyl., (Produced 1904-05-06)

Tr	950	3000	5000	10,000	17,500	25,000

Model K
40 hp, 6-cyl., (Produced 1905-06-07-08)

Tr	2650	8400	14,000	28,000	49,000	70,000
Rds	2650	8400	14,000	28,000	49,000	70,000

Model N
18 hp, 4-cyl., (Produced 1906-07-08)

Rbt	750	2400	4000	8000	14,000	20,000

Model R
4-cyl., (Produced 1907-08)

Rbt	750	2400	4000	8000	14,000	20,000

Model S
4-cyl.

Rbt	750	2400	4000	8000	14,000	20,000

1908
Model T, 4-cyl., 2 levers, 2 foot pedals (1,000 produced)

Tr	950	3000	5000	10,000	17,500	25,000

1909
Model T, 4-cyl.

Rbt	700	2150	3600	7200	12,600	18,000
Tr	650	2050	3400	6800	11,900	17,000
Trbt	700	2300	3800	7600	13,300	19,000
Cpe	650	2050	3400	6800	11,900	17,000
TwnC	850	2650	4400	8800	15,400	22,000
Lan'let	700	2300	3800	7600	13,300	19,000

1910
Model T, 4-cyl.

Rbt	550	1700	2800	5600	9800	14,000
Tr	550	1750	2900	5800	10,200	14,500
Cpe	550	1800	3000	6000	10,500	15,000
TwnC	650	2050	3400	6800	11,900	17,000
C'ml Rds	550	1800	3000	6000	10,500	15,000

1911
Model T, 4-cyl.

Rbt	600	1900	3200	6400	11,200	16,000
Tor Rds	600	1900	3200	6400	11,200	16,000
Tr	700	2300	3800	7600	13,300	19,000
Trbt	700	2150	3600	7200	12,600	18,000
Cpe	550	1800	3000	6000	10,500	15,000
TwnC	700	2300	3800	7600	13,300	19,000
C'ml Rds	500	1550	2600	5200	9100	13,000
Dely Van	500	1550	2600	5200	9100	13,000

1912
Model T, 4-cyl.

Rds	550	1800	3000	6000	10,500	15,000
Tor Rds	600	1900	3200	6400	11,200	16,000
Tr	650	2050	3400	6800	11,900	17,000
TwnC	700	2150	3600	7200	12,600	18,000
Dely Van	550	1700	2800	5600	9800	14,000
C'ml Rds	500	1550	2600	5200	9100	13,000

1913
Model T, 4-cyl.

Rds	550	1800	3000	6000	10,500	15,000
Tr	650	2050	3400	6800	11,900	17,000
TwnC	600	1900	3200	6400	11,200	16,000

1914
Model T, 4-cyl.

Rds	550	1700	2800	5600	9800	14,000
Tr	550	1800	3000	6000	10,500	15,000
TwnC	650	2050	3400	6800	11,900	17,000
Cpe	400	1200	2000	4000	7000	10,000

1915 & early 1916
Model T, 4-cyl., (brass rad.)

Rds	550	1700	2800	5600	9800	14,000
Tr	550	1800	3000	6000	10,500	15,000
Conv Cpe	650	2050	3400	6800	11,900	17,000
Ctr dr Sed	450	1450	2400	4800	8400	12,000
TwnC	550	1800	3000	6000	10,500	15,000

1916
Model T, 4-cyl., (steel rad.)

Rds	500	1550	2600	5200	9100	13,000
Tr	450	1450	2400	4800	8400	12,000
Conv Cpe	400	1200	2000	4000	7000	10,000
Ctr dr Sed	450	950	2100	4750	6650	9500
TwnC	450	1450	2400	4800	8400	12,000

1917
Model T, 4-cyl.

Rds	400	1300	2200	4400	7700	11,000
Tr	450	1450	2400	4800	8400	12,000

	6	5	4	3	2	1
Conv Cpe	400	1200	2000	4000	7000	10,000
TwnC	450	1400	2300	4600	8100	11,500
Ctr dr Sed	450	900	1900	4500	6300	9000
Cpe	350	700	1350	2800	4550	6500

1918
Model T, 4-cyl.

Rds	400	1300	2200	4400	7700	11,000
Tr	450	1450	2400	4800	8400	12,000
Cpe	350	700	1350	2800	4550	6500
TwnC	400	1300	2200	4400	7700	11,000
Ctr dr Sed	350	875	1700	4250	5900	8500

1919
Model T, 4-cyl.

Rds	400	1200	2000	4000	7000	10,000
Tr	400	1250	2100	4200	7400	10,500
Cpe	200	650	1250	2400	4200	6000
TwnC	450	1450	2400	4800	8400	12,000
Ctr dr Sed	350	825	1600	4000	5600	8000

1920-1921
Model T, 4-cyl.

Rds	400	1200	2000	4000	7000	10,000
Tr	400	1250	2100	4200	7400	10,500
Cpe	350	700	1350	2800	4550	6500
Ctr dr Sed	350	875	1700	4250	5900	8500

1922-1923
Model T, 4-cyl.

Rds	400	1200	2000	4000	7000	10,000
'22 Tr	400	1300	2200	4400	7700	11,000
'23 Tr	400	1250	2100	4200	7400	10,500
Cpe	200	650	1250	2400	4200	6000
4 dr Sed	200	600	1200	2200	3850	5500
2 dr Sed	200	550	1150	2100	3700	5300

1924
Model T, 4-cyl.

Rds	400	1200	2000	4000	7000	10,000
Tr	400	1250	2100	4200	7400	10,500
Cpe	350	700	1350	2800	4550	6500
4 dr Sed	200	600	1200	2200	3850	5500
2 dr Sed	200	600	1200	2300	4000	5700
Rds PU	450	900	1900	4500	6300	9000

1925
Model T, 4-cyl.

Rds	400	1200	2000	4000	7000	10,000
Tr	400	1250	2100	4200	7400	10,500
Cpe	350	700	1350	2800	4550	6500
2 dr	200	600	1200	2200	3850	5500
4 dr	200	650	1250	2400	4200	6000

1926
Model T, 4-cyl.

Rds	400	1300	2200	4400	7700	11,000
Tr	450	1450	2400	4800	8400	12,000
Cpe	350	700	1350	2800	4550	6500
2 dr	350	700	1350	2800	4550	6500
4 dr	200	600	1200	2200	3850	5500

1927
Model T, 4-cyl.

Rds	400	1300	2200	4400	7700	11,000
Tr	450	1450	2400	4800	8400	12,000
Cpe	350	700	1350	2800	4550	6500
2 dr	200	600	1200	2200	3850	5500
4 dr	200	650	1200	2300	4100	5800

1928
Model A, 4-cyl.
(Add 20 percent avg for early 'AR' features)

Rds	450	1450	2400	4800	8400	12,000
Phae	500	1550	2600	5200	9100	13,000
Cpe	350	875	1700	4250	5900	8500
Spec Cpe	450	900	1900	4500	6300	9000
Bus Cpe	450	925	2000	4600	6400	9200
Spt Cpe	450	950	2100	4750	6650	9500
2 dr	350	875	1700	4250	5900	8500
4 dr	350	875	1700	4300	6000	8600

1929
Model A, 4-cyl.

Rds	550	1700	2800	5600	9800	14,000
Phae	550	1800	3000	6000	10,500	15,000
Cabr	500	1550	2600	5200	9100	13,000
Cpe	450	950	2100	4750	6650	9500
Bus Cpe	450	900	1900	4500	6300	9000
Spec Cpe	450	950	2100	4750	6650	9500
Spt Cpe	400	1200	2000	4000	7000	10,000
2 dr	350	875	1700	4250	5900	8500
3W 4 dr Sed	450	900	1900	4500	6300	9000
5W 4 dr Sed	350	875	1700	4250	5900	8500
DeL 4 dr Sed	450	900	1900	4500	6300	9000
Twn Sed	450	950	2100	4750	6650	9500
Taxi	400	1300	2200	4400	7700	11,000
TwnC	700	2150	3600	7200	12,600	18,000
Sta Wag	500	1550	2600	5200	9100	13,000

1930
Model A, 4-cyl.

Rds	550	1750	2900	5800	10,200	14,500
DeL Rds	600	1850	3100	6200	10,900	15,500
Phae	650	2050	3400	6800	11,900	17,000
DeL Phae	700	2150	3600	7200	12,600	18,000
Cabr	550	1700	2800	5600	9800	14,000
Cpe	450	900	1900	4500	6300	9000
DeL Cpe	450	950	2100	4750	6650	9500

	6	5	4	3	2	1
Spt Cpe	400	1250	2100	4200	7400	10,500
Std 2 dr	350	875	1700	4250	5900	8500
DeL 2 dr	450	900	1900	4500	6300	9000
3W 4 dr	450	900	1900	4500	6300	9000
5W 4 dr	350	875	1700	4250	5900	8500
DeL 4 dr	400	1200	2000	4000	7000	10,000
Twn Sed	450	900	1900	4500	6300	9000
Vic	500	1550	2600	5200	9100	13,000
Sta Wag	500	1550	2600	5200	9100	13,000

1931

Model A, 4-cyl.

	6	5	4	3	2	1
Rds	550	1750	2900	5800	10,200	14,500
DeL Rds	600	1850	3100	6200	10,900	15,500
Phae	650	2050	3400	6800	11,900	17,000
DeL Phae	700	2150	3600	7200	12,600	18,000
Cabr	550	1700	2800	5600	9800	14,000
SW Cabr	550	1800	3000	6000	10,500	15,000
Conv Sed	650	2050	3400	6800	11,900	17,000
Cpe	450	900	1900	4500	6300	9000
DeL Cpe	450	950	2100	4750	6650	9500
Spt Cpe	400	1250	2100	4200	7400	10,500
Tudor	350	875	1700	4250	5900	8500
DeL Tudor	450	900	1900	4500	6300	9000
Fordor	450	900	1900	4500	6300	9000
DeL Fordor	400	1200	2000	4000	7000	10,000
Twn Sed	400	1250	2100	4200	7400	10,500
Vic	500	1550	2600	5200	9100	13,000
Sta Wag	500	1550	2600	5200	9100	13,000

1932

Model B, 4-cyl.

	6	5	4	3	2	1
Rds	700	2300	3800	7600	13,300	19,000
Phae	750	2450	4100	8200	14,400	20,500
Cabr	700	2150	3600	7200	12,600	18,000
Conv Sed	700	2300	3800	7600	13,300	19,000
Cpe	500	1550	2600	5200	9100	13,000
Spt Cpe	550	1700	2800	5600	9800	14,000
Tudor	400	1200	2000	4000	7000	10,000
Fordor	450	900	1900	4500	6300	9000
Vic	700	2150	3600	7200	12,600	18,000
Sta Wag	650	2050	3400	6800	11,900	17,000

Model 18, V-8

	6	5	4	3	2	1
Rds	800	2500	4200	8400	14,700	21,000
DeL Rds	850	2650	4400	8800	15,400	22,000
Phae	850	2750	4600	9200	16,100	23,000
DeL Phae	900	2900	4800	9600	16,800	24,000
Cabr	700	2300	3800	7600	13,300	19,000
Conv Sed	750	2400	4000	8000	14,000	20,000
Cpe	550	1700	2800	5600	9800	14,000
DeL Cpe	550	1800	3000	6000	10,500	15,000
Spt Cpe	600	1900	3200	6400	11,200	16,000
Tudor	450	1450	2400	4800	8400	12,000
DeL Tudor	500	1550	2600	5200	9100	13,000
Fordor	400	1300	2200	4400	7700	11,000
DeL Fordor	450	1450	2400	4800	8400	12,000
Vic	750	2400	4000	8000	14,000	20,000
Sta Wag	800	2500	4200	8400	14,700	21,000

1933

Model 40, V-8

	6	5	4	3	2	1
Phae	850	2650	4400	8800	15,400	22,000
DeL Phae	850	2750	4600	9200	16,100	23,000
Rds	850	2650	4400	8800	15,400	22,000
DeL Rds	850	2750	4600	9200	16,100	23,000
3W Cpe	400	1300	2200	4400	7700	11,000
3W DeL Cpe	450	1450	2400	4800	8400	12,000
5W Cpe	400	1300	2200	4400	7700	11,000
5W DeL Cpe	450	1450	2400	4800	8400	12,000
Cabr	700	2150	3600	7200	12,600	18,000
Tudor	400	1300	2200	4400	7700	11,000
DeL Tudor	450	1450	2400	4800	8400	12,000
Fordor	450	900	1900	4500	6300	9000
DeL Fordor	400	1200	2000	4000	7000	10,000
Vic	600	1900	3200	6400	11,200	16,000
Sta Wag	700	2300	3800	7600	13,300	19,000

Model 40, 4-cyl.

(All models deduct 20 percent avg from V-8 models)

1934

Model 40, V-8

	6	5	4	3	2	1
Rds	850	2650	4400	8800	15,400	22,000
Phae	850	2750	4600	9200	16,100	23,000
Cabr	750	2400	4000	8000	14,000	20,000
SW Cpe	400	1200	2000	4000	7000	10,000
DeL 3W Cpe	450	1450	2400	4800	8400	12,000
DeL 5W Cpe	400	1300	2200	4400	7700	11,000
Tudor	450	900	1900	4500	6300	9000
DeL Tudor	450	950	2100	4750	6650	9500
Fordor	450	900	1900	4500	6300	9000
DeL Fordor	450	950	2100	4750	6650	9500
Vic	600	1900	3200	6400	11,200	16,000
Sta Wag	700	2300	3800	7600	13,300	19,000

1935

Model 48, V-8

	6	5	4	3	2	1
Phae	950	3000	5000	10,000	17,500	25,000
Rds	900	2900	4800	9600	16,800	24,000
Cabr	800	2500	4200	8400	14,700	21,000
Conv Sed	850	2650	4400	8800	15,400	22,000
DeL 3W Cpe	550	1800	3000	6000	10,500	15,000
5W Cpe	500	1550	2600	5200	9100	13,000
DeL 5W Cpe	550	1700	2800	5600	9800	14,000
Tudor	450	900	1900	4500	6300	9000
DeL Tudor	450	950	2100	4750	6650	9500
Fordor	450	900	1900	4500	6300	9000
DeL Fordor	450	950	2100	4750	6650	9500
Sta Wag	750	2400	4000	8000	14,000	20,000
C'ham TwnC	850	2650	4400	8800	15,400	22,000

1936

Model 68, V-8

	6	5	4	3	2	1
Rds	950	3000	5000	10,000	17,500	25,000
Phae	1000	3100	5200	10,400	18,200	26,000
Cabr	850	2650	4400	8800	15,400	22,000
Clb Cabr	850	2750	4600	9200	16,100	23,000
Conv Trk Sed	900	2900	4800	9600	16,800	24,000
Conv Sed	850	2750	4600	9200	16,100	23,000
3W Cpe	550	1800	3000	6000	10,500	15,000
5W Cpe	500	1550	2600	5200	9100	13,000
DeL 5W Cpe	550	1700	2800	5600	9800	14,000
Tudor	450	900	1900	4500	6300	9000
Tudor Tr Sed	450	950	2100	4750	6650	9500
DeL Tudor	450	950	2100	4750	6650	9500
DeL Tr Sed	400	1200	2000	4000	7000	10,000
Fordor	450	950	2100	4750	6650	9500
Fordor Tr Sed	400	1200	2000	4000	7000	10,000
DeL Fordor	400	1250	2100	4200	7400	10,500
Sta Wag	800	2500	4200	8400	14,700	21,000

1937

Model 74, V-8, 60-hp

	6	5	4	3	2	1
Tudor	450	900	1900	4500	6300	9000
Tudor Tr Sed	450	950	2100	4750	6650	9500
Fordor	450	900	1900	4500	6300	9000
Fordor Tr Sed	450	950	2100	4750	6650	9500
Cpe	400	1200	2000	4000	7000	10,000
Cpe PU	400	1300	2200	4400	7700	11,000

V-8 DeLuxe

	6	5	4	3	2	1
Sta Wag	700	2150	3600	7200	12,600	18,000

Model 78, V-8, 85-hp

	6	5	4	3	2	1
Rds	800	2500	4200	8400	14,700	21,000
Phae	850	2650	4400	8800	15,400	22,000
Cabr	850	2650	4400	8800	15,400	22,000
Clb Cabr	850	2750	4600	9200	16,100	23,000
Conv Sed	900	2900	4800	9600	16,800	24,000
Cpe	400	1300	2200	4400	7700	11,000
Clb Cpe	450	1450	2400	4800	8400	12,000
Tudor	450	950	2100	4750	6650	9500
Tudor Tr Sed	400	1200	2000	4000	7000	10,000
Fordor	450	950	2100	4750	6650	9500
Fordor Tr Sed	400	1200	2000	4000	7000	10,000
Sta Wag	750	2400	4000	8000	14,000	20,000

1938

Model 81A Standard, V-8

	6	5	4	3	2	1
Cpe	400	1250	2100	4200	7400	10,500
2 dr	350	875	1700	4250	5900	8500
4 dr	350	875	1700	4250	5900	8500
Sta Wag	700	2300	3800	7600	13,300	19,000

Model 81A DeLuxe, V-8

	6	5	4	3	2	1
Phae	950	3000	5000	10,000	17,500	25,000
Conv	900	2900	4800	9600	16,800	24,000
Clb Conv	950	3000	5000	10,000	17,500	25,000
Conv Sed	1000	3100	5200	10,400	18,200	26,000
Cpe	400	1300	2200	4400	7700	11,000
Clb Cpe	450	1450	2400	4800	8400	12,000
2 dr	450	900	1900	4500	6300	9000
4 dr	450	900	1900	4500	6300	9000

NOTE: Deduct 10 percent avg. for 60 hp 82A Cord.

1939

Model 922A Standard, V-8

	6	5	4	3	2	1
Cpe	400	1300	2200	4400	7700	11,000
2 dr	450	900	1900	4500	6300	9000
4 dr	450	900	1900	4500	6300	9000
Sta Wag	750	2400	4000	8000	14,000	20,000

Model 91A DeLuxe, V-8

	6	5	4	3	2	1
Conv	1200	3850	6400	12,800	22,400	32,000
Conv Sed	1250	3950	6600	13,200	23,100	33,000
Cpe	400	1300	2200	4400	7700	11,000
Tudor	450	950	2100	4750	6650	9500
Fordor	450	950	2100	4750	6650	9500
Sta Wag	800	2500	4200	8400	14,700	21,000

NOTE: Deduct 10 percent avg. for V-60 hp models.

1940

Model 022A, V-8

	6	5	4	3	2	1
Conv	1250	3950	6600	13,200	23,100	33,000
Cpe	450	1400	2300	4600	8100	11,500
DeL Cpe	450	1450	2400	4800	8400	12,000
Tudor	450	900	1900	4500	6300	9000
DeL Tudor	450	950	2100	4750	6650	9500
Fordor	450	900	1900	4500	6300	9000
DeL Fordor	450	950	2100	4750	6650	9500
Sta Wag	800	2600	4300	8600	15,100	21,500

NOTE: Deduct 10 percent avg. for V-8, 60 hp models.

1941

Model 11A Special, V-8

	6	5	4	3	2	1
Cpe	350	875	1700	4250	5900	8500
Tudor	350	775	1500	3750	5250	7500
Fordor	350	775	1500	3750	5250	7500

DeLuxe

	6	5	4	3	2	1
3P Cpe	450	950	2100	4750	6650	9500
4P Cpe	400	1200	2000	4000	7000	10,000
Tudor	350	825	1600	4000	5600	8000
Fordor	350	825	1600	4000	5600	8000
Sta Wag	1000	3100	5200	10,400	18,200	26,000

Super DeLuxe

	6	5	4	3	2	1
Conv	1250	3950	6600	13,200	23,100	33,000
3P Cpe	400	1200	2000	4000	7000	10,000
4P Cpe	400	1300	2200	4400	7700	11,000
5P Cpe	400	1300	2200	4400	7700	11,000
Tudor	350	875	1700	4250	5900	8500
Fordor	350	875	1700	4250	5900	8500
Sta Wag	1000	3250	5400	10,800	18,900	27,000

NOTE: Deduct 10 percent average for 6-cyl.

1942

Model 2GA Special, 6-cyl.

	6	5	4	3	2	1
3P Cpe	350	825	1600	4000	5600	8000
Tudor	350	700	1350	2800	4550	6500
Fordor	350	700	1350	2800	4550	6500

Model 21A DeLuxe, V-8

	6	5	4	3	2	1
Cpe	350	875	1700	4250	5900	8500
5P Cpe	350	875	1700	4350	6050	8700
Tudor	350	750	1450	3300	4900	7000
Fordor	350	750	1450	3300	4900	7000

Super DeLuxe

	6	5	4	3	2	1
Conv	1000	3100	5200	10,400	18,200	26,000
3P Cpe	450	900	1900	4500	6300	9000
5P Cpe	450	950	2100	4700	6600	9400
Tudor	350	775	1500	3750	5250	7500
Fordor	350	775	1500	3750	5250	7500
Sta Wag	950	3000	5000	10,000	17,500	25,000

NOTE: Deduct 10 percent avg. for 6-cyl.

1946

Series 69A DeLuxe, V-8

	6	5	4	3	2	1
Cpe	350	875	1700	4250	5900	8500
Tudor	350	750	1450	3300	4900	7000
Fordor	350	750	1450	3300	4900	7000

Super DeLuxe

	6	5	4	3	2	1
Conv	1000	3100	5200	10,400	18,200	26,000
Sptman Conv	2050	6600	11,000	22,000	38,500	55,000

	6	5	4	3	2	1
3P Cpe	450	900	1900	4500	6300	9000
5P Cpe	450	925	2000	4600	6400	9200
Tudor	350	775	1500	3750	5250	7500
Fordor	350	775	1500	3750	5250	7500
Sta Wag	950	3000	5000	10,000	17,500	25,000
NOTE: Deduct 5 percent avg. for 6-cyl.						
1947						
Model 79A DeLuxe, V-8						
3P Cpe	450	950	2100	4750	6650	9500
Tudor	350	750	1450	3300	4900	7000
Fordor	350	750	1450	3300	4900	7000
Super DeLuxe						
Conv	1000	3250	5400	10,800	18,900	27,000
Sptman Conv	2050	6600	11,000	22,000	38,500	55,000
3P Cpe	400	1200	2000	4000	7000	10,000
5P Cpe	400	1200	2000	4000	7000	10,000
2 dr Sed	350	775	1500	3750	5250	7500
4 dr Sed	350	775	1500	3750	5250	7500
Sta Wag	1000	3100	5200	10,400	18,200	26,000
NOTE: Deduct 5 percent average for 6-cyl.						
1948						
Model 89A DeLuxe, V-8						
3P Cpe	450	950	2100	4750	6650	9500
2 dr Sed	350	750	1450	3300	4900	7000
Sed	350	750	1450	3300	4900	7000
Model 89A Super DeLuxe, V-8						
Conv	1000	3250	5400	10,800	18,900	27,000
Sptman Conv	2050	6600	11,000	22,000	38,500	55,000
3P Cpe	400	1200	2000	4000	7000	10,000
5P Cpe	400	1200	2000	4000	7000	10,000
2 dr Sed	350	775	1500	3750	5250	7500
4 dr Sed	350	775	1500	3750	5250	7500
Sta Wag	1000	3100	5200	10,400	18,200	26,000
NOTE: Deduct 5 percent avg. for 6-cyl.						
1949						
Model 8BA DeLuxe, V-8						
Cpe	350	825	1600	4000	5600	8000
Clb Cpe	350	850	1650	4100	5700	8200
2 dr Sed	350	725	1400	3200	4850	6900
4 dr Sed	350	725	1400	3100	4800	6800
Custom						
Conv	850	2650	4400	8800	15,400	22,000
Clb Cpe	450	900	1900	4500	6300	9000
2 dr Sed	350	775	1500	3750	5250	7500
4 dr Sed	350	775	1500	3700	5200	7400
Sta Wag	800	2500	4200	8400	14,700	21,000
NOTE: Deduct 5 percent avg. for 6-cyl.						
1950						
DeLuxe, V-8, 114" wb						
4 dr Sed	350	725	1400	3100	4800	6800
2 dr Sed	350	725	1400	3200	4850	6900
Bus Cpe	350	825	1600	4000	5600	8000
Custom DeLuxe, V-8, 114" wb						
4 dr Sed	350	775	1500	3700	5200	7400
2 dr Sed	350	775	1500	3750	5250	7500
Crest	400	1250	2100	4200	7400	10,500
Conv	850	2750	4600	9200	16,100	23,000
Sta Wag	850	2650	4400	8800	15,400	22,000
Clb Cpe	450	950	2100	4750	6650	9500
NOTE: Deduct 5 percent average for 6-cyl.						
1951						
DeLuxe, V-8, 114" wb						
4 dr Sed	350	725	1400	3000	4700	6700
2 dr Sed	350	700	1350	2800	4550	6500
Bus Cpe	350	800	1550	3850	5400	7700
Custom DeLuxe, V-8, 114" wb						
4 dr Sed	350	775	1500	3700	5200	7400
2 dr Sed	350	775	1500	3750	5250	7500
Crest	400	1250	2100	4200	7400	10,500
Clb Cpe	450	925	2000	4600	6400	9200
2 dr HdTp	400	1300	2200	4400	7700	11,000
Conv	900	2900	4800	9600	16,800	24,000
Sta Wag	850	2750	4600	9200	16,100	23,000
NOTE: Deduct 5 percent average for 6-cyl.						
1952						
Mainline, V-8, 115" wb						
4 dr Sed	200	600	1200	2200	3900	5600
2 dr Sed	200	600	1200	2200	3850	5500
Bus Cpe	350	700	1350	2800	4550	6500
Sta Wag	350	725	1400	3100	4800	6800
Customline, V-8, 115" wb						
4 dr Sed	350	725	1400	3100	4800	6800
2 dr Sed	350	725	1400	3000	4700	6700
Clb Cpe	350	775	1500	3750	5250	7500
Ctry Sed	350	800	1550	3900	5450	7800
Crestline, V-8, 115" wb						
2 dr HdTp	400	1300	2200	4400	7700	11,000
Conv	700	2300	3800	7600	13,300	19,000
Sta Wag	450	900	1900	4500	6300	9000
NOTE: Deduct 5 percent average for 6-cyl.						
1953						
Mainline, V-8, 115" wb						
4 dr Sed	200	550	1150	2100	3800	5400
2 dr Sed	200	550	1150	2100	3700	5300
Bus Cpe	350	700	1350	2800	4550	6500
Sta Wag	350	700	1350	2800	4550	6500
Customline, V-8, 115" wb						
4 dr Sed	350	725	1400	3200	4850	6900
2 dr Sed	350	700	1350	2900	4600	6600
Clb Cpe	350	750	1450	3500	5050	7200
Sta Wag	350	775	1500	3750	5250	7500
Crestline, 8-cyl., 115" wb						
2 dr HdTp	400	1300	2200	4400	7700	11,000
Conv	700	2300	3800	7600	13,300	19,000
Sta Wag	450	900	1900	4500	6300	9000
NOTE: Deduct 5 percent average for 6-cyl. Add 50 percent for Indy Pace Car replica convertible.						
1954						
Mainline, 8-cyl., 115.5" wb						
4 dr Sed	200	600	1200	2200	3850	5500
2 dr Sed	200	550	1150	2100	3800	5400
Bus Cpe	350	700	1350	2800	4550	6500
Sta Wag	350	700	1350	2900	4600	6600
Customline, V-8, 115.5" wb						
4 dr Sed	350	725	1400	3100	4800	6800
2 dr Sed	350	725	1400	3000	4700	6700
Clb Cpe	350	750	1450	3400	5000	7100
Sta Wag	350	750	1450	3300	4900	7000
Crestline, V-8, 115.5" wb						
4 dr Sed	350	750	1450	3300	4900	7000
Sky Cpe	550	1700	2800	5600	9800	14,000
2 dr HdTp	450	1400	2300	4600	8100	11,500
Conv	750	2350	3900	7800	13,700	19,500
Sta Wag	450	950	2100	4750	6650	9500
NOTE: Deduct 5 percent average for 6-cyl.						
1955						
Mainline, V-8, 115.5" wb						
4 dr Sed	200	650	1200	2300	4100	5800
Bus Sed	200	600	1200	2200	3900	5600
2 dr Sed	200	600	1200	2300	4000	5700
Customline, V-8, 115.5" wb						
4 dr Sed	200	675	1300	2500	4300	6100
2 dr Sed	200	650	1250	2400	4200	6000
Fairlane, V-8, 115.5" wb						
4 dr Sed	350	775	1500	3700	5200	7400
2 dr Sed	350	750	1450	3500	5050	7200
2 dr HdTp	550	1800	3000	6000	10,500	15,000
Crn Vic	950	3000	5000	10,000	17,500	25,000
Crn Vic Plexi-top	1050	3350	5600	11,200	19,600	28,000
Conv	1200	3850	6400	12,800	22,400	32,000
Station Wagon, V-8, 115.5" wb						
Ran Wag	350	750	1450	3300	4900	7000
Ctry Sed	350	825	1600	4000	5600	8000
Ctry Sq	400	1300	2200	4400	7700	11,000
NOTE: Deduct 5 percent average for 6-cyl.						
Thunderbird, 102" wb						
Conv	1800	5750	9600	19,200	33,600	48,000
NOTE: Add $1,800. for hardtop.						
1956						
Mainline, V-8, 115.5" wb						
4 dr Sed	200	650	1250	2400	4150	5900
2 dr Sed	200	650	1200	2300	4100	5800
Bus Sed	200	600	1200	2300	4000	5700
Customline, V-8, 115.5" wb						
4 dr Sed	200	675	1300	2600	4400	6300
2 dr Sed	200	675	1300	2500	4350	6200
2 dr HdTp Vic	400	1200	2000	4000	7000	10,000
Fairlane, V-8, 115.5" wb						
4 dr Sed	350	725	1400	3000	4700	6700
4 dr HdTp Vic	350	875	1700	4250	5900	8500
2 dr Sed	350	700	1350	2900	4600	6600
2 dr HdTp Vic	700	2300	3800	7600	13,300	19,000
Crn Vic	1000	3100	5200	10,400	18,200	26,000
Crn Vic Plexi-top	1200	3850	6400	12,800	22,400	32,000
Conv	1300	4200	7000	14,000	24,500	35,000
Station Wagons, V-8, 115.5" wb						
Ran Wag	350	800	1550	3850	5400	7700
Parklane	500	1550	2600	5200	9100	13,000
Ctry Sed	350	875	1700	4350	6050	8700
Ctry Sq	400	1300	2200	4400	7700	11,000
NOTE: Deduct 5 percent average for 6-cyl. Add 10 percent for "T-Bird Special" V-8.						
Thunderbird						
Conv	1850	5900	9800	19,600	34,300	49,000
NOTE: Add $1,800. for hardtop.						
1957						
Custom, V-8, 116" wb						
Sed	200	650	1250	2400	4150	5900
2 dr Sed	200	650	1200	2300	4100	5800
Bus Cpe	200	600	1200	2200	3900	5600
Custom 300, V-8, 116" wb						
4 dr Sed	200	675	1300	2500	4300	6100
2 dr Sed	200	650	1250	2400	4200	6000
Fairlane, V-8, 118" wb						
4 dr Sed	350	700	1350	2700	4500	6400
4 dr HdTp Vic	350	750	1450	3300	4900	7000
2 dr Sed	200	675	1300	2600	4400	6300
2 dr Vic HdTp	450	950	2100	4750	6650	9500
Fairlane 500, V-8, 118" wb						
4 dr Sed	350	725	1400	3000	4700	6700
4 dr HdTp Vic	350	775	1500	3750	5250	7500
2 dr Sed	350	700	1350	2900	4600	6600
2 dr HdTp Vic	450	1450	2400	4800	8400	12,000
Conv	1000	3250	5400	10,800	18,900	27,000
Sky HdTp Conv	1250	3950	6600	13,200	23,100	33,000
Station Wagons, 8-cyl., 116" wb						
Ctry Sed	350	875	1700	4250	5900	8500
Ctry Sq	400	1200	2000	4000	7000	10,000
Ran Wag	350	775	1500	3750	5250	7500
DeL Rio Ran	350	825	1600	4000	5600	8000
NOTE: Deduct 5 percent average for 6-cyl. Add 20 percent for "T-Bird Special" V-8 (Code E). Add 30 percent for Supercharged V-8 (Code F).						
Thunderbird, 102" wb						
Conv	1900	6000	10,000	20,000	35,000	50,000
NOTE: Add $1,800. for hardtop. Add 30 percent for super charged V-8 (Code F). Add 20 percent for "T-Bird Special" V-8 (Code E).						
1958						
Custom 300, V-8, 116.03" wb						
4 dr Sed	200	650	1200	2300	4100	5800
2 dr Sed	200	600	1200	2300	4000	5700
Bus Cpe	200	550	1150	2000	3600	5200
Fairlane, V-8, 116.03" wb						
4 dr Sed	200	650	1250	2400	4150	5900
4 dr HdTp	200	675	1300	2500	4350	6200
2 dr Sed	200	650	1200	2300	4100	5800
2 dr HdTp	450	950	2100	4750	6650	9500
Fairlane 500, V-8, 118.04" wb						
4 dr Sed	350	700	1350	2700	4500	6400
4 dr HdTp	350	775	1500	3750	5250	7500
2 dr Sed	200	675	1300	2500	4350	6200
2 dr HdTp	450	1450	2400	4800	8400	12,000
Sun Conv	850	2750	4600	9200	16,100	23,000
Sky HdTp Conv	1000	3250	5400	10,800	18,900	27,000
Station Wagons, V-8, 116.03" wb						
Ctry Sed	350	825	1600	4000	5600	8000
Ctry Sq	450	900	1900	4500	6300	9000
4 dr Ran	350	750	1450	3300	4900	7000
2 dr Ran	350	750	1450	3500	5050	7200
DeL Rio Ran	350	800	1550	3850	5400	7700
NOTE: Deduct 5 percent average for 6-cyl.						

Thunderbird	6	5	4	3	2	1
2 dr HdTp	850	2750	4600	9200	16,100	23,000
Conv	1150	3700	6200	12,400	21,700	31,000
1959						
Custom 300, V-8, 118" wb						
Sed	200	550	1150	2000	3600	5200
2 dr Sed	200	675	1300	2500	4300	6100
Bus Cpe	200	650	1250	2400	4200	6000
Fairlane, V-8, 118" wb						
4 dr Sed	200	550	1150	2100	3700	5300
2 dr Sed	200	550	1150	2000	3600	5200
Fairlane 500, V-8, 118" wb						
4 dr Sed	200	600	1200	2200	3850	5500
4 dr HdTp	200	650	1250	2400	4150	5900
2 dr Sed	200	550	1150	2100	3800	5400
2 dr HdTp	350	875	1700	4250	5900	8500
Sun Conv	900	2900	4800	9600	16,800	24,000
Sky HdTp Conv	1100	3500	5800	11,600	20,300	29,000
Galaxie, V-8, 118" wb						
4 dr Sed	200	600	1200	2300	4000	5700
4 dr HdTp	200	675	1300	2500	4350	6200
2 dr Sed	200	600	1200	2200	3900	5600
2 dr HdTp	450	950	2100	4750	6650	9500
Sun Conv	900	2900	4800	9600	16,800	24,000
Sky HdTp Conv	1100	3500	5800	11,600	20,300	29,000
Station Wagons, V-8, 118" wb						
4 dr Ran	200	650	1200	2300	4100	5800
Ctry Sed	350	825	1600	4000	5600	8000
Ctry Sq	350	875	1700	4250	5900	8500
2 dr Ran	200	650	1250	2400	4200	6000
DeL Rio Ran	350	750	1450	3300	4900	7000
NOTE: Deduct 5 percent average for 6-cyl.						
Thunderbird						
2 dr HdTp	850	2650	4400	8800	15,400	22,000
Conv	1100	3500	5800	11,600	20,300	29,000
1960						
Falcon, 6-cyl., 109.5" wb						
4 dr Sed	200	550	1150	2000	3600	5200
2 dr Sed	200	500	1100	1950	3600	5100
4 dr Sta Wag	200	550	1150	2100	3700	5300
2 dr Sta Wag	200	550	1150	2000	3600	5200
Fairlane, V-8, 119" wb						
Sed	200	550	1150	2000	3600	5200
2 dr Sed	200	500	1100	1950	3600	5100
Bus Cpe	200	500	1100	1900	3500	5000
Fairlane 500, V-8, 119" wb						
4 dr Sed	200	550	1150	2100	3800	5400
2 dr Sed	200	550	1150	2100	3700	5300
Galaxie, V-8, 119" wb						
4 dr Sed	200	650	1200	2300	4100	5800
4 dr HdTp	200	650	1250	2400	4200	6000
2 dr HdTp	400	1200	2000	4000	7000	10,000
2 dr Sed	200	600	1200	2300	4000	5700
Galaxie Special, V-8, 119" wb						
2 dr HdTp	500	1550	2600	5200	9100	13,000
Sun Conv	800	2500	4200	8400	14,700	21,000
Station Wagons, V-8, 119" wb						
4 dr Ran	200	600	1200	2200	3850	5500
2 dr Ran	200	650	1200	2300	4100	5800
Ctry Sed	200	650	1250	2400	4200	6000
Ctry Sq	350	700	1350	2800	4550	6500
NOTE: Deduct 5 percent average for 6-cyl.						
Thunderbird, 113" wb						
SR HdTp	900	2900	4800	9600	16,800	24,000
2 dr HdTp	850	2650	4400	8800	15,400	22,000
Conv	1100	3500	5800	11,600	20,300	29,000
1961						
Falcon, 6-cyl., 109.5" wb						
4 dr Sed	200	550	1150	2100	3700	5300
2 dr Sed	200	550	1150	2000	3600	5200
Futura	350	825	1600	4000	5600	8000
4 dr Sta Wag	200	550	1150	2100	3700	5300
2 dr Sta Wag	200	550	1150	2000	3600	5200
Fairlane, V-8, 119" wb						
4 dr Sed	200	550	1150	2100	3800	5400
2 dr Sed	200	550	1150	2100	3700	5300
Galaxie, V-8, 119" wb						
4 dr Sed	200	600	1200	2200	3850	5500
4 dr Vic HdTp	350	700	1350	2800	4550	6500
2 dr Sed	200	550	1150	2100	3800	5400
2 dr Vic HdTp	450	950	2100	4750	6650	9500
2 dr Star HdTp	450	1450	2400	4800	8400	12,000
Sun Conv	600	1900	3200	6400	11,200	16,000
Station Wagons, V-8, 119" wb						
4 dr Ran	200	600	1200	2200	3850	5500
2 dr Ran	200	600	1200	2300	4000	5700
6P Ctry Sed	200	650	1250	2400	4200	6000
Ctry Sq	350	700	1350	2800	4550	6500
Thunderbird, 113" wb						
2 dr HdTp	550	1800	3000	6000	10,500	15,000
Conv	1050	3350	5600	11,200	19,600	28,000
NOTE: Deduct 5 percent average for 6-cyl.						
1962						
Falcon, 6-cyl., 109.5" wb						
4 dr Sed	200	500	1100	1900	3500	5000
2 dr	200	500	1100	1850	3350	4900
Fut Spt Cpe	450	950	2100	4750	6650	9500
Sq Wag	200	600	1200	2200	3850	5500
Falcon Station Bus, 6-cyl., 109.5" wb						
Sta Bus	150	450	1050	1800	3300	4800
Clb Wag	200	500	1100	1850	3350	4900
DeL Wag	200	500	1100	1900	3500	5000
Fairlane, V-8, 115.5" wb						
4 dr Sed	200	500	1100	1850	3350	4900
2 dr Sed	150	450	1050	1800	3300	4800
Spt Sed	200	550	1150	2100	3800	5400
Galaxie 500, V-8, 119" wb						
4 dr Sed	200	500	1100	1950	3600	5100
4 dr HdTp	200	550	1150	2100	3700	5300
2 dr Sed	200	500	1100	1900	3500	5000
2 dr HdTp	400	1200	2000	4000	7000	10,000
Conv	550	1700	2800	5600	9800	14,000
Galaxie 500 XL, V-8, 119" wb						
2 dr HdTp	450	1450	2400	4800	8400	12,000
Conv	650	2050	3400	6800	11,900	17,000
Station Wagons, V-8, 119" wb						
Ranch	200	600	1200	2200	3850	5500
Ctry Sed	200	650	1250	2400	4200	6000
Ctry Sq	350	700	1350	2800	4550	6500

NOTE: Add 30 percent for 406 V-8.
Deduct 5 percent for 6-cyl.

Thunderbird	6	5	4	3	2	1
2 dr HdTp	600	1900	3200	6400	11,200	16,000
2 dr Lan HdTp	650	2050	3400	6800	11,900	17,000
Conv	1050	3350	5600	11,200	19,600	28,000
Spt Rds	1300	4200	7000	14,000	24,500	35,000
1963						
Falcon, 6-cyl., 109.5" wb						
4 dr Sed	200	550	1150	2000	3600	5200
2 dr Sed	200	500	1100	1950	3600	5100
2 dr Spt Sed	200	600	1200	2200	3900	5600
2 dr HdTp	450	900	1900	4500	6300	9000
2 dr Spt HdTp	400	1200	2000	4000	7000	10,000
Conv	450	1450	2400	4800	8400	12,000
Spt Conv	500	1550	2600	5200	9100	13,000
Squire Wag	200	600	1200	2200	3850	5500
4 dr Sta Wag	200	500	1100	1850	3350	4900
2 dr Sta Wag	150	450	1050	1800	3300	4800
Station Buses, 6-cyl., 90" wb						
Sta Bus	150	450	1050	1800	3300	4800
Clb Wag	200	500	1100	1850	3350	4900
DeL Clb Wag	200	500	1100	1900	3500	5000
Sprint, V-8, 109.5" wb						
HdTp	500	1550	2600	5200	9100	13,000
Conv	550	1800	3000	6000	10,500	15,000
Fairlane, V-8, 115.5" wb						
4 dr Sed	200	500	1100	1850	3350	4900
2 dr Sed	150	450	1050	1800	3300	4800
2 dr HdTp	200	650	1250	2400	4200	6000
Spt Cpe	350	750	1450	3300	4900	7000
Sq Wag	200	500	1100	1900	3500	5000
Cus Ran	200	500	1100	1850	3350	4900
NOTE: Add 20 percent for 271 hp V-8.						
Ford 300, V-8, 119" wb						
Sed	200	500	1100	1900	3500	5000
2 dr Sed	200	500	1100	1850	3350	4900
Galaxie 500, V-8, 119" wb						
Sed	200	500	1100	1950	3600	5100
4 dr HdTp	200	500	1100	1900	3500	5000
2 dr Sed	200	500	1100	1900	3500	5000
2 dr HdTp	400	1300	2200	4400	7700	11,000
FsBk	500	1550	2600	5200	9100	13,000
Conv	550	1700	2800	5600	9800	14,000
Galaxie 500 XL, V-8, 119" wb						
4 dr HdTp	350	700	1350	2800	4550	6500
2 dr HdTp	450	1450	2400	4800	8400	12,000
FsBk	550	1700	2800	5600	9800	14,000
Conv	700	2150	3600	7200	12,600	18,000
Station Wagons, V-8, 119" wb						
Squire	200	650	1250	2400	4200	6000
Ctry Sed	200	600	1200	2200	3850	5500
NOTE: Add 30 percent for 406 & add 40 percent for 427. Deduct 5 percent average for 6-cyl.						
Thunderbird, 113.2 wb						
2 dr HdTp	600	1900	3200	6400	11,200	16,000
2 dr Lan HdTp	650	2050	3400	6800	11,900	17,000
Conv	1050	3350	5600	11,200	19,600	28,000
Spt Rds	1300	4100	6800	13,600	23,800	34,000
NOTE: Add 5 percent for Monaco option.						
1964						
NOTE: Add 5 percent for V-8 except Sprint.						
Falcon, 6-cyl., 109.5" wb						
4 dr Sed	200	500	1100	1950	3600	5100
2 dr Sed	200	500	1100	1900	3500	5000
2 dr HdTp	350	775	1500	3750	5250	7500
2 dr Spt HdTp	450	950	2100	4750	6650	9500
Conv	450	1400	2300	4600	8100	11,500
Spt Conv	450	1500	2500	5000	8800	12,500
Squire Wag	200	600	1200	2200	3850	5500
DeL Wag	150	400	1000	1650	3150	4500
4 dr Sta	150	400	1000	1650	3150	4500
2 dr Sta	150	450	1050	1800	3300	4800
Station Bus, 6-cyl., 90" wb						
Sta Bus	150	400	1000	1650	3150	4500
Clb Wag	150	450	1050	1700	3200	4600
DeL Clb	150	450	1050	1800	3300	4800
Sprint, V-8, 109.5" wb						
2 dr HdTp	400	1250	2100	4200	7400	10,500
Conv	500	1550	2600	5200	9100	13,000
Fairlane, V-8, 115.5" wb						
Sed	200	550	1150	2000	3600	5200
2 dr Sed	200	500	1100	1950	3600	5100
2 dr HdTp	350	875	1700	4250	5900	8500
2 dr Spt HdTp	450	950	2100	4750	6650	9500
Ran Cus	200	675	1300	2500	4300	6100
NOTE: Add 20 percent for 271 hp V-8.						
Fairlane Thunderbolt						
2 dr Sed	5650	18,000	30,000	60,000	105,000	150,000
Custom, V-8, 119" wb						
Sed	200	550	1150	2000	3600	5200
2 dr Sed	200	500	1100	1950	3600	5100
Custom 500, V-8, 119" wb						
Sed	200	550	1150	2100	3700	5300
2 dr Sed	200	550	1150	2000	3600	5200
Galaxie 500, V-8, 119" wb						
Sed	200	600	1200	2200	3850	5500
4 dr HdTp	200	600	1200	2200	3850	5500
2 dr Sed	200	550	1150	2100	3800	5400
2 dr HdTp	450	1450	2400	4800	8400	12,000
Conv	550	1800	3000	6000	10,500	15,000
Galaxie 500XL, V-8, 119" wb						
4 dr HdTp	350	700	1350	2800	4550	6500
2 dr HdTp	550	1700	2800	5600	9800	14,000
Conv	750	2400	4000	8000	14,000	20,000
Station Wagons, V-8, 119" wb						
Ctry Sq	200	650	1250	2400	4200	6000
Ctry Sed	200	600	1200	2200	3850	5500
NOTE: Add 40 percent for 427 V-8.						
Thunderbird, 113.2" wb						
2 dr HdTp	500	1550	2600	5200	9100	13,000
2 dr Lan HdTp	550	1700	2800	5600	9800	14,000
Conv	950	3000	5000	10,000	17,500	25,000
NOTE: Add 25 percent for Tonneau convertible option.						
1965						
Falcon, 6-cyl., 109.5" wb						
4 dr Sed	150	450	1050	1800	3300	4800
2 dr Sed	150	450	1050	1750	3250	4700
2 dr HdTp	200	650	1250	2400	4200	6000

	6	5	4	3	2	1
Conv	450	950	2100	4750	6650	9500
Squire Wag	200	500	1100	1900	3500	5000
DeL Wag	150	450	1050	1750	3250	4700
4 dr Sta	150	450	1050	1750	3250	4700
2 dr Sta	150	450	1050	1700	3200	4600
Sprint V-8, 109.5" wb						
2 dr HdTp	400	1200	2000	4000	7000	10,000
Conv	450	1450	2400	4800	8400	12,000
Falcon Station Buses, 6-cyl., 90" wb						
Sta Bus	200	500	1100	1850	3350	4900
Clb Wag	200	500	1100	1950	3600	5100
DeL Wag	200	550	1150	2100	3700	5300
Fairlane, V-8, 116" wb						
Sed	200	500	1100	1950	3600	5100
2 dr Sed	200	500	1100	1900	3500	5000
2 dr HdTp	200	650	1250	2400	4200	6000
2 dr Spt HdTp	350	875	1700	4250	5900	8500
Sta Wag	200	500	1100	1900	3500	5000

NOTE: Add 10 percent for 271 hp V-8.
Add 50 percent for 427 Thunderbolt.

	6	5	4	3	2	1
Custom, V-8, 119" wb						
Sed	150	450	1050	1800	3300	4800
2 dr Sed	150	450	1050	1750	3250	4700
Custom 500, V-8, 119" wb						
Sed	200	500	1100	1850	3350	4900
2 dr Sed	150	450	1050	1800	3300	4800
Galaxie 500, V-8, 119" wb						
Sed	200	500	1100	1900	3500	5000
4 dr HdTp	200	550	1150	2000	3600	5200
2 dr HdTp	350	825	1600	4000	5600	8000
Conv	400	1300	2200	4400	7700	11,000
Galaxie 500 XL, V-8, 119" wb						
2 dr HdTp	350	875	1700	4250	5900	8500
Conv	450	1450	2400	4800	8400	12,000
Galaxie 500 LTD, V-8, 119" wb						
4 dr HdTp	200	650	1250	2400	4200	6000
2 dr HdTp	450	900	1900	4500	6300	9000
Station Wagons, V-8, 119" wb						
9P Ctry Sq	200	600	1200	2200	3850	5500
9P Ctry Sed	200	500	1100	1900	3500	5000
Ran	150	450	1050	1800	3300	4800

NOTE: Add 40 percent for 427 V-8.

	6	5	4	3	2	1
Thunderbird						
2 dr HdTp	500	1550	2600	5200	9100	13,000
2 dr Lan HdTp	550	1700	2800	5600	9800	14,000
Conv	950	3000	5000	10,000	17,500	25,000

NOTE: Add 5 Special Landau option.

1966

NOTE: Add 5 percent for V-8.

	6	5	4	3	2	1
Falcon, 6-cyl., 110.9" wb						
Sed	150	450	1050	1800	3300	4800
Clb Cpe	150	450	1050	1750	3250	4700
Spt Cpe	200	500	1100	1950	3600	5100
6P Wag	150	450	1050	1750	3250	4700
Squire Wag	200	600	1200	2200	3850	5500
Falcon Station Bus, 6-cyl., 90" wb						
Clb Wag	150	450	1050	1700	3200	4600
Cus Clb Wag	150	450	1050	1750	3250	4700
DeL Clb Wag	150	450	1050	1800	3300	4800
Fairlane, V-8, 116" wb						
Sed	200	500	1100	1850	3350	4900
Clb Cpe	150	450	1050	1800	3300	4800
2 dr HdTp Cpe	200	600	1200	2200	3850	5500
Conv	350	825	1600	4000	5600	8000
Fairlane 500 XL, V-8, 116" wb						
2 dr HdTp	350	775	1500	3750	5250	7500
Conv	400	1200	2000	4000	7000	10,000
Fairlane 500 GT, V-8, 116" wb						
2 dr HdTp	350	825	1600	4000	5600	8000
Conv	400	1300	2200	4400	7700	11,000
Station Wagons, V-8, 113" wb						
6P DeL	150	450	1050	1800	3300	4800
Squire	200	500	1100	1900	3500	5000
Custom, V-8, 119" wb						
Sed	200	500	1100	1900	3500	5000
2 dr Sed	200	500	1100	1850	3350	4900
Galaxie 500, V-8, 119" wb						
Sed	200	500	1100	1950	3600	5100
4 dr HdTp	200	550	1150	2100	3700	5300
2 dr HdTp	350	775	1500	3750	5250	7500
Conv	450	950	2100	4750	6650	9500
Galaxie 500, XL, V-8, 119" wb						
2 dr HdTp	350	875	1700	4250	5900	8500
Conv	450	1450	2400	4800	8400	12,000
LTD, V-8, 119" wb						
4 dr HdTp	200	600	1200	2200	3850	5500
2 dr HdTp	350	775	1500	3750	5250	7500
Galaxie 500 7-litre, V-8, 119" wb						
2 dr HdTp	450	1450	2400	4800	8400	12,000
Conv	600	1900	3200	6400	11,200	16,000
Station Wagons, V-8, 119" wb						
Ran Wag	150	450	1050	1800	3300	4800
Ctry Sed	200	500	1100	1900	3500	5000
Ctry Sq	200	550	1150	2000	3600	5200
Thunderbird, 113" wb						
2 dr HdTp Cpe	500	1550	2600	5200	9100	13,000
2 dr Twn Lan	550	1700	2800	5600	9800	14,000
2 dr HdTp Twn	500	1600	2700	5400	9500	13,500
Conv	850	2650	4400	8800	15,400	22,000

NOTE: Add 40 percent for 427 or 428 engine option.

1967

	6	5	4	3	2	1
Falcon, 6-cyl, 111" wb						
4 dr	150	450	1050	1800	3300	4800
2 dr	150	450	1050	1750	3250	4700
Sta Wag	150	450	1050	1800	3300	4800
Futura						
Sed	200	500	1100	1850	3350	4900
Clb Cpe	150	450	1050	1800	3300	4800
2 dr HdTp	200	500	1100	1950	3600	5100
Fairlane						
4 dr Sed	150	450	1050	1800	3300	4800
Cpe	150	450	1050	1750	3250	4700
Fairlane 500, V-8, 116" wb						
4 dr Sed	200	500	1100	1850	3350	4900
Cpe	150	450	1050	1800	3300	4800
2 dr HdTp	350	700	1350	2800	4550	6500
Conv	450	950	2100	4750	6650	9500
Wagon	150	450	1050	1800	3300	4800
Fairlane 500 XL V-8						
2 dr HdTp	350	750	1450	3300	4900	7000
Conv	400	1300	2200	4400	7700	11,000
2 dr GT HdTp	350	825	1600	4000	5600	8000
Conv GT	450	1450	2400	4800	8400	12,000
Fairlane Wagons						
Sta Wag	150	450	1050	1800	3300	4800
500 Wag	200	500	1100	1850	3350	4900
Squire	200	500	1100	1950	3600	5100
Ford Custom						
4 dr Sed	150	450	1050	1800	3300	4800
2 dr Sed	150	450	1050	1750	3250	4700
Ford Custom 500						
4 dr Sed	200	500	1100	1850	3350	4900
2 dr Sed	150	450	1050	1800	3300	4800
Galaxie 500, V-8, 119" wb						
4 dr Sed	200	500	1100	1950	3600	5100
4 dr HdTp	200	550	1150	2100	3700	5300
2 dr HdTp	350	875	1700	4250	5900	8500
Conv	450	1450	2400	4800	8400	12,000
Galaxie 500 XL						
2 dr HdTp	450	950	2100	4750	6650	9500
Conv	500	1550	2600	5200	9100	13,000
LTD, V-8, 119" wb						
4 dr HdTp	200	650	1250	2400	4200	6000
2 dr HdTp	400	1200	2000	4000	7000	10,000
Wagons						
Ranch	150	450	1050	1800	3300	4800
Ctry Sq	200	600	1200	2200	3850	5500
Ctry Sed	200	500	1100	1900	3500	5000
Thunderbird, 115" wb						
4 dr Lan	350	775	1500	3750	5250	7500
2 dr Lan	450	900	1900	4500	6300	9000
2 dr HdTp	450	925	2000	4600	6400	9200

NOTE: Add 5 percent for V-8.
Add 40 percent for 427 or 428 engine option.

1968

NOTE: Add 5 percent for V-8.

	6	5	4	3	2	1
Standard Falcon						
Sed	150	400	1000	1650	3150	4500
2 dr Sed	150	400	1000	1600	3100	4400
Sta Wag	150	400	1000	1550	3050	4300
Falcon Futura, 6-cyl, 110.0" wb						
Sed	150	450	1050	1700	3200	4600
2 dr Sed	150	400	1000	1650	3150	4500
Spt Cpe	150	450	1050	1800	3300	4800
Sta Wag	150	400	1000	1550	3050	4300
Fairlane						
4 dr Sed	150	450	1050	1700	3200	4600
2 dr HdTp	200	550	1150	2100	3700	5300
Sta Wag	150	400	1000	1600	3100	4400
Fairlane 500, V-8, 116" wb						
4 dr Sed	150	450	1050	1750	3250	4700
2 dr HdTp	200	650	1250	2400	4200	6000
2 dr FsBk	350	700	1350	2800	4550	6500
Conv	450	950	2100	4750	6650	9500
Sta Wag	150	400	1000	1550	3050	4300
Torino, V-8, 116" wb						
4 dr Sed	150	400	1000	1550	3050	4300
2 dr HdTp	350	700	1350	2800	4550	6500
Wagon	150	400	1000	1550	3050	4300
Torino GT V-8						
2 dr HdTp	350	825	1600	4000	5600	8000
FsBk	450	900	1900	4500	6300	9000
Conv	450	1400	2300	4600	8100	11,500
Custom						
4 dr Sed	150	400	1000	1650	3150	4500
2 dr Sed	150	400	1000	1600	3100	4400
Custom 500						
4 dr Sed	150	450	1050	1700	3200	4600
2 dr Sed	150	400	1000	1650	3150	4500
Galaxie 500, V-8, 119" wb						
4 dr Sed	150	450	1050	1750	3250	4700
4 dr HdTp	150	450	1050	1800	3300	4800
2 dr HdTp	350	750	1450	3300	4900	7000
FsBk	450	900	1900	4500	6300	9000
Conv	400	1300	2200	4400	7700	11,000
XL						
Fsbk	400	1200	2000	4000	7000	10,000
Conv	450	1450	2400	4800	8400	12,000
LTD						
4 dr Sed	200	500	1100	1900	3500	5000
4 dr HdTp	200	600	1200	2200	3850	5500
2 dr HdTp	350	775	1500	3750	5250	7500
Ranch Wag						
Std Wag	150	400	1000	1550	3050	4300
500 Wag	150	400	1000	1600	3100	4400
DeL 500 Wag	150	400	1000	1650	3150	4500
Country Sedan						
Std Wag	150	450	1050	1700	3200	4600
DeL Wag	150	450	1050	1750	3250	4700
Country Squire						
Sta Wag	200	500	1100	1900	3500	5000
DeL Wag	200	550	1150	2000	3600	5200

NOTE: Add 40 percent for 427 or 428 engine option.
Add 50 percent for 429 engine option.

	6	5	4	3	2	1
Thunderbird, 115" wb						
HdTp	450	900	1900	4500	6300	9000
Lan Cpe	450	925	2000	4600	6400	9200
Lan Sed	350	775	1500	3700	5200	7400

1969

NOTE: Add 10 percent for V-8.

	6	5	4	3	2	1
Falcon Futura, 6-cyl, 111" wb						
Spt Cpe	150	350	950	1450	2900	4100
2 dr	150	300	900	1250	2600	3700
Fairlane 500, V-8, 116" wb						
4 dr	125	250	750	1150	2500	3600
2 dr HdTp	200	600	1200	2200	3850	5500
FsBk	200	650	1250	2400	4200	6000
Conv	350	875	1700	4250	5900	8500
Wagon	150	350	950	1350	2800	4000
Torino, V-8, 116" wb						
4 dr	150	350	950	1350	2800	4000
2 dr HdTp	200	600	1200	2200	3850	5500
Torino GT V-8						
2 dr HdTp	350	750	1450	3300	4900	7000

	6	5	4	3	2	1
FsBk	450	900	1900	4500	6300	9000
Conv	400	1300	2200	4400	7700	11,000
Cobra						
2 dr HdTp	550	1800	3000	6000	10,500	15,000
FsBk	600	1900	3200	6400	11,200	16,000
Galaxie 500, V-8, 121" wb						
4 dr HdTp	150	350	950	1450	3000	4200
2 dr HdTp	150	450	1050	1750	3250	4700
FsBk	350	750	1450	3300	4900	7000
Conv	450	900	1900	4500	6300	9000
XL						
FsBk	350	875	1700	4250	5900	8500
Conv	400	1200	2000	4000	7000	10,000
LTD						
4 dr HdTp	200	500	1100	1900	3500	5000
2 dr HdTp	350	700	1350	2800	4550	6500

NOTE: Add 40 percent for 428 engine option.
Add 50 percent for 429 engine option.

Thunderbird, 117.2" wb						
4 dr Lan	200	550	1150	2100	3700	5300
2 dr Lan	350	725	1400	3000	4700	6700
2 dr HdTp	350	700	1350	2800	4550	6500

1970

Falcon, 6-cyl, 110" wb						
4 dr Sed	150	300	900	1350	2700	3900
2 dr Sed	150	300	900	1250	2650	3800
Sta Wag	150	300	900	1250	2650	3800
1970-1/2 Falcon, 6-cyl, 117" wb						
4 dr Sed	150	350	950	1450	2900	4100
2 dr Sed	150	300	900	1350	2700	3900
Sta Wag	150	350	950	1350	2800	4000
Futura, 6-cyl, 110" wb						
4 dr Sed	150	350	950	1450	3000	4200
2 dr Sed	150	350	950	1350	2800	4000
Sta Wag	150	350	950	1350	2800	4000

NOTE: Add 10 percent for V-8.

Maverick						
2 dr	150	300	900	1250	2600	3700
Fairlane 500, V-8, 117" wb						
4 dr Sed	150	400	1000	1550	3050	4300
2 dr HdTp	200	600	1200	2200	3850	5500
Sta Wag	150	350	950	1450	3000	4200
Torino, V-8, 117" wb						
4 dr Sed	150	400	1000	1600	3100	4400
4 dr HdTp	150	400	1000	1650	3150	4500
2 dr HdTp	350	700	1350	2800	4550	6500
2 dr HdTp Sports Roof	350	775	1500	3750	5250	7500
Sta Wag	150	400	1000	1650	3150	4500
Torino Brougham, V-8, 117" wb						
4 dr Sed	150	400	1000	1650	3150	4500
2 dr HdTp	350	700	1350	2800	4550	6500
Sta Wag	150	400	1000	1550	3050	4300
Torino GT, V-8, 117" wb						
2 dr HdTp	350	825	1600	4000	5600	8000
Conv	400	1200	2000	4000	7000	10,000
Cobra, V-8, 117" wb						
2 dr HdTp	700	2300	3800	7600	13,300	19,000
Custom, V-8, 121" wb						
4 dr Sed	150	350	950	1350	2800	4000
Sta Wag	150	350	950	1350	2800	4000
Custom 500, V-8, 121" wb						
4 dr Sed	150	350	950	1450	2900	4100
Sta Wag	150	350	950	1450	2900	4100
Galaxie 500, V-8, 121" wb						
4 dr Sed	150	350	950	1450	3000	4200
4 dr HdTp	150	400	1000	1650	3150	4500
2 dr HdTp	200	600	1200	2200	3850	5500
Sta Wag	150	400	1000	1650	3150	4500
2 dr FsBk HdTp	350	750	1450	3300	4900	7000
XL, V-8, 121" wb						
2 dr FsBk HdTp	350	775	1500	3750	5250	7500
Conv	450	950	2100	4750	6650	9500
LTD, V-8, 121" wb						
4 dr Sed	150	400	1000	1550	3050	4300
4 dr HdTp	150	450	1050	1750	3250	4700
2 dr HdTp	200	600	1200	2200	3850	5500
Sta Wag	150	450	1050	1700	3200	4600
LTD Brougham, V-8, 121" wb						
4 dr Sed	150	400	1000	1600	3100	4400
4 dr HdTp	200	500	1100	1900	3500	5000
2 dr HdTp	200	650	1250	2400	4200	6000

NOTE: Add 40 percent for 428 engine option.
Add 50 percent for 429 engine option.

Thunderbird, 117" wb						
4 dr Lan	200	675	1300	2600	4400	6300
2 dr Lan	350	700	1350	2700	4500	6400
2 dr HdTp	350	725	1400	3000	4700	6700

1971

Pinto						
Rbt	150	300	900	1250	2600	3700
Maverick						
2 dr	150	300	900	1250	2600	3700
4 dr	150	300	900	1250	2650	3800
Grabber	150	300	900	1350	2700	3900
Torino, V-8, 114" wb, Sta Wag 117" wb						
4 dr Sed	150	300	900	1350	2700	3900
2 dr HdTp	200	500	1100	1900	3500	5000
Sta Wag	150	300	900	1250	2650	3800
Torino 500, V-8, 114" wb, Sta Wag 117" wb						
4 dr Sed	150	350	950	1350	2800	4000
4 dr HdTp	150	350	950	1450	2900	4100
2 dr HdTp Formal Roof	350	775	1500	3750	5250	7500
2 dr HdTp Sports Roof	350	825	1600	4000	5600	8000
Sta Wag	150	300	900	1250	2600	3700
4 dr HdTp Brougham	150	350	950	1450	2900	4100
2 dr HdTp Brougham	200	650	1250	2400	4200	6000
Squire Sta Wag	125	250	750	1150	2500	3600
2 dr HdTp Cobra	700	2150	3600	7200	12,600	18,000
2 dr HdTp GT	400	1200	2000	4000	7000	10,000
Conv	450	1500	2500	5000	8800	12,500
Custom, V-8, 121" wb						
4 dr Sed	125	250	750	1150	2500	3600
Sta Wag	125	250	750	1150	2500	3600
Custom 500, V-8, 121" wb						
4 dr Sed	150	300	900	1250	2600	3700
Sta Wag	150	300	900	1250	2600	3700
Galaxie 500, V-8, 121" wb						
4 dr Sed	150	300	900	1250	2650	3800

	6	5	4	3	2	1
4 dr HdTp	150	350	950	1350	2800	4000
2 dr HdTp	150	450	1050	1750	3250	4700
Sta Wag	150	300	900	1250	2650	3800
LTD						
4 dr	150	300	900	1350	2700	3900
4 dr HdTp	150	350	950	1450	2900	4100
2 dr HdTp	200	500	1100	1900	3500	5000
Conv	350	825	1600	4000	5600	8000
Ctry Sq	150	350	950	1350	2800	4000
LTD Brougham, V-8, 121" wb						
4 dr Sed	150	350	950	1450	2900	4100
4 dr HdTp	150	400	1000	1600	3100	4400
2 dr HdTp	200	600	1200	2200	3850	5500

NOTE: Add 40 percent for 429 engine option.

Thunderbird						
4 dr HdTp	200	650	1250	2400	4150	5900
2 dr HdTp	200	675	1300	2500	4300	6100
2 dr Lan HdTp	200	675	1300	2500	4350	6200

1972

Pinto						
2 dr	125	250	750	1150	2400	3400
3 dr	125	250	750	1150	2450	3500
Wagon	125	250	750	1150	2500	3600
Maverick						
4 dr	125	250	750	1150	2400	3400
2 dr	125	250	750	1150	2450	3500
Grabber	150	300	900	1350	2700	3900

NOTE: Deduct 20 percent for 6-cyl.

Torino, V-8, 118" wb, 2 dr 114" wb						
4 dr Sed	125	250	750	1150	2400	3400
2 dr HdTp	150	400	1000	1650	3150	4500
Sta Wag	125	250	750	1150	2400	3400
Gran Torino						
4 dr	125	250	750	1150	2450	3500
2 dr HdTp	200	650	1250	2400	4200	6000
Custom, V-8, 121" wb						
4 dr Sed	125	250	750	1150	2500	3600
Sta Wag	125	250	750	1150	2500	3600
Custom 500, V-8, 121" wb						
4 dr Sed	150	300	900	1250	2600	3700
Sta Wag	150	300	900	1250	2600	3700
Galaxie 500, V-8, 121" wb						
4 dr Sed	150	300	900	1250	2650	3800
4 dr HdTp	150	350	950	1350	2800	4000
2 dr HdTp	200	600	1200	2200	3850	5500
Sta Wag	150	300	900	1250	2650	3800
LTD, V-8, 121" wb						
4 dr Sed	150	300	900	1350	2700	3900
4 dr HdTp	150	350	950	1450	3000	4200
2 dr HdTp	200	650	1250	2400	4200	6000
Conv	450	900	1900	4500	6300	9000
Sta Wag	150	350	950	1350	2800	4000
LTD Brougham, V-8, 121" wb						
4 dr Sed	150	350	950	1350	2800	4000
4 dr HdTp	150	450	1050	1750	3250	4700
2 dr HdTp	350	700	1350	2800	4550	6500

NOTE: Add 40 percent for 429 engine option.
Add 30 percent for 460 engine option.

Thunderbird						
2 dr HdTp	350	700	1350	2700	4500	6400

1973

Pinto, 4-cyl.						
2 dr	125	250	750	1150	2450	3500
Rbt	125	250	750	1150	2500	3600
Sta Wag	150	300	900	1250	2600	3700
Maverick V8						
2 dr	125	250	750	1150	2500	3600
4 dr	150	300	900	1250	2600	3700
2 dr Grabber	150	350	950	1450	3000	4200
Torino V8						
4 dr	125	250	750	1150	2400	3400
2 dr HdTp	150	400	1000	1650	3150	4500
Sta Wag	125	250	750	1150	2500	3600
Gran Torino V8						
4 dr	125	250	750	1150	2450	3500
2 dr HdTp	200	500	1100	1900	3500	5000
Sta Wag	150	300	900	1250	2600	3700
Gran Torino Sport V8						
2 dr SR HdTp	350	700	1350	2800	4550	6500
2 dr FR HdTp	350	750	1450	3300	4900	7000
Sq Wag	150	350	950	1350	2800	4000
Gran Torino Brgm V8						
4 dr	125	250	750	1150	2500	3600
2 dr HdTp	350	700	1350	2800	4550	6500
Custom 500 V8						
4 dr	125	250	750	1150	2500	3600
Sta Wag	150	300	900	1250	2600	3700
Galaxie 500 V8						
4 dr	150	300	900	1250	2600	3700
2 dr HdTp	150	450	1050	1700	3200	4600
4 dr HdTp	150	300	900	1250	2650	3800
Sta Wag	150	300	900	1250	2600	3700
LTD V8						
4 dr	150	300	900	1250	2650	3800
2 dr HdTp	150	450	1050	1800	3300	4800
4 dr HdTp	150	300	900	1350	2700	3900
Sta Wag	150	300	900	1250	2650	3800
LTD Brgm V8						
4 dr	150	300	900	1350	2700	3900
2 dr HdTp	200	500	1100	1950	3600	5100
4 dr HdTp	150	350	950	1350	2800	4000

NOTE: Add 30 percent for 429 engine option.
Add 30 percent for 460 engine option.

Thunderbird						
2 dr HdTp	200	600	1200	2200	3850	5500

1974

Pinto						
Cpe	125	250	750	1150	2500	3600
Htchbk	150	300	900	1250	2600	3700
Sta Wag	125	250	750	1150	2500	3600
Maverick, V-8						
Cpe	125	250	750	1150	2500	3600
Sed	150	300	900	1250	2600	3700
Grabber	150	300	900	1350	2700	3900
Torino, V-8						
4 dr Sed	125	250	750	1150	2500	3600
HdTp	150	450	1050	1750	3250	4700
Sta Wag	125	250	750	1150	2450	3500

Gran Torino, V-8	6	5	4	3	2	1
4 dr Sed	125	250	750	1150	2500	3600
2 dr HdTp	150	450	1050	1750	3250	4700
Sta Wag	125	250	750	1150	2500	3600
Gran Torino Sport, V-8						
2 dr HdTp	200	600	1200	2200	3850	5500
Gran Torino Brgm, V-8						
4 dr Sed	150	300	900	1250	2650	3800
2 dr HdTp	200	500	1100	1900	3500	5000
Gran Torino Elite, V-8						
2 dr HdTp	200	550	1150	2000	3600	5200
Gran Torino Squire, V-8						
Sta Wag	150	300	900	1250	2600	3700
Custom 500						
4 dr Sed	125	250	750	1150	2450	3500
Sta Wag	125	250	750	1150	2450	3500
Galaxie 500, V-8						
4 dr Sed	125	250	750	1150	2500	3600
2 dr HdTp	150	300	900	1350	2700	3900
4 dr HdTp	150	300	900	1250	2600	3700
Sta Wag	125	250	750	1150	2500	3600
LTD, V-8						
2 dr HdTp	150	350	950	1450	2900	4100
4 dr Sed	150	300	900	1250	2600	3700
4 dr HdTp	150	300	900	1250	2650	3800
Sta Wag	150	300	900	1250	2600	3700
Ltd Brgm, V-8						
4 dr Sed	150	300	900	1250	2600	3700
2 dr HdTp	150	350	950	1450	3000	4200
4 dr HdTp	150	300	900	1250	2650	3800
NOTE: Add 30 percent for 460 engine option.						
Thunderbird						
HdTp	200	600	1200	2200	3850	5500

1975

	6	5	4	3	2	1
Pinto						
Cpe	125	200	600	1100	2300	3300
Htchbk	125	250	750	1150	2400	3400
Sta Wag	125	200	600	1100	2300	3300
Maverick						
Cpe	125	250	750	1150	2400	3400
4 dr Sed	125	250	750	1150	2450	3500
Grabber	125	250	750	1150	2500	3600
Torino						
o/w Cpe	125	250	750	1150	2450	3500
4 dr Sed	100	175	525	1050	2100	3000
Sta Wag	125	200	600	1100	2200	3100
Gran Torino						
o/w Cpe	125	250	750	1150	2500	3600
4 dr Sed	125	200	600	1100	2250	3200
Sta Wag	125	200	600	1100	2250	3200
Gran Torino Brougham						
o/w Cpe	150	300	900	1250	2650	3800
4 dr Sed	125	200	600	1100	2250	3200
Gran Torino Sport						
2 dr HdTp	150	350	950	1350	2800	4000
Torino Squire						
Sta Wag	125	200	600	1100	2300	3300
Elite						
2 dr HdTp	150	350	950	1450	3000	4200
Granada						
Cpe	125	200	600	1100	2300	3300
4 dr Sed	100	150	450	1000	1750	2500
Ghia Cpe	125	250	750	1150	2500	3600
Ghia Sed	125	250	750	1150	2450	3500
Custom 500						
4 dr Sed	125	200	600	1100	2200	3100
Sta Wag	125	200	600	1100	2200	3100
LTD						
o/w Cpe	125	250	750	1150	2400	3400
4 dr Sed	125	200	600	1100	2250	3200
LTD Brougham						
o/w Cpe	125	250	750	1150	2450	3500
4 dr Sed	125	200	600	1100	2300	3300
LTD Landau						
o/w Cpe	150	300	900	1250	2600	3700
4 dr Sed	125	250	750	1150	2400	3400
LTD Station Wagon						
Sta Wag	125	200	600	1100	2250	3200
Ctry Squire	125	200	600	1100	2300	3300
NOTE: Add 30 percent for 460 engine option.						
Thunderbird						
HdTp	200	500	1100	1950	3600	5100

1976

	6	5	4	3	2	1
Pinto, 4-cyl.						
2 dr Sed	125	250	750	1150	2450	3500
2 dr Rbt	125	250	750	1150	2500	3600
Sta Wag	150	300	900	1250	2600	3700
Squire Wag	150	300	900	1250	2650	3800
NOTE: Add 10 percent for V-6.						
Maverick, V-8						
4 dr Sed	125	250	750	1150	2400	3400
2 dr Sed	125	200	600	1100	2300	3300
NOTE: Deduct 5 percent for 6-cyl.						
Torino, V-8						
4 dr Sed	125	250	750	1150	2450	3500
2 dr HdTp	125	250	750	1150	2500	3600
Gran Torino, V-8						
4 dr Sed	125	250	750	1150	2500	3600
2 dr HdTp	150	300	900	1250	2600	3700
Gran Torino Brougham, V-8						
4 dr Sed	150	300	900	1250	2600	3700
2 dr HdTp	150	300	900	1250	2650	3800
Station Wagons, V-8						
2S Torino	125	250	750	1150	2450	3500
2S Gran Torino	125	250	750	1150	2500	3600
2S Gran Torino Squire	150	300	900	1250	2600	3700
Granada, V-8						
4 dr Sed	125	200	600	1100	2250	3200
2 dr Sed	125	200	600	1100	2300	3300
Granada Ghia, V-8						
4 dr Sed	125	200	600	1100	2300	3300
2 dr Sed	125	250	750	1150	2400	3400
Elite, V-8						
2 dr HdTp	150	300	900	1250	2600	3700
Custom, V-8						
4 dr Sed	125	250	750	1150	2400	3400
LTD, V-8						
4 dr Sed	125	250	750	1150	2500	3600
2 dr Sed	150	300	900	1250	2650	3800

LTD Brougham V-8	6	5	4	3	2	1
4 dr Sed	150	300	900	1250	2650	3800
2 dr Sed	150	350	950	1350	2800	4000
LTD Landau, V-8						
4 dr Sed	150	350	950	1350	2800	4000
2 dr Sed	150	350	950	1450	3000	4200
Station Wagons, V-8						
Ranch Wag	125	250	750	1150	2500	3600
LTD Wag	150	300	900	1250	2650	3800
Ctry Squire Wag	150	350	950	1350	2800	4000
Thunderbird						
2 dr HdTp	150	450	1050	1800	3300	4800

1977

	6	5	4	3	2	1
Pinto, 4-cyl.						
2 dr Sed	125	250	750	1150	2500	3600
2 dr Rbt	150	300	900	1250	2600	3700
Sta Wag	150	300	900	1250	2650	3800
Squire Wag	150	300	900	1350	2700	3900
NOTE: Add 5 percent for V-6.						
Maverick, V-8						
4 dr Sed	125	250	750	1150	2450	3500
2 dr Sed	125	250	750	1150	2400	3400
NOTE: Deduct 5 percent for 6-cyl.						
Granada, V-8						
4 dr Sed	125	200	600	1100	2250	3200
2 dr Sed	125	200	600	1100	2300	3300
Granada Ghia, V-8						
4 dr Sed	125	250	750	1150	2400	3400
2 dr Sed	125	250	750	1150	2450	3500
LTD II "S", V-8						
4 dr Sed	125	200	600	1100	2300	3300
2 dr Sed	125	250	750	1150	2400	3400
LTD II, V-8						
4 dr Sed	125	250	750	1150	2400	3400
2 dr Sed	125	250	750	1150	2450	3500
LTD II Brougham, V-8						
4 dr Sed	125	250	750	1150	2500	3600
2 dr Sed	150	300	900	1250	2600	3700
Station Wagons, V-8						
2S LTD II	125	250	750	1150	2450	3500
3S LTD II	125	250	750	1150	2500	3600
3S LTD II Squire	150	300	900	1250	2650	3800
LTD, V-8						
4 dr Sed	150	300	900	1250	2600	3700
2 dr Sed	150	300	900	1250	2650	3800
LTD Landau, V-8						
4 dr Sed	150	300	900	1350	2700	3900
2 dr Sed	150	350	950	1350	2800	4000
Station Wagons, V-8						
2S LTD	150	300	900	1250	2650	3800
3S LTD	150	300	900	1350	2700	3900
3S Ctry Squire	150	350	950	1350	2800	4000
Thunderbird						
2 dr	150	450	1050	1700	3200	4600
2 dr Landau	150	450	1050	1750	3250	4700

1978

	6	5	4	3	2	1
Fiesta						
Hatch	100	175	525	1050	1950	2800
Pinto						
2 dr	100	175	525	1050	2050	2900
3 dr Rbt	125	250	750	1150	2500	3600
Sta Wag	150	300	900	1250	2600	3700
Fairmont						
4 dr Sed	125	200	600	1100	2200	3100
2 dr Sed	100	175	525	1050	2100	3000
Cpe Futura	125	250	750	1150	2450	3500
Sta Wag	125	200	600	1100	2250	3200
Granada						
4 dr Sed	125	200	600	1100	2250	3200
2 dr Sed	125	200	600	1100	2200	3100
LTD II 'S'						
4 dr	125	200	600	1100	2200	3100
2 dr	100	175	525	1050	2100	3000
LTD II						
4 dr	125	200	600	1100	2250	3200
2 dr	125	200	600	1100	2200	3100
LTD II Brougham						
4 dr	125	200	600	1100	2300	3300
2 dr	125	200	600	1100	2250	3200
LTD						
4 dr	125	250	750	1150	2500	3600
2 dr	150	300	900	1250	2600	3700
2S Sta Wag	125	250	750	1150	2450	3500
LTD Landau						
4 dr	150	300	900	1250	2650	3800
2 dr	150	300	900	1350	2700	3900
Thunderbird						
2 dr	200	500	1100	1900	3500	5000
2 dr Town Landau	200	650	1250	2400	4200	6000
2 dr Diamond Jubilee	350	750	1450	3300	4900	7000

1979

	6	5	4	3	2	1
Fiesta, 4-cyl.						
3 dr Hatch	100	175	525	1050	2050	2900
Pinto, V-6						
2 dr Sed	125	200	600	1100	2200	3100
Rbt	125	250	750	1150	2500	3600
Sta Wag	125	250	750	1150	2500	3600
Squire Wag	150	300	900	1250	2600	3700
NOTE: Deduct 5 percent for 4-cyl.						
Fairmont, 6-cyl.						
4 dr Sed	125	200	600	1100	2250	3200
2 dr Sed	125	200	600	1100	2200	3100
Cpe	125	250	750	1150	2500	3600
Sta Wag	125	200	600	1100	2300	3300
Squire Wag	125	250	750	1150	2400	3400
NOTE: Deduct 5 percent for 4-cyl. Add 5 percent for V-8.						
Granada, V-8						
4 dr Sed	125	200	600	1100	2300	3300
2 dr Sed	125	200	600	1100	2250	3200
NOTE: Deduct 5 percent for 6-cyl.						
LTD II, V-8						
4 dr Sed	125	200	600	1100	2250	3200
2 dr Sed	125	200	600	1100	2200	3100
LTD II Brougham, V-8						
4 dr Sed	125	200	600	1100	2300	3300
2 dr Sed	125	200	600	1100	2250	3200
LTD, V-8						
4 dr Sed	125	250	750	1150	2500	3600

	6	5	4	3	2	1
2 dr Sed	125	250	750	1150	2400	3400
2S Sta Wag	125	250	750	1150	2450	3500
3S Sta Wag	125	250	750	1150	2500	3600
2S Squire Wag	150	300	900	1250	2600	3700
3S Squire Wag	150	300	900	1250	2650	3800
LTD Landau						
4 dr Sed	150	300	900	1250	2650	3800
2 dr Sed	125	250	750	1150	2500	3600
Thunderbird, V-8						
2 dr	150	400	1000	1650	3150	4500
2 dr Landau	150	450	1050	1750	3250	4700
2 dr Heritage	200	500	1100	1900	3500	5000
1980						
Fiesta, 4-cyl.						
2 dr Hatch	125	200	600	1100	2200	3100
Pinto, 4-cyl.						
2 dr Cpe Pony	125	200	600	1100	2250	3200
2 dr Sta Wag Pony	125	250	750	1150	2400	3400
2 dr Cpe	125	200	600	1100	2300	3300
2 dr Hatch	125	250	750	1150	2400	3400
2 dr Sta Wag	125	250	750	1150	2450	3500
2 dr Sta Wag Squire	125	250	750	1150	2500	3600
Fairmont, 6-cyl.						
4 dr Sed	125	250	750	1150	2400	3400
2 dr Sed	125	200	600	1100	2300	3300
4 dr Sed Futura	125	250	750	1150	2500	3600
2 dr Cpe Futura	150	350	950	1450	2900	4100
4 dr Sta Wag	150	300	900	1250	2650	3800
NOTES: Deduct 10 percent for 4-cyl. Add 12 percent for V-8.						
Granada, V-8						
4 dr Sed	150	300	900	1350	2700	3900
2 dr Sed	150	300	900	1250	2650	3800
4 dr Sed Ghia	150	350	950	1450	2900	4100
2 dr Sed Ghia	150	350	950	1350	2800	4000
4 dr Sed ESS	150	350	950	1450	3000	4200
2 dr Sed ESS	150	350	950	1450	2900	4100
NOTE: Deduct 10 percent for 6-cyl.						
LTD, V-8						
4 dr Sed S	150	350	950	1450	3000	4200
4 dr Sta Wag S 3S	150	400	1000	1600	3100	4400
4 dr Sta Wag S 2S	150	400	1000	1550	3050	4300
4 dr Sed	150	400	1000	1550	3050	4300
2 dr Sed	150	350	950	1450	3000	4200
4 dr Sta Wag 3S	150	400	1000	1650	3150	4500
4 dr Sta Wag 2S	150	400	1000	1600	3100	4400
4 dr Sta Wag CS 3S	150	450	1050	1750	3250	4700
4 dr Sta Wag CS 2S	150	450	1050	1700	3200	4600
LTD Crown Victoria, V-8						
4 dr Sed	150	450	1050	1700	3200	4600
2 dr Sed	150	400	1000	1650	3150	4500
Thunderbird, V-8						
2 dr Cpe	200	600	1200	2200	3850	5500
2 dr Cpe Twn Lan	200	650	1200	2300	4100	5800
2 dr Cpe Silver Anniv	200	650	1250	2400	4200	6000
1981						
Escort, 4-cyl.						
2 dr Hatch	125	200	600	1100	2250	3200
4 dr Hatch	125	200	600	1100	2300	3300
2 dr Hatch L	125	200	600	1100	2300	3300
4 dr Hatch L	125	250	750	1150	2400	3400
2 dr Hatch GL	125	250	750	1150	2400	3400
4 dr Hatch GL	125	250	750	1150	2450	3500
2 dr Hatch GLX	125	250	750	1150	2450	3500
4 dr Hatch GLX	125	250	750	1150	2500	3600
2 dr Hatch SS	125	250	750	1150	2500	3600
4 dr Hatch SS	150	300	900	1250	2600	3700
Fairmont, 6-cyl.						
2 dr Sed S	125	250	750	1150	2400	3400
4 dr Sed	125	250	750	1150	2450	3500
2 dr Sed	125	250	750	1150	2450	3500
4 dr Futura	125	250	750	1150	2500	3600
2 dr Cpe Futura	150	350	950	1450	3000	4200
4 dr Sta Wag	150	300	900	1350	2700	3900
4 dr Sta Wag Futura	150	350	950	1350	2800	4000
NOTES: Deduct 10 percent for 4-cyl. Add 12 percent for V-8.						
Granada, 6-cyl.						
4 dr Sed L	150	300	900	1250	2650	3800
2 dr Sed L	150	300	900	1250	2600	3700
4 dr Sed GL	150	300	900	1350	2700	3900
2 dr Sed GL	150	300	900	1250	2650	3800
4 dr Sed GLX	150	350	950	1350	2800	4000
2 dr Sed GLX	150	300	900	1350	2700	3900
NOTES: Deduct 10 percent for 4-cyl. Add 12 percent for V-8.						
LTD, V-8						
4 dr Sed S	150	400	1000	1550	3050	4300
4 dr Sta Wag S 3S	150	400	1000	1650	3150	4500
4 dr Sta Wag S 2S	150	400	1000	1600	3100	4400
4 dr Sed	150	400	1000	1600	3100	4400
2 dr Sed	150	400	1000	1550	3050	4300
4 dr Sta Wag 3S	150	450	1050	1700	3200	4600
4 dr Sta Wag 2S	150	400	1000	1650	3150	4500
4 dr Sta Wag CS 3S	150	450	1050	1800	3300	4800
4 dr Sta Wag CS 2S	150	450	1050	1750	3250	4700
LTD Crown Victoria, V-8						
4 dr Sed	150	450	1050	1800	3300	4800
2 dr Sed	150	450	1050	1750	3250	4700
Thunderbird, V-8						
2 dr Cpe	200	600	1200	2200	3900	5600
2 dr Cpe Twn Lan	200	650	1200	2300	4100	5800
2 dr Cpe Heritage	200	650	1250	2400	4150	5900
NOTE: Deduct 15 percent for 6-cyl.						
1982						
Escort, 4-cyl.						
2 dr Hatch	125	200	600	1100	2300	3300
4 dr Hatch	125	250	750	1150	2400	3400
2 dr Hatch L	125	250	750	1150	2400	3400
4 dr Hatch L	125	250	750	1150	2450	3500
4 dr Sta Wag L	125	250	750	1150	2500	3600
2 dr Hatch GL	125	250	750	1150	2450	3500
4 dr Hatch GL	125	250	750	1150	2500	3600
4 dr Sta Wag GL	150	300	900	1250	2600	3700
2 dr Hatch GLX	125	250	750	1150	2500	3600
4 dr Hatch GLX	150	300	900	1250	2600	3700
4 dr Sta Wag GLX	150	300	900	1250	2650	3800
2 dr Hatch GT	150	300	900	1350	2700	3900

	6	5	4	3	2	1
EXP, 4-cyl.						
2 dr Cpe	150	400	1000	1650	3150	4500
Fairmont Futura, 4-cyl.						
4 dr Sed	100	175	525	1050	2100	3000
2 dr Sed	100	175	525	1050	2050	2900
2 dr Cpe Futura	125	200	600	1100	2300	3300
Fairmont Futura, 6-cyl.						
4 dr Sed	150	300	900	1250	2600	3700
2 dr Cpe Futura	150	400	1000	1550	3050	4300
Granada, 6-cyl.						
4 dr Sed L	150	300	900	1350	2700	3900
2 dr Sed L	150	300	900	1250	2650	3800
4 dr Sed GL	150	350	950	1350	2800	4000
2 dr Sed GL	150	300	900	1350	2700	3900
4 dr Sed GLX	150	350	950	1450	2900	4100
2 dr Sed GLX	150	350	950	1350	2800	4000
NOTE: Deduct 10 percent for 4-cyl.						
Granada Wagon, 6-cyl.						
4 dr Sta Wag L	150	350	950	1450	3000	4200
4 dr Sta Wag GL	150	400	1000	1550	3050	4300
LTD, V-8						
4 dr Sed S	150	400	1000	1600	3100	4400
4 dr Sed	150	400	1000	1650	3150	4500
2 dr Sed	150	400	1000	1600	3100	4400
LTD Crown Victoria, V-8						
4 dr Sed	200	500	1100	1850	3350	4900
2 dr Sed	150	450	1050	1800	3300	4800
LTD Station Wagon, V-8						
4 dr Sta Wag S 2S	150	400	1000	1650	3150	4500
4 dr Sta Wag S 3S	150	450	1050	1700	3200	4600
4 dr Sta Wag 2S	150	450	1050	1700	3200	4600
4 dr Sta Wag 3S	150	450	1050	1750	3250	4700
4 dr Sta Wag CS 2S	150	450	1050	1800	3300	4800
4 dr Sta Wag CS 3S	200	500	1100	1850	3350	4900
Thunderbird, V-8						
2 dr Cpe	200	650	1200	2300	4100	5800
2 dr Cpe Twn Lan	200	650	1250	2400	4200	6000
2 dr Cpe Heritage	200	675	1300	2500	4350	6200
NOTE: Deduct 15 percent for V-6.						
1983						
Escort, 4-cyl.						
2 dr Hatch L	125	250	750	1150	2400	3400
4 dr Hatch L	125	250	750	1150	2450	3500
4 dr Sta Wag L	125	250	750	1150	2500	3600
2 dr Hatch GL	125	250	750	1150	2450	3500
4 dr Hatch GL	125	250	750	1150	2500	3600
4 dr Sta Wag GL	150	300	900	1250	2600	3700
2 dr Hatch GLX	125	250	750	1150	2500	3600
4 dr Hatch GLX	150	300	900	1250	2600	3700
4 dr Sta Wag GLX	150	300	900	1250	2650	3800
2 dr Hatch GT	150	300	900	1250	2600	3700
EXP, 4-cyl.						
2 dr Cpe	150	400	1000	1650	3150	4500
Fairmont Futura, 4-cyl.						
4 dr Sed S	125	250	750	1150	2400	3400
2 dr Sed S	125	200	600	1100	2300	3300
4 dr Sed	125	250	750	1150	2450	3500
2 dr Sed	125	250	750	1150	2400	3400
2 dr Cpe	150	300	900	1250	2650	3800
Fairmont Futura, 6-cyl.						
4 dr Sed	150	300	900	1250	2600	3700
2 dr Sed	125	250	750	1150	2500	3600
2 dr Cpe	150	400	1000	1550	3050	4300
LTD, 4-cyl.						
4 dr Sed	150	350	950	1450	2900	4100
4 dr Sed Brgm	150	400	1000	1550	3050	4300
LTD, 6-cyl.						
4 dr Sed	150	350	950	1450	3000	4200
4 dr Sed Brgm	150	400	1000	1600	3100	4400
4 dr Sta Wag	150	450	1050	1700	3200	4600
LTD Crown Victoria, V-8						
4 dr Sed	200	500	1100	1900	3500	5000
2 dr Sed	200	500	1100	1850	3350	4900
4 dr Sta Wag 2S	200	500	1100	1900	3500	5000
4 dr Sta Wag 3S	200	500	1100	1950	3600	5100
Thunderbird, 4-cyl. Turbo						
2 dr Cpe	350	750	1450	3300	4900	7000
Thunderbird, V-8						
2 dr Cpe	350	775	1500	3750	5250	7500
2 dr Cpe Heritage	350	800	1550	3900	5450	7800
NOTE: Deduct 15 percent for V-6.						
1984						
Escort, 4-cyl.						
2 dr Hatch	125	200	600	1100	2250	3200
4 dr Hatch	125	200	600	1100	2250	3200
2 dr Hatch L	125	200	600	1100	2300	3300
4 dr Hatch L	125	200	600	1100	2300	3300
4 dr Sta Wag L	125	250	750	1150	2400	3400
2 dr Hatch GL	125	250	750	1150	2400	3400
4 dr Hatch GL	125	250	750	1150	2400	3400
4 dr Sta Wag GL	125	250	750	1150	2450	3500
4 dr Hatch LX	125	250	750	1150	2450	3500
2 dr Hatch LX	125	250	750	1150	2450	3500
4 dr Sta Wag LX	125	250	750	1150	2500	3600
2 dr Hatch GT	125	250	750	1150	2500	3600
2 dr Hatch Turbo GT	150	300	900	1250	2650	3800
EXP, 4-cyl.						
2 dr Cpe	150	350	950	1350	2800	4000
2 dr Cpe L	150	350	950	1450	3000	4200
2 dr Cpe Turbo	150	450	1050	1700	3200	4600
Tempo, 4-cyl.						
2 dr Sed	125	200	600	1100	2300	3300
4 dr Sed	125	200	600	1100	2300	3300
2 dr Sed GL	125	250	750	1150	2400	3400
4 dr Sed GL	125	250	750	1150	2400	3400
2 dr Sed GLX	125	250	750	1150	2450	3500
4 dr Sed GLX	125	250	750	1150	2450	3500
LTD, 4-cyl.						
4 dr Sed	150	350	950	1450	2900	4100
4 dr Sed Brgm	150	350	950	1450	3000	4200
LTD, V-6						
4 dr Sed	150	350	950	1450	3000	4200
4 dr Sed Brgm	150	400	1000	1550	3050	4300
4 dr Sta Wag	150	400	1000	1550	3050	4300
4 dr Sed LX, (V-8)	150	450	1050	1700	3200	4600
LTD Crown Victoria, V-8						
4 dr Sed S	150	450	1050	1750	3250	4700
4 dr Sed	200	500	1100	1850	3350	4900
2 dr Sed	200	500	1100	1850	3350	4900

	6	5	4	3	2	1
4 dr Sta Wag S, 8P	200	500	1100	1900	3500	5000
4 dr Sta Wag S, 6P	200	500	1100	1850	3350	4900
4 dr Sta Wag 8P	200	500	1100	1950	3600	5100
4 dr Sta Wag 6P	200	500	1100	1900	3500	5000
4 dr Sta Wag Squire 8P	200	550	1150	2000	3600	5200
4 dr Sta Wag Squire 6P	200	500	1100	1950	3600	5100
Thunderbird, V-6						
2 dr Cpe	200	675	1300	2500	4350	6200
2 dr Cpe Elan	350	700	1350	2700	4500	6400
2 dr Cpe Fila	350	700	1350	2800	4550	6500
Thunderbird, V-8						
2 dr Cpe	200	675	1300	2600	4400	6300
2 dr Cpe Elan	350	700	1350	2900	4600	6600
2 dr Cpe Fila	350	725	1400	3000	4700	6700
Thunderbird, 4-cyl.						
2 dr Cpe Turbo	350	725	1400	3100	4800	6800

MUSTANG

1964
	6	5	4	3	2	1
2 dr HdTp	450	1450	2400	4800	8400	12,000
Conv	850	2750	4600	9200	16,100	23,000

NOTE: Deduct 10 percent for 6-cyl.
Add 20 percent for Challenger Code "K" V-8.
First Mustang introduced April 17, 1964 at N.Y. World's Fair.

1965
2 dr HdTp	450	1450	2400	4800	8400	12,000
Conv	850	2750	4600	9200	16,100	23,000
FsBk	700	2150	3600	7200	12,600	18,000

NOTE: Add 30 percent for 271 hp Hi-perf engine.
Add 10 percent for "GT" Package.
Add 10 percent for original "pony interior".
Deduct 10 percent for 6-cyl.

1965 Shelby GT
GT-350 FsBk	1600	5150	8600	17,200	30,100	43,000

1966
2 dr HdTp	450	1450	2400	4800	8400	12,000
Conv	850	2750	4600	9200	16,100	23,000
FsBk	700	2150	3600	7200	12,600	18,000

NOTE: Same as 1965.

1966 Shelby GT
GT-350 FsBk	1400	4450	7400	14,800	25,900	37,000
GT-350H FsBk	1450	4700	7800	15,600	27,300	39,000
GT-350 Conv	1600	5150	8600	17,200	30,100	43,000

1967
2 dr HdTp	450	1450	2400	4800	8400	12,000
Conv	750	2400	4000	8000	14,000	20,000
FsBk	550	1800	3000	6000	10,500	15,000

NOTES: Same as 1964-65, plus;
Add 10 percent for 390 cid V-8 (code "Z").
Deduct 10 percent for 6-cyl.

1967 Shelby GT
GT-350 FsBk	1450	4550	7600	15,200	26,600	38,000
GT-500 FsBk	1550	4900	8200	16,400	28,700	41,000

1968
2 dr HdTp	450	1450	2400	4800	8400	12,000
Conv	750	2400	4000	8000	14,000	20,000
FsBk	550	1800	3000	6000	10,500	15,000

NOTES: Same as 1964-67, plus;
Add 10 percent for GT-390.
Add 50 percent for 427 cid V-8 (code "W").
Add 30 percent for 428 cid V-8 (code "Q").
Add 15 percent for "California Special" trim.

1968 Shelby GT
350 Conv	1900	6000	10,000	20,000	35,000	50,000
350 FsBk	1600	5050	8400	16,800	29,400	42,000
500 Conv	2350	7450	12,400	24,800	43,400	62,000
500 FsBk	1700	5400	9000	18,000	31,500	45,000

NOTE: Add 30 percent for KR models.

1969
2 dr HdTp	450	1450	2400	4800	8400	12,000
Conv	600	1900	3200	6400	11,200	16,000
FsBk	500	1550	2600	5200	9100	13,000

NOTE: Deduct 10 percent for 6-cyl.
Mach I	650	2050	3400	6800	11,900	17,000
Boss 302	1000	3100	5200	10,400	18,200	26,000
Boss 429	1900	6000	10,000	20,000	35,000	50,000
Grande	550	1700	2800	5600	9800	14,000

NOTES: Same as 1968; plus;
Add 30 percent for Cobra Jet V-8.
Add 40 percent for "Super Cobra Jet" engine.

1969 Shelby GT
350 Conv	1500	4800	8000	16,000	28,000	40,000
350 FsBk	1400	4450	7400	14,800	25,900	37,000
500 Conv	1600	5050	8400	16,800	29,400	42,000
500 FsBk	1450	4550	7600	15,200	26,600	38,000

1970
2 dr HdTp	450	1450	2400	4800	8400	12,000
Conv	600	1900	3200	6400	11,200	16,000
FsBk	500	1550	2600	5200	9100	13,000
Mach I	650	2050	3400	6800	11,900	17,000
Boss 302	1000	3100	5200	10,400	18,200	26,000
Boss 429	1900	6000	10,000	20,000	35,000	50,000
Grande	550	1700	2800	5600	9800	14,000

NOTE: Add 30 percent for Cobra Jet V-8.
Add 40 percent for "Super Cobra Jet".
Deduct 10 percent for 6-cyl.

1970 Shelby GT
350 Conv	1500	4800	8000	16,000	28,000	40,000
350 FsBk	1400	4450	7400	14,800	25,900	37,000
500 Conv	1600	5050	8400	16,800	29,400	42,000
500 FsBk	1450	4550	7600	15,200	26,600	38,000

1971
2 dr HdTp	450	950	2100	4750	6650	9500
Grande	400	1200	2000	4000	7000	10,000
Conv	600	1900	3200	6400	11,200	16,000
FsBk	550	1700	2800	5600	9800	14,000
Mach I	550	1800	3000	6000	10,500	15,000
Boss 351	1100	3500	5800	11,600	20,300	29,000

NOTE: Same as 1970.
Deduct 10 percent for 6-cyl.

1972
	6	5	4	3	2	1
2 dr HdTp	450	950	2100	4750	6650	9500
Grande	400	1200	2000	4000	7000	10,000
FsBk	550	1700	2800	5600	9800	14,000
Mach I	550	1800	3000	6000	10,500	15,000
Conv	600	1900	3200	6400	11,200	16,000

NOTE: Add 5 percent for engine and decor options.
Deduct 10 percent for 6-cyl.

1973
2 dr HdTp	450	900	1900	4500	6300	9000
Grande	400	1200	2000	4000	7000	10,000
FsBk	500	1550	2600	5200	9100	13,000
Mach I	550	1700	2800	5600	9800	14,000
Conv	650	2050	3400	6800	11,900	17,000

NOTE: Add 10 percent for engine and decor options.

1974
Mustang II
Mustang Four
HdTp Cpe	150	350	950	1350	2800	4000
FsBk	150	350	950	1450	2900	4100
Ghia	150	350	950	1450	3000	4200
Mustang Six						
HdTp Cpe	150	350	950	1350	2800	4000
FsBk	150	350	950	1450	2900	4100
Ghia	150	350	950	1450	3000	4200
Mach I Six						
FsBk	200	500	1100	1900	3500	5000

1975
Mustang
HdTp Cpe	150	350	950	1350	2800	4000
FsBk	150	350	950	1450	2900	4100
Ghia	150	350	950	1450	3000	4200
Mustang Six						
HdTp Cpe	150	350	950	1450	2900	4100
FsBk	150	350	950	1450	3000	4200
Ghia	150	400	1000	1550	3050	4300
Mach I	150	400	1000	1650	3150	4500
Mustang, V-8						
HdTp Cpe	200	600	1200	2200	3900	5600
FsBk Cpe	200	600	1200	2300	4000	5700
Ghia	200	650	1250	2400	4200	6000
Mach I	350	700	1350	2800	4550	6500

1976
Mustang II, V-6
2 dr	150	400	1000	1550	3050	4300
3 dr 2 plus 2	150	400	1000	1600	3100	4400
2 dr Ghia	150	450	1050	1750	3250	4700

NOTE: Deduct 10 percent for 4-cyl.
Add 20 percent for V-8.
Add 20 percent for Cobra II.
Mach I, V-6						
3 dr	200	500	1100	1900	3500	5000

1977
Mustang II, V-6
2 dr	150	350	950	1350	2800	4000
3 dr 2 plus 2	150	350	950	1450	3000	4200
2 dr Ghia	150	400	1000	1600	3100	4400

NOTE: Deduct 10 percent for 4-cyl.
Add 20 percent for Corba II option.
Add 20 percent for V-8.
Mach I, V-6						
2 dr	200	500	1100	1900	3500	5000

1978
Mustang II
Cpe	150	350	950	1450	2900	4100
3 dr 2 plus 2	150	400	1000	1550	3050	4300
Cpe Ghia	150	400	1000	1600	3100	4400
Mach I, V-6						
Cpe	200	500	1100	1900	3500	5000

NOTE: Add 20 percent for V-8.
Add 20 percent for Cobra II option.
Add 50 percent for King Cobra option.

1979
Mustang, V-6
2 dr Sed	150	350	950	1450	3000	4200
3 dr Sed	150	400	1000	1550	3050	4300
2 dr Ghia Sed	150	400	1000	1650	3150	4500
3 dr Ghia Sed	150	450	1050	1700	3200	4600

1980
Mustang, 6-cyl.
2 dr Cpe	150	400	1000	1550	3050	4300
2 dr Hatch	150	400	1000	1600	3100	4400
2 dr Cpe Ghia	150	450	1050	1700	3200	4600
2 dr Hatch Ghia	150	450	1050	1750	3250	4700

NOTES: Deduct 11 percent for 4-cyl.
Add 25 percent for V-8.

1981
Mustang, 6-cyl.
2 dr Cpe S	150	400	1000	1600	3100	4400
2 dr Cpe	150	450	1050	1700	3200	4600
2 dr Hatch	150	450	1050	1750	3250	4700
2 dr Cpe Ghia	150	450	1050	1750	3250	4700
2 dr Hatch Ghia	150	450	1050	1800	3300	4800

NOTES: Deduct 11 percent for 4-cyl.
Add 25 percent for V-8.

1982
Mustang, 4-cyl.
2 dr Cpe L	150	350	950	1350	2800	4000
2 dr Cpe GL	150	350	950	1450	2900	4100
2 dr Cpe GLX	150	350	950	1450	3000	4200
2 dr Cpe GLX	150	400	1000	1600	3100	4400
2 dr Hatch GLX	150	400	1000	1650	3150	4500
Mustang, 6-cyl.						
2 dr Cpe L	150	400	1000	1600	3100	4400
2 dr Cpe GL	150	400	1000	1650	3150	4500
2 dr Hatch GL	150	450	1050	1700	3200	4600
2 dr Cpe GLX	150	450	1050	1800	3300	4800
2 dr Hatch GLX	200	500	1100	1850	3350	4900
Mustang, V-8						
2 dr Hatch GT	200	600	1200	2300	4000	5700

1983
Mustang, 4-cyl.
2 dr Cpe L	150	350	950	1450	2900	4100
2 dr Cpe GL	150	350	950	1450	3000	4200
2 dr Hatch GL	150	400	1000	1600	3100	4400
2 dr Cpe GLX	150	400	1000	1650	3150	4500
2 dr Hatch GLX	150	450	1050	1700	3200	4600

	6	5	4	3	2	1
Mustang, 6-cyl.						
2 dr Cpe GL	150	450	1050	1700	3200	4600
2 dr Hatch GL	150	450	1050	1750	3250	4700
2 dr Cpe GLX	200	500	1100	1850	3350	4900
2 dr Hatch GLX	200	500	1100	1900	3500	5000
2 dr Conv GLX	200	650	1250	2400	4200	6000
Mustang, V-8						
2 dr Hatch GT	350	750	1450	3300	4900	7000
2 dr Conv GT	350	825	1600	4000	5600	8000
1984						
Mustang, 4-cyl.						
2 dr Cpe L	150	350	950	1450	3000	4200
2 dr Hatch L	150	400	1000	1550	3050	4300
2 dr Cpe LX	150	400	1000	1550	3050	4300
2 dr Hatch LX	150	400	1000	1600	3100	4400
2 dr Hatch GT Turbo	150	450	1050	1800	3300	4800
2 dr Conv GT Turbo	350	700	1350	2800	4550	6500
Mustang, V-6						
2 dr Cpe L	150	400	1000	1550	3050	4300
2 dr Hatch L	150	400	1000	1600	3100	4400
2 dr Cpe LX	150	400	1000	1600	3100	4400
2 dr Hatch LX	150	400	1000	1650	3150	4500
2 dr Conv LX	350	725	1400	3100	4800	6800
Mustang, V-8						
2 dr Hatch L	150	400	1000	1650	3150	4500
2 dr Cpe LX	150	450	1050	1700	3200	4600
2 dr Hatch LX	150	450	1050	1700	3200	4600
2 dr Conv LX	350	750	1450	3300	4900	7000
2 dr Hatch GT	150	450	1050	1800	3300	4800
2 dr Conv GT	350	750	1450	3500	5050	7200

NOTE: Add 30 percent for 20th Anniversary Edition.
Add 40 percent for SVO Model.

EDSEL

1958	6	5	4	3	2	1
Ranger Series, V-8, 118" wb						
Sed	350	700	1350	2800	4550	6500
4 dr HdTp	350	825	1600	4000	5600	8000
2 dr Sed	350	700	1350	2800	4550	6500
2 dr HdTp	400	1300	2200	4400	7700	11,000
Pacer Series, V-8, 118" wb						
Sed	350	750	1450	3300	4900	7000
4 dr HdTp	350	875	1700	4250	5900	8500
2 dr HdTp	450	1450	2400	4800	8400	12,000
Conv	850	2650	4400	8800	15,400	22,000
Corsair Series, V-8, 124" wb						
4 dr HdTp	450	950	2100	4750	6650	9500
2 dr HdTp	500	1550	2600	5200	9100	13,000
Citation Series, V-8, 124" wb						
4 dr HdTp	400	1200	2000	4000	7000	10,000
2 dr HdTp	550	1700	2800	5600	9800	14,000
Conv	1050	3350	5600	11,200	19,600	28,000

NOTE: Deduct 5 percent for 6 cyl.

	6	5	4	3	2	1
Station Wagons, V-8						
4 dr Vill	350	875	1700	4250	5900	8500
4 dr Ber	450	900	1900	4500	6300	9000
4 dr 9P Vill	350	875	1700	4350	6050	8700
4 dr 9P Ber	450	925	2000	4600	6400	9200
2 dr Rdup	350	750	1450	3300	4900	7000
1959						
Ranger Series, V-8, 120" wb						
Sed	350	700	1350	2800	4550	6500
4 dr HdTp	350	750	1450	3300	4900	7000
2 dr Sed	350	700	1350	2800	4550	6500
2 dr HdTp	400	1300	2200	4400	7700	11,000
Corsair Series, V-8, 120" wb						
Sed	350	750	1450	3300	4900	7000
4 dr HdTp	350	775	1500	3750	5250	7500
2 dr HdTp	450	1450	2400	4800	8400	12,000
Conv	800	2500	4200	8400	14,700	21,000
Station Wagons, V-8, 118" wb						
Vill	350	775	1500	3750	5250	7500
9P Vill	350	825	1600	4000	5600	8000

NOTE: Deduct 5 percent for 6 cyl.

	6	5	4	3	2	1
1960						
Ranger Series, V-8, 120" wb						
Sed	350	700	1350	2800	4550	6500
4 dr HdTp	350	775	1500	3750	5250	7500
2 dr Sed	350	700	1350	2800	4550	6500
2 dr HdTp	550	1700	2800	5600	9800	14,000
Conv	950	3000	5000	10,000	17,500	25,000
Station Wagons, V-8, 120" wb						
9P Vill	350	850	1650	4100	5700	8200
6P Vill	350	825	1600	4000	5600	8000

NOTE: Deduct 5 percent for 6 cyl.

LINCOLN

1920	6	5	4	3	2	1
Lincoln, V-8, 130" - 136" wb						
3P Rds	1700	5400	9000	18,000	31,500	45,000
5P Phae	1800	5750	9600	19,200	33,600	48,000
7P Tr	1750	5500	9200	18,400	32,200	46,000
4P Cpe	1250	4000	6700	13,400	23,500	33,500
5P Sed	1200	3900	6500	13,000	22,800	32,500
Sub Sed	1200	3900	6500	13,000	22,800	32,500
7P TwnC	1300	4150	6900	13,800	24,200	34,500
1921						
Lincoln, V-8, 130" - 136" wb						
3P Rds	1650	5300	8800	17,600	30,800	44,000
5P Phae	1750	5500	9200	18,400	32,200	46,000
7P Tr	1700	5400	9000	18,000	31,500	45,000
4P Cpe	1250	4000	6700	13,400	23,500	33,500
4P Sed	1200	3800	6300	12,600	22,100	31,500
5P Sed	1200	3900	6500	13,000	22,800	32,500
Sub Sed	1200	3900	6500	13,000	22,800	32,500
TwnC	1300	4150	6900	13,800	24,200	34,500
1922						
Lincoln, V-8, 130" wb						
3P Rds	1750	5650	9400	18,800	32,900	47,000
5P Phae	1700	5400	9000	18,000	31,500	45,000
7P Tr	1650	5300	8800	17,600	30,800	44,000

	6	5	4	3	2	1
Conv Tr	1700	5400	9000	18,000	31,500	45,000
4P Cpe	1300	4150	6900	13,800	24,200	34,500
5P Sed	1250	4000	6700	13,400	23,500	33,500
Lincoln, V-8, 136" wb						
Spt Rds	1750	5500	9200	18,400	32,200	46,000
DeL Phae	1750	5650	9400	18,800	32,900	47,000
DeL Tr	1700	5400	9000	18,000	31,500	45,000
Std Sed	1300	4150	6900	13,800	24,200	34,500
Jud Sed	1350	4250	7100	14,200	24,900	35,500
FW Sed	1350	4250	7100	14,200	24,900	35,500
York Sed	1350	4250	7100	14,200	24,900	35,500
4P Jud Sed	1350	4400	7300	14,600	25,600	36,500
7P Jud Limo	1450	4700	7800	15,600	27,300	39,000
Sub Limo	1550	4900	8200	16,400	28,700	41,000
TwnC	1600	5050	8400	16,800	29,400	42,000
FW Limo	1650	5300	8800	17,600	30,800	44,000
Std Limo	1600	5050	8400	16,800	29,400	42,000
FW Cabr	1850	5900	9800	19,600	34,300	49,000
FW Coll Cabr	2050	6500	10,800	21,600	37,800	54,000
FW Lan'let	1650	5300	8800	17,600	30,800	44,000
FW TwnC	1750	5500	9200	18,400	32,200	46,000
Holbrk Cabr	1850	5900	9800	19,600	34,300	49,000
Brn TwnC	1650	5300	8800	17,600	30,800	44,000
Brn OD Limo	1750	5500	9200	18,400	32,200	46,000
1923						
Model L, V-8						
Tr	1650	5300	8800	17,600	30,800	44,000
Phae	1700	5400	9000	18,000	31,500	45,000
Rds	1650	5300	8800	17,600	30,800	44,000
Cpe	1350	4400	7300	14,600	25,600	36,500
5P Sed	1350	4250	7100	14,200	24,900	35,500
7P Sed	1350	4400	7300	14,600	25,600	36,500
Limo	1550	4900	8200	16,400	28,700	41,000
OD Limo	1600	5050	8400	16,800	29,400	42,000
TwnC	1600	5150	8600	17,200	30,100	43,000
4P Sed	1300	4150	6900	13,800	24,200	34,500
Berl	1350	4250	7100	14,200	24,900	35,500
FW Cabr	1600	5150	8600	17,200	30,100	43,000
FW Limo	1600	5050	8400	16,800	29,400	42,000
FW TwnC	1600	5150	8600	17,200	30,100	43,000
Jud Cpe	1350	4400	7300	14,600	25,600	36,500
Brn TwnC	1600	5150	8600	17,200	30,100	43,000
Brn OD Limo	1650	5300	8800	17,600	30,800	44,000
Jud 2W Berl	1350	4400	7300	14,600	25,600	36,500
Jud 3W Berl	1350	4400	7300	14,600	25,600	36,500
Holbrk Cabr	1850	5900	9800	19,600	34,300	49,000
1924						
V-8						
Tr	1650	5300	8800	17,600	30,800	44,000
Phae	1700	5400	9000	18,000	31,500	45,000
Rds	1750	5500	9200	18,400	32,200	46,000
Cpe	1400	4500	7500	15,000	26,300	37,500
5P Sed	1350	4250	7100	14,200	24,900	35,500
7P Sed	1300	4150	6900	13,800	24,200	34,500
Limo	1350	4400	7300	14,600	25,600	36,500
4P Sed	1300	4150	6900	13,800	24,200	34,500
TwnC	1450	4700	7800	15,600	27,300	39,000
Twn Limo	1500	4800	8000	16,000	28,000	40,000
FW Limo	1550	4900	8200	16,400	28,700	41,000
Jud Cpe	1350	4250	7100	14,200	24,900	35,500
Jud Berl	1350	4400	7300	14,600	25,600	36,500
Brn Cabr	1600	5150	8600	17,200	30,100	43,000
Brn Cpe	1350	4400	7300	14,600	25,600	36,500
Brn OD Limo	1550	4900	8200	16,400	28,700	41,000
Leb Sed	1600	5050	8400	16,800	29,400	42,000
1925						
Model L, V-8						
Tr	1750	5650	9400	18,800	32,900	47,000
Spt Tr	1900	6100	10,200	20,400	35,700	51,000
Phae	1800	5750	9600	19,200	33,600	48,000
Rds	1750	5650	9400	18,800	32,900	47,000
Cpe	1450	4550	7600	15,200	26,600	38,000
4P Sed	1250	4000	6700	13,400	23,500	33,500
5P Sed	1200	3900	6500	13,000	22,800	32,500
7P Sed	1200	3900	6500	13,000	22,800	32,500
Limo	1450	4550	7600	15,200	26,600	38,000
FW Limo	1450	4700	7800	15,600	27,300	39,000
Jud Cpe	1300	4150	6900	13,800	24,200	34,500
Jud Berl	1350	4250	7100	14,200	24,900	35,500
Brn Cabr	1800	5750	9600	19,200	33,600	48,000
FW Coll Clb Rds	1750	5650	9400	18,800	32,900	47,000
FW Sed	1600	5050	8400	16,800	29,400	42,000
FW Brgm	1600	5150	8600	17,200	30,100	43,000
FW Cabr	1750	5500	9200	18,400	32,200	46,000
Jud 3W Berl	1600	5150	8600	17,200	30,100	43,000
Jud 4P Cpe	1600	5150	8600	17,200	30,100	43,000
Jud Brgm	1600	5050	8400	16,800	29,400	42,000
Mur OD Limo	1750	5500	9200	18,400	32,200	46,000
Holbrk Brgm	1650	5300	8800	17,600	30,800	44,000
Holbrk Coll	1700	5400	9000	18,000	31,500	45,000
Brn OD Limo	1700	5400	9000	18,000	31,500	45,000
Brn Spt Phae	1900	6100	10,200	20,400	35,700	51,000
Brn Lan Sed	1700	5400	9000	18,000	31,500	45,000
Brn TwnC	1750	5500	9200	18,400	32,200	46,000
Brn Pan Brgm	1700	5400	9000	18,000	31,500	45,000
Hume Limo	1750	5650	9400	18,800	32,900	47,000
Hume Cpe	1600	5150	8600	17,200	30,100	43,000
5P Leb Sed	1750	5500	9200	18,400	32,200	46,000
4P Leb Sed	1650	5300	8800	17,600	30,800	44,000
Leb DC Phae	2500	7900	13,200	26,400	46,200	66,000
Leb Clb Rds	2050	6500	10,800	21,600	37,800	54,000
Leb Limo	1650	5300	8800	17,600	30,800	44,000
Leb Brgm	1700	5400	9000	18,000	31,500	45,000
Leb Twn Brgm	1750	5500	9200	18,400	32,200	46,000
Leb Cabr	1850	5900	9800	19,600	34,300	49,000
Leb Coll Spt Cabr	2050	6500	10,800	21,600	37,800	54,000
Lke Cabr	1950	6250	10,400	20,800	36,400	52,000
Dtrch Coll Cabr	2000	6350	10,600	21,200	37,100	53,000
1926						
Model L, V-8						
Tr	1900	6100	10,200	20,400	35,700	51,000
Spt Tr	2100	6700	11,200	22,400	39,200	56,000
Phae	2050	6500	10,800	21,600	37,800	54,000
Rds	1950	6250	10,400	20,800	36,400	52,000
Cpe	1250	4000	6700	13,400	23,500	33,500
4P Sed	1200	3900	6500	13,000	22,800	32,500
5P Sed	1200	3900	6500	13,000	22,800	32,500

	6	5	4	3	2	1
7P Sed	1200	3800	6300	12,600	22,100	31,500
Limo	1300	4150	6900	13,800	24,200	34,500
FW Limo	1350	4250	7100	14,200	24,900	35,500
Jud Cpe	1550	4900	8200	16,400	28,700	41,000
Jud Berl	1500	4800	8000	16,000	28,000	40,000
Brn Cabr	1900	6000	10,000	20,000	35,000	50,000
Holbrk Coll Cabr	1900	6100	10,200	20,400	35,700	51,000
Hume Limo	1500	4800	8000	16,000	28,000	40,000
W'by Limo	1500	4800	8000	16,000	28,000	40,000
W'by Lan'let	1550	4900	8200	16,400	28,700	41,000
Dtrch Sed	1450	4550	7600	15,200	26,600	38,000
Dtrch Coll Cabr	1950	6250	10,400	20,800	36,400	52,000
Dtrch Brgm	1600	5050	8400	16,800	29,400	42,000
Dtrch Cpe Rds	1900	6100	10,200	20,400	35,700	51,000
Jud 3W Berl	1450	4700	7800	15,600	27,300	39,000
Jud Brgm	1450	4550	7600	15,200	26,600	38,000
Brn Phae	1900	6000	10,000	20,000	35,000	50,000
Brn Sed	1400	4500	7500	15,000	26,300	37,500
Brn Brgm	1450	4550	7600	15,200	26,600	38,000
Brn Semi-Coll Cabr	1900	6000	10,000	20,000	35,000	50,000
Leb 2W Sed	1400	4500	7500	15,000	26,300	37,500
Leb 3W Sed	1400	4500	7500	15,000	26,300	37,500
Leb Cpe	1450	4700	7800	15,600	27,300	39,000
Leb Spt Cabr	1900	6100	10,200	20,400	35,700	51,000
Leb A-W Cabr	1850	5900	9800	19,600	34,300	49,000
Leb Limo	1550	4900	8200	16,400	28,700	41,000
Leb Clb Rds	1950	6250	10,400	20,800	36,400	52,000
Lke Rds	2050	6500	10,800	21,600	37,800	54,000
Lke Semi-Coll Cabr	1850	5900	9800	19,600	34,300	49,000
Lke Cabr	1950	6250	10,400	20,800	36,400	52,000
Leb Conv Phae	2050	6500	10,800	21,600	37,800	54,000
Leb Conv	2050	6500	10,800	21,600	37,800	54,000

1927

Model L, V-8

	6	5	4	3	2	1
Spt Rds	2700	8650	14,400	28,800	50,400	72,000
Spt Tr	2650	8400	14,000	28,000	49,000	70,000
Phae	2800	8900	14,800	29,600	51,800	74,000
Cpe	1450	4700	7800	15,600	27,300	39,000
2W Sed	1350	4400	7300	14,600	25,600	36,500
3W Sed	1350	4250	7100	14,200	24,900	35,500
Sed	1300	4150	6900	13,800	24,200	34,500
FW Limo	1600	5050	8400	16,800	29,400	42,000
Jud Cpe	1550	4900	8200	16,400	28,700	41,000
Brn Cabr	2650	8400	14,000	28,000	49,000	70,000
Holbrk Cabr	2800	8900	14,800	29,600	51,800	74,000
Brn Brgm	1900	6000	10,000	20,000	35,000	50,000
Dtrch Conv Sed	2850	9100	15,200	30,400	53,200	76,000
Dtrch Conv Vic	2850	9100	15,200	30,400	53,200	76,000
Brn Conv	2700	8650	14,400	28,800	50,400	72,000
Brn Semi-Coll Cabr	2800	8900	14,800	29,600	51,800	74,000
Holbrk Coll Cabr	2850	9100	15,200	30,400	53,200	76,000
Leb A-W Cabr	2850	9100	15,200	30,400	53,200	76,000
Leb A-W Brgm	2850	9100	15,200	30,400	53,200	76,000
W'by Semi-Coll Cabr	2800	8900	14,800	29,600	51,800	74,000
Jud Brgm	1900	6000	10,000	20,000	35,000	50,000
Clb Rds	2050	6500	10,800	21,600	37,800	54,000
Jud 2W Berl	1450	4700	7800	15,600	27,300	39,000
Jud 3W Berl	1450	4700	7800	15,600	27,300	39,000
7P E d Limo	1600	5150	8600	17,200	30,100	43,000
Leb Spt Cabr	2850	9100	15,200	30,400	53,200	76,000
W'by Lan'let	2650	8400	14,000	28,000	49,000	70,000
W'by Limo	1650	5300	8800	17,600	30,800	44,000
Leb Cpe	1600	5050	8400	16,800	29,400	42,000
Der Spt Sed	1550	4900	8200	16,400	28,700	41,000
Lke Conv Sed	2850	9100	15,200	30,400	53,200	76,000
Dtrch Cpe Rds	2800	8900	14,800	29,600	51,800	74,000
Dtrch Spt Phae	2850	9100	15,200	30,400	53,200	76,000

1928

Model L, V-8

	6	5	4	3	2	1
164 Spt Tr	3150	10,100	16,800	33,600	58,800	84,000
163 Lke Spt Phae	3300	10,550	17,600	35,200	61,600	88,000
151 Lke Spt Rds	3250	10,300	17,200	34,400	60,200	86,000
154 Clb Rds	3100	9850	16,400	32,800	57,400	82,000
156 Cpe	1800	5750	9600	19,200	33,600	48,000
144A 2W Sed	1700	5400	9000	18,000	31,500	45,000
144B Sed	1700	5400	9000	18,000	31,500	45,000
152 Sed	1650	5300	8800	17,600	30,800	44,000
147A Sed	1650	5300	8800	17,600	30,800	44,000
147B Limo	1800	5750	9600	19,200	33,600	48,000
161 Jud Berl	1900	6000	10,000	20,000	35,000	50,000
161C Jud Berl	1900	6000	10,000	20,000	35,000	50,000
Jud Cpe	2050	6500	10,800	21,600	37,800	54,000
159 Brn Cabr	3150	10,100	16,800	33,600	58,800	84,000
145 Brn Brgm	2650	8400	14,000	28,000	49,000	70,000
155A Hlbrk Coll Cabr	3300	10,550	17,600	35,200	61,600	88,000
155 Leb Spt Cabr	3700	11,750	19,600	39,200	68,600	98,000
157 W'by Lan'let Berl	3300	10,550	17,600	35,200	61,600	88,000
160 W'by Limo	3550	11,300	18,800	37,600	65,800	94,000
162A Leb A-W Cabr	3400	10,800	18,000	36,000	63,000	90,000
162 Leb A-W Lan'let	3250	10,300	17,200	34,400	60,200	86,000
Jud Spt Cpe	3000	9600	16,000	32,000	56,000	80,000
Leb Cpe	3150	10,100	16,800	33,600	58,800	84,000
Dtrch Conv Vic	3550	11,300	18,800	37,600	65,800	94,000
Dtrch Cpe Rds	3600	11,500	19,200	38,400	67,200	96,000
Dtrch Conv Sed	3700	11,750	19,600	39,200	68,600	98,000
Holbrk Cabr	3600	11,500	19,200	38,400	67,200	96,000
W'by Spt Sed	1750	5500	9200	18,400	32,200	46,000
Der Spt Sed	1750	5500	9200	18,400	32,200	46,000
Brn Spt Conv	3250	10,300	17,200	34,400	60,200	86,000

1929

Model L, V-8

Standard Line

	6	5	4	3	2	1
Lke Spt Rds	3550	11,300	18,800	37,600	65,800	94,000
Clb Rds	3450	11,050	18,400	36,800	64,400	92,000
Lke Spt Phae	4050	12,950	21,600	43,200	75,600	108,000
Lke TWS Spt Phae	4450	14,150	23,600	47,200	82,600	118,000
Lke Spt Phae TC & WS	4650	14,900	24,800	49,600	86,800	124,000
Lke Spt Tr	3900	12,500	20,800	41,600	72,800	104,000
Lke Clb Rds	4300	13,700	22,800	45,600	79,800	114,000
4P Cpe	1850	5900	9800	19,600	34,300	49,000
Twn Sed	1800	5750	9600	19,200	33,600	48,000
5P Sed	1750	5500	9200	18,400	32,200	46,000
7P Sed	1750	5650	9400	18,800	32,900	47,000
7P Limo	1900	6000	10,000	20,000	35,000	50,000
2W Jud Berl	1950	6250	10,400	20,800	36,400	52,000
3W Jud Berl	1900	6100	10,200	20,400	35,700	51,000
Brn A-W Brgm	3300	10,550	17,600	35,200	61,600	88,000
Brn Cabr	3450	11,050	18,400	36,800	64,400	92,000
Brn Non-Coll Cabr	3300	10,550	17,600	35,200	61,600	88,000
Holbrk Coll Cabr	3700	11,750	19,600	39,200	68,600	98,000
Leb A-W Cabr	4050	12,950	21,600	43,200	75,600	108,000
Leb Semi-Coll Cabr	3300	10,550	17,600	35,200	61,600	88,000
Leb Coll Cabr	3700	11,750	19,600	39,200	68,600	98,000
W'by Lan'let	2800	8900	14,800	29,600	51,800	74,000
W'by Limo	2650	8400	14,000	28,000	49,000	70,000
Dtrch Cpe	2400	7700	12,800	25,600	44,800	64,000
Dtrch Sed	2400	7700	12,800	25,600	44,800	64,000
Dtrch Conv	3550	11,300	18,800	37,600	65,800	94,000
Leb Spt Sed	2500	7900	13,200	26,400	46,200	66,000
Leb Aero Phae	3550	11,300	18,800	37,600	65,800	94,000
Leb Sal Cabr	3450	11,050	18,400	36,800	64,400	92,000
Brn Spt Conv	3550	11,300	18,800	37,600	65,800	94,000
Dtrch Conv Sed	3700	11,750	19,600	39,200	68,600	98,000
Dtrch Conv Vic	4050	12,950	21,600	43,200	75,600	108,000

1930

Model L, V-8

Standard Line

	6	5	4	3	2	1
Conv Rds	3550	11,300	18,800	37,600	65,800	94,000
5P Lke Spt Phae	4300	13,700	22,800	45,600	79,800	114,000
5P Lke Spt Phae TC & WS	4650	14,900	24,800	49,600	86,800	124,000
7P Lke Spt Phae	4050	12,950	21,600	43,200	75,600	108,000
Lke Rds	4300	13,700	22,800	45,600	79,800	114,000
4P Cpe	1850	5900	9800	19,600	34,300	49,000
Twn Sed	1800	5750	9600	19,200	33,600	48,000
5P Sed	1750	5650	9400	18,800	32,900	47,000
7P Sed	1750	5500	9200	18,400	32,200	46,000
7P Limo	2050	6500	10,800	21,600	37,800	54,000

Custom Line

	6	5	4	3	2	1
Jud Cpe	1950	6250	10,400	20,800	36,400	52,000
2W Jud Berl	2350	7450	12,400	24,800	43,400	62,000
3W Jud Berl	2350	7450	12,400	24,800	43,400	62,000
Brn A-W Cabr	2950	9350	15,600	31,200	54,600	78,000
Brn Non-Coll Cabr	2400	7700	12,800	25,600	44,800	64,000
Leb A-W Cabr	4050	12,950	21,600	43,200	75,600	108,000
Leb Semi-Coll Cabr	3550	11,300	18,800	37,600	65,800	94,000
W'by Limo	2350	7450	12,400	24,800	43,400	62,000
Dtrch Cpe	2100	6700	11,200	22,400	39,200	56,000
Dtrch Sed	2100	6700	11,200	22,400	39,200	56,000
2W W'by Twn Sed	2100	6700	11,200	22,400	39,200	56,000
3W W'by Twn Sed	2200	7100	11,800	23,600	41,300	59,000
W'by Pan Brgm	2400	7700	12,800	25,600	44,800	64,000
Leb Cpe	2100	6700	11,200	22,400	39,200	56,000
Leb Conv Rds	3550	11,300	18,800	37,600	65,800	94,000
Leb Spt Sed	2800	8900	14,800	29,600	51,800	74,000
Der Spt Conv	3600	11,500	19,200	38,400	67,200	96,000
Der Conv Phae	3700	11,750	19,600	39,200	68,600	98,000
Brn Semi-Coll Cabr	3550	11,300	18,800	37,600	65,800	94,000
Dtrch Conv Cpe	3700	11,750	19,600	39,200	68,600	98,000
Dtrch Conv Sed	4050	12,950	21,600	43,200	75,600	108,000
Wolf Conv Sed	4050	12,950	21,600	43,200	75,600	108,000

1931

Model K, V-8

Type 201, V-8, 145" wb

	6	5	4	3	2	1
202B Spt Phae	4650	14,900	24,800	49,600	86,800	124,000
202A Spt Phae	4800	15,350	25,600	51,200	89,600	128,000
203 Spt Tr	4450	14,150	23,600	47,200	82,600	118,000
214 Conv Rds	4300	13,700	22,800	45,600	79,800	114,000
206 Cpe	1650	5300	8800	17,600	30,800	44,000
204 Twn Sed	1600	5050	8400	16,800	29,400	42,000
205 Sed	1600	5150	8600	17,200	30,100	43,000
207A Sed	1600	5150	8600	17,200	30,100	43,000
207B Limo	1750	5500	9200	18,400	32,200	46,000
212 Conv Phae	4450	14,150	23,600	47,200	82,600	118,000
210 Conv Cpe	4300	13,700	22,800	45,600	79,800	114,000
211 Conv Sed	4450	14,150	23,600	47,200	82,600	118,000
216 W'by Pan Brgm	2350	7450	12,400	24,800	43,400	62,000
213A Jud Berl	2050	6500	10,800	21,600	37,800	54,000
213B Jud Berl	2050	6500	10,800	21,600	37,800	54,000
Jud Cpe	2000	6350	10,600	21,200	37,100	53,000
Brn Cabr	4300	13,700	22,800	45,600	79,800	114,000
Leb Cabr	4300	13,700	22,800	45,600	79,800	114,000
W'by Limo	2350	7450	12,400	24,800	43,400	62,000
Lke Spt Rds	4450	14,150	23,600	47,200	82,600	118,000
Der Conv Sed	4800	15,350	25,600	51,200	89,600	128,000
Leb Conv Rds	4650	14,900	24,800	49,600	86,800	124,000
Mur DC Phae	5050	16,100	26,800	53,600	93,800	134,000
Dtrch Conv Sed	5050	16,100	26,800	53,600	93,800	134,000
Dtrch Conv Cpe	4950	15,850	26,400	52,800	92,400	132,000
Wtrhs Conv Vic	5050	16,100	26,800	53,600	93,800	134,000

1932

Model KA, V-8, 8-cyl., 136" wb

	6	5	4	3	2	1
Rds	3900	12,500	20,800	41,600	72,800	104,000
Phae	4300	13,700	22,800	45,600	79,800	114,000
Twn Sed	1850	5900	9800	19,600	34,300	49,000
Sed	1750	5500	9200	18,400	32,200	46,000
Cpe	1900	6100	10,200	20,400	35,700	51,000
Vic	1900	6000	10,000	20,000	35,000	50,000
7P Sed	1850	5900	9800	19,600	34,300	49,000
Limo	2050	6500	10,800	21,600	37,800	54,000

Model KB, V-12

Standard, 12-cyl., 145" wb

	6	5	4	3	2	1
Phae	4450	14,150	23,600	47,200	82,600	118,000
Spt Phae	4650	14,900	24,800	49,600	86,800	124,000
Cpe	1950	6250	10,400	20,800	36,400	52,000
2W Tr Sed	1900	6000	10,000	20,000	35,000	50,000
3W Tr Sed	1800	5750	9600	19,200	33,600	48,000
5P Sed	1900	6100	10,200	20,400	35,700	51,000
7P Sed	1950	6250	10,400	20,800	36,400	52,000
Limo	2100	6700	11,200	22,400	39,200	56,000

Custom, 145" wb

	6	5	4	3	2	1
Leb Conv Cpe	5450	17,400	29,000	58,000	101,500	145,000
2P Dtrch Cpe	2650	8400	14,000	28,000	49,000	70,000
4P Dtrch Cpe	2500	7900	13,200	26,400	46,200	66,000
Jud Cpe	2700	8650	14,400	28,800	50,400	72,000
Jud Berl	2350	7450	12,400	24,800	43,400	62,000
W'by Limo	2400	7700	12,800	25,600	44,800	64,000
Wtrhs Conv Vic	5650	18,000	30,000	60,000	105,000	150,000
Dtrch Conv Sed	5800	18,600	31,000	62,000	108,500	155,000
W'by Twn Brgm	2950	9350	15,600	31,200	54,600	78,000
Brn Brgm	2850	9100	15,200	30,400	53,200	76,000
Brn Non-Coll Cabr	3300	10,550	17,600	35,200	61,600	88,000
Brn Semi-Coll Cabr	5050	16,100	26,800	53,600	93,800	134,000
Leb Twn Cabr	5650	18,000	30,000	60,000	105,000	150,000

	6	5	4	3	2	1
Dtrch Spt Berl	4300	13,700	22,800	45,600	79,800	114,000
5P Rlstn TwnC	5050	16,100	26,800	53,600	93,800	134,000
7P Rlstn TwnC	5050	16,100	26,800	53,600	93,800	134,000
Brn Phae	5800	18,600	31,000	62,000	108,500	155,000
Brn dbl-entry Spt Sed	3700	11,750	19,600	39,200	68,600	98,000
Brn A-W Brgm	5450	17,400	29,000	58,000	101,500	145,000
Brn Clb Sed	3300	10,550	17,600	35,200	61,600	88,000
Mur Conv Rds	7900	25,200	42,000	84,000	147,000	210,000
1933						
Model KA, V-12, 12-cyl., 136" wb						
512B Cpe	1900	6100	10,200	20,400	35,700	51,000
512A RS Cpe	2050	6500	10,800	21,600	37,800	54,000
513A Conv Rds	4050	12,950	21,600	43,200	75,600	108,000
514 Twn Sed	1700	5400	9000	18,000	31,500	45,000
515 Sed	1650	5300	8800	17,600	30,800	44,000
516 Cpe	1950	6250	10,400	20,800	36,400	52,000
517 Sed	1650	5300	8800	17,600	30,800	44,000
517B Limo	1850	5900	9800	19,600	34,300	49,000
518A DC Phae	5650	18,000	30,000	60,000	105,000	150,000
518B Phae	5050	16,100	26,800	53,600	93,800	134,000
519 7P Tr	4800	15,350	25,600	51,200	89,600	128,000
520B RS Rds	4450	14,150	23,600	47,200	82,600	118,000
520A Rds	4300	13,700	22,800	45,600	79,800	114,000
Model KB, V-8						
12-cyl., 145" wb						
252A DC Phae	5800	18,600	31,000	62,000	108,500	155,000
252B Phae	5650	18,000	30,000	60,000	105,000	150,000
253 7P Tr	5650	18,000	30,000	60,000	105,000	150,000
Twn Sed	1850	5900	9800	19,600	34,300	49,000
255 5P Sed	1900	6000	10,000	20,000	35,000	50,000
256 5P Cpe	2050	6500	10,800	21,600	37,800	54,000
257 7P Sed	1850	5900	9800	19,600	34,300	49,000
257B Limo	2100	6700	11,200	22,400	39,200	56,000
258C Brn Semi-Coll Cabr	5050	16,100	26,800	53,600	93,800	134,000
258d Brn Non-Coll Cabr	4450	14,150	23,600	47,200	82,600	118,000
259 Brn Brgm	2800	8900	14,800	29,600	51,800	74,000
260 Brn Conv Cpe	7900	25,200	42,000	84,000	147,000	210,000
Dtrch Conv Sed	8050	25,800	43,000	86,000	150,500	215,000
2P Dtrch Cpe	2800	8900	14,800	29,600	51,800	74,000
4P Dtrch Cpe	2800	8900	14,800	29,600	51,800	74,000
Jud Berl	2350	7450	12,400	24,800	43,400	62,000
2P Jud Cpe	2500	7900	13,200	26,400	46,200	66,000
4P Jud Cpe	2500	7900	13,200	26,400	46,200	66,000
Jud Limo	2650	8400	14,000	28,000	49,000	70,000
Leb Conv Rds	6550	21,000	35,000	70,000	122,500	175,000
W'by Limo	2650	8400	14,000	28,000	49,000	70,000
W'by Brgm	2800	8900	14,800	29,600	51,800	74,000
1934						
Series K, V-12						
12-cyl., 136" wb						
4P Conv Rds	4050	12,950	21,600	43,200	75,600	108,000
4P Twn Sed	1750	5500	9200	18,400	32,200	46,000
5P Sed	1700	5400	9000	18,000	31,500	45,000
5P Cpe	2050	6500	10,800	21,600	37,800	54,000
7P Sed	1800	5750	9600	19,200	33,600	48,000
7P Limo	2100	6700	11,200	22,400	39,200	56,000
2P Cpe	2100	6700	11,200	22,400	39,200	56,000
5P Conv Phae	4800	15,350	25,600	51,200	89,600	128,000
4P Cpe	1850	5900	9800	19,600	34,300	49,000
V-12, 145" wb						
Tr	3700	11,750	19,600	39,200	68,600	98,000
Sed	1900	6000	10,000	20,000	35,000	50,000
Limo	2050	6500	10,800	21,600	37,800	54,000
2W Jud Berl	2400	7700	12,800	25,600	44,800	64,000
3W Jud Berl	2350	7450	12,400	24,800	43,400	62,000
Jud Sed Limo	2100	6700	11,200	22,400	39,200	56,000
Brn Brgm	2350	7450	12,400	24,800	43,400	62,000
Brn Semi-Coll Cabr	3150	10,100	16,800	33,600	58,800	84,000
Brn Conv Cpe	5050	16,100	26,800	53,600	93,800	134,000
W'by Limo	2050	6500	10,800	21,600	37,800	54,000
Leb Rds	5050	16,100	26,800	53,600	93,800	134,000
Dtrch Conv Sed	5450	17,400	29,000	58,000	101,500	145,000
Brn Conv Vic	5450	17,400	29,000	58,000	101,500	145,000
Leb Cpe	2350	7450	12,400	24,800	43,400	62,000
Dtrch Conv Rds	5050	16,100	26,800	53,600	93,800	134,000
W'by Spt Sed	2050	6500	10,800	21,600	37,800	54,000
Leb Conv Cpe	5050	16,100	26,800	53,600	93,800	134,000
Brn Conv Sed	5450	17,400	29,000	58,000	101,500	145,000
Brn Cus Phae	5450	17,400	29,000	58,000	101,500	145,000
Brwstr Non-Coll Cabr	3900	12,500	20,800	41,600	72,800	104,000
1935						
Series K, V-12						
V-12, 136" wb						
Leb Conv Rds	4500	14,400	24,000	48,000	84,000	120,000
Leb Cpe	2050	6500	10,800	21,600	37,800	54,000
Cpe	1950	6250	10,400	20,800	36,400	52,000
Brn Conv Vic	4650	14,900	24,800	49,600	86,800	124,000
2W Sed	1750	5500	9200	18,400	32,200	46,000
3W Sed	1700	5400	9000	18,000	31,500	45,000
Leb Conv Phae	4800	15,350	25,600	51,200	89,600	128,000
V-12, 145" wb						
7P Tr	4450	14,150	23,600	47,200	82,600	118,000
7P Sed	1750	5650	9400	18,800	32,900	47,000
7P Limo	2050	6500	10,800	21,600	37,800	54,000
Leb Conv Sed	5050	16,100	26,800	53,600	93,800	134,000
Brn Semi-Coll Cabr	3700	11,750	19,600	39,200	68,600	98,000
Brn Non-Coll Cabr	3550	11,300	18,800	37,600	65,800	94,000
Brn Brgm	2050	6500	10,800	21,600	37,800	54,000
W'by Limo	2100	6700	11,200	22,400	39,200	56,000
W'by Spt Sed	2050	6500	10,800	21,600	37,800	54,000
2W Jud Berl	2100	6700	11,200	22,400	39,200	56,000
3W Jud Berl	2050	6500	10,800	21,600	37,800	54,000
Jud Sed Limo	2200	7100	11,800	23,600	41,300	59,000
1936						
Zephyr, V-12, 122" wb						
4 dr Sed	1000	3200	5300	10,600	18,600	26,500
2 dr Sed	1050	3300	5500	11,000	19,300	27,500
12-cyl., 136" wb						
Leb Rds Cabr	3300	10,550	17,600	35,200	61,600	88,000
2P Leb Cpe	1650	5300	8800	17,600	30,800	44,000
5P Cpe	1600	5050	8400	16,800	29,400	42,000
Brn Conv Vic	3550	11,300	18,800	37,600	65,800	94,000
2W Sed	1350	4250	7100	14,200	24,900	35,500
3W Sed	1300	4150	6900	13,800	24,200	34,500
Leb Conv Sed	3700	11,750	19,600	39,200	68,600	98,000
V-12, 145" wb						
7P Tr	3700	11,750	19,600	39,200	68,600	98,000
7P Sed	1650	5300	8800	17,600	30,800	44,000
7P Limo	1850	5900	9800	19,600	34,300	49,000
Leb Conv Sed W/part	3900	12,500	20,800	41,600	72,800	104,000
Brn Semi-Coll Cabr	3550	11,300	18,800	37,600	65,800	94,000
Brn Non-Coll Cabr	2800	8900	14,800	29,600	51,800	74,000
Brn Brgm	1750	5650	9400	18,800	32,900	47,000
W'by Limo	1900	6100	10,200	20,400	35,700	51,000
W'by Spt Sed	1800	5750	9600	19,200	33,600	48,000
Jud 2W Berl	1900	6000	10,000	20,000	35,000	50,000
Jud 3W Berl	1900	6100	10,200	20,400	35,700	51,000
Jud Limo	1950	6250	10,400	20,800	36,400	52,000
1937						
Zephyr, V-12						
3P Cpe	1050	3400	5700	11,400	20,000	28,500
2 dr Sed	950	3050	5100	10,200	17,900	25,500
4 dr Sed	900	2950	4900	9800	17,200	24,500
Twn Sed	950	3050	5100	10,200	17,900	25,500
Conv Sed	1850	5900	9800	19,600	34,300	49,000
Series K, V-12						
V-12, 136" wb						
Leb Conv Rds	3150	10,100	16,800	33,600	58,800	84,000
Leb Cpe	1650	5300	8800	17,600	30,800	44,000
W'by Cpe	1750	5500	9200	18,400	32,200	46,000
Brn Conv Vic	3300	10,550	17,600	35,200	61,600	88,000
2W Sed	1350	4400	7300	14,600	25,600	36,500
3W Sed	1350	4250	7100	14,200	24,900	35,500
V-12, 145" wb						
7P Sed	1500	4800	8000	16,000	28,000	40,000
7P Limo	1600	5050	8400	16,800	29,400	42,000
Leb Conv Sed	3400	10,800	18,000	36,000	63,000	90,000
Leb Conv Sed W/part	3550	11,300	18,800	37,600	65,800	94,000
Brn Semi-Coll Cabr	3150	10,100	16,800	33,600	58,800	84,000
Brn Non-Coll Cabr	2500	7900	13,200	26,400	46,200	66,000
Brn Brgm	1900	6100	10,200	20,400	35,700	51,000
Brn Tr Cabr	3300	10,550	17,600	35,200	61,600	88,000
Jud 2W Berl	1850	5900	9800	19,600	34,300	49,000
Jud 3W Berl	1850	5900	9800	19,600	34,300	49,000
Jud Limo	2050	6500	10,800	21,600	37,800	54,000
W'by Tr	2350	7450	12,400	24,800	43,400	62,000
W'by Limo	2050	6500	10,800	21,600	37,800	54,000
W'by Spt Sed	1850	5900	9800	19,600	34,300	49,000
W'by Cpe	1900	6100	10,200	20,400	35,700	51,000
W'by Pan Brgm	1950	6250	10,400	20,800	36,400	52,000
Jud Cpe	1900	6100	10,200	20,400	35,700	51,000
1938						
Zephyr, V-12						
3P Cpe	1100	3550	5900	11,800	20,700	29,500
3P Conv Cpe	1650	5300	8800	17,600	30,800	44,000
4 dr Sed	750	2350	3900	7800	13,700	19,500
2 dr Sed	750	2450	4100	8200	14,400	20,500
Conv Sed	1850	5900	9800	19,600	34,300	49,000
Twn Sed	850	2700	4500	9000	15,800	22,500
Series K, V-12						
V-12, 136" wb						
Leb Conv Rds	3150	10,100	16,800	33,600	58,800	84,000
Leb Cpe	1600	5050	8400	16,800	29,400	42,000
W'by Cpe	1600	5150	8600	17,200	30,100	43,000
2W Sed	1350	4400	7300	14,600	25,600	36,500
3W Sed	1350	4250	7100	14,200	24,900	35,500
Brn Conv Vic	3250	10,300	17,200	34,400	60,200	86,000
V-12, 145" wb						
7P Sed	1450	4550	7600	15,200	26,600	38,000
Sed Limo	1450	4700	7800	15,600	27,300	39,000
Leb Conv Sed	3550	11,300	18,800	37,600	65,800	94,000
Leb Conv Sed W/part	3700	11,750	19,600	39,200	68,600	98,000
Jud 2W Berl	1500	4800	8000	16,000	28,000	40,000
Jud 3W Berl	1550	4900	8200	16,400	28,700	41,000
Jud Limo	1650	5300	8800	17,600	30,800	44,000
Brn Tr Cabr	3600	11,500	19,200	38,400	67,200	96,000
W'by Tr	2350	7450	12,400	24,800	43,400	62,000
W'by Spt Sed	1650	5300	8800	17,600	30,800	44,000
Brn Non-Coll Cabr	2200	7100	11,800	23,600	41,300	59,000
Brn Semi-Coll Cabr	3150	10,100	16,800	33,600	58,800	84,000
Brn Brgm	1650	5300	8800	17,600	30,800	44,000
W'by Pan Brgm	1700	5400	9000	18,000	31,500	45,000
W'by Limo	1650	5300	8800	17,600	30,800	44,000
1939						
Zephyr, V-12						
3P Cpe	1000	3250	5400	10,800	18,900	27,000
Conv Cpe	1750	5650	9400	18,800	32,900	47,000
2 dr Sed	800	2500	4200	8400	14,700	21,000
5P Sed	850	2650	4400	8800	15,400	22,000
Conv Sed	1950	6250	10,400	20,800	36,400	52,000
Twn Sed	850	2750	4600	9200	16,100	23,000
Series K, V-12						
V-12, 136" wb						
Leb Conv Rds	2800	8900	14,800	29,600	51,800	74,000
Leb Cpe	1700	5400	9000	18,000	31,500	45,000
W'by Cpe	1750	5500	9200	18,400	32,200	46,000
2W Sed	1550	4900	8200	16,400	28,700	41,000
3W Sed	1550	4900	8200	16,400	28,700	41,000
Brn Conv Vic	2800	8900	14,800	29,600	51,800	74,000
V-12, 145" wb						
Jud 2W Berl	1600	5150	8600	17,200	30,100	43,000
Jud 3W Berl	1600	5050	8400	16,800	29,400	42,000
Jud Limo	1700	5400	9000	18,000	31,500	45,000
Brn Tr Cabr	2400	7700	12,800	25,600	44,800	64,000
7P Sed	1600	5150	8600	17,200	30,100	43,000
7P Limo	1750	5500	9200	18,400	32,200	46,000
Leb Conv Sed	3550	11,300	18,800	37,600	65,800	94,000
Leb Conv Sed W/part	3700	11,750	19,600	39,200	68,600	98,000
W'by Spt Sed	1750	5650	9400	18,800	32,900	47,000
V-12, 145" wb, 6 wheels						
Brn Non-Coll Cabr	3150	10,100	16,800	33,600	58,800	84,000
Brn Semi-Coll Cabr	3550	11,300	18,800	37,600	65,800	94,000
Brn Brgm	1650	5300	8800	17,600	30,800	44,000
W'by Limo	1750	5650	9400	18,800	32,900	47,000
1940						
Zephyr, V-12						
3P Cpe	1000	3100	5200	10,400	18,200	26,000
OS Cpe	1000	3250	5400	10,800	18,900	27,000
Clb Cpe	1050	3350	5600	11,200	19,600	28,000
Conv Clb Cpe	1650	5300	8800	17,600	30,800	44,000
6P Sed	850	2650	4400	8800	15,400	22,000

	6	5	4	3	2	1
Twn Limo	1200	3850	6400	12,800	22,400	32,000
Cont Clb Cpe	1750	5650	9400	18,800	32,900	47,000
Cont Conv Cabr	2550	8150	13,600	27,200	47,600	68,000

Series K, V-12

Available on special request, black emblems rather than blue.

1941

Zephyr, V-12	6	5	4	3	2	1
3P Cpe	1000	3100	5200	10,400	18,200	26,000
OS Cpe	1000	3250	5400	10,800	18,900	27,000
Clb Cpe	1050	3350	5600	11,200	19,600	28,000
Conv Cpe	1650	5300	8800	17,600	30,800	44,000
Cont Cpe	1750	5650	9400	18,800	32,900	47,000
Cont Conv Cabr	2400	7700	12,800	25,600	44,800	64,000
6P Sed	850	2650	4400	8800	15,400	22,000
Cus Sed	850	2750	4600	9200	16,100	23,000
8P Limo	1100	3500	5800	11,600	20,300	29,000

1942

Zephyr, V-12	6	5	4	3	2	1
3P Cpe	550	1800	3000	6000	10,500	15,000
Clb Cpe	600	1900	3200	6400	11,200	16,000
Conv Clb Cpe	1700	5400	9000	18,000	31,500	45,000
Cont Cpe	1750	5650	9400	18,800	32,900	47,000
Cont Conv Cabr	2150	6850	11,400	22,800	39,900	57,000
6P Sed	500	1550	2600	5200	9100	13,000
Cus Sed	550	1700	2800	5600	9800	14,000
8P Limo	1000	3250	5400	10,800	18,900	27,000

1946

V-12, 125" wb	6	5	4	3	2	1
Clb Cpe	550	1800	3000	6000	10,500	15,000
Conv	1600	5050	8400	16,800	29,400	42,000
4 dr Sed	500	1550	2600	5200	9100	13,000
Cont Cpe	1500	4800	8000	16,000	28,000	40,000
Cont Conv	1950	6250	10,400	20,800	36,400	52,000

1947

V-12, 125" wb	6	5	4	3	2	1
Clb Cpe	550	1800	3000	6000	10,500	15,000
Conv	1600	5050	8400	16,800	29,400	42,000
4 dr Sed	500	1550	2600	5200	9100	13,000
Cont Cpe	1500	4800	8000	16,000	28,000	40,000
Cont Conv	1950	6250	10,400	20,800	36,400	52,000

1948

8th Series, V-12, 125" wb	6	5	4	3	2	1
Clb Cpe	550	1800	3000	6000	10,500	15,000
Conv	1600	5050	8400	16,800	29,400	42,000
4 dr Sed	500	1550	2600	5200	9100	13,000
Cont Cpe	1500	4800	8000	16,000	28,000	40,000
Cont Conv	1950	6250	10,400	20,800	36,400	52,000

1949

Model 9-EL, V-8, 121" wb	6	5	4	3	2	1
Spt Sed	400	1200	2000	4000	7000	10,000
Cpe	400	1300	2200	4400	7700	11,000
Conv	750	2400	4000	8000	14,000	20,000
Cosmopolitan, V-8, 125" wb						
Twn Sed	400	1300	2200	4400	7700	11,000
Spt Sed	450	1400	2300	4600	8100	11,500
Cpe	450	1450	2400	4800	8400	12,000
Conv	1050	3350	5600	11,200	19,600	28,000

1950

Model OEL, V-8, 121" wb	6	5	4	3	2	1
Spt Sed	400	1200	2000	4000	7000	10,000
Cpe	400	1300	2200	4400	7700	11,000
Lido Cpe	550	1700	2800	5600	9800	14,000
Cosmopolitan, V-8, 125" wb						
Spt Sed	400	1300	2200	4400	7700	11,000
Cpe	450	1450	2400	4800	8400	12,000
Capri	550	1700	2800	5600	9800	14,000
Conv	1000	3250	5400	10,800	18,900	27,000

1951

Model Del, V-8, 121" wb	6	5	4	3	2	1
Spt Sed	400	1200	2000	4000	7000	10,000
Cpe	450	1450	2400	4800	8400	12,000
Lido Cpe	550	1700	2800	5600	9800	14,000
Cosmopolitan, V-8, 125" wb						
Spt Sed	400	1300	2200	4400	7700	11,000
Cpe	500	1550	2600	5200	9100	13,000
Capri	550	1800	3000	6000	10,500	15,000
Conv	1050	3350	5600	11,200	19,600	28,000

1952

Model 2H, V-8, 123" wb	6	5	4	3	2	1
Cosmopolitan						
4 dr Sed	400	1200	2000	4000	7000	10,000
2 dr HdTp	550	1700	2800	5600	9800	14,000
Capri, V-8, 123" wb						
4 dr Sed	400	1300	2200	4400	7700	11,000
2 dr HdTp	550	1800	3000	6000	10,500	15,000
Conv	1050	3350	5600	11,200	19,600	28,000

1953

Model BH, V-8, 123" wb	6	5	4	3	2	1
Cosmopolitan						
4 dr Sed	400	1200	2000	4000	7000	10,000
2 dr HdTp	550	1700	2800	5600	9800	14,000
Capri, V-8, 123" wb						
4 dr Sed	400	1300	2200	4400	7700	11,000
2 dr HdTp	550	1800	3000	6000	10,500	15,000
2 dr Conv	1050	3350	5600	11.200	19,600	28,000

1954

V-8, 123" wb	6	5	4	3	2	1
4 dr Sed	450	975	2200	4850	6800	9700
2 dr HdTp	550	1700	2800	5600	9800	14,000
Capri, V-8, 123" wb						
4 dr Sed	400	1200	2000	4000	7000	10,000
2 dr HdTp	550	1800	3000	6000	10,500	15,000
Conv	1100	3500	5800	11,600	20,300	29,000

1955

V-8, 123" wb	6	5	4	3	2	1
4 dr Sed	400	1200	2000	4000	7000	10,000
HdTp	500	1550	2600	5200	9100	13,000
Capri, V-8, 123" wb						
4 dr Sed	400	1250	2100	4200	7400	10,500
2 dr HdTp	550	1700	2800	5600	9800	14,000
Conv	1000	3250	5400	10,800	18,900	27,000

1956

Capri, V-8, 126" wb	6	5	4	3	2	1
4 dr Sed	450	1450	2400	4800	8400	12,000
2 dr HdTp	600	1900	3200	6400	11,200	16,000
Premiere, V-8, 126" wb						
4 dr Sed	500	1550	2600	5200	9100	13,000
2 dr HdTp	700	2150	3600	7200	12,600	18,000
Conv	1150	3700	6200	12,400	21,700	31,000
Lincoln Continental Mark II, V-8, 126" wb						
2 dr HdTp	1200	3850	6400	12,800	22,400	32,000

1957

Capri, V-8, 126" wb	6	5	4	3	2	1
4 dr Sed	400	1250	2100	4200	7400	10,500
4 dr HdTp	400	1300	2200	4400	7700	11,000
2 dr HdTp	550	1700	2800	5600	9800	14,000
Premiere, V-8, 126" wb						
4 dr Sed	450	1400	2300	4600	8100	11,500
4 dr HdTp	450	1450	2400	4800	8400	12,000
2 dr HdTp	550	1800	3000	6000	10,500	15,000
Conv	1150	3700	6200	12,400	21,700	31,000
Lincoln Continental, V-8, 126" wb						
2 dr HdTp	1200	3850	6400	12,800	22,400	32,000

1958

Lincoln Capri, V-8, 131" wb	6	5	4	3	2	1
4 dr Sed	350	800	1550	3850	5400	7700
4 dr HdTp	350	800	1550	3900	5450	7800
2 dr HdTp	350	875	1700	4250	5900	8500
Lincoln Premiere, V-8, 131" wb						
4 dr Sed	350	825	1600	4000	5600	8000
4 dr HdTp	350	875	1700	4250	5900	8500
2 dr HdTp	400	1200	2000	4000	7000	10,000
Lincoln Continental Mark III, V-8, 131" wb						
4 dr Sed	450	950	2100	4750	6650	9500
4 dr HdTp	400	1200	2000	4000	7000	10,000
2 dr HdTp	500	1550	2600	5200	9100	13,000
Conv	1150	3600	6000	12,000	21,000	30,000

1959

Capri, V-8, 131" wb	6	5	4	3	2	1
4 dr Sed	350	825	1600	4000	5600	8000
4 dr HdTp	350	875	1700	4250	5900	8500
2 dr HdTp	400	1200	2000	4000	7000	10,000
Premiere, V-8, 131" wb						
4 dr Sed	350	875	1700	4250	5900	8500
4 dr HdTp	450	900	1900	4500	6300	9000
2 dr HdTp	400	1300	2200	4400	7700	11,000
Continental Mark IV, V-8, 131" wb						
4 dr Sed	400	1200	2000	4000	7000	10,000
4 dr HdTp	400	1250	2100	4200	7400	10,500
2 dr HdTp	550	1800	3000	6000	10,500	15,000
Conv	1150	3700	6200	12,400	21,700	31,000
TwnC	550	1700	2800	5600	9800	14,000
Limo	550	1800	3000	6000	10,500	15,000

1960

Lincoln, V-8, 131" wb	6	5	4	3	2	1
4 dr Sed	350	875	1700	4250	5900	8500
4 dr HdTp	450	900	1900	4500	6300	9000
2 dr HdTp	400	1300	2200	4400	7700	11,000
Premiere, V-8, 131" wb						
4 dr Sed	450	900	1900	4500	6300	9000
4 dr HdTp	450	950	2100	4750	6650	9500
2 dr HdTp	500	1550	2600	5200	9100	13,000
Continental Mark V, V-8, 131" wb						
4 dr Sed	400	1300	2200	4400	7700	11,000
4 dr HdTp	450	1450	2400	4800	8400	12,000
2 dr HdTp	550	1700	2800	5600	9800	14,000
Conv	1300	4100	6800	13,600	23,800	34,000
TwnC	550	1700	2800	5600	9800	14,000
Limo	550	1800	3000	6000	10,500	15,000

1961

Lincoln Continental, V-8, 123" wb	6	5	4	3	2	1
4 dr Sed	350	825	1600	4000	5600	8000
4 dr Conv	500	1550	2600	5200	9100	13,000

1962

Lincoln Continental, V-8, 123" wb	6	5	4	3	2	1
4 dr Sed	350	825	1600	4000	5600	8000
4 dr Conv	550	1700	2800	5600	9800	14.000

1963

Lincoln Continental, V-8, 123" wb	6	5	4	3	2	1
4 dr Sed	350	825	1600	4000	5600	8000
4 dr Conv	550	1700	2800	5600	9800	14,000
Exec Limo	450	1450	2400	4800	8400	12,000

1964

Lincoln Continental, V-8, 126" wb	6	5	4	3	2	1
4 dr Sed	350	825	1600	4000	5600	8000
4 dr Conv	550	1700	2800	5600	9800	14,000
Exec Limo	450	1450	2400	4800	8400	12,000

1965

Lincoln Continental, V-8, 126" wb	6	5	4	3	2	1
4 dr Sed	350	825	1600	4000	5600	8000
4 dr Conv	550	1700	2800	5600	9800	14,000
Exec Limo	450	1450	2400	4800	8400	12,000

1966

Lincoln Continental, V-8, 126" wb	6	5	4	3	2	1
4 dr Sed	350	825	1600	4000	5600	8000
2 dr HdTp	350	850	1650	4100	5700	8200
4 dr Conv	550	1700	2800	5600	9800	14,000

1967

Lincoln Continental, V-8, 126" wb	6	5	4	3	2	1
4 dr Sed	350	825	1600	4000	5600	8000
2 dr HdTp	350	850	1650	4100	5700	8200
4 dr Conv	550	1700	2800	5600	9800	14,000

1968

Lincoln Continental, V-8, 126" wb	6	5	4	3	2	1
4 dr Sed	350	825	1600	4000	5600	8000
2 dr HdTp	350	850	1650	4100	5700	8200
Continental Mark III, V-8, 117" wb						
2 dr HdTp	450	1450	2400	4800	8400	12,000

1969

Lincoln Continental, V-8, 126" wb	6	5	4	3	2	1
4 dr Sed	350	750	1450	3300	4900	7000
2 dr HdTp	350	775	1500	3750	5250	7500

Continental Mark III, V-8, 117" wb

	6	5	4	3	2	1
2 dr HdTp	450	1450	2400	4800	8400	12,000

1970
Lincoln Continental

	6	5	4	3	2	1
4 dr Sed	350	750	1450	3300	4900	7000
2 dr HdTp	350	775	1500	3750	5250	7500

Continental Mark III, V-8, 117" wb

2 dr HdTp	450	1450	2400	4800	8400	12,000

1971
Continental

4 dr Sed	350	700	1350	2800	4550	6500
2 dr	350	750	1450	3300	4900	7000

Mark III

2 dr	400	1300	2200	4400	7700	11,000

1972
Continental

4 dr Sed	350	700	1350	2900	4600	6600
2 dr	350	750	1450	3300	4900	7000

Mark IV

2 dr	400	1300	2200	4400	7700	11,000

1973
Continental V-8

2 dr HdTp	350	725	1400	3200	4850	6900
4 dr HdTp	350	700	1350	2700	4500	6400

Mark IV V-8

2 dr HdTp	400	1300	2200	4400	7700	11,000

1974
Continental, V-8

4 dr Sed	200	675	1300	2500	4350	6200
2 dr Cpe	350	725	1400	3100	4800	6800

Mark IV, V-8

2 dr HdTp	450	950	2100	4750	6650	9500

1975
Continental, V-8

4 dr Sed	200	675	1300	2500	4300	6100
2 dr Cpe	350	700	1350	2800	4550	6500

Mark IV, V-8

2 dr HdTp	450	900	1900	4500	6300	9000

1976
Continental, V-8

4 dr Sed	350	700	1350	2900	4600	6600
Cpe	350	725	1400	3100	4800	6800

Mark IV, V-8

Cpe	450	900	1900	4500	6300	9000

1977
Versailles, V-8

4 dr Sed	350	700	1350	2800	4550	6500

Continental, V-8

4 dr Sed	350	725	1400	3100	4800	6800
Cpe	350	750	1450	3300	4900	7000

Mark V, V-8

Cpe	450	900	1900	4500	6300	9000

1978
Versailles

4 dr Sed	200	650	1250	2400	4200	6000

Continental

4 dr Sed	150	450	1050	1750	3250	4700
Cpe	200	500	1100	1850	3350	4900

Mark V

Cpe	350	825	1600	4000	5600	8000

NOTE: Add 10 percent for Diamond Jubilee.
Add 5 percent for Collector Series.
Add 5 percent for Designer Series.

1979
Versailles, V-8

4 dr Sed	200	650	1250	2400	4200	6000

Continental, V-8

4 dr Sed	200	500	1100	1900	3500	5000
Cpe	200	550	1150	2000	3600	5200

Mark V, V-8

Cpe	350	775	1500	3750	5250	7500

NOTE: Add 5 percent for Collector Series.

1980
Versailles, V-8

4 dr Sed	200	675	1300	2500	4300	6100

Continental, V-8

4 dr Sed	200	650	1250	2400	4200	6000
2 dr Cpe	200	675	1300	2500	4350	6200

Mark VI, V-8

4 dr Sed	350	750	1450	3300	4900	7000
2 dr Cpe	350	750	1450	3500	5050	7200

1981
Town Car, V-8

4 dr Sed	200	650	1200	2300	4100	5800
2 dr Cpe	200	650	1250	2400	4150	5900

Mark VI

4 dr Sed	200	600	1200	2300	4000	5700
2 dr Cpe	200	650	1200	2300	4100	5800

1982
Town Car, V-8

4 dr Sed	350	700	1350	2800	4550	6500

Mark VI, V-8

4 dr Sed	200	675	1300	2500	4300	6100
2 dr Cpe	200	675	1300	2500	4350	6200

Continental, V-8

4 dr Sed	450	900	1900	4500	6300	9000

1983
Town Car, V-8

4 dr Sed	350	725	1400	3100	4800	6800

Mark VI, V-8

4 dr Sed	200	675	1300	2500	4300	6100
2 dr Cpe	200	675	1300	2500	4350	6200

Continental, V-8

4 dr Sed	450	900	1900	4500	6300	9000

1984
Town Car, V-8

4 dr Sed	350	725	1400	3200	4850	6900

Mark VII, V-8

2 dr Cpe	350	725	1400	3100	4800	6800

Continental, V-8

4 dr Sed	450	900	1900	4500	6300	9000

MERCURY

1939
Series 99A, V-8, 116" wb

	6	5	4	3	2	1
Conv	1150	3600	6000	12,000	21,000	30,000
Cpe	450	1500	2500	5000	8800	12,500
2 dr Sed	450	925	2000	4600	6400	9200
4 dr Sed	450	925	2000	4650	6500	9300

1940
Series O9A, V-8, 116" wb

Conv	1100	3500	5800	11,600	20,300	29,000
Conv Sed	1000	3250	5400	10,800	18,900	27,000
Cpe	450	1450	2400	4800	8400	12,000
2 dr Sed	450	925	2000	4650	6500	9300
4 dr Sed	450	950	2100	4700	6600	9400

1941
Series 19A, V-8, 118" wb

Conv	1050	3350	5600	11,200	19,600	28,000
Bus Cpe	450	900	1800	4400	6150	8800
5P Cpe	450	925	2000	4650	6500	9300
6P Cpe	450	975	2300	4900	6850	9800
2 dr Sed	450	900	1800	4400	6150	8800
4 dr Sed	450	900	1900	4500	6300	9000
Sta Wag	1100	3500	5800	11,600	20,300	29,000

1942
Series 29A, V-8, 118" wb

Conv	1000	3100	5200	10,400	18,200	26,000
Bus Cpe	450	975	2200	4850	6800	9700
6P Cpe	450	950	2200	4800	6700	9600
2 dr Sed	350	850	1650	4150	5800	8300
4 dr Sed	350	850	1650	4200	5850	8400
Sta Wag	1050	3350	5600	11,200	19,600	28,000

NOTE: Add 10 percent for liquamatic drive models.

1946
Series 69M, V-8, 118" wb

Conv	1000	3100	5200	10,400	18,200	26,000
6P Cpe	450	950	2100	4750	6650	9500
2 dr Sed	350	850	1650	4100	5700	8200
4 dr Sed	350	825	1600	4000	5600	8000
Sta Wag	1000	3250	5400	10,800	18,900	27,000
Sptsman Conv	2050	6600	11,000	22,000	38,500	55,000

1947
Series 79M, V-8, 118" wb

Conv	1000	3100	5200	10,400	18,200	26,000
6P Cpe	450	950	2100	4750	6650	9500
2 dr Sed	350	850	1650	4100	5700	8200
4 dr Sed	350	825	1600	4000	5600	8000
Sta Wag	1050	3350	5600	11,200	19,600	28,000
Sptsman Conv	2050	6600	11,000	22,000	38,500	55,000

1948
Series 89M, V-8, 118" wb

Conv	1000	3250	5400	10,800	18,900	27,000
Cpe	450	950	2100	4750	6650	9500
2 dr Sed	350	850	1650	4100	5700	8200
4 dr Sed	350	825	1600	4000	5600	8000
Sta Wag	1050	3350	5600	11,200	19,600	28,000

1949
Series 9CM, V-8, 118" wb

Conv	700	2300	3800	7600	13,300	19,000
Cpe	450	900	1900	4500	6300	9000
4 dr Sed	350	800	1550	3850	5400	7700
Sta Wag	800	2500	4200	8400	14,700	21,000

1950
Series OCM, V-8, 118" wb

Conv	750	2400	4000	8000	14,000	20,000
Cpe	450	900	1900	4500	6300	9000
Clb Cpe	450	925	1900	4550	6350	9100
Mon Cpe	450	975	2200	4850	6800	9700
4 dr Sed	350	800	1550	3900	5450	7800
Sta Wag	800	2500	4200	8400	14,700	21,000

1951
Mercury, V-8, 118" wb

4 dr Sed	350	775	1500	3750	5250	7500
Cpe	450	900	1900	4500	6300	9000
Conv	800	2500	4200	8400	14,700	21,000
Sta Wag	850	2650	4400	8800	15,400	22,000

Monterey, V-8, 118" wb

Clth Cpe	400	1300	2200	4400	7700	11,000
Lthr Cpe	450	1400	2300	4600	8100	11,500

1952
Mercury Custom, V-8, 118" wb

4 dr Sed	200	650	1250	2400	4200	6000
2 dr Sed	200	650	1250	2400	4150	5900
2 dr HdTp	400	1250	2100	4200	7400	10,500
Sta Wag	450	900	1900	4500	6300	9000

Mercury Monterey, V-8, 118" wb

4 dr Sed	350	750	1450	3300	4900	7000
2 dr HdTp	400	1300	2200	4400	7700	11,000
Conv	700	2300	3800	7600	13,300	19,000

1953
Mercury Custom, V-8, 118" wb

4 dr Sed	200	675	1300	2500	4300	6100
2 dr Sed	200	650	1250	2400	4200	6000
2 dr HdTp	400	1250	2100	4200	7400	10,500

Monterey Special Custom, V-8, 118" wb

4 dr Sed	350	750	1450	3400	5000	7100
2 dr HdTp	400	1300	2200	4400	7700	11,000
Conv	700	2300	3800	7600	13,300	19,000
Sta Wag	450	900	1900	4500	6300	9000

1954
Mercury Custom, V-8, 118" wb

4 dr Sed	350	700	1350	2700	4500	6400
2 dr Sed	200	675	1300	2600	4400	6300
2 dr HdTp	450	1450	2400	4800	8400	12,000

Monterey Special Custom, V-8, 118" wb

4 dr Sed	350	775	1500	3700	5200	7400
SV Cpe	700	2150	3600	7200	12,600	18,000
2 dr HdTp	500	1550	2600	5200	9100	13,000
Conv	800	2500	4200	8400	14,700	21,000
Sta Wag	400	1200	2000	4000	7000	10,000

NOTE: Overhead valve V-8 introduced.

1955
Custom Series, V-8, 119" wb

	6	5	4	3	2	1
4 dr Sed	350	700	1350	2700	4500	6400
2 dr Sed	200	675	1300	2600	4400	6300
2 dr HdTp	600	1900	3200	6400	11,200	16,000
Sta Wag	350	775	1500	3750	5250	7500
Monterey Series, V-8, 119" wb						
4 dr Sed	350	800	1550	3850	5400	7700
2 dr HdTp	650	2050	3400	6800	11,900	17,000
Sta Wag	350	825	1600	4000	5600	8000
Montclair Series, V-8, 119" wb						
4 dr Sed	350	875	1700	4250	5900	8500
2 dr HdTp	700	2300	3800	7600	13,300	19,000
2 dr HdTp SV	900	2900	4800	9600	16,800	24,000
Conv	1050	3350	5600	11,200	19,600	28,000

1956

	6	5	4	3	2	1
Medalist Series, V-8, 119" wb						
4 dr Sed	200	650	1250	2400	4200	6000
2 dr Sed	200	650	1250	2400	4150	5900
2 dr HdTp	450	1450	2400	4800	8400	12,000
Custom Series, V-8, 119" wb						
4 dr Sed	350	700	1350	2800	4550	6500
2 dr Sed	350	700	1350	2700	4500	6400
2 dr HdTp	550	1800	3000	6000	10,500	15,000
4 dr HdTp	400	1300	2200	4400	7700	11,000
Conv	1050	3350	5600	11,200	19,600	28,000
4 dr Sta Wag	350	775	1500	3750	5250	7500
2 dr Sta Wag	350	825	1600	4000	5600	8000
Monterey Series, V-8, 119" wb						
4 dr Sed	350	775	1500	3600	5100	7300
4 dr Spt Sed	350	775	1500	3750	5250	7500
2 dr HdTp	600	1900	3200	6400	11,200	16,000
4 dr HdTp	450	1400	2300	4600	8100	11,500
4 dr Sta Wag	350	875	1700	4250	5900	8500
Montclair Series, V-8, 119" wb						
4 dr Spt Sed	450	950	2100	4750	6650	9500
2 dr HdTp	700	2150	3600	7200	12,600	18,000
4 dr HdTp	450	1450	2400	4800	8400	12,000
Conv	1150	3600	6000	12,000	21,000	30,000

1957

	6	5	4	3	2	1
Monterey Series, V-8, 122" wb						
4 dr Sed	350	700	1350	2700	4500	6400
4 dr HdTp	350	825	1600	4000	5600	8000
2 dr Sed	200	675	1300	2600	4400	6300
2 dr HdTp	500	1550	2600	5200	9100	13,000
Conv	750	2400	4000	8000	14,000	20,000
Montclair Series, V-8, 122" wb						
4 dr Sed	350	700	1350	2800	4550	6500
4 dr HdTp	350	875	1700	4250	5900	8500
2 dr HdTp	600	1900	3200	6400	11,200	16,000
Conv	850	2650	4400	8800	15,400	22,000
Turnpike Cruiser, V-8, 122" wb						
4 dr HdTp	500	1550	2600	5200	9100	13,000
2 dr HdTp	700	2150	3600	7200	12,600	18,000
Conv	1000	3250	5400	10,800	18,900	27,000
Station Wagons, V-8, 122" wb						
Voy 2 dr HdTp	400	1250	2100	4200	7400	10,500
Voy 4 dr HdTp	400	1200	2000	4000	7000	10,000
Com 2 dr HdTp	400	1300	2200	4400	7700	11,000
Com 4 dr HdTp	400	1250	2100	4200	7400	10,500
Col Pk 4 dr HdTp	400	1300	2200	4400	7700	11,000

1958

	6	5	4	3	2	1
Mercury, V-8, 122" wb						
4 dr Sed	200	675	1300	2500	4300	6100
2 dr Sed	200	650	1250	2400	4200	6000
Monterey, V-8, 122" wb						
4 dr Sed	200	675	1300	2500	4350	6200
4 dr HdTp	350	725	1400	3100	4800	6800
2 dr Sed	200	675	1300	2500	4300	6100
2 dr HdTp	450	1450	2400	4800	8400	12,000
Conv	750	2400	4000	8000	14,000	20,000
Montclair, V-8, 122" wb						
4 dr Sed	200	675	1300	2600	4400	6300
4 dr HdTp	350	775	1500	3600	5100	7300
2 dr HdTp	500	1550	2600	5200	9100	13,000
Conv	750	2400	4000	8000	14,000	20,000
Turnpike Cruiser, V-8, 122" wb						
4 dr HdTp	450	1450	2400	4800	8400	12,000
2 dr HdTp	600	1900	3200	6400	11,200	16,000
Station Wagons, V-8, 122" wb						
Voy 2 dr HdTp	400	1250	2100	4200	7400	10,500
Voy 4 dr HdTp	400	1200	2000	4000	7000	10,000
Com 2 dr HdTp	450	1450	2400	4800	8400	12,000
Col Pk 4 dr HdTp	400	1300	2200	4400	7700	11,000
Com 4 dr HdTp	400	1250	2100	4200	7400	10,500
Parklane, V-8, 125" wb						
4 dr HdTp	450	1450	2400	4800	8400	12,000
2 dr HdTp	550	1800	3000	6000	10,500	15,000
Conv	850	2750	4600	9200	16,100	23,000

1959

	6	5	4	3	2	1
Monterey, V-8, 126" wb						
4 dr Sed	200	675	1300	2500	4350	6200
4 dr HdTp	350	750	1450	3300	4900	7000
2 dr Sed	200	675	1300	2500	4300	6100
2 dr HdTp	450	1450	2400	4800	8400	12,000
Conv	700	2150	3600	7200	12,600	18,000
Montclair, V-8, 126" wb						
4 dr Sed	350	700	1350	2700	4500	6400
4 dr HdTp	350	775	1500	3750	5250	7500
2 dr HdTp	500	1550	2600	5200	9100	13,000
Parklane, V-8, 128" wb						
4 dr HdTp	450	950	2100	4750	6650	9500
2 dr HdTp	550	1800	3000	6000	10,500	15,000
Conv	750	2400	4000	8000	14,000	20,000
Country Cruiser Station Wagons, V-8, 126" wb						
Com 2 dr HdTp	400	1200	2000	4000	7000	10,000
Com 4 dr HdTp	450	950	2100	4750	6650	9500
Voy 4 dr HdTp	400	1250	2100	4200	7400	10,500
Col Pk 4 dr HdTp	400	1300	2200	4400	7700	11,000

1960

	6	5	4	3	2	1
Comet, 6-cyl., 114" wb						
4 dr Sed	350	700	1350	2700	4500	6400
2 dr Sed	200	675	1300	2600	4400	6300
4 dr Sta Wag	200	675	1300	2500	4350	6200
2 dr Sta Wag	200	675	1300	2500	4350	6200
Monterey, V-8, 126" wb						
4 dr Sed	200	675	1300	2500	4300	6100
4 dr HdTp	350	775	1500	3750	5250	7500

	6	5	4	3	2	1
2 dr Sed	200	650	1250	2400	4200	6000
2 dr HdTp	450	900	1900	4500	6300	9000
Conv	650	2050	3400	6800	11,900	17,000
Country Cruiser Station Wagons, V-8, 126" wb						
Com 4 dr HdTp	350	875	1700	4250	5900	8500
Col Pk 4 dr HdTp	450	950	2100	4750	6650	9500
Montclair, V-8, 126" wb						
4 dr Sed	350	700	1350	2800	4550	6500
4 dr HdTp	350	825	1600	4000	5600	8000
2 dr HdTp	400	1300	2200	4400	7700	11,000
Parklane, V-8, 126" wb						
4 dr HdTp	350	875	1700	4250	5900	8500
2 dr HdTp	550	1700	2800	5600	9800	14,000
Conv	750	2400	4000	8000	14,000	20,000

1961

	6	5	4	3	2	1
Comet, 6-cyl., 114" wb						
4 dr Sed	200	550	1150	2100	3800	5400
2 dr Sed	200	550	1150	2100	3700	5300
S-22 Cpe	350	825	1600	4000	5600	8000
4 dr Sta Wag	200	550	1150	2100	3800	5400
2 dr Sta Wag	200	550	1150	2100	3700	5300
Meteor 600, V-8, 120" wb						
4 dr Sed	200	550	1150	2100	3700	5300
2 dr Sed	200	550	1150	2000	3600	5200
Meteor 800, V-8, 120" wb						
4 dr Sed	200	600	1200	2200	3850	5500
4 dr HdTp	200	600	1200	2200	3900	5600
2 dr Sed	200	550	1150	2100	3800	5400
2 dr HdTp	200	650	1250	2400	4200	6000
Monterey, V-8, 120" wb						
4 dr Sed	200	650	1250	2400	4150	5900
4 dr HdTp	200	650	1250	2400	4200	6000
2 dr HdTp	350	750	1450	3300	4900	7000
Conv	450	950	2100	4750	6650	9500
Station Wagon, V-8, 120" wb						
Col Pk	200	650	1200	2300	4100	5800
Com	200	600	1200	2300	4000	5700

1962

	6	5	4	3	2	1
Comet, 6-cyl.						
(Add 10 percent for Custom line)						
4 dr Sed	200	550	1150	2100	3800	5400
2 dr Sed	200	550	1150	2100	3700	5300
4 dr Sta Wag	200	550	1150	2100	3700	5300
2 dr Sta Wag	200	550	1150	2100	3800	5400
S-22 Cpe	350	825	1600	4000	5600	8000
Vill Sta Wag	200	600	1200	2200	3850	5500
Meteor, 8-cyl.						
(Deduct 10 percent for 6-cyl. Add 10 percent for Custom line).						
4 dr Sed	200	600	1200	2200	3850	5500
2 dr Sed	200	550	1150	2100	3800	5400
S-33 Cpe	350	750	1450	3300	4900	7000
Monterey, V-8						
(Add 10 percent for Custom line)						
4 dr Sed	200	600	1200	2200	3900	5600
4 dr HdTp Sed	200	600	1200	2300	4000	5700
2 dr Sed	200	550	1150	2100	3800	5400
2 dr HdTp	200	650	1250	2400	4200	6000
Sta Wag	200	600	1200	2200	3850	5500
Custom S-55 Sport Series, V-8						
2 dr HdTp	350	875	1700	4250	5900	8500
Conv	400	1300	2200	4400	7700	11,000

NOTE: Add 30 percent for 406.

1963

	6	5	4	3	2	1
Comet, 6-cyl.						
(Add 10 percent for Custom line)						
4 dr Sed	200	550	1150	2100	3800	5400
2 dr Sed	200	550	1150	2100	3700	5300
Cus HdTp	350	750	1450	3300	4900	7000
Cus Conv	450	900	1900	4500	6300	9000
S-22 Cpe	350	875	1700	4250	5900	8500
S-22 HdTp	450	900	1900	4500	6300	9000
S-22 Conv	400	1200	2000	4000	7000	10,000
4 dr Sta Wag	200	550	1150	2100	3700	5300
2 dr Sta Wag	200	550	1150	2100	3700	5300
Vill Sta Wag	200	600	1200	2300	4000	5700
Meteor, V-8						
(Deduct 10 percent for 6-cyl. Add 10 percent for Custom line).						
4 dr Sed	200	600	1200	2200	3850	5500
2 dr Sed	200	550	1150	2100	3800	5400
Sta Wag	200	550	1150	2100	3700	5300
Cus HdTp	200	650	1250	2400	4200	6000
S-33 HdTp	350	775	1500	3750	5250	7500
Monterey, V-8						
(Add 10 percent for Custom line)						
4 dr Sed	200	600	1200	2300	4000	5700
4 dr HdTp	200	650	1250	2400	4200	6000
2 dr Sed	200	600	1200	2200	3900	5600
2 dr HdTp	200	675	1300	2500	4300	6100
Cus Conv	350	750	1450	3500	5050	7200
S-55 2 dr HdTp	450	900	1900	4500	6300	9000
S-55 Conv	400	1300	2200	4400	7700	11,000
Maraud FsBk	350	825	1600	4000	5600	8000
Mar S-55 FsBk	450	950	2100	4750	6650	9500
Col Pk	200	650	1250	2400	4200	6000

NOTES: Add 30 percent for 406.
Add 40 percent for 427.

1964

	6	5	4	3	2	1
Comet, 6-cyl., 114" wb						
4 dr Sed	200	500	1100	1900	3500	5000
2 dr Sed	200	500	1100	1850	3350	4900
Sta Wag	150	450	1050	1800	3300	4800
Comet 404, 6-cyl., 114" wb						
4 dr Sed	200	500	1100	1950	3600	5100
2 dr Sed	200	500	1100	1900	3500	5000
2 dr HdTp	200	650	1250	2400	4200	6000
Conv	350	825	1600	4000	5600	8000
DeL Wag	150	450	1050	1800	3300	4800
Sta Wag	150	450	1050	1750	3250	4700
Comet Caliente, V-8 cyl., 114" wb						
4 dr Sed	200	550	1150	2000	3600	5200
2 dr HdTp	350	875	1700	4250	5900	8500
Conv	400	1200	2000	4000	7000	10,000
Comet Cyclone, V-8 cyl., 114" wb						
2 dr HdTp	400	1250	2100	4200	7400	10,500

NOTE: Deduct 25 percent for 6-cyl. Caliente.

	6	5	4	3	2	1
Monterey, V-8						
4 dr Sed	200	500	1100	1850	3350	4900

	6	5	4	3	2	1
4 dr HdTp	200	500	1100	1950	3600	5100
2 dr Sed	150	450	1050	1800	3300	4800
2 dr HdTp	200	550	1150	2100	3700	5300
FsBk	200	650	1200	2300	4100	5800
Conv	350	875	1700	4250	5900	8500
Montclair, V-8, 120" wb						
4 dr Sed	200	500	1100	1900	3500	5000
4 dr HdTp	200	550	1150	2100	3700	5300
2 dr HdTp	350	700	1350	2800	4550	6500
FsBk	350	750	1450	3300	4900	7000
Parklane, V-8, 120" wb						
4 dr Sed	200	550	1150	2000	3600	5200
4 dr HdTp	200	600	1200	2200	3850	5500
4 dr FsBk	200	650	1250	2400	4200	6000
2 dr FsBk	350	775	1500	3750	5250	7500
2 dr FsBk	350	875	1700	4250	5900	8500
Conv	400	1300	2200	4400	7700	11,000
Station Wagon, V-8, 120" wb						
Col Pk	200	550	1150	2100	3800	5400
Com	200	550	1150	2100	3700	5300

NOTES: Add 10 percent for Marauder.
Add 40 percent for 427 Super Marauder.

1965
Comet 202, V-8, 114" wb
(Deduct 20 percent for 6 cyl.)

	6	5	4	3	2	1
4 dr Sed	200	500	1100	1950	3600	5100
2 dr Sed	200	500	1100	1900	3500	5000
Sta Wag	200	500	1100	1950	3600	5100
Comet 404						
4 dr Sed	200	550	1150	2000	3600	5200
2 dr Sed	200	500	1100	1950	3600	5100
Vill Wag	200	550	1150	2000	3600	5200
Sta Wag	200	500	1100	1950	3600	5100
Comet Caliente, V-8, 114" wb						
(Deduct 20 percent for 6 cyl.)						
4 dr HdTp	200	550	1150	2100	3700	5300
2 dr HdTp	350	750	1450	3300	4900	7000
Conv	450	900	1900	4500	6300	9000
Comet Cyclone, V-8, 114" wb						
2 dr HdTp	400	1300	2200	4400	7700	11,000
Monterey, V-8, 123" wb						
4 dr Sed	200	600	1200	2200	3850	5500
4 dr HdTp	200	650	1200	2300	4100	5800
Brzwy	200	650	1250	2400	4150	5900
2 dr Sed	200	550	1150	2100	3800	5400
2 dr HdTp	200	650	1250	2400	4200	6000
Conv	450	950	2100	4750	6650	9500
Montclair, V-8, 123" wb						
Brzwy	200	675	1300	2500	4350	6200
4 dr HdTp	200	650	1250	2400	4200	6000
2 dr HdTp	350	700	1350	2800	4550	6500
Parklane, V-8, 123" wb						
Brzwy	350	700	1350	2800	4550	6500
4 dr HdTp	200	650	1250	2400	4200	6000
2 dr HdTp	350	750	1450	3300	4900	7000
Conv	450	950	2100	4750	6650	9500
Station Wagon, V-8, 119" wb						
Col Pk	200	600	1200	2200	3850	5500
Com	200	550	1150	2100	3800	5400

NOTE: Add 20 percent for 427 CI engine.

1966
Comet Capri, V8, 116" wb

	6	5	4	3	2	1
4 dr Sed	200	550	1150	2000	3600	5200
2 dr HdTp	200	650	1200	2300	4100	5800
Sta Wag	200	550	1150	2100	3700	5300
Comet Caliente, V8, 116" wb						
4 dr Sed	200	550	1150	2100	3700	5300
2 dr HdTp	350	825	1600	4000	5600	8000
Conv	450	900	1900	4500	6300	9000
Comet Cyclone, V8, 116" wb						
2 dr HdTp	350	875	1700	4250	5900	8500
Conv	400	1200	2000	4000	7000	10,000
Comet Cyclone GT/GTA, V8, 116" wb						
2 dr HdTp	400	1300	2200	4400	7700	11,000
Conv	500	1550	2600	5200	9100	13,000
Comet 202, V8, 116" wb						
4 dr Sed	200	500	1100	1900	3500	5000
2 dr Sed	200	550	1150	2000	3600	5200
Sta Wag	200	500	1100	1900	3500	5000
Monterey, V-8, 123" wb						
4 dr Sed	200	550	1150	2100	3700	5300
4 dr Brzwy Sed	200	600	1200	2200	3850	5500
4 dr HdTp	200	550	1150	2100	3700	5300
2 dr Sed	200	550	1150	2100	3700	5300
2 dr HdTp FsBk	200	650	1250	2400	4200	6000
Conv	350	775	1500	3750	5250	7500
Montclair, V-8, 123" wb						
4 dr Sed	200	550	1150	2100	3700	5300
4 dr HdTp	200	550	1150	2100	3800	5400
2 dr HdTp	200	600	1200	2200	3900	5600
Parklane, V-8, 123" wb						
4 dr Brzwy Sed	200	650	1250	2400	4200	6000
4 dr HdTp	200	600	1200	2200	3900	5600
2 dr HdTp	200	675	1300	2500	4350	6200
Conv	350	875	1700	4250	5900	8500
S-55, V-8, 123" wb						
2 dr HdTp	350	825	1600	4000	5600	8000
Conv	400	1200	2000	4000	7000	10,000
Station Wagons, V-8, 123" wb						
Comm	200	600	1200	2200	3850	5500
Col Pk	200	600	1200	2300	4000	5700

NOTE: Add 18 percent for 410 CI engine.
Add 40 percent for 428 CI engine.

1967
Comet 202, V-8, 116" wb

	6	5	4	3	2	1
2 dr Sed	200	550	1150	2100	3700	5300
4 dr Sed	200	550	1150	2100	3800	5400
Capri, V-8, 116" wb						
2 dr HdTp	200	600	1200	2300	4000	5700
4 dr Sdn	200	550	1150	2100	3700	5300
Caliante, V-8, 116" wb						
4 dr Sed	200	650	1200	2300	4100	5800
2 dr HdTp	350	775	1500	3750	5250	7500
Conv	450	950	2100	4750	6650	9500
Cyclone, V-8, 116" wb						
2 dr HdTp	400	1200	2000	4000	7000	10,000
Conv	450	1450	2400	4800	8400	12,000

Station Wagons, V-8, 113" wb	6	5	4	3	2	1
Voyager	200	550	1150	2100	3700	5300
Villager	200	550	1150	2100	3800	5400
Cougar, V-8, 11" wb						
2 dr HdTp	450	900	1900	4500	6300	9000
X-R7 HdTp	400	1200	2000	4000	7000	10,000
Monterey, V-8, 123" wb						
4 dr Sed	200	550	1150	2100	3700	5300
4 dr Brzwy	200	550	1150	2100	3800	5400
Conv	350	750	1450	3300	4900	7000
2 dr HdTp	200	600	1200	2200	3900	5600
4 dr HdTp	200	550	1150	2100	3800	5400
4 dr HdTp	200	550	1150	2100	3800	5400
Montclair, V-8, 123" wb						
4 dr Sed	200	550	1150	2100	3800	5400
4 dr Brzwy	200	600	1200	2200	3850	5500
2 dr HdTp	200	600	1200	2300	4000	5700
4 dr HdTp	200	600	1200	2200	3850	5500
Parklane, V-8, 123" wb						
4 dr Brzwy	200	600	1200	2200	3900	5600
Conv	350	875	1700	4250	5900	8500
2 dr HdTp	200	650	1200	2300	4100	5800
4 dr HdTp	200	650	1250	2400	4150	5900
Brougham, V-8, 123" wb						
4 dr Brzwy	200	650	1250	2400	4200	6000
4 dr HdTp	200	600	1200	2300	4000	5700
Marquis, V-8, 123" wb						
2 dr HdTp	350	700	1350	2800	4550	6500
Station Wagons, 119" wb						
Commuter	200	600	1200	2200	3850	5500
Col Park	200	600	1200	2300	4000	5700

NOTES: Add 10 percent for GT option.
Add 15 percent for S-55 performance package.
Add 40 percent for 427 C.I. engine.
Add 50 percent for 428 cubic inch V-8.

1968
Comet, V-8

	6	5	4	3	2	1
2 dr Hdtp	200	650	1250	2400	4200	6000
Montego, V-8						
4 dr Sed	150	350	950	1450	3000	4200
2 dr HdTp	150	400	1000	1650	3150	4500
Montego MX						
Sta Wag	150	400	1000	1550	3050	4300
Sed	150	400	1000	1550	3050	4300
2 dr HdTp	200	600	1200	2200	3850	5500
Conv	350	750	1450	3300	4900	7000
Cyclone, V-8						
Fsbk Cpe	450	900	1900	4500	6300	9000
2 dr HdTp	350	875	1700	4250	5900	8500
Cyclone GT 427, V-8						
Fsbk Cpe	750	2400	4000	8000	14,000	20,000
2 dr HdTp	700	2300	3800	7600	13,300	19,000
Cyclone GT 428, V-8						
Fsbk Cpe	550	1700	2800	5600	9800	14,000
Cougar, V-8						
HdTp Cpe	400	1200	2000	4000	7000	10,000
XR-7 Cpe	450	1450	2400	4800	8400	12,000

NOTE: Add 10 percent for GTE package.

Monterey, V-8

	6	5	4	3	2	1
4 dr Sed	150	400	1000	1550	3050	4300
Conv	350	825	1600	4000	5600	8000
2 dr HdTp	150	400	1000	1650	3150	4500
4 dr HdTp	150	400	1000	1550	3050	4300
Montclair, V-8						
4 dr Sed	150	400	1000	1600	3100	4400
2 dr HdTp	150	450	1050	1750	3250	4700
4 dr HdTp	150	400	1000	1650	3150	4500
Parklane, V-8						
4 dr Sed	150	400	1000	1650	3150	4500
Conv	450	950	2100	4750	6650	9500
2 dr HdTp	200	500	1100	1900	3500	5000
4 dr HdTp	150	450	1050	1800	3300	4800
Marquis, V-8						
2 dr HdTp	200	650	1250	2400	4200	6000
Station Wagons, V-8						
Commuter	150	400	1000	1650	3150	4500
Col Pk	150	450	1050	1750	3250	4700

NOTES: Deduct 5 percent for six-cylinder engine.
Add 5 percent for Brougham package.
Add 5 percent for 'yacht paneling'.
Add 40 percent for '427'.
Add 50 percent for 428.

1969
Comet, 6-cyl.

	6	5	4	3	2	1
2 dr HdTp	200	500	1100	1900	3500	5000
Montego, 6-cyl.						
Sed	150	300	900	1250	2650	3800
2 dr HdTp	150	350	950	1350	2800	4000
Montego MX, V8						
Sed	150	300	900	1350	2700	3900
2 dr HdTp	200	500	1100	1900	3500	5000
Conv	350	700	1350	2800	4550	6500
Sta Wag	150	300	900	1250	2650	3800
Cyclone, V-8						
2 dr HdTp	350	825	1600	4000	5600	8000
Cyclone CJ, V-8						
2 dr HdTp	450	900	1900	4500	6300	9000
Cougar, V-8						
2 dr HdTp	450	900	1900	4500	6300	9000
Conv	400	1250	2100	4200	7400	10,500
XR-7	400	1200	2000	4000	7000	10,000
XR-7 Conv	450	1400	2300	4600	8100	11,500

NOTE: Add 45 percent for Eliminator 428 V-8 option.

Monterey, V-8

	6	5	4	3	2	1
Sed	150	300	900	1250	2650	3800
4 dr HdTp	150	300	900	1350	2700	3900
2 dr HdTp	150	350	950	1450	3000	4200
Conv	200	600	1200	2200	3850	5500
Sta Wag	150	300	900	1250	2650	3800
Marauder, V-8						
2 dr HdTp	200	650	1250	2400	4200	6000
X-100 HdTp	350	825	1600	4000	5600	8000
Marquis, V-8						
Sed	150	300	900	1350	2700	3900
4 dr HdTp	150	350	950	1350	2800	4000
2 dr HdTp	150	400	1000	1650	3150	4500
Conv	350	775	1500	3750	5250	7500
Sta Wag	150	300	900	1350	2700	3900

Marquis Brgm, V-8	6	5	4	3	2	1
Sed	150	350	950	1350	2800	4000
4 dr HdTp	150	400	1000	1650	3150	4500
2 dr HdTp	200	500	1100	1900	3500	5000

NOTES: Add 10 percent for Montego/Comet V-8.
Add 15 percent for GT option.
Add 20 percent for GT Spoiler II.
Add 10 percent for bucket seats (except Cougar).
Add 10 percent for bench seats (Cougar only).
Add 40 percent for 'CJ' 428 V-8.
Add 50 percent for 429.

1970

Montego	6	5	4	3	2	1
4 dr	150	300	900	1350	2700	3900
2 dr	150	350	950	1350	2800	4000
Montego MX, V-8						
4 dr	150	400	1000	1550	3050	4300
2 dr HdTp	150	400	1000	1550	3050	4300
Sta Wag	150	350	950	1350	2800	4000
Montego MX Brgm, V-8						
4 dr	150	350	950	1450	3000	4200
4 dr HdTp	150	400	1000	1550	3050	4300
2 dr HdTp	150	450	1050	1800	3300	4800
Vill Sta Wag	150	350	950	1450	2900	4100
Cyclone, V-8						
2 dr HdTp	350	775	1500	3750	5250	7500
Cyclone GT, V-8						
2 dr HdTp	350	875	1700	4250	5900	8500
Cyclone Spoiler, V-8						
2 dr HdTp	450	950	2100	4750	6650	9500

NOTE: Add 40 percent for 429 V-8 GT and Spoiler.

Cougar, V-8	6	5	4	3	2	1
2 dr HdTp	350	875	1700	4250	5900	8500
Conv	400	1200	2000	4000	7000	10,000
Cougar XR-7, V-8						
2 dr HdTp	450	950	2100	4750	6650	9500
Conv	450	1400	2300	4600	8100	11,500

NOTE: Add 45 percent for Eliminator 428 V-8 option.

Monterey, V-8	6	5	4	3	2	1
4 dr	150	300	900	1350	2700	3900
4 dr HdTp	150	350	950	1350	2800	4000
2 dr HdTp	150	350	950	1450	2900	4100
Conv	350	700	1350	2800	4550	6500
Sta Wag	150	350	950	1350	2800	4000
Monterey Custom, V-8						
4 dr	150	350	950	1350	2800	4000
4 dr HdTp	150	350	950	1450	2900	4100
2 dr HdTp	150	350	950	1450	3000	4200
Marauder, V-8						
2 dr HdTp	200	650	1250	2400	4200	6000
Marauder X-100, V-8						
2 dr HdTp	350	750	1450	3300	4900	7000
Marquis, V-8						
4 dr	150	350	950	1450	2900	4100
4 dr HdTp	150	350	950	1450	3000	4200
2 dr HdTp	150	400	1000	1600	3100	4400
Conv	350	775	1500	3750	5250	7500
Sta Wag	150	350	950	1450	2900	4100
Col Pk	150	350	950	1450	3000	4200
Marquis Brgm, V-8						
4 dr	150	350	950	1450	3000	4200
4 dr HdTp	150	400	1000	1550	3050	4300
2 dr HdTp	200	500	1100	1900	3500	5000

NOTE: Add 30 percent for any 429 engine option.

1971

Comet, V-8	6	5	4	3	2	1
4 dr	125	200	600	1100	2200	3100
2 dr	125	200	600	1100	2250	3200
2 dr GT	150	350	950	1350	2800	4000
Montego, V-8						
4 dr	100	175	525	1050	2100	3000
2 dr HdTp	125	250	750	1150	2400	3400
Montego MX						
4 dr	125	200	600	1100	2200	3100
2 dr HdTp	150	300	900	1250	2600	3700
Sta Wag	125	200	600	1100	2200	3100
Montego MX Brgm						
4 dr	125	200	600	1100	2250	3200
4 dr HdTp	125	250	750	1150	2400	3400
2 dr HdTp	150	300	900	1350	2700	3900
Villager Sta Wag	125	200	600	1100	2250	3200
Cyclone, V-8						
2 dr HdTp	200	650	1250	2400	4200	6000
Cyclone GT, V-8						
2 dr HdTp	350	750	1450	3300	4900	7000
Cyclone Spoiler, V-8						
2 dr HdTp	350	775	1500	3750	5250	7500

NOTE: Add 40 percent for 429 V-8 GT and Spoiler.

Cougar, V-8	6	5	4	3	2	1
2 dr HdTp	350	750	1450	3300	4900	7000
Conv	350	825	1600	4000	5600	8000
Cougar XR-7, V-8						
2 dr HdTp	350	875	1700	4250	5900	8500
Conv	450	950	2100	4750	6650	9500
Monterey, V-8						
4 dr	100	175	525	1050	2100	3000
4 dr HdTp	125	200	600	1100	2200	3100
2 dr HdTp	125	200	600	1100	2250	3200
Sta Wag	100	175	525	1050	2100	3000
Monterey Custom, V-8						
4 dr	125	200	600	1100	2200	3100
4 dr HdTp	125	200	600	1100	2250	3200
2 dr HdTp	125	250	750	1150	2450	3500
Marquis, V-8						
4 dr	125	200	600	1100	2200	3100
4 dr HdTp	125	250	750	1150	2450	3500
2 dr HdTp	150	350	950	1350	2800	4000
Sta Wag	100	175	525	1050	2100	3000
Marquis Brgm						
4 dr	125	200	600	1100	2250	3200
4 dr HdTp	125	250	750	1150	2450	3500
2 dr HdTp	150	400	1000	1650	3150	4500
Col Pk	125	250	750	1150	2450	3500

NOTE: Add 30 percent for 429.

1972

Comet, V-8	6	5	4	3	2	1
4 dr	125	200	600	1100	2200	3100
2 dr	125	250	750	1150	2450	3500
Montego, V-8						
4 dr	100	175	525	1050	2100	3000
2 dr HdTp	125	250	750	1150	2400	3400
Montego MX, V-8						
4 dr	125	200	600	1100	2250	3200
2 dr HdTp	150	300	900	1350	2700	3900
Sta Wag	125	200	600	1100	2250	3200
Montego Brgm, V-8						
4 dr	125	200	600	1100	2300	3300
2 dr HdTp	150	350	950	1350	2800	4000
Sta Wag	125	200	600	1100	2300	3300
Montego GT, V-8						
2 dr HdTp Fsbk	150	400	1000	1650	3150	4500
Cougar, V-8						
2 dr HdTp	350	750	1450	3300	4900	7000
Conv	350	875	1700	4250	5900	8500
Cougar XR-7, V-8						
2 dr HdTp	350	875	1700	4250	5900	8500
Conv	400	1200	2000	4000	7000	10,000
Monterey, V-8						
4 dr	125	200	600	1100	2300	3300
4 dr HdTp	125	250	750	1150	2450	3500
2 dr HdTp	150	350	950	1350	2800	4000
Sta Wag	125	250	750	1150	2450	3500
Monterey Custom, V-8						
4 dr	125	250	750	1150	2400	3400
4 dr HdTp	150	350	950	1350	2800	4000
2 dr HdTp	150	400	1000	1650	3150	4500
Marquis, V-8						
4 dr	125	250	750	1150	2450	3500
4 dr HdTp	150	400	1000	1650	3150	4500
2 dr HdTp	200	500	1100	1900	3500	5000
Sta Wag	125	250	750	1150	2450	3500
Marquis Brgm, V-8						
4 dr	125	250	750	1150	2500	3600
4 dr HdTp	150	300	900	1250	2600	3700
2 dr HdTp	150	450	1050	1800	3300	4800
Col Pk	125	250	750	1150	2500	3600

1973

Comet, V-8	6	5	4	3	2	1
4 dr	125	200	600	1100	2200	3100
2 dr	125	250	750	1150	2450	3500
Montego, V-8						
4 dr	100	175	525	1050	2100	3000
2 dr HdTp	150	300	900	1250	2650	3800
Montego MX, V-8						
4 dr	125	200	600	1100	2200	3100
2 dr HdTp	150	350	950	1350	2800	4000
Montego MX Brgm, V-8						
4 dr	125	200	600	1100	2200	3200
2 dr HdTp	150	350	950	1450	3000	4200
Montego GT, V-8						
2 dr HdTp	200	500	1100	1900	3500	5000
Montego MX						
Village Wag	125	200	600	1100	2250	3200
Cougar, V-8						
2 dr HdTp	350	750	1450	3300	4900	7000
Conv	350	825	1600	4000	5600	8000
Cougar XR-7, V-8						
2 dr HdTp	350	825	1600	4000	5600	8000
Conv	450	900	1900	4500	6300	9000
Monterey, V-8						
4 dr	100	175	525	1050	2100	3000
2 dr HdTp	125	200	600	1100	2200	3100
Monterey Custom, V-8						
4 dr	125	200	600	1100	2200	3100
2 dr HdTp	150	350	950	1350	2800	4000
Marquis, V-8						
4 dr	125	200	600	1100	2300	3300
4 dr HdTp	125	250	750	1150	2450	3500
2 dr HdTp	150	400	1000	1650	3150	4500
Marquis Brgm, V-8						
4 dr	125	250	750	1150	2400	3400
4 dr HdTp	150	350	950	1350	2800	4000
2 dr HdTp	200	500	1100	1900	3500	5000
Station Wagon, V-8						
Monterey	125	200	600	1100	2300	3300
Marquis	125	250	750	1150	2400	3400
Col Pk	125	250	750	1150	2450	3500

1974

Comet, V-8	6	5	4	3	2	1
4 dr	125	200	600	1100	2200	3100
2 dr	125	250	750	1150	2450	3500
Montego, V-8						
4 dr	125	200	600	1100	2250	3200
2 dr HdTp	125	250	750	1150	2500	3600
Montego MX, V-8						
4 dr	125	200	600	1100	2300	3300
2 dr HdTp	150	300	900	1250	2600	3700
Montego MX Brgm, V-8						
4 dr	125	250	750	1150	2400	3400
2 dr HdTp	150	300	900	1350	2700	3900
Villager	125	250	750	1150	2400	3400
Cougar, V-8						
2 dr	200	600	1200	2200	3850	5500
Monterey, V-8						
4 dr	125	200	600	1100	2200	3100
2 dr HdTp	150	350	950	1350	2800	4000
Monterey Custom, V-8						
4 dr	125	200	600	1100	2250	3200
2 dr HdTp	150	400	1000	1650	3150	4500
Marquis, V-8						
4 dr	125	200	600	1100	2300	3300
4 dr HdTp	125	250	750	1150	2450	3500
2 dr HdTp	150	450	1050	1800	3300	4800
Marquis Brgm, V-8						
4 dr	125	250	750	1150	2400	3400
4 dr HdTp	150	350	950	1350	2800	4000
2 dr HdTp	200	500	1100	1900	3500	5000
Station Wagons, V-8						
Monterey	125	250	750	1150	2450	3500
Marquis	125	250	750	1150	2500	3600
Col Pk	150	300	900	1250	2600	3700

1975

	6	5	4	3	2	1
Bobcat 4-cyl.						
Htchbk	125	250	750	1150	2500	3600
Sta Wag	125	250	750	1150	2450	3500
Comet, V-8						
4 dr	125	200	600	1100	2200	3100
2 dr	125	200	600	1100	2250	3200
Monarch, V-8						
4 dr	125	250	750	1150	2400	3400
2 dr	125	250	750	1150	2450	3500
Monarch Ghia, V-8						
4 dr	125	250	750	1150	2450	3500
2 dr	125	250	750	1150	2500	3600
Monarch Grand Ghia, V-8						
4 dr	150	300	900	1250	2600	3700
Montego, V-8						
4 dr	125	200	600	1100	2300	3300
2 dr	125	250	750	1150	2400	3400
Montego MX, V-8						
4 dr	125	250	750	1150	2400	3400
2 dr	125	250	750	1150	2450	3500
Montego Brgm, V-8						
4 dr	125	250	750	1150	2450	3500
2 dr	125	250	750	1150	2500	3600
Station Wagons, V-8						
Villager	125	250	750	1150	2400	3400
Cougar, V-8						
2 dr HdTp	125	250	750	1150	2500	3600
Marquis, V-8						
4 dr	125	250	750	1150	2400	3400
2 dr	125	250	750	1150	2450	3500
Marquis Brgm, V-8						
4 dr	125	250	750	1150	2450	3500
2 dr	125	250	750	1150	2500	3600
Grand Marquis, V-8						
4 dr	125	250	750	1150	2500	3600
2 dr	150	300	900	1250	2600	3700
Station Wagons, V-8						
Marquis	150	300	900	1250	2600	3700
Col Pk	150	300	900	1250	2650	3800

1976

	6	5	4	3	2	1
Bobcat, 4-cyl.						
3 dr	125	250	750	1150	2500	3600
Sta Wag	150	300	900	1250	2600	3700
Comet, V-8						
4 dr Sed	125	250	750	1150	2450	3500
2 dr Sed	125	250	750	1150	2400	3400
Monarch, V-8						
4 dr Sed	125	200	600	1100	2300	3300
2 dr Sed	125	250	750	1150	2400	3400
Monarch Ghia, V-8						
4 dr Sed	125	250	750	1150	2450	3500
2 dr Sed	125	250	750	1150	2500	3600
Monarch Grand Ghia, V-8						
4 dr Sed	150	300	900	1350	2700	3900
Montego, V-8						
4 dr Sed	125	250	750	1150	2500	3600
Cpe	150	300	900	1250	2600	3700
Montego MX, V-8						
4 dr Sed	150	300	900	1250	2650	3800
Cpe	150	300	900	1350	2700	3900
Montego Brougham, V-8						
4 dr Sed	150	350	950	1350	2800	4000
Cpe	150	350	950	1450	2900	4100
Station Wagons, V-8						
Montego MX	150	300	900	1250	2600	3700
Montego Vill	150	300	900	1250	2650	3800
Cougar XR7, V-8						
2 dr HdTp	150	300	900	1250	2650	3800
Marquis, V-8						
4 dr Sed	125	250	750	1150	2500	3600
Cpe	150	300	900	1250	2600	3700
Marquis Brougham, V-8						
4 dr Sed	150	300	900	1250	2650	3800
Cpe	150	300	900	1350	2700	3900
Grand Marquis, V-8						
4 dr Sed	150	350	950	1350	2800	4000
Cpe	150	350	950	1450	2900	4100
Station Wagons, V-8						
Marquis	150	300	900	1250	2650	3800
Col Pk	150	300	900	1350	2700	3900

1977

	6	5	4	3	2	1
Bobcat, 4-cyl.						
3 dr	150	300	900	1250	2600	3700
Sta Wag	150	300	900	1250	2650	3800
Vill Wag	150	300	900	1350	2700	3900
NOTE: Add 5 percent for V-6.						
Comet, V-8						
4 dr Sed	125	250	750	1150	2500	3600
2 dr Sed	150	300	900	1250	2600	3700
Monarch, V-8						
4 dr Sed	125	250	750	1150	2400	3400
2 dr Sed	125	250	750	1150	2450	3500
Monarch Ghia, V-8						
4 dr Sed	125	250	750	1150	2500	3600
2 dr Sed	150	300	900	1250	2600	3700
Cougar, V-8						
4 dr Sed	150	300	900	1250	2650	3800
2 dr Sed	150	300	900	1350	2700	3900
Cougar Brougham, V-8						
4 dr Sed	150	300	900	1350	2700	3900
2 dr Sed	150	350	950	1350	2800	4000
Cougar XR7, V-8						
2 dr	150	350	950	1450	3000	4200
Station Wagons, V-8						
Cougar	150	300	900	1250	2650	3800
Vill	150	300	900	1350	2700	3900
Marquis, V-8						
4 dr Sed	150	300	900	1350	2700	3900
2 dr Sed	150	350	950	1350	2800	4000
Marquis Brougham, V-8						
4 dr Sed	150	300	900	1350	2700	3900
2 dr Sed	150	350	950	1350	2800	4000
Grand Marquis, V-8						
4 dr HdTp	150	350	950	1450	2900	4100
2 dr HdTp	150	350	950	1450	3000	4200
Station Wagons, V-8						
2S Marquis	150	300	900	1350	2700	3900
3S Marquis	150	350	950	1350	2800	4000

1978

	6	5	4	3	2	1
Bobcat						
3 dr Rbt	125	250	750	1150	2500	3600
Sta Wag	150	300	900	1250	2600	3700
Zephyr						
4 dr Sed	125	200	600	1100	2300	3300
2 dr Sed	125	200	600	1100	2250	3200
Cpe	125	250	750	1150	2450	3500
Sta Wag	125	250	750	1150	2400	3400
Monarch						
4 dr Sed	125	200	600	1100	2300	3300
2 dr Sed	125	250	750	1150	2400	3400
Cougar						
4 dr	125	250	750	1150	2450	3500
2 dr	125	250	750	1150	2500	3600
Cougar XR7						
2 dr	150	350	950	1450	2900	4100
Marquis						
4 dr	150	300	900	1250	2650	3800
2 dr	150	300	900	1350	2700	3900
Sta Wag	150	300	900	1250	2650	3800
Marquis Brougham						
4 dr	150	300	900	1350	2700	3900
2 dr	150	350	950	1350	2800	4000
Grand Marquis						
4 dr	150	350	950	1450	2900	4100
2 dr	150	350	950	1450	3000	4200

1979

	6	5	4	3	2	1
Bobcat, 4-cyl.						
3 dr Rbt	150	300	900	1250	2600	3700
Wag	125	250	750	1150	2500	3600
Villager Wag	150	300	900	1250	2600	3700
Capri, 4-cyl.						
Cpe	150	300	900	1250	2650	3800
Ghia Cpe	150	350	950	1350	2800	4000
NOTES: Add 5 percent for 6-cyl.						
Add 8 percent for V-8.						
Zephyr, 6-cyl.						
4 dr Sed	125	250	750	1150	2400	3400
Cpe	125	250	750	1150	2500	3600
Spt Cpe	150	300	900	1250	2650	3800
Sta Wag	125	250	750	1150	2450	3500
NOTE: Add 5 percent for V-8.						
Monarch, V-8						
4 dr Sed	125	250	750	1150	2400	3400
Cpe	125	250	750	1150	2500	3600
NOTE: Deduct 5 percent for 6-cyl.						
Cougar, V-8						
4 dr Sed	125	250	750	1150	2500	3600
2 dr	150	300	900	1250	2600	3700
2 dr XR7	150	350	950	1450	2900	4100
Marquis, V-8						
4 dr	150	300	900	1250	2650	3800
2 dr	150	300	900	1350	2700	3900
Marquis Brougham, V-8						
4 dr	150	300	900	1350	2700	3900
2 dr	150	350	950	1350	2800	4000
Grand Marquis, V-8						
4 dr	150	350	950	1350	2800	4000
2 dr	150	350	950	1450	2900	4100
Station Wagons, V-8						
3S Marquis	150	300	900	1250	2650	3800
3S Colony Park	150	350	950	1350	2800	4000

1980

	6	5	4	3	2	1
Bobcat, 4-cyl.						
2 dr Hatch	125	250	750	1150	2450	3500
2 dr Sta Wag	125	250	750	1150	2500	3600
2 dr Sta Wag Villager	150	300	900	1250	2650	3800
Capri, 6-cyl.						
2 dr Hatch	150	450	1050	1750	3250	4700
2 dr Hatch Ghia	200	500	1100	1900	3500	5000
NOTE: Deduct 10 percent for 4-cyl.						
Zephyr, 6-cyl.						
4 dr Sed	125	250	750	1150	2450	3500
2 dr Sed	125	250	750	1150	2400	3400
2 dr Cpe Z-7	150	350	950	1450	3000	4200
4 dr Sta Wag	150	300	900	1350	2700	3900
NOTE: Deduct 10 percent for 4-cyl.						
Monarch, V-8						
4 dr Sed	150	350	950	1450	3000	4200
2 dr Cpe	150	350	950	1450	2900	4100
NOTE: Deduct 10 percent for 4-cyl.						
Cougar XR7, V-8						
2 dr Cpe	200	650	1200	2300	4100	5800
Marquis, V-8						
4 dr Sed	150	400	1000	1600	3100	4400
2 dr Sed	150	400	1000	1550	3050	4300
Marquis Brougham, V-8						
4 dr Sed	150	450	1050	1700	3200	4600
2 dr Sed	150	400	1000	1650	3150	4500
Grand Marquis, V-8						
4 dr Sed	150	450	1050	1750	3250	4700
2 dr Sed	150	450	1050	1700	3200	4600
4 dr Sta Wag 2S	150	450	1050	1750	3250	4700
4 dr Sta Wag 3S	150	450	1050	1800	3300	4800
4 dr Sta Wag CP 2S	200	500	1100	1850	3350	4900
4 dr Sta Wag CP 3S	200	500	1100	1900	3500	5000

1981

	6	5	4	3	2	1
Lynx, 4-cyl.						
2 dr Hatch	125	200	600	1100	2300	3300
2 dr Hatch L	125	250	750	1150	2400	3400
4 dr Hatch L	125	250	750	1150	2450	3500
2 dr Hatch GL	125	250	750	1150	2450	3500
4 dr Hatch GL	125	250	750	1150	2500	3600
2 dr Hatch GS	125	250	750	1150	2500	3600
4 dr Hatch GS	150	300	900	1250	2600	3700
2 dr Hatch RS	150	300	900	1250	2600	3700
4 dr Hatch RS	150	300	900	1250	2650	3800
2 dr Hatch LS	150	300	900	1250	2650	3800
Zephyr, 6-cyl.						
4 dr Sed S	125	250	750	1150	2450	3500
4 dr Sed	125	250	750	1150	2500	3600
2 dr Sed	125	250	750	1150	2450	3500
2 dr Cpe Z-7	150	400	1000	1550	3050	4300
4 dr Sta Wag	150	350	950	1350	2800	4000
NOTE: Deduct 10 percent for 4-cyl.						

	6	5	4	3	2	1
Capri, 6-cyl.						
2 dr Hatch	150	400	1000	1650	3150	4500
2 dr Hatch GS	150	450	1050	1750	3250	4700
NOTE: Deduct 10 percent for 4-cyl.						
Cougar, 6-cyl.						
4 dr Sed	150	350	950	1450	3000	4200
2 dr Sed	150	350	950	1450	2900	4100
NOTE: Deduct 10 percent for 4-cyl.						
Cougar XR7, V-8						
2 dr Cpe	200	650	1250	2400	4150	5900
NOTE: Deduct 12 percent for 6-cyl.						
Marquis, V-8						
4 dr Sed	150	400	1000	1600	3100	4400
Marquis Brougham, V-8						
4 dr Sed	150	450	1050	1700	3200	4600
2 dr Sed	150	400	1000	1650	3150	4500
Grand Marquis, V-8						
4 dr Sed	150	450	1050	1800	3300	4800
2 dr Sed	150	450	1050	1750	3250	4700
4 dr Sta Wag 2S	150	450	1050	1800	3300	4800
4 dr Sta Wag 3S	200	500	1100	1850	3350	4900
4 dr Sta Wag CP 2S	150	450	1050	1800	3300	4800
4 dr Sta Wag CP 3S	200	500	1100	1850	3350	4900

1982

	6	5	4	3	2	1
Lynx, 4-cyl.						
2 dr Hatch	125	250	750	1150	2400	3400
4 dr Hatch	125	250	750	1150	2450	3500
2 dr Hatch L	125	250	750	1150	2450	3500
4 dr Hatch L	125	250	750	1150	2500	3600
4 dr Sta Wag L	150	300	900	1250	2600	3700
2 dr Hatch GL	125	250	750	1150	2500	3600
4 dr Hatch GL	150	300	900	1250	2600	3700
4 dr Sta Wag GL	150	300	900	1250	2650	3800
2 dr Hatch GS	150	300	900	1250	2600	3700
4 dr Hatch GS	150	300	900	1250	2650	3800
4 dr Sta Wag GS	150	300	900	1350	2700	3900
2 dr Hatch LS	150	300	900	1250	2650	3800
4 dr Hatch LS	150	300	900	1350	2700	3900
4 dr Sta Wag LS	150	350	950	1350	2800	3900
2 dr Hatch RS	150	300	900	1350	2700	3900
LN7, 4-cyl.						
2 dr Hatch	150	450	1050	1700	3200	4600
Zephyr, 6-cyl.						
4 dr Sed	150	300	900	1250	2600	3700
2 dr Cpe Z-7	150	400	1000	1550	3050	4300
4 dr Sed GS	150	300	900	1250	2650	3800
2 dr Cpe Z-7 GS	150	400	1000	1650	3150	4500
Capri, 4-cyl.						
2 dr Hatch	150	450	1050	1750	3250	4700
2 dr Hatch L	150	450	1050	1800	3300	4800
2 dr Hatch GS	200	500	1100	1900	3500	5000
Capri, 6-cyl.						
2 dr Hatch L	200	550	1150	2100	3700	5300
2 dr Hatch GS	200	600	1200	2200	3850	5500
Capri, V-8						
2 dr Hatch RS	200	600	1200	2200	3900	5600
Cougar, 6-cyl.						
4 dr Sed GS	150	350	950	1350	2800	4000
2 dr Sed GS	150	300	900	1350	2700	3900
4 dr Sta Wag GS	150	350	950	1450	3000	4200
4 dr Sed LS	150	350	950	1450	2900	4100
2 dr Sed LS	150	350	950	1350	2800	4000
Cougar XR7, V-8						
2 dr Cpe	200	650	1250	2400	4200	6000
2 dr Cpe LS	200	675	1300	2500	4350	6200
NOTE: Deduct 10 percent for 6-cyl.						
Marquis, V-8						
4 dr Sed	150	400	1000	1650	3150	4500
Marquis Brougham, V-8						
4 dr Sed	150	450	1050	1750	3250	4700
2 dr Cpe	150	450	1050	1700	3200	4600
Grand Marquis, V-8						
4 dr Sed	200	500	1100	1850	3350	4900
2 dr Cpe	150	450	1050	1800	3300	4800
4 dr Sta Wag 2S	200	500	1100	1850	3350	4900
4 dr Sta Wag 3S	200	500	1100	1850	3350	4900
4 dr Sta Wag CP 2S	200	500	1100	1900	3500	5000
4 dr Sta Wag CP 3S	200	500	1100	1900	3500	5000

1983

	6	5	4	3	2	1
Lynx, 4-cyl.						
2 dr Hatch L	125	250	750	1150	2500	3600
4 dr Hatch L	150	300	900	1250	2600	3700
4 dr Sta Wag L	150	300	900	1250	2650	3800
2 dr Hatch GS	150	300	900	1250	2600	3700
4 dr Hatch GS	150	300	900	1250	2650	3800
4 dr Sta Wag GS	150	300	900	1350	2700	3900
2 dr Hatch LS	150	300	900	1250	2650	3800
4 dr Hatch LS	150	300	900	1350	2700	3900

	6	5	4	3	2	1
4 dr Sta Wag LS	150	350	950	1350	2800	4000
2 dr Hatch RS	150	300	900	1350	2700	3900
4 dr Hatch LTS	150	350	950	1350	2800	4000
LN7, 4-cyl.						
2 dr Hatch	150	450	1050	1750	3250	4700
2 dr Hatch Sport	150	450	1050	1800	3300	4800
2 dr Hatch Grand Sport	200	500	1100	1900	3500	5000
2 dr Hatch RS	200	550	1150	2000	3600	5200
Zephyr, V-6						
4 dr Sed	150	300	900	1250	2650	3800
2 dr Cpe Z-7	150	400	1000	1600	3100	4400
4 dr Sed GS	150	300	900	1350	2700	3900
2 dr Cpe Z-7 GS	150	450	1050	1700	3200	4600
NOTE: Deduct 10 percent for 4-cyl.						
Capri, 4-cyl.						
2 dr Hatch	150	450	1050	1800	3300	4800
2 dr Hatch H-L	200	500	1100	1850	3350	4900
2 dr Hatch RS	200	500	1100	1950	3600	5100
Capri, 6-cyl.						
2 dr Hatch L	200	550	1150	2100	3800	5400
2 dr Hatch GS	200	600	1200	2200	3900	5600
Capri, V-8						
2 dr Hatch RS	200	600	1200	2300	4000	5700
Cougar, V-8						
2 dr Cpe	350	700	1350	2800	4550	6500
2 dr Cpe LS	350	725	1400	3000	4700	6700
NOTE: Deduct 15 percent for V-6.						
Marquis, 4-cyl.						
4 dr Sed	150	350	950	1450	3000	4200
4 dr Brougham	150	400	1000	1600	3100	4400
Marquis, 6-cyl.						
4 dr Sed	150	400	1000	1600	3100	4400
4 dr Sta Wag	150	450	1050	1750	3250	4700
4 dr Sed Brgm	150	450	1050	1800	3300	4800
4 dr Sta Wag Brgm	200	500	1100	1850	3350	4900
Grand Marquis, V-8						
4 dr Sed	200	550	1150	2000	3600	5200
2 dr Cpe	200	500	1100	1950	3600	5100
4 dr Sed LS	200	550	1150	2100	3800	5400
2 dr Cpe LS	200	550	1150	2100	3700	5300
4 dr Sta Wag 2S	200	550	1150	2100	3800	5400
4 dr Sta Wag 3S	200	600	1200	2200	3850	5500

1984

	6	5	4	3	2	1
Lynx, 4-cyl.						
2 dr Hatch	125	200	600	1100	2250	3200
4 dr Hatch	125	200	600	1100	2250	3200
2 dr Hatch L	125	200	600	1100	2300	3300
4 dr Hatch L	125	200	600	1100	2300	3300
4 dr Sta Wag L	125	200	600	1100	2300	3300
2 dr Hatch GS	125	250	750	1150	2400	3400
4 dr Hatch GS	125	250	750	1150	2400	3400
4 dr Sta Wag GS	125	250	750	1150	2400	3400
4 dr Hatch LTS	125	250	750	1150	2450	3500
2 dr Hatch RS	125	250	750	1150	2500	3600
2 dr Hatch RS Turbo	150	300	900	1250	2650	3800
Topaz, 4-cyl.						
2 dr Sed	125	200	600	1100	2300	3300
4 dr Sed	125	200	600	1100	2300	3300
2 dr Sed GS	125	250	750	1150	2400	3400
4 dr Sed GS	125	250	750	1150	2400	3400
Capri, 4-cyl.						
2 dr Hatch GS	150	400	1000	1600	3100	4400
2 dr Hatch RS Turbo	150	450	1050	1800	3300	4800
2 dr Hatch GS, V-6	150	450	1050	1700	3200	4600
2 dr Hatch GS, V-8	150	450	1050	1800	3300	4800
2 dr Hatch RS, V-8	200	500	1100	1900	3500	5000
Cougar, V-6						
2 dr Cpe	150	350	950	1450	3000	4200
2 dr Cpe LS	150	400	1000	1550	3050	4300
Cougar, V-8						
2 dr Cpe	150	400	1000	1650	3150	4500
2 dr Cpe LS	150	450	1050	1800	3300	4800
2 dr Cpe XR7	200	600	1200	2200	3850	5500
Marquis, 4-cyl.						
4 dr Sed	150	350	950	1450	2900	4100
4 dr Sed Brougham	150	350	950	1450	3000	4200
Marquis, V-6						
4 dr Sed	150	350	950	1450	3000	4200
4 dr Sed Brougham	150	400	1000	1550	3050	4300
4 dr Sta Wag	150	400	1000	1550	3050	4300
4 dr Sta Wag Brougham	150	400	1000	1600	3100	4400
Grand Marquis, V-8						
4 dr Sed	200	500	1100	1850	3350	4900
2 dr Sed	200	500	1100	1850	3350	4900
4 dr Sed LS	200	500	1100	1900	3500	5000
2 dr Sed LS	200	500	1100	1900	3500	5000
4 dr Sta Wag Colony Park 8P	200	500	1100	1900	3500	5000
4 dr Sta Wag Colony Park 6P	200	500	1100	1900	3500	5000

1939 Mercury Club Coupe.

1984 Mercury Marquis station wagon.

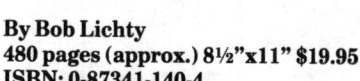

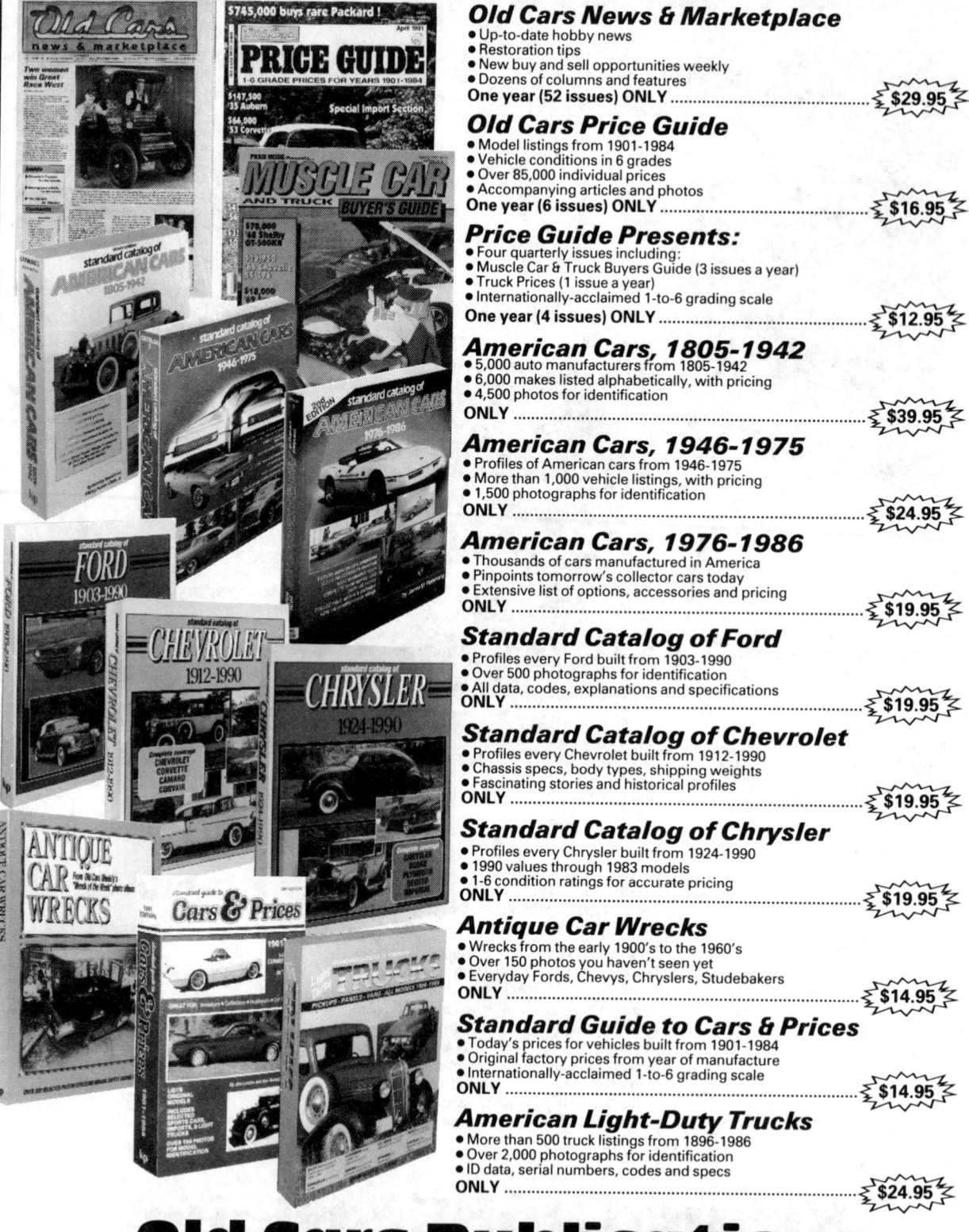
480